W9-BAX-009

lonely planet

Southeast Asia
on a Shoestring

Myanmar (Burma) p483

Laos p317

Thailand p656

Vietnam p821

Cambodia p71

Philippines p553

Brunei Darussalam p58

Malaysia p384

Singapore p620

Indonesia p159

Timor-Leste p796

Brett Atkinson, Lindsay Brown, Jayne D'Arcy, David Eimer, Paul Harding, Nick Ray, Tim Bewer, Joe Bindloss, Greg Bloom, Celeste Brash, Austin Bush, Ria de Jong, Michael Grosberg, Damian Harper, Ashley Harrell, Trent Holden, Anita Isalska, Mark Johanson, Hugh McNaughtan, Rebecca Milner, Simon Richmond, Iain Stewart, Andy Symington, Phillip Tang

PLAN YOUR TRIP

PROBOSCIS MONKEY, KOTA KINABALU P435

CORON ISLAND, PALAWAN P608

ON THE ROAD

Contents

Contents

Contents

Welcome to Southeast Asia

Wrapped in rainforests, edged by golden sands, crowned by volcanoes, studded with ruins of lost civilisations: this is Southeast Asia as you've always imagined it.

Elemental Forces

The soul of Southeast Asia has been forged by the elements. Mighty volcanoes have thrust the land up, and raging rivers have carved it down. Coral reefs have formed islands, and sea spray has sculpted them into surreal karst outcrops. Millennia of monsoon rain have created cultures defined by the seasons, and by the annual flooding of rivers, which double as super-highways through impenetrable jungles. In this region of rivers, oceans and islands, you're as likely to travel by boat as by road, following trade routes that were old when the great powers of Europe were young.

Epicurean Encounters

Southeast Asia is both a melting pot and a cooking pot, where the flavours of some of the world's greatest cuisines melt into one another, throwing up ever more mesmerising combinations. The region's spices were once valued more highly than gold, and combined with one notable import – the South American chilli – they've created a cooking palette that inflames the senses and leaves the taste buds begging for more. This is a region where humble hawker stalls come with Michelin stars, and where a meal at a roadside canteen or night market can be as memorable as a five-star, dim sum banquet.

Spiritual Spaces

Spirituality swirls around Southeast Asia like the smoke from incense swirls around its myriad temples. At dawn in Buddhist nations, monks flood the streets to gather alms. In Muslim countries, the call to prayer rises in a chorus above rooftops. In Taoist temples, devotees fill the morning air with thick incense smoke, while tribal people in remote villages mark the new day's arrival with animist rituals. Every aspect of life here has a spiritual dimension, from the food people eat to the religious geometry dictating the layout of centuries-old mosques and temples.

Urban Adventures

Southeast Asia's mighty megacities are stepping boldly towards the future with one foot planted firmly in the past. Skyscrapers rise above streets like crystal gardens, while at street level, traders hustle, food-hawkers hawk, and temples bustle with devotees toting their offerings. For many travellers, the first taste of the region is the urban chaos of Bangkok, or the organised modernity of Singapore, but each of Southeast Asia's capitals has its own unique character, defined by religion, culture, geography and, in most cases, centuries of colonialism and feuding dynasties. Learning the rhythms of each is part of the magic.

Why I Love Southeast Asia

By Joe Bindloss, Writer

Part of being a traveller is working out which places get your juices flowing. I first encountered Southeast Asia on a round-the-world trip in the early 1990s, and something clicked. It might've been the waft of incense, the gleam of gold leaf, lotus blossoms floating in a temple pool, or the roots of jungle trees thrusting through Angkor Wat's ruins. I've never stopped being amazed at how every country in Southeast Asia offers its own unique version of the East, but all drawn from the same narrative of faith, lost empires and the ebb and flow of the monsoon rains.

For more about our writers, see p992

Above: Ta Prohm (p109), Cambodia

Southeast Asia

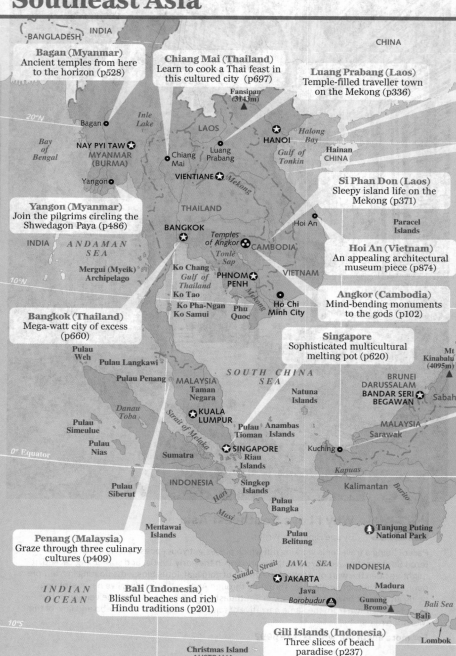

Bagan (Myanmar)
Ancient temples from here
to the horizon (p528)

Chiang Mai (Thailand)
Learn to cook a Thai feast in
this cultured city (p697)

Luang Prabang (Laos)
Temple-filled traveller town
on the Mekong (p336)

Yangon (Myanmar)
Join the pilgrims circling the
Shwedagon Paya (p486)

Si Phan Don (Laos)
Sleepy island life on the
Mekong (p371)

Hoi An (Vietnam)
An appealing architectural
museum piece (p874)

Bangkok (Thailand)
Mega-watt city of excess
(p660)

Angkor (Cambodia)
Mind-bending monuments
to the gods (p102)

Singapore
Sophisticated multicultural
melting pot (p620)

Penang (Malaysia)
Graze through three culinary
cultures (p409)

Bali (Indonesia)
Blissful beaches and rich
Hindu traditions (p201)

Gili Islands (Indonesia)
Three slices of beach
paradise (p237)

EAST CHINA SEA

Tropic of Cancer

Halong Bay (Vietnam)
Limestone towers anchoring a jewel-coloured bay (p841)

Phong Nha-Ke Bang National Park (Vietnam)
The world's biggest cave (p856)

Ifugao Rice Terraces (Philippines)
An emerald landscape (p576)

20°N

Batanes Islands

Luzon Strait
Babuyan Islands

Banaue

Luzon

Polillo Islands

MANILA

Catanduanes

PHILIPPINES

Mindoro

Calamian Group

Sibuyan Sea

Panay

Visayan Sea

Samar

Cebu Leyte

Bohol Dinagat
Siargao

Palawan Negros

Bohol Sea

SULU SEA

Mindanao

Basilan
Jolo Sulu Archipelago

Tawi-Tawi

Semporna Archipelago

CELEBES SEA

PHILIPPINE SEA

Palawan (Philippines)
Rugged, remote and oh-so-beautiful beaches (p601)

10°N

Malaysian Borneo
Jungle adventures galore (p435)

PALAU

PACIFIC OCEAN

Talaud

Sangir Islands

Morotai

Halmahera
Waigeo

Komodo & Flores (Indonesia)
Mystical beasts and magnificent beaches (p246)

Equator 0°

Togean Islands

Teluk Tomini

MALUKU SEA

Pulau Bacan

Sula Islands Obi

HALMAHERA SEA

Pulau Biak

Yapen

Teluk Cenderawasih

Sulawesi

Tana Toraja

Banggai Islands

SERAM SEA

Buru

Misool

Seram

Ambon

Banda Islands

Puncak Jaya (5030m)

INDONESIA
Papua

PAPUA NEW GUINEA

Teluk Bone

Butung (Buton)

BANDA SEA

Kai Islands

Aru Islands

Yos Sudarso

Selayar

FLORES SEA

Sumbawa Komodo

Alor Ataúro
Islands Island

Wetar

Leti Islands

Babar Islands

Tanimbar Islands

ARAFURA SEA

10°S

DILI

Flores

Solor Islands

TIMOR-LESTE

West Timor

TIMOR SEA

Ataúro Island (Timor-Leste)
Explore the less-seen Southeast Asia (p806)

SAWU SEA

Sumba Sawu Rote

120°E

AUSTRALIA

140°E

Southeast Asia's
Top 20

Temples of Angkor (Cambodia)

1 All your Indiana Jones fantasies will come alive at Angkor, where the walls of ancient temples are torn apart by the roots of towering jungle trees, and delicate bas reliefs of demons and angels peek out between the vines. From the geometric perfection of Angkor Wat (p102), to the more-jungle-than-temple ruins of Ta Prohm and the gigantic stone faces of Avalokiteshvara that grace the Bayon, Angkor feels even greater than the sum of its parts. Kick back in the local traveller hub of Siem Reap and enjoy days of glorious exploring. Bas relief in Angkor Thom (p103)

Hoi An (Vietnam)

2 Vietnam's most graceful outpost, beautiful Hoi An (p874) was once a busy port, and the streets of the old town are bejewelled with traditional houses and family chapels, built by its seafaring citizens. Today, these glorious structures have found new life as restaurants, bars, cafes, boutiques, tailors' shops and cooking schools. When you're done with history, rent a bicycle or motorcycle and drift along the coast to gorgeous beaches, or take a boat trip offshore to the idyllic Cham Islands. Consider it a sampling platter of Southeast Asia, in one handy location.

EARTH9566/SHUTTERSTOCK ©

YUSNIZAM YUSOF/SHUTTERSTOCK ©

MARK WOLTERS/SHUTTERSTOCK ©

Bangkok (Thailand)

3 This superstar city has it all, and in super-sized proportions: fabulous food and shopping, simple spirituality, hedonistic nightlife, and, at the base of it all, a profound sense of fun and irreverence. Bangkok (p660) may be a pressure cooker for new arrivals, but for travellers coming back from remote dusty corners of Southeast Asia, this is a comforting dose of civilisation. The city has monuments and monasteries to spare, but amid the sightseeing, build in time for regular snacking, swapping traveller tales over beers and calming boat rides down the Chao Phraya river. Th Yaowarat (p661)

Bali (Indonesia)

4 Although this Hindu island in the heart of the Indonesian archipelago is firmly on the traveller radar, its unique culture and epic surf breaks make it an essential stop on the Asia circuit. There's more to Bali (p201) than Kuta Beach, but most visitors swing by Kuta for at least a day or two to catch a wave and party before retreating to more peaceful parts of the island. With Kuta out of your system, you can enjoy Ubud's rich cultural heritage, sleepy Pemuteran's laid-back vibe and Jimbaran's seafood feasts. Jimbaran beach (p211)

Komodo & Flores (Indonesia)

5 Here there be dragons – literally, in the case of Komodo (p246), one of the last refuges of the prehistoric-looking Komodo dragon. Encountering these primordial predators in their natural habitat is just part of the appeal of this chilled-out corner of the Indonesian archipelago. Add in lazy days on deserted-island beaches, trips to some of Indonesia's best dive sites, and the upbeat traveller buzz in Labuanbajo on neighbouring Flores (p247), and it's easy to see the attraction. But word is getting out, so see Komodo and Flores now before runaway development alters their laid-back charm. Komodo dragon (p247)

Bagan (Myanmar)

6 Myanmar's proud retort to the temples of Angkor, the plains of Bagan (p528) are dotted with the remains of some 4000 Buddhist temples, many lovingly restored, but others still in ruins from the ravages of Kublai Khan's Mongol hordes. Explore the temples at your leisure on foot or by bicycle or horse-cart, avoiding the tour-bus crowds. The definitive view of Bagan is at dawn or sunset from Pyathada Paya (pictured below) or one of the other terraced pagodas, but consider looking down from above on a hot-air-balloon trip across the plain.

Halong Bay (Vietnam)

7 What's this? A pirate cove in the South China Sea? Nope, it's just Halong Bay (p841), where some 3000 limestone outcrops thrust out of the shimmering Gulf of Tonkin waters. Protected as a Unesco World Heritage Site, this atmospheric stretch of coastline is one of Vietnam's top drawcards, so take your pick from overnight tours by junk or guided kayak trips to wave-carved grottoes and hidden lagoons. If after all this you're still hungry for more karst action, move on to less touristy Lan Ha Bay, tumbling off the shore of Cat Ba island.

JAKOB FISCHER/SHUTTERSTOCK ©

DANNY IACOB/SHUTTERSTOCK ©

GWOEII/SHUTTERSTOCK ©

WATCHARIN TAOSANA/SHUTTERSTOCK ©

Penang (Malaysia)

8 The mists of time swirl around George Town (p410) on the island of Penang, like the incense smoke wafting around its Taoist temples and clanhouses. This seafaring city was forged by British colonists and Chinese and Indian migrant workers, and the melting pot still stirs today, with Chinese, Malay and Indian culture all playing their part in the island's attitude and cuisine. Added to the Unesco World Heritage list in 2008, Penang has taken steps to preserve its historic architecture, and today its atmospheric shophouses hide museums, boutique hotels and chic cafes. Street food sellers in Penang

Chiang Mai (Thailand)

9 Thailand's capital (p697) is the perfect antidote to the bustling modernity of Bangkok. Bound by a moat and crumbling city walls, the calm streets of Chiang Mai's Old City are filled with teak temples in the distinctive northern Thai style. It's a place to wander aimlessly, drifting from ancient wat to ancient wat, pausing for fresh fruit juices and some of Asia's finest street food. Many make a week of it, day-tripping to waterfalls and hill-tribe villages, indulging in Thai massages and learning to cook curries in Chiang Mai's famous cooking schools. Wat Chiang Man (p699)

Palawan (Philippines)

10 Once a backwater, Palawan (p601) has sky-rocketed in popularity as it gets added to travel-magazine lists of the world's best island escapes. The crown jewel is the Bacuit Archipelago near El Nido, a surreal seascape of limestone outcrops, dotted with hidden beaches and coral reefs offering some of the Philippines' most exciting diving. More sublime sand awaits further south at Port Barton and Sabang. The real treasure for divers lies to the north at Coron Bay, where the wrecks of dozens of Japanese warships lie in the murky gloom. Kayangan Lake (p608)

ADRIAN BAKER/SHUTTERSTOCK ©

Luang Prabang (Laos)

11 Hemmed in by the Mekong and Nam Khan rivers, the former royal capital of Luang Prabang (p336) is one of Southeast Asia's great temple cities, where the streets are crowded with Buddhist monks on the daily call to alms. Despite its growing popularity, Luang Prabang hasn't strayed far from its backpacker roots, so kick back for days or weeks, exploring temples, learning Lao cookery, pedalling around backstreets visiting ancient temples and unwinding even further with a massage at one of the city's affordable spas.

KENGPHOTOSTOCK/SHUTTERSTOCK ©

11

Si Phan Don (Laos)

12 The Mekong River sheds its characteristic muddy hue for a more tropical turquoise blue as it swirls around Laos' enigmatic 'Four Thousand Islands', collectively known as Si Phan Don (p371). This is Laos at its most laid-back, where the busiest way to spend a day is cycling from islet to islet, riding down the river on an inner tube, or kayaking in search of rare Irrawaddy dolphins. A sleepy traveller vibe prevails, so kick off your shoes, drop into a hammock and let the swoosh of the river lull you into a peaceful slumber. Waterfall on Don Khon (p373)

Malaysian Borneo

13 The *other* Malaysia, the states of Sabah (p435) and Sarawak (p453) share the island of Borneo with Brunei and Indonesia's Kalimantan. Here, on cruises along rainforest-cloaked rivers, you can encounter some of Southeast Asia's wildest inhabitants: chattering gibbons, ponderous orangutans and the myriad indigenous cultures who share their jungle home. But it's not all rivers and rainforest. There are the cosmopolitan cities of Kuching (Sarawak) and Kota Kinabalu (Sabah), and dive boats explore some of Southeast Asia's best stocked coral reefs. Gibbon in Kota Kinabalu (p435)

ANNA EWA BIENIEK/SHUTTERSTOCK ©

KJERSTI JOERGENSEN/SHUTTERSTOCK ©

Singapore Food

14 Little bigger than a cooking pot itself, the city-state of Singapore (p620) is one of Asia's great culinary melting pots – a great coming together of the best cooking know-how from China, India and the Malay peninsula. There's no shortage of things to do and see in this metropolis, from the futuristic Gardens by the Bay to the eccentric recreation of Taoist heaven and hell at Haw Par Villa, but somehow it's the meals that'll stay with you, whether you feast at the city's banquet restaurants or chow down in the abundant hawker courts.

Ataúro Island (Timor-Leste)

15 Often (unfairly) excluded on a typical Southeast Asian itinerary, Timor-Leste may be a young nation, but it offers old-school adventure for those bold enough to venture here. The story of the nation's struggle for independence is powerfully told in the capital, Dili, but most are drawn here by the untouched coral reefs off the north coast, and to hidden villages and misty mountains in the densely forested interior. Cap off your trip with a night on sleepy Ataúro Island (p806) to get a feel for what Southeast Asia was like in the 1960s.

Ifugao Rice Terraces (Philippines)

16 Hand-hewn by generations of Ifugao tribal people in the rugged Cordillera mountains, the Ifugao rice terraces are celebrated as one of the wonders of the Asian world. The plunging valleys were first cut into terraces some 2000 years ago, and trekking these emerald staircases – and sleeping among them in idyllic Batad (p576) – feels like skipping back centuries to the days before the Philippines caught the attention of colonial powers. Nearby, you can detour to the trekking hub of Bontoc, or cross the hills to Sagada, where hanging coffins spill eerily down the cliff-sides.

Gili Islands (Indonesia)

17 One of Indonesia's great pleasures is hopping on a fast boat from busy Bali and arriving at the calm, irresistible Gili Islands (p237). This is the Indonesia people dream of – sugar-white sand, turquoise waters, swishing palm fronds and relaxing beach hang-outs entreating you to extend your stay. Spend your days snorkelling and diving with sharks, rays and turtles on the fringing reefs, then after dark savour the dining and nightlife on Gili Trawangan, or just swing in a hammock and enjoy the sea breezes on Gili Air and Gili Meno. Gili Trawangan (p241)

LKPRO/SHUTTERSTOCK ©

JULIYABURNOS/SHUTTERSTOCK ©

Yangon (Myanmar)

18 A delightfully faded vision of the colonial Far East, executed in a palette of colours washed out to pastels by centuries of monsoon rains: Yangon (p486), formerly Rangoon, is changing rapidly as the outside world rushes in after decades of isolation, but in other ways it has hardly changed at all. The gilded spire of the Shwedagon Paya (pictured above) still rises above the city like a beacon, surrounded by an ever-swirling tide of Buddhist pilgrims, and monks flood the streets at dawn to gather alms as they have since time immemorial.

Phong Nha-Ke Bang National Park (Vietnam)

19 With jagged hills draped in a shroud of rainforest and mountain rivers charging through plunging ravines, Phong Nha-Ke Bang (p856) is one of Vietnam's most spectacular national parks. You can crawl underground through the reserve's twisting and turning cave systems. The cathedral-like chambers of Hang Son Doong (pictured above), are only open to expensive caving tours, but more accessible are the ziplining and kayaking thrills of Hang Toi (Dark Cave), and the ethereal beauty of aptly named Paradise Cave.

Phnom Penh (Cambodia)

20 The Cambodian capital is chaotic but charming, physically carrying the scars of the past, but looking towards a brighter future. The Tonlé Sap and Mekong River swirl together in the middle of Phnom Penh (p73), hinting at onward travel by river boat to Angkor Wat, but before you go, wander the backstreets, with their old-fashioned shophouses and colonial villas. Also make time for the sobering experience of the Choeung Ek killing fields and Tuol Sleng Genocide Museum (pictured above) – an essential step towards understanding modern Cambodia.

Need to Know

For more information, see Survival Guide (p939)

Currency
Brunei dollar (B$)
Cambodia riel (r)
Indonesia rupiah (Rp)
Laos kip (K)
Malaysia ringgit (RM)
Myanmar kyat (K)
Philippines peso (P)
Singapore dollar (S$)
Thailand baht (B)
Timor-Leste US dollar (US$), centavo (cv)
Vietnam dong (d)

Language
Brunei Bahasa Malaysia
Cambodia Khmer
Indonesia Bahasa Indonesia
Laos Lao
Malaysia Bahasa Malaysia
Myanmar Burmese
Philippines Tagalog
Singapore English, Malay, Mandarin, Tamil
Thailand Thai
Timor-Leste Portuguese, Tetun
Vietnam Vietnamese

Mobile Phones
All nations in the region have their own mobile phone companies and most have partnership deals with foreign operators, so roaming on your home phone package is easy, though expensive. It's usually cheaper to buy a local SIM.

When to Go

- Hanoi GO Oct–May
- Yangon GO Nov–Apr
- Bangkok GO Nov–Mar
- Ko Tao GO Feb–Oct
- Boracay GO Jan–Sep
- Kuching GO Jun–Sep
- Bali GO Apr–Aug

Tropical climate, rain year round
Tropical climate, wet & dry seasons
Highland areas, warm summers, cool winters

High Season
(Jun–Aug & Dec–Feb)

➡ Dry, cool winter months.

➡ Chilly in the mountains.

➡ Travel is difficult during Tet in Vietnam.

➡ Summer rains across most of the region.

Shoulder Season
(Mar & Nov)

➡ Hot, dry season begins in March.

➡ November sees lower prices, before the rush.

Low Season
(Apr–May, Sep–Oct)

➡ Travel difficult during April's new year festivals in Cambodia, Laos, Myanmar and Thailand.

➡ Wet season (Sep–Oct); flooding, typhoons, transport cancellations.

➡ Dry season begins in Indonesia (Apr–May).

Useful Websites

Lonely Planet (www.lonelyplanet.com/southeast-asia) Destination information, hotel bookings, traveller forum and more.

Travelfish (www.travelfish.org) Popular travel site specialising in Southeast Asia.

Agoda (www.agoda.com) Regional hotel booking website.

Bangkok Post (www.bangkokpost.com) In-depth analysis of current events in Southeast Asia.

Important Numbers

Each country in the region has its own emergency numbers. There is normally a single nationwide number for the police; ambulance services are often provided by individual hospitals and fire services may just have a local number.

Exchange Rates

Exchange rates fluctuate around the region, and political crises can send rates plummeting. The US dollar is the most useful foreign currency to carry; it's easy to exchange, and in many areas, shops and hotels will accept US bills in place of the local currency, though change may be given in local notes.

Time

GMT/UTC plus 6½ hours
Myanmar

GMT/UTC plus seven hours
Cambodia, Laos, Thailand, Vietnam, parts of Indonesia (Java, Sumatra, and west and central Kalimantan)

GMT/UTC plus eight hours
Brunei, Malaysia, Philippines, Singapore, parts of Indonesia (Bali, Nusa Tenggara, south and east Kalimantan and Sulawesi)

GMT/UTC plus nine hours
Timor-Leste, parts of Indonesia (Irian Jaya and Maluku)

Daily Costs

Budget:
Less than US$50

➡ Cheap guesthouse: US$10–20

➡ Night-market meal: US$1–5

➡ Local transport: US$1–5

➡ Bottled beer: US$1–5

Midrange:
US$50–100

➡ Midrange hotel room: US$20–75

➡ Restaurant meal: US$6–10

➡ Motorcycle hire: US$6–10

Top End:
More than US$100

➡ Boutique hotel or beach resort: US$100+

➡ Dive trip: US$50–100

➡ Hiring a car and driver: US$25–50

Opening Hours

Opening hours vary from country to country; the following is an overview.

Banks & Government Offices Open Monday to Friday, from around 9am to about 5pm (most close for an hour for lunch).

Restaurants Open early morning to late at night; only expensive restaurants have separate lunch and dinner opening times.

Bar & Nightclubs Closing times depend on local licensing laws, but tend to be earlier than in Western countries.

Shops These often double as the proprietor's home, so they open early and stay open late into the night, seven days a week.

Arriving in Southeast Asia

Changi International Airport (Singapore) Rail (45 minutes), bus (one hour) and taxis (one hour) go to the centre.

Kuala Lumpur International Airport (Kuala Lumpur, Malaysia) Take the KLIA Ekspres rail (30 minutes) to the centre.

Soekarno-Hatta International Airport (Jakarta, Indonesia) Taxis and buses (one hour) run to the centre.

Suvarnabhumi International Airport (Bangkok, Thailand) Taxis (one hour), bus (one hour) and rail (30 minutes) run to the centre.

Getting Around

Transport around Southeast Asia is frequent and inexpensive but not always fast. Private operators supplement government-run airlines, rail services and bus networks, often offering more comfort for a higher fare.

Air Budget airlines and national carriers offer flights all over the region, with competition keeping fares low.

Bus Buses go everywhere, at almost any time of day or night; fares depend on the level of comfort, but are rarely expensive.

Boat Ferries of all shapes and sizes connect islands and towns along the region's major rivers and seaboards.

Car & Motorcycle Useful for local exploring, but road conditions deter many from self-driving for longer trips.

Train Thailand, Malaysia, Myanmar, Laos, Cambodia and Indonesia have small but functional rail networks.

For much more on **getting around**, see p951

First Time Southeast Asia

For more information, see Survival Guide (p939)

Checklist

→ Make sure your passport is valid for at least six months past your arrival date.

→ Check if you need any visas before arrival.

→ Organise travel insurance and an international driving permit.

→ Visit a doctor to get any recommended vaccinations.

→ Inform your bank and credit-card provider of your travel plans.

→ Check your mobile phone is set up for international roaming.

What to Pack

→ A week's worth of lightweight clothes

→ Rain gear (jacket, breathable poncho, dry pack for electronics)

→ Comfortable sandals and walking shoes

→ Earplugs

→ Medicine/first-aid kit

→ USB drive for storing digital copies of documents and photos

→ GSM mobile phone

→ Refillable water bottle

→ Sunscreen and deodorant

Top Tips for Your Trip

→ Learn the scams (p947): phony guides, dodgy transport, touts.

→ Roads are crazy; drive defensively and cross the road even more carefully.

→ Most supplies (mosquito repellent, umbrella) can be bought locally.

→ Take your cue from the locals when it comes to appropriate dress.

→ Take digital pictures of important documents and cards in case of theft or loss.

→ Tell your bank where you are travelling, and keep their phone number handy in case they block your card.

→ Know your passwords! Many websites run security measures when accessed from a new location.

→ Keep your passport and other valuables in a hidden waist pouch or similar beneath your clothing.

→ Watch your bags while out and about; grab and run is a common form of theft.

→ Pay for accommodation first thing in the morning, or the night before if leaving early.

What to Wear

In general, lightweight, loose-fitting clothes are the most comfortable option. Swimwear is pretty much essential, but only appropriate for the beach. Shorts are ideal for the climate, but may be frowned on in rural areas; loose-fitting long cotton trousers work everywhere.

Bring comfortable thongs (flip-flops) or sandals – they're easy to slip on and kick off when entering homes, hostels and religious buildings – along with comfortable walking shoes (sneakers are generally fine) for hikes and motorcycle rides.

Wear clothes that cover down to your elbows and knees for visits to temples, mosques and rural villages. A sarong can be purchased locally and is handy for quick cover-ups. Bring a jacket or fleece for cool temperatures in the mountains and on heavily air-conditioned buses.

Bargaining

Outside of shops with marked prices, haggling is the norm in most Southeast Asian countries. Remember that it is an art, not a battle of wills, and the trick is to find a price that makes everyone happy. Avoid letting anger or frustration enter into the bargaining process. Typically, the vendor starts high, the buyer starts low, and eventually you'll reach a price that adds up for both parties.

Tipping

Hotels Not expected, but a small tip for carrying bags is appreciated.

Restaurants Not essential but a tip of around 10% will help top up low wages for servers.

Chartered Transport Prices are usually agreed through haggling, but a tip for good service will always be appreciated.

Guides If you hire guides, tip a little extra at the end for good service; 10% is a good start.

Eating

Rice is the foundation of Southeast Asian cooking, whether fragrant or sticky, molded into noodles or steamed into wraps for spring rolls. Add onto this base rich herbs and spices – lemongrass, lime leaves, galangal and the like – and exotic cooking techniques such as steaming in banana, pandanus and bamboo leaves, and you have the makings of half a dozen of the world's greatest cuisines, all waiting to be sampled as you travel around the region.

Hawkers in Hoi An (p874), Vietnam

Etiquette

Modesty Though fashions are changing in urban centres, modesty is still important in traditional areas, especially in Muslim-dominated countries. Avoid baring too much skin in general – avoid topless sunbathing and cover up when visiting religious buildings.

Taboos Politics and religion are often sensitive topics. Always treat both with deference and avoid being critical. Many Southeast Asian cultures are superstitious; it is wise to learn about these beliefs and act accordingly. Muslims don't drink alcohol or eat pork. Women shouldn't touch Buddhist monks or their belongings.

Save Face Southeast Asians, especially in Buddhist cultures, place a high value on harmonious social interactions. Don't get visibly angry, raise your voice or get into an argument – it will cause you and the other person embarrassment. When in doubt, smile.

Shoes Take them off when entering private homes, religious buildings and certain businesses. If there's a pile of shoes at the door, be sure to follow suit.

Money

Each country has its own currency. Cash is king, but ATMs are widespread and credit cards are increasingly accepted in cities in Thailand, Malaysia and Indonesia.

For more information see p946 and each country's Directory A-Z section.

If You Like...

Fabulous Food

Bangkok (Thailand) Food, glorious food! Anytime is dinner time in this non-stop grazing city. (p675)

Hanoi (Vietnam) Be an urban forager among Hanoi's street-food stalls. (p833)

Luang Prabang (Laos) Cafes and bakeries with a French flair preserve a delicious colonial connection. (p341)

Chiang Mai (Thailand) Don't just feast, learn to cook every delicious mouthful in Thailand's northern capital. (p705)

Singapore Five-star feasting at one end of the spectrum; bargain, Michelin-starred hawker food at the other. (p640)

Penang (Malaysia) This magical Malay melting pot offers an edible journey through India, China and the Malay Straits. (p413)

Phnom Penh (Cambodia) Marketplace feasts and a string of training restaurants where eating fab food helps Cambodia's most disadvantaged. (p79)

Bali (Indonesia) Enjoy some of Asia's most affordable and inventive cuisine at Kerobokan or Seminyak, or out on the Jimbaran sands. (p207)

Temples, Tombs & Towers

Temples of Angkor (Cambodia) The temple complex by which all others are judged, built by the Khmer god-kings in an incredible array of styles. (p102)

Bagan (Myanmar) The warrior hordes of Kublai Khan hardly made a dent in the architectural heritage of this stupa-studded plain. (p528)

Borobudur (Indonesia) A stunning Buddhist vision of heaven, ringed by mist and mountains. (p190)

Wat Phra Kaew (Thailand) Bangkok's dazzling royal temple is a mosaic-covered marvel, home to the revered Emerald Buddha. (p660)

Shwedagon Paya (Myanmar) A constant tide of humanity floats around this hilltop stupa that rises like a golden torch above Yangon. (p486)

Wat Xieng Thong (Laos) The jewel in the crown of temple-studded Luang Prabang, with its eaves sweeping majestically to the ground. (p336)

Hue (Vietnam) Emperors left their imperial mark here, from palaces and pagodas to the grand tombs of Tu Duc and Minh Mang. (p861)

George Town (Malaysia) The old streets of colonial George Town are studded with jewel-box Taoist temples and Hokkien clanhouses. (p410)

Beautiful Beaches

Phu Quoc Island (Vietnam) Vietnam's poster island, ringed by picture-perfect white crescents and sandy bays sheltered by rocky headlands. (p907)

Railay (Thailand) Rock-climbers gravitate to the karst cliffs, but the sands between the outcrops are snippets of paradise. (p777)

Bohol (Philippines) Natural and cultural wonders onshore, and a haven for sand and scuba addicts. (p596)

Pulau Tioman (Malaysia) Hollywood's stand-in for Bali Ha'i is castaway perfection, with added dive appeal. (p423)

Ko Pha-Ngan (Thailand) This backpacker legend rages during Full Moon parties, but its sun-kissed coves doze in between. (p751)

Lombok (Indonesia) The *other* Kuta, with a string of perfect sands, and the iconic Gili Islands just offshore. (p231)

Koh Rong (Cambodia) Good times rule at Cambodia's new favourite party islands, but you'll still find serene stretches of sand. (p128)

Top: Statue in Wat Phra Kaew (p660), Thailand
Bottom: Boat trip in Lombok (p231), Indonesia

Mui Ne (Vietnam) Squeaky sands, towering dunes and kitesurfing galore. (p882)

Spectacular Treks

Gunung Bromo (Indonesia) A night-time start is essential to reach this volcanic moonscape summit in time for sunrise views. (p197)

Mt Kinabalu (Malaysia) Borneo's highest mountain is conquered via a two-day march into the sky. (p443)

Sapa (Vietnam) Dirt paths wind through verdant rice terraces tended by ethnic minorities in this toothy mountainous region. (p847)

Batad (Philippines) Ancient hand-hewn rice terraces are carved into jagged mountains. (p576)

Khao Yai National Park (Thailand) Close to Bangkok but still jungle wild; home to elephants, monkeys and myriad bird species. (p730)

Kalaw (Myanmar) Off-beat treks through forested hills and minority villages fringing lovely Inle Lake. (p510)

Nam Ha NPA (Laos) Eco-oriented treks through an old-growth forest and high-altitude hill-tribe villages. (p355)

Mondulkiri (Cambodia) Experience 'walking with the herd' at the Elephant Valley Project in Cambodia's wild east. (p144)

Nightlife

Bangkok (Thailand) Bangkok after hours is fast-paced, frenetic and almost out of control; you'll need stamina to make it through until morning! (p679)

Phnom Penh (Cambodia) Crawl the buzzing bar strips, then take your pick from party clubs or the genteel Foreign Correspondents' Club. (p83)

Ko Pha-Ngan (Thailand) Home of the very first Full Moon parties in Southeast Asia and the ultimate beach-bum island. (p755)

Nha Trang (Vietnam) Ever since the GI days, Nha Trang has been top spot on the map for beachside R&R. (p881)

Boracay (Philippines) The party spills onto the sand in this pocket-sized island paradise. (p586)

Kuala Lumpur (Malaysia) Drink beneath the bright lights of towering skyscrapers, or up on the rooftop for giddying views over downtown. (p395)

Bali (Indonesia) Quaff a sundowner on the sand from Kuta north to Canggu, then head out to heaving all-night clubs. (p201)

Singapore Sky-high drinks served at sky-high prices, but oh, what views. (p643)

Markets & Shopping

Bangkok (Thailand) From the 8000 stalls at Chatuchak Weekend Market to streets that are more market than pavement. (p680)

Singapore Shopping is a national pastime, with everything from gleaming modern tech malls to pungent wet and dry markets. (p650)

Chiang Mai (Thailand) Weekend 'Walking Streets' transform Thailand's northern capital into an open-air food and crafts extravaganza. (p706)

Bogyoke Aung San Market (Myanmar) Yangon's Britishera covered market sells everything from gilded marionettes

to Burmese sapphires and rubies. (p491)

Can Tho (Vietnam) Get up early and experience the Mekong Delta's famous floating markets. (p904)

Jonker Walk Night Market (Malaysia) Melaka's weekly night market attracts legions of trinket sellers, food hawkers and fortune tellers. (p404)

Russian Market (Cambodia) This energetic market is Phnom Penh's top shopping spot: if it's available in Cambodia, it will be somewhere here. (p85)

Cultural Encounters

Ubud (Indonesia) Ubud is the spiritual home of Balinese dance, one of Asia's most vivid and colourful dance forms. (p216)

George Town (Malaysia) Young artists are upgrading the blank canvas of the old town with bright and brilliant street art. (p410)

Maubisse (Timor-Leste) Expect many surprises on a visit to an *uma lulik* (traditional sacred house) in the highlands around Maubisse. (p810)

Luang Prabang (Laos) Visit the Living Land farm to learn how to plant and grow sticky rice, the ubiquitous national dish. (p340)

Singapore Southeast Asia's most modern metropolis displays the best of modern Southeast Asian art at the celebrated National Gallery Singapore. (p624)

Chiang Mai (Thailand) Join a meditation retreat or 'monk chat' at a temple, or learn *moo·ay tai* (Thai boxing) from a local master. (p701)

Siem Reap (Cambodia) Roll up, roll up – catch a performance of Phare the Cambodia Circus, to see Asia's take on big-top showmanship. (p97)

Sulawesi (Indonesia) In Tana Toraja the dead live as house guests in one of Asia's most extraordinary funeral ceremonies. (p285)

Colonial-Era Architecture

Hanoi (Vietnam) The grand old dame of French Indochina is blessed with imposing civic buildings and leafy garden villas. (p823)

Yangon (Myanmar) Washed by centuries of monsoon rains, the former Rangoon has endless streets of British-era shophouses and civic buildings. (p486)

Luang Prabang (Laos) It may have been a mere Mekong outpost, but the French loved this town, leaving landmark buildings as their legacy. (p336)

George Town (Malaysia) This ethnic entrepôt has experienced a renaissance, with dilapidated mansions reborn as cafes, hotels and galleries. (p410)

Hoi An (Vietnam) The Portuguese, Spanish, Japanese, Chinese and French all imprinted their own design sensibilities in this stunning old port town. (p874)

Vigan (Philippines) A perfectly preserved Spanish colonial jewel under the shadow of a towering volcano. (p577)

Battambang (Cambodia) Ghosts of Indochine swirl through the sleepy streets lining the banks of the Sangker River. (p110)

Month by Month

TOP EVENTS

Buddhist New Year/ Water Festival, April

Deepavali, November

Rainforest World Music, July

Ork Phansaa, October

Festival of the Nine Emperor Gods, October

January

Peak tourist season, cool and dry weather in mainland Southeast Asia and the Philippines. The east coast of the Malay peninsula (Samui Archipelago, Pulau Perhentian) and Indonesia are wet thanks to the northeast monsoon; low season in Bali.

🎎 Ati-Atihan

The mother of all Filipino fiestas, Ati-Atihan celebrates Santo Niño (Infant Jesus) with colourful, Mardi Gras–like indigenous costumes and displays in Kalibo, on the island of Panay.

🎎 Bun Pha Wet

This Lao-Buddhist festival commemorates the story of the Buddha-to-be. It's considered an auspicious time to enter the monastery. Festivities are held in villages throughout Laos on varying dates.

🎎 Myanmar's Independence Day

The end of colonial rule in Burma is celebrated as a national holiday on 4 January.

🎎 Sultan of Brunei's Birthday

Colourful official ceremonies are held on 15 January to mark the birthday of Sultan Hassanal Bolkiah.

🎎 Thaipusam

Self-mortification, including the carrying of portable altars mounted on spikes, marks the Tamil festival of Thaipusam, held in the lunar month of Thai in Kuala Lumpur and Singapore. Sometimes falls in February.

February

Peak season continues in mainland Southeast Asia and beaches are packed. The east coast of the Malay peninsula starts to dry off as the rains move further east; still raining in Bali.

🎎 Chinese New Year

This lunar festival (sometimes occurring in January) is celebrated in Chinese-dominated towns. In Penang, it's a family affair and businesses close for one to two weeks. In Bangkok, Singapore, Phnom Penh and Kuching, there are dragon-dancing parades, food festivities and deafening fireworks.

🎎 Tet

Vietnam's lunar New Year (sometimes occurring in late January) is the country's biggest holiday, signalling the first day of spring. It involves family reunions, ancestor worship, gift exchanges, fireworks and lots of all-night luck-inducing racket. Travel is difficult; businesses close.

March

Mainland Southeast Asia is hot and dry; the beaches start to empty out. The winds kick up, ushering in kitesurfing season. In Bali, the northwest monsoon rains are subsiding to afternoon showers.

🎎 Easter Week

This Christian holiday (sometimes in April) is observed in the Philippines, Vietnam, Indonesia, Melaka and Timor-Leste. Holy Week (Semana Santa) in the Philippines starts on the Wednesday before Easter Sunday. Expect lots of Spanish-influenced rituals such as fasting, penance and church-going.

★★ Hindu New Year (Nyepi)

Bali's 'Day of Silence' is marked by fasting and meditation; businesses and beach access close. The next day is the Balinese New Year's Day, welcomed with night-time racket. Held 6 March 2019.

★★ Makha Bucha

One of three Buddhist holy days, Makha Bucha falls on the full moon of the third lunar month (usually in March, but sometimes in February) and commemorates Buddha preaching to 1250 enlightened monks. Celebrated at temples across Cambodia, Laos, Myanmar and Thailand.

April

The hottest time of year in mainland Southeast Asia makes inland sightseeing a chore. Cambodia, Laos, Myanmar and Thailand enjoy riotous traditional new year celebrations – make transport reservations in advance. Shoulder season in Bali.

★★ Buddhist New Year (Water Festival)

In mid-April, Buddhist countries celebrate their lunar new year with symbolic water-throwing and religious observances. Celebrated with particular aplomb in Chiang Mai, Thailand, and in larger cities in Cambodia, Laos and Myanmar.

★★ Vietnamese Liberation Day

The day US troops withdrew from Saigon (30 April) as North Vietnamese forces entered the city. Also called Reunification Day (and less complimentary names by overseas Vietnamese).

May

Still hot in mainland Southeast Asia but the end is in sight. May sees preparations for the upcoming rains and the start of rice-planting season. Northern Vietnam has spring-like weather and Bali is not yet crowded.

★★ Independence Day (Timor-Leste)

One of the planet's youngest nations, Timor-Leste celebrates Independence Day (20 May) with cultural events and sporting competitions.

★★ Ramadan

The Muslim fasting month is observed in Malaysia, Indonesia, Brunei and parts of southern Thailand in the ninth month of the Islamic calendar (May to early June in 2019). Muslims abstain from food, drink, cigarettes and sex between sunrise and sunset. Idul Fitri marks the end of Ramadan.

★★ Rocket Festival

Villagers fire off bamboo rockets (bang fai) to provoke rainfall for a bountiful rice harvest. Mainly celebrated in northeast Thailand and Laos; dates vary from village to village.

★★ Royal Ploughing Ceremonies

In Thailand and Cambodia, this royal ceremony employs astrology and ancient Brahman rituals to kick off rice-planting season, blending Hindu and Buddhist traditions.

★★ Visakha Bucha

This Buddhist holy day, the 15th day of the waxing moon in the sixth lunar month, commemorates Buddha's birth, enlightenment and parinibbana (death). Ceremonies, including the lighting of hundreds of candles, are held at temples throughout Cambodia, Laos, Myanmar and Thailand.

June

The southwest monsoon brings rain, usually an afternoon downpour, to most of mainland Southeast Asia and most of the Philippines. Summer holidays in Europe and China bring another tourist high season, especially in Bali.

★★ Gawai Dayak

The end of the rice-harvest season is celebrated on the first two days of June in Sarawak (Malaysian Borneo). City-dwelling Dayaks return to their longhouses to socialise, feast and down shots of tuak (rice wine).

★★ Hue Festival (Biennial)

Vietnam's biggest cultural event is held every two years (2020, 2022 etc) in the one-time royal capital. Art, theatre, music, circus and

Top: National Independence Day, Solo, Indonesia.
Bottom: Celebrating Buddhist New Year in Thailand

shippers offer candles and donations at temples, particularly in Thailand and Laos, and Ubon Ratchathani (Thailand) celebrates with a grand parade.

☆ Rainforest World Music

Sarawak (Malaysian Borneo) celebrates tribal music from around the world during this three-day music festival. Has also taken place in June and August.

August

The holiday season in Europe and China's summer holiday ensure crowds across the region. Expect afternoon showers in most of mainland Southeast Asia, with a few all-day soakers. However, weather in Indonesia (especially Bali) is just right.

🎏 HM the Queen's Birthday

Thailand celebrates its queen's birthday (and Mother's Day) on 12 August.

🎏 Independence Day (Indonesia)

The country celebrates liberation from the Dutch on 17 August with large parades in Jakarta.

September

The rains ratchet up a gear in mainland Southeast Asia – flooding and boat cancellations are common. Occasional typhoons sweep in across Vietnam and the Philippines, sometimes wreaking havoc. Shoulder season in Bali.

Islamic New Year

This lunar new year (known as Awal Muharram) in Indonesia and Malaysia is marked by fasting, self-reflection and commemoration of the martyrdom of Hussein ibn Ali. Held on 11 September 2018 and 1 September 2019.

Pchum Ben

In Cambodia, respects are paid to the dead through temple offerings. Many Khmers return to their home villages and try to visit seven temples in seven days. Most commonly held in September.

October

Mainland Southeast Asia prepares for the end of the rainy season and the end of Buddhist Lent. The northeast monsoon (affecting the east coast of the Malay peninsula and Indonesia) begins. Bali has occasional showers.

Festival of the Nine Emperor Gods

In Thailand, this Taoist event is called the Vegetarian Festival, and is marked by abstinence from meat and other purification rituals. The most extreme is Phuket's parade of entranced and pierced worshippers. Variations occur in Singapore, Malaysia and Myanmar. Sometimes held in September.

Ork Phansaa

The end of the Buddhist Lent occurs three lunar months after Khao Phansaa. Merit-makers present new robes to the monks. Mysteri-ous 'naga fireballs' are said to rise from the Mekong River, and riverside communities in Thailand and Laos celebrate with traditional boat races, particularly around Nong Khai.

November

The start of the month is shoulder season in mainland Southeast Asia, with cool, dry days and lush greenery all around. Northern altitudes see chilly nighttime temperatures. The east coast of the Malay peninsula and Indonesia are in the midst of the rainy season.

Bon Om Tuk

This Cambodian festival (sometimes held in October) celebrates Jayavarman VII's victory over the Chams in 1177 and the reversal of the Tonlé Sap river. Boat races stir local patriotism and crowds gather in Phnom Penh and Siem Reap.

Bun Pha That Luang

Laos pays tribute to its iconic stupa in Vientiane with a week-long festival coinciding with the full moon.

Deepavali

Hindus across the region celebrate the festival of lights to mark the triumph of good over evil. Tiny oil lamps are ceremoniously lit in Malaysia, Thailand and Bali, and Singapore's Little India hosts public festivities. Sometimes occurs in October.

Loi Krathong

During November's full moon, Thais launch illuminated banana-leaf boats in honour of the river goddess. In Chiang Mai, for the linked festival of Yi Peng, floating paper lanterns are released into the sky. A similar tradition is practised in Myanmar during the fire-balloon competitions in Taunggyi.

Prophet Mohammed's Birthday

The birthday of Islam's holy prophet is celebrated in the third month of the lunar-based Islamic calendar (21 November 2018 and 10 November 2019) with religious prayers and processions.

December

This is mainland Southeast Asia's busiest tourism season. The weather is fine; rain is tapering off on the Samui archipelago but still falling in Bali.

Christmas

Christmas is particularly important for Catholic communities in the Philippines, Timor-Leste, Indonesia and Vietnam. It's a serious celebration, with important religious services and ceremonies.

Lao National Day

On 2 December Laos celebrates the 1975 victory over the monarchy and the establishment of the Lao People's Democratic Republic.

Itineraries

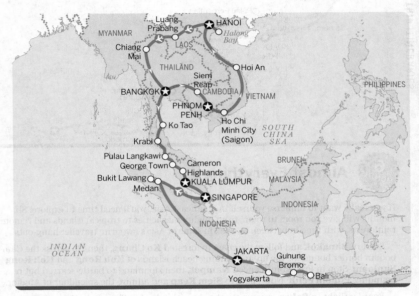

8 WEEKS The Best of Southeast Asia

This sampling platter for Southeast Asia hits all the highlights. Start in fun-filled **Bangkok**, then bus over to Cambodia to **Siem Reap** for Angkor's magnificent temples. Continue the party in **Phnom Penh**, then roll southeast to Vietnam's bustling **Ho Chi Minh City**. Head north to charming **Hoi An**, then hit the antique streets of **Hanoi** and the dramatic karst outcrops of **Halong Bay**.

Fly out of Vietnam to Laos' **Luang Prabang** for some laid-back river life, then fly on to chic **Chiang Mai** for fabulous food, terrific temples and jungle encounters. Loop back through Bangkok to **Ko Tao** and learn to dive before hitting the rock-climbing playground of **Krabi**. Cross the border from Ko Lipe to Malaysia's **Pulau Langkawi**, then tumble on to the foodie paradise of **George Town** (Penang) and overland to Malaysia's multi-ethnic capital **Kuala Lumpur**, with a stop in the lush **Cameron Highlands**.

Roll on to **Singapore**, for five-star food-court feasts, then fly to **Medan** in Sumatra and bus to **Bukit Lawang** to meet orangutans. Travel on by bus and boat to **Jakarta**, Indonesia's capital; soak up Java's renowned culture in **Yogyakarta**, then bus it to active volcano **Gunung Bromo**. Finally, leapfrog to **Bali** for sun, fun and surf.

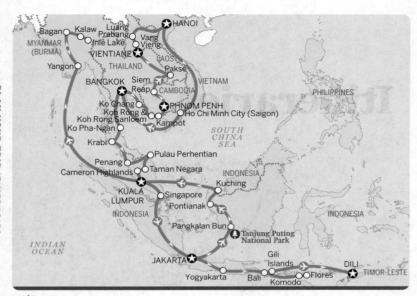

 6 MONTHS **Almost Everything**

If you really want to immerse yourself in Southeast Asia, you'll need time to explore. Six months will give you room to roam, from mighty megacities to tropical islands and remote rainforests, with time in between to relax in some of Asia's favourite traveller hang-outs.

Start in **Bangkok** and follow the coast to forested **Ko Chang**, then zip across the Cambodian border bound for the up-and-coming beach islands of **Koh Rong** and **Koh Rong Sanloem**. Stop in French-influenced **Kampot**, then zip inland to battle-scarred but rebounding **Phnom Penh**. Now bus it to **Siem Reap** and admire the splendour of Angkor.

Board a flight to **Pakse**, gateway to the river islands of Si Phan Don, then a bus to gentle **Vientiane** and on via **Vang Vieng** to **Luang Prabang**. Trundle to Nong Khiaw for tribal trekking and follow the rugged revolutionaries' trail to **Hanoi**.

Roll south through Vietnam, sampling history, culture and beaches, then fly from **Ho Chi Minh City** back to temple-studded **Bangkok**. Now start your journey south along the Malay peninsula, snorkelling or diving around **Ko Pha-Ngan** and climbing at **Krabi**.

Slip over to Malaysia for the street eats of **Penang** and teeming coral reefs at **Pulau Perhentian**. Seek terrestrial wildlife inland at **Taman Negara**, and detour to the mistshrouded hills of the **Cameron Highlands** before taking in the bright lights of **Kuala Lumpur**. A swift train ride will drop you in bright and bustling **Singapore**.

Fly on to **Jakarta** and admire the cultural treasures of **Yogyakarta** and Unescolisted Borobudur. Bask on the beach in **Bali** or the **Gili Islands**, spot real-life dragons on **Komodo** and escape the crowds in **Flores**, or in **Dili** in little-visited Timor-Leste.

Alternatively fly from Jakarta to **Pangkalan Bun** to spot orangutans at **Tanjung Puting National Park**, then fly from Banjarmasin to **Pontianak** and bus to the border to reach Malaysia's **Kuching**, a gateway to more nature and former headhunting cultures.

Take a connecting flight onwards to **Yangon** and the beautiful Buddhist temples of **Bagan**. Take a trek to **Kalaw** or relax by the placid waters of **Inle Lake**. Finish up back in Bangkok for some last-minute souvenir shopping before flying home.

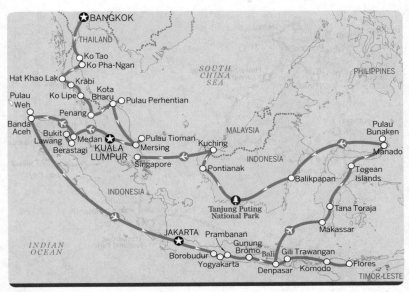

 Islands, Beaches Jungles

Become a beach connoisseur by splashing along the coastline of Thailand, Malaysia and Indonesia, with some cultural and wildlife detours to keep things interesting.

Start in **Bangkok** and make a beeline for the islands in the Gulf of Thailand: dive-crazy **Ko Tao** and hippy-trippy **Ko Pha-Ngan**. Get certified on Tao, then head to the Andaman coast. **Hat Khao Lak** is the base for dive trips to the world-class Surin and Similan islands. Skip down to adrenaline-charged **Krabi** for rock climbing and cave exploring, then island hop to beach-bum-vibed **Ko Lipe**. Cross the border at Pulau Langkawi and bus south to graze at the famous hawker centres of **Penang**.

From Penang, take a bus to **Kota Bharu**, jumping-off point for the fabulous dive islands of **Pulau Perhentian**. Head south to **Mersing**, the mainland port for sleepy, beachy **Pulau Tioman**, then head to **Kuala Lumpur** to pick up a flight to Indonesia.

From Indonesia's tip in **Medan**, visit the orangutan reserve of **Bukit Lawang** and hike up a volcano in Berastagi. From Medan fly to less-visited **Banda Aceh** and dive offshore near **Pulau Weh**.

Say goodbye to Sumatra and buzz over to Java, touching down in **Jakarta**, Indonesia's intense capital. Explore **Yogyakarta** and take a day-trip to the giant Buddhist stupa of **Borobudur** and the ancient Hindu temple of **Prambanan**. Continue eastwards to the volcano **Gunung Bromo** for a sunrise spectacle over a lunar landscape.

Leapfrog to **Denpasar** to nuzzle the sandy beaches of the Bukit Peninsula or get cultured in Ubud. Party in **Gili Trawangan**, spot dragons on **Komodo** and go rustic on the beaches of **Flores**. You may need to extend your visa in Denpasar before flying to **Makassar**. Pay your respects in **Tana Toraja**, famed for its surreal funeral rites travel to the remote and pristine **Togean Islands** and **Pulau Bunaken**; it's well worth the trip.

To close the loop, fly from **Manado** to **Balikpapan** on Kalimantan and head overland to reach the orangutan reserve at **Tanjung Puting National Park**. Roll on to Pontianak and cross the border to reach **Kuching** in Sarawak, Malaysia, for one last flight to finish up in calm and comfortable **Singapore**.

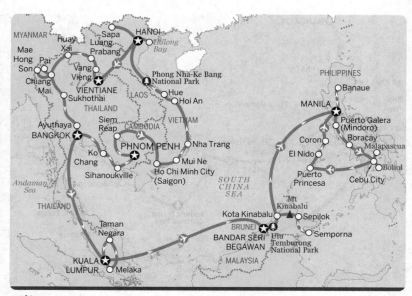

Mainland to Borneo the Philippines

An adventurous trip from mainland to islands, climbing to the heavens and diving the depths. Kick off in **Bangkok** and follow the overland trail through **Ko Chang** to **Sihanoukville** for detours to beach islands offshore. Roll on to shabby-chic **Phnom Penh**, and take the river boat to **Siem Reap** to gaze at the architectural wonder of Angkor Wat.

Fly on to full-throttle **Ho Chi Minh City**, and dial down the pace at the beaches of **Mui Ne** and **Nha Trang**. Drift north to the antique city of **Hoi An**, the imperial capital of **Hue** and the extensive caves of **Phong Nha-Ke Bang National Park**. Rest in mature capital **Hanoi**, and make detours to karst-filled **Halong Bay** and ethnic highland gateway **Sapa**.

Fly on from Hanoi to **Vientiane** (Laos), bus to **Vang Vieng** and on to **Luang Prabang**, a temple-studded World Heritage town. Ride the Mekong River to the Laos/Thailand border at **Huay Xai** and enter the fabled Golden Triangle.

Onwards to **Chiang Mai**; take in the temples then make detours to the mountains of **Pai** or **Mae Hong Son** for views and cultural encounters. Tumble south through the ancient capitals at **Sukhothai** and **Ayuthaya** before returning to **Bangkok**. Take a budget flight or bus south to **Kuala Lumpur**. Explore colonial **Melaka** and loop back to KL via the steamy rainforests of **Taman Negara**. Fly to Brunei's unassuming capital, **Bandar Seri Begawan (BSB)**, gateway to wildlife-rich **Ulu Temburong National Park**.

Cross the border into Malaysian Borneo by bus, bound for **Kota Kinabalu**, and ascend Mt Kinabalu, Borneo's highest peak. Detour out to the orangutan sanctuary at **Sepilok**, and scuba dive around **Semporna**, then return to Kota Kinabalu for a flight to the Philippines. After landing in fast-paced **Manila**, bus it to the spectacular Ifugao rice terraces near **Banaue** then return to Manila and hit up party isle **Boracay** via dive-tastic **Puerto Galera**. Spend a few days unwinding, then fly or bus to **Cebu City**, the Philippines' second city.

Cebu is an easy base for detours to dive at **Malapascua** and hill-hike on **Bohol**. Fly on from Cebu to **Puerto Princesa** on Palawan and drift north to **El Nido** via lonely beaches and pristine jungles. Take the all-day boat to wreck-diving playground **Coron** before flying back to Manila.

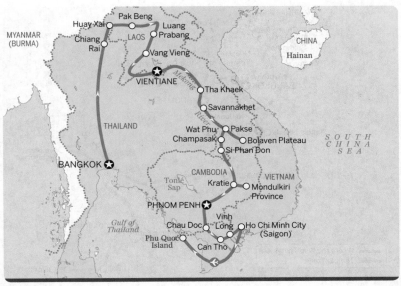

Mekong Meander

4 WEEKS

This trip follows Southeast Asia's signature river downstream from northern Laos all the way to Vietnam's Mekong Delta, offering a mesmerising window onto ever-changing landscapes and cultures.

From the bustling international gateway of **Bangkok**, make a beeline for **Chiang Rai**, near the Golden Triangle, where the borders of Laos, Myanmar and Thailand converge. Cross over into laid-back Laos at **Huay Xai** and step back in time. Take a slow boat down the Mekong to **Luang Prabang**, stopping overnight in **Pak Beng**. Soak up the magic before leaving the river for some relaxation in **Vang Vieng**.

Continue to **Vientiane** and reunite with the mighty waterway. The Lao capital has some great cafes, restaurants and even a sprinkling of nightlife (the last you'll encounter for a while after leaving). Board a bus and follow the river southeast, stopping off in **Tha Khaek** and **Savannakhet** before arriving in **Pakse**, jumping-off point for the imposing Khmer sanctuary of **Wat Phu Champasak**. Detour to the waterfalls and villages of the **Bolaven Plateau** then drift south to the laid-back islands of **Si Phan Don**.

Cross into Cambodia. If you missed the Irrawaddy dolphins near Si Phan Don, you'll get a second chance to spot them further south in the laid-back riverside town of **Kratie**. From Kratie, consider a visit to the mountains of **Mondulkiri province**, home to elephants, hill tribes and untamed jungles.

After weeks in rural provinces, it's back to big-city living in **Phnom Penh**, where the Mekong merges with another vital regional waterway, the Tonlé Sap, a riverine link to Siem Reap and the majestic temples of Angkor. See the waters turn gold on a sunset cruise and hit the bars for a well-deserved night on the town.

Suitably recharged, board a fast boat downstream to **Chau Doc** (Vietnam), gateway to the Mekong Delta. Continue to **Can Tho**, commercial heart of the Delta, then hotfoot it to **Ho Chi Minh City** for food and fun. Delve deeper into the Delta with a homestay around **Vinh Long**, or make for the tropical retreat of **Phu Quoc Island**, a well-earned reward. If you still have time and stamina, the rest of Vietnam beckons.

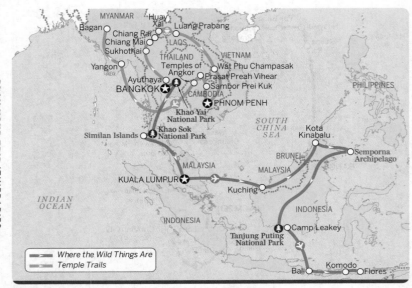

Where the Wild Things Are
Temple Trails

6 WEEKS Where the Wild Things Are

Southeast Asia is home to a magical menagerie of signature wildlife: tigers, elephants, whale sharks, orangutans and the Komodo dragon.

Start in **Bangkok**, and roam east to explore **Khao Yai National Park**, home to wild elephants and Asian black bears. Follow the peninsula south to **Khao Sok National Park** to see gibbons and macaques, then explore the underwater wonderland of the **Similan Islands**.

Continue to **Kuala Lumpur** to board a flight to **Kuching** in Borneo. See rare proboscis monkeys in Bako National Park and gentle orangutans in Semenggoh Wildlife Centre. Cross over to **Kota Kinabalu**, Sabah, to explore the Sungai Kinabatangan and perhaps see rare pygmy elephants. Wind down on the beaches and reefs of the **Semporna Archipelago**.

Head south into Kalimantan (Indonesia) and explore the jungle waterways of **Tanjung Puting National Park**. Stay overnight in a *klotok* riverboat and visit the orangutan research station at **Camp Leakey**. Fly on to **Bali** then head east to the rocky outcrops of **Komodo** and **Flores**, home to the Komodo dragon.

6 WEEKS Temple Trails

Southeast Asia sets the bar high when it comes to tremendous temples for travellers to explore.

Start out in **Bangkok**, home to iconic Wat Pho, Wat Phra Kaew and Wat Arun, before heading north to the stupa-studded former capital **Ayuthaya** and the ancient Khmer-era capital of **Sukhothai**.

See gems of the northern Lanna temple style in **Chiang Mai**, then continue through **Chiang Rai** to cross the Mekong River border at **Huay Xai**. Cruise on to **Luang Prabang**, Laos' gilded city of step-roofed temples and saffron-robed monks. Travel on to Laos' deep south to see the Khmer mountain temple of **Wat Phu Champasak**.

Continue into Cambodia, pass through **Phnom Penh** to the pre-Angkorian temples of **Sambor Prei Kuk**, and make an adventurous diversion north to the mountain temple of **Prasat Preah Vihear** before hitting the big league at the **temples of Angkor**.

Fly onwards from Siem Reap to **Yangon**, home to the shimmering Shwedagon Paya, then finish up the temple trail at **Bagan**, where a veritable garden of stupas stretches to the horizon.

Top: Bagan (p528), Myanmar

Bottom: Phong Nha cave (p857), Phong Nha-Ke Bang National Park, Vietnam,

Off the Beaten Track: Southeast Asia

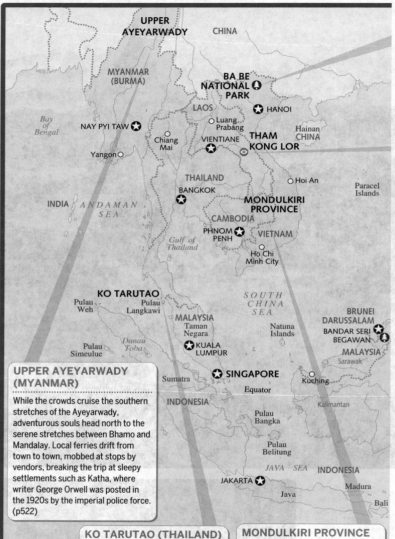

UPPER AYEYARWADY (MYANMAR)

While the crowds cruise the southern stretches of the Ayeyarwady, adventurous souls head north to the serene stretches between Bhamo and Mandalay. Local ferries drift from town to town, mobbed at stops by vendors, breaking the trip at sleepy settlements such as Katha, where writer George Orwell was posted in the 1920s by the imperial police force. (p522)

KO TARUTAO (THAILAND)

The island heart of a peaceful marine national park, Tarutao is so far south it's practically in Malaysia. But with gorgeous reefs and beaches, inexpensive national park lodgings and low-key backpacker bungalows, it's a top castaway contender. (p783)

MONDULKIRI PROVINCE (CAMBODIA)

Cambodia's up-and-coming adventure centre, Mondulkiri offers walking with a herd of elephants, ziplining over a waterfall, quad-biking, and authentic encounters with indigenous Bunong people. (p143)

0 500 km
0 250 miles

BA BE NATIONAL PARK (VIETNAM)

A stunning landscape of limestone mountains, sloping valleys, mist-shrouded lakes and evergreen forests provides a full dose of nature exploration. For a cultural hook, ethnic minorities host rustic homestays. (p845)

Tropic of Cancer

THAM KONG LOR (LAOS)

A watery underworld awaits at this 7.5km-long cave explored by longtail boat. Daylight recedes as you putter deep into the darkness and bulbous-shaped calcified sculptures decorate the vaulted ceiling. (p359)

SIARGAO (PHILIPPINES)

Famous for its surf breaks, this Catholic island in northern Mindanao is blessed with pretty coves, sand-dusted beaches and laid-back villages. Nearby Camiguin has hikes and off-road motorcycling on the slopes of four volcanoes, and reef dives offshore. (p599)

ULU TEMBURONG NATIONAL PARK (BRUNEI DARUSSALAM)

This pristine tract of primary rainforest, reachable only by boat, is one of the few remaining expanses of the truly wild jungle that once covered all of Borneo. (p67)

O Banaue
Luzon
PHILIPPINE SEA
★ MANILA
Catanduanes
PHILIPPINES
Mindoro
Samar
Panay
Cebu
Bohol
SIARGAO
Palawan
SULU SEA
Mindanao
PACIFIC OCEAN
Mt Kinabalu (4095m)
Jolo
Sabah
Tawi-Tawi
Talaud
ULU TEMBURONG NATIONAL PARK
Sangir Islands
Morotai
CELEBES SEA
Waigeo
TOGEAN ISLANDS
Sula Islands
Misool
Sulawesi
SERAM SEA
Seram
Tana Toraja
INDONESIA
Buru
Puncak Jaya (5030m)
Papua
Butung (Buton)
Kai Islands
Aru Islands
PAPUA NEW GUINEA
Selayar
BANDA SEA
Bali Sea
FLORES SEA
ATAÚRO ISLAND
Wetar
Yos Sudarso
Lombok
Flores
★ DILI
Babar Islands
Tanimbar Islands
TIMOR-LESTE
ARAFURA SEA

TOGEAN ISLANDS (INDONESIA)

The blissful Togean Islands are an unadulterated vision of the tropics. Wander blinding white-sand beaches fringed by coconut palms and enjoy world-class snorkelling and diving on majestic coral reefs. (p292)

TIMOR SEA

ATAÚRO ISLAND (TIMOR-LESTE)

If you've made it all the way to Timor-Leste, take one more hop over to this blissfully undeveloped isle off Dili for excellent snorkelling, diving, hiking and hammock-swinging. (p806)

AUSTRALIA

Plan Your Trip
Big Adventures, Small Budget

You don't need to be a high-roller to get the best from Southeast Asia – in fact you can live like a cheapskate and still bask on beautiful beaches, visit magnificent temples and delve into tropical jungles. But you do need to watch your spending and plan wisely.

Planning & Costs

Planning Timeline

12 months before Calculate a trip budget and start saving.

6 months Pick which countries to visit, when and for how long. Research long-haul flights.

8 to 6 weeks Make passport and visa arrangements as needed.

4 weeks Get vaccinations and travel insurance.

2 weeks Reserve high-season transport and accommodation for popular destinations and activities.

1 week Book accommodation for arrival city; start packing.

Average Costs

Bottle of beer US$1–3

Long-distance bus ticket US$10–30

Food-stall meal US$2–5

Guesthouse room US$5–20

Internet access per hour Free, or up to US$5

Domestic flight US$50–150

Budget Guide

It's no struggle to get by in Southeast Asia on a daily budget of about US$25 to US$50 a day. This covers the basics: food, shelter, local transport and the odd cold beer. Costs vary by country, the popularity of the destination and the time of year.

Factor any long-distance travel into your budget, and funds special activities, such as diving, wildlife tours or rock-climbing. Then add a buffer for unexpected expenses, such as increased costs during holiday periods.

Accommodation costs will be a big portion of your budget; luckily, cheap digs abound, and the more creature comforts (air-con, hot water, en suite) you can forsake, the more you'll save.

Public transport within each country is affordable, particularly if you travel mainly by boat and bus. Air travel, rail travel, chartering boats and using taxis will ramp up your costs.

Getting around some islands can be expensive because of price-fixing or lack of competition. Renting a motorcycle can be an affordable alternative to local transport. Even cheaper is bicycle hire, which is a great way to explore.

Tips by Destination

We posed the following question to our writers: What's the cheapest place for the best time in each country?

Brunei Darussalam Tiny, oil-rich Brunei can be a great budget destination if you arrive by bus from Malaysian Borneo. Stay in a hostel, dine in the open-air markets and tour the free cultural sights.

Cambodia You can have a great time living it up on the cheap on the islands of Koh Rong and Koh Rong Sanloem, Cambodia's new party beaches, where you can score dorm beds for around US$5.

Indonesia Do Bali on the cheap by opting for an Ulu Watu homestay. Enjoy a surfer-chic scene and epic views with enough spare cash to wash it all down with several Bintangs.

Laos Si Phan Don (Four Thousand Islands) is quintessential lotus-eating country: come for hammock-hanging, tubing down the river, river-dolphin-spotting, laid-back island life and the fun traveller scene.

Malaysia Pulau Perhentian is an awesome deal and has some of the cheapest diving in Asia, comparable to Ko Tao. Cherating is another budget-friendly beach.

Myanmar Although increasingly on the map, Hsipaw is still a charming traveller centre with plenty of budget food, activities and digs. Consider Kalaw or Kyaingtong for inexpensive tribal treks.

Philippines North Luzon and Palawan are inexpensive, off-the-beaten-track options. Sleep amid Batad's rice terraces or camp on the beach in Coron or El Nido.

Singapore It's tricky be a high-flyer in Singapore on a shoestring, but the city's food centres offer gourmet eating for bargain prices.

Thailand Ko Tao is still a cheap place for an Open Water diving certificate. Heading south, eastern Ko Pha Ngan remains a bargain, and Railay near Krabi offers plenty of cheap digs for climbers.

Timor-Leste Catch a *microlet* (local bus) heading to Liquiçá (US$1) and hop off at the rocky point near the Pope's monument. Welcome to Dili Rock West, a great spot for free snorkelling with amazing coral and fish.

Vietnam With some of the cheapest beer in the region (from US$0.30 a glass), Vietnam might win the budget showdown. Nha Trang is the backpackers' beach, with a rocking nightlife and affordable lodging.

Sticking to a Budget

➡ Eat like a local at street stalls and day or night markets.

➡ Opt for dorm rooms or share a room with a friend.

➡ Stay in fan (non-air-con) rooms with shared bathrooms.

➡ Travel by road or boat instead of flying.

➡ Go snorkelling instead of diving.

➡ Hire a bicycle instead of a motorbike.

➡ Choose which national parks to visit based on entry fees.

➡ Know the price of local transport and bargain accordingly.

➡ Leave souvenir shopping to the end of your trip to avoid blowing your budget.

➡ Track your daily expenses so you know your average daily costs.

Accommodation Tips

Accommodation will be one of your biggest expenses. Here are some tips for saving money:

➡ If the price is too high, ask if they have a cheaper room.

➡ Enquire about discounts in the low season.

➡ Once you've paid for a room, there's no refund, so pay by the day.

➡ When making bookings, don't rely on agents, as they'll charge a commission.

➡ Consider overnight bus and boat journeys to save the cost of a night's accommodation.

PACKING FOR YOUR TRIP

Take as little as possible in your luggage: you're going to have to carry it everywhere. Pack your bag once and then repack it with a third less stuff. Aim to make your pack small enough to fit into the aircraft's overhead compartment, which represents the average size of most stowage areas on buses and trains. The smaller your pack the easier it will be to climb on and off public transport and to explore a new place on foot – and you'll look like less of a target for touts and hustlers.

Mt Kinabalu (p443), Malaysia

Plan Your Trip
Activities

Mountains soar, rivers rage, caverns burrow and volcanoes bubble, and offshore, coral reefs teem with astounding marine life – welcome to the adventure playground of Southeast Asia. The activities on offer here are limitless: trekking, cycling, climbing, caving, rafting, surfing, diving – you name it, and there are almost as many options for relaxing afterwards.

THOSAPON.S/SHUTTERSTOCK ©

Top Activities

Best Diving

Indonesia & the Philippines When it comes to reefs, wrecks and drop-offs, these archipelago nations are the undisputed dive capitals of Southeast Asia.

Best Hiking & Trekking

Malaysia Welcome to trekking central: ascend the lunar landscape of Mt Kinabalu, tramp through virgin rainforests or explore the lush green hummocks of the Cameron Highlands.

Best Surfing

Indonesia Barrel through the breaks of Java and Bali to Nusa Tenggara's big waves on Sumbawa and Sumba, or brave the lefts and rights of the Mentawai Islands off Sumatra.

Best Wildlife-Watching

Malaysia Borneo is not known as the Amazon of Asia for nothing: meet orangutans, proboscis monkeys and pygmy elephants in the national parks of Sabah and Sarawak.

Best Caving

Vietnam There's no better place to head underground than Phong Nha-Ke Bang National Park, home to the world's longest cave system.

Hiking & Trekking

Trekking in Southeast Asia covers a lot of ground, from tramps through monkey-filled rainforests to hikes to the bare rocky summits of smouldering volcanoes. However, for anything more ambitious than short walks on marked trails, a guide is essential. Guides will also keep you informed about local laws, regulations and etiquette relating to wildlife and the environment.

Trekking on elephant back is discouraged because of the serious harm that this can cause to the elephants, but a number of organisations in Thailand, Cambodia and Laos offer treks where you walk alongside elephants. However, some careful research is required, as standards of animal welfare vary, and maltreatment of elephants is not unheard of.

On any trek, be prepared for the conditions with appropriate clothing: long trousers, adequate hiking shoes and leech socks during and after the rainy season. Bring along wet-weather gear (for yourself and your pack) even if the skies are clear. Drink lots of water and pace yourself, as the humidity can make even minimal exercise feel demanding. Note that volcano summit treks typically start before dawn and can be quite chilly, so bring a warm layer.

When to Go

Rain, not temperature, is the primary consideration when planning your trip. The monsoon can make trails impassable, and mosquitoes and leeches flourish in the damp undergrowth. The best months for trekking in mainland Southeast Asia are immediately after the rainy season (November to February), when the forest is lush and flooding is not a concern – although frost is possible at higher elevations, such as Sapa. Things can get busy on popular routes during the peak tourist season from December to January. Avoid the rain-soaked months from September to October.

If you're island-bound, the April–June shoulder season offers dry – or at least drier – weather for trekking to Indonesia's volcanic summits. July and August are peak season in many parts of the region, and popular treks such as the Mt Bromo climb can get very busy. For leech-free trekking, avoid January and February, the wettest months of the northeast monsoon in most of Brunei, Indonesia, Malaysia and Timor-Leste.

Where to Go

Mt Kinabalu (Malaysia; p443) Scramble over granite moonscapes for the ultimate Bornean sunrise atop 4095m-high Mt Kinabalu.

Ifugao Rice Terraces (Philippines; p572) Hiking the exquisitely carved rice terraces around Banaue and Batad is one of Southeast Asia's most fascinating walks.

Baliem Valley (Indonesia; p301) The wild Baliem Valley in Papua draws acolytes from around the world for encounters with some of the world's most unique tribal cultures.

> ## RESPONSIBLE TREKKING
> ....
>
> Tourism can bring many benefits to highland communities: cross-cultural understanding, improved infrastructure, cheaper market goods, employment opportunities and tourist money supporting handicraft industries. Conversely, it can also bring increased litter, pollution, water shortages, erosion of walking trails, increased hunting to provide food and souvenirs for tourists, exploitation by the dominant community at the expense of tribal peoples and the abandonment of local customs and traditions.
>
> To visit tribal villages responsibly, travel in small groups and hire indigenous guides to ensure your money goes directly to local communities. A local guide will also greatly improve your access to highland villages, overcoming language barriers and explaining taboos and traditions that might cause misunderstandings between tourists and local people. Be sure to take out any rubbish that you bring with you, particularly plastic waste that won't biodegrade.

Sapa (Vietnam; p847) Sapa is Vietnam's trekking hub, with spectacular scenery, majestic mountains, impossibly green rice paddies and fascinating tribal villages.

Hsipaw (Myanmar; p526) The laid-back traveller hub of Hsipaw is ringed by timeless, friendly Shan, Palaung and Lisu villages, and the ruins of lost kingdoms.

Mt Ramelau (Timor-Leste; p811) Rise at dawn to scale Timor-Leste's highest peak – just in time to watch the sun rise over the glittering ocean.

Cycling

The bicycle is a staple form of transport for rural communities across the region, and visiting cyclists will get a warm reception from locals. Bikes are available for hire in tourist towns and at archaeological sites for local exploring, and dozens of operators offer cross-country trips, from leisurely hill-village tours to rugged downhill trails.

For hard-core cyclists, the mountains of northern Vietnam and northern Laos are the ultimate destination, but Chiang Mai in northern Thailand is another mountain-biking hub, and Borneo offers some spectacular trails. For a gentler trip, meandering between villages is always memorable, particularly in the Mekong Delta in Vietnam. A bike is a glorious way to explore historic sites such as Angkor, Bagan and Sukhothai. With all the boat crossings, island-hopping across Indonesia is an ambitious proposition, but many islands are well set up for local cycling, including Bali and Lombok or, for the more adventurous, Flores and Sulawesi.

Throughout the region, basic Chinese-made bicycles can be rented for US$1 to US$5 per day; good-quality imported mountain bikes cost US$10 to US$20. Repair shops are found almost everywhere. Bangkok-based Spice Roads (www.spiceroads.com) is the acknowledged expert for cycle tours across Southeast Asia, but there are good local operators in each country.

When to Go

Cycling in the monsoon is no fun, and highland roads and trails are prone to landslides during the rains, so plan your trip for the dry season. The ideal months to tour mainland Southeast Asia are November to February, when the temperatures are lower and breezes provide natural air-conditioning for sweating cyclists.

Where to Go

Temples of Angkor (Cambodia; p102) The temples can get very busy in peak season, so pedal past the crowds and follow local jungle trails.

Bagan (Myanmar; p528) Temples sprawl across the Ayeyarwady plain, and a bike will get you to unrestored ruins between the famous *zedis*.

Chiang Mai (Thailand; p697) The mountains that climb above Chiang Mai are criss-crossed by epic mountain-biking trails.

Luang Prabang (Laos; p336) Cycling is perfectly in tune with the languorous mood of this riverside retreat, providing easy access to the surrounding countryside and villages.

Mekong Delta (Vietnam; p903) The flatlands of the Mekong Delta region are ideal for long-distance rides, linking villages off the tourist trail.

Motorcycling

The motorcycle is the official vehicle of Southeast Asia, used for everything from transporting pigs to market to shifting three generations of the same family through rush-hour traffic. The mad melee of motorcycles can seem daunting at first, but in urban areas at least, traffic moves slowly, and it doesn't take long to adjust to local riding conditions.

The big bonus of being on two wheels is mobility. Motorcycles can traverse trails that even the hardiest 4WD can't follow, and if the road is washed away, boats are on hand to transport you and your bike to the next stretch of hardtop. Motorcycling will also bring you closer to the countryside, and to local people, than being tucked away inside a car or bus.

Motorcycles are widely available for rent in traveller centres, particularly in Vietnam, Cambodia, Laos and Thailand. Daily charges start at US$5 to US$10 for 100cc bikes and rise to US$15 to US$50 for 250cc dirt bikes or road bikes. One-way bike rentals are often available for an extra fee. Specialist motorcycle-touring companies can organise multiday trips into remote areas, using suitable trail bikes. Repair shops are everywhere, and scooters with automatic gears are widely available for novice riders, but caution is advised, as many tourists are injured in accidents each year.

Hire firms often rent out bikes without asking to see a license, although you might be asked to show one in Brunei, Malaysia or Thailand. The law, however, may disagree: it pays to make sure you are licensed to ride any vehicle you hire. You almost always need to leave a passport to hire a bike; the shop should keep this safe, but it can cause problems if you get injured in a remote place and need to be evacuated.

When to Go

The rainy season creates perilous motorcycling conditions and extends stopping distances when braking, so stick to the dry season if you're on two wheels. In rural parts of Thailand, Cambodia, Laos and Vietnam, leave the trip a little later into January to give the remote jungle trails time to dry out after the rain.

Where to Go

Sapa (Vietnam; p847) Rumble through glorious mountain scenery, river valleys and tribal villages around Sapa, Bac Ha and Dien Bien Phu.

Vang Vieng (Laos; p331) Meander between the karst outcrops that pepper the west bank of the Nam Song River on this scenically stunning motorcycle ride.

TOP VOLCANO TREKS

Forming part of the Pacific Ring of Fire, Indonesia and the Philippines are together home to more than 100 active volcanoes, many of which can be climbed all the way to the summit, on anything from short jaunts to multiday camping expeditions. Some volcanoes have been dormant for centuries, while others are active, so enquire with local authorities before setting out. Lava encounters are possible on several volcanoes, but erupting volcanoes should only be approached with local guides.

Gunung Bromo (Indonesia; p197) One of three volcanic cones (one active) that emerge from an other-worldly caldera. Highly recommended.

Gunung Merapi (Indonesia; p186) Close to Yogyakarta, mighty Merapi is the most active cone in Indonesia, so there's a chance of fireworks if your visit coincides with an eruption.

Mt Mayon (Philippines; p578) The country's most iconic and postcard-perfect volcano, the conical-shaped Mt Mayon (2462m) is also one of the Philippines' most active – seek local advice before approaching live flows.

Gunung Batur (Indonesia; p226) This Balinese volcano's other-worldly scenery almost makes you forget about the tourist hubbub at the bottom.

Mt Pinatubo (Philippines; p571) Hiking around the bizarre lahar formations and up to the serene crater lake of Mt Pinatubo (1450m) is an unmissable experience.

Mae Hong Son (Thailand; p719) The classic northern route is the Mae Hong Son loop, a 600km ride that begins in Chiang Mai and takes in Pai, Mae Hong Son and Mae Sariang.

Boat Trips, Kayaking & Rafting

With the mighty Mekong and Ayeyarwady rivers slicing through mainland Southeast Asia, and any number of jungle rivers cutting across Borneo and other islands, the region was made for boat travel. Many cities were built on canals, so boats are even an option for downtown travel.

The trips everyone thinks about are long-distance journeys along Southeast Asia's major arteries – the cruise along the Tonlé Sap from Phnom Penh to Siem Reap, riding the Ayeyarwady from Mandalay to Bagan, cross-border hops from Laos to Thailand and Cambodia to Vietnam. These multiday odysseys offer a fantastic vantage point for observing life on the riverbanks.

Then there are backwater trips to remote jungle reserves and minority villages in Cambodia, Borneo and across Indonesia. Indeed, it is possible to travel right across the Indonesian and Philippines archipelagos by local ferry or chartered outrigger boats. There are even boat trips along subterranean rivers, and out over sleepy lakes where even markets take place on the water.

Kayaking has seen an explosion in popularity in recent years. Krabi Province in Thailand is the spiritual home of sea

kayaking and most Halong Bay tours in Vietnam also now include kayaking through the karsts. River kayaking to tribal villages in Indonesia, Laos and Malaysia is growing in popularity, as are lake trips around Ba Be National Park in Vietnam and the flooded forests and floating villages of the Tonlé Sap in Cambodia.

Though white-water rafting here is not as dramatic as in mountain areas such as Nepal, things get a little more vigorous in the wet season. Go with the flow and try rafting on the Pai River in Thailand or the Chico or Cagayan Rivers in the Philippines.

Stand-up paddleboarding (SUP) is also growing in popularity around the region as an easy option for beginners to test themselves on calm seas or gentle rivers.

When to Go

Whether you're after a mellow boat cruise on the Mekong or a white-water rafting trip on a raging river, the best time to go is during the rainy season. Rivers are high, lakes are full and the landscape is lush and green. During the dry season, some trips stop completely as rivers are too shallow for boats.

Where to Go

Halong Bay (Vietnam; p841) Take an overnight cruise among the karsts and paddle into a hidden lagoon, or try stand-up paddleboarding.

Krabi Province (Thailand; p776) Sea kayaking in Southeast Asia began here amid the region's iconic karst islands.

Tham Kong Lor (Laos; p359) This river cave might feel like the River Styx, but offers one of

---

KNOW YOUR MONSOON

The two monsoon seasons are deciding factors in determining when and where to go for adventure. From June or July to September or October, the southwest monsoon brings rain to mainland Southeast Asia and the west coast of the Malay peninsula (Phuket and Langkawi), creating soggy conditions for trekking and sometimes poor visibility for diving.

As the rains slow, the dry and comparatively cool season from November to February is peak time for tourism and diving, but the mercury soars from March to June. This is the start of typhoon season in the Philippines and parts of Myanmar and Vietnam, which can be a risky time to be out on the water.

The northeast monsoon starts in September, bringing rain to the east coast of the Malay peninsula (Ko Samui, Pulau Perhentian), before migrating east through Indonesia, hitting Timor-Leste by December. Many head to the west coast of Malaysia or Thailand's Andaman Coast to escape the worst of the downpours.

Top: Diving a shipwreck off Coron Island (p608), Philippines

Bottom: Kayaking near Krabi (p776), Thailand

the most memorable underground boat rides on Earth.

Bhamo to Mandalay (Myanmar; p522) Cruise the mighty Ayeyarwady River from remote Bhamo to Mandalay, then continue downstream to Bagan.

Ulu Temburong National Park (Brunei; p67) Approach this impressive national park by longboat for wildlife encounters from the water.

Diving & Snorkelling

Considering that many of the islands here were created by coral reefs, it should be no surprise to learn that Southeast Asia is one of the world's top diving and snorkelling playgrounds. Inexpensive dive centres, offering everything from dive certification to Nitrox, are found pretty much anywhere the land touches the ocean.

Thailand, Malaysia, Indonesia and the Philippines top the list of dive destinations, with everything from sunken islands and epic wall drifts to wartime wrecks and underwater caves. Be aware that diving and snorkelling put unique pressures on the

marine environment: use reputable and environmentally conscious operators, and follow best practice to minimise your own effect on the undersea environment.

When to Go

Diving depends on visibility, which depends on calm waters and storm-free days. Most diving locations have subpar conditions during the rainy season; luckily the double monsoon means you can always find high visibility somewhere in the region; the Gulf of Thailand offers good conditions for most of the year.

Where to Go

Komodo National Park (Indonesia; p247) Besides dragons, this national park boasts some of Indonesia's best and most varied diving.

Coron (Philippines; p608) The Calamian archipelago is festooned with dive sites, but perhaps the highlight is roaming the WWII wrecks in the murky gloom off Coron island.

Similan Islands (Thailand; p767) Keep an eye out for whale sharks on a live-aboard diving adventure to this stunning marine national park.

RESPONSIBLE DIVING

The popularity of Southeast Asia's diving industry places immense pressure on fragile coral sites. To help preserve the ecology, adhere to these simple rules:

➡ Don't feed the fish or allow your dive operator to dispose of excess food in the water. The fish become dependent on this food source and don't tend to the algae on the coral, causing harm to the reef.

➡ Avoid touching or standing on living marine organisms or dragging equipment across reefs.

➡ Never use anchors on reefs, and take care not to ground boats on coral.

➡ Be conscious of your fins: the surge from fin strokes near reefs can damage delicate organisms. Take care not to kick up clouds of sand, which can smother organisms.

➡ Practise and maintain proper buoyancy control: major damage can be done by divers descending too fast and colliding with reefs.

➡ Take great care in underwater caves. Spend as little time within them as possible – your air bubbles may be caught within the roof and leave organisms high and dry. Take turns to inspect the interior of small caves.

➡ Resist the temptation to collect or buy corals or shells or to remove objects from marine archaeological sites (mainly shipwrecks).

➡ Ensure that you remove all your rubbish, and any litter you may find. Plastics are a serious threat to marine life.

➡ Minimise your disturbance of marine animals. Never ride on the backs of turtles, whale sharks or dolphins.

➡ Join a coral clean-up campaign, sponsored by a local dive shop.

PICK YOUR BEACH

BEACH AREA	JAN & FEB	MAR & APR	MAY & JUN	JUL–SEP	OCT–DEC
Ko Tao (p757) (Thailand)	dry, high season	dry, shoulder season	dry, shoulder season	dry, high season	rain, low season
Phuket (p49) (Thailand)	dry, high season	dry, shoulder season	start of rains, shoulder season	rain, low season	dry, shoulder season
Bali (p49) (Indonesia)	rain, low season	end of rains, shoulder season	dry, shoulder season	dry, high season	start of rains, shoulder season
Nha Trang (p880) (Vietnam)	dry, high season	dry, high season	dry, high season	dry, high season	rain, low season
Koh Rong (p128) (Cambodia)	dry, high season	dry, shoulder season	start of rains, shoulder season	rain, low season	rain, shoulder season
Boracay (p49) (Philippines)	dry, high season	dry, high season	dry, shoulder season	rain, low season	end of rains, shoulder season
Timor-Leste (p49)	rain, low season	dry, high season	dry, high season	dry, high season	dry, high season

Pulau Sipadan (Malaysia; p451) Malaysia's only oceanic island boasts sea turtles, sharks, and schooling barracuda; it's often voted the world's best dive site.

Ataúro Island (Timor-Leste; p806) Dazzling, pristine reefs fringe Timor-Leste's north coast, and arguably the best lie off Ataúro Island.

Best-Value Places to Learn to Dive

Ko Tao (Thailand; p757) New to diving? Check out Ko Tao, the cheapest and best place to learn the basics.

Gili Trawangan (Indonesia; p241) Among the best places to get certified worldwide; accessible reefs are just a 10-minute boat ride away.

Perhentian Islands (Malaysia; p428) Plentiful competition ensures rock-bottom rates at this popular traveller hang-out off Malaysia's northwest coast.

Moalboal (Philippines; p594) The original hub for Philippines diving is still one of the best places to learn.

Water Sports

Surfing and kitesurfing are big draws in Southeast Asia, aided by the ample monsoon winds. Indonesia is the region's surf-

ing capital, though the Philippines isn't too far behind, while Vietnam and Thailand have consistent winds for seasonal kitesurfing. Laos has carved itself a unique niche as a centre for tubing and kayaking. Be sure to go with a company that has a good safety record, and respect the water conditions during the monsoon and typhoon seasons.

When to Go

May to September brings prime swells to Indonesia's Lombok and Sumbawa, while Bali always has good surf somewhere year-round. In the Philippines, surf season coincides with the typhoons (August to November), creating challenging barrels for experienced surfers. For beginners, Phuket (Thailand) has swells from April to September, and Cherating (Malaysia) from November to March.

Kitesurfing is popular on Boracay (Philippines), the east and west coast of Thailand (Hua Hin and Phuket), in Mui Ne (Vietnam) and at Hu'u and Pantai Lakey on Sumbawa (Indonesia). These beaches tend to have a long windy season through most of the year.

Where to Go

Sumatra (Indonesia; p258) You'll be up against the best in the surf capital of Southeast Asia, but the Mentawai Islands are pure perfection.

Phuket (Thailand; p768) As one of Thailand's top beach destinations, Phuket offers surfing, kitesurfing and more.

Mui Ne (Vietnam; p882) Mui Ne Beach is fast becoming a windchasers' hot spot in Asia.

Siargao (Philippines; p599) Home to Cloud Nine, the name of this legendary right-hander says it all: it's one of Asia's top reef breaks.

Rock Climbing

Across Southeast Asia, karst cliffs and limestone outcrops have been hung with bolted climbing routes that now have a reputation as some of the world's top sport climbs. Thailand, Laos and Vietnam are the focus of the scene, but there are also bolted crags in Malaysia, Indonesia, the Philippines and Myanmar.

When to Go

Climbing in the wet season is not advisable as the rocky surfaces are slippery and potentially dangerous. Carry plenty of chalk for the hot months from April to June.

Where to Go

Railay (Thailand; p777) Scaling beachside outcrops above azure seas makes Railay the number-one climbing site in Thailand, particularly for big-wall enthusiasts.

Cat Ba Island (Vietnam; p842) Instruction for beginners and dedicated trips for experienced rock stars, set against the backdrop of Halong Bay.

Vang Vieng (Laos; p331) Another set of stunning limestone cliffs with more than 200 rock-climbing routes – many bolted for sport route fans.

Caving

The term 'outdoors' in Southeast Asia extends to several spectacular networks of cave systems, offering some of the world's best caving experiences. However, spelunking through underground rivers, squeezing through narrow cracks and dropping into bottomless chasms is a dry-season-only activity – the risk of sudden floods rules out the monsoon season.

When to Go

Some caves are open year-round, but deeper systems are best avoided during the rainy seasons because of the risk of flash flooding and the difficulty of approaching entry points on waterlogged trails.

Where to Go

Phong Nha-Ke Bang National Park (Vietnam; p856) Stupendous caving trips delve underground in this national park; most trips combine hiking, swimming and climbing.

Vieng Xai Caves (Laos; p353) A different take on the caving experience, exploring the underground base and wartime capital of the Pathet Lao communists, beneath stunning limestone rock formations.

Gunung Mulu National Park (Malaysia; p470) Some of the world's largest and most spectacular caves pockmark the outcrops in this Sarawak national park.

Sagada (Philippines; p574) Explore fascinating burial caves or slog through underground rivers on a thrilling cave-to-cave excursion.

ZIPLINING

Ziplining has taken off in a big way in Southeast Asia, with lines snaking through the canopy like spider silk in dozens of locations around Cambodia, Laos, Indonesia, Thailand and Vietnam. Zip between islands in Malaysia and Thailand, over waterfalls in Cambodia and Laos or into the mouths of monster caves in Vietnam.

The Gibbon Experience (p357) in Laos blazed an aerial trail: visitors glide through forest where the gibbons roam, and can stay overnight in a treehouse. Cambodia's Angkor Zipline (p91) adds in temple views, while Chiang Mai's **Flight of the Gibbon** (Map p698; ☎053 010660; www.treetopasia.com; 29/4-5 Th Kotchasan; day tours 4000B; ⊙9.30am-6.30pm) takes in hill-tribe encounters. Newcomer Mayura Zipline (p145) offers a memorable flight over the Bou Sraa falls in northeast Cambodia's Mondulkiri Province.

VESPAFOTO/SHUTTERSTOCK ©

Top: Rock climbing at Railay Beach (p777), Thailand

Bottom: Spelunking at Sagada (p574), Philippines

KIZEL COTIW-AN/SHUTTERSTOCK ©

Watching Wildlife

It may not be as easy to spot wildlife in the steamy jungles of Southeast Asia as it is on the open plains of Africa, but there are some excellent wildlife-watching opportunities here. Most visitors crave encounters with large mammals such as wild elephants, Komodo dragons, proboscis monkeys and orangutans in Malaysia and Indonesia, but there are also amazing opportunities to spot rare bird life around lakes and rivers. Once common in the wild, tigers and big cats are more likely to be seen in wildlife sanctuaries and zoos in the region. Then there's the amazing underwater world, where megafauna such as whale sharks, dugongs and mantas rival the big beasts visible on land.

When to Go

Many of the best wildlife destinations are in protected forests or deep jungle, so plan a visit in the dry season, when trails are passable. Some national parks in the region are best visited by boat, so trips can run year-round. Birdwatching (p52) is seasonal due to migratory patterns, but the dry season offers the best visibility for birders.

Where to Go

Sungai Kinabatangan (Malaysia; p448) Cruise down this Sabah river to spot orangutans, proboscis monkeys, monitor lizards and even elephants.

BIRDWATCHING

Tram Chim National Park (Vietnam; p907) Home to the rare eastern sarus crane, a red-headed beauty depicted on the bas-reliefs of Angkor.

Khao Sok National Park (Thailand; p765) Fish eagles, hornbills and kingfishers are found in this beautiful national park.

West Papua (Indonesia; p299) Encounter the rainbow-hued birds of paradise, many species of which are endemic to the island of Papua.

Jurong Bird Park (Singapore; p633) See almost every bird under the sun at the world's largest bird park.

Khao Yai National Park (Thailand; p730) Elephants, monkeys, hornbills, blood-sucking leeches and other creepy-crawlies call this monsoon forest home.

Cat Tien National Park (Vietnam; p887) Meet primates in the jungles of Cat Tien on a wild gibbon trek, then swing into the Dao Tien Endangered Primate Species Centre.

Kratie Province (Cambodia; p137) Spot rare freshwater Irrawaddy dolphins in the Mekong River at Kampi in Kratie Province.

Tanjung Puting National Park (Indonesia; p282) Anchor along one of Kalimantan's iconic rivers and watch orangutans running wild.

Wellness

Many of the treatments and therapies that have become staples in spas worldwide were originally devised in the monasteries and villages of Southeast Asia. From meditation to traditional Thai massage, spa treatments are available everywhere, and at bargain prices, with some of the best centres providing work for ex-prisoners as part of their rehabilitation into mainstream life.

In Thailand, monasteries are important centres for traditional massage, but there are also some magnificent luxury spas that take indulgence to a new level. Beachside massage is available on almost every coast, particularly in tourist centres such as Bali, southern Thailand and resort islands in Malaysia and Indonesia.

However, in some places 'massage' is a smokescreen for sex tourism; the look of the establishment should give a clear indication of what kind of 'services' are really on offer (red lights or fairy lights usually mean the main business may not be wellness). Be aware that some traditional massages can be vigorous to the point of pain – make sure you know what is involved before you start.

Yoga and meditation are both also widely available on the beach, in forest retreats and at working monasteries, where people interested in Buddhism can fully immerse themselves in spiritual life for days, weeks, months or even years.

Outdoor yoga class in Ubud (p216), Indonesia

When to Go

Unless the yoga or meditation is in an outdoor setting, it really doesn't matter when you travel. Some wellness centres may offer more varied programs during the high season, as resident yoga instructors may move around from traveller centre to traveller centre over the course of the year. Plan ahead if you want a tailor-made experience, particularly for monastery stays.

Where to Go

Phuket (Thailand; p768) The island has numerous retreats aimed at foreigners, plus several leading yoga schools.

Ubud (Indonesia; p216) Ubud is the epicentre of wellness in Bali, and yoga, meditation and massage seem to be offered almost everywhere.

Siem Reap (Cambodia; p90) Foot massages to soothe your soul, loosening yoga classes, calm meditation retreats and some of the best spas in the country.

Luang Prabang (Laos; p336) Laos' spiritual and holistic hub, with some excellent spas and a small yoga community.

Mawlamyine (Myanmar; p502) The Pa-Auk-Taw-Ya Monastery is one of the largest and most welcoming meditation centres in Myanmar.

Countries at a Glance

Thailand

Culture/History
Beaches
Food

Religious Riches

The death of King Bhumibol marks a new chapter in the spiritual life of Thailand, where religion and royalty meld and mingle, but the pulse of the nation beats on in its spectacular shrines and temples.

Beach Perfection

With crystal waters, fringing palms and shimmering sand, Thailand's southern beaches are the real deal, with added party appeal. Expect late nights and lazy days of sun-soaking, scuba diving and spa indulgence.

Stellar Gastronomy

Feted as one of the world's top cuisines, Thai food draws on a fabulous palette of herbs, spices and seasonings. Don't just eat it, learn to cook it too – courses are offered in traveller towns across the kingdom.

p656

Brunei Darussalam

Food
Outdoor Activities
River Journeys

Foodie Surprises

Bruneian cuisine may not be well known, but we can guarantee you've never eaten anything like *ambuyat* (made from sago starch), or delicious *kueh* – Malay-style sweets made from rice, tapioca or mung-bean flour.

Jungle Encounters

Ulu Temburong National Park preserves 40% of Brunei's virgin rainforest, so there's a good chance of spotting wildlife on a jungle hike or elevated walkway.

Aquatic Adventures

River cruises penetrate the forested interior, but you'll see a different side to life in Brunei in Kampong Ayer, the world's largest stilt village, on the Brunei River.

p58

Cambodia

Culture/History
Community-based Tourism
Beaches

Amazing Angkor

While the scars of recent history are still visible – particularly at Tuol Sleng Prison and the Killing Fields near Phnom Penh – ancient history is the big drawcard, particularly at Angkor.

Meeting the Khmers

Community-based tourism projects are turning former poachers into trekking guides and rural village homes into captivating homestays.

Seductive Shores

A laid-back alternative to the crowded sands of southern Thailand, the squeaky-clean beaches and islands along Cambodia's short coastline are every bit as beautiful, but with lower costs and half the crowds.

p71

Indonesia

Culture/History
Outdoor
Activities
Beaches

Island Heritage

Empires too numerous to count have risen on the Indonesian archipelago, leaving behind majestic ruins such as Borobudur. Then there are Indonesia's rich and varied tribal cultures.

Volcanic Excursions

East Java's Gunung Bromo is just one of dozens of active volcanoes. The experience of bursting through the cloud layer to the smouldering summit of an Indonesian volcano will linger for a lifetime.

Seaside Splendour

Charming Bali blends rich culture with stupendous sands, and just across the channel are the Gili Islands for diving, Sumbawa for surfing, Flores for discovering and Sumba for simply getting lost.

p159

Laos

Culture/History
Outdoor
Activities
River Journeys

Green Escapes

Laos has an abundance of undisturbed wilderness and 20 designated reserves promising magical natural encounters. Eco-oriented programs such as the Gibbon Experience add ziplines and sleep-outs in the canopy.

River Highways

Rivers are the life-blood of Laos, and life moves to their ebb and flow. Laze beside the muddy waters, kayak deep into the hinterland or use the river as a highway from Luang Prabang to the Golden Triangle.

Royal Relics

The former royal capital of Luang Prabang is studded with historic temples and relics from French Indochina. Homestays in nearby mountain villages promise encounters with Laos' hill-tribe peoples.

p317

Malaysia

Food
Diving
Outdoor
Activities

Culinary Combinations

Malaysia is one of the world's great melting pots, and its kitchens fuse the spices of India, the cooking know-how of China and the rich culinary traditions of the Malay peninsula.

Sands & Sealife

Malaysia's beaches are postcard perfect, and the vibe is less frenetic than in Thailand. Hang-outs such as Tioman and Pulau Perhentian combine sparkling sand with stunning scuba dives.

Jungle Jamborees

The fabled jungles of Borneo are accessed by evocative boat rides along tea-coloured rivers, and encounters with orangutans are top of the bucket list. Rainforests even spill into downtown Kuala Lumpur.

p384

Myanmar

Culture/History
River Journeys
Festivals

Buddhist Brilliance

Across Myanmar, stupas gleam above the rooftops, a reminder of the nation's Buddhist soul. A tide of pilgrims swirls around Yangon's Shwedagon Paya, whisking visitors along too.

Wonderous Waters

From the surging Ayeyarwady to the mill-pond calm backwaters of Inle Lake, Myanmar's waterways call out to be explored. The overnight trip from Mandalay to Bagan offers a mesmerising glimpse of river communities.

Festival Fun

Myanmar's big festivals – the Thingyan water festival and Tazaungdaing, festival of lights – are show-stoppers, but just as fascinating are the *nat pwe* held in rural villages to propitiate animist spirits.

p483

Philippines

Culture/History
Outdoor
Activities
Beaches

Cultural Fusions

The Philippines is a stir-fry of ingredients from the powers who have coveted these shores: Catholicism and mysticism from Spain, bravado and bling from America, and beneath it, a complex native tribal culture.

Tectonic Treats

Volcanoes soar above the skyline across the Philippines, and trekking to their summits, or relaxing in the natural hot springs that surround their bases, are favourite pastimes.

Island Idylls

With 7000-plus islands to choose from, it's no trouble finding your own perfect strip of sand in the Philippines – typically with stunning scuba diving and boat rides to isolated islets offshore.

p553

Singapore

Culture/History
Food
Outdoor
Activities

Sophisticated History

East and West come together in sophisticated Singapore, where grand colonial mansions and traditional Chinese shophouses double as swish boutiques, restaurants and upbeat nightspots.

Fantastic Feasts

Banquet halls abound, but Singapore is the home of the Michelin-starred hawker. The city's food centres serve up treats to rival the showiest restaurants.

Surprising Greenery

When the shiny skyscrapers close in, break for the jungle. The Botanic Gardens and futuristic Gardens by the Bay serve up tame versions, or try Bukit Timah Nature Reserve or the Southern Ridges for real jungle experiences.

p620

Timor-Leste

Culture/History
Outdoor
Activities
Diving

A National Journey

Timor-Leste's journey from European colony to Indonesian province to independent nation is etched into the national psyche, and marked in the country's churches and shrines, and in Dili's moving museums and burial grounds.

Sacred Summits

Catholic Timor-Leste has mystical leanings, with mountains as spiritual sites. Sacred Mt Ramelau boasts a summit Virgin Mary statue and spectacular sunrise views over two coasts.

Destination Diving

Often overlooked in favour of its famous neighbours, Timor-Leste is gaining popularity for scuba diving on the pristine reefs off the north shore and Ataúro Island.

p796

Vietnam

Culture/History
Beaches
Food

Fusion Eating

Vietnam's cuisine almost dares to rival Thai cooking, mixing concepts from China, Southeast Asia and colonial France. Where else can you enjoy noodle soup with a baguette and a drip-filter coffee?

Empire Legacies

Everyone from China to France and the USA tried to claim Vietnam, but it still emerged as a proud independent nation. Martial history is painted large in its ancient monuments, imperial palaces and 20th-century battlegrounds.

Stunning Shores

Take your pick from built-up Nha Trang, dune-backed Mui Ne, or peaceful escapes at Con Dao and Phu Quoc.

p821

On the Road

Brunei Darussalam

☏ 673 / POP 429,000 / AREA 5765 SQ KM

Best Places to Eat

➡ Tamu Selera (p64)
➡ Pondok Sari Wangi (p64)
➡ Nasi Katok Corner (p64)

Best Places to Stay

➡ Ulu Ulu Resort (p68)
➡ Brunei Hotel (p64)
➡ Sumbiling Eco Village (p67)

Top Phrases

Hello Salam/Helo

Thank you Terima kasih

How much is it? Berapa harganya?

Why Go?

The tiny sultanate of Brunei is just a remnant of a naval empire that once ruled all of Borneo and part of present-day Philippines. Nevertheless, this quiet *darussalam* (Arabic for 'abode of peace') boasts the largest oilfields in Southeast Asia.

Look beneath the surface of this well-ordered and tightly regulated sultanate and you'll see the underlying warmth of Brunei's people and the wisely conserved wildness of its natural environment. Thanks to the money generated by the oilfields, Brunei hasn't turned its rainforests into oil palm plantations. Old-growth, primary forest abounds, especially in verdant Ulu Temburong National Park.

In the charming riverside capital, Bandar Seri Begawan (BSB), opulent palaces and magnificent mosques contrast with the haphazard and flimsy-looking water villages. Fringing this city's modest extents are lush forests and mangroves, home to proboscis monkeys, hornbills and crocs.

When to Go
Bandar Seri Begawan

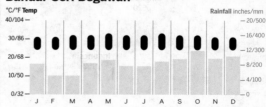

Oct–Dec The rainiest, ever-so-slightly coolest, months of the year.

Jan–May February and March are the driest months.

Jun–Aug It's *hot*. The sultan's birthday is celebrated around the country. in July.

Entering the Country

Direct flights connect various centres in Asia, Europe and Australia with Brunei International Airport. Daily buses link Sabah (KK) and Sarawak (Miri) with BSB. Ferries connect Pulau Labuan with Brunei (Seras Ferry Terminal, Muara).

REGIONS AT A GLANCE

Brunei Darussalam's capital Bandar Seri Begawan (BSB) is a quiet and rather sleepy capital when compared to other Asian cities. It's charm lies in its friendly inhabitants, picturesque stilt-supported water villages, pristine wilderness right on its doorstep of the CBD, and its colourful and pungent seafood hawker markets.

Spending time surrounded by the bustling, buzzing, chirping rainforests of Ulu Temburong National Park is one of the highlights of a visit to Brunei Darussalam. The journey is part of the adventure. Firstly, you are whizzed along palm-lined waterways on a speedboat from BSB, then you board a *temuai* (shallow-draft Iban longboat) and make you way upriver, dodging hanging vines and submerged boulders, deep into Borneo's renowned rainforest.

Essential Food & Drink

Ambuyat This gelatinous porridge-like goo made from the ground pith of the sago tree and dipped in spicy sauces is Brunei's unofficial national dish.

Kueh Garishly coloured and fiendishly sweet local cakes are sold at markets and street stalls.

Ayam Penyet A classic Indonesian dish of fried then smashed chicken served with sambal; it is popular in Brunei.

Teh Tarik Tea and condensed milk poured into the cup from a height; a spectacle not to be missed.

Top Tips

➡ Dress appropriately in discreet, loose-fitting clothing that covers the shoulders and knees. Avoid shorts and flip-flops unless you're at the beach.

➡ Bring or purchase an umbrella, because it can rain at any time.

➡ Get acquainted with Friday business hours – restaurants close between noon and 2pm.

➡ Pick up a local prepaid SIM for B$15.

➡ Bring a UK-style electrical adapter.

AT A GLANCE

Currency Brunei dollar (B$), Singapore dollar (S$)

Visas 14- to 90-day visas free on arrival to most nationalities

Money ATMs easy to find in towns, except in Temburong District

Time Brunei Darussalam Time (GMT/UTC plus eight hours)

Police ☑993

Language Bahasa Malaysia, English

Exchange Rates

Australia	A$1	B$1.07
Canada	C$1	B$1.08
Euro zone	€1	B$1.62
Japan	¥100	B$1.24
New Zealand	NZ$1	B$0.98
Singapore	S$1	B$1.00
UK	UK£1	B$1.75
USA	US$1	B$1.35

For current exchange rates, see www.xe.com.

Daily Costs

Dorm bed B$10–50

Food-stall meal B$1–4

Water taxi B$1–2 per trip

Museum admission: free

Resources

Lonely Planet (www.lonelyplanet.com/brunei-darussalam)

Brunei Tourism (www.bruneitourism.travel)

Borneo Guide (www.borneoguide.com)

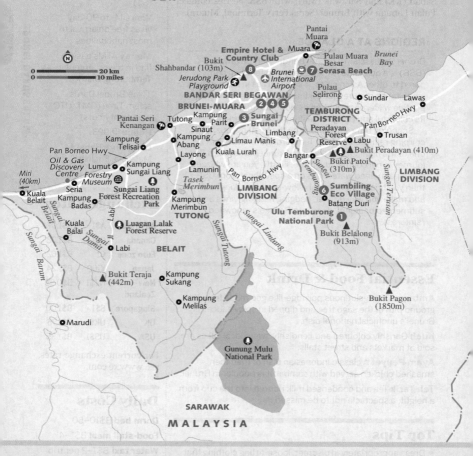

Brunei Darussalam Highlights

1 Ulu Temburong National Park (p67) Climbing high into the rainforest canopy and cooling off in a jungle stream.

2 Bandar Seri Begawan (p61) Visiting a mosque, museum or shopping mall and exploring the restaurant scene.

3 Sungai Brunei (p62) Spotting proboscis monkeys

and glimpsing royal palaces from a water taxi.

4 Kampong Ayer (p61) Water taxing to this charming village and learning about Brunei's heritage.

5 Ambuyat (p64) Educating your taste buds with the culinary curiosity that is Brunei's signature dish.

6 Sumbiling Eco Village (p67) Experiencing the culture and forests of Temburong District.

7 Diving (p62) Exploring the reefs and wrecks of unspoilt dive sites off Serasa Beach.

8 Empire Hotel & Country Club (p64) Wondering at the extravagance before cooling off in the pool.

BANDAR SERI BEGAWAN

POP 279,924

Cities built on oil money tend to be flashy ostentatious places, but with the exception of a palace you usually can't enter, a couple of enormous mosques and one wedding cake of a hotel, Bandar (as the capital is known, or just BSB) is a very understated place. Urban life pretty much revolves around shopping malls and restaurants; there is virtually no nightlife. BSB does boast a few museums and the biggest water village in the world, a little slice of vintage that speaks to the Bruneian love of cosiness and nostalgia.

⊙ Sights

Kampong Ayer   VILLAGE

Home to around 30,000 people, Kampong Ayer consists of 42 contiguous stilt villages built along the banks of the Sungai Brunei (Brunei River). A century ago, half of Brunei's population lived here, and even today many Bruneians still prefer the lifestyle of the water village to residency on dry land. The village has its own schools, mosques, police stations and fire brigade. To get across the river, stand somewhere a water taxi can dock and flag one down (the fare is B$1).

Kampong Ayer Cultural & Tourism Gallery   GALLERY

(south bank, Kampong Ayer; ⊙9am-5pm Sat-Thu, 9-11.30am & 2.30-5pm Fri) FREE A good place to start a visit to Kampong Ayer (p61) – and get acquainted with Brunei's pre-oil culture – is the Cultural & Tourism Gallery, directly across the river from Sungai Kianggeh (the stream at the eastern edge of the city centre). Opened in 2009, this riverfront complex focuses on the history, lifestyle and crafts of the Kampong Ayer people. A square, glass-enclosed **viewing tower** offers panoramic views of the scene below.

Old Customs House   HISTORIC BUILDING

(Jln McArthur; ⊙9am-4.30pm Sat-Thu, 9-11.30am & 2.30-4.30pm Fri) The waterfront building, completed in the 1950s, is now a gallery space, Galleri Seni, for temporary art exhibitions, as well as housing the Tourist Information Centre (p66).

Omar Ali Saifuddien Mosque   MOSQUE

(Jln Stoney; ⊙interior 8.30am-noon, 1.30-3pm & 4.30-5.30pm Sat-Wed, closed Thu & Fri, exterior compound 8am-8.30pm daily except prayer times) FREE Completed in 1958, Masjid Omar Ali Saifuddien – named after the 28th Sultan of Brunei (the late father of the current sultan) – is surrounded by an artificial lagoon that serves as a reflecting pool. This being Brunei, the interior is pretty lavish. The floor and walls are made from the finest Italian marble, the chandeliers were crafted in England and the luxurious carpets were flown in from Saudi Arabia. A 3.5-million-piece glass mosaic overlaying real gold leaf covers the main dome.

Royal Regalia Museum   MUSEUM

(Jln Sultan; ⊙9am-5pm Sun-Thu, 9-11.30am & 2.30-5pm Fri, 9.45am-5pm Sat, last entry 4.30pm) FREE When called upon to present a gift to the sultan of Brunei, you must inevitably confront the question: what do you give a man who has everything? At this entertaining museum you'll see how heads of state have solved this conundrum (hint: you'll never go wrong with gold and jewels). Family photos and explanatory texts offer a good overview of the life of the sultan, who is himself depicted in myriad forms (including a hologram) in a series of portraits.

Brunei Darussalam Maritime Museum   MUSEUM

(Muzium Maritim; Simpang 482, Jln Kota Batu; ⊙9am-5pm Sun-Thu, 9-11.30am & 2.30-5pm Fri, 9.45am-5pm Sat, last entry 30min before closing; P; ☐39) FREE A gleaming building, ship-like in both style and proportion, houses this museum opened in 2015 at Kota Batu, 5km east of the city centre (take the 39 bus). On display are some of the more than 13,000 artefacts excavated from a shipwreck discovered by divers in 1997. The ship is believed to have set sail from China sometime in the late 15th or early 16th centuries before being struck by stormy weather as it approached Brunei.

Brunei Museum   MUSEUM

(Jln Kota Batu; ⊙9am-5pm Sat-Thu, 9-11.30am & 2.30-5pm Fri, last entry 30min before closing; P; ☐39) FREE Brunei's national museum, with its Islamic-art gallery, exhibits depicting Brunei's role in Southeast Asian history from the arrival of the Spanish and Portuguese in the 1500s, and a natural-history gallery, is a decent place to blow an hour of your time. It is situated 4.5km east of central BSB along the coastal road, at Kota Batu. At research time the museum was closed for renovations.

Jame'Asr Hassanil Bolkiah Mosque   MOSQUE

(Sultan Hassanal Bolkiah Hwy, Kampung Kiarong; ⊙8am-noon, 2-3pm & 5-6pm Mon-Wed & Sat, 10.45am-noon, 2-3pm & 5-6pm Sun, closed Thu & Fri;

Bandar Seri Begawan

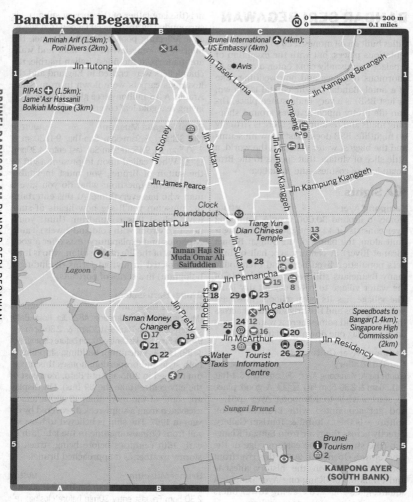

P; **1)** **FREE** Built in 1992 to celebrate the 25th year of the current sultan's reign, Brunei's largest mosque and its four terrazzo-tiled minarets dominate their surroundings. It's impossible to miss as you head towards Gadong, about 3km from the city centre. It's certainly an impressive building; because the sultan is his dynasty's 29th ruler, the complex is adorned with 29 golden domes. At night the mosque is lit up like a gold flame.

Istana Nurul Iman   PALACE
(Jln Istana Nurul Iman) Istana Nurul Iman (Palace of the Light of Faith), the official residence of the sultan, is one of the largest habitations of any sort in the world – more than four times the size of the Palace of Versailles.

The palace is open to the public only during the three-day Hari Raya Aidil Fitri festivities at the end of Ramadan. The best way to check it out on the other 362 days of the year is to take a water-taxi cruise.

🏃 Activities

Water-Taxi Cruise   BOATING
(1hr B$30-40) The best way to see BSB's water villages and the sultan's fabled palace, Istana Nurul Iman (p62), is from a water taxi,

Bandar Seri Begawan

which can be chartered along the waterfront for about B$30 to B$40 (a bit of negotiating will occur, but at least you know the locals can't claim the petrol is expensive).

Finding a boat won't be a problem, as the boatmen will have spotted you before you spot them. After you admire the palace's backyard, your boatman can take you further upriver into the mangrove to see proboscis monkeys. Head out in the late afternoon if you can; the monkeys are easiest to spot around sunset.

Poni Divers DIVING
(☎ 223 3655; www.ponidivers.com; Watersports Complex, Simpang 287, Pantai Serasa; 2 fun dives B$180; ☉9am-5pm) Brunei's largest dive centre offers a full range of PADI certification courses, recreational dives and various water sports including water skiing and banana boating. Operates from Serasa Beach, with a booking office in BSB. Also puts together dive packages including airport transfers and accommodation at the dive centre's homestay.

A typical itinerary for fun dives includes three dives a day combining shallower reef dives with deeper wreck dives in locations chosen depending on water conditions and diving experience.

⟳ Tours

★**Borneo Guide** TOURS
(☎718 7138, 242 6923; www.borneoguide.com; Unit 204, Kiaw Lian Building, Jln Pemancha; ☉9am-5pm Mon-Thu, 9am-noon & 2-5pm Fri, 9am-1pm Sat & Sun) Excellent service, good prices and a variety of packages around Brunei and Borneo are available. A day trip to Ulu Temburong National Park costs B$135 per person from BSB. Also offers overnight trips to Temburong with accommodation at Sumbiling Eco Village (p67) just outside the park (two days and one night from B$185). The office serves as a useful tourism information centre.

🛏 Sleeping

Budget options are thin on the ground. Upscale places often offer discounts online. For homestays in village areas contact Borneo Guide.

Youth Hostel HOSTEL $
(Pusat Belia; ☎899 8852, 887 3066; Jln Sungai Kianggeh; dm B$10; ❄🛜❄) Popular with backpackers, despite the fact that couples can't stay together. The sex-segregated accommodation includes 13 four-bed dorms for males and two four-bed dorms and two 10-bed dorms for females. Expect functional furnishings and passable bathrooms. Dorms are at the southern end of the Youth Centre complex.

Enter from Jln Sungai Kianggeh at the centre's Kafe Belia and turn right. If the gate is locked try and enter from Jln Kampung Berangah. Reception is supposed to be open 8am to noon, 2pm to 4pm Monday to Thursday and Saturday, and 8am to 11.30am, 2.30pm to 4pm Friday. But staffing can be intermittent. If the office is locked, hang around and someone should (eventually) find you. The hostel may fill up with government guests or school groups, so call ahead to check availability. The adjacent swimming pool costs B$1.

KH Soon Resthouse GUESTHOUSE $
(✆ 222 2052; http://khsoon-resthouse.tripod.com; 2nd fl, 140 Jln Pemancha; dm B$18, s/d B$30/50; 🅰🛜) This basic guesthouse is one of the few hotels offering budget rates in a central location. Rooms are large but spartan. The reception-level rooms that have been renovated (either with share and attached bathrooms) are a much better bet than the old ones upstairs, which have private facilities positioned awkwardly behind low partitions or squat share toilets.

★ **Capital Residence Suites** HOTEL $$
(✆ 222 0067; www.capitalresidencesuites.com; Simpang 2, Kampong Berangan; d/ste incl breakfast B$80/180-280; 🅰🛜) This good-value, rather blandly decorated hotel is lifted by friendly, helpful staff and a free shuttle service from 9am to 9pm, which transports guests all around BSB city and to the beaches and attractions beyond. The spacious suites are like small apartments with sofas, a kitchen and washing machine. Standard rooms, though comfortably furnished, are a little cramped with tiny bathrooms.

★ **Brunei Hotel** HOTEL $$
(✆ 224 4828; www.thebruneihotel.com; 95 Jln Pemancha; r/ste incl breakfast B$140-175/240-320;

SPLURGE

Pharaonic in its proportions and opulence, the 522-room **Empire Hotel & Country Club** (✆ 241 8888; www.theempirehotel.com; Lebuhraya Muara-Tutong, Jerudong; d B$250-300, ste from B$980, villas from B$2200; 🅰🅰🛜🏊) was commissioned by Prince Jefri at a cost of US$1.1 billion as lodging for guests of the royal family and quickly transformed into an upscale resort. It's worth a visit if only to gawp at the extravagance of the lobby. For B$25 you can use the seafront swimming pool complex or visit the three-screen cinema complex. The hotel is 26km northwest of BSB's city centre. To get there take bus 57 (B$1) from central BSB, or a taxi (B$35 each way).

🅰🅰🛜) A chic, dare we say hip, hotel with clean lines, monochromatic colour schemes, geometric patterns and a general up-to-date style that is pretty unexpected in the sultanate. There's a decent breakfast buffet thrown into the deal served in the downstairs **Choices Cafe**.

🍴 Eating

In the city centre, restaurants can be found along the waterfront and on Jln Sultan (south of Jln Pemancha). The big shopping malls, including those out in Gadong, have food courts and restaurants.

★ **Tamu Selera** HAWKER $
(cnr Jln Tasek Lama & Jln Stoney; mains B$2-7; ◷5pm-midnight) At this bustling, makeshift hawker centre, set in a shady park, diners eat excellent, cheap Malaysian and Indonesian dishes under colourful tarps and ceiling fans. Options include fresh seafood, satay, fried chicken – particularly *ayam penyet* (Indonesian fried chicken with sambal), *ambuyat*, rice and noodle dishes, and iced drinks. Situated 1km north of the waterfront.

★ **Nasi Katok Corner** BRUNEIAN $
(Seri Mama Express; Cnr Jln Sultan & Jln Cator; nasi katok B$1; ◷24hr) Locals queue at night for cheap snack of *nasi kotok* – rice and meat (or tofu) plus sambal – at this tiny shopfront. Rice, sambal and piece of fried meat (or fishball or tofu) are placed in a paper cone, you hand over a dollar and off you go.

Tamu Kianggeh HAWKER $
(Kianggeh market; Jln Sungai Kianggeh; mains from B$1; ◷5am-5pm) The food stalls here serve Brunei's cheapest meals, including *nasi katok* (B$1) and *nasi lemak* (B$1). Many stalls are closed by 4pm.

★ **Pondok Sari Wangi** INDONESIAN $
(✆ 244 5403; Block A, No 12-13, Abdul Razak Complex, Jln Gadong; mains B$5-6.50; ◷10am-10pm; 🅰) Located in Gadong, Pondok Sari Wangi is a beloved Bandar institution. The extensive menu includes a variety of tasty noodle and rice dishes, stir-fries and curries. *Nasi ayam bakar sari wang*, grilled chicken and rice, is one of the signature dishes. It's in a separate block, north of the Mall.

Aminah Arif BRUNEIAN $$
(✆ 223 6198; Unit 2-3, Block B, Rahman Bldg, Simpang 88, Kiulap; mains B$5-28, set meals for two from B$22; ◷7am-10pm; 🅰🍴) Aminah Arif is synonymous with *ambuyat* (thick, starchy

---

ℹ️ GETTING TO MALAYSIA

BSB to Miri

Getting to the border Two buses a day link BSB with Miri (B$20 from BSB, RM50 from Miri, 3½ hours). Tickets are sold on-board.

At the border Most travellers to Malaysia are granted a 30- or 60-day visa on arrival.

Moving on The bus will leave you at Miri's Pujut Bus Terminal, a 4km taxi ride from the city centre.

BSB to Pulau Labuan & Kota Kinabalu

Getting to the border Travelling by sea to Sabah is the easiest option, avoiding the hassles and delays of land borders. There are five ferries (adult/child/car B$17/10/58, 1½ hours) each day departing from Serasa Ferry Terminal in Muara, about 25km north-east of BSB, to Pulau Labuan. At 8am daily a bus runs to Kota Kinabalu (B$45, eight to nine hours) via Limbang, Bangar, Lawas and various towns in Sabah and stopping at eight passport checkpoints.

At the border Most travellers to Malaysia are granted a 30- or 60-day visa on arrival.

Moving on From Pulau Labuan, twice-daily ferries go to Kota Kinabalu (RM40, 3hr).

For more details see p70. To make this crossing in reverse see p469.

---

porridge), Brunei's signature dish. If you're up for a generous serving of wiggly white goo, this is a good spot to do so. Meals can be washed down with iced *kasturi ping* (lime juice). There are five branches of Aminah Arif in town; this one – located in Kiulap about 3km northwest of the waterfront – is the most central.

🍷 Drinking & Nightlife

The sale and public consumption of alcohol is banned and nightlife is virtually unknown. Cafes are on the rise and decent espresso is readily available. Locals are fond of the soft drink *air batu campur* (ice mix), usually called ABC, which includes ice, little green noodles, grass jelly, sago pearls and red beans.

Piccolo Café CAFE
(📋224 1558; Lot 11, Jln McArthur; coffee RM3-450, sandwiches RM3.50-6.90; ⊙7.30am-11pm Mon-Wed, 7.30am-1am Thu-Sat, 9.30am-11pm Sun; 🛜) This cafe serves up lavender lattes (an original, if not completely delicious, drink) as well as more conventional coffees, teas and smoothies and a range of sandwiches, wraps, waffles and cakes, including an extremely tasty sea-salt chocolate tart (B$3.20).

Another CAFE
(📋222 3012; G8, ground fl, Wisma Jaya, Jln Pemancha; coffee B$4.50-6, cakes B$5; ⊙7am-7pm Mon-Sat; 🛜) Corrugated metal walls, polished concrete floors and a wooden counter lend an industrial feel to this small, urban cafe.

Coffee lovers (even the fussy ones) should be more than satisfied by the aromatic brews served here, and there is a tempting selection of pastries, cakes (chocolate brownies and Dutch apple pie) and sandwiches.

🛍️ Shopping

The Mall SHOPPING CENTRE
(Gadong; ⊙10am-10pm) Sure, BSB's much-touted shopping mall is sleek, and the ceiling mural of a Royal Brunei airlines plane careering across the sky is an interesting touch. Here you'll find a collection of local and international-brand outlets, a useful supermarket, an inexpensive food court and an eight-screen **cineplex** (📋242 2455; www.themallcineplex.com; 3rd fl, The Mall, Gadong; adult B$4-10, child B$3-6; ⊙11am-midnight), the most popular cinema in Brunei!

**Hua Ho
Department Store** DEPARTMENT STORE
(Yayasan Complex, Jln McArthur; ⊙10am-10pm) A four-floor department store with a decent supermarket on the basement level.

ℹ️ Information

Banks and international ATMs are sprinkled around the city centre, especially along Jln McArthur and Jln Sultan. The airport also has ATMs.

Brunei Tourism (📋220 0874; www.bruneitourism.travel; Kampong Ayer Cultural & Tourism Gallery; ⊙9am-12.15pm & 1.30-4.30pm Mon-Thu & Sat, 9-11.30am & 2-4.30pm Fri) Free maps, brochures and information about Brunei. The website has oodles of useful information.

Isman Money Changer (Shop G14, ground fl, Block B, Yayasan Complex, Jln Pretty; ⊙10am-8pm) Changes major currencies. Just off the central atrium.

Main Post Office (cnr Jln Sultan & Jln Elizabeth Dua; ⊙ 8am-4.30pm Mon-Thu & Sat, 8-11am & 2-4pm Fri) The Stamp Gallery displays some historic first-day covers and enlargements of colonial-era stamps.

Paul & Elizabeth Cyber Cafe (G7, ground fl, Teck Guan Plaza, 56-60 Jln Sultan; per hr B$1.50; ⊙ 8.30am-8.30pm) Old-style cyber-cafe with decent connections.

RIPAS Hospital (☑ 224 2424; www.moh.gov.bn; Jln Putera Al-Muhtadee Billah; ⊙24hr) Brunei's main hospital, with fully equipped, modern facilities. Situated about 2km west of the centre (across the Edinburgh Bridge).

Tourist Information Centre (Pusat Maklumat Pelacong; www.tourismbrunei.com; Old Customs House, Jln McArthur; ⊙ 9am-4.30pm Sat-Thu, 9-11.30am & 2.30-4.30pm Fri) Has free maps, suggested walking tours and lists of accommodation providers as well as bus and ferry information.

Getting Around

TO/FROM THE AIRPORT

The airport, about 8km north of central BSB, is linked to the city centre, including the bus terminal on Jln Cator, by buses 23, 36 and 38 (B$1) until about 5.30pm. A taxi to/from the airport costs B$25; pay at the taxi counter. Some hotels offer airport pick-up.

BUS

Brunei's limited public bus system, run by a variety of companies, is somewhat erratic, at least to the uninitiated, so getting around by public transport takes effort. Buses (B$1) operate daily from 6.30am to about 6pm; after that, your options are taking a cab or hoofing it. If you're heading out of town and will need to catch a bus back, ask the driver if and when he's coming back and what time the last bus back is.

Finding stops can be a challenge – some are marked by black-and-white-striped uprights or a shelter, others by a yellow triangle painted on the pavement, and yet others by no discernible symbol. Fortunately, numbers are prominently displayed on each 20- or 40-passenger bus.

The bus station lacks an information office or a ticket counter, though there is a schematic route map which, while it's hard to decipher, explains what buses (routes are numbered) go where. It may be best to ask about transport options at your hotel before heading to the bus station.

CAR

Hiring a car is a good way to explore Brunei's hinterland. Prices start at about B$85 a day. Surcharges may apply if the car is taken into Sarawak. Most agencies will bring the car to your hotel and pick it up when you've finished, and drivers can also be arranged, though this could add B$100 to the daily cost.

Avis (☑ 222 7100; www.avis.com; Radisson Hotel, Jln Tasek Lama 2203; ⊙8am-noon & 1.30-5pm Mon-Thu, 8am-noon & 2-5pm Fri, 8am-noon & 1.30-4pm Sat, 9am-noon & 1.30-3pm Sun) Also has an office at the **airport** (☑ 233 3298; Arrival Hall, Brunei International Airport; ⊙8.30am-5.30pm).

Hertz (☑ airport 872 6000; www.hertz.com; Arrival Hall, Brunei International Airport; ⊙8am-5pm) The international car-rental company has a counter at Brunei airport.

TAXI

Taxis are a convenient way of exploring BSB – if you can find one, that is, as there are about 50 in the country. There is no centralised taxi dispatcher, and it's difficult or impossible to flag down a taxi on the street. Hotels can provide drivers' mobile-phone numbers. Most taxis have yellow tops; a few serving the airport are all white. BSB's only proper taxi rank (Jln Cator) is two blocks north of the waterfront at the bus terminal on Jln Cator. Some taxis use meters, although many drivers will just try to negotiate a fare with you. Fares go up by 50% after 10pm; the charge for an hour of wait time is B$30 to B$35. Sample day-time taxi fares from the city centre include the Brunei Museum (B$25), Gadong (B$15), the airport (B$20-25), the Serasa Ferry Terminal in Muara (B$40), the Empire Hotel & Country Club (B$35) and the Jerudong Park Playground (B$35).

WATER TAXI

If your destination is near the river, water taxis – the same little motorboats that ferry people to and from Kampung Ayer – are a good way of getting there. You can hail a water taxi anywhere on the waterfront a boat can dock, as well as along Venice-esque Sungai Kianggeh. Crossing straight across the river is supposed to cost B$1 per person; diagonal crossings cost more.

TEMBURONG DISTRICT

POP 10,500

Brunei's 1288-sq-km Temburong District is physically separated from the rest of the nation by Sarawak's Limbang division, and happens to contain one of the best preserved tracts of primary rainforest in all of Borneo. The main draw is the brilliant Ulu Temburong National Park.

Bangar

POP 4000

Bangar, perched on the banks of Sungai Temburong, is the gateway to, and administrative centre of, Temburong District. It can be visited as a day trip from BSB if you catch an early speedboat, but most visitors are here to explore the rainforests upriver.

Sleeping & Eating

Youth Hostel HOSTEL $
(Pusat Belia; ☑ 522 1694; Jln Bangar Puni-Ujong, Bangar; dm B$10; ☉ office staffed 7.30am-4.30pm, closed Fri & Sat; ❄) This basic hostel is in a bright-orange building across the road (walk under the road bridge) about 50m from the Bangar ferry terminal. The sex-segregated dorms, each with six beds (bunks), are clean and have air-con. The office is upstairs.

Stoneville Hotel HOTEL $$
(☑ 522 2252; stonevillehotel@yahoo.com; 1532 Kampong Sungai Tanam; r from B$78; ❄ 🛜) Bangar's first (and only) hotel is a modern if modest establishment with simple, clean, comfortable rooms with TVs and cable channels. In the lobby the restaurant is open for breakfast, lunch and dinner. It is about 500m northwest of the ferry terminal, along the road running parallel to the river's west bank.

RR Max Cafe MALAYSIAN $
(Bangar; mains B$1-3; ☉ 7.30am-8pm) This cafe north of the jetty has inexpensive meals, such as *nasi katok* (B$1) and egg (B$1.80) or tuna (B$2.50) sandwiches and fresh fruit juice (B$3.50). Also the owners are very helpful with travellers new to Bangar.

ℹ Information

3 in 1 Services (Shop A1-3, 1st fl, Kompleks Utami Bumiputera; per hr B$1; ☉ 8am-5.30pm, closed Sun) Internet access on the 1st floor of the Kompleks Utami Bumiputera building.
Bank Islam Brunei Darussalam (☉ 8.45am-3.45pm Mon-Thu, 8.45-11am & 2.30-4pm Fri, 8.45-11.15am Sat) The only bank in town has two ATMs and they accept foreign cards. Non-account holders cannot change money. On the west bank of the river 150m north of the bridge.
Chop Hock Guan Minimarket (☉ 8am-8pm) Exchanges Malaysian ringgits for Brunei dollars. In the second row of shops northwest of Bangar ferry terminal.

ℹ Getting There & Away

By far the fastest way to and from BSB is by speedboat (B$7, 45 minutes, hourly from 6.15am to at least 5pm). Bangar's ferry terminal, Terminal Perahu Dan Penumpang, is on the western bank of the river just south of the road bridge.

Boats depart at a scheduled time or when they're full, whichever comes first. When you get to the ticket counters, check which company's boat will be the next to leave and then pay and add your name and passport number to the passenger list.

Buses run by **Jesselton** (☑ 719 3835, 717 7755, in BSB 718 3838) pick up passengers heading towards Limbang and BSB (B$10, 2 hours) in the early afternoon; its bus to KK (B$25, 6 hours) via Lawas (B$10, 3 hours) passes through town at about 10am (can be up to an hour late). Buses stop on Jln Labu, just across the bridge on the west side of the river beside the produce market.

Ulu Temburong National Park

Ulu Temburong National Park, located in the heart of a 500-sq-km area of pristine rainforest covering most of southern Temburong, is a highlight of a visit to Brunei. It's odd that a small country such as Brunei should contain a sizable chunk of true untamed wilderness. Only about 1 sq km of the park is accessible to tourists, who are only admitted as part of guided-tour packages. To protect it, the rest is off-limits to everyone except scientists, who flock here from around the world. Permitted activities include a canopy walk, some short jungle walks, and swimming in the cool mountain waters of Sungai Temburong.

☞ Tours

For all intents and purposes, the only way to visit the park is by booking a tour; several BSB-based agencies (p63) organise tours and guides.

Sleeping

★ **Sumbiling Eco Village** CABIN $$
(☑ 718 7138, 242 6923; www.borneoguide.com/ecovillage; Kampong Sumbiling Lama, Jln Batang Duri; per person day trips from US$105, 2-day, 1-night incl meals & guided hikes from US$138) 🌿 If you're looking for Brunei's version of a jungle camp with basic amenities and a chilled-out atmosphere that encourages slipping into a state of utterly relaxed Zen,

come to Sumbiling. This eco-friendly rustic camp in a beautiful riverside location offers tasty Iban cuisine and accommodation in bamboo huts or tents, which have beds, mosquito nets and fans.

UNDERSTAND BRUNEI DARUSSALAM

Brunei Darussalam Today

The implementation of the first of a three-phase process of the introduction of sharia law in Brunei made global headlines in 2014, but a few years later it has made minimal impact on life in the quiet, law-abiding sultanate. The new penal code applies to both Muslims and non-Muslims.

Brunei's oil and gas wealth affords its citizens one of the highest standards of living in Asia, with a GDP per capita of US$71,000. Literacy stands at 96%, average life expectancy is 79 years, and generous state benefits include free healthcare and education, cheap loans and subsidised housing. It's not surprising that most Bruneians, happy with their lot, prefer not to ponder the question of what will happen when the oil runs out (recent reports suggest that at current rates of extraction it will last only another 20 years).

History

The earliest recorded references to Brunei concern China's trading connections with 'Pu-ni' in the 6th century. Prior to the region's embrace of Islam in the 1400s, Brunei was within the boundaries of the Sumatran Srivijaya empire, then the Majapahit empire of Java. By the late 15th and early 16th centuries, the so-called Golden Age of Sultan Bolkiah (the fifth sultan), Brunei had become a considerable regional power, with its sea-faring rule extending throughout Borneo and deep into the Philippines.

The Spanish and Portuguese arrived in the 16th century and at times confronted the sultanate with force, though in the long term the European powers' disruption of traditional patterns of trade proved more damaging. In the mid- and late 19th century, internal divisions and the policies of Sarawak's first White Rajah, a British adventurer named James Brooke, led to a series of treaties ceding land and power. To save itself, Brunei became a British protectorate in 1888. Despite this, two years later Limbang was lost to Sarawak, dividing the sultanate into two parts.

In 1929 oil was discovered, turning the tiny state into an economic power overnight. The present sultan's father, Sultan Omar Saifuddien, kept Brunei out of both the Federation of Malaya and Malaysia, preferring that his country remain a British protectorate – and that oil revenues stay on home soil.

Saifuddien abdicated in 1967, leaving the throne to his popular son and heir, Sultan Hassanal Bolkiah. In 1984 he reluctantly led his tightly ruled country to complete independence from Britain and later adopted a national ideology known as Melayu Islam Beraja (MIB; Malay Islamic Monarchy), which stresses Malay culture, Islam (the official religion) and the legitimacy of the sultan.

People & Culture

Ethnic Malays make up two-thirds of the sultanate's 429,000 inhabitants, people of Chinese heritage account for 10%, and Iban, Kelabit and other Dayak groups constitute around 3.4%. Temporary workers make up the rest. The state religion is Islam.

Traditional crafts have almost disappeared in modern Brunei. In its heyday, Brunei produced brassware – gongs, kettles, betel containers and, most famously, ceremonial cannons – that was prized throughout Borneo and beyond. *Jong sarat* sarongs, handwoven using gold thread, are still worn at formal ceremonial occasions.

SURVIVAL GUIDE

ℹ Directory A–Z

ACCOMMODATION
The following price ranges refer to a double room with bathroom.

ELECTRICITY
Brunei uses 240V, 50Hz AC electricity; power outlets have three flat sockets (UK style).

EMBASSIES & CONSULATES
Australian High Commission (☑ 222 9435; Level 6, Dar Takaful IBB Utama, Jln Pemancha; ⊙ 8am-5pm Mon-Thu, 8am-1pm Fri)

British High Commission (☑ 222 2231; Unit 2.01, 2nd fl, Block D, Yayasan Complex, Jln Pretty; ⊙ 8am-4.30pm Mon-Thu, 8am-noon Fri)

Canadian High Commission (☑ 222 0043; www.brunei.gc.ca; 5th fl, Jalan McArthur Bldg, 1 Jln McArthur; ⊙ 8am-4.45pm Mon-Thu, 8am-12.30pm Fri)

French Embassy (☑ 222 0961; www.amba france-bn.org; 51-55, 3rd fl, Kompleks Jalan Sultan, Jln Sultan; ⊙ 8.30am-12.30pm & 2-6pm Mon-Fri)

German Embassy (☑ 222 5547; www.bandar-seri-begawan.diplo.de; Unit 2.01, 2nd fl, Block A, Yayasan Complex, Jln Pretty; ⊙ 8.15am-12.30pm & 1.15-4.30pm Mon-Thu, 8.15am-12.15pm & 1-3pm Fri)

Malaysian Embassy (☑ 238 1095-7; www.kln. gov.my/web/brn_begawan; No 61, Simpang 336, Jln Kebangsaan; ⊙ 9am-noon & 3-4pm Mon-Fri)

New Zealand Consulate (☑ 222 5880/2422; www.mfat.govt.nz; c/o Deloitte & Touche, 5th fl, Wisma Hajjah Fatimah, 22-23 Jln Sultan; ⊙ 7.45am-4.30pm Mon-Thu, 7.45am-4.30pm Sat)

Singapore High Commission (☑ 226 2741; www.mfa.gov.sg/brunei; No 8, Simpang 74, Jln Subok; ⊙ 9am-noon & 1.30-4pm Mon-Fri)

US Embassy (☑ 238 4616; http://brunei.usem bassy.gov; Simpang 336-52-16-9, Jln Duta; ⊙ 8am-4.30pm Mon-Thu, 8am-noon Fri)

INTERNET ACCESS
Wi-fi is available at virtually all top-end and midrange hotels and most budget hotels. Western-style cafes in BSB also offer wi-fi.

LEGAL MATTERS
In May 2014, Brunei began phasing in a new criminal code based on sharia law. Offences in this first phase are punishable with a fine, imprisonment or both. Subsequent phases will introduce more severe penalties including corporal and capital punishments. As the laws could be applied to non-Muslims, ensure you're on the right side of them.

The sale and public consumption of alcohol is forbidden in Brunei. Drug trafficking is punishable by the death penalty.

FOOD PRICE RANGES
The following price ranges refer to the cost of the cheapest non-vegetarian main dish on the menu.

$ less than B$6

$$ B$6–16

$$$ more than B$16

LGBT TRAVELLERS
Homosexual activity is illegal in Brunei.

MEDIA
The *Borneo Bulletin* (www.borneobulletin.com. bn) covers local and international news, none of it controversial.

MONEY
ATMs are widely available in BSB and larger towns. Credit cards are usually accepted at top-end establishments.

OPENING HOURS
On Fridays all businesses and offices – including restaurants, cafes, museums, shops and even parks – are closed by law between noon and 2pm for Friday prayers. During Ramadan, business and office hours are often shortened and restaurants are closed during daylight hours.

Banks 9am–4pm Monday to Thursday, 9am-noon and 2–4pm Friday, 9am–11am Saturday

Restaurants Variable hours, generally 11am–11pm Saturday to Thursday, 11am–noon and 2–11pm Friday

Cafes Variable hours, generally 8am–6pm Saturday to Thursday, 8am–noon and 2–6pm Friday

Shops 10am–9.30pm Saturday to Thursday, 10–noon and 2–9.30pm Friday

Government offices 7.45am–12.15pm and 1.30pm–4.30pm Monday to Thursday, Saturday.

PUBLIC HOLIDAYS
The dates of Muslim holidays follow lunar calendars and so vary relative to the Gregorian (Western) calendar. Muslim holidays fall 11 or 12 days earlier each year; their final dates are determined by the sighting of the moon and therefore may vary slightly relative to the dates below. The dates we give for some other religious holidays are also approximate. For details on public and

---

SLEEPING PRICE RANGES

$ less than B$60

$$ B$60–150

$$$ more than B$150

BRUNEI DARUSSALAM SURVIVAL GUIDE

religious holidays (as well as cultural events), see the events calendars posted by **Brunei Tourism** (www.tourismbrunei.com). Some of the holidays include:

New Year's Day 1 January

Chinese New Year 5 February 2019, 25 January 2020

Brunei National Day 23 February

First Day of Ramadan 6 May 2019, 23 April 2020

Royal Brunei Armed Forces Day 31 May

Hari Raya Aidil Fitri (End of Ramadan); three-day holiday begins 4 June 2019, 24 May 2020

Islamic New Year 31 August 2019, 19 August 2020

Christmas Day 25 December

TELEPHONE

Prepaid SIM cards (B$15, including B$5 credit) are available at DST (www.dst.com.bn) stores. Bring your passport.

TOURIST INFORMATION

Borneo Guide (p63) Private tour company in BSB can supply up-to-date information including land transport to Miri (Sarawak) and Sabah.

Brunei Tourism (p65) A useful website, containing information on transport, business hours, accommodation, tour agencies and more.

Tourist information (⊙ 9am-5pm) Counter on the ground floor at Brunei International Airport.

Tourist Information Centre (p66) In the Old Customs House on BSB's waterfront.

VISAS

Travellers from the US and European Union, Switzerland and Norway are granted a 90-day visa-free stay; travellers from New Zealand, Singapore, South Korea and Malaysia, among others, receive 30 days; Japanese and Canadians get 14 free days. Chinese can apply for a 14-day single-entry visa (B$20). Australians can apply for the following visas upon arrival: a 72-hour transit (B$5), a 30-day single-entry (B$20) or a multiple-entry (B$30).

WOMEN TRAVELLERS

Discreet clothing is appropriate here – you don't have to cover your hair, but walking around in a tank top is a bad idea. Loose fitting clothes that cover the shoulders and knees are best, especially when visiting any kind of official or religious building.

❶ Getting There & Away

AIR

There are international flights to Malaysia, the Philippines, Thailand, Australia and Singapore.

Brunei International Airport (☎ 233 1747; www.civil-aviation.gov.bn), about 8km north of central BSB, has an ATM and a tourist information kiosk (p70) in the arrivals hall.

AirAsia (www.airasia.com) has two flights a day to Kuala Lumpur.

Cebu Pacific (www.cebupacificair.com) has flights from BSB to Manila on Tuesday, Friday, Saturday and Sunday.

Malaysia Airlines (☎ 233 2655; www.malaysiaairlines.com; 2nd level Departure Hall, Brunei International Airport; ⊙ 9am–9pm Mon–Fri, 9.30am–noon Sat) flights are operated by Royal Brunei Airlines.

Royal Brunei Airlines (☎ 221 2222; www.flyroyalbrunei.com; RBA Plaza, Jln Sultan; ⊙ 8am-4pm Mon-Thu & Sat, 8am-noon & 2-4pm Fri) has direct flights from BSB to destinations including Bangkok, Kota Kinabalu, Kuala Lumpur, Melbourne and Singapore.

Singapore Airlines (☎ 224 4901; www.singaporeair.com; 38 Sultan Omar Ali Saifuddien, Bandar Seri Begawan) has five flights a week from BSB to Singapore.

BOAT

Passenger ferries depart from the Serasa Ferry Terminal in Muara, about 20km northeast of BSB, to Pulau Labuan (adult/child B$17/10, 1½ hours) at 8am, 8.30am, 9am (car ferry), 1pm and 4.30pm. Moving on to Sabah, there are two ferries a day from Labuan to Kota Kinabalu (RM40, three hours).

PHLS run an express service from BSB bus station to the Serasa Ferry Terminal departing at 6.45am, 9am, noon, 2pm, 4.15pm and 7pm.

BUS

At 8am daily a **Jesselton Express** (☎ 016-830 0722, www.sipitangexpress.com.my) bus runs to Kota Kinabalu (B$45, eight to nine hours) via Limbang, Bangar, Lawas and various towns in Sabah. In the other direction, the bus leaves Kota Kinabalu's Jalan Tugu Bus Station at 8am. Reservations can be made at www.busonlineticket.com. Make sure your passport has plenty of unstamped pages; the trip will add eight new stamps.

Twice a day **PHLS Express** (☎ 277 1668) links BSB with Miri (B$20 from BSB, RM50 from Miri, 3½ hours). Departures from BSB's waterfront are at 7am and 1pm and from Miri's Pujut Bus Terminal at 8.15am and 3.45pm. Tickets are sold on-board.

Another option for travel between BSB and Miri is a private transfer (which may be shared with other travellers) run by **Ah Pau** (B$25/100 or RM70/300 per person/car, three hours). Call Ah Pau on ☎ 016-8072893 (Malaysian mobile) or 866 8109 (Brunei mobile). Departures from BSB are usually at 1pm or 2pm; departures from Miri are generally at 9am or 10am but may be earlier.

Cambodia

🎧 855 / POP 16 MILLION / AREA 181,035 SQ KM

Includes ➡

Best Temples

➡ Angkor Wat (p102)
➡ Bayon (p103)
➡ Beng Mealea (p109)
➡ Prasat Preah Vihear (p118)
➡ Ta Prohm (p109)

Top Khmer Phrases

Hello johm riab sua

Goodbye lia suhn hao-y

Thank you aw kohn

Does anyone speak English? tii nih mian niak jeh phiasaa awngle te?

Why Go?

Ascend to the realm of the gods at Angkor Wat, a spectacular fusion of spirituality, symbolism and symmetry. Descend into the darkness of Tuol Sleng to witness the crimes of the Khmer Rouge. This is Cambodia, a country with a history both inspiring and depressing, a captivating destination that casts a spell on all those who visit.

Fringed by beautiful beaches and tropical islands, sustained by the mother waters of the Mekong River and cloaked in some of the region's few remaining emerald wildernesses, Cambodia is an adventure as much as a holiday. This is the warm heart of Southeast Asia, with everything the region has to offer packed into one bite-sized chunk.

Despite the headline attractions, Cambodia's greatest treasure is its people. The Khmers have been to hell and back, but thanks to an unbreakable spirit and infectious optimism they have prevailed with their smiles and spirits largely intact.

When to Go
Phnom Penh

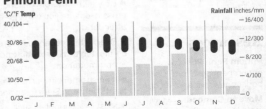

Nov–Feb The best all-round time to visit with relatively cool climes.

Mar–Jun Khmer New Year falls in mid-April and the mercury regularly hits 40°C.

Jul–Oct Green season: rice paddies shimmer, clouds bring some relief and prices plummet.

AT A GLANCE

Currency riel (r);
US dollars (US$)
universally accepted

Money ATMs are widely
available. Credit cards
accepted in larger cities.

Visas A one-month tourist visa costs US$30 on
arrival and requires one
passport-sized photo.

Language Khmer

Exchange Rates

Australia	A$1	3113r
Canada	C$1	3158r
Euro zone	€1	4775r
Japan	¥100	3554r
New Zealand	NZ$1	2777r
Thailand	1B	122r
UK	UK£1	5363r
USA	US$1	4042r

Daily Costs

Cheap guesthouse room
US$5–10

**Local meals and street
eats** US$1–3

Local buses (per 100km)
US$2–3

Resources

Phnom Penh Post (www.
phnompenhpost.com) Cam-
bodia's newspaper of record.

Move to Cambodia (www.
movetocambodia.com)
Insightful guide to living and
working in Cambodia.

**Cambodia Tribunal Moni-
tor** (www.cambodiatribunal.
org) Detailed coverage of
the Khmer Rouge trials.

Entering the Country

The majority of visitors enter or exit Cambodia by air through the popular international gateways of Phnom Penh or Siem Reap. Lots of independent travellers enter or exit the country via the numerous land borders shared with Thailand, Vietnam and Laos. There is also the option to cross via the Mekong River between Vietnam and Cambodia.

REGIONS AT A GLANCE

Phnom Penh, Cambodia's resurgent capital, is the place to check the pulse of contemporary life. Siem Reap, gateway to the majestic temples of Angkor, is starting to give the capital a run for its money with sophisticated restaurants, funky bars and chic boutiques. World Heritage Site Angkor houses some of the most spectacular temples on earth.

Down on the South Coast are several up-and-coming beach resorts and a smattering of tropical islands that are just beginning to take off, unlike those of neighbouring countries. Northwestern Cambodia is home to Battambang, a slice of more traditional life, and several remote jungle temples. The country's wild east is where elephants roam, waterfalls thunder and freshwater dolphins can be found.

Essential Food & Drink

Amok The national dish, aromatic steamed fish curry in banana leaf.

Angkor Beer The national beer, drunk in copious quantities.

Bobor A rice-based soup like Chinese congee.

Prahoc Fermented fish paste, almost a biological weapon.

Spiders Just like it sounds, deep-fried tarantulas.

Top Tips

➡ Do your homework on land-border crossings before you cross to ensure you don't great stranded in a remote location after dark.

➡ Overnight sleeper buses are generally pretty comfortable in Cambodia and will save the cost of a night's accommodation.

➡ If time is more important than money, consider domestic flights between Siem Reap and Sihanoukville; the road is long.

➡ Most basic supplies such as toiletries, sanitary pads, shaving foam, insect repellent and sunscreen can be purchased cheaply in major towns in Cambodia.

➡ Dress appropriately around the countryside, as Cambodia remains a conservative country and not a beach destination.

➡ Buy a *krama*, a checked traditional scarf, as it is a multipurpose towel that can be used in a multitude of ways.

PHNOM PENH

♩ 023 / POP 2 MILLION

Phnom Penh (ភ្នំពេញ): the name can't help but conjure up an image of the exotic. The glimmering spires of the Royal Palace, the fluttering saffron of the monks' robes and the luscious location on the banks of the mighty Mekong – this is the Asia many dreamed of from afar. Once the 'Pearl of Asia', Phnom Penh's shine was tarnished by war and revolution. But that's history and the city has risen from the ashes to take its place among the hip capitals of Asia, with an alluring cafe culture, bustling bars and a world-class food scene. Whatever your flavour, no matter your taste, it's all here in Phnom Penh.

◉ Sights

Most sights are fairly central and lie within walking distance or a short remork-moto (tuk tuk) ride from the riverfront Sisowath Quay.

★ National Museum of Cambodia   MUSEUM

(សារមន្ទីរជាតិ; Map p78; www.cambodiamuseum.info; cnr Sts 13 & 178; US$10; ⊙8am-5pm) Located just north of the Royal Palace, the National Museum of Cambodia is housed in a graceful terracotta structure of traditional design (built from 1917 to 1920), with an inviting courtyard garden. The museum is home to the world's finest collection of Khmer sculpture: a millennium's worth and more of masterful Khmer design.

★ Tuol Sleng Genocide Museum MUSEUM

(សារមន្ទីរប្រល័យពូជសាសន៍ទួលស្លែង; Map p80; www.tuolsleng.gov.kh; cnr Sts 113 & 350; adult/child US$5/3, guide US$6, audio tour US$3; ⊙8am-5pm) In 1975, Tuol Svay Prey High School was taken over by Pol Pot's security forces and turned into a prison known as Security Prison 21 (S-21); it soon became the largest centre of detention and torture in the country. S-21 has been turned into the Tuol Sleng museum, which serves as a testament to the crimes of the Khmer Rouge.

Killing Fields of Choeung Ek   MEMORIAL

(វាលពិឃាតជើងឯក; admission incl audio tour US$6; ⊙7.30am-5.30pm) Between 1975 and 1978 about 17,000 men, women, children and infants who had been detained and tortured at S-21 were transported to the extermination camp of Choeung Ek. It is a peaceful place today, where visitors can learn of the horrors that unfolded here decades ago. Admission to the Killing Fields includes an excellent audio tour, available in several languages.

Wat Phnom   BUDDHIST TEMPLE

(វត្តភ្នំ; Map p78; Norodom Blvd; temple US$1, museum US$2; ⊙7am-6.30pm, museum 7am-6pm) Set on top of a 27m-high tree-covered knoll, Wat Phnom is on the only 'hill' in town. According to legend, the first pagoda on this site was erected in 1372 to house four statues of Buddha deposited here by the waters of the Mekong River and discovered by Lady Penh. Hence the city name Phnom Penh or 'hill of Penh'.

Independence Monument   MONUMENT

(វិមានឯករាជ្យ; Map p80; cnr Norodom & Sihanouk Blvds) FREE Modelled on the central tower of Angkor Wat, Independence Monument was built in 1958 to commemorate the country's independence from France in 1953. It also serves as a memorial to Cambodia's war dead. Wreaths are laid here on national holidays.

DON'T MISS

ROYAL PALACE   ព្រះបរមរាជវាំង

With its classic Khmer roofs and ornate gilding, the **Royal Palace** (Map p80; Samdech Sothearos Blvd; admission incl camera 40,000r, guide per hour US$10; ⊙7.30-11am & 2-5pm) dominates the diminutive skyline of Phnom Penh. It's a striking structure near the riverfront, bearing a remarkable likeness to its counterpart in Bangkok. Being the official residence of King Sihamoni, parts of the massive palace compound are closed to the public. Visitors are allowed to visit only the throne hall and a clutch of buildings surrounding it.

Adjacent to the palace, the Silver Pagoda complex is also open to the public. From the palace compound you enter the Silver Pagoda complex through its north gate. The Silver Pagoda was so named in honour of the floor, which is covered with more than 5000 silver tiles weighing 1kg each, adding up to five tonnes of gleaming silver. You can sneak a peek at some near the entrance – most are covered for their protection. It is also known as Wat Preah Keo (Pagoda of the Emerald Buddha).

Cambodia Highlights

❶ Temples of Angkor (p102) Discovering the eighth wonder of the world.

❷ Phnom Penh (p73) Enjoying the 'Pearl of Asia', with its impressive museums, a sublime riverside setting and happening nightlife.

❸ Southern Islands (p128) Island-hopping around Cambodia's next big thing.

❹ Battambang (p110) Delving into the lush countryside, climbing hilltop temples, exploring caves and riding the 'Bamboo Train'.

❺ Mondulkiri (p143) Exploring this wild land of rolling hills, thundering waterfalls, indigenous minorities and adrenaline activities.

❻ Kampot (p130) Slipping into the soporific pace of the riverside, with French-era architecture, cave temples and pepper plantations.

❼ Prasat Preah Vihear (p118) Making a pilgrimage to the awe-inspiring mountain temple.

❽ Kratie (p137) Exploring the bucolic Mekong islands and dolphin pools by bicycle and boat.

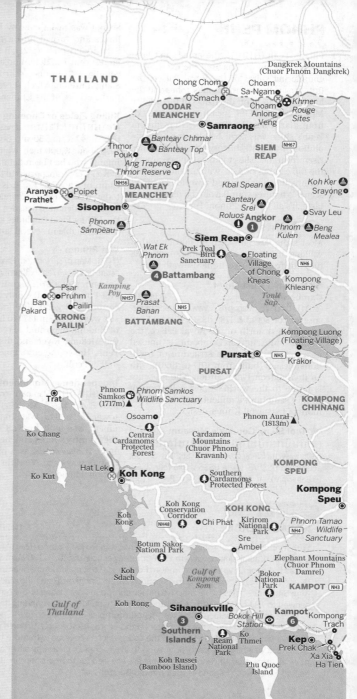

🏃 Activities

Don't miss the quirky and colourful aerobics sessions that take place in parks around the city at dawn and again at dusk. The riverfront and Olympic Stadium are two good places to jump in and join the fun. Most boutique hotels with pools will let you swim for about US$5, sometimes free with the purchase of food. The great pool at the **Himawari Hotel** (Map p80; ☎023-214555; 313 Sisowath Quay; weekday/weekend US$7/8) is another option.

Boat Cruises   BOATING
(Map p77) Boat trips on the Tonlé Sap and Mekong River are very popular with visitors. Sunset cruises are ideal, the burning sun sinking slowly behind the glistening spires of the Royal Palace. A slew of cruising boats are available for hire on the riverfront about 500m north of the tourist-boat dock. Just rock up and arrange one on the spot for around US$20 an hour, depending on negotiations and numbers. You can bring your own drinks or buy beer and soft drinks on the boat.

Cambodia Cooking Class   COOKING
(Map p80; ☎023-220953; www.frizz-restaurant.com; booking office 67 St 240; half-/full day US$15/23) Learn the art of Khmer cuisine through Frizz Restaurant on St 240. Classes are held on a breezy rooftop near the Russian embassy. Reserve one day ahead.

Vicious Cycle   CYCLING
(Map p78; ☎012 430622; www.grasshopperadventures.com; 23 St 144; road/mountain bike per day US$4/8) Plenty of excellent mountain and other bikes are available here. Kiddie seats can be attached to your mountain bike for US$3. Vicious represents well-respected Grasshopper Adventures in Phnom Penh.

SPLURGE

Tucked away down discreet St 830, **You Khin Art House** (Map p80; ☎061 828577; ykarthouse@gmail.com; St 830; r US$20-35; 🕸@🛜🏊) has the feel of a large private home and, tardis-like, is considerably bigger on the inside. The Franco-Khmer owners display their own artwork on the walls and the ample public spaces include a pool table and table tennis. 'Kitchen' rooms are suite-like, great value and a good choice for families.

Daughters   SPA
(Map p78; ☎077 657678; www.daughtersofcambodia.org; 321 Sisowath Quay; 1hr foot spa US$10; ⏱9am-5.30pm Mon-Sat) 🖐 Hand and foot massages are administered by participants in this NGO's vocational training program for at-risk women. Shorter (15- to 30-minute) treatments are also available.

Nail Bar   MASSAGE
(Map p78; www.mithsamlanh.org; Friends n' Stuff store, 215 St 13; 30/60min massages US$4/7; ⏱11am-9pm) 🖐 Provides cheap manicures, pedicures, foot massages, hand massages and nail painting, all to help Mith Samlanh train street children in a new vocation.

👉 Tours

Cyclo Centre   TOURS
(Map p78; ☎097 700 9762; www.cyclo.org.kh; 95 St 158; per hour/day from US$3/12) 🖐 Dedicated to supporting *cyclo* (bicycle rickshaw) drivers in Phnom Penh, these tours are a great way to see the sights. Themed trips such as pub crawls or cultural tours are also available.

🛏 Sleeping

There are several mini Khao San Rd backpacker colonies scattered around the centre. St 172 between St 19 and St 13 has emerged as the most popular area for budget accommodation. For walk-in guests, this is a great area to target. South of St 172 and closer to the river, St 258 has a clutch of budget guesthouses. In the O Russei Market area west of busy Monivong Blvd there is a mix of discount high-rise hotels and backpacker-oriented guesthouses. The trendy Boeng Keng Kang (BKK) district south of Independence Monument is the flashpacker zone.

⭐Eighty8 Backpackers   HOSTEL $
(Map p78; ☎023-500 2440; www.88backpackers.com; 98 St 88; dm US$6.40-8, r US$24-34; 🕸@🛜🏊) A hostel with a swimming pool means party time, and this place hosts a big one on the first Friday of every month. The extensive villa has a variety of dorms and private rooms. The courtyard has a central bar with a pool table, and there are plenty of spots to lounge around the pool.

⭐Mad Monkey   HOSTEL $
(Map p80; ☎023-987091; www.madmonkeyhostels.com; 26 St 302; dm US$5-7, r from US$18-25; 🕸@🛜) This colourful and vibrant hostel is justifiably popular. The spacious dorms have air-con and sleep six to 20; the smaller ones

Phnom Penh

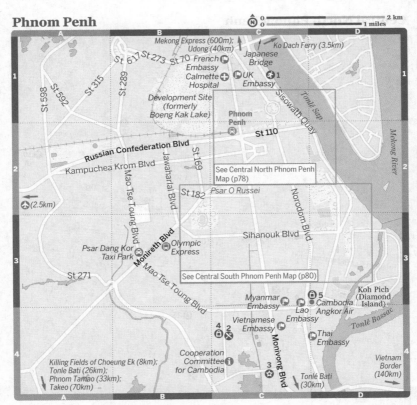

have double-width bunk beds that can sleep two. The private rooms are swish for the price but lack TVs and, often, windows. The rooftop bar above quiet St 302 serves free beer on Mondays from 6pm to 8pm.

Top Banana Guesthouse HOSTEL $
(Map p80; ☎ 012 885572; www.topbananahostels. weebly.com; 9 St 278; dm from US$4, r US$12-16; ❄ @ 🛜) The rooms are in good shape by hostel standards, and there are some dorms available, including a four-bed female dorm. The main draw is the strategic location overlooking Wat Langka and St 278, plus the open-air chill-out area. It can get noisy as the rooftop bar is raucous most nights. Book way ahead.

Narin Guesthouse GUESTHOUSE $
(Map p80; ☎ 023-991955; 50 St 125; r with fan/air-con US$12/17; ❄ @ 🛜) One of the stalwarts of the Phnom Penh guesthouse scene (we first stayed here back in 1995) run by a friendly family. Rooms are smart, bathrooms

Phnom Penh

🟢 Activities, Courses & Tours
1 Boat Cruises...C1

❌ Eating
2 Café Yejj..C4

🟢 Entertainment
3 Sovanna Phum Arts Association.......C4

🔵 Shopping
Rajana..(see 2)
4 Russian Market..................................C4
5 Watthan Artisans...............................D3

smarter still and the price is right. There is a super-relaxed, open-air restaurant-terrace where you can take some time out.

Panorama Mekong Hostel HOSTEL $
(Map p78; ☎ 018 950 0400; www.facebook.com/ panorama.mekong.hostel; 357 Sisowath Quay; dm

Central North Phnom Penh

US$3; 🛜) There's good news and bad news here. The good news is this place has panoramic views of the Mekong and you can even look down on the iconic Foreign Correspondents' Club (FCC), something that is unique for a backpacker pad. The bad news is there is no lift and there are four flights of stairs. Get fit and enjoy the views!

Blues Hostel
HOSTEL **$**

(Map p78; 📞010 302210; www.blueshostel.com; 149 St 19; dm US$3.50-4.50, r from US$10; ⚒🛜) This impressive hostel opened its doors in the summer of 2017 and has some pretty at-

tractive rates, even by hostel standards, and includes private rooms with attached bathroom. Downstairs is a lively bar and a pool table where the occasional free beer is on offer.

Mini Banana Guesthouse
GUESTHOUSE **$**

(Map p80; 📞023-726854; www.mini-banana.asia; 136 St 51; dm US$6, r US$8-20; ⚒🛜) It's almost a banana republic in this part of town, with three guesthouses playing on the name. Renovated dorms with sturdy bunks, comfortable rooms with fan or air-con and a lively little bar-restaurant make this one of the most likeable of the bunch.

Number 9 Guesthouse   HOSTEL **$**
(Map p80; ☎023-984999; www.number9hotel.com; 7C St 258; r US$15-35; ❄@🛜🏊) The first of Phnom Penh's old-school backpacker pads to be transformed into a flashpacker hotel, Number 9 Guesthouse is still going strong thanks to great rates, a rooftop pool and a lively bar-restaurant with generous happy hours (4pm to 8pm). Worth a splash for backpackers who have been exploring rural Cambodia.

Tat Guesthouse   GUESTHOUSE **$**
(Map p80; ☎012 921211; tatcambodia@yahoo.com; 52 St 125; s without bathroom US$4, r US$7-15;

❄@🛜) A super-friendly spot with a breezy rooftop hang-out that's perfect for chilling. The rooms aren't going to wow you but they are functional. For US$12 you get air-con. They also own nearby **Tattoo Guesthouse** (Map p80; ☎011 801000; 62A St 125; r US$5-10; ❄🛜), which has a great name and smarter rooms.

✕ Eating

For foodies, Phnom Penh is a delight, boasting a superb selection of restaurants that showcase the best in Khmer cooking, as well as the greatest hits from all over the globe.

Central South Phnom Penh

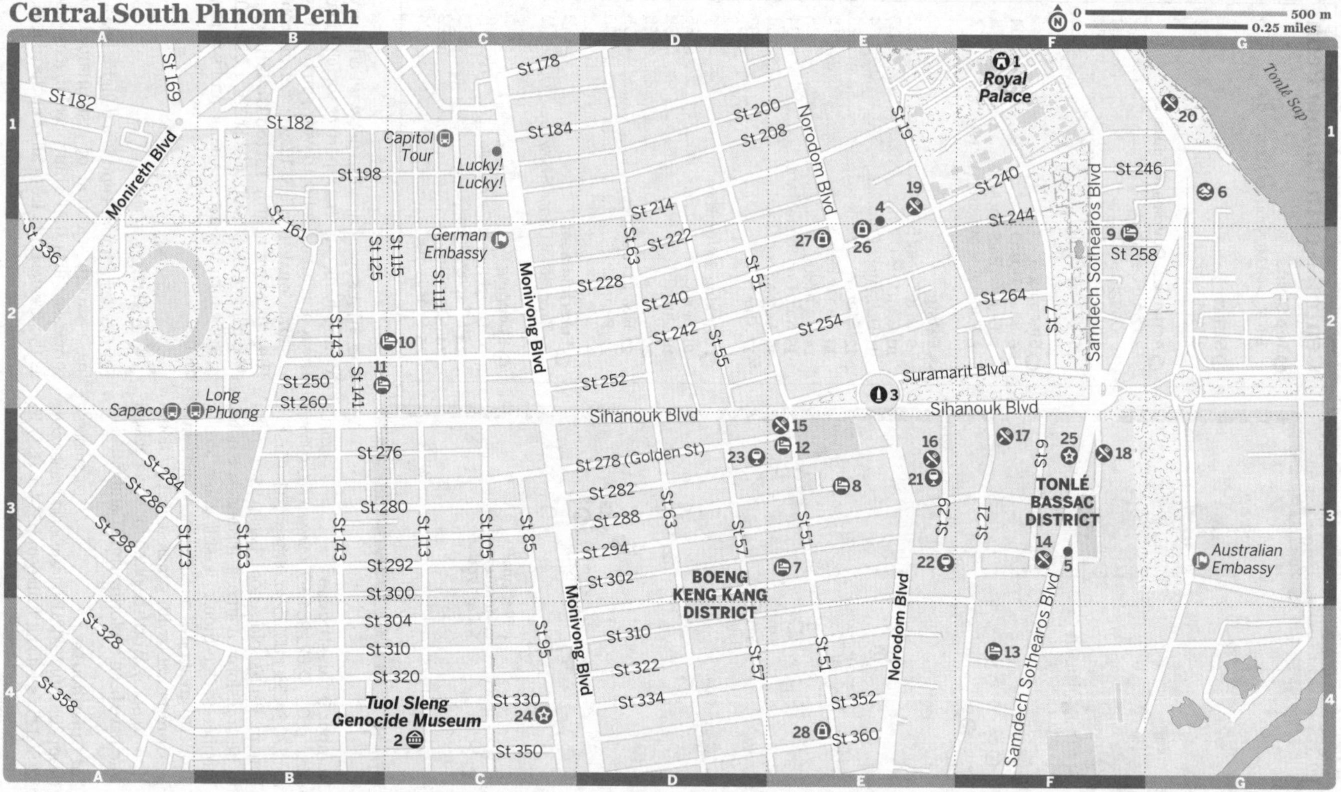

500 m
0.25 miles

Tonlé Sap

Australian Embassy

Royal Palace

TONLÉ BASSAC DISTRICT

BOENG KENG KANG DISTRICT

Tuol Sleng Genocide Museum

German Embassy

Lucky! Lucky!

Capitol Tour

Long Phuong

Sapaco

Monireth Blvd

Monivong Blvd

Norodom Blvd

Sihanouk Blvd

Suramarit Blvd

Samdech Sothearos Blvd

Samdech Sothearos Blvd

St 7
St 19
St 21
St 29
St 51
St 51
St 55
St 57
St 57
St 63
St 63
St 85
St 95
St 105
St 111
St 113
St 115
St 125
St 141
St 143
St 143
St 161
St 163
St 169
St 173
St 178
St 182
St 182
St 184
St 198
St 200
St 208
St 214
St 222
St 228
St 240
St 240
St 242
St 244
St 246
St 250
St 252
St 254
St 258
St 260
St 264
St 276
St 278 (Golden St)
St 280
St 282
St 284
St 286
St 288
St 292
St 294
St 298
St 300
St 302
St 304
St 310
St 310
St 320
St 322
St 328
St 330
St 334
St 336
St 350
St 352
St 358
St 360

Central South Phnom Penh

✖ Central North

Cam Cup Cafe CAFE $
(Map p78; ☎ 093 771577; Main Post Office, St 13; US$2-5; ☺7am-9pm; ☎) This elegant little cafe is the perfect way to make the iconic main post office relevant once more for a new generation of travellers. It offers fresh brews, herbal teas and some of the best value Khmer dishes you will hope to find in this sort of setting.

Sorya Food Court ASIAN $
(Map p78; 11 St 63; 5000-10,000r; ☺9am-9pm) The top-floor food court is a sanitised, air-cooled way to experience a variety of local fare, with stalls serving a wide range of affordable Cambodian, Chinese, Vietnamese, Malaysian and Korean dishes. It works on a coupon system.

Thai Huot SUPERMARKET $
(Map p78; 103 Monivong Blvd; ☺7.30am-8.30pm) This is the place for French travellers who are missing home as it stocks many French products, including Bonne Maman jam and the city's best cheese selection. There are several branches around the city.

★**Sam Doo Restaurant** CHINESE $$
(Map p78; ☎ 017 427688; 56-58 Kampuchea Krom Blvd; mains US$2.50-15; ☺7am-2am; ☎) Many Chinese Khmers swear that this upstairs eatery near Central Market has the best Middle Kingdom food in town. Choose from the signature Sam Doo fried rice, *trey chamhoy* (steamed fish with soy sauce and ginger), fresh seafood, hotpots and dim sum.

Happy Herb Pizza PIZZA $$
(Map p78; ☎ 012 921915; 345 Sisowath Quay; medium pizzas US$6-9; ☺8am-11pm; ☎) Another Phnom Penh institution. No, happy doesn't mean it comes with free toppings, it means pizza à la ganja. The non-marijuana pizzas are also pretty good, but don't involve the free trip. It's a good place to sip a cheap beer and watch the riverfront action unfold.

✖ Central South

★**Boat Noodle Restaurant** THAI $
(Map p80; ☎ 012 774287; 57 Samdech Sothearos Blvd; mains US$3-7; ☺7am-9pm; ☎) This long-running Thai-Khmer restaurant has some of the best-value regional dishes in town. Choose from the contemporary but traditionally decorated space at the front or a traditional wooden house behind. There are delicious noodle soups and local specialities ranging from fish cakes to spicy curries.

★**The Shop** CAFE $
(Map p80; ☎ 023-986964; 39 St 240; mains US$3.50-6; ☺7am-7pm, to 3pm Sun; ☎☑) If you

DON'T MISS

DINING FOR A CAUSE

These fantastic eateries act as training centres for young staff and help fund worthy causes in the capital.

Friends (Map p78; ☑ 012 802072; www.tree-alliance.org; 215 St 13; tapas US$4-7, mains US$6-10; ⊙ 11am-10.30pm; 🛜) One of Phnom Penh's best-loved restaurants, this place is a must, with tasty tapas bites, heavenly smoothies and creative cocktails. Take two tapas or one main for a filling meal. It offers former street children a head start in the hospitality industry. Book ahead.

Daughters Cafe (Map p78; www.daughtersofcambodia.org; 321 Sisowath Quay; meals US$4-8; ⊙ 9am-6pm Mon-Sat; 🛜) This fantastic cafe on the top floor of the Daughters of Cambodia visitors centre features soups, smoothies, original coffee drinks, cupcakes and fusion-ish mains served by former victims of trafficking, who are being retrained with a new set of skills.

Romdeng (Map p78; ☑ 092 219565; www.tree-alliance.org; 74 St 174; mains US$5-9; ⊙ 11am-9pm; 🛜) Set in a gorgeous colonial villa with a small pool, Romdeng specialises in Cambodian country fare, including a famous baked-fish *amok*, two-toned pomelo salad and tiger-prawn curry. Sample deep-fried tarantulas or stir-fried tree ants with beef and holy basil if you dare. It is staffed by former street youths and their teachers.

are craving the local deli back home, make for this haven, which has a changing selection of sandwiches and salads with healthy and creative ingredients such as wild lentils, forest mushrooms and lamb. The pastries, cakes and chocolates are delectable and well worth the indulgence.

Feel Good Cafe II CAFE $
(Map p80; ☑ 077 694702; www.feelgoodcoffee. com.kh; 11B St 29; dishes US$2-5; ⊙ 7.30am-4.30pm) 🍃 One of the only cafes in town to roast and grind its own coffee, with responsibly sourced blends that are a fusion of Cambodian, Lao and Thai coffee beans. The menu is international with influences from the Med to Mexico, including wraps and burgers.

Dosa Corner INDIAN $
(Map p80; 5E St 51; mains US$1.50-5; ⊙ 8.30am-2pm & 5-10pm) Fans of Indian dosas will be pleased to discover this place does just what it says on the label – namely, a generous variety of savoury pancakes from the south. Vegetarian thalis are a bargain at US$4.

★**Yi Sang Riverside** CHINESE $$
(Map p80; Sisowath Quay; mains US$3-20; ⊙ 6am-11pm; 🛜) The riverfront location is one of the few places in the city where you can dine right on the riverside, perfect for a relaxing sunset cocktail. The menu here includes a mix of well-presented Cambodian street flavours such as *naom bunchok* (rice noodles with curry), plus plenty of dim sum and some international flavours.

Piccola Italia Da Luigi PIZZA $$
(Map p80; ☑ 017 323273; 36 St 308; pizzas US$5-10; ⊙ 11am-2pm & 6-10pm; 🛜) This is the place where it all began and it's hard to believe this was just a quiet residential street just a few years ago. A bustling kerbside eatery just like you'd find in Italy, Luigi's certainly has a claim to making some of the best pizza in Phnom Penh. After dark, reservations are recommended.

🍴 Russian Market Area

Café Yejj CAFE $
(Map p77; ☑ 092 600750; 170 St 450; mains US$3.50-6; ⊙ 8am-9pm; 🛜☑) 🍃 An air-con escape from the Russian Market (walk upstairs), this bistro-style cafe uses organic ingredients to prepare pasta, salads and wraps, as well as a few more-ambitious dishes such as Moroccan lamb stew and chilli con carne. Promotes fair trade and responsible employment.

Super Duper SUPERMARKET $
(Map p80; www.super-duper.biz; 3 Samdech Sothearos Blvd; ⊙ 24hr) Phnom Penh's only 24-hour supermarket, this could be handy if the midnight munchies strike. It has one of the best product ranges in town, as the owners import containers direct from the US and Australia.

🏺 Drinking & Nightlife

Phnom Penh has some great bars and clubs, so it's definitely worth one big night out here. There are lots of late-night spots clustered around the intersection of Sts 51 and 172, appropriately nicknamed 'Area 51'. 'Golden St' (St 278) is also popular, and the riverfront has its share of bars as well. St 308 and Bassac Lane have emerged as the hipster areas of town.

Happy hours are a big thing in Phnom Penh, so it pays to get started early, when even such storied watering holes as the Foreign Correspondents' Club offers two-for-one specials. Wednesday is 'Ladies' Night' at some of the smarter bars around town, with two-for-one deals all night or even free drinks. Most bars are open until at least midnight, which is about the time that Phnom Penh's clubs swing into action. There are now some good micro-breweries around town turning out homegrown craft beer and these are well worth seeking out.

There are some great hostel bars in Phnom Penh, so keep these in mind if you want to meet other travellers on a big night out. Top Banana (p77) is one of the liveliest rooftop bars, as is the rooftop bar at Mad Monkey (p76), in the same part of town. Eighty8 Backpackers (p76) has a 'first Friday of the month' party that sees the expat and backpacker worlds collide.

★**FCC** BAR

(Foreign Correspondents' Club; Map p78; 363 Sisowath Quay; ⊘ 6am–midnight; 🛜) A Phnom Penh institution, the 'F' is housed in a colonial gem with great views and cool breezes. It's one of those must-see places in Cambodia. Happy hours are 5pm to 7pm and 10pm to midnight. If the main bar is too crowded, head up to the rooftop, which often sees live music at weekends. Renovations were scheduled during 2018.

★**Botanico Wine &**
Beer Garden CRAFT BEER

(Map p80; ☑ 077 943135; www.facebook.com/botanicowineandbeergarden; 9B St 29; ⊘ 9am–10pm Mon–Sat; 🛜) Bringing US-style craft-brewing to Phnom Penh, this great little hideaway stocks Irish Red, IPA and other homebrewed beers. It is set in a verdant garden tucked down a winding alley. Monthly specials include yoga and beer, plus pork-knuckle nights.

★**Score** BAR

(Map p80; ☑ 023-221357; www.scorekh.com; 5 St 282; ⊘ 8am–late; 🛜) With its cinema-sized screen and television banks on every wall, this cavernous bar is the best place to watch a big game. It's not just the usual footy and rugby, as almost all sports are catered for here. Several pool tables tempt those who would rather play than watch.

LOCAL FLAVOURS

Khmer Barbecues

After dark, Khmer eateries scattered across town illuminate their Cambodia Beer signs, hailing locals in for grilled strips of meat or seafood and generous jugs of draught beer. Khmer barbecues are literally all over the place, so it won't be hard to find one. Some recommended local eateries:

Sovanna II (Map p80; 2C St 21; mains US$2–8; ⊘ 6–11am & 3–11pm; 🛜) Sovanna II is always jumping with locals and a smattering of expats who have made this their barbecue of choice thanks to the huge menu and cheap local beer. It's also as good a place as any to sample the national breakfast, *bei sait chrouk* (pork and rice).

18 Rik Reay BBQ (Map p78; ☑ 095 361818; 3 St 108; US$2–8; ⊘ 5pm–midnight) One of the best local barbecue restaurants near the riverfront, the Rik Reay is packed with locals every night, partly thanks to its convenient location near the Night Market, but more so it is a testament to the quality of its food. Choose from grilled beef, ribs, chicken, squid, shrimp and much more, all with signature dipping sauces.

Markets

Phnom Penh's many markets all have large central eating areas where stalls serve up local faves like noodle soup and fried noodles during daylight hours. Most dishes cost a reasonable 4000r to 8000r. The best market for eating is Russian Market (p85), with an interior food zone that's easy to find and with a nice variety of Cambodian specialities. Psar Thmei (p85) is another great option with a large food court.

DON'T MISS

BASSAC LANE BARS

Bassac Lane is the moniker given to an alley that leads south off St 308. The brainchild of Kiwi brothers the Norbert-Munns, who have a flair for drinks and design, there are half a dozen or more hole-in-the-wall boozers in this eclectic spot. Choose from fusion wraps and burgers at the original **Meat & Drink** (Map p80; ☑ 089 666414; mains US$5-10; ⊙ 5pm-1am), tiny and intimate **Seibur** (Map p80; St 308; ⊙ 5pm-1am), the refined **Library** (Map p80; Bassac Lane; ⊙ 5pm-1am; 🛜), newcomer **Harry's Bar** (Map p80; ⊙ 5pm-1am) or custom-bike tribute bar, **Hangar 44** (Map p80; ⊙ 5pm-1am). There's even a gin palace, the tiny **Cicada Bar** (Map p80; ⊙ 5pm-1am). From out of nowhere, Bassac Lane has become the new Bohemian district of Phnom Penh and is well worth a visit.

★ **Pontoon**　　　　　　　　　　CLUB
(Map p78; www.pontoonclub.com; 80 St 172; weekends US$3-5, weekdays free; ⊙ 9.30pm-late; 🛜) After floating around from pier to pier for a few years (hence the name), the city's premier nightclub found a permanent home on terra firma. It draws top local DJs and occasional big foreign acts. Thursday is gay-friendly night, with a 1am lady-boy show. Adjacent Pontoon Pulse is more of a lounge-club, with electronica and ambient music.

Dusk Til Dawn　　　　　　　　BAR
(Map p78; 46 St 172; ⊙ 5pm-late) Also known as Reggae Bar thanks to the laid-back beats, Dusk Til Dawn's rooftop setting makes it a great spot for a sundowner, but the party lasts well into the night. The bar is split over two levels, so continue upstairs if it's quiet. Ride the lift to the top floor in the tall building opposite Pontoon club.

Blue Chili　　　　　　　　　　GAY
(Map p78; 36 St 178; ⊙ 6pm-late; 🛜) The owner of this long-running, gay-friendly bar stages his own drag show every Friday and Saturday at 10.30pm.

Heart of Darkness　　　　　CLUB
(Map p78; 26 St 51; ⊙ 8pm-late) This Phnom Penh institution with an alluring Angkor theme has evolved more into a nightclub than a bar over the years. It goes off every night of the week, attracting all – and we

mean *all* – sorts. Everybody should stop in at least once just to bask in the aura and atmosphere of the place.

☆ Entertainment

For news on what's happening in town, AsiaLife is a free monthly with entertainment features and some listings. Online, try www.lengpleng.com.

★ **Traditional Dance Show**　PERFORMING ARTS
(Map p78; ☑ 017 998570; www.cambodianliving arts.org; National Museum, St 178; adult/child from US$15/10; ⊙ 7pm daily Oct-Mar, Mon-Sat Jun-Aug, Mon, Wed, Fri & Sat Apr, May & Sep) 🖉 The Traditional Dance Show is a series of must-see performances put on by **Cambodian Living Arts** (CLA; Map p80; 128 Samdech Sothearos Blvd). There are three rotating shows, each lasting about an hour: *Shadow & Light* (Monday to Wednesday); *Grace & Grandeur* (Thursday and Saturday); and *Heaven & Earth* (Friday and Sunday). Set in the attractive grounds of the National Museum, there's also an optional dinner show (US$30, 5.30pm).

★ **Meta House**　　　　　　　CINEMA
(Map p80; www.meta-house.com; 37 Samdech Sothearos Blvd; ⊙ 4pm-midnight Tue-Sun; 🛜) This German-run cinema screens art-house films, documentaries and shorts from Cambodia and around the world most evenings at 4pm (admission free) and 7pm (admission varies). Films are sometimes followed by Q&As with those involved. Order German sausages, pizza-like 'flamecakes' and beer to supplement your viewing experience.

Sovanna Phum Arts Association　　PERFORMING ARTS
(Map p77; ☑ 010 337552; 166 St 99, btwn Sts 484 & 498; adult/child US$5/3) 🖉 Regular traditional shadow-puppet performances and occasional classical dance and traditional drum shows are held here at 7.30pm every Friday and Saturday night. Audience members are invited to try their hand at the shadow puppets after the 50-minute performance. Classes are available in the art of shadow puppetry, puppet making, classical and folk dance, and traditional Khmer musical instruments.

Flicks　　　　　　　　　　CINEMA
(Map p80; www.theflicks-cambodia.com; 39B St 95; tickets US$3.50; 🛜) It shows at least two movies a day in an uber-comfortable, air-conditioned screening room. You can watch both films on one ticket.

🛍 Shopping

An affirmation of identity, the *krama* (chequered scarf) is worn around the necks, shoulders and waists of nearly every Khmer. The scarves make superb souvenirs, as do Cambodia's sculptures and handicrafts. Bargains galore can be found at Phnom Penh's vibrant markets. Navigating the labyrinths of shoes, clothing, bric-a-brac and food is one of the most enjoyable ways to earn a foot massage.

⭐ Psar Thmei   MARKET
(ផ្សារធំថ្មី, Central Market; Map p78; St 130; ⊙6.30am-5.30pm) A landmark building in the capital, the art-deco Psar Thmei (literally 'New Market') is often called the Central Market, a reference to its location and size. The huge domed hall resembles a Babylonian ziggurat and some claim it ranks as one of the 10 largest domes in the world.

Russian Market   MARKET
(Psar Tuol Tom Pong; Map p77; St 155; ⊙6am-5pm) This sweltering bazaar is the market all visitors should come to at least once during a trip to Phnom Penh. It is *the* place to shop for souvenirs and discounted name-brand clothing. We can't vouch for the authenticity of everything, but along with knock-offs you'll find genuine locally made articles.

Night Market   MARKET
(Psar Reatrey; Map p78; cnr St 108 & Sisowath Quay; ⊙5-11pm daily) A cooler, alfresco version of the Russian Market, this night market takes place every evening if it's not raining. Bargain vigorously, as prices can be on the high side. Interestingly, it's probably more popular with Khmers than foreigners.

Monument Books   BOOKS
(Map p80; 111 Norodom Blvd; ⊙7am-8.30pm) The best-stocked bookshop in town, with almost every Cambodia-related book available and a superb maps-and-travel section.

D's Books   BOOKS
(Map p80; 79 St 240; ⊙9am-9pm) The largest chain of secondhand bookshops in the capital, with a good range of titles.

ℹ Orientation

Phnom Penh's sequentially numbered streets may be a paragon of logic, but when it comes to house numbering, utter chaos reigns. It's not uncommon to find a row of adjacent buildings numbered, say, 13A, 34, 7, 26. Worse, several buildings on the same street, blocks apart, may have adopted the same house number! When you're given an address, try to get a cross-street, such as 'on St 240 near St 51'.

SHOPPING FOR A CAUSE

The stores here sell high-quality silk items and handicrafts to provide the disabled and disenfranchised with valuable training for future employment, plus a regular flow of income to improve lives.

Daughters of Cambodia (Map p78; www.daughtersofcambodia.org; 321 Sisowath Quay; ⊙9am-5.30pm Mon-Sat) Daughters is an NGO that runs a range of programs to train and assist former prostitutes and victims of sex trafficking. The fashionable clothes, bags and accessories here are made with ecofriendly cotton and natural dyes by program participants.

Rajana (Map p77; www.rajanacrafts.org; 170 St 450; ⊙7am-6pm Mon-Sat, 10.30am-5pm Sun) One of the best all-round handicraft stores, Rajana aims to promote fair wages and training. It has a beautiful selection of cards, some quirky metalware products, jewellery, bamboo crafts, lovely shirts, gorgeous wall hangings, candles: you name it, they probably have it.

Mekong Blue (Map p78; http://mekongblue.com; 9 St 130; ⊙8am-6pm) This is the Phnom Penh boutique for Stung Treng's best-known silk cooperative to empower women. Produces beautiful scarves and shawls, as well as jewellery.

Tabitha (Map p80; 239 St 360; ⊙7am-6pm Mon-Sat) A leading NGO shop with a good collection of silk bags, tableware, bedroom decorations and children's toys. Proceeds go towards rural community development, such as well drilling.

Watthan Artisans (Map p77; www.wac.khmerproducts.com; 180 Norodom Blvd; ⊙8am-6.30pm) Located at the entrance to Wat Than, it sells silk and other products, including wonderful contemporary handbags, made by a project-supported cooperative of land mine and polio victims. You can visit the on-site woodworking and weaving workshops.

CAMBODIA PHNOM PENH

ℹ Information

EMERGENCY

In the event of a medical emergency it may be necessary to be evacuated to Bangkok.

Ambulance	☎ 119 in emergency; ☎ 023-723840 in English
Fire	☎ 118 in emergency
Police	☎ 117 in emergency; ☎ 097 778 0002 in English

INTERNET ACCESS

Pretty much all hotels and most cafes, restaurants and bars offer free wi-fi. Internet cafes are less common than they used to be, but usually charge US$0.50 to US$1 per hour.

MEDICAL SERVICES

Calmette Hospital (Map p77; ☎ 023-426948; www.calmette.gov.kh; 3 Monivong Blvd; ☺24hr) The best of the local hospitals, with the most comprehensive services and an intensive-care unit, but it really helps to go with a Khmer speaker.

Tropical & Travellers Medical Clinic (Map p78; ☎ 023-306802; www.travellersmedical-clinic.com; 88 St 108; ☺9.30-11.30am & 2.30-5pm Mon-Fri, to 11.30am Sat) Well-regarded clinic, run by a British general practitioner for more than two decades.

U-Care Pharmacy (Map p78; 26 Samdech Sothearos Blvd; ☺8am-10pm) International-style pharmacy with a convenient location.

ℹ WARNING: BAG SNATCHING

Bag snatching has become a real problem in Phnom Penh, with foreigners often targeted. Hot spots include the riverfront and busy areas around popular markets, but there is no real pattern; the speeding motorbike thieves, usually operating in pairs, can strike any time, any place. Countless expats and tourists have been injured falling off their bikes in the process of being robbed. Wear close-fitting bags (such as backpacks) that don't dangle from the body temptingly. Don't hang expensive cameras around the neck and keep things close to the body and out of sight, particularly when walking along the road, crossing the road or travelling by remork-moto (tuk tuk) or especially by moto. These people are real pros and only need one chance.

MONEY

Phnom Penh's airport has a few ATMs. The city has plenty of banks and exchange services, including the following:

ANZ Royal Bank (Map p78; 265 Sisowath Quay; ☺8.30am-4pm Mon-Fri, to noon Sat) ANZ has ATMs galore all over town, including at supermarkets and petrol stations, but there is a US$5 charge per transaction.

Canadia Bank (Map p78; cnr St 110 & Monivong Blvd; ☺8am-3.30pm Mon-Fri, to 11.30am Sat) Has ATMs around town, with a US$4 charge. At its flagship branch you can also get cash advances on MasterCard and Visa. Also represents MoneyGram.

POST

The **Central Post Office** (Map p78; St 13; ☺8am-6pm) is housed in a French-colonial classic just east of Wat Phnom.

TOURIST INFORMATION

There is not much in the way of official tourist information in the Cambodian capital, but private travel agencies are everywhere and are usually happy to dispense advice.

The Phnom Penh Visitors' Guide (www.canbypublications.com) has good maps and is brimming with useful information on the capital. Also, look out for the free Phnom Penh Pocket Guide (www.cambodiapocketguide.com).

ℹ Getting There & Away

AIR

Many international air services operate to/from **Phnom Penh International Airport** (PNH; ☎ 023-862800; www.cambodia-airports.com). Domestically, there are now several airlines connecting Phnom Penh and Siem Reap. **Cambodia Angkor Air** (Map p77; ☎ 023-666 6786; www.cambodiaangkorair.com; 206A Norodom Blvd) flies four to six times daily to Siem Reap (from US$35 to US$110 one way, 30 minutes), while **Bassaka Air** (☎ 023-217613; www.bassakaair.com), **JC Airlines** (www.jcairline.com) and **Cambodia Bayon Airlines** (☎ 023-231555; www.bayonairlines.com) have at least one flight a day, from US$20 to US$75 one way. Healthy competition has really driven down prices recently, so it pays to book ahead for special promotions.

BOAT

Between August and March, speedboats depart daily to Siem Reap (US$35, five to six hours) at 7.30am from the tourist-boat dock at the eastern end of St 104, but the tickets are overpriced compared with the bus.

Following the river to Chau Doc in Vietnam is a gorgeous way to go; see the boxed text 'Getting to Vietnam: Mekong Delta Borders'.

ℹ GETTING TO VIETNAM: MEKONG DELTA BORDERS

Phnom Penh to Ho Chi Minh City

The original Bavet/Moc Bai land crossing between Vietnam and Cambodia has seen steady traffic for two decades.

Getting to the border The easiest way to get to Ho Chi Minh City (HCMC; Saigon) is to catch an international bus (US$8 to US$13, six hours) from Phnom Penh. Numerous companies make this trip.

At the border Long lines entering either country are not uncommon, but otherwise it's a straightforward crossing.

Moving on If you are not on the international bus, it's not hard to find onward transport to HCMC or elsewhere.

For information on making this crossing in reverse, see p902.

Phnom Penh to Chau Doc

The most scenic way to end your travels in Cambodia is to sail the Mekong to Kaam Samnor, about 100km south-southeast of Phnom Penh, cross the border to Vinh Xuong in Vietnam, and proceed to Chau Doc on the Tonlé Bassac River via a small channel. Chau Doc has onward land and river connections to points in the Mekong Delta and elsewhere in Vietnam. Various companies do trips all the way through to Chau Doc using a single boat (US$25 to US$35, about four hours) or a cheaper bus/boat combo (US$19). Prices vary according to speed and level of service. Departures are from the tourist-boat dock in Phnom Penh. For information on making this crossing in reverse, see p908.

Takeo to Chau Doc

The remote and seldom-used Phnom Den/Tinh Bien border crossing (open 7am to 5pm) between Cambodia and Vietnam lies about 50km southeast of Takeo town in Cambodia and offers connections to Chau Doc.

Getting to the border Take a share taxi (10,000r), a chartered taxi (US$25) or a moto (US$10) from Takeo to the border (48km).

At the border Formalities are minimal here, as international traffic is light.

Moving on On the other side, travellers are at the mercy of Vietnamese xe om (moto) drivers and taxis for the 30km journey from the border to Chau Doc. Prepare for some tough negotiations. Expect to pay around US$10 by bike, and more like US$20 for a taxi.

For information on making this crossing in reverse, see p908.

BUS

All major towns in Cambodia are accessible by air-conditioned bus from Phnom Penh. Most buses leave from company offices, which are generally clustered around Psar Thmei or located near the corner of St 106 and Sisowath Quay. Buying tickets in advance is a good idea for peace of mind, although it's not always necessary.

Not all buses are created equal, or priced the same. Buses run by Capitol Tour and Phnom Penh Sorya are usually among the cheapest, while Giant Ibis and Mekong Express buses are better and pricier.

Most of the long-distance buses drop off and pick up in major towns along the way, such as Kompong Thom en route to Siem Reap, Pursat on the way to Battambang, or Kompong Cham en route to Kratie. However, full fare is usually charged anyway.

Express minivans are generally faster than buses on most routes, but some travellers prefer the size and space of a large bus.

To book bus tickets online, visit www.camboticket.com.

Capitol Tour (Map p80; ☑ 023-724104; 14 St 182; US$19) Cheap buses to popular destinations such as Siem Reap, Sihanoukville and Battambang.

Giant Ibis (Map p78; ☑ 023-999333; www.giantibis.com; 3 St 106) 'VIP' bus and express-van specialist. Big bus to Siem Reap has plenty of legroom and wi-fi. A portion of profits goes towards giant ibis conservation.

GST (Map p78; ☑ 023-218114; 13 St 142) Buses nationwide.

Long Phuong (Map p80; ☑ 097 311 0999; www.longphuongcambodia.com; 274 Sihanouk Blvd) Buses to Ho Chi Minh City.

Mekong Express (Map p78; ☑ 023-427518; www.catmekongexpress.com; Sisowath Quay)

VIP buses to Ho Chi Minh City, plus Siem Reap and Sihanoukville.

Phnom Penh Sorya (Map p78; ☎ 023-210359; cnr Sts 217 & 67, Psar Thmei area) Bus services all over the country.

Sapaco (Map p80; ☎ 023-210300; www. sapacotourist.com; 309 Sihanouk Blvd) Buses to Ho Chi Minh City.

Virak Buntham (Map p78; ☎ 016-786270; 1 St 106) Night-bus specialist with services to Siem Reap, Sihanoukville and Koh Kong.

CAR & MOTORCYCLE

Guesthouses and travel agencies can arrange a car and driver for US$25 to US$75 a day, depending on the destination.

SHARE TAXI & MINIBUS

Share taxis serve most destinations. They save time and offer flexible departure times. Local minibuses and pickups tend to be slow and packed, but they will save you a buck or two if you're pinching pennies and offer a true 'local' experience (especially if somebody vomits on you). Taxis to Kampot, Kep and Takeo leave from **Psar Dang Kor** (Map p77; Mao Tse Toung Blvd), while local minibuses and share taxis for most other places leave from the northwest corner of **Psar Thmei** (Map p78).

🛈 Getting Around

TO/FROM THE AIRPORT & BUS STATION

Phnom Penh International Airport is 7km west of central Phnom Penh, via Russian Confederation

BUSES FROM PHNOM PENH

DESTINATION	DURATION (HR)	COST (US$)	COMPANIES	FREQUENCY
Ban Lung	11	12	PP Sorya	6.45am
Bangkok	12	18-23	Mekong Express, PP Sorya, Virak Buntham	1 daily
Battambang (day)	5-6	5-6	GST, PP Sorya	frequent
Battambang (night)	6	8-10	Virak Buntham	4 per night
Ho Chi Minh City	7	8-13	Capitol Tour, Long Phuong, Mekong Express, PP Sorya, Sapaco, Virak Buntham (night bus)	frequent
Kampot (direct)	3	5-6	Capitol Tour	2 daily
Kampot (via Kep)	4	6	PP Sorya	7.30am, 9.30am, 2.45pm
Kep	3	5	PP Sorya	7.30am, 9.30am, 2.45pm
Koh Kong	5½	7	Olympic Express, PP Sorya, Virak Buntham	2-3 daily (before noon)
Kompong Cham	3	5	PP Sorya; GST	hourly to 4pm
Kratie	6-8	8	PP Sorya	regularly in the morning
Poipet (day)	8	9-11	Capitol Tour, PP Sorya	frequently to noon
Poipet (night)	7	10-11	Virak Buntham	at least 1 daily
Preah Vihear City	7	10	GST, PP Sorya	morning only
Sen Monorom	8	9	Minivans only	regular
Siem Reap (day)	6	6-8	most companies	frequent
Siem Reap (VIP)	6	13-15	Giant Ibis, Mekong Express	regular
Siem Reap (night)	6	10	Virak Buntham	6pm, 8pm, 11pm, 12.30am
Sihanoukville	5½	5-6	Capitol Tour, GST, Mekong Express, PP Sorya, Virak Buntham	frequent
Stung Treng	9	10	PP Sorya	6.45am, 7.30am

Blvd. There are ATMs for US dollars withdrawals on arrival or departure.

When arriving by air at Phnom Penh International Airport, there is an official booth outside the airport arrivals area to arrange taxis to the centre for US$12; a remork-moto costs a flat US$9. You can get a remork for US$5 to US$7 and a moto (motorcycle taxi) for about US$3 if you exit the airport and arrange one on the street.

The cheapest option to the city is the Bus No 3 (1500r) which has a stop right outside the airport and runs to the Night Market and riverfront. It can be slow with 20 or more stops along the way.

If you arrive in town by bus, chances are you'll be dropped off near Psar Thmei (aka Central Market), a short ride from most hotels and guesthouses. Figure on US$0.50 to US$1 for a moto, and US$2 to US$3 for a remork. Prices are about the same from the tourist-boat dock on Sisowath Quay, where arriving boats from Vietnam and Siem Reap incite *moto*-madness.

BICYCLE
Simple bicycles can be hired from some guesthouses and hotels from US$1 a day, or contact Vicious Cycle (p76) for something more sophisticated.

MOTO, REMORK & CYCLO
Motos are everywhere and the drivers of those hanging out around tourist areas can generally speak good street English. Short rides around the city cost 2000r rising to US$1 for a longer ride of 2km. At night these prices double. To charter one for a day, expect to pay around US$10 in town. Remorks usually charge double the price of a moto, possibly more if you pile on the passengers. Cyclos can be tougher to find but cost about the same as motos.

MOTORCYCLE
Exploring Phnom Penh and the surrounding areas on a motorbike is a very liberating experience if you are used to chaotic traffic conditions. You generally get what you pay for when choosing a steel variety.

Lucky! Lucky! (Map p80; ☑ 023-212788; 413 Monivong Blvd) Motorbikes are US$4 to US$7 per day, less for multiday rentals. Trail bikes from US$12.

Vannak Bikes Rental (Map p78; ☑ 012 220970; 46 St 130) Has high-performance trail bikes up to 600cc for US$15 to US$30 per day, and smaller motorbikes for US$5 to US$7.

TAXI
Taxis are cheap at 3000r per kilometre but don't expect to flag one down on the street. Call **Global Meter Taxi** (☑ 011 311888) or **Choice Taxi** (☑ 010 888010, 023-888023) for a pickup.

AROUND PHNOM PENH

There are several sites close to Phnom Penh that make for rewarding excursions by car or motorbike. Tonlé Bati and Phnom Tamao are near each other on NH2 and make a great day trip together.

Koh Dach កោះដាច់

Known as 'Silk Island' by foreigners, this is actually a pair of islands lying in the Mekong River about 5km northeast of the Japanese Friendship Bridge. They make for an easy half-day DIY excursion for those who want to experience the 'real Cambodia'. The hustle and bustle of Phnom Penh feels light years away here. The name derives from the preponderance of silk weavers who inhabit the islands, and you'll have plenty of chances to buy from them.

Remork drivers offer half-day tours to Koh Dach; US$12 should do it, but be ready to negotiate. Daily boat tours from the tourist boat dock, departing at 8.30am, 9.30am and 1pm, are another option (minimum four people).

Tonlé Bati ទន្លេបាទី

Locals love to come to **Tonlé Bati** (US$3, incl lake & temples) for picnics, as along the way they can stop off at two 12th-century temples: Ta Prohm and Yeay Peau. Ta Prohm is the more interesting of the two and it has some fine carvings in good condition, depicting scenes of birth, dishonour and damnation.

The well-marked turn-off to Tonlé Bati is on the right, 33km south of central Phnom Penh. The Takeo-bound Phnom Penh Sorya bus (8000r, four daily – shoot for the 7am or 10.30am one) can drop you here; find a moto to the temples (1.8km from the highway). Returning to Phnom Penh, buy a ticket in advance on Sorya's Takeo–Phnom Penh bus. Otherwise, hire a moto.

Phnom Tamao Wildlife Sanctuary
មជ្ឈមណ្ឌលសង្គ្រោះសត្វព្រៃភ្នំតាម៉ៅ

This **centre** (adult/child US$5/2; ☉ 8am-5pm) for rescued animals is home to gibbons, sun bears, elephants, tigers, deer and a bird enclosure. All were taken from poachers or abusive owners and receive care and shelter here as part of a sustainable breeding program.

The access road to Phnom Tamao is clearly signposted on the right 6.5km south of the turn-off to Tonlé Bati on NH2. If coming by bus, have the driver let you off at the turn-off, where motos await to whisk you the final 5km to the sanctuary.

SIEM REAP & THE TEMPLES OF ANGKOR

✔ 063 / POP 185,000 (TOWN)

Siem Reap is the life-support system for the temples of Angkor, the eighth wonder of the world. Although in a state of slumber from the late 1960s until a few years ago, the town has woken up with a jolt and is now one of the regional hotspots for wining and dining, shopping and schmoozing. The ultimate fusion of creative ambition and spiritual devotion, the temples of Angkor are a source of inspiration and profound pride to all Khmers. No traveller to the region will want to miss their extravagant beauty and spine-tingling grandeur. One of the most impressive ancient sites on earth, Angkor has the epic proportions of the Great Wall of China, the detail and intricacy of the Taj Mahal and the symbolism and symmetry of the Egyptian pyramids, all rolled into one. Angkor is a place to be savoured, not rushed, and Siem Reap is the perfect base from which to plan your adventures.

ℹ Getting Around

There are endless options when it comes to exploring Angkor. Bicycles are a great way to get to and around the temples, which are linked by flat roads that are in good shape. Just make sure you drink plenty of water at every opportunity.

Another environmentally friendly option is to explore on foot. There are obvious limitations, but exploring Angkor Thom's walls or walking to and from Angkor Wat are both feasible. Don't forget to buy an entrance ticket.

Zippy and inexpensive motos (about US$10 per day, more for distant sites) are the most popular form of transport around the temples. Drivers accost visitors from the moment they set foot in Siem Reap, but they often end up being friendly and knowledgeable. Guesthouses are also a good source of experienced driver-guides.

Remorks (around US$15 a day, more for distant sites) take a little longer than motos but offer protection from the rain and sun.

Even more protection is offered by cars, though these tend to isolate you from the sights, sounds and smells. Hiring a car in Siem Reap costs about US$30 for a day cruising around Angkor; US$50

to Kbal Spean and Banteay Srei; US$70 to Beng Mealea; and US$90 out to Koh Ker.

Siem Reap សៀមរាប

Siem Reap is the comeback kid of Southeast Asia. It has reinvented itself as the epicentre of the new Cambodia, with more hotels and guesthouses than temples, world-class wining and dining, and sumptuous spas. At its heart, it remains a charming town with rural qualities. Old French shophouses, shady tree-lined boulevards and a winding river are attractive remnants of the past, while five-star hotels, air-con buses and international restaurants point to a glitzy future.

⊙ Sights

★ **Angkor National Museum**   MUSEUM
(សារមន្ទីរជាតិអង្គរ; Map p92; ✔063-966601; www.angkornationalmuseum.com; 968 Charles de Gaulle Blvd; adult/child under 1.2m US$12/6; ⊙8.30am-6pm May-Sep, to 6.30pm Oct-Apr; ☎) Looming large on the road to Angkor is the Angkor National Museum, a state-of-the-art showpiece on the Khmer civilisation and the majesty of Angkor. Displays are themed by era, religion and royalty as visitors move through the impressive galleries. After a short presentation, visitors enter the Zen-like Gallery of a Thousand Buddhas, which has a fine collection of images. Other exhibits include the pre-Angkorian periods of Funan and Chenla; the great Khmer kings; Angkor Wat; Angkor Thom; and the inscriptions.

★ **Artisans Angkor –
Les Chantiers Écoles**   ARTS CENTRE
(សិប្បករអង្គរ; Map p92; www.artisansdangkor. com; ⊙7.30am-6.30pm) 🖉 **FREE** Siem Reap is the epicentre of the drive to revitalise Cambodian traditional culture, which was dealt a harsh blow by the Khmer Rouge and the years of instability that followed its rule. Les Chantiers Écoles teaches wood- and stone-carving techniques, traditional silk painting, lacquerware and other artisan skills to impoverished young Cambodians. Free guided tours explaining traditional techniques are available daily from 7.30am to 6.30pm. Tucked down a side road, the school is well signposted from Sivatha St.

★ **Cambodia Landmine Museum**   MUSEUM
(សារមន្ទីរគ្រាប់មីនកម្ពុជា និងមូលនិធិស ្រ្តា៖; www.cambodialandminemuseum.org; US$5; ⊙7.30am-5pm) Established by DIY de-miner

WORTH A TRIP

FLOATING VILLAGES

The famous floating village of **Chong Kneas** is an easy excursion to arrange yourself. The village moves depending on the season and you will need to rent a boat to get around it properly. Unfortunately, large tour groups tend to take over and Sou Ching, the company that runs the tours, has fixed boat prices at an absurd US$20 per person, plus US$3 entry. Contact **Tara Boat** (☑092 957765; www.taraboat.com; per person incl lunch/dinner US$29/36) for an all-inclusive trip. The small, floating **Gecko Centre** (www.greengecko-project.org; ⊙8.30am-5.30pm) has displays on the Tonlé Sap's remarkable annual cycle.

To get to Chong Kneas from Siem Reap costs US$3 by moto each way (more if the driver waits), or US$15 by taxi. The trip takes 20 minutes. Alternatively, you can rent a bicycle in town, as it's a leisurely 11km ride through pretty villages and rice fields.

More memorable than Chong Kneas, but also harder to reach, is the friendly village of **Kompong Pluk**, an other-worldly place built on soaring stilts. In the wet season you can explore the nearby flooded forest by canoe. Similar to Chong Kneas, prices have been set at between US$20 and US$30 per person for a boat, but again it may be possible to negotiate this as a per-boat cost split between a group. To get here, travel via the small town of Roluos by a 60- to 90-minute combination of road and boat.

Aki Ra, this museum has eye-opening displays on the curse of landmines in Cambodia. The collection includes mines, mortars, guns and weaponry, and there is a mock minefield where visitors can attempt to locate the deactivated mines. Proceeds from the museum are ploughed into mine-awareness campaigns. The museum is about 25km from Siem Reap, near Banteay Srei.

**Banteay Srei
Butterfly Centre**　　　WILDLIFE RESERVE
(មជ្ឈមណ្ឌលសួនមេអំបៅបន្ទាយស្រី; www.angkorbutterfly.com; adult/child US$5/2; ⊙9am-5pm) The Banteay Srei Butterfly Centre is one of the largest fully enclosed butterfly centres in Southeast Asia, with more than 30 species of Cambodian butterflies fluttering about. It is a good experience for children, as they can see the whole life cycle from egg to caterpillar to cocoon to butterfly.

Cambolac　　　ARTS CENTRE
(ខេមប៉ូឡាក់; Map p92; ☑088 355 6078; http://cambolac.com; Wat Polanka; ⊙8-11.30am & 1-5pm Mon-Sat) FREE Cambodia has a long tradition of producing beautiful lacquerware, although the years of upheaval resulted in some of the skills being lost. Cambolac is a social enterprise helping to restore Cambodia's lacquer tradition and create a new contemporary scene. You can tour the workshop to learn more about the perfectionist approach required to produce a piece. Most of the guides are hearing-impaired and a tour allows some great interaction and the opportunity to learn some basic sign language.

Wat Bo　　　BUDDHIST TEMPLE
(វត្តបូ; Map p92; Tep Vong St; ⊙6am-6pm) FREE This is one of the town's oldest temples and has a collection of well-preserved wall paintings from the late 19th century depicting the *Reamker,* Cambodia's interpretation of the *Ramayana.* The monks here regularly chant sometime between 4.30pm and 6pm and this can be a spellbinding and spiritual moment if you happen to be visiting.

 ## Activities

Foot massage is a big hit in Siem Reap, hardly surprising given all those steep stairways at the temples. There are half a dozen or more places offering a massage for about US$6 to US$8 an hour on the strip running northwest of Psar Chaa. Some are more authentic than others, so dip your toe in first before selling your sole. For an alternative foot massage, try a fish spa, which sees cleaner fish nibble away at your dead skin – heaven for some, tickly as hell for others. Places have sprung up all over town, including along Pub St.

★ Angkor Zipline　　　ZIPLINE
(Map p104; ☑096 999 9100; www.angkorzipline.com; short/full course US$60/100; ⊙6am-5pm) Angkor provides the ultimate backdrop for this zipline experience, although you won't actually see the temples while navigating the course. Formerly Flight of the Gibbon Angkor, the Angkor Zipline is located inside the Angkor protected area. The course includes 10 ziplines, 21 treetop platforms, four skybridges and an abseil finish. There is a panoramic rest stop halfway and highlights include a tandem line for couples.

Siem Reap

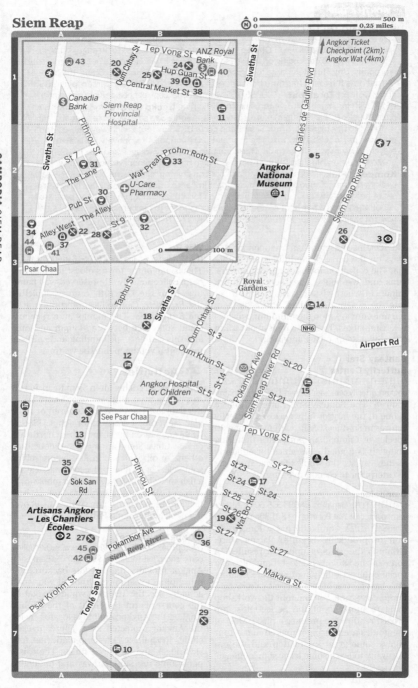

0   500 m
0   0.25 miles

Angkor Ticket
Checkpoint (2km);
Angkor Wat (4km)

Tep Vong St

ANZ Royal
Bank

Oum Chhay St

Central Market St

Hup Guan St

Sivatha St

Charles de Gaulle Blvd

Canadia
Bank

Siem Reap
Provincial
Hospital

Angkor
National
Museum

Siem Reap River Rd

Pithnou St

Sivatha St

St 7

The Lane

Wat Preah Prohm Roth St

U-Care
Pharmacy

Pub St

The Alley

Alley West

St 9

Psar Chaa

0   100 m

Royal
Gardens

Taphul St

Sivatha St

Oum Chhay St

St 3

NH6

Airport Rd

Oum Khun St

St 20

Angkor Hospital
for Children

St 14

St 5

Pokambor Ave

Siem Reap River Rd

St 21

See Psar Chaa

Pithnou St

Tep Vong St

Sok San
Rd

St 23

St 22

St 24

St 24

St 25

Wat Bo Rd

St 26

Artisans Angkor
– Les Chantiers
Écoles

St 27

Pokambor Ave

St 27

Siem Reap River

Psar Krohm St

Tonlé Sap Rd

7 Makara St

Siem Reap

Angkor Wat Putt GOLF
(Map p104; ☑ 012 302330; www.angkorwatputt.
com; Chreav District; adult/child US$5/4; ◷8am-
8pm) Crazy golf to the Brits among us, this
home-grown minigolf course contrasts with
the big golf courses out of town. Navigate
minitemples and creative obstacles for 14
holes and win a beer for a hole-in-one. Recently relocated to a more remote location,
it is well worth seeking out.

Krousar Thmey MASSAGE
(Map p104; www.krousar-thmey.org; Charles de
Gaulle Blvd; 1hr massage US$7; ◷9am-9pm) ⊘
Massages here are performed by blind masseurs. In the same location is the free Tonlé
Sap Exhibition, which includes a 'Seeing in
the Dark' interactive exhibition exploring
what it is like to be blind, guided by a vision-
impaired student.

Peace Cafe Yoga YOGA
(Map p92; ☑ 063-965210; www.peacecafeangkor.
org; Siem Reap River Rd East; per session US$6)
This popular community centre and cafe has

daily morning and evening yoga sessions, including ashtanga and hatha sessions.

Seeing Hands Massage 4 MASSAGE
(Map p92; ☑ 012 836487; 324 Sivatha St; per fan/
air-con US$5/7) ⊘ Seeing Hands trains blind
people in the art of massage. Watch out for
copycats, as some of these are just exploiting
the blind for profit.

Happy Ranch HORSE RIDING
(Map p104; ☑ 012 920002; www.thehappyranch.
com; 1hr/half-day US$28/59) Forget the Wild
West – try your hand at horse riding in the
Wild East. Happy Ranch offers the chance to
explore Siem Reap on horseback, taking in
surrounding villages and secluded temples.
This is a calm way to experience the countryside, far from the traffic and crowds.

Popular rides take in Wat Athvea, a modern pagoda with an ancient temple on its
grounds, and Wat Chedi, a temple set on a
flood plain near the Tonlé Sap lake. Riding
lessons are available for children and beginners. Book directly for the best prices.

Courses

Le Tigre de Papier
COOKING
(Map p92; ☑ 012 265811; www.angkor-cook-ing-class-cambodia.com; Pub St; per person US$15) Classes include a visit to the market and the chance to prepare an *amok* degustation, a variation on the national dish. Daily classes are held at 10am, 1pm and 5pm.

Vegetarian Cooking Class
COOKING
(Map p92; ☑ 092 177127; http://peacecafeangkor.org; Siem Reap River Rd East; per person US$20) A vegetarian cooking class with tofu *amok*, papaya salad and vegie spring rolls on the menu.

Khmer Ceramics Fine Arts Centre
ART
(សេរាមិចិ; Map p92; ☑ 017 843014; www.khmer-ceramics.com; Charles de Gaulle Blvd; pottery course US$20; ⊙ 8am-8pm) ◢ Located on the road to the temples, this ceramics centre is dedicated to reviving the Khmer tradition of pottery, which was an intricate art during the time of Angkor. It's possible to visit and try your hand at the potter's wheel, and courses in traditional techniques, including pottery and ceramic painting, are available.

Tours

★ KKO Bike Tours
CYCLING
(Khmer for Khmer Organisation; Map p92; ☑ 093 903024; www.kko-cambodia.org; Taphul Rd; tours US$35-60) ◢ Cycling and moto tours around the paths of Angkor or into the countryside beyond the Western Baray. Proceeds go towards the Khmer for Khmer Organisation, which supports education and vocational training.

Quad Adventure Cambodia
ADVENTURE SPORTS
(Map p104; ☑ 092 787216; www.quad-adven-ture-cambodia.com; Country Rd Laurent; sunset ride US$30, full day US$170) The original quad-bike operator in town. Rides around Siem Reap involve rice fields at sunset, pretty temples and back roads through traditional villages.

SUPPORTING RESPONSIBLE TOURISM IN SIEM REAP
ConCERT (www.concertcambodia.org) works to build bridges between tourists and worthy projects in the Siem Reap/Angkor area and offers information on anything from ecotourism initiatives to volunteering opportunities.

★ Siem Reap Food Tours
FOOD & DRINK
(☑ 012 505542; www.siemreapfoodtours.com; per person US$75) Operated by an American food writer and an experienced Scottish chef with a penchant for stand-up comedy, these tours are a recipe for engaging food encounters. Choose from a morning tour that takes in local markets and the *naom banchok* noodle stalls of Preah Dak or an evening tour that takes in street stalls and local barbecue restaurants.

Sleeping

While accommodation is spread throughout town, three areas hold the bulk of budget choices: the Psar Chaa area; the area to the west of Sivatha St; and north of Wat Bo on the east bank of the river. Psar Chaa is the liveliest part of town, brimming with restaurants, bars and boutiques. Staying here can be a lot of fun, but it's not the quietest part of town. The area to the west of Sivatha St includes a good selection of budget guesthouses and midrange boutique hotels. There is a great guesthouse ghetto in a backstreet running parallel to the north end of Wat Bo Rd, which is good for on-the-spot browsing.

★ Onederz Hostel
HOSTEL $
(Map p92; ☑ 063-963525; https://onederz.com; Angkor Night Market St; dm US$8.50-9.50, r US$26; ❋ @ 🛜 ⛱) Winner of several 'Hoscars' (Hostelworld's Oscars), this is one of the smartest hostels in Siem Reap. Facilities include a huge cafe-bar downstairs, which acts as a giant waiting room for all those coming and going from Siem Reap. Dorms are a little pricey but don't forget this is because they include access to the rooftop swimming pool.

★ Green Home I
HOMESTAY $
(Map p104; ☑ 095 334460; www.thegreenhome.org; Chreav Commune; r with fan/air-con US$8/10; ❋ 🛜) Setting the standard for the homestay experience around Siem Reap, the Green Home is set up like a family guesthouse and offers beautiful garden views over the surrounding rice fields. Bathrooms are shared but meticulously clean and the downstairs rooms include air-con. Cooking classes are available, as well as village walks, farm visits and birding trips.

Seven Candles Guesthouse
GUESTHOUSE $
(Map p92; ☑ 063-963380; www.sevencan-dlesguesthouse.com; 307 Wat Bo Rd; r US$20-38; ❋ @ 🛜) ◢ Seven Candles uses profits to help a local foundation that seeks to

promote education in rural communities. Rooms include hot water, TV and fridge, plus some decorative flourishes.

Siem Reap Hostel
HOSTEL $

(Map p92; ☑063-964660; www.thesiemreaphostel.com; 10 Makara St; dm US$8-10, r incl breakfast US$30-45; ❋@🛜🏊) Angkor's original backpacker hostel is pretty slick. The dorms are well tended, while the rooms are definitely flashpacker and include breakfast. There is a lively bar-restaurant and a covered pool, plus a well-organised travel desk.

Mad Monkey
HOSTEL $

(Map p92; www.madmonkeyhostels.com; Sivatha St; dm US$7-9, r US$16-26; ❋@🛜) The Siem Reap outpost of an expanding Monkey business, this classic backpacker has deluxe dorms with air-con and extra-wide bunk beds, good-value rooms for those wanting privacy and the obligatory rooftop bar, only this one's a beach bar!

Ivy Guesthouse 2
GUESTHOUSE $

(Map p92; ☑012 800860; www.ivy-guesthouse.com; Psar Kandal St; r with fan US$6-8, with air-con US$15; ❋@🛜) An inviting guesthouse with a chill-out area and bar, the Ivy is a lively place to stay. The restaurant is as good as it gets among the guesthouses in town, with a huge vegetarian selection and US$1.25 'Tapas Fridays'.

Funky Flashpacker
HOSTEL $

(Map p92; ☑070 221524; www.funkyflashpacker.com; Funky Lane; dm US$5-8, r US$10-40; ❋@🛜🏊) Siem Reap's number-one party address among backpackers. The entire downstairs courtyard is taken up with a swimming pool where regular bouts of water polo take place, while the rooftop bar sizzles with inebriated youth hopped up on cheap shooters. Great hostel, but it's no place for quiet time.

HI Siem Reap Deluxe
HOSTEL $

(Map p92; ☑063-765569; www.hisiemreap.com; 319 Siem Reap River Rd East; dm US$4-6, r US$15-30; ❋🛜🏊) The official Hostelling International property in Siem Reap, the 'Deluxe' offers great services and facilities at rock-bottom prices. Dorm beds include two pillows and a reading light, while private rooms are definitely flashpacker. Throw in a rooftop pool and it's a steal.

Rosy Guesthouse
GUESTHOUSE $

(Map p92; ☑063-965059; www.rosyguesthouse.com; Siem Reap River Rd East; d US$9, with bath-

SPLURGE

A hotel with a heart, promoting local causes to help the community, thie-boutique **Soria Moria Hotel** (Map p92; ☑063-964768; http://thesoriamoria.com; Wat Bo Rd; s US$45-65, d US$60-80; ❋@🛜🏊) has attractive rooms with smart bathroom fittings. There's a fusion restaurant downstairs, sky hot tub upstairs and a swimming pool. Half the hotel was transferred to staff ownership in 2011, a visionary move.

room & air-con US$16-35; ❋🛜) 🌿 A Brit-run establishment whose 13 value-for-money rooms come with TV and DVD, plus tasteful touches like silk furnishings. The lively pub downstairs has great grub and hosts regular events to support community causes, including a popular quiz night.

✗ Eating

Worthy restaurants are sprinkled all around town but Siem Reap's culinary heart is the Psar Chaa area, whose focal point, the Alley, is literally lined with mellow eateries offering great atmosphere. It is wall-to-wall good Cambodian restaurants, many family owned.

For self-caterers, markets sell fruit and veg. **Angkor Market** (Map p92; Sivatha St; ⏱8am-9pm), a supermarket, can supply international treats.

★ Marum
INTERNATIONAL $

(Map p92; ☑017 363284; www.marum-restaurant.org; Wat Polanka area; mains US$3.25-6.75; ⏱11am-10.30pm; 🛜✏🏠) 🌿 Set in a delightful wooden house with a spacious garden, Marum serves up lots of vegetarian and seafood dishes, plus some mouth-watering desserts. Menu highlights include beef with red ants and chilli stir-fry, and mini crocodile burgers. Marum is part of the Tree Alliance group of training restaurants; the experience is a must.

★ Pot & Pan Restaurant
CAMBODIAN $

(Map p92; ☑017 970780; www.thepotandpan-restaurant.com; Stung Thmei Rd; meals US$2-5; ⏱10am-10pm; 🛜) One of the best-value Khmer restaurants in the downtown area, Pot & Pan specialises in well-presented, authentic dishes at affordable prices. The menu includes spicy soups and subtle salads, and rice is beautifully served in a lotus leaf. Some

EXPLORING THE CENTRAL CARDAMOMS PROTECTED FOREST

Although the Central Cardamoms Protected Forest (CCPF) and adjacent wildlife sanctuaries are slowly opening to ecotourism, the opportunities to explore these areas are still somewhat limited, as the ranger stations mostly exist to combat illegal logging, poaching and encroaching. Pursat is emerging as the Cardamoms' northern gateway.

Osoam Cardamon Community Centre (016 309075, 089 899895; http://osoamccc. weebly.com) is a great base to explore the region and can organize hiking, dirt-bike and boat trips in the surrounding countryside, as well as day trips and overnights to **Phnom Samkos**, where elephants roam. The property has seven well-kept rooms (US$6) along with connections to simple guesthouses and homestays (single/double US$5/6) nearby. Electricity is limited and showers come from buckets, but this is about as close to real Cambodia as you can get. Mr. Lim, the enigmatic, self-made Cambodian who runs the place, is becoming a legend among travellers.

Roads and bridges in the area have been upgraded to service a new hydro-dam in Osoam, and you can now get into the park year round. Areas in and near the CCPF are still being de-mined, so stay on roads and well-trodden trails.

From Psar Chaa in Pursat, share taxis and pick-ups serve Kravanh (one hour), Rovieng (two hours) and Pramoay (three hours) year-round. From Pramoay, the track south to Osoam is in rougher shape. It's passable by moto year-round, but taxis can't handle it during the height of the wet season. The road south from Osoam to Koh Kong is much better and can accommodate taxis year-round.

---

of the cheapest pizzas in town are, somewhat surprisingly, also available here.

★ Bloom Cafe   CAFE $

(Map p92; www.bloomcakes.org; St 6; cupcakes US$1.50; ⊙10am-5pm Mon-Sat; 🖘) 🍴 Cupcakes are elevated to an art form at this elegant cafe, with beautifully presented creations available in a rotating array of 48 flavours. Creative coffees, teas and juices are also on offer. Profits assist Cambodian women in vocational training.

★ Gelato Lab   ICE CREAM $

(Map p92; www.facebook.com/gelatolabsiemreap; 109 Alley West; 1/2 scoops US$1.50/2.50; ⊙9am-11pm; 🖘) The great ice cream scooped up here is thanks to the state-of-the-art equipment, all-natural ingredients and – most importantly – plenty of passion courtesy of the Italian owner. Also pours some of the best hand-roasted coffee in town.

Little Red Fox   CAFE $

(Map p92; www.thelittleredfoxespresso.com; Hup Guan St; dishes US$2-8; ⊙7am-5pm Thu-Tue) This foxy little cafe is incredibly popular with long-term residents in Siem Reap, who swear that the regionally sourced Feel Good coffee is the best in town. Add to that designer breakfasts, bagels, salads, creative juices and air-con and it's easy to while away some time here. The slick upstairs wing is popular with the laptop crowd.

Psar Chaa   CAMBODIAN $

(Map p92; mains US$1.50-4; ⊙7am-9pm) When it comes to cheap Khmer eats, Psar Chaa market has plenty of food stalls on the northwestern side, all with signs and menus in English. These are atmospheric places for a local meal at local-ish prices. Some dishes are on display, others are freshly wok-fried to order, but most are wholesome and filling.

Road 60 Night Market   MARKET $

(Map p104; Rd 60; snacks US$1-4; ⊙4-11pm) For a slice of local life, head to the Road 60 Night Market located on the side of the road near the main Angkor ticket checkpoint. Stallholders set up each night, and it's a great place to sample local Cambodian snacks, including the full range of deep-fried insects, barbecue dishes such as quail, and plenty of cheap beer.

Bugs Cafe   CAMBODIAN $

(Map p92; 017 764560; www.bugs-cafe.com; Angkor Night Market St; dishes US$2-8; ⊙5-11pm; 🖘) Cambodians were onto insects long before the food scientists started bugging us about their merits. Choose from a veritable feast of crickets, water bugs, silkworms and spiders. Tarantula doughnuts, pan-fried scorpions, snakes – you won't forget this menu in a hurry.

Banllé Vegetarian Restaurant VEGETARIAN $
(Map p92; www.banlle-vegetarian.com; St 26; dishes US$2-4; ⊙11am-9.30pm Wed-Mon; 🕾🖉) Set in a traditional wooden house with its own organic vegetable garden, this is a great place for a healthy bite. The menu offers a blend of international and Cambodian dishes, including a vegetable *amok* and zesty fruit and vegetable shakes.

★**Haven** FUSION $$
(Map p92; ☑078-342404; www.haven-cambodia. com; Chocolate Rd, Wat Dam Nak area; mains US$6-8; ⊙11.30am-2.30pm & 5.30-9.30pm Mon-Sat, closed Aug; 🕾) 🖉 A culinary haven indeed. Dine here for the best of East meets West; the fish fillet with green mango is particularly zesty. Proceeds go towards helping young adult orphans make the step from institution to employment.

★**Spoons Cafe** CAMBODIAN $$
(Map p92; ☑076 277 6667; www.spoonscambodia. org; Bamboo Rd; mains US$5.50-8; ⊙11.30am-10pm Tue-Sun; 🕾) 🖉 This excellent contemporary-Cambodian restaurant supports local community EGBOK (Everything's Gonna Be OK), which offers education, training and employment opportunities in the hospitality sector. The menu includes some original flavours such as *trey saba* (whole mackerel) with coconut-turmeric rice, tiger-prawn curry and *tuk kroeung*, a pungent local fish-based broth. Original cocktails are shaken, not stirred.

★**Mamma Shop** ITALIAN $$
(Map p92; www.facebook.com/mammashop. italian.restaurant; Hup Guan St; mains US$5-9; ⊙11.30am-10.30pm Mon-Sat; 🕾) A compact menu of terrific homemade pasta is the signature of this bright, friendly Italian corner bistro in the up-and-coming Kandal Village district. Add a selection of *piadina romagnola* (stuffed flatbread) pizza, a nice wine list and delicious desserts, and this place is highly recommended.

🍷 Drinking & Nightlife

Siem Reap is now firmly on the nightlife map of Southeast Asia. The Psar Chaa area is a good hunting ground, and one street is now known as 'Pub St': dive in, crawl out.

★**Asana Wooden House** BAR
(Map p92; www.asana-cambodia.com; The Lane; ⊙11am-late; 🕾) This is a traditional Cambodian countryside home dropped into the backstreets of Siem Reap, which makes for an atmospheric place to drink. Lounge on *kapok*-filled rice sacks while sipping a classic cocktail made with infused rice wine. Khmer cocktail classes (US$15 per person) with Sombai spirits are available.

★**Laundry Bar** BAR
(Map p92; www.facebook.com/laundry.bar.3; St 9; ⊙4pm-late; 🕾) One of the most chilled, chic bars in town thanks to low lighting and discerning decor. This is the place to come for electronica and ambient sounds; it heaves on weekends or when guest DJs crank up the volume. Happy hour until 9pm.

Soul Train Reggae Bar BAR
(Map p92; www.facebook.com/soultrainreggaebar; 35 New St; ⊙5pm-late) One of the most lively late-night spots in town, this bar is tucked away down the side street that passes Wat Preah Prohm Roth, so hopefully the reggae beats are subtle enough not to disturb the monks. Great tunes, cheap drinks and a party atmosphere that is more chilled than Pub St.

Angkor What? BAR
(Map p92; www.facebook.com/theangkorwhatbar; Pub St; ⊙5pm-late; 🕾) Siem Reap's original bar claims to have been promoting irresponsible drinking since 1998. The happy hour (to 9pm) lightens the mood for later when everyone's bouncing along to dance anthems, sometimes on the tables, sometimes under them.

X Bar BAR
(Map p92; www.facebook.com/Xbar.Asia; Sivatha St; ⊙4pm-sunrise; 🕾) One of *the* late-night spots in town, X Bar draws revellers for the witching hour when other places are closing up. Early-evening movies on the big screen, pool tables and even a skateboard pipe – take a breath test first!

☆ Entertainment

Classical dance shows take place all over the town, but only a few are worth considering.

★**Phare the Cambodian Circus** CIRCUS
(Map p104; ☑015 499480; www.pharecircus.org; west end of Sok San Rd; adult/child US$18/10, premium seats US$38/18; ⊙8pm daily) Cambodia's answer to Cirque du Soleil, Phare the Cambodian Circus is so much more than a conventional circus, with an emphasis on performance art and a subtle yet striking social message behind each production. Cambodia's leading circus, theatre and performing arts organisation, Phare Ponleu Selpak opened its big top for nightly shows in 2013 and the results are a unique form of

Siem Reap

Siem Reap is known as gateway to the temples of Angkor; however, there is much going on in and around town to warrant a visit on its own merit. Floating villages on the nearby Tonlé Sap, a superb selection of restaurants and bars, first-class shopping, first-rate cooking classes and a host of other activities as diverse as birdwatching and Vespa tours are all on offer.

1. Ta Prohm (p109)
The temple ruins of Ta Prohm remind us of the power of nature.

2. Tonlé Sap (p91)
The 'floating villages' of Tonlé Sap are fascinating though expensive places to tour.

3. Psar Chaa (p100)
Souvenirs are sold at the market in Siem Reap.

4. Nightlife (p97)
Siem Reap is now firmly on the nightlife map of Southeast Asia and Pub St is a firm favourite with backpackers looking to bar hop.

entertainment that should be considered unmissable when staying in Siem Reap.

Beatocello CLASSICAL MUSIC
(Map p104; www.beatocello.com; Charles de Gaulle Blvd; ⊙7.15pm Sat) 🕊 Better known as Dr Beat Richner, Beatocello performs cello compositions at Jayavarman VII Children's Hospital. Entry is free, but donations are welcome as they assist the hospital in offering free medical treatment to the children of Cambodia.

🛍 Shopping

Siem Reap has an excellent selection of Cambodian-made handicrafts. **Psar Chaa** is well stocked and there are bargains to be had if you haggle patiently and humorously. **Angkor Night Market** (Map p92; https://angkornightmarket.com; ⊙4pm-midnight) is packed with silks, handicrafts and assorted souvenirs. Up-and-coming Alley West is also a great strip to browse socially responsible fashion boutiques. Several shops, such as the exquisite Artisans Angkor (p90), support Cambodia's disabled and disenfranchised.

⭐**AHA Fair Trade Village** ARTS & CRAFTS
(Map p104; ☎078 341454; www.aha-kh.com; Rd 60, Trang Village; ⊙10am-7pm) 🕊 For locally produced souvenirs (unlike much of the imported stuff that turns up in Psar Chaa) drop in on this handicraft market. It's a little out of the way, but there are more than 20 stalls selling a wide range of traditional items. There's a Khmer cultural show every second and fourth Saturday of the month, with extra stalls, traditional music and dancing.

⭐**trunkh.** GIFTS & SOUVENIRS
(Map p92; www.trunkh.com; Hup Guan St; ⊙10am-6pm) The owner here has a great eye for the quirky, stylish and original, including beautiful shirts, throw pillows, jewellery, poster art, and T's, plus some offbeat items such as genuine Cambodian water-buffalo bells.

Sra May FASHION & ACCESSORIES
(Map p92; 640 Hup Guan St; ⊙10am-6pm Mon-Sat) Sra May is a social enterprise that uses traditional local materials such as palm leaves to create boxes and artworks. They also specialise in handwoven *krama*. This is also the drop-in office to book the **PURE! Countryside Bicycle Tour** (Map p92; ☎097 2356862; Hup Guan St; per person US$25-35) 🕊.

Smateria FASHION & ACCESSORIES
(Map p92; www.smateria.com; Alley West; ⊙10am-10pm) 🕊 Recycling rocks here with funky bags made from construction nets, plastic bags, motorbike seat covers and more. It's a fair-trade enterprise employing some disabled Cambodians.

Made in Cambodia MARKET
(Map p92; www.facebook.com/madeincambodia-market; Siem Reap River Rd East; ⊙noon-10pm) King's Rd hosts the daily Made in Cambodia community market, bringing together many of the best local craftsfolk and creators in Siem Reap, many promoting good causes.

ⓘ Information

The free Siem Reap Angkor Visitors Guide (www.can bypublications.com) and Siem Reap Pocket Guide (www.cambodiapocketguide.com) are both widely available in Siem Reap.

There are ATMs at the airport and in banks and minimarts all over central Siem Reap, especially along Sivatha St. The greatest concentration of internet shops is along Sivatha St and around Psar Chaa. Free wi-fi is available at many of the leading cafes, restaurants and bars, not forgetting most guesthouses and hotels.

Angkor Hospital for Children (AHC; Map p92; ☎063-963409; www.angkorhospital.org; cnr Oum Chhay & Tep Vong Sts; ⊙24hr) This international-standard paediatric hospital is the place to take your children if they fall sick. They will also assist adults in an emergency for up to 24 hours. Donations accepted.

ANZ Royal Bank (Map p92; Achar Mean St; ⊙8.30am-3.30pm Mon-Fri, to 11.30am Sat) Offers credit-card cash advances. Several branches and many ATMs (US$5 per withdrawal) are spotted around town.

Canadia Bank (Map p92; Sivatha St; ⊙8.30am-3.30pm Mon-Fri, to 11.30am Sat) Offers credit-card cash advances (US$4) and changes travellers cheques in most major currencies at a 2% commission.

Main Post Office (Map p92; Pokambor Ave; ⊙7am-5.30pm) Services are more reliable these days, but it doesn't hurt to see your stamps franked. Includes a branch of EMS express mail.

Royal Angkor International Hospital (Map p104; ☎063-761888; www.royalangkorhospital.com; Airport Rd) This international facility affiliated with the Bangkok Hospital is on the expensive side as it's used to dealing with insurance companies.

Tourist Police (Map p104; ☎012 402424; Rd 60) Located at the main ticket checkpoint (Map p104; Rd 60; ⊙5am-6pm) for the Angkor area, this is the place to lodge a complaint if you encounter any serious problems while in Siem Reap.

U-Care Pharmacy (Map p92; ☑ 063-965396; Pithnou St; ⊙ 8am-10pm) Smart pharmacy and shop similar to Boots in Thailand (and the UK). English spoken.

❶ Getting There & Away

AIR

Siem Reap International Airport (Map p104; ☑ 063-962400; www.cambodia-airports.com) is a work of art set 7km west of the centre and offers regular connections to most neighbouring Asian cities, plus domestic flights to Phnom Penh and Sihanoukville.

BOAT

Boats for the incredibly scenic trip to Battambang (US$20, five to nine hours depending on water levels) and the faster ride to Phnom Penh (US$35, six hours, August to March only) depart at 7am from the tourist-boat dock at Chong Kneas, 11km south of town.

Tickets are sold at guesthouses, hotels and travel agencies, including pickup from your hotel or guesthouse around 6am.

BUS

All buses depart from the **bus station** (Map p104), which is 3km east of town and nearly 1km south of NH6. Tickets are available at guesthouses, hotels, bus offices, travel agencies and ticket kiosks. Some bus companies send a minibus around to pick up passengers at their place of lodging. Upon arrival in Siem Reap, be prepared for a rugby scrum of eager moto drivers when getting off the bus.

Tickets to Phnom Penh via NH6 cost anywhere from US$5 for basic air-con buses to US$15 for the business-class buses run by Giant Ibis.

Several companies offer direct services to Kompong Cham (US$5, five or six hours), Battambang (US$5 to US$8, three hours) and Poipet (US$5 to US$8, three hours). There are no through buses to Ho Chi Minh City, but it is possible to change in Phnom Penh.

Bus companies in Siem Reap:

Asia Van Transfer (AVT; Map p92; ☑ 063-963853; www.asiavantransfer.com; Hup Guan St) A daily express minivan departs at 8am to Stung Treng (US$20, five hours) via Preah Vihear City, with onward services from Stung Treng to Don Det (Laos), Ban Lung and Kratie.

Giant Ibis (Map p92; ☑ 095 777809; www.giantibis.com) The smartest bus operator serving Phnom Penh (US$15, daily) has free wi-fi on board.

Mekong Express (Map p92; ☑ 063-963662; https://catmekongexpress.com; 14 Sivatha St) Upmarket bus company with hostesses and drinks.

Phnom Penh Sorya (Map p92; ☑ 096 766 6577; https://ppsoryatransport.com.kh; Sivatha St) Most extensive bus network in Cambodia.

CAMBODIA SIEM REAP

❶ GETTING TO THAILAND: SIEM REAP TO BANGKOK

The original land border crossing (open from 7am to 8pm) between Cambodia and Thailand is by far the busiest and the one most people take when travelling between Bangkok and Siem Reap. It has earned itself a bad reputation over the years, with scams galore to help tourists part with their money, especially coming in from Thailand.

Getting to the border Frequent buses and share taxis run from Siem Reap and Battambang to Poipet. Buying a ticket all the way to Bangkok (usually involving a change of buses at the border) can expedite things and save you the hassle of finding onward transport on the Thai side. The 8am through-bus to Mo Chit bus station in Bangkok run by **Nattakan** (Map p104; ☑ 078 795333; www.nattakan-transport.com; Concrete Drain Rd) in Siem Reap costs an inflated US$28, but is the only bus service that allows you to continue to Bangkok without a change of bus.

At the border Waits of two or more hours are not uncommon, especially in the high season. Show up early to avoid the crowds. You can pay a special 'VIP fee' (aka a bribe) of 200B on either side to skip the lines. There is no departure tax to leave Cambodia despite what Cambodian border officials might tell you. Entering Thailand, most nationalities are issued 30-day entry free of charge.

Moving on Minibuses wait just over the border on the Thai side to whisk you to Bangkok (300B, four hours, every 30 minutes). Or make your way 7km to Aranya Prathet by túktúk (80B) or sŏrng·tăa·ou (pickup truck; 15B), from where there are regular buses to Bangkok's Mo Chit station (223B, five to six hours) between 4am and 6pm. The 1.55pm train is another option to Bangkok.

For making this crossing in reverse see p742.

TRANSPORT FROM SIEM REAP

DESTINATION	CAR & MOTORCYCLE	BUS	BOAT	AIR
Bangkok, Thailand	8hr	US$15-28, 10hr, frequent	N/A	US$50-150, 1hr, 8 daily
Battambang	3hr	US$5-8, 4hr, frequent	US$20, 6-8hr, 7am	N/A
Kompong Thom	2hr	US$5, 2hr, frequent	N/A	N/A
Phnom Penh	4-5hr	US$6-15, 5-6hr, frequent	US$35, 5hr, 7am	US$20-100, 30min, frequent
Poipet	3hr	US$5-8, 3hr, frequent	N/A	N/A

Virak Buntham (Map p92; ☑ 017 790440; www.virakbuntham.com) The night-bus specialist to Phnom Penh and Sihanoukville.

SHARE TAXI

Share taxis stop along NH6 just north of the bus station. Destinations include Phnom Penh (US$10, five hours), Kompong Thom (US$5, two hours), Sisophon (US$5, two hours) and Poipet (US$7, two hours).

❶ Getting Around

From the airport, an official taxi costs US$9, while remork-motos (US$7) are also available.

From the bus station a moto/remork to the city centre should cost about US$1/2. If you're arriving on a bus service sold by a guesthouse, the bus will head straight to a partner guesthouse.

If arriving by boat, a moto into town should cost about US$3 from the dock in Chong Kneas. Short moto trips around the centre of town cost 2000r or 4000r, more at night. A remork starts from US$2 and up.

Most guesthouses and small hotels can usually help with bicycle rental for about US$2 per day. Look out for guesthouses and hotels supporting the **White Bicycles** (www.thewhitebicycles. org; per day US$2) project, whose proceeds go to local development projects. otorbike hire is currently prohibited in Siem Reap.

Temples of Angkor

ប្រាសាទអង្គរ

Where to begin with Angkor? There is no greater concentration of architectural riches anywhere on Earth. Choose from the world's largest religious building, Angkor Wat, one of the world's weirdest, Bayon, or the riotous jungle of Ta Prohm. All are global icons and have helped put Cambodia on the map as the temple capital of Asia.

Beyond the big three are dozens more temples, each of which would be the star were it located anywhere else in the region: Banteay Srei, the art gallery of Angkor; Preah Khan, the ultimate fusion temple uniting Buddhism and Hinduism; or Beng Mealea, the Titanic of temples suffocating under the jungle. The most vexing part of a visit to Angkor is working out what to see, as there are simply so many spectacular sites. One day at Angkor? Sacrilege! Don't even consider it.

The hundreds of temples surviving today are but the sacred skeleton of the vast political, religious and social centre of the ancient Khmer empire. Angkor was a city that, at its zenith, boasted a population of one million when London was a small town of 50,000. The houses, public buildings and palaces of Angkor were constructed of wood – now long decayed – because the right to dwell in structures of brick or stone was reserved for the gods.

Angkor Wat   អង្គរវត្ត

The traveller's first glimpse of **Angkor Wat** (Map p104; incl in Angkor admission 1/3/7 days US$37/62/72; ☉ 5am-5.30pm), is simply staggering and is matched by only a few select spots on Earth, such as Machu Picchu or Petra.

Angkor is heaven on earth, namely the symbolic representation of Mt Meru, the Mt Olympus of the Hindu faith and abode of ancient gods. It is the perfect fusion of creative ambition and spiritual devotion. The Cambodian 'god-kings' of old each strove to better their ancestors in size, scale and symmetry, culminating in the world's largest religious building, Angkor Wat.

Angkor Wat is the Khmers' national symbol, the epicentre of their civilisation and a source of fierce national pride. Unlike the other Angkor monuments, it was never abandoned to the elements and has been in virtually continuous use since it was built.

The temple is surrounded by a moat, 190m wide, which forms a giant rectangle measuring 1.5km by 1.3km. Stretching around the outside of the central temple complex is an 800m-long series of bas reliefs, designed to be viewed in an anticlockwise direction. Rising 31m above the third level is the central tower, which gives the whole ensemble its sublime unity.

Angkor Wat was built by Suryavarman II (r 1113–52), who unified Cambodia and extended Khmer influence across much of mainland Southeast Asia. He also set himself apart religiously from earlier kings by his devotion to the Hindu deity Vishnu, to whom he consecrated the temple, built around the same time as European Gothic heavyweights such as Westminster Abbey and Chartres.

The upper level of Angkor Wat is once again open to modern pilgrims, but visits are strictly timed to 20 minutes.

Angkor Thom అంగ్రం

It is hard to imagine any building bigger or more beautiful than Angkor Wat, but in Angkor Thom (Great Angkor, or Great City) the sum of the parts add up to a greater whole. It is the gates that grab you first, flanked by a monumental representation of the Churning of the Ocean of Milk, 54 demons and 54 gods engaged in an epic tug of war on the causeway. Each gate towers above the visitor, the magnanimous faces of the Bodhisattva Avalokiteshvara staring out over the kingdom. Imagine being a peasant in the 13th century approaching the forbidding capital for the first time: it would have been an awe-inspiring yet unsettling experience to enter such a gateway and come face to face with the divine power of the god-kings.

The last great capital of the Khmer empire, Angkor Thom took monumental to a whole new level, set over 10 sq km. It was built in part as a reaction to the surprise sacking of Angkor by the Chams. Jayavarman VII (r 1181–1219) decided that his empire would never again be vulnerable at home. Beyond the formidable walls is a massive moat that would have stopped all but the hardiest invaders in their tracks.

⊙ Sights

At the heart of Angkor Thom is the 12th-century **Bayon** (បាយ័ន; Map p104; ⊙7.30am-5.30pm). The mesmerising if slightly mind-bending state temple of Jayavarman VII epitomises the creative genius and in-

flated ego of Cambodia's most celebrated king. Its 54 gothic towers are famously decorated with 216 gargantuan smiling faces of Avalokiteshvara that bear more than a passing resemblance to the great king himself.

It's known as the 'face temple' thanks to its iconic visages. These huge heads glare down from every angle, exuding power and control with a hint of humanity – precisely the blend required to hold sway over such a vast empire, ensuring the disparate and far-flung population yielded to the king's magnanimous will.

The Bayon is decorated with 1.2km of extraordinary bas-reliefs incorporating more than 11,000 figures, depicting everyday life in 12th-century Cambodia. You may notice something that looks much like the 'Thai' kickboxing of today depicted in these bas-reliefs; much of Thailand's culture is linked to the Cambodian artisans, dancers, scholars and fighters with whom the Thais made off after they sacked Angkor in 1432. The history of Angkor remains a seriously sensitive topic between the two cultures, fuelling a bitter rivalry that's lasted centuries.

Baphuon HINDU TEMPLE
(បាពួន; Map p104; ⊙7.30am-5.30pm) Some have called Baphuon the 'world's largest jigsaw puzzle'. Before the civil war the Baphuon was painstakingly taken apart piece-by-piece by a team of archaeologists, but their meticulous records were destroyed during the Khmer Rouge regime, leaving experts

TOP ANGKOR EXPERIENCES

Angkor Wat (p102) Watching the sun rise over the holiest of holies, Angkor Wat, the world's largest religious building.

Bayon (p103) Contemplating the serenity and splendour of Bayon, its 216 enigmatic faces staring out into the jungle.

Ta Prohm (p109) Witnessing nature reclaiming the stones at this mysterious ruin, the *Tomb Raider* temple.

Banteay Srei (p109) Staring in wonder at the delicate carvings adorning Banteay Srei, the finest seen at Angkor.

Kbal Spean (p109) Trekking deep into the jungle to discover the 'River of a Thousand Lingas'.

Beng Mealea (p109) Exploring the tangled vines, crumbling corridors and jumbled sandstone blocks.

Temples of Angkor

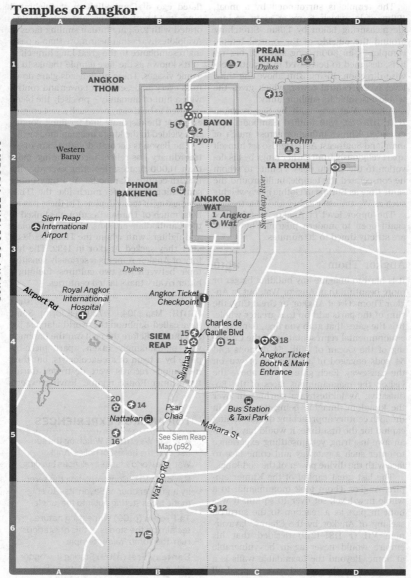

with 300,000 stones to put back into place. After years of excruciating research, this temple has been partially restored. In the 16th century, the retaining wall on the western side of the second level was fashioned into a 60m reclining Buddha.

Terrace of Elephants   ARCHAEOLOGICAL SITE
(ម៉ី លានដំរី; Map p104; ☼7.30am-5pm) The 350m-long Terrace of Elephants was used as a giant viewing stand for public ceremonies and served as a base for the king's grand audience hall. Try to imagine the pomp and

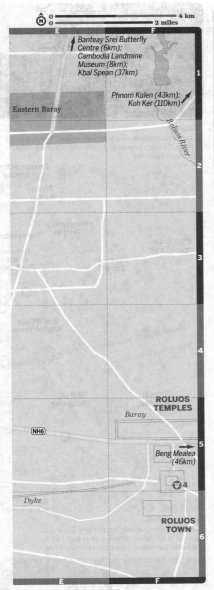

Temples of Angkor

attended by mandarins and handmaidens bearing gold and silver utensils.

Terrace of the Leper King   ARCHAEOLOGICAL SITE
(ព្រះលានស្តេចគម្លង់; Map p104; ⊙7.30am-5.30pm) The Terrace of the Leper King is just north of the Terrace of Elephants. Dating from the late 12th century, it is a 7m-high platform, on top of which stands a nude, though sexless, statue. The front retaining walls of the terrace are decorated with at least five tiers of meticulously executed carvings. On the southern side of the Terrace of the Leper King, there is access to a hidden terrace with exquisitely preserved carvings.

Around Angkor Thom

◎ Sights

Phnom Bakheng   HINDU TEMPLE
(ភ្នំបាខែង; Map p104; incl in Angkor admission 1/3/7 days US$37/62/72; ⊙5am-7pm) Located around 400m south of Angkor Thom, the

grandeur of the Khmer empire at its height, with infantry, cavalry, horse-drawn chariots and elephants parading across Central Square in a colourful procession, pennants and standards aloft. Looking on is the god-king, shaded by multi-tiered parasols and

Temples of Angkor

THREE-DAY EXPLORATION

The temple complex at Angkor is simply enormous and the superlatives don't do it justice. This is the site of the world's largest religious building, a multitude of temples and a vast, long-abandoned walled city that was arguably Southeast Asia's first metropolis, long before Bangkok and Singapore got in on the action.

Starting at the Roluos group of temples, one of the earliest capitals of Angkor, move on to the big circuit, which includes the Buddhist-Hindu fusion temple of ❶ **Preah Khan** and the ornate water temple of ❷ **Preah Neak Poan**.

On the second day downsize to the small circuit, starting with an early visit to ❸ **Ta Prohm**, before continuing to the temple pyramid of Ta Keo, the Buddhist monastery of Banteay Kdei and the immense royal bathing pond of ❹ **Sra Srang**.

Next venture further afield to Banteay Srei temple, the jewel in the crown of Angkorian art, and Beng Mealea, a remote jungle temple.

Saving the biggest and best until last, experience sunrise at ❺ **Angkor Wat** and stick around for breakfast in the temple to discover its amazing architecture without the crowds. In the afternoon, explore ❻ **Angkor Thom**, an immense complex that is home to the enigmatic ❼ **Bayon**.

Three days around Angkor? That's just for starters.

TOP TIPS

➡ To avoid the crowds, try dawn at Sra Srang, post-sunrise at Angkor Wat and lunchtime at Banteay Srei.

➡ Three-day passes can be used on non-consecutive days over the course of a week, but be sure to request this.

Bayon
The surreal state temple of legendary king Jayavarman VII, where 216 faces bear down on pilgrims, asserting religious and regal authority.

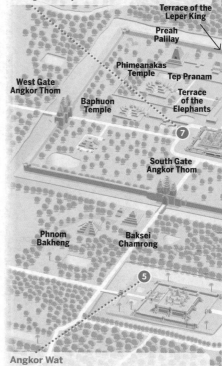

Angkor Wat
The world's largest religious building. Experience sunrise at the holiest of holies, then explore the beautiful bas-reliefs – devotion etched in stone.

Angkor Thom

The last great capital of the Khmer empire conceals a wealth of temples and its epic proportions would have inspired and terrified in equal measure.

Preah Khan

A fusion temple dedicated to Buddha, Brahma, Shiva and Vishnu; the immense corridors are like an unending hall of mirrors.

Preah Neak Poan

If Vegas ever adopts the Angkor theme, this will be the swimming pool; a petite tower set in a lake, surrounded by four smaller ponds.

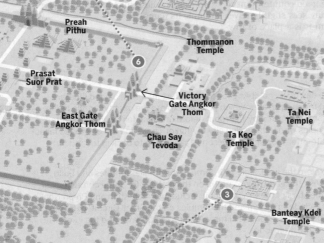

North Gate, Angkor Thom

Preah Pithu

Thommanon Temple

❶

❻

Prasat Suor Prat

Victory Gate Angkor Thom

East Gate Angkor Thom

Chau Say Tevoda

Ta Keo Temple

Ta Nei Temple

❷

Banteay Srei

❸

Banteay Kdei Temple

Roluos, Beng Mealea

Prasat Kravan

Bat Chum Temple

❹

Ta Prohm

Nicknamed the *Tomb Raider* temple; *Indiana Jones* would be equally apt. Nature has run riot, leaving iconic tree roots strangling the surviving stones.

Sra Srang

Once the royal bathing pond, this is the ablutions pool to beat all ablutions pools and makes a good stop for sunrise or sunset.

main attraction at Phnom Bakheng is the sunset view over Angkor Wat. For many years, the whole affair turned into a circus, with crowds of tourists ascending the slopes of the hill and jockeying for space. Numbers are now restricted to just 300 visitors at any one time, so get here early (4pm) to guarantee a sunset spot. The temple, built by Yasovarman I (r 889–910), has five tiers, with seven levels.

Preah Khan
BUDDHIST TEMPLE

(ប្រះខ័ន; Sacred Sword; Map p104; incl in Angkor admission 1/3/7 days US$37/62/72; ⏰7.30am-5.30pm) The temple of Preah Khan is one of the largest complexes at Angkor, a maze of vaulted corridors, fine carvings and lichenclad stonework. It is a good counterpoint to Ta Prohm and generally sees slightly fewer visitors. Like Ta Prohm it is a place of towered enclosures and shoulder-hugging corridors. Unlike Ta Prohm, however, the temple of Preah Khan is in a reasonable state of preservation thanks to the ongoing restoration efforts of the World Monuments Fund (WMF).

Preah Neak Poan
BUDDHIST TEMPLE

(នាគព័ន្ធ, Temple of the Intertwined Nagas; Map p104; incl in Angkor admission 1/3/7 days US$37/62/72; ⏰7.30am-5.30pm) The Buddhist temple of Preah Neak Poan is a petite yet perfect temple constructed by Jayavarman VII in the late 12th century. It has a large square pool surrounded by four smaller square pools. In the middle of the central pool is a circular 'island' encircled by the two *nagas* whose intertwined tails give the temple its name.

EXPLORING THE TEMPLES

One Day

If you've got only one day to spend at Angkor, that's unfortunate, but a good itinerary would be Angkor Wat for sunrise, after which you can explore the mighty temple before the crowds arrive. From there, drop by Ta Prohm before breaking for lunch. In the afternoon, explore the temples within the walled city of Angkor Thom and the enigmatic faces of the Bayon in the late-afternoon light. Biggest mistake: trying to pack in too much.

Three Days

With three days to explore the area, start with some of the smaller temples and build up to the big hitters. Visit the early Roluos group on the first day for some chronological consistency and try the stars of the Grand Circuit, including Preah Khan and Preah Neak Poan. Day two might include Ta Prohm and the temples on the Small Circuit, plus the distant but stunning Banteay Srei. Then the climax: Angkor Wat at dawn and the immense city of Angkor Thom in the afternoon.

One Week

Angkor is your oyster, so relax, enjoy and explore at will. Make sure you visit Beng Mealea and Kbal Spean. Do at least one overnight trip further afield, to Koh Ker, Banteay Chhmar or Prasat Preah Vihear. For a change of pace, take a boat to the stilted village of Kompong Pluk.

Tickets

The Angkor ticket checkpoint is on the new road from Siem Reap to Angkor. Three day passes can be used on any three days over a one-week period, and one-week passes are valid over the course of a month. Tickets issued after 5pm (for sunset viewing) are valid the next day. Tickets are not valid for Phnom Kulen, Beng Mealea or Koh Ker. Get caught ticketless in a temple and you'll be fined US$100.

Eating

There are dozens of local noodle stalls just near the Terrace of the Leper King, and a village with a cluster of restaurants opposite Sra Srang (Pool of Ablutions; Map p104; incl in Angkor admission 1/3/7 days US$37/62/72; ⏰5am-5.30pm), the former royal bathing pond. Angkor Wat has full-blown cafes and restaurants. Try to be patient with the hordes of children selling food, drinks and souvenirs, as they're only doing what their families have asked them to do to survive. You'll find that their ice-cold bottled water and fresh pineapples are heavenly in the heat.

DON'T MISS

TA PROHM   តាព្រហ្ម

The ultimate Indiana Jones fantasy, **Ta Prohm** (Map p104; incl in Angkor admission 1/3/7 days US$37/62/72; ⊙7.30am-5.30pm) is cloaked in dappled shadow, its crumbling towers and walls locked in the slow muscular embrace of vast root systems. If Angkor Wat is testimony to the genius of the ancient Khmers, Ta Prohm reminds us equally of the awesome fecundity and power of the jungle. There is a poetic cycle to this venerable ruin, with humanity first conquering nature to rapidly create, and nature once again conquering humanity to slowly destroy.

Built from 1186 and originally known as Rajavihara (Monastery of the King), Ta Prohm was a Buddhist temple dedicated to the mother of Jayavarman VII. Ta Prohm is a temple of towers, closed courtyards and narrow corridors. Ancient trees tower overhead, their leaves filtering the sunlight and casting a greenish pall over the whole scene. It is the closest most of us will get to the discoveries of the explorers of old.

Bakong   HINDU TEMPLE

(បាគង; Map p104; ⊙7.30am-5.30pm) Bakong is the largest and most interesting of the Roluos group of temples. Built and dedicated to Shiva by Indravarman I, it's a representation of Mt Meru, and it served as the city's central temple. The east-facing complex consists of a five-tier central pyramid of sandstone, 60m square at the base, flanked by eight towers of brick and sandstone, and by other minor sanctuaries. A number of the lower towers are still partly covered by their original plasterwork.

Further Afield

⊙ Sights

★Banteay Srei   HINDU TEMPLE

(បន្ទាយស្រី; incl in Angkor admission 1/3/7 days US$37/62/72; ⊙7.30am-5.30pm) Considered by many to be the jewel in the crown of Angkorian art, Banteay Srei is cut from stone of a pinkish hue and includes some of the finest stone carving anywhere on Earth. Begun in AD 967, it is one of the smallest sites at Angkor, but what it lacks in size it makes up for in stature. The art gallery of Angkor, Banteay Srei, a Hindu temple dedicated to Shiva, is wonderfully well preserved and many of its carvings are three-dimensional.

★Beng Mealea   BUDDHIST TEMPLE

(បេងមាលា; US$5; ⊙7.30am-5.30pm) A spectacular sight to behold, Beng Mealea, located about 68km northeast of Siem Reap, is one of the most mysterious temples at Angkor, as nature has well and truly run riot. Exploring this titanic of temples, built to the same floor plan as Angkor Wat, is the ultimate Indiana Jones experience. Built in the

12th century under Suryavarman II, Beng Mealea is enclosed by a massive moat measuring 1.2km by 900m.

Kbal Spean   HINDU SHRINE

(ក្បាលស្ពាន, River of a Thousand Lingas; incl in Angkor admission 1/3/7 days US$37/62/72; ⊙7.30am-5.30pm) A spectacularly carved riverbed, Kbal Spean is set deep in the jungle to the northeast of Angkor. More commonly referred to in English as the 'River of a Thousand Lingas', the name actually means 'bridgehead', a reference to the natural rock bridge here. Lingas (phallic symbols) have been elaborately carved into the riverbed, and images of Hindu deities are dotted about the area. It was 'discovered' in 1969, when ethnologist Jean Boulbet was shown the area by a hermit.

Phnom Kulen   MOUNTAIN

(ភ្នំគូលែន; www.adfkulen.org; US$20; ⊙6-11am to ascend, noon-5pm to descend) Considered by Khmers to be the most sacred mountain in Cambodia, Phnom Kulen is a popular place of pilgrimage on weekends and during festivals. It played a significant role in the history of the Khmer empire, as it was from here in AD 802 that Jayavarman II proclaimed himself a *devaraja* (god-king), giving birth to the Cambodian kingdom. Attractions include a giant reclining Buddha, hundreds of lingas carved in the riverbed, an impressive waterfall and some remote temples.

Koh Ker   HINDU TEMPLE

(កោះកេរ; US$10; ⊙7.30am-5.30pm) Abandoned to the forests of the north, Koh Ker, capital of the Angkorian empire from AD 928 to AD 944, is within day-trip distance of Siem Reap. Most visitors start at Prasat Krahom where impressive stone carvings grace lintels, doorposts and slender window columns. The principal monument is Mayan-looking Prasat Thom, a 55m-wide, 40m-high sandstone-faced pyramid whose seven tiers offer spectacular views across the forest. Koh Ker is 127km northeast of Siem Reap.

NORTHWESTERN CAMBODIA

Offering highway accessibility and outback adventure in equal measure, northwestern Cambodia stretches from the Cardamom Mountains to the Dangkrek Mountains, with Tonlé Sap lake at its heart. Battambang attracts the most visitors thanks to an alluring blend of mellowness, colonial-era architecture and excellent day-tripping. Northwestern Cambodia's remote plains and jungles conceal some of the country's most inspired temples, including spectacular Prasat Preah Vihear, declared a World Heritage site in 2008, and the pre-Angkorian temples of Sambor Prei Kuk near Kompong Thom, added to the World Heritage list in 2017.

Battambang ឋត់ដំបង

 053 / POP 147,000

The elegant riverside town of Battambang is home to Cambodia's best-preserved French-period architecture. The stunning boat trip from Siem Reap lures travellers here, but it's the remarkably chilled atmosphere that makes them linger. Battambang is an excellent base for exploring nearby temples and villages that offer a real slice of rural Cambodia.

◉ Sights

Much of Battambang's charm lies in its early 20th-century French architecture. Some of the finest colonial buildings are along the waterfront (St 1), especially just south of Psar Nath, itself an architectural monument, albeit a modernist one. The two-storey Governor's Residence, with its balconies and wooden shutters, is another handsome legacy of the early 1900s. Designed by an Italian architect for the last Thai governor, who departed in 1907, it has imposing balconies and a grand reception room with 5m ceilings.

ⓘ GETTING TO THAILAND: REMOTE NORTHERN BORDERS

There are a couple of seldom-used crossings along Cambodia's northern border with Thailand. The usual 30-day entry to Thailand and Cambodian visas on arrival are available at both borders.

Anlong Veng to Chong Sa-Ngam

The remote Choam/Chong Sa-Ngam crossing (open from 7am to 8pm) connects Anlong Veng in Oddar Meanchey Province with Thailand's Si Saket Province.

Getting to the border A moto from Anlong Veng to the border crossing (16km) costs US$3 or US$4. Share taxis link Anlong Veng with Siem Reap (20,000r, 1½ hours).

At the border Formalities here are straightforward.

Moving on On the Thai side, find a motorcycle taxi or taxi to take you to the nearest town, Phusing (30 minutes), where buses and sŏrng·tăa·ou (pickup trucks) head to Si Saket and Kantharalak. Or try to hop on a casino shuttle from the border to Phusing, Ku Khan or Si Saket.

Samraong to Surin

The remote O Smach/Chong Chom crossing connects Cambodia's Oddar Meanchey Province and Thailand's Surin Province.

Getting to the border Share taxis link Siem Reap with Samraong (30,000r, two hours) via NH68. From Samraong, take a moto (US$5) or a charter taxi (US$15) for the smooth drive to O Smach (40km, 30 minutes) and its frontier casino zone. A private taxi from Siem Reap all the way to the border should cost US$60 to US$70.

At the border The crossing itself is easy.

Moving on On the Thai side walk to the nearby bus stop, where regular buses depart to Surin throughout the day (60B, 70km, 1½ hours).

BETREED ADVENTURES

Secluded in the Cambodian wilderness, the eco-stay **BeTreed Adventures** (☏078 960420, 012 765136; http://betreed.com; Phnom Tnout, Ta Bos Village; bungalows US$60, treehouse US$40; 🛜 🅿️) is the brainchild of two conservation-minded expats who left jobs with NGOs to save 70 sq km of forestland and all the creatures calling it home. Accommodations include two comfy bungalows on stilts and a treehouse built from reclaimed hardwood around a wild rain tree. Book ahead as early as possible and call for detailed directions.

In addition to sleeping in the canopy, guests go on guided zipline and hiking adventures, and return to camp for delicious, mostly vegetarian meals (US$15 per day). It's US$10 for a guide, and there's also a US$15-per-person fee for community development and preservation. Note that access in the wet season can be quite challenging, as the trails out here are easily flooded.

Battambang Museum
MUSEUM

(សារមន្ទីរខេត្តបាត់ដំបង; ☏012 238320; St 1; US$1; ⏰8-11am & 2-5.30pm) This small and rather dusty museum displays a trove of fine Angkorian lintels and statuary from all over Battambang Province, including pieces from Prasat Banan and Sneng. Signs are in Khmer, English and French.

A museum enlargement and renovation project was under way during our last visit.

🏃 Activities

Soksabike
CYCLING

(☏012 542019; www.soksabike.com; St 1½; half-day US$23-27, full day US$34-40; ⏰departs 7.30am) 🌿 Soksabike is a social enterprise aiming to connect visitors with the Cambodian countryside and its people. The half- and full-day trips cover 25km and 40km respectively, and include stops at family-run industries such as rice-paper making and the **prahoc factory**, as well as a visit to a local home. Tour prices depend on group size.

Green Orange Kayaks
KAYAKING

(☏012 207957; www.fedacambodia.org; Ksach Poy; half-day US$12) 🌿 Kayaks can be rented from Green Orange Kayaks, part of the Friends Economic Development Association (FEDA), a local NGO which runs a community centre in Ksach Poy village, 8km south of Battambang. Half-day, self-guided kayaking trips begin at Ksach Poy's Green Orange Cafe. From there you paddle back to the city along the Sangker River. A FEDA student guide (US$5) is optional. Booking ahead is recommended.

Heritage Walking Trail
WALKING

Phnom Penh–based **Khmer Architecture Tours** (www.ka-tours.org; tours US$10-55) is highly regarded for its specialist tours in and around the capital and has collaborated with Battambang Municipality to create heritage walks in Battambang's historic centre. The walks concentrate both on the French period and on the modernist architecture of the '60s. The company's website has two downloadable PDFs including a colour map and numbered highlights.

Coconut Lyly
COOKING

(☏016 399339; St 111; per person US$10) These classes are run by Chef Lyly, a graduate from Siem Reap's Paul Dubrule Cooking School. Three-hour classes (start times 9am and 3.30pm) include a visit to Psar Nath market, preparing four typical Khmer dishes (recipe book included) and then eating your handiwork afterwards. The excellent restaurant here is open from 9am to 10pm.

🛏 Sleeping

⭐ Here Be Dragons
HOSTEL $

(☏089 264895; www.herebedragonsbattambang. com; St 159D; fan/air-con dm US$4/6, r from US$12/15; ❄🛜) A funky fun bar, leafy front garden for relaxing and free beer on arrival make Here Be Dragons a top backpacker base. Six- and eight-bed dorms come with lock-boxes, while sunny private rooms are cheerfully decked out with brightly coloured bedding. The quiet location next to the riverside park on the east bank is a bonus.

⭐ Angkor Comfort Hotel
HOTEL $

(☏077 306410; www.angkorcomforthotel.com; St 1; r with air-con US$15-25; ❄🛜) Offering serious bang for your buck, the Angkor's huge rooms are sparkling clean and come with midrange amenities on a backpacker budget. White linens on the beds, flat-screen TVs, enough powerpoints to charge all your devices at once, and modern bathrooms with walk-in showers all feature.

Battambang

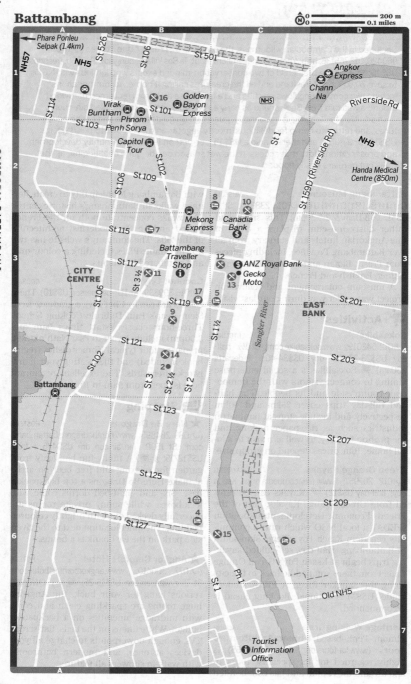

← Phare Ponleu
Selpak (1.4km)

NH57

NH5

St 526

St 106

St 501

NH5

Angkor
Express

Chann
Na

Riverside Rd

St 114

16

Golden
Bayon
Express

Virak
Buntham

St 101

St 103

Phnom
Penh Sorya

Capitol
Tour

St 102

St 109

St 106

St 1

NH5

St 159D (Riverside Rd)

Handa Medical
Centre (850m)

3

8

10

Mekong
Express

Canadia
Bank

St 115

7

Battambang
Traveller
Shop

12

ANZ Royal Bank

Gecko
Moto

13

Sangker River

St 117

St 3½

11

EAST
BANK

St 201

St 106

17

St 119

5

9

St 1½

CITY
CENTRE

St 102

St 121

14

2

St 3

St 2½

St 2

St 203

Battambang

St 123

St 207

St 125

St 209

1

4

St 127

15

6

St 1

Ph 1

Old NH5

Tourist
Information
Office

Battambang

Ganesha Family Guesthouse GUESTHOUSE **$**
(☑092 135570; www.ganeshaguesthouse.com;
St 1½; dm US$4.50, r US$11-25; 🛜) The best
of Battambang's cheapies, Ganesha has a
light-filled dorm with double-wide beds,
and small private rooms with bamboo furniture and tiled bathrooms (cold water only).
Downstairs is a funky cafe with a pool table.

Seng Hout Hotel HOTEL **$**
(☑012 530327; www.senghouthotel.com; St 2; r
with fan US$10-15, with air-con US$15-35; ❄🛜🏊)
Known for its on-the-ball staff who are quick
to help with traveller queries, the Seng Hout
has a variety of nicely decorated rooms.
Some can be a bit poky, so check out a few
before deciding. The open-air rooftop space
is a key drawcard, and the third-floor pool
has great views as well.

Royal Hotel HOTEL **$**
(☑016 912034; www.royalhotelbattambang.com;
St 115; s/d with fan US$7/10, r with air-con from
US$15; ❄@🛜) An old-timer on the Battam-
bang scene, the Royal is deservedly popular.
Some rooms may be faded but the air-con
rooms are decently sized and come with
fridge and TV. Staff here are some of the
most clued-up in town, and there's a new
bar and Jacuzzi on the rooftop.

🍴 Eating & Drinking

Cheap dining is available in and around Psar
Nath. There's a **riverside night market** (St
1; mains 4000-8000r; ☺3pm-midnight) opposite
the Battambang Museum.

★**Lonely Tree Cafe** CAFE **$**
(www.thelonelytreecafe.com; St 121; mains US$4-
5.50; ☺10am-10pm; 🛜) 🖉 Upstairs from the
shop of the same name, this uber-cosy cafe
serves Spanish tapas-style dishes and a few
Khmer options under a soaring, bamboo-in-
laid ceiling. Its mascot is an actual tree on
the road to Siem Reap. Proceeds support
cultural preservation and people with disabilities, among other causes.

Kinyei CAFE **$**
(www.kinyei.org; 1 St 1½; coffee US$1.50-2.50,
mains US$2.75-5.25; ☺7am-4pm; 🛜) 🖉 Be-
sides having the best coffee in town (national barista champs have been crowned here),
teensy-weensy Kinyei does surprisingly good
Mexican food, vegie burgers, energy salads
and some of the best breakfasts in town.
Aussies will appreciate the long blacks and
flat whites among the coffee selection.

Choco l'art Café CAFE **$**
(☑010 661617; St 117; mains US$1.50-5; ☺8am-
11pm; 🛜) Run with gusto by local painter
Ke and his partner, Soline, this inviting
gallery-cafe sees foreigners and locals alike
gather to drink and eat Soline's wonderful
bread, pastries and breakfast crêpes. Occasional open-mic nights, live painting sessions and musical performances.

Vegetarian Foods Restaurant VEGETARIAN **$**
(St 102; mains 1500-3000r; ☺6.30am-2pm; 🖉)
This hole-in-the-wall eatery serves some
of the most delicious vegetarian dishes in
Cambodia, including rice soup, homemade
soy milk and dumplings for just 1000r. Tremendous value.

About the World INTERNATIONAL **$**
(☑086 920476; St 2½; mains US$2.50-4; ☺8am-
10pm Mon-Sat; 🖉) Travellers love this cosy
spot for its relaxed ambience and tasty
vegetarian options, including the recommended Spanish omelette and tofu burger.
Those who sit indoors, where art and photography festoon the walls, do so barefoot
and perched atop floor pillows. The homebrewed jackfruit rice wine (US$1) is deli-
ciously potent.

ALL ABOARD THE BAMBOO TRAIN

One of the world's unique rail journeys, Battambang's bamboo train was finally dismantled in late 2017 to make way for plans to upgrade the railway.

The train used to trundle from O Dambong, a few kilometres east of Battambang's old French bridge (Wat Kor Bridge), to O Sra Lav along warped, misaligned rails and vertiginous bridges left by the French. Each bamboo train – known in Khmer as a *norry* – consisted of a 3m-long wooden frame, covered lengthwise with slats made of ultralight bamboo, resting on two barbell-like bogies, connected by belts to a 6HP gasoline engine. With a pile of 10 or 15 people, or up to 3 tonnes of rice, it could cruise along at about 15km/h.

The genius of the system is that it offers a solution to the most ineluctable problem faced on any single-track line: what to do when two trains going in opposite directions meet. In the case of bamboo trains, the answer is simple: one car is quickly disassembled and set on the ground beside the tracks so that the other can pass.

With the advent of good roads, the bamboo train would have become defunct sooner if it hadn't been for its reinvention as a tourist attraction. Due to its past popularity, the government has created a new track about 20km away near Prasat Banan (p116), to reconstruct the bamboo-train experience. It remains to be seen whether the new train will be as popular as the original.

★ **Jaan Bai**　　　　　　　　　FUSION $$

(📞078 263144; www.cambodianchildrenstrust. org/projects/social-enterprise/jaan-bai; cnr Sts 1½ & 2; small plates US$3, mains US$4-10; ⊙11am-9pm; 🖥🌿) 🍴 Jaan Bai ('rice bowl' in Khmer) is Battambang's foodie treat, with a sleekly minimal interior offset by beautiful French-Khmer tilework lining the wall. The menu likewise is successfully bold. Order a few of the small plates to experience the range of flavours, or go all out with the tasting menu: seven plates plus wine for US$15 per person (minimum two people).

Cafe Eden　　　　　　　　　CAFE $$

(📞053-731525; www.cafeedencambodia.com/ main; St1; mains US$4-7; ⊙7.30am-9pm Wed-Mon; 🖥) 🍴 This American-run social enterprise offers a relaxed space for a hearty breakfast or an afternoon coffee. The compact lunch-and-dinner menu is Asian-fusion style, with burgers, Mexi flaves, the best chips in town and superior jam-jar shakes, all amid blissful air-con.

Libations Bar　　　　　　　　BAR

(📞077 531562; 112 St 2; ⊙5-9pm; 🖥) Downstairs in the Bric-à-Brac hotel, this classy streetside bar caters to a relatively refined crowd with creative cocktails, craft beer, and wine and champagne by the glass. The chatty owners are a great source of information on the area. Upstairs are three arty, designed rooms.

☆ Entertaiment

★ **Phare Ponleu Selpak**　　　　　CIRCUS

(📞077 554413; www.phareps.org; adult/child US$14/7) Battambang's signature attraction is the internationally acclaimed circus (*cirque nouveau*) of this multi-arts centre for Cambodian children. Although it also runs shows in Siem Reap, it's worth timing your visit to Battambang to watch this amazing spectacle where it began. Shows are held two to four nights per week, depending on the season (check the website), and kick off at 7pm.

❶ Information

For information on what's happening in town, look out for copies of the free, biannual *Battambang Buzz* magazine, and the handy *Battambang Traveller* (www.battambangtraveler.com), which comes out four times a year.

Free wi-fi access is the norm at hotels and most cafes and restaurants.

ANZ Royal Bank (St 1; ⊙8am-4pm Mon-Fri, ATM 24hr)

Canadia Bank (Psar Nath; ⊙8am-3.30pm Mon-Fri, to 11.30am Sat, ATM 24hr)

Handa Medical Centre (📞095 520654; https://thehandafoundation.org/programs/ medical-center; NH5; ⊙emergency 24hr) Has two ambulances and usually an English-speaking doctor or two in residence.

Tourist Information Office (📞012 534177; www.battambangtourism.org; St 1; ⊙7.30-11.30am & 2-5.30pm Mon-Fri) Battambang's tourist office is of little use even when it's open, but it does sometimes stock a great free map.

ⓘ Getting There & Away

BOAT

The boat to Siem Reap (US$20, 7am) squeezes through narrow waterways and passes by protected wetlands, taking from five hours in the wet season to nine or more hours at the height of the dry season. Cambodia's most memorable boat trip, it's operated on alternate days by **Angkor Express** (☑ 012 601287) and **Chann Na** (☑ 012 354344). In the dry season, passengers are driven to a navigable section of the river.

BUS

Most bus companies are clustered in the centre just south of the intersection of NH5 and St 4. For Phnom Penh, Capitol Tour and Phnom Penh Sorya have the most services, but for quicker day travel to the capital, consider express minivans run by Golden Bayon Express (US$10, 4½ hours) or Mekong Express (US$12, 4½ hours). Sleeper buses arrive at an ungodly hour so are not recommended.

Capitol Tour (☑ 012 810055; St 102)

Golden Bayon Express (☑ 070 968966; St 101)

Mekong Express (☑ 088 576 7668; St 3) Minivans to Phnom Penh, Ho Chi Minh City and Bangkok. Handy minibus to Siem Reap.

Phnom Penh Sorya (☑ 092 181804; St 106)

Virak Buntham (St 106)

TAXI

At the taxi station (NH5), share taxis to Phnom Penh (40,000r, 4½ hours) leave from the southeast corner, while taxis to Poipet (20,000r, 1¾ hours) and Siem Reap (26,000r, three hours) leave from north of the market out on NH5.

Share taxis to Pailin (20,000r, 1¼ hours) near the Psar Pruhm/Pong Nam Ron border leave from the east edge of Psar Leu.

ⓘ Getting Around

English- and French-speaking remork drivers are commonplace in Battambang, and all are eager to whisk you around on day trips. A half-day trip out of town to a single sight such as Phnom Sampeau might cost US$12, while a full-day trip taking in three sights costs US$16 to US$20, depending on your haggling skills. A moto costs about half that.

A moto ride in town costs around 2000r, while a remork ride starts from US$1.50.

Gecko Moto (☑ 089 924260; St 1; ⏰8am-10pm) and the Royal Hotel (p113) rent out motorbikes for US$6 to US$8 per day. Bicycles can be rented at the Royal Hotel, Soksabike (p111), **Battambang Bike** (☑ 095 578878; www.thebattambangbike.com; St 2½; tours half-/full-day US$18/38; ⏰7am-7pm) and several guesthouses for about US$2 per day.

Around Battambang

The countryside around Battambang is littered with old temples, bamboo trains and other worthwhile sights. Admission to Phnom Sampeau, Phnom Banan and Wat Ek Phnom costs US$3. If you purchase a ticket at one site, it's valid all day long at the other two.

Prasat Banan   TEMPLE

(ប្រាសាទភ្នំបាណន់; US$3; ⏰6am-sunset) It's a 358-stone-step climb up Phnom Banan to reach Prasat Banan, but the incredible

BUSES FROM BATTAMBANG

DESTINATION	DURATION (HR)	COST (US$)	COMPANIES	FREQUENCY
Bangkok, Thailand	9	15-16	Mekong Express, PP Sorya, Virak Buntham, Capitol	7.45am, 8.30am, 10.30am, 11.30am, noon
Ho Chi Minh City, Vietnam	10-11	26	Mekong Express	7.30am
Kompong Cham	8	9	Rith Mony	9am
Pailin	1¼	4	Rith Mony	1pm, 3pm
Phnom Penh (day)	4½-7	5-12	All companies	frequent
Phnom Penh (night)	5-6	6-15	Capitol, Mekong Express, TSS, Virak Buntham	frequent, 10pm to midnight
Poipet	2¼	4	Capitol, PP Sorya, Rith Mony, TSS	regular to 4pm
Siem Reap	3-4	4-10	Capitol, Golden Bayon Express, Mekong Express, PP Sorya, Rith Mony	regular to 3pm

WORTH A TRIP

KOMPONG LUONG   កំពង់លួង

Kompong Luong has all the amenities you'd expect to find in a large fishing village – cafes, mobile-phone shops, chicken coops, ice-making factories, a pagoda, a church – except that here everything floats. The result is an ethnic-Vietnamese Venice without the dry land. In the dry season, when water levels drop and the Tonlé Sap shrinks, the entire aquapolis is towed, boat by boat, a few kilometres north.

The way to explore Kompong Luong, naturally, is by boat. The official tourist rate to charter a four-passenger wooden motorboat (complete with life jackets) is US$10 per hour for one to three passengers. **Homestays** (per person US$4-6) are available with local families and meals are available for US$1 to US$2 per person. This is an interesting way to discover what everyday life is really like on the water. You can book a homestay when you arrive at the boat landing.

The jumping-off point to Kompong Luong is the town of Krakor, 32km east of Pursat. From Krakor to the boat landing where tours begin is 1.5km to 6km, depending on the time of year. From Pursat, a moto/remork costs about US$10/20 return. From Phnom Penh, take any Pursat- or Battambang-bound bus.

views across surrounding countryside from the top are worth it. Udayadityavarman II, son of Suryavarman I, built Prasat Banan in the 11th century; some locals claim the five-tower layout here was the inspiration for Angkor Wat, although this seems optimistic. There are impressive carved lintels above the doorways to each of the towers and bas-reliefs on the upper parts of the central tower.

Wat Ek Phnom   BUDDHIST TEMPLE
(វត្តឯកភ្នំ; US$2) Hidden behind a colourful modern pagoda and a gargantuan Buddha statue is this atmospheric, partly collapsed 11th-century temple. Wat Ek Phnom measures 52m by 49m and is surrounded by the remains of a laterite wall and an ancient *baray* (reservoir). A lintel showing the Churning of the Ocean of Milk can be seen above the eastern entrance to the central temple, whose upper flanks hold some fine bas-reliefs. It's about 10km north of central Battambang.

Phnom Sampeau   BUDDHIST TEMPLE
(ភ្នំសំពៅ; US$1) This fabled limestone outcrop 12km southwest of Battambang along NH57 (towards Pailin) is known for its gorgeous views and mesmerising display of bats, which pour out of a massive cave in its cliff face.

Between the summit and the mobile-phone antenna, a deep canyon descends steeply through a natural arch to a 'lost world' of stalactites, creeping vines and bats.

About halfway up the hill, a turn-off leads 250m up to the Killing Caves of Phnom Sampeau. An enchanted staircase, flanked by

greenery, leads into a cavern where a golden reclining Buddha lies peacefully next to a glass-walled memorial filled with the bones and skulls of some of the people bludgeoned to death by Khmer Rouge cadres, before being thrown through the overhead skylight.

Access to the summit is via a cement road or a steep staircase. The road is too steep for remorks. Moto drivers hang out near the base of the hill and can whisk you up and back for US$4.

Kompong Thom   កំពង់ធំ
☑ 062 / POP 68,000

A bustling commercial centre, Kompong Thom is mainly a base from which to explore dazzling Sambor Prei Kuk.

Arunras Hotel   HOTEL $
(☑ 062-961294; NH6; s/d with fan US$5/8, d with air-con US$15; ❄ 🛜) Dominating Kompong Thom's accommodation scene, this central establishment has 58 good-value rooms with Chinese-style decoration and on-the-ball staff. The popular restaurant downstairs dishes up tasty Khmer fare. They also operate the 53-room **Arunras Guesthouse** (☑ 012 865935; NH6; s/d with fan US$6/8, with air-con US$10/13; ❄ 🛜) next door.

Vimean Sovann Guesthouse   HOTEL $
(☑ 078 220333; St 7; s/d with fan US$6/7, with air-con US$12/14; ❄ 🛜) It may not look like much from the outside, but hiding inside are the smartest budget rooms in town, all with fresh paint, modern bathroom fixtures and cute wall art. Opt for the spacious double

rooms (with two beds), which come with private balcony.

★ Kompong Thom

Restaurant CAMBODIAN **$$**
(NH6; mains US$3-8; ⊙7am-10pm; 🕑🅿) With delightful waiters and a pocket-sized terrace overlooking the river, this restaurant is also Kompong Thom's most adventurous. Unique concoctions featuring Kampot pepper, water buffalo and stir-fried eel appear on the menu of Khmer classics, which come in generous portions.

Canadia Bank BANK
(NH6; ⊙8am-3.30pm Mon-Fri, to 11.30am Sat, ATM 24hr)

❶ Getting There & Around

Dozens of buses travelling between Phnom Penh (US$5, four hours) and Siem Reap (US$5, two hours) pass through Kompong Thom and can easily be flagged down outside the Arunras Hotel. Heading north to Preah Vihear City, share taxis (US$5, two hours) depart in the morning only.
Im Sokhom Travel Agency (☑012 691527; St 3) rents bicycles (US$1 a day) and motorbikes (US$5 a day).

Around Kompong Thom

Sambor Prei Kuk

Cambodia's most impressive group of pre-Angkorian monuments, Sambor Prei Kuk (សំបូរព្រៃគុក; www. samborpreikuk. com; US$10) encompasses more than 100 brick temples scattered throughout the forest. Originally called Isanapura, it served as the capital of Chenla during the reign of the early-7th-century King Isanavarman. To the delight of Cambodians, the attraction recently became the country's third Unesco World Heritage site.

Forested and shady, Sambor Prei Kuk has a serene atmosphere. The main temple area consists of three complexes: **Prasat Sambor**, dedicated to Gambhireshvara, one of Shiva's many incarnations; **Prasat Yeay Peau**, which feels lost in the forest, its eastern gateway smothered by an ancient tree; and **Prasat Tao** (Lion Temple), the largest of the Sambor Prei Kuk complexes, boasting two large and elaborately coiffed stone lions.

Isanborei (☑017 936112; www.samborpreikuk.com) 🌿 runs a community-based

CAMBODIA AROUND KOMPONG THOM

---

❶ GETTING TO THAILAND: WESTERN BORDERS

Pailin to Chanthaburi

The laid-back Psar Pruhm/Ban Pakard border (open from 7am to 8pm) is 102km southwest of Battambang and 18km northwest of Pailin via good sealed roads.

Getting to the border From Battambang, the daily Ponleu Angkor buses to Pailin continue on to this border. Alternatively, take a share taxi to Pailin from Psar Leu in Battambang, then continue to the border by moto (US$5) or private taxi (US$10).

At the border Formalities are extremely straightfoward and quick on both sides.

Moving on Onward transport on the Thai side dries up mid-morning so cross early. In the morning you should be able to find a motorcycle taxi (50B) to the nearby sŏrng·tǎa·ou (pickup truck) station, where two morning minibuses head to Chanthaburi (150B, 1½ hours), offering frequent buses to Bangkok.

For information on making this crossing in reverse, see p739.

Koh Kong to Trat

Getting to the border To cross at the Cham Yeam/Hat Lek border, take a taxi (US$10 plus toll) or moto (US$3 plus toll) from Koh Kong across the toll bridge to Cham Yeam at the border.

At the border Departing Cambodia via the Hat Lek border is actually pretty straightforward, as there are no visa scams for immigration to benefit from.

Moving on Once in Thailand, catch a minibus to Trat (120B), from where there are regular buses to Bangkok (from 254B, five to six hours). Arrange onward transport to Ko Chang in Trat.

For information on making this crossing in reverse, see p739.

OFF THE BEATEN TRACK

PRASAT PREAH VIHEAR ប្រាសាទព្រះវិហារ

The 800m-long temple of **Prasat Preah Vihear** (adult/child US$10/free; ⊙ tickets 7.30am-4.30pm, temple to 5.30pm) is the most dramatically situated of all the Angkorian monuments. It sits high atop the Dangkrek escarpment on the Thai border, with stupendous views of Cambodia's northern plains.

Prasat Preah Vihear consists of a series of four cruciform *gopura* (sanctuaries) decorated with exquisite carvings, including some striking lintels. Starting at the **Monumental Stairway**, a walk south takes you to the **Gopura of the Third Level**, with its early rendition of the Churning of the Ocean of Milk, and finally, perched at the edge of the cliff, the **Central Sanctuary**. Stick to well-marked paths, as the Khmer Rouge laid huge numbers of landmines around Prasat Preah Vihear as late as 1998.

Prasat Preah Vihear and the lands surrounding it were ruled by Thailand in the 19th century, but were returned to Cambodia during the French protectorate. In 1959 the Thai military seized the temple from Cambodia, but the International Court of Justice (ICJ) in the Hague recognised Cambodian sovereignty in a 1962 ruling.

In July 2008 Prasat Preah Vihear was declared Cambodia's second Unesco World Heritage site. Thai troops soon crossed into Cambodian territory, sparking an armed confrontation. In July 2011 the ICJ ruled that both sides should establish a demilitarised zone. Then in November 2013 the ICJ confirmed its 1962 ruling that the temple belongs to Cambodia. The border area remains tense, but is considered safe.

Driving in from Sra Em, stop at the **information centre** (Kor Muy; ⊙ 7am-4.30pm) in the village of Kor Muy. This is where you pay your entry fee, secure an English-speaking guide (US$15), and arrange transport via moto (US$5 return) or 4WD (US$25 return, maximum six passengers) up the 6.5km temple access road, the final 1.5km of which is extremely steep.

Budget lodging is plentiful in the burgeoning town of Sra Em, 23km south of the information centre. Try **Sok San Guesthouse** (⏾ 097 715 3839; s/d with fan US$8/10, with air-con from US$13/15; ✳ ☜), 1km west of Sra Em's central roundabout.

With a private car you can get to Prasat Preah Vihear (not to be confused with Preah Vihear City, 110km south) in about three hours from Siem Reap (about US$140 round trip). It makes more sense to break up the long trip with a night in Sra Em, which is just 30km from the temple. Share taxis (US$10 per person, three hours) link Sra Em with Siem Reap. From Sra Em's central roundabout, you can find a moto to the information centre in Kor Muy (US$10 return).

homestay program, offers cooking courses, rents bicycles (US$2 per day) and organises ox-cart rides. It also operates a stable of remorks to whisk you safely to/from Kompong Thom (US$15 one way).

You'll find plenty of restaurants (mains US$2 to US$4) serving local fare around the large open-air handicrafts market near the temple entrance.

Sambor Prei Kuk is 30km northeast of Kompong Thom via smooth roads. A round-trip moto ride out here should cost US$10, a remork about US$20.

SOUTH COAST

Cambodia's south coast is an alluring mix of clear blue water, castaway islands, pristine mangrove forests, time-worn colonial towns and jungle-clad mountains, where bears and elephants lurk. Adventurers will find this region of Cambodia just as rewarding as sunseekers do.

Koh Kong City ក្រុងកោះកុង

⏾ 035 / POP 36,053

Once Cambodia's Wild West, its frontier economy dominated by smuggling, prostitution and gambling, the city of Koh Kong, eponymous capital of the province, is striding towards respectability as ecotourists scare the sleaze away.

◉ Sights & Activities

Koh Kong's main draw is for those seeking adventure in and around the Cardamom Mountains and the Koh Kong Conservation Corridor.

Peam Krasaop
Wildlife Sanctuary NATURE RESERVE

(ដែនជំរកសត្វព្រៃពាមក្រសោប; 5000r; ⊙6am-6pm) Anchored to alluvial islands – some no larger than a house – this 260-sq-km sanctuary's magnificent mangroves protect the coast from erosion, offer vital breeding and feeding grounds for fish, shrimp and shellfish, and are home to myriad birds.

☞ Tours

Boat tours are an excellent way to view Koh Kong's many coastal attractions. English-speaking **Teur** (✆016 278668) hangs around the boat dock and can help you hire six-passenger (40-horsepower) and three-passenger (15-horsepower) outboards (speedboats). Destinations include Koh Kong Island's western beaches (big/small boats US$80/50), around Koh Kong Island (US$120/90) and Peam Krasaop Mangrove Sanctuary (US$40/30).

Ritthy Koh Kong
Eco Adventure Tours ADVENTURE

(✆012 707719; www.kohkongecoadventure.com; St 1; ⊙8am-9pm) A one-stop shop for all your tour needs in Koh Kong, this is the longest-running ecotourism operator in town. Ritthy's excursions include excellent Koh Kong Island boat tours, birdwatching, and multiday jungle trekking and camping in the Areng Valley within the Koh Kong Conservation Corridor (p120). Check the website for pricing.

🛏 Sleeping

Some places pay moto drivers a commission, leading to a whole lot of shenanigans.

Ritthy's Retreat GUESTHOUSE $

(✆097 555 2789; ritthy.info@gmail.com; St 1; dm US$4, r US$6-15; ❋🛜) Long-time tour operator Ritthy has opened a welcoming guesthouse and restaurant on the riverfront. It features spacious en-suite dorms with double-wide beds and a nice variety of roomy doubles. The fancier air-con rooms upstairs have semi-private balconies with river views, while the downstairs bar-restaurant, with a pool table, is a top hang-out.

Koh Kong City Hotel HOTEL $

(✆035-936777; St 1; r US$15-20; ❋@🛜) Ludicrous value for what you get: each squeaky-clean room includes a huge bathroom, two double beds, 50 TV channels, a full complement of toiletries, free water and – in the US$20 rooms – a river view. Friendly staff top off the experience.

★ Oasis Bungalow Resort BUNGALOW $$

(✆092 228342; http://oasisresort.netkhmer.com; d/tr US$35/40; ❋🛜❋) Surrounded by lush forest, 2km north of Koh Kong centre, Oasis really lives up to its name. Five large, airy bungalows set around a gorgeous infinity pool with views of the Cardamom Mountains provide a tranquil base in which to chill out and reset your travel batteries. To get here, follow the blue signs from **Acleda Bank** (St 3).

🍴 Eating & Drinking

★ Happy Beach CAMBODIAN $

(✆097 744 4454; mains US$2-5; ⊙24hr) Northeast of town, this place offers a unique slice of Cambodian life with seaside, covered decks on stilts where families and friends laze about with their shoes off, taking down heaping portions of Khmer food served off a wooden block on the ground.

Crab Shack SEAFOOD $

(✆081 447093; Koh Yor Beach; mains US$4-8; ⊙hours vary) A family-run place over the bridge on Koh Yor Beach, this spot is known for perfect sunsets and heaping portions of fried crab with pepper (on request). If Crab Shack isn't open, the neighbouring restaurant also serves delicious crab and coconut water in little beach huts strung with hammocks.

Café Laurent INTERNATIONAL $$

(✆088 829 0410; St 1; mains US$4-15; ⊙10.30am-9.30pm Wed-Mon; 🛜) This chic waterfront cafe and restaurant offers atmospheric dining in over-water pavilions where you can sit back and watch the sunset while feasting on refined Western and Khmer cuisine. As well as French-accented steaks and a decent pasta menu, there's a huge range of fresh seafood and Asian classics, all served with fine-dining panache.

❶ Information

Guesthouses, hotels and pubs are the best places to get the local low-down. You can also look for the free Koh Kong Visitors Guide (www.kohkong.com), which is mostly advertisements.

Canadia Bank (St 1; ⊙8am-3.30pm Mon-Fri, to 11.30am Sat, ATM 24hr)

❶ Getting There & Around

Most buses drop passengers at Koh Kong's unpaved bus station (St 12), on the northeast edge of town, where motos and remorks await, eager

Koh Kong City

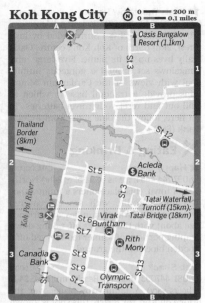

Oasis Bungalow Resort (1.1km)

St 3

St 1

Thailand Border (8km)

St 12

Acleda Bank

St 5

Koh Pol River

St 3

Tatai Waterfall Turnoff (15km); Tatai Bridge (18km)

St 6 Virak Buntham

St 7

Rith Mony

Canadia Bank

St 8

St 9

St 1

St 2

Olympic Transport

St 13

Koh Kong City

☺ Activities, Courses & Tours

Ritthy Koh Kong Eco
Adventure Tours .... (see 2)

🛌 Sleeping

1 Koh Kong City Hotel A2
2 Ritthy's Retreat A3

✖ Eating

3 Café Laurent A3
4 Happy Beach A1

to overcharge tourists. Don't pay more than US$1/2 for the three-minute moto/remork ride into the centre. From the taxi lot next to the bus station, share taxis head to Phnom Penh (US$11, five hours) and occasionally to Sihanoukville (US$10, four hours).

Virak Buntham (☎ 089 998760; St 3) Virak Buntham offers bus (US$8, six hours, 7.45am) and minivan (US$12, five hours, two daily) services to Phnom Penh, and an 8am direct bus to Sihanoukville (US$8, five hours). Services to Kampot (US$11, 8am) and to Bangkok (US$20, 1pm) via Ko Chang (US$15 including boat to island) involve a bus change.

Ritthy Koh Kong Eco Adventure Tours (p119) rents out bicycles for half-/full day US$1/2, as well as motorbikes.

Koh Kong Conservation Corridor

Stretching along both sides of NH48 from Koh Kong to the Gulf of Kompong Som, the Koh Kong Conservation Corridor encompasses many of Cambodia's most outstanding natural sites, including the most extensive mangrove forests on mainland Southeast Asia and the southern reaches of the fabled Cardamom Mountains, an area of breathtaking beauty and astonishing biodiversity.

The next few years will be critical in determining the future of the Cardamom Mountains. NGOs such as Conservation International (www.conservation.org), Fauna & Flora International (www.fauna-flora. org) and Wildlife Alliance (www.wildlife alliance.org) are working to help protect the region's 16 distinct ecosystems from loggers and poachers. Ecotourism is playing a huge role in their plans – Wildlife Alliance is promoting several enticing projects in the **Southern Cardamoms Protected Forest** (1443 sq km).

Tatai Waterfall

Tatai Waterfall   WATERFALL
(ទឹកធ្លាក់តាតៃ; US$1) Tatai Waterfall is a thundering set of rapids during the wet season, plunging over a 4m rock shelf. Water levels drop in the dry season, but you can swim year-round in the surrounding refreshing pools. The water is fairly pure as it comes down from the isolated high Cardamom Mountains. Access to the waterfall is by car or motorbike. The clearly marked turn-off is on NH48 about 15km southeast of Koh Kong, or 2.8km northwest of the Tatai Bridge.

From the highway it's about 2km to the falls along a rough access road. There's a stream crossing about halfway – at the height of the wet season you may have to cross it on foot and walk the last kilometre. From Koh Kong, a half-day moto/remork excursion to Tatai Waterfall costs US$10/15 return, or less to go one way to the bridge.

Sihanoukville   ក្រុងព្រះសីហនុ

☏ 034 / POP 91,000

Sure, Sihanoukville would never win first prize in a pretty-town competition, and much of it is now dominated by casinos and tacky commercial centres. But despite the rapid and mostly unwanted development, it has remained the jumping-off point for the best of Cambodia's white-sand beaches and castaway-cool southern islands. The **Serendipity Beach** area is a decompression chamber for backpackers, who flock here to rest up between travels and party through the night.

Away from the hustle south of town is relaxed **Otres Beach**, where cheap bungalow joints and bohemian-flavoured guesthouses are now neighbours with rather swish boutique resorts. Although much of the beachfront will likely be cleared for large-scale development in the future, for now the mellow scene still allows for lazy days of sunbathing and whirlwind nights of bar-hopping.

⊙ Sights & Activities

Coastal Ream National Park, 15km east of Sihanoukville, offers invigorating boat trips through coastal mangroves and long stretches of unspoiled beach, not to mention trekking in primary forest.

Beaches

Sihanoukville's beaches all have wildly different characters, offering something for just about everyone. Most central is **Occheuteal Beach**, lined with ramshackle restaurants, whose northwestern end – a tiny, rocky strip – has emerged as a happy, easygoing travellers' hang-out known as **Serendipity Beach**.

South of Occheuteal Beach, beyond a small headland, lies **Otres Beach**, lined with dozens of bungalow-style restaurants and resorts. Otres has cleaner water and is more relaxed than anything in Sihanoukville proper, and is lengthy enough that finding your own patch of private sand is not a challenge...just walk south. Otres Beach is about 5km south of the Serendipity area. It's a US$2/5 moto/remork ride to get here (more at night).

One beach north of Serendipity lies Sihanoukville's prettiest beach, 1.5km-long **Sokha Beach**. Its fine, silicon-like sand squeaks loudly underfoot. The tiny eastern end of Sokha Beach is open to the public and rarely crowded. The rest is part of the exclusive Sokha Beach Resort.

Moving north from Sokha Beach, you'll hit **Independence Beach** near the classic Independence Hotel, most of which has been taken over by a huge new development, and the original backpacker beach, **Victory Beach**, not the best beach in town due to the looming backdrop of the Sihanoukville Port development.

Diving

The diving near Sihanoukville isn't Southeast Asia's finest. It gets better the further out you go, although you still shouldn't expect anything on a par with the western Gulf of Thailand or the Andaman Sea. Most serious trips will hit **Koh Rong Sanloem**, while overnight trips target the distant islands of **Koh Tang** and **Koh Prins**. Overnight trips cost about US$100 per day including two daily dives, food, accommodation on an island, and equipment. Two-tank dives out of Sihanoukville average US$80 including equipment. PADI open-water courses average about US$400 to US$450, pretty competitive by world standards.

Scuba Nation   DIVING
(Map p127; ☑012 604680; www.divecambodia. com; Serendipity Beach Rd; 2-dive package US$85, PADI Open Water Diver course US$445; ⊙9am-8pm) The longest-running dive operator in Sihanoukville, Scuba Nation is a PADI five-star IDC (instructor development centre) with a comfortable boat for day and live-aboard trips.

Dive Shop   DIVING
(Map p127; ☑097 723 2626, 034-933664; www. diveshopcambodia.com; Serendipity Beach Rd; PADI Discover Scuba course US$95, 2-dive package US$80; ⊙7am-9pm) A PADI five-star dive centre offering the full gamut of PADI courses, as well as fun dives, out of its bases at Sunset Beach (high season) and Saracen Bay (low season) on Koh Rong Sanloem. Also runs snorkelling tours.

> **OFF THE BEATEN TRACK**
>
> ## KOH KONG ISLAND
>
> Cambodia's largest island towers over seas so crystal-clear you can make out individual grains of sand in a couple of metres of water. At the sixth beach from the north, a narrow channel leads to a Gilligan's Island–style lagoon. A strong military presence on the island means access is tightly controlled. You must visit on a guided boat tour out of Koh Kong or Tatai. These cost US$21 per person, including lunch and snorkelling equipment, or US$55 for overnight trips with beach camping or homestay accommodation. The island is only accessible from October to May.

CHI PHAT

Once notorious for land-grabbing, illegal logging and poaching, the river village of Chi Phat (www.chi-phat.org) is now home to a popular community-based ecotourism project (CBET) launched by Wildlife Alliance (www.wildlifealliance.org) to transform the Southern Cardamoms Protected Forest (1443 sq km), into a source of jobs and income for local people.

Chi Phat offers travellers an opportunity to explore the Cardamoms ecosystems while contributing to their conservation and providing an alternative livelihood to the former poachers who now act as the landscape's protectors and guides. Accommodation is in basic homestays and guesthouses, and there's a menu of activities on offer, from bird-watching kayak trips to combo hike-and-mountain-bike expeditions.

All activities in Chi Phat are controlled through **CBET Community Visitor Centre** (035-675 6444, 092 720925; www.chi-phat.org; Chi Phat; 7am-7pm), a two-minute walk from the river pier, although there's not a lot of English spoken. All tours must be booked at the visitor centre by 5pm the day before. Prices for tours range from US$25 to US$35 per person including lunch, transport and equipment.

Chi Phat only has limited electricity and there is no bank or ATM, although there is a credit-card machine.

Chi Phat is on the scenic Preak Piphot River, 21km upriver from Andoung Tuek, which is on NH48, 98km from Koh Kong. All buses travelling between Koh Kong and Phnom Penh or Sihanoukville pass through here. A longtail boat (US$30) makes the two-hour trip from Andoung Tuek when reserved in advance and is the most atmospheric option. A moto is faster (45 minutes; 17km) and costs US$7. Travelling from Chi Phat, a boat or moto can be booked the night before to return to Andoung Tuek in the morning, in time to catch onward buses.

Massage

NGO-trained blind and disabled masseurs deftly ease away the tension at **Seeing Hands Massage 3** (Map p124; 034-679 2555; 95 Ekareach St; per hr US$6; 8am-9pm) and Starfish Bakery & Café (p125).

📖 Courses

Don Bosco Hotel Khmer Cooking Course
COOKING

(016 919834; www.donboscohotelschool.com/cooking; Ou Phram St, Don Bosco Hotel School; per person US$30) The cooking classes here provide a great opportunity to learn some Khmer culinary skills. They include a slap-up three-course lunch (which you've helped create), as well as a tour of the hotel school. Classes run from 8.30am to 1.30pm every weekday and start with a market trip, but guests can also join at 10am after the market (for US$5 less).

🧭 Tours

Popular day tours go to some of the closer islands and to Ream National Park. Booze cruises are popular.

Party Boat
BOATING

(Map p127; 034-666 6106; Serendipity Beach Pier; per person US$25) The daily cruise (9.30am to 5pm) to Koh Rong Sanloem includes snacks, lunch, snorkelling and a free drink. This outfit also runs return transport to Koh Rong Island's full-moon parties, leaving Sihanoukville at 5pm and returning around 8am.

Suntours
BOATING

(096 379 4133; per adult/child US$25/12.50; departs at 10am, back at 5pm) Suntours offers island cruises aboard a motor yacht, with day trips to Koh Rong Sanloam that get rave reviews. Trips include snacks, buffet lunch, coffee and tea, as well as snorkelling, kayaking and fishing equipment. Pick-up points vary.

🛏 Sleeping

Most backpackers shoot for the Serendipity area if they want to party, or Otres Beach if they want to chill. Other decent options exist in the town centre (for those who want to escape tourists) and on long-running Victory Hill, a former backpacker ghetto that is now one of Sihanoukville's sleazier strips. There are popular bungalow resorts popping up all over the islands off Sihanoukville.

🏨 Serendipity & Occheuteal

The road to Serendipity is the main backpacker hang-out, while down the hill tiny Serendipity Beach offers a string of mellow midrange resorts perched over the rocky shoreline.

★**Chochi Garden**   GUESTHOUSE $

(Map p127; ☎ 096 274 7674; chochiguesthouse@ gmail.com; Serendipity Beach Rd; r with fan/air-con US$15/25; ❄✳🛜) Run by a friendly expat couple, this boutique backpacker pad is the closest Serendipity gets to a tranquil oasis right in the heart of the action. Out front is a cool bar-restaurant while simple rooms, some with palm-thatch roofs and pretty painted window-grills, are in a plant-filled garden strewn with comfy seating areas.

Onederz Hostel   HOSTEL $

(Map p127; ☎ 096 339 0005; onestophostelsshv@ gmail.com; Golden Lions Roundabout; dm US$8; ✳@🛜❄) The six- and eight-bed dorms here are decked out in lashings of white-on-white and centred on a floor-to-ceiling glassed courtyard with a small pool, proving slick styling doesn't have to cost the earth. The 68 beds have individual reading lamps and luggage lock-boxes, and all dorms are air-conditioned. One quibble is that the bottom bunks are basically on the floor.

Big Easy   HOSTEL $

(Map p127; ☎ 081 943930; Serendipity Beach Rd; dm US$4, r US$8-10; 🛜) This classic backpacker joint offers accommodation, comfort food and a lively rock bar, all rolled into one. The dorms are basic but have some amenities: air-con, hot water, privacy curtains and plentiful power outlets. Still, you'll most likely spend your time in the bar. There's a great vibe with occasional live music, live English Premier League games and beer pong.

CAMBODIA SIHANOUKVILLE

Sihanoukville

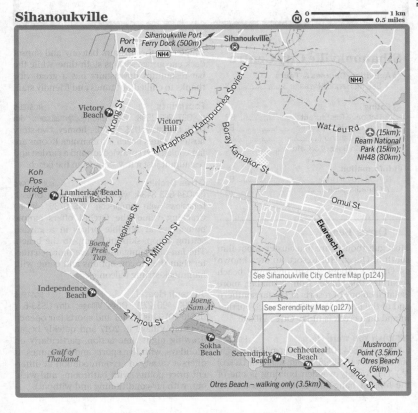

Sihanoukville City Centre

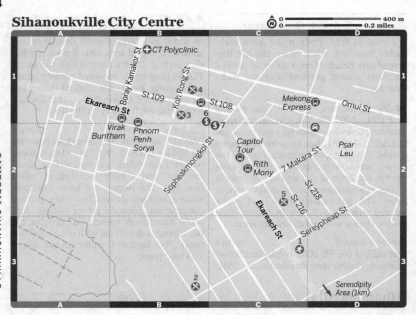

🛏 Otres Beach

Most guesthouses are in a cluster about 1km south of Queen Hill Resort, an area known as Otres 1. About 2.5km of empty beach separates this cluster from a smaller, more isolated colony of resorts at the far southern end of the beach, known as Otres 2. Further inland on a creek is funky Otres Village.

★ Wish You Were Here   HOSTEL $
(☎097 241 5884; Otres 1; dm from US$6, r without bathroom US$12-16, r with bathroom US$20; 🛜) This rickety wooden building is one of the hippest hang-outs in Otres. Rooms are

simple but the upstairs balcony and sunset deck encourage serious sloth-time, while the bar-restaurant downstairs has a great vibe thanks to chilled-out tunes and friendly staff.

Footprints   HOSTEL $
(☎097 262 1598; footprintotres@gmail.com; dm US$5, bungalows US$25) This homey, two-story hostel in Otres Beach is a charmer. Rooms are fan-cooled and sprawled around a garden and restaurant just a few steps from the beach.

Otres Orchid   BUNGALOW $
(☎034-633 8484; www.otresorchid.com; Otres 1; bungalows with fan/air-con US$20/35; ❄🛜) Cracking value, the Orchid offers simple bungalows at sensible prices in a garden setting a hop, skip and jump to the beach. The fan-only bungalows have more character than the air-con options and come with hammock-strung balconies.

Jumanji Hostel   HOSTEL $
(☎096 490 2711; Otres Village; dm US$3-6, r US$10-20) This hostel and sports bar opened in Otres Village in 2017 and quickly began drawing night time crowds, particularly on Mondays, with live sports and bar games. It offers a variety of accommodation at different price points (with bathrooms and without, with air-conditioning and without).

Eating

Sihanoukville's centre of culinary gravity is the Serendipity area.

Starfish Bakery & Cafe
CAFE $

(Map p124; ☎ 012 952011; www.starfishcambodia.org; off 7 Makara St; sandwiches US$3.50-4.75; ⊙ 7am-5.30pm; ☎🥢) 🍴 This relaxing, NGO-run garden cafe specialises in filling Western breakfasts, baked cakes and tarts, and healthy, innovative sandwiches heavy on Mexican and Middle Eastern flavours. Sitting down for coffee here on the shady terrace is a peaceful reprieve from Sihanoukville's hustle. Income goes to sustainable development projects.

Cabbage Restaurant
CAMBODIAN $

(Chamka Spai; Map p124; mains 8000-15,000r; ⊙ 11am-10pm) Known to locals as Chamka Spai, this restaurant gets rave reviews for its seafood and spicy seasonings. An authentic Khmer dining experience. A sign in English on Sereypheap St points the way, but look out for nearby, imposter restaurants with the same name.

Espresso Kampuchea
CAFE $

(Map p124; Boray Kamakor St; mains US$2-4; ⊙ 8am-10pm) Serious caffeine aficionados should definitely make the trip down a nondescript side street in Sihanoukville centre to get to Espresso Kampuchea. The owner, Sophal, personally sources her coffee from Thailand and serves up excellent double-shot cappuccinos and espresso. There's a small menu of baguettes, fried noodles and other breakfasts – and draught beer for US$0.75.

Gelato Italiano
ICE CREAM $

(Map p124; St 109; mains US$2-5, gelati US$1; ⊙ 7.30am-9pm; ☎) 🍴 Run by students from Don Bosco Hotel School, this cafe specialises in gelato (Italian-style ice cream) but offers so much more, including coffee, pizza and full-blown Asian-fusion meals in a bright, airy space. Wonderful value.

Mushroom Point Beach
INTERNATIONAL $$

(Otres 1; mains $3.50-12; ⊙ 8am-10pm) Mushroom Point's breakfasts, featuring homemade baguettes with mango jam and homemade muesli, are a winner. The barbecued seafood and Italian plates that come out later in the day get plaudits from travellers, too. There's an excellent wine list to boot.

★ Chez Paou
INTERNATIONAL $$

(Otres 1; mains US$5-22; ⊙ 8am-11pm; ☎) This is fine dining Otres style: right on the beach. The menu contains a good selection of steaks, pasta and burgers, but it's the Khmer specials (order in advance) – stingray cooked on embers with fresh Kampot pepper, prawns flambéed in pastis, and crabs cooked two different ways – that make this place really stand out.

★ Amareina
ITALIAN $$

(☎ 070 900306; pizzas US$6-8) This Italian restaurant and guesthouse has quickly gained a reputation for the best party pool in town, which is free for nonguests as well, and its pizzas and pastas are divine. There's also a small but decent selection of wine and the best carpaccio in Otres Beach.

★ Manoha
FRENCH $$

(Map p127; ☎ 034-657 2666; www.facebook.com/pg/restaurant.manoha; mains from US$5; ⊙ 24hr) At this charming but modest-looking place on Serendipity Rd, the French and Khmer menu is enormous – with 130 dishes, to be exact. And whether it's a sandwich, a salad, an omelette, some frogs' legs or even barracuda carpaccio you're after, this place will nail it. And it's always open.

🍷 Drinking & Nightlife

The party tends to start up on the road to Serendipity before heading downhill (literally and figuratively) to the all-night beach discos along Occheuteal Beach. A few long-standing regular bars remain amid the hostess bars of Victory Hill, but the overall impression is Sinville rather than the more relaxed beach vibe of Sihanoukville.

SPLURGE

Ropanha Boutique Hotel (Map p127; ☎ 012 556654; www.ropanha-boutiquehotel.com; 23 Tola St; r incl breakfast US$45-55; ❀☎📶) is the pick of the pack when it comes to affordable atmosphere in the Serendipity area. Set around a lush courtyard garden and pool, Ropanha's rooms include flat-screen TVs and accompanying DVD players, plus rain showers in the bathrooms. Deluxe rooms have pool views but all have lashings of white and are exceptionally well cared for.

Some of the guesthouses have lively bars, including Monkey Republic, the Big Easy and Wish You Were Here.

Maybe Later BAR
(Map p127; Serendipity Beach Rd; ⊗11am-11pm) This popular little Mexican taco restaurant that doubles as a bar serves top-notch margaritas and some refined tequilas for those who prefer sips to shots. It's a civilised escape from the beachside party scene.

La Rhumerie BAR
(Map p127; Serendipity Beach Rd; ⊗9am-2am) Pull up a bar stool at La Rhumerie for salsa music and yummy rum infused with ingredients such as Kampot pepper, ginger and coffee. The rum selection hails from 17 countries and pairs well with many of the food items on the menu, including barbecue. Not a rum fan? The bar also whips up mean cocktails, such as a spicy mango margarita.

Last Hippie Standing BAR
(Otres Corner; ☑097 579 5329; Otres 1; ⊗24hr) The first place you'll see when you enter the Otres area and, often, the last place you'll have been seen on particularly rowdy nights. DJs play dance and trance music 'til the wee hours and the owners offer basic, US$10 accommodation to guests who decide they never want to leave.

JJ's Playground BAR
(Map p127; Ochheuteal Beach; ⊗6pm-6am) The go-to spot for those seeking late-night debauchery. The scene here is pretty much summed up by JJ's slogan: 'Let's get wasted'. Expect shots, loud techno music, a fire show or two, and a lot of chaos. And don't say we didn't warn you about the toilets.

🛍 Shopping

Tapang ARTS & CRAFTS
(www.mloptapang.org; Otres 2; ⊗11am-9pm) 🖋 Run by a local NGO that works with at-risk children, this shop sells good-quality bags, scarves and T-shirts made by street kids (and their families) so that they can attend school instead of peddling on the beach. Tapang has another outlet at Sandan (Map p127; ☑034-452 4000; 2 Thnou St; mains US$4-10; ⊗11.30am-11pm; 🛜🪑) 🖋 restaurant.

ℹ Information

Internet cafes (per hour 4000r) are sprinkled along the road to Serendipity and, in the city centre, along Ekareach St near Sopheakmongkol St.

Theft is a problem, especially on Occheuteal Beach, so leave your valuables in your room. As in Phnom Penh, drive-by bag-snatchings occasionally happen and are especially dangerous when you're riding a moto. Hold your shoulder bags tightly in front of you. At night, both men and women should avoid walking alone along dark, isolated beaches and roads.

Ana Travel (Map p127; ☑034-933929; Serendipity Beach Rd; ⊗8.30am-8.30pm) Organises buses to Ha Tien (Vietnam) via Kampot and Kep, and also does the usual tours and visas.

ANZ Royal Bank (Map p124; 215 Ekareach St; ⊗8am-4pm Mon-Fri, to 11.30am Sat, ATM 24hr)

Canadia Bank (Map p124; 197 Ekareach St; ⊗8am-3.30pm Mon-Fri, to 11.30am Sat, ATM 24hr)

CT Polyclinic (Map p124; ☑034-936666, 081 886666; 47 Boray Kamakor St; ⊗emergency 24hr) The best medical clinic in town. Can administer rabies shots, and antivenin in the event of a snake bite.

ℹ Getting There & Away

AIR
There are now several flights daily between Sihanoukville and Siem Reap, so it is usually possible to hop to temple town at short notice. The airport is 15km east of town, just off the NH4. Figure on US$5/10 for a one-way moto/remork.

Cambodia Angkor Air (☑in Phnom Penh 023 666 6786; www.cambodiaangkorair.com) Has one daily direct flight from Sihanoukville Airport to Siem Reap.

BUS
All of the major bus companies have frequent connections with Phnom Penh (US$5 to US$11, four to five hours) from early morning until at least 2pm, after which trips are sporadic.

Virak Buntham has morning buses to Bangkok (US$28, change buses on the Thai side) via Koh Kong (US$8, four hours). GST and Virak Buntham have night buses to Siem Reap (US$13 to US$17).

Most bus departures originate at the company terminals on Ekareach St and stop at the **bus station** (Map p124; St 109) on the way out of town. The main bus companies:

Capitol Tour (Map p124; ☑034-934042; 169 Ekareach St)

Champa Mekong Tourist Bus (Map p127; ☑069 698282; Mithona St) Departures to Ha Tien, Vietnam (US$13, 3½ hours), via Kampot (US$5) and Kep (US$7) at 8am, 11am, 1.30pm and 3.30pm.

Giant Ibis (Map p127; ☑023 999333; www.giantibis.com; Thnou St) Luxury buses to

Serendipity

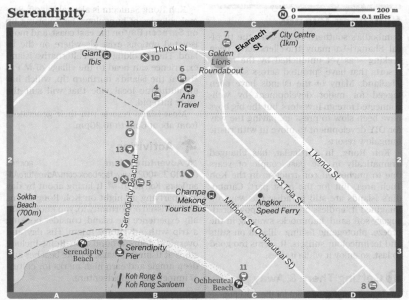

Phnom Penh, Siem Reap, Ho Chi Minh City and Bangkok.

Mekong Express (Map p124; ☑ 010 833329; Omui St)

Phnom Penh Sorya (Map p124; ☑ 034-933888; 236 Ekareach St)

Virak Buntham (Map p124; ☑ 016 754358; Ekareach St)

SHARE TAXI

Cramped share taxis (US$6 per person, US$45 per car) to Phnom Penh depart from the new bus station until about 8pm. Share taxis to Kampot (US$5, 1½ hours) leave mornings only from an open lot on 7 Makara St, across from Psar Leu. This lot and the new bus station are good places to look for rides to Koh Kong or the Thai border (US$45 to US$60 to charter).

❶ Getting Around

Arriving in Sihanoukville, most buses terminate at the bus station and do not continue to their central terminals. Prices to the Serendipity Beach area from the bus station are fixed at a pricey US$2/6 for a moto/remork. You can do better by walking out to the street.

A moto/remork should cost about US$1/2 from the city centre to Serendipity, but over-charging is rife.

Motorbikes can be rented from many guest-houses for US$5 to US$7 a day. For fundraising

Serendipity

⊙ Activities, Courses & Tours

1 Dive Shop	B2
2 Party Boat	B3
3 Scuba Nation	B2

⊜ Sleeping

4 Big Easy	B1
5 Chochi Garden	B2
6 Monkey Republic	B1
7 Onederz Hostel	C1
8 Ropanha Boutique Hotel	D3

⊗ Eating

9 Manoha	B2
10 Sandan	B1

⊜ Drinking & Nightlife

11 JJ's Playground	C3
12 La Rhumerie	B2
13 Maybe Later	B2

purposes, the police sometimes 'crack down' on foreign drivers. Common violations: no driving licence, no helmet, or driving with the lights on during the day.

Bicycles can be hired from many guesthouses for about US$2 a day, or try Eco-Trek Tours (p117) for mountain bikes.

Southern Islands

Cambodia's southern islands are the tropical Shangri-La many travellers have been seeking – as yet untouched by the mega-resorts that have sprouted across southern Thailand. Many of the islands have been tagged for major development by well-connected foreign investors, but the big boys have been slow to press go, paving the way for DIY development to move in with rustic bungalow resorts.

Koh Rong, in particular, has changed dramatically in the past couple of years due to unchecked construction in the Koh Tuch area. But for the most part, Cambodia's islands are still paradise the way you imagined it: endless crescents of powdered-sugary-soft sand, hammocks swaying in the breeze, photogenic fishing villages on stilts and technicolour sunsets. It seems too good to last, so enjoy it while it does.

ℹ Getting There & Away

The logical jumping-off point for the most popular islands is Sihanoukville. Scheduled boat services link Sihanoukville with Koh Rong and Koh Rong Sanloem. Other islands are reached by private boats, usually owned by the resort you're visiting.

Koh Rong & Koh Rong Sanloem កោះរ៉ុង កោះរ៉ុងសន្លឹម

These deceptively large neighbouring islands are the rapidly emerging pearls of the South Coast. They boast isolated white-sand beaches and heavily forested interiors populated by an incredible variety of wildlife.

The epicentre of the action is rapidly developing Koh Tuch Beach on Koh Rong's southeastern corner, which hosts a fabled full-moon party once a month. If you want to hang out with fellow travellers, hit an all-night rave and crash out on the sand during the day, Koh Rong's the spot. Those looking for a more relaxed vibe would be wise to pick a bungalow-resort well away from Koh Tuch village (on lovely Long Beach or the even-less-imaginatively named 4km Beach) or head to Koh Rong Sanloem.

However, be aware that security can be an issue on Koh Rong, with incidents of theft and occasional attacks on female tourists in remote parts of the island, so do not go walking in the jungle interior alone.

Koh Rong Sanloem is also taking off. Several colonies of bungalows have sprung up on Saracen Bay on the east coast, and more isolated options exist elsewhere on the island. Those looking for an alternative island experience can head to the village of M'Pai Bay at the island's northern tip, which has an authentic local vibe that will suit the more intrepid.

Most island resorts run their generators from about 6pm to 10.30pm.

🏃 Activities

★ Adventure Adam   BOATING
(☑ 010 354002; www.facebook.com/AdventureAdamTours; Koh Rong) 🚩 If lazing about by day and partying all night on Koh Rong seems like a missed opportunity to, you know, actually experience the island, consider booking a trip with Adventure Adam. His day and overnight tours around Koh Rong include stops at fishing villages, remote beaches and deep jungle and earn high marks for cultural immersion and adventure.

High Point
Rope Adventure   ADVENTURE SPORTS
(☑ 016 839993; www.high-point.asia; Koh Tuch village; per person US$35; ⊙ 9am-6pm) A collection of ziplines, swing bridges and walking cables takes thrill-seekers on an adrenaline-packed, 400m-long journey through the forest canopy, not far from Koh Tuch. Your ticket gets you unlimited access to the course for the entire day. From April to October, tickets are US$5 cheaper.

Koh Rong Dive Centre   DIVING
(☑ 096 560 7362; www.kohrongdivecenter.com; Koh Rong pier; ⊙ 9am-6pm) Koh Rong's main dive centre organises trips in the waters around Koh Rong, Koh Rong Sanloem and a few other islands nearby. Also offers boat trips to other islands, snorkelling excursions and diving courses.

ℹ Information

Bring all the cash you think you'll need with you as there are no banks or ATMs on Koh Rong, or any of the other southern islands. If you do run out of money, some guesthouses offer money-lending services for a 10% fee.

Wi-fi is still largely elusive (and when available, sporadic) on Koh Rong Samloem.

Emergency Services Centre (☑ whatsapp 1-912-663-1640; Koh Tuch Beach; ⊙ walk-in 9.30am-4pm, emergency 24hr) is the best medical facility on Koh Rong.

ⓘ Getting There & Away

Several companies – including **Island Speed Ferry Cambodia** (TBC Speed Boat; ☑ 069 811711; www.islandspeedboatcambodia.com), **Speed Ferry Cambodia** (www.speedferrycambodia.com), **Buva Sea** (☑ 015 888970; www.buvasea.com) and **GTVC Speedboat** (www.gtvcspeedboat.com) – operate ferries and catamarans that transport people from Koh Rong Sanloem's Saracen Bay and M'Pai Bay to Koh Rong and Sihanoukville. Note that schedule changes, unpredictable delays and cancellations are common, meaning you'll need to check up on the details of your ferry directly with the company.

Tickets cost around US\$20 return between Koh Rong and Sihanoukville. Hopping to Koh Rong Sanloem costs US\$5.

Tickets for boats can be purchased from most guesthouses and travel agencies, or booked online via www.bookmebus.com. Transport to more remote resorts and beaches on Koh Rong is by day-trip boats or on private boats owned by resorts.

KOH RONG

★Nest   HOSTEL $
(dm US\$10; ❄ 🛜) On the southern end of Long Set Beach is this new flashpacker crash pad, and it's a step up from anything you'll find in Koh Tuch. The well-designed dorms feature private bunks divided by walls and curtains, and the restaurant has a stunner of an open-air, oceanfront terrace with delicious Khmer battered chicken, vegie wraps and sweet-potato chips.

Suns of Beaches   GUESTHOUSE $
(☑ 010 550355; Vietnamese Beach; dm US\$5, r US\$10-20) On a glorious private beach a little north of Long Set Beach, this newer expat-owned hostel is for shoestringers who are into serious chilling. The huge and airy fan-cooled dorms are things of beauty, while a well-stocked bar means you won't go thirsty. Hammocks are everywhere and the beach is just wow. This is backpacker bliss.

Monkey Island   BUNGALOW $$
(☑ 081 830992; www.monkeyisland-kohrong.com; Koh Tuch Beach; dm from US\$5, bungalows US\$25-40; 🛜) Linked to the popular **Monkey Republic** (Map p127; ☑ 012 490290; www.monkeyrepublic.info; Serendipity Beach Rd; dm US\$6, r with fan US\$15-22, with air-con US\$18-30; ❄ @ 🛜 ≋) in Sihanoukville, Monkey Island's action revolves around its bamboo-and-thatch bar, which is always jam-packed with backpackers. Some of the basic bungalows can fit up to five people at a squeeze and

come with hammocks on the porches; the cheapest ones share bathrooms.

Koh Lanta   INTERNATIONAL $
(Koh Tuch; mains US\$3-6; ⏰24hr) Named after the famous French version of *Survivor*, which is filmed on Koh Rong, this place offers some of the best pizzas on the island.

Dragon Den Pub   PUB
(Koh Tuch; ⏰9am-late) In addition to a convivial atmosphere nourished by proprietor Jay, the Dragon Den serves excellent craft beer from Sihanoukville's Five Men Microbrewery – and it's a good deal at US\$1.50 to US\$2.50 a glass. There are rooms (from US\$10) upstairs if stumbling somewhere else seems too hard.

KOH RONG SANLOEM

Dragonfly Guesthouse   HOSTEL $
(☑ 069 493914; dm US\$7, r US\$15, bungalows US\$25) This chilled-out spot in M'Pai Bay operates at a languid pace, with a scenic check-in area and papasan chairs overlooking the frothy sea. Accommodation is airy and clean, and restaurant and bar are beloved for wine and cheeseboards. Live music and movie nights are hosted frequently.

★Huba-Huba   HOSTEL $$
(☑ 088 554 5619; www.huba-huba-cambodia.com; Sunset Beach; dm US\$7-8, bungalows US\$30-60) Perched on secluded Sunset Beach and flanked by the jungle, this small collection of thatched-roof bungalows and glistening hardwood common spaces looks like an island fantasy land. During high season, a beach restaurant with a bar constructed from the bow of a boat serves up cold beers, wine, cocktails and barbecue, and everybody goes snorkelling on a nearby reef.

★Mad Monkey Island Resort   HOSTEL $$
(☑ 016 762654; www.madmonkeyhostels.com; dm US\$9-10, bungalows US\$40; 🛜) The latest addition to the Mad Monkey hostel empire wins big with its secluded private cove and beaches to the north of Saracen Bay. Dorms of varying size and private bungalows are oceanfront, simple and fan-cooled, and the atmosphere is laid-back and convivial. A big, open-air bar and restaurant overlooks the sea, where people laze about in hammocks all day.

Fishing Hook   INTERNATIONAL $
(M'Pai Bay; mains US\$1.25; ⏰8am-9pm) Some of the finest food on Koh Rong Sanloem is being served up at a food stall near M'Pai

Bay pier. The menu waltzes from Khmer-influenced curries to chilli onion rings to more global offerings. Keep an eye out for a bigger and better Fishing Hook up the hill from Dragonfly Guesthouse (p129).

Tree Bar BAR
(Saracen Bay; ⊙10am-late; 🔊) Travellers regularly perch at this locally owned tiki bar until late into the night, playing drinking games and sizing up who might be interested in a skinny-dip in the plankton. There's also a sign for free Khmer lessons here.

Other Islands

Closer to Sihanoukville, Koh Ta Kiev and Koh Russei appear on most island-hopping itineraries out of Sihanoukville, with day trips running from US$12 to US$15 depending on whether you launch from Otres Beach or Serendipity Beach. Both islands have accommodation, although both are slated for development.

Kampot កំពត
📞033 / POP 39,500
There is something about this little charmer that encourages visitors to linger. It might be the lovely riverside setting or the ageing French buildings, or it could be the great little guesthouses and burgeoning bar scene. Whatever the magic ingredient, this is the perfect base from which to explore nearby caves and the beautiful Kompong Bay River.

◎ Sights & Activities

This is not a town where you come and do, but a place to come and be. Sit on the riverbank and watch the sun set beneath the mountains, or stroll among the town's fine French shophouses (in the triangle delineated by 7 Makara St, the central roundabout and the post office).

★**La Plantation** FARM
(📞017 842505; www.kampotpepper.com; guided tours US$18-20; ⊙9am-6pm) 🏷FREE This sprawling, lovely organic pepper farm offers guided walks in French, English and Khmer, explaining how several varieties of pepper are grown, harvested and processed. The farm also grows fruits, chillis, herbs and peanuts, and there's a restaurant and shop where you can buy pepper at steep prices. (The money helps pay for children's English classes at local schools.)

Kampot Traditional Music School CULTURAL CENTRE
(📞010 223325; www.kcdi-cambodia.org; St 724; ⊙2-5pm Mon & Tue, 5-7pm Fri) 🏷FREE During set hours, visitors are welcome to observe traditional music and dance training sessions and/or performances at this school that teaches children who are orphaned or have disabilities. Donations are very welcome.

Khmer Roots Cafe COOKING
(📞088 356 8016; www.khmerrootscafe.com; off NH33; US$20; ⊙10am-4pm) More than just a cooking class, Khmer Roots Cafe is a slice of Cambodian rural life set amid owner Soklim's shady trees and organic vegetable gardens about an hour east of Kampot. Classes usually involve preparing two dishes (including gathering the ingredients), eating lunch and having the opportunity to explore the tranquil countryside by bicycle afterwards.

Climbodia CLIMBING
(📞070 255210; www.climbodia.com; St 710; half day US$35-40, full day US$80; ⊙3-8pm Tue-Sun, from 5pm Mon) Cambodia's first outdoor rock-climbing outfit offers highly recommended half-day and full-day programs of climbing, abseiling and caving amid the limestone formations of Phnom Kbal Romeas, 5km south of Kampot. Cabled routes (via ferratas) have been established across some of the cliffs and the program offerings cater for both complete novices and the more experienced.

⤵ Tours

Love the River BOATING
(📞016 627410; per person US$15-19) Offers longtail boat charters and cruises from the Green House along the river, with stops for beach swimming and exploring a durian plantation. Captain Bjorn earns high marks for local knowledge and foresight (he brings fresh fruit and cold beer to go with the sunset).

SUP Asia WATER SPORTS
(📞093 980550; www.supasia.org; Old Market; 2½hr tour US$25, half-day tour US$55; ⊙daily, closed Sep) SUP (stand-up paddleboarding) has come to Kampot in a big way; this company offers it as an alternative form of touring the river. Daily tours depart at 8.30am, 2.30pm and 3.30pm, taking in the riverbank sights of the local area (with a SUP lesson

beforehand). There's also a two-day (18km) trip that traverses the Kampong Bay River to the sea.

Bart the Boatman   BOATING
(☑ 092 174280; 2-person tour US$40) Known simply as Bart the Boatman, this expat runs original private boat tours along the small tributaries of the Kampong Bay River. His backwater tour is highly recommended by travellers.

Captain Chim's   BOATING
(☑ 012 321043; St 724, Captain Chim's Guesthouse; sunset boat trip per person US$5) A sunset cruise with firefly-watching on a traditional boat, including a cold beer, is one of Captain Chim's popular excursions. Also on offer are fishing trips for US$11 including lunch, and bicycle hire (US$2 per day).

Sok Lim Tours   TOURS
(☑ 012 796919, 010 796919; www.soklimtours. com; St 730; ⊗ 8am-7pm) Kampot's longest-running tour outfit is well regarded and organises all the usual day tours and river cruises. For private countryside tours there are good English-speaking remork-moto (tuk tuk) driver-guides who understand the process and history behind Kampot pepper. If there's no one in the actual office, check the neighbouring **Jack's Place** (St 730; mains US$2.50-6; ⊗ 6.30am-10.30pm; ☎✐) restaurant.

🛏 Sleeping

You can stay in the centre of the old town, or stay a little out of town in one of several places strung out along the riverbank.

Naga House   HOSTEL $
(☑ 012 289916; nagahousekampot@gmail.com; Tek Chhouu Rd; dm US$4, bungalows US$9-14; ☎) This classic backpacker hang-out offers basic ground-level and stilted thatched bungalows (all with shared bathrooms) amid lush foliage, and coveted four- and eight-bed dorms in the main house on the river. There's an attractive and extremely social bar-restaurant that often rocks into the night, especially on Saturdays when it hosts DJ sets.

Arcadia Backpackers &
Water Park   HOSTEL $
(☑ 097 519 7902; www.arcadiabackpackers.com; Tek Chhouu Rd; dm US$7-10, r US$20; ☎) One of Kampot's great backpacker party scenes, riverside Arcadia offers a wide range of accommodations, from large, mixed dorms by

> ### KAMPOT PEPPER
> In the years before the Cambodian civil war took its toll, no self-respecting French restaurant in Paris would be without Kampot pepper on the table. Pepper plantations are once again a common sight in the Kampot region and come in a variety of colours, including white, black, green and red.

the bar to quiet, private doubles by the water. All beds come with mosquito nets and free entry to the water park, which includes a Russian swing, a 50m water slide, a climbing wall, a diving platform and a zipline.

Banyan Tree Guesthouse   HOSTEL $
(☑ 078 665094; www.banyantreekampot.com; Tek Chhouu Rd; dm US$3, r US$6-12; ☎) Boat sports by day, booze by night, and plenty of downtime in between on the sublime riverside chill-out deck. Choose from a 20-bed dorm, simple rooms above the bar or pleasing rattan bungalows out back. Fridays are party nights with live music from top local band Kampot Playboys or visiting Phnom Penh acts. This is no place for light sleepers.

Monkey Republic Kampot   HOSTEL $
(☑ 012 848390; monkeyrepublickampot@gmail. com; St 730; dm with air-con US$5-7, r with fan US$8-12; ❄☎) This 100-bed backpacker mecca in a restored villa features Kampot's nicest dorm rooms. Choose from large dorms in the main building, or brand-new, six-bed 'pods' in the neighbouring house. Think individual lockers, privacy curtains and charging stations. There's an upstairs hammock lounge, while French tiles and big booths add character to the lively bar downstairs.

★ Green House   BUNGALOW $$
(☑ 088 886 3071; www.greenhousekampot.com; Tek Chhouu Rd; bungalows US$25-35; ☎) This gorgeously conceived riverfront pad is all about tranquillity, with the best of its palm-thatch bungalows and colourful wooden cottages (with balconies) right on the riverbank. The historic teak-wood main building, which houses the restaurant, was once home to the legendary Phnom Penh bar Snowy's (aka Maxine's), transported lock, stock, and barrel here in 2011. No children under age 12.

Kampot

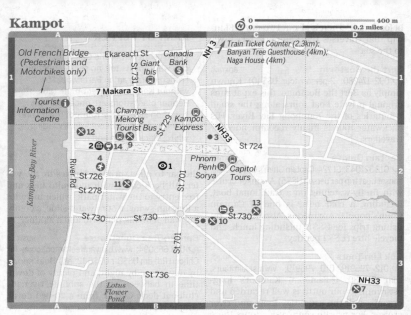

Kampot

◎ Sights

⊕ Activities, Courses & Tours

⊜ Sleeping

⊗ Eating

⊙ Drinking & Nightlife

⊕ Entertainment

✗ Eating & Drinking

★ Ciao
ITALIAN $

(St 722; mains US$2.75-4; ⊗ from 6pm) Kampot's most beloved Western street-food vendor is an Italian who cooks delicious pizzas one at a time in a modified dustbin out of this ram-shackle space on Kampot's street-food row. The pizzas take awhile but are *sooo* worth it. Also serves homemade gnocchi and pasta.

★ Thai Fire
THAI $

(☏ 081 364559; www.facebook.com/ThaiFire-Kampot; Guesthouse Rd; mains US$4.50-5; ⊗ noon-10.30pm Mon-Sat) Guests here are in the capable hands of Nalee, a culinary ge-nius from Laos who taught herself to cook in Thailand and opened this restaurant with her husband Rhett, who handles non-cooking details. Don't miss the excellent whole fried fish, enormous and Thai-style, with crispy skin, delicate flakes and chilli, lemongrass and cashews galore. Just dig in.

Epic Arts Café
CAFE $

(www.epicarts.org.uk; St 724; mains US$2-4; ⊗ 7am-4pm; 🛜) 🍃 A great place for break-fast, homemade cakes, infused tea and light lunches, this mellow eatery is staffed by young people who are deaf or have a disability. Profits fund arts workshops for Cambodians with disabilities and there's an upstairs shop that sells art, bags, jewellery, stuffed toys and the like.

Cafe Espresso
CAFE $

(NH33; mains US$4-6; ☺8.30am-4pm Tue-Fri, 9am-4.30pm Sat & Sun; 🖥🍴) It's worth the trip to this cafe on the outskirts of town. The owners are real foodies and offer a global menu that traipses from vegetarian quesadillas to Brazilian-style pork sandwiches with some especially tempting breakfast options. But it is caffeine-cravers who will really be buzzing, thanks to the regionally grown coffee blends, roasted daily on-site.

KAMA Cafe
CAFE $

(St 726; mains US$3.50-4; ☺8am-7.30pm; 🖥) Inside the art space of the same name, KAMA is delightfully situated in an elegant old townhouse – perfect for an atmospheric breakfast or happy hour. The food – especially breakfast – is scrumptious, featuring light bites, curries and exciting daily specials prepared by Soon, who co-runs the place with her partner, Julien of the band Cambodian Space Project. Hours can be unpredictable.

Rusty Keyhole
INTERNATIONAL $$

(☑095 212485; River Rd; ribs US$5-10; ☺8am-11.30pm Nov-May, 11am-11pm Jun-Oct; 🖥) This popular riverfront bar-restaurant turns out a global menu of comfort food and Khmer home cooking. Most people are here for its famous ribs; order in advance, but beware of the enormous, extra-large portions. Three more Rusty restaurants have opened in the last few years, with varying ownership.

Moi Tiet
BAR

(Old Market) This artsy little enclave in the **Old Market** (Riverfront Rd) specialises in 'brews and tattoos' according to its signage, but also does things like home-brewed ginger beer and tasty French dishes. It's beloved most for its garden setting, intriguing patrons and delicious cocktails.

❶ Information

The free and often hilarious Kampot Survival Guide takes a tongue-in-cheek look at local expat life, and there's also the free guide Coastal (www.coastal-cambodia.com).

Canadia Bank (Durian Roundabout; ☺8am-3.30pm Mon-Fri, to 11.30am Sat, ATM 24hr)

Sonja Kill Memorial Hospital (☑emergency 078 265782, outpatient clinic 077 666752;

www.skmh.org; NH3) The best hospital in the area, with state-of-the-art medical facilities and highly trained local and expat doctors. It's 7km west of Kampot.

Tourist Information Centre (☑097 899 5593; lonelyguide@gmail.com; River Rd; ☺7am-5pm) Led by the knowledgeable Mr Pov, Kampot's tourist office doles out free advice, sells tours and can arrange transport to area attractions such as caves, falls and Kompong Trach.

❶ Getting There & Away

Kampot is 105km from Sihanoukville and 148km from Phnom Penh.

Capitol Tours (☑092 665001; NH33) and **Phnom Penh Sorya** (NH33) sell bus tickets from offices opposite the Total petrol station near the Four Nagas Roundabout. Both have daily trips to Phnom Penh (US$5 to US$6, 2½ hours) until lunchtime. **Giant Ibis** (☑095 666809; www.giantibis.com; 7 Makara St) and **Kampot Express** (☑078 555123; NH33) run comfortable express vans to Phnom Penh (US$8 to US$9, two hours).

Champa Mekong Tourist Bus (☑087 630036; St 724) has five minivan departures daily to Sihanoukville and twice-daily departures to Ha Tien, Ho Chi Minh City, Phnom Penh and Bangkok.

A moto/remork to Kep should cost about US$6/12.

❶ Getting Around

Bicycles (US$2) and motorbikes (from US$5) can be rented from guesthouses in town.

Around Kampot

The limestone hills east towards Kep are honeycombed with fantastic caves, some of which can be explored with the help of local kids and a reliable torch (flashlight).

Phnom Chhnork
CAVE

(ភ្នំឆ្នោក; US$1; ☺7am-6pm) Phnom Chhnork is a short walk through a quilt of rice paddies from Wat Ang Sdok, where a monk collects the entry fee and a gaggle of friendly local kids offer their services as guides. From the bottom, a 203-step staircase leads up the hillside and down into a cavern as graceful as a Gothic cathedral. The view from up top is especially magical in the late afternoon, as is the walk to and from the wat.

Phnom Sorsia
CAVE

(ភ្នំសសៀរ, Phnom Sia; ☺7am-5pm) FREE Phnom Sorsia is home to several natural caves. From the parking area, a stairway leads up the hillside to a gaudy modern temple. From there, steps lead left up to **Rung Damrey Saa** (White Elephant Cave). A slippery, sloping staircase (where one false step will send you into the abyss) leads down and then up and then out through a hole in the other side. Exit the cave and follow the right-hand path which leads back to the temple.

Kep កែប

♫ 036 / POP 35,000

Kep was founded as a seaside retreat for the French elite in 1908 and was a favoured haunt of Cambodian high-rollers during the 1960s. Today tourists are being drawn back to Kep (Krong Kep, also spelled Kaeb) thanks to its spectacular sunsets and splendid seafood. Some travellers find Kep a tad soulless because it lacks a centre. Others are oddly charmed by its torpid pace.

Most of Kep's beaches are too shallow and rocky to make for good swimming. The best is centrally located Kep Beach, but it's still somewhat pebbly and tends to fill up with locals on weekends. The best place for sunset viewing is the long wooden pier in front of Knai Bang Chat's Sailing Club.

◎ Sights & Activities

★ Kep National Park NATIONAL PARK

(ឧទ្យានជាតិកែប; 4000r) The interior of Kep peninsula is occupied by Kep National Park, where an 8km circuit, navigable by foot and mountain bike, winds through thick forest passing by wats and viewpoints. Quirky yellow signs point the way and show trailheads to off-shooting walking paths that lead into the park's interior. The 'Stairway to Heaven' trail is particularly worthwhile, leading up the hill to a pagoda, a nunnery and the Sunset Rock viewpoint. The main park entrance is behind Veranda Natural Resort.

Koh Tonsay ISLAND

(កោះទន្សាយ, Rabbit Island) If you like the rustic beachcomber lifestyle, Koh Tonsay's 250m-long main beach is for you, but come now as the island is tagged for development. The beach is one of the nicest of any of the Kep-area islands, but don't expect sparkling white sand. This one has shorefront flotsam, chickens and wandering cows. Restaurant shacks and rudimentary bungalows (from US$7 per night) rim the sand. Boats to Rabbit Island (30 minutes) leave from **Rabbit Island pier** at 9am and 1pm.

Kep Beach BEACH

(ឆ្នេរកែប) This handkerchief-sized strip of sand is Kep's only proper beach. In the prewar period, powder-white sand was trucked in from other beaches and this practice began again in 2013, ensuring the beach is now in better shape than it has been for years. It's still somewhat pebbly and can get packed on weekends. The eastern end of the shaded promenade along the beach is marked by **Sela Cham P'dey**, a statue depicting a nude fisherman's wife awaiting her husband's return.

Wat Kiri Sela BUDDHIST TEMPLE

(វត្តគីរីសេលា; US$1; ⊙7am-6pm) This Buddhist temple sits at the foot of Phnom Kompong Trach, a dramatic karst formation riddled with more than 100 caverns and passageways. From the wat, an underground passage leads to a fishbowl-like formation, surrounded by vine-draped cliffs and open to the sky. Various stalactite-laden caves shelter reclining Buddhas and miniature Buddhist shrines. The closest town is Kompong Trach. From here, take the dirt road opposite the old Acleda Bank, on NH33 in the town centre, for 2km.

⨇ Sleeping

Botanica Guesthouse BUNGALOW $

(☏ 097 899 8614; www.kep-botanica.com; NH33A; r with fan/air-con US$22/29; ❄ � 🛜 ❄) A little way from the action (if Kep can be said to have any action), Botanica offers exceptional value for money with attractive bungalows boasting contemporary bathrooms. There's a well-shaded pool and guests can use free bicycles to pedal into town. Renovations have only improved what was already a good thing.

Bacoma BUNGALOW $

(☏ 088 411 2424; www.bacoma.weebly.com; NH33A; r US$15-30; 🛜) Cheap and cheerful rondavels (circular dwellings with conical thatched roofs) in the garden all have mosquito nets and fan, with a generous helping of sparkling-clean shared bathrooms. There are also roomy bungalows and traditional Khmer houses with private bathrooms, and the owner is a super-nice guy.

Bird of Paradise BUNGALOW $

(☏ 090 880413; www.birdofparadisebungalows. com; bungalows incl breakfast with fan/air-con from US$14/20; ❄ 🛜) Set in a relaxed, peaceful garden, Bird of Paradise offers

ℹ️ **GETTING TO VIETNAM: KEP TO HA TIEN**

The Prek Chak/Xa Xia border crossing (open 6am to 5.30pm) has become a popular option for linking Kampot and Kep with Ha Tien and the popular Vietnamese island of Phu Quoc.

Getting to the border The easiest way to get to Prek Chak and on to Ha Tien, Vietnam, is on a bus or van from Sihanoukville (US$16, five hours), Kampot (US$8, 1½ hours) or Kep (US$5, one hour). Several companies ply the Sihanoukville–Kampot–Kep–Ha Tien route. A more flexible alternative from Phnom Penh or Kampot is to take any bus to Kompong Trach, then a moto (about US$3) for 15km to the border. In Kep, tour agencies and guesthouses can arrange a direct remork (US$13, one hour) or taxi (US$20, 30 minutes). Rates are almost double from Kampot.

At the border Pick up motos on the Vietnamese side of the border to Ha Tien (7km). You'll save money walking across no-man's land and picking up a moto on the other side for about US$3.

Moving on Travellers bound for Phu Quoc should arrive in Ha Tien no later than 12.30pm to secure a ticket on the 1pm ferry (230,000d or about US$11, 1½ hours). Extreme early risers may be able to make it to Ha Tien in time to catch the 8am ferry.

For information on making this crossing in reverse, see p908.

stupendous value and is well located just uphill from the main road, within walking distance of the crab market. Simple but sweet wooden bungalows, with hammocks strung from the porch, are delightfully rustic, while the air-con concrete cottages are more spacious.

🍴 Eating & Drinking

Eating fresh crab fried with Kampot pepper at the Crab Market – a row of wooden waterfront shacks next to a wet fish market – is a quintessential Kep experience. There are lots of great places to choose from. **Kimly** (📞097 255 5596; Crab Market; mains US$2.75-11.85; ⏱9am-11pm) has a good reputation with crab prepared 27 different ways. The crab shacks also serve prawns, squid, fish and terrestrial offerings.

Deli's Kep   DELI **$**
(📞088 470 7952; NH33A; sandwiches US$3.50-4; ⏱7am-7pm) This new gourmet food store in Kep is earning high praise for its *coppa*, *lomo*, *saucisson* and other imported meats, along with top-notch pepper (100g for US$5 to US$8), coffee and craft booze. Grab a sandwich on the way to a pepper farm, or plop down for a relaxing meal in the airy, modern space.

⭐ **Sailing Club**   COCKTAIL BAR
(mains US$7-12.50; ⏱10am-10pm; 📶) With a small beach, a breezy wooden bar and a wooden jetty poking out into the sea, this is

one of Cambodia's top sundowner spots. The Asian-fusion food is excellent and you can get your crab fix here too. There's now an outdoor cocktail lounge and a vastly expanded seafront terrace.

ℹ️ Getting There & Away

Kep is 25km from Kampot and 41km from the Prek Chak/Xa Xia border crossing to Vietnam. Phnom Penh Sorya and Hua Lian buses link the town with Kampot (US$2, 45 minutes) and Phnom Penh (US$5, four hours). A private taxi to Phnom Penh (three hours) costs US$40 to US$45. A moto/remork to Kampot costs about US$6/12. Guesthouses can arrange minibus/bus combos to Sihanoukville and Koh Kong. Motorbike rental is US$5 to US$7 per day and can be organised through guesthouses.

Bokor Hill Station   កស្ថានីយភ្នំបូកគោ

The 1581-sq-km **Bokor National Park** (ឧទ្យានជាតិភ្នំបូកគោ, Preah Monivong National Park; motorbike/car 2000/10,000r) has impressive wildlife, lush primary forests and a refreshingly cool climate, but is most famous for its once-abandoned **Bokor Hill Station**, established atop Phnom Bokor (1080m) in the 1920s.

Until recently the main attraction here was the the abandoned shell of the grand, four-storey hotel, the Bokor Palace, opened in 1925 and the old Catholic church. The

WORTH A TRIP

MEKONG DISCOVERY TRAIL

It's well worth spending a couple of days exploring the various bike rides and activities on offer along the Mekong Discovery Trail (www.mekongdiscoverytrail. com), an initiative designed to open up stretches of the Mekong River around Stung Treng and Kratie to community-based tourism. Once managed by the government with foreign development assistance, the project is now being kept alive by private tour companies, such as **Cambodia Mekong Trail** (Xplore-Asia; ☑ 011 433836; www.cambodiamekongtrail. com) in Stung Treng and CRDTours (p138) in Kratie.

hill station was abandoned to the howling winds in the 1970s when Khmer Rouge forces infiltrated the area. The once-grand buildings became eerie, windowless shells. Unfortunately it is now becoming more famous for the ugly casino that blights the summit, part of a massive development project that has sadly destroyed the atmosphere of bygone Bokor.

To visit the park you can rent a motorbike or join an organised tour (US$10 to US$15 per person). The road is in incredible shape making for a great ride.

EASTERN CAMBODIA

If it's a walk on the wild side that fires your imagination, then the northeast is calling. It's home to forest elephants, freshwater dolphins and funky gibbons. Peppering the area are thundering waterfalls, crater lakes and meandering rivers. Trekking, biking, kayaking and ziplining are all beginning to take off. The rolling hills and lush forests provide a home to many ethnic minority groups. Do the maths: it all adds up to an amazing experience.

Kompong Cham កំពង់ចាម

☑ 042 / POP 125,000

This quiet Mekong city, an important trading post during the French period, serves as the gateway to Cambodia's northeast. Most of the action is on the riverfront.

◉ Sights & Activities

Koh Paen ISLAND
(កោះប៉ែន) For a supremely relaxing bicycle ride, it's hard to beat Koh Paen, a rural island in the Mekong River, connected to the southern reaches of Kompong Cham town by an elaborate **bamboo bridge** (foreigner US$1) in the dry season or a local ferry (with/without bicycle 1500/1000r) in the wet season.

Wat Nokor Bachey BUDDHIST TEMPLE
(វត្តនគរបាជ័យ; US$2) The original fusion temple, Wat Nokor is a modern Theravada Buddhist pagoda squeezed into the walls of a 12th-century Mahayana Buddhist shrine of sandstone and laterite. It's located down a pretty dirt road just off the highway to Phnom Penh, about 2.5km west of the centre.

🛏 Sleeping & Eating

★ **Moon River Guesthouse** GUESTHOUSE $
(☑ 016 788973; moonrivermekong@gmail.com; Sihanouk St; r with fan US$7-15, with air-con US$12-25; ❄ 🛜) The best of the riverfront guesthouses, Moon River is a great all-rounder with smart, spacious rooms, including some triples. Downstairs is a popular restaurant-bar (mains US$2 to US$4) that serves hearty breakfasts and draws a crowd by night.

Mekong Bamboo Hut
Guesthouse HOSTEL $
(☑ 015 905620; mekongbamboohut@gmail.com; Koh Paen; hammock US$3; 🛜) This French-run riverside guesthouse has the feel of a hippy commune and is a great place to get away from it all if the pace of life is too fast back on the mainland. Accommodation is very basic with hammocks strung across bamboo pavilions with mosquito nets, but it certainly has a chilled vibe. It has a little restaurant on-site.

★ **Smile Restaurant** CAMBODIAN $
(www.bsda-cambodia.org; Sihanouk St; mains US$3-5; ⊙ 6.30am-10pm; 🛜) 🌱 Run by the Buddhism and Society Development Association (BSDA), this handsome nonprofit restaurant is a huge hit with the NGO crowd for its big breakfasts and authentic Khmer cuisine, such as *char k'dau* (stir-fry with lemongrass, hot basil and peanuts) and black-pepper squid. Western dishes are on the menu as well, and it sells BSDA-made *krama* (checked scarves) and trinkets.

Lazy Mekong Daze INTERNATIONAL **$**
(Sihanouk St; mains US$3-5.50; ⏰7.30am-last cus-
tomer; 🛜) One of the go-to places to gather
after dark thanks to a mellow atmosphere,
a pool table and a big screen for sports
and movies. The menu includes a range of
Khmer, Thai and French food, plus the best
pizzas in town, chilli con carne and tempting ice creams.

ℹ️ Information

Lazy Mekong Daze hands out a decent map that
highlights the major sights in and around Kompong Cham.
Canadia Bank (Preah Monivong Blvd; ⏰8am-
3.30pm Mon-Fri, 8-11.30am Sat, ATM 24hr)
ATM plus cash advances on credit cards.

ℹ️ Getting There & Around

Phnom Penh is 120km southwest. If you are
heading north to Kratie or beyond, secure transport via the sealed road to Chhlong rather than
taking a huge detour east to Snuol on NH7.
Phnom Penh Sorya (Preah Monivong Blvd)
is the most reliable bus company operating
and serves Phnom Penh (20,000r, three
hours), Kratie (20,000r, two hours), Ban
Lung (32,000r, seven hours) and Siem Reap
(24,000r, five hours).

Share taxis (15,000r, 2½ hours) and overcrowded local minibuses (10,000r) also make
the run to Phnom Penh, departing from the taxi
park near the New Market (Psar Thmei).

Morning share taxis and minibuses to Kratie
(US$5, 1½ hours) depart when full from the Cal-
tex station at the main roundabout, and there are
morning minibuses from the taxi park as well.

Kratie ឃ្លាំង

📞072 / POP 45,000
The most popular place in Cambodia to
glimpse Southeast Asia's remaining freshwater Irrawaddy dolphins, Kratie (kra-cheh)
is a lively riverside town with a rich legacy
of French-era architecture and some of the
best Mekong sunsets in Cambodia.

Lying just across the water from Kratie
is the island of **Koh Trong**, an almighty
sandbar in the middle of the river. Cross
here by boat and enjoy a slice of rural island
life. Catch the little ferry from the port or
charter a local boat (around US$2) to get
here. Bicycle rental is available on the island
near the ferry landing for US$1, or do the
loop around the island on a moto (US$2.50)
steered by a female *motodup* (moto driver) –
a rarity for Cambodia.

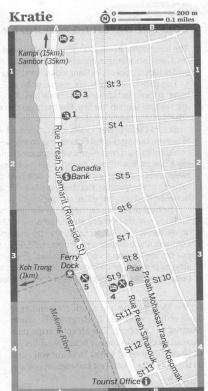

Kratie

🅐 **Activities, Courses & Tours**
  CRDTours...(see 3)
1 Sorya Kayaking Adventures................A1

🅑 **Sleeping**
2 Balcony Guesthouse.............................A1
3 Le Tonlé Tourism Training Center......A1
4 U-Hong II Guesthouse B3

🅧 **Eating**
5 Jasmine Boat Restaurant A3
  Pete's Pizza Pasta & Cafe............(see 1)
6 Tokae Restaurant.................................B3

🏃 Activities

⭐ **Sorya Kayaking
Adventures** KAYAKING
(📞090 241148; www.soryakayaking.com; Rue
Preah Suramarit; US$24-52, depending on numbers;
⏰7am-9pm) Sorya has a fleet of seven tandem
kayaks and runs memorable half-day trips

DON'T MISS

DOLPHIN-WATCHING AROUND KRATIE

The freshwater Irrawaddy dolphin (trey pisaut) is an endangered species throughout Asia, with shrinking numbers inhabiting stretches of the Mekong in Cambodia and Laos, and isolated pockets in Bangladesh and Myanmar.

The dark blue to grey cetaceans grow to 2.75m long and are recognisable by their bulging foreheads and small dorsal fins. They can live in fresh or saltwater, although they are seldom seen in the sea. For more on this rare creature, see www.worldwildlife.org/species/irrawaddy-dolphin.

Before the civil war, locals say, Cambodia was home to as many as 1000 dolphins. However, during the Pol Pot regime, many were hunted for their oils, and their numbers continue to plummet even as drastic protection measures have been put in place, including a ban on fishing and commercial motorised boat traffic on much of the Mekong between Kratie and Stung Treng. The dolphins continue to die off at an alarming rate, and experts now estimate that there are fewer than 85 Irrawaddy dolphins left in the Mekong between Kratie and the Lao border.

The best place to see them is at Kampi, about 15km north of Kratie, on the road to Sambor. A moto/remork should be around US$7/10 return depending on how long the driver has to wait. Motorboats shuttle visitors out to the middle of the river to view the dolphins at close quarters. It costs US$9 per person for one to two persons and US$7 per person for groups of three to four. Encourage the boat driver to use the engine as little as possible once near the dolphins, as the noise is sure to disturb them. It is also possible to see the dolphins near the Lao border in Stung Treng province.

on the Mekong north of Kratie (November to June only), or on the Te River to the south (August to October). The Mekong trips pass through secluded sandbar beaches and areas of beautiful flooded forest to bring you close to the dolphins – without the engine noise.

CRDTours TOURS
(Cambodia Rural Discovery Tours; ☑ 099 834353; www.crdtours.org; St 3; ⊙ 8am-noon & 2-5.30pm; 🛜) 🏃 Run by the Cambodian Rural Development team, this company focuses on sustainable tours along the Mekong Discovery Trail (p136). Homestays, volunteer opportunities and various excursions are available on the Mekong island of Koh Pdao, 20km north of Kampi. The typical price is US$38 to US$60 per day, including all meals and tours.

🛌 Sleeping

There are homestays available on the island of Koh Trong opposite Kratie town.

⭐ **Le Tonlé Tourism
Training Center** GUESTHOUSE $
(☑ 072-210505; www.letonle.org; St 3; r without bathroom US$10-20; ❄🛜) 🏃 CRDT runs this fantastic budget guesthouse in a beautiful wooden house in the centre. With silk pillows and bed runners, agreeable art and photos, wood floors and a great hang-out

area, it puts plenty of care into the design. Rooms are somewhat dark but share boutique-quality bathrooms. It doubles as a training centre for at-risk locals.

U-Hong II Guesthouse GUESTHOUSE $
(☑ 085 885168; 119 St 10; r US$4-13; ❄@🛜) A lively little shoes-off guesthouse between the market and the riverfront. There are eight rooms here, plus 11 more in a nearby annex, some with air-con. There is a buzzing bar-restaurant that boasts the most extensive cocktail list in town.

Balcony Guesthouse GUESTHOUSE $
(☑ 016 604036; www.balconyguesthouse.net; Rue Preah Suramarit; dm US$5, r US$5-15; ❄@🛜) This long-running backpacker place has a few tasteful private rooms, a four-bed dorm, a popular bar overlooking the Mekong and a huge balcony on the 3rd floor for prime river views. The bar has a gigantic snooker table, which is a lot harder to master than a standard pool table.

🍴 Eating

⭐ **Tokae Restaurant** CAMBODIAN $
(☑ 097 297 2118; St 10; mains US$2-4; ⊙ 6am-11pm; 🛜) Look out for Cambodia's largest tokae (gecko) on the wall and you've found this excellent little eatery. The menu offers a good mix of cheap Cambodian food such as

curries and *amok* (a baked fish dish), plus equally affordable Western breakfasts and comfort food.

Pete's Pizza Pasta & Cafe   INTERNATIONAL $

(☑090 241148; www.petescafekratie.com; Rue Preah Suramarit; US$1-5; ☺7am-9pm daily; 📶) Get your home fix of pizza, pasta, toasties and salads at this internationally run riverfront cafe; it is also the base for Sorya Kayaking Adventures. The menu includes homemade bakery items such as pumpkin bread, muffins and cookies. By night it doubles as a small riverside bar with a flat-screen television and will stay open later for big games.

Jasmine Boat Restaurant   INTERNATIONAL $$

(☑096 331 1998; Rue Preah Suramarit; mains US$4-22; ☺7am-10pm; 📶) Occupying a prime location overlooking Kratie's busy ferry dock, this is the only place on the riverbank in town. The boat-shaped restaurant has a mixed menu of affordable Khmer specials and pricey international cuts of meat. It really shines at sunset but is a good perch any time of day.

ℹ Information

All of the recommended guesthouses are pretty switched-on to travellers' needs and U-Hong II Guesthouse has public internet access.

Canadia Bank (Rue Preah Suramarit; ☺8.30am-3.30pm Mon-Fri, ATM 24hr) has an ATM offering cash withdrawals, plus currency exchange.

ℹ Getting There & Away

Kratie is 348km northeast of Phnom Penh (250km via Chhlong) and 141km south of Stung Treng.

Phnom Penh Sorya runs three buses per day to Phnom Penh (US$8, five to seven hours). Sorya buses to Siem Reap involve a change in Suong.

Going the other way, Sorya's bus from Phnom Penh to Pakse, Laos (US$20, eight hours), hits Kratie around 11.30am. Sorya also has a 1pm bus to Ban Lung (US$8, five hours), and a 3pm bus to Stung Treng (US$5, three hours).

Express vans, which pick you up from your guesthouse, are a faster way to Phnom Penh (US$7, four hours, about six per day). There's also an express van to Siem Reap (US$13, six hours, 7.30am).

For Sen Monorom, take a local minibus from the taxi park (30,000r, four hours, two or three early morning departures). Local minibuses also serve Ban Lung, with most departures between 11am and 2pm.

Most guesthouses can arrange bicycle (from US$1) and motorbike hire (from US$5). An English-speaking motodup will set you back US$10 to US$15 per day, or a remork about US$25.

Stung Treng   ស្ទឹងត្រែង

☑074 / POP 35,000

Located on the Tonlé San near its confluence with the Mekong, Stung Treng is a quiet town with limited appeal, but sees a lot of transit traffic passing through between Laos and Cambodia.

🛏 Sleeping & Eating

4 Rivers Hotel   HOTEL $

(☑070 507822; www.fourrivershotel.com; US$15-30; ❋@📶) In no way affiliated with the floating 4 Rivers in Koh Kong, this is most definitely located on dry land overlooking the Tonlé San and Mekong River. Rooms

CAMBODIA STUNG TRENG

ℹ GETTING TO LAOS: STUNG TRENG TO SI PHAN DON

The remote Trapeang Kriel/Nong Nok Khiene border (open 6am to 6pm) is 60km north of Stung Treng.

Getting to the border There are no longer any through buses between Phnom Penh and Pakse. You'll need to get yourself to Stung Treng, from where there are at least two minivans per day (at noon and 2pm) that run across the border and onward to the 4000 Islands and Pakse. The only other option to the border is a private taxi (around US$35 to US$40) or moto (motorcycle taxi; around US$15) from Stung Treng.

At the border Both Lao and Cambodian visas are available on arrival. Entering Laos, you'll pay US$30 to US$42 for a visa, depending on nationality, plus a US$2 fee. Cambodian immigration usually overcharge by up to US$5 for a visa on arrival and all the associated paperwork.

Moving on Aside from the Sorya bus, there's virtually zero traffic on either side of the border. If you're dropped at the border, expect to pay 150,000r/50,000K (US$12/4) for a taxi/săhmlór heading north to Ban Nakasang (for Don Det).

feature a contemporary trim and it is worth paying a little extra for the river-view rooms.

Riverside Guesthouse GUESTHOUSE $
(☑ 012-257207; kimtysou@gmail.com; r with fan/ air-con US$6/12; @ 🛜) Overlooking the riverfront area, the Riverside has long been a popular travellers' hub. Rooms are basic, but then so are the prices. It's a good spot for travel information and there's a bar-restaurant downstairs.

ℹ Information

Canadia Bank (⊙ 8.30am-3.30pm Mon-Fri, ATM 24hr) Has an international ATM.

ℹ Getting There & Away

Phnom Penh Sorya (☑ 092 181805) has a 6.30am bus to Phnom Penh (40,000r, nine hours) via Kratie (20,000r, three hours). Sorya's bus from Laos to Phnom Penh comes through Stung Treng around 11.30am. There is a comfortable tourist van to Ban Lung (US$6, two hours, 8am).

The new highway west from Thala Boravit to Preah Vihear via Chhep is in great shape. **Asia Van Transfer** (☑ in Siem Reap 063-963853; www.asiavantransfer.com; Riverside Guesthouse) has an express minibus to Siem Reap at 2pm daily (US$23, five hours), with a stop in Preah Vihear City (US$12, three hours).

Riverside Guesthouse rents out motorbikes (from US$8) and bicycles (US$1 to US$2).

Ratanakiri Province

ខេត្តរតនគិរី

Popular Ratanakiri Province is a diverse region of natural beauty that provides a remote home for a mosaic of minority peoples – Jarai, Tompuon, Brau and Kreung – with their own languages, traditions and customs. Adrenaline-pumping activities abound. Swim in clear volcanic lakes, show-

WARNING: DANGER UXO

The Ho Chi Minh Trail once passed through the hills of Ratanakiri, where it was nicknamed the Sihanouk Trail in reference to Cambodia's then head of state. This region was heavily bombed by the Americans and there is still some unexploded ordnance (UXO) around. Never touch anything that looks vaguely like UXO.

er under waterfalls, or trek in the vast Virachey National Park, it's all here.

Ban Lung បានលុង

☑ 075 / POP 45,000
Affectionately known as *dey krahorm* (red earth) after its rust colour, Ban Lung provides a popular base for a range of Ratanakiri romps. It is one of the easiest places in Cambodia to arrange a jungle trek and has several beautiful lakes and waterfalls nearby.

◎ Sights & Activities

★**Boeng Yeak Lom** LAKE
(បឹងយក្សឡោម; US$2) At the heart of the protected area of Boeng Yeak Lom is a beautiful, emerald-hued crater lake set amid the vivid greens of the towering jungle. It is one of the most peaceful, beautiful locations Cambodia has to offer and the water is extremely clear. Several wooden piers are dotted around the perimeter, making it perfect for swimming. A small Cultural and Environmental Centre has a modest display on ethnic minorities in the province and hires out life jackets for children.

Virachey National Park PARK
(ឧទ្យានជាតិវីរជ័យ; ☑ 097 333 4775; leamsou@ gmail.com; US$5; ⊙ office 8-11am & 2-5pm Mon-Fri) This park is one of the largest protected areas in Cambodia, stretching for 3325 sq km east to Vietnam, north to Laos and west to Stung Treng Province. Virachey has one of the most organised ecotourism programs in Cambodia, focusing on small-scale culture, nature and adventure trekking. The program aims to involve and benefit local minority communities. All treks into the park must be arranged through the Virachey National Park Eco-Tourism Information Centre (p142) in Ban Lung.

Waterfalls WATERFALL
Tucked amid the sprawling cashew and rubber plantations just west of Ban Lung are three waterfalls (per waterfall 2000r) worth visiting: Chaa Ong, Ka Tieng and Kinchaan. All are within a 20-minute moto ride of town, and visits to all three are usually included in tour companies' half- and full-day excursions. The turn-offs to all three are 200m west of the new bus station, just beyond a Lina petrol station. There's signage but it's barely visible.

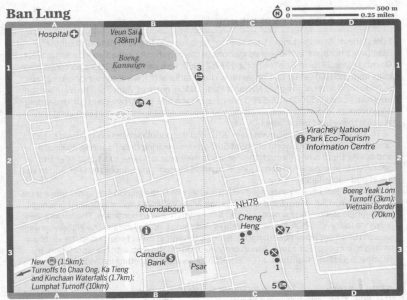

Ban Lung

☞ Tours

Overnight treks with nights spent camping or staying in minority villages north of Veun Sai or Ta Veng are popular. Figure on US$50 per person per day for a couple (less for larger groups). Backpacker Pad and Tree Top Ecolodge are good at arranging tours, but there are also several dedicated tour companies in town.

DutchCo Trekking Cambodia TOURS
(☑097 679 2714; www.trekkingcambodia.com) One of the most experienced trekking operators in the province, run by – wait for it – a friendly Dutchman. Runs four- to five-day treks north of Veun Sai through Kavet villages and community forests, and one- to two-day trips around Kalai (south of Veun Sai), among many other tours.

Highland Tours TOURS
(☑097 658 3841; highland.tour@yahoo.com) Kimi and Horng are husband-and-wife graduates of Le Tonlé Tourism Training Center in Stung Treng, who have moved to the highlands to run a range of tours, including fun day trips and a multiday tour between Veun Sai and Ta Veng that combines trekking with floating down the Tonlé San on a bamboo raft. Horng is one of the only female guides in Ratanakiri.

Ban Lung

🛏 Sleeping

★ Tree Top Ecolodge BUNGALOW $
(☑012 490333; www.treetop-ecolodge.com; d US$7, cottage with cold/hot water US$12/15; 🛜) This is one of the best places to stay in Cambodia's 'wild east', with oodles of atmosphere. 'Mr T's' place boasts rough-hewn walkways leading to huge bungalows featuring mosquito nets, thatch roofs and hammock-strewn verandahs with verdant valley vistas. Like the bungalows, the restaurant is fashioned from hardwood and dangles over a lush ravine.

THE REAL GIBBON EXPERIENCE

Spend the night in the jungle, then rise well before dawn to spend time with semi-habituated northern buff-cheeked gibbons at the community-based ecotourism project **Cambodian Gibbon Ecotours** (☏ 097 752 9960; www.cambodiangibbons.wordpress.com; tours from US$100) set up by Conservation International (CI; www.conservation.org) just outside the border of Virachey National Park (p140), north of Veun Sai. The high-season-only tours cost US$100 to US$200 per person for a one-night/two-day tour, depending on group size and which tour company you choose. Most companies in Ban Lung can arrange these trips on behalf of CI.

This species was only discovered in 2010 and the population here is believed to be one of the largest in the world at about 500 groups. Hearing their haunting dawn call and seeing them swing through the canopy is memorable. These tours also offer the opportunity to experience dense jungle, open savannah, rivers and waterfalls, and to visit Kavet and Lao villages.

CI has an exclusive arrangement with the village near the gibbon site to run these tours within the Veun Sai–Siem Pang Conservation Area (VSSPCA). You stay at least one night in the jungle sleeping in hammocks or in a community-based homestay. The fee includes entrance to the VSSPCA, guide, homestays and camps, and all meals. The gibbon-viewing season runs from November to mid-June – it's too wet at other times – and the visits are limited to six people at a time. For an organised tour to the area with transportation, try **Gibbon Spotting Cambodia** (☏ 063-966355; www.gibbonspottingcambodia.com).

Banlung Balcony
GUESTHOUSE $

(☏ 097 809 7036; www.balconyguesthouse.net; Boeng Kansaign; dm US$2, r US$5-20; @ 🛜) Under super-friendly French management, this long-standing backpackers has upped its game with a tip-top renovation of both the atmospheric main house and the enviably placed bar and restaurant, which features sunset views over the lake. The upstairs rooms, all polished wood and high ceilings, are borderline boutique, only at budget prices.

Flashpacker Pad
HOTEL $

(☏ 093 785259; flashpackerpad@gmail.com; Boeng Kansaign; r US$8-15; ❄ 🛜) Quite literally a flashpacker pad, the rooms here have a touch of class, with flat-screen TVs and indigenous-made runners on white bedspreads. Go for a room with a view for misty mornings on the lake. Owner Sophat is a great source of info and runs a tour company.

✖ Eating & Drinking

★ Cafe Alee
INTERNATIONAL $

(mains US$1.50-5.50; ⊙ 7am-9pm; 🛜🅿) 🍴 This friendly cafe has one of the more interesting menus in town, including a generous smattering of vegetarian options, a hearty lasagne and the full gamut of Khmer food. Be sure to check the exciting specials board. It often stays open later if there is drinking to be done.

★ Green Carrot
INTERNATIONAL $

(mains US$2-6; ⊙ 7am-10pm; 🛜) A great little hole-in-the-wall restaurant that turns out surprisingly sophisticated food, including healthy salads, sandwiches and wraps, plus a good range of Khmer favourites. It even does a decent burger and some very affordable pizzas. Happy hour has two-for-one cocktails from 6pm to 8pm.

ℹ Information

Canadia Bank (⊙ 8.30am-3.30pm Mon-Fri, ATM 24hr) Full-service bank with an international ATM.

Virachey National Park Eco-Tourism Information Centre (☏ 097 333 4775; leamsou@gmail.com; ⊙ 8-11am & 2-5pm Mon-Fri) The place to organise trekking in Virachey National Park.

ℹ Getting There & Away

There is a vast bus station on the western outskirts of town, 2.5km west of Ban Lung's main roundabout, but guesthouses and tour companies can arrange pickups in town.

Phnom Penh Sorya and Thong Ly run early-morning buses to Phnom Penh (US$9 to US$10, 11 hours) via Kratie and Kompong Cham.

Speedy express-van services pick you up at your guesthouse and head to Phnom Penh (US$15, eight hours, 6am and 1pm) and Stung Treng (US$7, two hours, around 8am). Organise these through your guesthouse. Call Backpacker

Pad or Tree Top Ecolodge to arrange an express van pickup if coming from Phnom Penh.

There is also a daily minivan south to Sen Monorom (US$8, two hours, 8am) in Mondulkiri. Various local slow minibuses also depart in the morning to Phnom Penh (50,000r), Stung Treng (20,000r) and O'Yadaw (12,000r), and throughout the day to Lumphat (10,000r, one hour) and Kratie (25,000r, four hours).

ℹ️ Getting Around

Bicycles (US$1 to US$3), motorbikes (US$5 to US$7), cars (from US$30) and 4WDs (from US$50) are available for hire from most guesthouses in town.

Motodups hang out around the market and some double as guides. Figure on US$15 to US$20 per day for a good English-speaking driver-guide. A moto to Yeak Lom costs about US$5 return; to Veun Sai is US$15 return; to any waterfall is about US$6 return.

Cheng Heng (📞 088 8516104; ⏰ 6am-8pm) has some 250cc trail bikes for rent (US$25) in addition to a stable of well-maintained smaller motorbikes (US$6 to US$8).

Mondulkiri Province
ខេត្តមណ្ឌលគិរី

Mondulkiri (Meeting of the Hills), the original 'wild east' of the country, is a world apart from the lowlands with not a rice paddy or palm tree in sight. Home to the hardy Bunong people and their noble elephants, this upland area is a seductive mix of grassy hills, pine groves and jade-green rainforests. Activities are taking off in a big way with a new zipline and quad-biking adventures on tap.

Conservationists have grand plans for the sparsely populated province, with wildlife encounters such as walking with the herd at Elephant Valley Project and spotting doucs and gibbons in the Seima Protected Forest, but are facing off against loggers, poachers and speculators.

Sen Monorom   សែនមនោរម្យ
📞 073 / POP 10,000

The provincial capital of Mondulkiri, Sen Monorom is really an overgrown village, a charming community set in the spot where

CAMBODIA MONDULKIRI PROVINCE

WORTH A TRIP

MONKEY BUSINESS IN MONDULKIRI

A recent Wildlife Conservation Society (WCS) study estimated populations of 20,600 black-shanked doucs and more than 1000 yellow-cheeked crested gibbons in Seima Protected Forest (p144); these are the world's largest known populations of both species. **Jahoo Gibbon Camp** (📞063-963710; https://samveasna.org/category/jahoo-gibbon-camp/; Andong Kroloeng; per person incl meals US$125-200) 🍃 offers the chance to trek into the wild and try to spot these primates, along with other elusive animals, thanks to an exciting project supported by the Sam Veasna Center (SVC) in the Bunong village of Andong Kraloeng.

The Jahoo Gibbon Camp provides local villagers with an incentive to conserve the endangered primates and their habitat through providing a sustainable income. Treks wind their way through mixed evergreen forest and waterfalls, with an excellent chance of spotting the doucs and macaques along the way. Gibbons are very shy and harder to see, but thanks to recent field research by WCS and the community, the local gibbon families are more used to people than gibbons elsewhere. You'll need to be up before dawn to spot them, however, so sleeping at the camp is highly recommended.

Many other species are present in this area; there is an enormous diversity of bird life, including the spectacular giant hornbill, as well as chances to find the tracks and signs of more elusive species, such as bears, gaur (wild cattle) and elephants.

Registered guides, together with local Bunong guides, accompany visitors along the trails. A conservation contribution is included in the cost of the trip, which supports community development projects; an additional contribution is paid by each visitor and by SVC if doucs and/or gibbons are spotted, providing a direct incentive for the village to protect these rare wildlife species.

For information and booking, contact the **Sam Veasna Center** (📞 071 553 9779, 012 520828; www.samveasna.org; Hefalump Cafe, Sen Monorom) 🍃 team at the Hefalump Cafe in Sen Monorom.

the legendary hills meet. The area around Sen Monorom is peppered with minority villages and picturesque waterfalls, making it the ideal base to spend some time. It's set at 800m; when the winds blow it's notably cooler than the rest of Cambodia, so bring warm clothing.

👁 Sights & Activities

Multiday forest treks taking in minority villages are the big draw. We recommend securing indigenous Bunong guides for these trips. They know the forests intimately and can break the ice with the locals in any Bunong villages you visit.

★**Seima Protected Forest** NATIONAL PARK (https://cambodia.wcs.org/Saving-Wild-Places/ Seima-Forest.aspx; Andong Kroloeng; wildlife-spotting tours US$70-125; Jahoo Gibbon Camp per night US$115-200) 🕊 The 3000-sq-km Seima Protected Forest hosts the country's greatest treasure trove of mammalian wildlife. Besides unprecedented numbers of black-shanked doucs and yellow-cheeked crested gibbons, an estimated 150 wild elephants – accounting for around half of the total population in Cambodia – roam the park, along with bears and cats.

The Wildlife Conservation Society (WCS; www.wcscambodia.com) in partnership with ecotourism specialist Sam Veasna Center (p143) helps to manage the forest, and there are a range of ecotourism initiatives under way, including primate spotting in Andong Kroloeng.

Bou Sraa Waterfall WATERFALL (ទឹកជ្រោះប្រីស្រា; US$2.50) Plunging into the dense jungle below, this is one of Cambodia's most impressive falls. Famous throughout the country, this double-drop waterfall has an upper tier of some 10m and a spectacular lower tier with a thundering 25m drop. Getting here is a 33km, one-hour journey east of Sen Monorom on a mostly sealed road.

★**Elephant Valley Project** WILDLIFE RESERVE (EVP; ☏ 099 696041; www.elephantvalleyproject. org; ⊙ Mon-Fri) For an original elephant experience, visit the Elephant Valley Project, a pioneering 'walking with the herd' project in Mondulkiri. The project entices local mahouts to bring their overworked or injured elephants to this 1600-hectare sanctuary. It's very popular, so make sure you book well ahead. You can visit for a whole day (US$85) or a half day (US$55). It does not take overnight visitors on Friday and Saturday nights and is not open to day visitors on Saturday and Sunday.

RESPONSIBLE TREKKING AROUND NORTHEAST CAMBODIA

Treks taking in the remote forests and minority villages of Ratanakiri and Mondulkiri are very popular these days. Where possible, we recommend using indigenous guides for organised treks and other excursions around the provinces. They speak the local dialects, understand tribal taboos and can secure permission to visit cemeteries that are off-limits to Khmer guides. Their intimate knowledge of the forests is another major asset.

More tips on visiting indigenous communities responsibly:

➡ Try to spend some real time in minority villages – at least several hours if not overnight. If you don't have a few hours to invest, don't go.

➡ Travel in small, less disruptive groups.

➡ Do not photograph without asking permission first – this includes children. Some hill tribes believe the camera will capture their spirit.

➡ Dress modestly.

➡ Taste traditional wine if you are offered it, especially during a ceremony. Refusal will cause offence.

➡ Individual gifts create jealousy and expectations. Instead, consider making donations to the local school, medical centre or community fund.

➡ Honour signs discouraging outsiders from entering a village, for instance during a spiritual ceremony. A good local guide will be able to detect these signs.

➡ Never give children sweets or money.

➡ Don't buy village treasures, such as altarpieces or totems, or the clothes or jewellery locals are wearing.

ⓘ GETTING TO VIETNAM: EASTERN BORDERS

Kompong Cham to Tay Ninh

The Trapeang Plong/Xa Mat crossing (open 7am to 5pm) is convenient for those using private transport to travel between northeast Cambodia or Siem Reap and Ho Chi Minh City.

Getting to the border From Kompong Cham take anything heading east on NH7 toward Snuol, and get off at the roundabout in Krek (Kraek) on NH7. From there, it's 13km south by moto (US$3) along NH72 to snoozy Trapeang Plong.

At the border This border is a breeze; just have your Vietnam visa ready.

Moving on On the Vietnamese side, motorbikes and taxis go to Tay Ninh, 45km to the south.

Snuol to Binh Long

The Trapeang Sre/Loc Ninh crossing (open 7am to 5pm) is useful for those trying to get straight to Vietnam from Kratie or points north.

Getting to the border First get to Snuol by bus, share taxi or minibus from Sen Monorom, Kratie or Kompong Cham. In Snuol catch a moto (US$5) for the 18km trip southeastward along smooth NH74.

At the border Some nationalities need a prearranged visa to enter Vietnam.

Moving on On the Vietnamese side, the nearest town is Binh Long, 40km to the south. Motorbikes wait at the border.

Ban Lung to Pleiku

The O Yadaw/Le Thanh crossing (open 7am to 5pm) is 70km east of Ban Lung along smooth NH19.

Getting to the border From Ban Lung, guesthouses advertise a 6.30am van to Pleiku (US$12, 3½ hours) involving a change of vehicle at the border. This picks you up at your guesthouse.

At the border Formalities are straightforward and lines nonexistent; just make sure you have a Vietnam visa if you need one.

Moving on On the Vietnamese side of the frontier, the road is nicely paved. Motos await to take you to Duc Co (20km), where there are buses to Pleiku, Quy Nhon and Hoi An. For information on making this crossing in reverse, see p891.

Mayura Zipline ZIPLINE
(☑071 888 0800, 011 79 77 79; http://mondulkresort.com; Bou Sraa Waterfall; US$45; ⏱9am-4pm) The Mayura Zipline is an adrenaline rush in the extreme, as the longest 300m-line passes right over the top of the spectacular Bou Sraa falls. The zipline course starts on the far bank of the river; there are six lines to navigate, plus a suspension bridge. The first four zips are warm-ups for the high-speed flight over the waterfall; the course finishes with a short tandem line for couples or new friends.

ᒐ Tours

Hefalump Cafe (p146) This NGO-run cafe doubles as a 'drop-in centre' for Bunong people and is the best source of information on sustainable tourism in Mondulkiri Province, including the Elephant Valley Project,

the Seima Protected Forest and responsible tours to Bunong communities. It is advisable to try and book two to three days in advance to best ensure availability.

Green House TOURS
(☑017 905659; www.greenhouse-tour.blogspot.com; NH76) One of the longest-running tour operators in Mondulkiri, Green House organises the full range of forest treks and waterfall trips, and there are motorbikes for hire (per day US$6 to US$8).

🛏 Sleeping

★**Nature Lodge** GUESTHOUSE $
(☑012 230272; www.naturelodgecambodia.com; r US$10-30; 🛜) Sprawling across a windswept hilltop near town are 30 solid wood bungalows with private porches, hot showers and mosquito nets. Among them are Swiss

Family Robinson–style chalets with sunken beds and ante-rooms. The magnificent restaurant has comfy nooks, a pool table and an enviable bar where guests chill out and swap travel tales.

Indigenous Peoples Lodge BUNGALOW $
(📞 012 725375; indigenouspeopleslodge@gmail.com; d US$5-15, q US$20; @🖹) Run by a Bunong family, this is a great place to stay, with a whole range of accommodation set in minority houses, including a traditional thatched Bunong house with an upgrade or two. The cheapest rooms involve a share bathroom, but are good value. Perks include free internet and free drop-offs in town.

Tree Lodge BUNGALOW $
(📞 097 723 4177; www.treelodgecambodia.com; d US$7-10, q US$12-15; 🖹) Sixteen bungalows of various shapes and sizes drip down a hillside at the back of the reception. Rooms have balconies and attractive open-air bathrooms, but lack any shelf space or furniture besides a bed. Hang out at the restaurant, where hammocks and tasty Khmer food await.

✗ Eating & Drinking

⭐ **Coffee Plantation Resort** CAMBODIAN $
(📞 012 666542; www.chormkacafe.com; mains US$2.50-7; ⊘7am-9pm; 🖹) As the name suggests, this place is set in the grounds of an extensive coffee plantation, but offers some excellent local flavours, as well as the homegrown coffee. The *banh chaeuv* savoury pancakes are a wholesome meal for just US$2.50. There's also delicious honey-roasted chicken.

Hefalump Cafe CAFE $
(www.helalumpcafe-tourismhub.com; NH76; cakes US$1-3; ⊘7am-6pm Mon-Fri, 9am-4pm Sun; 🖹) 🖉 A collaboration of various NGOs and conservation groups in town, this cafe doubles as a hospitality training centre for Bunong people. Local coffee or Lavazza, teas, cakes and healthy breakfasts make this a great spot to plan your adventures over a cuppa.

Khmer Kitchen CAMBODIAN $
(NH76; mains US$2-5; ⊘6am-10pm; 🖹) This unassuming streetside eatery whips up some of the most flavoursome Khmer food in the hills. The *kari saik trey* (fish coconut curry) and other curries are particularly noteworthy, plus they also offer a smattering of international dishes.

⭐ **The Hangout** BAR
(📞 088 721 9991) The bar at this backpacker guesthouse is the most happening spot in town. There are bar sports including table football, occasional jam sessions and some of Sen Monorom's best Western food to complement the Khmer menu. It's run by an affable Tasmanian-Khmer couple and has dorms and private rooms downstairs.

ℹ Information

The recommended guesthouses are all very good sources of information and run the full gamut of tours.

Acleda Bank (NH76; ⊘8.30am-3.30pm, ATM 24hr) changes major currencies and has a Visa-only ATM.

ℹ Getting There & Away

Phnom Penh Sorya runs a 7.30am bus to Phnom Penh (35,000r, eight hours). Kim Seng Express runs comfortable minivans (US$11) that do the trip in five hours and has six departures daily between 7am and 2pm. Virak-Buntham also operates a minibus to Phnom Penh (US$12), with departures at 7.15am and 1.30pm.

Local minibuses are the way to get to Kratie (30,000r, four hours). Count on at least one early-morning departure and two or three departures around lunchtime.

There are now minibuses plying the new road to Ban Lung in Ratanakiri, which cost US$8 and take about two hours.

ℹ Getting Around

English-speaking moto drivers cost about US$15 to US$20 per day. Most guesthouses rent out motorbikes for US$6 to US$8 and a few have bicycles for US$2.

UNDERSTAND CAMBODIA

Cambodia Today

Cambodia's political landscape shifted dramatically in the 2013 election, with major gains by the opposition Cambodia National Rescue Party (CNRP) further cemented in the 2017 commune elections. This set the scene for an unpredictable general election in 2018, but the Cambodian People's Party (CPP) manoeuvered to protect its future, and the opposition was dissolved in late 2017. Meanwhile, the economy continues to grow at a dramatic pace, but many observers are beginning to question the cost to the environment.

The overall political climate has deteriorated rapidly from 2015 beginning with the threatened arrest and subsequent self-imposed exile of then-CNRP leader Sam Rainsy. His deputy, Kem Sokha, took over the leadership of the party going into the commune elections, but was himself arrested on treason charges in late 2017 that many observers claim were politically motivated by government paranoia about a 'colour revolution' in Cambodia. There were many heated topics on the agenda as the country headed towards the national poll, including huge inflows of Chinese investment and people, the sensitive shared border with Vietnam and land reform.

The governing Cambodian People's Party (CPP) controls most of the national television stations, radio stations and most newspapers. However, social media is plugging the gap and a new generation of young Cambodians are avid Facebook and YouTube users. In 2017 there was a dramatic clampdown on the free press in Cambodia with the closure of the long-running *Cambodia Daily* under the duress of an unpaid tax bill.

Badly traumatised by decades of conflict, Cambodia's economy was long a gecko amid the neighbouring dragons. However, China has come to the table to play for big stakes, and annually pledges as much as all the other international donors put together, with no burdensome strings attached. There is huge investment from China and other Asian neighbours changing the urban landscape in the capital Phnom Penh. However, Cambodia remains one of Asia's poorest countries and income is desperately low for many families, with the official minimum wage set at only US$153 per month.

Cambodia's pristine environment may be a big draw for adventurous ecotourists, but much of it is currently under threat. Ancient forests are being razed to make way for plantations, rivers are being sized up for major hydroelectric power plants and the South Coast is being stripped of sand and explored by leading oil companies. Places like the Cardamom Mountains are on the front line, and it remains to be seen whether the environmentalists or the investors will win the debate. All this economic activity adds up to some impressive statistics, but it's unlikely to encourage the ecotourism that is just starting to take off.

History

The good, the bad and the ugly is a simple way to sum up Cambodian history. Things were good in the early years, culminating in the vast Khmer empire, unrivalled in the region during four centuries of dominance. Then the bad set in, from the 13th century, as ascendant neighbours steadily chipped away at Cambodian territory. In the 20th century it turned downright ugly, as a brutal civil war culminated in the genocidal rule of the Khmer Rouge (1975–79), from which Cambodia is still recovering.

Funan & Chenla

The Indianisation of Cambodia began in the 1st century AD as traders plying the sea route from the Bay of Bengal to southern China brought Indian ideas and technologies to what is now southern Vietnam. The largest of the era's nascent kingdoms, known to the Chinese as Funan, embraced the worship of the Hindu deities Shiva and Vishnu and, at the same time, Buddhism.

From the 6th to 8th centuries Cambodia seems to have been ruled by a collection of competing kingdoms. Chinese annals refer to 'Water Chenla', apparently the area around the modern-day town of Takeo, and 'Land Chenla', further north along the Mekong and around Sambor Prei Kuk.

The Rise & Fall of Angkor

The Angkorian era lasted from AD 802 to 1432, encompassing periods of conquest, turmoil and retreat, revival and decline, and fits of remarkable productivity.

In 802 Jayavarman II (reigned c 802–50) proclaimed himself a *devaraja* (god-king). He instigated an uprising against Javanese domination of southern Cambodia and, through alliances and conquests, brought the country under his control, becoming the first monarch to rule most of what we now call Cambodia.

In the 9th century Yasovarman I (r 889–910) moved the capital to Angkor, creating a new centre for worship, scholarship and the arts. After a period of turmoil and conflict, Suryavarman II (r 1113–52) unified the kingdom and embarked on another phase of territorial expansion, waging successful but costly wars against both Vietnam and Champa (an Indianised kingdom that occupied what is now southern and central Vietnam).

His devotion to the Hindu deity Vishnu inspired him to commission Angkor Wat.

The tables soon turned. Champa struck back in 1177 with a naval expedition up the Mekong, taking Angkor by surprise and putting the king to death. But the following year a cousin of Suryavarman II – soon crowned Jayavarman VII (r 1181–1219) – rallied the Khmers and defeated the Chams in another epic naval battle. A devout follower of Mahayana Buddhism, it was he who built the city of Angkor Thom.

During the twilight years of the empire, religious conflict and internecine rivalries were rife. The Thais made repeated incursions into Angkor, sacking the city in 1351 and again in 1431, and making off from the royal court with thousands of intellectuals, artisans and dancers, whose profound impact on Thai culture can be seen to this day.

From 1600 until the arrival of the French, Cambodia was ruled by a series of weak kings whose intrigues often involved seeking the protection of either Thailand or Vietnam – granted, of course, at a price.

French Colonialism

The era of yo-yoing between Thai and Vietnamese masters came to a close in 1864, when French gunboats intimidated King Norodom I (r 1860–1904) into signing a treaty of protectorate. An exception in the annals of colonialism, the French presence really did protect the country at a time when it was in danger of being swallowed by its more powerful neighbours. In 1907 the French pressured Thailand into returning the northwest provinces of Battambang, Siem Reap and Sisophon, bringing Angkor under Cambodian control for the first time in more than a century.

Led by King Norodom Sihanouk (r 1941–55 and 1993–2004), Cambodia declared independence on 9 November 1953.

Independence & Civil War

The period after 1953 was one of peace and prosperity, and a time of creativity and optimism. Dark clouds were circling, however, as the war in Vietnam began sucking in

THE KHMER ROUGE TRIAL

The Vietnamese ousted the Khmer Rouge on 7 January 1979, but it wasn't until 1999 – after two decades of civil war – that serious discussions began about a trial to bring to justice those responsible for the deaths of about two million Cambodians. After lengthy negotiations, agreement was finally reached on establishing a war crimes tribunal to try the surviving leaders of the Khmer Rouge.

It took another decade for the first verdict in the Extraordinary Chambers in the Courts of Cambodia (ECCC) trial. In that time one of the key suspects, the one-legged general Ta Mok ('The Butcher'), died in custody. Case 001, the trial of Kaing Guek Eav, aka Comrade Duch, finally began in 2009. Duch was seen as a key figure as he provided the link between the regime and its crimes in his role as head of S-21 prison. Duch was sentenced to 35 years in 2010, a verdict that was later extended on appeal to life imprisonment.

Case 002 began in November 2011, involving the most senior surviving leaders of the Democratic Kampuchea (DK) era: Brother Number 2 Nuon Chea (age 84), Brother Number 3 and former foreign minister of DK Ieng Sary (age 83), and former DK head of state Khieu Samphan (age 79). Justice may prove elusive, however, due to the slow progress of court proceedings and the advancing age of the defendants. Ieng Sary died in 2013, and his wife and former DK Minister of Social Affairs Ieng Thirith (age 78) was ruled unfit to stand trial because of dementia. Both Nuon Chea and Khieu Samphan received life sentences for crimes against humanity in August 2014, but are currently facing additional charges of genocide.

Case 003 against head of the DK navy, Meas Muth, and head of the DK air force, Sou Met, is meant to follow Case 002. However, investigations into this case stalled back in 2009 under intense pressure from the Cambodian government. Although Prime Minister Hun Sen is opposed to Case 003, the international judges went ahead and charged Meas Muth with genocide, crimes against humanity and war crimes in 2015.

To keep abreast of developments in the trial, visit the official ECCC website at www.eccc.gov.kh or the Cambodian Tribunal Monitor at www.cambodiatribunal.org.

neighbouring countries. As the 1960s drew to a close, the North Vietnamese and the Viet Cong were using Cambodian territory in their battle against South Vietnam and US forces, prompting devastating American bombing and a land invasion into eastern Cambodia.

In March 1970 Sihanouk, now serving as prime minister, was overthrown by General Lon Nol, and took up residence in Beijing. Here he set up a government-in-exile that allied itself with an indigenous Cambodian revolutionary movement that he dubbed the Khmer Rouge. Violence engulfed large parts of the country.

Khmer Rouge Rule

Upon taking Phnom Penh on 17 April 1975, two weeks before the fall of Saigon, the Khmer Rouge implemented one of the most radical and brutal restructurings of a society ever attempted. Its goal was to transform Cambodia, renamed Democratic Kampuchea, into a giant peasant-dominated agrarian cooperative, untainted by anything that had come before. Within days, the entire populations of Phnom Penh and provincial towns, including the sick, elderly and infirm, were forced to march into the countryside and work as slaves for 12 to 15 hours a day. Intellectuals were systematically wiped out – wearing glasses or speaking a foreign language was reason enough to be killed. The advent of Khmer Rouge rule was proclaimed Year Zero.

Leading the Khmer Rouge was Saloth Sar, better known as Pol Pot. Under his rule, Cambodia became a vast slave labour camp. Meals consisted of little more than watery rice porridge twice a day, meant to sustain men, women and children through a back-breaking day in the fields. Disease stalked the work camps, malaria and dysentery striking down whole families. Khmer Rouge rule was brought to an end by the Vietnamese, who liberated the almost-empty city of Phnom Penh on 7 January 1979. It is estimated that around two million people perished at the hands of Pol Pot and his followers. The Documentation Center of Cambodia (www.dccam.org) records the horrific events of the period.

A Sort of Peace

The Vietnamese installed a new government led by several former Khmer Rouge officers, including current Prime Minister Hun Sen,

who had defected to Vietnam in 1977. In the dislocation that followed liberation, little rice was planted or harvested, leading to a massive famine.

The Khmer Rouge continued to wage civil war from remote mountain bases near the Thai border throughout the 1980s. In February 1991 all parties, including the Khmer Rouge, signed the Paris Peace Accords, according to which the UN Transitional Authority in Cambodia (UNTAC) would rule the country for two years before elections were held in 1993. But the Khmer Rouge boycotted the elections and re-established a guerrilla network throughout Cambodia.

The last Khmer Rouge hold-outs, including Ta Mok, were not defeated until the capture of Anlong Veng and Prasat Preah Vihear by government forces in the spring of 1998. Pol Pot cheated justice by dying a sorry death near Anlong Veng during that year; he was cremated on a pile of old tyres.

People & Culture

Population

Around 16 million people live in Cambodia. With a rapid growth rate of about 2% a year, the population is predicted to reach 20 million by 2025. More than 40% of the population is under the age of 16. According to official statistics, around 96% of the people are ethnic Khmers, making the country the most homogeneous in Southeast Asia, but in reality anywhere between 10% and 20% of the population is of Cham, Chinese or Vietnamese origin. Cambodia's diverse Khmer Leu (Upper Khmer) or Chunchiet (minorities), who live in the country's mountainous regions, probably number between 75,000 and 100,000.

The official language is Khmer, spoken by 95% of the population. English has taken over from French as the second language of choice, although Chinese is also growing in popularity. Life expectancy is currently 64 years.

BOTTOMS UP

When Cambodians propose a toast, they usually stipulate what percentage must be downed. If they are feeling generous, it might be just *ha-sip pea-roi* (50%), but more often than not it is *moi roi pea-roi* (100%). This is why they love ice in their beer, as they can pace themselves over the course of the night. Many a *barang* (foreigner) has ended up face down on the table at a Cambodian wedding when trying to outdrink the Khmers without the help of ice.

Lifestyle

For many older Cambodians, life is centred on faith, family and food, an existence that has stayed the same for centuries. Faith is a rock in the lives of many older Cambodians, and Buddhism helped them to survive the terrible years and then rebuild their lives after the Khmer Rouge. Family is more than the nuclear family we now know in the West; it's the extended family of third cousins and obscure aunts – as long as there is a bloodline, there is a bond. Families stick together, solve problems collectively, listen to the wisdom of the elders, and pool resources. The extended family comes together during times of trouble and times of joy, celebrating festivals and successes, mourning deaths and disappointments. Whether the Cambodian house is big or small, there will be a lot of people living inside.

However, the Cambodian lifestyle is changing as the population gets younger and more urbanised. Cambodia is experiencing its very own '60s swing, as the younger generation stands ready for a different lifestyle from the one their parents had to swallow. This creates plenty of friction in the cities, as rebellious teens dress as they like, date whoever they wish and hit the town until all hours. More recently this generational conflict spilled over into politics as the Facebook generation helped deliver a shock result that saw the Cambodian People's Party majority slashed in half in the 2013 general elections.

Corruption remains a way of life in Cambodia. It is a major element of the Cambodian economy and exists to some extent at all levels of government. Sometimes it is overt, but increasingly it is covert, with private companies often securing very favourable business deals on the basis of their connections. It seems everything has a price, including ancient temples, national parks and even genocide sites.

Religion

The majority of Khmers follow the Theravada branch of Buddhism. Buddhism in Cambodia draws heavily on its predecessors, incorporating many cultural traditions from Hinduism for ceremonies such as birth, marriage and death, as well as genies and spirits, such as Neak Ta, which link back to a pre-Indian animist past.

Under the Khmer Rouge, the majority of Cambodia's Buddhist monks were murdered and nearly all of the country's wat (more than 3000) were damaged or destroyed. In the late 1980s Buddhism once again became the state religion.

Other religions found in Cambodia include Islam, practised by the Cham community; animism, among the hill tribes; and Christianity, which is making inroads via missionaries and Christian NGOs.

Arts

The Khmer Rouge regime not only killed the living bearers of Khmer culture, it also destroyed cultural artefacts, statues, musical instruments, books and anything else that served as a reminder of a past it was trying to efface. The temples of Angkor were spared as a symbol of Khmer glory and empire, but little else survived. Despite this, Cambodia is witnessing a resurgence of traditional arts and a growing interest in cross-cultural fusion. Cambodia's royal ballet is a tangible link with the glory of Angkor and includes a unique *apsara* (heavenly nymphs) dance. Cambodian music, too, goes back at least as far as Angkor. To get some sense of the music that Jayavarman VII used to like, check out the bas-reliefs at Angkor.

In the mid-20th century a vibrant Cambodian pop-music scene developed, but it was killed off by the Khmer Rouge. After the war, overseas Khmers established a pop industry in the USA and some Cambodian-Americans, raised on a diet of rap, are now returning to their homeland. The Los Angeles–based sextet Dengue Fever, inspired by 1960s Cambodian pop and psychedelic rock, is the ultimate fusion band.

The people of Cambodia were producing masterfully sensuous sculptures – much more than mere copies of Indian forms – in the age of Funan and Chenla. The Banteay Srei style of the late 10th century is regarded as a high point in the evolution of Southeast Asian art.

Food & Drink

Some traditional Cambodian dishes are similar to those of neighbouring Laos and Thailand (though not as spicy), others closer to Chinese and Vietnamese cooking. The French left their mark, too.

Thanks to the Tonlé Sap, freshwater fish – often *ahng* (grilled) – are a huge part of the Cambodian diet. The legendary national dish, *amok*, is fish baked with coconut and lemongrass in banana leaves. *Prahoc* (fermented fish paste) is used to flavour foods, with coconut and lemongrass making regular cameos.

A proper Cambodian meal almost always includes *samlor* (soup), served at the same time as other courses. *Kyteow* is a rice noodle soup that will keep you going all day. *Bobor* (rice porridge), eaten for breakfast, lunch or dinner, is best sampled with some fresh fish and a dash of ginger.

Tap water must be avoided, especially in rural areas. Bottled water is widely available but coconut milk, sold by machete-wielding street vendors, is more ecological and may be more sterile.

Beer is immensely popular in the cities, while rural folk drink palm wine, tapped from the sugar palms that dot the landscape. *Tukaloks* (fruit shakes) are mixed with milk, sugar and sometimes a raw egg.

Environment

The Land

Cambodia's two dominant geographical features are the mighty Mekong River and a vast lake, the Tonlé Sap. The rich sediment deposited during the Mekong's annual wet-season flooding has made central Cambodia incredibly fertile. This low-lying alluvial plain is where the vast majority of Cambodians live, fishing and farming in harmony with the rhythms of the monsoon. In Cambodia's southwest quadrant, much of the land mass is covered by the Cardamom Mountains and, near Kampot, the Elephant Mountains. Along Cambodia's northern border with Thailand, the plains collide with the Dangkrek Mountains, a striking sandstone escarpment more than 300km long and up to 550m high. One of the best places to get a sense of this area is Prasat Preah Vihear. In the northeastern corner of the country, in the provinces of Ratanakiri and Mondulkiri, the plains give way to the Eastern Highlands, a remote region of densely forested mountains and high plateaus.

Wildlife

Cambodia's forest ecosystems were in excellent shape until the 1990s and, compared with its neighbours, its habitats are still relatively healthy. The years of war took their toll on some species, but others thrived in the remote jungles of the southwest and northeast. Ironically, peace brought increased threats as loggers felled huge areas of primary forest and the illicit trade in wildlife targeted endangered species.

Still, with more than 200 species of mammal, Cambodia has some of Southeast Asia's best wildlife-watching opportunities. Highlights include spotting gibbons and black-shanked doucs in Ratanakiri and Mondulkiri provinces, and viewing some of the last remaining freshwater Irrawaddy dolphins in Kratie and Stung Treng provinces. The country is a birdwatcher's paradise – feathered friends found almost exclusively in Cambodia include the giant ibis, Bengal florican, sarus crane and three species of vulture. The marshes around Tonlé Sap are particularly rich in bird life. The Siem Reap-based Sam Veasna Center runs birding trips.

TONLÉ SAP: THE HEARTBEAT OF CAMBODIA

During the wet season (June to October) the Mekong River rises dramatically, forcing the Tonlé Sap river to flow northwest into Tonlé Sap (Great Lake). During this period the lake swells from around 3000 sq km to almost 13,000 sq km, and from the air Cambodia looks like one almighty puddle. As the Mekong falls during the dry season, the Tonlé Sap river reverses its flow, and the lake's floodwaters drain back into the Mekong. This unique process makes Tonlé Sap one of the world's richest sources of freshwater fish.

Globally threatened species that you stand a slight chance of seeing include the Asian elephant, banteng (a wild ox), gaur, clouded leopard, fishing cat, marbled cat, sun bear, Siamese crocodile and pangolin. Asian tigers were once commonplace but are now exceedingly rare – the last sighting was in about 2007.

Environmental Issues

Cambodia's pristine environment is a big draw for adventurous ecotourists, but much of it is currently under threat. Ancient forests are being razed to make way for plantations, rivers are being sized up for major hydroelectric power plants, and the south coast is being explored by leading oil companies. Places like the Cardamom Mountains are in the front line and it remains to be seen whether the environmentalists or the economists will win the debate.

The greatest threat is illegal logging, carried out to provide charcoal and timber, and also to clear land for cash-crop plantations. The environmental watchdog Global Witness (www.globalwitness.org) publishes meticulously documented exposés on corrupt military and civilian officials and their well-connected business partners. In the short term, deforestation is contributing to worsening floods along the Mekong, but the long-term implications of deforestation are mind-boggling. Silting, combined with overfishing and pollution, may lead to the eventual death of Tonlé Sap lake, a catastrophe for future generations of Cambodians.

Throughout the country, pollution is a problem, and detritus of all sorts, especially plastic bags and bottles, can be seen in distressing quantities everywhere.

The latest environmental threats to emerge are dams on the Mekong River. Environmentalists fear that damming the mainstream Mekong may disrupt the flow patterns of the river and the migratory patterns of fish, as well as the critically endangered freshwater Irrawaddy dolphin. Work on the Don Sahong (Siphandone) Dam just north of the Cambodia–Laos border has begun, and plans under consideration include the Sambor Dam, a massive 3300MW project 35km north of Kratie.

RESPONSIBLE TRAVEL IN CAMBODIA

Cambodia has been to hell and back and there are many ways that you can put a little back into the country. Staying longer, travelling further and avoiding package tours is obvious advice. For those on shorter stays, consider spending money in local markets and in restaurants and shops that assist disadvantaged locals. If visiting minority villages, pay attention to a few basic rules such as those in the Responsible Trekking box (p144).

The looting of stone carvings has had a devastating impact on many ancient temples. Don't contribute to this cultural plunder by buying antiquities of any sort. Classy reproductions are available in Phnom Penh and Siem Reap, complete with export certificates.

Cambodians dress very modestly and may be offended by skimpily dressed foreigners. Just look at the Cambodians frolicking in the sea – most are fully dressed. Wearing bikinis on the beach is fine but cover up elsewhere. Topless or nude bathing is a definite no-no.

The sexual exploitation of children is now taken very seriously in Cambodia. Report anything that looks like child-sex tourism to the ChildSafe hotlines listed here. Tourism establishments that sport the ChildSafe logo have staff trained to protect vulnerable children and, where necessary, intervene.

Phnom Penh (☑ 012 311112)

Siem Reap (☑ 017 358758)

Sihanoukville (☑ 012 478100)

Police Hotline (☑ 023-997919)

Friends International (www.friends-international.org) Has lots of practical ideas for responsible travel.

SURVIVAL GUIDE

ℹ Directory A–Z

ACCOMMODATION

Accommodation in Cambodia is terrific value. In popular tourist destinations, budget guesthouses generally charge US$5 to US$10 for a room with a cold-water bathroom. Dorm beds usually cost US$3 to US$10, but you can get a whole room for these prices at locally run guesthouses. Rooms with air-con start at US$10. Spend US$15 or US$20 and you'll be living in style. Spend US$30 and up and we're talking boutique standards with a swimming pool.

Accommodation is busiest from mid-November to March. There are substantial low-season rates available at major hotels in Phnom Penh, Siem Reap and Sihanoukville, although this tends to affect midrange and top-end places more than budget digs.

Homestays are popular in more rural areas and on Mekong islands. These are a good way to meet the local people and learn about Cambodian life.

ACTIVITIES

Cambodia is steadily emerging as an ecotourism destination. Activities on offer include the following:

→ Jungle trekking in Ratanakiri, Mondulkiri and the Cardamom Mountains of the south coast

→ Walking with elephants in Mondulkiri

→ Scuba diving and snorkelling near Sihanoukville

→ Cycling around Battambang, in Mondulkiri, along the Mekong Discovery Trail between Kratie and Stung Treng, and around the temples of Angkor

→ Adventurous dirt biking all over the country (for those with some experience)

BOOKS

A whole bookcase-worth of volumes examine Cambodia's recent history, including the French-colonial period, the spillover of the war in Vietnam into Cambodia, the Khmer Rouge years and the wild 1990s. The best include the following:

→ Cambodia's Curse by Joel Brinkley (2011). Pulitzer Prize–winning journalist pulls no punches in his criticism of the government and donors alike.

→ Hun Sen's Cambodia by Sebastian Strangio (2015). A no-holds-barred look at contemporary Cambodia and the rule of Prime Minister Hun Sen.

→ River of Time by John Swain (1995). Takes readers back to an old Indochina, lost to the madness of war.

→ The Gate by François Bizot (2003). Bizot was kidnapped by the Khmer Rouge, and later held by them in the French embassy.

→ First They Killed My Father by Loung Ung (2001). Covers the destruction of an urban Cambodian family through execution and disease during the Khmer Rouge period.

CUSTOMS REGULATIONS

A 'reasonable amount' of duty-free items is allowed into the country. Alcohol and cigarettes are on sale at well below duty-free prices on the streets of Phnom Penh.

It is illegal to take antiquities out of the country.

ELECTRICITY

The usual voltage is 220V, 50 cycles, but power surges and power cuts are common, particularly in the provinces. Electrical sockets are usually two-prong, mostly flat but sometimes round pin.

EMBASSIES & CONSULATES

Australian Embassy (Map p80; ☎ 023-213470; 16 National Assembly St, Phnom Penh)

French Embassy (Map p77; ☎ 023-430020; 1 Monivong Blvd, Phnom Penh)

German Embassy (Map p80; ☎ 023-216381; 76-78 St 214, Phnom Penh)

Lao Embassy (Map p77; ☎ 023-997931; 15-17 Mao Tse Toung Blvd, Phnom Penh)

Myanmar Embassy (Map p77; ☎ 023-223761; 181 Norodom Blvd, Phnom Penh)

Thai Embassy (Map p77; ☎ 023-726306; 196 Norodom Blvd, Phnom Penh)

UK Embassy (Map p77; ☎ 023-427124; 27-29 St 75, Phnom Penh)

US Embassy (Map p78; ☎ 023-728000; 1 St 96, Phnom Penh)

INSURANCE

Make sure your medical insurance policy covers emergency evacuation: limited medical facilities mean that you may have to be airlifted to Bangkok for problems such as a traffic accident or dengue fever.

INTERNET ACCESS

Internet access is widespread, but there are not as many internet shops as there used to be now that wi-fi is more prevalent. Charges range from 1500r to US$2 per hour. Many hotels,

FOOD PRICE RANGES

The following price ranges refer to the average price of a main course.

$ US$5

$$ US$5 to US$10

$$$ US$10

guesthouses, restaurants and cafes now offer free wi-fi, even in the most out-of-the-way provincial capitals.

LEGAL MATTERS

All narcotics, including marijuana, are illegal in Cambodia. However, marijuana is traditionally used in food preparation, so you may find it sprinkled across some pizzas. Many Western countries have laws that make sex offences committed overseas punishable at home.

LGBT TRAVELLERS

Cambodia is a very tolerant country when it comes to sexual orientation and the scene is slowly coming alive in the major cities. But as with heterosexual couples, displays of public aff ection are a basic no-no. Handy websites:

Cambodia Gay (http://cambodia-gay.com) Promoting the LGBT community in Cambodia.

Sticky Rice (www.stickyrice.ws) Gay travel guide covering Cambodia and Asia.

MAPS

The best all-round map is Gecko's Cambodia Road Map at a 1:750,000 scale.

MONEY

➺ Cambodia's currency is the riel (r).

➺ The US dollar is accepted everywhere and by everyone, though change may arrive in riel (handy when paying for things such as moto rides and drinks).

➺ When calculating change, the US dollar is usually rounded off to 4000r.

➺ Near the Thai border, many transactions are in Thai baht.

➺ Avoid ripped banknotes, which Cambodians often refuse.

ATMs

ATMs that accept debit cards and credit cards are found in all major cities and a growing number of provincial towns, and at border crossings. Machines dispense US dollars or riel. Most banks charge a withdrawal fee of US$4 to US$5 per transaction. Acleda Bank has the largest network of ATMs countrywide, closely followed by ANZ Royal Bank and Canadia Bank.

Bargaining

Bargaining is expected in local markets, when travelling by share taxi or moto and, sometimes, when taking a cheap room. The Khmers are not ruthless hagglers, so a persuasive smile and a little friendly quibbling is usually enough to get a good price.

Tipping

Tipping is not traditionally expected here, but in a country as poor as Cambodia, a dollar tip (or 5% to 10% on bigger bills) can go a long way.

OPENING HOURS

Most Cambodians get up very early and it's not unusual to see people out exercising at 5.30am if you're heading home – ahem, sorry, getting up – at that time.

Banks Most keep core hours of 8am to 3.30pm Monday to Friday, plus Saturday morning.

Government offices Open from Monday to Friday and on Saturday mornings. They theoretically begin the working day at 7.30am, break for a siesta from 11.30am to 2pm, and end the day at 5pm.

Local markets Operate seven days a week and usually open and close with the sun, running from 6.30am to 5.30pm. They close for a few days during major holidays.

Shops Tend to open from about 8am until 6pm, sometimes later.

POST

➺ The postal service is hit-and-miss. Letters and parcels sent further afield than Asia can take up to two or three weeks to reach their destination.

➺ Send anything valuable by courier service, such as **EMS** (☑ 023-723511; www.ems.com.kh; Main Post Office, St 13, Phnom Penh), or from another country.

➺ Ensure postcards and letters are franked before they vanish from your sight.

➺ Phnom Penh's main post office has the most reliable poste-restante service.

PUBLIC HOLIDAYS

Banks, ministries and embassies close down during public holidays and festivals, so plan ahead if visiting Cambodia during these times. Cambodians also roll over holidays if they fall on a weekend and take a day or two extra during major festivals. Add to this the fact that they take a holiday for international days here and there, and it soon becomes apparent that Cambodia has more public holidays than any other nation on Earth!

International New Year's Day 1 January

Victory over the Genocide 7 January

International Women's Day 8 March

International Workers' Day 1 May

International Children's Day 8 May
King's Birthday 13–15 May
King Mother's Birthday 18 June
Constitution Day 24 September
Commemoration Day 15 October
Independence Day 9 November
International Human Rights Day 10 December

SAFE TRAVEL

Mines & Mortars

Cambodia is one of the most heavily mined countries in the world, especially in the north-west of the country near the Thai border. Many mined areas are unmarked, so do not stray from well-worn paths and never, ever touch any unexploded ordnance (UXO) you come across, including mortars and artillery shells. If you find yourself in a mined area, retrace your steps only if you can clearly see your footprints. If not, stay where you are and call for help. If someone is injured in a minefield, do not rush in to help even if they are crying out in pain – find someone who knows how to enter a mined area safely

Crime

Given the number of guns in Cambodia, there is less armed theft than one might expect. Still, hold-ups and motorcycle theft are a potential danger in Phnom Penh and Sihanoukville. There is no need to be paranoid, just cautious. Walking or riding alone late at night is not ideal, certainly not in rural areas. Bag-snatching has become an increasing problem in Phnom Penh in recent years and the motorbike thieves don't let go, dragging passengers off motos and endangering lives. If riding a moto carry your shoulder bag in front of you and be careful when riding on re-morks as well. Should anyone be unlucky enough to be robbed, it is important to note that the Cambodian police are the best that money can buy! Any help, such as a police report, is going to cost you. The going rate depends on the size of the claim, but anywhere from US$5 to US$50 is a common charge.

Scams

Most scams are fairly harmless, involving a bit of commission here and there for taxi or moto drivers, particularly in Siem Reap. There have been one or two reports of police set-ups in Phnom Penh involving planted drugs.This seems to be very rare, but if you fall victim to the ploy, it may be best to pay them off before more police get involved at the local station, as the price will only rise when there are more offi cials to pay off.

Beggars in places such as Phnom Penh and Siem Reap are asking for milk powder for an infant in arms. Some foreigners succumb to the urge to help, but the beggars usually request the most expensive milk formula available and return it to the shop to split the proceeds after the handover.

Moto and remork drivers will always try to get an extra buck or two out of you. Some price inflation for foreigners is natural, but you are being gouged if they charge three times the prices we quote. Fares are pretty cheap and don't tend to rise much year on year.

TELEPHONE

In many areas landline service is spotty. Mobile phones, whose numbers start with 01, 06, 07, 08 or 09, are hugely popular with both individuals and commercial enterprises. Buying a local SIM card is highly recommended to avoid expensive roaming charges. SIM cards are widely available and cost almost nothing. Mobile-phone calls and 3G internet access are also quite cheap. Foreigners usually need to present a valid passport to purchase a local SIM card.

If you don't have a phone, the easiest way to make a local call in most urban areas is to head to one of the many small private booths on the kerbside, with prices around 300r.

For listings of businesses and government offices, check out www.yp.com.kh.

TIME

Cambodia, like Laos, Vietnam and Thailand, is seven hours ahead of Greenwich Mean Time or Universal Time Coordinated (GMT/UTC).

TRAVELLERS WITH DISABILITIES

Although Cambodia has one of the world's highest rates of limb loss (due to mines), the country is not designed for people with impaired mobility. Few buildings have lifts/elevators, footpaths and roads are riddled with potholes, and the staircases and rock jumbles of many Angkorian

DANGEROUS DRUGS 101

Watch out for *yaba*, the 'crazy' drug from Thailand, known rather ominously in Cambodia as *yama* (the Hindu god of death). Known as ice or crystal meth elsewhere, it's not just any old diet pill from the pharmacist but homemade meth-amphetamines produced in labs in Cambodia and the region beyond. The pills are often laced with toxic substances, such as mercury, lithium or whatever else the maker can find. *Yama* is a dirty drug and more addictive than users would like to admit, provoking powerful hallucinations, sleep deprivation and psychosis. Steer clear of the stuff unless you plan on an indefinite extension to your trip.

temples are daunting even for the able-bodied. Transport-wise, chartering is the way to go and is a fairly affordable option. Also affordable is hired help if you require it, and Khmers are generally very helpful should you need assistance.

VISAS
Visa on Arrival
➡ For most nationalities, one-month tourist visas (US$30) are available on arrival at Phnom Penh and Siem Reap airports and all land border crossings. If you are carrying an African, Asian or Middle Eastern passport, there are some exceptions.

➡ One passport-sized photo is required and you'll be 'fined' US$2 if you don't have one. Citizens of ASEAN member countries do not require a visa.

➡ Visas are issued extremely quickly at the airports and lines are usually minimal, so it's not really worth paying US$5 extra for an e-visa. However, you might consider the e-visa option if you plan to cross at the Poipet or Koh Kong land borders. Overcharging for visas is rampant at these crossings, and with an e-visa you'll avoid these potential charges.

E-Visas
➡ One-month tourist e-visas cost US$30 plus a US$5 processing fee.

➡ E-visas are available from www.mfaic.gov.kh and take three business days to process.

➡ E-visas can be used at all airports and at the Bavet, Koh Kong and Poipet land border crossings. They cannot be used at the more remote land crossings, so you are on your own dealing with corrupt border officials at remote Thai and Lao land borders (corruption is less of a problem at Vietnamese borders).

Visa Extensions
➡ Tourist visas can be extended once for one month only. If you're planning a longer stay, upon arrival request a one-month business visa (US$35), which can be extended for up to a year through any travel agent in Phnom Penh. Bring a passport photo.

➡ Extensions for one/three/six/12 months cost about US$45/75/155/285 and take three working days.

➡ For one-month extensions, it may be cheaper to do a 'visa run' to Thailand, getting a fresh visa when you cross back into Cambodia.

➡ Overstayers are charged US$5 per day at the point of exit.

Visa Regulations for Neighbouring Countries
Vietnam One-month single-entry visas cost US$60/70 for one-day/one-hour processing in Phnom Penh, Sihanoukville or Battambang. Many visitors no longer need visas following a 2015 change in regulations.

Laos Most visitors can obtain a visa on arrival, costing US$3 to US$42 depending on nationality.

Thailand Most visitors do not need a visa.

VOLUNTEERING
Cambodia hosts a huge number of NGOs, some of which do require volunteers from time to time. The best way to find out who is represented in the country is to drop in on the **Cooperation Committee for Cambodia** (CCC; Map p77; ☑ 023-214152; www.ccc-cambodia.org; 9-11 St 476) in Phnom Penh.

Professional Siem Reap–based organisations helping to place volunteers include **ConCERT** (www.concertcambodia.org) and **Globalteer** (www.globalteer.org); the latter program involves a weekly charge.

WORK
Jobs are available throughout Cambodia, but apart from teaching English or helping out in guesthouses, bars or restaurants, most are for professionals and are arranged in advance. There is a lot of teaching work available for English-language speakers; those with an English-language teaching certificate can earn considerably more than those with no qualifications.

Places to look for work include the classifieds sections of the *Phnom Penh Post* and the *Cambodia Daily*, and noticeboards at guesthouses. For information about work opportunities with NGOs, call into the CCC, which posts vacant positions.

❶ Getting There & Away
AIR
Cambodia's two major international airports, **Phnom Penh International Airport** (p86) and **Siem Reap International Airport** (p101), have frequent flights to destinations all over eastern Asia. Both airports have a good range of services, including restaurants, bars, shops and ATMs.

Sihanoukville International Airport (☑ 012-333524; www.cambodia-airports.com) currently offers very limited international connections to a handful of neighbouring countries. Note that e-visas are not accepted at Sihanoukville's airport.

Flights to Cambodia are expanding, but most connect only as far as regional capitals. **Cambodia Angkor Airways** (www.cambodiaangkorair. com) is the national airline and offers the most international flight connections to destinations around the region, including Bangkok, Danang, Guangzhou, Ho Chi Minh City, Seoul and Shanghai. **Thai Airways** (www.thaiair.com) and **Bangkok Airways** (www.bangkokair.com) offer the most daily international flights connections, all via Bangkok. **Vietnam Airlines** (www.vietnamairlines.com) has several useful connections, including from both Phnom Penh and Siem Reap to both Hanoi and Ho Chi Minh City, as well as from Phnom Penh to Vientiane and Siem Reap to Luang Prabang, Danang and Phu Quoc.

Budget airlines have taken off in recent years and are steadily driving down prices. Useful budget airlines include **Air Asia** (www.airasia.com), with daily flights connecting Phnom Penh and Siem Reap to Kuala Lumpur and Bangkok; **Jetstar** (www.jetstar.com), with daily flights from both Phnom Penh and Siem Reap to Singapore; and **Cebu Pacific** (www.cebupacificair.com), with three or four weekly flights from Siem Reap to Manila.

Other regional centres with direct flights to Cambodia include Pakse, Hong Kong and Taipei. Longer-haul flights are currently limited to Doha and Tokyo.

LAND

There are land border crossings shared with Laos, Thailand and Vietnam. These are covered throughout this chapter.

Getting Around

AIR

There are several domestic airlines in Cambodia operating flights between Phnom Penh and Siem Reap (up to 10 flights a day) and Siem Reap and Sihanoukville (several flights daily).

Bassaka Air (023-217613; www.bassakaair.com)

Cambodia Angkor Air (023-212564; www.cambodiaangkorair.com)

Cambodia Bayon Airlines (023-231555; www.bayonairlines.com)

JC International Airlines (023-989707; www.jcairline.com)

BICYCLE

Some guesthouses and hotels rent out bicycles for US$1 to US$2 per day. If you'll be doing lots of cycling, bring along a bike helmet, which can also provide some protection on a moto.

Cambodia is a great country for cycle touring as travelling at gentle speeds allows for lots of interaction with locals. Much of Cambodia is pancake flat or only moderately hilly. Safety, however, is a considerable concern on paved roads as trucks, buses and cars barrel along at high speed. Usually flat unpaved trails run roughly parallel to the highways, allowing for a more relaxed journey and much more interaction with the locals.

Cycling around Angkor is an incredible experience, as it really gives you a sense of the size and scale of the temple complex. Adventure mountain biking is likely to take off in the Cardamom Mountains and in Mondulkiri and Ratanakiri provinces over the coming years.

AIRPORT TAXES

International departure tax of US$25 is included in the ticket price at the point of purchase so there is no need for cash dollars when you leave the country.

BOAT

Long-distance public boats are increasingly rare as the roads improve, but fast boats still ply the Tonlé Sap from Phnom Penh to Siem Reap, while smaller boats take on the sublime stretch between Siem Reap and Battambang.

BUS AND MINIVAN

About a dozen bus companies serve all corners of the country. Comfort levels and prices vary wildly, so shop around. Booking bus tickets through guesthouses and travel agents is convenient, but often incurs a commission. Also note that travel agents tend to work with only a handful of preferred companies, so won't always offer your preferred company and/or departure time.

Express minivans (usually modern Ford Transits or Toyota Hiaces) are an option between most major cities. They operate a one seat/one passenger policy. They cost about the same as the big buses, but are much faster, often too fast for many people's taste. Also, they don't have much legroom; big buses are considerably more comfortable.

Older local minibuses serve most provincial routes but are not widely used by Western visitors. They are very cheap but often uncomfortably overcrowded (you are almost guaranteed to be vomited on) and sometimes driven by maniacs. Only really consider them if there is no alternative.

CAR & MOTORCYCLE

Renting a (self-drive) motorbike is a great way to get around provincial cities and their surrounding sights (although tourists are forbidden from renting motorbikes in Siem Reap). Basic 100cc to 125cc motorbikes are widely available and cheap (about US$5 per day). No one will ask you for a driving licence except, occasionally, the police. Make sure you have a strong lock and always leave the bike in guarded parking where possible.

For longer-distance travel, motorcycles and cars offer travellers flexibility to visit out-of-the-way places and to stop when they choose. Cambodia's main national highways (NH) are generally in good shape but can be quite dangerous due to the prevalence of high-speed overtaking/passing.

While major national highways are too heavily trafficked for happy motorcycling, many of

Cambodia's less-travelled tracks are perfect for two-wheeled exploration. However, forays on motorcycles into the remote and diabolical roads of the northwest and northeast should only be attempted by experienced riders. In all cases, proceed cautiously, as outside Phnom Penh and Siem Reap medical facilities are rudimentary and ambulances are rare.

CYCLO

A few cyclos (pedicabs) can still be seen on the streets of Phnom Penh and Battambang. They are a charming and environmentally friendly, if slow, way to get around, and cost about the same as a moto.

REMORK, MOTO & CYCLO

Motos, also known as motodups (meaning moto driver), are small motorcycle taxis. They are a quick way of making short hops around towns and cities. Prices range from 2000r to US$1.50 or more, depending on the distance and the town. Chartering a moto for the day costs around US$10, but can cost more if a greater distance is involved or the driver speaks good English.

The vehicle known in Cambodia as a remork-moto (tuk tuk) is a canopied two-wheeled trailer hitched to the back of a motorbike. These generally cost a bit more than double what a moto costs. Still, for two or more people a remork can be cheaper than a moto, not to mention safer and much more comfortable if you've got luggage or it's raining.

Although locals rarely agree on a price in advance for a moto or remork, it's best for tourists to agree to a price beforehand. Many optimistic drivers have gotten into the habit of overcharging foreigners, or trying to charge per passenger (you should never let them do this, although paying an extra dollar or two is fair if you are stuffing four to six people into a remork).

Taxis can be ordered via guesthouses and hotels to get around Phnom Penh, Siem Reap and Sihanoukville, and usually cost a bit more than a remork. Expect to pay around US$30 per day and up depending on the itinerary.

SHARE TAXIS

Share taxis (usually Toyota Camrys) are faster, more flexible in terms of departure times, and a bit more expensive than buses. They leave when full, which is usually rather quickly on popular routes. For less-travelled routes, you may have to wait a while (possibly until the next day if you arrive in the afternoon) before your vehicle fills up, or pay for the vacant seats yourself.

Share taxis can be pretty cramped. In addition to the driver, each one carries four to seven passengers, with the price fluctuating according to how many people are in the car. It's not uncommon to see two in the front seat, four in the back, and a seventh passenger squished between the driver and his door! Pay double the regular fare and you get the front seat all to yourself; pay six fares and you've got yourself a private taxi. Haggle patiently, with a smile, to ensure fair prices.

Indonesia

POP 261 MILLION / AREA 1,904,600 SQ KM

Best Activities

➡ Diving & Snorkelling, Pulau Weh (p266)

➡ Surfing, Mentawai Islands (p278)

➡ Trekking Baliem Valley (p301)

➡ Wildlife-watching Tanjung Puting National Park (p283)

Top Indonesian Phrases

Hello Salam

Thank you Terima kasih

Do you speak English? Anda bisa Bahasa Inggris?

Why Go?

Indonesia defines adventure: the only limitation is how many of its 17,000-odd islands you can reach before your visa expires. Following the equator, Indonesia stretches between Malaysia and Australia in one long, intoxicating sweep. The nation's natural diversity is staggering: snow-capped peaks in Papua, sandalwood forests in Sumba, dense jungle in Borneo and impossibly green rice paddies in Bali and Java. Indonesian reefs are a diver's fantasy, while the surf breaks above are the best anywhere.

But even as the diversity on land and sea run like a traveller's dream playlist, it's the mash-up of people and cultures that's the most appealing. Bali justifiably leads off, but there are also Papua's stone-age folk, the many cultures of Flores and West Timor, the artisans of Java, mall-rats of Jakarta, orangutans of Sumatra and much more. Whether it's an idyllic remote beach, a glorious discovery underwater or a Bali all-nighter, Indonesia scores.

When to Go
Jakarta

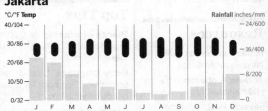

°C/°F Temp		Rainfall inches/mm
40/104 —		— 24/600
30/86 —		— 16/400
20/68 —		— 8/200
10/50 —		
0/32 —		— 0
	J F M A M J J A S O N D	

Sep–Mar Rainy season; starts later in the southeast. Rain everywhere in January and February.

Apr–Jun Dry days and high temps that aren't withering. Hill towns like Bali's Ubud can be chilly at night.

Aug High season. Prices peak on Bali and the Gilis; book ahead. Remote spots may also fill up.

AT A GLANCE

Currency Rupiah (Rp)

Money ATMs and moneychangers are widespread across Indonesia's cities but may be hard to find once you get off the beaten track.

Visas 30 days on arrival for most visitors

Language Bahasa Indonesian

Exchange Rates

Australia	A$1	10,575Rp
Canada	C$1	10,820Rp
Euro	€1	15,800Rp
Japan	¥100	12,120Rp
New Zealand	NZ$1	9680Rp
UK	UK£1	17,320Rp
US	US$1	13,140Rp

For current exchange rates, see www.xe.com.

Daily Costs

Budget Less than 500,000Rp

Simple rooms less than 200,000Rp

Cheap street meals less than 30,000Rp

Local transport such as becaks from 20,000Rp

Resources

Inside Indonesia (www.insideindonesia.org)

Jakarta Globe (www.thejakartaglobe.com)

Jakarta Post (www.thejakartapost.com)

Lonely Planet (www.lonelyplanet.com/indonesia)

Entering the Country

There are many ways into Indonesia: by boat from Malaysia and Singapore, and overland to Kalimantan, Papua and West Timor. But most people will fly, landing at – or transiting through – Jakarta or Bali.

REGIONS AT A GLANCE

Java Indonesia's most populous island; monuments, mosques and temples exist alongside a spectacular tropical landscape spiked with smoking volcanoes..

Bali Indonesia's most popular island; excellent dining and nightlife, famous beaches, epic surfing and a gracious welcome.

Nusa Tenggara A stunning chain of eastern islands; from Lombok to Timor via Flores you will be tempted by diving, surfing, Komodo dragons and ancient cultures.

Sumatra Wild and largely untamed, Sumatra is epic travel with dense rainforest, pristine reefs and unmatched surf.

Kalimantan Cut by countless rivers, Borneo's legendary rainforest attracts wildlife enthusiasts and hardened trekkers.

Sulawesi Wind your way through this crazy-shaped island of elaborate funeral ceremonies, trails through terraced rice fields and tarsier-filled jungles.

Maluku Push past isolation of the legendary Spice Islands to discover brilliant coral gardens and jungle-swaddled volcanoes.

Papua Remote Papua is an adventurer's fantasy. From high-mountain valleys and snaking jungle rivers to translucent coastal waters teeming with life, it offers superb trekking and world-class diving among proud indigenous peoples.

Top Tips

Places of worship Be respectful. Remove shoes and dress modestly when visiting mosques; wear a sash and sarong at Bali temples.

Body language Use both hands when handing somebody something. Don't display affection in public or talk with your hands on your hips.

Clothing Avoid showing a lot of skin, although many local men wear shorts. Don't go topless if you're a woman (even in Bali).

Photography Before taking photos of someone, ask – or mime – for approval

Indonesia Highlights

1 Bali (p201) Surfing by day, partying at night and absorbing amazing culture.

2 Borobudur (p190) Ascending the ancient Buddhist stupa.

3 Yogyakarta (p179) Trawling the batik markets.

4 Komodo National Park (p247) Gazing at the iconic dragons.

5 Nusa Tenggara (p231) Rocking on in hopping Labuanbajo.

6 Sumatra (p260) Paying primate-to-primate respects to the orangutans.

7 Pulau Bunaken (p295) Diving the pristine walls and coral canyons beneath seas of dimpled glass.

8 Maluku's Banda Islands (p298) Exploring the lovely time capsule.

9 Baliem Valley (p302) Hiking along raging rivers and scaling exposed ridges to reach interior Papua's remote tribal villages.

10 Gili Islands (p238) Diving and lazing following fun-filled nights.

JAVA

The heart of the nation, Java is an island of megacities, mesmerising natural beauty, magical archaeological sites and profound traditions in art, music and dance.

Boasting a dazzling array of bewitching landscapes – iridescent rice paddies, smoking volcanoes, rainforest and savannah, not to mention virgin beaches – most journeys here are defined by scenic excesses. The island is at its most excessive in the cities: crowded, polluted, concrete labyrinths that buzz and roar. Dive into Jakarta's addictive mayhem, soak up Yogyakarta's soul and stroll though Solo's batik laneways en route to the island's all-natural wonders.

Home to 140 million people and the most populated island on earth, Java travel can be slow going, particularly in the west. However, the rail network is generally reliable and efficient, and flights are inexpensive. Your endurance will be rewarded with fascinating insights into Indonesia's most complex and culturally compelling island.

❶ Getting There & Away

AIR

Jakarta has numerous international and domestic connections. Other useful international gateway Javanese cities are Surabaya, Solo, Bandung, Yogyakarta and Semarang. Domestic flights can be very convenient and affordable: Jakarta, Yogyakarta, Bandung and Surabaya are all well connected to neighbouring islands of Bali, Sumatra and Lombok; if your time is short, it's worth booking a few internal flights to cut down on those hours on the road.

SEA

Very few travellers now use Pelni passenger ships, but there are connections between Jakarta and most ports in the nation. Ferries run round the clock between Banyuwangi/Ketapang

Java

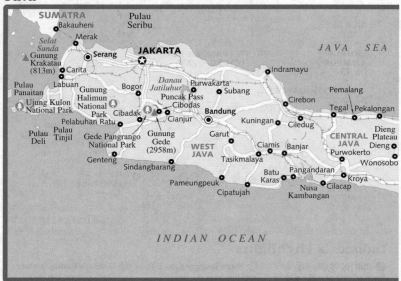

harbour in east Java and Gilimanuk in Bali and also between the Javanese port of Merak and Bakauheni in south Sumatra. Surabaya also has a harbour that offers regular passenger services to destinations such as Kalimantan and Sulawesi.

ℹ️ Getting Around

The traditional east–west route across Java is Jakarta–Bogor–Bandung–Pangandaran–Yogyakarta–Solo–Surabaya–Gunung Bromo–Gunung Ijen and on to Bali. However, flight connections mean that there are now many more potential points of entry (and exit), such as flying into Semarang and heading down to Yogyakarta from there.

Java has a fairly punctual and efficient rail service running right across the island. Overall, train travel certainly beats long bus journeys, so try to take as many as you can. You can check timetables and make online bookings at www.kereta-api.co.id; it's in Bahasa Indonesia, so you may need to use Google Translate.

Jakarta

♩ 021 / POP 10.2 MILLION

One of the world's greatest megalopolises, Jakarta is a dynamic city of daunting extremes – one that's developing at a pace that offers challenges and surreal juxtapositions on every street corner. An organism unto itself, this is a town in the midst of a very public metamorphosis, and despite the maddening traffic, life here is lived at an allout rush, driven by an industriousness and optimism that's palpable. Dysfunction be damned. Translation: it's no oil painting, yet beneath the unappealing facade of newly built high-rises, relentless concrete and gridlocked streets, fringed with rickety slums and shrouded in a persistent blanket of smog, Jakarta has many faces and plenty of surprises.

⦿ Sights

👁️ Kota & Glodokbog

Kota is Jakarta's old town where you'll find the vestiges of old Batavia, the colonial Dutch city of the 18th century. The centrepiece is Taman Fatahillah, Kota's central cobblestone square, surrounded by imposing colonial buildings. This area includes the historic port of Sunda Kelapa to the north. Just south of Kota, Glodok is the heart of old Chinatown and offers great opportunities to explore in a compact and vibrant area.

★ **Museum Bank Indonesia**   MUSEUM
(Map p166; Pintu Besar Utara III; 5000Rp; ⊘8am-3.30pm Tue-Fri, 8am-4pm Sat & Sun) This museum presents an engaging and easily consumed history of Indonesia from a loosely

financial perspective, in a grand, expertly restored, neoclassical former bank headquarters that dates from the early 20th century. All the displays (including lots of zany audiovisuals) are slickly presented, with exhibits about the spice trade and the financial meltdown of 1997 (and subsequent riots) as well as a gallery dedicated to currency, with notes from every country in the world.

★ Jin De Yuan   BUDDHIST TEMPLE
(Vihara Dharma Bhakti Temple; Map p166; Jl Kemenangan; ⊙ dawn-dusk) FREE This large Chinese Buddhist temple compound dates from 1755 and is one of the most important in the city. The main structure has an unusual roof crowned by two dragons eating pearls, while the interior is richly atmospheric: dense incense and candle smoke waft over Buddhist statues, ancient bells and drums, and some wonderful calligraphy.

Museum Wayang   MUSEUM
(Puppet Museum; Map p166; ☑ 021-692 9560; Taman Fatahillah; adult/child 5000/2000Rp; ⊙ 8am-5pm Tue-Sun; ☎) This puppet museum has one of the best collections of *wayang* (flat wooden puppets) in Java and its dusty cabinets are full of a multitude of characters from across Indonesia, as well as China, Vietnam, India, Cambodia and Europe.

The building itself dates from 1912. Watch for free *wayang* performances on Sunday (10am to 2pm), which are very popular and crowded. There are also often more elaborate performances on weekends which can be very worthwhile.

Jembatan Kota Intan   BRIDGE
(Kota Intan Bridge; Map p166; Kali Besar) At the northern end of Kali Besar is the last remaining Dutch drawbridge, originally called Hoenderpasarbrug (Chicken Market Bridge). Now restored, it dates from the 17th century and is an ideal photo stop.

Museum Bahari   MUSEUM
(Maritime Museum; Map p166; ☑ 021-669 3406; Jl Pakin 1; adult/child 5000/2000Rp; ⊙ 9am-3pm Tue-Sun) Near the entrance to Sunda Kelapa (p165), several old VOC (Vereenigde Oost-Indische Compagnie; the Dutch East India Company) warehouses, dating back to 1652, comprise the Museum Bahari. This is a good place to learn about the city's maritime history, with a sprawling series of galleries covering anything from nautical legends, famous explorers to WWII history in the archipelago. Parts of the museum were damaged in a fire in January 2018 and are being restored; the unaffected areas of the museum remain open to visitors.

Jakarta

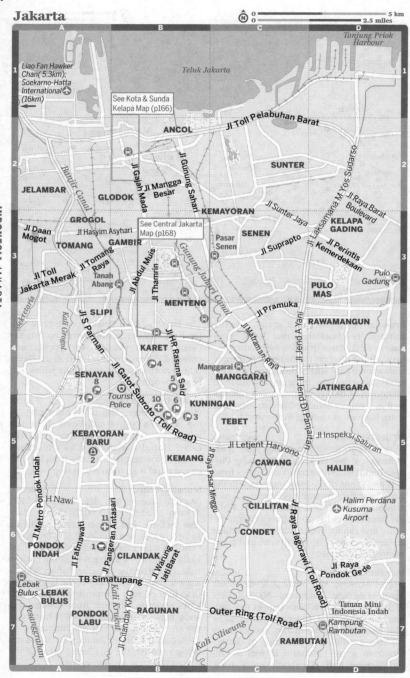

0 — 5 km
0 — 2.5 miles

INDONESIA JAKARTA

Tanjung Priok Harbour

Teluk Jakarta

Liao Fan Hawker Chan(5.3km); Soekarno-Hatta International (16km)

See Kota & Sunda Kelapa Map (p166)

ANCOL

Jl Toll Pelabuhan Barat

SUNTER

Jl Gajah Mada

Jl Gunung Sahari

Jl Mangga Besar

Banjir Canal

JELAMBAR

GLODOK

KEMAYORAN

Jl Sunter Jaya

Jl Laksamana M Yos Suoarso

Jl Raya Barat Boulevard

KELAPA GADING

GROGOL

Jl Hasyim Asyhari

See Central Jakarta Map (p168)

SENEN

Jl Suprapto

Jl Perintis Kemerdekaan

Jl Daan Mogot

TOMANG

GAMBIR

Pasar Senen

Pulo Gadung

Jl Toll Jakarta Merak

Jl Tomang Raya

Tanah Abang

Jl Abdul Muis

Jl Thamrin

Gunung Jabni Canal

PULO MAS

Sekretaris

Jl SLIPI

MENTENG

Jl Pramuka

RAWAMANGUN

Kali Grogol

Jl S Parman

Jl HR Rasuna Said

KARET

4

Jl Mataman Raya

Jl Jend A Yani

JATINEGARA

SENAYAN

8

Jl Gatot Subroto (Toll Road)

Manggarai

MANGGARAI

Tourist Police

7

10

6

KUNINGAN

Jl Jend DI Panjaitan

5

9

3

TEBET

Jl Inspeksi Saluran

KEBAYORAN BARU

2

KEMANG

Jl Letjent Haryono

CAWANG

HALIM

Jl Raya Pasar Minggu

Jl Metro Pondok Indah

H Nawi

CILILITAN

Halim Perdana Kusuma Airport

Jl Pangeran Antasari

11

CONDET

Jl Raya Jagorawi (Toll Road)

PONDOK INDAH

Jl Fatmawati

1

CILANDAK

Jl Warung Jati Barat

Jl Raya Pondok Gede

TB Simatupang

Lebak Bulus

LEBAK BULUS

Kali Krukut

Taman Mini Indonesia Indah

pesanggrahan

PONDOK LABU

RAGUNAN

Outer Ring (Toll Road)

Kampung Rambutan

Jl Cilandak KKO

Kali Ciliwung

RAMBUTAN

Jakarta

◉ Drinking & Nightlife

◉ Shopping

ℹ Information

Museum Bank Mandiri   MUSEUM
(Map p166; Jl Pintu Besar Utara; adult/child 10,000/2000Rp; ⊙9am-3pm Tue-Sun) **FREE** One of two bank museums within a block of each other might have you scratching your head, but it's worthwhile popping in to explore the behind-the-scenes inner workings of a bank, and the interior of this fine 1930s art deco structure. Marvel at the marble counters and vintage counting machines, abacuses, old ATMs and colossal cast-iron safes. Pause on the terrace overlooking the Kota hubbub, before taking the grand staircase up to admire stained-glassed panels and the lavish board room.

Museum Sejarah Jakarta   MUSEUM
(Jakarta History Museum; Map p166; Taman Fatahillah; adult/child 5000/2000Rp; ⊙9am-5pm Tue-Sun) Also known as Museum Kesejarahan Jakarta, the Jakarta History Museum is housed in the old town hall of Batavia, a stately Dutch colonial structure that was once the epicentre of an empire. This bell-towered building, built in 1627, served the administration of the city and was also used by the city law courts. Today it presents a grand white-washed facade to Taman Fatahillah, while inside it has a collection of artefacts.

Museum Seni Rupah Dan Keramik   MUSEUM
(Museum of Fine Arts and Ceramics; Map p166; Taman Fatahillah; adult/child 5000/2000Rp; ⊙8am-5pm Tue-Sun) Built between 1866 and 1870, the former Palace of Justice building is now a fine arts museum. It houses contemporary paintings with works by prominent artists, including Affandi, Raden Saleh and Ida Bagus Made. Part of the building is also a ceramics museum, charging separate admission, with Chinese ceramics and Majapahit terracottas. Pause and relax in the palm-shaded grounds.

Pasar Kemenangan   MARKET
(Map p166; Jl Kemenangan; ⊙dawn-dusk) Be sure to wander down the narrow Kemenangan Market off Jl Pancoran, lined with crooked houses with red-tiled roofs. It's an assault on the senses, with skinned frogs and live bugs for sale next to vast piles of produce. Stalls extend down even narrower neighbouring alleys.

Sunda Kelapa   PORT
(Map p166) A kilometre north of **Taman Fatahillah** (Map p166), the old port of Sunda Kelapa still sees the magnificent Makassar schooners *(pinisi)*. In some respects the dock scene here has barely changed for centuries, with porters unloading cargo from sailing ships by hand and trolley, though it's far less busy today. The much more modern main harbour can also be seen in the distance from here. This entire area is rundown and its waters grotesquely polluted. The many tracts of landfill suggest that redevelopment may not be far off.

◉ Merdeka Square & Central Jakarta

The huge grassy expanse of **Merdeka Square** is home to Sukarno's monument to the nation, and is surrounded by good museums and some fine colonial-era buildings. This part of Jakarta is not about atmospheric streets or idiosyncratic sights, rather its where the nation makes a statement about its stature and prominence.

★ Museum Nasional   MUSEUM
(National Museum; Map p168; ☎021-386 8172; www.museumnasional.or.id; Jl Medan Merdeka Barat 12; admission 10,000Rp; ⊙8am-4pm Tue-Fri, 8am-5pm Sat & Sun) The National Museum is the best of its kind in Indonesia and an essential visit. The enormous collection begins around an open courtyard of the 1862 building which is stacked with magnificent millennia-old statuary including a colossal 4.5m stone image of a Bhairawa king from Rambahan in Sumatra, who is shown trampling on human skulls. The ethnology section is superb, with Dayak puppets and wooden statues from Nias sporting beards (a sign of wisdom) plus some fascinating textiles.

Kota & Sunda Kelapa

N 0 ————— 400 m
   0 ————— 0.2 miles

ian marble, and is topped with a sculpted flame, gilded with 50kg of gold leaf.

Monumen Irian Jaya Pembebasan   MONUMENT
(Irian Jaya Liberation Monument; Map p168; Lapangan Banteng) The twin towers of this monument with a dodgy provenance soar over grassy Banteng Sq and are topped by a sculpture of a human breaking his chains. It dates to the Sukarno era and was designed as anti-Imperialist propaganda, even as Indonesia took over Irian Jaya (Timor and Papua) despite local protests in 1963. These days some call it the 'Freedom Monument'.

Mesjid Istiqlal   MOSQUE
(Independence Mosque; Map p168; Jl Veteran I)
FREE The striking, modernist Mesjid Istiqlal, highlighted by geometrically grated windows, was designed by Catholic architect Frederich Silaban and completed in 1978. It's the largest mosque in Southeast Asia, with five levels representing the five pillars of Islam; its dome is 45m across and its minaret tops 90m. During Ramadan more than 200,000 worshippers can be accommodated here. Non-Muslim visitors are welcome. You have to sign in first and then you'll be shown around by an English-speaking guide on a 20-minute tour.

Lapangan Banteng   SQUARE
(Banteng Square; Map p168) Just east of Merdeka Square, Lapangan Banteng is surrounded by some of Jakarta's best colonial architecture. It

Monumen Nasional   MONUMENT
(Monas; National Monument; Map p168; Merdeka Sq; adult/student/child 5000/3000/2000Rp, to the top 15,000/5000/2000Rp; ⏱8.30am-5pm, closed last Mon of month) Ingloriously dubbed 'Sukarno's final erection', the 132m-high National Monument (aka Monas), which rises into the shroud of smog and towers over Merdeka Square, is both Jakarta's principal landmark and the most famous architectural extravagance of the former president. Begun in 1961, Monas was not completed until 1975, when it was officially opened by Suharto. The monument is constructed from Ital-

was designed by the Dutch in the early 19th century, and called Waterlooplein.

Welcome Monument   MONUMENT
(Salamat Datang; Map p168; Jl Thamrin) Set in the centre of a fountain on one of central Jakarta's most prominent *alun-alun* (public square) is the Salamat Datang, or Welcome Monument. Built in 1962, it's just across from the Hotel Indonesia Kempinski, the city's original luxury hotel.

Tours

★ Hidden Jakarta Tours   TOURS
(0812 803 5297; www.realjakarta.blogspot.com; per person US$50) Hidden Jakarta offers tours of the city's traditional *kampung*, the urban villages of the poor. These warts-and-all tours take you along trash-choked riverways, into cottage-industry factories and allow you to take tea in residents' homes.

Festivals & Events

★ Independence Day   CULTURAL
(Hari Kemerdekaan; 17 Aug) Indonesia's independence is celebrated; the parades in Jakarta are the biggest in the country.

Jakarta Anniversary   FAIR
(22 Jun) Marks the establishment of the city in 1527. Celebrated with fireworks and the Jakarta Fair, a celebration of commerce and culture held at the Jakarta International Expo complex in Kemayoran.

Java Jazz Festival   MUSIC
(www.javajazzfestival.com; early Mar) Held at the Jakarta International Expo in Kemayoran. Attracts acclaimed international artists, including jazz heavyweights like Ramsey Lewis and Brad Mehldau.

Sleeping

Jakarta's central budget options are slowly improving and midrange choices are plentiful; book ahead for both. Jalan Jaksa was once Jakarta's backpacking hub, but travellers are thin on the ground these days, probably because most hotels on Jl Jaksa are grungy (if not outright sleazy).

★ Packer Lodge   HOSTEL $
(Map p166; 0878 8790 3650, 021-629 0162; www.thepackerlodge.com; Jl Kermunian IV 20-22; dm/s/d from 135,000/200,000/300,000Rp;) This owner-operated boutique hostel set in Glodok offers hip, Ikea-chic environs and plenty of amenities close to Kota.

Choose among the four- and eight-bed dorms where the bunks are curtained pods with electrical outlets, lights and USB charger. There are also very compact singles and doubles. All share common Western baths and a spacious common kitchen.

★ Wonderloft Hostel   HOSTEL $
(Map p166; 021-2607 2218; www.wonderloft.id; Jl Bank 6; dm/d incl breakfast 100,000/275,000Rp;) Well located for all the sights and sounds around colonial Kota is this lively hostel with cheerful staff and social set-up. In the evenings the lobby is abuzz with backpackers playing pool, beer in hand, to go with darts, foosball and a kitchen busy with guests cooking up food. The dorms have icy air-con and beds equipped with curtains, powerpoints and lamps. It offers walking tours, pub crawls and good info on all things to do in Jakarta.

Hostel 35   GUESTHOUSE $
(Map p168; 021-392 0331; Jl Kebon Sirih Barat I 35; r with fan & shared/private bathroom 120,000/130,000Rp, with air-con from 250,000Rp;) In a vibrant neighborhood that's a bit of an old-school backpacker enclave is this atmospheric and well-priced hostel. The clean, if aged, tiled rooms have high ceilings and a faded colonial ambience, and the lobby area with rattan sofas is inviting and decorated with fine textiles and tasteful photography.

Six Degrees   HOSTEL $$
(Map p168; 021-314 1657; www.jakarta-backpackers-hostel.com; Jl Cikini Raya 60B-C, Cikini; incl breakfast, dm 115,000-160,000Rp, d with shared/private bathroom 280,000/310,000Rp;) Run by a helpful and friendly Irish/English/Sumatran team, Six Degrees rightfully remains popular with travellers. There's a relaxed, sociable atmosphere, a pool table and TV room, a guests' kitchen and roof garden – complete with bar and gym. Dorms are tight but clean; breakfast is included. The staff here are a good source for local info and onward travel plans.

Hotel Ibis Budget Tanah Abang   HOTEL $$
(www.accorhotels.com; Jl Tanah Abang II 35; r incl breakfast from 380,000Rp;) Excellent-value budget chain that's clean, modern and run by friendly, professional staff. The contemporary lobby is decorated with colour and style, and rooms, though squashy, have good air-con, cable TV and floating bathroom sinks. It's popular with Western travellers due to its proximity to the main sights, and has a small gym, a coffee shop and complimentary breakfast.

Central Jakarta

0 — 500 m
0 — 0.25 miles

Stadium (1.5km);
Kota (3km)
Jl Batu Ceper Raya
Jl Batu Tulis Raya
Pelni
Ticketing
Office
Jl Hayam Wuruk
Jl Gajah Mada
Sawah
Besar
Jl Ceylan
Jl Pintu Air V
Kemayoran

Jl Pecenongan
Jl Dr Sutomo
Jl Bungur Besar

Jl Ir H Juanda
Juanda
Jl Antara
Jl Pos
Jl Gedung
Kesenian 1
Jl Budi
Utomo
Jl Gunung Sahari

Jl Majapahit
Jl Veteran
Jl Veteran I
Jl Veteran III
Jl Kathedral
Jl Banteng
Timur
2
4

Jl Tanah Abang I
GAMBIR
Jl Medan Merdeka Utara
Jl Perwira
Jl Banteng
Selatan

Jl Medan Merdeka Barat
Jl Abdul Muis
Jl Medan Merdeka Timur
Jl Tanah Abang II
Jl Tanah Abang Timur
Hotel Ibis
Budget Tanah
Abang
(200m)
Museum
Nasional
1
Merdeka Square
(Lapangan Merdeka)
5
Jl Pejambon
Jl Abul Rachman
Saleh Raya
Jl Kalilio
Jl Senen
Raya III
Jl Pasar Senen
Jl Senen Raya

Gambir
Damri
Jl Medan Merdeka Utara

Jl Budi Kemuliaan
Jl Merdeka Selatan
US Embassy
Jl Prapatan
Jl Kwitang

Jl Thamrin
Jl Agus Salim (Jl Sabang)
Jl Kebon Sirih Raya
12
Jl Menteng
8
Jl Jaksa
Jl Wahid Hasyim
Jl Menteng Raya
Kali Krukut

Jakarta Visitor
Information Office
10
Day Trans
Gondangdia
Jl Johar
Jl Cikini VI

Jl Kebon Kacang 11
14
Jl Sunda
French
Embassy
Jl Gereja Theresia
Jl Dr Sam Ratulangi
7
CIKINI

Jl Thamrin
Jl Kebon Sirih
Jl Jusuf Adiwinata
Jl Cokroaminoto
Jl Teuku Umar
Jl Cut Nyak Dien
Suroso
17
Cikini
Hospital
Jl Cikini Raya

Jl Kebon Kacang Raya
6
Jl Sultan Syahrir
9
Jl Raden
Saleh Raya

16
15
German
Embassy
Jl Prof Mohammad Yamin SH
11
Jl Teuku Cik Ditiro
Jl Pegangsaan
Timur

Jl Kusuma Atmaja
Jl Imam Bonjol
MENTENG
Jl Sumenep
Jl Taman
Suropati
Cikini
18

Dukuh
Jl Sumahi
Jl Sunda
Kelapa
Jl Diponegoro
Jl Surabaya

INDONESIA JAKARTA

Central Jakarta

INDONESIA JAKARTA

Gondia International Guesthouse
GUESTHOUSE **$$**
(Map p168; ☎021-390 9221; www.gondia-guest house.com; Jl Gondiangdia Kecil 22; r incl breakfast 300,000-400,000Rp; ❇🛜) This modest-looking guesthouse, with hostel-esque signage, occupies a leafy garden plot on a quiet suburban street and has 12 spacious tiled rooms. It's a good low-key choice.

✕ Eating

Jakarta is a world-class eating destination. You'll find amazing options, including oh-so-refined Javanese Imperial cuisine, hit-the-spot street grub and, if you're pining for something familiar, even Western faves.

★ Historia
INDONESIAN **$**
(Map p166; ☎021-3176 0555; Jl Pintu Besar Utara 11; mains 35,000-51,000Rp; ⊗10am-9pm Sun-Thu, to 10pm Fri & Sat; 🛜) Historia's tasty dishes from around the archipelago include fried fish with a Sumatran sambal *(Ikan goreng sambal adaliman)*, Javanese mixed rice and all manner of oxtail – in soup, grilled, deep fried or braised with ground chilli. Served in hip, tiled, warehouse environs with soaring ceilings and a retro-industrial vibe.

Liao Fan Hawker Chan
SINGAPOREAN **$**
(2nd fl Rukan Crown Golf Bldg Jl 8-10, Pantai Indah Kapuk, North Jakarta; mains 28,000-52,000Rp; ⊗8am-10pm) Famed as the only street-food outlet to be awarded a Michelin Star is this Singaporean eatery that opened in Jakarta in 2017. Its famous dish here is the rather humble soy-sauce chicken and rice (28,000Rp); tasty, but it won't blow your mind. It's a simple affair on the 2nd floor above its Michelin

Star–sibling Tim Ho Wan (from Hong Kong), a part of the same franchise.

Santong Kuo Tieh 68
CHINESE **$**
(Map p166; ☎021-692 4716; Jl Pancoran; 10 dumplings 45,000Rp; ⊗10am-9pm) You'll see cooks preparing fried and steamed Chinese pork dumplings out front of this humble but highly popular little place. The *bakso ikan isi* (fish balls) are also good. There are myriad more choices within a few steps.

Serbaraso
INDONESIAN **$**
(Map p168; ☎0812 6896 8910; www.serbaraso. com; Jl Batu Tulis Raya 41; dishes from 15,000Rp; ⊗11am-10pm; 🛜) A much more refined version of your usual Padang restaurant is this modern, air-con eatery that originated in Pekanburu, Sumatra. Specialising in Riau food, Serbaraso is most famous for its smoky charcoal-grilled beef *rendang* (26,000Rp).

Lara Djonggrang
INDONESIAN **$$**
(Map p168; ☎021-315 3252; www.tuguhotels. com; Jl Teuku Cik Ditiro 4; mains 50,000-130,000Rp; ⊗12.30-11pm; 🛜) While many Jakartan restaurants lack atmosphere, that accusation could never be levelled at Lara Djonggrang. As you enter it's easy to think you've stumbled across some lost temple – one that serves perfectly executed and creatively presented imperial Indonesian cuisine from across the archipelago.

Café Batavia
INTERNATIONAL **$$**
(Map p166; ☎021-691 5531; www.cafebatavia. com; Jl Pintu Besar Utara 14; mains 55,000-350,000Rp; ⊗9am-midnight Sun-Thu, to 1am Fri & Sat; 🛜) In a 200-year-old building overlooking Kota's old Dutch quarter is this classy

bistro styled with a colonial decor of old parlour floors, marble table tops and art-deco furnishings. Its jazz soundtrack adds to the atmosphere and makes it an essential stop for a cocktail or a long lunch or dinner. There's Indonesian and Western mains, live music and a great coffee selection.

Waha Kitchen ASIAN $$
(Map p168; ☑ 021-3193 6868; www.wahakitchen. com; Jl Wahid Hasyim 127, Kosenda Hotel; mains from 68,000Rp; ⊘ 24hr) A fittingly fashionable bistro occupies the lobby of the designer Kosenha Hotel, with a 24-hour bar and a menu of modern Asian dishes. Expect the likes of *char kway teow* or salt-and-pepper squid, while in the morning it does Melbourne-inspired brekkies of smashed avocado and poached egg on sourdough etc.

Garuda INDONESIAN $$
(Map p168; ☑ 021-6262 9440; Jl Agus Salim 59; mains from 30,000Rp; ⊘ 24hr; 🎅) A smoky, fluorescent-lit, all-day, all-night depot of locally loved Padang food goodness, throbbing with Bollywood tunes and Indo-pop, and packed with locals. Little dishes of tempting flavours are piled on your table with lightning speed: jackfruit curry, chilli prawns, *tempe penyet* (fried tempe with spicy sauce), *rendang* (beef coconut curry), potato and corn fritters. All of it made fresh.

Sate Khas Senayan INDONESIAN $$
(Map p168; ☑ 021-3192 6238; www.sarirasa.co.id; Jl Kebon Sirih Raya 31A; mains 30,000-110,000Rp; ⊘ 8am-11pm Sun-Thu, to midnight Fri & Sat; 🎅) Upmarket air-conditioned restaurant renowned for its superb *sate* (skewers of chicken, beef and lamb), plus Indonesian favourites such as *ayam goreng kremes* (fried chicken in batter), *gurame bakar* (grilled fish) and *nasi campur* (rice with a choice of side dishes). Look for well-prepared regional specialities, which go well with an iced durian juice or Bintang on tap.

🍷 **Drinking & Nightlife**

If you're expecting the capital of the world's largest Muslim country to be a sober city with little in the way of drinking culture, think again. Bars are spread throughout the city, with casual places grouped around Jl Jaksa, fancy-pants rooftop lounge bars and beer gardens in central and south Jakarta and many more places in between. Cafe culture has really taken off in the last few years.

⭐**Tanamera Coffee** COFFEE
(Map p168; ☑ 021-2962 5599; www.tanameracoffee.com; Jl Kebon Kacang Raya Blok AA07; coffee from 30,000Rp; ⊘ 7am-8pm; 🎅) A real contender for Jakarta's best cup of coffee is this third-wave roaster that offers a range of single-origin beans from around Indonesia. It now has five branches, but this is the original, and where it roasts its beans. Coffee is prepared either as V60 pour-overs or espresso machine, along with tasty breakfasts and dishes such as soft-shell crab burgers.

⭐**Awan Lounge** BAR
(Map p168; www.awanlounge.com; Jl Wahid Hasyim 127; ⊘ 5pm-1am Sun-Thu, to 2am Fri & Sat) Set on the top floor of Kosenda Hotel is this lovely rooftop garden bar that manages to be both understated and dramatic. There's a vertical garden, ample tree cover, plenty of private nooks flickering with candlelight and a vertigo-inducing glass skylight that plummets nine floors down. They have a tasty bar menu, electronica thumps at a perfect volume and the crowd is mixed local and expat. Weekends can get overly crowded. Midweek it's an ideal date-night rendezvous. Cocktails average 120,000Rp.

⭐**Jakarta Coffee House** COFFEE
(Map p164; ☑ 021-7590 0570; www.jakartacoffeehouse.com; Jl Cipete Raya 2; coffee from 26,000Rp; ⊘ 8am-midnight Sun-Thu, to 1am Fri & Sat; 🎅) One of the city's best spots for Indonesian single-origin coffee is this intimate micro-roastery with knowledgeable baristas who can prepare coffee to your tastes. They roast all their beans onsite, sourced from Aceh to Papua.

Paulaner Bräuhaus PUB
(Map p168; ☑ 021-2358 3871; Jl Thamrin 1, Grand Indonesia East Mall; beer 300mL/500mL/1L 79,000/94,000/155,000Rp; ⊘ 11.30am-12.30am Sun-Thu, to 1am Fri & Sat) In a country not known for its diversity of beer options, this German-themed pub offers a point of difference with its house-brewed unfiltered lager, dunkel and wheat beer. There's a menu of hearty Bavarian cuisine, or grab a freshly baked pretzel to enjoy live sports showing on their TVs.

☆ **Entertainment**

⭐**Taman Ismail Marzuki** PERFORMING ARTS
(TIM; Map p168; ☑ 021-3193 7530, 021-230 5146; http://tamanismailmarzuki.jakarta.go.id/; Jl Cikini Raya 73) Jakarta's premier cultural centre has a great selection of cinemas, theatres and exhibition spaces. Performances (such as Sun-

danese dance and gamelan music events) are always high quality and the complex has a couple of good casual restaurants too.

Shopping

Pasar Jl Surabaya   MARKET
(Map p168; Jl Surabaya; ⊙8am-6pm) Jakarta's famous street market is in Menteng. It has woodcarvings, furniture, textiles, jewellery, old vinyl records and many (dubious) antiques. Bargain like crazy.

Pasaraya   DEPARTMENT STORE
(Map p164; www.pasaraya.co.id; Jl Iskandarsyah II/2; ⊙10am-10pm) Opposite the Blok M mall, this department store has two huge floors that seem to go on forever. The slogan here is 'The pride of Indonesia', and you'll see why when you discover the enormous range of handicrafts, such as batik, from throughout the archipelago. It's a fascinating place to browse; watch for sales.

ⓘ Information

MEDICAL SERVICES
Cikini Hospital (Map p168; ☑ emergency 021-3899 7744, urgent care 021-3899 7777; www.rscikini.com; Jl Raden Saleh Raya 40) Caters to foreigners and has English-speaking staff.

SOS Medika Klinik (Map p164; ☑ 021-750 5980, emergency 021-750 6001; Jl Puri Sakti 10, Cipete; ⊙24hr) Offers English-speaking GP appointments, dental care, and emergency specialist healthcare services. Also has a clinic in **Kuningan** (Map p164; ☑ 021-5794 8600; 2nd fl Menara Prima bldg, Jl Dr Ide Anak Agung Gde Agung, Kuningan; ⊙8am-6pm Mon-Fri, to 2pm Sat).

POST
Main Post Office (Map p168; Jl Gedung Kesenian I; ⊙8am-7pm Mon-Fri, to 1pm Sat). Smaller branches are common. International service is somewhat reliable.

TOURIST INFORMATION
Jakarta Visitor Information Office (Map p168; ☑ 021-314 2067, 021-316 1293; www.jakarta-tourism.go.id; Jl KH Wahid Hasyim 9; ⊙7.30am-5.30pm) Inside the Jakarta Theatre building. A helpful office; the staff here can answer queries and set you up with tours. Practical information can be lacking, but it does have several excellent city-produced publications and maps. There are also desks at the airport.

ⓘ Getting There & Away

Jakarta is the main international gateway to Indonesia. It's a hub for domestic and international flights as well as train services from across Java. Though train travel is the preferred choice for many, bus routes also radiate out in all directions, and there are even some boat services.

AIR
Soekarno-Hatta International Airport (CGK; http://soekarnohatta-airport.co.id) is 35km west of the city centre. All international flights and most domestic flights operate from CGK. Surging passenger numbers mean that it can get chaotic, give yourself plenty of time for formalities.

Halim Perdana Kusuma Airport (HLP; Map p164; www.halimperdanakusuma-airport.co.id) is 11km south of Jakarta's Cikini district. It has a limited domestic service.

BOAT
Pelni shipping services operate on sporadic schedules to ports all over the archipelago. The **Pelni ticketing office** (Map p168; ☑ 021-2188 7000, 021-162, 021-633 4342; www.pelni.co.id; Jl Gajah Mada 14) is 1.5km northwest of the Monumen Nasional in central Jakarta.

Pelni ships all arrive at and depart from Pelabuhan Satu (dock No 1) at Tanjung Priok, 13km northeast of the city centre. Transjakarta koridor 10 and 12 provides a direct bus link; a taxi from Jl Jaksa is around 120,000Rp.

BUS
The city's four major bus terminals – Kalideres, Kampung Rambutan, Pulo Gadung and Lebak Bulus – are all a long way from the city centre. Take the TransJakarta busway to these terminals as the journey can take hours otherwise. Tickets (some including travel to the terminals) for the better buses can be bought from agencies. Note that train travel is a faster, safer, more comfortable and often cheaper option.

Kampung Rambutan (Map p164; Rambutan) mainly handles buses to points south and southwest of Jakarta such as Bogor (normal/air-con 10,000/20,000Rp, 45 minutes); Cianjur (air-con 35,000Rp, three hours); Bandung (from 65,000Rp, four to five hours); Pangandaran (normal/air-con 85,000/95,000Rp, eight to nine hours) and Pelabuan Ratu (60,000Rp, four hours via Bogor).

Take Transjakarta bus line 7 to get here.

Pulo Gadung (Map p164; Jl Raya Bekasi) covers Bandung, central and east Java, Sumatra, Bali and even Nusa Tenggara. Bandung buses travel the toll road (from 60,000Rp, three hours), as do the long-haul Yogyakarta coaches (150,000Rp to 275,000Rp, 12 hours). Sumatra is another long haul from Jakarta by bus, destinations include Bengkulu (from 330,000Rp) and Palembang (from 230,000Rp).

Take Transjakarta bus lines 2 or 4 to get there.

Lebak Bulus (Map p164; Jl Lebak Bulus Raya) runs long-distance deluxe buses to Yogyakarta (from 130,000Rp to 300,000Rp), Surabaya and Bali (prices for both vary by time and season).

Take Transjakarta bus line 8 to get there.

Door-to-door travel minibuses are not a good option in Jakarta because it can take hours to pick up or drop off passengers in the traffic jams. Unless you've the patience of a saint, take a train, plane or bus.

Day Trans (Map p168; ☑ 021-2967 6767; www. daytrans.co.id; Jl Thamrin; ☺ 6am-8pm) Runs hourly minibuses to Bandung (115,000Rp to 125,000Rp) from Jl Thamrin; keep an eye out for sales on its website.

TRAIN

Jakarta's four main train stations are quite central. Schedules (www.kereta-api.co.id) to cities around Jakarta and across Java are convenient. You can even get a train–ferry–bus connection to Bali. Fares are cheap, so it can be worth buying the best available class of service.

Gambir (Jl Medan Merdeka Utara) is the most convenient and important of Jarkarta's train stations. It's on the eastern side of Merdeka Square, a 15-minute walk from Jl Jaksa. It handles express trains to Bandung, Yogyakarta, Solo, Semarang and Surabaya. It is a well-run and modern facility with full services; it's a good place to buy tickets.

Jakarta Kota (Map p166; Jl Asemka) An art-deco gem in its namesake neighbourhood, it has limited services to points as far afield as Surabaya.

Pasar Senen (Jl Let Jen Suprapto-Kramat Bunder) To the east, mostly economy-class trains to the east and south.

Tanah Abang (Jl Jati Baru Raya) Has economy trains to the west.

ⓘ Getting Around

Jakarta's notorious traffic means that there are no great options for getting around that avoid long delays. TransJakarta Busway is the quickest way of getting around.

A new subway system, the Jakarta MRT, is sorely needed and will run along a spine from Kota in the north via Jl Thamrin to Blok M in the south. However the first section won't open before 2019.

TO/FROM THE AIRPORT

A toll road links **Soekarno-Hatta International Airport** (CGK) to the city and the journey takes 45 minutes to two hours depending on traffic and final destination. Taxis cost 150,000Rp to 220,000Rp to central Jakarta. Uber and Grab can drop off passengers, but are prohibited from airport pickups – however, you can arrange to meet a bit up from the taxi rank. A new train service links the airport with Sudirman and Manggarai stations within 45 minutes. Otherwise

Damri (Map p168; ☑ 021-550 1290, 021-460 3708; www.busbandara.com; Gambir Station; 40,000Rp; ☺ every 15 to 30 minutes) buses run to major train stations. Eventually the Transjakarta bus will also be another option along koridor 13.

Halim Perdana Kusama Airport has limited domestic service, a taxi to central Jakarta costs 100,000Rp.

All the major **train stations** in Jakarta have metered taxis available.

BUS

TransJakarta Busway is a network of air-conditioned buses that run on reserved busways (designated lanes that are closed to all other traffic). They are the quickest way to get around the city. One of the most useful routes is Koridor 1, which runs north to Kota, past Monas and along Jl Sudirman. Stations display maps (www. transjakarta.co.id/peta-rute/).

Fares cost 3500Rp to 9000Rp, which covers any destination in the network (regardless of how many koridor you use). Payment is via a stored value card (40,000Rp, including 20,000Rp credit) which is available from station ticket windows.

TAXI

➡ Taxis are inexpensive in Jakarta. All are metered and flagfall is 7500Rp, costing around 300Rp for each subsequent 100m after the first kilometre.

➡ Tipping is greatly appreciated.

➡ Not all taxi drivers speak any English. It helps to have your destination written in Bahasa.

➡ Not all taxis provide good service. The most reliable taxis are run by **Bluebird** (☑ 021-794 1234; www.bluebirdgroup.com); they can be found cruising, at taxi stands and at many hotels. Order one using their handy app.

➡ Uber (www.uber.com) and Singapore-based Grab (www.grab.com) offer ride services that can be remarkably cheap (less than US$20 for eight hours driving around town). Order and manage your rides through their apps. Note that there's no guarantee your driver will speak any English. Tolls and parking fees are extra.

Bogor

☑ 0251 / POP 1.04 MILLION

'A romantic little village' is how Sir Stamford Raffles described Bogor when he made it his country home during the British interregnum. As an oasis of unpredictable weather – it is credited with 322 thunderstorms a year – cool, quiet Bogor was the chosen retreat of colonials escaping the stifling, crowded capital.

Today, the long arm of Jakarta reaches the whole way to Bogor, infecting this satelite city with the overspill of the capital's perennial traffic and air-quality problems. The city

Bogor

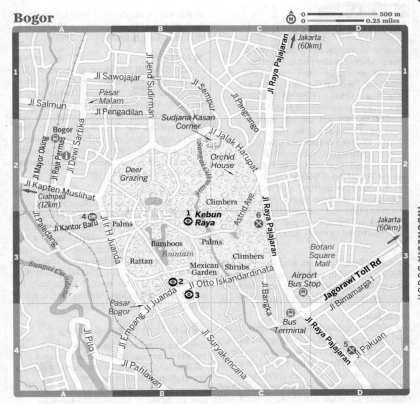

itself isn't charmless, however. The local people are quite warm and friendly, the world-class botanical gardens are still beautiful and the two are certainly worthy of a sleepover.

⊙ Sights

Tours of Bogor can be arranged through the **tourist office** (☏081 6195 3838; Jl Dewi Sartika 51; ⊙8am-6pm) for around 200,000/300,000Rp per half-day/day. The tours take in a working-class *kampung*, and various cottage industries including the gong factory and tofu and *krupuk* (prawn cracker) kitchens. Speak to them about hiking trips into Halimun National Park. For trips to the nearby Gunung Salak, an active volcano, get in touch with Ridwan Guide Bogor (www.ridwanguidebogor.com).

★ Kebun Raya
GARDENS
(Great Garden; www.krbogor.lipi.go.id; admission 25,000Rp, car 30,000Rp; ⊙8am-7pm) At the

Bogor

⊙ **Top Sights**

⊙ **Sights**

🛏 **Sleeping**

🍽 **Eating**

heart of Bogor are the fabulous botanical gardens, known as the Kebun Raya, the city's green lung of around 87 hectares. Governor General Raffles first developed a garden here, but the spacious grounds of the Istana Bogor (Presidential Palace) were expanded by Dutch botanist Professor Reinwardt, with

WORTH A TRIP

SUNDANESE EXPERIENCE

Author Yudhi Suryana (who for years lived in New Zealand) is building the tourism industry in Cianjur, one guest at a time. Through the wonderful **Chill Out Guest House** (☑ 0813 2172 9004; www.cianjuradventure.com; r incl 3 meals 250,000Rp; 🛜), and through his rare agenda of treks and driving tours, his goal is to offer independent travellers a slice of authentic Sundanese life.

The most popular of several trips is the **Traditional Village Tour** (175,000Rp per person, lunch included). Guests will take local *angkot* transport from the centre of Cianjur into the hills, where you'll follow a concrete *gang* (footpath) until it flakes away into earth.

assistance from London's Kew Gardens, and officially opened in 1817. Colonial cash crops, such as tea, cassava, tobacco and cinchona, were first developed here by Dutch botanists.

Pasar Baru MARKET
(cnr Jl Otto Iskandardinata & Suryakencana; ⊙ 6am-1pm) Jl Suryakencana, steps from the garden gates, is a whirlwind of activity as shoppers spill en masse from within the byzantine concrete halls of Pasar Baru onto the street. Inside, the morning market is awash with all manner of produce and flowers, meat and fish, second-hand clothes and more. Hot, sweltering and loud, it's a hell of a browse.

🛏 Sleeping & Eating

Tom's Homestay GUESTHOUSE $
(☑ 0877 7046 7818; www.tomshomestay.com; r incl breakfast 100,000Rp; 🛜) Offering a great local experience is this character-filled family home of Tom, who has lived here his entire life. It's a basic affair, but rooms are spacious and there's a back verandah to relax while looking onto its jungle-like backyard. It's a 10-minute walk from the train station. Tom is a wealth of knowledge on what to do in the area.

Cendana Mulia Hostel Bogor HOSTEL $
(☑ 0812-8662 795; Jl Cendana Mulia 9; dm/r incl breakfast 120,000/230,000Rp; ❄🛜) In a quiet residential street to the north of town is this popular and chilled-out guesthouse. The whole place is spotless, while the staff are super-friendly. The CCTV in the dorms is a tad off-putting but will ensure your

stuff is safe; though you'll need to change in the bathroom! Prices go up by 10,000Rp to 20,000Rp on weekends.

★**De' Leuit** INDONESIAN $$
(☑ 0251-839 0011; Jl Pakuan III; mains 40,000-105,000Rp; ⊙ 10am-10pm; 🛜🚭) The most happening eatery in Bogor. There's seating on three floors beneath a soaring, pyramid-shaped thatched roof, though the best tables are on the first two levels. It does *sate* (satay), mixed rice dishes, fried *gurame* (fish), and fried chicken, as well as a variety of local vegie dishes. Come with a group and eat Sundanese family style.

Grand Garden Café INTERNATIONAL $$
(☑ 0251-857 4070; inside Kebun Raya; mains 45,000-105,000Rp; ⊙ 8am-11pm Sun-Thu, to midnight Fri & Sat) The cafe-restaurant in the botanical gardens is a wonderfully civilised place for a bite or a drink, with sweeping views down to the water-lily ponds. It's a little pricey (especially as you need to pay the 25,000Rp entry fee; though it's free after 4pm), but the tasty international and Indonesian food and sublime setting make it an essential stop.

ⓘ Getting There & Away

Every 15 minutes or so, buses depart from Jakarta's Kampung Rambutan bus terminal (10,000Rp to 15,000Rp, 45 minutes) for Bogor's **bus station**, located in the centre of town.

Buses depart frequently to Bandung (air-con, 65,000Rp, 3½ hours), Pelabuhan Ratu (50,000Rp, three hours) and Labuan (50,000Rp, four hours). For Cianjur (25,000Rp to 30,000Rp, two hours), white minibuses (called *colt*) depart regularly from Jl Raya Pajajaran. Door-to-door *travel* minibuses go to Bandung for 100,000Rp.

Damri buses head direct to Jakarta's Soekarno-Hatta International Airport (55,000Rp, two to three hours) every 40 minutes from 2am to 8.30pm from **Jl Raya Pajajaran**.

Express trains (6000Rp to 16,000Rp, one hour) connect Bogor with the capital roughly every hour, though try to avoid travelling during rush hour. Economy trains are more frequent, but they are packed with people – some clinging to the roof.

Bandung

☑ 022 / POP 2.8 MILLION
A city of punks and prayer, serious religion and serious coffee. Here are teeming markets and good shopping, thriving cafes in reclaimed Dutch relics, palpable warmth and camaraderie on street corners and mind-numbing, air-trashing traffic almost everywhere you

look. Almost everything great and terrible about Indonesia can be found in Bandung. You may cringe at the young teens smoking and systemic poverty, and nod with respect at the city's thriving and growing middle class. Yes, Bandung has everything, except nature, and after the bottle-green hills of Cibodas, the sprawling bulk of Bandung is quite the urban reality check. But even if the local mountains are cloaked in smog, the city does make a good base for day trips to the surrounding countryside – high volcanic peaks, hot springs and tea plantations are all within reach.

There are some fine Dutch art deco structures to admire on Jl Jenderal Sudirman and Jl Asia Afrika, two of the best being the **Prama Grand Preanger** (www.preanger.aerowisata.com; Jl Asia Afrika 181) and the **Savoy Homann Hotel** (www.savoyhomann-hotel.com; Jl Asia Afrika 112), both of which have imposing facades. In the north of the city, Villa Isola is another wonderful Dutch art deco structure.

Freelance English-speaking **Enoss** (✆ 0852 2106 3788; enoss_travellers@yahoo.com) is a good-natured tour guide who runs one-day tours (400,000Rp per person) of the sights to the north and south of the city. The tours get you away from the more predictable touristy locations. He can also set up trips to Pangandaran (800,000Rp) via Garut.

🛏 Sleeping

The Attic   HOSTEL $
(✆ 0856 2101 500; www.facebook.com/theatticbedandbreakfast; Jl Juanda 130; incl breakfast; dm 120,000, d with shared/private bathroom 200,000/250,000Rp; ❄🕸) While it's 4km north of the city, the Attic remains Bandung's best budget option. It's run by friendly owners who are helpful in assisting with local travel info and offer tours in the area. The dorms and private rooms are basic, but spotlessly maintained with comfortable beds, and there's a homely kitchen for self-caterers.

Chez Bon   HOSTEL $
(✆ 0811 2015 333, 022-426 0600; www.chez-bon.com; Jl Braga 45; dm incl breakfast 150,000Rp; ❄🕸) In the heart of the action is this popular, but institutional-feeling hostel, located up a flight of scruffy marble stairs from Jl Braga. Bunks are set up in two-bed, six-bed and 16-bed arrangements. All are air-conditioned and come with lockers and wi-fi.

ℹ Getting There & Away

Five kilometres south of the city centre, Leuwi Panjang bus terminal has buses west to places such as Cianjur (normal/air-con 20,000/30,000Rp, two hours), Bogor (air-con 70,000Rp, 3½ hours) and to Jakarta's Kampung Rambutan bus terminal (50,000Rp to 65,000Rp, three hours). Buses to Bogor take at least an hour longer on weekends because of heavy traffic. There are daily trains to Jakarta, Surabaya and Yogyakarta.

Pangandaran

📶 0265 / POP 52,163

Situated on a narrow isthmus, with a broad stretch of sand on either side and a thickly forested national park on the nearby headland, Pangandaran is west Java's premier beach resort. It's built up, especially toward the south end where a jumble of concrete block towers stand shoulder to shoulder across the channel from the national park.

A 6000Rp admission charge is officially levied at the gates on entering Pangandaran.

◉ Sights

Pangandaran National Park   NATIONAL PARK
(Taman Nasional Pangandaran; weekday/weekend 215,000/315,000Rp; ⊙ 7am-5pm) The Pangandaran National Park, which takes up the entire southern end of Pangandaran, is a wild expanse of dense forest. Within its boundaries live porcupines, *kijang* (barking deer), hornbills, monitor lizards and monkeys (including Javan gibbons). Small bays within the park enclose pretty tree-fringed beaches. The park is divided into two sections: the recreation park and the jungle.

Due to environmental degradation, the jungle is usually off limits. Well-maintained paths allow the recreation park to be explored, passing small caves (including Gua Jepang, which was used by the Japanese in WWII), the remains of a Hindu temple, Batu Kalde, and a nice beach on the eastern side. English-speaking guides hang around both entrances and charge around 100,000Rp (per group of four) for a two-hour walk or up to 200,000Rp for a five-hour trip. Pangandaran's best swimming beach, white-sand Pasir Putih, lies on the western side of the national park.

☞ Tours

It's still possible to do the once-popular backwater boat trip east of Pangandaran, via Majingklak harbour to Cilacap on the Citandui River, but there are no scheduled connections so you'll have to charter your own *compreng* (wooden boat). Boatmen

Pangandaran

in Majingklak will do the three-hour trip for 550,000Rp. Alternatively, you can call ahead through a tour agent in Pangandaran to Kalipucang harbour and organise a boat from there for the same price.

Popular Green Canyon and Green Valley tours (350,000Rp per person) depart from Pangandaran and usually combine 'home industry' visits that take in a sugar, *tahu* (tofu) or *krupuk* (prawn cracker) kitchen factory, as well as a *wayang golek* (three-dimensional wooden puppet) maker. There are also tours to Paradise Island, an uninhabited nearby island with good beaches (including a 5km white-sand beach) and waves.

Mas Rudin (📱 0813 8005 6724; www.pangandaran-guide.com) is a tremendous local guide who operates out of **MM Books** (Jl Pasanggrahan; ⊙9am-7pm) and offers fair prices on a range of tours. His website is a wealth of information. The guesthouses can organise guides for you as well.

🛏 Sleeping & Eating

Rinjani Homestay   GUESTHOUSE **$**
(📱 0813 2302 0263, 0265-639757; rinjanipnd@gmail.com; s/d incl breakfast with fan 100,000/130,000Rp, with air-con 130,000/160,000Rp; ❇🛜) A welcoming family-run place with 10 pleasant, tiled rooms with wood furnishings, private porches and clean but cold-water bathrooms. Sweet, quiet and good value. Holiday periods see price increases of up to 100,000Rp.

Mini Tiga Homestay   GUESTHOUSE **$**
(📱0265-639436; www.minitigahomestay.weebly.com; off Jl Pamugaran Bulak Laut; s/d/tr incl breakfast with fan 125,000/175,000/195,000Rp, with air-con 216,000/270,000/295,000Rp; @🛜) Great brick and wood chalets with reasonable rates. The 13 rooms are clean, spacious and have nice decorative touches – including bamboo walls and batik wall hangings. All have en-suite bathrooms and Western toilets. Good tours and transport tickets are also offered, including a popular tour of the nearby Green Canyon (300,000Rp).

★ **Adam's Homestay**   HOTEL **$$**
(📱0265-639396, 0813 2146 1636; www.adamshomestay.com; off Jl Pamugaran Bulak Laut; r incl breakfast 350,000/488,000Rp; ❇🛜🏊) Pangandaran's only real gem is a wonderfully relaxed and stylish guesthouse with artistically presented rooms (many with balconies, beamed ceilings and outdoor bathrooms) spread around a luxurious pool and land-

scaped verdant Balinese garden bursting with exotic plants, lotus ponds and birdlife. There's good international and local food available, too, including wonderful breakfasts cooked by German owner, Kirsten.

Rumah Makan Christi   INDONESIAN **$**
(Jl Pamugaran; meals 20,000-40,000Rp; ⊘7am-10pm) This clean, orderly *rumah makan* (restaurant), with a large interior and bench seating outside, is a good bet for local food. It fries, grills and stews tofu, chicken and fish, and offers a range of vegetarian dishes too. All authentic Javanese. Pick and mix to your pleasure, then sit at the common table and dine with your new friends.

⭐**Pasar Ikan**   SEAFOOD **$$**
(Fish Market; Jl Raya Timor; fish around 90,000Rp; ⊘11am-10pm) Pangandaran's terrific fish market consists of more than a dozen large, open-sided restaurants just off the east beach. **Karya Bahari** is considered the best – which is why it's so crowded – but all operate on exactly the same basis.

⭐**Bamboo Beach Café**   BAR
(Jl Pamugaran; ⊘8.30am-late) This fine beach bar lines up nicely with the waves, and is the perfect location to scout the swell with a cold Bintang in hand, particularly at sunset. Benches and tables with thatched umbrellas wander all the way to the beach. At the time of writing they (and many other beach warung) were about to relocate to the beach 5km west of town.

❶ Getting There & Away

Pangandaran can be a frustratingly slow and complicated place to get to. The nearest train station, Sidareja, is 41km away. Speak to Mas Rudin (p176) about organising train tickets. You'll need to pay a 6000Rp tourist levy upon entering town.

Most *patas* (express) buses to Jakarta and Bandung leave from the **main bus terminal**, 1.5km north from the beach and tourist centre. The **Budiman** (☑0265-339854; www.budimanbus.com) bus depot, about 2km west of Pangandaran along Jl Merdeka also have regular departures, but most swing by the main terminal too. Buses run to Bandung roughly every hour (65,000Rp to 78,000Rp, six hours) and to Jakarta's Kampung Rambutan terminal (85,000Rp to 95,000Rp, eight to nine hours). To Bandung, there are also two daily **Sari Harum** (☑0265-607 7065) door-to-door *travel* minibuses (100,000Rp, six hours).

To Yogyakarta, Budiman runs five or so minibus services daily (90,000Rp nine hours), while

Estu Travel (☑0812 2679 2456, 027-4668 4567) has minibuses (130,000Rp, nine hours) leaving at 9am and 8pm. Both leave from the main bus terminal.

From the main bus terminal **Sari Bakti Utama Bus Depot** there are hourly buses to both Banjar (30,000Rp, two hours) and Sidareja (30,000Rp, 1½ hours) for train connections.

❶ Getting Around

Pangandaran's brightly painted becak start at around 10,000Rp and require heavy negotiation; expect to pay around 20,000Rp from the bus terminal to the main beach area. Bicycles can be rented for 20,000Rp per day, and motorcycles cost around 70,000Rp per day.

Batu Karas
☑0265 / POP 3000

The idyllic fishing village and surfing hot spot of Batu Karas, 32km west of Pangandaran, is one of the most enjoyable places to kick back in west Java. It's as pretty as a picture – a tiny one-lane fishing settlement, with two beaches that are separated by a wooded promontory.

The main surfing beach is the smaller one, and it's a sweet bay tucked between two rocky headlands. The other is a long black-sand arc parked with pontoon fishing boats that shove off each night looking for fresh catch in the tides. There's good swimming, with sheltered sections that are calm enough for a dip, but many visitors are here for the breaks, and there's a lot of surf talk.

On weekends, however, it can become inundated with domestic tourists. The best time to surf and relax here is midweek.

This is one of the best places in Java to learn to surf. The Point (offshore from Java Cove) is perfect for beginners with paddle-in access from the beach, and slow, peeling waves over a sandy bottom. Other waves include The Reef, a deep-water reef break, and Bulak Bender, a challenging right-hander in the open ocean that's a 40-minute ride away by bike or boat.

🛏 Sleeping & Eating

⭐**Treehouse**   GUESTHOUSE **$**
(☑0821 3087 6531, 0822 2000 9155; Jl Pantai Indah; r 150,000-250,000Rp) Offering a unique choice is this charming, double-storey matchbox house with colourful painted Mediterranean-style shutters, and named after the gigantic tree that grows within the

building. Its two floors are managed by separate owners, but both have a rustic, vibrant feel and comfy beds. The upper floor has an additional loft space and can sleep six – making it exceptional value.

Bonsai Bungalow　　　　　GUESTHOUSE $
(✆ 0812 2197 8950; Jl Pantai Indah; r with fan/air-con 200,000/250,000Rp; @) An upgrade from the other beach bungalows is this laid-back choice across the road from the beach, with spartan rooms with attached bathroom, a porch to hang out and an option of air-con. There's no food here but they can arrange beer.

BK Homestay　　　　　HOMESTAY $
(✆ 0265-7015 708, 0822 6023 7802; www.batu-karashomestay.com; Jl Pantai Indah; r incl breakfast 200,000Rp; 🛜) Terrific-value, fan-cooled rooms, all with floor-to-ceiling glass on one side, high ceilings, wood floors and wi-fi in the restaurant below. No hot water, but that won't matter much here. It's set off the main beach parking lot, right in the centre of things.

Beach Corner　　　　　INDONESIAN $
(mains 15,000-40,000Rp; ⊗6am-10pm) Plonked directly on the sand on the edge of the surf beach is this aptly named warung, serving Indonesian and Western mains, cold beer and strong Javanese coffee.

❶ Getting There & Away

There's no public transport to Batu Karas but it can be reached from Pangandaran by taking a bus to Cijulang (10,000Rp) then an *ojek* for 20,000Rp to 30,000Rp. Or you can hire a motorbike in Pangandaran (per day 50,000Rp) and drive yourself, or book a pricey private car transfer (300,000Rp). An outrageous rate given the distances involved, but that's the going rate in high season; bargain for low-season discounts.

Wonosobo

✆ 0286 / POP 113,000

Bustling Wonosobo is the main gateway to the Dieng Plateau. At 900m above sea level in the central mountain range, it has a comfortable climate and is a typical country town with a busy market.

If you value comfort, it's easy to base yourself here in one of the town's good-quality hotels and get up to Dieng, which is just over an hour away and served by regular buses.

Duta Homestay (✆ 0813-9337 9954, 0286-321674; Jl Rumah Sakit III; d incl breakfast 200,000-300,000Rp; ✳🛜) is a rather elegant guesthouse that's been hosting travellers for

years. The attractive rooms have exposed stonework and are decorated with antiques.

Locals rate **Shanti Rahayu** (Jl A Yani 122; meals 12,500-35,000Rp; ⊗8am-9pm) as one of the best for authentic central Javanese cuisine; the chicken curries are great.

❶ Getting There & Away

Wonosobo's bus terminal is 4km out of town on the Magelang road. There are buses connecting Wonosobo with Yogyakarta (60,000Rp, four hours), Bandung (80,000Rp, 8½ hours), Jakarta (100,000Rp, 10 to 12 hours), Borobudur (25,000Rp, three hours) and Magelang (15,000Rp, 40 minutes) until about 4pm.

Hourly buses go to Semarang (45,000Rp, four hours), passing through Ambarawa (25,000Rp, 2½ hours). Frequent buses to Dieng (15,000Rp, one hour) leave throughout the day (the last at 5pm) and continue on to Batur; you can catch them on Jl Rumah Sakit, 100m from Duta Homestay. **Sumber Alam** (✆ 0286-321589; www.sumberalam.co.id) has door-to-door minibuses to Yogyakarta (60,000Rp, 3½ hours) via Borobudur (50,000Rp, 2½ hours),

Dieng Plateau

✆ 0286

The spectacular, lofty volcanic plateau of Dieng (Abode of the Gods), a glorious, verdant, fertile landscape laced with terraced potato and tobacco fields, is home to some of the oldest Hindu architecture in Java. More than 400 temples, most dating from the 8th and 9th centuries, originally covered this 2000m-high plain, but they were abandoned and forgotten and only rediscovered in 1856 by the archaeologist Van Kinsbergen.

These squat, simple temples, while of great archaeological importance, can be slightly underwhelming for non-experts. Rather, Dieng's beautiful scenery is the main reason to make the long journey to this isolated region. Any number of walks across the volcanically active plateau are possible – to mineral lakes, steaming craters or even the highest village in Java, Sembungan. Dieng is also base camp for the popular climb to Gunung Prau peak. Most start hiking in the wee hours to catch the sunrise on the summit.

❍ Sights & Activities

Arjuna Complex　　　　　HINDU TEMPLE
(incl Candi Gatutkaca & Kawah Sikidang 30,000Rp; ⊗7am-6pm) The five main temples that form the Arjuna Complex are clustered together on the central plain. They are Shiva temples,

but like the other Dieng temples they have been named after the heroes of the *wayang* (Javanese puppet theatre performance) of the Mahabharata epic: Arjuna, Puntadewa, Srikandi, Sembadra and Semar. All have mouth-shaped doorways and strange bell-shaped windows and some locals leave offerings, burn incense and meditate here.

Telaga Warna
LAKE

(weekdays/weekends 100,000/150,000Rp; ⊙7am-5pm) Exquisitely beautiful and ringed by highland forest, the lake has turquoise and cobalt hues from the bubbling sulphur deposits around its shores. To lose the crowds, follow the trail counterclockwise to the adjoining lake, Telaga Pengilon, and past holy Gua Semar, a meditation cave. Then for a lovely prospect of the lakes return to the main road via a narrow trail that leads around Telaga Pengilon and up a terraced hillside.

Gunung Prau
HIKING

A popular, steep, three-hour trek to Gunung Prau (2565m) begins in the village at 3am. The top isn't a defined peak but a rolling savannah with views of five volcanoes and eight mountains. Several outfitters offer the trek. Losmen Budjono does the deal for 250,000Rp. Bring extra water.

🛏 Sleeping

Losmen Budjono
GUESTHOUSE $

(☑0852 2664 5669, 0286-642046; Jl Raya Dieng, Km26; r with shared/private bathroom 100,000/200,000Rp; 🛜) This simple, social place has been hosting backpackers for years and has a certain ramshackle charm with basic, clean, economy rooms. The pleasant, orderly restaurant downstairs (mains 12,000Rp to 25,000Rp) has tablecloths and lace curtains. Good three-hour tours to Gunung Prau are offered for 250,000Rp per person, departing at 2.30am. It's close to the turn-off for Wonosobo.

Homestay Flamboyan
HOMESTAY $

(☑0852 2744 3029, 0813-2760 5040; www.flamboyandieng.com; Jl Raya Dieng 40; r 200,000Rp; 🛜) One of three homestays on this corner, and all are decent value. The carpets may be stained, but the cubist paint jobs are creative. All rooms have private bathrooms, high ceilings and homely furnishings.

❶ Getting There & Away

Dieng is 26km from Wonosobo, which is the usual access point by bus (15,000Rp, 45 minutes

to one hour). It's possible to reach Dieng from Yogyakarta in one day (including a stop at Borobudur) by public bus, provided you leave early enough (around 6am) to make the connection; the route is Yogyakarta–Borobudur–Magelang–Wonosobo–Dieng.

Travel agents including **Jogja Trans** (☑0816 426 0124, 0274-439 8495; www.jogjatrans.com) in Yogyakarta offer day trips including to Borobudur for around 750,000Rp to 800,000Rp per car.

Yogyakarta
☑0274 / POP 636,660

If Jakarta is Java's financial and industrial powerhouse, Yogyakarta is its soul. Central to the island's artistic and intellectual heritage, Yogyakarta (pronounced 'Jogjakarta' and called Yogya, 'Jogja', for short), is where the Javanese language is at its purest, the arts at their brightest and its traditions at their most visible.

Fiercely independent and protective of its customs – and still headed by its sultan, whose *kraton* (walled city palace) remains the hub of traditional life – contemporary Yogya is nevertheless a huge urban centre (the entire metropolitan area is home to more than 3.3 million people) complete with shiny malls, fast-food chains and traffic jams, even as it remains a stronghold of batik, gamelan and ritual.

Put it all together and you have Indonesia's coolest, most liveable and lovable city, with street art, galleries, coffee shops and cultural attractions everywhere you look. It's also a perfect base for Indonesia's most important archaeological sites, Borobudur and Prambanan.

◎ Sights

★ Affandi Museum
MUSEUM

(☑0274-562593; www.affandi.org; Jl Laksda Adisucipto 167; adult/student/child under 6yr 75,000/35,000Rp/free, camera phone 20,000Rp, mobile phone with camera 10,000Rp; ⊙9am-4pm Mon-Sat) One of Indonesia's most celebrated artists, Affandi (1907–90) lived and worked in a wonderfully quirky self-designed riverside home studio, about 6km east of the town centre. Today it's the Affandi Museum, a must for any self-respecting art lover. It has an extensive collection of his abstract paintings, an expressionist style featuring his distinctive curled strokes reminiscent of Van Gogh. Check out his car, a real boy-racer's dream: a lime-green and yellow customised 1967 Galant with an oversized rear spoiler.

Yogyakarta

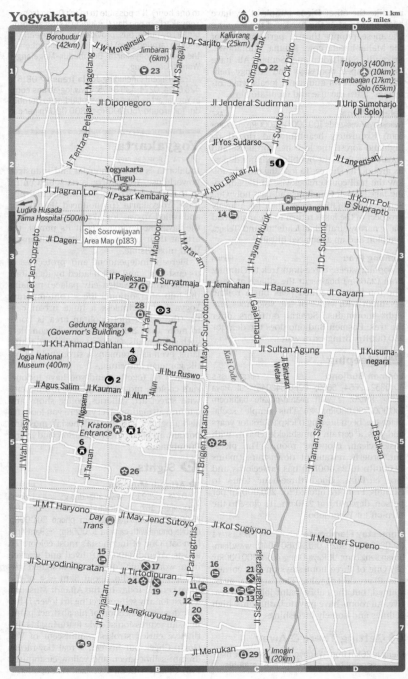

0 ——— 1 km
0 ——— 0.5 miles

Borobudur (42km)
Jl W Monginsidi
Jimbaran (6km)
Jl Dr Sarjito
Kaliurang (25km)
Jl Cik Ditiro
Jl AM Sangaji
Jl Simanjuntak
23
22
Jl Magelang
Jl Diponegoro
Jl Jenderal Sudirman
Jl Urip Sumoharjo (Jl Solo)
Tojoyo 3 (400m); (10km); Prambanan (17km); Solo (65km)
Jl Tentara Pelajar
Jl Suroto
Jl Yos Sudarso
Jl Langensari
5
Jl Abu Bakar Ali
Yogyakarta (Tugu)
Jl Jlagran Lor
Jl Pasar Kembang
Jl Kom Pol B Suprapto
Lempuyangan
Ludira Husada Tama Hospital (500m)
14
Jl Dagen
Jl Hayam Wuruk
Jl Let Jen Suprapto
Jl Maliobroro
Jl Mataram
Jl Dr Sutomo
See Sosrowijayan Area Map (p183)
Jl Pajeksan
27
Jl Suryatmaja
Jl Jeminahan
Jl Bausasran
Jl Gayam
28
3
Jl A Yani
Gedung Negara (Governor's Building)
Jl Mayor Suryotomo
Jl Gajahmada
Jl KH Ahmad Dahlan
4
Jl Senopati
Jl Sultan Agung
Jl Kusuma-negara
Jogja National Museum (400m)
Jl Ibu Ruswo
Kali Code
Jl Bintaran Wetan
Jl Agus Salim
Jl Kauman
2
Jl Alun
Jl Ngasem
Alun
Jl Taman Siswa
18
Kraton Entrance
1
25
Jl Brigjen Katamso
Jl Batikan
6
26
Jl Wahid Hasyim
Jl Taman
Jl MT Haryono
Day Trans
Jl May Jend Sutoyo
Jl Kol Sugiyono
Jl Menteri Supeno
Jl Suryodiningratan
15
17
Jl Tirtodipuran
16
21
24
19
11
7
12
8
10 13
Jl Panjaitan
Jl Parangtritis
Jl Mangkuyudan
20
Jl Sisingamangaraja
Jl Menukan
9
29
Imogiri (20km)

Taman Sari
PALACE

(Map p180; Jl Taman; admission 15,000Rp, camera 2000Rp; ⏱9am-3pm) Just southwest of the *kraton* is this complex, which once served as a splendid pleasure park of palaces, pools and waterways for the sultan and his entourage. It's said that the sultan had the Portuguese architect of this elaborate retreat executed, to keep his hidden pleasure rooms secret. Built between 1758 and 1765, the complex was damaged first by Diponegoro's Java War, and an earthquake in 1865 helped finish the job.

Stadion Kridosono
PUBLIC ART

(Map p180; Jl Yos Sudarso) When it comes to street art, Yogya is one giant gallery with every wall covered in graffiti, stencils, murals and pasteups. A good spot to see some of this work is the circular concrete wall of this old football stadium, which is a canvas for edgy, political and irreverent subject matter.

Jogja National Museum
GALLERY

(☑0274-586105; www.jogjanationalmuseum.com; Jl Amri Yahya 1; ⏱10am-9pm) FREE Yogyakarta's premier contemporary art gallery is located within a massive multistorey building that was built as an art faculty back in the 1950s. Today it exhibits diverse shows by Indonesian artists that change monthly; check its website for details. There are also regular local bands who play here and a cool **record store** (☑0856 3425 7226).

Kraton
PALACE

(Map p180; ☑0274-373321; Jl Rotowijayan Blok 1; admission 15,000Rp, camera 1000Rp, guided tour by donation; ⏱8.30am-2pm Sat-Thu; to 1pm Fri) The cultural and political heart of this fascinating city is the huge palace of the sultans of Yogya, the *kraton*. Effectively a walled city, this unique compound is home to around 25,000 people, and has its own market, shops, batik and silver cottage industries, schools and mosques. Around 1000 of its residents are employed by the sultan. Alas, the treasures here are poorly displayed.

Pasar Beringharjo
MARKET

(Map p180; Jl A Yani; ⏱9am-5pm) Yogya's main market, 800m north of the *kraton,* is a lively and fascinating place. The front section has a wide range of batik – mostly inexpensive *batik cap* (stamped batik). More interesting is the old section towards the back. Crammed with warungs (food stalls) and a huge variety of fruit and vegetables, this is still very much a traditional market. The range of *rempah rempah* (spices) at the rear of the ground floor is quite something. Come early in the morning for maximum atmosphere.

Sono-Budoyo Museum
MUSEUM

(Map p180; ☑0274-376775; www.sonobudoyo.com; Jl Pangurakan 6; 5000Rp; ⏱8am-3.30pm Tue-Thu, Sat & Sun, to 2.30pm Fri) This treasure chest is the pick of Yogya's museums, with a first-class collection of Javanese art, including *wayang kulit* puppets, *topeng* (masks), kris and batik. It also has a courtyard packed with Hindu statuary and artefacts from further afield, including superb Balinese carvings. Wayang kulit performances are held here.

☞ Tours

Tour agents on Jl Prawirotaman and in the Sosrowijayan area offer a host of tour options at similar prices. Typical day tours are Dieng, Gedung Songo and Ambarawa; Prambanan; Borobudur and Parangtritis; and Solo and Candi Sukuh.

★ Via Via Tours
TOURS
(Map p180; ☎ 0274-386557; www.viaviajogja.com; Jl Prawirotaman I 30) This famous cafe-restaurant (p184) offers a dozen different tours, including some really creative options. There are numerous bike and motorbike tours, including a backroad trip to Prambanan (135,000Rp), foodie tours (from 250,000Rp), city walks (120,000Rp to 135,000Rp) and even a *jamu* (herbal medicine) and massage tour (235,000Rp to 275,000Rp) that takes in a visit to a specialist market. Tours to east Java are also offered. It also offers yoga classes in the morning (9am or 9.30am) and evening (6.30pm). All cost 60,000Rp per person.

Kaleidoscope of Java
TOURS
(Map p180; ☎ 0812 2711 7439; www.kaleidoscopeofjavatour.com; Gang Sartono 823, Rumah Eyang) Fascinating tours of the Borobudur region. The day trip (300,000Rp) from Yogya involves visits to Borobudur, Pawon and Mendut temples and a monastery, cottage industries and Javanese gamelan performance. Tours include meals, guide and transport, but not the entrance fee to the temples.

✿✿ Festivals & Events

Jogja Art Weeks
ART
(www.jogjaartweeks.com; ⊙ mid May–mid Jun) Another example of why Yogya is one of the hippest cities in Asia is this month-long arts festival featuring hundreds of events hosted in galleries and art spaces around the city. Expect art shows, music performances, poetry and film screenings. Check its website for dates and schedule of events.

Gerebeg
CULTURAL
Three Gerebeg festivals are Java's most colourful and grand processions. In traditional court dress, palace guards and retainers, not to mention large floats of decorated mountains of rice, all make their way to the **Mesjid Besar** (Map p180; Grand Mosque; off Jl Alun-Alun Utara), west of the *kraton,* to the sound of prayer and gamelan music. The dates change each year, so contact the tourist information centre for an exact schedule.

🛏 Sleeping

Yogya has Java's best range of hostels, guesthouses and hotels, many offering excellent value for money. During the high season – July, August and Christmas and New Year – you should book ahead.

🛏 Sosrowijayan Area

This area is very popular with backpackers as most of Yogya's cheap guesthouses are in the souk-like maze of *gang* (alleys) within this traditional neighbourhood. But the best part about staying in what feels like a *bule* (foreigner) ghetto is that those little lanes spill out onto Jl Sosrowijayan and are within a short stroll of the more authentic Jl Malioboro.

Andrea Hotel
GUESTHOUSE $
(Map p183; ☎ 0274-563502; www.andreaholteljogja.wordpress.com; Sosrowijayan/140 Gang II; incl breakfast s/d with fan & shared bathroom 140,000/160,000Rp, r with fan & private bathroom 175,000Rp, r with air-con from 230,000Rp; ❄🛜) The Swiss-owned Andrea is a charming guesthouse with rooms fitted with stylish fixtures and good-quality beds. Even the rooms without an en-suite still have a bathroom allocated for their private use. There's a slim street terrace where you can watch the Sosrowijayan world go by with a drink in your hand.

Wakeup Homestay
HOSTEL $
(Map p183; ☎ 0274-514762; www.wakeuphomestay.com; Jl Gandekan 44; 4-/10-bed dm 150,000/135,000Rp; ❄@🛜) Not a homestay at all; instead Wakeup is a multistory hostel that's well run, functional and immaculately presented. All the dorms (mixed and female-only) are pod-style and air-conditioned, though it's BYO padlock for lockers. It's well placed in a touristy locale, close to all the action. Breakfast is served on its rooftop terrace.

Laura's Backpackers 523
HOSTEL $
(Map p180; ☎ 0812 2525 6319; www.facebook.com/backpackers523; Jl Hansip Karnowaluyo 523; dm incl breakfast 95,000Rp; ❄🛜) Located down a narrow street in an appealing local neighborhood is this popular backpackers split between its two nearby properties. The main building is its main hangout area with

Sosrowijayan Area

a leafy courtyard that doubles as a vegetarian cafe. Dorms have curtains for privacy, air-con, power points and lamps. Staff are very friendly and Laura's an excellent source of local info.

Tiffa GUESTHOUSE $
(Map p183; ☑ 0274-512841; tiffaartshop@yahoo. com; Jl Sosrowijayan Wetan Gt II 12; s/d/tr incl breakfast with fan 100,000/150,000/175,000Rp, with aircon 150,000/175,000/200,000Rp; ❋☎) A tidy little losmen owned by a hospitable family, with a handful of smallish, quirky and charming rooms, each with private *mandi*. There's a communal balcony where you can tuck into your free (but basic) jam-and-toast breakfast and slurp wonderful Javanese coffee.

Dewi Homestay HOMESTAY $
(Map p183; ☑ 0274-516014; dewihomestay@hotmail.com; Jl Sosrowijayan 115; r incl breakfast with fan/air-con 150,000/250,000Rp; ❋☎) An attractive, long-running place that has character with a lovely leafy, shady garden and Javanese adornments. Rooms are charming and spacious, and many have four-poster beds draped with mosquito nets. At reception there's a book exchange and cold Bintang in the fridge.

★1001 Malam HOTEL $$
(Map p183; ☑ 0274-515087; www.1001malamhotel. com; Sosrowijayan Wetan I/57, Gang II; s/d incl breakfast from 350,000/400,000Rp; ❋☎) A beautifully built Moroccan-style structure complete with hand-carved wooden doorways and a lovely Moorish courtyard decked out with palm trees and classy craftsman tiles. The rooms themselves aren't nearly as stylish as the common areas, but are clean and comfortable enough, and livened up with murals on the walls.

Sosrowijayan Area

Activities, Courses & Tours

Pawon Cokelat Guesthouse HOTEL $$
(Map p183; ☑ 0878 7880 9008; www.pawoncokelat. com; Gang 1 102; r incl breakfast weekday/weekend 320,000/370,000Rp; ❋☎) An unexpected change up from the humble losmen in the area is this hipster-style guesthouse with a facade draped in a vertical garden and industrial-chic touches. Its hotel-standard rooms have exposed brick, comfy beds and ice-cold air-con, but are slightly overpriced. There's a lobby cafe for meals and coffee, and a rooftop hangout. Not much English is spoken.

Jalan Prawirotaman

This area has both tasteful budget places mixed in with some boutique midrange choices. Plenty have pools and the choice of restaurants is excellent. But it does feel like a tourist enclave within an Indonesian city.

★ Abrabracadabra
HOSTEL $

(Map p180; ☑0857 2792 6925, 0274-287 2906; Jl Minggiran Baru 19; incl breakfast dm from 70,000Rp, r 200,000-240,000Rp; ❀ ❒ ☀) Arty, vibrant and original, this tiny hostel is a cool choice to suit those looking for something a bit different. Its small plunge pool is surrounded by leafy plants, and its rooms are individually decorated in styles ranging from street art and surfer theme, to jungle room or junkyard-industrial. The dorms are also nice, offering full privacy with curtains and power points.

Omah Jegok Homestay
GUESTHOUSE $

(☑0821 3374 9524; www.omahjegok.weebly. com; Jl Plataran, Kashian; r incl breakfast from 130,000Rp; ❒) One for cat- and dog-lovers is this arty homestay that doubles as a shelter for rescued animals. It's a basic set up with only a couple of rooms in a forested residential area on the confluence of two small rivers, 5km from downtown Yogya.

Via Via
GUESTHOUSE $

(Map p180; ☑0274-374748; www.viaviajogja. com; Prawirotaman 3/514A; d/r incl breakfast from 110,000/195,000Rp; ❀ ❒ ☀) Part of the expanding Via Via empire, this fine guesthouse enjoys a quiet side-street location not far from the mothership **cafe-restaurant** (Map p180; ☑0274-386557; Jl Prawirotaman I 30; mains 27,000-86,000Rp; ⏱7.30am-10pm; ❒). It has seven stylish rooms with high ceilings, good-quality beds and semi-open bathrooms, as well as two clean, air-conditioned dorms. Out back there's a garden and a swimming pool, which features a wall mural by renowned local street artist Anagard.

Kampoeng Djawa Hotel
GUESTHOUSE $

(Map p180; ☑0274-378318; Jl Prawirotaman I 40; incl breakfast r with fan & shared/private bathroom 125,000Rp/200,000Rp, with private bathroom & air-con 235,000Rp; ❀ @ ❒) Occupying a long, thin house, this place has character to spare. The Javanese-influenced rooms (in five price categories) have artistic touches including exposed brick walls, mosaic tiling and pebble-walled bathrooms. There's a peaceful rear garden for your complimentary tea or coffee (available all day) and afternoon snack. Staff are eager to help.

Rumah Eyang
GUESTHOUSE $

(Map p180; ☑0812 2711 7439; Gang Sartono 823, off Jl Parangtritis; r incl breakfast from 200,000Rp; ❀ @ ❒) A stylish suburban house that's been converted into an inviting guesthouse and art space. Rooms are simple and comfortable, but the real benefit here is that Atik, the Javanese author, owner and tour guide, is a font of knowledge about the region and offers great tours (p182) to Borobudur. There's great Javanese coffee and a library full of cultural books.

Delta Homestay
GUESTHOUSE $

(Map p180; ☑0274-327051; www.dutagardenhotel. com/en/homestay; Jl Prawirotaman II 597A; s/d with shared bathroom from 150,000/175,000Rp, s/d with bathroom 225,000/250,000Rp, with bathroom & air-con 275,000/300,000Rp; ❀ ❒ ☀) A sunny backstreet guesthouse with a selection of small but perfectly formed rooms built from natural materials, each with a porch, grouped around a pool. It's peaceful here, staff are welcoming and breakfast is included.

★ Adhisthana
BOUTIQUE HOTEL $

(Map p180; ☑0274-413888; www.adhisthanahotel. com; Jl Prawirotaman II 613; dm/r incl breakfast from 135,000/425,000Rp; @ ❒ ☀) Featuring an intriguing juxtaposition of colonial house and designer hotel is this elegant option. Its facade is decorated with colourful Mediterranean-style window shutters, and within lies plenty of boutique touches intertwined with a classic motel configuration of rooms and dorms (both stylish and comfortable) built around a small pool lined with palm trees.

Ostic House
HOSTEL $

(Map p180; ☑0877 3955 4438, 0274-378930; www. ostichostel.com; Jl Suryodiningratan 10B; dm/d incl breakfast from 118,000/288,000Rp; ❀ ❒) Occupying a stunning space that was a former art gallery is this unique hostel that's run by Oscar and his friendly team. Dorm beds have full privacy with curtains, lamps and power points, while private rooms are spacious and well furnished. The enormous common area has a soaring ceiling and plenty of couches, board games, foosball table and large TV.

★ Greenhost
BOUTIQUE HOTEL $$$

(Map p180; ☑0274-389777; www.greenhosthotel. com; Jl Prawirotaman II 629; r incl breakfast from 675,000Rp; ❀ @ ❒ ☀) This raw, natural-wood and polished-concrete structure dripping with vines is a terrific boutique hotel. The lobby is the ground floor of a dramatic atrium, and its lemongrass-scented rooms offer polished-concrete floors, raw-wood furnishings and floating beds. In the lobby there's an indoor saltwater pool, and stylish restaurant doing seasonal farm-to-table cuisine. Its ritzy rooftop bar (p186) is another highlight.

Eating

Wanderlust Coffee Division   CAFE $
(Map p183; ☑ 0274- 2921 902; Gang I 96; mains from 30,000Rp; ☺10am-10pm; ☑) This Dutch-owned cafe is a cool little hang-out, with awesome coffee, cold beers and an interesting menu of vegetarian fusion cuisine. Choose from original items such as *tempe rendang* to its signature pulled jackfruit burger, which comes with sweet-potato fries and chilli mayo.

Simple Plant   VEGAN $
(Map p180; ☑ 0821 3374 9524, 0821 7217 8303; www.facebook.com/simpleplantvegetarianrestoandartspace; Jl Prawirotaman I 32; mains 28,000-32,000Rp; ☺10am-10pm; ☎☑) Set up by a young couple is this vegan diner serving *tempe* burgers, crispy mushrooms and Javanese dishes, along with fresh juices and cold beer. It's affiliated with various animal-rights groups and the co-owner is the bassist from Shaggy Dog (a well-known Yogya ska band) who also has Omah Jegok Homestay.

Superman II Resto   INDONESIAN, WESTERN $
(Map p183; Gang 2; mains 20,000-32,000Rp; ☺8am-11pm; ☎) Just like the movie, the sequel is better than the original, with Superman II opening up in the next street along. At this open-air restaurant you'll encounter rabbits bouncing about, and a miniature banana grove at the back with random sheep and chickens. Both the Western and Indo mains and breakfasts are cheap and tasty.

Tojoyo 3   INDONESIAN $
(☑0274-552750; Jl Urip Sumoharjo 133; dishes 4000-12,500Rp; ☺11am-10.30pm) A smoky, salty, tiled den of turmeric-rubbed, fried-chicken iniquity. Dishes are impossibly cheap and that lean-yet-juicy *kampung* chicken is improbably good. No wonder all the tables and benches are packed with locals, here to get their deep-fried fix. It's set on a commercial strip east of Jl Malioboro.

Oxen Free   PUB FOOD $
(Map p183; www.oxenfree.net; Jl Sosrowijayan 2; mains 30,000-60,000Rp; ☺11am-2am Sun-Thu, to 3am Fri & Sat; ☎) A popular drinking spot in an old colonial building, Oxen also has a menu of pub food enjoyed in its beer garden or front bar. It does all-day Western breakfasts and brunch, burgers, Indo mains, roast dinners, and a mean *tempe* steak for vegos.

Bu Ageng   INDONESIAN $
(Map p180; ☑0274-387191; Jl Tirtodipuran 13; mains 13,000-32,000Rp; ☺11am-10pm Tue-Sun) Traditional Javanese dishes like *eyem penggeng*, chicken simmered in spiced coconut cream then grilled, are served in a tasteful interior space with wood columns and a bamboo-mat ceiling twirling with fans. Bu Ageng's adventurous array of mixed rice platters includes dishes such as beef tongue, smoked fish or beef stewed in coconut milk. It even does a durian bread pudding.

Tempo del Gelato   GELATO $
(Map p180; ☑0274-373272; www.facebook.com/tempogelato; Jl Prawirotaman I 43; small/medium/large 20,000/40,000/60,000Rp; ☺10am-11pm) A stone-and-glass chapel to Italian ice cream. Flavours on rotation include ginger, *kemangi* (lemon basil), dragon fruit, 'hot and spicy', lemongrass and green tea, to go with all the better known varieties.

Milas   VEGETARIAN $
(Map p180; ☑0851-0142 3399; Jl Prawirotaman IV 127; dishes 18,000-45,000Rp; ☺3-9pm Tue-Fri, noon-9pm Sat & Sun; ☑🏠) A great retreat from the streets, this secret-garden vegetarian restaurant is part of a project centre for street youth. It offers meat-free cooking including Indonesian mains, burgers, sandwiches, salads and desserts. There's no alcohol but there's an excellent choice of juices, smoothies and coffee. Every Wednesday and Saturday there's an organic farmers market here from 10am to 1pm.

Bedhot Resto   INTERNATIONAL $
(Map p183; ☑0274-512452; Gang II; mains 23,000-44,000Rp; ☺8am-11pm; ☎☑) *Bedhot* means 'creative' in old Javanese and this place is one of the more stylish warungs in Sosrowijayan. There's tasty Indonesian and international food – a cut above usual tourist fare – plus cold beer, fresh juices and wi-fi.

★ Mediterranea   MEDITERRANEAN $$
(Map p180; ☑0274-371052; www.restobykamil.com; Jl Tirtodipuran 24A; pizza 44,000-62,000Rp, mains 45,000-210,000Rp; ☺8am-11pm Tue-Sun; ☎) This French-owned kitchen is a delight in every sense. Everything here is homemade, including the bread which is baked twice daily. Staff also smoke their own salmon, slice a paper-thin beef carpaccio, offer a tasty tuna tataki, and grill kebabs, steaks and chops. The traditional range of wood-fired pizzas are marvellous, too.

Gadri Resto   INDONESIAN $$
(Map p180; ☑0274-373520; Jl Rotowijayan 5; mains 34,000-110,000Rp; ☺9am-8pm) Just outside the *kraton* is this place, where you can literally eat like royalty: within the residence of Prince Gusti Jaryo Haju Joyouksumo, a

WORTH A TRIP

GUNUNG MERAPI & KALIURANG

Few of Southeast Asia's volcanoes are as evocative, or as destructive, as Gunung Merapi (Fire Mountain). Towering 2930m over Yogyakarta, Borobudur and Prambanan, this immense Fuji-esque peak is a threatening, disturbingly close presence for thousands. Merapi has erupted dozens of times over the past century; the massive 2010 eruption killed 353 and forced the evacuation of 360,000 more. It's officially Indonesia's most active volcano – quite an accolade in a nation with 127 active cones – and some observers have theorised it was responsible for the mysterious evacuation of Borobudur and the collapse of the old Mataram kingdom during the 11th century.

Merapi is frequently declared off-limits to visitors. But if conditions permit, climbing the cone is possible in the dry season (April to September). Access is via the small village of Selo, on the northern side of the mountain. Extreme caution is advised.

The hill resort of Kaliurang, 25km north of Yogyakarta, is the main access point for views of Merapi. It has two good museums: **Ullen Sentalu** (☑0274-895161; www.ullensentalu.com; Jl Boyong Km25; adult/child 60,000/40,000Rp; ⏱8.30am-4pm Tue-Sun), with a rich collection of Javanese fine art, and **Merapi Volcano Museum** (☑0274-896498; www.mgm.slemankab.go.id; Jl Kaliurang Km25.7; 10,000Rp; ⏱8am-3.30pm Tue-Thu & Sat-Sun, to 2pm Fri), which has exhibits on all things volcanic.

While many tourists use Yogyakarta as their base to visit Merapi, spending a night at **Vogels Hostel** (☑0274-895208; www.vogelshostel.net; Jl Astamulya 76, Kaliurang; dm 30,000Rp, d with shared bathroom 100,000Rp, d/tr with bathroom 150,000/200,000Rp, bungalows with bathroom & hot water 125,000-200,000Rp; @🛜) in Kaliurang is highly recommended – and will ensure you get fantastic morning vistas. For those wanting to climb to the summit, there are a handful of homestays and guesthouses in Selo, north of Merapi.

Take an *angkot* (small minibus) to Kaliurang (20,000Rp, one hour) from Condong Catur terminal, 7km north of downtown Yogyakarta. For Selo, taxi is your only realistic choice; expect to pay around 250,000Rp to 300,000Rp one way from Yogyakarta.

son of the current sultan. Many of his favourite dishes are on offer, including *nasi campur* among other rice and chicken dishes. It's worth a wander about to have a look at the family's antiques and belongings.

🍸 Drinking & Nightlife

★ Taphouse   PUB
(Map p183; ☑0812 2444 2255; www.facebook.com/taphouse.jogja; Jl Jlagran 18; ⏱7pm-2am Sun-Thu, to 3am Fri & Sat; 🛜) One of the best spots for a beer in town is this atmospheric bar, set within a stylised, ruined-brick courtyard, which feels a bit like a bombed-out village. It's a sprawling, eclectic space worthy of exploration before settling on a spot, whether at a bench table or bean bags on the grass. There's a big screen showing movies and sports, a menu of pub food and a lengthy drinks list. There's live music and DJs most nights from 10pm.

★ Sakapatat Social House   BAR
(Map p180; ☑0274-2921354; www.sakapatat.com; Jl Pakuningratan 34; ⏱11am-1am Sun-Thu, to 2am Fri & Sat; 🛜) A little out of the way in a residential area north of town is this hip, contemporary Belgian-owned gastropub. It has

several local beers on tap along with Belgian beers (albeit pricey!) and cocktails to enjoy in its leafy beer garden or atmospheric interior with exposed brick. There's a menu of Belgian fries, great burgers and Philly steak sandwiches on homemade bread.

Agenda   BAR
(Map p180; ☑0878 3890 6088; www.agenda-id.com; Jl Prawirotaman II 629, Greenhost; cocktails 80,000-150,00Rp; ⏱11am-midnight Sun-Thu, to 2am Fri & Sat) Atop of the boutique Greenhost (p184) hotel is this stylish rooftop bar and restaurant that's one of Yogya's coolest spots for a cocktail. Its decor is a mishmash of contemporary flair and design, and features a flashy bar where bartenders mix original and classic cocktails; happy hour is 11am to 8pm. There's Bintang on tap, a great wine list and DJs most nights.

Awor Gallery & Coffee   COFFEE
(Map p180; ☑0821 3561 8881; www.facebook.com/awor.gallery; Jl Simanjuntak 2; ⏱9am-midnight) One for those who take their coffee seriously. Grab a stool at the counter and watch aficionado baristas painstakingly prepare Indonesian coffees to an exact science, using v-60, Kalita wave, Aeropress, siphon or traditional

INDONESIA YOGYAKARTA

tubruk methods. It has a smart decor, a menu of contemporary cafe fare and art on its walls.

☆ Entertainment

Asmara Art & Coffee Shop
LIVE MUSIC
(Map p180; ☎0274-4221017; www.facebook.com/asmaracoffee; Jl Tirtodipuran 22; ☻5pm-1am; 🛜) It calls itself an art and coffee shop, but this split-level joint feels like a restaurant and bar with frequent live bands from 9pm. Regulars include a really good reggae band on Thursdays and there's a fun, mixed crowd every night. Locals call it 'Ascos'.

Sono-Budoyo Museum
PUPPET THEATRE
(Map p180; ☎0274-376775; admission 20,000Rp, camera 3000Rp; ☻8-10pm Mon-Sat) Popular two-hour performances; the first half-hour involves reading the story in Javanese, so most travellers arrive later.

Ramayana Ballet Purawisata
DANCE
(Map p180; ☎0274-371333, 0274-375705; www.purawisata-jogja.rezgo.com; Jl Brigjen Katamso; adult/child 5-10yr 300,000/150,000Rp; ☻8pm) Nightly traditional dance performances of the Ramayana at 8pm, which goes for around 1½ hours. You can dine and watch the show (420,000Rp).

Sasono Hinggil
PUPPET THEATRE
(Map p180; South Main Sq; 7500-20,000Rp) Most of the tourist centres, hotels etc offer shortened versions for tourists, but here in the *alun-alun* of the *kraton*, marathon all-night performances are held every second Saturday of the month from 9pm to 5am.

🛍 Shopping

Via Via
GIFTS & SOUVENIRS
(Map p180; www.viaviajogja.com/shop.php; Jl Prawirotaman 30; ☻7.30am-11pm) 🍃 This is a great place to pick up souvenirs, with an interesting range of locally made, sustainable, fair-trade crafts and accessories, as well as organic coffee, spices, Indonesian books and postcards.

Lana Gallery
ART
(Map p180; ☎0818 0412 8277, 0877 3929 3119; rl-hwildan@yahoo.com; Jl Menukan 276; ☻9am-8pm Tue-Sun) A great range of contemporary art by new and emerging artists from across the archipelago, many of them graduates of Yogya's fine arts school. The gallery is split over two art-filled houses. It's run by Wildan, one of the friendliest people you'll ever meet.

Hamzah Batik
CLOTHING
(Map p180; ☎0274-588524; Jl A Yani 9; ☻8am-9pm) An excellent place to browse for cheap clothes, leatherwork, batik bags, *topeng* (wooden masks used in funerary dances) and *wayang golek* (3D wooden puppets). When you're done shopping here try the traditional Javanese food on the roof terrace.

Batik Keris
CLOTHING
(Map p180; www.batikkeris.co.id; Jl A Yani 71; ☻9am-8pm) Excellent-quality batik at fixed prices. Best for traditional styles – men's shirts start at about 200,000Rp.

ℹ Information

Hassles from smooth-talking batik salesmen are a constant issue for every traveller in town. A time-honoured scam is to pressure you to visit a 'fine-art student exhibition' or a 'government store' – there are no official shops or galleries in the city.

There are numerous banks (and a few money-changers) in the tourist areas. **BNI Bank** (☎0274-376287; Jl Trikora I; ☻8am-4pm Mon-Sat) is opposite the main post office. **Mulia** (Jl Malioboro 60, Inna Garuda Hotel; ☻7am-7pm Mon-Fri, to 3pm Sat) has the best money-changing rates in Yogya.

Yogyakarta's **tourist information office** (☎0274-566000; ticmalioboro@yahoo.com; Jl Malioboro 16; ☻7.30am-7pm Mon-Thu, to 6pm Fri & Sat) is the most well organised in the country, with delightful, helpful staff, free maps and good transport information. It has a number of publications (including a calendar of events and a great map), and can book any and all transport, as well as local attractions and performances. They have gamelan performances here at 1.30pm on Friday and Saturday.

Ludira Husada Tama Hospital (☎0274-620333, 0274-620373; Jl Wiratama 4; ☻24hr) is open 24 hours.

BUSES FROM GIWANGAN

DESTINATION	FARE (RP)	DURATION (HR)	FREQUENCY
Bandung	air-con 140,000	10	3 daily
Borobudur	normal 25,000	1½	every 30min
Denpasar	air-con 325,000	19	3 daily
Jakarta	normal/air-con 210,000/270,000	12	10-12 daily

TRAINS FROM YOGYAKARTA

DESTINATION	FARE (RP)	DURATION (HR)	FREQUENCY (DAILY)
Bandung	215,000–320,000	7½-8½	6
Banyuwangi	94,000	14	1
Sidareja (for Pangandaran)	94,000–320,000	3½	3
Jakarta	335,000–430,000	7½-8	6
Malang	190,000–375,000	7-8	4
Probolinggo	74,000-315,000	8½-9	3
Solo	40,000–320,000	1	19
Surabaya	120,000-300,000	4¼-5¼	8

ⓘ Getting There & Away

AIR

Yogyakarta Adisucipto International Airport (www.yogyakartaairport.com; Jl Raya Solo, Km 9) has international connections to Singapore and Kuala Lumpur, plus many domestic connections.

BUS & MINIBUS

Yogya's main bus terminal, **Giwangan** (Jl Timur), is 5km southeast of the city centre; bus 3B connects it with Yogyakarta train station and Jl Malioboro. Buses run from Giwangan to points all over Java, and also to Bali. For long trips make sure you take a luxury bus. It's cheaper to buy tickets at the bus terminal, but it's less hassle to simply check fares and departures with the ticket agents along Jl Mangkubumi, Jl Sosrowijayan or Jl Prawirotaman. These agents can also arrange pick-up from your hotel.

To go to Prambanan (3500Rp) take a 1A city bus from Jl Malioboro. Buses to/from Borobudur (25,000Rp, every 30 minutes, 1¼ hours) use the **Jombor terminal** (Jl Magelang). To get there take a Trans Jogja bus 3A from Jl Malioboro to Jl Ahmad Dahlan, and change to a 2B for Jombor.

Door-to-door travel minibuses run to all major cities from Yogya. Sosrowijayan and Prawirotaman agents sell tickets. Prices are similar to air-conditioned buses. Journeys of more than four hours can be cramped – trains and buses offer more comfort. Due to traffic patterns, it's much faster to get to Solo, Surabaya or Probolinggo by train.

TRAIN

Centrally located, Yogyakarkta train station handles most long-distance destinations. Economy-class trains also depart from and arrive at Lempuyangan station, 1km to the east, including the two morning trains to Probolinggo and Banyuwangi.

ⓘ Getting Around

TO/FROM THE AIRPORT

Situated 10km east of the centre, the airport is very well connected to the city by public transport. Bus 1A (3500Rp) runs there from Jl Malioboro. Pramek trains stop at Maguwo station, which is right by the airport as well. Rates for taxis from the airport to the city centre are fixed at 70,000Rp.

BICYCLE

Bikes cost about 30,000Rp a day from hotels. Always lock your bike.

BUS

Yogya's reliable bus system, Trans Jogja consists of modern air-conditioned buses running from 5.30am to 9pm on 11 routes around the city to as far away as Prambanan. Tickets cost 3500Rp per journey. Trans Jogja buses only stop at the designated bus shelters. Bus 1A is a very useful service, running from Jl Malioboro past the airport to Prambanan. Trans Jogja route maps can be accessed at the tourist office.

LOCAL TRANSPORT

Yogyakarta has an oversupply of becak (bicycle rickshaws); most drivers are quite pushy, but it can be a fun way to get around. Watch out for drivers who offer cheap hourly rates, unless you want to do the rounds of all the batik galleries that offer commission. A short trip is about 15,000Rp. To go from Jl Prawirotaman to Jl Malioboro costs around 25,000Rp.

TAXI

Online ride-hailing apps **Go-Jek** (www.go-jek.com), **Grab** (www.grab.com) and **Uber** (www.uber.com) are the cheapest, quickest and safest way to get around town. Otherwise metered taxis are also cheap, costing 10,000Rp to 30,000Rp for short trips. If you call any of the taxi companies for a ride around town, the minimum fee is 25,000Rp. **Citra Taxi** (☑ 0274-373737) is considered the most reliable. From Jl Prawirotaman to the airport, the fare is fixed at 70,000Rp.

Prambanan

📷 0274

Jaw-dropping and mystical, the spectacular temples of Prambanan, set in the plains, are the best remaining examples of Java's extended period of Hindu culture and are an absolute must.

All the temples in the Prambanan area were built between the 8th and 10th centuries AD, when Java was ruled by the Buddhist Sailendras in the south and the Hindu Sanjayas of Old Mataram in the north. Possibly by the second half of the 9th century, these two dynasties were united by the marriage of Rakai Pikatan of Hindu Mataram and the Buddhist Sailendra princess Pramodhavardhani. This may explain why a number of temples, including those of the Prambanan temple complex and the smaller Plaosan group, reveal both Shivaite and Buddhist elements in architecture and sculpture. But this is a Hindu site first and foremost, and the wealth of sculptural detail on the great Shiva temple here is the nation's most outstanding example of Hindu art.

👁 Sights

⭐ **Prambanan Temple**   HINDU TEMPLE
(📱0274-496402; www.borobudurpark.com; adult/ child under 10yr US$25/15, guide 100,000Rp; ⊙6am-5.15pm) Comprising the remains of some 244 temples, World Heritage–listed Prambanan is Indonesia's largest Hindu site. The highlight is its central compound, where its eight main and eight minor temples rise up majestically like ornate 9th-century skyscrapers. Erected in the middle of the 9th century – around 50 years later than Borobudur – little is known about its early history. It's thought that it was built by Rakai Pikatan to commemorate the return of a Hindu dynasty to sole power in Java.

Candi Sambisari   TEMPLE
(Jl Candi Sambisari; 10,000Rp; ⊙8am-5pm) Candi Sambisari is a Shiva temple and possibly the latest temple at Prambanan to be erected by the Mataram dynasty. It was discovered by a farmer in 1966. Excavated from under ancient layers of protective volcanic ash and dust, it lies almost 6m below the surface of the surrounding fields and is remarkable for its perfectly preserved state. The inner sanctum of the temple is dominated by a large lingam and yoni (stylised penis and vagina), typical of Shiva temples.

Candi Kalasan   TEMPLE
(Jl Raya Yogya-Solo; 10,000Rp; ⊙8am-5pm) One of the oldest Buddhist temples on the Prambanan Plain, Candi Kalasan stands just off the main highway 13km east of Yogyakarta en route to Prambanan. It's been partially restored and features some fine detailed carvings on its southern side, where a huge, ornate *kala* (demonic face) glowers over the doorway. At one time it was completely covered in coloured, shining stucco, and traces of the hard, stonelike 'diamond plaster' that provided a base for paintwork can still be seen.

Candi Sari   TEMPLE
(off Jl Raya Solo; 10,000Rp; ⊙8am-3pm) The 8th-century Candi Sari is about 200m north from Candi Kalasan (4.5km west of Prambanan), in the middle of coconut and banana groves. This temple has the three-part design of the larger Plaosan temple but is probably slightly older. Some experts believe that its 2nd floor may have served as a dormitory for the Buddhist priests who took care of Candi Kalasan. The sculptured reliefs around the exterior are similar to those of Kalasan but are in much better condition.

Kraton Ratu Boko   TEMPLE
(www.borobudurpark.com; admission adult/child under 10yr US$25/15; ⊙6am-5.30pm) Kraton Ratu Boko (Palace of King Boko) is a partly ruined Hindu palace complex dating from the 9th century. Perched on a hilltop overlooking Prambanan, it is believed to have been the central court of the mighty Mataram dynasty. You can see the large gateway and the platform of Candi Pembakaran (the Royal Crematorium), as well as a series of bathing places staggered on different levels leading down to the village. The sunset view over the Prambanan Plain is magnificent.

Plaosan Temples   TEMPLE
(admission 3000Rp; ⊙7am-5pm) Built around the same time as the Prambanan temple group, the Plaosan temples also combine both Hindu and Buddhist religious symbols and carvings. **Plaosan Lor** (Plaosan North) comprises two restored, identical main temples, surrounded by some 126 small shrines and solid stupas, most of which are now just a jumble of stone. **Plaosan Kidul** (Plaosan South) has more stupas and the remnants of a temple, but little renovation work has been done.

☆ Entertainment

Ramayana Ballet DANCE
(📞0274-496408, 024-8646 2345; www.borobudu-rpark.com; tickets from 125,000Rp; ⏰7.30-9.30pm Tue, Thu & Sat) Held at the outdoor theatre just west of the main Prambana temple complex, the famous Ramayana Ballet is Java's most spectacular dance-drama. The story of Rama and Sita takes place three nights a week on Tuesday, Thursday and Saturday; from May to October it takes place on the open-air stage (weather pending), while other times it's held indoors.

❶ Getting There & Away

You can visit all the temples by bicycle from Yogyakarta, 17km away. The most pleasant route, though it's a longer ride, is to take Jl Senopati out past the zoo to the eastern ring road, where you turn left. Follow this right up to Jl Solo, turn right and then left at Jl Babarsari. Go past the Sahid Garden Hotel and follow the road counterclockwise around the school to the Selokan Mataram. This canal runs parallel to the Solo road, about 1.5km to the north, for around 6km to Kalasan, about 2km before Prambanan. From Yogyakarta, take TransYogya bus 1A (3500Rp, 40 minutes) from Jl Malioboro.

Borobudur

📋0293

Along with Angkor Wat in Cambodia and Bagan in Myanmar, Java's Borobudur makes the rest of Southeast Asia's spectacular sites seem almost incidental. Looming out of a patchwork of bottle-green paddies and swaying palms, this colossal Buddhist monument has survived Gunung Merapi's eruptions, terrorist bombs and the 2006 earthquake to remain as enigmatic and as beautiful as it must have been 1200 years ago.

It's well worth planning to spend a few days in the Borobudur region, which is a supremely beautiful landscape of impossibly green rice fields and traditional rice-growing *kampung* (villages), all overlooked by soaring volcanic peaks. Locals call it the Garden of Java.

This region is establishing itself as Indonesia's most important centre for Buddhism, and there are now three monasteries in the surrounding district. Visitors are welcome and you can even join the monks at prayer time for chanting.

◉ Sights

★ Borobudur Temple BUDDHIST TEMPLE
(www.borobudurpark.com; adult/child US$25/15, sunrise or sunset 450,000Rp, 90min guided tour 1-5 people 100,000Rp; ⏰6am-5pm) The world's largest Buddhist temple and one of Indonesia's biggest attractions is Unesco World Heritage-listed Borobudur Temple. It's built from two million stone blocks in the form of a massive symmetrical stupa, literally wrapped around a small hill. Standing on a 118m by 118m base, its six square terraces are topped by three circular ones, with four stairways leading up through carved gateways to the top. Viewed from the air, the structure resembles a colossal three-dimensional tantric mandala (symbolic circular figure).

It has been suggested, in fact, that the people of the Buddhist community that once supported Borobudur were early Vajrayana or Tantric Buddhists who used it as a walk-through mandala. Though the paintwork is long gone, it's thought that the grey stone of Borobudur was once coloured to catch the sun.

The monument was conceived as a Buddhist vision of the cosmos in stone, starting in the everyday world and spiralling up to nirvana, or enlightenment. At the base of the monument is a series of reliefs representing a world dominated by passion and desire, where the good are rewarded by reincarnation as a higher form of life, while the evil are punished with a lower reincarnation. These carvings and their carnal scenes are covered by stone to hide them from view, but they are partly visible on the southern side.

Starting at the main eastern gateway, go clockwise (as one should around all Buddhist monuments) around the galleries of the stupa. Although Borobudur is impressive for its sheer bulk, the delicate sculptural work is exquisite when viewed up close. The pilgrim's walk is about 5km long and takes you along narrow corridors past nearly 1460 richly decorated narrative panels and 1212 decorative panels in which the sculptors have carved a virtual textbook of Buddhist doctrines as well as many aspects of Javanese life 1000 years ago – a continual procession of ships and elephants, musicians and dancing girls, warriors and kings.

On the third level there's a lengthy panel sequence about a dream of Queen Maya, which involved a vision of white elephants with six tusks. Monks and courtiers interpret this as a premonition that her son would become a Buddha, and the sequence continues until the birth of Prince Siddhartha and his journey to enlightenment. Many other panels are related to Buddhist concepts of cause and effect or karma.

Some 432 serene-faced Buddha images stare out from open chambers above the galleries, while 72 more Buddha images (many now headless) sit only partly visible in latticed stupas on the top three terraces – one is considered the lucky Buddha. The top platform is circular, signifying neverending nirvana.

Admission to the temple includes entrance to the **Karmawibhangga Museum**, featuring 4000 original stones and carvings from the temple, and the **Borobudur Museum** with more relics, interesting photographs and gamelan performances at 9am and 3pm. The ticket also allows a visit to the **Samudra Raksa Museum**, which houses a full-size replica of an 8th-century spice-trading ship, that was remarkably designed and built based on an image depicted on one of the panels that adorn Borobudur Temple.

Tickets for the temple can be purchased from its website, along with a combined Borobudur–Prambanan package (adult/child US$40/25) that brings discounts – but it's only valid for two days. Take note that the Borobudur–Prambanan discount ticket isn't available for those wanting to visit Borobudur at sunrise or sunset.

★ Mendut Temple & Monastery
BUDDHIST TEMPLE

(Jl Mayor Kusen 92; 3500Rp, incl entry to Candi Pawon; ⊙ 6am-5.30pm) This exquisite temple, set within a cute neighbourhood around 3.5km east of Borobudur, may look insignificant compared with its mighty neighbour, but it houses the most outstanding statue in its original setting of any temple in Java. The magnificent 3m-high figure of Buddha is flanked by bodhisattvas: Lokesvara on the left and Vairapana on the right. The Buddha is also notable for his posture: he sits Western-style with both feet on the ground.

☞ Tours

★ Jaker
TOURS

(📞 0293-788845; jackpriyana@yahoo.com.sg; Jl Balaputradewa 54, Lotus II Homestay) Jaker is a group of guides and local activists based in the small settlement of Borobudur that surrounds the world's largest Buddhist monument. All Jaker members were born in the area, can provide expert local knowledge and speak fluent English.

🛏 Sleeping & Eating

Rajasa Hotel & Restoran
GUESTHOUSE $

(📞 0293-788276; Jl Badrawati II; r incl breakfast with fan & cold water/air-con & hot water 200,000/400,000Rp; ❄ 🛜) A popular, welcoming guesthouse with rooms that face rice fields (through railings) about 1.5km south of the bus terminal. The fan-cooled rooms are the best value, as you pay a lot more for air-conditioning and slightly smarter furniture. It has a lovely restaurant (mains 25,000Rp to 35,000Rp) with plenty of Javanese specialties, vegetarian dishes and cold beer.

Lotus II Homestay
GUESTHOUSE $$

(📞 0293-788845; jackpriyana@yahoo.com.sg; Jl Balaputradewa 54; r incl breakfast 225,000-300,000Rp; ❄ @ 🛜) This popular, friendly place is owned by one of the founders of Jaker, so there's great local information and everyone speaks English. The spacious upstairs rooms are the pick with classy furnishings and are well positioned along the rear balcony overlooking rice fields; perfect for your breakfast or an afternoon tea or beer. Rooms downstairs are less appealing, but are clean with decent beds and high ceilings.

Alea Coffee Shop
CAFE $

(📞 0877 0548 8561; Jl. Balaputradewa 58; mains 25,000Rp; ⊙ 7am-10pm; 🛜) A tranquil cafe with outdoor decking that juts out to the rice paddies is a great spot for strong Javanese coffee, cold beer (not always available) or tasty Indonesian dishes. At night it's lit up with fairy lights and there's an attached art gallery, too.

❶ Getting There & Away

From Yogyakarta, buses leave Jombor terminal (25,000Rp, every 30 minutes, 1¼ hours) to Borobudur. The last bus to/from Borobudur is at 4.30pm. From Borobudur terminal buses go regularly to Magelang (10,000Rp) until 4pm. In Borobudur, becak cost 10,000Rp to 15,000Rp anywhere in the village. Bicycles (25,000Rp) and motorbikes (around 75,000Rp) can be hired from hotels. Day tours of Borobudur are easily arranged in Yogyakarta, which is 42km southeast of town.

Solo (Surakarta)

🎵 0271 / POP 555,308

Arguably the epicentre of Javanese identity and tradition, Solo is one of the least Westernised cities on the island. The city's distinguished past as a seat of the great Mataram empire means it competes with its rival Yogyakarta as the hub of Javanese culture, though this conservative town often plays second fiddle to its more contemporary neighbour.

But with backstreet *kampung* (neighbourhoods) and its elegant *kraton*, traditional markets and gleaming malls, Solo has more than enough to warrant at least an overnight visit. Two nights is better, and as there are some fascinating temples close by, it also makes a great base for forays into the lush hills of central Java.

Solo attracts students and scholars to its music and dance academies, and it's an excellent place to see traditional performing arts, as well as traditional crafts – especially batik, which is a local staple.

⊙ Sights

Kraton Surakarta   PALACE
(Kraton Kasunanan; ☎0271-656432; Jl Sidikoro; 15,000Rp, photography 3500Rp, guide 30,000-50,000Rp; ⊙9am-2pm Mon-Fri, to 3pm Sat & Sun) Once the hub of an empire, today the 18th-century Kraton Surakarta is a faded memorial of a bygone era. It's worth a visit, but much of the *kraton* was destroyed by fire in 1985. Many of the inner buildings were rebuilt, but today the allure of this once-majestic palace has largely vanished and its structures are left bare and unloved – though restoration work will hopefully improve things. The main sight for visitors is the Sasono Sewoko museum.

Mangkunegaran Palace   PALACE
(Istana Mangkunegaran; www.puromangkunegaran.com; Jl Ronggowarsito; admission 20,000Rp; ⊙8.30am-3pm Mon-Wed, Fri & Sat, to 2.30pm Thu & Sun) Dating to 1757, the Mangkunegaran Palace is in better condition than the kraton and is the home of the second house of Solo. The centre of the compound is the *pendopo*, a pavilion built in a mix of Javanese and European architectural styles. Its high, rounded ceiling was painted in 1937 and is intricately decorated with a central flame surrounded by figures of the Javanese zodiac, each painted in its own mystical colour.

House of Danar Hadi   MUSEUM
(☎0271-714326; Jl Slamet Riyadi 261; adult/child 35,000/15,000Rp; ⊙9am-4.30pm, showroom to 9pm) Danar Hadi is one of the world's best batik museums. A terrific collection of antique and royal textiles from Java, China and beyond are housed within an elegant white-washed colonial building. Entry includes an excellent guided tour (around 1½ hours, in English), which explains the history of the

many pieces (11,000 in the collection). You'll also get to visit its workshop where you can watch craftswomen at work creating new masterpieces, an upmarket storeroom and a souvenir shop. No photography.

🛏 Sleeping & Eating

Warung Baru Homestay   GUESTHOUSE $
(☎0812 2687 443, 0271-656369; off Jl KH Ahmad Dahlan; r incl breakfast with fan/air-con from 100,000/150,000Rp; ❄🛜) Hidden down a small *gang* (alley) off Jl KH Ahmad Dahlan is this unique guesthouse offering four exceptional-value rooms in a rather lavish Javanese home. The more expensive rooms have hot water and bathtubs. Check in at their restaurant around the corner, which is a great little hangout.

Cakra Homestay   HOMESTAY $
(☎0271-634743, 0878 3636 3686; www.cakrahomestay.com; Jl Cakra II 15; r incl breakfast with shared/private bathroom from 125,000/175,000Rp, r with air-con & private bathroom from 200,000Rp; ❄🛜🏊) This atmospheric place scores highly for those interested in Javanese culture (and the welcoming staff are keen to promote it). There's an amazing gamelan room with free performances on Tuesday, and sometimes Thursday evenings. It also has a gorgeous pool area. However, the rooms are pretty simple. Shared bathrooms are Western and mandi-style.

Red Planet   HOTEL $$
(☎0271-788 9333; www.redplanethotels.com; Jl Dr Supomo 49; r from 280,000Rp; ❄@🛜) A competitively priced, dressed-up three-star chain with branches in a handful of Indonesian cities. Rooms have wood floors, high ceilings, wall-mounted flatscreens, rain showers and security boxes, but they aren't huge and can feel slightly soulless despite the good value.

Galabo   STREET FOOD $
(Jl Slamet Riyadi; ⊙5-11pm) Galabo is a kind of open-air food court with dozens of stalls – tuck into local specialities including *nasi gudeg* (unripe jackfruit served with rice, chicken and spices), *nasi liwet* (rice cooked in coconut milk and eaten with a host of side dishes) or the *timlo solo* (beef noodle soup). It's open during the day too, but these dishes are only cooked in the evenings.

Ramayana   INDONESIAN $
(☎0271-666900; Jl Imam Bonjol 49-51; mains 20,000-80,000Rp; ⊙8am-9.30pm) This smart, air-conditioned restaurant offers tasty east Javanese specialities such as *ayam penyet*

Solo (Surakarta)

(flattened fried chicken) and *empal penyet* (fried, marinated beef), which both go fantastically with a cold beer – a rarity in Solo.

Nasi Liwet Wongso Lemu　INDONESIAN $
(Jl Teuku Umar; meals 12,000-30,000Rp; ⊙4pm-2am) Solo street dining at its best, this evening-only stall, run by an *ibu* (mother; older woman) in traditional batik, specialises in *nasi liwet*: coconut-flavoured rice served on a banana leaf topped with shredded chicken, chicken liver (optional), egg, turmeric-cooked tofu and special seasonings. Tables are set up with pickled vegetables, tofu fried in turmeric and chicken feet. This is cultural dining deluxe!

Warung Baru　INTERNATIONAL $
(☏0271-656369; Jl Ahmad Dahlan 23; mains 10,000-18,000Rp; ⊙6am-10pm; 🖋) An old-school backpackers' hang-out, the Baru is also a good spot to try local Solonese specialities such as *nasi liwet*, along with vegetari-

an dishes, home-baked bread and the usual Western fare. Cold beer is another reason to visit. The friendly owners can arrange tours and batik classes.

Omah Sinten
INDONESIAN $$

(☑ 0271-641160; www.omahsinten.com; Jl Diponegoro 34-54; mains 25,000-55,000Rp; ☺ 8am-10pm; 🛜) A rather attractive restaurant where you can dine on quality Javanese fare including lots of local Solonese specialities, like beef sliced and stewed in herbs and green chillies, or duck stewed in coconut milk. Why not enjoy both while listening to the tinkle of fountains and the calming waft of classical Javanese music? It's opposite the entrance to the Istana Mangkunegaran (p192).

❶ Information

Tourist Office (☑ 0271-716501; Jl Slamet Riyadi 275; ☺ 8am-4pm Mon-Sat) Staff are only moderately helpful here. They have maps, brochures and information on cultural events. They also peddle (slightly pricey) tours.

❶ Getting There & Away

AIR
Solo's **Adi Sumarmo international Airport** (☑ 0271-780715; www.adisumarmo-airport.com/en; Jl Bandara Adi Sumarmo) has regular flights to Jakarta with **Garuda** (☑ 0271-737500; www.garuda-indonesia.com; Hotel Riyadi Palace, Jl Slamet Riyadi 335), **Lion Air** (☑ 0271-780400; www.lionair.co.id) and **Citilink** (☑ 0271-7889352; www.citilink.co.id/en), while **AirAsia** (☑ 021-2927 0999; www.airasia.com) has cheap flights to Kuala Lumpur.

BUS
The **Tirtonadi bus terminal** (Jl Yani) is 3km from the centre of the city. Only economy buses leave from here to destinations such as Prambanan (20,000Rp, 1½ hours) and Semarang (35,000Rp, 3¼ hours), plus Surabaya (from 31,000Rp) and Malang (100,000Rp, 10 hours).

Otherwise near the bus terminal, the **Gilingan minibus terminal** (Jl Ahmad Yani) has express air-con *travel* minibuses to Semarang (75,000Rp), Surabaya (140,000Rp) and Malang (150,000Rp).

It's fastest to reach Yogyakarta (and Prambanan) by train. Prambanan is best accessed via catching a train to Maguwo station near Yogyakarta's airport, from where you'll transfer to bus 1A to reach the temple.

TRAIN
Solo is located on the main Jakarta–Yogyakarta–Surabaya train line and most trains stop at **Balapan** (☑ 0271-714039; Jl Monginsidi 112), the principal train station. Jebres train station, in the northeast of Solo, also has a few economy-class services to Surabaya and Jakarta.

❶ Getting Around

Air-conditioned Batik Solo Trans buses connect Adi Sumarmo airport (20,000Rp), 10km northwest of the centre, with Jl Slamet Riyadi. A taxi costs around 90,000Rp; **Kosti Solo taxis** (☑ 0271-856300) are reliable, but as everywhere the likes of Uber, Grab and Go-Jek are cheaper.

Becak cost about 20,000Rp from the train station or bus terminal into the centre. Homestays can arrange bike hire for 25,000Rp or a motorcycle for around 100,000Rp per day.

Around Solo

In a magnificent position 900m above the Solo plain, **Candi Sukuh** (25,000Rp; ☺ 7am-5pm) is one of Java's most enigmatic and striking temples. It's not a large site, but it has a large, truncated pyramid of rough-hewn stone, and there are some fascinating reliefs and Barong statues. It's clear that a fertility cult was practised here: several explicit carvings have led it to be dubbed the 'erotic' temple. It's a quiet, isolated place with a potent atmosphere.

On clear days the view of the terraced emerald valley and the volcano looming above are magical. Built in the 15th century during the declining years of the Majapahit kingdom, Candi Sukuh seems to have nothing whatsoever to do with other Javanese Hindu and Buddhist temples. The origins of its builders and strange sculptural style (with crude, squat and distorted figures carved in the *wayang* style found in east Java) remain a mystery and it seems to mark a reappearance of the pre-Hindu animism that existed 1500 years earlier.

Virtually all travellers get here on a tour from Solo or Yogyakarta. Public transport is very tricky: take a bus bound for Tawangmangu from Solo as far as Karangpandan

TRAINS FROM SOLO

DESTINATION	FARE (RP)	DURATION (HR)	FREQUENCY (DAILY)
Jakarta	380,000-535,000	8¼-9	4-5
Surabaya	120,000–280,000	3¾-4½	6-8
Yogyakarta	40,000-320,000	1	19

(10,000Rp to 15,000Rp), then a Kemuning minibus (3000Rp) to the turn-off to Candi Sukuh; from here it's a steep half-hour walk uphill (2km) to the site or a 50,000Rp *ojek* ride. For around 80,000Rp, *ojek* will take you to both Sukuh and Cetho.

Malang

📞 0341 / POP 887,443

With leafy, colonial-era boulevards and a breezy climate, Malang moves at a far more leisurely pace than the regional capital, Surabaya. It's a cultured city with several important universities, and is home to a large student population. The central area is not too large and quite walkable.

Established by the Dutch in the closing decades of the 18th century, Malang earned its first fortunes from coffee, which flourished on the surrounding hillsides. Today, the city's colonial grandeur is quickly disappearing behind the homogenous facades of more modern developments, but there's still much to admire for now. And with a number of Hindu temples and sights outside the city, Malang makes an ideal base to explore this intriguing corner of east Java.

◉ Sights

Hotel Tugu Malang   MUSEUM
(📞 0341-363891; www.tuguhotels.com/hotels/malang; Jl Tugu III; tour per person incl snacks 90,000Rp; ⊘ 6pm; 🛜) Malang's most impressive museum isn't actually a museum at all, but a hotel: the boutique, four-star Hotel Tugu Malang. A showcase for its owner, arguably Indonesia's foremost collector of Asian art and antiquities, the exhibit includes 10th-century ceramics, jade carvings from the 13th century, Ming dynasty porcelain, Qing dynasty wood carvings and even the complete facade of a Chinese temple. English-speaking tours of the collection take place at 6pm; it's complimentary for guests staying here.

Jalan Besar Ijen   AREA
Malang has some wonderful colonial architecture. Just northwest of the centre, Jl Besar Ijen is Malang's millionaires' row, a boulevard lined with elegant whitewashed mansions from the Dutch era. Many have been substantially renovated, but there's still much to admire. On Sunday mornings it's closed to traffic and a market is set up along here; in late May it becomes the setting for the city's huge Malang Kembali festival.

🛏 Sleeping

★ Kampong Tourist   HOSTEL $
(📞 0341-345797; www.kampongtourist.com; Hotel Helios, Jl Patimura 37; s/d/tr dm 65,000/120,000/150,000Rp; 🛜) The owners of this superb backpacking place have fashioned an excellent hostel on the rooftop of Hotel Helios. Dorm beds are comfy (and interestingly include double and triple-sized beds), as are the bamboo gazebo-style rooms, and there's a great shared shower block and guests' kitchen, too. They offer a bunch of tours in the region, including Bromo, cooking classes and free city walks.

Jona's Homestay   HOMESTAY $
(📞 0341-324678; Jl Sutomo 4; s/d with fan & shared bathroom 85,000/130,000Rp, d/tr including breakfast, aircon & private bathroom 225,000/260,000Rp; ❄🛜) This long-running homestay in a colossal colonial villa, with a digital ticker out front, is run by a sweet family that looks after guests well and offers tours. The location in an affluent neighbourhood is also convenient and quiet, though the rooms have aged somewhat. Some of the air-con options are huge and great value. Breakfast is available, as is cheap, cold beer. It hires bicycles (per day 25,000Rp) and scooters (80,000Rp).

Same Hotel   HOTEL $$
(📞 0341-3031999; Jl Patimura 19; r incl breakfast from 375,000Rp; ❄🛜) With its rather grand colonnaded Italianate facade and large sparkling lobby, there's nothing same-same about this hotel. It sets the scene nicely for what offers an excellent-value stay, with professional staff, comfortable, spacious rooms, fast wi-fi, cable TV, room service and inclusive buffet breakfast.

🍴 Eating & Drinking

Mie Tomcat   NOODLES $
(📞 0812 3369 7450; Jl Trunijoyo 31; dishes 9000-12,000Rp; ⊘ 9am-11pm) A cool designer warung popular with young locals, with a Jenga-like exterior and cherry-wood furnishings inside and out. The staff speak little English but they do know how to make some tasty noodle soup, ramen and *mie goreng* (fried noodles). Use the helpful chalkboard spice-meter to stretch your personal heat index.

Bebek Gong   INDONESIAN $
(📞 0341-365055; www.bebekgong.com; Jl Cokroaminoto 2d; dishes 5000-23,000Rp; ⊘ 10am-10pm) A dressed-up warung dangling with

TEMPLES AROUND MALANG

Candi Singosari (Jl Kertanegara 148; admission by donation; ⊘7.30am-4pm) Situated right in the village of Singosari, 12km north of Malang, this temple stands 500m off the main Malang–Surabaya road. One of the last monuments erected to the Singosari dynasty, it was built in 1304 in honour of King Kertanegara, the fifth and last Singosari king, who died in 1292 in a palace uprising.

To reach Singosari, take an *angkot* (6000Rp) from Malang's Arjosari bus terminal and get off at the Singosari market on the highway.

Candi Sumberawan (admission by donation; ⊘7.30am-4pm) This small, squat Buddhist stupa lies in the terraced, cultivated foothills of Gunung Arjuna, about 5km northwest of Singosari. It was built to commemorate the 1359 visit of Hayam Wuruk, the great Majapahit king. Within the temple grounds are a lingam stone and the crumbling origins of additional stupa along with the remains of recent offerings. But what makes it special is the approach. Take an *angkot* (5000Rp) from Singosari *pasar* (market) on the highway to Desa Sumberawan, then walk 500m down the road to the canal and the dirt path.

Candi Jago (Jajaghu; Jl Wisnuwardhana; admission by donation; ⊘7.30am-4pm) Along a small road near the market in Tumpang, 22km from Malang, Candi Jago was built between 1268 and 1280 and is thought to be a memorial to the fourth Singosari king, Vishnuvardhana. The temple has some interesting decorative carving from the Jataka and the Mahabharata, in the three-dimensional, wayang kulit (shadow puppet) style typical of east Java. Take a white angkot from Malang's Arjosari bus terminal to Tumpang (10,000Rp).

Candi Kidal (Jl Candi Kidal; admission by donation; ⊘7am-noon & 1-4pm) Set in the village of Kidal, with houses rising all around, this graceful temple was built around 1260 as the burial shrine of King Anusapati (the second Singosari king, who died in 1248). Now 12m high, it originally topped 17m and is an example of east Javanese architecture. Its slender form has pictures of the Garuda (mythical man-bird) on three sides, plus bold, glowering *kala* (demonic face often seen over temple gateways). From Tumpang market it's best to take an *ojek* (passenger motorcycle; 10,000Rp) to Candi Kidal.

lovely rattan lanterns and lined with bamboo wallpaper, serving fried chicken and duck meals to the Malang masses. Platters come with raw cabbage and long beans on the side. Rice is 5000Rp extra.

Legipait   COFFEE
(Jl Patimura 24; ⊘7am-midnight; 🛜) A popular hangout for Malang hipsters is this corner cafe serving local coffees, juices and meals to a soundtrack of indie tunes.

❶ Getting There & Away

Due to dangers driving on the sandy volcanic road, the shortcut to Bromo via the easterly route from Malang is only permissable for those who've signed up with a jeep tour. If you have your own vehicle you'll need to take the much longer northerly route via Probolinggo.

BUS & ANGKOT

Malang has three bus terminals. Arjosari, 5km north of town, is the main one with regular buses to Surabaya, Probolinggo and Banyuwangi. Long-distance buses to Solo, Yogyakarta, Denpasar and even Jakarta mostly leave in the early

evening. Minibuses (called *angkot* or *mikrolet* locally) run from Arjosari to nearby villages such as Singosari and Tumpang.

Gadang bus terminal is 5km south of the city centre, and sends buses along the southern routes to destinations such as Blitar (25,000Rp to 30,000Rp, two hours).

Buses depart Landungsari bus terminal, 5km northwest of the city, to destinations west of the city, such as Batu (10,000Rp, 40 minutes).

MINIBUS

Plenty of door-to-door *travel* companies operate from Malang, and hotels and travel agencies can book them. **Wijaya Travel** (☎0341-327072) is a reliable agency and can arrange shuttles to Solo, Yogyakarta and Probolinggo. **Abimanyu Travel** (☎0812 3007 1652, 0341-3041 382; www. abimanyutravel.id) has minibuses to Surabaya (100,000Rp) that will drop you off at hotels in Surabaya or the airport (thus saving the long haul from Surabaya's bus terminal).

TRAIN

Malang train station is centrally located but not well connected to the main network. There are three daily trains to Yogyakarta

(150,000Rp to 355,000Rp, eight hours) via Solo. There's a train to Probolinggo (62,000Rp, 2¾ hours) leaving at 4pm. Surabaya (35,000Rp to 60,000Rp, two hours) is only served by very slow and crowded economy trains. There is also a daily service to Banyuwangi (62,000Rp, 7½ hours), where you can hop on a ferry to Bali.

ⓘ Getting Around

Mikrolet (small taxis) run all over town. Most buzz between the bus terminals via the town centre. These are marked A–G (Arjosari to Gadung and return), A–L (Arjosari to Landungsari) or G–L (Gadang to Landungsari). Trips cost 4000Rp; or 8000Rp if you have a large bag.

Go-Jek online taxi and motorbikes offers a cheap means of getting around town.

Gunung Bromo

☑ 0335

A lunarlike landscape of epic proportions and surreal beauty, the volcanic Bromo region is one of Indonesia's most breathtaking sights.

Rising from the guts of the ancient Tengger caldera, Gunung Bromo (2329m) is one of three volcanoes to have emerged from a vast crater, stretching 10km across. Flanked by the peaks of Kursi (2581m) and Batok (2440m), the smouldering cone of Bromo stands in a sea of ashen, volcanic sand, surrounded by the towering cliffs of the crater's edge. Just to the south, Gunung Semeru (3676m), Java's highest peak and one of its most active volcanoes, throws its shadow – and occasionally its ash – over the whole scene.

The vast majority of independent travellers get to Bromo via the town of Probolinggo and stay in Cemoro Lawang where facilities are good. There are other options in villages on the road up from Probolinggo. Additional approaches via Wonokitri and Ngadas are possible.

◉ Sights & Activities

The classic Bromo tour peddled by all hotels and guides in Cemoro Lawang (and other villages) involves pick-up at around 3.30am and a 4WD journey up to the neighbouring peak of Gunung Penanjakan (2770m). This viewpoint offers the best vistas (and photographs) of the entire Bromo landscape, with Gunung Semeru puffing away on the horizon. After sunrise, 4WDs head back down the steep lip of the crater and then over the Laotian Pasir (Sea of Sand) to the base of Bromo. It's usually easy to hook up with others for this tour to share costs. Private jeeps cost 500,000Rp,

but sometimes you can negotiate a cheaper price. If you pay for a single seat, expect to be crammed in with four or five others, though the price (150,000Rp) is right.

Alternatively, it's a two-hour hike to the top of Gunung Penanjakan, the so-called second viewpoint, from Cemoro Lawang. But King Kong Hill – perched just 20 minutes beyond the first viewpoint, and also on Penanjakan, set on a ledge jutting out from the main trail – has even better views than the top. From here looking toward the west you'll see Bromo bathed in that dawn light, along with Gunung Batok, with Gunung Semeru photo bombing from behind. It can take up to an hour to reach it, but it's a stunning walk. Just up from the village, the slopes are planted with scallions, potatoes and cauliflower. You won't see them in the dark, but they make a lovely vista on the easy downhill stroll. Trekkers can also take an interesting walk across the Laotian Pasir to the village of Ngadas (8km), below the southern rim of the Tengger crater. From here, motorbikes and 4WDs descend to Tumpang, which is connected by regular buses to Malang.

🛏 Sleeping

Accommodation in the Bromo area is notoriously poor value for money. Given it's proximity to Bromo, the village of Cemoro Lawang is the most convenient place to stay, and offers a choice of rudimentary guesthouses or overpriced hotels. Around 5km eastwards towards Probolinggo is another enclave of guesthouses that also has some OK spots, including Yoschi's Hotel.

🛏 Cemora Lawag

Tengger Indah   HOMESTAY $
(☑ 0858 5357 4021; Cemoro Lawang; r incl breakfast 250,000Rp; 🛜) An east-facing double-storey homestay in town, a stone's throw from the rim at the junction. Prim and painted with murals on the exterior, the interiors are simple, tiled and affordable. There are superb views from its balcony, and it's perfectly located for the jaunts into Bromo.

Cafe Lava Hostel   HOTEL $$
(☑ 0812 3584 1111, 0335-541020; www.cafelava. lavaindonesia.com; Cemoro Lawang; r without bathroom from 175,000Rp, with bathroom & breakfast from 450,000Rp; ❄🛜) With a sociable vibe thanks to its streetside cafe and attractive layout (rooms are scattered down the side of

a valley), this is first choice for most travellers, despite the steep prices. Economy rooms are very small but neat, and have access to a shared verandah and clean communal bathrooms (fitted with all-important hot showers).

Ngadisari

Yoschi's Hotel GUESTHOUSE **$$**
(☑ 0813 3129 8881, 0335-541018; www.hotelyoschi. com; Wonokerto St 117, Km2; incl breakfast, r with shared/private bathroom 300,000/540,000Rp, cottages from 900,000Rp; @ 🛜) This rustic place has lots of character, with bungalows and small rooms dotted around a large, leafy garden compound. However, many lack hot water and cleanliness standards could be better. There's a huge restaurant that serves up pricey Western and Indonesian food (subject to a stiff 20% service charge), along with a bar and wi-fi access.

Probolinggo

Sinar Harapan HOTEL **$**
(☑ 0823 3110 0222, 0335-7010335; Jl Bengawan Solo 100; r with fan/air-con from 100,000/150,000Rp; ❄🛜) An OK hotel with a contemporary feel, but its shine is fading and little English is spoken. Also it's a little out of town, 6km from the bus station, but it's in a relaxed neighbourhood. It rents out motorbikes to guests for 100,000Rp per day. An *ojek* from the bus station is around 25,000Rp.

ℹ Information

Information about trails and mountain conditions is available from the **PHKA post** (☑ 0335-541038; ☺ 8am-3pm Tue-Sun) in Cemoro Lawang and also at the **PHKA post** (☑ 034-357 1048; ☺ 8am-3pm Tue-Sun) on the southern outskirts of Wonokitri. Both extend their opening hours during busy periods. The park's official office is located in Malang.

ℹ Getting There & Away

Probolinggo is the main gateway to Bromo. From Probolinggo there are public minibuses to Cemoro Lawang (35,000Rp to 40,000Rp, two hours) at the foot of Bromo, but they only leave when they're full. Otherwise there are shuttles run by tour operators for around 60,000Rp to 100,000Rp

For the return trip you can try to take the public minibus (which again, have no set schedules) or otherwise there's a shuttle (50,000Rp to 60,000Rp) that leaves around 9.30am to Probol-

inggo, from where you can catch long-distance buses to Yogyakarta and Denpasar. Many people arrive on tours from Yogyakarta, which involves a punishing overland journey, usually in a cramped minibus. **Great Tours** (Map p183; ☑ 0274-583221; www.greattoursjogja.com; Jl Sosrowijayan 29; ☺ 8am-8pm) is one recommended company that offers this trip for around 180,000Rp.

Alternatively you can take the train from Yogyakarta to Probolinggo (74,000Rp to 315,000Rp, 8½ to nine hours, three times daily), and then take the minibus up to Cemoro Lawang. Yogyakarta to Surabaya by train is another option, and then a train or bus to Probolinggo.

Tours to Bromo are also easily organised in Malang, where you can arrange 4WD hire in hotels and travel agencies. If you've got your own vehicle you'll have to take the long route via Probolinggo; only 4WD jeeps can make the pass over the soft volcanic sand roads via Malang.

Bondowoso

☑ 0332 / POP 69,780

Bondowoso, suspended between the highlands of Tengger and Ijen, is the gateway to Bromo and Ijen and home to some of the island's best *tape*, a tasty, sweet-and-sour snack made from boiled and fermented cassava. It is mainly a transit and market town, but tours to Ijen can be organised here.

Just south of the huge, grassy *alun-alun* (main public square), **Palm Hotel** (☑ 0332-421201; www.palm-hotel.net; Jl A Yani 32; r incl breakfast with fan & cold shower 219,000Rp, with air-con from 341,000Rp; ❄🛜🛁) has a huge, heat-busting pool, spacious air-conditioned rooms and an open-air restaurant.

ℹ Getting There & Away

To get to Ijen there are many (cramped) minibuses to Sempol (around 30,000Rp, 2½ to 3½ hours), a gateway village to tackle the volcano; all leave Bondowoso's **bus terminal** (Jl Imam Bonjol) before 1pm. From Sempol you can take an *ojek* (50,000Rp) to Pos Paltuding, the starting point for treks to Ijen. Otherwise **Palm Hotel** can arrange trips for 750,000Rp.

Other destinations from Bondowoso include Jember (7000Rp, one hour), Probolinggo (25,000Rp to 35,000Rp, two hours) and Surabaya (normal/air-con 38,000/70,0000Rp, five hours).

Ijen Plateau

The fabled Ijen Plateau is a vast volcanic region dominated by the three cones of Ijen (2368m), Merapi (2800m) and Raung

INDONESIA IJEN PLATEAU

SURABAYA

Polluted, congested and business-driven, Surabaya is mainly a transport hub for most travellers. Attractions are slim on the ground, and against the calm of rural east Java, it is pandemonium writ large. And yet if you've the patience to explore, Surabaya has quixotic little corners of interest. Its historic **Arab quarter** is fascinating: a labyrinthine warren of lanes leading to historic **Mesjid Ampel** (Jl Ampel Suci) FREE that's a place of pilgrimage. Surabaya also has one of Indonesia's biggest Chinatowns and impressive, though disintegrating, Dutch buildings. For locals, Surabaya is closely linked to the birth of the Indonesian nation, as it was here that the battle for independence began.

If you get stuck, head for **Hotel Paviljoen** (031-534 3449; www.hotelpaviljoen.com/id; Jl Genteng Besar 94-98; r incl breakfast with fan/air-con from 148,000/198,000Rp;), in a colonial villa that still has a twinkle of charm, or **The Hostel** (0812 3517 4233; Jl Simpang Dukuh 38-40; dm incl breakfast 120,000Rp;), with dorm beds and friendly managment.

(3332m). Virtually everyone comes purely for Ijen and the hike up to its spectacular sulphur crater lake and to experience the unworldly sight of its 'blue fire' phenomenon.

The rest of the area is also worthy of exploration, and its sweeping vistas combined with a temperate climate make the plateau a great base for a few days. A beautiful, forested alpine area, the most dramatic scenery is yours as you wind through the rubber and clove groves, climbing up and over a pass, before dropping into an extinct crater (the so-called plateau), now home to evocative, shade-grown coffee plantations, threaded with streams and gurgling with hot springs. Along with the plantations and their company *kampung* (village), there are a few isolated settlements here.

Sights & Activities

The magnificent turquoise sulphur lake of Kawah Ijen lies at 2148m above sea level and is surrounded by the volcano's sheer crater walls. At the edge of the lake, sulphurous smoke billows from the volcano's vent and the lake bubbles when activity increases. Ijen's last major eruption was in 1936, though due to an increased threat access was closed in late 2011, and again in March 2012 for a few weeks.

Ijen is a major sulphur-gathering centre and you'll pass the collectors as you hike up the trail. Most now ask for a fee for photographs, though a cigarette will usually be accepted as payment.

The starting point for the trek to the crater is the **PHKA post** (weekdays/weekends 100,000/150,000Rp) at Pos Paltuding, which can be reached from Bondowoso or Banyuwangi. Sign in and pay your entry fee here.

The steep 3km path up to the observation post (where there's a teahouse) takes just over an hour. From the post it's a further 30-minute walk to the lip of the wind-blasted crater and its stunning views.

From the crater rim, an extremely steep, gravelly path leads down to the sulphur deposits and the steaming lake. Most climbers make the effort to set out in the middle of the night in order to witness the stunning and eerie spectacle of its 'blue fire', which blazes on the shore of the crater lake. Only visible in the darkness of night (generally best viewed before 4am – which is when most people arrive to coincide with sunrise), this phenomenon of glowing electric-blue flame is explained through the combustion of sulphurous gases, an effect seen only in a few places on Earth; Iceland is another. The walk down takes around 30 minutes; the path is slippery in parts and the sulphur fumes towards the bottom can be overwhelming. Expect burning lungs and streaming eyes if you do make it to the bottom. Take great care – a French tourist fell and died here some years ago. A gas mask is essential, available for hire for 50,000Rp at Pos Paltuding; make sure you test it works before setting off. Those with respiratory illnesses should avoid making the descent into the crater. Bringing along a guide (100,000Rp to 150,000Rp) is highly recommended.

Back at the lip of the crater, turn left for the climb to the highest point (2368m) and magnificent views at sunrise, or keep walking counterclockwise for even more expansive vistas of the lake. On the other side of the lake, opposite the vent, the trail disappears into crumbling volcanic rock and deep ravines.

WORTH A TRIP

SURFING G-LAND

Occupying the whole of the remote Blambangan Peninsula on the southeastern tip of Java, **Alas Purwo National Park** has spectacular beaches and good opportunities for wildlife-spotting. Surfers head here for Plengkung, on the isolated southeastern tip of the peninsula, where one of the best left-handed waves in the world breaks over a shallow reef in perfect barrels. Surfers have dubbed it G-Land. It's best between April and September.

Grajagan Surf Charter (☑ 0813 5808 0565, 0853 3092 9851; kenrofish72@gmail. com; 4-person boat trip US$90) can get you out on the waves and arrange fishing and ecotrips. **Wana Wisata** (☑ 0821 4397 3873; Grajagan Beach; ☺ r with fan/air-con from 200,000/250,000Rp; ✳) is a laid-back losmen over the bay in Grajagan Beach (outside the national park), while **G-Land Joyo's Surf Camp** (☑ 0812 380 5899, bookings in Bali 0817 939 9777; www.g-land.com; 3-night incl food & transport from Bali from US$625; ✳ ☎) is a more upmarket resort offering package trips from Bali.

The ideal time to make the Kawah Ijen hike is in the dry season between April and October. However, while the path is steep, it's usually not too slippery, so the hike is certainly worth a try in the rainy season if you have a clear day.

🛏 Sleeping

⭐**Catimor Homestay**   LODGE $
(☑ 0823 3262 8342; catimor_n12@yahoo.com; Blawan; r 200,000-400,000Rp; ☎ ✳) This budget lodge boasts an excellent location in the Kebun Balawan coffee plantation, close to hot springs and a waterfall. Rooms are divided between its original wooden Dutch lodge (c 1894), which features a fantastic sitting area, or better maintained and cleaner rooms around its sparkling, chilly pool. Be sure to indulge yourself in the spring-fed hot tub (from 4pm).

Arabika Homestay   LODGE $
(☑ 0852 5959 5955; arabica.homestay@gmail. com; Jl Kawah Ijen, Sempol; r incl breakfast 200,000-400,000Rp; ☎) This dated, usually chilly mountain lodge is managed by the Kebun Kalisat coffee plantation, which is a short walk away. While general cleanliness could be better it remains an atmospheric place with lovely views of Ijen from its restaurant patio. The cheapest rooms are in the main building, or nicer options in its rows of cottage-style accommodation.

ℹ Getting There & Away

It is possible to travel nearly all the way to Kawah Ijen by public transport, but most visitors charter transport. Both access roads are badly potholed and slow going.

FROM BONOWOSO

From Wonosari, 8km from Bondowoso towards Situbondo, a rough, potholed road runs via Sukosari and Sempol to Pos Paltuding. It's normally passable in any high-clearance vehicle, but sometimes a 4WD is necessary. Sign in at the coffee-plantation checkpoints (around 5000Rp) on the way. Hotels in Bondowoso can arrange day tours to Ijen for around 750,000Rp.

By public transport, several angkot run from Bondowoso to Sempol (30,000Rp, 2½ hours), most in the late morning, but there's a final one at 1pm. If passengers want to continue on to Pos Paltuding, drivers will sometimes do so, though foreigners are regularly overcharged on this route. Otherwise ojek in Sempol charge around 50,000Rp one way. At Pos Paltuding, there are usually a few drivers to take you back.

FROM BANYUWANGI

The Banyuwangi–Ijen road was in good condition at research time, though it has been known to be impossibly rutted in the past. Check locally for current conditions before setting off. There's no public transport all the way from Banyuwangi to Pos Paltuding, which is a sparsely populated region.

The best option is to take a tour with **Green Ijen Homestay** who run trips to see the blue fire for 200,000Rp per person (excluding entry fee). Otherwise jeep-style cars (700,000Rp per vehicle) can be arranged through the Banyuwangi tourist office. Chartering an ojek from Banyuwangi to Ijen is possible for around 200,000Rp (including a wait of four hours). Ojek drivers hang around the ferry terminal in Ketapang and Banyuwangi bus station, or ask at your guesthouse.

Heading back down the mountain, ojek charge around 100,000Rp for a one-way ride to Banyuwangi from Pos Paltuding.

Banyuwangi

📞 0333 / POP 116,000

Java's land's end is a pleasant, growing city, home to a large number of Osig people, whose roots reach back centuries in southeast Java. Most travellers simply pass through on their way to or from Bali by ferry, but the city does make a reasonable and comfortable base to explore the Ijen Plateau and other national parks along the east coast. It's worthy of a night or two.

Point of clarification: the ferry port for Bali, the bus terminal and the train station are all some 8km north of town in Ketapang, though all transport states 'Banyuwangi' as their destination.

🛏 Sleeping

Green Ijen Homestay GUESTHOUSE **$**
(📱 0823 3255 5077; greenijen@gmail.com; Jl Opak 7; r incl breakfast, with shared bathroom & fan/ air-con 125,000/200,000Rp; 🛜) Easily one of Banyuwangi's best budget choices is this relaxed, lime-green guesthouse, tucked down a residential street in town. Rooms here are both spotless and comfortable. It's run by Johan who's very helpful with all local tourist info, and is *the* place to arrange Ijen volcano tours (per person 200,000Rp, excluding entrance ticket) to see the 'blue flame'.

If you book a tour to Ijen there's free pickup from the harbor, train station or bus terminal. Snorkelling tours are also popular here.

🛈 Getting There & Away

BOAT

Ferries depart around the clock for Gilimanuk in Bali (every 45 minutes, one hour). The ferry costs 6500Rp for passengers, 24,000Rp for a motorbike and 159,000 for a car (including four pasesengers). Through-buses between Bali and Java include the ferry fare in the bus ticket. Pelni ships no longer call at Banyuwangi.

BUS

Banyuwangi has two bus terminals. The Sri Tanjung terminal is 3km north of Ketapang ferry terminal, 11km from the centre. Buses from here head along the north coast road to Baluran (12,000Rp, one hour), Probolinggo (normal/ *patas* 36,000/60,000Rp, five hours) and Surabaya (54,000/90,000Rp, seven hours). Buses to Denpasar (40,000/ 70,000Rp, five hours) include the ferry trip.

Brawijaya terminal (also known as Karang Ente), 4km south of town, covers buses along the southern highway to Kalibaru

(15,000/22,000Rp, two hours) and Jember (35,000Rp, three hours).

TRAIN

The main Banyuwangi train station is just a few hundred metres north of the ferry terminal. There are about five trains a day to Probolinggo (27,000Rp to 160,000Rp, 4¼ to five hours), four trains to Surabaya (56,000Rp to 170,000Rp, 6¼ to 7¼ hours) and one train to Yogyakarta (94,000Rp, 13 to 14 hours) at 6.30am.

BALI

Impossibly green rice terraces, pulse-pounding surf, enchanting Hindu temple ceremonies, mesmerising dance performances, ribbons of beaches, truly charming people: there are as many images of Bali as there are flowers on the ubiquitous frangipani trees. This small island looms large for any visit to Indonesia. No place is more visitor-friendly. Hotels range from surfer dives to lavish retreats in the lush mountains. You can dine on local foods bursting with flavours fresh from the markets or let world-class chefs take you on a culinary journey around the globe. From a cold Bintang beer at sunset to an epic night out clubbing, your social whirl is limited only by your fortitude. And small obviously doesn't mean homogeneous. Manic Kuta segues into glitzy Seminyak. The artistic swirl of Ubud is a counterpoint to misty treks amid the volcanoes, including Mt Agung which erupted several times in 2017, forcing thousands to evacuate and disrupting air travel. Mellow beach towns such as Bingin, Amed and Pemuteran are found right round the coast.

History

Bali's first prehistoric tourists strolled out of the spume and onto the island's western beaches around 3000 BC. Perhaps distracted by primitive beach life, however, they got off to a relaxed start and it was only in the 9th century that an organised society began to develop around the cultivation of rice. Hinduism followed hot on the heels of wider cultural development, and as Islam swept through neighbouring Java in the following centuries, the kings and courtiers of the embattled Hindu Majapahit kingdom began crossing the straits into Bali, making their final exodus in 1478. The priest Nirartha brought many of the complexities of the Balinese Hindu religion to the island. In the 19th century the Dutch began to form alliances with local princes in northern Bali. A dispute over the ransacking of wrecked ships was the pretext for the 1906 Dutch invasion of the south, which climaxed in a suicidal *puputan* (fight to the death). The Denpasar nobility burnt their own palaces, dressed in their finest jewellery and, waving golden kris (traditional daggers), marched straight into the Dutch guns. In later years, Bali's rich and complex culture was actually encouraged by many Dutch officials. International interest was aroused and the first Western tourists arrived in the 1930s. The tourism boom, which started in the early 1970s, has brought many changes, and has helped pay for improvements in roads, telecommunications, education and health. Though tourism and Bali's sizzling economic development has have had marked adverse environmental and social effects, Bali's unique culture has proved to be remarkably resilient, even as visitor numbers approach four million per year.

ⓘ Dangers & Annoyances

Persistent hawkers are the bane of most visitors to Bali. The best way to deal with them is to ignore them from the first instance. 'Temporary' tattoos in any colour may cause permanent damage due to the use of toxic chemicals, and *arak* (alcohol typically distilled from the sap of the coconut palm or from rice) should always be viewed with suspicion. There's also an ongoing rabies problem. The beaches on the west side of the island, including Kuta and Seminyak, are subject to heavy surf and strong currents. The sea water near touristed areas is commonly contaminated by run-off from both built-up areas and surrounding farmland, especially after heavy rains. You can smell it. Bali's economic and tourism boom means that traffic is now a huge problem across South Bali. It's also a menace: someone dies on Bali's choked roads every day, reason enough to wear a helmet while riding your motorcycle.

ⓘ Getting There & Away

AIR
Ngurah Rai International Airport (http://bali-airport.com), just south of Kuta, is the only airport in Bali. It is sometimes referred to internationally as Denpasar or on some internet flight-booking sites as Bali.

International airlines flying to and from Bali have myriad flights to Australia and Asian capitals. The present runway is too short for planes flying nonstop to/from Europe. Domestic airlines serving Bali from other parts of Indonesia change frequently.

BOAT
Pelni (www.pelni.co.id), the national shipping line, operates large boats on infrequent long-distance runs throughout Indonesia. For Bali, Pelni ships stop at the harbour in Benoa. Schedules and fares are found on the website. You can enquire and book at the **Pelni ticket office** (☑ 0361-763963, 0623 6175 5855; www.pelni.co.id; Jl Raya Kuta 299; ⊙ 8am-noon & 1-4pm Mon-Fri, 8am-1pm Sat) in Tuban.

You can reach Java, just west of Bali, via the ferries that run between Gilimanuk in west Bali and Ketapang (Java), and then take a bus all the way to Jakarta.

Public car ferries travel slowly between Padangbai and Lembar on Lombok. There are also fast boats from various ports in Bali to the Gilis and Lombok.

BUS
Any trip to Bali over land will require a ferry crossing.

The ferry crossing from Bali is included in the services offered by numerous bus companies, many of which travel overnight to Java. It's advisable to buy your ticket at least one day in advance from a travel agent or at the terminals in Denpasar (Ubang) or Mengwi. Note that flying can be almost as cheap as the bus.

Fares vary between operators; it's worth paying extra for a decent seat (all have air-con). Destinations include Yogyakarta (350,000Rp, 20 hours) and Jakarta (500,000Rp, 24 hours). You can also get buses from Singaraja in north Bali.

ⓘ Getting Around

TO/FROM THE AIRPORT
A taxi from Ngurah Rai International Airport to Kuta is 80,000Rp, to Seminyak it's 130,000Rp and to Ubud it's 300,000Rp.

BEMO & BUS
Bemos are normally a minibus or van with a row of low seats down each side and which carry about 12 people in very cramped conditions. They were once the dominant form of public transport in Bali, but widespread motorbike ownership (which is often cheaper than daily bemo use) has caused the system to wither. Expect to find that getting to many places is both time-consuming and inconvenient. It's uncommon to see visitors on bemos in Bali.

Larger minibuses and full-size buses ply the longer routes, particularly on routes linking Denpasar, Singaraja and Gilimanuk. They operate out of the same terminals as bemos. However, with everybody riding motorbikes, there are long delays waiting for buses to fill up at terminals before departing.

Bali

20 km
10 miles

Gili Trawangan (30km)

Lombok (25km)

Lombok (30km)

Lombok Strait

JAVA

Betekan
Selogiri
Gunung Agung (310m)
Prapat
Labuhan
Pulau Menjangan
Gilimanuk
Cekik
Banyuwangi
Ketapang
Rogodjampi

Bali Strait

Pemuteran
Banyuwedang
Lalang
Gunung Kelatakan
Gunung Musi (1224m)
Taman Nasional Bali Barat
Gunung Sanglang (1004m)
Gunung Merbuk (13388m)
Gunung Gede
Pura Gede Perancak
Perancak
Melaya

Tanjung Sembulungan

JAWA TIMUR

Taman Nasional Alas Purwo

Blambangan Peninsula

Plengkung

INDIAN OCEAN

Bali Sea

Celukanbawang
Serirt
Lovina
Pengastulen
Rangdu
Mayong
Munduk
Pujungan
Medewi
Mendoyo
Negara
Pura Rambut Siwi

Balian Beach

Sembireteng
Tembok
Pacung
Tejakula
Sangsit
Jagaraga
Sawan
Sukasade
Gitgit
Singaraja
Kubutambahan
Yeh Sanih

Gunung Penulisan (1745m)
Gunung Catur Penulisan (2096m)
Catur
Kintamani
Danau Bratan
Gunung Batukau (2276m)
Candikuning
Pupuan
Bedugul
Pelaga
Batur
Penelokan
Danau Buyan
Danau Bratan (Candikuning)
Tamblingan
Pura Ulun Danu

Kubu
Culik
Tianyar
Tirta Gangga
Amed
Gunung Seraya (1175m)
Gunung Aas
AMLAPURA
Ujung
Tenganan
Candidasa
Padangbai
Tulamben

Gunung Agung (3142m)
Besakih
Pampatan
Muncan
Duda
Iseh
Sidemen
Semarapura (Klungkung)
Rendang
Toya Bungkah
Songan
Gunung Batur (1717m)
Danau Batur

Kayuanbua
Kayubihi
Petang
Pujung
Tampaksiring
Pejeng
Ubud
Mas
Batuan
Celuk
Sukawati
Batubulan
Bangli
Sidan
Jambu
Bukit
Lebih
Pura Masceti
Gianyar
Ketewel
Kusamba
Nusa Lembongan
Ped
Toyapakeh
Jungutbatu
Lembongan
Nusa Ceningan
529m
Nusa Penida
Sampalan
Karangsari
Semaya

Badung Strait

Pelaga
Payangan
Marga
Sangeh
Mengwi
Bedulu
Pura Taman Ayun
Kediri
Antosari
Tabanan
Penebel
Jatiluwih
Pacung
Wongayegede
Pura Luhur Batukau

Sempidi
Canggu
Seminyak
Kerobokan
Legian
Kuta
Denpasar
Sanur
Serangan
Pulau Serangan
Benoa Harbour
Tanjung Benoa
Nusa Dua
Ngurah Rai International Airport
Bukit Peninsula
Jimbaran
Bingin
Pecatu
Pura Luhur Ulu Watu

Pura Tanahlot

Tourist buses are economical and convenient ways to get around. You'll see signs offering services in major tourist areas. Typically a tourist bus is an eight- to 20-passenger vehicle. Service is not as quick as with your own car and driver but it's far easier than trying to use public bemos and buses.

BICYCLE

Increasingly, people are touring the island by *sepeda* (bike) and many visitors are using bikes around towns and for day trips.

There are plenty of bicycles for rent in tourist areas, but many are in poor condition. Ask at your accommodation. Prices are from 30,000Rp per day.

BOAT

Fast boats linking Bali, Nusa Lembongan, Lombok and the Gili Islands have proliferated, especially as the latter places have become more popular.

CAR & MOTORCYCLE

Renting a car or motorbike can open up Bali for exploration – and can also leave you counting the minutes until you return it; there can be harrowing driving conditions on the islands at certain times and south Bali traffic is often awful. But it gives you the freedom to explore myriad back roads and lets you set your own schedule.

Most people don't rent a car for their entire visit but rather get one for a few days of meandering.

Motorbikes are a popular way of getting around – locals ride pillion almost from birth. A family of five all riding cheerfully along on one motorbike is called a Bali minivan.

Rentals cost 50,000Rp a day, less by the week. This should include minimal insurance for the motorcycle but not for any other person or property. Some have racks for surfboards.

Think carefully before renting a motorbike. It is dangerous and every year visitors go home with lasting damage – this is no place to learn to ride. Helmet use is mandatory.

If you plan to drive a car, you're supposed to have an International Driving Permit (IDP). You can obtain one from your national motoring organisation if you have a normal driving licence. Bring your home licence as well. Without an IDP, add 50,000Rp to any fine you'll have to pay if stopped by the police.

An excellent way to travel anywhere around Bali is by hired vehicle with a driver, allowing you to leave the driving and inherent frustrations to others. Costs for a full day should average 500,000Rp to 800,000Rp.

TAXI & OJEK

Metered taxis are common in south Bali and Denpasar (but not Ubud). They are essential for getting around and you can usually flag one down in busy areas. They're often a lot less hassle than haggling with drivers offering 'transport!' The best taxi company by far is **Blue Bird Taxi** (☑ 0361-701111; www.bluebirdgroup.com), which uses blue vehicles with a light on the roof bearing a stylised bluebird.

Around towns and along roads, you can always get a lift by *ojek* (a motorcycle or motorbike that takes a paying passenger). Fares are negotiable, but about 30,000Rp for 5km is fairly standard.

Kuta & Legian

☑ 0361

Loud and frenetic, Kuta and Legian are the epicentre of mass tourism in Bali. The grit and wall-to-wall cacophony have become notorious through often overhyped media reports of tourists behaving badly. Although this is often the first place many visitors hit in Bali, the region is not for everyone. Kuta has ugly narrow lanes jammed with cheap cafes, surf shops, incessant motorbikes and an uncountable number of T-shirt vendors and bleating offers of 'massage'. But flash new shopping malls and chain hotels show that Kuta's allure may continue to grow.

◎ Sights & Activities

Kuta and Legian's main appeal is, of course, the beaches. And on the streets and back alleys, wanderers will find much to fascinate, delight and irritate amid the constant hubbub.

Low-key hawkers will sell you soft drinks and beer, snacks and other treats, and you can rent surfboards, lounge chairs and umbrellas (negotiable at 10,000Rp to 20,000Rp), or just crash on the sand. The sunsets are legendary.

Dream Museum Zone   MUSEUM
(Map p206; ☑ 0361-849 6220; http://dmzbali.com/eng; Jl Nakula 33X; 110,000Rp, child under 3 free; ☺ 9am-10pm) Fun for the whole family, it features a collection of around 120 interactive life-size murals that come to life – or rather, can be viewed in 3D – once photographed. It's divided into 14 sections so you can take your pick from Indonesia, Jurassic Park, Egypt and others.

Waterbom Park   WATER PARK
(Map p206; ☑ 0361-755676; www.waterbom-bali.com; Jl Kartika Plaza; adult/child 520,000/370,000Rp; ☺ 9am-6pm) This watery amusement park covers 3.8 hectares of landscaped tropical gardens. It has assorted water

slides (a couple dozen in total, including the 'Climax'), swimming pools, a FlowRider surf machine and a 'lazy river' ride. Other indulgences include a food court, a bar and a spa.

Pro Surf School
SURFING
(Map p206; 📞0361-751200; www.prosurfschool.com; Jl Pantai Kuta; lessons per day from 675,000Rp; 🕾) Right along Kuta Beach, this well-regarded school has been getting beginners standing for years. It offers all levels of lessons, including semi-private ones, plus gear and board rental. There are dorm rooms (from 150,000Rp), a pool and a cool cafe.

Rip Curl School of Surf
SURFING
(Map p206; 📞0361-735858; www.ripcurlschoolofsurf.com; Jl Arjuna; lessons from 700,000Rp) Usually universities sell shirts with their logos; here it's the other way round: the beachwear company sponsors a school. Lessons at all levels are given across the south; there are special courses for kids. It has a location for kitesurfing, windsurfing, diving, wakeboarding and stand-up paddle boarding (SUP) in Sanur.

🛏 Sleeping

★ Kuta Bed & Breakfast
GUESTHOUSE $
(KBB; Map p206; 📞0818 568 364, 0821 4538 9646; kutabnb@gmail.com; Jl Pantai Kuta 1E; r from 250,000Rp; ❄🕾) There are nine comfortable rooms in this excellent guesthouse right across from Bemo Corner – it has all the basics. It's a 10-minute walk from the beach and a 10-minute ride from the airport. It has a wonderful rooftop with views over the Kuta skyline; nightlife is close too.

★ Hotel Ayu Lili Garden
HOTEL $
(Map p206; 📞0361-750557; ayuliligardenhotel@yahoo.com; off Jl Lebak Bene; r with fan/air-con from 195,000/250,000Rp; ❄🕾🏊) In a *relatively* quiet area near the beach, this vintage family-run hotel has 22 bungalow-style rooms. Standards are high and for a little bit extra you can add amenities such as a fridge.

La Costa Central
HOTEL $
(Map p206; 📞0812 8041 7263; Jl Nakula; r incl breakfast 280,000Rp; ❄🕾🏊) In a multistorey building off a relatively quiet side street in Legian, this comfy and economical new hotel will wow backpackers with its sparkling clean rooms, lush garden and refreshing swimming pool. Rooms contain midrange amenities such as minifridge and bath products, and staff members are kind and helpful. Those seeking a bit more privacy will prefer the 3rd floor.

Cheeky Piggy Hostel
HOSTEL $
(Map p206; 📞0361-475 3919; Poppies Lane 1; dm/r 75,000/170,000Rp; ❄🕾🏊) In a tourist-thronged location in the back alleys of Kuta, close to **Poppies Restaurant** (Map p206; 📞0361-751059; www.poppiesbali.com; Poppies Gang I; mains 40,000-130,000Rp; ⊙8am-11pm; 🕾), this homely and intimate hostel is a top place to meet fellow travellers. There's a small pool, free pancakes and cheap beer.

Kayun Hostel Downtown
HOSTEL $
(Map p206; 📞0361-758442; www.kayun-downtown.com; Jl Legian; dm from 100,000Rp; ❄🕾🏊) In the heart of Kuta, close to all the nightlife, this hostel is the place to be if you're here to party. Set in an elegant colonial building, it has a sense of style and a small plunge pool. Dorm rooms have between four and 20 beds, with curtains for privacy.

Island
GUESTHOUSE $$
(Map p206; 📞0361-762722; www.theislandhotelbali.com; Gang Abdi; dm/r incl breakfast from 150,000/500,000Rp; ❄@🕾🏊) One of Bali's few flashpacker options, Island is a real find – literally. Hidden in the attractive maze of tiny lanes west of Jl Legian, this stylish place with a sparkling pool lies at the confluence of Gang 19, 21 and Abdi. It has a deluxe dorm room with 12 beds.

🍴 Eating & Drinking

Saleko
INDONESIAN $
(Map p206; Jl Nakula 4; meals from 15,000Rp; ⊙8am-1am Mon-Sat, 9am-1am Sun; 🍴) If you haven't tried Masakan Padang food yet, you haven't eaten proper Indonesian. Saleko is a great place to sample this simple, delicious and cheap Sumatran street food. Spicy grilled chicken and fish dare you to ladle on the volcanic sambal – not despiced for timid tourist palates. For vegetarians there's also tasty tofu, cooked jack fruit and flavourful eggplant.

Warung Asia
ASIAN $
(Map p206; Jl Werkudara; mains from 32,000Rp; ⊙10.30am-11pm; 🕾) Staffed by waiters cheery even by Bali standards, this popular upstairs warung serves both Indo classics and Thai fare. It gets boozy and raucous at night.

Fat Chow
ASIAN $$
(Map p206; 📞0361-753516; www.fatchowbali.com; Poppies Gang II; mains from 60,000Rp; ⊙10am-10.20pm; 🕾) A stylish, modern take on the

Kuta & Legian

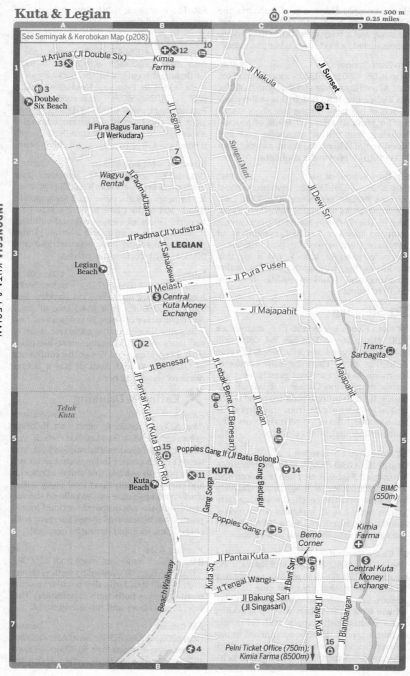

See Seminyak & Kerobokan Map (p208)

0
0

500 m
0.25 miles

Jl Arjuna (Jl Double Six)
13

Kimia
Farma
12
10

Jl Nakula

Jl Sunset

3
Double
Six Beach

1

Jl Legian

Jl Pura Bagus Taruna
(Jl Werkudara)

7

Stungai Mati

Jl Dewi Sri

Wagyu
Rental

Jl Padmautara

Jl Padma (Jl Yudistra)

LEGIAN

Jl Sahadewa

Legian
Beach

Jl Pura Puseh

Jl Melasti
Central
Kuta Money
Exchange

Jl Majapahit

Trans-
Sarbagita

Jl Benesari

2

Jl Pantai Kuta (Kuta Beach Rd)

Jl Lebak Bene (Jl Benesari)

Jl Legian

6

Jl Majapahit

Teluk
Kuta

8

15

Poppies Gang II (Jl Batu Bolong)

Gang Bedugul

14

BIMC
(550m)

Kuta
Beach

11

KUTA

Gang Sorga

Poppies Gang I

5

Kimia
Farma

Bemo
Corner

Beach Walkway

Kuta Sq

Jl Pantai Kuta

Jl Buni Sari

9

Central Kuta
Money
Exchange

Jl Tengal Wangi

Jl Bakung Sari
(Jl Singasari)

Jl Raya Kuta

Jl Blambangan

4

Pelni Ticket Office (750m);
Kimia Farma (8500m)

16

INDONESIA KUTA & LEGIAN

Kuta & Legian

traditional open-fronted cafe, Fat Chow serves Asian-accented fare at long picnic tables, small tables and lounges. The food is creative, with lots of options for sharing. Among the favourites: crunchy Asian salad, pork buns, Tokyo prawns and authentic pad Thai.

Sky Garden Lounge CLUB
(Map p206; www.skygardenbali.com; Jl Legian 61; from 115,000Rp; ⊙5pm-4am) This multilevel palace of flash flirts with height restrictions from its rooftop bar where all of Kuta twinkles around you. Look for top DJs, a ground-level cafe and paparazzi-wannabes. Possibly Kuta's most iconic club, with hourly drink specials and a buffet. Gets backpackers, drunken teens, locals on the make etc.

🛍 Shopping

Beachwalk MALL
(Map p206; www.beachwalkbali.com; Jl Pantai Kuta; ⊙10.30am-10.30pm Mon-Thu, 10am-midnight Fri-Sun) This vast open-air mall, hotel and condo development across from Kuta Beach is filled with international chains: from Gap to Starbucks. Water features course amid the generic retail glitz. Dig deep for the odd interesting find.

Joger GIFTS & SOUVENIRS
(Map p206; ☎0361-752523; Jl Raya Kuta; ⊙10am-8pm) This Bali retail legend is the most popular store in the south. Mobs come for doe-eyed plastic puppies or one of thousands of T-shirts bearing wry, funny or simply inexplicable phrases (almost all are limited edition). In fact the sign out front says 'Pabrik Kata-Kata', which means 'factory of words'. Warning: conditions inside the cramped store are insane.

ℹ Getting There & Away

A minivan from the airport costs 100,000Rp to Tuban, 150,000Rp to Kuta and 160,000Rp to Legian. When travelling to the airport, get a metered taxi for savings. A motorbike taxi will usually cost about half of a regular taxi.

Bemos (minibuses) travel between Kuta and the Tegal terminal in Denpasar – the fare should be around 8000Rp.

Seminyak & Kerobokan
☎0361

Seminyak is the centre of life for hordes of the island's expats, many of whom own boutiques, design clothes, surf, or do seemingly nothing at all. It may be immediately north of Kuta and Legian, but in many respects, not the least of which is its intangible sense of style, Seminyak feels almost like it's on another island.

Seminyak seamlessly merges with Kerobokan, which is immediately north and combines some of Bali's best restaurants and shopping with still more beach. One notable landmark is the notorious Kerobokan jail.

A sunset lounger and an ice-cold Bintang on **Seminyak Beach** (Map p208) at sunset is simply magical. A good stretch can be found near Pura Petitenget, and it tends to be less crowded than further south in Kuta.

🛏 Sleeping & Eating

Raja Gardens GUESTHOUSE $
(Map p208; ☎0361-934 8957; www.jdw757.wixsite.com/rajagardens; off Jl Camplung Tanduk; r with fan/air-con from 500,000/600,000Rp; ❀🕱🗷) Here since 1980, this old-school guesthouse has spacious, grassy grounds with fruit trees and a quiet spot located almost on the beach. The eight rooms are fairly basic but there are open-air bathrooms and plenty of potted plants. The large pool is a nice spot to lounge by, and it's generally a mellow place.

Seminyak & Kerobokan

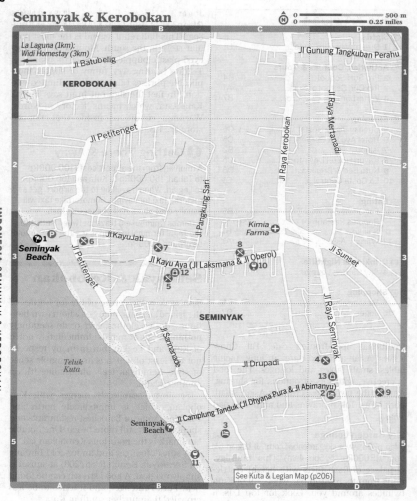

INDONESIA SEMINYAK & KEROBOKAN

Seminyak & Kerobokan

Ned's Hide-Away   GUESTHOUSE $
(Map p208; ☑0361-731270; waynekelly1978@
gmail.com; Gang Bima 3; r with fan/air-con from
180,000/300,000Rp; ✳🖟) While its standards have slipped, Ned's remains a good
budget choice with 16 rooms, some basic
and others more plush. Wi-fi is only available in reception.

⭐**Revolver**   CAFE $
(Map p208; ☑0851 0088 4968; off Jl Kayu Aya;
coffee 28,000-55,000Rp, mains from 35,000Rp;
🕓7am-midnight; 🖟) Wander down a tiny
gang and push through narrow wooden
doors to reach this matchbox coffee bar that
does an excellent selection of brews. There
are just a few tables in the creatively retro
room that's styled like a Wild West saloon;
nab one and enjoy tasty fresh bites for
breakfast and lunch.

Warung Taman Bambu   BALINESE $
(Map p208; ☑0361-888 1567; Jl Plawa 10; mains
from 28,000Rp; 🕓10am-10pm; 🖟) This classic
warung may look simple from the street but
the comfy tables are – like the many fresh
and spicy dishes on offer – a cut above the
norm. There's a small stand for *babi guling*
(suckling pig) right next door.

Warung Aneka Rasa   INDONESIAN $
(Map p208; ☑0812 361 7937; Jl Kayu Aya; meals
from 25,000Rp; 🕓7am-7pm) Keeping things
real in the heart of Seminyak's upmarket retail strip, this humble warung cooks up all
the Indo classics in an inviting open-front
cafe. It's a refuge from the buzz.

⭐**Shelter Cafe**   AUSTRALIAN $$
(Map p208; ☑0813 3770 6471; www.shelterca-
febali.com; Jl Drupadi; mains 55,000-80,000Rp;
🕓8am-6pm; 🖟) This second-storey cafe
brims daily with the young, beautiful people
of Seminyak, their coffee strong, their acai
bowls piled high. Those are actually from
Nalu Bowls (Map p208; ☑0812 3660 9776;
www.nalubowls.com; Jl Drupadi; 60,000-85,000Rp;
🕓7.30am-6pm), the acai bar downstairs, and
next door is also a third restaurant, Papitos
(the triumvirate is under joint ownership).
This is the top brunch spot in Seminyak, and
a cultural hub and host of things like pop-up
fashion stores and weekend parties.

⭐**Sisterfields**   CAFE $$
(Map p208; ☑0361-738454; www.sisterfieldsbali.
com; Jl Kayu Cendana 7; mains 80,000-150,000Rp;
🕓7am-10pm; 🖟) Trendy Sisterfields does
classic Aussie breakfasts such as smashed

avocado, and more-inventive dishes such as
salmon Benedict and maple-roasted-pump-
kin salad. There are also hipster faves such
as pulled-pork rolls and shakshuka poached
eggs. Grab a seat at a booth, the counter or
in the rear courtyard. Several other good coffee cafes are nearby.

Sea Circus   INTERNATIONAL $$
(Map p208; ☑0361-738667; http://seacircus-bali.
com; 22 Jl Kayu Aya; mains from 80,000Rp; 🕓7.30am-
10pm; 🖉) Adorned in cartoonish, pastel circus
murals, this fabulous spot offers up fresh and
delicious dishes inspired by cuisines in Asia,
Australia and the Americas. Brunch is hugely
popular and includes favourites such as acai
bowls, chilli scrambled eggs and the 'hang-
over happy meal'; the cocktails, taco bar and
dinner selections, including a summer tuna
poke bowl, are also exquisite.

🍷 **Drinking & Nightlife**

⭐**La Favela**   BAR
(Map p208; ☑8124 697 7410; www.lafavela.com;
Jl Kayu Aya 177X; 🕓5pm-late; 🖟) A mysterious
entry lures you into full bohemian flair at La
Favela, one of Bali's coolest and most origi-
nal nightspots. Themed rooms lead you on
a confounding tour from dimly lit speakeasy
cocktail lounges and antique dining rooms to
graffiti-splashed bars. Tables are cleared after
11pm to make way for DJs and a dance floor.

La Plancha   BAR
(Map p208; ☑0878 6141 6310; off Jl Camplung
Tanduk; 🕓8.30am-midnight) The most substan-
tial of the beach bars along the beach walk
south of Jl Camplung Tanduk, La Plancha
has its share of ubiquitous brightly coloured
umbrellas and beanbags on the sand, plus
a typical beach menu (pizzas, noodles etc).
After sunset, expect DJs and beach parties.

🛍 **Shopping**

⭐**Drifter Surf Shop**   FASHION & ACCESSORIES
(Map p208; ☑0361-733274; www.driftersurf.com; Jl
Kayu Aya 50; 🕓9am-11pm) High-end surf fash-
ion, surfboards, gear, cool books and brands
such as Obey and Wegener. Started by two
savvy surfer dudes, the shop stocks goods
noted for their individuality and high quality.

Duzty   CLOTHING
(Map p208; ☑0831 1460 4558; Jl Raya Seminyak
67; 🕓9am-10pm) Casual wear designed by
Rahsun, an up-and-coming Balinese talent.
Features edgy rock-and-roll and countercul-
ture themes.

❶ Getting There & Away

Metered taxis are easily hailed. A trip from the airport with the airport taxi cartel costs about 150,000Rp; a regular taxi to the airport, about 100,000Rp. You can beat the traffic, save the ozone and have a good stroll by walking along the beach; Legian is only about 15 minutes away.

Canggu & Around

More a state of mind than a place, Canggu is the catch-all name given to the villa-filled stretch of land between Kerobokan and Echo Beach. It's packed with an ever-more alluring collection of businesses, especially casual cafes. Three main strips have emerged, all running down to the beaches: two along meandering Jl Pantai Berawa and one on Jl Pantai Batu Bolong.

Batu Bolong Beach (parking motorbike/car 2000/5000Rp) is the most popular in the Canggu area. There's almost always a good mix of locals, expats and visitors hanging out in the cafes, surfing the breaks or watching it all from the sand. There are rental loungers, umbrellas and beer vendors.

🛏 Sleeping

Serenity Eco Guesthouse GUESTHOUSE $
(☑ 0361-846 9251, 0361-846 9257; www.serenityecoguesthouse.com; Jl Nelayan; dm/s/d incl breakfast 175,000/205,000/495,000Rp; ❄ 🛜 🛋) 🏊 This hotel is an oasis among the sterility of walled villas, run by young and inexperienced (though lovable) staff members. Rooms range from shared-bath singles to nice doubles with bathrooms (some with fans, others with air-con). The grounds are eccentric; Nelayan Beach is a five-minute walk. There are yoga classes (from 110,000Rp) and you can rent surfboards and bikes. his place makes an effort to minimise its carbon footprint.

Widi Homestay HOMESTAY $
(☑ 0819 3626 0860; widihomestay@yahoo.co.id; Jl Pantai Berawa; r from 250,000Rp; ❄ 🛜) There's no faux-hipster vibe here with fake nihilist bromides, just a spotless, friendly family-run homestay. The four rooms have hot water and air-con; the beach is barely 100m away.

🍴 Eating & Drinking

Betelnut Cafe CAFE $
(☑ 0821 4680 7233; Jl Pantai Batu Bolong; mains from 45,000Rp; ⏱ 7am-10pm; 🛜 🍴) There's a hippy-chic vibe at this thatched cafe with a mellow open-air dining room upstairs. The menu leans towards healthy, but not too healthy – you can get fries. There are juices and lots of mains featuring veggies. It has good baked goods and nice shakes.

⭐ **Old Man's** INTERNATIONAL $$
(☑ 0361-846 9158; www.oldmans.net; Jl Pantai Batu Bolong; mains from 50,000Rp; ⏱ 7am-midnight) You'll have a tough time deciding just where to sit down to enjoy your drink at this popular coastal beer garden overlooking Batu Bolong Beach. The self-serve menu is aimed at surfers and surfer-wannabes: burgers, pizza, fish and chips, salads. Wednesday nights are an institution, while Fridays (live rock and roll) and Sundays (DJs) are also big.

⭐ **La Laguna** COCKTAIL BAR
(☑ 0812 3638 2272; www.facebook.com/lalagunabali; Jl Pantai Kayu Putih; ⏱ 11am-midnight; 🛜) A sibling of Seminyak's La Favela (p209), La Laguna is one of Bali's most alluring bars. It combines a beatnik look with Moorish trappings and sparkling tiny lights. Explore the eclectic layout, and sit on a couch, sofa bed, a table inside or a picnic table in the garden. The drinks are good and the food is delicious (mains from 75,000Rp).

Gimme Shelter Bali BAR
(☑ 0812 3804 8867; www.facebook.com/gimmeshelterbali; Jl Lingkar Nelayan 444; ⏱ 7pm-3am) The perfect hang-out for those who like their music with an extra dose of loud, Gimme Shelter regularly stages alternative gigs by the island's rock and roll, rockabilly and punk bands. This is one of the only venues in Canggu that stays open past midnight.

❶ Getting There & Around

The airport taxi cartel charges 250,000Rp for a taxi. Getting to the Canggu area can cost 150,000Rp or more by taxi from Kuta or Seminyak. Don't expect to find taxis cruising anywhere, although any business can call you one.

Bukit Peninsula

Hot and arid, the southern peninsula is known as Bukit (meaning 'hill' in Bahasa Indonesia). It's popular with visitors, from the cloistered climes of Nusa Dua to the sybaritic retreats along the south coast. The booming west coast (often generically called Pecatu) with its string-of-pearls beaches is a real hot spot. Accommodation sits precariously on the sand at Balangan Beach while the cliffs are dotted with idiosyncratic lodges at Bingin and elsewhere. New places sprout daily and most have views of the turbulent waters here, which have world-famous surf breaks all the way south to the important temple of Ulu Watu.

❶ Getting There & Away

You'll need your own wheels – whether taxi, hire car or motorbike – to explore the Bukit. Expect to pay upwards of 5000Rp per vehicle to use the beach-access roads.

Jimbaran

Just south of Kuta and the airport, Teluk Jimbaran (Jimbaran Bay) is an alluring crescent of white-sand beach and blue sea, fronted by a long string of seafood warungs (food stalls) and ending at the southern end in a bushy headland, home to the Four Seasons Jimbaran Bay.

A popular morning stop on a Bukit Peninsula amble is the Jimbaran Fish Market. Brightly painted boats bob along the shore while huge cases of everything from small sardines to fearsome langoustines are hawked. Buy your seafood here and have one of the warungs cook it up.

Balangan Beach

Balangan Beach is a long, low strand at the base of rocky cliffs. It's covered with palm trees and fronted by a ribbon of near-white sand, picturesquely dotted with sun umbrellas. Surfer bars, cafes in shacks and even slightly more permanent guesthouses precariously line the shore where buffed First World bods soak up rays amid Third World sanitation. Think of it as a bit of the Wild West not far from Bali's glitz.

Santai Bali Homestay (☑0338-695942; www.facebook.com/santaiwarungbalihomestay; r from 250,000Rp; ☎) has 19 bare-bones rooms that are perfect for surfers and beach bums wanting easy access to the water.

Bingin

An ever-evolving scene, Bingin comprises scores of unconventionally stylish lodgings scattered across cliffs and on the strip of white-sand Bingin Beach below. Smooth Jl Pantai Bingin runs 1km off Jl Melasti (look for the thicket of accommodation signs) and then branches off into a tangle of lanes. The beach is a five-minute walk down fairly steep paths.

🛏 Sleeping & Eating

This is one of the Bukit's coolest places to stay. Numerous individual places are scattered along and near the cliffs, well off the main road. You can also get basic accommodation down the cliff at a string of bamboo and thatch surfer crash pads near the water.

Chocky's Place GUESTHOUSE $
(☑0818 0530 7105; www.chockysplace.com; Bingin Beach; r 150,000-400,000Rp; ☎) Down the bottom of the stairs and right on Bingin Beach, this classic surfer hang-out has cosy rooms varying from charming with awesome views to rudimentary with shared bathrooms. Its bamboo restaurant looks out to the beach; it's a great place to meet fellow travellers over a few cold ones.

Bingin Garden GUESTHOUSE $
(☑0816 472 2002; tommybarrell76@yahoo.com; off Jl Pantai Bingin; r with fan/air-con 280,000/400,000Rp; ❄☎☎) There's a relaxed hacienda feel to Bingin Garden, where eight bungalow-style rooms are set among an arid garden and a large pool. It's back off the cliffs and about 300m from the path down to the beach. It's run by gun local surfer Tommy Barrell and his lovely wife.

Olas Homestay HOMESTAY $
(☑0857 3859 5257; http://olashomestaybali.com; Jl Labuansait; r 350,000Rp; ☎) This new, family-run surfer crash pad is excellent value in Bingin, with lush landscaping and five private rooms offering air-con and hot water. The owners are super-nice, and can arrange airport pickups, surf lessons, tours and rental vehicles.

★**Temple Lodge** BOUTIQUE HOTEL $$
(☑0857 3901 1572; www.thetemplelodge.com; off Jl Pantai Bingin; r incl breakfast US$80-230; ☎☎) 'Artsy and beautiful' just begins to describe this collection of huts and cottages made from thatch, driftwood and other natural materials. Each sits on a jutting shelf on the cliffs above the surf breaks, and there are superb views from the infinity pool and some of the 10 units. You can arrange for meals, and there are morning yoga classes.

★**Cashew Tree** CAFE $
(☑0813 5321 8157; www.facebook.com/the-cashew-tree; Jl Pantai Bingan; meals from 40,000Rp; ☺8am-10pm; ☎☎) *The* place to hang out in Bingin. Surfers and beach-goers gather in this large garden for tasty vegetarian meals. Expect the likes of burritos, salads,

sandwiches and smoothies. It's also a good spot for a drink; Thursday nights especially go off, attracting folk from up and down the coast with live bands.

Padang Padang

Padang Padang Beach and Impossibles Beach are the stuff tropical surf dreams are made of. The backdrop of rocky cliff faces gives them an isolated feel you won't get in Kuta or Seminyak. A very cool scene has developed, with groovy cafes, oddball sleeps and iconoclastic surf shops.

On Saturdays and full-moon nights there's a party on the beach at Padang Padang, with grilled seafood and tunes until dawn.

The namesake beach here is near Jl Labuan Sait. It's fairly easily reached. Immediately east, Impossibles Beach is more of a challenge. Rocks and tide may prevent you from coming over from Padang Padang.

For a heaping plates of Australian-style brunch composed of fresh, local ingredients, **Bukit Cafe** (☑ 0813 3749 8745; www.bukitcafe. com; Jl Labuan Sait; mains 40,000-75,000Rp; ◷ 7am-9.30pm; ✔) is unbeatable. Standout dishes include vegan pancakes, smoothie bowls and smashed avocado, and the open-air, convivial setting has loads of appeal.

Ulu Watu & Around

Ulu Watu has become the generic name for the southwestern tip of the Bukit Peninsula. It includes the much-revered temple and the fabled namesake surf breaks.

About 2km north of the temple there is a dramatic cliff with steps leading to the water and Suluban Beach. All manner of cafes and surf shops spill down the nearly sheer face to the water below. Views are stellar and it's quite the scene.

⊙ Sights & Activities

★**Pura Luhur Ulu Watu**   HINDU TEMPLE
(off Jl Ulu Watu; adult/child 30,000/20,000Rp, parking 2000Rp; ◷ 7am-7pm) This important temple is perched precipitously on the southwestern tip of the peninsula, atop sheer cliffs that drop straight into the ceaseless surf. You enter through an unusual arched gateway flanked by statues of Ganesha. Inside, the walls of coral bricks are covered with intricate carvings of Bali's mythological menagerie.

★**Ulu Watu**   SURFING
On a top day Ulu Watu is Bali's biggest and most powerful wave. It's the stuff of dreams and nightmares, and definitely not one for beginners! Since the early 1970s when it fea-

Ulu Watu & Around

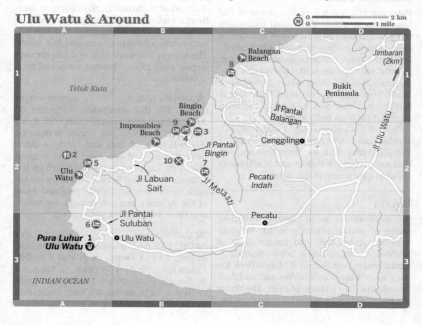

tured in the legendary surf flick *Morning of the Earth,* Ulu Watu has drawn surfers from around the world for left breaks that seem to go on forever.

🛏 Sleeping & Eating

Gong Accommodation   GUESTHOUSE $
(✆0361-769976; www.thegonguluwatubali.com; Jl Pantai Suluban; r 250,000-500,000Rp; 🛜🏊) The 13 tidy rooms here have good ventilation and hot water, and face a small compound with a lovely pool. Some 2nd-floor units have distant ocean views, TVs and air-con. It's about 1km south of the Ulu Watu cliffside cafes; the host family is lovely. Recent renovations have raised rates.

Delpi Uluwatu Beach Rooms   GUESTHOUSE $
(balibrook@juno.com; Ulu Watu; r US$45) Six basic cliffside rooms rattle to the beat of the surf day and night. Set in the rocks amid the various bars, this is the place if all you want is a 24-hour view of the breaks. Closed between surf seasons. Prices negotiable for longer stays.

★ Single Fin   BAR
(✆0361-769941; www.singlefinbali.com; Jl Mamo; mains 65,000-150,000Rp; ⊙8am-9pm Mon-Sat, to 1am Sun; 🛜) From this triple-level cafe, you can watch the never-ending swells march in across the Indian Ocean from this cliff-side perch, and the surfers carve it right up when the waves are big. Drinks here aren't cheap (or very good), but the food is tasty, the sunsets are killer and the Sunday night party

is the best one on the peninsula. A new, attached, poke-bowl joint, Coco & Poke is under the same ownership. The bowls start at 75,000Rp and are available from 11am to 7pm Monday through Saturday, and to 9pm Sunday. There's a tofu bowl for vegetarians.

Denpasar
✆0361 / POP 834,881

Sprawling, hectic and ever-growing, Bali's capital has been the focus of a lot of the island's growth and wealth over the last five decades. It can seem a daunting and chaotic place, but spend a little time on its tree-lined streets in the relatively affluent government and business district of Renon and you'll discover a more genteel side.

◉ Sights

Museum Negeri Propinsi Bali   MUSEUM
(✆0361-222680; Jl Mayor Wisnu; adult/child 50,000/25,000Rp; ⊙7.30am-3.30pm Sat-Thu, to 1pm Fri) Think of this as the British Museum or the Smithsonian of Balinese culture. It's all here, but unlike those world-class institutions, you have to work at sorting it out – the museum could use a dose of curatorial energy (and some new light bulbs). Most displays are labelled in English. The museum comprises several buildings and pavilions, including many examples of Balinese architecture, housing prehistoric pieces, traditional artefacts, Barong (mythical lion-dog creature), ceremonial objects and rich displays of textiles.

🛏 Sleeping & Eating

Nakula Familiar Inn   GUESTHOUSE $
(✆0361-226446; www.nakulafamiliarinn.com; Jl Nakula 4; r 200,000-300,000Rp; ❄🛜) The eight rooms at this sprightly urban family compound, a long-time traveller favourite, are clean and have small balconies. There is a nice courtyard and cafe in the middle. Tegal–Kereneng bemos go along Jl Nakula.

★ Depot Cak Asmo   INDONESIAN $
(✆0361-256246; Jl Tukad Gangga; mains from 15,000Rp; ⊙9.30am-11pm) Join the government workers and students from the nearby university for superb dishes cooked to order in the bustling kitchen. Order the buttery and crispy *cumi cumi* (calamari) battered in *telor asin* (a heavenly mixture of eggs and garlic). Fruity ice drinks are a cooling treat.

Denpasar

An English-language menu makes ordering a breeze. It's halal, so there's no alcohol.

🔒 Shopping

Pasar Badung   MARKET
(Jl Gajah Mada; ⊘24hr) Bali's largest food market is still recovering from a 2016 fire. While rebuilding continues, there are ad hoc stalls in the surrounding area. Busy in the mornings and evenings, it's a great place to browse and bargain, with food from all over the island, including fruits and spices.

❶ Getting There & Away

Denpasar is a hub of public transport in Bali – you'll find buses and minibuses bound for all corners of the island.

The city has several bemo and bus terminals – if you're travelling by bemo around Bali you'll often have to go via Denpasar, and transfer from one terminal to another by bemo (7000Rp).

Sanur

📞 0361

Many consider Sanur 'just right', as it lacks most of the hassles found to the west while maintaining a good mix of restaurants and bars that aren't all owned by resorts. The beach, while thin, is protected by a reef and breakwaters, so families appreciate the limpid waves. Sanur has a good range of places to stay and it's well placed for day trips. Really, it doesn't deserve its local moniker, 'Snore'.

Sanur's **beachfront walk** was the first in Bali and has been delighting locals and visitors alike from day one. More than 4km long, it curves past resorts, beachfront cafes, wooden fishing boats under repair and quite a few elegant old villas.

A large number of paintings by Adrien-Jean Le Mayeur de Merpres (1880–1958) are on display at his former home in the **Muse-**

um Le Mayeur (☑0361-286201; JI Hang Tuah; adult/child 50,000/25,000Rp; ⊙8am-3.30pm Sat-Thu, 8.30am-12.30pm Fri).

🛏 Sleeping & Eating

Agung & Sue Watering Hole I   GUESTHOUSE $
(☑0361-288289; www.wateringholesanurbali.com; JI Hang Tuah 35; r 275,000-400,000Rp; ❄🛜) Ideally located for an early fast boat to Nusa Lembongan or the Gilis, this long-running guesthouse has a veteran conviviality. Rooms are standard, but the beer is indeed cold and Sanur Beach is a five-minute walk. A good place if you have that early fast boat to catch.

Pollok & Le Mayeur Inn   HOMESTAY $
(☑0812 4637 5364; sulaiman.mei1980@gmail.com; JI Hang Tuah, Museum Le Mayeur; r with fan/air-con from 250,000/350,000Rp; ❄🛜) The grandchildren of the late artist Le Mayeur de Merpres and his wife Ni Polok run this small homestay. It's within the Museum Le Mayeur compound, and offers a good budget option on the beachfront. The 17 rooms vary in size; ask to see a few.

★Genius Cafe   CAFE
(☑0821 4415 8854; http://geniuscafebali.com; Mertasari Beach) This new hub for entrepreneurship, which is part of a growing, membership-based network of beach clubs, also serves up delicious food and drinks from a stunning seafront perch. Yes to the ginger latte, yes to the fresh coconut water with lavender and dragon fruit, yes to the happiness bowl of raw salad, avocado, fresh herbs, nuts, seed and other goodness.

Warung Pantai Indah   CAFE $$
(Beachfront Walk; mains 30,000-110,000Rp; ⊙9am-9pm) Sit at battered tables and chairs with your toes in the sand at this timeless beach cafe. It specialises in fresh barbecue-grilled seafood and cheap local dishes.

❶ Getting There & Away

The myriad boats to Nusa Lembongan, Nusa Penida, Lombok and the Gilis depart from a strip of beach south of JI Hang Tuah. None of these services use a dock – be prepared to wade to the boat. Most companies have shady waiting areas facing the beach. The Kura-Kura bus has a route linking Sanur with Kuta and Ubud. Buses run every hour and cost 80,000Rp.

Nusa Lembongan
☑0366

Once the domain of shack-staying surfers, Nusa Lembongan has hit the big time. Yes, you can still get a simple room with a view of the surf breaks and the gorgeous sunsets, but now you can also stay in a boutique hotel and have a fabulous meal.

◉ Sights & Activities

Surfing here is best in dry season (April to September), when the winds come from the southeast. It's not for beginners, and can be dangerous even for experts. This is also a good bases for divers and snorkellers.

Pura Puseh   TEMPLE
At the north end of town where the island's main road passes, you can ascend a long stone staircase to Pura Puseh, the village temple, which has great views.

Pantai Tanjung Sanghyang   BEACH
(Mushroom Bay) This beautiful bay, unofficially named Mushroom Bay after the mushroom corals offshore, has a crescent of bright white beach. By day, the tranquillity can be disturbed by banana-boat riders or parasailers. Otherwise, this is a dream beach. The most interesting way to get here from Jungutbatu is to walk along the trail that starts from the southern end of the main beach and follows the coastline for a kilometre or so. Alternatively, take a boat or a motorbike from Jungutbatu.

★World Diving   DIVING
(☑0812 390 0686; www.world-diving.com; Jungutbatu Beach; introductory dive 940,000Rp, open-water course 5,500,000Rp) World Diving, based at Pondok Baruna, is very well regarded. It offers a complete range of courses, plus diving trips to dive sites all around Nusa Penida and Nusa Penida. Equipment is first-rate.

Thabu Surf Lessons   SURFING
(http://thabusurflessons.webs.com; adult/child from 350,000/300,000Rp based on skill level & group size) Very professional surf instruction outfit that offers private and group lessons, with prices including return boat transfer to the surf break, booties and rash vests.

🛏 Sleeping & Eating

★Pondok Baruna   GUESTHOUSE $
(☑0812 394 0992; www.pondokbaruna.com; Jungutbatu Beach; r from 400,000Rp; ❄🛜🅿)

Associated with World Diving, a local dive operator, this place offers fantastic rooms with terraces facing the ocean. Six plusher rooms surround a dive pool behind the beach. There are another eight rooms at sister site Pondok Baruna Frangipani, set back in the palm trees around a large pool. Staff members, led by Putu, are charmers.

★ **Green Garden Warung** INDONESIAN $
(☑0813 374 1928; Jungutbatu; 20,000-50,000Rp; ⏱7am-10pm; 🅿) Tucked into a lovely garden on a side street off Jungutbatu Beach, this locally owned warung serves up tasty smoothie bowls and creative Indonesian dishes, many of which are vegetarian-friendly (ie crumbed tempe with a mushroom-cream sauce). The owners donate a portion of their proceeds to local schools, and are in the process of adding five guest rooms.

ℹ Getting There & Away

Public Fast Boats (Jungutbatu Beach; one-way 200,000Rp) Leave from the northern end of Sanur Beach for Nusa Lembongan 10 times daily, between 8.30am and 5.30pm, and take 30 minutes.

Rocky Fast Cruises (☑0361-283624; www.rockyfastcruise.com; Jungutbatu Beach; one-way/return 300,000/500,000Rp) Runs several large boats daily that take 30 minutes.

Scoot (☑0812 3767 4932, 0361-285522; www.scootcruise.com; Jungutbatu Beach; one-way adult/child 400,000/280,000Rp) Makes a few trips daily; each takes 30 minutes.

Nusa Penida

Just beginning to appear on visitor itineraries, Nusa Penida still awaits proper discovery. It's an untrammelled place that answers the question: what would Bali be like if tourists never came?

There are just a handful of formal activities and sights; instead, you go to Nusa Penida to explore and relax, to adapt to the slow rhythm of life here. It's an unforgiving area: Nusa Penida was once used as a place of banishment for criminals and other undesirables from the kingdom of Klungkung (now Semarapura).

The island is a limestone plateau with a strip of sand on its north coast, and views over the water to the volcanoes in Bali. The south coast has 300m-high limestone cliffs dropping straight down to the sea and a row of offshore islets – it's rugged and spectacular scenery. Beaches are very few although some are spectacular.

Basic guesthouses can be found in Crystal Bay, Sampalan, Toyapakeh and now Ped. Top choices include **Namaste** (☑0813 3727 1615; www.namaste-bungalows.com; r with fan/air-con from 450,000/600,000Rp; 🕸🛜🛏) in Crystal Bay Beach and **Full Moon Bungalows** (☑0813 3874 5817; www.facebook.com/fullmoonbungalows; Bodong; dm/r from 125,000/300,000Rp; 🕸🛜) in Ped.

Various speedboats leave from the beach at Sanur, and make the run in less than an hour. There are also fast boats from Pandangbai and public boats between Lembongan Town and Toyapakeh.

Ubud

☑0361

Ubud is culture, yes. It's also home to good restaurants, cafes and streets of shops, many selling goods from the region's artisans. There's somewhere to stay for every budget, and no matter what the price you can enjoy lodgings that reflect the local Zeitgeist: artful, creative and serene.

Ubud's popularity continues to grow, adding on the hoopla created by the bestselling *Eat, Pray, Love*. Tour buses with day trippers can choke the main streets and incite chaos. Fortunately, Ubud adapts and a stroll away from the intersection of Jl Raya Ubud and Monkey Forest Rd, through the nearby verdant rice fields, can quickly make all right with the world.

Spend a few days in Ubud to appreciate it properly. It's one of those places where days can become weeks and weeks become months, as the noticeable expat community demonstrates.

◉ Sights

★**Sacred Monkey Forest Sanctuary** PARK
(Mandala Wisata Wanara Wana; Map p220; ☑0361-971304; www.monkeyforestubud.com; Monkey Forest Rd; adult/child 50,000/40,000Rp; ⏱8.30am-6pm) This cool and dense swath of jungle, officially called Mandala Wisata Wanara Wana, houses three holy temples. The sanctuary is inhabited by a band of more than 600 grey-haired and greedy long-tailed Balinese macaques who are nothing like the innocent-looking doe-eyed monkeys on the brochures. Nestled in the forest is the interesting **Pura Dalem Agung** (Map p218; Sacred Monkey Forest Sanctuary).

★ **Museum Puri Lukisan**   MUSEUM
(Museum of Fine Arts; Map p220; ☑0361-975136; www.museumpurilukisan.com; off Jl Raya Ubud; adult/child 85,000Rp/free; ⊙9am-5pm) It was in Ubud that the modern Balinese art movement started, when artists first began to abandon purely religious themes and court subjects for scenes of everyday life. This museum displays fine examples of all schools of Balinese art, and all are well labelled in English. It was set up by Rudolf Bonnet, with Cokorda Gede Agung Sukawati (a prince of Ubud's royal family) and Walter Spies.

★ **Neka Art Museum**   GALLERY
(Map p218; ☑0361-975074; www.museumneka.com; Jl Raya Sanggingan; adult/child 75,000Rp/free; ⊙9am-5pm) The creation of Suteja Neka, a private collector and dealer in Balinese art, Neka Art Museum has an excellent and diverse collection. It's a good place to learn about the development of painting in Bali. You can get an overview of the myriad local painting styles in the **Balinese Painting Hall**. Look for the *wayang* works.

★ **Agung Rai Museum of Art**   GALLERY
(ARMA; Map p218; ☑0361-976659; www.armamuseum.com; Jl Raya Pengosekan; incl drink adult 80,000Rp, child under 10 free; ⊙9am-6pm, Balinese dancing 3-5pm Mon-Fri, classes 10am Sun) Founded by Agung Rai as a museum, gallery and cultural centre, the impressive ARMA is the only place in Bali to see haunting works by influential German artist Walter Spies, alongside many more masterpieces. The museum is housed in several traditional buildings set in gardens with water coursing through channels. The collection is well labelled in English.

Ubud Palace   PALACE
(Map p220; cnr Jl Raya Ubud & Jl Suweta; ⊙8am-7pm) FREE The palace and its temple, **Puri Saren Agung** (Map p220), share a space in the heart of Ubud. The compound was mostly built after the 1917 earthquake and the local royal family still lives here. You can wander around most of the large compound and explore the many traditional, though not excessively ornate, buildings.

🏃 Activities

Ubud brims with salons and spas where you can heal, pamper, rejuvenate or otherwise focus on your personal needs, physical and mental. Many shops and hotels in central Ubud display mountain bikes for hire for around 35,000Rp per day.

★ **Yoga Barn**   YOGA
(Map p220; ☑0361-971236; www.theyogabarn.com; off Jl Raya Pengosekan; classes from 130,000Rp; ⊙6am-9pm) The chakra for the yoga revolution in Ubud, the life force that is the Yoga Barn sits in its own lotus position amid trees back near a river valley. The name exactly describes what you'll find: a huge range of classes in yoga, Pilates, dance and life-affirming offshoots are held through the week.

Bali Botanica Day Spa   SPA
(Map p218; ☑0361-976739; www.balibotanica.com; Jl Raya Sanggingan; massage from 190,000Rp; ⊙9am-9pm) Set beautifully on a lush hillside past little fields of rice and ducks, this spa offers a range of treatments, including Ayurvedic. The herbal massage is popular. Transport is provided if needed.

🎓 Courses

★ **Casa Luna Cooking School**   COOKING
(Map p218; ☑0361-973282; www.casalunabali.com; Honeymoon Guesthouse, Jl Bisma; classes from 400,000Rp) Regular cooking courses are offered at Ubud's Honeymoon Guesthouse and/or **Casa Luna restaurant** (Map p220; ☑0361-977409; www.casalunabali.com; Jl Raya Ubud; meals from 50,000Rp; ⊙8am-10pm). Half-day courses cover ingredients, cooking techniques and the cultural background of the Balinese kitchen (note, not all courses include a market visit). Each day has a different focus so you can return for more instruction. Tours are also offered, including a good one to the Gianyar night market.

Pondok Pekak Library & Learning Centre   LANGUAGE
(Map p220; ☑0361-976194; www.facebook.com/pg/pondokpekak; Monkey Forest Rd; classes per hr from 100,000Rp; ⊙9am-9pm) On the far side of the football field, this centre offers painting, dance, music and woodcarving classes; some are geared to kids.

🛌 Sleeping

Ubud has the best and most appealing range of places to stay on Bali, including fabled resorts, artful guesthouses and charming, simple homestays.

Ubud Area

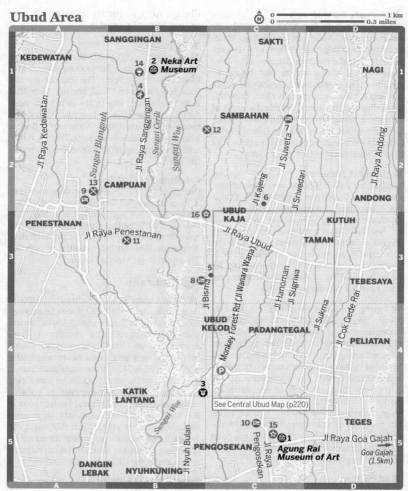

INDONESIA UBUD

Nirvana Pension GUESTHOUSE **$**

(Map p220; ☑ 0361-975415; www.nirvanaku.com; Jl Goutama 10; s with fan/air-con 250,000/350,000Rp, d with fan/air-con 350,000/450,000Rp; ❋ ☜) Nirvana has a plethora of paintings, ornate doorways and eight rooms with modern bathrooms, all set in a shady, secluded locale next to a large family temple. Batik courses and offering workshops are also held here. It's a great location, back off popular Goutama.

d'Rompok House GUESTHOUSE **$**

(Map p220; ☑ 0813 5334 4837; drompokhouse@ yahoo.com; Jl Hanoman 39; r incl breakfast 250,000-350,000Rp; ❋ ☜) Tucked down a tight *gang* (alley), the well-priced d'Rompok is more suave than your usual homestay, with five large, modern rooms decorated with contemporary art. Go for one of the top-floor rooms with views of the rice fields.

Happy Mango Tree HOSTEL **$**

(Map p218; ☑ 0812 3844 5498; www.thehappymangotree.com; Jl Bisma 27; dm/d from 100,000/250,000Rp; ☜) This bright and bubbly hostel revels in its hippie vibe. Bright colours abound inside the rooms and out on the various terraces, some of which have

Ubud Area

rice-field views. Mixed dorms have four or five beds; doubles come with names (and matching decor) such as Love Shack and Ceiling Museum. There's a social bar and a restaurant, too.

Santra Putra GUESTHOUSE $
(Map p218; ☑0812 8109 9940, 0361-977810; www.santraputra.com; Jl Pacekan 18, off Jl Raya Campuan; r incl breakfast 350,000-450,000Rp; ☞) Run by internationally exhibited abstract artist I Wayan Karja – whose **studio-gallery** (Map p218; ☑0361-977810; Jl Pacekan 18, Penestanan, off Jl Raya Campuan; classes from 300,000Rp) is also on-site – this place has 15 big, open, airy rooms with hot water. Enjoy paddy-field views from all vantage points. Painting and drawing classes are offered by the artist.

Biangs HOMESTAY $
(Map p220; ☑0361-976520; wah_oeboed@yahoo.com; Jl Sukma 28; s/d with fan 100,000/200,000Rp, with air-con 200,000/350,000Rp; ❈☞) In a little garden, Biangs (meaning 'mama') homestay has six well-maintained rooms, with hot water. Three generations of the family make this a genuine family homestay. Jl Sukma is one of Ubud's most atmospheric streets.

Han Snel Siti Bungalows GUESTHOUSE $
(Map p220; ☑0361-975699; www.sitibungalow.com; Jl Kajeng 3; r incl breakfast with fan/air-con from 250,000/350,000Rp; ❈☞✦) Owned by the family of the late Han Snel, a well-known Dutch painter, Siti Bungalows is one of Ubud's original guesthouses. While its standards have slipped, it remains excellent value and a wonderful choice for those seeking somewhere with character. There's a delightful garden and eight spacious bungalows – some of which overlook the river gorge.

Bali Asli Lodge HOMESTAY $$
(Map p218; ☑0361-970537; www.baliaslilodge.com; Jl Sweta; r incl breakfast from 300,000Rp; ☞) Escape the central Ubud hubbub here. Made is your friendly host, and her five rooms are in traditional Balinese stone-and-brick houses set in verdant gardens. There are terraces where you can let the hours pass; interiors are clean and comfy. Town is a 15-minute walk away.

Tegal Sari HOTEL $$
(Map p218; ☑0361-973318; www.tegalsari-ubud.com; Jl Raya Pengosekan; r 300,000-1,500,000Rp; ❈@☞✦) Though literally a stone's throw from the hectic main road, here rice fields (along with ducks) miraculously materialise. Go for a superdeluxe multilevel cottage (770,000Rp) with bathtub looking out to soul-calming bucolic views. Units in the new brick buildings, on the other hand, are stark. It has two pools, including one on the rooftop, and a yoga space.

★**Bambu Indah** BOUTIQUE HOTEL $$$
(☑0361-977922; www.bambuindah.com; Banjar Baung; incl breakfast tent US$100, r US$200-400; ☞✦) ✿ Famed expat entrepreneur John Hardy sold his jewellery company in 2007 and became a hotelier. On a ridge near Sayan and his beloved Sungai Ayung (Ayung River), he's assembled a compound of 100-year-old royal Javanese houses, a stunning Sumbanese thatched house and a couple of new glamping tents; each space is furnished with style and flair.

✕ Eating

Ubud's cafes and restaurants are some of the best in Bali. Local and expat chefs

INDONESIA UBUD

Central Ubud

INDONESIA UBUD

N	0 — 200 m
	0 — 0.1 miles

UBUD KAJA

9 🏠

1 **Museum Puri Lukisan** 🏛

Jl Kajeng

Jl Suweta

22 ☆

17 🍴

11 🍴

Jl Anggada

Jl Bisma

3 🛕
4 🏠 Kura-Kura Bus

Ubud Tourist Information ℹ

Jl Arjuna

Market

19 🍴

Jl Sriwedari

Jl Sandat

TAMAN

Jl Raya Ubud

13 🍴

10 🍴

Jl Gootama

23 🏠

21 ☆

Jl Karna

Jl Maruti

Jl Dewi Sita

15 🍴   14 🛕   16 🍴   8 🍴

5 ●

20 🍴

18 🍴

Football Field

Monkey Forest Rd (Jl Wanara Wana)

12 🍴

Jl Sugriwa

Jl Jembawan

7 🍴

PADANGTEGAL

UBUD KELOD

Jl Hanoman

Jl Sukma

P 🅿

2 **Sacred Monkey Forest Sanctuary** 🐒

Perama 🏠

6 🏠

Jl Raya Pengosekan

produce a bounty of authentic Balinese dishes, plus inventive Asian and other international cuisines.

★ Warung Bodag Maliah
HEALTH FOOD $

(Sari Organik; Map p218; ☑ 0361-972087; Subak Sok Wayah; mains from 40,000Rp; ☺ 8am-8pm) 🍃 In a beautiful location on a plateau overlooking rice terraces, this attractive cafe is in the middle of a big organic farm. The food's healthy and the drinks are amazing; there's even homemade dragon-fruit wine. The walk through the rice fields means half the fun is getting here, and the owners also have delicious restaurants in Penestanan and Batur.

Waroeng Bernadette at Toko Madu
INDONESIAN $

(Map p220; ☑ 0821 4742 4779; Jl Goutama; mains from 35,000Rp; ☺ 11am-11pm; 🛜) It's not called the 'Home of Rendang' for nothing. The west Sumatran classic dish of long-marinated meats (beef is the true classic, but here there's also a vegie jackfruit variety) is pulled off with colour and flair. Other dishes have a zesty zing that is missing from lacklustre versions served elsewhere. The elevated dining room is a vision of kitsch.

Earth Cafe & Market
VEGETARIAN $

(Map p220; www.earthcafebali.com; Jl Gotama Selatan; meals from 30,000Rp; 🛜🍴) 'Eliminate free radicals' is but one of many healthy drinks at this hard-core outpost for vegetarian organic dining and drinking. The seemingly endless menu has a plethora of soups, salads and platters that are heavy on Med flavours. There's a market on the main floor.

Warung Sopa
VEGETARIAN $

(Map p220; ☑ 0851 0076 5897; Jl Sugriwa 36; mains from 30,000Rp; ☺ 8am-9.30pm; 🛜🍴) This popular open-air place in a residential street captures the Ubud vibe with creative and (more importantly) tasty vegetarian fare with a Balinese twist. Look for specials of the day on display; the ever-changing *nasi campur* is a treat.

Yellow Flower Cafe
INDONESIAN $

(Map p218; ☑ 0812 3889 9695; off Jl Raya Campuan; mains from 59,000Rp; ☺ 7.30am-9pm; 🛜) New Age Indonesian right up in Penestanan along a little path through the rice fields. Organic mains such as *nasi campur* or rice pancakes are good; snackers will delight in the decent coffees, cakes and smoothies. From 5pm Sunday evenings there's an excellent Balinese buffet (94,000Rp). Great views.

Tutmak Cafe
CAFE $

(Map p220; ☑ 0361-975754; Jl Dewi Sita; mains 40,000-100,000Rp; ☺ 8am-11pm; 🛜) This smart, breezy multilevel terrace restaurant is a popular place for a refreshing drink or something to munch on from the menu of Indo classics. The *nasi campur* (rice with a choice of side dishes) with fresh tuna is one of Ubud's finest.

INDONESIA UBUD

★ **Hujon Locale** INDONESIAN $$

(Map p220; ☑0813 3972 0306; www.hujanlocale.
com; Jl Sriwedari 5; mains 120,000-200,000Rp;
☺noon-10pm; 🖥) From the team of the criti-
cally acclaimed Mama San in Seminyak, Hu-
jon Locale is one of Ubud's most enjoyable
restaurants. The menu mixes traditional In-
donesian dishes with modern, creative flair,
from salt-grilled whole fish to lamb shoulder
simmered in Javanese spice. The setting with-
in a chic colonial-style two-storey bungalow
is made for a balmy evening. Great cocktails.

Alchemy VEGAN $$

(Map p218; ☑0361-971981; www.alchemybali.
com; Jl Raya Penestanan 75; mains from 60,000Rp;
☺7am-9pm; 🖥🚭) 🍷 A prototypical 100%
vegan Ubud restaurant, Alchemy features a
vast customised salad menu as well as cash-
ew-milk drinks, smoothie bowls, ice cream,
fennel juice and a lot more. The raw-choco-
late desserts are addictive.

Warung Ibu Oka BALINESE $$

(Map p220; ☑0851 0007 7490; Jl Suweta; mains
from 55,000Rp; ☺11am-7pm) Opposite Ubud
Palace, lunchtime crowds are waiting for
one thing: Balinese-style roast *babi guling*
(suckling pig). Order a *spesial* to get the best
cut. Plenty of tourist hype means that prices
are more than double the norm.

🍷 Drinking & Nightlife

★ **Night Rooster** COCKTAIL BAR

(Map p220; ☑0361-977733; www.locavore.co.id/
nightrooster; 10B Jalan Dewi Sita; ☺4pm-midnight
Mon-Sat) From the same folks who do **Loca-
vore** (Map p220; ☑0361-977733; www.restau-
rantlocavore.com; Jl Dewi Sita; 5-/7-course menu
675,000/775,000Rp; ☺noon-2pm & 6-10pm; 🖥),
this neighbouring, 2nd-storey cocktail bar
boasts a talented mixologist and some fas-
cinating flavour combos. Inventive cocktails
include things such as jackfruit-infused dry
gin, homemade bitters and flaming cassia
bark, and the selection of appetisers and
cheese and charcuterie platters make for
rich pairings.

★ **Room 4 Dessert** LOUNGE

(Map p218; ☑0821 4429 3452; www.room4dessert.
asia; Jl Raya Sanggingan; treats from 90,000Rp;
☺noon-midnight Tue-Sun) Celebrity chef Will
Goldfarb, who gained fame as *the* dessert
chef in Manhattan, runs what could be a
nightclub except that it just serves dessert.
Get some friends and order the sampler. Pair
everything with his line-up of classic and ex-

traordinary cocktails and wines, then let the
night pass by in a sugary glow.

★ **Coffee Studio Seniman** CAFE

(Map p220; ☑0361-972085; www.senimancoffee.
com; Jl Sriwedari 5; coffee from 30,000Rp; ☺8am-
10pm; 🖥) That 'coffee studio' moniker isn't
for show; all the equipment is on display
at this temple of single-origin coffee. Take
a seat on the designer rocker chairs and
choose from an array of pour-overs, syphon,
Aeropress or espresso using a range of qual-
ity Indonesian beans. It's also popular for
food (mains from 50,000Rp) and drinks in
the evening.

☆ Entertainment

Pura Dalem Ubud DANCE

(Map p218; Jl Raya Ubud) At the west end of
Jl Raya Ubud, this open-air venue has a
flame-lit carved-stone backdrop and is one
of the most evocative places to see a dance
performance.

Pura Taman Saraswati DANCE

(Ubud Water Palace; Map p220; Jl Raya Ubud) The
beauty of the setting may distract you from
the dancers, although at night you can't see
the lily pads and lotus flowers that are such
an attraction by day.

Oka Kartini PERFORMING ARTS

(Map p220; ☑0361-975193; Jl Raya Ubud; adult/
child 100,000/50,000Rp; ☺8pm Wed, Fri & Sun)
Regular shadow-puppet shows are held at
Oka Kartini, which also has an art gallery.

Ubud Palace DANCE

(Map p220; Jl Raya Ubud; 100,000Rp) Perfor-
mances are held here almost nightly against
a beautiful backdrop.

Arma Open Stage DANCE

(Map p218; ☑0361-976659; Jl Raya Pengosekan)
Has some of the best troupes performing
Kecak and Legong dance.

🛍 Shopping

★ **Threads of Life Indonesian
Textile Arts Center** TEXTILES

(Map p218; ☑0361-972187; www.threadsoflife.com;
Jl Kajeng 24; ☺10am-7pm) This small, profes-
sional textile gallery and shop sponsors the
production of naturally dyed, handmade
ritual textiles from around Indonesia. It ex-
ists to help recover skills in danger of being
lost to modern dyeing and weaving meth-
ods. Commissioned pieces are displayed in
the gallery, which has good explanatory ma-

BALINESE DANCE & MUSIC

Few travel experiences are more magical than watching Balinese dance, especially in Ubud. Ubud is the perfect base for nightly cultural entertainment and for events in surrounding villages. In Ubud you can see Kecak, Legong and Barong dances, Mahabharata and Ramayana ballets, *wayang kulit* (shadow-puppet plays) and gamelan (traditional Javanese and Balinese orchestras). There are eight or more performances each night.

Excellent troupes who regularly perform in Ubud include the following.

Semara Ratih High-energy, creative Legong interpretations. The best local troupe musically.

Gunung Sari Legong dance; one of Bali's oldest and most respected troupes.

Semara Madya Kekac dance; especially good for the hypnotic chants. A mystical experience for some.

Tirta Sari Legong dance.

Cudamani One of Bali's best gamelan troupes. They rehearse in Pengosekan, run a school for children and tour internationally. You have to seek them out, though, as they no longer perform in tourist venues.

terial. Also runs regular textile-appreciation **courses** (classes from 75,000Rp).

★**Ganesha Bookshop** BOOKS
(Map p220; www.ganeshabooksbali.com; Jl Raya Ubud; ⊗9am-8pm) A quality bookshop with an excellent selection of titles on Indonesian studies, travel, arts, music, fiction (including used books) and maps. Great staff recommendations.

ⓘ Information

Visitors will find every service they need and then some along Ubud's main roads. Bulletin boards at Bali Buda and Kafe have info on housing, jobs, classes and much more.

Ubud is home to many nonprofit and volunteer groups.

Ubud Tourist Information (Fabulous Ubud; Map p220; ☑0361-973285; www.fabulousubud. com; Jl Raya Ubud; ⊗8am-9pm) is run by the Ubud royal family and is the one really useful tourist office in Bali. It has a good range of information and a noticeboard listing current happenings and activities. The staff can answer most regional questions and it has up-to-date information on ceremonies and traditional dances held in the area; dance tickets and tours are sold here.

ⓘ Getting There & Away

Ubud is on two bemo routes. Bemo travel to Gianyar (10,000Rp) and Batubulan terminal in Denpasar (20,000Rp). Ubud doesn't have a bemo terminal; there are bemo stops on Jl Suweta near the market in the centre of town.

Perama (Map p220; ☑0361-973316; www. peramatour.com; Jl Raya Pengosekan; ⊗7am-10pm) is the major tourist-shuttle operator, but its terminal is inconveniently located in Padangtegal; to get to/from your destination in Ubud will cost another 15,000Rp. Destinations include Sanur (50,000Rp, one hour), Padangbai (75,000Rp, two hours) and Kuta (60,000Rp, two hours).

Kura-Kura Bus (Map p220; www.kura2bus. com) runs from near the Ubud Palace to its hub in Kuta five times daily (80,000Rp, two hours).

ⓘ Getting Around

With numerous nearby attractions, many of which are difficult to reach by bemo, renting a vehicle is sensible. Ask at your accommodation or hire a car and driver.

There are no metered taxis based in Ubud – those that honk their horns at you have usually dropped off passengers from southern Bali in Ubud and are hoping for a fare back. Instead, you'll use one of the ubiquitous drivers with private vehicles hanging around on the streets hectoring passers-by (the better drivers politely hold up signs that say 'transport').

Around Ubud

Some 2km southeast of Ubud on the road to Bedulu, **Goa Gajah** (Elephant Cave; Jl Raya Goa Gajah; adult/child 30,000/15,000Rp, parking motorcycle/car 2000/5000Rp; ⊗7.30am-5pm) is carved into a rock face and you enter through the cavernous mouth of a demon. Inside the T-shaped cave you can see fragmentary remains of the lingam, the phallic

AMED & THE FAR EAST COAST

Stretching from Amed to Bali's far eastern tip, this semiarid coast long drew visitors with its succession of small, scalloped, grey-sand beaches (some more rocks than sand), relaxed atmosphere and excellent diving and snorkelling. In late 2017 when nearby Gunung Agung was threatening to erupt, the tourists fled and the area's economy suffered greatly.

'Amed' is actually a misnomer for the area, as the coast is a series of seaside *dusun* (small villages) that starts with the actual Amed in the north and then runs southeast to Aas. Now more than ever, if you're looking to get away from crowds this is the place to come and try some yoga.

Snorkelling is excellent along the coast. Jemeluk is a protected area where you can admire live coral and plentiful fish within 100m of the beach. The coral gardens and colourful marine life at Selang are highlights. Snorkelling equipment rents for about 30,000Rp per day. Divers should head to one of many dive operators such as **Eco-Dive** (🖉 0363-23482; www.ecodivebali.com; Jemeluk Beach; 🕾) 🖉 .

Meditasi (🖉 0363-430 1793; meditasibali@yahoo.com; Aas; r incl breakfast 400,000-900,000Rp) 🖉 is a chilled-out and charming hideaway. Meditation and yoga help you relax and the 10 rooms are well situated for good swimming and snorkelling.

Straddling the road amid nice gardens, the 11 rooms at **Galang Kangin Bungalows** (🖉 0363-23480; bali_amed_gk@yahoo.co.jp; Jemeluk; r incl breakfast with fan/air-con from 300,000/500,000Rp; 🕸🕾) mix and match fans, cold water, hot water and air-con. Near the beach, **Hoky Home Stay & Cafe** (🖉 0819 1646 3701; Jemeluk; r incl breakfast from 200,000Rp; 🕾) offers great cheap rooms with fans and hot water.

Most people drive here via the main highway from Amlapura and Culik. The spectacular road going all the way around the twin peaks from Aas to Ujung makes a good circle. You can arrange for a driver and car to/from south Bali and the airport for about 500,000Rp.

symbol of the Hindu god Shiva, and its female counterpart the yoni, plus a statue of Shiva's son, the elephant-headed god Ganesha. In front of the cave are two square bathing pools with waterspouts held by six female figures.

Tampaksiring is a small village about 18km northeast of Ubud with a large and important temple, Tirta Empul, and the most impressive ancient site in Bali, **Gunung Kawi** (adult/child incl sarong 15,000/7500Rp, parking 2000Rp; ⊙7am-5pm). The site consists of 10 *candi* (shrines) – memorials cut out of the rock face in imitation of actual statues. Part of a region nominated for Unesco Heritage status, they stand in awe-inspiring 8m-high sheltered niches cut into the sheer cliff face. The views as you walk through ancient terraced rice fields are as fine as any in Bali.

Semarapura (Klungkung)

A tidy regional capital, Semarapura is worthwhile for its fascinating Kertha Gosa complex, a relic of Bali from the time before the Dutch. Once the centre of Bali's most important kingdom, Semarapura is still commonly called by its old name, Klungkung. Formerly the seat of the Dewa Agung dynasty, **Klungkung Palace** (Jl Puputan; adult/child 12,000/6000Rp; ⊙6am-6pm) has now largely crumbled away, but history and architecture buffs will enjoy a wander past the **Kertha Gosa** (Hall of Justice; Klungkung Palace).

Sideman

The Sideman region is getting more popular as a verdant escape every year, where a walk in any direction is a communion with nature. Winding through one of Bali's most beautiful river valleys, the road to Sideman offers marvellous paddy-field scenery, a delightful rural character and extraordinary views of Gunung Agung (when the clouds permit). Its proximity to that volcano, which was threatening to erupt in late 2017, led to an influx of residents fleeing the danger zone.

Khrisna Home Stay (🖉 0815 5832 1543; pinpinaryadi@yahoo.com; Jl Tebola; r incl breakfast 300,000-1,000,000Rp; 🕾🖵) is a wonderful 10-room guesthouse surrounded by organic trees and plants growing guava, bananas, passion-fruit, papaya, oranges and more.

Padangbai

☑ 0363

There's a real traveller vibe about this little beach town that is also the port for the public ferry connecting Bali with Lombok and many of the fast boats to the Gilis.

When not inundated by the travellers in transit, Padangbai is an attractive stop: it sits on a small bay and has a nice little curve of beach. A compact seaside backpacker hub offers cheap places to stay and some fun cafes.

Should ambition strike there's good snorkelling and diving plus some easy walks and a couple of great beaches. Meanwhile you can soak up the languid air between ferry arrivals and departures, which clog the narrow streets and incite general chaos.

🛏 Sleeping & Eating

Fat Barracuda   GUESTHOUSE $
(☑ 0812 3682 8686, 0822 3797 1212; www.facebook.com/fatbarracuda; Jl Segara; dm/r incl breakfast from 115,000/310,000Rp; ❄ 🛜) Run by the same owner from nearby Bamboo Paradise (p225), this popular backpacker pad next to the harbour overlooks the water. It has 10 beds in an air-conditioned dorm and hot water.

Bamboo Paradise   GUESTHOUSE $
(☑ 0363-438 1765, 0822 6630 4330; Jl Penataran Agung; dm/r incl breakfast from 120,000/280,000Rp; ❄ 🛜) Away from the main strip, 200m up a gentle hill from the ferry port, this popular backpackers has the cheapest crash in town (in four-bed, air-con dorms). Regular rooms are comfortable (some fan only) and it has a nice, large lounging area with hammocks and beanbags.

Topi Inn   GUESTHOUSE $
(☑ 0363-41424; www.topiinn.com; Jl Silayukti; dm/r from 70,000/170,000Rp; @ 🛜) Sitting at the east end of the strip in a serene location, Topi has six charming but rudimentary cold-water rooms. Some share bathrooms, others are literally a mattress on the outdoor deck. There's a popular restaurant downstairs, plus various cultural workshops on offer.

★ Bloo Lagoon Village   HOTEL $$
(☑ 0363-41211; www.bloolagoon.com; Jl Silayukti; r incl breakfast US$145-222; ❄ 🛜 ⛱) 🌿 The recently revamped, 25 open-air bungalows that overlook Blue Lagoon Beach are se-cluded, relaxing and full of character. Stylish units come with one, two or three bedrooms. The grounds are lush and the walls adorned with interesting local art, and yoga classes (inclusive in rates) are held in a space with inspiring ocean views. Good-value diving packages and spa treatments available.

ℹ Getting There & Away

Perama (☑ 0361-751875; www.peramatour.com) offers services around the east coast. Destinations include Kuta (75,000Rp, three hours), Sanur (75,000Rp, two hours) and Ubud (75,000Rp, 1½ hours). Other buses go direct to Kuta, whereas Perama makes a stop in Ubud.

Several companies link Padangbai to the Gilis and Lombok. Fares are negotiable and average 300,000Rp to 600,000Rp one-way. Travel times will be more than the 90 minutes advertised. Public ferries travel nonstop between Padangbai and Lembar on Lombok (four to six hours). Passenger tickets are sold near the pier.

Tirta Gangga & Around

☑ 0363

Tirta Gangga (Water of the Ganges) is the site of a holy temple, some great water features and some of the best views of rice fields and the sea beyond in east Bali. Capping a sweep of green flowing down to the distant sea, it is a relaxing place to stop for an hour. With more time you can hike the surrounding terraced countryside, which ripples with coursing water and is dotted with temples. A small valley of rice terraces runs up the hill behind the parking area. It is a majestic vision of emerald steps receding into the distance.

◉ Sights & Activities

Hiking in the surrounding hills transports you far from your memories of frenetic south Bali.

★ Taman Tirta Gangga   PALACE
(adult/child 30,000/15,000Rp, parking 5000Rp; ⊙ 6am-6pm) Amlapura's water-loving raja, after completing his lost masterpiece at Ujung, had another go at building the water palace of his dreams in 1948. He succeeded at Taman Tirta Gangga, which has a stunning crescent of rice-terrace-lined hills for a backdrop. The multilevel aquatic fantasy features two swimming ponds that are popular on weekends and ornamental water features filled with huge koi and lotus blossoms.

Sleeping

★ Side by Side Organic Farm HOMESTAY $
(☏ 0812 3623 3427; balipamela@yahoo.com;
Dausa; r from 150,000Rp, minimum 2 nights) Set
amid lush rice fields near Tirta Gangga in
the tiny village of Dausa, Side by Side Organic Farm serves bounteous and delicious buffet lunches (150,000Rp) and *nasi campur*
(100,000Rp, overnight guests only). Meals
use organic foods grown in the village farms.
International volunteers are welcome; call
at least one day before for directions and to
book lunch.

Pondok Lembah Dukuh GUESTHOUSE $
(☏ 0813 3829 5142; dukuhstay@gmail.com; s/d
from 150,000/200,000Rp; 🕸) Atop a hill with
divine views over the rice fields, this guesthouse has charming bungalows. Rooms are
basic but a stay here is a good chance to get
close to local life.

❶ Getting There & Away
Bemos and minibuses making the east-coast
haul between Amlapura (7000Rp) and Singaraja stop at Tirta Gangga, 6km northwest of
Amlapura.

Gunung Batur Area
☏ 0366

The Gunung Batur area is like a giant bowl,
with its bottom half covered by water and a
set of volcanic cones jutting out of the middle. Sound a bit spectacular? It is. On clear
days – vital to appreciating the spectacle –
the turquoise waters wrap around the newer volcanoes, which have paths of old lava
flows snaking down their sides.

Don't miss **Pulu Mujung Warung** (☏ 0853
3842 8993; Penelokan; mains 40,000-65,000Rp;
🕙 9am-5pm) 🍴, easily the best option for a
meal in the area, with epic volcano views.
It's affiliated with the much-loved Warung
Bodag Maliah restaurant in Ubud.

❶ Getting There & Around
From Batubulan terminal in Denpasar, bemo
(minibuses) travel regularly to Kintamani
(25,000Rp). Buses on the Denpasar–Singaraja
route (via Batubulan, where you may need to
change) will stop in Penelokan and Kintamani
(about 20,000Rp). Alternatively, you can hire
a car or use a driver but be sure to rebuff buf-
fet-lunch entreaties.

If you arrive by private vehicle, you will be
stopped at Penelokan or Kubupenelokan to buy
an entry ticket (30,000/5000Rp per vehicle/
person, beware of scams demanding even more)
for the entire Gunung Batur area. You shouldn't
be charged again – save your receipt.

Bemos shuttle between Penelokan and Kintamani (20,000Rp for tourists). Bemos from
Penelokan down to the lakeside villages go in
the morning (about 15,000Rp to Toya Bungkah).
Later in the day, you may have to hire transport
(40,000Rp or more).

Toya Bungkah
Perched at the edge of Lake Batur, tourist
enclave Toya Bungkah (also known as Tirta)
boasts lovely volcano views and steaming
hot springs (*tirta* and *toya* both mean water). It's a very small village and one of the
places people stay before climbing Gunung
Batur early in the morning.

FPPGB (Mt Batur Tour Guides Association;
☏ 0366-52362; 🕙 3am-9pm), formerly HP-
PGB, has a monopoly on guided climbs up
Gunung Batur. It requires trekking agencies
to hire at least one of its guides for trips
up the mountain, and has a reputation for
tough tactics in requiring climbers to use
its guides. A simple ascent at 4am (sunrise)
costs 400,000Rp; exploration of the main
crater 500,000Rp and additional volcanic
cones 650,000Rp.

Tucked in the hills of Toya Bungkah,
Black Lava Hostel (☏ 0813 3755 8998; www.
facebook.com/blacklavahostel123; Jl Raya Penda-
kian Gunung; dm 150,000Rp, r from 400,000Rp;
🕸🌀) offers basic, affordable dorm accommodation and a toasty dipping pool filled
with mineral water from the nearby hot
springs. **Under the Volcano III** (☏ 0813 3860
0081; s/d incl breakfast from 200,000/250,000Rp;
🕸) features a lovely, quiet lakeside location
opposite chilli plots.

Munduk & Around
☏ 0362

The simple village of Munduk, west of Danau
Bratan, is one of Bali's most appealing mountain retreats. It has a cool misty ambience
set among lush hillsides covered with jungle,
rice fields, fruit trees and pretty much anything else that grows on the island. Waterfalls
tumble off precipices by the dozen. There are
hikes and treks galore and a number of really
nice places to stay, from old Dutch colonial
summer homes to retreats where you can
plunge full-on into local culture. Many people
come for a day and stay for a week.

GUNUNG BATUKAU AREA

Gunung Batukau is Bali's second-highest mountain (2276m), the third of Bali's three major mountains and the holy peak of the island's western end. It's often overlooked, which is probably a good thing given what the vendor hordes have done to Gunung Agung. You can climb its slippery slopes from one of the island's holiest and most underrated temples, **Pura Luhur Batukau** (adult/child 20,000/10,000Rp; ⏰8am-6.30pm).

At **Jatiluwih** (adult/child 40,000/30,000Rp, plus car 5000Rp), which means 'Truly Marvellous', you'll be rewarded with vistas of centuries-old rice terraces that exhaust your ability to describe green. The terraces have received Unesco World Heritage status in recognition of the ancient rice-growing culture. You'll understand why by viewing the panorama from the narrow, twisting 18km road leading in and out of town, but do get out for a rice-field walk. Follow the water as it runs through channels and bamboo pipes from one plot to the next. The only realistic way to explore the Gunung Batukau area is with your own transport.

This is a good base for visiting **Pura Ulun Danu Bratan** (off Jl Raya Denpasar-Singaraja; adult/child 50,000/25,000Rp, parking 5000Rp; ⏰7am-4pm) in Candikuning. This important Hindu-Buddhist temple was founded in the 17th century. It is dedicated to Dewi Danu, the goddess of the waters, and is built on small islands.

🛏 Sleeping & Eating

⭐**Puri Lumbung Cottages**   GUESTHOUSE **$$**
(📱0812 387 4042; www.purilumbung.com; cottages incl breakfast US$80-175; @🖳) 🥾 Founded by Nyoman Bagiarta to develop sustainable tourism, this lovely hotel has 43 bright, two-storey thatched cottages and rooms set among rice fields. Enjoy intoxicating views (units 32 to 35 have the best) from the upstairs balconies. Dozens of trekking options and courses are offered.

Meme Surung Homestay   GUESTHOUSE **$$**
(📱0812 387 3986; www.memesurung.com; r incl breakfast from 400,000Rp; 🖳) Two atmospheric old Dutch houses adjoin to form a compound of six rooms, immersed amid an English-style garden. The decor is traditional and simple; the view from the long wooden verandah is both the focus and joy here. It's located along the main strip of Munduk's township.

Don Biyu   CAFE **$**
(📱0812 3709 3949; www.donbiyu.com; mains 22,000-87,000Rp; ⏰7.30am-10pm; 🖳) Catch up on your blog, enjoy good coffee, zone out before the sublime views, and choose from a mix of Western and interesting Asian fare. Dishes are served in mellow open-air pavilions. It also has six double **rooms** (600,000Rp), all with balconies and views. It's on the main road leading into Munduk.

ℹ Getting There & Away

Minibuses leave Ubung terminal in Denpasar for Munduk (20,000Rp) a few times a day. Driving to the north coast, the main road west of Munduk goes through a number of picturesque villages to Mayong (where you can head south to west Bali). The road then goes down to the sea at Seririt in north Bali.

Lovina

📞0362

'Relaxed' is how people most often describe Lovina, and aside from the pushy touts, they are correct. This low-key, low-rise, low-priced beach resort is a far cry from Kuta. The waves are calm, the beach thin and overamped attractions nil.

Lovina is sun-drenched, with patches of shade from palm trees. A highlight every afternoon at fishing villages such as Anturan is watching *prahu* (traditional outrigger canoes) being prepared for the night's fishing; as sunset reddens the sky, the lights of the fishing boats appear as bright dots across the horizon.

The Lovina tourist area stretches over 8km, and consists of a string of coastal villages – Kaliasem, Kalibukbuk, Anturan and Tukad Mungga – collectively known as Lovina. The main focus is Kalibukbuk, 10.5km west of Singaraja and the heart of Lovina. Daytime traffic on the main road is loud and fairly constant.

DON'T MISS

JOSHUA DISTRICT

Set amid rice fields near the iconic temple of Tanah Lot, **Joshua District** (☏ 0819 1668 7263; www.joshuadistrict. com; Pangkung Tibah, Kediri, Tabanan Regency; ⊘ 8am-10pm Tue-Sun) **FREE** is a creative complex – coffee shop, gallery, fashion concept store and a number of villas – made out of shipping containers. With the motto 'recycle or die', the community space promotes environmental awareness and sustainable lifestyles. Cash only.

⊙ Sights & Activities

Sunrise boat trips to see dolphins are Lovina's much-hyped tourist attraction, so much so that they have a monument in their honour.

★ **Komang Dodik**   HIKING
(☏ 0877 6291 5128; lovina.tracking@gmail.com; hikes 350,000-600,000Rp) Komang Dodik leads hikes in the hills along the north coast. Trips can last from three to six hours. The highlight of most trips is a series of waterfalls, more than 20m high, in a jungle grotto. Routes can include coffee, clove and vanilla plantations. Komang also leads custom tours around the island.

⨼ Sleeping & Eatiing

★ **Funky Place**   HOSTEL $
(☏ 0878 6325 3156; Jl Seririt-Singaraja; tent 130,000Rp, tree house 170,000Rp, dm 150,000-170,000Rp, r from 230,000Rp) From the unicycle bar stools to the affordable tree house to the free foot massage (and with heaps of reclaimed wood, clever signage and weird antiques scattered throughout) this new compound is basically a backpacker's dream. There's a path directly to the beach, and it also holds barbecues, Balinese dancing events and beer-pong competitions. Live music happens every weekend.

Sea Breeze Lovina   GUESTHOUSE $
(☏ 0362-41138; off Jl Bina Ria, Kalibukbuk; r/bungalow incl breakfast 350,000/450,000Rp; ❄ 🛜 🏊) One of the best choices in the heart of Kalibukbuk, the Sea Breeze has five bungalows and two rooms by the pool and the beach, some with sensational views from their verandahs. The only downside is that it can get noisy from nearby bars at night.

Harris Homestay   HOMESTAY $
(☏ 0362-41152; Gang Binaria, Kalibukbuk; s/d incl breakfast from 130,000/150,000Rp; 🛜) Sprightly, tidy and white, Harris avoids the weary look of some neighbouring cheapies. The charming owner lives in the back; guests enjoy four bright, modern rooms up the front.

★ **Global Village Kafe**   CAFE $
(☏ 0362-41928; Jl Raya Lovina, Kalibukbuk; mains from 27,000Rp; ⊘ 8am-10pm; 🛜) Che Guevara, Mikhail Gorbachev and Nelson Mandela are just some of the figures depicted in the paintings lining the walls of this artsy cafe. The baked goods, fruit drinks, pizzas, breakfasts, Indo classics and much more are excellent. There are free book and DVD exchanges, plus a selection of local handicrafts. Profits go to a foundation that funds local health care.

Akar   VEGETARIAN $
(☏ 0362-343 5636; Jl Bina Ria, Kalibukbuk; mains 45,000-70,000Rp; ⊘ 7am-10pm; 🛜 🌿) 🍃 The many shades of green at this vegetarian cafe aren't just for show. They reflect the earth-friendly ethics of the owners. Enjoy organic smoothies, house-made gelato, and fresh and tasty international dishes, such as chargrilled aubergine filled with feta and chilli.

❶ Getting There & Away

To reach Lovina from south Bali by public transport, take a bus from Denpasar to the Sangket terminal in Singaraja. Once there take a bemo to Singaraja's Banyuasri terminal. Finally, get another bemo to the Lovina area. This will take most of a day.

Perama (☏ 0362-41161; www.peramatour. com; Jl Raya Lovina, Anturan) buses stop in Anturan. Passengers are then ferried to other points on the Lovina strip (15,000Rp). There's a daily bus to/from the south, including Kuta, Sanur and Ubud (all 130,000Rp). To Amed, it's 150,000Rp and to Pemuteran it's 100,000Rp.

West Bali

Even as development from south Bali creeps ever further west (via hot spots such as Canggu), Bali's true west, which is off the busy main road from Tabanan to Gilimanuk, remains infrequently visited. It's easy to find serenity amid its wild beaches, jungle and rice fields.

Balian Beach

Ever more popular, Balian Beach is a rolling area of dunes and knolls overlooking pounding surf. It attracts both surfers and those looking to escape the bustle of south Bali.

Much of the accommodation is fairly close together and near the beach, but there are also some comfortable homestays set back from the water. **Surya Homestay** (✉ 0813 3868 5643; wayan.suratni@gmail.com; r incl breakfast 200,000-350,000Rp; ✳ 🛜) is a sweet little family-run homestay with seven rooms in bungalow-style units. At **Made's Homestay** (✉ 0812 396 3335; r 150,000-200,000Rp) three basic bungalow-style units are surrounded by banana trees back from the beach.

Sushi Surf (✉ 0812 3709 0980; Jl Pantai Balian; rolls from 20,000Rp; ⏲ 10am-10pm) is *the* place for a sunset cocktail and bite of sushi. The surf action is arrayed out right in front of the quirky multilevel seating area.

Gilimanuk

Gilimanuk is the terminus for ferries that shuttle back and forth across the narrow strait to Java. Most travellers to or from Java can get an onward ferry or bus straightaway, and won't hang around.

Frequent buses run between Gilimanuk's large depot and Denpasar's Ubung terminal (45,000Rp, three hours), or along the north-coast road to Singaraja (40,000Rp). Smaller, slightly more comfortable minibuses serve both routes for 5000Rp more.

Car ferries to and from Ketapang on Java (30 minutes, adult/child 7000/5000Rp, motorbike/car 25,000/225,000Rp) run around the clock. Their safety record has been fair at best. The pedestrian terminal is 300m north of the large bus station.

Taman Nasional Bali Barat

Most visitors to Bali's only national park, Bali Basrat National Park (Taman Nasional Bali Barat), are struck by the mellifluous sounds emanating from the myriad birds darting among the rustling trees.

The park covers 190 sq km of the western tip of Bali, including almost 32 sq km of coral reef and coastal waters. Taking up 3% of Bali, this represents a significant commitment to conservation on such a densely populated island.

It's a place where you can enjoy Bali's best diving at Pulau Menjangan, hike through forests and explore coastal mangroves.

Pemuteran

✉ 0362

This popular oasis in the northwest corner of Bali has a number of artful resorts set on a little dogbone-shaped bay that's incredibly calm, thanks to its location within an extinct volcano crater protected by flourishing coral reefs. The beach is decent, but most people come to view the undersea wonders just offshore and at nearby Pulau Menjangan.

The busy Singaraja–Gilimanuk road is the town's spine and ever more businesses aimed at visitors can be found along it. Despite its popularity, Pemuteran's community and tourism businesses have forged a sustainable vision for development that should be a model for the rest of Bali.

Right on the beach in a large compound, **Reef Seen** (✉ 0362-93001; www.reefseenbali.com; 2-tank dives from 1,200,000Rp) is a PADI dive centre and has a full complement of classes. It also offers pony rides on the beach for kids, and some dive packages include accommodation at the dive complex (rooms from 525,000Rp). The company is active in local preservation efforts.

> **WORTH A TRIP**
>
> ### DIVING PULAU MENJANGAN
>
> With its great selection of lodgings, Pemuteran is the ideal base for diving and snorkelling Pulau Menjangan. Banyuwedang's harbour is just 7km west of town, so you have only a short ride before you're on a boat for the relaxing and pretty 30-minute journey to Menjangan. Dive shops and local hotels run snorkelling trips that cost US$45 to US$75; two-tank dive trips cost from US$75. That includes a 200,000Rp park entrance fee, but note that on Sundays and other national holidays, the price for entering the park increases to 300,000Rp.
>
> Some tours to Menjangan leave by boat right from Pemuteran Beach; this is best. Other trips involve a car ride and transfer at Banyuwedang.

🛏 Sleeping & Eating

Pande Guest House
GUESTHOUSE $

(☑ 0818 822 088; Jl Singaraja-Gilimanuk; r from 250,000Rp; ❀🛜) This newer guesthouse is well run and charming, with immaculate, comfy rooms featuring open-air bathrooms with lovely garden showers. It's by far the best budget option in town.

★ Taman Selini
Beach Bungalows
BOUTIQUE HOTEL $$

(☑ 0362-94746; www.tamanselini.com; Jl Singaraja-Gilimanuk; r incl breakfast from 850,000Rp; ❀🛜🏊) The 11 bungalows here recall an older, refined Bali, from the quaint thatched roofs down to the antique carved doors and detailed stonework. Rooms, which open on to a large garden running down to the beach, have four-poster beds and large outdoor bathrooms. The outdoor daybeds can be addictive, and the beachfront restaurant – with Indonesian and Greek dishes – is fantastic.

Kubuku Ecolodge
GUESTHOUSE $$

(☑ 0813 3857 5384; www.kubukuhotel.com; Jl Singaraja-Gilimanuk; r incl breakfast from 750,000Rp; ❀🛜) A slice of modern style in Pemuteran, Kubuku has a smallish pool with a bar and an inviting patch of lawn. The 21 comfortable rooms are decent value, and the restaurant serves tasty organic meals. The compound is down a lane on the mountain side of the main road.

★ Santai Warung
INDONESIAN $

(☑ 0852 3737 0220; Jl Hotel Taman Sari; mains from 35,000Rp; ⏰ 11am-9pm; 🚲) Follow the glowing lanterns off Pemuteran's main road to this adorable Indonesian restaurant, which serves up spicy, authentic dishes – including lots of great vegetarian options – in a wonderful garden setting. The restaurant also features rice tables (banquets involving dozens of Balinese dishes that must be ordered 24 hours in advance), along with a traditional Javanese *joglo* house and cooking classes.

ℹ Getting There & Away

Pemuteran is served by buses on the Gilimanuk–Lovina–Singaraja run. To Pemuteran from Gilimanuk or Lovina, you should be able to negotiate a fare of around 20,000Rp. There's no stop, so just flag one down. It's a three- to four-hour drive from south Bali, either over the hills or around the west coast. A private car and driver costs 600,000Rp to either Ubud or Seminyak, among other destinations.

NUSA TENGGARA

If you're seeking white sand, spectacular diving, frothing hot springs and hidden traditional villages, Nusa Tenggara is your wonderland. Spreading west from the Wallace Line dividing Asia from Australasia, this archipelago is lush and jungle-green in the north, tending to drier savannah in the south and east. In between are some of the world's best diving spots, limitless surf breaks, Technicolor volcanic lakes, pink-sand beaches and swaggering dragons.

You'll also find a human diversity that is unmatched even in multicultural Indonesia. Animist rituals and tribal traditions still thrive alongside minarets, temples, convents and chapels, and though Bahasa

Nusa Tenggara

Indonesia is the lingua franca, each main island has at least one native language, often subdivided into dialects. Whether your wish is to drop into the easy, tourist-ready life of a car-free Gili island, or you crave, somewhere less comfortable, more challenging and a shade deeper, you're exactly where you're supposed to be.

ⓘ Getting There & Away

Lombok International Airport is the principal port of entry in West Nusa Tenggara, connecting with Kuala Lumpur and Singapore internationally, and Jakarta, Denpasar and other airports within Indonesia. While nominally an international airport, El Tari in Kupang is really a domestic hub for East Nusa Tenggara. All the important towns and cities have regular – and expanding – air service. Lombok and Kupang are hubs, while airports such as Labuanbajo in Flores and Tambolaka in Sumba boast new and improved facilities.

Regular ferries and fast boats also connect Lombok and the Gili Islands with Bali.

ⓘ Getting Around

Overland travel is slow in mountainous Nusa Tenggara. Busy Lombok, Sumbawa, Flores and Timor have fairly decent surfaced main roads and relatively comfortable bus services. Get off the highways, and things slow down considerably. Ferry services are regular and consistent in the dry season, but in the wet season, when seas get rough, your ship may be cancelled for days on end. Overland travel across all of Nusa Tenggara is time-consuming, with stretches of tedium offset by areas of interest.

Several airlines cover interisland routes, many of which start in Bali.

Lombok

As beguiling, beach-blessed and downright blissful as its near neighbour Bali, Lombok is now much more than just a surfers' paradise.

Lombok is an easy hop from Bali. It has a spectacular, mostly deserted coastline with palm coves, Balinese Hindu temples, looming cliffs and epic surf. The majestic and sacred Gunung Rinjani rises from its centre – a challenging and rewarding climb. The Gilis, a car-free collection of islands infused with a sun-drenched party vibe, are Lombok's biggest draw, although the beautiful surf breaks and beaches of Kuta are fast gaining popularity.

ⓘ Getting There & Away

Flying into Lombok International Airport near Praya, from a range of domestic and international cities, is the most commonly used method of entry to the island, followed by arriving on boat, via tourist-focused ferries from Bali to the west coast and Gilis, or on the more workaday ferries between neighbouring Sumbawa and Labuhan Lombok on the east coast.

Flights, cars and tours can be booked online at lonelyplanet.com/bookings.

ⓘ Getting Around

Moving around Lombok is easy, with a good – though often traffic-clogged – road across the middle of the island between Mataram and Labuhan Lombok.

Almost every corner of Lombok can be reached by bus, and *bemo* (small, cheap, public minibuses) operate around population centres, often radiating out along pre-determined routes from dedicated terminals.

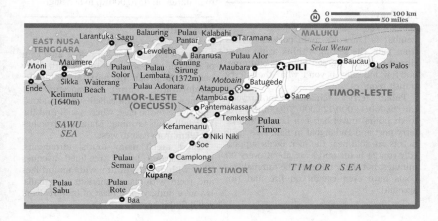

Lombok

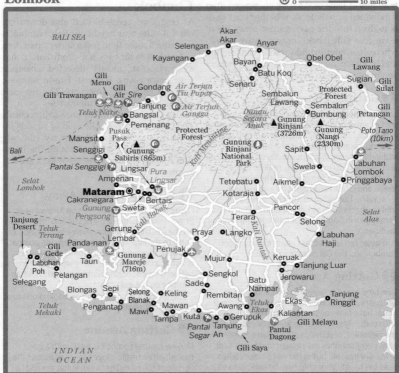

Cheap motorbike rentals can be a good way to explore short distances, while *ojeks* (motorbike taxis) are ubiquitous. Metered taxis operate from the airport and other transport hubs.

Lembar

📞 0370 / POP 44,426

Lembar is Lombok's main port for ferries from Bali. The setting – think azure inlets ringed by soaring green hills – is stunning, but few folk stay beyond what their ferry transit requires.

Public ferries (child/adult/motorcycle/car 29,000/44,000/123,000/879,000Rp, five to six hours) travel between Lembar's large ferry port and Padangbai in Bali. Passenger tickets are sold near the pier. Boats supposedly run 24 hours and leave about every 90 minutes, but the service can be unreliable – boats have even caught on fire and run aground.

Bemo (minibus) and bus connections are abundant and bemos run regularly to the Mandalika Terminal (15,000Rp), so there's no reason to linger. Taxis cost around 80,000Rp to Mataram and 170,000Rp to Senggigi.

Mataram

📞 0370 / POP 402,843

Lombok's capital is a sprawling amalgam of several, once-separate towns with fuzzy borders: Ampenan (the port), Mataram (the administrative centre), Cakranegara (the business centre, often called simply 'Cakra') and Sweta to the east, where you'll find the Mandalika bus terminal. Mataram stretches for 12km from east to west.

There aren't many tourist attractions, yet Mataram's broad tree-lined avenues buzz with traffic, thrum with motorbikes and teem with classic markets and malls. If you're hungry for a blast of Indo realism, you'll find it here.

Pura Meru (Jl Selaparang; 6000Rp; ⊙ 8am-5pm) is the largest and second-most important Hindu temple on Lombok. Built in 1720, it's dedicated to the Hindu trinity of Brahma, Vishnu and Shiva.

Lombok Epicentrum Mall (☑ 0370-617 2999; www.lombokepicentrum.com; Jl Sriwijaya 333; ⊙ 9am-10pm), with a cinema, food courts and the full spread of consumer pleasures, is Lombok's biggest and fanciest.

🛏 Sleeping & Eating

Hotel Melati Viktor   GUESTHOUSE $
(☑ 0370-633830; Jl Abimanyu 1; r incl breakfast 250,000Rp; ※ 🕏) The high ceilings, 37 clean rooms and Balinese-style courtyard, complete with Hindu statues, make this one of the best-value places in town. The cheapest rooms have fans.

Ikan Bakar 99   SEAFOOD $
(☑ 0370-643335, 0819 3313 8188; Jl Subak III 10; mains 30,000-55,000Rp; ⊙ 11am-10pm) Think squid, prawns, fish and crab, brushed with chilli sauce, perfectly grilled or fried, and drenched in spicy Padang or sticky sweet-and-sour sauce. You will eat alongside the Mataram families who fill the long tables in the arched, tiled dining room. It's in a Balinese neighbourhood.

ℹ Information

Kantor Imigrasi (Immigration Office; ☑ 0370-632520; Jl Udayana 2; ⊙ 8am-noon & 1-4pm Mon-Fri) Government office for renewing your visa.

ℹ Getting There & Away

The chaotic **Mandalika Terminal** (Jl Pasar Bertais B8), 3km from the centre and surrounded by the city's main market, is Lombok's biggest bus and bemo hub. Use the official ticket office to avoid touts and take yellow bemos for the centre (5000Rp). Buses and bemos departing hourly from the Mandalika Terminal include the following:

DESTINATION	FARE (RP)	DURATION
Airport (Damri Bus)	15,000	45min
Kuta (no-change shuttle bus)	45,000	1¼hr
Kuta (via Praya & Sengkol)	45,000	2-3hr
Labuhan Lombok	35,000	2½hr
Lembar	30,000	45min
Senggigi (via Ampenan)	15,000	1hr

Senggigi
☑ 0370

Lombok's traditional tourist resort, Senggigi enjoys a fine location along a series of sweeping bays, with light-sand beaches sitting pretty below a backdrop of jungle-clad mountains and coconut palms. In the late afternoon a setting blood-red sun sinks into the surf next to the giant triangular cone of Bali's Gunung Agung.

Senggigi is now usurped by the Gilis and Kuta; tourist numbers are relatively modest here and you'll find some excellent-value hotels and restaurants. Still, the tacky main strip could be more appealing, the noticeable influx of bar girls is sleazy, the garish billboards are ugly and the resident beach hawkers can be over-persistent. If you want a quieter beach experience, head north.

The Senggigi area spans 10km of coastal road; the upscale neighbourhood of **Mangsit** is 3km north of central Senggigi, while just beyond lie the picturesque beaches of **Malimbu** and **Nipah**.

◉ Sights & Activities

There's reasonable snorkelling off the point in Senggigi, 3km north of the town. You can rent gear (per day 50,000Rp) from several spots on the beach. Diving trips from Senggigi usually visit the Gili Islands.

Local dive outfits include **Blue Coral** (☑ 0370-693441; Jl Raya Senggigi; 2 dives 850,000Rp, open-water course 4,950,000Rp; ⊙ 8am-9pm) and **Blue Marlin** (☑ 0817 571 2389, 0370-693719; www.bluemarlindive.com; Holiday Resort Lombok, Jl Raya Senggigi; 2-tank dive 1,100,000Rp, open-water course 5,750,000Rp).

Taman Wisata Alam Kerandangan   NATURE RESERVE
(off Jl Wisata Alam) This pleasant, little-visited nature reserve is ideal for escaping the tourist bustle of Senggigi and indulging in a few hours of strolling in the rainforest. The Princess Twin and Swallow Cave waterfalls lie on the marked trail (which can get a little indistinct in parts) and there's the chance of seeing rare butterflies and black monkeys (alongside the common kind). To get here, head north of town to Mangsit, then take Jalan Wisata Alam inland through the Kerandangan Valley.

Rinjani Trekking Club   TREKKING
(☑ 0817 573 0415, 0370-693202; www.info2lombok. com; Jl Raya Senggigi; 3-day/2-night trek $US225;

Senggigi

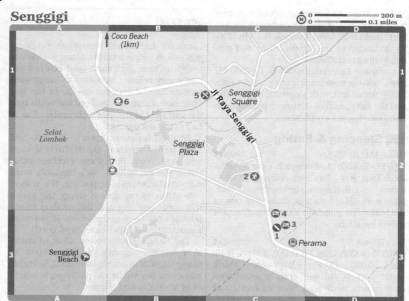

Senggigi

Activities, Courses & Tours

Sleeping

Eating

Transport

⊘ 9am-8pm) Responsible, knowledgeable and run by the friendly Ronnie, this well-established outfit is the best of the many hawking Rinjani treks along Senggigi's main strip. There is a wide choice of guided hikes available; all include entrance fees, three meals a day, camping equipment and a donation towards Rinjani clean-up efforts.

🛏 Sleeping & Eating

BC Inn   GUESTHOUSE $
(☑ 0370-619 7880, 0876 595 0549; http://bcinnsenggigi.com; Jl Raya Senggigi; d & tw 200,000Rp; 🛜) Spick and span, relatively new, comfortable and right in the heart of Senggigi, BC is named for the Blue Coral dive shop, which it sits behind. All rooms have satellite TV, wi-fi, decent beds, walk-in showers and lime, caramel and cream decor. Two people buying a dive package get a night free.

Sendok Hotel   HOTEL $
(☑ 0370-692270; Jl Raya Senggigi; r with fan/air-con from 250,000/400,000Rp; 🌢🛜🏊) Fronted by a friendly bar-restaurant, this hotel offers 28 rooms amid lovingly tended gardens nibbled by sunburnt rabbits and embellished with Hindu shrines and statues. The rooms are basic and not all have hot water, but they're comfortable and have private front porches.

★ Cafe Tenda Cak Poer   INDONESIAN $
(Jl Raya Senggigi; mains 20,000-30,000Rp; ⊘ 6pm-midnight Tue-Sun) This roadside warung feeds the locals with hot-outta-the-wok Indo classics. Grab a plastic stool at a battered metal table, open a pack of *krupuk* (Indonesian crackers) and order the nasi goreng, made extra hot *(ekstra pedas)* and with extra garlic *(bawang putih ekstra)*. You'll be smiling (and sweating) through tears.

★ **Coco Beach** INDONESIAN **$$**
(☑ 0817 578 0055; off Jl Raya Senggigi, Pantai Kerandangan; mains 55,000-70,000Rp; ☺ noon-10pm; ♪) This wonderful beachside restaurant 2km north of Senggigi has a blissfully secluded setting off the main road. Dining is at individual thatch-covered tables, with many choices for vegetarians. The nasi goreng and madras curry are locally renowned and the seafood is the best in the area. It has a full bar and blends its own authentic *jamu* tonics (herbal medicines).

❶ Getting There & Away

BEMO

Regular bemos (minibuses) travel between Senggigi and Ampenan's Kebon Roek terminal (5000Rp), where you can connect to Mataram (10,000Rp). Wave them down on the main drag.

BOAT

Fast boats to Bali leave from the large **pier** right in the centre of the beach. Some companies sell tickets from an office out on the pier; others from the shore nearby.

Gili Getaway (☑ 0813 3707 4147; http://giligetaway.com; Senggigi Pier; one-way 200,000-250,000Rp) has useful services to Gili T and Gili Air as well as Gili Gede.

Perama (☑ 0370-693008; www.peramatour.com; Jl Raya Senggigi; ☺ 7am-10pm) has an economical shuttle-bus service that connects with the public ferry from Lembar to Padangbai, Bali (125,000Rp), from where there are onward shuttle-bus connections to Sanur, Kuta and Ubud (all 175,000Rp). These trips can take eight or more hours. It also offers a bus-and-boat connection to the Gilis for a reasonable 150,000Rp (two hours). It saves some hassle at Bangsal Harbour.

Scoot (☑ 0828 9701 5565; www.scootcruise.com; Senggigi Pier; one-way from 675,000Rp) has daily fast boats to Nusa Lembongan and Sanur on Bali.

For those going on adventures further into Nusa Tenggara, **Kencana Adventure** (☑ 0812 2206 6066; www.kencanaadventure.com; Jl Raya Senggigi; one-way deck/shared cabin 1,650,000/2,000,000Rp; ☺ 10am-8pm) has an office where you can get info about heading east on a boat.

Gunung Rinjani

Lording over the northern half of Lombok, the active Gunung Rinjani (3726m) is Indonesia's second-tallest volcano. It's an astonishing peak, and sacred to Hindus and Sasaks who make pilgrimages to the summit and lake to leave offerings for the gods and spirits. To the Balinese, Rinjani is one of three sacred mountains, along with Bali's Agung and Java's Bromo. Sasaks ascend throughout the year around the full moon.

The mountain has climatic significance. Its peak attracts a steady stream of swirling rain clouds, while its ash emissions bring fertility to the surrounding crops of rice, tobacco, cashews and mangoes.

Rinjani also attracts many trekkers who thrill to the other-worldly vistas. In fact the volcano has become so popular that the number of annual trekkers now exceeds 100,000.

Senaru

The scenic villages that make up Senaru merge into one along a steep road with sweeping volcano and sea views. Most visitors here are Gunung Rinjani–bound but beautiful walking trails and spectacular waterfalls beckon to those who aren't.

Senaru derives its name from *sinaru,* which means light. As you ascend the hill towards the sky and clouds, you'll see just why this makes sense.

From Mandalika Terminal in Bertais (Mataram), catch a bus to Anyar (25,000Rp to 30,000Rp, 2½ hours). Bemos don't run from Anyar to Senaru, so you'll have to charter an *ojek* (motorcycle taxi; per person from 30,000Rp, depending on your luggage).

Kuta

☑ 0370

What could be a better gateway to the wonderful beaches of south Lombok? Imagine a crescent bay, turquoise in the shallows and deep blue further out. It licks a huge, white-sand beach, as wide as a football pitch and framed by headlands. Now imagine a coastline of nearly a dozen such bays, all backed by a rugged range of coastal hills spotted with lush patches of banana trees and tobacco fields, and you'll have a notion of Kuta's immediate appeal.

Kuta's original attraction was the limitless world-class breaks, and now even as developers lick their chops, the sets still keep rolling in. Meanwhile, the town itself is an appealing mix of guesthouses, cafes, restaurants and low-key places for a beer.

Kimen Surf (☑ 0878 6590 0017; www.kuta-lombok.net; Jl ke Mawan; board rental per day 100,000Rp, lessons per person from 525,000Rp;

TREKKING GUNUNG RINJANI

Treks to the rim, lake and peak should not be taken lightly, and guides are mandatory. Climbing Rinjani during the wet season (January to April) is usually completely forbidden due to the risk of landslide. June to August is the only time you are (almost) guaranteed minimal rain or clouds. Be prepared with layers and a fleece because it can get cold at the rim (and near freezing at the summit) at any time of year.

Roughly the same trek packages and prices are offered by all operators, though some outfitters have a 'luxury' option. Typical itineraries include:

Crater Rim (two days) An up-and-back to see the caldera lake view from Senaru.

Rim & Lake Return (four days) A return trip from either Senaru or Sembalun Lawang to the crater rim and then down into the caldera to the lake. Note that a three-day variation on this trip involves an exhausting and potentially dangerous 12-hour (or more) marathon on the last day.

Senaru–Rim–Lake–Sembalan Lawang (five days) The classic trek takes in everything with little repetition and at a humane pace.

Trek prices get cheaper the larger the party. Costs (including food, equipment, guide, porters, park fee and transport back to Senaru) average US$100 per person per day, although this is generally negotiable. Any posted prices are just an opening gambit.

The easiest way to organise a trip is through your accommodation. You will also find numerous independent operators.

In Senaru:

John's Adventures (☑ 0817 578 8018; www.rinjanimaster.com)

Rudy Trekker (☑ 0818 0365 2874; www.rudytrekker.com)

Rinjani Trek Centre (RTC; ☑ 0819 0741 1211; www.rinjanitrekcentre.com; ⊙ 6am-4pm)

Senaru Trekking (☑ 0818 540673; http://senarutrekking.com; Jl Pariwisata; 3-day/2-night trek per person from US$200) ✎

In Sembalun Lawang:

Rinjani Information Centre (RIC; ☑ 0818 540 673; www.rinjaniinformationcentre.com; Sembalun Lawang; ⊙ 6am-6pm)

Agencies in Kuta, Senggigi and beyond can organise Rinjani treks, too, with return transport from the point of origin.

⊙ 9am-9pm) is a well-regarded local surf shop that provides swell forecasts, tips, kitesurfing, board rental, repairs and lessons. It also runs guided excursions to breaks such as Gerupuk (500,000Rp). For diving, **Scuba Froggy** (☑ 0878 6454 1402; www.scubafroggy. com; Jl ke Mawan; open-water course US$390; ⊙ 9am-7pm) runs local trips to a dozen dive sites, most no deeper than 18m.

🛏 Sleeping

⭐ **Bombara Bungalows**   GUESTHOUSE $
(☑ 0370-650 2571; bomborabungalows@yahoo.com; Jl Raya Kuta; standard/superior r 425,000/575,000Rp; ❇ ⛱ ☀) One of the best places for a low-cost stay in Kuta, these eight bungalows (some fan-cooled, all with bathrooms) are built around a lovely pool area. Coconut palms shade loungers, pink-flamingo floatation devices stand ready and the entire place feels like an escape from the hubbub of town. The staff understand the needs of surfers, and pretty much everyone.

Mimpi Manis   B&B $
(☑ 0818 369950; www.mimpimanis.com; Jl Raya Kuta; dm/d 125,000/350,000Rp; ❇ ⛱) Run by Made and Gemma, a friendly Balinese/British couple, 'Sweet Dreams' is an inviting B&B offering spotless dorms and private rooms, some with air-con and showers. Located 1km inland, it's more peaceful than central Kuta options, with plenty of good books and DVDs to borrow. There's also a free drop-off service to the beach and town, plus bike and motorbike rental.

Bule Homestay
GUESTHOUSE $

(📱0819 1799 6256; Jl Raya Bypass; r 250,000-
320,000Rp; ❋ 🛜) About 2km back from the
beach, near the junction of Jl Raya Kuta and
Jl Raya Bypass, this nine-bungalow complex
is worth considering for the quiet surrounds
and snappy way it's run. Shoes are left on
the front steps and dirt doesn't dare enter
the small compound, where rooms gleam
with a hospital white.

✗ Eating & Drinking

Full Moon Cafe
INDONESIAN $

(Jl Raya Pantai Kuta; mains 35,000-45,000Rp;
🕑8am-11pm; 🛜) Right across from the beach,
the 2nd-floor cafe here is like a tree house
built of driftwood, with killer ocean views
(although development threatens to partially
obscure these). The menu has all the standards, from grilled whole fish to nasi goreng
and, yes, pizza! Come for the views at sunset, then hang out. Cheap accommodation is
also available.

Sea Salt
SEAFOOD $$

(📱0819 3674 3650; Jl Raya Pantai Kuta; mains
65,000-75,000Rp; 🕑11am-10pm) That a Scot-
tish-owned, vaguely Greek seafood restau-
rant is one of Kuta's best speaks volumes for
where the current dining scene here is at.
Be fussed over by super-enthusiastic, bare-
foot staff in a small, arched dining room
open to the beach and hung with bird cages
and shrimp traps, as you tuck into the day's
catch with your choice of sides and accom-
panying sauce.

Warung Bule
SEAFOOD $$

(📱0370-615 8625; http://warungbulelombok.
com; Jl Raya Pantai Kuta; mains 66,000-72,000Rp;
🕑10am-11pm; 🛜) Tucked away from the main
thoroughfares, on a quiet stretch of Kuta
beach, this friendly, spotlessly tiled warung
is one of the best in town. The grilled barracuda with Sasak spices is fantastic, while
the trio of lobster, prawns and mahi-mahi
(385,000Rp, expensive by local standards)
is a full seafood fix. It can get very busy in
high season.

Surfer's Bar
BAR

(📱0853 3849 7038; www.facebook.com/surfers
barkutalombok; Jl Raya Pantai Kuta; 🕑5pm-mid-
night) 'No Shirt, No Shoes, No Worries!'
proclaims the up-ended surfboard at the
entrance to this beachside bar, giving some
flavour of its laid-back party vibe. Coco-
nut-thatch and palms shade tables wedged

into the sandy floor, while cover bands and
DJs bring the noise on Friday nights, which
don't end until around 3am.

ℹ️ Getting There & Away

You'll need at least three bemos to get here just
from Mataram. Take one from Mataram's Mandalika Terminal to Praya (15,000Rp), another to
Sengkol (5000Rp) and a third to Kuta (5000Rp).

Simpler are the daily tourist buses serving
Mataram (125,000Rp), plus Senggigi and Lembar (both 150,000Rp).

A taxi to the airport costs 100,000Rp.

Ride-share cars are widely advertised around
town. Destinations include: Bangsal for Gili Islands public boats (160,000Rp), Seminyak (Bali)
via the public ferry (200,000Rp) and Senaru
(400,000Rp).

Gili Islands

Floating in a turquoise sea and fringed by
white sand and coconut palms, the Gilis are
a vision of paradise. And they're booming
like nowhere else in Indonesia – speedboats
zip visitors direct from Bali and hip new hotels are rising like autumnal mushrooms.

The lure of big tourist dollars tugs against
the traditionally laid-back culture of the
islands, the alternative spirit imported by
Western party goers and a buoyant green
sensibility. While the outcome is uncertain,
for now the Gilis retain their languorous
charm (partly due to local efforts to exclude
dogs and motorbikes from the islands).

Each island has its own special character.
Gili Trawangan (aka Gili T) is the most cosmopolitan, with a raucous party scene and
plenty of upscale dining and accommodation. Gili Air has the strongest local character and an appealing mix of buzz and bliss,
while little Gili Meno is only just waking
from its pre-development slumber.

🏃 Activities

The Gili Islands are a superb dive destination, with plentiful and varied marine life
to be encountered across around 25 closely
packed sites. Safety standards are reasonably high on the Gilis, but with the proliferation of new dive schools, several have
formed the Gili Island Divers Association
(GIDA). Rates incllude 900,000Rp for an
introductory dive and 5,500,000 for a PADI
Open Water course.

Ringed by coral reefs, the Gilis also offer
superb snorkelling. Masks, snorkels and

INDONESIA GILI ISLANDS

fins are widely available and can be hired for about 50,000Rp per day. Snorkelling trips – many on glass-bottomed boats – are very popular. Typically, you'll pay about 100,000Rp to 150,000Rp per person or about 650,000Rp for the entire boat.

ℹ Information

The drug trade remains endemic in Trawangan. You'll get offers of mushrooms, meth and other drugs. But remember, Indonesia has a strong anti-drugs policy; those found in possession of or taking drugs risk jail or worse.

Tourists have been poisoned by adulterated arak (colourless, distilled palm wine) on the Gilis, as happens in Bali and Lombok. Skip it, and beware cut-price cocktails.

ℹ Getting There & Away

Most hotels and many guesthouses will help you sort out your transport options to and from the Gilis as part of your reservation. If you use an online booking website, contact the hotel directly afterwards. Some high-end resorts have their own boats for transporting guests.

FROM BALI

Fast boats advertise swift connections between Bali and Gili Trawangan (45 minutes to 2½ hours, depending on destination). They leave from several departure points in Bali, including Benoa Harbour, Sanur, Padangbai and Amed. Some go via Nusa Lembongan. Many dock at Teluk Nare/ Teluk Kade on Lombok north of Senggigi before continuing on to Air and Trawangan (you'll have to transfer for Meno). The website Gili Bookings (www.gilibookings.com) presents a range of boat operators and prices in response to your booking request. It's useful for getting an idea of the services offered, but it is not comprehensive and you may get a better price by buying direct from the operator.

Operators include the following:

Amed Sea Express (☑ 0853 3925 3944, 0878 6306 4799; www.gili-sea-express.com) Makes 45-minute crossings to Amed on a large speedboat. This makes many interesting itineraries possible.

Blue Water Express (☑ 0813 3841 8988, 0361-895 1111; www.bluewater-express.com; one-way from 790,000Rp) From Serangan and Padangbai (Bali) to Teluk Kade, Gili T and Gili Air.

Gili Getaway (☑ 0821 4489 9502, 0813 3707 4147; www.giligetaway.com; one-way Bali to Gilis adult/child 675,000/525,000Rp) Very professional; links Serangan on Bali with Gili T and Gili Air as well as Senggigi and Gili Gede.

Perama (☑ 0361-750808; www.peramatour. com; per person one-way from 225,000Rp) Links Padangbai, the Gilis and Senggigi by a not-so-fast boat.

Scoot (☑ 0823 4002 9679; www.scootcruise. com; one-way 750,000Rp) Boats link Sanur, Padangbai, Nusa Lembongan, Senggigi and the Gilis.

Semaya One (☑ 0361-877 8166, 0819 9997 1078; www.semayacruise.com; one-way adult/ child 700,000/650,000Rp) Network of services linking Sanur, Nusa Penida, Padangbai, Teluk Kade, Gili Air and Gili T.

FROM LOMBOK

Coming from Lombok, you can travel by fast boat from Teluk Nare/Teluk Kade north of Senggigi. Many of these services are operated by hotels and dive outfits based in the Gilis (making pre-arranged diving/accommodation and transfer options appealing), but private charters with local owners are also possible. Most people still use the public boats that leave from Bangsal Harbour.

Public boats run to all three islands before 11am; after that you may only find one to Gili T or Gili Air. These leave, in both directions, only when full – about 45 people. If the seas are high and the boat (over)loaded, riding these battered outriggers can be a hair-raising experience. When no public boat is running to your Gili, you may have to charter a boat (400,000Rp to 500,000Rp, for up to 25 people), or decide this is the safer option in any case. One-way public fares are 12,000Rp to Gili Air, 14,000Rp to Gili Meno and 15,000Rp to Gili Trawangan. Boats often pull up on the beaches; be prepared to wade ashore.

ℹ Getting Around

There's no motorised transport on the Gilis – one of their greatest charms.

Introduced relatively recently, public fast boats run almost hourly in the daytime on a route linking Gili T, Gili Meno, Gili Air and Bangsal; they cost 85,000Rp. This makes it easy to hop from one Gili to another.

There's also a slow, daily, island-hopping boat service that loops between all three islands (15,000Rp to 50,000Rp). Check the latest timetable at the islands' docks. You can always charter boats between the islands (350,000Rp to 400,000Rp).

The Gilis are flat and easy enough to get around on by foot. Bicycles, available for hire on all three islands (40,000Rp to 70,000Rp per day), can be a fun way to get around, but sandy stretches of path mean that you will spend time pushing your bike in the hot sun.

Gili Air

📱 0370 / POP 1800

Closest of the Gilis to Lombok, Gili Air blends Gili T's buzz and bustle with Meno's minimalist vibe, and, for many, is just right. The white-sand beaches here are arguably the best of the Gili bunch and there's just enough nightlife to keep the sociable happy. Accommodation right from the main strip along the east coast – a lovely sandy lane dotted with bamboo bungalows and little restaurants where you can eat virtually on top of a turquoise sea.

Though tourism dominates Gili Air's economy, coconuts, fishing and creating the fake-distressed fishing-boat wood vital to any stylish Gili guesthouse are important income streams. Buzzy little strips have developed along the beaches in the southeast and the west, although the lanes are still more sandy than paved.

🏃 Activities

⭐ **H2O Yoga**   YOGA

(📱 0877 6103 8836; www.h2oyogaandmeditation. com; class/3hr workshop 120,000/300,000Rp) This wonderful yoga and meditation centre is found down a well-signposted track leading inland from Gili Air's eastern shore. Top-quality classes (at 9am, or 5pm for 'can-

dlelight yoga') are held in a lovely circular *beruga* (open-sided pavilion) and massage is also available. H2O also offers a pool (and aqua yoga classes), accommodation (doubles from 270,000Rp) and seven-day retreats (from US$765).

7 Seas   DIVING

(📱 0878 6570 3510; www.7seasdivegili.com; 4-day TEC diving package 7,100,000Rp; ⊘ 7.30am-7pm) 🏊 A vast dive shop with a range of accommodation and a good pool for training (or just playing), 7 Seas is also a local leader in environmental care, offering free clean-up dives to certified divers.

Gili Air

➕ **Activities, Courses & Tours**
1 7 Seas C3
2 Blue Marine Dive Centre C1
3 H2O Yoga C2

🛏 **Sleeping**
4 7 Seas C3
5 Bintang Beach 2 .... B1
6 Gili Air Hostel C3

🍴 **Eating**
7 Eazy Gili Waroeng C3

🍸 **Drinking & Nightlife**
8 Coffee & Thyme B3

INDONESIA GILI ISLANDS

Gili Air

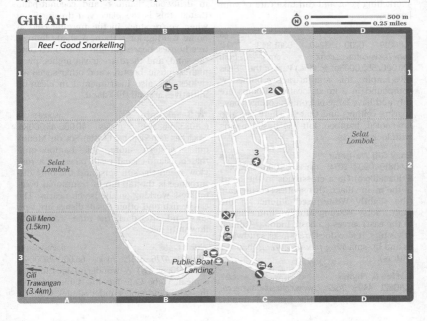

Blue Marine Dive Centre   DIVING
(☑0811 390 2550; www.bluemarinedive.com; night
dive/10 dives 600,000/4,165,000Rp; ☺8am-8pm)
✎ Blue Marine has a nice location on the
beautiful northeast corner of the island,
and also offers freediving, stand-up paddleboarding and yoga (100,000Rp per class).
The owner is very active in reef preservation
efforts.

🛏 Sleeping & Eating

★ Gili Air Hostel   HOSTEL $
(www.giliairhostel.com;   dm/r   from
150,000/350,000Rp;   ☺reception 7.30am-7pm;
❄🛜) Beds at this fun hostel are in two- to
seven-bed rooms, all of which share bathrooms. The decor defines cheery, and there's
a cool bar, hot showers, free breakfast, movie nights, a huge frangipani tree and even a
climbing wall.

Bintang Beach 2   BUNGALOW $
(☑0819   742   3519;   r/bungalow
250,000/550,000Rp; ❄🛜) On Gili Air's quiet
northwest coast, this sandy but tidy compound has 25 basic rooms and bungalows
(ranging from budget-friendly and fan-
cooled to mildly snazzy) and an open-sided
beachbar/restaurant that's a delightful place
to linger. This enterprising clan has a few
other guesthouses nearby, rents bikes and
snorkelling gear, and can take care of your
laundry.

7 Seas   HOTEL $$
(☑0819   0700   3240,   0361-849   7094;
www.7seas-cottages.com;   dm/r   from
120,000/550,000Rp; ❄🛜🛏) Part of the 7 Seas
dive empire, this is an attractive bungalow
compound in a great location. Rooms are
tidy and have large balconies; cottages have
soaring ceilings and thatch. There are also
fan-cooled, bamboo, loft-like hostel rooms
with lockers.

Eazy Gili Waroeng   INDONESIAN $
(☑0819 0902 2074; mains 35,000-40,000Rp;
☺10am-10pm) On a crossroads in the heart
of the main village, this spotless corner cafe
(the slightly Westernised adjunct of the
more rootsy Warung Muslim, immediately
to the east) serves up basic Indo fare aimed
at visitors. It also does breakfasts, sandwiches and lip-smacking *pisang goreng* (banana
fritters).

Coffee & Thyme   CAFE
(☑0821 4499 3622; www.coffeeandthyme.co;
☺7am-7pm) Right in the thick of things,
where boats to Gili Air disgorge their
sun-seeking seafarers, Coffee & Thyme is a
bustling, part open-air cafe that makes some
of the best coffee in the Gilis. Also good if
you're craving a Western-style breakfast,
lunch wrap or muffin.

Gili Meno
☑0370 / POP 500
Gili Meno is the smallest of the three Gili
Islands and a good setting for your desert-
island fantasy. Ringed by gorgeous beaches
and teeming reefs, Meno is also the quietest
and most traditional of the three, beloved
more of honeymooners and mature travellers than the full-moon-party set. Most accommodation is strung out along the east
coast, near the most picturesque beach. Inland you'll find scattered homesteads, coconut plantations and a salty lake.
   Gili Meno Divers (☑0878 6409 5490; www.
gilimenodivers.com; Kontiki Cottages; introductory dive from 900,000Rp; ☺9am-5pm) offers a
range of courses including freediving and
some good ones in underwater photography.

🛏 Sleeping & Eating

★ Gili Meno Eco Hostel   HOSTEL $
(☑0853   3738   3071;   hammock/dm/r
95,000/110,000/250,000Rp; 🛜) ✎ A fantasy
in driftwood, bamboo and coconut-palm
thatch, this is the place you dream about
when you're stuck in the freezing cold at
home waiting for a train. A shady lounge,
tree houses, beach bar and more open onto
the sand, and there are trivia nights, pizza
nights, music, bonfires and other social activities. It's also instrumental in clean-up
initiatives around the island.

★ Sasak Cafe   INDONESIAN $
(☑0332-662379;   mains   40,000-45,000Rp;
☺kitchen 7am-9pm, bar till late) Set on Meno's
quiet western shore, this bamboo-and-
thatch, island-casual resto takes on a rosy
glow when the sun sets, and the only disturbance is the tap-tap of traditional boat-
builders working on the beach nearby. The
crispy fish and other Sasak dishes are very
good and, after dark, the tunes and drinks
flow until late.

Webe Café   INDONESIAN $$
(☑0821 4776 3187; mains 65,000-75,000Rp;
☺8am-10pm; 🛜) A wonderful location for
a meal, Webe Café has low tables sunk in
the sand (and tables under shade), with the

Gili Meno

Reef - Good Snorkelling

Selat Lombok

Webe Café

Gili Meno Eco Hostel

Salt Lake

Public Boat Landing

Sasak Cafe

Selat Lombok

Gili Meno Divers

Gili Air (2.5km)

Gili Trawangan (800m)

turquoise water just a metre away. It scores well for Sasak and Indonesian food such as *kelak kuning* (snapper in yellow spice); staff fire up a seafood barbecue most nights, too. There are also basic bungalows for rent (from 400,000Rp).

Gili Trawangan

0370 / POP 1500

Gili Trawangan is a tropical playground of global renown, ranking alongside Bali and Borobudur as one of Indonesia's top destinations. Trawangan's heaving main drag, busy with bikes, *cidomo* (horse-drawn carts) and mobs of scantily clad visitors, can surprise those expecting a languid island retreat. Instead, a bustling string of lounge bars, hip guesthouses, ambitious restaurants, convenience stores and dive schools clamours for attention.

And yet behind this glitzy facade, a bohemian character endures, with rickety warungs (cheap eating houses) and reggae joints surviving between the cocktail tables, and quiet retreats dotting the much-less-busy north coast. Even as massive 200-plus-room hotels begin to colonise the gentrifying west coast, you can head just inland to a village laced with sandy lanes roamed by free-range roosters, fussing *ibu* (mothers)

and wild-haired kids playing hopscotch. Here the call of the muezzin, not happy hour, defines the time of day.

🏃 Activities

Gili T is ringed by the sort of powdery white sand people expect to find on Bali, but don't. It can be crowded along the bar-lined main part of the strip, but walk just a bit north or south and east and you'll find some of Gili T's nicest swimming and snorkelling beaches.

Trawangan is a major diving and snorkelling hot spot, with more than a dozen professional scuba and freediving schools. Most dive schools and shops have good accommodation for clients who want to book a package.

⭐ Lutwala Dive   DIVING

(☑ 0877 6549 2615; www.lutwala.com; divemaster course 14,000,000Rp; ⊙ 8am-6pm) A nitrox and five-star PADI centre, this dive shop is a member of GIDA (Gili Islands Divers Association) and rents top-quality snorkelling gear. There's accommodation on-site (rooms from 800,000Rp) plus a very nice garden cafe-bar to relax in post-plunge. Make sure you say hello to the parrots.

Freedive Gili   DIVING

(☑ 0370-614 0503; www.freedivegili.com; beginner/ advanced course 3,900,000/5,275,000Rp; ⊙ 9am-8pm) Freediving is a breath-hold technique that allows you to explore greater depths than snorkelling (to 30m and beyond). Owned by an expert diver who has touched 108m on a single breath, Freedive Gili offers two-day beginner and three-day advanced courses. After a two-day course many students are able to get down to 20m. There's also yoga and accommodation on-site.

Big Bubble   DIVING

(☑ 0811 390969; www.bigbubblediving.com; fun dive day/night 490,000/600,000Rp) 🏄 The original engine behind the island's notable green-crusading NGO, Gili Eco Trust, and a long-running dive school. Hidden behind a whitewashed cafe, it's a GIDA (Gili Island Divers Association) member.

The Gili Eco Trust works to preserve, restore and clean the reefs around the islands.

Gili Yoga   YOGA

(☑ 0370-614 0503; www.giliyoga.com; per person from 100,000Rp; ⊙ 7am-8pm) Runs daily vinyasa flow and hatha classes, and is attached to Freedive Gili.

🛏 Sleeping

Gili T has more than 5000 rooms and an astonishing 675 registered places to stay, ranging from thatched huts to sleek, air-conditioned villas with private pools. Yet, in peak season (July and August) the entire island is often booked out; reserve well ahead.

Mango Tree Homestay HOMESTAY **$**
(📞 0823 5912 0421; Jl Karang Biru; d 300,000Rp)
This friendly homestay in a quieter part of the village offers eight simple doubles facing each other across a shady, fern-filled courtyard. The young staff are relaxed but competent, ukelele music frequently sweetens the air and bikes can be hired for 40,000Rp per day.

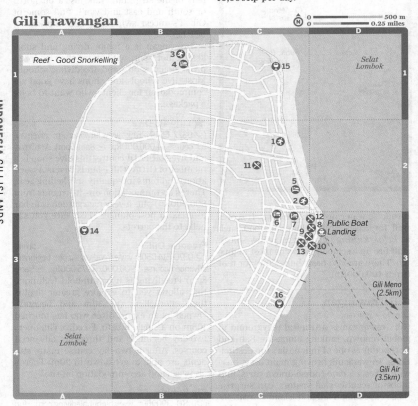

Gili Trawangan

Pondok Gili Gecko   GUESTHOUSE $
(☑0818 0573 2814; r from 400,000Rp; 🖫) An
inviting guesthouse with a charming gecko
motif. The four rooms here are clean, and
have ceiling fans and private tiled patios
overlooking the garden.

★**Gili Beach Bum Hotel**   HOSTEL $$
(☑0877 6526 7037; www.gilibeachbum.com; dm/
tr 260,000/600,000Rp; ✻🖫≋) Formerly the
Gili Hostel, this co-ed dorm and hotel com-
plex has 18 triple rooms under thatched
Torajan-style roofs. The rooms have concrete
floors, high ceilings, lockers and a sleeping
loft (dorms share bathrooms). Out front
is the Lava Bar (open until 1am and often
raucous) and there are parties in the on-site
pool every Friday. Breakfast is included.

★**Eden Cottages**   COTTAGE $$
(☑0819 1799 6151; www.edencottages.com; cottages
from 750,000Rp; ✻🖫≋) Eden takes the form
of six clean, thatched concrete bungalows
wrapped around a pool, fringed by a garden
and shaded by a coconut grove. Rooms have
tasteful furnishings, stone baths, TV-DVD and
(cold) fresh-water showers. The charming
expat owner does all she can to ensure her
guests' serenity (including installing wi-fi).

✗ **Eating**

★**Warung Dewi**   INDONESIAN $
(☑0819 0763 3826; Jl Cardinal; mains 25,000-
35,000Rp; ⊙7am-8pm) The best traditional
warung on Gili T is just a few steps back from
the high-priced bustle of the main strip, behind a few small fresh-produce stands. The
nasi campur is fantastic (coconut sambal,
jackfruit curry, fried chicken and several
vegetable sides is a common combination)
while vegetarians will like the *nasi pecel*
(rice, vegetables and peanut sauce).

★**Pasar Malam**   MARKET $
(mains 20,000-35,000Rp; ⊙6pm-midnight, last
stall 3am; 🖉) Blooming every evening in
front of Gili T's market, this night market
is the place to indulge in a galaxy of Lombok flavours, including tangy noodle salads,
savoury fried treats, smoky grilled chicken,
grilled fresh catch and heaps of veggie options. Just wander around until you find
something that appeals, and grab a chair at
the shared trestle tables.

Warung Kiki Novi   INDONESIAN $
(mains from 20,000Rp; ⊙8am-10pm) Some islanders insist this is the best place for *nasi*

campur (rice with a choice of side dishes)
in the Gilis, and they may be right – it's a
basic, open-sided warung that's budget-din-
ing nirvana. Besides the spot-on Indo mains
there's a smattering of Western sandwiches
and salads, if you must.

★**Pituq Café**   VEGAN $$
(☑0812 3677 5161; mains 55,000-65,000Rp;
⊙9am-10pm Sat-Thu, 3-10pm Fri; 🖉) More life-
style choice than food choice, this hippie-
trail-to-Kerala place combines yoga, dread-
locks and exquisite vegan fare (think rösti
with cauliflower puree, lime, shallots and
coriander) in a chilled-out open-air com-
pound. Lounge around on raised platforms
and discover the heights Gili T's vegetables
can reach when given a chance by the tal-
ents in the kitchen. Meditation classes are
held daily (150,000Rp).

★**Kayu Café**   CAFE $$
(☑0878 6239 1308; mains 65,000-70,000Rp;
⊙7am-9pm; 🖫) The main cafe here, on the
inland side of the strip, has a lovely array
of healthy baked goods, salads, sandwiches,
rice bowls and the island's best juices, all
served in air-con comfort. Across the road,
the beach cafe is all open air and exposed
wood. Service on the sand can be slow –
head inside to order.

La Dolce Vita   ITALIAN $$
(☑0813 1772 0228; piadinas 50,000Rp, mains
100,000-110,000Rp; ⊙7.30am-10pm) There
comes that moment when another nasi
goreng will just make you turn nasty. Don't
delay, hop right on over to this expanded
cafe that's not much bigger than one of its
excellent espressos. Slices of authentic piz-
za and a whole range of pastries are joined
by daily specials cooked by the Italian
chef-owner.

🍺 **Drinking & Nightlife**

★**Casa Vintage Beach**   LOUNGE
(www.casavintagebeach.com; ⊙10am-midnight)
Facing Bali's Gunung Agung and some su-
perb sunsets, Casa Vintage is the best place
to enjoy a sundowner on Trawangan. A bro-
chure-perfect beach is littered with cushions
and loungers, trees shelter hammocks and
trestles, the Swedish-Jamaican owners do
great Caribbean food (mains 79,000Rp to
115,000Rp), the soundtrack is just right (Bil-
lie Holiday, reggae, latin) and bonfires keep
the atmosphere warm past sundown.

La Moomba BAR

(⊗7am-10pm) This friendly beach-bar straddles the road just north of Turtle Point. The Western and Indo fare is good (mains 65,000Rp to 85,000Rp), tables and loungers are dotted about the sand and there are great views across to Gili Meno and the cloud-capped heights of Gunung Rinjani beyond. After sundown the squid-fishing boats light up the nearby waters in eerie phosphorescent green.

Tir na Nog PUB

(☑0370-613 9463; www.tirnanogbar.com; ⊗7am-2am Thu-Tue, to 3am Wed; ☎) Known simply as 'the Irish', this hangar of hangovers has a sports-bar interior with big screens. Its shoreside open-air bar is probably the busiest meeting spot on the island. Serving bar chow such as fajitas and spicy wings (mains 68,000Rp to 82,000Rp), it has DJs every night, but jovial mayhem truly reigns on 'party night' every Wednesday.

Sumbawa

Elaborately contorted and sprawling into the sea, Sumbawa is all volcanic ridges, terraced rice fields, dry expanses and sheltered bays. Though well connected to Bali and Lombok, it's a very different sort of place – far less developed, mostly very dry, much poorer, extremely conservative and split between two distinct peoples. Those who speak Sumbawanese probably reached the west of the island from Lombok. Bimanese speakers dominate the Tambora Peninsula and the east. Although Sumbawa is an overwhelmingly Islamic island, in remote parts underground *adat* (traditional law and lore) still thrives.

Mostly traffic-free and in great shape, the Trans-Sumbawa Hwy is excellent for getting quickly between Lombok and Flores. Transport connections off this trunk road are infrequent and uncomfortable, and most overland travellers don't even get off the bus in Sumbawa as they float and roll from Lombok to Flores. For now, it's the domain of surfers, miners and mullahs.

❶ Dangers & Annoyances

➔ Most Sumbawans are hospitable, albeit taciturn, but you may encounter some tension. In the past, protests against foreign-owned mining operations have turned violent.

➔ The island is also much more conservative in terms of religion than neighbouring Lombok or Flores; behave modestly at all times.

➔ Indonesia's anti-terrorism police make raids and arrests around Bima.

❶ Getting There & Around

Sumbawa's main highway is in good condition and runs from Taliwang (near the west coast) through Sumbawa Besar, Dompu and Bima to Sape (the ferry port on the east coast). It's relatively traffic-free – a relief if you've made the trek through Java, Bali and Lombok. Fleets of long-distance buses, most of them air-conditioned, run between the west-coast ferry port of Poto Tano and Sape, serving all the major towns between.

You'll need private transport to navigate Sumbawa's outskirts effectively.

Car hire is possible through hotels: depending on your destination, the cost will be about 800,000Rp to 1,000,000Rp per day, including a driver and fuel. Motorcycles cost 60,000Rp to 80,000Rp a day.

Poto Tano

Poto Tano, the main port for ferries to/from Lombok, is a ramshackle harbour, fringed by stilt-fishing villages with tremendous views of Gunung Rinjani. It's a pretty place, but there's no need to sleep here.

Ferries run hourly, 24 hours a day, between Labuhan Lombok and Poto Tano (passengers 19,000Rp, 1½ hours). Cars cost 466,000Rp, motorcycles 54,000Rp. Through buses to Lombok, Bali and Java include the ferry fare.

Buses meet the ferry and go to Taliwang (20,000Rp, one hour) and Sumbawa Besar (30,000Rp, two hours).

Maluk

South of Taliwang, the beaches and bays try to outdo one another. Your first stop is the working-class commercial district of Maluk, 30km south of Taliwang. Yes, the town is ugly, but the beach is superb. The sand is a blend of white and gold, and the bay is buffered by two headlands. There's good swimming in the shallows, and when the swell hits, the reef further out sculpts perfect barrels.

Directly south of Maluk, within walking distance of the beach (though it is a long walk) is **Supersuck**, consistently rated as the best left in the world. Surfers descend regularly from Hawaii's North Shore to surf here – which should tell you something – and many lifelong surfers have proclaimed it the finest barrel of their lives. It really pumps in the dry season (May to October).

ALOR ARCHIPELAGO

The final link of the Lesser Sunda Islands – the chain stretching east of Java – is wild, volcanic and drop-dead gorgeous. There are crumbling red-clay roads, jagged peaks, white-sand beaches, and crystal-clear bays offering remarkable diving – with plenty of pelagics and sheer walls draped in vast eye-popping coral gardens.

Isolated from the outside world and one another by rugged terrain, the 200,000 inhabitants of this tiny archipelago are divided into 100 tribes speaking eight languages and 52 dialects. Although the Dutch installed local rajas along the coastal regions after 1908, they had little influence over the interior, where people were still taking heads into the 1950s. Here, indigenous animist traditions endure.

Though a network of simple roads now covers Pulau Alor, boats are still a common form of transport. The few visitors who land here tend to linger on nearby Pulau Kepa or dive these waters from liveaboards.

Dive resorts offer the choicest, best-located and most logical places for travellers to sleep in the archipelago. The highest density of guesthouses and low-budget hotels is found in Kalabahi.

Bemos travel between Taliwang and Maluk (20,000Rp, two hours) almost hourly from 7am to 6pm. Three daily buses leave Terminal Maluk, north of town across from the entrance to the Newmont mine (look for the big gates and massive parking area), for Sumbawa Besar (40,000Rp, four hours).

From Benete Harbour, just north of Maluk, a fast ferry run by the Newmont mine (125,000Rp, 90 minutes) goes to/from Labuhan Lombok one or two times daily. Check times with the Rantung Beach guesthouses.

Sumbawa Besar

☑ 0371 / POP 54,000

Sumbawa Besar, often shortened to 'Sumbawa', is the principal market town of the island's west. It's leafy, devoutly Muslim (oversupply of karaoke bars notwithstanding), and runs on the bushels of beans, rice and corn cultivated on the outskirts.

The airport is very close to the centre. Garuda and Wings Air fly direct to Lombok daily.

Sumbawa Besar's main long-distance bus station is Terminal Sumur Payung, 5.5km northwest of town on the highway.

Pantai Lakey

☑ 0373

Pantai Lakey, a gentle crescent of golden sand, is where Sumbawa's tourist pulse beats, thanks to seven world-class surf breaks that curl and crash in one massive bay, and a string of modest beach guesthouses, all linked by a sandy path studded with

bars that contribute to the perfect beach-bum ambience.

Lakey Beach Inn (☑ 0373-623576; www.lakey-beach-inn.com; Jl Raya Hu'u; s/d with fan 100,000/170,000Rp, s/d with air-con 200,000/260,000Rp; ✳ ☎), is a good budget option. Overlooking two legendary breaks, Lakey Pipe and Lakey Peak, its open-sided, driftwoody cafe-bar is a great place to enjoy a post-surf beer, pizza and Indo classics.

Vivi's Lakey Peak Homestay (☑ 0878 6698 1277; www.lakeypeakhomestay.com; Jl Pantai Lakey; s/d/tr 250,000/350,000/450,000Rp; ✳ ☎) offers the area's warmest welcome, with Vivian and her Sumbawanese-Australian family your generous hosts. Rooms are modern and large with nice furnishings.

Set amid tropical gardens, the six new rooms at **Rock Pool Home Stay** (☑ 0813 3733 6856; http://rockpoolhomestay.com; Jl Pantai Nunggas Lakey; bungalow 400,000Rp; ✳ ☎) are some of the nicest on Pantai Lakey, with air-con, decent wi-fi and fabulous views across the breaks towards the rolling hills of Sumbawa.

Unremarkable externally, **Fatmah's** (off Jl Raya Hu'u; mains 40,000-55,000Rp; ☺ 7am-10pm) nonetheless turns out quality fare throughout the day and night.

❶ Getting There & Away

From Dompu there are two daily (slow) buses as far as Hu'u (25,000Rp, 1½ hours), where you can hire an *ojek* (20,000Rp) to Pantai Lakey. *Ojeks* to/from Dompu on the trans-Sumbawa highway start at 100,000Rp.

Try doing this with a surfboard and you'll see why so many people take a taxi from Bima airport (800,000Rp for up to four people). Buses to/from Bima cost from 50,000Rp (two daily, at 6am and noon).

The *ojek* cartel is omnipresent in Lakey; rates to the breaks range from 30,000Rp to 80,000Rp.

Bima

♩ 0374 / POP 149,000

East Sumbawa's largest metropolitan centre is a conservative Islamic place. It has few sights, the streets can be traffic-choked, the architecture is charmless and crumbling, and the vibe is unappealing after dark. It's only worth overnighting here if it suits your flight plans. If you're heading to Pantai Lakey there's no need to stop, and if you want a morning ferry to Flores, you're better off staying in Sape.

ⓘ Getting There & Away

Bima is the main airport for travellers to Pantai Lakey. During peak season (June to August), when flights from Labuanbajo (Flores) to Bali are often fully booked, you can make the 10-hour ferry and bus trip from Labuanbajo to Bima, then find a seat on a less-packed Bima–Bali flight. Services include the following:

Bali Nam Air, Wings Air; 1¼ hours; daily

Makassar Wings Air, 1¼ hours, daily

Buses heading west leave from the Bima bus terminal, a 10-minute walk south along Jl Sultan Kaharuddin from the centre of town. You can buy a ticket in advance from bus company offices on Jl Sultan Kaharuddin. Buses for Sape depart from the Kumbe terminal in Raba (a 3000Rp bemo ride away). Routes include the following:

Dompu 25,000Rp; two hours; almost hourly from 6am to 5pm

Mataram 250,000Rp; 11 to 14 hours; two daily

Sape 35,000Rp; two hours; almost hourly from 6am to 5pm

Sumbawa Besar 80,000Rp; seven hours; several daily

Sape

Sape's got a tumbledown port-town vibe, perfumed with the conspicuous scent of drying cuttlefish. The outskirts are quilted in rice fields backed by jungled hills, and the streets are busy with *benhur* (horse-drawn carts) and early morning commerce. There's decent food and doable lodging here too, so if you are catching a morning ferry, consider this an alternative to Bima.

The ferry port is 3km east of Sape's diminutive centre. Regular breakdowns and rough seas disrupt ferry services – always double-check the latest schedules in Bima and Sape. Ferries from Sape include the following:

Labuanbajo (Flores) 60,000Rp, six hours, one daily

Waikelo (Sumba) 69,000Rp, eight hours, three weekly

Express buses with service to Lombok and Bali meet arriving ferries.

Buses leave every hour for Bima (35,000Rp, two hours), where you can catch local buses to other Sumbawa destinations.

Taxi drivers may claim that buses have stopped running and you must charter their vehicle to Bima (350,000Rp, 1½ hours); this is usually not true.

Komodo & Rinca

Spectacular Komodo, its steep hillsides jade in the short wet season, frazzled by the sun and winds to a deep rusty red for most of the year, is the largest island in Komodo National Park. A succession of peninsulas spreads east, fringed in pink sand, thanks to the abundance of red coral offshore. The main camp of **Loh Liang** and the PHKA office, where boats dock and guided walks and treks start, is on the east coast.

The fishing village of **Kampung Komodo** is an hour-long walk south of Loh Liang. It's a friendly, stilted Bugis village that's full of goats, chickens and children. The inhabitants, said to be descendants of convicts exiled to the island in the 19th century by the Sultans of Sumbawa, are used to seeing tourists. You can spend your time simply absorbing village life and gazing out over the water.

Rinca is slightly smaller than nearby Komodo, close to Labuanbajo, and easily done in a day trip. It packs a lot into a small space and for many it is more convenient but just as worthy a destination as Komodo. The island combines mangroves, light forest and sun-drenched hills, as well as – of course – Komodo dragons.

One of Indonesia's greatest natural treasures, **Komodo National Park** (www.komodonationalpark.org), established in 1980, encompasses Komodo, Rinca, Padar, plenty of lesser islands and a rich marine ecosystem within its 1817 sq km (future plans may see it extended to 2321 sq km). Admission is 150,000Rp per person per day (225,000Rp on weekends and public holidays) and subsequent fees accrue from there: 25,000Rp to

KOMODO DRAGONS

The Komodo dragon (ora) is a monitor lizard, albeit one on steroids. Growing up to 3m in length and weighing up to 100kg, they are an awesome sight and make a visit to Komodo National Park well worth the effort. Lounging about lethargically in the sun, they are actually as fearsome as their looks imply. Park rangers keep them from attacking tourists; random encounters are a bad idea.

At both Komodo and Rinca your odds of seeing dragons are very good. Although claims are made that there is no feeding of the ora, invariably you'll see a few specimens hanging around the ranger stations, especially at the kitchens. There are further opportunities on the actual walks, where you are likely to see the animals in purely natural surroundings. Rangers carry a forked staff as their only protection; you may get quite close to ora. A telephoto lens is handy but not essential. Still, treat the seemingly slow-moving ora with great respect: two villagers have been killed in the last two decades. Peak months for komodo-spotting are September to December, when both sexes are out and about. The worst months are June to August, which is mating season, which causes the females to go into hiding.

dive, 15,000Rp to snorkel and 250,000Rp for a guided walk for up to four people.

🏃 Activities

The 150,000Rp entrance fee at Komodo includes a choice of three walks: the **short walk** (1.5km, 45 minutes), which includes a stop at an artificial waterhole that attracts the diminutive local deer, and Komoda dragons; the **medium walk** (2.5km, 90 minutes), which includes a hill with sweeping views and a chance to see colourful cockatoos; and the **long trek** (4km, two hours), which includes the features of the shorter hikes and gets you much further from the peak-season crowds.

You can also negotiate for adventure treks (from 500,000Rp for up to five people). These walks are up to 9km long and can last four or more hours. Bring plenty of water. Highlights can include a climb to the 538m-high **Gunung Ara**, with expansive views from the top. **Poreng Valley** is another potential dragon haunt, and has an out-in-the-wild feeling. Watch for wildlife, such as buffalo, deer, wild boar and Komodo's rich bird life, including the fabled megapodes.

A great hike goes over **Bukit Randolph**, passing a memorial to 79-year-old Randolph Von Reding, who disappeared on Komodo in 1974, and on to **Loh Sebita**. It's challenging, the sea views are spectacular, you'll likely see a dragon or two, and you can organise your boat to pick you up in Loh Sebita so you don't have to retrace your steps.

❶ Getting There & Away

Competition for Komodo day trips from Labuanbajo is fierce. Join one of the many tours hawked by operators in town, which cost 400,000Rp to 500,000Rp per person, including a light lunch and stops for beach fun and snorkelling. As it takes 3½ hours to reach Komodo, day trips leave around 5.30am and return around 6pm. Overnight charters leave a little later (around 7am) and cost 5,000,000Rp for up to four people. They return around 4pm the next day – altogether a more leisurely trip.

You can also charter your own speedboat, which will cover the distance to Komodo in under an hour. Prepare to bargain but expect to pay around 3,000,000Rp for up to four people for a full day out (which can include stops at both Komodo and Rinca).

The many liveaboard schemes almost always include a stop at Komodo at some point, as do the private boats making the run between Flores, and Lombok and Bali.

Flores

Flores, the island given an incongruous Portuguese name by its 16th-century colonists, has become Indonesia's 'Next Big Thing'. The serpentine, 670km Trans-Flores Hwy runs the length of the island, skirting knife-edge ridges, brushing by paddy-fringed traditional villages, and opening up dozens of areas few tourists explore.

In the far west, Labuanbajo is a booming tourist town that combines tropical beauty with nearby attractions such as Komodo National Park, superb dive spots and stunning waterways speckled with little islands.

Beyond, the generally lush interior is attracting an ever-greater number of travellers chasing smoking volcanoes, emerald rice fields, prehistoric riddles, exotic cultures and hidden beaches. You'll even see plenty of steeples, as away from the port towns most people are nominally Catholic. Many more are part of cultures and groups that date back centuries, and live in traditional villages seemingly unchanged in millennia.

ⓘ Information

Foreign aid money has funded a string of useful tourist offices in key towns across Flores. Their enthusiastic assistance is backed by an excellent website (www.florestourism.com), free town maps and several publications well worth their modest prices, including a huge, detailed island map, and books covering activities and culture.

ⓘ Getting There & Away

AIR
You can easily get flights connecting Flores and Bali, Lombok and Kupang (West Timor), among other destinations. Labuanbajo is the main gateway, while Maumere and Ende are also serviced by daily flights. It's easy to fly into, say Labuanbajo, tour the island, and fly out of Maumere. However, note that the booming popularity of Flores means that flights are booked solid at peak times.

BOAT
Daily ferries connect Labuanbajo with Sape (Sumbawa), while weekly services go to Bira (Sulawesi) and Pulau Jampea. From Larantuka, two weekly ferries go to Kupang (West Timor). From Ende and Aimere, weekly boats will take you to Waingapu (Sumba).

ⓘ Getting Around

Regular buses run between Labuanbajo and Maumere. They're cheap and cramped. Much more comfortable and only somewhat more expensive are public minibuses (often a Toyota Kijang), which link major towns in air-con comfort. Many travellers hire a car and driver, which costs from 800,000Rp to 1,000,000Rp per day.

BOAT TOURS BETWEEN LOMBOK & FLORES

Travelling by sea between Lombok and Labuanbajo is a popular way to get to Flores, as you'll glimpse more of the region's spectacular coastline and dodge the slog by bus across Sumbawa. Typical three- and four-day itineraries take in snorkelling at Pulau Satonda or Pulau Moyo off the coast of Sumbawa, and a dragon-spotting hike on Komodo or Rinca.

But note, this is usually no luxury cruise – a lot depends on the boat, the crew and your fellow travellers. Some operators have reneged on 'all-inclusive' deals en route, and others operate decrepit old tugs without life jackets or radio. And this crossing can be hazardous during the rainy season (October to January), when the seas are rough.

Most travellers enjoy the journey though, whether it involves bedding down on a mattress on deck or in a tiny cabin. The cost for a three- to four-day itinerary ranges from about US$170 to US$400 per person and includes all meals, basic beverages and use of snorkelling gear.

Other considerations:

➡ Carefully vet your boat for safety: check for safety equipment, locate exits and avoid overcrowded vessels.

➡ Understand what's included and not included in the price. For instance, if drinking water is included, how much is provided? If you need more, can you buy it on the boat or do you need to bring your own?

➡ If you are flexible, you can often save money by travelling west from Flores, as travelling eastwards to Flores is more popular. Look for deals at agents once you're in Labuanbajo.

Providers include:

Kencana Adventure (☑ 0812 2206 6065; www.kencanaadventure.com; Jl Soekarno Hatta, Beta Bajo Hotel; one-way deck/shared cabin per person 1,650,000/2,000,000Rp) Offers basic boat trips between Lombok and Labuanbajo with deck accommodation as well as cabins that sleep two.

Perama Tour (☑ 0376-42016, 0376-42015; www.peramatour.com; Jl Soekarno Hatta; one-way deck/cabin 2,200,000/3,300,000Rp) Runs basic boat trips between Lombok and Labuanbajo with deck accommodation as well as small two-person cabins.

If you have a group of six, this is a fair deal. Some drivers also work as guides, and can arrange fascinating and detailed island-wide itineraries. Your accommodation will usually have details on all the above options.

Labuanbajo

🌐 0385 / POP 3000

Ever more travellers are descending on this gorgeous, slightly ramshackle harbour town, orbited by stunning islands and blessed with idyllic views towards unsurpassed tropical sunsets.

Labuanbajo's main drag, Jl Soekarno Hatta, is lined with cafes, guesthouses, travel agents, dive shops and a few hopping bars. The waterfront is busy and connections to other parts of Indonesia are excellent. With so many beguiling islands and Komodo National Park so close, you may find Labuanbajo (or Bajo as it's commonly called) hard to leave, even as the jungled hills of inland Flores lure you east.

Traditionally a low-key fishing town, the capital of Manggarai Barat regency is today full of new developments and tourist money. Whether Bajo remains a traveller's idyll or becomes just another trashed hot spot is a question very much in the balance.

🏃 Activities

Uber Scuba   DIVING
(📞 0813 3961 9724; www.uberscubakomodo.com; Jl Soekarno Hatta; 3-dive fun dive 1,500,000Rp; ⏰8.30am-8pm) This dive shop is one of the best that's riding the wave of ever-increasing visitor numbers to the Komodo area. Besides an extensive range of fun dives and courses, it offers all-inclusive liveaboard diving packages (three nights with 10 dives and all meals costs US$815). The *Iona* and the *Amalia*, Uber's two vessels, are owned by the operation, not chartered from third parties.

Wicked Diving   DIVING
(📞 0812 3964 1143; www.wickeddiving.com/komodo; Jl Soekarno Hatta; ⏰9am-7pm) 🌿 Wicked offers popular multiday liveaboard excursions, scouring the best dive sites of Komodo National Park on a *phinisi* (Sulawesan schooner). Three-night trips cost US$695; six nights cost US$1295. Its day trips are also justifiably popular and the company wins plaudits for nurturing local guides and divers, promoting strong green practices and giving back to the community.

CNDive   DIVING
(📞0823 3908 0808; www.cndivekomodo.com; Jl Mutiara; per person per day from US$150; ⏰8am-8pm) 🌿 Condo Subagyo, the proprietor of CNDive, is the area's original Indonesian dive operator and a former Komodo National Park ranger. The staff are all locals who have been thoroughly trained and have intimate knowledge of more than 100 dive sites, some of which were first 'discovered' and named by this outfit. Three-day liveaboard excursions are US$546 per person.

🛏 Sleeping

Bajo Beach Hotel   GUESTHOUSE $
(📞 0812 3764 3139, 0385-41008; Jl Soekarno Hatta; r with fan/air-con 150,000/300,000Rp; ❄️🛜) A fine cheapie in the city centre with 16 basic but spacious tiled older rooms that are clean and well tended, with plywood cladding on the walls and private seating areas out front. Breakfast is a simple toast-and-jam affair.

⭐ **Palulu Garden Homestay**   HOMESTAY $$
(📞0822 3658 4279; https://palulugarden.wordpress.com; Jl Ande Bole; dm 170,000Rp, r with fan/air-con 250,000/350,000Rp; ❄️) Long-time local guide Kornelis Gega and his family run this four-room homestay, a short walk above the town centre. The cheapest rooms share a bathroom, while the top room has aircon. It's pure Flores throughout, and utterly spick and span. Kornelis can help with your trip planning, transport arrangements and motorbike hire (75,000Rp per day). Contact them by phone.

Green Hill Hotel   GUESTHOUSE $$
(📞0385-41289; www.greenhillboutiquehotel.com; Jl Soekarno Hatta; s/d/tr 484,000/514,000/635,000Rp; ❄️🛜) The view of the town, bay and sunsets, together with clean and quiet rooms set back from the main-street hubbub make this an excellent choice. Reception is in the centre of town, but the 13 rooms are a brief climb uphill and come with TVs, aircon, hot water, balconies and decent beds. Breakfasts are excellent.

Bajo Sunset Hostel   HOSTEL $$
(📞0812 3645 2244; Jl Reklamasi Pantai; s/d 250,000/500,000Rp; ❄️🛜) This welcoming hostel/guesthouse sits on reclaimed land on the waterfront. There is a modest cafe and a large open-air common area with great views out to sea. Accommodation is spread across a 14-bed dorm and four-bed rooms.

✕ Eating & Drinking

★ Warung Mama
INDONESIAN $
(☑ 0822 3926 4747; Jl Soekarno Hatta; mains 35,000-50,000Rp; ⊙10am-10pm; 🖘) Set on stilts above Bajo's main drag, this bamboo haven offers cheap and cheerful fare at communal tables beneath sepia photos of aromatics and village scenes. Piece your meal together from superior renditions of local fare such as fish cutlets in coconut-turmeric sauce, jackfruit curry, perky-fresh vegetable dishes and the excellent *daging rendang* (dry beef curry).

★ Pasar Malam
INDONESIAN $
(Night Market; Jl Soekarno Hatta; mains 25,000-60,000Rp; ⊙6pm-midnight) At sunset, grab a tarp-shaded table at Bajo's waterfront night market, as a dozen stalls come alive with all manner of Indo classics, fried delights and spanking-fresh grilled seafood. Get cold beer from the convenience store across the road.

★ MadeInItaly
ITALIAN $$
(☑ 0385-244 0222; www.miirestaurants.com; Jl Pantai Pede; mains 70,000-120,000Rp; ⊙11am-11pm; 🖘) A fun and stylish indoor–outdoor dining room known the island over for its fantastic pizza and pasta. Despite its unlikely location, it's some of the best pizza we've ever had anywhere – wafer thin and crunchy, with perfectly delectable toppings. The dining room is darkly stylish, and some of the ingredients are imported from the mother country.

★ Paradise Bar
BAR
(☑ 0822 6640 7569; Jl Binongko; ⊙4pm-1am Sun-Fri, to 2am Sat; 🖘) Perched on a cliff overlooking Labuanbajo's diadem of islands, Paradise is a preposterously lovely place for an *arak* cocktail at sundown. There's a breezy deck, plentiful wicker armchairs, snacks such as chips and nuggets (35,000Rp), a decent range of cold drinks and that mesmerising sea view. Saturday is party night, with two bands playing reggae and rock, plus DJs.

Le Pirate
BAR
(☑0361-733493, 0385-41962; https://lepirate.com/labuan-bajo; Jl Soekarno Hatta; ⊙7am-11pm; 🖘) This colourful 1st-floor bar in downtown Labuanbajo is a popular space to kick back after a day's diving or island-hopping, and offers cold beer, cocktails, a rooftop bar, live music (8pm to 10pm Tuesday, Thursday and Saturday) and film screenings (Wednesday night). There's also an excellent kitchen (7am to 11pm; mains 70,000Rp to 80,000Rp; last orders 10.15pm) and very good accommodation nearby (from 650,000Rp).

ℹ Information

PHKA Information Booth (☑ 0385-41005; Jl Soekarno Hatta; ⊙7-11am & 2-4pm Mon-Fri, 7-10am Sat & Sun) PHKA administers the Komodo National Park, and provides information and permits for Komodo and Rinca islands.
Tourist Office (☑ 0361-271145; www.flores-tourism.com; Jl Mutiara; ⊙8am-4.30pm Mon-Sat) Friendly and helpful, this official office is set just back from Bajo's main drag.

ℹ Getting There & Away

AIR
Labuanbajo's **Komodo Airport** has a huge new terminal as well as a newly lengthened runway, which gives some idea of the expected tourism growth.

Garuda, Nam Air, Transnusa and Wings Air serve destinations including Denpasar, Jakarta and Kupang and have counters in the terminal. There are several daily flights to/from Bali, although these are booked solid at busy times. Don't expect to just turn up and go. While the daily Wings Air flight to Kupang is less heavily subscribed, prebooking is still a good idea.

BOAT
The ASDP ferry from Labuanbajo to Sape (60,000Rp, six hours) runs every morning at 10am. Confirm all times carefully. Buy your tickets the day of departure at the **ferry port office** (Jl Soekarno Hatta; ⊙7am-5pm).

Agents for the boats running between Labuanbajo and Lombok (p248) line Jl Soekarno Hatta.

BUSES FROM LABUANBAJO

DESTINATION	TYPE	FARE (RP)	DURATION (HR)	FREQUENCY
Bajawa	bus	160,000	10	several daily
Denpasar (Bali)	bus & ferry	500,000	38	1 daily
Mataram (Lombok)	bus & ferry	350,000	24	1 daily
Ruteng	bus	80,000	4	every 2hr, 6am-6pm

Easily missed on a side street leading uphill from Jl Mutiara, the **Pelni Agent** (☎0385-41106; off Jl Mutiara; ⏰9am-6pm) is the place to get tickets for long-distance boat travel. Schedules posted in the windows outline services, including Makassar and the east coast of Sulawesi as well as Bima, Lembar and Benoa (Bali).

Kencana Adventure (p248) offers basic three-day/two-night boat trips between Lombok and Labuanbajo.

BUS

There's no bus terminal in Labuanbajo, so most people book their tickets through a hotel or agency such as **Varanus Travel** (☎0385-41709; Jl Soekarno Hatta; ⏰8am-6pm). If you get an advance ticket, the bus will pick you up from your accommodation. All eastbound buses run via Ruteng.

Ticket sellers for long-distance buses to Lombok and Bali work the ferry port office. The fares include all ferries (three to Bali) and air-con buses in between.

Bajawa

☎0384 / POP 44,000

Framed by forested volcanoes and blessed with a pleasant climate, Bajawa is a laid-back and predominantly Catholic hill town. Perched at 1100m above sea level, it's the de facto trading post of the local Ngada people, a great base from which to explore dozens of traditional villages and a relaxed place in which to mingle with the locals as you stroll dusty streets edged by blooming gardens. Gunung Inerie (2245m), a perfectly conical volcano, looms to the south, where you'll also find active hot springs. The recently emerged volcano, Wawo Muda, with its Kelimutu-esque lakes, is another favourite.

🛏 Sleeping & Eating

★**Hotel Happy Happy** GUESTHOUSE $$
(☎0853 3370 4455, 0384-421763; www.hotelhappyhappy.com; Jl Sudirman; r 475,000Rp; 🛜) This simple yet classy guesthouse offers six immaculate tiled rooms, brushed with lavender walls and furnished with decent linen – a scarcity in Bajawa. There's a sociable sitting area on the patio, free water-bottle refills and an excellent breakfast included. It's a short walk from the main cluster of tourist businesses.

Sanian Hotel Bajawa HOTEL $$
(☎0384-220006; www.sanianhotelbajawa.com; Jl DI Panjaitan; r from 350,000Rp; 🛜) This new-

ish hotel offers 11 rooms in a two-storey building near the town centre and market. Rooms are refreshingly spare of extraneous decor, and those upstairs have nice views of Bajawa and the surrounding hills from the shared balcony.

Anugerah INDONESIAN $
(☎0812 1694 7158; Jl Sudirman; mains 25,000-40,000Rp; ⏰8am-10.30pm) This simple family-run *rumah makan* (eating house) is a great choice for a cheap lunch in Bajawa. Menu items such as wontons, noodles and soups veer into almost-Chinese territory, while others such as the *nasi babi rica rica* (spicy pork with rice) steer things back to the archipelago. Save room for sweets from the cabinet in the entrance.

ℹ Information

Tourist Office (☎0823 3907 0178; www.florestourism.com; Jl Ahmad Yani 2; ⏰8.30am-4.30pm Mon-Sat) Small but highly useful; good for Ngada info. Various trekking and travel agencies have shops nearby.

ℹ Getting There & Away

There are buses and bemos to various destinations including Ende (80,000Rp) and Labuanbajo (160,0000Rp).

Ende

☎0381 / POP 80,253

The most immediately apparent merit of this muggy port town is its spectacular setting. The eye-catching cones of Gunung Meja (661m) and Gunung Iya (637m) loom over the city and the nearby black-sand and cobblestone coastline. The views get even better just northeast of Ende as the road to Kelimutu rises along a ridge opposite misty peaks, overlooking a roaring river and gushing with ribbons of waterfalls in the wet season. Throw in the jade rice terraces and you have some of Flores' most jaw-dropping scenery.

But Ende itself is worth more than a pause at its traffic circles, offering a compact and atmospheric centre and an intriguing grittiness. Plus, its central airport is a useful hub for connections to Labuanbajo, Kupang (West Timor) and Tambolaka (Sumba).

Worth are look are the **Ikat Market** (cnr Jls Pabean & Pasar; ⏰9am-5pm), selling hand-woven tapestries, and the waterfront *pasar* (produce market)

🛌 Sleeping & Eating

Guesthouse

Alhidayah GUESTHOUSE $
(📞 0381-23707; Jl Yos Sudarso; r from 200,000Rp;
❄️) This solid budget choice in the centre of
Ende offers seven sparkling, but otherwise
basic, tiled rooms with high ceilings and a
private porch area. The priciest rooms have
air-con and hot water, and are decent value.

★ **Dasi Guest House** GUESTHOUSE $$
(📞 0852 1863 8432, 0381-262 7049; yosdam@ya-
hoo.co.id; Jl Durian Atas 2; r from 250,000Rp; ❄️ 🛜)
This excellent family-run guesthouse has 15
rooms in a modern building. Some are dark,
some are bright, but all have air-con and TV.
Located about 3km east of the centre, it also
has a pleasant common room with views
south. Don't miss the *nasi pecel* (greens
with rice cake and spicy peanut sauce) at the
nameless warung over the road.

★ **Sari Rasa** INDONESIAN $
(Jl Ahmad Yani; mains 25,000-30,000Rp; ⏰ 6.30-
10pm) Looks are deceiving: this bare-walled
restaurant offers just a few plastic stools at
fluorescent-lit metal tables, but is one of
the best not only in Ende, but in all of Nusa
Tenggara. The whiteboard-scrawled menu
is short, but shows the incredible care of
the genial owner, Martin, and his talented
chef-wife.

ℹ️ Information

Tourist Office (📞 0381-23141; www.florestour-
ism.com; Jl Soekarno; ⏰ 8.30am-3pm Mon-Fri)
The enthusiastic staff here dispense up-to-date
transport information.

ℹ️ Getting There & Away

Air and ferry schedules in East Nusa Tenggara
are historically fluid, and it's best to confirm all
times and carriers prior to planning your trip.
Wings, Garuda and Nam Air serve **Ende Airport**
(H Hasan Aroeboesman Airport; Jl Ahmad
Yani), which is located almost in the centre of
town.

Pelni has boats every two weeks to Waingapu,
Benoa and Surabaya, then east to Kupang and
Sabu. Visit the helpful **Pelni office** (📞 0381-
21043; Jl Kathedral 2; ⏰ 8am-noon & 2-4pm
Mon-Sat) for tickets to Waingapu (65,000Rp,
nine hours).

East-bound buses leave from the Wolowana
terminal, 5km from town. Buses heading west
leave from the Ndao terminal, 2km north of town
on the beach road.

Kelimutu

Kelimgutu, a sacred (extinct) volcano, is
the centrepiece of the mountainous, jun-
gle-clad **national park** (admission per person
Mon-Sat/Sun 150,000/225,000Rp, per ojek/car
5000/10,000Rp; ⏰ ticket office 5am-5pm) of the
same name. There aren't many better rea-
sons to wake up before dawn than to wit-
ness the sun cresting Kelimutu's western
rim, filtering mist into the sky and revealing
three deep, volcanic lakes – nicknamed the
tri-coloured lakes because for years each one
was a different striking shade.

Less than an hour's drive from either
Moni or Detusoko, the park shelters en-
dangered flora and fauna (including 19 rare
avian species) and other peaks such as Mt
Kelibara (1731m).

The ticket office is 8.5km up the paved
access road, which connects to the Trans-
Flores Hwy 2km west of Moni. The park-
ing area for the lake is another 4km. From
the car park it's a nice 20-minute walk up
through the pines to Inspiration Point. To
get here from Moni, hire an *ojek* (50,000Rp
one way) or car (350,000Rp return, maxi-
mum five people).

Moni
📞 0361
Moni is a lovely, picturesque hill town afloat
in a sea of rice fields, ringed by lush volcan-
ic peaks and blessed with distant sea views.
It's a slow-paced, easygoing, cool breeze of
a town that serves as the main gateway to
Kelimutu, mainland Flores's biggest draw-
card. The Monday market, held on the soc-
cer pitch, is a major local draw and a good
place to snare local ikat (patterned textiles).

🛌 Sleeping & Eating

Watugana Bungalow GUESTHOUSE $
(📞 0813 3916 7408; Jl Trans Flores; r 150,000-
350,000Rp) The four downstairs rooms at
Watugana are older and kept reasonably
clean, though they are dark and the bath-
rooms are a bit moist. The two upstairs
rooms are newer, brighter and have hot wa-
ter, and are priced accordingly. For 75,000Rp
per person the owners can prepare a sev-
en-dish feast of fish, chicken, rice, veggies
and cheesy mashed potato.

Bintang Lodge GUESTHOUSE $$
(📞 0852 3790 6259, WhatsApp 0823 4103 6979;
www.bintang-lodge.com; Jl Trans Flores; s/d from

330,000/385,000Rp; ❄@) One of the best of Moni's guesthouses, Bintang offers four large, clean rooms in the centre of town. They also have hot water, which is nice on chilly mornings and evenings. The cafe (mains 30,000Rp to 45,000Rp) has a great open terrace with views over the green surrounds. Owner Tobias is a super-friendly fount of local information.

★ **Mopi's Place** CAFE $
(☎0813 3736 5682; Jl Trans Flores; mains 40,000-45,000Rp; ⏰8am-10pm; 🖉) The cafe Moni deserves, this open-sided Indo-Australian affair is an absolute winner. It starts with great coffee (made with beans from Kelimutu and house-made soy milk, if you like), progresses to exceptional gado gado made with squeaky-fresh local vegetables, and ends, via fresh tropical juices and baked goods, with great live music and company, as it morphs into a nocturnal bar.

ℹ Getting There & Away

It's always best to travel in the morning, when buses are often half empty; afternoon buses are usually overcrowded. Don't book through your homestay – hail the bus as it passes through town.

Bintang Lodge rents motorbikes (per day 100,000Rp) and cars (per day 750,000Rp, with driver).

Paga

POP 15,598

Halfway between Moni and Maumere are a string of beaches that are the stuff of Flores fantasy. The Trans-Flores Hwy swoops down to the shore at this rice-farming and fishing hamlet, where the wide rushing river meets the placid bay. As accommodation options grow, Paga may soon be another must-stop town on the trans-Flores shuffle.

A highlight is **Pantai Koka** (entry per car 20,000Rp), about 5km west of Pantai Naga, and one of the nicest beaches in Flores.

Don't miss **Restaurant Laryss** (☎0852 5334 2802; www.floresgids.com; Jl Raya Maumere-Ende; mains 50,000-60,000Rp; ⏰kitchen 8am-10pm), a fabulously situated beachside fish shack: a clutch of tree-shaded tables on the sand that make up one of the best restaurants in Flores. Owner and Flores guide Agustinus Naban serves freshly caught snapper and tuna, rubbed generously with turmeric and ginger, squeezed with lime and roasted on an open flame flavoured with coconut shells.

Maumere

☎0382 / POP 54,000

Blessed with a long, languid coastline backed by layered hills and fringed with islands, Maumere is a logical terminus to a trans-Flores tour. With good air connections to Bali and Timor, it's a gateway to Flores Timur (East Flores). Largely razed in the devastating earthquake of 1992, it's been thoroughly rebuilt, and is now a busy, dusty urban hub. Thankfully, you don't have to stay in the city, as there are pleasant options along the coast in both directions.

Hotel Wini Rai II (☎0382-21362; Jl Soetomo 7; fan-only s/d 100,000/150,000Rp, air-con s/d 150,000/200,000Rp; ❄) is a central budget option, bare-bones but very friendly. More upmarket, **Wailiti Hotel** (☎0821 4717 5576, 0382-23416; Jl Da Silva; r/bungalow from 450,000/550,000Rp; ❄📶🏊) is Maumere's most pleasant accommodation with tidy rooms and bungalows in spacious grounds with a large pool.

ℹ Getting There & Away

Maumere is connected to Bali and Kupang. Airline offices and travel agents are clustered in the centre on Jl Pasar Baru Timur.

Maumere's **Frans Seda Airport** (Wai Oti Airport) is 3km east of town, 800m off the Maumere–Larantuka road.

A taxi to/from town is a non-negotiable, flat fee of 60,000Rp.

There are two bus terminals. Buses and Kijang heading east to Larantuka leave from **Terminal Lokaria** (Jl Raja Centis), 3km east of town. **Terminal Madawat** (Jl Gajah Mada), 1km southwest of town, is the place for westbound departures. Schedules are rarely precise – be prepared to wait around until there are sufficient passengers, and watch out for buses that pick up passengers from the streets adjoining the terminals, without actually entering them.

Larantuka

☎0383 / POP 37,348

A bustling, predominantly Catholic little port of rusted tin roofs at the easternmost end of Flores, Larantuka rests against the base of **Gunung Ili Mandiri** (1510m), separated by a narrow strait from Pulau Solor and Pulau Adonara. Once a significant colonial entrepôt and base for missionary activity, today it's the low-key capital of Flores Timur (East Flores). It has a fun street-market vibe at dusk, when streets come alive with the commerce of fresh fruit and fish, but most visitors stay just one night on their way to Kupang or Alor. The Easter Semana Santa (Holy Week) is a particularly good time to visit, as Catholic pilgrims from across Indonesia come for the huge processions of penitents and cross-bearers. On Good Friday these even extend to the water, where a statue-bearing boat is followed by a flotilla of canoes.

Larantuka's best place to stay, **Asa Hotel & Restaurant** (📞 0383-232 5018; https://asahotel-larantuka.com; Jl Soekarno Hatta; d from 400,000Rp; ✳✳) has an impressive complex overlooking Weri beach, 5km northeast of the centre. The 27 modern and well-designed rooms are in one- and two-storey blocks, and have fridges and balconies.

🛈 Getting There & Away

Ferries run to Kupang (105,000Rp, 15 hours) on Monday and Friday at noon. Two Pelni ships also run to Kalabahi in the Alor Archipelago (78,000Rp, 15 hours).

The main bus terminal is 5km west of town. Buses (60,000Rp, four hours) and cars (80,000Rp, three hours) to Maumere run frequently between 7am and 5pm.

West Timor

With amazing traditional villages, rugged countryside and empty beaches, West Timor is an undiscovered gem. Deep within its mountainous, *lontar* palm–studded interior, animist traditions persist alongside tribal dialects, and ikat-clad, betel-nut-chewing chiefs preserve *adat* (traditional law) in bee-hive-hut villages. Hit one of the many weekly markets in tribal country and you'll get a feel for rural Timor life, while eavesdropping on several of the 14 different languages spoken on the island. In West Timor, even Bahasa Indonesia is often a foreign tongue. Except, of course, in Kupang, the coastal capital and East Nusa Tenggara's top metropolis, which buzzes to a frenetic Indonesian beat.

🛈 Getting There & Around

West Timor is easily accessed through the principal city, Kupang, site of El Tari Airport, the regional gateway to Nusa Tenggara Timur. Technically an international airport, it actually offers daily flights to Jakarta, Denpasar, the Alor Islands, Sumba and Flores. Ferries also sail to Kalabahi, Larantuka, Rote and Waingapu.

Kupang

📞 0380 / POP 315,768

Kupang is the capital of Nusa Tenggara Timur (NTT). Despite the city's scruffy waterfront, its sprawling gnarl of traffic, and the almost total lack of endearing cultural or architectural elements, this is a place you can get used to. Chalk it up to sheer chaotic energy – it's a university town, after all, and it has the palpable buzz of a place on the move.

Kupang's a regional transport hub, so you will do time here. Just don't be surprised if between trips to the interior, Alor or Rote, you discover that you actually dig it. England's Captain Bligh had a similar epiphany when he spent 47 days here after that unfortunate mutiny on the *Bounty* incident in 1789.

🛈 GETTING TO TIMOR-LESTE: KUPANG TO DILI

Besides pure tourism, many head to Timor-Leste from West Timor to renew their Indonesian visa. If you decide to go, be aware that Timor-Leste is considerably more expensive than Indonesia, and the return trip normally takes more than a week by the time you get to Dili, wait for your Indonesian visa and return to West Timor.

Getting to the border Direct minibuses (10 to 11 hours) to Dili from Kupang are operated by **Timor Tour & Travel** (📞 0380-881543, 0852 1708 5378). Call for a hotel pickup.

At the border Apply for your visa to Timor-Leste at the **Timor-Leste Consulate** (📞 0813 3936 7558, 0380-855 4552; Jl Frans Seda; ⊙ 8am-4pm Mon-Thu, to 2pm Fri) in Kupang with a valid passport, a photocopy and passport photos. It costs US$30 and takes one to three working days to process. There are no buses waiting on either side of the border if you arrive independently; you'll have a long wait hoping for one to show up. The through minibus is by far the best option.

Moving on The through minibuses take you direct to Dili, where most people start their Timor-Leste visit. They do drop-offs at guesthouses and hotels.

For information on making this crossing in reverse see p820.

Kupang

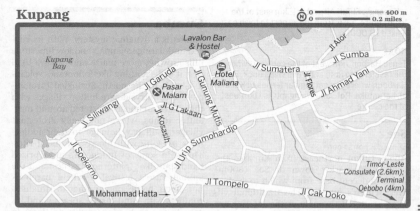

🛏 Sleeping & Eating

⭐ Lavalon Bar & Hostel
HOSTEL $

(📲 0812 377 0533, 0380-832256; www.lava lontouristinfo.com; Jl Sumatera 44; dm/r from 70,000/160,000Rp; ❀🛜) Run by the much-loved living Nusa Tenggara encyclopedia and former Indonesian film star Edwin Lerrick, Lavalon is a natural meeting place for West Timor travellers, and Kupang's best-value accommodation. Rooms are worn but clean (some with Western-style bath-rooms), and excellent meals and cold beer are served in the seaside common area. Ask for the corner room, for sea views.

Edwin runs the attached (private) visitor information office, arranges cars, motorcycles and drivers and can advise on onward connections. Phone or message ahead to guarantee a booking.

Hotel Maliana
GUESTHOUSE $

(📲 0380-821879; Jl Sumatera 35; r with fan/air-con 175,000/250,000Rp; ❀🛜) These 13 basic yet comfy and clean motel rooms are a popular budget choice. There are ocean glimpses from the vine-shrouded front porch.

⭐ Pasar Malam
MARKET $

(Night Market; Jl Garuda; fish from 50,000Rp; ⏰6-11pm) Kupang was never considered a good eating town until this wonderful, lamp-lit market launched and turned a lane off Jl Garuda over to streetside grill and wok chefs, who expertly prepare inexpensive dishes. The selection is vast, the fish flapping fresh and the grilling, in a sticky *kecap manis*—based glaze, superb.

ℹ Information

Edwin Lerrick (📲 0812 377 0533, 0380-832256; lavalonbar@gmail.com; per day from 300,000Rp), the proprietor of Lavalon Bar & Hostel, is a vital source for the latest transport information, as well as cultural attractions throughout Nusa Tenggara. His Lavalon website is a must-read for information.

ℹ Getting There & Away

AIR
Kupang is the most important hub for air travel in Nusa Tenggara. There are frequent flights to Bali and a web of services across the region.

BUSES FROM KUPANG
Buses from Kupang to further destinations in West Timor leave from **Terminal Oebobo** (Jl Frans Seda).

DESTINATION	FARE (RP)	DURATION (HR)	FREQUENCY
Kefamenanu	50,000	5½	several times daily
Niki Niki	35,000	3½	hourly 5am-6pm
Soe	30,000	3	hourly 5am-6pm

Kupang's El Tari Airport is 15km east of the town centre. Taxis from the airport to town cost a fixed 70,000Rp.

BOAT

Tenau Harbor, 7km west of the centre, is where the fast ferry to Rote and Pelni ships dock. Bolok Harbour, where you get regular ferries to Kalabahi, Larantuka, Rote and Waingapu, is 11km west of the centre.

Soe

☑0388 / POP 32,000

About 110km northeast from Kupang, the cool, leafy market town of Soe (800m) makes a decent base from which to explore West Timor's interior. The traditional villages scattered throughout the interior are some of the most intriguing sights in NTT.

Hotel Bahagia I (☑0853 3830 3809; Jl Diponegoro; standard/VIP r 150,000/300,000Rp; ✱) offers a range of rooms, from small, dark cold-water cubbies to spacious, air-conditioned suites. No English is spoken. Sprawling **Timor Megah Hotel** (☑0852 5301 5444, 0388-22280; www.timormegah.com; Jl Gajah Mada 56; standard/VIP r 250,000/350,000Rp; ✱ 🛜) is Soe's best place to stay with a range of large rooms in an L-shaped three-storey block.

None

None is Kefamenanu's last headhunting village and one of the area's best attractions. A trail runs for 900m from where the bemo drops you off on the main road. Stroll past corn and bean fields and hop over a meandering stream (often dry) and you'll reach scattered *ume bubu* (traditional beehive huts), home to 56 families who have lived here for nine generations. Parents still bury their baby's placenta in the centre of their hut, and the village is protected by a native rock fort, which abuts a sheer cliff.

Villagers are warm and welcoming, and break out their looms at the village *lopo* (meeting place) for weaving demonstrations upon request. It is so peaceful here that it's hard to believe they were taking heads just two generations ago. You can arrange for traditional dances or even stay the night. BLeave an offering of at least 20,000Rp per person.

You can reach None, 18km east of Soe, on an *ojek* (30,000Rp), or hop on a Soe–Niki Niki bemo for 5000Rp. If driving, you can get close to the village, but consider doing the access walk from the main road to soak up the atmosphere.

Sumba

Sumba is a dynamic mystery. With its rugged undulating savannah and low limestone hills growing more maize and cassava than rice, it looks nothing like Indonesia's volcanic islands to the north. Sprinkled throughout the countryside are hilltop villages with thatched clan houses clustered around megalithic tombs, where nominally Protestant villagers still pay homage to their indigenous *marapu* with bloody sacrificial rites. Throw in some of Indonesia's most prized hand-spun ikat (patterned textiles) and the annual Pasola festival – where bareback horsemen 'battle' one another in ritualised conflicts with hand-carved spears – and it's easy to see that *adat* (traditional lore) in Sumba runs deep.

It's one of the poorest islands in Indonesia, but an influx of investment has brought improvements in infrastructure and change that's trickled down to traditional villages – thatched roofs have been switched to tin, tombs are now made from concrete, traditional dress is rare and remote villagers expect larger donations from visitors.

Sumba's links to greater Indonesia are improving. Airports in Tambolaka and Waingapu have daily flights to Denpasar (Bali), Kupang (West Timor) and Ende (Flores). Ferries run to Flores and Kupang.

Waingapu

☑0387 / POP 55,000

Waingapu is a leafy, laid-back town that is plenty walkable and makes a decent base from which to explore the surrounding villages. It became an administrative centre after the Dutch military 'pacified' the island in 1906 and has long been Sumba's main trading post for textiles, prized Sumbanese horses, dyewoods and lumber. Waingapu has a few ikat (patterned textiles) shops and workshops, and the old harbour provides some camera fodder and becomes redolent with the smell of grilled fish after sundown, when the Pasar Malam (night market) kicks off. Traders with bundles of textiles and carvings hang around hotels or walk the streets touting for rupiah.

🛏 Sleeping

⭐ **Tanto Hotel**   GUESTHOUSE **$$**
(☑0387-61048, 0387-62500; http://tantohotel.com; Jl Prof Yohanes 14; r/ste 380,000/680,000Rp;

✳✿) Bright, fresh rooms and good service set the Tanto apart from most of the competition in Waingapu. The decor is primarily white, with natural wood and vivid-red accents, many rooms have fridges and the breakfast is good. They can arrange car hire from 500,000Rp for 12 hours, and there's a decent lobby restaurant (open 9am to 9pm, mains 35,000Rp to 60,000Rp).

Padadita Beach Hotel　　　HOTEL **$$**
(📶 0812 3899 5246; Jl Erlangga Padadita; superior/deluxe r 465,000/475,000Rp) This gleamingly tiled three-storey hotel, nestled between swathes of mangrove on Waingapu's waterfront, is a nice midrange option outside the centre of town. The airport shuttle is free and the buffet breakfast, spread out in an open-sided pavilion overlooking the water, is pretty good.

ℹ️ Getting There & Away

The airport is 6km south on the Melolo road. A taxi into town costs a standard 60,000Rp, but most hotels offer a free pick-up and drop-off service for guests. It's 3000Rp for a bemo ride to any destination around town, and 5000Rp to the western bus terminal.

TX Waingapu (📶 0387-61534; www.txtravel.com; Jl Beringin 12; ⏰ 9am-6pm) is a travel agency that books airline tickets.

Pelni ships leave from the newer Darmaga dock to the west of town but their **ticket office** (📶 0387-61665; www.pelni.co.id; Jl Hasanuddin; ⏰ 9am-4pm) is at the old port. Ferry schedules are subject to change: check with **ASDP** (📶 0214-288 2233; www.indonesiaferry.co.id) or see the schedules at the port.

The terminal for eastbound buses is in the southern part of town, close to the market. The West Sumba terminal (aka Terminal Kota) is about 5km west of town.

Waikabubak
📶 0387 / POP 22,000

A country market town, home to both thatched clan houses and rows of concrete shops, administrative buildings and tin-roof homes sprouting satellite dishes, Waikabubak makes Waingapu feel like a metropolis. It's a welcoming place, surrounded by thick stands of mahogany, and at about 600m above sea level, it's a little cooler than the east and a good base for exploring the traditional villages of West Sumba. The big market is on Saturday.

Yuliana Leda Tara (📶 0822 3621 6297; yuli.sumba@gmail.com; Kampung Tarung; per day from 500,000Rp) is a wonderful local English- and French-speaking guide who lives in Tarung – Waikabubak's hilltop traditional village. Yuliana can organise tours of traditional villages throughout West Sumba, where she finds out about funerals and sacrifices, takes horse tours through rice fields, and can arrange village homestays.

🛏️ Sleeping & Eating

Hotel Karanu　　　GUESTHOUSE **$**
(📶 0387-21645; Jl Sudirman 43; standard/VIP r per person 150,000/250,000Rp; 🅿️) A bright garden hotel east of the downtown swirl and within view of nearby rice fields, Karanu offers clean (if timeworn) rooms. The VIP ones have air-con and TVs, and there's wi-fi (and a fading *Last Supper* rug) in the lobby.

D' Sumba Ate　　　INTERNATIONAL **$$**
(📶 0812 3868 3588; Jl Ahmad Yani 148; mains 40,000-70,000Rp; ⏰ 11am-11pm) A welcome find in Waikabubak, this very good restaurant cooks up wood-fired pizzas, pasta and burgers alongside flapping-fresh grilled fish and the usual Indo suspects. There's a cool open-air bamboo vibe, a competent bar, and perhaps Sumba's cleanest toilets.

ℹ️ Getting There & Away

Tambolaka, 42km northwest of Waikabubak, has the closest airport. A bus to the terminal at Waitabula (an older town being swallowed by Tambolaka) and a bemo or *ojek* from there is the cheapest way, but most people get a taxi from Waitabula or charter a bemo (around 120,000Rp) from Waikabubak.

Bemos, trucks and minibuses service most other towns and villages in West Sumba. Generally, it's best to leave early in the day, when they tend to fill up and depart most quickly. There are several daily buses to Waingapu (60,000Rp, five hours).

Waikabubak is the place to rent a motorcycle for exploring West Sumba. Expect to pay 80,000Rp per day. Hotels can set you up with car rental (800,000Rp with driver).

Tambolaka
📶 0387

Located 42km northwest of Waikabubak, this once sleepy market town has become West Sumba's main transport hub – it's booming and it's going by a whole new name, Tambolaka, at least in tourism brochures and other government literature. We've followed suit, even if many locals of a certain age still refer to it as Waitabula.

INDONESIA SUMBA

While still in the early stages of growth, Tambolaka is easily accessible from Bali, and is the gateway to the island's sensational western half.

Future visitor growth seems inevitable; beachfront 'for sale' signs are common and a new school to train locals in tourism is opening east of the airport.

Experienced guide Philip Renggi at **Sumba Adventure Tours & Travel** (☑ 0813 3710 7845; http://sumbaadventuretours.com; Jl Timotius Tako Gely 3; per day guide services 300,000Rp, per day with car & driver 800,000-1,000,000Rp; ☺8am-5pm), is one of the best in West Sumba. He and his team of guides lead trips into seldom-explored villages, including his native Manuakalada and Waiwarungu, where there are several sacred marapu houses that only shaman can enter. He can arrange itineraries, set you up for Pasola, rent cars and more.

🛏 Sleeping & Eating

Penginapan Melati   GUESTHOUSE $
(☑ 0813 5396 6066, 0387-24055; Jl Saputra; r with fan/air-con 200,000/300,000Rp; ✱ 🛜) Shaded by a huge tree, with 15 rooms that are simple but immaculate with fresh paint and tiling throughout, and plenty of images of the holy family, the Virgin Mother and Il Papa to brighten things up. They even have rain shower heads in the *mandi* (bath). There's a simple Padang-style restaurant right next door.

★ Oro Beach Houses &
Restaurant   BUNGALOW $$
(☑ 0812 3608 9096, 0813 3978 0610; www. oro-beachbungalows.com; Weepangali; bungalow/villa 665,000/850,000Rp) Think: three wild beachfront acres where you can nest in a circular thatched bungalow with canopied driftwood beds and outdoor baths. Oro offers excellent meals, mountain bikes and snorkelling (50,000Rp each) just off their stunning 200m-long beach. Tambolaka Airport is 20 minutes away by potholed road; transfers can be arranged for 120,000Rp per car.

Warung Gula Garam   INTERNATIONAL $$
(☑ 0387-252 4019; Jl Soeharto; mains 50,000-60,000Rp; ☺10am-10pm; 🛜) Run by expat Frenchman Louis, this open-air cafe near the airport does very good wood-fired pizza and pasta, plus other Western dishes such as chicken cordon bleu and sausages with mash and veg. There's also good Indo fare and more-than-passable coffee and juices.

ⓘ Getting There & Away

Tambolaka's airport terminal is shiny and modern. There are daily flights to Denpasar (Bali) and Kupang (West Timor) with Garuda, Nam Air and Wings Air. Note that on some airline/booking websites the destination is listed as 'Waikabubak'.

Waikelo, a small and predominantly Muslim town north of Tambolaka, has a little, picturesque harbour that is the main port for West Sumba and offers ferry service to Sape (Sumbawa) three times a week (52,000Rp, nine hours).

Buses leave throughout the day for Waikabubak (10,000Rp to 15,000Rp, one hour), departing from the centre of town.

SUMATRA

POP 50.37 MILLION

Few isles tempt the imagination with the lure of adventure quite like the wild land of Sumatra. An island of extraordinary beauty, it bubbles with life and vibrates under the power of nature. Eruptions, earthquakes and tsunamis are Sumatran headline grabbers. Steaming volcanoes brew and bluster while standing guard over lakes that sleepily lap the edges of craters. Jungles host not only orangutans, but also tigers, rhinos and elephants. And down at sea level, idyllic deserted beaches are bombarded by clear barrels of surf.

As varied as the land, the people of Sumatra are a spicy broth of mixed cultures, from the devout Muslims in Aceh to the hedonistic Batak Christians around Danau Toba and the matrilineal Minangkabau of Padang. All are unified by a fear, respect and love of the wild and wondrous land of Sumatra.

ⓘ Getting There & Away

These days, most travellers reach Sumatra via budget-airline flight or ferry from Java. The old sea routes are largely redundant. Sumatra is one hour behind Singapore and Malaysia.

AIR

Medan is Sumatra's primary international hub, with frequent flights from its new airport to mainland Southeast Asian cities such as Singapore, Kuala Lumpur and Penang with Silk Air (www. silkair.com), AirAsia (www.airasia.com) and Malaysia Airlines (www.malaysiaairlines.com), respectively. In West Sumatra, Padang has flights from Kuala Lumpur. Banda Aceh, Palembang, Pulau Batam and Pekanbaru also have international flights from mainland Southeast Asia.

You can hop on a plane from Jakarta to every major Sumatran city aboard Garuda

Sumatra

200 km
100 miles

ANDAMAN SEA

MALAYSIA

KUALA LUMPUR

SINGAPORE

Pelabuhan (Port Klang)

Melaka

Pulau Rapat

Strait of Melaka

Pulau Penang

Tanjung Balai

Tebing-tinggi

Langsa

Bireuen

Pulau Weh Marine National Park

Pulau Weh

Pulau Breueh

Banda Aceh

Meulaboh

Tangkahan

ACEH

Bukit Lawang

Gunung Leuseur (3404m)

Gunung Leuseur National Park

Medan

Berastagi

Gunung Sibayak (2094m)

Gunung Sinabung (2450m)

Parapat

Rantauparapat

NORTH SUMATRA

Danau Toba

Trans-Sumatran Hwy

Singkil

Sinabang

Pulau Simeulue

Pulau Banyak

Kepulauan Banyak

Sibolga

Gunung Sitoli

Pulau Nias

Teluk Dalam

Pulau Telo

Sikabaluan

Pulau Rangsang

Pulau Kalimun

Pulau Bengkalis

Dumai

Duri

Pekanbaru

RIAU

Pulau Batam

Pulau Bintan

Pulau Karimun

Pulau Kundur

Pulau Mendol

Pulau Singkep

Pulau Lingga

LINGGA ISLANDS

Pulau Galang

Pulau Sebangka

Selat Berhala

Equator

Jambi

JAMBI

Bukit Duabelas National Park

Bukit Tigapuluh National Park

Sungaipagar

Muarabungo

Bangko

Lubuklinggau

Sungai Penuh

Gunung Kerinci (3805m)

WEST SUMATRA

Bukittinggi

Bonjol

Solok

Padang

Danau Maninjau

Danau Singkarak

Tua Pejat

Muara Siberut

Pulau Siberut

Pulau Sipora

Pulau Pagai Utara

Pulau Pagai Selatan

Siobau

Sikakap

MENTAWAI ISLANDS

INDIAN OCEAN

Equator

Pegunungan Bukitbarisan

Peregunungan Bukitbarisan

SOUTH SUMATRA

Palembang

Mentok

Belinyu

Pangkal Pinang

Pulau Bangka

Pulau Belitung

Tanjung Pandan

Prabumulih

Kotabumi

Baturaja

Lahat

Manna

Mukomuko

Ipuh

Bengkulu

BENGKULU

Bintuhan

Danau Ranau

Krui

Pulau Enggano

Bukit Barisan Selatan National Park

Bandarlampung

Bakauheni

Kota Krakatau

Gunung Agung

LAMPUNG

Way Kambas National Park

Pulau Seribu

Merak

Sunda Strait

JAVA

Gunung Krakatau

(www.garuda-indonesia.com), **Lion Air** (www.lionair.co.id) or **Sriwijaya Air** (www.sriwijayaair.co.id), among others. Flights from Sumatra to other parts of Indonesia typically connect through Jakarta. A warning: when palm-oil plantations on Sumatra's east coast are burned (annually, usually during dry season), the smoke frequently results in the closure of Pekanbaru and Jambi airports.

BOAT

Budget airlines have signalled the end of some international ferries, such as the Penang–Medan route. Ferries run between Dumai on Sumatra's east coast and Melaka and Klang (for Kuala Lumpur) in Malaysia, Singapore and Pulau Batam, but Dumai is only useful if you have your heart set on an international boat journey or if you're transporting a motorbike between Sumatra and Malaysia.

From Singapore, ferries make the quick hop to Pulau Batam and Pulau Bintan, the primary islands in the Riau archipelago. From Batam, boats set sail for Dumai, Palembang and Pekanbaru, but few travellers use these routes.

Ferries cross the narrow Sunda Strait, which links the southeastern tip of Sumatra at Bakauheni to Java's westernmost point of Merak. The sea crossing is a brief dip in a day-long voyage that requires several hours' worth of bus transport from both ports to Jakarta and, on the Sumatra side, Bandarlampung.

ⓘ Getting Around

Most travellers bus around northern Sumatra and then hop on a plane to Java, largely avoiding Sumatra's highway system. Most of the island is

mountainous jungle and the poorly maintained roads form a twisted pile of spaghetti on the undulating landscape. Don't count on getting anywhere very quickly on Sumatra.

AIR

Short plane journeys can be a good alternative to spending an eternity on packed buses. Competition between domestic carriers means internal flights are inexpensive and largely reliable, except for Susi Air and their small planes, which are quite susceptible to bad weather. Dry-season smog affects planes along the east coast. Medan to Pulau Weh, Medan to Padang, Palembang to Jambi, Medan to Banda Aceh, and Pulau Batam to Padang and Bengkulu are useful air hops.

BOAT

Most boat travel within Sumatra connects the main island with the many satellite islands lining the coast. The most commonly used routes link Banda Aceh with Pulau Weh; Singkil and Sibolga with Pulau Nias; and Padang with the Mentawai Islands. Most long-distance ferries have several classes, ranging from dilapidated and crowded to air-conditioned, dilapidated and less crowded. The Mentawai Islands are now served by a comfortable large speedboat.

BUS & MINIBUS

Bus is the most common mode of transport around Sumatra, and in some cases it's the only option for intercity travel. But it is far from efficient or comfortable, since all types of buses – from economy sardine cans to modern air-con coaches – are subject to the same traffic snarls along Sumatra's single carriageways, potholes and endless stops to pick up or drop off passengers. At the top of the class structure are super-executive or VIP buses with reclining seats, deep-freeze air-con, toilets and an all-night serenade of karaoke. Smart passengers come prepared with a jacket and earplugs.

In some towns, you can go straight to the bus terminal to buy tickets and board buses, while other towns rely on bus-company offices outside the terminals. Ticket prices vary greatly depending on the quality of the bus and the perceived gullibility of the traveller; ask at your guesthouse how much a ticket is supposed to cost.

For midrange and shorter journeys, many locals and travellers use minibus and shared car services, which can be more convenient than hustling out to the bus terminal as they run intercity and door-to-door. They are not necessarily faster or more comfortable, but are convenient.

TRAIN

The only three useful train services in Sumatra run from Medan's new airport to the centre of Medan, and from Bandarlampung to Palembang and Lahat (for the Pasemah Highlands).

ⓘ GETTING TO SINGAPORE: RIAU ARCHIPELAGO TO SINGAPORE

Getting to the border Although backpackers seldom visit Sumatra's Riau Archipelago, some do transit through Pulau Batam on their way to Singapore. Ferry operators on this route include BatamFast (www.batamfast.com). You can get to Pulau Batam by boat and bus connections from Dumai, Palembang and Pekanbaru.

At the border Citizens of most countries will be granted a 30-day visa when they arrive in Singapore.

Moving on Ferry services from the Riau Islands serve several terminals in Singapore, where it's easy to get onward public transport connections.

For information on making this crossing in reverse see p647.

Medan

📞 061 / POP 2.2 MILLION

Sumatra's major metropolis, and Indonesia's third-largest city, is seen as a necessary evil by many Sumatra-bound travellers. It suffers from poor geography: it's not on the coast, there's no mountain backdrop or even a grand river. It's inevitably a transport hub en route to more exciting destinations and, for some, a welcome return to the trappings of 'civilisation' in the shape of modern malls and restaurants. But it's a city with real Indonesian urban character and it perks up in the evening with backstreet food stalls. So get over the culture shock, give Medan a bit of time and discover an amenity-filled, modern city with more than a hint of crumbling Dutch colonial-era charm and a couple of worthwhile museums.

⊙ Sights

Ghosts of Medan's colonial-era mercantile past are still visible along Jl Ahmad Yani from Jl Palang Merah north to Lapangan Merdeka, a former parade ground surrounded by handsome colonial-era buildings, such as **Bank Indonesia** (Jl Balai Kota; ⊙8am-4pm Mon-Fri), **Balai Kota** (Town Hall; Jl Balai Kota) and the **main post office** (Jl Bukit Barisan; ⊙8am-6pm).

★**Museum of North Sumatra**   MUSEUM
(Museum Negeri Privinci Sumatera Utara; Jl HM Joni 51; Indonesian/foreigner 2000/10,000Rp; ⊙8am-4pm Tue-Thu, to 3.30pm Fri-Sun) Housed in a striking traditional building, this museum has a well-presented collection ranging from early North Sumatran civilisations to Hindu, Buddhist and Islamic periods to Dutch colonial-era and military history. Highlights include fine stone carvings and extravagantly carved wooden dragon coffins from Nias, Batak scrolls for fending off misfortune, fine textiles and a *keris* (ornamental dagger) collection. It's a short way southeast of the centre.

Istana Maimoon   PALACE
(Jl Katamso; 5000Rp; ⊙8am-5pm) The grand, 30-room Maimoon Palace was built by the sultan of Deli in 1888 and features Malay, Mughal and Italian influences. Only the main room, which features the lavish inauguration throne, is open to the public. Here you can check out a modest collection of ceremonial *kerises* and dress up in traditional Malay costume.

Mesjid Raya   MOSQUE
(cnr Jl Mesjid Raya & SM Raja; by donation; ⊙9am-5pm, except during prayer times) The impressive Grand Mosque was commissioned by the sultan in 1906. The Moroccan-style building has a grand entrance, towering ceilings, ornate carvings, Italian marble and stained glass from China.

Tjong A Fie Mansion   HISTORIC BUILDING
(www.tjongafiemansion.org; Jl Ahmad Yani 105; 35,000Rp; ⊙9am-5pm) The former house of a famous Chinese merchant who died in 1921 – formerly the wealthiest resident of Medan – mixes Victorian and Chinese style. The original hand-painted ceilings, Tjong's huge bedroom, imported dark-wood furniture inlaid with marble and mother-of-pearl, interesting art pieces, an upstairs ballroom and Taoist temples help to make it one of the most impressive historic buildings in town.

🛏 Sleeping

K77 Guest House   GUESTHOUSE $
(📞061-736 7087, 0813 9653 8897; www.k77guest housemedan.blogspot.com; Jl Seto 6B; dm/s/d/f 125,000/200,000/250,000/350,000Rp; ✳🛜) The only budget hotel in Medan that we really recommend, this backpacker haven is in a quiet residential street east of the centre. Spotlessly clean rooms, comfy beds and friendly, helpful hosts, Johan and Lola, add up to all the things a budget guesthouse should be. The dorm has four single beds; all rooms share bathrooms and have air-con.

Pondok Wisata Angel   GUESTHOUSE $
(📞061-732 0702; pondokwisataangelangel@yahoo. com; Jl SM Raja 70; s with fan 80,000Rp, d with fan/air-con 130,000/150,000Rp; ✳🛜) A central backpacker choice near the Grand Mosque, Angel's pokey rooms on several floors are tiny and in serious need of some TLC but passably clean. A highlight is the sociable downstairs **cafe** (📞061-732 0702; Jl SM Raja 70; mains 10,000-50,000Rp; ⊙7am-midnight; 🛜) where you can use wi-fi, strum a guitar and get a cold beer.

D'Prima Hotel   HOTEL $$
(📞061-456 1077; www.dprimahotelmedan.com; Jl Stasiun Kereta Api 1; r 550,000-750,000Rp; ➌✳🛜) Occupying the top floors of the train station, you'd expect this hotel would be noisy and drab but it's not. Super-central for airport-train departures and close to Merdeka Sq. Rooms are ultraclean and come with flat-screen TV, soft bed and powerful hot shower.

INDONESIA MEDAN

Medan

✖ Eating

Medan has Sumatra's most varied selection of cuisines, from basic Malay-style *mie* (noodle) and nasi (rice) joints, to top-class hotel restaurants.

Simple warungs (food stalls) occupy the front courtyards of the houses in the lanes around Mesjid Raya. Evening food stalls on Jl Selat Panjang are worth visiting. Medan's modern malls have decent food courts and world-food restaurants. Centre Point mall has an excellent Lotte supermarket.

★ **Merdeka Walk**   SOUTHEAST ASIAN **$**
(Lapangan Merdeka, Jl Balai Kota; dishes 10,000-45,000Rp; ⊙11am-11pm; 🔊) Inspired by Singapore's alfresco dining, this contemporary collection of outdoor eateries in Lapangan Merdeka offers everything from doughnut stalls to breezy sit-down restaurants serving grilled seafood and Malaysian-style noodles, to fast-food chains. Hours vary but it's live-

liest after 5pm – come for the atmosphere rather than low prices.

Mie Tiong Sim Selat Panjang
NOODLES **$**

(Jl Selat Panjang 7; mains 26,000-38,000Rp; ⏰3pm-midnight) On a little street packed with night food stalls, this bustling canteen is locally (and justifiably) famous for its *mie tiong sim* (soft, handmade noodles topped with sweet, flavourful char siu pork). The chicken noodle is also good, as are the wontons.

Pasar Ramai
MARKET **$**

(Ramani Market; Jl Thamrin; ⏰7am-midnight) The main fruit market is a profusion of colour and smells, and has an impressive selection of local and imported tropical fruit. It's next to Thamrin Plaza.

Bollywood Food Centre
INDIAN **$**

(☎061-453 6494; Jl Muara Takus 7; mains 15,000-45,000Rp; ⏰noon-9pm; 🖉) Locals are adamant that this tucked-away little place, which is more like someone's front room with a family atmosphere to match, serves the most authentic North Indian cuisine in the city. There are several Malay-Indian roti shops located nearby.

Tip Top Restaurant
INTERNATIONAL **$$**

(☎061-451 4442; Jl Ahmad Yani 92; mains 26,000-73,000Rp; ⏰8am-11pm; 🖉) Only the prices have changed at this colonial-era relic. Medan's oldest restaurant dates to 1934 and is great for a taste of bygone imperialism with an array of Indonesian, Chinese and international dishes, but it's the old-school ice cream and the adjoining bakery and cake shop that are worth a try.

🍷 Drinking & Nightlife

Healy Mac's Irish Pub
IRISH PUB

(☎0822 7785 3333; Jl Timor 23; ⏰11am-midnight Mon-Thu, noon-2am Fri-Sun; 🖉) Street-facing but part of the Centre Point complex, Healey Mac's is a typically convivial Irish bar with Guinness on tap, big servings of Western food such as pizza, burgers and steak, sports on the big screen and live music from Thursday to Sunday.

🛍 Shopping

Centre Point Medan
MALL

(www.centrepoint.co.id; Jl Jawa & Jl Timor; ⏰9am-10pm; 🖉) The biggest, brashest and most central of Medan mega shopping malls, Centre Point is just east of the train station. As well as brand-name stores, restaurants and a cinema, there's a supermarket on the basement level.

ℹ️ Information

Kantor Imigrasi Kelas 1 Polonia (☎061-845 2112; medan.imigrasi.go.id; 2nd fl, Jl Mangkubumi 2; ⏰8am-4pm Mon-Fri) processes visa extensions. Technically it takes three days, costs 350,000Rp and cannot be processed until a few days before your current visa expires. Bring photocopies of your passport data and Indonesian visa, as well as your onward ticket. The office is on the 2nd floor.

Rumah Sakit Columbia Asia (☎061-456 6368; www.columbiaasia.com; Jl Listrik 2A; ⏰24hr) The best hospital in the city, with a 24-hour walk-in clinic and pharmacy, as well as English-speaking doctors and specialists. For an ambulance, dial 118.

ℹ️ Getting There & Away

Medan is Sumatra's main international arrival and departure point.

AIR

Kualanamu International Airport (☎061-8888 0300; www.kualanamu-airport.co.id), which opened in 2014, is 39km from the city centre and connected to central Medan by frequent trains and buses.

There are flights from Medan to Jakarta, Denpasar, major Sumatran cities as well as Malaysia and Singapore.

BUS

There are two major bus terminals in Medan. Purchase tickets from ticket offices outside the terminals.

The **Amplas bus terminal** (Jl SM Raja), which serves Parapat (for Danau Toba) and other southern destinations, is 6.5km south of the city centre. Almost any *angkot* heading south on Jl SM Raja will get you to Amplas (5000Rp).

The **Pinang Baris bus terminal** (Jl Gatot Subroto), 10km west of the city centre, serves Bukit Lawang, Berastagi and Banda Aceh.

Singkil Raya (Jl Bintan), near the caged-bird shops, is one of the companies running daily morning and evening trips to Singkil, the departure point for boats to the Banyak Islands. Nearby you'll also find a **bus** at 7.30pm to Ketambe. Take *angkot* 53 from Jl SM Raja to Medan Mall.

Most lodgings and numerous travel agencies along Jl Katamso can arrange a space for you on a shared door-to-door taxi to popular destinations such as Bukit Lawang (100,000Rp), Berastagi and Danau Toba (60,000Rp); it's pricier than a bus but faster and more comfortable.

ⓘ GETTING TO MALAYSIA: DUMAI TO MELAKA

Getting to the border Dumai is a busy and charmless port on Sumatra's north coast. Bus services to Dumai include those from Bukittinggi (160,000Rp, 10 hours, 7pm daily) and Padang (170,000Rp, 12 hours, frequent). High-speed ferries make the trip from Dumai to Melaka daily (one way about 335,000Rp, 1¾ hours).

At the border Nationals of most countries are given a 30- or 60-day visa on arrival, depending on the expected length of stay.

Moving on Melaka is a large and popular city with connections to the rest of Malaysia.

For information on making this crossing in reverse see p403.

ⓘ Getting Around

The cheapest way to get from the airport to the city is on the frequent Damri shuttle buses departing from in front of the terminal. There are buses to central Medan (20,000Rp), Amplas (15,000Rp) and Binjai (40,000Rp). Going to the airport, the Damri shuttle departs from Medan Fair Plaza every 15 minutes.

The fastest and most comfortable way to reach central Medan from the airport is by air-conditioned Railink train (100,000Rp, 45 minutes, 4.40am to 11.40pm). From Medan city centre, trains run roughly hourly between 3.30am and 9.10pm.

Taxis from the airport charge a basic fare of 6000Rp, with an additional 3500Rp per kilometre. A journey to the city centre will cost around 200,000Rp and take an hour depending on traffic.

Hundreds of *angkot* zip around Medan's streets and charge 5000Rp per ride. A few helpful routes include the white Mr X from Jl SM Raja to Kesawan Sq, Lapangan Merdeka and the train station, and the yellow 64 from Maimoon Palace to Sun Plaza. Becak journeys across the city centre cost between 20,000Rp and 30,000Rp.

Banda Aceh

♪ 0651 / POP 223,500

Forget what you've heard about Aceh and its hardline religious stance – Banda Aceh is a surprisingly relaxed and charming provincial capital that more than deserves a day or two en route to Pulau Weh.

Given that Banda Aceh bore the brunt of the 2004 tsunami, with 61,000 killed here, and that much of the city had to be rebuilt, it's little wonder that it looks well maintained and affluent, with broad streets, pavements and parks. The magnificent central mosque – Indonesia's best – still stands as the city's crowning glory, along with the poignant Tsunami Museum.

Banda Aceh is still a fiercely religious city and the ornate mosques are at the centre of daily life. Respectfully dressed visitors shouldn't face any hassles and most travellers find the Acehnese to be friendly and extremely hospitable.

◉ Sights

★ Mesjid Raya Baiturrahman
MOSQUE

(by donation; ⊙5am-10pm) With its brilliant-white walls, ebony-black domes and towering minaret, this 19th-century mosque is a dazzling sight. The best time to visit is during Friday-afternoon prayers, when the entire building and courtyard are filled with people. A recent addition to the tiled courtyard is a series of retractable shades, offering all-weather protection for worshippers. A headscarf is required for women.

★ Tsunami Museum
MUSEUM

(Jl Iskandar Muda; ⊙9am-noon & 2-4.45pm) FREE A visit to this beautifully designed, hard-hitting museum commences with a walk through a dark, dripping tunnel that symbolises the tsunami waves. This is followed by a powerful set of images of the devastation projected from tombstone-like receptacles, and a circular chamber engraved with the names of the lost. Upstairs a very graphic short film is shown, along with photographs of rebuilding, loss, hopefulness, displacement and reunited families.

Lampulo Boat
MEMORIAL

FREE The most famous of the tsunami sights is the fishing boat resting on the house in Lampulo village, about 2km north of the city and 1km from where it was docked. It's said that 59 villagers survived the tsunami by climbing into the stuck boat.

🛏 Sleeping & Eating

There's not much in the way of budget accommodation in Banda, but there are some very reasonable central midrange places in the market area around Jl Khairil Anwar.

Siwah Hotel
HOTEL $$

(☑ 0651-22126; Jl Twk Daud Syah 18-20; d 250,000-465,000Rp; ※⑤) In the market area just north of the river, Siwah is good value compared to other hotels in the area. Clean, bright air-con rooms, hot water, helpful staff and a reasonable price tag.

Linda's Homestay
HOMESTAY $$

(☑ 0823 6436 4130, 0811 680 305; www.lin-das-homestay.blogspot.com; Jl Mata Lorong Rahmat 3, Lambneu Barat; r incl breakfast 350,000-500,000Rp; ※⑤) Staying in the home of hospitable Linda, 4km out of town, is a good way to experience local life in a family home. Many travellers rave about the hospitality and Aceh-nese home cooking. Linda also offers a full-day tour of the city (700,000Rp per person). Some travellers report misunderstandings about prices and ensuing bad feelings.

Pasar Malam Rek
MARKET $

(cnr Jl Ahmad Yani & Jl Khairil Anwar; mains 8000-20,000Rp; ⊙ 5-10pm) The square at the junction of Jl Ahmad Yani and Jl Khairil Anwar is the setting for the Pasar Malam Rek, Banda Aceh's lively night food market featuring noodle and *sate* stalls.

Mie Razali
NOODLES $

(Jl Panglima Polem; mains 10,000-30,000Rp; ⊙ 11am-1am) The best place in town to sample *mie Aceh* (Achenese noodles), spicy noodles served with chicken or seafood. Razali gets busy in the evening so you may have to wait for a table.

★ La Piazza
ITALIAN $$

(☑ 0651-805 7041; Jl Iskandar Muda 308 & 309; mains 25,000-75,000Rp; ⊙ 11am-11pm; ⑤ ✐) Authentic Italian food is on the menu at this 3rd-floor garden restaurant started by Freddie from Pulau Weh. It's not limited to pasta and pizza, though; the seafood dishes, Thai curries, Vietnamese beef and steaks are also strong points. Beer is served discreetly. It's about 2km west of the centre.

ⓘ Information

Regional Tourist Office (Dinas Parawisata; ☑ 0651-26206; www.bandaacehtourism.com; Jl Chik Kuta Karang 3; ⊙ 9am-5pm Mon-Fri) On the 1st floor of a government building; the staff are exceptionally friendly and have free copies of an excellent guidebook to the province.

ⓘ Getting There & Away

AIR

Sultan Iskandar Muda International Airport (http://sultaniskandarmuda-airport.co.id) is 16km southeast of the centre.

There are direct daily flights to/from Jakarta, Medan and Kuala Lumpur.

BOAT

Express boats and car ferries serving Pulau Weh depart at least twice daily from the port at Uleh-leh, 5km west of Banda Aceh's city centre. Express boats depart at 10am and 4pm daily, with an additional 8am service from Friday to Sunday. Car ferries depart at 11am and 4pm Saturday, Sunday and Wednesday, and at 2pm Monday, Tuesday, Thursday and Friday.

BUS

Terminal Bus Bathoh (Jl Mohammed Hasan) is 4km south of the city centre. Large buses to Medan depart from here.

There are hourly buses throughout the day and evening to Medan (180,000Rp to 330,000Rp, 12 hours).

ⓘ Getting Around

➡ Taxis from the airport charge 100,000Rp to the city centre and 140,000Rp to Uleh-leh port.

➡ *Labi-labi* are the local minibuses and cost 2500Rp for trips around town, though sights in the central area can easily be covered on foot or by becak. The most useful services are the blue *labi-labi* for Uleh-leh (10,000Rp, 35 minutes) and the white one to Lhok Nga and Lampu'uk (16,000Rp). The **labi-labi terminal** (Jl Diponegoro; ⊙ 7am-5pm) is just north of the Grand Mosque.

➡ From the bus terminal, a becak into town will cost around 30,000Rp. A becak around town should cost between 15,000Rp and 30,000Rp, depending on your destination. A becak to Uleh-leh from the city centre is 40,000Rp and a taxi 70,000Rp.

➡ For a reliable becak or a city tour aboard a deluxe wi-fi-enabled becak, call or look out for **Little John** (0813 6023 1339).

Pulau Weh

☑ 0652 / POP 32,000

Tiny Pulau Weh has been drawing travellers – mostly divers and in-the-know backpackers – for a couple of decades now, but its charm hasn't faded. It's too remote for that. Ferrying out to this tiny island is an adventure, and exploring its beaches, jungles and clear waters, or just chilling in a hammock at your budget bungalow, rewards travellers who've journeyed up through the turbulent greater mainland below (though you can now fly here direct from Medan). Both figuratively and geographically, Pulau Weh is the cherry on top for many visitors to Sumatra.

Sabang is the tiny island capital but most travellers head to the dive resorts at Gapang Beach or the sweet backpacker enclave at Iboih, but at the northwest end of the island.

◉ Sights & Activities

Most travellers come to Weh for the diving and snorkelling, which is considered some of the best in the Indian Ocean. On an average day, you're likely to spot morays, lionfish and stingrays. During plankton blooms, whale sharks come to graze. Unlike at other dive sites, the coral fields take a back seat to the sea life and landscapes. There are close to 20 dive sites around the island, mostly in and around Iboih and Gapang. Dive operators are based in Gapang and Iboih.

Snorkelling gear can be hired almost anywhere for around 30,000Rp per day.

Recommended dive outfits:

Lumba Lumba Diving Centre (☑ 0811 682 787; www.lumbalumba.com; discover dive 680,000Rp, Open Water Diver course 4,500,000Rp; ⊙ dive shop 8am-8pm; ⊛)

Monster Divers (☑ 0812 6960 6857; www.monsterdivers.com; discover scuba dive 650,000Rp, 1/2 dives 390,000/780,000Rp)

Rubiah Tirta Divers (☑ 0652-332 4555; www.rubiahdivers.com; 1/3/5 dives with equipment 360,000/1,020,000/1,600,000Rp)

Hire a scooter or taxi in Iboih to visit **Kilometer Nol** (5000Rp; ⊙ 8am-sunset), an impressive 44m-high globe monument marking the westernmost-tip of Indonesia, and to wander the path to the lovely swimming hole at **Pria Lot Falls**.

🛌 Sleeping & Eating

Iboih, with its simple palm-thatch bungalows, many built on stilts and overlooking crystal-clear water, is Pulau Weh's backpacker hang-out par excellence. Walk along the jungle path past the village to check out a few places.

★**Olala**   HUT **$**
(☑ 0852 332 4199; eka.enk@gmail.com; r 80,000-150,000Rp; ⊛) Offering cheap and cheerful huts on stilts, Olala caters both to shoestringers (basic huts with shared bathrooms) and those who want their own bathroom and

fan. The best huts are over the water. The restaurant is a popular traveller hang-out and one of the best on the jungle strip.

Oong's Bungalows   HUT **$**
(☑ 0813 6070 0150; r 80,000-130,000Rp, with air-con 250,000Rp) Good-value rooms in basic tin-roof cottages hover back from the water. Cheaper options share bathrooms. The on-site restaurant, **Norma's**, serves seafood and beer amid diving chat.

Yulia's   HUT **$$**
(☑ 0821 6856 4383; r without bathroom 290,000-310,000Rp, with bathroom 400,000-650,000Rp; ⊛⊛) The last resort at the end of the bungalow strip, Yulia's has grown and blossomed into easily Iboih's most upmarket accommodation. Like tropical Swiss chalets, quality, spacious timber bungalows are scattered along the hillside and down to the water's edge. The best have air-con, sea views and breakfast included. The overwater restaurant is a charm.

Lumba Lumba   RESORT **$$**
(☑ 0811 682 787; www.lumbalumba.com; d 300,000Rp, without bathroom 200,000Rp, bungalow 470,000Rp; @⊛) Behind the dive shop of the same name, Lumba Lumba offers some of the best-quality accommodation in Gapang. Wood-decked cottages have tiled rooms, fans and Western toilets, while simpler budget rooms have shared bathrooms. Accommodation is mostly for divers, but it will happily rent out any spare rooms.

ⓘ Information

BRI Bank (Jl Perdagangan) in Sabang has an ATM, as do a couple of other banks.

ⓘ Getting There & Away

AIR
The small **Maimun Saleh Airport**, 2km south of Sabang, is connected to Medan by Garuda Indonesia and Wings four times a week.

BOAT
Slow car ferries and express passenger ferries ply the route between Uleh-leh, 5km northwest of Banda Aceh on the mainland, and Balohan port, around 8km south of Sabang on Pulau Weh. You should get to the port at least 45 minutes before departure to get a ticket. Ferry service is weather dependent.

Car ferries (economy/air-con 27,000/60,000Rp, two hours) leave Pulau Weh daily at 8am, returning from Uleh Leh on the mainland at 11am. On Wednesday, Saturday and Sunday, there's an additional service from Pulau Weh at 1.30pm, returning from Uleh Leh at 4pm.

The **Express Ferry** (☎ 0651-43791, 0652-332 4800; economy/executive/VIP 75,000/85,000/105,000Rp) runs from Pulau Weh to Uleh-leh at 8am and 2.30pm daily (45 minutes to one hour), with an additional service at 4pm Friday to Sunday in high season. Services from the mainland to Pulau Weh depart at 10am and 4pm, with the additional weekend service at 10am.

❶ Getting Around

There is no regular public bus service on the island, but from the Balohan port, a handful of *labi-labi* (minibuses) meet the boats and head to Sabang (25,000Rp, 15 minutes) and Gapang and Iboih (60,000Rp, 40 minutes). Becaks and taxis charge around 150,000Rp from the port to Gapang and Iboih, and 50,000Rp to Sabang. A taxi from Sumur Tiga to the airport is 35,000Rp; from Gapang/Iboih it's around 100,000Rp. Many lodgings rent out motorbikes for around 100,000Rp per day.

Bukit Lawang
☑ 061 / POP 30,000

Bukit Lawang, 96km northwest of Medan, is not so much a town as a sprawling tourist village laced along the fast-flowing Bohorok River and bordered by the dense jungle of Gunung Leuser National Park. Its legend is built around the orangutan rehabilitation centre set up here in 1973 and, although the feeding platform has closed, this is still the best place in Sumatra to spot semi-wild orangutans on a trek.

Trekking aside, it's a very traveller-friendly place where you can while away a few days lounging in hammocks, splashing or tubing in the river and enjoying some of the best-value jungle resorts in Sumatra.

☆ Activities

Treks into the Gunung Leuser National Park require a permit and guide and can last anywhere from three hours to several days. Most people opt for two days so they can spend the night in the jungle, which increases the likelihood of seeing orangutans and other wildlife. It's best to hike in the smallest group possible and to set off early. Take your time choosing a guide as jungle practices are not as regulated as they should be, and don't feel pressured to book a guide before you arrive in Bukit Lawang or as soon as you get off the bus. Guide rates are fixed by the Sumatra Guide Association (quoted in euros) and are based on a three-person minimum. A half-day trek is €35 per person, one-/two-/three-days costs €45/80/110.

Tubing on the fast-flowing Sungai Bohorok river is another popular activity. You can rent tubes along the riverside strip for 20,000Rp per day.

🛏 Sleeping & Eating

The further upriver you go, the more likely you are to spot wildlife from your porch hammock. Only a few guesthouses have hot water; some provide fans.

Most guesthouses have their own restaurants and serve beer.

★ Garden Inn GUESTHOUSE $
(☎ 0813 9600 0571; www.bukitlawang-garden-inn.com; r 150,000-350,000Rp; ☜) A popular backpacker choice, the ever-growing Garden Inn spreads over several buildings, from fabulous wooden jungle shacks to pristine, modern rooms. The excellent river-facing cafe is a sociable spot for swapping ape-spotting tales and singalongs with friendly staff.

Rainforest Guesthouse GUESTHOUSE $
(☎ 0813 62199018; www.rainforestguesthouse.com; d 50,000-200,000Rp; ☜) This cluster of wooden rooms set close to the gurgling river is built with backpackers in mind. Cheaper rooms have shared bathrooms, but pricier rooms come with bathrooms and fans. There's a little restaurant with river views and it's a super place to hook up with other budget travellers.

Green Hill GUESTHOUSE $
(☎ 0813 7034 9124; www.greenhillbukitlawang.com; d/tr/q 200,000/250,000/300,000Rp, d without bathroom 100,000Rp; ☜) 🗗 Run by an English conservation scientist and her Sumatran husband, Green Hill has three lovely stilt-high rooms ideal for couples and families, with en suite bamboo-shoot showers that afford stunning jungle views while you wash, as well as a budget room. Various conservation and volunteering programs can be arranged.

Sam's Bungalows GUESTHOUSE $
(☎ 0813 7009 3597; www.samsbukitlawang.com; r 150,000-300,000Rp; ☜) There's an excellent range of wooden tree houses here as well as more solidly built rooms painted in sunny Mediterranean colours. Rooms have four-poster bed, huge bathroom and Italian rain shower.

★ On the Rocks
BUNGALOW $$

(☑ 0812 6303 1119; www.ontherocksbl.com; r 200,000-500,000Rp; 🛜) More on the hill than on the rocks, the seven 'tribal' huts here verge on being luxurious in a rustic way. Each hut has a verandah and sunken bathroom, and all are shrouded in peace and beautiful views. It's across the river and a fair hike from the main strip, so it's a good thing the restaurant serves decent meals.

Jungle Hill
INDONESIAN $

(mains 17,000-50,000Rp, pizza 50,000-90,000Rp; ⊙ 8am-10pm; ✒) This chilled-out, family-run spot overlooking the river is good for chowing down on curry, *rendang* and sambal dishes. It's also one of the better pizza places on the strip.

Brown Bamboo Cafe
INDONESIAN $

(mains 22,000-50,000Rp; ⊙ 6am-10pm; 🛜) Next to the guides association office, Brown Bamboo is a good place to chill out and get some local information on arrival (come here if the office is closed). The menu runs from coconut curry to tacos and cold Bintang.

ℹ Information

There are no banks, but you'll find moneychangers along the strip in the nearby village of Gotong Royong. There's a BRI ATM in Bohorok town, 15km away.

The nearby village of Gotong Royong is where most facilities can be found. If you arrive by public bus it's about a 1km walk north to where the Bukit Lawang accommodation begins.

Bukit Lawang Guide Association (☑ 0813 7696 3787; ⊙ 7am-3pm) The yellow riverside building in the village doubles as the visitor centre, where you can pick up a town map and book guides. If it's closed, head next door to Brown Bamboo Cafe, owned by the head of the guides association.

ℹ Getting There & Away

Direct public buses go from Gotong Royong village to Medan's Pinang Baris bus terminal (30,000Rp, four hours, half-hourly) between 5.30am and 5pm. There are also tourist minibuses (120,000Rp, three hours, daily at 8am). For Berastagi, there's a daily public bus (50,000Rp, six to seven hours, 8am) and tourist minibus (170,000Rp, four to five hours, daily 8.30am). Tourist minibuses also go to Medan Airport (190,000Rp, around four hours, daily 8am) and Parapat (for Danau Toba; 230,000Rp, six hours, daily 8.30am).

Berastagi
☑ 0628 / POP 44,800

At 1300m, Berastagi is a cool mountain retreat and market town, established by colonial Dutch traders escaping the heat of sea-level Medan. Since it's only two hours out of Medan, it's still a popular weekend retreat, when main-street traffic almost comes to a standstill. For travellers the main attraction is climbing active volcano Mt Sibayak and exploring the surrounding Karo Highlands and villages.

⊙ Sights & Activities

★ Gunung Sibayak
VOLCANO

(4000Rp) At 2094m, Gunung Sibayak is one of Indonesia's most accessible volcanoes. A guide is only really essential if you're taking the route through the jungle, but if you're trekking alone it's still a good idea – a German tourist got lost and perished in 2017. The hike can be done in five hours return, and you should set out as early as possible. Guides can be booked at the tourist office and cost from 250,000Rp per person along the road, 320,000Rp through the jungle.

Lingga
VILLAGE

The most visited of the villages around Berastagi, Lingga, a few kilometres northwest of Kabanjahe, has just a couple of traditional houses with characteristic soaring thatched roofs topped with cattle horns. To get here, take a yellow KT minibus from Berastagi (7000Rp, 45 minutes). Some only go as far as Kabanjahe, so check first if you'll have to change.

🛏 Sleeping & Eating

Wisma Sibayak
GUESTHOUSE $

(☑ 0628-91104; Jl Udara 1; r 150,000Rp, without bathroom 60,000-80,000Rp; @ 🛜) Centrally located guesthouse with a prim old-school feel – there's a 10pm curfew and extra cost for hot showers – but the cheapest rooms really are cheap, and the better ones are clean and spacious.

Losmen Sibayak Guesthouse
GUESTHOUSE $

(☑ 0628-91122; dicksonpelawi@yahoo.com; Jl Veteran 119; r with/without bathroom from 100,000/75,000Rp; @ 🛜) Behind Sibayak Trans Tour & Travel, rooms here have a lot of Indonesian personality, making the place feel more like a homestay. The best rooms come with hot water. Wi-fi in the lobby.

Berastagi

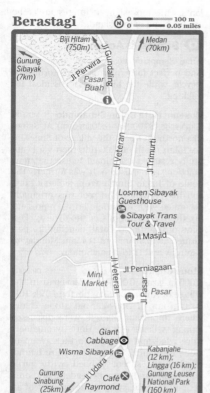

★ **Nachelle Homestay** HOMESTAY $$
(☑ 0813 6242 9977, 0821 6275 7658; nachelle-homestay@gmail.com; Jl Veteran; r 280,000-400,000Rp, without bathroom 220,000Rp; 🛜) By far the most traveller-friendly place in Berastagi is run by Mery and Abdy, who speak excellent English and will issue you with a map. Rooms are super-clean and comfortable and there are plans to create appealing common areas, including the rooftop terrace which has views of Sinabung. It's set back from the main road; call for directions.

Café Raymond INTERNATIONAL $
(Jl Trimurti; mains 12,000-30,000Rp; ⊗ 7am-midnight; 🛜) Berastagi's local bohemians hang out at tiny Café Raymond, which serves fruit juices, beer and a mix of Indonesian and Western food, with a few Indian dishes thrown in for good measure. Ask here about shared cars to Bukit Lawang, Medan and Lake Toba.

Biji Hitam COFFEE
(Jl Kolem Renang; coffee 12,000-25,000Rp; ⊗ 1pm-midnight Tue-Thu, Sat & Sun, 2pm-midnight Fri) Pull up a rugged bar stool and enjoy a strong coffee and the hum of locals in conversation. Plenty of choice, from espresso to Nutella latte, along with several types of tea and bar snacks.

ⓘ Information

Tourist Information Centre (☑ 0628-91084; Jl Gundaling 1; ⊗ 7.30am-6pm) Has maps and can arrange trekking guides, day tours and private transport to Medan, Danau Toba and Kutacane.

A good place for almost any onward travel advice as well as local tours is **Sibayak Trans Tour & Travel** (☑ 0628-91122; dicksonpelawi@yahoo.com; Jl Veteran 119; ⊗ 7am-10pm).

ⓘ Getting There & Away

The **bus terminal** (Jl Veteran) is conveniently located in the town centre. Long-distance buses pass through Berastagi en route to Kabanjahe, the local hub. You can catch buses to Medan's Padang Bulan (15,000Rp, three to four hours) anywhere along the main street between 6am and 8pm.

The cheapest way to reach Danau Toba is to catch an *angkot* to Kabanjahe (5000Rp, 20 minutes), change to a bus for Pematangsiantar (30,000Rp, three hours), then connect with a Parapat-bound bus (15,000Rp, 1½ hours). For Bukit Lawang, take a bus to Medan's Pinang Baris (15,000Rp, two hours) and change for Bukit Lawang (30,000Rp, three hours). Berastagi is the southern approach for visits to Gunung Leuser National Park; catch a bus to Kutacane.

Several private companies run a shared minibus or car service, connecting Berastagi to Bukit Lawang (150,000Rp, three to four hours), Danau Toba (to Parapat; 150,000Rp, 3½ to four hours), Medan's Padang Bulan (100,000Rp, 2½ hours) and Medan airport (150,000Rp, three hours).

Danau Toba

☑ 0625

Danau Toba has been part of traveller folklore for decades. This grand ocean-blue lake, found up among Sumatra's volcanic peaks, is where the amiable Christian Batak people reside. The secret of this almost mythical place was opened up by intrepid travellers years ago but these days Tuk Tuk – the knobby village on the lake's inner island – is well on the beaten Sumatran overland path and still one of the undisputed highlights of central Sumatra.

Danau Toba is the largest lake in Southeast Asia, covering a massive 1707 sq km. In the middle of this huge expanse is Pulau Samosir, a wedge-shaped island almost as big as Singapore that was created by an eruption between 30,000 and 75,000 years ago. In fact, Samosir isn't actually an island at all. It's linked to the mainland by a narrow isthmus at the town of Pangururan – and then cut again by a canal.

Parapat

The mainland departure point for Danau Toba, Parapat is a cramped lakeside town with a handful of hotels, restaurants and travel agents that seem designed only to trap wayward travellers on their way to or from Samosir Island. Unless you get here too late to catch a boat to Tuk Tuk, there's no reason to overnight here.

The commercial sector of the town is clumped along the Trans-Sumatran Hwy (Jl SM Raja) and has banks, ATMs and plenty of basic eateries. Most buses pick up and drop off passengers at ticket agents along the highway or at the pier.

❶ Getting There & Away

The **bus terminal** (Jl SM Raja) is about 2km east of town on the way to Bukittinggi, but it's infrequently used by travellers. From here you could, however, make your way by public bus to Berastagi (48,000Rp, with two changes), Medan (35,000Rp, five to six hours) and Sibolga (70,000Rp, seven hours).

PT Bagus Holiday (☎ 0813 9638 0170) is one of several operators next to the ferry pier that arranges tourist minibuses and car transfers to the most popular destinations. Don't think these are quick trips though – the long-distance journeys are longer and more cramped than equivalent bus journeys. Tourist minibuses go to Berastagi (150,000Rp, three hours), Bukittinggi (350,000Rp, 19 hours), Bukit Lawang (200,000Rp, six hours), Medan (100,000Rp, four hours), Padang (400,000, 18 hours) and Sibolga (150,000Rp, six hours).

If you're heading as far as Padang, seriously consider a minibus back to Medan airport and a cheap flight from there.

Pulau Samosir

The large island in the middle of Toba is where everyone is headed. The village of Tuk Tuk, where the ferry arrives, has plentiful waterfront guesthouses and restaurants, while most sights of interest are at the northern end of the island.

◉ Sights & Activities

Pulau Samosir's sleepy roads make the island perfect for exploring by motorbike or bicycle, while the hilly interior is ideal for trekking.

Museum Huta Bolon Simanindo MUSEUM
(Simanindo; 50,000Rp; ⊙10am-5pm) At Samosir's northern tip, in the village of Simanindo, 15km north of Tuk Tuk, there's a beautifully restored traditional house that now functions as a museum. It was formerly the home of Rajah Simalungun, a Batak king, and his 14 wives. The roof was originally decorated with 10 buffalo horns, representing the 10 generations of the dynasty. Displays of traditional Batak dancing are performed at 10.30am and 11.45am Monday to Saturday and 11.45am on Sunday.

Stone Chairs HISTORIC SITE
(3000Rp, guide 50,000Rp; ⊙8am-6pm) In the village of Ambarita, 5km north of Tuk Tuk, is a group of 300-year-old stone chairs where important matters were discussed among village elders. Here wrongdoers were tried and led to a further group of stone furnishings where they were bound, blindfolded, sliced, rubbed with garlic and chilli, and then beheaded. Rumours abound that the story is the product of an overactive imagination and that the chairs are just 60 years old. There are eight Batak houses here.

King Sidabutar Grave HISTORIC SITE
(Tomok; by donation; ⊙dawn-dusk) The Batak king who adopted Christianity is buried in Tomok village, 5km southeast of Tuk Tuk. The king's image is carved on his tombstone, along with those of his bodyguard and Anteng Melila Senega, the woman the king is said to have loved for many years without fulfilment. The tomb is also decorated with carvings of *singa* (mythical creatures with grotesque three-horned heads and bulging eyes).

🛏 Sleeping

⭐**Liberta Homestay** GUESTHOUSE $
(☎0625-451035; liberta_homestay@yahoo.com.co.id; r 66,000-88,000Rp, without bathroom 44,000Rp; 🛜) This backpacker fave close to the ferry dock has limited lake views, but a chill universe is created by a lush garden

Danau Toba

INDONESIA DANAU TOBA

and arty versions of traditional Batak houses. Crawling around the garden paths, balconies and shortened doors of the rooms is cool, there's a good cafe and the popular Mr Moon is a great source of travel information.

Gokhon Guesthouse   GUESTHOUSE $
(☑0852 6169 1642; d 200,000Rp; 🛜) This friendly double-storey waterfront place is one of several simple, clean guesthouses along this strip. Walk out from your veranda to a lawn area and enjoy the views. Ask at the Gokhon Library across the road.

Bagus Bay Homestay   GUESTHOUSE $
(☑0823 6822 9003, 0625-451287; www.bagus-bay.com; Tuk Tuk; s/d without bathroom from 60,000/75,000Rp; d 150,000-300,000Rp; 🛜) Rooms in traditional Batak houses overlook avocado trees, a children's playground and a volleyball court at this excellent budget resort. The more expensive rooms (and shared bathrooms) come with hot water, lake views

and pot plants that add a nice green touch. At night its restaurant, which has frequent film evenings, is a lively spot for travellers to congregate.

Danau Toba

🛏 Sleeping
1	Bagus Bay Homestay	C2
2	Gokhon Guesthouse	D1
3	Liberta Homestay	C2
4	Tabo Cottages	C2

🍽 Eating
5	Jenny's Restaurant	C1
6	Juwita Cafe	D2
	Today's Cafe	(see 6)

🍷 Drinking & Nightlife
7	Brando's Blues Bar	C1

🎭 Entertainment
8	Roy's Pub	D2

WORTH A TRIP

PULAU NIAS

The Indian Ocean roars on to Indonesia, arriving in one of the world's most spectacular surf breaks here on remote Pulau Nias: a sizeable but solitary rock off the northern Sumatran coast. Surfers have been coming here for decades for the waves on superb Teluk Sorake, which has deservedly kept this far-flung island on the international surfing circuit.

For nonsurfers the island also has much to offer: the traditional hill villages, such as **Tundrumbaho** and **Bawomataluo**, will captivate even casual cultural tourists as well as ethno-architectural buffs. The waves of Teluk Lagundri (or more correctly Pantai Sorake), on the southwest corner of the island, are best between April and October. On smaller days it's a fairly accessible wave for all but total beginners, but as soon as the swell starts to pick up, it becomes an experts-only barrel machine. The point here is lined by a string of basic and almost identical losmen. The going rate is about 100,000Rp per night, but you're expected to eat at your losmen, too. The owner of **Lagundri Beach House** (☑0813 9656 7202; r 200,000-300,000Rp; ✳🔊) can arrange local tours.

These days most travellers fly to Nias' Bimaka airport from Medan or Padang but there are still regular ferries from the mainland port of Sibolga. Ferries run daily except Sunday from Sibolga to Gunung Sitoli (economy/VIP 100,000/120,000Rp, 11 to 13 hours) and twice-weekly to Teluk Dam (economy/VIP 100,000/150,000Rp, 12 to 14 hours) in the south of Nias (which is much closer to the surf).

★ **Tabo Cottages**　　　　BUNGALOW **$$**
(☑0625-451318; www.tabocottages.com; r incl breakfast 390,000-490,000Rp, cottage 680,000-750,000Rp; ✳@🔊⛴) The swankiest accommodation on the island, this German-run lakeside place has beautiful traditional-style Batak houses, with huge bathrooms and hammocks and a superb lakefront pool. Owner Annette is a treasure trove of information on Batak culture, and the homemade bread and cakes at the attached German Bakery are worth a stop.

✖ Eating

★ **Jenny's Restaurant**　　　INTERNATIONAL **$**
(Tuk Tuk; mains 30,000-65,000Rp; ☺8am-10pm) Jenny's has long been a standout on the northern edge of Tuk Tuk, with all kinds of breakfasts, noodles, curries and rice dishes. But the one dish that really shines is the lake fish grilled right in front of you and served with chips and salad. Follow it up with the generously portioned fruit pancake.

Today's Cafe　　　　　INTERNATIONAL **$**
(Tuk Tuk; mains 30,000-70,000Rp; ☺8am-10pm; 🔊☑) This little wooden shack has a laid-back vibe in keeping with Tuk Tuk life. It's run by a couple of friendly ladies who whip up some fabulous and eclectic dishes such as *sak sang* (chopped pork with brown coconut sauce, cream and a wealth of spices), aubergine curry and chapatis with guacamole. Homemade yoghurt is a hit for breakfast.

Juwita Cafe　　　　　　INDONESIAN **$**
(☑0625-451217; mains 20,000-45,000Rp; ☺8am-10pm; 🔊) This cosy lakefront family restaurant and garden does Batak and other Indonesian dishes extremely well. Friendly matriarch Heddy also hosts cooking courses (one-/two-/three dishes 250,000/325,000/350,000Rp). Book a day in advance.

🍺 Drinking & Entertainment

Brando's Blues Bar　　　　　　BAR
(☑0625-451084; Tuk Tuk; ☺noon-late) One of a handful of genuine bars with pool tables and occasional live bands that gets particularly lively on weekends. Happy hour is a civilised 6pm to 10pm and you can take to the small dance floor during the reggae and house sets.

Roy's Pub　　　　　　LIVE MUSIC
(☑0821 7417 4576; Tuk Tuk; ☺9pm-1am Sat, Tue & Thu) The best night out on Samosir, Roy's has live music (normally local rock bands) on Tuesday, Thursday and Saturday nights in a graffiti-splattered building with a dancing vibe. Great, alcohol-fuelled fun.

❶ Information

There are BRI ATMs in **Ambarita** (Ambarita; ☺24hr), Tomok and Panguruan, but they may not accept all foreign cards. The nearest BNI ATM is at Parapat – bring cash as exchange rates at the island's hotels and moneychangers are pretty awful.

ℹ Getting There & Away

BOAT

Ferries between Parapat and Tuk Tuk (15,000Rp, 11 daily) operate about every hour from 8.30am to 7pm. Ferries stop at Bagus Bay (35 minutes), then continue north stopping on request. The first and last ferries from Tuk Tuk leave at 7am and 5.30pm respectively; check exact times with your lodgings. When leaving for Parapat, stand on your hotel jetty and wave a ferry down. Fourteen ferries a day shuttle motorbikes and people between Parapat and Tomok (10,000Rp), from 7am to 7pm.

BUS

To get to Berastagi from Samosir via public bus, catch a bus from Tomok to Pangururan (15,000Rp, 45 minutes), then take another bus to Berastagi (50,000Rp, three hours). This bus goes via Sidikalang, which is also a transfer point to Kutacane. Most guesthouses and travel agencies can prebook the pricier, direct shared minibus tickets from Parapat for you.

ℹ Getting Around

Local buses serve the whole of Samosir except Tuk Tuk. Minibuses run between Tomok and Ambarita (5000Rp), continuing to Simanindo (10,000Rp) and Pangururan (15,000Rp); flag them down on the main road. Services dry up after 5pm. The peaceful, generally well-maintained (yet narrow) island roads are good for travelling by motorbike (80,000Rp to 100,000Rp per day) or bicycle (30,000Rp per day), both easily rented in Tuk Tuk.

Bukittinggi

📞 0752 / POP 117,000

The market town of Bukittinggi sits high above the valley mists as three sentinels – fire-breathing Merapi, benign Singgalang and distant Sago – all look on impassively. Sun-ripened crops grow large in the rich volcanic soil, *bendis* (two-person horse-drawn carts) haul goods to the *pasa* (market), and the muezzin's call is heard through the town. Modern life seems far removed – until 9am – then the traffic starts up, and there's soon a mile-long jam around the bus terminal. The air turns the colour of diesel and the mosques counter the traffic by cranking up their amps. Such is the incongruity of modern Bukittinggi, blessed by nature, choked by mortals. Still, it's a popular traveller base on the road between Padang and Danua Toba and, at 930m above sea level, refreshingly temperate all year round.

👁 Sights

Local tours fall into two categories – culture and nature – and can range from a half-day meander through neighbouring villages to a three-day jungle trek to Danau Maninjau, or an overnight assault on Gunung Merapi.

Full-day tours start at around 150,000Rp per person (minimum 300,000Rp). Some tours have a minimum quota, though some guides and agencies also run solo tours by motorbike. If approached by a freelance guide, be clear about what you want, and what is and isn't included.

Try **Armando** (📞 0812 674 1852; arisna_sejati@yahoo.co.id; day tour 300,000Rp) or **Roni's Tours** (📞 0812 675 0688; www.ronistours.com; Jl Teuku Umar, Orchid Hotel).

Taman Panorama (Panorama Park; Jl Panorama; 20,000Rp; ⏰ 7.30am-5.30pm), on the southern edge of town, overlooks the deep **Ngarai Sianok** (Sianok Canyon), where fruit bats swoop at sunset. Friendly guides will approach visitors to lead you through **Gua Jepang** (Japanese Caves), wartime defensive tunnels built by Japanese slave labour; settle on a price (around 30,000Rp) before continuing. Another path gives you access to the **Koto Gadang** (Great Wall), a cheesy scaled-down Great Wall of China.

🛏 Sleeping & Eating

⭐ **Hello Guesthouse**   GUESTHOUSE $
(📞 0752-21542; www.helloguesthouse.net; Jl Teuku Umar 6B; dm/s/d/f from 75,000/150,000/175,000/350,000Rp; 📶) This bright and modern guesthouse is run by thoughtful owner Ling, who understands the needs of budget travellers. She is happy to provide maps of town, has displays on town attractions, and has fitted the town rooms with super-comfy mattresses and hot-water showers. Earplugs (10,000Rp) are available to counter the nearby mosque. It's often full so book ahead.

Orchid Hotel   HOTEL $
(📞 0752-32634; roni_orchid@hotmail.com; Jl Teuku Umar 11; r 150,000-180,000Rp; 📶) This popular budget inn has a good travel desk, helpful staff and a sociable downstairs space. Rooms on three levels are pretty basic but all have attached bathrooms and the more expensive ones come with hot water.

Rajawali Homestay   HOMESTAY $
(📞 0752-31095; ulrich.rudolph@web.de; Jl Ahmad Yani 152; r 80,000Rp) The eight rooms at this friendly but basic homestay come with

Bukittinggi

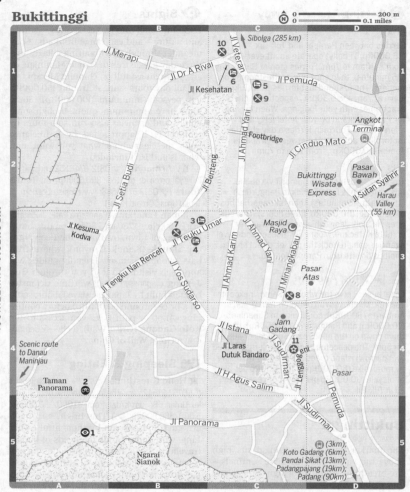

Bukittinggi

⊙ Sights
1 Gua Jepang A5
2 Taman Panorama A4

✦ Activities, Courses & Tours
    Roni's Tours ....(see 4)

🛏 Sleeping
3 Hello Guesthouse B3
4 Orchid Hotel B3
5 Rajawali Homestay C1
6 Treeli Hotel C1

✗ Eating
7 De Kock Cafe B3
8 Simpang Raya C3
9 Turret Cafe C1
10 Waroeng Jalal Spesifik
    Sambal C1

✪ Entertainment
11 Gedung Medan Nan
    Balinduang C4

Indonesian bathrooms and creaky beds. Owner Ulrich is a good source of local (and regional) information.

★ Treeli Hotel BOUTIQUE HOTEL $$
(☑0752-625350; treeliboutiquehotel@gmail.com; Jl Kesehatan 36A; d incl breakfast 350,000-790,000Rp; ❄️ 🛜) An excellent addition to Bukittinggi's rather tired midrange bunch, contemporary Treeli gets a lot of things right. Rooms are compact and quiet, with modern bathrooms and all sorts of mod cons. An excellent breakfast is served on the breezy roof terrace and the restaurant specialises in Chinese-style seafood dishes.

De Kock Cafe INTERNATIONAL $
(☑0821 7492 9888; www.dekock.id; Jl Teuku Umar 18; mains 15,000-50,000Rp; ⊗7am-midnight; 🛜) De Kock (cannon) serves a fine mixture of Western and Indonesian dishes in arty, stone-walled surroundings. Baked potatoes, steak and pizza are some of the comfort-food offerings, along with good breakfast fare. Live music on Saturday.

Waroeng Jalal Spesifik Sambal INDONESIAN $
(Jl Kesehatan; mains 12,000-25,000Rp; ⊗11am-10pm; 🛜🅿️) Fans of spicy dishes will love this shady garden warung specialising mostly in sambal dishes. Squid, prawns, chicken, tofu, tempeh and aubergine are all cooked in a rich, fiery chilli sauce, with *kangkung* (water spinach) providing a mild accompaniment. The beer may well be Bukittinggi's coldest.

Turret Cafe CAFE $
(Jl Ahmad Yani 140-142; mains 25,000-60,000Rp; ⊗9am-10pm; 🛜) This Bukittinggi standby offers a smattering of Western dishes with the odd inclusion of *mie goreng* (fried noodles), beef *rendang* and green curry, cold beer and the best guacamole in town.

Simpang Raya INDONESIAN $
(Jl Minangkabau; meals around 50,000Rp; ⊗11am-10pm) The best place in town to sample the famous Padang cuisine. The usual array of spicy, flavourful dishes is on display, with a particularly savoury *rendang* (beef coconut curry). Just ask for the assortment of what's on offer.

☆ Entertainment

Gedung Medan Nan Balinduang DANCE
(Jl Lenggogeni; tickets 70,000Rp; ⊗8.30pm) Medan Nan Balinduang presents one-hour Minangkabau dance performances. It's usually at night but check with your lodgings for the latest schedule.

ℹ️ Information

Guesthouses on Jl Teuku Umar are a good source of tour information and minibus bookings.

ℹ️ Getting There & Away

The chaos of the main bus terminal, Aur Kuning, 3km south of town can be reached by *angkot* (3000Rp) or *ojek* (15,000Rp); ask for 'terminal'. Heading to central Bukittinggi on arrival ask for 'Kampung China'.

The main bus terminal is useful for some bus departures but not all. Minibuses to Sibolga (200,000Rp, 12 hours) depart from offices on Jl Veteran as do minibuses to Parapat (350,000Rp, 18 hours); scheduled door-to-door transfers to Padang (70,000Rp, three hours) are more convenient than waiting for a bus at the terminal. Most lodgings can point you in the right direction and assist with booking passage.

The best way to get to Dumai – for ferries to Melaka and Kuala Lumpur in Malaysia – is with **BWE Travel** (BWE; ☑0752-625139, 0752-625140; Jl Pemuda 81). Minibuses leave Bukittinggi nightly at 8pm (160,000Rp, nine hours), to link with the ferry from Dumai to Batam (332,000Rp, 6am) and Melaka (335,000Rp, 10am). Prebooking is required. BWE can also book the ferry; you'll need to drop in the day before departure with your passport.

ℹ️ Getting Around

Angkot around town cost 3000Rp. *Bendi* rides start from 20,000Rp; bargain hard. An *ojek* from the bus terminal to the hotels costs 15,000Rp and a taxi costs 30,000Rp but takes up to 30 minutes. Transfers to Padang airport can be arranged by any travel agent for around 60,000Rp. A private taxi to Padang airport is around 300,000Rp. Some guesthouses hire mopeds for 75,000Rp per day, or contact **Roni's Tours** (p273) at Orchid Hotel.

Danau Maninjau
☑0752

The first glimpse of this perfectly formed volcanic lake sucks your breath away as you lurch over the caldera lip and hurtle towards the first of the 44 (numbered) hairpin bends down to the lakeshore. Monkeys watch your progress from the crash barriers as the road takes you down from the lush rainforest of the highlands to the ever-expanding farms and paddies of the lowlands.

When the traveller tide receded from Bukittinggi, Danau Maninjau was left high and dry. The locals looked to more sustainable sources of income and aquaculture to fill the void. Fish farms now dot the lake foreshore, outnumbering tourists.

The lake is 460m above sea level and encircled by a 60km road. Most places of interest spread out north from Maninjau village to Bayur (3.5km) and beyond. If coming by bus, tell the conductor where you're staying and you'll be dropped off at the right spot. Swimming and canoeing in the lake (warmed by subterranean springs) are still the main drawcards but there are plenty of other options.

The caldera, covered in rainforest that hides waterfalls and traditional villages, is a hiker's dream. Hike to the rim from Bayur, or cheat by catching the bus up the hill to Matur, then walking back down via the lookout at **Puncak Lawang**. Check out the map at Beach Guest House for more good trekking information.

It takes roughly three hours to circumnavigate the lake on a moped. Beach Guest House organises both guided hikes and motorbike tours.

🛏 Sleeping & Eating

⭐ **Beach Guest House**   GUESTHOUSE $
(☑ 0752-861799, 0813 6379 7005; www.beachguesthousemaninjau.com; Jl Raya Maninjau; dm 45,000Rp, d 85,000-150,000Rp; 🛜) Run by a friendly, energetic local couple, this hostel and cafe is Danau Maninjau's bona fide traveller central. Bunk in the four-bed dorm or go for one of the lakefront rooms with private bathroom and hot showers. Owners organise excursions, from round-the-lake bicycle or motorbike jaunts to hiking the caldera (seven hours).

Muaro Beach Bungalows   BUNGALOW $$
(☑ 0813 3924 0042, 0752-61189; neni967@yahoo.com; Jl Muaro Pisang 53, Maninjau; r 180,000-300,000Rp; 🛜) Down a maze of footpaths about 300m northwest of the main intersection, these beachfront bungalows are a good deal in central Maninjau. The small beach area is (almost) free of aquaculture, and there's a good restaurant.

⭐ **Waterfront Zalino**   INDONESIAN $$
(☑ 0815 3454 6280; mains 30,000-85,000Rp; ⊙ 8am-9pm; 🛜) A great lakeside location showcases some exotic local specialities such as *dendeng kijang balado* (fried deer with chilli and red pepper), *udang* (freshwater lake shrimp) and grilled catfish. Zal – AKA 'Mr Porcupine' – is the deer hunter and can take you trekking. It's around 1km north of Maninjau's main intersection.

ℹ Getting There & Around

Buses run hourly between Maninjau and Bukittinggi (20,000Rp, 1¾ hours). Taxis from Bukittinggi start from 160,000Rp.

Rent mountain bikes (per day 45,000Rp), motorcycles (per day 100,000Rp) and canoes (per day 40,000Rp) from **Beach Guest House** or **Waterfront Zalino**.

Minibuses (3000Rp) travel the lake road during daylight hours. An *ojek* from the intersection to Bayur will cost around 10,000Rp.

Padang

🗐 0751 / POP 1 MILLION

Padang is an urban-Indonesian sprawl sandwiched between the Indian Ocean and the Minangkabau hills. It is to West Sumatra what Medan is to the North (but with better scenery) – a handy transport hub with air, boat and road connections to major regional attractions, including Mentawai islands, Bukittinggi, Danau Maninjau and the Kerinci Highlands. Due to the sheer volume of backpacker and surfer traffic passing through, it also has an above-average amount of good budget accommodation and an excellent dining scene, with regional food the most globally famous of Indonesian culinary offerings.

Padang sits astride one of the planet's most powerful seismic zones, centrally located on the tectonic hotspot where the Indo-Australian plate plunges under the Eurasian plate. Significant tremors occur on an almost annual basis, the most recent being in 2012.

⊙ Sights & Activities

Colonial Quarter   AREA
Although damaged in the 2009 earthquake, Padang's colonial-era quarter around Jl Batang Arau is still worth a lazy stroll. Old Dutch and Chinese warehouses back on to a river brimming with fishing boats. The beach along Jl Samudera is the best place to watch the sunset.

Adityawarman Museum   MUSEUM
(☑ 0751-31523; Jl Diponegoro 10; adult/child 3000/2500Rp; ⊙ 8am-4pm Tue-Sun) Adityawarman Museum, built in the Minangkabau tradition, has pleasant grounds and the exhibits are a thorough introduction to everyday Minangkabau life. A healthy imagination helps, since the exhibits are in Bahasa Indonesia. The entrance is on Jl Gereja.

Padang

INDONESIA PADANG

Padang

◉ Sights

1	Adityawarman Museum	B2
2	Colonial Quarter	C4

✪ Activities, Courses & Tours

3	Sumatran Surfariis	C3

🛏 Sleeping

4	Brigitte's House	B4
5	Golden Homestay	A3
6	New House Padang	B3
7	Riverside Hostel	B4
8	Yani's Homestay	A4

◆ Eating

9	Beach Safari	A2
10	Hoya Bakery	B3
11	Pagi Sore	C3
12	Pondok Indah Jaya	C3
13	Safari Garden	B4
14	Sari Raso	C2
15	Simpang Raya	B2

◉ Drinking & Nightlife

16	Bat & Arrow	C4

★ Regina Adventures   TOURS, SURFING
(☑ 0751-781 0835, 0812 6774 5464; www.regi-naadventures.com; Jl Pampangan 54; 8-day Mentawai surf packages per person from US$515) Reliable local operator Elvis offers trekking and surfing on the Mentawai Islands, boat charters, trips to Danau Maninjau and Bukittinggi, and ascents of Gunung Merapi and Gunung Kerinci. Check the website for good-value surf trips to Mentawai and Krui further south.

🛏 Sleeping

★ New House Padang
GUESTHOUSE **$**

(📞 0751-25982; https://newhousepadang.com; Jl HOS Cokroaminoto 104; dm/s/d from 100,000 /125,000/250,000Rp, d with bathroom 330,000Rp; ❄🛜) This friendly and relaxed six-room guesthouse is the perfect mix of budget with style. A compact Zen garden combines with colourful rooms (some with terrace), contemporary artwork and a vast common area. Shared bathrooms are spotless and have hot water. The owners are on hand to advise about surfing and onward travel.

Riverside Hostel
HOSTEL **$**

(dm 125,000-145,000Rp, d 270,000Rp; ❄🛜) This new hostel, down a lane near the boat dock, has three spacious boutique rooms with lots of polished timber, a huge country-style kitchen and a comfy lounge. Friendly owners are just getting established but it's a cut above most backpacker places.

MENTAWAI ISLANDS

It was surfing that put the Mentawais on the tourism radar: nowhere else on earth has such a dense concentration of world-class surf spots in such a small area. Today, dozens of wave-hunting liveaboards run from Padang harbour year-round and a growing number of dedicated surf camps populate the banner spots. Surfing is big business here year-round, but the season peaks between April and October. Like many Indonesian surf areas, the Mentawais are not suitable for learners. The waves, which break over shallow reefs, tend to be fast, hollow, heavy and unforgiving.

Note that in 2016 the Mentawai government introduced a 'retribution' tax on visiting surfers, with proceeds to be directed to local communities. Surfers now pay 1,000,000Rp (around AUD\$100) for up to 15 days, or 100,000Rp per day for short stayers. Most surf-tour companies can arrange payment.

The most consistent cluster of waves is in the Playground area, but things can get rather crowded during peak season. **Bintang Surf Camp** (📞 0812 6617 4454; www.bintangsurfcamp.com; Pulau Masokut; per person incl meals 460,000Rp) is the best of the local budget lot, with basic thatched huts and shared rooms.

It's not just surfers who come out here; more and more ecotourists are also braving the rugged ocean crossing and muddy jungle of this remote archipelago to trek, glimpse traditional tribal culture and spot endemic primates. The economic, and culturally responsible, choice for touring is to take a public boat to Siberut and seek out a Mentawai guide. You pay less and directly benefit the community you've come to experience. As far as surfing tours go, the vast majority of surfers pre-arrange boat charters or surf camp accommodation with a surf travel company in their home country. These are ideal if all you want to do is get off a plane and surf your guts out. However, it's a real bubble-like existence and the only Indonesians you're actually likely to meet will be your boat crew. If you've got lots of time then it's perfectly possible, and much closer to the true spirit of old-school surf travel, to take the public ferry out to the islands and once there arrange local boat transport and accommodation in one of the cheap and simple losmen that can be found close to many of the breaks.

Getting There & Away

Twelve-seater **Susi Air** (www.susiair.com) planes link Padang to Rokot airport on Pulau Sipora, but flights are unreliable.

Most independent travellers use the 200-seater speedboat, **Mentawai Fast** (📞 0751-893489; www.mentawaifast.com; one-way from 295,000Rp, surfboard 230,000-690,000Rp) from Padang. There are also ferries that make the overnight journey from the Sumatran mainland to the islands; they leave from the Teluk Kabang port at Bungus, around 20km south of Padang, and take around 10 to 12 hours, depending on sea conditions. In Padang, ferry operators to the Mentawais include Ambu Ambu and Gambolo. Fares range from 50,000Rp to 180,000Rp, depending upon route and travel class. Tickets can be booked through most surfer-friendly homestays, as well as tour agencies such as **Sumatran Surfariis** (📞 0751-34878; www.sumatransurfariis.com; Komplek Pondok Indah B 12, Parak Gadang).

SOUTHERN SUMATRA

Aside from Krakatau and the ferry crossing to Java, southern Sumatra is something of a blank on the backpacker map, but the region holds a few enticing little secrets for intrepid travellers. Chief among these are the wild forests and swamps of the **Way Kambas National Park** to the northeast of Bandarlampung. It's home to very endangered elephants, rhinos and tigers. If sun, sand and surf is more your thing, the laid-back village of **Krui** has your name all over it. Five hours' drive from Bandarlampung, Krui has recently gained a serious name for itself among travelling surfers thanks to a coastline littered with world-class spots (many of them not beginner-friendly).

The main city in the south is Bandarlampung. There's nothing much to see here but if you need to stay try the **Grand Citihub Hotel @Kartini** (☑0721-240420; www.citihub-hotels.com; Jl Kartini 41; r 315,000-385,000Rp; ☺❈☎). The most convenient bus service from here to Java is the **Damri** (☑0751-780 6335) bus-boat-bus combination ticket to Jakarta (200,000Rp, eight to 10 hours). Buses leave from Bandarlampung's train station at 9am, 10am, 8pm and 9pm. Heading north through Sumatra there are a number of buses to Padang, Medan or elsewhere – all very long bus rides.

Yani's Homestay
HOMESTAY $

(☑0852 6380 1686; yuliuz.caesar@gmail.com; Jl Nipah 1; d 90,000Rp, r 150,000-180,000Rp; ❈☎) Run by friendly young owner Yuliuz, this central homestay provides bona fide backpacker digs in the form of an air-con dorm with lockers and rooms with colourful bedspreads. The best rooms have private bathroom. Motorbikes for rent (60,000Rp per day).

Brigitte's House
HOSTEL $

(☑0813 7425 7162; https://brigitteshousepadang.com; Jl Kampung Sebalah 1/14; dm/s/d from 95,000/100,000/250,000Rp, d with air-con 250,000-330,000Rp; ❈☎) Down a backstreet just off Jl Nipah, Brigitte's is a great backpacker pad with relaxed ambience and chilled lounge and kitchen areas. The singles are pokey but the doubles and dorms are spacious, while the air-con rooms are in a separate apartment building a block away. Brigitte is a treasure trove of information on buses, ferries and Mentawai adventures.

Golden Homestay
HOMESTAY $

(☑0821 7438 8002; Jl Nipah Berok 1B; r without/with bathroom from 150,000/275,000Rp; ❈☎) More midrange hotel than homestay – but at an affordable price – the rooms here are very clean with comfortable beds, air-con and hot water. If you've been roughing it for a while, splash out on one of the three spacious rooms with private bath – room 1 has a massive bathroom with corner bathtub.

✗ Eating & Drinking

Padang is the mother of the cuisine that migrated across Indonesia. Pay homage to the native cooks by visiting a famous franchise: **Pagi Sore** (☑0751-32490; Jl Pondok 143; dishes from 9000Rp; ☺11am-10pm), **Sari Raso** (☑0751-33498; Jl Karya 3; dishes from 10,000Rp; ☺10am-9pm) and **Simpang Raya** (Jl Bundo Kandung; dishes from 8000Rp; ☺10am-9pm).

Cheap warungs on Jl Batang Arau spring to life at night, while discerning foodies visit Jl Pondok and Jl HOS Cokroaminoto. Beachfront shacks lining Jl Sumadera have cheap *sate,* grilled seafood and cold Bintangs at sunset.

Hoya Bakery
BAKERY $

(☑0751-27540; Jl HOS Cokroaminoto 48; pastries from 8000Rp, mains 15,000-30,000Rp; ☺8am-10pm) Padang's go-to spot for freshly baked sweet and savoury goodies. Friendly shop assistants will guide you around the selection before steering you to a colourful table. There are also good burgers, sandwiches and pasta, and the juices and smoothies are soothing antidotes to Padang's tropical buzz.

Pondok Indah Jaya
INDONESIAN $

(Jl Niaga 138; meals around 40,000Rp; ☺9am-9pm) This warung is an excellent intro to Padang cuisine; staff will talk you through the selection of dishes including spicy tofu, beef *rendang, ayam* sambal and tempe. Cool the fire in your mouth with some *sirsak* (soursop), cucumber or mango juice.

★ Safari Garden
STEAK $$

(☑0751-36055; http://safarigarden.net; Jl Nipah 21; mains 30,000-315,000Rp; ☺10am-midnight Mon-Fri, to 1am Sat & Sun; ☎) This stylish, convivial steakhouse with exposed brick walls and rustic log-lined booths is a fine place for a splurge or just good coffee. The speciality is Wagyu beef steaks (from 200,000Rp) but there's a big menu of Western, Japanese, Indonesian and seafood dishes.

It's a newer sibling to **Beach Safari** (Jl Samudera 16; mains 50,000-350,000Rp; ⊙4-10pm; 🛜) restaurant.

★ Bat & Arrow PUB

(Jl Batang Arau; ⊙2pm-midnight; 🛜) Overlooking the river in the colonial quarter, this barn-sized pub and live-music venue is Padang's top traveller hangout. The beer garden fills up nightly with surfers, backpackers and locals. Pizzas and bar snacks available.

ℹ Information

Padang Imigrasi Office (🖉 0751-705 5113; http://imigrasipadang.com; Jl Khatib Sulaiman 50; ⊙8am-4pm Mon-Fri) 30-day visa extensions can be obtained for US$35. It's about 5km north of the centre.

Tourism Padang (🖉 0751-34186; Dinas Kebudayaan Dan Pariwisata, Jl Samudera 1; ⊙8am-4pm) This little hut near the beach is not always staffed but has maps of town and a few English-language regional brochures.

ℹ Getting There & Away

AIR

Padang's airport, **Bandara Internasional Minangkabau** (BIM; Jl Adinegoro), is 20km north of town.

BUS

Tranex (🖉 0751-705 8577) buses depart for Bukittinggi (30,000Rp) from the city's northern fringes, outside the Wisma Indah building. It's half the price of a door-to-door minibus but it means you have to catch any white *angkot* (3000Rp) heading north on Jl Permuda (ask for 'Tranex' or 'Wisma Indah'), and then find transport from Bukittinggi bus terminal, which is miles from the centre. In reality you save very little money.

Minibuses to Bukittinggi (60,000Rp) and other destinations depart from a variety of offices scattered around the city and offer a door-to-door service. Ask your lodgings to arrange a pickup.

The minibuses most relevant to travellers depart from Jl Jhoni Anwar. **PO Sinar Kerinci** (🖉 0751-783 1299; Jl Jhni Anwar) has regular departures to Sungai Penuh (for Kerinci Seblat National Park). **Putra Mandau** (🖉 0812 8130 3039; Jl Jhoni Anwar) links Padang to Dumai if you're travelling to/from Sumatra by sea from Malaysia or Singapore. Catch an *angkot* (3000Rp) north along Jl Permuda and Jl S Parman, get off at the

white mosque around 5km north of central Padang, and turn right into Jl Jhoni Anwar.

ℹ Getting Around

Taxis charge around 150,000Rp to/from the airport. If you're travelling light, step outside the airport boundaries and hail an *ojek* (motorcycle that takes passengers) to central Padang. White **Damri** (🖉 0751-780 6335) airport buses (26,000Rp) are the cheapest option, running roughly hourly between 4.30am and 5pm. Tell the conductor your accommodation and street and they'll drop you at the right stop.

There are numerous *angkot* (3000Rp) around town, operating out of the **Angkot terminal** (Jl M Yamin), but it helps to know where you're going. Padang has no becaks but there are plenty of *ojeks* – if you're walking they'll often beep to get your attention.

KALIMANTAN

POP 14.9 MILLION

Skewered by the equator, the steamy forests and snaking rivers of Kalimantan – the Indonesian part of Borneo – serve up endless opportunities for epic jungle exploration. The island has no volcanoes and is protected from tsunamis, which has allowed its ancient forests to grow towering trees that house some of the world's most memorable species. The noble orangutan shares the canopy with acrobatic gibbons, while prehistoric hornbills patrol the air above.

The indigenous people, collectively known as Dayak, have long lived in concert with this rich, challenging landscape. Their longhouses dot the banks of Kalimantan's many waterways, creating a sense of community unmatched elsewhere in the country.

Kalimantan's natural resources have made it a prime target for exploitation; just three-quarters of Borneo's lowland forests remain, and its once abundant wildlife and rich traditional cultures are rapidly disappearing. Visit this awesome wilderness while you still can.

ℹ Getting There & Away

The only entry points to Kalimantan that issue visas on arrival are Balikpapan's Sepinggan Airport, Pontianak's Supadio Airport, Tarakan's Juwata airport and the Tebedu–Entikong land crossing between Kuching (Sarawak) and Pontianak. All other entry points require a visa issued in advance.

Kalimantan

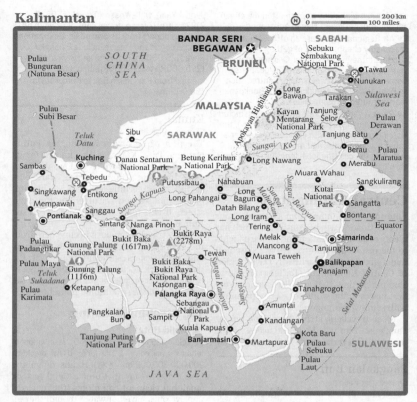

INDONESIA KALIMANTAN

AIR

Most major cities can be reached from Jakarta or Surabaya. Pontianak connects with Kuching (Malaysia), while Balikpapan has direct flights to Kuala Lumpur, Malaysia and Singapore, as well as Makassar in Sulawesi. There are no direct flights from Europe or the Americas to Kalimantan.

BOAT

Major ferry ports in Kalimantan include Balikpapan, Samarinda, Banjarmasin, Pontianak and Kumai. Pelni (www.pelni.co.id) and other carriers connect to Jakarta, Semarang and Surabaya on Java, as well as Makassar and Pare Pare on Sulawesi. There is an infrequent ferry between Tawau (Sabah) and Tarakan, with more regular speedboat service from Tawau to Nunukan.

BUS

Air-con buses link Pontianak with Kuching (230,000Rp, nine hours), as well as with other cities along Sarawak's central coast, and even Brunei (750,000Rp, 25 hours). Bus travel between Putussibau and Sarawak requires switching carriers at the border.

❶ Getting Around

Kalimantan is both immense and relatively undeveloped. River travel is as common as road travel, and transport options can form a complex picture. To assess the ever-changing transport options it is often easiest to visit a local travel agent.

By Road Highways between major cities are improving rapidly, and range from excellent to pockmarked and unsealed. Buses are fairly ubiquitous, except in East and North Kalimantan. Most major routes offer air-con for an extra cost. A Kijang (4WD minivan) or 'travel' (shared taxi) often operates between towns and cities and can be chartered for six times the single-seat fare. Intracity travel usually involves a minibus known as an *angkot* or *opelet* that charges a flat fee per trip. To really go native, take an *ojek* (motorcycle taxi). Ride-sharing apps such as Gojek and Grab are increasingly popular in major cities and are often the cheapest and most efficient way to get around.

By Air Regional flights are an efficient (and reasonably cheap) means of getting from one hub to another, while smaller Cessnas may be your only option for some remote locations. Domestic flights between major centres such as Pontianak and Palangkan Bun or Balikpapan may be routed through Jakarta.

By River A variety of craft ply the rivers, including the *kapal biasa* (large two-storey ferry), the *klotok* (smaller boat with covered passenger cabins), speedboats, and motorised canoes, including the *ces* (the local longtail). Bring your earplugs.

Central Kalimantan

Entering Kalimantan from Sarawak, your first destination will be Pontianak, which has plenty of accommodation and forward flights to the rest of the country. We've focused on major highlights on the heavily Dayak region of Central Kalimantan (KalTeng), home to Tanjung Puting National Park, among the best places in the world for close encounters with semi-wild orangutans.

Most travellers arrive by air or bus at Pangkalan Bun but the actual access to the national park is the nearby village of Kumai.

Pangkalan Bun

🖵 0532 / POP 200,000

Pangkalan Bun is largely a transit city for travellers heading to Tanjung Puting National Park and it has the biggest range of accommodation and restaurants, but most travellers skip it and head straight to Kumai.

Hotel Tiara (🖵 0532-22717; JI P Antasari 16; incl breakfast d with fan/air-con 150,000/200,000Rp, deluxe 225,000-350,000; ❋ 🛜) is the best budget bet in town. Around the corner, **Iduna Cafe** (🖵 0532-21031; JI Rangga Santrek 42; mains 18,000-60,000Rp; ⏱ 10am-9pm) is a modern aircon place offering burgers, pasta and espresso coffee.

ℹ Getting There & Away

Trigana (🖵 0532-27115; JI Iskandar 3) and **NAM Air** fly to Jakarta, Surabaya and Semarang from Pangkalan Bun's **Iskandar Airport** (🖵 0532-27399), while **Wings Air** and **Garuda** offer short hops to Sampit and Ketapang. Flights to Balikpapan go via Jakarta.

The **DAMRI** (🖵 0812 5186 3651; Nantai Suka Terminal) service to Pontianak (450,000Rp, 13 hours, 7am daily) and all **Logos** (🖵 0532-24954) buses depart from **Terminal Nantai Suka** (JI

Jend A Yani), while **Yessoe Travel** (🖵 0532-21276; http://yessoetravel.com; JI Kawitan 68) services depart from its own office. Destinations aboard Logos and Yessoe include Palangka Raya (125,000Rp, 12 hours) and Banjarmasin (205,000Rp to 290,000Rp, 16 hours).

A taxi from Pangkalan Bun to Kumai costs 150,000Rp.

Kumai

🖵 0532 / POP 26,500

The port of departure for Tanjung Puting National Park, Kumai is also known for its bird's-nest industry, which endows the town with towering Chinese-owned warehouses full of screeching swiftlets. A handful of guesthouses and warungs line the main street, JI HM Idris, running parallel to the Kumai river.

Many travellers make a beeline here from the airport or Pangkalan Bun bus terminal, and backpackers sometimes meet at the national-park dock on the northern edge of town to hook up with a guide and share the price of a *klotok* (traditional houseboats).

🛏 Sleeping & Eating

⭐ **Majid Hotel** HOTEL $$
(🖵 0852 4859 0487, 0532-61740; reservationhoteltour@gmail.com; JI HM Idris; d incl breakfast 200,000-300,000Rp; ❋ 🛜) Hands down the best place to stay in Kumai, Majid has six small but clean air-con rooms (the more expensive ones have hot water, though they all lack wash basins). Helpful English-speaking owners Majid and Liesa have several *klotok* so can arrange good-value trips to Tanjing Puting National Park and help solo travellers find shared boats.

⭐ **Acil Laila** INDONESIAN $
(JI Gerilya 5; mains 10,000-40,000Rp; ⏱ 8am-10pm) Don't let the displays of offal (hearts, livers, brains) throw you off: this place does a mean grilled chicken and a divine *nasi bakar* (seasoned rice wrapped in a banana leaf and charred to perfection).

Tanjung Puting National Park

Tanjung Puting is the most popular tourist destination in Kalimantan, and for good reason. A near guarantee you'll see free-roaming orangutans, combined with a storybook journey up a winding jungle river, give this adventure world-class appeal. And though remote, the park is easily reached by direct flights from Jakarta and Surabaya.

The park is best seen from a *klotok,* a ramshackle, multistorey romantic live-aboard boat that travels up Sungai Sekonyer from Kumai to the legendary rehabilitation centre at Camp Leakey. During the day you lounge on deck surveying the jungle for wildlife with binoculars as the boat chugs along its narrowing channel, and stopping to convene with semi-wild orangutans at the three main feeding stations.

Despite an increase in visitor numbers in recent years, the trip is still a fine introduction to the rainforest, and one of the most memorable experiences you'll have in Kalimantan

◉ Sights & Activities

Orang-utan Feedings   WILDLIFE
(Tanjung Puting National Park; ⊗ feeding 9am, 2pm & 3pm daily) Orang-utan feedings at Tanjung Puting National Park are part of an ongoing rehabilitation process but also allow visitors a guaranteed opportunity to see the great apes in semi-wild surroundings. Feedings take place at three camps: Tanjung Harapan, Pondok Tangui and Camp Leakey. Times are generally fixed and scheduled to allow boat-bound tourists to visit all three. Reaching camp feeding stations requires a short walk through jungle from the dock. Wear enclosed shoes, and bring sun protection and insect repellent.

⌕ Tours

Guides are mandated for all visitors to Tanjung Puting, and while it's possible to organise a guide and *klotok* yourself, it's easier, quicker and not much more expensive to go with a local operator. The ideal journey length is three days and two nights, giving you ample time to see everything. If you only have one day, you should take a speedboat from Kumai to Camp Leakey (3,000,000Rp). A *klotok* can reach Camp Leakey in 4½ hours, making a return trip possible in one day if you leave at 6am, but it's not recommended.

The cost of hiring a *klotok* varies with its size. They range from small (two to four passengers, from 650,000Rp per day) to large (eight to 10 passengers, from 1,200,000Rp per day), including captain, mate and fuel. Cooks are an additional 100,000Rp per day, with food on top of that. When you factor in a guide (150,000Rp to 300,000Rp per day), permits (150,000Rp per person per day)

and boat parking fees (100,000Rp per boat per day) the total cost for a three-day, two-night guided trip for two people easily tops 5,000,000Rp.

Recommended local operators include:

Borneo Wild Orangutan (☑ 0812 507 2343, 0852 4859 0487; www.liesatanjungputing.com; Jl HM Idris 600) Leisa and Majid are widely regarded as the go-to people in Kumai when it comes to organising budget river tours.

Orangutan Green Tours (☑ 0812 508 6105, 0532-203 1736; www.orangutangreentours.com; Jl Utama Pasir Panjang, Pangkalan Bun) Long-established operator with distinctive green boats.

Orangutan House Boat Tours (☑ 0857 5134 9756; www.orangutanhouseboattour.com) Kumai-born Fardi is hard-working and passionate about both his homeland and orangutans.

Borneo Hiju Travel (☑ 0852 4930 9250; www.orangutantravel.com; Jl Kawitan 1) Run by the excellent Ahmad Yani, the first official guide in the area.

Jenie Subaru (☑ 0857 6422 0991; jeniesubaru@gmail.com) ⬒ Long-running guide.

East Kalimantan

Balikpapan

☑ 0542 / POP 701,000

Balikpapan is Kalimantan's only truly cosmopolitan city, which makes it worth a look in its own right, but it's still seen largely as a stepping stone to Samarinda or Derawan. A long history of oil money and foreign workers has had a tremendous impact, bringing Western aesthetics to this Eastern port town. The city is clean and vibrant, with several enormous shopping plazas and some decent beaches – head to **Kemala Beach** (Jl Sudirman) with its cafes or to the **Ruko Bandar** (Jl Sudirman, waterfront) area. Note that Balikpapan is on Central Indonesian Standard Time, one hour ahead of Jakarta and West Kalimantan.

⊨ Sleeping & Eating

Wisma Polda Kaltim   HOTEL $
(☑ 0542-421260, 0812 5490 2392; Jl Sudirman 6; r 200,000-320,000Rp; ✸) Formerly the residence of the police chief (now living next

WORTH A TRIP

PULAU MARATUA

If you're willing to go a little further out than Derawan, Maratua is a slice of heaven. This enormous U-shaped atoll is only now beginning to feel the reach of tourism. Four tiny fishing villages are evenly spaced along the narrow strip of land. Central to the island, the large village of Tanjung Harapan offers several homestays, bicycle rental and access to the island's only upscale lodging options. Bohe Silian, at the southern end of both road and island, also has a few homestays, pleasant sea views and Sembat cave – the coolest swimming hole on the island.

The new airport and tourism port are likely to rapidly change the character of the place forever – go now.

Although not cheap, the best place to stay is **Maratua Guesthouse** (www.maratuaguesthouse.com; d & tw cabins US$69-109), nestled in a limestone forest between the island's cleanest beach and an inland tidal pond.

door), this motel-style place is good value for its 12 clean and simple ground-level rooms backing on to Kemala beach. Don't come expecting luxury (there is no hot water), and it can feel a little forlorn and quiet, but the location is handy with beach cafes accessed off the back lawn.

Ibis Hotel HOTEL $$
(0542-820821; www.ibishotels.com; Jl Suparjan 2; r incl breakfast 440,000Rp; ❄@🛜🏊) Balikpapan's great bargain, especially if you get a discounted online rate. The cosy, design-conscious rooms are stylish and sophisticated, with funky space-station bathrooms. Best of all, guests are welcome to use the considerable amenities (pool, gym) of the adjoining five-star **Novotel** (0542-820820; www.novotel.com/asia; Jl Suparjan 2; r incl breakfast 670,000-800,000Rp; ❄🛜🏊). Breakfast may cost extra if you book the lowest rate online.

✖ Eating

⭐ **Warung Soto Kuin Abduh** INDONESIAN $
(Jl Ahmad Yani; soto Banjar 16,000Rp; ⏰11am-11pm)
Soto Banjar (chicken soup seasoned with a delicate blend of spices including cinnamon) is naturally the dish of choice at this popu-

lar little warung, but you can also try satay chicken and *nasi sop* (soup with rice). You may have to wait for a seat or share a table.

⭐ **Ocean's Resto** SEAFOOD $$$
(0542-739439; Ruko Bandar; mains 60,000-300,000Rp; ⏰10am-2am; 🛜) An entire reef's worth of fresh fish and crustaceans (the menu is a book in itself), along with steaks, burgers, pizza and Indonesian dishes, all served in a fine open-air waterfront space. Ocean's anchors a row of cafes along the waterfront, and is (deservedly) the most popular. The tiny open-air 2nd-floor curry house, Aquarium, is a good place for appetisers.

ℹ Getting There & Away

The modern airport has flights to major Indonesian cities, as well as Singapore. Buses to Samarinda (30,000Rp, three hours, departing every 15 minutes 5.30am to 8pm) and minibuses to points north leave from Batu Ampar Terminal on *angkot* route 3 (light blue). Your best company for Banjarmasin (150,000Rp to 205,000Rp, 15 hours, eight times daily, noon to 8pm) is **Pulau Indah** (0542-423688; www.pulauindahjaya.com; Jl Soekarno-Hatta 58, Km2.5).

ℹ Getting Around

Taxis to the city centre from the airport cost 70,000Rp. Alternatively, walk 150m to the road, and hail a green-and-white *angkot* 7 heading west (5000Rp). City *angkot* run regular routes converging at Balikpapan Plaza, and charge 5000Rp a ride.

Berau

📞 0554 / POP 63,000

Berau is a sprawling east-Kalimantan town that serves as a transit point for the Derawan Archipelago to the east, or the karst wonderland of Merabu to the south. Most travellers fly in and arrange transport out.

Although you shouldn't need to overnight here, Berau has a decent selection of hotels, including long-standing budget favourite **Hotel Mitra** (0812 5315 0715; Jl Gajah Mada 531A; s/d incl breakfast 255,000/285,000Rp; ❄🛜) and modern midranger **Neotel Hotel** (0821 7733 1961, 0554-202 2235; www.neotel-hotel.com; Jl Durian 1; s/d incl breakfast from 350,000/490,000Rp; ❄🛜).

ℹ Getting There & Away

Destinations serviced from Berau's Kalimaru airport include Balikpapan (one hour; eight daily), Samarinda (45 minutes, one daily) and Tarakan

(25 minutes, four times weekly). Susi Air flies to Maratua on Wednesday.

To get to Derawan, look for a shared taxi to Tanjung Batu (100,000Rp, three hours). You can charter the whole vehicle for 500,000Rp. A taxi from the airport to Berau costs 80,000Rp.

Pulau Derawan

The closest island to the mainland, Derawan is tiny – you can walk it end to end in under half an hour. As a result it is also increasingly crowded, especially on weekends and holidays. Along the waterfront newer guesthouses clamber over the old, reaching out into the ocean like tentacles. However, the locals still maintain a friendly attitude, there's decent snorkelling off the stilted boardwalks and you can easily arrange transport to other islands from here.

There are no ATMs on the island.

🏃 Activities

The diving and snorkelling rank among the best in Indonesia, offering an assortment of reef and pelagic species including barracuda, sharks, mantas, turtles and whale sharks. A full-day snorkelling trip in the area runs from 1,500,000Rp to 2,000,000Rp, depending on how far you go. It is four hours of spine-compressing travel from Derawan to the popular snorkelling areas around Kakaban and Sangalaki, return. Organise diving at **Derawan Dive Resort** (📞0811 542 4121; www.divederawan. com; discover dive 650,000Rp, 3-dive package 1,500,000Rp) or **Tasik Divers** (📞0431-824445; www.derawandivelodge.com).

🛏 Sleeping & Eating

There are lots of village homestays (look for signs) on the island charging around 200,000Rp for a room but the best accommodation is the waterfront places, some with rooms on stilted overwater boardwalks.

There are just a handful of restaurants on the main village strip. Fresh seafood is the local speciality.

Penginapan 88   GUESTHOUSE $
(📞0813 4660 3944; r with fan/air-con 200,000/300,000Rp; ❄) Roughly halfway along the village strip, this waterfront place has 10 simple but good-value rooms and a couple of 'penthouse' rooms way out on the end of the pier with unobstructed water views.

Derawan Beach Cafe & Cottages   GUESTHOUSE $$
(📞0853 4679 7578; r 300,00-500,000Rp; ❄) Towards the end of the village strip, this group of waterfront cottages, including two premium overwater bungalows, boasts one of the longest jetties on the island and a small private beach. The best rooms have air-con and hot water.

Sari Cottages   GUESTHOUSE $$
(📞0813 4653 8448; r 400,000Rp; ❄) Centrally located Sari has 22 compact rooms, strung along two parallel piers connected by a footbridge. All have air-con, cold-water showers and private back verandahs with at least partial water views. Turn off the street at the sign for 'Pinades,' and keep walking the plank.

❶ Getting There & Away

Most trips to the islands leave from the coastal village of Tanjung Batu, accessible from Berau by road (500,000Rp charter, 100,000Rp regular seat, three hours). From there, a regular morning boat takes passengers to Pulau Derawan (100,000Rp per person, 30 minutes); if you arrive later in the day you may have to charter a speedboat (400,000Rp, seats four). Returning from Derawan, boats leave between 7am and 8am.

SULAWESI

This splay-limbed enigma of a tropical island, the 11th-largest in the world, is one of Indonesia's most fascinating. It is tied physically and historically to the sea and ringed with teeming waters and reefs; its interior is mountainous and cloaked in dense jungle. Here rare species such as nocturnal tarsiers and flamboyantly colourful maleo birds survive, as do proud cultures, isolated by impenetrable topography, who guard their customs against the onslaughts of modernity. Meet the Toraja highlanders, with their elaborate funeral ceremonies in which buffaloes are sacrificed and *balok* (palm sugar wine) flows freely; the Minahasans in the far north, who offer spicy dishes of everything from stewed forest rat to grilled fish; and the Bugis, who are mainly found inhabiting Sulawesi's coastal regions and are Indonesia's most famous seafarers.

❶ Getting There & Around

AIR
The two main transport hubs are Makassar and Manado, which are well connected with the rest

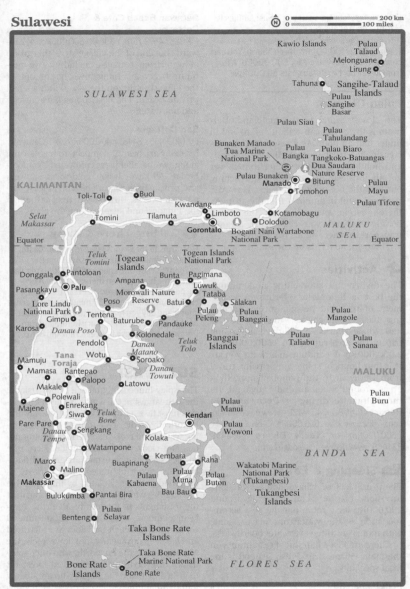

of Indonesia. Palu is the third most important airport.

Silk Air flies between Manado and Singapore four days a week (from around US$170, 3¾ hours). Air Asia flies from Makassar to Kuala Lumpur, Malaysia (from US$70, 3¼ hours).

BOAT

Sulawesi is well connected, with around half the Pelni ferry fleet calling at Makassar, Bitung (the seaport for Manado), Pare Pare and Toli-Toli, as well as a few other minor towns.

BUS

Excellent air-conditioned buses connect Rantepao with Makassar. Elsewhere you're looking at pretty clapped-out local buses that stop every few minutes. There are some decent long-distance bemo (minibus) services, particularly on the road across Central Sulawesi connecting Luwuk and Palu.

Makassar

☑ 0411 / POP 1.71 MILLION

The gritty metropolis of Makassar is one of Indonesia's primary ports. It's a seething maelstrom of commerce and shipping, with a polyglot population of Makassarese, Bugis and Chinese residents. But as the city has few sights, and the tropical heat and pollution are unremitting, few travellers stay more than a night or two.

Makassar was the gateway to eastern Indonesia for centuries, and it was from here that the Dutch controlled much of the trade that passed between the West and the East. You can investigate the city's historical core, which retains considerable colonial charm, around Fort Rotterdam, which includes the remains of an ancient Gowanese fort and some striking Dutch buildings.

Note that the one-time name for Makassar, Ujung Pandang, is still in common use. Look for both names when arranging flights and other transport.

◉ Sights

Fort Rotterdam   FORT

(Benteng Rotterdam; Jl Ujung Pandang; suggested donation 10,000-20,000Rp; ⊙ 7.30am-6pm) One of the best-preserved examples of Dutch military architecture in Indonesia, Fort Rotterdam was built on the site of a Gowanese fort, itself built to repel the Dutch East India Company. Having failed to keep out the *orang belanda*, it was rebuilt by the new masters of Makassar after their 1667 conquest, and includes many fine, well-restored colonial structures. You can walk the enclave's stout ramparts, see sections of the original walls and visit the **Museum Negeri La Galigo** (10,000Rp), inside.

Masjid Amirul Mukminin   MOSQUE

(Jl Penghibur) FREE Rising above the sea at the southern end of Pantai Losari, this futuristic twin-domed house of worship (constructed using concrete piles driven into the seabed) is known as the 'floating mosque'. Visitors of all faiths are welcome. Built in 2009, it enjoys fine coastal views, and the landscaped area around the mosque is *the* place to break the daily fast during Ramadan.

🛏 Sleeping & Eating

★ Dodo's Homestay   HOMESTAY $

(☑ 0812 412 9913; www.dodopenman.blogspot.co.uk; Jl Abdul Kadir, Komplex Hartaco Indah Blok 1Y/25; s/d 100,000/120,000Rp; ❈🛜) An excellent homestay owned by Dodo, a super-friendly local who's been assisting travellers for more than 20 years. His home is a spacious, air-conditioned house in a quiet neighbourhood 4km south of the centre; one of the rooms has an en-suite bathroom. There's free tea and coffee, and Dodo arranges transport (including motorbike and car rental) and tours around Sulawesi.

★ Ge Jac Mart   HOMESTAY $$

(☑ 0411-859421; www.ge-jacmart-homestay.blogspot.co.uk; Jl Rambutan 3; r incl breakfast 290,000Rp; ❈🛜) This wonderful homestay lies down a quiet lane, just off the seafront. It's run by the Pongrekun family (originally from Tana Toraja), who are hospitable, speak good English and enjoy looking after guests. Their tiled, immaculately clean home has whitewashed walls splashed with art, and seven very comfortable rooms, each with a private bathroom and hot water.

★ Rumah Makan Pate'ne   INDONESIAN $

(☑ 0411-361 5874; Jl Sulawesi 48; mains 30,000-35,000Rp; ⊙ 8am-10pm) Serving up super-fresh Makassarese and Indonesian classics, Pate'ne offers fine value and authentic flavours. The *lele goreng* (deep-fried catfish with sambal, shredded green papaya, lemon basil and fresh veggies) and *rujak manis* (tropical-fruit salad with a spicy-sweet palm-sugar, tamarind and shrimp-paste dressing) are delicious, especially washed down with fresh melon, mango, apple or avocado juice.

Lae Lae   SEAFOOD $$

(☑ 0411-334326; Jl Datu Museng 8; fish from 60,000Rp; ⊙ 10am-midnight) A locally famous seafood restaurant, Lae Lae is a no-frills, no-fuss magnet for lovers of grilled fish. Enter past a smoking streetside barbecue, choose your piscine pleasure from deep tubs of super-fresh iced fish, and eat at long, battered metal tables, rubbing shoulders with the locals. Three sambals, rice and squeaky-fresh raw vegetables are the standard accompaniments.

Makassar (Ujung Pandang)

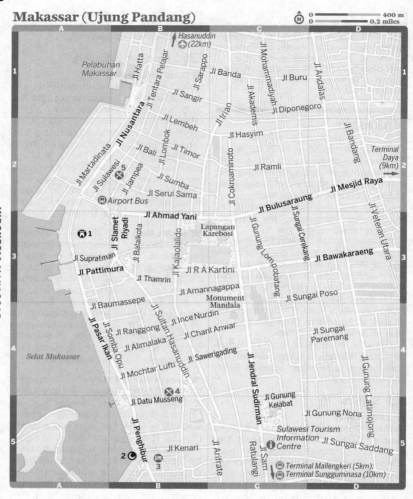

Makassar (Ujung Pandang)

◉ Sights
1 Fort Rotterdam.....................................A3
2 Masjid Amirul Mukminin B5
  Museum Negeri La Galigo ....(see 1)

🛏 Sleeping
3 Ge Jac Mart...B5

🍴 Eating
4 Lae Lae B4
5 Rumah Makan Pate'ne B2

ℹ️ Information

Sulawesi Tourism Information Centre
(📞0411-872336; cnr Jl Sam Ratulangi & Jl Sungai Saddang; ⏰8am-4pm) There's little printed, English-language information available here, but the staff are helpful and some speak excellent English. Take any red *pete-pete* (a type of *mikrolet* or bemo) travelling south along Jl Jendral Sudirman to get here.

ℹ️ Getting There & Away

AIR

Makassar's Hasanuddin Airport is well connected with other cities in Sulawesi and with Java,

Kalimantan and Maluku. International flights include Air Asia to Kuala Lumpur and Silk Air to Singapore.

BUS & KIJANG

The most useful terminals are Terminal Daya for points north such as Rantepao (150,000Rp to 200,000Rp, nine hours); Terminal Mallengkeri for points southeast such as Bulukumba (60,000Rp, four hours); and Terminal Sungguminasa for services to Malino (24,000Rp, 1½ hours).

 Getting Around

Airport buses (27,000Rp) with Damri run every 20 to 30 minutes between 8am and 9pm daily from the basement level of the airport to Jl Ahmad Yani in central Makassar.

Prepaid taxis are available in the arrivals area of the airport. Taxis between the airport and city cost from 110,000Rp to 150,000Rp.

The main *pete-pete* terminal is at the site of the old Makassar Mall. The standard fare around town is 5000Rp.

Tana Toraja

With its vibrant tribal culture and stunning scenery, the fascinating highland region of Tana Toraja is rightly a mecca for travellers. Its visual allure is immediate, with its villages of elaborately painted houses with boat-shaped roofs, and towering terraces of emerald-green rice paddies, all of which is overseen by a protective necklace of jagged jungle-clad hills.

While most people consider attending a funeral here to be a highlight of their visit, Tana Toraja also offers some great do-it-yourself trekking, cycling and motorbiking through its evergreen landscape of spell-binding beauty.

INDONESIA TANA TORAJA

TORAJA CULTURE

The Toraja inhabit the vast, rugged landscape of the South Sulawesi highlands. Their name is derived from the Bugis word *toriaja*, which once had negative connotations similar to 'hillbilly' or 'bumpkin'. Despite the strength of traditional beliefs, Christianity in Toraja is a very active force.

Traditional Houses

One of the most noticeable aspects about Tana Toraja is the size and grandeur of the *tongkonan* (traditional Torajan house). It is the place for family gatherings and may not be bought or sold.

The towering roof, which rears up at either end, is the most striking aspect of a *tongkonan*. Some believe the roof represents the horns of a buffalo; others suggest it represents the bow and stern of a boat. The more buffalo horns visible, the higher the household's status.

Funerals

Of all Torajan ceremonies, the most important is the *tomate* (funeral; literally 'deceased'). Without proper funeral rites the soul of the deceased will cause misfortune to its family.

The Toraja generally have two funeral ceremonies: one immediately after death and an elaborate second funeral after preparations have been made. The bigger funerals are usually scheduled during the dry months of July and August, but there are funerals year-round.

Until the time of the second funeral, the deceased remains in the family house. An invitation to visit the deceased is an honour. If you accept, remember to thank the deceased and ask permission of the deceased when you wish to leave – as you would of a living host.

The second funeral can be spread over several days and involve hundreds of guests. The Toraja believe that the souls of animals should follow their masters to the next life, hence the importance of animal sacrifices. Festivities often start with bullfights, where lots of lively betting takes place, and some famous fighting bulls may be imported for the event from the distant reaches of the country. Animal lovers are likely to find the bullfights disturbing and the sacrifices very traumatic; these two kinds of events are best avoided if you cringe at the sight of blood.

Visitors attending a funeral should wear black or dark-coloured clothing and bring gifts of sugar or cigarettes for the family of the deceased.

Rantepao

☎ 0423 / POP 26,500

Something of an overgrown village, Rantepao is an easy-to-manage town that lies within striking distance of the region's major sites, and offers a good range of accommodation and restaurants. The centre is a tad scruffy, but traffic isn't too heavy and the streets quickly merge with farmers' fields on Rantepao's outskirts; you're never far from the crow of a rooster. Nights can be cool and there is rain throughout the year, even in the dry season.

🏃 Activities

Most of the area's activities lie in the hills beyond Rantepao. Hotels that have **swimming pools** allow nonguests to swim for a fee (from 15,000Rp).

There are many independent guides based in Rantepao. Agencies can also arrange tours (including trekking and cultural tours), vehicles and guides.

Indo' Sella (☎ 0813 4250 5301, 0423-25210; www.sellatours.com; Jl Limbong Ba'lele 7) is run by long-time guide Agustinus Lamba. This reliable, experienced tour company organises good hiking, white-water rafting and cultural excursions. A rafting day trip on the Sungai Mai'ting is US$85 per person, including meals, portage and transport, while two days on the Sungai Sa'dan is US$350 per person. Agus can also organise longer trips including to the Togean Islands and elsewhere.

🛏 Sleeping & Activities

★ **Pia's Poppies Hotel**   GUESTHOUSE **$**
(☎ 0813 4202 6768, 0423-21121; poppiestoraja@ yahoo.co.id; Jl Pongtiku 22; s/d 135,000/175,000Rp; ☏) This welcoming place in a tranquil location 10 minutes' walk from the centre has very helpful staff. Rooms face a verdant

Tana Toraja

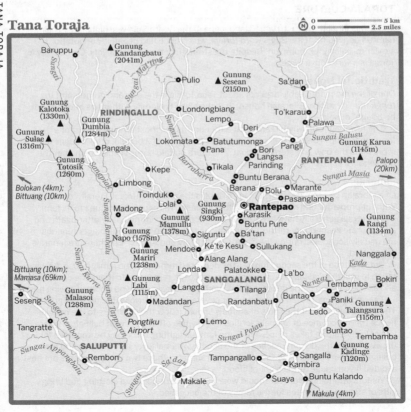

garden, have quirky details such as stone bathrooms and en suites have hot water. Be sure to eat in the charming cafe, which serves excellent local food. Breakfast is an extra 33,000Rp and wi-fi only works in the public areas.

Rosalina Homestay   HOMESTAY $
(☑ 0852 5572 5432, 0423-25530; http://rosalina-homestayrantepao.blogspot.co.uk; Jl Pongitiku Karassik; s/d 175,000/250,000Rp; ☏) Opened in 2015, this fine place is owned by Enos, a highly experienced Torajan guide, and his family. They take really good care of their guests, including the preparation of filling breakfasts. The spacious rooms are on the upper floor of the family's home, and overlook an ocean of rice paddies from a large shared balcony.

Wisma Monika   GUESTHOUSE $$
(☑ 0423-21216; Jl Ratulangi 36; r 250,000-400,000Rp; ✱☏) A grandiose-looking cream villa in a central spot, close to plenty of eating options and with a choice of plain but well-maintained and clean rooms, all with bedside reading lights. The staff prepare a good breakfast, incuding pancakes, nasi goreng and fresh fruit juices.

Rimiko Restoran   INDONESIAN $
(☑ 0813 5339 2779, 0423-23366; Jl Andi Mappanyukki 115; dishes 30,000-50,000Rp; ⊙ 8am-10pm) A long-running, very friendly place that serves authentic local food, including Torajan specialties such as buffalo, pork and eel in black sauce (50,000Rp), alongside Indo staples such as gado gado. Book ahead for the *pa'piong* – pork or chicken slow-cooked with wild local herbs in bamboo over a fire.

❶ Information

Government Tourist Office (☑ 0423-21277; off Jl Ahmad Yani; ⊙ 9am-2pm Mon-Sat) The friendly staff here can provide accurate, independent information about local ceremonies and festivals, and recommend guides.

❶ Getting There & Away

Transnusa schedules four flights per week between Makassar and Rantepao, but be warned they'll only fly when demand is sufficient. The 50-minute one-way flights cost 410,000Rp and leave from Makassar at 8.45am each Tuesday, Wednesday, Thursday and Saturday, returning at 10.05am the same days.

Most long-distance buses leave from the bus company offices along Jl Andi Mappanyukki.

Buses often run at night. Prices vary according to speed and the level of comfort and space. Rantepao to Makassar costs 110,000Rp to 220,000Rp and takes nine hours.

Chartering a private car and driver between Makassar and Rantepao costs from 1,200,000Rp each way.

❶ Getting Around

Rantepao is small and easy to walk around. A becak (bicycle-rickshaw) should cost around 5000Rp in town. Motorbikes cost from 70,000Rp per day to hire; many guesthouses, including **Wisma Maria I** (☑ 0423-21165; adespasaka1@yahoo.com; Jl Sam Ratulangi 23; s/d incl breakfast 115,000/137,000Rp, r with hot water bathroom from 170,000Rp; ☏), rent out bikes.

Around Rantepao

About 2km west across the river from Rantepao, **Gunung Singki** (930m) is a steep hill with a slippery, overgrown hiking trail to the summit. From the top you'll get panoramic views across Rantepao and the surrounding countryside. Return to the road and head to **Siguntu** (7km from Rantepao), which offers more superb views of the valleys and Rantepao.

The 3km walk from Siguntu to the Rantepao–Makale road at **Alang Alang** is also pleasant. Stop on the way at the traditional village of **Mendoe**. From Alang Alang, where a covered bridge crosses the river, head a few hundred metres to **Londa**, back to Rantepao, or remain on the western side of the river and continue walking south to the villages of **Langda** and **Madandan**.

Poso

☑ 0452 / POP 49,300

Poso is the main town, port and terminal for road transport on the northern coast of Central Sulawesi. For years, violence between Muslims and Christians made it a no-go zone, but tensions have eased. However, there's still no reason to visit other than to catch a flight, change buses, or break up a trip to/from Ampana and the Togean Islands.

Armada Losmen (☑ 0452-23070; Jl Sumatera 17; r with shared/private bathroom 100,000/200,000Rp) has a wide selection of bland but clean rooms, all of them good value.

Poso's Kasiguncu airport, 15km west of town, is fast growing in popularity with travellers as flight connections multiply. Wings Air flies daily to Makassar (from 816,000Rp).

From the bus terminal, 5km out of town, there are services to Ampana (75,000Rp, five hours) and Palu (80,000Rp, six hours).

Ampana

📞 0464 / POP 22,367

The main reason for travellers to come to Ampana is to catch a boat to/from the Togean Islands. It's a laid-back, pleasant coastal town with a vibrant market and makes a good stopover while you recover from, or prepare for, an assault on the Togeans.

Oasis Hotel (📞 0464-21058; Jl Kartini 5; r with fan/air-con from 150,000/250,000Rp; ❄🛜) benefits from a central location, close to the ferry for the Togean Islands, and has shabby yet functional rooms. It's worth travelling to Labuan, 3km northeast of central Ampana, to **Marina Cottages** (📞 0823 4995 1833, 0464-21280; www.marina-cottages.com; Jl Tanjung Api 33, Labuan; cottage with fan/AC from 160,000/300,000Rp; ❄🛜), 20 rustic, very well-maintained cottages situated on a lovely pebble-strewn beach.

❶ Getting There & Away

Access to Ampana will really take off when direct flights to Makassar commence. At the time of research, this connection (and others to Manado, Gorontalo and Luwuk) require transit through Palu on a Wings Air twin-propeller plane. Tanjung Api airport is 7km east of central Ampana.

Boats to Poso, Wakai (in the Togean Islands) and beyond leave from the main boat terminal at the end of Jl Yos Sudarso, in the centre of Ampana. Boats to Bomba in the Togeans leave from a jetty in Labuan village, next to **Marina Cottages** (p292) (check https://infotogian.weebly.com for schedules).

Minibuses travel each day to Luwuk (150,000Rp, six hours, 8am), Poso (75,000Rp, five hours, 10am and 5pm) and Palu (150,000Rp, 12 hours, 10am and 5pm). There are also additional but much slower and less comfortable buses on these routes.

Togean Islands

If it takes determination to get to the Togean Islands, it's even harder to leave. You'll hop from one forested golden-beach island to the next, where hammocks are plentiful, worries

scarce and the welcome genuine. Most islands have only a few family-run guesthouses, while popular Kadidiri has a small but lively beach scene with night-time bonfires and cold beers all around.

❶ Getting There & Away

There are many ways to get to the Togeans, but all of them are time-consuming and none of them straightforward. Firstly, the islands have no airport, so the only access is by boat. The two gateway cities are Ampana and Gorontalo. Consult the excellent https://infotogian.weebly.com for up-to-date information as schedules change regularly.

If you're travelling overland from South Sulawesi (including Tana Toraja), Ampana is the logical gateway. Several daily ferries run from Gorontalo, in North Sulawesi, is the other main gateway. KM *Tuna Tomini* sails directly to Wakai (economy class/air-con cabin for four 64,000Rp/500,000Rp, 13 hours) at 5pm on Tuesday and Friday and is the easiest option from this direction if you want to get to Katupat, Kadidiri or Bomba. On the way back, the boat departs Wakai on Monday, Thursday and Sunday at 4pm..

❶ Getting Around

Use the Ampana–Dolong ferries to island-hop, or charter local boats. Public boats also connect Wakai with Una Una (40,000Rp, three hours, three per week).

Finding a charter is relatively easy in Wakai, Bomba and Kadidiri, but it's more difficult to arrange in smaller settlements. Rates are fairly standard among the cartel of local operators (around 500,000Rp from Wakai or Kadidiri to Bomba). Ask at your accommodation.

Pulau Kadidiri

Beautiful, thickly wooded Kadidiri, a 30-minute boat trip from Wakai, is definitely the island to go to if you're feeling social. Its popular lodging options are all close together, so you can stroll along a fine strip of sand for a drink elsewhere if your place has run out of beer. It's a 15-minute walk from the hotels, through coconut groves, to a lovely sandy cove, **Barracuda Beach** (where you could camp).

Kadidiri Paradise Resort (📞 0813 4372 2072, 0464-21058; www.kadidiriparadise.com; s/d incl all meals from 348,000/580,000Rp) enjoys a stunning location on a lovely beach and has extensive grounds that hug the coastline. Wooden bungalows are spacious and have good beds, mosquito nets, generous front decks and either beach frontage or easy access to the beach. The well-run dive centre offers single dives for 450,000Rp, open-water certification for 5,250,000Rp and discounts of up to 10% on multiple dives.

Togean & Katupat

Pulau Togean is large, forested island, fringed by mangroves; Pulau Katupat is much smaller, and has a small village for supplies. Some of the best diving at the islands can be found off Togean's northern coast.

Fadhila Cottages (☑ 0852 4100 3685; www.fadhilacottage.com; standard/superior d incl all meals 500,000/700,000Rp) has 18 clean, wooden bungalows with terraces and hammocks lining a palm-shaded beach facing either Katupat village or the ocean. There's a good PADI dive centre here (one boat dive is €30) and a breezy restaurant.

Pulau Batu Daka

The largest and most accessible island of the Togeans is Pulau Batu Daka, which is home to the two main villages, Bomba and Wakai.

Bomba is a tiny outpost at the southwestern end of the island, which most travellers sail past on the way to and from Wakai. It's an appealing alternative to social Pulau Kadidiri, as it has some of the Togean's best beaches, good snorkelling and is social in a very mellow way. It's a pleasant walk to the **bat caves** in the hills behind Bomba village, but you'll need a guide and a torch (flashlight).

The largest settlement in the Togeans, **Wakai** is a small port that's mainly used as the departure point for boats to Pulau Kadidiri, but there are several well-stocked general stores and a lively market. A small **waterfall**, a few kilometres inland from Wakai, is a pleasant hike; ask for directions in the village.

Gorontalo

☑ 0435 / POP 186,000

Gorontalo has the feel of an overgrown country town, where all the locals seem to know each other. The compact town centre features some of the best-preserved Dutch houses in Sulawesi and retains a languid colonial feel.

New Melati Hotel (☑ 0435-822934; yfvelberg@yahoo.com; Jl Monginsidi 1; r incl breakfast 130,000-325,000Rp; ❄@🗲) is a long-time backpacker favourite with English-speaking staff who are very well informed about

transport connections. It's based around a lovely home, built in the early 1900s for the harbour master.

ℹ Getting There & Away

There are daily flights to Makassar divided between the carriers Garuda, Citilink, Batik Air, Lion Air and Sriwijaya. Wings Air and Garuda fly several times per day to Manado; Wings also has connections to Palu.

Gorontalo has two harbours, both about 4km from the town centre: Talumolo port for the Togean Islands boats and Leato port for Pelni ferries. Both are easily accessible by *mikrolet* (small taxis) along Jl Tantu.

Every two weeks the Pelni liner *Tilongkabila* links Gorontalo with Bitung, and the *Sangiang* tackles the same route monthly. The **Pelni office** (☑ 0435-821089; Jl 23 Januari) is efficient and convenient.

The main bus terminal is 3km north of town and accessible by bemo, *bendi* (two person horse-drawn cart) or *ojek*. There are direct buses to Palu (180,000Rp, 18 hours) and Manado (regular/air-con 100,000/130,000Rp, 11 hours), departing every hour. Most people make the Manado trip by minibus or Kijang (150,000Rp to 200,000Rp).

Manado

☑ 0431 / POP 458,500

Manado is a prosperous, well-serviced and friendly place, with a decent selection of comfortable hotels and an excellent dining scene. This is despite the fact that appearances do deceive, as it doesn't immediately register as one of North Sulawesi's highlights, with its overabundance of shopping malls and cavernous holes in the sidewalk. Adventures lie nearby around the city at Bunaken, Tomohon, the Lembeh Strait and Tangkoko-Batuangas Dua Saudara Nature Reserve; to get to these places most travellers will have to spend a night or more in Manado.

🛏 Sleeping & Eating

Manado Grace Inn HOTEL $
(☑ 0431-888 0288; Jl Sam Ratulangi 113H; r from 175,000Rp; ❄🗲) This good-value, modern hotel offers smallish, no-frills, cream-and-white rooms, with air-con, private bathrooms (with hot water) and in-room wi-fi. Breakfast is very basic – just a bread roll and tea or coffee.

★Libra Homestay HOMESTAY $$
(☑ 0821 9268 6320; Jl Pramuka XI 16; r 300,000-350,000Rp; ❄🗲) An excellent place in a

spacious whitewashed villa on a quiet street, where the kindly Chinese owner (who studied in London and speaks excellent English) looks after guests well. There are five rooms, all with air-con, cable TVs, desks and private bathrooms with hot water. It's in the south of the city, a five-minute walk from restaurants.

Hotel Celebes HOTEL **$$**
(☑ 0431-870425; www.hotelcelebesmdo.com; Jl Rumambi 8A; r from 310,000Rp; ❉ ☎) Hotel Celebes is a big block that looms over the market and port, so is very handy for boats to Pulau Bunaken. Rooms are functional and kept pretty clean; angle for one on an upper floor with a view of the sea, and note that online rates can be lower.

★ Maminon INDONESIAN **$**
(☑ 0431-880 5777; Jl Sarapung 38; mains 35,000-50,000Rp; ☺ 9am-9pm Mon-Sat; ☎) The gleaming, tiled dining room and beaming, uniformed staff show a pride in hospitality that's matched by the kitchen in this delightful Minahasan restaurant. Go the *cakalang fufu* (local smoked tuna), perhaps with *sous rica tomat* (tomato/chilli sambal) or *santan* (in an almost-Thai sauce of coconut milk, kaffir lime and aromatics), and you'll eat like royalty.

Rumah Makan Green Garden CHINESE, INDONESIAN **$**
(☑ 0431-870089; Jl Sam Ratulangi 173; mains 47,000-65,000Rp; ☺ 9am-midnight) This popular Indo-Chinese restaurant does excellent pork dishes (try it barbecued or go for the pork belly) and seafood (perhaps crab, plucked live from the tank and served in corn soup, or grouper with salted mustard leaf). There's also fresh juice and cold beer.

❶ Getting There & Away

AIR
Tickets for domestic flights often cost about the same at travel agencies as they do online.

A number of airlines have offices in town.
XpressAir (www.xpressair.co.id) and **Batik Air** (www.batikair.com) also fly to Manado.

Garuda (☑ 0431-877737; Jl Sam Ratulangi 212; ☺ 8.30am-5pm Mon-Sat) flies from Manado to Denpasar and Jakarta.

Lion Air (☑ 0431-847000; www.lionair.co.id; Jl Piere Tendean 19; ☺ 9am-5pm Mon-Fri, to 3pm Sat, to noon Sun) flies from Manado to Jakarta, Makassar, Surabaya and Luwuk.

Silk Air (☑ 0431-863744; Jl Sarapung; ☺ 9am-4pm Mon-Fri, to 1pm Sat) flies from Manado to Singapore.

Sriwijaya Air (☑ 0431-888 0988; www.sriwijayaair.co.id; Jl Piere Tendean, Manado Town Sq 12A; ☺ 8am-6.30pm) flies from Manado to Ambon and Ternate.

BOAT
Speed ferries operate daily to Siau (200,000Rp, four hours) and on to Tahuna (240,000Rp, 6½ hours) in the Sangihe-Talaud Islands. Tickets and information are available from **Majestic Kawanua** (☑ 0851 0540 5499; majestickawanua@gmail.com; Jl Piere Tendean, Komplek Marina Plaza; ☺ 8am-5pm).

There are also local boats to Maluku. Tickets are available from the stalls outside the port. Boats to Pulau Bunaken leave from a harbour near Pasar Jengki fish market. There's a daily service leaving from 2pm, when full and depending on tides (one-way fare 50,000Rp).

BUS
There are three reasonably orderly terminals for long-distance buses and the local *mikrolet*.
Terminal Karombasan (5km south of the city) Connections to Tomohon (10,000Rp) and other places south of Manado.
Terminal Malalayang (far south of the city) Buses to Kotamobagu (60,000Rp) and Gorontalo (from 100,000Rp, 11 hours).
Terminal Paal 2 (eastern end of Jl Martadinata) Varied public transport runs to Bitung (11,000Rp) and to the airport (10,000Rp).

❶ Getting Around

Mikrolet from Sam Ratulangi International Airport go to Terminal Paal 2 (10,000Rp), where you can change to a *mikrolet* for elsewhere. There are also four daily air-conditioned buses (30,000Rp) to/from Jl Piere Tendean. Fixed-price taxis cost around 100,000Rp from the airport to the city (13km).

Pulau Bunaken
☑ 0431

This tiny, coral-fringed isle is North Sulawesi's top tourist destination, yet it has managed to maintain a rootsy island soul. Tourist accommodation is spread out along two beaches and beyond that, the isle belongs to the islanders. These friendly folk have a seemingly endless reserve of authentically warm smiles and there are no hassles here – just laid-back beachy bliss.

Most people come to Bunaken for the diving. The marine biodiversity is extraordinary, with more than 300 types of coral and 3000 species of fish, abundant sponges and phenomenally colourful life on vertical walls. The 808-hectare island is part of the 891-sq-km **Bunaken Manado Tua Marine National Park** (Taman Laut Bunaken Manado Tua), which includes Manado Tua (Old Manado), the dormant volcano that can be seen from Manado and climbed in about four hours; Nain and Mantehage islands; and Pulau Siladen, which also has accommodation.

Trips around Bunaken and nearby islands, including two dives and equipment rental, will cost around 1,400,000Rp; PADI Open Water courses are about 6,000,000Rp. Snorkellers can go along with the dive boats for around 80,000Rp per person.

🛏 Sleeping

Novita Homestay   GUESTHOUSE **$$**
(☑ 0812 443 0729; r per person incl all meals 250,000Rp) Owned and operated by Vita, a terrific cook, Novita is a delightful old-fashioned homestay right in Bunaken village (at the southern end of the island, where the ferries dock). Vita also organises tours, rents snorkelling gear (50,000Rp per day) and raises turtle hatchlings for release into the wild. Rooms with outside bathrooms are 50,000Rp cheaper.

Froggies   DIVE RESORT **$$**
(☑ 0812 430 1356; www.froggiesdivers.com; s/d bungalow incl all meals from 529,000/1,058,000Rp; ❇ 🛜) Froggies, one of the first dive centres on Bunaken, is still going strong. It offers a fine beachfront location with sunset views and the perfect cone of Pulau Manadotua, and 14 bungalows, some with two bedrooms, and all with terraces. Wi-fi is available in the restaurant and laundry service is free.

Lorenso's Cottages   GUESTHOUSE **$$**
(☑ 0852 5697 3345; r per person incl all meals from 250,000Rp; 🛜) Lorenso's is an excellent choice for travellers; it has a good selection of accommodation on a pretty mangrove-lined bay, and there's world-class snorkelling offshore. The staff are very helpful, there's a good communal vibe, and when the tin-can band rocks up, great live music.

❶ Getting There & Away

Daily public boats leave for Bunaken village and Pulau Siladen from Manado (50,000Rp, one hour); they leave from 2pm when full, tides depending, from the harbour near Pasar Jengki fish market in Manado. They return at around 8am to 9am the next day. There are also several unscheduled boats (which leave when full) at other times of the day, or you can charter a boat for around 300,000Rp.

MALUKU

POP 2.8 MILLION

Welcome to the original Spice Islands. Back in the 16th century when nutmeg, cloves and mace were global commodities that grew nowhere else, money really did 'grow on trees'. It was the search for the Moluccas' (Maluku's) valuable spices that kick-started European colonialism and, thanks to a series of wrong turns and one auspicious land swap, shaped the modern world. When the islands' monopoly on cloves and nutmeg was broken in the 18th century, Maluku settled into gentle obscurity.

Today Maluku is a scattering of idyllic islands where the complex web of cultures envelops visitors with an effusive, almost Polynesian charm. Interisland transport can prove infuriatingly inconvenient, but with flexibility and patience you can explore pristine reefs, stroll empty stretches of powdery white sand, book idyllic overwater bungalows, view perfectly formed volcanoes, and revel in a tropical discovery that seems almost too good to be true.

❶ Getting There & Around

AIR
Ambon and Ternate are the region's air hubs. Both have several daily connections to Jakarta, some direct and some via Makassar, Manado (Sulawesi) or Surabaya. There are several connections from Ambon to Papua.

BOAT
Pelni's patchy North Maluku services change each month, but you can usually count on the routes that connect Ambon with the Banda Islands and onwards to the Kei Islands. Some medium-range hops are served by uncomfortable ASDP ferries or by wooden boats known as *kapal motor*. Perintis cargo boats are bigger but not at all designed with passengers in mind (bring waterproof clothes). Speedboats link nearby islands and roadless villages.

Regular speedboats connect short and midrange destinations (eg Ternate–Tidore, Ternate–Halmahera, Ambon–Lease Islands, Ambon–Seram). The longer rides are only available in the dry season and are best early in the morning when seas are calmest. Chartering is widely available.

PUBLIC TRANSPORT
In mountainous Maluku, the few asphalted roads can be surprisingly good, but some areas have only mud tracks or no roads at all. Ambon is encircled by a good ring road and has plenty of taxis. Shorter routes are generally operated

Maluku

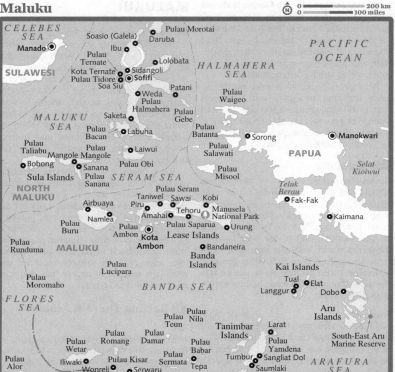

by bemo (minibus), also known as *mobil*. On Halmahera and Seram, shared Kijangs (fancy seven-seat Toyotas) predominate. Renting an *ojek* (motorcycle taxi) can be an inexpensive way to travel without luggage.

Pulau Ambon

POP 441,000

Maluku's most prominent and populous island is lush and gently mountainous, indented with two great hoops of bay. Around the busy capital Kota Ambon, villages merge into a long, green, suburban ribbon. West of the airport, this gives way to a string of charming coastal villages where, if you take the time to explore, you'll discover Ambon is not just an unavoidable step on the road to the lovely Lease, Kei and Banda Islands. The bay is known for excellent muck-diving, while the southern coast has clear waters and intact coral.

Kota Ambon

☑ 0911 / POP 331,000

By the region's dreamy tropical standards, Maluku's capital is a sprawling metropolis. Sights are minimal and the architecture wins no prizes, but there is a unique cafe culture, decent accommodation and some very good restaurants. This is the place to chill out and do business while you plan your travels to the Banda and Kei Islands or beyond.

🛏 Sleeping & Eating

⭐ **Momoa Michael Guesthouse** HOMESTAY $
(☑ 0813 4302 8872; erenst_michael@yahoo.co.id; Jl Propinsi, Laha; r with fan/air-con incl breakfast 150,000/200,000Rp; ❄ 🐠) On the main road opposite the airport runway, this cosy homestay is run by the ever-warm and welcoming Michael, Ambon's finest tourism ambassador. He offers three clean and tidy

rooms with shared bathroom, just a short *ojek* ride, or longer stroll, to the terminal. This is a fine base for exploring dive sites or arranging transport to other islands.

Penginapan the Royal   GUESTHOUSE $

(✒ 0911-348077; Jl Anthony Rhebok 1D; s/d 220,000/248,000Rp; ❄ 🛜) A decent budget option, with Ikea-chic wardrobes and desks, hot water, small flat-screens and wi-fi. The walls are a touch grubby and some rooms smell of stale smoke, but overall it's clean, central and well run.

★ Hero Hotel Ambon   HOTEL $$

(✒ 0911-342898; http://hero-hotel-ambon.booked. net; Jl Wim Reawaru 7B; d 415,000-510,000Rp; ❄ 🛜) Deluxe rooms are good value at this contemporary 10-room hotel, with floating desks, big beds and 32-inch, wall-mounted LCD flat-screens. Standard rooms are slightly smaller and have twin beds, but share the same slick, modern styling. The downstairs restaurant serves breakfast (30,000Rp) and meals throughout the day.

★ Beta Rumah   INDONESIAN $

(✒ 0822 4840 5481; Jl Said Perintah 1; mains 25,000-60,000Rp; ⊙ 9am-9pm Mon-Sat; ✐) The Beta is the Alpha and Omega of real Ambonese food. Laid out in simple *rumah makan* style beneath a glass sneeze shield, you'll find local delicacies such as *kohu-ko-hu*, made with smoked skipjack tuna, green beans and shaved coconut, or squid with papaya leaves, steamed in a banana leaf with *kenari* nuts and *colo colo* (citrus dip).

Sarinda   BAKERY $

(✒ 0911-355109; Jl Sultan Hairun 11; pastries from 7000Rp; ⊙ 8am-8pm; 🛜) With its lovely Dutch-colonial windows, ample garden seating and central location, this bakery is a great place to start the day with fresh bread, pastries and decent coffee. There's a second branch on Jl Sam Ratulangi.

★ Sibu-Sibu   CAFE

(✒ 0911-312 525; Jl Said Perintah 47A; coffee 10,000-15,000Rp, snacks & meals 5000-30,000Rp; ⊙ 7am-10pm; 🛜) Ambonese stars of screen and song deck the walls of this sweet little open-fronted coffee shop and bar, which plays live Malukan and Hawaiian music while serving snacks such as *koyabu* (cassava cake), and *lopis pulut* (sticky rice with palm jaggery). It has cold Bintang, free wi-fi, good full breakfasts and the signature strong ginger coffee mixed with spices and nuts.

ⓘ Information

Maluku Province Tourist Office (Dinas Parawisata; ✒ 0911-312300; Jl Jenderal Sudirman; ⊙ 8am-4pm Mon-Fri) A handy source of info on Ambon, the Bandas, Seram and other neighbouring islands, some in English.

A good source of Maluku information is Ernest Michael, who can be found at Momoa Michael Guesthouse, near the airport.

ⓘ Getting There & Around

The Damri **airport bus** (per person 35,000Rp) leaves from landward side of the Peace Gong four times daily (4.30am, 5am, 10am and 1pm – timed to feed airline departures). It departs from the airport for the city centre after inbound flights land (approximately 7am, 8am, 1pm and 4pm).

Hatu- and Liliboi-bound bemos pass the airport gates (10,000Rp, 40 minutes from Mardika Market). A small passenger ferry (3000Rp) operates from Mardika Market across the bay to Wayame village from where you can pick up a bemo or *ojek* for the 9km to the airport – if you're travelling light it's the quickest way. A taxi costs 150,000Rp to/from the airport.

Road transport (including buses to Seram via the Hunimua car ferry) starts from various points along Jl Pantai Mardika. For Natsepa (5000Rp), Tulehu-Momoking (7000Rp) and Tulehu-Hurnala (10,000Rp) take Waai or Darussalam bemos. Latuhalat (5000Rp) and Amahusu bemos also pick up passengers beside the Trikora monument on Jl Dr Latumenten.

Banda Islands

✒ 0910 / POP 22,000

Combining raw natural beauty, a warm local heart, and a palpable and fascinating history, this remote cluster of 10 picturesque islands isn't just Maluku's choice travel destination, it's one of the best in Indonesia. Particularly impressive undersea drop-offs are vibrantly plastered with multicoloured coral gardens offering superlative snorkelling and tasty diving. The central islands – Pulau Neira and Pulau Banda Besar (the great nutmeg island) – curl in picturesque crescents around a pocket-sized tropical Mt Fuji (Gunung Api, 656m). Outlying Hatta, Ai and Neilaka each have utterly undeveloped picture-postcard beaches. The fast-boat service from Ambon has made Banda more accessible, at least in the dry season; it's time to get there before everyone else does!

ℹ️ Getting There & Around

Dimonim Air (www.dimonimair.com) flies from Ambon to Bandaneira on Wednesday (351,000Rp, 40 minutes). Cancellations are likely in bad weather.

Express Bahari 2B ferry leaves Tulehu for Bandaneira at 9am on Tuesday and Saturday, returning at the same time on Wednesday and Sunday (regular/VIP 415,000/650,000Rp, six hours).

Pelni ships leave Ambon fortnightly on Monday, taking about nine hours to Banda.

Bandaneira

Little Bandaneira is the Bandas' main port and administrative centre. In the Dutch era the *perkeniers* virtually bankrupted themselves maintaining a European lifestyle, even after the lost nutmeg monopoly made it untenable. Today, Bandaneira's sleepy, flower-filled streets are so quiet that two becak count as a traffic jam. It's a charming place to wander aimlessly, admire tumbledown Dutch villas, ponder mouldering ruins, watch glorious cloudscapes over Gunung Api and trip over discarded cannon lolling in the grass.

Bandaneira has a handful of mosques, historic buildings and fortresses. Stop by **Benteng Belgica** (by donation) and **Benteng Nassau** for a slice of colonial history.

Dive Bluemotion (✆0823 9933 0106; www.dive-bluemotion.com; Jl Baba Village, Baba Lagoon Hotel; dives 500,000Rp; equipment per day 150,000Rp; ⊙Feb-May & Sep-Dec) is one of only two land-based dive operations in the Bandas. It has new, well-maintained gear, a good speedboat and fair prices (cheaper as more dives are taken). Surcharges for Run and Hatta apply, and trips include lunch. It's closed during the unsettled months of January and June to September.

🛏️ Sleeping & Eating

Mutiara Guesthouse   GUESTHOUSE $
(✆0813 3034 3377, 0910-21344; www.banda-mutiara.com; r with fan/air-con from 250,000/275,000Rp; ❄️🛜) A special boutique hotel disguised as a homestay, Mutiara is the first venture of Abba Rizal, the tirelessly helpful and well-connected owner of Cilu Bintang. The front garden is a wonderful spot for an afternoon snooze, or to catch the resident cuscus raiding the cinnamon tree at night.

Delfika   GUESTHOUSE $
(✆0910-21027; delfika1@yahoo.com; Jl Gereja Tua; r with fan/air-con 250,000/350,000Rp; ❄️) Built around a shady courtyard, the charming Delfika has a range of mostly well-renovated rooms on the main village drag. There's also a sitting room stuffed with bric-a-brac and an attached **cafe** (Jl Gereja Tua; mains 20,000-80,000Rp; ⊙10am-9pm), one of Banda's best.

Vita Guesthouse   GUESTHOUSE $
(Fita; ✆0910-21332, 0812 4706 7099; allandarman@gmail.com; Jl Pasar; d with fan/air-con from 190,000/220,000Rp; ❄️) Popular with Euro backpackers, Vita offers a great bayside location with seven comfortable rooms set in a colonnaded L-shape around a waterfront palm garden (ideal for an evening beer, contemplating Gunung Api). The beds are adequate, and it has some decent wooden furniture in the rooms and Western-style toilets.

★**Cilu Bintang Estate**   BOUTIQUE HOTEL $$
(✆0813 3034 3377, 0910-21604; www.cilubintang.com; Jl Benteng Belgica; d 400,000-800,000Rp; ❄️🛜♿) After storming the charts with his first guesthouse, the still-excellent Mutiara, Abba (Rizal, the owner) has outdone himself with the difficult sophomore release. Cilu Bintang is head and shoulders above any other accommodation in all the Banda Islands – an immaculate, breezy Dutch-colonial reproduction with superb rooms, beds, food and company.

Other Islands

Pulau Banda Besar is the largest of the Banda Islands, and the most important historical source of nutmeg. You can explore nutmeg groves or the ruins of fort Benteng Hollandia (c 1624). Arrange a spice tour with your Bandaneira lodging.

Pulau Hatta has crystal waters and a mind-expanding, coral-encrusted vertical drop-off near Lama village.

Pulau Ai is also blessed with rich coral walls and postcard beaches. It has a few very simple homestays, from which you can explore the empty white-sand beaches. Simple guesthouses near the dock have fine views. Enjoy pure tropical fantasy at **CDS Bungalow** (per person incl meals r 250,000-300,000Rp), which has two secluded rooms perched over a nearly deserted beach; book through Cilu Bintang Estate).

PAPUA (IRIAN JAYA)

Even a country as full of adventure as Indonesia has its final frontier. And here it is: Papua, half of the world's second-biggest island, New Guinea. It may be the youngest part of Indonesia, but Papua's rich tribal traditions span centuries. This is a place where some people still hunt their food with bows and arrows. A place where roads are so scarce, that to travel between towns you often have no choice but to take to the air or the water. So unlike any other part of Indonesia, the province formerly known as Irian Jaya can feel like a different country – which is what many Papuans, who are Melanesian and ethnically distinct from other Indonesians, would like it to be.

Travel here is a challenge, and it's not cheap. But those who do so are awed by the charm of Papua's peoples, the resilience of its cultures and the grandeur of its dramatic landscapes and idyllic seascapes.

ℹ Getting There & Around

Intercity roads are still a thing of the future for Papua. Boats are an option for travelling to Papua and between its coastal towns if you have enough time, or along its rivers if you have enough money. Flying is the common way to reach Papua and to travel between its cities and towns.

Jayapura

✔ 0967 / POP 315,872

Downtown Jayapura is hot and busy with traffic, but it has a beautiful setting between steep, forested hills opening on to Teluk Imbi and tropical air that some find appealing.

A small settlement named Hollandia was established here by the Dutch in 1910. In 1944, 80,000 Allied troops landed here to dislodge the Japanese in the largest amphibious operation of WWII in the southwestern Pacific. After WWII, Hollandia became capital of Dutch New Guinea. Following the Indonesian takeover in 1963, it was renamed Jayapura ('Victory City') in 1968. A public consultation exercise in 2010 favoured changing the name to Port Numbay, a name popular with indigenous Papuans, but this has yet to be officially ratified.

Cenderawasih University's recently redesigned **Museum Loka Budaya** (✔ 0852 4438 0693; Jl Abepura, Abepura; 25,000Rp; ⊙ 8am-4pm Mon-Fri) contains a fascinating range of Papuan artefacts including the best collection of Asmat carvings and 'devil-dance' costumes outside Agats, most of which were selected by Michael Rockefeller and his team in the 1950s for exhibition in New York City's Metropolitan Museum of Art. The art remained in Papua after Rockefeller's canoe capsized near the Asmat region and he was eaten by cannibals.

ℹ PAPUA TRAVEL PERMIT

In the past couple of years permit restrictions have been eased for many areas of Papua. At the time of research in mid-2017, exactly where a *surat jalan* (permit) was required seemed to depend on whom you asked. The police in Jayapura insisted one was required for almost every town and area in Papua, but the reality was that in all but the remotest areas you now very rarely get asked to produce a *surat jalan*. To be on the safe side, however, if you're heading to the Baliem Valley, Yali country, Agats and the Korowai region it's better to get one.

A *surat jalan* is usually easily obtained from the police in the capitals of Papua's 30-odd *kabupaten* (regencies). Take your passport, two passport photos, and photocopies of your passport's personal details page and your Indonesian visa. The procedure normally takes about an hour and no payment should be requested. The duration of the permit depends on how long you request and the expiry date of your visa. The best place to obtain a wide-ranging *surat jalan* is Polresta in Jayapura, where you can present a list of every place that you intend to visit.

When you apply for a surat jalan, the police will tell you if anywhere on your itinerary is off-limits. Some Indonesian embassies may tell you that in order to visit Papua you must obtain a special permit from the Indonesian immigration authorities and/or the police department in Jakarta – some have even reportedly refused visas to applicants who said they planned to visit Papua. This is not true. In practice, as long as you have an Indonesian visa then you're free to travel to and around Papua.

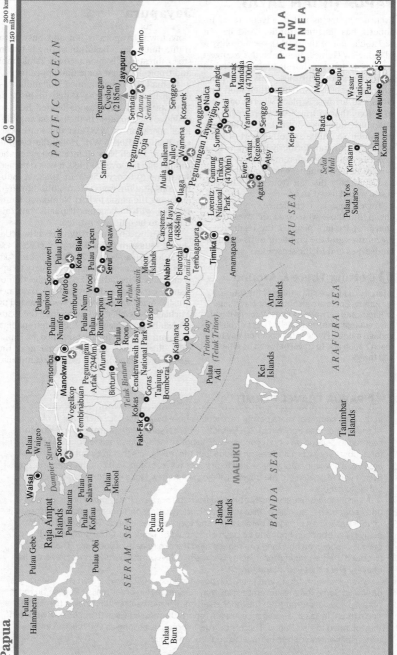

Antoni Sitepu (☎0812 488 0304; www.
papuajayatours.com) has been guiding trips
around Papua and beyond since 1993. He
speaks excellent English and is well versed
in the ways of the local tribes.

🛏 Sleeping & Eating

Amabel Hotel   HOTEL $
(☎0967-522102; Jl Tugu 100; s/tw/d
253,000/297,000/363,000Rp; ❄🌐) Easily the
best budget option, the Amabel has neat
little rooms with windows and its own inexpensive restaurant. It's up a small, leafy
side street, a block before the **Mal Jayapura**
(Jl Sam Ratulangi 46; ⊙10am-10pm) shopping
mall.

Hotel Grand View   HOTEL $$
(☎0967-550646; Jl Pasifik Permai 5; r incl breakfast 450,000-750,000Rp; ❄🌐) A very good
deal. This place is plain but bright, modern, no-frills rooms, half of which peer directly out over the waters of the bay. The
downstairs cafe-restaurant is a delightfully
cheery strawberry red.

Duta Cafe   SEAFOOD $$
(Duta Dji Cafe; ☎0853 4414 5982; Jl Raya Kelapa
Dua, Entrop; vegetable dishes from 40,000Rp, whole
fish 90,000Rp; ⊙8am-11pm) Open-air and riverfront, Duta Cafe serves up excellent *ikan
bakar* (grilled fish) and offers a lively scene
in the evenings.

ℹ Information

Immigration Office (☎0967-533647; Jl Perce-
takan 15; ⊙8am-4pm Mon-Fri) This office will
issue one 30-day extension to a visa on arrival
(VOA): apply at least one week before your visa
expires. Travellers with VOAs must come here
for a (free) exit stamp before crossing the land
border to Vanimo, Papua New Guinea.

ℹ Getting There & Away

Jayapura airport, actually located at Sentani,
36km west, is the hub of Papuan aviation. Most
flights arrive and depart between 7am and
1pm. Tickets are available online and at travel
agencies, as well as at the airport and Jayapura
offices of the airlines. Official airport taxis from
the airport at Sentani to central Jayapura cost
300,000Rp. If you organise a taxi yourself
without going through the taxi booths, they will
quote you the same fare but with bargaining will
drop as low as 200,000Rp.

Sentani
☎0967 / POP 44,779
Sentani, the growing airport town 36km
west of Jayapura, sits between the forested
Pegunungan Cyclop and beautiful Danau
Sentani, where authentic island fishing villages can be visited by boat.

Rasen Hotel (☎0967-594455; rasenhotel_
papua@yahoo.com; Jl Penerangan; s incl breakfast
250,000Rp, d incl breakfast 350,000-400,000Rp;
❄🌐) is the best choice near the airport,
with small, clean rooms with hot showers
and TV, plus a decent restaurant, free airport drop-offs and even a small fish pond.
Unsurprisingly it fills up, so try to call ahead.
Some staff speak English.

Sentani's most charming dining is at
Yougwa Restaurant (☎0822 3952 7778; Jl
Raya Sentani; mains 25,000-60,000Rp; ⊙9am-
7pm Mon-Sat, 11am-5pm Sun), over the lake
13km east of town. Try ikan gabus (snake-
skin fish), a tasty lake fish that doesn't fill
your mouth with little bones.

Baliem Valley

The legendary Baliem Valley is the most
popular and most accessible destination in
Papua's interior. The Dani people who live
here were still dependent on tools of stone,
bone and wood when a natural-history expedition led by American Richard Archbold
chanced upon the valley in 1938. Dani life
has since changed enormously with stone
axes being replaced by mobile phones and
age-old belief systems with Christianity, but
even so the changes are often only skin-deep
and the valley and surrounding highlands
remain one of the world's last fascinatingly
traditional areas. Visiting the Baliem Valley
and trekking through high mountain scenery, past neat and orderly Dani villages,
takes you to a world far removed from Jakarta and is an honour and an experience to
be savoured. For most people it is the highlight of Papua.

Wamena
☎0969 / POP 45,000
The obligatory base for travels around
the valley, Wamena is a sprawling Indonesian creation peppered with authentic
attractions such as farmers' markets and
surrounding Dani villages, some of which

display their 200-year-old, mummified ancestors. The population is a mix of Papuans and non-Papuans, and the latter run most of the businesses.

Penis gourds worn by the Dani tribesmen were once banned here, during Indonesia's 'Operasi Koteka' (an attempt to force the men to wear clothes) in the 1970s. But some old men who come into town for supplies or to hawk their wares are regularly seen wearing them.

🛏 Sleeping & Eating

★ Baliem Pilamo Hotel   HOTEL $$
(☑ 0969-31043; baliempilamohotel@yahoo.co.id; Jl Trikora 114; r incl breakfast from 456,000Rp; 🛜) The hotel of choice for most visitors. The more expensive rooms are tasteful, contemporary, brown-and-white affairs in the newer section at the rear. Of the cheaper ones, the standards are smallish and plain but acceptable, and the superiors have a semi-luxury feel and quirky garden-style bathrooms.

Putri Dani Hotel   HOTEL $$
(☑ 0969-31223; Jl Irian 40; r incl breakfast from 650,000Rp) This small family-run place offers nine spotless, comfortable rooms with hot showers and endless tea and coffee. The back rooms surround Japanese garden complete with a fish-filled water feature. From December to July it's often home to Wamena's Persiwa football team, so may be booked out.

Mas Budi   INDONESIAN $
(☑ 0969 31214; Jl Patimura; mains from 75,000Rp) Run by the same owners as the Baliem Pilamo, this restaurant offers a smorgasbord with local specialities such as deer meat, fried shrimp, corn fritters and delicious *tamarela* juice. An attached hotel also offers rooms starting at 350,000Rp.

ℹ Information

Papua.com (☑ 0969-34488; fuj0627@yahoo.co.jp; Jl Ahmad Yani 49; per hour 12,000Rp; ⊘ 8am-6pm Mon-Sat) This efficient internet cafe has fax and scanning services. Its owner is a highly experienced Papua traveller and a willing mine of information. He sometimes runs trips up the mountain to search for wild dogs.
Police Station (☑ 0969-112, 0969-110; Jl Safri Darwin; ⊘ 7am-2pm) Come here to obtain a *surat jalan*.

ℹ Getting There & Away

Flights can be heavily booked, especially in August. The carriers between Jayapura (Sentani) and Wamena are **Wings Air** (☑ 0811 420 757, 0804 177 8899; www.lionair.co.id; Bandar Udara Airport; ⊘ 5am-3pm), **Trigana** (☑ 0969 34590; www.trigana-air.com; airport; ⊘ 6am-3pm) and **Xpress Air** (☑ 0821 9937; www.xpressair.co.id; Bandar Udara Airport; ⊘ 6am-3pm), and all operate out of Wamena's **airport terminal** (Jl Gatot Subroto).

Overcrowded bemos head out along the main roads from several starting points around Wamena. Most just leave when they are full. The main terminals – Terminal Jibama, Terminal Misi and Sinakma – are at Wamena's three markets.

Sorong
☑ 0951 / POP 219,958

Papua's second-biggest city, Sorong sits at the northwestern tip of the Vogelkop. It's a busy port and base for oil and logging operations in the region. Few travellers stay longer than it takes to get on a boat to the Raja Ampat Islands, but Sorong can be interesting for a day or two, and there are some worthwhile destinations in the surrounding region.

Waigo Hotel (☑ 0951-333500; Jl Yos Sudarso; r 489,000-705,600Rp, ste from 1,029,000Rp, all incl breakfast; ⊞🛜) offers fair value, large and bright rooms. The in-house restaurant (mains 25,000Rp to 65,000Rp) is good value. JE Meridien Hotel is handily located opposite the airport, with nicely aged, slightly old-fashioned rooms of generous proportions.

ℹ Information

Polresta Sorong (☑ 0811 487 2016, 0951-321929; http://polressorongkota.com; Jl Yani I) Head to this police station, 1km west of the airport, for a *surat jalan* (travel permit).
Raja Ampat Tourism Management Office (☑ 0811 485 2033; Jl Basuki Rahmat; ⊘ 9am-5pm Mon-Fri, to 1pm Sat) This incredibly helpful office can tell you almost anything you need to know about the Raja Ampat Islands, and it's the best place to buy the tag permitting you to visit the islands (it's 1,000,000Rp and is good for one year).

ℹ Getting There & Around

Flights serve Ambon, Jakarta, , Makassar and regional destinations.

Boats for the Raja Ampat Islands depart regularly from Pelabuhan Feri.

Official airport taxis charge 100,000Rp to hotels at the western end of town; on the street outside you can charter a public *taksi* for half that or less. Using the yellow public *taksi* (minibuses; 5000Rp), first get one going west outside the airport to Terminal Remu (600m), then change there to another for Jl Yos Sudarso. Short *ojek* (motorcycle) rides of 2km to 3km are 10,000Rp; between the western end of town and the airport is 20,000Rp.

Raja Ampat Islands

POP 49,048

The sparsely populated Raja Ampat Islands comprise more than 1500 islands just off Sorong. With their sublime scenery of steep, jungle-covered islands, scorching white-sand beaches, hidden lagoons, spooky caves, weird mushroom-shaped islets and pellucid turquoise waters, Raja Ampat has to be one of the most beautiful island chains in Southeast Asia.

Unadulterated beauty isn't the only thing drawing people here, though. Raja Ampat also has abundant wildlife, with a couple of species of birds of paradise dancing in the trees and a diversity of marine life and coral reef systems that are a diver's dream come true (and fantastic for snorkellers, too). So great is the quantity and variety of marine life here that scientists have described Raja Ampat as a biological hotspot and believe that the reef systems here restock reefs throughout the South Pacific and Indian Oceans.

✖ Activities

★ Blue Magic
DIVING

The runaway favourite among local dive professionals who have seen it all, this submerged seamount teems with life, including tassled wobbegong sharks, schools of barracuda, massive manta rays and plenty of corals and smaller creatures such as pygmy seahorses. Best to dive here with stronger current and an advanced certification.

★ Wayag Islands
DIVING

These small, uninhabited and incredibly picturesque islands, 30km beyond Waigeo, feature heavily in Raja Ampat promotional material. It's mainly liveaboards that dive here, but Wayag also attracts nondivers for its scenery, snorkelling and the challenge of scaling its highest peak, Pindito. An all-day speedboat round trip from Waisai for six to 10 people costs around 13,000,000Rp.

★ KLM Insos Raja Ampat
DIVING

(📱 0812 9940 9148; www.yenkoranurajaampat.com/budget-liveaboard; 2,500,000Rp per person per day) This locally owned *phinisi*, a traditional Indonesian wooden ship, recently became the first budget-friendly liveaboard in the Raja Ampat Islands. It's an unbeatable option for those looking to remain solvent while exploring the best of the islands above and below the sea, including far-flung islands like Wayag and Piaynemo, and top dive sites including Melissa's Garden, Blue Magic, Cape Kri and Sardine Reef.

Cape Kri
DIVING

The fish numbers and variety at the eastern point of Pulau Kri have to be seen to be believed. A world-record 374 fish species in one dive was counted in 2012. Schools of barracuda, jacks, batfish and snapper coexist with small reef fish, rays, sharks, turtles and groupers. Beautiful coral too. Currents can be strong, so you'll need a minimum of 50 logged dives.

Sardine Reef
DIVING

Sardine, 4km northeast of Kri, slopes down to 33m, and has so many fish that it can get quite dark. The fish-and-coral combination is great for photographers. Currents can be strong.

Fam Islands
DIVING

Calm waters, stunning coral and masses of fish, notably at the Melissa's Garden spot.

☞ Tours

★ Kayak4Conservation
KAYAKING

(K4C; 📱 0811 483 4617, 0811 485 7905; www.kayak4conservation.com; packages from €1270 per person) 🖉 Established by the forward-thinking folk at Papua Diving and the Raja Ampat Research and Conservation Centre (RARCC) on Pulau Kri, Kayak4Conservation runs exciting multiday expeditions around the Raja Ampat islands by kayak, staying at locally owned guesthouses and guided by a local community member.

🛏 Sleeping & Eating

★ Yenkoranu Homestay
HOMESTAY $$

(📱 082198498519; www.yenkoranurajaampat.com; Pulau Kri; s/d full board from 300,000/500,000Rp) A well-run homestay sandwiched between a couple of dive shops on the northern stretch of Kri, with burgeoning coral reefs right off the jetty. The place offers a range of accommodation and a waterfront restaurant featuring cold Bintang. The highly competent general manager speaks perfect English, is a divemaster and knows about activities in the region.

Kordiris Homestay & Diving
GUESTHOUSE $$

(📱 0852 4412 4338; kordirisrajaampat@gmail.com; Pulau Gam; per person full board 300,000-350,000Rp) This well-organised homestay, which sits in a secluded, dreamy bay dotted with tiny coral islands, is one of the best around. The rooms are made of palm thatch, and while some are in the cool shade of trees, others are over the crystal-clear water or on the salty white sand. There's a dive center on-site, but no certification program.

Kri Eco Resort
RESORT $$$

(📱 0811 483 4614; www.papua-diving.com; Pulau Kri; 7-night unlimited diving package from €1667; 🖥) ✎ Operating since 1994, Kri Eco is the original Raja Ampat dive lodge. It's a professional operation with a gorgeous setting. Baby black-tip reef sharks are frequently seen swimming in the shallows below the restaurant. All 13 rooms are on stilts at the edge of the crystal-clear water but most have on-land, shared bathrooms (with *mandis* and hot-water showers).

ⓘ Getting There & Away

Waisai has an airport, but its runway is very short – too short for full-sized passenger planes. Instead there are Susi Air (www.susiair.com) flights on Monday and Friday at 10am between Sorong and Waisai, Wings Air (www.lionair.co.id) flights every afternoon and Nam Air is set to open a flight as well. But it's just as quick (after all the messing around at the airport) to get the ferry.

Fast Marina Express passenger boats (economy/VIP 125,000/220,000Rp, two hours) depart at 9am and 2pm daily for Waisai from Sorong's **Pelabuhan Feri** (Pelabuhan Rakyat; Jl Feri, off Jl Sudirman). The boats head back from Waisai at 9am and 2pm as well.

Ojeks to Pelabuhan Feri cost around 15,000Rp from the western end of Sorong or outside the airport; a taxi is around 50,000Rp. *Ojeks* between port and town in Waisai (2km) are 20,000Rp.

An overnight Fajar Indah boat to Waigama and Lilinta on Misool leaves Pelabuhan Feri at 11pm every Friday (economy/VIP 200,000/300,000Rp) arriving in Misool Saturday around 8am. The boat returns Thursday morning at 8am, arriving in Sorong at 4pm.

Marina Express runs a boat twice weekly between Sorong and Misool, for 250,000Rp each way. It leaves Monday at noon from Sorong, returns on Tuesday, then leaves again for Misool on Wednesday and returns to Sorong Thursday morning. The journey takes about five hours.

Other passenger boats to and around the islands are irregular. To arrange transport around the islands once there, your best bet is to ask at your accommodation or the **Waisai Tourism Information Centre** (Waisai; ⊙ 8am-4pm Mon-Thu, to 3pm Fri, limited hours Sat & Sat). Prices depend on boat, distance and petrol prices and are usually negotiable.

UNDERSTAND INDONESIA

Indonesia Today

Nothing ever seems settled in Indonesia, whether it's the land, the sea, tourists and traffic in Bali or society itself. Yet there was justifiable cause for celebration after the 2014 national elections continued the almost entirely peaceful precedent set during elections five years earlier. Not bad for a country with a violent political past, including a 1965 political genocide. Still, economic, religious and environmental challenges remain hugely significant as the nation feels its way to the future.

As the site of the modern world's greatest explosion (Gunung Tambora in 1815) and other cataclysms such as the tsunami in 2004, Indonesia has more than its fair share of natural disasters. More recent concern was the threat of eruption from Bali's Gunung Agung in September 2017. More than 100,000 residents from the volcano's fringes were forced to evacuate and the tourism industry was on high alert as authorities monitored the situation.

The tourism dollar accounts for just a bit more than 3% of Indonesia's GDP but it's a vital source of foreign income and investment, especially in Bali. The Indonesian government has made no secret of wanting to increase this little cash cow and has plans to attract foreign investment and develop 'new Balis' in places such as Nusa Tenggara, Thousand Islands off Java, Danau Toba in Sumatra, and parts of Sulawesi and Maluku.

History

Until the last few years it was widely believed that the first humanoids (Homo erectus) lived in Central Java around 500,000 years ago – having reached Indonesia across land bridges from Africa – before either dying off or being wiped out by the arrival of Homo sapiens. But the discovery in 2003 of the remains of a tiny islander, dubbed the 'hobbit', seems to indicate that Homo erectus survived much longer than was previously thought, and that previously accepted timelines of Indonesia's evolutionary history need to be re-examined (though many scientists continue to challenge the 'hobbit theory'). Most Indonesians are descendents of Malay people who began migrating around 4000 BC from Cambodia, Vietnam and southern China. They steadily developed small kingdoms and by 700 BC these settlers had developed skilful rice-farming techniques.

Hinduism & Buddhism

The growing prosperity of these early kingdoms soon caught the attention of Indian and Chinese merchants, and along with silks and spices came the dawn of Hinduism and Buddhism in Indonesia. These religions quickly gained a foothold in the archipelago and soon became central to the great kingdoms of the 1st millennium AD. The Buddhist Srivijaya empire held sway over the Malay Peninsula and southern Sumatra, extracting wealth from its dominion over the strategic Straits of Melaka. The Hindu Mataram and Buddhist Sailendra kingdoms dominated Central Java, raising their grandiose monuments, Borobudur and Prambanan, over the fertile farmland that brought them their prosperity. When Mataram slipped into mysterious decline around the 10th century AD, it was fast replaced with an even more powerful Hindu kingdom. Founded in 1294, the Majapahit empire made extensive territorial gains under its ruler, Hayam Wuruk, and prime minister, Gajah Mada, and while claims that they controlled much of Sulawesi, Sumatra and Borneo now seem fanciful, most of Java, Madura and Bali certainly fell within their realm. But things would soon change. Despite the Majapahit empire's massive power and influence, greater fault lines were opening up across Indonesia, and Hinduism's golden age was swiftly drawing to a close.

Rise of Islam

With the arrival of Islam came the power, the reason and the will to oppose the hegemony of the Majapahits, and satellite kingdoms soon took up arms against the Hindu kings. In the 15th century the Majapahits fled to Bali, where Hindu culture continues to flourish, leaving Java to the increasingly powerful Islamic sultanates. Meanwhile, the influential trading kingdoms of Melaka (on the Malay Peninsula) and Makassar (in southern Sulawesi) were also embracing Islam, sowing the seeds that would later make modern Indonesia the most populous Muslim nation on earth.

European Expansion

Melaka fell to the Portuguese in 1511 and European eyes were soon settling on the archipelago's riches, prompting two centuries of unrest as the Portuguese, Spanish, Dutch and British wrestled for control. By 1700 the Dutch held most of the trump cards, with the Dutch East India Company (Vereenigde Oost-Indische Compagnie; VOC) controlling the region's lucrative spice trade and becoming the world's first multinational company. Following the VOC's bankruptcy, however, the British governed Java under Sir Stamford Raffles between 1811 and 1816, only to relinquish control again to the Dutch after the end of the Napoleonic wars; they then held control of Indonesia until its independence 129 years later. It was not, however, a trouble-free tenancy: the Dutch had to face numerous rebellions. Javan prince Diponegoro's five-year guerrilla war was finally put down in 1830, costing the lives of 8000 Dutch troops.

Road to Independence

By the beginning of the 20th century, the Dutch had brought most of the archipelago under their control, but the revolutionary tradition of Diponegoro was never truly quashed, bubbling beneath the surface of Dutch rule and finding a voice in the young Sukarno. The debate was sidelined as the Japanese swept through Indonesia during WWII, but with their departure came the opportunity for Sukarno to declare Indonesian independence, which he did from his Jakarta home on 17 August 1945. The Dutch, however, were unwilling to relinquish their hold over Indonesia and – supported by the British, who had entered Indonesia to accept the Japanese surrender – moved quickly to reassert their authority over the country. Resistance was stiff and for four bitter years the Indonesian resistance fought a guerrilla war. But American and UN opposition to the reimposition of colonialism and the mounting casualty toll eventually forced the Dutch to pack it in, and the Indonesian flag – the *sang merah putih* (red and white) – was finally hoisted over Jakarta's Istana Merdeka (Freedom Palace) on 27 December 1949.

Depression, Disunity & Dictatorship

Unity in war quickly became division in peace, as religious fundamentalists and nationalist separatists challenged the fledgling central government. After almost a decade of political impasse and economic depression, Sukarno made his move in 1957, declaring Guided Democracy (a euphemism for dictatorship) with army backing and leading Indonesia into nearly four decades of authoritarian rule. Despite moves towards the one-party state, Indonesia's three-million-strong Communist Party (Partai Komunis Indonesia; PKI) was the biggest in the world by 1965 and Sukarno had long realised the importance of winning its backing. But as the PKI's influence in government grew, so did tensions with the armed forces. Things came to a head on the night of 30 September 1965, when elements of the palace guard launched an attempted coup. Quickly put down by General Suharto, the coup was blamed – perhaps unfairly – on the PKI and became the pretext for an army-led purge that left as many as 500,000 communist sympathisers dead. Strong evidence later emerged from declassified documents that both the US (opposed to communism) and the UK (seeking to protect its interests in Malaysia) aided and abetted Suharto's purge by drawing up hit lists of communist agitators. By 1968 Suharto had ousted Sukarno and was installed as president. Suharto brought unity through repression, annexing Papua in 1969, and reacting to insurgency with an iron fist. In 1975 Portuguese Timor was invaded, leading to tens of thousands of deaths; separatist ambitions in Aceh and Papua were also met with a ferocious military response. But despite endemic corruption, the 1980s and 1990s were Indonesia's boom years, with meteoric economic growth and a starburst of opulent building ventures transforming the face of the capital.

Suharto's Fall

As Asia's economy went into freefall during the closing years of the 1990s, Suharto's house of cards began to tumble. Indonesia went bankrupt overnight and the country found an obvious scapegoat in the cronyism and corruption endemic in the dictator's regime. Protests erupted across Indonesia in 1998, and the May riots in Jakarta left thousands, many of them Chinese, dead. After three decades of dictatorial rule, Suharto resigned on 21 May 1998. Passions cooled when Vice President BJ Habibie took power on a reform ticket, but ambitious promises were slow to materialise, and in November of the same year riots again rocked many Indonesian cities. Promises of forthcoming elections succeeded in closing the floodgates, but separatist groups took advantage of the weakened central government and violence erupted in Maluku, Papua, East Timor and Aceh. East Timor won its independence after a referendum in August 1999, but only after Indonesian-backed militias had destroyed its infrastructure and left thousands dead.

Democracy & Reform

Against this unsettled backdrop, the June 1999 legislative elections passed surprisingly smoothly, leaving Megawati Sukarnoputri (Sukarno's daughter) and her reformist Indonesian Democratic Party for Struggle (PDI-P) as the largest party, with 33% of the vote. But months later the separate presidential election was narrowly won by Abdurrahman Wahid (Gus Dur), whose efforts to undo corruption met with stiff resistance. Megawati was eventually sworn in as president in 2001, but her term proved a disappointment for many Indonesians, as corrupt infrastructures were left in place, the military's power remained intact, poverty levels remained high and there were high-profile terrorism attacks such as the 2002 Bali bombings. Megawati lost the 2004 presidential elections to Susilo Bambang Yudhoyono (aka 'SBY'), an ex-army officer who served in East Timor. His successes included cracking down on Islamic militants and pumping more money into education and health. SBY's term was also marked by a series of disasters, beginning with the 2004 Boxing Day tsunami that ravaged Aceh in northern Sumatra. In 2006, a quake shook Yogyakarta, killing 6800 people, and in 2009 a quake devastated Padang in Sumatra. Elections in 2009 were largely peaceful. SBY cruised to an easy re-election on a platform of continuing moderate policies. Extremist Islamic parties have fared poorly against more moderate parties. In the years following, the nation enjoyed a good run of peace and prosperity.

People & Culture

The old Javanese saying *bhinneka tunggal ika* (they are many; they are one) is said to be Indonesia's national dictum, but with a population of over 255 million, 300-plus languages and more than 17,000 islands it's not surprising that many from the outer islands resent Java, where power is centralised. Indonesia is loosely bound together by a single flag (which is increasingly flown with pride during national holidays) and a single language (Bahasa Indonesia), but in some ways can be compared to the EU – a richly diverse confederacy of peoples.

The world's most populous Muslim nation is no hardline Islamic state. Indonesians have traditionally practised a relaxed form of Islam, and though there's no desire to imitate the West, most see no conflict in catching a Hollywood movie in a Western-style shopping mall after prayers at the mosque. The country is becoming more cosmopolitan; Facebook usage is epic. Millions of Indonesians now work overseas – mainly in the Gulf, Hong Kong and Malaysia – bringing back external influences to their villages when they return. A boom in low-cost air travel has enabled a generation of Indonesians to travel internally and overseas conveniently and cheaply for the first time, while personal mobility is much easier today – it's possible to buy a motorcycle on hire purchase with as little as a 500,000Rp deposit. But not everyone has the cash or time for overseas jaunts and there remains a yawning gulf between the haves and the havenots. Indonesia is much poorer than many of its Asian neighbours, with over 40% surviving on US$2 a day, and in many rural areas opportunities are few and far between.

Religion

Indonesia's constitution affirms that the state is based on a belief in 'the One and Only God'; yet it also, rather contradictorily, guarantees 'freedom of worship, each according to his/her own religion or belief'. In practice, this translates into a requirement to follow one of the officially accepted 'religions', of which there are now six: Islam, Catholicism, Protestantism, Hinduism, Buddhism and Confucianism.

Islam is the predominant religion, with followers making up about 88% of the population. In Java, pilgrims still visit hundreds of holy places where spiritual energy is believed to be concentrated. Christians make up about 10% of the population, in scattered areas spread across the archipelago. Bali's Hindus comprise about 1.5% of the population.

Nevertheless, old beliefs persist. The earliest Indonesians were animists who practised ancestor and spirit worship. When Hinduism and Buddhism and, later, Islam and Christianity spread into the archipelago, they were layered on to this spiritual base.

Arts

DANCE

Indonesia has a rich heritage of traditional dances. In Yogyakarta there's the Ramayana Ballet, a spectacular dance drama; Lombok has a mask dance called the *kayak sando* and war dances; Malaku's *lenso* is a handkerchief dance; while Bali has a multitude of elaborate dances, a major reason to visit the island.

MUSIC

Indonesia has a massive contemporary music scene that spans all genres. The popular *dangdut* is a melange of traditional and modern, Indonesian and foreign musical styles that features instruments such as electric guitars and Indian tablas (a type of drum), and rhythms ranging from Middle Eastern pop to reggae or salsa. Among the best performers and bands of late are Neonomora, Frau, Glovves and Banda Neira. Gamelan is the best-known traditional Indonesian music: besides Bali, Java has orchestras composed mainly of percussion instruments, including drums, gongs and *angklung* (bamboo tubes shaken to produce a note), along with flutes and xylophones

Environment

It makes sense that Indonesians call their country Tanah Air Kita (literally, 'Our Land and Water'), as it is the world's most expansive archipelago. Of its 17,500-plus islands, about 6000 are inhabited. These diverse lands and surrounding waters have an impressive collection of plant and animal life. Yet this very bounty is its own worst enemy, as resource exploitation threatens virtually every corner of Indonesia.

The Land

About 30 million years ago, the Australian plate (carrying Papua and the Mulukus) careened into the Sunda Shelf (carrying Sumatra, Java and Borneo) from the south, while the twirling Philippine plate was pushed in from the east by the Pacific plate. The result: a landscape and ecology as diverse and dynamic as the people who live here. Much of Indonesia is defined by its 150 volcanoes: spectacular peaks towering above the forests and people below.

Wildlife

From tiny tarsiers to enormous stinking flowers, Indonesia's natural diversity is astounding, and we still don't know the complete story. Scientists continually discover new species such as a fanged frog in Sulawasi in 2015, an owl in Lombok in 2013, and three walking sharks since 2007 in the Malukus. Meanwhile, the 'lost world' of Papua's Foja mountains is a constant source of firsts, including the world's smallest wallaby, recorded in 2010.

Great apes (endemic orangutans), tigers, elephants and monkeys – lots of monkeys – plus one mean lizard are just some of the more notable critters you may encounter in Indonesia. Here you can find an astonishing 12% of the world's mammal species and 17% of its bird species.

National Parks

Despite a constant nipping at the edges by illegal loggers and farmers, Indonesia still has large tracts of protected forest and parks, and many new protected areas have been gazetted in recent years. National parks receive greater international recognition and funding than nature, wildlife and marine reserves, of which there are also many in Indonesia.

Environmental Issues

The side effects of deforestation and resource extraction are felt across the nation and beyond: floods and landslides wash away valuable topsoil, rivers become sluggish and fetid, and haze from clearing fires blankets Malaysia and Singapore every dry season, increasing international tensions. The carbon released from deforestation and fires is a significant contributor to global climate change, which in a vicious cycle creates a longer dry season, allowing for more fires.

The problems flow right through to Indonesia's coastline and seas, where more than 80% of reef habitat is considered to be at risk. A long history of cyanide and bomb fishing has left much of Indonesia's coral lifeless or crumbled. Shark finning and manta hunting have taken their toll on populations, while overfishing threatens to disrupt the marine ecosystem. Meanwhile, the burgeoning middle class is straining the nation's infrastructure. Private vehicles clog urban streets, creating choking air pollution; waste-removal services have difficulty coping with household and industrial refuse; and a lack of sewage disposal makes water from most sources undrinkable without boiling, putting further pressure on kerosene and firewood supplies.

Food & Drink

When you eat in Indonesia you savour the essence of the country. The abundance of rice reflects Indonesia's fertile landscape, the spices are reminiscent of a time of trade and invasion, and the fiery chilli echoes the passion of the people. Indonesian cuisine is really one big food swap. Chinese, Portuguese, colonists and traders have all influenced the ingredients that appear at the Indonesian table, and the cuisine has been further shaped over time by the archipelago's diverse landscape, people and culture.

Indonesian cooking is not complex, and its ingredients maintain their distinct flavours. Coriander, cumin, chilli, lemon grass, coconut, soy sauce and palm sugar are all important flavourings; sambal is a crucial condiment. Fish is a favourite and the seafood restaurants are often of a good standard. Indonesians traditionally eat with their fingers, hence the stickiness of the rice. *Sate* (skewered meat), nasi goreng (fried rice) and gado gado (vegetables with peanut sauce) are some of Indonesia's most famous dishes.

Java

The cuisine of the Betawi (original inhabitants of the Jakarta region) is known for its richness. Gado gado is a Betawi original, as is *ketoprak* (noodles, bean sprouts and tofu with soy and peanut sauce; named after a musical style, as it resembles the sound of ingredients being chopped).

Central Javan food is sweet, even the curries *gudeg* (jackfruit curry). Yogyakarta specialities include *ayam goreng* (fried chicken) and *kelepon* (green rice-flour balls with a palm-sugar filling). In Solo, specialities include *nasi liwet* (rice with coconut milk, unripe papaya, garlic and shallots, served with chicken or egg) and *serabi* (coconut-milk pancakes topped with chocolate, banana or jackfruit).

Bali

Balinese specialities are easy to find, as visitor-friendly warungs offer high-quality Balinese dishes, with several options of spiciness. Many restaurants offer the hugely popular Balinese dish, *babi guling* (spit-roast pig stuffed with chilli, turmeric, garlic and ginger) on a day's notice, but look out for any of many warungs that specialise in it. Look for the pig's head drawn on the sign or a real one in a display case. Also popular is *bebek betutu* (duck stuffed with spices, wrapped in banana leaves and coconut husks, and cooked in embers).

The local *sate, sate lilit,* is made with minced, spiced meat pressed on to skewers. Look for spicy dishes such as *lawar* (salad of chopped coconut, garlic and chilli with pork or chicken meat and blood).

Nusa Tenggara

In dry east Nusa Tenggara you'll eat less rice (although much is imported) and more sago, corn, cassava and taro. Fish is popular and one local dish is Sumbawa's *sepat* (shredded fish in coconut and mango sauce). The Sasak people of Lombok (and visitors!) like spicy *ayam Taliwang* (roasted chicken served with a peanut, tomato, chilli and lime dip) and *pelecing* sauce (made with chilli, shrimp paste and tomato).

Sumatra

In West Sumatra, beef is used in *rendang* (beef coconut curry). The region is the home of spicy Padang cuisine, among the most famous of Indonesian cuisines. The market in Bukittinggi is a great place to sample *nasi Kapau* (cuisine from the village of Kapau) – it's similar to Padang food but uses more vegetables. There's also *bubur kampiun* (mung-bean porridge with banana and rice yoghurt). In North Sumatra, the Acehnese love their *kare* or *gulai* (curry). The Bataks have a taste for pig and, to a lesser extent, dog. Pork features in *babi panggang* (pork boiled in vinegar and pig blood, and then roasted).

Kalimantan

Dayak food varies, but you may sample *rembang*, a sour fruit that's made into *sayur asem rembang* (sour vegetable soup). In Banjarmasin, the Banjar make *pepes ikan* (spiced fish cooked in banana leaves with tamarind and lemon grass). Kandangan town is famous for *ketupat Kandangan* (fish and pressed rice with lime-infused coconut sauce). The regional soup, *soto Banjar*, is a chicken broth made creamy by mashing boiled eggs into the stock. Chicken also goes into *ayam masak habang*, cooked with large red chillies.

Sulawesi

South Sulawesi locals love seafood, especially *ikan bakar* (grilled fish). Another popular local dish is *coto Makassar* (soup of beef innards, pepper, cumin and lemon grass). For sugar cravers, there's *es pallubutun* (coconut custard and banana in coconut milk and syrup). The Toraja people have their own distinct cuisine with a heavy emphasis on indigenous ingredients, many of them odd to Western palates. You can easily find *pa'piong*, which is meat or fish cooked in bamboo tubes with spices. Also look for *pamarasan*, a spicy black sauce used to cook meat. If a North Sulawesi dish has the name *rica-rica*, it's prepared with a paste of chilli, shallots, ginger and lime.

Maluku

A typical Maluku meal is tuna and *dabu-dabu* (raw vegetables with a chilli and fish-paste sauce). Sometimes fish is made into *kohu-kohu* (fish salad with citrus fruit and chilli). Sago pith is used to make porridge, bread and *mutiara* (small, jelly-like 'beans' that are added to desserts and sweet drinks).

Boiled cassava *(kasbi)* is a staple in peoples' homes as it's cheaper than rice.

In the Banda Islands you'll find nutmeg jelly on bread and pancakes, which is fitting as these were the original Spice Islands, where nutmeg was first cultivated.

Papua (Irian Jaya)

Little rice is grown here: indigenous Papuans get their carbs from other sources and the rice eaten by migrants from elsewhere in Indonesia is mostly imported. In the highlands of Papua the sweet potato is king. The Dani people grow around 60 varieties, some of which can only be eaten by the elders.

In the lowlands the sago palm provides the starchy staple food: its pulped-up pith is turned into hard, moist sago cakes, to which water is added to make *papeda,* a kind of gluey paste usually eaten with fish in a yellow turmeric-and-lime sauce. You may find the fish tastier than the *papeda.* Some lowlanders also eat the sago beetle grubs found in rotting sago palms.

Drinks

Indonesia's most popular brew is black tea with sugar. If you don't want sugar ask for *teh pahit* (bitter tea), and if you want milk buy yourself a cow. Indonesian coffee, especially from Sulawesi, is of exceptional quality, though most of the best stuff is exported. Warungs serve a chewy concoction called *kopi tubruk* (ground coffee with sugar and boiling water).

Indonesia's *es* (ice drinks) are not only refreshing, they are visually stimulating, made with syrups, fruit and jellies.

Islam is the predominant religion in Indonesia and restrictions on alcohol sales are increasing. In early 2015 a law was enacted that banned the sale of alcoholic beverages in minimarkets and shops across Indonesia (except in Bali, of course).

You will see traditional spirits for sale, including *tuak* (palm-sap wine), *arak* (rice or palm-sap wine) and Balinese *brem* (rice wine). Be careful when buying *arak.* In recent times, there have been cases where it has been adulterated with chemicals that have proved deadly. Of the domestic breweries, iconic Bintang, a clean, slightly sweet lager, is the preferred choice for many.

SURVIVAL GUIDE

 **Directory A–Z**

ACCOMMODATION
Accommodation in Indonesia ranges from a basic box with a mattress to the finest five-star luxury resorts. Costs vary considerably across the archipelago, but in general Indonesia is one of the better bargains in Southeast Asia.

Accommodation attracts a combined tax and service charge (called 'plus plus') of 21%. In budget places, this is generally included in the price, but check first.

Budget: The cheapest accommodation is in small places that are simple but usually reasonably clean and comfortable. Names often include the word losmen, homestay, inn, *penginapan* or *pondok*. Standards vary widely. You should expect air-con (in some rooms), usually wi-fi, maybe hot water, sometimes no window, private bathroom with shower and sometimes a Western-style toilet, often a pool (on Bali) and a simple breakfast.

Midrange: Many hotels have a range of rooms, from budget to midrange. The best may be called VIP, deluxe or some other moniker. In addition to what you'll get at a budget hotel, expect a a balcony/porch/patio, satellite TV, a small fridge and wi-fi.

CUSTOMS REGULATIONS
Indonesia has the usual list of prohibited imports, including drugs, weapons, fresh fruit and anything remotely pornographic. Items allowed include the following:
➡ 200 cigarettes (or 50 cigars or 100g of tobacco)
➡ a 'reasonable amount' of perfume
➡ 1L of alcohol

Surfers with more than two or three boards may be charged a 'fee', and this could apply to other items if the officials suspect that you aim to sell them in Indonesia. If you have nothing to declare, customs clearance is usually quick.

ELECTRICITY
Voltage is 30V/50Hz. Plugs have two round pins.

EMBASSIES & CONSULATES
Bali
Australian Consulate (☑ 0361-200 0100; www.bali.indonesia.embassy.gov.au; Jl Tantular 32, Denpasar; ⊘ 8am-4pm Mon-Fri) Has a consular sharing agreement with Canada.
US Consulate (☑ 0361-233605; https:// id.usembassy.gov; Jl Hayam Wuruk 310, Renon, Denpasar; ⊘ 9am-noon & 1-3.30pm Mon-Fri)

Jakarta

Australian Embassy (Map p164; ☑ 021-2550 5555; www.indonesia.embassy.gov.au; Jl Patra Kuningan Raya Kav 1-4)

Brunei Darussalam Embassy (☑ 021-3190 6080; www.mofat.gov.bn; Jl Patra Kuningan IX, 3-5, Kumingan Timur; ⊙8am-4pm Mon-Fri)

Canadian Embassy (Map p164; ☑ 021-2550 7800; www.jakarta.gc.ca; 6th fl, World Trade Centre, Jl Jenderal Sudirman Kav 29-31; ⊙7.30am-4.30pm Mon-Thu, 7.30am-3pm Fri)

Dutch Embassy (Map p164; ☑ 021-524 8200; www.netherlandsworldwide.nl/countries/indonesia; Jl HR Rasuna Said Kav S-3; ⊙9.30am-noon Mon, 8am-noon Tue-Fri)

French Embassy (Map p168; ☑021-2355 7600; www.ambafrance-id.org; Jl MH Thamrin No 20, Menteng)

German Embassy (Map p168; ☑ 021-3985 5000; www.jakarta.diplo.de; Jl MH Thamrin No 1, Menteng)

Malaysian Embassy (Map p164; ☑ 021-522 4974; www.kln.gov.my/web/idn_jakarta/home; Jln HR Rasuna Said Kav X/6, No 1-3, Kuningan; ⊙8am-4pm Mon-Fri)

New Zealand Embassy (Map p164; ☑ 021-2995 5800; www.nzembassy.com; 10th fl, Sentral Senayan 2, Jl Asia Afrika No 8; ⊙7.30am-4pm Mon-Thu, 7.30am-3pm Fri)

Papua New Guinea Embassy (Map p164; ☑021-725 1218; www.kundu-jakarta.com; 6th fl, Panin Bank Centre, Jl Jenderal Sudirman 1; ⊙8.30am-11.30am Mon-Fri)

Singaporean Embassy (Map p164; ☑021-2995 0400; www.mfa.gov.sg; Jl HR Rasuna Said, Block X/4 Kav 2, Kuningan)

UK Embassy (Map p164; ☑021-2356 5200; http://ukinindonesia.fco.gov.uk; Jl Patra Kuningan Raya Blok L5-6)

US Embassy (Map p168; ☑021-3435 9000; https://id.usembassy.gov; Jl Medan Merdeka Selatan No 3-5)

Medan

Malaysian Consulate (☑061-453 1342; www.kln.gov.my/web/idn_medan; Jl Diponegoro 43; ⊙8am-4pm Mon-Fri)

FESTIVALS & EVENTS

Religious events and official holidays are a vital part of Indonesian life. There are many through the year and they're often cause for celebrations and festivals. With such diversity among the people in the archipelago, there are many local holidays, festivals and cultural events. This is especially true on Bali, where religious events can easily occupy a third of the typical person's calendar. The Muslim fasting month of Ramadan requires that Muslims abstain from food, drink, cigarettes and sex between sunrise and sunset. Many bars and restaurants close and it is impor-

SLEEPING PRICE RANGES

The following price ranges refer to a double room with bathroom. Unless otherwise stated, relevant taxes are included in the price.

Bali & Lombok

$ less than 450,000Rp
$$ 450,000–1,500,000Rp
$$$ more than 1,500,000Rp

Rest of Indonesia

$ less than 250,000Rp
$$ 250,000–1,000,000Rp
$$$ more than 1,000,000Rp

tant to avoid eating or drinking publicly in Muslim areas during this time. For the week before and after Lebaran (Idul Fitri), the festival to mark the end of the fast, transport is often fully booked and travelling becomes a nightmare – plan to stay put at this time. Ramadan, Idul Fitri and Idul Adha (Muslim day of sacrifice) move back 10 days or so every year, according to the Muslim calendar. Although some public holidays have a fixed date, the dates for many events vary each year depending on Muslim, Buddhist or Hindu calendars.

January/February

New Year's Day Celebrated on 1 January.

Imlek (Chinese New Year) Special food is prepared, decorations adorn stores and homes, and **barongsai** (lion dances) are performed; held in January or February.

Muharram (Islamic New Year) The date varies each year; it's usually in late January.

March/April

Hindu New Year (Nyepi) Held in March or April; in Bali and other Hindu communities, villagers make as much noise as possible to scare away devils. Virtually all of Bali shuts down.

Good Friday In March or April.

April/May

Waisak (Buddha's Birthday) Mass prayers are said at the main Buddhist temples, including Borobudur.

May/June

Ascension of Christ Occurs in May or June.

Ascension of Mohammed Special prayers are held in mosques.

August

Independence Day Celebrated on 17 August with plenty of pomp and circumstance; government

EATING PRICE RANGES

The following ranges represent the average cost of standard meals.

Bali & Lombok

$ less than 60,000Rp

$$ 60,000–250,000Rp

$$$ more than 250,000Rp

Rest of Indonesia

$ less than 50,000Rp

$$ 50,000–200,000Rp

$$$ more than 200,000Rp

buildings are draped in huge red-and-white flags and banners, and there are endless marches.

Lebaran (Idul Fitri) Everyone returns to their home village for special prayers and gift giving; it's also a time for charity donations.

October

Idul Adha The end of the Haj is celebrated with animal sacrifices, the meat of which is given to the poor.

Galungan One of Bali's major festivals, Galungan celebrates the death of the legendary tyrant Mayadenawa.

November/December

Maulid Nabi Muhammad (Mohammed's Birthday) Celebrated in November in 2018 and 2019; prayers are held in mosques throughout the country, and there are street parades in Solo and Yogyakarta.

INTERNET ACCESS

Indonesia is getting wired, though speed varies from fast to painfully slow.

➤ Wi-fi (pronounced 'wee-fee' in Indonesia) is commonly available in hotels except in rural areas. It is often free but watch out for hotels that may charge ridiculous rates by the hour or by data use.

➤ Cafes and restaurants in tourist areas often have free wi-fi.

➤ Data through your smartphone is often the fastest way to connect to the internet. 3G service is widespread.

LEGAL MATTERS

Drugs, gambling and pornography are illegal; the executions of two Australian nationals of the so-called 'Bali Nine' in 2015 for drug offences serve as a grim reminder. Generally, you are unlikely to have any encounters with the police unless you are driving a rented car or motorcycle, in which case you may be stopped for a dubious

reason and asked to pay an impromptu 'fine' of about 50,000Rp, but up to 500,000Rp may be demanded in Bali.

Visa limits are strictly enforced; many a careless tourist has seen the inside of an immigration detention facility or paid large fines.

LGBT TRAVELLERS

Gay travellers in Indonesia should follow the same precautions as straight travellers: avoid public displays of affection. This is especially important in conservative areas such as Aceh, where two women hugging were sent for 're-education' by religious police in 2015. Bali is especially LGBT-friendly, with a large community of expats and people from elsewhere in Indonesia.

Indonesian LGBT organisations include:

GAYa Nusantara (www.gayanusantara.or.id) Publishes the monthly magazine *GAYa Nusantara*.

Gaya Dewata (YGD, www.gayadewata.com) Bali's oldest and only community-run LGBT organisation.

MONEY

The unit of currency used in Indonesia is the rupiah (Rp).

➤ ATMs are common across Indonesia except in rural areas; most now accept cards affiliated with international networks. Bank BNI, with ATMs across the nation, is reliable.

➤ ATMs in Indonesia have a maximum limit for withdrawals; sometimes it is 2,000,000Rp, but it can be as low as 500,000Rp, which is not much in foreign-currency terms.

➤ In cities and touristed areas (eg Bali), credit cards will be accepted at midrange and better hotels and resorts. More expensive shops as well as travel agents will also accept them but often there will be a surcharge of around 3%.

➤ The US dollar is the most widely accepted foreign currency in Indonesia. Australian, British, euros and Japanese currencies are exchangeable only in the most touristed areas of Bali and Jakarta.

➤ Tipping a set amount is not expected but for good service leave 5000Rp or 10% or more (this is expected on Bali).

➤ Most midrange and all top-end hotels and restaurants add 21% to the bill for tax and service (known as 'plus plus').

OPENING HOURS

The following are typical opening hours across Indonesia.

Banks 8am–2pm Monday to Thursday, to noon Friday, to 11am Saturday

Government offices Generally 8am–3pm Monday to Thursday, to noon Friday

Post offices 8am–2pm Monday to Friday (in tourist centres, main post offices are often open longer and/or on weekends)

Private business offices 8am–4pm or 9am–5pm Monday to Friday; many open to noon Saturday

Restaurants 8am–10pm

Shopping 9am or 10am–5pm; larger shops and tourist areas to 8pm; many closed Sunday

PUBLIC HOLIDAYS

Following are the national public holidays in Indonesia. Unless stated, they vary from year to year. Also, there are many regional holidays.

Tahun Baru Masehi (New Year's Day) 1 January

Tahun Baru Imlek (Chinese New Year) Late January to early February

Wafat Yesus Kristus (Good Friday) Late March or early April

Nyepi (Balinese New Year) Bali closes down for one day, usually in March, sometimes April

Hari Buruh (Labour Day) 1 May

Hari Waisak May

Kenaikan Yesus Kristus (Ascension of Christ) May

Hari Proklamasi Kemerdekaan (Independence Day) 17 August

Hari Natal (Christmas Day) 25 December

The following Islamic holidays have dates that change each year.

Muharram Islamic New Year

Maulud Nabi Muhammad Birthday of the Prophet Muhammad

Isra Miraj Nabi Muhammad Ascension of the Prophet Muhammad

Idul Fitri Also known as Lebaran, this two-day national public holiday marks the end of Ramadan; avoid travel due to crowds.

Idul Adha Islamic feast of the sacrifice.

SAFE TRAVEL

It's important to note that, compared with many places in the world, Indonesia is fairly safe. There are some hassles from the avaricious, but most visitors face many more dangers at home. Petty theft occurs, but it is not prevalent.

Outside of reputable bars and resorts, it's best to avoid buying *arak*, the locally produced fermented booze made from rice or palm.

Indonesia has demonstrated its zero-tolerance policy towards drugs with a spate of high-profile arrests and convictions. The law does not provide for differentiation of substance types or amounts, whether a full bag of heroin or a few specks of marijuana dust in your pocket.

TELEPHONE

Cheap SIM cards and internet calling make it easy to call from Indonesia at reasonable prices.

Mobile Phones

➤ SIM cards for mobile phones cost only 5000Rp. They come with cheap rates for calling other countries, starting at US$0.20 per minute.

➤ SIM cards are widely available and easily refilled with credit.

➤ Watch out for vendors who sell SIM cards to visitors for 50,000Rp or more. If they don't come with at least 45,000Rp in credit you are being ripped off.

➤ Reasonably fast 3G data networks are found across the nation.

➤ Data plans average about 200,000Rp for 5GB of data.

➤ Mobile numbers start with a four-digit prefix that begins with 08 and has a total of 10 to 12 digits.

Phone Codes

Directory assistance	☏ 108
Indonesia country code	☏ 62
International call prefix	☏ 001
International operator	☏ 102

TIME

There are three time zones in Indonesia.

➤ Java, Sumatra, and West and Central Kalimantan are on Western Indonesian Time (GMT/UTC plus seven hours).

➤ Bali, Nusa Tenggara, South and East Kalimantan, and Sulawesi are on Central Indonesian Time (GMT/UTC plus eight hours).

➤ Papua and Maluku are on Eastern Indonesian Time (GMT/UTC plus nine hours).

In a country straddling the equator, there is no daylight-saving time.

Allowing for variations due to summer or daylight-saving time, when it is noon in Jakarta it is 9pm the previous day in San Francisco, midnight in New York, 5am in London, 1pm in Singapore, Bali and Makassar, 2pm in Jayapura and 3pm in Melbourne and Sydney.

VISAS

Unless you're on brief holiday, visas are the biggest headache many travellers face in their Indonesian trip. They are not hard to obtain, but the most common – 30 days – is very short for such a big place. Many travellers find even the 60-day visa restrictive.

The visa situation is constantly in flux. It is essential that you confirm current formalities before you arrive. Failure to meet all the entrance requirements can see you on the first flight out or subject to heavy fines.

No matter what type of visa you are going to use, your passport must be valid for at least six months from the date of your arrival.

At the time of research, the main visa options for visitors to Indonesia are as follows.

Visa in Advance Visitors can apply for a visa before they arrive in Indonesia. Typically this is a visitor's visa, which is usually valid for 60 days. Details vary by country; contact your nearest Indonesian embassy or consulate to determine processing fees and times. Note: this is the only way to obtain a 60-day visitor visa, even if you qualify for Visa on Arrival.

Visa Free Citizens of some 150 countries can receive a 30-day visa for free upon arrival. But note that this visa cannot be extended and you may be limited to which airports and ports you can use to exit the country, eg the Timor-Leste visa run may not work with this visa.

Visa on Arrival This 30-day extendable visa is available at major airports and harbours (but not most land borders). The cost is US$35; be sure to have the exact amount in US currency. Eligible countries include Australia, Canada, much of the EU including France, Germany, Ireland, the Netherlands and the UK, plus New Zealand and the USA. VOA renewals for 30 days are possible. If you don't qualify for VOA, you must get a visa in advance.

Fines for overstaying your visa expiration date are 300,000Rp per day and include additional hassles.

VOLUNTEERING

There are excellent opportunities for aspiring volunteers in Indonesia, but Lonely Planet does not endorse any organisations that we do not work with directly, so it is essential that you do your own thorough research before agreeing to volunteer with or donate to any organisation. A three-month commitment is recommended for working with children.

For many groups, fundraising and cash donations are the best way to help. Some also can use skilled volunteers to work as English teachers and provide professional services such as medical care. A few offer paid volunteering, whereby volunteers pay for room and board and perform often menial tasks.

A good resource to find NGOs and volunteer opportunities on Bali is www.balispirit.com/ngos.

Alam Sehat Lestari (www.alamsehatlestari. org/volunteer) Accepts skilled medical and conservation volunteers to help protect and restore Kalimantan's rainforest.

Borneo Orangutan Survival Foundation (www.orangutan.or.id) Accepts volunteers for its orangutan and sun-bear rehabilitation and reforestation programs.

East Bali Poverty Project (www.eastbalipovertyproject.org) Works to help children in the impoverished mountain villages of east Bali. Uses English teachers and has a solid child-protection policy.

Friends of the National Parks Foundation (www.fnpf.org) Has volunteer programs on Nusa Penida off Bali and Kalimantan.

IDEP (www.idepfoundation.org) The Indonesian Development of Education & Permaculture has projects across Indonesia; works on environmental projects, disaster planning and community improvement.

ProFauna (www.profauna.net) A large nonprofit animal-protection organisation operating across Indonesia; has been active in protecting sea turtles.

Sea Sanctuaries Trust (www.seasanctuaries. org) Diving-based marine conservation volunteering in Raja Ampat.

Smile Foundation of Bali (www.senyumbali. org) Organises surgery to correct facial deformities; operates the Smile Shop in Ubud to raise money.

Yayasan Bumi Sehat (www.bumisehatfoundation.org) Operates an internationally recognised clinic and gives reproductive services to disadvantaged women in Ubud; accepts donated time from medical professionals. Founder Robin Lim has received international recognition.

Yayasan Rama Sesana (www.yrsbali.org) Dedicated to improving reproductive health for women across Bali.

Getting There & Away

AIR

Indonesia is well connected to the rest of the world by numerous airlines. Many international flights, especially those to Bali, stop first in Singapore or Kuala Lumpur due to runway restrictions at Bali.

The principal gateways for entry to Indonesia are Jakarta's Soekarno-Hatta International Airport and Bali's Ngurah Rai International Airport (which is sometimes shown as Denpasar in schedules).

LAND

There are four possible land crossings into Indonesia.

Regular buses between Pontianak (Kalimantan) and Kuching (Sarawak, eastern Malaysia) pass through the border post at Entikong. You can get a visa on arrival on this route. A crossing is possible between Lubok Antu, Sarawak, and Badau, West Kalimantan provided you have a visa in advance.

The border crossing between West and East Timor (Timor-Leste) is open. Get a Timor-Leste visa at the consulate in Kupang; a visa is required when travelling from East to West Timor.

The road from Jayapura or Sentani in Indonesia to Vanimo in Papua New Guinea can be crossed, depending on the current political situation. A visa is required if travelling into Indonesia.

SEA

Malaysia and Singapore are linked to Sumatra by boats and ferries, although the links are inconvenient and most travellers fly. Boats make the Melaka (Malaysia) to Dumai (Indonesia) crossing. From Singapore, ferries make the quick hop to Pulau Batam and Bintan, the primary islands in the Riau Archipelago. There is a link on Borneo from Nunukan in East Kalimantan to Tawau in Malaysian Sabah. There is currently no sea travel between the Philippines and Indonesia.

ⓘ Getting Around

AIR

With almost a dozen carriers flying all over Indonesia, inexpensive domestic flights are the best way to avoid long overland or ferry trips. Getting reliable information on Indonesian domestic flights can be a challenge – some airlines on minor routes don't show up on travel websites, although www.traveloka.com and www.skyscanner.com are fairly complete. You can also check with local airline offices and travel agents; local hotel and tour operators are often the best sources. The domestic flight network continues to grow; schedules and rates are in a constant state of flux. Small carriers servicing remote routes often operate cramped and dated aircraft.

Tickets

The larger Indonesian-based carriers have websites listing fares, however, it may be difficult to purchase tickets over the internet using non-Indonesian credit cards. Consider the following methods.

Travel Agents A good way to buy domestic tickets once you're in Indonesia. This is often the best way to get the lowest fares.

Travel websites Many general sites accept international cards.

Friends Get an Indonesian friend or guesthouse owner to buy you a ticket using their credit card, then pay them back.

Airport Some airlines will sell you a ticket at the airport, although travel agents and airline city offices are more reliable.

BICYCLE

If reasonably fit, and with a bit of preparation and a ton of common sense, a cyclist will enjoy an incomparable travel experience almost anywhere in the archipelago. The well-maintained roads of Bali, Lombok, East Java and South Sulawesi are suitable for cyclists of all ability levels, while the adventuresome can head for the hills along the length of Sumatra or Nusa Tenggara.

Bicycling is gaining popularity among Indonesians and bicycle clubs will be delighted to aid a foreign guest. Bike to Work (www.b2w-indonesia.or.id) has an extensive national network.

BOAT

Sumatra, Java, Bali, Nusa Tenggara and Sulawesi are all connected by regular car ferries, and you can use them to island-hop all the way from Sumatra to West Timor. Local ferries run several times a week or daily (or even hourly on the busy Java–Bali–Lombok–Sumbawa routes). Check with shipping companies, the harbour office, travel agents or hotels for current schedules and fares.

Going to and between Kalimantan, Maluku and Papua, the main connections are provided by Pelni, the government-run passenger line.

Pelni

Pelni (www.pelni.co.id) has a fleet of large vessels linking all of Indonesia's major ports and the majority of the archipelago's outlying areas. Pelni's website is a good resource, showing arrivals and departures about a month in advance. Its ships operate set routes around the islands, either on a fortnightly or monthly schedule. The ships usually stop for a few hours in each port, so there's time for a quick look around. Note that sailing times can be in flux until the last moment. Economy fares can be quite cheap but at higher levels of accommodation, budget airlines are competitive if not cheaper.

Pelni ships have two to six classes. Economy class, which is the modern version of deck class, is a bare-bones experience. As you move up the price ladder, you exchange a seat on the deck for small accommodations until you reach a level that may give you your own private cabin with two beds (this is some variation of 1st class). These are functional at best and far from lavish.

Other Boats

There's a whole range of boats you can use to hop between islands, down rivers and across lakes. Just about any sort of vessel can be rented in Indonesia.

Fast Ferries When available, these are a great alternative to the slow car ferries that link many islands.

Fishing boats Small boats can be chartered to take you to small offshore islands.

Longboat The *longbot* is a long, narrow boat powered by a couple of outboard motors, with bench seats on either side of the hull for passengers to sit on. They are mainly used in Kalimantan where they are also called *klotok*.

Outrigger boats Used for some short interisland hops, such as the trip from Manado in North Sulawesi to the coral reefs surrounding nearby Pulau Bunaken. On Lombok they serve the Gilis while Komodo National Park is served from Labuanbajo. On Bali they are called *jukung*.

River ferries Commonly found on Kalimantan, where the rivers *are* the roads. They're large,

INDONESIA GETTING AROUND

ESSENTIAL FOOD & DRINK

Gado gado vegetables with peanut sauce, a Javanese speciality

Sate ayam Skewered chicken with peanut satay sauce

Nasi goreng/mie goreng Fried rice/ noodles

Padang food The spicy dishes of West Sumatra include beef *rendang*

Babi guling Spit-roast pig, a Balinese favourite

Ikan kuah assam Tamarind fish soup from Nusa Tenggara

bulky vessels that carry passengers and cargo up and down the water network.

Tourist boats Often very fast speedboats outfitted to carry 40 or more passengers, most commonly used for quick trips between Bali, Nusa Lembongan, Lombok and the Gilis.

BUS

Buses are the mainstay of Indonesian transport (excepting Papua and Maluku). At any time of day, thousands of buses in all shapes and sizes move thousands of people throughout Indonesia. The 'leave-when-full' school of scheduling applies to almost every service, and 'full' sometimes means the aisles are occupied too. Consider the following.

➡ On major runs across Indonesia, air-con buses are at least tolerable.

➡ Crowded roads mean that buses are often stuck in traffic.

➡ On major routes, such as the 24-hour run from Bali to Jakarta, budget airlines are competitive price-wise.

➡ Buses on nonmajor routes are usually not air-conditioned.

➡ Bring as little luggage as possible – there is rarely any room for storage. Large bags will ride on your lap.

➡ Take precautions with your personal belongings and keep your passport, money and any other valuables secure and concealed.

CAR & MOTORCYCLE

Small self-drive cars can be hired for as little as 100,000Rp to 300,000Rp a day with limited insurance in tourist areas.

It is very common for tourists to hire a car with a driver and this can usually be arranged for 400,000Rp to 1,400,000Rp per day (600,000Rp per day is average in popular places like Bali).

With a small group, a van and driver is not only economical but also allows maximum travel and touring freedom. Hotels can always arrange drivers.

Motorcycles and motorbikes are readily available for hire throughout Indonesia.

➡ Motorcycles and scooters can be hired for 60,000Rp to 100,000Rp per day.

➡ Wearing a helmet is required by law and essential given road conditions.

➡ In popular surfing areas, many motorbike rentals come with a surfboard rack.

➡ A licence is required by law, though you'll rarely need to show it unless stopped by the police, who may be looking for a 'tip'.

➡ Some travel-insurance policies do not cover you if you are involved in an accident while on a motorcycle and/or don't have a licence. Check the small print.

LOCAL TRANSPORT

Public minibuses are used for local transport around cities and towns, short intercity runs and the furthest reaches of the transport network. Minibuses are known as bemos or *angkot*, although they are called *taksi* in many parts of Papua, Kalimantan and East Java. Other names include *opelet*, *mikrolet*, *angkudes* and *pete-pete*.

Ojeks (or *ojegs*) are motorcycle riders who take pillion passengers for a bargainable price. They are found at bus terminals and markets, or just hanging around at crossroads.

Becak are three-wheeled cycle rickshaws either peddle- or motor-powered. The becak is banned from the main streets of some large cities, but you'll still see them swarming the backstreets, moving anyone and anything.

TRAIN

In Java, trains are one of the most comfortable, fastest and easiest ways to travel. In the east, the railway service connects with the ferry to Bali, and in the west with the ferry to Sumatra. Sumatra's limited rail network runs in the south from Bandarlampung to Lubuklinggau, and in the north from Medan to Tanjung Balai and Rantau Prapat.

Laos

POP 6.9 MILLION

Includes ➡

Best Places to Eat

➡ Doi Ka Noi (p326)

➡ Coconut Garden (p342)

➡ Tamarind (p342)

➡ Il Tavolo (p334)

➡ Lao Kitchen (p327)

Top Laos Phrases

Hello sábại-děe

Goodbye sábại-děe

Yes/No maan/bor

Thank you kòrp jại

Do you speak English? jôw bàhk páh-săh ạng·kít dâi bor

Why Go?

A land of the lotus eaters amid the bloated development of its neighbours, Laos brings together the best of Southeast Asia in one bite-sized destination. It's no accident that Laos appears as a favourite in many Southeast Asian odysseys, for this landlocked country lays claim to incredibly genuine people and the chance for your inner adventurer to let rip. The 'Land of a Million Elephants' oozes magic from the moment you spot a Hmong tribeswoman looming through the mist; trek through a glimmering rice paddy; or hear the dawn call of the endangered gibbon. But it's also a place to pamper yourself in a spa like a French colonial, or chill under a wood-blade fan in a delicious Gallic restaurant. The country offers green tourism with excellent forest treks and tribal homestays operated by eco-responsible outfits. Be it flying along forest ziplines, exploring creepy subterranean river caves or tackling the jungle on motocross adventures, Laos will burn itself into your memory.

When to Go
Vientiane

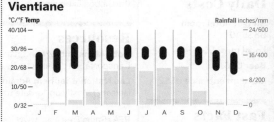

Nov–Feb A great time to visit, with the magical Bun Pha That Luang (Full Moon Festival) in November.

Mar–May Temperatures and humidity levels climbs, but hotel prices fall.

Jun–Nov The monsoon brings fresh air and river festivals like Bun Awk Phansa and Bun Nam.

AT A GLANCE

Currency Lao kip (K)

Money ATMs in major centres. Credit cards accepted in Luang Prabang and Vientiane.

Visas On arrival (valid for 30 days; US$30 to US$42 depending which passport you hold).

Mobile phones Prepaid SIMs available for as little as 10,000K. Decent connections.

Language Lao

Exchange Rates

Australia	A$1	6512K
Canada	C$1	6439K
Euro zone	€1	9750K
Japan	¥100	7554K
New Zealand	NZ$1	5807K
Thailand	10B	2484K
UK	UK£1	10665K
US	US$1	8250K
Vietnam	10,000d	3629K

For current exchange rates, see www.xe.com.

Daily Costs

Budget hotel room US$5-10

Local meal US$2-4

Beer US$1

Museum entrance US$2

Fast Facts

Area 236,000 sq km

Capital Vientiane

Emergency Police 191

Entering the Country

There are more than a dozen border crossings into Laos from Cambodia, China, Thailand and Vietnam. Frequent flights also connect Laos with neighbouring countries.

REGIONS AT A GLANCE

For many short-stay visitors, Luang Prabang is their Laos experience. And a mighty impressive one it is too, thanks to its deserved World Heritage status. Laos' other main city, its capital Vientiane, may be bucolic for an Asian city, but it hits home on the charm stakes, with attractive cafes, stylish restaurants and lively little bars.

Beyond lies northern Laos, a landscape of towering mountains and dense forests that is home to extensive national parks, rare wildlife and some of the most colourful minorities in the region.

The middle of the country is one of the least travelled regions. Some of the most dramatic cave systems in Asia are found here, together with spectacular scenery and crumbling colonial-era towns. Head south to live life in the slow lane. The Mekong islands of Si Phan Don suck people in for longer than expected, and there is a real buzz on the Bolaven Plateau – not just from the coffee.

Essential Outdoor Activities

National Protected Areas Trek the dense forests of 20 national protected areas spread across Laos.

Vang Vieng Go ape with the latest craze of ziplines.

The Loop This two-day adventure by motorbike through jungle and karst, frontier town and dam country, gets under Laos' skin.

Tha Khaek One of the most beautiful places in the country to climb limestone karsts.

Gibbon Experience Zipline through the jungle canopy with the Gibbon Experience.

Resources

Hobo Maps (http://hobomaps.com) Up-to-date maps and transportation details, mostly regarding northern Laos.

Lao National Tourism Administration (www.tourismlaos.org) Mostly up-to-date travel information from the government.

RFA (Radio Free Asia; www.rfa.org/english/news/laos) Unbiased, censorship-free news on Laos from Asia-based journalists.

Lonely Planet (www.lonelyplanet.com/laos) Destination information, hotel bookings, traveller forum and more.

VIENTIANE

🎵 021 / POP 997,000

From its sleepy tuk-tuk drivers to its cafe society and affordable spas, this former French trading post is languid to say the least. Eminently walkable, the historic old quarter of Vientiane (ວຽງຈັນ) beguiles with glittering temples, lunging *naga* (river serpent) statues, wandering Buddhist monks, and boulevards lined with frangipani and tamarind. Meanwhile, with most of its old French villas now stylishly reincarnated into restaurants and small hotels, Vientiane is achieving an unprecedented level of panache with a distinctly Gallic flavour. For the well-heeled traveller and backpacker the city acquits itself equally well, be it with low-cost digs and street markets, or upscale boutique accommodation and gastronomic eateries.

History

Through 10 centuries of history Vientiane was variously controlled, ravaged and looted by the Vietnamese, Burmese, Siamese and Khmer. When Laos became a French protectorate at the end of the 19th century, Vientiane was renamed as the capital, rebuilt and became one of the classic Indochinese cities, along with Phnom Penh and Saigon (Ho Chi Minh City). By the early 1960s and the onset of the war in Vietnam, the city had taken on a vastly different face. In 2009 the city hosted the Southeast Asian Games, a major illustration of the country's new profile. In 2015 China's Kunming to Vientiane express route started in earnest.

⊙ Sights

★ Pha That Luang   BUDDHIST STUPA

(ພະທາດຫລວງ, Great Sacred Reliquary, Great Stupa; Map p323; Th 23 Singha; 10,000K, rental of long skirt to enter temple 5000K; ⊙ 8am-5pm) Svelte and golden Pha That Luang is the most important national monument in Laos; a symbol of Buddhist religion and Lao sovereignty. Legend has it that Ashokan missionaries from India erected a *tâht* (stupa) here to enclose a piece of Buddha's breastbone as early as the 3rd century BC. Pha That Luang is about 4km northeast of the city centre.

★ Wat Si Saket   BUDDHIST TEMPLE

(ວັດສີສະເກດ; Map p324; cnr Th Lan Xang & Th Setthathirath; 10,000K; ⊙ 8am-5pm, closed public holidays) Built between 1819 and 1824 by Chao Anou, Wat Si Saket is believed to be Vientiane's oldest surviving wat. And it is starting to show, as this beautiful temple is in need of a facelift. Along the western side

of the cloister is a pile of buddhas that were damaged during the 1828 Lao Rebellion.

COPE Visitor Centre   CULTURAL CENTRE

(ສູນພື້ນຟູຄົນພິການແຫ່ງຊາດ; Cooperative Orthotic & Prosthetic Enterprise; Map p323; 🎵 021-241972; www.copelaos.org; Th Khu Vieng; donations welcome; ⊙ 9am-6pm) FREE COPE is the main source of artificial limbs, walking aids and wheelchairs in Laos. Its excellent Visitor Centre, part of the organisation's National Rehabilitation Centre, offers myriad interesting and informative multimedia exhibits about prosthetics and the unexploded ordnance (UXO) that sadly make them necessary.

Xieng Khuan   MUSEUM

(ຊຽງຂວັນ, Suan Phut, Buddha Park; 5000K; camera 3000K, motorbike parking 5000K; ⊙ 8am-5pm; 🚌 14) Located 25km southeast of central Vientiane, eccentric Xieng Khuan, aka Buddha Park, thrills with other-worldly Buddhist and Hindu sculptures, and was designed and built in 1958 by Luang Pu, a yogi-priest-shaman who merged Hindu and Buddhist philosophy, mythology and iconography into a cryptic whole. Bus 14 (6000K, one hour, 24km) leaves Talat Sao Bus Station every 20 minutes for Xieng Khuan. Alternatively, charter a tuk-tuk (200,000K return).

Patuxai   MONUMENT

(ປະຕູໄຊ, Victory Gate; Map p323; Th Lan Xang; 3000K; ⊙ 8am-5pm) Vientiane's Arc de Triomphe replica is a slightly incongruous sight, dominating the commercial district around Th Lan Xang. Officially called 'Victory Gate' *and* commemorating the Lao who died in prerevolutionary wars, it was built in the 1960s with cement donated by the USA intended for the construction of a new airport. Climb to the summit for panoramic views over Vientiane.

DOS & DON'TS IN LAOS

➡ Always ask permission before taking photos.

➡ Don't prop your feet on chairs or tables while sitting.

➡ Refrain from touching people on the head, or having any physical contact with monks.

➡ Remove your shoes before entering homes or temple buildings.

➡ Don't hold hands or kiss in a Buddhist temple.

Laos Highlights

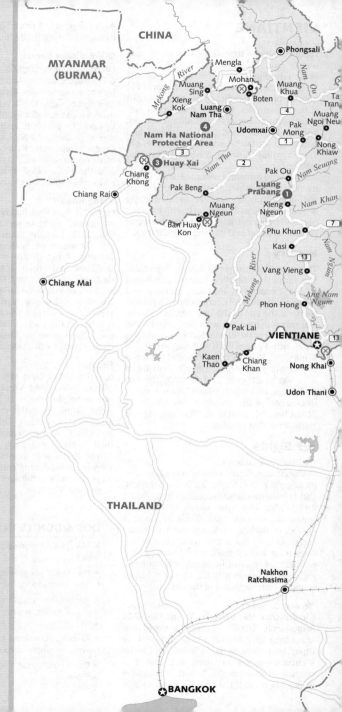

1 Luang Prabang (p336) Experiencing the ancient city of temples that has it all: royal history, Indochinese chic, colourful monks, waterfalls, stunning river views and world class French cuisine.

2 Tham Kong Lor (p359) Taking a boat ride through this exhilaratingly spooky 7.5km cave, home to fist-sized spiders and stalactite woods.

3 Gibbon Experience (p357) Trekking and zipping across the forest by day at the Gibbon Experience in Huay Xai and sleeping in cosy treehouses at night.

4 Nam Ha National Protected Area (p355) Trekking through some of the wildest, densest jungle in the country, home to a rich variety of ethnic tribes.

5 Si Phan Don (p371) Relaxing at Four Thousand Islands, hammock capital of Laos; a steamy traveller's idyll where the Mekong turns turquoise.

6 Vieng Xai (p353) Exploring the war-shelter cave complexes, set in beautiful gardens backed by fabulous karst scenery.

7 Plain of Jars (p351) Touring the mysterious plain of jars near Phonsavan.

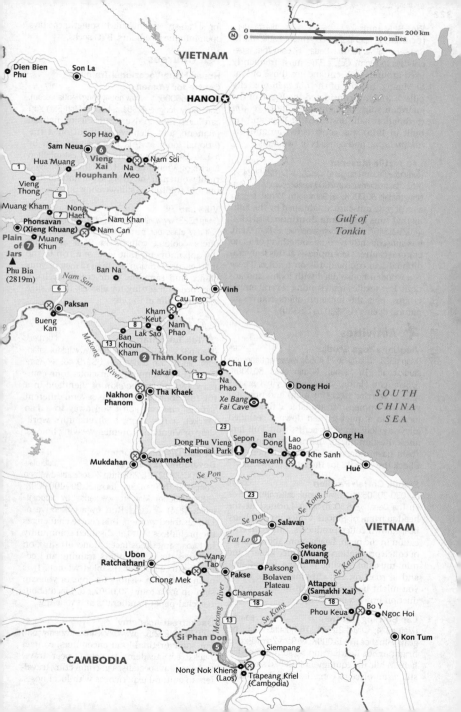

Wat Si Muang   BUDDHIST TEMPLE

(ວັດສີເມືອງ; Map p323; cnr Th Setthathirath, Th Samsènethai & Th Tha Deua; ⊗6am-7pm, special days to 10pm) FREE The most frequently used grounds in Vientiane are those of Wat Si Muang, the site of the *lák méuang* (city pillar), which is considered the home of the guardian spirit of Vientiane. The large *sĭm* (ordination hall; destroyed in 1828 and rebuilt in 1915) was constructed around the *lák méuang*, and consists of two halls.

Lao Textile Museum   MUSEUM

(ພິພິດທະພັນຜ້າໄໝບູຮານລາວ; ☑021-562454; http://laotextilemuseum2003.weebly.com; Ban Nongthatai; 30,000K; ⊗9am-4pm) What began as a private museum, established by the family that runs **Kanchana Boutique** (Map p324; ☑021-213467; 140 Th Samsenethai; ⊗8am-9pm), has subsequently become something of a Lao cultural centre. The emphasis at this leafy traditional Lao compound is on textiles. There is a wooden house filled with looms and antique Lao textiles representing several ethnic groups, plus the museum offers courses in natural dyeing (US$20 to US$30).

🏃 Activities

Vientiane Yoga Studio   YOGA

(Map p323; ☑020-5698 4563; www.vientianeyogastudio.com; Th Nerhu; 80min class 80,000K; ⊗5am-7pm) Hatha, vinyasa and yin yoga, as well as warrior yoga (for men) and prenatal yoga (for women), are available at this studio, located in a quiet garden down a secluded alleyway (look for signs across from Fuji Japanese Restaurant 2). Instructors Nanci and Toshi have more than 10 years' experience. Check the website for the latest schedule.

Sinouk Coffee Pavilion   COFFEE

(☑030-2000654; www.sinouk-cafe.com; Km 9, Th Tha Deua; ⊗8.30am-5pm) Located at the headquarters of Sinouk Coffee, one of Laos' best-known coffee producers, this is an education in the bean. Learn more about the art of coffee production at the coffee gallery and mini-museum paying homage to caffeine, and in roasting and cupping rooms, where you might be lucky enough to see the production process underway.

Lao Bowling Centre   BOWLING

(Map p324; ☑021-218661; Th Khounboulom; per game with shoe hire 13,000K; ⊗9am-2am) Expect bright lights, Beerlao and boisterous bowlers here. While the equipment is in bad shape, it's still a fun place to come later in the evening for a Lao-style night out. It sometimes stays open into the wee hours. BYO socks.

🍴 Courses

Houey Hong Vocational Training Centre for Women   WEAVING

(☑021-560006; www.houeyhongvientiane.com; Ban Houey Hong; ⊗8.30am-4.30pm Mon-Sat) You can learn how to dye textiles using natural pigments and then weave them on a traditional loom at this NGO centre, run by a Lao-Japanese woman. It was established north of Vientiane to train disadvantaged rural women in the dying art of natural dyeing and traditional silk-weaving practices.

Villa Lao   COOKING

(Map p323; www.villalaos.com; off Th Nong Douang; half-day class per person US$25-30) Villa Lao offers cooking courses at 9am and 1pm (by appointment) that involve a trip to the market, preparation of three dishes of your choice and sampling your creations. It's a very peaceful setting for classes, like a slice of country life in the city.

🧭 Tours

★ Tuk Tuk Safari   CULTURAL

(Map p323; ☑020-54333089; www.tuktuksafari.com; adult/child under 12yr US$70/40; ⊗8am-5pm) This community-conscious tour company gets under the skin of Vientiane in a tuk-tuk. Tour guide Ere has several different 'safaris' and can spirit you away to a Lao market, a rice farm, a silversmith's workshop or Vientiane's premier weaving houses.

★ Lao Disabled Women's Development Centre   CULTURAL

(LDWDC; ☑021-812282; http://laodisabledwomen.com; 100 Th Tha Deua; tours 50,000-100,000K; ⊗8am-4.30pm Mon-Fri, weekends by appointment; 🚍14) 🖋 FREE Run by a collective of Lao disabled women, this centre challenges the prejudices that the disabled community in Laos sometimes faces. Concentrating on abilities, the centre offers training and education to empower disabled women. It is open to drop-in visitors for free, or you can sign up for a tour (50,000K) to learn about recycled-paper handicrafts and weaving.

Backstreet Academy   TOURS

(☑020-58199216; www.backstreetacademy.com) For some original local encounters, contact Backstreet Academy, a peer-to-peer travel website that specialises in connecting travellers to cultural experiences with local hosts.

Vientiane

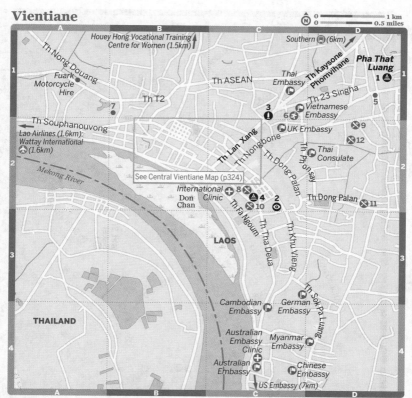

See Central Vientiane Map (p324)

LAOS VIENTIANE

Choose from a *muay Lao* (kickboxing) class, a traditional dance lesson, a Lao cooking class in a private home, a clay art class, Zen meditation and a whole lot more.

✨ Festivals & Events

Bun Nam   SPORTS
(Bun Suang Héua; ⊘ Oct) A huge annual event at the end of *pansăh* (the Buddhist rains retreat) in October, during which boat races are held on the Mekong River. Rowing teams from all over the country, as well as from Thailand, China and Myanmar (Burma), compete; the river bank is lined with food stalls, temporary discos, carnival games and beer gardens for three days and nights.

Bun Pha That Luang   CULTURAL
(That Luang Festival; ⊘ Nov) Bun Pha That Luang, usually held in early November, is the largest temple fair in Laos. Festivities begin with a *wéean téean* (circumambulation)

Central Vientiane

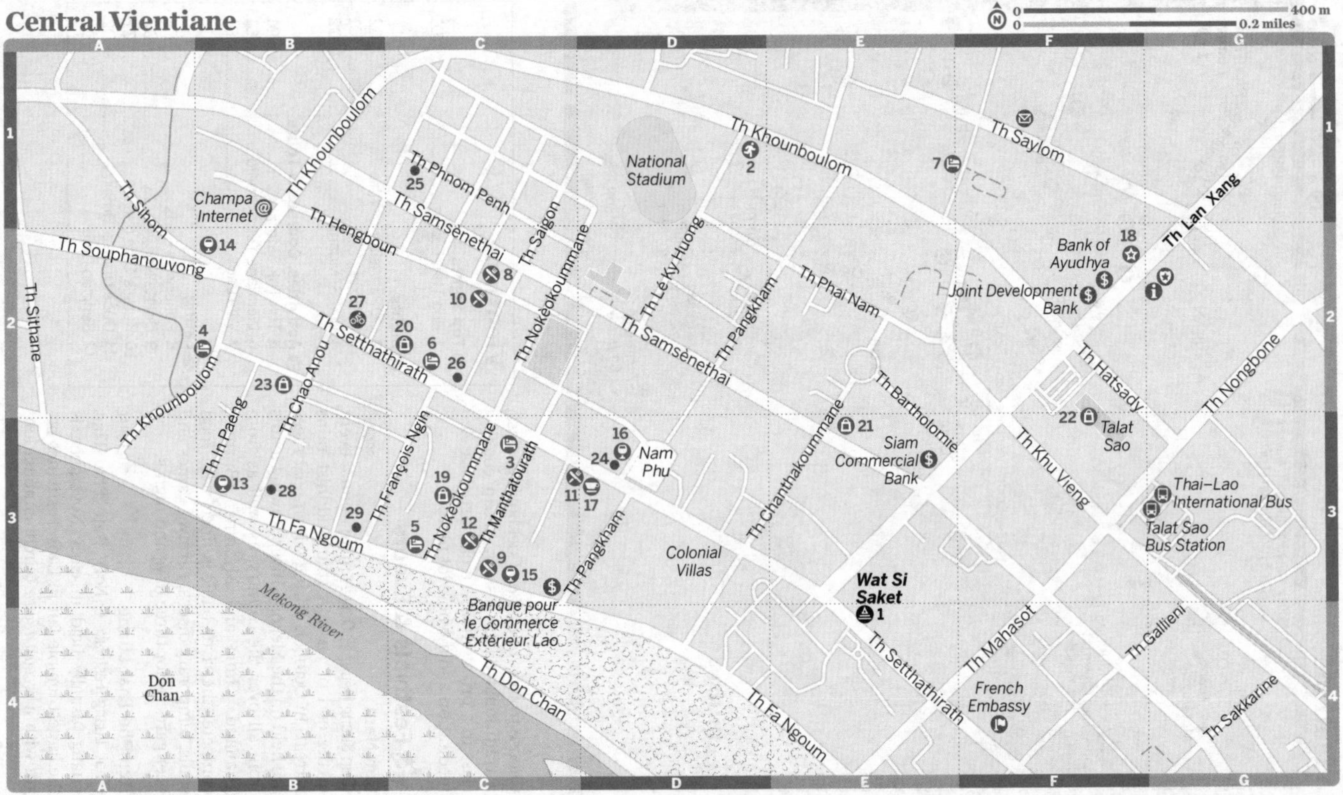

LAOS VIENTIANE

400 m
0.2 miles

Th Lan Xang

Th Nongbone

Th Sakkarine

Thai–Lao International Bus

Talat Sao Bus Station

Th Hatsady

Bank of Ayudhya

Joint Development Bank

Talat Sao

Th Saylom

Th Khu Vieng

Th Mahasot

French Embassy

Th Setthathirath

Th Bartholomie

Th Phai Nam

Siam Commercial Bank

Wat Si Saket

Th Khounboulom

Th Chanthakoumane

Th Fa Ngoum

Th Pangkham

Th Samsenethai

Th Le Ky Huong

National Stadium

Colonial Villas

Th Don Chan

Nam Phu

Th Pangkham

Th Nokeokoummane

Th Manthatourath

Th Saigon

Th Phnom Penh

Th Samsenethai

Th Hengboun

Th Setthathirath

Th François Ngin

Th Nokeokoummane

Banque pour le Commerce Extérieur Lao

Mekong River

Th Chao Anou

Th In Paeng

Th Fa Ngoum

Champa Internet

Th Sihom

Th Souphanouvong

Th Khounboulom

Th Sithane

Don Chan

Central Vientiane

LAOS VIENTIANE

around Wat Si Muang, followed by a procession to Pha That Luang, which is illuminated all night for a week.

Pi Mai CULTURAL
(☺ Apr) Lao New Year is celebrated in mid-April with a mass water fight and tourists are considered fair game. Be warned, drunk driving and theft go through the roof at these times so remain vigilant!

🛏 Sleeping

Vientiane is bursting with a wide range of accommodation, from cheap backpacker digs to beautiful boutique hotels.

★ **Sailomyen Hostel** HOSTEL $
(Map p324; ☑ 021-214246; www.facebook.com/sailomyenhostel; Th Saylom; dm incl breakfast 80,000K; ⊝❋☎) Perhaps it's the chic design, the luxurious rain showers or the trendy ground-floor **cafe**? Maybe it's the friendly touches (such as personal lights and outlets in each bunk) or the Siberian air-con (which invites you to snuggle beneath your fluffy duvet and hide behind your privacy curtain)? Whatever the reason, Sailomyen is a hostel connoisseur's dream come true.

Hive Hostel HOSTEL $
(Map p324; ☑ 020-98132074; www.facebook.com/hivelao; Th Setthathilath; dm incl breakfast 60,000-90,000K; ❋☎) This new hostel has a great

central location and three exceptionally cold air-con dorms with curtained-off bunks, lockers and sparklingly clean toilets. There's a funky little **cafe** on the ground floor where you'll eat your (simple) breakfast.

Mixay Paradise Guesthouse GUESTHOUSE $
(Map p324; ☑ 021-254223; laomixayparadise@yahoo.com; Th François Ngin; s/d with fan & shared bathroom 90,000/100,000K; r with air-con & bathroom 130,000-140,000K; ⊝❋☎) Mixay Paradise has 50 rooms with pastel-coloured walls, some of which have balconies, bathrooms and air-con; spotless floors; a bright lobby cafe with lime-green walls; and a lift. One of the best, most hygienic budget options in the city. Safety deposit lockers cost 50,000K.

★ **LV City Riverine Hotel** HOTEL $$
(Map p324; ☑ 021-214643; www.lvcitylaos.com; 48 Th Fa Ngoum; r incl breakfast 220,000-390,000K; ⊝❋☎) Not to be confused with various other 'city' hotels in the capital, the LV has a great location near the riverfront. Rooms are spacious and well appointed, although it is worth the ego-massage of VIP just for the four-poster bed and extra space. Rooms include free laundry, so will be even better value if you are returning from a jungle trek.

★ **Hotel Khamvongsa** HOTEL $$
(Map p324; ☑ 021-218415; www.hotelkhamvongsa.com; Th Khounboulom; s/d/tr incl breakfast

ITINERARIES

One Week

After spending a few days in riverside Vientiane sampling its Soviet-Franco architecture, sophisticated bars and Asian-fusion cuisine, travel north three hours to the beautiful karst country of Vang Vieng, a former party town turned outdoor activity haven for cycling, climbing, trekking and ziplining. From here catch a bus to unforgettable Luang Prabang to experience its temples, crumbling villas, pampering spas, bike rides and Gallic cuisine.

Two Weeks

Follow the one-week itinerary, then take a two-day slow boat up the Mekong River to Huay Xai, having already booked yourself in for the memorable Gibbon Experience and its overnight stays in jungle tree-houses. If you've got time head up to Luang Namtha for a trek in the wild Nam Ha National Protected Area, where you can also kayak and homestay with a number of great tour providers. From here you can fly back to Vientiane to catch your flight out.

US$40/45/80; ⊖❄🛜) Lovely French-era building lovingly reincarnated as a welcoming boutique hotel; think belle-époque touches like glass-tear lightshades, chequerboard-tiled floors, and softly lit simple rooms with two-poster beds, wood floors and Indo-chic decor. Rooms on the 3rd and 4th floors have masterful views. There's also a restful courtyard and restaurant. Breakfast is a treat.

🍴 Eating

For such a small capital city, Vientiane boasts a range of culinary options and is an exceptional spot for fine dining on a budget.

★ Doi Ka Noi   LAOTIAN $

(Map p323; ☑020-55898959; 242 Sapang Mor; mains 25,000-50,000K; ⊙10am-2.30pm Tue-Thu, 10am-9pm Fri-Sun; 🛜) An authentic and unmissable Lao restaurant near That Luang that is guaranteed to spice up your life. The menu changes daily and focuses on home recipes and seasonal ingredients. Sample dishes include fish curry with hummingbird-tree flowers and bamboo curry with mushrooms. Co-owned by a photographer, there are some stunning food shots adorning the walls.

★ The State of Pasta   FUSION $

(Map p324; ☑021-253322; www.thestateofpasta. com; Th Manthatourath; mains 20,000-45,000K; ⊙11am-10pm Sun-Thu, to 11.30pm Fri & Sat; ❄🛜) Imagine fresh Italian pasta paired with traditional Lao flavours. That's the concept behind this new fusion restaurant, which has dishes you won't find anywhere else on the planet. Take the humdrum Bolognese sauce, re-imagined here with the ingredients of *láhp* (minced meat, local herbs and spices). Chill music, draft beers and an upstairs cocktail bar will have you lingering long after the meal.

★ Naked Espresso   CAFE $

(Map p324; ☑020-56222269; Th Manthatourath; dishes 25,000-50,000K; ⊙7am-5pm; ❄🛜) One of the best-loved coffee shops in Vientiane, Naked specialises in home-grown Lao coffee and selected gourmet imports from places as diverse as Ethiopia and Indonesia. Light meals are also available, including salads and sandwiches, plus some impressive homemade baked goods. Australian Prime Minister Malcolm Turnbull dropped by for a coffee in 2016.

Bakery By Boris   BAKERY $

(Map p323; ☑020-77792228; www.facebook. com/bakerybyboris; off Th Setthathirath; snacks 10,000-25,000K, meals 30,000-50,000K; ⊙7am-7pm; ❄🛜) With high glass ceilings and a minimalist design, this sleek new cafe is like a giant fishbowl marooned in a leafy oasis next to Wat Si Muang. Paris-trained chef Boris Luangkhot makes drool-worthy macarons, croissants and homemade ice creams in flavours such as durian and passion fruit. There are also quiches, coffees and baguette sandwiches for a midday pick-me-up.

Noy's Fruit Heaven   CAFE $

(Map p324; Th Hengboun; mains 20,000-30,000K; ⊙7am-9pm; ❄🛜) Noy's is a homely, colourful juice bar with Chinese paper lanterns hanging from the ceiling. Stop in to pick up a few of your 'five a day' or decimate your hangover with one of its dragonfruit, coconut, mango, or tomato-juice shakes (15,000K). It also turns out super-fresh fruit salads and burgers.

Kung's Cafe Lao
LAOTIAN $
(Map p323; ☑021-219101; near Ministry of Health, Phiawat Village; mains 12,000-20,000K; ⊙7am-4pm; ☑) Approaching cult status with Vientiane residents in the know, Kung's Cafe is hard to find, but well worth the effort. Affable Kung has decorated the local diner with hanging gourds and has a simple and effective menu that is superb value. Try the sticky-rice pancake or *phat Lao* and wash it down with a signature coffee and coconut.

Once Upon a Time
CAFE $
(Map p323; ☑030-5809988; Th Dong Palan; mains 20,000-60,000K; ⊙7am-6pm; ✳☎) Feed your inner princess with a trip to this fairy-tale-themed cafe in the Phonthan part of town. The owner-barista here has won multiple awards in Thailand and the breakfasts are a cut above the guesthouse and budget-hotel offerings.

★ Senglao Cafe
FUSION $$
(Map p323; ☑030-5880588; mains 30,000-200,000K; ⊙11am-10pm Mon-Sat, 9am-4pm Sun; ✳☎) Named after a now-defunct cinema in the centre of town, this contemporary restaurant has a cinematic theme and restored leather chairs from the old movie hall. The fusion menu is ambitious but executed with some panache and includes everything from fusion squid-ink pasta with scallops to stone-baked pizzas. Films are shown at weekends.

★ Lao Kitchen
LAOTIAN $$
(Map p324; ☑021-254332; Th Hengboun; mains 25,000-70,000K; ⊙11am-10pm; ✳☎☑) This superb contemporary Lao restaurant is unfailingly creative in its execution of trad Lao dishes. Colourful walls, alt tunes and good service complement a menu spanning stews, Luang Prabang sausage, *láhp* variations, stir-fried morning glory (water spinach), spring rolls, Mekong fish soup and palate-friendly sorbets. Choose the level of spice with chilli gradings of one to three.

Sputnik Burger
BURGERS $$
(Map p324; ☑030-9376504; www.facebook.com/SputnikBurger; Th Setthathirath; mains 45,000-110,000K; ⊙11am-10pm Mon-Sat; ✳☎) A contemporary burger joint featuring great beef burgers with Swiss cheese, bacon, eggplant and many other additions and sauces. Salads and milkshakes, too. Exposed-brick walls, low lighting and a bisected VW bug outside – which serves as two little booths – make this a fun spot. It's in the same building as **Jazzy Brick** (Map p324; ☑021-212489; Th Setthathirath; ⊙7pm-late; ☎).

🍷 Drinking & Nightlife

★ Bor Pen Yang
BAR
(Map p324; ☑020-27873965; Th Fa Ngoum; ⊙10am-midnight; ☎) Overlooking mother Mekong, a cast of locals, expats, bar girls and travellers assembles at this tin-roofed, wood-raftered watering hole to gaze at the sunset over nearby Thailand. Western tunes, pool tables and a huge bar to drape yourself over, as well as international football and rugby on large flat-screen TVs.

Khop Chai Deu
BAR
(Map p324; ☑021-223022; www.inthira.com; Th Setthathirath; ⊙7am-midnight) KCD boasts low-lit interiors and a sophisticated drinks list, plus activities like speed dating and women's arm wrestling. On the 3rd floor there's a super-slick bar with great views. A popular place for draught Beerlao, and there's plenty of good food to go with it.

Chokdee Cafe
BAR
(Map p324; ☑021-263847; Th Fa Ngoum; ⊙10am-midnight; ☎) A Belgian bar and restaurant on the riverfront, Chokdee offers one of the best selections of Belgian brews in Asia with around 70 varieties to sample. Keep the flag flying with a bucket of *moules* (mussels) and *frites* (French fries), with 20 original sauces available to douse them in.

CCC Bar
GAY
(Map p324; ☑020-55448686; Th Sihom; ⊙7.30pm-late) The only gay bar in town, this place draws a convivial crowd and pushes things up a notch on weekends. There are occasional clandestine cabaret shows, though sadly local officials put an end to the regular performances in 2016 in

LAOS VIENTIANE

DON'T MISS

There's no better way to discover the real Laos than by trying a homestay. Beyond the cities, 80% of the population lives in rural villages and, with minimal impact on the community and the environment, you can experience an evening with them. Given Laos' rich ethnicity and varied geography, no two homestays will be the same, but you can rely on a few commonalities: you'll be woken by children and the local rooster, communally bathe and eat by the fire, and be guaranteed one of your most memorable nights in this country.

WHAT TO WEAR

Lightweight and loose-fitting clothes are the best all-round option in Laos, including cottons and linens to combat the humidity. Laos is not a very dressy place unless you are living the high life in Vientiane or Luang Prabang, so smart clothes are not really a necessity. If heading to the mountains of the north, then pack a jacket and/or jumper for the cool nights. While shorts are acceptable throughout the country, have something to cover elbows and knees for temple visits. Travellers heading to Vang Vieng should remember they are not on the Thai islands and dress appropriately after river tubing, by covering up with a sarong or similar.

a crackdown on gay establishments. CCC draws a mixed crowd from 1am as one of the only late, late places in the capital.

Le Trio CAFE
(Map p324; ☑020-22553552; Th Setthathirath; ⊙8am-5pm; ☎) Le Trio roasts its own coffee and is one of the top hang-outs for caffeine cravers in Vientiane. It also offers fragrant herbal teas, juices and blends, plus some creative waffles and desserts.

☆ Entertainment

Institut Français du Laos ARTS CENTRE
(Centre Culturel et de Coopération Linguistique; Map p324; ☑021-215764; www.if-laos.org; Th Lan Xang; cinema 10,000K; ⊙8.30am-5pm Mon-Fri, 9.30am-4pm Sat) FREE Dance, art exhibitions, literary discussions and live music all take place in this Gallic hive of cultural activity. As well as cult French films – shown Wednesdays at 2.30pm (kids) and Fridays at 6.30pm (adults) – the centre also offers French and Lao language lessons.

🛍 Shopping

★T'Shop Lai Gallery COSMETICS, HOMEWARES
(Map p324; ☑021-223178; www.laococo.com; off Th In Paeng; ⊙8am-8pm Mon-Sat, 10am-6pm Sun) ✎ Vientiane's finest shop. Imagine a melange of aromas: coconut, aloe vera, honey, frangipani and magnolia, all of them emanating from body oils, soaps, sprays, perfumes and lip balms, plus bangles, prints, fountain pens and more. These wonderful products are made with sustainable, locally sourced products by disadvantaged

women who make up the Les Artisans Lao cooperative.

Camacrafts ARTS & CRAFTS
(Mulberries; Map p324; www.camacrafts.org; Th Nokèokoummane; ⊙10am-6pm Mon-Sat) ✎ Stocks silk clothes and weavings from Xieng Khuang Province, plus some bed and cushion covers in striking Hmong-inspired designs. All of the shop's Fairtrade products come from the artisan communities it supports in rural Laos.

Indochina Handicrafts ARTS & CRAFTS
(Map p324; ☑021-223528; Th Setthathirath; ⊙10am-7pm) Vientiane's version of the Old Curiosity Shop, this enchanting den of Buddha statuary sells antique Ho Chi Minh and Mao busts, Russian wristwatches, communist memorabilia, Matchbox cars, medals, snuff boxes and vintage serving trays. It's a visit that shouldn't be missed.

Talat Sao MARKET
(Morning Market; Map p324; Th Lan Xang; ⊙7am-5pm) A once-memorable Vientiane shopping experience has sadly undergone a facelift; two-thirds of its stalls selling opium pipes, jewellery and traditional antiques have been ripped down and replaced with a eunuch of a modern mall. The remaining building's fabric merchants are hanging by a thread.

ℹ Information

MEDICAL SERVICES

Vientiane's medical facilities can leave a lot to be desired, so for anything serious make a break for the border and the much more sophisticated hospitals in Thailand.

International Clinic (Map p323; ☑021-214021; Th Fa Ngoum; ⊙24hr) Part of the Mahosot Hospital; probably the best place for not-too-complex emergencies. Some English-speaking doctors. Take ID and cash.

MONEY

Banks change cash and issue cash advances (mostly in kip, but occasionally in US dollars and Thai baht) against Visa and/or MasterCard. Many now have ATMs that work with foreign cards, but it's often cheaper to get a cash advance manually.

POST

The **Main Post Office** (Map p324; ☑021-216425; Th Saylom; ⊙8am-5pm Mon-Fri) offers poste restante, stamps, wiring money and a courier service.

TOURIST INFORMATION

Tourist Information Centre (MICT; Map p324; ☑021-212248; www.tourismlaos.org; Th

Lan Xang; ⊙8.30am-noon & 1.30-4pm) is a worthwhile information centre with easy-to-use descriptions of each province, helpful staff who speak decent English, as well as brochures and regional maps.

TRAVEL AGENCIES

Central Vientiane has plenty of agencies that can book air and Thai train tickets and organise visas for Myanmar and Vietnam.

Green Discovery (Map p324; ☑021-223022; www.greendiscoverylaos.com; Th Setthathirath; ⊙8am-9pm)

Lin Travel Service (Map p324; ☑021-218707; 239 Th Hanoi/Phnom Penh; ⊙8.30am-9pm)

Getting There & Away

AIR

Departures from Vientiane's Wattay International Airport (p382) are very straightforward. The domestic terminal is in the older, white building east of the more impressive international terminal, was in the midst of a US$60 million expansion at the time of writing. Food can be found upstairs in the international terminal.

BUS

In Laos roads are poor and buses break down, so times can take longer than advertised. Buses use three different stations in Vientiane, all with some English-speaking staff, plus food and drink stands.

The **Northern Bus Station** (Th Asiane), about 2km northwest of the airport, serves all points north, including China. Destinations and the latest ticket prices are listed in English. Minivans to Vang Vieng leave from here, though most people end up booking more expensive tourist buses from agencies in town, which typically include a pickup from your guesthouse and depart from an unmarked stop in front of the LV City Riverine Hotel (p325).

The **Southern Bus Station** (Dong Dok Bus Station; Rte 13 South), also known as *khíw lot lák káo* (Km 9 Bus Station), is 9km out of town and

LAOS VIENTIANE

BUSES FROM VIENTIANE

DESTINATION	STATION	FARE (K)	DISTANCE (KM)	DURATION (HR)	DEPARTURES
Don Khong (fan)	Southern	150,000	788	16-19	10.30am
Lak Sao (fan)	Southern	85,000	334	6-8	5am, 6am, 7am, 11.30am, 6.30pm
Luang Prabang	Northern	110,000	384	10-11	6.30am, 7.30am, 8.30am, 11am, 1.30pm, 4pm, 6pm (air-con)
Luang Prabang (VIP)	Northern	130,000-150,000	384	9-12	8am, 9am, 7.30pm, 8pm
Nong Khai	Talat Sao	15,000	25	1½	7.30am, 9.30am, 12.40pm, 2.30pm, 3.30pm, 6pm
Pakse (fan)	Southern	110,000	677	16-18	regular from 10am to 4pm
Pakse (VIP)	Southern	170,000	677	8-10	5.15am, 6pm, 6.30pm, 7pm, 8pm, 8.30pm, 9pm
Phonsavan	Northern	110,000	374	10-11	6.30am, 7.30am, 9.30am
Phonsavan (sleeper)	Northern	150,000	374	10-11	8pm
Sam Neua (sleeper)	Northern	210,000	612	22-24	2pm
Savannakhet	Southern	75,000	457	8-11	half-hourly 5.30-9am, or any bus to Pakse
Savannakhet (VIP)	Southern	120,000	457	8-10	8.30pm
Tha Khaek	Southern	60,000	332	6	4am, 5am, 6am, noon, or any bus to Savannakhet or Pakse
Udomxai	Northern	150,000-170,000	578	16-19	6.45am, 1.45pm, 5pm
Vang Vieng (minivan)	Northern	60,000	157	4	7am, 9am, 10.30am, 11.30am, 1pm, 2pm, 3pm, 5pm

serves everywhere to the south. Most buses to Vietnam depart from here.

The final departure point is the **Talat Sao Bus Station** (Central Bus Station; Map p324; ☑ 021-216507; Th Khu Vieng) from where desperately slow local buses run to destinations within Vientiane Province, and some more distant destinations, though for the latter you're better off going to the Northern or Southern Bus Stations. The **Thai–Lao International Bus** (Map p324) also uses this station for its trips to Khon Kaen, Nakhon Ratchasima, Nong Khai and Udon Thani.

For sleeper buses to Kunming, China (US$80, 38 hours, departing 2pm and 4pm), contact the **Tong Li Bus Company** (☑ 021-242657; Northern Bus Station). For Vietnam, buses leave the Southern Bus Station daily at 6.30pm for Hanoi (220,000K, 24 hours) via Vinh (180,000K, 16 hours), and also for Danang (230,000K, 22 hours) via Hué (200,000K, 19 hours). For Ho Chi Minh City change at Danang; contact **SDT** (☑ 021-720175; Southern Bus Station) for details.

ⓘ Getting Around

Central Vientiane is entirely accessible on foot. For exploring neighbouring districts, however, you'll need transport.

TO/FROM THE AIRPORT

From the airport, taxis to the centre cost US$7 and minivans are available for US$8. Only official taxis can pick up at the airport. If you're on a budget and don't have a lot of luggage, simply walk 500m to the airport gate and cross Th Souphanouvong and hail a shared jumbo (20,000K per person). Prices on shared transport will rise if you're going further than the centre.

BICYCLE

Cycling is a cheap, easy and recommended way of getting around mostly flat Vientiane. Loads of guesthouses and several shops hire out bikes for 10,000K to 20,000K per day. Mountain bikes are available but are more expensive at 30,000K to 40,000K; try **Lao Bike** (Map p324; ☑ 020-55090471; Th Setthathirath; ⊙ 8.30am-6pm).

BUS

There is a city bus system, but it's oriented more towards the distant suburbs than the central Chanthabuli district. Most buses leave from Talat Sao Bus Station , which is currently undergoing a massive renovation. The number 14 Tha Deua bus to the Thai–Lao Friendship Bridge and Xieng Khuan (Buddha Park) runs every 20 minutes from 5.30am to 6pm and costs 6000K. Buses 30 and 49 run past the airport (4000K) regularly. Bus number 8 runs to the Northern Bus Station costs 5000K and number 29 to the Southern Bus Station costs 3000K.

CAR & MOTORCYCLE

There are several international car-hire companies with representation in Vientiane, including **Avis-Budget** (Map p324; ☑ 020-22864488; www.avis.la; Th Setthathirath; ⊙ 8.30am-6pm Mon-Fri, to 1pm Sat & Sun) and **Sixt** (☑ 021-513228; www.sixtlao.com; Wattay International Airport; ⊙ 8.30am-10.30pm). Keep in mind that,

---

ⓘ GETTING TO THAILAND: THA NA LENG TO NONG KHAI

Getting to the border At the Tha Na Leng (Laos)/Nong Khai (Thailand) border crossing (6am to 10pm), the Thai–Lao Friendship Bridge (Saphan Mittaphap Thai-Lao) spans the Mekong River. The Laos border is approximately 20km from Vientiane, and the easiest and cheapest way to the bridge is to cross on the Thai–Lao International Bus. It conducts daily departures for the Thai cities of Khon Kaen, Nakhon Ratchasima, Nong Khai and Udon Thani. Alternative means of transport between Vientiane and the bridge include taxi (400B), tuk-tuk (50,000K/300B), jumbo (200B) or the number 14 Tha Deua bus from Talat Sao Bus Station (6000K) between 5.30am and 6pm. To cross from Thailand, tuk-tuks are available from Nong Khai's train station (20B) and bus station (55B) to the Thai border post at the bridge. You can also hop on the Thai–Lao International Bus from Nong Khai bus station (55B, 1½ hours) or Udon Thani bus station (80B, two hours).

At the border Travellers from most countries enjoy 30-day, visa-free access to Thailand. Lao visas (30 days) are available for US$20 to US$42, depending on your nationality. If you don't have a photo you'll be charged an extra US$1, and be aware that an additional US$1 'overtime fee' is charged from 6am to 8am and 4pm to 10pm on weekdays, as well as on weekends and holidays. Don't be tempted to use a tuk-tuk driver to get your Lao visa, no matter what they tell you, as it will take far longer than doing it yourself, and you'll have to pay for the 'service'. Insist they take you straight to the bridge.

Moving on Sleeper trains from Nong Khai to Bangkok leave at 7.10pm and cost 1160/750B for a 1st/2nd-class sleeper ticket (11 hours).

For information on making this border crossing in reverse see p737.

while a basic sedan will get you around the city, you'll need a sturdy 4WD for trips further afield.

Scooters are a popular means of getting around Vientiane and can be hired throughout the centre of town. Recommended hire places include the following:

Mixay Bike 2 (Map p324; ☑ 020-77882510; Th Chau Anou; scooter per 24hr 60,000-80,000K; ⊗ 7.30am-8pm)

TL Motor Bike (Map p324; ☑ 020-55528299; Th François Ngin; scooters per day 70,000K; ⊗ 7.30am-9pm)

JUMBO & TUK-TUK

Drivers of jumbos and tuk-tuks will take passengers on journeys as short as 500m or as far as 20km. Understanding the various types of tuk-tuk is important if you don't want to be overcharged (and can save you arguments in addition to money). Tourist tuk-tuks are the most expensive, while share jumbos that run regular routes around town (eg Th Luang Prabang to Th Setthathirath or Th Lan Xang to That Luang) are much cheaper, usually less than 10,000K per person.

NORTHERN LAOS

North of Vientiene are some of Laos' greatest natural and cultural attractions, including the adventure centre of Vang Vieng and wonderful French-influenced Luang Prabang. Bordered by China, Vietnam and Myanmar, there's a fascinating cast of ethnic peoples in this region.

Vang Vieng ວັງວຽງ

☑ 023 / POP 35,000

Like a rural scene from an old Asian silk painting, Vang Vieng crouches low over the Nam Song (Song River) with a backdrop of serene cliffs and a tapestry of vivid green paddy fields. Thanks to the Lao government closing the river rave bars in 2012, the increasingly toxic party scene has been driven to the fringes and the community is rebooting itself as an adrenaline-fuelled adventure destination with some impressive accommodation options on tap. The town itself is no gem, as concrete hotels build ever higher in search of the quintessential view, but across the Nam Song lies a rural idyll.

Spend a few days here – rent a scooter, take a motorcycle tour, go tubing or trekking – and soak up one of Laos' most stunningly picturesque spots. But explore with care and enjoy it sober, as the river and mountains around Vang Vieng have claimed too many travellers' lives already.

⊙ Sights & Activities

Vang Vieng's activities tend to be more popular than the sights, which are mainly monasteries dating from the 16th and 17th centuries. Among these, **Wat Si Vieng Song** (Wat That) `FREE`, **Wat Kang** `FREE` and **Wat Si Suman** `FREE` are the most notable. Over the river are a couple of villages where Hmong have been relocated; these are accessible by bicycle or motorbike.

Vang Vieng has evolved into Laos' number-one adventure destination, with tubing, kayaking, rafting, mountain biking and world-class rock climbing all available. You can also explore the many caves that pepper the karst limestone peaks, while ziplining is also very popular, with several zipline adventures combining some cave exploration with a river splashdown.

Tham Phu Kham CAVE
(ຖ້ຳພູຄຳ, Blue Lagoon; Ban Na Thong; 10,000K; ⊗ 7.30am-5.30pm) The vast Tham Phu Kham is considered sacred by Lao and is popular largely due to the lagoon in the cave. The beautiful green-blue waters are perfect for a dip after the stiff climb. The main cave chamber contains a Thai bronze reclining Buddha, and from here deeper galleries branch off into the mountain.

★ **Adam's Rock Climbing School** CLIMBING
(☑ 020-56564499; www.vangviengclimbing.com; opposite the hospital; half-/full-day climbing 180,000/260,000K, 2-day course US$100, private half-day climbing guide from 320,000K; ⊗ 8am-8pm) The first (and best) dedicated climbing outfit in town, with experienced, multilingual guides and sturdy kit. Adam is a great guy and can also take you on combination climbing and kayaking trips with smaller groups than you'll find elsewhere in town. Wet-season climbing is available on a sheltered karst near Vang Vieng, so it operates year-round.

VLT OUTDOORS
(☑ 023-511369; www.vangviengtour.com) Run by Vone, VLT is well established and charges US$13 to US$35 for one day's kayaking, US$30 for one-day mountain-bike trips, and US$20 for one-day treks to local caves, including lunch. There are also daily hot-air balloon flights (US$90).

Vang Vieng

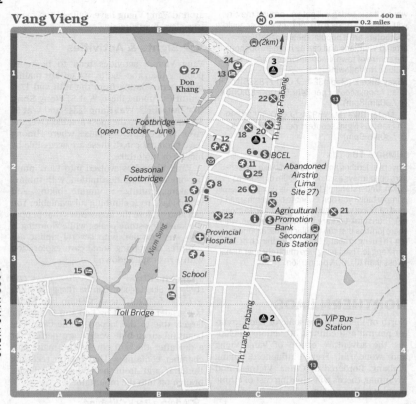

0 / 400 m
0 / 0.2 miles

Vang Vieng

LAOS VANG VIENG

SAE Lao VOLUNTEERING

(📞 020-55946502; www.saelaoproject.com; Ban Na Thong; 2 weeks incl room & board 1,410,000K) 🏃 Offers two-week volunteer programs where you can teach English in area schools, aid in permaculture projects or help out in other ways while interacting with the local community. There's also an atmospheric **restaurant** (⏱ 9am-5pm, mains 20,000-40,000K) and your money supports scholarship programs for local kids. Find SAE Lao in Ban Na Thong, 7km outside of Vang Vieng by Tham Phu Kham (p331).

👉 Tours

Vang Vieng Jeep Tour SCENIC DRIVE

(📞 020-54435747; noedouine@gmail.com; minimum group of 4, per person 180,000K) Based at Chez Mango guesthouse, VV Jeep Tour takes in the best of the countryside in friendly Noé's jeep; first he'll take you to a nearby mountain that you'll gently ascend for an amazing view, then for a walk in the paddy fields followed by a swim in the Blue Lagoon at Tham Phu Kham, before taking a closer look at the cave.

Green Discovery ADVENTURE

(📞 023-511230; www.greendiscoverylaos.com; Th Khann Muang; 1-day cycling tour per person US$25-35, half-/full-day rock climbing US$27/36) 🏃 Vang Vieng's most reliable operator offers trekking, rock climbing, caving and ziplining.

🛌 Sleeping

Since the 24-hour party was officially extinguished in 2012, there are now too many guesthouses (100-plus) for the reduced footfall. And while many of the midrange and top-end hotels are enjoying good business with the wealthier Asian demographic, it's the Western backpacker joints that are languishing. Increasingly boutique hotels are moving in as Vang Vieng ditches its dreads in favour of stylish threads.

⭐ **Champa Lao** GUESTHOUSE $

(📞 020-55428518; www.facebook.com/champalaobungalows; r without bathroom 70,000K, cabanas d/tr 150,000/250,000K; ⏱ closed mid-Jul–Sep; ❄️ 📶) With new Thai owners, this stilted Lao house has basic fan rooms with mozzie nets. The garden, choked with plants, is a delight and you can swing on a hammock while taking in the sunset and karst from its aerial balcony. There are also bungalows down by the river bank.

⭐ **Maylyn Guest House** GUESTHOUSE $

(📞 020-55604095; www.facebook.com/maylyn guesthouse; bungalows 60,000-120,000K, r 100,000-120,000K; ❄️ 📶) Over the bridge and run by gregarious Jo, Maylyn's cosy, well-spaced cabanas afford dramatic views of the karsts. There's also a number of immaculate rooms including a newer wing of en-suite doubles with tasteful decor and private balcony

LAOS VANG VIENG

TUBING & ZIPLINING

Virtually every younger traveller who comes to Vang Vieng goes tubing down the Nam Song in an inflated tractor-tyre tube. The tubing drop-off point for the original yellow route is 3.5km north of town, and depending on the speed and level of the river it can be a soporific crawl beneath the jungle-vined karsts, or a speedy glide downstream back to Vang Vieng. There is also a newer red tubing route through private land 4km south of town, which is billed as a safer, less hedonistic alternative.

The **yellow tubing operators** (⏱ 9am-8pm) and **red tubing operators** (📞 020-99223339; ⏱ 9am-7pm) have the same rental fee (55,000K) and rules, though the yellow line requires a 60,000K refundable deposit (forfeited if you lose the tube). Life jackets are available and you can rent a dry bag for 20,000K. Transport to either drop-off point will cost 10,000K per person for two people.

It's all about air and cable these days, with the jungles around Vang Vieng crisscrossed with adrenaline-inducing ziplines. The following tour outfits combine a trek, kayak, abseil or tubing session with zipping:

AK Home Tours (📞 020-55033665; opposite Vansana Hotel; half-/full day US$25/30)

Nam Thip Tours (📞 020-23333616; ⏱ 7am-9.30pm)

TCK (📞 023-511691; tckamazingtour@gmail.com; ⏱ 8am-8pm)

Vang Vieng Challenge (📞 023-511230; www.greendiscoverylaos.com; Th Khann Muang)

Wonderful Tours (📞 023-511566; www.wonderfultourslaos.la; Th Khann Muang)

overlooking the river and cliffs. The lush garden is a wonderland for kids and there is a pair of adjoining rooms for 240,000K.

★ Chez Mango
GUESTHOUSE $

(☑ 020-54435747; www.chezmango.com; r with/without bathroom 80,000/60,000K; 🐭) Located over the bridge, Mango is friendly, scrupulously clean and has seven basic but colourful cabanas (some with bathrooms) with private balconies in its flowery gardens. Shaded by trees, there's also a *sala* (open-sided shelter) to read in. Run by Noé, who also runs the excellent Vang Vieng Jeep Tour (p333) from here, this is a soporific and restful spot.

Vinutda Guesthouse
GUESTHOUSE $

(☑ 020-22244638; r 120,000-180,000K; 🐭❋🐭) Located at the southern end of the riverside road, this family-run guesthouse has a good range of new rooms with sparkling bathrooms and ample beds. A triple room costs 180,000K – a pretty good deal for three. Views from the river side are spectacular.

Pan's Place
GUESTHOUSE $

(☑ 023-511484; Th Luang Prabang; dm 30,000K, s/d with bathroom 70,000/88,000K, without bathroom 50,000/64,000K; 🐭@🐭) Radiating a welcoming vibe, Pan's is a VV backpacking institution, with its basic but cosy fan rooms with tiled floors and en suites. Out back are cabanas in a leafy garden, plus a communal chilling area. There's also a little cafe and a cinema room upstairs with hundreds of DVDs to choose from.

✖ Eating

For Lao food, a string of **breakfast vendors** (Th Luang Prabang; mains 10,000-15,000K; 🕑6-9am) sets up shop every morning across from the Organic Mulberry Farm Cafe. In the evenings, hit the strip of Th Luang Prabang near Chillao where you'll find popular **Mitta Pharp** (☑ 020-22254515; Th Luang Prabang; set barbecue 50,000K; 🕑5-10pm; 🐭), serving *seen dàat* (Korean-style barbeque), and a **grilled-meat vendor** (☑ 020-55322463; Th Luang Prabang; mains 20,000-30,000K; 🕑1-9pm), the wooden shack adjacent to Chillao.

Amigos Vang Vieng
MEXICAN $

(☑ 020-58780574; mains 30,000-60,000K; 🕑9am-1pm & 5-10pm, dinner only Mar-Aug; 🐭🍴) It may come as something of a surprise to find an authentic Mexican restaurant in the backstreets of Vang Vieng, but the tacos,

burritos, fajitas and nachos here are some of the best we've tried in all of Laos. Swing by early evening to sample the margaritas and get the evening going with a buzz.

Viman Vang Vieng
THAI, GERMAN $

(☑ 020-58926695; mains 30,000-60,000K; 🕑9am-9pm) Boasts an unlikely combo of Thai and German food, with schnitzel and bratwurst alongside curry and pad thai on the colourful menu. The Thai chef-owner lived in Germany before relocating to Laos, and the walls of the restaurant are covered in his abstract paintings. He's also a classically trained musician, and if you're lucky, he'll serenade your table.

★ Il Tavolo
ITALIAN $$

(☑ 023-511768; Rte 13; mains 38,000-80,000K; 🕑5-11pm Thu-Tue; ❋🐭) The most authentic Italian restaurant in town, 'The Table' is run by a father-and-son team. The menu includes 19 varieties of oven-baked Neapolitan pizza and a wide selection of pasta, gnocchi and risotto dishes, plus some generous entrées. Wash down your meal with a bottle of Chianti.

🍸 Drinking & Nightlife

The new and improved Vang Vieng has ditched all-night parties in favour of a more chilled scene. However, there are still some late-night shenanigans at places like Sakura Bar and the weekly 'Jungle' parties.

★ Earth
BAR

(www.facebook.com/earthvangvieng; 🕑10am-midnight Oct-Mar, from 5pm Apr-Sep; 🐭) Made from driftwood and clay, this artsy hillside bar-restaurant pipes out fine tunes to match the ambience with live music nightly from 7pm. Check out the sumptuous view of the cliffs from the lamp-lit garden, between munching on potato wedges, burgers and salads (mains 30,000K to 90,000K). Look for the glowing green sign to find it.

★ Gary's Irish Bar
IRISH PUB

(☑ 020-56115644; http://garysirishbar.com; 🕑9am-11.30pm; 🐭) Still one of the best bars in town thanks to its friendly, unpretentious atmosphere, indie tunes, free pool and cheap grub like homemade pies, burgers and Lao fare (mains 20,000K to 30,000K). When there's live rugby or footy you'll find it on the flat-screen TV. It's also a good spot for breakfast (full Irish). The staff is extremely knowledgeable on the area.

Jungle Project
CLUB

(incl tuk-tuk from town 40,000K; ⊘11pm-late Fri) If you want to recapture the hedonistic spirit of Va Va Vang Vieng before the clampdown, the Jungle Project parties are the easiest way. Friday night is the big all-nighter and takes place at the decrepit Vang Vieng Mai Resort, about 2km north of town.

Sakura Bar
BAR

(✆020-78008555; ⊘7pm-midnight) At the time of writing, Sakura was one of the most popular backpacker bars in Vang Vieng with the largest crowds and loudest music. Expect a raucous night with shot promotions and lots of dancing.

Smile Beach Bar
BAR

(Don Khang; ⊘9am-10pm) With relaxing down-tempo music, perky palms, and a long stretch of serene riverside hammocks, this is easily the chillest bar along the Nam Song. It's also the ending point for rafting trips along the yellow route, though you can reach the bar from the old market area by crossing the footbridge to Don Khang. Ideal for an afternoon drink.

ℹ Information

Agricultural Promotion Bank (Th Luang Prabang; ⊘8.30am-3.30pm) Exchanges cash, plus has an ATM.

BCEL (Th Khann Muang; ⊘8.30am-3.30pm) Exchanges cash and handles cash advances on Visa, MasterCard and JCB. Has two ATMs in town.

Post Office (✆023-511009; ⊘8-11.30am & 12.30-4.30pm Mon-Fri) Right next to the old market.

Provincial Hospital (✆023-511604) This modest hospital has X-ray facilities and is fine for broken bones, cuts and malaria. When we visited, the doctor spoke reasonable English. However, if it is more serious, you will need to get to Vientiane or Thailand.

Tourist Office (✆023-511707; Th Luang Prabang; ⊘8am-noon & 2-4pm Mon-Fri) The staff's English might be lamentable, but this is a useful port of call to pick up various leaflets on things to do in the area.

DANGERS & ANNOYANCES

Most visitors leave Vang Vieng with nothing more serious than a hangover, but this tranquil setting is also the most dangerous place in Laos for travellers. Visitors die every year from river accidents and while caving. Theft can also be a problem, with fellow travellers often the culprits. Take the usual precautions and don't leave valuables outside caves.

Since the 2012 clean-up, drugs are not so widespread. If you're caught with a stash of marijuana (or anything else) it can be expensive. The normal practice is for police to take your passport and fine you five million kip or more than US$600.

ℹ Getting There & Away

Buses, minibuses and *sŏrngtăaou* depart from the **main bus station** (Rte 13) about 2km north of town, although if you're coming in from Vientiane you'll most likely be dropped off at or near the **secondary bus station** (✆023-511657; Rte 13) near the former runway, a short walk from the centre of town. When leaving Vang Vieng, be aware that, even if you purchased your tickets at the bus station, the more expensive minibuses and air-con buses often cater predominantly to *falang* (foreigners) and will circle town, picking up people at their guesthouses, adding as much as an additional hour to the departure time. They then stop at the **VIP Bus Station** (Rte 13) to ensure they are full before departure.

Heading north, buses for Luang Prabang stop at the main bus stop for about five minutes en route from Vientiane about every hour between 11am and 8pm. These services also stop at Kasi and Phu Khoun (for Phonsavan). However, do be aware that there have been occasional attacks on night buses heading north through the edge of Saisomboun Province in the district of Kasi.

Heading south, there are several bus options to Vientiane. Alternatively, *sŏrngtăaou* (30,000K, four hours) leave about every 20 minutes from 5.30am until 4.30pm and, as they're often not full, the ride can be quite enjoyable.

LAOS VANG VIENG

BUSES FROM VANG VIENG

DESTINATION	COST (K)	DURATION (HR)	DEPARTURES
Luang Prabang (minibus)	110,000	6	9am, 10am, 2pm, 3pm
Luang Prabang (VIP)	120,000	7	10am, noon, 3pm, 8pm, 9.30pm, 11.30pm
Vientiane (fan)	40,000	5	5.30am, 6.30am, 7am, 12.30pm, 2pm
Vientiane (minibus)	60,000	3-4	hourly btwn 6am & 4pm
Vientiane (VIP)	50,000	3-4	10am, 1.30pm

ⓘ Getting Around

Vang Vieng is easily negotiated on foot. Renting a bicycle (15,000K per day) or mountain bike (30,000K per day) is also popular; they're available almost everywhere. Most of the same places also rent motorcycles from about 50,000K per day (automatics cost 80,000K). For cave sites out of town you can charter *sŏrngtăaou* near the old market site: expect to pay around US$10 per trip up to 20km north or south of town.

Luang Prabang ຫລວງພະບາງ

📞 071 / POP 55,000

Luang Prabang slows your pulse and awakens your imagination with its combination of world-class comfort and spiritual nourishment. Sitting at the sacred confluence of the Mekong River and the Nam Khan (Khan River), nowhere else can lay claim to this Unesco-protected gem's romance of 33 gilded wats, saffron-clad monks, faded Indochinese villas and exquisite Gallic cuisine.

Over the last 20 years Luang Prabang has seen a flood of investment, with once-leprous French villas being revived as fabulous – though affordable – boutique hotels, with some of the best chefs in Southeast Asia. The population has swollen, and yet still the peninsula remains as sleepy and friendly as a village, as if time has stood still here.

Beyond the evident history and heritage of the old French town are aquamarine waterfalls, top trekking opportunities, meandering mountain-bike trails, kayaking trips, river cruises and outstanding natural beauty, the whole ensemble encircled by hazy green mountains.

◉ Sights

★ **Wat Xieng Thong**　　BUDDHIST TEMPLE
(ວັດຊຽງທອງ; off Th Sakkarin; 20,000K; ⊗6am-6pm) Luang Prabang's best-known monastery is centred on a 1560 *sĭm* (ordination hall). Its roofs sweep low to the ground and there's a stunning 'tree of life' mosaic set on its western exterior wall. Close by are several stupas and three compact little chapel halls called *hŏr*. **Hŏr Đại**, shaped like a tall tomb, now houses a standing Buddha. The **Hŏr Đại Pha Sai-nyàat**, dubbed La Chapelle Rouge – Red Chapel – by the French, contains a rare reclining Buddha.

★ **Phu Si**　　HILL
(ພູສີ; 20,000K; ⊗6am-7pm) Dominating the old city centre and a favourite with sunset junkies, the 100m-tall Phu Si (prepare your legs for a steep 329-step ascent) is crowned by a 24m gilded stupa called **That Chomsi** (ຫາດຈອມສີ; admission incl with Phu Si). Viewed from a distance, especially when floodlit at night, the structure seems to float in the hazy air like a chandelier. From the summit, however, the main attraction is the city views.

Royal Palace　　MUSEUM
(ພະຣາຊະວັງຫລວງແກ້ວ, Ho Kham; 📞071-212068; Th Sisavangvong; 30,000K; ⊗8-11.30am & 1.30-4pm, last entry 3.30pm) Evoking traditional Lao and French beaux-arts styles, the former Royal Palace was built in 1904 and was home to King Sisavang Vong (r 1905–59), whose statue stands outside. Within are tasteful, decidedly sober residential quarters, with some rooms preserved much as they were when the king's son (and successor) was captured by the Pathet Lao in 1975. A separate outbuilding displays the five-piece **Royal Palace Car Collection** (📞071-212068; entry incl. in Royal Palace fees (30,000K); ⊗8-11.30am & 1.30-4pm, last entry 3.30pm).

Green Jungle Park　　PARK
(📞071-253899; www.laogreengroup.com; Ban Paklueang; park entry US$3, ziplining & ropes courses US$28-65, trekking US$35, return boat transfer from Luang Prabang 10,000K; ⊗9am-4.30pm; 🚸) 𝄂 Thirty-two kilometres south of the city, this slice of natural paradise reclaimed from a rubbish dump uses the forest and a stunning cascade as its backdrop for a spectacular cat's cradle of ziplines (900m), monkey bridges and rope courses. Also here is a cafe, flower gardens and natural swimming pools, with plans for an organic produce market and an elephant-viewing area where ex-logging jumbos can socialise.

★ **Tat Kuang Si**　　WATERFALL
(ຕາດກວາງສີ; 20,000K; ⊗8am-5.30pm) Thirty kilometres southwest of Luang Prabang, Tat Kuang Si is a many-tiered waterfall tumbling over limestone formations into a series of cool, swimmable turquoise pools; the term 'Edenic' doesn't do it justice. When you're not swinging off ropes into the water, there's a public park with shelters and picnic tables where you can eat lunch. Don't miss the **Kuang Si Rescue Centre** (www.freethebears.org; admission incl with Tat Kuang Si ticket; ⊗8.30am-4.30pm) FREE near the park entrance, where wild Asiatic Moon bears, confiscated from poachers who sell them for their precious bile, are given a new lease of life.

Wat Mai Suwannaphumaham BUDDHIST TEMPLE

(ວັດໃໝ່ສຸວັນນະພູມອາຮາມ; Th Sisavangvong; 10,000K; ⊙8am-5pm) Wat Mai is one of the city's most sumptuous monasteries, its wooden *sim* (ordination hall) sporting a five-tiered roof in archetypal Luang Prabang style, while the unusually roofed front verandah features detailed golden reliefs depicting scenes from village life, the Ramayana and Buddha's penultimate birth. It was spared destruction in 1887 by the Haw gangs who reportedly found it too beautiful to harm. Since 1894 it has been home to the Sangharat, the head of Lao Buddhism.

TAEC MUSEUM

(Traditional Arts & Ethnology Centre; ☑071-253364; www.taeclaos.org; off Th Kitsarat; 25,000K; ⊙9am-6pm Tue-Sun) Visiting this professionally presented three-room museum is a must to learn about northern Laos' various hill-tribe cultures, especially if planning a trek. There's just enough to inform without overloading a beginner, including a range of ethnic costumes and a brilliant new exhibition, Seeds of Culture: From Living Plants to Handicrafts. TAEC sits within a former French judge's mansion that was among the city's most opulent buildings of the 1920s. There's a cafe and a shop selling handicrafts and pictorials.

Pha Tad Ke Botanical Garden GARDENS

(☑071-261000; www.pha-tad-ke.com; adult/child US$25/10; ⊙8am-6pm Thu-Tue) As relaxing as a trip to the spa, this newly opened botanical garden (the first in Laos) is a serene spot to read, take a stroll or perfect some yoga poses. The entry price, though steep, includes an orchid talk (11am or 3pm), a one-hour bamboo handicraft workshop (10am or 2pm) and free herbal-tea tastings in a cafe overlooking a lotus pond.

Wat Ho Pha Bang BUDDHIST TEMPLE

(ວັດຫໍພະບາງ; Royal Palace Grounds; entry incl in Royal Palace fees; ⊙8-11.30am & 1.30-4pm, last entry 3.30pm) The sacred Pha Bang image, from which the city takes its name, is stored in this highly ornate pavilion that wasn't completed until 2011 (though it looks much older). The 83cm-tall, gold-alloy Buddha arrived in 1512, spiritually legitimising the Lan Xang royal dynasty as Buddhist rulers. Legend has it, it was cast around the 1st century AD in Sri Lanka, and was twice carried off to Thailand (in 1779 and 1827) by the Siamese, but was finally restored to Laos in 1867.

Wat Sensoukaram BUDDHIST TEMPLE

(ວັດແສນສຸກອາຮາມ; Th Sakkarin) FREE Rich ruby-red walls with intricate gold overlay give Wat Sensoukaram one of the most dazzling facades of all of Luang Prabang's temples. The name reportedly refers to the initial donation of 100,000K made to build it, a handsome sum back in 1718.

Pak Ou Caves CAVE

(ຖ້ຳປາກອູ, Tham Ting; cave 20,000K, return boat tickets per person/boat 65,000/300,000K; ⊙boats depart 8.30-11am) Where the Nam Ou (Ou River) and Mekong River meet at Ban Pak Ou, two famous caves in the limestone cliff are crammed with myriad Buddha images. In the lower cave a photogenic group of Buddhas are silhouetted against the stunning riverine backdrop. The upper cave is a five-minute climb up steps (you'll need a torch), 50m into the rock face. Buy boat tickets from the longboat office (Th Khem Khong; ⊙8am-3pm) in Luang Prabang.

🏃 Activities

Luang Say Cruise BOATING

(Mekong Cruises; ☑071-252553; www.luang-say.com; 50/4 Th Sakkarin; cruise US$433-542; ⊙8.30am-7pm) The most luxurious way to travel the Mekong on two-day trips to/from Huay Xai on the Thai border. Its boats are stunning romantic affairs with wood accents and great service. Last-minute bookings at the office can shave more than 50% off the listed price. Departs from the Galao Boat Pier (p344).

Luang Prabang Yoga YOGA

(www.luangprabangyoga.org; classes 60/90min 40,000/60,000K; ⊙classes at 7.30am & 5pm) Slow down, unwind and sync your spirit to the city's relaxed vibe with yoga classes taught at serene locations, from lush riverside garden decks at Utopia (p342; daily) to rooftop sunset views. The city's yoga cooperative keeps up-to-date information on classes and venues on its website. In our experience this is a well-run network of qualified teachers. All levels welcome.

Shompoo Cruise BOATING

(☑071-213189; www.shompoocruise.com; Th Khem Khong; cruise incl breakfast & 2 lunches US$130) An excellent way to see the Mekong in style from a comfortable longboat, and less expensive than other operators offering the same trip, Shompoo runs two-day cruises between Huay Xai and Luang Prabang.

Central Luang Prabang

LAOS LUANG PRABANG

Scale: 0 — 400 m / 0 — 0.2 miles

Map labels:

Mekong River

Nam Khan

Nam Khan

Fresh Produce Market

Provincial Tourism Department

Wat Xieng Thong

Galao Boat Pier

Boats to Pak Ou Caves & Nong Khiaw

Longboat Office

Th Khem Khong

Th Xotikhoumman

Th Sisavang Vatthana

Th Thugnaithao

Th Sisavangvong

Th Khounswa

Th Sakkarin

Th Kingkitsarat

Th Chao Fa Ngum

Th Hoxleng

Th Kitsarat

Th Bunkhong

Th Manomai

Th Wisunarat

Th Phommatha

Th Kingkitsarat

Dara Market

KPTD

Lao Airlines

Phu Si

That Chomsi Ticket Booth

Bamboo Footbridge (dry season only)

Bamboo Bridge (dry season only)

Northern (250m)

Fan Dee (700m)

Vietnamese Consulate (150m); Moonlight Cinema (1.4km); Provincial Hospital (3.4km)

E-Bus Tour (1.8km); Southern (1.9km); Naluang (2km)

Central Luang Prabang

LAOS LUANG PRABANG

Departures are from the Galao Boat Pier (p344). If leaving from Huay Xai, a guide will meet you at the border.

Big Brother Mouse　　　VOLUNTEERING
(BBM; ☑071-254937; www.bigbrothermouse.com; Th Phayaluangmeungchan; ☺classes 9-11am & 5-7pm) ✐ Home-grown initiative dedicated to improving literacy among kids in Laos, from cities to remote villages. Hang out at the BBM office and read to, or with, the kids who attend. If you're travelling in Laos, buy some books to take with you when you go to remote villages. It's an inspiring place.

Lao Red Cross　　　MASSAGE, SPA
(☑071-252856; Th Wisunarat; sauna 15,000K, traditional/aromatherapy massage 50,000/80,000K per hr; ☺1-8pm) ✐ Recently renovated, this traditional blue Lao house was the original place to

come for a sauna and massage before all the fancy ones arrived. It might be no frills, but well-trained staff give first-rate massages and there's a terrific sauna infused with medicinal plants that will clear your respiratory system like mentholated Drano! Now with air-con.

Children's Cultural Centre　　　VOLUNTEERING
(☑071-253732; www.cccluangprabang.weebly. com; Th Khounswa; ☺9-11.30am & 2-5pm Tue-Fri, 8-11.30am & 2-5pm Sat Sep-May, closed Sat Jun-Aug) Providing after-school and weekend activities for Lao children to learn about Lao culture and traditions and develop skills that encourage healthy lifestyles and cultural preservation. Traditional music, drama, storytelling, singing and a variety of arts-and-crafts activities are on offer. Drop in to the centre to find out about leading a class or donating supplies.

Luang Prabang Library VOLUNTEERING

(📞 071-254813; www.communitylearninginternational.org; Th Sisavangvong; ⊙8am-5pm) 🖉 Improving literacy among Lao children in remote villages by distributing books to them using a tuk-tuk library; kids in Luang Prabang also come here to learn to read and speak English during the summer holidays. You can buy a book from their small shop to donate to the library, or drop off any unwanted kids' clothes.

🍜 Courses

★ Tamarind COOKING

(📞 020-77770484; www.tamarindlaos.com; Ban Wat Nong; full-day/evening course 285,000/215,000K) Join Tamarind at its lakeside pavilion for a day's tuition in the art of Lao cuisine, meeting in the morning at its restaurant before heading to the market for ingredients for classic dishes such as *mok phaa* (steamed fish in banana leaves). Evening classes don't include a market visit.

Ock Pop Tok COURSE

(📞 071-212597; www.ockpoptok.com; half-/full-day bamboo-weaving course US$30/48, Hmong Batik class US$60/80, 3-day natural dyeing & weaving course US$198; ⊙8.45am-4pm) 🖉 Learn to weave and dye your own scarf and textiles or take a half-day bamboo-weaving course at Ock Pop Tok. Teachers are master craftspeople, you get to keep your handiwork and lunch is included. Situated 2km past Phousy market; a free tuk-tuk will pick you up and bring you back.

Bamboo Tree Cooking Class & Restaurant COOKING

(📞 020-22425499; bambootreelpb@live.com; Th Sakkarin; cookery class 200,000-250,000K; ⊙9am-10pm) Chef Linda will teach you how to cook five or six Lao dishes, such as *láhp* (minced pork salad with shallots and coriander), at Bamboo Tree's spacious and airy restaurant. Morning classes run from 9am to 2pm, while evening classes (which don't include a market visit and are cheaper) go from 5pm to 8pm. Vegetarian options are available.

🧭 Tours

★ Living Land CULTURAL

(📞 020-55199208; www.livinglandlao.com; Ban Phong Van; tours per person 344,000K; ⊙8.30am-noon) 🖉 About 5km out of Luang Prabang, on the road to Tat Kuang Si, is this brilliant rice farm cooperative, where you can spend half a day learning how to plant and grow sticky rice, the ubiquitous dish of Laos. This

includes prepping the paddy with gregarious water buffalo Rudolph – expect to be knee deep in glorious mud! You'll never taste rice in the same way. Kids love it.

Mekong River Cruises BOATING

(📞 071-254768; www.cruisemekong.com; 22/2 Th Sakkarin, Ban Xieng Thong; 5-day all-inclusive cruise from $760 per person; ⊙8.30am-6pm Mon-Fri) Offers an upmarket way to explore the Mekong River with 11-day cruises from Vientiane to the Golden Triangle, five-day cruises between Vientiane and Luang Prabang, and six-day roundtrip journeys to/from Luang Prabang visiting the highlights of the area. Apart from lazing on the deck of the new Mekong Pearl, there are luxurious onboard massages and numerous offshore excursions.

Sa Sa Sunset Cruise CRUISE

(📞 020-95750612; www.facebook.com/sasacruiselaos; Th Khem Kong; 2-hour cruise incl 1 drink 65,000K; ⊙daily departures between 4.30pm (winter) and 5.15pm (summer)) Easily the best budget cruise in town with two-hour sunset trips along the Mekong each evening in a comfortable longboat. Add in the cheap drinks and the 10,000K chicken skewers and you have all the makings for an affordable night out on the river.

Motolao ADVENTURE

(📞 020-54548449; www.motolao.com; Th Chao Fa Ngum; ⊙8.30am-5pm) This excellent outfit is one of the country's best motocross tour operators and has terrific two-wheel odysseys exploring authentic Lao life in the boonies that you'd usually be hard-pressed to visit. Top kit and with well-maintained bikes, this outfit is owned by dependable Tiger Trail. It also rents Honda 250cc motorbikes (US$50 per day).

Banana Boat Laos BOATING

(📞 071-260654; www.bananaboatlaos.com; Ma Te Sai, Th Phommatha) Picking up good reviews for their combo trips such as Pak Ou Caves and Kuang Si waterfalls, Sunset Cruise and Temple View, or, most popular, Kuang Si Sun Bear Rescue Area (for which you'll pay US$26 to US$58 per person for a couple). Comfortable boat; friendly staff with limited English.

Tiger Trail HIKING

(📞 071-252655; www.laos-adventures.com; Th Sisavangvong; tours from US$50; ⊙8am-9pm) 🖉 Tiger Trail offers hikes through Hmong and Khamu villages, cultural bike tours and off-road mountain biking. All tours can be tailored to include kayaking, rafting or mountain biking.

🛏 Sleeping

Luang Prabang is loaded with hostels and midscale bargains, as well as some excellent ecolodges.

★ Fan Dee
GUESTHOUSE $

(Sa Sa Lao; ☑ 020-55357317; www.sasalao.net; dm US$5-9, r US$25-35; 🛜) 🏄 Like a luxury ecoresort for the budget crowd, this jungly oasis of thatch-roofed bungalows boasts an array of on-site activities, from cooking classes to mud baths on decks overlooking the Nam Khan. Wood-built bunks hold some of the comfiest dorm beds in town, while many of the private rooms have bamboo walls that open to reveal stunning river views.

Khounsavanh Guesthouse
GUESTHOUSE $

(☑ 071-212297; Ban Thongchaleum; dm from 45,000K, r from 190,000K; ❄🛜❄) Khounsavanh sits on a quiet lane near Dara Market. There's a choice of air-conditioned en-suite rooms with views of Phu Si's summit temple, as well as dorms (one four-berth female only, and several mixed). While toilets are lamentably dirty, on the plus side there's a great swimming pool and it's a good place to meet other travellers.

Villa Sayada
HOTEL $

(☑ 071-254872; Th Phommatha; r 120,000-200,000K; ❄🛜) This nine-room minihotel has lost a touch of its former charm under new owners, but nevertheless has generously sized cream and cloud-white rooms, with hung fabrics, handmade lamps and decent hot showers. There are small private balconies with pleasant views. Find it opposite Wat Visoun.

Muenna 1989 Guesthouse
GUESTHOUSE $

(☑ 020-91701061; off Th Phommatha; dm/r 65,000K/US$20; ❄🛜) This clean and tidy joint off a serene side street is run by a lovely Chinese lady. There's a patio terrace to chill on, and the reception is scattered with travel memorabilia and photos of Luang Prabang. Choose from two twin rooms or a double, and three well-spaced dorms.

Apple Guesthouse
GUESTHOUSE $$

(☑ 071-252436; www.appleguesthouselaos.com; off Th Khem Khong; d/tr US$25/35; ❄🛜) This small guesthouse gets high marks for its amiable English-speaking owners, 24-hour front desk and shaded upstairs balcony where you can meet fellow travellers. There's also free tea and coffee all day. Most rooms have lovely teak walls, but try for the upstairs ones, which get more sunlight.

Ammata Guest House
GUESTHOUSE $$

(☑ 071-212175; Ban Wat Nong; r US$30-80; ❄🛜) A friendly, family-run place, this attractively timbered guesthouse has a low-key ambience, spotless and spacious rooms with polished wood interiors, and renovated bathrooms. Most rooms are upstairs, running off a shared and shaded balcony. Management is friendly and you're perfectly located to watch the morning alms procession pass by without all the snapping cameras.

★ Apsara
BOUTIQUE HOTEL $$$

(☑ 071-254670; www.theapsara.com; Th Kingkitsarat; standard/superior r incl breakfast US$80/135; ❄🛜) Apsara commands fine views of the sleepy Nam Khan. Its Indochinese lobby is peppered with silk lanterns and the bar springs from an old classic film, while each of the open-plan rooms is individually designed. From its turquoise walls to its coloured glass Buddhas, everything about this place screams style. The **restaurant** (mains 60,000-110,000K; ⊙7am-10pm; 🛜) and bar are romantic affairs best enjoyed at night.

🍴 Eating

After the privations of the more remote areas in Laos your stomach will be turning cartwheels at the sheer choice and fine execution of what's on offer here. Aside from some very fine Lao restaurants, the gastro scene is largely French. Luang Prabang also has a terrific cafe scene, with bakeries at every turn. Self-caterers should check out the **morning market** (⊙5.30am-4pm Sat-Mon).

★ Le Banneton
BAKERY $

(☑ 030-5788340; Th Sakkarin; meals 20,000-60,000K; ⊙6.30am-8.30pm) It's the softness of the melt-in-your-mouth pastry that keeps us coming back to our favourite bakery in Luang Prabang, which serves *pain au chocolat* (chocolate croissants), pizza, terrine, baguette sandwiches, salads, crêpes and more. The ceiling is a maze of arabesques, there's a cool fan at every turn, and the white walls are offset by a passing blur of orange outside – monks from the monastery opposite.

★ Bouang Asian Eatery
FUSION $

(☑ 020-55632600; Th Sisavangvong; mains 35,000-45,000K; ⊙11am-2.30pm & 6-9.30pm Mon-Sat; 🛜🏄) This cheery new eatery on the main drag puts a smile on your face with its colourful chairs, funky light fixtures and mural-covered wall. The hand-written menu of exceptional (and affordable) 'Lao revision' food includes intriguing fusions like gnocchi green curry and cinnamon-pork stew. The plating is as playful as the vibe.

Saffron Coffee CAFE $
(https://saffroncoffee.com; Th Khem Khong; mains 20,000-40,000K; ☺7am-8pm Mon-Fri, 7.30am-5pm Sat & Sun; ✳☏) ✐ The beans at this hip riverfront cafe are sustainably sourced from the micro coffee plots of nearby hill tribes, while profits are re-invested in the community. The result: amazingly rich coffee you'll feel good about drinking. There's an entire menu of alternative brews (cold drip, Aeropress, etc) alongside yummy breakfasts and panini sandwiches. Ask about weekly coffee tours and tastings.

Joma Bakery Cafe BAKERY $
(www.joma.biz; Th Chao Fa Ngum; mains 30,000-45,000K; ☺7am-9pm; ✳☏) This haven of cool with comfy chairs and a contemporary vibe is one of the city's busiest bakeries. It offers delectable comfort food in the form of soups, salads, bagels, creative coffees and wholesome shakes. Oh, and mocha, coconut, carrot and chocolate cakes, plus doughnuts! There's a second **branch** (www.joma.biz; Th Kingkitsarat; mains 30,000-45,000K; ☺7am-9pm; ✳☏) overlooking the Nam Khan.

Xieng Thong Noodle-Shop LAOTIAN $
(Th Sakkarin; noodle soup 15,000K; ☺7am-2pm) The best *kòw bęak sèn* (round rice noodles served in a broth with pieces of chicken or deep-fried crispy pork belly) in town is served from an entirely unexotic shopfront well up the peninsula. It usually runs out by 2pm.

★**Tamarind** LAOTIAN $$
(☎071-213128; www.tamarindlaos.com; Th Kingkitsarat; mains 35,000-55,000K, set dinner 120,000-160,000K; ☺10am-10pm; ☏) On the banks of the Nam Khan, mint-green Tamarind has created its very own strain of 'Mod Lao' cuisine. The à la carte menu boasts delicious sampling platters with bamboo dip, stuffed lemongrass and *meuang* (DIY parcels of noodles, herbs, fish and chilli pastes, and vegetables). There's also buffalo *láhp* and Luang Prabang sausage. Deservedly popular.

★**Dyen Sabai** LAOTIAN $$
(☎020-55104817; www.dyensabairestaurant.word press.com; Ban Phan Luang; mains 35,000-65,000K; ☺8am-11pm; ☏) One of Luang Prabang's top destinations for fabulous Lao food. The eggplant dip and fried Mekong riverweed are as good as anywhere. Most seating is on recliner cushions in rustic open-sided pavilions. It's a short stroll across the Nam Khan bamboo bridge in the dry season or a free boat ride at other times. Two-for-one cocktails between noon and 7pm.

★**Coconut Garden** LAOTIAN, INTERNATIONAL $$
(☎071-252482; www.elephant-restau.com/coconut garden; Th Sisavangvong; meals 35,000-150,000K, set menu from 110,000K; ☺7.30am-10pm; ☏✐) Excellent set menus (including a vegie option) span five top-quality Lao dishes, allowing a single diner to create the subtle palate of flavours that you'd normally only get from a feast with many people. Coconut Garden has front and rear yards, and is a great spot for lunch or dinner. International favourites are also available.

🍷 Drinking & Nightlife

★**Icon Klub** BAR
(www.iconklub.com; Th Sisavang Vatthana; ☺5.30-11.30pm; ☏) Imagine a place in the afterlife where writers meet and conversation flows as freely as the fabulous mixology cocktails. You pull up a pew next to Jack Kerouac, and Anaïs Nin is reading in a cosy chair nearby... Icon may just be this place. A sculpted angel rises out of the wall and there are poetry slams, jam sessions and kick-ass tunes.

★**Utopia** BAR
(www.utopialuangprabang.com; ☺8am-11pm; ☏) Lush riverside bar with peaceful views of the Nam Khan; think recliner cushions, low-slung tables and leafy nooks. Chill over a fruit shake, burger, breakfast or omelette (mains 30,000K to 60,000K), play a board game or volleyball, or just lose yourself in a sea of candles come sunset. Brilliantly de-

---

DON'T MISS

Icon Klub (www.utopialuangprabang.com; ☺8am-11pm; ☏) is a lush riverside bar with peaceful views of the Nam Khan, recliner cushions, low-slung tables and leafy nooks. Chill over a fruit shake, burger, breakfast or omelette (mains 30,000K to 60,000K), play a board game or volleyball, or just lose yourself in a sea of candles come sunset. Brilliantly designed with faux Khmer ruins and creeper vines; surely the city's liveliest outdoor bar.

signed with faux Khmer ruins and creeper vines; surely the city's liveliest outdoor bar.

Bar 525   BAR
(📋071-212424; www.525.rocks; ⊙5-11.30pm; 📶)
Parked down a quiet street, there's nothing retiring about this chic, urban bar. Sit outside stargazing on the terrace, inside at the long bar in low-lit style, or chill in the comfy lounge. Cocktails galore, glad rags, stunning photography on the walls and a sophisticated crowd. Snacks like buffalo sliders and quesadillas are also available. Prices match the ambience.

☆ Entertainment

Garavek Storytelling   THEATRE
(📋020-96777300; www.garavek.com; Th Khounswa; tickets 50,000K; ⊙6.30pm) *Garavek* means 'magical bird', and this enchanting hour-long show – comprising an old man dressed in tribal wear playing a haunting *khene* (Lao-style lyre) alongside an animated storyteller (in English) recalling local Lao folk tales and legends – takes your imagination on a flight of fancy. Held in an intimate 30-seat theatre. Book ahead in high season.

Moonlight Cinema   CINEMA
(http://ockpoptok.com/eat/moonlight-cinema; Ock Pop Tok Living Crafts Centre; ticket incl return tuk-tuk & dinner 70,000K; ⊙9am-10pm; 📶) The latest films are shown at the Ock Pop Tok centre every Thursday at 7.30pm, screened after 7pm dinner. Tuk-tuk is included; pickup is from in front of the Joma Bakery Cafe on Th Chao Fa Ngum at 6.45pm. Book via email.

Phrolak-Phralam Theatre   DANCE
(Royal Palace Grounds; tickets 100,000-150,000K; ⊙shows 6pm Mon, Wed, Fri & Sat) The misleadingly named Royal Lao Ballet puts on slow-moving traditional dances accompanied by a 10-piece Lao 'orchestra'. Performances last about 1¼ hours and include a Ramayana-based scene. It's well worth reading the typewritten notes provided at the entrance to have an idea of what's going on. If all the seats are full (rare), guests who bought the very cheapest tickets could end up standing.

🔒 Shopping

★ Queen Design Lao   CLOTHING
(queendesignlao@gmail.com; Th Sakkarin, 1/17 Ban Khili; ⊙10am-6pm Mon-Sat; 📶) This stylish Aussie-run boutique has a choice selection of hand-woven linen, silk and cotton dresses, chemises, skirts, and beach shawls made by Chris Boyle, a renowned designer in Oz. Most are one-off pieces. As well as pashminas and scarves, it also sells organic face scrubs and wooden designer glasses, and is the sole distributor for Article 22 Bomb Jewellery.

★ Handicraft Night Market   MARKET
(Th Sisavangvong; ⊙5.30-10pm) Every evening this tourist-oriented but highly appealing market assembles along Th Sisavangvong and is deservedly one of Luang Prabang's biggest tourist lures. Low-lit, quiet and devoid of hard selling, it has myriad traders hawking silk scarves and wall hangings, plus Hmong appliqué blankets, T-shirts, clothing, shoes, paper, silver, bags, ceramics, bamboo lamps and more.

Ock Pop Tok Boutique   CLOTHING, HANDICRAFTS
(📋071-254406; www.ockpoptok.com; Th Sakkarin; ⊙8am-9pm) 🌿 Ock Pop Tok works with a wide range of different tribes to preserve their handicraft traditions. Fine silk and cotton scarves, chemises, dresses, wall hangings and cushion covers make perfect presents. Weaving courses (p340) are also available. Hop across Th Sakkarin to visit Ock Pop Tok's newer **Heritage Shop** for more classical textiles.

Kopnoi   ARTS & CRAFTS
(www.madeinlaos.com; Th Kingkitsarat; ⊙7am-10pm Mon-Sat, 10am-10pm Sun; 📶) 🌿 Kopnoi sells stunning handicrafts from ethnic-minority craftsmen; Akha bracelets, silk pashminas, fine jewellery, packaged spices and teas, and local art. If you're 'shopped out' by the night market, this is a restful alternative; the quality is good, and there's no chance of you buying Chinese copies. Find it at **L'Etranger Books & Tea** (www.facebook.com/booksandtea; Th Kingkitsarat; ⊙7am-10pm Mon-Sat, 10am-10pm Sun; 📶) FREE.

ℹ Information

MONEY
There are lots of ATMs in town. Several tour companies on Th Sisavangvong offer cash advances on Visa or MasterCard for around 3% commission. They'll also change money but rates tend to be poor.

BCEL (Th Sisavangvong; ⊙8.30am-3.30pm Mon-Fri) Changes major currencies in cash, has a 24-hour ATM and offers cash advances against Visa and MasterCard.

Lao Development Bank (Th Wisunarat; ⊙8.30am-3.30pm Mon-Fri) Has a 24-hour ATM.

Minipost Booth (Th Sisavangvong; ⊘8.30am-9pm) Changes most major currencies at fair rates and is open daily.

POST

Post office (Th Chao Fa Ngum; ⊘8am-4pm & 5-8pm) Phone calls, DHL and Western Union facilities.

TOURIST INFORMATION

Provincial Tourism Department (☑071-212487; www.tourismluangprabang.org; Th Sisavangvong; ⊘9-11.30am & 1.30-3.30pm Mon-Fri; ☎) General information on festivals and ethnic groups. Also offers some maps and leaflets, plus information on buses or boats on a new hi-tech touchscreen computer. Great office run by helpful staff.

In addition to booking tours, many agencies – notably those lining Th Sisavangvong – also book flights, rent bicycles, change money and arrange visas (but note that Vietnamese visas and Lao visa extensions are easy and cheaper to arrange yourself).

ⓘ Getting There & Away

AIR

There has been a boom in international routes into the city ever since Luang Prabang International Airport (p382) got a smart new building and an expanded runway in 2013. Bangkok Airways (www.bangkokair.com) and Air Asia (www.airasia.com) both fly daily to Bangkok, while the latter also serves Kuala Lumpur. **Lao Airlines** (☑071-212172; www.laoairlines.com; Th Pha Mahapatsaman; ⊘8am-noon & 1-5pm Mon-Fri) serves Vientiane several times daily, as well as Pakse, Chiang Mai and Hanoi once daily. It also has frequent flights to Jinghong and Chengdu in China. **Vietnam Airlines** (☑071-213049; www.vietnamairlines.com) flies to both Siem Reap (codeshare with Lao Airlines) and Hanoi daily; buy tickets through **All Lao Travel** (☑071-253522, 020-55571572; www.alllaoservice.com; Th Sisavangvong; ⊘8am-9pm).

BOAT

For slowboats to Pak Beng (130,000K, nine hours, 8.30am), it will likely be cheaper and easier to buy tickets from an agent in town than to take a tuk-tuk to the **navigation office** (⊘8-11am & 2-4pm) at the new **slowboat landing**, located an inconvenient 10km north of the city in Ban Donemai. Through tickets to Huay Xai (250,000K, two days) are also available, but you'll have to sleep in Pak Beng. This allows you to stay a little longer in Pak Beng should you like the place.

The more upscale Luang Say Cruise (p337) departs on two-day rides to Huay Xai from the **Galao boat pier** (Th Khem Khong) near Wat Xieng Thong. Rates include an overnight stay at the Luang Say Lodge in Pak Beng. A cheaper alternative is Shompoo Cruise (p337), a two-day cruise aboard a smart boutique boat; accommodation in Pak Beng is not included.

Fast, uncomfortable and seriously hazardous speedboats can shoot you up the Mekong to Pak Beng (190,000K, three hours) and Huay Xai (310,000K, seven hours). Boats depart when full with six or seven passengers, so your best bet is to arrive at the new speedboat landing (next to the slowboat landing) at around 8am and form a group.

From June to February, Mekong River Cruises (p340) makes lazy eight-day trips from Luang Prabang to Thailand's Golden Triangle on an innovative new two-storey German–Lao riverboat with a small sun deck and 15 cabins in which you sleep as well as travel (from US$1710, all inclusive).

BUS & MINIBUS

Predictably enough, the **Northern Bus Station** (☑071-252729; Rte 13) and **Southern Bus Station** (Bannaluang Bus Station; ☑071-252066; Rte 13, Km 383) are at opposite ends of town. Several popular bus routes are duplicated by minibuses/minivans from the **Naluang minibus station** (☑071-212979; www.naluangstation.com; Rte 13), diagonally opposite the latter. Typical fares include Vientiane (150,000K, seven hours) with departures at 7.30am, 8.30am and 4pm; Vang Vieng (110,000K, five hours) at 8am, 9.30am, 10am, 2pm and 3pm; Luang Namtha (120,000K, eight hours) at 8.30am; and Nong Khiaw (55,000K, three hours) at 9.30am.

For less than double the bus fare, another option is to gather your own group and rent a comfortable six-seater minivan. Prices include photo stops and you'll get there quicker. Directly booked through the minibus station, prices are about 1,000,000K to Phonsavan or Vang Vieng and 800,000K to Nong Khiaw, including pick-up from the guesthouse.

Sainyabuli & Hongsa

Buses to Sainyabuli depart from the Southern Bus Station. The new Tha Deua bridge over the Mekong River is now open and has reduced the journey time to Sainyabuli to two hours or so by private vehicle. There is also a direct minibus service to the **Elephant Conservation Center** (ECC; ☑020-96590665; www.elephantconservation-center.com; 2-day discovery US$205, 3-day exploration US$265, 7-day eco-volunteering US$420) in Sainyabuli, which picks you up outside the post office and is included in the price of your tour. For Hongsa, the new bridge means it is easiest to travel to Sainyabuli and connect from there.

Nong Khiaw & Sam Neua

An alternate route for Nong Khiaw and Sam Neua leaves from the northern bus station.

Take the *sŏrngtăaou* (pick-up trucks fitted with benches in the back for passengers; 40,000K) at 9am, 11am and 2pm or the 8.30am bus that continues to Sam Neua (140,000K, 17 hours) via Vieng Thong (120,000K, 10 hours). Another Sam Neua–bound bus (from Vientiane) should pull in sometime around 5.30pm.

China & Vietnam

The sleeper bus to Kunming (500,000K, 24 hours) in China departs from the southern bus station at 7am, sometimes earlier. Pre-booking, and checking the departure location, is wise.

Head to the Naluang minibus station for buses to Dien Bien Phu (200,000K, 10 hours, leaves 6.30am) and Hanoi (350,000K, 24 hours, leaves 6pm) in Vietnam.

ℹ️ Getting Around

Compact Luang Prabang is easily walkable and best appreciated on foot. A satisfying way to get around is by bicycle. Numerous shops and some guesthouses hire bikes for 15,000K to 30,000K per day.

TO/FROM THE AIRPORT

Taxi-vans at the airport charge a standardised 50,000K into the city centre (4km away). These will cost more if more than three people share the ride. From town back to the airport you might pay marginally less.

BUS

E-Bus (www.laogreengroup.com; per ride 10,000-20,000K) is an electric zero-emission tuk-tuk (green and yellow) that used to circulate around the old town as a form of public transportation, but now acts like a normal tuk-tuk. The catch: prices are generally a fraction of what the old-school tuk-tuks charge, at about 10,000K for a short hop or 20,000K to the bus stations. Simply wave one down as it passes by.

The company also offers an **E-Bus Tour** (☑ 071-253899; www.laogreengroup.com; tour US$40, child under 10 free; ⊙ tours 8.30am-12.30pm, 1-4.30pm), which takes passengers around the city on a guided visit to local attractions.

TUK-TUK

Luang Prabang has no motorbike taxis, only tuk-tuks, plus the odd taxi-van from the airport charging a standardised 50,000K into town. These will cost more if more than three people share the ride. From town back to the airport you might pay marginally less.

Around town locals often pay just 5000K for short tuk-tuk rides, but foreigners are charged a flat 20,000K per hop. To the slowboat landing or speedboat landing reckon on at least 50,000K for the vehicle.

Nong Khiaw ໜອງຂຽວ
☑ 071 / POP 3500

Nong Khiaw is a traveller's haven in the truest sense, offering pampering, good food, decent accommodation and bags of activities with established adventure-tour operators. Nestled on the west bank of the Nam Ou (the river almost currentless since the building of the dam upstream), spanned by a vertiginous bridge and bookended by towering limestone crags, it's surely one of the most photogenic spots in Laos. On the river's scenic east bank (officially called Ban Sop Houn) is the lion's share of guesthouses and restaurants.

Be aware that Nong Khiaw is alternatively known as Muang Ngoi (the name of the surrounding district), creating obvious confusion with Muang Ngoi Neua, a 75-minute boat ride further north.

⊙ Sights & Activities

Pha Daeng Peak Viewpoint VIEWPOINT (ຈຸດຊົມວິວຜາແດງ; Pha Daeng Peak, Ban Sop Houn; 20,000K; ⊙5am-6pm) Reached by a testing though thoroughly doable 1½-hour walk (with a decent path) up Pha Daeng mountain, directly above the town, this viewpoint offers an unforgettable panorama. Drink up the sunset view (but bring a strong torch for your descent) or head here at 6am to witness the valley below veiled in mist, with the mountain peaks painted gold.

Recently opened **Sleeping Woman Viewpoint** (Pha Nang None Mountain View; ☑ 020-55377400; Rte 1C, heading northwest from Nong Khiaw, roughly 1km out of town; 15,000K; ⊙7am-6pm) is a good alternative.

⭐ **Nong Khiaw Jungle Fly** ADVENTURE SPORTS (☑ 020-22256151; http://nongkhiawjunglefly.com; Rte 1C; half-day/full-day tour US$37/49; ⊙8:30am-5pm) This highly recommended new adventure park 10km out of town offers half-day and full-day tours that include canopy walks, 'Tarzan swings' and zipping through the jungle on 10 lines up to 400m long. There's also abseiling and trekking through the bamboo forest. Expect quality equipment and an emphasis on safety from the professional English-speaking guides.

Green Discovery HIKING, CYCLING (☑ 071-810081; www.greendiscoverylaos.com; ⊙8am-9pm) Reliable Green Discovery has a range of trips, including a two-day trek to a Hmong village involving a homestay, with five hours' trekking per day (US$66 per person in a group of four). It also has challenging one-day cycling trips on forest dirt tracks covering 18km (US$39 per person in a group of four).

Tiger Trail HIKING, CYCLING
(☑ 030-4507049, 020-54395686; www.laos-adventures.com; Delilah's Place, Main St; ⊘ 7.30am-11pm) 🖉 This ecoconscious outfit has treks and homestays around the local area, including memorable one-day trips to the '100 waterfalls', one-day trekking and boat rides, plus the new pursuit of paddleboarding on the now-becalmed Nam Ou. These trips, as with most of Tiger Trail's activities, cost US$35-45 per person in a group of four. The excellent office is run by amiable Harp.

🛏 Sleeping & Eating

In the low season, accommodation prices are definitely negotiable. Nong Khiaw offers mainly budget options, plus a few deluxe digs.

Sengdao Chittavong Guesthouse GUESTHOUSE $
(☑ 030-9237089; Rte 1C; bungalows 50,000-80,000K, r 200,000K; 🖥) This family-run spot on the west bank (next to the start of the bridge) has wooden bungalows with rattan-walls, mozzie nets, clean linen and balconies, located in a garden looking out onto the river. Even closer to the water is a new block of more upscale air-con rooms. There's also a restaurant with river-garden views. The wi-fi is patchy. Popular with families.

Delilah's Place HOSTEL $
(☑ 020-54395686; www.delilahscafenongkhiaw. wordpress.com; Main St; dm/r 35,000/55,000K; 🖥) Delilah's Place has clean shared-bathroom rooms and cosy dorms with mozzie nets, super-thick matresses and safety lockers. Tiger Trail is also based here and there's a **cafe** (Main St; mains 15,000-35,000K; ⊘ 7am-10pm; 🖥) to 'carb-up' before activities, so one-stop-shop Delilah's is deservedly the main traveller hub in town. Thanks to the goodwill of eccentric owner Harp, it is also a great resource for info.

★**Mandala Ou Resort** BOUTIQUE HOTEL $$
(☑ 030-5377332; www.mandala-ou.com; r US$41-65; 🅿🖥🏊) This stunning boutique accommodation in cinnamon-coloured chalets – six facing the river – has imaginative features like inlaid glass bottles in the walls that allow more light, contemporary bathrooms and swallow-you-up beds. The own-

ers are friendly and there's a terrific Thai and Western menu, the town's only swimming pool and a yoga deck used by Luang Prabang Yoga (p337), which runs monthly retreats here.

Deen INDIAN $
(Ban Sop Houn; mains 15,000-35,000K; ⊘ 7am-10pm; 🖥) A superbly friendly Indian eatery with wood-fired naan bread, freshly made tandoori dishes, zesty curries and a homely atmosphere, Deen is deservedly packed every night.

★**Coco Home Bar & Restaurant** LAOTIAN, INTERNATIONAL $$
(☑ 020-23677818; Main St; mains 25,000-70,000K; ⊘ 8am-11pm; 🖥) Run by new owners Sebastien and Chok, this leafy riverside oasis has a great menu, with dishes like papaya salad, mango sticky rice, *mok phaa* (steamed fish in banana leaves) and duck in orange sauce. It's arguably the best place in town to delight your taste buds. Eat in the lush garden or upstairs.

🍷 Drinking & Nightlife

Q Bar BAR
(☑ 020-99918831; Rte 1C, Ban Sop Houn; ⊘ 7am-11.30pm; 🖥) Chilled Q sits on the main road with an ox-blood, rattan interior, a little roof terrace, good tunes and a friendly owner. Cocktails are 35,000K to 40,000K, with a two-for-one happy hour from 5pm to 7pm. If hungry, you can transform your tabletop into a barbecue grill and cook up a traditional Lao meal.

Hive Bar BAR
(☑ 030-5377990; Rte 1C; ⊘ 7am-11pm) Recently moved to a new location 1km outside of town (heading towards Pak Mong), Hive Bar is run by a friendly Lao, has a downstairs disco and karaoke for those inclined, plus a chilled terrace to sink a beer and watch the sunset explode in pinks and oranges behind the karsts. Great indie tunes; happy hour is from 6pm to 7.30pm.

ℹ️ Information

BCEL has two 24-hour ATMs: one (⊘ 24hr) at the end of the bridge on the Ban Sop Houn side, and another (⊘ 24hr) 100m after the bridge on the road heading to Pak Mong.

Tourist Information Office (⊘ 8-11am & 2-4pm Mon-Fri) is located above the boat landing and rarely open. Much better is reliable Harp at Delilah's Place; a one-stop travel resource for bus and boat tickets, the home of Tiger Trail and also decent budget digs.

❶ Getting There & Away

BOAT

Riverboat rides are a highlight of visiting Nong Khiaw; however, since the Nam Ou was dammed, the trip to Luang Prabang is no longer possible. **Boats to Muang Ngoi Neua** (25,000K, 1¼ hours) leave at 11am and 2pm (in high season extra departures are possible), taking you through some of the most dramatic karst country in Laos. The 11am boat continues all the way to Muang Khua (150,000K, seven hours) for connections to Phongsali or Dien Bien Phu in Vietnam.

There needs to be a minimum of eight people (on all the above journeys) before the boatman leaves, otherwise you will have to club together to make up the difference. This is typically only an issue on the Muang Khua journey.

BUS & SŎRNGTǍAOU

The journey to Luang Prabang is possible in three hours but in reality usually takes at least four. Minivans or *sŏrngtǎaou* (40,000K) run at 9am, 11am and 12.30pm, while air-con minibuses leave from around 1.30pm (50,000K). Tickets are sold at the **bus station**, but the 11am service will wait for folks arriving off the boat(s) from Muang Ngoi. When a boat arrives from Muang Khua there'll usually be additional Luang Prabang minivans departing at around 3pm from either the bus station or **boat office** (☉ 8:30-11:30am & 1-3pm).

For Udomxai, a direct minibus (50,000K, three hours) leaves at 11am. Alternatively, take any westbound transport and change at Pak Mong (25,000K, 50 minutes).

Originating in Luang Prabang, the **minibus to Sam Neua** (150,000K, 11 hours) via Vieng Thong (100,000K, five hours) makes a quick lunch stop in Nong Khiaw at around 11.30am, leaving at about noon or 1pm. Another Sam Neua bus (arriving from Vientiane) passes through around 7pm. Both of these arrive at an unmarked bus stand on the Nong Khiaw side just before the start of the bridge. Try and get on the lunchtime bus as this is usually a larger vehicle compared to the cramped minibus in the evening. Plus there's the view you'll want to catch by daylight; it's one of the most beautiful mountain rides in Laos.

❶ Getting Around

Bicycle rental makes sense for exploring local villages or reaching the caves. Town bicycles cost 20,000K per day and mountain bikes cost 30,000K. Alternatively, hire a scooter (80,000/100,000K for a manual/automatic) from **Motorbike Rental Donkham Service** (☑ 030-9005476; Ban Sop Houn; ☉ 8am-7pm). Tuk-tuks to the nearby bus station cost 5000K.

Muang Ngoi Neua ເມືອງງອຍເຫນືອ

☒ 071 / POP 1000

Muang Ngoi Neua is deliciously bucolic, a place to unwind and reset your soul. As the Nam Ou (Ou River) slides sedately beneath the shadow of sawtoothed karsts, cows wander the village's unpaved 500m-long road, while roosters strut past villagers mending fishing nets. Packed with cheap guesthouses and eateries, here there's enough competition to keep prices down. And while hammock-swinging on balconies is still de rigueur, there's plenty more to do if you have the energy, be it short, unaided hikes into timeless neighbouring villages, exploring caves, tubing and kayaking on the now pacified Nam Ou, or fishing and mountain biking.

☞ Tours

★ **Lao Youth Travel** KAYAKING
(☑ 030-5140046; ☉ 7.30-10.30am & 1.30-6pm) This long-established local outfit run by the friendly Mr Ping provides trekking, fishing and kayaking in the surrounding area. A half-day trip combining all three costs 145,000K for a group of four or more.

Gecko Tours & Cooking Class COOKING, TREKKING
(☑ 020-58886295; muangngoihandmade@gmail. com; ☉ 7am-9pm) ⬤ The friendly team at Gecko Bar (p348) has branched out to offer tours, massages (from 60,000K) and even a cooking class (150,000K for one person, less per person for groups). The latter involves a half-day trip to the restaurant's organic garden (15km away) where you'll pick ingredients and visit a nearby waterfall before retuning to town to cook your dishes.

🛏 Sleeping & Eating

Uniquely for such a tiny place, budget accommodation abounds and English is widely spoken, so you get the experience of a remote village without the inconvenience. The only drawback is that the accommodation is showing its age compared with up-and-coming Nong Khiaw just down the river.

PDV Riverview Guesthouse GUESTHOUSE $
(☑ 020-22148777; pdvbungalows@gmail.com; dm/r/tr 30,000/100,000/100,000K, bungalows 50,000-120,000K; ☎) This place halfway down Main St offers fine riverside accommodation, with five fresh rooms and a

LAOS MUANG NGOI NEUA

six-berth dorm in a new orange building with a sweeping Nam Ou panorama. The bungalows are nothing extraordinary but have great karst views and the usual balcony and hammock. The owner is super-helpful. Rates plummet off season.

★ **Ning Ning Guest House** GUESTHOUSE $$
(☑ 030-5140863, 020-23880122; ningning_guesthouse@hotmail.com; bungalows 220,000K, r 250,000K; ☜) Nestled around a peaceful garden, Ning Ning offers 10 immaculate wooden bungalows with mosquito nets, verandahs, en suites, lily-white bed linens and walls draped in ethnic tapestries. There's also a stunning new riverfront block with a stylish **restaurant** and rooms that have a decidedly more upscale look (and sumptuous views!). The only complaint: internet access doesn't extend to all rooms.

★ **Gecko Bar & Shop** LAOTIAN $
(☑ 020-58886295; muangngoihandmade@gmail. com; mains 15,000-30,000K; ☺ 7am-9pm; ☜) Handmade woven gifts and tea are for sale at this delightful, memorable little cafe (two-thirds of the way down the main drag, on your left heading south). There's a nice terrace to sit and read on, the owners are charming and the food, spanning noodles to soups, and pancakes to curries, is among the most raved about in the village.

Riverside Restaurant LAOTIAN $
(☑ 030-5329920; meals 25,000-40,000K; ☺ 7am-11pm; ☜) Since being damaged by a storm, Riverside has come back better than ever. In the evening its Chinese lanterns sway in the breeze on the decked terrace, beneath the sentinel arms of an enormous light-festooned mango tree. Riverside has gorgeous cliff views, and its menu encompasses noodles, fried dishes, *láhp* and Indian fare.

ℹ Information

Most restaurants and guesthouses have wi-fi, while Ning Ning Guest House has access via a machine that allows you to use your credit and debit cards.

There are no banks or ATMs here so bring plenty of cash from either Muang Khua (upriver) or Nong Khiaw (downriver). In an emergency you could exchange US dollars at a few of the guesthouses but rates are unsurprisingly poor.

ℹ Getting There & Away

Boats to Nong Khiaw (25,000K, one hour) leave around 9.30am, with tickets on sale from 8am at

the boat office beside **Ning Ning Guest House**. At Nong Khiaw tuk-tuks will wait above the boat landing for your arrival to take you to the bus station.

There is a boat from Muang Khua that runs if there is demand and it will pick up in Muang Ngoi Neua for Nong Khiaw around 1.30pm. Going to Muang Khua (120,000K, five hours), a boat leaves at 9.30am provided enough people sign up the day before on the list at the boat office. The first hour of the ride cuts through particularly spectacular karst scenery.

A new road running alongside the Nam Ou connecting Muang Ngoi Neua to Nong Khiaw has been created. However, it is still unsealed and passes through tributaries that have not yet been bridged; pretty useless for travellers unless you can hitch a lift with a boatman who happens to be there.

Phonsavan   ໂພນສະຫວັນ

☑ 061 / POP 37,500

Phonsavan is a popular base from which to explore the Plain of Jars. The town itself has an unfinished feel and is very spread out, with its two parallel main boulevards stretching for about 3km east–west. Fortunately a very handy concentration of hotels, restaurants and tour agents is crammed into a short if architecturally uninspired central 'strip'. More shops, markets and facilities straggle along Rte 7. But the town is best appreciated from the surrounding hills, several of which are pine-clad and topped with small resorts. Keep an eye out too for wooden powder-blue Hmong cottages on the mountain roads with firewood neatly stacked outside.

The region has long been a centre of Phuan language and culture (part of the Tai-Kadai family). There's also a strong Vietnamese presence.

⊙ Sights & Activities

★ **Xieng Khouang UXO-Survivors' Information Centre** CULTURAL CENTRE
(www.laos.worlded.org; donations encouraged; ☺ 8am-8pm Mon-Fri, from noon Sat & Sun) ✐ **FREE** This unexploded ordnance (UXO) information centre and colourful, upbeat shop sells silk laptop bags, purses and handicrafts made by UXO survivors. Aside from displays including bomb parts and harrowing stories of recent victims, there's also a reading room with a wealth of information on the Secret War and the different kinds of UXO that still present a danger in Laos to-

day. Ask to see the video *Surviving Cluster Bombs*. Note that 90% of your donations go towards the treatment of UXO survivors.

UXO Information Centre (MAG)   CULTURAL CENTRE

(📞061-211010; www.maginternational.org/laos; donations encouraged; ⏱10am-8pm) **FREE** Decades after America's Secret War on Laos, unexploded bombs and mines remain a devastating problem throughout this region. Visit the thought-provoking UXO Information Centre, run by British organisation MAG (Mines Advisory Group) that's been helping to clear Laos' unexploded ordnance since 1994. The centre's information displays underline the enormity of the bomb drops, and there are also examples of (defused) UXO to ponder. Donations are encouraged: US$15 pays for the clearing of around 10 sq metres and a commemorative T-shirt.

Lone Buffalo   VOLUNTEERING

(📞020-77159566; www.facebook.com/lonebuffalo; Highway 1D) Named after Manophet 'Lone Buffalo', a visionary community leader, this nonprofit is dedicated to providing free English classes to rural youth, as well as filmmaking workshops and football coaching. There are several ways to help out, from coaching the football team on weekends to purchasing the students' guide to Phonsavan or buying Lone Buffalo T-shirts at restaurants in town.

★ Sousath Travel   TOURS

(📞020-22967213; rasapet_lao@yahoo.com; Rte 7; ⏱8am-8pm) Sousath is the man who helped open the Plain of Jars to tourists, and the trips run by his son, Mr Nouds, are the most informative in town. Extremely knowledgeable about the region, Mr Nouds can also organise tours of the Ho Chi Minh Trail,

homestays in Hmong villages and multiday treks (including the Phakeo Trek).

🛏 Sleeping & Eating

Rooms in Phonsavan span basic guesthouse digs to midrange hotel rooms. Booking ahead is not usually necessary, nor is air-conditioning. There are also several smarter lodge-style hotels spread around town, including some imperiously perched atop pine-clad hills.

★ Kong Keo Guesthouse   GUESTHOUSE $

(📞020-285858; dm 50,000K; r in outside block 80,000K, chalets 120,000K; 🕸) Run by the charming and extremely knowledgeable Kong; at the time of writing he was building six balconied brick chalets. While the seven-berth dorm is slightly cramped, the outdoor block has large clean rooms with mint-green walls and private bathrooms. The UXO-decorated **restaurant-bar** has occasional barbecues, and Kong runs highly recommended **tours** to the Plain of Jars.

White Orchid Guesthouse   GUESTHOUSE $

(📞061-312403; r incl breakfast with fan/air-con 80,000/200,000K; 🕸🕸) The menthol-green rooms enjoy en-suite bathrooms, double beds, cable TV and welcome blankets. The price includes a pick-up from the airport or bus station and there's also a little **tour office** that can arrange trips to see the Plain of Jars. Basic and clean.

Anoulack Khen Lao Hotel   HOTEL $$

(📞061-213599; www.anoulackkhenlao.com; Rte 7; r incl breakfast 250,000K; 🕸🕸) This glass Lego tower has easily the best rooms in town, with wood floors, thick mattresses, white linen, cable TV, fridges, kettles and swish hot-water en suites. There's a great **restaurant** on the 5th floor where you can take

LAOS PHONSAVAN

PHAKEO TREK

Organised through Phonsavan agencies or the Xieng Khuang Tourist Office (p350), the excellent two-day **Phakeo trek** combines many essential elements of the Xieng Khuang experience. On the long first day, hike across secondary forested mountain ridges to a three-part jar site with about 400 ancient jars and jar fragments, many moss-encrusted and shaded by foliage. The trek then descends into the roadless Hmong village of Ban Phakeo, whose shingle-roofed mud-floor homes huddle around a central rocky knoll. A purpose-built, Hmong-style guest shack provides a basic sleeping platform with space for eight hikers. There's no electricity. The next day, the hike descends into attractive semi-agricultural valleys then climbs up the cascades of a multi-terraced waterfall to arrive in the famous 'Bomb Village', which no longer has many bombs after extensive clearance work.

❶ GETTING TO VIETNAM: PANG HOK TO TAY TRANG

Getting to the border Daily buses (60,000K, departing 5.30am in either direction) between Muang Khua and Dien Bien Phu cross at the Pang Hok (Laos)/Tay Trang (Vietnam) border crossing 26km east of Muang Mai. The road has been entirely rebuilt on the Lao side right up to the Pang Hok border post, but is still surprisingly rough in places on the Vietnamese side. It's a picturesque route, particularly down in the Dien Bien Phu valley, which is often a blanket of emerald rice paddies. Making the trip in hops is definitely not recommended, as it will cost far more than the bus fare and it's easy to end up stranded along the way.

At the border This remote crossing sees a handful of travellers. Laos visas are available on arrival for the usual price, but you will likely be asked to pay up to 50,000K in random 'processing fees', 'tourist fees' and health checks as you pass from window to window. Vietnamese visas are definitely not available on arrival, so plan ahead to avoid getting stranded.

Moving on There are no facilities or waiting vehicles at either of the border posts, which are separated by about 4km of no-man's land. From the Tay Trang side of the border it's about 31km to Dien Bien Phu.

breakfast and use the wi-fi. Conveniently the hotel also has a lift. Worth the extra spend.

Nisha Restaurant INDIAN $
(☑ 020-98266023; Rte 7; meals 20,000-30,000K; ⊙7am-10pm; 🛜🍴) Cream-interiored Nisha is tidy and simple but the real colour is found in its excellent cuisine. The menu includes all the usual suspects like tikka masala and rogan josh, curries and a wide range of vegetarian options. However, it's the perfect application of spice and the freshness of the food that'll keep you coming back.

Bamboozle Restaurant & Bar INTERNATIONAL $$
(☑ 030-9523913; www.facebook.com/BamboozleRestaurantBar; Rte 7; meals 20,000-60,000K; ⊙7-10.30am & 3.30-10.30pm, kitchen closes 9.30pm; 🛜) 🌿 True to its name, with bamboo walls plus pretty lanterns strung from its ceiling, Bamboozle dishes up thin-crust pizza, salads, pasta dishes, good-sized cheeseburgers and terrific Lao cuisine. Add to this chilled beers and a rock-and-roll soundtrack and it's a winner. A percentage of the profits goes towards the Lone Buffalo Foundation (p349), which supports the town's youth.

Cranky-T Café & Bar FUSION $$
(☑ 030-5388003; www.facebook.com/CrankyTLaos; Rte 7; mains 35,000-130,000K; ⊙7am-10.30pm Mon-Sat, to 5pm Sun, happy hour 4-7pm; ❄️🛜) Cranky-Ts has a stylish red-wine-coloured and exposed-brick interior, with the eponymous owner creating mouth-watering salads, sashimi, smoked-salmon crêpes and

hearty fare like NZ sirloin with mash to fill you up after trekking the jar sites. Add to this cinnamon muffins, brownie cheesecake and a good selection of cocktails (35,000K), and you may spend all day here.

❶ Information

Currency exchange is available at **Lao Development Bank** (☑ 061-312188; ⊙8.30am-3.30pm Mon-Fri), at **BCEL** (☑ 061-213297; Rte 7; ⊙8.30am-3.30pm Mon-Fri) and from several travel agents. There are three ATMs along Rte 7.

Lao-Mongolian Friendship Hospital (☑ 061-312166) May be able to assist with minor health concerns.

Post Office (☑ 061-312005; ⊙8am-noon & 1-4.30pm Mon-Fri) Also has a domestic phone service and Western Union.

Xieng Khuang Tourist Office (☑ 061-312217; www.xiengkhouangtourism.com; ⊙8-11.30am & 1.30-4pm) Impractically located in the middle of nowhere (on the road to the airport), this otherwise helpful office has English-speaking staff, a small exhibit and souvenirs recycled from war junk. Find free maps for Phonsavan and Xieng Khuang district, plus the brochure entitled *Hidden Stories of Xieng Khoung*, for alternative ideas on things to do aside from the jar sites.

Many tours stop here on the way to the jar sights to view the impressive pile of war remnants sitting behind the office.

❶ Getting There & Away

Airline and bus timetables usually call Phonsavan 'Xieng Khuang', even though that was originally the name for Muang Khoun.

AIR

Lao Airlines (☑ 020-22228658; www.laoair-lines.com) has daily flights to/from Vientiane (US$75). Sometimes a weekly flight to/from Luang Prabang operates in peak season.

BUS

From the **Northern Bus Station** (☑ 030-5170148), located 4km west of the centre, Vietnam-bound buses depart to Vinh (150,000K, 11 hours) at 6.30am on Tuesday, Thursday, Friday and Sunday, continuing seasonally on Mondays to Hanoi (320,000K). For Vientiane (110,000K, 11 hours) there are air-con buses at 7am, 8am, 10.30am, 4.30pm, 6.30pm and a VIP bus (130,000K) at 8.30pm. These all pass through Vang Vieng, to where there's an additional 7.30am departure (95,000K). For Luang Prabang (10 hours) both minivans (95,000K) and VIP buses (120,000K) depart at 8.30am and 6pm.

The **Southern (Bounmixay) Bus Station** (Highway 1D), 4km south of town, has a 6.45am bus every other day to Savannakhet (150,000K) that continues on to Pakse (170,000K). Buses to Paksan (100,000K, eight hours) via the newly completed road depart daily at 6.30am and 8.30am. Local buses and *sŏrngtăaou* also depart for Muang Khoun (20,000K, hourly).

Phoukham Garden Minibus & Bus Station (☑ 020-99947072; Th Xaysana; ☺ 7am-8pm) in the east-central side of town (by the tourist strip), has minibuses leaving at 8.30am for Luang Prabang (110,000K), Vang Vieng (100,000K) and Nong Khiaw (150,000K) with 5am, 8am and 5pm minibuses for Vientiane (130,000K).

❶ Getting Around

Tuk-tuks, if and when you can find them, cost from 15,000K for a short hop to about 30,000K to the airport. **Lao Falang Travel Service** (☑ 020-23305614; Rte 7; 1-day all-inclusive trip US$150) rents 100cc and 150cc motorbikes (100,000K to 150,000K), ideal for reaching a selection of jar sites. Fill up at the petrol station in town.

Chauffeured six-seater vans or 4WDs can be chartered through the minibus station (or most guesthouses); you're looking at US$200 to Sam Neua or Luang Prabang.

Plain of Jars ທົ່ງໄຫຫິນ

Mysterious giant stone jars of unknown ancient origin are scattered over hundreds of hilly square kilometres around Phonsavan, giving the area the misleading name of Plain of Jars. Remarkably, little is known about the Austro-Asiatic civilisation that created them, although archaeologists estimate they date from the Southeast Asian iron age (500 BC to AD 200) and were likely used for elaborate burial rituals.

Smaller jars have long since been carted off by collectors but around 2500 larger jars, jar fragments and 'lids' remain. As the region was carpet-bombed throughout the Indochina wars, it's miraculous that so many artefacts survived. Only nine of the 90 recorded jar sites have so far been cleared of unexploded ordnance (UXO), and then only within relatively limited areas. These sites, and their access paths, are delineated by easily missed red-and-white marker stones: remain vigilant.

Sites 1, 2 and 3 form the bases of most tour loops.

The biggest and most easily accessible, **Site 1** (Thong Hai Hin; 15,000K) features more than 300 jars relatively close-packed on a pair of hilly slopes pocked with bomb craters. The biggest, Hai Jeuam, weighs around 25 tonnes, stands more than 2.5m high and is said to have been the mythical victory cup of Khun Jeuam. The bare, hilly landscape is appealing, although in one direction the views of Phonsavan airport seem discordant. There is a small cafe, a gift shop and toilets near the entrance.

Site 2 (Hai Hin Phu Salato; 10,000K) is a pair of hillocks divided by a shallow gully that forms the access lane. This rises 700m from the ticket desk in what becomes a muddy slither in wet conditions. To the left in thin woodlands, look for a cracked stone urn through which a tree has managed to grow. To the right another set of jars sits on a grassy knoll with panoramas of layered hills, paddies and cow fields. It's very atmospheric.

The 150-jar **Site 3** (Hai Hin Lat Khai; 10,000K) sits on a scenic hillside in pretty woodland near Ban Lat Khai village. The access road to Lat Khai leads east beside a tiny motorbike repair hut just before Ban Xiang Di (Ban Siang Dii). The ticket booth is beside a simple local restaurant that offers somewhat overpriced *fĕr* (rice noodles; 30,000K). The jars are accessed by a little wooden footbridge and an attractive 10-minute walk (or wade, depending on the season) through rice fields.

❶ Getting There & Away

All three main jar sites can be visited by rented motorbike from Phonsavan in around five hours, while Site 1 is within bicycle range. Site 1 is just 8km southwest of central Phonsavan, 2.3km west of the Muang Khoun road (1D): turn at the signed junction in Ban Hay Hin. For Sites 2 and 3, turn west off the Muang Khoun road just past Km

HISTORY OF THE JARS

Lao folklore tells of a race of giants ruled by a powerful king named Khun Jeuam who ordered his people to make jars here to brew and store rice wine for celebrations of their victories on the battlefield. Modern archaeologists believe that the bone fragments, beads and burnt charcoal found in and around the jumbo-sized jars suggest that they were instead used as part of an elaborate funeral ceremony (for normal-sized people). Alternatively looted and carpet bombed over the years, very little remains today of the burial offerings that may have once been hidden in these rolling hills. There are believed to be nearly 90 recorded jar sites in Xiangkhouang Province, each with as many as 300 stone ruins between 1m and 2.5m tall. Some 80% of the jars were carved from quarried sandstone, with the rest made of granite, limestone or conglomerate rock. The first jar sites didn't open to the public until 1992 following a bootstraps effort by locals to remove UXO. Six years later, Unesco initiated a decades-long project to safeguard the archaeological ruins, promote safe (and sustainable) tourism, and get the site on the World Heritage List.

8. Follow the newly paved road for 10km/14km to find the turnings for Sites 2/3, then follow muddy tracks for 0.5/1.8km respectively.

Alternatively, sign up the night before to join one of several regular guided minibus tours. It really is worth the extra money to hear the war stories and get some context on both the jars and their creators. Most throw in a noodle-soup lunch at Site 2 or 3 and a quick stop to see the lumpy rusting remnant of an armoured vehicle in a roadside copse at Ban Nakho: its nickname, the 'Russian Tank', exaggerates the appeal.

Sam Neua   ຊຳເໜືອ

📞 064 / POP 39,000

While Sam Neua (Xam Neua) is something of a nostalgic Soviet oddity, with its well-spaced concrete modernity, spartan communist monument and old boys with Muscovite hats, the real draw is the stunning countryside in which it sits. The town is a logical transit point for visiting nearby Vieng Xai or catching the daily bus to Vietnam, and remains one of Laos' least-visited provincial capitals. It is perched at an altitude of roughly 1200m, so some warm clothes are advisable in the dry winter period, at least by night and until the thick morning fog burns off. From April to October the lush landscapes are contrastingly warm and wet.

The eye-widening, photogenic produce markets here are worth visiting for the colourful ethnic diversity on display.

🛏 Sleeping & Eating

Phonchalern Hotel   HOTEL $

(📞 064-312192; r 80,000-110,000K; ❄🖥) This palatially sized hotel has a mix of rooms; some are dark and uninviting while those facing the river are full of light and have a communal balcony out front. Rooms have fridge, TV and clean en suite. Downstairs there's a lobby the size of a bowling alley. It's a sure bet for one night. It was the first place in Sam Neua to install a lift.

Xayphasouk Hotel   HOTEL $

(📞 064-312033; xayphasoukhotel@gmail.com; r 150,000-200,000K; ❄🖥) Currently the smartest hotel in Sam Neua. The huge lobby-restaurant is woefully underused, but the rooms are very comfortable for such a remote region of Laos. All include piping-hot showers, flat-screen TVs, tasteful furnishings and crisp linen.

★ Yuni Coffee   CAFE $

(📞 020-52221515; https://yunicoffeeco.com; mains 30,000K; ⏱7.30am-5.30pm Tue-Sat, 8am-2pm Sun; ❄) A blessing for coffee snobs: if you're missing standard lattes your caffeine privations are over. Now in a new, more spacious location with a modern industrial look and a choice selection of breakfast items and casual Western fare, as well as kick-ass locally grown coffee. Yuni is the only way to kick-start your day.

ℹ Information

Provincial Tourist Office (📞 064-312567; hp_pto@yahoo.com; ⏱8-11.30am & 1.30-4pm Mon-Fri) An excellent tourist office with English-speaking staff eager to help.

ℹ Getting There & Away

AIR

Sam Neua's little **Nathong Airport** (NEU) is 3km east of the centre towards Vieng Xai. **Lao Skyway** (📞 020-99755556, 064-314268; www.

laoskyway.com; Nathong Airport; ⊘8am-4pm) runs morning flights on Cessnas to Vientiane (899,000K) Tuesday to Saturday, with an afternoon flight on Monday. All too frequently the flights get cancelled just before departure. At the time of writing, there was no flight to Phonsavan.

BUS

The **main bus station** (☑064-314270) is on a hilltop 1.2km south of the central monument, just off the Vieng Thong road. From here buses leave to Vientiane (190,000K, 20 hours) via Phonsavan (80,000K, 10 hours) at 10am, 1pm, 3pm and 5pm. An additional 7.30am Vientiane bus (190,000K) goes via Vieng Thong (50,000K, five hours), Nong Khiaw (140,000K, 12 hours) and Luang Prabang (150,000K, 17 hours). There are also daily minibuses to Luang Prabang (130,000K to 150,000K, 15 hours) at 7.30am and 4pm. Finally there is a Vieng Thong bus (50,000K) at 7.30am and 4pm.

The **Nathong bus station** is 1km beyond the airport on the Vieng Xai road at the easternmost edge of town (a tuk-tuk here costs 20,000K). There is now just one daily bus to Vieng Xai (20,000K, 50 minutes), which leaves at 9.30am and continues to Sam Tai (Xamtay; 40,000K, five hours).

Vieng Xai ວຽງໄຊ

☑064 / POP 10,000

The thought-provoking 'bomb-shelter caves' of Vieng Xai are set amid dramatic karst outcrops and offer a truly inspirational opportunity to learn about northern Laos' painful 20th-century history. Imagine Vang Vieng, but with a compelling historical twist instead of happy tubing. Or think of it as Ho Chi Minh City's Cu Chi Tunnels cast in stone. The caves were shrouded in secrecy until they were opened to the world in 2007.

⦿ Sights

⭐ **Vieng Xai Caves**   CAVE
(ຖ້ຳວຽງໄຊ; ☑064-315022; entry incl audio tour 60,000K, bicycle rental per tour/day 15,000/30,000K; ⊘9am-noon & 1-4pm) Joining a truly fascinating 18-point tour is the only way to see Vieng Xai's seven most important war-shelter cave complexes, set in beautiful gardens backed by fabulous karst scenery. A local guide unlocks each site while an audio guide gives a wealth of first-hand background information and historical context. The **Kaysone Phomvihane Cave** still has its air-circulation pump in working order and is the most memorable of the caves.

Tham Nok Ann   CAVE
(ຖ້ຳນົກແອນ, Nok Ann Cave; 10,000K; ⊘8am-5pm) Tham Nok Ann is a soaring well-lit cavern through which a river passes beneath awesome rock formations. It's dripping, creepy and very atmospheric, with a set of stairs leading up to an adjacent cave complex that once housed a Vietnamese military hospital. You could previously kayak into the cave, however, when we passed through it was only open for viewing.

🛏 Sleeping & Eating

Sailomyen Guesthouse   GUESTHOUSE $
(☑020-56596688; r 70,000K; 🛜) Built on stilts atop a serene artificial lake with a communal balcony that's perfect for daydreaming. The rooms may be small with wonky carpeted floors, but there are hot showers, fans and mosquito nets. And did we mention the view? Picture jungle-clad hills with watercolour reflections.

Naxay II Guesthouse   GUESTHOUSE $
(☑064-314330; r 80,000K) Opposite the cave office, these bamboo-accented bungalows are set around a manicured garden backed by an impressive split-toothed crag. Beds are comfy, hot water flows, lino floors are clean and fans keep you cool. They also have private verandahs and bathrooms, and if you're in luck the attached beach-style cafe occasionally serves up food.

Sabaidee Odisha   INDIAN $
(☑020-55577202; mains 15,000-35,000K; ⊘7am-9pm; 🛜) Don't be fooled by the less than impressive exterior, cement floor and bare walls of this hole-in-the-wall joint, for the food is terrific. Prepared fresh and with care, it comes with a smile and the menu offers different levels of spiciness. It's in the northernmost corner of the Viengsai market, facing the main road.

ℹ Information

Vieng Xai Cave Tourist Office (☑064-315022; ⊘8-11.30am & 1-4pm) Around 1km south of the market, the cave office organises all cave visits, rents bicycles and has maps and a useful information board. There's even a display case full of old Lenin busts and assorted socialist iconograpy.

ℹ Getting There & Away

There is just one daily bus to Sam Neua (20,000K, 50 minutes) leaving at approximately 1pm on the road parallel to the market (the bus station was closed for a rebuild at the time of writing). Buses between Sam Neua and Thanh Hoa (one bus daily to each) can be flagged down on Rte 6. The bus for Thanh Hoa (180,000K) should pass by around 8.45am, while the bus for Sam Neua (20,000K) passes through around 4pm.

Visiting Vieng Xai by rented taxi from Sam Neua (including return) costs around 250,000K per vehicle.

NORTHWESTERN LAOS

Northern Udomxai and Luang Namtha provinces form a mountainous tapestry of rivers, forests and traditional villages that are home to almost 40 classified ethnicities in Laos' furthest northern corner.

Udomxai   ອຸດົມໄຊ

📞 081 / POP 35,000

Booming Udomxai (also known as Muang Xai) is a Laos–China trade centre and cross-roads city, and with its cast of migrant truck drivers and Mandarin signage at every turn it certainly feels like it. The dusty, brash main street and lack of a traveller vibe puts off many short-term visitors, and you might think the highlight is the bus that spirits you out of here; however, it takes minimal effort to find the real Laos nearby. The well-organised tourist office – one of the best in the country – has many ideas to tempt you to stay longer, from cooking courses to treks through ethnic villages, ziplining and cycling.

Around 15% of Udomxai's population is Chinese (with many more transient work-ers), and the Yunnanese dialect is as common as Lao in some businesses and hotels.

For cycling, trekking, ziplining, rock climbing, abseiling, swimming and massage head to **Nam Kat Yorla Pa Adventure Park** (📞 081-219666, 020-55564359; www.namkatyorlapa.com; Faen village, Xay District) 🏍, 17km north of Udomxai by the picturesque Nam Kat (Kat River).

🛏 Sleeping & Eating

Lithavixay Guesthouse   GUESTHOUSE $
(📞 081-212175; Rte 1; r 60,000-120,000K; ❄ 🛜) A long-time traveller fave, with a large lobby and super-cheap breakfast (10,000K). Although some rooms look tired, they include TVs, couches and homely touches. Old showers suffer from slow drainage, and recently service has dropped a little. It's close to the old bus station and very central.

Villa Keoseumsack   GUESTHOUSE $$
(📞 081-312170; Rte 1; r 130,000-220,000K; 🅿 ❄ 🛜) Udomxai's best guesthouse is set back from the road in a handsome Lao house with large, inviting rooms. They come with crisp linen, decent fittings, springy beds and varnished floors. Hmong bed runners, TV, free wi-fi and a communal reading balcony finish them off. There's even complimentary toothbrush and toothpaste.

⭐**Souphailin Restaurant**   LAOTIAN $
(📞 081-211147; mains 20,000-50,000K; ⊙ 7am-10pm) Don't be fooled by the modest bamboo exterior of this backstreet gem – easily the tastiest Lao food in the city is served here. Friendly Souphailin creates culinary magic

---

ℹ GETTING TO CHINA: BOTEN TO MÓHĀN

Getting to the border The Lao immigration post at the Boten (Laos)/Móhān (China) border crossing (7.30am to 4.30pm Laos time, 8.30am to 5.30pm China time) is a few minutes' walk north of Boten market. Tuk-tuks shuttle across no-man's land to the Chinese immigration post in Móhān (Bohan) or it's an easy 1km walk. Alternatively, take one of the growing number of handy Laos–China bus connections such as Udomxai–Mengla, Luang Namtha–Jinghong and Luang Prabang–Kunming.

At the border Northbound it is necessary to have a Chinese visa in advance. On arrival in Laos, 30-day visas are available.

Moving on From the Chinese immigration post it's a 1km walk up Móhān's main street to the stand where little buses depart for Mengla (RMB16, one hour) every 20 minutes or so until mid-afternoon. These arrive at Mengla's bus station No. 2. Nip across that city to the northern bus station for Jinghong (RMB42, 2½ hours, frequent until 6pm) or Kunming (mornings only).

On the Lao side minibuses shuttle regularly in the morning from Boten to Luang Namtha (one hour, 25,000K)

with her *mok phaa* (steamed fish in banana leaves), *láhp*, perfectly executed spring rolls, beef steak, fried noodles, and chicken and mushroom in banana leaf. Everything is fresh and seasonal. Check out the guest logs!

❶ Information

Tourist Office (Provincial Tourism Department of Oudomxay; ☑ 081-212483; www.oudomxay.info; ⊙ 8am-noon & 2-4.30pm) Has masses of information about onward travel, accommodation and local sights. It has free town maps and sells GT-Rider Laos maps. There are 12 different tours on offer, including the two-day/one-night tour to an impressive local cave, and three-day/two-night treks and homestays with local ethnic villages. It's best to book by email and re-confirm at the office when you arrive.

❶ Getting There & Away

Lao Airlines (☑ 081-312047; www.laoairlines.com; ⊙ 8-11am & noon-5pm) flies daily to/from Vientiane (US$90) to Udomxai's **airport** (Oudomxay Airport), while **Lao Skyway** (☑ 020-23112219; www.laoskyway.com; Udomxai Airport; ⊙ 8-11am & noon-5pm) flies to Vientiane as well (US$60) on Tuesday, Thursday and Saturday. Tickets are also available from Lithavixay Guesthouse.

There are two bus stations in Udomxai: the old **Northern Bus Station** in the centre of town, and the newer Long-Distance Bus Station, aka **Southern Bus Terminal** (☑ 081-312200), 5km southwest from the centre.

Luang Namtha   ຫລວງນ້ຳທາ

☑ 086 / POP 21,000

Welcoming travellers like no other town in northern Laos, Luang Namtha packs a powerful green punch with its selection of eco-minded tour companies catering for trekking to ethnically diverse villages, and cycling, kayaking and rafting in and around the stunning Nam Ha NPA. Locally there's bags to do before you set out into the boonies, such as exploring the exotic night market, or grabbing a rental bike and tootling around the gently undulating rice-bowl valleys to waterfalls and temples.

The 2224-sq-km **Nam Ha NPA** (ປ່າສະຫງວນແຫງຊາດນ້ຳທາ; www.namha-npa.org) 🖋 is one of Laos' most accessible natural preserves and home to clouded leopard and possibly a few unpoached tigers. Both around and within the mountainous park, woodlands have to compete with pressure from villages of various ethnicities, including Lao Huay, Akha and Khamu. Since 1999, an ecotouristic vision has tried to ensure tour operators and villagers work together to provide a genuine experience for trekkers while ensuring minimum impact on local communities and the environment.

☞ Tours

★ **The Hiker**   TREKKING
(☑ 020-59294245, 086-212343; www.thehikerlaos.com; Main St; ⊙ 8am-9pm) 🖋 This new outfit is garnering some glowing feedback. Cycling and kayaking trips are available but its main focus is trekking, with one- to seven-day options; the longest one is more hard-core (eight hours' trekking per day) and promises to take you into untouched areas deep in the Nam Ha jungle, while one-day treks are much easier.

Forest Retreat Laos   ECOTOUR
(☑ 020-55560007, 020-55680031; www.forestretreatlaos.com; Main St; ⊙ 8am-9pm) 🖋 Based at the **Minority Restaurant** (mains 35,000K; ⊙ 7am-10.30pm; 🛜) 🖋, this ecotourism outfit offers kayaking, trekking, homestays and mountain biking on one- to seven-day multi-activity adventures, and recruits staff and guides from ethnic-minority backgrounds where possible. It also runs a gruelling 60km one-day cycle trip to Muang Sing and back. Another option here is to take a cooking class.

Green Discovery   ECOTOUR
(☑ 086-211484; www.greendiscoverylaos.com; Main St; ⊙ 8am-9pm) 🖋 The grandaddy of ecotourism in Laos offers a combo of boat trips, mountain biking, kayaking, homestays and one- to three-day treks in Nam Ha NPA. Safety is a given and staff are helpful. The most popular trip is a two-day walk through Nam Ha Valley combining culture and nature (US$62 for a group of six).

🛏 Sleeping & Eating

The lively **night market** (Rte 3A; ⊙ 7-11.30pm) is a good place for snack grazing. Find noodle stands galore in the **morning market** (noodles 10,000K; ⊙ 7am-5pm).

★ **Zuela Guesthouse**   GUESTHOUSE $
(☑ 020-22391966; www.zuela.asia; r old block with fan/air-con 70,000/100,000K, new block with air-con with/without balcony US$38/25; ᴘ🌀🛜) Located in a leafy courtyard, Zuela has an old block of spotless – though dim – rooms with exposed-brick walls and en suites. The newer block has better rooms with glazed rattan ceilings, lemon walls (some with

balcony), desks and vivid art. Located off the main drag down a quiet lane. Besides its great **restaurant**, it also offers scooter rental and tours.

Thoulasith Guesthouse
GUESTHOUSE $

(☑086-212166; www.thoulasith-guesthouse.com; Rte 3A; r with fan/air-con 70,000/100,000K; P❀❅) This traveller-friendly place offers clean rooms with bedside lamps, art on the walls, free tea and inviting balconies. There's also a new block of swish rooms with baths. It's set back from the main strip so makes for a peaceful spot to wind down before or after a trek.

Phou Iu III Bungalows
GUESTHOUSE $$

(☑020-22390195; www.luangnamtha-oasis-resort. com; bungalow incl breakfast US$25; ❅❆) This place is cracking value and sits in pretty, flowering gardens, though a new swimming pool with watersides and jungle gyms makes it slightly less serene for couples. Bungalows are spacious and nicely fitted out with lumber-wood beds, brick floors, fireplaces and inviting terraces. It's well signposted from the centre of town. Note that in December it's a little on the chilly side.

★Lai's Place
LAOTIAN $

(☑086-23939111; mains 15,000-40,000K; ☉6.30am-9.30pm; ❅☑) No other restaurant in northern Laos offers such a tourist-friendly introduction to the diverse cuisines of the region's ethnic minorities than this simple eatery with sturdy wooden tables and walls lined in groceries. There's a long list of *jqaou* dipping sauces for sticky rice alongside traditional Akha and Tai Dam dishes like *aw lahm*, a stew of banana flower, rattan shoot, eggplant and pumpkin.

Manikong Bakery Cafe
BAKERY, CAFE $

(mains 10,000-35,000K; ☉6.30am-10.30pm; ❅) A hole-in-the-wall bakery/cafe serving tasty salads, bagels, panini, croissants, juices, sandwiches and homemade cakes. There are good-value breakfast sets and inventive shakes and iced coffees, too.

★Bamboo Lounge
INTERNATIONAL $$

(☑020-29643190; www.bambooloungelaos.com; mains/pizzas 40,000/75,000K; ☉7am-11.30pm, happy hour 5-7pm; ❅) 𝒫 With its moss-green facade this place is the favourite in town for travellers, offering employment to young people from remote villages and donating more than 2800 books to local schools. It's alluring by night with its winking fairy lights, thumping tunes and outdoor terrace piping delicious aromas from its wood-fired oven – there are myriad thin-crust pizza choices. And unusually for Laos, it's completely nonsmoking.

❶ Information

BCEL (☉8.30am-3.30pm Mon-Fri) Changes major currencies (commission-free) and has a 24-hour ATM.

Lao Development Bank (☉8.30am-noon & 2-3.30pm Mon-Fri) Exchanges major currencies and has Western Union.

Post Office (☑086-312007; ☉8-11.30am & 1-4pm Mon-Fri)

Provincial Hospital (Rte 3A; ☉24hr) Adequately equipped for X-rays, dealing with broken limbs and dishing out antibiotics. Ask for English-speaking Dr Veokham.

Provincial Tourism Office (☑086-211534; www.luangnamtha-tourism-laos.org; ☉8-11.30am & 1.30-4pm Mon-Fri) Helpful resource for things local, including trekking advice.

❶ Getting There & Away

AIR

Both **Lao Airlines** (☑086-212072; www.laoairlines.com; ☉8am-noon & 1-5pm; US$85) and **Lao Skyway** (☑020-99990011; Luang Namtha Airport; ☉8am-noon & 1-5pm; US$50) fly to Vientiane daily.

BUS & SŎRNGTĂAOU

There are two bus stations. The **district bus station** is walking distance from the traveller strip. The main **long-distance bus station** is 10km south of town. For buses at either station, prebooking a ticket doesn't guarantee a seat – you just have to arrive early and claim one in person.

Destinations include Luang Prabang (100,000K, eight hours), Boten (25,000K, two hours), Huay Xai (60,000K, four hours) and Nong Khiaw (100,000K, six hours).

❶ Getting Around

Chartered tuk-tuks charge 20,000K per person between the long-distance bus station or airport and the town centre, more if you're travelling solo. Most agencies and guesthouses sell ticket packages for long-distance buses that include a transfer from the guesthouse and cost around 20,000K above the usual fare.

Cycling is the ideal way to explore the wats, waterfalls, villages and landscapes surrounding Luang Namtha. There are a couple of **bike shops** (per day bicycle 10,000-25,000K, motorcycle 30,000-60,000K; ☉9am-6.30pm) in front of the Zuela Guesthouse. Choose from a bicycle or motorcycle depending on how energetic you are feeling.

LAOS LUANG NAMTHA

THE GIBBON EXPERIENCE

At the long-running ecotourism project **Gibbon Experience** (☏ 084-212021, 030-5745866; www.gibbonexperience.org; 2-day Express US$190, 3-day Classic or Waterfall US$310; ⊙ 7am-5pm) a series of ziplines criss-cross the canopy in the Nam Kan NPA – home to tigers, clouded leopards, black bears and the black-crested gibbon – giving you the chance to soar across valleys and stay in 40m-high tree houses, claimed to be the world's tallest. There are three tour options (two-day Express, or three-day Classic and Waterfall), each involving some trekking. Well-cooked meals are ziplined in by your guide.

The guides are helpful, though make sure you're personally vigilant with the knots in your harness. It's optional to wear a helmet, but we recommend asking for one given the speed you travel along the cable. Also check that your karabiner actually closes. Should it rain when you're ziplining, remember you need more time to slow down with your brake (a humble bit of bike tyre). For all three tour options, we recommend being in good shape.

Pre-payment online through PayPal works well but do be patient as communication isn't always immediate. One day before departure, check in at the Huay Xai **Gibbon Experience Office** (☏ 084-212021; www.gibbonexperience.org; Th Saykhong; ⊙ 8am-5pm) on Th Saykhong. Gloves (essential for using the ziplines) are provided. It's also advisable to bring a torch (flashlight), water bottle, toilet paper and earplugs to deflect the sound of a million crickets, but otherwise leave most of your baggage in the office storeroom. Everything you bring you must carry on your back over some steep hikes and on the ziplines. As there'll be no electricity, don't forget to pre-charge camera batteries.

Tragically, an accident here in March 2017 resulted in the death of one traveller and tours were temporarily suspended. Following investigations, the Gibbon Experience resumed services and began implementing a range of stricter safety protocols.

Huay Xai ຫ້ວຍຊາຍ

☏ 084 / POP 20,000

Separated from Thailand by the mother river that is the Mekong, Huay Xai is, for many, their first impression of Laos. While that used to be a bad thing, this oddly charming town has perked up in recent years. By night roadside food vendors take to the streets, and there are some welcoming traveller guesthouses and cafes serving tasty food.

Huay Xai was allegedly home to a US heroin-processing plant during the Secret War, but these days the only things trafficked through are travellers en route to Luang Prabang or the fabled Gibbon Experience, the most talked-about adventure in the country. Yet, with new day trips to nearby ethnic villages, worthwhile voluntourism opportunities and kayaking tours down the Mekong, there are good reasons to stick around for a while.

New Challenge Discovery (☏ 030-5209858, 020-97720313; www.newchallengediscovery.com; Th Saykhong; 2-day trekking US$120 per person, 1-day kayaking US$70 per person, steep discounts for groups of three or more; ⊙ 8am-5:30pm) 🖉, run by former Gibbon Experience guides, offers authentic one- to three-day trekking tours to nearby Khmu villages on the edge of the Nam Kan NPA, as well as kayaking trips on the Mekong. Your money goes to support rural education projects and the empowerment of local people to restore and protect the fragile ecosystem.

🛏 Sleeping & Eating

Gateway Villa Hotel GUESTHOUSE $
(☏ 084-212180; gatewayconsult@hotmail.com; Th Saykhong; r incl breakfast & air-con 140,000K; ❄🖥) Gateway Villa has tastefully furnished rooms with hardwood floors, wicker chairs, TVs and comfy beds. Some rooms are more prettified than others and have Mekong views. You'll get a good night's sleep, an OK breakfast, fast internet and helpful English-speaking staff.

Daauw Home BUNGALOW $
(☏ 030-9041296; http://daauwvillagelaos.com; bungalows 100,000K, dm 30,000K) 🌱 Daauw Home is run by lovely Hmong folk, and your stay in a cosy bungalow near the heart of town enables you to contribute something to women's empowerment and minority rights, as this place is a grassroots initiative run by Project Kajsiab. Simple rooms (one of which was recently converted into a dorm) come with hammock, balcony and private bathroom.

Terrasse Restaurant & Chill Place LAOTIAN $
(mains 15,000-30,000K; ⊙ 8.30am-10.30pm) This
relaxing hilltop spot just off the stairs to Wat
Jom Khao Manilat offers simple Lao food
cooked to perfection using market-fresh
ingredients. With comfy cotton hammocks
and views of the tangerine sun setting over
the Mekong, it makes a great spot for a long,
lazy dinner. Try the garlic chicken!

Bar How BAR
(⌨ 020-55167220; Th Saykhong; ⊙ 6.30am-11pm;
🖥) Decked in rice-paddy hats and old mus-
kets, Bar How is darkly atmospheric. By night
a row of sinister-looking homemade *lòw-lów*
(rice wine), infused with anyything from blue-
berry to lychee, catches the low light and resembles a Victorian apothecary. It also serves
pizza, steak, *láhp* and spring rolls (mains
30,000K to 60,000K). However, the service is
very slack – you may have to seek out staff.

ⓘ Information

BCEL (Th Saykhong; ⊙ 8.30am-4.30pm Mon-
Fri) Has a 24-hour ATM, exchange facility and
Western Union.

Lao Development Bank Exchange Booth
(⊙ 8am-5pm Mon-Fri) Handy booth beside the pedestrian immigration window. Most
major currencies exchanged into kip. US-dollar
bills must be dated 2006 or later.

Post Office (Th Saykhong; ⊙ 8am-noon &
1-4pm Mon-Fri) Also contains a telephone
office.

Tourist Information Office (⌨ 084-211162; Th
Saykhong; ⊙ 8am-4.30pm Mon-Fri) Has free
tourist maps of the town and some suggestions
for excursions around the province.

ⓘ Getting There & Away

For years, streams of Luang Prabang–bound
travellers have piled into Huay Xai and jumped
straight onboard a boat for the memorable
descent of the Mekong. Today, improving roads
mean an ever-increasing proportion opt instead
for the overnight bus. But while slightly cheaper
than the slowboat, it's far less social, less attractive and, at around 15 hours of travel, leaves
most travellers exhausted on arrival.

AIR

Huay Xai's airport is oddly perched on a hillside
off the city bypass, 1.5km northwest of the bus
station. **Lao Skyway** flies to/from Vientiane
daily with tickets from 800,000K.

BOAT

Slowboats currently depart from Huay Xai at
11.30am daily. Purchase tickets at the **slowboat ticket booth** (⌨ 084-211659) for Pak
Beng (150,000K, one day) or Luang Prabang
(210,000K excluding accommodation, two days).
Sales start at 8am on the day of travel. Avoid
buying a ticket from a travel company – you'll
get an overpriced tuk-tuk transfer to the pier and
then have to sit around awaiting departure.

'Seats' are typically uncomfortable wooden
benches for which you'll value the expenditure of
10,000K on a cushion (sold at many an agency in
town). Some boats also have a number of more
comfy airliner-style seats. If the boat operators
try to cram on too many passengers (more than
70 or so), a tactic that really works is for later
arrivals to simply refuse to get aboard until a
second boat is provided.

The **speedboat landing** (⌨ 084-211457; Rte
3, 200m beyond Km 202) is directly beneath
Wat Thadsuvanna Phakham, 3km south of town.
Six-passenger speedboats *(héua wái)* zip thrilling-

ⓘ GETTING TO THAILAND: HUAY XAI (HOKSAY) TO CHIANG KHONG

Getting to the border Since the completion of the Thai-Lao Friendship Bridge 4 at the
Huay Xai/Chiang Khong border crossing in late 2013, the former ferry-boat crossing is for
locals only. Tuk-tuks cost about 30,000K per person to the immigration post. Alternatively,
many agencies in Huay Xai sell tickets to Chiang Khong or Chiang Rai that include a tuk-tuk to
the border, bus across the bridge and onward transport for about the same price as DIY.

At the border A bus (25B) crosses the bridge to Thailand where a 30-day visa waiver
is automatically granted to residents of most countries. There are ATMs and exchange
counters at the heavily trafficked border post in Chiang Khong.

Moving on Most buses to Chiang Mai and Chiang Rai booked in Huay Xai will pick up
at the border. Alternatively, buses for Chiang Rai (from 65B, 2½ hours) typically depart
from Chiang Khong's bus station every hour from 6am to 5pm. **Greenbus** (⌨ in Thailand
0066 5324 1933; www.greenbusthailand.com) has a service to Chiang Mai at 9.45am. Several overnight buses for Bangkok (650B to 800B, 14 hours) leave at 3pm and 3.30pm.

For information on making this border crossing in reverse see p708.

ly but dangerously and with great physical discomfort to Pak Beng (180,000K, three hours) and Luang Prabang (350,000K, seven hours including lunch stop), typically departing around 10.30am.

Due to a section of the Nam Tha (Tha River) being dammed it's no longer possible to catch a boat all the way up to Luang Namtha.

BUS & SŎRNGTĂAOU

Note that Huay Xai–bound buses are usually marked 'Borkeo'. The bus station is 5km southeast of town. Buses to Luang Prabang (120,000K, 14 to 17 hours) depart at 10am and 4pm; for Luang Namtha (60,000K, four hours) they leave at 9am and 12.30pm; for Udomxai (90,000K, eight hours) there is one at 9.30am and 1pm. For Vientiane (230,000K, 25 hours) catch the 11.30am. There is also a bus to Mengla (120,000K) at 8.30am.

Travel-agency minibuses to Luang Namtha leave from central Huay Xai at around 9am (100,000K, four hours) but still arrive at Namtha's inconveniently out-of-town bus station.

Sŏrngtăaou to Tonpheung (30,000K, two hours) leave when full from beside the main market, very occasionally continuing to Muang Mom.

ⓘ Getting Around

Bicycles (30,000K per day) are available from **Little Hostel** (☑ 030-5206329; https:// littlehostel.wordpress.com; Th Saykhong; dm 40,000K; 🛜), while **Phonevichith Guesthouse** (☑ 084-211765; www.houayxairiverside.com; Ban Khonekeo; r incl breakfast US$45; 🌫🛜) rents motorbikes for 125,000K.

Tuk-tuks, if you can find them, charge about 20,000K per person to the airport, bus station, speedboat or slowboat landings.

CENTRAL & SOUTHERN LAOS

This part of the country claims the most forest cover and highest concentrations of wildlife, including some species that have disappeared elsewhere in Southeast Asia. With its rugged, intrepid travel, and stylish pockets of comfort in Savannakhet and Tha Khaek, central Laos makes for a great place to combine your inner Indiana Jones with a Bloody Mary.

Tham Kong Lor & Around   ຖ້ຳກອງລໍ

Tham Kong Lor is one of central Laos', if not the country's, most vivid highlights. A journey into this preternatural underworld is like a voyage into the afterworld itself, with a 7.5km river passing through the cathedral-high limestone cave.

Ban Kong Lor (Kong Lor Village) is the most convenient base for visiting the cave and has seen an explosion of guesthouses and small resorts in the last few years.

★ **Tham Kong Lor**   CAVING, BOATING
(cave entrance 10,000K, parking fee 5000K; boat trip 1/2/3 persons 110,000/120,000/130,000K; ⊙8am-4pm) A boat trip through the other-worldly Tham Kong Lor is an absolute must. Situated in the 1580-sq-km wilderness of Phu Hin Bun NPA, the 7.5km river cave runs beneath an immense limestone mountain. Your imagination will be in overdrive as the boat takes you further into the bat-black darkness and the fear dial will ratchet up as if on some natural Gothic ghost ride. The experience is unforgettable.

A section of Kong Lor has now been atmospherically lit, allowing you a greater glimpse of this epic spectacle; your longtail docks in a rocky inlet to allow you to explore a stalactite wood of haunting pillars and sprouting stalagmites like an abandoned *Star Trek* set.

Boat trips through Tham Kong Lor take up to an hour each way, and in dry season when the river is low, you'll have to get out while the boatman and point man haul the wooden craft up rapids. At the other end of the cave, a brief five minutes upstream takes you to a refreshment stop. Catch your breath and then head back in for more adrenaline-fuelled excitement.

Life jackets are provided. Be sure to bring a torch (flashlight) as the ones for rent are inadequate, and wear rubber sandals; the gravel in the riverbed is sharp and it's often necessary to disembark and wade at several shallow points.

🛏 Sleeping & Eating

Ban Kong Lor has eclipsed Ban Khoun Kham as the preferred base to visit Tham Kong Lor thanks to its location right on the doorstep and good range of accommodation.

Kong Lor Eco Lodge   GUESTHOUSE $
(☑ 030-9062772; r 50,000K; 🅿🛜) Kong Lor Eco Lodge has 12 spartan but clean rooms set back from the road. The small **restaurant** here is one of the more popular in town.

★ **Spring River Resort**   BUNGALOW $$
(☑ 020-59636111; www.springriverresort.com; Ban Tiou; bungalows US$15-50; ⊙closed Jun &

Jul; ✳ 🐾) These stilted bungalows sit in an immaculately landscaped garden and range from basic (without bathroom) to superior (with bathroom) and sit by the beautiful Nam Hin Bun. En-suite triple rooms include mozzie nets and private balconies to enjoy the lush river view, and breakfast is included with the more expensive room. There's a clear-water creek nearby to cool off in.

Khounmee Restaurant   LAOTIAN $
(☎ 020-58190652;   mains   20,000-40,000K; 🕐 7.30am-9pm; 🐾) Cheap local and Western dishes, combined with friendly service, make this simple new spot the favourite of most travellers. The English-speaking owner, Mr Dam, has put together a helpful information board on the region, from bus times to tours and tips. He also offers clean, no-frills **rooms** across the street (50,000K).

Tha Khaek   ທ່າແຂກ

☎ 051 / POP 80,000

This ex-Indochinese trading post is a delightful melange of crumbling French villas and warped Chinese merchant's shopfronts, with an easy riverside charm which, despite the bridge over to nearby Thailand, shows few signs of change. It's from here that you begin **the Loop** (http://tourismkhammouane.org), a three-day motorbike journey through shape-shifting landscapes, and you can also use Tha Khaek as a base from which to make organised day trips to Tham Kong Lor. There are more than a dozen other caves nearby, some with swimmable lagoons, that can be accessed by scooter or tuk-tuk.

While you shouldn't expect Luang Prabang levels of sophistication from Tha Khaek, you will find a historically appealing old town and slice of authentic Lao life. The epicentre (if you can call it that) of the old town is the modest Fountain Sq at the western end of Th Kuvoravong near the river.

◉ Sights

★ **Phu Hin Bun NPA**   NATIONAL PARK
(ປ່າສະຫງວນແຫ່ງຊາດພູຫິນບູນ) Phu Hin Bun NPA is a huge (1580 sq km) wilderness area of turquoise streams, monsoon forests and striking karst topography across central Khammuan. It was made a protected area in 1993 and it's no overstatement to say this is some of the most breathtaking country in the region.

Passing through on foot or by boat, it's hard not to feel awestruck by the very scale of the limestone cliffs that rise almost vertically for hundreds of metres into the sky. Although much of the NPA is inaccessible by road, local people have reduced the numbers of key forest-dependent species through hunting and logging. Despite this, the area remains home to the endangered (red-shanked) douc langur, François' langur and several other primate species, as well as elephants, tigers and a variety of rare species of deer. Khammuan Province runs five different community-based treks of varying lengths. From Tha Khaek, the popular two-day trip (1,700,000K for one person, 950,000K each for two, 650,000K for six or more) into the Phu Hin Bun NPA is especially good. The route includes plenty of karst scenery, a walk through Tham Pa Chan and overnight accommodation in an ethnic village. Bookings can be made through the Tourist Information Centre (p362) in Tha Khaek.

ℹ GETTING TO VIETNAM: THA KHAEK TO DONG HOI

Getting to the border Despite the fact that Rte 12 is now fully paved, for *falang* (Westerners) the Na Phao (Laos)/Cha Lo (Vietnam) border crossing (7am to 4pm) remains one of the least used of all Laos' borders. This is partly because transport on both sides is slow and infrequent, though there's a bus from Tha Khaek to Dong Hoi (90,000K, 10 to 14 hours) at 7am Monday, Wednesday, Friday and Sunday. If you're determined to cross here, take this bus as there's no accommodation in the border area.

At the border The Lao border offers 30-day tourist visas on arrival. Some nationalities require a Vietnam visa in advance, so check with the Vietnamese consulate (p380). Most regional visitors and Scandinavian, British, French, German, Italian and Spanish visitors do not need a visa for short stays.

Moving on Get back on the same bus, which will wait for you to complete your paperwork before continuing to Dong Hoi.

For information on making the border crossing in the reverse direction see p860.

THA KHAEK LOOP

This awe-inspiring three-day motorbike journey, known as the 'The Loop', has become the stuff of legends on the Southeast Asia backpacker circuit. If you're up to the challenge of navigating all 450km – and it is quite challenging – your reward is a highlights reel of rural Laos with verdant jungles, raging rivers and soaring karst walls that hide subterranean wonderlands.

The trip starts and ends in Tha Khaek, where you can arrange for a sturdy motorbike and backpack storage with a number of respected rental companies. Most travellers then set off on The Loop counter-clockwise, taking in the swimming holes and minor caves east of town before zipping past the impregnable karst to overnight by the Nam Theun (Theun River) in Ban Tha Lang. Day two will have you biking past flooded valleys (and eerie dead forests) to the frontier town of **Lak Sao** before you cut south to the river cave of **Tham Kong Lor** (p359), the highlight of the entire trip. Though much of day three is spent on the highway returning to Tha Khaek, the road that leads you there is the most spectacular yet, zigzagging through the pristine jungle of **Phu Hin Bun NPA**.

Tham Pa Seuam
CAVE

(ຖ້ຳປາເຊືອມ) The recently discovered river cave of Tham Pa Seuam runs for 3km. A much smaller version of Tham Kong Lor, it features impressive stalactites and stalagmites and is conveniently only 15km from Tha Khaek. A day trip to multiple caves, including Tham Pa Seuam, with the Tourist Information Centre (p362) costs from 350,000K per person (for a group of six or more) and includes a 400m boat ride into the main chamber.

Tham Pa Fa
CAVE

(Buddha Cave; entry 5000K, parking 3000K; ⊙8am-noon & 1-5pm) When Mr Bun Nong used a vine to scramble up a sheer 200m-high cliff in 2004, he discovered a narrow cave mouth and was greeted by 229 bronze Buddha images. The Buddhas, ranging from 15cm to about 1m tall, were sitting as they had been for centuries facing the entrance of a cave of impressive limestone formations.

Activities

Green Climbers Home
CLIMBING

(☎020-56105622; www.greenclimbershome.com; Ban Kouanphavang; courses per person 140,000-500,000K; ⊙Oct-May) This efficiently run training school set in a valley in soaring karst country 18km from Tha Khaek is hugely popular, and often booked up thanks to its cosy cabanas, great food and excellent courses. It also boasts one of the easiest overhangs in the world to learn on and has beginner-, intermediate- and expert-level climbs, with more than 320 routes from class 4 to 8C.

Green Discovery
ADVENTURE SPORTS

(☎051-251390; www.greendiscoverylaos.com; Inthira Hotel, Th Chao Annou; ⊙8am-9pm) Green Discovery is the country's most experienced ecotourism outfit and runs a number of interesting trips around central Laos. A range of treks and kayaking excursions in the lush Phu Hin Bun NPA are available, including Tham Kong Lor (from US$70 for a day trip to US$155 for an overnight trip). Also arranges cycling and kayaking.

Sleeping & Eating

Thakhek Travel Lodge
GUESTHOUSE $

(☎051-212931; thakhektravellodge@gmail.com; Rte 13; dm 50,000K; r 60,000-130,000K; ⊛❄🤶) It might be an inconvenient five minutes out of town by tuk-tuk, but this place has a great vibe thanks to its nightly garden firepit, drawing travellers together. Rooms vary from basic fan options to expansive air-con bungalows, and a cafe serves *láhp*, salads and juices. Check out the logbook for updated news from the Loop.

★ Inthira Hotel
BOUTIQUE HOTEL $$

(☎051-251237; www.inthira.com; Th Chao Anou; r incl breakfast US$26-49; ⊛❄@🤶) Set in an old French villa with a pretty facade, Inthira offers the most romantic, stylish digs in town. Its restaurant fronts the old fountain, and its chic wine-hued rooms, with exposed-brick walls, rain showers, cable TV, dark wood furniture, air-con and safety deposit boxes, are a delight for weary travellers. The best rooms face the street and have balconies.

DD Bistro & Cafe
INTERNATIONAL $

(☑ 051-212355; Fountain Sq; mains 20,000-80,000K; ⊙ 7am-9pm; ✳ 🕾) This new glass-fronted cafe overlooking Fountain Sq offers a fusion menu of Lao, Thai and international dishes in a cool atmosphere, both figuratively and literally, thanks to the powerful air-con. Twinings teas, coffees with a kick and fresh juices are also available.

★ Khop Chai Deu
FUSION $$

(Inthira Hotel, Th Chao Anou; mains 30,000-90,000K; ⊙ 7am-10pm; ✳ 🕾 ☑) Classy and low-lit, this fine restaurant is as sophisticated as sleepy Tha Khaek gets. Based in a pretty French colonial-era building, the open-range kitchen, visible but behind glass, dishes up tasty Lao salad, burgers, substantial tenderised steak and decent cocktails from the sleek wooden bar. You can eat on the street if it's cool out.

ℹ Information

BCEL (Th Vientiane; ⊙ 8.30am-3:30pm Mon-Fri) Changes major currencies and offers cash advances on debit or credit card.

Lao Development Bank (Th Vientiane; ⊙ 8.30-11.30am & 1.30-3.30pm) Cash exchange only, plus an ATM.

Post Office (☑ 051-212004; Th Kuvorawong) Offers expensive international phone calls.

Tourist Information Centre (☑ 030-5300503, 020-55711797; www.tourismkhammouane.org; Th Vientiane; ⊙ 8.30am-5pm) This excellent tourist office offers exciting one- and two-day treks in Phu Hin Boun NPA, including a homestay in a local village. There are also treks to the waterfall by Ban Khoun Kham and Tham Kong Lor (900,000K). Offers advice on journeying the Loop as well.

ℹ Getting There & Away

BUS

Tha Khaek's **bus station** (☑ 051-251519; Rte 13) is about 3.5km from the town centre and has a sizeable market and basic guesthouses to complement the regular services going north and south. Buses for Vientiane (60,000K, six hours) depart hourly from 5.30am to midnight. There is a VIP service at 9.15am (80,000K) and a sleeper VIP at 1am (110,000K). Any bus going north stops at Vieng Kham (Thang Beng; 30,000K, 1½ hours), Pak Kading (40,000K, three hours) or Paksan (50,000K, four hours).

Heading south, buses for Savannakhet (30,000K, two to three hours) depart every hour, and there's an air-con departure for Pakse (85,000K, six to seven hours) at 8.30am and regular local buses every hour during the day (70,000K). There are two daily departures to Attapeu (90,000K, about 10 hours) at 3.30pm and 11pm. Buses originating in Vientiane leave at around 5.30pm for Don Khong (90,000K, about 12 to 13 hours) and around 5.30pm for Non Nok Khiene (90,000K, about 15 hours), on the Cambodian border. They stop at Tha Khaek between 5pm and 6pm, but this is only recommended if you're in a hurry to get to Cambodia.

If you're heading to Vietnam, a bus for Hué (90,000K, 12 to 13 hours) leaves every Monday, Wednesday, Friday and Sunday at 7am and 8pm. There are also departures for Danang (120,000K, 15 to 17 hours) at 8pm every Monday and Friday; for Dong Hoi (90,000K, 10 to 14 hours) at 7am on Monday, Wednesday, Friday and Sunday; and for Hanoi (160,000K, 15 to 17 hours) at 12.30pm on Tuesday, Thursday and Saturday.

SŎRNGTǍAOU

Sŏrngtǎaou (passenger trucks) regularly depart when full from **Talat Phetmany** (Th Kuvorawong) to Mahaxai Mai (20,000K, one hour). Departures

ℹ GETTING TO THAILAND: THA KHAEK TO NAKHON PHANOM

Getting to the border Crossing the Mekong at the Tha Khaek (Laos)/Nakhon Phanom (Thailand) border is now only possible for locals. Travellers can catch an international bus (18,000K/70B, around 1½ hour) to Nakhon Phanom via the Friendship Bridge from the main bus station in Tha Khaek. Buses run every hour or so from 8am to 4.30pm. If crossing the border after 4pm you'll have to pay an overtime fee.

At the border In Tha Khaek, Lao immigration issues 30-day tourist visas on arrival and there's a BCEL money-exchange service and 24-hour ATM at the immigration office. In Thailand, travellers from most countries are given visa-free, 30-day entry.

Moving on Once in Nakhon Phanom, buses depart regularly for Udon Thani and head to Bangkok at 7.30am and then regularly from 4.30pm to 7.30pm. Faster and almost as cheap are the budget flights to Bangkok offered by Air Asia and Nok Air, with several flights per day.

For information on making this border crossing in reverse see p735.

❶ GETTING TO VIETNAM: SAVANNAKHET TO DONG HA

Getting to the border Crossing the Dansavanh (Laos)/Lao Bao (Vietnam) border (7am to 7.30pm) is a relative pleasure. From Savannakhet's bus terminal, buses leave for Dansavanh (40,000K, five to six hours) at 7am and noon. Alternatively, consider breaking the journey for a night in Sepon, which you can use as a base for seeing the Ho Chi Minh Trail. The bus station in Dansavanh is about 1km short of the border; Vietnamese teenagers on motorbikes are more than happy to take you the rest of the way for about 10,000K.

At the border The Lao border offers 30-day tourist visas on arrival and has an exchange booth. Some nationalities require a Vietnam visa in advance, so check with the **Vietnamese consulate** (p380) in Savannakhet. Most regional visitors, Scandinavian visitors, and British, French, German, Italian and Spanish visitors do not need a visa for short stays.

Moving on Once through, take a motorbike (40,000d or US$2) 2km to the Lao Bao bus terminal and transport to Dong Ha (50,000d, two hours) on Vietnam's main north–south highway and railway. Entering Laos, there are buses to Savannakhet (40,000K, five to six hours) at 7am and 9am, as well as regular *sŏrngtǎaou* (passenger trucks) to Sepon (30,000K, one hour) from 7am to 5pm. Simple accommodation is available on both sides of the border.

If you're in a hurry, an alternative is to take one of the various direct buses from Savannakhet bound for the Vietnamese cities of Dong Ha, Hué and Danang.

For information on making this border crossing in reverse see p868.

---

for Ban Kong Lor (60,000K, four hours) are at 7am, 2.30pm and 3.30pm.

Talat Lak Sǎam (Sook Som Boon Bus Terminal) serves buses into the Khammuan Province interior. There's a daily departure at 8am for Lang Khang (40,000K, two to three hours), and one at 8pm for Na Phao (60,000K, 3½ hours), 18km short of the Vietnam border.

❶ Getting Around

It should cost about 20,000K to hire a jumbo (motorised three-wheeled taxi) to the bus terminal, though you'll have to negotiate. From the bus terminal, jumbos don't budge unless they're full or you're willing to fork out 30,000K or more to charter the entire vehicle. Rides around town can cost around 15,000K per person.

Savannakhet ສະຫວັນນະເຂດ

☑ 041 / POP 120,000

Languid, time-trapped and somnolent during the sweltering days that batter the old city's plasterwork, Savannakhet is an attractive blend of past and present Laos. The highlight is the historic quarter with its impressive display of decaying early-20th-century architecture. Leprous and listing, these grand old villas of Indochina's heyday now lie unwanted like aged dames crying out for a makeover. There's little to do in town but wander the riverfront and cool off in one of a clutch of stylish restaurants and bijou cafes that are steadily growing in number.

That said, there's plenty to do nearby and Savannakhet has a dedicated Tourist Information Centre (p365), which can help you plan intrepid trips into the nearby NPAs.

Wat Sainyaphum (ວັດໄຊຍະພູມ; Th Tha He) **FREE** is one of the oldest and largest monasteries in southern Laos and an important centre of local Buddhism. Museums in town include **Musee Des Dinosaures** (ຫໍພິພິດທະພັນໄດໂນເສົາ, Dinosaur Museum; ☑041-212597; Th Khanthabuli; 10,000K; ⊘8-11:30am & 1-4pm), containing 110-million-year-old dinosaur fossils, and **Savannakhet Museum** (ຫໍພິພິດທະພັນແຂວງສະຫວັນນະເຂດ; Th Khanthabuli; 10,000K; ⊘8am-noon & 1:30-4pm Mon-Fri), where you can see war relics, artillery and inactive UXO.

🛏 Sleeping & Eating

Savannakhet has high-quality budget and midrange options; most guesthouses are located within walking distance of the attractive old town. The riverside snack and drink vendors are a great place for sundowners, serving cheap big bottles of Beerlao (10,000K) and *sìn daat* (Lao hotpot barbecue) sizzling away on charcoal grills.

★**Hostel Savan Cafe** HOSTEL $
(☑020-91243402; Th Si Muang; dm 65,000K, r 200,000K; ❄🔊) This swanky new hostel by the tourism office will make you feel like a million bucks on just a few thousand kip with a trendy floor-level cafe, leafy lounge

Savannakhet

⬆ N 0 —— 200 m
0 —— 0.1 miles

LAOS SAVANNAKHET

Savannakhet

you feel at home. Guacamole-green rooms feature clean beds, air-con and attached bathrooms with hot water. The current five rooms are set to expand to seven rooms and include some larger family-friendly options.

★ **Vivanouk Homestay**   HOMESTAY **$$**
(☏ 020-91606030; www.vivanouk.com; Th Khantabouly; r without bathroom US$20-40; ❂✴🖥) This funky little place is akin to a boutique homestay and is a great new addition to the Savan scene. There are just three rooms sharing two bathrooms – one with an alfresco outdoor shower – and delightfully decorated in a contemporary-colonial fusion style. Breakfast is available downstairs in an artsy venue that doubles as a bar by night.

★ **Lin's Café**   INTERNATIONAL **$**
(☏ 030-5332188; Th Phetsalat; mains 30,000-60,000K; ⊗8am-10pm; ✴🖥✐) Savannakhet's original travellers' cafe, this delightful spot has outgrown its former home and relocated to a new open-plan house near St Theresa's Cathedral. It's popular for its easy vibe, friendly staff, reservoir of local information, eclectic interior furnishings and gallery upstairs. But best of all are the cappuccinos, Thai green curry, tasty burgers, fruit salad and fresh pastries.

★ **Savannakhet Plaza
Food Market**   MARKET, LAOTIAN **$**
(Savannakhet Plaza; meals 10,000-30,000K; ⊗5-10pm) An excellent new addition to the Savan dining scene, this nightly food market brings 20 or more stalls to the Savannakhet Plaza area in the heart of the old town. This is street-food surfing at its best, with a choice of freshly barbecued skewers, steam

zones and a tiled rooftop patio with sweeping sunset views of the Mekong. The dorm beds are cushy and the bathrooms spotless. Friendly service is the only thing missing.

Pilgrim's Inn   B&B **$**
(☏ 020-22133733; www.facebook.com/pilgrimskitchenandinn; 106 Th Latsaphanith; r US$20-25; ✴🖥) Pilgrim's Inn is a small B&B-style place attached to the popular **Pilgrim's Kitchen** (☏ 020-22133733; www.facebook.com/pilgrimskitchenandinn; 106 Th Latsaphanith; mains 20,000-60,000K; ⊗7.30am-9pm Mon-Sat; ✴🖥) with caring English-speaking staff who make

ing noodle soups, dim-sum-sushi-tapas confusion and more. Plus Beerlao in plentiful supply.

Cafe Chai Dee   JAPANESE, INTERNATIONAL $
(☑ 030-5003336; www.cafechaidee.com; Th Ratsavongsouk; mains 20,000-50,000K; ☺ 9am-3pm & 5-9pm Mon-Sat; ✸ 🛜 ☑) This spotless Japanese-owned cafe has rattan mats to lounge on, a book exchange and a wide menu of Japanese classics such as ramen and *tonkatsu* (pork coated in breadcrumbs and fried), plus samosas, homemade yoghurt, Thai food and healthy shakes. Great breakfasts, too. Expect super-fresh, well-presented food, fast wi-fi and warm service.

ℹ Information

BCEL (Th Ratsavongseuk; ☺ 8.30am-3.30pm) and **Lao Development Bank** (Th Udomsin; ☺ 8.30-11.30am & 1.30-3.30pm) both have cash exchange, credit-card advances and an ATM. **Phongsavanh Bank** (☑ 041-300888; Th Ratsavongseuk; ☺ 8.30am-4pm Mon-Fri, to 11.30am Sat) has cash exchange, Western Union and an ATM.

Post Office (☑ 041-212205; Th Khanthabuli) International calls here are overpriced; make calls via an internet connection instead.

Tourist Information Centre (☑ 041-212755; Th Si Muang; ☺ 8am-noon & 1-4pm Mon-Fri) A useful stop for a selection of well-produced brochures on Savannakhet and its surrounds.

ℹ Getting There & Away

Most travellers arrive and depart Savannakhet by road, with convenient bus links to all points in Laos and international destinations in Thailand and Vietnam. The airport offers limited flight connections to Vientiane, Pakse and Bangkok.

AIR

Savannakhet's airport (p382) is served solely by Lao Airlines, with connections to Vientiane (710,000K to 875,000K, 55 minutes, four weekly), Pakse (420,000K to 580,000K, 30 minutes, four weekly) and Bangkok (US$110 to US$150, 80 minutes, four weekly). Tickets can be purchased at the **Lao Airlines office** (☑ 041-212140; http://laoairlines.com; Savannakhet Airport; ☺ 8.30am-4pm Sun, Mon, Wed & Fri) at the airport, online or with travel agents in town.

An alternative option for those wanting to save money on the Bangkok route is to cross the Friendship Bridge and connect with the Fly-Drive services offered with Air Asia or Nok Air via Nakhon Phanom Airport; tickets are available from less than 1000B.

The airport is located at the southeastern edge of town; jumbos make the trip downtown for 30,000K, although they may start higher for new arrivals fresh off the plane.

BUS

Savannakhet's orderly **bus terminal**, usually called the *khíw lot*, is near the Talat Savan Xai at the northern edge of town. Buses leave here for Vientiane (75,000K, eight to 11 hours) roughly every half-hour from 6am to 11.30am. From

ℹ GETTING TO THAILAND: SAVANNAKHET TO MUKDAHAN

Since the construction of the second Thai/Lao Friendship Bridge back in 2006, non-Thai and non-Lao citizens are not allowed to cross between Mukdahan and Savannakhet by boat.

Getting to the border The Thai–Lao International Bus crosses the Savannakhet (Laos)/Mukdahan (Thailand) border crossing (6am to 10pm) in both directions. From Savannakhet's bus terminal, the Thai–Lao International Bus (14,000K, 45 minutes) departs approximately every hour from 8am to 7pm. It leaves Mukdahan's bus station (50B, 45 minutes) roughly every hour from 7.30am to 7pm and also stops at the border crossing to pick up passengers.

At the border Be sure not to board the Savan Vegas Casino staff bus at the border, as this also stops at the international bus stop but heads out of town to the eponymous casino resort. The Lao border offers 30-day tourist visas on arrival. If you don't have a photo you'll be charged the equivalent of US$1. An additional US$1 'overtime fee' is charged from 6am to 8am and 6pm to 10pm on weekdays, as well as on weekends and holidays. Most nationalities do not require a visa to cross into Thailand; check with the Thai consulate (p380) in Savannakhet.

Moving on Onward from Mukdahan, there are at least five daily buses bound for Bangkok. Alternatively, to save time, consider a fly-drive option with Air Asia or Nok Air, including an express minivan to Nakhon Phanom Airport and a budget flight to Bangkok.

For information on making this border crossing in reverse see p734.

1.30pm to 10pm you'll have to hop on a bus passing through from Pakse, which stop at Tha Khaek (30,000K, 2½ to four hours). Hourly *sŏrngtǎaou* and minivans also head to Tha Khaek (30,000K) from 8am to 7pm. A VIP sleeper bus (120,000K, seven to eight hours) to Vientiane leaves at 10.30pm, or you could try to pick up a seat on one of the VIP buses coming through from Pakse.

Four daily buses to Pakse (40,000K, five to six hours) originate in Savannakhet; the first is at 7am and the last at 12.30pm. Otherwise, jump on one of the regular buses passing through from Vientiane. There's also a daily bus to Attapeu (75,000K, eight to 10 hours) at 9am.

Buses leave for the Laos/Vietnam border at Dansavanh (40,000K, five to six hours) at 7am and noon, stopping at Sepon (40,000K, four to five hours).

To Vietnam, there's a daily bus to Dong Ha (110,000K, about seven hours) departing at 8am. For Hué, there's a local bus (110,000K, about 10 hours) daily at 8am. There's also a sleeper bus to Danang (150,000K, about 12 hours) at 9am on Tuesday, Thursday and Saturday. Buses depart for Hanoi (250,000K, about 24 hours) at 10am Monday (sleeper bus), Wednesday, Thursday (sleeper bus) and Saturday, but we reckon you'd have to be a masochist to consider this journey.

ⓘ Getting Around

Savannakhet is just big enough that you might occasionally need a jumbo. A charter around town costs about 15,000K and more like 20,000K to the bus station.

Motorcycles can be hired at **Souannavong Guest House** (☑041-212600; Th Saenna) for 70,000K to 80,000K per day. There are also a few places to rent bicycles; most are along Th Ratsavongseuk and charge about 10,000K per day.

Pakse   ປາກເຊ

☑031 / POP 88,330

Pakse, the capital of Champasak Province and the gateway to southern Laos, sits at the confluence of the Mekong and the Se Don (Don River). Most travellers don't linger long because there's not much to do. The city lacks the sort of Mekong River–town lethargy found in Savannakhet and Tha Khaek further north and fewer colonial-era buildings remain.

Pakse serves mostly as a launching pad for forays to surrounding attractions such as the Bolaven Plateau and Wat Phu Champasak (p370), and the many good restaurants, stylish hotels and clued-in tour companies make it a comfortable and convenient one.

There are about 20 wats in Pakse, among which the riverside **Wat Luang** (ວັດຫຼວງ; Th 11) is one of the largest. The old monastic school, built in 1935, features a commanding tiled roof and ornate concrete pillars while two newer buildings have modern murals telling the Buddha's life story and other tales.

The **Talat Dao Heuang** (ຕະຫຼາດດາວເຮືອງ; ⊙5am-6pm) market near the Lao–Japanese Bridge is one of the biggest in the country. It's at its most chaotic in the food zones, but just about anything a person might need – from medicinal herbs to mobile phones – is sold here. It's highly worth a wander.

ⓒ Tours

Most people organise their southern Laos tours and treks in Pakse.

Green Discovery   ADVENTURE
(☑031-252908; www.greendiscoverylaos.com; Th 10; 2-day Tree Top Explorer tour 2-/4-person group per person US$308/240; ⊙8am-8pm) Green Discovery is a solid all-around tour company offering private and small group tours. It goes places and does things no other company does. Its signature trip is the Tree Top Explorer adventure in **Dong Hua Sao NPA** (ປ່າສະຫງວນແຫ່ງຊາດດົງຫົວສາວ) near Paksong on the Bolaven Plateau. It consists of two or three days' ziplining, canopy walking and jungle trekking around waterfalls beyond any roads.

Xplore-Asia   ADVENTURE
(☑031-251983; www.xplore-laos.com; Th 21; ⊙7.30am-7.30pm) Xplore-Asia specialises in multiday adventures, but also runs the standard day trips to the Bolaven Plateau and Wat Phu (with English-speaking guides) alongside nonstandard trips like a one-day, 54km mountain-biking loop from Pakse to Don Kho island and back. There's a good selection of books and guidebooks to the region for sale.

🛏 Sleeping

★ **Alisa Guesthouse**   HOTEL $
(☑031-251555; www.alisa-guesthouse.com; Rte 13; r 130,000-160,000K, f 210,000K; ➔❄@🛜) Perhaps the best-value lodging in Pakse, Alisa has sparkling rooms, tiled floors, solid wood beds, armoires, working satellite TV and a fridge. Service is good, too. The only significant knock is that some rooms barely catch a wi-fi signal. No surprise, it's often full.

Pakse

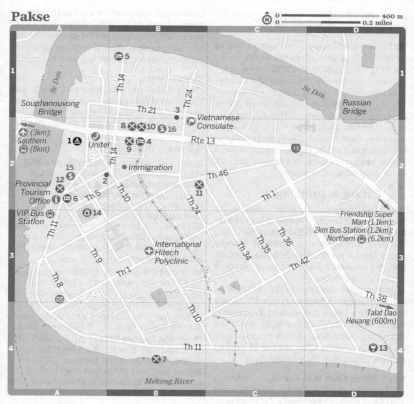

Pakse

◎ Sights
1 Wat Luang A2

⊕ Activities, Courses & Tours
2 Green Discovery A2
3 Xplore-Asia B1

🛏 Sleeping
4 Alisa Guesthouse B2
5 Khaemse Guest House B1
6 Residence Sisouk A2

✖ Eating
7 Banlao B4
8 Friendship Minimart B2
9 Lankham Noodle Shop B2

10 Noodle Shop Mengky B2
11 Pon Sai B2
12 Rahn Naem Khao Mae Fuean A2

⊙ Drinking & Nightlife
13 Champahom D4

🛍 Shopping
14 Champasak Shopping Centre A3

ℹ Information
15 BCEL A2
   Lankham Hotel Currency
   Exchange Counter .... (see 9)
16 Lao Development Bank B2

Khaemse Guest House   GUESTHOUSE **$**
(📞 020-56359292; Th 12; r with fan 40,000-70,000K; with air-con 100,000K; ❄🛜) With its riverside position and rickety sun deck shipwrecked over the bank, this friendly house at the end of a lane feels far from the city and has a lazy tumbledown charm. The rooms offer great value for money (they're

simple but clean, with river views) and the owners are extremely friendly.

★ Residence Sisouk
BOUTIQUE HOTEL $$

(☑ 031-214716; www.residence-sisouk.com; cnr Th 9 & Th 11; r incl breakfast US$50-100; ❷❄@☎) This exquisite boutique hotel occupies a lovely old house and evokes a bit of old France. The rooms enjoy polished hardwood floors, flat-screen TVs, verandahs, Hmong bed runners, stunning photography and fresh flowers everywhere. Breakfast is in the penthouse cafe with great views. Paying extra gets you a bigger, brighter room with a balcony in front. Rates drop 30% out of season.

✗ Eating & Drinking

Two good morning spots for delicious *fĕr* (rice noodles) are the **Noodle Shop Mengky** (Rte 13; noodles 20,000K; ❂6am-1pm) and the more tourist-friendly **Lankham Noodle Shop** (Rte 13; noodles 15,000-25,000K; ❂6am-2pm; ☎) across the road. The latter also does baguette sandwiches.

Self-caterers can head to the centrally located **Friendship Minimart** (Rte 13; ❂8am-8pm) or the larger but distant **Friendship Super Mart** (Rte 13; ❂9am-9pm) inside the Friendship Mall. Several fruit vendors open early to late next to **Champasak Shopping Centre** (Champasak Plaza; ❂8am-7pm).

Rahn Naem Khao Mae Fuean
LAOTIAN $

(Th 11; mains 25,000-40,000K; ❂9am-10.30pm) This local joint (hidden behind a Pepsi sign) offers a rare combination: real-deal Lao food and an English-language menu. Well, something close to English anyway...the 'fried chicken power' is really stir-fried holy basil with chicken. It's well-known for *pan mîiang baa* (a sort of make-your-own fish sandwich) and also serves Mekong River algae soup. The deck on the Se Don is a big bonus.

Pon Sai
LAOTIAN $

For a wonderful local experience, head to Pon Sai at the junction of Th 34 and Th 46, which bustles with small shops and street vendors selling *fĕr*, baguette sandwiches, *kòw nĕeo bîng* (grilled, egg-dipped sticky rice patties) and many doughy delights (including waffles). Best in the morning, some shops stay open through the day and into the night.

★ Banlao
THAI, LAOTIAN $$

(Th 11; mains 20,000-80,000K; ❂10am-10pm) One of several floating restaurants in Pakse, Banlao has a reliable menu of expected favourites but also many dishes you might not

have encountered before, such as the seasonal ant-egg *gôy* (*gôy kài mót sòm – gôy* is similar to *láhp* but with added blood). For the less adventurous there's mild, central-Thai papaya salad and grilled fish with herbs.

Champahom
BAR

(Th 11) A chill place to drink and snack, this Thai-owned bar has live music (usually Carabao-style Thai country music) most nights except Sunday from about 7.30pm to 9pm.

❶ Information

Banks, such as the conveniently located **BCEL** (Th 11; ❂8.30am-3.30pm Mon-Fri) and **Lao Development Bank** (Rte 13; ❂8.30am-3.30pm Mon-Fri), have the best currency-exchange rates, though the exchange counter at the **Lankham Hotel** (❂7am-7pm) is good too. All three give cash advances (3% commission) on credit cards. LDB also has Western Union and can exchange US dollar travellers cheques (1%).

ATMs are plentiful in the city centre.

Main Post Office (Th 8; ❂8am-noon & 1-5pm Mon-Fri) A short walk from the tourist strip.

Miss Noy (☑ 020-22272278; noy7days@hotmail.com; Rte 13; internet per hour 10,000K; ❂8am-8pm) The gang here are seriously clued in to the region, especially the Bolaven Plateau.

Provincial Tourism Office (☑ 031-212021; Th 11; ❂8am-4pm Mon-Fri) Mostly exists to hand out maps and brochures, but some staff can answer questions or help you make bookings for homestays and activities at Kiet Ngong, Don Kho and Don Daeng.

❶ Getting There & Away

AIR

The Pakse International Airport (p382) is 2.5km northwest of the Souphanouvong Bridge. A tuktuk to/from the airport will cost about 40,000K.

Lao Airlines (☑ 031-212252; www.laoairlines.com; Pakse Airport; ❂8am-5pm) has direct flights to the following cities in Asia:

Bangkok US$115, four weekly

Ho Chi Minh City US$105, three weekly

Luang Prabang 1,010,000K, three weekly

Savannakhet 375,000K, four weekly

Siem Reap US$100, five weekly

Vientiane 770,000K, two daily

A cheaper way to fly to Bangkok is to travel overland to Ubon Ratchathani and catch a budget flight from there.

BOAT

A tourist boat motors from Pakse to Champasak (one way per person 70,000K) at 8.30am, provided there are enough punters – in the low season there usually aren't. The return trip from Champasak is at 2.30pm. It's two hours downstream to Champasak, and a bit longer on the return. Book through Miss Noy (p368) or call **Mr Khamlao** (☑ 020-22705955; per boat US$80, per person for 10 people US$8), who runs his own separate boat.

BUS & SŎRNGTĂAOU

Pakse, frustratingly, has many bus and sŏrngtăaou (passenger truck) stations. The vast majority of tourists simply book bus journeys through their guesthouse or a travel agency, and since these are either special tourist buses that pick you up in the centre or include a free transfer to the relevant departure point, the prices are usually reasonable.

Note that on long-distance routes to Cambodia and Vietnam you'll want to be careful which company you use: choosing the wrong one could cost you several hours and cause a lot of pain. Buy your ticket from a travel agency that actually knows the details of the route, rather than a guesthouse, which probably does not. The main station is the **Southern Bus Terminal** (Rte 13), with departures to most places. It is also known as khĭw lot lák pæt (8km bus terminal) because it's 8km out of town on Rte 13.

Most travellers prefer the comfortable 'VIP' night sleeper buses to Vientiane (170,000K, 10 hours). You can book these through your guesthouse or head to the conveniently located **VIP Bus Station** (Th 11), from where there are several nightly departures, all leaving at 8.30pm; or the **2km Bus Station** (Sengchalern Bus Station; ☑ 031-212428; Rte 13), with one departure at 8pm. It's possible to take these buses to Tha Khaek (130,000K, 4½ hours) and Seno (for Savannakhet; 100,000K, three hours).

If you prefer day travel, slower-moving, ordinary air-con buses (110,000K, 12 to 14 hours) depart throughout the day from the Southern Bus Terminal, stopping occasionally to pick up more passengers at the **Northern** (Rte 13) station. These buses also go to Tha Khaek (50,000K, five hours) and Seno (60,000K, seven hours).

Regular sŏrngtăaou leave **Talat Dao Heuang** (morning market) for Champasak (20,000K, one hour) until noon or so – sometimes even as late as 2pm. There's also a morning tourist bus-boat combo to Champasak (55,000K, 1½ hours) offered by most travel agencies. Be sure your ticket includes the boat crossing from Ban Muang. The regular price for the boat is 10,000K per person or 30,000K if you're alone.

For Si Phan Don, tourist buses and minivans – including pick-ups in town and boat transfer to Don Khong (60,000K, 2½ hours), Don Det (70,000K, three hours) and Don Khon (70,000K, 3¼ hours) – are most comfortable and conven-

ient. Book these through any guesthouse or travel agent. All departures are in the morning around 8am.

If you want to leave later in the day, take a sŏrngtăaou from the Southern Bus Terminal (p369) to Ban Nakasang (for Don Det and Don Khon; 40,000K, 3½ hours). These depart hourly until 5pm and go via Hat Xai Khun (for Don Khong).

One sŏrngtăaou services Kiet Ngong (30,000K, two hours), leaving at 1pm.

ⓘ Getting Around

Local transport in Pakse is expensive by regional standards. Figure on about 10,000K for a short sähm-lór (three-wheels) trip (including between Talat Dao Heuang and the city centre) if you're one person – more if you're in a group or use a tuk-tuk. A ride to the Northern or Southern Bus Terminal costs 15,000K per person shared and 50,000K for a whole tuk-tuk.

Champasak   จำปาสัก

☑ 031 / POP 14,000

It's hard to imagine Champasak as a seat of royalty, but from 1713 until 1946 it was just that. These days the town is a somnolent place, the fountain circle (that no longer hosts a fountain) in the middle of the main street alluding to a grandeur long since departed, along with the former royal family. Scattered French colonial-era buildings share space with traditional Lao wooden stilt houses, and the few vehicles that venture down the narrow main street share it with chickens and cows.

With a surprisingly good range of accommodation and several attractions in the vicinity – most notably the Angkor-period ruins of Wat Phu Champasak (p370) – it's easy to see why many visitors to the region prefer staying in Champasak over bustling Pakse.

Just about everything in Champasak is spread along the riverside road, both sides of the fountain circle.

Champasak Spa (☑ 020-56499739; www.champasak-spa.com; massages 80,000-160,000K; ⊙10am-noon & 1-7pm, closed Mon May-Oct, all of Jun) ⌀ is a fragrant oasis of free tea and sensitively executed treatments using locally grown and sourced organic bio products. And it creates jobs for local residents. A full-day spa package (reservations required) comprising facial, body scrub, hair spa, massage and lunch costs 550,000K.

📖 Sleeping & Eating

★ Nakorn Guest House GUESTHOUSE $
(📱 020-98177964; r with air-con 200,000K; ❄) This new Lao–Belgian-owned spot on the river a tad south of the main drag has the cleanest rooms in town, with private balconies, beautifully tiled interiors and luxurious rain showers. Plans are in the works for a second unit of rooms overlooking a Zen garden in front of the Mekong.

Dokchampa Guesthouse GUESTHOUSE $
(📱 020-55350910; r with fan/air-con 50,000/ 200,000K; ❄ 🛜) Porches in front of all rooms, a well-placed restaurant along the river, a helpful English-speaking owner and a good mellow vibe make this one of Champasak's best choices. The fan rooms are typical, though we have no clue what they were thinking when building glass-walled bathrooms in the recently renovated air-con rooms. There are big discounts in the low season.

Nakorn Restaurant LAOTIAN, INTERNATIONAL $
(mains 20,000-53,000K; 🕐 7.30am-9.30pm; 🛜✍) A pleasant melange of classy and casual, this riverside restaurant has a small mixed menu that covers duck *láhp* to chicken green curry to tuna sandwiches. There's also plenty of local advice available from the affable owners.

Champasak with Love THAI, LAOTIAN $
(📱 030-9786757; mains 20,000-40,000K; 🕐 8am-9pm; 🛜✍) The marvellous riverfront patio shaded by a big old ficus tree is alone worth a visit, but the food and service are also good. It has the biggest menu in town, with mostly Thai food but also Lao standards and good brownies, fruit salad, sandwiches and breakfasts. The basic and slightly overpriced **guest rooms** (with fan/air-con 50,000/80,000K) in the creaky old house have shared bathrooms.

ℹ Information

Champasak District Visitor Information Centre (📱 030-9239673; 🕐 8am-4.30pm Mon-Fri, also open weekends Sep-Apr) Can arrange boats to, and accommodation on, Don Daeng. Local guides, some of whom speak English, lead day walks around Wat Phu and can accompany you to Uo Moung. You can also arrange boats to Uo Moung here (350,000K), taking in Don Daeng and Wat Muang Kang.

Lao Development Bank (🕐 8.30am-3.30pm Mon-Fri) Has an ATM, changes cash and does Western Union.

ℹ Getting There & Away

Champasak is 30km from Pakse along a beautiful, almost empty sealed road running along the west bank of the Mekong. *Sŏrngtǎaou* to Pakse (20,000K, one hour) depart only in the morning, up to around 8am. There are also the tourist buses and boats direct to/from Pakse, but they don't run often due to lack of demand.

The regular morning tourist buses from Pakse to Champasak (55,000, 1½ hours) are actually the buses heading to Si Phan Don and these drop you at Ban Muang on the eastern bank of the Mekong where a small ferry (10,000K per person, 20,000K for motorbikes) crosses to the village of Ban Phaphin just north of Champasak. Be sure you know whether your ticket includes the ferry or not. (The ferrymen won't rip you off over this, but some of the ticket agents in Pakse have been known to.) None of the tickets include the final 2km into Champasak, so you'll probably need to walk it.

To reach Si Phan Don you can also use the Ban Muang ferry route or travel by boat (US$240 private; the Champasak District Visitor Information Centre will know if others are interested in sharing the cost).

Wat Phu World Heritage Area

A visit to the ancient Khmer religious complex of Wat Phu is one of the highlights of southern Laos. Stretching 1400m up the slopes of Phu Pasak (also known more colloquially as Phu Khuai or Mt Penis), Wat Phu is small compared with the monumental Angkor-era sites near Siem Reap in Cambodia. However, you know the old adage about location, location, location! The tumbledown pavilions, ornate Shiva-lingam sanctuary, enigmatic crocodile stone and tall trees that shroud much of the upper walkway in soothing shade give Wat Phu an almost mystical atmosphere. These, and a layout that is unique in Khmer architecture, led to Unesco declaring the Wat Phu complex a World Heritage site in 2001.

An electric cart shuttles guests from the ticket office area past the *baray* (ceremonial pond; *nǎwng sá* in Lao). After that, you must walk.

◉ Sights

★ Wat Phu Champasak RUINS
(ວັດພູຈຳປາສັກ; 50,000K, motorbike parking 5000K; 🕐 site 8am-6pm, museum to 4.30pm) Bucolic Wat Phu sits in graceful decrepitude, and while it lacks the arresting enormity of Angkor in Cambodia, given its few visitors

and more dramatic natural setting, these small Khmer ruins evoke a more soulful response. While some buildings are more than 1000 years old, most date from the 11th to 13th centuries. The site is divided into six terraces on three levels joined by a frangipani-bordered stairway ascending the mountain to the main shrine at the top.

Wat Phu Exhibition Hall   MUSEUM
(ຫໍພິພິດທະພັນວັດພູ; admission with Wat Phu ticket; ⊙8am-4.30pm) The Exhibition Hall near the ticket office showcases dozens of lintels, *naga* (mythical water serpents), Buddhas and other stone work from Wat Phu and its associated sites. Detailed descriptions are in English, plus the building includes clean bathrooms.

✦ Festivals & Events

Bun Wat Phu Champasak   BUDDHIST
(Wat Phu Champasak Festival) The highlight of the year in Wat Phu Champasak is this three-day festival, held as part of Magha Puja (Makha Busa) during the full moon of the third lunar month, usually in February. The central ceremonies performed are Buddhist, culminating on the full-moon day with an early-morning parade of monks receiving alms from the faithful, followed that evening by a candlelit *wéean téean* (circumambulation) of the lower shrines.

SI PHAN DON

Si Phan Don (ສີພັນດອນ) is where Laos becomes the land of the lotus-eaters, an archipelago of islands where the pendulum of time swings slowly and postcard-worthy views are the rule rather than the exception. Many a traveller has washed ashore here, succumbed to its charms and stayed longer than expected.

Down here the Mekong bulges to a breadth of 14km – the river's widest reach along its 4350km journey from the Tibetan Plateau to the South China Sea – and if you count every islet and sandbar that emerges in the dry months the name, which literally means 'Four Thousand Islands', isn't that much of an exaggeration.

Don Khong   ດອນໂຂງ
☐ 031 / POP 60,000
Life moves slowly on Don Khong (Khong Island), like a boat being paddled against the flow on the Mekong. It's a pleasant place to spend a day or two, wandering past fishing nets drying in the sun, taking a sunset boat ride, pedalling about on a bicycle or just chilling and reading by the river.

Don Khong measures 18km long by 8km at its widest point. Most of the roughly 60,000 islanders live on the perimeter and there are only two proper towns: lethargic Muang Khong on the eastern shore and the charmless market town of Muang Saen on the west; an 8km road links the two.

Khamtay Siphandone, the postman who went on to serve as president of Laos from 1998 to 2006, was born in Ban Hua Khong at the north end of Don Khong in 1924.

🛏 Sleeping & Eating

The island has a good selection of quality accommodation, pretty much all of it in Muang Khong where the ferry boats from Hat Xai Khun land. Most places have attached restaurants.

Pon's Riverside Guesthouse   GUESTHOUSE $
(☐020-55406798; www.ponarenahotel.com; Muang Khong; r 100,000K; ❄🗢) The most popular spot in town for sleeping and eating, Pon's has pleasant lemon-hued rooms with tiled floor, cable TV and a relaxed atmosphere. There's a riverside restaurant deck across the road. Good value.

Done Khong Guesthouse   GUESTHOUSE $
(☐020-98789994; donekhong.gh@gmail.com; Muang Khong; r with fan/air-con 70,000/100,000K; ❄🗢) The first place you'll see when you get off the boat, Done Khong has dark rooms with tiled floors and homely furnishings in an old house run by an English-speaking man. Try to bag a 2nd-floor room with a river-facing balcony. The riverside restaurant, with a mostly Lao menu, is a good place to chill and the staff are a good source of island info.

Senesothxeune Hotel   HOTEL $$
(☐031-515021; www.ssx-hotel.com; Muang Khong; incl breakfast r US$50-60, ste US$90; ❄@🗢) This modern hotel a short distance from the tourist strip has comfortable rooms and a pleasant restaurant with views of the river through its blossoming garden. The pricier rooms have balconies and hardwood floors. It's been around a while, but the French–Lao owners keep it shipshape. A sparkling new pool makes the price tag easier to swallow.

Si Phan Don

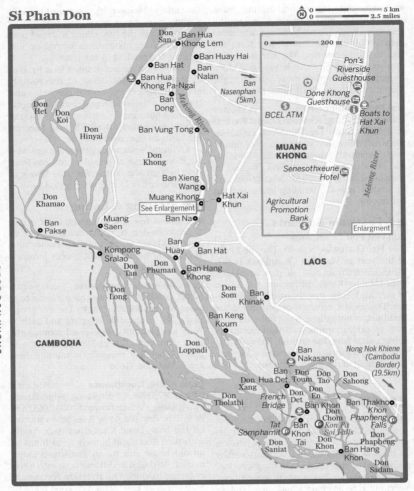

LAOS DON KHONG

ℹ️ Information

Agricultural Promotion Bank (Muang Khong; ⊘8am-3.30pm Mon-Fri) Exchanges major currencies, does Western Union and has an ATM out front.

BCEL ATM (Muang Khong) Below the Lao Telecom tower.

Don Khong Tourist Information Centre (☑029-250303; panhdonkhong25@gmail.com; Muang Khong; ⊘8am-4pm Mon-Fri) Near the boat landing, this office is run by helpful Mr Phan. There's information for the whole Si Phan Don region and he can set you up with a local guide for 60,000K per day.

ℹ️ Getting There & Away

The Don Khong boatmen's association runs a boat most days to Don Det and Don Khon (one way/return per person 40,000/60,000K) at 8.30am and departing Don Det at 3pm. It's 1½ hours downstream and two hours back. The rate rises if there are fewer than six people as there is a fixed price per boat of 250,000K. You can book this through any guesthouse.

The vast majority of travellers ride the tourist bus, which always includes getting dropped off on Rte 13 with a connecting leg to the island. Sometimes you will get dropped off at the road to the bridge and head to Muang Khong by tuk-tuk. Other times you will be dropped off at Hat

Xai Khun on the mainland (1km from the highway) and then squeezed into a small **ferry** boat. If you need the **boat** or tuk-tuk on your own, the price is 15,000K per head with a 30,000K minimum.

For leaving the island, tourist transport heading south to Don Det (70,000K) and Don Khon (80,000K including boat transfers, two hours) passes by about 10am while pickup for going north to Pakse (70,000K, two hours) is about noon.

There are also non-air-conditioned buses (50,000K, three hours) from Muang Khong to Pakse's **Southern Bus Terminal** (p369) leaving between 6am and 9.30am. They pick up passengers in Muang Khong on the way. At other times, you can go to Rte 13 and wait for the hourly Pakse–Nakasang *sŏrngtăaou*.

ⓘ Getting Around

Motorbikes (from 60,000K to 80,000K per day) that are real clunkers and newish bicycles (10,000K per day) can be hired at several places on the tourist strip in Muang Khong.

Don Det & Don Khon
ດອນເດດ/ດອນຄອນ

The vast majority of travellers to Si Phan Don end up on these twin islands. Don Det is defined by its hippyesque party scene, though it's really quite mild and there's nothing stronger than grass in the 'happy' snacks sold openly at some bars.

Of course there's much more to these two islands. Heading south from Ban Hua Det (Hua Det Village), the guesthouses thin out and the icons of rural island life – fishermen, rice farmers, weavers, buffalo, sugar palms – are on full display. Chill in a hammock, wander aimlessly around the islands or languidly drift downstream in an inner tube in the turquoise arms of the Mekong.

The serenity continues across the French bridge on Don Khon (ດອນຄອນ), but down here there are also some gorgeous waterfalls to visit, sandy beaches to lounge on, dolphins to spot and even a little patch of wilderness to explore.

⊙ Sights & Activities

These twin islands are famous for soaking up low-key village life rather than ticking off a list of attractions, but the dolphins and waterfalls on Don Khon are genuinely wonderful destinations.

When you cross the French bridge to Don Khon, you will be asked to pay a 35,000K tourism tax at the little blue shack. This is not a scam (the money helps pay for local projects) and it covers the entrance fee to Tat Somphamit. If you're sleeping on Don Khon and you want to go north, you don't need to pay it. Just check in before you cross to Don Det and hope they remember you when you return.

A pod of severely endangered Irrawaddy dolphins lives along the southern shore of Don Khon and spotting these rare creatures in the wild is a highlight of any trip to southern Laos. The population has dropped to just three as some have died and others have gone south. Though nothing in nature is guaranteed, sightings here are virtually certain.

Boats are chartered (70,000K, maximum four people) from the old French landing pier in Ban Hang Khon. Where you go depends on where the dolphins are. In the hot season they stay close to village, but when the river runs high they can travel further away. You may be able to see them from your boat, or you may need to disembark in Cambodia and walk to a spot that overlooks the conservation zone. This may require a 20,000K payment to the officials there. Try to go in the early morning or early evening to avoid the heat.

The boat trips from Bang Hang Khon can combine dolphin-watching with **Khon Phapheng Falls** (ຕາດຄອນພະເພັ້ງ; 55,000K; ⊙8am-5pm) (250,000K) or little **Nook Xume** (100,000K) waterfalls.

★ Tat Somphamit   WATERFALL
(ຕາດສົມພະມິດ, Li Phi Falls; Don Khon; 35,000K; ⊙ticket booth 8am-5pm) Located on Don Khon, 1.5km downriver from the French bridge, vast Tat Somphamit is a gorgeous set of raging rapids. Its other name, Li Phi, means 'Spirit Trap' and locals believe the falls act as just that: a trap for bad spirits as they wash down the river. Local fishermen risk their skin edging out onto rocks in the violent flow of the cascades to empty bamboo traps. Don't try this stunt yourself – travellers have died slipping off the rocks beyond the barrier.

⌁ Sleeping

The common wisdom is to stay on Don Det to party, and Don Khon to get away from it all. But this is not how things really work, as the party is confined to the northern tip of Don Det. In fact, the quietest and most isolated guesthouses in all of Si Phan Don are actually on the southern portion of Don Det.

Many places offer low-season discounts; sometimes it's automatic and sometimes you need to ask.

🛏 Don Det

★ Mekong Dream Guesthouse
GUESTHOUSE $

(✆020-55275728; Don Det; r 50,000K; ☎) At the south of Don Det, facing the strip on Don Khon, Mekong Dream is one of the homiest, best-value guesthouses on the islands. The 11 rooms, all with private bathrooms and comfortable king-size beds, are the antidote to claustrophobic rooms elsewhere (except for the three inferior concrete rooms downstairs) and share a roomy balcony/hammock lounge.

Mama Piang
GUESTHOUSE $

(✆020-58186049; sunrise side, Don Det; r 50,000K) If there is a more fun and friendly host in Si Phan Don than Mama Piang – who proudly calls herself 'crazy' – we didn't meet her. There are six cold-water fan rooms across the road from her riverfront **restaurant**. She's rightfully pretty proud of her cooking.

Crazy Gecko
GUESTHOUSE $

(✆020-97193565; www.crazygecko.ch; sunrise side, Don Det; r 80,000K-170,000K; ☎) In a stilted structure made of solid wood, Crazy Gecko's three tidy rooms surround a balcony that's equal parts funky and functional. Festooned with hammocks and random decoration, it's a superior place to relax (if a bit overpriced). There's a pool table and board games down below and across the road is a recommended **restaurant** on a deck over the water.

★ Baba Guesthouse
GUESTHOUSE $$

(✆020-98893943; www.dondet.net; sunrise side, Ban Hua Det; r 350,000K; ❄☎) This beautiful guesthouse looks out on the Mekong on one side, and emerald paddy fields on the other. The price is well above average for this area, but you really do get more for your money here. Rooms are sleekly white and almost luxurious, with private balcony, tasteful decor, mosquito net and spotless bathroom.

🛏 Don Khon

Souksan Guesthouse
GUESTHOUSE $

(✆020-22337722; Don Khon; r with fan/air-con 50,000/100,000K; ☎) Souksan has so-so rooms set in a bungalow block with a great

shared river-view terrace. Next door is the restaurant with cushion seating right over the water. Bathrooms have only cold water. Mr Souksan's barbecue boat tours are popular and fun.

★ Pomelo Guesthouse
GUESTHOUSE $$

(✆020-97925893; Don Khon; r US$25; ☎) Run by a Thai chef and his Swiss girlfriend, this new guesthouse boasts a stunning location over the river in Ban Hang Khon. The two spacious rooms sit in a traditional stilt home with mosquito nets, rain showers and sweeping views. Read under the shade of the pomelo tree, daydream on the private swimming platforms or set off in the free kayak.

★ Sala Done Khone
BOUTIQUE HOTEL $$

(✆031-260940; www.salalaoboutique.com; Don Khon; r incl breakfast US$60-80; ❄❋❄❄) 🅿 Five hotels in one, Sala Done Khone has both the classiest and the most original rooms in Si Phan Don. Its signature unit, the French Residence, is a renovated 1896 timber trading headquarters with tiled floors and louvred blinds, while out on the river the Sala Phae wing features floating cottages with bio-safe toilets and private decks.

🍴 Eating & Drinking

★ Chez Fred et Lea
INTERNATIONAL, LAOTIAN $

(✆020-22128882; Don Khon; mains 20,000-50,000K; ⊙7am-10pm; ☎) This new cafe and 'salon de thé' serves organic coffees and teas, as well as top-quality Lao and Western cuisine that you won't find elsewhere on island. There are no river views, but the Lao–French couple who runs the place makes up for it with sleek hardwood floors, inviting tunes and the freshest of ingredients.

★ Garden
LAOTIAN, THAI $

(Don Khon; mains 20,000-65,000K; ⊙7am-10pm; 🖊) Taking freshness seriously, this thatched-roof, open-kitchen restaurant is a good place for the uninitiated to sample Laotian foods, such as spicy papaya salad and grilled Mekong River fish. It also serves all the usual traveller comfort foods and the cook's personal version of lemon-grass chicken.

Street View Restaurant
PIZZA $$

(✆020-98779177; sunrise side, Don Det; mains from 25,000-65,000K; ⊙8am-11pm; ☎) This attractive wooden riverside haunt has decks for chilling on; a long, well-stocked bar; and a good reputation. Tuck into mouth-water ing wood-fired pizza, barbecued chicken, Mekong fish, pork chops, burgers, salads and healthy breakfasts. Prices are higher than average, but worth it.

4000 Island Bar BAR
(☎ 020-96476088; sunrise side, Ban Hua Det; ⏰ 7am-11pm; 🛜) Good Western and Indian food, cold drinks, friendly service and a soothing vibe combine to make this a perennial favourite among travellers. You can make new friends around the pool table, throw some darts, play your favourite tunes or just kick back, relax and enjoy the view.

ℹ Information

There are no banks on the islands, though an increasing number of businesses accept plastic. Cash can be exchanged, at generally poor rates, at most guesthouses and some, including **Baba** on Don Det, do cash advances on credit cards for a 6% commission. There's an Agricultural Promotion Bank and a BCEL with ATMs on the main drag in Ban Nakasang. Kayaking tours budget enough time at the end of the trip for people to make an ATM stop.

ℹ Getting There & Away

Boat prices between Ban Nakasang and the islands are fixed by a local boat association, and there are very few running each day on a shared basis. Expect to pay 15,000K per person (or 30,000K if travelling on your own) to Don Det, and 20,000K per person (or 60,000K if travelling alone) to Don Khon.

For Pakse, most travellers book tickets on the island, which includes the local boat and a noon bus or minibus (60,000K, three hours). If you want to leave at another time there are *sŏrngtǎaou* from Ban Nakasang to the Southern Bus Terminal in Pakse (40,000K, 3½ hours) every hour until noon. One shared boat always leaves the islands in time for the 8am *sŏrngtǎaou*. These all stop in Hat Xai Khun (for Don Khong).

River travel to Don Khong (500,000K) and Champasak (US$200) is only available by chartered boat, but very often there are other people willing to join together to share the cost.

ℹ Getting Around

With virtually no traffic and only a few small hills, Don Det and Don Khon are ideally explored by bicycle (hired from just about any guesthouse for 10,000K per day) though they are small enough that everything is also walkable.

There are some *sǎhm-lór* available in Ban Hua Det and Ban Khon. It's 100,000K for a trip from Ban Hua Det to see the dolphins and Tat Somphamit, including sufficient waiting time, and 70,000K just to travel between Ban Hua Det and Ban Khon.

ℹ GETTING TO CAMBODIA: NONG NOK KHIENE TO TRAPAENG KRIEL

Getting to the border The Nong Nok Khiene (Laos)/Trapaeng Kriel (Cambodia) border (open 6am to 6pm) is a popular route for backpackers on the Indochina overland circuit, and it is always a real hassle. The Cambodian company Sorya Transport runs the Pakse–Phnom Penh route from the Southern Bus Terminal (7.30am, 220,000K) and is the best choice. Sengchalern bus company provides daily service from Pakse to Phnom Penh (230,000K, 12 to 14 hours) via Stung Treng (120,000K, six hours) and Kratie (160,000K, nine hours). Sengchalern also sells tickets to Siem Reap (280,000K), but this extra long trip is not recommended. Better to use reliable Asia Van Transfer, which departs from the border at 11.30am and takes the new northern route to Siem Reap (US$20) arriving at about 7pm.

At the border Both Lao and Cambodian visas are available on arrival, while bribes, scams and rudeness are a mandatory part of the process. In Laos, you'll pay a US$2 (or the equivalent in kip or baht) 'overtime' or 'processing' fee, depending on when you cross, upon both entry and exit. In Cambodia, they jack up the price of a visa to US$35 from the actual US$30.

Moving on Aside from the buses mentioned here, there's virtually zero traffic here. If you're dropped at the border, expect to pay about US$45 for a private taxi heading south to Stung Treng, or 150,000/60,000K for a taxi/sǎhm-lór (three-wheels) heading north to Ban Nakasang.

For information on making this border crossing in reverse see p139.

UNDERSTAND LAOS

Laos Today

Laos sits on one of the world's major geo-political crossroads, where Southeast Asia meets China, and this is a huge challenge for such a small country. Hemmed in by the Asian tigers of China, Vietnam and Thailand, Laos often looks like vulnerable prey. Traditionally, Vietnam has held political sway, China wields financial clout and Thailand has a dominant cultural influence. While the government tries to parry these competing influences, the Lao people are ever more plugged into a global world and this contributes to domestic tension.

History

The Kingdom of Lan Xang

Before the French, British, Chinese and Siamese drew a line around it, Laos was a collection of disparate principalities subject to an ever-revolving cycle of war, invasion, prosperity and decay. Laos' earliest brush with nationhood was in the 14th century, when Khmer-backed Lao warlord Fa Ngum conquered Wieng Chan (Vientiane). It was Fa Ngum who gave his kingdom the title still favoured by travel romantics and businesses – Lan Xang, or (Land of a) Million Elephants. He also made Theravada Buddhism the state religion and adopted the symbol of Lao sovereignty that remains in use today, the Pha Bang Buddha image, after which Luang Prabang is named. Lan Xang reached its peak in the 17th century, when it was the dominant force in Southeast Asia.

French Rule

By the 18th century the nation had crumbled, falling under the control of the Siamese, who coveted much of modern-day Laos as a buffer zone against the expansionist French. It was to no effect. Soon after taking over Annam and Tonkin (modern-day Vietnam), the French negotiated with Siam to relinquish its territory east of the Mekong, and Laos was born. The first nationalist movement, the Lao Issara (Free Lao), was created to prevent the country's return to French rule after the invading Japanese left at the end of WWII. In 1953, without any regard for the Lao Issara, sovereignty was granted to Laos by the French. Internecine struggles followed with the Pathet Lao (Country of the Lao) Army forming an alliance with the Vietnamese Viet Minh (which opposed French rule in their own country). Laos was set to become a chessboard on which the clash of communist ambition and US anxiety over the perceived Southeast Asian 'domino effect' played itself out.

The Secret War

In 1954 at the Geneva Conference, Laos was declared a neutral nation – as such neither Vietnamese nor US forces could cross its borders. Thus began a game of cat and mouse as a multitude of CIA operatives secretly entered the country to train anticommunist Hmong fighters in the jungle. From 1964 to 1973 the US, in response to the Viet Minh funnelling massive amounts of war munitions down the Ho Chi Minh Trail, devastated eastern and northeastern Laos with nonstop carpet-bombing (reportedly a planeload of ordnance dropped every eight minutes). The intensive campaign exacerbated the war between the Pathet Lao and the Royal Lao armies and, if anything, increased domestic support for the communists. The US withdrawal in 1973 saw Laos divided up between Pathet Lao and non-Pathet Lao, but within two years the communists had taken over and the Lao People's Democratic Republic (PDR) was created under the leadership of Kaysone Phomvihane. Around 10% of Laos' population fled, mostly to Thailand. The remaining opponents of the government – notably tribes of Hmong (highland dwellers) who had fought with and been funded by the CIA – were suppressed, often brutally, or sent to re-education camps for indeterminate periods.

A New Beginning

Laos entered the political family of Southeast Asian countries known as Asean in 1997, two years after Vietnam. Politically, the Party remains firmly in control. And with neighbours like one-party China and Vietnam, there seems little incentive for Laos to move towards any meaningful form of democracy. While still heavily reliant on foreign aid (some 8.5% of its GDP), Laos has committed to income-generating projects in recent years in a bid to increase its prosperity. The year 2012 saw the international press starting to ask questions over the disappearance of Sombath Somphone, an award-winning civil-society activist and land-rights campaigner, with fingers directly pointed at the Lao government as the main culprit. In 2015, in an effort to counterbalance China's growing influence over the region, President Obama met with the Laos premier in New York.

People & Culture

National Psyche

Laos is a patchwork of different beliefs, ranging from animism to the prevailing presence of Thervada Bhuddism – and often both combined. But, certainly, there's a commonality in the laid-back attitude you'll encounter. Some of this can be ascribed to Buddhism, with its emphasis on controlling extreme emotions by keeping *jai yen* (cool heart), making merit and doing good in order to receive good. You'll rarely hear a heated argument, and can expect a level of kindness seldom experienced in neighbouring countries.

Etiquette

Touching another person's head is taboo, as is pointing your feet at another person or at a buddha image. Strong displays of emotion are also discouraged. The traditional greeting gesture is the *nop* or *wâi*, a prayerlike placing together of the palms in front of the face or chest, although in urban areas the handshake is becoming more commonplace. For all temple visits, dress conservatively.

Population

Laos has one of the lowest population densities in Asia, but the number of people has more than doubled in the last 30 years, and continues to grow quickly. One-third of the country's seven million inhabitants live in cities in the Mekong River valley, chiefly Vientiane, Luang Prabang, Savannakhet and Pakse. Another one-third live along other major rivers. This rapid population growth comes despite the fact that about 10% of the population fled the country after the 1975 communist takeover. Vientiane and Luang Prabang lost the most inhabitants, with approximately a quarter of the population of Luang Prabang going abroad. During the last couple of decades this emigration trend has been reversed so that the influx of immigrants (mostly repatriated Lao, but also Chinese, Vietnamese and other nationalities) now exceeds the number of émigrés.

Religion

Most lowland Lao are Theravada Buddhists and many Lao males choose to be ordained temporarily as monks, typically spending anywhere from a month to three years at a wat (temple). After the 1975 communist victory, Buddhism was suppressed, but by 1992 the government had relented and it was back in full swing, with a few alterations. Monks are still forbidden to promote *phî* (spirit) worship, which has been officially banned in Laos along with *săiyasàht* (folk magic). Despite the ban, *phî* worship remains the dominant non-Buddhist belief system. Even in Vientiane, Lao citizens openly perform the ceremony called *sukhwăn* or *bạsî*, in which the 32 *kwăn* (guardian spirits of the body) are bound to the guest of honour by white strings tied around the wrists (you'll see many Lao people wearing these). Outside the Mekong River valley, the phî cult is particularly strong among tribal Thai, especially among the Thai Dam. The Khamu and Hmong-Mien tribes also practise animism.

Arts

The true expression of Lao art is found in its religious sculpture, temples, handicrafts and architecture. Distinctively Lao is the Calling for Rain Buddha, a standing image with hands held rigidly at his sides. Wat in Luang Prabang feature *sĭm* (chapels), with steep, low roofs. The typical Lao *tâht* (stupa) is a four-sided, curvilinear, spirelike structure. Upland crafts include gold- and silversmithing among the Hmong and Mien tribes, and tribal Thai weaving (especially among the Thai Dam and Thai Lü). Classical music and dance have all but evaporated, partly due to the vapid tentacles of Thai pop and the itinerant nature of Laos' young workforce.

Food & Drink

Food

The standard Lao breakfast is *fĕr* (rice noodles), usually served in a broth with vegetables and meat of your choice. *Lahp* is the most distinctively Lao dish, a delicious spicy salad made from minced beef, pork,

LAOS PEOPLE & CULTURE

duck, fish or chicken, mixed with fish sauce, small shallots, mint leaves, lime juice, roasted ground rice and lots and lots of chillies. In lowland Laos almost every dish is eaten with *khào nǐaw* (sticky rice), which is served in a small basket. Take a small amount of rice and, using one hand, work it into a walnut-sized ball before dipping it into the food.

Drink

Beerlao remains a firm favourite with 90% of the nation, and, although officially illegal, *lào-láo* (Lao liquor, or rice whisky) is a popular drink among lowland Lao. It's usually taken neat and offered in villages as a welcoming gesture. Water purified for drinking purposes is simply called *nâm deum* (drinking water), whether it's boiled or filtered. All water offered to customers in restaurants or hotels will be purified, and purified water is sold everywhere. Juice bars and cafes proliferate in cities. Lao coffee is usually served strong and sweet.

Environment

The Land

With a landmass of 236,800 sq km, Laos is a little larger than the UK and, thanks to its relatively small population and mountainous terrain, is one of the least altered environments in Southeast Asia. Unmanaged vegetation covers an estimated 85% of the country, and a dwindling 10% of Laos is original-growth forest. A hundred years ago this last statistic was nearer 75%, which provides a clear idea of the detrimental effects of relentless logging and slash-and-burn farming. In 1993 the government set up 18 National Protected Areas (NPAs) comprising a total of 24,600 sq km, just over 10% of the land. An additional two were added in 1995 (taking the total coverage to 14% of Laos). Despite these conservation efforts, illegal timber felling and the smuggling of exotic wildlife are still significant threats to Laos' natural resources. The WWF claims that in 2014 China imported US$1 billion worth of timber from Laos, up from US$45 million in 2008.

Wildlife

Laos is home to Asian elephants, jackals, Asiatic black bears, black-crested gibbons, langurs, clouded leopards, pythons, king cobras, 437 kinds of bird and the rare Irrawaddy dolphin. Tigers are all but extinct. The illegal wildlife trade is flourishing, driven by neighbours – particularly China – who seek body parts of endangered animals for traditional medicine and aphrodisiac purposes. Almost two-thirds of Lao people live in rural areas and rely on wildlife as a source of protein to supplement their diet.

SURVIVAL GUIDE

❶ Directory A–Z

ACCOMMODATION

It's worth booking in advance in popular destinations like Luang Prabang and Vientiane during peak-season months of November to February and around Lao New Year in April.

Guesthouses There are a good range of guesthouses around the country from the budget to the boutique.

Homestays A homestay is a great option for immersing yourself in the Lao way of life and there is an increasing number of homestay options all over the country, particularly in or near National Protected Areas (NPAs).

Hostels There aren't a whole lot of hostels in upcountry Laos, but there are plenty of options in popular places like Vientiane, Vang Vieng and Luang Prabang.

Hotels Laos has a good range of hotels these days, including everything from cheap business pads to luxury heritage hotels.

ACTIVITIES

Cycling

Laos is slowly but steadily establishing itself as a cycling destination. For hard-core cyclists, the mountains of northern Laos are the ultimate destination. For those who like a gentler workout, meandering along Mekong villages is memorable, particularly in southern Laos around Si Phan Don.

In most places that see a decent number of tourists, simple single-speed bicycles can be hired for around 20,000K per day. Better mountain bikes will cost from 40,000K to 80,000K per day or US$5 to US$10. Serious tourers should bring their own bicycle. The choice in Laos is fairly limited compared with neighbouring Thailand or Cambodia.

Several tour agencies and guesthouses offer mountain-biking tours, ranging in duration from a few hours to several weeks.

Kayaking & Rafting

With the Mekong cutting a swathe through the heart of the country, it is hardly surprising to find that boat trips are a major drawcard here. There are also opportunities to explore small jungled tributaries leading to remote minority villages.

Kayaking has exploded in popularity in Laos in the past few years, particularly around Luang Prabang, Nong Khiaw and Vang Vieng, all popular destinations for a spot of paddling. Kayaking trips start from around US$25 per person and are often combined with cycling.

Tubing down the river has long been a popular activity in Vang Vieng and is now a more sedate affair with the clampdown on riverside bars, rope swings and aerial runways. Tubing is a lot of fun, but it's a safer experience sober.

Rock Climbing & Caving

When it comes to organised climbing, Vang Vieng and Tha Khaek have some of the best climbing in Southeast Asia, along with excellent instructors and safe equipment. Climbing costs from about US$25 per person for a group of four and rises for more specialised climbs or for instruction.

Real caving of the spelunker variety is not really on offer unless undertaking a professional expedition. However, there are many extensive cave systems that are open to visitors.

Trekking

Trekking in Laos is all about exploring the National Protected Areas (NPAs) and visiting the colourful ethnic-minority villages, many of which host overnight trekking groups. Anything is possible, from half-day hikes to weeklong expeditions that include cycling and kayaking. Most treks have both a cultural and an environmental focus, with trekkers sleeping in village homestays and money going directly to some of the poorest communities in the country. There are now a dozen or more areas you can choose from. Less strenuous walks include jungle hikes to pristine waterfalls and village walks in remote areas. The scenery is often breathtaking, featuring plunging highland valleys, tiers of rice paddies and soaring limestone mountains.

Treks are mostly run by small local tour operators and have English-speaking guides. Prices, including all food, guides, transport, accommodation and park fees, start at about US$25 per person per day for larger groups. For more specialised long treks into remote areas, prices can run into several hundred dollars. In most cases you can trek with as few as two people, with per-person costs falling with larger groups.

Ziplining

Ziplining has, well, quite literally taken off in Laos. The **Gibbon Experience** (p357) in Nam Kan NPA pioneered the use of ziplines to glide through the forest where the gibbons roam. Now, chords are going up at an astounding pace in forests across the country.

Ecotourism pioneer **Green Discovery** (p366) offers an alternative zipline experience for thrill-seekers in southern Laos. Its Tree Top Explorer tour is an exciting network of vertiginous ziplines passing over the semi-evergreen canopy of the south's Dong Hua Sao NPA. Ride so close to a giant waterfall you can taste the spray on your lips.

Vang Vieng, Nong Khiaw and Udomxai have all emerged recently as the latest zipline centres with several companies offering aerial adventures through jaw-dropping mountainous terrain.

BOOKS

The Coroner's Lunch (Colin Cotterill; 2004) Delve into the delightful world of Dr Siri, full-time national coroner in the 1970s and part-time supersleuth. The first installment in a 12-part Siri series.

Ant Egg Soup (Natacha Du Pont de Bie; 2004) Subtitled *The Adventures of a Food Tourist in Laos,* the author samples some local delicacies (including some that aren't suitable for a delicate stomach).

One Foot in Laos (Dervla Murphy; 1999) Renowned Irish travel writer explores Laos back in the early days of the 1990s and discovers a country undergoing profound change.

A Great Place to Have a War (Joshua Kurlantzick; 2017) A fresh look at America's 'secret war' in Laos, why it transformed the nation and how it emboldened a fledgling CIA.

CUSTOMS REGULATIONS

Customs inspections at ports of entry are lax, as long as you're not bringing in more than a moderate amount of luggage. You're not supposed to enter the country with more than 500 cigarettes or 1L of distilled spirits. All the usual prohibitions on drugs, weapons and pornography apply.

EMBASSIES & CONSULATES

There are about 25 embassies and consulates in Vientiane. Many nationalities are served by their embassies in Bangkok (eg New Zealand and The Netherlands), Hanoi (eg Ireland) or Beijing.

Australian Embassy (Map p323; ☑ 021-353800; www.laos.embassy.gov.au; Th Tha

LAOS DIRECTORY A–Z

Deua, Ban Wat Nak, Vientiane; ⊙8.30am-5pm Mon-Fri) Also represents nationals of Canada.

Cambodian Embassy (Map p323; ☑021-314952; Th Tha Deua, Km 3, Ban That Khao, Vientiane; ⊙8.30-11.30am & 2.30-5pm Mon-Fri) Issues visas for US\$30.

Chinese Embassy (Map p323; ☑021-315105; http://la.china-embassy.org/eng; Th Wat Nak Nyai, Ban Wat Nak, Vientiane; ⊙8-11.30am Mon-Fri) Issues visas in four working days (less for a fee). Some travellers report sudden and unannounced 'changes in policy' preventing them from applying for visas.

French Embassy (Map p324; ☑021-267400; www.ambafrance-laos.org; Th Setthathirath, Ban Si Saket, Vientiane; ⊙9am-12.30pm & 2-5.30pm Mon-Fri)

German Embassy (Map p323; ☑021-312110; www.vientiane.diplo.de; Th Sok Pa Luang, Vientiane; ⊙9am-noon Mon-Thu)

Myanmar Embassy (Map p323; ☑021-314910; Th Sok Pa Luang, Vientiane; ⊙8.30am-noon Mon-Fri) Issues tourist visas in three working days for US\$40, but can turn a visa around the same day on request if you already have a ticket to travel.

Thai Embassy (Map p323; ☑021-453916; www.thaiembassy.org/vientiane; Th Kaysone Phomvihane, Vientiane; ⊙8.30am-noon & 1-4pm Mon-Fri) For visa renewals and extensions, head to the consulates in **Vientiane** (Map p323; ☑021-415335; 15 Th Bourichane, Vientiane; ⊙8.30-11.30am & 1.30-4pm) or **Savannakhet** (☑041-212373; Rte 9 West, Savannakhet; ⊙8.30am-4.30pm Mon-Fri), which issue tourist and non-immigrant visas (1000B).

UK Embassy (Map p323; ☑030-7700000; www.gov.uk; Th Yokkabat; ⊙8.30-11.30am Mon-Fri)

US Embassy (☑021-487000; https://la.usembassy.gov; Th Tha Deua, Ban Somvang Thai, Km 9, Hatsayfong District, Vientiane; ⊙7.30am-4pm Mon-Fri) Based in a new building to the south of the city.

Vietnamese Embassy (Map p323; ☑021-451990; www.mofa.gov.vn/vnemb.la; Th 23 Singha, Vientiane; ⊙8.30-11.30am & 1.30-5pm Mon-Fri) Issues tourist visas in three working days for US\$55, or in one day for US\$65. The **Luang Prabang consulate** (www.vietnam-consulate-luangprabang.org; Th Phothisarat; ⊙8-11.30am & 1.30-5pm Mon-Fri) issues tourist visas for US\$50 in 24 hours or US\$40 if you wait three days. At the consulates in **Pakse** (☑031-252947; https://vnconsulate-pakse.mofa.gov.vn; Th 21; ⊙7.30-11.30am & 2-4.30pm Mon-Fri) and **Savannakhet** (☑041-212418; Th Sisavangvong, Savannakhet), visas cost US\$60.

LEGAL MATTERS

Although Laos guarantees certain rights, the reality is that you can be fined, detained or deported for any reason, as has been demonstrated repeatedly in cases involving foreigners.

If you stay away from anything you know to be illegal, you should be fine. If not, things might get messy and expensive. Drug possession and using prostitutes are the most common crimes for which travellers are caught, often with the dealer or consort being the one to inform the authorities. Sexual relationships between foreigners and Lao citizens who are not married are illegal; penalties for failing to register a relationship range from fines of US\$500 to US\$5000, and possibly imprisonment or deportation.

If you are detained, ask to call your embassy or consulate in Laos, if there is one. A meeting or phone call between Lao officers and someone from your embassy/consulate may result in quicker adjudication and release.

Police sometimes ask for bribes for traffic violations and other petty offences.

LGBT TRAVELLERS

For the most part Lao culture is pretty tolerant of homosexuality, although lesbianism is often either denied completely or misunderstood. In any case, public displays of affection, whether heterosexual or homosexual, are frowned upon.

Use these helpful resources to find the latest on Laos' gay scene:

Sticky Rice (www.stickyrice.ws) Gay travel guide covering Laos and Asia.

Utopia (www.utopia-asia.com) Gay travel information and contacts, including some local gay terminology.

MAPS

The best all-purpose country map that's generally available is GT-Rider.com's *Laos*, which has a scale of 1:1,650,000. It's available at bookshops in Thailand and at many guesthouses in Laos, as well as online at www.gt-rider.com.

MEDIA

Vientiane Times (www.vientianetimes.org.la) The country's only English-language newspaper follows the party line. Published Monday to Saturday.

FOOD

Virtually all restaurants in Laos are inexpensive by international standards. The following price ranges refer to a main course.

\$ less than US\$5 (40,000K)

\$\$ US\$5–15 (40,000–120,000K)

\$\$\$ more than US\$15 (120,0000K)

Le Rénovateur (www.lerenovateur.la) A government mouthpiece in French; similar to the *Vientiane Times*.

Lao National Radio (LNR; www.lnr.org.la) Broadcasts sanitised English-language news twice daily.

Radio Short-wave radios can pick up BBC, VOA, Radio Australia and Radio France International.

TV Lao National TV is so limited that most people watch Thai TV and/or karaoke videos.

MONEY

The official national currency in Laos is the Lao kip (K). Although only kip is legally negotiable in everyday transactions, in reality three currencies are used for commerce: kip, Thai baht (B) and US dollars (US$).

ATMs

ATMs are now found all over Laos. But before you get too excited, ATMs dispense a maximum of 700,000K to 2,000,000K (about US$85 to US$250) per transaction, depending on the bank, not to mention a variable withdrawal fee. If you also have to pay extortionate charges to your home bank on each overseas withdrawal, this can quickly add up.

Tipping & Bargaining

Tipping is not customary in Laos except in tourist-oriented restaurants, where 10% of the bill is appreciated, but only if a service charge hasn't already been added.

Bargaining in most places in Laos is not nearly as tough as in other parts of Southeast Asia. Lao-style bargaining is generally a friendly transaction where two people try to agree on a price that is fair to both of them. Good bargaining, which takes practice, is one way to cut costs.

Exchanging Money

Licensed moneychangers maintain booths around Vientiane (including at Talat Sao) and at some border crossings. Their rates are similar to the banks, but they stay open longer. There's no real black market in Laos and unless there's an economic crash that's unlikely to change.

OPENING HOURS

Bars & Clubs 5pm to 11.30pm (later in Vientiane)

Government Offices 8am to noon and 1pm to 5pm Monday to Friday

Noodle Shops 7am to 1pm

Restaurants 10am to 10pm

Shops 9am to 6pm

PUBLIC HOLIDAYS

Schools and government offices are closed on the following official holidays, and the organs of state move pretty slowly, if at all, during festivals.

International New Year 1 January

Army Day 20 January

International Women's Day 8 March

Lao New Year 14–16 April

International Labour Day 1 May

International Children's Day 1 June

Lao National Day 2 December

SAFE TRAVEL

Over the last couple of decades Laos has earned a reputation among visitors as a remarkably safe place to travel, with little crime reported and few of the scams often found in more touristed places such as Vietnam, Thailand and Cambodia. And while the vast majority of Laotians remain honest and welcoming, things aren't quite as idyllic as they once were. The main change has been in the rise of petty crimes, such as theft and low-level scams, which are more annoying than dangerous.

Large areas of eastern and southern Laos are contaminated by unexploded ordnance (UXO).

TELEPHONE

With a local SIM card and a 3G or wi-fi connection, the cheapest option is to use internet-based messaging and call apps via a mobile device. Topping up a phone for as little as 50,000K can give you enough data to last a month.

International calls can be made from Lao Telecom offices or the local post office in most provincial capitals and are charged on a per-minute basis, with a minimum charge of three minutes. Calls to most countries cost about 2000K to 4000K per minute. Office hours typically run from about 7.30am to 9.30pm.

The country code for calling Laos is 856. For long-distance calls within the country, dial 0 first, then the area code and number. For international calls dial 00 first, then the country code, area code and number.

All mobile phones have a 020 code at the beginning of the number. Similar to this are WIN satellite phones, which begin with 030.

TOURIST INFORMATION

The Department of Tourism Marketing, part of the Ministry of Information, Culture and Tourism (MICT), has tourist offices all over Laos, with the ones in Vientiane and Luang Prabang particularly helpful.

The MICT also runs three very good websites that offer valuable pre-departure information:

Central Laos Trekking (www.trekkingcentral-laos.com)

Ecotourism Laos (www.ecotourismlaos.com)

Ministry of Information, Culture and Tourism (www.tourismlaos.org)

TRAVELLERS WITH DISABILITIES

With its lack of paved roads or footpaths (sidewalks), Laos presents many physical obstacles for people with mobility impairments. Rarely do public buildings feature ramps or other access points for wheelchairs, nor do most hotels make efforts to provide access for the physically disabled, the few exceptions being at the top end in Vientiane and Luang Prabang. Most sights have no disabled access. Public transport is particularly crowded and difficult, even for the fully ambulatory.

VISAS

Thirty-day tourist visas are readily available on arrival at international airports and most land borders.

VOLUNTEERING

Volunteers have been working in Laos for years, usually on one- or two-year contracts that include a minimal monthly allowance. Volunteers are often placed with a government agency and attempt to 'build capacity'. These sort of jobs can lead to non-volunteer work within the non-government organisation (NGO) community.

WOMEN TRAVELLERS

Laos is an easy country for women travellers, although it is necessary to be more culturally aware or sensitive than in many parts of neighbouring Thailand. Laos is very safe and violence against women travellers is extremely rare.

WORK

With a large number of aid organisations and a fast-growing international business community, especially in energy and mining, the number of jobs available to foreigners is increasing, but still relatively small. The greatest number of positions are in Vientiane. Possibilities include teaching English privately or at one of the handful of language centres in Vientiane. Certificates or degrees in English teaching aren't absolutely necessary, but they do help.

ⓘ Getting There & Away

AIR

There are four international airports in Laos: **Wattay International Airport** (VTE; ☑ 021-512165; www.vientianeairport.com) in Vientiane, **Luang Prabang International Airport** (LPQ; ☑ 071-212173; www.luangprabangairport. com; 🛜), **Savannakhet International Airport** (☑ 041-212140; Th Kaysone Phomvihane) and **Pakse International Airport** (Rte 13).

Air Asia (www.airasia.com) Flights from Vientiane to Bangkok daily and Kuala Lumpur three times per week, plus Luang Prabang to Bangkok and Kuala Lumpur.

Bangkok Airways (www.bangkokair.com) Daily flights between Bangkok and Vientiane and Luang Prabang.

China Eastern Airlines (www.ce-air.com) Flies daily to Kunming and Nanning from Vientiane, plus Luang Prabang to Kunming three times per week.

Jin Air (www.jinair.com) Daily connections between Vientiane and Seoul.

Lao Airlines (www.laoairlines.com) National carrier. The extensive international flight network includes Vientiane to Bangkok, Busan, Changsha, Changzhou, Guangzhou, Hanoi, Kunming and Seoul; Luang Prabang to Bangkok, Chengdu, Chiang Mai, Hanoi and Jinghong; Pakse to Ho Chi Minh City and Siem Reap; and Savannakhet to Bangkok.

Thai Airways (www.thaiairways.com) Vientiane to Bangkok daily.

Vietnam Airlines (www.vietnamairlines.com) Connects Vientiane with Hanoi and Phnom Penh, plus Luang Prabang with Hanoi and Siem Reap.

LAND

Laos shares land and/or river borders with Thailand, Myanmar (Burma), Cambodia, China and Vietnam. Border-crossing details change regularly, so ask around and check the Thorn Tree (lonelyplanet.com/thorntree) before setting off.

It's possible to bring a car or motorcycle into Laos from Cambodia and Thailand with the right paperwork and Lao customs don't object to visitors bringing bicycles into the country, but it is not currently possible from Vietnam, China or Myanmar.

ⓘ Getting Around

AIR

Domestic flights to smaller airports suffer fairly frequent cancellations due to fog and, in March, heavy smoke during the slash-and-burn season. During the holiday season it's best to book ahead as flights can fill fast. At other times, when flights are more likely to be cancelled, confirm the flight is still departing a day or two before.

Lao Airlines (www.laoairlines.com) The main airline in Laos handling domestic flights, including between Vientiane and Luang Prabang, Luang Nam Tha, Pakse, Phonsavan, Savannakhet and Udomxai.

Lao Skyway (www.laoskyway.com) A newer domestic airline with flights from Vientiane to Udomxai, Luang Prabang, Huay Xai, Phonsavan and Luang Namtha.

BICYCLE

The stunningly beautiful roads and light, relatively slow traffic in most towns and on most highways make Laos arguably the best country for cycling in Southeast Asia.

Simple single-speed bicycles can be hired in most places that see a decent number of tourists, usually costing about 20,000K per day. Better mountain bikes will cost from 30,000K to 80,000K per day.

BOAT

More than 4600km of navigable rivers are the highways and byways of traditional Laos, the main thoroughfares being the Mekong, Nam Ou, Nam Khan, Nam Tha, Nam Ngum and Se Kong. The Mekong is the longest and most important route and is navigable year-round between Luang Prabang in the north and Savannakhet in the south, though new dams make this increasingly difficult. Smaller rivers accommodate a range of smaller boats, from dugout canoes to 'bomb boats' made from war detritus.

Whether it's on a tourist boat from Huay Xai to Luang Prabang or on a local boat you've rustled up in some remote corner of the country, it's still worth doing at least one river excursion while in Laos.

The slowboat between Huay Xai and Luang Prabang is the most popular river trip in Laos. It is still a daily event and relatively cheap at about 250,000K or US$30 per person for the two-day journey. From Huay Xai, these basic boats are often packed, while travelling in the other direction from Luang Prabang there seems to be more room. Passengers sit, eat and sleep on the wooden decks. The toilet (if there is one) is an enclosed hole in the deck at the back of the boat.

For shorter river trips, such as Luang Prabang to the Pak Ou Caves, it's usually best to hire a river taxi. The *héua hǎng nyáo* (longtail boats) are the most common and cost around US$10 an hour.

Along the upper Mekong River between Huay Xai and Vientiane, Thai-built *héua wái* (speedboats) are common. They can cover a distance in six hours that might take a ferry two days or more. Charters cost at least US$30 per hour, but some ply regular routes so the cost can be shared among passengers. They are, however, rather dangerous and we recommend taking one only if absolutely necessary.

BUS, SŎRNGTĂAOU, JUMBO, SĂHM-LÓR, SAKAI-LÀEP & TUK-TUK

The various pick-ups and three-wheeled taxis found in Vientiane and provincial capitals have different names depending on where you are.

Largest are the *sŏrngtăaou,* which double as buses in some areas and as local buses around bigger towns. Larger three-wheelers are called *jąmbǫh* (jumbo) and can hold four to six passengers on two facing seats. In Vientiane they are sometimes called tuk-tuks as in Thailand (though traditionally in Laos this refers to a slightly larger vehicle than the jumbo). These three-wheeled conveyances are also labelled simply *taak-see* (taxi) or, usually for motorcycle sidecar-style vehicles, *săhm-lór* (three-wheels). The old-style bicycle *săhm-lór* (pedicab), known as a *cyclo* elsewhere in Indochina, is an endangered species in Laos.

CAR & MOTORCYCLE

Driving in Laos is easier than it looks. Sure, the road infrastructure is pretty basic, but outside of the large centres there are so few vehicles that it's a doddle compared to Vietnam, China or Thailand.

Motorcyclists planning to ride through Laos should check out the wealth of information at Golden Triangle Rider (www.gt-rider.com). Doing some sort of motorbike loop out of Vientiane, Vang Vieng or Tha Khaek is becoming increasingly popular among travellers.

Chinese- and Japanese-made 100cc and 110cc step-through motorbikes can be hired for approximately 40,000K to 120,000K per day in most large centres and some smaller towns, although the state of the bikes can vary greatly. No licence is required, though you will have to leave your passport as collateral. Try to get a Japanese bike if travelling any distance out of town. In Vientiane, Luang Prabang, Vang Vieng, Tha Khaek and Pakse, 250cc dirt bikes are available from around US$25 to US$50 per day.

It's possible to hire a self-drive vehicle, but when you consider that a driver usually costs little more, takes responsibility for damage and knows where he's going, it looks risky. Costs run from US$40 to US$100 per day, depending on the route.

Vientiane-based Avis-Budget (p330) is a reliable option for car hire. When it comes to motorbikes, try **Drivenbyadventure** (☏ 020-58656994; www.hochiminhtrail.org; rental per day US$38-95, tours per day US$160-200) or **Fuark Motorcycle Hire** (Map p323; ☏ 021-261970; fuarkmotorcross@yahoo.com; Th T2, Ban Nakham) in Vientiane.

Malaysia

Includes ➜

Best for Regional Specialities

➜ Penang (p409), for *asam laksa*

➜ Melaka (p398) for *satay celup*

➜ Kuching (p453) for Sarawak laksa

➜ Cameron Highlands (p405) for tea

Top Phrases

Hello Salam/Helo

Thank you Terima kasih

How much is it? Berapa harganya?

Why Go?

Buzzing cities, culinary sensations, beautiful beaches, idyllic islands and wildlife-packed rainforests – all of this can be found in Malaysia. The catchy slogan 'Malaysia, Truly Asia' continues to ring true. The multicultural peninsula tantalises all five senses with Malay, Chinese and Indian influences. The photogenic landscapes continue across the South China Sea to Malaysian Borneo with its remote tribes, orangutans, colourful birds and amazing limestone caves. Architecture ranges from the soaring skyscrapers and glitzy shopping malls of Kuala Lumpur to the jungle-surrounded longhouse villages of Sarawak. The supreme expression of the national diversity is its amazing range of delicious culinary offerings featuring tropical fruits and vegetables and an impressive bounty of seafood. Start with Chinese-Malay 'Nonya' fare, then move on to Indian curries, Chinese buffets and Malay food stalls. The icing on the cake is that Malaysia is one of the safest, most stable and manageable countries in Southeast Asia.

When to Go
Kuala Lumpur

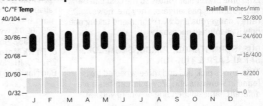

Dec–Feb High season: school holidays and Chinese New Year. Prices rise; bookings essential.

Nov–Mar Monsoon season sees many east-coast peninsular islands shut; Cherating fills with surfers.

Mar–Jun Low season: plenty of rain and fewer tourists. Ramadan food bazaars open at night.

Entering the Country

The bulk of international flights arrive at Kuala Lumpur. There are also direct flights from Asia and Australia into Penang, Kuching, Kota Kinabalu and a few other cities. There are rail and road connections with Thailand and Singapore, and buses connect Malaysia's Sabah and Sarawak with both Brunei Darussalam and Indonesia (Kalimantan). Ferries connect Malaysia with Indonesia, Brunei Darussalam, Singapore and Thailand.

REGIONS AT A GLANCE

Peninsular Malaysia's west coast features the modern capital of Kuala Lumpur, multicultural Melaka and the colourful colonial heritage of Penang's George Town. All cities boast a thriving street-food scene. To escape the city hustle, head to the tea-infused Cameron Highlands or a picture-perfect beach resort.

Malaysian Borneo lures travellers with the chance to climb one of Southeast Asia's tallest mountains and come face to face with gentle orangutans. Exploring beneath Borneo's surface reveals Sarawak's world-heritage limestone caves and the fabled scuba diving surrounding Sabah's Semporna Archipelago.

Essential Food & Drink

Breakfast *Nasi lemak* (coconut rice with a variety of accompaniments), *roti canai* (Indian flat bread), *won ton mee* (egg noodles and wontons), dim sum or *congee* (savoury rice porridge).

Barbecue Fish, lobster, prawns, squid, cockles and stingrays. Point to it and then see it get slathered in *sambal* and grilled in a banana leaf.

Noodles Fried or in soup. Top dishes include *char kway teow* (fried noodles with egg, soy sauce, chilli and a variety of additions), laksa, *curry mee* (curry noodles), Hokkien mee (fried noodles with chicken, pork and a variety of additions) and *won ton mee*.

Rice *Nasi campur* is a lunch favourite of rice and a buffet of toppings.

Dessert Malaysians drink their sweets via sugared fruit juices, sweetened condensed milk in hot beverages and icy concoctions like ABC (shaved ice covered in coconut cream, coloured syrups, jellies and sweet red beans).

Daily Costs

→ Dorm bed: RM15–50

→ Hawker centres and food-court meals: RM5–7

→ Metro ticket: RM1–2.50

AT A GLANCE

Currency Malaysian ringitt (RM)

Language Bahasa Malaysia (official), Chinese (Hakka and Hokkien), Tamil, English

Money ATMs in large towns

Visas Most nationalities get a 30- to 90-day visa on arrival

Exchange Rates

Australia	A$1	RM3.07
Euro zone	€1	RM4.68
Singapore	S$1	RM3.06
Thailand	10B	RM1.21
UK	UK£1	RM6.63
USA	US$1	RM4.30

MALAYSIA

Top Tips

→ Dress modestly, especially in the northeastern states of Peninsula Malaysia.

→ When visiting mosques, cover your head and limbs with a headscarf and sarong (many mosques lend these out at the entrance).

→ Compare the cost of flying into Singapore versus flying into Malaysia. From Singapore you can cheaply travel overland to Peninsular Malaysia, and Singapore also has direct flights to Malaysian Borneo.

→ If time is limited, consider Malaysia's very reasonably priced domestic flights.

→ Credit-card fraud is a growing problem. Use your cards only at established businesses.

→ Seek treatment if bitten by any animals (Rabies risk).

Malaysia Highlights

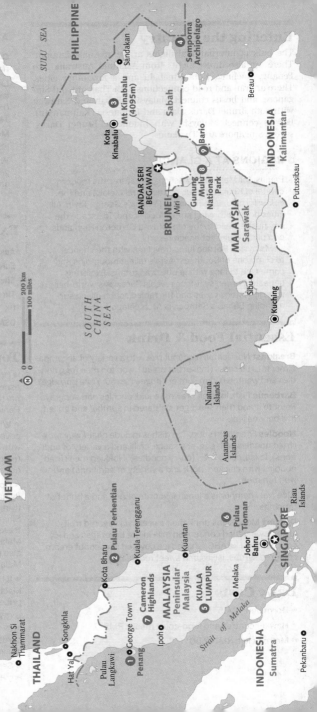

1 Penang (p409) Exploring George Town's heritage district while grazing on street food.

2 Pulau Perhentian (p428) Swimming, lying on the beach, snorkelling, eating and snoozing.

3 Mt Kinabalu (p443) Hiking past moonscapes for sunrise atop the granite peak.

4 Semporna Archipelago (p451) Diving technicolour coral gardens with sealife.

5 Kuala Lumpur (p387) Admiring the view from the KL Tower or the Heli Lounge Bar.

6 Pulau Tioman (p423) Hopping between idyllic beach villages and diving reefs.

7 Cameron Highlands (p405) Admiring the verdant, rolling tea plantations.

8 Gunung Mulu National Park (p470) Exploring the World Heritage limestone caverns.

9 Bario (p472) Sipping wild tea on a longhouse verandah.

KUALA LUMPUR

☑ 03 / POPULATION 1.73 MILLION

From a humble tin-mining base over 150 years ago, Kuala Lumpur (KL) has evolved into an affluent 21st-century metropolis remarkable for its cultural diversity. Indigenous Malays, Chinese prospectors, Indian immigrants and British colonials all helped shape the city and bestowed a assortment of cultural traditions. Temples and mosques rub shoulders with space-age towers and shopping malls, traders' stalls are piled high with pungent durians and counterfeit handbags, and locals sip cappuccinos or feast on delicious hawker food.

KL's city centre is surprisingly compact – from Chinatown to Masjid India takes little more than 10 minutes on foot; it's often quicker to walk than take public transport. Merdeka Sq is the focus of colonial-era KL. Southeast across the river, Chinatown is popular with travellers for its budget accommodation and lively night market.

⊙ Sights

◉ Chinatown, Merdeka Square & Bukit Nanas

★ **Sin Sze Si Ya Temple** TEMPLE
(Map p390; Jln Tun HS Lee; ⊙ 7am-5pm; LRT Pasar Seni) FREE Kuala Lumpur's oldest Chinese temple (1864) was built on the instructions of Kapitan Yap Ah Loy and is dedicated to Sin Sze Ya and Si Sze Ya, two Chinese deities believed instrumental in Yap's ascension to Kapitan status. Several beautiful objects decorate the temple, including two hanging carved panels, but the best feature is the almost frontier-like atmosphere.

★ **Merdeka Square** SQUARE
(Dataran Merdeka; Map p390; LRT Masjid Jamek) The huge open square where Malaysian independence was declared in 1957 is ringed by heritage buildings, such as the magnificent **Sultan Abdul Samad Building** (Map p390; Jln Raja) and **St Mary's Anglican Cathedral** (Map p390; ☑ 03-2692 8672; www.stmaryscathedral.org.my; Jln Raja; ⊙ 8am-5pm), both designed by AC Norman. It also has an enormous flagpole and a fluttering Malaysian flag. In the British era, the square was used as a cricket pitch and called the Padang (field).

KL Forest Eco Park NATURE RESERVE
(Taman Eko Rimba KL; Map p394; ☑ 03-2026 4741; www.forestry.gov.my; ⊙ 8am-6pm; ☐ KL Tower)

WORTH A TRIP

BATU CAVES

Hindu deities rule over the Batu Caves, a system of three caves 13km northwest of the capital. The main focus is **Temple Cave** (⊙ 8am-8.30pm; ☐ Batu Caves) FREE, which contains a Hindu shrine reached by a straight flight of 272 steps, guarded by a 42.7m golden statue of Murugan, said to be the largest in the world. The caves are busy every day, but hundreds of thousands of pilgrims converge on the caves every year during Thaipusam (January/February) to engage in or watch the spectacularly masochistic feats of the devotees.

Take KTM Komuter Trains to Batu Caves (RM2.60, 30 minutes, every 15 to 30 minutes). A taxi costs RM20 to RM30.

FREE KL's urban roar is replaced by buzzing insects and cackling birdlife at this forest of tropical hardwoods, covering 9.37 hectares in the heart of the city. One of the oldest protected jungles in Malaysia (gazetted in 1906), the park is commonly known as Bukit Nanas (Pineapple Hill). Don't miss traversing the lofty **canopy walkway**, which is easily reached from the Menara KL car park; signposts display walking routes. For longer forays, pick up a basic map to the trails from the **Forest Information Centre** (Jln Raja Chulan; ⊙ 9am-5pm) – trails lead directly from here.

Menara Kuala Lumpur TOWER
(KL Tower; Map p394; ☑ 03-2020 5444; www.menarakl.com.my; 2 Jln Punchak; observation deck adult/child RM52/31, open deck adult/child RM105/55; ⊙ observation deck 9am-10pm, last tickets 9.30pm; ☐ KL Tower) Although the Petronas Towers are taller, the 421m Menara KL, rising from the crest of Bukit Nanas, offers the best city views. The bulb at the top contains a revolving restaurant, an interior **observation deck** at 276m and, most thrilling of all, an **open deck** at 300m, access to which is weather dependent. Here (if you dare) you can take your photo in the **sky box**, which puts nothing but glass between you and the ground below (no young children allowed).

Masjid Jamek MOSQUE
(Friday Mosque; Map p390; off Jln Tun Perak; ⊙ 9am-noon & 2.30-4pm Sat-Thu; LRT Masjid Jamek) FREE Gracefully designed by British architect AB Hubback, this onion-domed mosque borrows

Mogul and Moorish styles with its brick-and-plaster banded minarets and three shapely domes. Located at the confluence of the Gombak and Klang rivers, Masjid Jamek was the first brick mosque in Malaysia when completed in 1907. It remained the city's centre of Islamic worship until the opening of the National Mosque in 1965.

Sri Mahamariamman Temple HINDU TEMPLE
(Map p390; 163 Jln Tun HS Lee; ⊙6am-8.30pm; LRT Pasar Seni) FREE Rising almost 23m above this lively temple is a tower colourfully decorated with Hindu gods. Founded in 1873, this Hindu temple is thought to be the oldest in Malaysia. Decorated in South Indian style, the temple is named for Mariamman, the South Indian mother goddess (also known as Parvati). Her shrine is at the back of the complex. On the left sits a shrine to the elephant-headed deity Ganesh, and on the right, one to Lord Murugan.

◉ Bukit Bintang & KLCC

★Petronas Towers TOWER
(Map p394; ☎03-2331 8080; www.petronastwintowers.com.my; Jln Ampang; adult/child RM85/35; ⊙9am-9pm Tue-Sun, closed 1-2.30pm Fri; 🚹; LRT KLCC) Resembling twin silver rockets plucked from an episode of *Flash Gordon,* the Petronas Towers are the perfect allegory for the meteoric rise of the city from tin-miners' hovel to 21st-century metropolis. Half of the 1500 tickets for 45-minute tours are sold in advance online. Otherwise turn up early to be sure of scoring a ticket to go up.

★ILHAM GALLERY
(Map p394; www.ilhamgallery.com; 3rd & 5th fl, Ilham Tower, 8 Jln Binjai; ⊙11am-7pm Tue-Sat, to 5pm Sun; LRT Ampang Park) FREE This thought-provoking contemporary-art gallery is an excellent excuse to step inside the glossy, 60-storey ILHAM Tower. The artwork selected for ILHAM's rotating exhibitions spans various media and is curated to provoke debate: expect anything from black-and-white photography to neon-coloured *kampung* houses.

KLCC Park PARK
(Map p394; Jln Ampang, KLCC; ⊙7am-10pm; 🚹; LRT KLCC) The park is the best vantage point for eyeballing the Petronas Towers (p388). In the early evening it can seem like everyone in town has come down here to watch the glowing towers punching up into the night sky. Every night at 8pm, 9pm and 10pm the Lake Symphony fountains play in front of the Suria KLCC.

◉ Lake Gardens, Brickfields & Bangsar

★Islamic Arts Museum MUSEUM
(Muzium Kesenian Islam Malaysia; Map p390; ☎03-2092 7070; www.iamm.org.my; Jln Lembah Perdana; adult/child RM14/7; ⊙10am-6pm; 🚇 Kuala Lumpur) Inhabiting a building every bit as impressive as its collection, this museum showcases Islamic decorative arts from around the globe. Scale models of the world's best Islamic buildings, fabulous textiles, carpets, jewellery and calligraphy-inscribed pottery all vie for attention; the 19th-century recreation **Damascus Room** is a gold-leaf-decorated delight. Don't forget to gaze up at the building's intricate domes and tile work.

KL Bird Park WILDLIFE RESERVE
(Map p389; ☎03-2272 1010; www.klbirdpark.com; Jln Cenderawasih; adult/child RM67/45; ⊙9am-6pm; 🚹; 🚇 Kuala Lumpur) More than 3000 birds flutter and soar through this 21-hectare aviary. Some 200 species of (mostly) Asian birds can be spotted here, from strutting flamingos to parakeets. The park is divided into four sections: in the first two, birds fly freely beneath an enormous canopy. Section three features the native hornbills (so-called because of their enormous beaks), while section four offers the less-edifying spectacle of caged species.

Perdana Botanical Garden PARK
(☎03-2617 6404; www.klbotanicalgarden.gov.my; ⊙7am-8pm; 🚹; 🚇 Kuala Lumpur) FREE Strolling around KL's oldest public park, established in the 1880s, you'll admire native and introduced flora from around Malaysia, including 800 species of orchid, mahogany trees more than 300 years old, and countless hibiscus blooms (the country's national flower). Ferns, rare trees, medicinal herbs and aquatic plants each have their own gardens, all prettily arranged with gazebos and boardwalks (though there's only limited signage to identify the plants). Pick up a map at the **information booth** (⊙7am-8pm; LRT Masjid Jamek).

National Museum MUSEUM
(Muzium Negara; ☎03-2267 1111; www.muzium negara.gov.my; Jln Damansara; adult/child RM5/2; ⊙9am-6pm; 🚇KL Sentral) This excellent modern museum offers a good primer on Malaysia's history, from prehistoric to present-day. The country's geological features and prehistory are tackled in one gallery (which features a replica of the 11,000-year-old Perak Man, Malaysia's most celebrated archaeological

Kuala Lumpur

N

| 0 | | 1 km |
| 0 | | 0.5 miles |

Sentul Park

↑ Batu Caves (7km)

Sungai Gombak

Jln Sentul

Sentul LRT

Jln Pahang

Lake Titiwangsa

Sungai Bunus

Titiwangsa Lake Gardens

National Visual Arts Gallery

TITIWANGSA

Jln Ipoh

Sungai Batu

Titiwangsa LRT

Titiwangsa Monorail

Jln Tun Razak

Pekeliling Bus Station

Hospital Kuala Lumpur

Jalan Kuching

Jln Ipoh

PWTC LRT

Jln Putra

Chow Kit Monorail

Jln Raja Muda Abdul Aziz

Putra KTM

Jln Raja Laut

CHOW KIT

Kampung Baru

KAMPUNG BARU

Sultan Ismail LRT

Medan Tuanku Monorail

Kampung Baru LRT

Ampang Elevated Hwy

Jln Yap Kwan Seng

KLCC LRT

Bandaraya LRT

Jln Raja Abdullah

Dang Wangi LRT

Kuala Lumpur City Centre (KLCC) Park

Bank Negara KTM

Jln Dang Wangi

Capital Café

Dang Wangi Monorail

Bukit Nanas Monorail

Jln Sultan Salahuddin

Masjid India Pasar Malam

MASJID INDIA

Jln Ampang

KL Forest Eco Park

Raja Chulan Monorail

National Monument

Jln Parlimen

Masjid Jamek LRT

Jln Raja Chulan

Immigration Office (7km)

MERDEKA SQUARE

Jln Kuching

Forest Information Centre

AirAsia-Bukit Bintang Monorail

BUKIT BINTANG

Perdana Botanical Garden

Perdana Botanical Garden Information Booth

COLONIAL DISTRICT

Jln Cheng Lock

Plaza Rakyat LRT

Jln Pudu

Bukit Bintang MRT

Jln Imbi

KL Bird Park

Pasar Seni LRT

CHINATOWN

Pasar Seni MRT

Imbi Monorail

Tasik Perdana

National Museum

Kuala Lumpur

Maharajalela Monorail

Merdeka MRT

Hang Tuah Monorail
Hang Tuah LRT

Muzium Negara MRT

See Chinatown, Merdeka Square & Masjid India Map (p390)

See Golden Triangle & KLCC Map (p394)

PUDU

BRICKFIELDS

Jln Istana

Jln Travers

KL Sentral

Jln Lapangan Terbang

Pudu LRT

Jln Pasar

Jln Tun Sambanthan

Tun Sambanthan Monorail

Jln Syed Putra

Jln San Peng

Jln Loke Yew

RAIL SYSTEMS
KTM
LRT
MRT

Sungai Klang

Jln Sungai Besi

Chan Sow Lin LRT

Terminal Bersepadu Selatan (TSB) (10km) ↓

MALAYSIA KUALA LUMPUR

Chinatown, Merdeka Square & Masjid India

MASJID INDIA

Jln Sultan Salahuddin

Jln Kuching

Sungai Gombak

Jln Raja Laut

Lg Gombak

Jln Tuanku Abdul Rahman (TAR)

Lg Tuanku Abdul Rahman

Jln Masjid India

Jln Parlimen

Jln Tun Perak

Jln Tangsi

Visit KL ℹ️

7 ✝️

Jln Raja

Royal Selangor Club

Jln Melaka

Sungai Klang

Masjid Jamek LRT 🚇

Merdeka Square ⊚ 2

8 🏛️

MERDEKA SQUARE

Jln Raja

Jln Makhamah Persekutuan

🌙 4

Lebuh Ampang

13 🏨

Jln Raja

Jln Kinabalu

Central Market Annexe

17 🔒

Bangkok Bank Bus Stop

Lebuh Pudu

COLONIAL DISTRICT

Sin Sze Si ⊚ Ya Temple 3

Jln Cenderasari

Jln Sultan Hishamuddin

Kompleks Dayabumi

Sungai Klang

Jln Hang Kasturi

CHINATOWN

6 🕌

Jln Lembah Perdana

✉️ 🔲

Rapid KL Information Booth ℹ️

⊚ 9

Pasar Seni LRT Ⓜ️

Jln Panggong

MALAYSIA KUALA LUMPUR

Islamic Arts 🏛️ 1 Museum

🌙 5

Jln Tun Tan Cheng Lock

Jln Tun HS Lee

Jln Lembah Perdana

Jln Tugu

Jln Kinabalu

Tun Abdul Razak Heritage Park

🍴 Nice

Jln Tun Sambanthan

Kuala 🏛️ Lumpur

KL Sentral Station (1km)

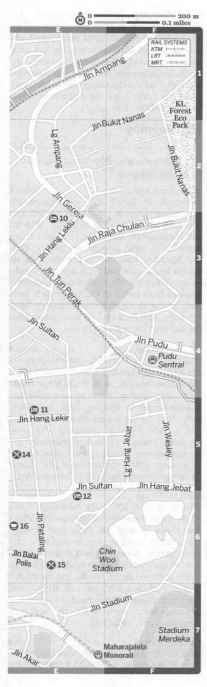

discovery). The gallery of modern history is even more interesting, with recreations of temple walls, royal beds and ceremonial garb from across the centuries.

Outside, look for a traditional raised house; ancient burial poles from Sarawak; a regularly changing exhibition (extra charge); and two excellent small side galleries, the **Orang Asli Craft Museum** (☑ 03-2282 6255; www.jmm.gov.my) and **Museum of Malay World Ethnology** (☑ 03-2267 1000; www.jmm.gov.my).

National Monument MONUMENT
(Tugu Negara; Plaza Tugu Negara, Jln Parlimen; ⊙ 7am-6pm; LRT Masjid Jamek) **FREE** On a palm-fringed plaza with fine views of KL's skyscrapers stands this bombastic monument. Commemorating military sacrifices in the name of Malaysian freedom, the National Monument's centrepiece is a bronze sculpture of soldiers (one of them holding aloft the Malaysian flag), created in 1966 by Felix de Weldon, the artist behind the Iwo Jima monument near Washington, DC. A royal-blue

MALAYSIA KUALA LUMPUR

pool and curved pavilion heighten the grand impression. Get a taxi from Masjid Jamek.

Masjid Negara
MOSQUE

(National Mosque; Map p390; www.masjidnegara. gov.my; Jln Lembah Perdana; ⊙9am-noon, 3-4pm & 5.30-6.30pm, closed Fri morning; 🚇Kuala Lumpur) **FREE** The main place of worship for KL's Malay Muslim population is this gigantic 1960s mosque, inspired by Mecca's Masjid al-Haram. Able to accommodate 15,000 worshippers, it has an umbrella-like blue-tile roof with 18 points symbolising the 13 states of Malaysia and the five pillars of Islam. Rising above the mosque, a 74m-high minaret issues the call to prayer, which can be heard across Chinatown. Non-Muslims are welcome to visit outside prayer times; robes are available for those who are not dressed appropriately.

◉ Masjid India, Kampung Baru & Northern KL

★ Kampung Baru
AREA

(LRT Kampung Baru) In this neighbourhood of traditional Malay wooden houses, village life unfolds despite the surrounding skyscrapers. Gazetted by the British in 1899, Kampung Baru's low-slung charms are best revealed by simply wandering its streets, ideally with a guide on the city's **Kampung Baru walking tour** (Jalan-Jalan at Kampung Baru; ☏03-2698 0332; www.visitkl.gov.my; ⊙4.15-7pm Tue, Thu & Sun; Medan Tuanku) **FREE**. Along the way enjoy tasty home-cooked Malay food at unpretentious roadside cafes and stalls.

★ National Visual Arts Gallery
GALLERY

(NVAG, Balai Seni Lukis Negara; ☏03-4026 7000; www.artgallery.gov.my; 2 Jln Temerloh; ⊙10am-6pm; Titiwangsa) **FREE** For their inventive-

---

SPLURGE

Checking in to the neon-accented **Wolo Bukit Bintang** (Map p394; ☏03-2719 1333; www.thewolo.com; cnr Jln Bukit Bintang & Jln Sultan Ismail; d from RM230; ❀🗺; AirAsia-Bukit Bintang) feels like sashaying into a nightclub. Mirror-clad elevators whisk you to corridors dimly lit by cloud-shaped lanterns. In the rooms, mattresses sit on a blonde-wood base, like a futon, and the shower and toilet are hidden behind padded-leather doors. This is the place to party like a pop star (but on a midrange budget).

---

ness and sheer scale, the artworks on display at the NVAG are worth a trip out of central KL. In rotating exhibitions by regional artists, themes of Malaysian politics and local identity positively leap from canvases. Upper galleries are accessed by a spiral-shaped ramp that recalls the Guggenheim Museum, while the lower level has a permanent collection of 4000 pieces.

🛏 Sleeping

🛏 Chinatown, Merdeka Square & Bukit Nanas

★ Reggae Mansion
HOSTEL $

(Map p390; ☏03-2072 6877; www.reggaehostels malaysia.com/mansion; 49-59 Jln Tun HS Lee; dm RM48-58, d RM140-150, tr RM200; ❀❀🗺; LRT Masjid Jamek) Grooving to a beat that's superior to most backpacker places, Reggae Mansion instantly impresses with its faux-colonial style and contemporary touches, including a lively rooftop bar, mini-cinema and flash cafe-bar. Container-style beds feel private, though one dorm is very large (24 beds). Ask for a quieter room away from the bar if you're not a night owl.

★ BackHome
HOSTEL $

(Map p390; ☏03-2022 0788; www.backhome.com. my; 30 Jln Tun HS Lee; dm RM50-80, d RM138-144, tr RM156, all incl breakfast; ❀@🗺; LRT Masjid Jamek) This chic pitstop for flashpackers offers polished-concrete finishes, Zen decoration, rain showers (all rooms share bathrooms) and a blissful central courtyard with spindly trees. There are mixed, women-only and couples' dorms (sleeping four). Also on site is pleasant **LOKL Coffee** (Map p390; http:// loklcoffee.com; mains RM16-30; ⊙8am-6pm; 🗺).

Mingle Hostel
HOSTEL $

(Map p390; ☏03-2022 2078; www.minglekl.com; 53 Jln Sultan; mixed/female dm from RM55/58, r from RM108; ❀@🗺; LRT Pasar Seni) Occupying a 1920s building once owned by a Chinese tycoon, Mingle Hostel has a natural feel with venerable stone walls and lounge zones open to the air. Dorms and rooms feel ample, each bed with its own air-con and electrical sockets. Occasional antiques and old brass lamps hark back to the building's glory days as a social hall.

Lantern Hotel
HOTEL $

(Map p390; ☏03-2020 1648; www.lanternhotel. com; 38 Jln Petaling; d RM95-115, tr RM125, all incl breakfast; ❄️ 📶; LRT Pasar Seni) You can't get more central to Chinatown than this slickly designed, contemporary hotel. Simple, whitewashed rooms have lime or tangerine feature walls and private bathrooms – the cheapest ones have no windows. A huge plus is the terrace with a cityscape mural, creeper plants and a view of Petaling Street Market.

Paloma Inn   HOTEL **$$**
(Map p394; 📞 03-2110 6677; www.hotelpaloma inn.com.my; 12-14 Jln Sin Chew Kee; dm/s/d/tr RM40/100/105/170; ❄️@📶;   Hang Tuah) Set on a backstreet of painted pre-war shophouses, Paloma is well run and quiet, with simple, mostly wooden-floored rooms, featuring occasional flashes of magenta, and pleasingly modern bathrooms. The nightlife of Changkat Bukit Bintang is a 10-minute walk away. Rates are slightly higher Friday to Sunday. Breakfast is an extra RM10, and there's a laundry service from RM12.

🛏️ Bukit Bintang & KLCC

Classic Inn   GUESTHOUSE **$$**
(Map p394; 📞 03-2148 8648; www.classicinn.com. my; 36 & 52 Lg 1/77A; d incl breakfast RM118-138; ❄️@📶;   Imbi) Check-in is at the newer, more upmarket branch of Classic Inn at No 36, where there are spotless rooms all with private bathrooms and a pleasant verandah cafe. The original yellow-painted shophouse at No 52 continues to be a retro-charming choice with plain but perfectly agreeable private rooms, a small grassy garden and welcoming staff.

🍴 Eating

🍴 Chinatown, Merdeka Square & Bukit Nanas

Madras Lane Hawkers   HAWKER **$**
(Map p390; Madras Lane; noodles RM5-6; ⏱️8am-4pm Tue-Sun; LRT Pasar Seni) Enter beside the Guandi Temple to find this alley of hawker stalls. It's best visited for breakfast or lunch. One of its stand-out operators offers 10 types of *yong tau fu* (vegetables stuffed with tofu and a fish-and-pork paste). The *bak kut teh* (pork and medicinal-herbs stew) and curry laksa stalls are also good.

Merchant's Lane   FUSION **$$**
(Map p390; 📞 03-2022 1736; www.facebook.com/ merchantslane/home; Level 1, 150 Jln Petaling; mains RM20-30; ⏱️11.30am-10pm Mon, Tue, Thu & Fri, 9.30am-10pm Sat & Sun; 📶;   Maharajalela)

DON'T MISS

JALAN ALOR

The collection of roadside restaurants and stalls lining **Jln Alor** (Map p394; ⏱️24hr;   AirAsia-Bukit Bintang) is the great common denominator of KL's food scene, hauling in everyone from sequinned society babes to penny-strapped backpackers. From around 5pm till late every evening, the street transforms into a continuous open-air dining space with hundreds of plastic tables and chairs and rival caterers shouting out to passers-by to drum up business (avoid the pushiest ones!). Most places serve alcohol and you can sample pretty much every Malay Chinese dish imaginable, from grilled fish and satay to *kai-lan* (Chinese greens) in oyster sauce and fried noodles with frogs' legs. Thai food is also popular.

Stairs lead up from a narrow doorway to this high-ceilinged charmer of a cafe. Staff nurture an easygoing vibe and punters are a mix of tourists and locals, united by enthusiasm for Instagramming the greenery-draped venue and its fusion cuisine. East-meets-West dishes like chicken with green-stained pandan rice and 'Italian chow mein' are hit and miss, but the venue is a delight.

🍴 Bukit Bintang & KLCC

Nasi Kandar Pelita   FOOD HALL **$**
(Map p394; 📞 03-2162 5532; www.pelita.com. my; 149 Jln Ampang; mains RM8-15; ⏱️24hr; LRT KLCC) There's round-the-clock eating at the Jln Ampang branch of this chain of excellent *mamak* (Muslim Indian-Malay) food courts. It's cheap, clean and offers plenty of choice: browse *roti canai* (flat, flaky bread), chicken cooked in the tandoor (cylindrical oven) and biryani (spiced rice dishes) before you decide.

Lot 10 Hutong   HAWKER **$**
(Map p394; www.lot10hutong.com; basement, Lot 10, 50 Jln Sultan Ismail; dishes RM9-18; ⏱️10am-10pm;   AirAsia-Bukit Bintang) Lot 10 Hutong was the first mall to encourage top hawkers to open branches in a basement food court. In its well-designed space it has pulled in names such as Soong Kee, which has served beef noodles since 1945. Look also for Kong Tai's oyster omelettes, Hon Kee's Cantonese porridge, Kim Lian Kee's Hokkien *mee* and Penang Famous Fried Koay Teow.

MALAYSIA KUALA LUMPUR

Golden Triangle & KLCC

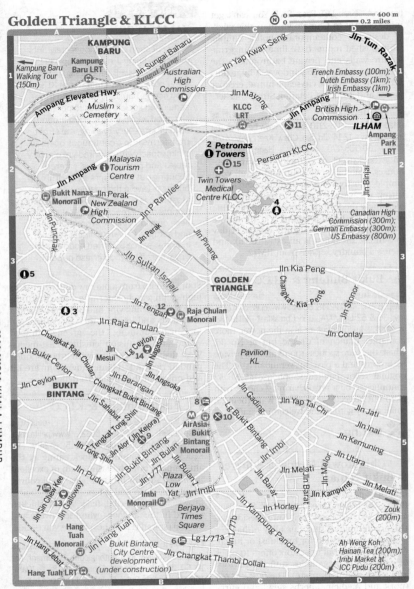

Imbi Market at ICC Pudu HAWKER $
(Jln 1/77C; dishes RM5-10; ⊗6am-2pm; LRT
Pudu) The rather clinical grey-and-white,
purpose-built food court at ICC Pudu might
lack the colour and atmosphere of the old
Imbi market, but many old vendors are here
serving the same mouthwatering food (with
more expected to join them). Top eats include the freshly made rice-flour noodles at
Ah Fook Chee Cheong Fun; rice with rich,
spicy *sambal* at Ann Nasi Lemak; and sticky
treats at Nyonya Kuih sweet stall.

Golden Triangle & KLCC

Several stalls are located in a separate *kopitiam*, **Ah Weng Koh Hainan Tea** (www.facebook.com/AhWengKohHainanTea/; lot G85 ICC Pudu, Jln 1/77C; dishes RM3-10; ⏱5.30am-2pm; LRT Pudu), situated just outside the main food court. Here you'll find Sisters Crispy Popiah serving exquisite wraps, and stalls selling *kaya* toast, tea and coffee.

✕ Masjid India, Kampung Baru & Northern KL

Capital Café   MALAYSIAN $
(213 Jln TAR; dishes RM4-6; ⏱7.30am-7.30pm Mon-Sat; LRT Bandaraya) In a formula little-changed since it opened in 1956, Capital Café has no frills, only fabulously old-fashioned Malay food. Chinese, Malay and Indian chefs work together to rush plates of mee goreng, *rojak* (salad doused in a peanut-sauce dressing) and satay (evenings only) to hungry diners; on busy days, you may have to share a table.

Masjid India Pasar Malam   HAWKER $
(Night Market; Lg Tuanku Abdul Rahman; street food RM5-10; ⏱3pm-midnight Sat; LRT Masjid Jamek) Stalls pack out the length of Lg Tuanku Abdul Rahman, the alley between Jln TAR and Masjid India. Amid the headscarf and T-shirt sellers are plenty of stalls serving excellent Malay, Indian and Chinese snacks and colourful soya- and fruit-based drinks.

🍷 Drinking & Nightlife

🍷 Chinatown, Merdeka Square & Bukit Nanas

★ **Aku Cafe & Gallery**   CAFE
(Map p390; ☎03-2857 6887; www.oldchina.com.my/aku.html; 1st fl, 8 Jln Panggong; ⏱11am-8pm Tue-Sun; 📶; LRT Pasar Seni) This intimate, art-filled

cafe serves good hand-drip brews, ice-blended drinks and juices from pressed apple to banana smoothie. Light meals and pasta dishes are outshone by the inventive dessert menu (try the pandan panna cotta). There are some unusual craft souvenirs for sale, too.

★ **Pahit**   COCKTAIL BAR
(Map p394; ☎03-2110 0776; www.facebook.com/barpahit; 3 Jln Sin Chew Kee; ⏱5pm-1am Tue-Sun; Hang Tuah) Tucked inside an unassuming gateway, Pahit immortalises its 'juniper and joy' ethos with a neon sign. Inside the brick-lined bar, skilled mixologists combine their favourite gins with gingerflower, pomelo and all manner of exotic flavours.

VCR   CAFE
(Map p394; ☎03-2110 2330; www.vcr.my; 2 Jln Galloway; ⏱8.30am-11pm; 📶; Hang Tuah) Set in an airy pre-war shophouse, VCR serves first-rate coffee, all-day breakfasts (RM19 to RM35) and desserts to a diverse crowd of backpackers and laptop-wielding locals.

🍷 Bukit Bintang & KLCC

★ **Heli Lounge Bar**   COCKTAIL BAR
(Map p394; ☎03-2110 5034; www.facebook.com/Heliloungebar; Level 34, Menara KH, Jln Sultan Ismail; ⏱5pm-midnight Mon-Wed, to 2am Thu, to 3am Fri & Sat, to 11am Sun; 📶; Raja Chulan) With exhilarating 360-degree views, this dizzying rooftop bar is the best place for sundowners in KL. Steady your hands carrying your daiquiri or lychee martini upstairs from the gleaming bar to the helipad, where bird's-eye views prompt selfies galore.

★ **Zouk**   CLUB
(www.zoukclub.com.my; TREC, 436 Jln Tun Razak; RM25-45; ⏱10pm-3am Sun-Tue, to 4am Thu, to 5am Fri & Sat; AirAsia-Bukit Bintang) If you're going

MALAYSIA KUALA LUMPUR

to visit one club in KL, make it Zouk at TREC. Among its seven party spaces are the Main Room, which reverberates to electro, techno and trance; Ace, a hip-hop and R&B club; and the surprisingly green balcony deck. Wear your flashiest threads (no T-shirts or sandals). Get a taxi from AirAsia-Bukit Bintang.

Taps Beer Bar   MICROBREWERY
(Map p394; ☑ 03-2110 1560; www.tapsbeerbar.my; One Residency, 1 Jln Nagasari; ⊙ 5pm-1am Mon-Sat, noon-1am Sun; 🛜🚻; Raja Chulan) Taps specialises in ale from around the world, with some 80 different microbrews on rotation, 14 of them on tap. There's live music Thursday to Saturday at 9.30pm and regular beer festivals and events. There's also a menu of Malay and American-style comfort food (mains RM15 to RM50).

🛍 Shopping

Museum of Ethnic Arts   ANTIQUES
(Map p390; ☑ 03-2301 1468; 2nd fl, the Annexe, 10 Jln Hang Kasturi; ⊙ 11am-7pm; LRT Pasar Seni) Although this place is billed as a museum, almost everything is for sale in this extraordinary private collection of tribal arts from Borneo. You'll also find Nonya ceramics, Tibetan *thangka* paintings, Chinese paintings and porcelain, embroidered wall hangings, hand-carved boxes and doors, and all manner of delights from Malaysia and the region. There's also a gallery of contemporary artworks.

Petaling Street Market   MARKET
(Map p390; Jln Petaling; ⊙ 10am-10.30pm; LRT Pasar Seni) Malaysia's relaxed attitude towards counterfeit goods is well illustrated at this heavily hyped night market bracketed by fake Chinese gateways. Traders start to fill Jln Petaling from midmorning until it is jam-packed with market stalls selling everything from fake Mulberry handbags to jackfruit. Visit in the afternoon if you want to take pictures or see the market without the crowds.

ℹ Information

IMMIGRATION OFFICE
Immigration Office (☑ 03-6205 7400; www.imi.gov.my; 69 Jln Sri Hartamas 1, off Jln Duta; ⊙ 7.30am-1pm & 2-5.30pm Mon-Thu, 7.30am-12.15pm & 2.45-5.30pm Fri; 🚉 U83, Ⓜ Semantan) Handles visa extensions; offices are opposite Publika mall.

INTERNET ACCESS
Kuala Lumpur is blanketed with hot spots for wi-fi connections (usually free). Internet cafes are less common these days, but a few still exist.

MEDICAL SERVICES
Hospital Kuala Lumpur (☑ 03-2615 5555; www.hkl.gov.my; Jln Pahang; Titiwangsa, LRT Titiwangsa) City's main hospital, north of the centre.

Twin Towers Medical Centre KLCC (Map p394; ☑ 03-2382 3500; http://ttmcklcc.com.my; Level 4, Suria KLCC, Jln Ampang; ⊙ 8.30am-6pm Mon-Sat; LRT KLCC) Located in the mall (Map p394; ☑ 03-2382 2828; www.suriaklcc.com.my; KLCC, Jln Ampang; ⊙ 10am-10pm; LRT KLCC) attached to the Petronas Towers, with a second clinic near KL Sentral.

MONEY
Most banks and shopping malls provide international ATMs (typically on the ground floor or basement level). Money changers frequently offer better rates than banks for changing cash and (at times) travellers cheques; they're usually open later and at weekends and are found in shopping malls.

POST
Main Post Office (Map p390; ☑ 03-2267 2267; www.pos.com.my; Jln Tun Tan Cheng Lock; ⊙ 8.30am-6pm Mon-Fri, to 1pm Sat; LRT Pasar Seni) Across the river from the Central Market.

TOURIST INFORMATION
Visit KL (Kuala Lumpur Tourism Bureau; Map p390; ☑ 03-2698 0332; www.visitkl.gov.my; 11 Jln Tangsi; ⊙ 8.30am-5.30pm Mon-Fri; 🛜; LRT Masjid Jamek) In addition to supplying tons of useful brochures and maps, Visit KL runs free walking tours, including a 2½-hour tour of KL's heritage sites (at 9am on Mondays, Wednesdays and Saturdays).

Malaysia Tourism Centre (MaTiC; Map p394; ☑ 03-9235 4900; www.matic.gov.my/en; 109 Jln Ampang; ⊙ 8am-10pm; Bukit Nanas) Provides information on KL and tourism across Malaysia. There's also a cultural dance show staged at the theatre here (at 3pm Monday to Saturday; free).

ℹ Getting There & Away

Kuala Lumpur is a major transport hub, with direct flights connecting Kuala Lumpur International Airport with cities all over the world. The city is also easily reached on a host of short-haul local flights, many of them with budget airlines such as AirAsia and Firefly; most of these flights arrive at the SkyPark Subang Terminal, which is also known as Sultan Abdul Aziz Shah Airport.

The city has rail connections to Singapore in the south and Thailand in the north, with stops at Butterworth (for Penang) and Alor Setar (for Langkawi) along the way. Long-distance buses connect KL with major cities all over Malaysia and beyond; most of these now leave from the **Terminal Bersepadu Selatan** (TBS; ☑ 03-9051 2000; www.tbsbts.com.my; Jln Terminal Selatan, Bandar Tasik Selatan; 🚉 Bandar Tasik Selatan, LRT

Bandar Tasik Selatan). Flights, cars and tours can be booked online at lonelyplanet.com/bookings.

AIR

Kuala Lumpur International Airport (KLIA; ☑ 03-8777 7000; www.klia.com.my; ⓡ KLIA) Kuala Lumpur's main airport has two terminals and is about 55km south of the city.

SkyPark Subang Terminal (Sultan Abdul Aziz Shah Airport; ☑ 03-7842 2773; www.subang-skypark.com; M17, Subang) Firefly, Berjaya Air and some AirAsia and Malindo Air flights land here, around 23km west of the city centre.

BUS

Connected to the Bandar Tasik Selatan train-station hub, about 15 minutes south of KL Sentral, is Terminal Bersepadu Selatan, which was built to replace Pudu Sentral as KL's main long-distance bus station. TBS operators, including **Plusliner** (☑ 03-4047 7878; www.plusliner.com.my), serve destinations to the south and northeast of KL. This vast, modern transport hub has a centralised ticketing service (CTS) selling tickets for nearly all bus companies – including services offered by major operator Transnasional Express – at counters on level 3 or online (up to three hours before departure).

Pudu Sentral (Map p390; Jln Pudu; LRT Plaza Rakyat) Only a handful of destinations are still served by Pudu Sentral Bus Station, including Genting Highlands, Seremban and Kuala Selangor. Note that nearly all long distance buses from KL now leave from **Terminal Bersepadu Selatan** (p396), a 20-minute journey from Plaza Rakyat station (just behind Pudu Sentral) on the LRT.

Pekeliling Bus Station (off Jln Pekeliling Lama; LRT Titiwangsa, Titiwangsa) Bus station serving central Pahang towns including Jerantut, Temerloh and Kuala Lipis, as well as east-coast destinations such as Kuantan.

Buses from Kuala Lumpur:

DESTINATION	FARE (RM)	DURATION (HR)
Alor Setar	43-55	5
Butterworth	35-45	4½
Cameron Highlands	23-35	4
Ipoh	21-33	2½
Johor Bahru	34-55	4
Kuantan	24-29	4
Melaka	10-17	2
Penang	30-40	5
Singapore	45-50	6

TRAIN

All long-distance trains depart from **KL Sentral** (☑ 1300-889 933; www.ktmb.com.my), hub of the **KTM** (Keretapi Tanah Melayu; ☑ 03-2267 1200; www.ktmb.com.my; ⊙ call centre 7am-10pm) national railway system. The information office in the main hall can advise on schedules and check seat availability.

There are daily connections with Butterworth, Johor Bahru, Hat Yai (Thailand) and Singapore. Fares are cheap, especially if you opt for a seat rather than a berth (for which there are extra charges), but journey times are slow.

ⓘ Getting Around

TO/FROM THE AIRPORT
Kuala Lumpur International Airport (KLIA) Trains RM55; every 15 minutes from 5am to 1am; 30 minutes to KL Sentral. Buses RM10; every hour from 5.30am to 12.30am; one hour to KL Sentral. Taxis from RM75; one hour to central KL.

SkyPark Subang Terminal Shuttles RM10; hourly between 9am and 9pm; one hour to KL Sentral.

BUS
Most buses are provided by either **Rapid KL** (☑ 03-7885 2585; www.rapidkl.com.my; RM1-5; ⊙ 6am-11.30pm) or **Metrobus** (☑ 03-5635 3070). There's an **information booth** (Map p390; Jln Hang Kasturi; ⊙ 7am-9pm; LRT Pasar Seni) at the Jln Sultan Mohammed bus stop in Chinatown. Rapid KL buses have their destinations clearly displayed. Fares are from RM1 to RM3.80.

Local buses leave from half-a-dozen small bus stands around the city – useful stops in Chinatown include Jln Sultan Mohamed by Pasar Seni, **Bangkok Bank** (Map p390) on Lebuh Pudu, and Medan Pasar on Lebuh Ampang.

The **GO-KL free city bus** (☑ 1800-887 723; www.facebook.com/goklcitybus; ⊙ 6am-11pm Mon-Thu, to 1am Sat, 7am-11pm Sun) has four circular routes around the city, with stops at KLCC, KL Tower, KL Sentral, the National Museum and Merdeka Sq. Buses run every five minutes during peak hours and every 10 to 15 minutes at other times.

TAXI
KL has plenty of air-conditioned taxis, which queue up at designated taxi stops across the city. Fares start at RM3 for the first three minutes, with an additional 25 sen for each 36 seconds. From midnight to 6am there's a surcharge of 50% on the metered fare. Some drivers refuse to use the meter, even though this is a legal requirement.

One of the easiest ways to use taxis in KL is to download an app such as **Uber**, **Easy Taxi** or **Grab** (formally known as My Teksi) to your smartphone or tablet.

TRAIN
Rapid KL runs the **Light Rail Transit** (LRT; ☑ 03-7885 2585; www.myrapid.com.my; from

RM1.30; ⊘ every 6-10min 6am-11.45pm Mon-Sat, to 11.30pm Sun) system. There are three lines: the Ampang line from Ampang to Sentul Timur; the Sri Petaling line from Sentul Timur to Putra Heights; and the Kelana Jaya line from Gombak to Putra Heights. Buy single-journey tokens or MyRapid cards from the cashier or electronic ticket machines.

KTM Komuter (www.ktmb.com.my; from RM1.40; ⊘ 6.45am-11.45pm) train services run every 15 to 20 minutes from 6am to 11.45pm and use KL Sentral as a hub. There are two lines: Tanjung Malim to Pelabuhan Klang and Batu Caves to Pulau Sebang/Tampin.

The air-conditioned **monorail** (www.myrapid. com.my; RM1.20-4.10; ⊘ 6am-midnight) zips from KL Sentral to Titiwangsa, linking many of the city's sightseeing areas.

PENINSULAR MALAYSIA – WEST COAST

Melaka City

📞 06 / POP 484,885

The peacock of Malaysian cities, Melaka City preens with its wealth of colourful trishaws, homegrown galleries and crimson colonial buildings. The city's historic centre achieved Unesco World Heritage status in 2008 and since then Melaka City's tourism industry has developed at breakneck pace. Old shophouses and mansions have enjoyed makeovers as galleries and hotels and Melaka City's kaleidoscope of architectural styles – spanning Peranakan, Portuguese, Dutch and British elements – is well preserved.

Inevitably, a strong whiff of commercialism has accompanied this success. However, it's easy to feel the town's old magic (and get a seat at popular restaurants) on quiet weekdays. Melaka City, as it has for centuries, continues to exude tolerance and welcomes cultural exchange.

◉ Sights

◉ Town Square & Bukit St Paul

Stadthuys HISTORIC BUILDING

(📞 06-282 6526; Dutch Sq; foreign/local visitor RM10/4; ⊘ 9am-5.30pm Sat-Thu, to 12.15pm & 2.45-5.30pm Fri) Melaka's favourite trishaw pick-up spot is the cerise-coloured Stadthuys. This former town hall and governor's residence dates to the 1650s and is believed to be the oldest Dutch building in the East. Erected after the Dutch captured Melaka in 1641, it's a reproduction of the former Stadhuis (town hall) of the Frisian town of Hoorn in the Netherlands. Today it's a museum complex exhibiting colourful artefacts like record-breaking trishaws and bird-shaped longboats; the **History & Ethnography Museum** is the highlight.

Admission covers all the small museums within the complex. There is no fee for guided tours, which take place at 10.30am and 2.30pm on Saturday and Sunday.

For in-depth acquaintance with Melaka past and present, peruse the **Governor's House, Democratic Government Museum**, a **Literature Museum** focusing on Malaysian writers, **Cheng Ho Gallery** and the **Education Museum**.

Maritime Museum & Naval Museum MUSEUM

(📞 06-283 0926; Jln Merdeka; adult/child RM10/6; ⊘ 9am-5pm Mon-Thu, to 6.30pm Fri-Sun) Embark on a voyage through Melaka's maritime history at these linked museums. The most enjoyable of the museum's three sections (one ticket covers them all) is housed in a huge re-creation of the *Flor de la Mar*, a Portuguese ship that sank off the coast of Melaka. The fun of posing on the deck and clambering between floors rather eclipses the displays and dioramas.

St Paul's Church RUINS

(Jln Kota; ⊘ 24hr) FREE The evocative ruin of St Paul's Church crowns the summit of Bukit St Paul overlooking central Melaka. Steep stairs from Jln Kota and Jln Chang Koon Cheng lead up to this faded sanctuary, originally built by a Portuguese captain in 1521. The church was regularly visited by St Francis Xavier, whose marble statue – minus his right hand and a few toes – stands in front of the ruin.

Porta de Santiago RUINS

(A'Famosa; Jln Kota; ⊘ 24hr) FREE Most visitors pause for a photo at Porta de Santiago before hiking to the ruined church (p398) on Bukit St Paul. It was built as a Portuguese fortress in 1511; the British took over in 1641 and destroyed it in 1806 to prevent it falling into Napoleon's hands. Fortunately Sir Stamford Raffles arrived in 1810 and saved what remains today.

◉ Chinatown

Chinatown is Melaka City's most interesting area. Jln Tun Tan Cheng Lock, formerly

Peninsular Malaysia

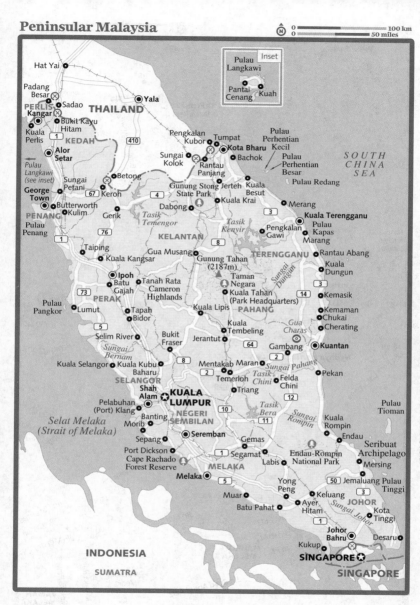

called Heeren St, was the preferred address for wealthy Peranakan (also known as Straits Chinese) traders. Jln Hang Jebat, formerly known as Jonker St, is dominated by souvenir shops and restaurants; every weekend it hosts the Jonker Walk Night Market (p404). Jln Tokong, which changes name to Jln Tokang Emas and Jln Tokang Besi as you head from north to south, is home to several Chinese temples, a mosque and an Indian temple – the reason it is also known as Harmony St.

400

Melaka

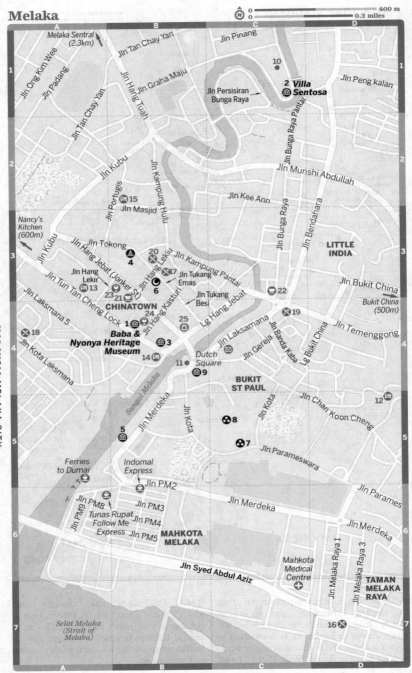

★ Baba & Nyonya Heritage Museum
MUSEUM

(☑ 06-283 1273; http://babanyonyamuseum.com; 48-50 Jln Tun Tan Cheng Lock; adult/child RM16/11; ⊙ 10am-1pm & 2-5pm Mon-Thu, to 6pm Fri-Sun) Touring this traditional Baba-Nonya (Peranakan) townhouse transports you to a time when women peered at guests through decorative partitions and every social situation had its specific location within the house. The captivating museum is arranged to look like a typical 19th-century Baba-Nonya residence. Tour guides enliven the setting with their arch sense of humour. Book ahead or arrive just before the strike of the hour. Last tour of the day is an hour before closing time.

8 Heeren Street
HISTORIC BUILDING

(8 Jln Tun Tan Cheng Lock; ⊙ 11am-4pm) **FREE** This 18th-century, Dutch-period residential house was restored as a model conservation project. A guide is on hand to explain the features and history behind this airy two-storey building. Entry is free, but donations are appreciated. Opening hours can be spotty.

Cheng Hoon Teng Temple
BUDDHIST TEMPLE

(Qing Yun Ting or Green Clouds Temple; ☑ 06-282 9343; www.chenghoonteng.org.my; 25 Jln Tokong; ⊙ 7am-7pm) **FREE** Malaysia's oldest still-operating Chinese temple, constructed in 1673, remains a central place of worship for the Buddhist community in Melaka City. It's also a testament to the perseverance of the local Chinese community who funded its restoration following traditional methods, from the ornate roof ceramics to the painted tigers by

the door. The temple is dedicated to Kuan Yin, the goddess of mercy.

Masjid Kampung Kling
MOSQUE

(cnr Jln Hang Lekiu & Jln Tokong Emas) **FREE** While the mosque oiginally dates back to 1748, the 19th-century rebuild you see today mingles a number of styles. Its multi-tiered *meru* roof (a stacked form similar to that seen in Balinese Hindu architecture) owes its inspiration to Hindu temples, the Moorish watchtower minaret is typical of early mosques in Sumatra, while English and Dutch tiles bedeck its interior.

◉ Elsewhere

★ Villa Sentosa
HISTORIC BUILDING

(Peaceful Villa; ☑ 06-282 3988; Jln Kampung Morten; entry by donation; ⊙ hr vary, usually 9am-1pm & 2-6pm) The highlight of visiting the charming Malay village of **Kampung Morten** (Jln Kampung Morten; ⊙ 4pm Mon, Wed & Fri) **FREE** is this living museum within a 1920s *kampung* house. Visitors (or rather, guests) are welcomed by a member of the household who points out period objects, including photographs of family members, Ming dynasty ceramics and a century-old Quran. You're unlikely to leave without a photo-op on plush velvet furniture or a few strikes of the lucky gong.

Bukit China
CEMETERY

(Jln Puteri Hang Li Poh) More than 12,500 graves, including about 20 Muslim tombs, cover the 25 grassy hectares of serene 'Chinese Hill'. In the middle of the 15th century, the sultan of

DON'T LEAVE MELAKA WITHOUT TRYING ...

Chicken rice balls Steamed chicken paired with small balls of glutinous rice, often greased with stock or fat and served with a piquant dipping sauce.

Asam fish Freshwater fish doused in a mouth-burning stew of chilli and tamarind.

Nonya laksa Melaka's version of this coconut-milk and noodle soup, infused with a powerful lemongrass flavour.

Satay celup Submerge your choice of tofu, fish or meat into a spicy, bubbling soup.

Curry debel Hot chicken curry that marries Portuguese and Malay flavours.

Cendol An addictive shaved-ice dessert with green tentacles (sorry, noodles), syrups, fruit and coconut milk.

Melaka imported the Ming emperor's daughter from China as his bride in a move to seal relations between the two countries. She brought with her a vast retinue, including 500 handmaidens, who settled around Bukit China. It has been a Chinese area ever since.

☞ Tours

Melaka River Cruise CRUISE
(☎ 06-286 5468, 06-281 4322; Jln Laksamana; adult/child RM17/6; ⊙ 9am-11pm) The most convenient place to board this 40-minute riverboat cruise along Sungai Melaka is at the quay near the Maritime Museum (p398). Cruises go 9km upriver past Kampung Morten and old *godown* (river warehouses) with a recorded narration explaining the riverfront's history.

Eco Bike Tour CYCLING
(☎ 019-652 5029; www.melakaonbike.com; half-day per person RM100) Explore the fascinating landscape around Melaka City with Alias on his three-hour bike tour (minimum two people) through 20km of oil-palm and rubber-tree plantations and *kampung* communities. Book at least three days in advance and flag your level of fitness. Pickups are from your accommodation.

🛏 Sleeping

★ **Nomaps** HOSTEL $
(☎ 06-283 8311; www.thenomaps.com; 11 Jln Tun Tan Cheng Lock; dm/d RM80-100/150 all incl breakfast;

🅿 ✳ @ ⊚) A real step up for Melaka's hostel options. The attractive street art of Kenji Chai decorates the walls of this otherwise minimalist flashpackers in a key Chinatown location. Six- and four-bed dorms are tiny but have colourful duvets and quality mattresses. Free laundry and a comfy TV room are other pluses. Rates are slightly cheaper on weekdays (dorm beds from RM55).

Apa Kaba Home & Stay GUESTHOUSE $
(☎ 012-798 1232, 06-283 8196; www.apa-kaba.com; 28 Kg Banda Kaba; d/tr with shared bathroom from RM50/90, tw/tr RM90/135, all incl breakfast; ✳ ⊚) This tranquil homestay has a low-key *kampung* (village) setting, but is within easy walking distance of central Melaka City. The ramshackle 1912 building is a mishmash of Malay and Chinese styles. Rooms are simple, arranged on the ground-floor around the reception (the more expensive have aircon). Completing the idyllic picture are the large garden with dangling mango trees and strutting house cat.

Ringo's Foyer GUESTHOUSE $
(☎ 06-281 6393, 016-668 8898; www.ringosfoyer.com; 46A Jln Portugis; dm/d/d incl breakfast from RM38/80/140; ✳ ⊚) The friendly owners do a great job of keeping the atmosphere sociable at Ringo's Foyer, particularly in the rooftop cafe and hang-out areas. Beds in the 18-bed dorm are pod-style, allowing reasonable privacy. With bike rental, free lockers, laundry (RM8) and guitars, this place has everything a weary backpacker could want.

★ **Hotel Puri** HOTEL $$
(☎ 06-282 5588; www.hotelpuri.com; 118 Jln Tun Tan Cheng Lock; d RM188-299, tr from RM310, q from RM380, all incl breakfast; ✳ @ ⊚) Why merely tour one of Melaka's heritage buildings when you can stay overnight? Elegant Hotel Puri inhabits a superbly renovated Peranakan mansion dating to 1822. Its elaborate lobby, decked out with beautiful old cane and inlaid furniture, opens to a fountained courtyard garden. A small on-site museum holds lavish antiques. Rooms have crisp sheets, shuttered windows and a regal colour scheme.

✗ Eating

Peranakan cuisine is Melaka City's most famous type of cooking. It's also known as Nonya (or Nyonya), an affectionate term for a Peranakan wife (often the family chef). You'll also find Portuguese Eurasian food, Indian, Chinese and more.

★**Nancy's Kitchen**   MALAYSIAN $
(☑06-283 6099; www.eatatnancyskit.com; 13 Jln KL 3/8, Taman Kota Laksamana; mains from RM10; ⊙11am-5pm Sun, Mon, Wed & Thu, to 9pm Fri & Sat) The mouth-watering Peranakan cuisine stirred up in Nancy's Kitchen lives up to local hype. Service can be curt, and a wait is inevitable at weekends, but it's worth it for the juicy pork fried with bean curd, or signature dish candlenut chicken – simmered in a nutty sauce, fragrant with lemongrass. Buy some *kuih* (sticky-rice sweets) on your way out.

★**Pak Putra Restaurant**   PAKISTANI $
(☑012-601 5876; 58 Jln Kota Laksmana 4; mains RM10-12; ⊙5.30pm-1am, closed alternate Mon; ☑) Tikka chickens rotate hypnotically on skewers, luring diners to this excellent Pakistani restaurant. With aromatic vegetarian dishes, seafood and piquant curries, there's no shortage of choice. The unchallenged highlights are oven-puffed naan bread and chicken fresh from the clay tandoor. Portions are generous and service is speedy.

Selvam   INDIAN $
(☑06-281 9223; 2 Jln Temenggong; mains RM5-11; ⊙7am-10pm; ☑) This well-loved banana-leaf restaurant is excellent value, with efficient (if not always warm) staff. Generous servings of aromatic chicken biryani are eclipsed by the vegetarian offerings, in particular the Friday-afternoon veggie special. Selvam is also an excellent stop for a breakfast *dosa* or *idli* (rice-and-lentil cake).

Shui Xian Vegetarian   CHINESE $
(☑012-635 8052; 43 Jln Hang Lekiu; mains RM3-6; ⊙7.30am-2.30pm Mon-Sat; ☑) In a city where vegetable dishes so often arrive strewn with shrimp or pork, vegetarians can breathe a sigh of relief here. This no-frills canteen whips up meat-free versions of *char kway teow*, laksa and even 'chicken' rice balls.

Low Yong Moh   CHINESE $
(☑06-282 1235; 32 Jln Tokong Emas; dim sum RM2.40-3.70; ⊙5.30am-noon Wed-Mon) Famous across Melaka for its large and delectably well-stuffed *pao* (steamed pork buns), this place is Chinatown's biggest breakfast treat. With high ceilings, plenty of fans running and a view of Masjid Kampung Kling, the atmosphere oozes charm. It's usually packed with talkative, newspaper-reading locals by around 7am. Food offerings thin out by 11am, so arrive early.

Amy Heritage Cuisine   PERANAKAN $$
(☑06-286 8819; Jln Melaka Raya 24; mains RM22-28; ⊙noon-2.30pm & 6-9pm Tue-Sun) Nipping at the heels of Melaka's long-time Peranakan favourite Nancy's Kitchen (p403), Amy Heritage Cuisine dishes up sensational food in a no-frills restaurant, 1km southeast of Dutch Sq. Melt-in-the-mouth candlenut chicken, spicy asam fish and *kangkung belacan* (spinach flavoured with shrimp and chilli) make this perennially busy place worth booking.

🍸 Drinking & Nightlife

On Friday, Saturday and Sunday nights, Jonker Walk Night Market (p404) in Chinatown closes Jln Hang Jebat to traffic and the handful of bars along the lane become a mini street party with live music and tables spilling beyond the sidewalks.

★**Daily Fix**   CAFE
(☑06-283 4858; www.facebook.com/thedailyfix cafe; 55 Jln Hang Jebat; ⊙9am-11pm Mon-Fri, from 8.30am Sat & Sun; ☜) You may have to wait patiently for a spot in Melaka City's trendiest cafe, hidden away behind a Chinatown souvenir shop. Most of Daily Fix's fans are here for the impressive brunches (RM18 to RM29), such as banana French toast and eggs Benedict. The signature rose latte, sprinkled with petals, looks as good as it tastes.

★**Geographér Cafe**   BAR
(☑06-281 6813; www.geographer.com.my; 83 Jln Hang Jebat; ⊙10am-1am Sun-Thu, from 9am Fri & Sat; ☜) A swinging soundtrack of Eurotrash, jazz and classic pop keeps the beers

---

ⓘ GETTING TO INDONESIA: MELAKA TO DUMAI

Getting to the border High-speed **Indomal Express** (☑019-665 7055, 06-286 2506; G35, Jln PM2, Plaza Mahkota,) ferries make the trip from Melaka to **Dumai** (Jln Merdeka) in Sumatra daily at 10am (one way/return RM110/170, two hours; child tickets are half price). The quay is walking distance or a short taxi ride from most hotels and guesthouses. Tickets are available at **Tunas Rupat Follow Me Express** (☑06-283 2506; www.tunasrupat.com; G-29, Jln PM10, Plaza Mahkota) near the wharf.

At the border Citizens of most countries can obtain a 30-day visa on arrival (US$35).

Moving on Dumai is on Sumatra's east coast and is a 10-hour bus ride from Bukittinggi.

BUSES FROM MELAKA

DESTINATION	PRICE (RM)	DURATION (HR)	FREQUENCY
Cameron Highlands	65	5	1 daily
Ipoh	34-38	5	5 daily
Johor Bahru	18-21	3½	more than hourly
KLIA	24-28	2	more than hourly
Kota Bharu	57	10	1 daily
Kuala Lumpur	10-14	2	half-hourly
Mersing	25	4½	3 daily
Penang	49-55	7	3 daily
Singapore	24-27	4½	almost hourly

flowing at this traveller magnet. It's a well-ventilated cafe-bar, strewn with greenery. Despite bordering busy Jonker St, it feels like a haven. Monday nights have live jazz while Fridays and Saturdays bring a father-daughter vocal-keyboard duet (both 8.30pm). Geographér also serves decent food ranging from American-style fast food to *nasi lemak* (mains RM15), though it doesn't compare favourably against the cheap and delicious street food outside.

Me & Mrs Jones PUB
(☑016-234 4292; 3 Jln Hang Kasturi; ⊙7pm-midnight Tue-Sun) This cosy pub is staunchly unhip and all the more enjoyable for it. At weekends there's live blues and rock, often with retired co-owner Mr Tan leading a jam session. Relax into the atmosphere and grab a beer or juice (long menus are not the Jones' style).

🛍 Shopping

★ **Jonker Walk Night Market** MARKET
(Jln Hang Jebat; ⊙6-11pm Fri-Sun) Food hawkers, trinket sellers and fortune tellers pile into Jln Hang Jebat for Melaka City's weekly extravaganza of street food and shopping. The street closes to traffic, shops stay open late, and a party atmosphere prevails. Graze on barbecued quail eggs and *kuih* (sticky-rice sweets) as you squeeze between souvenir and T-shirt stalls, pausing to watch the occasional Chinese karaoke performance. The night market is unashamedly commercial but this riotously colourful experience shouldn't be missed.

ℹ Information

There are plenty of ATMs at shopping malls but fewer in Chinatown.

Mahkota Medical Centre (☑06-285 2999, emergency 06-285 2999; www.mahkotamedical. com; Jln Merdeka; ⊙24hr) A private hospital offering a full range of services including accident and emergency care.

Post Office (Jln Laksamana; ⊙8.30am-5pm Mon-Fri, to 1pm Sat)

ℹ Getting There & Away

Melaka City is 149km south from Kuala Lumpur, 220km northwest from Johor Bahru and 80km southeast from Port Dickson, and is served by regular direct buses from major cities around Peninsular Malaysia.

Melaka Sentral (☑06-288 1324; www.melaka sentral.com.my; Jln Sentral), the huge, modern long-distance bus station, is 5km north of the city. Luggage deposit at Melaka Sentral is RM2 per bag. You'll also find an ATM and restaurants here.

A medley of privately run bus companies make checking timetables a herculean feat; scout popular routes at www.expressbusmalaysia. com/coach-from-melaka or book ahead (not a bad idea on busy weekends or if you have a plane to catch) on www.busonlineticket.com. You can also buy bus tickets in advance at **Discovery Cafe** (☑012-683 5606, 06-292 5606; www. discovery-malacca.com; 3 Jln Bunga Raya) in downtown Melaka City – there's a small commission, dependent on the ticket fare.

ℹ Getting Around

Melaka City is small enough to walk around or, for the traffic fearless, you can rent a bike for between RM5 and RM10 per day from guesthouses.

Taking to Melaka City's streets by trishaw is a must – rates are supposedly fixed at RM40 per hour, but you'll still have to bargain. A one-way trip within town should cost roughly RM20.

Taxis should cost around RM10 to RM15 for a trip anywhere around town.

Cameron Highlands

☑ 05

Emerald tea plantations unfurl across valleys, and the air is freshened by eucalyptus – Malaysia's largest hill-station area feels instantly restorative. Temperatures in these 1300m to 1829m heights rarely top 30°C, inspiring convoys of weekenders to sip tea and eat strawberries here. Though in Pahang, the highlands are accessed from Perak.

From north to south, the Cameron Highlands roughly encompass Tringkap, Brinchang, Tanah Rata, Ringlet and their surrounds. Named after explorer Sir William Cameron, who mapped the area in 1885, the highlands were developed during the British colonial period. Gardens, bungalows and even a golf course sprang up during the 1930s, making the Cameron Highlands a refuge for heat-addled Brits to mop their brows.

Tourism is big business, so expect views to be occasionally obscured by construction sites for yet another megaresort. But between eco-conscious trekking, temples and genteel tea culture, you can find serenity amid the tourist hubbub.

◉ Sights & Activities

Besides getting in touch with your inner Englishman via tea and strawberries, the main pastime in the Cameron Highlands is hiking. Maps are available at most guesthouses and tour offices. Yellow-and-black signboards mark the trails, many of which aren't maintained very well and can be treacherous, steep and unclear. Before setting out on any trail, always ask locally about its safety; the folk at Father's Guest House (p406) are seriously on the ball when it comes to the ever-changing picture of trails, routes and safety advice. Always carry water, some food, and rain gear to guard against unpredictable weather, and don't set out in the mid-afternoon (darkness descends quickly). Let your guesthouse know your planned route and predicted return time. Better yet, get a local guide.

Boh Sungei Palas Tea Estate   PLANTATION
(☑ 05-496 2096; www.boh.com.my; ⊙ 8.30am-4.30pm Tue-Sun) FREE Touristy but thoroughly good fun, the Cameron Highlands' most famous tea plantation has a modern visitors centre and a cafe with spectacular views over undulating, tea-clad valleys. Watch a short video on the estate's history, then browse every imaginable version of Boh tea in the giftshop. Free 15-minute tours showing the tea-making process are conducted half-hourly; wait for a staff member to collect you from the visitors centre.

Sam Poh Temple   BUDDHIST TEMPLE
(Brinchang) FREE This scarlet-and-yellow temple complex, just below Brinchang about 1km off the main road, leaves visitors rubbing their eyes. Inside, look for the burnished statues of the defenders of Buddhist law, then continue to the inner temple building (remove your shoes) where hundreds of ceramic tiles feature intricate Buddha images, each one hand-painted. The temple is dedicated to medieval admiral and eunuch Zheng Ho and is allegedly the fourth-largest Buddhist temple in Malaysia.

☞ Tours

★ Eco Cameron   TOURS
(☑ 05-491 5388; www.ecocameron.com; 72-A Persiaran Camellia 4, Tanah Rata; tours RM50-120; ⊙ 8am-9.30pm) This outfit specialises in nature tours of the Cameron Highlands: hiking, orchid walks, birdwatching and insect-spotting. Most enthralling are guided hikes through the Mossy Forest – Eco Cameron has exclusive access to a protected trail.

Jason Marcus Chin   TOURS
(☑ 010-380 8558; jason.marcus.chin@gmail.com; half-/full-day tour from RM50/70) Exceptional nature guide Jason Marcus Chin leads guided group hikes (from two to 10 people). Jason's observational skills are impressive, as is his knowledge of local flora and fauna.

BUSES FROM TANAH RATA

DESTINATION	PRICE (RM)	DURATION	FREQUENCY
Brinchang	2	20min	every 2hr, 6.30am-6.30pm
Ipoh	20	2hr	7 daily
Kuala Lumpur	35	4hr	8 daily, 8.30am-5.30pm
Melaka	65	6hr	1 daily
Penang	32	5hr	5 daily
Singapore	125-140	10hr	1 daily

Cameron Highlands

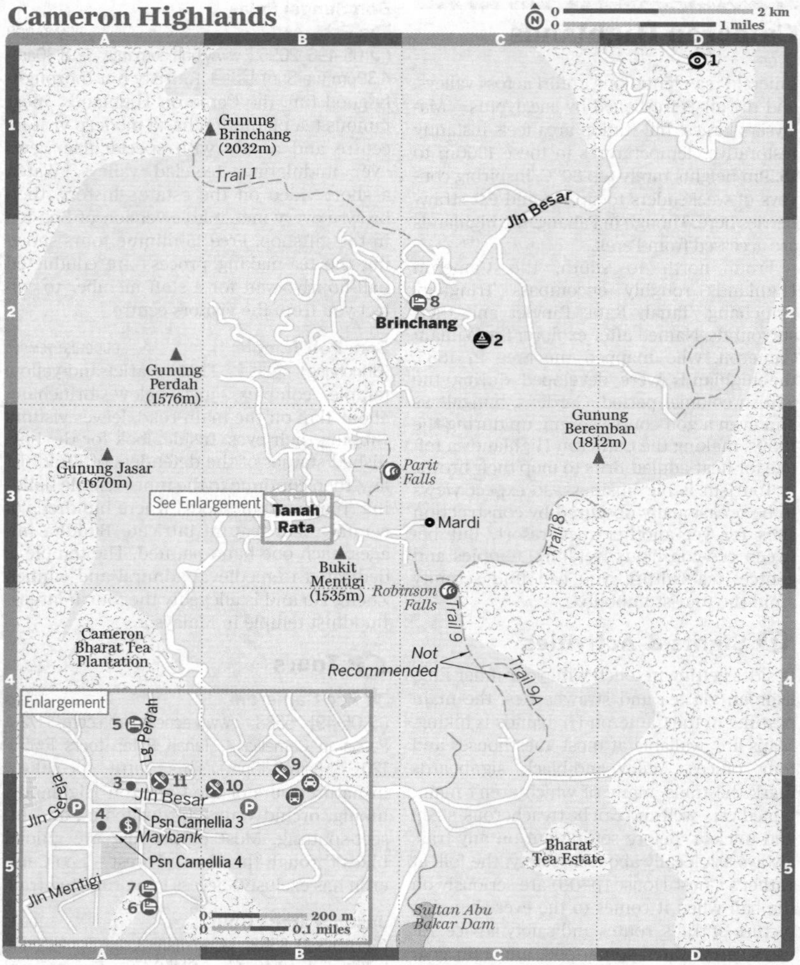

CS Travel & Tours TOURS
(☎05-491 1200; www.cstravel.com.my; 47 Jln Besar, Tanah Rata; ⏲7.30am-7.30pm) This agency leads popular half-day 'countryside tours' (adult/child RM25/20) around the highlands' main sights. More worthwhile are the 'sunrise tours' (adult/child RM65/55), which include breakfast along with the golden-hour views.

Sleeping

The highlands are busy during school holidays in April, August and December; book well in advance. Prices rise by around 25% at weekends and during holidays.

★ **Father's Guest House** GUESTHOUSE $
(☎016-566 1111; www.fathersguesthouse.net; 4 Jln Mentigi, Tanah Rata; dm RM30, d RM95, d/tr/q without bathroom from RM74/95/127; P@🛜) Pleasant private rooms and clean 10-person dorms elicit sighs of relief from travellers checking in at Father's. A merry vibe prevails and friendly staff ooze local knowledge, and there are handy perks like hairdryers, free tea and coffee, and an on-site cafe (breakfast from RM3).

Cameron Highlands

Eight Mentigi   HOSTEL $

(☑05-491 5988; www.eightmentigi.com; 8A Jln
Mentigi, Tanah Rata; dm/d/tr from RM25/70/100;
🅿@🛜) The digs, from six-bed dorms to
spacious private rooms, are simple. But the
host Smith cultivates a welcoming ambience
in this fuss-free hostel, only a stone's throw
from Tanah Rata's main drag. Bonus: you
can buy beers from the front desk.

Snooze   GUESTHOUSE $

(☑014-669 0108, 016-666 2102; www.facebook.
com/SnoozeCH; 4 Jln Besar, Brinchang; d/tr/q from
RM88/120/145; 🛜) The bright and cheery
rooms at Snooze are excellent value. The
cupcake wallpaper and buttercup bedsheets
might be a little kitsch for some, but this
clean guesthouse is one of Brinchang's better
places to stay. There are colourful sitting areas at which to chill, plus a fridge and laundry.

Daniel's Lodge   HOSTEL $

(☑05-491 5823; www.daniels.cameronhighlands.
com; 9 Lg Perdah, Tanah Rata; dm RM18, d RM70,
without bathroom RM40-70; @🛜) The backpacker force remains strong at this long-
standing hostel, also known as Kang's. The
accommodation won't win prizes for comfort, but despite the grungy feel, it's a functional place with perks like lockers (RM2),
laundry service and a jungle-themed bar
(with occasional bonfires).

✖ Eating

★**Singh Chapati**   INDIAN $

(cnr Lg Perdah & Jln Besar, Tanah Rata; mains RM7-20;
⊙1-9pm; 🖋) On a lofty perch behind Tanah
Rata's main drag, Singh's is the sweetest In-

dian joint in town. Dig in to fragrant biryanis,
excellent veggie mains like butter paneer, its
famous smoky chapati (flatbreads), and wash
it down with mango lassi or masala tea. This
no-frills restaurant benefits from a slightly secluded setting; try to bag a terrace table looking towards hills and mock-Tudor mansions.

Restoran Sri Brinchang   INDIAN $

(25 Jln Besar, Tanah Rata; mains RM4-20; ⊙7am-
10pm; 🖋) This busy place heaps spiced aubergine, pappadams and rice onto banana leaves
for its filling lunches; it prides itself on spring
chicken served straight from the *tandoor*.

Lord's Cafe   CAFE $

(Jln Besar, Tanah Rata; mains RM2.50-4.90;
⊙10am-9pm Wed-Fri & Mon, to 6pm Sat) Despite
the neon threat from the chain restaurants
encroaching on Tanah Rata, Lord's Cafe
prevails...possibly protected by the prayers
decorating it inside and out. Skip the so-
so breakfasts, omelettes and savoury pies:
Lord's specialities include thick mango and
banana lassi and apple pie. There's a community atmosphere, and it's reassuringly
decorated like your grandma's living room.

❶ Getting There & Around

Tanah Rata's **bus station** (Jln Besar) is also
known as Terminal Freesia. Buy tickets a day in
advance for popular destinations. Daily bus and
boat transfer packages also reach Taman Negara and the Perhentian Islands.

Taxi services (☑05-491 2355; Jln Besar)
from Tanah Rata include Brinchang (RM10),
Ringlet (RM25) and Boh Sungei Palas (RM30).
For prices on additional destinations, including
hiking trailheads and tea estates, see the price
list posted at the taxi stop at Terminal Freesia.
For touring around, a taxi costs RM25 per hour.

Ipoh

☑05 / POP 710,000

Travellers rushing from Kuala Lumpur to
Penang are missing a trick if they don't stop
in historic Ipoh. This pleasant, mid-sized
town is rising to prominence as an attractive
city-break destination among in-the-know
Malaysians (particularly food fans). It's an
exciting place for an urban interlude, as well
as a convenient gateway for travel to the
Cameron Highlands.

A self-guided walking tour is the best way
to cover all of the colonial-era architecture
(and modern street art) in Ipoh's old town.
Use the excellent *Ipoh Heritage Trail* maps

1 and 2, available at Ipoh's **tourist information centre** (☑05-208 3155; http://ipohtourism.mbi.gov.my; 1 Jln Tun Sambanthan; ⊙10am-5pm), or simply check out the billboards around the **Kong Heng Block** (75 Jln Panglima; ⊙9am-10pm Wed-Mon) area.

🛏 Sleeping

★ Container Hotel   HOSTEL $
(☑05-243 3311; http://containerhotel.my/ipoh; 89-91 Jln Sultan Yussuf; per pod standard/deluxe RM45/65; ❀☎) Hostelling is done differently at Ipoh's Container Hotel: metal girders and concrete establish an industrial theme, evoking Ipoh's tin-mining heyday. Instead of bunk beds, guests tuck into one of several 'pods' in each dorm; there's a curtain for privacy and 'deluxe' pods have windows overlooking the street. Even more intriguing is the slide between floors – who needs stairs, anyway?

Abby by the River   HOSTEL $
(☑05-292 2999; www.abbyhotel.my; cnr Jln Laxamana & Jln Sultan Iskandar; 8-bed/6-bed dm RM25/30, d RM90, tr RM120; ℗❀☎) Perched next to Sultan Iskandar bridge, Abby's is neatly positioned for access to Ipoh's old and new towns. Dorms are cramped but clean; private rooms are a little comfier. The decor in both is somewhat reminiscent of a hospital.

🍴 Eating

★ Lim Ko Pi   CHINESE $
(☑05-253 2898; 10 Jln Sultan Iskandar; mains RM12-17; ⊙8.30am-5.30pm) From its colourful tiles to the secluded inner dining chambers, this relaxing cafe has a strong whiff of Ipoh's glory days. Breakfasts are excellent value (from RM5 for eggs, toast and white coffee), while lunches include generous portions of prawn fried rice, curry noodles and smoky-but-sweet stewed pork. Service is wonderfully unrushed compared to many of Ipoh's eateries.

★ Restaurant Lou Wong   MALAYSIAN $
(☑05-254 4190; 49 Jln Yau Tet Shin; mains RM13; ⊙11am-9.30pm Sat-Thu) Ipoh's culinary pride and joy may not seem like much, with brisk staff and streetside plastic stools. But this is the place to try Ipoh's signature dish, *tauge ayam* (chicken with beansprouts). Lou Wong has perfected the recipe: smooth poached chicken on soy-drenched cucumber; plump, blanched bean sprouts sprinkled with pepper; and your choice of rice or noodles on the side.

Concubine Lane Tau Fu Fa   CHINESE $
(www.facebook.com/concubinelanetff; 8 Jln Panglima; per bowl RM2.50; ⊙10.30am-4.30pm; ☑) A brimming bowlful of *tau fu fah* (beancurd pudding) at this hole-in-the-wall canteen is the perfect excuse to linger on historic Jalan Panglima, aka 'Concubine Lane'. Freshly prepared each morning, each pudding is topped with sugar or ginger and black sesame.

Sri Ananda Bahwan Banana Leaf   INDIAN $
(☑05-253 9798; 7 Persiaran Bijeh Timah; mains from RM5; ⊙7am-11pm; ☑) Some of Ipoh's best Indian food is cooked up in this simple cafeteria in Little India. Mop up chutney and dhal with a fluffy *dosa* or order the gen-

BUSES FROM IPOH

DESTINATION	PRICE (RM)	DURATION (HR)	FREQUENCY
Alor Setar	24-29	3½-4	10 daily, 9am-4pm
Butterworth/George Town (Penang)	16-25	2	frequent, 9am-9pm
Cameron Highlands	20-24	2	7 daily, 9.30am-5.30pm
Hat Yai (Thailand)	65	6-7	1-2 daily
Johor Bahru	55-70	7¼	At least 8 daily, morning & evening only
Kota Bharu	34-39	7	At least 4 daily, morning & evening only
Kuala Lumpur (also KLIA/LCCT)	20-35	3-3½	half-hourly, 4.30am-10pm
Melaka	36-40	5	every 2hr, 8.30am-11pm
Singapore	65-85	8	frequent, 8.30-10.30am & 8.30-11pm

erous banana-leaf special, with mountains of rice and spiced okra. Leave space to take away a box of the excellent *barfi*, fudge-like confectionery in flavours from cashew to chocolate.

ℹ Getting There & Away

Most travellers will arrive in Ipoh's intercity bus station, **Terminal Amanjaya** (📞 05-526 7818, 05-526 7718; www.peraktransit.com.my; Persiaran Meru Raya 5), approximately 8km north of Ipoh. Bus 116 (RM2.40) goes between Amanjaya and the city centre until 8pm, while taxis cost roughly RM20 to RM25.

It's worthwhile checking timetables or booking ahead using an online ticket service such as www.easybook.com.

Trains run to Kuala Lumpur (RM25 to RM40, 2½ to 3½ hours, eight daily) and Butterworth (RM30 to RM42, 2½ to four hours, four daily). Check www.ktmb.com.my for the latest info on fares and schedules.

Penang

POP 1.75 MILLION / AREA 1031 SQ KM

If there's a more thrilling cocktail of eastern cultures than Penang, we've yet to find it. Penang has long served as the link between Asia's great kingdoms and an important outlet to the markets of Europe and the Middle East. At its heart is diverse, cosmopolitan George Town, Penang Island's main city and an urban centre that delivers old-world Asia in spades; think trishaws pedalling past watermarked Chinese shophouses and blue joss smoke perfuming the air. The freshest aspects of modern culture are present, too, in an exceptional art scene and free-spirited carnivals, all fed by an infectious local enthusiasm for Penang's long history and kaleidoscope of cultures.

If you can tear yourself away, the rest of the island is rich in palm-fringed beaches and fishing villages, mountainous jungle and farms growing nutmeg and durian. And

Penang Island

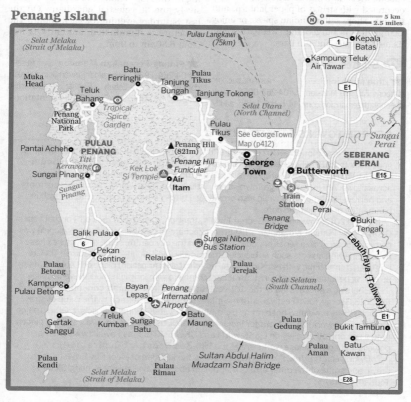

MALAYSIA PENANG

there's even more of the state to explore across in Penang's mainland section, Seberang Perai.

George Town

 04 / POP 740,200

Combine three distinct and ancient cultures, indigenous and colonial architecture, shake for a few centuries, and garnish with some of the best food in Southeast Asia, and you've got the irresistible urban cocktail that is George Town.

The time-worn shophouses of the Unesco World Heritage Zone will likely spark a desire in some visitors to move straight to Pulau Penang's most attractive city. Even more impressive is the movie set–like mishmash of Chinese temples in Little India, mosques in Chinatown, and Western-style skyscrapers and shopping complexes gleaming high above British Raj–era architecture.

The eclectic jumble makes this a city that rewards explorers. Get lost in the maze of chaotic streets and narrow lanes, past shrines decorated with strings of paper lanterns and fragrant shops selling Indian spices; or enjoy George Town's burgeoning street-art scene, its modern cafes and fun bars.

◉ Sights

★ Blue Mansion   HISTORIC BUILDING
(Cheong Fatt Tze Mansion; ☑04-262 0006; www. cheongfatttzemansion.com; 14 Lebuh Leith; adult/ child RM17/8.50; ☺tours 11am, 2pm & 3.30pm) The most photographed building in George Town is this magnificent 38-room, 220-window mansion, built in the 1880s and rescued from ruin in the 1990s. Its distinctive blue-hued exterior (once common in George Town) is the result of an indigo-based limewash.

Hour-long guided tours (included in the admission fee) explain the building's feng shui and unique features, and relate stories about Cheong Fatt Tze, the rags-to-riches Hakka merchant-trader who commissioned the mansion for his seventh (and favourite) wife.

★ Khoo Kongsi   HISTORIC BUILDING
(☑04-261 4609; www.khookongsi.com.my; 18 Cannon Sq; adult/child RM10/1; ☺9am-6pm) This spectacular clanhouse is one of the most impressive in George Town. Gorgeous ceramic sculptures of immortals, carp, dragons, and carp becoming dragons dance across the roof ridges. The interior is dominated by incredible murals depicting birthdays, weddings and, most impressively, the 36 celestial guardians. On the last Saturday evening of each month the structure is illuminated and entry is free from 6.30pm to 9pm.

★ Pinang Peranakan Mansion   MUSEUM
(☑04-264 2929; www.pinangperanakanmansion. com.my; 29 Lebuh Gereja; adult/child RM21.20/10.60; ☺9am-5pm) This ostentatious,

---

GEORGE TOWN'S STREET ART

The current craze for street art in George Town shows no sign of abating. It's a trend that goes back to 2010, when Penang's state government commissioned the studio **Sculpture At Work** (http://sculptureatwork.com) to do a series of cartoon steel art pieces across town. Affixed to George Town street walls, these 3D artworks detail local customs and heritage with humour, while also providing a quirky counterpoint to the natural urban beauty of the historic core.

It was in 2012, however, that George Town's street-art scene really took off. For that year's George Town Festival, Lithuanian artist Ernest Zacharevic (www.ernestzacharevic.com) was commissioned to do a series of public paintings in the city centre, some of which he chose to combine with objects such as bicycles, motorcycles and architectural features. The art has been a smash hit, with his **Kids on a Bicycle** (Lebuh Armenian) piece on Lebuh Armenian having become a major tourist attraction, complete with long lines and souvenir stalls.

Zacharevic's success led to the '101 Lost Kittens' series of murals commissioned for the 2013 George Town Festival, with the intent of bringing attention to the issue of stray animals; there have also been many examples of privately funded public art. Other major street artists' works to look out for include Russian artist Julia Volchkova's striking pieces (you'll see one off an alley on Lg Stewart) and UK artist Thomas Powell (www.thomas powellartist.com), whose works are at the **Hin Bus Depot Art Centre** (p411).

'Marking George Town', a free map showing the location of pieces by Ernest Zacharevic and some of the other artists mentioned above, is available at Penang Global Tourism (p415).

mint-green structure is among the most stunning restored residences in George Town. Every door, wall and archway is carved and often painted in gold leaf, and the grand rooms are furnished with majestic wood furniture with intricate mother-of-pearl inlay. There are displays of charming antiques, and fascinating black-and-white photos of the family in regal Chinese dress grace the walls. Self-guided visits are possible, or enquire with staff about the timing of occasional guided tours (included in the ticket price).

Cheah Kongsi   HISTORIC BUILDING

(☑ 04-261 3837; www.cheahkongsi.com.my; 8 Lebuh Armenian; adult/child RM10/5; ⊙ 9am-5pm, to 1pm Sat) Looking splendid after a major restoration, Cheah Kongsi is home to the oldest Straits Chinese clan association in Penang. The ornate front of the clanhouse can be seen clearly across a grassy lawn from Lebuh Pantai, but the official entrance where you need to buy a ticket is on Lebuh Armenian.

Besides serving as a temple and assembly hall, this building has also been the registered headquarters of several clans.

Hin Bus Depot   GALLERY

(http://hinbusdepot.com; 31A Jln Gurdwara; ⊙ noon-8pm Mon-Fri, from 11am Sat & Sun) FREE The elegant remains of this former bus station have become a vibrant hub for George Town's burgeoning contemporary-art scene. Half a dozen artist studios and a gallery host exhibitions (ranging from sculpture to photography), an arts-and-crafts market every Sunday (11am to 5pm), and art-house movies and documentaries on Tuesdays. The open-air areas are bedecked with street art.

Chew Jetty   AREA

(Pengkalan Weld) The largest and most intact of the clan jetties, Chew Jetty consists of 75 elevated houses, several Chinese temples, a community hall and lots of tourist facilities, all linked by elevated wooden walkways. It's a fun place to wander around admiring docked fishing boats while the scent of frying fish wafts across the walkways. There are numerous places to browse souvenirs and nibble snacks.

☞ Tours

There's a huge variety of self-guided George Town tours, from food walks to those focusing on traditional trades or architecture – pick up a pamphlet of the routes at Penang Global Tourism (p415). Likewise,

the **Penang Global Ethic Project** (www.globalethicpenang.net) has put together a World Religion Walk that takes you past the iconography and houses of worship of Christians, Muslims, Hindus, Sikhs, Buddhists and Chinese traditional religion.

If walking isn't your thing, consider the **Hop-On Hop-Off** (www.myhoponhopoff.com/pg; single trip adult/child RM20/10, 3-day pass adult/child RM55/30; ⊙ 9am-8pm) city bus route, which winds its way around the perimeter of the Unesco Protected Zone. It's a good way to get a quick overview of the town, and you can get on and off at one of 17 stops.

🛏 Sleeping

Ryokan Muntri   HOSTEL $

(☑ 04-250 0287; www.ryokanmuntri.com; 62 Jln Muntri; dm/r incl breakfast from RM39/158; ❋@☎) This flashpacker hostel boasts a minimalist feel – though not an especially Japanese one, despite the name. The dorms, ranging from four to six beds (including women-only rooms), are awash in muted greys, and each bed has its own USB and plug socket. There are bean-bag-strewn chill zones, a TV room and reading spaces, plus a colourful, convivial bar.

80's Guesthouse   HOSTEL $

(☑ 04-263 8806; www.the80sguesthouse.com; 46 Love Lane; incl breakfast dm RM35, r RM80-95; ❋@☎) With 1950s film posters and old radios, the nostalgic theme extends much further back than the '80s, but it'd be rude to quibble when the dorms and private rooms are spotless and common areas pleasantly attired with greenery and bookshelves. Single-sex four-bed and mixed six-bed dorms all share bathrooms, as do the minimalist private rooms. Lockers and towels included.

MALAYSIA PENANG

George Town

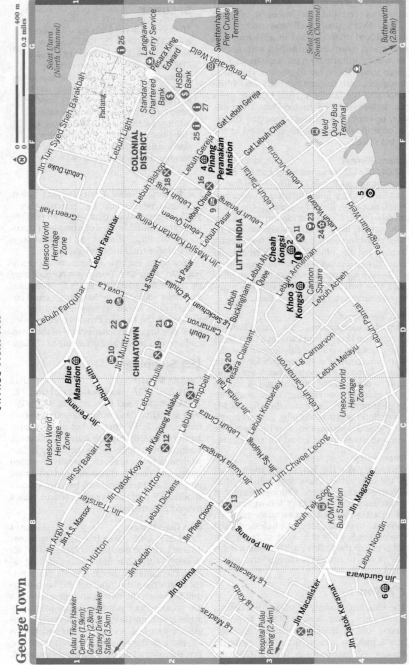

MALAYSIA PENANG

George Town

🍴 Eating

You'll soon realise why locals are so passionate about the food here. The diversity of George Town's food scene is breathtaking: Chinese dim sum, Indian banana-leaf meals, and Malaysian curries, through to sourdough bakeries and paleo (grain-free) cakes. Whether you choose to dine at hawker stalls or the finest white-tablecloth restaurants, you're sure to find quality food.

Wai Kei Cafe CHINESE $
(Lebuh Chulia; mains from RM7; ⊙11am-2pm & 6-9pm) This gem sits in the middle of the greatest concentration of travellers in George Town, yet is somehow almost exclusively patronised (in enthusiastic numbers) by locals. Come early for *char siew* (barbecued pork) and *siew yoke* (pork belly), considered among the best in town.

Hameediyah MALAYSIAN $
(☑04-261 1095; 164 Lebuh Campbell; mains RM5.50-25; ⊙10am-10pm) Dating back to 1907 and allegedly the oldest *nasi kandar* (Indian-influenced curries served over rice) place in Penang, a renovation belies Hameediyah's many years. Brave long lines and a rather dreary dining room for rich, meaty curries or *murtabak* – a *roti prata* (flaky, flat bread) stuffed with minced mutton, chicken or vegetables, egg and spices.

Tho Yuen Restaurant CHINESE $
(92 Lebuh Campbell; dim sum RM1.60-8, mains from RM4.50; ⊙6am-3pm Wed-Mon) Packed with newspaper-reading loners and chattering locals all morning long, it's best to arrive early for Tho Yuen's widest array of breakfast dim sum. Mid-morning, plump pork *bao* and shrimp dumplings give way to chicken rice and *hor fun* (vermicelli with beef and bean sprouts). Servers speak minimal English but do their best to explain the contents of dim sum carts.

Sri Ananda Bahwan INDIAN $
(☑04-264 4204; www.srianandabahwan.com.my; 53-55 Lebuh Penang; mains from RM3; ⊙7am-11.30pm; ❄☑) This busy and buzzy chain restaurant whips up filling *masala dosa* (lentil-and-rice pancake stuffed with spiced potato), lip-smacking tandoori chicken and countless vegetarian Indian dishes. There's also a counter of glistening sweets, such as *laddu* (tiny cannonballs of syrup, coconut and gram flour), for takeaway nibbles.

Veloo Villas INDIAN $
(☑04-262 4369; 22 Lebuh Penang; set meals RM5-13.50; ⊙7am-10pm; ☑) Service is amiable and unfussy at this cheap, cheerful banana-leaf restaurant. Rice is scooped onto your leaf, along with ladlefuls of dhal and tangy pickled veggies. Come between 11am and 4pm for hearty rice-based set meals, or outside

MALAYSIA PENANG

HAWKER-STALL HEAVEN

Not eating at a hawker stall in George Town is like skipping the Louvre in Paris – unthinkable! Prices are cheap and most places serve beer.

Lorong Baru (New Lane) Hawker Stalls (cnr Jln Macalister & Lg Baru; mains from RM3; ⊘5-10.30pm Thu-Tue) Ask locals where their favourite hawker stalls are, and they'll generally mention this night-time street extravaganza. Just about everything is available here: oyster omelette, *otak otak* (steamed fish curry), Chinese congee, grilled satay skewers... We especially enjoyed the *char koay kak* (wok-fried rice cakes, egg, preserved radish and bean sprouts) and a version of *Hokkien mee* (mixed noodles in a piquant prawn broth). Prepare to battle for a spot if you're visiting at the weekend.

Pulau Tikus Hawker Centre (cnr Solok Moulmein & Jln Burma; ⊘6am-2pm) Before yet another bland guesthouse breakfast gets you down, consider a visit to this busy morning market area. A cluster of cafes sell *chee cheong fun* (flat rice noodles drowned in soya sauce, bean paste and chilli), *mee goreng* (spicy fried noodles) and other dishes that have earned die-hard fans.

Joo Hooi Cafe (475 Jln Penang; mains RM3-5.50, desserts from RM2.50; ⊘11am-5pm) The hawker-centre equivalent of one-stop shopping, this hectic place assembles all of Penang's best dishes: laksa, *rojak*, *char kway teow* (broad noodles, clams and eggs fried in chilli and black-bean sauce) and *cendol*.

Kafe Kheng Pin (80 Jln Penang; mains from RM4; ⊘7am-2pm Tue-Sun) The must-eats at this old-school-feeling hawker joint include a legendary *lor bak* (deep-fried meat rolls dipped in sauce), rice porridges and an exquisite Hainanese chicken rice (steamed chicken with broth and rice).

Gurney Drive Hawker Stalls (Persiaran Gurney; mains from RM4; ⊘5pm-midnight) One of Penang's most famous hawker complexes sits amid modern high-rise buildings bordered by the sea. Tourists rush in for both Muslim and Chinese-Malay dishes including laksa, *rojak* (a mixed vegetable dish with a thick shrimp-based sauce) and crushed-ice dessert *cendol*, though the harried atmosphere and crowds prompt many locals to give it a wide berth.

of these hours for *dosa* (paper-thin rice-and-lentil crepes) and other made-to-order meals.

Yin's Sourdough Bakery BAKERY $
(☑011-2419 5118; www.yinssourdough.com; 11 Pesara Claimant; pastries from RM2.30, sandwiches from RM12.50; ⊘7am-6pm Mon-Fri, to 1pm Sat; ✳☑) Tired of rice? Weary of noodles? Head here for freshly baked, additive-free bread, alongside cranberry buns, cinnamon rolls and focaccia. Buy baked goods to go, or stick around for a sandwich, breakfasts or pizza.

🍷 Drinking & Nightlife

★**Gravity** BAR
(☑04-219 0000; www.ghotelkelawai.com.my/dining-gravity.html; G Hotel Kelawei, 2 Persiaran Maktab; ⊘5pm-1am) Yes, it's a hotel pool bar. But the breezy rooftop location and spectacular views, both out to sea and across to Penang Hill, make Gravity one of the island's top sundowner destinations. Time a visit for the 5pm to 7pm happy hour, or enjoy free-flow house wines (RM75 per hour).

★**Mish Mash** COCKTAIL BAR
(☑017-536 5128; www.mishmashpg.com; 24 Jln Muntri; ⊘5pm-midnight Tue-Sun) Mixology magic takes place between the whisky- and wine-bottle-lined walls of Mish Mash. Japanese flavours come to the fore in cocktails like the 'Pandan Paloma', with tequila and pandan sugar. We also appreciated well-blended mocktails like the pear and rosemary smash.

Micke's Place BAR
(☑012-493 8279; www.facebook.com/mickesplacelovelane; 94 Love Lane; ⊘noon-3am Sat-Thu, from 2pm Fri) Graffitied walls, shisha and free-flowing booze: this classic formula has allowed Micke's Place to remain one of the most popular backpacker bars in George Town. Sure, Micke's lacks panache, but its crowd of travellers makes for easy mingling, so it's a good place to start your night.

ℹ️ Information

Branches of major banks are on Lebuh Pantai and Lebuh Downing, near the main post office.

Most have 24-hour ATMs. At the northwestern end of Lebuh Chulia there are a few money changers open longer hours than banks and with more competitive rates.

Nearly all lodging options offer wi-fi, and some have a computer terminal for guest use. Wi-fi is also widely available at restaurants, cafes and in shopping malls.

Hospital Pulau Pinang (☑04-222 5333; http://jknpenang.moh.gov.my; Jln Residensi) The island's largest public hospital, with general health-care and emergency services.

Penang Global Tourism (☑04-264 3456; www.mypenang.gov.my; Whiteways Arcade, Lebuh Pantai; ☺9am-5pm Mon-Fri, to 3pm Sat, to 1pm Sun) The visitors centre of the state tourism agency is the best all-round place to go for maps, brochures and local information.

ⓘ Getting There & Away

AIR

Penang International Airport (☑04-252 0252; www.penangairport.com; 11900 Bayan Lepas; ⬚401), 18km south of George Town, is served by plenty of international and domestic flights.

BOAT

Langkawi Ferry Service (LFS; ☑04-264 2088, 016-419 5008; www.langkawi-ferry.com; PPC Bldg, Pesara King Edward; adult/child 1-way RM70/51.30; ☺7am-5.30pm Mon-Sat, to 3pm Sun) boats leave for Langkawi, the resort island in Kedah, at 8.30am and 2pm and return from Langkawi at 10.30am and 3pm. The journey each way takes between 1¾ and 2½ hours. Book a few days in advance to ensure a seat.

BUS

Most interstate and international buses to George Town arrive and depart from **Sungai Nibong Bus Station** (☑04-659 2099; www.rapidpg.com.my; Jln Sultan Azlan Shah, Kampung Dua Bukit; ⬚401, 303), just to the south of Penang Bridge. A taxi from Sungai Nibong to George Town costs around RM25.

Before heading out to Sungai Nibong, check whether you can board your long-distance bus at KOMTAR Bus Station (www.rapidpg.com.my; Jln Ria). Note that transport to Thailand (except to Hat Yai) is via minivan. Transport can also be arranged to Ko Samui and Ko Phi Phi via a transfer in Surat Thani and Hat Yai respectively.

Buses around Penang island are run by the government-owned **Rapid Penang** (☑bus times 04-238 1313; www.rapidpg.com.my). Fares range from RM1.40 to RM4. Most routes originate at **Weld Quay Bus Terminal** (www.rapidpg.com.my; 19-24 Pengkalan Weld) and most also stop at KOMTAR.

ⓘ Getting Around

TO/FROM THE AIRPORT

Bus 401 runs to and from the airport (RM4) every half hour between 6am and 11pm daily, and stops at KOMTAR Bus Station and Weld Quay Bus Terminal, taking at least an hour. The fixed taxi fare to central George Town is RM44.70; expect the journey to take around 30 minutes depending on traffic.

BICYCLE

There are several places near the intersection of Gat Lebuh Armenian and Lebuh Victoria offering one-day rental of city bikes for around RM10. You can also find bicycles for rent at many places along Lebuh Chulia.

BUS

Rapid Penang runs public transport buses around the state. Fares range from RM1.40 to RM4. Most routes originate at Weld Quay Bus Terminal and most also stop at KOMTAR and along Jln Chulia as well.

TAXI

Penang's taxis all have meters, which most drivers refuse to use, so negotiate the fare before you set off. Typical fares to places just outside the city centre start at around RM15. Taxis can be found on Jln Penang, near Cititel Hotel, at

---

SPLURGE

You can't really say you've been to George Town unless you've stepped inside **China House** (☑04-263 7299; www.chinahouse.com.my; 153 & 155 Lebuh Pantai; ☺9am-midnight). This block-wide amalgamation of shophouses is home to a variety of dining, drinking and shopping options. It all starts splendidly with the buzzy cafe/bakery, **Kopi C** (desserts from RM10; ☺9am-midnight; ☎) serving scrumptious bakes, serious coffee and great light meals, and just gets better from there.

Return in the evening to experience the elegant yet relaxed restaurant **BTB** (☑04-262 7299; www.chinahouse.com.my; 155 Lebuh Pantai; mains RM42-84; ☺6.30-10.30pm; ✳☑), the cocktail and wine bar **Vine & Single** (☑04-263 7299; ☺5pm-midnight) and the live-music venue **Canteen** (183B Lebuh Victoria; ☺9am-11pm). And don't forget about the boutique shop and art gallery upstairs!

the Weld Quay Bus Terminal (p415) and near KOMTAR Bus Station (p415). Ride-sharing apps including Grab are used in George Town.

TRISHAW

Bicycle rickshaws are a fun, if touristy, way to negotiate George Town's backstreets and cost between RM20 and RM40 per hour depending on your negotiating skills. As with taxis, it's important to agree on the fare before departure.

Greater Penang

◉ Sights

★ **Penang National Park**   NATIONAL PARK
(Taman Negara Pulau Pinang; ☎04-881 3500; ⊙8am-5pm; P; ☐101) FREE The old saying about good things in small packages suits dainty Penang National Park well. At 2300 hectares it's Malaysia's smallest national park, but you can fill a day with activities as diverse as jungle walks, fishing, and sunbathing on quiet, golden-sand beaches. Private guides and boat operators amass near the entrance and parking lot. A one-way trip should cost RM50 from Teluk Duyung (Monkey Beach), RM90 from Pantai Kerachut and RM100 from Teluk Kampi. Sign in at the park entrance.

★ **Tropical Spice Garden**   GARDENS
(☎04-881 1797; www.tropicalspicegarden.com; Jl Teluk Bahang; adult/child RM29/17, incl tour RM45/25; ⊙9am-6pm; ☐101) ✔ This beautifully landscaped oasis of tropical flora, more than 500 species in all, unfurls across 500 fragrant acres. Armed with an audioguide, you can wander independently among lily ponds and terraced gardens, learning about local spices and medicinal plants. Alternatively, join one of four daily guided tours at 9am, 11.30am, 1.30pm and 3.30pm, or book a kid-friendly educational tour. Take bus 101

from George Town (RM4) and inform the driver that you want to get off here. Last admission 5.15pm.

The garden offers well-regarded **cooking courses** (☎04-881 1797; http://tsgcooking school.com; adult/child RM250/130; ⊙lessons 9am-1pm Tue-Sun) and its **restaurant** (☎04-881 3493; www.treemonkey.com.my; mains RM18-80-58.80; ⊙9am-10.30pm; 🔊), though pricey, is worth a visit for its relaxing terrace area and refreshing herb-infused lemonades. There's also a good shop, and just across the road from the gardens is a beautiful white-sand beach.

Kek Lok Si Temple   BUDDHIST TEMPLE
(Temple of Supreme Bliss; http://kekloksitemple. com; Jln Balik Pulau, Air Itam; ⊙8am-6.30pm; ☐204) FREE Staggered on hillside terraces overlooking Air Itam, around 8km from the centre of George Town, Malaysia's largest Buddhist temple is a visual delight. Built between 1890 and 1905, Kek Lok Si is the cornerstone of the Malay-Chinese community, which provided the funding for its two-decade-long construction (and ongoing additions). Its key features are the seven-tier **Ban Po Thar** (Ten Thousand Buddhas Pagoda; ☎04-828 3317; http://kekloksitemple.com; Kek Lok Si Temple, Air Itam; RM2; ⊙8am-6pm; ☐204) pagoda and an awesome 36.5m-high bronze statue of Kuan Yin, goddess of mercy.

To reach the temple's main entrance, you'll have to run the gauntlet of souvenir stalls on the uphill path. You'll also pass a pond packed with turtles, and the complex's **vegetarian restaurant** (☎04-828 8142; Air Itam; mains RM10; ⊙9am-6pm; ✔; ☐204). There are a lot of stairs involved, but the final stretch up to the statue of Kuan Yin is covered by a **funicular** (one-way/return RM8/16; ⊙8.30am-5.30pm).

MALAYSIA PENANG

BUSES FROM PENANG

DESTINATION	PRICE (RM)	DURATION (HR)	FREQUENCY
Hat Yai (Thailand)	35	3	4 daily, 5am-5.30pm
Ipoh	16-25	2½	7 daily, 7am-9pm
Johor Bahru	65-90	9	8 daily, 8am-11.30pm
Kota Bharu	41	7	2 daily
Kuala Lumpur	36-50	5	every 30min, 7am-midnight
Kuala Terengganu	51	8	5 daily
Melaka	50	7	2 daily
Singapore	65-100	10	3, morning & evening only
Tanah Rata (for Cameron Highlands)	32-40	5	5 daily

ℹ️ GETTING TO/FROM BUTTERWORTH

Butterworth, the city on the mainland part of Penang, is home to Penang's main train station and is the departure point for ferries to Penang Island. Unless you're taking the train or your bus has pulled into Butterworth's busy bus station from elsewhere, you'll probably not need to spend any time here.

The cheapest way to get to George Town is via the **ferry** (foot passenger adult/child/bicycle/motorbike/car RM1.20/0.60/1.40/2/7.70; ⊘ 5.20am-12.40am); the Pangkalan Sultan Abdul Halim Ferry Terminal is linked by walkway to Butterworth's bus and train stations. Ferries take passengers and cars every 20 to 30 minutes from 5.20am to 10pm, and then roughly every hour until the last ferry at 12.40am. The journey takes 10 minutes and fares are charged only for the journey from Butterworth to Penang; returning to the mainland is free.

Taxis to/from Butterworth (approximately RM50) cross the 13km Penang Bridge. There's a RM7 toll payable at the toll plaza on the mainland, but no charge to return.

At least five daily trains connect **Butterworth Train Station** (☑ 04-323 7962; www.ktmb.com.my) with Kuala Lumpur (RM59, 3½ to four hours).

To reach Thailand, take a Komuter Train (RM11.40, 1¾ hours, 14 daily) to the border at Padang Besar. There you can connect to the International Express to Hat Yai, or take a Shuttle Train across the border.

Check www.ktmb.com.my and www.train36.com for the latest info on fares and schedules.

Alor Setar

☑ 04 / POP 405,523

Most travellers use the capital of Kedah, also known as Alor Star, as a jumping-off point to Langkawi or southern Malaysia. But it's worth lingering long enough to admire its architectural treasures. Alor Setar is generally a welcoming place for foreign visitors, though it's rooted in a conservative mindset that references a fairly strict interpretation of Islam and carries a reverence for the local monarchy.

🛏️ Sleeping & Eating

Comfort Motel   HOTEL $
(☑ 04-734 4866; 2C Jln Kampung Perak; r incl breakfast RM45; 🅿️❄️) This is a good-value, Chinese-style budget hotel, located in a renovated wooden house across from **Masjid Zahir** (Jln Sultan Muhammad Jiwa; ⊘ 7am-7pm) FREE. The rooms are tidy and come equipped with TV and air-con, but are otherwise bare, and have shared bathrooms.

Nasi Lemak Ong   MALAYSIAN $
(☑ 012-498 3660; www.facebook.com/NasiLemakOngAlorSetar; 24, ground fl, Jln Putra; mains RM5-12; ⊘ 10.30am-3.30pm Thu-Tue; ❄️☑) This efficient, family-run canteen is the most popular *nasi lemak* place in Alor Setar. At the counter, select your rice and choice of accompaniments from the wide array of dishes

laid out, including rich, spicy *sambal*, dried anchovies, curried prawns or mutton, and various vegetable dishes. Worth the queue.

ℹ️ Getting There & Away

The main bus terminal, **Shahab Perdana** (Lebuhraya Bahiyah), is 4km north of the town centre. A local bus links Shahab Perdana and Kuala Kedah (RM3, one hour, frequent departures from 7am to 10pm), passing through the city centre on the way. There is a **bus stop** (Jln Langgar) next to the taxi stand on Jln Tunku Ibrahim.

The bus to Shahab Perdana from the city centre costs RM1.30 and a taxi there costs around RM10.

The train station (www.ktmb.com.my; Jln Stesyen) is 850m southeast of the town centre. There is one daily northbound train to Hat Yai (RM9 to RM48, 3½ hours) in Thailand and one to Bangkok (about RM110, 18½ hours). Southbound trains head to Tasik Gelugor for Penang (RM18 to RM22, one hour, two daily) and Kuala Lumpur (RM70 to RM93, five hours, seven daily).

Pulau Langkawi

☑ 04 / POP 94,777

Dominating an archipelago of more than 100 islands and islets, Pulau Langkawi is synonymous with sandy shores, jungle-cloaked valleys and bargain shopping. The island's official name is 'the jewel of Kedah', and its rugged beauty is evident in waterfalls, hot springs and forest parks – all excellent reasons to peel yourself off your beach towel.

◉ Sights

Move on briskly from **Kuah**, the major town and the arrival point for ferries, to **Pantai Cenang** (cha-nang). This gorgeous 2km-long strip of sand on Langkawi's west coast has the biggest concentration of hotels and tourist facilities. The water is good for swimming, but jellyfish are common. If you're looking for somewhere a bit quieter try adjacent **Pantai Tengah**.

In Pantai Kok, northwest of Pantai Cenang, it's also worth riding the **Panorama Langkawi** (☑ 04-959 4225; www.panoramalangkawi.com; Oriental Village, Burau Bay; basic package of SkyCab & 3D Art Museum adult/child RM55/40; ☺ 9.30am-7pm) cable car to the top of Gunung Machinchang to enjoy spectacular views.

☳ Sleeping

During school holidays and peak tourist season (approximately November to February), advance bookings are generally necessary for all budgets. At other times, supply outstrips demand and prices are negotiable.

☳ Pantai Cenang

There are dozens of backpacker places along the small roads leading away from the beach.

Langkawi Dormitorio HOSTEL $
(☑ 017-236 2587; www.facebook.com/lgkdormitorio; 1556 Jln Pantai Cenang, Pantai Cenang; dm RM50, r RM120-500; ❄ 🛜) Feeling a little weary of party hostels? Dormitorio offers a more sedate, grown-up experience with its clean, pastel-hued dorm rooms, each with its own bathroom. Rooms feature solid, capsule-style bunk beds.

Rainbow Lodge HOSTEL, GUESTHOUSE $
(☑ 04-955 8103; www.rainbowlangkawi.com; Pantai Cenang; dm RM18-22, r RM40-120; ❄ @ 🛜) Set 300m back from Pantai Cenang, this cheerfully painted place has non-bunk dorm beds with partitions and curtains, allowing better repose than the average hostel. Cheaper private rooms have fans, the pricier ones have air-con and fridges.

★ Tubotel HOSTEL $$
(☑ 014-240 7022; www.tubotel.com; Kuala Cenang; incl breakfast dm RM45-50, r RM128-188; 🅿 ❄ 🛜) At thrillingly distinctive Tubotel, rooms are individual concrete pipes whose snug interiors house surprisingly comfy beds (bathrooms are in a separate block). Occupying a slim peninsula north of Pantai Cenang, Tubotel rooms are framed by overhanging greenery. A deck with sun loungers overlooks glittering sea.

ⓘ GETTING TO THAILAND

Alor Setar to Hat Yai

Getting to the border The border at Bukit Kayu Hitam, 48km north of Alor Setar, is the main road crossing between Malaysia and Thailand. There are no taxis or local buses at this border; the only practical way to cross here is on a through bus from points elsewhere in Malaysia (eg Alor Setar or KL).

At the border The Malaysian border post is open every day from 6am to midnight. All passengers must disembark to clear customs and immigration (both Thai and Malaysian) before reboarding.

Moving on The lack of local transport means that you'll most likely pass this border on a bus already bound for Hat Yai.

Kangar to Hat Yai

Getting to the border There are four buses a day from Kangar to Padang Besar (RM4.20), stopping at a bus stop by a roundabout about 500m from the border.

At the border The Malaysian border post is open every day from 6am to 10pm. Few people walk the more-than-2km of no-man's land between the Thai and Malaysian sides of the border. Motorcyclists shuttle pedestrian travellers back and forth for less than RM5 each way. For train passengers, customs and immigration are dealt with at Padang Besar station.

Moving on Once in Thailand there are frequent buses to Hat Yai, 60km away (THB44). There are trains at 10.30am and 6.40pm connecting Padang Besar and Hat Yai (RM6 to RM13, 50 minutes).

🛏 Pantai Tengah

Pantai Tengah is quieter and more relaxed than Pantai Cenang, with a main drag bursting with upscale restaurants and bars.

Zackry Guest House GUESTHOUSE $
(zackryghouse@gmail.com; Lot 735, Jln Teluk Baru, Pantai Tengah; dm RM35, r RM70-110; ❄@🛜) This ramshackle, family-run guesthouse has a sociable atmosphere. Rooms are basic, yet clean and cosy, and communal areas include a fridge, vending machines and places to lounge. Note that there's a two-night minimum, no phone bookings, and only about half of the rooms have an attached bathroom.

✕ Eating

The roving night market *(pasar malam)* is held at various points across the island and is Pulau Langkawi's stand-out (and best value) food experience. Restaurants can be found scattered along the main roads in Pantai Cenang and Pantai Tengah. Kuah is home to several very good Chinese and Indian restaurants.

Wonderland Food Store CHINESE $
(Lot 179-181, Pusat Perniagaan Kelana Mas, Kuah; mains from RM10; ◷6-11pm Sat-Thu) Of the string of Chinese-style seafood restaurants in Kuah, Wonderland has been around longer than most and gets the best reviews. It's an informal, open-air place where the food (steamed fish, giant prawns, fried rice) is cheap and tasty.

Melayu MALAYSIAN $$
(☑04-955 4075; Jln Teluk Baru, Pantai Tengah; mains RM10-20; ◷3-10.30pm; ❄) The comfortable dining room, pleasant outdoor seating area and efficient service here belie the reasonable prices. A good place to go for authentic Malaysian food in the evening, since most of the island's local restaurants are lunchtime buffets.

Alcohol isn't served, but you can bring your own for no charge.

🍷 Drinking & Nightlife

Langkawi's duty-free status makes it one of the cheapest places to buy booze in Malaysia, and alcohol at many restaurants and hotels is half the mainland price.

Smiling Buffalo CAFE
(www.facebook.com/Smilingbuffalocafe; Jln Pantai Cenang, Pantai Cenang; ◷8am-6pm) Superb cof-

fee and freshly pressed juices are served in shady grounds at this idyllic, friendly cafe.

Cliff BAR
(☑04-953 3228; www.theclifflangkawi.com; Jln Pantai Cenang, Pantai Cenang; ◷noon-11pm) Perched on a wave-lashed rocky outcrop between Pantai Cenang and Pantai Tengah, the Cliff is an exhilarating spot for a sundowner. Expect a full bar, a good wine selection, and cocktails a class above those mixed on the beach below (from RM18).

Yellow Café BAR
(www.facebook.com/yellowbeach.cafe; Pantai Cenang; ◷noon-1am Sat & Sun, from 3pm Mon, Wed-Fri; 🛜) The best bar on Pantai Cenang has a mellow soundtrack, shaded seating and swinging yellow hammocks (don't spill your margarita). Come between 4pm and 6pm when beers are buy one, get one free. Cocktails from RM20.

ℹ Information

The only banks are at Kuah and Telaga Harbour Park, but there are ATMs at the airport, the jetty, at **Cenang Mall** (Jln Pantai Cenang) and at **Underwater World** (Jln Pantai Cenang). There are a couple of money changers at Pantai Cenang.
Tourism Malaysia (☑04-966 7789; www.malaysia.travel; Jln Persiaran Putra, Kuah; ◷9am-5pm) This office is on Jln Persiaran Putra, next to the mosque in Kuah town, and offers comprehensive information on the whole island. There are two other offices, one located opposite the ferry terminal entrance at Kuah jetty, and one in the airport arrivals hall (open until 10pm).

ℹ Getting There & Away

AIR

Langkawi International Airport (☑04-955 1311; www.langkawiairport.com) is located in the west of the island near Padang Matsirat. It's well stocked with ATMs, currency-exchange booths, car-rental agencies, travel agencies,

ⓘ GETTING TO THAILAND: PULAU LANGAKAWI TO SATUN & KO LIPE

Getting to the border There are three daily ferries from Kuah on Pulau Langkawi to Satun (one way RM30, 1¼ hours) on the Thai mainland. Tropical Charters also runs two ferries daily between Langkawi and Ko Lipe in Thailand.

At the border You'll get stamped out of Malaysia at immigration at the ferry terminal then get stamped into Thailand when you arrive at the ferry terminal in Satun. Most visitors can get a Thai visa for 15 days or more on arrival.

Moving on From Satun there are more bus and boat connections. From Ko Lipe there are onward services available to as far as Ko Lanta.

For information on making the crossing in reverse see p782.

and a Tourism Malaysia office. A half-dozen airlines offer flights from Langkawi.

BOAT

All passenger ferries operate from the busy terminal at **Kuah Jetty** (Kuah). Several ferry providers, including **Langkawi Ferry Service** (LFS; ☎ 04-966 9439; www.langkawi-ferry.com; Kuah Jetty, Kuah), have merged to operate a shared ferry service to the destinations below, with the exception of Ko Lipe, which is operated by **Tropical Charters** (☎ 012-316 5466; www.tropicalcharters.com.my; Pantai Tengah; cruises from adult/child RM245/145), from October to June only.

DESTINATION	PRICE (RM, ADULT/CHILD)	DURATION (HR)
George Town	60/45	2¾
Ko Lipe (Thailand)	245/145	1½
Kuala Kedah	23/17	1¾
Kuala Perlis	18/13	1¼
Satun (Thailand)	35/28	1¼

ⓘ Getting Around

A good option is to rent your own vehicle: rates are around RM70 to RM100 per day for a car, RM35 per day for a motorcycle. Otherwise, taxis are the main way of getting around. Fixed taxi fares from the airport include Kuah jetty (RM30), Pantai Cenang or Pantai Kok (RM20), Tanjung Rhu (RM30) and Teluk Datai (RM60). Buy a coupon at the desk before leaving the airport terminal and use it to pay the driver. The taxi fare from Kuah jetty to Pantai Cenang is RM30. It's also possible to hire a taxi for four hours for RM120.

PENINSULAR MALAYSIA – SOUTH & EAST COAST

As you travel around the south of Peninsular Malaysia and up the east coast, the communities you encounter become more laid-back, more Malay and more Islamic. Headscarves, skullcaps and the hauntingly melodious call to prayer are as ubiquitous here as the white-sand beaches that fringe the coast and jewel-like islands.

Johor Bahru

☑ 07 / POP 1,448,000

After years of being criticised as a dirty, chaotic border town, Johor's capital city of Johor Bahru (JB for short) has been repaved and replanted and is well on the way to rebranding itself. Most travellers skip southern Malaysia's largest city, but for intrepid souls there's a handful of worthwhile museums, temples and mosques, shopping and party zones.

⊙ Sights

Arulmigu Sri Rajakaliamman   HINDU TEMPLE
(Glass Temple; 22 Lorong 1; RM10; ⊙ 1-5pm) FREE
Step through the looking glass into this wonderland of a temple built from mirrors, glass and metal – not a single inch of the vaulted roof or wall has been left unadorned. The temple is dedicated to Kali, known as the goddess of time, change, power and destruction.

Heritage District   ARCHITECTURE
Wandering around the heritage area between Jln Ibrahim and Jln Ungku Puan is a real highlight of Johor Bahru. Walk past colourful old shophouses filled with barbers, Ayurvedic salons, sari shops, gorgeous temples, a few modern-art galleries and old-style eateries.

Royal Abu Bakar Museum   MUSEUM
(☎ 07-223 0555; Jln Ibrahim) The marvellous Istana Besar, once the Johor royal family's principal palace, was built in Victorian style by Anglophile sultan Abu Bakar in 1866. It

was opened as a museum to the public in 1990 and displays the incredible wealth of the sultans. It's now the finest museum of its kind in Malaysia, and the 53-hectare palace grounds (free entry) are beautifully manicured. At the time of research the museum was getting an extensive remodelling..

🛏 Sleeping & Eating

Replacement Lodge   HOSTEL $$
(www.facebook.com/thereplacementlodgeand kitchen; 33-34 Jln Dhoby; d RM170; ❄🛜) This small hostel (there are only six rooms) is one of the only hostels in the old heritage area of Johor Bahru. With Nordic-inspired interiors (think whitewashed walls, light wooden furnishings and sporadic pot plants), rooms are light-filled and comfy. Its location near a mosque can mean an early morning wake-up call for light sleepers. Breakfast is served in the great little cafe on the bottom floor.

Restoran Reaz Corner   INDIAN $
(www.facebook.com/pg/restoranreazcorner; 24A Jln Dhoby, cnr Jln Duke; RM3-12.50; ⏲24hr) You can't go wrong with the yellow rice topped with spicy chicken curry at this clean, open-air curry joint. The ginger tea is a not-to-be-missed-nor-soon-forgotten accompaniment. If you're here for breakfast, it's hard to go past the lovely flaky roti.

Medan Selera Meldrum Walk   HAWKER $
(Meldrum Walk; meals from RM3; ⏲5pm-late) Every late afternoon, the little food stalls crammed along this alley (parallel to Jln Meldrum) start frying up everything from *ikan bakar* (grilled fish) to laksa. Wash down your meal with fresh sugar-cane juice or a Chinese herbal jelly drink. Nothing here is excellent, but it's all good.

ℹ Information

Tourism Malaysia (☏07-224 4133; www. malaysia.travel; JB Sentral; ⏲10am-10pm) At the CIQ complex, right after you pass through immigration from Singapore.

ℹ Getting There & Away

AIR
JB is served by the **Senai International Airport** (☏07-599 4500; www.senaiairport.com), 32km northwest of JB. Senai International Airport is linked to the city centre by regular shuttle buses (RM8, 45 minutes) that run from the bus station at Kotaraya 2 Terminal. A taxi between the

---

ℹ GETTING TO INDONESIA: JOHOR BAHRU TO BATAM & BINTAN (RIAU ISLANDS)

Getting to the border There are several daily departures to Batam (one way RM69, 1½ hours) and Tanjung Pinang Bintan (one way RM86, 2½ hours), part of Indonesia's Riau Islands. Ferries depart from the **Berjaya Waterfront Ferry Terminal** (☏07-221 1677; www.berjayawaterfront.com.my; 88 Jln Ibrahim Sultan, Zon Ferry Terminal), which is serviced by several buses from downtown Johor Bahru.

At the border You'll be charged a RM10 seaport tax, RM2 insurance and RM3 fuel surcharge (total RM15) on top of your ticket price and stamped out of Malaysia before you board the boat in JB.

---

airport and JB is RM50, taking 30 to 45 minutes depending on traffic.

BUS
Larkin Sentral (Larkin Bus Terminal; Jln Garuda) is about 5km north of town and is the main terminal for long-distance buses departing to greater Malaysia.

DESTINATION	PRICE (RM)	DURATION (HR)
Butterworth	80	9
Melaka	21	3
Muar	17	3
Kuala Lumpur	35	4½
Mersing	13	2½
Kuantan	29	6
Kuala Terengganu	49	9

JB Sentral Bus Terminal (Jln Jim Quee) is located beside the JB Sentral Railway, and services local and regional buses as well as buses to and from Singapore.

TAXI
JB's long-distance taxi station is at **Larkin Sentral** (p421), 5km north of town, from where **taxis to Singapore** (Larkin Sentral, Jln Garuda) leave (S$48 per taxi).

Some other taxi destinations and approximate costs (share taxi with four passengers) include:
➡ Kuala Lumpur (RM440)
➡ Kukup (RM80)
➡ Melaka (RM280)
➡ Mersing (RM170)

🛈 GETTING TO SINGAPORE: JOHOR BAHRU TO SINGAPORE

At JB Sentral (p421) you can clear immigration and travel across the Causeway to Singapore.

Getting to the border From central JB, board your bus after clearing Malaysian immigration just before the Causeway – you can buy your tickets on board. There are also frequent buses between JB's Larkin Sentral bus station (p421), 5km north of the city, and Singapore's Queen St bus station. **Causeway Link** (www.causewaylink.com.my; from JB/Singapore RM3.40/S$3.30; ⏱ 4am-midnight) is the most convenient service. **Trans Star Cross Border Coaches** (www.regentstar.travel/crossborder) run between Johor Bahru CIQ and Singapore's Changi Airport, embarking in the Terminal 2 coach area.

Registered Taxis depart from Larkin Sentral (p421), with taxis to Orchard Rd or Queen St terminal costing around RM60. Local city taxis cannot cross the Causeway.

KTM Intercity (p422) has trains (RM5) to take you from JB Sentral to Woodlands in Singapore; these run every few hours between 8am and 11pm. You'll go through passport checks and switch to the Singapore metro system at Woodlands.

At the border All buses and taxis stop at **Malaysian immigration**. You'll need to disembark from your vehicle with your luggage (and ticket), clear immigration and reboard. Vehicles then stop at Singapore immigration; again, clear immigration with your luggage, before getting back in your vehicle for the last leg to Queen St bus station. There are tourism information offices and money exchanges at the border.

Moving on At Queen St there are buses, taxis and an MRT (light rail) system that can take you almost anywhere you need to go in the city.

For more information on making this crossing in reverse see p648.

TRAIN

Daily express trains on **KTM Intercity** (☎ 03-2267 1200; www.ktmb.com.my; JB Sentral) leave from the sparkling JB Sentral station in the CIQ complex. You'll have to catch the rather old, slow, single-track line to Gemas, before boarding the new fast-train ETS service, which runs all the way to Padang Besar. ETS operates as part of KTM Intercity so tickets can be purchased at the KTM counter. The line passes through Tampin (for Melaka), Seremban, KL Sentral, Tapah Rd (for Cameron Highlands), Ipoh, Taiping and Butterworth. Ekspres Rakyat Timuran, known as the 'jungle train', runs daily to Tumpat: you can board this service for Jerantut (for Taman Negara) and Kuala Lipis.

Mersing

☎ 07 / POP 70,000

This busy, compact fishing town has everything that travellers passing through on their way to the islands might need: OK sleeping options, shops, cold beers, even a laundry. Take an afternoon to revel in views of the hilltop mosque, hike out to the nearby green areas or just reconnect with mainland life.

🛏 Sleeping & Eating

Hotel Embassy   HOTEL $

(☎ 07-799 3545; 2 Jln Ismail; r RM60; ❄ 🛜) A fabulous choice compared with the other cheapies in town, this is a great place to clean up and get back to reality after bumming it on island beaches. All rooms are huge and bright, and have cable TV, turbo-charged aircon and attached bathrooms.

Zeeadam Backpackers   HOSTEL $

(☎ 019-740 3456, 07-7991280; ahmadzamani_77@yahoo.com; 1C-1 Jln Abu Bakar; dm RM20; @ 🛜) The only true backpacker place in town, the Zeeadam has just two dorm rooms, sleeping six to eight people on ultra-firm beds. There's a little TV and a hangout chill area at this second-storey spot that is short on charms but long on value.

Loke Tien Yuen Restaurant   CHINESE $

(55 Jln Abu Bakar; mains RM8-20; ⏱ 12.30-3pm & 6.45-8.30pm Sat-Wed; ❄) Mersing's oldest Chinese restaurant is one of the friendliest and busiest places in town. You may have to wait for a marble table to enjoy the deliciously prepared prawn and pork dishes. The speciality, whole steamed fish that you'll see the locals eating, isn't on the menu so ask your server.

❶ Getting There & Away

Most buses as well as long-distance taxis depart from the **bus station** near the bridge on the river, although a few long-distance buses leave from bus-company offices near the pier. Some buses will drop you off at the pier when you arrive in Mersing if you ask nicely. For buses to Cherating, travel first to Kuantan.

DESTINATION	PRICE (RM)	DURATION (HR)
Johor Bahru	13	2½
Kuala Lumpur	40	5½
Kuala Terengganu	38	9
Kuantan	19	5
Melaka	25	4
Singapore	16	3
Penang	80	10

You can connect by **ferry** for Tioman and other islands. Purchase tickets and pay the marine park entrance fee (RM30) at the new **Mersing Harbour Centre** (Jln Abu Bakar; ⊘ 5am-10pm) opposite the jetty entrance.

Pulau Tioman

📋 09 / POP 4000

Sitting like an emerald dragon guarding the translucent waters of the South China Sea, Tioman Island offers every possible shade of paradise. There's cascading waterfalls, rigorous jungle hikes, laid-back villages, and then there's the sea, beckoning you to paddle, snorkel, dive and sail. At 20km long and 11km wide, the island is so spacious that your ideal holiday spot is surely here somewhere. Tekek, Tioman's largest village and its administrative centre, is where ferries arrive from Mersing (in Johor) and Tanjung Gemok (in Pahang).

◉ Sights & Activities

Beaches

Most budget accommodation is clustered in Air Batang (ABC) and Salang on the northern end of the west coast. Salang has wider stretches of sand and is the most backpacker-esque of Tioman's *kampung*, while ABC is slightly more upscale. On Tioman's east coast Juara has a stunning beach, surfing during the monsoon, and affordable accommodation. Other small beaches reachable only by boat run south along the west coast.

Juara Turtle Project　　　VOLUNTEERING
(📞 09-419　3244; www.juaraturtleproject.com; Mentawak beach, Kampung Juara; tour RM10, dm RM120; ⊘ 10am-5pm) 🌿 This voluntourism operation works to protect declining sea-turtle populations by collecting eggs and moving them to a hatchery, and patrolling the beaches for poachers and predators. Anyone can tour the facility to learn more about the area's turtles, which nest here February to October, with public releases June through November.

Volunteers (accepted March to October) get basic dorm accommodation and full board. When you're not working on patrols and participating in information seminars, activities including sea kayaking, treks and cooking classes. There's a minimum four-night stay in dorm accommodation.

Diving & Snorkelling

There is good snorkelling off the rocky points on the west coast of the island, particularly those just north of ABC, but the best snorkelling is around nearby Pulau Tulai, better known as Coral Island. Snorkelling equipment for hire is easy to find (masks and snorkels are typically RM15 per day) at many places on the island. Snorkelling trips with boat transfers cost RM40 to RM100.

Pulau Tioman

There are plenty of excellent dive centres on Tioman, and Open Water Diver (OWD) certification courses are priced competitively. Expect to pay about RM1100 to RM1200 for a four-day PADI OWD course and RM120 to RM130 for fun dives. Discover dives (beginner dives that do not require pre-certification and include basic instruction) cost RM200 to RM250 for a half-day course.

Hiking

Jungle-swathed Tioman offers plenty of excellent hikes to keep the intrepid landlubber exhausted and happy. While you can easily take on most hikes by yourself, guided jungle trips (arranged through your accommodation) give you a curated look at the island's unique flora and fauna, and cost around RM100 for a half-day.

🛏 Sleeping & Eating

Budget accommodation largely comprises small wooden chalets, typically with a bathroom, fan and mosquito net. More expensive rooms have air-con and hot showers. Most operations have larger family rooms for those with children.

Johan's Resort   BUNGALOW $
(☑ 09-419 1359; Kampung Air Batang/ABC; dm/chalet/f RM25/60/120) A friendly, welcoming place offering tons of information. The two four-bed dorms up the hillside are decent value; the chalets are pretty much the same as other cheapies on the beach.

Mokhtar's Place   BUNGALOW $
(☑ 019-704 8299; www.mokhtarplace.blogspot.com; Kampung Air Batang/ABC; s & d with fan RM40-60, d with air-con RM100-220; ❄🛜) Great budget value, this cluster of 16 bungalows along the beach south of town features little patios and mozzie nets. If the wind's just right, you can catch a cooling ocean breeze at night.

Bushman   CHALET $
(☑ 09-419 3109; bushmanchalets@outlook.my; Barok beach, Kampung Juara; r RM100-150; ❄🛜) Nabbing one of Bushman's eight varnished wood bungalows, with their inviting wicker-furnished terraces, is like winning the Juara lottery – reserve in advance! The location is right up against the boulder outcrop at the southern end of Barok beach.

Ella's Place   CHALET $
(☑ 014-844 8610, 09-419 5004; Kampung Salang; chalets RM60-200; ❄🛜) There's usually a lounge-able patch of sand at this cute-as-a-button, family-run place at the quiet northern end of the beach. There are 10 clean bungalows (some with air-con) and a small cafe.

★ Rainbow Chalets   CHALET $$
(☑ 012 989 8572; rainbow.chalets1980@gmail.com; Barok beach, Kampung Juara; s or d RM120, tr RM160; ❄🛜) Eight colourful bungalows await you at this friendly place. All come with wooden porches, decorated with shells and coral, which provide direct access to the beach and glorious views of the South China Sea.

Nazri's Place   GUESTHOUSE $$
(☑ 017-490 1384; www.nazrisplace.net; Kampung Air Batang/ABC; r incl breakfast RM120-200; ❄🛜) At the far southern end of the beach, which has some of ABC's best sand, this place has clean rooms and a wide range of accommodation. The sea-view rooms are cheaper and more basic, while the upscale rooms have an almost business vibe, save for the pleasant patios that look onto a lush garden.

ℹ Information

Tioman's sole **ATM** (Tekek; ⊙ 24 hrs) is across from Tekek's airport and takes international cards. It's been known to run dry, so consider getting cash in Mersing. There's a money-changer at the airport.

ℹ Getting There & Away

Ferries (☑ 014-988 4281; https://tiomanferry ticket.com; 38 Jln Jeti; return RM70; ⊙ 10am-6pm Mon-Sat, 11am-6pm Sun) from Mersing tend only to run early in the morning and are very much dependent on the tides. Several operators run boats, but only **Gemilang/Bluewater Express** (☑ 09-413 1363; Tanjong Gemok Ferry Terimnal; one-way/return RM35/70) have services both from Mersing and Tanjong Gemok – you can go from one port and return to another which can be useful depending on your travel plans.

Book online to be sure of a ticket at busy times of year, such as during public and school holidays in Malaysia or Singapore. Also call for up-to-date sailing schedules – these tend to be erratic during monsoon season (November to February). Aim to be at the jetty at least one hour prior to departure – particularly if you haven't pre-booked your ticket.

ℹ Getting Around

Typical sea-taxi fares from Tekek:
➡ ABC/Panuba (RM25)
➡ Genting (RM50)
➡ Nipah (RM120)
➡ Mukut (RM150)

- Paya Beach (RM35)
- Salang (RM35).

Most hotels can arrange boat charter. Expect to pay around RM600 for a full day on a boat, and expect waters to be far rougher on the Juara side of Tioman.

If you have the time, you can explore some of the island on foot. Bicycles can be hired at guesthouses on all the main beaches (per hour/day RM5/30), and mopeds (per hour/day RM15/40) are a good bet for trips to Juara.

Taxis from Tekek to Juara cost RM70 to RM90.

Kuantan

09 / POP 354,400

Most travellers pause briefly in Pahang's capital and Malaysia's second-biggest port, to break up long bus trips. This is a shame; while the city isn't especially geared towards tourism, it is definitely interesting enough to warrant a day or two of exploration. There's the excellent **Pahang Museum** (010 924 7134; www.pahangmuseums.com; Jln Masjid; adult/child RM4/free; 9.30am-5pm Mon-Thu, 9.30am-12.15pm & 2.45-5pm Fri), the impressive **Masjid Sultan Ahmad Shah** (State Mosque; 014 840 3802; Jln Masjid), many good places to eat and the nearby beach of Teluk Chempedak with upmarket resort accommodation.

Sleeping & Eating

★**Classic Hotel**   BOUTIQUE HOTEL **$$**
(09-516 4599; www.classhotelkuantan.com; 7 Bangunan LKNP, Jln Besar; r incl breakfast RM100-180;) All rooms are spacious and clean (ask for a river view), with large bathrooms and all the mod cons. Central location, ample Malay-style breakfasts and considerate staff make this a top pick.

East Coast Mall   FOOD HALL
(09-565 8600; www.eastcoastmall.com.my; Jln Putra Sq; 10am-10pm) An option for eating in a spick-and-span, air-conditioned Malay-style food court.

Information

Lots of banks (many with 24-hour ATMs), including **HSBC** (1 Jln Mahkota) and **Standard Chartered Bank** (1-3 Jln Haji Abdul Aziz;) are on or near the aptly named Jln Bank.

Getting There & Away

AIR

Sultan Ahmad Shah Airport (09-531 2123; www.malaysiaairports.com.my) is 17km west of

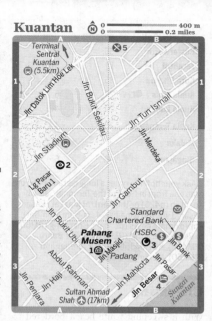

Kuantan

Top Sights
1 Pahang Musem A3

Sights
2 Central Market A2
3 Masjid Sultan Ahmad Shah B3

Sleeping
4 Classic Hotel B3

Eating
5 East Coast Mall B1

the city centre; a taxi here costs RM35. **Malaysia Airlines** (p481) has several daily direct flights to KLIA with plenty of onward connections from there. **Firefly** (p481) has two daily flights to/from Subang Airport in KL and four weekly flights to Singapore.

BUS & TAXI

Long-distance buses leave from **Terminal Sentral Kuantan** (TSK; Jln Pintasan Kuantan), about 20 minutes from the city centre (taxi RM20). The ticket offices, food court and left-luggage centre (RM2 per piece) are on the 2nd floor of the building.

Head to the **local bus station** (Hentian Bas Bandar Kuantan; 2704 Jln Stadium) for services to Pekan (RM4), Balok (RM4) and Beserah (RM2).

DESTINATION	PRICE (RM)	DURATION (HR)
Butterworth	56	8½
Jerantut	18	3½
Kota Bharu	35	6
Kuala Lipis	29	6
Kuala Lumpur	24	4
Kuala Terengganu	20	4
Melaka	31	6
Singapore	48	6

Ask your hotel to order a long-distance taxi or grab one from in front of the Terminal Sentral Kuantan (p425) or the **Central Market** (Pasar Besar; 3 Jln Tun Ismail; ⊘4am-6pm Mon-Sat). Approximate costs (per car): Cherating (RM60 to RM70), Jerantut (RM320), Johor Bahru (RM450), KL (RM350), Kuala Terengganu (RM250), Mersing (RM250).

Cherating

☑09

With a sweeping white beach bordered by coconut palms, this small village of guesthouses and shops is a popular spot for surfing, windsurfing and general beachfront slacking. It has several beach bars and the best nightlife on Pahang's coast. You can also see fireflies flicker at night on cruises along the Sungai Cherating and go turtle watching.

◎ Sights & Activities

Cherating's bay has a long sandy shelf, making this a peaceful spot for swimming most of the year. Watch out for jellyfish in June and July.

Cherating's beach isn't great for snorkelling but places all around town offer half-day snorkelling tours to the aptly named Coral Island for around RM60.

Turtle Sanctuary   ANIMAL SANCTUARY
(☑09-581 9087; Bukit Cherating; RM30; ⊘9.30am-4.30pm Tue-Sun) The turtle sanctuary next to Club Med has a few basins with baby and rehabilitating green turtles, and can offer information about the laying and hatching periods.

⊨ Sleeping & Eating

★**Ku Mimi Cablet**   CHALET $
(☑019-927 3871; https://m.facebook.com/kumimi cablet; r fan/air-con from RM60/90; ❋ ⊛) Cablet stands for cabin and chalet and that's

just what you'll find at this sweet place located a short walk from the main road. The whitewashed wood chalets with attached bathrooms are simple and clean, while converted shipping containers make the cabins. Pluses are a shared kitchen and cool central hang-out.

★**Tanjung Inn**   BUNGALOW $
(☑09-581 9081; www.tanjunginn.com; safari tents RM50-70, r with fan RM106, r with air-con RM223-318; ❋ ⊛) This highly recommended place offers wooden bungalows with decks set around a stunning lilypad-bedazzled pond surrounded by tall grass and fruit trees. All the bungalows have hot showers, and there's an excellent lending library. There's also a second landscaped pond surrounded by safari-style tents over mattresses on wooden palates for those who prefer to glamp.

Don't Tell Mama Eco Bar   INTERNATIONAL $$
(☑012 630 2543; Cherating Beach; mains RM25-55; ⊘5.30pm-late) 🏄 Don't Tell Mama is best known for its legendary burgers but there are plenty of other options on the menu, including vegetarian ones. With its cool beachside shack set-up, reggae music and friendly service it's easy to see why this is a top spot to relax in the evening.

❶ Getting There & Away

Whether travelling from the north or south by long-distance bus, you'll first arrive at **Terminal** Sentral Kuantan (p425). From there take bus 303 to Kuantan's local bus station (p425; RM2, 30 minutes) and transfer to bus 600 to Batok (RM4, 40 minutes), followed by bus 604 to Cherating Lama (Old Cherating; RM2, 20 minutes). Ask the driver to let you know when to get off.

It's simpler and speedier to take a taxi from Kuantan (RM60; 45 minutes).

Kuala Terengganu

☑09 / POP 406, 317

A microcosm of Malaysia's economic history: fishing village strikes oil, modernity ensues. Kuala Terengganu retains its charm despite the newly built skyscrapers. There's a boardwalk, a couple of decent beaches, a few old *kampong*-style houses hidden among the high-rises, and one of eastern Peninsular Malaysia's prettiest and most interesting Chinatowns. With seafood-heavy local cuisine and good transport links, KT is worth a day or two in between the islands and jungles.

Kuala Terengganu

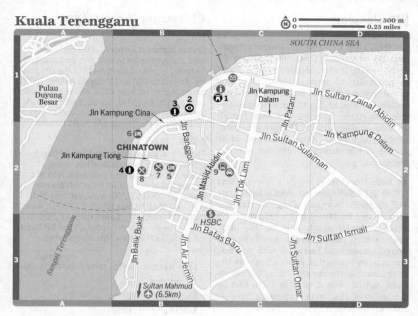

◉ Sights

Centred on Jln Kampung Cina (also known as Jln Bandar), KT's compact Chinatown features heritage buildings and temples, as well as watermarked buildings and alleys jazzed up with contemporary and quirky street art. Gentrification is in full swing with cafes, bars and gift shops opening up, but sleepy hardware shops and traditional Chinese medicinal-herb shops can also be found.

Worth seeking out are **Turtle Alley** (off Jln Kampung Cina), with mosaics telling the story of KT's now-endangered turtles, and **Pasar Payang Alley** (Memory Lane), which commemorates local Chinese community leaders and famous Malays. Pick up the *Chinatown Heritage Trail* brochure at the tourist information office (p428).

Central Market   MARKET
(Pasar Payang; cnr Jln Kampung Cina & Jln Sultan Zainal Abidin; ◷ 6am-5pm) The Central Market is a lively place to graze on exotic snacks, and the floor above the fish section has a wide collection of batik and *kain songket* (traditional handwoven fabric). Many stalls don't operate on Fridays.

Bukit Puteri   FORT
(Princess Hill; Jln Sultan Zainal Abidin; adult/child RM1/0.50; ◷ 9am-5pm Sat-Thu, to 3pm Fri)

Across the road from the Central Market, look for an escalator and steep flight of steps leading up to Bukit Puteri, a 200m-high hill with good views of the city. On top are the scant remains of a mid-19th-century fort, some cannons and a bell.

🛌 Sleeping

KT Chinatown Lodge   GUESTHOUSE $
(📞 09-6221 938, 013-9316 192; lawlorenz@gmail.
com; 113 Jln Kampung Cina; r RM75-150; ❋ 🛜)
Right in the heart of Chinatown – and
in proximity to nesting swiftlets – this
two-storey guesthouse features simple but
spotless rooms, and a warm welcome. The
cheapest rooms have no windows, but all
include multi-channel TV, private bathrooms and air-con. Retro black-and-white
photos of Chinatown bolster the heritage
ambience.

⭐ Jen's Homestay   APARTMENT $$
(📞 019-957 8368; www.jenhomestay.weebly.com;
8-12 Pangsapuri Kampung Tiong, Jln Kampung
Tiong; r from RM100; ❂ ❋ 🛜) Friendly Jen's
has four rental apartments in this high-
rise building, each with three bedrooms, a
shared lounge, and balconies with washing
machine and sweeping views across the riv-
er or towards the ocean. The entire apart-
ment can be rented, or rent them just by
the bedroom (the more expensive have an
attached bathroom).

🍴 Eating

T Homemade Cafe   CHINESE, MALAY $
(214 Jln Kampung Cina; mains from RM5;
⊙10am-5pm) Take a shaded pavement seat
and revive yourself during your Chinatown
exploration at this buzzy cooperative of a
few food stalls. You can try tasty Chinese
dishes here, such as yummy roast chicken,
duck and pork with rice, as well as fresh
juices.

Chinatown Hawker Centre   HAWKER $
(off Jln Kampung Tiong; ⊙7am-11pm) China-
town's outdoor hawker centre is divided
into Chinese and Malay sections, and sizzles
with cooking and socialising by day and
night. You can get a chilled beer here and
there's a small morning craft and produce
market too – well worth visiting for take-
away foods.

ℹ️ Information

You'll find plenty of banks on Jln Sultan Ismail,
including **HSBC** (📞 09-622 3100; 57 Jln Sultan
Ismail), most have 24-hour ATMs that accept
international cards.

  Tourist Information Office (📞 09-622 1553;
http://beautifulterengganu.com; Jln Sultan
Zainal Abidin; ⊙9am-5pm Sat-Thu) has helpful
staff and good brochures and maps.

ℹ️ Getting There & Away

AIR
Sultan Mahmud Airport (📞 09-667 3666;
www.malaysiaairports.com.my; Jln Lapangan
Terbang) is around 11km north of the city cen-
tre. AirAsia (p481) and Malaysia Airlines (p481)
have services to/from KLIA, while Firefly (p481)
and Malindo Air (p481) connect with SkyPark
Subang Terminal (also known as Sultan Abdul
Aziz Shah Airport), closer to Kuala Lumpur.

BUS & TAXI
The central **bus station** (Jln Masjid Abidin)
is the terminus for both local buses and
longer-distance express buses. Express bus
companies at the station include **Transna-
sional** (📞 09-622 2700; www.transnasional.
com.my), **MARA Liner** (📞 09-622 2097; www.
maralinergroup.my), **Sani Express** (📞 09-622
2717; www.saniexpress.com.my) and **SP Bumi**
(📞 09-623 7789; www.spbumi.com.my).

DESTINATION	PRICE (RM)	DURATION (APPROX HR)
Johor Bahru	80	9
Kota Bharu	10	3
Kuala Besut (Perhentians)	10.80	2
Kuala Lumpur	44.20	8
Kuantan	9	5
Melaka	48	8

Kuala Terengganu's **main taxi stand** is near
the local bus station, but taxis can be found
throughout the city.

Kuala Besut

Boats to Pulau Perhentian leave from the
attractive seaside town of Kuala Besut. A
bus from Kota Bharu is RM6, a taxi around
RM70; both take two hours. The bus from
Kuala Terengganu is RM10.80, and a taxi
around RM120; again it takes around two
hours. There is at least one daily bus from
Kuala Lumpur (RM45, nine hours). Many
travel agents run minibus services to Kuala
Besut from tourist hotspots around Malaysia.

Pulau Perhentian
📞 09 / POP 1300

Imagine crystal-clear waters, reflecting
turquoise skies and perfect for diving and
snorkelling, jungles thick and fecund, and
beaches with blindingly white sand. At
night, beach bonfires and phosphorescence

in the water illuminate the velvety black fabric of darkness, and myriad stars are mirrored above. The Perhentians offer all this and more.

Your biggest dilemma on the Perhentians may well be choosing the right beach as your base. There are two main islands, Kecil ('Small'), popular with the younger backpacker crowd, and Besar ('Large'), with higher standards of accommodation and a more relaxed ambience. Boats can take you out to five smaller islands for day trips.

🏃 Activities

With relatively shallow and calm waters, great visibility, and largely gentle currents, the Perhentian Islands are an ideal place to snorkel or learn to dive.

Most guesthouses organise snorkelling trips for around RM40 per person. Highlights include Turtle Point at the northern end of Besar's Main Beach, and Shark Point on the island's southwestern tip. For scuba divers, competition between many dive centres keeps prices keen. A PADI open-water course costs around RM1000.

There's plenty of hiking on both islands. Some tracks can get washed out in heavy rains, so use common sense. Hot and humid is the norm, so bring plenty of water, and don't hike at night without a torch (flashlight).

🛌 Sleeping & Eating

🛌 Pulau Kecil

Long Beach (Pulau Perhentian Kecil) offers the best variety of accommodation from barebones backpacker hostels to spiffy upmarket resorts – but it can get very noisy here with all the bars and beach parties. **Coral Bay** (Pulau Perhentian Kecil) has a good variety of accommodation in all budget brackets.

A 45-minute walk south takes you via RainForest Camping to **Petani Beach** (Pulau Perhentian Kecil) which offers a couple of upmarket resorts.

★**D'Lagoon Chalet & Restaurant** CHALET $
(☎019-985 7089; www.dlagoon.my; Teluk Kerma, Pulau Perhentian Kecil; camp site RM15, dm RM25, r RM70-220, mains RM8-15; ⊙restaurant 7.45am-4pm & 7-10.30pm; ❄☎) Family-run D'Lagoon is the sole property on a tranquil bay with fine coral a short swim from the beach. Accommodation ranges from camping and a longhouse with dorm beds to simple stilt chalets. Activities include snorkelling, shark-

and turtle-watching trips, jungle hikes to remote beaches and a free 200m flying fox.

The restaurant serves decent international and Malay food. Live local music can be arranged on request. Take a water taxi to reach here, otherwise it's an hour's hike from the Long Beach jetty.

Lemon Grass Chalet BUNGALOW $
(☎012-956 2393; Long Beach, Pulau Perhentian Kecil; chalet RM60) At the southern tip of Long Beach, Lemongrass offers a pair of no-frills wooden bungalows with shared bathrooms. There are great views from the verandah at reception and nice secluded spots to sit and gaze out to sea. All huts are the same price; try to get one with a sea view.

RainForest Camping CAMPGROUND $
(rainforestcamping.perhentian@gmail.com; Kampung Pasir Karang, Pulau Perhentian Kecil; camping RM50) Simple tents resting on bamboo decks sit in a shady (and buggy) rainforest glade. Shared toilets and bathrooms are rudimentary, but the real attractions here are the perfect arc of beach and chilled vibe in the attached cafe.

★**Crocodile Rock Villas** VILLAS $$
(www.crocodilerockvillas.com; Kampung Pasir Karang, Pulau Perhentian Kecil; tent/villa from R250/315; ⊙restaurant 9-11am & 6.30-10pm; ❄☎) Run by a Malaysian-English couple, this is one heavenly crocodile. It's a short walk south of Coral Beach; glampers will swoon over the three spacious safari-tents while flashpackers are just as well served by the handful of luxe wooden chalets, raised on stilts and with sea-facing balconies. An excellent restaurant serving Malay and international cuisine rounds out the package.

Panorama Chalet CHALET $$
(☎09-6911590; www.panoramaperhentianisland. com; Long Beach, Pulau Perhentian Kecil; r RM120-250; ❄☎) A favourite with divers and snorkellers, Panorama is set back a short way from the sand. Rooms range from fan-cooled doubles to air-conditioned chalets. The family room has two queen-sized beds, near-wraparound windows, and a balcony.

🛌 Pulau Besar

The big island's two main bases are **Main Beach** (Pulau Perhentian Besar) and **Teluk Dalam** (Pulau Perhentian Besar). Both are more family-orientated than the sleeping locations on Kecil and offer a good range of accommodation to suit all budgets.

Samudra Beach Chalet
BUNGALOW $

(📞09-691 1677; www.samudrabeachchalet.com; Teluk Dalam, Pulau Perhentian Besar; r RM60-160; 🌬🛜) Samudra has traditional Malaysian A-frame bungalows. They are slightly dark on the inside, but the cheaper ones have fans. The air-conditioned family room with two double beds is a decent deal.

EcoMarine Perhentian Island Resort
RESORT $$

(📞011-1083 4729, 013-396 2245; https://eco marineperhentian.com; Teluk Dalam, Pulau Perhentian Besar; camping per person RM20, dm/r from RM82/210; 🌬) At the far southwest end of the beach, EcoMarine offers one of the best accommodation deals in the Perhentians, if you're up for camping. There's also an air-conditioned dorm with a hot-water shower, as well as comfortable rooms in concrete bungalows facing the beach.

Reef Chalets
CHALET $$

(📞09-691 1762; http://thereefperhentian.com; Main Beach, Pulau Perhentian Besar; chalet RM140-408; 🌬🛜) This family-owned resort offers a wide range of pleasant wood chalets set along the beach, and surrounding a beautifully maintained jungle garden featuring trees filled with occasional lemurs, monkeys, birds and bats. Many chalets have sea views; the cheapest are fan-cooled, the more expensive have air-conditioning.

The friendly owners rent out canoes and snorkelling equipment and can help you plan your stay.

ℹ Information

The RM30 conservation fee for entering the marine park around the Perhentians is payable at the jetty in Kuala Besut.

There are no banks or ATMs on the islands. Free wi-fi is ubiquitous on both islands at accommodation and restaurants. If you're planning on using your own smartphone, Celcom has the best 3G broadband coverage in the islands.

ℹ Getting There & Around

Speedboats run several times a day between Kuala Besut and the Perhentians (return trip adult/child RM70/35, 30 to 40 minutes) from 8.30am to 5.30pm. Tickets are sold by travel agents around Kuala Besut. The boats will drop you off at any of the beaches. Expect delays or cancellations if the weather is bad or if there aren't enough passengers.

In the other direction, speedboats depart from the islands daily at 8am, noon and 4pm. Let your guesthouse owner know a day before you plan on leaving so they can arrange a pickup. If the water is rough or tides are low, you may be ferried from the beach on a small boat to your mainland-bound craft; you'll have to pay around RM5 for this.

While there are some trails around the islands, the easiest way to go from beach to beach or island to island is by boat. From island to island, the trip costs around RM15 to RM30, and a jaunt from one beach to another on the same island usually costs RM10 to RM15. There's a minimum of two passengers (so double the rate if you're a solo passenger). Prices also double after sunset.

Kota Bharu
📞09 / POP 491,200

Kota Bharu (KB) has the energy of a mid-sized city, the compact feel and friendly vibe of a small town, plus superb food and a good spread of accommodation. A logical overnight stop between Thailand and the Perhentians, KB is a good base for exploring Kelantan. The state's villages are within day-tripping distance, and its crafts, cuisine and culture are present in the city itself.

⊙ Sights

★ Streetart Gallery
PUBLIC ART

(off Jln Ismail) FREE Not to be missed is this colourful display of street art covering a back alley between Jln Ismail and Jln Dato Pati. The depictions of smiling locals at work and play and idyllic jungle scenes are contrasted with graphic displays of conflict and suffering in Palestine.

Istana Jahar
MUSEUM

(Royal Ceremonies Museum; 📞09-748 2266; www. muzium.kelantan.gov.my; Jln Istana; adult/child RM3/1.50; ⏱8.30am-4.45pm Sat-Wed, to 3.30pm Thu) Kota Bharu's best museum focuses on Kelatanese rituals and crafts. It's also housed in a beautiful chocolate-brown building that dates back to 1887 and which is easily one of the most attractive traditional buildings in the city.

Istana Batu
MUSEUM

(Royal Museum, Muzium Diraja; 📞09-748 7737; www.muzium.kelantan.gov.my; Jln Istana; adult/child RM4/2; ⏱8.30am-4.45pm Sat-Wed, to 3.30pm Thu) The pale-yellow building, constructed in 1939, was the crown prince's palace until donated to the state. The richly furnished rooms of this museum give a surprisingly intimate insight into royal life,

Kota Bharu

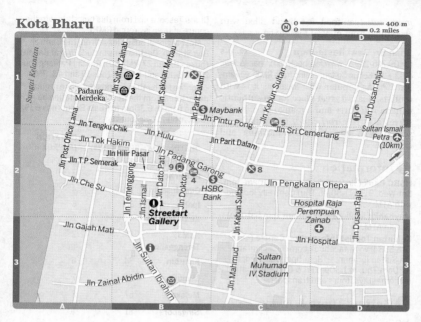

with family photos and personal belongings scattered among the fine china, chintzy sofas, and the late sultan's collection of hats.

🛏 Sleeping

My Place Guest House GUESTHOUSE $
(☑013-9011 463; myplacekb@yahoo.com; 4340-R2 Jln Kebun Sultan; s/d RM35/50; 🖼🛜) Just a short stroll from Chinatown, My Place Guest House is a welcoming and friendly spot. Retro posters, including the Beatles and Che Guevara, punctuate the eclectically furnished interior, and the rooms are simple but clean.

KB Backpackers Lodge HOSTEL $
(☑019-944 5222, 09-748 8841; www.facebook. com/kbbackpackerslodge; 1872-D Tingat 1, Jln Padang Garong; dm/r from RM15/35; 🖼@) Owner Pawi is a wealth of information, dorms and rooms are simple but clean, there's a rooftop terrace, and local city tours can be arranged.

Zeck's Travellers Inn HOMESTAY $
(☑019-946 6655; http://zecktravellers.blogspot.my; 7088-F Jln Sri Cemerlang; dm/s/d from RM15/25/30, r with air-con RM50-80; 🖼@🛜) Zeck and Miriam Zaki's home, located in a peaceful nook north of the city centre, is a great way to get a feel for genuine Malaysian *kampung* (village) life in the heart of Kota Bharu. Light meals and drinks are always at hand.

🍴 Eating

Night Market MARKET $
(Jln Parit Dalam; mains from RM5; ⊙5-9pm) The most popular spot for the best Malay food in town is KB's night market. Specialities include *ayam percik* (marinated chicken on bamboo skewers) and *nasi kerabu* (blue rice with coconut, fish and spices), squid-on-a-stick and

MALAYSIA KOTA BHARU

murtabak (pan-fried flat bread filled with everything from minced meat to bananas).

Shan Sri Dewi Restaurant   INDIAN $
(☑09-746 2592; www.facebook.com/shansridewi; 4213-F Jln Kebun Sultan; mains from RM8; ☺7am-9pm; ☑) As popular with locals as it is with tourists, this is a great place for an authentic banana-leaf curry and a mango lassi. It also serves a terrific *roti canai* (flaky flatbread served with curry) in the morning and evening.

ℹ Information

HSBC Bank (Jln Padang Garong; ☺10am-3pm Sat-Wed, 9.30-11.30am Thu) Centrally located with ATM.

Maybank (Jln Pintu Pong; 10am-7pm Sat-Thu) Has an ATM.

Kelantan Tourist Information Centre (☑09-748 5534; www.facebook.com/tic.kelantan; Jln Sultan Ibrahim; ☺8am-5pm Sun-Wed, to 3.30pm Thu, to 1.30pm Fri & Sat) Information on homestays, tours and transport.

ℹ Getting There & Away

AIR
Sultan Ismail Petra Airport (☑09-773 7400; www.malaysiaairports.com.my; Sultan Ismail Petra Airport Darul Naim) Kota Bharu's airport is 10km northeast of the city centre.

BUS
Local buses and Transnasional express buses operate from the **Central Bus Station** (☑09-747 5971, 09-747 4330; Jln Padang Garong). Other express and long-distance buses leave from the **Interstate Bus Terminal** (Terminal Bas Kota Bharu; Jln Datuk Wan Halim) near the Kota

Bharu Tesco; a taxi from this bus station to the centre of town is around RM15.

Most regional buses leave from the Central Bus Station. Destinations include Wakaf Baharu (buses 19 and 27, RM1.60), Rantau Panjang (bus 29, RM5.10) and Tumpat (bus 19 and 43, RM3).

For the Perhentian Islands there are regular departures from the Central Bus Station between 6am to 6.30pm to Kuala Besut (bus 639, RM6, around two hours).

DESTINATION	PRICE (RM)	DURATION (APPROX HR)
Alor Setar	39	7
Butterworth	37	7
Gua Musang	17	4
Ipoh	36	6
Kuala Lumpur	44	7
Kuala Terengganu	17	3
Kuantan	34	6
Lumut	44	7
Melaka	57	8
Singapore	81	10

TAXI
The **taxi stand** (Jln Hilir Pasar) is on the southern side of the central bus station. Avoid the unlicensed cab drivers who will pester you around town, and take an official taxi as these are cheaper and safer.

TRAIN
The nearest railway station is **Wakaf Baharu** (☑09-719 6986; Jln Stesen), around 10km west of Kota Bharu; it can be reached by local buses 19 or 17.

ℹ GETTING TO THAILAND: KOTA BHARU TO SUNGAI KOLOK

Getting to the border The Thailand border is at Rantau Panjang; bus 29 (RM5, 1½ hours) departs on the hour from Kota Bharu's Central Bus Station (p432). Share taxis, also departing from the Central Bus Station, cost around RM50 per car and take 45 minutes.

There's another border crossing at Pengkalan Kubor, on the coast, but transport links aren't as good and crossing here can be dodgy during periods of sectarian violence in southern Thailand. Enquire at the tourist information centre (p432) before using this crossing. During the day a large car ferry (RM1 for pedestrians) crosses the river to busy Tak Bai in Thailand. From Kota Bharu, take bus 27 or 43 (RM2.40) from the central bus station.

At the border From Rantau Panjang you can walk across the border to Sungai Kolok, where you can arrange ongoing transport to Bangkok.

Moving on Trains to Bangkok depart at 11.30am and 2.20pm, buses at 11.30am. There are also hourly minibuses from Sungai Kolok to Hat Yai.

For information on making the crossing in the reverse direction see p760.

Destinations on what is sometimes called the 'jungle line' include Jerantut (8½ hours, daily) and Johor Bharu (18 hours, daily). For Kuala Lumpur you'll need to change lines at Gemas.

Check with KB's **tourist information centre** (p432) or see **Keretapi Tanah Melayu** (p397) for the latest times and fares.

PENINSULAR INTERIOR

Separating the two peninsular coasts is a thick band of jungle featuring Taman Negara, the peninsula's most famous national park, and the 'jungle railway', an engineering feat.

Jerantut

📞 09 / POP 90,000

Sleepy Jerantut is the gateway to Taman Negara and an access point for the 'jungle railway' connecting with Kota Bharu in the north. If you have to spend a night here before heading into the jungle, it's a pleasant enough place to wander around and has good accommodation and places to eat.

🛏 Sleeping & Eating

★ **Hotel Firdaus** HOTEL **$**

(📞09-266 1409; www.facebook.com/hfjerantut; 2-5 Jln Kuantan; s/d/q RM38/55/90; ❄🛜) This new hotel offers clean rooms (mostly with no windows) that are spacious, well equipped and reasonably priced. Throw in its brightly decorated ground-floor cafe Kopi Chantek and bakery Dania Cakes Corner, and you have an almost irresistible combination.

ℹ Getting There & Away

BUS

All buses arrive and depart from **Jerantut Bus Station** (120 Jln Bandar Baru).

DESTINATION	PRICE (RM)	DURATION (HR)
Kuala Lipis	5	1½
Kuala Lumpur (Pekeliling)	18.40	4
Kuantan	17.80	3
Temerloh	6.20	1

Public buses go to the jetty at Kuala Tembeling for boats to Taman Negara (RM4, 45 minutes) usually every hour from 10.30am to 3.30pm. The schedule is unreliable and doesn't coincide with boat departures.

NKS Hotel & Travel (📞09-266 4488; www.taman-negara-nks.com; 21-22 Jln Besar, Bandar Lama; ⏰7.30am-6pm; 🛜) arranges minibuses and buses to a variety of destinations, including Tembeling jetty (RM10), KL (RM40), Kuala Besut (RM70) and the Cameron Highlands (RM60). Buses leave from outside theNKS cafe. NKS can also arrange a river trip to the national park from the jetty in Kuala Tembeling (RM45). If you want to skip the riverboat, take one of the minibuses directly from Kuala Tahan for Taman Negara (RM25, 8am and sometimes 4.30pm).

TRAIN

Jerantut train station is on the Tumpat–Gemas line (also known as the East Line or 'jungle railway'). Going north, the 4am train stops at Kuala Lipis and Gua Musang before arriving at Wakaf Baharu close to Kota Bharu (RM20, nine hours). Going south, the 1am sleeper train heads to Johor Bahru (seat/sleeper RM19/44, nine hours), where you can transfer to either the shuttle train or bus to Singapore.

For an up-to-date timetable and list of fares, consult **KTM** (p397).

Taman Negara

📞 09

Malaysia's oldest, largest and most popular national park straddles the borders of Pahang, Kelantan and Terengganu. Since 1939 Taman Negara (which means national park in Bahasa Malaysia) has been a haven for amazing tropical flora and a vast variety of wildlife, including elephants, tigers, leopards and flying squirrels.

Join a tour or hire a guide – and head well away from the park headquarters at Kuala Tahan – to stand even a slim chance of spotting such large fauna. Or set aside nine days to scale the peninsula's highest peak, 2186m Gunung Tahan. Even if you can only spend a day or two here, it's still a great place to experience, on foot or by riverboat, and will give you a taste of how most of Malaysia once looked.

🏃 Activities

Hikes & Treks

Consider an overnight trek or at least a long boat-trip up one of the park's rivers. Whether coming for an afternoon hike or a multi-day trek, you'll need to buy a permit at the Park Information Counter (p435).

★ Canopy Walk & Around   HIKING

(adult/child RM5/3; ⊙9am-3pm Sat-Thu, to noon Fri) Taman Negara's most popular hike is to the Canopy Walk, a 500m bridge, suspended between huge trees, and around 45m above the forest floor. The easy-to-follow board-walk starts east park headquarters and leads along the Sungai Tembeling to the turn off to the canopy walk, 30 minutes away. Get here early for the best birding and wildlife watching.

Kuala Trenggan   HIKING

The well-marked main trail along the bank of Sungai Tembeling leads 9km to Kuala Trenggan, a popular trail for those heading to the Bumbun Kumbang hide. Allow five hours. From here, boats go back to Kuala Tahan, or it's a further 2km walk to Bumbun Kumbang.

Kuala Keniam   HIKING

The trail from Kuala Trenggan to Kuala Keniam is a popular day hike. It's normally done by chartering a boat to Kuala Keniam and then walking back to Kuala Trenggan (six hours). The trail is quite taxing and hilly in parts, and passes a series of limestone caves.

Lata Berkoh   HIKING

North from park headquarters, it's an easy two-hour hike to Lata Berkoh, a set of cascading rapids on Sungai Tahan. The trail

passes the **Lubok Simpon** swimming hole and **Bumbun Tabing**, and ultimately leads up to **Gunung Tahan**.

There is one river crossing before you reach the falls, which can be treacherous if the water is high. Do not attempt the river crossing in high water – you should hail one of the boat operators waiting on the opposite side to ferry you across.

River Bus & Boat Trips

At either **Mutiara Taman Negara Resort** (☑09-266 3500, in KL 03-2782 2222; www.mutiarahotels.com; Kampung Kuala Tahan; camp site RM10, dm/chalet/ste/bungalow incl breakfast RM100/450/650/1500; ⊙❀🛜), or with the boats that gather at Kuala Tahan's jetty, you can enquire about trips along the river to the following destinations. Departures are on request and there's often a minimum number of passengers.

DESTINATION	PRICE PER BOAT (RM)	TRIP DURATION (MIN)
Bunbun Yong	120	20
Canopy Walkway	100	15
Gua Telinga	120	30
Kuala Tembeling	220	180
Lata Berkoh	200	45
Kuala Kenian	450	60-90

Tours

There is a wide variety of thematic tours offered by nearly every hotel and a few independent operators in town. Some activities are easily doable on your own (such as the walk to the Canopy Walkway) but for longer treks, or if you really want to learn about the jungle, a tour is the way to go.

Good options are night jungle trips, on foot or by four-wheel drive (RM25 to RM45), a boat trip to the rapids at Lata Berkok via the *kelah* fish sanctuary (RM200), and motorboating through Class I rapids (RM40 to RM80).

Inside Taman Negara are around nine villages of the Batek, a subgroup of the indigenous people of the peninsula known collectively as Orang Asli. On tours to their settlements (around RM80), tribal elders give a general overview of life there and you'll learn how to use a long blow-pipe and start a fire. While local guides insist that these tours provide essential income

---

❶ GEAR HIRE & LEECHES

Leeches are everywhere inside the park (but are rarely found in Kampung Kuala Tahan). Wearing boots with gaiters or long socks tucked over your trousers and doused in DEET will make hiking more pleasant.

You can hire camping, hiking and fishing gear at several places in Kuala Tahan and also at Mutiara Taman Negara Resort. Approximate asking prices per day:

➡ sleeping bag RM10

➡ rucksack RM30

➡ tent RM10 to RM25

➡ fishing rod RM30

➡ sleeping pad RM8 to RM10

➡ stove RM8

➡ boots RM8

for the Orang Asli, most of your tour money will go to the tour company. A handicraft purchase in the village will help spread the wealth.

🛏 Sleeping & Eating

Kampung Kuala Tahan, directly across the river from park headquarters and the Mutiara Resort, is where most of Taman Negara's lodging, restaurants and shops are found. There are a handful of secluded places just 10 minutes' walk south and north of Kampung Kuala Tahan that are worth checking out if you are looking for a little more tranquillity.

Wild Lodge HOSTEL $
(☑016-665 7844; www.pahangoutdoor.com; Kampung Kuala Tahan; dm R25-30; ❉🛜) This new hostel overlooks the river and is close to the jetty. All rooms are simply furnished and have views into the park; the more expensive ones have beds rather than bunks.

There's free tea and coffee, beer (RM10 to RM13) and an outdoor lounge area, also with river views. They also offer a variety of guided tours and activities into the park, including a night river safari (RM65).

Mahseer Chalet BUNGALOW $
(☑019-383 2633; mahseerchalet@gmail.com; Kampung Kuala Tahan; dm RM13, r RM100-140; ❉🛜) This clutch of jungle bungalows occupies a quiet part of the village above the river. The rooms and bungalows are well-maintained and there's a restaurant on site serving breakfast and dinner. Cats patrol the grounds and there's a cool vibe that's wide-grinning friendly.

ℹ Information

Park Information Counter (Mutiara Taman Negara Resort; park entrance/camera/fishing/canopy/hides/camping RM1/5/10/5/5/1; ☉8am-10pm Sun-Thu, 8am-noon & 3-10pm Fri) You must register here and buy various permits before heading into the park. The counter is located in the building 100m north of the Mutiara Taman Negara Resort's reception. Pick up the good leaflet and map *Taman Negara Kuala Tahan* (free).

ℹ Getting There & Away

A recommended option is to head to Taman Negara by minibus or taxi from Jerantut and return by boat. The bold of spirit can get here on foot.

BOAT
The 60km boat trip from Kuala Tembling (18km north of Jerantut) to Kuala Tahan is a beautiful journey and a highlight for many visitors. The boat ride is three hours to the park and two hours in the other direction.

Boats (one way RM45) depart daily at 2pm. Extra boats are laid on during the busy season, and service can be irregular from November to February.

BUS & TAXI
Minibus services go directly from several tourist destinations around Malaysia to Kampung Kuala Tahan. **Han.Travel** (Map p390; ☑03-2031 0899; www.han-travel.com; ground Fl, Bangunan Mariamman, Jln Hang Kasturi; LRT Pasar Seni), **NKS** (p433) and **Danz Travel & Adventures** (☑09-266 3036, 013-655 4789; http://danzecoresort.com; Kuala Tahan; ☉8am-10pm; 🛜) run several useful private services, including daily buses from Kuala Tahan to Jerantut (RM25), Cameron Highlands (RM85), Kuala Besut, for the Perhentians (RM95), Kota Bharu (RM105) and Penang (RM140). These minibuses can also drop you en route anywhere in between.

MALAYSIAN BORNEO – SABAH

Most visitors come to Sabah to experience nature in all its riotous glory: the spectacular reefs of Sipadan; climbers paradise Mt Kinabalu, reaching 4095m into the clouds; the jungle-clad banks of Sungai Kinabatangan teeming with monkeys, hornbills and other creatures; and Sepilok, one of the only places in the world where you can see semi-wild orangutans in their native habitat. And while Sabah's cities are not as pretty as their Sarawakian counterparts, cosmopolitan Kota Kinabalu (known as KK) will soon win you over.

Kota Kinabalu
☑088 / POP 452,058
Kota Kinabalu (KK) won't immediately overwhelm you with its beauty, but the centre is compact and walkable. Alongside swanky new malls, old KK happily endures, with its markets stocked to the gills with sea creatures, pearls, and busy fishermen shuttling about the waterfront. KK is an ideal base to book your Sabah adventure, whether it be diving, wildlife watching, or Mt Kinabalu trekking.

Malaysian Borneo

Map labels:

SOUTH CHINA SEA

BANDAR SERI BEGAWAN

Kuala Baram · Seria
Sungai Tujoh ⊗ **Miri** · **BRUNEI**
Lambir Hills · Marudi
National Park · Long Terawan
Batu Niah
Niah National Park · Sungai Baram
Simalajau National Park
Bintulu · Batang Kemena · Tubau
Mukah · Batang Belaga
Pan Borneo Highway · Lumut Range
SARAWAK · Belaga
Sibu · Pelagus Rapids
Kubah National Park & Matang Wildlife Centre
Gunung Gading National Park · Santubong Peninsula · Bako National Park
Sarikei · Batang Rejang · Pegunungan Hose
Kanowit · Song · Kapit · Batang Baleh
Kuching
Lundu
Semenggoh Nature Reserve
Annah's (Rais Longhouse)
Batang Ai National Park
⊗ Tebedu · Sri Aman
Entikong · Lubuk Antu · Putussibau · Long Apari

⦿ Sights

Tunku Abdul Rahman National Park   NATIONAL PARK
(www.sabahparks.org.my; adult/child RM10/6) Just west of Kota Kinabalu, the five islands of Manukan, Gaya, Sapi, Mamutik and Sulug (and the reefs in between) make up the Tunku Abdul Rahman National Park, covering a total area of just over 49 sq km. Only a short boat ride from the Kota Kinabalu city centre, the islands have some nice beaches and the water in the outer areas is usually clear, offering ideal day-trip material for anyone wanting to escape the city and unwind.

Sunday Market   MARKET
(Jln Gaya; ⊙ 6am-about noon Sun) On Sundays a lively Chinese street fair takes over a section of Jln Gaya. It's vividly chaotic, with stalls cheek by jowl hawking batik sarongs, umbrellas, fruit and antiques.

Sabah Museum   MUSEUM
(Kompleks Muzium Sabah; ☑ 088-253 199; www.museum.sabah.gov.my; Jln Muzium; RM15; ⊙ 9am-5pm; P) About 2km south of the city centre, this refurbished museum is the best place to go in KK for an introduction to Sabah's ethnicities and environments, with clear signage and explanations. Expect tribal and

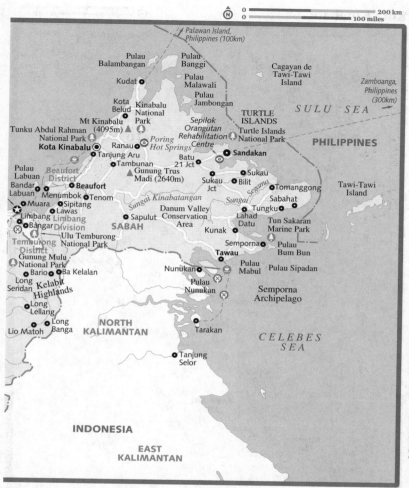

historical artefacts, including ceramics and a centrepiece whale skeleton, and a replica limestone cave. The **Heritage Village** has traditional tribal dwellings, including Kadazan bamboo houses and a Chinese farmhouse, all nicely set on a lily-pad lake.

🏃 Activities

⭐ Borneo Divers

DIVING

(📞088-222226; www.borneodivers.info; 9th fl, Menara Jubili, 53 Jln Gaya; ⊙9am-6pm) A topnotch dive outfit, with a strong pedigree as the longest operator in Sabah, offering PADI

dive courses. Also based on Mabul island, Borneo Divers can take you diving all over Sabah.

Borneo Dream

DIVING

(📞088-811 8149; www.borneodream.com; G27 Wisma Sabah, Jln Tun Fuad Stephens; ⊙9am-6pm) Operating out of Kota Kinabalu and at the **Gaya Island Resort** (📞KL 03-2783 1000; www.gayaislandresort.com; villas from RM1520; ❄🛜🏊), on Pulau Gaya, this outfit has a good name and can take you diving on a try dive excursion or take you through your PADI paces to become an Open Water Diver.

Kota Kinabalu

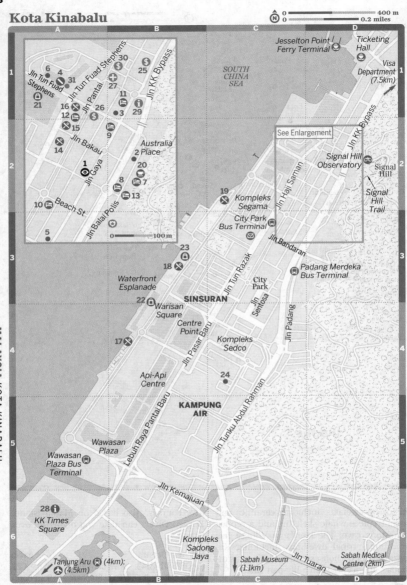

☞ Tours

There are many tour companies based in KK, enough to suit every taste and budget. Head to Wisma Sabah (p449) – this office building on Jln Haji Saman is full of agents and operators.

★ Sticky Rice Travel   ADVENTURE
(☏088-251654; www.stickyricetravel.com; 3rd fl, 134 Jln Gaya; ⊙9am-6pm) 🌿 *National Geographic* prefers this outfit for a reason; it's organised, original in its choice of tours and has excellent knowledgeable guides.

Kota Kinabalu

Responsible community-based tourism: expect adventure, culture and something very different. Sticky Rice will sit down with you and tailor your experience around your interests, fitness and budget; your trip may last four days or a few weeks.

Adventure Alternative Borneo ADVENTURE
(☏198726355; www.adventurealternative.com; Lg Dewan; ☉9am-6pm) ✐ Sustainable and ethical travel are key to this British-owned company, which works closely with Sabah Tourist Board, and runs tours to Lupa Masa rainforest camp, close to Mt Kinabalu. If you're looking for remote natural immersion, it also operates trips to Sapulot.

🛏 Sleeping

Hostels and cool cafes tend to congregate on Lg Dewan, aka Australian Place. Check out the **Sabah Backpacker Operators Association** (www.sabahbackpackers.com), which was set up in an effort to help shoestring travellers in the region.

★ **Borneo Backpackers** HOSTEL $
(☏088-234009; www.borneobackpackers. com; 24 Lg Dewan; dm/s/d incl breakfast from RM37/60/80; ❄🤙) Turquoise and chic with Hoi An lanterns, choice art, wood floors, and an excellent **cafe** (24 Lg Dewan; mains RM11-19; ☉11am-late) down below firing up Asian fusion cuisine, this is one of KK's

best backpacker haunts. Dorms and rooms are immaculate, with art-stencilled walls, a balcony and reading room to chill in, and constantly whirring fans. Better still, it's the HQ of Sticky Rice Travel.

B&B@21 HOSTEL $
(☏016-883 3763, 088-210632; bookingbb21@ gmail.com; lot 21, Lg Dewan; dm RM40, r RM93; ❄🤙) This welcoming hostel has large double rooms, uncramped dorms, a great kitchen area and chilling/TV lounge with loads of DVDs. The staff can help you book trips around Sabah. There is a garden and air-con throughout.

Borneo Gaya Lodge HOSTEL $
(☏088-242477; www.borneogayalodge.com; 1st fl, 78 Jln Gaya; dm incl breakfast RM30-35, d with bath from RM85; ❄@🤙) This comfortable hostel pipes air-con through its entirety – phew! With a cosy communal lounge, the place is quiet and clean. Note that two of the private-bath doubles have no windows. The friendly staff are happy to help you book tours and provide tourist information.

D'Beach Street Lodge HOSTEL $
(☏088-258228; www.dbeachstreet.com; 48 Jln Pantai; dm/s/d RM35/60-90/70-150; ❄🤙) Located in the swinging centre of the 'Beach Street' complex, D'Beach Street Lodge is all

of a stairward stumble from some of KK's best nightlife. Rooms are refreshingly chic and modern, and many have cool balconies that look onto the Beach St parade below. Just be warned: it gets loud at night.

Lucy's Homestay HOSTEL $
(Backpacker's Lodge; ☎ 088-261495; backpacker kk@yahoo.com; Lot 25, Lg Dewan, Australia Place; dm/s/d with shared bathroom incl breakfast RM25/52/62; ☎) Lucy's welcomes with brightly muralled walls, a book exchange (lots of travel tomes) and a plant-filled balcony to flop on. There's a house-proud kitchen and natural wood floor, fan-only rooms and dorms. It's calm, quiet and without a hint of laddish noise (midnight curfew). Check out the 100-year-old banyan tree towering above you out the back.

★Hotel Sixty3 HOTEL $$
(☎ 088-212663; www.hotelsixty3.com; 63 Jln Gaya; r RM298-558, ste RM668; ✳@☎) This fabulous award-winning hotel has an international feel in its 100 rooms, with glossy floors, evocative black-and-white photos of Kota Kinabalu and Sabah on the walls, subtle down-lighting, flat-screen TVs, a smoke-free policy and refillable glass bottles for drinking water. Stylish, fresh and sustainable. There's no restaurant, but there are plenty of options in the neighbourhood.

Kinabalu Daya Hotel HOTEL $$
(☎ 088-240000; Lot 3 & 4, Block 9, Jln Pantai; r from RM144; ✳☎) A totally smoke-free hotel, attentive staff and a hip street-level bar are just part of the appeal here. Colourful, carpeted halls lead to cool, tiled, neutral-toned rooms. Drinking water is provided in re-useable containers and there are refilling stations throughout the hotel. It's worth upgrading to the deluxe category (RM175) for the larger room and bathroom. Standard rooms are tiny.

✗ Eating

KK is one of the few cities in Borneo with an eating scene diverse enough to refresh the noodle-jaded palate. Besides the ubiquitous Chinese *kedai kopi* (coffee shops) and Malay halal restaurants, you'll find plenty of interesting options around the city centre.

★El Centro INTERNATIONAL $
(☎ 014-862 3877, 019-893 5499; www.elcentro.my; 32 Jln Haji Saman; mains RM18-25; ⊙11am-midnight Tue-Sun; ☎) ✐ Tiny El Centro is super-casual, with a menu free of palm oil and focussing on delicious and authentic Mexican fare: soft tacos, burritos, etc, but also featuring hummus, pizza, chorizo wraps, chicken and beef burgers. It even does bangers and mash. There's a good bar. Note that it's popular and seating is limited, and smokers are not discouraged from smoking inside.

Todak Waterfront SEAFOOD $
(Jln Tun Fuad Stephens; from RM3-4 per 100g; ⊙5-10pm) Flaming woks, crowds of customers and tables of glistening fish and squid, crabs, prawns and lobster. All within a few metres of the fishing boats bobbing on their moorings. This is a nicer alternative to enjoy a fresh seafood dinner than the very smoky Filipino barbecue stalls further south. Choose your seafood and cooking style and take a plastic seat.

On the tables are a box of utensils, hand-washing water and bottles of drinking water (RM1). Several stall holders here are unfussed about providing beer. It's located between the Central Market and the Todak (aka spearfish/marlin) roundabout on jln Tun Fuad Stephens.

Night Market HAWKER $
(Jln Tun Fuad Stephens; fish/prawn per 100g from RM3/15, satay RM1.50; ⊙5-11pm) The night market is the best, cheapest and most interesting place in KK for barbecued squid, ray and a vast selection of delicious seafood cooked up right before your eyes. Vegetarian options available. The presence of the mosque in the vicinity means alcohol is not served.

Kedai Kopi Fatt Kee CHINESE $
(28 Jln Bakau; mains from RM8; ⊙noon-10pm Mon-Sat) The woks are always flamin' and sizzlin' at this popular Cantonese joint below Ang's Hotel. Look out for sweet-and-sour shrimp, jungle fern, and oyster-sauce chicken wings.

★Mother India INDIAN $$
(☎ 088-276 136; Ground fl, Lot G-40A, Oceanus Waterfront Mall; mains RM18-55; ⊙11am-3pm & 5.30-10pm; ✳✐) The enticing aromas lead you into this beautifully decorated restaurant accented with ochre and golden tones, pendant lighting and carved screens. With attentive staff, sparkling white china and linen napkins, Mother India is a cut above the rest. The food is Mughal-style Indian, with rich creamy sauces accompanying the main ingredients, be they vegetables, fish, prawns, mutton or chicken.

Little Italy
ITALIAN $$

(☑088-232231; 23 Jln Haji Saman, ground fl, Hotel Capital; ⊙10am-11pm Mon-Thur, 10am-11.30pm Fri-Sun) This very popular restaurant fairly buzzes with an army of bandanna-wrapped staff waiting on your every need. Great pasta, great pizzas, Roman statues – what more could you want? Italian coffee, cold beer, wine by the glass? Check, check, check.

Drinking & Nightlife

The Workshop
CAFE

(☑088-274810; Lg Dewan; ⊙8am-10pm; 🛜) A cafe, art gallery and bar, The Workshop is industrial chic, with cool sounds, local art for sale and fair-trade coffee brewing. If the fresh juices and smoothies don't cool you down, there's also a shady beer garden out the back with cold bottles of Guinness. Happy hour is 3pm to 7pm.

El Centro
BAR

(☑014-862 3877; 32 Jln Haji Saman; ⊙5pm-midnight, closed Mon) El Centro is understandably popular; it's friendly, the food is good and it makes for a great spot to meet other travellers. With cool tunes and a laid-back vibe, El Centro also hosts impromptu quiz nights, costume parties and live-music shows.

Shopping

Borneo Shop
BOOKS

(☑088-538689; www.theborneoshop.com; shop 26, ground fl, Wisma Merdeka Phase 2, Jln Haji Saman; ⊙10am-8pm) Borneo shop stocks books, gifts, prints and postcards. There's a wealth of wildlife and flora books all focused on Borneo.

Borneo Trading Post
ARTS & CRAFTS

(☑088-232 655; lot 16, Waterfront Esplanade, Jln Tun Fuad Stephens; ⊙10am-8pm) Selling upmarket tribal art, contemporary art and Borneo souvenirs, this is a great place for that last-minute mementos.

Handicraft Market
MARKET

(Filipino Market; Jln Tun Fuad Stephens; ⊙8am-9pm) The Handicraft Market is a good place to shop for inexpensive souvenirs. Offerings include pearls, textiles, seashell crafts, jewellery and bamboo goods, some from the Philippines, some from Malaysia and some from other parts of Asia. Needless to say, bargaining is a must!

ⓘ Information

EMERGENCY

Ambulance	☑088-218 166, ☑999
Fire	☑994
Police	☑999

MEDICAL SERVICES
Permai Polyclinics (☑088-232100; www.permaipolyclinics.com; 4 Jln Pantai; consultation weekday RM60, Sat & Sun RM80; ⊙doctors on duty 8am-6pm, emergency 24hr) Excellent private outpatient clinic.

Sabah Medical Centre (☑088-211333; www.sabahmedicalcentre.com; Lg Bersatu, off Jln Damai; ⊙24hr) Good private hospital care, located about 6km southeast of the city centre.

MONEY
Central KK is chock-a-block with 24-hour ATMs.

HSBC (☑088-212 622; 56 Jln Gaya; ⊙9am-4.30pm Mon-Thu, to 4pm Fri)

Standard Chartered Bank (☑088-298111; 20 Jln Haji Saman; ⊙9.15am-3.45pm Mon-Fri)

Maybank (☑088-254295; 9 Jln Pantai; ⊙9am-4.30pm Mon-Thu, to 4pm Fri)

POST
Main Post Office (Jln Tun Razak; ⊙8am-5pm Mon-Sat) Western Union cheques and money orders can be cashed here.

TOURIST INFORMATION
Free maps of central KK and Sabah are available at almost every hostel or hotel.

Sabah Parks (☑088-486430, 088-523500; www.sabahparks.org.my; 1st-5th fl, lot 45 & 46, block H, Signature Office KK Times Sq; ⊙8am-1pm & 2-4.30pm Mon-Thu, 8-11.30am & 2-4.30pm Fri, 8am-12.50pm Sat) Information on the state's parks.

Sabah Tourism Board (☑088-212121; www.sabahtourism.com; 51 Jln Gaya; ⊙8am-5pm Mon-Fri, 9am-4pm Sat, closed Sun & holidays) Housed in the historic post office building, KK's tourist office has plenty of brochures, maps and knowledgeable staff keen to help you with advice tailored around your needs – they won't just try and sell you a package tour! Their website, packed with helpful information from accommodation to sights, is equally worth a visit.

Immigration Office (☑088-488700; Kompleks Persekutuan Pentadbiran Kerajaan, Jln UMS; ⊙7am-1pm & 2-5.30pm Mon-Fri) In an office complex near the Universiti Malaysia Sabah (UMS), 9km north of town. Also open on weekends, but only for Malaysian passport processing.

ⓘ Getting There & Away

AIR

KK is well served by Malaysia Airlines (www.malaysiaairlines.com) and AirAsia (www.airasia.com), which offer the following international flights to/from KK: Brunei, Shenzhen, Jakarta, Manila, Singapore and Taipei. Within Malaysia, flights go to/from Johor Bahru, Kuala Lumpur and Penang in Peninsular Malaysia, and Kuching, Labuan, Lawas, Miri, Kudat, Sandakan, Lahad Datu and Tawau in Borneo. Jetstar (www.jetstar.com) and **Tiger Airways** (www.tigerairways.com) offer flights to Singapore.

The **Kota Kinabalu International Airport** (KKIA; www.kotakinabaluairport.com; Tanjung Aru) is in Tanjung Aru, 7km south of central KK; it takes around 25 to 40 minutes by taxi or bus.

BOAT

All passengers must pay an adult/child RM3.82/RM1.91 terminal fee for ferries departing from KK. Passenger boats connect KK to Pulau Labuan (3½ hours) twice daily at 8am and 1.30pm (adult first/economy class RM41/36, child first/economy class RM28/RM23), with onward service to Brunei.

Speedboats (RM31) link Jesselton Point with the five islands of Tunku Abdul Rahman National Park (p436). Tickets can be bought at the Jesselton Wharf **ticketing hall** (Jesselton Point Ferry Terminal; ⊙8am-6pm). Ferries depart from **Jesselton Point** (Jln Haji Saman, 500m northeast of Wisma Sabah), located a little way north of the Suria Sabah shopping mall.

BUS

Several different stations around KK serve a variety of out-of-town destinations.

In general, land transport heading east departs from **Utara Terminal** (Inaman), 9km north of the city, while those heading north on the west coast leave from **Padang Merdeka** (Merdeka Field; Jln Tunku Abdul Rahman) Bus Station (also called 'old bus station'; in the middle of town). Those heading south on the west coast leave from both Padang Merdeka and Wawasan Plaza, while the latter is being redeveloped. BSB services leave the **City Park Bus Terminal** (Jln Haji Saman).

Local buses (RM2) from Wawasan Plaza can take tourists to Inanam if you don't want to splurge on the RM20 taxi. Have your hotel call ahead to the bus station to book your seat in advance. Same-day bookings are usually fine, although weekends are busier than weekdays. It's always good to ring ahead because sometimes transport will be halted due to flooding caused by heavy rains.

ⓘ Getting Around

TO/FROM THE AIRPORT

Airport shuttle buses (adult/child RM5/RM3) leave Padang Merdeka station every 45 minutes to an hour between 7.30am to 7.15pm daily. From the airport to the city buses depart from 8am until 8.30pm. It's usually 45 mins between services but some gaps are longer.

Taxis heading from terminals into town operate on a voucher system (RM30) sold at a taxi desk on the terminal's ground floor. Taxis heading to the airport should also charge RM30, if you catch one in the city centre.

Bus

Minibuses operate from several stops, including Padang Merdeka Bus Station, **Wawasan Plaza** (Wawasan Plaza), and the car park outside Milimewa Superstore (near the intersection of Jln Haji Saman and Beach St). They circulate the town looking for passengers. Most destinations within the city cost RM4 to RM6.

Taxi

Expect to pay a minimum of RM15 for a ride in the city centre. Taxis can be found throughout the city ,and bus stations and shopping centres.

BUSES FROM KOTA KINABALU

This bus and minivan transport information was provided to us by the **Sabah Tourism Board** (p441) and should be used as an estimate only: transport times can fluctuate due to weather, prices may change and the transport authority has been known to alter departure points.

DESTINATION	DURATION (HR)	PRICE	TERMINAL	DEPARTURES
Bandar Seri Begawan (Brunei)	8½	RM100	City Park Bus Terminal	8am
Mt Kinabalu NP	2	RM15-20	Inanam & Padang Merdeka	7am-8pm (very frequent)
Ranau	2	RM20	Padang Merdeka	7am-5pm
Sandakan	6	RM45	Inanam	7am-2pm (frequent) & 8pm
Semporna	9	RM75	Inanam	7.30am, 2pm & 7.30pm
Tawau	9	RM50	Inanam	7.30am, 8am, 10am, 12.30pm, 4pm & 8pm

Mt Kinabalu & Kinabalu National Park

Gunung Kinabalu, as it is known in Malay, is the highest mountain on the world's third-largest island. It is also the highest point between the Himalayas and the island of New Guinea. Rising almost twice as high as its Crocker Range neighbours, and culminating in a crown of wild granite spires, it is a sight to behold. Amazingly, the mountain is still growing, increasing in height by about 5mm a year.

The 4095m Mt Kinabalu may not be a Himalayan sky-poker, but Malaysia's first Unesco World Heritage Site is a major drawcard attracting thousands of climbers every year. The climb, by no means an easy jaunt, is essentially a long walk up a very steep hill, through jungle then barren moonscapes, with a little scrambling thrown in for good measure. On a clear day you can see the Philippines from the summit; often, though, the mountain is wreathed in cloud.

◉ Sights & Activities

Climbing Mt Kinabalu

The only way to get to the top of the mountain is to book a two-day package that includes a bed at Laban Rata (elevation 3272m), the predawn launch point for the summit. It is not possible to do a one-day hike to the summit.

If you're aiming for a specific date, especially one that falls in July or August or around Christmas, it's recommended that you make reservations two or more months ahead. Almost any tour operator in Sabah – including those with offices in the downtown KK office building known as Wisma Sabah – can organise a trip to the mountain. However, it's cheaper to book directly through **Sutera Sanctuary Lodges** (☏088-287887; www.suterasanctuarylodges.com.my; ground fl, lot G15, Wisma Sabah, Jln Haji Saman; ⊙9am-6pm), the company that has a monopoly on accommodation within the national park. If you don't have your reservations squared away before arriving in KK, drop by its office to check last-minute options. The more lead time you allow and the more flexible your travel itinerary, the better the chance that a window will open up.

If you book through Sutera, additional fees have to be paid (cash only) at the Sabah Parks Visitor Centre:

➡ entry fee (adult/child RM15/10 per day)

➡ climbing permit (adult/child RM200/80)

➡ guide fee (RM230 for one to five people)

➡ insurance (RM7)

All this does not include at least RM978 for dorm and board, or RM1927 for private room and board, on the mountain at Laban Rata. With said lodging, plus buses or taxis to the park, you're looking at spending around RM1500 for the common two day, one-night trip to the mountain.

You can try your luck and just show up at the park to see if there's a last-minute cancellation – spaces at Laban Rata do open up. Do not attempt an 'unofficial' climb – permits are scrupulously checked at three points along the trail.

No special equipment is required to summit Mt Kinabalu. However, a headlamp is strongly advised for the predawn jaunt to the top – you'll need your hands free to negotiate the ropes on the summit massif. Expect freezing temperatures near the top, not to mention strong winds and the occasional rainstorm, so it's a good idea to bring along a quick-drying fleece jacket and a waterproof shell to go over it. Don't forget a water bottle, which can be refilled en route.

Via Ferrata

The *via ferrata* ('iron road' in Italian) is a permanent network of mountaineering cables, rungs and rails attached to Mt Kinabalu's dramatic granite walls. After ascending the mountain in the usual way, climbers can use the *via ferrata*, managed by **Mountain Torq** (www.mountaintorq.com; Kinabalu Park Headquarters; per person, 2-3 climbers: Low's Peak Circuit RM1760, Walk the Torq RM1935), to return from 3766m to the Laban Rata rest camp. The Low's Peak Circuit is a four- to five-hour scramble along Mt Kinabalu's sheer flanks. The route's threadlike tightrope walks and swinging planks will have you convinced that the course designers are sadistic, but that's what makes it such fun – testing your limits without putting your safety in jeopardy.

Hikes Around the Base

If you're not up for an ascent to the summit, can't afford an expensive package and/ or didn't reserve ahead for the dates you need, it's still well worth coming here to explore the interconnected nature trails that wend their way through the beautiful jungles around the base of Mt Kinabalu. A climbing permit and a guide are required if you go above Timpohon Gate.

MALAYSIA MT KINABALU & KINABALU NATIONAL PARK

🛏 Sleeping

It's generally preferable to stay in the park, mainly because the lodging is reasonable value and it's more convenient for the mountain and walking trails. However, there are places to stay outside the park, most on the road between the park HQ and Kundasang (6km east of the park's main entrance).

Sleeping options located at the base of the mountain are operated by **Sutera Sanctuary Lodges** (www.suterasanctuarylodges.com; Kinabalu Park Headquarters; ⏰8.30am-4.30pm Mon-Sat, to 12.30pm Sun). They're expensive compared to sleeping spots outside the park. Options range from a hostel, to cabins costing from RM965, to apartments that sleep four, costing RM1632.

Grace Hostel HOSTEL $$
(http://suterasanctuarylodges.com.my; Kinabalu Park Headquarters; dm incl breakfast RM372) Clean, comfortable 20-bed dorm with fireplace and drink-making area.

Rock Twin Share HOSTEL $$
(http://suterasanctuarylodges.com.my; Kinabalu Park Headquarters; tw incl breakfast RM520) Small clean twin rooms that share common bathrooms. There is an inviting common lounge.

Hill Lodge CABIN $$$
(http://suterasanctuarylodges.com.my; Kinabalu Park Headquarters; cabins incl breakfast RM965) These semi-detached cabins are a good option for those who can't face a night in the hostel or in a twin with a share bathroom. They're clean and comfortable, with private bathrooms.

ℹ Getting There & Away

Park headquarters is 88km by road, northeast of KK. Express buses (RM30) leave KK from the Utara Terminal bus station every hour on the hour from 7am to 10am and at 12.30pm, 2pm and 3pm. Alternatively, take a Ranau-bound minivan (RM25) from central KK at Padang Merdeka bus terminal, asking the driver to drop you at a **bus shelter** outside the gate at Kinabalu National Park. Minivans leave when full and run from early morning till around 2pm. We recommend leaving before 7am for the two-hour trip, in order to check in at Park Headquarters by 9am.

To get from the park to KK or Sandakan (RM40), you can flag down a bus from the park turn-off.

Share taxis leave KK from Inanam and Padang Merdeka Bus Stations (RM30 per person, RM120 per vehicle).

Share 4WDs park just outside of the park gates and leave when full for KK (RM200 per 4WD) and Sandakan (RM500); each 4WD can hold around four to five passengers, and they can be chartered by individuals.

Around Mt Kinabalu

◉ Sights & Activities

Kundasang War Memorial MEMORIAL
(Kota Kinabalu–Ranau Hwy, Kundasang; adult/child RM10/1; ⏰8.30am-5pm) At Kundasang, beside the KK–Ranau Hwy, 10km east of Kinabalu National Park headquarters, is this poignant memorial conceived in 1961. It commemorates the Australian and British prisoners who died on the infamous Sandakan Death Marches and at the Sandakan and Ranau POW camps, as well as the those from Borneo who died while assisting the prisoners. Four modest gardens individually represent the Australians, the British and the people of Borneo, plus a colonnaded Contemplation Garden.

In the Contemplation Garden is a list of the deceased and at the back of this garden there is a stunning vista of Mt Kinabalu.

Poring Hot Springs HOT SPRINGS
(Poring, Ranau; adult/child incl Kinabalu National Park RM15/10; ⏰entrance gate 7am-5pm, park until 8pm, Butterfly Garden & Canopy Walk closed Mon) One of the legacies of the Japanese invasion of Borneo during WWII, Poring Hot Springs has become a popular weekend retreat for locals. Located in a well-maintained forest park with nature paths that the elderly and children can enjoy, the springs steam with hot sulphurous water channelled into pools and tubs, some of which feel a little rundown. Remember your towel and swimming trunks.

🛏 Sleeping

Mountain Rest House GUESTHOUSE $
(☎016-837 4060; Km 53, Jln Tinompok, off Kinabalu Park, Kundasang; dm/s/d incl breakfast from RM20/30/40; ❄🐾) This friendly, clean guesthouse is endearingly ramshackle and spans different levels up the side of the mountain. About five minutes' walk from the park entrance, house-proud though very basic rooms have a few sticks of furniture and clean bathrooms. Breakfast included and vegetarian dinners are available.

★ **Lupa Masa** CAMPGROUND $$
(☑012-845 1987, 016-806 8194; http://lupamasa.
com; Poring; per person incl meals tent/chalet
RM90/250) 🏊 This eco-camp is surround-
ed by forest and has two gin-clear rivers to
bathe in, with waterfalls and natural jacuz-
zis. Lupa Masa isn't for everyone though...
no electricity or wi-fi, but bugs and leeches
at no extra cost. Accommodation is on mat-
tresses in tents on raised platforms, or the
delightful new chalets with striking river
views.

Wind Paradise YURT $$
(☑019-800 0201, 088-714 563; http://mongo
lianyurt.mrsabah.com; Jln Mesilau, Cinta Mata, Kundasang; d/tr RM170/200, 4-person yurt RM300; 🅿)
With staggeringly pretty views of the valley
and town of Kundasang far below, these Mon-
golian yurts, and rooms in a central lodge –
both set in pleasant lawns – are delightful.
There's self-catering and a great lounge, and
barbecue facilities to lap up the mountain
view. Yurts have comfy beds and make for a
great sleep with natural ventilation.

ℹ️ Getting There & Around

KK roundtrip buses stop in front of Kinabalu
National Park headquarters and in Ranau (RM25
to RM30, two hours) from 7am to 8pm. Minibuses operate from a blue-roofed shelter in Ranau
servicing the nearby attractions (park HQ, Por-
ing etc) for RM5.

Sandakan

☑089 / POP 157,330
Sabah's second city has long been a major
trading port, but today it feels quite provincial compared to bustling KK. The main
draw here is that it's the gateway to the Sungai Kinabatangan and Sepilok. Curiously, a
completely new city centre is planned to be
built 2.5km west of the city.

◎ Sights

Sandakan Memorial Park HISTORIC SITE
(◎9am-5pm) A beautiful rainforest garden
marks the site of a Japanese POW camp and
starting point for the infamous WWII 'death
marches' to Ranau. Of the 1800 Australian
and 600 British troops imprisoned here, the
only survivors by July 1945 were six Australian escapees. A concrete water tank and a
few rusting machines of the erstwhile British agricultural station that became a prison
comprise the only physical remains. A pavil-

ion recounts the horrors and heroism and
includes photographs and accounts from
survivors.

To reach the park, take any Batu 8 (or
higher-numbered) bus from the local bus
station on the waterfront in the city centre
(RM1.50); get off at the 'Taman Rimba' sign-
post and walk down Jln Rimba. A taxi from
downtown costs about RM80 return with
one hour waiting time.

See http://sandakandeathmarch.com for
more details of the death march route.

Agnes Keith House MUSEUM
(☑089-221140; www.museum.sabah.gov.my; Jln
Istana; RM15; ◎9am-5pm) This atmospheric
two-storey wooden villa, and former British colonial quarters, is now renovated as a
museum. Living in Sandakan in the 1930s,
American Agnes Keith wrote several books
about her experiences here, including the
famous *Land Below the Wind*. The villa
documents Sandakan in all its colonial
splendour.

To reach the museum, head up the Tangga
Seribu (100 Steps) to Jln Istana and turn left,
then immediately right. Also on the grounds
is the **English Tea House & Restaurant**
(☑089-222 544; www.englishteahouse.org; Jln
Istana; mains RM16.50-55, cocktails RM18-20;
◎10am-9pm).

🛏️ Sleeping

If you're only passing through Sandakan
to see the orangutans, it's better to stay at
Sepilok itself. Sandakan has several budget
hostels and a few upscale midrange options.

Sandakan Backpackers Hostel HOSTEL $
(☑089-211213; www.sandakanbackpackershostel.
com; Lot 109, Sandakan Harbour Square; dm RM35,
d RM70, d with bath RM75; 🌀🛜) Decorated with
murals by the former owner and former
guests, this friendly and clean hostel has
rooms with sea views and a rooftop area
with even more watery vistas. It's close to
the waterfront restaurants (and an occasionally noisy karaoke bar). Note that the front
door is locked at 11pm.

Borneo Sandakan Backpackers HOSTEL $
(☑089-215754; www.borneosandakan.com; 1st fl,
54 Harbour Sq; dm/s/d RM35/60/75; 🌀🛜) This
superclean, welcoming hostel boasts warm
orange walls, air-con in every room and a
lobby with a flat-screen TV. It also serves up
a decent, complimentary breakfast (eggs).
There are six rooms and two well-sized

MALAYSIA SANDAKAN

dorms (though some rooms lack windows). It has a relaxed vibe and helpful staff who are also qualified guides and run a number of tours.

✗ Eating

★ **Harbour Bistro Cafe** INTERNATIONAL $
(Waterfront; Mains RM8-30; ☺ 2pm-2am; ☑) Regarded by many as the best of the gaggle of casual eateries that line the waterfront, the Harbour Bistro offers plenty of Asian options using beef, chicken and local seafood, plus Western-style mains such as fish 'n' chips and steaks. Vegetarians will find plenty of options, but be wary of the addition of dried shrimp.

Sandakan Central Market HAWKER $
(Jln Dua; mains RM1-8; ☺ 7am-3pm) Despite being located in what looks like a multi-storey car park, this is the best spot in town for cheap eats and food stalls. Upstairs you'll find strictly halal food stalls, with a mix of Chinese, Malay, Indonesian and Filipino fare. Hours given for the food stalls are a bit flexible, but by 3pm most are empty.

★ **Ba Lin Roof Garden** INTERNATIONAL $$
(☑ 089-272 988; www.nakhotel.com; 18th fl, Nak Hotel, Jln Pelabuhan Lama; mains RM26-45, cocktails RM20-25; ☺ 7.30am-1am, happy hour 2-8pm; ✻ ☺) A hidden treat at the top of the Nak Hotel, this stylish restaurant/bar has retro paper light shades, wicker swing-chairs, and swallow-you-up couches. Eat inside or out; on the pot-plant shaded verandah or, in the evenings, up on the rooftop. Pizza, soups, marinated NZ lamb, grass-fed Angus steaks and a wealth of fresh juices and original cocktails. Check the blackboard for specials.

ⓘ BORDER CROSSING WARNING

Standard Marine (☑ 089-216 996; Block G, Lot 1, 1st fl, Bandar Ramai-Ramai Jalan Leila) links Sandakan with Zamboanga (economy/cabin RM280/300) on the Philippine island of Mindanao. Ferries depart Sandakan harbour at 6pm every Tuesday, arriving at 4pm the next day (22 hours). Because of lawlessness, including kidnappings of foreign nationals, and Islamist insurgency, Western embassies warn against travel to or through Zamboanga, so check local conditions before you sail.

ⓘ Information

Duchess of Kent Hospital (☑ 089-248600; http://hdok.moh.gov.my; Batu 2/Mile 2, Jln Utara; ☺ 8am-10pm) Provides hospital care.

Maybank (Lebuh Tiga) In addition to a full-service bank and ATM, a sidewalk currency-exchange window is open 9am to 5pm daily for changing cash and travellers cheques.

ⓘ Getting There & Away

AIR

Malaysia Airlines (☑ 1300-883000, Sandakan airport 089-660525; www.malaysiaairlines.com; ground fl, Terminal Building, Sandakan Airport; ☺ 8am-5pm) and **MASwings** (☑ 1300 88 3000, Sandakan airport 089-675980; www.maswings.com; ground fl, Terminal Building, Sandakan Airport; ☺ 7am-10pm) have several flights per day to/from KK and KL; two per day to/from Tawau and two per week to Kudat.
AirAsia (☑ 089-222737; www.airasia.com; 2nd fl, Sandakan Airport) operates direct daily flights to/from KL and KK.

BUS

Buses and minibuses to KK, Lahad Datu, Semporna and Tawau leave from the long-distance bus station in a large car park at Batu 2.5, 4km north of town. Most express buses to KK (RM43, six hours) leave between 7am and 2pm, plus one evening departure around 8pm. All pass the turn-off to Kinabalu National Park headquarters.

Buses depart regularly for Lahad Datu (RM22, 2½ hours) and Tawau (RM43, 5½ hours) between 7am and 8am. There's also a bus to Semporna (RM45, 5½ hours) at 8am. If you miss it, head to Lahad Datu, then catch a frequent minibus to Semporna.

Minibuses depart throughout the morning from Batu 2.5 for Ranau (RM30, four hours) and Lahad Datu (some of those continuing to Tawau). Minibuses for Sukau (RM15) leave from a lot behind Centre Point Mall in town.

ⓘ Getting Around

TO/FROM THE AIRPORT

Sandakan Airport is 11km from the city centre. Batu 7 Airport bus (RM1.80) stops on the main road about 500m from the terminal. A coupon taxi to the town centre costs RM30; and going the other way is the same.

BUS

Terminal Bas Sandakan (Minibus Stand), behind the Centre Point Plaza, is Sandakan's bus terminal. Buses run from 6am to 6pm on the main road to the north, Jln Utara. Buses display a sign indicating how far from town they go, eg Batu 2.5 (the long-distance bus station,

RM1.50), Batu 14 (the turn-off to Sepilok), Batu 32 (the end of the line on the KK–Semporna Highway). Fares range from RM2 to RM5.

To reach the long-distance bus station, you can also catch a local bus (RM1.50) from the **local bus station** at the waterfront.

Sepilok

📞 089

A visit to the world's most famous place to see orangutans in their natural rainforest habitat is all the more compelling thanks to the outdoor nursery for orangutan youngsters in the same complex, and the nearby Sun Bear Conservation Centre and Rainforest Discovery Centre. In addition, the Labuk Bay Proboscis Monkey Sanctuary is only a short drive away. There are also some beautiful places to stay here on the edge of the jungle.

👁 Sights

⭐ Sepilok Orangutan
Rehabilitation Centre ANIMAL SANCTUARY
(SORC; 📞089-531189, emergency 089-531180; www.wildlife.sabah.gov.my; Jln Sepilok; adult/child RM30/15, camera fee RM10; ⊙9am-noon & 2-4pm Sat-Thu, 9-11.30am & 2-4pm Fri) 🚗 Around 25km north of Sandakan, and covering some 40 sq km of the Kabili-Sepilok Forest Reserve, this inspiring, world-famous centre welcomes orphaned and injured orangutans for rehabilitation before returning them to forest life. In 2017 we were told there are around 200 living in the reserve, many more than the website suggests, though only a few are regular visitors to the feeding platform. At the **outdoor nursery**, a short walk from the feeding platform, you can watch orphaned toddlers at play.

Rainforest
Discovery Centre NATURE RESERVE
(RDC; 📞089-533780; www.forest.sabah.gov.my/rdc; adult/child RM15/7; ⊙ticket counter 8am-5pm, night walk 6-8pm) The RDC, about 1.5km from SORC, offers an engaging education in tropical flora and fauna. Outside the exhibit hall filled with child-friendly displays, a botanical garden presents samples of tropical plants. There's a gentle 1km lakeside walking trail, and a series of eight canopy towers connected by walkways to give you a bird's-eye view of the treetops; by far the most rewarding element of a trip here.

Borneo Sun Bear
Conservation Centre ANIMAL SANCTUARY
(BSBCC; 📞089-534491; www.bsbcc.org.my; Jln Sepilok; adult/child 12-17 yr/under 12 yr RM31.80/15.90/free; ⊙9am-3.30pm) 🚗 The Borneo Sun Bear Conservation Centre (BSBCC), which opened in 2014, provides care to rescued sunbears: 44 bears at the time of writing. The centre has full access for the disabled, and it's possible to see the bears from an elevated glassed viewing area as they climb up trees close by you. There are also telescopes set up for micro examination. A gift shop sells t-shirts, fridge magnets, souvenirs etc, and screens an educational video.

Labuk Bay Proboscis
Monkey Sanctuary ANIMAL SANCTUARY
(📞089-672133; www.proboscis.cc; adult/child RM60/30, camera & video RM10; ⊙8am-6pm) A local palm-plantation owner has created a private proboscis monkey sanctuary, attracting the floppy-conked locals with sugar-free pancakes at 9.30am and 2.30pm feedings at Platform A, and 11.30am and 4.30pm at Platform B, a kilometre away. An estimated 300 wild monkeys live in the 6 sq km reserve. The proboscis monkeys are enticed onto the main viewing platform so tourists can get better pictures, which may put you off if you're looking for a more ecologically minded experience.

🛏 Sleeping

Sepilok B&B HOSTEL $
(📞019-833 0901, 089-534050; www.sepilokbednbreakfast.com.my; Jln Fabia; camping RM20, dm with fan/air-con RM35/45, d with air-con RM138-195; ❄🛜) Located about 400m from the Rainforest Discovery Centre, this place has an authentic, relaxed hostel vibe. Dorms are spartan but clean and comfortable and supplied with fresh linen. Pitta Lodge has self-catering facilities for families. Camping here is better in March and April when there's less rain. Wi-fi is available only in the reception/restaurant and the eight rooms of Hornbill Lodge. Transport to SORC can be arranged at a very reasonable RM5 per person.

Sepilok Jungle Resort RESORT $
(📞089-533031; www.sepilokjungleresort.com; Jln Rambutan; dm RM37.10, r fan only RM84.80, r with air-con RM148.40-190.80, all include breakfast; 🅿❄@🛜🏊) Rooms are tile-floored with desk, bathroom, TV and fan or air-con; all are adequate

though many are in need of refurbishment and updating. Similarly, the complimentary breakfast is not quite up to scratch; however, the restaurant's seafood and local vegetables and fruits are excellent. The resort's best features are the large pool and its proximity to the Orangutan Rehabilitation Centre.

★ **Sepilok Nature Resort** RESORT $$
(✆089-673999, 089-674999; http://sepilok.com; d RM318; ❇@🖙) Beside an ornamental pond, this beautiful wood-accented hotel is a study in comfort: mature rubber plants shade its two-tiered central lodge, carriage lamps cast their glow on its welcoming lounge and restaurant. Chalets are roomy with sumptuous bathrooms, huge beds and private balconies. The cuisine and romantic candlelit setting at the resort's **Lake Bistro & Bar** (✆089-674999; Jln Sepilok; mains RM19-29; ⊙7am-10pm) are exquisite.

Sepilok Forest Edge Resort RESORT $$
(✆013-869 5069, 089-533190; www.sepilokforest-edgeresort.com; Jln Rambutan; dm/d RM44.70/100, chalets RM318-678.40; ❇🖙▨) Set within manicured lawns, this stunning accommodation is choking on plants and flowers and has chalets fit for a colonial explorer, with polished-wood floors, choice art, and private balconies with wrought-iron chairs. There's also a dorm and double rooms located in a pretty longhouse, **Labuk Longhouse B&B**, plus a tiny, relaxing pool/jacuzzi.

It's around 2km or 15-minutes' walk from the Sepilok Orangutan Rehabilitation Centre (p447).

ⓘ Getting There & Away

Sepilok is located at 'Batu 14' – 14 miles (23km) from Sandakan.

BUS

A shuttle bus (RM4) operates between Sandakan (departing 9.30am, 11.30am, 2pm and 5pm) and Sepilok (departing 6.30am, 10.30am, 12.30pm and 4pm). The departure point in Sandakan is the bus terminal.

If coming from KK, board a Sandakan-bound bus and ask the driver to let you off at 'Batu 14' (RM43). You will pay the full fare, even though Sandakan is 23km away.

TAXI

If you are coming directly from Sandakan, a taxi should cost no more than RM50 (RM40 from the airport). If you want one to wait and return you to Sandakan, you're looking at RM120.

Sungai Kinabatangan

⏺089

The 560km-long Kinabatangan River, Sabah's longest waterway, is one of the best places in Southeast Asia to see jungle wildlife in its native habitat. The reason, tragically, is that creatures such as orangutans, proboscis monkeys, macaques, hornbills (all eight species) and blue-eared kingfishers have been pushed to the banks of the Kinabatangan by encroaching palm-oil plantations.

The easiest way to explore the Kinabatangan is to purchase a one- or two-night package that includes transfers from KK or Sandakan, sights such as the Gomantong Caves, river cruises and full board. However, it is possible to book transport, accommodation and river cruises independently.

◉ Sights

Gomantong Caves CAVE
(✆089-230 189; www.sabah.gov.my/jhl; Gomantong Hill, Lower Kinabatangan; adult/child RM30/15, camera/video RM30/50; ⊙8am-noon & 2-4.30pm, closing periods apply) Imagine a massive crack in a mountain, a cathedral-like inner chamber shot with splinters of sunlight and a cave floor that's swarming with cockroaches, long-legged centipedes and scorpions, and you have the Gomantong Caves. Yes, the smell is disgusting thanks to the ubiquity of bird and bat shit, and yes, you will want covered shoes and a hat, but these caves are magnificent. Moreover, the forested area around the caves conceals plenty of wildlife – including orangutans.

🏃 Activities

The best way to see wild rainforest creatures is to take guided river cruises run by local lodges. Most take place early in the morning and around sunset, when the animals are most active. The cost is from RM100 for a two-hour river cruise, although most cruises are included in a tour package.

🛏 Sleeping

★ **Tungog Rainforest Eco Camp** CABIN $
(✆089-551070, 019-582 5214; www.mescot.org; per night incl 3 meals RM95, river cruises per boat RM95 or per person RM40 (minimum 3)) 🍃 This eco camp faces a pretty oxbow lake by the Kinabatangan River. Luxurious it isn't – expect wooden shelters with mattress, fragrant

sheets and pillows, plus a mozzie net and shared bathrooms. However, the immersion in nature and chance to put something back by planting trees is magical. Given there are no other camps for miles, you have the wildlife to yourself.

Sukau Greenview B&B
B&B **$**

(☑ 013-869 6922, 089-565 266; www.sukaugreenview.net; dm/r incl breakfast RM45/60, 3-day, 2-night package incl breakfast & 3 x 2hr river trips per person RM499) Run by locals, this lime-green wooden affair has OK dorms and basic rooms. There's also a pleasant cafe looking out on the river. Greenview runs special elephant-sighting trips priced at RM250 per person (minimum two).

★ Myne Resort
RESORT **$$**

(☑ 089-216093; www.myne.com.my; 2-day, 1-night package ex Sandakan in longhouse/chalet RM895/948; ❋ ⏾) Situated on a sweeping bend of the river, Myne has an open, breezy reception, games room and restaurant festooned with lifeguard rings, and is vaguely reminiscent of an old wooden ship. Chalets are beautiful with peach drapes, river-facing balcony, polished-wood floors, comfy beds, dresser and flat-screen cable TV. Packages include river cruises and jungle walks. Extra activities include nocturnal walks and cruises.

❶ Getting There & Away

Transfers are usually arranged with your lodging as part of your package.

From KK, board a Tawau- or Lahad Datu–bound bus and ask the driver to let you off at 'Sukau Junction', also known as 'Meeting Point' – the turn-off road to reach Sukau. If you are on a Sandakan-bound bus, ask your driver to stop at the Tawau-Sandakan junction – it's called 'Batu 32' or 'Checkpoint' (sometimes it's known as Sandakan Mile 32).

From Sepilok or Sandakan, expect to pay around RM20 to reach 'Batu 32', and around RM35 if you're on a Sandakan–Tawau bus and want to alight at 'Meeting Point'.

Semporna

☑ 089 / POP 133,164

The mainland town of Semporna is rather ugly and chaotic, but it's the gateway to some of the world's most stunning scuba diving, off legendary Sipadan and other islands of the storied Semporna Archipelago.

SPLURGE

One of National Geographic's 'Top 30 Lodges in the World', **Sukau Rainforest Lodge** (☑ 088-438300; www.sukau.com; 3-day, 2-night package RM1820; ❋ ⏾) is the most upscale digs on the Kinabatangan river. Beautifully appointed split-level rooms have wood and terrazzo floors, rain shower, lounge area and mozzie nets. There's a fine restaurant, an onsite naturalist who gives wildlife talks and night walks, plus a welcome plunge pool to cool off in. Romantic.

🏃 Activities

A variety of scuba operators have offices around the Semporna seafront complex and/or in KK.

★ Scuba Junkie
DIVING

(☑ 089-785 372; www.scuba-junkie.com; Lot 36, Block B, Semporna seafront; 2 dives from RM250; ⏰ 9am-6pm) 🌿 The most proactive conservationist outfit on Mabul, Scuba Junkie employs two full-time environmentalists and recycles much of its profits into its turtle hatchery and rehab centre and 'shark week' initiative. It's also a favourite with Westerners thanks to its excellent divemasters and comfortable digs at Mabul Beach Resort (p452). Accommodation-plus-dive packages available.

Sipadan Scuba
DIVING

(☑ 012-813 1688, 089-781 788; www.sipadanscuba.com; lot 28, block E, Semporna seafront; 3-day & 2-night package incl dives, accommodation, transfer & equipment RM1200) Over 20 years' experience and an international staff makes Sipadan Scuba a reliable, recommended choice. You can take your PADI Open Water course here for RM870.

Seaventures
DIVING

(☑ 088-251 669, 017-811 6023; www.seaventuresdive.com; lot 28, block E, Semporna seafront; 4-day, 3-night package incl meals & transfers to island & airport RM3050) Based out of their funky blue and orange ocean platform close to Mabul Island, this is a well-regarded outfit with several packages available. Offices in Semporna and in KK's **Wisma Sabah building** (cnr Jln Haji Saman & Jln Tun Fuad Stephens).

Seahorse Sipadan
DIVING

(📞 089-782 289, 012-279 7657; www.seahorse-sipadanscuba.org; 1st fl, lot 1, Semporna seafront; 4-day, 3-night package incl 3 dives per day, accommodation, equipment & boat transfer RM690) Backpacker-oriented outfit with accommodation on Mabul Island.

🛏 Sleeping

⭐ Scuba Junkie Dive Lodge
HOSTEL $

(📞 089-785372; www.scuba-junkie.com; block B 36, 458 Semporna seafront; diver or snorkeller/nondiver dm RM25/50, r without bathroom RM80/160, r with bathroom RM100/200; ✳ 🕿) Walls peppered with underwater shots of marine life, clean bathrooms and a variety of air-con rooms to choose from make this a sure bet. Also it's directly opposite Scuba Junkie's office, and next to the **Diver's Bar** (Semporna seafront; mains RM18-32; ⊘7-9am & 1pm-midnight), a good spot for breakfast before you head of to the Semporna Archipelago.

Borneo Global Sipadan BackPackers
HOSTEL $

(📞 089-785 088; www.bgbackpackers.com/semporna; Jln Causeway; dm/tr/f incl breakfast RM40/130/150; ✳ @ 🕿) There are nine rooms comprising dorm, triples and family options with bathroom. There's a friendly lobby area to chill in. It also runs three-day PADI Open Water courses.

Holiday Dive Inn
HOTEL $$

(📞 089-919148; www.holidaydiveinn.com; lot A5-A7, Semporna seafront; r from RM154, f RM217; ✳ 🕿) This 24-room, fully air-conditioned hotel has spotless accommodation featuring a bright colour scheme, fresh bathrooms, TVs and some rooms with a balcony. It's affiliated with **Sipadan Scuba** nearby. There's also a nice sundowner roof lounge.

Sipadan Inn
HOTEL $$

(📞 089-781766; www.sipadaninn-hotel.com; block D, lot 19-24, Semporna seafront; d/f from RM110/170; ✳ @ 🕿) A slice of air-conditioned comfort, the Sipadan Inn has simple but tidy rooms with wood-lined walls, fresh linen, coffee-making facilities, spotless bathrooms and very friendly staff. **Sipadan Inn 2** is nearby (Block B Semporna seafront) with pricier sea-view rooms.

🍴 Eating

⭐ Fat Mother Seafood Restaurant
SEAFOOD $

(Semporna seafront; mains RM15-30; ⊘5-10pm) Bustling Fat Mother's gets terrific reviews for its warm service and wide-ranging seafood menu – your dinner will be glowering

---

ℹ GETTING TO INDONESIA: TAWAU TO TARAKAN & NUNUKAN

Getting to the border Tawau is the only crossing point with Kalimantan where foreigners can get a visa to enter Indonesia. The local **Indonesian consulate** (📞089-752969, 089-772052; Jln Sinn Onn, Wisma Fuji; ⊘8am-noon & 1 or 2pm-4pm Mon-Fri, closed Indonesian and Malaysian public holidays) is known for being fast and efficient – many travellers are in and out in an hour. The consulate is in Wisma Fuji, on Jln Sinn Onn. Flag down a taxi (RM15) and ask the driver to drop you off in front of the consulate.

Visa applications are processed between 9.30am and 2pm Monday to Friday. You technically need to either provide proof of onward travel or a credit card, which consulate staff will make a copy of. A 60-day tourist visa will cost RM170 and require two passport photos. Bank on spending at least one night in town before shipping off to Indonesia, given the ferry departure schedule, and bring extra cash to the consulate, as there are no ATMs nearby.

Ferry companies Tawindo Express and Indomaya Express make the three- to four-hour trip to Tarakan (RM140; 11.30am Monday, Wednesday and Friday, 10.30am Tuesday, Thursday and Saturday) and the one-hour trip to Nunukan (RM65; 10am and 3pm daily except Sunday). We recommend showing up at least 60 minutes before departure to get a ticket; less than that is cutting it fine. A taxi ride to the ferry terminal costs RM10. MAS-Wings flies from Tawau to Tarakan (RM225) on Saturday, Monday and Thursday.

At the border Blue minibusess in Tarakan can get you around the city for Rp3000; expect to pay around Rp20,000 to get to the airport.

Moving On Ferry company **Pelni** (www.pelni.co.id) has boats to Balikpapan and the Sulawesi ports of Toli-Toli, Pare-Pare and Makassar..

at you from the glass tanks. They'll even prepare your own fish if you've caught it. Grouper and mango sauce, fish porridge, salted egg and squid, Malay curries and noodle dishes, plus free Chinese tea and melon dessert. Cold beer available.

ℹ Information

If you're arriving in Semporna under your own steam, leave the bus and minivan drop-off area and head towards the waterfront. This is the way to the waterfront. Follow the grid of concrete streets to the right until you reach 'Semporna Seafront' – home to the diving operators, each stacked one next to the other in a competitive clump.

Semporna has several ATMs.

ℹ Getting There & Away

AIR

Flights to Tawau from KK and KL land at **Tawau Airport**, roughly 28km from town. A taxi from Tawau airport to Semporna costs RM100 (30 minutes), while Tawau–Semporna buses (RM20, 50 minutes) will stop at the airport if you ask the driver nicely. Buses that do not stop at the airport will let you off at Mile 28, where you will have to walk a few (unshaded) kilometres to the terminal.

Remember that flying less than 24 hours after diving can cause serious health issues, even death.

BUS

The '**terminal**' is vaguely around the Milimewa supermarket not too far from the mosque. All buses run from early morning until 4pm (except Kota Kinabalu) and leave when full.

Kota Kinabalu (RM75, nine hours) leaves at around 7am or 7pm.

Lahad Datu (RM30, 2½ hours)

Sandakan (RM45, 5½ hours)

Tawau (RM25, 1½ hours)

Semporna Archipelago

The stunning sapphire waters and emerald isles of the Semporna Archipelago, home to Bajau sea gypsies in crayola-coloured boats, are plucked from your most vivid dreams of tropical paradise. Of course few visitors come this way for the islands – rather, it is the ocean and everything beneath its glassy surface, that appeals. This is first and foremost a diving destination – one of the best in the world.

ℹ MEN IN BLACK: SEMPORNA SECURITY SITUATION

If staying in Mabul, you'll inevitably notice the presence of black-clad armed police patrolling the beach and the fact that there's a 6pm curfew to be back in your resort. Try not to be alarmed, they're here for your safety and as a powerful deterrent. Their presence is a response to a number of incidents involving kidnap-for-ransom groups from southern Philippines.

But is it now safe in the archipelago? While kidnappers continue to be active in the region, the beefed-up police numbers on the islands appears to have forced them to look elsewhere for their ransoms. For now, the curfew remains and many international embassies recommend reconsidering your need to travel here. Always check the latest security warnings with your home country's travel advisories.

🏃 Activities

In local speak 'Semporna' means perfect, but there is only one island in the glittering Semporna Archipelago that takes this title. **Sipadan**, aka Pulau Sipidan, 36km off the southeast coast, is perfection. Roughly a dozen delineated dive sites orbit the island – the most famous dive being **Barracuda Point**, where chevron and blacktail barracuda merge to form impenetrable walls of undulating fish.

There are many other reefs in the archipelago worth exploring. The macro-diving around **Mabul** (or 'Pulau Mabul') is world-famous. The submerged sites around **Kapalai**, **Mataking** and **Sibuan** are also of note.

The government issues 120 passes (RM40) to Sipadan each day. Each dive company is issued a predetermined number of passes per day depending on the size of its operation and the general demand for permits. Advance booking is, therefore, highly advised.

A three-dive day trip costs between RM300 and RM500, and equipment rental comes to about RM60 per day. Although most of the diving in the area is 'fun diving', Open Water certifications are available. A three-day Open Water course will set you back at least RM975.

MALAYSIA SEMPORNA ARCHIPELAGO

Several dive operators are based at their respective resorts, while others have shopfronts and offices in Semporna and/or KK.

🛏 Sleeping

The archipelago's only relatively inexpensive accommodation is on Mabul, 26km southeast of Semporna and 14km north of Sipadan. Prices rise and places fill fast in July and August. Mabul is endowed with a white-sand beach, fantastically blue waters, a marine police base and two small settlements: on the northeast coast, a hamlet of Bajau sea gypsies, known for their colourful, pointy-prowed boats called *jonkong*; on the southwest coast, a Suluk and Malay stilt village is home to several guesthouses.

Seahorse Sipadan Scuba Lodge   RESORT $
(☑ Semporna 089-782 289; www.seahorse-sipadanscuba.org; Mabul Island; packages incl room, meals, dives from RM518) Seahorse has a few rooms showing their age with patchy lino floors, yellow walls and an open deck to catch the breeze but nice little touches like conch shells on tables. There's also a dependable dive outfit here.

Uncle Chang's   GUESTHOUSE $
(☑ 017-895 002, 089-786 988, 089-781 002; www.ucsipadan.com; Mabul; dm RM75, d without/with air-con RM90/110; ❄) If Chang's was an avuncular connection, he'd be a rough old seadog, shipwrecked amid the stilted weaveworld of the Malay village. Think banana-yellow basic

rattan-walled rooms in small chalets, a lively threadbare communal deck with occasional jam sessions and a happy, sociable vibe. There's also a well-known dive school here with seven daily dive permits to Sipadan.

Sipadan Dive Centre (SDC)   RESORT $
(☑ 088-240 584, 012-821 8288; www.sdclodges.com; Mabul; 3-day packages incl 5 dives dm/r RM885/1045; ❄) Simple rainbow-coloured huts with attached bathroom, air-con, Caribbean-blue walls, fresh linen, wood floors, and a dive outfit – and less-cramped quarters compared to other budget digs thanks to its spacious compound – make this a winner. Friendly management too; they cook up barbecue feasts by night.

⭐ Scuba Junkie Mabul Beach Resort   RESORT $$
(☑ 089-785 372; www.scuba-junkie.com; Mabul; dm RM142, d with fan/air-con from RM184232; ❄ 🛜)
🍴 Run by a lovely American couple, this place attracts a younger international crowd with a little cash to splash on semi-luxe digs. Superfresh rooms come with porches and bathrooms, polished wood floors and choice decor. Dorms are airy and of a good size, plus there's a welcoming central gazebo which houses the lively restaurant/bar. Prices above include generous buffet meals.

ℹ Getting There & Away

Your accommodation will arrange any transport needs from Semporna or Tawau airport (sometimes included, sometimes for an extra fee – ask!).

> ### ℹ GETTING TO BRUNEI: PULAU LABUAN TO BANDAR SERI BEGAWAN
>
> **Getting to the border** Ferries depart Bandar Labuan for the Bruneian port of Muara (RM40, 1¼ hours), daily at 9am, 1.30pm, 3.30pm and 4pm.
>
> **At the border** In Brunei, most visitors are granted a visa on arrival for free, although Australians and Chinese must pay a fee.
>
> **Moving on** You'll be dropped at Serasa Ferry Terminal; from here buses 37 or 39 can take you to central Bandar Seri Begawan for B$1 (one hour). Express buses (B$2) to BSB are supposed to coincide with the ferry arrivals. A taxi should cost around B$30.

Pulau Labuan

☑ 087 / POP 86,910

The island of the Federal Territory of Labuan lies some 115km southwest of KK and only 50km northeast of BSB (Brunei). Shopping here is duty free, alcohol is cheap and the ferry connections are convenient, making Labuan an attractive destination for local travellers.

The sultan of Brunei ceded Labuan to the British in 1846 and it remained part of the empire for 115 years. The only interruption came during WWII, when the Japanese held the island for three years.

Bandar Labuan is the main town and the transit point for ferries linking Kota Kinabalu and Brunei – the best way to travel between the two countries.

🛏 Sleeping

Labuan Homestay Programme   HOMESTAY $
(🖉 Bukit Kuda 013-851 1907, Patau Patau 2 016-824 6193, Sungai Labu 016-804 1147; www.tourism.gov.my/niche/homestay; 1/2 days incl full board RM70/150) This excellent service matches visitors with a friendly local in one of three villages around the island: Patau Patau 2, Kampong Sungai Labu and Kampong Bukit Kuda. If you want to be near Bandar Labuan, ask for accommodation at Patau Patau 2 – it's a charming stilt village out on the bay. If you want to enrol in the program, book at least a few days in advance.

★ Tiara Labuan   HOTEL $$
(🖉 087-414300; www.tiaralabuan.com; Jln Tanjung Batu; r incl breakfast from RM368; ❋ 🛜) Pulau Labuan's favourite hotel is a cut above the rest with its cobalt-blue outdoor pool nestled in manicured gardens at Tanjung Batu. There's an excellent Asian-fusion restaurant, courtyard bar and open-range kitchen, plus large and alluring wood-signatured rooms with bed runners, snow-white linen, spotless bathrooms and recessed lighting.

ℹ Getting There & Away

Kota Kinabalu Passenger ferries (business/economy class RM31-44/RM26-39, 3¼ hours) depart KK for Labuan from Monday to Saturday at 8am and 1.30pm (3pm Sunday). In the opposite direction, they depart the **Labuan Ferry Terminal** (Jln Merdeka) for KK from Monday to Saturday at 8am and 1pm, and 10.30am and 3pm on Sundays.

Sarawak There are ferries to Limbang (two hours, RM17-31) and Lawas (2¼ hours, RM18-33) in Sarawak's Limbang Division.

MALAYSIAN BORNEO – SARAWAK

Sarawak makes access to Borneo's natural wonders and cultural riches a breeze. From Kuching, the capital of Sarawak, pristine rainforests – where you can spot orangutans, proboscis monkeys and the world's largest flower, the rafflesia – can be visited on day trips, with plenty of time in the evening for a delicious meal and a drink in a chic bar. Adventurous travellers can take a 'flying coffin' riverboat up the Batang Rejang, 'the Amazon of Borneo', on your way to visit the spectacular caves and extraordinary rock formations of Gunung Mulu National Park, a Unesco World Heritage Site.

Kuching

🖉 082 / POP 618,000

Sarawak's sophisticated capital brings together a kaleidoscope of cultures, crafts and cuisines. The bustling streets - some wide and modern, others narrow alleys lined with carpenter shops, cafes and bars - reward visitors with a penchant for exploring on foot. Attractions include time-capsule museums, Chinese temples decorated with dragons, a weekend market, shophouses from the time of the White Rajahs, and that postcard riverfront esplanade that draws people out for a warm evening stroll and a delicious meal.

Kuching's proximity to several first-rate national parks makes it the perfect base for day trips to wild coastal and rainforest destinations.

◎ Sights

★ Ethnology Museum   MUSEUM
(www.museum.sarawak.gov.my; Jln Tun Abang Haji Openg; ⊘ 9am-4.45pm Mon-Fri, 10am-4pm Sat, Sun & holidays) 𝗙𝗥𝗘𝗘 At the top of the hill, on the eastern side of Jln Tun Abang Haji Openg, the Ethnology Museum (the Old Building) – guarded by two colonial cannons – spotlights Borneo's incredibly rich indigenous cultures. Upstairs the superb exhibits include an Iban longhouse, masks and spears; downstairs is an old-fashioned natural-history museum.

★ Art Museum   MUSEUM
(www.museum.sarawak.gov.my; Jln Tun Abang Haji Openg; ⊘ 9am-4.45pm Mon-Fri, 10am-4pm Sat, Sun & holidays) 𝗙𝗥𝗘𝗘 This museum features an exhibit called Urang Sarawak, which deftly and succinctly describes the people and culture of Sarawak, especially indigenous lifestyles and traditional mythology, historical periods such as the Brooke era and World War II, as well as contemporary Sarawak. Other exhibits feature prehistoric archaeology including important finds from the Niah Caves, and Chinese ceramics.

Chinese History Museum   MUSEUM
(opp cnr Main Bazaar & Jln Temple; ⊘ 9am-4.45pm Mon-Fri, 10am-4pm Sat, Sun & holidays) 𝗙𝗥𝗘𝗘 Housed in the century-old Chinese Court building, the Chinese History Museum provides an excellent introduction to the nine major Chinese communities – each with its own dialect, cuisine and temples – who began settling in Sarawak around

MALAYSIA KUCHING

Kuching

400 m
0.2 miles

KAMPUNG BOYAN

Sungai Sarawak

Jln Brooke

Astana (200m)

Footbridge

Kuching Mosque

Jln Market

18

30

Jln Gambier

Indian Mosque Ln

Jln India

Jln Khoo Hun Yeang

Jln Mosque (Jln Masjid)

Gurdwara Sahib Kuching

Jln P Ramlee

Jln Barrack

24

Main Bazaar

Jln China

Jln Carpenter

14

Jln Pearl

25 21 11
22

Jln Bishopsgate

13

3
Klinik Chan

Jln Wayang

12 19

15

Tua Pek Kong Temple

Jln Temple

Jln Green Hill

8

An Hui Motor

26

Padang Merdeka

Jln Tun Abang Haji Openg

1 Art Museum

2 Ethnology Museum

Museum Garden

Jln Tun Haji Openg

Jln Satok

Jln McDougall

Jln Reservoir

Reservoir Park

Jln Tabuan

5

Jln Ban Hock

4

Jln Tunku Abdul Rahman

28

27

Jln Borneo

BUKIT MATA

Jln Bukit Mata Kuching

Jln Bukit Mata

Jln Padungan

Bukit Mata

Jln Matthies

Sarawak Plaza

Mohamed Yahia & Sons

Tun Jugah Shopping Centre

5

Jln Chan Chin Ann

29

Jln Abell

6

20

i

9

Jln Padungan

PADUNGAN

Jln Song Thian Cheok

23

16

Persiaran Ban Hock

Jln Ban Hock

7 10

17

Kuching

1830. Highlights include ceramics, musical instruments, historic photographs and some fearsome dragon- and lion-dance costumes. The entrance is on the river side of the building.

Fort Margherita   MUSEUM
(The Brooke Gallery; Kampung Boyan; adult/child RM20/10; ⊙9am-4.45pm Mon-Fri, 10am-4pm Sat & Sun) Built by Charles Brooke in 1879 and named after his wife, Ranee Margaret, this hilltop fortress long protected Kuching against surprise attack by pirates. Inside, the Brooke Gallery illustrates the remarkable story of the White Rajahs of Sarawak with fascinating artefacts and story boards. You can explore the ramparts, inspect the cells and see where executions took place.

To get here take a *tambang* (wooden boat; RM1) from the waterfront promenade to Kampung Boyan and then follow the signs up through the abandoned and derelict school for 500m.

☞ Tours

Borneo Experiences   TOURS
(☑082-429239; www.borneoexperiences.com; ground fl, No. 1 Jln Temple; ⊙10am-7pm Mon-Sat, may also open Sun) Singgahsana Lodge's trav-el agency. Destinations include a remote Bidayuh 'village in the clouds' and an Iban longhouse in the Batang Ai area (three days/two nights RM1450, minimum two guests). Also offers cycling tours. Gets excellent reviews.

Adventure Alternative Borneo   ADVENTURE
(☑082-248000, 019-892 9627; www.adventure aalternativeborneo.com; Lot 37 Jln Tabuan; ⊙9am-5pm Mon-Sat) ∅ Offers ethical and sustainable trips that combine 'culture, nature and adventure'. Can help you design and coordinate an itinerary for independent travel to remote areas, including the Penan villages of the Upper Baram.

🛏 Sleeping

★ Singgahsana Lodge   GUESTHOUSE $
(☑082-429277; www.singgahsana.com; 1 Jln Temple; dm/d incl breakfast RM35/RM113-158; ✳@☎) Setting the Kuching standard for backpacker digs, this hugely popular guesthouse, decked out with stylish Sarawakian crafts, has an unbeatable location, a great chill-out lobby and a sociable rooftop bar. Free bicycle hire is available to room guests. Dorms have 10 beds and lockers.

MALAYSIA KUCHING

Threehouse B&B
GUESTHOUSE $

(082-423499; www.threehousebnb.com; 51 Jln China; incl breakfast dm RM22, d without bathroom RM65-70; 🛜) A spotless, family-friendly guesthouse in a great Old Chinatown location that is warm and welcoming – everything a guesthouse should be. All nine rooms are spaced over three creaky wooden floors and share a bright-red colour scheme. Amenities include a common room with TV, DVDs and books, a laundry service and a kitchen.

Radioman
HOSTEL $

(082-238801, 082-248816; 1 Jln Wayang; incl breakfast dm RM20, d without bathrooms RM60; 🌐🛜) This centrally located, self-styled 'heritage hostel' occupies a century-old shophouse that was once used for radio repairs. The building still has the original ceilings, floors and fiendishly steep stairs and it has been thoughtfully decorated. As well as a 12-bed mixed dorm there is a 4-bed women's dorm. Dorms and private rooms share a shower and toilet.

Marco Polo's
GUESTHOUSE $

(082-246679, Samuel Tan 019-888 8505; www.marcopolokuching.com; 1st fl, 236 Jln Padungan; incl breakfast dm RM27, d without bathrooms RM58-62; 🌐🛜) A well-run, comfortable place with a breezy verandah and cosy indoor living room. The breakfast of fresh fruit, banana fritters and muffins is a popular bonus. Only some rooms have windows. Owner Sam is happy to give travel advice and sometimes takes guests to the market. Situated about 15 minutes' walk (1.5km) from the waterfront.

Beds
GUESTHOUSE $

(082-424229; www.bedsguesthouse.com; 229 Jln Padungan; dm RM22, s/d without bathroom RM45/58; 🌐@🛜) This guesthouse has attracted a loyal following thanks to comfy couches in the lobby, a well-equipped kitchen you can cook in and 12 spotless rooms, nine with windows. Dorm rooms have six metal bunks of generous proportions. Located in New Chinatown, about 15 minutes' walk (1.5km) from the Main Bazaar.

Le Nomade
HOSTEL $

(082-237831; www.lenomadehostel.com; 3 Jln Green Hill; dm incl breakfast 8-bed/4-bed RM25/28, s/d with shared bathroom RM35/70, d with bathroom RM75; 🌐@🛜) There's a buzzing backpacker vibe at this relaxed, Iban-run place – guests often hang out in the lounge area with the friendly management. Breakfast times are flexible to suit late risers and there is a kitchen that guests can use. Of the 12 rooms, most have windows (the others make do with exhaust fans).

⭐ The Marian
BOUTIQUE HOTEL $$

(082-252777; www.themarian.com.my; Jln Wayang; incl breakfast dm RM80, d from RM290; ✳@🛜⛱) Delightfully different, the Marian is a converted mansion once owned by a Chinese merchant before it became a convent attached to nearby St Thomas's Cathedral. Great care has been taken to preserve the old building's long and varied historical legacy while providing modern comforts. The 40 rooms are divided into eight categories, reflecting the highly individual nature of the design.

Batik Boutique Hotel
BOUTIQUE HOTEL $$

(082-422845; www.batikboutiquehotel.com; 38 Jln Padungan; d incl breakfast RM280; ✳🛜) A superb location, classy design and superfriendly staff make this a top midrange choice. The swirling batik design used on the hotel's facade is continued in the lobby and the 15 spacious, colour-coordinated rooms. On the ground floor you'll find the **restaurant** featuring Scandinavian cuisine, plus a bar that is handy to the comfy outdoor courtyard at the back.

Lime Tree Hotel
HOTEL $$

(082-414600; www.limetreehotel.com.my; Lot 317, Jln Abell; d incl breakfast RM158-278; ✳@🛜) Dashes of lime green – a pillow, a bar of soap, a staff member's tie, the lobby's **Cafe Sublime** – accent every room of this well-run boutique hotel. The family who owns it also owns a lime orchard. The 50 nonsmoking rooms are sleek and minimalist. The rooftop bar has river views and a good selection of meals including vegan and vegetarian options.

🍴 Eating

Kuching is the ideal place to explore the entire range of Sarawak-style cooking. You can pick and choose from a variety of Chinese and Malay hawker stalls, while Jln Padungan is home to some of the city's best noodle houses. The question of where to find the city's best laksa is sure to spark a heated debate. The only way to get a definitive answer is to try them all yourself.

⭐ Fig Tree Cafe
MALAYSIAN $

(017-818 6636; 29 Jln Wayang; mains RM6-10; 🕙10.30am-8.30pm, closed Mon; ✳🍽) This innovative cafe features Malay-Chinese dishes served with flair and enthusiasm. There are plenty of vegetarian choices, and vegan options are available. The adventurous should try the *lui cha*, rice and vegetables accompanied by a deep-green soup of Sarawak herbs. Carnivores can opt for the *ka-cangma*, rice wine chicken. Also available: waffles, smoothies and a glowing green-tea cheesecake.

★**Choon Hui**   MALAYSIAN $
(☑ 082-893709; 34 Jln Ban Hock; laksa RM6-10; ⊗ 7-11am Tue-Sun) This old-school *kopitiam* (coffee shop) gets our vote for the most delicious laksa in town, and we're not alone – the place can get crowded, especially at weekends. There is also a stall here selling excellent *popiah*, a kind of spring roll made with peanuts, radish and carrot (RM3).

Kim Food Court   BAKERY $
(Jln Padungan, New Chinatown; tarts RM2.20; ⊗ 7am-9pm) Egg tarts are the speciality here. Delicious egg tarts with the flakiest of bases are available as traditional, pandan-flavoured, coconut-flavoured, or Portuguese style.

Open-Air Market   HAWKER $
(Tower Market; Jln Khoo Hun Yeang; mains RM3-8; ⊗ most stalls 6am-4pm, Chinese seafood 3pm-4am) Cheap, tasty dishes to look for include laksa, Chinese-style *mee sapi* (beef noodle soup), red *kolo mee* (noodles with pork and a sweet barbecue sauce), tomato *kueh tiaw* (a fried rice-noodle dish) and shaved-ice desserts (ask for 'ABC' at stall 17). The Chinese seafood stalls that open in the afternoon are on the side facing the river.

★**The Dyak**   MALAYSIAN $$
(☑ 082-234068; Jln Mendu & Jln Simpang Tiga; mains RM25-35; ⊗ noon-11pm, last order 8.30pm; ✿ 🥕) This elegant restaurant is the first to treat Dayak home cooking as true cuisine. The chef, classically trained in a Western style, uses traditional recipes, many of them Iban (a few are Kelabit, Kayan or Bidayuh), and fresh, organic jungle produce to create mouth-watering dishes unlike anything you've ever tasted. It's 2km southeast of Old Chinatown.

The Granary   BRASSERIE $$
(www.thegranary.my; 23 Jln Wayang; lunch mains RM14-24, dinner mains RM24-58; ⊗ 7am-11pm) Housed in an old, you guessed it, granary that has been renovated with minimalist flair. This breezy restaurant serves up superb burgers, pizzas and pasta plus some pricier meat options. Check the specials board and

pencil in Happy Hour (5pm to 8pm) for good deals on cocktails, beer and spirits.

Top Spot Food Court   SEAFOOD $$
(Jln Padungan; fish per kg RM30-70, vegetable dishes RM8-12; ⊗ noon-11pm) A perennial favourite among local foodies, this neon-lit courtyard and its half-dozen humming seafooderies sits, rather improbably, on the roof of a concrete parking garage – look for the giant backlit lobster sign. Grilled white pomfret is a particular delicacy. **Ling Loong Seafood** and the **Bukit Mata Seafood Centre** are especially good.

🍷 Drinking & Nightlife

★**Drunken Monkey**   BAR
(☑ 082-242048; 68 Jln Carpenter; ⊗ 2pm-2am) This bar attracts a relaxed crowd of local professionals and tourists. Although it's a bar only, you will find menus from several nearby restaurants scattered about, and a variety of food can be delivered to your table. Drinks include draught Guinness (RM19 per pint), a decent range of imported wines and a whole page of whiskies.

Black Bean Coffee & Tea Company   CAFE
(Jln Carpenter; drinks RM3-6; ⊗ 9.30am-6pm Mon-Sat; 🥕) The aroma of freshly ground coffee assaults the senses at this tiny shop, believed

by many to purvey Kuching's finest brews. Specialities, roasted daily, include Arabica, Liberica and Robusta coffees grown in Java, Sumatra and, of course, Sarawak. Also serves Oolong and green teas from Taiwan. Has just three tables. Decaf not available.

Monkee Bar BAR
(www.monkeebars.com; Jln Song Thian Cheok; beer RM6.50-13, spirit & mixer RM13; ☺3pm-2am; 🛜) At Monkee Bar, 50% of profits go to the Orangutan Project, a wildlife conservation NGO that works at Matang Wildlife Centre (p462). If the idea of 'drinking for conservation' doesn't entice you, the prices might: Monkee Bar has some of the cheapest drinks in town. It's a smoky joint with a young local crowd interspersed with volunteers enjoying downtime from cage-cleaning.

🛍 Shopping

Main Bazaar ARTS & CRAFTS
(☺some shops closed Sun) The row of old shophouses facing the Waterfront Promenade is chock-full of handicrafts shops, some outfitted like art galleries, others with more of a 'garage sale' appeal, and yet others (especially along the Main Bazaar's western section) stocking little more than kitschy-cute cat souvenirs.

Juliana Native Handwork ARTS & CRAFTS
(☑016-809-5415, 082-230144; ground fl, Sarawak Textile Museum, Jln Tun Abang Haji Openg; ☺9am-4.30pm) As well as her own Bidayuh

---

ℹ GETTING TO INDONESIA: KUCHING TO PONTIANAK

Getting to the border A number of bus companies ply the route between Kuching Sentral bus terminal (and other cities along the Sarawak coast) and the West Kalimantan city of Pontianak (economy RM60, 1st class RM80, seven/10 hours via the new/old road), passing through the Tebedu-Entikong crossing 80km south of Kuching.

At the border Travellers from 64 countries can get a one-month Indonesian visa on arrival at the road crossing between Tededu (Malaysia) and Entikong (Indonesia), the only official land border between Sarawak and Kalimantan.

Moving on Pontianak is linked to other parts of Indonesia and to Singapore by airlines such as Batavia Air (www.batavia-air.com).

---

beadwork pieces – most of which have been displayed in an exhibition in Singapore – Juliana sells quality rattan mats made by Penan artists (RM780) and *pua kumbu* Iban woven cloths. The intricate, 50cm-long beaded table runners she sells (RM680) take her three months to complete.

Ting & Ting SUPERMARKET
(30A Jln Tabuan; ☺9am-9pm, closed Sun & holidays) A good selection of wine, snack food, chocolate, toiletries and nappies.

ℹ Information

EMERGENCY

Ambulance	999
Fire	999
Police	999

MEDICAL SERVICES
Klinik Chan (☑082-240307; 98 Main Bazaar; ☺8am-noon & 2-5pm Mon-Fri, 9am-noon Sat, Sun & holidays) Conveniently central. A consultation for a minor ailment costs from RM40.

Normah Medical Specialist Centre (☑082-440055, emergency 082-311999; www.normah.com.my; 937 Jln Tun Abdul Rahman, Petra Jaya; ☺emergency 24hr, clinics 8.30am-4.30pm Mon-Fri, to 1pm Sat; 🖥1) Widely considered Kuching's best private hospital. Has a 24-hour ambulance. Situated north of the river, about 6km by road from the centre. Served by the 1 bus from Saujana Bus Station, departures on the hour from 7am to 5pm.

Sarawak General Hospital (Hospital Umum Sarawak; ☑082-276666; http://hus.moh.gov.my/v3; Jln Hospital; ☺24hr) Kuching's large public hospital has modern facilities and remarkably reasonable rates but is often overcrowded. Situated about 2km south of the centre along Jln Tun Abang Haji Openg. To get there, take bus K6, K8 or K18.

MONEY
The majority of Kuching's banks and ATMs are on Jln Tunku Abdul Rahman.

Mohamed Yahia & Sons (basement, Sarawak Plaza, Jln Tunku Abdul Rahman; ☺10am-9pm) charges no commission, has good rates and accepts over 30 currencies (including US$100 bills), as well as traveller's cheques in US dollars, euros, Australian dollars and pounds sterling. Situated inside the bookshop.

TOURIST INFORMATION
Visitors Information Centre (☑082-410942, 082-410944; www.sarawaktourism.com; UTC Sarawak, Jln Padungan; ☺8am-5pm Mon-Fri, closed public holidays) On the first floor of the

UTC building on Jln Padungan. The office is usually helpful with well-informed staff, brochures and oodles of practical information (eg bus schedules).

VISA EXTENSIONS

Visa Department (Bahagian Visa; ☑ 082-245661; www.imi.gov.my; 2nd fl, Bangunan Sultan Iskandar, Kompleks Pejabat Persekutuan, cnr Jln Tun Razak & Jln Simpang Tiga; ⏱ 8am-5pm Mon-Thu, 8-11.45am & 2.15-5pm Fri) Situated in a 17-storey federal office building about 3km south of the centre (along Jln Tabuan). Served by City Public Link buses K8 or K11, which run every half-hour or so. A taxi from the centre costs RM15.

❶ Getting There & Away

AIR

Kuching International Airport (www.kuching airportonline.com), 11km south of the city centre, has direct air links with Singapore, Johor Bahru (the Malaysian city across the causeway from Singapore), Kuala Lumpur (KL), Penang, Kota Kinabalu (KK), Bandar Seri Begawan (BSB) and Pontianak.

MASwings, a subsidiary of Malaysia Airlines, flies from its hubs in Miri and Kuching to 14 destinations around Sarawak, including the lowland cities of Sibu, Bintulu, Limbang and Lawas and the upland destinations of Gunung Mulu National Park, Bario and Ba Kelalan.

The airport has three departure halls: 'Domestic Departures' for flights within Sarawak; 'Domestic Departures (Outside Sarawak)' for travel to other parts of Malaysia; and 'International Departures'.

BOAT

Ekspress Bahagia (☑ 016-800 5891, 016-889 3013, in Kuching 082-412 246, in Sibu 084-319228; one-way RM55) runs a daily express ferry from Kuching's Express Wharf, 6km east of the centre, to Sibu. Departures are at 8.30am from Kuching and at 11.30am from Sibu (RM55, five hours). It's a good idea to book a day ahead. A taxi from town to the wharf costs RM35.

BUS

Every half-hour or so from about 6am to 6.30pm, various buses run by **City Public Link** (☑ 082-239178) (eg K9) and STC (eg 3A, 4B, 6 and 2) link central Kuching's **Saujana Bus Station** (Jln Masjid & Jln P Ramlee) with **Kuching Sentral** (cnr Jln Penrissen & Jln Airport), the Regional Express Bus Terminal (RM2). Saujana's ticket windows can point you to the next departure. A taxi to Kuching Sentral from the centre costs RM35 (25 minutes).

Buses for many destinations can be booked online via www.busonlineticket.com.

To Central Sarawak

From 6.30am to 10.30pm, a dozen different companies send buses at least hourly along Sarawak's northern coast to Miri (RM100, 14½ hours), with stops at Sibu (RM50 to RM60, 7½ hours), Bintulu (RM80, 11½ hours), Batu Niah Junction (jumping-off point for Niah National Park) and Lambir Hills National Park. **Bus Asia** (☑ 082-411111; www.busasia.my; cnr Jln Abell & Jln Chan Chin Ann; ⏱ Mon-Fri 8am-8pm, 8am-5pm Sat; 6am-10pm), for instance, has seven departures a day, the first at 8am, the last at 10pm; unlike its competitors, the company has a city centre office and, from Monday to Saturday, runs shuttle buses out to Kuching Sentral. Luxurious 'VIP buses', eg those run by **Asia Star** (☑ 082-610111), have just three seats across (28 in total), and some come with on-board toilets, and yet cost a mere RM10 to RM20 more than regular coaches. To get to Brunei, Limbang or Sabah, you have to change buses in Miri.

To Western Sarawak

Buses to the Semenggoh Wildlife Centre, Bako National Park, Kubah National Park and the Matang Wildlife Sanctuary depart from town at or near Saujana Bus Station. Buses to Lundu (including the Wind Cave and Fairy Cave) use Kuching Sentral.

TAXI

For some destinations, the only transport option – other than taking a tour – is chartering a taxi. Hiring a red-and-yellow cab for an eight-hour day should cost about RM300 to RM350. If you'd like your driver to wait at your destination and then take you back to town, count on paying about RM35 per hour of wait time.

Sample taxi fares from Kuching (prices are 50% higher at night):

DESTINATION	PRICE (RM)
Annah Rais Longhouse	80-90 one-way
Bako Bazaar (Bako National Park)	60 one-way
Express Wharf (ferry to Sibu)	35
Fairy Cave (with Wind Cave)	180 return incl wait
Kubah National Park	60
Matang Wildlife Centre	60
Santubong Peninsula Resorts	80
Sarawak Cultural Village	80
Semenggoh Nature Reserve	140 return incl 1hr wait
Wind Cave (with Fairy Cave)	180 return incl wait

ℹ️ Getting Around

TO/FROM THE AIRPORT

The price of a red-and-yellow taxi from the airport into Kuching is fixed at RM26 (RM39 for late-night arrivals), including luggage; a larger *teksi eksekutiv* (executive taxi), painted blue, costs RM43 (RM64 late night). Coupons are sold inside the terminal next to the car-rental counters.

BOAT

Bow-steered wooden boats known as *tambang*, powered by an outboard motor, shuttle passengers back and forth across Sungai Sarawak, linking jetties along the Waterfront Promenade with destinations such as Kampung Boyan (for Fort Margherita) and the Astana. The fare for Sarawak's cheapest cruise is RM1 (more from 10pm to 6am); pay as you disembark. If a *tambang* isn't tied up when you arrive at a dock, just wait and one will usually materialise fairly soon.

MOTORCYCLE

An Hui Motor (📋 016-886 3328, 082-240508; 29 Jln Tabuan; ⊗ 8am-6pm Mon-Sat, 8am-10.30am Sun) is a motorcycle repair shop that charges RM30/RM175 per day/week for a Vespa-like Suzuki RG (110cc) or RM40/RM210 per day/week for a 125cc scooter (including helmet), plus a deposit of RM100. Insurance covers the bike but not the driver and may be valid only within an 80km radius of Kuching, so check before you head to Sematan, Lundu or Annah Rais.

TAXI

Taxis can be hailed on the street, found at taxi ranks (of which the city centre has quite a few, eg at larger hotels) or ordered by phone 24 hours a day from the following:

ABC Radio Call Service (📋 082-611611, 016-861 1611)

Kuching City Radio Taxi (📋 082-348898, 082-480000)

T&T Radio Call Taxi (📋 082-343343, 016-888 2255)

Kuching taxis are required to use meters; though, in our experience most won't. Overcharging, however, is not common. Be aware that fares go up by 50% from midnight to 6am.

Around Kuching

Western Sarawak offers a dazzling array of natural sights and indigenous cultures, most within day-trip distance of Kuching.

Bako National Park

Occupying a jagged peninsula jutting into the South China Sea, Sarawak's oldest **national park** (📋 Bako terminal 082-370434, Kuching 082-248 088; www.sarawakforestry.com; adult/child RM20/7; ⊗ park office 8am-5pm) is just 37km northeast of downtown Kuching but feels worlds away. Bako is notable for its incredible biodiversity, which encompasses everything from orchids and pitcher plants to proboscis monkeys and bearded pigs. Bako is one of the best places in Borneo to observe these endemics up close.

The coastline of the 27sqkm peninsula consists of secluded beaches and bays interspersed with wind-sculpted cliffs, forests and stretches of tangled mangroves. The interior of the park features a range of distinct ecosystems, including classic lowland rainforest (mixed dipterocarp forest) and *kerangas* (heath forest), streams and waterfalls. Hiking trails traverse the central sandstone plateau and connect with several of the beaches.

Bako is an easy day trip from Kuching, but we recommend staying a night or two to fully experience the wild beauty.

🎯 Sights & Activities

Bako's hiking trails – colour-coded and clearly marked with stripes of paint – are suitable for all levels of fitness and motivation, with routes ranging from short nature strolls to strenuous all-day hikes. The ranger-led **night walk** (per person RM10; ⊗ 8pm) gets great reviews. At park headquarters it's possible to hire a boat to one of the more distant beaches and then hike back, or to hike to one of the beaches and arrange for a boat to meet you there.

🛏️ Sleeping

Bako's accommodation is basic, although it's well run and adequately equipped.

Accommodation often fills up, especially from May to September, so it's best to book ahead. Some travel agencies reserve rooms that they release a week ahead if their packages remain unsold, and individual travellers also sometimes cancel, so week-before and last-minute vacancies are common. There is a RM10 key deposit and unlocked storage (free) is available at reception.

Accommodation includes the following options:

Camping (per person RM5)

Forest Hostel (dm RM15, q RM40)

Forest Lodge Type 4 (d RM150, cabin RM225; ❄)

Forest Lodge Type 5 (r RM100)

Forest Lodge Type 6 (d RM50, 2-room cabin RM75)

Eating

Kerangas Café
CAFETERIA $

(canteen; Bako National Park; meals RM8–12; ⊙7.30am-10.30pm) The cafeteria, designed to be macaque-proof, serves a varied and tasty selection of fried rice, chicken, fish, cakes, fresh fruit and packaged snacks. Buffet meals (where you pay by the scoop) are available from 11.30am to 2pm and 6.30pm to 8pm.

❶ Getting There & Away

Getting to the park by public transport is a cinch. First take one of the hourly buses from Kuching to Bako Bazaar, then hop on a motorboat to Teluk Assam jetty, about 400m along a wooden boardwalk from park HQ.

Kuching travel agencies charge from RM310 per person for a tour, including the boat ride.

Boat transfers to Bako park HQ from Bako Terminal (at Bako Bazaar) are managed by **Koperasi Warisan Pelancongan Bako Berhad** (Bako boat transfers; ☑ 011-2513 2711, 011-2509 5070; RM20 per person one-way, RM100 private hire; ⊙7.30am-4pm), which has a counter at the terminal and at park HQ. The 20-minute journey from the terminal at Bako Bazaar to the park costs RM20 per person (private hire of boat RM100 – in case you don't want to wait around for a boat to collect enough passengers). From May to September, transfers are usually every hour from 8am to 4pm (ask at the counter for the day's schedule). The last boat back from Bako is at 4pm.

When the tide is low, boats may not be able to approach the jetty at Teluk Assam, so you may have to wade ashore. Boatmen may insist on an early afternoon return time to beat a late-afternoon low tide – but bold outboard jockeys have been known to make the trip back to Bako Bazaar even at the lowest of tides.

From late November to February or March, the sea is often rough and scheduled boat trips may be less frequent.

Santubong Peninsula

☑ 082

The Santubong Peninsula (also known as Damai) is a 10km-long finger of land jutting into the South China Sea. The main drawcards are the Sarawak Cultural Village, some of Malaysian Borneo's best beaches, and Gunung Santubong (880m), which can be climbed from a point about 1km south of Damai Central.

◉ Sights & Activities

Access to **Damai Central Beach** FREE, across the parking lot from the Sarawak Cultural Village, is free. For a small fee, non-guests can hang out on the sand and in the waves at **Permai Rainforest Resort** (☑ 082-846490; www.permairainforest.com; Damai Beach; adult/child RM8/5; ⊙7am-7pm) .

Sarawak Cultural Village
MUSEUM

(SCV; ☑ 082-846411; www.scv.com.my; Damai Central; adult/child RM63.60/31.80; ⊙9am-4.45pm) This living museum is centred on seven traditional dwellings: three longhouses, a Penan hut, a Malay townhouse and a Chinese farmhouse. It may sound contrived but the SCV is held in high esteem by locals for its role in keeping their cultures and traditions alive.

Twice a day (at 11.30am and 4pm) a cultural show presents traditional music and dance. The lively Melanau entry involves whirling women and clacking bamboo poles, while the Orang Ulu dance features a blowpipe hunter.

🛏 Sleeping & Eating

BB Bunkers
HOSTEL $

(☑ 082-846835; www.bbbunkers.com; Damai Central; dm RM53; ❉🛜) Situated a few metres from Damai Central Beach in the Damai Central mall, this hostel has the peninsula's only dorm beds. The industrial-type space is subdivided by curtains, creating not-so-private spaces for one to three beds, either twins or queens. Secure storage is available.

Village House
GUESTHOUSE $$

(☑ 016-860 9389, 082-846166; www.villagehouse.com.my; Lot 634, off Jln Pantai Puteri, Kampung Santubong; incl breakfast dm RM102, d RM334-627 ; ❉⊠) Tucked away in the quiet Malay village of Santubong, this place has an air of serenity and relaxation to it. Rooms with *belian* wood floors and four-poster beds are arranged around a gorgeous pool with frangipani trees at either end. A well-stocked bar and menu of local dishes (mains RM18 to RM60) means there is really no reason to leave.

❶ Getting There & Away

Kuching is linked to the Santubong Peninsula (45 minutes) by the slow K15 bus from **Saujana Bus Station** (p459) and minibuses operated by **Damai Shuttle** (☑ 082-423111; 1-way adult/child RM20/10).

Damai Shuttle has departures from Kuching's Grand Margherita Hotel to Damai Beach and Sarawak Cultural Village four times a day (9.15am, 10.15am, 12.15pm, 2.15pm). The departures from Damai back to Kuching leave the Sarawak Cultural Village at 11.15am, 1.15pm, 3.15pm and 5.15pm.

Semenggoh Nature Reserve

One of the best places in the world to see semi-wild orangutans in their natural habitat, the **Semenggoh Wildlife Center** (082-618325; www.sarawakforestry.com; Jln Puncak Borneo; adult/child RM10/5; 8-10am & 2-4pm, feeding 9am & 3pm) can be visited on a half-day trip from Kuching or combined with a visit to Annah Rais Longhouse. The shaggy creatures often swing by park HQ to dine on bananas, coconuts and eggs at daily feeding sessions. There's no guarantee that any orangutans will show up, but even when there are plenty of fruits in the forest the chances are excellent. Sometimes they arrive a little late, so don't rush off straight away even if everything seems quiet.

ⓘ Getting There & Away

Two bus companies provide reliable public transport from Kuching's Saujana Bus Station to the park gate, which is 1.3km down the hill from park HQ (RM4, 45 minutes):

City Public Link (p459) Bus K6 (RM4.30) departs from Kuching at 7.15am, 10.15am and 1pm, and from Semenggoh at 8.45pm, 11.15am, 2.15pm and 4.15pm.

Sarawak Transport Company (STC; 082-233579; Jln P Ramlee) Bus 6 (RM4) has Kuching departures at 6.45am and 12.15pm; buses back to Kuching pass by Semenggoh at 10am and 3.45pm.

A taxi from Kuching costs RM60 to RM70 one-way or RM140 return, including one hour of wait time.

Tours are organised by Kuching guesthouses and tour agencies.

Annah Rais

Although this Bidayuh longhouse village has been on the tourist circuit for decades, it is still a good place to get a sense of what a longhouse is and experience what longhouse life is like. It's possible to visit as a day guest and eat a meal here or stay overnight in one of the several homestays.

The 500 or so residents of **Annah Rais** (adult/student RM8/4) are as keen as the rest of us to enjoy the comforts of modern life, but they've made a conscious decision to preserve their traditional architecture and the social interaction it engenders.

Once you pay your entry fee (in a pavilion next to the parking lot), you're free to explore Annah Rais' three longhouses, either with a guide or on your own. The most important feature is the *awah*, a long, covered common verandah – with a springy bamboo floor – used for economic activities, socialising and celebrations.

🛏 Sleeping

Half-a-dozen families run homestays with shared bathrooms, either in one of the three longhouses or in an adjacent detached house. Standard rates, agreed upon by the community, are RM298 per person for accommodation and delicious Bidayuh board. It is also possible to arrange a package including activities such as hiking, rafting, fishing, (mock) blowgun hunting, soaking in a natural hot spring and a dance performance.

Akam Ganja HOMESTAY $$
(010-984 3821; winniejagig@gmail.com; per person incl meals RM298) Akam, a retired forestry official, and his wife Winnie, an English teacher, run a welcoming homestay at their comfortable detached house on the riverbank.

ⓘ Getting There & Away

Annah Rais is about 55km south of Kuching. A taxi from Kuching costs RM80 to RM90 one-way (about 90 minutes).

A variety of Kuching guesthouses and tour agencies offer four-hour tours to Annah Rais (per person from RM250).

Kubah National Park & Matang Wildlife Centre

Mixed dipterocarp forest, among the lushest and most threatened habitats in Borneo, is front and centre at 22sqkm **Kubah National Park** (082-845033; www.sarawakforestry.com; incl Matang Wildlife Centre adult/child RM20/7; 8am-5pm), which makes an ideal day or overnight trip from Kuching.

When you pay your entry fee, you'll receive a hand-coloured schematic map of the park's interconnected trails. They're well marked, so a guide isn't necessary, and also offer a good degree of shade, making them ideal for the sun averse. And when you're hot and sweaty from walking you can cool off under a crystal-clear waterfall.

A 3.8km trail (or 3½ hours' walk) leads from Kubah National Park to **Matang Wildlife Centre** (082-374869; www.sarawak

forestry.com; incl Kubah National Park adult/child RM20/7; ⊙8am-5pm, animal enclosure trail 8.30am-3.30pm), which lies within the park boundaries. The centre has had remarkable success rehabilitating jungle animals rescued from captivity, especially orangutans and sun bears. The highly professional staff do their best to provide their abused charges with natural living conditions, but there's no denying that the centre looks like a low-budget zoo plopped down in the jungle. Because of the centre's unique role, there are endangered animals here that you cannot see anywhere else in Sarawak.

🛏 Sleeping & Eating

Accommodation, available at both Kubah and Matang, is of a better standard at Kubah. Attractive, inexpensive options include the **forest hostel** (☑082-370422, Kuching 082-248088; http://ebooking.sarawak.gov.my; dm RM15); **forest lodge type 4** (☑082-370422, Kuching 082-248088; http://ebooking.sarawak.gov.my; 6-bed cabin RM225; ✱) and **forest lodge type 5** (☑082-370422, Kuching 082-248088; http://ebooking.sarawak.gov.my; 10-bed cabin RM150). Cooking is allowed in the chalets, which have fully equipped kitchens, but there's nowhere to buy food, so bring everything you'll need.

ℹ Getting There & Away

Kubah National Park is 22km northwest of Kuching. A taxi from Kuching costs RM60/120 one way/return. Your taxi driver may charge RM35 per hour of waiting.

From Kuching's **Saujana Bus Station** (p459), bus K21 to the Politeknik stops on the main road 400m from park HQ, next to the Kubah Family Park (RM4, one hour). Departures from Kuching are at 8am, 11am, 2pm and 5pm, and from the main road (opposite the turn-off for Kubah), at 6.30am, 9.30am, 12.30pm and 3.30pm (be there at 3pm, the bus sometimes leaves early).

Wind Cave & Fairy Cave

About 26km southwest of Kuching, the town of **Bau** is a good access point to two interesting cave systems. Situated 5km southwest of Bau, the **Wind Cave** (Gua Angin; ☑082-765472; adult/child RM5/2; ⊙8.30am-4.30pm) is essentially a network of underground streams, while nearby **Fairy Cave** (Gua Pari Pari; adult/child RM5/2; ⊙8.30am-4pm) – almost the size of a football pitch and as high as it is wide – is an extraordinary chamber whose entrance is 30m above the ground in the side of a cliff.

ℹ Getting There & Away

Bau is 43km southwest of Kuching. The town is linked to Kuching's **Saujana Bus Station** (p459) (RM5, 1½ hours) by bus 2 (every 20 minutes from 6.20am to 6pm). A taxi from Kuching costs around RM80 (50 minutes).

To get from Bau to the Wind Cave turn-off (a 1km walk from the cave), take BTC bus 3A. Departures are at 9am, 11am and 3pm. To get from Bau to the Fairy Cave turn-off (a 1.5km or 30-minute walk from the cave), take BTC bus 3, which departs at 8.40am, 10.30am, 11.40am and 3pm.

From Kuching, a taxi to both caves costs RM180 return, including three hours of wait time. A tour from Kuching to both caves costs from RM150 per person (minimum two).

Gunung Gading National Park

The best place in Sarawak to see the world's largest flower, the renowned Rafflesia, **Gunung Gading National Park** (☑082-735144; www.sarawakforestry.com; adult/child RM20/7; ⊙8am-5pm) makes a fine day trip from Kuching. Its old-growth rainforest covers the slopes of four mountains *(gunung)* – Gading, Lundu, Perigi and Sebuloh – and is traversed by **hiking trails**.

The star attraction at 41sqkm Gunung Gading is the *Rafflesia tuan-mudae*, a species that's endemic to Sarawak. Up to 75cm in diameter, they flower pretty much year-round but unpredictably, and each flower lasts no more than five days. So to see one you'll need some luck. To find out if a Rafflesia is in bloom – something that happens here only about 25 times a year – contact the park or call the National Park Booking Office on 082-248088.

🛏 Sleeping & Eating

The park has a **hostel** (☑Kuching 082-248088, park HQ 082-735144; http://ebooking.sarawak.gov.my; Gunung Gading National Park HQ; dm/r without bathrooms RM15/40) with four fan rooms and two three-bedroom **forest lodges** (☑Kuching 082-248088, park HQ 082-735144; http://ebooking.sarawak.gov.my; Gunung Gading National Park HQ; per cabin RM150; ✱) that can sleep up to six people. **Camping** (☑Kuching 082-248088, park HQ 082-735144; http://ebooking.sarawak.gov.my; Gunung Gading National Park HQ; per person RM5) is possible at park headquarters. Cooking is permitted in park accommodation. There are restaurants, food stalls and a large market in the town of Lundu, a walkable 2.5km from the park.

❶ Getting There & Away

Gunung Gading National Park is 85km northwest of Kuching.

Four public buses a day link **Kuching Sentral** (p459) long-distance bus station with Lundu, but from there you'll either have to walk north 2.5km to the park, or hire an unofficial taxi (about RM5 per person).

A tour from Kuching costs about RM350 per person including lunch (minimum two people). Groups could consider hiring a taxi for around RM300 including waiting time.

Sibu

📞 084 / POP 162,676

Gateway to the Batang Rejang, Sibu has grown rich from trade with Sarawak's interior since the time of James Brooke. These days, although the 'swan city' does not rival Kuching in terms of charm, it's not a bad place to spend a day or two before or after a boat trip into Borneo's wild interior.

◉ Sights

⭐ **Tua Pek Kong Temple**   TAOIST TEMPLE
(Jln Temple; ⊙ 6.30am-8pm) FREE A modest wooden structure existed on the site of this colourful riverfront Taoist temple as far back as 1871; it was rebuilt in 1897 but badly damaged by Allied bombs in 1942.

For panoramic views over the town and the muddy Batang Rejang, climb the seven-storey **Kuan Yin Pagoda**, built in 1987; the best time is sunset, when a swirl of swiftlets buzzes around the tower at eye level. Ask for the key at the ground-floor desk.

Sibu Heritage Centre   MUSEUM
(Jln Central; ⊙ 9am-5pm, closed Mon & public holidays) FREE Housed in an airy, circular municipal complex built in 1960, this excellent museum explores the captivating history of Sarawak and Sibu. Panels, rich in evocative photographs, take a look at the various Chinese dialect groups and other ethnic groups, Sarawak's communist insurgency (1965–90), Sibu's Christian (including Methodist) traditions, and local opposition to Sarawak's incorporation into Malaysia in 1963.

🛏 Sleeping

⭐ **Li Hua Hotel**   HOTEL $
(📞 084-324000; www.lihuahotel.com.my; cnr Jln Maju & Jln Teo Chong Loh; s/d/ste RM50/65/150; ❄@🛜) Sibu's best-value hotel has 68 spotless, tile-floor rooms spread out over nine

storeys, and staff that are professional and friendly. It's especially convenient if you're arriving or leaving by boat. Light sleepers should avoid the rooms above the karaoke bars on Jln Teo Chong Loh that blare out music late into the night.

River Park Hotel   HOTEL $
(fax 084-316688; 51-53 Jln Maju; d RM50-65; ❄🛜) A friendly, well-run, 30-room budget hotel in a convenient riverside location. The cheapest rooms don't have windows and are best avoided.

🍴 Eating

⭐ **Sibu Central Market**   HAWKER $
(Pasar Sentral Sibu; Jln Channel; mains RM3-7; ⊙ food stalls 3am-midnight) Malaysia's largest fruit-and-veg market has more than 1000 stalls. Upstairs, Chinese, Malay and Iban-run food stalls serve up local specialities, including porridge (available early in the morning and at night), *kampua mee* (dry plate noodles) and *kompia* (a local bagel). Most of the noodle stalls close around noon.

Night Market   HAWKER $
(Pasar Malam; Jln Market; ⊙ 5-11pm or midnight) Chinese stalls (selling pork and rice, steamed buns etc) are at the western end of the lot, while Malay stalls (with superb satay and barbecue chicken) are to the northeast. Also has a few Iban-run places.

Payung Café   MALAYSIAN $$
(📞 016-890 6061; 20F Jln Lanang; mains RM8-19; ⊙ 10am-11pm Mon-Sat, 5.30-11pm Sun) This is a delightful cafe where diners feast on healthy (no re-used oil, deep frying or MSG) local food such as mushroom rolls, spicy *otak-otak* barbecued fish, deliciously fresh herb salad, and generous servings of the volcano-like Mulu icecream. Drinks include fresh pineapple-and-ginger soda (very refreshing) and local Sibu coffee.

❶ Information

Rejang Medical Centre (📞 084-323333; www.rejang.com.my; 29 Jln Pedada; ⊙ emergency 24hr) Has 24-hour emergency services, including an ambulance. Situated about 1.5km east of the city centre.

Visitors Information Centre (📞 084-340980; www.sarawaktourism.com; Sublot 3a & 3b, Sibu Heritage Centre, Jln Central; ⊙ 8am-5pm Mon-Fri, closed public holidays) Well worth a stop. Has friendly and informative staff, plenty of maps, bus and ferry schedules, and brochures on travel around Sarawak.

ℹ️ Getting There & Away

AIR

MASwings (📞 084-307888, ext 2; www.mas-wings.com.my; Sibu Airport, Jln Durin; ⏰ 6am-8.30pm) has inexpensive services to Kuching, Bintulu, Miri and KK. **Malaysia Airlines** (📞 084-307799; www.malaysiaairlines.com; Sibu Airport, Jln Durin) flies to KL, and **AirAsia** (📞 084-307808; www.airasia.com; Departure Area, Level 1, Sibu Airport; ⏰ 7am-8pm) flies to Kuching, KL and Johor Bahru (across the causeway from Singapore).

BOAT

Unless you fly, the quickest way to get from Sibu to Kuching is by boat. **Ekspress Bahagia** (📞 016-800 5891, in Kuching 082-429242, in Sibu 084-319228; Rejang Esp; ⏰ from Sibu 11.30am, from Kuching 8.30am) runs a daily express ferry to/from Kuching's Express Wharf (RM55, five hours), which passes through an Amazonian dystopia of abandoned sawmills and rust-bucket tramp steamers. Departures are 11.30am from Sibu and 8.30am from Kuching. It's a good idea to book a day ahead.

'Flying coffin' express boats head up the Batang Rejang to Kapit (RM25 to RM35, 140km, three hours) hourly from 5.45am to 2.30pm. Water levels at the Pelagus Rapids permitting, one boat a day, departing at 5.45am, goes all the way to Belaga, 155km upriver from Kapit (RM55, 11 hours).

All boats leave from the **Express Ferry Terminal** (Terminal Penumpang Sibu; Jln Kho Peng Long; 📶). Make sure you're on board 15 minutes before departure time – boats have been known to depart early.

BUS

Sibu's **long-distance bus station** (Jln Pahlawan) is about 3.5km northeast of the centre along Jln Pedada. A variety of companies send buses to Kuching (RM50 to RM60, seven to eight hours, regular departures between 7am and 4am), Miri (RM50, 6½ hours, roughly hourly from 6am to 3.30am) and Bintulu (RM27, 3¼ hours, roughly hourly from 6am to 3.30am).

ℹ️ Getting Around

To get from the **local bus station**, in front of the Express Ferry Terminal, to the long-distance bus station, take Lanang Bus 21 (RM2, 15 minutes, once or twice an hour 6.30am to 5.15pm).

Batang Rejang

A trip up the tan, churning waters of 640km-long Batang Rejang (Rejang River) – the 'Amazon of Borneo' – is one of Southeast Asia's great river journeys. Express ferries barrel through the currents, eddies and whirlpools, the pilots expertly dodging angular black boulders half-hidden in the roiling waters. Though the area is no longer the jungle-lined wilderness it was in the days before Malaysian independence, it retains a frontier, *ulu-ulu* (upriver, back-of-beyond) vibe, especially in towns and longhouses accessible only by boat.

Kapit

📞 084 / POP 16,000

The main upriver settlement on the Batang Rejang, Kapit is a bustling trading and transport centre dating back to the days of the White Rajahs. Kapit's lively markets reveal its importance as a trading hub for the surrounding longhouse communities.

👁️ Sights

Fort Sylvia MUSEUM
(Jln Kubu; ⏰ 10am-noon & 2-5pm, closed Mon & public holidays) FREE Built by Charles Brooke in 1880 to take control of the Upper Rejang, this wooden fort – built of *belian* – was renamed in 1925 to honour Ranee Sylvia, wife of Charles Vyner Brooke.

The exhibits inside offer a good introduction to the traditional lifestyles of the indigenous groups of the Batang Rejang and include evocative colonial-era photographs. Also on show is the peace jar presented during the historical 1924 peacemaking ceremony between previously warring Iban, Kayan and Kenyah groups.

Pasar Teresang MARKET
(Jln Penghulu Gerinang; ⏰ 5.30am-6pm) Some of the goods unloaded at the waterfront end up in this colourful covered market. It's a chatty, noisy hive of grass-roots commerce, with a galaxy of unfamiliar edibles that grow in the jungle, as well as handicrafts. Orang Ulu people sell fried treats and steamed buns.

🛏️ Sleeping & Eating

New Rejang Inn HOTEL $
(📞 084-796600, 084-796700; 104 Jln Teo Chow Beng; d RM98-108; ❄️📶) A welcoming and well-run hotel whose 15 spotless, good-sized rooms come with comfortable mattresses, hot water, TV, phone and minifridge. The best-value accommodation in town. A discount of RM10 on the rack rates is there for the asking.

Hiap Chiong Hotel HOTEL $
(📞 084-796314; 33 Jln Temenggong Jugah; d RM50; ❄️📶) Not much to look at from the outside,

the 15 rooms have outdated furniture but are passably clean and have tiny flat-screen TVs. Accepts cash only.

Night Market MALAYSIAN $

(Taman Selera Empurau; mains RM2.50-6; ⊙5-11pm or midnight) Delicious satay and barbecue chicken are the highlight of this night market, which has tables to eat at. Situated a block up the slope from Kapit Town Square.

ⓘ Information

Kapit has a couple of banks with ATMs.

ⓘ Getting There & Away

Express boats to Sibu (RM25 to RM35, 2½ to three hours, once or twice an hour) depart between 6.40am and 3.15pm from the **Kapit Passenger Terminal** (Jln Panglima Balang; 🛜), which has a pleasant verandah cafe with breezy river views. Purchase tickets next door inside the Petronas petrol station.

Water levels permitting (for details, call Daniel Levoh in Belaga), an express boat heads upriver to Belaga (RM55, 4½ hours) from the **Kapit Town Square jetty** (Kapit Town Sq), two blocks downriver from the Kapit Passenger Terminal, once a day at about 9.30am. Be on board by 9.15am.

Belaga

🎵 086 / POP 36,114

There's not much to do in Belaga except soak up the frontier outpost vibe, but nearby rivers are home to quite a few Kayan, Kenyah and Penan longhouses.

☞ Tours

Daniel Levoh TOURS

(🗷 013-848 6351, 086-461198; daniellevoh@hotmail.com; Jln Teh Ah Kiong) A Kayan former school headmaster, Daniel is friendly and knowledgeable. Possible excursions include walking to Sihan, a Penan settlement across the river and stopping at a waterfall (this can be done unguided at a cost of RM20 for the boat and a gift for the longhouse; Daniel will call ahead). Can also arrange private transport around Belaga and Bintulu.

🛏 Sleeping

Daniel Levoh's Guesthouse GUESTHOUSE $

(🗷 013-848 6351, 086-461198; daniellevoh@hotmail.com; Jln Teh Ah Kiong; dm RM20, d without bathroom RM40; 🛜) The four simple rooms sharing a bathroom are on the 2nd floor, opening off a large open verandah decorated with a traditional Kayan mural. Owner Daniel Levoh is happy to share stories of longhouse life. Situated two blocks behind Main Bazaar.

Belaga B&B HOTEL $

(🗷 013-842 9760; freeland205@gmail.com; Main Bazaar; with fan dm/d RM15/25, with air-con d RM35; ❄) Has seven basic rooms, some with air-con, all with shared bathroom facilities. Don't let the name fool you: breakfast isn't included. Owned by Hasbee, a former longhouse guide who now runs the eponymous **cafe** downstairs. He is happy to help arrange longhouse visits.

ⓘ Information

The town's only ATM is often out of order; bring plenty of cash.

ⓘ Getting There & Away

If the water levels at the Pelagus Rapids (32km upriver from Kapit) are high enough, you can take an express boat to Kapit (RM55, 4½ hours) departing at about 7.30am. To find out if the boat is running, call tour guide Daniel Levoh. When the river is too low, the only way to get out of Belaga is by 4WD to Bintulu.

4WD Toyota Land Cruisers link Belaga with Bintulu (RM50 to RM60 per person, RM400 for the whole vehicle, four hours) on most days, with departures from Belaga at about 7.30am and from Bintulu in the early afternoon (between noon and 2pm). If you're coming from Miri or Batu Niah Junction or heading up that way (ie northeast), you can arrange to be picked up or dropped off at Simpang Bakun (Bakun Junction), which is on the inland (old) highway 53km northeast of Bintulu and 159km southwest of Miri.

Bintulu

🎵 086 / POP 114,058

Roughly midway between Sibu and Miri (about 200km from each), the gritty port of Bintulu owes its existence to offshore gas fields. Most visitors will be planning to visit Similajau National Park or travel overland to or from Belaga.

🛏 Sleeping & Eating

Kintown Inn HOTEL $

(🗷 086-333666; 93 Jln Keppel; r RM92; ❄🛜) The carpeted rooms in this centrally located hotel, though small and rather musty, are a reasonable option for those on a budget who aren't put off by a bit of well-worn patina.

Riverfront Inn
HOTEL $$

(☑086-333111; riverfrontinn@hotmail.com; 256 Taman Sri Dagang; s/d from RM104/116; ❋❂) A long-standing favourite with business and leisure visitors alike, the Riverfront is low-key but has a touch of class. Try to get a deluxe room (RM121) overlooking the river – the view is pure Borneo.

Night Market
MALAYSIAN $

(Pasar Malam; off Jln Abang Galau; mains RM2-6; ☺4-10pm) A good place to pick up snacks, fresh fruit and Malay favourites such as satay and *nasi lemak*.

❶ Getting There & Away

AirAsia (www.airasia.com; Jln Bintulu, Bintulu Airport; ☺6am-6.30pm) and **Malaysia Airlines** (☑086-331349; www.malaysiaairlines.com; Jln Masjid; ☺9am-6pm Mon-Sat) have direct flights to Kuching and Kuala Lumpur. **MASwings** (☑086-331349; www.maswings.com. my; Bintulu airport; ☺7am-7pm) flies to Kota Kinabalu, Miri, Sibu and Kuching.

The long-distance bus station is at Medan Jaya, 5km northeast of the centre (aka Bintulu Town); a taxi costs RM20. About a dozen companies have buses approximately hourly to the following:

Kuching (RM80, 11 hours) via Sibu (RM27, four hours), from 6am to midnight.

Miri (RM27, four hours) via Niah Junction (RM20, 2¾ hours), from 6am to 9.30pm.

To arrange transport by 4WD Toyota Land Cruiser from Bintulu to Belaga (per person RM50, four hours) on some pretty rough logging roads, call Daniel Levoh. Departures are generally in the early afternoon (between noon and 2pm).

Niah National Park

Near the coast about 115km south of Miri, 31 sq km **Niah National Park** (☑085-737450, 085-737454; www.sarawakforestry.com; adult/child RM20/7; ☺park office 8am-5pm) is home to one of Borneo's gems, the Niah Caves. In addition to lots of bats and swiftlets, they shelter some of the oldest evidence of human habitation in Southeast Asia.

Across the river from park HQ, **Niah Archaeology Museum** (motor launch per person RM1, 5.30-7.30pm RM1.50; ☺9am-4.45pm Tue-Fri, 10am-4pm Sat & Sun) has informative displays on Niah's geology, ecology and prehistoric archaeology, including an original burial canoe that's at least 1200 years old.

◉ Sights

Great Cave
CAVE

(park entry fee adult/child RM20/7; ☺park office 8am-5pm) A raised boardwalk leads 3.1km (3½ to four hours return) through swampy, old-growth rainforest to the mouth of the Great Cave, a vast cavern approximately 2km long, up to 250m across and up to 60m high. Inside, the trail splits to go around a massive central pillar, but both branches finish at the same point, so it's impossible to get lost if you stick to the boardwalk. The stairs and handrails are usually covered with guano, and can be slippery.

🛏 Sleeping

Bookings for the **hostel** (Niah National Park HQ; r RM40, towel rental RM6) and **forest lodges** (Niah National Park HQ; q with fan RM100, d/q with air-con RM250/150) can be made at park headquarters or through one of the **National Park Booking Offices** (☑in Kuching 082-248088, in Miri 085-434184). Camping (RM5 per person) is permitted near the park headquarters.

Rumah Patrick Libau Homestay
HOMESTAY $

(☑Asan 014-596 2757; Niah National Park; per person incl meals RM70; ❂) The traditional,100-door Iban longhouse Rumah Patrick Libau, which is home to about 400 people, operates an informal homestay program. Accommodation is basic but the longhouse has wi-fi and 24-hour electricity. To get here, take the signposted turn off the main trail that leads to the caves. Villagers often sit at the junction selling cold drinks and souvenirs.

> ### ❶ UPRIVER TRAVEL PERMITS
>
> An outdated permit system is in place for tourists travelling from Kapit to Belaga, or up the Batang Belah. A permit for upriver travel takes just a few minutes to issue at the **Resident's Office** (☑084 796 230; www.kapit.sarawak.gov.my; 9th fl, Kompleks Kerajaan Negeri Bahagian Kapit, Jln Bleteh; ☺8am-1pm & 2-5pm Mon-Thu, 8-11.45am & 2.15-5pm Fri). Staff cannot provide information on visiting longhouses and we have yet to hear of a traveller being asked to show their permit when travelling upriver. The office is 2km west of the centre; to get there, take a minibus (RM2) from the southeast corner of Pasar Teresang.

MALAYSIA NIAH NATIONAL PARK

ℹ Getting There & Away

Niah National Park is about 115km southwest of Miri and 122km northeast of Bintulu and can be visited as a day trip from either city.

Park HQ is 15km north of **Batu Niah Junction**, a major transport hub on the inland (old) Miri–Bintulu highway. This makes getting to the park by public transport a tad tricky.

All long-haul buses linking Miri's **Pujut Bus Terminal** (p470) with Bintulu, Sibu and Kuching stop at Batu Niah Junction, but the only way to get from the junction to the park is to hire an unofficial taxi. The price should be RM30 to RM40, but you'll have to nose around the junction to find one. A good place to check: the bench in front of Shen Yang Trading, at the corner of Ngu's Garden Food Court. National park staff (or, after hours, park security personnel) can help arrange a car back to the junction.

From Miri, a taxi to Niah costs RM160 one-way or RM250 return, including waiting time.

Lambir Hills National Park

The 69-sq-km **Lambir Hills National Park** (☑ 085-471609; www.sarawakforestry.com; Jln Miri-Bintulu; adult/child RM20/7; ⊙ 8am-5pm, last entry 4pm) shelters dozens of jungle waterfalls, plenty of cool pools where you can take a dip, and a network of walking trails through mixed dipterocarp and *kerangas* forests. A perennial favourite among locals and an important centre of scientific research, Lambir Hills makes a great day or overnight trip out of Miri.

🛏 Sleeping & Eating

The park's accommodation is in reasonably comfortable, two-room **cabins** (☑ 085-471609; https://ebooking.sarawak.gov.my; Jln Miri-Bintulu; r with fan & share bathroom RM50, r with air-con & private bathroom RM100). **Camping** (☑ 085-471609; https://ebooking.sarawak.gov.my; Jln Miri-Bintulu; per person RM5) is permitted near the park HQ. Cabins are sometimes booked out at weekends and during school holidays. If you get in before 2pm (check-in time), bags can be left at the camp office.

A small **canteen** (Jln Miri-Bintulu; mains RM4-6; ⊙ 8am-5pm) serves fried rice and noodles. Cooking facilities are not available but you can rent an electric kettle (RM5) to boil water for instant noodles.

ℹ Getting There & Away

Park HQ is 32km south of Miri on the inland (old) highway to Bintulu.

All the buses that link Miri's Pujut Bus Terminal with Bintulu, Sibu and Kuching pass by here (RM10 from Miri) – just ask the driver to stop. There is a bus stand on the main road by the turn-off for the park, from where you can flag down a bus to Miri for the return journey.

A taxi from Miri costs RM50 one-way (RM100 to RM120 return, including two hours of wait time).

Miri

☑ 085 / POP 358,020

Miri, Sarawak's second city, is a thriving oil town that is vibrant and modern. Thanks to the offshore oil there's plenty of service industries and money sloshing around, so the eating is good, the broad avenues are brightly lit, and there's plenty to do when it's raining.

Miri serves as a major transport hub, so if you're travelling to/from Brunei, Sabah, the Kelabit Highlands or the national parks of Gunung Mulu, Niah or Lambir Hills, chances are you'll pass this way.

⊙ Sights

Miri City Fan   PARK
(Jln Kipas; ⊙ 24hr) An attractive open, landscaped park with Chinese- and Malay-style gardens and ponds that is a popular spot for walking and jogging. The complex also comprises a **library**, an **indoor stadium** and an Olympic-sized public **swimming pool** (RM1).

🛏 Sleeping

★**Dillenia Guesthouse**   GUESTHOUSE $
(☑ 085-434204; www.sites.google.com/site/dilleniaguesthouse; 1st fl, 846 Jln Sida; dm/s/d/f incl breakfast, with shared bathroom RM30/50/80/110; ❄@⋒) This welcoming hostel, with 11 rooms and lots of sweet touches like plants in the bathroom, lives up to its motto, 'a home away from home'. Incredibly helpful Mrs Lee, whose beautiful embroidered quilts adorn the walls, is an artesian well of travel information and tips – and even sells leech socks (RM20).

Coco House   GUESTHOUSE $
(☑ 085-417051; www.cocohouse.com.my; Lot 2117 Block 9, Jln Miri Pujut; incl breakfast dm/s/d RM30/55/90; ❄@⋒) Coco House has bright, modern dorms with pod-like bunks and

private rooms that are small but functional with splashes of colour. The spotless bathrooms have rainwater shower heads and there is a comfy common area with books, board games, DVDs and a microwave for heating food. There is a barbecue on the roof terrace for communal feasts.

My Homestay
GUESTHOUSE $

(☑085-429091; http://staymyhomestay.blogspot.com; Lot 1091, Jln Merpati; dm incl breakfast RM35, d RM55-60; ✴@☎) A friendly place in a good location, it has a spacious balcony with comfy chairs overlooking the bustling street below. Most rooms, though clean and colourful, are windowless and a little stuffy. Prices are higher at weekends.

Next Room Guesthouse
GUESTHOUSE $

(☑085-411422, 085-322090; 1st & 2nd fl, Lot 637, Jln North Yu Seng; incl breakfast dm per person RM32, d with shared bathroom RM60-65, with bathroom RM85-95; ✴@☎) In the heart of Miri's dining and drinking district, this cosy establishment offers 13 rooms, a small kitchen, a DVD lounge and a great rooftop sundeck. Dorm rooms are pretty packed, with 10 beds. Light sleepers be warned: the nightclub across the street pumps out music until 2am. Prices are higher on weekends.

✗ Eating

★ Madli's Restaurant
MALAYSIAN $

(☑085-426615; www.madli.net; Lot 1088 ground fl, Block 9, Jln Merpati; mains RM6-24; ◷8am-midnight Sun-Thu, 8am-1am Fri & Sat; ✴) A long-running family business that started off as a satay stall in the 1970s; read the history on the wall above the kitchen. Madli's is open on two sides for ventilation and is spotlessly clean. As well as lip-smackingly good chicken-fillet and Australian-beef satay (RM1.30 per stick), the menu includes Malaysian dishes like *nasi lemak* and *kampung* fried rice.

Summit Café
MALAYSIAN $

(☑019-885 3920; Lot 1245, Centre Point Commercial Centre, Jln Melayu; meals RM7-15; ◷7am-4pm Mon-Sat; ✐) If you've never tried Kelabit cuisine, this place will open up whole new worlds for your tastebuds. Queue up and choose from the colourful array of 'jungle food' laid out at the counter, including *dure* (fried jungle leaf), minced tapioca leaves, and *labo senutuk* (wild boar). The best selection is available before 11.30am – once the food runs out, it closes.

Miri Central Market
HAWKER $

(Pasar Pusat Miri; Jln Brooke; mains RM2-6; ◷24hr, most stalls 6am-noon) Of the Chinese food purveyors selling *kari ayam* (chicken curry), porridge and the usual rice and noodle dishes, stall 6 (open 3.30am to 10am) is particularly popular. Stall 20 serves up vegetarian fare.

★ Ming Cafe
INTERNATIONAL $$

(☑085-422797; cnr Jln North Yu Seng & Jln Merbau; mains RM5-40; ◷10am-2pm) This very popular cafe-bar serves excellent food in

MALAYSIA MIRI

ⓘ GETTING TO BRUNEI: MIRI TO BANDAR SERI BEGAWAN

Getting to the border The only company that's allowed to take passengers from Miri's Pujut Bus Terminal to destinations inside Brunei is **PHLS Express** (☑in Brunei +673 277 1668, in Miri 085-438301; Pujut Bus Terminal), which sends buses to BSB (RM70, three hours) via Kuala Belait (RM52) and Seria (RM52) at 8.15am and 3.45pm. Tickets are sold at the Bintang Jaya counter. Another option for travel between BSB and Miri is a private transfer (which may be shared with other travellers) run by Mr Ah Pau (RM70 per person, three hours). Call Ah Pau on 016-8072893 (Malaysian mobile) or 866 8109 (Brunei mobile). Departures from Miri are generally at 9am or 10am but may be earlier; departures from BSB to Miri are usually at 1pm or 2pm.

At the border Border formalities are usually quick, and for most nationalities Bruneian visas are free, but the process can slow down buses. If you're eventually headed overland to Sabah, make sure you have enough pages in your passport for 10 new chops (stamps).

Moving on Brunei's Serasa Ferry Terminal, 20km northeast of BSB, is linked by ferry with Pulau Labuan, from where boats go to Kota Kinabalu in Sabah. Several buses a day go from BSB to Sarawak's Limbang Division and destinations in Sabah.

For information on making this crossing in reverse see p65.

a relaxed casual, open-sided restaurant. There is an indoor air-conditioned section but the pot plants and fans keep the outdoor section comfortable and a great place to socialise. The menu features Chinese, Malay, pizzas (from RM19) and burgers (RM6 to RM40), plus particularly good Indian fare.

ⓘ Information

ATMs can be found at the airport and all over the city centre.

Miri City Medical Centre (☑ 085-426622; 916-920 Jln Hokkien; ☺ emergency 24hr) Has an ambulance service, a 24-hour accident-and-emergency department and various private clinics. Located in the city centre.

National Park Booking Office (☑ 085-434184; www.sarawakforestry.com; 452 Jln Melayu; ☺ 8am-5pm Mon-Fri) Inside the Visitors Information Centre. Has details on Sarawak's national parks and can book beds and rooms at Niah, Lambir Hills and Similajau (but not Gunung Mulu).

Visitors Information Centre (☑ 085-434181; www.sarawaktourism.com; 452 Jln Melayu; ☺ 8am-5pm Mon-Fri, 9am-3pm Sat, Sun & public holidays) The helpful staff can provide city maps and information on accommodation in and around Miri, including the national parks.

ⓘ Getting There & Away

Miri is 212km northeast of Bintulu and 36km southwest of the Brunei border.

AIR

Miri's **airport** (www.miriairport.com; Jln Airport) is 10km south of the town centre and is served by **AirAsia** (☑ 600 85 8888; www.airasia.com; ground fl, Miri Airport; ☺ 7.30am-8.30pm), **Malaysia Airlines** (☑ 085-414155; www.malaysiaairlines.com; Lot No 10635 Airport Commercial Centre, Jln Airport) and **MASwings** (☑ 085-423500; www.maswings.com.my; ground fl, Miri Airport; ☺ 6am-9pm).

There is a separate check-in area for MASwings 'Rural Air Service' which includes flights to Bario. If you are flying on a Twin Otter plane you'll be asked to weigh yourself on giant scales while holding your carry-on.

BUS

Long-distance buses use the **Pujut Bus Terminal** (Jln Miri Bypass), about 4km northeast of the centre.

About once an hour, buses head to Kuching (RM80 to RM90, 12 to 14 hours, departures from 7.15am to 8.30pm) via the inland (old) Miri–Bintulu highway, with stops at Lambir Hills

National Park, Batu Niah Junction (access point for Niah National Park; RM12, 1½ hours), Bintulu (RM27, 3½ hours) and Sibu (RM50, seven to eight hours). This route is highly competitive, and the spacious 'VIP' buses are worth the extra spend. Companies include **Bintang Jaya** (☑ Kuching 082-531133, Miri 085-432178; www.bintangjayaexpress.com) and **Miri Transport Company** (MTC; ☑ in Kuching 082-531161, in Miri 085-434161; www.mtcmiri.com; Pujut Bus Terminal).

Bintang Jaya also has services northeast to Limbang (RM45, four hours), Lawas (RM75, six hours) and Kota Kinabalu (KK; RM90, 10 hours). Buses leave Miri at 8.30am; departures from KK are at 7.30am. Borneo Express serves the same destinations at 7.45am; departures from KK are also at 7.45am. With both these companies, getting off in Brunei is not allowed.

Gunung Mulu National Park

Few national parks anywhere in the world pack so many natural marvels into such a small area. From caves of mind-boggling proportions to other-worldly geological phenomena such as the Pinnacles to brilliant old-growth rainforest, 529 sq km **Gunung Mulu National Park** (Gunung Mulu World Heritage Area; ☑ 085-792300; www.mulupark.com; Gunung Mulu National Park; 5-day pass adult/child RM30/10; ☺ HQ office 8am-5pm) is truly one of our planet's wonders.

ⓞ Sights & Activities

When you register at park HQ, you will receive a map of the park to help you plan your activities. HQ staff are generally helpful in planning itineraries and accommodating special interests.

The park's website and the brochures available at HQ have details of the tours and activities available. Note that some cave tours and treks may be booked out well in advance.

Mulu's 'show caves' (the park's name for caves that can be visited without specialised training or equipment) are its most popular attraction and for good reason: they are, quite simply, awesome. Cave routes that require special eqpment

All of the caves and some of the rainforest hikes require a certified guide. Advance reservations are a must, especially if you've got your heart set on adventure caving, or on hiking to the Pinnacles or the summit of Gunung Mulu. July, August and September are the park's busiest months, but even then spots do open up if you're able to hang out at the park for a few days. Tour agencies charge more than the park itself, but may be able to find a guide on short notice.

Deer Cave & Lang Cave
CAVE

(Gunung Mulu National Park; per person RM35; ⊙2pm & 2.30pm) A 3km walk through the rainforest takes you to these adjacent caverns. The Deer Cave – over 2km in length and 174m high – is the world's largest cave passage open to the public, while the Lang Cave – more understated in its proportions – contains interesting stalactites and stalagmites. Be sure to stay on for the 'bat exodus' at dusk.

Wind Cave & Clearwater Cave
CAVE

(Gunung Mulu National Park; per person incl boat ride RM65; ⊙8.45am & 9.15am) Zipping along a jungle river in a longboat on your way to the caves is not a bad way to start the day. The Wind Cave, named for the cool breezes blowing through it, has several chambers, including the cathedral-like King's Chamber, filled with dreamlike forests of stalagmites and columns. There is a sweaty 200-step climb up to Clearwater Cave and the subterranean river there. The cave itself is vast: more than 200km of passages have been surveyed so far.

Mulu Canopy Skywalk
WALKING

(Gunung Mulu National Park; per person RM45; ⊙7am, 8.30am, 10am, 10.30am, 1pm & 2pm) Mulu's 480m-long skywalk, unforgettably anchored to a series of huge trees, has excellent signage and is one of the best in Southeast Asia. Often gets booked out early – for a specific time slot, reserve as soon as you've got your flight.

Pinnacles
TREKKING

(Gunung Mulu National Park; per person RM415; ⊙Tue-Thu & Fri-Sun) The Pinnacles are an incredible formation of 45m-high stone spires protruding from the forested flanks of Gunung Api. Getting there involves a boat ride and, in between two overnights at Camp 5 (⊉park HQ 085-792300; www.mulupark.com; Gunung Mulu National Park; per person incl boat ride RM200), an unrelentingly steep 2.4km ascent. Coming down is just as taxing, so by the time you stagger back to camp, the cool, clear river may look pretty enticing.

Gunung Mulu Summit
TREKKING

(Gunung Mulu National Park; per person RM650, 3-8 people) The climb to the summit of Gunung Mulu (2376m) – described by one satisfied ascendee as 'gruelling' and, near the top, 'treacherous' – is a classic Borneo adventure. If you're very fit and looking for a challenge, this 24km, three-day, four-night trek may be for you. The climb must be booked at least one month in advance.

Headhunters' Trail
TREKKING

(Gunung Mulu National Park) The physically undemanding Headhunters' Trail continues on from Camp 5 (p471) for 11km in the direction of Limbang and is an overland alternative to flying in or out of Mulu. The park does not offer guided trips along this trail, but several private tour operators do, and it is also (theoretically) possible to do it without a guide.

🛏 Sleeping

Options at park headquarters – a truly lovely spot – include a **hostel** (⊉085-792300; www.mulupark.com; dm incl breakfast RM55) that has 20 beds in a clean, spacious dormitory-style room (lockers available), as well as **longhouse rooms** (⊉085-792300; www.mulupark.com; s/d/tr/q incl breakfast RM221/260/293/331; ❄), **rainforest lodge** (⊉085-792300; www.mulupark.com; s/d incl breakfast RM268/312; ❄) and **garden bungalows** (⊉085-792300; www.mulupark.com; s/d/tr incl breakfast RM253/294/341; ❄🕏). Several budget places, unaffiliated with the park, can be found across the bridge from park headquarters, along the banks of Sungai Melinau. There are plenty of beds, so if you don't mind very basic digs, you can fly up without worrying about room availability.

Mulu Backpackers
GUESTHOUSE $

(⊉Helen 012-871 2947, Peter 013-846 7250; mulu backpackers@gmail.com; dm/d incl breakfast RM35/80) Mulu Backpackers, situated just past the airport, occupies a picturesque spot by the river but is a 15-minute walk from the park. There is a pleasant sheltered outdoor dining area with views of the water and electricity from 6pm to 6am. The 11 beds here are arranged in a large, barn-like space with some randomly positioned partition walls.

D'Cave Homestay
HOMESTAY $

(☑ Dina 012-872 9752; beckhamjunior40@yahoo. com; incl breakfast dm RM30, d without bathroom RM80) A very friendly, rather ramshackle place with beds crammed into small rooms and basic, outdoor bathrooms. Owner Dina cooks buffet-style lunches (RM15) and dinners (RM18), and partner Robert is a licensed guide. There's always boiled water for water-bottle refills. Situated between the airport and the turning for the park – about a 10-minute walk from each.

Mulu River Lodge
HOSTEL $

(Edward Nyipa Homestay; ☑ 012-852 7471; dm/d/q incl breakfast RM35/70/140) Has 30 beds, most in a giant, non-bunk dorm room equipped with clean showers and toilets at one end. Electricity flows from 5pm to midnight. One of the few guesthouses outside the park, if not the only one, with a proper septic system. Just a two-minute walk from park HQ, its kitchen supplies simple meals and beer.

✖ Eating

Café Mulu
INTERNATIONAL $$

(mains RM12-21; ⊙ 7.30am-8.30pm) This cafe-restaurant serves excellent breakfasts (eggs, pancakes, muesli) and a varied lunch and dinner menu with a few Western items, Indian curries and local dishes including Mulu laksa and *umai* (Sarawak sushi). A beer costs RM13 and wine is available. Staff are happy to prepare packed lunches.

Good Luck Cave'fe Mulu
MALAYSIAN $

(mains RM8-10; ⊙ 11.30am-3pm & 5pm-midnight, kitchen closes at 9.15pm) The Good Luck 'Cave'fe' Mulu (geddit?) is located right outside the park gates and stays open later than the park cafe, making it a good dinner option if you come back late from a night walk. Serves the usual noodle and fried-rice dishes. A beer costs RM9. Also good for transport to the airport (RM5).

ℹ Information

For sums over RM100, the park accepts Visa and MasterCard. Staff can also do cash withdrawals of RM100 to RM300 (one transaction per day) for a 2% fee, but this depends on the available cash in the financial department, so try to bring enough cash to cover your expenses (there is no ATM in Mulu).

The shop and cafe area at park HQ has an excruciatingly slow and unreliable wi-fi connection (RM5 per day).

ℹ Getting There & Away

Unless you hike in via the Headhunters' Trail, the only way to get to Mulu is by **MASwings** (☑ 085-206900; www.maswings.com.my; ground fl, Mulu Airport; ⊙ 8.30am-5pm) plane.

MASwings flies 68-seat ATR 72-500 turboprops to Miri (daily at 10.15am and 2.40pm), Kuching (Monday, Wednesday, Thursday and Saturday at 1.40pm; Tuesday, Friday and Sunday at 2.15pm) and Kota Kinabalu (daily except Friday at 2.40pm via Miri; Sunday, Tuesday and Friday at 12.25pm).

Park HQ is a walkable 1.5km from the airport. Minibuses and SUVs run by **Melinau Transportation** (☑ 012-852 6065, 012-871 1372; RM5 per person) and other companies meet incoming flights at the airport; transport to park HQ and the adjacent guesthouses costs RM5 per person.

Kelabit Highlands

Nestled in Sarawak's remote northeastern corner, the mountains and rainforests of the Kelabit (keh-*lah*-bit) Highlands are sandwiched between Gunung Mulu National Park and the Indonesian state of East Kalimantan. The area is home to the Kelabits, an Orang Ulu group, and the semi-nomadic Penan. The main activity here is hiking from longhouse to longhouse on old forest trails to meet the locals.

Bario

POP 1200

The 'capital' of the highlands, Bario consists of about a dozen 'villages' spread over a beautiful valley, much of it given over to rice growing. Some of the appeal lies in the mountain climate (the valley is 1500m above sea level) and splendid isolation (the only access is by air and torturous 4WD track), but above all it's the unforced hospitality of the Kelabit people that will quickly win you over.

◉ Sights & Activities

The area around Bario offers plenty of opportunities for jungle exploration even if you're not a hardcore hiker. The nearby forests are a great place to spot pitcher plants, butterflies and even hornbills – and are an excellent venue for tiger leeches to spot you. Most guesthouses are happy to pack picnic lunches. The cost of a local guide is RM150 per day.

Bario Asal Longhouse   HOUSE

(RM5) This all-wood, 22-door longhouse has the traditional Kelabit layout. On the *dapur* (enclosed front verandah) each family has a hearth, while on the other side of the family units is the *tawa'*, a wide back verandah – essentially an enclosed hall over 100m long – used for weddings, funerals and celebrations and decorated with historic family photos.

Pa' Umor Megaliths   HISTORIC SITE

From Bario it's a 1½-hour walk to Pa' Umor, and another 15 minutes to Arur Bilit Farm, home to **Batu Narit**, an impressive stone carving featuring a human in a spread-eagled position among its designs.

Take the log bridge across the small river to reach **Batu Ipak**. According to legend, this stone formation was created when an angry warrior named Upai Semering pulled out his *parang* (machete) and took a wrathful swing at the rock, cutting it in two.

Prayer Mountain   HIKING

From the Bario Asal Longhouse, it's a steep, slippery ascent (two hours) up to the summit of Prayer Mountain, which has a cross that was erected in 1973, thickets of pitcher plants and amazing views of the Bario Valley and of the mixed Penan and Kelabit hamlet of Arur Dalan, with its three defunct wind turbines. Two-thirds of the way up is an extremely rustic church.

🛏 Sleeping & Eating

Bario's various component villages are home to 19 guesthouses. Almost all rooms have shared bathroom facilities. There is usually no need to book ahead – available rooms outstrip the space available on flights, and guesthouse owners meet incoming flights at the airport.

Most guesthouses offer full board – almost always tasty local cuisine – but Bario also has several modest eateries.

Libal Paradise   GUESTHOUSE $

(📞019-807 1640; roachas@hotmail.com; per person incl all meals RM85) 🍃 Surrounded by a verdant fruit and vegetable garden where you can pick your own pineapples, this sustainably run farm offers accommodation in two neat wooden cabins, each occupying its own idyllic spot in the greenery. From the airport terminal, walk eastward along the road that parallels the runway. Management prefers text messaging to email for contact.

Junglebluesdream   GUESTHOUSE $

(📞019-884 9892; www.junglebluesdream.weebly.com; Ulung Palang Longhouse, Bario; per person incl meals RM100) Owned by artist and one-time guide Stephen Baya, a Bario native, and his friendly Danish wife Tine, this super-welcoming lodge (and art gallery) has four mural-decorated rooms, good-quality beds and quilts, a library of books on local culture and wildlife, and fantastic Kelabit food. Guests can consult Stephen's extraordinary hand-drawn town and trekking maps. Airport pickup is free.

Bario Asal Longhouse   HOMESTAY $

(📞 Julian 011-2508 1114; http://rangshomestay-handicraft.blogspot.com.au; per person incl meals RM90) There are various homestays in this traditional longhouse, including a six-room guesthouse at **Sinah Rang Lemulun**. Staying at Bario Asal – which is home to 22 families – is a great way to experience longhouse living. Also available here are various 'farmstay' packages offering different rural experiences. Transport from the airport costs RM35.

ℹ Information

At research time there were no banks, ATMs or credit-card facilities in the Kelabit Highlands, so bring plenty of small-denomination banknotes for accommodation, food and guides, plus some extra in case you get stranded.

The airport has free wi-fi and there's's internet access at the **Bario Telecentre** (www.unimas.my/ebario; Gatuman Bario; per hr RM4; ⊙ 9.30-11.30am & 2-4pm, closed Sat afternoon & Sun). The best Malaysian mobile-phone company to have up here is Celcom.

ℹ Getting There & Away

Bario Airport (📞 013-835 9009; 🛜) is linked with Miri twice a day by Twin Otters, operated by **MASwings** (📞1300-88 3000; www.maswings.com.my). Weather, especially high winds, can sometimes cause delays and cancellations. Checked baggage is limited to 10kg, hand luggage to 5kg and passengers themselves are weighed on a giant scale, along with their hand luggage when they check in.

The airport is about a 30-minute walk south of the shop-houses, but you're bound to be offered a lift on arrival.

The overland trip between Bario and Miri, possible only by 4WD (per person RM150), takes 12 hours at the very least and sometimes a lot more.

UNDERSTAND MALAYSIA

Malaysia Today

National tragedies and political troubles have impacted Malaysia in recent years. Passenger airplanes have fallen from the sky and an earthquake struck Sabah killing 18 people. For several years, former Prime Minister Najib Razak battled allegations of corruption and a faltering economy. The 2018 general election flipped Malaysian politics on its head when the Barisan Nasional party (BN; National Front) lost to the opposition party led by Dr. Mahathir Mohamad. The oldest prime minister in the world, 92-year-old Mahathir took his seat as head of government for his second tenure. Anwar Ibrahim, a Malaysian politician jailed twice, first by former nemesis Mahathir then again by former Prime Minister Najib, is expected to succeed Mahathir within two years, having received a royal pardon by the king for his alleged crimes.

History

Early Influences

The earliest evidence of human life in the region is a 40,000-year-old skull found in Sarawak's Niah Caves. But it was only around 10,000 years ago that the aboriginal Malays, the Orang Asli, began moving down the peninsula from a probable starting point in southwestern China.

By the 2nd century AD Europeans were familiar with Malaya, and Indian traders had made regular visits in their search for gold, tin and jungle woods. Within the next century Malaya was ruled by the Funan empire, centred in what's now Cambodia, but more significant was the domination of the Sumatra-based Srivijayan empire between the 7th and 13th centuries.

In 1405 Chinese admiral Cheng Ho arrived in Melaka with promises to the locals of protection from the Siamese encroaching from the north. With Chinese support, the power of Melaka extended to include most of the Malay Peninsula. Islam arrived in Melaka around this time and soon spread through Malaya.

European Influence

Melaka's wealth and prosperity attracted European interest and it was taken over by the Portuguese in 1511, then the Dutch in 1641 and the British in 1795.

In 1838 James Brooke, a British adventurer, arrived to find the Brunei sultanate fending off rebellion from inland tribes. Brooke quashed the rebellion and in reward was granted power over part of Sarawak. Appointing himself Raja Brooke, he founded a dynasty that lasted 100 years. By 1881 Sabah was controlled by the British government, which eventually acquired Sarawak after WWII when the third Raja Brooke realised he couldn't afford the area's upkeep. In the early 20th century the British brought in Chinese and Indians, which radically changed the country's racial make-up.

Independence to the Current Day

Malaya achieved *merdeka* (independence) in 1957, but it was followed by a period of instability due to an internal Communist uprising and an external confrontation with neighbouring Indonesia. In 1963 the north Borneo states of Sabah and Sarawak, along with Singapore, joined Malaya to create Malaysia.

The results of the 1969 election were used as a pretext for the subsequent violent interracial riots across the country, but particularly in Kuala Lumpur, where hundreds of people were killed. In the aftermath the government moved to dissipate the tensions, which existed mainly between the Malays and the Chinese.

In 1973 Barisan Nasional (BN; National Front), a coalition of right-wing and centre parties, was formed – it has ruled Malaysia ever since. Under outspoken, dictatorial Prime Minister Dr Mahathir Mohamad, Malaysia's economy grew at a rate of over 8% per year until mid-1997, when the whole of Southeast Asia plunged into recession. In October 2003 Dr Mahathir Mohamad retired, handing power to Abdullah Badawi, who won the general election in March 2004.

In the next election in 2008, BN saw its parliamentary dominance slashed. The inroads were made by Pakatan Rakyat (PR), the opposition People's Alliance, later dismantled and succeeded by the Pakatan Harapan (PH), led by Anwar Ibrahim, a former deputy PM who had been jailed on corruption and sodomy charges that were widely regarded as politically motivated. Abdullah Badawi resigned in favour of Najib Razak, who would go on to win the 2013 election for BN, although it was the coalition's poorest showing in the polls since 1969.

In 2014 Malaysian Airlines lost two of its passenger aeroplanes in tragic circumstances, with a combined death toll of 537. An earthquake struck Sabah on 5 June 2015 and claimed the lives of 18 people on Mt Kinabalu, shutting down the mountain to tourists for months.

People & Culture

Lifestyle

The *kampung* (village) is at the heart of the Malay world and operates according to a system of *adat* (customary law) that emphasises collective rather than individual responsibility. Devout worship of Islam and older spiritual beliefs go hand in hand with this precept. However, despite the mutually supportive nature of the *kampung* environment, and growing Westernisation across Malaysia, some very conservative interpretations of Islam continue in certain areas, particularly along the peninsula's east coast.

Population

Malaysians come from a number of different ethnic groups: Malays, Chinese, Indians, the indigenous Orang Asli (literally, 'Original People') of the peninsula, and the various tribes of Sarawak and Sabah in Malaysian Borneo. The mixing of these groups has created the colourful cultures and delicious cuisine that makes Malaysia such a fabulous destination.

It's reasonable to generalise that the Malays control the government while the Chinese dominate the economy. Approximately 85% of the country's population of 32 million people lives in Peninsular Malaysia and the other 15% in Sabah and Sarawak on Borneo.

There are still small, scattered groups of Orang Asli in Peninsular Malaysia. Although most of these people have given up their nomadic or shifting-agriculture techniques and have been absorbed into modern Malay society, a few such groups still live in the forests.

Dayak is the term used for the non-Muslim people of Borneo. It is estimated there are more than 200 Dayak tribes in Borneo, including the Iban and Bidayuh in Sarawak and the Kadazan in Sabah. Smaller groups include the Kenyah, Kayan and Penan, whose way of life and traditional lands are rapidly disappearing.

Religion

Malays are almost all Muslims. But despite Islam being the state religion, freedom of religion is guaranteed. The Chinese are predominantly followers of Taoism and Buddhism, though some are Christians. The majority of the region's Indian population comes from the south of India and are Hindu and Christian, although a sizeable percentage are Muslim.

While Christianity has made no great inroads into Peninsular Malaysia, it has had a much greater impact in Malaysian Borneo, where many indigenous people have converted and carry Christian as well as traditional names. Others still follow animist traditions.

THE PERANAKANS

One of Malaysia's most celebrated cultures is that of the Peranakans, descendants of Chinese immigrants who, from the 16th century onwards, settled in Singapore, Melaka and Penang. While these arrivals often married Malay women, others imported their wives from China; all of them like to refer to themselves as Straits-born or Straits Chinese to distinguish themselves from later arrivals from China. Another name you may hear for these people is Baba-Nonyas, after the Peranakan words for males (*baba*) and females (*nonya*).

The Peranakans took the religion of the Chinese, but the customs, language and dress of the Malays. The Peranakans were often wealthy traders who could afford to indulge their passion for sumptuous furnishings, jewellery and brocades. Today they are most famous for their delicious fusion cooking that's best experienced in Melaka and Penang.

Arts

It's along the predominantly Malay east coast of Peninsular Malaysia that you'll find Malay arts and crafts, culture and games at their liveliest. Malaysian Borneo is replete with the arts and crafts of the country's indigenous peoples.

ARTS & CRAFTS

A famous Malaysian Bornean art is *pua kumbu,* a colourful weaving technique used to produce both everyday and ceremonial items.

The most skilled woodcarvers are generally held to be the Kenyah and Kayan peoples, who used to carve enormous, finely detailed *kelirieng* (burial columns) from tree trunks.

Originally an Indonesian craft, the production of batik cloth is popular in Malaysia and has its home in Kelantan. A speciality of Kelantan and Terengganu, *kain songket* is a handwoven fabric with gold and silver threads through the material. *Mengkuang* is a far more prosaic form of weaving using pandanus leaves and strips of bamboo to make baskets, bags and mats.

DANCE

Menora is a dance-drama of Thai origin performed by an all-male cast in grotesque masks; *mak yong* is the female version. The upbeat *joget* (better known around Melaka as *chakuncha*) is Malaysia's most popular traditional dance, often performed at Malay weddings by professional dancers.

Rebana kercing is a dance performed by young men to the accompaniment of tambourines. The *rodat* is a dance from Terengganu and is accompanied by the *tar* drum.

MUSIC

Traditional Malay music is based largely on the *gendang* (drum), of which there are more than a dozen types. Other percussion instruments include the gong, *cerucap* (made of shells), *raurau* (coconut shells), *kertuk* and *pertuang* (both made from bamboo), and the wooden *celampang.*

Wind instruments include a number of types of flute (such as the *seruling* and *serunai*) and the trumpetlike *nafiri,* while stringed instruments include the *biola, gambus* and *sundatang.*

The *gamelan,* a traditional Indonesian gong-orchestra, is also found in the state of Kelantan, where a typical ensemble will comprise four different gongs, two xylophones and a large drum.

Food & Drink

Food

The delicious food you'll enjoy in Malaysia strongly reflects the country's Malay, Chinese and Indian influences.

There are fewer culinary choices outside the cities, where staple meals of *mee goreng* (fried noodles) and *nasi goreng* (fried rice) predominate. Vegetarian dishes are usually available at both Malay and Indian cafes, but are hardly sighted at *kedai kopi* (coffee shops). You can also find an excellent selection of fruit and vegetables at markets.

Roti canai (flaky flat bread dipped in a small amount of dhal and potato curry) is probably the cheapest meal (around RM1.50). But really everything, from seafood laksa to the freshly caught and cooked wild cat or mouse deer you may be offered at a longhouse, is good and often cheap.

Halfway between a drink and a dessert is *ais kacang,* something similar to an old-fashioned snow-cone, except that the shaved ice is topped with syrups and condensed milk, and it's all piled on top of a foundation of beans and jellies (sometimes corn kernels). It tastes terrific.

Drink

Tap water is safe to drink in many big cities, but check with locals if you're unsure.

With the aid of a blender and crushed ice, simple and delicious juice concoctions are whipped up in seconds. Lurid soybean drinks are sold at street stalls and soybean milk is also available in soft-drink bottles. Medicinal teas are a big hit with the health-conscious Chinese.

A mug of beer at a *kedai kopi* will cost around RM7, and around RM15 at bars and clubs. Anchor and Tiger beers are popular, as

---

TRAVEL HINTS

➡ Malaysia is a Muslim country, so dress appropriately by covering everything to the knees and over the shoulders.

➡ Airfares can be so cheap around Borneo that flying is sometimes cheaper than bussing.

are locally brewed Carlsberg and Guinness. Indigenous people have a soft spot for *tuak* (rice wine), which tends to revolt first-timers but is apparently an acquired taste. Another rural favourite is the dark-coloured spirit *arak*, which is smooth and potent.

Environment

The Land

Malaysia covers 329,874 sq km and consists of two distinct regions. Peninsular Malaysia is the long finger of land extending south from Asia and though the mountainous northern half has some dense jungle coverage, unprotected forests are getting cut down at an alarming rate, mostly to create oil palm plantations. The peninsula's western side has a large fertile plain running to the sea, while the eastern side is fringed with sandy beaches. Malaysian Borneo consists of Sarawak and Sabah; both states are covered in thick jungle and have extensive river systems. Sabah is crowned by Mt Kinabalu (4095m), the highest mountain between the Himalaya and New Guinea.

Wildlife

Malaysia's ancient rainforests are endowed with a cornucopia of life forms. In Peninsular Malaysia alone there are over 8000 species of flowering plants, including the world's tallest tropical tree species, the *tualang*. In Malaysian Borneo, where hundreds of new species have been discovered since the 1990s, you'll find the world's largest flower, the *Rafflesia,* measuring up to 1m across, as well as the world's biggest cockroach. Mammals include elephants, tapirs, tigers, leopards, honey bears, *tempadau* (forest cattle), pangolins (scaly anteaters) and monkeys, gibbons and apes (including, in Borneo, the proboscis monkey and orangutans). Colourful bird species include kingfishers, sunbirds, woodpeckers, barbets, spectacular pheasants and sacred hornbills. Snakes include cobras, vipers and pythons. Of the world's seven species of turtle, four are native to Malaysia: the hawksbill, green, olive Ridley and giant leatherback.

National Parks

Malaysia's 23 national parks cover barely 5% of the country's landmass. The country's major national park is Taman Negara, on the peninsula, while Gunung Mulu and Kinabalu are the two main parks in Sarawak and Sabah, respectively. Especially on Borneo, the rarity and uniqueness of local flora and fauna is such that scientists – from dragonfly experts to palm-tree specialists – are regular visitors and vocal proponents of new parks and reserves both on land and in the surrounding waters. There are also 13 marine parks in Malaysia, notably around Pulau Perhentian, Tioman and Sipadan, although enforcement of protection measures is very loose.

Environmental Issues

There's a disparity between government figures and those of environmental groups, but it's probable that up up to 80% of Malaysia's rainforests have been logged. There have also been huge environmental consequences as vast swathes of land have been razed and planted with lucrative oil palm; Malaysia accounts for over 40% of global production of palm oil.

The crown of eco and social irresponsibility goes to Bakun Dam in Sarawak, which flooded some 690 sq km (the size of Singapore) of some of the world's most diverse rainforest in late 2010 and forced up to 10,000 indigenous peoples from their homes. The dam has been criticised as being corrupt, ill-planned and unnecessary, but the state already has plans to build more dams in the region.

SURVIVAL GUIDE

🛈 Directory A–Z

CUSTOMS REGULATIONS

The following can be brought into Malaysia duty free:
- 1L of alcohol
- 225g of tobacco (200 cigarettes or 50 cigars)
- souvenirs and gifts not exceeding RM200 (RM500 when coming from Labuan or Langkawi)

Cameras, portable radios, perfume, cosmetics and watches do not incur duty. Prohibited items include weapons (including imitations), fireworks and 'obscene and prejudicial articles' (pornography, for example, and items that may be considered inflammatory, or religiously offensive) and drugs. Drug smuggling carries the death penalty in Malaysia.

SLEEPING PRICE RANGES

The following price ranges refer to a double room with attached bathroom:

$ less than RM100

$$ RM100–RM400

$$$ more than RM400

Visitors can carry no more than the equivalent of US$10,000 in ringgit or any other currency in and out of Malaysia.

ELECTRICITY

Malaysia's electricity is 240V, 50Hz; power outlets have three flat pins.

EMBASSIES & CONSULATES

For a full list of Malaysian embassies and consulates outside the country check out www.kln. gov.my. Most foreign embassies are in Kuala Lumpur and are generally open 8am to 12.30pm and 1.30pm to 4.30pm Monday to Friday.

Australian High Commission (Map p394; 03-2146 5555; http://malaysia.highcommission.gov.au; 6 Jln Yap Kwan Seng; 8.30am-4.30pm Mon-Fri; LRT KLCC)

Canadian High Commission (03-2718 3333; www.canadainternational.gc.ca; 17th fl, Menara Tan & Tan, 207 Jln Tun Razak; 8am-noon & 1-4.30pm Mon-Thu, 8am-12.30pm Fri; LRT Ampang Park)

Dutch Embassy (03-2168 6200; www. nederlandwereldwijd.nl/landen/maleisie; 7th fl, South Block, The Amp Walk, 218 Jln Ampang; 8.30-11am Mon-Thu; LRT Ampang Park)

French Embassy (03-2053 5500; www. ambafrance-my.org; 348 Jln Tun Razak; 8.45am-1pm & 2-5.15pm Mon-Fri; LRT Ampang Park)

German Embassy (03-2170 9666; www. kuala-lumpur.diplo.de; 26th fl, Menara Tan & Tan, 207 Jln Tun Razak; 9am-noon Mon-Fri & 1-3pm Thu; LRT Ampang Park)

Irish Embassy (03-2167 8200; www.dfa.ie/ irish-embassy/malaysia; 5th fl, South Block, The Amp Walk, 218 Jln Ampang; 9.30am-12.30pm & 2.30-3.30pm Mon-Thu, 9.30am-12.30pm Fri; LRT Ampang Park)

New Zealand High Commission (Map p394; 03-2078 2533; www.nzembassy.com/mala ysia; Level 21, Menara IMC, 8 Jln Sultan Ismail; 8.30am-12.30pm Mon-Fri; Bukit Nanas)

UK High Commission (Map p394; 03-2170 2200; www.gov.uk/world/malaysia; Level 27 Menara Binjai, 2 Jln Binjai; 8am-12.30pm daily, 1.15-4.30pm Mon-Thu; LRT Ampang Park)

US Embassy (03-2168 5000; https:// my.usembassy.gov; 376 Jln Tun Razak; 7.45am-4.30pm Mon-Fri; LRT Ampang Park)

FESTIVALS & EVENTS

There are many cultures and religions coexisting in Malaysia, which means there are many occasions for celebration throughout the year.

Ramadan is the major annual Muslim event – 30 days during which Muslims cannot eat, drink, smoke or have sex from sunrise to sunset. The dates of Ramadan change every year; in 2019 it starts on 5 May and in 2020 on 23 April.

Chinese New Year (January/February) The most important celebration for the Chinese community is marked with dragon dances and street parades.

Thaipusam (January/February) One of the most dramatic Hindu festivals, in which devotees honour Lord Subramaniam with acts of amazing physical resilience. Self-mutilating worshippers make the procession from Sri Mahamariamman Temple in KL to the Batu Caves.

Malaysian Grand Prix (March/April) Formula One's big outing in Southeast Asia is held at the Sepang International Circuit in Selangor either at the end of March or early April.

Gawai Dayak (late May/early June) Festival of the Dayaks in Sarawak, marking the end of the rice season. War dances, cock fights and blowpipe events take place.

Festa de San Pedro (June) Christian celebration on 29 June in honour of the patron saint of the fishing community; notably celebrated by the Eurasian-Portuguese community of Melaka.

Dragon Boat Festival (June to August) Celebrated in Penang.

Rainforest World Music Festival (July/ August) Held for three days at the Sarawak Cultural Village, this music and arts festival features musicians from around the world and highlights indigenous music from Borneo.

National Day (Hari Kebangsaan) (August) Malaysia celebrates its independence on 31 August with events all over the country, but particularly in KL where there are parades and a variety of performances in the Lake Gardens.

Moon Cake Festival (September) Chinese festival celebrating the overthrow of Mongol warlords in ancient China with the eating of moon cakes and the lighting of colourful paper lanterns.

Festival of the Nine Emperor Gods (October) Involves nine days of Chinese operas, processions and other events honouring the nine emperor gods.

Deepavali (October/November) The Festival of Lights, in which tiny oil lamps are lit outside Hindu homes; celebrates Rama's victory over the demon King Ravana.

LGBT TRAVELLERS

Conservative political parties and religious groups make a regular habit of denouncing gays and lesbians in Malaysia, a country where it is illegal for men of any age to have sex with other men. This said, outright persecution of gays and lesbians in the country is rare. Nonetheless, while in Malaysia, gay and lesbian travellers (particularly the former) should avoid any behaviour that attracts unwanted attention.

Visit www.utopia-asia.com, which provides good coverage of gay and lesbian events and activities in the country.

INTERNET ACCESS

Malaysia is blanketed with hot spots for wi-fi connections (usually free). Internet cafes are much less common these days, but do still exist if you're not travelling with a wi-fi enabled device. Only in the jungles and the most remote reaches of the peninsula and Malaysian Borneo are you likely to be without any internet access.

LEGAL MATTERS

In any dealings with the local police it will pay to be deferential. You're most likely to come into contact with them either through reporting a crime (some of the big cities in Malaysia have tourist police stations for this purpose) or while driving. Minor misdemeanours may be overlooked, but don't count on it.

Drug trafficking carries a mandatory death penalty. A number of foreigners have been executed in Malaysia, some of them for possession of amazingly small quantities of heroin. Even possession of tiny amounts can bring down a lengthy jail sentence and a beating with the *rotan* (cane). Just don't do it.

MONEY

Bargaining is not usually required for everyday goods in Malaysia, but feel free to bargain when purchasing souvenirs, antiques and other tourist items, even when the prices are displayed. Transport prices are generally fixed, but negotiation is required for trishaws and taxis around town or for charter.

Tipping is not common in Malaysia.

OPENING HOURS

Banks 10am–3pm Monday to Friday, 9.30am–11.30am Saturday
Cafes 8am–10pm
Restaurants noon–2.30pm and 6pm–10.30pm
Shops 9.30am–7pm, malls 10am–10pm

In the more Islamic-minded states of Kedah, Perlis, Kelantan and Terengganu, government offices, banks and many shops close on Friday and on Saturday afternoon.

POST

Post offices are open from 8am to 5pm daily except Sunday and public holidays (also closed on Friday in Kedah, Kelantan and Terengganu districts).

Aerograms and postcards cost 50 sen to send to any destination, letters from RM1.20, parcels from RM20 for 1kg.

PUBLIC HOLIDAYS

In addition to national public holidays, each state has its own holidays, usually associated with the sultan's birthday or a Muslim celebration. Muslim holidays move forward 10 or 11 days each year. Hindu and Chinese holiday dates also vary, but fall roughly within the same months each year.

As well as fixed secular holidays, various religious festivals (which change dates annually) are national holidays. These include Chinese New Year (in January/February), the Hindu festival of Deepavali (in October/November), the Buddhist festival of Wesak (April/May) and the Muslim festivals of Hari Raya Haji, Hari Raya Puasa, Mawlid al-Nabi and Awal Muharram (Muslim New Year).

Fixed annual holidays include the following:
New Year's Day 1 January
Federal Territory Day 1 February (in Kuala Lumpur and Putrajaya only)
Good Friday March or April (in Sarawak & Sabah only)
Labour Day 1 May
Yang di-Pertuan Agong's (King's) Birthday 1st Saturday in June
Governor of Penang's Birthday 2nd Saturday in July (in Penang only)
National Day (Hari Kebangsaan) 31 August
Malaysia Day 16 September
Christmas Day 25 December

SAFE TRAVEL

Malaysia is generally a safe country to travel in, and compared with Indonesia or Thailand it's extremely safe.
➡ Theft and violence are not particularly common, although it pays to keep a close eye on your belongings, especially your travel

---

EATING PRICE RANGES

The following price ranges refer to a two-course meal including a soft drink.

$ less than RM15
$$ RM15–RM60
$$$ more than RM60

documents (passport, traveller's cheques etc), which should be kept with you at all times.

➡ Credit-card fraud is a growing problem. Use your cards only at established businesses and guard your credit-card numbers closely.

➡ The main thing to watch out for is animal and insect bites.

TELEPHONE

If you have arranged global roaming with your home provider, your GSM digital phone will automatically tune into one of the region's networks. If not, buy a prepaid SIM card (passport required) for one of the local networks on arrival.

The rate for local calls and text messages is around 36 sen.

There are three main mobile-phone companies, all with similar call rates and prepaid packages:

Celcom (www.celcom.com.my) This is the best company to use if you'll be spending time in remote regions of Sabah and Sarawak.

DiGi (http://new.digi.com.my)

Maxis (www.maxis.com.my)

TOILETS

Although there are still some places with Asian squat-style toilets, you'll most often find Western-style ones these days. At public facilities toilet paper is not usually provided. Instead, you will find a hose which you are supposed to use as a bidet or, in cheaper places, a bucket of water and a tap. If you're not comfortable with this, remember to take packets of tissues or toilet paper wherever you go.

TOURIST INFORMATION

Tourism Malaysia (www.tourism.gov.my) has a network of overseas offices, which are useful for pre-departure planning. Unfortunately, its domestic offices are less helpful. Nonetheless, they do stock some decent brochures as well as the excellent *Map of Malaysia*.

Within Malaysia there are also a number of state tourism-promotion organisations, which often have more detailed information about specific areas.

Sabah Tourism (www.sabahtourism.com)

Pahang Tourism (www.pahangtourism.org.my)

Perak Tourism (www.peraktourism.com.my)

Sarawak Tourism (http://sarawaktourism.com)

Penang Tourism (www.visitpenang.gov.my)

Tourism Johor (http://tourism.johor.my)

Tourism Selangor (www.tourismselangor.my)

Tourism Terengganu (http://tourism.terengganu.gov.my)

TRAVELLERS WITH DISABILITIES

For the mobility impaired, Malaysia can be a nightmare. In many cities and towns there are often no footpaths, kerbs are very high, construction sites are everywhere, and crossings are few and far between. On the upside, taxis are cheap and both Malaysia Airlines and KTM (the national rail service) offer 50% discounts on travel for travellers with disabilities.

VISAS

Visitors must have a passport valid for at least six months beyond the date of entry into Malaysia. The following gives a brief overview of other requirements – full details of visa regulations are available at www.kln.gov.my.

Depending on the expected length of their stay, most visitors are given a 30- or 60-day visa on arrival. As a general rule, if you arrive by air you will be given 60 days automatically, though coming overland you may be given 30 days unless you specifically ask for a 60-day permit. It's possible to get an extension at an immigration office in Malaysia for a total stay of up to three months.

Only under special circumstances can Israeli citizens enter Malaysia.

Both Sabah and Sarawak retain a certain degree of state-level control of their borders. Tourists must go through passport control and have their passports stamped whenever they:

➡ arrive in Sabah or Sarawak from Peninsular Malaysia or the federal district of Pulau Labuan;

➡ exit Sabah or Sarawak on their way to Peninsular Malaysia or Pulau Labuan;

➡ travel between Sabah and Sarawak.

When entering Sabah or Sarawak from another part of Malaysia, your new visa stamp will be valid only for the remainder of the period left on your original Malaysian visa. In Sarawak, an easy way to extend your visa is to make a 'visa run' to Brunei or Indonesia (through the Tebedu–Entikong land crossing).

WOMEN TRAVELLERS

Dressing modestly and being respectful, especially in areas of stronger Muslim religious sensibilities such as the northeastern states of Peninsula Malaysia, will ensure you travel with minimum hassle. When visiting mosques, cover your head and limbs with a headscarf and sarong (many mosques lend these out at the entrance). At the beach, most Malaysian women swim fully clothed in T-shirts and shorts, so don't even think about going topless.

Be proactive about your own safety. Treat overly friendly strangers, both male and female, with a good deal of caution. Take taxis after dark and avoid walking alone at night in quiet or seedy parts of town.

❶ Getting There & Away

AIR

The bulk of international flights arrive at Kuala Lumpur International Airport (KLIA; www.klia. com.my), 75km south of Kuala Lumpur (KL); it has two terminals, with KLIA2 being used mainly by budget airlines (KLIA2 is AirAsia's hub). There are also direct flights from Asia and Australia into Penang, Kuching, Kota Kinabalu and a few other cities. Malaysia Airlines (www.malaysiaairlines.com) is the national carrier.

LAND

Visas on arrival are available for land crossings into Brunei, Indonesia, Singapore and Thailand.

SEA
Indonesia

The following are the main ferry routes between Indonesia and Malaysia.

➡ Bengkalis (Sumatra) to Melaka
➡ Pulau Batam to Johor Bahru
➡ Dumai (Sumatra) to Melaka
➡ Medan (Sumatra) to Penang
➡ Pekanbaru (Sumatra) to Melaka
➡ Tanjung Pinang Bintan to Johor Bahru
➡ Tanjung Balai (Sumatra) to Pelabuhan Klang and Kukup
➡ Tarakan (Kalimantan) to Tawau

Singapore

Singapore has a number of regular ferry connections to Malaysia. Cruise trips in the region are also very popular with locals.

Thailand

Ferries connect Kuah on Pulau Langkawi with Satun on the Thai coast and, from November to mid-May, with Ko Lipe; make sure you get your passport stamped going in either direction.

❶ Getting Around

AIR

The two main domestic operators are **Malaysia Airlines** (MAS; ☑1300 883 000, international 03-7843 3000; www.malaysiaairlines.com) and **AirAsia** (☑600 85 8888; www.airasia.com).

The Malaysia Airlines subsidiary **Firefly** (☑03-7845 4543; www.fireflyz.com.my) has flights from KL (SkyPark Subang Terminal) to Ipoh, Johor Bahru, Kerteh, Kota Bharu, Kuala Terengganu, Langkawi and Penang. It also runs connections between Penang and Langkawi, Kuantan and Kota Bharu, Ipoh and JB, and JB and Kota Bharu. **Malindo Air** (☑03-7841 5388; www.malindoair.com) also has a wide range of connections between many Malaysian cities and towns.

In Malaysian Borneo, Malaysia Airlines' subsidiary MASwings (p473) offers local flights within and between Sarawak and Sabah; it's main hub is Miri.

BICYCLE

Bicycle touring around Malaysia and neighbouring countries is an increasingly popular activity. The main road system is well engineered and has good surfaces, but the secondary road system is limited. Road conditions are good enough for touring bikes in most places, but mountain bikes are recommended for forays off the beaten track.

KL Bike Hash (http://klmbh.org) has a whole load of useful information and links to other cycling-connected sites in Malaysia. Also see Bicycle Touring Malaysia (www.bicycletouring malaysia.com).

BOAT

There are no services connecting Peninsular Malaysia with Malaysian Borneo. On a local level, there are boats and ferries between the peninsula and offshore islands, and along the rivers of Sabah and Sarawak. Note that some ferry operators are notoriously lax about observing safety rules, and local authorities are often nonexistent. If a boat looks overloaded or otherwise unsafe, *do not board it* – no one else will look out for your safety.

BUS

Bus travel in Malaysia is economical and generally comfortable. Seats can be paid for and reserved either directly with operators or via online sites such www.easybook.com. Some bus drivers speed recklessly, resulting in frequent, often fatal, accidents.

Konsortium Transnasional Berhad (www. ktb.com.my) is Malaysia's largest bus operator running services under the **Transnasional** (☑03-4047 7878; www.transnasional.com.my), **Nice** (Map p390; ☑013-220 7867; www.nice-coaches. com.my; ☒ Kuala Lumpur), **Plusliner** (p397) and **Cityliner** (☑03-4047 7878; www.cityliner. com.my) brands. Its services tend to be slower than rivals, but its buses have also been involved in several major accidents. It has competition from a variety of privately operated buses on the longer domestic routes, including Aeroline (www. aeroline.com.my) and Super Nice (www.super nice.com.my). There are so many buses on major runs that you can often turn up and get a seat on the next bus.

Most long-distance buses have air-con, often turned to frigid, so bring a sweater!

In larger towns there may be a number of bus stations; local/regional buses often operate from one station and long-distance buses from another; in other cases, KL for example, bus stations are differentiated by the destinations they serve.

Bus travel off the beaten track is relatively straightforward. Small towns and *kampung* (villages) all over the country are serviced by public buses. Unfortunately, they are often poorly signed and sometimes the only way to find your bus is to ask a local. These buses are invariably dirt cheap and provide a great sample of rural life. In most towns there are no ticket offices, so buy your ticket from the conductor after you board.

CAR & MOTORCYCLE

Driving in Malaysia is fantastic compared with most Asian countries. There has been a lot of investment in the country's roads, which are generally of a high quality. New cars for hire are commonly available and fuel is inexpensive (around RM2.20 per litre).

It's not all good news, though. Driving in the cities, particularly KL, can be a nightmare, due to traffic and confusing one-way systems. Malaysian drivers aren't always the safest when it comes to obeying road rules – they mightn't be as reckless as drivers elsewhere in Southeast Asia, but they still take risks. For example, hardly any of the drivers keep to the official 110km/h speed limit on the main highways and tailgating is a common problem.

Unlimited distance rental rates for a 1.3L Proton Saga, one of the cheapest and most popular cars in Malaysia, are posted at around RM190/RM1320 per day/week, including insurance and collision-damage waiver.

HITCHING

Keep in mind hitching is never entirely safe, and we don't recommend it. Travellers who decide to hitch should understand that they are taking a small but potentially serious risk. People who do choose to hitch will be safer if they travel in pairs and let someone know where they are planning to go.

LOCAL TRANSPORT

Taxis are found in all large cities, and most have meters – although you can't always rely on the drivers to use them.

Bicycle rickshaws (trishaws) supplement the taxi service in George Town and Melaka and are definitely handy ways of getting around the older parts of town, which have convoluted and narrow streets.

In major cities there are also buses, which are extremely cheap and convenient once you figure out which one is going your way. KL also has commuter trains, a Light Rail Transit (LRT) and a monorail system.

In Malaysian Borneo, once you're out of the big cities, you're basically on your own and must either walk or hitch. If you're really in the bush, of course, riverboats and aeroplanes are the only alternatives to lengthy jungle treks.

TRAIN

Malaysia's national railway company is Keretapi Tanah Melayu (p397). It runs a modern, comfortable and economical railway service, although there are basically only two lines.

One line runs up the west coast from Johor Bharu, through KL on into Thailand; there's a short spur off this line for Butterworth – the jumping-off point for the island of Penang. Line two branches off the first line at Gemas and runs through Kuala Lipis up to the northeastern corner of the country near Kota Bharu in Kelantan. Often referred to as the 'jungle railway', this line is properly known as the 'East Line'.

On the west-coast line, a speedy electric train service now runs between Gemas and Padang Besar on the Thai border. Full electrification on this side of the peninsula is expected to be completed by 2020.

Myanmar (Burma)

Best Places to Stay

➡ Ostello Bello (p508)

➡ Pickled Tea Hostel (p487)

➡ La Maison Birmane (p508)

➡ Mr Charles Guest House (p527)

Top Burmese Phrases

Hello ming·guh·la·ba

Goodbye thwà·me·naw

Thank you jày·zù ding·ba·de

Do you speak English?
ìng·guh·lay'·loh byàw·da'·thu·h·là

Why Go?

Now is the time to visit this extraordinary, little-known land, dotted with golden pagodas and monasteries, where the traditional ways of Asia endure. Myanmar is fizzing with a new, hopeful energy following the end of 40-odd years of repressive military rule, even if the country's transition to democracy is very much a work in progress. But for all the recent changes, Myanmar remains a unique, magical place still unused to mass tourism.

Travelling in Myanmar offers the chance to suspend the demands of modern life and to immerse yourself in serene landscapes that range from lush jungle, to meandering rivers, mountains and pristine, palm-fringed beaches. Journeys and daily life unfold at a leisurely pace, allowing plenty of time for contemplation. Best of all, you'll meet locals who are gentle, humorous, engaging, considerate, inquisitive and passionate.

When to Go
Yangon

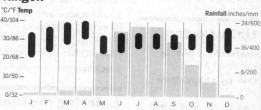

Dec–Feb The best time to visit (cooler weather) but it's high season, so prebook hotels and transport.

Apr The hottest time of the year, so head for the hills of Chin and Shan State where it's cooler.

May–Oct The rainy season means fewer visitors, although roads in remote areas can be impassable.

AT A GLANCE

Currency Burmese kyat (K)

Language Burmese

Money Cash mainly

Visas 28 days

Mobile Phones Prepaid SIM cards are widely available.

Fast Facts

Area 261,228 sq miles

Capital Nay Pyi Taw

Emergency Police (Yangon) 199

Exchange Rates

The US dollar is the only foreign currency that's readily exchanged and/or accepted as payment for goods and services.

Australia	A$1	K1075
Canada	C$1	K1101
Europe	€1	K1622
Japan	¥100	K1213
New Zealand	NZ$1	K988
UK	UK£1	K1842
US	US$1	K1358

For current exchange rates, see www.xe.com.

Daily Costs

Hostel or guesthouse US$10-40

One day's bicycle hire US$1-2

Two-course meal in mid-range restaurant US$5-15

Trekking Kalaw to Inle Lake US$30 per person per day

Don't Miss

Myanmar is one of the most devout Buddhist countries in the world. Yangon's Shwedagon Paya, Mandalay's Mahamuni Paya and Bagan's plain of temples are all must-sees, but across the country you'll find Buddhist religious sites that will impress you with their beauty and spirituality. The towering Shwemawdaw Paya looms over Bago; little-visited Mrauk U, former capital of Rakhine State, is studded with centuries-old temples and monasteries; or join the pilgrims who flock to Mt Kyaiktiyo to worship at the gravity-defying golden boulder.

REGIONS AT A GLANCE

Yangon offers iconic temples, bustling markets and the best selection of restaurants in the country while Southwestern Myanmar has easy to reach beaches, temples and unique handicrafts. Southeastern Myanmar has the finest beaches in the country, as well as the magical Mt Kyaiktiyo (Golden Rock) pilgrimage site while Bagan & Central Myanmar is home to thousands of temples scattered across one vast plain and famed lacquerware. In Eastern Myanmar you can float around Inle Lake and trek through minority villages. Mandalay, Myanmar's cultural capital, offers dance and puppet performances, as well as monasteries and temples. Northern Myanmar – Minorities and mountains galore plus boat trips down the Ayeyarwady River. In Western Myanmar you can get way off the grid in the Chin Hills, or laze on the palm-fringed beach at Ngapali.

Essential Food & Drink

Ăthouq Light, tart and spicy salads made with raw vegetables or fruit tossed with lime juice, onions, peanuts, and chillies. A common one is *leq-p'eq thouq*, which includes fermented tea leaves.

Mohinga (moun-hinga) A popular breakfast dish of rice noodles served with fish soup.

Shan khauk-swe Shan-style noodle soup; thin wheat noodles in a light broth with meat or tofu, available across the country but most common in Mandalay and Shan State.

Htamin chin A turmeric-coloured rice salad from Shan State.

Black tea Brewed in the Indian style: sweet with lots of milk.

Entering the Country

International flights land at Yangon and Mandalay airports. You can enter Myanmar overland from Mae Sai, Mae Sot, Ranong and Phu Nam Ron in Thailand. It's also possible to cross overland from China, at Ruili, and India, at Moreh, but you'll need a permit for those crossings.

Myanmar Highlights

1 Shwedagon Paya (p486) Being dazzled by the country's most important Buddhist temple and the buzz of Yangon.

2 Inle Lake (p507) Spending longer than you planned at this magical landscape of floating villages, stilted monasteries and aquatic gardens.

3 Bagan (p528) Witnessing the beauty of a misty dawn breaking over 4000 Buddhist temples from the upper terraces of one of the *paya* (temples).

4 Kalaw (p510) Trekking or mountain-biking your way to Inle Lake through hills, forests and villages.

5 Mrauk U (p537) Getting lost amid the hundreds of ruined temples and fortifications in the timeless former grand capital of Rakhine.

6 Mawlamyine (p502) Exploring this tranquil city that's home to colonial-era architecture, historic pagodas and nearby beaches.

7 Hsipaw (p526) Chilling out in laidback and historic Hsipaw in between hikes to surrounding ethnic minority villages.

8 Sagaing (p523) Touring the former royal capital and its cave monastery.

9 Rih Lake (p541) Taking the road less travelled to this mystical lake in remote Chin State.

YANGON

♪ 01 / POP 4,728,524

Yangon (ရန်ကုန်), Myanmar's largest city, is by far the most exciting place in the country to be right now, as former political exiles, Asian investors and foreign adventurers flock in. As Myanmar's commercial and artistic hub, it's Yangon that most reflects the changes that have occurred since the country reopened to the world. There's a rash of new restaurants, bars and shops. And there are building sites – and traffic jams – everywhere.

But in many ways Yangon, formerly known as Rangoon, has hardly changed at all. The city remains focused on Shwedagon Paya, an awe-inspiring golden Buddhist monument around which everything else revolves. Close to it are the parks and lakes that provide Yangonites with an escape from the surrounding chaos. Then there's downtown, its pavements one vast open-air market, which is home to some of the most impressive colonial architecture in all Southeast Asia.

◉ Sights

★ Shwedagon Paya   BUDDHIST TEMPLE
(ရွှေတိဂုံဘုရား; Map p496; www.shwedagonpago da.com; Singuttara Hill, Dagon; K8000; ⊙4am-10pm) One of Buddhism's most sacred sites, the 325ft *zedi* (stupa) here is adorned with 27 metric tons of gold leaf, along with thousands of diamonds and other gems, and is believed to enshrine strands of the Gautama Buddha's hair as well as relics of three former buddhas.

Four entrance stairways lead to the main terrace. Visit at dawn if you want tranquil-

---

ⓘ MYANMAR DOS AND DON'TS

Do

➜ Remove shoes on entering a Buddhist site or home.

➜ Dress respectfully: no shorts, short skirts or exposed shoulders.

➜ Ask before you photograph anyone.

Don't

➜ Touch anybody on the head (including a child).

➜ Pose with or sit on Buddha images.

➜ Point your feet at anyone or anything – apologise if you accidentally brush someone with your foot.

---

lity; otherwise, pay your respects when the golden stupa flames crimson and burnt orange in the setting sun.

★ Botataung Paya   BUDDHIST TEMPLE
(ဗိုလ်တထောင်ဘုရား; Map p492; Strand Rd, Botataung; US$5/K6000; ⊙6am-9pm) Botataung's spacious riverfront location and lack of crowds give it a more down-to-earth spiritual feeling than Shwedagon or Sule Paya. Its most original feature is the dazzling zigzag corridor, gilded from floor to ceiling, that snakes its way around the hollow interior of the 131ft golden *zedi* (stupa). Look out for a bronze buddha that once resided in the royal palace in Mandalay, and a large pond full of hundreds of terrapins.

Sule Paya   BUDDHIST STUPA
(ဆူးလေဘုရား; Map p492; cnr Sule Pagoda & Mahabandoola Rds, Pabedan; K3000; ⊙5am-9pm) It's not every city where a primary traffic circle is occupied by a 2000-year-old golden temple. This 46m *zedi*, said to be older than Shwedagon Paya, is an example of modern Asian business life melding with ancient Burmese tradition. Just after the sun has gone down is the most atmospheric time to visit the temple.

★ Chaukhtatgyi Paya   BUDDHIST TEMPLE
(ခြောက်ထပ်ကြီးဘုရား; Map p496; Shwegondine Rd, Tamwe; ⊙6am-8pm) Housed in a large metal-roofed shed, this beautiful 215ft-long reclining buddha is hardly publicised at all, even though it's larger than a similar well-known image in Bago. The statue's placid face, with glass eyes, is topped by a crown encrusted with diamonds and other precious stones.

★ Ngahtatgyi Paya   BUDDHIST TEMPLE
(ငါးထပ်ကြီးဘုရား; Map p496; Shwegondine Rd, Tamwe; ⊙6am-8pm) One of Yangon's, if not Myanmar's, most gorgeous Buddha images is this 46ft-tall seated one at the Ngahtatgyi Paya, sitting in calm gold-and-white repose and adorned with a healthy splash of precious stones. It's worth seeing for its carved wooden backdrop alone.

National Museum (Yangon)   MUSEUM
(အမျိုးသားပြတိုက်; Map p494; ☎01-371 540; 66/74 Pyay Rd, Dagon; K5000; ⊙9.30am-4.30pm Tue-Sun) Even though the museum's collection is appallingly labelled and often badly lit, the treasures that lie within this cavernous building deserve a viewing. The highlight is the spectacular 26ft-high, jewel-encrusted Sihasana (Lion Throne), which belonged to King Thibaw Min, the last king of Myanmar. It's actually more of an entrance

doorway than a throne, but let's not quibble – it's more impressive than your front door.

Mahabandoola Garden
PARK

(မဟာဗန္ဓုလပန်းခြံ; Map p492; Mahabandoola Garden St, Kyauktada; ⊗6am-6pm) FREE This park offers pleasant strolling in the heart of the downtown area and views of surrounding heritage buildings, including City Hall, the High Court and the old Rowe & Co department store, now a bank.

The park's **Independence Monument** (လွတ်လပ်ရေးကျောက်တိုင်; Map p492; Mahabandoola Garden, Kyauktada) FREE, a 165ft white obelisk surrounded by two concentric circles of *chinthe* (half-lion, half-dragon deities) is the park's most notable feature. There's also a children's playground.

Musmeah Yeshua Synagogue
SYNAGOGUE

(Map p494; ☑01-252 814; 85 26th St, Pabedan; ⊗10am-1pm Mon-Sat) The lovingly maintained interior of this 1896 building contains a *bimah* (platform holding the reading table for the Torah) in the centre of the main sanctuary and a women's balcony upstairs. The wooden ceiling features the original blue-and-white Star of David motif. It's best to contact Sammy Samuels at info@myanmarshalom.com to be sure of gaining access to the synagogue.

Kandawgyi Lake
LAKE

(ကန်တော်ကြီး; Map p496; Kan Yeik Thar Rd, Dagon; K3000) Also known as Royal Lake, this artificial lake, built by the British as a reservoir, is most attractive at sunset, when the glittering Shwedagon Paya is reflected in its calm waters. The boardwalk, which runs mainly along the southern and western sides of the lake (and which is free to wander), is also an ideal place for an early-morning jog or stroll.

Tours

★ Uncharted Horizons
CYCLING

(Map p492; ☑09 97117 6085; www.uncharted-ho rizons-myanmar.com; 109 49th St, Botataung; half-/full-day tour from K42,000/65,000) This adventure-tours operation is run by enthusiastic and knowledgeable Austrian Jochen Meissner. It offers four biking itineraries around Yangon, including a fantastic trip to Dalah and nearby Seikgyi island, where you'll pedal around idyllic rural villages.

Sleeping

★ Pickled Tea Hostel
HOSTEL $

(Map p496; ☑09-25090 3363; www.pickledtea hostel.com; 11 Myaynigone Zay St, Sanchaung; dm US$15-18, s/d US$38/54; ❄⑤) On the edge of

happening Sanchaung and a 15-minute walk from Shwedagon Paya, this appealing hostel has large, posh dorms, with proper beds and lockers. There's also an attractive terrace and a small communal area inside. The cheaper private rooms share bathrooms.

★ 21 Hostel
HOSTEL $

(Map p494; ☑09 77518 5358; 21hostelmyanmar@ gmail.com; 21 Bo Ywe Rd, Latha; s/d US$10-20; ❄⑤) A new hostel unique to Yangon, 21 dispenses with dorms in favour of 'pods': cubicle-like spaces that give travellers their own private experience. The pods aren't big – they're mostly taken up with the comfortable beds – and all share clean and modern bathrooms. The downstairs cafe and communal area is a cool hang-out and the overall vibe is mellow.

★ Lil Yangon Hostel
HOSTEL $

(Map p492; ☑09 79167 7731; www.littleyangon-hostel.com; 102 39th St, Kyauktada; dm US$12-16; ❄❄⑤) Popular hostel in the heart of downtown. Dorms only, ranging from four to eight beds in size, and with female-only ones too. The cheapest rooms lack windows, but all are big with high ceilings, and beds have thick mattresses. Pleasant, helpful staff. Reception and the communal area are on one side of the street; the dorms are in a building opposite.

Scott
HOSTEL $

(Map p494; ☑01-246 802; http://scotthostelyangon.com; 198 31st St, Pabedan; dm/tr US$12/15; ❄❄@⑤) You'll need the thighs of a mountain climber to negotiate the stairs up to the dorms *and* the upper-level bunks in this appealing, upmarket hostel. It's just steps from the old Scott Market after which it's

WORTH A TRIP

TWANTE တွံ‌တေး

An easy day trip from Yangon, Twante is a drowsy, spread-out town a 40-minute drive west of Dalah into the Ayeyarwady Delta past seemingly endless paddy fields. Its main claim to fame is the 2500-year-old **Shwesandaw Paya** (ရွှေဆံတော်ဘုရား; K2000; ⊙6am-9pm), said to contain strands of Buddha's hair, and the interesting **Oh-Bo Pottery Sheds** (အိုးဘို အိုးလုပ်ငန်း; ⊙8am-6pm) **FREE**, where you can see pots of various sizes being made.

To get to Twante, first catch the ferry (K2000/4000 one way/return, 5am to 9pm, every 15 minutes) that shuttles between Yangon's Pansodan Jetty and Dalah. Motorcycle-taxi drivers wait at Dalah's jetty and charge K10,000 for a return trip, including stops at the sights. A taxi from Dalah will cost K30,000.

named. A conversion of an old warehouse, the place has bags of charm, including a flock of wooden birds presiding over the cool ground-floor cafe.

4 Rivers Youth Hostel   HOSTEL $
(Map p494; ☑09 79988 7215; www.fourrivershostel.com; 79 12th St, Lanmadaw; dm US$10-15; ☯❋🛜) It's dorms only at this hostel in a two-storey house in the heart of downtown. Don't expect windows, but the dorms are clean, if compact, with comfortable beds. There's a small communal area and kitchen, and the staff is eager to please.

★ **Loft Hotel**   HOTEL $$
(Map p494; ☑01-372 299; www.theloftyangon.com; 33 Yaw Min Gyi St, Dagon; s/d/ste from US$135/150/280; ❋@🛜) Designer fairy dust has been cast over a 1960s warehouse, transforming it into this appealing boutique hotel in a very handy location. New York City–style loft rooms and split-level suites sport exposed-brick walls, floor-to-ceiling windows, arty black-and-white prints and contemporary furnishings. The garden area to the rear is a small oasis.

Yama Hotel   HOSTEL $$
(Map p492; ☑01-203 712; info.yamahotel@gmail.com; 195 Bo Myat Tun St, Botataung; s/d/s/d/tw K25,000/65,000/78,000/91,000; ❋@🛜) There isn't much of a traveller vibe at this hotel, but you do get high-quality bunk-bed dorms with privacy curtains, big lockers and

their own bathrooms. Private rooms are spacious and simply designed. There's an affable staff and good facilities, including DIY laundry and panoramic rooftop bar.

🍴 Eating

★ **Lucky Seven**   BURMESE $
(Map p492; ☑01-292 382; 138-140 49th St, Pazundaung; tea & snacks from K400; ⊙6am-5.30pm Mon-Sat, to noon Sun) The most central of this small chain of high-class traditional tea shops, Lucky Seven is much more than a pit stop for a cuppa. Its streetside tables are fringed by greenery and a small ornamental pond. The *mohinga* (thin rice noodles in a spicy fish broth; K600) is outstanding – order it with a side of crispy gourd or flaky-pastry savoury buns.

★ **Green Gallery**   THAI $
(Map p492; ☑09 3131 5131; www.facebook.com/yangongreengallery; 58 52nd St, Botataung; dishes K2300-6000; ⊙noon-3pm & 6-9pm Mon-Fri, 1-3pm & 6-9pm Sat; 🛜) The hippest Thai restaurant in town – book ahead in the evening – this cosy but artfully designed place has bags of atmosphere and is run by Bo, a friendly young Myanmar woman who used to live in Thailand. The food, including curries, soups and salads, is super fresh, authentically spicy and generously portioned.

Taing Yin Thar   BURMESE $
(Map p489; ☑01-966 0792; www.taingyinthar.com.mm; cnr May Kha & Parami Rds, Mayangone; mains K3000-6000; ⊙10am-midnight; 🛜) An airy wood-beamed dining hall with verandahs for outdoor dining is the setting for this pan-Myanmar restaurant. On the menu is a wide range of ethnic dishes that you're unlikely to find elsewhere, including plenty of vegetarian options.

Feel Myanmar Food   BURMESE $
(Map p494; ☑01-511 6872; www.feelrestaurants.com; 124 Pyidaungsu Yeiktha St, Dagon; dishes from K1500, curries from K2200; ⊙6am-11pm; 🛜) Something of an institution now, Feel is a fine place to start discovering quality Burmese cuisine. There's a big choice of freshly made dishes on display – just go up to the counter and point out what you'd like. All meals come with soup, a plate of salad vegies and a small dessert. Outside, more stalls sell sweets and other takeaways.

Nilar Biryani & Cold Drink   INDIAN $
(Map p494; ☑01-253 131; 216 Anawrahta Rd, Pabedan; biryani from K2600; ⊙4am-11pm) Giant cauldrons full of spices, broths and rice bubble away at the front of this Indian joint.

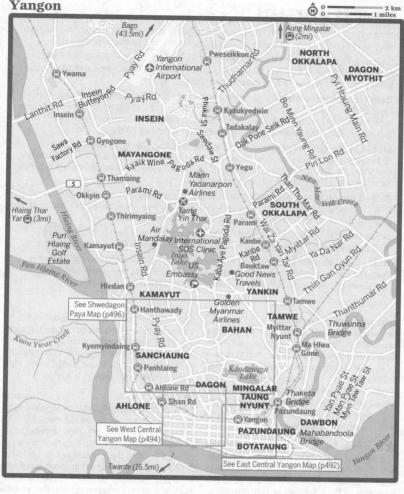

It's always packed, and with good reason: for this price, these biryanis are probably among the best your lips will meet. There are plenty of other delicious options on the picture menu at the counter. Your meal will be brought to you.

Cherry Mann BURMESE **$**
(Map p494; 78-80 Latha St, Latha; dishes K1500-7500; ⊙10.30am-11pm) Excellent and friendly Muslim restaurant; a fine spot for kebabs, curries and biryanis, with *paratha* (Indian-style bread) to accompany them. The kebabs are especially good, but all the food

is clean and tasty. You may have to wait for a table at busy times. No alcohol is served.

999 Shan Noodle Shop NOODLES **$**
(Map p492; 130B 34th St, Kyauktada; noodle dishes from K1500; ⊙6am-7pm) The tables are spread across two cramped floors at this always-busy eatery behind City Hall. The menu includes *Shàn k'auq swèh* (thin rice noodles in a slightly spicy chicken broth) and *myi shay* (Mandalay-style noodle soup), and tasty non-noodle dishes such as Shan tofu (actually made from chickpea flour) and delicious Shan yellow rice with tomato.

YANGON'S STREET EATS

Yangon's street-food options can be both overwhelming and challenging (pork offal on a skewer, anyone?). Here are the best places to sample some favourite street eats.

Samusa Thoke Vendor (Map p492; Merchant St, Pabedan; dishes K500; ⏰7am-6pm) Get *samusa thoke* (tasty samosas chopped up and served with fresh herbs and a thin lentil gravy) from this vendor near Mahabandoola Park.

Bein Mont Vendor (Map p492; cnr Bogyoke Aung San & Yay Kyaw Rds, Pazundaung; pancakes K200; ⏰6.30-10.30am) Head to this vendor for *bein mont* (delicious sweet pancakes topped with nuts and seeds). They're served fresh off the grill by an *amay* (mother) who reputedly makes the best ones in Yangon. Ideal for breakfast on the go.

Mote Lin Ma Yar Vendor (Map p492; cnr Anawrahta Rd & 37th St, Kyauktada; K300; ⏰8am-9pm) Come here for *mote lin ma yar*, nicknamed the 'couple's snack' because the two small mounds of the sticky rice-flour, ginger, salt, onion and sugar mixture are grilled separately and then combined into a single piece.

Grilled Snack Stalls (Map p494; 19th St, Latha; barbecue skewer from K300; ⏰5-11pm) Every night the strip of 19th St between Mahabandoola and Anawrahta Rds hosts dozens of stalls and open-air restaurants serving delicious grilled snacks.

Shwe Bali (Map p494; 112 Bo Sun Pat Rd, Pabedan; lassi per glass from 600K; ⏰10am-10.30pm) Deliciously curdy glasses of lassi (the Indian yoghurt drink) are served here.

Buthi Kyaw Vendor (Map p492; cnr Anawrahta & Thein Byu Rds, Pazuntaung; K1000; ⏰4-9pm) For some of Yangon's crispiest battered and deep-fried chunks of gourd, head to this vendor. The snack is served with a spicy-sour tamarind dipping sauce.

Aung Mingalar Shan Noodle Restaurant

NOODLES $

(Map p494; Bo Yar Nyunt St, Dagon; mains K2000-4500; ⏰7am-9pm) Open to the street on two sides, this is an excellent spot to indulge simultaneously in people-watching and noodle-slurping. It's a simple and easygoing restaurant with a cafe-like feel that's especially popular at lunchtime. The Shan tofu here is also worth sampling.

★ Rangoon Tea House

BURMESE $$

(Map p492; ☎01-122 4534; www.rangoonteahouse.com; 77-79 Pansodan Rd, Kyauktada; snacks from K2500, meals from K7500; ⏰8am-10pm Sun-Thu, to midnight Fri & Sat; ☎) This stylishly designed hipster teahouse is as popular with cashed-up locals as it is with travellers and expats. It serves traditional Burmese cuisine, locally inspired cocktails, and curries and biryanis. All the usual teahouse snacks are available – tea-leaf salads, samosas, *paratha* (Indian-style bread) and *bao* – but in bigger portions (hence the higher prices). And they're less oily than you'll get elsewhere.

★ Rau Ram

FUSION $$

(Map p492; ☎09 45516 0657; www.rauram.com; 64B Yay Kaw St, Pazundaung; mains K12,000-25,000; ⏰5-11pm Tue-Sun; ☎) Effortlessly channelling Southeast Asian chic, this place

east of downtown hits the mark with its Vietnamese-inspired menu made for sharing. The Hokkaido scallop crudo is a refreshing starter, the root-vegetable *rendang* and *bo kho* (beef brisket and oxtail stew with garlic bread) both satisfying mains.

★ Gekko

FUSION $$

(Map p492; ☎01-254 041; www.gekkoyangon.com; 535 Merchant St, Kyauktada; mains K12,000-28,000; ⏰11am-11pm; ☎) This stylish, justly popular restaurant and lounge bar is on the ground floor of the historic Sofaer building. It offers its own take on Japanese and Korean food, including *yakitori* (barbecue), *ramen* and spicy Korean-style noodles, as well as sushi, all prepared in the open kitchen. Also does decent cocktails, and there's live jazz every Friday from 7pm until 10pm.

★ Pansuriya

BURMESE $$

(Map p492; ☎09 77894 9170; www.facebook.com/pansuriyamyanmar; 102 Bo Galay Zay St, Botataung; ⏰7am-10pm) An inspired addition to Yangon's growing number of modern, more upmarket Burmese restaurants, Pansuriya trades on its evocative building's heritage and is plastered with memorabilia and art, some of it for sale. The traditional curries and salads (try the tamarind-leaf one) are excellent and will draw you back again.

Kaung Myat
BURMESE $$

(Map p494; ☑09 3000 2687; 110 19th St, Latha; mains from K4000, barbecue from K400; ☻noon-11.30pm) This is where Anthony Bourdain dined when he passed through Yangon, and it's still the most popular of the many barbecue restaurants on busy 19th St. The barbecue is available in the evenings only; pick from the skewers on display, which include meat, seafood and vegie options, or order dishes from the menu.

🍷 Drinking & Nightlife

★ Blind Tiger
COCKTAIL BAR

(Map p492; ☑09 78683 3847; www.blindtiger-yangon.com; 93/95 Seikkan Thar St, Kyauktada; cocktails from K6500; ☻4-11pm Mon-Sat; 🛜) Giant paintings of Myanmar girls, faces daubed in *thanakha,* dominate the walls of Blind Tiger's new, roomier digs. The one-time speakeasy has emerged from the shadows to lead the way as one of Yangon's top cocktail bars. Selected drinks are half-price during the daily happy hour (5pm to 7pm). It has great burgers and tapas too.

★ Penthouse
COCKTAIL BAR

(Map p496; ☑09 77123 9924; www.facebook.com/the-penthouse-201548120201732; 271-273 Bargaryar St, Sanchaung; ☻11am-1am; 🛜) This sophisticated rooftop space draws the local elite. You'll have to cram into one small corner of its spacious outdoor area to get a view of Shwedagon Paya, but otherwise the soft-cushioned horseshoe seating around low tables creates a mellow vibe for cocktail sipping.

7th Joint Bar & Grill
BAR

(Map p492; ☑09 26369 0876; www.facebook.com/7thjoint; 6-a10 Shwe Asia Bldg, cnr 48th St & Mahabandoola Rd, Botataung; beers K2000, cocktails K5000; ☻4pm-2am) The most popular of the handful of Yangon venues that stay open past midnight, 7th Joint gets so crowded at weekends that you can barely move. It's more of a cashed-up locals' place than it once was, although plenty of foreigners still roll up. During the week, when it stages various event nights, it's much more manageable.

Kosan Double Happiness Bar
BAR

(Map p494; ☑09 42803 8032; www.kosanmyanmar.com; 19th St, Latha; cocktails from K900, beers from K1200; ☻11am-midnight) At the quieter northern end of 19th St, this second branch of Kosan is much more of a bar than its original nearby **venue** (Map p494; ☑09 42803 8032; www.kosanmyanmar.com; 108 19th St, La-

tha; ☻1-11pm; 🛜). Cheap beers and cocktails draw in both locals and travellers to create that double-happy atmosphere.

Anya Ahtar
BAR

(Map p492; 136 37th St, Kyauktada; beers K800; ☻7am-10.30pm) With its black walls decorated with paintings by Burmese artists, this relaxed, upmarket beer station attracts hipster locals. Apart from alcohol, another draw is the carefully thought out menu of food from the central region of Myanmar. Decent salads and breakfast bowls of *mohinga* too.

50th Street Bar & Grill
BAR

(Map p492; ☑01-397 060; www.50thstreetyangon.com; 9-13 50th St, Botataung; beers from K2200, cocktails from K5500; ☻11am-midnight; 🛜) One of Yangon's longest-established Western-style bars, in a handsomely restored colonial building, 50th Street continues to draw in a largely expat crowd with its mix of event nights, free pool table and sport on the TVs. Happy hour is 6am to 8pm Monday to Friday and all day Sunday. The pizzas and burgers are decent, if a little pricey.

🛍 Shopping

★ Hla Day
ARTS & CRAFTS

(Map p492; ☑09 45224 1465; www.hladaymyanmar.org; 1st fl, 81 Pansodan St, Kyauktada; ☻10am-9.30pm) Meaning 'beautiful' in Burmese, Hla Day is a welcome addition to Yangon's growing band of social-enterprise shops. It offers quality contemporary and traditional handicrafts sourced from local producers often struggling to overcome disability, exclusion and poverty. You'll find colourful women's and kids' clothing, soft toys, stationery, jewellery, homewares and more here.

★ Bogyoke Aung San Market
MARKET

(Map p494; Bogyoke Aung San Rd, Dagon; ☻10am-5pm Tue-Sun) Half a day could easily be spent wandering around this sprawling covered market, sometimes called by its old British name, Scott Market. It has more than 2000 shops and the largest selection of Myanmar handicrafts and souvenirs you'll find, from lacquerware and Shan shoulder bags to puppets and jewellery.

Theingyi Zei
MARKET

(Map p494; Shwedagon Pagoda Rd, Pabedan; ☻9am-7pm) Most of the merchandise in downtown Yangon's largest market is ordinary housewares and textiles, but it's also renowned for its large selection of traditional herbs, cosmetics and medicines, which can

East Central Yangon

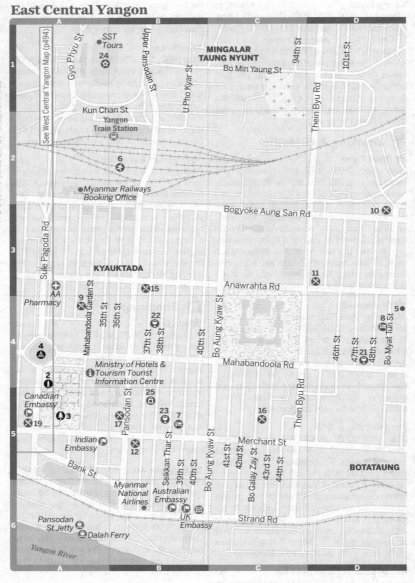

be found on the ground floor of the eastern-most building.

Bagan Book House   BOOKS
(Map p492; ☎ 01-377 227; 100 37th St, Kyauktada; ⊙ 8.30am-6.30pm) This Yangon institution

has one of the most extensive selections of English-language books on Myanmar and Southeast Asia. Genial owner U Htay Aung really knows his stock, which includes copies of tomes dating to the 19th century.

East Central Yangon

There isn't always an English-speaking operator on the following numbers; you might need the help of a Burmese speaker.

Ambulance	☏ 192
Fire	☏ 191
Police	☏ 199

INTERNET ACCESS

Nearly all hotels and many restaurants, cafes and bars offer free wi-fi; there's even free wi-fi at Shwedagon Paya. There are also plenty of internet shops around town. It's inexpensive to pick up a SIM card and data package for your smartphone.

Server speeds have improved but are still slower than those in the West.

ℹ Information

EMERGENCY

Your home embassy may be able to assist with advice during emergencies or serious problems.

West Central Yangon

DAGON

Pyidaungsu Yeiktha St

French
Embassy

See Shwedagon Paya Map (p496)

Myoma Kyaung Rd

Ziwaca St

Kin Won Min
Gyi St

Padonma Rd

Za Ga War Rd

Thantaman Rd

Za Ga War Rd

Myoma
Ground

U Wisara Rd

Pyay Rd

Samon Rd

Min Ye Kyaw Swar Rd

Pyay Rd

Lanmada

Bogyoke Aung San Rd

Phone Gyi St

Lanma Daw St

LANMADAW

Wadan St

Yangon
General
Hospital

Anawrahta Rd

4th St
5th St
Kaingdan St
7th St
Lan Thit St
9th St
Hledan St
11th St
Phone Gyi St
13th St
15th St
17th St
19th St

14
11
12
10

Latha St
21st St
22nd St

Madaw Rd

Mahabandoola Rd

8

Bo Ywe Rd
23rd St

IWT Ticket Office

LATHA

3

Lan Thit
Jetty

Shwe Pyi
Tan Express

Strand Rd

Yangon River

MEDICAL SERVICES

There are several private and public hospitals in Yangon, but fees, service and quality of treatment may vary. There are also some useful pharmacies in town, including those in CityMart supermarkets – you'll find these at **Marketplace by CityMart** (Map p496; Dhammazedi Rd, Bahan; ⊙9am-9pm).

AA Pharmacy (Map p492; ☏01-253 231; 142-146 Sule Pagoda Rd, Kyauktada; ⊙8am-9pm) Just north of Sule Paya.

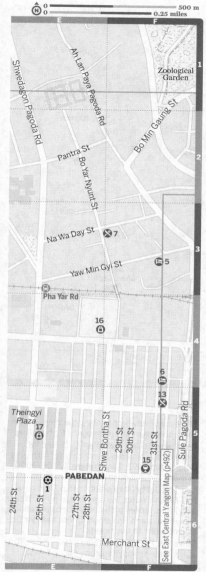

N
0 — 500 m
0 — 0.25 miles

West Central Yangon

Sights
1 Musmeah Yeshua Synagogue E6
2 National Museum (Yangon) B1

Sleeping
3 21 Hostel D6
4 4 Rivers Youth Hostel B5
5 Loft Hotel F3
6 Scott F4

Eating
7 Aung Mingalar Shan Noodle
   Restaurant F3
8 Cherry Mann D6
9 Feel Myanmar Food B1
10 Grilled-Snack Stalls D5
11 Kaung Myat D5
12 Kosan Cafe D5
13 Nilar Biryani & Cold Drink F5

Drinking & Nightlife
14 Kosan Double Happiness Bar D5
15 Shwe Bali F5

Shopping
16 Bogyoke Aung San Market E4
17 Theingyi Zei E5

MONEY
You'll get the best rates for changing money at the airport and at official bank exchange counters in places such as Bogyoke Aung San Market.

There are many ATMs dotted around Yangon that accept international Visa and MasterCards; there's a K5000 charge for using these ATMs.

POST
Central Post Office (Map p492; 39-41 Bo Aung Kyaw St, Kyauktada; 7.30am-6pm Mon-Fri) Stamps are for sale on the ground floor, but go to the 1st floor to send mail.

DHL (Map p494; 01-215 516; www.dhl.com; 58 Wadan St, Lanmadaw; 8am-6pm Mon-Fri, to 2pm Sat) Courier and logistics company that sends parcels and mail worldwide.

TOURIST INFORMATION
Ministry of Hotels & Tourism Tourist Information Centre (MTT; Map p492; 01-252 859; www.myanmartourism.org; 118 Mahabandoola Garden St, Kyauktada; 9am-4.30pm) Can answer some of your questions about Yangon and travel around Myanmar and has some official leaflets and free maps. It no longer offers its own tourism products and will refer you to other travel agents for specific assistance.

International SOS Clinic (Map p489; 01-657 922; www.internationalsos.com; Inya Lake Hotel, 37 Kaba Aye Pagoda Rd, Mayangone) Your best bet in Yangon for emergencies, this clinic claims to be able to work with just about any international health insurance and has a 24-hour emergency centre.

Shwedagon Paya

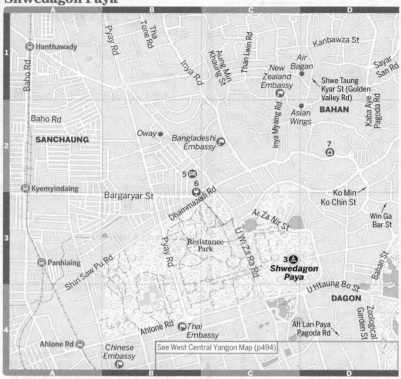

MYANMAR (BURMA) YANGON

❶ Getting There & Away

AIR

Yangon International Airport (Map p489; 📞 01-533 031; Mingalardon; 🛜) is Myanmar's main international gateway and hub for domestic flights.

Airlines here include **Air Bagan** (Map p496; 📞 01-504 888; www.airbagan.com; 56 Shwe Taung Kyar St, Bahan), **Air KBZ** (📞 01-372 977; www.airkbz.com), **Air Mandalay** (Map p489; 📞 01-525 488; www.airmandalay.com; 1 (A) Pyay Rd, Hlaing), **Asian Wings** (Map p496; 📞 01-512 140; www.asianwingsairways.com; 41 Shwe Taung Kyar St, Bahan), **Golden Myanmar Airlines** (Map p489; 📞 09 97799 3000; www.gmairlines.com; Sayar San Plaza, University Ave, Bahan), **Mann Yadanarpon Airlines** (Map p489; 📞 01-656 969; www.airmyp.com; 3 Thalarwaddy St, Mayangone), **Myanmar National Airlines** (Map p492; 📞 01-378 603; www.flymna.com; 104 Strand Rd, Kyauktada) and **Yangon Airways** (Map p496; 📞 01-383 100; www.yangonair.com; 8th fl, MMB Tower, Pansodan St, Mingalar Taung Nyunt).

BOAT

There are several jetties along the Yangon River. The following are the most useful for travellers.

Pansodan St Jetty (Map p492; Strand Rd, Kyauktada) The jumping-off base for ferries to **Dalah** (Map p492; 1 way/return K2000/4000; ⏱ every 15min 5.30am-9.30pm).

Lan Thit Jetty (Map p494; Latha) From here, **IWT** (Inland Water Transport; Map p494; Wadan jetty) runs ferries to the delta towns of Labutta, Myaungmya and Hpayapon. Check here for the schedule and to buy tickets.

Shwe Pyi Tan Express (Map p494; 📞 01-230 3003; www.shwepyitan.com; Phone Gyi St, Latha) Runs daily express boats to Bogalay from Yangon's Phone Gyi Jetty.

BUS

Two major bus terminals service Yangon: Allow plenty of time to get to them.

Aung Mingalar Bus Terminal (Aung Mingalar St, Mingaladon) In the city's northeast and for bus lines leaving for the northern part of My-

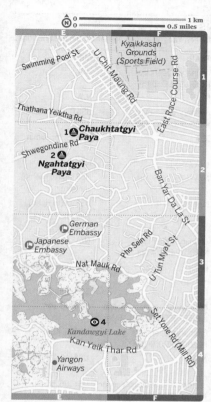

Myanmar Railways Booking Office (Map p492; Bogyoke Aung San Rd, Mingalar Taung Nyunt; ⊙7am-3pm), where you can also check the latest timetables.

Though inexpensive, trains are slow, uncomfortable and almost always delayed, often by hours.

❶ Getting Around

TO/FROM THE AIRPORT

Taxi drivers cluster just outside the departures area of the airport terminal. The fare to downtown Yangon (12 miles) is K8000, although some drivers will ask for K10,000. The journey can take up to an hour, or more if traffic is heavy.

BUS

Yangon has scores of competing private buses. New Chinese-made ones are slowly replacing the old wrecks, but all are packed to the rafters. Routes are confusing and there's virtually no English, spoken or written. If you're determined, the typical fare within central Yangon is K200 (use small bills – bus conductors don't tend to have change). Prices often double at night, but the buses are still cheap (and still crowded).

TAXI

Yangon taxis are still one of the best deals in Asia, even though drivers do not use a meter. Many drivers speak at least some English (although it's advisable to have someone write out your destination in Burmese), and they're mostly honest and courteous. Some will ask foreigners for higher fares. But if you negotiate with a smile, they will normally reduce their initial quote.

All licensed taxis have a visible taxi sign on the roof. The following should give you an idea of what to pay: a short hop (such as from the Strand to Bogyoke Market) will be K1500; double this distance will be K2000; from downtown to

anmar, as well as for Kyaiktiyo (Golden Rock), Mawlamyine (Moulmein) and destinations to the south. A taxi here from downtown Yangon costs K7000 and takes around 45 minutes to one hour outside rush hour.

Hlaing Thar Yar Bus Terminal (Pathein Rd, Hlaing Thar Yar) For travel to Ayeyarwady Division and destinations west of Yangon including Chaung Tha Beach, Ngwe Saung Beach and Pathein. By taxi (K8000) the terminal is 45 minutes to one hour west of the city centre across the Hlaing River.

Most hotels and travel agencies can book tickets for you, and several agents and bus companies have offices alongside **Bogyoke Aung San Stadium** (Map p492; 🕾 09 97207 6383; Gyo Phyu St, Dagon); expect to pay K1000 commission.

TRAIN

Yangon train station (🕾 01-251 181; Khun Chan St, Mingalar Tuang Nyunt; ⊙6am-4pm) is a short walk north of Sule Paya; advance tickets should be purchased at the adjacent

YANGON TRANSPORT CONNECTIONS

The following table shows travel costs and times between Yangon and Myanmar's main destinations.

DESTINATION	BUS	TRAIN	AIR
Bago	K1000, 2½hr	ordinary/upper class K1200/2400, 2hr	N/A
Chaung Tha Beach	K10,000, 7hr	N/A	N/A
Dawei	ordinary/VIP K15,300-23,500, 16hr	ordinary/upper class K5000/10,000, 24hr	US$110, 1hr 5min
Heho (for Inle Lake & Kalaw)	N/A	N/A	US$95, 1hr 10min
Hpa-an	K8000, 7-8hr	N/A	N/A
Hsipaw	ordinary/VIP K15,000/21,500, 15hr	N/A	US$145 (to Lashio), 1hr 45min
Kalaw	ordinary/VIP K15,000/18,500, 10-12hr	N/A	US$95 (to Heho), 1hr 10min
Kyaikto	K8000, 5hr	ordinary/upper class K1200/2400, 4-5hr	N/A
Lashio	ordinary/VIP K15,000/20,300, 15hr	N/A	US$145, 1hr 45min
Loikaw	K13,300, 15hr	N/A	$95, 50min
Mandalay	ordinary/VIP K11,000/20,500, 9hr	ordinary/upper class/sleeper K4650/9300/12,750, 15½hr	US$100, 1hr
Mawlamyine	ordinary/VIP K6000/10,000, 7hr	ordinary/upper class K2200/4200, 9-11hr	US$93, 40min
Myitkyina	ordinary/VIP K38,000/48,000, 22hr	N/A	US$140, 1½hr
Nay Pyi Taw	ordinary/VIP K5000/8000, 5-6hr	ordinary/upper class/sleeper K2800/5600/7700, 9hr	US$106, 50min
Ngwe Saung Beach	K11,000, 6hr	N/A	N/A
Nyaung U (for Bagan)	ordinary/VIP K13,000/23,000, 10hr	ordinary/upper class/sleeper K4500/6000/16,500, 16hr	US$105, 70min
Pathein	K7000, 4hr	N/A	N/A
Pyay	K5500, 6hr	ordinary K1950, 7-8hr	N/A
Sittwe	K20,500, 24hr	N/A	US$95, 50min
Taunggyi (for Inle Lake)	ordinary/VIP K14,000/17,500, 12hr	N/A	US$95 (to Heho), 1hr 10min
Taungoo	K4500, 6hr	ordinary/upper class/sleeper K2000/4000/12,750, 7hr	N/A
Thandwe (for Ngapali)	K15,000, 12hr	N/A	US$85, 50min

Shwedagon Paya and the southern half of Bahan township will be K3000 depending on the state of traffic; from downtown to the Inya Lake area will be K4000.

You can also hire a taxi for about K5000 an hour. For the entire day, you should expect to pay K40,000 to K50,000, depending on the quality of the vehicle and your negotiating skills.

TRISHAW

Trishaws (saiq-ka, as in 'sidecar') are slowly being pushed off the roads by the influx of cars. In downtown Yangon they can be found mostly around markets, near train stations and at points along main roads. Trishaw passengers ride with the driver, but back to back (one facing forward, one backward). Drivers charge around K1000 for a short journey. They're not very comfortable, especially if you're tall or broad.

AYEYARWADY & BAGO REGIONS

South and west of Yangon is the Ayeyarwady Delta (ဧရာဝတီ), a stunning patchwork of greenery floating on rivers, tributaries and lakes that stretches to the Bay of Bengal. In the far west of the delta are the beach resorts of Chaung Tha and Ngwe Saung, long-time favourite sea-and-sand escapes for Yangonites.

A couple of hours east of Yangon is Bago (ပဲခူး), once the capital of southern Myanmar and home to many historic pagodas, monasteries and palaces that date back more than a thousand years. Bago can be visited as a day trip from Yangon, or it makes an easy first stop as you set out on your tour of the country.

Chaung Tha Beach

ချောင်းသာကမ်းခြေ

042 / POP c 2000

Chaung Tha Beach is the closest thing Myanmar has to a holiday resort for ordinary folks – it's where the locals come to play. At this very Burmese beach party there's bobbing about on rubber rings, plodding along the beach on ponies, endless guitar playing, boisterous beach-football games, happy family picnics and evening fireworks.

Six-odd hours from Yangon, Chaung Tha gets especially busy at weekends and on holidays. It's not the most awe-inspiring coastline – parts of the beach can get dirty in high season – and the resorts are not aimed at foreigners. But if you're looking to squeeze some sand and sun into your visit to Myanmar, it's a relatively convenient and affordable option.

★ Hill Garden Hotel   HOTEL $

(09 4957 6072; r incl breakfast US$20-60; ❄ 🛜) The Hill Garden's elevated, lush location – the chalets are scattered throughout a large and appealing garden – make this an excellent choice for getting away from it all. The cheaper digs feature a bamboo design, are fan only and share bathrooms; the more expensive are cement bungalows with air-con. All have balconies. It's more popular with foreigners than locals.

★ Shwe Ya Min Restaurant   CHINESE, BURMESE $

(Main Rd; mains from K3500; ⏰ 7am-10pm; 🛜) This roofed, open-air place across the road from the beach is the best place in town to eat, apart from the swish resort restaurants. It has a big menu of reasonably priced Chinese-Burmese dishes and plenty of seafood. Everything is tasty, prepared with care and served with more style than you'd expect.

ⓘ Getting There & Away

A number of buses leave for Yangon at 9.30am every day (K10,000, six hours). They terminate at Sule Paya or Aung San Stadium downtown. Book tickets at your hotel. Buses leave from the hotels, or from the bus station opposite Azura Beach Resort. There's also an earlier departure at 5.30am that goes to Hlaing Thar Yar Bus Terminal in the far west of Yangon.

Ngwe Saung Beach

ငွေဆောင်ကမ်းခြေ

042 / POP c 2500

More sophisticated than nearby Chaung Tha Beach, and with finer sand and clearer, deeper water, palm-fringed Ngwe Saung Beach has emerged as a hip destination for Yangon's new rich. These days the northern end of the beach is occupied by a succession of upscale resorts. But backpackers have long found a home here too – the southern end has budget bungalows and an agreeably laid-back vibe. Foreign visitors tend to prefer this to Chaung Tha's more raucous atmosphere. Dividing the north and south of the 13 miles of beach here is Ngwe Saung Village, where there's an increasing crop of decent restaurants. Given Ngwe Saung's relative proximity to Yangon – it's a six-hour bus ride away – this is perhaps the best place in Myanmar for a beach getaway that won't break the bank.

Shwe Hin Tha Hotel   HOTEL $$

(042-40340; bungalows incl breakfast US$33-60; ❄) Set at the southern end of the beach, this place has a magnetic pull for backpackers, who agonise over whether to choose a simple bamboo hut or a more solid bungalow with air-con. Both options are clean and well maintained, and hot water appears on request. There's no wi-fi, and power only after 6pm.

★ Ume Restaurant & Bar   ASIAN $$

(09 42532 4652; mains from K4500; ⏰ 10am-10pm; 🛜) Run by a Japanese woman and her Burmese husband, this cool place is lit up spectacularly at night (check out the lights 50ft up at the top of the surrounding palm trees). The menu spans Chinese-Burmese, Thai and Japanese, with pizza as well. There's a nightly fire-dance show and the bar stays open until midnight serving OK cocktails.

ℹ️ Getting There & Away

Air-con buses to Yangon (K11,000, five to six hours) leave at 6.30am, 8am and noon from Ngwe Saung Village. During the rainy season (May to September), only the 8am bus runs. For Pathein (K4000, two hours), buses go at 6.30am, 7.30am, 9am, noon and 3pm. The buses leave and arrive at the junction between the village and the beach resorts.

Bago

📞 052 / POP C 254,424

If it weren't for Bago's abundance of religious sites and the remains of its palace, it would be hard to tell that this scrappy town – 50 miles northeast of Yangon on the old highway to Mandalay – was once the capital of southern Myanmar. The much-delayed opening of the new Hanthawaddy International Airport in 2022, which will take over from Yangon as Myanmar's main air hub, is set to revive Bago's fortunes.

Until then, the great density of blissed-out buddhas and treasure-filled temples makes Bago (ပဲခူး; formerly known as Pegu) an appealing and simple day trip from Yangon, or the ideal first stop when you leave the city behind.

👁️ Sights

Shwemawdaw Paya　　　BUDDHIST STUPA
(ရွှေမော်တောဘုရား; Shwemawdaw Paya Rd; with Bago Archaeological Zone ticket K10,000; ☉ daylight hours) A *zedi* (stupa) of washed-out gold in the midday haze and glittering perfection in the evening, the 376ft-high Shwemawdaw Paya stands tall and proud over the town. The stupa reaches 46ft higher than Shwedagon Paya in Yangon.

At the northeastern corner of the stupa is a huge section of the *hti* (pinnacle) toppled by an earthquake in 1917. Shwemawdaw is a

particularly good destination during Bago's annual pagoda festival in March or April.

Shwethalyaung Buddha　　BUDDHIST TEMPLE
(ရွှေသာလျောင်းဘုရား; with Bago Archaeological Zone ticket K10,000; ☉ daylight hours) Legend has it that this gorgeous reclining buddha, measuring 180ft long and 53ft high, was built by the Mon king Mgadeikpa in the 10th century. The monument's little finger alone extends 10ft. Following the destruction of Bago in 1757, the huge buddha was overgrown by jungle and not rediscovered until 1881, when a contractor unearthed it while building the Yangon–Bago railway line.

Hintha Gon Paya　　　　BUDDHIST STUPA
(ဟင်္သာကုန်း; ☉ daylight hours) **FREE** Located a short walk behind Shwemawdaw Paya (p500), this shrine was once the only place in this vast area that rose above sea level, and so it was the natural spot for the *hamsa* of legend to land. Images of this mythical bird decorate the stupa, which was built by U Khanti, the hermit monk who was the architect of Mandalay Hill.

Kyaik Pun Paya　　　BUDDHIST MONUMENT
(ကျိုက်ပွန်ဘုရား; Kyaikpon Pagoda Rd; with Bago Archaeological Zone ticket K10,000; ☉ daylight hours) Built in 1476 by King Dhammazedi, Kyaik Pun Paya consists of four 100ft-high sitting buddhas (Gautama Buddha and his three predecessors) placed back to back around a huge, square pillar that's about a mile south of Bago, just off the Yangon road.

🛏️ Sleeping & Eating

Hotel Mariner　　　　　　　HOTEL $
(📞 052-220 1034; hotelmariner.hm@gmail.com; 330 Shwemawdaw Paya Rd; r incl breakfast US$35-45; ❄️ 🤶) Still the pick of Bago's not very impressive budget and midrange accommodation offerings, the Hotel Mariner has modern, clean rooms in reasonable

BAGO TRANSPORT CONNECTIONS

The following table shows travel times and costs between Bago and several main destinations. The range in train fares is between ordinary and upper class.

DESTINATION	BUS	TRAIN
Kyaikto	3hr, K6000	3hr, K650-1300
Mandalay	9-10hr, from K13,000	13hr, K2100-8150
Mawlamyine	6hr, K9000	8hr, K1600-3150
Taungoo	7hr, from K6000	5hr, K1450-2900
Yangon	2hr, K1000	2hr, K600-1150

condition. The more expensive are big and light, and some offer grandstand views of Shwemawdaw Paya (p500).

San Francisco Guest House   HOTEL $

(☎ 052-2222265; 14 Main Rd; r US$15-20; 🏢🞉) This is the best of the cheapies, if you choose a double room. Bathrooms are small but clean, the owner is friendly, and you can rent bicycles (K3000 per day) and motorbikes (K8000 per day). There's a curfew from 11pm to 5am, although you'll be hard-pressed to find anywhere in Bago open after 10pm.

Hanthawaddy   CHINESE, BURMESE $

(192 Hintha St; mains K3000-8000; ☺10am-10pm) The food here isn't amazing, but it's solid enough, the place is clean and this is the only restaurant in central Bago with a bit of atmosphere. The open-air upper level is breezy and offers great views of Shwemawdaw Paya (p500).

Three Five Restaurant   CHINESE, BURMESE $

(10 Main Rd; mains K2200-6000; ☺7.30am-10pm; 🞉) This shabby but friendly place offers a menu spanning Burmese and Chinese cuisine, with a few European dishes. At night it's a popular spot for a beer.

ℹ️ Information

CB Bank (Yangon-Mandalay Rd; ☺9.30am-3pm) has an ATM that takes foreign cards. There are a few other ATMs scattered around town.

ℹ️ Getting There & Away

BUS

Bago's scruffy **bus station** (Yangon-Mandalay Rd) is about halfway between the town centre and the Bago Star Hotel, located across from the Hindu temple.

Buses to Yangon leave from along the main road opposite the bus station and depart approximately every 30 minutes from 6.30am to 5.30pm.

Buses to Kinpun, the starting point for Mt Kyaiktiyo (Golden Rock), leave at 7.30am, 8.30am and 2.30pm. During the rainy season (May to September), most buses go only as far as Kyaikto, 10 miles from Kinpun.

Sea Sar (☎ 09 530 0987; myothitsar86@gmail.com; ☺6am-6pm), which has an office at the bus station, can book tickets.

TRAIN

Bago is connected by train to Yangon and Mawlamyine and stops north towards Mandalay. Most trains do not run to schedule.

ℹ️ Getting Around

Motorcycle taxi and *thoun bein* (trishaw) are the main forms of local transport. A one-way trip in the central area should cost no more than K500. If you're going further afield – say from Shwethalyaung Buddha, at one end of town, to Shwemawdaw Paya, at the other – you should hire a trishaw or motorcycle for the day, either of which will cost around K7000.

SOUTHEASTERN MYANMAR

🎦 057

Strangely neglected by many travellers, southern Myanmar offers some of the finest natural sights in the entire country. In the space of a couple of days, you can descend into the Buddha-packed caves around sleepy Hpa-an and ascend the winding road to the sacred golden boulder perched on Mt Kyaiktiyo (Golden Rock). Then there's the historic city of Mawlamyine, once Myanmar's capital, which has almost as fine a collection of colonial-era buildings as Yangon, while Dawei, mixing traditional wooden architecture with brick mansions and buildings constructed during British rule, can boast of centuries of history as a port. Best of all, the lack of visitors means there's plenty of space to enjoy the region.

Mt Kyaiktiyo   ကျိုက်ထီးရိုးတောင်

Mt Kyaiktiyo (p501), the Golden Rock, sounds bizarre: an enormous, precariously balanced boulder covered in gold and topped with a stupa. But this monument is a major pilgrimage site for Burmese Buddhists and it's the presence of so many devotees that makes the place so special.

During the rainy season (May to October), the mountain is mostly covered in a chilly coat of mist and rain, although people still flock here. The area's hotels are open during this period, but some restaurants shut down.

💿 Sights

Mt Kyaiktiyo   BUDDHIST TEMPLE

(Golden Rock; K6000) The excursion to this incredible balancing-golden-boulder stupa is a must-do, especially during the peak pilgrimage season (November to March) and when the sun is shining. The small stupa, just 24ft high, sits atop the Golden Rock, a massive, gold-leafed boulder delicately balanced on the edge of a cliff at the top of Mt Kyaiktiyo.

BUSES FROM MT KYAIKTIYO

DESTINATION	BUS	TRAIN
Bago	K5000, 3hr, frequent 8.45am-4pm	ordinary/upper class K650/1300, 3hr, noon & midnight
Hpa-an	K7000, 3hr, frequent 9am-3pm	N/A
Mawlamyine	K7000, 4hr, frequent 9am-4pm	ordinary/upper class K1300/2550, 4hr, noon & 11.30pm
Yangon	K7000, 5hr, frequent 8.30am-4pm	ordinary/upper class K1200/2400, 4½hr, noon & midnight

When the boulder is bathed in the purple, sometimes misty, light of dawn and dusk, it looks stunning.

🛏 Sleeping

Golden Sunrise Hotel HOTEL $
(☏09 25075 8198; www.goldensunrisehotel. com; Golden Rock Rd, Kinpun; s/d incl breakfast US$42/47; 🌣🛜) A few minutes' walk outside the centre of Kinpun village in the direction of the highway, the Golden Sunrise has 16 semi-detached, sizeable, bungalow-style rooms with verandahs set around a secluded garden. It's something of an oasis, but the rooms themselves haven't been upgraded for a few years and the beds could be better, while the fixtures are old.

Bawga Theiddhi Hotel HOTEL $
(☏09 77807 6097; www.bawgatheiddhihotel. com; Kinpun; r incl breakfast US$25-65; 🌣🛜) Kinpun's flashest hotel has rooms that are clean, modern, and equipped with TV and fridge, although oddly only the most expensive have their own bathroom (the shared bathrooms are well maintained).

Mountain Top Hotel HOTEL $$
(☏09 871 8392, in Yangon 01-502 479; www.mountaintop-hotel.com; r incl breakfast US$110-135; 🌣🛜) The pick of the hotels on the summit, the Mountain Top has overpriced but clean and well-maintained rooms. There's good service, and the location means stunning views. The attached restaurant is reliable. Wi-fi in the lobby only.

ℹ Getting There & Away

The major transport hub for Mt Kyaiktiyo is the similar-sounding town of Kyaikto. Frequent pick-ups cruise the road between Kyaikto's train station and Kinpun (K500, 20 minutes, 7am to 4pm), which is the base camp for Mt Kyaiktiyo. A motorcycle taxi from Kyaikto will cost K2000.

Tickets for buses can be purchased in Kinpun across from Sea Sar Hotel and restaurant. The ticket price includes the transfer by pick-up to Kyaikto.

Mawlamyine

☏057 / POP C 253,730

With a ridge of stupa-capped hills on one side, the Thanlwin River on the other and a centre filled with crumbling colonial-era buildings, churches and mosques, Mawlamyine is a unique combination of landscape, beauty and melancholy. The setting inspired both George Orwell and Rudyard Kipling, two of the English-language writers most associated with Myanmar.

But it's not all about history; the area around Mawlamyine has enough attractions, ranging from beaches to caves, to keep a visitor happy for several days.

◉ Sights

⭐**Kyaikthanlan Paya** BUDDHIST TEMPLE
(ကျိုက်သံလွန်ဘုရား; Kyaik Than Lan Phayar St; ⏱daylight hours) FREE Rudyard Kipling's visit to Myanmar spanned just three days, but it resulted in a poem, 'Mandalay', that turned Burma into an oriental fantasy and began with the lines 'By the old Moulmein Pagoda, lookin' lazy at the sea...' The pagoda Kipling cited was most likely **Kyaikthanlan Paya**, the city's tallest stupa. It's a great sunset-viewing spot, with fine vistas over the city. To reach it, approach via the long covered walkway that extends from Kyaik Than Lan Phayar St.

Bilu Kyun ISLAND
(ဘီလူးကျွန်း) Bilu Kyun (Ogre Island) isn't a hideaway for nasty monsters. Rather, it's a beautiful island directly west of Mawlamyine. Roughly the size of Singapore, Bilu Kyun comprises 78 villages that are home to more than 200,000 people. It's a green, fecund place, home to palm-studded rice fields and fruit

plantations, and it has the vibe of a tropical island, only without the beaches. A brand-new bridge now links Bilu Kyun to the mainland, allowing travellers to drive there themselves.

Mon Cultural Museum MUSEUM
(မွန်ယဉ်ကျေးမှုပြတိုက်; cnr Baho & Dawei Jetty Rds; K5000; ⏱10am-4.30pm Tue-Sun) Unlike most of Myanmar's regional museums, Mawlamyine's is actually worth a visit, even if the collection here isn't huge. It's dedicated to the Mon history of the region, and the exhibits include stelae with Mon inscriptions, 100-year-old wooden sculptures depicting old age and sickness (used as *dhamma*-teaching devices in monasteries), ceramics, silver betel boxes, royal funerary urns and Mon musical instruments, with most exhibits accompanied by English-language descriptions.

🛏 Sleeping & Eating

Pann Su Wai GUESTHOUSE $
(📞057-22921; 333A Lower Main Rd; r K13,000-39,000; ⌨ 🕸) None of the rooms here is huge – the singles are tight – and they don't get a lot of natural light, but they're clean and come with OK bathrooms, making them a reasonable deal for the money. The friendly owner speaks English. There's no kitchen here, so no breakfast.

★ Ngwe Moe Hotel HOTEL $$
(📞057-24703; www.ngwemoehotel.com; cnr Kyaikthoke Paya & Strand Rds; r incl breakfast US$45-60; ⌨ 🕸) The spacious, modern rooms here are excellent value, with very comfortable beds; the more expensive rooms have decent river views. The staff is keen and helpful, and the expansive breakfast buffet sets you up for a day of sightseeing. There are KBZ Bank and CB Bank ATMs outside the lobby.

MYANMAR (BURMA) MAWLAMYINE

MAWLAMYINE TRANSPORT CONNECTIONS

DESTINATION	AIR	BUS	TRAIN	VAN (SHARE TAXI)
Bago	N/A	K5500, 5hr, frequent 6.30am-midnight	ordinary/upper class K1660/3150, 7hr, 8am	N/A
Dawei	N/A	K12,000, 8-9hr, 6pm, 5.30pm & 6.30pm	ordinary/upper class K2950/5900, 16hr, 4.30am	N/A
Hpa-an	N/A	K1000, 2hr, hourly 6am-4pm	N/A	N/A
Kawthoung	US$165, 1hr 50min, Mon	K40,000-45,000, 25hr, 5.30pm, 6pm & 6.30pm	N/A	N/A
Kyaikto (for Mt Kyaiktiyo, Golden Rock)	N/A	K3000, 4hr, frequent 6.30am-midnight	ordinary/upper class K1300/2250, 8am	N/A
Mandalay	N/A	K15,500, 13hr, 6pm & 7pm	N/A	N/A
Myawaddy	N/A	N/A	N/A	K10,000, 4hr, frequent 6am-4pm
Myeik	N/A	K18,000-20,000, 16hr, 6am, 5.30pm & 6.30pm	N/A	N/A
Nay Pyi Taw	N/A	K10,500, 8hr, 6pm	ordinary/upper class K3400/6750, 15hr, 6.15am	N/A
Pyin Oo Lwin	N/A	K17,000, 17hr, 5pm	N/A	N/A
Yangon	US$91, 40min, Mon	K6000-10,000, 7hr, frequent 8am-midnight	ordinary/upper class K2300/5550, 10hr, 8am	N/A
Ye	N/A	K3000, 4hr, 7am, 9am, 11am, 1pm, 2pm & 4pm	K1100/2200, 6hr, 4.30am	K3000, 3hr, frequent 6am-1.30pm

★ **Daw Yee**   BURMESE $

(☑ 09 42111 9556; U Ze Na Pagoda St; curries from K3000; ⊙ 8am-10pm) Humble Daw Yee does some of the best Burmese food you'll find. It has a great selection of curries, including an insanely fatty prawn curry. Be sure to order one of the vegetable side dishes (K500) that change daily. It's off the southern end of Strand Rd, about 10 minutes' walk south of the Ngwe Moe Hotel (p503).

Bone Gyi   CHINESE, BURMESE $$

(☑ 057-26528; cnr Strand Rd & Main Kha Lay Kyaung St; mains from K3500; ⊙ 9am-9pm) There's a big menu here, mostly featuring Chinese-inspired dishes but also including a few Thai ones and even some spicy Rakhine State–style soups. It's especially good for fish, grilled or steamed. There's an outside area and efficient service, and it's determinedly foreigner friendly, so it's a little pricier than other restaurants of its type.

❶ Information

Skip the basic accommodation at **Breeze Guest House** (☑ 057-22919, 057-21450; breeze.guesthouse@gmail.com; 6 Strand Rd), but the staff can arrange reliable guides and trips to Bilu Kyun and rent bicycles (K3000 per day) and motorbikes (K10,000 per day), and charter boats for the trip to Hpa-an by river (K10,000 per person).

❶ Getting There & Away

Buses for destinations north of Mawlamyine use the **Mye Ni Gone bus station**, located near the train station; a motorcycle taxi to/from the centre should cost K500. For routes south of Mawlamyine, head to the **Zay Gyo bus station**, a couple of miles south of the city centre; a motorcycle taxi to/from here should cost K1000. Vans (actually share taxis) to Myawaddy depart from opposite the entrance to Zay Gyo bus station.

Mawlamyine's train station is about 1.5km east of the city centre, a K500 ride on a motorcycle taxi. At the time of research, trains were not running south of Dawei.

Hpa-an ဘားအံ

☑ 058 / POP C 75,140

Hpa-an, Kayin State's scruffy riverside capital, isn't going to inspire many postcards home. But the people are friendly, and the city is the logical base from which to explore the Buddhist caves, sacred mountains, and rivers and lakes of the stunning surrounding countryside.

◉ Sights

★ **Saddan Cave**   CAVE

(ဆဒ္ဒန်ဂူ; K1000; ⊙ daylight hours) This football-stadium-sized cave is simply breathtaking, its entrance dominated by dozens of buddha statues, a couple of pagodas and some newer clay wall carvings. In absolute darkness (bring a torch; otherwise, for a donation of K3000 they'll turn on the lights for you), you can scramble for 15 minutes through chambers as high as a cathedral, past truck-sized stalactites and, in places, walls of crystal.

🏃 Activities

★ **Mt Zwegabin**   HIKING

(ဇွဲကပင်တောင်) The tallest of the limestone mountains that ring Hpa-an is Mt Zwegabin, about 7 miles south of town, which as well as being a respectable 2372ft is home to spirits and saintly souls. The two-hour hike to the summit is demanding – up many steps and with aggressive monkeys as constant adversaries – but once you're at the top the rewards are plentiful.

Mt Hpan Pu   HIKING

(ဖားပုတောင်) Mt Hpan Pu is a craggy, pagoda-topped peak that can be scaled in one sweaty morning. To get here, hop on a boat across the Thanlwin River (p506) from the informal jetty near Shweyinhmyaw Paya. After reaching the other side, you'll walk through a quiet village before the steep but relatively short ascent to the top.

TRANSPORT FROM HPA-AN

DESTINATION	BUS	VAN (SHARE TAXI)
Bago	K5000, 6hr, 6-11am & 6-8pm	N/A
Kyaikto	K5000, 4hr, 6-11am & 6-8pm	N/A
Mandalay	K15,000, 12hr, 5pm & 6pm	N/A
Mawlamyine	K1000, 2hr, hourly 6am-4pm	N/A
Myawaddy	N/A	K10,000, 4-6hr, hourly 6-11am
Yangon	K5000-8000, 7-8hr, 6-11am & 6-8pm	N/A

ℹ️ GETTING TO THAILAND

Hpa-an to Mae Sot

The Myawaddy/Mae Sot border crossing is 93 miles southeast of Hpa-an. If you have an e-visa, you are able to enter and exit Myanmar here.

Getting to the border Vans (share taxis) and buses linking Myawaddy with Hpa-an, Mawlamyine and Yangon terminate a short walk from the Friendship Bridge.

At the border The **Myanmar immigration office** (☎058-50100; AH1; ⊗6am-6pm) is at the foot of the Friendship Bridge. After you walk across the 0.25-mile bridge, the **Thai Immigration office** (☎in Thailand +066 55 56 3004; AH1, Mae Sot; ⊗6.30am-6.30pm) will grant you permission to stay in Thailand for up to 15 days if you don't have a Thai visa, or 30 days if you hold a passport from one of the G7 countries (Canada, France, Germany, Italy, Japan, the UK and the US).

Moving on Mae Sot's bus station is located 2 miles east of the border and has two buses a day to Chiang Mai and frequent connections to Bangkok. Mae Sot's airport is 2 miles east of the border, from where Nok Air (www.nokair.com) operates four daily flights to Bangkok. Both bus station and airport can be reached by frequent sŏrng·tǎa·ou (pick-ups) that run between the Friendship Bridge and Mae Sot from 6am to 6pm (20B).

Kawthoung to Ranong

Kawthoung (formerly known as Victoria Point) is at the far southern end of Tanintharyi Region. If you have an e-visa, you can enter/exit Myanmar here.

Getting to the border The bright-green **Myanmar border post** (Strand Rd; ⊗7am-4pm) is located a few steps from Kawthoung's jetty.

At the border If you've arrived in Kawthoung from elsewhere in Myanmar, you're free to exit the country here. After clearing Myanmar immigration, you'll be herded to a boat (100B per person) for the 20-minute ride to Ranong. On the Thai side, the authorities will issue you permission to stay in Thailand for up to 15 days – 30 days if you hold a passport from a G7 country – or you can enter with a Thai visa obtained overseas.

Moving on Ranong is a 50B motorcycle-taxi ride or 20B sŏrng·tǎa·ou (pick-up) ride from Saphan Pla Pier. **Nok Air** (☎in Thailand 1318; www.nokair.com) offers daily flights between Ranong and Bangkok, while major bus destinations include Bangkok, Hat Yai and Phuket.

For information on making this crossing in reverse see p765.

🛏️ Sleeping & Eating

Galaxy Motel GUESTHOUSE **$**
(☎09 566 1863, 058-21347; cnr Thitsar & Thida Sts; r incl breakfast US$22; ❄️🛜) The Galaxy is the sort of guesthouse Myanmar needs more of: tidy and clean, with spacious rooms that feature air-con, wi-fi and modern bathrooms. The friendly owner and staff get great feedback and can organise tickets and trips, as well as bicycle (K2000 per day) and motorbike (K7000 per day) hire.

Soe Brothers II Guesthouse GUESTHOUSE **$**
(☎058-22748, 09 7924 98664; soebrothers05821372@gmail.com; 4/820 Engyin St; r incl breakfast US$15-40; ❄️🛜) More upmarket than the original **guesthouse** (☎058-21372, 09 4977 1823; soebrothers05821372@gmail.com; 2/146 Thitsar St; dm US$5, r US$6-25; ❄️🛜), the latest addition to the Soe Brothers family's accommodation offerings features modern, fresh rooms in pastel pink. The cheaper singles aren't huge and are fan-only, but there's a nice roof terrace for breakfast, and the staff is solicitous. The riverside location means it's a 20-minute walk to the centre of town.

★San Ma Tau Myanmar Restaurant BURMESE **$**
(1/290 Bo Gyoke St; curries from K2500; ⊗10am-9pm) This local institution is one of the most appealing Burmese restaurants anywhere in the country. Friendly and popular, it serves a vast selection of rich curries, hearty soups and tart salads, all accompanied by platters of fresh veggies and herbs, and an overwhelming 10 types of local-style dips to eat with them.

① GETTING TO THAILAND: HTEE KHEE TO PHU NAM RON

The Htee Khee/Phu Nam Ron crossing is 100 miles east of Dawei. It's the most remote and least used of Myanmar's open borders with Thailand. You can exit Myanmar here with an e-visa (p550), but you cannot enter Myanmar here with one.

Getting to the border From Dawei, minivans (K13,000, five hours, 6am and 7am) make the run to the tiny outpost of Htee Khee.

At the border After being stamped out of Myanmar, catch the shuttle bus (50B) or take a motorcycle taxi (100B) across the 6 miles of no-man's land that separates the Myanmar border post from the Thai one. On the Thai side, the authorities will issue you permission to stay in Thailand for up to 15 days – 30 days if you hold a passport from a G7 country (Canada, France, Germany, Italy, Japan, the UK or the US) – or you can enter with a Thai visa obtained overseas.

Moving on From Phu Nam Ron, there are four buses daily to Kanchanaburi, from where there are frequent daily buses to Bangkok (120B, 2½ hours).

① Getting There & Away

BUS

Hpa-an's bus station is located about 4 miles east of town, but tickets can be bought and buses boarded at the **ticket stalls** (Bo Gyoke St; ⊙ 6am-9pm) near the clock tower. Buses to **Mawlamyine** (Bo Gyoke St; K1000; ⊙ hourly 6am-4pm) also stop here and at other spots around town. All hotels and guesthouses can arrange tickets.

Vans (share taxis) to Myawaddy depart from a **stall** (Bo Gyoke St; K10,000; ⊙ hourly 6am-9am) near the clock-tower intersection.

BOAT

There is no official ferry between Hpa-an and Mawlamyine, but private boats that carry 10 to 14 people can be chartered for K7500 to K8500 per person. Galaxy Motel (p505) and Soe Brothers Guesthouse (p505) can arrange this.

① Getting Around

Pick-ups to Eindu (K1000; ⊙ 7am-3pm), for Saddan Cave, depart near the corner of Thitsar and Zaydan Sts. **Boats to Mt Hpan Pu** (K500; ⊙ every 30min 6am-6pm) leave from a jetty at the end of Thidar St. The English-speaking

owner at **Good Luck Motorbike Rent** (Thitsar St; ⊙ 6am-10pm) hires out semi-automatic (K6000 per day) and automatic (K8000 per day) motorbikes.

Dawei

🚩 059 / POP C 80,120

The area near the mouth of the Dawei River has been inhabited for five centuries or more, mostly by Mon and Thai mariners. The present town dates from 1751, when it was a minor port for the Ayuthaya empire in Thailand (then Siam). From this point, it bounced back and forth between Burmese and Siamese rule until the British took over in 1826. Dawei remains a sleepy town, despite being the administrative capital of Tanintharyi Region.

Coconut Guesthouse & Restaurant GUESTHOUSE $
(🚩 09 42371 3681; www.coconutguesthouse.com; Phaw Taw Oo St, Maungmagan; r incl breakfast US$25-35; ❋ 🗐 🛜) This friendly Burmese- and French-run place is a 10-minute walk from Maungmagan beach. The 10 rooms and three

DAWEI TRANSPORT CONNECTIONS

DESTINATION	AIR	BUS
Htee Khee (for Thailand)	N/A	K20,000 (minivan), 5hr, 6am & 7am
Kawthoung	from US$100, 80min, daily	K30,000-35,000, 22hr, 5am
Mawlamyine	N/A	K12,000-13,000, 8hr, 5am, 1pm & 5pm
Myeik	N/A	K8000-10,000, 8hr, 5am, 10am, 3pm & 5pm
Yangon	from US$110, 65min, daily	K15,000, 16hr, 5am, 1pm, 2pm, 3pm & 5pm
Ye	N/A	K6000-8000, 4hr, 5am, 1pm & 5pm

WORTH A TRIP

BEACHES NEAR DAWEI

Dawei's most accessible beach is **Maungmagan**, a wide, sandy strip spanning approximately 7 miles along a pretty bay. On weekdays and outside holiday periods you're likely to have it mostly to yourself.

Maungmagan is around 11 miles west of Dawei. There's a daily, very crowded **truck** that departs from near Dawei's **Si Pin Tharyar Zei** (Arzani Rd; ⏰5am-6pm) at around 7am; otherwise motorcycles go to Maungmagan for K5000, *thoun bein* (motorised trishaws) for K12,000 and taxis for K25,000. From Maungmagan village, trucks depart, when bursting, for Dawei from the market area from 7am to 8am (K1000).

Several stunning and very empty white-sand beaches can be reached on day trips from Dawei or Maungmagan. For now, facilities are virtually non-existent, bar the odd simple restaurant. The few travellers who venture here normally do so on motorbikes that can be hired at Coconut Guesthouse & Restaurant in Maungmagan.

About 13 miles north of Maungmagan is **Nabule**, a lovely strip of sand with a golden pagoda at its northern end. Access is via a bad road.

Around 25 miles south of Dawei is **Teyzit**, a wide white-sand beach that's perhaps the prettiest in the area. There's a small fishing village here where you can find food, but the last stretch of the road to the beach is poor.

bungalows are set around a large garden and are comfortable enough and good value for the price. There's also a pleasant communal area and a reasonable restaurant serving Burmese, Thai and a few Western dishes, as well as more expensive seafood options.

★**Hotel Zayar Htet San** HOTEL **$$**
(☎059-23902; hotelzayarhtetsan@gmail.com; 566 Ye Yeik Thar St; r incl breakfast US$40-60; ❄🛜) This eye-catching hotel is easily the most stylish and contemporary accommodation in Dawei, as well as the best value. Rooms are a decent size, well equipped and feature the most comfortable beds in southern Myanmar. The attached restaurant serves OK Burmese-Chinese dishes.

Tavoy Kitchen BURMESE, CHINESE **$**
(☎09 45519 2525; 234 Phayar St; dishes from K2000; ⏰10am-3pm & 5-11pm) Simple but cute restaurant-cafe with a friendly English-speaking owner. The vegetarian-friendly menu ranges from noodle and rice dishes to more adventurous options like a fish-ball coconut curry. It's fine for a coffee or juice stop too. No alcohol served.

❶ Getting There & Away

Dawei's bus station is inconveniently located a couple of miles northeast of the city centre, but tickets can be purchased in advance from the various vendors near the canal on Ye Rd (although you'll still have to board your bus at the station). Minivans depart from their offices on Ye St or will pick you up at your hotel.

The daily truck to **Maungmagan beach** (Arzarni Rd; per person K1000) departs from the centre of town around 7am. It's possible to catch a minivan from Dawei to Htee Khee, where you can cross the border to Thailand.

INLE LAKE & SHAH STATE

Travellers to eastern Myanmar get the chance to experience both beautiful Inle Lake and some of the finest trekking in the country. Then there's the intriguing opportunity of getting right off the tourist trail in areas that see very few foreigners.

Inle Lake

The Inle Lake region is one of Myanmar's most anticipated destinations, and all the hype is justified. Picture a vast, serene lake – 13.5 miles long and 7 miles wide – fringed by marshes and floating gardens, where stilt-house villages and Buddhist temples rise above the water, and Intha fisher folk propel their boats along via their unique technique of leg-rowing. Surrounding the lake are hills that are home to myriad minorities: Shan, Pa-O, Taung Yo, Danu, Kayah and Danaw, who descend from their villages for markets that hopscotch around the towns of the region on a five-day cycle.

Nyaungshwe is the area's accommodation. It's a scrappy place, but once you've experienced the watery world that sits right by it and explored the environs of Inle Lake, that won't matter. Few people leave here disappointed with what they've seen and done.

The jumping-off point for Inle Lake is Nyaungshwe. But the town has no formal bus terminal or airport. If travelling to Inle Lake by air, you'll need to fly to Heho. Coming by land, you'll need to head to Taunggyi, hopping off in Shwenyaung, the junction leading to Nyaungshwe. A few bus and minivan services are now arriving in and departing from Nyaungshwe.

Nyaungshwe ညောင်ရွှေ

☑ 081 / POP C 80,000 (INCLUDING INLE LAKE)

Scruffy, busy Nyaungshwe is the main access point for Inle Lake. Located at the northern end of the lake, the town was once the capital of an important Shan kingdom (the former palace of the *saophas* (sky princes), who ruled here is now a museum). These days, Nyaungshwe has become a bustling travellers' centre, with dozens of guesthouses and hotels, an increasing number of restaurants, a few bars and a pleasantly relaxed vibe. If Myanmar can be said to have a backpacker scene at all, it can be found here.

◉ Sights

Yadana Man Aung Paya　BUDDHIST TEMPLE
(ရတနာမာန်အောင်ဘုရား; Phoung Taw Site St; ☺daylight hours) FREE The oldest and most important Buddhist shrine in Nyaungshwe, this handsome gilded stupa is hidden away inside a square compound south of Mingala Market. The stepped stupa is unique in Myanmar, and the surrounding pavilion contains a museum of treasures amassed by the monks over the centuries, including carvings, lacquerware and dance costumes.

Shwe Yaunghwe Kyaung　BUDDHIST TEMPLE
(ရွှေရောင်ဝဲကျောင်း; Nyaungshwe-Shwenyaung Rd; ☺daylight hours) FREE This is probably the most photographed monastery in

---

ⓘ INLE LAKE ENTRANCE FEE

There is a compulsory K13,500 fee to enter the Inle Lake area, which you must pay on arrival at the **permit booth** (☺6am-9pm) located by the bridge at the entrance to Nyaungshwe. Tickets are valid for one week, although you're unlikely to be asked to pay again if you stay longer.

Nyaungshwe: the unique oval windows in the ancient teak *thein* (ordination hall) create a perfect frame for portraits of the novices. The monastery is 1½ miles north of town on the road to Shwenyaung.

🛏 Sleeping

★ **La Maison Birmane**　HOTEL $$
(☑081-209 901; www.lamaisonbirmane.com; bungalows US$85-150; ❈@⏳) Nyaungshwe's only true boutique hotel is this charming compound of 10 wooden bungalows with thatched roofs set around a peaceful organic garden. The bungalows aren't huge, but they are attractive, with marble bathrooms in the more expensive rooms, and beds raised off the floor in all of them. You can laze around in the communal area, and the staff is attentive. Book ahead.

★ **Ostello Bello**　HOSTEL $
(☑081-209 302; www.ostellobello.com; Yone Gyi Rd; dm US$15-20, r US$80; ☺❈@⏳) This very well-organised new hostel – part of an expanding new chain – has become the go-to place for backpackers in Nyaungshwe. A variety of dorms is on offer, from four to 14 beds, all fair-sized with decent mattresses, bathrooms inside and cage lockers. Private rooms are comfortable, with TVs, fridges and spotless bathrooms.

★ **Song of Travel Hostel**　HOSTEL $
(☑081-209 731; www.songoftravel.com; Aung Chan Tha 5 St; dm US$17; ❈⏳) Nyaungshwe's original hostel remains an excellent choice. Artfully designed, with large roof terrace and big communal area, it has no private rooms, only identical light and spotless 14-bed dorms. Beds are curtained off for privacy and come with lockers, and the communal bathrooms are clean. It's a 20-minute walk to the centre of town, but free bikes are available.

Nawng Kham – Little Inn　GUESTHOUSE $
(☑081-209 195; noanhom@gmail.com; Phaung Daw Pyan Rd; r US$15-35; ❈⏳) The seven fan-only rooms here go quick, but the more expensive rooms with air-con and small balconies are almost as good a deal, featuring high ceilings and reasonably sized bathrooms. All look out on a pleasant garden. There's a small communal area and a good breakfast, and the staff is helpful.

Hotel Maineli　HOTEL $
(☑081-209 958; www.hotelmaineli.com; 66 Maine Li Quarter; r incl breakfast US$40-60; ❈⏳) This

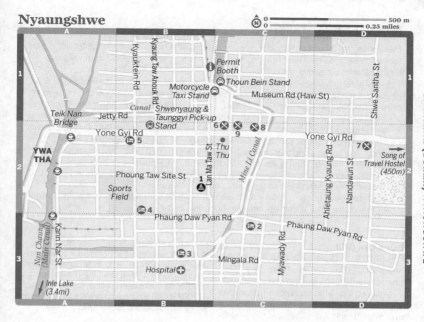

Nyaungshwe

impressive newcomer has big, wood-floored rooms that come with TVs, fridges, safety boxes and comfy beds. Bathrooms are plainer, but it's still a snip at the price. Rounding out the deal are professional staff, a peaceful location in a residential area and free bicycles.

✕ Eating

★ Lin Htett Myanmar
Traditional Food   BURMESE $

(☑ 09 42832 6575; Yone Gyi Rd; curries K3000-3500; ⏰10.30am-9.30pm) This is hands down the most appealing Burmese restaurant in Nyaungshwe, and one of the best curry houses in all Myanmar, where the service is as friendly as the food is delicious. Choose from a range of curries and salads, all accompanied by soup, dips and rice. Staff can also arrange cooking classes for K20,000 per person.

★ Live Dim Sum House   CHINESE $
(Yone Gyi Rd; dim sum K2000, mains K4500; ⏰11am-9pm) More and more people are making the walk to this laid-back place for the tasty and inventive dim sum – like prawn, bamboo shoot and water chestnut, or grilled pumpkin and mushroom – as well as for the other dishes on offer, such as Shanghai beef noodles or Kung Pao chicken (a spicy chicken, peanut and vegetable dish that's a Chinese staple).

Nyaungshwe

◎ Sights
1 Yadana Man Aung Paya B2

🛏 Sleeping
2 Hotel Maineli C3
3 La Maison Birmane B3
4 Nawng Kham – Little Inn................. B2
5 Ostello Bello B2

✕ Eating
6 Lin Htett Myanmar Traditional
  Food C2
7 Live Dim Sum House D2
8 One Owl Grill C2
9 Sin Yaw Bamboo Restaurant............ C2

★ Sin Yaw Bamboo
Restaurant   CHINESE, SHAN $

(Kyaung Daw A Shae St; mains K4000-4500; ⏰10am-10pm) The closest thing to an authentic Shan restaurant that you'll find in Nyaungshwe, run by a pleasant Shan-Chinese couple, Sin Yaw is now one of the most popular places in town. The food is good and flavoursome – they'll tone down the spices for Western palates if you want. Attentive service, and a passable mojito and Mandalay rum sour too.

INLE LAKE BOAT TRIPS

Every morning, a flotilla of slender wooden canoes fitted with long-tailed outboard motors surges across the lake, transporting visitors to various natural, cultural, religious, historical or commercial sites.

Every hotel, guesthouse and travel agent in Nyaungshwe can arrange motorboat trips, or you can make your own arrangements directly with the boat drivers at one of the piers or near Teik Nan Bridge – they'll most likely find you before you can find them. Prices for the standard day-long boat trip start at around K15,000, which typically includes visits to the famous sights in the northern part of the lake such as Phaung Daw Oo Paya in Tha Lay, the Nga Hpe Kyaung (Jumping Cat Monastery) in Nga Phe village and the floating gardens. Tacking on a trip to Inthein will raise the cost to K20,000. Other destinations further afield include Thaung Thut (K20,000, 1½ hours), Hmaw Be (K25,000, two hours) and Samkar (K50,000, three hours). The fee covers the entire boat; drivers will carry up to five passengers, who get padded seats and life jackets.

The boats have no roof, so be sure to wear sunscreen. Some people complain of wind chill while on the lake; if that sounds like you, bring a coat or wrap.

★ **One Owl Grill** INTERNATIONAL $$
(☑ 09 45209 6741; 1 Yone Gyi St; tapas from K2000, mains K6000-11,000; ⊙9am-11pm; 🗢) This French-owned bistro has proved a hit with its tapas-style, Mediterranean-influenced dishes, including the best hummus in Shan State, as well as its breakfasts, salads, burgers, pizza and pasta. It's a little more pricey than is usual for Nyaungshwe, but it stays open later than anywhere else. Also does potent cocktails and has a solid wine list.

ⓘ Getting There & Away

For such a popular destination, not that much transport arrives at, or departs from, Nyaungshwe. Instead, planes, many buses and all trains leave and arrive from nearby places such as Heho (the airport) and Shwenyaung.

AIR

The nearest airport is at Heho, an hour away by car. Taxis charge K25,000 from the airport to Nyaungshwe and K18,000 to go to the airport from Nyaungshwe.

BUS & PICK-UP TRUCKS

Any bus bound for Taunggyi can drop you at Shwenyaung – located at the junction for Nyaungshwe/Inle Lake – for the full Taunggyi fare. From Shwenyaung, *thoun bein* (three-wheeled taxi) drivers will take you the remaining 7 miles to Nyaungshwe for around K6000.

Nyaungshwe-based travel agents such as **Thu Thu** (☑ 081-209 258; thuthua79@gmail.com; Yone Gyi Rd; ⊙7am-9pm; 🗢) can sell tickets and arrange hotel pick-ups.

TRAIN

The train rumbling through the hills from Shwenyaung to Thazi is slow, but the scenery en route is stunning. From Shwenyaung's tiny station, trains depart at 8am and 9.30am, arriving in Kalaw after three hours (ordinary/upper class K500/1150) and reaching Thazi at least another six hours later (ordinary/upper class K1500/3000). *Thoun bein* drivers go to Shwenyaung's train station for K6000.

ⓘ Getting Around

Several shops on Yone Gyi Rd and Phaung Daw Pyan Rd rent out clunky Chinese bicycles for K1500 per day, as do some guesthouses and hotels.

Motorcycle taxis at the stand near the market go to Shwenyaung for around K6000.

Kalaw ကလော

☑ 081C 57,800 / POP C 57,800

Kalaw was founded as a hill station by British civil servants fleeing the heat of the plains. The town still feels like a high-altitude holiday resort – the air is cool, the atmosphere is calm and the tree-lined streets still contain a smattering of colonial-era architecture – while the surrounding hills are fine for relatively easy day or overnight treks to Danu, Danaw, Palaung, Pa-O and Taung Yo villages.

One of the few destinations in Myanmar that genuinely caters for backpackers rather than tour groups, Kalaw is an easy place to kick back for a few days. The town is also notable for its significant population of Nepali Gurkhas and Indians, whose ancestors came here to build the roads and railway during the colonial era.

Kalaw

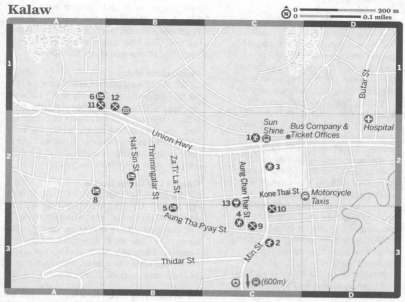

🏃 Activities

Almost everyone who comes to Kalaw goes trekking in the hills. The town is surrounded by Buddhist pagodas, hilltop viewpoints and the peaceful villages of the Palaung, Danu, Pa-O, Taung Yo and Danaw peoples, all set in a gorgeous landscape of forest-capped hills.

The most popular overnight trek is undoubtedly the two- to four-day trek to Inle Lake. You can also do a two-day mountain-bike trek along a similar route; contact **Naing Naing** (☑ 09 94283 12267, 09 54283 12265; naing.cc@gmail.com; Min St; bike hire per day K3000-5000; ☺ 8.30am-7pm) for details. A more adventurous overnight route is the multiday trek to Pindaya via Taung Ni (တောင်နီ).

On single-day treks, the only equipment you need is a pair of good walking shoes. Meals are usually included in the price of the trek, but you should buy and carry your own drinking water. Trekking goes on year-round, but expect muddy conditions during the rainy season (approximately June to October).

Trekking without a guide is not recommended – the trails are confusing and the terrain challenging, and few people in the hills speak English. The going rate for a day hike is around US$10 per person (in a group of four); overnight treks start at K32,000 per person, per day, in groups of two or more.

Green Hill Valley   WILDLIFE
(☑ in Yangon 09 7310 7278, 09 78514 5838; www.gh-velephant.com; Magway village; per person US$100) 🐘 Twelve fortunate elephants no longer fit for work in the government's timber camps have come to retire at Green Hill Valley, founded in 2011 by a family with a history of working with elephants. All visitors interact

DON'T MISS

KHAUNG DAING

Just because you've been on a boat trip doesn't mean you're finished with Inle Lake. The countryside that surrounds all that water is also worth a visit, and a half-day cycling trip from Nyaungshwe to Khaung Daing (ခေါင်တိုင်), an Intha village located at the northwestern corner of the lake, is an easy and worthwhile way to experience it. Make sure to check out **Phwar Ya Thay Paya** (ဖားရသေ့ဘုရား; ☉daylight hours) FREE, a hilltop temple on the road to Khaung Daing with amazing views over Inle Lake and the surrounding countryside. You can also take a dip in the **Hot Springs** (ခေါင်တိုင်ရေပူစမ်း; ☏09 4936 4876; hotspringinle@gmail.com; public pools US$7-10, private bath US$10; ☉5am-6pm), which are located on the road from Nyaungshwe to Khaung Daing.

Khaung Daing is a 45-minute bicycle ride from Nyaungshwe. To get here from Nyaungshwe, cross Teik Nan Bridge and follow the tree-lined, bone-shaking dirt track through the rice fields until you reach the sealed road, then turn left.

with the elephants, helping to feed and bathe them, and also get to plant a tree as part of the camp's reforestation project.

🛏 Sleeping

Genesis Motel   GUESTHOUSE $
(☏081-50842; genesismotel7@gmail.com; 18 Shwe Hin Thar St; incl breakfast r US$25-35, f US$50-60; ☻☏) There are only 10 compact but spotless rooms at this new place behind **Thiri Gay Har** (Union Hwy) restaurant, all

KALAW TREKKING COMPANIES

Sam's Trekking Guide (☏09 4580 40368, 081-50377; samtrekking@gmail. com; 21 Aung Chan Thar St; ☉7am-7pm)

Ever Smile (☏081-50683; toe1111@ gmail.com; Yuzana St; ☉7am-8pm)

Rural Development Society (RDS; ☏09 7861 16871, 081-50747; http://rural-developmentsociety.wordpress.com; Min St; ☉9am-6pm)

Naing Naing (p511)

with comfy beds and modern bathrooms. There's a professional staff, a couple of terraces to lounge on and a choice of breakfast options. The two family rooms also act as three-bed dorms and share bathrooms.

Pine Breeze Hotel   HOTEL $
(☏081-50459; www.pinebreezehotel.com; 174 Thittaw St; r incl breakfast US$35-45; ❋☏) Located just west of 'downtown' Kalaw, this baby-blue hilltop structure has four floors of comfortable, well-maintained rooms equipped with TV, fridges and heaters for cold nights. Upper-floor rooms are bigger and have little balconies for great views over the town.

Golden Lily Guest House   HOTEL $
(☏081-50108; 5/88 Nat Sin St; r K15,000-30,000; ☏) Kalaw's budget perennial looks its age and could do with a refit, especially the cell-like cheapest rooms that share grotty bathrooms. But the more expensive rooms are bigger and bearable, with wooden walls and floors and access to a large, wide communal balcony that overlooks the town.

★ **Dream Villa Hotel Kalaw**   HOTEL $$
(☏081-50144; dreamvilla@myanmar.com.mm; 5 Za Ti' La St; r incl breakfast US$50-65; ☏) A cut above your average Myanmar hotel, and still the best midrange option in Kalaw, the Dream Villa is a spotless three-storey home with 24 tasteful, attractively decorated wood-panelled rooms with a few local design touches. Efficient, English-speaking staff.

🍴 Eating & Drinking

★ **Thu Maung Restaurant**   BURMESE $
(Myanmar Restaurant; ☏081-50207; Union Hwy; curries K3500; ☉10am-9pm) Located in a bright-green building just past the post office, Thu Maung is one of the best Burmese curry restaurants in this part of the country, serving up rich, meaty chicken, pork, mutton and fish curries coupled with exceptionally delicious dips, sides, salads, pickles and trimmings. The tomato salad, made from crunchy green tomatoes, is a work of art.

Everest Nepali Food Centre   NEPALI $
(☏081-50348; Aung Chan Thar St; curries K4000-5500; ☉9.30am-9.30pm; ☏) Ever-popular, Nepali restaurant that serves up tasty curry spreads, complete with a good selection of side dishes, in pleasant surroundings.

★ **Red House**   ITALIAN $$
(☏09 77135 7407; redhousekalaw@gmail.com; 4/111 Min St; mains K6000-12,000; ☉11am-10pm;

TRANSPORT FROM KALAW

DESTINATION	BUS	MINIBUS	PICK-UP	TRAIN
Aungban (for Pindaya)	N/A	K1000, 20min, frequent 7am-3pm	K1000, 40min, frequent 7am-3qm	ordinary/upper class K250/K550, 1hr, 11.30am
Heho (airport)	N/A	K3000, 3hr, frequent 7am-3am	N/A	N/A
Loikaw	N/A	K4500, 6hr, 5am	N/A	ordinary/upper class K1550/2050, 13hr, 7am
Mandalay	K12,000, 7-8hr, 9.30am, 10.30am & 9pm	K13,000, 7hr, 9am & 10.30am	N/A	N/A
Meiktila	N/A	K7000, 4-5hr, frequent 8am-3pm	K4000, 4-5hr, frequent 7am-noon	N/A
Nay Pyi Taw	K11,000, 7-8hr, 9pm	N/A	N/A	ordinary/upper class K1500/K3050, 11hr, 12.49pm
Nyaung U (Bagan)	K12,000-18,000, 8hr, 9.30am & 8pm	K13,000, 7hr, 8.30am	N/A	N/A
Shwenyaung (for Inle Lake)	N/A	K3000, 3hr, frequent 7am-3pm	N/A	K500/K1150 (ordinary/ upper class), 3hr, 11.30am
Taunggyi	N/A	K3000, 3hr, frequent 7am-3pm	N/A	N/A
Thazi	N/A	K5000, 4hr, frequent 8am-3pm	K4000, 4hr, frequent 7am-3pm	ordinary/upper class K850/K1850, 7hr, 12.49pm
Yangon	K14,000-26,000, 10-12hr, 9.30am, 7pm, 8pm & 9pm	N/A	N/A	N/A

🔊) Very sophisticated for Kalaw, or anywhere in rural Myanmar, this new and worthwhile Italian-run restaurant offers homemade pasta, ravioli and wood-fired pizzas, as well as a smattering of local food. Set over two floors, it has a rooftop terrace to dine on, proper service and an impressive liquor selection, making for good cocktails, as well as wine.

★ **Hi Snack & Drink** BAR
(Kone Thai St; ⊙5-11pm) That rare thing: a genuine bar in a provincial Burmese town, Hi is the size of a closet and boasts a fun, speakeasy feel. If you haven't had its trademark rum sour (K2000), you haven't been to Kalaw. No beer served; just the hard stuff.

❶ Getting There & Away

Several **bus ticket offices** (Union Hwy) across from the market, including **Sun Shine** (☎09 3620 1202; Union Hwy; ⊙7am-9pm), book seats on the long-distance buses between Taunggyi

and various destinations. Air-con buses, fan-cooled minivans and pick-ups to other destinations in and around Shan State also stop along this stretch of the Union Hwy (NH4).

Kalaw is served via flights to Heho, about 16 miles away. Taxis waiting at the airport charge K20,000 to Kalaw (1½ hours); a cheaper option is to hike the near mile to the Union Hwy and wait for a westbound bus or pick-up, although you may face a long wait.

Pindaya ပင်းတယ

The road to sleepy Pindaya cuts across one of the most densely farmed areas in Myanmar. But it's the Danu, Palaung and Pa-O villages, rather than the farms, around Pindaya that draw travellers for treks through less-visited areas than elsewhere in western Shan State. Local guide **Sai Win Htun** (☎09 7883 26316, 09 2507 84688; shwegue.pdy@gmail.com; Golden Cave Hotel, Shwe U Min Padoga Rd) comes

INLE LAKE TRANSPORT CONNECTIONS

Air

Destinations to/from Heho include the following:

DESTINATION	PRICE	DURATION	FREQUENCY
Kyaingtong	from US$142	55min-2¾hr	daily
Lashio	from US$80	45min-1hr	daily via Mandalay
Mandalay	from US$62	30min	daily
Nyaung U (Bagan)	from US$70	75min	daily
Tachileik	from US$105	45min-1¾hr	daily via Mandalay
Yangon	from US$93	1-2¾hr	daily

Bus

From Inle Lake, some bus companies now make stops in Nyaungshwe, or run morning mini-vans to the following destinations:

DESTINATION	PRICE	DURATION (HR)	FREQUENCY
Hpa-an	K26,000	15	4.30pm
Loikaw	K12,000	10	8am
Mandalay	K11,000-18,000	10	9am, 6.30pm & 7.30pm
Myawaddy	K31,000	17	4.30pm
Nyaung U (Bagan)	K11,000-22,000	11	7.30am, 8am, 9am, 7pm & 8pm
Yangon	K14,500-28,000	12	8.30am, 9am, 5.30pm, 6.30pm & 7.30pm

recommended for leading hikes. Another good reason to make the journey here is to visit the famous **Shwe Oo Min Natural Cave Pagoda** (ရွှေဦးမင်သဘာဝလိုဏ်ဂူဘုရား; Shwe U Min Pagoda Rd; K3000, camera fee K300; ☺6am-6pm), a massive limestone cavern filled with thousands of gilded buddha statues.

The immaculate **Conqueror Resort Hotel** (☎081-66106; www.conquerorresorthotel.com; r US$70-100; ❋☞☎) is the pick of Pindaya's accommodation.

To get here catch the vans or pick-up trucks that run from near the clock-tower intersection in Aungban, a few miles east of Kalaw, from 7.30am to 11am. Waiting motorcycle taxis (K6000 one way, K10,000 return) and taxis (K30,000 one way, K50,000 return) are another option.

MANDALAY REGION

The Mandalay region is the major population centre of upper Burma and the cradle of Burmese arts, culture and civilisation. Whereas Yangon is a diverse microcosm of the nation, Mandalay – for all its traffic and construction – remains an urban expression of Burmese ethnic identity. Throw in Upper Burmese cuisine, friendly locals and sunsets over the Ayeyarwady (Irrawaddy) River, and you have a region worthy of careful exploration.

Mandalay   မန္တလေး

☑02 / POP C 1,225,546

Mandalay will never win any beauty contests. Myanmar's second city is a relatively new creation, founded at the foot of Mandalay Hill in 1857 by King Mindon as his royal capital. The hill, its slopes studded with pagodas, still looms over the city. But Mandalay was bombed flat in WWII and the palace disappeared, along with much else. The palace was rebuilt in the 1990s, and since then Mandalay has undergone a haphazard construction boom that was never about aesthetics. An ever-growing number of motorbikes and cars clog the roads, too, making for a sometimes smoggy city.

But if you can shut out all the honking, Mandalay has its own charm. There are splendid markets, many monasteries, Indian temples, mosques, gold workshops and a bustling, working riverside to explore, as well as a thriving teahouse culture that offers visitors the chance to mingle with the exceptionally friendly locals.

> ℹ **GETTING TO THAILAND: TACHILEIK TO MAE SAI**
>
> The Tachileik/Mae Sai broder crossing is 95 miles south of Kyaingtong. It's possible to enter/exit Myanmar here with an e-visa.
>
> **Getting to the border** The border is a short walk from 'downtown' Tachileik, or 1.2 miles and a K1500/50B motorcycle-taxi ride from the town's five bus stations.
>
> **At the border** If you've arrived in Kyaingtong or Tachileik via air from elsewhere in Myanmar, you can freely exit the country at Tachileik. The Myanmar border post is open from 6am to 6pm, and when you cross to Thailand the authorities will issue you permission to stay in Thailand for up to 15 days, or 30 days if you have a passport from one of the G7 countries (Canada, France, Germany, Italy, Japan, the UK or the US).
>
> **Moving on** Mae Sai's bus station is 4km from the border; pick-ups ply the route between the bus station and Soi 2, Th Phahonyothin (15B, 15 minutes, 6am to 9pm). Alternatively, it's a 40B motorcycle-taxi ride. From Mae Sai, major bus destinations include Bangkok, Chiang Mai and Chiang Rai.
>
> For information on making the crossing in reverse see p715.

◉ Sights

Several of Mandalay's top attractions are covered by a K10,000 Archaeological Zone ('combo') ticket valid for one week from first purchase. Currently the ticket is checked (and sold) at Mandalay Palace and Shwenandaw Kyaung. It's also sold in **Inwa**.

★ Mandalay Hill   LANDMARK

(မန္တလေးတောင်; Map p516; camera fee K1000) To get a sense of Mandalay's pancake-flat sprawl, climb the 760ft hill that breaks it. The walk up covered stairways on the hill's southern slope is a major part of the experience; note that you'll need to go barefoot in places, as you pass through numerous temples and pagodas. The climb takes a good 30 minutes, but much longer if you allow for stops en route. The summit viewpoint is especially popular at sunset, when young monks converge on foreigners for language practice.

★ Shwe In Bin Kyaung   BUDDHIST MONASTERY

(ရွှေအင်းပင်းကျောင်း; Map p518; 37/38; with Archaeological Zone ticket K10,000; ⊙7am-6.30pm) A meditative departure from the usual Burmese 'douse-it-all-in-gold-and-pastels' aesthetic, this gorgeously carved teak monastery is beloved by tourists and locals. Commissioned in 1895 by a pair of wealthy Chinese jade merchants, the central building stands on tree-trunk poles and the interior has a soaring dark majesty. Balustrades and roof cornices are covered in detailed engravings, a few of them mildly humorous.

★ Mahamuni Paya   BUDDHIST TEMPLE

(မဟာမုနိဘုရား; 83rd St; ⊙complex 24hr, museum sections 8am-5pm) FREE Every day, thousands of colourfully dressed faithful venerate Mahamuni's 13ft-tall **seated buddha**, a nationally celebrated image that's popularly believed to be some 2000 years old. Centuries of votary gold leaf applied by male devotees (women may only watch) has left the figure knobbly with a 6in layer of pure gold...except on his radiantly gleaming face, which is ceremonially polished daily at 4am.

Jade Market   MARKET

(ကျောက်ဝိုင်း; Map p518; 87th St, 39/40; K2500; ⊙8am-4pm) Rock dust and cheroot smoke fill the air in this heaving grid of cramped walkways, where you'll find a mass of jade traders haggling, hawking and polishing their wares. There's a K2500 entry fee (not always collected), but you could always sit outside the market and observe craftspeople cutting and polishing jade in the area around 87th St. Be on the lookout for merchants furtively discussing deals over cigarettes and tea at spots such as the **Unison Teahouse** (Map p518; 38th St at 88th St; tea K300; ⊙5am-1am).

Shwenandaw Kyaung   BUDDHIST MONASTERY

(ရွှေနန်းတော်ကျောင်း; Golden Palace Monastery; Map p516; 62nd St, at 14th St; with Archaeological Zone ticket K10,000) Lavished with carved panels, this fine teak monastery-temple is noted for its carvings, particularly the interior gilded scenes from the Jataka (past-life stories of the Buddha). The building once stood within the Mandalay Palace complex as the royal apartment of King Mindon, who died inside it in 1878.

Mandalay Palace　　　　　PALACE
(မန္တလေးနန်းတော်; Map p516; East Gate, 66th St; with Archaeological Zone ticket K10,000; ⊙7.30am-4.30pm) The 1990s reconstruction of Man-

dalay's royal palace features more than 40 timber buildings built to resemble the 1850s originals. Climb the curious spiral, timber-walled **watchtower** for a good general view. The palace's most striking structure is a soaring multilayered pyramid of gilt filigree

Royal Mandalay

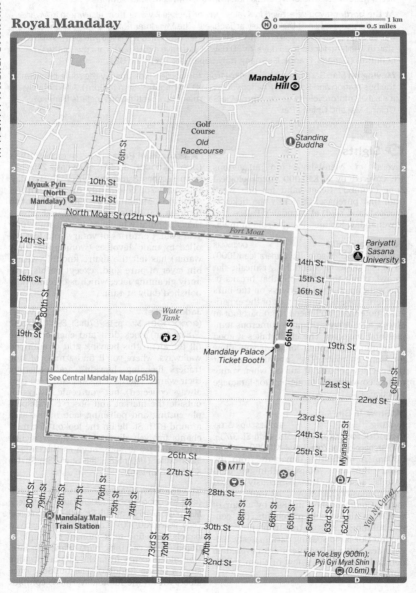

above the main **throne room**. Parts of the complex are now in need of repair.

Palace access for foreigners is only via the east gate and you may be asked for ID.

🛏 Sleeping

⭐ Ostello Bello   HOSTEL $
(Map p518; ☎ 02-64530; www.ostellobello.com; 28th St, 73/74; dm US$10-24, r US$70; ⊖ ❉ @ 🛜)
The least impressive of the Ostello Bello brood, mainly because it lacks the space of the branches in New Bagan (p533) and Nyaungshwe (p508), this is still the best hostel in Mandalay by some distance. Comfy dorms with their own bathrooms, free pasta snacks, a rooftop terrace, a busy bar and communal area, and solicitous service mean you'll need to book ahead.

Yoe Yoe Lay   GUESTHOUSE $
(☎ 09-44404 1944; nanbwe1@gmail.com; 58th St, 35/36; 4- & 6-bed dm US$8-11, s & d US$18-22; ❉ @ 🛜) Dorms at this friendly place are cramped but come with air-con, decent mattresses and small lockers. Private rooms are also compact, but they're comfortable enough; the cheapest share bathrooms. There's an outside communal area. The only drawback is the inconvenient location in eastern Mandalay that's a K1000 motorcycle-taxi ride to anywhere (bicycles can be hired for K2000 per day).

79 Living Hotel   HOTEL $
(Map p518; ☎ 02-32277; www.79livinghotel.com; 79th St, 29/30; r/f incl breakfast US$35/70; ❉ 🛜)
This sensibly priced hotel is handily placed behind the train station. Rooms come with TVs, fridges and safes, and have gleaming clean floors, high ceilings and maybe a (fake) welcome rose on the bed. There's a rooftop terrace-bar for breakfast and happy hour (6pm to 8pm) and free bicycle hire.

Ayarwaddy River View Hotel   HOTEL $$
(Map p518; ☎ 02-64945; http://ayarwaddyriverviewhotel.net; Strand Rd, 22/23; r incl breakfast US$70-150; ❉ @ 🛜 ⊠) Luxurious for the price, this sizeable, professional hotel has tasteful decor and large, fully equipped rooms sporting parquet floors and decent bathrooms. The best rooms have superb views, either across the river towards Mingun or overlooking the city, Mandalay Hill and the Shan uplands. The rooftop bar is famed for its daily happy hour and stages marionette shows in high season.

Hotel 8   HOTEL $$
(Map p518; ☎ 02-31448; www.hotel8mandalay.com; 29th St, 82/83; r incl breakfast US$40-60; ❉ 🛜) This multistorey glass tower is decent value for money. The staff is smiley and helpful, the location is central, the rooms are clean and comfortable with some splashes of colour to liven them up, and there's free bike hire.

🍴 Eating

⭐ Aye Myit Tar   BURMESE $
(Map p518; 530, 81st St; curries K4000-6500; ⏱ 9am-10pm; ❉) Brightly lit, this simple but historic thick-walled colonial-era merchant's building houses central Mandalay's most popular upmarket curry eatery. There's a big range of chicken, fish and pork curries; all come with sides, soup and rice. Alternatively, boost your meal by choosing from the salad and vegetable dishes on the menu.

⭐ Shan Ma Ma   SHAN $
(Map p518; ☎ 02-71858; 81st St, 29/30; meals K1500-4000; ⏱ 11am-9.30pm; 🍴) Plastic stools and chairs? Check. Delicious aroma of food awaiting your inspection? Check. And the friendly sisters who run it will offer you a taste of what's on offer before you decide. This is Southeast Asian budget dining at its best, with a range of meat, fish and vegetable dishes served in a semi-open-air dining area that buzzes come nightfall.

Lashio Lay   SHAN $
(Map p518; ☎ 02-22653; 23rd St, 83/84; per plate K2000-3000; ⏱ 10am-9.30pm) This simple, long-running restaurant is known for

Central Mandalay

consistently good, Shan-inspired dishes. Point and pick, and pay per dish – a couple of curries and some rice ought to fill you up. Popular for cold beers as the evening goes on.

Marie-Min   VEGETARIAN **$**
(Map p518; mains K2000-3000; ☉9am-10pm; 🛜🖉) An all-vegetarian menu fits the owners' stated principle: 'Be kind to animals by not eating them'. The food largely references Sri Lanka, India and Myanmar; highlights

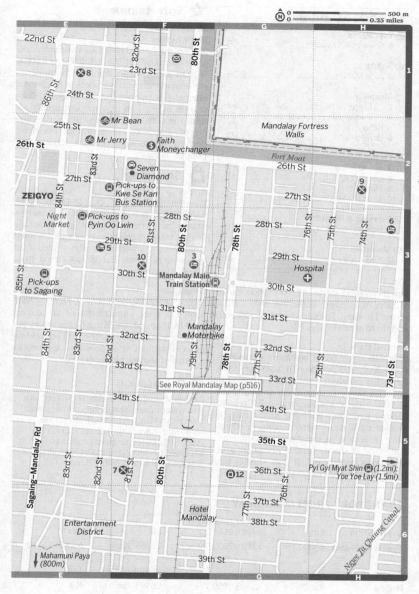

0   500 m
0   0.25 miles

22nd St

8

86th St

24th St

23rd St

82nd St

80th St

25th St   Mr Bean

26th St

Mr Jerry

Faith Moneychanger

Mandalay Fortress Walls

Fort Moat

26th St

ZEIGYO

33rd St

27th St

Seven Diamond

Pick-ups to Kwe Se Kan Bus Station

84th St

27th St

9

Night Market

Pick-ups to Pyin Oo Lwin

28th St

28th St

28th St

76th St

75th St

74th St

6

81st St

29th St

5

80th St

78th St

29th St

29th St

Hospital

85th St

Pick-ups to Sagaing

30th St

10

3

Mandalay Main Train Station

30th St

31st St

84th St

83rd St

82nd St

32nd St

Mandalay Motorbike

79th St

78th St

77th St

75th St

32nd St

73rd St

33rd St

33rd St

See Royal Mandalay Map (p516)

34th St

34th St

35th St

Sagaing–Mandalay Rd

83rd St

82nd St

81st St

7

80th St

36th St

76th St

Pyi Gyi Myat Shin (1.2mi); *Yoe Yoe Lay* (1.5mi)

12

77th St

37th St

Entertainment District

38th St

Hotel Mandalay

Mahamuni Paya (800m)

39th St

Ngoe Ta Chaung Canal

---

include tofu curry, a meal-sized aubergine 'dip', and avocado milkshakes (K2000) that are as 'fabulous' as promised. Very popular with backpackers. It's off 27th St, between 74th and 75th Sts.

Ko's Kitchen   THAI **$$**
(Map p516; ☎02-69576; 80th St at 19th St; mains K4000-10,000; ☺11am-2.30pm & 5-9pm; ✦) Popular with cashed-up locals and sometimes tour groups, this place set in an attractive art-deco building with simple,

Central Mandalay

◎ Top Sights
1 Shwe In Bin Kyaung C6

◎ Sights
2 Jade Market D6

⬤ Sleeping
3 79 Living Hotel F3
4 Ayarwaddy River View Hotel B1
5 Hotel 8 ....E3
6 Ostello Bello H3

✖ Eating
7 Aye Myit Tar F5
8 Lashio Lay E1
9 Marie-Min H2
10 Shan Ma Ma F3

◎ Drinking & Nightlife
11 Unison Teahouse C6

⬤ Shopping
12 King Galon G5

peach-coloured decor offers a wide range of tasty, reasonably authentic dishes from across Thailand. Spice levels can be adjusted and there are daily specials.

Central Park BAR
(Map p516; 27th St, 68/69; beer from K900, cocktails from K3000; ☺3-11pm Mon-Fri, 11am-11pm Sat & Sun) This convivial semi-open-air bar combines the best points of a beer-and-barbecue station with a low-key, musically eclectic cocktail bar, while adding a tourist-friendly food menu – pizza, burgers, wings and nachos – to boot. It's a sociable place to unwind, and some of the decorative Myanmar artefacts are a century old. It does shishas too. Happy hour is 6pm to 7.30pm.

☆ Entertainment

★ Myanmar Marionettes PUPPET THEATRE
(Map p516; ☑02-34446; www.myanmarmarionettes.com; 66th St at 27th St; K15,000; ☺8.30pm; 🖥) On a tiny stage, colourful marionettes expressively recreate snippets of traditional tales at this puppet theatre. Occasionally a curtain is lifted so that you can briefly admire the deft hand movements of the puppeteers (one's an octogenarian), who have performed internationally. You can also buy puppets here.

🔒 Shopping

Rocky GIFTS & SOUVENIRS
(Sein Win Myint; Map p516; ☑02-284 4106; 27th St, 62/63; ☺8am-8pm) Excellent, family-run, reputable handicrafts shop; the goods include lacquerware, puppets, carvings and stuffed 'gold-thread' appliqué tapestries, plus a lot of jewellery, gems and jade, sourced from across Myanmar.

King Galon ARTS & CRAFTS
(Map p518; ☑02-32135; 36th St, 77/78; ☺8am-6pm) The most sophisticated of Mandalay's gold-leaf workshops, King Galon offers patient explanations of the gold-pounding process without sales pressure. Also stocks a range of souvenir handicrafts.

❶ Orientation

Central Mandalay city streets are laid out on a grid system. East–west streets are numbered from 1st to 49th. North–south streets are numbered above 50th. A street address that reads 66th, 26/27, means a location on 66th St between 26th and 27th Sts. Corner addresses are given in the form 26th at 82nd.

TRANSPORT FROM MANDALAY

DESTINATION	BUS	TRAIN (ORDINARY/ UPPER CLASS)	AIR	BOAT
Nyaung U (Bagan)	K9000, 8hr	K1450/2900, 9hr	US$65, 30min	from US$18, 10-14hr
Bhamo	N/A	N/A	US$101, 50min	N/A
Hsipaw	K5000, 7hr	K2700/3950, 11hr	US$93, 45min to Lashio +2hr taxi	N/A
Inle Lake	K12,500-16,500, 11hr	N/A	US$77, 30min via Heho +1hr taxi	N/A
Nay Pyi Taw	K8500, 5hr	K1900/3700, 5hr	N/A	N/A
Yangon	K14,500-20,500, 11hr	K4700/9300 sleeper 12,750, 15½-16½hr	US$100, 90min	N/A

BOATS FROM MANDALAY

Taking a boat on the Ayeyarwady River is one of Mandalay's delights. Flits to Mingun (US$8, one hour) or all-day rides to Bagan (from US$42, 10 hours) are the most popular, though a return service to Inwa is a great alternative. Prebooking one day ahead is usually fine for Bagan – bring plenty of drinking water.

Boats to Mingun depart at 9am; boats to Bagan leave around 7am.

IWT Ferries (Map p518; ☑ 02-36035, 01-381 912; www.iwt.gov.mm/en; Gawein Jetty) Ferries to Bagan on Wednesday and Sunday. Boats leave at 5.30am and tickets cost K18,000. Buy them at the **IWT Ticket Office** (Map p518; 35th St; ⊙ 9am-5pm).

Malikha (Map p518; ☑ 02-72279; www.malikha-rivercruises.com; to Bagan/Mandalay US$47/33) Comfy tourist boats do the Bagan run. Buy tickets through hotels or agencies or online.

MGRG (Map p518; ☑ 09-9100 6098; www.mgrgexpress.com; Strand Rd; to Bagan US$42) Bagan express ferries. Buy tickets from a booth at the **jetty** (Map p518).

Nmai Hka (Map p518; ☑ 09 40270 0072; nmaihkamdy@gmail.com; 35th St at 92nd St; to Bagan US$42) Shwei Keinnery ferries to Bagan (tourist season). Buy tickets from its office just south of Strand Rd, close to where the IWT boats depart. Departures are from Gawein Jetty.

Tourist Boat Association (Mayan Chan Jetty; Map p518; to Mingun US$8) Departs for Mingun at 9am from a jetty at the end of 26th St. No prebooking; just show up.

Information

MONEY

Pristine euro and US-dollar notes can be changed for excellent rates at Mandalay Airport and at downtown moneychangers and banks. There are numerous ATMs.

TOURIST INFORMATION

Seven Diamond (Map p518; ☑ 02-72939, 02-72868; www.sevendiamondtravels.com; 82nd St, 26/27; ⊙ 8.30am-6pm, closed Sun) Helpful, major agency that can book flights and hotels, and organise airport-bound shared taxis.

Getting There & Away

AIR

All international and domestic flights use **Mandalay International Airport** (MDL; ☑ 02-27048, 02-27027), which is just over 20 miles south of the city.

BUS

Mandalay has three major bus stations. **Thiri Mandalar bus station** (Map p518; 89th St at 23rd St) is relatively central. **Pyi Gyi Myat Shin bus station** (60th St) is 2 miles east of the centre and has buses for Hsipaw and Lashio. The main **Kwe Se Kan bus station** (Highway Bus Station, Chan Mya Shwe Pyi) is 5 miles south of the centre. The K3000/6000 motorbike/taxi ride from central Mandalay can take 45 minutes; **pick-ups** (Map p518; K500), which leave from 27th St, just east of the intersection with 83rd St, can take even longer. Allow plenty of time

once you're there to find the right bus in the mayhem.

Prebooking bus tickets for longer-distance routes (over four hours) is wise. Booking through backpacker hotels will usually incur a commission, but that's rarely more than the motorbike-taxi fare you'd incur when buying your own. **Academy** (☑ 02-78699 02-78885; K25,300) provides a bus service connecting Mandalay with Mrauk U. The bus departs Kwe Se Kan bus station daily at 4pm and gets to Mrauk U the next day around 1pm.

TRAIN

The **train station** (30th St, 78/79) is relatively central, but trains rarely run to schedule.

Getting Around

GETTING TO/FROM THE AIRPORT

There's a fixed rate of US$10/K12,000 for a private taxi, US$5/K4000 for a shared taxi. Cheaper guesthouses will order you an airport car for about the same price as a shared taxi, but big hotels ask for a fair bit more. Taxis on the street typically want a double fare, as they'll find it hard to get a return ride.

BICYCLE

Several rental agents in the central backpacker area charge around K2000/10,000 per day for bicycles/motorbikes including long-established **Mr Jerry** (Map p518; ☑ 02-65312; 83rd St, 25/26; ⊙ 8am-8pm) and **Mr Bean** (Map p518; ☑ 02-31770; 83rd St, 24/25). Several hotels

CRUISING THE UPPER AYEYARWADY

At the time of research, foreigners were barred from taking IWT ferries between Mandalay and Bhamo and north from Bhamo to Myitkyina. However, foreigners can fly into Bhamo and then travel south by IWT ferries or fast boats to Katha and Mandalay.

IWT ferries are cheap and the best for interacting with locals, but they're slow and unreliable. Ferries run three times a week (Monday, Wednesday and Friday) between Bhamo and Mandalay, with stops in Shwegu, Katha, Ti-Kyaing, Tagaung and Kyaukmyaung. Boats can be a day or more late. Tickets need to be booked at the relevant IWT office and paid for in pristine US-dollar bills. You'll generally need to sleep aboard at least one night. A few simple cabins are available (US$60, shared toilet), but most folk travel deck class (maximum fare US$12), for which you'll need your own mat and bedding. Pricey snacks and drinks are sold aboard. Food can also be bought at the boat stops.

Fast boats are long, covered motorboats. Fast boats make daily one-day hops along the following sections, always by day: Bhamo–Shwegu–Katha and Katha–Mandalay. Buy tickets just before departure, or one day before for Katha–Mandalay. They are more expensive than the IWT ferries. The wooden bench seats are small. Life jackets may not be available. You'll need to sleep at local guesthouses. You can buy food at the brief intermediate halts.

Boats run all year but journeys are fastest in autumn, when water levels are high. April is difficult due to Burmese New Year, when locals pack out the boats. Between May and October, rain and high winds can make the passage very uncomfortable.

The most eye-catching part of the journey is the section between Bhamo and Shwegu, when the scenery reaches a modest climax in the short second defile, where the Ayeyarwady passes through a wooded valley with a rocky cliff face at one point, often described misleadingly as a gorge. Further south, Katha is popular for its George Orwell connection, while you can disembark at the interesting pottery town of Kyaukmyaung and travel to Bagan overland.

The minimum time from Bhamo to Mandalay by IWT ferry will be two to three days. You can save time by jumping ship at Katha and catching the express boat or train to Mandalay.

rent bicycles too. Cyclists are advised to carry a head torch at night.

To go further afield, expat-run **Mandalay Motorcycle** (Map p518; ☑ 09 44402 2182; www.mandalaymotorbike.com; 32nd St, 79/80; per day city bike from K10,000, trail bike from K40,000) and **Myanmar Bike Rental** (☑ 09 4211 30276; www.myanmarbikerental.com; 59th St, 22/19; city bikes K5000-15,000, 200cc K25,000, motorcyle K50,000) have city bikes and trail bikes. Call ahead or shoot them an email to set up your rental and plan your route.

MOTORCYCLE & TAXI

Motorcycle taxis lurk near hotels and on city corners. Expect to pay K1000 for a short hop, K1500 across the centre, and K10,000 for all-day hire within Mandalay (K15,000 including Amarapura, Inwa and Sagaing); double these rates for a regular taxi.

Seven Diamond Express (Map p518; ☑ 02-22365; 82nd St, 26/27) is a local taxi service.

Amarapura   အမရပူရ

Myanmar's penultimate royal capital, Amarapura (amu-*ra*-pu-*ra*) means 'City of Immortality', though its period of prominence lasted less than 70 years (from 1783). These days leafy Amarapura is essentially a spread-out suburb of Mandalay, attractively set on a wide, shallow lake, named for an ogre who supposedly came looking for the Buddha here.

The wide roads and twisting alleyways make Amarapura feel less aggressively modern than Mandalay. The main attraction is the iconic wooden U-Bein footbridge that crosses the lake. Several other minor sights are widely scattered – you'll need a bike or taxi to see them all.

Crammed-full pick-up trucks leave from 84th St at 29th St in Mandalay (K500, 45 minutes) and pass along the main Sagaing road. For U-Bein Bridge, get off just after the road crosses the railway and walk east or take a horse cart (K2000).

A return taxi from Mandalay with an added 90 minutes of sightseeing should run around K10,000, or K7000 on a motorbike.

Inwa အင်းဝ

Since 1364, Inwa, formerly known as Ava, has had four stints as the royal capital of the Burmese people. Indeed, upper Burma was often referred to as the 'Kingdom of Ava', even well after the royal court abandoned Inwa for Amarapura in 1841. Despite its rich history, the site today is a remarkably rural backwater sparsely dotted with ruins, monastic buildings and stupas. It's a world away from the hustle of Mandalay, which is a big part of its charm. Many visitors like to explore by horse cart, and while this can be appealing, cycling allows more flexibility, village stops and human interactions.

The Mandalay 'combo ticket' is theoretically required to visit Inwa, but it's only checked if you enter Bagaya Kyaung or Maha Aungmye Bonzan.

★ **Bagaya Kyaung** BUDDHIST MONASTERY (ဘားကရာကျောင်း; with Mandalay combo ticket K10,000; ⊙daylight hours) This lovely 1834 teak monastery is Inwa's most memorable individual attraction. It's supported on 267 teak posts, the largest 60ft high and 9ft in circumference, creating a cool and dark prayer hall that feels genuinely aged. Stained timbers are inscribed with repeating peacock and lotus-flower motifs. Despite the constant flow of visitors, this remains a living monastery, with globes hung above the little school section to assist in the novices' geography lessons. Beware of protruding floorboard nails.

Shwezigon Paya BUDDHIST SITE (ရွှေစည်းခုံဘုရား) This golden stupa rises photogenically above the overgrown southwestern corner of Inwa's city walls. The best view is from across the moat, especially in September, when the water level is high. The main access is from the northwestern city gate, but there's also a small pathway at the back of the associated monastery, allowing you to continue east by bicycle or motorbike.

🛈 Getting There & Around

Sagaing–Mandalay pick-ups can drop you at Inwa Lanzou junction just west of Ava Bridge. From there it's a 15-minute walk or a 10-minute **trishaw** (Inwa Lanzou Junction; K200) ride to the Myitnge river crossing. A covered wooden longboat shuttles across to Inwa's eastern jetty (K800, with bicycle/motorbike K1000/1500 return, two minutes) around every 15 minutes according to demand, with last departures at 6pm.

Unless you specify otherwise, most taxis and motorbike taxis will drop you at the Myitnge Jetty.

Within Inwa there are no taxis or motorbike taxis (unless you hire your own in Mandalay).

The most popular way to get around is by **horse cart** (K10,000). Dozens of carts wait at Inwa's eastern jetty.

Sagaing စစ်ကိုင်း

A crest of green hills studded with white and gold pagodas marks the 'skyline' of Saigang, a religious pilgrimage centre that resembles Bagan with elevation. This pretty, friendly town is a major monastic centre and a somewhat serene escape from Mandalay's constant hum. No individual pagoda stands out as a particular must-see, but taken together the whole scene is enthralling. A highlight is walking the sometimes steep covered stairways that lead past monasteries and nunneries to viewpoints from where you can survey the river and an undulating landscape of emerald hills and stupas.

🛈 Getting There & Away

Pick-ups from Mandalay (K500, one hour) drop off passengers in the market area but return from outside Aye Cherry Restaurant, by the Ava Bridge's south slip road.

If the river is behaving, **longboats** (Strand Rd; per person/boat K400) will shuttle you across to Inwa from the end of Zeya St. Charter one or be prepared to wait many hours.

> **WORTH A TRIP**
>
> ### ANISAKAN FALLS
>
> Just north of Anisakan village the plateau disappears into an impressive, deeply wooded amphitheatre, its sides ribboned with several waterfalls. The most spectacular of the **Anisakan Falls** (အနီးစခန်းရေတံခွန်) is the gorgeous three-step Dat Taw Gyaik, whose last stage thunders into a shady splash pool beside a small pagoda on the valley floor. It's best visited in the early morning or late afternoon.

DON'T MISS

COLONIAL BUILDINGS

Most of Pyin Oo Lwin's trademark colonial-era buildings are dotted amid the southeastern woodland suburbs on and off Circular Rd. Many look like classic 1920s British homes, while the biggest have the feel of a St Trinian's–style boarding school. There's also a number of decaying but still impressive mansions on Nan Myaing St heading towards the Naval College.

Check out the splendid **Former Croxton Hotel** (Gandamar Myaing Hotel; Circular Rd) FREE, as well as the **Number 4 High School** (Circular Rd) FREE and the **Survey Training Centre** (Multi-Office Rd) FREE. Up near the Shan Market, a fine half-timbered mansion is a **Seventh Day Adventist Church** (Cherry St) FREE.

Mingun　　　　မင်းကွန်း

Home to several unique sites – as well as the foundations for what would have been the largest temple in the world – Mingun is a compact riverside village that makes a popular half-day excursion from Mandalay. The journey is part of the attraction, whether puttering up the wide Ayeyarwady or roller-coastering along a rural lane from Sagaing.

A Sagaing–Mingun fee (K3000) is half-heartedly collected on the eastern side of Mingun Paya. In peak season this might be checked at the Mingun Bell.

Mingun Paya　　　　BUDDHIST STUPA
(မင်းကွန်းဘုရား; Pahtodawgyi) FREE Begun in 1790, Mingun Paya would have been the world's biggest stupa if it had been completed. Work stopped in 1819 when King Bodawpaya died, and at that point only the bottom third of the structure was finished. But what's there is still huge: a roughly 240ft cube on a 460ft lower terrace. It's often described as the world's largest pile of bricks. There's a steep staircase to the top, where you can enjoy amazing views of the countryside.

ⓘ Getting There & Away

Mingun is a pleasant 35-minute drive from Sagaing, easily added to an 'ancient capitals' motorcycle or taxi tour from Mandalay.

You can also get here by boat (one hour out, 40 minutes back, passport required). From Mandalay's 26th St 'tourist jetty' (Mayan Chan), boats depart at 9am (foreigner US$8), returning at 1.30pm.

Pyin Oo Lwin　　　ပြင်ဦးလွင်
☑ 085 / POP C 158,800

Founded by the British in 1896, Pyin Oo Lwin was originally called Maymyo ('Maytown'), after Colonel May of the 5th Bengal Infantry, and was designed as a place to escape the Mandalay heat. After the construction of the railway from Mandalay, Maymyo became the summer capital for the British colonial administration, a role it held until the end of British rule in 1948. The name was changed after the British departed, but numerous colonial mansions and churches remain, as do the descendants of the Indian and Nepali workers who came here to lay the railway line.

More recently, Pyin Oo Lwin has become famous for its fruit, jams and fruit wines. With the rise of the Myanmar version of the nouveau riche, Pyin Oo Lwin is once again a popular weekend and hot-season getaway, so get here sharpish to experience what's left of the old charm and calm.

◉ Sights

★ National Kandawgyi Gardens　PARK
(အမျိုးသားကန်တော်ကြီးဥယျာဉ်; Nanda Rd; adult/child under 12yr US$5/3; ⊙ 8am-6pm, aviary to 5pm, orchid garden & butterfly museum 8.30am-5pm, Nan Myint Tower lift to 5pm) Founded in 1915 and carved into an existing park by Turkish prisoners captured by the British during WWI, this lovingly maintained 435-acre botanical garden features more than 480 species of flower, shrub and tree. The most appealing aspect is the way flowers and overhanging branches frame views of Kandawgyi Lake's wooden bridges and small gilded pagoda. Admission includes the swimming pool, the **aviary**, the **orchid garden and butterfly museum** and the bizarre **Nan Myint Tower**.

Aung Htu Kan Tha Paya　BUDDHIST TEMPLE
(အံ့ထူးကံသာဘုရား) Finished in March 2000, this dazzling pagoda is by far the region's most impressive religious building. It en-

shrines an enormous 17-ton white-marble buddha statue that fell off a truck bound for China in April 1997. After several attempts to retrieve the buddha failed, it was decided that the statue 'had decided to stay in Myanmar'.

Peik Chin Myaung CAVE
(ပိတ်ချင်းမြောင်; camera fee K300; ⊙6.30am-4.30pm) FREE Many Buddhist caves are little more than rocky niches or overhangs, but Peik Chin is much more extensive. It takes around 15 minutes to walk to the cave's end, following an underground stream past a series of colourful scenes from Buddhist scriptures interspersed with stupas and buddha images.

🛏 Sleeping & Eating

★ Hotel Maymyo HOTEL $
(☑085-28440; hotelmaymyo@gmail.com; 12 Yadanar St; r incl breakfast US$45-65; ❄❀🛜) The best-value option in town, this slick, centrally located, business-style hotel has 40 spacious, spick-and-span rooms with all the amenities of a more expensive property, including flat-screen TVs, minibars, safes and swish bathrooms (for Myanmar). Breakfast is served at the rooftop restaurant, which offers panoramic views of town. Pleasant, helpful staff.

★ Hotel Pyin Oo Lwin BOUTIQUE HOTEL $$
(☑085-21226; www.hotelpyinoolwin.com; 9 Nanda Rd; r incl breakfast US$150; ❀@🛜❄) This excellent hotel has bungalows scattered around a 5-acre site that feels like a suburban cul-de-sac and comes with a miniature

version of the Purcell Tower FREE. The smart, roomy bungalows all have terraces and fireplaces. Efficient, English-speaking staff, an Asian-fusion restaurant and a heated indoor pool complete the picture.

★ Lake Front Feel EUROPEAN, ASIAN $$
(☑085-22083; mains K3700-13,600; ⊙9.30am-9.30pm; 🛜) The upmarket yet casual lakeside setting is an obvious attraction here, while the menu spans dishes from Europe, China, Thailand and Japan, making it the only place in town where you can sate your sushi craving. The waterside terrace is a relaxed spot for a sundowner, or juices, coffee and cakes during the day. Dinner reservations are advisable on weekends and holidays.

★ Taj INDIAN $$
(☑09 78404 9880; 26 Nanda Rd; mains K4600-9,000; ⊙10am-10pm; ❀🛜) Best by night, this standout lakeside eatery is much more reasonably priced than its extravagant look suggests. The curries, tikkas and baltis are superb and quite literally melt in the mouth. There are plenty of vegie options, a decent alcohol selection and the most attentive service in town.

❶ Getting There & Away
Yangon and Nay Pyi Taw buses leave from the inconvenient main bus station Thiri Mandala, 2 miles east of the Shan Market.

All other buses leave from behind the San Pya Restaurant, 600m south of the bus station, as do some shared taxis and pick-ups to Mandalay.

MYANMAR (BURMA) PYIN OO LWIN

TRANSPORT FROM PYIN OO LWIN

DESTINATION	BUS	SHARED TAXI	PICK-UP TRUCK	TRAIN
Hsipaw	K5000, 3hr, aircon 3pm	back/front K13,000/15,000, 3hr, frequent	N/A	ordinary/upper class K1200/2750, 7hr, 8.22am
Kyaukme	K4000, 2hr, aircon 3pm	back/front K12,000/13,000, 2hr, frequent	N/A	ordinary/upper class K950/2150, 5hr, 8.22am
Lashio	K5500, 5hr, aircon 3pm	back/front K12,000/13,000, 4hr, frequent	N/A	ordinary/upper class K1900/4400, 11hr, 8.22am
Mandalay	K2000, 2hr, 7am & 8am	back/front K4500/5000, 2hr, frequent	K2000, 2-3hr, frequent until 6pm	ordinary/upper class K550/1200, 6hr, 4.40pm
Yangon	K12,000-18,500, 11hr, 5pm, 6pm & 7pm	N/A	N/A	N/A

Pick-ups to Mandalay leave from near the gas station at the roundabout at the entrance to town, as well as less frequently from outside the train station, north of the town centre. **Shared taxis** (4th St) to Mandalay leave from 4th St.

ⓘ Getting Around

Crown Bicycle Rental (46 Mandalay-Lashio Rd; bicycles/motorbikes per day from K2000/8000; ☺7.30am-7pm) rents bicycles and motorbikes. It also has some automatic motorbikes for K15,000 per day.

Pyin Oo Lwin's signature horse-drawn carts can be found near the Central Market. Reckon on K1500 to K2000 for a short trip across town and K15,000 for an all-day tour.

Hsipaw   သီပေါ

📄 082 / POP C 20,900

Increasing numbers of foreigners are finding their way to delightful Hsipaw (pronounced 'see-paw' or 'tee-bor'), drawn by the possibilities of easily arranged hill treks that are more authentic than those around Kalaw or anywhere in northern Thailand. Many people, though, find the town's laid-back vibe and intriguing history as a Shan royal city as much of an attraction and spend far longer here than they intended. With just enough tourist infrastructure to be convenient, Hsipaw remains a completely genuine northern Shan State town. Be sure to check it out before this changes.

◉ Sights

Myauk Myo   AREA
(မြောက်မြို့) FREE At the northern edge of town, Hsipaw's oldest neighbourhood has a village-like atmosphere, two delightful old teak monasteries and a collection of ancient brick stupas known locally as **Little Bagan**. Though this name blatantly overplays the size and extent of the sites, the area is undoubtedly charming. The multifaceted wooden **Madahya Monastery** looks especially impressive when viewed from across the palm-shaded pond of the **Bamboo Buddha Monastery** (Maha Nanda Kantha).

Sunset Hill   VIEWPOINT
FREE For sweeping views across the river and Hsipaw, climb to **Thein Daung Pagoda**, also known as Nine Buddha Hill or, most often, Sunset Hill. It's part of a steep ridge that rises directly behind the Lashio road, just over a mile south of Hsipaw.

Bawgyo Paya   BUDDHIST TEMPLE
(တော်ကြီးဘုရား) FREE Five miles west of Hsipaw, beside the Hsipaw–Kyaukme road, this pagoda is of great significance to Shan people and gets overloaded with pilgrims who arrive en masse during the annual **Bawgyo Paya Pwe**, culminating on the full-moon day of Tabaung (February/March). The pagoda's current incarnation is an eye-catching 1995 structure of stepped gilded

TRANSPORT FROM HSIPAW

DESTINATION	BUS	MINIBUS	SHARED TAXI	TRAIN
Bagan	K17,300, 10hr, 7pm	N/A	N/A	N/A
Kyaukme	K1000, 1hr, noon & 3.30pm	K1500, 7am & 10am	K2000	ordinary/upper class K300/650, 3hr, 9.30am
Lashio	K2000, 2hr, 5am, 6am & 7.30am	N/A	K5000	ordinary/upper class K700/1650, 4hr, 2.38pm
Mandalay	K5000-8000, 5½hr, 5.30am, 7.30am, 4pm & 7.30pm	K8000, 5hr, 7am & 9am	back/front seat K13,000/15,000, whole car K50,000	ordinary/upper class K2700/3950, 11hr, 9.30am
Pyin Oo Lwin	K5000, 3hr, 5.30am, 7.30am, 4pm & 7.30pm	N/A	back/front seat K13,000/15,000, whole car K50,000	ordinary/upper class K1200/2750, 7hr, 9.30am
Taunggyi	K15,500, 12hr, 3.30pm & 4.30pm	N/A	N/A	N/A
Yangon	K17,500-20,300, 14hr, 5.30pm & 6.30pm	N/A	N/A	N/A

MYANMAR (BURMA) HSIPAW

KYAINGTONG ကျိုင်းတုံ

Set around the attractive **Nyaung Toung** (ညောင်တန်း; Kan Rd) lake, Kyaingtong, also known as Kengtung, is one of the most pleasant towns in Myanmar. In culture and appearance, Kyaingtong feels closer to the hill towns of northern Thailand than elsewhere in Shan State.

The rugged terrain of eastern Shan State contributes to a palpable sense of isolation: Kyaingtong is an outpost of development amid largely deforested mountains that are home to Wa, Akha, Palaung and Lahu villages where little has changed in centuries. Unsurprisingly, hill treks are a major attraction here.

Kyaingtong's **central market** (ြ္ဗဈေး; Zeigyo Rd; ⊙ 5am-3pm, closed full-moon days) is one of the most exotic and fascinating in all Myanmar, playing host to a diverse mix of hill peoples, especially in the early morning. In the evening, Nyaung Tong is the most lively place in town, with locals flocking to the restaurants that surround the lake.

Long-standing backpacker favourite **Harry's Trekking House** (☑ 084-22909; harry. guesthouse@gmail.com; 67 Mai Yang Rd; r US$10-25; ⊛ 🛜) offers basic but clean digs and can organise treks and transport. The centrally located **Sam Yweat Hotel** (☑ 084-21235; samywethotel@gmail.com; cnr Kyaing Lan 1 & Kyaing Lan 4 Rds; s/d US$30/35; ⊛ 🛜) is more upmarket.

The only access to Kyaingtong by road is from Tachileik. Buses make the run in four to five hours to/from Tachileik in the morning (K12,000). Myanmar National Airlines (www. flymna.com) connects Kyaingtong with destinations around Myanmar.

---

polygons, within which the dome supposedly incorporates genuine rubies.

Produce Market   MARKET

(⊙ 4.30am-1pm) Most interesting before dawn, when the road outside is jammed with hill villagers selling their wares; all will have cleared away by 7am, although the market continues until 1pm.

🛏 Sleeping & Eating

★ Mr Charles Guest House   HOTEL $

(☑ 082-80105; www.mrcharleshotel.com; 105 Auba St; incl breakfast dm US$7-12, r US$18-55; ⊛ 🛜) Still the most efficient, comfortable and traveller-friendly guesthouse in town, the large, Shan-owned Mr Charles operation encompasses everything from simple mattresses on the floor in the dorms to swish suites with heating and air-con. Book ahead in peak periods.

Lily The Home Hotel   GUESTHOUSE $

(☑ 082-80318; www.lilythehome.com; 108 Aung Tha Pyay Rd; r US$15-70; ⊜ ⊛ 🛜) This smart, friendly hotel offers 33 rooms spread across a jumble of buildings. Cheapies are fan only and share bathrooms, but all are clean. Rooms from US$30 are sizeable, with air-con and modern bathrooms, and are in the main building (with Hsipaw's only lift). Treks can

be organised, and there's bike (K2000 per day) and motorbike (K10,000 per day) hire.

★ Club Terrace   SOUTHEAST ASIAN $

(35 Shwe Nyaung Pin St; mains K3500-6000; ⊙ 10am-10pm) Dine alfresco in a gorgeous 90-year-old teak house with a lovely riverside terrace. The menu mixes Thai and Chinese flavours, with a few Shan dishes such as minced-chicken curry with basil leaves. It has a decent wine list, splendid service and a peaceful, evocative setting.

★ Mrs Popcorn's Garden   CAFE $

(snacks K1000-3000; ⊙ 9am-9pm) Although Mrs Popcorn passed away in 2016, her equally irrepressible daughter makes this all-organic outdoor cafe a definitive stop on a tour of the Myauk Myo area of town. Choose from homemade snacks, some traveller favourites and, of course, popcorn. Cold beer is available, so it's easy to kick back and while away a couple of hours in the late afternoon.

ⓘ Information

The guesthouses are the best sources of reliable advice about things to do and see. Another mine of local information and history is Ko Zaw Tun, who is known as Mr Book because he runs a small **bookstall** (Namtu Rd; ⊙ 9am-7pm) oppo-

---

ℹ️ GETTING TO CHINA: MU-SE TO RUILI

Getting to the border While no documents are required to travel to Mu-se itself, people planning to cross the border need a permit from MHT, which will take 10 days to two weeks to process and is most easily arranged via a recommended tour operator. Border crossers will also need a pre-booked guide and car (US$200) to make the four-hour journey from Lashio to Mu-se.

At the border You must have a Chinese visa already, as they are not available at the border.

Moving on From Ruili (China) there are five buses a day (¥295 to ¥331, 12 hours, 8.30am to 7.30pm) to Yunnan's capital, Kunming.

---

site the entrance to the Central Pagoda, which his family helped to build.

ℹ️ Getting There & Away

Buses and minibuses leave from the **RC bus station** (Mandalay-Lashio Rd) and other ticket offices on the Mandalay–Lashio road and the Duhtawadi Cafe on Lanmataw St opposite the market. Lashio-bound buses can be picked up from the Mandalay–Lashio road opposite the RC bus station. The train station is in the west of town.

BAGAN & AROUND

Bagan   ပုဂံ

📋 061

This temple town is one of Myanmar's main attractions. Once the capital of a powerful ancient kingdom, the area known as Bagan or, bureaucratically, as the 'Bagan Archaeological Zone' occupies an impressive 26-sq-mile area. The Ayeyarwady (Irrawaddy) River drifts past its northern and western sides.

The area's most active town and main transport hub is Nyaung U, in the northeastern corner. About 2.5 miles west, Old Bagan is the former site of the village that was relocated 2 miles south to New Bagan in 1990. Between the two is Myinkaba, a village boasting a long-running lacquerware tradition.

Bagan has been hit by earthquakes over the centuries. The most recent, in August 2016, damaged 400 temples; work on re-

pairing them is ongoing. Bear in mind that Bagan is not a traveller destination with nightlife like Siem Reap (Cambodia) or even Luang Prabang (Laos). It's an overgrown village, so party elsewhere.

👁️ Sights

There are more than 3000 temples spread across the Bagan plain. Despite the 2016 earthquake, which damaged several hundred temples, Bagan's majesty can't be diminished. Seeing the soaring centuries-old structures from a prime spot is dazzling – particularly at sunrise or sunset.

👁️ Old Bagan

⭐ **Ananda Pahto**   BUDDHIST TEMPLE
(အာနန္ဒာပုထိုး; Map p530) With its 170ft-high, gold corn-cob *hti* (decorated pinnacle) shimmering across the plains, Ananda is one of the finest, largest, best preserved and most revered of all Bagan temples. Thought to have been built between 1090 and 1105 by King Kyanzittha, this perfectly proportioned temple heralds the stylistic end of the early Bagan period and the beginning of the middle period. Ananda Pahto was damaged during the 2016 earthquake and under repair at the time of research; it remains open to visitors.

Nathlaung Kyaung   HINDU TEMPLE
(နတ်လျောင်ကျောင်း; Map p530) Between Pahtothamya and Thatbyinnyu, this stubby building – the only Hindu temple remaining in Bagan – has a fascinating history. Named 'Shrine Confining Nat', it's where King Anawrahta stored non-Buddhist images, particularly ones for local *nat* (spirit beings), as he tried to enforce Buddhism. The king himself described the temple as 'where the *nat* are kept prisoner'. The structure was severely damaged in the 1975 earthquake; only the main hall and superstructure (with seven original Gupta-style reliefs) still stand.

Gawdawpalin Pahto   BUDDHIST TEMPLE
(ကန်တော့ပလ္လင်ဘုရား; Map p530) Standing 197ft tall, Gawdawpalin is one of the largest and most imposing Bagan temples, although by no means the most inspiring, with its modernised altar and tile floors inside. Built during the reign of Narapatisithu and finished under that of Nantaungmya, it's considered the crowning achievement of the late Bagan period. Its name means 'Platform to which Homage Is Paid'. The stairs to the top terrace are closed to visitors.

Archaeological Museum MUSEUM

(ကျောက်စာသိမ်းပြတိုက်; Map p530; Bagan-Nyaung U Rd; adult/child under 10yr K5000/free; ◷9am-4.30pm Tue-Sun) Housed in a sprawling complex, this government-run museum features many fine pieces from Bagan (reclining buddhas, original images, inscribed stones and mural re-creations) and an unexpected room of modern-art renderings of the temples. Other curiosities include a room of 55 kinds of women's hair knots (and five men's hairstyles), models of major temples with architectural details, and a model of an 11th-century village.

Tharabar Gate ARCHAEOLOGICAL SITE

(သရပါတံခါး; Map p530) Do stop on the eastern side of this former entrance to the original palace site. The gate is the best-preserved remains of the 9th-century wall and the only gate still standing. Traces of old stucco can still be seen on the arched gateway, and on either side are two niches, home not to buddha images but to *nat* (spirit beings) who guard the gate and are treated with profound respect by locals.

Thatbyinnyu Pahto BUDDHIST TEMPLE

(သဗ္ဗညုပုထိုး; Map p530) Named for 'omniscience', Bagan's highest temple is built of two white-coloured boxy storeys, each with three diminishing terraces rimmed with spires and leading to a gold-tipped *sikhara*, 207ft high. Its monumental size and looming height make it a classic example of Bagan's middle period. Built in 1144 by Alaungsithu, the temple has terraces encircled by indentations for 539 Jataka (stories from the Buddha's past lives).

Shwegugyi BUDDHIST TEMPLE

(ရွှေဂူကြီး; Map p530) Built by Alaungsithu in 1131, this smaller but elegant *pahto* (temple), 650ft north of Thatbyinnyu (p529), is an example of Bagan's middle period of temple building, a transition in architectural style from the dark and cloistered to the airy and light. Its name means 'Great Golden Cave' and its corn-cob *sikhara* is a scaled-down version of the one at Ananda.

Mimalaung Kyaung BUDDHIST MONASTERY

(မီးမလောင်ကျောင်း; Map p530) A nice set of *chinthe* (half-lion/half-dragon deities) guards the stairway leading up to this small, square monastery platform, constructed in 1174 by Narapatisithu. It's about 650ft south of Gawdawpalin (p528), on the other side of the road. In front of the monastery is a brick-

and-stucco Tripitaka (scripture) library next to a large acacia tree. Atop the steps, a tiered roof (with a newer gold-capped *hti*, an umbrella-like decorated pinnacle) contains a large sitting buddha.

Ananda Ok Kyaung BUDDHIST SITE

(အာနန္ဒာအုတ်ကျောင်း; Map p530) Just west of Ananda's northern entry, this small *vihara* (sanctuary or chapel), built in 1137, features some detailed 18th-century murals bursting with bright red and green, showing details of everyday life from the Bagan period. In the southeastern corner you can see a boat with a design depicting Portuguese figures engaged in trade. The temple's name means 'Ananda Brick Monastery'.

Ananda Ok Kyaung was damaged in the 2016 earthquake and was under repair at research time, but it's open to visitors.

👁 Myinkaba

Gubyaukgyi BUDDHIST TEMPLE

(ဂုဘြောက်ကြီး; Map p530) Just to the left of the road as you enter Myinkaba, Gubyaukgyi (Great Painted Cave Temple) draws visitors to see the well-preserved, richly coloured paintings inside. These are thought to date from the temple's original construction in 1113, when Kyanzittha's son Rajakumar built it following his father's death. In Indian style, the monument consists of a large vestibule attached to a smaller antechamber. The temple was damaged in the 2016 earthquake and remains under repair.

Manuha Paya BUDDHIST TEMPLE

(မနူဟာဘုရား; Map p530) In Myinkaba village stands this active and rather modern-looking pagoda (although it dates to 1059). It is named after Manuha, the Mon king from Thaton who was held captive here by King Anawrahta. In the front of the building are three seated buddhas; in the back is a huge reclining buddha. All seem too large for their enclosures – supposedly representing the stress and discomfort the king had to endure.

Mingalazedi Paya BUDDHIST TEMPLE

(မင်္ဂလာစေဒီဘုရား; Map p530) Close to the riverbank, towards Myinkaba from Old Bagan, Mingalazedi Paya (Blessing Stupa) represents the final flowering of Bagan's architectural outburst, as displayed in its enormous bell-like dome and the beautiful glazed Jataka (stories from the Buddha's past lives) tiles around each terrace. Although many of the 1061 original tiles have been damaged

Bagan

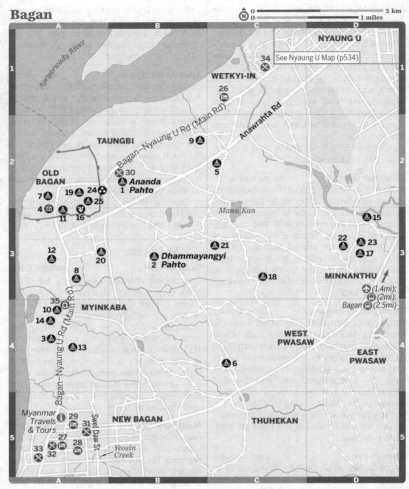

See Nyaung U Map (p534)

or stolen, 561 remain (in various states of decay). The smaller square building in the grounds is one of the few Tripitaka (scripture) libraries made of brick.

◉ North, Central & South Plain

★ **Dhammayangyi Pahto**   BUDDHIST TEMPLE
(ဓမ္မရံကြီးပုထိုး; Map p530) Visible from all parts of Bagan, this massive, walled, 12th-century temple (about 1600ft east of Shwesandaw (p530)) is infamous for its mysterious, bricked-up inner passageways and cruel history. It's said that King Narathu

built the temple to atone for his sins: he smothered his father and brother to death and executed one of his wives, an Indian princess, for practising Hindu rituals. The best preserved of Bagan's temples, it features detailed mortar work in its upper levels.

Shwesandaw Paya   BUDDHIST TEMPLE
(ရွှေဆံတော်ဘုရား; Map p530) Bagan's most famous sunset-viewing spot, Shwesandaw is a graceful white pyramid-style pagoda with steps leading past five terraces to the circular stupa top, with good 360-degree views. Its top terrace is roomy, which is just as well

Bagan

considering the numbers of camera-toting travellers who arrive before sunset. If you go during the day, you'll likely be alone. As it was badly damaged in the 2016 earthquake and by heavy rain in 2017, it wasn't possible to climb Shwesandaw at research time.

Sulamani Pahto
BUDDHIST TEMPLE

(စူဠာမဏိပုထိုး; Map p530) This temple with five doorways is known as the Crowning Jewel and was constructed around 1181 by Narapatisithu. It is one of Bagan's most attractive temples, with lush grounds (and ample vendors) behind the surrounding walls. It's a prime example of later, more sophisticated temple styles, with better internal lighting. Sulamani suffered significant damage during the 2016 earthquake and was closed at the time of writing.

Nan Paya
BUDDHIST TEMPLE

(နန်းဘုရား; Map p530) Just south of Manuha Paya (p529) by dirt road, this shrine is said to have been used as Manuha's prison, although there is little evidence supporting the legend. In this story the shrine was originally Hindu, and captors thought using it as a prison would be easier than converting it to a Buddhist temple. It's worth visiting for its interior masonry work – sandstone block facings over a brick core, certainly some of Bagan's finest detailed sculpture.

Nandamannya Pahto
BUDDHIST TEMPLE

(နန္ဒပညာပုထိုး; Map p530) Dating from the mid-13th century, this small, single-chambered temple has fine frescoes and a ruined seated buddha. It's about 650ft north of **Thambula** (သမ္ဗူလပုထိုး; Map p530); a sign leads down a short dirt road. The murals' similarity with those at Payathonzu has led some art historians to suggest that they were painted by the same hand.

Payathonzu
BUDDHIST TEMPLE

(ဘုရားသုံးဆူ; Map p530) Across the main road from **Tayok** (တရုတ်ပြေးဘုရား; Map p530), this complex of three interconnected shrines (the name means Three Stupas) is worth seeing for its 13th-century murals. It was abandoned shortly before construction was completed. Each square cubicle is topped by a fat *sikhara;* a similar structure appears only at Salay. The design is remarkably like Khmer Buddhist ruins in Thailand.

Dhammayazika Paya
BUDDHIST TEMPLE

(ဓမ္မရာဇိကဘုရား; Map p530) Sitting in lush garden grounds with a gilded bell, the Dhammayazika dates from 1196. Set in the south-central end of Bagan on the main road, it has lovely views from its highest terrace. The pentagonal *zedi* (stupa) is similar to the Shwezigon (p532) but with a more unusual design. An outer wall has five gateways.

Dhammayazika Paya suffered serious damage during the 2016 earthquake but is now open again.

Abeyadana Pahto
BUDDHIST TEMPLE

(အဘ၀ယ်ရတနာပုထိုး; Map p530) About 1300ft south of Manuha Paya (p529), this 11th-century temple with a Sinhalese-style stupa was supposedly built by Kyanzittha's Bengali wife Abeyadana, who waited for him here as he hid for his life from his predecessor King Sawlu. It's famed for its original frescoes, which were cleaned in 1987 by Unesco staff. Ask at the caretaker's house, to the south, if the temple is locked.

Pyathada Paya
BUDDHIST TEMPLE

(ပြဿဒါးဘုရား; Map p530) Dating from the 13th century, during the latter period of temple building at Bagan, this huge, impressive pagoda is a superb sunset-viewing spot, with a giant open terrace (Bagan's largest) atop the steps, and another small deck further up. Pyathada Paya suffered serious damage in the 2016 earthquake and is currently not open to visitors.

Nagayon
BUDDHIST TEMPLE

(နဂါးရုံ; Map p530) Slightly south of Abeyadana and across the road, this elegant and well-preserved temple was built by Kyanzittha. The main buddha image is twice life-size and shelters under the hood of a huge *naga* (dragon serpent). This reflects the legend that in 1192 Kyanzittha built the temple on the spot where he was sheltered while fleeing from his angry brother and predecessor Sawlu, an activity he had to indulge in on more than one occasion.

Htilominlo Pahto
BUDDHIST TEMPLE

(ထီးလိုမင်းလိုပုထိုး; Map p530) This 150ft-high temple (built in 1218) marks the spot where King Nantaungmya was chosen (by a leaning umbrella, that timeless decider), among five

> **ⓘ BAGAN ENTRANCE FEE**
>
> All foreign visitors to the Bagan Archaeological Zone are required to pay a K25,000 entrance fee. If you arrive by boat or air, the fee will be collected at the river jetty or airport. If you arrive by bus, the fee is collected at a toll booth as you head into town. The fee covers a one-week visit, but it's unlikely that you'll be asked to pay again if you stay longer.

brothers, to be the crown prince. It's more impressive from the outside, with a terraced design similar to that of Sulamani Pahto (p531). Unfortunately, it's vendor central here. Htilominlo Pahto suffered significant damage during the 2016 earthquake.

Buledi
BUDDHIST TEMPLE

(ဗူးလ၀သိး; Map p530) Great for its views, this steep-stepped, pyramid-style stupa looks ho-hum from afar, but the narrow terrace has become something of an alternative sunset spot. It's about 2000ft south of Htilominlo, across Anawrahta Rd. It's also known as Temple 394 (not correctly labelled on some maps). Buledi was one of many temples in Bagan badly damaged in the 2016 quake, but it's now open again.

⊙ Nyaung U

Shwezigon Paya
BUDDHIST TEMPLE

(ရွှေစည်းခုံဘုရား; Map p534; ☉ daylight hours) At the western end of Nyaung U, this big, beautiful *zedi* (stupa) is the town's main religious site, and is most famous for its link with Myanmar's main *nat* (spirits). Lit up impressively at dusk, the gilded *zedi* sits on three rising terraces. Enamelled plaques in panels around the base of the *zedi* illustrate scenes from the Jataka (stories from the Buddha's past lives). At the cardinal points, facing the terrace stairways, are four shrines, each housing a 13ft-high bronze standing buddha.

🏃 Activities

Balloons over Bagan
BALLOONING

(Map p534; ☏ 061-60713; www.balloonsoverbagan. com; per person from US$340; ☉ 9am-8pm Oct-Mar) One of the best ways to see Bagan is on a hot-air balloon ride with this highly reputable company. The office is near Thiripyitsayar St.

🛏 Sleeping

There are three distinct accommodation bases around Bagan. Old Bagan has only high-end hotels, while New Bagan and Nyaung U have a mix of midrange and budget choices.

🛏 New Bagan

Northern Breeze
GUESTHOUSE $

(Map p530; ☏ 061-65472; www.northernbreezeguesthouse.com; 162 Cherry St; dm/r incl breakfast US$15/40; ❈ 🅏) This friendly place on a quiet, leafy street offers good value. Rooms are set around a small courtyard and aren't huge, but they are nicely maintained and have all the essentials (mini fridge, electric kettle with coffee, TV). The three-bed dorms share a bathroom. There are plenty of dining options a short stroll away.

★**Ostello Bello** HOSTEL $$
(Map p530; ☎061-65069; www.ostellobello.com; Khaye St; incl breakfast dm US$39-59, d US$116-149; ❄️🛜) This cleverly designed, Italian-owned flashpacker hostel is the best place in town for socialising and meeting other travellers. The buzzing courtyard eatery and drinking space hosts events throughout the week (bingo nights, trivia nights), and there are loads of activities on offer (sunrise and sunset tours, boat trips). The big, comfortable dorms have their own bathrooms.

Thurizza Hotel HOTEL $$
(Map p530; ☎061-65229; thirimarlarhotelbagan@gmail.com; Ingin St; r incl breakfast US$38-60; ❄️@🛜) Teak walkways lead to a mix of rooms wrapped around a small pagoda-style dining room, although most guests eat breakfast on the roof deck with its temple views. Standard rooms are compact and have smaller bathrooms, but the superior rooms are a decent deal: bigger, with shiny wood floors and better light – some also have temple views.

🛏 Nyaung U

★**New Wave Guesthouse** GUESTHOUSE $
(Map p530; ☎061-60731; www.newwavebagan.com; Bagan-Nyaung U Rd, Wetkyi-in; r incl breakfast US$50; ❄️🛜) This smart guesthouse has attractive, modern rooms that overlook a back garden. Each has a bright and appealing design with tall ceilings, handcrafted wooden beds and decent bathrooms, even if they're not huge. It's a big step up from most of Bagan's guesthouse options.

Saw Nyein San GUESTHOUSE $
(Map p534; ☎061-60651; www.sawnyeinsanguesthousebagan.wordpress.com; Main Rd; r incl breakfast US$30-50; ❄️🛜) This popular, family-run guesthouse on Nyaung U's main road earns high marks for its spotless accommodation and kind-hearted service. The rooms have tile floors and light pastel colour schemes, although some are a bit on the small side. Staff members go out of their way to make you feel at home. Breakfast is served on the rooftop.

DON'T MISS

TOP BAGAN TEMPLES

➡ Ananda Pahto (p528)

➡ Dhammayangyi Pahto (p530)

➡ Shwesandaw Paya (p530)

➡ Abeyadana Pahto (p532)

➡ Shwezigon Paya (p532)

➡ Htilominlo Pahto (p532)

New Park Hotel HOTEL $
(Map p534; ☎061-60322; www.newparkmyanmar.com; 4 Thiripyitsaya; r incl breakfast US$25-55; ❄️🛜) One of the best all-round budget hotels, the New Park is tucked away in the leafy backstreets off Yarkinthar Rd. The older rooms, with bungalow-style front decks, are comfortable, wooden-floored set-ups, with reasonable bathrooms. The newer wing brings more space, a fridge, a TV and even a rain shower. The cheapest rooms are cramped.

Eden III Motel GUESTHOUSE $
(Map p534; ☎09 2042 061; Anawrahta Rd; incl breakfast dm US$9, r US$18-40; ❄️🛜) Spread over three buildings (Eden I, II and III) and split in two by the busy road to the airport, Eden isn't exactly paradise. The best rooms are found in the newer Eden III, although the bathrooms are old-fashioned. The 16-bed dorm is fan only. The staff is quite attuned to backpacker needs.

🍴 Eating

🍴 New Bagan

Mother's House BURMESE, CHINESE $
(Map p530; Chauk Rd; mains K1000-5000; ⏰6am-10pm Mon-Sat) Big, busy and popular with the locals, this teahouse has plenty of outdoor seating and an attached restaurant. It's good for a traditional Burmese breakfast before exploring the temples or after catching sunrise somewhere nearby. Try the Shan noodles or the deep-fried doughnuts. The restaurant serves up standard Burmese-Chinese dishes.

Ma Mae Naing BURMESE $
(Map p530; ☎09 40273 0712; Khayea St (Main Rd); mains K3000; ⏰9am-10pm; 🍴) Ma Mae Naing (also known as 'Unforgettable') serves delicious fare, with good choices for vegetarians. The small menu consists mostly of curries served with rice and a variety of

MYANMAR (BURMA) BAGAN

Nyaung U

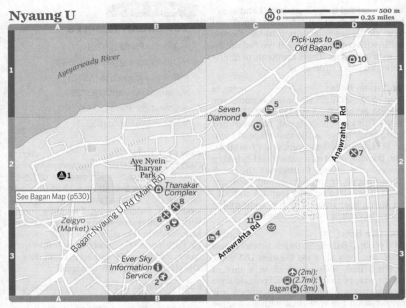

Nyaung U

◎ Sights
1 Shwezigon Paya A2

◎ Activities, Courses & Tours
2 Balloons over Bagan B3

◎ Sleeping
3 Eden III Motel D2
4 New Park Hotel C3
5 Saw Nyein San C1

◎ Eating
6 Bagan Zay B3
7 Sanon D2
8 Weather Spoon's Bagan B2

◎ Drinking & Nightlife
9 Shwe Yar Su B3

◎ Shopping
10 Mani-Sithu Market D1
11 MBoutik C3

vegetable side dishes. It all goes nicely with fresh fruit juices (a bargain at K1000 each).

Mingalabar Food Corner　　ASIAN $
(Map p530; Bagan-Nyaung U Rd; mains K3000-5000; ⊘9am-10pm) Offers the usual combo of Chinese, Thai and Burmese cooking, with ever-flowing draught beer and sizzling barbecue as well. In the evening, an outdoor table on the raised terrace is the place to be.

★ Kyaw Kitchen　　FUSION $$
(Map p530; ☑09 25975 4811; High School Rd, Hti Min Yin Quarter; mains K300-10,000; ⊘11am-3pm & 5-10pm; ☑) Tucked away a few blocks north of the main road, Kyaw Kitchen earns high marks for its good-quality cooking, friendly

service and appealing, garden-like setting. Highlights from the creative and wide-ranging menu include a Burmese-style seafood risotto, a butterfish curry, grilled river prawns and a juicy vegie burger.

✖ Old Bagan

**Be Kind to Animals
the Moon**　　BURMESE, VEGETARIAN $
(Map p530; mains K3000-4500; ⊘9am-10pm; ☑) The original among the vegetarian restaurants clustered near Tharabar Gate (p529), this garden-like eatery off Bagan-Nyaung U Rd offers a friendly welcome and delicious food, including pumpkin curry with ginger, sautéed vegetables with vermicelli, spicy

chapati wraps and creamy lassis. Don't overlook the homemade ice cream for dessert.

Starbeam Bistro INTERNATIONAL $
(Map p530; ☑ 09 40250 2614; mains K4000-7500; ⊙8.30am-9.30pm; 🛜) Located close to Ananda Pahto (p528), this garden bistro was set up by chef Tin Myint, who spent several years working with the Orient Express hotel group. Dishes include Rakhine fish curry, market-fresh specials, traditional salads such as avocado or tea leaf, and classic baguettes and sandwiches. Best accompanied by a healthy blend or fresh juice.

🍴 Nyaung U

★ Weather Spoon's Bagan INTERNATIONAL $
(Map p534; Yarkinthar Rd; mains K3700-5900; ⊙10am-10.30pm; 🛜🍽) Brits will be familiar with the name, borrowed by amiable owner Win Tun from a UK discount-pub chain, and there are plenty of Western classics – fish and chips, pasta, pancakes – on the menu here, as well as Thai and Chinese choices. It's justly famous for its decadent burger, and this is the most popular spot on Restaurant Row.

Bagan Zay FUSION $
(Map p534; Yarkinthar Rd; mains K2900-5900; ⊙11am-11pm; 🛜🍽) Bagan Zay serves up attractively presented and creative curries, as well as dishes with Middle Eastern influences: try the Burmese-style falafals or the grilled-eggplant sandwich. There are ample vegetarian choices, including a vegan curry (with pumpkin, cauliflower and broccoli) and lentil galettes, and it does OK cocktails too. Look for the distinctive grass roof.

Myo Myo Myanmar Rice Food BURMESE $
(Map p530; Bagan-Nyaung U Rd; curries from K1000, side dishes K200-500; ⊙6am-8pm) Deservedly popular, this restaurant specialises in the tabletop buffets that characterise the national cuisine. But here they really go to town, with up to 25 small dishes appearing alongside the curry of your choice, including seasonal specials such as asparagus. English is spoken. Bring a crowd to share. You only pay for what you eat.

★ Sanon BURMESE, FUSION $$
(Map p534; ☑ 09 45195 1950; www.facebook.com/sanonrestaurant; Pyu Saw Hit St; mains K4000-8700; ⊙11am-10pm Mon-Sat; 🛜🍽) 🌿 A charming addition to the Nyaung U restaurant scene, Sanon has a classy but casual setting, with tropical plants surrounding an open-sided dining room. You'll find inventive Burmese small plates that are meant for sharing: river-prawn and catfish curry, pan-seared squid stuffed with pork, and crispy watercress and onion pakora. It has delicious juices, too (try the mint and pomelo freeze).

🍺 Drinking & Nightlife

Shwe Yar Su BEER STATION
(Map p534; Yarkinthar Rd; beer K750, mains K3000-6000, barbecue from K500; ⊙7am-10pm) Thanks to endless draught Myanmar Beer, this place with a large outside area and a menu of Chinese-inspired favourites has become quite the local hang-out. It's a good spot to watch some football (soccer), and the barbecue on offer is tasty too.

🛍 Shopping

Golden Cuckoo ARTS & CRAFTS
(Map p530; ⊙6am-8.30pm) Pho Htoo and his brother run this workshop, which has been in their family for four generations and focuses on high-quality 'traditional' designs. In addition to exquisite bowls and cylinders, there are such unusual objects as a motorbike helmet and guitar (both US$1200). Located just behind Manuha Paya (p529); a

---

WORTH A TRIP

MT POPA ပုပ္ပားတောင်

Like a Burmese Mt Olympus, Mt Popa is the spiritual HQ to Myanmar's infamous '37 nat' and the most popular location in the country for nat worship.

Mt Popa is now the official name of the famous Popa Taung Kalat, a tower-like 2418ft volcanic plug infested with monkeys and crowned with a gilded Buddhist temple accessed by 777 steps.

From the temple there are mammoth views back towards the Myingyan Plain and beyond. It's stunning (if a little kitsch), yet relatively few visitors make the half-day trip from Bagan.

Most travellers visit in half a day by shared taxi or organised tour from their hotel. In Nyaung U, a space in a shared taxi is K10,000 per person (without guide); a whole taxi is K35,000 to K40,000. A pick-up truck departs Nyaung U's bus station at 8.30am for Mt Popa (K3500, three hours); on the return leg, it departs Popa for Nyaung U at 1pm.

second branch has opened on the main road a few blocks away.

★ MBoutik
ARTS & CRAFTS

(Map p534; Anawrahta Rd; ⊙9am-5.30pm Mon-Sat, to 9pm Nov-Mar) 🖉 This colourful boutique has gorgeous textiles, bags, toys, handicrafts and clothing that are entirely produced by a women's cooperative started by the international NGO ActionAid. Some 600 artisans based in more than 130 villages across the country incorporate traditional designs and patterns in their expertly made works.

Mani-Sithu Market
MARKET

(Map p534; Main Rd; ⊙6am-5pm Mon-Sat) Near the roundabout at the eastern end of the main road, this market offers a colourful display of fruit, vegetables, flowers, fish and textiles. It's best visited early in the day to see it at its liveliest. There are plenty of traveller-oriented goods (woodcarvings, T-shirts, lacquerware) at its northern end.

🛈 Information

Ever Sky Information Service (Map p534; ☑061-60895; everskynanda@gmail.com; 5 Thiripyitsaya St; ⊙7.30am-9.30pm) Just off the restaurant strip, this highly recommended place can book tickets and organise tours; it also has a secondhand bookshop. Staff can arrange shared taxis (around Bagan, to Kalaw, Salay, and Mt Victoria in Chin State) for the best available rates. Ask about shared taxis to Mt Popa, which cost K8000 to K9000 and depart daily at 9am and 3pm.

🛈 Getting There & Away

The main hub for Bagan is Nyaung U, which is the closest town to the airport and the bus station.

Taxis between Nyaung U airport and hotels in Nyaung U, Old Bagan and New Bagan cost between K5000 and K8000. Taxis to/from the train station, about 2.5 miles southeast of Nyaung U, cost about K7000.

If you arrive by boat, it will cost between K2000 and K5000 for horse carts and taxis from the Old Bagan or Nyaung U jetties to hotels in Nyaung U, Old Bagan and New Bagan.

AIR

Nyaung U Airport is about 2 miles southeast of the market. Airlines connect Bagan daily with Mandalay (US$65, 30 minutes), Heho (US$70, 40 minutes) and Yangon (US$105, 70 minutes).

Travel agencies sometimes have cheaper tickets than the airline offices. Try **Seven Diamond** (Map p534; ☑061-61184; www.sevendiamondtravels.com; Main Rd; ⊙9am-8pm).

BOAT

Boats to Mandalay go from either Nyaung U or Old Bagan, depending on water levels. The Nyaung U jetty is about half a mile northeast of the Nyaung U market.

BUS

Shwe Pyi bus station is Bagan's main coach station, located 3 miles southeast of Nyaung U (and half a mile north of the train station), on the highway to Kyaukpadaung. A taxi here costs K5000 to K8000, depending on which part of Bagan you are coming from.

During peak season, it's wise to book bus tickets for Mandalay, Taunggyi (for Inle Lake) and Yangon a couple of days in advance.

TRANSPORT FROM NYAUNG U (BAGAN)

TO/FROM YANGON	DURATION	COST	FREQUENCY
Air	70min	US$105	frequent
Bus	10hr	K13,000-23,000	frequent
Car	9hr	K150,000	charter
Train	16hr	K6000-16,500 (sleeper)	daily

TO/FROM MANDALAY	DURATION	COST	FREQUENCY
Air	30min	US$65	frequent
Boat	10-14hr	from US$18	daily in high season
Bus	8hr	K9000	frequent
Car	6hr	K75,000	charter
Train	9hr	K1450-2900	daily

TRAIN

The elaborate and over-the-top Bagan train station is located in splendid isolation about 2.5 miles southeast of Nyaung U. Train tickets are only sold at the station.

ℹ Getting Around

E-bikes, which operate much like motorbikes but are powered by electric batteries, are widely available and an ideal way of getting around. Drive slowly on dusty, sandy roads and always wear a helmet. The going rate is about K8000 per day, with e-bikes available at nearly every hotel and at many travel agencies.

Bicycles are also available from accommodation places, with rates running from K2000 to K5000 per day, depending on the bikes' condition and model.

WESTERN MYANMAR

Remote, rugged and rewarding, Myanmar's westernmost states – Rakhine (also known as Arakan) and Chin – remain staunchly untouristed.

Few travellers make it to the old Rakhine capital of Mrauk U, an amazing archaeological site studded with hundreds of temples, or the current capital, scrappy Sittwe.

But if you really want to get off the grid, then head to largely unknown and undeveloped Chin State, where breathtaking mountains, forests and traditional villages await.

Sittwe   စစ်တွေ

☑ 043 / POP C 100,750

Rakhine State's capital, Sittwe (still known sometimes by its former name, Aykab), sits in an incredible spot where the wide, tidal Kaladan River kisses the big, fat Bay of Bengal. The impact of ongoing sectarian violence in Rakhine State, along with the town's generally scrappy vibe, means that most visitors approach the city as little more than a transit point to the ruins at Mrauk U.

Yuzana Aung Guest House   GUESTHOUSE **$**
(☑ 043-24275; Nga Pain St; r incl breakfast K35,000-40,000; ❈ 🛜) This newish guesthouse spread over four floors is the best budget option in Sittwe. Rooms are compact, but they are light, clean and well equipped and come with comfortable beds. The staff is conscientious and there are good sunset views from the roof terrace.

ℹ Getting There & Away

AIR

Sittwe's airport is about 1.5 miles west of the centre. *Thoun bein* (motorised trishaws; K3000 to K4000) and motorcycle taxis (K2000) await flights.

BOAT

The cheapest and slowest way to reach Mrauk U by boat are the double-decker boats run by the government's **Inland Water Transport** (IWT; ☑ 043-23382). There's an office west of Sittwe's jetty, though there's no need to buy tickets in advance. Ferries depart Sittwe Tuesday and Friday at 8am, and return from Mrauk U on Wednesday and Saturday at 8am (US$7, four to seven hours).

By far the quickest and best option is the 'speedboats' run by **Shwe Pyi Tan** (☑ 09 4959 2709, 043-22719; cnr Main Rd & U Ottama St; ◷ 8am-8pm), with departures from Sittwe on Wednesday, Friday and Sunday at 7am, and from Mrauk U on Monday and Thursday at 7am (K25,000, two hours).

Sittwe's jetty is 1 mile north of town, a K2000 ride in a *thoun bein*.

BUS

Sittwe's bus station is about 3 miles northwest of the centre. A *thoun bein* between the station and the centre will cost K4000, a motorcycle taxi K2500.

There are daily buses to Mrauk U (K4000, 3½ hours, 6.30am and noon), Yangon (K20,500, 24 hours, 6am) and Mandalay (K25,300, 24 hours, 6am).

Mrauk U   မြောက်ဦး

☑ 043 / POP C 36,140

Mrauk U (pronounced 'mrau-oo'), Myanmar's second-most-famous archaeological site, is very different from Bagan. The temples are smaller and newer and, unlike Bagan's, predominantly made from stone, not brick. Mrauk U's temples, too, are dispersed throughout a still-inhabited and fecund landscape of small villages, rice paddies, rounded hillocks and grazing cows.

Best of all, you're likely to have the temples all to yourself: only about 5000 foreigners make it to Mrauk U annually.

◉ Sights

The original site of Mrauk U is spread over 17.5 sq miles, although the town today and the bulk of the temples to visit cover a 2.7-sq-mile area.

The sights are not always marked, and this is where an experienced guide can come in

MYANMAR (BURMA) SITTWE

Mrauk U

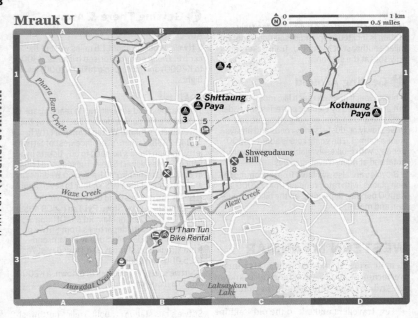

Mrauk U

handy. Many of the guides in the **Regional Guides Society – Mrauk U** (☏ 09 78240 4790, 09 25024 2844; jimes.htun@gmail.com; per day US$35) speak English well and have a good grasp of the region's history and culture.

Foreign visitors to Mrauk U are required to pay an archaeological-site 'entry fee' of K5000. There's only one place to pay it – Shittaung Paya – but it's sometimes collected at the jetty when you arrive or depart. On the government ferry, you may be asked to show proof of payment before leaving.

★**Shittaung Paya** BUDDHIST TEMPLE
(ရှစ်သောင်းဘုရား; K5000; ⊙7am-5pm) 'Shittaung' means 'Shrine of the 80,000 Images', a reference to the number of holy images inside. King Minbin, the most powerful of Rakhine's kings, built Shittaung in 1535. This is Mrauk U's most complex temple – it's a frenzy of stupas of various sizes; some 26 surround a central stupa. Thick walls, with windows and nooks, encircle the two-tiered structure, which has been highly reconstructed over the centuries – in some places rather clumsily.

★**Kothaung Paya** BUDDHIST TEMPLE
(ကိုးသောင်းဘုရား; ⊙daylight hours) FREE One of Mrauk U's star attractions, Kothaung Paya is also the area's largest temple. It was built in 1553 by King Minbin's son, King Mintaikkha, to outdo his dad's Shittaung by 10,000 images ('Kothaung' means 'Shrine of 90,000 Images'). Kothaung Paya is located a mile or so east of the palace; follow the road directly north of the market, veering left on the much smaller road before the bridge.

Dukkanthein Paya BUDDHIST TEMPLE
(ထုက္ကန်သိမ်ဘုရား; ⊙daylight hours) FREE Built by King Minphalaung in 1571, Dukkanthein Paya smacks of a bunker (with stupas). Wide stone steps lead up the southern and eastern

side of the building considered to be an ordination hall; take the east-side steps to reach the entrance. The interior features spiralling cloisters lined with images of buddhas and ordinary people (landlords, governors, officials and wives) sporting all of Mrauk U's 64 traditional hairstyles. The passageway nearly encircles the centre three times before reaching the sun-drenched buddha image.

Mahabodhi Shwegu   BUDDHIST TEMPLE
(မဟာတော်ရွှေဂူ; ⊙daylight hours) `FREE` The highlight of this squat, little-visited temple is its passageway with bas-relief illustrations of the *tribumi* – Buddhist visions of heaven, earth and hell – including acrobats, worshippers and animals. At the end there's a 6ft central buddha and four buddhas in niches; the throne of the former includes some erotic carvings. Mahabodhi Shwegu is largely hidden behind shrubbery on a hilltop northeast of Ratanabon Paya. To get here, proceed up the barely discernible uphill path that starts behind the covered water well.

🛏 Sleeping & Eating

Royal City Guest House   HOTEL **$**
(☏09 4307 3323, 043-50257; r US$10-25, bungalows US$40-55; ❋) On offer here are lean and reasonably comfortable rooms with cold-water showers in the main building for the budget crowd (the cheapest are very small indeed and lack bathrooms), and bungalows with air-con (if the electricity's working) and hot water across the road for those who can afford a bit more. The staff gives out a map of the main sites.

⭐**Nawarat Hotel**   HOTEL **$$**
(☏043-50073, in Yangon 01-298 543; mraukoonawarathotel@gmail.com; r US$55-98; ❋🕸) It's neither new nor sexy, but this is probably Mrauk U's best-value digs. Located a short walk from the main sights, the semidetached concrete bungalows here are big and comfortable, with decent beds, and are well kitted out with satellite TV, fridge and balcony. There's also an OK attached restaurant.

Happy Garden   CHINESE, BURMESE **$**
(dishes from K2500; ⊙8am-10pm) This beergarden joint is the most lively spot in town come nightfall. The Chinese-sounding dishes are tasty enough, and there are a few Burmese options. It's fine for a beer, too. It also rents out a few basic bungalows (K8000 to K30,000).

Moe Cherry   BURMESE **$$**
(mains from K4500; ⊙9am-9.30pm) More sophisticated than the other restaurants in Mrauk U – a shaded terrace to eat on, and tablecloths! – this is also the best place in town for both Rakhine-style curries and Chinese-Burmese fusion food. There's an extensive English menu and beer as well.

❶ Getting There & Away

BOAT

Mrauk U's jetty is about half a mile south of the market. Come here on the day of departure to buy tickets.

Double-decker boats run by the government's Inland Water Transport (p537) depart from Mrauk U for Sittwe on Wednesday and Saturday at 8am (US$7, four to seven hours). The faster 'speedboats' run by Shwe Pyi Tan (p537) leave Mrauk U for Sittwe on Monday and Thursday at 7am (K25,000, three hours).

BUS

There are two buses daily to Sittwe (K4000, 3½ hours, 6am and 7am), although you can always try to get a ride on the buses passing through later from Mandalay and elsewhere.

A daily bus leaves for Mandalay (K25,000, 20 hours, 8.30am). If you're heading to Bagan or Pakokku, take this bus and get off in Magwe, spend the night there and then catch one of the many vans or buses from Magwe to those destinations.

A sole minivan runs daily to Thandwe (for Ngapali Beach; K35,000, 22 hours, 4pm).

❶ Getting Around

Bicycles can be hired from **U Than Tun Bike Rental** (per day K2000; ⊙7am-7pm), just south of the bridge leading to the central market.

Mt Victoria   ဝိတိုရိယတောင်

Chin State's most-visited destination is Mt Victoria (p540), roughly 80 miles west of Bagan. The peak stands amid a 279-sq-mile national park and is a prime spot for birdwatching. It's best visited November to February, when the rhododendron bushes that cover the slopes are in full bloom. During the rainy season (mid-May to mid-October), the mountain is normally inaccessible and many hotels shut down.

The base for the trek is the tiny town of Kanpetlet, a six-hour drive from Nyaung U.

◉ Sights

★ Mt Victoria
MOUNTAIN

(Nat Ma Taung; K10,000; ☺ Oct-May) The high-est peak in Chin State – 10,016ft high – and the third highest in all Myanmar, stunning and little-visited Mt Victoria is the principal attraction of southern Chin State. Located within Nat Ma Taung National Park, the mountain is covered in large rhododendron trees that bloom in a delightful riot of red, yellow and white flowers between November and February. It's an easy two- to three-hour climb to the twin summits from the trail-head, accessed from the town of Kanpetlet.

🏃 Activities

The start of the trail to Mt Victoria's twin summits is 14 miles from Kanpetlet. There are many other trails across the mountain, and fascinating villages in the area to visit, so you could easily spend a few days here.

A guide is necessary to explore properly. For that reason, and due to the lack of public transport in the area, most people visit on three- or four-day tours run out of Bagan. Prices start at US$80 per person per day for a group of four, not including accommodation and food. There's a K10,000 entrance fee for the national park, although it's not always collected.

🛏 Sleeping & Eating

Mountain View Hill Resort   HOTEL $
(☎ 09 4923 2963; Mt Victoria St, Kanpetlet; r incl breakfast US$45-50) This new-ish place on the outskirts of Kanpetlet has 25 simple brick bungalows with wooden floors and reason-able beds, although they're not very warm in the winter months. There's also an OK at-tached restaurant. It's a fair step uphill from the centre of Kanpetlet.

Eden Guesthouse   GUESTHOUSE $
(☎ 09 4717 0420; Thitsar St, Kanpetlet; r K10,000) The cheapest digs in Kanpetlet, the Eden is a typical Chin State budget guesthouse: box-like rooms separated by thin wooden parti-tions, shared bathroom, cold water, no wi-fi, and electricity from 6pm to 10pm only. But the genial owner speaks some English and can arrange local transport to Mt Victoria. It's also clean and there are plenty of blan-kets for the chilly nights.

Maymyo Snack Shop   BURMESE, CHINESE $
(Kanpetlet; dishes from K700; ☺ 6.30am-8pm) Simple noodle and rice dishes and better

salads are on offer here at Kanpetlet's best restaurant. No alcohol is served, but there's a pleasant outside area to eat in. It's just off the main road through town, opposite the Taung Tarn Guesthouse. Everyone knows it.

ℹ Information

There are no banks or ATM's in Kanpetlet. Bring cash.

ℹ Getting There & Around

Tours to Mt Victoria start in Bagan, a six-hour drive away, where your transport will meet you. It's also possible to hike here from Mindat, a three-day journey. If you just want transport to and from Mt Victoria, Ever Sky (p536) in Nyaung U can arrange a car and driver for three days for around US$200.

There's a minibus from Pakokku to Kanpetlet (K9000, six hours, 10am Monday to Saturday).

From Kanpetlet, there's a minibus to Pakokku (K9000, six hours, 7am Monday to Saturday) and a bus to Mandalay (K17,500, 12 hours, 8am Monday to Saturday).

A return trip from Kanpetlet to the trailhead by motorbike will cost K25,000.

Mindat   မင်းတပ်မြို့

☑ 070 / POP C 10,000

Sitting at almost 5000ft above sea level, Min-dat is strung out along a ridge top, with its houses perched above and below the single road running through town. It's a stunning setting and Mindat is a jumping-off point for treks to surrounding traditional hill villages and Mt Victoria.

The higher altitude means that this is one of the few places in Myanmar where you'll see people wearing socks (with thongs). Most Westerners find the cooler weather (bring a fleece) a huge relief after the baking central plains.

Se Naing Family Guest House   GUESTHOUSE $
(☎ 070-70149, 09 44200 2645; mindatfgh@gmail. com; Main Rd; r incl breakfast K15,000-40,000) Run by the charming Monica, who speaks reason-able English, this cosy guesthouse has simple but clean rooms. The more expensive ones have their own small bathrooms, but there's hot water for everyone here, a luxury in Chin State, and fine views from the roof. The guest-house is close to the village entrance.

Myo Ma Restaurant   CHINESE, BURMESE $
(Main Rd; mains from K2500; ☺ 7am-9.30pm) The best and most popular place in Mindat

RIH LAKE ရိဟ်ရေအိုင်

Way up on the Myanmar–India border, mystical Rih Lake is an idyllic, heart-shaped lake with a magical, tranquil setting: the water shines a deep blue and the lake is surrounded by rice paddies and forested hills. The lake is of immense spiritual significance to the local Mizo people, who are spread across Chin State, Mizoram State in India and eastern Bangladesh. Rih Lake is accessed from nearby Rihkhawdar (ရိဟ်ခေါ်ဒါးလ်), a small but hectic border town separated from Mizoram State by a 100yd-long bridge. Rih Lake is a 15-minute motorcycle-taxi ride (K5000 return) from Rihkhawdar.

Sleeping options are limited: try **Rih Shwe Pyi Guest House** (☑09 647 2400; r K15,000-25,000; ❄), a three-minute walk from the bridge to India, just off the main drag through Rihkhawdar. **Rih Restaurant & Bungalows** (☑+91 81198 79086; Rih Lake; bungalows K20,000) right by the lake is fine place to eat, but the bungalows are very basic.

There are no banks or ATMs in Rihkhawdar, so bring cash. Uncomfortable, packed jeeps run to Rihkhawdar Monday to Saturday. From Kalaymyo, they leave from a bus ticket office a mile west of the main bus station (K15,000, nine hours). Get here at 6am to look for a ride, and preferably buy your ticket the day before.

A much better option is to catch one of the minivans to Tiddim (K7000, four hours) that leave around 7am from Kalaymyo's bus station and break the journey there. From Tiddim there are jeeps (K8000, four hours) to Rihkhawdar from 9am to noon. Jeeps return from Rihkhawdar to Kalaymyo via Tiddim from 7am to 9am (K15,000, nine hours).

to eat (though there's not much competition), Myo Ma offers reasonable Chinese-Burmese dishes and serves up draught beers. It does takeaway as well. Find it five minutes' walk uphill from the market; look for the blue building with the Myanmar Lager sign.

Market
MARKET

(⊙6am-5pm) Mindat's small market is just off the main road. It's mostly produce – you'll see tattoo-faced elderly women bent double under their food shopping – but a couple of shops sell traditional Chin clothes, bags and purses, which make good souvenirs.

ℹ Information

GUIDES

A recommended guide to the area around Mindat and beyond, Naing Kee Shing speaks excellent English, can arrange permits and is a mine of information about the region. He charges US$60 per day, excluding food, transport and accommodation. He can be contacted on 09 45463 1280 but is often away on treks, so email him first at chinlion93@gmail.com.

MONEY

There are no banks or ATMs in Mindat. Bring cash.

ℹ Getting There & Away

Public transport doesn't run on Sunday in Chin State.

Buses and minivans go to Mindat from Pakkoku in Magwe Region. They leave from the Moe Pi bus station, which is 500yd from the main bus station, between 6am and 8am (K7000, six hours).

Going in the opposite direction, buses and minivans depart from near the market in Mindat for Pakokku between 6am and 8.30am (K7000, six hours). There's also a bus to Mandalay (K12,000, 12 hours, 8am).

Kalaymyo ကလေးမြို့

☑073 / POP C 130,500

The gateway to northern Chin State, Kalaymyo, mostly known by its former name of Kalay, has a claim to be the true capital of Chin State, even though it's located just across the border in neighbouring Sagaing Region. More than half its population is Chin, far outnumbering the people who live in the actual Chin capital, Hakha.

Shin Hong Hotel
HOTEL $

(☑073-22714; shinhonghotel.kalay@gmail.com; Bo Gyoke Rd; r US$30; ❄✿) The Shin Hong isn't the best hotel in town, but it's the closest to the bus station. It feels a little institutional, but the rooms are large and comfortable enough, although the bathrooms are poky. But if you're coming from Chin State, you'll consider the 24-hour hot water to be worth the price alone.

Flow

THAI $

(☎ 09 42002 2526; Bo Gyoke Rd; dishes from K2000; ◷10am-10pm) Flow bills itself as a cocktail bar and restaurant, and foreign liquors and beers are available, but the real reason to come here is to sample its local but OK take on classic Thai dishes. It's rather more sophisticated than the beer gardens that dominate Kalaymyo's nightlife and dining scene. It's 10 minutes' walk east of the Shin Hong Hotel.

🛈 Information

KBZ Bank (Bo Gyoke Rd; ◷9.30am-3pm) You can exchange money here, and it has an ATM that takes foreign cards. It's 10 minutes' walk east of the Majesty Hotel. There are other ATMs around town, too.

🛈 Getting There & Away

Kalaymyo is the closest place with an airport to northern Chin State. **Air KBZ** (Bo Gyoke Rd; ◷9am-5pm) and **Myanmar National Airlines** (www.flymna.com; Bo Gyoke Rd; ◷9am-5pm) fly on alternate days to Yangon (from US$165) and Mandalay (from US$100). Their offices are near KBZ Bank, about 10 minutes' walk east of the Majesty Hotel.

Kalaymyo's scruffy bus station is off Bo Gyoke Rd, a 10-minute walk from the Shin Hong Hotel. There are crowded minivans Monday to Saturday to Hakha (K10,000, eight hours), Falam (K5000, four hours) and Tiddim (K7000, four hours). Most leave between 6am and 8am.

There are also daily buses to Yangon (K25,000, 22 hours, 2pm) and Mandalay (K15,000, 10 hours, 2pm).

If you're heading directly to Rih Lake, uncomfortable jeeps to Rihkhawdar (K15,000, nine hours) leave Monday to Saturday when full from an office about a mile west of the bus station on Bo Gyoke Rd. They depart between 6am and 9am.

Tiddim

တီးတိန်မြို့

☎ 070 / POP C 15,000

About two hours' drive from Kalaymyo into the Chin Hills, the road forks: south to Falam and Hakha, north to Tiddim and the Myanmar–India border. This part of northern Chin State is even less visited than the regions further south, despite the fact that the area around Tiddim is home to Kennedy Peak, Chin State's second-highest mountain. Tiddim, also known as Tedim or Teddim, is the ideal place to break the journey to mystical Rih Lake.

Siang Sawn

VILLAGE

(ရှောင်ဆောန်း) This rather strange, impeccably tidy village is an oddity in that it remains animist despite its proximity to heavily Christian Tiddim. In fact, all its inhabitants (many of whom wear traditional Chin costume) follow an animist religion that's overseen by the village spiritual leader. It's about 2 miles northeast of Tiddim; follow the main road almost to the end of town, turn right and head downhill – the locals will point the way.

Tedim Guesthouse

GUESTHOUSE $

(☎ 09 76756 3907; Kam Hau St; s/d US$15/30) A big step up from most Chin State guesthouses, this brand-new place offers clean and comfortable enough rooms with private bathrooms – a real rarity in this part of the world. There are great views of Kennedy Peak from the balcony. It's opposite the Cope Memorial Baptist Church on the main road through Tiddim; you can't miss the purple and tinted-glass exterior.

Power Win Restaurant

BURMESE, CHINESE $

(Kam Hau St; dishes from K2000; ◷7am-10pm) Run by friendly John and his wife, this beer station and restaurant serves standard Burmese-Chinese dishes, as well as draught beer (K1000). John speaks excellent English, is a mine of information about the Tiddim area and can help organise transport to outlying sights. Power Win is on the main road through town, almost opposite the minivan ticket offices.

🛈 Information

Tiddim is home to a new **KBZ Bank** (Kam Hau St; ◷9.30am-3pm), one of only two banks in Chin State. It has an ATM, but you can't change money here.

🛈 Getting There & Away

Minivans and jeeps to/from Tiddim run Monday to Saturday only.

There are minivans to Tiddim from Kalaymyo's bus station (K7000, four hours), most leaving 6am to 9am.

From Tiddim, a number of minivans to Kalaymyo (K7000, four hours) run at 7am from the bus ticket offices opposite Mangala Restaurant, at the junction of the main road through town and the road to Rihkhawdar.

If you're heading to Rih Lake, very uncomfortable jeeps to Rihkhawdar (K8000, four hours) pass through Tiddim from Kalaymyo from 9am to noon. Be sure to reserve a seat the day before at the stall at the junction of the main road and the road to Rihkhawdar.

UNDERSTAND MYANMAR

Myanmar Today

State Counsellor Aung San Suu Kyi and her colleagues have their work cut out for years to come tackling Myanmar's key problems: negotiating an end to the many ethnic conflicts, boosting an economy that has been mismanaged for decades, and overhauling the country's decrepit infrastructure. Worldwide criticism of the harsh treatment of the Rohingya Muslim minority has severely dented Myanmar's reputation, just a few years after the country was welcomed back into the global community.

History

Long before the British took control of Burma in three successive wars in the 19th century, the area was ruled over by several major ethnic groups, with the Bamar only coming into prominence in the 11th century. Britain managed the mountainous border regions separately from the fertile plains and delta of central and lower Burma, building on a cultural rift between the lowland Bamar and highland ethnic groups that lingers today. Civil war erupted between minority groups after independence in 1948, and continues still in pockets of the country.

General Ne Win wrested control from the elected government in 1962 and began the world's longest-running military dictatorship, which pursued xenophobic policies, leading Burma to full isolation. State socialism ruined the economy, necessitating several major currency devaluations, the last of which sparked massive protests in 1988.

The pro-democracy marches saw Aung San Suu Kyi, daughter of independence hero General Aung San, emerge as the leader of the National League for Democracy (NLD). The military allowed a national election in 1990 in which the NLD won 82% of the assembly seats, but refused to transfer power, placed Aung San Suu Kyi under house arrest and imprisoned many elected politicians and student leaders.

Despite Western sanctions, the generals continued to rule for the next two decades. An election in October 2010 brought in the quasi-civilian Union Solidarity and Development Party (USDP) to replace the junta. The USDP guaranteed to undertake political and economic reforms in return for the West lifting sanctions.

The NLD won a historic landslide victory in the November 2015 general election. Aung San Suu Kyi remains barred from the presidency under a law that bans people with foreign spouses from taking power (her late husband was British). Instead, she rules Myanmar under the title of State Counsellor.

But her time in power has been difficult, with the military retaining control of three key ministries and making up 25% of all MPs. The army's brutal response to terrorist attacks in Rakhine State in August 2017 by militant members of the Rohingya minority, which resulted in an estimated 600,000 Rohingya fleeing to Bangladesh, has made her the subject of fierce criticism around the world. Myanmar's economic development too, remains very much a work in progress.

People & Culture

Myanmar people are as proud of their country and culture as any nationality on Earth. Locals gush over ancient kings, *pwe* (theatre), *mohinga* (noodles with chicken or fish) breakfasts, great temples and Buddhism. A typical Burmese Buddhist values meditation, gives alms freely and sees their lot as the consequence of sin or merit in a past life. The social ideal for most Burmese is a standard of behaviour commonly termed *bamahsan chin* (Burmese-ness). The hallmarks of *bamahsan chin* include showing respect for elders, acquaintance with Buddhist scriptures and discretion in behaviour towards the opposite sex. Most importantly, *bamahsan chin* values the quiet, subtle and indirect over the loud, obvious and direct.

Lifestyle

About three-quarters of Myanmar's population are rural-dwellers, where life revolves around villages and farming. Here, national politics pale in comparison to the season, the crop or the level of the river (used for bathing, washing and drinking water). People are known for helping each other when in need, and call each other 'brother' and 'sister' affectionately.

Families tend to be large; you might find three or four generations of one family living in a two- or three-room house. The birth of a child is a big occasion. Girls are as equally welcome as boys, if not more so, as they're expected to look after parents later in life. Some thatched huts in the countryside have generators, powering electric light and pumping life into the TV a couple of hours a night; many don't. Running water outside the cities and bigger towns is rare.

Life is much more 21st century in Yangon and Mandalay but even these big cities suffer power outages. The extremes of Myanmar's wealth and poverty are very apparent too in the urban centres.

Population

A 2014 census listed the population of Myanmar as 51,419,420. But this total included estimates for regions – parts of Kachin, Rakhine and Shan States – that were not surveyed. It is likely that the real figure is closer to 60 million.

There are 135 officially recognised ethnic groups in Myanmar. The most numerous of those groups is the Bamar, making up around 68% of the population. Other major groups include the Shan, Kayin, Rakhine, Mon, Kayah and Kachin. There are also large numbers of Burmese Indians and Chinese, whose ancestors arrived mostly in the colonial era.

Under the 2008 constitution Myanmar is divided into seven regions (they used to be called divisions; these are where the Bamar are in the majority) and seven states (minority regions, namely Chin, Kachin, Kayah, Kayin, Mon, Rakhine and Shan States). In addition, there are six ethnic enclaves

BURMA OR MYANMAR?

In 1989, the military junta ditched Burma in favour of Myanmar.

During the years of military dictatorship, what to call the country was highly politicised, democracy supporters favouring Burma. Today, that polarisation is fading into the past. In 2016, Aung San Suu Kyi, addressing diplomats, said they could call the country either Burma or Myanmar. Although accustomed to calling it Burma herself, she vowed to sometimes use Myanmar – all in the spirit of diplomacy!

We use Myanmar as the default name for the country, with Burma used for periods before 1989. 'Burmese' is used for the Bamar people, the food and the language.

(Danu, Kokang, Naga, Palaung, Pa-O and Wa) with varying degrees of self-governance.

Religion

Freedom of religion is guaranteed under the country's constitution. But around 89% of Myanmar's citizens are Theravada Buddhists and the religion is given special status. The other major religions are Islam and Christianity. Many rural people believe also in *nat* spirits, a relic of the animist religions followed before Buddhism.

There has been an alarming upsurge in religious intolerance since Myanmar's opening up, driven by extreme Buddhist nationalists. Muslims have been the main target. In July 2015 a controversial new law was passed requiring Buddhist women to obtain official permission before marrying someone of a different faith.

BUDDHISM

For the average Burmese Buddhist much of life revolves around the merit (*kutho*, from the *Pali kusala*, meaning 'wholesome') that is accumulated through rituals and good deeds. One of the more common rituals performed by individuals visiting a stupa is to pour water over the buddha image at their astrological post (determined by the day of the week they were born) – one glassful for every year of their current age plus one extra to ensure a long life.

Every Burmese male is expected to take up temporary monastic residence twice in his life: once as a *samanera* (novice monk), between the ages of five and 15, and again as a *pongyi* (fully ordained monk), some time after the age of 20. Almost all men or boys under 20 years of age participate in the *shinpyu* (initiation ceremony), through which their family earns great merit.

While there is little social expectation that they should do so, a number of women live monastic lives as *dasasila* ('ten-precept' nuns). Burmese nuns shave their heads, wear pink robes and take vows in an ordination procedure similar to that undertaken by monks.

NAT WORSHIP

Buddhism in Myanmar has overtaken, but never entirely replaced, the pre-Buddhist practice of *nat* worship. The 37 *nat* figures are often found side by side with Buddhist images. The Burmese *nat* are spirits that can inhabit natural features, trees or even people. They can be mischievous or beneficent.

The *nat* cult is strong. Mt Popa is an important centre. The Burmese divide their devotions and offerings according to the sphere of influence: Buddha for future lives, and the *nat* – both Hindu and Bamar – for problems in this life. A misdeed might be redressed with offerings to the *nat* Thagyamin, who annually records the names of those who perform good deeds in a book made of gold leaves. Those who commit evil are recorded in a book made of dog skin.

Arts

For centuries the arts in Myanmar were sponsored by the royal courts, mainly through the construction of major religious buildings that required the skills of architects, sculptors, painters and a variety of craftspeople. Such patronage was cut short during British colonial rule and has not been a priority since independence. This said, there are plenty of examples of traditional art to be viewed in Myanmar, mainly in the temples that are an ever-present feature of town and countryside. There's also a growing contemporary art scene, particularly in Yangon.

MARIONETTE THEATRE

Yok-thei pwe (Burmese marionette theatre) was the forerunner of Burmese classical dance. Marionette theatre declined following WWII and is now mostly confined to tourist venues in Yangon, Mandalay and Bagan.

MUSIC

Traditional Burmese music relies heavily on rhythm and is short on harmony, at least to the Western ear. Younger Burmese listen to Western-influenced sounds – you will often hear Burmese-language covers of classic oldies, as well as sappy love or pop tunes. A number of Burmese rock musicians, such as Lay Phyu of the band Iron Cross, produce serious songs of their own, and in Yangon there is a small but vibrant punk scene.

PWE

The *pwe* (show) is everyday Burmese theatre. A religious festival, wedding, funeral, celebration, fair, sporting event – almost any gathering – is a good excuse for a *pwe*. Once underway, a *pwe* traditionally goes on all night. If an audience member is flaking at some point during the performance, they

---

MYANMAR READING LIST

Burma's Spring (Rosalind Russell; 2016) Lively memoir with a broad cast of characters from girl-band singers and domestic workers to opposition politicians.

Golden Parasol (Wendy Law-Yone; 2013) An insider's view of key events in modern Myanmar's history; the author's father, Ed Law-Yone, an influential newspaper editor, was exiled from the country in the 1960s.

River of Lost Footsteps (Thant Myint-U; 2006) Must-read historical review by the grandson of former UN secretary-general U Thant.

---

simply fall asleep. To experience one, ask a trishaw driver if a *pwe* is on nearby.

Myanmar's truly indigenous dance forms are those that pay homage to the *nat*. In a special *nat pwe*, one or more *nat* are invited to possess the body and mind of a medium. Sometimes members of the audience seem to be possessed instead, an event greatly feared by most Burmese.

Environment

Myanmar covers an area of 261,000 sq miles, which is roughly the size of Texas or France. From the snowcapped Himalaya in the north to the coral-fringed Myeik (Mergui) Archipelago in the south, Myanmar's length of 1250 miles crosses three distinct ecological regions, producing what is probably the richest biodiversity in Southeast Asia.

Unfortunately, that wildlife – which includes a third of the world's Asiatic elephants and the largest tiger reserve on the planet – is threatened by habitat loss. Rampant deforestation by the timber industry, which occurs in order to feed demand in China and Thailand, is a primary cause. Optimistically, about 7% of the country is protected in national parks and other protected areas, but most of these are just lines on maps. Wildlife laws in Myanmar are seldom enforced, due to a desperate lack of funding.

For travellers, seeing wildlife will be more a matter of luck than design. And without some serious cash, forget about visiting national parks.

Food & Drink

Food

Mainstream Burmese cuisine represents a blend of Bamar, Mon, Indian and Chinese influences. A typical meal has *htamin* (rice) as its core, eaten with a choice of *hin* (curry dishes), most commonly fish, chicken, pork, prawns or mutton. Soup is always served, along with a table full of condiments (including pickled vegies as spicy dipping sauces).

Most Burmese food is pretty mild on the chilli front, with cooks favouring a simple masala of turmeric, ginger, garlic, salt and onions, plus plenty (and we mean loads!) of peanut oil and shrimp paste. *Balachaung* (chillies, tamarind and dried shrimp pounded together) or the pungent *ngapi kyaw* (spicy shrimp paste with garlic) is always nearby to add some kick. Almost everything savoury in Burmese cooking is flavoured with *ngapi* (a salty paste concocted from dried and fermented shrimp or fish).

Noodle dishes are often eaten for breakfast or as light snacks between meals. The seafood served along the coasts is some of the best and cheapest you'll find in the entire region.

Drink

NON-ALCOHOLIC DRINKS

Tea shops, a national institution, are good places to meet people over a drink and inexpensive snacks such as *nam-bya* and *pal-ata* (flat breads) or Chinese fried pastries. Burmese tea (about K300 a cup), brewed Indian-style with lots of condensed milk and sugar, is the national drink. Ask for *lahpeq ye* (tea with a dollop of condensed milk); *cho bouk* is less sweet, and *kyauk padaung* is very sweet. Most restaurants will provide as much free Chinese tea as you can handle. Real coffee is limited to modern, Western-style cafes in Yangon and other large cities. Sugar-cane juice is a very popular streetside drink.

ALCOHOL

Myanmar beer is a little lighter in flavour and alcohol than other Southeast Asian beers. Mandalay beer is weaker still.

There are a variety of stronger liquors, including the harsh local version of whisky. Then there's the rum produced in Mandalay, and the fermented palm juice known as toddy.

Popular in Shan State is a pleasant-tasting orange brandy called *shwe leinmaw* that packs quite a punch. There are a couple of vineyards making wine, and in Pyin Oo Lwin there are several sweet, fruit-based wines.

SURVIVAL GUIDE

❶ Directory A–Z

ACCOMMODATION

Myanmar's range and overall capacity of accommodation is steadily increasing, leading to more affordable rates across the board. Unless you're planning on travelling in major holiday seasons it's usually unnecessary to book more than a week or so ahead.

Guesthouses More and more of these are opening in popular destinations across the country.

Hostels Found in the major cities and tourist centres and squarely aimed at the budget crowd.

Hotels Very common, but outside the big cities don't expect much luxury or anything boutique.

Resorts Confined mainly to the beaches at Ngapali, Chaung Tha and Ngwe Saung.

CLIMATE

Myanmar has two seasons: the wet and the dry. The rainy season runs roughly from May to October. It doesn't rain nonstop, but there are daily downpours. From November to April, the weather is dry, becoming progressively more hot and humid as the rainy season approaches. November to February are the most pleasant months weather-wise.

ELECTRICITY

When it's working, the electricity supply is 230V, 50Hz AC. Many hotels have generators (some run at night only). Local power sources in many towns are scheduled for night hours only.

EMBASSIES & CONSULATES

Most foreign embassies and consulates are based in Yangon. Check the government's Ministry of Foreign Affairs (www.mofa.gov.mm) for more information.

SLEEPING PRICE RANGES

The following price ranges refer to a double room or dorm bed.

$ less than US$50

$$ US$50–150; in Yangon US$50–200

$$$ more than US$150; in Yangon more than US$200

Australian Embassy (Map p492; ☑ 01-251 810; www.burma.embassy.gov.au; 88 Strand Rd, Kyauktada)

Bangladeshi Embassy (Map p496; ☑ 01-515 275; www.bdembassyyangon.org; 11B Than Lwin Rd, Kamayut)

Canadian Embassy (Map p492; ☑ 01-384 805; www.canadainternational.gc.ca; 9th fl, Centrepoint Towers, 65 Sule Pagoda Rd, Kyauktada)

Chinese Embassy (Map p496; ☑ 01-221 281; http://mm.china-embassy.org/eng; 1 Pyidaungsu Yeiktha St, Dagon)

French Embassy (Map p494; ☑ 01-212 520; www.ambafrance-mm.org; 102 Pyidaungsu Yeiktha Rd, Dagon)

German Embassy (Map p496; ☑ 01-548 952; www.rangun.diplo.de; 9 Bogyoke Aung San Museum Rd, Bahan)

Indian Embassy (Map p492; ☑ 01-391 219; www.indiaembassyyangon.net; 545-547 Merchant St, Kyauktada)

Japanese Embassy (Map p496; ☑ 01-549 644; www.mm.emb-japan.go.jp; 100 Nat Mauk Rd, Bahan)

New Zealand Embassy (Map p496; ☑ 01-230 5805; yangonoffice@mft.net.nz; 43 Inya Myiang Rd, Bahan)

Thai Embassy (Map p496; ☑ 01-226 721; www.thaiembassy.org/yangon/en; 94 Pyay Rd, Dagon)

UK Embassy (Map p492; ☑ 01-370 867, 01-370 865; www.gov.uk/government/world/burma; 80 Strand Rd, Kyauktada)

US Embassy (Map p489; ☑ 01-536 509; http://mm.usembassy.gov; 110 University Ave Rd, Kamayut)

FESTIVALS & EVENTS

Myanmar follows a 12-month lunar calendar, and most festivals are on the full moon of the Burmese month in which they occur – hence shifting dates. The build-up to festivals can go on for days.

February/March

Shwedagon Festival Myanmar's largest *paya* festival takes place in Yangon.

March/April

Full Moon Festival Biggest event of the year at Shwemawdaw Paya in Bago.

April/May

Buddha's Birthday The full moon also marks the day of Buddha's enlightenment and his entry to nirvana. One of the best places to observe this ceremony is at Yangon's Shwedagon Paya.

Thingyan (Water Festival) The Burmese New Year is the biggest holiday of the year, celebrated with a raucous nationwide water fight. It is impossible to go outside without getting

> **EATING PRICE RANGES**
>
> The following prices ranges refer to a two-course meal with a soft drink.
>
> **$** less than K5500; in Yangon less than K10,000
>
> **$$** K5500–16,500; in Yangon K10,000–25,000
>
> **$$$** more than K16,500; in Yangon more than K25,000

drenched, so just join the fun. Businesses close and some transport – especially buses – stops running for around a week.

June/July

Buddhist Lent Start of the Buddhist Rains Retreat. Laypeople present monasteries with new robes, because during the three-month Lent period monks are restricted to their monasteries.

July/August

Wagaung Festival Nationwide exercise in alms-giving.

September/October

Thadingyut Celebrates Buddha's return from a period of preaching.

October/November

Tazaungdaing The biggest 'festival of lights' sees all Myanmar lit by oil lamps, fire balloons, candles and even mundane electric lamps.

Kathein A one-month period at the end of Buddhist Lent during which new monastic robes and requisites are offered to the monastic community.

December/January

Kayin New Year Karen communities throughout Myanmar celebrate by wearing their traditional dress and by hosting folk-dancing and singing performances. Big celebrations are held in the Karen suburb of Insein, just north of Yangon, and in Hpa-an.

Ananda Festival Held at the Ananda Pahto in Bagan at the full moon.

INTERNET ACCESS

Wi-fi is the norm in big cities – most hotels and guesthouses and some restaurants and cafes will have it and it's normally free. There are also internet cafes in the cities, although they are usually used for online gaming. Internet access can even be found in relatively remote locations, such as Mrauk U.

However, with low bandwidth and power outages, it can often be a frustrating exercise to send and receive large files over the internet, particularly in rural areas.

LEGAL MATTERS

You have absolutely no legal recourse in case of arrest or detainment by the authorities, regardless of the charge. If you are arrested, you will most likely be permitted to contact your consular agent in Myanmar for possible assistance.

If you purchase gems or jewellery from persons or shops that are not licensed by the government, you run the risk of having them confiscated if customs officials find them in your baggage when you're exiting the country.

Drug-trafficking crimes are punishable by death.

LGBT TRAVELLERS

➡ Homosexuality is seen as a bit of a cultural taboo, though most locals are known to be tolerant of it, for both men and women.

➡ Gay and transgendered people in Myanmar are rarely 'out', except for 'third sex' spirit mediums who channel the energies of *nat* spirits.

➡ Public displays of affection, whether heterosexual or homosexual, are frowned upon; a local woman walking with a foreign man will raise more eyebrows than two same-sex travellers sharing a room.

➡ For more information on LGBT issues in Myanmar, see Colours Rainbow (www.colorsrainbow.com). Also check Utopia-Asia (www.utopia-asia.com).

MEDIA

Newspapers and magazines Read the English-language newspaper *Myanmar Times* (www.mmtimes.com), published Monday to Friday, and the weekly current-affairs magazines *Frontier Myanmar* (http://frontiermyanmar.net) and *Mizzima Weekly* (http://mizzima.com).

Radio Bring a short-wave radio and listen to BBC and VOA broadcasts.

TV Watch satellite TV – you'll often find CNN, BBC World, Al Jazeera, and other news and entertainment channels at hotels.

ⓘ BRING NEW DOLLAR BILLS

Bringing to Myanmar pristine 'new' bills – bills issued in 2006 or later that have colour and are in perfect condition: no folds, stamps, stains, writing marks or tears – is still recommended.

You will get the best exchange rates from US$100 bills, but it's also a good idea to bring some small dollar bills – ones, fives and 10s.

MONEY

Cash mainly. ATMs accepting international cards are increasingly available in cities, towns and tourist areas. Bring pristine US bills for exchange.

ATMs & Banks

There are now hundreds of ATMs across the country. There is a withdrawal fee of K5000 and a withdrawal limit of K300,000 per transaction.

Don't rely solely on ATMs: the machines don't always work.

The most useful of the local banks (open 9.30am to 3pm Monday to Friday) are CB and KBZ.

Credit Cards & Travellers Cheques

Travellers cheques are useless. However, in Yangon and other major tourist spots you'll increasingly find credit cards accepted by top-end hotels, restaurants and some shops.

Money Changers

You'll find official bank and private licensed exchange booths at places such as Yangon and Mandalay airports, Bogyoke Aung San Market and Shwedagon Paya in Yangon.

Never hand over your money until you've received the kyat and counted them. Honest money changers will expect you to do this. Considering that K10,000 is the highest denomination, you'll get a lot of notes. Money changers give ready-made, rubber-banded stacks of a hundred K1000 bills. It's a good idea to check each note individually. Often you'll find one or two (or more) with a cut corner or taped tears, neither of which anyone will accept.

Tipping

Tipping is not customary in Myanmar, though little extra 'presents' are sometimes expected (even if they're not asked for) in exchange for a service.

Airport If someone helps you with your bags, a small tip is welcomed.

Restaurants As wages are low, it's a good idea to leave change for waiters.

Temples A small donation is appreciated if a caretaker is required to unlock a temple.

OPENING HOURS

Government Offices and Post Offices 9.30am to 4.30pm Monday to Friday

Shops 9am to 6pm

Restaurants 11am to 9pm

Cafes and Tea Shops 6am to 6pm

Banks 9.30am to 3pm Monday to Friday

PHOTOGRAPHY & VIDEO

Photo-processing shops and internet cafes can burn digital photos onto a CD, but you should have your own adapter. Avoid taking photographs of military facilities, uniformed individuals, road blocks and strategic locations, such as bridges.

Some sights, including some *paya* and other religious sites, charge a small camera or video fee.

POSTAL SERVICES

Most mail out of Myanmar gets to its destination quite efficiently. International-postage rates are a bargain: a postcard is K500, a 1kg package to Australia/the UK/the US K16,200/18,900/20,700.

Post offices are supposed to be open from 9.30am to 4.30pm Monday to Friday, but you may find some keep shorter hours.

DHL (p495) is a more reliable but expensive way of sending out bigger packages.

PUBLIC HOLIDAYS

Major fixed public holidays:

Independence Day 4 January
Union Day 12 February
Peasants' Day 2 March
Armed Forces Day 27 March
Workers' Day 1 May
Martyrs' Day 19 July
Christmas 25 December

The following public-holiday dates vary according to the lunar calendar:

Thingyan Three days in April
National Day Mid-November to late December

SAFE TRAVEL

For the vast majority of visitors, travel in Myanmar is safe and should pose no serious problems.

➡ Some areas of the country remain off-limits due to ongoing civil war and/or landmines.

➡ In off-the-beaten-track places, where authorities are less used to seeing foreigners, local officials may ask you what you are up to. Saying you're a tourist normally satisfies them.

➡ If you have any tattoos of Buddha on your body, keep them covered up.

Crime

While not unheard of, crimes such as mugging are rare in Myanmar. Locals know that the penalties for stealing, particularly from foreigners, can be severe. Most travellers' memories of locals grabbing their money are of someone chasing them down to return a K500 note they dropped. If someone grabs your bag at a bus station, it's almost certainly just a motorcycle-taxi driver hoping for a fare.

Transport & Road Hazards

The poor state of road and rail infrastructure plus lax safety standards and procedures for flights and boats mean that travelling can sometimes be dangerous.

Safety often seems to be the last consideration of both drivers and pedestrians. Proceed with caution when crossing any road, particularly in cities. Do not expect drivers to follow road rules.

TELEPHONE
Local Calls

To dial long distance within Myanmar, dial the area code (including the '0') and the number.

International Calls

Via a landline, it costs about US$5 per minute to call Australia or Europe and US$6 per minute to phone North America.

To call Myanmar from abroad, dial your country's international-access code, then 95 (Myanmar's country code), the area code (minus the '0'), and the five- or six-digit number.

Mobile Phones

There are three mobile networks: government-owned MPT (www.mpt.com.mm) and the private operators Telenor Myanmar (www.telenor.com.mm) and Ooredoo (www.ooredoo.com.mm). All offer pay-as-you go SIM cards (from K1500), which can be used with unlocked smartphones.

For call and text fees and internet plans, top-up cards of between K1000 and K10,000 are widely available.

TIME

The local Myanmar Standard Time (MST) is 6½ hours ahead of Greenwich Mean Time (GMT/UTC). When coming in from Thailand, turn your watch back half an hour; coming from India, put your watch forward an hour. The 24-hour clock is often used for train times.

TOILETS

In most out-of-the-way places, Burmese toilets are often squat toilets, generally in a cobweb-filled outhouse that is reached by a dirt path behind a restaurant. In guesthouses and hotels you will usually find Western-style toilets. Toilet paper is widely available but consider carrying an emergency stash. Either way, don't flush it.

TOURIST INFORMATION

Ministry of Hotels & Tourism Tourist Information (p495) Located in Yangon. This office is quiet, and often the staff has sketchy knowledge on restricted areas of the country.

Myanmar Travels & Tours (MTT; Map p530; ☑ 061-65040; ☺8.30am-4.30pm) Located in New Bagan.

MTT (Myanmar Travel & Tours; Map p516; ☑ 02-60356; 68th St, 26/27; ☺9.30am-6pm) Located in Mandalay. Efficient and generally helpful staff.

Travellers who want to arrange a driver, or have hotel reservations awaiting them, would do well to arrange a trip with the help of private travel agents (p495) in Yangon and other major cities. Many Myanmar 'travel agents' outside Yangon only sell air tickets.

TRAVELLERS WITH DISABILITIES

With its lack of paved roads or footpaths (even when present, the latter are often uneven), Myanmar presents many physical obstacles for those with impaired mobility. Rarely do public buildings (or transport) feature ramps or other access points for wheelchairs, and hotels make inconsistent efforts to provide access for travellers with disabilities.

USEFUL WEBSITES

Go-Myanmar.com (www.go-myanmar.com) Plenty of up-to-date travel-related information and advice.

Myanmar Tourism Federation (http://myanmar.travel) Inspirational pictures, good backgroun=d information and travel tips.

Online Burma/Myanmar Library (www.burmalibrary.org) Database of books and past articles on Myanmar.

Ministry of Hotels & Tourism (http://tourism.gov.mm/en_US) Government department with some useful information.

Myanmar Now (www.myanmar-now.org) News and features site.

Lonely Planet (www.lonelyplanet.com/myanmar-burma) Destination information, hotel bookings, traveller forum and more.

VISAS

Everyone requires a visa. Single-entry tourist visas last 28 days.

E-Visa

Citizens of 100 countries can apply online for tourist visas via Myanmar's Ministry of Immigration and Population website: http://evisa.moip.gov.mm.

The cost is US$50. After your application is processed, you'll be emailed an approval letter. Print it out and give it to the passport official on arrival at the airport or designated land borders with Thailand and you'll be stamped into the country.

E-visas can be used at Yangon, Mandalay and Nay Pyi Taw international airports; and at three Thailand–Myanmar land border crossings: Tachileik, Myawaddy and Kawthoung. You can exit the country at any overland border crossing bar the remote Htee Khee crossing (although you will need a permit and permission to exit to China and India).

Citizens of 51 countries can also apply online for business visas (US$70, valid 70 days), but

you'll need a letter of invitation from a sponsoring company and proof of your company's registration of business.

Applications

Tourist visas (28 days) are valid for up to three months from the date of issue. Starting the process a month in advance is the safe bet; these days the processing can take anything between a day and a week.

If you're already travelling, it's possible to get a tourist visa at short notice from the Myanmar Embassy (p792) in Bangkok; the cost is 1260B for same-day processing (application 9am to noon, collection 3.30pm to 4.30pm), 1035B for the next day.

Visa Extensions & Overstaying

It is not possible to extend a tourist visa.

Some travellers extend their trips by overstaying their visa. This is not normally a problem, as long as you don't overstay for more than 14 days. You will be charged US$3 a day, plus a US$3 registration fee, at the airport or land border as you exit the country. The fine can be paid in kyat as well, but it's important to have the correct amount, as receiving change is unlikely.

However, some hotels won't take guests who have overstayed their visas, and domestic airlines may be unwilling to let you on planes. If you're overstaying, it's wise to stick with land routes and places within easy reach of Yangon. There have been cases in the past of tourists being instructed to leave the country immediately if their visa has expired.

VOLUNTEERING

Volunteering opportunities in Myanmar include teaching, medicine, and assisting entrepreneurs and fledgling social businesses with skills and administration.

Be very wary about visiting or volunteering to teach at orphanages – see www.thinkchildsafe.org/thinkbeforerevisiting for more details.

Organisations in Myanmar that often look for volunteers include the following:

KT Care Foundation Myanmar (www.ktcare.org)

Myanmore (www.myanmore.com)

UN Volunteers (http://unv.org/how-to-volunteer)

VIA (Volunteers in Asia; http://viaprograms.org)

WOMEN TRAVELLERS

Women travelling alone are more likely to be helped than harassed, although there have been a few reports of sexual harassment. In some areas you'll be regarded with friendly curiosity – and asked, with sad-eyed sympathy, 'Are you only one?' – because Burmese women tend to travel in mobs. At remote religious sites, a single foreign woman may be 'adopted' by a Burmese woman, who will take you and show you the highlights. At some sites, such as Mandalay's Mahamuni Paya and Golden Rock, 'ladies' are not permitted to the central shrine; signs will indicate if this is the case.

ℹ Getting There & Away

Flights, tours and rail tickets can be booked online at lonelyplanet.com/bookings.

AIR

Most international flights arrive at Yangon International Airport (p496). You can also fly directly into Mandalay International Airport (p521) from China, Hong Kong, India, Singapore and Thailand, and **Nay Pyi Taw International Airport** (NYT; ☏ 09 79900 0196) from China and Thailand.

LAND

Arriving in and departing Myanmar by land to/from China, India and Thailand is possible, although for Chinese and Indian crossings you will need a permit.

ℹ Getting Around

A few remote destinations are accessible only by plane or boat, but many others, including key tourist sites, can be reached by road or rail. Poor, overstretched infrastructure means travellers must have patience and a tolerance for discomfort.

Air Fast; reasonably reliable schedules; the safety record of local airlines is much better than it was.

Car Total flexibility but can be expensive; some destinations require a government-approved guide and driver.

Boat Chance to interact with locals and pleasant for sightseeing, but slow, uncomfortable and only covers a few destinations.

Bus Frequent; reliable services; speed depends on state of road and bus; overnight trips save on accommodation.

Train Interaction with locals and countryside views, but uncomfortable, slow and with long delays.

AIR

Following is the contact information for airline offices in Yangon. These airlines all serve the same major destinations (ie Yangon to/from Nay Pyi Daw, Mandalay, Bagan, Inle, Sittwe). Myanmar National Airlines serves the most extensive range of destinations.

Air Bagan (☏ 01-504 888; www.airbagan.com)
Air KBZ (☏ 01-372 977; www.airkbz.com)

Air Mandalay (☏ 01-525 488; www.airmanda lay.com)
Asian Wings (☏ 01-516 654; www.asianwings airways.com)
Golden Myanmar Airlines (☏ 09 97799 3000; www.gmairlines.com)
Mann Yadanarpon Airlines (☏ 01-656 969; www.airmyp.com)
Myanmar National Airlines (☏ 01-378 603; www.flymna.com)
Yangon Airways (☏ 01-383 100; www.yangon air.com)

BOAT

A great variety of boats – from creaky old government-run ferries to luxurious private cruise ships – ply Myanmar's waterways.

In addition to the rivers, it's possible to travel along the Bay of Bengal between Sittwe and Taunggok (north of Ngapali Beach).

BUSES

Almost always faster and cheaper than trains, Myanmar buses range from luxury air-conditioned express buses to less luxurious but pleasant buses (without air-con), local buses and mini 32-seaters.

From November to February it's wise to book buses a couple of days in advance for key routes, such as Bagan–Inle Lake. Seat reservations are made for all buses – you should be able to check the seating plan with the reservation agent.

ℹ BORDER CROSSINGS

At the time of research there were entry and exit points at six locations along Myanmar's land borders.

➡ Mae Sai in northern Thailand to/from Tachileik in Shan State

➡ Mae Sot in Thailand to/from Myawaddy in Kayin State

➡ Ranong in Thailand to/from Kawthoung at far southern end of Tanintharyi Region

➡ Phu Nam Ron in Thailand to/from Htee Khee in Tanintharyi Region

➡ Ruili in Yunnan Province, China, to/from Mu-se in Shan State

➡ Moreh in India's Manipur state to/from Tamu in Sagaing Region

E-visas (p550) are currently only available at the following Myanmar–Thailand borders: Tachileik, Myawaddy and Ka-wthoung.

CAR & MOTORCYCLE

Hiring a car and driver for part or all of a trip is a good way to go. To drive yourself, permission must be arranged via the government-run MTT and Road Transport Administration Department (RTAD; www.myanmarrtad.com).

For a car and driver outside Yangon, expect to pay US$70 and up per day, depending on the quality of the vehicle. Most hotels and guest-houses can organise one. In a few places, such as Hpa-an and Dawei, it's possible to hire manual or automatic 100cc to 125cc motorbikes, but motorbikes are generally not available for hire in Myanmar. In Bagan you can hire electric bikes.

LOCAL TRANSPORT

Small towns rely heavily on motorcycle taxis and trishaws as the main modes of local transport. However, in big cities public buses take regular routes along the main avenues for a fixed per-person rate, usually K200.

Standard rates for taxis, motorcycle taxis, trishaws and horse carts are sometimes 'boosted' for foreigners. Generally a ride from the bus station to a central hotel – often a distance of 1.25 miles or more – is between K500 and K1500 on a motorbike. Short rides around the city centre can be arranged for between K500 and K1000. You will likely have to bargain a bit.

PICK-UP TRUCKS

Japanese-made pick-up trucks feature three rows of bench seats in the covered back. Most pick-ups connect short-distance destinations, making many stops along the way to pick up people or cargo. They are normally packed. Pick-ups trace some useful or necessary routes, such as from Mandalay to Amarapura, from Bagan to Mt Popa, and up to the Golden Rock at Kyaiktiyo. Unlike buses, they go regularly during the day.

TRAIN

A train ride on Myanmar's narrow-gauge tracks is like going by horse, with the carriages rocking back and forth and bouncing everyone lucky enough to have a seat into the air – sleep is practically impossible. Compared to bus trips on the same routes, taking the train means extra travel time, on top of which likely delays (of several hours, if you're unlucky) have to be factored in.

However, train travel is cheap now that foreigners pay the same as locals. Routes sometimes get to areas not reached by road and the services provide a chance to interact with locals.

Reservations

Tickets can be bought directly at the train stations.

A day's notice is usually enough to book a seat, but if you want a coveted sleeper, you'll need at least a couple of days' notice – longer during high season (November to March).

Philippines

Includes ➜

Best Places to Eat

➜ Van Gogh is Bipolar (p569)

➜ Kalui (p603)

➜ Cafe by the Ruins Dua (p573)

➜ Lab-as Seafood Restaurant (p588)

➜ Angelina (p596)

Top Filipino Phrases

Good day *Magandáng araw pô*

Goodbye *Paalam na pô*

Thank you *Salamat pô*

Do you speak English? *Marunong ka ba ng Inglés?*

Why Go?

Just when you thought you had Asia figured out, you get to the Philippines. Instead of monks you have priests; instead of túk-túk you have tricycles; instead of *pho* you have *adobo*. At first glance the Philippines will disarm you more than charm you, but peel back the country's skin and there are treasures aplenty to be found. This far-flung archipelago is defined by its emerald terraced rice fields, teeming mega-cities, mountain tribes, smouldering volcanoes, bug-eyed tarsiers, fuzzy water buffalo and laid-back people. Explore desert islands, descend into world-class dive sites, and venture deep into the mountains to visit remote tribes.

The Philippines possesses a quirky streak that takes a little time to appreciate. But in amongst the secret potions and healing lotions, wheezing bangkas (outrigger boats), crooked politicians, graffiti-splashed jeepneys, blaring karaoke and cheap beer, you'll find a diverse land that fully rewards your travels.

When to Go
Manila

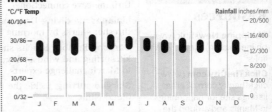

| Dec–Apr High season is dry season for most of the country; December to February are peak months. | May & Nov Shoulder season. Gets hot in May ahead of the wet season. | Jun–Oct Monsoon in most parts of the country and typhoons likely. Accommodation prices drop. |

AT A GLANCE

Currency Peso (P)

Languages Tagalog (Filipino), English

Money ATMs abound in cities, but are scarce in remote areas

Visas Visa waivers on arrival (30 days) the norm.

Exchange Rates

Australia	A$1	P40
Canada	C$1	P40
Euro zone	€1	P60
Japan	¥100	P46
New Zealand	NZ$1	P37
Thailand	10B	P15
UK	£1	P66
USA	US$1	P50

For current exchange rates see www.xe.com

Daily Costs

Dorm bed P450

Bottle of San Miguel beer P40

Two-tank scuba dive P2500

Short taxi ride P60

Resources

Philippine Newslink (www.philnews.com) News, views, links

ClickTheCity.com (www.clickthecity.com) A great listings site for happenings in Manila and around the country

Lonely Planet (www.lonelyplanet.com/philippines) Destination information, hotel bookings, traveller forum and more.

Don't Miss

Filipinos revel in colourful fiestas, and it's worth scheduling your travels around one. The granddaddy of them all is the Ati-Atihan festival in Kalibo in January. Cebu's Sinulog Festival, also in January, sees revellers dancing a unique two-steps-forward, one-step-back shuffle, while Baguio's Panagbenga involves a grand procession of floral floats. The Easter crucifixion ceremony in San Fernando, north of Manila, produces a more macabre tableau, with Catholic devotees being physically nailed to crosses. Every little town holds a fiesta, so your odds of seeing one are pretty good.The Filipino *joie de vivre* also manifests itself in other ways – namely, singing. A karaoke night out is essential. Or pay homage to Filipino cover bands worldwide with some live music. Cover-band shows in Malate can be lively, or head up to Quezon City or Makati for more original fare.

REGIONS AT A GLANCE

The Philippines consists of three main island groups: Luzon, the Visayas and Mindanao. You can rub shoulders with them in the megacity madness in Manila, the hill tribes in North Luzon, and indigenous village life in Mindanao. And you can go surfing along the eastern seaboard of the entire country, or enjoy good snorkelling practically everywhere. The Visayas most embody the defining image of the Philippines: a dreamy desert island festooned with palm trees and ringed by white sand. Palawan is a region apart, a fantastic otherworld of unspoiled rainforests and surreal seascapes.

Essential Outdoor Activities

Whale sharks Snorkelling with the gentle butanding of Donsolis the quintessential Philippine adventure.

Sagada caving Dodge stalactites, slither through crevasses and swim in crisp underground pools on the thrilling cave connection.

Malapascua diving Drop onto Monad Shoal to view thresher sharks by morning and manta rays by day.

Boracay Bulabog Beach's shallow lagoon is perfect for kitesurfing and windsurfing; stiff winds from December to March challenge experts.

Siargao surfing Tackle the Philippines' ultimate wave, Cloud Nine.

Entering the Country

Entering the country is straightforward and usually done by air through Manila, Cebu, Clark or Kalibo airports.

LUZON

The Philippines' main island is a vast expanse of misty mountains, sprawling plains, simmering volcanoes and endless coastline – with Manila at the centre of it all. The island's trophy piece is the northern mountainous area known as the Cordillera, where the *Ifugao* built their world-famous rice terraces in and around Banaue more than 2000 years ago. Along Luzon's northwest coast, historic Vigan is the country's best-preserved Spanish colonial-era town. Elsewhere, the southeast region of Bicol is home to fiery food and two of the country's top attractions: the whale sharks of Donsol and the perfect cone of Mt Mayon.

Manila

☑ 02 / POP 12.95 MILLION

Manila's moniker, the 'Pearl of the Orient', couldn't be more apt – its cantankerous shell reveals its jewel only to those resolute enough to pry. No stranger to hardship, the city has endured every disaster both humans and nature could throw at it, and yet today the chaotic metropolis thrives as a true Asian megacity.

As well as outstanding sightseeing, visitors who put in the effort will discover its creative soul – from edgy galleries to a lively indie music scene. Combine this with a penchant for speakeasy bars, artisan markets and single-origin coffees, and it's clear to see that Manila's not only one of Asia's most underrated cities, but one of its coolest.

History

The Spanish brushed aside a Muslim fort here in 1571 and founded the modern city as the capital of their realm. Spanish residents were concentrated around the walled city of Intramuros until 1898, when the Spanish governor surrendered to the Filipinos at San Agustin Church. After being razed to the ground during WWII, the city grew exponentially during the postwar years as migrants left the countryside in search of new opportunities.

◉ Sights

Manila has a lot to see but if you're short on time, focus on the downtown area, metro Manila's epicentre.

◉ Intramuros

From its founding in 1571, Intramuros was the exclusive preserve of the Spanish ruling classes. Fortified with bastions, the wall enclosed an area of some 64 hectares. Start your walking tour at the **Intramuros Visitors Center** (Map p562; ☑ 02-527 2961; Fort Santiago; ☺ 8am-6pm) 🖉 just inside the gate to Fort Santiago. It has an excellent free guided map of the walled city, available on request. Next door is a cinema inside a bomb-shelter cellar that screens a short film on the history of the area.

Guarding the entrance to the Pasig River is Intramuros' premier tourist attraction: **Fort Santiago** (Map p562; Santa Clara St, Intramuros; adult/student P75/50; ☺ 8am-9pm). Within the fort grounds is an oasis of lovely manicured gardens, plazas and fountains leading to an arched gate and a pretty lily pond. Within is the beautifully presented **Rizal Shrine museum** (Map p562; Fort Santiago; adult/student P75/50; ☺ 9am-6pm Tue-Sun, 1-5pm Mon), where Dr José Rizal was incarcerated as he awaited execution in 1896.

The **San Agustin Church** (Map p562; ☑ 02-527 4060; General Luna St, Intramuros) was the only building left intact after the

---

TOP MANILA MUSEUMS

Manila boasts an eclectic bunch of museums. Some of the best include:

Ayala Museum (Map p568; www.ayalamuseum.org; Greenbelt 4, Ayala Centre, Makati; adult/student P425/300; ☺ 9am-6pm Tue-Sun) Features four floors of superbly curated exhibits on Filipino culture, art and history.

Marikina Shoe Museum (Map p558; www.marikina.gov.ph/#!/museum; JP Rizal St, Marikina City; P50; ☺ 8am-noon & 1-5pm, closed holidays) A must for Imelda Marcos junkies, with over 800 pairs of the former First Lady's shoes plus footwear from other Filipino luminaries.

Metropolitan Museum of Manila (Map p566; ☑ 02-523 7855; www.metmuseum.ph; Roxas Blvd, Bangko Sentral ng Pilipinas, Central Bank, Pasay; P100; ☺ 10am-5.30pm Mon-Sat, gold exhibit to 4.30pm) World-class gallery tracing the evolution of Filipino art from the early 20th century to the present.

Philippines Highlights

1 Drifting among the limestone cathedrals and azure lagoons of the Bacuit Archipelago around **El Nido** (p605)

2 Trekking through the skyscraping rice terraces around Banaue and Bontoc in North Luzon's **Cordillera** (p572)

3 Having a night out in **Manila** (p555), a city that never sleeps

4 Exploring sunken WWII wrecks and kayaking amid myriad islands around **Coron** (p608)

5 Enjoying sun, seasports and dancing till dawn on the stunning beaches of **Boracay** (p584)

6 Hopping from natural spring to coral reef to volcano to waterfall around

200 km
100 miles

PHILIPPINE SEA

Batanes Islands
Sabtang

Luzon Strait

Babuyan Channel

Aparri ● Santa Ana
Gonzaga
Claveria ● Gattaran

Babuyan Islands

LUZON
Kabugao ●
Laoag ● Banguéd ● Tuguegarao ●
Tabuk ● Cordillera
Vigan ● Bontoc **2** Ilagan ● Palanan
Sagada ● Banaue Dinapigue
Cervantes ● Batad Casiguran
Tagudin ● Kabayan ● Lagawe
Abatan ● Solano
San Fernando Kabayan ● La Trinidad
(La Union) ● Baguio City
Bolinao ● Dagupan ● *Pantabangan Lake*
Hundred Islands Baler ●
National Park **4**
San Carlos ● Tarlac ● Cabanatuan ●

Clark Airport ✈
Mt Pinatubo ▲ Angeles
(1450m) ● San Fernando
Olongapo ● (Pampanga)
Balanga ● **3** MANILA

Mariveles ● Pagsanjan ●
Lake Taal
Lubang Anilao ● Batangas ● Lucena
Island *Verde Island*
Puerto Galera ● **10** *Passage* ● Boac
Abra de Ilog ● Calapan MARINDUQUE
Mamburao ●

SOUTH CHINA SEA

Lemon Bay
Polillo Islands

Calagua Islands

Catanduanes Island
Daet ●
Caramoan Peninsula Caramoan
Naga ● Virac ●
Mt Mayon ▲

the lush island of **Camiguin** (p601)

7 Discovering unheralded **Dumaguete** (p588), in an enviable mix of adventures and getaways

8 Taking Cebu by storm: party in **Cebu City** (p590), then detox on idyllic **Malapascua Island** (p596).

9 Swimming with whale sharks in the waters over **Donsol** (p579).

10 Scuba diving and partying around busy **Puerto Galera** (p580).

Philippines Trench

Laoang
Catarman
Sablayan Colintaan
MINDORO
Pinamalayan
Matnog
Cervantes
Irosin
Sorsogon
Apo Reef National Park
Bulalacao
Busuanga Island
Buluanga
San José
Calauit Island
Salvacion
Senirara Islands
CALAMIAN GROUP
Coron Island
Culion Island
Tablas Island
Sibuyan Island
Roxas
Caticlan
Boracay Island
Sibuyan Sea
Burias Island
Masbate
MASBATE
SAMAR
Calbayog
Catbalogan
Borongan
Homonhon Island
Sohoton Caves & Natural Bridge National Park
Siargao Island
Dinagat Island
Caraga
Tandag
Prosperidad
Bislig
Butuan
Surigao
Lake Mainit
Padre Burgos
Tacloban
LEYTE
Maasin
Baybay
Ormoc
Donsol
Bulan
Pinamalayan
Biliran Island
Visayan Sea
Camiguin Island
Balingoan
Siquijor Island
Cadiz
Silay
Bacolod
San Carlos
Cebu
Toledo
Mt Kanlaon Natural Park
Moalboal
BOHOL
Tagbilaran
Dumaguete
NEGROS
Guimaras Island
Jordan
Iloilo
Roxas
Batad
PANAY
Kalibo
San José (Antique)
Cuyo Islands
Cagayan Islands
Kabankalan
Sipalay
Cagayan Islands
Cagayan de Oro
MINDANAO
Mt Apo (2954m)
Malaybalay
Tagum
Davao
Mati
Digos
Lake Buluan
Malita
Kidapawan
General Santos
Alabel
Glan
Alah Valley
Cotabato
Moro Gulf
Lake Lanao
Iligan
Oroquieta
Tubod
Dipolog
Zamboanga Peninsula
Liloy
Pagadian
Ipil
Zamboanga City
Basilan Island
Isabela
Sulu Archipelago
Pangutaran Island
Jolo
Jolo Island
Bongao
Tawi-Tawi Island
Mindanao Sea
Celebes Sea
Turtle Islands
Cagayan Sulu Island
Sandakan
MALAYSIA
Balabac Island
Bugsuk Island
Mt Mantalingajan (2086m)
Quezon
Brooke's Point
Narra
PALAWAN
Puerto Princesa Subterranean River National Park
Puerto Princesa
Roxas
Port Barton
Dumaran Island
Taytay
Liminangcong
El Nido
Taytay Bay
Tubbataha Reefs
Tubbataha Reefs National Park
Sulu Sea
KALAYAAN GROUP
Spratly Islands
Palawan Passage
Mindanao Sea
Mindanao Sea
Davao Gulf
Moro Gulf

Metro Manila

2 km
1 mile

Commonwealth Ave

Marikina 2 Shoe Museum

Santolan

Katipunan Ave

UP Diliman

QUIRINO

Katipunan

University Ave

Maginhawa St 12

Anonas Ave

Anonas

CUBAO

Cubao 25 26

Cubao-Araneta Center 32

Kalayaan Ave

Quezon Memorial Circle

V Luna Ave

Kamias Rd

29 40

Gilmore

People Power Monument

Ortigas

Visayas Ave

North Ave

QUEZON CITY

North Avenue

GMA

Kamuning

Timog Ave East Ave

34 EDSA

31

Betty Go Belmonte

NEW MANILA

Ruiz

SAN JUAN

Ortigas Ave

Shaw Blvd

Wack-Wack Golf & Country Club

West Ave

Quezon Avenue

Don Alejandro Roces Ave

T Morato Ave Kamuning Rd

19

E Rodriguez St

V Mapa (Araneta)

New Panaderos

Roosevelt Ave

Quezon Ave

Pureza

BALINTAWAK

Quirino Hwy

North Luzon Expwy

Baguio (180km)

Roosevelt (Muñoz)

Balintawak

North Ave

Del Monte Ave

18

SANTA MESA HEIGHTS

Mayon St

Blumentritt St

España St

PANDACAN

CALOOCAN CITY

Monumento (North Terminal)

GRACE PARK

Bonifacio St

1 Chinese Cemetery

Bonifacio Ave

Antipolo St

33

UST

MacArthur Hwy

5th Avenue

R Papa

Abad Santos

5

10

Blumentritt

España Blvd

Quezon Blvd

Recto (Isetan)

39

Legarda

Carriedo

See Intramuros & Rizal Park Map (560;2)

CITY OF MANILA

Central

MALABON CITY

C-3 Rd

Mabini Ave

Juan Luna St

Paul Luna Blvd

José Abad Santos St

Tayuman

Doroteo José Ave

Bambang

Tutuban

BINONDO

3

7

C M Recto

Honoratio Lopez Blvd

Velasquez St

Morienes St

27

SOUTH HARBOR DISTRICT

NORTH HARBOR DISTRICT

Manila North Harbor Port

38

Manila North Harbor District

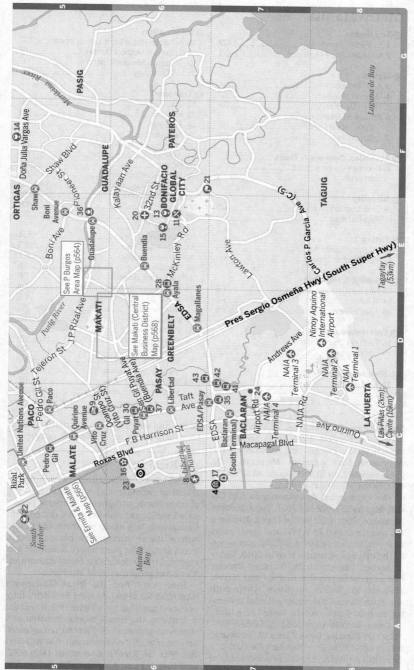

Metro Manila

◎ Top Sights
1	Chinese Cemetery	C2
2	Marikina Shoe Museum	G3

◎ Sights
3	Arch of Goodwill	B4
4	Galleon Museum	B7
5	North Cemetery	C2
6	Philippine International Convention Center	C6
7	Quiapo Church	C4

⊕ Activities, Courses & Tours
8	Prestige Cruises	C6
	Sun Cruises	(see 8)

⊜ Sleeping
9	Pink Manila Hostel	C5
10	Red Carabao	C3

⊗ Eating
11	Mercato Centrale	E6
12	Van Gogh is Bipolar	F2

⊕ Drinking & Nightlife
13	Nectar	E6
14	O Bar	F5
15	Tap Station	E6

⊛ Entertainment
16	Cultural Center of the Philippines	C6

⊕ Shopping
17	Mall of Asia	C7

ℹ Information
18	Advance Hyperbaric Life Support	C2
19	St Luke's Medical Center	D3
20	St Luke's Medical Center	E6
21	UK Embassy	F6

ℹ Transport
22	2GO Travel	B5
23	Air Juan	B6
24	Air Swift	C7
25	Araneta Bus Terminal	F3
26	Araneta Center Busport	F3
27	Atienza Shipping Lines	B4
28	BGC Bus	E6
29	Bicol Isarog Cubao	E3
	BSC San Agustin	(see 35)
	Cagsawa Cubao	(see 26)
30	Ceres	C6
31	Coda Lines	E3
32	Dimple Star	F3
33	Florida Bus Lines	C4
34	Genesis Cubao	E3
35	Genesis Pasay	C7
36	Guadalupe Ferry Station	E5
37	Jam Liner Buendia	C6
38	Manila North Harbor Port	B4
39	Maria de Leon Trans	C3
	Ohayami	(see 33)
40	Partas Cubao	E3
41	Partas Pasay	C7
	Pasay Rotunda	(see 35)
42	Philtranco	D7
	Roro Bus	(see 32)
	Victory Liner Cubao	(see 34)
43	Victory Liner Pasay	D6
	Victory Liner Sampaloc	(see 33)

destruction of Intramuros in WWII. Built between 1587 and 1606, it is the oldest church in the Philippines. Attached is the renovated **San Agustin Museum** (Map p562; General Luna St, Intramuros; adult/student P200/160; ⊗8am-noon & 1-6pm).

The once-grand **Ayuntamiento** (Old City Hall; Map p562; ☑02-524 7007; Plaza de Roma, Intramuros; P50; ⊗1hr tours at 11am & 4pm Tue & Fri) was destroyed in WWII and spent years as a parking lot before a faithful recreation of the original structure rose in 2010. Today it houses the country's Treasury Bureau, but its most impressive rooms – the Marble Hall and the Sala de Sessiones, where both the Spanish and American colonial governments held court – can be visited on a tour.

Casa Manila (Map p562; ☑02-527 4084; Plaza Luis Complex, General Luna St, Intramuros; adult/student P75/50; ⊗9am-6pm Tue-Sun) is a beautiful reproduction of a Spanish colonial house, and offers a window into the opulent lifestyle of the gentry in the 19th century.

◎ Rizal Park

Still widely known as 'Luneta', Manila's iconic central park is spread out over 60 hectares of open lawns, ornamental gardens, ponds, paved walks and wooded areas, dotted with monuments to a whole pantheon of Filipino heroes. It's an atmospheric place to take a stroll, and, as the place where José Rizal was executed by the Spanish colonial authorities, it's also of great historical significance.

Here you'll find the **Rizal Monument** (Map p562; Rizal Park), fronted by a 46m flagpole and guarded by sentries in full regalia; it contains the hero's mortal remains and stands as a symbol of Filipino nationhood. To one side of the monument you will find the **Site of Rizal's Execution** (Map p562; Rizal Park; admission incl tour P20; ⊗8am-5pm

Wed-Sun); at the entrance is a black granite wall inscribed with Rizal's 'Mi Ultimo Adios' (My Last Farewell).

In the middle of the park is the **Central Lagoon**, a pool lined with busts of Filipino heroes and martyrs, and a dancing musical fountain that erupts in colourful explosions in the evening. Just north of the lagoon is the **open-air auditorium**, where the long-running (and free) classical Concert at the Park kicks off at 6pm on Sunday. There's a free Filipino rock concert here at the same time every Saturday night.

The **visitors centre** (Map p562; Kalaw Ave, Rizal Park; ⊙8am-5pm) has a good map detailing the park's attractions and info on upcoming concerts and events.

★ National Museum of the Filipino People

MUSEUM

(Map p562; www.nationalmuseum.gov.ph; T Valencia Circle, Rizal Park; ⊙10am-5pm Tue-Sun) FREE Within a resplendent neoclassical building, this superb museum houses a vast and varied collection, including the skullcap of the Philippines' earliest known inhabitant, Tabon Man (said by some to actually be a woman), who lived around 24,000 BC. A large section of the museum is devoted to the wreck of the *San Diego,* a Spanish galleon that sank off the coast of Luzon in 1600, with salvaged items such as shell-encrusted swords, coins, porcelain plates and jewellery on display.

◎ Binondo & Quiapo

After centuries of suppression by the Spanish, Manila's Chinese population quickly rose on the economic and social ladder under more liberal administrations. Today the centre of the vibrant Chinese community is Chinatown, demarcated by the **Arch of Goodwill** (Map p558; Chinatown) and the **Filipino–Chinese Friendship Arch** (Map p562; Paredes St, Chinatown). The main street is Ongpin St, which straddles Binondo and Santa Cruz. It's lined with teahouses, goldsmiths, herbalists, and shops selling moon cakes, incense, paper money to burn for ancestors and other curios. The **Chinese Cemetery** (Map p558; Rizal Ave Extension, Santa Cruz; ⊙7.30am-7pm) FREE is worth a visit for its gaudy and outlandish mausoleums.

☞ Tours

Sun Cruises (Map p558; ☑02-831 8140; www.corregidorphilippines.com; Esplanade Seaside Terminal, Seaside Blvd, Pasay; ferry only week-day/weekend P1400/1500, excursion incl lunch & tram tour weekday/weekend P2550/2750, walking tours P1800; ⊙6.30am-4.15pm) and **Prestige Cruises** (Map p558; ☑02-832 8200; www.manilabaycruise.com; Esplanade Seaside Terminal, Seaside Blvd, Pasay; without/with buffet dinner P350/750) run evening boat trips on Manila Bay, with an optional dinner, at 6pm and 8pm (extra trips on weekends).

Sun Cruises also runs the day trips to historic Corregidor Island.

★ Walk This Way

TOURS

(Map p562; ☑0920 909 2021; https://carloscelderanwalks.wordpress.com; adult/student P1350/650) Carlos Celdran's walking tour of Intramuros is a hilariously eccentric one-man show of Filipino history and trivia. Highly recommended for those with a sense of humour and an open mind. His Intramuros headquarters is in his sort-of souvenir shop, La Monja Loca, opposite San Agustin Church. He is also active in efforts to revive downtown Manila through **VivaManila** (Map p562; www.vivamanila.org; Room 500, First United Bldg, Escolta St, Binondo), which he co-founded.

Old Manila Walks

WALKING

(☑02-711 3823, 0918 962 6452; www.oldmanilawalks.com; tours P1000-1400) Tour leader Ivan Man Dy has a deep knowledge of Manila and its history and culture. He's an expert at ferreting out the city's often overlooked secrets, and is most known for his all-you-can-eat Chinatown foodie tours (P1200, 3½ hours), as well as a Chinese Cemetery tour (P650, two hours).

Smokey Tours

TOUR

(☑02-622 1325, 0917 578 5398; www.smokeytours.com; tours per person P950-1200) Smokey's signature slum tours are highly educational, experiential, interactive forays into the *baryos* of Tondo, Manila's poorest district. This is not voyeurism; tours are led by underprivileged guides, and proceeds go to an NGO assisting with disaster relief and preparedness in slum areas. The operator has expanded and now does tours of the **North Cemetery** (Map p558; Santa Cruz; tour guides approx P300), plus lighter market and bicycle tours.

Bambike

CYCLING

(Map p562; ☑02-525 8289; www.bambike.com; Plaza Luis Complex, General Luna St, Intramuros; 1/2½hr tours P600/1200; ⊙10am & 3pm) Bambike runs guided cycling tours around Intramuros on handmade bicycles constructed

Intramuros & Rizal Park

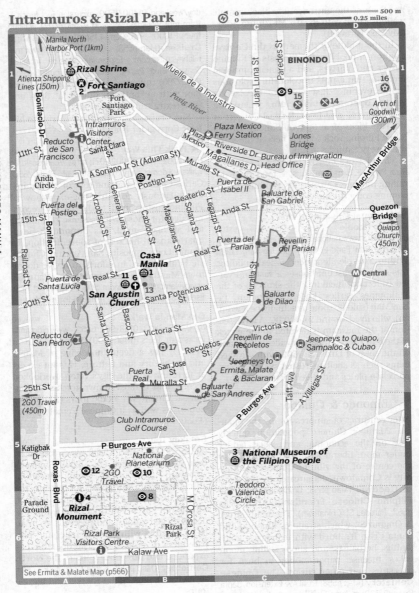

0   500 m
0   0.25 miles

PHILIPPINES MANILA

BINONDO

Manila North Harbor Port (1km)

Atienza Shipping Lines (150m)

5 **Rizal Shrine**

2 **Fort Santiago**

Muelle de la Industria

Pasig River

Fort Santiago Park

Juan Luna St

Paredes St

16

Arch of Goodwill (300m)

MacArthur Bridge

9

15

14

Intramuros Visitors Center

Santa Clara St

Reducto de San Francisco

11th St

Bonifacio Dr

Anda Circle

A Soriano Jr St (Aduana St)

Plaza Mexico Ferry Station

Plaza Mexico

Riverside Dr

Magallanes Dr

Jones Bridge

Bureau of Immigration Head Office

7 Postigo St

Muralla St

Puerta de Isabel II

Baluarte de San Gabriel

Quezon Bridge

Quiapo Church (450m)

Puerta del Postigo

15th St

Beaterio St

Solana St

Legazpi St

Anda St

Railroad St

Bonifacio Dr

General Luna St

Arzobispo St

Cabildo St

Magallanes St

Puerta del Parian

Real St

Revellin del Parian

Muralla St

M Central

Puerta de Santa Lucia

Casa Manila

11 6

13

San Agustin Church

Santa Potenciana St

Baluarte de Dilao

20th St

Santa Lucia St

Basco St

Victoria St

Recoletos St

Victoria St

Revellin de Recoletos

Jeepneys to Quiapo, Sampaloc & Cubao

Reducto de San Pedro

17

San Jose St

Jeepneys to Ermita, Malate & Baclaran

Taft Ave

A Villegas St

25th St

2GO Travel (450m)

Puerta Real

Muralla St

Baluarte de San Andres

P Burgos Ave

Club Intramuros Golf Course

Katigbak Dr

Roxas Blvd

P Burgos Ave

National Planetarium

12

2GO Travel

10

3 **National Museum of the Filipino People**

Teodoro Valencia Circle

8

Parade Ground

4 **Rizal Monument**

Rizal Park Visitors Centre

Rizal Park

M Orosa St

Kalaw Ave

See Ermita & Malate Map (p566)

using bamboo frames. Pedalling the laid-back backstreets of the walled city makes for a great way to cover expansive Intramuros, taking in all the main stops plus some less-visited gems. Prices include entrance fees, helmets and water.

🎊 Festivals & Events

Black Nazarene Procession RELIGIOUS
(⊙9 Jan & Holy Week) The Black Nazarene, a life-size and highly revered statue of Christ in **Quiapo Church** (Map p558; Quezon Blvd, Quiapo), is paraded through the streets in

Intramuros & Rizal Park

massive processions on 9 January and again during the week before Easter (Holy Week). Thousands of devotees crowd the streets carrying the image, believed to be miraculous, on their shoulders.

🛏 Sleeping

🛏 Malate, Ermita & Pasay

Like a smaller version of Bangkok's Khao San Rd, Malate's Adriatico St is Manila's traditional stamping ground for backpackers. However, there's also some classy higher-end and midrange accommodation around too.

★ Makabata Guesthouse & Cafe
GUESTHOUSE $

(Map p566; ☎02-254 0212; www.makabata.org; 2218 Leveriza St, Malate; incl breakfast dm P495-720, s P1050, d P1400-1800; ❄❅) This training hotel provides at-risk youth with a chance to get a start in the hospitality industry. But it's more than just a feel-good story. Rooms boast an impressive traditional-meets-modern design, capiz-shell windows offsetting boutique wash basins and plasma TVs. Most rooms have balconies overlooking a colourful local neighbourhood, at 700m south of Remedios Circle. The cafe serves tasty light bites.

★ Pink Manila Hostel
HOSTEL $

(Map p558; ☎02-484 3145; www.pinkmanilahostel. com; 5th fl, cnr Bautista St & San Pedro St, Pasay; dm fan/air-con P450/570, d P1600; ❄❅❆) Newly renovated and looking smarter than ever, Pink is a sociable hostel where on any given afternoon you might find bikini-clad or shirtless backpackers lazing around the

pools drinking and playing guitar. There's a nice mix of dorms with beds swathed in trademark pink linen, a hammock-strewn roof deck, and rocking monthly parties. The somewhat random location is equally convenient to Malate and Makati.

Bahay Kubo Hostel
HOSTEL $

(Map p566; ☎02-243 7537; 1717 M Orosa St, Malate; dm P400-500, d P1500-3600; ❄❅) Helpful owners and homey if busy common spaces are the hallmarks of this popular Malate crash pad. The downstairs common area, open to the street, lends it a friendly neighbourhood feel, while upstairs is for lounging. Most of the six- to 14-bed dorms are air-conditioned; they are roomy enough, with big wooden lockers.

Tambayan Capsule Hostel
HOSTEL $

(Map p566; ☎02-521 8835; www.tambayanhostel. com; 1602 Bocobo St, Malate; dm P550, s/d/q from P1250/1450/2850; ❄❅❆) The dorms are the highlight here. Picture beds (capsules) with roll-up privacy blinds, personal charging stations, private safety boxes, bright reading lights and crisp air-con. Alas, the 'capsule' concept is less effective with the window-less private rooms, which feel cramped and overpriced. Bonus points for the beautiful antique house, once a wealthy Chinese merchant's mansion.

Chill-Out Guesthouse
HOSTEL $

(Map p566; ☎02-218 7227; chilloutmanila63@ gmail.com; 612 Remedios St, Malate; dm P350, r with fan P650-850, r with air-con P1200-1450; ❄❅❆) P350 air-con dorms? Works for us. They are plenty liveable, too, if a bit cramped. But what really makes this French-managed place stick out are the air-con private rooms,

P Burgos Area

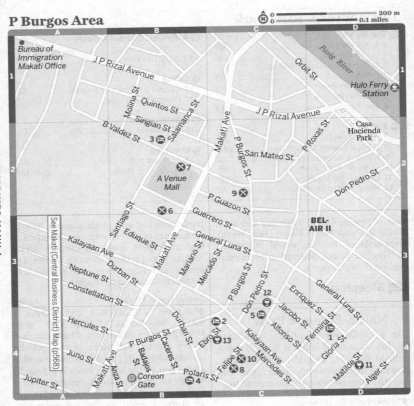

P Burgos Area

🛏 Sleeping

1 La Casita Mercedes	D4
2 Lokal Hostel	C4
3 MNL Boutique Hostel	B2
4 Our Melting Pot	B4
5 Z Hostel	C4

🍴 Eating

6 A Venue Food Market	B2
7 Beni's Falafel	B2
8 El Chupacabra	C4
9 Friends & Neighbors	C2
10 Tambai	C4

🍷 Drinking & Nightlife

11 Joe's Brew	D4
Polilya	(see 12)
12 Pura Vida	C3
13 Social	C4
Z Roofdeck	(see 5)

which are downright roomy and have touches like couches, bedside tables and art on the walls. Hang out, cook and eat in the kitchen/common area.

Wanderers Guest House   HOSTEL **$**
(Map p566; ☎02-525 1534; www.wanderersguesthouse.com; 1750 Adriatico St, Malate; dm with fan/air-con P350/400, s/d from P690/790, tr P1350-1800; ✳@🖥) In the heart of Malate, Wanderers knows precisely what backpackers want and delivers beautifully with a mix of clean dorms and private rooms (some with balconies), excellent travel info and cooking facilities. The highlight is its grungy rooftop bar-restaurant–chill-out lounge, perfect for socialising with other travellers over cheap booze.

★ Amélie Hotel
BOUTIQUE HOTEL **$$**

(Map p566; ☎02-875 7888; www.ameliehotelmanila. com; 1667 Bocobo St, Malate; r incl breakfast P3900-5100; ❄🕸@📶🏊) A shot in the arm for Malate's hopeful revival, Amélie's grey-stone minimalism is the perfect antidote to the sweaty, steamy metropolis. The throwback art-deco furniture barely fills the immense rectangular space of rooms. Head up to the rooftop plunge pool for happy hour and dial up drinks from the lobby bar, 10 stories below.

1775 Adriatico Suites
HOTEL **$$**

(Map p566; ☎02-524 5402; www.adriaticosuites. com; 1775 Adriatico St, Malate; d/tw incl breakfast from P2200/2500, apt from P5000; ❄🕸📶🏊) Down a side street near Remedios Circle, this is your best bet for a quiet yet central mid-ranger in Malate. There's a brand-new wing with snazzy doubles featuring attractive bed frames, cosy mattresses, desks and Netflix-enabled smart TVs. The pleasant pool and Jacuzzi are welcome amenities at this price point. The older wing consists mainly of apartments.

🛌 Makati

Makati's hip Poblacion area has emerged as Manila's flashpacker district, with more than a dozen hostels and poshtels and loads of happening bars and restaurants.

★ Our Melting Pot
HOSTEL **$**

(OMP; Map p564; ☎0915 105 9459; www.our meltingpotmakati.com; 37 Polaris St, 3rd fl, Poblacion, Makati; dm P500-600, s/d without bathroom P1000/1450, d with bathroom P1750; ❄🕸@📶) Makati's original backpacker relocated to a larger space in 2016 and added more beds, a fully equipped kitchen and a guests-only roof deck, while retaining its trademark friendly service and good vibes. Dorms feature turbo-charged air-conditioning, individual electrical sockets and thin privacy-protecting curtains on the beds. The shoes-off policy (slippers provided) ensures cleanliness, and basic breakfast is included.

MNL Boutique Hostel
HOSTEL **$**

(Map p564; ☎02-511 7514; www.mnlboutiquehos tel.com; 4688 B Valdez St, Poblacion, Makati; incl breakfast dm P400-600, r without bathroom P1500; ❄🕸@📶) Incorporating industrial decor such as polished concrete and colourful plywood doors, arty MNL prides itself on being a creative, comfy backpackers. The rooms are cramped and lack natural light, but the beds are quality, unsavoury smells are absent, and the street-level locale is a plus.

Lokal Hostel
HOSTEL **$**

(Map p564; ☎02-890 0927; www.lokalhostel.com; 3rd fl, 5023 P Burgos St, Poblacion, Makati; dm with fan/air-con from P400/500, s/d from P900/1400; 🕸@📶) In the middle of Makati's red-light district, this hostel offers respite from within. The dorms lack windows but are spacious and have big beds and murals, and include a simple breakfast. The private doubles are the best value you'll find in Makati.

★ La Casita Mercedes
B&B **$$**

(Map p564; ☎02-887 4385; http://lacasita mercedes.com; 5956 Enriquez St, Poblacion, Makati; incl breakfast s P1500-2200, d P2500-2900; ❄🕸📶) 🍃 This sophisticated addition to Poblacion occupies a beautifully restored 1930s house. Step into an Old-World lobby of antique mirrors, filigreed transoms and gorgeous *machuka* (Mediterranean–style) tiles. The eight rooms, each with its own character, have touches like four-poster beds and original art-deco furniture. The neighbourhood wakes up early, so bring earplugs.

Z Hostel
HOSTEL **$$**

(Map p564; ☎02-856 0851; www.zhostel.com; 5660 Don Pedro St, Poblacion, Makati; dm P650-850, d incl breakfast P2430; 🕸@📶) This is Manila's number-one party address for groovy backpackers thanks to its rocking rooftop bar and chic ground-floor cafe. It's a huge space, with 130 beds over seven floors. The airy dorms are all en suite and boast sturdy iron-framed beds with personal charging stations.

🍴 Eating

Most of the best (and priciest) restaurants are in Makati and the Fort (BGC). Malate has plenty of neighbourhood colour around Remedios Circle and J Nakpil St. Self-caterers will find large supermarkets in the malls, or try outdoor markets such as Malate's **San Andres Public Market** (Map p566; San Andres St, Malate; ⏱7am-6pm) and the weekend pop-up **Mercato Central** (Map p558; 7th Ave cnr 25th St, BGC; mains P100-300; ⏱6pm-3am Thu-Sat).

🍴 Malate, Ermita & Paco

Shawarma Snack Center
MIDDLE EASTERN **$**

(Map p566; 485 R Salas St, Ermita; shawarma P60-75, meals P85-300; ⏱24hr; 🕸) It doesn't sound like much, but this streetside eatery serves the richest and most flavourful falafel, *mutabal* (eggplant dip), hummus and kebabs in downtown Manila.

Ermita & Malate

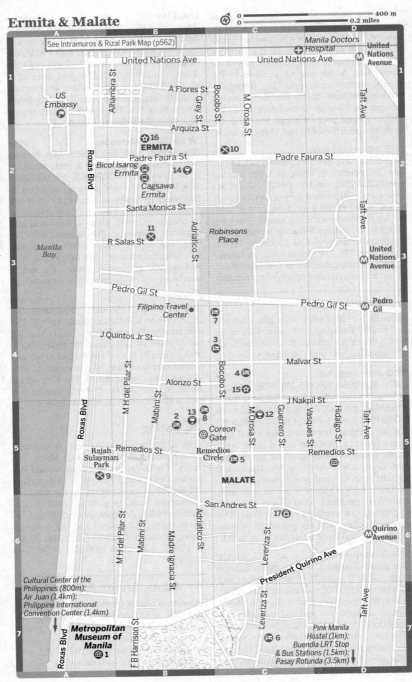

0 ____ 400 m
0 ____ 0.2 miles

See Intramuros & Rizal Park Map (p562)

United Nations Ave

United Nations Ave

Manila Doctors Hospital

United Nations Avenue

US Embassy

Alhambra St

A Flores St

Grey St

Bocobo St

M Orosa St

Arquiza St

Taft Ave

ERMITA

16

10

Padre Faura St

Padre Faura St

Bicol Isarog Ermita

14

Cagsawa Ermita

Santa Monica St

Roxas Blvd

Adriatico St

Robinsons Place

11

R Salas St

Manila Bay

United Nations Avenue

Pedro Gil St

Pedro Gil St

Pedro Gil

Filipino Travel Center

7

J Quintos Jr St

3

M H del Pilar St

Mabini St

Bocobo St

Malvar St

4

Alonzo St

15

J Nakpil St

2   13

8

12

Coreon Gate

Remedios St

Remedios Circle

5

M Orosa St

Guerrero St

Vasques St

Hidalgo St

Taft Ave

Rajah Sulayman Park

9

MALATE

Remedios St

San Andres St

17

Leveriza St

Quirino Avenue

Madre Ignacia St

Adriatico St

President Quirino Ave

Cultural Center of the Philippines (800m); Air Juan (1.4km); Philippine International Convention Center (1.4km)

Roxas Blvd

Metropolitan Museum of Manila

1

F B Harrison St

Leveriza St

6

Taft Ave

Pink Manila Hostel (1km); Buendia LRT Stop & Bus Stations (1.5km); Pasay Rotunda (3.5km)

Ermita & Malate

◎ Top Sights
1 Metropolitan Museum of Manila...........A7

🛏 Sleeping
2 1775 Adriatico Suites.............................B5
3 Amélie Hotel C4
4 Bahay Kubo Hostel C4
5 Chill-Out Guesthouse C5
6 Makabata Guesthouse & Cafe..............C7
7 Tambayan Capsule Hostel....................C4
8 Wanderers Guest House........................B5

🍴 Eating
9 Aristocrat A5

10 Midtown Diner.......................................C2
11 Shawarma Snack Center.......................B3

🍷 Drinking & Nightlife
12 Che'lu..C5
13 Erra's Vest Ramen in Town..................B5
14 Tap Station B2

🎭 Entertainment
15 FAB/The Library....................................C4
16 Hobbit House B2

🛍 Shopping
17 San Andres Public Market....................C6

PHILIPPINES MANILA

Midtown Diner FILIPINO, AMERICAN $
(Map p566; 551 Padre Faura St, Ermita; meals P115-180; ⊙7am-9pm Mon-Fri, to 2pm Sat; ❋ 🛜) Filipino take on an old-school meat-and-potatoes American diner. Home in on the budget set meals, which include a soup and iced tea.

Aristocrat FILIPINO $$
(Map p566; www.aristocrat.com.ph; cnr Roxas Blvd & San Andres St, Malate; mains P200-400; ⊙24hr) Aristocrat began life in 1936 as a mobile snack cart and is so iconic that it has its own historical marker. A replica of the old Ford canteen is incorporated into the front window. It serves a huge range of Filipino food, but chicken barbecue is the speciality. Branches have sprung up all over the country but you want this one.

🍴 Makati

Beni's Falafel MIDDLE EASTERN $
(Map p564; 📞02-621 6163; A Venue Mall, B Valdez St Entrance, Poblacion, Makati; dishes P130-225; ⊙24hr; ❋ 🛜) Everything on the menu of this unassuming Yemeni-owned eatery is original and done to perfection. The *shakshuka* (eggs poached in a spicy tomato sauce) and Beni's falafel are our faves. Shawarmas are served out of neighbouring Beni's Grill. There's another Beni's branch in Mall of Asia (p570).

Tambai FUSION $
(Map p564; Felipe St, Makati; dishes P70-300; ⊙6pm-midnight; ❋ 🛜) Quick but highly original Japanese-infused Filipino snacks served on the street or in a small air-conditioned room at the back. Try the to-die-for beef-rib *laki-tori* sticks.

Friends & Neighbors FILIPINO $
(Map p564; 5070 P Burgos St, Poblacion, Makati; dishes P70-100; ⊙9am-9pm Mon-Sat; ❋) This slightly upscale *turu-turò* (point-point, or fast food) restaurant is a great introduction to home-cooked Filipino food, in an air-conditioned setting.

A Venue Food Market FILIPINO $
(Baga Manila; Map p564; A Venue Mall, Makati Ave, Makati; dishes P75-85; ⊙1pm-midnight) This outdoor food court next to A Venue Mall is a great introduction to Filipino food, including many regional specialities.

★**Corner Tree Cafe** CAFE $$
(Map p568; 📞02-897 0295; www.cornertreecafe.com; 150 Jupiter St, Makati; mains P250-350; ⊙11am-10pm; ❋ 🛜🍴) 🌿 Corner Tree provides a tranquil escape from busy Jupiter St, not to mention heavenly vegetarian fare that even diehard meat-eaters will love. The soups, stews, spinach filo triangles and smoothies are our favourites, or try the tofu walnut burger or vego chilli. Vegan and gluten-free options available.

Yardstick CAFE $$
(Map p568; 📞02-624 9511; www.yardstickcoffee.com; 106 Esteban St, Legazpi Village, Makati; mains P300; ⊙7am-11pm Mon-Sat, 8am-6pm Sun; ❋ 🛜) This serious coffee shop doubles as a wholesaler of single-origin beans and La Marzocco equipment. It's in a bright, airy space out back and a glassed-in facility for frequent cuppings and coffee workshops. Brewed coffee is steam pumped and there's a simple blackboard menu of pasta, waffles and rice bowls.

★**El Chupacabra** MEXICAN $$
(Map p564; 5782 Felipe St, Poblacion, Makati; tacos P110-170; ⊙11am-3am Mon-Thu, to 4am Fri-Sun; ❋) Bringing the Mexican street-food craze to Makati, El Chupacabra is a grungy open-air taqueria cooking up a mouthwatering

Makati (Central Business District)

N ↑   0 ——————— 400 m
   0 ——————— 0.2 miles

Makati (Central Business District)

selection of soft corn tortilla tacos. Go for the spicy chipotle shrimp or *sisig* (sizzling grilled pork) tacos. It's wildly popular so expect to wait in the evenings (no reservations). Grab a margarita in the meantime.

TimHoWan   HONG KONG **$$**
(Map p568; Glorietta 3, Makati; small plates P120-170; ⊙10am-9.40pm; ✷) Michelin-starred in Hong Kong, this dim sum institution was an instant smash upon opening in Manila in

2014. It's a more sanitised experience than its hole-in-the-wall parent, but the signature BBQ pork buns leave nothing to be desired. We also love the vermicelli rolls, but really you can't go wrong here.

Restock Coffee & Curiosities
CAFE $$

(Map p568; 7365 Guijo St, Makati; mains P250-325; ⊙1-9pm Mon-Sat; ✸ 🛜) This hip little cafe is home to the pizzadilla, the bastard child of pizza and the quesadilla. Paintings and vintage bric-a-brac are on sale, and many creatives fuel up on the espresso-based coffee drinks and use the place as a work space.

✕ Binondo

Escolta Ice Cream & Snacks
ICE CREAM, FILIPINO $

(Map p562; 275 Escolta St, Binondo; mains P100-150, ice cream scoops P30; ⊙8.30am-8pm; ✸) Opened in 2009, this unassuming eatery has acquired cult status and is a de-rigueur stop on any tour of historic Escolta St. In addition to ice cream (try the nine-scoop Mt Everest if you dare), it serves good-value Filipino lunch meals to keep the area's struggling artists happy.

Polland Hopia Cafe
BAKERY $

(Map p562; Escolta St, Binondo; snacks from P35; ⊙7am-7pm; ✸) A classic *Tsinoy* (Chinese Filipino) bakery marked by an awesome 1950s-style neon sign on Escolta St. Thin-crust *hopia* – dense sweet cakes filled with mung beans or *ube* (purple yam) – is the name of the game. Plenty of savoury surprises await too, plus crisp air-con.

🍷 Drinking & Nightlife

Malate is popular with university kids and backpackers and, along with the Fort (BGC), is the centre of Manila's gay nightlife. Makati is where the expats hang out, along with more and more travellers. Music lovers focus their love on Quezon City.

★Long Bar
COCKTAIL BAR

(Map p568; 1 Raffles Dr, Makati; ⊙noon-2am) Inspired by the Singapore original, this lobby-level watering hole at the **Raffles Makati** (Map p568; ☎02-795 0755; www.raffles.com/makati) has an unbeatable happy hour – all-you-can-drink beer, wine and cocktails (including the signature Singapore Sling) for P870 from 5pm to 8pm. The lacquered, suitably lengthy bar is a real treasure. Discarded peanut husks pile up on the floor.

SPLURGE

Every bit as interesting as it sounds, this chaotic **Van Gogh is Bipolar** (Map p558; ☎0922 824 3051; 154 Maginhawa St, Quezon City; mains P300-500; ⊙noon-5pm & 6pm-midnight; ✸) inhabits a tiny space packed with curios and artworks. It's run by artist Jetro, who cooks entirely original, delicious food in a riotous atmosphere that'll likely see you dine wearing a flamboyant hat (grab one from the hatstand). Dinners are three- to five-course set meals, while lunch is à la carte.

★Pura Vida
BAR

(Map p564; Don Pedro St cnr Jacobo St, Poblacion, Makati; ⊙6.30pm-2am Mon-Sat) Owned by a Costa Rican, Pura Vida brings a dash of laid-back Caribbean attitude to the heart of Poblacion, with occasional reggae bands, *arroz con camarones* (rice with prawns), mojitos and a decidedly global crowd lapping it all up. Downstairs is **Polilya** (Map p564; ⊙6.30pm-2am Tue-Sun; 🛜), the uber-classy new taproom of craft brewer Engkanto.

Z Roofdeck
BAR

(Map p564; 5660 Don Pedro St, Poblacion, Makati; ⊙5pm-late) There's no doubt where the top backpacker party spot is in Manila. Z Hostel's (p565) roof deck draws hot local and foreign DJ talent and is popular with locals and expats too. Happy hour (5pm to 8pm Monday to Thursday) brings P58 local beers – purchase credit on an RFID bracelet to pay for your drinks.

Tap Station
BAR

(Map p558; Forbestown Rd, BGC; ⊙5pm-late) A happening, down-to-earth craft-beer specialist nestled in an open-air nook near Burgos Circle. There are 25 beers on tap (P225 to P295), including a few Belgian varieties. Happy hour (6pm to 9pm) means two-for-one on the house pilsner. It's related to **Tap Station** (Map p566; Adriatico St cnr Padre Faura St, Ermita; 330ml beer P120-200; ⊙5pm-2am Mon-Sat, to 11pm Sun) in Malate but has a much larger beer selection.

Erra's Vest Ramen in Town
BAR

(Map p566; 1755 Adriatico St, Malate; ⊙24hr) Erra's is your classic Southeast Asian streetside shack luring folk from all corners of the galaxy to quaff cheap San Miguel and – as its quirky name implies – slurp the house ramen (P60 to P90).

Social
BAR

(Map p564; Ebro St, Poblacion, Makati; ⊘5pm-2am) A new concept for Manila's trendiest bar district, the Social is a mini food-park infused with pumping beats and centred around a bar that specialises in reasonably priced craft beer. There are pizza and Indian food eateries on the premises, but the focus is on music and drinking and it can really rock on weekends.

Joe's Brew
BAR

(Map p564; Mathilde St cnr Jacobo St, Poblacion, Makati; ⊘5pm-1am Tue-Sun) This minute space is the taproom of one of Manila's leading craft brewers. Try the Fish Rider Pale Ale accompanied by brisket or poutine (French-Canadian dish of chips with gravy) from the attached **Holy Smokes** smoke house.

☆ Entertainment

It's worth making it up to Quezon City one evening for quality live music. The **Cultural Center of the Philippines** (Map p558; ☑02-832 1125; www.culturalcenter.gov.ph; CCP Complex, Roxas Blvd, Pasay; performance prices vary; ⊘box office 9am-6pm Tue-Sat, 1-5pm Sun performance days) jn Pasay is the place for theatre and classical music. Manila is quickly becoming

a major international gambling destination; the casino zone is on reclaimed land in Parañaque.

★ SaGuijo
LIVE MUSIC

(Map p568; ☑02-897 8629; www.facebook.com/saGuijo.Cafe.Bar.Events; 7612 Guijo St, Makati; admission after 10pm incl one drink P150-200; ⊘6pm-2am) A wonderfully decrepit dive bar with a jam-packed roster of indie, punk and new-wave bands that kick off at 10.30pm. Check Facebook for the schedule.

★ Hobbit House
LIVE MUSIC

(Map p566; www.hobbithousemanila.com; 1212 MH del Pilar St, Ermita; admission P150-175; ⊘5pm-2am; ☎) This quality blues bar has been attracting some of Manila's finest musos since 1973. Beloved American founder Jim Turner passed away in 2016, leaving the bar in the hands of his height-challenged staff. Also has an impressive imported and craft-beer selection.

🛍 Shopping

Huge malls such as **Mall of Asia** (Map p558; Manila Bay, Pasay; ⊘10am-10pm) and **Greenbelt** (Map p568; Ayala Centre, Makati; ⊘11am-9pm) stock everything imaginable in air-con comfort.

★ Silahis Arts & Artifacts
GIFTS & SOUVENIRS

(Map p562; 744 General Luna St, Intramuros; ⊘10am-7pm) This is almost more of a cultural centre than a shop. Intricately woven baskets, wooden Ifugao *bulol* statues for guarding rice, textiles and other crafts from around the country are sold next to beautiful antiques. Upstairs **Tradewinds Books** (Map p562; 744 General Luna St, Intramuros; ⊘10am-7pm) specialises in Philippine history, culture and biography.

ℹ Information

MEDICAL SERVICES

Metro Manila has several large private hospitals that are gaining traction for medical tourism.

Makati Medical Center (☑02-888 8999; www.makatimed.net.ph; 2 Amorsolo St, Makati)

Manila Doctors Hospital (Map p566; ☑02-558 0888; www.maniladoctors.com.ph; 667 United Nations Ave, Ermita)

St Luke's Medical Center (Map p558; ☑02-789 7700, emergency 02-789 7810; www.stluke.com.ph; 32nd St, BGC) Metro Manila's most modern hospital. Also in **Quezon City** (Map p558; ☑02-723 0101, emergency 02-727 2328; 279 E Rodriguez Sr Ave, Quezon City).

WORTH A TRIP

VOLCANO TREKKING

You don't have to go far out of Manila to find adventure. Head 60km south to the cool hill town of Tagaytay, with spectacular views over Taal Lake and the island **Taal Volcano** (adult/child P50/100; ◷6am-6pm). Charter a bangka to the volcano itself, which can be climbed in just 45 minutes. Many hostels in Manila arrange day tours here, or stay overnight at **Tagaytay Garden Mountain Breeze** (☑0977-816 0773; 730 Calamba Rd; dm/d/tr P450/1000/1400).

Another popular tour is a 4WD ride (followed by a two-hour climb) to the stunning emerald crater lake of **Mt Pinatubo**, site of a cataclysmic volcanic eruption in 1991. The mountain is a couple of hours' drive north of Manila and tours leave at around 4.30am. Otherwise stay a night at **Alvin & Angie Mt Pinatubo Guesthouse** (☑0929 249 0865, 0919 861 4102; www.mt-pinatubo.weebly.com; Santa Juliana; dm P350-500; s/d incl breakfast P1000/1200; ✳🛜) in Santa Juliana.

TOURIST INFORMATION

Department of Tourism Information Centre (Map p568; DOT; ☑02-459 5200; www.visitmyphilippines.com; JB Bldg, 351 Sen Gil Puyat Ave, Makati; ◷7am-6pm Mon-Sat) The tourism office has helpful staff, city maps and information for trips around Manila. There are also smaller DOT offices at the various Ninoy Aquino International Airport (NAIA) terminals.

TRAVEL AGENCIES

Filipino Travel Center (Map p566; ☑02-528 4507; www.filipinotravel.com.ph; cnr Adriatico & Pedro Gil Sts, Malate; ◷8am-6pm Mon-Fri, 9am-5pm Sat) Catering to foreign tourists, this helpful and knowledgable agency organises city tours and day tours around Manila and beyond. It can also do visa extensions and buy advance bus tickets to Banaue.

❶ Getting There & Away

AIR

All international flights in and out of Manila use one of the three main terminals (Terminal 1, Terminal 2, Terminal 3) of **Ninoy Aquino International Airport** (p618) in Manila's south, while many domestic flights use a fourth, domestic, terminal (Terminal 4). For more information see the Transport chapter p950.

BOAT

The flashy **Manila North Harbor Port** (Map p558; ☑02-588 9000; www.mnhport.com.ph; Piers 4 & 6, Tondo), northwest of Binondo, is the departure and arrival point for all domestic ferry travel. The South Harbor is now used for cargo and international cruise ships.

It's best to take a taxi to/from North Harbor, as Tondo district isn't a place for a foreigner to be wandering around with luggage, and public transport routes are complicated.

2GO Travel (Map p558; ☑02-528 7000; http://travel.2go.com.ph; Pier 4, Manila North Harbor Port) is the major shipping line handling inter-island boat trips from Manila. It has an excellent website for checking schedules and reserving tickets. Tickets can be purchased online, and through travel agents, major malls or its main branch in **Rizal Park** (Map p562; The Hub @ Kilometer Zero, Rizal Park). For ferries to Caticlan (for Boracay), you'll need to head to Batangas pier.

Atienza Shipping Lines (Map p558; ☑0999 881 7266; 1st St, cnr Muelle de Tacoma, Tondo) has ferries to Coron town, Palawan, Tuesday at 8pm and on Thursday and Saturday at 4pm (P1000 to P1150, 16 hours). Atienza also sails to El Nido on Friday at 4pm (P1700 to P1850, 25 hours) via Linapacan in the southern Calamian Islands.

BUS

Getting out of Manila by bus is harder than you might expect, as there is no central bus terminal. Instead, many private operators serve specific destinations from their own terminals.

The two main 'clusters' of terminals are known as **Cubao**, which is in Quezon City near the corner of EDSA and Aurora Blvd; and **Pasay**, which is along EDSA near the LRT/MRT interchange at **Pasay Rotunda** (Map p558; cnr EDSA & Taft Ave).

Two harder-to-reach clusters are **Sampaloc**, north of Quiapo near the University of Santo Tomas (UST); and **Caloocan** in the far north of Metro Manila.

Wherever you are heading, it's worth paying a little extra for buses that take the modern expressways heading north and south out of Manila. Getting stuck on a 'local' bus could add several hours to your trip.

Better yet, shoot for the comfortable 27-seat 'deluxe' express and/or sleeper buses that serve major Luzon hubs including Baguio, Vigan, Laoag, Tuguegarao, Naga and Legazpi. It's recommended to book these, and the direct night buses to Banaue, a day or more ahead.

BUSES FROM MANILA

DESTINATION	DURATION (HR)	PRICE (P)	COMPANY	FREQUENCY
Baguio	4-7	air-con/deluxe 450/750	Genesis, Victory Liner (Cubao, Pasay)	frequent
Banaue	8-9	490-530	Florida (seasonal), Ohayami	2-4 night buses
Batangas	2-2½	170	Ceres, DLTB, Jam	every 20 mins
Clark Airport	2-3	350	Philtranco	8 daily
Dau (Angeles)	1½-2½	139-150	Victory Liner, many others	frequent
Legazpi	10-12	850-1100	Amihan, Bicol Isarog, Cagsawa, DLTB, Philtranco	mostly night buses
Sagada (via Banaue)	11	720-980	Coda Lines	8pm & 9pm
Tagaytay	3	83-92	BSC San Agustin, DLTB	every 30 mins
Vigan	8-11	air-con/deluxe 550/850	Dominion, Partas	hourly

ⓘ Getting Around

TO/FROM THE AIRPORT

As there are no direct public transport routes from any of the four terminals to Malate or Makati, bite the bullet and take a taxi, especially if you have a bit of luggage. The airport is quite close to the city and, barring traffic, you can get to Malate or Makati by taxi in 20 minutes. Uber is also a good option from the airport.

The 'Airport Loop' shuttle bus takes you to Pasay Rotunda in Baclaran (P20, every 20 minutes), from where you can find onward public transport (taxi, jeepney or MRT/LRT). At the three main terminals, walk straight and then to the right for Airport Loop buses.

JEEPNEY

Heading south from Quiapo Church, jeepneys to 'Baclaran' pass City Hall, then traverse Ermita/Malate along MH del Pilar St, continue close to the CCP, cross EDSA and end up at the Baclaran LRT stop. From Quiapo Church you can also take 'Kalaw' jeepneys to Ermita.

Heading north from Baclaran, jeepneys pass along Mabini St or Taft Ave, heading off in various directions from Manila City Hall.

LRT & MRT

The LRT and MRT trains are an excellent way to soar over and past traffic. Unfortunately, coverage of the city is far from comprehensive, and they are basically unusable at rush hour, when hour-long lines are common. If you do manage to get on a train, it can be a tight squeeze to say the least, and pickpocketing is common.

The LRT (Light Rail Transit) has two elevated lines. The LRT-1 runs from Monumento in the north to Baclaran in the south, interchanging with the MRT at the corner of EDSA and Taft Ave near Pasay Rotunda. The LRT-2 runs from Recto in the west to Santolan in the east, interchanging with the MRT in Cubao.

The MRT (Metro Rail Transit) travels a south–north route along EDSA. It is handy for getting to and from the Ayala Centre in Makati and to Quezon City.

Fares are P12 to P15, depending on distance. Transferring between train lines means leaving the station and lining up anew for another ticket. 'Stored-value' cards are a good idea if you're going to be using the trains a lot, but these can be hard to find.

The Cordillera

To many travellers, North Luzon is simply the Cordillera. These spiny mountains, which top out at around 2900m, are beloved, worshipped and feared in equal doses by those who witness them and those who live among them.

The tribes of the Cordillera, collectively known as the Igorot, have distinct traditions that have survived both Spanish and American occupation and that add a culturally rich dimension to the already bounteous attractions of the region. Banaue's renowned rice terraces have been dubbed 'the eighth wonder of the world', while lesser-known but no less spectacular terraces exist throughout Ifugao, Mountain Province and Kalinga. Rice terraces aside, the mountains throw down the gauntlet to hikers, bikers, cavers and other fresh-air fiends.

Baguio

📞 074 / POP 345,370 / ELEV 1540M

This is the Philippine's upland, pine-clad retreat from the heat and dust of the lowlands, albeit not a very tranquil one. Baguio (bah-gee-oh) is a university town that boasts one of the Philippines' largest student populations (250,000), and is also a crossroads between hill-tribe culture and lowland settlers. For most travellers, Baguio serves as the primary gateway to backpacker bliss up north in Sagada, Banaue and Kalinga.

👁 Sights & Activities

⭐ BenCab Museum
MUSEUM

(www.bencabmuseum.org; Km 6 Asin Rd, Tadiangan; adult/student P120/100; ⏰ 9am-6pm Tue-Sun) This superb museum dedicated to the life, times and work of artist Benedicto Reyes Cabrera (BenCab) is as fascinating as the man himself. The gallery is a mix of high glass panes that slant light into modern art colonnades offset by walls of traditional animist wood carvings, *bulol* (sacred wood figures), psychedelic works by Leonard Aguinaldo and ceremonial *hagabi* (carved wooden benches).

⭐ St Louis University Museum
MUSEUM

(Magsaysay Ave; ⏰ 8am-12.30pm & 1.30-5pm Mon-Sat) FREE This campus museum is run by Isekias 'Ike' Picpican, one of the country's foremost authorities on the history and culture of the Cordillera people. You can spend hours examining weapons, funereal artefacts, tribal costumes, musical instruments such as the nose flute, woodcarvings, and photographs of various rituals and sacrifices, but it helps if Ike is around to explain their context.

Tam-awan Village
ARTS CENTRE

(📞 074-446 2949, 0921 588 3131; www.tam-awan-village.com; Long-Long Rd, Pinsao; adult/student P50/30, workshops per person P450; ⏰ 8am-6pm) 🌿 Nine traditional Ifugao homes and two Kalinga huts were taken apart then reassembled on the side of a hill at this artists colony. Spending the night in one of these huts (single/double P500/P1000) is a rare treat. You can participate in art workshops, learn dream-catcher or bead making, and enjoy indigenous music and dance demonstrations.

🛏 Sleeping & Eating

Upstairs Bed & Bath
HOSTEL $

(📞 074-446 4687; www.upstairsbedandbath.com; GSP Bldg, Leonard Wood Rd; dm P400, d P1200-1600; @🛜) This place just southeast of SM Mall has 90 beds spread over a variety of spotless dorm rooms. Note, the four-bed dorms cost the same as the 20-bed dorms. There's no kitchen and the common spaces aren't super-inviting but the rest is a win.

Baguio Village Inn
GUESTHOUSE $

(📞 074-442 3901; 355 Magsaysay Ave; s/d from P400/750; 🛜) Beyond the Slaughterhouse Terminal, this warm and inviting backpacker special is reminiscent of cosy pinewood guesthouses in Sagada. Rooms in the new annex at the back are pricier but quieter.

Mile Hi Inn
HOSTEL $$

(📞 074-446 6141; Mile Hi Center, Loacan Rd; dm/d/tr P650/2300/2700; 🛜) Mile Hi's motto is 'clean, cosy, comfy', and frankly it would be hard to argue with that. Located in Camp John Hay's duty-free shopping centre, it has simple, tiled, four-bed dorm rooms and golden-hued doubles.

Oh My Gulay!
VEGETARIAN $

(📞 0939 912 7266; 4th fl, La Azotea Bldg, Session Rd; mains P130-155; ⏰ 11am-8pm Tue-Thu, to 9pm Fri & Sat, to 7pm Sun & Mon; 🌿) Step into an enchanted, multi-level garden, with wooden carvings, plants, bridges, water features and little nooks to hide in. The delicious vegetarian menu tempts with veggie burgers, open-faced sandwiches, salads, omelettes, pastas and more. Mediterranean flavours dominate. It's a bit hard to find on the 4th floor of the La Azotea Building (and there's no sign).

⭐ Cafe by the Ruins Dua
FUSION $$

(📞 074-442 4010; 225 Upper Sessions Rd; P120-380; ⏰ 7am-9pm; 🛜🌿) The clean white, vaguely colonial decor makes one of North Luzon's best meals taste even swankier. Local specialities such as carabao (water buffalo) cheese, *etag* (smoked pork), mountain rice and jackfruit are woven into a seasonal

MUMMIES OF KABAYAN

A road heading north out of Baguio for 50km leads to picturesque Kabayan, the site of several caves containing eerie mummies entombed centuries ago by the Ibaloi people. Some of these caves can be visited, while others are known only to Ibaloi elders. Even if mummified mortal remains aren't your thing, Kabayan is a great place to hike around the dramatically sloped rice terraces and marvel at the star-filled night sky.

menu inspired by dishes from around the world. Live music and poetry readings pop up on occasion and there's an all-round intellectual, bohemian vibe.

 Drinking & Entertainment

Baguio Craft Brewery MICROBREWERY
(Palispis (Marcos) Hwy; ⊙5pm-2am; 🛜) Baguio's entry on the ever-growing ledger of Philippine craft-brew houses is worth the mild slog out of the centre. You'll be rewarded by around 20 different types of expertly crafted beers (from P160), fine mountain views from the rooftop terrace, and toothsome wings, fish tacos and other bar snacks (mains P300 to P350).

18 BC LIVE MUSIC
(16 Legarda Rd; ⊙6.30pm-late) In a city where live music seemingly wafts out of every window, this dive opposite Prince Plaza Hotel consistently features Baguio's best original live music, from jazz and blues to reggae. Annoyingly, no shorts or flip-flops allowed.

🛍 **Shopping**

Baguio is a shopping mecca where you can pick up all manner of indigenous crafts, from antique *bulol* (sacred wood figures) to all manner of traditional weaving, baskets, silver, Kalinga spears and mass-produced, glossy woodcarvings. Check out the **city market** (Magsaysay Ave; ⊙6am-7pm) for souvenirs.

ℹ **Information**

Cordillera Regional Tourist Office (☎074-442 7014; Governor Pack Rd; ⊙8am-5pm Mon-Fri) Information on tours and treks throughout the Cordillera, and maps of town.

ℹ **Getting There & Away**

The nonstop, 25-seater buses run by **Victory Liner** (☎074-619 0000; Utility Rd) to Pasay (P750, five hours, one to five daily) are a quick and comfortable option. Just as nice are the 29-seater Joybuses run by **Genesis** (☎074-422 7763; Governor Pack Rd) that run both to Pasay (P730, six hours, frequent) and Cubao (Manila; P720, six hours, frequent). All these buses take the fast SCTEX (Subic–Clark–Tarlac Expressway). Victory and Genesis also have slower buses to Manila about every 20 minutes (P455, seven hours); Victory accepts credit cards.

Lizardo Trans (☎074-304 5994) has hourly trips to Sagada (P250, five to seven hours) departing from 6am to 1pm from the **Dangwa Terminal** (Magsaysay Ave), and four buses to Baler (P312 to P360, eight hours) via San Jose

departing from 4am and 1pm from the **Slaughterhouse Terminal** (Magsaysay Ave).

Ohayami (Shanum St) and **KMS** (Shanum St) each have daily trips to Banaue (P490, nine to 11 hours) along the paved southern route, via San Jose, departing around 7am and from 6pm or 7pm. A faster way to Banaue is to take a direct air-con van from the Dangwa terminal (P360, seven hours) via Ambuklao Rd.

Sagada
🗐074 / POP 1670 / ELEV 1477M

Sitting among mist-shrouded mountains, tiny Sagada is the closest thing the Philippines has to a Southeast Asian backpacker mecca. Still, it's possible to find tranquillity along its many hiking trails and get your adrenalin pumping on adventures in the depths of its caves. There's a mystical element to this village, a former refuge for intelligentsia fleeing dictatorship. Sagada's most popular attractions are the **Echo Valley Hanging Coffins**: some are centuries old, while others are only a few years old. Most are high up the sheer rock face, leading you to wonder how this was originally done. It's a short trek (P200) of less than half an hour to get down to the coffins via the trail that runs by the cemetery, but people do get lost without a guide.

Perhaps the best local tour is the thrilling **Cave Connection** (P800; 3-4 hrs) underground adventure, which links the Samaging and Lumiang caves, while **Sagada Outdoors** (☎0919 698 8361; www.sagadaoutdoors.com; rafting trips per person from P2500) runs rafting-season trips between September and December. There are numerous hikes to local mountains and waterfalls.

If you're lucky, your visit will coincide with a *begnas* (traditional Kankanay community celebration), when women wear *tapis* (woven wraparound skirts) and older men don G-strings and gather in the *dap-ay* (outdoor patio).

🛏 **Sleeping & Eating**

⭐**Misty Lodge & Cafe** LODGE $
(☎0926 123 5186; mistylodgeandcafe@rocketmail.com; r without bathroom per person P300; 🛜) It's definitely worth the 15-minute walk east out of town to stay (or dine) at this gem. The eight rooms are sizeable and swathed in radiant blond wood, and the owner is a fountain of smiles and helpful information. A fireplace crackles in the cafe, where you can enjoy gourmet pizzas, real Australian beef burgers, good wine, coffees and desserts.

PHILIPPINES THE CORDILLERA

Canaway Resthouse GUESTHOUSE $
(☑0918 291 5063; r per person P300; ☏) You'll find exceptional-value, bright, big rooms here, with friendly service, clean sheets and reliable hot showers in the attached bathrooms. Wi-fi comes and goes.

Green House GUESTHOUSE $
(☑0999 903 7675; r per person P200; ☏) Not only is this about the cheapest guesthouse we've found here, but it's also one of the warmest and quietest, set up on the hill over the south road. The simple rooms have plenty of rustic charm.

Bana's Cafe CAFE $
(mains P100-170; ◷6.30am-8pm; ☏🍴) Oriented towards trekkers, Bana's specialises in coffee, omelettes and delicious home-made yoghurt. Its narrow balcony overlooks a gorge and catches the morning sun.

Gaia Cafe VEGETARIAN $
(mains P125-175; ◷7am-7pm; 🍴) Hidden in the woods 1.6km south of the centre past the Lumiang Cave entrance, Gaia serves locally sourced vegan fare (plus a few egg dishes) amid pine trees and with a view of rice terraces. It's easily the most pleasant setting for a meal in Sagada, and the food is good enough to please carnivores as long as no one's too hungry.

★**Sagada Brew** FUSION $$
(meals P200; 🍴) All clean lines, floor-to-ceiling glass and blond-wood furnishings, Sagada Brew strives to be the most sophisticated cafe in the village, which it does well. Stuffed peppers sit alongside rosemary pepper chicken and waffles on its diverse menu. You may find yourself lingering over a freshly brewed coffee or beautifully steeped wild herb tea – it's that kind of place.

★**Log Cabin** INTERNATIONAL $$
(☑0915 671 7949; mains P190-290; ◷6-9pm) One of Sagada's many wonderful surprises is this aptly named restaurant that feels like a cosy ski lodge, with a roaring log fire and a fleece-clad foreign crowd. Treat yourself to the likes of roast meats with local vegies or pasta, complemented by a short wine list. Place your order before 3pm during peak season, and always reserve in advance.

Yoghurt House FUSION $$
(snacks P100, mains P160-240; ◷8am-8.30pm; 🍴) Enjoy your banana pancake out on the balcony at breakfast; get some of the great oat-

meal cookies to go; or linger over pasta and chunky sandwiches on home-made bread or baguettes. If you've been craving veggies, the tangy yoghurt sauce is the best thing in town to top the locally grown, seasonal crop.

ℹ Information

Sagada Genuine Guides Association (SAGGAS; ☑0916 559 9050; www.saggas.org) Head here for help with serious hikes.

Tourist Information Center (Municipal Building; ◷7am-5pm) Pay your P35 environmental fee here. Rates are fixed for guides and private jeepney hire.

ℹ Getting There & Away

Jeepneys run hourly to Bontoc (P45, one hour); the last one leaves at 1pm. **GL Lizardo** (Sagada Public Market) has hourly buses to Baguio (P250, seven hours) until 1pm.

Coda Lines (☑0929 521 3247; Sagada Public Market) runs a bus to Manila (P720, 13 hours) via Banaue at 2pm.

One direct van to Banaue leaves daily at around 1pm. Otherwise connect in Bontoc for more transport to Banaue.

Bontoc

☑074 / POP 3790 / ELEV 900M

Bustling Bontoc is one of the most important market towns and transport hubs in the Cordillera. It's an excellent place to arrange a guide if you're looking to get out to the rice terraces of Maligcong and Mainit or stay in the former headhunter villages of Kalinga, so you'll likely find yourself staying a day or two. Today you can still glimpse the occasional elderly woman with tattooed arms and snake vertebrae headgear or elderly men wearing a traditional G-string, particularly during the **Lang-Ay Festival** in the first week of April, when locals parade through the streets wearing traditional clothing.

At the wonderful **Bontoc Museum** (P70; ◷8am-noon & 1-5pm Mon-Sat), powerful black-and-white photos are interspersed with indigenous art, representing each of the region's main tribes. You may spot Kalinga headhunter axes, *gansa* (gong) handles made with human jawbones, and *fanitan* (baskets used for carrying severed heads).

Churya-a Hotel & Restaurant (☑0999 994 6726; Halsema Hwy; d without bathroom P300, d/tr with bathroom from P700/1000; ☏) is a centrally located guesthouse with a social common area and cafe overlooking the main street. Friendly **Anayah's** (Halsema

Hwy; P60-135; ⊘ 7am-7pm Mon, Tue & Thu-Sat; ✍) offers local dishes jazzed up with additional vegetables and flair.

Jeepneys depart every hour to Sagada (P60, one hour) from 8am to 5.30pm. Jeepneys to Banaue leave when full, usually around noon (P150). D'Rising Sun has hourly buses to Baguio (P240, six hours) from 5.30am until 4pm.

Banaue

📞 074 / POP 1390 / ELEV 1200M

Hemmed in on all sides by dramatic rice terraces, Banaue is directly accessible from Manila and can sometimes get overwhelmed by visitors. It's hard to blame them: the local mud-walled rice terraces are pleasingly different from the stone-walled terraces in most of the Cordillera. World Heritage listed, they're impressive not only for their chiselled beauty but because they were introduced around 2000 years ago by the Chinese.

Museum of Cordillera Sculpture (P100; ⊘ 8am-6pm) showcases an excellent collection of Ifugao woodcarvings, and what a collection it is. There are fine examples of ritual objects and antique *bulol*.

🛏 Sleeping & Eating

★ **Banaue Homestay**   GUESTHOUSE $
(📞 0920 278 7328, 0929 197 4242; www.banaue-homestay.weebly.com; d P600-1200; 🛜) Staying at this spotless, homey guesthouse up from the main town is like staying with family. You get to know your fellow guests and get plenty of individual attention and advice; the views from the rooms are splendid; and the meals rival anything you'll sample elsewhere in Banaue. Very popular year-round; book well in advance.

Randy's Brookside Inn   GUESTHOUSE $
(📞 0917 577 2010; r per person incl breakfast P250; 🛜) Not only is Randy a great and knowledgeable host whose brain you may wish to pick about all things Banaue, but he runs a shipshape guesthouse with some of the cheapest rooms in town, and throws in a free breakfast.

7th Heaven's   GUESTHOUSE $
(📞 0908 467 4854; d P1000) Located 500m up the road from the main town, 7th Heaven's has rooms that are basic but clean and cheery. Each has its own bathroom outside the rooms, not en suite. Angle for a room with a view! The wonderful cafe (open from 7am to 8pm) has the best views in town.

ⓘ Information

Banaue Tourist Information Center (📞 0906 770 7969; ⊘ 5.30am-5pm Mon-Fri, to 3pm Sat & Sun) Manages a network of accredited guides and maintains the definitive list of guide and private-transport prices to selected locations. Guides average P1200 for full-day hikes.

ⓘ Getting There & Away

Ohayami buses depart at 6.30pm and 7pm for Manila (P490, nine hours) via Cubao. It's a P25 tricycle ride from the Ohayami bus station to the town centre. **Dangwa** (📞 0918 522 5049; www.phbus.com/florida-bus) also runs a more comfortable bus to Manila (P530, nine hours) departing at 8pm in high season only. The earliest Manila-bound bus of the day is the 5pm Coda Lines (P490, nine hours).

If you prefer daytime travel, take a frequent jeepney to Lagawe (P40, one hour), then another to Solano (P80, 1¼ hours), and from there catch a frequent Manila (Sampaloc)-bound bus (P355, seven hours).

For Baguio, Ohayami has a 5am departure and Coda Lines a 6pm (both P430, eight hours). Vans also run to Baguio from the main square between 7am and 1pm, and there's an unreliable 5pm departure (P415, eight hours).

Batad

📞 074 / POP 1150

Given the proliferation of hugely picturesque rice terraces all over the Cordillera, winning the 'best terrace' competition is no mean feat. While these particular rice terraces are not necessarily the most beautiful, it's difficult not to gawp in awe when you reach the ridge overlooking Batad's 'amphitheatre' of rice, because as far as stages go, it's certainly very dramatic.

This backpacker hot spot is for now only accessible on foot (hence the lack of crowds from Manila), but this may soon change, as a road towards the village is being paved. If Batad is too 'on the beaten track', you can also escape to remoter surrounding villages such as Pula and Kambulo.

There are many hikes in the area, and the Banaue Tourist Information Center or any guide can recommend longer treks. Good options include the 40-minute trek to **Tappia Waterfall** or the 2½-hour hike to **Bangaan** with its Unesco rice terraces and some fantastic vistas en route.

Mobile phone reception barely reaches Batad, and most of its guesthouses usually cannot be contacted by phone. Most lodgings are on the ridge overlooking the rice terraces, and are nicer, breezier places to stay than the options in the village proper below. Try **Hiker's Homestay** (☑0939 6357 055; Cambulo; r per person P250) or **Batad Pension & Restaurant** (☑0918 964 3368; r per person P250).

ⓘ Getting There & Away

From Banaue, it's 12km to Batad junction, where a beautifully paved road runs right up to the 'saddle' high above Batad and continues towards the village. From the end of the paved road, it's a 20-minute hike downhill to Batad. Work on the road paving continues at a slow pace, and will eventually link to the village, so walking time may decrease in future.

The easiest and most popular method to get to Batad is to hire a tricycle in Banaue; get it to drop you at the end of the paved road and have it pick you up again at a set time when you plan to leave (P1400 return trip). You can organise a tricycle at the Banaue Tourist Information Center (p576) the moment you step off your bus in Banaue (during daylight hours).

Another option is to take the jeepney that heads from Banaue to Batad Saddle at 3pm (P150). From there you'll have to walk 40 minutes to the village. To return to Banaue, the same jeepney runs from Batad Saddle at 9am.

Vigan

☑077 / POP 53,880

One of the oldest towns in the Philippines, Vigan is a Spanish Colonial fairy tale of dark-wood mansions, cobblestoned streets and clattering *kalesa* (horse-drawn carriages). In fact, it is the finest surviving example of a Spanish Colonial town in Asia and a Unesco World Heritage Site. But outside of well-restored Crisologo St (closed to vehicular traffic) and a few surrounding blocks, it's also a noisy Filipino town like many others. In the places where history feels alive, you can smell the aroma of freshly baked empanadas wafting past antique shops, explore pottery collectives and watch sunlight flicker off capiz-shell windows.

Vigan weavers are known for using *abel*, a locally produced cotton fabric, to handweave shawls, tablecloths, napkins and *barong* (traditional Filipino shirts). You can watch *abel* hand-weavers in action at **Rowilda's Weaving Factory** or **Cristy's Loom Weaving**.

High-quality *binakol* (blankets), including some antique blankets from nearby Abra Province, are for sale at many shops lining Crisologo St.

🛏 Sleeping & Eating

The Ilocos region of the Cordillera is known for its food, and local specialities include *pinakbét* (mixed vegetable stew), *bagnet* (deep-fried pork knuckle) and *poqui-poqui* (a roasted eggplant dish).

Henady Inn HOTEL $
(☑077-722 8001; National Hwy; dm P250, d P800-1375; ❋) Out on the highway right where the buses drop you off, the Henady has four-bed dorms that will please those on a budget and/or early-morning arrivals looking for a few extra hours of shut-eye.

★Villa Angela HISTORIC HOTEL $$
(☑077-722 2914; 26 Quirino Blvd; d/q incl breakfast from P1600/3800; ❋🛜) This hotel is more than 135 years old and retains every morsel of its old-world charm. The spacious rooms, fabulous antique furniture – which includes wooden harps and king-sized *nara*-wood canopy beds – and colonial-style lounge were good enough for Tom Cruise and Willem Dafoe when filming *Born on the Fourth of July* near Vigan in 1989.

★Lilong & Lilang Restaurant ILOCANO $
(Hidden Garden; ☑077-722-1450; www.hiddengardenvigan.com; Barangay Bulala; mains P40-120; ⊙noon-9pm) Nestled at the heart of lush gardens crossed with a nature trail, this thatched-roofed, plant-festooned restaurant is a great bet for Ilocano dishes such as Vigan empanadas, *poqui-poqui* (a roasted eggplant dish), *warek-warek* (pork innards with mayo) and the more conventional *bagnet, pinakbét* and mega fruit shakes. During busy weekends it has set meals only (P180) and you'll have to queue.

Street Stalls STREET FOOD $
(Plaza Burgos; snacks P50) For quick, cheap Ilocano fare, check out the collection of street stalls that lines Florentino St along Plaza Burgos. These specialise in local empanadas filled with cabbage, green papaya and *longganisa* (sausage); *okoy* (deep-fried shrimp omelettes) and *sinanglao* (beef soup).

ⓘ Information

Ilocos Sur Tourism Information Centre
(☑077-722 8520; www.ilocossur.gov.ph; 1 Crisologo St; ⊙8am-noon & 1-5pm) Highly informative staffers give out maps of Vigan in the ancestral home of poet Leona Florentino.

MT MAYON

The perfect cone of Mt Mayon (2462m), the Philippines' most active volcano, rises dramatically from the flat Albay terrain and has been responsible for over 40 deadly eruptions since 1616.

The summit of Mt Mayon is presently off limits to climbers, but at the time of writing it was possible to trek to Camp 2 (1400m) and beyond to 'Rabbit's Ear' at around 1750m. A guide for a Mayon hiking package costs from P6000 for a two-day climb and P4500 for a one-day climb. This fee covers all food, transport, gear and porters: **Bicol Adventure ATV** (☑0919 228 7064, 0917 571 4357; www.bicoladventureatv.com) and **Your Brother Travel & Tours** (☑052-742 9871; www.mayonatvtour.com; Pawa Rd; ATV tours P599-4000) can arrange guides, equipment and transport.

ⓘ Getting There & Away

Buses to Manila (P700, nine hours) are plentiful. Try **Dominion Bus Lines** (☑077-722 2084; cnr Liberation Blvd & Quezon Ave) to Cubao and Sampaloc, or **Partas** (☑077-722 3369; Alcantara St) to Cubao and Pasay. Partas has three nightly 29-seat deluxe express buses (P805, eight hours), as well as frequent buses to Laoag (P165, two hours), a daily bus to Pagudpud (P245, five hours) and buses to Baguio (P334, five to seven hours, three daily). It also runs buses south to San Fernando (La Union; P235, four hours).

Bicol

The Bicol region, in Southeast Luzon, is famous among Filipinos for its spicy food, while among travellers it's best known for its active volcanoes and the whale sharks of Donsol.

Legazpi

☑052 / POP 196,560

Legazpi is a pleasant enough harbour city but its real claim to fame is its location at the foot of spectacular active Mt Mayon (2462m), and its proximity to Donsol. The nearby suburb of Albay is a better place to stay than the city proper, while easy half-day trips to **Daraga Church** (Santa Maria St; ☺5am-6pm) and the **Cagsawa Church & Ruins** (adult/child P20/10; ☺6am-7.30pm) should definitely be on the to-do list. Cag-

sawa is popular for ATV (quad bike) tours around the foot of Mt Mayon.

Mayon is visible from many places in and around the city; for the best views head up to **Lignon Hill** (☑0922 883 6722; P25; ☺5am-10pm) or to Daraga and Cagsawa.

🛏 Sleeping

Head about 3km west of Legazpi City for the best of the accommodation.

★**Mayon Backpackers Hostel** HOSTEL $
(☑052-742 2613; http://mayonbackpackers.wordpress.com; Diego Silang St; dm with fan/air-con P350/450, d/q P1200/1400; ❄@�) The only legitimate hostel in Legazpi is clearly the top budget choice, with cramped but comfy four-, six- and eight-bed dorm rooms with en suite and lockers, and a few highly sought-after private rooms in a separate building. There's a basic common kitchen and free breakfast is served in the upstairs dining room. Good views of Mt Mayon from the tiny rooftop area.

Legazpi Tourist Inn INN $
(☑052-480 6147; legazpitouristinn@yahoo.com.ph; V&O Bldg, Quezon Ave; s/d with fan P600/700, with air-con P1200/1400; ❄GED) The 3rd-floor Tourist Inn is the best of the budget places in Legazpi City, with cramped but clean rooms with private bathrooms, TVs and lots of mirrors. The attached Veranda Cafe (7am to 7pm) makes up for a lack of common areas.

★**Balai Tinay Guesthouse** B&B $$
(☑0917 841 3051, 052-742 3366; http://balaitinay.weebly.com; 70 Gapo St; d/tr/f incl breakfast P1500/2000/3000; ❄GED) This welcome family-run oasis of peace sits on a quiet little street in Albay and is easily the best mid-range guesthouse around. The eight compact en-suite rooms are spotless and the tranquil common areas are great for meeting other guests. Naturally there's a balcony for Mayon viewing. Head right along the riverside path from Albay Central School.

🍴 Eating & Drinking

Legazpi has some of the best Bicolano food in the region. Must-try dishes include *pinangat* (taro leaves wrapped around minced fish or pork), 'Bicol *exprés*' (spicy minced pork dish), *laing* (a leafy green vegetable) and *pili* nuts mixed with minuscule, red-hot *sili* peppers.

The best place for a sunset or evening drink is the collection of ramshackle restaurants and bars lining the seafront south of the city centre along Legazpi Blvd.

★ **Chachi's Inn**   INDIAN $
(☑ 0977 429 6379; Tandang Sora St; mains P90-250; ☺ noon-9pm) The simplicity of this little kitchen-dining room with plastic chairs belies the quality of the Indian cooking. Friendly hosts Cecil and Doris chat with guests while preparing authentic North Indian dishes such as butter chicken, *palak paneer* and even *kulfi* (Indian ice cream). Highly recommended.

★ **Smalltalk Cafe**   BICOLANO $$
(Doña Aurora St; mains P120-290; ☺ 11.30am-10pm; ❋ 🛜 ☑) This quaint little Albay eatery defines the notion of Bicol-fusion cooking and draws in travellers and locals like a tractor beam. The menu covers 'small talk', 'big talk' and, of course, 'sweet talk'. Consider the Bicol *exprés* pasta, the Mayon stuffed pizza or paella Valencia. Save room for the *pili*-nut pie or the apocalyptic Red Hot Lava: with *sili* ice cream.

★ **Waway Albay**   BICOLANO $$
(cnr Balintawak St & Gov Locsin St; buffet P250; ☺ 10.30am-2pm & 5.30-9pm; ❋) The newly opened Albay branch of Legazpi's longstanding favourite buffet (☑ 052-480 8415; Peñaranda St) is a good deal classier than the original, and conveniently located in central Albay. Come for the excellent Bicolano dishes served buffet-style and enjoy the contemporary dining room. Large groups sometimes book it out on weekends.

🛈 **Information**

Provincial Tourism Office (☑ 052-481 0250; www.albay.gov.ph; Aquende Dr; ☺ 8am-5pm Mon-Fri) Adjacent to the Astrodome Complex in Albay.

🛈 **Getting There & Away**

Cebu Pacific and PAL each fly at least once daily to/from Manila (1¼ hours).

From the **Legazpi Grand Central Terminal** (Terminal Rd; ☺ 24hr), overnight air-con and deluxe services to Manila (around P800 to P1100, 12 to 15 hours) depart between 6.30pm and 8.30pm. 'Ordinary' (non air-con) buses depart throughout the day, both to Manila (P500) and to local destinations such as Sorsogon and Tabaco. Frequent minivans run during daylight hours to Donsol (P75, 1¼ hours) and Naga (P140, 2½ hours).

Donsol
☑ 056 / POP 47,560

Until the 'discovery' of whale sharks off the coast here in 1998, Donsol, about 45km southwest of Legazpi, was an obscure, sleepy fishing village in one of Sorsogon's more remote areas. In 1998 a local diver shot a video of the whale sharks and a newspaper carried a story about Donsol's gentle butanding. Since then Donsol has become one of the Philippines' most popular tourist locations, though the permanence of its shark population is uncertain.

The string of guesthouses and resorts on the coast road north of the village are the best places to stay and most have restaurants. Try **Victoria's Guest House** (☑ 0936 153 6990; www.victorias-guesthouse-donsol.com; Purok 1; d with shared bath P600, cottages P1000; 🛜), **Dancalan Beach Resort** (☑ 0999 445 0030; dm P500, d/tr with fan P800/1200, with air-con P1500/2000; ❋🛜) or the fancier **Vitton & Woodland Resorts** (☑ 0917 544 4089; Woodland dm P500, r from P1800, Vitton d/f P2300/3700; ☺ closed Jul-Oct; ❋🛜☒).

For whale shark info head straight to the **Butanding Visitors Center** (Donsol Whaleshark Interaction Center; ☑ 0919 707 0394, 0927 483 6735; ☺ 7am-4.30pm). There's one ATM in Donsol town.

There are direct air-con minivans to and from Legazpi (P75, one hour) that leave when full until about 2pm.

SWIMMING WITH DONSOL'S WHALE SHARKS

Whale sharks migrate to the Donsol waters between November and June, with the peak months generally being March and April. Whale-shark spotting is also subject to the vagaries of weather – if the sea is rough or a typhoon is on the way, the boats will not go out.

When you get to Donsol, head to the **Butanding Visitors Center** (p580), along the coast road about 1.5km north of the river bridge (P40 by tricycle from town). There are three spotting sessions daily at 7.30am, 11am and 2pm, depending on visitor numbers. Register a day ahead (P300). The boat costs P3500 for six people for a three-hour tour; if you're a solo traveller, staff will try to add you to a group. Each boat has a spotter and a Butanding Interaction Officer (BIO) on board – tip them a couple of hundred pesos, especially if you've had a good day. While multiple sightings are common in season, they're not guaranteed and interactions can often be fleeting.

MINDORO

Bisected by a virtually impassable mountain range – aptly named the High Rolling Mountains – rugged Mindoro is part tropical paradise, part provincial backwater. Forming a dramatic backdrop almost everywhere, the mountains separate the island's two provinces: rough and rugged Mindoro Occidental to the west, and more prosperous Mindoro Oriental to the east.

Most visitors head to the dive resorts around Puerto Galera on the north coast, but there is much more to Mindoro. If you prefer remote to resort, venture into Mindoro Occidental, where virtually tourist-free Sablayan, jumping-off point for the pristine dive mecca of Apo Reef, awaits. Improvements to roads are making this once hard-to-reach province more accessible than ever.

Mindoro's south coast has excellent island-hopping, while in the mountainous interior you can hike to remote villages populated by the indigenous Mangyan tribespeople.

Puerto Galera

☑ 043 / POP 32,520

Just a few hours' travel from Manila, this gorgeous collection of bays and islands is one of the country's top dive destinations. Puerto Galera is Spanish for 'port of the galleons'. Its deep natural harbour, sheltered on all sides, was a favoured anchorage well before the Spanish arrived in 1572, and today it remains a favoured anchorage for long-term yachties and short-term vacationers.

Puerto Galera (PG) typically refers to the town of Puerto Galera and the resort areas surrounding it – namely Sabang, 5km to the east, and White Beach, 7km to the west. Each area has its own distinct character, spanning the range from sleaze to sophistication; you'd be well advised to choose carefully.

A number of waterfalls can be visited, including **Tukuran Falls** (P50), **Talipanan Falls** and **Tamaraw Falls** (P30; ⊘ 7am-5pm).

🏃 Activities

Around Puerto Galera, diving reigns supreme (with drinking a close second). Dive prices vary wildly, so shop around. Expect to pay between P1000 and P1800 for a dive, including equipment, with discounts available if you do six or more dives. Many of the top dive sites are well suited for snorkelling.

Recommended outfits include **Capt'n Gregg's Dive Shop** (☑ 0917 540 4570; www. captngreggs.com; Sabang; fun dives incl equipment P1400), **EACY Dive** (Environmental Awareness for Children & Youth; ☑ 0916 794 5624; www.eacy dive.org; Aninuan) 🏖 and **Asia Divers** (☑ 0917 814 5107; www.asiadivers.com; Small La Laguna).

🛏 Sleeping

Location is everything in PG. Sabang is the noisy party zone but is closest to the dive sites; adjoining Small La Laguna and Big La Laguna are much quieter. Puerto Galera town is noisy by day, quiet by night. White Beach draws mostly local tourists as well as a smattering of loyal expats and the odd lost backpacker. Aninuan and Talipanan feel the most remote and have the best beaches.

★ **Capt'n Gregg's Dive Resort**　　　LODGE $
(☑ 043-287 3070, 0917 540 4570; www.captngreggs. com; Sabang; r with fan P800-1200, with air-con P1200-1900; ❄ 🛜) This Sabang institution has been the best value in town for more than 25 years. The compact but cosy wood-lined 'old' rooms, right over the water, still have the most charm and are also the cheapest.

Puerto Galera & Around

Puerto Galera & Around

Escarceo
Point

Simanidigan 1

Simandigan
10

Sabang
Beach

Coral Cove

Batangas

See Enlargement

Sabang

Markoe Cove

Varadero Bay

Batangas

Coco
Beach

16

Encenada
Beach

Daluruan

Medio Island

Dulangan
Beach

Dulangan

Manila Channel

Muelle
Pier

Balete Beach

Tabinay
Beach

Boquete Island

Muelle
Bay

Air Juan

13

Puerto Galera
Grand Terminal

Tamaraw Falls (4.5km);
Calsapa (15km);
Calapan (50km)

Halige
Beach

Puerto Galera

Puerto Galera
Hospital

Balatero
Pier

MINDORO
ORIENTAL

Balatero

Enlargement

11

Minolo

Balatero

Big La Laguna
Beach

Sabang
Beach

Minolo
Bay

12

7

Small La
Laguna
Beach

15

6

San
Isidro

14

9

5

3

8

White
Beach

4

Aninuan

Aninuan
Beach

Talipanan
Point

Talipanan
Beach

2

Mt Malasimbo
(2km)

0 ___ 2 km
0 ___ 1 mile

0 ___ 500 m
0 ___ 0.25 miles

★**Reynaldo's Upstairs** GUESTHOUSE $
(☎0917 489 5609; rey_purie@yahoo.com; Sabang; r P900-1200; ❄️🛜) Run by the nicest family you'll ever meet, Reynaldo's has a splendid mix of more-than-passable budget fan rooms and large 'view' rooms with kitchenettes and private balconies on a hillside. Some rooms even have extras such as DVDs and wicker love seats.

Paddy's Bar &
Backpacker Hostel GUESTHOUSE $
(☎0977 184 5540; Sinandigan; dm/d with fan P250/400, d with air-con P450-700; 🛜🏊) About 1km east of Sabang (P20 by motorbike), Paddy's is Puerto Galera's only legitimate hostel. It has basic doubles, spacious if stuffy five-bed dorms in stand-alone huts, and a well-stocked Irish bar overlooking a ravine. Two slightly fancier rooms are fronted by a newly added plunge pool.

Cataquis COTTAGE $
(☎0916 297 8455; Big La Laguna; r with fan/air-con from P1000/1500; ❄️🛜) The tidy, brightly painted concrete cottages here are flush with the Sabang area's best beach. A few larger rooms are tucked among the trees at the back. The Filipino restaurant (mains P160 to P350) is excellent value.

★**El Galleon Beach Resort** RESORT $$
(☎043-287 3205; www.elgalleon.com; Small La Laguna; d incl breakfast US$59-110, villas US$110-315; ❄️🛜🏊) Elegant hut-style rooms with wicker furniture and verandahs creep up a beachfront cliff and slink around a pool. There's a fine restaurant and a top technical dive school on the premises, not to mention the Point Bar, one of the country's best bars. For a modest splurge, ask about the incredible villas at their neighbouring Waimea Suites.

★**La Laguna Villas** RESORT $$
(☎043-287 3696; www.llv.ph; Small La Laguna; r from P3100, ste from P6000; ❄️🛜🏊) These luxury hillside villas are a steal, especially when low-season discounts kick in. Most rooms have working kitchenettes and at least two rooms are outfitted with quality beds, polished wood floors and flat-screen TVs (although not all rooms have balconies to take full advantage of the luscious views).

Blue Ribbon Dive Resort RESORT $$
(☎0917 893 2791, 043-287 3561; www.blueribbon divers.com; Small La Laguna; r P2000-2200, bungalows P2400; ❄️🛜🏊) This place is popular with divers, who get a 10% discount on accommodation. The large rooms are set around a small pool at the back. They are more functional than fashionable, but have TVs, and most have private terraces. Out the front a lively beachfront bar and restaurant sometimes has live acoustic music.

🍴 Eating & Drinking

Puerto Galera has a great dining scene, with the waterfront restaurants of Sabang leading the way, although prices are high by Philippine standards. Almost everywhere has a happy hour, any time between 2pm and 7pm.

Teo's Native Sizzling House FILIPINO $
(Sabang; mains P85-300; ⏰24hr) Open-air place with a comprehensive menu of sizzling dishes, Filipino classics, steaks and budget meals.

★**Arcobaleno Pizzeria**
& Ristorante ITALIAN $$
(National Hwy, Minolo; ⏰9am-9pm) It doesn't look like much – basically a lean-to with just a few tables – but the medium-crust pizza here is the best in Puerto Galera, heaped with mozzarella and fresh toppings. There's a tall Italian staffing the kitchen and a simple menu of pizza, pasta and salads. The pizzas feed two, making this excellent value.

★**Puerto Galera**
Yacht Club INTERNATIONAL $$
(Puerto Galera Town; meals P290-450; ⏰noon-9pm, closed Mon in low season) This is a hidden gem, perched among the trees on the west edge of Muelle Bay. Sunset drinks and a barbecue are the traditional way to celebrate Friday, while 'Wet Wednesdays' mean all-you-can-eat curry for just P289.

Rumulus FUSION $$
(White Beach; meals P245; ⏰10am-10pm) The eponymous Filipino chef at Rumulus serves some of PG's best food out of a nondescript shack 100m behind White Beach. It's all about the specials here – three new ones per day, usually consisting of fresh fish and/or meat and potatoes, plus an Asian curry or stir-fry. Fresh ingredients are bought each morning from the local market.

★**Point Bar** BAR
(El Galleon Beach Resort, Small La Laguna) Our favourite bar, the Point Bar is a mellow sunset-and-beyond meeting place with great views and eclectic music. It's one of the few bars in town where solo women travellers can feel comfortable.

View Point

BAR

(⊙9am-9pm) Atop a ridge on the winding road between PG town and Sabang, View Point overlooks jaw-droppingly beautiful Dalaruan Cove, about 2km west of Sabang. Come for the views and stay for English faves such as steak and mushroom pies (mains P200 to P300).

❶ Getting There & Away

Air Juan (☑0917 625 9628; Puerto Galera Town) sea planes now connect Puerto Galera with Manila (from P4500, 20 minutes).

Frequent bangka ferries connect Batangas on Luzon with all three Puerto Galera resort hubs (P230 to P250, one to 1½ hours). Be aware that the last trip to Batangas from Sabang Pier leaves at 2pm. From White Beach the last trip is usually 3pm, and from Muelle Pier in Puerto Galera town it's 3.30pm.

The irregular roll-on, roll-off (RORO) to Batangas was working during our last visit. It departs from the Balatero Pier, 2.2km west of PG town,

at 5am and 3pm. Also from Balatero, there's a 10.30am bangka every day to Abra de Ilog (P200, one to 1½ hours).

Heavy winds or bad weather often close the Verde Island Passage to Batangas-bound bangkas, especially during windy months from December to February. In such a situation pray for space on the RORO, or high-tail it down to Calapan and catch a ferry from there.

THE VISAYAS

If it's white sand, rum and coconuts you're after, look no further than the jigsaw puzzle of central islands known as the Visayas. From party-mad Boracay and Cebu to mountainous Negros, to dreamy Siquijor and Malapascua, the Visayas have about everything an island nut could ask for. Hopping among paradisiacal, palm-fringed isles, you'll inevitably wonder why you can't go on doing this forever. Indeed, many foreigners do give it

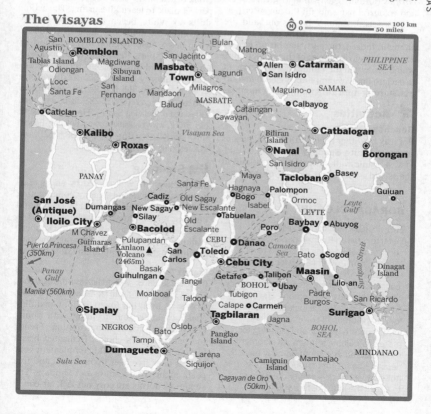

The Visayas

all up and live out their years managing this resort or that dive centre on some exquisite patch of white sand. Others merely end up extending their trip for weeks – or months. This is one area of the country where you can dispense with advanced planning. Just board that first ferry and follow your nose.

Boracay

📞 036 / POP 30,100

While only 7km tall and at its bikini line 500m wide, tiny Boracay is the Philippines' top tourist draw, fuelled by explosive growth and a tsunami of hype. The centre of the action is dreamy White Beach, a 4km, postcard-perfect stretch of sand lined from one end to the other with hotels, restaurants, bars and dive shops several blocks deep. The beach path is typically awash with visitors, including large groups of package tourists from across Asia. The ocean is full of romantic *paraws* (an outrigger sailboat) giving rides; and colourful parasails fill the air. After perfect sunsets, live music breaks out, and fire dancers twirl their batons. The party goes on all night. Indeed, the party has begun to take a toll on the environment of this small island, which prompted the Philippines government to declare Boracay temporarily closed to tourists, starting April 2018 for up to six months.

🏃 Activities

Beaches

Boracay has other beaches that are almost as pretty as **White Beach**, if not quite so endless. A scenic walk around the headland at the island's north end brings you to lovely

BORACAY CLOSURE

Early in 2018, Philippine President Duterte ordered that the popular resort island of Boracay be closed to all tourists from 26 April 2018 for up to six months, declaring it had become a 'cesspool' after years of mass tourism and unchecked development. The stated aims of the closure included allowing for rehabilitation of the environment, infrastructure repairs, and planning for more sustainable tourism development. It is expected that some Boracay businesses – so reliant on tourists – may not survive the closure period. Be sure to check the latest before you travel.

and secluded **Diniwid Beach**, where you'll find excellent accommodation and dining. On the north tip of the island, pretty **Puka Beach** is popular in off-season and has a few good places to eat.

Sailing

Sunset *paraw* (traditional outrigger sailboat) trips are a quintessential Boracay experience. Trips start at P800 per hour for up to five or six passengers, and you can usually haggle. Boats depart from Station 1 and 3 in season (October to June), and from Bulabog Beach in the off-season (June to October). **D'Boracay Sailing** (📞0906 308 8614; www.boracay-sailing.com) offers a much more personalised and luxurious experience.

Kitesurfing & Windsurfing

During the height of the *amihan* (northeast monsoon; December to March), excellent conditions and decent prices (about P19,000 for a 12-hour certification course) make Bulabog Beach on the east side of the island the perfect place to learn kitesurfing. The action shifts to White Beach during the *habagat* (southwest monsoon; June to October), when heavy onshore chop makes it more of an expert's sport. Recommended operators for rental and instructions include **Freestyle Academy** (📞0915 559 3080; www.freestyle-boracay.com; Bulabog Beach), **Funboard Center Boracay** (📞036-288 3876; www.windsurfasia.com; Bulabog Beach), **Hangin'** (📞036-288 3766; www.hanginkite.com; Bulabog Beach) and **Isla Kitesurfing** (📞036-288 5352; www.islakitesurfing.com; Bulabog Beach).

🛏 Sleeping

Backpackers are well served by an increasing number of hostels, many congregating in the area between the pond by D'Mall and Bulabog Beach. Rates everywhere drop 20% to 50% in the low season (June to October). Walking in often nets a discount, and bargaining might bear fruit at any time of year.

Frendz Resort   HOSTEL $
(📞036-288 3803; www.frendzresortboracay.com; Station 1; dm P300, r with fan/air-con P1200/1600; ❄@🛜) A lively bar (open to 11pm) peddling cheap cocktails and teeming with young backpackers makes long-running Frendz the party people's choice. Dedicated beach beds (a two-minute walk) complement your stay, as does free beer upon arrival and free pasta nights Wednesdays and Sundays. The single-sex dorms are cosy but lack air-con.

Chillax Flashpackers
HOSTEL **$**

(☑ 0908 603 7463; www.chillaxflashpackers.com; Diniwid Rd; dm P450-550, d P1500; ❄ ❅ ⊠) Far from the White Beach action, especially if travelling by vehicle, Chillax, true to its name, is a hostel best considered by those looking for peace and quiet. White, minimalistic and stylish, Chillax is built out of shipping containers with a great rooftop pool. Not carrying any baggage? You can reach Chillax walking north from White Beach.

W Hostel Boracay
HOSTEL **$**

(☑ 036-288 9059; 2nd fl, Gill & Park Bldg, Rd 1-A; dm P500-950, d incl breakfast P2300; ❅) You'll think you're travelling in an alien spaceship at this sleek addition to the Bulabog hostel scene. It has washed concrete hallways, fluorescently lit room numbers and efficiently designed, if bare-bones, bunk rooms (trippy spray-painted wall murals add colour). An equally slick kitchen and the large flat-screen TV with video games are a nice touch.

Mad Monkey Hostel
HOSTEL **$**

(www.madmonkeyhostels.com/boracay; Bulabog Beach Rd; dm/d P800/3000; ❄ ❅) The party rarely stops at this fun and raucous hostel with whitewashed, simply furnished rooms a short walk from Bulabog Beach. Because of its popularity and relatively large size for a hostel, service can feel impersonal. But for the socially minded you can't beat the pool and bar area and daily activities and trips – many involve drinking.

Box & Ladder
HOSTEL **$**

(☑ 0917 881 0598; www.boxandladder.com; 3rd & 4th fl, Boracay Midway Bldg; dm incl breakfast P700; ❄ ❅) Crawling into bed at this hostel on the noisy main road feels a bit like crawling into a human-sized cubby hole, but they are nothing if not cosy, and all sleeping 'pods' have electrical sockets, lockers and curtains.

★ Hey! Jude South Beach
HOTEL **$$**

(☑ 036-288 2401, 0917 861 6618; www.heyjude-boracay.com; Angol, White Beach; d incl breakfast P3200-7000; ❄ ❅) The clean minimalist style and variety of rooms – the priciest of which open to the sea – are just right. The low-key breakfast by the White Beach Path is an ideal start to the day. Add helpful staff and an attractive price and you simply can't beat this for value.

Jeepney Hostel & Boracay Kite Resort
HOSTEL **$$**

(☑ 0947 777 3551; www.jeepneyhostelboracay.com; Bulabog Rd; incl breakfast dm P400-700, d P1200-2000; ❄ ❅) Just off Bulabog Beach, Canadian-owned Jeepney caters to hard-living kitesurfers with regular parties, a kitesurfing centre and a sports bar (open 24 hours). Choose from polished-bamboo dorm beds – a step above others in terms of character – in the hostel or the kite resort's clean and colourful private rooms. A small above-ground pool occupies the central courtyard.

✕ Eating

White Beach Path is one long fantastic food court – half the fun of dining is taking a walk here at sunset.

Kubo Resto Bar & Grill
FILIPINO **$**

(Bulabog Rd; mains P120-250; ⊙ 11am-3am) Avoid the oft-inflated White Beach prices at this local, open-air nipa-hut-style eatery serving a wide selection of noodle, meat and seafood dishes. The vegie curry and tuna *kinilaw* are good and there's live acoustic music most nights.

Smoke 2
FILIPINO **$**

(Bulabog Beach; P120-180; ⊙ 7am-11pm) There's no competition if you want a good-value Filipino-style dining experience on Bulabog Beach. Caters to locals and budget-minded travellers with grilled fish, steak, noodle and soup dishes.

English Bakery
BAKERY **$**

(breakfasts P100-200; ⊙ 7am-11pm) Geared to locals and backpackers on a budget, this is a good spot for freshly baked bread and on-the-run breakfasts such as bacon, egg and cheese sandwiches (P130).

★ Plato D'Boracay
SEAFOOD **$$**

(D'Talipapa Market; cook to order P150-250; ⊙ 8am-9pm) Choose fish, lobster, prawns and other freshly caught shellfish from the D'Talipapa wet market just a few feet away and this family-style grill will cook them. While the resulting prices don't necessarily undercut the White Beach seafood barbecues on the beach by much, it feels satisfying to cut out at least one step on the food-production chain.

★ Nagisa Coffee Shop
JAPANESE **$$**

(Angol, White Beach; mains P140-330; ⊙ 6.30-11pm) Open-air nipa-style Nagisa fronts the attached Surfside Resort, serving affordable sashimi, okonomiyaki and a big P100 snack menu.

★ Sunny Side Cafe
CAFE **$$**

(☑ 036-288 2874; www.thesunnysideboracay.com; White Beach; meals P225-395; ⊙ 7.30am-10pm;

Boracay

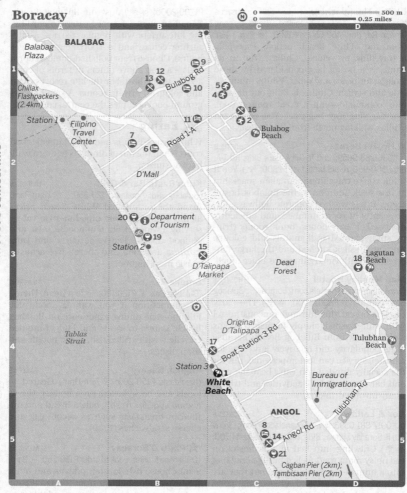

(🛜) Make a beeline here in the morning for large, fluffy pancakes (a half-order is all you'll need) and the sunny-side cafe *roesti* (crumbled chorizo, poached eggs, sour cream and arugula on a fried potato frittata) and strong espresso drinks. Repeat visits will likely follow for inventive twists on classics such as the bacon and mango grilled-cheese sandwiches or shrimp and spinach ravioli.

🍷 Drinking & Nightlife

Follow thumping beats to find the discos. Five of them carry momentum into the wee hours, even in low season; Epic and **Summer Place**

(Station 2, White Beach; P200; ⏰ 11am-late) are the only clubs open till 4am or 5am.

⭐ Epic
CLUB

(www.epicboracay.com; MOS nights P100; ⏰ 10pm-3am) This flashy club with its world-class DJs remains the most popular of the beach discos, and is also known for its Wednesday-night table-football matches. During the day, it's a bar and grill; happy hour lasts from noon to 10pm – far longer than you will.

⭐ Area 51 Secret Party Facility
CLUB

(📞 0917 886 2548; Lugutan Beach; cover P100-200) Apart from having one of the greatest

Boracay

◉ Top Sights
1 White Beach.............................C4

◉ Activities, Courses & Tours
2 Freestyle Academy...................C2
3 Funboard Center Boracay..................B1
4 Hangin'.....................................C1
5 Isla Kitesurfing........................C1

◉ Sleeping
6 Box & Ladder B2
7 Frendz Resort B2
8 Hey! Jude South Beach..................... C5
9 Jeepney Hostel & Boracay Kite Resort B1
10 Mad Monkey Hostel.................B1
11 W Hostel Boracay.....................B2

◉ Eating
12 English Bakery.........................B1
13 Kubo Resto Bar & Grill.......................B1
14 Nagisa Coffee Shop C5
15 Plato D'Boracay........................B3
16 Smoke 2...................................C1
17 Sunny Side Cafe C4

◉ Drinking & Nightlife
18 Area 51 Secret Party Facility D3
19 Club Summer Place...........................B3
20 Epic B3
21 Red Pirates..............................C5

club names ever, Area 51 is (low voice) the only underground party spot on the island. Its schedule is appropriately linked to the phases of the moon, ie there are full-moon and black-moon parties each month, as well as others in high season.

Red Pirates   PUB
(Angol, White Beach; ⊙10am-2pm) Way down at the south end of White Beach, this supremely mellow bar throws funky driftwood furniture on to the sand and best captures the spirit of the 'Old Boracay'. Stargazing is even a possibility here.

ⓘ Information

Department of Tourism (DOT; ☏ 036-288 3689; dotr6@boracay@gmail.com; D'Mall; ⊙8am-5pm) Has a few brochures and updated ferry schedules out of Caticlan, Kalibo and Iloilo. Otherwise of limited use.

Filipino Travel Center (☏ 036-288 6499; www.filipinotravel.com.ph; G/F Plaza Santa Fe Commercial Bldg, Balabag; ⊙9am-6pm) One-stop shop for all air, boat and land transport questions; can book tickets. Also offers smooth

transfers from Kalibo (P650) and Caticlan (P550) airports. Possibly worth considering for Kalibo, but not for Caticlan.

ⓘ Getting There & Away

AIR

The island of Boracay has no commercial airport. **Caticlan Airport** (Boracay Airport) is just across the strait on the mainland of Panay, only a 10- to 15-minute boat ride away. **Cebu Pacific** (www.cebupacificair.com) and **Philippine Airlines** (www.philippineairlines.com) offer many flights daily to Manila and Cebu. And two small airlines, **Air Swift** (www.air-swift.com) and **Air Juan** (www.airjuan.com) service important routes to Palawan.

Flights fill up during high season and so the alternative is the airport in Kalibo, 1½ to two hours by road to Caticlan.

BOAT

A fleet of bangkas shuttles people back and forth between Caticlan and Boracay (P25 for pumpboat, P75 environmental fee and P100 terminal fee; 15 minutes) every 15 minutes between 5am and 7pm, and then as the need arises between 7pm and 10pm (sometimes later if a ferry is late). All boats arrive at Boracay's **Cagban Pier**, where a queue of tricycles awaits to take you to your hotel. They cost P25 per person or P150 per tricycle (more if you are going north of Station 1).

From June to November, brisk southwesterly winds mean you'll often be shuttled round the northern tip of Caticlan to Tabon, where the same fleet of boats will take you to Boracay's alternative pier at **Tambisaan**.

If you arrive after the last regular bangka has departed, you will have to charter a private bangka or sleep at one of the basic pension houses in town.

Negros

With its rugged mountain interior, unspoiled beaches, underwater coral gardens and urban grooves, Negros has the most to offer in western Visayas after Boracay. This is particularly true of its southern coast, stretching from Danjugan Island around the tip to Bais, where diving is big business. Here the natural base is Dumaguete, a funky college town and expat hangout. In the north, Bacolod has culinary treats, nearby Silay is a living museum of historic homes and the cool mountain resorts of Mt Kanlaon are a refreshing alternative to the beach.

Dumaguete

📞 035 / POP 131,000

Dumaguete is a convenient base for exploring all that southern Negros has to offer. The harbour-front promenade, lined with upmarket bars, restaurants and food stalls, and blessed with peaceful sea views, is an undeniable draw. After becoming familiar with the city – one only needs a couple of days – it becomes a comfortable place to return after short stints diving, hiking or swimming nearby.

There's plenty to do in the surrounding area, from visiting waterfalls and adventure parks, to snorkelling and trekking. Most dive centres are in the resorts south of town. **Scuba Ventures** (📞 035-225 7716; www.dumaguetedive.com; Hibbard Ave) is a long-running dive shop in town.

🛏 Sleeping & Eating

GO Hotel   HOTEL $
(📞 035-522 1100; www.gohotels.ph; South Rd, behind Robinsons Mall; r P1000; ❇ 🛜) Outpost of nationwide chain with clean and simple rooms. A good budget choice for travellers in transit, if style and character aren't important.

Island's Leisure   BOUTIQUE HOTEL $$
(📞 0915 349 1132; www.facebook.com/islandsleisurehotel; Hibbard Ave; d incl breakfast with/without bathroom from P1600/990; ❇ 🛜 ❄) This alluring property combines Zen modernism with indigenous Philippine elements: woven lamps, contemporary art, stone love seats and plasma TVs. The central courtyard has several stylish cabanas and there are spa services on-site.

★**Two Story Kitchen**   KOREAN $
(📞 035-522 0126; Santa Catalina St; Korean meals P189-250; ⊙ 10am-11pm Sun-Thu, to midnight Fri & Sat) The upstairs teahouse is the draw, with elevated floor seating in semi-private stalls

WHALE SHARKS OF OSLOB

A popular trip from Dumaguete is swimming with whale sharks in Oslob on Cebu. Many people return with memories of an unforgettable experience. Others find it unsettling. The whale sharks are fed in order to attract them and it can get extremely crowded with boats. We recommend the more natural experience in southern Leyte.

cushioned by cosy floor pillows. The menu is double-sided: standard cafe fare (sandwiches, pasta, pizza etc) on one side and Korean meals on the other. A fun and popular hang-out.

Qyosko   FILIPINO $
(cnr Santa Rosa St & Perdices St; mains P60-120; ⊙ 7am-3am; 🛜) This local legend serves up sticky ribs and hot Filipino dishes, plus delicious shakes and coffee from its air-conditioned adjoining coffee shop.

★**Lab-as Seafood Restaurant**   SEAFOOD $$
(📞 035-225 3536; Flores Ave; meals around P250; ⊙ 10am-2pm) Loud and lively, this Dumaguete institution has expanded from a small seafood restaurant in 1988 to a diverse culinary, drinking and entertainment complex that includes Hayahay and Taco Surf (you can order from any of three menus). Tanks of fresh seafood are on hand, and there's a steakhouse and sushi bar. It's a one-stop evening, and it's all well done.

★**Hayahay Treehouse Bar**   BAR
(201 Flores Ave; ⊙ 4pm-late) Cosy up to the bar or grab a plastic chair at this two-storey pavilion made of driftwood and nipa roof, part of a complex of bars and restaurants on the waterfront 2km north of the town centre. Known for delicious fresh seafood and rockin' reggae Wednesdays. On weekends the live music continues until 4am.

❶ Getting There & Away

From Dumaguete Airport Cebu Pacific (www.cebupacificair.com) and Philippine Airlines (www.philippineairlines.com) serve Manila several times per day.

The main wharf is downtown. The Sibulan ferry terminal is 4km beyond the airport. The Tampi port is 22km north of the city; Ceres buses leave for Tampi hourly from 2am to 2.15pm. Boats to Siquijor are generally most relevant to travellers – try to get the **Oceanjet** (📞 0923 725 3734; www.oceanjet.net; fastcraft to Larena, Siquijor P230-380) fast ferry to Siquijor Town; **GL Shipping** (📞 0915 891 1426; ⊙ Sun-Fri) also has two daily departures. To get to the northern coast of Mindanao, try **Aleson Shipping Lines** (📞 035-422 8762; www.aleson-shipping.com; ⊙ 6am-4am) boats to Dipolog.

Apo Island

📞 035 / POP 920

This tiny 12-hectare volcanic island, with its one beachfront village, is known for having some of the best diving and snorkelling in the Philippines thanks to a vigorously defended community-run protected **marine sanctuary** (P100, additional snorkelling/diving fee P50/300) established in 1985. There are 400 species of coral (one side of the island's reef was severely damaged by a typhoon) and 650 species of fish, including five types of clownfish and green-sea and hawksbill turtles. You'll also find gorgeous white coral-sand beaches, some fine short walks, a friendly island community and excellent views back to Negros, crowned by Mt Talinis.

Mario Scuba (📞0906 361 7254; www.mariosscubadivinghomestay.com; dm P300, d P500-1000; 🕙) is the budget option, while **Apo Island Beach Resort** (📞0917 701 7150, in Dumaguete 035-226 3716; www.apoislandresort.com; dm P800, d P2700-3400) and **Liberty's Lodge & Dive** (📞0920 238 5704; www.apoisland.com; dm/s/d incl full board from P900/1650/2100; ❄🕙) are midrange dive resorts.

Apo Island is about 25km south of Dumaguete as the crow flies. Departures are from Malatapay Beach (look for the shed where the road ends), where boats (P300, 30 minutes) depart three to four times per day from 7am to 4pm. You can hire your own boat too (four/eight people P2000/3000).

Sugar Beach

With just a handful of eclectic, homespun resorts, a gorgeous stretch of beach and psychedelic sunsets, Sugar Beach remains one of Negros' best-kept secrets, helped along by a tidal river that cuts it off from the road network. It's the simple pleasures, such as quiet lazy days spent combing the beach and peaceful evenings gazing up at the stars, that reward those who journey here. There are some hikes in the area, plus scuba diving and trips to **Danjugan Island Marine Reserve & Sanctuary** (📞0915 234 7145; www.danjuganisland.ph), one of the more intelligently designed protected areas.

Resorts are strung along the beautiful wide beach. Try **Sulu Sunset** (📞0919 716 7182; www.sulusunset.com; r P650-1350), **Driftwood Village** (📞0920 900 3663; www.driftwood-village. com; dm P250-300, d from P450; 🕙) or wacky **Takatuka Lodge & Dive Resort** (📞0920 230 9174; www.sipalay.net; d P1275-2400; ❄🕙).

Sipalay, a sprawling coastal town 21km to the southeast of Sugar Beach, is the area's transport hub. If the weather is good, the quickest and easiest way is to take a bangka (P300 to P350, 10 minutes) from Poblacion Beach in Sipalay, 3km to the south.

Siquijor

📍035 / POP 96,000

For most Filipinos, Siquijor is a mysterious other-world of witchcraft and the unknown. True, this tiny island province is famous for its mountain-dwelling *mangkukulam* (healers) who brew traditional ointments for modern ailments. But these days Siquijor's most popular healing practice involves a cocktail and a deckchair at any number of its laid-back and wonderfully affordable beach resorts. Attractions include great diving, waterfalls, caves and forest walks in the hilly interior. Just about everywhere on Siquijor is great for snorkelling – find the nearest beach and dive in. Like many beaches in the Visayas, swimming is only possible during high tide, and wearing thongs (flip-flops) is recommended as protection against sea urchins.

🛏 Sleeping & Eating

Most accommodation is on the stretch of waterfront between Solangon and Tagi-ibo with San Juan at the centre. Another much smaller group is found between Larena and Sandugan at the northern tip of the island. If you stay anywhere other than the San Juan side you'll be far from other conveniences.

Kiwi Dive Resort   RESORT **$**
(📞035-424 0534, 0908 889 2283; www.kiwidiveresort.com; Km 16.9, Sandugan; d with fan P500-1290, with air-con P800-1600; ❄@🕙) It's a lovely walk down a trellis-covered pathway from the simple and clean hillside rooms to this long-running resort's beach and lounge area. It's a hodgepodge of accommodation in a mix of bamboo, nipa and stone; check several before booking. Bathrooms are cramped and beds less than forgiving. There's a dive centre and house reef just offshore.

Charisma Beach Resort   RESORT **$**
(📞0908 861 9689; www.charismabeachresort.com; Km 64.8, Solangon; dm P450, d with fan/air-con P1000/1750; ❄🕙) This compact place, popular with European families and backpackers, is set on a pleasant stretch of beach with rooms abutting a concrete pool area. The rooms could use some work and are simply furnished. It's especially good value for backpackers staying in the fan-cooled dorms.

★ Coco Grove Beach Resort   RESORT **$$**
(📞0939 915 5123, 0917 325 1292; www.cocogrovebeachresort.com; Km 60.5, Tubod; d P3500-5500,

ste P8000, all incl breakfast; ✳🛜🏊) A well-oiled machine (if you can call a perfectly coiffed Spanish-style beachfront resort a machine), Coco Grove has doubled in size from its original incarnation without losing any of its charm or personality. Two wings of the property are separated by a mini 'fishing village' with accommodation in a variety of buildings, from bungalows to a boutique-hotel-style stucco building.

ℹ️ Getting There & Away

Fastcraft to Dumaguete are run by **Oceanjet** (📞 0923 725 3732; www.oceanjet.net; P230 to P380, one hour, 1.50pm) and GL Shipping (P160, 1¼ hours, several daily). In heavy seas, opt for the more stable, twice-daily RORO run by Aleson Lines (P100, two hours).

Note that Seventh-day Adventist GL Shipping does not run trips on Saturday, while Oceanjet sometimes schedules additional trips; all schedules are fluid.

Oceanjet boats continue on to Tagbilaran (P700, three hours) and Cebu (P1500, six hours).

From Larena, Montenegro Lines has two RORO trips daily to Dumaguete (P136, two hours) in Negros. **Lite Ferries** (📞 Cebu 032-255 1721; www.liteferries.com; Larena Pier) services Cebu (P365, eight hours) via Tagbilaran, Bohol (from P225, 3½ hours) on Tuesday, Thursday and Sunday at 7pm; and Plaridel, Mindanao, three times a week (from P350).

Cebu

Cebu is the hub around which the Visayas revolve. It is the most densely populated island in the Philippines and is second only to Luzon in its strategic and economic importance to the country. This is one of the most prosperous regions in the country – the 2016 growth rate was 8.8%, considerably above the national average. Tourism numbers are booming: Cebu draws almost two million foreign travellers a year. The island's prime attractions are its white-sand beaches and spectacular diving, chiefly off the northern tip of Cebu at Malapascua and down on the southwest coast at Moalboal. And don't ignore much-maligned Cebu City, which has lively bars, emerging eateries and burgeoning retail appeal.

Cebu City

📞 032 / POP 936,200

The capital of the Southern Philippines, Cebu City is a bustling metropolis, the hub of a three-million-strong conurbation. Aestheti-

cally, it's gritty and not exactly easy on the eye, but the city is also relatively cosmopolitan thanks to a surging English-language school industry and well-regarded universities. Historic sights are slim on the ground, though there are some colonial-era gems, and the traffic is notorious – but you'll still find plenty to do. Cebu City's energy is infectious: its bar and club scene is justly famous throughout the archipelago and dining out is a delight, with a dizzying choice of restaurants.

👁️ Sights & Activities

In addition to its historic sights and churches, Cebu has a few worthwhile museums, including **Museo Sugbo** (MJ Cuenco Ave; adult/child P75/50; 🕐 9am-5.30pm Mon-Sat), with fascinating historical exhibits in the old provincial jail; the archaeology-oriented **University of San Carlos Museum** (Del Rosario St; P30; 🕐 8am-noon & 1.30-5pm Mon-Fri, 8am-noon Sat); and the lovely **Casa Gorordo Museum** (35 L Jaena St; P80-180; 🕐 10am-6pm Tue-Sun), in a house dating to the mid-1800s.

Tops Lookout (Cebu Tops Rd; P100; 🕐 10am-11pm), a viewpoint high above the city, is best visited at sunset.

The city's adventure-sport tour operators will get you out of Cebu's smog in no time. Recommended companies include Bugoy Bikers and **Island Buzz Philippines** (📞 0917 885 7515; www.islandbuzzphilippines.com; half-day tours for 1/2 people P3500/2500).

⭐**Basilica Minore del Santo Niño**   CHURCH

(Pres Osmeña Blvd; 🕐 5am-9pm; 24hr during Jan pilgrimage season) Cebu's holiest church houses a revered Flemish statuette of the Christ child (Santo Niño) that dates to Magellan's time. The church is no stranger to hardship: established in 1565 (the first church in the Philippines), three earlier structures were destroyed by fire, before the existing baroque structure was built in 1737. Its facade and belfry were badly damaged by the 2013 earthquake but have been restored.

Fort San Pedro   FORT

(A Pigafetta St; student/adult P20/30; 🕐 8am-8pm) Established in 1565 under the command of Miguel López de Legazpi, conqueror of the Philippines, Fort San Pedro has served as an army garrison, a rebel stronghold, prison camp and the city zoo. Today's partly ruined structure, dating from the late 18th century, includes an impressive gateway, a small section of ramparts and a small museum. Its peaceful walled garden is a perfect retreat from the chaos and madness of downtown Cebu, especially at sunset.

Sky Experience
ADVENTURE SPORTS
(☑032-418 8888; www.skyexperienceadventure.com; Crown Regency Hotel & Tower, Fuente Osmeña Circle; 2 rides incl buffet dinner P900; ⊙2pm-midnight Mon-Fri, 10am-1am Sat, 10am-midnight Sun) Thrill seekers with a head for heights will love this mile-high (well, 37th-floor) experience which allows you to 'walk' using a safety harness around the summit of the Crown Plaza hotel, ride an 'Edgecoaster' (tilting rollercoaster) and zipline across the night sky. Phones and cameras aren't allowed; pictures and videos must be purchased. Ride packages include a buffet dinner.

🛏 Sleeping

★ Elicon House
HOTEL $
(☑032-255 0300; www.elicon-house.com; cnr Del Rosario & Junquera Sts; s/d P600/850; ✴@🛜)
🍃 This inviting, genuinely ecofriendly place has clean, spacious rooms, delightful common spaces loaded with games, a vegie-heavy cafe and slogans on permaculture philosophy plastered on the brightly painted walls. No chemicals are used for cleaning and there's a lot of recycling going on. Daily, weekly and monthly rates are available.

★ Mayflower Inn
HOTEL $
(☑032-255 2800; www.mayflower-inn.com; Villalon Dr; s/d/tr/q P900/1200/1400/1800; ✴🛜)
🍃 The Mayflower's location, on the north side of uptown, and though they lay on the 'eco' vibe a bit thick, its green credentials are legit. Brightly painted rooms are tidy, and you get a garden cafe and lounge-library with ping pong, foosball, stacks of *National Geographic* mags and board games.

Bugoy Bikers Bed & Breakfast
B&B $
(☑0918 908 9594; www.bugoybikers.com; 5a Wright Brothers, off Upper Fulton St; dm P500, d P800-1000; ✴🛜) This **biking-tour operator** (☑032-321 6348; www.bugoybikers.com; 5a Wright Brothers, off Upper Fulton St; full-day bike tour 1/2 people P4500/3500) also has a little guesthouse, with cosy bamboo rooms (with aircon or fan, and shared or en-suite bathroom) and a six-bed dorm. The Lahug location, down a quiet lane, is tranquil and there's a kitchen and garden to enjoy. The owners look after guests well and help out with travel plans and renting a bike or scooter.

★ Montebello Villa Hotel
HOTEL $$
(☑032-231 3681; www.montebellovillahotel.com; Gov M Cuenco Ave, Banilad; r from P2700; ✴🛜🏊) Built in a Spanish-Colonial style reminiscent of a Mexican hacienda, the Montebello enjoys a tranquil location 3km north of the Ayala Center in leafy Banilad. The glorious 30m pool and stunning tropical gardens are a delight, and rooms are spacious and well appointed, if a little dated in terms of decor.

★ Zen Rooms Don Mariano
HOTEL $$
(☑032-231 3338; www.zenrooms.com; Don Mariano Cui St; r from P1400; ✴🛜) A fine no-frills hotel that enjoys a terrific uptown location with cafes, restaurants and shopping options on your doorstep. Rooms are smallish, but perfectly formed with crisp white linen, quiet air-con, laminate flooring, hot-shower en suites, fast wi-fi and flat-screen TV with cable channels.

🍴 Eating & Drinking

Cebu has a wide choice of restaurants and cafes. Lahug is foodie central – in particular Asiatown IT Park and the Crossroads strip mall. There's also a wide selection of cuisines in the Terraces and Ayala Center. For budget food stalls head to **Carbon Market** (⊙6am-7pm). The city is considered the home of *lechón* (spit-roasted pork); meat eaters should try this delicious local speciality.

★ Healthy U
VEGETARIAN $
(☑032-401 1386; http://healthyuvg.weebly.com; A Tormis St; meals P60-110; ⊙9am-10pm Mon-Sat; 🍃) This quirky, inexpensive little place is a haven for vegetarians, with tasty tofu and vegan dishes (most costing P30 to P40). For really cheap eats you can't beat the P59 meal deal which includes soup, rice, a main dish and a drink. It's down a little lane near the University of San Carlos (south campus) and popular with Cebuano yogis.

Barbecue Boss
FILIPINO $
(☑0933 722 2677; Pope John Paul 2 Ave; meals P100-170) A lively open-sided place where groups of students and young office workers come to eat, drink and socialise. Grab one of the large wooden tables and tuck into pepper steak, chicken or spicy pork kebabs. Beer is P50 or so a bottle.

Cora's Lechon
FILIPINO $
(Robinson's Place mall, Fuente Osmeña; portions from P115; ⊙9am-8pm) Delicious *lechón* from a tiny stand in the basement food court of

Cebu City

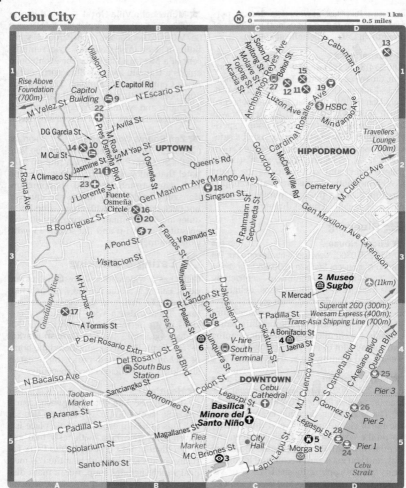

Robinson's (www.robinsonsmalls.com; Fuente Osmeña; ⊙10am-8.30pm). For a true pig-out, a full kilogram costs P460.

★Abaca   CAFE **$$**
(www.theabacagroup.com; Terraces; snacks & meals P130-300; ⊙7am-10pm) Superstylish cafe where you can dine overlooking the Terraces or in the air-con interior. Great for breakfast with healthy and not-so-healthy options – try the eggs Benedict, or a sandwich. Also very popular for coffee; its croissants and pastries are some of the best in town.

★Cafe Laguna   FILIPINO **$$**
(☑032-231 0922; level 1, Ayala Center; mains P195-345; ⊙9.30am-10pm) The cosmopolitan Ayala Center (Lahug district; meals P70-120; ⊙10am-9pm) does not have many options for good local food, but highly popular Cafe Laguna is an exception. Excellent, relatively affordable dishes such as chicken cooked in pandan leaves, crispy *pata* (pork leg) and seafood *kare kare* (prepared with peanuts and coconut) really hit the spot. There's an air-conditioned interior and terrace seating.

Cebu City

PHILIPPINES CEBU

Bucket Shrimps　　　　　　SEAFOOD **$$**
(☏ 032-260 6520; Orchard St; mains P150-350; ☺11am-10pm) A fun place where you don goofy cling-wrap gloves and a bib and attack buckets of Cajun-butter shrimp (or ribs, mussels, crab or pork belly) while guzzling buckets of beer.

🍷 Drinking & Nightlife

★ The Social　　　　　　　　BAR
(www.thesocial.com.ph; Ayala Center; ☺11am-midnight, to 2am Fri & Sat; ☎) This stylish, buzzing outdoor/indoor bar is a great place to warm up before continuing the night further uptown. Abundant big screens are conducive to sports viewing and the huge terrace is perfect for al fresco quaffing. It draws a good mix of locals and expats and there's great food available.

Liv Super Club　　　　　　　CLUB
(City Time Sq, Mantawe Ave, Mandaue; weekends P300-400; ☺8pm-6am Wed-Sun) Styling itself as a 'superclub', this smart, upmarket venue draws a moneyed crowd who lap up the commercial EDM and dancefloor bangers. Internationally renowned DJs play every month or so. Dress to impress and pack plenty of pesos. It's 5km west of the centre in Mandaue.

Bamboozers Bar　　　　　　　BAR
(http://bamboozersbar.com; General Maxilom Ave; ☺7pm-5am; ☎) A small, sociable Canadian-owned bar that draws a good mix of expats, locals and visitors. Musically things are far better and more up-to-date than most on this strip, with house and electronica, funk and soul, and a dash of hip-hop and R&B.

ℹ Information

Cebu Doctors Hospital (☏ 032-255 5555; www.cduh.com.ph; Pres Osmeña Blvd; ☺24hr)

Central Post Office (Quezon Blvd; ☺8am-5pm Mon-Sat) On the harbourfront.

Cebu City Tourism Commission (☏ 032-412 4355; www.facebook.com/cebucitytourism; 2nd fl, Rizal Memorial Library & Museum, Pres Osmeña Blvd; ☺8am-5pm Mon-Fri) Centrally located; good for city information.

Travellers' Lounge (☏ 032-232 0293; ☺6am-8pm; ☎) Located just outside SM City Mall, this handy lounge has a bag-drop (P30, same-day pickup only), showers (P50), free wi-fi and sells certain ferry tickets.

ℹ Getting There & Away

AIR

AirAsia, Cebu Pacific, PAL, Air Juan and Air Swift have regular flights to Manila and many additional domestic and international destinations.

BOATS FROM CEBU CITY

DESTINATION	COMPANY	PRICE (P)	DURATION (HR)	FREQUENCY
Manila	2GO, Philippine Span Asia	1310	22	7 weekly
Tagbilaran (Bohol)	Oceanjet, Weesam, Supercat 2GO	400-650	2	frequent
Cagayan de Oro (Mindanao)	2GO, Super Shuttle Ferry, Trans Asia	650-980	8-12	1-2 daily
Dumaguete (Negros)	Cokaliong Shipping, Trans Asia	310	6	daily
Siquijor Town	Oceanjet	1410	6	1-2 daily

BOAT

Cebu's vast, multi-piered port is linked with the rest of the country by scores of speedy fastcraft passenger ferries, slower roll-on, roll-off (RORO) car ferries and large multi-decked passenger vessels. The *Cebu Daily News* publishes a schedule that is generally reliable, but doublecheck directly with the shipping companies. Major operators include **2GO Travel** (☑ 032-233 7000; http://travel.2go.com.ph; Pier 1, Quezon Blvd) and **Super Shuttle Ferry** (☑ 032-345 5581; http://supershuttleroro.com; Pier 8, FE Zuellig Ave).

BUS

There are two bus stations in Cebu. Most buses are ordinary/standard class but there are a few air-conditioned buses (costing around 20% more) on all the main routes.

Heading south there are buses to Bato (P170, four hours, frequent) either via Moalboal (P118, three hours), or via Argao (P85, two hours) and Oslob (P155, 3½ hours) from the **South Bus Station** (Bacalso Ave; ☑ 24hr). Quicker air-con vans (V-hires) for southern destinations including Moalboal (P150, 2¼ hours) and Toledo (P100, 1½ hours) leave from the separate **V-hire South Terminal** (Junquera St; ☑ 5am–11pm). Note the latter terminal has moved several times in the last few years, so double check its location before you head here.

All buses and vans heading north use the **North Bus Station** (☑ 032-345 8650/59; M Logarta Ave; ☑ 24hr) next to SM City Mall. From here there are buses to Hagnaya (P135, 3½ hours, every 30 minutes) for Bantayan Island, and to Maya (P170, 4½ hours, every 30 minutes) for Malapascua Island. Vans also operate from this terminal, and are air-conditioned and quicker, if more cramped. Destinations include Hagnaya (P165, three hours, every 30 minutes) and Maya (P200, 3½ hours, every 30 minutes).

Moalboal

☑ 032 / POP 32,300

Wildly popular with travellers, Moalboal is a small but lively coastal resort around 90km southwest of Cebu City. There's a lot to love about the place, its craggy coastline lined with shoreside bars and restaurants where you can sip a sundowner and gaze over the azure waters of the Tañon Strait to the distant hills of Negros. Directly offshore is a stupendous coral wall, so you can amble out of your hotel room, don snorkelling gear and encounter outstanding marine life (including Moalboal's world-renowned sardine run).

The actual settlement of Moalboal is a humdrum town on the highway, 6km west of the coast. The tourist resort is officially Panagsama Beach. Glorious **White Beach**, where there's a broad stretch of sand and several midrange and luxury hotels, is 6km north of Panagsama.

⊙ Sights & Activities

Located 17km south of Moalboal, **Kawasan Falls** (local/foreigner P20/40) comprise a series of three waterfalls; the largest cascades 15m into a massive, milky-blue swimming hole.

While diving, freediving and snorkelling are Moalboal's raison d'être, a great choice of terrestrial activities are also on offer in the area including canyoning, climbing and mountain biking. For yoga sessions ask at **Freediving Planet** (☑ 0908 608 7864; www.freediving-planet.com) and for cooking classes check out Ven'z.

Recommended dive operators include **Quo Vadis Divers** (☑ 0917 519 4050; www.quovadisresort.com), **Blue Abyss Dive Shop** (☑ 032-474 3036; www.blueabyssdiving.com), **Nelson's Dive Shop** (Ocean Safari Philippines; ☑ 032-474 3023; www.ibara.ne.jp/~bitoon) and **Neptune Diving** (☑ 032-495 0643; www.neptunediving.com).

🛏 Sleeping

Pacitas　　　　　　　　　　　　HOTEL **$**
(☑ 0910 858 7222, 032-474 3017; Panagsama Beach; r with fan/air-con from P800/1200; ❄ 🛜) One of Panagsama's original places to stay, with simple, inexpensive bungalows (some with two bedrooms) and rooms dotted around a shady seaside plot. It's owned by

a friendly team and the location is quiet (except on Saturday night when it hosts a disco in the grounds).

Le Village Hostel Moalboal
HOSTEL $

(☑ 0933 153 2719; www.facebook.com/levillage hostelmoalboal; Panagsama Rd; dm/d from P300/600; ❀ ☎) A basic, inexpensive hostel with choice of air-con (good move) or fan (hot) dorms and three private rooms – all with shared bathrooms. There's a chill-out deck for chatting and a restaurant for tasty, cheap local food. It's a kilometre inland from the beach. Cash only.

Moalboal Backpacker Lodge
HOSTEL $

(☑ 0917 751 8902; www.moalboal-backpacker lodge.com; dm/s/d/cottage from P300/450/700/ 950; ☎) This hostel's location on the noisy main drag is not great, but step inside and you'll find airy mixed and women's dorms and a couple of semi-private rooms. The converted VW camper out front doubles as a kooky coffee shop. There are discounted weekly rates and, like all good hostels, there's a sociable vibe.

★ Tipolo Beach Resort
RESORT $$

(☑ 0917 583 0062; www.tipoloresort.com; d P1700-2000; ❀ @) This small seaside resort has fine-value, well-constructed accommodation with clean tiled floors and sturdy bamboo furniture, along with mod cons such as hot water, fridge and a safe. But the balconies are what win us over, amply furnished and with partial sea views. Staff are well trained, helpful and chatty and the in-house restaurant is excellent too.

✖ Eating & Drinking

★ Last Filling Station
INTERNATIONAL $$

(☑ 032-474 3016; meals P175-345; ⏰ 7am-10pm; ☎ ✎) An enjoyable little restaurant with efficient service (though with street views rather than ocean vistas). Famous for its energy-boosting breakfasts, replete with yoghurt, muesli and protein shakes. Lunchtime and dinner dishes include baguettes and pita-bread sandwiches (from P195), sizzlers and spicy garlic shrimps (P275).

Cafe Cebuano
CAFE $$

(www.facebook.com/cafe.cebuano; mains P160-320; ⏰ 9am-midnight; ☎) Boasts a great shoreside deck perfect for quaffing a glass of red or sipping on a cappuccino and soaking up the ocean views. There's a full food menu too, featuring Western and Asian dishes – try the Singapore fried noodles (P250).

Ven'z Kitchen
FILIPINO $$

(☑ 032-474 3981; www.facebook.com/venzkitchen; Panagsama Beach; mains P130-260; ⏰ 10am-10pm; ✎) Everything is prepared with love and attention at this simple place run by two friendly local ladies; there's always a daily special and vegans and vegetarians are well catered for. Filipino classics include pork *sisig*, *kare kare* and *adobo*. As the board outside says, 'We don't serve fast food we serve food fast'. It also offers **cooking lessons** (per person P500-1300; ⏰ 11am & 3pm).

Chilli Bar
BAR

(⏰ 9.30am-last customer) A Panagsama institution where the mantra on the wall proclaims, 'The liver is evil and it must be punished'. Yes, this is the liveliest bar in town: expect party tunes and dancing, plenty of banter and competitive games on the pool tables. Draws an incongruous, gregarious mix of local ladyboys, backpackers, dive crews and hard-drinking expats. Also offers pub-grub-style food.

❶ Getting There & Away

There are no direct buses to Panagsama Beach. Buses from Moalboal to Cebu City (standard/ air-con P110/P130, 3½ hours) depart every 30 to 45 minutes between 6am and 8pm, plus additional night buses. Cramped air-con vans (P120, 2½ hours) depart every 30 minutes until 5pm. Buses and vans arrive at and depart from the highway in Moalboal, from where a tricycle to Panagsama Beach is P80.

A taxi to/from Cebu is around P2500.

Continuing south from Moalboal, very frequent buses terminate a few kilometres beyond the RORO pier in Bato (standard/air-con P65/P76, 1½ hours). Ferries from Bato depart every 1½ hours or so to Tampi, Negros (P70, 30 minutes), where you can pick up transport to Dumaguete.

Malapascua Island

☑ 032 / POP 4700

This idyllic island off the north coast of Cebu is famous for its world-class diving: above all, the chance to dive with thresher sharks at **Monad Shoal**, which are present year-round. But even if you've no interest in reefs and marine life, Malapascua makes a beautiful beach destination, the southern part of the island is fringed with gorgeous sandy bays and there's an excellent choice of hotels and guesthouses. Malapascua is justifiably a very popular escape for travellers and Cebuanos. There are no ATMs on the island.

◉ Sights & Activities

A good four-hour **walk** will take you around the entire coast of the island, with plenty of photo opportunities. Attractions include a waterside **cemetery** with sun-bleached graves, the boat-building village of **Pasil** on the east side of the island where locals construct outriggers, a **lighthouse** in Guimbitayan and a 12m-high **lookout** on the island's northwestern tip which some brave souls treat as a cliff jump. Bring water. You can also tour most of the island by motorcycle, widely available for rent for a hefty P200 or so per hour.

🛏 Sleeping & Eating

Hiltey's Hideout Home GUESTHOUSE $
(☑ 0905 832 5954, 0918 287 0999; www.hiltey-shideout.com; Logon village; r with fan/air-con P900/1600; 🔆 🛜) Run by a jovial German, this backpackers' stronghold has small rooms grouped around a grassy compound, each with bright bedspreads and en-suite bathrooms. Long-term deals are available.

Malapascua Budget Inn HOSTEL $
(☑ 0977 820 3111; www.exploremalapascua.com.ph; Logon village; dm/r from P400/2000; 🔆 🛜) This locally run hostel is well set up, with a choice of dorms (four, 10 or 14 beds) each with reading light and privacy curtain – though bunks are tightly packed together. There are private rooms too, but they're not great value. It's pretty secure thanks to CCTV and lockers and there's a great common area for chilling, drinks and meals.

**Mike & Diose's Aabana
Beach Resort** RESORT $
(☑ 0905 263 2914; www.aabana.de; east end of Bounty Beach; d P500-2150; 🔆 🛜) This friendly, rambling place fringing the boat-building barangay of Pasil has a range of accommodation, from budget rooms to big air-con options with kitchens. The decor is a little dated, but the German-Filipino family who runs the place looks after guests well. There's a basic beach-facing restaurant for meals (which would really benefit from a fan or two!).

★ Tepanee Beach Resort RESORT $$
(☑ 032-317 0124; www.tepanee.com; Logon Beach; d P3300-4700; 🔆 🛜) The classiest place in Malapascua, this Italian-run hillside resort above Logon Beach is a cut above the competition. Attractive cottages feature soaring Balinese-style thatched roofs, wooden floors

and excellent beds. All accommodation has private balconies and vistas, but the ocean-view deluxe rooms, perched over a private white-sand cove, are sublime. There's a little bar, a small gym, spa and Jacuzzi.

★ Angelina B&B $$
(☑ 0977 469 5801; http://angelinabeach.com; Logon Beach; r P3000; 🔆 🛜) Above the owners' Italian restaurant (http://angelinabeach.com; Logon Beach; mains P275-695; ⏱ 8am-10pm), these four units represent a great deal – all are spacious, with polished-wood flooring, exposed stone walls, sofas and modish bathrooms, and decorated with handmade textiles and art. Two have stunning bay views.

ℹ Getting There & Away

Bangkas from Maya (P100, 45 minutes) to Malapascua leave roughly every hour until 5.30pm or so (until 4.30pm from Malapascua). The usual **drop-off and departure point** on Malapascua is Logon Beach, where there's a ticket office and schedule board you can check. However, during the *habagat* (southwest monsoon; June to October) you may be dropped off on Bounty Beach or even in Pasil.

Especially late in the day, boaters in Maya are notorious for trying to get tourists to pay extra for a special trip, claiming they don't have any passengers. Relax – there's always a last trip that leaves at 5.30pm or so.

Vans (P200, 3½ hours, every 30 minutes) and buses (standard/air-con P170/P195, 4½ hours) depart Maya pier for Cebu City until mid-evening.

Bohol

☑ 038 / POP 1.33 MILLION

Bohol offers independent travellers a wealth of options both on and off the beaten track. This island province is promoted almost exclusively through images of cute bug-eyed tarsiers and the majestic Chocolate Hills, but there's much more to experience. Offshore there's superb diving, and when you throw in jungle-fringed rivers perfect for kayaking and paddle-boarding, and pristine white-sand beaches, it's easy to understand the Bohol appeal.

ℹ Getting There & Away

Jagna is where you catch the useful ferry to Camiguin, Mindanao. **Super Shuttle Ferry** (☑ in Jagna 0916 568 2236; http://supershuttleroro.com) has a RORO to Balbagon, Camiguin, on Monday, Wednesday and Friday at 1pm (P400, 3½ hours). In addition, **Lite Shipping** (☑ 0977 822 5483; www.liteferries. com) sends a RORO to Cagayan de Oro on Tuesday, Thursday, Saturday and Sunday at 10pm (from P620, seven hours), and another RORO to Butuan (also in Mindanao) on Monday, Wednesday and Friday at 10pm and at 10am on Sunday.

Sailings do sometimes get cancelled, so be sure to confirm departures directly with the ferry companies; many update their Facebook pages more regularly than their websites.

V-hire vans connect Tagbilaran and Jagna (P100, 1½ hours, hourly).

Loboc & Around

☑ 038 / POP 16,312

Fast emerging as one of the Visayas' hottest destinations for independent travellers, the tranquil town of Loboc makes an idyllic base for a few days. The settlement's main appeal is its bucolic forest-fringed river, which is perfect for kayak and paddleboarding excursions. Many travellers base themselves here for day trips up to the Chocolate Hills.

In Canapnapan you can see saucer-eyed tarsiers in the wild at the **Philippine Tarsier Sanctuary** (☑ 0927 541 2290; www.tarsier foundation.org; Canapnapan; P60; ⊙ 9am-4pm). Over 100 of these territorial primates hang out in the immediate vicinity of the centre, though only eight are in the viewing area. The guides will bring you right to them via a short jungle trail; no flash photography is permitted. The visitors centre includes good information boards and the whole forested sanctuary is well managed and a pleasure to visit.

One of Bohol's premier tourist attractions, and certainly its most hyped, the **Chocolate Hills** are a series of majestic grassy hillocks that span far into the horizon. The hills get their name from the lawn-like vegetation that roasts to chocolate brown in the driest months (February to July). Their exact origin is still debated, but most scientists believe they were formed over time by the uplift of coral deposits and the effects of rainwater and erosion.

The largest and most visited concentration is 4km south of Carmen, site of the **Chocolate Hills Main Viewpoint** (P50; ⊙ 6am-6pm). For a less touristy experience, there's another range of Chocolate Hills northeast of Sagbayan on the road to Danao.

🛏 Sleeping & Eating

★ **Fox & The Firefly Cottages**   HOSTEL $

(☑ 0947 893 3022; www.facebook.com/foxandthe fireflycottages; dm/cottage from P450/1200; 🛜) Virtually on the riverbank, this small, supremely chilled guesthouse has delightful nipa cottages and a well-set-up dorm (with shared bathroom). It's very much a base for paddleboarding on the Loboc with **SUP Tours** (☑ 0947 893 3022; www.suptoursphilip pines.com; 2hr/half-day tour per person P950/1650), but birdwatching walks and mountain-biking trips (from P500) are also offered. There's a great cafe-restaurant for delicious meals. It's a little southwest of Loboc's centre.

★ **Nuts Huts**   HOSTEL $

(☑ 0920 846 1559; www.nutshuts.org; dm P400, nipa huts P900-1400) This near-legendary place polarises opinion. Ensconced in tropical forest on the Loboc River, it's perfect for those eager to experience and explore the jungle and who don't mind roughing it a bit – the huts are very rustic. If you hate creepy-crawlies and dislike exercise (it's a stiff walk up to the entrance) this isn't the place for you. Book ahead.

❶ Getting There & Away

Loboc is 25km east of Tagbilaran, accessed by very regular jeepneys and buses (P30, 50 minutes). Very frequent buses also head to Carmen (P34, one hour) for the Chocolate Hills.

Panglao Island

☑ 038 / POP 83,700

Low-lying sun-baked Panglao Island is generally associated with **Alona Beach**, a busy holiday resort renowned for its nightlife, while neighbouring **Danao Beach** is far more mellow. The underwater scene around Alona is exceptional, and divers can score nifty package deals by combining dives with accommodation. Just 15km from Tagbilaran, Alona works just fine as a base for exploring the rest of Bohol.

🏃 Activities

Everything is water-related in Panglao. Offshore diving and boat trips are the main draw and there's good swimming around the coast, including the sea cave at **Hinagdanan** (P50, swimming fee P75; ⊙ 7.30am-6pm).

You can arrange early-morning dolphin-watching tours around Pamilacan

Island through most resorts and dive centres, though some of these resemble 'dolphin chasing'. Consider organising a more respectful trip via **Pamilacan Island Dolphin & Whale Watching Tours** (PIDWWT; 038-540 9279, 919 730 6108; http://whales.bohol.ph; group of 1-4 P3300, lunch per person P300) out of Baclayon, 6km from Tagbilaran. Figure on paying P1500 for a four-person boat out of Alona – more if you want to extend that into an island-hopping trip, taking in Pamilacan, Virgin and Balicasag islands.

Diving draws many to Panglao, in particular the underwater paradise of Balicasag Island. Pamilacan Island also has reefs but they're less visited as its corals are recovering from years of dynamite fishing. Recommended operators include **Bohol Bee Diving** (038-502 2288; www.boholbeefarm.com/diving; Southern Coastal Rd, Km 11), **Philippine Fun Divers** (038-416 2336; www.boholfundivers.com; Lost Horizon Beach Resort) and **Tropical Divers** (038-502 9031; www.tropicaldivers-alona.com; Alona Tropical).

🛌 Sleeping

★ Bohol Coco-Farm HOSTEL $
(0917 304 9801; www.facebook.com/boholcfarm; Southern Coastal Rd, Km 13; dm/d incl breakfast P350/800; 🌐) 🍃 The best base for backpackers in Panglao, if you don't mind being inland, with nipa huts that are entirely appropriate for the rustic setting. There's a gregarious vibe, with staff and visitors mixing well. The organic cafe (mains P100 to P190) features produce from its 2.5-hectare grounds. Located 5km east of Alona Beach, it's P60 in a *habal-habal* (motorcycle taxi).

Calypso Resort RESORT $
(038-502 8184; www.philippins.info; Danao Beach; r P890-1500; 🌀🌐♨️) Set well back from Danao Beach, this place would be a good deal even without a free motorcycle. If you don't ride, hang out at the pool all day and order cocktails from the cosy bar, equipped with billiards and other games.

Alona Grove Tourist Inn HUT $
(038-502 8857; www.facebook.com/alonagrovetouristinn; off Southern Coastal Rd; hut with fan/air-con P750/1300; 🌀🌐) This place has some of the cheapest beds near the beach, with 10 nipa huts scattered among its pleasant garden with manicured grass. It's located up a little alley and run by helpful folk.

★ Sunshine Village RESORT $$
(0928 552 3431; http://panglaosunshinevillage.com; Barangay Bolod; r P1500-1900) This fine-value resort complex boasts a stupendous pool (around 30m) and attractive gardens, which more than make up for its inland location, 4km east of Alona Beach. Rooms are immaculately clean, with fast wi-fi and modern bathrooms and there's an excellent restaurant on-site. Rent a scooter (available here but cheaper elsewhere) and you're sorted.

🍴 Eating & Drinking

★ Gavroche CAFE $$
(http://gavroche.ph; Southern Coastal Rd; meals P130-260; ⏰6.30am-8.30pm) One of the best places in Alona for breakfast, with fresh croissants, Filipino (P150) and French (from P130) sets plus lots of à la carte options. Also great for sandwiches on home-made bread with smoked hams and imported cheeses. Serves smoothies, shakes, juices and espresso coffee; and the premises are air-conditioned.

Cafe Lawis CAFE $$
(Dauis Convent, Dauis; dishes P95-185; ⏰11am-9pm; 🅿️) In a rectory, on the southern side of Borja bridge next to Our Lady of the Assumption church, this healthy waterside cafe serves up tasty meals (panini, pasta, *adobo*), snacks, espresso coffee and ice cream.

Reggae Bar Aliahailey BAR
(Alona Beach; 7am-1am) Shack on the beach with a friendly bar crew. DJs spin dread Jamaican tunes from morning until...morning.

ℹ️ Getting There & Away
Slow buses head from Alona to Tagbilaran roughly every 30 minutes until 7pm (P25, 50 minutes). The quicker and easier option is to hire a tricycle (P300) or taxi (P450).

MINDANAO

Despite beautiful beaches, killer surf, rugged mountains, and indigenous cultures living much as they have for centuries, Mindanao, with the exception of Siargao and to an extent Camiguin, remains off the tourism industry's radar. Of course, the conflict that has simmered for several generations (and the 2017 declaration of martial law in the region) bears much of the responsibility for this. That's not to say, however, that there isn't development and the woes that go with it – the city of Davao is, for example, fairly cosmopolitan.

Siargao

Initially drawn to Siargao (shar-gow) by good year-round waves and a tranquillity and beauty lost in other Philippine islands, a small group of passionate Aussie, American, European and now Filipino surfers are still living the good life. Even with a marked surge in development over the last several years, more hotels and flights and better roads, the island's laid-back resorts are still the norm.

The port is in the main township of Dapa. On arrival you'll probably make for one of the resorts located along the road between General Luna (known locally as GL) and 'Cloud Nine'.

❶ Getting There & Away

Skyjet (✆ Manila 02-863 1333, mobile 0997 503 5654; www.flyskyjetair.com) offers daily morning flights to Manila (two hours, 7.50am) and **Cebu Pacific** (✆ Cebu 032-230 8888, Manila 02-702 0888; www.cebupacificair.com; cnr Hayes & Rizal Sts, Cagayan de Oro) has three daily direct flights to Cebu (50 minutes). Siargao's Sayak airport is out near Del Carmen.

Four morning boats leave from Dapa to Surigao (all departure times are approximate): the 5.30am Fortune Angel (2½ hours) with an indoor air-con cabin is most recommended; the 6am Montenegro Lines boat is a roll-on, roll-off (RORO) ferry, which needs to be booked several days in advance. The 11am Yohan and 11.30 LQP are the least comfortable. You can purchase tickets (P270) the morning of departure. The early-morning boats allow you to connect to flights in Surigao or travel by bus to Cagayan de Oro and Davao in a single day (these would be long, tiring days); however, it means leaving Cloud Nine extremely early. Arrange a motorcycle to Dapa through your accommodation.

❶ Getting Around

Jeepneys run from Dapa to GL (one hour); a better option is to hop on a *habal-habal* (motorcycles large enough to seat more than one passenger with bags) to GL or the nearby resorts (P150 to P250, 20 minutes) or Cloud Nine (P200 to P300, 30 minutes).

A new venture, **Binggo** (✆ 0977 642 3765; www.binggoride.com), offers mini-multicabs available for self-drive (P1200 per day) or with a driver (P1500 per day). One can hold three to four passengers comfortably.

PHILIPPINES SIARGAO

Cloud Nine & General Luna

📞 086 / POP 16,800

Solidly ensconced in the international surfing circuit, the surf break at Cloud Nine is unmistakably marked by the raised walkway and three-storey wood pavilion offering front-row seats to the action. It's a friendly and open surfing community, with plenty of up-and-coming local Filipinos welcoming foreigners and beginners alike. Only 3.5km to the south, GL is a relaxed small town with a few resorts and transport links.

All the resorts here can help organise island-hopping and lagoon day tours, as well as arrange surf lessons (P500 per hour, including equipment) and board rental (P300 per half-day). Or stop by **Hippie's Surf Shop** (⊙ 6am-6pm); Hippie also teaches yoga classes on many mornings.

🛏 Sleeping & Eating

⭐ **Kermit Surf Resort**   HOTEL $
(✆ 0917 655 0648; www.kermitsiargao.com; d with fan/air-con P950/1200, bungalow P1800; ❇ 🛜) Located down a quiet road just northeast and inland from the centre of GL, Swiss–Italian-owned Kermit is a deservedly popular choice for budget-minded surfers closed out of Cloud Nine. The 10 rooms include several large stand-alone thatch-roofed cottages with tile floors and large, modern bathrooms. The restaurant has candlelit tables in a sandy garden, and pizza, pasta and fish (mains P230 to P300) are the specialities.

Ocean 101 Beach Resort   HOTEL $
(✆ 0910 848 0893; www.ocean101cloud9.com; d with fan P900-1500, with air-con P1700-2500;

⊞⧉) No longer the backpacking surfer's HQ, Ocean 101, spread over a manicured lawn facing a sea wall just north of the Cloud Nine break, has evolved over the years. Basic budget rooms are part of the older 101; the pricier beachfront quarters with high ceilings and big bathrooms are part of the new. A two-storey waterfront pavilion provides scenic lounging space.

Paglaom Hostel HOSTEL **$**
(www.paglaomhostel.com; dm P350; ⧉) At this price, it's the vibe not the creature comforts that matters. And Paglaom gets it right. It is laid-back but socially inclined, with an open lounge area where bunkmates get to know another. The open-air dorms with bunk beds draped in mosquito nets are cooled by a few fans. There are cold showers and a separate kitchen area for guests to use.

★ Bravo Surf Resort BUNGALOW **$$**
(☑0999 877 8518; www.bravosiargao.com; dm/d incl breakfast P1200/P3400; ⊞⧉⛱) Young, Spanish-owned Bravo has become one of GL's happening spots. This is thanks in part to its attractive, closely spaced nipa-roofed cottages with brushed concrete floors and tasteful furniture, and in part to its large open-air restaurant (mains P180 to P320), which is run by a Basque chef. The four-person surfer bunk is a luxurious version of a dorm.

★ Harana BUNGALOW **$$**
(☑0998 849 5461; www.haranasurf.com; dm P800, d P3200; ⊞⧉) Boasting typical Filipino use of wood with contemporary architectural flourishes, Harana's aesthetic is a sophis-

---

RAFTING IN CAGAYAN DE ORO

If you're travelling between Siargao and Camiguin, consider detouring to Cagayan de Oro (CDO) to take on the year-round white-water rafting rapids. The standard three-hour rafting trip (P1200) takes you through 14 Class II to III rapids; several Class IV rapids are part of an alternative longer trip (P1800, six hours); plus P200 for a grilled lunch. Much of the trip is spent floating past bucolic scenery, and enthusiastic guides and excited first-timers add to the fun. **CDO Bugsay River Rafting** (☑088-850 1580; www.cdorafting.com; Everlasting St; per person P1200-1800) is a recommended operator.

---

ticated combination of the traditional and modern. The coed dorm villa is beautiful and the open-air restaurant, which serves innovative Filipino dishes like shwarma *sisig* (mains P150 to P300), and lounge area is one of the area's best hang-outs. Beach and Tuason surf break are directly out front.

Kawayan Gourmand CAFE **$**
(pastries P80-200; ⊙6am-6pm; ⧉) For the island's best croissants, other pastries and espresso drinks, head to this comfortable oasis of cool, both in terms of temperature and style.

Mama's Grill BARBECUE **$**
(skewers P50-70; ⊙6-9pm) Every evening the surfing herd converges to feed on skewered pork chops, chicken and beef at this modest BBQ shack about 1.5km north of GL. And then, just like that, they're gone...until the next evening.

Shaka Siargao HEALTH FOOD **$$**
(mains P250; ⊙6.30am-5pm; ⧉) To maintain the healthy vibe after hours out in the surf, try one of the delicious bowls and smoothies at this postage-stamp-sized spot. The super bowl (quinoa, yoghurt, fruit, granola and honey) is especially good.

Camiguin
☑088 / POP 88,000

Relatively unspoiled and an ideal size for exploration, Camiguin (cah-mee-geen) is notable for its imposing silhouette – drop it down next to Hawaii or Maui and it wouldn't look out of place. With over 20 cinder cones 100m-plus high, Camiguin has more volcanoes per square kilometre than any other island on earth. And because it's untouched by large-scale tourism and one of the more tranquil islands around – the 10km of Gingoog Bay separating the island from the mainland are partly responsible – those who do come feel proprietorial about this little jewel and guard news of its treasures like a secret. Besides the usual diving, snorkelling and sandy beaches (except for offshore ones, beaches have brown sand), Camiguin offers a chance to climb a volcano and a seeming endless supply of jungle waterfalls and hot and cold springs.

Kuguita, Bug-ong, Agoho and Yumbing are the most developed of the northern beaches, and where much of the accommodation is located. Some of the best diving is probably off **Jigdup Reef**, **White Island** and **Mantigue Island**; **Old Volcano** has interesting rock formations.

🛏 Sleeping & Eating

Camiguin Souldivers
HOSTEL **$**

(📱 0947 411 1189; www.camiguinsouldivers.com; Tupsan; dm/s/d/cottage P200/300/350/600; 🔊) The simple, fan-cooled, cave-like dorms and rooms here cater to shoestring divers. It abuts the highway where the road divides about 6km southeast of Mambajao.

⭐ Casa Roca Inn
GUESTHOUSE **$$**

(📱 088-387 9500; www.casarocacamiguin.com; Naasag; r with shared bathroom P1000-1500; 🔊) Gnarly tree branches serve as pillars holding up this two-storey home perched on a rocky headland with waves breaking below. Just three rooms here. The gorgeous sea-facing room, with its sprawling mahogany balcony, is the pick of the island. The two rooms at the back are more modest but terrific value. The international restaurant (mains P200) is highly recommended.

Volcan Beach Eco Retreat & Dive Resort
COTTAGE **$$**

(📱 088-387 9551; www.camiguinvolcanbeach.com; Naasag; r with fan/air-con P1500/2500; ❀🔊) A line of well-constructed thatch-roofed cottages face one another across a palm-tree-filled garden (with several hammocks) that ends on a rocky shore battered by waves – there's a neat bamboo platform for sunbathing. Each has its own small private balcony, high ceilings and mosquito nets. German-owned Volcan has its own full-service dive shop. Service can be inconsistent.

⭐ Beehive
CAFE **$**

(📱 0939 932 0334; Catibac; mains P95-215; ⊙ 8am-7pm) 🍽 Made from recycled wood, shells, rocks and a hotchpotch of other materials a la Robinson Crusoe, this eccentrically designed oceanfront cafe is a good place for a pit stop on a round-the-island motorbike tour. Healthy items such as vegie burgers, salads, pizzas with crusts made from wholewheat, dragonfruit juice and herbs are on the menu.

⭐ Guerrera
SOUTHEAST ASIAN **$$**

(📱 mobile 0917 311 9859; www.guerrera.ph; Pearl St, Yumbing; mains P250-325; ⊙ noon-2pm & 4-9pm; 📱) Camiguin's culinary profile is given a big boost by this restaurant housed in a large yellow villa on an isolated bit of waterfront. The culinary-school-trained Filipino owner-chef focuses mostly on versions of Thai and Vietnamese street food but also does daily specials like Indonesian–style chicken, Bangkok pork and Indian *dal tadka* (smoked yellow lentil and chickpea soup).

ℹ Getting There & Away

Camiguin has two functioning ports relevant to travellers: Benoni, 18km south of Mambajao, where ferries connect to Balingoan on the mainland; and Balbagon, only 2km southeast of Mambajao, with connections to Cebu and Jagna on Bohol.

Eight to 10 boats ply the channel between Benoni and Balingoan roughly hourly from 4.30am until 5.30pm (P170, 1¼ hours). If white caps are visible, the crossing can be unpleasant in the smaller and less-seaworthy-looking ferry. Before leaving, local kids climb up the outside of the boats and leap into the water soliciting tips. Heading to Camiguin from the mainland, you purchase ferry tickets at the bus terminal in Balingoan (and then pay a nominal terminal fee at the port entrance itself 200m away).

PALAWAN

Nothing defines Palawan more than the water around it. With seascapes the equal of any in Southeast Asia, and terrestrial and aquatic wildlife, the Philippines' most sparsely populated region is also the most beguiling. Because of the silhouette of its main island – a long sliver stretching 650km all the way to Borneo – there's a certain liberating logic to travel here.

Puerto Princesa

📱 048 / POP 255,116

Palawan's bustling capital is mainly a gateway to El Nido and the beaches of the west coast, but 'Puerto' does have enough diversions to warrant a day or two if you're passing through. A decent food scene, some nightlife along main drag Rizal Ave, and a growing number of boutique hotels increase the appeal.

⊙ Sights & Activities

The **Environmental Enforcement Museum** (p602) displays confiscated chainsaws, boats, dynamite and (sometimes) animals such as civets. The **World War II Museum** (Rizal Ave; ⊙ 8am-5pm Mon-Sat) is chock-full of war memorabilia and has tributes to the Fighting 1000 and to the 143 Americans who died in the Palawan Massacre at Plaza Cuartel.

Popular **island-hopping tours** (P1300 to P1500 for up to six people) in scenic Honda Bay are run out of Sta Lourdes, 12km north of Puerto proper. Booking these through tour agencies in Puerto costs an exorbitant P1500 or so per person including lunch and various entrance fees. Instead, put your own group together or show up at the pier and try to join one.

★ **Pasyar Travel & Tours**   OUTDOORS
(☑ 048-433 5525; http://pasyarpalawantravel. weebly.com; Gabinete Rd) ✆ Genuinely dedicated to conservation and community-based tourism, Pasyar runs a unique, multiday old growth forest-trekking tour that involves tagging along with enforcement officers on the look-out for illegal loggers around Palawan. It also runs the important **Environmental Enforcement Museum** (Gabinete Rd; P20; ⏲ 8am-6pm) ✆ out of its headquarters.

Dolphins & Whale Sharks   WILDLIFE WATCHING
(☑ 0915 263 2105; www.dolphinandwhales.com; Rizal Ave; whale-shark tours per person P1800, dolphin tours per person P1000; ⏲ Apr-Oct only; whale sharks 7am-2pm, dolphins 6.20-10.30am) The effusive Toto Kayabo runs separate tours to spot these creatures in Honda Bay. This is your best chance to spot wild (ie non-handfed) whale-sharks during the country's southwest monsoon (May to October). Weather permitting, the whale shark tours (minimum six people) usually only take place in the 10 days before and the two days after a full moon, while the dolphin tours (minimum 14 people) are daily.

🛌 Sleeping

★ **Casa Linda Inn**   INN $
(☑ 0917 749 6956, 048-433 2606; casalindainn@ gmail.com; Trinidad Rd; s/d with fan P650/750, with air-con P850/1000; ❄ 🛜) The meticulously maintained garden courtyard and pergola make centrally located Casa Linda feel like a country refuge. The surrounding wood-floored rooms are clean and simply furnished, though they lack hot water and have thin walls. Yet noise isn't really a problem, as it's set 100m back from Rizal Ave. Easily the best-value hotel in town.

★ **Sheebang Hostel**   HOSTEL $
(☑ 048-433 0592, 0915 370 0647; judy.sheebang@ gmail.com; 118 Libis Rd; dm/d P350/850; ❄ 🛜) Sheebang quickly emerged as Puerto's leading hostel after the legendary Banwa Art

House burned down in 2014. In a gorgeous wooden house, it has three air-con dorms with sturdy bunk beds and big lockers, plus some basic en-suite private rooms with aircon. An open-air bar, sprawling garden and competent travel desk make up for the out-of-the-way location.

Pagdayon Traveler's Inn   INN $
(☑ 048-434 9102; off Rizal Ave; d P950-1100; ❄ 🛜) Central but quiet, native-style Pagdayon has six well-kept rooms, each with individual verandahs, set around a thatched open-air common-dining area. It's just off Rizal Ave next to the giant new Best Western.

Edam & Ace Hostel   HOSTEL $
(☑ 0935 118 5909; edamandace@gmail.com; off Rizal Ave; dm P250-300, d P500-945) This colourful, maze-like house is a budget special. While it's not a particularly social hostel, the simple air-conditioned dorms do not have any major flaws considering the bargain-basement price. Breakfast is P80.

★ **Puerto Pension**   HOTEL $$
(☑ 048-433 2969; www.puertopension.com; 35 Malvar St; s P1280-2080, d P1380-2180; ❄ 🛜) ✆ An impressive-looking four-storey wood-and-bamboo building, located close to the Baywalk, with sweeping views of the bay from the top-floor restaurant. Rooms are masterpieces of tasteful native-style design. Swathed in rattan, with wood floors, they practically define 'cosy'. The standard rooms are tiny, so spend just a few hundred pesos extra on a plush 'superior' double. Discounts available on request.

🍽 Eating & Drinking

Aloeha Mercato de Runway   FOOD HALL $
(National Hwy; ⏲ 5pm-2am) You'll find a nice variety of stands at this open-air food market – the best of several in the immediate area. Highlights include **Crystal Sands Bar & Grill**, which serves burgers, Mexican and cheesy baked clams; and tasty bread pizzas at **Sheebang**. Beer towers and live music give the whole place a party vibe on weekend nights.

Ima's Vegetarian   VEGETARIAN $
(Fernandez St; dishes P85-140; ⏲ 11am-9pm Sun-Thu, to 3pm Fri, 6.30-9pm Sat; 🍴) ✆ A decidedly healthy and delicious option run by Seventh-Day Adventists. Try the spicy bean burrito or vegan-cheese pizza for *meryenda* (a daytime snack).

Scribbles & Snacks
CAFE $

(off Rizal Ave; dishes P50-100; ⊙ noon-9pm) This mural-splashed, open-air *kubo* (native-style shelter) hidden behind a Best Western hotel is a hang-out for the local 'Art on the Move' group. Struggling creative types lap up the budget pizza breads (P35), pasta and other light meals while sipping San Miguel or iced tea.

★ Kalui
FILIPINO $$

(☑ 048-433 2580; 369 Rizal Ave; mains P245-265; ⊙ 11am-noon & 6-10.30pm Mon-Sat; 🐾) An institution, this shoes-off eatery has a lovely Balinese ambience – colourful paintings, sculptures and masks adorn the walls, and there's a general air of conviviality. Choose from a few varieties of seafood, all served with vegies, a seaweed salad, or opt for the sumptuous set meal (P695), which includes coconut flan for dessert. Reservations recommended, especially for dinner and groups.

★ Artisans
INTERNATIONAL $$

(Rizal Ave; mains P150-250; ⊙ 11.30am-10pm) The Scottish owner calls the style here 'obscurity'; it basically consists of anything he fancies. The menu is a best-of-the-world affair, where *tikka masala* mingles with Mexican, Indonesian *rendang*, sloppy joes, giant salad bowls and – for drinkers – margaritas. An unorthodox approach yet somehow he pulls it off.

★ Palaweño Brewery
BREWERY

(☑ 048-434 0709; www.palawenobrewery.com; 82 Manalo St; ⊙ 1-9pm Mon-Sat) Producer of Ayahay craft beers, Palaweño offers free tours and has an attractive tap room for tasting and lounging. A glass costs P150 to P170 or it's P400 for a five-beer flight.

Kinabuchs Grill & Bar
BAR

(Rizal Ave; ⊙ 5pm-1am) This is where a good chunk of Puerto goes at night. It's a large open-air restobar with a billiard table, a giant outdoor TV showing sports, and cheap beer. The extensive menu (mains P200 to P400) features many exotic offerings, including *tamilok* (woodworm), which is said to taste like oyster.

ⓘ Information

Palawan Provincial Tourism Office (☑ 048-433 2968; www.palawan.gov.ph; ground fl, Provincial Capital Bldg, Rizal Ave; ⊙ 8am-5pm Mon-Fri) This helpful office is a good first stop for all things Palawan. Ask for Rosalyn or Maribel.

Subterranean River National Park Office (☑ 048-434 2509; City Coliseum, National Hwy; ⊙ 8am-4pm Mon-Fri, to noon & 1-4pm Sat & Sun) Underground River permits (adult/child P500/150) issued here for those not booking with an agency; can usually get a day in advance. Note: You can secure your permit in Sabang only if you can show proof of accommodation in Sabang or points north. If visiting from Puerto Princesa, you must secure your permit here or in the **satellite office** (2nd fl, Robinson's Place; ⊙ 10am-6pm Mon-Fri). The office is about 2km north of the centre.

Tubbataha Management Office (☑ 048-434 5759; www.tubbatahareef.org; Manalo St Ext) Provides information on trips to Tubbataha Reefs Natural Park.

ⓘ Getting There & Away

AIR

Cebu Pacific (www.cebupacificair.com) and PAL (www.philippineairlines.com) have flights to Puerto Princesa from both Manila and Cebu, while AirAsia (www.airasia.com) serves Manila. Cebu Pacific also has thrice-weekly flights to Iloilo on Panay.

Air Juan (www.airjuan.com) flies little six-seaters to Coron (Busuanga) on Thursday and Sunday, and to the Cuyo Islands on Wednesday and Friday.

BOAT

2GO (☑ 043-433 0039; Malvar St) has trips from Puerto Princesa to Manila (P2000 to P2800, 31 hours) on Wednesday and Saturday at 11.59pm. These go via Coron (P1450 to P2280, 15 hours).

Milagrosa Shipping (☑ 048-433 4806; Rizal Ave) serves Iloilo via the Cuyo Islands with departure at 3pm Thursday (P870 to P1450, 36 hours), as does sturdier **Montenegro Lines** (☑ 048-434 9344; Malvar St) at 6pm Monday (P1220 to P1590, 26 hours).

All departures are from the **Ferry Port** (Malvar St).

BUS

Buses, jeepneys and most minivans leave from the San Jose Bus Terminal – otherwise known as the 'New Public Market' – 5km north of Puerto city centre, off the National Hwy.

ⓘ Getting Around

Multicabs ('multis') clog the city's arteries; it's P10 to P13 for short hops, including from the centre of town to Robinson's Place or Santa Monica; grab multis to either location at the corner of National Hwy and Rizal Ave.

Sabang

♪048

Tiny Sabang has a beautiful, wind-lashed beach, huge tracts of pristine jungle and a famous underground river that draws van-loads of day-tripping tourists from Puerto Princesa. While the underground river is certainly worth visiting, Sabang's main appeal lies in its wild setting. The surrounding rainforest is part of the **Puerto Princesa Subterranean River National Park** (Underground River; park permit incl paddle boat adult/child P500/150, plus environmental fee P150; ☉8am-3.30pm), and offers world-class hiking and birdwatching.

At 8km in length, Sabang's famous underground river is one of the longest navigable river-traversed caves in the world and draws scores of tourists. Trips aboard unmotorised paddle boats proceed about 1.5km upstream into the cave (45 minutes return) and now include audioguide headsets. Book a bangka through the Sabang Information Office (P1120 for up to six people, 15 minutes) to get you from the wharf to the cave entrance, or walk 5km via the **Jungle Trail** (P200 incl guide).

🛏 Sleeping & Eating

★**Cafe Sabang** GUESTHOUSE $
(☎0905 592 8947; dm/s/d P250/350/700) Budget travellers finally have a go-to place to congregate in Sabang thanks to this warm and welcoming place in a wooden house. Nothing pretentious at all here, just rustic little private rooms with shared facilities, a cosy five-bed dorm and an earthy cafe. It's about a five-minute walk south of the beach on the road to Puerto.

The French-Filipino proprietors run a **cafe** (Sabang Beach; dishes P75-175; ☉4-10pm; ✍) of the same name on Sabang Beach.

Dab Dab Resort BUNGALOW $
(☎0949 469 9421; cottage with/without bathroom P800/500, with air-con P1800; ☎) This place, 200m northwest of Sabang pier, is an appealing haven. There's no beach here, only a rocky shoreline, but the seven hardwood cottages, equipped with ceiling fans, private porches and hammocks, are much nicer than those on the beach. Generator-powered until midnight (all night for air-con rooms).

Blue Bamboo Cottages BUNGALOW $
(☎0946 085 2134; www.bluebamboo-sabang.com; d P300-600, f P1000; ☎) A mix of basic budget rooms and charmingly dilapidated all-bamboo cottages with private porches. It fronts a rocky shoreline around 250m northwest of Sabang pier.

Agkarawan BARBECUE $$
(Sabang Beach; mains P150-500; ✍) If you're looking for a square meal, this is the best of the dedicated eateries on the beachfront. Lots of grilled seafood, fresh sashimi, a good vegetarian selection and some Thai and North African flavours.

ℹ Information

Sabang Information Office (☎048-723 0904; ☉8am-4pm) is your first stop for visits to the underground river. If you're not on a group tour, this is where you pay all fees and arrange your boat.

ℹ Getting There & Away

Coming from Puerto, the turn-off to Sabang along the main highway is in Salvacion, from where it's a scenic 35km drive over a winding, sealed road.

Port Barton

POP 5000

Essentially a two-road town where the jungle drops precipitously into the bay, Port Barton offers simple pleasures. It's the kind of place where, after just a few strolls down the beach, you don't want to share the tranquillity with outsiders. Several islands with good beaches and snorkelling lurk offshore, surrounded by rows and rows of buoys, the sign of working pearl farms.

Island-hopping tours (P700 per head) take in a mix of islands, beaches, reefs and **Bigaho Falls** (suggested donation P50), with lunch and snorkel stops along the way. You can arrange visits to nearby mangroves (P700 for two, three hours) through the **Tourist Assistance Center** (☎0949 770 9597, 0909 151 1769; Ballesteros St; ☉8am-5pm).

🛏 Sleeping & Eating

Budget-friendly resorts on offshore islands include **Coconut Garden Island Resort** (☎0918 370 2395; www.coconutgardenislandresort.com; Cacnipa Island; basic s/d P860/995, cottages P1700-2200; ☎) and **Blue Cove Island Resort** (☎0908 562 0879; www.bluecoveresort.com; Albaguen Island; cottages P1200-1800; ❄☎), while **Thelma & Toby's Island Camping Adventure** (Palawan Camping;

0998 983 3328, 0999 486 3348; www.palaw-ancamping.com; per person incl full board P1600) offers glamping on a divine mainland beach, 20 minutes north by boat from Port Barton.

★ Dragon House   HOSTEL $

(0919 322 3054; dm P400-450) Easily the coolest and most creative hostel in Port Barton. Practical adds include personal battery fans for every bed to combat Port Barton's power issues; and huge, clutter-eliminating storage drawers under the bunks. Showers have pressure, and hammocks are inverted and turned into chairs on the common balcony. It's at the back of **Deep Moon Resort** (0919 322 3054; www.deepgoldresorts.com; fan cottages P1000-1600, f with air-con P2000-2500; ❀ ✿): book through Deep Moon.

Besaga Beachfront Cottages   BUNGALOW $

(0918 570 4665; besagabeachresort@gmail. com; r P1200-2500) With the best resort food in Port Barton, solar-powered fans (usually available all night) and a quiet location at the north end of the beach, Besaga is a cut above most of the beachfront places. The seven cottages are concrete but tasteful, adorned with bamboo and Filipino rattan.

Harmony Haven Hostel   HOSTEL $

(0917 711 0069; Pamuayan sitio; dm incl breakfast P500, d/q P1200/2400; ✿) If Port Barton is too buzzing for you, then this somewhat isolated hostel 2km north of the centre might suit. It consists of a large concrete house and a few cottages, all set back from a narrow beach. You can kayak fairly easily to absurdly idyllic beaches and islands just offshore; kayak hire is P300 per day.

Hashtag Tourist Inn   HOTEL $

(0917 993 4115; Mabini St; r P1000; ✿) It's off the beach, but Hashtag has two features that most beachfront places lack: 24-hour electricity and hot water. The seven rooms are standard concrete affairs, arranged in a row with private balconies. If it's full, neighbouring Pisces has a similar profile and is owned by the same extended family.

Gacayan   FILIPINO, EUROPEAN $

(Bonafacio St; meals P50-250; ⏲6.30am-midnight; ✿) Backpackers flock here, and it's no wonder: Gacayan is as reliable as it gets for cheap, tasty meals. It offers backpacker staples like banana pancakes mixed with local specialities such as grilled stuffed squid. A free drink is thrown in with most meals – even the popular budget rice meals (P50).

★ Jambalaya Cajun Cafe   INTERNATIONAL $$

(0948 520 4811; mains P200-400; ⏲8am-9pm; ✿) A quirky vibe and huge portions of steaming jambalaya (the Cajun version of paella, properly spiced, P240 to P350) make this the best of Port Barton's beachfront restaurants. Authentic gumbo, Thai curries, good breakfasts and imported coffee round out the mix. Shakes are available all day thanks to the generator.

❶ Getting There & Away

There are seven or eight daily van trips to Puerto Princesa (P350, 2½ hours, last trip 5pm) and six direct trips to El Nido (P500, four hours, last trip 1pm). Recaro Transport, Santolis and Nature Island are the companies for El Nido, while Recaro and SBE serve Puerto. A private van to El Nido/Sabang/Puerto costs P4500/4000/3500 (negotiate hard).

For Sabang, take a Puerto-bound vehicle and hop off in Salvacion; arrange a pickup in Salvacion through Lexus Shuttle, or flag down the thrice-daily Puerto-Sabang jeepney.

El Nido

048 / POP 41,606

El Nido is the primary base for exploring Palawan's star attraction, the stunning Bacuit Archipelago. Tiny swiftlets build edible nests out of saliva in the immense limestone cliffs that surround the ramshackle town proper – hence the name, El Nido ('nest' in Spanish). The town proper has an ordinary beach, but is home to an emerging restaurant and bar scene. Brooding Cadlao Island looms just offshore.

The El Nido area is blessed with arguably the best beaches in the country, both onshore and on islands offshore. Standouts include **Nacpan Beach**, around 20km from El Nido, the jungle-backed surfing magnet **Duli Beach** and the easily accessible **Maremegmeg Beach**.

🏃 Activities

Tours of Bacuit Bay are universally available and cost P1200 to P1400 per person including lunch, mask and snorkel. Don't miss Miniloc Island's **Big Lagoon**, **Small Lagoon** and **Secret Lagoon**, three of the more photographed sights in all of Palawan. Or DIY to some of the closer attractions, like Seven Commandos Beach and **Cadlao Island**, by sea kayak, which are available for rent (P600 to P800 per day) all along El Nido Beach and Corong Corong Beach. **Tao Philippines** (www.taophilippines.com; National Hwy, Corong Corong) runs multi-day bangka trips through the Bacuit Archipelago.

El Nido has outstanding **diving**, and more than a dozen dive shops are ready to take you there. Dives range from shallow reefs to deep wall and drift dives, and it's a popular destination for PADI certification courses.

🛏 Sleeping

In a nutshell, stay in El Nido proper if you want to be close to the action; Caalan is central yet has a secluded feel; Corong Corong has variety, beach bars and the sunset; off-shore is for private-island opulence; and the north peninsula or east coast is where to escape the tourist scene. Low-season discounts average 30% wherever you stay.

★ Eda Beach Campsite   BUNGALOW $
(📞 0905 572 0646; edabeach@gmail.com; Km 316, National Hwy, Sibaltan; cottages P500-1500; 🛜) This delightfully rustic collection of bungalows has a real castaway feel. It's south of, and isolated from, the other Sibaltan resorts. Despite the name, it's a significant step up from camping. Owner Randy is, simply, the man. He cooks well and leads superb boat trips to the many remote islands off El Nido's east coast.

★ Where 2 Next   HOSTEL $
(📞 0917 804 0434; www.where2nexthostel.com; Nacpan Beach; dm P550, r P1200-1700, d in tent Mar-May only P800; 🛜) Enviably placed just off Nacpan Beach, peaceful Where 2 Next is well positioned to ride Nacpan's surging popularity. The dorm rooms are charmingly rustic, or you can opt for a snug private. Solar power, great food, friendly management and the most beautiful common bathroom in Palawan round out the package.

Cavern Pod Hotel & Specialty Cafe   HOSTEL $
(📞 0915 102 3272; National Hwy, Corong Corong; dm P675; ❄🛜) Simply the nicest dorm beds in El Nido. The Japanese-inspired design of the 'pods' features a colour scheme of slate grey and black, beautiful linens, boutique reading lights and a staircase to the top bunk (yes, really). There are just four beds to a room, and each room has its own beautiful bathroom with rain shower and designer-shampoo dispensers.

★ Bulskamp Inn   GUESTHOUSE $
(📞 0956 648 2901; www.bulskampinn.com; Osmeña St; r P1400-2200; ❄🛜) Under new management, this old-timer has spruced up its outdoor common area and restaurant while supplying the same friendly service and good value that it has long been known for. The compact rooms, which can be fan-cooled or air-conditioned, have small beds but are spotless.

Hammock Homestay   HOSTEL $
(📞 0917 935 4027; hammockhomestay@gmail. com; Nacpan Beach; dm/nipa hut P450/1000; 🛜) A very chilled-out spot 300m off Nacpan Beach with a sociable vibe and a bit of reggae spirit. A diminutive place, it has a comfy common area and snug dorms. It's near the guardhouse where you enter Nacpan Beach.

Pawikan Hostel   HOSTEL $
(📞 0943 438 5397; www.pawikanhostel.com; San Joaquin St; incl breakfast dm P700, r P1500-2000; ❄🛜) A super-friendly, locally run hostel with a generous breakfast (for a hostel) in a three-storey high-rise a five-minute walk from Hama St. The private rooms are a tad small for the price, but the dorms are great – tidy four-bed affairs with personal charging stations and pleasant lighting.

★ Duli Beach Resort   COTTAGE $$
(📞 0947 969 8210; www.dulibeach.com; Duli Beach; bungalow P2500) Duli features six thoughtfully conceived bungalows mixing European (the owners are Dutch) and local styles on what is essentially a private beach. The bungalows are enclosed by thin screens that bring you closer to the raw nature that surrounds you. A generator provides electricity for a few hours at night. Great food and surfing from November to March.

Jack's Place   BUNGALOW $$
(📞 0995 237 4811; Nacpan Beach; d/q cottage incl breakfast P1600/1800; 🛜) Walk towards the north end of Nacpan Beach and you'll encounter this castaway-style gem. It consists of five basic ensuite cottages on stilts, all fashioned of wood and equipped with beach-facing balconies. Kayak rental available (per hour/day P150/500).

Outpost Beach Hostel   HOSTEL $$
(📞 0977 373 5229; www.outpostbeachhostel. com; sitio Lugadia, Corong Corong; 4-/9-bed dm P1200/900, r P4000-5500; ❄🛜) There's really no debate as to where the top party hostel

is in El Nido. Outpost ticks all the boxes for hedonistic backpackers, provided they can afford the lofty prices. Beautiful young crowd mingling gleefully in contemporary dorm rooms? Check. Rockin' beach bar with shooter specials and regular beer pong tourneys? Check. Social island tours by day? Of course.

✗ Eating

Gusto Gelato   ICE CREAM $
(Hama St; 1/2 scoops P100/150; ⊘7am-11.30pm) Fabulous gelato stop offers a variety of flavours in the middle of busy Hama St.

IBR   FILIPINO $
(Hama St; mains P95-180; ⊘24hr) A Filipino greasy spoon where backpackers (often nursing a hangover) and locals chow down on soups and rice and meat dishes. Streetside fan seating and an air-con dining room out the back.

★ Bulalo Plaza   FILIPINO $$
(mains P150-200; ⊘24hr) In-the-know travellers flock to this nondescript open-air eatery on the road to Corong Corong for the best fresh-cooked Pinoy eats in town. It's all *sarap* (delicious), but the black squid *adobo*, sizzling pork *bulgogi* and seafood curry stand out. Cheap breakfasts and lots of vegetarian choices.

★ El Nido Boutique & Art Café   INTERNATIONAL $$
(☑0920 902 6317; www.elnidoboutiqueandartcafe.com; Sirena St; mains P220; ⊘7am-11pm;) Everyone ends up here at some point. Rightfully so. The large 2nd-storey dining room is a warm and relaxed place to eat, drink and get your bearings. Especially good are the salads (using lettuce and arugula from its own organic farm), home-made bread, seafood curry, pizza, pineapple upside-down cake, and chocolate and mango tarts. It has a bar and live music four nights a week.

★ Trattoria Altrove   ITALIAN $$
(☑0947 775 8653; Hama St; mains P240-450; ⊘5-10pm) This upstairs Slovenian–owned place does the best pizza in El Nido, made with imported mozzarella in the street-level brick oven. There are a dozen types of pasta from Italy, plus T-bone steak and other meat dishes on the menu. It's very popular, so get here early (or late) during the high season to avoid a long wait.

🍷 Drinking & Nightlife

★ Beach Shack   BAR
(Maremegmeg Beach) The ubercool beach bar that makes Maremegmeg Beach (aka Las Cabanas Beach) tick. In the high season it assumes a Miami Beach vibe around sunset as it turns up the tunes and the pretty people flock to it.

★ Bella Vita   BEACH BAR
(Corong Corong) Quite simply our favourite sunset bar. It has dangerous mojitos, groovy tunes and two-for-one San Miguel during happy hour (3pm to 5pm), plus superb pizza and fresh-baked bread. But most importantly it has that elusive sunset view, unlike many places in El Nido.

Pukka Bar   BAR
(Hama St; ⊘4pm-4am;) Long the most happening place in El Nido, this reggae bar suddenly has a lot more competition and has responded by expanding. It now has two entrances – one on Hama St, one on the beach. Live reggae music and buckets of beer are what make it tick.

Lucky Alofa   BAR
(Hama St; mains P170-300; ⊘3pm-midnight, closed Jul-Aug;) Burgers, bar snacks, '90s tunes and quality cocktails are the hallmarks of this buzzing Swedish-owned bar on the main drag.

ⓘ Information

Credit cards are accepted at some of the fancier resorts and at one restaurant **SAVA** (Hama St; ⊘8am-2am), but they incur at least a 4% surcharge.

BPI (Real St) El Nido's only reliable ATM is here.

City Tourism Office (☑0917 775 6036; www.elnidotourism.com; Real St; ⊘8am-8pm Mon-Fri, to 5pm Sat & Sun)

ⓘ Getting There & Away

AIR

Air Swift (http://air-swift.com) has at least daily flights to Manila, Caticlan (for Boracay), Cebu and Clark. One-way fares range from P4500 to P7000, depending on the season. All flights are into **Lio Airport**, 7km north of town (P200 by tricycle). Air Swift and the airport are both owned by El Nido Resorts, and guests of that company's resorts have priority on the flights, although there is usually plenty of room for outsiders.

Many people heading to El Nido take a cheaper flight to Puerto Princesa, then drive north five hours by van. The newly opened airport in **San Vicente** (Poblacion Rd) will potentially cut that van trip in half, but at the time of writing there were no commercial flights. **Sandoval Airport** in Taytay, just an hour from El Nido, is in the process of upgrading in the hope of landing commercial flights.

BOAT

All public boats use **El Nido Port** at the west end of Sirena St in the town proper.

The most important boat service for visitors to northern Palawan is the El Nido–Coron connection. **Montenegro Lines** (☎0905 371 0787; Real St) runs a daily fastcraft at 6am (adult/student P1760/1500; 4½ to 5½ hours). Book this ahead in the high season via a travel agent or www.biyaheroes.com). **M/Bca Bunso** (☎0910 720 8443; Real St) runs a slower bangka ferry that's a better option if you want to take in the scenery (P1200 including lunch, eight hours, 8am). **Atienza Shipping** (☎0998 881 7226; El Nido Port) has a Tuesday 2am departure to Manila (P1700 to P1850, 25 hours) via Linapacan (P500, five hours). It's a big cargo boat with rudimentary bunk beds for passengers – a real experience. Additional departures to Linapacan (a few weekly) are via bangka ferry from barangay San Fernando on the east coast.

There are no longer any public bangkas heading south to Port Barton or Sabang.

BUS, JEEPNEY & MINIVAN

All ground transport leaves from the **Bus Station** (Km 270, National Hwy, Corong Corong), 1km south of town in Corong Corong (P50 by tricycle).

The vast majority of visitors to El Nido arrive on cramped minivans from Puerto Princesa (P500, five hours, frequent), but buses are more comfortable and there is no need to book them ahead. **Cherry Bus** and **Roro Bus** alternate trips every hour until 10pm, with a mix of air-con and standard buses (P350 to P450, 6½ hours). **Nature Island** (☎0915 644 1630), **Recaro Transport** (☎0920 502 5797) and **Santolis** run direct vans to Port Barton, each with at least a morning and an early-afternoon departure (P700, four hours). Alternatively, take a 7am or earlier bus to Roxas (P250, four hours) and catch the noon jumbo jeepney to Port Barton. For San Vicente, you must also transfer to a jeepney in Roxas. **Lexus Shuttle** (☎0917 686 1110) vans head to Sabang with a change in Salvacion (P700, six hours, 4am, 8am & 11am).

Minivans can be booked everywhere, and a few, such as pricier VIP carrier **Daytripper** (☎0917 848 8755, 048-723 0533; www.daytripperpalawan.com), offer hotel pick-ups. **El Nido Boutique & Art Café** (p607) has a useful booking service for select van companies on its website; you can pay via PayPal or direct bank deposit.

Privately hired vans to Puerto Princesa cost P7000 to P10,000, depending on your negotiation skills. For Port Barton/Sabang, prices start at P4500/5500.

Busuanga & the Calamian Islands

☎048

This group of islands in the far north of Palawan, also known simply as the Calamianes, is a bona fide adventurer's paradise, with wreck diving, kayaking, island-hopping and motorbiking leading the way. It's a bountiful region filled with white-sand beaches, coral reefs, dense rainforests, mangrove swamps and the crystal-clear lakes of Coron Island.

Busuanga is the largest and most developed island. It comprises just two municipalities: Busuanga town (pop 22,046) covers the northwestern half, while more touristy Coron town (51,803) covers the southeastern half. Most of Busuanga Island is extremely rural, but newly sealed roads are bringing development even to more remote parts.

Sights & Activities

★Coron Island ISLAND

This island, only a 20-minute bangka ride from Coron, has an imposing, mysterious skyline that wouldn't be out of place in a King Kong film. Flying over Coron, you see that the fortresslike, jungle-clad interior is largely inaccessible terrain pockmarked with lakes, two of which, **Kayangan Lake** (Coron Island; P300) and **Barracuda Lake** (Coron Island; P200), can be visited. The entire island is the ancestral domain of the Tagbanua indigenous group, who are primarily fishers and gatherers of the very lucrative *balinsasayaw* (birds' nests).

Mt Tapyas VIEWPOINT

FREE Grunt your way up 700+ steps to Mt Tapyas for astounding views of Coron Bay. It's a quintessential Coron experience.

Red Carabao Travel Hub OUTDOORS

(☎0905 338 1314; www.redcarabaophilippines.com; National Hwy; ⏲8am-8pm) The culturally immersive **Manila hostel** (Map p558; ☎0998 573 3884; www.redcarabaophilippines.com; 2819 Felix Huertas St, Santa Cruz; dm P450-500, r per person with fan/air-con P650/1050; ⏲Sep-May; ❄@📶; 🚌) has created a space in Coron for travellers to find alternatives to the area's predominant but almost inescapable 'alphabet tours' (A, B, C, etc). It offers its own tours and provides a venue for others with unique tour ideas to see and be seen. For independent travellers looking to hook up with a group for a great tour, it's the perfect spot. Upstairs is a common area for games and mingling. Great stuff all around.

Diving

Coron Bay is a world-class wreck-diving destination, and Coron town proper is the main base for dive trips (though they're easier to access from Concepcion). More than two dozen Japanese navy and merchant ships can be found in the waters off Busuanga, sunk by US Navy aircraft on 24 September 1944.

Recommended dive operators include:

Coron Divers (☑ 0998 953 0430; www.coron divers.com.ph; Zuric Pension, National Hwy; 🖼)

Freediving Coron (☑ 0915 172 6809; http:// freediving-coron.com; GMG Hotel, National Hwy)

Neptune Dive Center (☑ 0927 418 4118; www.neptunedivecenter.com; National Hwy)

D'Divers (☑ 0935 403 1816; www.ddivers.com; Km 37, National Hwy, Concepcion)

Pirate Divers (☑ 0905 237 3758; www. piratedivers.org; Concepcion; 2/3 dives incl gear P3000/4000)

Island Hopping

Full-day island-hopping tours are all the rage in Coron, with scores of bangkas departing the town pier every morning on set tours of the main islands and snorkelling sites. Many of the sites are more easily accesible from Busuanga town but Coron town has the bulk of the operators.

A good way to avoid the crowds is to get a small group together and tailor an affordable private tour through the **Calamian Tourist Boat Association** (☑ 0920 403 7965; town pier) in Coron proper or the alternative Red Carabao Travel Hub.

Kayaking

Coron Bay and the islands around Busuanga offer world-class sea kayaking. Several places in the town proper offer day rentals for P500 to P1000. Coron Island is a reasonable target only for strong kayakers; others should stick to the bay.

You'll find even better kayaking in Dipuyai Bay off Concepcion, or in Maricaban Bay on the northeast coast, with kayak rental locally available.

To really experience the Calamianes, consider a multiday trip run by **Calamianes Expeditions Eco Tour** (☑ 0920 254

6553; www.corongaleri.com.ph; San Augustin St) or **Tribal Adventures** (☑ in Boracay 0998 999 3049; www.tribaladventures.com; Palawan Sandcastles Resort, barangay Lakdayan, Cheey).

🛏 Sleeping

🛏 Coron Town

Coron town proper has the highest concentration of hotels on Busuanga Island, and chances are you'll spend at least a night here during your stay in the Calamianes.

★ **Vicky's Place**   GUESTHOUSE $
(☑ 0946 433 5257, 0935 105 7428; www.facebook. com/Guesthouse.Vickys; Maricaban Bay, San Jose; r with/without bathroom P800/600; 🖼) This quiet budget option on luscious Maricaban Bay, run by eco-conscious local dive instructor Brenda, is a wonderful place to chill out. She maintains a small dive shop and leads boat excursions around the bay, including dugong-spotting trips (per person P2500 including lunch). It has no beach per se, but you can easily kayak to a few good ones.

Fat Monkey Hostel   HOSTEL $
(☑ 📱 0998 271 4111; www.fatmonkeyhostel.com; Km 5, National Hwy; dm P380) This simple, sociable hostel 2km north of town has some of the cheapest dorms on Busuanga, and guests are eligible to take the 'Fat Monkey Tour' of the islands, which focuses on drinking and aims to avoid the notorious crowds at hotspots like Kayangan Lake.

Marley's Guesthouse   GUESTHOUSE $
(☑ 0956 143 0399; marleysguesthouse@yahoo.com; National Hwy; r without bathroom P400-500; 🖼) On the main road near the centre, Marley's is susceptible to street noise, but its arty kitchen and common areas are the best in town.

Happy Camper Hostel   HOSTEL $
(☑ 0926 503 9616; happycamper.hostel@gmail. com; dm P350) This hidden place is like a wealthy uncle's living room converted into a spacious en-suite dorm room. Just seven single beds, each with its own nightstand, electrical socket and fan. Lovely wood floor, a few antique chairs for kicking back in, and a long wooden desk. The downside is no service whatsoever.

Krystal Lodge   BUNGALOW $
(☑ 0908 357 3309; s/d P500/800, cottage P1200-1600; 🖼) This long-running bamboo complex, built on stilts over the water, is the

quietest place in town. Rooms range from passable boxes to unique overwater 'apartments' with their own bars and sitting areas. Great views, but maintenance is a problem and service is not a hallmark. You'll either love it or hate it.

Sunz en Coron Resort HOTEL $$
(☑0999 659 1891; www.sunzencoron.com; d P2400-2950, f 3600-5200; ❈ 🛜 🌊) Coron has a dearth of quality at the midrange, but Sunz en Coron fills that void with its collection of compact but efficient rooms set around an elegant pool, and with a restaurant serving the best Korean food in town. The drawback is the location – it's on a dark backstreet about 1.5km north of the centre.

Seahorse Guest House HOSTEL $$
(☑0927 497 7559; www.seahorsecoron.com; Don Pedro St; dm/d incl breakfast P600/2000; ❈ 🛜) This tidy, narrow high-rise houses six cool, crisp, four-bed mixed dorms and just two private rooms. The dorm beds, with personal plugs, lights and cabinets, are the nicest in town. The complimentary breakfast is on the 4th-floor rooftop, which looks out to Coron Bay and Coron Island beyond. Noise is the only concern – it's right in the centre of town.

🛏 Busuanga Town

Busanga town makes a fine alternative base for those looking to escape the crowds of Coron town proper. Most accommodation is in Concepcion.

Ann & Mike's Guesthouse GUESTHOUSE $
(☑0929 582 4020; mcbare13@gmail.com; town pier, Concepcion; r with fan P800-1000, with air-con P1500) This friendly little place near the pier in Concepcion has a simple nipa hut with shared bathroom, and a newer duplex with two mural-splashed air-con rooms. It has the best food in town, including delicious curries, and is a good source of information on the area.

Busuanga Backpackers LODGE $
(☑0916 401 8703; Km 36, National Hwy, Concepcion; d P500) This rustic place just off the highway has four simple fan-cooled rooms with shared bathrooms and a kitchen for self-caterers. Walk up a small hill to a hut with sea views – a good spot for a sunset drink. The food is good and it has an eco-friendly tour arm (http://tourbusuanga.com) for island-hopping and other fun excursions.

🍴 Eating & Drinking

🍴 Coron Town

★Winnie's FUSION $$
(National Hwy; mains P180-380; ⊘9am-9.30pm) On the main road just east of the centre, this unassuming restaurant surprises with creative specials written on a chalkboard and a permanent menu heavy on pretty good Thai food. Specials might include steamed slipper lobster or meatloaf or octopus salad. Wonderful.

★Get Real Cafe CAFE $$
(Real St; mains P175-280; ⊘9am-2pm & 5pm-midnight) This place works equally well for drinks or a meal. It's sort of a TexMex menu with more emphasis on the Tex (marbled Angus rib-eye steak) than the Mex (*ellotos callejeros*, or street corn). Sausages are another speciality. The drink highlight is top-notch imported tequila, taken straight or in a margarita. Pretty cheap beer too (P55).

Brujita INTERNATIONAL $$
(National Hwy; mains P170-300; ⊘9am-10pm; 🛜🅿) Various global delights emerge from the kitchen here: squid done several ways, beef goulash, and pork and red beans. Mung-bean curry is the highlight of the impressive vegetarian menu, or choose from the exciting chalkboard specials menu, which might include fresh fish or Thai tastes. Its location on the noisy main road is a drawback.

Island Boy Grill BARBECUE $$
(cnr Real & Rosario Sts; mains P150-300; ⊘10am-midnight) Most evenings BBQ smoke and live music waft out in harmony at this popular and prominent street-side barbecue. It specialises in grilled-meat skewers and sizzling dishes, but also does pasta and vegetable kebabs.

Hangover Bar BAR
(Rosario St; ⊘3pm-2am) Hangover Bar has quickly become the most raucous place in Coron. Cheap shots lure backpackers, flashpackers and locals alike. Once a critical mass of booze has been consumed, the tiny dance floor starts heaving with sweaty bodies. Upstairs is a tad more mellow.

🍴 Busuanga Town

**Laura's Garden
Tropical Restaurant** FILIPINO $
(Km 36, National Hwy, Concepcion; mains P100-165; ⊘7am-7pm) This simple eatery adjoins a

beautiful garden near the resorts of Dipuyai Bay. Just a few items on the menu, including pesto pasta, seaweed salad and *kinilaw* (raw fish cured in vinegar).

Airplane Bar BAR
(Dipuyai Bay, Concepcion) Gunter of D'Divers (p609) was fitting out this old Albatross plane sitting in Dipuyai Bay as a floating bar at the time of research, it should be open by the time you read this. The story of how the plane ended up at Busuanga in the early 1990s is the stuff of legend (you'll just have to ask).

ℹ Information

There are reliable ATMs in Coron Town.

ℹ Getting There & Around

Busuanga's **Francisco B Reyes Airport** (USU; www.franciscoreyesairport.com; Santa Cruz) is 20km north of Coron town proper. PAL, Cebu Pacific and SkyJet fly to/from Manila, while small Air Juan planes fly to/from Caticlan (for Boracay).

All boat departures are from Coron Port, 1.5km east of the town proper (P50 by tricycle), and include **2Go** (☑ 0977 849 5305) for Manila, **Montenegro Lines** (☑ 0915 176 9095) for fastcraft to El Nido and **M/Bca Bunso** (☑ 0910 371 0621) for a bangka to El Nido.

There's a public boat service between Coron town proper and Culion Island. Regular buses traverse the southwest coastal road of Busuanga Island between Coron town proper and Salvacion. Motorbike hire is widely available in Coron town, with rates starting at P400 to P500 per day.

UNDERSTAND THE PHILIPPINES

Philippines Today

Epic city traffic jams, a 'war on drugs' and martial law. Upheavals – natural and political – are par for the course for this country situated in the typhoon belt and the Pacific Ring of Fire. As a result, Filipinos are resolute and adept survivors. Political intrigue, corruption scandals and shifting foreign alliances are often splashed across newspaper headlines. However, for many, it's mostly white noise. Scratch the surface, and Filipinos' thoughts are elsewhere: on migration, traditions, superstitions, and the next generation.

Rodrigo Duterte (aka 'Digong'), who was oft referred to as the 'Death Squad Mayor' when he was mayor of the city of Davao for over two decades, ran a populist campaign for the presidency in 2016, promising to fight crime, drugs and corruption. According to Human Rights Watch, quoting official police statistics, more than 7000 people were killed in the so-called war on drugs in the first six months after Duterte took office, many of them suspected dealers and users of *shabu* (methamphetamine).

The situation in Mindanao, which has been festering for decades, changed trajectory radically in 2017 when nearly 600 ISIS-affiliated militants seized the Islamic City of Marawi. The Philippine military's response, involving bombing raids, artillery and urban warfare, was intense; however, the rebels still controlled parts of the city several months later.

History

Ancient Filipinos stuck to their own islands until the 16th century, when Ferdinand Magellan claimed the islands for Spain and began the bloody process of Christianisation. Filipinos revolted and won their independence in 1898, only to have the Americans take over, whereupon they revolted again and lost. Out of the bloody ashes of WWII rose an independent republic. However, the defining moment of modern Filipino history is the overthrow of elected hardliner President Ferdinand Marcos in the 1986 'People Power' revolution.

Spanish Colonialists

In the early 16th century all signs pointed to the archipelago universally adopting Islam, but in 1521 Portuguese explorer Ferdinand Magellan changed the course of Filipino history by landing at Samar and claiming the islands for Spain. Magellan set about converting the islanders to Catholicism and winning over various tribal chiefs before he was killed by Chief Lapu-Lapu on Mactan Island near Cebu City. In 1565, Miguel de Legazpi returned to the Philippines and, after conquering the local tribes one by one, declared Manila the capital of the new Spanish colony. But outside Manila real power rested with the Catholic friars – the notoriously unenlightened *friarocracia* (friarocracy), who acted as sole rulers over what were essentially rural fiefdoms.

The Philippine Revolution

At the end of the 19th century, as Spain grew weaker and as the friars grew ever more repressive, the Filipino people started to resist.The Spanish sealed their fate in 1896 by executing Rizal for inciting revolution. A brilliant scholar and poet, Rizal had worked for independence by peaceful means. His death galvanised the revolutionary movement. With aid from the USA, already at war with Spain over Cuba, General Emilio Aguinaldo's revolutionary army drove the Spanish back to Manila. American warships defeated the Spanish fleet in Manila Bay in May 1898, and independence was declared on 12 June 1898.

American Rule

Alas, the Americans had other ideas. They acquired the islands from Spain and made the Philippines an American colony. War inevitably broke out in February 1899. But the expected swift American victory didn't materialise, and as the Philippine–American War dragged on, public opposition mounted in the US. The character of the American home-front debate, and the ensuing drawn-out guerrilla war, would have parallels to Vietnam and Iraq wars many decades later. It was only on 4 July 1902 that the US finally declared victory in the campaign. The Americans quickly set about healing the significant wounds their victory had wrought, instituting reforms aimed at improving the Filipinos' lot and promising eventual independence. The first Philippine national government was formed in 1935 with full independence pencilled in for 10 years later. This schedule was set aside when Japan invaded the islands in WWII. For three years the country endured a brutal Japanese military regime before the Americans defeated the Japanese in the Battle for Manila in February 1945. The battle destroyed a city that had been one of the finest in Asia and resulted in the deaths of over 100,000 civilians.

People Power

The 1983 assassination of Ferdinand Marcos' opponent Benigno 'Ninoy' Aquino pushed opposition to Marcos to new heights. Marcos called elections for early 1986 and the opposition united to support Aquino's widow, Corazon 'Cory' Aquino. Both Marcos and Aquino claimed to have won the election, but 'people power' rallied behind Cory Aquino, and within days Ferdinand and his profligate wife, Imelda, were packed off by the Americans to Hawaii, where the former dictator later died. Cory Aquino failed to win the backing of the army but managed to hang on through numerous coup attempts. She was followed by Fidel Ramos, Ferdinand Marcos' second cousin. In 1998 Ramos was replaced by movie actor Joseph 'Erap' Estrada, who promised to redirect government funding towards rural and poor Filipinos. Estrada lasted only 2½ years in office before being ousted over corruption allegations in a second 'people power' revolt and replaced by his vice-president, Gloria Macapagal Arroyo, who would somehow serve nine years, battling her own corruption allegations and threats of a third 'people power' revolt.

The Moro Problem

Muslim dissent emanating out of Mindanao has been the one constant in the Philippines' roughly 450 years of history as a loosely united territory. The country's largest separatist Muslim group, the Moro Islamic Liberation Front (MILF), has fought the government from its base in the Autonomous Region in Muslim Mindanao (ARMM) since the 1980s, conducting periodic bombings and abductions. In October 2012 the MILF and the government signed the Bangsamoro Framework Agreement (BFA), a preliminary peace deal meant to hand the MILF more autonomy and end decades of conflict and poverty in Mindanao. The agreement was finally signed by the two parties in 2014. However, violence has continued apace throughout the peace process, as the agreement excluded the MILF's main rivals, the Moro National Liberation Front (MNLF),as well as other Muslim splinter groups. In 2013 the MNLF orchestrated a siege of the southern city of Zamboanga, resulting in the deaths of more than 200 people. Kidnappings and abductions in Muslim-dominated areas of Mindanao remained common in 2014 and 2015. At the time of writing, peace in Mindanao seemed as tenuous as ever.

Promising to end corruption, crime and reset relations with China, Rodrigo Duterte, the former long-time mayor of the southern city of Davao, beat his closest rival by more than 6 million votes in the 2016 presidential elections.

People & Culture

Lifestyle

It's impossible to deny it: Filipinos have a zest for life that may be unrivalled on our planet. The national symbol, the jeepney, is an apt metaphor for the nation. Splashed with colour, laden with religious icons and festooned with sanguine scribblings, the jeepney flaunts the fact that, at heart, it's a dilapidated pile of scrap metal. No matter their prospects in life, Filipinos face them with a laugh and a wink. Whatever happens...'so be it'. This fatalism has a name: *bahala na*, a phrase that expresses the idea that all things shall pass and in the meantime life is to be lived.

For centuries the two most important influences on the lives of Filipinos have been family and religion. The Filipino family unit extends to distant cousins, multiple godparents and one's *barkada* (gang of friends). Filipino families, especially poor ones, tend to be large. It's not uncommon for a dozen family members to live together in a tiny apartment, shanty or *nipa* hut. Filipinos are a superstitious lot. In the hinterland, a villager might be possessed by a wandering spirit, causing them to commit strange acts. In urban areas, faith healers, psychics, fortune tellers, tribal shamans, self-help books and evangelical crusaders can all help cast away ill-fortune. Another vital thread in the fabric of Filipino society is the Overseas Filipino Worker (OFW) – the nurse in Canada, the construction worker in Qatar, the entertainer in Japan, the cleaner in Singapore. Combined, they send home billions of dollars a year.

Population

A journey from the northern tip of Luzon to the southern tip of the Sulu islands reveals a range of ethnic groups speaking some 170 different dialects. Filipinos are mainly of the Malay race, although there's a sizeable and economically dominant Chinese minority and a fair number of *mestizos* (Filipinos of mixed descent). The country's population is thought to be about 102 million and expanding at a rapid clip of almost 2% per year – one of the fastest growth rates in Asia. The median age is only 23.2 and almost a quarter of the population lives in or around metro Manila.

Arts

CINEMA

The Philippines has historically been Southeast Asia's most prolific film-making nation. The movie industry's 'golden age' was the 1950s, when Filipino films won countless awards. In the 1980s and '90s the industry surged again thanks to a genre called 'bold' – think sex, violence and dudes with great hair in romantic roles. Today the mainstream studios are in decline, but the quality of films is improving with the proliferation of independent films such as Jeffrey Jeturian's Kubrador (2006), Ekstra (2013) and Lav Diaz' epic four-hour masterpiece, Norte, the End of History. Another important indie director is Brillante Mendoza, who won Best Director at the 2009 Cannes Film Festival for his graphic, controversial film *Kinatay* (Slaughtered).

MUSIC

Filipinos are best known for their ubiquitous cover bands and their love of karaoke, but 'OPM' (Filipino rock) is wildly popular too. Original Pinoy Music ('Pinoy' is what Filipinos call themselves) encompasses a wide spectrum of rock, folk and New Age genres – plus a subset that includes all three.The big three of Pinoy rock are slightly grungy eponymous band Bamboo, agreeable trio Rivermaya (formerly fronted by Bamboo), and sometimes sweet, sometimes surly diva Kitchie Nadal, who regularly tours internationally. One veteran band worth checking out in the bars of Manila is Kalayo, which plays a sometimes-frantic fusion of tribal styles and modern jam-band rock. Other good bands, currently thriving, that are part of this legacy are Parokya ni Edgar, Moonstar 88, Silent Sanctuary and Brownman Revival, the latter a reggae band. Alternative rock fans should give quintet Taken by Cars a listen. Two other names to look out for are Mumford & Sons–esque folk rockers Ransom Collective, and jazzy vocalist Jireh Calo.

Food & Drink

Kain na tayo – 'let's eat'. It's the Filipino invitation to eat, and if you travel here, you will hear it over and over again. The phrase reveals two essential aspects of Filipino people: one, that they are hospitable, and two, that they love to, well, eat. Three meals a day isn't enough, so they've added two *merienda*. The term means 'snack', but don't let that fool you – the afternoon *merienda* can include filling *goto* (Filipino congee) or *bibingka* (fluffy rice cakes topped with cheese). Other favourite Filipino snacks and dishes:

Adobo Chicken, pork or fish in a dark tangy sauce.

Balut Half-developed duck embryo, boiled in the shell.

Crispy pata Deep-fried pork hock or knuckles.

Halo-halo A tall, cold glass of milky-crushed ice with fresh fruit and ice cream.

Kare-kare Meat (usually oxtail) cooked in peanut sauce.

Kinilaw Delicious Filipino-style ceviche.

Lumpia Spring rolls filled with meat or vegetables.

Mami Noodle soup, like mee soup in Malaysia or Indonesia.

Pancit Stir-fried bihon (white) or canton (yellow) noodles with meat and vegetables.

Pinakbet Vegetables with shrimp paste, garlic, onions and ginger.

The national brew, San Miguel, is very palatable and, despite being a monopolist, eminently affordable at around P30. Tanduay rum is the national drink and is usually served with cola. Popular nonalcoholic drinks include *buko* juice (young coconut juice with floating pieces of jelly-like flesh) and sweetened *calamansi* (small local lime) juice.

Environment

An assemblage of 7107 tropical isles scattered about like pieces of a giant jigsaw puzzle, the Philippines stubbornly defies geographic generalisation. The typical island boasts a jungle-clad, critter-infested interior and a sandy coastline flanked by aquamarine waters and the requisite coral reef. About 25% of the Philippines is forested, but only a small percentage of that is primary tropical rainforest. Endangered animal species include the mouse deer, the tamaraw (a species of dwarf buffalo) of Mindoro, the Philippine crocodile of Northeast Luzon, the Palawan bear cat and the flying lemur. As for the country's national bird, there are thought to be about 500 pairs of haribon (Philippine eagles) remaining in the rainforests of Mindanao, Luzon, Samar and Leyte. There's an unbelievable array of fish, shells

and corals, as well as dwindling numbers of the *duyong* (dugong, or sea cow).If your timing's right, you can spot wild whale sharks in Donsol, Puerto Princesa and southern Leyte.

National Parks

The Philippines' national parks, natural parks and other protected areas comprise about 10% of the country's total area, but most lack services such as park offices, huts, trail maps and sometimes even trails. The most popular national park is surely Palawan's Subterranean River National Park.

Environmental Issues

Given its extraordinary geography of 7107 tropical islands and population of 100 million people, many of whom live well below the poverty line, it seems inevitable that environmental issues will arise. Deforestation, soil erosion, improper waste disposal, air and water pollution, overfishing, destructive fishing and coral-reef loss are all of concern. Not all the damage is self-inflicted, however. The Philippine environment is also suffering from some well-known external pressures, from plastic bottles floating ashore from the rest of Southeast Asia to the many impacts of climate change.

There is an ongoing battle between the many sources of these problems, and the many conservation organisations, both governmental and non-governmental, arrayed against them. The environment of the Philippines today is basically the product of this conflict, whose shifting frontline is everywhere to be seen.

SURVIVAL GUIDE

❶ Directory A–Z

ACCOMMODATION

Within the budget category, rooms for less than P500 are generally dorms or private fan-cooled rooms with a shared cold-water bathroom. Rooms between P700 and P1000 usually have a fan and private bathroom. Anything higher (and some within this range) should have both air-conditioning and a private bathroom.

High-season rates are from November to April or May. While prices in resort areas go down around 20% to 50% in the low season, they may double, triple or even quadruple during the 'superpeak' periods of Holy Week (Easter) and New Year.

Chinese New Year (usually in February) and the Japanese holiday period of Golden Week (29 April to 5 May) are additional times of heavy travel that may cause price spikes in resort areas.

CLIMATE

➤ For most of the country, the dry season is during the *amihan* (northeast monsoon), roughly November to May. Rains start once the *habagat* (southwest monsoon) arrives in June, peak in August, and taper off in October.

➤ On the country's eastern seaboard, the seasons are flipped. Siargao, Bicol, eastern Samar etc are rainy from December to February and, unless there's a typhoon stirring up trouble, relatively dry.

➤ Typhoons are common from June to early December. Use the website of PAGASA (www. pagasa.dost.gov.ph) or www.typhoon2000.ph to avoid meteorological trouble spots.

ELECTRICITY

Philippines uses 225V, 60Hz electricity; power outlets most commonly use two square pins, although variations are found.

EMBASSIES & CONSULATES

The **Philippines Department of Foreign Affairs** (DFA; www.dfa.gov.ph) website lists all Philippine embassies and consulates abroad, and all foreign embassies and consulates in the Philippines.

Some countries that require Western visitors to have visas for entry maintain embassies in Manila, including China, India, Myanmar and Vietnam.

Australian Embassy (Map p568; ☑02-757 8100; www.philippines.embassy.gov.au; 23rd fl, Tower 2, RCBC Plaza, 6819 Ayala Ave, Makati)

Canadian Embassy (Map p568; ☑02-857 9000; www.manila.gc.ca; Levels 6-8, Tower 2, RCBC Plaza, 6819 Ayala Ave, Makati)

Canadian Consulate (☑032-254 4749; cebu@ international.gc.ca; RD Corporate Center, 96 Governor MC Cuenco Ave, Banilad; ☺9-11am Mon-Fri)

Dutch Embassy (Map p568; ☑02-786 6666; www.netherlandsworldwide.nl; 26th fl, BDO Equitable Tower, 8751 Paseo de Roxas, Makati)

Dutch Consulate (☑032-346 1823; zeny. monterola@aboitiz.com; Metaphil Bldg, Tipolo, Mandaue; ☺9am-noon Mon-Fri)

French Embassy (Map p568; ☑02-857 6900; www.ambafrance-ph.org; 16th fl, Pacific Star Bldg, cnr Gil Puyat & Makati Aves, Makati)

German Embassy (Map p568; ☑02-702 3000; www.manila.diplo.de; 25/F Tower 2, RCBC Plaza, 6819 Ayala Ave, Makati)

German Consulate (☑032-236 1318, 0929 667 6386; www.honorarkonsul-cebu.com; Ford's Inn Hotel, AS Fortuna St; ☺9am-noon Tue-Thu)

Indonesian Consulate (☑082-297 2930; www.kemlu.go.id/davaocity/id/default. aspx; General Ecoland Subdivision, Matina; ☺8.30am-4.30pm Mon-Fri)

Malaysian Consulate (☑082-221 4050; www. kln.gov.my/web/phl_davao-city; 3rd fl, Florentine Bldg, A Bonifacio St; ☺8am-4pm Mon-Fri)

New Zealand Embassy (Map p568; ☑02-234 3800; www.nzembassy.com; 35th fl, Zuellig Bldg, Makati Ave, Makati City)

UK Embassy (Map p558; ☑02-858 2200; www.gov.uk; 120 Upper McKinley Rd, McKinley Hill, Taguig)

US Embassy (Map p566; ☑02-301 2000; http://manila.usembassy.gov; 1201 Roxas Blvd, Ermita)

INTERNET ACCESS

Theoretically, wi-fi and 4G internet access is available in much of the Philippines. For smartphone users, local SIM cards with data (4G) are easy to purchase, and data is cheap at less than P50 per day.

LGBT TRAVELLERS

Bakla (gay men) and *binalaki* or *tomboy* (lesbians) are almost universally accepted in the Philippines. Harrassment is rare and you can usually be as 'out' as you want to be.

Online gay and lesbian resources for the Philippines include Outrage Magazine (www. outragemag.com), Utopia Asian Gay & Lesbian Resources (www.utopia-asia.com) and Travel Gay Asia (www.travelgayasia.com). B-Change (ww.b-change.org) is a social enterprise group that works to promote LGBT rights.

For Manila-related events, the best site is www.thegaypassport.com/gay-manila.

MONEY

ATMs
→ Prevalent in any decent-sized provincial city; dispense pesos.

→ More remote towns do not have ATMs.

→ The most prevalent ATMs that accept most Western bank cards belong to Banco de Oro (BDO), Bank of the Philippine Islands (BPI) and Metrobank.

→ Standard ATM charge is P200 per withdrawal.

→ Most ATMs have a P10,000 to P15,000 per-transaction withdrawal limit. Exception: HSBC ATMs in Manila and Cebu let you take out P40,000 per transaction.

Cash
→ Cash in US dollars is a good thing to have in case you get stuck in an area with no working ATM. Other currencies, such as the euro or UK pound, are more difficult to change outside of the bigger cities.

→ 'Sorry, no change' becomes a very familiar line in the provinces. Stock up on coins and P20, P50 and P100 notes at every opportunity.

Credit Cards
→ Major credit cards are accepted by most hotels, high-end restaurants and businesses in Manila, Cebu City and other large cities.

→ Outside of large cities, you may be charged an extra 3% to 5% for credit-card transactions.

→ Most Philippine banks will let you take a cash advance on your card.

OPENING HOURS

Banks 9am to 4.30pm Monday to Friday (most ATMs operate 24 hours)

Bars 6pm to late

Public Offices 8am to 5pm Monday to Friday

Restaurants 7am or 8am to 10pm or 11pm

Shopping Malls 10am to 9.30pm

Supermarkets 9am to 7pm or 8pm

PUBLIC HOLIDAYS

New Year's Day 1 January

People Power Day 25 February

Maundy Thursday Varies; around March or April

Good Friday Varies; the day after Maundy Thursday

Araw ng Kagitingan (Bataan Day) 9 April

Labour Day 1 May

Independence Day 12 June

Ninoy Aquino Day 21 August

National Heroes Day Last Sunday in August

All Saints' Day 1 November

End of Ramadan Varies; depends on Islamic calendar

Bonifacio Day 30 November

Christmas Day 25 December

Rizal Day 30 December

New Year's Eve 31 December

TELEPHONE

The Philippine Long-Distance Telephone Company (PLDT) operates the Philippines' fixed-line network. International calls can be made from any PLDT office for US$0.40 per minute. Local calls cost almost nothing, and long-distance domestic calls are also very reasonable.

Mobile Phones

Mobile (cell) phones are ubiquitous, and half the country spends much of its time furiously texting the other half. Local SIM cards are widely available and can be loaded up cheaply with data and phone credit. Roaming is possible but expensive.

→ Prepaid SIM cards cost as little as P40 and come pre-loaded with about the same amount of text credits.

→ The two companies with the best national coverage are **Globe** (www.globe.com.ph) and **Smart** (www.smart.com.ph).

→ Text messages on all mobile networks cost P1 to P2 per message; local calls cost P7.50 per minute (less if calling within a mobile network).

→ International text messages cost P15, and international calls cost US$0.40 per minute.

→ To dial a landline or mobile number from a mobile phone dial 0 or +63 followed by the three-digit prefix and the seven-digit number.

→ Mobile prefixes always begin with a 9 (eg 917, 906).

→ Roaming with your home phone is another, though likely very expensive, option.

Phone Codes

For domestic long-distance calls or calls to mobile numbers, dial 0 followed by the city code (or mobile prefix) and then the seven-digit number.

Useful dialling codes from land lines include:

Philippines country code 63

International dialling code 00

PLDT directory 101171

International operator 108

Domestic operator 109

TOILETS

→ Toilets are commonly called a 'CR', an abbreviation of the delightfully euphemistic 'comfort room'.

→ Other than at some bus terminals and ports, public toilets are virtually nonexistent, so aim for one of the ubiquitous fast-food restaurants should you need a room of comfort.

→ In Filipino, men are *lalake* and women are *babae*.

TRAVELLERS WITH DISABILITIES

Steps up to hotels, tiny cramped toilets, narrow doors and dysfunctional lifts are the norm outside of three-star-and-up hotels in Manila, Cebu and a handful of larger provincial cities. The same goes for restaurants, although mall restaurants tend to be more accessible.

On the flip side, most Filipinos are more than willing to lend a helping hand, and the cost of hiring a taxi for a day, and possibly an assistant as well, is not excessive.

VISAS

A free 30-day visa is issued on arrival for most nationalities. You can extend, for a fee, in major provincial centres, or extend upon arrival at the airport.

Visa Extensions

Visa rules and fees changed in early 2017. The situation remains fluid, so check the latest rules and regulations on the website of the Bureau of Immigration, whose head office is in **Manila** (BOI; Map p562; ☏02-465 2400; www.immigration.gov.ph; Magallanes Dr, Intramuros; ◷8am-5.30pm Mon-Fri), with a second office in **Makati** (Map p564; ☏02-899 3831; JP Rizal Ave, Lasala Bldg, 3rd fl, Makati; ◷8am-5pm).

➔ It is easy to extend your initial 30-day visa (technically a visa 'waiver') for an additional 29 days. This costs about P3030 for most nationalities.

➔ Thereafter, you may apply for additional one-month, two-month or six-month extensions. The cost for the first month is P4400 and includes purchase of an 'ACR-I card' valid for one year; subsequent extensions cost P500 to P1430 per month.

➔ You can apply for visa extensions at the head office in Manila or at any BOI provincial office. Most regional hubs and touristy areas such as Boracay have BOI offices; a full list of the regional offices can be found on the BOI website (http://immigration.gov.ph).

➔ Apply for extensions at least a week before your visa expires, or you may have to pay a modest fine (about P1000).

➔ The visa process is generally painless, especially in provincial offices, but you can also pay a travel agent to handle everything for you.

VOLUNTEERING

Coral Cay Conservation (www.coralcay.org) Works to protect coral reefs in Southern Leyte.

Gawad Kalinga (☏in Manila 02-533 2217; www.gk1world.com/ph) GK's mission is building not just homes but entire communities for the poor and homeless. Volunteers can build houses or get involved in a host of other activities. Contact the volunteer coordinator, Fatima Amamo (maamano@gawadkalinga.com).

Habitat for Humanity (☏02-846 2177; www.habitat.org.ph) Builds houses for the poor all over the country, concentrating on disaster-affected areas.

Hands On Manila (☏02-843 7044; www.handsonmanila.org) Always looking for volunteers to help with disaster assistance and other projects throughout the Philippines.

Haribon Foundation (☏02-911 6088; http://haribon.org.ph) A longstanding conservation organisation focused on scientific research and community empowerment programs.

Rise Above Foundation (☏032-255 1063; www.riseabove-cebu.org; 252 I Limkakeng St, Happy Valley Subd, V Rama Ave, Cebu City) Housing, education and vocational training projects in Cebu. We've had positive feedback from recent volunteers.

Save Palawan Seas (☏0917 824 1488; www.savepalawanseasfoundation.org) NGO owned by one of the largest pearl producers in Philippines and supported by **Flower Island Beach Resort** (☏0917 504 5567; www.flower-island-resort.com; cottages incl all meals per person with fan/air-con from P7000/8500; ❄☞), dedicated to educating local fishers in Palawan about the dangers of destructive fishing and agricultural practices.

Volunteer for the Visayas (☏0917 846 6967; www.visayans.org) Runs various volunteer programs around Tacloban, Leyte.

ⓘ Getting There & Away

Most people enter the Philippines via one of the three main international airports: Manila, Cebu or Clark. A handful of international flights also go straight to Kalibo, near Boracay; Iloilo City on the island of Panay; and Davao in southern Mindanao.

AIR
Airports & Airlines

Ninoy Aquino International Airport (p618) The busiest international airport in the country and where you're most likely to fly in to and out of.

Mactan-Cebu International Airport (www.mactan-cebuairport.com.ph) Cebu's airport is second only to Manila in terms of air traffic, but way ahead in terms of user-friendliness.

Clark International Airport (http://crk.clarkairport.com) Near Angeles, a two-hour bus ride north of Metro Manila; traditionally a hub for low-cost airlines.

Kalibo International Airport (www.kaliboint-ernational.com) Useful direct flights to Kalibo, near Boracay, from Beijing, Kunming, Hong Kong, Seoul, Shanghai, Singapore and other Asian hubs.

TERMINAL CHAOS

Navigating Manila's convoluted **Ninoy Aquino International Airport** (NAIA; Map p558; www.manila-airport.net) is a nightmare. NAIA's four terminals are linked only by busy public roads, and shuttle vans linking them are unreliable, so take a taxi between terminals if you're in a hurry.

Pay close attention to which terminal your airline uses and allow plenty of time between connecting flights if you have to switch terminals. Most international flights use recently upgraded but still dismal Terminal 1. However, international flights run by Cebu Pacific, ANA, Cathay Pacific, Delta, Emirates Air, KLM and Singapore Airlines use newer Terminal 3.

Some domestic flights run by Philippine Airlines (PAL), and all domestic flights run by Cebu Pacific, also use Terminal 3. Meanwhile, all PAL international and some PAL domestic flights use yet another terminal, the Centennial Terminal 2.

Lastly, all AirAsia and Skyjet flights, and 'Cebgo'-branded Cebu Pacific flights, use the ancient Manila Domestic Terminal (Terminal 4), located near Terminal 3.

The following regional budget and Philippine carriers are worth checking out for flights in to and out of the country:

AirAsia (www.airasia.com)

Cebu Pacific (www.cebupacificair.com)

Jetstar (☑ 02-810 4744; www.jetstar.com)

Philippine Airlines (www.philippineairlines.com)

Tigerair (☑ 02-798 4499; www.tigerair.com)

SEA

The only international route open to foreigners is Zamboanga to Sandakan in the Malaysian state of Sabah. **Aleson Shipping Lines** (☑ 062-991 2687; www.aleson-shipping.com; 172 Veterans Ave, Zamboanga) leaves Zamboanga on Monday and (sometimes) Thursday, and departs Sandakan on Tuesday and (sometimes) Friday (economy/cabin P2900/P3300, 23 hours).

Cruise ships frequently dock in Manila and elsewhere.

ⓘ Getting Around

AIR

AirAsia (☑ 02-722 2742; www.airasia.com; NAIA Terminal 4), **Philippine Airlines** (PAL; ☑ 02-855 8888; www.philippineairlines.com; NAIA Terminal 2) and **Cebu Pacific** (☑ 02-702 0888; www.cebupacificair.com) are the main domestic carriers. **Skyjet** (☑ in Manila 02-863 1333; www.skyjetair.com; NAIA Terminal 4) is a newer carrier with good deals on some key routes such as Manila–Caticlan and Manila–Busuanga.

➡ Pay attention to baggage allowances – some routes and airlines are more restrictive than others.

➡ If you book a month or so in advance, you'll rarely pay more than P1500 (about US$30) for a one-way ticket on the main carriers (exceptions on touristy routes such as Manila–

Caticlan and Manila–Siargao, and during peak domestic travel periods).

➡ Flight routes are skewed towards Manila and (to a lesser extent) Cebu. If you want to fly between any other cities you'll likely have to purchase two tickets and transfer through one of those hubs.

➡ Typhoons and other adverse weather often ground planes from July to December.

BOAT

The islands of the Philippines are linked by an incredible network of ferry routes, and prices are generally affordable. Ferries usually take the form of motorised outriggers (known locally as bangkas), speedy 'fastcraft' vessels, roll-on, roll-off ferries (ROROs; car ferries) and, for long-haul journeys, vast multi-decked passenger ferries. Mega company 2GO Travel (www. travel.2go.com.ph) serves the majority of major destinations in the Philippines.

Most ferry terminals have a small fee (P20 on average); Manila's is P95.

You can check out the real-time locations of the various larger ferries plying the waters at www.marinetraffic.com. The website www. schedule.ph is not entirely comprehensive but it's a good place to start for ferry schedules.

➡ Booking ahead is essential for long-haul liners and can be done at ticket offices or travel agencies in most cities.

➡ For fastcraft and bangka ferries, tickets can usually be bought at the pier before departure (exception: book El Nido–Coron ferries ahead in the high season).

➡ Passenger ferries offer several levels of comfort and cost. Bunks on or below deck in 3rd or 'economy' class should be fine, as long as the ship isn't overcrowded. First class nets you a two-person stateroom.

→ Before purchasing your ticket, it pays to ask about 'promo rates' (discounts). Student and senior-citizen discounts usually only apply to Filipino citizens.

BUS & VAN
→ Bus depots are dotted throughout towns and the countryside, and most buses will stop if you wave them down.

→ More services run in the morning – buses on unsealed roads may *only* run in the morning, especially in remote areas.

→ Night services, including deluxe 27-seaters, are common between Manila and major provincial hubs in Luzon and in Mindanao.

→ Air-con minivans (along with jeepneys) shadow bus routes in many parts of the Philippines (especially Bicol, Leyte, Cebu, Palawan and Mindanao) and in some cases have replaced buses altogether.

→ Minivans are a lot quicker than buses, but also more expensive and cramped.

→ Reservations aren't usually necessary; however, they're essential on the deluxe night buses heading to/from Manila (book these at least two days in advance, if possible, at the bus terminal).

→ Bus and van tickets on some popular routes – such as Manila–Banaue (North Luzon), Manila–Bicol (Southeast Luzon) and Puerto Princesa–El Nido (Palawan) – can be reserved online through booking sites such as www.pinoytravel.com.ph or www.biyaheroes.com.

LOCAL TRANSPORT
Jeepney
The first jeepneys were modified army jeeps left behind by the Americans after WWII. They have been customised with Filipino touches such as chrome horses, banks of coloured headlights, radio antennae, paintings of the Virgin Mary and neon-coloured scenes from action comic books.

→ Jeepneys form the main urban transport in most cities and complement the bus services between regional centres.

→ Within towns, the starting fare is usually P8, rising modestly for trips outside of town. Routes are clearly written on the side of the jeepney.

→ Jeepneys have a certain quirky cultural appeal, but from a tourist's perspective they have one humongous flaw: you can barely see anything through the narrow open slats that pass as windows. The best seats are up the front next to the driver.

Taxi
Metered taxis are common in Manila and most major provincial hubs. Flagfall is P40, and a 15-minute trip rarely costs more than P150. Airport taxi flagfall is usually P70.

Most taxi drivers will turn on the meter; if they don't, politely request that they do. If the meter is 'broken' or your taxi driver says the fare is 'up to you', the best strategy is to get out and find another cab (or offer a low-ball price). Rigged taxi meters are also becoming more common, although it must be said that most taxi drivers are honest.

Tricycle
Found in most cities and towns, the tricycle is the Philippine rickshaw – a little, roofed sidecar bolted to a motorcycle. The standard fare for local trips in most provincial towns is P10. Tricycles that wait around in front of malls, restaurants and hotels will attempt to charge five to 10 times that for a 'special trip'. Many towns also have nonmotorised push tricycles, alternately known as pedicabs, *put-put* or *padyak*, for shorter trips.

Habal-habal are essentially motorcycle taxis with extended seats (literally translated as 'pigs copulating', after the level of intimacy attained when sharing a seat with four people). Known as 'singles' in some regions, they function like tricycles, only cheaper. They are most common in the Visayas and northern Mindanao.

Singapore

📞 65 / POP 5.6 MILLION / AREA 719 SQ

Best Places to Eat

➡ Gluttons Bay (p640)

➡ A Noodle Story (p641)

➡ Ah Chiang's (p642)

➡ Hong Kong Soya Sauce Chicken Rice & Noodle (p642)

➡ National Kitchen by Violet Oon (p641)

Top Singlish Phrases

lah Generally an ending for any phrase or sentence; can translate as 'OK', but has no real meaning.

can! 'Yes! That's fine.'

aiyo! 'Oh, dear!'

Why Go?

Singapore is perhaps best known as a transit hub for long-haul flights, a gateway to Asia and a stopover for travellers intent on a shopping spree. However, beyond the transit lounges and shopping malls, Singapore's multicultural pedigree, Chinese, Malay, Indian and Peranakan, provides travellers with a rich milieu in which to explore, experience and savour all the flavours of Southeast Asia.

One of Asia's economic success stories, Singapore consistently ranks as one of the wealthiest countries in the world. Glass skyscrapers may dominate the tiny island and its rooftop bars are world famous, but at ground level pretty heritage shophouses line the riverfront while grand imperial edifices grace the Colonial District. Affluent, high-tech and occasionally a little snobbish, Singapore's great leveller is its steamy and smoky hawker centres. The ubiquitous and raucous food markets where everyone mucks in together to indulge in cheap eating and drinking.

When to Go
Singapore

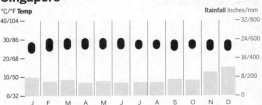

Jan & Feb Chinese New Year and Chingay are the events to catch.

Apr & May Lots of events, and just before the local school holidays start.

Dec The northeast monsoons bring lashing rains, but they also cool Singapore down.

Entering the Country

Singapore is one of Asia's major air hubs, serviced by both full-service and budget airlines. The city state has excellent and extensive regional and international connections. You can also catch trains and buses to Malaysia and Thailand.

NEIGHBOURHOODS AT A GLANCE

The Colonial District and CBD boast a treasure of colonial architecture, museums and parks, nearby Chinatown features hawker stalls and fine-dining restaurants. Fans of futuristic architecture will be wowed by the Marina Bay Sands development with its floating ship-like hotel at Marina Bay. Just next door, marvel at high-tech Gardens by the Bay and its Supertrees and space-like conservatories. The Singapore River weaves through it all, connecting the three quays – Robertson, Clarke and Boat – home to restaurants, clubs and bars.

Self-dubbed 'a city in a garden', Singapore prides itself on its green spaces. Just moments from the glitzy emporia of Orchard Rd, you'll find the ever-peaceful Singapore Botanic Gardens. In Singapore's north are the highly acclaimed Singapore Zoo, River Safari and Night Safari.

Essential Food & Drink

Hainanese chicken rice Tender poached chicken served on a bed of fragrant rice (cooked in chicken stock) with accompanying garlic chilli sauce.

Char kway teow Flat rice noodles wok-fried with bean sprouts, cockles, prawns and Chinese sausage in dark soy sauce and chilli sauce.

Roti prata Fried flour-based pancake served with chicken or fish curry; variations include mushroom, egg and banana.

Nasi padang Steamed white rice served with your choice of meats and vegetables. Lots of curries available.

Fried carrot cake Not a sweet dessert, but steamed rice flour, water and white radish cake stir-fried with eggs and preserved radish. Dark version is cooked in soy sauce.

Top Tips

➡ Buy an EZ-Link card, an electronic travel card accepted on MRT trains, local buses and the Sentosa Express monorail, and by most taxis. Options include one-, two- or three-day 'Singapore Tourist Pass' cards, which offer unlimited travel on buses and trains.

➡ Leave rigorous outdoor activities for early morning or late afternoon to avoid the sweltering midday heat.

➡ Party early: there's no shortage of bars offering good-value happy-hour deals, mostly between 5pm and 8pm or 9pm.

➡ Carry a packet of tissues: you won't find serviettes at hawker centres, use these to save your seat before lining up for food.

AT A GLANCE

Currency Singapore dollar (S$)

Visas Citizens of most countries are granted 90-day entry on arrival.

Money ATMs widely available. Credit cards are accepted in most shops and restaurants.

Language English (primary), Mandarin, Bahasa Malaysia, Tamil

SINGAPORE

Exchange Rates

Australia	A$1	S$1.01
Euro	€1	S$1.56
Malaysia	RM10	S$3.36
UK	UK£1	S$1.77
US	US$1	S$1.33

For current exchange rates, see www.xe.com.

Daily Costs

Budget Less than S$200

Dorm bed S$20-45

Meals at hawker centres & food courts around S$6

One-hour foot reflexology at People's Park Complex S$25

Ticket to a major museum S$6–20

Resources

Lonely Planet (www.lonely planet.com/singapore)

Your Singapore (www.yoursingapore.com)

Honeycombers (www.the honeycombers.com)

City Nomads (www.city nomads.com)

Sistic (www.sistic.com.sg)

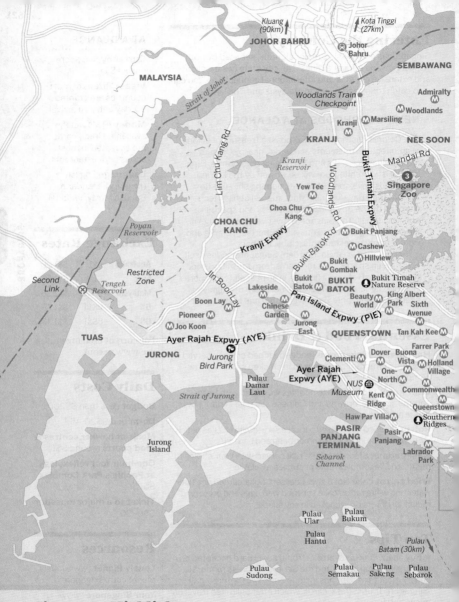

Singapore Highlights

1 **Gardens by the Bay**
(p625) Getting lost in this
futuristic green oasis, where
nature and design collide.

2 **Little India** (p629)
Navigating a jumble of gold,

textiles, temples and cheap
eats.

3 **Singapore Zoo** (p632)
Experiencing one of three
outstanding open-concept
zoos.

4 **National Gallery
Singapore** (p624) Immersing
yourself in Southeast Asian
art.

5 **Sentosa Island** (p633)
Eating, drinking and playing

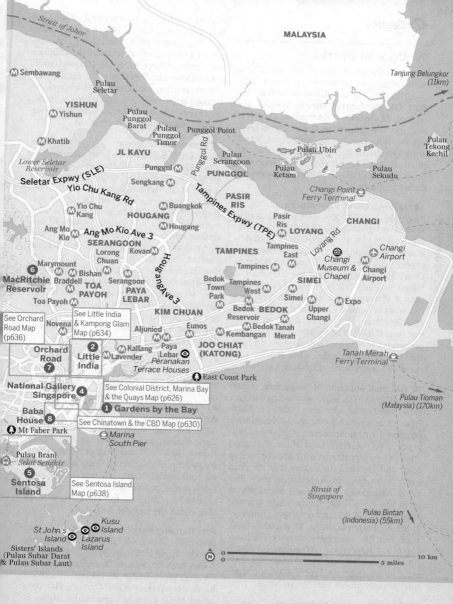

MALAYSIA

Strait of Johor

Tanjung Belungkor
(11km)

Ⓜ Sembawang
Pulau Seletar

YISHUN
Ⓜ Yishun

Pulau
Punggol
Barat

Pulau
Punggol
Timor

Punggol Point

Pulau
Tekong
Kechil

Ⓜ Khatib

JL KAYU

Lower Seletar
Reservoir

Seletar Expwy (SLE)

Ⓜ Punggol

Pulau
Serangoon

Pulau Ubin

Pulau
Ketam

Pulau
Sekudu

Yio Chu Kang Rd

Ⓜ Sengkang

PUNGGOL

Changi Point
Ferry Terminal

Yio Chu
Kang

Ang Mo
Kio

Ang Mo Kio Ave 3

SERANGOON

Lorong
Chuan

Ⓜ Kovan

Ⓜ Buangkok

PASIR
RIS

Pasir
Ris

CHANGI

Ⓜ Hougang

HOUGANG

Tampines Expwy (TPE)

LOYANG

Loyang Rd

Changi
Airport

Ⓜ Marymount

Ⓜ Bishan

Braddell

Ⓜ Serangoon

TAMPINES

Tampines
East

Changi
Museum &
Chapel

Changi
Airport

❻
MacRitchie
Reservoir

TOA
PAYOH

PAYA
LEBAR

Houng Ave 3

Ⓜ Tampines

SIMEI

Ⓜ Toa Payoh

KIM CHUAN

Bedok
Town
Park

Tampines
West

Ⓜ Simei

Ⓜ Expo

Upper
Changi

See Orchard
Road Map
(p636)

Ⓜ Novena

See Little India
& Kampong Glam
Map (p634)

Ⓜ Aljunied

Bedok
Reservoir

BEDOK

Ⓜ Bedok

❷

Ⓜ Eunos

Ⓜ Kembangan

Ⓜ Bedok
Tanah
Merah

Orchard
Road

❼

Little
India

Ⓜ Kallang

Ⓜ Lavender

Paya
Lebar ◉

JOO CHIAT
(KATONG)

Tanah Merah
Ferry Terminal

National Gallery
Singapore

❹

Peranakan
Terrace Houses

See Colonial District, Marina Bay
& the Quays Map (p626)

★ East Coast Park

Baba
House ❽

❶ Gardens by the Bay

Ⓜ Mt Faber Park

See Chinatown & the CBD Map (p630)

Pulau Tioman
(Malaysia) (170km)

◉ Marina
South Pier

Pulau Brani
Selat Sengkir

❺

Sentosa
Island

See Sentosa Island
Map (p638)

Strait of
Singapore

Pulau Bintan
(Indonesia) (55km)

St John's
Island

Kusu
Island

Lazarus
Island

Sisters' Islands
(Pulau Subar Darat
& Pulau Subar Laut)

Ⓝ 0
0

10 km

5 miles

in Singapore's all-ages
playground.

❻ MacRitchie Reservoir
(p632) Getting among nature
on the treetop walk.

❼ Orchard Road (p631)
Shopping, shopping, shopping
at this mesmerising maze of
malls.

❽ Baba House (p629)
Joining the detailed tour
through this gorgeously
restored Peranakan house.

◉ Sights

◎ Colonial District

The Colonial District is where you'll find many imposing remnants of British rule, including the **Victoria Concert Hall & Theatre**, **Old Parliament House** (now an arts centre), **St Andrew's Cathedral**, **City Hall** and the **Old Supreme Court** (now housing the National Gallery Singapore), which are arranged around the **Padang**, a cricket pitch. Rising above them is the spaceship of the Norman Foster–designed **Supreme Court** building.

★ National Gallery Singapore   GALLERY
(Map p626; ☑ 6271 7000; www.nationalgallery.sg; St Andrew's Rd; adult/child S$20/15; ☉ 10am-7pm Sat-Thu, to 9pm Fri; ☎; M City Hall) Connected by a striking aluminium and glass canopy, Singapore's historic City Hall and Old Supreme Court buildings now form the city's breathtaking National Gallery. Its world-class collection of 19th-century and modern Southeast Asian art is housed in two major spaces, the DBS Singapore Gallery and the UOB Southeast Asia Gallery. The former delivers a comprehensive overview of Singaporean art from the 19th century to today, while the latter focuses on the greater Southeast Asian region.

★ National Museum of Singapore   MUSEUM
(Map p626; ☑ 6332 3659; www.nationalmuseum. sg; 93 Stamford Rd; adult/child S$15/10; ☉ 10am-7pm, last admission 6.30pm; ☎; M Dhoby Ghaut, Bencoolen) Imaginative and immersive, Singapore's rebooted National Museum is good enough to warrant two visits. At once cutting edge and classical, the space ditches staid exhibits for lively multimedia galleries that bring Singapore's jam-packed biography to vivid life. It's a colourful, intimate journey, spanning ancient Malay royalty, wartime occupation, nation-building, food and fashion. Look out for interactive artwork *GoHead/ GoStan: Panorama Singapura*, which offers an audiovisual trip through the city-state's many periods. Free guided tours are offered daily; check website for times.

★ Asian Civilisations Museum   MUSEUM
(Map p626; ☑ 6332 7798; www.acm.org.sg; 1 Empress Pl; adult/child under 6yr S$20/free, 7-9pm Fri half price; ☉ 10am-7pm Sat-Thu, to 9pm Fri; M Raffles Place, City Hall) This remarkable museum houses the region's most comprehensive collection of pan-Asian treasures. Its galleries

explore the history, cultures and religions of Southeast Asia, China, the Asian subcontinent and Islamic West Asia. Having just completed a radical transformation, the galleries are curated to emphasise the cross-cultural connections developed due to Singapore's history as a port city. The Tang Shipwreck exhibition showcases over 500 pieces of recovered booty – look out for the Chinese bronze mirrors, one is over 1000 years old.

★ Peranakan Museum   MUSEUM
(Map p626; ☑ 6332 7591; www.peranakanmuseum. org.sg; 39 Armenian St; adult/student & child under 7yr S$10/6, 7-9pm Fri half price; ☉ 10am-7pm, to 9pm Fri; M City Hall, Bras Basah) This is the best spot to explore the rich heritage of the Peranakans (Straits Chinese descendants). Thematic galleries cover various aspects of Peranakan culture, from the traditional 12-day wedding ceremony to crafts, spirituality and feasting. Note the intricately detailed ceremonial costumes and beadwork, beautifully carved wedding beds and rare dining porcelain. An especially curious example of Peranakan fusion culture is a pair of Victorian bell jars in which statues of Christ and the Madonna are adorned with Chinese-style flowers and vines.

Raffles Hotel   NOTABLE BUILDING
(Map p626; ☑ 6337 1886; www.raffleshotel.com; 1 Beach Rd; M City Hall, Esplanade) Although its resplendent lobby is only accessible to hotel guests, Singapore's most iconic slumber palace is worth a quick visit for its magnificent ivory frontage, famous Sikh doorman and lush, hushed tropical grounds. The hotel started life in 1887 as a modest 10-room bungalow fronting the beach (long gone thanks to land reclamation). It was undergoing renovations at the time of research which should be completed by the time you read this: check the website for details.

Fort Canning Park   PARK
(Map p626; ☑ 1800 471 7300; www.nparks.gov.sg; bounded by Hill St, Canning Rise, Clemenceau Ave & River Valley Rd; M Dhoby Ghaut, Clarke Quay, Fort Canning) When Raffles rolled into Singapore, locals steered clear of Fort Canning Hill, then called Bukit Larangan (Forbidden Hill) out of respect for the sacred shrine of Sultan Iskandar Shah, ancient Singapura's last ruler. Today, the hill is better known as Fort Canning Park, a lush retreat from the hot streets below. Take a stroll in the shade of truly enormous trees, amble through the spice garden

or ponder Singapore's wartime defeat at the **Battlebox Museum** (Map p626; ☑ 6338 6133; www.battlebox.com.sg; 2 Cox Tce; adult/child 7-12 yrs S\$18/9, not suitable for under 6 yrs; ☺ tours 1.30pm, 2.45pm & 4pm Mon, 9.45am, 11am, 1.30pm, 2.45pm & 4pm Tue-Sun; Ⓜ Dhoby Ghaut).

Singapore Art Museum   MUSEUM
(SAM; Map p626; ☑ 6589 9580; www.singaporeart-museum.sg; 71 Bras Basah Rd; Ⓜ Bras Basah, Bencoolen) Formerly the St Joseph's Institution – a Catholic boys school – SAM now sings the praises of contemporary Southeast Asian art. Currently undergoing a S\$90 million facelift, the museum's renovation is due for completion in 2021. The new, much larger space will house the museum's permanent collection as well as pieces from private collections: from painting and sculpture to video art and site-specific installations.

Around the corner from the museum is its younger sibling, **8Q SAM** (Map p626; ☑ 6589 9580; www.singaporeartmuseum.sg; 8 Queen St; adult/student & senior S\$6/3, 6-9pm Fri free; ☺ 10am-7pm Sat-Thu, to 9pm Fri; Ⓜ Bras Basah, Bencoolen), which will remain open during the revamp works.

◉ Marina Bay & the Quays

South of the Colonial District lies Marina Bay, Singapore's glittering new financial district and home to the now-iconic Marina Bay Sands and Gardens by the Bay.

★ Gardens by the Bay   GARDENS
(☑ 6420 6848; www.gardensbythebay.com.sg; 18 Marina Gardens Dr; gardens free, conservatories adult/child under 13yr S\$28/15, OCBC Skyway adult/child under 13yr S\$8/5; ☺ 5am-2am, conservatories & OCBC Skyway 9am-9pm, last ticket sale 8pm; 🛜; Ⓜ Bayfront) Singapore's 21st-century botanic garden is a S\$1 billion, 101 hectare fantasy land of space-age biodomes, high-tech Supertrees and whimsical sculptures. The Flower Dome replicates the dry Mediterranean climates found across the world, while the even more astounding Cloud Forest is a tropical montane affair, complete with waterfall. Connecting two of the Supertrees is the OCBC Skyway, with knockout views of the gardens, city and South China Sea. At 7.45pm and 8.45pm the Supertrees twinkle and glow for the spectacular Garden Rhapsody show.

★ Marina Bay Sands   AREA
(Map p626; www.marinabaysands.com; 10 Bayfront Ave, Marina Bay; 🛜; Ⓜ Bayfront) Designed by Israeli-born architect Moshe Safdie, Marina Bay Sands is a sprawling hotel, casino, mall, theatre, exhibition and museum complex. Star of the show is the **Marina Bay Sands hotel** (Map p626; ☑ 6688 8888; www.marinabaysands.com; 10 Bayfront Ave; r from S\$550; ✳@🛜🌊; Ⓜ Bayfront), its three 55-storey towers connected by a cantilevered **SkyPark** (Map p626; ☑ 6688 8826; www.marinabaysands.com/sands-skypark; Level 57, Marina Bay Sands Hotel Tower 3, 10 Bayfront Ave; adult/child under 13yr S\$23/17; ☺ 9.30am-10pm Mon-Thu, to 11pm Fri-Sun; Ⓜ Bayfront). Head up for a drink and stellar views at CÉ LA VI (p646), before catching a show at the MasterCard Theatres or doing serious damage to your credit card at the **Shoppes** (Map p626; ☑ 6688 8868; www.marinabaysands.com; 10 Bayfront Ave; ☺ 10.30am-11pm Sun-Thu, to 11.30pm Fri & Sat; 🛜; Ⓜ Bayfront).

Clarke Quay   AREA
(Map p626; 🛜; Ⓜ Clarke Quay, Fort Canning) Named after Singapore's second colonial governor, Sir Andrew Clarke, this is the busiest and most popular of Singapore's three quays. How much time you spend in its plethora of bars, restaurants and clubs depends upon your taste in aesthetics. This is Singapore at its most hyper-touristy, a kitsch, pastel-coloured sprawl of mostly run-of-the-mill eateries and lad-and-ladette drinking holes.

Boat Quay   AREA
(Map p626; Ⓜ Raffles Place, Clarke Quay) Closest to the river mouth, this was once Singapore's centre of commerce, and it remained an important economic area into the 1960s. By the mid-1980s many of the shophouses were in ruins, businesses having shifted to

---

SINGAPORE ON THE CHEAP

➡ Stick to eating at hawker centres or food courts.

➡ If you drink at a bar, go during happy hour (for discounted booze or one-for-one specials).

➡ To cool off, dive into one of Singapore's impressive public pools.

➡ Pack a picnic and spend a day at the beach in East Coast Park (p632) or Sentosa.

➡ Hike in Bukit Timah Nature Reserve (p632), around the MacRitchie Reservoir (p632) or along the Southern Ridges (p633).

Colonial District, Marina Bay & the Quays

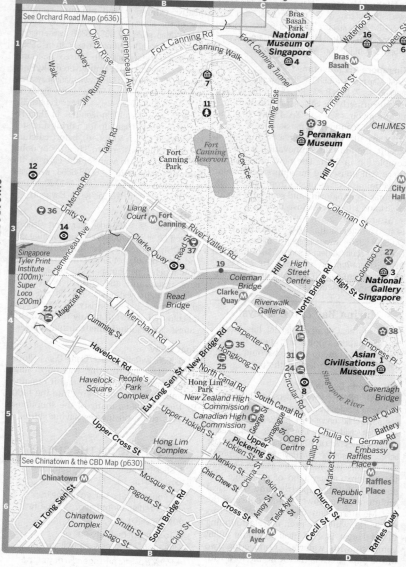

SINGAPORE SIGHTS

See Orchard Road Map (p636)

See Chinatown & the CBD Map (p630)

Bras Basah Park
National Museum of Singapore 4

CHIJMES

5 **Peranakan Museum**

City Hall

National Gallery Singapore 3

Asian Civilisations Museum 1

Fort Canning Park

Fort Canning Reservoir

Fort Canning

Liang Court

Clarke Quay

Coleman Bridge

Read Bridge

Riverwalk Galleria

Coleman Street

High Street Centre

Singapore Tyler Print Institute (100m); Super Loco (200m)

Havelock Square

People's Park Complex

Hong Lim Park

Hong Lim Complex

New Zealand High Commission

Canadian High Commission

Upper Pickering St

OCBC Centre

Boat Quay

Cavenagh Bridge

Empress Pl

Raffles Place

Republic Plaza

Chinatown Complex

Telok Ayer

German Embassy

---

high-tech cargo centres elsewhere on the island. Declared a conservation zone by the government, the area is now crammed with pubs, touristy eateries and persistent restaurant touts.

Robertson Quay

AREA

(Map p626; M Clarke Quay, Fort Canning) The most remote and least visited of the quays, Robertson Quay is home to some of the best eateries and bars along the river, including Mexican 'It kid' **Super Loco** (✆6235 8900;

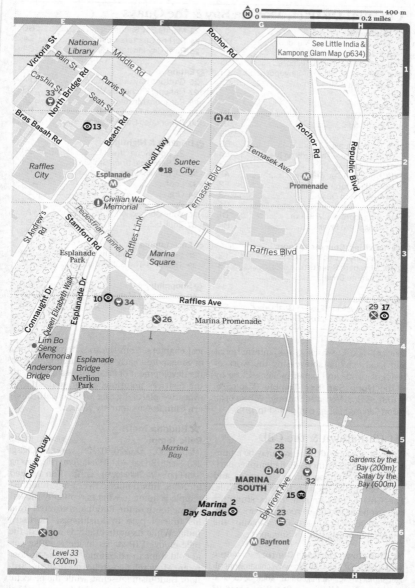

SINGAPORE SIGHTS

www.super-loco.com; 01-13, 60 Robertson Quay; tacos S$8-12, quesadillas S$14-16; ⊙ 5-10.30pm Mon-Thu, to 11pm Fri, 10am-3.30pm & 5-11pm Sat, to 10pm Sun; M Fort Canning) and well-priced wine bar **Wine Connection** (Map p626; ☑ 6235 5466; www.wineconnection.com.sg; 01-

19/20 Robertson Walk, 11 Unity St; ⊙ 11.30am-2am Mon-Thu, to 3am Fri & Sat, 11.30am-11pm Sun; 🛜; M Fort Canning). The precinct is also home to the **Singapore Tyler Print Institute** (STPI; ☑ 6336 3663; www.stpi.com.sg; 41 Robertson Quay; ⊙ 10am-7pm Mon-Fri, 9am-6pm Sat; M Fort

Colonial District, Marina Bay & the Quays

Canning) **FREE**, which hosts international and local exhibits showcasing the work of resident print- and paper-makers. Close by is the **Hong San See Temple** (Map p626; ☑ 6737 3683; 31 Mohamed Sultan Rd; ☉ 8am-6pm; Ⓜ Fort Canning) **FREE**, completed in 1913.

⊙ Chinatown & the CBD

While Singapore's Chinatown may be a tamer version of its former self, its temples, heritage centre, and booming restaurant and bar scene make the trip there worthwhile. The CBD is best known for its stunning, ever-evolving skyline: rooftop bars jostle with old-school temples, all set against the financial heart that funds Singapore.

★**Chinatown Heritage Centre**   MUSEUM
(Map p630; ☑ 6224 3928; www.chinatownheritagecentre.com.sg; 48 Pagoda St; adult S$15, child under 13yr/7yr S$11/free; ☉ 9am-8pm, closed 1st Mon of month; Ⓜ Chinatown) Delve into Chinatown's gritty, cacophonous backstory at the recently revamped Chinatown Heritage Centre. Occupying several levels of a converted shophouse, it holds interactive exhibitions that shed light on numerous histor-

ical chapters, from the treacherous journey of Singapore's early Chinese immigrants to the development of local clan associations to the district's notorious opium dens. It's an evocative place, digging well beneath modern Chinatown's touristy veneer.

★**Buddha Tooth
Relic Temple**   BUDDHIST TEMPLE
(Map p630; ☑ 6220 0220; www.btrts.org.sg; 288 South Bridge Rd; ☉ 7am-7pm, relic viewing 9am-6pm; Ⓜ Chinatown) **FREE** Consecrated in 2008, this hulking, five-storey Buddhist temple is home to what is reputedly the left canine tooth of the Buddha, recovered from his funeral pyre in Kushinagar, northern India. While its authenticity is debated, the relic enjoys VIP status inside a 420kg solid-gold stupa in a dazzlingly ornate 4th-floor room. More religious relics await at the 3rd-floor Buddhism museum, while the peaceful rooftop garden features a huge prayer wheel inside the Ten Thousand Buddhas Pagoda.

★**Thian Hock Keng Mural**   PUBLIC ART
(Map p630; www.yipyc.com; Amoy St; Ⓜ Telok Ayer) Spanning 44m, this mural, painted by Singaporean artist Yip Yew Chong (accountant by

weekday, artist by weekend), tells the story of Singapore's early Hokkien immigrants. You'll find it on the outside rear wall of the **Thian Hock Keng Temple**; start from the right end and follow the immigrants' story, from leaving China to arriving in Singapore, and the sacrifices, hardships and joys they experienced along the way. Discover the mural's hidden secrets via the LocoMole app: instructions are on the far left of the mural.

Baba House MUSEUM
(Map p630; ✆ 6227 5731; http://babahouse.nus. edu.sg; 157 Neil Rd; S$10, children must be 12yrs and above; ⏰ 1hr tour 10am Tue-Fri, self-guided tour 1.30pm, 2.15pm, 3.15pm & 4pm Sat; Ⓜ Outram Park) Baba House is one of Singapore's best-preserved Peranakan heritage homes. Built in the 1890s, it's a wonderful window into the life of an affluent Peranakan family living in Singapore a century ago. Its loving restoration has seen every detail attended to, from the carved motifs on the blue facade down to the door screens. The only way in is on one of the excellent guided tours, held daily Tuesday through Friday, or via a self-guided tour on Saturdays. The guided tour is best. Bookings, by telephone, are essential.

Sri Mariamman Temple HINDU TEMPLE
(Map p630; ✆ 6223 4064; www.smt.org.sg; 244 South Bridge Rd; take photos/videos S$3/6; ⏰ 5.30am-noon & 6-9pm; Ⓜ Chinatown) FREE Paradoxically in the middle of Chinatown, this is the oldest Hindu temple in Singapore, originally built in 1823, then rebuilt in 1843. You can't miss the fabulously animated, Technicolor 1930s *gopuram* (tower) above the entrance, the key to the temple's South Indian Dravidian style. Sacred cow sculptures grace the boundary walls, while the *gopuram* is covered in kitsch plasterwork images of Brahma the creator, Vishnu the preserver and Shiva the destroyer.

◉ **Little India & Kampong Glam**

Little India bursts with vibrancy. This is a world where goods crowd the five-foot ways (covered pedestrian walkways), shophouses are all the colours of crayons and men in *dhotis* (loincloths) gossip over authentic *dosa* (paper-thin lentil-flour pancakes) at the marketplace. After soaking up the atmosphere of its bustling temples, walk 15 minutes southeast and you'll hit calmer Kampong Glam with its beautiful mosques and many-hued shophouses.

★**Indian Heritage Centre** MUSEUM
(Map p634; ✆ 6291 1601; www.indianheritage.org. sg; 5 Campbell Lane; adult/child under 6yr S$6/ free; ⏰ 10am-7pm Tue-Thu, to 8pm Fri & Sat, to 4pm Sun; Ⓜ Little India, Jalan Besar) Delve into the heritage of Singapore's Indian community at this showpiece museum. Divided into five themes, its hundreds of historical and cultural artefacts explore everything from early interactions between South Asia and Southeast Asia to Indian cultural traditions and the contributions of Indian Singaporeans to the development of the island nation. Among the more extraordinary objects is a 19th-century Chettinad doorway, intricately adorned with 5000 minute carvings.

★**Sultan Mosque** MOSQUE
(Map p634; ✆ 6293 4405; www.sultanmosque. sg; 3 Muscat St; ⏰ 10am-noon & 2-4pm Sat-Thu, 2.30-4pm Fri; Ⓜ Bugis) FREE Seemingly pulled from the pages of the *Arabian Nights,* Singapore's largest mosque is nothing short of enchanting, designed in the Saracenic style and topped by a golden dome. It was originally built in 1825 with the aid of a grant from Raffles and the East India Company, after Raffles' treaty with the sultan of Singapore allowed the Malay leader to retain sovereignty over the area. In 1928 the original mosque was replaced by the present magnificent building, designed by an Irish architect.

Sri Veeramakaliamman Temple HINDU TEMPLE
(Map p634; ✆ 6295 4538; www.sriveeramakaliamman.com; 141 Serangoon Rd; ⏰ 5.30am-12.30pm & 4-9.30pm; Ⓜ Little India, Jalan Besar) FREE Little India's most colourful, visually stunning temple is dedicated to the ferocious goddess Kali, depicted wearing a garland of skulls, ripping out the insides of her victims, and sharing more tranquil family moments with her sons Ganesh and Murugan. The bloodthirsty consort of Shiva has always been popular in Bengal, the birthplace of the labourers who built the structure in 1881. The temple is at its most evocative during each of the four daily *puja* (prayer) sessions.

Malay Heritage Centre MUSEUM
(Map p634; ✆ 6391 0450; www.malayheritage. org.sg; 85 Sultan Gate; adult/child under 6yr $6/ free; ⏰ 10am-6pm Tue-Sun; Ⓜ Bugis) The Kampong Glam area is the historic seat of Malay royalty, resident here before the arrival of Raffles, and the *istana* (palace) on this site was built for the last sultan of Singapore, Ali Iskander Shah, between 1836 and 1843. It's

SINGAPORE SIGHTS

Chinatown & the CBD

See Colonial District,
Marina Bay &
the Quays Map (p626)

400 m
0.2 miles

MARINA SOUTH

Raffles Place

Ocean Financial Centre

Republic Plaza

Singapore International Chamber of Commerce

Robinson Rd

Market St

Market St

Church St

China Square Food Court

Cross St

Raffles Quay

Maxwell Link

Robinson Rd

Cecil St

Stanley St

Boon Tat St

Telok Ayer St

McCallum St

Treasury Building

Choon Guan St

International Plaza

Tanjong Pagar

Wallich St

Peck Seah St

Maxwell Rd

URA Centre

Ann Siang Rd

Kadayanallur St

Erskine Rd

Murray St

Duxton Hill

Tanjong Pagar Rd

Craig Rd

Yan Kit Rd

Tanjong Pagar Plaza

Cantonment Rd

Neil Rd

Asia Gardens

Everton Park

Singapore (350m)

New Bridge Rd

Eu Tong Sen St

Bukit Pasoh Rd

Kreta Ayer Rd

Teck Lim Rd

Keong Saik Rd

Banda St

Sago Ln

Trengganu St

Smith St

Temple St

Pagoda St

Mosque St

Sago St

Buddha Tooth Relic Temple

Chinatown Heritage Centre

Chinatown

Thian Hock Keng

Mural by Yip Yew Chong

Telok Ayer

Far East Square

Pekin St

China St

Nankin St

Chin Chew St

Upper Cross St

Amoy St

Telok Ayer St

Hong Lim Complex

South Bridge Rd

Chin Swee Rd

Outram Park

Pearl's Hill City Park

Pearl's Centre

Pearl Bank

Outram Rd

Outram Park

Eu Tong Sen St

New Bridge Rd

Second Hospital Ave

Third Hospital Ave

Singapore General

Outram Park

COO (200m);
Ah Chiang's (375m)

Raffles Place

Church St

now a museum, its recently revamped galleries exploring Malay-Singaporean culture and history, from the early migration of traders to Kampong Glam to the development of Malay-Singaporean film, theatre, music and publishing.

⊙ Orchard Road

No one visits Orchard Rd for the sights alone, though the Christmas-light displays are breathtaking. The only major historical site is the President's digs, the **Istana** (Map p636; www.istana.gov.sg; Orchard Rd; Ⓜ Dhoby Ghaut), but it's only open on select public holidays; check the website for details.

★ **Singapore Botanic Gardens** GARDENS
(📞 1800 471 7300; www.sbg.org.sg; 1 Cluny Rd; ⊙ 5am–midnight; 🚌 7, 75, 77, 105, 106, 123, 174, Ⓜ Botanic Gardens) FREE Singapore's 74-hectare botanic wonderland is a Unesco World Heritage Site and one of the city's most arresting attractions. Established in 1860, it's a tropical Valhalla peppered with glassy lakes, rolling lawns and themed gardens. The site is home to the National Orchid Garden (adult/child under 12 years S$5/free; 8.30am to 7pm, last entry 6pm), as well as a rare patch of dense primeval rainforest. The latter is home to over 300 species of vegetation, over half of which are now (sadly) considered rare in Singapore.

★ **ION Sky** VIEWPOINT
(Map p636; 📞 6238 8228; www.ionorchard.com/en/ion-sky.html; Level 56, ION Orchard, 2 Orchard Turn; ⊙ 2-8.30pm; Ⓜ Orchard) FREE Observation deck on Level 56 of the ION Orchard complex. Last entry 5.30pm.

Emerald Hill Road ARCHITECTURE
(Map p636; Emerald Hill Rd; Ⓜ Somerset) Take time out from your shopping to wander up frangipani-scented Emerald Hill Rd, graced with some of Singapore's finest terrace houses. Special mentions go to No 56 (one of the earliest buildings here, built in 1902), Nos 39 to 45 (unusually wide frontages and a grand Chinese-style entrance gate), and Nos 120 to 130 (art deco features dating from around 1925). At the Orchard Rd end of the hill is a cluster of popular bars housed in fetching shophouse renovations.

⊙ Eastern Singapore

While most people head to Geylang to eat, this gritty suburb is actually home to Singapore's highest concentration of heritage-listed shophouses, so it's worth arriving before nightfall to check them out. You'll find more in Joo Chiat (Katong), as well as some cool street art, while in Changi it's all about the poignant Changi Museum & Chapel.

★ **Peranakan Terrace Houses**   AREA
(Koon Seng Rd and Joo Chiat Pl; 🚌 10, 14, 16, 32)
Just off Joo Chiat Rd, Koon Seng Rd and Joo
Chiat Pl feature Singapore's most extraordinary Peranakan terrace houses, joyously
decorated with stucco dragons, birds, crabs
and brilliantly glazed tiles. *Pintu pagar*
(swinging doors) at the front of the houses
are a typical feature, allowing cross breezes
while retaining privacy. Those on Koon Seng
Rd are located between Joo Chiat and Tembeling Rds, while those on Joo Chiat Pl run
between Everitt and Mangis Rds.

★ **Changi Museum & Chapel**   MUSEUM
(🖉 6214 2451; www.changimuseum.sg; 1000 Upper Changi Rd N; audio guide adult/child S$8/4;
⊙ 9.30am-5pm, last entry 4.30pm; 🚌 2) **FREE**
The Changi Museum and Chapel poignantly
commemorates the WWII Allied POWs who
suffered horrific treatment at the hands of
the invading Japanese. The museum includes full-size replicas of the famous Changi
Murals painted by POW Stanley Warren in
the old POW hospital, and a replica of the
original Changi Chapel built by inmates as
a focus for worship and sign of solidarity.
Tours run daily at 9.45am, 11am, 1pm, 2pm
and 3pm, but are subject to availability.

East Coast Park   PARK
(🖉 1800 471 7300; www.nparks.gov.sg; 🚌 36, 43,
48, 196, 197, 401) This 15km stretch of seafront
park is where Singaporeans come to swim,
windsurf, wakeboard, kayak, picnic, bicycle,
in-line skate, skateboard and – of course
– eat. You'll find swaying coconut palms,
patches of bushland, a lagoon, sea-sports
clubs, and some excellent eateries. Renting
a bike, enjoying the sea breezes, watching
the veritable city of container ships out in
the strait, and capping it all off with a beachfront meal is one of the most pleasant ways
to spend a Singapore afternoon.

◉ Northern & Central Singapore

★ **Singapore Zoo**   ZOO
(🖉 6269 3411; www.wrs.com.sg; 80 Mandai Lake
Rd; adult/child under 13yr S$33/22; ⊙ 8.30am-
6pm; 🛜; 🚌 138) The line between zoo and botanic oasis blurs at this pulse-slowing sweep
of spacious, naturalistic enclosures and interactive attractions. Get up close to orangutans, dodge Malaysian flying foxes, even
snoop around a replica African village. Then
there's *that* setting: 26 soothing hectares on
a lush peninsula jutting out into the waters
of the Upper Seletar Reservoir.

★ **Night Safari**   ZOO
(🖉 6269 3411; www.wrs.com.sg; 80 Mandai Lake Rd;
adult/child under 13yr S$47/31; ⊙ 7.15pm-midnight;
🛜; 🚌 138) Electric trams glide past over 130
species, including tigers and elephants, with
more docile creatures often passing within
centimetres of the trams. Walking trails lead
to enclosures inaccessible by tram, though
sighting the animals can be a little hit-and-
miss. (In truth, many are better seen at
neighbouring Singapore Zoo.) If you've got
kids in tow, the 20-minute **Creatures of the
Night** (🖉 6269 3411; www.wrs.com.sg; Night Safari;
⊙ 7.15pm, 8.30pm & 9.30pm Sun-Thu, plus 10.30pm
Fri & Sat; 🚌 138) show will thrill. Admission is
timed and later slots are less crowded; last
entry is at 11.15pm. Restaurants, shops and
ticket counter open at 5.30pm.

★ **MacRitchie Reservoir**   NATURE RESERVE
(🖉 1800 471 7300; www.nparks.gov.sg; Lornie Rd;
🚌 130, 132, 162, 166, 167, 980) MacRitchie Reservoir makes for a calming, evocative jungle
escape. Walking trails skirt the water's edge
and snake through the mature secondary
rainforest spotted with long-tailed macaques
and huge monitor lizards. You can rent kayaks at the **Paddle Lodge** (🖉 6258 0057; www.
scf.org.sg; per hr from S$15; ⊙ 9am-noon & 2-6pm;
🚌 130, 132, 162, 166, 167, 980), but the standout is
the excellent 11km walking trail – and its various well-signposted offshoots. Aim for the
TreeTop Walk (🖉 1800 471 7300; www.nparks.
gov.sg; ⊙ 9am-5pm Tue-Fri, 8.30am-5pm Sat & Sun;
🚌 130, 132, 162, 166, 167, 980), the highlight of
which is traversing a 250m-long suspension
bridge, perched 25m up in the forest canopy.

River Safari   ZOO
(🖉 6269 3411; www.wrs.com.sg; 80 Mandai Lake Rd;
adult/child under 13yr S$32/21; ⊙ 10am-7pm; 🛜;
🚌 138) This wildlife park re-creates the habitats of numerous world-famous rivers, including the Yangtze, Nile and Congo. While most
are underwhelming, the Mekong River and
Amazon Flooded Forest exhibits are impressive, their epic aquariums rippling with giant
catfish and stingrays, electric eels, red-bellied
piranhas, manatees and sea cows. Another
highlight is the Giant Panda Forest enclosure,
home to rare red pandas and the park's famous black-and-whiters, KaiKai and JiaJia.

Bukit Timah Nature Reserve   NATURE RESERVE
(🖉 1800 471 7300; www.nparks.gov.sg; end of
Hindhede Dr; ⊙ 7am-7pm; Ⓜ Beauty World) Singapore's steamy Bukit Timah Nature Reserve
is a 163-hectare tract of primary rainforest

clinging to Singapore's highest peak, Bukit Timah (163m). The reserve holds more tree species than the entire North American continent, and its unbroken forest canopy shelters what remains of Singapore's native wildlife, including long-tailed macaques (monkeys), pythons and dozens of bird species. The recently revamped visitors centre (8.30am to 5pm) showcases the area's flora and fauna, including two Sumatran tigers who once roamed Singapore.

◉ Southern & Western Singapore

For a beautiful view, walk up 116m **Mt Faber** (🕿 1800 471 7300; www.nparks.gov.sg; Mt Faber Rd; ☺ 24hr; 🚇 Mt Faber), then catch the **cable car** (🕿 6377 9688; www.onefabergroup.com; adult/child return S$33/22; ☺ 8.45am-9.30pm; 🚇 HarbourFront) to the Harbour Front Centre or across to Sentosa Island. Mt Faber is connected to Kent Ridge Park via Telok Blangah Park and Hort Park in a 9km-long chain known as the **Southern Ridges** (🕿 1800 471 7300; www.nparks.gov.sg; ☺ 24hr; 🚇 Pasir Panjang), arguably Singapore's best walking trail. The walk takes visitors along shady forested paths and across amazing bridges that pass through the forest canopy.

Jurong Bird Park   BIRD SANCTUARY
(🕿 6269 3411; www.wrs.com.sg; 2 Jurong Hill; adult/child under 13yr S$30/20; ☺ 8.30am-6pm; 🚌 194) Home to some 400 species of feathered friends – including spectacular macaws – Jurong is a great place for young kids. Highlights include the wonderful Lory Loft forest enclosure, where you can feed colourful lories and lorikeets, and the interactive High Flyers (11am and 3pm) and Kings of the Skies (10am and 4pm). We must note, however, that some birds are made to perform for humans, which is discouraged by animal-welfare groups. The park is set to relocate to Mandai by 2020.

Gillman Barracks   GALLERY
(www.gillmanbarracks.com; 9 Lock Rd; ☺ 11am-7pm Tue-Sun; 🚇 Labrador Park) FREE Built in 1936 as a British military encampment, Gillman Barracks is now a rambling art outpost with 11 galleries scattered around verdant grounds. Among these is New York's **Sundaram Tagore** (🕿 6694 3378; www.sundaramtagore.com; 01-05, 5 Lock Rd, Gillman Barracks; ☺ 11am-7pm Tue-Sat; 🚇 Labrador Park) FREE, whose stable of artists includes award-winning photographers Edward Burtynsky and Annie Leibovitz. Also on site is the **NTU Centre for Contemporary Art** (🕿 6339 6503; www.ntu.ccasingapore.

org; Block 43, Malan Rd, Gillman Barracks; ☺ noon-7pm Tue-Thu, Sat & Sun, noon-9pm Fri; 🚇 Labrador Park) FREE, a forward-thinking art-research centre hosting art talks, lectures and contemporary exhibitions from dynamic regional and international artists working in a variety of media. Individual gallery hours vary.

NUS Museum   MUSEUM
(🕿 6516 8817; www.museum.nus.edu.sg; National University of Singapore, 50 Kent Ridge Cres; ☺ 10am-6pm Tue-Sat; 🚌 96) FREE Located on the lush campus of the NUS, this museum is one of the city's lesser-known cultural delights. Ancient Chinese ceramics and bronzes, as well as archaeological fragments found in Singapore, dominate the ground-floor Lee Kong Chian Collection; one floor up, the South and Southeast Asian Gallery showcases paintings, sculpture and textiles from the region. The Ng Eng Teng Collection is dedicated to Ng Eng Teng (1934–2001), Singapore's foremost modern artist, best known for his figurative sculptures.

◉ Sentosa Island

Sentosa's sights might be human-made, but that doesn't make them any less fun. Unleash your inner child (or your actual kids) at the amusement parks, spend a day at the beach (or in a bar beside one) or get a dose of history at Fort Siloso.

★ SEA Aquarium   AQUARIUM
(Map p638; 🕿 6577 8888; www.rwsentosa.com; Resorts World, 8 Sentosa Gateway; adult/child under 13yr S$39/29; ☺ 10am-7pm; Waterfront) You'll be gawking at more than 800 species of aquatic creatures at Singapore's impressive, sprawling aquarium. The state-of-the-art complex recreates 49 aquatic habitats found between Southeast Asia, Australia and Africa. The Open Ocean habitat is especially spectacular, its 36m-long, 8.3m-high viewing panel one of the world's largest. The complex is also home to an interactive, family-friendly exhibition exploring the history of the maritime Silk Route.

★ Universal Studios   AMUSEMENT PARK
(Map p638; 🕿 6577 8888; www.rwsentosa.com; Resorts World, 8 Sentosa Gateway; adult/child under 13yr S$76/56; ☺ 10am-6pm; 🕿; Waterfront) Universal Studios is the top draw at Resorts World. Shops, shows, restaurants, rides and roller coasters are all neatly packaged into fantasy-world themes based on blockbuster Hollywood films. Top attractions include

Little India & Kampong Glam

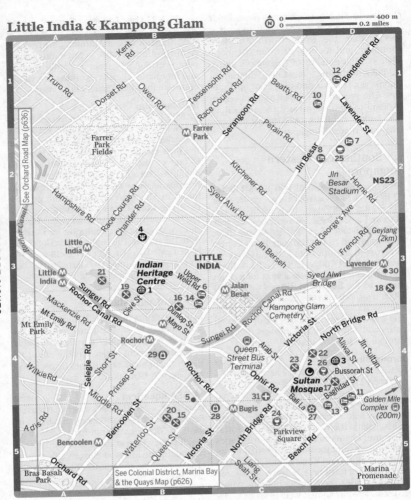

See Orchard Road Map (p636)

See Colonial District, Marina Bay & the Quays Map (p626)

SINGAPORE SIGHTS

Transformers: The Ride, a next-generation thrill ride deploying 3D animation, and Battlestar Galactica: Human vs Cylon, the world's tallest duelling roller coasters. Opening times are subject to slight variations across the year, so always check the website before heading in.

Pulau Ubin

A rural, unkempt expanse of jungle full of fast-moving lizards, strange shrines and a cacophony of bird life. Tin-roofed buildings bake in the sun, chickens squawk and panting dogs slump in the dust, while in the for-est, families of wild pigs run for cover as visitors pedal past on squeaky rented bicycles. Get to Tanah Merah MRT, then take bus 2 to Changi Village Ferry Terminal. There boats depart for the island (one way S$3, 10 minutes, sunrise to sunset) whenever there are 12 people aboard.

Southern Islands

Three other islands popular with castaway-fantasising locals are **St John's** (☎ 6323 9829; www.sla.gov.sg/Islands; ☐ Singapore Island Cruises), **Lazarus** and **Kusu**. They're quiet and great

Little India & Kampong Glam

for fishing, swimming and picnicking. The islands have changing rooms and toilets. Kusu Island is culturally interesting; devotees come to pray for health, wealth and fertility at its Taoist temple and Malay *kramat* (shrine). There's nowhere to buy food or drink on any of the islands, so come prepared. Catch a ferry from the **Marina South Pier** (www.mpa.gov.sg; 31 Marina Coastal Dr; Ⓜ Marina South Pier).

🏃 Activities

Singapore is jam-packed with fun and exciting things to do. Stretch your legs discovering the island's green spaces, shopping strips and beaches or, if adrenaline-pumping rides are more your thing, head straight to Sentosa. For those looking to slow things down, book in for a day of pampering at a luxury spa or head to one of the excellent local pools.

Wave House   SURFING
(Map p638; ☑ 6238 1196; www.wavehousesentosa. com; 36 Siloso Beach Walk; admission from S$30; ⊙ 11.30am-9.30pm Mon-Fri, from 10.30am Sat & Sun; 🚌 Siloso Beach) Two specially designed wave pools allow surfer types to practise their gashes and cutbacks at ever-popular

Wave House. The non-curling Double Flow-rider (30-minute session S$30) is good for beginners, while the 3m FlowBarrel (one-hour session from S$35) is more challenging. Wave House also includes beachside eating and drinking options.

Ultimate Drive   ADVENTURE SPORTS
(Map p626; ☑ 6688 7997; www.ultimatedrive.com; Tower 3, 01-14 Marina Bay Sands Hotel, 10 Bayfront Ave; ride as driver/passenger from S$375/300; ⊙ 9am-10pm; Ⓜ Bayfront) Dress to kill, then make a show of getting into a Ferrari California (red), Lamborghini Gallardo Spyder (orange) or McLaren MP4-12 (white) before tearing out for a spin. A taste of luxury can be yours, if only for 15 to 60 minutes. One can dream, right? Rides also depart from Suntec City (p637) at the convention centre entrance (01-K27) between 10am and 8pm.

🍴 Courses

Food Playground   COOKING
(Map p630; ☑ 9452 3669; www.foodplayground. com.sg; 24A Sago St; 3hr class from S$119; ⊙ 9.30am-12.30pm Mon-Fri; Ⓜ Chinatown) You've been gorging on Singapore's famous food, so why not learn to make it? This

Orchard Road

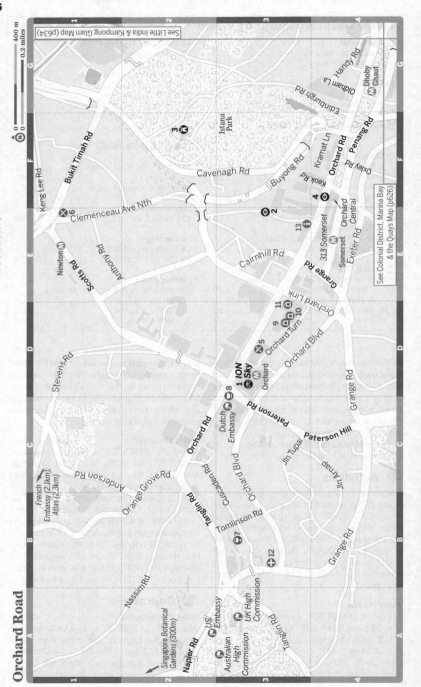

See Little India & Kampong Glam Map (p634)

400 m
0.2 miles

N

SINGAPORE

Istana Park

Handy Rd

Oldham La

Dhoby Ghaut

Edinburgh Rd

Penang Rd

Orchard Rd

Bukit Timah Rd

Kramat Ln

Keok Rd

Oxley Rd

Cavenagh Rd

Buyong Rd

Keng Lee Rd

Clemenceau Ave Nth

313 Somerset

Orchard Central

Somerset

Exeter Rd

See Colonial District, Marina Bay & the Quays Map (p626)

Cairnhill Rd

Grange Rd

Newton

Scotts Rd

Anthony Rd

Orchard Link

Stevens Rd

Orchard Turn

Orchard Blvd

ION Sky

Orchard

Grange Rd

Dutch Embassy

Paterson Rd

Paterson Hill

Orchard Rd

Cuscaden Rd

Orchard Blvd

Jln Tupai

Jln Arnap

Grange Rd

Anderson Rd

Orange Grove Rd

French Embassy (2.1km); Atlas (2.3km)

Tanglin Rd

Tomlinson Rd

Nassim Rd

Singapore Botanical Gardens (300m)

Napier Rd

US Embassy

Australian High Commission

UK High Commission

Tanglin Rd

Orchard Road

fantastic hands-on cooking school explores Singapore's multicultural make-up and sees you cook up classic dishes like laksa, *nasi lemak* (coconut rice) and Hainanese chicken rice. Courses usually run for three hours and can be tailored for budding cooks with dietary restrictions.

☞ Tours

Original Singapore Walks   WALKING
(✆ 6325 1631; www.singaporewalks.com; adult S$32-60, child 7-12yr S$15-30; ⊙ 9am-6pm Mon-Fri) Original Singapore Walks conducts irreverent but knowledgable off-the-beaten-track walking tours through Chinatown, Little India, Kampong Glam, the Colonial District and war-related sites. Rain-or-shine tours last from 2½ to three hours. Bookings aren't necessary; check the website for departure times and locations.

Singapore River Cruise   BOATING
(Map p626; ✆ 6336 6111; www.rivercruise.com.sg; bumboat river cruise adult/child S$25/15; Ⓜ Clarke Quay) This outfit runs 40-minute bumboat tours of the Singapore River and Marina Bay. Boats depart about every 15 minutes from various locations, including Clarke Quay, Boat Quay and Marina Bay. A cheaper

option is to catch one of the company's river taxis – commuter boats running a similar route on weekdays; see the website for stops and times. River-taxi payment is by EZ-Link transport card only.

Singapore Ducktours   BOATING
(Map p626; ✆ 6338 6877; www.ducktours.com. sg; 01-330 Suntec City, 3 Temasek Blvd; adult/child under 13yr S$43/33; ⊙ 10am-6pm; Ⓜ Esplanade, Promenade) An informative, kid-friendly, one-hour romp in the 'Wacky Duck', a remodelled WWII amphibious Vietnamese war craft. The route traverses land and water, with a focus on Marina Bay and the Colonial District. You'll find the ticket kiosk and departure point in Tower 5 of **Suntec City** (Map p626; ✆ 6266 1502; www.sunteccity.com.sg; 3 Temasek Blvd; ⊙ 10am-10pm; ☎; Ⓜ Promenade, Esplanade), directly facing the Nicoll Hwy.

✵ Festivals & Events

Singapore's multicultural population celebrates an amazing number of festivals and events. For a calendar, check out www. yoursingapore.com. **Chinese New Year** (⊙ Feb) is the major festival, held in January/February. Look out for parades throughout Chinatown and festive foods in shops. During the **Great Singapore Sale** (www. greatsingaporesale.com.sg; ⊙ early Jun–mid-Aug) in June and July, merchants drop prices to boost Singapore's image as a shopping destination.

⌂ Sleeping

Staying in Singapore is expensive. Budget travellers can stay in hostel rooms for S$25 a night. Newer midrange hotels are lifting the game with better facilities and good, regular online deals. Luxury digs are expensive but plentiful and among the world's best, with options from colonial and romantic to architecturally cutting-edge.

⌂ Colonial District, Marina Bay & the Quays

Port by Quarters Hostel   HOSTEL $
(Map p626; ✆ 6816 6960; www.stayquarters. com; 50A Boat Quay; s/q capsules from S$35/85; ❋ @ ☎; Ⓜ Clarke Quay, Raffles Place) Smack bang on the Singapore River, the Port by Quarters Hostel has raised the bar for capsule hostels in Singapore. The sleek single and queen capsules offer under-bed storage, folding workstation, power points and roll-down privacy screen. The best bit,

Sentosa Island

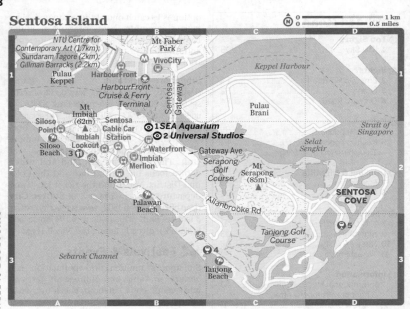

however, is the views – straight over to Parliament and the skyline beyond.

5Footway.Inn Project Boat Quay HOSTEL $
(Map p626; ☎6557 2769; www.5footway-inn.com; 76 Boat Quay; dm/s/d/tr/q from S$36/70/90/110/136; ✳@❂; ⓂClarke Quay, Raffles Place) Right on Boat Quay, the white-washed dorms come in one-, two-, three- and four-bed configurations, and though rooms are small (superior rooms have windows), they're modern and comfortable, with wooden bunks and handy bedside power sockets and lights. Bathrooms are modern, reception operates round the clock, and the chic breakfast lounge comes with an amazing river view.

River City Inn HOSTEL $
(Map p626; ☎6532 6091; www.rivercityinn.com; 33C Hong Kong St; dm from S$26; ✳@❂; ⓂClarke Quay) Its location, on the 4th floor of a shophouse, hasn't deterred backpackers from booking beds here en masse. The communal areas are well done but the 4th-floor location can be a bit tiresome, especially if you're carting heavy luggage.

Holiday Inn Express Clarke Quay HOTEL $$
(Map p626; ☎6589 8000; www.hiexpress.com; 2 Magazine Rd; r from S$250; ✳@❂❈; ⓂClarke Quay) This smart hotel delivers modern, earthy-hued rooms with high ceilings, massive floor-to-ceiling windows and comfortable beds with both soft and firm pillows. Small bathrooms come with decent-sized showers. Best of all is the rooftop garden, home to a tiny gym and impressive glass-sided pool with spectacular city views. The hotel's self-service laundry room is a handy touch.

🛏 Chinatown & the CBD

★Adler Hostel HOSTEL $
(Map p630; ☎6226 0173; www.adlerhostel.com; 259 South Bridge Rd; cabin s/d S$40/80; ✳@❂; ⓂChinatown) Hostelling reaches sophisticated new heights at this self-proclaimed

'poshtel'. Chinese antiques grace the tranquil lobby lounge, and fresh towels and feather-down duvets and pillows the beds. Airy, air-con dorms consist of custom-made cabins, each with lockable storage and curtains that can be drawn for privacy. Some even feature king-size beds for couples. Book around three weeks ahead for the best rates.

★ COO
HOSTEL $

(☑ 6221 5060; www.staycoo.com; 259 Outram Rd; dm from S$44; ✳@☎; M Outram Park) Looking more like a funky dance club with its graphic artwork, neon lighting and cage walls, this self-proclaimed 'sociatel' is all about everything social – social media, socialising – you get the drift. A great place to make new friends and Snapchat about it; dorms come in four-, six- or eight-bed configurations. Super-clean and super-comfy, there's a bistro on-site and free bike rental.

Beary Best Hostel
HOSTEL $

(Map p630; ☑ 6222 4957; www.bearybesthostel.com; 16 Upper Cross St; dm/tw from S$28/82; ✳@☎; M Chinatown) In a restored heritage building just steps from Chinatown MRT, this fun, brightly coloured affair offers clean dorms and private rooms. Bathrooms are unisex or women only, and you can book discounted attraction tickets via the online shop, a beary nice touch. Staff are super-helpful and if you've a teddy needing a new home, they'll happily take him in.

Wink Hostel
HOSTEL $

(Map p630; ☑ 6222 2940; www.winkhostel.com; 8A Mosque St; pod s/d S$40/72; ✳@☎; M Chinatown) Located in a restored shophouse in the heart of Chinatown, flashpacker favourite Wink merges hostel and capsule-hotel concepts. Instead of bunks, dorms feature private, soundproof 'pods', each with comfortable mattress, coloured mood lighting, adjacent locker and enough room to sit up in. Communal bathrooms feature rain shower heads, while the in-house kitchenette, laundry and lounge areas crank up the homey factor.

★ Amoy
BOUTIQUE HOTEL $$

(Map p630; ☑ 6580 2888; www.stayfareast.com; 76 Telok Ayer St; s/d S$270/325; ✳@☎; M Telok Ayer) Not many hotels are accessed through a historic Chinese temple, but the Amoy is no ordinary slumber pad. History inspires this contemporary belle, from the lobby feature wall displaying old Singaporean Chinese surnames to custom-made opium

beds in the cleverly configured 'Cosy Single' rooms. Plush doubles include Ming-style porcelain basins, and all rooms please with designer bathroom, Nespresso machine and complimentary minibar.

🛏 Little India & Kampong Glam

★ Bunc@Radius
HOSTEL $

(Map p634; ☑ 6262 2862; www.bunchostel.com; 15 Upper Weld Rd; dm from S$28, d S$100; ✳@☎; M Rochor, Jalan Besar) Fresh, clean, new-school Bunc@Radius is the coolest flashpacker hostel in town. A concrete floor, art installations and monochromatic colour scheme give the spacious lobby a hip, boutique feel. Dorms – in four-, six-, eight-, 12- and 16-bed configurations – offer both single and double beds, with each thick mattress wrapped in a hygiene cover (no bed bugs!).

Pod
HOSTEL $

(Map p634; ☑ 6298 8505; www.thepodcapsule-hotel.com; 289 Beach Rd; pod s/d from S$56/88, pod suite s/d from S$75/110; ✳@☎; M Bugis, Nicoll Hwy) Riding the new wave of capsule hotels, the Pod offers sleek accommodation steps from vibrant Kampong Glam. Dorms are modern and sleep 10 to 12 in single or queen pods; privacy comes in the form of roll-down screens. These new pods give you your own space; however, they're not soundproof. A free Nespresso coffee, hot breakfast and laundry service cement its popularity.

Five Stones Hostel
HOSTEL $

(Map p634; ☑ 6535 5607; www.fivestoneshostel.com; 285 Beach Rd; dm from S$28, tw/d S$95/105; ✳@☎; M Bugis, Nicoll Hwy) This upbeat, no-shoes hostel comes with polished-concrete floors and both Wii and DVDs in the common lounge, plus complimentary use of washing machines and dryers. While not all dorms have windows, all feature steel-frame bunks, personal power sockets and lamps, and bright, mood-lifting murals depicting local themes. There's an all-women floor, plus private rooms with bunks or a queen-size bed.

Dream Lodge
HOSTEL $

(Map p634; ☑ 6816 1036; www.dreamlodge.sg; 172 Tyrwhitt Rd; dm from S$53; ✳@; M Bendemeer, Farrer Park, Lavender) This popular hostel is spick and span, with comfy beds in a trendy pod formation and super-helpful staff. The location is quiet but hip (you'll find cool coffeeshops and bars just steps away), moments from three MRT stations and hyperactive

REFLEXOLOGY

This Chinese form of relaxation involves lying in a chair and letting the masseur knead and press all the pressure points on your feet. In theory, the different bits of your foot are connected to vital organs, and getting the circulation going is good for you. In reality, it can be bloody painful. Most malls have a foot reflexology place. One Chinatown favourite is **People's Park Complex** (www.peoplesparkcomplex. sg; 1 Park Rd; ⊙9am-10pm, shop hours vary; MᏟChinatown), a mall packed with cheap, no-frills reflexology stalls.

Little India. Choose from 12- to 14-bed mixed dorms, or six-bed women-only dorms.

Kam Leng Hotel
BOUTIQUE HOTEL $

(Map p634; ☑6239 9399; www.kamleng.com; 383 Jln Besar; r from S$95; ❋ⓐ; MᏟBendemeer, Farrer Park) Hipster meets heritage at Kam Leng, a revamped retro hotel in the up-and-coming Jalan Besar district. Common areas are studiously raw, with distressed walls, faded Chinese signage, colourful wall tiles and modernist furniture. Rooms are tiny and simple yet cool, with old-school terrazzo flooring and pastel accents. A word of warning: rooms facing Jln Besar can get rather noisy.

Fisher BnB
HOSTEL $

(Map p634; ☑6297 8258; www.fisherbnb.com; 127 Tyrwhitt Rd; dm from S$36; ❋@ⓐ; MᏟBendemeer, Lavender, Farrer Park) With simple, industrial interiors, this squeaky-clean hostel in up-and-coming heritage neighbourhood Jalan Besar is a great bet for a good night's sleep. The mixed dorm sleeps 16 in metal bunk beds and the women-only dorm fits 12 – the pink walls are a fun touch. Lockers are huge and the owner James is a wealth of information.

Rucksack Inn
HOSTEL $

(Map p634; ☑6295 2495; www.rucksackinn.com; 280 Lavender St; dm from S$19, pods from S$31, private r from S$80; ❋@ⓐ; MᏟBendemeer, Farrer Park) An easy walk from the hipster pocket of Jalan Besar is this popular, well-air-conditioned option. Low-frills dorms (including a women-only room) feature bunks or pods; private rooms sleeping up to 14 are also available. Perks include laundry service (from S$10), friendly staff and a leafy rooftop garden.

Shophouse the Social Hostel
HOSTEL $

(Map p634; ☑6298 8721; www.shophousehostel. com; 48 Arab St; dm/d from S$20/70; ❋@ⓐ; MᏟBugis, Nicholl Hwy) This well-located, well-designed hostel has a fantastic rooftop lounge and terrace with great views. Rooms feature dark-wood bunks and industrial elements such as raw-concrete floors. There's a women-only floor, and guests enjoy a 20% discount at Working Title, the cafe on the ground floor.

★Wanderlust
BOUTIQUE HOTEL $$

(Map p634; ☑6396 3322; www.wanderlusthotel. com; 2 Dickson Rd; r from S$210; ❋@ⓐ; MᏟRochor, Jalan Besar) Wanderlust delivers wow factor with its insanely imaginative accommodation, ranging from seriously bright Pantone-coloured rooms to calm comic-book 'mono' rooms, to those with themes including 'Tree' and 'Space'. Take some time to chillax in the rooftop garden, complete with rainbow Jacuzzi, guarded by a herd of tiny elephants. Early bookings and online deals deliver great rates.

✖ Eating

Singaporeans are obsessed with *makan* (food), from talking incessantly about their last meal, to feverishly photographing, critiquing and posting about it online. It's hardly surprising – food is one of Singapore's greatest drawcards, the nation's mix of cultures creating one of the world's most diverse, drool-inducing culinary landscapes.

✖ Colonial District, Marina Bay & the Quays

★Gluttons Bay
HAWKER $

(Map p626; www.makansutra.com; 01-15 Esplanade Mall, 8 Raffles Ave; dishes from S$4.50; ⊙5pm-2am Mon-Thu, to 3am Fri & Sat, 4pm-1am Sun; MᏟEsplanade, City Hall) Selected by the *Makansutra Food Guide,* this row of alfresco hawker stalls is a great place to start your Singapore food odyssey. Get indecisive over classics like oyster omelette, satay, barbecue stingray and carrot cake (opt for the black version). Its central, bayside location makes it a huge hit, so head in early or late to avoid the frustrating hunt for a table.

Satay by the Bay
HAWKER $

(☑6538 9956; www.sataybythebay.com.sg; Gardens by the Bay, 18 Marina Gardens Dr; dishes from S$4; ⊙stall hrs vary, drinks stall 24hr; MᏟBayfront) Gardens by the Bay's own hawker centre has an enviable location, alongside Marina Bay and far from the roar of city traffic. Especially evocative at night, it's known for its satay, best devoured under open skies on the spacious wooden deck. As you'd expect, prices are a little higher than at more local hawker centres, with most dishes costing S$8 to S$10.

Singapore Food Treats HAWKER $
(Map p626; Singapore Flyer, 30 Raffles Ave; dishes S$6-15; ⊙11am-10pm; ✳Ⓜ Promenade) This spot is a retro-inspired recreation of the hawker stalls from 1960s Singapore, except with air-conditioning. Located under the shadow of the **Singapore Flyer** (Map p626; ☑6333 3311; www.singaporeflyer.com), you'll find an array of local favourites, including chicken rice and laksa.

Rasapura Masters HAWKER $
(Map p626; ☑6688 6888; www.marinabaysands. com; B2-50 Shoppes at Marina Bay Sands, 2 Bayfront Ave; dishes from S$5; ⊙24hr, stall hrs vary; 🛜✳; Ⓜ Bayfront) If you prefer your hawker grub with a side of air-con, head to this bustling, gleaming food court in the basement of the Marina Bay Sands mall. Its stalls cover most bases, from Japanese ramen and Korean kimchi to Hong Kong roast meats and local *bak kut teh* (pork-bone tea soup).

★**National Kitchen by Violet Oon** PERANAKAN $$
(Map p626; ☑9834 9935; www.violetoon.com; 02-01 National Gallery Singapore, 1 St Andrew's Rd; dishes S$15-42; ⊙noon-2.30pm & 6-9.30pm, high tea 3-4.30pm; Ⓜ City Hall) Chef Violet Oon is a national treasure, much loved for her faithful *Peranakan* (Chinese-Malay fusion) dishes – so much so that she was chosen to open her latest venture inside Singapore's showcase National Gallery (p624). Feast on made-from-scratch beauties like sweet, spicy *kueh pie ti* (pastry cups stuffed with prawns and yam beans), dry laksa and beef rendang. Bookings two weeks in advance essential.

Super Loco Customs House MEXICAN $$
(Map p626; ☑6532 2090; www.super-loco.com/customshouse; 01-04 Customs House, 70 Collyer Quay; dishes S$8-38, set lunch from S$35; ⊙noon-3pm & 5-10.30pm Mon-Thu, noon-11pm Fri, 5pm-11pm Sat; ✐; Ⓜ Raffles Place, Downtown) With a perfect harbourside location and fashionable string lights, this Mexican restaurant injects a laid-back vibe into Singapore's super-corporate CBD. Tacos are the house speciality and the *de cangrejo* with tangy soft-shell crab and pineapple is a winner; wash it down with a margarita while admiring the in-your-face Marina Bay Sands view.

✕ Chinatown & the CBD

★**Maxwell Food Centre** HAWKER $
(Map p630; cnr Maxwell & South Bridge Rds; dishes from S$2.50; ⊙stall vary; ✐; Ⓜ Chinatown) One of Chinatown's most accessible hawker centres, Maxwell is a solid spot to savour some of the city's street-food staples. While stalls slip in and out of favour with Singapore's fickle diners, enduring favourites include **Tian Tian Hainanese Chicken Rice** (Map p630; 01-10 Maxwell Food Centre; chicken rice from S$3.50; ⊙10am-5pm Tue-Sun) and **Rojak, Popiah & Cockle** (Map p630; 01-56 Maxwell Food Centre,; popiah S$1.30, rojak S$3-8; ⊙10am-10pm).

★**Chinatown Complex** HAWKER $
(Map p630; 335 Smith St; dishes from S$3; ⊙stall hrs vary; Ⓜ Chinatown) Leave Smith St's revamped 'Chinatown Food Street' to the out-of-towners and join old-timers and foodies at this nearby labyrinth, now home to Michelin-starred hawker stall Hong Kong Soya Sauce Chicken Rice & Noodle (p642). You decide if the three-hour wait is worth it. Other standouts include mixed claypot rice at **Lian He Ben Ji Claypot Rice** (Map p630; ☑6227 2470; 02-198/199 Chinatown Complex; dishes S$2.50-5, claypot rice S$5-20; ⊙4.30-10.30pm Fri-Wed) and the rich, nutty satay at **Shi Xiang Satay** (Map p630; 02-79 Chinatown Complex; 10 sticks S$6; ⊙4-9pm Fri-Wed).

For a little TLC, opt for Ten Tonic Ginseng Chicken Soup at **Bonne Soup** (Map p630; www.facebook.com/SingaporeBestHawkerSoup; 02-05, Chinatown Complex; soups S$3.20-7; ⊙10am-8pm). After 6pm head over to Smith Street Taps (p647) and Good Beer Company (p648) for craft and premium beers on tap

★**A Noodle Story** NOODLES $
(Map p630; ☑9027 6289; www.anoodlestorydotcom. wordpress.com; 01-39 Amoy Street Food Centre, cnr Amoy & Telok Ayer Sts; noodles S$7-9; ⊙11.15am-

SINGAPORE EATING

MUST-READ FOOD BOOKS

➡ *Makansutra Singapore* (KF Seetoh)

➡ *Only the Best! The ieatishootipost Guide to Singapore's Shiokest Hawker Food* (Leslie Tay)

➡ *Singapore Tatler: Best Restaurants Guide* (https://sg.asiatatler.com)

➡ *Michelin Guide Singapore* (https://guide.michelin.com)

THE HEARTLANDS

Orchard Rd and the CBD area offer plenty for the tourist, but the city's residential neighbourhoods proffer a stronger dose of local culture. Pick any MRT station to stop at and you'll usually emerge in a local mall. Wander away from the mall and you'll see local life in a big way: wet markets, local coffeeshops, tailors, barbers, Chinese medical halls and the like. Lively neighbourhoods include Tampines, Jurong, Bishan, Toa Payoh and Ang Mo Kio.

2.30pm & 5.30-7.30pm Mon-Fri, 10.30am-1.30pm Sat; M Telok Ayer) With a snaking line and proffered apology that 'we may sell out earlier than stipulated timing' on the facade, this one-dish-only stall is a magnet for Singapore foodies. The object of desire is Singapore-style ramen created by two young chefs, Gwern Khoo and Ben Tham. It's Japanese ramen meets wanton *mee* (noodles): pure bliss in a bowl, topped with a crispy potato-wrapped prawn.

★ Hong Kong Soya Sauce
Chicken Rice & Noodle   HAWKER $
(Map p630; 02-126 Chinatown Complex, 335 Smith St; dishes S$2-3; ⊙10.30am-7pm Mon, Tue, Thu & Fri, from 8.30am Sat & Sun; M Chinatown) With its newly bestowed Michelin star, this humble hawker stall has been thrust into the culinary spotlight. The line forms hours before Mr Chan Hon Meng opens for business, and waiting times can reach three hours. Standout dishes are the tender soy sauce chicken and the caramelised pork *char siew* ordered with rice or noodles. Worth the wait? You bet.

Capitalising on the stall's success, hawker Chan Hong Meng has already opened three new outlets. The closest is just outside the Chinatown Complex on Smith St (Map p630; 78 Smith St; dishes S$3-10; ⊙10am-7pm Thu-Tue; M Chinatown); look for the bright red and blue sign. Here you'll find a larger menu, higher prices and a more sterile environment – we say stick with the original.

Ah Chiang's   CHINESE $
(☑6557 0084; www.facebook.com/ahchiangporridgesg; 01-38, 65 Tiong Poh Rd; porridge S$4-5; ⊙6am-11pm; M Outram Park) Join gossiping uncles and Gen-Y hipsters for a little Cantonese soul food at Ah Chiang's. The star turn at this retro corner *kopitiam* (coffeeshop) is fragrant, charcoal-fired congee (a rice-based porridge). While it's all soul-coaxingly good, do not go past the raw sliced fish, delectably drizzled with sesame oil. Do not lick the bowl.

Little India & Kampong Glam

★ Zam Zam   MALAYSIAN $
(Map p634; ☑6298 6320; www.zamzamsingapore.com; 697-699 North Bridge Rd; murtabak from S$5; ⊙7am-11pm; M Bugis) These guys have been here since 1908, so they know what they're doing. Tenure hasn't bred complacency, though – the touts still try to herd customers in off the street, while frenetic chefs inside whip up delicious *murtabak*, the restaurant's speciality savoury pancakes, filled with succulent mutton, chicken, beef, venison or even sardines. Servings are epic, so order a medium between two.

Hill Street Tai Hwa Pork Noodle   HAWKER $
(Map p634; www.taihwa.com.sg; 01-12, Block 466, Crawford Lane; noodles S$6-10; ⊙9.30am-9pm; M Lavender) Locals have tried to keep this second-generation hawker stall – famous for Teochew-style *bak chor mee* (minced pork noodles) – secret, but with its new Michelin star, that's now impossible. It's best to arrive early; before opening, you can grab a number instead of joining the forever-lengthening queue. Bowls come in four sizes; the S$8 option will fill you right up.

Tekka Centre   HAWKER $
(Map p634; cnr Serangoon & Buffalo Rds; dishes S$3-10; ⊙7am-11pm, stall hrs vary; ☑; M Little India) There's no shortage of subcontinental spice at this bustling hawker centre, wrapped around the sloshed guts and hacked bones of the wet market. Queue up for real-deal biryani, *dosa* (paper thin, lentil-flour pancake), *roti prata* (wheat-flour pancake) and *teh tarik* (pulled tea). Well worth seeking out is Ah Rahman Royal Prata (Map p634; 01-248 Tekka Centre; murtabak from S$5; ⊙7am-10pm Tue-Sun; M Little India), which flips some of Singapore's finest *murtabak* (stuffed savoury pancake).

QS269 Food House   HAWKER $
(Map p634; Block 269B, Queen St; dishes from S$2.50; ⊙stall hrs vary; M Bugis) This is not so much a 'food house' as a loud, crowded undercover laneway lined with cult-status stalls. Work up a sweat with a bowl of award-winning coconut-curry noodle soup from Ah Heng (Map p634; www.facebook.com/AhHengChickenCurryNoodles; 01-236 QS269 Food House; soup S$4.50-6.50; ⊙9.30am-10pm; M Bugis) or

join the queue at **New Rong Liang Ge** (Map p634; ☑ 01-235 QS269 Food House; dishes from S$2.50; ⊙ 9am-8pm, closed first Wed of the month; Ⓜ Bugis), with succulent roast-duck dishes that draw foodies from across the city. The laneway is down the side of the building.

Bismillah Biryani INDIAN $
(Map p634; ☑ 9382 7937; www.facebook.com/bismillahbiryanisg; 50 Dunlop St; kebabs from S$6, biryani from S$8.50; ⊙ 11.30am-3pm & 5.30-9pm; Ⓜ Rochor) This place is often touted as having the best biryani in Singapore, and the owners have taken it one step further by declaring that it's 'probably the best biryani anywhere!' Mutton biryani is the speciality – and it is special – but even that's surpassed by the melt-in-the-mouth mutton kebab. Get here early: the best dishes are often long gone before closing.

Moghul Sweets SWEETS $
(Map p634; ☑ 6392 5797; 01-16 Little India Arcade, 48 Serangoon Rd; sweets from S$1; ⊙ 9.30am-9.30pm; Ⓜ Little India) If you're after a subcontinental sugar rush, tiny Moghul is the place to get it. Bite into luscious *gulab jamun* (syrup-soaked fried dough balls), harder-to-find *rasmalai* (paneer soaked in cardamom-infused clotted cream) and *barfi* (condensed milk and sugar slice) in flavours including pistachio, chocolate...and carrot.

Warong Nasi Pariaman MALAYSIAN, INDONESIAN $
(Map p634; ☑ 6292 2374; www.pariaman.com. sg; 736-738 North Bridge Rd; dishes from S$3; ⊙ 7.30am-8pm; Ⓜ Bugis) This no-frills corner *nasi padang* (rice with curries) stall is the stuff of legend. Top choices include the delicate *rendang* beef, *ayam bakar* (grilled chicken with coconut sauce) and spicy sambal goreng (long beans, tempeh and fried beancurd). Get here by 11am to avoid the lunch hordes, and by 5pm for the dinner queue. And be warned: most of it sells out well before closing time.

★ Cicheti ITALIAN $$
(Map p634; ☑ 6292 5012; www.cicheti.com; 52 Kandahar St; pizzas S$18-25, mains S$22-56; ⊙ noon-2.30pm & 6.30-10.30pm Mon-Fri, 6-10.30pm Sat; Ⓜ Bugis, Nicoll Hwy) Cool-kid Cicheti is a slick, friendly, buzzing scene of young-gun pizzaioli, trendy diners and seductive, contemporary Italian dishes made with hand-picked market produce. Tuck into beautifully charred wood-fired pizzas, made-from-scratch pasta and evening standouts like *polpette di carne grana* (slow-cooked meatballs topped with shaved Grana Padana). Book early in the week if heading in on a Friday or Saturday night.

✖ Orchard Road

Food Republic FOOD HALL $
(Map p636; www.foodrepublic.com.sg; Level 4, Wisma Atria, 435 Orchard Rd; dishes S$5-15; ⊙ 10am-10pm; ☎; Ⓜ Orchard) A cornucopia of street food in air-conditioned comfort. Muck in with the rest of the crowd for seats before joining the longest queues for dishes spanning Japan, Korea and Thailand, to India, Indonesia and, quite rightly, Singapore.

Takashimaya Food Village FOOD HALL $
(Map p636; ☑ 6506 0458; www.takashimaya. com.sg; B2 Takashimaya Department Store, Ngee Ann City, 391 Orchard Rd; dishes S$4-17; ⊙ 10am-9.30pm; ☎; Ⓜ Orchard) In the basement of Japanese department store Takashimaya, this polished, expansive food hall serves up a *Who's Who* of Japanese and other Asian culinary classics. If comfort food is on the agenda, order a fragrant bowl of noodles from the Tsuru-koshi stand. The hall is also home to a large Cold Storage supermarket.

Newton Food Centre HAWKER $
(Map p636; 500 Clemenceau Ave Nth; dishes from S$2; ⊙ noon-2am, stall hrs vary; Ⓜ Newton) Reopened in April 2016 after a mini facelift, this famous hawker centre still has a great atmosphere. You could eat here for a whole year and never get bored. Well-known stalls include Sheng Da BBQ seafood (01-02), Hup Kee oyster omelette (01-73) and Kwee Heng (01-13). Touts can be a problem for foreigners, but ignore them. The best stalls don't need to tout.

▼ Drinking & Nightlife

From speakeasy cocktail bars to boutique beer stalls to artisan coffee roasters, Singapore is discovering the finer points of drinking. The clubbing scene is no less competent, with newcomers including a futuristic club in the clouds, a basement hot spot fit for the streets of Tokyo, and a techno refuge in Boat Quay.

Colonial District, Marina Bay & the Quays

You'll find no shortage of touristy bars and pubs on Boat Quay and Clarke Quay, with a small handful of more discerning cocktail bars behind Boat Quay. There are loads of rooftop options too, with many of the best skirting Marina Bay.

KANUMAN/SHUTTERSTOCK ©

CHATCHAWAT PRASERTSOM/SHUTTERSTOCK ©

2

. **Gardens by the Bay (p625)**
ngapore's S$1-billion botanic garden is
101-hectare fantasy land of space-age
odomes, high-tech Supertrees and
himsical sculptures.

. **ION Orchard Mall (p650)**
uturistic ION is the cream of the
rchard Rd malls, with designer labels, a
nge of dining options and the viewing
allery ION Sky.

. **Street Food**
ood is one of Singapore's major
rawcards and the Satay Street market in
oon Tat St is a street food lovers' delight.

. **Merlion sculpture**
he official mascot of Singapore, the
erlion is a mythical creature with a
on's head and the body of a fish. It's
cated in the Merlion Park that fronts
arina Bay.

★ 28 HongKong Street   COCKTAIL BAR

(Map p626; www.28hks.com; 28 Hongkong St; ⏱5.30pm-1am Mon-Thu, to 3am Fri & Sat; ⓂClarke Quay) Softly lit 28HKS plays hide and seek inside an unmarked 1960s shophouse. Slip inside and into a slinky scene of cosy booths and passionate mixologists turning grog into greatness. Marked with their alcohol strength, cocktails are seamless and sublime, among them the refreshing 'planter's punch' with rum, grenadine, citrus and Darjeeling tea. House-barreled classics, hard-to-find beers and lip-smacking grub seal the deal.

★ Zouk   CLUB

(Map p626; ☑6738 2988; www.zoukclub.com; 3C River Valley Rd; women/men from S$30/35 redeemable for drinks; ⏱Zouk 10pm-4am Fri, Sat & Wed, Phuture 10pm-3am Wed & Fri, 10pm-2am Thu, 10pm-4am Sat, Red Tail 6-11pm Sun-Tue & Thu, 7pm-3am Wed & Fri, 7pm-4am Sat, Capital 10pm-2am Thu, 10pm-3am Fri, 10pm-4am Sat; ⓂClarke Quay, Fort Canning) After a massive farewell to Zouk's original location, this legendary club has settled in to its new home in pumping Clarke Quay. Drawing some of the world's biggest DJs and Singapore's seen-to-be-seen crowd, this is the place to go to if you want to let loose. Choose between the main, two-level club with pumping dance floor and insane lighting, or the hip-hop-centric, graffiti-splashed Phuture.

Ah Sam Cold Drink Stall   COCKTAIL BAR

(Map p626; ☑6535 0838; www.facebook.com/AhSamColdDrinkStall; 60A Boat Quay; ⏱6pm-midnight Mon-Thu, to 2am Fri & Sat; ⓂClarke Quay, Raffles Place) Get that in-the-know glow at this sneaky cocktail den, perched above the tacky Boat Quay pubs. Adorned with vintage Hong Kong posters and feeling more like a private party than a bar, Ah Sam specialises in Asian mixology. Simply tell the bartender your preferences, and watch them twist, shake and torch up clever creations.

CÉ LA VI SkyBar   BAR

(Map p626; ☑6508 2188; www.sg.celavi.com; Level 57, Marina Bay Sands Hotel Tower 3, 10 Bayfront Ave; admission S$20, redeemable on food or drinks; ⏱noon-late; ⓂBayfront) Perched on Marina Bay Sands' cantilevered SkyPark, this bar offers a jaw-dropping panorama of the Singapore skyline and beyond. A dress code kicks in from 6pm (no shorts, singlets or flip-flops) and live DJ sets pump from 7pm. Tip: skip the entry fee to the Sands SkyPark Observation Deck (p625) – come here, order a cocktail and enjoy the same view!

Loof   BAR

(Map p626; ☑6337 9416; www.loof.com.sg; 03-07, Odeon Towers Bldg, 331 North Bridge Rd; ⏱5pm-1am Mon-Thu, to 2am Fri & Sat; ☎; ⓂCity Hall, Bras Basah) Red neon warmly declares 'Glad you came up' at upbeat Loof, its name the Singlish mangling of the word 'roof'. Sit on the leafy rooftop deck and look out over the Raffles Hotel and Marina Bay Sands with a *calamansi*-spiked 'Singapore sour' in hand. The great-value weekday happy hour lasts from 5pm to 8pm.

Orgo   BAR

(Map p626; ☑6336 9366; www.orgo.sg; 04-01 Esplanade Theatres on the Bay, Roof Terrace, 8 Raffles Ave; ⏱6pm-1am Sun-Wed, to 2am Thu-Sat; ⓂEsplanade) It's hard not to feel like the star of a Hollywood rom-com at rooftop Orgo, its view of the skyline so commanding you'll almost feel obliged to play out a tear-jerking scene. Don't. Instead, slip into a wicker armchair, order a vino (you'll get better cocktails elsewhere) and Instagram the view to the sound of soft conversation and sultry tunes.

KOPI TO COFFEE

While old-school *kopitiams* (coffeeshops) have been serving *kopi* (coffee) for generations, Singapore's speciality coffee scene is a more recent phenomenon. Inspired by Australia's artisanal coffee culture, contemporary cafes such as **Ronin** (Map p626; http://ronin.sg; 17 Hongkong St; ⏱8am-6pm; ⓂClarke Quay, Raffles Place), **Atlas** (☑6314 2674; www.atlascoffeehouse.com.sg; 6 Duke's Rd; ⏱8am-7pm Tue-Sun; ⓂBotanic Gardens) and **Maison Ikkoku** (Map p634; ☑6294 0078; www.maison-ikkoku.net; 20 Kandahar St; ⏱cafe 9am-9pm Mon-Thu, to 11pm Fri & Sat, to 7pm Sun, bar 4pm-1am Sun-Thu, to 2am Fri & Sat; ☎; ⓂBugis) are brewing ethically sourced seasonal beans, using either espresso machines or 'third wave' brewing techniques such as Japanese siphons and AeroPress. Also on the increase are cafes sourcing and roasting their own beans, the best of which include Chye Seng Huat Hardware (p648) and Nylon Coffee Roasters (p647).

> ℹ **GETTING TO INDONESIA: SINGAPORE TO THE RIAU ARCHIPELAGO**
>
> **Getting to the borders** Direct ferries run between the Riau Archipelago islands of Pulau Batam and Pulau Bintan and Singapore. The ferries are modern, fast and air-conditioned. Expect to pay around S$25 for a one-way ticket to Batam, and S$45 to Bintan. Ferries to Batam Centre, Sekupang, Harbour Bay and Waterfront City (all on Batam) depart from HarbourFront ferry terminal. Ferries to Bintan and Batam's Harbour Bay, Batam Centre and Nongsapura depart from the Tanah Merah ferry terminal. There are also cheaps daily flights to Medan.
>
> **At the borders** Border posts on Bintan and Batam are open during ferry operational hours and immigration on both sides is straightforward. Many countries receive a 30-day Indonesian free visa on arrival or are able to apply for a US$35 visa on arrival; it is advisable to check your visa status with the Indonesian Consulate prior to travel.
>
> For information on making this crossing in reverse see p260.

Level 33
MICROBREWERY

(☑ 6834 3133; www.level33.com.sg; Level 33, Marina Bay Financial Tower 1, 8 Marina Blvd; ☺ 11.30am-midnight Mon-Thu, to 2am Fri & Sat, noon-midnight Sun; ☏ ; Ⓜ Downtown) In a country obsessed with unique selling points, this one takes the cake – no, keg. Laying claim to being the world's highest 'urban craft brewery', Level 33 brews its own lager, pale ale, stout, porter and wheat beer. It's all yours to slurp alfresco with a jaw-dropping view over Marina Bay. Bargain hunters, take note: beers are cheaper before 8pm.

🍷 Chinatown & the CBD

Club Street and adjacent Ann Siang Rd are the heart of Singapore's booming bar scene, with both streets closed to traffic from 7pm on Friday and Saturday. Just over the hill, on Amoy and Telok Ayer streets, are many hidden watering holes, but you'll need to find them first. South of Chinatown, Tanjong Pagar and the Duxton Hill area offer an ever-expanding number of in-the-know cafes and drinking spots, while Chinatown's hawker centres are always a good standby for a no-frills beer.

★ Operation Dagger
COCKTAIL BAR

(Map p630; ☑ 6438 4057; www.operationdagger. com; 7 Ann Siang Hill; ☺ 6pm-late Tue-Sat; Ⓜ Chinatown, Telok Ayer) From the 'cloud-like' light sculpture to the boundary-pushing cocktails, 'extraordinary' is the keyword here. To encourage experimentation, libations are described by flavour, not spirit, the latter shelved in uniform, apothecary-like bottles. Sample the sesame-infused *gomashio,* or the textural surprise of the

'hot & cold'. Head up the hill where Club Street and Ann Siang Hill meet; a symbol shows the way.

★ Employees Only
COCKTAIL BAR

(Map p630; http://employeesonlysg.com; 112 Amoy St; ☺ 5pm-1am Mon-Fri, to 2am Sat, 6pm-1am Sun; Ⓜ Telok Ayer) This outpost of the famous New York cocktail bar of the same name has brought a slice of big-city buzz to Singapore, along with a dazzling array of innovative drinks. Some of the sting from the eye-watering prices is soothed by the free-pour mixing method; lightweights may be knocked from their perch. A pink neon 'psychic' sign marks the entrance.

★ Native
BAR

(Map p630; ☑ 8869 6520; www.tribenative.com; 52A Amoy St; ☺ 6pm-midnight Mon-Sat; Ⓜ Telok Ayer) It's best not to think about bug-eating reality TV shows when ordering your 'antz' cocktail. This hidden bar, in hot-spot-heavy Amoy St, is the brainchild of bartender extraordinaire Vijay Mudaliar, formerly of Operation Dagger, and his concoctions have everyone talking. Spirits are sourced from around the region, such as Thai rum and Sri Lankan arak, paired with locally foraged ingredients – expect the unexpected.

★ Nylon Coffee Roasters
CAFE

(Map p630; ☑ 6220 2330; www.nyloncoffee.sg; 01-40, 4 Everton Park; ☺ 8.30am-5.30pm Mon & Wed-Fri, 9am-6pm Sat & Sun; Ⓜ Outram Park, Tanjong Pagar) Hidden away in the Everton Park public housing complex, this pocket-sized, standing-room-only cafe and roastery has an epic reputation for phenomenal seasonal blends and impressive single origins. At the helm is a personable, gung-ho crew of coffee fanatics, chatting away with customers about their latest coffee-sourcing trip (they deal directly with the farmers), or the virtues of French-press brewing.

Good Beer Company CRAFT BEER
(Map p630; ☑9430 2750; www.facebook.com/goodbeersg; 02-58 Chinatown Complex, 335 Smith St; ⊙6-10pm Mon-Sat; Ⓜ Chinatown) Injecting Chinatown Complex with a dose of new-school cool, this hawker-centre beer stall has an impressive booty of bottled craft suds, sourced from far-flung corners of the world. A few stalls down is the co-owned **Smith Street Taps** (Map p630; ☑9430 2750; www.facebook.com/smithstreettaps; 02-62 Chinatown Complex; ⊙6.30-10.30pm Tue-Thu, 5-11pm Fri, 2-10.30pm Sat; Ⓜ Chinatown), run by a friendly dude and offering a rotating selection of craft and premium beers on tap.

Little India & Kampong Glam

★**Chye Seng Huat Hardware** CAFE
(CSHH Coffee Bar; Map p634; ☑6396 0609; www.cshhcoffee.com; 150 Tyrwhitt Rd; ⊙9am-10pm Tue-Thu & Sun, to midnight Fri & Sat; Ⓜ Bendemeer, Farrer Park, Lavender) An art-deco former hardware store provides the setting and name for Singapore's coolest cafe and roastery, its third-wave offerings including on-tap Nitro Black Matter, a malty, cold-brew coffee infused with CO_2. Get your coffee geek on at one of the education sessions (from S$26); see www.papapalheta.com/education/classes for details.

★**Atlas** BAR
(Map p634; ☑6396 4466; www.atlasbar.sg; Lobby, Parkview Sq, 600 North Bridge Rd; ⊙10am-1am Mon-Thu, to 2am Fri, 3pm-2am Sat; Ⓜ Bugis) Straight out of 1920s Manhattan, this cocktail lounge is an art deco–inspired extravaganza, adorned with ornate bronze ceilings and low-lit plush lounge seating, and a drinks menu filled with decadent Champagnes, curated cocktails and some mean martinis. However, it's the 12m-high gin wall, displaying over 1000 labels, that really makes a statement – make sure you ask for a tour.

Druggists BEER HALL
(☑6341 5967; www.facebook.com/DruggistsSG; 119 Tyrwhitt Rd; ⊙4pm-midnight Mon-Thu, to 2am Fri & Sat, 2-10pm Sun; Ⓜ Bendemeer, Farrer Park, Lavender) Druggists is indeed addictive for beer aficionados. Its 23 taps pour a rotating selection of craft brews from cognoscenti favourites like Denmark's Mikkeller and Britain's Magic Rock. The week's beers are scribbled on the blackboard, with the option of 250mL or 500mL pours. Sud-friendly grub is also available, though the place is better for drinking than for eating.

Orchard Road

Manhattan BAR
(Map p636; ☑6725 3377; www.regenthotels.com/en/Singapore; Level 2, Regent, 1 Cuscaden Rd; ⊙5pm-1am Sun-Thu, to 2am Fri & Sat, noon-3pm Sun; Ⓜ Orchard) Step back in time to the golden age of fine drinking at this handsome *Mad Men*–esque bar, where long-forgotten cocktails come back to life. Grouped by New

---

ⓘ GETTING TO MALAYSIA: SINGAPORE TO JOHOR BAHRU OR TANJUNG BELUNGKOR
. . . .

While you can enter Malaysia via Tanjung Belungkor by boat, the following options provide better onward transport connections.

Getting to the borders The easiest way to reach the border is on the Causeway Link Express (www.causewaylink.com.my). Buses run every 15 to 30 minutes between 6am and 11.45pm; fares are S$3.50/RM3.40 one way. There are several routes, with stops including Queen Street Bus Terminal (Map p620; cnr Queen & Arab Sts; mBugis), Newton Circus, Jurong East Bus & MRT Interchange, and Kranji MRT station.

At the borders At the Singapore checkpoint, disembark from the bus with your luggage to go through immigration, and reboard the next bus (keep your ticket). After repeating the process on the Malaysian side, it's a quick walk into central JB.

Moving on Most routes also stop at Larkin Bus Terminal (Larkin Sentral), 5km from central JB. From here, long-distance buses depart to numerous Malaysian destinations, including Melaka, Kuala Lumpur and Ipoh.

For information on making this crossing in reverse see p422.

LIVE MUSIC

Sure, a lot of average Pinoy cover bands grace hotel bars, but an enthusiastic local music scene also thrives (to a point). **Esplanade – Theatres on the Bay** (Map p626; ☑6828 8377; www.esplanade.com; 1 Esplanade Dr; ◷box office noon-8.30pm; ☎; Ⓜ Esplanade, City Hall) hosts regular free performances, and is the performing home of the **Singapore Symphony Orchestra** (SSO; Map p626; ☑6602 4245; www.sso.org.sg; 01-02 Victoria Concert Hall, 9 Empress Pl; ◷9am-6.30pm Mon-Fri; Ⓜ Raffles Place, City Hall).

Singapore is on the map for a growing number of international acts, with top-tier talent showcased at both the **Singapore International Jazz Festival** (www.sing-jazz. com; ◷Mar-Apr) and the indie-music favourite **St Jerome's Laneway Festival** (http:// singapore.lanewayfestival.com; ◷Jan/Feb).

York neighbourhoods, the drinks menu is ever changing; however, waistcoated bartenders are only too happy to guide you. Sunday brings freshly shucked oysters, and an adults-only cocktail brunch (S$150) during which you can make your own bloody Marys.

Privé CAFE
(Map p636; ☑6776 0777; www.theprivegroup.com. sg; 01-K1 Wheelock Place, 501 Orchard Rd; ◷9am-1am Mon-Fri, from 8am Sat & Sun; Ⓜ Orchard) With its pedestrian sidewalk location and terraced seating, this Parisian style cafe is the perfect ringside spot to watch the masses strutting up and down Orchard Rd. Serving decent cafe fare, plus burgers, pastas and all-day breakfasts, Privé has a good cocktail and wine list and more than 15 whiskies. Happy hour is 5pm to 8pm; book for the best seats.

🍺 Sentosa Island

Tanjong Beach Club BAR
(Map p638; ☑6270 1355; www.tanjongbeachclub. com; 120 Tanjong Beach Walk; ◷11am-10pm Tue-Fri, from 10am Sat, from 9am Sun, from noon Mon; ☑Tanjong Beach) Generally cooler than the bars on Siloso Beach, Tanjong Beach Club is an evocative spot, with striped deckchairs on the sand, a small, stylish pool for guests, and a sultry, lounge-and-funk soundtrack. The restaurant serves trendy beachside fare, and a kick-ass weekend-brunch menu. Some of the island's hottest parties happen on this shore.

Woobar BAR
(Map p638; ☑6808 7258; www.woobar.wsingaporesentosacove.com; W Singapore, 21 Ocean Way; ◷11.30am-1am Mon-Fri, from 9am Sat & Sun; ☎; ☑B) The W Singapore's hotel bar is glam and camp, with suspended egg-shaped pods, gold footrests and floor-to-ceiling windows looking out at palms and pool. The afternoon 'high tea' (from S$65/75 for two on

weekdays/weekends) is served in dainty birdcages, while the Wednesday Ladies' Night (from S$36) comes with free-pour bubbly between 7.30pm and 9pm, followed by half-price drinks until midnight.

☆ Entertainment

You're never short of a hot night out in Singapore. There's live music, theatre and adrenalin-pumping activities year-round, while at certain times of the year the Little Red Dot explodes into a flurry of car racing, cultural festivals and hot-ticket music events. Tickets and an events calendar can be found on the Sistic website (www.sistic.com.sg).

Chinese Theatre Circle OPERA
(Map p630; ☑6323 4862; www.ctcopera.com; 5 Smith St; show & snacks S$25, show & dinner S$40; ◷7-9pm Fri & Sat; Ⓜ Chinatown) Teahouse evenings organised by this nonprofit opera company are a wonderful, informal introduction to Chinese opera. Every Friday and Saturday at 8pm there is a brief talk on Chinese opera, followed by a 45-minute excerpt from an opera classic, performed by actors in full costume. You can also opt for a pre-show Chinese meal at 7pm. Book ahead.

Timbrè @ The Substation LIVE MUSIC
(Map p626; ☑6338 8030; www.timbre.com.sg; 45 Armenian St; ◷5pm-1am Mon-Thu, to 3am Fri & Sat; Ⓜ City Hall, Bras Basah) Some are content to queue for seats at this popular live-music venue, whose rotating roster features local bands and singer-songwriters playing anything from pop and rock to folk. Hungry punters can fill up on soups, salads, tapas and passable fried standbys like buffalo wings and truffle fries.

BluJaz Café LIVE MUSIC
(Map p634; ☑6292 3800; www.blujazcafe.net; 11 Bali Lane; ◷9am-12.30am Mon & Tue, to 1am Wed & Thu, to 2.30am Fri & Sat, noon-midnight Sun; ☎;

Bugis) Bohemian pub BluJaz is one of the best options in town for live music, with regular jazz jams and other acts playing anything from blues to rockabilly. Check the website for the list of events, which includes DJ-spun funk, R&B and retro nights, as well as 'Talk Cock' open-mic comedy nights on Wednesday and Thursday. Cover charge for some shows.

Shopping

While its shopping scene mightn't match the edge of Hong Kong or Bangkok, Singapore is no retail slouch. Look beyond the malls and you'll find everything from sharply curated local boutiques to vintage-map peddlers and clued-in contemporary galleries.

Orchard Road

ION Orchard Mall   MALL
(Map p636; ☑ 6238 8228; www.ionorchard.com; 2 Orchard Turn; ◷ 10am-10pm; ☏; Ⓜ Orchard) Rising directly above Orchard MRT station, futuristic ION is the cream of Orchard Rd malls. Basement floors focus on mere-mortal high-street labels like Zara and Uniqlo, while upper-floor tenants read like the index of *Vogue*. Dining options range from foodcourt bites to posher nosh, and the attached 56-storey tower offers a top-floor viewing gallery, ION Sky (p631).

Ngee Ann City   MALL
(Map p636; ☑ 6506 0461; www.ngeeanncity. com.sg; 391 Orchard Rd; ◷ 10am-9.30pm, restaurants till 11pm; Ⓜ Somerset) It might look like a forbidding mausoleum, but this marble-and-granite behemoth promises retail giddiness on its seven floors. International luxury brands compete for space with sprawling bookworm nirvana **Kinokuniya** (Map p636; ☑ 6737 5021; www.kinokuniya.com.sg; 04-20/21 Ngee Ann City; ◷ 10am-9.30pm Sun-Fri, to 10pm Sat; Ⓜ Orchard) and upmarket Japanese department store **Takashimaya** (Map p636; ☑ 6738 1111; www.takashimaya.com.sg; Ngee Ann City; ◷ 10am-9.30pm; ☏; Ⓜ Somerset), home to Takashimaya Food Village, one of the strip's best food courts.

Little India & Kampong Glam

Little India's streets are a browser's delight, laced with art, antiques, textiles, food and music. Quieter and more relaxed, Kampong Glam is even more eclectic – head to Arab St for textiles, rugs and bespoke perfumes, or Haji and Bali Lanes for independent fashion and hipster-approved accessories.

Bugis Street Market   MARKET
(Map p634; ☑ 6338 9513; www.bugisstreet.com. sg; 3 New Bugis St; ◷ 11am-10pm; Ⓜ Bugis) What was once Singapore's most infamous sleaze pit – packed with foreign servicemen on R&R and gambling dens – is now its most famous undercover street market. It's crammed with cheap clothes, shoes, accessories and manicurists, and is especially popular with teens and 20-somethings. In a nod to its past, there's even a sex shop.

Sim Lim Square   ELECTRONICS, MALL
(Map p634; ☑ 6338 3859; www.simlimsquare.com. sg; 1 Rochor Canal Rd; ◷ 10.30am-9pm; Ⓜ Rochor, Jalan Besar) A byword for all that is cut-price and geeky, Sim Lim is jammed with stalls selling laptops, cameras, soundcards and games consoles. If you know what you're doing, there are deals to be had, but the untutored are likely to be out of their depth. Bargain hard (yet politely) and always check that the warranty is valid in your home country.

UNDERSTAND SINGAPORE

Singapore Today

Ecofriendly architectural wonders, a billion-dollar super-park and a swell of world-class bars and eateries – Singapore is shining its way into the future. Yet the city-state's ascent from tiny shipping village to global powerhouse is not without its challenges. Driven by an influx of foreign workers, massive population growth is straining infrastructure, affordability, and the patience of many Singaporeans. Simultaneously, the gag on the LGBT community's annual Pink Dot festival has a lot of people talking.

History

Singapore was originally a tiny sea town squeezed between powerful neighbours Sumatra and Melaka. According to Malay legend, a Sumatran prince spotted a lion while visiting the island of Temasek, and on the basis of this good omen he founded a city there called Singapura (Lion City).

Sir Thomas Stamford Raffles arrived in 1819 to secure a strategic base for the British

Empire in the Strait of Melaka. He decided to transform the sparsely populated, swampy island into a free-trade port. The layout of central Singapore is still as Raffles drew it.

WWII

The glory days of the empire came to an abrupt end on 15 February 1942, when the Japanese invaded Singapore. For the rest of WWII the Japanese ruled the island harshly, jailing Allied prisoners of war at Changi Prison and killing thousands of locals. Although the British were welcomed back after the war, their days in the region were numbered.

Foundation for the Future

The socialist People's Action Party (PAP) was founded in 1954, with Lee Kuan Yew as its secretary general. Lee led the PAP to victory in elections held in 1959, and hung onto power for more than 30 years. Singapore was kicked out of the Malay Federation in 1965, but Lee pushed through an ambitious, strict and successful industrialisation program.

His successor in 1990 was Goh Chok Tong, who loosened things up a little, but maintained Singapore on the path Lee had forged. In 2004 Goh stepped down to make way for Lee's son, Lee Hsien Loong.

Lee the Younger faces the huge challenge of positioning Singapore to succeed in the modern, globalised economy. As manufacturing bleeds away to cheaper competitors, the government is focused on boosting its population, attracting more 'foreign talent' and developing industries such as tourism, financial services, digital media and biomedical research.

People & Culture

Singapore is the ultimate melting pot. With no less than four official languages, it's a place where mosques sidle up to Hindu and Taoist temples, where European chefs experiment with Chinese spices, and where local English is peppered with Hokkien, Tamil and Malay words. Since Sir Stamford Raffles set up a free trading port on the island in 1819, the Little Red Dot has been defined and redefined by its wave of migrants, from early Chinese workers to modern-day expats seeking their corporate fortunes.

Population

The majority of the 5.6 million people are Chinese (74% of the population). Next come the Malays (13%), Indians (9%) and Eurasians and 'others' (4%). Western expats are a very visible group. Also visible is the large population of domestic maids and foreign labourers. Contrary to popular belief, English is the first language of Singapore. Many Singaporeans speak a second language or dialect (usually Mandarin, Malay or Tamil).

Religion

The Chinese majority are usually Buddhists or Taoists, and Chinese customs, superstitions and festivals dominate social life.

The Malays embrace Islam as a religion and a way of life. *Adat* (customary law) guides important ceremonies and events, including birth, circumcision and marriage.

More than half the Indians are Hindus and worship the pantheon of gods in various temples across Singapore. Christianity, including Catholicism, is also popular in Singapore, with both Chinese and Indians pledging their faith to this religion.

SURVIVAL GUIDE

❶ Directory A–Z

ACCOMMODATION

Hostels offer competitive prices (S$20 to S$45 for a dorm bed) and facilities such as free internet, breakfast and laundry use. Cheaper ensuite hotel rooms (S$50 to S$100) are cramped and often windowless. Most places offer air-con rooms. Establishments usually quote net prices, which include all taxes. If you see ++ after a price, you'll need to add a 10% service charge and 7% GST.

CUSTOMS REGULATIONS

You are permitted 1L each of wine, beer and spirits duty free. Alternatively, you are allowed 2L of wine and 1L of beer, or 2L of beer and 1L of wine. You need to have been out of Singapore for more than 48 hours and to anywhere but Malaysia.

ELECTRICITY

Electricity is 230V, 50Hz; plugs usually have three flat pins.

EMERGENCY

Country Code	☑ 65
Ambulance & Fire	☑ 995
Police	☑ 999

EMBASSIES & CONSULATES

For a full list of foreign embassies and consulates in Singapore, check out the website of the Ministry of Foreign Affairs (www.mfa.gov.sg).

Australian High Commission (Map p636; ☑ 6836 4100; www.singapore.embassy.gov.au; 25 Napier Rd; ⊗ 8.30am-4pm Mon-Fri; ☐ 7, 75, 77, 105, 106, 123, 174)

Canadian High Commission (Map p626; ☑ 6854 5900; www.singapore.gc.ca; Level 11, 1 George St; ⊗ 8am-4.30pm Mon-Thu, to 1.30pm Fri; Ⓜ Clarke Quay, Raffles Place)

Dutch Embassy (Map p636; ☑ 6737 1155; www.netherlandsworldwide.nl; 13-01 Liat Towers, 541 Orchard Rd; ⊗ 9am-noon Mon-Fri; Ⓜ Orchard)

French Embassy (☑ 6880 7800; www.sg.ambafrance.org; 101-103 Cluny Park Rd; ⊗ 9am-noon & 2.30-3.30pm Mon-Fri; Ⓜ Botanic Gardens)

German Embassy (Map p626; ☑ 6533 6002; www.singapur.diplo.de; Level 12, Singapore Land Tower, 50 Raffles Pl; ⊗ 8.30-11.30am Mon-Fri; Ⓜ Raffles Place)

New Zealand High Commission (Map p626; ☑ 6235 9966; www.nzembassy.com/singapore; Level 21, 1 George St; ⊗ 9am-1pm Mon-Fri; Ⓜ Clarke Quay, Raffles Place)

UK High Commission (Map p636; ☑ 6424 4200; www.gov.uk/world/singapore; 100 Tanglin Rd; ⊗ 9-11am Mon, Wed-Fri; ☐ 7, 75, 77, 105, 106, 111, 123, 132, 174)

US Embassy (Map p636; ☑ 6476 9100; https://sg.usembassy.gov; 27 Napier Rd; ⊗ 8.30am-5.15pm Mon-Fri; ☐ 7, 75, 77, 105, 106, 123, 174)

FOOD

Bear in mind that most restaurant prices will have 17% added to them at the end: a 10% service charge plus 7% for GST. You'll see this indicated by ++ on menus.

EATING PRICE RANGES

The following price ranges represent the cost of a single dish or a main course, including service charge and GST.

$ less than S$10

$$ S$10–30

$$$ more than S$30

INTERNET ACCESS

Singapore has an ever-expanding network of around 10,000 wireless hot spots – and most cafes, pubs, libraries and malls operate them. In Chinatown you'll find 20 wi-fi hot spots within just a few blocks of the MRT station – simply choose the wireless@chinatown wi-fi network. You don't need a local number to access the free wi-fi – just download the wireless@sg app, fill in your details and you'll be able to locate the nearest free hot spots.

LGBT TRAVELLERS

Sex between men is illegal in Singapore, carrying a minimum sentence of 10 years. In reality, nobody is ever likely to be prosecuted, but the ban remains as a symbol of the government's belief that the country is not ready for the open acceptance of homosexuality.

Despite that, Singapore has a string of popular LGBT bars. A good place to start looking for information is on the websites of Travel Gay Asia (www.travelgayasia.com), PLUguide (www.pluguide.com) or Utopia (www.utopia-asia.com), which provide coverage of venues and events.

LEGAL MATTERS

The law is extremely tough in Singapore, but also relatively free from corruption. Possession and trafficking of drugs is punishable by death. Smoking in all public places, including bars, restaurants and hawker centres, is banned unless there's an official smoking 'area'.

MEDICAL SERVICES

Your hotel or hostel should be able to direct you to a local GP: there are plenty around.

International Medical Clinic (Map p636; ☑ 6733 4440; www.imc-healthcare.com; 14-06 Camden Medical Centre, 1 Orchard Blvd; ⊗ 8am-5.30pm Mon-Fri, 9am-1pm Sat; Ⓜ Orchard) Specialising in family and travel medicine.

Raffles Medical Clinic (Map p634; ☑ 6311 2233; www.rafflesmedicalgroup.com; Level 2, Raffles Hospital, 585 North Bridge Rd; ⊗ 8am-10pm; Ⓜ Bugis) A walk-in clinic at Raffles Hospital.

Singapore General Hospital (☑ 6222 3322; www.sgh.com.sg; Block 1, Outram Rd; Ⓜ Outram Park) Also has an emergency room.

MONEY

The country's unit of currency is the Singapore dollar (S$), locally referred to as the 'singdollar', which is made up of 100 cents. Singapore uses 5¢, 10¢, 20¢, 50¢ and S$1 coins, while notes come in denominations of S$2, S$5, S$10, S$50, S$100, S$500 and S$1000. The Singapore dollar is a highly stable and freely convertible currency.

Cirrus-enabled ATMs are widely available at malls, banks, MRT stations and commercial areas. Banks change money, but virtually nobody uses them for currency conversion because the rates are better at the money changers dotted all over the city. These tiny stalls can be found in just about every shopping centre (though not necessarily in the more modern malls). Rates can be haggled a little if you're changing amounts of S$500 or more.

OPENING HOURS

Banks 9.30am to 4.30pm Monday to Friday (some branches open at 10am and some close at 6pm or later); 9.30am to noon or later Saturday.

Government and Post Offices Between 8am and 9.30am to between 4pm and 6pm Monday to Friday; between 8am and 9am to between 11.30am and 1.30pm Saturday.

Restaurants Top restaurants generally noon–2.30pm for lunch and 6pm to 11pm for dinner. Casual restaurants and food courts open all day.

Shops 10am or 11am to 6pm; larger shops and department stores open until 9.30pm or 10pm. Some smaller shops in Chinatown and Arab St close Sunday.

POST

Postal delivery in Singapore is very efficient. Call 1605 to find the nearest post office or check www.singpost.com.sg.

PUBLIC HOLIDAYS

The only holiday that has a major effect on the city is Chinese New Year, when virtually all shops shut down for two days. Public holidays are as follows:

New Year's Day 1 January

Chinese New Year Three days in January/February

Good Friday March/April

Labour Day 1 May

Vesak Day June

Hari Raya Puasa July

National Day 9 August

Hari Raya Haji September

Deepavali October

Christmas Day 25 December

SAFE TRAVEL

Singapore is one of the world's safest and easiest travel destinations, but be aware of the following:

➡ Penalties for the illegal import or export of drugs are severe and include the death penalty.

➡ Outbreaks of mosquito-borne illnesses, such as dengue fever do occur, especially during the wet season. There have also been a number of zika cases confimed in Singapore; the National Environment Board (www.nea.gov.sg) monitors any outbreaks. Wear mosquito repellent, especially if visiting nature reserves.

➡ Eating and drinking is prohibited on public transport.

> ### SLEEPING PRICE RANGES
>
> The following price ranges refer to the price of a double room including taxes.
>
> **$** less than S$150
>
> **$$** S$150 to S$350
>
> **$$$** more than S$350

TELEPHONE

➡ Singapore's country code is 65.

➡ There are no area codes within Singapore; telephone numbers are eight digits unless you are calling toll-free (1800).

➡ Mobile-phone numbers start with a 9 or 8.

You can buy a tourist SIM card for around S$15 from post offices, convenience stores and telco stores – by law you must show your passport. Local carriers include:

M1 (www.m1.com.sg)

SingTel (www.singtel.com)

StarHub (www.starhub.com)

TOURIST INFORMATION

Before your trip, a good place to check for information is the website of the Singapore Tourism Board.

Singapore Visitors Centre @ Orchard (Map p636; ☑1800 736 2000; www.yoursingapore. com; 216 Orchard Rd; ⊗8.30am-9.30pm; Ⓜ Somerset) Singapore's main tourist-information centre, with brochures, customised itineraries and design-savvy souvenirs. Check out the Event Space on level two, which often holds exhibitions showcasing Singapore's heritage and culture.

Singapore Visitors Centre @ ION Orchard (Map p636; ☑1800 736 2000; www.yoursingapore.com; Level 1 Concierge, ION Orchard, 2 Orchard Turn; ⊗10am-10pm; Ⓜ Orchard)

Singapore Visitor Centre@Chinatown (Map p630; ☑1800 736 2000; www.yoursingapore. com; 2 Banda St; ⊗9am-9pm; Ⓜ Chinatown) Offers maps of Chinatown and Singapore, books various tours, and has a small range of quality souvenirs, including books, reproduction watercolours of Singapore street scenes, and T-shirts.

TRAVELLERS WITH DISABILITIES

A large government campaign has seen ramps, lifts and other facilities progressively installed around the island. The footpaths in the city are nearly all immaculate, all MRT stations have lifts and there are some buses and taxis equipped with wheelchair-friendly equipment.

The **Disabled People's Association Singapore** (www.dpa.org.sg) can provide information on accessibility in Singapore. Download Lonely

Planet's free Accessible Travel guide from http://lptravel.to/AccessibleTravel.

VISAS

Citizens of most countries are granted 90-day entry on arrival. Citizens of India, Myanmar and certain other countries must obtain a visa before arriving. Visa extensions can be applied for at the **Immigration & Checkpoints Authority** (Map p634; ✆ 6391 6100; www.ica.gov.sg; Level 4, ICA Bldg, 10 Kallang Rd; ☉8am-4pm Mon-Fri; Ⓜ Lavender).

VOLUNTEERING

Volunteering in their local community is very important to Singaporeans. The website of **SG Cares** (www.sgcares.org) lists activities requiring assistance.

WOMEN TRAVELLERS

There are few problems for women travelling in Singapore. In Kampong Glam and Little India skimpy clothing may attract unwanted stares. Tampons and pads are widely available across the island, as are over-the-counter medications.

ⓘ Getting There & Away

AIR

Changi Airport (✆ 6595 6868; www.changiairport.com; Airport Blvd; Ⓜ Changi Airport), 20km northeast of Singapore's central business district (CBD), has four main terminals (the latest opened in 2017) and a fifth already in the works. Regularly voted the world's best airport, it is a major international gateway, with frequent flights to all corners of the globe. You'll find free internet, courtesy phones for local calls, foreign-exchange booths, medical centres, left luggage, hotels, day spas, showers, a gym, a swimming pool and no shortage of shops.

BOAT

Ferry services from Malaysia and Indonesia arrive at various ferry terminals in Singapore.

Changi Point Ferry Terminal (✆ 6545 2305; 51 Lorong Bekukong; ☉24hr; ⛴2)

HarbourFront Cruise & Ferry Terminal (Map p638; ✆ 6513 2200; www.singaporecruise.com; 1 Maritime Sq; Ⓜ HarbourFront)

Tanah Merah Ferry Terminal (✆ 6513 2200; www.singaporecruise.com.sg; 50 Tanah Merah Ferry Rd; ⛴35)

To/From Indonesia & Malaysia

Direct ferries run between the Riau Archipelago islands of Pulau Batam and Pulau Bintan and Singapore. The ferries are modern, fast and air-conditioned. A small ferry also runs between Singapore and Tanjung Belungkor in Malaysia.

BatamFast (✆ HarbourFront terminal 6270 2228, Tanah Merah terminal 6542 6310; www.batamfast.com) Ferries from Batam Centre,

Sekupang and Harbour Bay in Pulau Batam terminate at HarbourFront Ferry Terminal. Ferries from Nongsapura, also in Pulau Batam, terminate at the Tanah Merah Ferry Terminal.

Bintan Resort Ferries (✆ 6542 4369; www.brf.com.sg; 01-21 Tanah Merah Ferry Terminal, 50 Tanah Merah Ferry Rd; ☉7am-8pm Mon-Fri, 6.30am-8pm Sat & Sun; Ⓜ Tanah Merah, then bus 35) Ferries to Bandar Bentan Telani in Pulau Bintan depart from Tanah Merah Ferry Terminal.

Sindo Ferries (✆ HarbourFront terminal 6331 4123, Tanah Merah terminal 6331 4122; www.sindoferry.com.sg; 01-15 Tanah Merah Ferry Terminal, 50 Tanah Merah Ferry Rd; ⛴35) Ferries to Batam Centre, Sekupang, Waterfront and Tanjung Balai depart from HarbourFront Ferry Terminal. Ferries to Tanjung Pinang depart from Tanah Merah Ferry Terminal.

Limbongan Maju Ferry Services (✆ Tangjung Belungkor 07-827 8001; www.tanjungbelungkor.com) Ferries from Tanjung Belungkor, Malaysia, arrive at Changi Point Ferry Terminal.

BUS

If you are travelling beyond Johor Bahru, Malaysia, the simplest option is to catch a bus straight from Singapore, though there are more options and lower fares travelling from JB.

Numerous private companies run comfortable bus services to Singapore from many destinations in Malaysia, including Melaka and Kuala Lumpur, as well as from destinations such as Hat Yai in Thailand. Many of these services terminate at **Golden Mile Complex Bus Terminal** (5001 Beach Rd; Ⓜ Bugis, Nicoll Hwy), close to Kampong Glam. Golden Mile Complex houses numerous bus agencies specialising in journeys from Singapore to Malaysia or Thailand. You can book online at www.busonlineticket.com.

TRAIN

As of July 2015, it's no longer possible to catch a direct train from Singapore to Kuala Lumpur. Instead, Malaysian company Keretapi Tanah Melayu Berhad (www.ktmb.com.my) operates a shuttle train from **Woodlands Train Checkpoint** (11 Woodlands Crossing; ⛴170, Causeway Link Express from Queen St terminal) to JB Sentral with a connection to Kuala Lumpur. Tickets for the shuttle (S$5) can be bought at the counter. Trains leave from here to Kuala Lumpur, with connections on to Thailand. You can book tickets at the Woodlands or JB Sentral stations or via the dreadful KTM website.

ⓘ Getting Around

TO/FROM THE AIRPORT

MRT trains run into town from **Changi Airport** from 5.30am to 11.18pm; public buses run from 6am to midnight. Both the train and bus trips cost from S$1.69. The airport shuttle bus (adult/child S$9/$6) runs 24 hours a day.

A taxi into the city will cost anywhere from S$20 to S$40, and up to 50% more between midnight and 6am, plus airport surcharges. A four-seater limousine taxi is S$55, plus a S$15 surcharge per additional stop.

BICYCLE

Avoid cycling on roads. Drivers are sometimes aggressive and the roads themselves are uncomfortably hot. A much safer and more pleasant option for cyclists is Singapore's large network of parks and park connectors, not to mention the dedicated mountain-biking areas at Bukit Timah Nature Reserve, Tampines and Pulau Ubin.

Other excellent places for cycling include East Coast Park, Sentosa, Pasir Ris Park and the route linking Mt Faber Park, Telok Blangah Hill Park and Kent Ridge Park.

BUS

Singapore's extensive bus service is clean, efficient and regular, reaching every corner of the island. The two main operators are **SBS Transit** (1800 287 2727; www.sbstransit.com.sg) and **SMRT** (1800 336 8900; www.smrt.com.sg). Both offer similar services. For information and routes, check the websites. Alternatively, download the 'SG Buses' smartphone app, which will give you real-time bus arrivals.

Bus fares range from S$1 to S$2.10 (less with an EZ-Link card). When you board the bus, drop the exact money into the fare box (no change is given), or tap your EZ-Link card or Singapore Tourist Pass on the reader as you board, then again when you get off.

MASS RAPID TRANSIT (MRT)

The efficient Mass Rapid Transit (MRT) subway system is the easiest, quickest and most comfortable way to get around Singapore. The system operates from 5.30am to midnight, with trains at peak times running every two to three minutes, and off-peak every five to seven minutes. You'll find a map of the network at www.smrt.com.sg.

Single-trip tickets cost from S$1.40 to S$2.50 (plus a 10¢ refundable deposit), but if you're using the MRT a lot it can become a hassle buying and refunding tickets for every journey. A lot more convenient is the EZ-Link card. Alternatively, a **Singapore Tourist Pass** (www.thesingaporetouristpass.com.sg) offers unlimited train and bus travel (S$10 plus a S$10 refundable deposit) for one day.

TAXI

You can flag down a taxi any time, but in the city centre taxis are technically not allowed to stop anywhere except at designated taxi stands.

The fare system is complicated but thankfully it's all metered, so there's no haggling over

TRANSPORT MADE EZ

→ If you're staying in Singapore for more than a day or two, the easiest way to pay for travel on public transport is with the EZ-Link card (www.ezlink.com.sg). The card allows you to travel by train and bus by simply swiping it over sensors as you enter and leave a station or bus.

→ EZ-Link cards can be purchased from the customer service counters at MRT stations for S$12 (this includes a S$5 non-refundable deposit).

→ The card can also be bought at 7-Elevens for S$10 (including the S$5 non-refundable deposit).

→ Cards can be topped up with cash or by ATM cards at station ticket machines. The minimum top-up value is S$10 while the maximum stored value allowed on your card is S$500.

fares. The basic flagfall is S$3 to S$3.40 then S$0.22 for every 400m.

There's a whole raft of surcharges to note, among them:

→ 50% of the metered fare from midnight to 6am

→ 25% of the metered fare between 6am and 9.30am Monday to Friday, and 6pm to midnight daily

→ S$5 for airport trips from 5pm to midnight Friday to Sunday, and S$3 at all other times

→ S$3 city-area surcharge from 5pm to midnight

→ S$2.30 to S$8 for telephone bookings

Payment by credit card incurs a 10% surcharge. You can also pay using your EZ-Link transport card. For a comprehensive list of fares and surcharges, visit www.taxisingapore.com.

Comfort Taxi & CityCab (6552 1111; www.cdgtaxi.com.sg)

Premier Taxis (6363 6888; www.premiertaxi.com.sg)

SMRT Taxis (6555 8888; www.smrt.com.sg)

TRISHAW

Trishaws peaked just after WWII when motorised transport was practically nonexistent and trishaw drivers could make a tidy income. Today there are only around 250 trishaws left in Singapore, mainly plying the tourist routes. Trishaws have banded together and are now managed in a queue system by **Trishaw Uncle** (Map p634; 6337 7111; www.trishawuncle.com.sg; Albert Mall Trishaw Park, Queen St; 30min tour adult/child from S$39/29, 45min tour S$49/39; Bugis).

Thailand

🎵 66 / POP 68.4 MILLION / AREA 514,000 SQ KM

Best Activities

➡ Diving in the Similan Islands Marine National Park (p767)

➡ Amita Thai Cooking Class (p666)

➡ Rock climbing at Railay (p777)

➡ Trekking at Chiang Rai (p710)

Top Thai Phrases

Hello sà-wàt-dee

Thank you kòrp kun

Do you speak English? kun pôot pah-săh ang-grìt dâi măi

Why Go?

Thailand is an abundant land with naturally good looks and warm hospitality. A stunning coastline lapped at by cerulean seas invites winter-weary travellers, while the northern mountains that cascade into the misty horizon invite scenic journeys. In between are emerald-coloured rice fields and busy, prosperous cities built around sacred temples. The markets are piled high with pyramids of colourful fruits and tasty treats can be found on every corner.

You'll suffer few travelling hardships, save for a few pushy touts, in this land of comfort and convenience. Bangkok reigns as an Asian superstar, Chiang Mai excels in liveability and the tropical islands are up all night to party. It is relatively cheap to hop around by plane or leapfrog anywhere else in the region, though once you leave you'll miss the fiery curries and simple stir-fries that earn Thai cuisine global acclaim.

When to Go
Bangkok

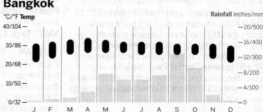

Nov–Feb Cool and dry season; peak tourist season is December to January.

Mar–Jun Hot season is hot but a good shoulder season for the beaches.

Jul–Oct Wet season begins with a drizzle and ends with a downpour; July to August is a mini high season.

Entering the Country

Bangkok is the main flight hub, with two airports, but international flights also arrive and depart from Chiang Mai, Chiang Rai, Hat Yai, Ko Samui, Krabi, Pattaya and Phuket. There are overland border crossings with Cambodia, Laos, Malaysia and Myanmar. You can also travel by sea between Thailand and Malaysia.

REGIONS AT A GLANCE

The major cities of Bangkok and Chiang Mai offer an exhilarating mix of temples and palaces, buzzing night-life and fantastic food. Central Thailand has mellow ancient capitals and national parks. Head to northern and north-eastern Thailand for hill treks and outdoor adventures. Ko Chang and the eastern seaboard has islands and charming rural towns.

Come to Hua Hin and the the southern gulf for family-friendly resort towns and super seafood. Further south, the islands of Ko Samui and the lower gulf have legendary beach parties, while on the opposite coast, Phuket and the idyllic islands of the Andaman Sea have some of the best diving and snorkelling in Southeast Asia, as well as dreamy beaches and plenty of nightlife.

Essential Food & Drink

Pàt gàprow gài Fiery stir-fry of chopped chicken, chillies, garlic and fresh basil.

Kôw pàt Fried rice, garnish it with ground chillies, sugar, fish sauce and a squirt of lime.

Pàt prík tai krà-thiam gài/mǒo Stir-fried chicken or pork with black pepper and garlic.

Pàt tai Thailand's famous dish of rice noodles fried with egg and prawns garnished with bean sprouts, peanuts and chillies.

Pàt pàk kanáh Stir-fried Chinese greens, often fried with meat (upon request), served over rice; simple but delicious.

Top Tips

➡ Eat at markets or street stalls for true Thai flavor.

➡ Hop aboard local transport – it's cheap and a great way to hang out with the locals.

➡ Hire a bicycle to tour towns and neighbourhoods.

➡ Learn a few Thai phrases and always smile.

➡ Avoid the first-timer scams: one-day gem sales in Bangkok, insanely low (or high) transport prices, dodgy tailors etc.

➡ Learn how to bargain without being rude.

➡ Avoid touching the Thais on the head.

➡ Don't point with your feet.

AT A GLANCE

Currency Baht (B)

Visas For visitors from most countries, visas are generally not required for stays of up to 90 days.

Money Most places in Thailand deal only with cash. Some foreign credit cards are accepted in high-end establishments.

Language Thai

Exchange Rates

Australia	A$1	26B
Canada	C$1	25B
China	Y10	50B
Euro	€1	37B
Japan	¥100	32B
New Zealand	NZ$1	24B
South Korea	1000W	30B
UK	£1	44B
US	US$1	34B

THAILAND

Daily Costs

Basic guesthouse room 600B to 1000B

Market/street stall meal 40B to100B

Small bottle of beer 100B

Public transport around town 20B to 50B

Resources

Thaivisa (www.thaivisa. com)

Lonely Planet (www.lonely planet.com/thailand)

Tourism Authority of Thailand (TAT; www.tourism thailand.org)

Thai Language (www. thai-language.com)

Thailand Highlights

1 Bangkok (p660)
Joining the crowds and the chaos in the hyperactive capital.

2 Ko Pha-Ngan (p751) Overdosing on sunsets.

3 Ko Tao (p757) Getting dive certified.

4 Chiang Mai (p697) Learning to cook like a Thai auntie.

5 Sukhothai (p691) Pedalling around the ruined capital.

6 Khao Yai National Park (p730) Crawling around with the critters.

7 Mae Hong Son (p719) Trekking to the remote villages.

8 Nong Khai (p735) Hanging out on the Mekong River.

9 Hua Hin (p743) Eating like royalty.

VIETNAM

★ **PHNOM PENH**

Tonlé Sap

Pursat

Pailin ◉ ◉Battambang

Trat ◉ ◉ Chanthaburi

Pong Nam Ron ◉ Koh Kong

3

Laem Ngop ◉ ◎ Hat Lek

Ko Chang ◎ Ko Kut

Mu Ko Chang Marine National Park

Sihanoukville ◉

GULF OF THAILAND

Rayong ◉ ◉ Sattahip

Ban Phe ◎ Ko Samet

Thap Sakae ◎ Bang Saphan

Prachuap Khiri Khan ◉

9 Hua Hin ◉

Cha-am ◉

4

Myeik ◉

ANDAMAN SEA

Isthmus of Kra

Ranong ◉ ✕

Kawthoung ✕

Chaiya ◉

Chumphon ◉

Ang Thong Marine National Park

3 Ko Tao

2 Ko Pha-Ngan

◎ Ko Samui

◎ Don Sak

Surat Thani ◉

41

Thung Song ◎

Nakhon Si Thammarat ◉

◎ Hua Sai

408

◎ Ranot

Phatthalung ◉

Songkhla ◉

Hat Yai ◉

4

Satun ◉

Perlis ◎

Kubala ◎

Yala ◉ ✕

Pattani ◉

42

Narathiwat ◉

Kota ◎ ◎ Bharu

Sungai Kolok ✕ ◎ Rantau Panjang

Betong ◉

Pengkalan Hulu ◎

MALAYSIA

Alor Setar ◎

Pulau Langkawi ◎

Sungai Petani ◉

Ko Tarutao Marine National Park

Trang ◉

Krabi ◉ **10 Railay**

◎ Ko Lanta

◎ Ko Muk

Phang-Nga ◉

Ko Yao Yai ◎

Ko Phi Phi ◎

Phuket Town ◉

Hat Noppharat Thara-Mu Ko Phi Phi Marine National Park

Khao Lak/Lam Ru National Park

Takua Pa ◉

Similan Marine Islands National Park

Surin Islands Marine National Park

Khao Sok National Park

Laem Son National Park

401

INDIAN OCEAN

BANGKOK

♪ 02 / POPULATION 9.27 MILLION

Bored in Bangkok? You've got to be kidding. This high-energy city loves neon and noise, chaos and concrete, fashion and the future. But look beyond the modern behemoth and you'll find an old-fashioned village napping in the shade of a narrow soi (lane). It's an urban connoisseur's dream: a city with vibrant markets, historic temples and palaces, the hidden lanes of Chinatown and fantastic shopping and nightlife. And did we mention the food? For adventurous foodies, there is probably no finer or better-value dining destination in the world. You'll probably pass through Bangkok en route to some place else as it is such a convenient and major transport hub. At first you'll be confounded, then relieved and pampered when you return, and slightly sentimental when you depart for the last time.

◉ Sights

Cultural and religious destinations form the bulk of Bangkok's most popular sights. If you're open to self-guided exploration, then you can add fresh markets and neighbourhoods to this list.

◉ Ko Ratanakosin & Around

With its royal and religious affiliations, this area hosts many Thai Buddhist pilgrims as well as many foreign sightseers. The temples with royal connections enforce a strict dress code – clothes should cover to the elbows and knees and foreigners should not wear open-toed shoes. Behave respectfully and remove shoes when instructed. Do your touring early in the morning to avoid the heat and the crowds. And ignore anyone who says that the sight is closed.

★ Wat Phra Kaew & Grand Palace   BUDDHIST TEMPLE

(วัดพระแก้ว, พระบรมมหาราชวัง; Map p670; Th Na Phra Lan; 500B; ⊙8.30am-3.30pm; ⚓Chang Pier, Maharaj Pier, Phra Chan Tai Pier) Also known as the Temple of the Emerald Buddha, Wat Phra Kaew is the colloquial name of the vast, fairy-tale compound that also includes the former residence of the Thai monarch, the Grand Palace.

This ground was consecrated in 1782, the first year of Bangkok rule, and is today Bangkok's biggest tourist attraction and a pilgrimage destination for devout Buddhists and nationalists. The 94.5-hectare grounds encompass more than 100 buildings that represent 200 years of royal history and architectural experimentation.

★ Wat Pho   BUDDHIST TEMPLE

(วัดโพธิ์/วัดพระเชตุพน, Wat Phra Chetuphon; Map p670; Th Sanam Chai; 100B; ⊙8.30am-6.30pm; ⚓Tien Pier) You'll find (slightly) fewer tourists here than at Wat Phra Kaew, but Wat Pho is our favourite among Bangkok's biggest sights. In fact, the compound incorporates a host of superlatives: the city's largest reclining Buddha, the largest collection of Buddha images in Thailand and the country's earliest centre for public education.

Almost too big for its shelter is Wat Pho's highlight, the genuinely impressive **Reclining Buddha**.

★ Wat Arun   BUDDHIST TEMPLE

(วัดอรุณฯ; Map p670; www.watarun.net; off Th Arun Amarin; 50B; ⊙8am-6pm; ⚓cross-river ferry from Tien Pier) After the fall of Ayuthaya, King Taksin ceremoniously clinched control here on the site of a local shrine and established a royal palace and a temple to house the Emerald Buddha. The temple was renamed after the Indian god of dawn (Aruna) and in honour of the literal and symbolic founding of a new Ayuthaya. Today the temple is one of Bangkok's most iconic structures – not to mention one of the few Buddhist temples one is encouraged to climb on.

Museum of Siam   MUSEUM

(สถาบันพิพิธภัณฑ์การเรียนรู้แห่งชาติ; Map p670; www.museumsiam.org; Th Maha Rat; 300B; ⊙10am-6pm Tue-Sun; ⚓Tien Pier) Although temporarily closed for renovation when we stopped by, this fun museum's collection employs a variety of media to explore the origins of the Thai people and their culture. Housed in a European-style 19th-century building that was once the Ministry of Commerce, the exhibits are presented in a contemporary, engaging and interactive fashion not typically found in Thailand's museums. They are also refreshingly balanced and entertaining, with galleries dealing with a range of questions about the origins of the nation and its people.

National Museum   MUSEUM

(พิพิธภัณฑสถานแห่งชาติ; Map p670; 4 Th Na Phra That; 200B; ⊙9am-4pm Wed-Sun; ⚓Chang Pier, Maharaj Pier, Phra Chan Tai Pier) Often touted as Southeast Asia's biggest museum, Thailand's National Museum is home to an impressive, albeit occasionally dusty, collection of items, best appreciated on one of the museum's free twice-weekly guided **tours** (Map p670; National Museum, 4 Th Na Phra That; free with museum admission; ⏰9.30am Wed & Thu; ⛴Chang Pier, Maharaj Pier).

Most of the museum's structures were built in 1782 as the palace of Rama I's viceroy, Prince Wang Na. Rama V turned it into a museum in 1874, and today there are three permanent exhibitions spread out over several buildings. When we visited, several of the exhibition halls were being renovated.

Amulet Market
MARKET

(ตลาดพระเครื่องวัดมหาธาตุ; Map p670; Th Maha Rat; ⏰7am-5pm; ⛴Chang Pier, Maharaj Pier, Phra Chan Tai Pier) This arcane and fascinating market claims both the footpaths along Th Maha Rat and Th Phra Chan, as well as a dense network of covered market stalls that runs south from Phra Chan Pier; the easiest entry point is clearly marked 'Trok Maha That'. The trade is based around small talismans carefully prized by collectors, monks, taxi drivers and people in dangerous professions.

◉ Chinatown

Cramped and crowded Chinatown is a beehive of commercial activity. Th Yaowarat is fun to explore at night when it's lit up like a Christmas tree and packed with food vendors. The area has undergone a renaissance in recent years, with new and artsy businesses opening.

Wat Traimit (Golden Buddha)
BUDDHIST TEMPLE

(วัดไตรมิตร, Temple of the Golden Buddha; Map p664; Th Mittaphap Thai-China; 100B; ⏰8am-5pm; ⛴Ratchawong Pier, Ⓜ Hua Lamphong exit 1) The attraction at Wat Traimit is undoubtedly the impressive 3m-tall, 5.5-tonne, **solid-gold Buddha image**, which gleams like, well, gold. Sculpted in the graceful Sukhothai style, the image was 'discovered' some 60 years ago beneath a stucco/plaster exterior, when it fell from a crane while being moved to a new building within the temple compound.

Talat Mai
MARKET

(ตลาดใหม่; Map p664; Soi Yaowarat 6/Charoen Krung 16; ⏰6am-6pm; ⛴Ratchawong Pier, Ⓜ Hua Lamphong exit 1 & taxi) With nearly two centuries of commerce under its belt, New Market is no longer an entirely accurate name for this strip of commerce. Regardless, this is Bangkok's, if not Thailand's, most Chinese

market, and the dried goods, seasonings, spices and sauces will be familiar to anyone who's ever spent time in China. Even if you're not interested in food, the hectic atmosphere (be on guard for motorcycles squeezing between shoppers) and exotic sights and smells create something of a surreal sensory experience.

◉ Other Areas

★Jim Thompson House
HISTORIC BUILDING

(เรือนไทยจิมทอมป์สัน; Map p674; www.jimthompsonhouse.com; 6 Soi Kasem San 2; adult/student 150/100B; ⏰9am-6pm, compulsory tours every 20min; ⛴klorng boat to Sapan Hua Chang Pier, Ⓢ National Stadium exit 1) This jungly compound is the former home of the eponymous American silk entrepreneur and art collector. Born in Delaware in 1906, Thompson briefly served in the Office of Strategic Services (the forerunner of the CIA) in Thailand during WWII. He settled in Bangkok after the war, when his neighbours' handmade silk caught his eye and piqued his business sense; he sent samples to fashion houses in Milan, London and Paris, gradually building a steady worldwide clientele.

★Lumphini Park
PARK

(สวนลุมพินี; Map p664; bounded by Th Sarasin, Rama IV, Th Witthayu/Wireless Rd & Th Ratchadamri; ⏰4.30am-9pm; Ⓜ Lumphini exit 3, Si Lom exit 1, Ⓢ Sala Daeng exit 3, Ratchadamri exit 2) Named after the Buddha's place of birth in Nepal, Lumphini Park is the best way to escape Bangkok without actually leaving town. Shady paths, a large artificial lake and swept lawns temporarily blot out the roaring traffic and hulking concrete towers.

Bangkokian Museum
MUSEUM

(พิพิธภัณฑ์ชาวบางกอก; Map p664; 273 Soi 43, Th Charoen Krung; admission by donation; ⏰10am-4pm Wed-Sun; ⛴Si Phraya/River City Pier) A collection of three antique structures built

Wat Phra Kaew & Grand Palace

EXPLORE BANGKOK'S PREMIER MONUMENTS TO RELIGION & REGENCY

The first area tourists enter is the Buddhist temple compound generally referred to as Wat Phra Kaew. A covered walkway surrounds the area, the inner walls of which are decorated with the **1 2 murals of the Ramakian**. Originally painted during the reign of Rama I (r 1782–1809), the murals, which depict the Hindu epic the *Ramayana*, span 178 panels that describe the struggles of Rama to rescue his kidnapped wife, Sita.

After taking in the story, pass through one of the gateways guarded by **3 yaksha** to the inner compound. The most important structure here is the **4 bòht (ordination hall)**, which houses the **5 Emerald Buddha**.

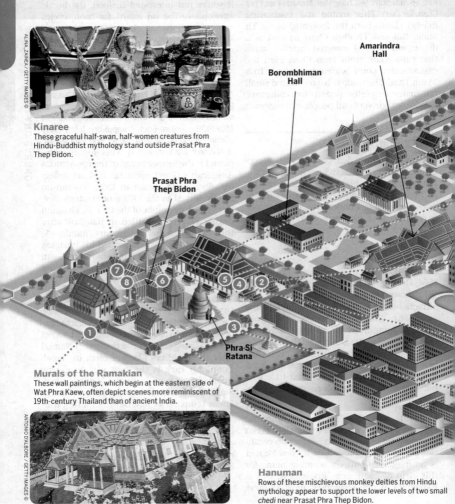

Kinaree
These graceful half-swan, half-women creatures from Hindu-Buddhist mythology stand outside Prasat Phra Thep Bidon.

Amarindra Hall

Borombhiman Hall

Prasat Phra Thep Bidon

Phra Si Ratana

Murals of the Ramakian
These wall paintings, which begin at the eastern side of Wat Phra Kaew, often depict scenes more reminiscent of 19th-century Thailand than of ancient India.

Hanuman
Rows of these mischievous monkey deities from Hindu mythology appear to support the lower levels of two small *chedi* near Prasat Phra Thep Bidon.

ALINA_ZIENKA / GETTY IMAGES ©

ANTONIO DALBORE / GETTY IMAGES ©

Head east to the so-called Upper Terrace, an elevated area home to the **6 spires of the three primary chedi**. The middle structure, Phra Mondop, is used to house Buddhist manuscripts. This area is also home to several of Wat Phra Kaew's noteworthy mythical beings, including beckoning **7 kinaree** and several grimacing **8 Hanuman**.

Proceed through the western gate to the compound known as the Grand Palace. Few of the buildings here are open to the public. The most noteworthy structure is **9 Chakri Mahaprasat**. Built in 1882, the exterior of the hall is a unique blend of Western and traditional Thai architecture.

The Three Spires
The elaborate seven-tiered roof of Phra Mondop, the Khmer-style peak of Prasat Phra Thep Bidon, and the gilded Phra Si Ratana *chedi* are the tallest structures in the compound.

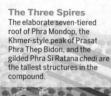
LEPNEVA IRINA / SHUTTERSTOCK ©

Emerald Buddha
Despite the name, this diminutive statue (it's only 66cm tall) is actually carved from nephrite, a type of jade.

ALEXEY STIOP / GETTY IMAGES ©

The Death of Thotsakan
The panels progress clockwise, culminating at the western edge of the compound with the death of Thotsakan, Sita's kidnapper, and his elaborate funeral procession.

Chakri Mahaprasat
This structure is sometimes referred to as *fa·ràng sài chá·dah* (Westerner in a Thai crown) because each wing is topped by a *mon·dòp*: a spire representing a Thai adaptation of a Hindu shrine.

DESIGN PICS / BLAKE KENT / GETTY IMAGES ©

Dusit Hall

Bòht (Ordination Hall)
This structure is an early example of the Ratanakosin school of architecture, which combines traditional stylistic holdovers from Ayuthaya along with more modern touches from China and the West.

Yaksha
Each entrance to the Wat Phra Kaew compound is watched over by a pair of vigilant and enormous *yaksha*, ogres or giants from Hindu mythology.

ZZVET / GETTY IMAGES ©

Central Bangkok

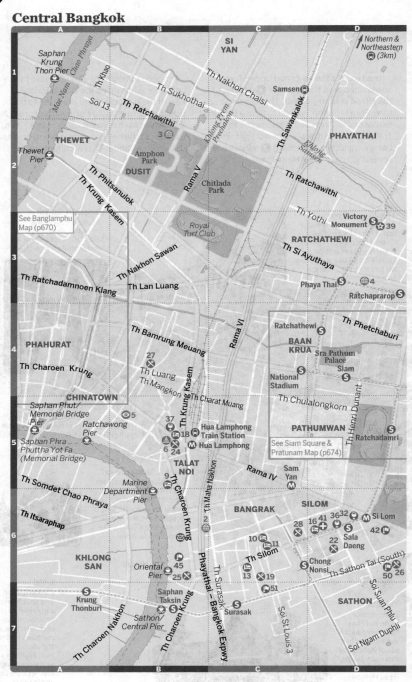

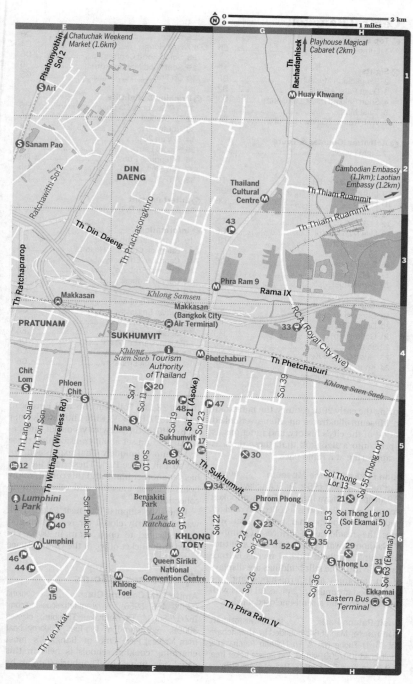

0   2 km
0   1 miles

Phahonyothin Soi 2

🚇 Ari

🚇 Sanam Pao

Chatuchak Weekend Market (1.6km)

Th Rachadaphisek

Playhouse Magical Cabaret (2km)

Ⓜ Huay Khwang

DIN DAENG

Ratchawithi Soi 2

Th Din Daeng

Th Prachasongkhro

Th Ratchaprarop

Cambodian Embassy (1.1km); Laotian Embassy (1.2km)

Th Thiam Ruammit

Th Thiam Ruammit

Thailand Cultural Centre Ⓜ

43

Ⓜ Phra Ram 9

Rama IX

Khlong Samsen

Ⓜ Makkasan

Makkasan (Bangkok City Air Terminal)

RCA (Royal City Ave)

33

PRATUNAM

SUKHUMVIT

Chit Lom 🚇

Phloen Chit 🚇

ℹ Tourism Authority of Thailand

Ⓜ Phetchaburi

Th Phetchaburi

Khlong Suen Saeb

Khlong Suen Saeb

Th Lang Suan

Th Ton Son

Th Witthayu (Wireless Rd)

Soi 7

Soi 11

20

Soi 19

48

Soi 21 (Asoke)

Soi 23

47

Soi 39

🚇 Nana

🚇 Sukhumvit

17

Ⓜ Asok

Th Sukhumvit

30

Soi 55 (Thong Lor)

12

Soi 10

8

34

Lumphini Park

49

40

Ⓜ Lumphini

46

44

15

Soi Phlukchit

Benjakiti Park

Lake Ratchada

Soi 16

Queen Sirikit National Convention Centre

Ⓜ Khlong Toei

Th Yen Akat

Soi 22

KHLONG TOEY

7

Soi 24

23

Soi 26

14

52

Soi 26

Soi 36

Th Phra Ram IV

Phrom Phong 🚇

Soi Thong Lor 13

21

Soi 53

Soi Thong Lor 10 (Soi Ekamai 5)

38

35

29

31

🚇 Thong Lo

Soi 63 (Ekamai)

Eastern Bus Terminal 🚇 Ekamai

Central Bangkok

during the early 20th century, the Bangkokian Museum illustrates an often-overlooked period of the city's history, and functions as a peek into a Bangkok that, these days, is disappearing at a rapid pace.

Suan Pakkad Palace Museum MUSEUM
(วังสวนผักกาด; Map p664; Th Si Ayuthaya; 100B; ⊙9am-4pm; ⑤Phaya Thai exit 4) An overlooked treasure, Suan Pakkad is a collection of eight traditional wooden Thai houses that was once the residence of Princess Chumbon of Nakhon Sawan and before that a lettuce farm (in Thai, Suan Pakkad means Lettuce Farm). Within the stilt buildings are displays of art, antiques and furnishings, and the landscaped grounds are a peaceful oasis with ducks, swans and a semi-enclosed garden.

Dusit Palace Park MUSEUM, HISTORIC SITE
(วังสวนดุสิต; Map p664; bounded by Th Ratchawithi, Th U Thong Nai & Th Nakhon Ratchasima; adult/child 100/20B, with Grand Palace ticket free; ⊙9.30am-4pm Tue-Sun; 🚢Thewet Pier, ⑤Phaya

Thai exit 2 & taxi) Following his first European tour in 1897, Rama V (King Chulalongkorn; r 1868–1910) returned with visions of European castles and set about transforming these styles into a uniquely Thai expression, today's Dusit Palace Park. These days the king has yet another home and this complex now holds a house museum and other cultural collections.

When we stopped by, Dusit Palace Park was temporarily closed for renovation and was expected to open again in 2018; enquire at the ticket office of the Grand Palace (p660).

🏃 Courses & Tours

Amita Thai Cooking Class COOKING
(📞02 466 8966; www.amitathaicooking.com; 162/17 Soi 14, Th Wutthakat, Thonburi; classes 3000B; ⊙9.30am-1pm Thu-Tue; 🚢klorng boat from Maharaj Pier) One of Bangkok's most charming cooking schools is held in this canal-side house in Thonburi. Taught by

the delightfully enthusiastic Piyawadi 'Tam' Jantrupon, a course here includes a romp through the garden and instruction in four dishes. The fee covers transport, which in this case takes the form of a boat ride from Maharaj Pier.

Grasshopper Adventures — CYCLING

(Map p670; ☑02 280 0832; www.grasshopperadventures.com; 57 Th Ratchadamnoen Klang; half-/full-day tours from 1350/2400B; ⊗8.30am-6.30pm; ⬒klorng boat to Phanfa Leelard Pier) This lauded outfit runs a variety of unique bicycle tours in and around Bangkok, including a night tour and a tour of the city's historic zone.

✱ Festivals & Events

Chinese New Year — CULTURAL

(⊗Jan or Feb) Thai-Chinese celebrate the Lunar New Year with a week of house-cleaning, lion dances and fireworks. Most festivities centre on Chinatown. Dates vary.

Songkran — CULTURAL

(⊗mid-Apr) The celebration of the Thai New Year has morphed into a water war with high-powered water guns and water balloons being launched at suspecting and unsuspecting participants. The most intense water battles take place on Th Silom and Th Khao San.

Royal Ploughing Ceremony — CULTURAL

(⊗May) His Majesty the King commences rice-planting season with a ceremony at Sanam Luang. Dates vary.

Vegetarian Festival — FOOD & DRINK

(⊗Sep or Oct) This 10-day Chinese-Buddhist festival wheels out yellow-bannered streetside vendors serving meatless meals. The greatest concentration of vendors is found in Chinatown. Dates vary.

Loi Krathong — CULTURAL

(⊗early Nov) A beautiful festival where, on the night of the full moon, small lotus-shaped boats made of banana leaf and containing a lit candle are set adrift on Mae Nam Chao Phraya.

🛏 Sleeping

🛏 Th Khao San, Banglamphu & Thewet

Banglamphu still holds the bulk of Bangkok's budget places. Lots of eating, drinking and shopping options are other clever reasons to stay in Banglamphu, although it can feel somewhat isolated from the rest of Bangkok.

★Chern — HOSTEL $

(Map p670; ☑02 621 1133; www.chernbangkok.com; 17 Soi Ratchasak; dm 400B; r 1400-1900B; ❄@🛜; ⬒klorng boat to Phanfa Leelard Pier) The vast, open spaces and white, overexposed tones of this hostel converge in an almost afterlife-like feel. The eight-bed dorms are above average, but we particularly like the private rooms, which are equipped with attractively minimalist touches, a large desk, TV, safe, fridge and heaps of space, and are a steal at this price.

NapPark Hostel — HOSTEL $

(Map p670; ☑02 282 2324; www.nappark.com; 5 Th Tani; dm 440-600B; ❄@🛜; ⬒Phra Athit/Banglamphu Pier) This popular hostel features dorm rooms of various sizes, the smallest and most expensive of which boasts six pod-like beds outfitted with power points, mini-TV, reading lamp and wi-fi. Cultural-based activities and inviting communal areas ensure that you may not actually get the chance to plug in.

Suneta Hostel Khaosan — HOSTEL $

(Map p670; ☑02 629 0150; www.sunetahostel.com; 209-211 Th Kraisi; incl breakfast dm 470-570B, r 1180B; ❄@🛜; ⬒Phra Athit/Banglamphu Pier) A pleasant, low-key atmosphere, a unique, retro-themed design (some of the dorm rooms resemble sleeping-car carriages), a location just off the main drag and friendly service are what make Suneta stand out.

Niras Bangkoc — HOSTEL $

(Map p670; ☑02 221 4442; www.nirasbankoc.com; 204-206 Th Mahachai; dm 450-500B, r 1300-1500B; ❄🛜; ⬒klorng boat to Phanfa Leelard Pier) A counterpart to Bangkok's predominately modern-feeling hostels, Niras takes advantage of its location in an antique shophouse to arrive at a charmingly old-school feel. Both the four- and six- bed dorms and private rooms (some of which share bathrooms) feature dark woods and vintage furniture, with access to friendly staff, a cosy ground-floor cafe and an atmospheric location.

Fortville Guesthouse — HOTEL $

(Map p670; ☑02 282 3932; www.fortvilleguesthouse.com; 9 Th Phra Sumen; r 820-1190B; ❄@🛜; ⬒Phra Athit/Banglamphu Pier) With an exterior that combines elements of a modern

Food Spotter's Guide

Spanning four distinct regions, influences from China to the Middle East, a multitude of ingredients and a reputation for spice, Thai food can be more than a bit overwhelming. So to point you in the direction of the good stuff, we've put together a shortlist of the country's must-eat dishes.

1. Đôm yam
The 'sour Thai soup' moniker featured on many menus is a feeble description of this mouth-puckeringly tart and intensely spicy herbal broth.

2. Pàt tai
Thin rice noodles fried with egg, tofu and shrimp, and seasoned with fish sauce, tamarind and dried chilli, have emerged as the poster child for Thai food.

3. Gaang kĕe·o wăhn
Known outside of Thailand as green curry, this intersection of a piquant, herbal spice paste and rich coconut milk is single-handedly emblematic of Thai cuisine's unique flavours and ingredients.

4. Yam
This family of Thai 'salads' combines meat or seafood with a tart and spicy dressing and fresh herbs.

5. Lâhp
Minced meat seasoned with roasted rice powder, lime, fish sauce and fresh herbs is a one-dish crash course in the rustic flavours of Thailand's northeast.

6. Bà·mèe
Although Chinese in origin, these wheat-and-egg noodles, typically served with roast pork and/or crab, have become a Thai hawker-stall staple.

7. Kôw mòk
The Thai version of biryani couples golden rice and tender chicken with a sweet and sour dip and a savoury broth.

8. Sôm·đam
'Papaya salad' hardly does justice to this tear-inducingly spicy dish of strips of crunchy unripe papaya pounded in a mortar and pestle with tomato, long beans, chilli, lime and fish sauce.

9. Kôw soy
Even outside of its home in Thailand's north, there's a cult following for this soup that combines flat egg-and-wheat noodles in a rich, spice-laden, coconut-milk-based broth.

10. Pàt pàk bûng fai daang
Crunchy green vegetables, flash-fried with heaps of chilli and garlic, is Thai comfort food.

NARIN NONTHAMAND/SHUTTERSTOCK ©

NENEULTIMATE/SHUTTERSTOCK ©

3

CHOOKGEE RONKAEW/SHUTTERSTOCK ©

PAUL BRIGHTON/SHUTTERSTOCK ©

5

MOXUMBIC/SHUTTERSTOCK ©

CBENJASUWAN/SHUTTERSTOCK ©

10

PIYATO/SHUTTERSTOCK ©

Banglamphu

THAILAND BANGKOK

Map Labels

- Phra Athit/ Banglamphu Pier
- Phra Pin Klao Bridge Pier
- Saphan Phra Pin Klao
- Th Phra Athit
- 15 20
- Soi Ram Buttri
- Th Chao Fa
- Bangkok Information Center
- Th Somdet Phra Pin Klao
- Th Rongmai
- Bangkok Noi (Thonburi) Train Station
- Khlong Bangkok Noi
- THONBURI
- Thonburi Railway Station Pier
- Siriraj Hospital
- Mae Nam Chao Phraya
- Phra Chan Pier
- Thammasat University
- 6
- Th Na Phra That
- Sanam Luang
- Wang Lang/ Siriraj Pier
- Th Phra Chan
- Th Phrannok
- 4
- Soi Tambon Wanglang 1
- Th Maha Rat
- Maharaj Pier
- Silpakorn University
- Th Ratchadamnoen Nai
- Wat Rakhang Pier
- BANGKOK NOI
- Chang Pier
- Th Na Phra Lan
- Th Lak Meuang
- Mae Nam Chao Phraya
- Wat Phra Kaew & Grand Palace
- 3
- Th Sanam Chai
- Th Maha Rat
- KO RATANAKOSIN
- Saranrom Royal Garden
- Khlong Mon
- Th Thai Wang
- Tien Pier
- Wat Pho 2
- Th Arun Amarin
- Th Chetuphon
- Wat Arun Pier
- Soi Pratu Nokyung
- Th Sanam Chai
- Wat Arun 1
- 5

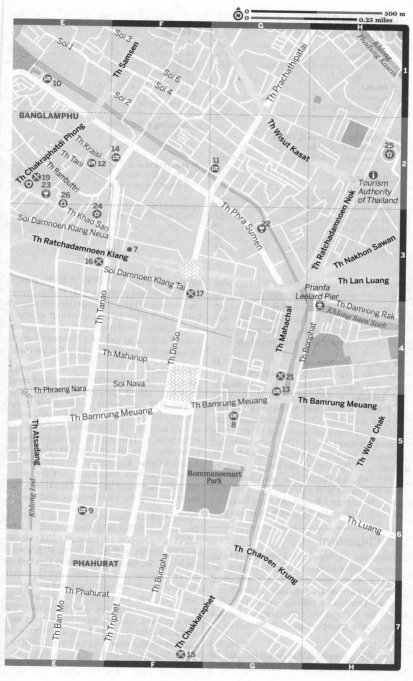

Banglamphu

church and/or castle, and an interior that relies on mirrors and industrial themes, the design concept of this hotel is tough to pin down. The rooms themselves are stylishly minimalist, and the more expensive ones include perks such as a fridge and balcony.

★**Lamphu Treehouse**　HOTEL $$
(Map p670; ☑02 282 0991; www.lamphutreehotel.com; 155 Wanchat Bridge, off Th Prachathipatai; incl breakfast r 1650-2500B; ste 3500-4500B; ✳@⊙✳; ☒klorng boat to Phanfa Leelard Pier) Despite the name, this attractive midranger has its feet firmly on land, and as such represents brilliant value. The wood-panelled rooms are attractive, inviting and well maintained, and the rooftop sun lounge, pool, internet cafe, restaurant and quiet canal-side location ensure that you may never want to leave. An annexe a few blocks away increases the odds of snagging an elusive reservation.

⌂ Chinatown

Chinatown is home to some good-value budget and midrange accommodation options; access to some of the city's best street food and its main train station are additional pluses. Downsides include noise, pollution and the neighbourhood's relative distance from public transport and 'new' Bangkok.

Loftel 22　HOSTEL $
(Map p664; www.loftel22bangkok.com; 952 Soi 22, Th Charoen Krung; dm 250-300B; r with shared bathroom 850-1300B; ✳@⊙; ☒Marine Department Pier, MHua Lamphong exit 1) Stylish, inviting dorms and private rooms (all with shared bathrooms) have been coaxed out of these two adjoining shophouses. Friendly service and a location in one of Chinatown's most atmospheric corners round out the package.

Wanderlust　HOSTEL $
(Map p664; ☑083 046 8647; www.facebook.com/onederlust; 149-151 Rama IV; dm 450B, r 1300-1800B; ✳@⊙; ☒, MHua Lamphong exit 1) An almost clinical-feeling industrial vibe rules at this new hostel. The dorms span four to eight beds, and the private rooms are on the tight side, with the cheapest sharing bathrooms. These are united by a hyper-chic ground-floor cafe-restaurant. Not the greatest value accommodation in Chinatown, but quite possibly the most image-conscious.

Feung Nakorn Balcony　HOTEL $$
(Map p670; ☑02 622 1100; www.feungnakorn.com; 125 Th Fuang Nakhon; incl breakfast r 2200-4400B, ste 4300-4800B; ✳@⊙; ☒Saphan Phut/Memorial Bridge Pier, Pak Klong Taladd Pier) Located in a former school, the 42 rooms here surround an inviting garden courtyard and are generally large, bright and cheery. Amenities such as a free minibar, safe and flat-screen TV are standard, and the hotel has a quiet and secluded location away from the strip, with capable staff. A charming and inviting (if not exceedingly great-value) place to stay.

🛏 Siam Square

Siam Square and the surrounding area offers a good selection of budget and mid-range accommodation. Added benefits include a central location and easy access to food, shopping and public transport.

★ Lub*d   HOSTEL $
(Map p674; ☎02 612 4999; www.siamsquare.lubd. com; Rama I; dm 550B, r 1900-2500B; ❄@🛜; ⓢNational Stadium exit 1) A modern-feeling hostel with diversions including an inviting communal area stocked with games and a bar, and thoughtful facilities range from washing machines to a theatre room. If this one's full, there's another branch off Th Silom.

Chao Hostel   HOSTEL $
(Map p674; ☎02 217 3083; www.chaohostel. com; 8th fl, 865 Rama I; incl breakfast dm 550B, r 1600-1800B; ❄@🛜; ⓢNational Stadium exit 1) Blending modern minimalist and Thai design elements, not to mention tonnes of open space, the new Chao is one of the most sophisticated hostels we've encountered in Bangkok. Dorms are roomy, with six beds and en-suite bathrooms, and include access to several inviting communal areas.

Bed Station Hostel   HOSTEL $
(Map p674; ☎02 019 5477; www.bedstationhostel.com; 486/149-150 Soi 16, Th Phetchaburi; incl breakfast dm 500-650B, r 1350-1550B; ❄@🛜; ⓢRatchathewi exit 3) A handsome industrial-chic theme unites the dorms and private rooms at this hostel. The former range from four to eight beds and include access to tidy toilet facilities and a laundry room, while the latter are stylish and functional, if basic, and mostly lacking windows.

🛏 Sukhumvit

Th Sukhumvit is home to a significant slice of Bangkok's accommodation, and as such there's a bit of everything here.

Pause Hostel   HOSTEL $
(Map p664; ☎02 108 8855; www.onedaybkk.com; Oneday, 51 Soi 26, Th Sukhumvit; incl breakfast dm 450-600B, r 1300-1500B; ❄@🛜; ⓢPhrom Phong exit 4) Attached to a cafe/co-working space is this modern, open-feeling hostel. Dorms span four to eight beds and, like the private rooms (only some of which have en-suite bathrooms), share an industrial-design theme and inviting, sun-soaked communal areas.

FU House Hostel   HOSTEL $
(Map p664; ☎098 654 5505; www.facebook.com/ fuhouseghostel; 77 Soi 8, Th Sukhumvit; dm/r incl breakfast 500/1650B; ❄🛜; ⓢNana exit 4) Great for a quiet, low-key stay is this two-storey wooden villa on a residential street. Choose between attractive bunk beds in one of two spacious, private-feeling dorms, or rooms with en-suite bathrooms.

★ Tints of Blue   HOTEL $$
(Map p664; ☎099 289 7744; www.tintsofblue. com; 47 Soi 27, Th Sukhumvit; r incl breakfast 1800-2000B; ❄🛜; Ⓜ Sukhumvit exit 2, ⓢAsok exit 6) The location in a leafy, quiet street is reflected in the rooms here, which manage to feel secluded, homey and warm. Equipped with kitchenettes, lots of space and natural light, and balconies, they're also a steal at this price.

🛏 Silom, Lumphini & Riverside

Lub*d   HOSTEL $
(Map p664; ☎02 634 7999; www.silom.lubd.com; 4 Th Decho; dm 350B, r 950-1500B; ❄@🛜; ⓢChong Nonsi exit 3) The title is a play on the Thai làp dee, meaning 'sleep well', but the fun atmosphere here might make you want to stay up all night. Only double rooms have en suite bathroom. If this one's full, there's another branch near Siam Sq.

ⓘ OUTSMARTING THE SCAM ARTISTS

Gem scam We're begging you – if you aren't a gem trader, don't buy unset stones in Thailand. Period.

Closed today Ignore any 'friendly' local who tells you that an attraction is closed for a Buddhist holiday or for cleaning.

Túk-túk rides for 20B These alleged 'tours' bypass the sights and instead cruise to all the fly-by-night gem and tailor shops that pay commissions.

Flat-fare taxi ride Flatly refuse any driver who quotes a flat fare, which will usually be three times more expensive than the reasonable meter rate.

Friendly strangers Be wary of smartly dressed men who approach you asking where you're from and where you're going.

Siam Square & Pratunam

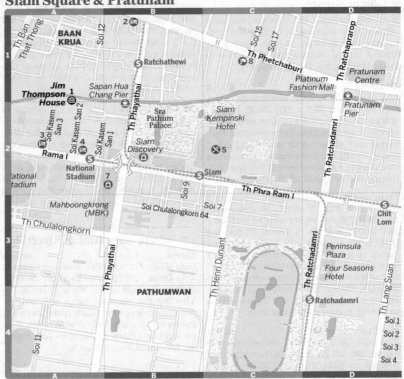

S1 Hostel HOSTEL **$**
(Map p664; ☎02 679 7777; www.facebook.com/ s1hostelbangkok; 35/1-4 Soi Ngam Du Phli; dm 330-380B, r 700-1300B; ❄@🛜; Ⓜ Lumphini exit 1) A huge hostel with dorm beds and private rooms decked out in a simple yet attractive primary-colour scheme. A host of facilities (laundry, kitchen, rooftop garden) and a convenient location within walking distance of the MRT make it great value.

Mile Map Hostel HOSTEL **$**
(Map p664; ☎02 635 1212; 36/4 Th Pan; dm 250-285B, r 600-900B; ❄@🛜; Ⓢ Chong Nonsi exit 3) Despite the quasi-industrial theme, this hostel feels inviting, warm and fun. The 10-bed dorms are one of the best deals in town, and the private rooms have a modern, minimalist feel, although not much natural light.

★ Smile Society HOTEL **$$**
(Map p664; ☎081 442 5800, 081 444 1596; www. smilesocietyhostel.com; 30/3-4 Soi 6, Th Silom; incl breakfast dm 450-600B, r 1100-2200B; ❄@🛜; Ⓜ Si Lom exit 2, Ⓢ Sala Daeng exit 1) Part boutique hotel, part hostel, this four-storey shophouse combines small but comfortable and well-equipped rooms, and dorms with spotless shared bathrooms. A central location, overwhelmingly positive guest feedback, and helpful, English-speaking staff are other perks. A virtually identical annexe next door helps with spillover.

LUXX HOTEL **$$**
(Map p664; ☎02 635 8844; www.staywithluxx.com; 6/11 Th Decho; r 1060-1445B, ste 1570B; ❄@🛜; Ⓢ Chong Nongsi exit 3) LUXX, the Th Decho branch of **LUXX XL** (Map p664; ☎02 684 1111; 82/8 Th Lang Suan; incl breakfast r 1500-2400B, ste 3700-7700B; ❄@🛜; Ⓢ Ratchadamri exit 2), flaunts the same hip minimalist vibe of its big sibling, and though rooms here can be a bit tight, and some lack natural light, they are all decked out with appropriately stylish furnishings.

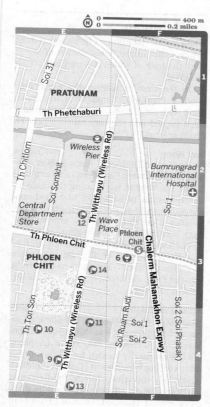

noodles in town. Note that Thip Samai is closed on alternate Wednesdays.

Kimleng
THAI $

(Map p670; 158-160 Th Tanao; mains 60-150B; ⊙10am-10pm Mon-Sat; 🛥klorng boat to Phanfa Leelard Pier) This tiny family-run restaurant specialises in the dishes and flavours of central Thailand. It's a good place to dip your toes in the local cuisine via an authentic *yam* (Thai-style salad), such as *yam plah dùk foo*, a mixture of catfish deep-fried until crispy and strands of tart, green mango.

Khun Daeng
THAI $

(Map p670; Th Phra Athit, no roman-script sign; mains 45-55B; ⊙11am-9.30pm Mon-Sat; 🛥Phra Athit/Banglamphu Pier) This popular place does *gŏo·ay jáp yoo·an,* identified on the English-language menu as 'Vietnamese noodle'. Introduced to north-eastern Thailand via Vietnamese immigrants, the dish combines peppery pork sausage, a quail egg, thin rice noodles and a garnish of crispy fried shallots in a slightly viscous broth.

There's no English-language sign here; look for the white-and-green shopfront.

Soy
CHINESE $

(Map p670; 100/2-3 Th Phra Athit, no roman-script sign; mains 80-100B; ⊙7am-5.30pm; 🛥Phra

✗ Eating

✗ Th Kao San & Banglamphu

Banglamphu is famous for its old-school central Thai food – the predominant cuisine in this part of town. For something more international, head to Th Khao San, where you'll find a few international fast-food franchises as well as foreign and vegetarian restaurants.

Thip Samai
THAI $

(Map p670; 313 Th Mahachai; mains 50-250B; ⊙5pm-2am; 🛥klorng boat to Phanfa Leelard Pier) Brace yourself: you should be aware that the fried noodles sold from carts along Th Khao San have little to do with the dish known as *pàt tai*. Luckily, less than a five-minute túk-túk (pronounced *đúk đúk*; a type of motorised rickshaw) ride away lies Thip Samai, home to some of the most legendary fried

Athit/Banglamphu Pier) Long-standing and lauded Soy serves big, hearty bowls of beef noodle soup. Choose between the fall-apart tender braised beef, fresh beef, beef balls, or all of the above. There's no English-language sign here; look for the open-fronted shophouse with red plastic chairs.

★**Krua Apsorn**   THAI $$
(Map p670; www.kruaapsorn.com; Th Din So; mains 100-450B; ⊙10.30am-8pm Mon-Sat; ☒klorng boat to Phanfa Leelard Pier) This cafeteria-like dining room is a favourite of members of the Thai royal family and restaurant critics alike. Just about all of the central and southern Thai dishes are tasty, but regulars never miss the chance to order the decadent stir-fried crab with yellow pepper chilli or the *tortilla Española*—like fluffy crab omelette.

Shoshana   ISRAELI $$
(Map p670; 88 Th Chakraphatdi Phong; mains 80-320B; ⊙10am-midnight; ☑; ☒Phra Athit/Banglamphu Pier) One of Khao San's longest-running Israeli restaurants, Shoshana resembles your grandparents' living room right down to the tacky wall art and plastic placemats. Feel safe in ordering anything deep-fried – staff do an excellent job of it – and don't miss the deliciously garlicky eggplant dip.

SPLURGE

Australian chef-author David Thompson is the man behind one of Bangkok's – and if you believe the critics, the world's – best Thai restaurants. **nahm** (Map p664; ☑02 625 3388; www.comohotels.com; ground fl, Metropolitan Hotel, 27 Th Sathon Tai/South; set lunch 600-1600B, set dinner 2500B, mains 310-800B; ⊙noon-2pm Mon-Fri, 7-10.30pm daily; Ⓜ Lumphini exit 2). Using ancient cookbooks as his inspiration, Thompson has given new life to previously extinct dishes with descriptions such as 'smoked fish curry with prawns, chicken livers, cockles, chillies and black pepper'.

Dinner is best approached via the multicourse set meal, while lunch means *kà·nŏm jeen*, thin rice noodles served with curries.

If you're expecting bland, gentrified Thai food meant for foreigners, prepare to be disappointed. Reservations essential.

✖ Chinatown

When you mention Chinatown, most Bangkokians immediately dream of street food, the bulk of which is found just off Th Yaowarat.

On the western side of the neighbourhood is Phahurat, Bangkok's Little India, filled with small Indian and Nepali restaurants tucked into the tiny soi (lane) off Th Chakkaraphet.

Nay Hong   STREET FOOD $
(Map p664; off Th Yukol 2; mains 35-50B; ⊙4-10pm; ☒Ratchawong Pier, Ⓜ Hua Lamphong exit 1 & taxi) The reward for locating this hole-in-the-wall is one of Bangkok's best fried noodle dishes – *gŏo·ay dĕe·o kôo·a gài* (flat rice noodles fried with garlic oil, chicken and egg). No English-language menu.

There's no English-language sign. To find Nay Hong, proceed north from the corner of Th Suapa and Th Luang, then turn right into the first side street; it's at the end of the narrow alleyway.

Khun Yah Cuisine   THAI $
(Map p664; off Th Mittaphap Thai-China, no roman-script sign; mains from 40B; ⊙6am-1.30pm Mon-Fri; ☒Ratchawong Pier, Ⓜ Hua Lamphong exit 1) Strategically located for a lunch break after visiting Wat Traimit (Golden Buddha), Khun Yah specialises in the full-flavoured curries, relishes, stir-fries and noodle dishes of central Thailand. Be sure to get here early; come noon many dishes are already sold out.

Khun Yah has no English-language sign (nor an English-language menu) but is located just east of the Golden Buddha, in the same compound.

Royal India   INDIAN $$
(Map p670; 392/1 Th Chakkaraphet; mains 135-220B; ⊙10am-10pm; ☑; ☒Saphan Phut/Memorial Bridge Pier, Pak Klong Taladd Pier) Yes, we're aware that this hole-in-the-wall has been in every edition of our guide since the beginning, but after all these years it's still the most reliable place to eat in Bangkok's Little India. Try any of the delicious breads or rich curries, and don't forget to finish with a home-made Punjabi sweet.

✖ Siam Square

You're largely at the mercy of shopping-mall food courts and chain restaurants here. However, the food can often be quite good.

FLOATING MARKETS

Photographs of Thailand's floating markets – wooden canoes laden with multicoloured fruits and vegetables – have become an iconic image of the kingdom. The following are all an easy half-day or day trip from Bangkok.

Tha Kha Floating Market (ตลาดน้ำท่าคา; Tha Kha, Samut Songkhram; ⏰7am-noon, 2nd, 7th & 12th day of waxing & waning moons plus Sat & Sun) This, the most real-feeling floating market, is also the most difficult to reach. A handful of vendors coalesce along an open rural *klorng* (canal, also spelt *khlong*) lined with coconut palms and old wooden houses. Boat rides (20B per person, 45 minutes) can be arranged along the canal, and there are lots of tasty snacks and fruits for sale. Contact Amphawa's tourist office (☏034 752 847; 71 Th Prachasret; ⏰8.30am-4.30pm) to see when the next market is.

Damnoen Saduak Floating Market (ตลาดน้ำดำเนินสะดวก; Damnoen Saduak, Ratchaburi; ⏰7am-noon) This 100-year-old floating market – the country's most famous – is now essentially a floating souvenir stand filled with package tourists. This in itself can be a fascinating insight into Thai culture, as the vast majority of tourists here are Thais and watching the approach to this cultural 'theme park' is instructive. But beyond the market, the residential canals are quite peaceful and can be explored by hiring a boat (per person 100B) for a longer duration.

Taling Chan Floating Market (ตลาดน้ำตลิ่งชัน; Khlong Bangkok Noi, Thonburi; ⏰7am-4pm Sat & Sun; Ⓢ Wongwian Yai exit 3 & taxi) Located just outside of Bangkok on the access road to Khlong Bangkok Noi, Taling Chan looks like any other fresh food market busy with produce vendors from nearby farms. But the twist emerges at the canal where several floating docks serve as informal dining rooms and the kitchens are boats tethered to the docks.

★ **MBK Food Island**   THAI $
(Map p674; 6th fl, MBK Center, cnr Rama I & Th Phayathai; mains 35-150B; ⏰10am-9pm; 🖊; Ⓢ National Stadium exit 4) With dozens of vendors offering exceedingly cheap and tasty regional Thai, international and even vegetarian dishes, MBK Food Island fiercely clings to its crown as the grandaddy of Bangkok food courts.

Gourmet Paradise   THAI $
(Map p674; ground fl, Siam Paragon, 991/1 Rama I; mains 35-500B; ⏰10am-10pm; 🖊; Ⓢ Siam exits 3 & 5) The perpetually busy Gourmet Paradise unites international fast-food chains, domestic restaurants and food-court-style stalls, with a particular emphasis on the sweet stuff.

✕ Sukhumvit

With the city's largest selection of international restaurants, this seemingly endless ribbon of a road is where to go if, for the duration of a meal, you wish to forget that you're in Thailand.

Gokfayuen   CHINESE $
(Map p664; www.facebook.com/wuntunmeen; 161/7 Soi Thong Lor 9; mains 70-140B; ⏰11am-

11.30pm; Ⓢ Thong Lo exit 3 & taxi) Gokfayuen has gone to great lengths to re-create classic Hong Kong dishes in Bangkok. Couple your house-made wheat-and-egg noodles with roasted pork, steamed vegetables with oyster sauce, or the Hong Kong–style milk tea.

★ **Soul Food Mahanakorn**   THAI $$
(Map p664; ☏02 714 7708; www.soulfood-mahanakorn.com; 56/10 Soi 55/Thong Lor, Th Sukhumvit; mains 140-290B; ⏰5.30pm-midnight; 🖊; Ⓢ Thong Lo exit 3) This contemporary staple gets its interminable buzz from its dual nature as both an inviting restaurant – the menu spans tasty interpretations of rustic Thai dishes – and a bar serving deliciously boozy, Thai-influenced cocktails. Reservations recommended.

★ **Sri Trat**   THAI $$
(Map p664; www.facebook.com/sritrat; 90 Soi 33, Th Sukhumvit; mains 180-450B; ⏰noon-11pm Wed-Mon; Ⓢ Phrom Phong exit 5) This new restaurant specialises in the unique fare of Thailand's eastern provinces, Trat and Chanthaburi. What this means is lots of rich, slightly sweet, herbal flavours, fresh seafood and dishes you won't find anywhere else in town. Highly recommended.

ℹ️ LGBT BANGKOK

Bangkok has a notable LGBT-friendly vibe to it. From kinky underwear shops to gay bars and lesbian-only get-togethers – you could eat, shop and play here for days without ever leaving the comfort of welcoming venues. Unlike elsewhere in Southeast Asia, homosexuality is not criminalised in Thailand and the general attitude remains extremely laissez-faire.

The following are some of Bangkok's best LGBT venues.

DJ Station (Map p664; www.dj-station.com; 8/6-8 Soi 2, Th Silom; admission from 150B; ⊙10pm-2am; Ⓜ Si Lom exit 2, Ⓢ Sala Daeng exit 1) One of the most iconic gay nightclubs in Asia.

Telephone Pub (Map p664; www.telephonepub.com; 114/11-13 Soi 4, Th Silom; ⊙6pm-1am; 🖥; Ⓜ Si Lom exit 2, Ⓢ Sala Daeng exit 1) Long-standing bar right in the middle of Bangkok's queerest zone.

Playhouse Magical Cabaret (🗹 090 287 2660; www.playhousethailand.com; 481 Yaowarat Rd, Khwaeng Samphanthawong; 1200B; ⊙show times 8pm & 9.30pm; Ⓢ Lat Phrao exit 1) The city's premier drag show.

Jidori Cuisine Ken
JAPANESE $$

(Map p664; 🗹02 661 3457; www.facebook.com/jidoriken; off Soi 26, Th Sukhumvit; mains 60-350B; ⊙5pm-midnight Mon-Sat, to 10pm Sun; Ⓢ Phrom Phong exit 4) This cosy Japanese restaurant does tasty tofu dishes, delicious salads and even excellent desserts; basically everything here is above average, but the highlight is the smoky, perfectly seasoned chicken skewers. Reservations recommended.

Daniel Thaiger
AMERICAN $$

(Map p664; 🗹084 549 0995; www.facebook.com/danielthaiger; Soi 11, Th Sukhumvit; mains from 140B; ⊙11am-late; Ⓢ Nana exit 3) Bangkok's best burgers are served from this American-run stall that, at the time of research, had a long-standing location on Soi 11. Check the Facebook page to see where the food truck will be when you're in town.

🍽️ Silom, Lumphini & Riverside

Th Silom has a bit of everything, from old-school Thai to some of the city's best upmarket international dining.

Soi 10 Food Centres
THAI $

(Map p664; Soi 10, Th Silom; mains 20-60B; ⊙8am-3pm Mon-Fri; Ⓜ Si Lom exit 2, Ⓢ Sala Daeng exit 1) These two adjacent hangar-like buildings tucked behind Soi 10 are the main lunchtime fuelling stations for the area's office staff. Choices range from southern-style *kôw gaang* (point-and-choose curries ladled over rice) to just about every incarnation of Thai noodle.

Jay So
THAI $

(Map p664; 146/1 Soi Phiphat 2; mains 45-80B; ⊙10am-4pm Mon-Sat; Ⓜ Si Lom exit 2, Ⓢ Sala Daeng exit 2) Jay So has no menu, but a mortar and pestle and a huge grill are the telltale signs of ballistically spicy *sôm-dam* (green papaya salad), sublime herb-stuffed, grilled catfish and other north-eastern Thai specialities.

There's no English signage (nor an English-language menu), so look for the ramshackle, white and green, Coke-decorated shack about halfway down Soi Phiphat 2.

Muslim Restaurant
THAI $

(Map p664; 1354-6 Th Charoen Krung; mains 40-140B; ⊙6.30am-5.30pm; 🚢Oriental Pier, Ⓢ Saphan Taksin exit 1) Plant yourself in any random wooden booth of this ancient eatery for a glimpse into what restaurants in Bangkok used to be like. The menu, much like the interior design, doesn't appear to have changed much in the restaurant's 70-year history, and the biryanis, curries and samosas remain more Indian-influenced than Thai.

Chennai Kitchen
INDIAN $

(Map p664; 107/4 Th Pan; mains 70-150B; ⊙10am-3pm & 6-9.30pm; 🗹; Ⓢ Surasak exit 3) This thimble-sized mum-and-dad restaurant puts out some of the best southern Indian vegetarian food in town. The metre-long *dosai* (crispy southern Indian pancake) is always a good choice, but if you're feeling indecisive (or exceptionally famished) go for the banana-leaf thali (set meal) that seems to incorporate just about everything in the kitchen.

🍸 Drinking & Nightlife

As in any big international city, the drinking and partying scene in Bangkok ranges from trashy to classy and touches on just about everything in between.

Perhaps most famously, Bangkok is one of the few big cities in the world where nobody seems to mind if you slap a bar on top of a skyscraper (most rooftop bars enforce a dress code – no shorts or sandals).

Bangkok bars generally close at midnight, dance clubs go to 2am (at the time of research, some of the bigger places were stretching this to 3am).

Cover charges can run as high as 600B in clubs but usually include a drink or two. At the bigger places you'll need ID to prove you're legal (20 years old). To find out what club is bumping on any night, check out Dudesweet (www.dudesweet.org) and Paradise Bangkok (www.facebook.com/paradisebangkok), organisers of hugely popular monthly parties.

★ WTF   BAR
(Map p664; www.wtfbangkok.com; 7 Soi 51, Th Sukhumvit; ⊙6pm-1am Tue-Sun; 🛜; Ⓢ Thong Lo exit 3) Wonderful Thai Friendship (what did you think it stood for?) is a funky and friendly neighbourhood bar that also packs in a gallery space. Arty locals and resident foreigners come for the old-school cocktails, live music and DJ events, poetry readings, art exhibitions and tasty bar snacks. And we, like them, give WTF our vote for Bangkok's best bar.

★ Tep Bar   BAR
(Map p664; www.facebook.com/tepbar; 69-71 Soi Nana; ⊙5pm-midnight Tue-Sun; Ⓜ Hua Lamphong exit 1) We never expected to find a bar this sophisticated – yet this fun – in Chinatown. Tep does it with a Thai-tinged, contemporary interior, tasty signature cocktails, Thai drinking snacks, and raucous live Thai music performances from Thursday to Sunday.

A R Sutton & Co Engineers Siam   BAR
(Map p664; Parklane, Soi 63/Ekamai, Th Sukhumvit; ⊙6pm-midnight; Ⓢ Ekkamai exit 2) Skeins of copper tubing, haphazardly placed one-of-a-kind antiques, zinc ceiling panels, and rows of glass vials and baubles culminate in one of the most unique and beautifully fantastical bars in Bangkok – if not anywhere. An adjacent distillery provides fuel for the bar's largely gin-based cocktails.

Ku Bar   BAR
(Map p670; www.facebook.com/ku.bangkok; 3rd fl, 469 Th Phra Sumen; ⊙7pm-midnight Thu-Sun) Tired of buckets and cocktails that revolve around Red Bull? Head to Ku Bar, in almost every way the polar opposite of the Khao San party scene. Climb three floors of stairs (look for the tiny sign) to emerge at an almost comically minimalist interior where sophisticated fruit- and food-heavy cocktails (sample names: Lychee, Tomato, Pineapple/Red Pepper) and obscure music augment the underground vibe.

Sky on 20   ROOFTOP BAR
(Map p664; 📞02 009 4999; www.novotelbangkoksukhumvit20.com; 26th fl, Novotel, 19/9 Soi Sukhumvit 20; ⊙5pm-2am; 🛜; Ⓢ Phrom Phong) With drinks averaging 250B, Sky on 20 has a reputation as a laid-back place for bargain sundowners. Electro house beats fill the open-air bar that has circular couches and lounge chairs overlooking Sirikit Lake and Benjasiri Park. Drinks made with local fruit juices rule the menu, and there is a retractable roof to keep the rainy season downpours at bay.

Hair of the Dog   BAR
(Map p674; www.hairofthedogbkk.com; 1st fl, Mahathun Plaza, 888/26 Th Phloen Chit; ⊙5pm-midnight; Ⓢ Phloen Chit exit 2) The craft-beer craze that has swept Bangkok over the last few years is epitomised at this semi-concealed bar. With a morgue theme, dozens of bottles and 13 rotating taps, it's a great place for a weird, hoppy night.

SPAS & MASSAGE

Bangkok could mount a strong claim to being the massage capital of the world. Exactly what type of massage you're after is another question. Variations range from storefront traditional Thai massage to an indulgent 'spa experience' with service and style. Some spas now focus more on the medical than the sensory, while plush resort-style spas offer a menu of appealing beauty treatments.

Prices for massages in small parlours are 200B to 350B for a foot massage and 300B to 600B for a full-body massage. Spa experiences start at about 1000B and climb like a Bangkok skyscraper.

Studio Lam   BAR, CLUB
(Map p664; www.facebook.com/studiolambangkok;
3/1 Soi 51, Th Sukhumvit; ⊘6pm-1am Tue-Sun;
⑤Thong Lo exit 3) Studio Lam is an extension
of uberhip record label ZudRangMa, and
boasts a Jamaican-style sound system cus-
tom-built for world and retro-Thai DJ sets
and the occasional live show. For a night
of dancing in Bangkok that doesn't revolve
around Top 40 cheese, this is the place.

Route 66   CLUB
(Map p664; www.route66club.com; 29/33-48 RCA/
Royal City Ave; 300B; ⊘8pm-2am; Ⓜ Phra Ram 9
exit 3 & taxi) This vast club has been around
just about as long as RCA has, but frequent
facelifts and expansions have kept it relevant. Top 40 hip-hop rules the main space
here, although there are several differently
themed 'levels', featuring anything from
Thai pop to live music.

The Club   CLUB
(Map p670; www.facebook.com/theclubkhaosanbkk;
123 Th Khao San; admission Fri & Sat 120B; ⊘9pm-
2am; ⊕Phra Athit/Banglamphu Pier) Located
right in the middle of Th Khao San, this cav-
ern-like dance hall hosts a good mix of locals
and backpackers; check the Facebook page
for upcoming events and guest DJs.

☆ Entertainment

★**Brick Bar**   LIVE MUSIC
(Map p670; www.brickbarkhaosan.com; basement,
Buddy Lodge, 265 Th Khao San; admission Sat &
Sun 150B; ⊘7pm-1.30am; ⊕Phra Athit/Banglam-
phu Pier) This basement pub, one of our favourite destinations in Bangkok for live music, hosts a nightly revolving cast of bands
for an almost exclusively Thai crowd – many
of whom will end the night dancing on the
tables. Brick Bar can get infamously packed,
so be sure to get there early.

Saxophone Pub & Restaurant   LIVE MUSIC
(Map p664; www.saxophonepub.com; 3/8 Th
Phayathai; ⊘7.30pm-1.30am; ⑤Victory Monument exit 2) After 30 years, Saxophone remains Bangkok's premier live-music venue
– a dark, intimate space where you can pull
up a chair just a few metres away from the
band and see their every bead of sweat. If
you prefer some mystique in your musicians, watch the blues, jazz, reggae or rock
from the balcony.

Rajadamnern Stadium   SPECTATOR SPORT
(สนามมวยราชดำเนิน; Map p670; www.rajadamn-
ern.com; off Th Ratchadamnoen Nok; tickets 3rd

class/2nd   class/ringside   1000/1500/2500B;
⊘matches 6.30-11pm Mon-Thu, 3pm & 6.30pm
Sun; ⊕Thewet Pier, ⑤Phaya Thai exit 3 & taxi) Rajadamnern Stadium, Bangkok's oldest and
most venerable venue for *moo·ay tai* (Thai
boxing; also spelt *muay Thai*), hosts matches throughout the week. Be sure to buy tickets from the official ticket counter or online,
not from the touts and scalpers who hang
around outside the entrance.

🔒 Shopping

★**Chatuchak Weekend Market**   MARKET
(ตลาดนัดจตุจักร, Talat Nat Jatujak; www.chatuchak-
market.org; 587/10 Th Phahonyothin; ⊘7am-6pm
Wed & Thu plants only, 6pm-midnight Fri wholesale
only, 9am-6pm Sat & Sun; Ⓜ Chatuchak Park exit
1, Kamphaeng Phet exits 1 & 2, ⑤Mo Chit exit 1)
Among the largest markets in the world,
Chatuchak seems to unite everything buy-
able, from used vintage sneakers to baby
squirrels. Plan to spend a full day here, as
there's plenty to see, do and buy. But come
early, ideally around 10am, to beat the
crowds and the heat.

MBK Center   SHOPPING CENTRE
(Map p674; www.mbk-center.com; cnr Rama I &
Th Phayathai; ⊘10am-10pm; ⑤National Stadium
exit 4) This eight-storey market in a mall has
emerged as one of Bangkok's top attractions.
On any given weekend half of Bangkok's
residents (and most of its tourists) can be
found here combing through a seemingly
inexhaustible range of small stalls, shops
and merchandise.

Siam Discovery   SHOPPING CENTRE
(Map p674; www.siamdiscovery.co.th; cnr Rama I &
Th Phayathai; ⊘10am-10pm; ⑤Siam exit 1) With
an open, almost-market-like feel and an
impressive variety of unique goods ranging
from housewares to clothing (including lots
of items by Thai designers), the recently renovated Siam Discovery is hands down the
most design-conscious mall in town.

**Thanon Khao San
Market**   GIFTS & SOUVENIRS
(Map p670; Th Khao San; ⊘10am-midnight;
⊕Phra Athit/Banglamphu Pier) The main
guesthouse strip in Banglamphu is a day-
and-night shopping bazaar peddling all the
backpacker 'essentials': profane T-shirts,
bootleg MP3s, hemp clothing, fake student
ID cards, knock-off designer wear, selfie
sticks, orange juice and, of course, those
croaking wooden frogs.

ℹ Information

EMERGENCY

Police (☎191) The police contact number functions as the de-facto universal emergency number in Thailand and can also be used to call an ambulance or report a fire.

Tourist Police (24-hr hotline ☎1155) The best way to deal with most problems requiring the police is to contact the tourist police, who are used to dealing with foreigners and can be very helpful in cases of arrest.

MEDICAL SERVICES

The following hospitals have English-speaking doctors.

Bangkok Christian Hospital (Map p664; ☎02 625 9000; www.bch.in.th; 124 Th Silom; Ⓜ Si Lom exit 2, Ⓢ Sala Daeng exit 1) Modern hospital in central Bangkok.

Bumrungrad International Hospital (Map p674; ☎02 667 1000; www.bumrungrad.com; 33 Soi 3, Th Sukhumvit; ⊗24hr; Ⓢ Phloen Chit exit 3) An internationally accredited hospital.

POST

Main Post Office (Map p664; ☎02 233 1050; Th Charoen Krung; ⊗8am-8pm Mon-Fri, to 1pm Sat & Sun; 🚢 Oriental Pier)

TOURIST INFORMATION

Bangkok Information Center (Map p670; ☎02 225 7612-4; www.bangkoktourist. com; 17/1 Th Phra Athit; ⊗8am-7pm Mon-Fri, 9am-5pm Sat & Sun; 🚢 Phra Athit/ Banglamphu Pier) City-specific tourism office providing maps, brochures and directions. Seldom-staffed kiosks and booths are found around town; look for the green-on-white symbol of a mahout on an elephant.

Tourism Authority of Thailand (TAT; Map p664; ☎02 250 5500, nationwide 1672; www. tourismthailand.org; 1600 Th Phetchaburi; ⊗8.30am-4.30pm; Ⓜ Phetchaburi exit 2) The head TAT office has brochures and maps covering the whole country.

VISAS & IMMIGRATION

Bangkok Immigration Office (☎02 141 9889; www.bangkok.immigration.go.th; Bldg B, Government Centre, Soi 7, Th Chaeng Watthana; ⊗8.30am-noon & 1-4.30pm Mon-Fri; Ⓜ Chatuchak Park exit 2 & taxi, Ⓢ Mo Chit exit 3 & taxi) In Bangkok, visa extensions are filed at this office.

ℹ Getting There & Away

AIR

Located 30km east of central Bangkok, **Suvarnabhumi International Airport** (☎02 132 1888; www.suvarnabhumiairport.com), pronounced

SHOPPING BY NEIGHBOURHOOD

Banglamphu Home to a couple of souvenir shops, not to mention the streetside wares of Th Khao San.

Chinatown Street markets with a flea-market feel.

Siam Square, Pratunam, Phloen Chit & Ratchathewi Simply put: malls, malls and more malls.

Riverside, Silom & Lumphini The place to go for antiques and art.

Sukhumvit Upscale malls and touristy street markets.

sù·wan·ná·poom, handles international and domestic flights. Its airport code is BKK.

Bangkok's other airport, **Don Mueang International Airport** (☎02 535 2111; www.donmueangairportthai.com), 25km north of central Bangkok, is used by budget airlines. Terminal 1 handles international flights, while Terminal 2 is for domestic destinations.

BUS

Buses using government bus stations are far more reliable and less prone to incidents of theft than those departing from Th Khao San or other tourist centres.

Eastern Bus Terminal (Map p664; ☎02 391 2504; Soi 40, Th Sukhumvit; Ⓢ Ekkamai exit 2) is the departure point for buses to Pattaya, Rayong, Chanthaburi and other points east, except for the border crossing at Aranya Prathet. Most people call it *sà·tǎh·nee èk·gà·mai* (Ekamai station). It's near the Ekkamai BTS station.

Northern & Northeastern Bus Terminal (Mo Chit; ☎ northeastern routes 02 936 2852, ext 602/605, northern routes 02 936 2841, ext 325/614; Th Kamphaengphet; Ⓜ Kamphaeng Phet exit 1 & taxi, Ⓢ Mo Chit exit 3 & taxi) is located just north of Chatuchak Park. This hectic bus station is also commonly called *kǒn sòng mǒr chít* (Mo Chit station) – not to be confused with Mo Chit BTS station. Buses depart from here for all northern and north-eastern destinations, as well as international destinations including Pakse (Laos), Phnom Penh (Cambodia), Siem Reap (Cambodia) and Vientiane (Laos). To reach the bus station, take BTS to Mo Chit or MRT to Kamphaeng Phet and transfer onto city bus 3, 77 or 509, or hop on a taxi or motorcycle taxi.

Southern Bus Terminal (Sai Tai Mai; ☎02 422 4444, call centre 1490; Th Boromaratchachonanee), commonly called *sǎi đâi mài*, lies a long way west of the centre of Bangkok. Besides serving as the departure point for all buses south of Bangkok, transport to Kanchanaburi and western Thailand also departs from here. The easiest way to reach the station is by taxi, or you can take bus 79, 159, 201 or 516 from Th Ratchadamnoen Klang.

MINIVAN

Privately run minivans, called *rót dôo*, are a fast and relatively comfortable way to get between Bangkok and its neighbouring provinces. The various routes depart from their respective bus stations (for example, minivans to Ayuthaya depart from the Northern & Northeastern Bus Terminal, those to Ban Phe from the Eastern Bus Terminal).

TRAIN

The city's main train terminus is known as **Hualamphong** (☑ 02 220 4334, call centre 1690; www.railway.co.th; off Rama IV; Ⓜ Hua Lamphong exit 2). It's advisable to ignore all touts here and avoid the travel agencies. To check timetables and prices for destinations call the State Railway of Thailand or look at its website.

Bangkok Noi (☑ 02 418 4310, call centre 1690; www.railway.co.th; off Th Itsaraphap; 🚆Thonburi Railway Station, Wang Lang/Siriraj Pier, Ⓢ Wongwian Yai exit 4 & taxi), also known as Thonburi, is a miniscule train station with (overpriced) departures for Kanchanaburi.

❶ Getting Around

Bangkok may seem chaotic and impenetrable at first, but its transport system is gradually improving, and although you'll almost certainly find

yourself stuck in traffic at some point, the traffic jams aren't as legendary as they used to be.

BTS The elevated Skytrain runs from 6am to midnight. Tickets 16B to 44B.

MRT The Metro runs from 6am to midnight. Tickets 16B to 42B.

Taxi Outside of rush hours, Bangkok taxis are a great bargain. Flagfall 35B.

Chao Phraya Express Boat Runs 6am to 8pm, charging 10B to 40B.

Klorng boat Bangkok's canal boats run from 5.30am to 8pm most days. Tickets 9B to 19B.

Bus Cheap, but a slow and confusing way to get around Bangkok. Tickets 5B to 30B.

TO/FROM THE AIRPORTS
Suvarnabhumi International Airport

Airport Rail Link (☑ call centre 1690; www.srtet.co.th) connects Suvarnabhumi International Airport with the BTS (Skytrain) stop at Phaya Thai (45B, 30 minutes, from 6am to midnight) and the MRT (Metro) stop at Phetchaburi (45B, 25 minutes, from 6am to midnight).

Local Bus A public transport centre is 3km from the airport and houses a bus terminal with buses to a handful of provinces, and inner-city-bound buses and minivans. A free airport shuttle connects the transport centre with the passenger terminals. Bus lines that city-bound tourists are likely to use include line 551 to BTS Victory Monument station (40B, frequent from 5am to 10pm) and 552 to BTS On Nut (20B, frequent from 5am to 10pm). From these points, you can continue by public transport or taxi to your hotel.

Taxi Metered taxis are available kerbside at Floor 1 – ignore the 'official airport taxi' touts who approach you inside the terminal. Typical metered fares from Suvarnabhumi include 200B to 250B to Th Sukhumvit; 250B to 300B to Th Khao San; and 400B to Mo Chit. Toll charges (paid by passengers) vary between 25B and 70B. Note that there's a 50B surcharge added to all fares departing from the airport, payable directly to the driver.

Don Muang Airport

Airport Bus From outside the arrivals hall, there are four bus lines:
➡ A1 makes stops at BTS Mo Chit (50B, frequent from 7.30am to 11.30pm)
➡ A2 makes stops at BTS Mo Chit and BTS Victory Monument (50B, every 30 minutes from 7.30am to 11.30pm)
➡ A3 makes stops at Pratunam and Lumphini Park (50B, every 30 minutes from 7.30am to 11.30pm)
➡ A4 at Th Khao San and Sanam Luang (50B, every 30 minutes from 7.30am to 11.30pm)

Local Buses Buses stop on the highway in front of the airport.

GETTING AROUND BANGKOK

❶ ➡ Take advantage of the city's public transport networks – the BTS and MRT – as much as possible, saving taxis for short jaunts from the stations to your destination.

➡ If you're not in a rush and your destination is riverside, consider taking the Chao Phraya Express Boat.

➡ If you need to take a taxi during peak traffic hours (from approximately 7am to 9am and 5pm to 7pm), be sure to set aside enough time – often at least 45 minutes for relatively close destinations.

➡ For distances too far to walk but too far to justify a taxi, consider a ride on one of Bangkok's numerous motorcycle taxis.

→ Bus 29, with a stop at Victory Monument BTS station, before terminating at Hualamphong Train Station (24 hours)

→ Bus 59, with a stop near Th Khao San (24 hours)

Taxi Public taxis leave from outside both arrival halls and there is a 50B airport charge added to the meter fare.

Train The walkway that crosses from the airport to the Amari Airport Hotel also provides access to Don Muang Train Station, which has trains to Hualamphong Train Station every one to 1½ hours from 4am to 11.30am and then roughly every hour from 2pm to 9.30pm (from 5B to 10B).

BOAT

Chao Phraya Express Boat (☑ 02 623 6001; www.chaophrayaexpressboat.com) operates the main ferry service along Mae Nam Chao Phraya. The central pier is known as Tha Sathon, Saphan Taksin or sometimes Sathon/Central Pier, and connects to the BTS at Saphan Taksin station.

Boats run from 6am to 8pm. You can buy tickets (10B to 40B) at the pier or on board; hold on to your ticket as proof of purchase.

Pay attention to the colour-coded flags during rush hour.

→ **Express** Indicated by an orange flag. They run between Wat Rajsingkorn, south of Bangkok, to Nonthaburi, north, stopping at most major piers (15B, frequent from 6am to 7pm).

→ **Tourist** Indicated by a blue flag. They run from Sathon/Central Pier to Phra Athit/Banglamphu Pier, with stops at eight major sightseeing piers (40B, every 30 minutes from 9.30am to 5pm).

Klorng, or canal, taxi boats run along Khlong Saen Saep (Banglamphu to Ramkhamhaeng) and are an easy way to get between Banglamphu and Jim Thompson House, the Siam Sq shopping centres (get off at Sapan Hua Chang Pier for both) and other points further east along Th Sukhumvit.

Fares range from 9B to 19B and boats run during daylight hours. Be careful when boarding: the boats stop at the piers for only a few seconds.

BTS & MRT

The elevated **BTS** (Skytrain; ☑ 02 617 6000, tourist information 02 617 7341; www.bts.co.th), also known as the Skytrain (*rót fai fáa*), whisks you through 'new' Bangkok (Silom, Sukhumvit and Siam Sq). The interchange between the two lines is at Siam station and trains run frequently from 6am to midnight. Fares range from 16B to 44B or 140B for a one-day pass. Most ticket machines only accept coins, but change is available at the information booths.

Bangkok's Metro, the **MRT** (☑ 02 354 2000; www.bangkokmetro.co.th) is most helpful for people staying in the Sukhumvit or Silom area to reach the train station at Hualamphong. Fares cost from 16B to 42B or 120B for a one-day pass. The trains run frequently from 6am to midnight.

BUS

Bangkok's public buses are run by the **Bangkok Mass Transit Authority** (☑ 02 246 0973, call centre 1348; www.bmta.co.th). They are slow and confusing, unless you speak and read Thai.

→ Air-con bus fares range from 10B to 23B and fares for fan-cooled buses start at 6.50B.

→ Most of the bus lines run between 5am and 10pm or 11pm, except for the 'all-night' buses, which run from 3am or 4am to midmorning.

→ You'll most likely require the help of Think-net's *Bangkok Bus Guide*.

TAXI

All taxis are required to use their meters, which start at 35B, and fares to most places within central Bangkok cost 60B to 90B. Freeway tolls – 25B to 70B depending on where you start – must be paid by the passenger. Ignore taxis parked outside hotels and tourists areas who quote you a flat fare instead of using their meters. Cabs are normally plentiful, unless it is raining. Few taxi drivers speak much English: have your destination written in Thai if possible.

App-based alternatives to traditional taxis include Grab Taxi and Uber.

Motorcycle taxis (known as *motorsai*) camp out at the mouth of a soi to shuttle people from the main road to their destinations down the lane. Riders wear coloured, numbered vests and usually charge 10B to 20B for the trip (without a helmet unless you ask).

Their other purpose is as a means of beating the traffic. You tell your rider where you want to go, negotiate a price (from 20B for a short trip up to about 150B going across town), strap on the helmet (they will insist for longer trips) and say a prayer to whichever god you're into. Accidents do happen.

TÚK-TÚK

Bangkok's iconic túk-túk (pronounced *đúk đúk;* a type of motorised rickshaw) overcharge foreigners outrageously (expats never use them). If you feel the need to try one out, and most first-time visitors use them at least once, ignore anyone offering too-good-to-be-true 20B trips: you'll be detoured via commission-paying gem and silk shops and massage parlours.

Expect to be quoted a 100B fare, if not more, for even the shortest trip. Try bargaining them down to about 60B for a short trip. Never take a túk-túk without agreeing the fare in advance.

THAILAND BANGKOK

CENTRAL THAILAND

Thailand's heartland, the central region is a fertile river plain that birthed the country's history-shaping kingdoms of Ayuthaya and Sukhothai, and crafted the culture and language that defines the mainstream Thai identity. The nationally revered river Mae Nam Chao Phraya is the lifeblood of the region and connects the country's interior with the Gulf of Thailand. Geographically, central Thailand is a necessary thoroughfare for any Chiang Mai–bound traveller, but culturally it is a must-see region.

Ayuthaya   อยุธยา

☑ 035 / POPULATION 18,600

Enigmatic temple ruins are strewn across Ayuthaya, whispering of its glory days as a royal capital. Once replete with gilded temples and treasure-laden palaces, the city was the capital of Siam from 1350 until 1767, when the city was brutally sacked by the Burmese. Dozens of crumbling temples evoke Ayuthaya's past grandeur. Standing among towering stupas, it's easy to imagine how they looked in their prime.

A day trip is enough to tour temple ruins and catch the flavour of Ayuthaya's faded majesty. But linger for a couple of days and you'll fully experience its otherworldly atmosphere of sloshing riverboats, temple silhouettes drawn sharp against the setting sun, and ruins illuminated at night.

⊙ Sights

At its zenith, Ayuthaya was home to more than 400 temples. Ayuthaya's river-encircled island houses most of the city's major sights and it's easy to get between them by bicycle. On the opposite side of the water are several famous temples. You can reach some by bicycle, but others require a motorbike or car. Evening boat tours are another option.

Most sites are open from 8am to 4pm; the most famous charge an entrance fee. A one-day pass for six major ruins costs 220B and can be bought at each site. The ruins are symbols of royalty and religion, and require utmost respect and proper attire (cover to elbows and knees).

⊙ On the Island

★ **Wat Phra Si Sanphet**   RUINS
(วัดพระศรีสรรเพชญ์; 50B; ⊙8am-6pm) At this captivating ruined temple, three wonderful-

ly intact stupas form one of Ayuthaya's most iconic views; unlike at many other ruins, it's possible to clamber up the stairs for a lofty vantage point (and epic selfie). Built in the late 15th century, this was a royal temple inside palace grounds; these were the model for Bangkok's Wat Phra Kaew and Royal Palace. This temple once contained a 16m-high standing Buddha (Phra Si Sanphet) covered with at least 143kg of gold.

Wat Mahathat   RUINS
(วัดมหาธาตุ; Th Chee Kun; 50B; ⊙8am-6.30pm) Ayuthaya's most photographed attraction is in these temple grounds: a sandstone Buddha head tangled within a bodhi tree's entwined roots. Founded in 1374, during the reign of King Borom Rachathirat I, Wat Mahathat was the seat of the supreme patriarch and the kingdom's most important temple. The central *prang* (Hindi/Khmer-style stupa) once stood 43m high and it collapsed on its own long before the Burmese sacked the city. It was rebuilt in more recent times, but collapsed again in 1911.

Wat Ratchaburana   RUINS
(วัดราชบูรณะ; off Th Naresuan; 50B; ⊙8am-6pm) The *prang* in this sprawling temple complex is one of the best extant versions in the city, with detailed carvings of lotus flowers and mythical creatures; it's surrounded by another four stupas. If you aren't afraid of heights, small spaces or bats, you can climb inside the *prang* to visit the crypt (the largest in Thailand), decorated with faint murals of the Buddha from the early Ayuthaya period.

Wihan Phra Mongkhon Bophit   BUDDHIST TEMPLE
(วิหารพระมงคลบพิตร; ⊙8am-5pm) FREE Next to Wat Phra Si Sanphet (p684), this sanctuary hall houses one of Thailand's largest bronze Buddha images, dating to 1538. Coated in gold, the 12.5m-high figure (17m with the base) was badly damaged by a lightning-induced fire around 1700, and again when the Burmese sacked the city. The Buddha and the building were repaired in the 20th century.

Chao Sam Phraya National Museum   MUSEUM
(พิพิธภัณฑสถานแห่งชาติเจ้าสามพระยา; ☑035 244570; cnr Th Rotchana & Th Si Sanphet; adult/child 150B/free; ⊙9am-4pm Wed-Sun) The most impressive treasure of Ayuthaya's largest museum is the haul of royal gold (jewellery, utensils, gourds, spittoons) unearthed from

the crypts of Wat Mahathat (p684) and Wat Ratchaburana (p684). Beautifully carved teak friezes, some flecked with gold leaf, and numerous Buddha statues (some sculpted in the 7th century) are also on display.

Ayutthaya Tourist Center   MUSEUM
(ศูนย์ท่องเที่ยวอยุธยา; ☑035 246076; off Th Si Sanphet; ⊗8.30am-4.30pm) FREE Two floors of historical exhibitions contextualise Ayuthaya's history from ancient to present-day within this impressive building crowned with militaristic statues. Downstairs is the tourist information centre (p688).

◉ Off the Island

★**Wat Chai Wattanaram**   RUINS
(วัดไชยวัฒนาราม; Ban Pom; 50B; ⊗8am-6pm) Glorious at sunset, this temple is Ayuthaya's most impressive off-island site thanks to its 35m-high Khmer-style central *prang* and fine state of preservation. Relief panels are heavily eroded, but you can make out carved scenes from the Buddha's life.

Wat Phanan Choeng   BUDDHIST TEMPLE
(วัดพนัญเชิง; Khlong Suan Plu; 20B; ⊗daylight hours) This lively temple, believed to date to 1324, is a fascinating place to observe merit-making ceremonies, which unfold beneath the gaze of the 19m-high Phra Phanan Choeng Buddha. This enormous statue, a guardian for seafarers, is the focus of most visits. He sits within a soaring *wí·hăhn* (sanctuary; open 8am to 5pm) surrounded by 84,000 small Buddha images lining the walls.

Wat Yai Chai Mongkhon   RUINS
(วัดใหญ่ชัยมงคล; 20B; ⊗6am-6pm) Visitors to this photogenic ruin can climb stairs up the bell-shaped *chedi* (another term for stupa) for a view of sculpted gardens and dozens of stone Buddhas. There's a 7m-long reclining Buddha near the entrance and the local belief is that if you can get a coin to stick to the Buddha's feet, good luck will come your way.

It's 2km east of the island's south-east corner.

🛏 Sleeping

Most backpackers head for Soi 2, Th Naresuan (known as 'foreigner street'); the area in front of the train station also has plenty of low-priced rooms.

★**Ayothaya Riverside House**   GUESTHOUSE $
(☑081 644 5328; www.facebook.com/ayothayariversidehouse; 17/2 Mu 7, Tambon Banpom; d

---

ⓘ TOURING OFF THE ISLAND

Most guesthouses are happy to arrange tours, though you may get more options and flexibility by talking to a travel agency such as **Tour With Thai** (☑086 982 6265, 035 958226; http://tour-with-thai.business.site; Soi 2, Th Naresuan; ⊗8am-7pm).

One of the most common itineraries is a two-hour boat tour (around 250B) taking in Wat Phanan Choeng, **Wat Phutthai Sawan** (วัดพุทไธศวรรย์; Samphao Lom; ⊗8am-5.30pm) FREE and Wat Chai Wattanaram; it's worthwhile if you don't have private transport. **Ayutthaya Boat & Travel** (☑081 733 5687; www.ayutthaya-boat.com; cnr Th Chee Kun & Th Rotchana; ⊗9am-5pm Mon-Sat) offers dinner cruises on a teak rice barge, as well as longer cycling and paddling tours with homestay accommodation.

---

with shared bathroom 400B, d on boat 1500B; ❄🛜) Across Mae Nam Chao Phraya on the west side of Ayuthaya, this wonderful guesthouse offers a choice between pleasant rooms with fans and mosquito nets or satin-and-wood-decorated rooms on a boat (with air-con).

Chantana House   GUESTHOUSE $
(☑035 323200; chantanahouse@yahoo.com; 12/22 Soi 2, Th Naresuan; d with fan/air-con incl breakfast from 400/500B; ❄🛜) Rooms are plain, but modern Chantana House arguably offers the best value on the backpacker strip. Staff are friendly, though English is limited.

11:11 Hostel   HOSTEL $
(☑035 950138; www.facebook.com/11.11hostel; Th U Thong; dm incl breakfast 200B; ❄🛜) If you prefer modern dorm rooms to teak houses, you'll sigh with delight upon entering the cheerful and efficient 11:11 Hostel. Monochrome dorms have iron-frame bunks, each with its own light and plug socket, plus there's a dining area and a small terrace where you can look out over the river.

★**Promtong Mansion**   GUESTHOUSE $$
(☑089 165 6297; www.promtong.com; off 23 Th Pa Thon; d 1100B; ❄❄🛜) Extending the warmest welcome in Ayuthaya, Promtong Mansion is filled with fabulous wood-carved sculptures. Large, comfortable rooms are decked with elephant-shaped bedside lamps and other

THAILAND AYUTHAYA

Ayuthaya

Th Dusit

Main Terminal (5km)

Train Station

Th Watkluay

Chao Phrom Ferry Pier

Saphan Pridi Damrong

Th U Thong

Ko Lai

Soi 2

Bus Stop

Minivans to Bangkok

Th Khlong Makhamriang

Th Panaphrao

Bus Ticket Office

Th Ho Rattanachai

Th Bang Ian

Th Rotchana

Mae Nam Chao Phraya

Th Chee Kun

Th Naresuan

Bueng Phra Ram

Th Pa Thon

Th U Thong

Ayuthaya Historical Park

Th Si Sanphet

Wat Phra Si Sanphet

Mae Nam Lopburi

Th Ayuthaya – Pa Mok

Wat Worachetharam

Th Khlong Thaw

Mae Nam Chao Phraya

Wat Chai Wattanaram

Ayuthaya

local trimmings. The owner is a fount of local knowledge, complimentary fruit platters are offered throughout guests' stays, and the location is quiet but convenient.

Tamarind Guesthouse   GUESTHOUSE **$$**
(☑ 089 010 0196, 081 655 7937; tamarindthai2012@ gmail.com; off Th Chee Kun; d & tw incl breakfast 650-1200B; ❈ 🔊) Service couldn't be friendlier at this guesthouse within an attractively modified wooden building. Hidden in a back street across from Wat Mahathat (p684), Tamarind feels like a retreat despite being close to major attractions. As in many wooden guesthouses, creaky floors and thin walls aren't ideal for light sleepers; we think the traditional decor (stained glass, colourfully painted wood) amply compensates.

Tony's Place   GUESTHOUSE **$$**
(☑ 035 252578; Soi 2, 8 Th Naresuan; d 850-1200B, f 1500B; ❈🔊🔊) Tony's remains a prime destination for flashpackers thanks to its large outdoor **restaurant** (mains 70-300B; ⊙8am-10pm; 🔊🔊) area (ideal for mingling), mini-pool and spacious, characterful rooms. Lodgings on the upper floor are the most attractive.

🍴 Eating

★**Malakor**   THAI **$**
(www.facebook.com/malakorrestaurant; Th Chee Kun; mains 40-200B; ⊙restaurant noon-10pm, coffee shop 8am-4pm; 🔊) Touristy but satisfying, Malakor has a big menu, a great cook whipping up catfish curry and *pàd gàprow gài* (chicken with basil), and a relaxing wooden hut to enjoy it in. You will need to be patient with the service.

★**Sainam Pomphet**   THAI **$**
(Th U Thong; mains 100-150B; ⊙10am-10pm; 🔊) Spider crab – either steamed or whipped into fried rice – is the house speciality at this excellent riverside restaurant. Fish 'steamboat' dishes (in a simmering tureen) are immensely popular too. Those who aren't fans of seafood can tuck into a range of other Thai fare (try the pineapple spare ribs).

Bang Ian Night Market   MARKET **$**
(Th Bang Ian; snacks from 10B, mains 30-100B; ⊙5-8.30pm) This big, busy night market on its namesake street is a great destination for noshing on barbecued river fish, glass noodles, curry and rice dishes, rainbow-coloured *kà·nŏm chan* (layered coconut jellies) and much more besides.

Lung Lek   NOODLES **$**
(Th Chee Kun; mains 30-50B; ⊙8.30am-4pm) This locally adored noodle emporium serves some of the most notable *gŏo·ay dĕe·o mŏo đŭn* (stewed pork noodles, aka boat noodles) in town.

Bann Kun Pra   THAI **$$**
(☑ 035 241978; www.bannkunpra.com; Th U Thong; mains 70-350B; ⊙11am-9.30pm) More intimate than most of Ayuthaya's riverside restaurants, this century-old teak house is a great place to sit and watch river life pass by. Service quality varies, but the menu is loaded with seafood – including multiple preparations of local river prawns and fresh, tasty shrimp omelettes – and features other dishes such as chicken with cashew nuts.

THAILAND AYUTHAYA

TRANSPORT FROM AYUTHAYA

Bus

DESTINATION	FARE (B)	DURATION (HR)	FREQUENCY
Bangkok (Rangsit)	40	¾	frequent (minivan)
Bangkok Northern (Mo Chit) bus terminal	55-70	1-1½	frequent (minivan)
Chiang Mai	419-837	8½-10	at least eight daily
Lopburi	80	1½-1¾	every 30min (minivan)
Saraburi	45	1½	frequent
Sukhothai	266-342	7	at least 10 daily
Suphanburi	50-80	1½	more than hourly (minivan)

Train

DESTINATION	FARE (B)	DURATION (HR)	FREQUENCY
Bang Pa In	3-12	¼	16 daily
Bangkok Hualamphong station	20-65	1½-2½	frequent
Chiang Mai	396-1848	10-14	5 daily
Nong Khai	202-1750	9-11	3 daily
Pak Chong	53-465	2-3	12 daily

ℹ Information

Main Post Office (Th U Thong; ⊘8.30am-4.30pm Mon-Fri, 9am-noon Sat)

Phra Nakorn Si Ayutthaya Hospital (☑035 211888; www.ayhosp.go.th/ayh; Th U Thong) Has an emergency centre and English-speaking doctors.

Tourism Authority of Thailand (TAT; ☑035 246076; tatyutya@tat.or.th; Th Si Sanphet; ⊘8.30am-4.30pm) Has an information counter with maps and good advice at the Ayutthaya Tourist Center (p685).

Tourist Police (☑035 241446, 1155; Th Si Sanphet)

ℹ Getting There & Away

BUS

Ayuthaya's minivan **bus stop** (Th Naresuan) is just south of the backpacker strip (ask for the *dà·làht tâh rót jôw prom*). Minivans to Suphanburi (transfer here for Kanchanaburi), Saraburi (transfer here for Pak Chong and Khorat) and various places in Bangkok leave from here. There's a second Bangkok **departure point** (Th Naresuan) one block west.

The **main bus terminal** (off Hwy 32) is 3km east of the island, off Hwy 32, though you can buy tickets for Chiang Mai and Sukhothai from a town-centre **bus ticket office** (Th Naresuan; ⊘6.30am-5pm) for a fee (from 20B). A túk-túk

between the terminal and the island will cost 100B to 150B. Motorcycle taxis will charge 50B to 75B. Or take the purple *sŏrng·tăa·ou* (7B; passenger pick-up truck).

TRAIN

Ayuthaya's train station is just across the river from the town's main island. For Khao Yai National Park, catch the train to Pak Chong. For Bangkok, get off at Bang Sue if you're headed for Th Khao San.

ℹ Getting Around

Many guesthouses hire bicycles (40B to 50B per day) and motorcycles (250B to 300B per day).

Lopburi ลพบุรี

☑036 / POPULATION 161,000

In Thailand's 'Monkey City', imposing Khmer-style temples are assailed by an army of furry menaces. These mischief-makers have the run of the town and are impossible to avoid – and for many, monkeys are the headline attraction of Lopburi.

One of Thailand's oldest cities, Lopburi is home to an array of palaces and temples from the Khmer and Ayuthaya empires that still stand, though in various states of decay.

◉ Sights

All of Lopburi's main sites can be visited in a leisurely day.

★ Prang Sam Yot
RUINS

(ปรางค์สามยอด; cnr Th Wichayen & Th Prang Sam Yot; 50B; ⊙8.30am-6pm) As well known for its resident monkeys as its looming towers, this is Lopburi's most famous attraction. The three linked towers were built from laterite and sandstone by the Khmer in the 13th century as a Buddhist temple. It was later converted to Shiva worship but was returned to Buddhism by King Narai in the 17th century. There are two ruined headless Buddha images inside; a third, more complete Buddha sits photogenically in front of the main *prang* (Hindi/Khmer-style stupa).

Phra Narai Ratchaniwet
MUSEUM

(วังนารายณ์ราชนิเวศน์, Somdet Phra Narai National Museum; ☑036 414372; entrance Th Sorasak; 150B; ⊙8.30am-4.30pm Wed-Sun) An excellent museum is enclosed within these ruins of a 17th-century palace. Built from 1665 with help from French and Italian engineers, the palace was originally used to welcome foreign dignitaries. A trim promenade leads between King Narai's elephant stables, banquet rooms, wells and dozens of storage buildings to the Somdet Phra Narai National Museum. Allow a couple of hours to explore this 7-hectare historical site inside and out.

Wat Phra Si Ratana Mahathat
RUINS

(วัดพระศรีรัตนมหาธาตุ; Th Na Phra Kan; 50B; ⊙8.30am-4pm) For a peaceful, monkey-free experience of a Khmer *wát*, stroll around this beautiful site opposite the train station. Built in the 12th century and heavily modified over the centuries, this now-ruined temple has the tallest central *prang* in Lopburi and retains a good amount of original stucco, including gorgeous lotus-shaped detailing and intricate Buddha images.

🛏 Sleeping & Eating

★ Noom Guesthouse
GUESTHOUSE $

(☑036 427693; www.noomguesthouse.com; Th Phraya Kamjat; s/d/tr with shared bathroom & fan 250/350/450B; d with air-con 500B; ❄🛜) Weary backpackers sigh with relief upon arrival at family-run Noom, easily the most *fa-ràng*-friendly spot in town. Even if you aren't staying in one of the clean, simple rooms (or the comfy garden bungalows out back), it's worth swinging by to rent a motorbike (from 250B), book a climbing tour

or swap travel stories with the backpackers at the **bar**.

Pee Homestay
HOMESTAY $

(☑086 164 2184; www.lopburimassage.com; Soi Promachan; d with fan 280B, d with air-con 340-500B; ❄🛜) On the wrong side of the tracks (in a good way), this homestay behind the train station is run by the super-friendly Kanaree, a beautician and massage therapist. It's a laid-back local experience. Spicand-span rooms are priced by size.

Matini
INTERNATIONAL, THAI $$

(18 Th Phraya Kamjat; mains 50-350B; ⊙9amlate; 🛜🍴) Free pool, a Blues Brothers motif on the wall and good food (both Thai and Western) plant Matini firmly in the sights of backpackers. With indoor and outdoor areas, this is a great spot to tuck into sizeable portions of richly spiced curries (including veggie options), sip on smoothies or kick back late with a few beers.

Baan Sahai
THAI $

(Soi Sorasak; mains 40-250B; ⊙11am-10pm; 🛜) With a touch of European flair, this little spot styles itself as a bistro, serving Thai main courses and a range of loosely French desserts. It's as good for a full-blown meal as for a fresh, ice-blended pineapple shake.

ℹ Information

King Narai Hospital (☑036 785444; www.kingnaraihospital.go.th; Th Phahonyothin) For

MONKEY MAYHEM

Grown men arm their catapults, old women grab 2m-long poles and tourists alternately shriek and pose for photos. Welcome to Lopburi, a town that fights a losing battle to keep its iconic monkeys at bay.

Many locals loathe their simian neighbours, but the monkeys are never harmed due to the belief that they are disciples of the Hindu god Hanuman and so to injure one would be seriously bad karma.

Most of the monkeys live at Prang Sam Yot and **San Phra Kan** (ศาลพระกาฬ; Th Wichayen; ⊙5.30am-6pm) FREE. Exercise caution around them: they are wild animals, not pets. Don't carry anything they can grab, especially food and bags. If they do mug you, don't resist. They will bite.

TRANSPORT FROM LOPBURI

Bus

DESTINATION	FARE (B)	DURATION (HR)	FREQUENCY
Ayuthaya	80	1½	every 30min (minivan)
Bangkok	110-120	2	frequent (minivan)
Chiang Mai	502-582	9-12	four daily
Nakhon Ratchasima (Khorat)	130-164	3½	every 30min (minivan & bus)
Pak Chong	70	2	every 30min (minivan)

Train

DESTINATION	FARE (B)	DURATION (HR)	FREQUENCY
Ayuthaya	13-58	½-1½	18 daily
Bangkok Hualamphong	28-123	2-3½	16 daily
Chiang Mai	236-1800	9-12	5 daily
Phitsanulok	49-1046	3-5	11 daily

monkey bites and other health needs. Ideally, bring a local if you can't speak Thai. It's 5km east of the old town.

Post Office (Th Prang Sam Yot; ⊙8.30am-7pm Mon-Fri, 9am-noon Sat & Sun)

Tourism Authority of Thailand (TAT; ☑036 770096; tatlobri@tat.or.th; Th Na Phra Kan; ⊙8.30am-4.30pm) Kiosk in the train station.

❶ Getting There & Away

Lopburi's **bus station** (Sa Kaew Circle) is 2km east of the old town. For Kanchanaburi, you'll need to change buses in Ayuthaya or Suphanburi (50B, two hours). Minivans to Bangkok depart from Th Na Phra Kan. The **train station** (Th Na Phra Kan) is in the old town. It has luggage storage if you're just passing through.

Phitsanulok   พิษณุโลก

☑055 / POPULATION 84,000

Phitsanulok sees relatively few independent travellers, although the city is a convenient base from which to explore the attractions of nearby Sukhothai and Kamphaeng Phet. But this friendly city also boasts some interesting sites and museums of its own, including one of Thailand's most revered Buddha images.

◉ Sights

Sergeant Major Thawee Folk Museum   MUSEUM

(พิพิธภัณฑ์พื้นบ้านจ่าทวี; Th Wisut Kasat; adult/child 50/25B; ⊙8.30am-4.30pm) This fascinating museum displays a remarkable collec-

tion of tools, textiles and photographs from Phitsanulok Province. It's spread throughout five traditional-style Thai buildings with well-groomed gardens, and the displays are all accompanied by informative and legible English descriptions. Those interested in cooking will find much of interest in the display of a traditional Thai kitchen and the various traps used to catch game.

Wat Phra Si Ratana Mahathat   TEMPLE

(วัดพระศรีรัตนมหาธาตุ; Th Phutta Bucha; ⊙temple 6am-9pm, museum 9am-5.30pm Wed-Sun) The main *wi·hǎhn* (sanctuary) at this temple, known by locals as Wat Yai, appears small from the outside, but houses the **Phra Phuttha Chinnarat**, one of Thailand's most revered and copied Buddha images. This famous bronze statue is probably second in importance only to the Emerald Buddha in Bangkok's Wat Phra Kaew.

🛏 Sleeping & Eating

Lithai Guest House   HOTEL $

(☑055 219626; 73/1-5 Th Phayarithai; r incl breakfast 300-580B; ❋🛜) The light-filled 60 or so rooms here don't have much character but they are clean. Air-con rooms include perks such as large private bathrooms with hot water, cable TV, fridge and breakfast, while the cheapies are fan-cooled and share bathrooms.

Ayara Grand Palace   HOTEL $$

(☑055 909993; www.ayaragrandpalacehotel.com; Th Authong; incl breakfast r 1200-1500B, ste 1800-3500B; ❋@🛜❄) The '90s-era pastels, fake fireplaces and relentless flower theme of this hotel give it an undeniably cheesy feel. But it's all in good fun, and the vast suites – the most expensive of which is decked out with an electric massage chair – are pretty good value.

Rim Nan
THAI $

(5/4 Th Phutta Bucha; mains 20-35B; ⊙9am-4pm) Just north of Wat Phra Si Ratana Mahathat, Rim Nan is one of a few similar restaurants along Th Phutta Bucha that offer *gŏoay-đĕe-o hôy kăh*, literally 'legs-hanging' noodles, named for the benches that make eating a bowl an even more informal endeavour.

★ Ban Mai
THAI $$

(93/30 Th Authong; mains 100-290B; ⊙11am-10pm) Dinner at this local favourite is like a meal at your grandparents' place: opinionated conversation resounds, frumpy furniture abounds and an overfed cat appears to rule the dining room. The likewise homey dishes include *gaang pèt bèt yâhng* (grilled duck curry) and *yam đà krái* (herbal lemongrass salad). There's no roman-script sign; look for the yellow compound across from Ayara Grand Palace Hotel.

❶ Getting There & Away

Phitsanulok's **airport** (☑055 301002) is about 5km south of town; a taxi counter can arrange trips to/from town for 150B. **Air Asia** (☑Phitsanulok 094 7193645, nationwide 02 515 9999; www.airasia.com; Phitsanulok Airport; ⊙7am-6.30pm), **Nok Air** (☑055 301051, nationwide 1318; www.nokair.co.th; Phitsanulok Airport; ⊙6am-7pm) and **Thai Lion Air** (☑call centre 02 529 9999; www.lionairthai.com; Phitsanulok Airport; ⊙7am-7pm) conduct flights to/from Bangkok's Don Mueang International Airport (from 640B, 55 minutes, seven daily).

The city's **bus station** (☑055 212090; Rte 12) is 2km east of town on Hwy 12; túk-túk and motorcycle taxis to/from town cost 60B. There are hourly buses to Sukhothai between 7am and 6pm (39B, one hour), as well as frequent minivans. There are also hourly departures to Bangkok (263B to 361B, five to six hours, 8.45am to 11pm) and frequent buses to Chiang Mai (202B to 304B, six hours, 5.40am to 12.40pm).

Phitsanulok's **train station** (☑055 258005, nationwide 1690; www.railway.co.th; Th Akatossaroth) is within walking distance of accommodation and offers a left-luggage service. Destinations include Bangkok (69B to 1664B, five to seven hours, 10 daily) and Chiang Mai (65B to 1645B, seven to nine hours, five daily).

Sukhothai
สุโขทัย

☑055 / POPULATION 37,000

The Sukhothai (Rising of Happiness) Kingdom flourished from the mid-13th century to the late 14th century. This period is often viewed as the golden age of Thai civilisation. The remains of the kingdom, known as *meu-ang gòw* (old city), feature around 45 sq km of partially rebuilt ruins, making up one of the most visited ancient sites in Thailand.

Located 12km east of the historical park on Mae Nam Yom, the market town of Sukhothai makes a pleasant base from which to explore the old city ruins.

◎ Sights

★ Sukhothai Historical Park
HISTORIC SITE

(อุทยานประวัติศาสตร์สุโขทัย; ☑055 697527; Central, Northern & Western zones 100B, per bicycle/motorcycle/car 10/20/50B; ⊙Central Zone 6.30am-6pm Sun-Fri, to 9pm Sat, Northern Zone 7.30am-5.30pm, Western Zone 8am-4.30pm) The Sukhothai Historical Park ruins are one of Thailand's most impressive World Heritage Sites. The park includes the remains of 21 historical sites and four large ponds within the old walls, with an additional 70 sites within a 5km radius. The ruins are divided into five zones; the central, northern and western zones have a separate 100B admission fee.

The architecture of Sukhothai temples is most typified by the classic lotus-bud *chedi*, featuring a conical spire topping a square-sided structure on a three-tiered base. Some sites exhibit other rich architectural forms introduced and modified during the period, such as bell-shaped Sinhalese and double-tiered Srivijaya *chedi*.

Despite the popularity of the park, it's quite expansive and solitary exploration is usually possible. Some of the most interesting ruins are outside the city walls, so a bicycle or motorcycle is essential to fully appreciate everything.

➡ Central Zone

The historical park's **main zone** (โซนกลาง; 100B, plus per bicycle/motorcycle/car 10/20/50B; ⊙6.30am-6pm Sun-Fri, to 9pm Sat) is home to what are arguably some of the park's most impressive ruins. On Saturday night much of the central zone is illuminated and remains open until 9pm.

THAILAND SUKHOTHAI

Sukhothai Historical Park

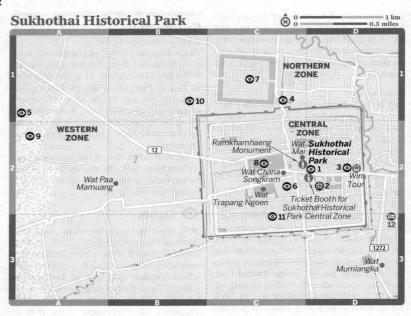

Wat Mahathat (วัดมหาธาตุ; Central Zone, Sukhothai Historical Park; 100B, plus per bicycle/motorcycle/car 10/20/50B; ⊙ 6.30am-6pm Sun-Fri, to 9pm Sat) was completed in the 13th century.The largest wát in Sukhothai is surrounded by brick walls (206m long and 200m wide) and a moat that is believed to represent the outer wall of the universe and the cosmic ocean.

Just south of Wat Mahathat, **Wat Si Sawai** (วัดศรีสวาย; Central Zone, Sukhothai Historical Park; 100B, plus per bicycle/motorcycle/car 10/20/50B; ⊙ 6.30am-6pm Sun-Fri, to 9pm Sat), a Buddhist shrine dating from the 12th and 13th centuries, features three Khmer-style towers and a picturesque moat. It was

originally built by the Khmers as a Hindu temple.

Wat Sa Si (วัดสระศรี, Sacred Pond Monastery; Central Zone, Sukhothai Historical Park; 100B, plus per bicycle/motorcycle/car 10/20/50B; ⊙ 6.30am-6pm Sun-Fri, to 9pm Sat) sits on an island west of the bronze monument of King Ramkhamhaeng (the third Sukhothai king). It's a simple, classic Sukhothai-style wát containing a large Buddha, one *chedi* and the columns of the ruined *wí-hǎhn* (sanctuary).

Near the entrance of the Central Zone, the **Ramkhamhaeng National Museum** (พิพิธภัณฑสถานแห่งชาติรามคำแหง; Sukhothai Historical Park; 150B; ⊙ 9am-4pm) this museum is a decent starting point for exploring the historical park ruins. A replica of the famous Ramkhamhaeng inscription, said to be the earliest example of Thai writing, is kept here among an impressive collection of Sukhothai artefacts. Admission to the museum is not included in the ticket to the central zone.

➡ **Northern Zone**

The **northern zone** (โซนเหนือ; 100B, plus per bicycle/motorcycle/car 10/20/50B; ⊘7.30am-5.30pm), 500m north of the old city walls, is easily reached by bicycle.

The **Wat Si Chum** (วัดศรีชุม; Northern Zone, Sukhothai Historical Park; 100B, plus per bicycle/motorcycle/car 10/20/50B; ⊘7.30am-5.30pm) is north-west of the old city and contains an impressive *mon-dòp* with a 15m brick-and-stucco seated Buddha. This Buddha's elegant, tapered fingers are much photographed. Archaeologists theorise that this image is the 'Phra Atchana' mentioned in the famous Ramkhamhaeng inscription. A passage in the *mon-dòp* wall that leads to the top has been blocked so that it's no longer possible to view the *Jataka* inscriptions that line the tunnel ceiling.

The somewhat isolated **Wat Phra Phai Luang** (วัดพระพายหลวง; Sukhothai Historical Park; 100B, plus per bicycle/motorcycle/car 10/20/50B; ⊘7.30am-5.30pm) features three 12th-century Khmer-style towers, bigger than those at Wat Si Sawai in the Central Zone. This may have been the centre of Sukhothai when it was ruled by the Khmers of Angkor prior to the 13th century.

➡ **Western Zone**

The **western zone** (โซนตะวันตก; 100B, plus per bicycle/motorcycle/car 10/20/50B; ⊘8am-4.30pm), at its furthest extent 2km west of the old city walls, has several mostly featureless ruins. A bicycle or motorcycle is necessary to explore this zone.

Located on the crest of a hill that rises about 200m above the plain, the name of **Wat Saphan Hin** (วัดสะพานหิน; Western Zone, Sukthothai Historical Park; 100B, plus per bicycle/motorcycle/car 10/20/50B; ⊘8am-4.30pm), which means 'stone bridge', is a reference to the slate path and staircase that lead up to the temple, which are still in place.

All that remains of the original temple are a few *chedi* and the ruined *wí-hǎhn*, consisting of two rows of laterite columns flanking a 12.5m-high standing Buddha image on a brick terrace. The site is 3km west

SANGKHALOK MUSEUM

The small but comprehensive **Sangkhalok Museum** (พิพิธภัณฑ์สังคโลก; Rte 1293; adult/child 100/50B; ⊘8am-5pm) is an excellent introduction to ancient Sukhothai's most famous product and export, its ceramics.

The ground floor displays an impressive collection of original Thai pottery found in the area, plus some pieces traded from Vietnam, Burma and China. The 2nd floor features examples of non-utilitarian pottery made as art, including some beautiful and rare ceramic Buddha statues.

The museum is about 2.5km east of the centre of New Sukhothai; a túk-túk here is about 100B.

of the former city wall and gives a good view of the Sukhothai ruins to the southeast and the mountains to the north and south.

☞ Tours

Cycling Sukhothai CYCLING
(☎085 083 1864, 055 612519; www.cycling-sukhothai.com; off Th Jarodvithithong; half/full day 800/990B, sunset tour 450B) A resident of Sukhothai for nearly 20 years, Belgian cycling enthusiast Ronny Hanquart offers themed bike tours, such as the Historical Park Tour, which also includes stops at lesser-seen *wát* and villages.

The office is about 1.2km west of Mae Nam Yom, off Th Jarodvithithong in New Sukhothai; free transport can be arranged.

🛏 Sleeping

New Sukhothai has some of the best-value budget accommodation in northern Thailand.

Ban Thai GUESTHOUSE $
(☎055 610163; banthai_guesthouse@yahoo.com; 38 Th Prawet Nakhon; r & bungalows 250-800B; ✳🖥) The rooms here range from plain to stylish, but the convergence of a friendly atmosphere, an attractive garden setting and low prices makes for a winner.

Sila Resort HOTEL $
(☎055 620344; www.silaresort-sukhothai.com; 3/49 Th Kuhasuwan; incl breakfast r 230-500B, bungalows 750-1200B; ✳@🖥) We couldn't

SUBURBS OF THE SUKHOTHAI EMPIRE

The Sukhothai empire expanded to the satellite cities of Si Satchanalai and Chaliang (อุทยานประวัติศาสตร์ศรีสัชนาลัย-เชลียง), 50km north of Sukhothai.

Set among peaceful hills, the 13th- to 15th-century ruins of these old cities are now part of the 720 hectare **Si Satchanalai-Chaliang Historical Park** (อุทยาน ประวัติศาสตร์ศรีสัชนาลัย-เชลียง; off Rte 101; 100B; ☉8.30am-4.30pm). A visit here is a more pastoral experience than at old Sukhothai.

The Park is off Rte 101 between Sawankhalok and Ban Hat Siaw. From New Sukhothai, take a Si Satchanalai bus (45B, 1½ hours, hourly 6.40am to 5pm) or one of four buses to Chiang Rai between 6.40am and 11.30am (46B) and ask to get off at *meu·ang gòw* (old city).

A combined ticket of 250B allows entry to all the sites below. Bicycles (30B) can be rented near the entrance gates to the park.

Si Satchanalai

Wat Chang Lom (วัดช้างล้อม; Si Satchanalai-Chaliang Historical Park; 100B; ☉8.30am-4.30pm) has a *chedi* (stupa) surrounded by Buddha statues set in niches and guarded by the remains of well-preserved elephant buttresses. Climb to the top of the hill supporting **Wat Khao Phanom Phloeng** (วัดเขาพนมเพลิง; Si Satchanalai-Chaliang Historical Park; 100B; ☉8.30am-4.30pm) for a view over the town and river. **Wat Chedi Jet Thaew** (วัด เจดีย์เจ็ดแถว; Si Satchanalai-Chaliang Historical Park; 100B; ☉8.30am-4.30pm) has a group of stupas in classic Sukhothai style.

Chaliang

Chaliang is an older city site, dating to the 11th century, and sits 1km from Si Satchanalai. **Wat Phra Si Ratana Mahathat** (วัดพระศรีรัตนมหาธาตุ; Si Satchanalai-Chaliang Historical Park; 20B; ☉8am-4.30pm) contains a bas-relief of the classic walking Buddha, a hallmark of the Sukhothai era. **Wat Chao Chan** (วัดเจ้าจันทร์; Si Satchanalai-Chaliang Historical Park; 100B, combined entry with Si Satchanalai & Si Satchanalai Centre for Study & Preservation of Sangkalok Kilns 250B; ☉8am-5pm) has a large Khmer-style tower probably constructed during the reign of Khmer King Jayavarman VII (1181–1297). The roofless *wí·hǎhn* (sanctuary) contains the laterite outlines of a large standing Buddha that has all but melted away from exposure.

Sangkhalok Kilns

This area was famous for its beautiful pottery, much of which was exported to China and Indonesia. **Si Satchanalai Centre for Study & Preservation of Sangkalok Kilns** (ศูนย์ศึกษาและอนุรักษ์เตาสังคโลก; 100B, combined ticket with Si Satchanalai & Wat Chao Chan 250B; ☉8am-4.30pm), 5km north-west of Si Satchanalai, has large excavated kilns and intact pottery samples documenting the area's pottery traditions.

help but think of Disneyland when we first encountered this compound of flowering trees, a gingerbread Thai villa, wood bungalows, statues, resort-like A-frames and a restaurant. And like Disneyland, it comes together in a cheerful, colourful package looked after by smiling people. The only downside is that it's a fair hike from the centre of New Sukhothai.

4T Guesthouse HOTEL **$**
(☎055 614679; fourhouse@yahoo.com; 122 Soi Mae Ramphan; r 300-1000B; ❄☞🛋) An expansive budget 'resort'. There's a smorgasbord of spacious yet plain rooms to consider, and the swimming pool makes the decision even easier.

★**Orchid Hibiscus Guest House** HOTEL **$$**
(☎055 633284; www.orchidhibiscus-guesthouse. com; 407/2 Rte 1272; r/bungalows 900/1400B; ❄☞🛋) This collection of rooms and bungalows is set in relaxing, manicured grounds with a swimming pool as a centrepiece and the self-professed 'amazing breakfast' (100B) as a highlight. Rooms are

spotless and fun, featuring colourful design details and accents. It's on Rte 1272, about 500m off Rte 12; the turn-off is between the Km 48 and Km 49 markers.

TR Room & Bungalow GUESTHOUSE $$
(☑ 055 611663; www.sukhothaibudgetguesthouse.com; 27/5 Th Prawet Nakhon; r/bungalow 600/850B; ❊@🖧) The rooms here were renovated in 2016, with new furniture and eclectic interior-design elements bumping them up to midrange level. For those needing a bit more space, there are five wooden bungalows out the back.

🍴 Eating & Drinking

★ Jayhae THAI $
(Th Jarodvithithong; dishes 30-120B; ⊘8am-4pm) You haven't been to Sukhothai if you haven't tried the noodles at Jayhae, an extremely popular restaurant that serves Sukhothai-style noodles, *pàt tai* and tasty coffee drinks. Located about 1.3km west of Mae Nam Yom, off Th Jarodvithithong.

Night Market MARKET $
(Th Ramkhamhaeng; mains 30-60B; ⊘6-11pm) A wise choice for cheap eats is New Sukhothai's tiny night market. Most vendors here are accustomed to accommodating foreigners and even provide bilingual menus.

Dream Café THAI $$
(86/1 Th Singhawat; mains 120-350B; ⊘5-11pm; 🖉) A meal at Dream Café is like dining in an antique shop. Eclectic but tasteful furnishings and knick-knackery abound, staff members are competent and friendly and,

most importantly of all, the food is good. Try one of the well-executed *yam* (Thai-style 'salads').

Chopper Bar BAR
(Th Prawet Nakhon; ⊘10am-12.30am; 🖧) Travellers and locals congregate at this restaurant-bar from morning till hangover for food (mains 30B to 150B), drinks and live music. Take advantage of Sukhothai's cool evenings on the rooftop terrace.

ℹ Information

Sukhothai Hospital (☑ 055 610280; Th Jarodvithithong) Located just west of New Sukhothai.

Tourism Authority of Thailand (TAT; ☑ 055 616228, nationwide 1672; www.tourismthailand.org; Th Jarodvithithong; ⊘8.30am-4.30pm) In new digs since 2016 and about 750m west of the bridge in New Sukhothai, this office has a pretty good selection of maps and brochures.

ℹ Getting There & Away

Sukhothai's airport is located a whopping 27km north of town off Rte 1195. **Bangkok Airways** (☑ 055 647224, nationwide 1771; www.bangkokair.com; Sukhothai Airport; ⊘7am-6pm) is the only airline operating here, with three daily flights to/from Bangkok's Suvarnabhumi International Airport (from 1890B, one hour and 15 minutes).

Sukhothai's minivan and **bus station** (☑ 055 614529; Rte 101) is almost 1km north-west of the centre of New Sukhothai; a motorcycle taxi between here and central New Sukhothai should cost around 50B, or you can hop on any *sŏrng·tăa·ou* (passenger pick-up truck) bound

BUSES FROM SUKHOTHAI

DESTINATION	FARE (B)	DURATION (HR)	FREQUENCY
Bangkok	241-310	6-7	half-hourly 7.50am-10.40pm
Chiang Mai	195-374	5-6	frequent 6.20am-2am
Chiang Rai	231	9	4 departures 6.40-11.30am
Kamphaeng Phet	53-68	1½	every 30 min 7.50am-10.40pm
Khon Kaen	221-334	7	frequent 10.30am-12.40am
Lampang	155-205	3	frequent 6.20am-2am
Mae Sot	130-176	3	3 departures 9.15am-2.30am
Mukdahan	476	10	7.50pm & 9.40pm
Nan	176	4	3pm
Phitsanulok	39-50	1	every 30 min 7.50am-10.40pm
Sawankhalok	27	1	hourly 6.40am-5pm
Si Satchanalai	45	1½	hourly 6.40am-5pm

for Sukhothai Historical Park (20B, 10 minutes, frequent from 6am to 5.30pm).

If you're staying near the historical park, **Win Tour** (☎ 099 135 5645; Rte 12; ⏱ 6am-9.40pm) has an office where you can board buses to Bangkok (310B, six hours, 8am, noon and 9.50pm) and Chiang Mai (210B, five hours, six departures from 6am to 2pm).

❶ Getting Around

A *sǎhm·lór* (also spelt *sǎamláw*; three-wheeled pedicab) ride within New Sukhothai should cost no more than 40B.

Relatively frequent **sǒrng·tǎa·ou** (Th Jarodvithithong; 30B; ⏱ 6am-5.30pm) run between New Sukhothai and Sukhothai Historical Park (30B, 30 minutes, 6am to 5.30pm), leaving from a stop on Th Jarodvithithong. Motorcycle taxis go between the town or bus station and the historical park for 120B.

Bicycles can be hired at shops outside the park entrance for 30B per day (6am to 6pm).

Motorbikes (from 250B for 24 hours) can be hired at nearly every guesthouse in New Sukhothai.

Kamphaeng Phet   กำแพงเพชร

☑ 055 / POPULATION 30,000

Kamphaeng Phet translates as 'Diamond Wall', a reference to the apparent strength of this formerly walled city's protective barrier. The city helped to protect the Sukhothai and, later, Ayuthaya kingdoms against attacks from Burma or Lanna. Parts of the wall can still be seen today, as well as fascinating ruins of several religious structures.

◉ Sights

Kamphaeng Phet Historical Park   HISTORIC SITE

(อุทยานประวัติศาสตร์กำแพงเพชร; 100B, with walled city 150B; ⏱ 8am-6.30pm) A Unesco World Heritage Site, the Kamphaeng Phet Historical Park features the ruins of structures dating back to the 14th century, roughly the same time as the better-known kingdom of Sukhothai. Kamphaeng Phet's Buddhist monuments continued to be built up until the Ayuthaya period, nearly 200 years later, and thus possess elements of both Sukhothai and Ayuthaya styles, resulting in a school of Buddhist art quite unlike anywhere else in Thailand.

Kamphaeng Phet National Museum   MUSEUM

(พิพิธภัณฑสถานแห่งชาติกำแพงเพชร; Th Pindamri; 100B; ⏱ 9am-4pm Wed-Sun) Kamphaeng Phet's visit-worthy museum has undergone an extensive renovation. It's home to an expansive collection of artefacts from the Kamphaeng Phet area, including an immense Shiva statue that is the largest bronze Hindu sculpture in the country. The image was formerly located at the nearby **Shiva Shrine** (ศาลพระอิศวร; off Th Pindamri) **FREE** until a German missionary stole the idol's hands and head in 1886 (they were later returned). Today a replica stands in its place.

🛏 Sleeping & Eating

Three J Guest House   GUESTHOUSE $

(☎ 081 887 4189, 055 713129; www.threejguesthouse.com; 79 Soi 1, Soi Ratchavitee; r 300-900B; ❄ @ 🛜) The cheapest rooms at this homey

BUSES FROM KAMPHAENG PHET

DESTINATION	PRICE (B)	DURATION (HR)	DEPARTURES
Bangkok	200-400	5	frequent 9am-10pm
Chiang Mai	256-298	5	hourly 9.30am-11pm
Chiang Rai	265-397	7	5 departures noon-10.30pm
Lampang	147-225	4	5 departures noon-10.30pm
Mae Hong Son	466-544	11	10pm & 10.30pm
Mae Sot	164	3	2am & 4am
Phayao	212-326	6	5 departures noon-10.30pm
Phitsanulok	73	2½	hourly 5am-6pm
Sukhothai	57-74	1	hourly noon-4am

guesthouse are fan-cooled and share a clean bathroom, while the more expensive have air-con. There's heaps of local information, and bicycles and motorcycles are available for hire (per day bicycle/motorcycle 50B/200B).

★**Navarat Heritage Hotel**   HOTEL $$
(☑055 711211; www.navaratheritage.com; 2 Soi 21, Th Tesa 1; incl breakfast r 1100-3200B, ste 15,000B; ❀❀☎) The '70s-era Navarat has undergone a renovation, erasing most signs of the hotel's true age. Rooms are modern, spacious, cosy and well equipped, some with views of the river.

★**Bamee Chakangrao**   THAI $
(cnr Soi 9 & Th Rachadumnoen 1; mains 30-35B; ☺8.30am-3pm) Thin wheat-and-egg noodles (bà·mèe) are a speciality of Kamphaeng Phet, and this famous restaurant is one of the best places to try them. The noodles are made fresh every day behind the restaurant, and pork satay is also available. There's no roman-script sign; look for the green banners on the corner.

Night Market   THAI $
(Th Thesa 1; mains 30-60B; ☺4-10pm) For cheap Thai eats, a busy night market sets up every evening near the river just north of the Navarat Hotel.

ℹ **Getting There & Around**

Kamphaeng Phet's **bus station** (☑055 799103; Rte 101) is about 1km west of the Mae Nam Ping. Motorcycles (50B) and sŏrng·tăa·ou (passenger pick-up trucks, 20B, frequent from 7.30am to 3pm) run between the station and town. If coming from Sukhothai or Phitsanulok, get off in the old city or at the roundabout on Th Thesa 1 to save yourself the trouble of having to get a sŏrng·tăa·ou back into town.

NORTHERN THAILAND

What can't you do in northern Thailand?

The region's premier draw is its nature, and its rugged geography is a playground for outdoor pursuits ranging from rafting excursions to hill treks to visiting minority villages.

Then there's northern Thailand's buffet of cultural attractions. The region is regarded as the birthplace of much of Thai culture, and had its capital at temple- and market-laden Chiang Mai.

Chiang Mai   เชียงใหม่

☑053 / POPULATION 201,000

The former seat of the Lanna kingdom is a blissfully calm and laid-back place. Yes, you'll be surrounded by other amazed travellers but that scarcely takes away from the fabulous food and leisurely wandering. Participate in a vast array of activities on offer, or just stroll around the backstreets, and discover a city that is still firmly Thai in its atmosphere, and attitude.

A sprawling modern city has grown up around ancient Chiang Mai. Despite this, the historic centre of Chiang Mai still feels more like a sleepy country town than a bustling capital. If you drive in any direction, you'll soon find yourself in the lush green countryside and pristine rainforests dotted with churning waterfalls, serene wát, and peaceful country villages – as well as a host of markets and elephant sanctuaries.

👁 **Sights**

Chiang Mai overflows with temples, markets and museums, but don't overlook the sights outside the old city, both inside and outside the fringing highways.

★**Wat Phra Singh**   BUDDHIST TEMPLE
(วัดพระสิงห์; Th Singharat; 20B; ☺5am-8.30pm) Chiang Mai's most revered temple, Wat Phra Singh is dominated by an enormous, mosaic-inlaid wí·hăhn (sanctuary). Its prosperity is plain to see from the lavish monastic buildings and immaculately trimmed grounds, dotted with coffee stands and massage pavilions. Pilgrims flock here to venerate the famous Buddha image known as **Phra Singh** (Lion Buddha), housed in Wihan Lai Kham, a small chapel immediately south of the chedi (stupa) to the rear of the temple grounds.

Wat Chedi Luang   BUDDHIST TEMPLE
(วัดเจดีย์หลวง; Th Phra Pokklao; adult/child 40/20B; ☺7am-10pm) Wat Chedi Luang isn't as grand as Wat Phra Singh, but its towering, ruined Lanna-style chedi (built in 1441) is much taller and the sprawling compound around the stupa is powerfully atmospheric. The famed Phra Kaew (Emerald Buddha), now held in Bangkok's Wat Phra Kaew, resided in the eastern niche until 1475; today, you can view a jade replica.

Chiang Mai

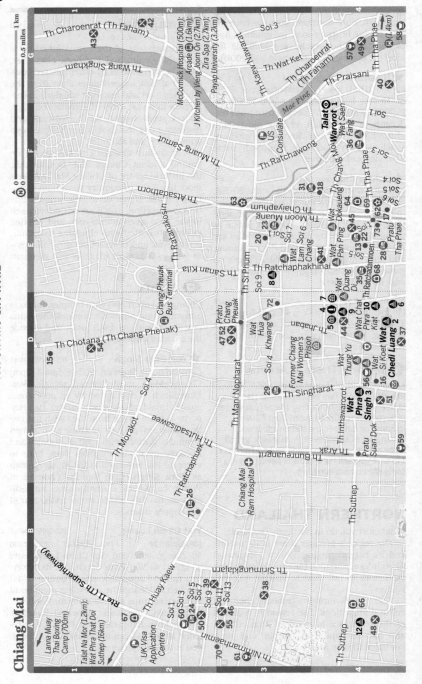

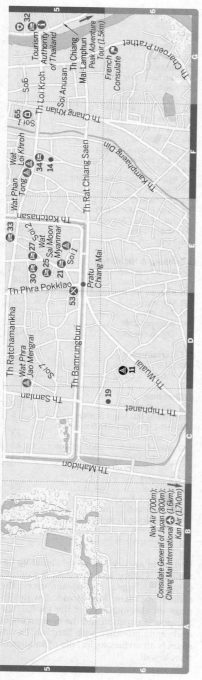

Lanna Folklife Museum
MUSEUM

(พิพิธภัณฑ์พื้นถิ่นล้านนา; Th Phra Pokklao; adult/child 90/40B; ⊗8.30am-5pm Tue-Sun) Set inside the Thai-colonial-style former Provincial Court, dating from 1935, this imaginative museum re-creates Lanna village life in a series of life-size dioramas. They explain everything from *lai·krahm* pottery stencilling and *fon lep* (a mystical Lanna dance featuring long metal fingernails) to the intricate symbolism of different elements of Lanna-style monasteries.

★Wat Phra That Doi Suthep
BUDDHIST TEMPLE

(วัดพระธาตุดอยสุเทพ; Th Huay Kaew, Doi Suthep; 30B; ⊗6am-6pm) Overlooking the city from its mountain throne, Wat Phra That Doi Suthep is one of northern Thailand's most sacred temples, and its founding legend is learned by every schoolkid in Chiang Mai. The wát is a beautiful example of northern Thai architecture, reached via a 306-step staircase flanked by *naga* (serpents); the climb is intended to help devotees accrue Buddhist merit.

Wat Phan Tao
BUDDHIST TEMPLE

(วัดพันเถา; Th Phra Pokklao; donations appreciated; ⊗daylight hours) Without doubt the most atmospheric wát in the old city, this teak marvel sits in the shadow of Wat Chedi Luang. Set in a compound full of fluttering orange flags, the monastery is a monument to the teak trade, with an enormous prayer hall supported by 28 gargantuan teak pillars and lined with dark teak panels, enshrining a particularly graceful gold Buddha image.

Wat Chiang Man
BUDDHIST TEMPLE

(วัดเชียงมั่น; Th Ratchaphakhinai; donations appreciated; ⊗daylight hours) Chiang Mai's oldest temple was established by the city's founder, Phaya Mengrai, sometime around 1296. In front of the *ubosot* (ordination hall), a stone slab, engraved in 1581, bears the earliest-known reference to the city's founding. The main *wí·hǎhn* also contains the oldest-known Buddha image created by the Lanna kingdom, cast in 1465.

Chiang Mai City Arts & Cultural Centre
MUSEUM

(หอศิลปวัฒนธรรมเชียงใหม่; www.cmocity.com; Th Phra Pokklao; adult/child 90/40B; ⊗8.30am-5pm Tue-Sun) Set in the former Provincial Hall, a handsome Thai-colonial-style building from 1927, this museum provides an excellent primer on Chiang Mai history. Dioramas,

THAILAND CHIANG MAI

Chiang Mai

photos, artefacts and audiovisual displays walk visitors through the key battles and victories in Chiang Mai's story, from the first settlements to the arrival of the railroad. Upstairs is a charming re-creation of a wooden Lanna village.

Chiang Mai Historical Centre MUSEUM
(หอประวัติศาสตร์เมืองเชียงใหม่; Th Ratwithi; adult/child 90/40B; ⊗8.30am-5pm Tue-Sun)

Housed in an airy Lanna-style building behind the Chiang Mai City Arts & Cultural Centre, this appealing museum covers the history of Chiang Mai Province, with displays on the founding of the capital, the Burmese occupation and the modern era of trade and unification with Bangkok. Downstairs is an archaeological dig of an ancient temple wall.

Wat Suan Dok
BUDDHIST TEMPLE

(วัดสวนดอก; Th Suthep; donations appreciated; ☉daylight hours) Built on a former flower garden in 1373, this important monastery enshrines one half of a sacred Buddha relic; the other half was transported by white elephant to Wat Phra That Doi Suthep (p699). The main *chedi* is a gilded, bell-shaped structure that rises above a sea of white memorial *chedi* honouring the Thai royal family, with the ridge of Doi Suthep soaring behind.

Wat Inthakhin Saduemuang
BUDDHIST TEMPLE

(วัดอินทขิลสะดือเมือง; donations appreciated; ☉6am-6pm) Tucked to the side of the Chiang Mai City Arts & Cultural Centre, this was the original location of the Làk Meuang (city pillar). Marooned in the middle of Th Inthwarorot, its gilded teak *wí·hăhn* is one of the most perfectly proportioned monuments in the city. The free onsite museum tells the *wát's* history.

🏃 Activities

Outdoor escapes are easy in Chiang Mai, with tropical rainforests, looming mountains, rushing rivers, hill-tribe villages, and sanctuaries and camps full of elephants all within an hour's drive of the city. Dozens of operators offer adventure tours, exploring the forested mountains and waterways on foot, or by bike, raft, all-terrain-vehicle and even zipline.

★ Chiang Mai on Three Wheels
TOURS

(www.chiangmaionthreewheels.com; Don Kaeo, Saraphi; 4hr tours for 2 people 1700B) 🖉 There are few better ways to tour Chiang Mai than by slow, quiet, culturally immersive săhm·lór (three-wheel pedicabs). This organisation helps promote this dying industry by connecting tourists with the often non-English-speaking drivers and pairs you with an English-speaking guide. Profits go entirely to the drivers and to support their industry.

Zira Spa
SPA

(☎053 222288; www.ziraspa.com; 8/1 Th Rajvithi; treatments 700-6000B; ☉10am-10pm) Located on one of the main streets in the centre of Chiang Mai, Zira Spa offers some of the best spa treatments and massages in the region, all for a decent price. You need to book in advance for the larger spa packages, but same-day service is available for one or two of the 30-, 60- or 90-minute treatments.

Chiang Mai Mountain Biking & Kayaking
MOUNTAIN BIKING

(☎053 814207; www.mountainbikingchiangmai.com; 1 Th Samlan; tours 1250-2700B; ☉8am-8pm) This specialist operator offers recommended kayaking trips on Mae Ping and full-day guided mountain-biking tours (using imported bikes) to Doi Suthep-Pui National Park and further afield, including the popular ascent to Wat Phra That Doi Suthep.

Green Trails
ADVENTURE

(☎053 141356; www.green-trails.com; treks for 2 people from 2900B) A very reliable, eco and socially responsible outfit that can arrange trekking trips to Doi Inthanon, overnight trips to Ban Mae Kampong and much more.

Peak Adventure Tour
ADVENTURE

(☎053 800567; www.thepeakadventure.com; 302/4 Th Chiang Mai-Lamphun; tours 1600-2800B) The Peak offers a variety of adventure trips, including quad biking, abseiling, trekking, white-water rafting and rock climbing, plus photography tours of Chiang Mai by săhm·lór.

Thai Elephant Care Center
ELEPHANT INTERACTION

(☎053 206247; www.thaielephantcarecenter.com; Mae Sa; half-/full day 2000/3000B) This small centre at Mae Sa, about 25km north-west of Chiang Mai, was set up to provide care for elderly elephants retired from logging camps and elephant shows. There are no rides and visitors feed the old-timers with ground grass, herb balls and bananas. You can also help out at bath-time, and visit the cemetery for elephants who have died of old age.

MONK CHAT

If you're curious about Buddhism, many Chiang Mai temples offer popular Monk Chat sessions, where novice monks get to practise their English and tourists get to find out about the inner workings of monastery life.

Wat Suan Dok has a dedicated room for Monk Chats from 5pm to 7pm Monday, Wednesday and Friday. **Wat Srisuphan** (วัดศรีสุพรรณ; Soi 2, Th Wualai; donations appreciated; ☉6am-6pm) holds its sessions from 5.30pm to 7pm just before a meditation course. Wat Chedi Luang (p697) has a table under a shady tree where monks chat from 9am to 6pm daily.

🍴 Courses

Cooking

Chiang Mai is the most popular place in the country to learn Thai cooking. You'll learn about the ingredients as well as the techniques, with trips to local markets to buy herbs and spices. The best courses take place in bespoke communal kitchens at country farmhouses around Chiang Mai.

★ Small House Chiang Mai
Thai Cooking School   COOKING
(☑ 095 674 4550; www.chiangmaithaicooking. com; 19/14 Th Thipanet; 1-day/evening-only classes 1500/1300B) Arm teaches Thai cookery at the eponymous dwelling outside Chiang Mai. Courses include transport, a visit to a local market, and span northern Thai dishes. The small two- to four-person classes are intimate and the experience feels more local than touristy. She also offers day-long private classes from 3500B.

Thai Farm Cooking School   COOKING
(☑ 081 288 5989; www.thaifarmcooking.com; 38 Soi 9, Th Moon Muang; courses 1500B) Cooking classes at a beautiful and serene organic farm, 17km outside of Chiang Mai; includes return transport from Chiang Mai.

Language

Chiang Mai is a popular place to learn the Thai language.

American University Alumni   LANGUAGE
(AUA; ☑ 053 214120; www.learnthaiinchiangmai. com; 73 Th Ratchadamnoen; group courses 5300B) Conducts 60-hour Thai courses, with two hours of classes daily, Monday to Friday. Private instruction is also available.

Payap University   LANGUAGE
(☑ 053 851478; http://ic.payap.ac.th; Th Kaew Nawarat, Kaew Nawarat Campus; Thai courses from 3000B) A private university founded by the Church of Christ of Thailand; offers intensive Thai-language courses in 60-hour modules.

Thai Massage

Lanna Thai
Massage School   MASSAGE
(☑ 053 232547; http://en.lannathaimassageschool. net; 37 Th Chang Moi Kao; 10-day course 9500B) Close to Wat Chomphu, this reputable school is recognised by the Thai Ministry of Education and Public Health; training includes the preparation of herbal treatments using fresh ingredients.

Chetawan Thai Traditional
Massage School   MASSAGE
(☑ 053 410360; www.watpomassage.com; 7/1-2 Soi Samud Lanna, Th Pracha Uthit; general courses 9500B) Bangkok's respected Wat Pho massage school established this Chiang Mai branch outside of town near Rajabhat University.

Art of Massage   MASSAGE
(☑ 083 866 2901; www.artofmassage.webs.com; Soi 3, Th Loi Kroh; courses 1500-3000B) Khun Wanna gets rave reviews for her practical training sessions, limited to a maximum of two people, lasting two to three days.

Moo-ay Tai (Thai Boxing)

Lanna Muay
Thai Boxing Camp   MARTIAL ARTS
(☑ 053 892102; 161 Soi Chang Khian, Th Huay Kaew; day/week/month 400/2200/8000B) Offers instruction to foreigners and Thais. The gym is famous for having trained the title-winning, transgender boxer Parinya Kiatbusaba.

Chai Yai Muay Thai   MARTIAL ARTS
(☑ 082 938 1364; www.muaythaicampsthailand. com; Th Sunpiliang, Nong Hoi; day/week/month 600/1900/5500B) 🌿 This school has been training Thai and foreign fighters of all levels for 30 years. It's south-east of the city, off Rte 11 near the Chiang Mai 700 Years Park.

🎉 Festivals & Events

Flower Festival   CULTURAL
(🕑 early Feb) A riot of blooms, held over a three-day period. There are flower displays, cultural performances and beauty pageants, plus a floral parade from Saphan Nawarat to Suan Buak Hat.

★ Songkran   NEW YEAR
(🕑 mid-Apr) The traditional Thai New Year (13 to 15 April) is celebrated in Chiang Mai with infectious enthusiasm that's made it one of the best places in the country to be for the occasion. Thousands of revellers line all sides of the moat to throw water on passers-by and each other, while more restrained Songkran rituals are held at Wat Phra Singh.

Loi Krathong   RELIGIOUS
(🕑 Oct/Nov) Also known as Yi Peng, this lunar holiday is celebrated along Mae Ping with the launching of small lotus-shaped boats honouring the spirit of the river, and the release of thousands of illuminated lanterns into the night sky.

🛌 Sleeping

Make reservations far in advance if visiting during Chinese New Year, Songkran and other holiday periods.

★ Diva Guesthouse
GUESTHOUSE $

(☑ 053 273851; www.divaguesthouse.com; 84/13 Th Ratchaphakhinai; dm 120-180B; r 300-800B; ✳@☎) An energetic, vaguely bohemian spot on busy Th Ratchaphakhinai, Diva offers the full backpacker deal – dorm beds, budget boxrooms, adventure tours, net access, ambient tunes and fried rice and *sà-đé* (grilled meat with peanut sauce) in the downstairs cafe. Accommodation ranges from dorms to family rooms and comes with either fan or air-con.

60 Blue House
GUESTHOUSE $

(☑ 053 206120; www.60bluehouse.com; 32-33 Th Ratchaphakhinai; dm 250B, s/d from 350/400B; ✳☎) This appealing, clean and colourful hostel has one eight-bed dorm and clean private rooms with shared bathroom. Owner Khun Tao is a mine of local information, so guests always know where to go and what to do. A great bargain for high standards.

Banjai Garden
GUESTHOUSE $

(☑ 085 716 1635; www.banjai-garden.com; 43 Soi 3, Th Phra Pokklao; r with fan 450B, with air-con 550-1400B; ✳☎) Set in an orderly wooden house, Banjai Garden has a calm air and a pleasant garden for hanging out. Take your pick from simple but clean and great-value fan rooms or better air-con rooms. Staying here feels a little like staying in a Thai home.

Gap's House
GUESTHOUSE $

(☑ 053 278140; www.gaps-house.com; 3 Soi 4, Th Ratchadamnoen; r incl breakfast 420-1000B; ✳☎) The overgrown garden at this old backpacker favourite is a veritable jungle, providing plenty of privacy in the relaxing communal spaces. Modest budget rooms are set in old-fashioned wooden houses, and the owner runs cooking courses and dishes up a delicious vegetarian buffet from Monday to Saturday (closed June). No advance reservations.

Smile House 1
GUESTHOUSE $

(☑ 053 208661; www.smilehousechiangmai.com; 5 Soi 2, Th Ratchamankha; r with fan/air-con 350/700B; ✳☎🏊👪) There's a hint of the 1950s motel about this popular and friendly guesthouse, with a splash pool for kids and a bigger pool for grown-ups. It's very relaxed and the simply furnished rooms (with big windows) offer good value for money.

Bunk Boutique
HOSTEL $

(☑ 091 859 9656; bunkboutique@hotmail.com; 8/7 Th Ratchaphuek; dm 250-500B; r 900-1200B; ✳☎) Bunk Boutique offers superior accommodation in four-bed dorms in a large apartment block behind Th Huay Kaew. Blonde-wood bunks have curtains for privacy and everyone gets a locker. You can rent a dorm as a private room if there's space.

SoHostel
HOSTEL $

(☑ 053 206360; sohostel.chiangmai@gmail.com; 64/2 Th Loi Kroh; dm/r from 219/1500B; ✳☎) Loi Kroh is better known for girlie bars than backpacker bunks, but this huge modern hostel is a good deal, just an easy stroll from the old city and the Night Bazaar. The two-tone red-and-white dorms (with six to 12 beds) are better value than the somewhat overpriced private rooms.

Virgo Hostel
HOSTEL $

(☑ 053 234292; www.hit-thapae.com; Soi 2, Th Tha Phae; dm 350B; ✳☎) One of a cluster of spick-and-span backpacker hostels just east of the old city walls, Virgo has neat dorms with lockers, towels and a rooftop cafe. There's a women-only dorm on the 2nd floor.

Julie Guesthouse
HOSTEL $

(☑ 053 274355; www.julieguesthouse.com; 7 Soi 5, Th Phra Pokklao; dm 100-150B; r with/without bathroom from 260/150B; ☎) Julie is perennially popular, though this is as much about budget as facilities. For not much more than the price of a fruit smoothie you can get a basic dorm bed, and tiny boxrooms cost only a little more. In the evenings travellers congregate on the covered roof terrace.

SPLURGE

Effortlessly refined, the atmospheric Lanna-style **Tamarind Village** (☑ 053 418 8969; www.tamarindvillage.com; 50/1 Th Ratchadamnoen; r incl breakfast from 5200B, ste 8200-10,700B; ✳☎🏊👪) sprawls across the grounds of an old tamarind orchard in a prime location off Th Ratchadamnoen. Walkways covered by tiled pavilions lead to secluded and beautiful spaces, and tall mature trees cast gentle shade around the huge pool and gardens. Design-magazine-worthy rooms are full of gorgeous tribal fabrics and artefacts.

CHIANG MAI'S FOOD MARKETS

The best food in Chiang Mai is served on the street, and the city's night markets are fragrant, frenetic and fabulous. Every evening from about 5pm, hawker stalls set up around the old city. You'll find everything from grilled river fish and *pàt gà prow* (chicken or meat fried with chilli and holy basil) to Western-style steaks, grilled prawns, and 'Tornado potato' (a whole potato, corkscrew sliced and deep fried).

The city's day markets are also thronged by food stalls, who prepare *gàp kôw* (premade stews and curries served with rice) for busy city workers.

Here's a guide to Chiang Mai's best market eats.

Talat Pratu Chiang Mai (Th Bamrungburi; mains from 40B; ⊙4am-noon & 6pm-midnight) Ready-made packed lunches by day and night-market treats after dark.

Talat Pratu Chang Pheuak (Th Mani Nopharat; mains from 30B; ⊙5-11pm) Hugely popular, serving the city's finest *kôw kăh mŏo* (slow-cooked pork leg with rice), prepared with a flourish by the 'Cowboy Hat Lady' – you can't miss her stall.

Talat Warorot (ตลาดวโรรส; cnr Th Chang Moi & Th Praisani; ⊙6am-5pm) The grandmother of Chiang Mai markets has northern Thai food stalls tucked in all sorts of corners (mains from 30B).

Talat Thanin (Siri Wattana; mains from 30B; ⊙5am-7pm) Specialises in takeaway meals, with vendors serving fish stews, curries and stir-fries.

Talat Na Mor (Malin Plaza, Th Huay Kaew; mains from 40B; ⊙5-10pm) A cheerful night market for the college set, with low prices and lots of choice.

★ Awana House
HOTEL **$$**
(☑053 419005; www.awanahouse.com; 7 Soi 1, Th Ratchadamnoen; r with fan 500B, with air-con 700-1000B; ❄@🕾☀🚲) The pick of the guesthouses around the medieval city gate of Pratu Tha Phae, with rooms for every budget – all kept spotless – and a mini swimming pool under cover on the ground-floor terrace. Rooms get more comfortable and better decorated as you move up the price scale and there's a rooftop chill-out area with views across old Chiang Mai.

Baan Hanibah Bed & Breakfast
HOTEL **$$**
(☑053 287524; www.baanhanibah.com; 6 Soi 8, Th Moon Muang; s/d from 1000/1400B; ❄🕾) Protected by a garden of fragrant frangipani trees, Baan Hanibah is a relaxed boutique escape on a quiet lane in the heart of the old city. Behind an ornate gateway, in a converted teak house, you'll find small, quite stylish rooms with floaty drapes and Thai trim.

Riverside House
GUESTHOUSE **$$**
(☑053 241860; www.riversidehouse-chiangmai.com; 101 Th Chiang Mai-Lamphun; r incl breakfast 800-1500B; ❄@🕾☀) Plain yet spotless and rather large rooms are spread across three blocks; you pay top dollar for the central block, by the pool and away from the traffic noise, but all the rooms are good for the money. It's great value and a fine choice for families. Note that despite the name and location, there are no river views.

Baan Say-La
GUESTHOUSE **$$**
(☑053 894229; www.baansaylaguesthouse.com; 4 Soi 5, Th Nimmanhaemin; r with fan/air-con 600/900B; ❄🕾) Set in a Nimmanhaemin shophouse, this boutique guesthouse has pleasant rooms in a mixture of styles – modernist, heritage, flowery colonial – and the owners keep the place looking immaculately clean and prim. Prices are as low as you'll find this close to the action.

Hostel by Bed
HOSTEL **$$**
(☑053 217 215; www.hostelbybed.com; Th Singharat; dm 450-700B, d from 1250B; @🕾) Although you can find a room in Chiang Mai for the same price as these dorm beds, you get a lot of flashy facilities for your baht here, including a good breakfast, a chic kitchen, high standards of cleanliness and a big bed with a curtain. Common areas inspire meeting people and it's in a decent location near cheap street food.

Nat Len
Boutique Guesthouse
GUESTHOUSE **$$**
(www.natlenboutiqueguesthouse.com; 2/4 Soi Wat Chompu, Th Chang Moi; r 750-1200B; ❄🕾☀) Quirky rooms are spread over several colourful houses at this low-key guesthouse

just outside the city walls. Our favourite feature is the pale blue pool with its bubbling whirlpools, and there are lots of interesting wát in the surrounding alleyways. It's a five-minute walk to Thapae Gate.

✕ Eating

★ SP Chicken
THAI $

(9/1 Soi 1, Th Samlan; mains 50-170B; ☺11am-9pm) Chiang Mai's best chicken emerges daily from the broilers at this tiny cafe near Wat Phra Singh. The menu runs to salads and soups, but most people just pick a half (90B) or whole (170B) chicken, and dip the moist meat into the spicy, tangy dipping sauces provided.

★ Lert Ros
THAI $

(Soi 1, Th Ratchadamnoen; mains 30-160B; ☺noon-9pm) As you enter this local-style hole in the wall, you'll pass the main course: delicious whole tilapia fish, grilled on coals and served with a fiery Isan-style dipping sauce. Eaten with sticky rice, this is one of the great meals of Chiang Mai. The menu also includes fermented pork grilled in banana leaves, curries and *sôm·đam* (spicy green papaya salad).

Kiat Ocha
CHINESE, THAI $

(Th Inthawarorot; mains 50-90B; ☺6am-3pm) This humble Chinese-style canteen throngs daily with locals who can't get enough of the *kôw man gài* (Hainanese-style boiled chicken). Each plate comes with soup, chilli sauce and blood pudding and the menu also includes wok-fried chicken and pork and *sà·đé* (grilled skewers of pork or chicken). There's no English sign but you'll know it when you see it.

I-Berry
ICE CREAM $

(off Soi 17, Th Nimmanhaemin; single scoop 69B; ☺10am-10pm; ☺) Mobbed day and night, this shop creates fantastic ice cream and sorbets using local fruits and creative ingredients such as black beans and sticky rice; the *saraka* (snake fruit) sorbet is quite possibly the best ice cream in Thailand. There are also fancy cakes and desserts. I-Berry is owned by Thai comedian Udom Taepanich (nicknamed 'Nose' for his signature feature).

J Kitchen by Vieng Joom On
VEGETARIAN $

(☎053 851815; www.facebook.com/jkitchencm; Green Plus Mall 2; mains 100-250B; ☺10.30am-8.30pm, closed Sun; ☝) Perhaps Chiang Mai's best vegetarian restaurant, J Kitchen uses home-made tofu and some of the best brown rice in Thailand. Its curries are incredibly creamy, full of fresh Thai vegetables, and not overly sweet – unlike those in other vegetarian restaurants. Start with fried shiitake mushrooms and wash it all down with one of the hot or cold teas on offer.

Pun Pun
VEGETARIAN $

(www.punpunthailand.org; Wat Suan Dok, Th Suthep; mains 40-85B; ☺8am-4pm Thu-Tue; ☝) 🌿 Tucked away at the back of Wat Suan Dok, this student cafe is a great place to sample Thai vegetarian food prepared using little-known herbs and vegetables and lots of healthy whole grains grown on its concept farm, which doubles as an education centre for sustainable living.

Huen Phen
THAI $

(☎053 277103; 112 Th Ratchamankha; mains lunch 30-100B, dinner 80-200B; ☺9am-4pm & 5-10pm) Huen Phen restaurant serves a comprehensive, and usually quite delicious, selection of northern Thai food in an antique bric-a-brac, plant-filled house that feels more like a garden. It's phenomenally popular, so come early or face a long wait for a table. We loved the 'Pork Curry in Burmese Style'.

LOCAL KNOWLEDGE

KÔW SOY SAMPLER

Chiang Mai's unofficial city dish is *kôw soy* (khao soi), wheat-and-egg noodles in a curry broth, served with pickled vegetables and sliced shallots, and garnished with deep-fried crispy noodles.

These are the best places to sample *kôw soy*.

Kao Soi Fueng Fah (Soi 1, Th Charoen Phrathet; mains 40-60B; ☺7am-9pm) We love the flavourful bowls here.

Khao Soi Islam (Chang Moi Soi 1; mains from 50B; ☺8am-5pm) Serves a simple and salty broth that the locals crave.

Khao Soi Lam Duan Fah Ham (352/22 Th Charoenrat/Th Faham; mains from 40B; ☺9am-4pm) A deliciously rich *kôw soy*.

Khao Soi Samoe Jai (391 Th Charoenrat/Th Faham; mains 50-70B; ☺8am-5pm) Tasty, superior and with all the trimmings.

STREET MARKETS

Chiang's Mai's most entertaining shopping experiences are all outdoors. Make sure to check out the following markets.

Saturday Walking Street (ถนนเดินวันเสาร์; Th Wualai; ⊘ 4pm-midnight Sat) The Saturday Walking Street takes over Th Wualai, running south-west from Pratu Chiang Mai at the southern entrance to the old city. There is barely space to move as locals and tourists from across the world haggle vigorously for carved soaps, novelty dog collars, woodcarvings, Buddha paintings, hill-tribe trinkets, Thai musical instruments, T-shirts, paper lanterns and umbrellas, silver jewellery and herbal remedies.

Sunday Walking Street (ถนนเดินวันอาทิตย์; Th Ratchadamnoen; ⊘ 4pm-midnight Sun) On Sunday afternoon Th Ratchadamnoen is taken over by the boisterous Sunday Walking Street. It feels even more animated than Th Wualai's Saturday Walking Street because of the energetic food markets that open up in wát courtyards along the route, in addition to the usual selection of handmade items and northern Thai–themed souvenirs.

Chiang Mai Night Bazaar (Th Chang Khlan; ⊘ 7pm-midnight) Chiang Mai Night Bazaar is one of the city's main night-time attractions, especially for families, and is the legacy of the original Yunnanese trading caravans that stopped here along the ancient route between Simao (China) and Mawlamyaing (on Myanmar's Gulf of Martaban). Today the night bazaar sells the usual tourist souvenirs, similar to what you'll find at Bangkok's street markets.

Neau-Toon Rod Yam THAI $
(Soi 11, Th Nimmanhaemin; mains 60-100B; ⊘ 9am-8pm Mon-Fri, to 6pm Sat & Sun) Build your own soup at this yummy corner-shop cheaply. Choose between rice or several types of noodles, spice level, then meat, ranging from basic chicken to beef entrails. It also makes a decent *kôw soy* and hotpot.

Party Buffet KOREAN $
(Th Mani Nopharat; buffet 169B; ⊘ 4pm-6am) Don't be put off by the name – this all-night Korean BBQ and hotpot buffet is where Chiang Mai's night owls come to play. It's all-you-can-eat, so pay once and feast at traditional mealtime or until the wee hours on boiled and barbecued meat, fish and veg.

★ **Italics** ITALIAN $$
(☑ 05 321 6219; www.theakyra.com; 22/2 Nimmana Haeminda Soi 9; pizzas 260-550B; ⊘ 7am-11pm) Yes the modern black decor interspersed with gigantic, golden candelabra-style chandeliers is interesting, the pastas and mains are innovative and the cocktails are addictive, but it's the perfect pizzas here that makes this a top choice in Chiang Mai. We are still dreaming of the 'Akyra Pizza' with mozzarella, mushrooms, salami, bacon, blue cheese and truffle paste.

Kebab House INDIAN $$
(☑ 097 356 8006; 40/12 Th Ratvithi; mains 60-250B; ⊘ 1pm-midnight) This budget-friendly Indian restaurant has a wide range of curries and vegetarian options. Its chicken kebabs are very popular, and the *palak paneer* is equally good. It's in a clutch of bars and other Indian restaurants, so good for a night out.

Tong Tem Toh THAI $$
(Soi 13, Th Nimmanhaemin; mains 50-170B; ⊘ 11am-9pm) Set in an unpretentious garden of a teak house, this trendy cafe serves deliciously authentic northern Thai cuisine. The menu roams beyond the usual to specialities such as *nám prík ong* (chilli paste with vegetables for dipping), *gaang hang lay* (Burmese-style pork curry with peanut and tamarind) plus a few more adventurous dishes using snake heads and ant eggs.

Rustic & Blue INTERNATIONAL $$
(☑ 053 216420; www.rusticandblue.com; Soi 7, Th Nimmanhaemin; mains 180-360B; ⊘ 8.30am-9.30pm; ☎) With an interior looking like a Pinterest spread of farmhouse-chic and an outdoor patio complete with hammocks, Rustic & Blue's photogenic, farm-to-table dishes are in perfect harmony with the decor. Think eggs served with an array of greens, fresh breads like baguettes or croissants and granola bowls topped with seasonal local fruit.

Riverside Bar & Restaurant INTERNATIONAL, THAI $$
(Th Charoenrat; mains 100-370B; ⊘ 10am-1am) Almost everyone ends up at Riverside at some point in their Chiang Mai stay. Set in an old teak house, it feels like a boondocks reima-

gining of a Hard Rock Cafe, and bands play nightly until late. Stake out a claim on the riverside terrace or the upstairs balcony to catch the Mae Ping breezes.

🍷 Drinking & Nightlife

★ Good View
BAR

(www.goodview.co.th; 13 Th Charoenrat/Th Faham; ☺10am-2am) Good View attracts plenty of locals, with a big menu of Thai standards and sushi platters (mains 100B to 250B) and a nightly program of bands with rotating line-ups (meaning the drummer starts playing guitar and the bass player swaps to piano).

Zoe in Yellow
BAR

(40/12 Th Ratwithi; ☺11am-2am) Part of a complex of open-air bars at the corner of Th Ratchaphakhinai and Th Ratwithi, Zoe is where backpackers come to sink pitchers of cold Chang, sip cocktails from buckets, rock out to cheesy dance-floor fillers, canoodle and swap travel stories until the wee hours. There's also a few Indian food places between the bar joints.

Mixology
BAR

(61/6 Th Arak; ☺3pm-midnight Tue-Fri, 11am-midnight Sat & Sun) A tiny, eclectic bar with a huge selection of microbrews, a thick menu of fruity house drinks, burgers and northern Thai eats, and a lounging dog. Even if you drink too many chilli-infused 'prick me ups', you probably won't regret it the next day.

Warmup Cafe
CLUB

(www.facebook.com/warmupcafe1999; 40 Th Nimmanhaemin; ☺6pm-2am) A Nimmanhaemin survivor, cavernous Warmup has been rocking since 1999, attracting a young, trendy and beautiful crowd as the evening wears on. Hip-hop spins in the main room, electronic beats reverberate in the lounge, and rock bands squeal out solos in the garden.

☆ Entertainment

Inter
LIVE MUSIC

(271 Th Tha Phae; ☺4pm-1am) This small wooden house packs in a lively line-up of local talent. It has that beach-shack vibe beloved by travellers everywhere and a popular pool table – though we recommend against challenging the multiple-trophy-winning lady who owns the place!

Nabé
LIVE MUSIC

(Th Wichayanon; ☺6pm-1am) A happening spot for Chiang Mai 20-somethings, with cold beers, hot snacks and rocking live bands who can actually play their instruments, singing Thai songs for a Thai audience.

🔒 Shopping

Chiang Mai is Thailand's handicraft centre.

★ Studio Naenna
CLOTHING, HOMEWARES

(www.studio-naenna.com; 138/8 Soi Chang Khian; ☺9am-5pm Mon-Fri, plus Sat Oct-Mar only) The colours of the mountains have been woven into the naturally dyed silks and cottons here, part of a project to preserve traditional weaving and embroidery. You can see the whole production process at this workshop.

Hill-Tribe Products Promotion Centre
CLOTHING, HANDICRAFTS

(21/17 Th Suthep; ☺9am-5pm) Hill-tribe textiles, bags, boxes, lacquerware and other crafts are sold at this large store near Wat Suan Dok; profits go to hill-tribe welfare programs.

Backstreet Books
BOOKS

(2/8 Th Chang Moi Kao; ☺8am-8pm) Backstreet, a rambling shop along 'book alley' (Th Chang Moi Kao), has a good selection of guidebooks and stacks of crime and thriller novels.

COFFEE CRAZY CHIANG MAI

Cafes are everywhere in central Chiang Mai, and best of all most places are local, selling coffee sourced from the hill tribes and forest communities around the city.

Here are our picks for the most snob-worthy coffees in Chiang Mai.

Akha Ama Cafe (www.akhaama.com; 175/1 Th Ratchadamnoen; ☺8am-6pm; 📶) A cute local coffee shop founded by an enterprising Akha who was the first in his village to graduate from college.

Ristr8to (www.ristr8to.com; Th Nimmanhaemin; espresso drinks 88B; ☺8.30am-7pm, closed Tue) Drinks come with a caffeine rating and are often topped with award-winning latte art.

Khagee (Chiang Mai-Lamphun Soi 1; espresso drinks 75B; ☺10am-5pm Wed-Sun; 📶) A Japanese-style place that's insanely popular. Pair basic but near-perfect brews with their fresh breads and pastries.

Maya Lifestyle
Shopping Center SHOPPING CENTRE
(Th Huay Kaew; ☉11am-10pm Mon-Fri, 10am-10pm Sat & Sun) Chiang Mai's flashiest shopping centre hides behind a geometric facade, with all the big international brands, a whole floor of electronics, a good supermarket, a multi-screen cinema, and excellent eating options on the 4th floor.

ℹ Information

EMERGENCY
Police Station (☑053 276040, 24hr emergency 191; 169 Th Ratchadamnoen)
Tourist Police (☑053 247318, 24hr emergency 1155; 608 Rimping Plaza, Th Charoenraj; ☉6am-midnight) Volunteer staff speak a variety of languages.

MEDICAL SERVICES
Chiang Mai Ram Hospital (☑053 920300; www.chiangmairam.com; 8 Th Bunreuangrit) The most modern hospital in town.
McCormick Hospital (☑053 921777; www.mccormick.in.th; 133 Th Kaew Nawarat) Former missionary hospital; good for minor treatments.

TOURIST INFORMATION
Tourism Authority of Thailand (TAT; ☑053 248604; www.tourismthailand.org; Th Chiang Mai-Lamphun; ☉8.30am-4.30pm) English-speaking staff provide maps and advice on travel across Thailand.

ℹ Getting There & Away

AIR
Domestic and international flights arrive and depart from **Chiang Mai International Airport** (☑05 327 0222; www.chiangmaiairportthai.com), 3km south-west of the old city.

The bulk of the domestic routes are handled by **Air Asia** (☑053 234645, nationwide 02 515 9999; www.airasia.com; 416 Th Tha Phae; ☉10am-8.30pm), **Bangkok Airways** (☑053 289338, nationwide 1771; www.bangkokair.com; Room A & B, Kantary Terrace, 44/1 Soi 12, Th Nimmanhaemin; ☉8.30am-noon & 1-6pm Mon-Sat), **Kan Air** (☑053 283311, nationwide 02 551 6111; www.kanairlines.com; 2nd fl, Chiang Mai International Airport; ☉8am-5.30pm), **Nok Air** (☑053 922183, nationwide 02 900 9955; www.nokair.com; ground fl, Central Airport Plaza; ☉8am-5pm), **Thai Smile** (☑nationwide 02 118 8888; www.thaismileair.com; 35-41 Th Ratchadamnoen; ☉9am-9pm) and **Thai Airways International** (THAI; ☑023 561111, 053

ℹ GETTING TO LAOS: NORTHERN BORDERS

Chiang Khong to Huay Xai
The Chiang Khong/Huay Xai border is the most popular crossing for travellers moving from Chiang Mai to Luang Prabang in Laos.

Getting to the border The jumping-off point is the Friendship Bridge, around 10km south of Chiang Khong, via a 120B chartered săhm·lór ride or a 60B white passenger-truck ride from downtown.

At the border After the Thai immigration office, you'll board a shuttle bus (from 20B, 8am to 6pm) for Lao immigration, where visas are available on arrival.

Moving on From the Lao side of the bridge, it's a 100B/25,000K per person săhm·lór ride to the boat pier or Huay Xai's bus terminal, where buses leave for all the major Laos destinations and Kunming and Mengla in China (you must have a Chinese visa already).

There is also a daily **slowboat** (1350B or 220,000K, two days, around 10.30am) to Luang Prabang. Tickets can be booked through Chiang Khong–based agents such as **Easy Trip** (☑089 635 5999, 053 655174; www.discoverylaos.com; 183 Th Sai Klang; ☉9am-7pm).

For information on making this crossing in reverse see p358.

Ban Huay Kon to Muang Ngeun
140km north of Nan, the Ban Huay Kon/Muang Ngeun border is well off the beaten track.

Getting to the border To Ban Huay Kon, five daily minivans start in Phrae between 5am and noon (95B, three hours) and stop in Nan en route to Ban Huay Kon.

At the border After passing the Thai immigration booth, foreigners can purchase a 30-day visa for Laos for US$30 to US$42, depending on nationality. Surcharges may apply.

Moving on Proceed 2.5km to the Lao village of Muang Ngeun, from where sŏrng·tăa·ou leave for Hongsa (40,000K, 1½ hours) between 2pm and 4pm.

BUSES FROM CHIANG MAI'S ARCADE TERMINAL

DESTINATION	FARE (B)	DURATION (HR)	FREQUENCY
Bangkok	488-759	9-10	frequent
Chiang Khong	202-451	6½	1 daily
Chiang Rai	166-288	3-4	frequent
Chiang Saen	165-220	3½-4	2 daily
Khon Kaen	535	12	5 daily
Khorat (Nakhon Ratchasima)	540-662	12	11 daily
Lampang	66-143	2	hourly
Lampang (minivan)	75	1	hourly
Lamphun	30	1	hourly
Luang Prabang (Laos)	1200	20	9am (Mon, Wed, Fri-Sun)
Mae Hong Son	192-346	8	3 daily
Mae Hong Son (minivan)	250	5	hourly
Mae Sai	205-234	5	7 daily
Mae Sariang	104-187	4-5	6 daily
Mae Sot	290	6	3 daily
Nan	197-254	6	6 daily
Nong Khai	820	12	2 daily
Pai	80	4	hourly
Pai (minivan)	150	3	hourly
Phayao	142-249	3	hourly
Phrae	133-266	4	4 daily
Phuket	1646	22	1 daily
Phrae	133-266	4	4 daily
Sukhothai	207	5-6	hourly
Ubon Ratchathani	872	12	2 daily
Udon Thani	545-767	12	3 daily

THAILAND CHIANG MAI

211044; www.thaiair.com; 240 Th Phra Pokklao; ⊙8.30am-4.30pm Mon-Fri). Tickets to Bangkok start at around 1200B. Heading south, expect to pay from 2400B to Phuket, 1650B to Surat Thani.

There are also many international flights, including to Kuala Lumpur (Malaysia), Yangon (Myanmar) and many destinations around China. **Lao Airlines** (🗹 053 223401; www.laoairlines. com; ground fl, Nakornping Condominium, 2/107 Th Huay Kaew; ⊙8.30am-5pm Mon-Fri, to noon Sat) has direct flights to Luang Prabang and Vientiane.

BUS

Chiang Mai has two bus stations, and *sŏrng·tăa·ou* (minibuses) run from fixed stops to towns close to Chiang Mai. About 3km north-east of the city centre, near the junction of Th Kaew Nawarat and Rte 11, the **Arcade Bus Terminal** (Th Kaew Nawarat) handles all services, except for buses to Northern Chiang Mai Province. A chartered *rót daang* ('red truck' shared taxi) from the centre to the bus stand will cost about 60B; a túk-

túk will cost 80B to 100B. Just north of the old city on Th Chotana, the **Chang Pheuak Bus Terminal** (Th Chang Pheuak) is the main departure point for journeys to the north of Chiang Mai Province.

TRAIN

Chiang Mai Train Station (🗹 053 245363, nationwide 1690; Th Charoen Muang) is about 2.5km east of the old city on Th Charoen Muang. Trains run five times daily on the main line between Bangkok and Chiang Mai. Most comfortable are the overnight special express services leaving Chiang Mai at 5pm and 6pm, arriving in Bangkok at 6.15am and 6.50am.

At the time of research, fares to Bangkok were as follows.

2nd-class sleeper berth (fan cooled) 601B to 671B

2nd-class sleeper berth (air-con) 1071B to 1131B

1st-class sleeper berth (air-con) 1453B to 1903B

ⓘ Getting Around

Rót daang (literally 'red trucks') operate as shared taxis. There are no fixed routes so the easiest thing to do is to ask if the driver will take you where you want to go. Journeys start from 20B for a short trip of a few blocks and 40B for a longer trip.

Túk-túk rides start at 60B for short trips and creep up to 100B at night, although you'll have to bargain hard for these rates.

Bicycles (50B to 400B per day) and motorcycles (150B to 350B per day) can be rented from many agencies and guesthouses.

Around Chiang Mai

To the immediate south of Chiang Mai is the Ping Valley, a fertile agricultural plain that runs out to densely forested hills. Southwest is Thailand's highest peak, Doi Inthanon (2565m).

★ Doi Inthanon
National Park   NATIONAL PARK

(☑ 053 286730; adult/child 400/200B, car/motorcycle 30/20B; ⊙ 4am-6pm) Thailand's highest peak is Doi Inthanon (often abbreviated to Doi In), which is 2565m above sea level, an impressive altitude for the kingdom, but a tad diminutive compared to its cousins in the Himalaya. The 1000-sq-km national park surrounding the peak has hiking trails, waterfalls and two monumental stupas erected in honour of the king and queen.

It is a popular day trip from Chiang Mai for tourists and locals, especially during the New Year's holiday when there's the rarely seen phenomenon of frost.

Mae Sa Valley Loop

You don't have to roam far from the city limits to get into the jungle. Branching west off Rte 107 at Mae Rim, Rte 1096 winds past a

---

CHIANG RAI TREKKING

Nearly every guesthouse and hotel in Chiang Rai offers hiking excursions in hill-tribe country, some of which have grassroots, sustainable or nonprofit emphases. In general, trek pricing depends on the type of activities and the number of days and participants. Rates per person, for two people for a two-night trek, range from 2300B to 6000B. Generally, everything from accommodation to transport and food is included in this price.

---

string of tacky day-trip attractions – crocodile and monkey shows, orchid farms, shooting ranges, all-terrain-vehicle-hire companies, even a cobra farm – before climbing steadily into forested **Mae Sa Valley** (หุบเขาแม่สา). The road continues in a winding loop past charging waterfalls and a series of Royal Project farms and then morphs into Rte 1269 at the turn-off to the sleepy country village of **Samoeng** (สะเมิง). It makes for a thoroughly enjoyable 100km round-trip from Chiang Mai by rented motorcycle or chartered *rót daang*.

Chiang Rai   เชียงราย

☑ 053 / POPULATION 70,000

Chiang Rai Province has such a diversity of attractions that its capital is often overlooked. But small and delightful Chiang Rai is worth getting to know, with its relaxed atmosphere, good-value accommodation and great local food. It's also the logical base from which to plan excursions to the more remote corners of the province or abroad.

⊙ Sights

★ Hilltribe Museum &
Education Center   MUSEUM

(พิพิธภัณฑ์และศูนย์การศึกษาชาวเขา; www.pdacr.org; 3rd fl, 620/25 Th Thanalai; 50B; ⊙ 8.30am-6pm Mon-Fri, 10am-6pm Sat & Sun) This museum and cultural centre is a good place to visit before undertaking any hilltribe village trek. Run by the nonprofit Population & Community Development Association (PDA), the venue has displays that are underwhelming in their visual presentation but contain a wealth of information on Thailand's various tribes and the issues that surround them.

★ Mae Fah Luang Art &
Culture Park   MUSEUM

(ไร่แม่ฟ้าหลวง; www.maefahluang.org/rmfl; 313 Mu 7, Ban Pa Ngiw; adult/child 200B/free; ⊙ 8.30am-4.30pm Tue-Sun) In addition to a museum that houses one of Thailand's biggest collections of Lanna artefacts, this vast, meticulously landscaped compound includes antique and contemporary art, Buddhist temples and other structures. It's located about 4km west of the centre of Chiang Rai; a túk-túk or taxi here will run to around 100B.

Wat Phra Kaew   BUDDHIST TEMPLE
(วัดพระแก้ว; Th Trairat; donations appreciated; ⊙ temple 7am-7pm, museum 9am-5pm) Originally called Wat Pa Yia (Bamboo Forest

Chiang Rai

THAILAND CHIANG RAI

Chiang Rai

Monastery) in the local dialect, this is the city's most revered Buddhist temple. The main prayer hall is a medium-sized, well-preserved wooden structure. The octagonal *chedi* (stupa) behind it dates from the late 14th century and is in typical Lanna style. The adjacent two-storey wooden building is a museum housing various Lanna artifacts.

WORTH A TRIP

WAT RONG KHUN & BAAN DUM

Just outside Chiang Rai are Wat Rong Khun and Baandam, two of the province's most bizarre and worthwhile destinations.

Wat Rong Khun (วัดร่องขุ่น; White Temple; off Rte 1/AH2; ⊙8am-5pm Mon-Fri, to 5.30pm Sat & Sun) FREE is the brainchild of noted Thai painter-turned-architect Chalermchai Kositpipat. Seen from a distance, the temple appears to be made of glittering porcelain; a closer look reveals that the appearance is due to a combination of whitewash and clear-mirrored chips. Inside are contemporary scenes representing samsara (the realm of rebirth and delusion) featuring Keanu Reeves, Elvis, Hello Kitty and Superman, among others. The temple is about 13km south of Chiang Rai. To get here, hop on one of the regular buses that run from Chiang Rai to Wiang Pa Pao (20B, hourly from 6.15am to 6.10pm).

Baandam (บ้านดำ, Black House; off Rte 1/AH2; adult/child 80B/free; ⊙9am-5pm) is a rather sinister counterpart to Wat Rong Khun, uniting several structures, most of which are stained black and ominously decked out with animal pelts and bones. The centrepiece is a black, cavernous, temple-like building holding a long wooden dining table and chairs made from deer antlers – a virtual Satan's dining room.

The site is located 13km north of Chiang Rai in Nang Lae; any Mae Sai–bound bus will drop you off here for around 20B.

Oub Kham Museum MUSEUM

(พิพิธภัณฑ์อูบคำ; www.oubkhammuseum.com; Th Nakhai; adult/child incl tour 300/200B; ⊙8am-5pm) This slightly zany private museum houses an impressive collection of paraphernalia from virtually every corner of the former Lanna kingdom. The items, some of which truly are one of a kind, range from a monkey-bone food taster used by Lanna royalty to an impressive carved throne from Chiang Tung, Myanmar. It's located 2km west of the town centre and can be a bit tricky to find; túk-túk will take you here for about 60B.

Tham Tu Pu &
Buddha Cave BUDDHIST TEMPLE

(ถ้ำตู้ปู่/ถ้ำพระ; Th Ka Salong; ⊙daylight hours) FREE Cross the Mae Fah Luang Bridge (located just north-west of the city centre) to the northern side of Mae Nam Kok and you'll come to a turn-off for both Tham Tu Pu and the Buddha Cave. Neither attraction is particularly amazing on its own, but the surrounding country is beautiful and would make an ideal destination for a lazy bike or motorcycle ride.

🏃 Activities

⭐**Rai Pian Karuna** TREKKING

(☎062 246 1897; www.facebook.com/raipiankaruna) This community-based social enterprise conducts one-day and multi-day treks and homestays at Akha, Lahu and Lua villages in Mae Chan, north of Chiang Rai. Other activities, from week-long volunteering stints to cooking courses, are also on offer.

PDA Tours & Travel TREKKING

(☎053 740088; Hilltribe Museum & Education Center, 3rd fl, 620/25 Th Thanalai; ⊙8.30am-6pm Mon-Fri, 10am-6pm Sat & Sun) One- to three-day treks are available through this NGO. Profits go back into community projects that include HIV/AIDS education, mobile health clinics, education scholarships and the establishment of village-owned banks.

Mirror Foundation TREKKING

(☎053 737616; www.thailandecotour.org) Although its rates are higher, trekking with this nonprofit NGO helps support the training of its local guides. Treks range from one to three days and traverse the Akha, Karen and Lahu villages of Mae Yao District, north of Chiang Rai.

🛏 Sleeping

Baan Warabordee HOTEL $

(☎053 754488; baanwarabordee@hotmail.com; 59/1 Th Sanpanard; r 500-600B; ✳🗖) A handsome, good-value hotel has been made from this three-storey Thai villa. Rooms are decked out in dark woods and light fabrics, and are equipped with air-con, fridge and hot water.

FUN-D Hostel HOSTEL $

(☎053 712123; www.facebook.com/FunDHostelChiangRai; 753 Th Phahonyothin; incl breakfast dm 200-300B, r 600B; ✳@🗖) A lively hostel located, appropriately, above a restaurant-bar-cafe. Dorms are spacious and bright and range from six to eight beds, the more expensive of which have semi-private, en-suite bathroom facilities.

Orchids Guest House
GUESTHOUSE $

(☑ 053 718361; www.orchidsguesthouse.net; 1012/3 Th Jetyod; r 400-500B; ✳ ☎) This collection of spotless rooms in a residential compound is a good budget catch. In addition to accommodation, various services are available, including internet, laundry, taxi transfer and trekking.

Baan Bua Guest House
GUESTHOUSE $

(☑ 053 718880; www.baanbua-guesthouse.com; 879/2 Th Jetyod; r 250-550B; ✳ @ ☎) This quiet guesthouse consists of a strip of 17 bright green rooms with small porches looking out on an inviting garden. Rooms are simple, but unanimously clean and cosy, the cheapest of which are fan-cooled.

Moon & Sun Hotel
HOTEL $

(☑ 053 719279; 632 Th Singhaclai; r 399-499B, ste 699B; ✳ ☎) Bright and sparkling clean, this little hotel offers large, modern, terrific-value rooms. Some feature four-poster beds, while all come with desk, cable TV and refrigerator. Suites have a separate, spacious sitting area.

Ben Guesthouse
GUESTHOUSE $$

(☑ 053 716775; www.benguesthousechiangrai.com; 351/10 Soi 4, Th Sankhongnoi; r 500-700B, ste 1000-1500B; ✳ @ ☎ ☒) One of the best budget-to-midrange places in the north. The spotless compound has a bit of everything, from fan-cooled cheapies to immense suites, not to mention a pool. It's 1.2km from the town centre, at the end of Soi 4 on Th Sankhongnoi (the street is called Th Sathanpayabarn where it intersects with Th Phahonyothin).

🍴 Eating

★ Lung Eed
NORTHERN THAI $

(Th Watpranorn; mains 40-100B; ⏲ 11.30am-9pm Mon-Sat, 3-7pm Sun) One of Chiang Rai's most delicious dishes is available at this simple shophouse restaurant. There's an English-language menu on the wall, but don't miss the sublime *lâhp gài* (minced chicken fried with local spices and topped with crispy deep-fried chicken skin, shallots and garlic). The restaurant is about 150m east of Rte 1/AH2.

THAILAND CHIANG RAI

BUSES FROM CHIANG RAI

DESTINATION	FARE (B)	DURATION (HR)	FREQUENCY
Bangkok	423-958	11-12	frequent 7am-7pm (new bus station)
Bokeo (Laos)	240	3	4pm (new bus station)
Chiang Khong	65	2	frequent 6.30am-4.30pm (interprovincial bus station)
Chiang Mai	129-258	3-7	frequent 6am-7pm (interprovincial bus station)
Chiang Saen	37	1½	frequent 5.30am-7pm (interprovincial bus station)
Lampang	98-137	4-5	5 departures 12.45-4.30pm (new bus station)
Lampang	137	5	hourly 7am-3.15pm (interprovincial bus station)
Luang Prabang (Laos)	950	16	1pm (new bus station)
Mae Chan (for Mae Salong/Santikhiri)	25	45min	frequent 5am-7.30pm (interprovincial bus station)
Mae Sai	39	1½	frequent 6am-6.30pm (interprovincial bus station)
Mae Sot	416	12	8.15am & 8.45am (new bus station)
Nakhon Ratchasima (Khorat)	569-664	12-13	6 departures 6.30am-7.20pm (new bus station)
Phayao	43	1½-2	hourly 10am-3.30pm (new bus station)
Phayao	66	2	frequent 7.30am-3.30pm (interprovincial bus station)
Phitsanulok	260-335	6-7	hourly 6.15am-7.20pm (new bus station)
Phrae	144	4	half-hourly 6am-6pm (new bus station)
Sukhothai	231	8	hourly 7.30am-noon (new bus station)
Ubon Ratchathani	884	12	4pm (new bus station)

SLOW BOATS FROM CHIANG RAI

A boat journey along Mae Nam Kok is a much more pleasant way of travelling between Chiang Rai and Chiang Mai than taking a bus or minivan.

Passenger boats stop at Ban Ruam Mit, a village of mixed hill-tribe groups, along the way to Tha Ton, which is north of Chiang Mai. Boats depart from the **CR Pier** (☑ 053 750009; ⊙ 7am-4pm), 2km northwest of town; a túk-túk to the pier should cost about 80B.

Passenger boats depart from CR Pier at 10.30am daily; the trip to Tha Ton takes about three hours (400B), to Ruam Mit around an hour (100B). Alternatively, you can charter a boat for 800B for around three hours.

★ **Paa Suk**   NORTHERN THAI **$**
(Th Sankhongnoi; mains 10-25B; ⊙ 8.30am-3pm) Paa Suk does big, rich bowls of *kà·nŏm jeen nám ngée·o* (a broth of pork or beef and tomatoes served over fresh rice noodles). The restaurant is located between Soi 4 and Soi 5 of Th Sankhongnoi (the street is called Th Sathanpayabarn where it intersects with the southern end Th Phahonyothin). There's no roman-script sign; keep an eye out for the yellow sign.

Khao Soi Phor Jai   NORTHERN THAI **$**
(Th Jetyod; mains 40-50B; ⊙ 7am-4pm) Phor Jai serves mild but tasty bowls of the eponymous curry noodle dish, as well as a few other northern Thai staples. There's no roman-script sign, but look for the open-air shophouse with the white-and-blue interior.

Muang Thong   CHINESE, THAI **$**
(cnr Th Sanpanard & Th Phahonyothin; mains 30-100B; ⊙ 24hr) Comfort food for Thais and travellers alike: this long-standing open-air place serves the usual repertoire of satisfyingly salty and spicy Chinese-Thai dishes.

🍷 Drinking

★ **BaanChivitMai Bakery**   CAFE
(www.bcmthai.com; Th Prasopsook; ⊙ 8am-7pm Mon-Fri, to 6pm Sat & Sun; 🛜) In addition to a proper cup of joe made from local beans, you can snack on surprisingly authentic Swedish-style sweets and Western-style meals and sandwiches at this popular bakery. All the profits go to BaanChivitMai, an organisation that runs homes and education projects for vulnerable, orphaned or AIDS-affected children.

Cat Bar   BAR
(1013/1 Th Jetyod; ⊙ 5pm-1am) Long-standing Cat Bar has a pool table and, on some nights, live music from 10.30pm.

🛍 Shopping

Walking Street   MARKET
(Th Thanalai; ⊙ 4-10pm Sat) If you're in town on a Saturday evening, be sure not to miss the open-air Walking Street, an expansive street market focusing on all things Chiang Rai, from handicrafts to local dishes. The market spans Th Thanalai from the Hilltribe Museum to the morning market.

ℹ Information

Overbrook Hospital (☑ 053 711366; www.overbrook-hospital.com; Th Singhaclai) English is spoken at this modern hospital.

Tourism Authority of Thailand (TAT; ☑ Chiang Rai 053 744674, nationwide 1672; tatchrai@tat.or.th; Th Singhaclai; ⊙ 8.30am-4.30pm) English is limited, but staff here do their best to give advice and can provide a small selection of maps and brochures.

Tourist Police (☑ Chiang Rai 053 740249, nationwide 1155; Th Uttarakit; ⊙ 24hr) English is spoken and police are on standby around the clock.

ℹ Getting There & Away

Chiang Rai International Airport (Mae Fah Luang International Airport; ☑ 053 798 000; www.chiangraiairportthai.com) is approximately 8km north of the city. Taxis run into town from the airport for 200B.

There are 13 daily flights to Bangkok's Don Mueang International Airport (from 690B, one hour and 20 minutes). At the time of writing the only international flight was to Kunming (China).

Buses bound for destinations within Chiang Rai Province depart from the **interprovincial bus station** (☑ 053 715952; Th Prasopsook) in the centre of town. If you're heading beyond Chiang Rai, you'll have to go to the **new bus station** (☑ 053 773989; Rte 1/AH2), 5km south of town. Frequent *sŏrng·tăa·ou* (passenger pick-up trucks) linking the new bus station and the interprovincial station run from 6am to 5.30pm (15B, 15 minutes).

Frequent minivans head to local destinations like Chiang Saen, Mae Sai and Sop Ruak (Golden Triangle).

Golden Triangle

The three-country border between Thailand, Myanmar and Laos forms the legendary Golden Triangle, once a mountainous frontier where the opium poppy was a cash crop for the region's ethnic minorities. Thailand has successfully stamped out its cultivation through infrastructure projects, crop-substitution programs and aggressive law enforcement. But the porous border and lawless areas of the neighbouring countries have switched production to the next generation's drug of choice: methamphetamine and, to a lesser extent, heroin. Much of this illicit activity is invisible to the average visitor and the region's heyday as the leading opium producer is now marketed as a tourist attraction.

Mae Sai   แม่สาย

📞 053 / POPULATION 22,000

At first glance, Thailand's northernmost town can appear to be little more than a large open-air market. But Mae Sai serves as a convenient base for exploring the Golden Triangle and Doi Mae Salong, and its position across from Myanmar also makes it a jumping-off

point for those wishing to explore some of the more remote parts of Shan State.

Maesai Momhome   GUESTHOUSE $
(📞053 731537; haritchayahana@gmail.com; off Th Sailomjoy; r 300-500B; ❋ 🛜) A shiny new three-storey building holding nine rooms equipped with TV, refrigerator and hot-water showers; the price depends on whether you go with fan or air-con. Call in at the signed office at the three-way junction on Th Sailomjoy.

Night Market   THAI $
(Th Phahonyothin; mains 30-60B; ⊙5-11pm) An expansive night market unfolds every evening along Th Phahonyothin.

ℹ Getting There & Away

Mae Sai's **bus station** (📞053 646403; Th Phahonyothin) is 4km from the border; **shared sŏrng·tǎa·ou** (Th Phayhonyothin) ply the route between the bus station and a stop on Soi 2, Th Phahonyothin (15B, five minutes, 6am to 6pm). Alternatively, it's a 40B **motorcycle taxi** (Th Phahonyothin) ride to/from the stand at the corner of Th Phahonyothin and Soi 4.

If you're headed to Bangkok, you can avoid going all the way to the bus station by buying your tickets at **Siam First** (📞053 731504; near

THAILAND GOLDEN TRIANGLE

ℹ GETTING TO MYANMAR: MAE SAI TO TACHILEIK

Getting to the border The border and **Thai immigration office** (📞053 733261; Th Phahonyothin; ⊙6am-9pm) are a short walk from most accommodation in Mae Sai.

At the border If you haven't already obtained a Myanmar visa, it's straightforward to cross to Tachileik for the day and slightly more complicated to get a two-week border pass to visit Kyaingtong.

Day-trippers must pay a fee of 500B for a temporary ID card; your passport will be kept at the border. There is little to do in Tachileik apart from sample Burmese food and shop; everyone accepts baht.

If you'd like to visit Kyaingtong but don't have a Myanmar visa, proceed directly to the Myanmar Travels & Tours (MTT) office. There you'll need to inform the authorities exactly where you're headed. You'll need three photos and US$10 or 500B for a border pass valid for 14 days; your passport will be kept at the border ensuring that you return the way you came. It's also obligatory to hire a guide for the duration of your stay. Guides cost 1000B per day (plus a 400B 'guiding tax'), and if you haven't already arranged for a Kyaingtong-based guide to meet you at the border, you'll be assigned one by MTT and will also have to pay for your guide's food and accommodation during your stay. Recommended Kyaingtong-based guides include **Leng** (📞+95 9490 31470; sairoctor.htunleng@gmail.com) and **Freddie** (Sai Yot; 📞+95 9490 31934; yotkham@gmail.com).

Moving on Buses bound for Kyaingtong (K10,000, five hours, around 8am to 8.30am and around 11.30am to 12.30pm) depart from Tachileik's bus station, 2km and a 20B sŏrng·tǎa·ou ride (passenger pick-up truck) or a 50B motorcycle taxi ride from the border. Alternatively, you can charter a taxi from the same station from K100,000 or, if you're willing to wait until it's full, a seat in a share taxi for K12,000 or K15,000.

For information on making this crossing in reverse see p515.

WORTH A TRIP

HALL OF OPIUM

The borders of Myanmar, Thailand and Laos meet at Sop Ruak (สบรวก), the so-called centre of the Golden Triangle, at the confluence of Nam Ruak and the Mekong River. Sop Ruak is 9km east of Chiang Saen and most notable for its opium museum.

One kilometre north of Sop Ruak on a 40-hectare plot opposite the Anantara Golden Triangle Resort & Spa, the Mae Fah Luang Foundation has established the 5600-sq-metre **Hall of Opium** (หอฝิ่น; Rte 1290; adult/child 200B/free; ⌚8.30am-4pm Tue-Sun). The multimedia exhibitions include a fascinating history of opium, as well as engaging and informative displays on the effects of its abuse on individuals and society. Well balanced and worth investigating.

cnr Soi 9 & Th Phahonyothin; ⌚8am-5.30pm) – it's on the corner of Soi 9, Th Phahonyothin, next door to the motorcycle dealership.

On Th Phahonyothin, by Soi 8, is a sign saying 'bus stop'; this is where you'll find the **stop** (Th Phahonyothin) for *sŏrng·tăa·ou* bound for Sop Ruak and Chiang Saen.

Mae Salong คอยแม่สลอง

☎053 / POPULATION 20,000

Doi Mae Salong, an atmospheric village perched on the back hills of Chiang Rai, was originally settled by Chinese soldiers who fled communist rule in 1949. Generations later, the descendants and culture of this unique community persists. The Yunnanese dialect of Chinese remains the lingua franca and you'll find more Chinese than Thai food. The distinctly Chinese vibe, hilltop setting and abundance of hill tribes and tea plantations make this a destination unlike anywhere else in Thailand.

Shin Sane Guest House GUESTHOUSE $
(☎053 765026; www.maesalong-shinsane.blogspot.com; r 200-400B, bungalows 400-500B; @☎) The rooms in the original building of Mae Salong's oldest hotel are bare but spacious with shared bathrooms, while those in the new annexe and the bungalows are much more comfortable, with en-suite bathrooms and TV. Located near the morning market intersection.

★**Little Home Guesthouse** GUESTHOUSE $$
(☎053 765389; www.maesalonglittlehome.com; Rte 1130; r & bungalows 500-800B; @☎) Located near the market intersection is this recently renovated, large yellow building backed by a handful of attractive, great-value bungalows. Rooms are spacious, tidy and sunny, and the owners are extremely friendly and helpful.

Salima Restaurant CHINESE $
(Rte 1130; mains 60-220B; ⌚7am-8pm) One of the friendliest restaurants in town also happens to be the one serving the most delicious food. Salima does tasty Muslim-Chinese dishes, including a rich Yunnan-style beef curry and a deliciously tart, spicy tuna and tea-leaf salad. The noodle dishes are equally worthwhile and include a beef *kôw soy* (wheat-and-egg noodles in a curry broth).

ℹ Getting There & Away

The easiest way to get to Doi Mae Salong from Chiang Rai is to take a bus to Mae Chan, from where there are frequent green *sŏrng·tăa·ou* to Doi Mae Salong (60B, one hour, four departures daily). Alternatively, it's also possible to take a Mae Sai–bound bus to Ban Pasang, from where blue *sŏrng·tăa·ou* can be chartered for around 400B.

You can also reach Doi Mae Salong by road from Tha Ton, in Chiang Mai. Yellow *sŏrng·tăa·ou* bound for Tha Ton stop near Little Home Guesthouse four times daily (60B, one hour).

Chiang Saen เชียงแสน

☎053 / POPULATION 11,000

A sleepy river town, Chiang Saen is the site of a former Thai kingdom thought to date back to as early as the 7th century. Today huge river barges from China moor at Chiang Saen, keeping the old China–Siam trade route open.

Wat Pa Sak HISTORIC SITE
(วัดป่าสัก; off Rte 1290; historical park admission 50B; ⌚8.30am-4.30pm Wed-Sun) FREE About 200m from the Pratu Chiang Saen (the historic main gateway to the town's western flank) are the remains of Wat Pa Sak, where the ruins of seven monuments are visible in a historical park. The main mid-14th-century *chedi* combines elements of the Hariphunchai and Sukhothai styles with a possible Bagan influence, and still holds a great deal of attractive stucco relief work.

Jay Nay GUESTHOUSE $
(☎081 960 7551; Th Nhongmoon; r 400-1000B; ❄☎) Jay Nay consists of 13 nearly identi-

cal rooms in a two-storey complex. They're plain but new, clean and comfy. Look for the 'Rooms For Rent' sign. A great budget catch.

Kiaw Siang Hai
CHINESE $

(44 Th Rimkhong; mains 50-200B; ⊙8am-8pm) Serving the workers of Chinese boats that dock at Chiang Saen, this authentic Chinese restaurant prepares a huge menu of dishes in addition to the namesake dumplings. Try the spicy Sichuan-style fried tofu or one of the Chinese herbal soups.

There's no English-language sign, but the restaurant can be identified by the giant ceramic jars out front.

❶ Getting There & Away

Blue sŏrng·tăa·ou (Th Phahonyothin) bound for Sop Ruak (20B) and Mae Sai (50B) wait at a stall at the eastern end of Th Phahonyothin from 7.20am to 3pm. For Chiang Khong, you'll need to board one of the **green sŏrng·tăa·ou** (Th Rimkhong) bound for Hat Bai (50B, one hour, 9am to 2pm) at a stall on Th Rimkhong, and transfer to another sŏrng·tăa·ou from there.

Chiang Saen has a covered **bus shelter** (Th Phahonyothin) at the eastern end of Th Phahonyothin where buses pick up and drop off passengers. There are frequent buses to Chiang Rai (37B, 1½ hours, 5.30am to 5.30pm) and a daily bus to Chiang Mai (222B, five hours, 9am).

Chiang Khong
เชียงของ

❷ 053 / POPULATION 12,000

Chiang Khong has historically been an important market town for local hill tribes and for trade with northern Laos. Today, the riverside town is a sleepy travellers' gateway to Laos and onto China.

★ Namkhong Resort
HOTEL $

(❷053 791055; www.namkhongriverside.com/boutique-resort; 94/2 Th Sai Klang; r 200-800B; ❋ 🛜 ☲) Just off the main drag is this semi-secluded compound of tropical plants and handsome wooden structures. Even the fan-cooled, shared-bathroom cheapies are charming, and the swimming pool is a bonus.

Funky Box
HOSTEL $

(❷082 7651839; Soi 2, Th Sai Klang; dm 100B, s/d 250/300; ❋ 🛜) Pretty much what the label says: a box-like structure holding 16, fan-cooled dorm beds. Five shared-bathroom rooms have been added to the main building and all are united by a fun bar/restaurant.

Khao Soi Pa Orn
THAI $

(Soi 6, Th Sai Klang; mains 30-40B; ⊙8am-4pm) You may think you know kôw soy, the famous northern curry noodle soup, but the version served in Chiang Khong forgoes the curry broth and replaces it with clear soup topped with a rich, spicy minced-pork mixture. A few non-noodle dishes are also available. There's no roman-script sign, but it's located next to the giant highway-distance marker.

Bamboo Mexican House
INTERNATIONAL $$

(Th Sai Klang; mains 70-250B; ⊙7.30am-8.30pm; 🛜 🍴) Run by the manager of a now-defunct guesthouse who learned to make Mexican dishes from her American and Mexican guests. To be honest, though, we never got past the coffee and tasty home-made breads and cakes. Opens early and also does boxed lunches for the boat ride to Luang Prabang.

❶ Getting There & Away

Head to the new **bus station** (❷053 792000; Rte 1020) located 3km south of town, if you're bound for a destination in Laos. Otherwise, buses pick up and drop off passengers at various points near the market. For Chiang Saen, take a **sŏrng·tăa·ou to Hat Bai** (Th Sai Klang) from a stall on Th Sai Klang (50B, one hour, around 8am), and then transfer to another Chiang Saen–bound sŏrng·tăa·ou.

THAILAND GOLDEN TRIANGLE

BUSES FROM CHIANG KHONG

DESTINATION	PRICE (B)	DURATION (HR)	DEPARTURES
Bangkok	592-921	13	7am, 7.25am & frequent departures 3-4pm
Chiang Mai	254-395	6-7	7.15am, 9.45am & 10.30am
Chiang Rai	65-126	2½	hourly 5am-4pm
Luang Namtha (Laos)	280	4	2.30pm (Mon, Wed, Fri & Sat)
Luang Prabang (Laos)	730	13	2.30pm (Mon, Wed, Fri & Sat)
Phayao	151	3	10.30am
Udomxai (Laos)	460	10	2.30pm (Mon, Wed, Fri & Sat)

Pai ปาย

📞 053 / POPULATION 2000

Over the last decade Pai has started to resemble a Thai island getaway – without the beaches. Guesthouses, trekking agencies and restaurants are everywhere in 'downtown' and the nights buzz with live music and partying.

Despite the town's popularity, the setting in a mountain valley is near picture-perfect and there's a host of natural, lazy activities to keep visitors entertained. The town's Shan roots can still be seen in its temples, quiet backstreets and fun afternoon market.

👁 Sights & Activities

Most of Pai's sights are found outside the city centre, making motorcycle-hire a necessity. They can be hired all over town from 100B per day.

Tha Pai Hot Springs HOT SPRINGS
(บ่อน้ำร้อนท่าปาย; adult/child 300/150B; ⊙7am-6pm) Across Mae Nam Pai and 7km southeast of town via a paved road is this well-kept local park. Through it flows a scenic stream, which mixes with the hot springs in places to make pleasant bathing areas. The water is also diverted to a couple of nearby spas.

Thai Adventure Rafting RAFTING
(📞053 699111; www.thairafting.com; Th Chaisongkhram; ⊙10am-9pm) This experienced, French-run outfit leads one- and two-day rafting excursions. On the way, rafters visit a waterfall, a fossil reef and hot springs; one night is spent at the company's permanent riverside camp.

Duang Trekking TREKKING
(📞053 699101; Duang Guesthouse, Th Chaisongkhram; ⊙7am-9pm) An established local agency for trekking and day trips around town.

Pai Traditional Thai Massage HEALTH & WELLBEING
(PTTM; 📞083 577 0498; 68/3 Soi 1, Th Wiang Tai; massage per 1/1½/2hr 200/300/380B, sauna per visit 100B, 3-day massage course 3000B; ⊙9am-9pm) This long-standing and locally owned outfit offers very good northern Thai massage, and a sauna (cool season only) where you can steam yourself in medicinal herbs. Three-day massage courses begin every Monday and Friday and last three hours per day.

🛏 Sleeping

Pai Country Hut HOTEL $
(📞087 779 6541; www.paicountryhut.com; Ban Mae Hi; bungalows incl breakfast 400-650B; 🛜) The bamboo bungalows here are simple, but they're tidy and most have en-suite bathrooms and inviting hammocks. Although it's not exactly riverside, it's the most appealing of similar budget places close to the water.

Tayai's Guest House GUESTHOUSE $
(📞053 699579; off Th Raddamrong; r & bungalows 400-700B; ❄🛜) Simple but clean fan and aircon rooms and bungalows in a quiet, leafy compound just off the main drag. The friendly elderly hosts here make the decision easy.

★ Pairadise HOTEL $$
(📞053 698065; www.pairadise.com; Ban Mae Hi; bungalows 900-1300B; ❄🛜⊠) This neat resort looks over the Pai Valley from atop a ridge just outside town. The bungalows are stylish and spacious and include gold-leaf lotus mu-

---

BUSES & MINIVANS FROM PAI

Pai's tiny **bus station** (Th Chaisongkhram) is the place to catch slow, fan-cooled buses.

DESTINATION	PRICE (B)	DURATION (HR)	FREQUENCY
Chiang Mai	80	3-4	noon
Mae Hong Son	80	3-4	11am
Soppong (Pangmapha)	80	1½	11am

More frequent and efficient minivans to Chiang Mai and destinations in Mae Hong Son also depart from here.

DESTINATION	PRICE (B)	DURATION (HR)	FREQUENCY
Chiang Mai	150	3	hourly 7am-5pm
Mae Hong Son	150	2½	8.30am
Soppong (Pangmapha)	100	1	8.30am

rals, beautiful rustic bathrooms and terraces with hammocks. All surround a spring-fed pond that's suitable for swimming. You'll find it about 750m east of Mae Nam Pai; look for the sign just after the bridge.

★**Bueng Pai Farm** GUESTHOUSE **$$**
(☐089 265 4768; www.paifarm.com; Ban Mae Hi; bungalows 1000-2000B; 🛜🏊) In a rural setting about 2.5km east of Pai, the 12 spacious, fan-cooled bungalows here are strategically and attractively positioned around a vast pond stocked with freshwater fish. There's a camp-fire during the winter months, and a pool, communal kitchen and fishing equipment available year-round. Located off the road that leads to Tha Pai Hot Springs; look for the sign.

🍴 Eating & Drinking

★**Larp Khom Huay Poo** NORTHERN THAI **$**
(Ban Huay Pu; mains 50-100B; ⊙9am-8pm) Escape the wheatgrass-and-tofu crowd and get your meat on at this unabashedly carnivorous local restaurant. The house special (and the dish you must order) is *'larp moo kua'*, northern-style *lâhp* (minced pork fried with herbs and spices). Accompanied by a basket of sticky rice, a plate of bitter herbs and an ice-cold beer, it's easily the best meal in Pai.

Evening Market NORTHERN THAI **$**
(Th Raddamrong; mains 30-60B; ⊙3-7pm) For tasty take-home, local-style eats, try the market that unfolds every afternoon from about 3pm to sunset.

Maya Burger Queen AMERICAN **$**
(www.facebook.com/MayaBurgerQueen; Th Wiang Tai; mains 90-165B; ⊙1-10pm; 🖊) Burgers are a big deal in Pai, and our arduous research has concluded that Maya does the best job. Everything is home-made, from the soft, slightly sweet buns to the rich garlic mayo that accompanies the thick-cut fries.

Don't Cry BAR
(Th Raddamrong; ⊙6pm-late) Located just across the river, this is the kind of reggae bar you thought you left behind on Ko Phang-an. Soporifically chilled out, featuring both live music and a club, it's open until the last punter goes home.

ℹ️ Getting There & Away

Pai's airport is around 1.5km north of town along Rte 1095, it has daily flights to/from Chiang Mai.

WATERFALLS NEAR PAI

There are a few waterfalls around Pai that are worth visiting, particularly after the rainy season (October to early December). The closest and the most popular, **Nam Tok Mo Paeng** (น้ำตก หมอแปง), has a couple of pools that are suitable for swimming. The waterfall is about 8km from Pai along the road that also leads to Wat Nam Hoo – a long walk indeed, but suitable for a bike ride or short motorcycle trip. Roughly the same distance in the opposite direction is **Nam Tok Pembok** (น้ำตกแพมบก), just off the road to Chiang Mai. The most remote is **Nam Tok Mae Yen** (น้ำตกแม่ เย็น), a couple of hours' walk down the rough road east of Pai.

Mae Hong Son แม่ฮ่องสอน

⏱053 / POPULATION 7000

With its remote setting and surrounding mountains, Mae Hong Son fits many travellers' preconceived notion of how a northern Thai town should be. Best of all, there's hardly a túk-túk or tout to be seen. Mae Hong Son isn't uncharted territory, but the city's potential as a base for trekking ensures that your visit can be quite unlike anyone else's.

◉ Sights & Activities

With their bright colours, whitewashed stupas and glittering zinc fretwork, Mae Hong Son's Burmese- and Shan-style temples will have you scratching your head, wondering which country you're in.

PAI'S YUNNAN RESTAURANTS

Several open-air restaurants in Ban Santichon, 4km west of Pai, serve the traditional dishes of the town's Yunnanese residents. Choices include *màntŏ* (steamed buns), here served with pork leg stewed with Chinese herbs, hand-pulled noodles and several dishes using unique local crops and exotic ingredients such as black chicken. Mains cost 30B to 250B and most places are open from 7am till 8pm.

BOAT TRIPS

Long-tail boat trips on the nearby Mae Nam Pai are popular, and the same guesthouses and trekking agencies that organise hikes from Mae Hong Son can arrange river excursions. The most common trip sets off from Tha Pong Daeng, 4km south-west of Mae Hong Son. Boats travel 15km downstream to the 'long-neck' village of Huay Pu Keng (700B, one hour) or all the way to the border outpost of Ban Nam Phiang Din (800B, 1½ hours), 20km from the pier, before returning. Boats can accommodate a maximum of eight passengers.

★ **Wat Phra That Doi Kong Mu**   BUDDHIST TEMPLE

(วัดพระธาตุดอยกองมู; ☉daylight hours) Climb the hill west of town, Doi Kong Mu (1500m), to visit this temple compound, also known as Wat Plai Doi. Two Shan *chedi,* erected in 1860 and 1874, enshrine the ashes of monks from Myanmar's Shan State. Around the back of the wát you can see a tall, slender, standing Buddha and catch views west of the ridge. There's also a cafe and a small tourist market.

Nature Walks   TREKKING

(☎089 552 6899; www.naturewalksthai-myanmar. com) Treks here might cost more than elsewhere, but John, a Mae Hong Son native, is the best guide in town. Hikes range from day-long nature walks to multi-day journeys across the province. John can also arrange custom nature-based tours, such as the orchid-viewing tours he conducts from March to May. Email or call John to get in touch with him.

Friend Tour   TREKKING

(☎053 611 647, 086 1807031; 21 Th Pradit Jong Kham; ☉8am-6.30pm) With nearly 20 years' experience, this recommended outfit offers trekking and rafting excursions, as well as day tours.

Maehongson Living Museum   MUSEUM

(27 Th Singha-nat Barm Rung; ☉8.30am-4.30pm) An attractive wooden building – formerly Mae Hong Son's bus depot – has been turned into a museum on local culture, food and architecture, though the bulk of information is only in Thai. There are a few maps and brochures in English, free wi-fi and a free city tour every day at 4pm.

🛏 Sleeping

Palm House   GUESTHOUSE $

(☎053 614022; 22/1 Th Chamnansatit; r 300-700B; ❈ ☎) The original building here offers several characterless but large, clean rooms with TV, fridge, hot water and fan/air-con. A new annexe offers much of the same, but in a much more modern, spacious and attractive package. The helpful owner speaks English and can arrange transport.

Friend House   GUESTHOUSE $

(☎053 620119; 20 Th Pradit Jong Kham; r 150-500B; ☎) The super-clean though characterless rooms here run from the ultra-basic (think mattress on the floor), which share hot-water bathrooms, to larger rooms with private bathrooms. All rooms are fan-cooled.

★ **Sang Tong Huts**   HOTEL $$

(☎053 611680; www.sangtonghuts.org; Th Maka Santi; bungalows 1200-2500B; @ ☎ ⛱) This clutch of rustic, fan-cooled, TV-free bungalows in a wooded area just outside town is one of Mae Hong Son's more character-filled places to stay. Accommodation is spacious, comfortable and well designed, and the tasty baked goods and pool make up for the relative distance from the town centre.

Piya Guesthouse   HOTEL $$

(☎053 611 260; piyaguesthouse@hotmail. com; 1/1 Th Khunlumprapas; bungalows 700B; ❈ ☎ ⛱) Steps from Mae Hong Son's central lake is this compound of bungalows ringing a garden and a tiny pool. Rooms come equipped with air-con, fridge, TV and hot showers. It's all clean and inviting, if not brand new, and couldn't be more conveniently located.

🍴 Eating & Drinking

★ **little good things**   THAI, INTERNATIONAL $

(www.facebook.com/littlegoodthings; off Th Khunlumprapas; mains 30-70B; ☉9am-3pm Wed-Mon; ✔) In a town with such unique and tasty local food, we were reluctant to risk a meal at this new vegan cafe/restaurant. But 'little good things' is probably one of the better restaurants in town. A short menu lists appetising breakfast options and light, Thai-influenced meals, all of which are meat-free, wholesome, embarrassingly cheap and, most importantly, delicious.

Morning Market
THAI $

(off Th Phanich Wattana; mains 10-30B; ☺6-9am)
Mae Hong Son's morning market is a fun
place to have breakfast. Several vendors at
the northern end of the market sell unusual
fare such as *tòo·a poo ùn*, a Burmese noodle
dish supplemented with thick split pea porridge and deep-fried 'Burmese tofu'.

Chom Mai Restaurant
THAI $

(off Rte 108; mains 40-290B; ☺8.30am-3.30pm;
☎🖵) The English-language menu here
is limited, but don't miss the deliciously
rich *kôw soy* (northern-style curry noodle
soup) or *kôw mòk gài* (the Thai version of
biryani).

Chom Mai is located about 4km south of
Mae Hong Son, along the road that leads to
Tha Pong Daeng – there's no roman-script
sign, but look for the Doi Chaang coffee sign.

Night Market
THAI $

(Th Phanich Wattana; mains 20-60B; ☺4-8pm)
Popular among locals, this night market
is the place to go for takeaway Shan- and
northern Thai-style dishes.

Crossroads
BAR

(61 Th Khunlumprapas; ☺8am-1am; ☎) This
friendly bar-restaurant is a crossroads in
every sense, from its location at one of Mae
Hong Son's main intersections to its clientele that ranges from wet-behind-the-ears
backpackers to hardened locals. And there's
steak (180B to 250B).

ⓘ Information

Tourist Police (☑053 611812, nationwide 1155;
Th Singha-nat Barm Rung; ☺8.30am-4.30pm)

ⓘ Getting There & Around

For many people the time saved flying from Chiang
Mai to Mae Hong Son versus bus travel is worth
the extra baht. There are two flights daily to/from
Chiang Mai (from 990B, 35 minutes), operated
by **Bangkok Airways** (☑053 611426; www.
bangkokair.com; Mae Hong Son Airport; ☺8am-
5.30pm). A túk-túk into town costs about 80B.

Mae Sariang
แม่สะเรียง

☑053 / POPULATION 20,000

Little-visited Mae Sariang is gaining a low-
key buzz for its attractive riverside setting
and potential as a launching pad for sustainable tourism and hiking opportunities.
There are several hill-tribe settlements in
the greater area, particularly around Mae
La Noi, 30km north of the city, and the area
south of Mae Sariang is largely mountainous
jungle encompassing both Salawin and Mae
Ngao National Parks.

Salawin National Park
NATIONAL PARK

(อุทยานแห่งชาติสาละวิน; ☑053 071429; 200B)
This national park covers 722 sq km of protected land in Mae Sariang and Sop Moei
districts. The park is heavily forested with
teak and Asian redwood and is home to
what is thought to be the second-largest teak
tree in Thailand. There are numerous hiking

THAILAND MAE SARIANG

BUSES & MINIVANS FROM MAE HONG SON
Bus

Mae Hong Son's bus and minivan station is 1km south of the city; a túk-túk or motorcycle ride
to/from here costs 60B.

DESTINATION	FARE (B)	DURATION (HR)	FREQUENCY
Bangkok	675-1050	15	3pm, 4pm & 4.30pm
Chiang Mai	185-450	8-9	8am, 8pm & 9pm
Khun Yuam	43-200	2	8am, 8pm & 9pm
Mae Sariang	97-250	4	8am, 8pm & 9pm

Minivan

DESTINATION	FARE (B)	DURATION (HR)	FREQUENCY
Chiang Mai	250	6	hourly 7am-3pm
Mae Sariang	200	3½	2pm
Pai	150	2½	hourly 7am-3pm
Soppong (Pangmapha)	100	1½	hourly 7am-3pm

BUSES & MINIVANS FROM MAE SARIANG

DESTINATION	FARE (B)	DURATION (HR)	FREQUENCY
Bangkok	536-834	12	4 departures 4-8pm
Chiang Mai	100-350	4-5	12.30am, 1am & 1pm
Khun Yuam	150	3	4 departures 10.30am-4.30pm
Mae Hong Son	150	4	4am & 5pm

trails and it's also possible to travel by boat along Mae Nam Salawin to the park's outstation at Tha Ta Fang.

🍴 Sleeping & Eating

Northwest Guest House　　GUESTHOUSE $
(☑ 098 368 3867; patiat_1@hotmail.com; 81 Th Laeng Phanit; r 250-350B; ※ @ 🛜) The seven rooms in this cosy wooden house are mattress-on-the-floor simple, and only half have en-suite bathrooms, but they get natural light and are relatively spacious. Trekking and other excursions can be arranged here.

★ Riverhouse Hotel　　HOTEL $$
(☑ 053 621201; www.riverhousehotels.com; 77 Th Laeng Phanit; r incl breakfast 1000-1300B; ※ @ 🛜) The combination of teak and stylish decor – not to mention the riverside location – makes this boutique hotel the best spot in town. Rooms have air-con, huge balconies overlooking the river, and floor-to-ceiling windows. Guests here can use the pool at the **Riverhouse Resort** (☑ 053 683066; r incl breakfast 1500-2800B; ※ @ 🛜 ≋), just south on Th Laeng Phanit and run by the same folks.

★ Muu Thup　　NORTHERN THAI $
(Th Wiang Mai; mains 50-80B; ⊙ 8am-7pm) An authentic – and utterly delicious – northern Thai–style grilled-meat shack. You can't go wrong with the eponymous *mǒo đúp* (pork that's been grilled then tenderised with a mallet). Located at the junction of the road that leads to Mae Sariang; there's no roman-script sign, but look for the grill.

Intira Restaurant　　THAI $
(Th Wiang Mai; mains 50-200B; ⊙ 8am-10pm) Probably the town's best all-round restaurant, this place features a thick menu of dishes using unusual ingredients such as locally grown shiitake mushrooms and fish from Mae Nam Moei.

WESTERN THAILAND

Tall rugged mountains rise up from the central plains to meet Thailand's western border with Myanmar. Though the distances from population centres are minor, much of the region remains remote and undeveloped with an undercurrent of border intrigue. Kanchanaburi, just a few hours' bus ride from Bangkok, is a convenient and historical gateway to the region.

Kanchanaburi　　กาญจนบุรี

☑ 034 / POPULATION 94,600

Kanchanaburi has a dark history as the site of the so-called 'Death Railway', a rail route between Thailand and Myanmar built by Allied prisoners of war and conscripted Asian labourers during WWII. It was made famous by the book and movie, *The Bridge Over the River Kwai*. Kanchanaburi is also an ideal gateway to national parks in Thailand's wild west, and home to a range of lush riverside resorts.

👁 Sights

★ Death Railway Bridge　　HISTORIC SITE
(สะพานข้ามแม่น้ำแคว, Bridge Over the River Kwai; ⊙ 24hr) FREE This 300m-long bridge is heavy with the history of the Thailand–Burma Railway, the construction of which cost thousands of imprisoned labourers their lives. Its centre was destroyed by Allied bombs in 1945; only the outer curved spans are original. You're free to roam over the bridge; stand in a safety point if a train appears. Food and souvenir hawkers surround the bridge, so the site can have a jarring, funfair-like atmosphere; come early or late to avoid the scrum.

★ Thailand–Burma Railway Centre　　MUSEUM
(ศูนย์รถไฟไทย-พม่า; ☑ 034 512721; www.tbrconline.com; 73 Th Jaokannun; adult/child 140/60B;

⊘9am-5pm) This excellent museum balances statistics and historical context with personal accounts of the conditions endured by POWs and other imprisoned labourers forced to build the Thailand–Burma Railway. Kanchanaburi's role in WWII is thoroughly explained, but most of the museum traces the journey of railway workers from transport in cramped boxcars to disease-ridden labour camps in the jungle, as well as survivors' fates after the war. Allow time for the poignant video with testimony from both POWs and Japanese soldiers.

Kanchanaburi War Cemetery CEMETERY
(สุสานทหารพันธมิตรดอนรัก, Allied War Cemetery; Th Saengchuto; ⊘24hr) Immaculately maintained by the Commonwealth War Graves Commission, this, the largest of Kanchanaburi's two war cemeteries, is right in town. Of the 6982 soldiers buried here, nearly half were British; the rest came mainly from Australia and the Netherlands. As you stand at the cemetery entrance, the entire right-hand side contains British victims, the front-left area contains Australian graves, the rear left honours Dutch and unknown soldiers, and those who were cremated lie at the furthest spot to the left.

JEATH War Museum MUSEUM
(พิพิธภัณฑ์สงคราม; cnr Th Wisuttharangsi & Th Pak Phraek; 50B; ⊘8.30am-4.30pm) This small, open-air museum displays correspondence and artwork from former POWs involved in the building of the Death Railway. Their harsh living conditions are evident in the

many photos on display alongside personal effects and war relics, including an unexploded Allied bomb dropped to destroy the bridge. One of the three galleries is built from bamboo in the style of the shelters (called *attap*) the POWs lived in; another has a 10-minute video presentation.

Kanchanaburi

THAILAND KANCHANABURI

SIGHTS OUTSIDE KANCHANABURI

Tours are a convenient way to explore the wonderful countryside outside Kanchanaburi. Many tours include bamboo rafting and short jungle treks. Day trips generally cost 800B to 1100B per person, usually including admission fees and lunch.

Erawan National Park (อุทยานแห่งชาติเอราวัณ; ☑ 034 574222; adult/child 300/200B, car/motorbike 30/20B; ⏰ 8am-4.30pm) Splashing in cerulean pools under **Erawan Falls** is the highlight of this 550-sq-km park. Seven tiers of waterfall tumble through the forest, and bathing beneath these crystalline cascades is equally popular with locals and visitors. Reaching the first three tiers is easy; beyond here, walking shoes and some endurance are needed to complete the steep 2km hike (it's worth it to avoid the crowds in the first two pools). There are hourly buses from Kanchanaburi (50B, 1½ hours).

Hellfire Pass Memorial (พิพิธภัณฑ์ช่องเขาขาด; ☑ 034 919605; Hwy 323; ⏰ museum 9am-4pm, grounds 7.30am-6pm) A poignant museum and memorial trail pay tribute to those who died building the Thailand–Burma Railway in WWII. Begin at the museum and ask for the free audio guide, which provides historical detail and fascinating first-person accounts from survivors. Then descend behind the museum to a trail following the original rail bed. The infamous cutting known as Hellfire Pass was the largest along the railway's length and the most deadly for the labourers forced to construct it.

🛏 Sleeping

Blue Star Guest House　　GUESTHOUSE $
(☑ 064 984 4329, 034 512161; www.bluestar-guesthouse.com; 241 Th Mae Nam Khwae; d with fan/aircon 350/450B, bungalow 550-750B; ✳ 🛜) Nature wraps itself around Blue Star's waterside lodgings, which range from simple rooms and thatch-roofed huts to more solid, bungalow-style accommodation. With a jungly vibe and helpful staff, this family-run guesthouse is one of the best budget choices in town.

Sugar Cane 2 Guesthouse　　GUESTHOUSE $
(☑ 034 514988; Th Cambodia; d with fan/air-con 300/550B; ✳ 🛜) Though it feels way out in the countryside, Sugar Cane 2 is just a 10-minute walk from the restaurants and bars of Th Mae Nam Khwae. A spot of renovation wouldn't hurt, but both land-side rooms and the bamboo-made raft rooms are a fair price.

★ Sabai@Kan　　RESORT $$
(☑ 034 521559; www.sabaiatkan.com; 317/4 Th Mae Nam Khwae; incl breakfast d 1400-1700B, tr 2100B; ✳ 🛜 🏊) Hospitable and impeccably managed, this boutique resort has modern cream-and-mahogany rooms arranged around a swimming pool. Rooms have huge windows overlooking the pretty poolside garden, and it has the feel of a haven despite being close to Kanchanaburi's main tourist drag.

Ban Sabai Sabai　　GUESTHOUSE $$
(☑ 089 040 5268; www.bansabaisabai.com; 102/3 Mu 4, Nong Bua; d 400-800B, f from 1650B; ✳ 🛜)

Out in the countryside, 7km or so west of town along Hwy 323, this friendly place lives up to its name: 'Relaxation House'. Tile-floored rooms arranged around the florid garden are simple but very well maintained, and hosts can arrange anything from cooking classes to onward transport.

You can ask ahead for a free pick-up from town, but it's best to have your own wheels if staying here for a few days.

🍴 Eating

★ Blue Rice　　THAI $
(www.applenoikanchanaburi.com; 153/4 Mu 4, Ban Tamakahm; mains from 135B; ⏰ noon-2pm & 6-10pm; 🛜 🅿) Masterful spice blends, a creative menu and peaceful river views make this one of the most irresistible restaurants in Kanchanaburi. The signature massaman curry is perfectly balanced, and the menu is packed with reinvented Thai classics such as *yam sôm oh* (pomelo salad) and chicken-coconut soup with banana plant. The eponymous rice is stained with pea-flower petals, if you're wondering.

On's Thai-Issan　　VEGETARIAN $
(☑ 087 364 2264; www.onsthaiissan.com; Th Mae Nam Khwae; mains from 70B; ⏰ noon-10pm; 🅿) At this casual restaurant, vegetarian and vegan recipes borrow Isan flavours and reinvent classic Thai dishes from entirely plant-based ingredients, with other healthy flourishes such as brown rice. Banana flower salad, ginger tofu and 'morning glory' (pan-seared

greens) are cooked before your eyes on fryers outside and served in generous portions.

JJ Market
MARKET $

(Th Saengchuto; snacks from 15B; ☺5.30-10pm) One of Kanchanaburi's most popular night markets for food, clothes and souvenir shopping. Graze to your stomach's content on banana fritters, griddled quail eggs, barbecued cuttlefish, mango sticky rice and deep-fried everything.

ℹ Information

Main Post Office (Th Saengchuto; ☺8.30am-4.30pm Mon-Fri, 9am-noon Sat & Sun)

Thanakarn Hospital (☑034 622366; off Th Saengchuto) The best-equipped hospital to deal with foreign visitors.

Tourism Authority of Thailand (TAT; ☑034 511200; www.tourismthailand.org/Kanchanaburi; Th Saengchuto; ☺8.30am-4.30pm) Provides free maps of the town and province, along with bus timetables.

Tourist Police (☑034 512795; Th Saengchuto)

ℹ Getting There & Away

BUS

Kanchanaburi's **bus station** (☑034 515907; Th Lak Meuang) is in the centre of town just off Th Saengchuto, and minivans outnumber buses. There are also minivans to Bangkok catering to tourists; these pick up passengers along Th Mae Nam Khwae.

TRAIN

Kanchanaburi is on the Bangkok Noi–Nam Tok rail line, which includes a portion of the Death Railway. The SRT promotes this as a historic route, and so charges foreigners 100B for any one-way journey along the line, regardless of the distance.

Trains to Bangkok Noi (three hours) depart at 7.19am and 2.48pm.

ℹ Getting Around

Motorcycles can be rented at guesthouses and shops along Th Mae Nam Khwae for around 200B per day. Bicycle rentals cost from 50B per day.

Yellow and blue *sŏrng·tǎa·ou* (passenger pickup trucks) run up and down Th Saengchuto (get off at the cemetery if you want the guesthouse area) for 10B per passenger. A motorcycle taxi from the bus station to the guesthouse area will cost around 50B.

Sangkhlaburi
สังขละบุรี

☑034 / POPULATION 8000

Remote Sangkhlaburi is girded by forest and has the Khao Laem Reservoir almost entirely surrounding the town. Short-term visitors spend their days canoeing, trekking or shopping for handicrafts. Sangkhlaburi is also one of the most multicultural places in Thailand, with Thai, Karen and Mon locals mingling with Lao and Burmese.

◉ Sights & Activities

★ Saphan Mon
BRIDGE

(สะพานมอญ) Sangkhlaburi's iconic, 440m-long wooden bridge, the largest in Thailand, was dubbed the 'bridge of faith' after being built largely through manual labour. Saphan Mon connects the main town, home mostly to Thai and Karen, with the **Mon settlement**. This village is a striking place to explore, peopled by cheroot-smoking women, sarong-wearing men and faces covered in *thanaka* (a yellow paste made from tree bark, used both as sunblock and decoration). Parts of the bridge are uneven, so watch your step.

Khao Laem Reservoir
LAKE

(เขื่อนเขาแหลม) Backed by fuzzy green hills, the gigantic lake wrapped almost entirely around

THAILAND SANGKHLABURI

BUSES FROM KANCHANABURI

DESTINATION	FARE (B)	DURATION (HR)	FREQUENCY
Bangkok Khao San Rd	120	2½	frequent (minivan)
Bangkok Northern (Mo Chit) bus terminal	100-150	2½	frequent (minivan)
Bangkok Southern (Sai Tai Mai) bus terminal	100	2½	every 20min (minivan)
Chiang Mai	594	10-11	three daily (8.30am, 6pm, 7pm)
Hua Hin	220	3½	every two hours (5am-6pm)
Nong Khai	495-829	11	one daily (7pm)
Ratchaburi	50	2½	every 20min
Sangkhlaburi (via Thong Pha Phum)	145-175	3½-5	every 30min (7am-5pm
Suphanburi	48-65	2½	every 30min

WORTH A TRIP

SAI YOK NATIONAL PARK

Sai Yok National Park (อุทยานแห่งชาติ
ไทรโยค; ☑ 034 686024; www.dnp.go.th;
adult/child 300/200B; ⊘ daylight hours)
Caves, waterfalls and forest trails draw
walkers to Sai Yok National Park (958 sq
km). The main sights are easily reached
from the **visitors centre**, including
the park's best known attraction, **Sai
Yok Yai Waterfall** (Nam Tok Sai Yok
Yai, น้ำตกไทรโยคใหญ่). Here, a stream
makes a short, graceful drop into Mae
Nam Khwae Noi. Trails are well marked
and maintained; most are open to bikes.
This mixed forest, home to rare wildlife
including hog-nosed bats and unusual
freshwater crabs, never gets nearly as
crowded as **Erawan**.

The park is halfway between
Kanchanaburi and Sangkhlaburi – buses (60B, 1½ hours, every 30 minutes)
going in either direction will drop you at
the park turn-off by request.

Sangkhlaburi was formed in the 1980s by the
Vajiralongkorn Dam (Khao Laem Dam, เขื่อน
วชิราลงกรณ์; ⊘ 6am-6pm) **FREE**. Two of the
villages submerged under the new lake were
moved up to their present location; Saphan
Mon (p725) was built to connect them. About
all that remains now are ruined buildings
from three temples. A **boat ride** (Saphan Mon;
per person 500B) allows you to see them up
close, as well as feel the pace of life on the lake.

Sangkhlaburi Jungle Trekking   TREKKING
(☑ 085 425 4434; jarunsaksri1@gmail.com) The
forest around Sangkhlaburi is wilder and
less visited than most trekking destinations
in northern Thailand. 'Jack', who has years
of experience as a guide, can tailor trips for
different fitness levels and for family groups,
but the most adventurous option is a week
hiking the Myanmar border from Sangkhlaburi to Um Phang, staying in Karen villages
along the way.

🛏 Sleeping & Eating

P Guesthouse   GUESTHOUSE $
(☑ 081 450 2783, 034 595061; www.p-guesthouse.
com; off Th Si Suwankhiri; d with fan 300B, d/tr with
air-con 400/600B; ❄ 🛜) You don't often get
views like this on a budget. Stone and log-
built rooms gaze upon tranquil waters at this
family-run spot. Fan rooms share cold-water

bathrooms, while air-conditioned rooms
have en suites and the best views. The **restaurant** is a fantastic place to lounge. You
can rent a canoe almost from your door.

★ **Phu Chom Mork Resort**   RESORT $$$
(☑ 064 964 7767; www.phuchommorkresort.com;
32/6 Mu 3, Nong Lu; d incl breakfast 1500-2000B;
❄ 🛜) Delightful service and verdant sur-
rounds set Phu Chom Mork apart as Sang-
khlaburi's fanciest place to stay. Spacious
rooms with sumptuous stone-effect bath-
rooms are spread across banan-tree-hemmed
parkland, where your only soundtrack is
crickets and the pounding rain.

★ **Baan Unrak Bakery**   VEGETARIAN, BAKERY $
(☑ 034 595 006; www.baanunrak.org; Th Si Suwankh-
iri; snacks 25-90B, mains 80-150B; ⊘ 8am-7.30pm
Mon-Sat; 🛜 ☑) 🍜 This mostly vegan cafe, part
of the nonprofit Baan Unrak organisation, is
a crowd-pleaser for its meat-free *pad thai*,
green curry and freshly baked pizzas, not to
mention the home-made baked goods, from
banana sponge cake to chocolate doughnuts.

Toy's   THAI $
(Th Sangkhlaburi; mains 50-150B; ⊘ 9am-8pm Sat-
Thu) Superb Isan-style dishes are served with
a smile at Toy's. Offerings vary according to
what's in season, but you can expect *gài tôrt*
(crispy-coated fried chicken) and *lâhp kôo·a*
(spicy, herb-speckled mincemeat salad) as
well as thick, flavourful massaman curry.

🛈 Getting There & Away

From a **parking lot** (off west end of Thetsaban
1) on the west side of the town centre, old red
buses depart for Kanchanaburi (130B, four
hours, 6.30am, 8am, 9.30am and 1pm) and
air-conditioned buses go to Bangkok's Mo Chit
terminal (281B, seven hours, 8.30am). Minivans
to Kanchanaburi (175B, 3½ hours, almost hour-
ly) depart near **Blend Cafe** (Soi Thetsaban 1;
⊘ 8am-8pm; 🛜), where you can buy bus tickets
and check schedules at a kiosk window.

Mae Sot   แม่สอด

📞 055 / POPULATION 52,000

Remote Mae Sot is among the most cultur-
ally diverse cities in Thailand. Walking the
town's streets you'll see a fascinating ethnic
mixture of Burmese men in their *longyi* (sa-
rongs), Hmong and Karen women in tradi-
tional hill-tribe dress, bearded Muslims, Thai
army rangers and foreign NGO workers.

Although there aren't many formal sights
in Mae Sot, many visitors end up staying

BUSES FROM MAE SOT

DESINATION	FARE (B)	DURATION (HR)	FREQUENCY
Bangkok	290-580	7-8	frequent 8am-9.50pm
Chiang Mai	290	5-6	6.15am & 10pm
Chiang Rai	374	9	7am
Lampang	223	4	6am, 7am & 10am
Mae Sai	416	12	7am
Phitsanulok	172	4	4 departures 7am-2.40pm
Sukhothai	133	3	4 departures 7am-2.40pm

longer than expected. The multicultural vibe, fun activities and good food have become attractions in their own right.

◎ Sights & Activities

Border Market   MARKET
(ตลาดริมน้ำเมย; Rte 12/AH1; ⊙7am-7pm) Alongside Mae Nam Moei on the Thai side is an expansive market that sells a mixture of workaday Burmese goods, black-market clothes, cheap Chinese electronics and food, among other things. It's located 5km west of Mae Sot; *sŏrng·tăa·ou* depart from a spot on Th Chid Lom between approximately 6am and 6pm (20B).

Herbal Sauna   BATHHOUSE
(Wat Mani, Th Intharakhiri; 20B; ⊙3-7pm) Wat Mani has separate herbal sauna facilities for men and women. The sauna is towards the back of the monastery grounds, past the monks' *gù·đì* (living quarters).

🛏 Sleeping & Eating

Sleep Nest Hostel   HOSTEL $
(☑081 845 5579; www.facebook.com/sleepnest hostel; Th Intharakhiri; dm 300-450B; ✳🔊) Pod-like dorm beds in a roomy, young, artsy hostel. The more expensive pods are at ground level and offer much more leg room. The shared facilities have a bar-like feel, and bathrooms are clean and convenient.

Phan Nu House   GUESTHOUSE $
(☑081 972 4467; 563/3 Th Intharakhiri; r 300-500B; ✳🔊) This place consists of 29 large rooms in a residential strip just off the street. Most rooms are equipped with air-con, TV, fridge and hot water, making them a good deal.

Lucky Tea Garden   BURMESE $
(Th Suksri Rat-Uthit; mains 10-50B; ⊙6am-6pm) For the authentic Burmese teashop experience without crossing over to Myawaddy, visit this friendly cafe equipped with sweet tea, tasty snacks and, of course, Burmese pop music.

★Khaomao-Khaofang   THAI $$
(www.khaomaokhaofang.com; 382 Rte 105; mains 120-490B; ⊙11am-10pm; 🌱) Like dining in a gentrified jungle, Khaomao-Khaofang replaces chandeliers with hanging vines, and interior design with orchids and waterfalls.

ⓘ GETTING TO MYANMAR: MAE SOT TO MYAWADDY

The 420m Friendship Bridge links Mae Sot and Myawaddy, in Myanmar's Kayin State.

Getting to the border *Sŏrng·tăa·ou* make frequent trips between Mae Sot and the Friendship Bridge from 6am to 6pm (20B).

At the border After the **Thai immigration booth** (☑055 563004; Rte 12/AH1; ⊙5.30am-8.30pm) cross to the **Myanmar immigration booth** (☑95 0585 0100; Bayint Naung Rd; ⊙5am-8pm (Myanmar time)), from where, if you have a Myanmar visa, you are free to proceed to onward destinations. Otherwise you must pay a fee of 500B for a temporary ID card at the Myanmar immigration booth, which allows you to stay in Myawaddy until 8pm the same day; your passport will be kept at the border.

Moving on About 200m from the border are white share taxis. Destinations include Mawlamyine (10,000K, four to six hours) and Hpa-an (9000K, six hours) and Yangon (K25,000, 14 hours). There's also a daily bus to Yangon (15,000K, 14 hours, 5am).

For information on making this crossing in reverse see p505.

ℹ GETTING TO MYANMAR: PHU NAM RON TO DAWEI

Myanmar visas are not available at this remote border. Note that you cannot enter Myanmar here with an e-visa.

Getting to the border There are around six daily buses (70B to 80B, two hours) and minivans (100B, 1½ hours) from Kanchanaburi's bus station (p725) right to the border starting at 9am. If you leave early you can make it to Dawei in a day, though there are guesthouses in Phu Nam Ron if you need them.

At the border After getting stamped out of Thailand, wait for the shuttle (50B) or take a motorcycle taxi to Myanmar immigration. Formalities are hassle-free, though a bit slow, on both sides.

Moving on Not far from immigration, you'll be introduced to minivan drivers who will take you to Dawei for 800B per person, though this is sometimes negotiable. It's five hours through the beautiful mountains to Dawei on what is still a mostly dirt – and sometimes rough – road, though improvements are under way.

For information on making this crossing in reverse see p506.

Try one of the several delicious-sounding *yam* (Thai-style spicy salads) featuring ingredients ranging from white turmeric to local mushrooms.

The restaurant is north of town between the Km 1 and Km 2 markers on Rte 105, which leads to Mae Ramat.

Khrua Canadian INTERNATIONAL, THAI **$$**
(www.facebook.com/KruaCanadianRestaurant; 3 Th Sri Phanit; dishes 40-280B; ☺7am-3pm & 7-10pm; 🛜🅿) This is the place to go if you want to forget you're in Asia for one meal. Dave, the eponymous Canadian, brews his own coffee and also offers home-made bagels, deli meats and cheeses. The servings are large, the menu is varied and, when you finally remember you're in Thailand again, local information is also available.

🛍 Shopping

Municipal Market MARKET
(off Th Prasatwithi; ☺6am-6pm) Mae Sot's municipal market is among the largest and most vibrant we've encountered anywhere in Thailand. There's heaps of exotic stuff from Myanmar, including Burmese bookshops, sticks of *thanaka* (the source of the yellow powder you see on many faces), bags of pickled tea leaves and velvet thong slippers from Mandalay.

Borderline Shop ARTS & CRAFTS
(www.borderlinecollective.org; 674/14 Th Intharakhiri; ☺9am-7pm Tue-Sun) Selling arts and crafts made by refugee women, Borderline gives its profits back to a women's collective and a child-assistance foundation. The upstairs

gallery sells paintings, and the house is also home to a tea garden and cookery course.

ℹ Getting There & Away

Mae Sot's tiny **airport** (☑ 055 563620; Rte 12/AH1) is about 2km west of town. At research time, **Nok Air** (☑ Mae Sot 055 563883, nationwide 1318; www.nokair.co.th; Mae Sot Airport, Rte 12/AH1; ☺9am-5.30pm), with four daily flights to/from Bangkok's Don Muang International Airport (from 1649B, 65 minutes), was the only airline operating out of Mae Sot.

All long-distance *sŏrng·tăa·ou*, minivans and buses leave from Mae Sot's **bus station** (☑ 055 563435; Rte 12/AH1), located 1.5km west of town; a motorcycle taxi to/from here should cost about 50B.

NORTHEASTERN THAILAND

The northeast is Thailand's forgotten backyard. Isan (*ee-săhn*), as it's usually called, offers a glimpse of the Thailand of old: rice fields run to the horizon, water buffalo wade in muddy ponds, silk weavers work looms under their homes, and pedal-rickshaw drivers pull passengers down city streets.

Spend even just a little time here and you'll discover as many differences as similarities to the rest of Thailand. The language, food and culture are more Lao than Thai, with hearty helpings of Khmer and Vietnamese thrown into the mix. Yet, Isan is also home to some of Thailand's best historic sites, national parks and festivals. Thailand's tourist trail is at its bumpiest here (English is rarely spoken), but the fantastic attractions and daily interactions could end up being highlights of your trip.

Nakhon Ratchasima (Khorat) โคราช

044 / POPULATION 151,450

Nakhorn Ratchasima is a big, busy city that serves as the gateway to Isan. Khorat, as most people call the city, is at its best in its quieter nooks, where local life goes on in a fairly traditional way and you are more likely to run into a meter-long monitor lizard than another traveller.

Sansabai House HOTEL $

(044 255144; www.sansabai-korat.com; Th Suranaree; r with fan 300B, with air-con 500-800B; ❄ ⊛ 🛜) This clean, quiet and friendly place has long been supplying the best budget beds in Khorat. Rooms have good mattresses, mini-fridges and little balconies.

Wat Boon Night Bazaar THAI $

(Th Chomphon; ⊙5-9.30pm) This is the largest night market inside the old town. All the usual Thai and Isan dishes are available for takeaway.

Laap Loy THAI $

(Th Yommarat; mains 50-150B; ⊙11am-8.30pm; 🛜) A contemporary Isan restaurant in front of the Thai Inter Hotel with a mix of the classic, including *kôoa nòr mái dong* (roasted fermented bamboo shoot) and a fantastic *đôm sâap*, and the modern, like fried *làhp* and fish *lăam* cooked in a pan rather than a bamboo tube. Unfortunately there's no English menu, but there are lots of pictures on the wall to point at.

ℹ️ Information

Bangkok Hospital (044 429999; www. bangkokhospital.com; Th Mittaphap) Has a 24-hour casualty department and many English-speaking doctors.

Tourism Authority of Thailand (TAT; 044 213666; tatsima@tat.or.th; 2102-2104 Th Mittaphap; ⊙8.30am-4.30pm) Khorat's branch of TAT is inconveniently located outside the centre of town next to the Sima Thani Hotel.

ℹ️ Getting There & Away

Khorat has two bus terminals. **Terminal 1** (bor kŏr sŏr nèung; 044 242899; Th Burin) in the city centre serves Bangkok (191B, 3½ to four hours, frequent) and most towns within the province, including Pak Chong (56B to 72B, 1½ to two hours, frequent from 5.30am to 6.30pm). Buses to most other destinations use the confusing and

Nakhon Ratchasima (Khorat)

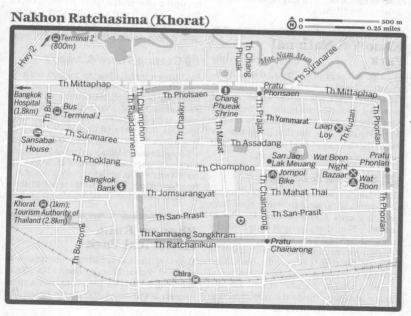

BUSES & MINIVANS FROM NAKHON RATCHASIMA (KHORAT)

DESTINATION	FARE (B)	DURATION (HR)	FREQUENCY
Aranya Prathet (border with Cambodia)	150	4	7 departures 5.30am-6pm
Ayuthaya (minivan)	132	3½-4	frequent 5.40am-6.20pm
Bangkok	148-508	4	frequent
Bangkok (minivan)	171	4	frequent 6.30am-7.30pm
Chiang Mai	526-613	13	7 departures 3am-8.30pm
Lopburi	149	4-4½	6am, 10.45am, 1.30pm
Lopburi (minivan)	130	3½-4	every 40min 4.50am-6.30pm
Nang Rong	60-95	2	hourly
Nang Rong (minivan)	64	2	every 30min 4.30am-8.10pm
Nong Khai	257-409	6	11 departures, most in the afternoon
Surin	115-218	4	every 30min
Trat	297-409	8-9	7 departures
Ubon Ratchathani	248-386	7-8	hourly
Vientiane (must already have Lao visa)	900	6	11.30am

chaotic **Terminal 2** (bor kŏr sŏr sŏrng; ☑044 256007; Hwy 2), north of the centre.

Khorat Train Station (☑044 242044) has 10 daily trains to/from Bangkok (50B to 425B, five to seven hours), via Ayuthaya. There are also nine trains to Ubon Ratchathani (58B to 453B, five to six hours). Khorat's smaller **Chira Train Station** (Jira Train Station; ☑044 242363) is closer to the old city, so it may be more convenient to get off there.

Khao Yai National Park
อุทยานแห่งชาติเขาใหญ่

Khao Yai is Thailand's oldest and most visited national park. Covering 2168 sq km, Khao Yai incorporates one of the largest intact monsoon forests remaining in mainland Asia, which is why it was named a Unesco World Heritage site. But despite its size, it's one of the easiest national parks in Thailand for independent travellers to visit.

🛏 Sleeping & Eating

There are campsites and a variety of rooms and bungalows around the park; none have air-con. There's a 30% discount Monday to Thursday. Note that you must book from the annoying national-park website (http://nps. dnp.go.th/reservation.php) or in person at the park. Lodging is often fully booked except for low-season weekdays. Tent rental is almost always available. There are also many restaurants inside the park, and outside the park on Th Thanarat.

Khao Yai Garden Lodge HOTEL $
(☑094 191 9176, 044 936352; www.khaoyaigardenlodge.com; Th Thanarat, Km 7; tw/tr with fan and shared bathroom 350/450B, incl breakfast d & tw with air-con 1150-2450B; ❄❅@☎❄) One of Khao Yai's veteran resorts, this vast place is in need of TLC. For midrange rooms you can do better elsewhere, but these are just about the only truly budget rooms between Pak Chong city and the park that you can take without having to join a tour – although most do join because the tours are very good.

ℹ Getting There & Away

Pak Chong is the base town for the park and is served by frequent minivans (66B, 1½ hours) and occasional buses (56B, two hours) from Nakhon Ratchasima (Khorat) and Bangkok (160B, three hours, every 30 minutes). If you're coming from Ayuthaya, the train to Pak Chong (23B to 363B, two to three hours, 10 daily) is a good option.

Sŏrng·tăa·ou (Th Mittaphap) travel the 30km from Pak Chong down Th Thanarat to the park's northern gate (40B, one hour) every 30 minutes from 6am to 5pm. The last sŏrng·tăa·ou from the park gate back to Pak Chong departs around 3pm.

Phanom Rung Historical Park

The most spectacular Khmer monument in Thailand, Prasat Phanom Rung ('Big Mountain Temple') sits on the summit of a spent volcano 200m above the paddy fields. The dramatic entrance and beautiful design make it a must-visit attraction for anyone in the area. Down below is the wonderful but often overlooked Prasat Muang Tam ('Lower City Temple'), which is also part of the historical park. It's smaller and less complete, but the peaceful setting – you'll often have it to yourself – and unique design make many people prefer it over its more famous neighbour.

🛏 Sleeping

Phanom Rong can be visited on a day trip from Nakhon Ratchasima or Surin, although some people spend the night in Nang Rong, the nearest town to the temple.

Thanyaporn Homestay　　GUESTHOUSE $
(☎087 431 3741; r incl breakfast 500-800B; ❁❀❈) This modern and cosy guesthouse is just 500m southwest of Prasat Muang Tam ruins, and staying here lets you enjoy village life without needing to rough it. It's the big orange house where the road curves.

ⓘ Getting There & Away

There's no public transport to Phanom Rung or Muang Tam. The best budget option is hiring a motorcycle from **P California Inter Hostel** (☎081 808 3347; www.pcalifornianangrong. webs.com; Th Sangkakrit; dm 150B, r 250-650B; ❁❀❈) in Nang Rong. You can also go by motorcycle-taxi (600B return) or car and driver (1000B) from Nang Rong. It costs 100B/200B for the motorcycle/car to add Muang Tam.

Otherwise, catch a bus from Nang Rong, Surin or Nakhon Ratchasima to the busy Ban Tako (20B to 30B, 20 minutes, every 30 minutes) junction 14km east of town, where motorcycle taxis usually charge 300B to Phanom Rung, including waiting time.

Surin　　สุรินทร์

🄳 044 / POPULATION 40,100

Surin city doesn't have much to say for itself until November, when the provincial capital explodes into life for the Surin Elephant Round-up, during which it hosts giant scrums of both pachyderms and tourists. It does, however, make the most comfortable base for exploring the sites further afield.

⊙ Sights & Activities

★**Chansoma**　　ART STUDIO
(จันทร์โสมา; ☎081 726 0397; ⊗8am-5pm) **FREE** You may find the village of Ban Tha Sawang, 8km west of Surin along Rte 4026, a fascinating stop, even if you're not particularly turned on by weaving. Chansoma, a family-run business in a cooling garden, has made it one of the most renowned silk villages in Thailand. Its exquisite brocade fabrics (pâh yók torng) incorporate threads made of real gold and silver, but the weaving process is just as impressive as the finished cloth.

Surin Elephant Round-up　　CULTURAL
(⊗Nov) Surin celebrates its famous and controversial festival for 11 days in mid-November with the main attraction being a 300-elephant battle reenactment. Elephant 'shows' of all kinds are contentious because the elephants are forced to undergo torturous training to become tamed enough, which is worth considering if you are thinking of attending.

TREKKING IN KHAO YAI NATIONAL PARK

There are five hiking trails through the forest that visitors can walk on their own. All other forest hiking requires a guide. Park rangers can be hired as guides (500B to 1000B per group depending on the time) through the visitors centre. They can also lead you on longer off-trail treks, but deep forest exploration is best done with a private guide arranged through tour companies and hotels. **Bobby's Apartments & Jungle Tours** (☎086 262 7006; www.bobbysjungletourkhaoyai.com; off Mittraphap Rd, Pak Chong) and **Greenleaf Guesthouse & Tour** (☎089 424 8809; www.greenleaftour.com; Th Thanarat, Km 7.5) both come recommended. The **Khao Yai National Park Visitors Centre** (☎086 092 6529; Khao Yai National Park; ⊗6am-9pm, staffed from 8am) has details of all the trails.

No matter where you hike, you should wear boots and long trousers. During the rainy season leeches are a problem. Mosquito repellent helps keep them away, but the leech socks sold in the visitors centre work much better.

BUSES FROM SURIN

DESTINATION	FARE (B)	DURATION (HR)	FREQUENCY
Bangkok	275-353	7-8	hourly 7.30am-11pm
Khon Kaen	160-205	5	every 45min 3.30am-3pm
Nakhon Ratchasima (Khorat)	115-218	4	every 30min 3.30am-8pm
Nang Rong	80-100	2	every 30min 3.30am-8pm
Roi Et	90	2½	hourly 5am-5pm
Ubon Ratchathani	130-202	3½	12 departures 3.20am-10.30pm

🛏 Sleeping & Eating

⭐ Baan Chang Ton HOMESTAY $
(☎ 087 459 8962; www.baanchangton.com; Th Suriyarart; r incl breakfast 400-500B; ❄ @ 🛜) The friendly owners here have rescued an old wooden house and created one of Isan's most charming places to stay. It's quite simple (shared bathrooms, mattresses on the floor and air-con in only one room) but the atmosphere makes it special. Guests can use the kitchen or, if arranged in advance, join the family for dinner. There are also free bikes to use.

Maneerote Hotel HOTEL $
(☎ 044 539477; www.maneerotehotel.com; Soi Poi Tunggor, Th Krungsri Nai; r 450-500B; ❄ @ 🛜) This quiet hotel southwest of the fresh market is hands-down the best-value place in town. Rooms are clean and modern and there's an attached restaurant and coffee shop.

⭐ Som Tam Petmanee 2 THAI $
(Th Murasart; mains 30-100B; ⊙ 8am-4pm) AKA Som Tom Mae Pet, this simple Isan restaurant by Wat Salaloi (there's no roman-script sign, but look for the large chicken grill) is Surin's most famous purveyor of sôm·đam (spicy green-papaya salad) and gài yâhng (grilled chicken). The súp nòr mái (bamboo-shoot dipping sauce) is good, too. There's little English, spoken or written, but the food is so good it's worth stumbling through an order.

Surin Green Market THAI
(Th Jitrbumrung; ⊙ 5am-noon Sat-Sun) Foodies in town on a weekend should make this popular market their breakfast destination. Although there's a variety of food available, Isan dishes are the most common. This is one place to sample the local speciality, gòp yát sâi (herb-stuffed frog). Silk fabric and other handicrafts are sold here too.

ℹ Getting There & Away

In addition to buses to distant destinations, there are also sŏrng·tǎa·ou and minivans to local destinations such as Chong Chom (for the Cambodian border; 45B, 1½ hours, frequent from 5.30am to 6.30pm) departing from Surin's **bus terminal** (☎ 044 511756; Th Jitrbumrung).

Ubon Ratchathani อุบลราชธานี

✓ 045 / POPULATION 86,800

Ubon Ratchathani, the 'Royal City of the Lotus', is a medium-sized city with a small town feel. It was a site of a US air base during the Vietnam War; most travellers who come here are on their way to and from the nearby Thai–Lao border crossing at Chong Mek.

⦿ Sights & Festivals

⭐ Wat Thung Si Meuang BUDDHIST TEMPLE
(วัดทุ่งศรีเมือง; Th Luang; ⊙ daylight hours) FREE Built during the reign of Rama III (1824–51), Wat Thung Si Meuang has a classic hŏr đrai (Tripitaka hall) in excellent shape. Like many hŏr đrai, it rests on stilts in the middle of a pond to protect the precious scriptures (written on palm-leaf paper) from termites. It's kept open so you can look inside. The original murals in the little bòht (ordination hall) beside the hŏr đrai show life in that era and are in remarkably good condition.

Candle Parade CULTURAL
(Kabuan Hae Tian; ⊙ usually Jul) Ubon's famous Candle Parade began during the reign of King Rama V, when the appointed governor decided the rocket festival was too dangerous. The original simple designs have since grown (with the help of internal frames) to gigantic, elaborately carved wax sculptures. The parade is part of Khao Phansaa (the start of Buddhist Lent).

🛏️ Sleeping & Eating

Phadaeng Hotel
HOTEL $

(☏ 045 254600; thephadaen@gmail.com; Th Phadaeng; r 500B; ❄@🛜) One of the best-value hotels in Ubon, the Phadaeng has well-maintained rooms (they look almost brand new) with good furnishings including large TVs and desks. It's located just minutes from Thung Si Meuang park, and the large parking area separates it from street noise. The hotel is livened up with copies of classic paintings. Bike hire costs 50B per day.

⭐ Outside Inn
GUESTHOUSE $$

(☏ 088 581 2069; www.theoutsideinnubon.com; 11 Th Suriyat; r incl breakfast 650-799B; ➖❄@🛜) A nice little garden lounge area sets the relaxed, communal vibe here. The rooms are large, comfy and fitted with tastefully designed reclaimed-timber furnishings. Owners Brent and Tun are great hosts, cook some good **food** (mains 50-225B; ⏰11am-2.30pm & 5-9pm Wed-Mon; 🛜🅿️), and have lots of advice on what to see and do in the area.

⭐ Rung Roj
THAI $

(Th Nakhonban; mains 50-290B; ⏰9.30am-8.30pm Mon-Sat) An Ubon institution serving excellent food using family recipes and only fresh ingredients. Many people swear by the ox-tongue stew. From the outside it looks more like a well-to-do house than a restaurant, and inside it has 1950s and '60s classic rock 'n' roll music and decor to match.

ℹ️ GETTING TO LAOS: UBON RATCHATHANI TO PAKSE

The busy Chong Mek/Vangtao crossing connects Ubon Ratchathani to Pakse in Laos.

Getting to the border Direct Ubon Ratchathani–Pakse buses (200B, three hours, 9.30am and 2.30pm) stop at the border so travellers can buy Lao visas.

At the border The border is open from 6am to 8pm and the crossing is largely hassle free, although surcharges to the visa fee are sometimes applied.

Moving on Pakse is about an hour away in one of the frequent minivans (20,000K, 45 minutes) or sŏrng·tăa·ou that wait beyond the Lao immigration office.

Peppers
INTERNATIONAL, BAKERY $$

(297/2-3 Uppalisan Rd; mains 80-495B; ⏰8am-9pm; 🛜) Peppers, popular with both fa·ràng and Thai, features a broad international menu with everything from nachos to schnitzel to pizza to đôm yam gûng and all-day breakfast. The bakery offerings, its real speciality, are downright delicious. There are also wines and international beers.

BUSES FROM UBON RATCHATHANI

DESTINATION	FARE (B)	DURATION (HR)	FREQUENCY
Bangkok	414-556	10	hourly 4am-midnight, frequent 4-8pm
Chiang Mai	707-790	12-14	7.30am, 12.45pm, 1.45pm, 2.45pm, 3.45pm, 5.45pm, 6.30pm
Chong Mek (Lao border)	100	2	every 30min 5am-6pm
Khon Kaen	176-244	4½-5	every 30min 5.30am-5.40pm
Mukdahan	130	2½	5.45am, 7.30am, 8.40am, 11.30am, 1pm
Mukdahan (minivan)	111	2½	every 30min 6am-5.30pm
Nakhon Ratchasima (Khorat)	248-386	7-8	hourly 5am-8pm
Nang Rong	144-265	5-6	hourly 5am-8pm
Pakse (Laos)	200	3	9.30am & 2.30pm
Rayong	515-801	13	7am, 7.15am, 5pm, 6pm, 7.30pm, 7.45pm, 8pm, 8.15pm
Surin	130-202	3½	hourly 5am-8pm
Udon Thani	284-332	7	every 30min 5.30am-5.40pm
Yasothon	66-99	2	hourly 5.30am-5.30pm
Yasothon (minivan)	80	2	hourly 5.30am-5.30pm

ⓘ GETTING TO CAMBODIA: CHONG CHOM TO O SMACH

Getting to the border Because of the casino, there are plenty of public minibuses (45B, 1½ hours, frequent from 5.30am to 6.30pm) from Surin's bus terminal (p732) to the border at Chong Chom.

At the border The Cambodian border is open from 7am to 10pm and visas are available on the spot. There's a 5B fee at Thai immigration on weekends and early mornings/late afternoons.

Moving on There are two buses from O Smach to the City Angkor Hotel in Siem Reap (350B, three hours, 8am and 5pm). Chartering a 'taxi' (drivers wait at the border looking for passengers) for the drive to Siem Reap should cost 2000B or less, and you can wait for others to share the costs, though this is generally only possible in the morning.

ⓘ Information

Tourism Authority of Thailand (TAT; ☑ 045 243770; tatubon@tat.or.th; 264/1 Th Kheuan Thani; ☻8.30am-4.30pm) Has helpful staff and a free city map.

Ubonrak Thonburi Hospital (☑ 045 429100; Th Phalorangrit) The best private hospital in Ubon; it has a 24-hour casualty department.

ⓘ Getting There & Around

Air Asia (☑ 045 255762, nationwide 02 515 9999; www.airasia.com; Ubon Ratchathani Airport; ☻7am-7pm), **Nok Air** (☑ nationwide 02 900 9955; www.nokair.com; Ubon Ratchathani Airport; ☻7am-7pm) and **Thai Lion Air** (☑ nationwide 02 529 9999; www.lionairthai.com; Ubon Ratchathani Airport; ☻6am-7pm) fly to/from Bangkok's Don Mueang Airport (one hour) a dozen times daily with prices well under 1000B usually available. **THAI Smile** (☑ 087 776 2266, nationwide 1181; www.thaismileair.com; Ubon Ratchathani Airport; ☻7am-7.30pm) has four flights to/from Bangkok's Suvarnabhumi Airport (one hour) for a little bit more. Air Asia also has one daily flight each to Pattaya and Chiang Mai.

Ubon's **bus terminal** (☑ 045 316085; Hwy 231) is north of town; take sŏrng·tăa·ou 2, 3 or 10 to the city centre. The best service to Bangkok is with **Nakhonchai Air** (☑ 045 955999).

Ubon's **train station** (☑ 045 321004; Th Sathani) is in Warin Chamrap; take sŏrng·tăa·ou 2. There are 10 daily trains between Ubon and Bangkok.

Mukdahan   มุกดาหาร

☑ 042 / POPULATION 34,294

On the banks of the Mekong, directly opposite the Lao city of Savannakhet, Mukdahan – just plain múk to locals – sees few visitors despite being the home of the Thai–Lao Friendship Bridge 2, which connects Thailand to Laos and Vietnam by road.

Huanum Hotel   HOTEL $
(☑ 042 611137; Th Samut Sakdarak; d/tw with fan & cold-water shared bathroom 200/350B, d/tw 350/450B; ❀ ☎) This Mukdahan classic is a friendly, reliable and clean old-timer that has been pleasantly spruced up recently. It's the first choice of most backpackers.

Mukdahan Night Market   THAI, VIETNAMESE $
(Th Song Nang Sathit; ☻4-9pm) Mukdahan's night market has all the Thai and Isan classics, but it's the Vietnamese vendors that set it apart. A few sell băhn dah (they'll tell you it's 'Vietnamese pizza'), which combines soft noodles, pork, spring onions and an optional egg served on a crispy cracker.

ⓘ Getting There & Away

Mukdahan's bus terminal is on Rte 212, west of town. There are frequent evening departures to

ⓘ GETTING TO LAOS: MUKDAHAN TO SAVANNAKHET

Getting to the border Thai and Lao citizens can use the boats that cross the Mekong from Mukdahan's city centre, while everyone else must use the bridge. The easiest way to cross is with the direct buses to Savannakhet (45B to 50B, hourly 7.30am to 7pm) from Mukdahan's bus station. There's a 5B fee during weekend, holidays and non-business hours.

At the border The border is open from 6am to 10pm. The crossing to Savannakhet can take from one to two hours, depending on the length of the immigration queues. There's time enough at the border to get a Lao visa.

Moving on From Savannakhet there are buses to various points in Laos, as well as Vietnam.

For information on making this crossing in reverse see p365.

Bangkok (439B to 717B, 10 to 11 hours), as well as many minivans to Nakhon Phanom (80B, 2½ hours), Ubon Ratchathani (100B to 135B, 2½ hours) and That Phanom (40B, one hour).

Nakhon Phanom นครพนม

☑ 042 / POPULATION 22,710

Nakhon Phanom means 'City of Mountains', but the undulating sugar loaf peaks all lie across the river in Laos, so you'll be admiring rather than climbing them. There are unexpected French colonial buildings here too, while Ho Chi Minh, who led Vietnam to independence, spent time near here in the late 1920s. Travellers can cross to Laos from here.

Lai Reua Fai   CULTURAL

(☉ late Oct/early Nov) Nakhon Phanom is famous for this illuminated boat procession. A modern twist on the ancient tradition of sending rafts loaded with food, flowers and candles down the Mekong as offerings for the *naga*, today's giant bamboo rafts hold up to 20,000 handmade lanterns, and some designers add animation to the scenes.

Ho Chi Minh House   MUSEUM

(บ้านโฮจิมินห์; ☑ 042 522430; Ban Na Chok; donations appreciated; ☉ daylight hours) FREE The best of the three Ho Chi Minh–related attractions in Ban Na Chok village, this is a replica of the simple wooden house where 'Uncle Ho' sometimes stayed in 1928 and 1929 while planning his resistance movement in Vietnam. A few of the furnishings are believed to be originals. It's a private affair in the back of a family home and they're very proud of it.

❶ Getting There & Away

Nahon Phanom's airport is located 20km west of town. **Nok Air** (☑ 082 790 7961, nationwide 02 900 9955; www.nokair.com; Nakhon Phanom Airport; ☉ 8am-8pm) and **Air Asia** (☑ 042 531571, nationwide 02 515 9999; www.airasia.com; Nakhon Phanom Airport; ☉ 8am-5pm) fly several times daily to/from Bangkok's Don Mueang Airport with one-way prices typically costing 1100B.

Nakhon Phanom's **bus terminal** (☑ 042 513444; Th Fuang Nakhon) is west of the town centre. There are buses to Nong Khai (200B, seven to eight hours, 11am), Udon Thani (147B to 200B, four hours, every 45 minutes from 7.15am to 5pm), Khon Kaen (212B, five hours, 13 departures from 5.50am to 9.30pm), Ubon Ratchathani (155B to 200B, 4½ hours, 7am, 8.30am and 2pm) and Bangkok (554B to 862B, 11 to 12 hours, three daily).

> ❶ **GETTING TO LAOS: NAKHON PHANOM TO THA KHAEK**
>
> **Getting to the border** Direct buses run to Tha Khaek in Laos from Nakhon Phanom's bus station (70B/75B weekdays/weekends, eight departures from 8am to 5pm).
>
> **At the border** The Thai border is open from 6am to 10pm. Lao visas are available at the border.
>
> **Moving on** Savannakhet is a two-hour bus ride from Tha Khaek.
>
> For information on making this crossing in reverse see p362

Nong Khai หนองคาย

☑ 042 / POPULATION 47,600

Sitting on the banks of the Mekong, just across from Vientiane in Laos, Nong Khai has been a popular destination for years, thanks to its proximity to Vientiane, the capital of Laos. But with its dreamy pink sunsets and relaxed traveller vibe, many visitors who mean to stay one night end up bedding down for many more.

Nong Khai's **rocket festival** (*bun bâng fai*) begins on Visakha Bucha day in late May to early June.

◉ Sights

★ Sala Kaew Ku   SCULPTURE

(ศาลาแก้วกู่, Wat Khaek; 20B; ☉ 7am-6pm) One of Thailand's most enigmatic attractions, Sala Kaew Ku can't fail to impress. Built over 20 years by Luang Pu Boun Leua Sourirat, a mystic who died in 1996, the park features a weird and wonderful smorgasbord of bizarre cement statues of Buddha, Shiva, Vishnu and other celestial deities. The main shrine building is packed with hundreds of smaller sculptures of various description and provenance, photos of Luang Pu at various stages throughout his life, and his corpse lying under a glass dome ringed by flashing lights.

Tha Sadet Market   MARKET

(ตลาดท่าเสด็จ; Th Rimkhong; ☉ 8.30am-6pm) The most popular destination in town. Almost everyone loves a stroll through this covered market despite it being a giant tourist trap. It offers the usual mix of clothes, electronic equipment, food and assorted bric-a-brac,

WAT PHRA THAT PHANOM

Towering over the small, peaceful town of That Phanom (ธาตุพนม), the spire of the colossal namesake *chedi* at Wat Phra That Phanom is one of the great pillars of Isan identity. Visitors from all over Thailand and Laos descend on the town during the **That Phanom Festival** (⊘ late Jan/early Feb) to make merit. There are frequent buses and minivans to That Phanom from nearby Nakhon Phanom, as well as destinations across Isan and Bangkok.

Wat Phra That Phanom (วัดพระธาตุพนม; Th Chayangkun; ⊘ 5am-9pm) is a potent and beautiful place – even if you're feeling templed out, you'll likely be impressed. At its hub is a stupa *(tâht)*, more imposing than any in present-day Laos and highly revered by Buddhists from both countries. It's 53.6m high, and a 16kg real-gold umbrella laden with precious gems adds 4m more to the top. A visit in the evening is extra-special.

most of it imported from Laos and China, but there are also a few shops selling quirky and quality stuff.

🛌 Sleeping & Eating

⭐ **Mut Mee Garden Guesthouse**　　GUESTHOUSE $$
(☎ 042 460717; www.mutmee.com; Soi Mutmee; r 200-1650B; ⊜❄🔊) Nong Khai's budget classic has a riverfront garden so relaxing it's intoxicating, and most nights it's packed with travellers. Mut Mee caters to many budgets, with a huge variety of rooms (the cheapest with shared bathroom, the most expensive with an awesome balcony) clustered around a thatched-roof lounge, where

owner Julian freely shares his wealth of knowledge about the area.

E-San Guesthouse　　GUESTHOUSE $
(☎ 086 242 1860; 538 Soi Srikhunmuang; r with fan & shared bathroom 250B, with air-con 450B; ❄🔊) Just off the river in a small, beautifully restored wooden house ringed by a long verandah, this is an atmospheric place for backpackers to stay. The air-con rooms in a new building are fine, though they lack the character of the original house. Bikes are free. There are two other wooden guesthouses on the same street.

Khiangkhong Guesthouse　　HOTEL $
(☎ 042 422870; Th Rimkhong; r with fan/air-con 400/500B; ❄🔊) Catch a refreshing breeze and snag some river views from the 3rd-floor terrace (and some of the rooms) at this family-run concrete tower that falls between guesthouse and hotel. Bicycles are free.

Daeng Namnuang　　VIETNAMESE $
(Th Rimkhong; mains 50-250B; ⊘ 8am-8pm; 🔊) This massive river restaurant has grown into an Isan institution, and hordes of out-of-towners head home with car boots and carry-on bags (there's an outlet at Udon Thani's airport) stuffed with their *năam neu·ang* (DIY pork spring rolls).

Hospital Food Court　　THAI $
(Th Meechai; mains 40-80B; ⊘ 6am-3pm) Don't be put off by the name – it isn't 'hospital food'. Located across from the hospital, this food court whips up Thai standards at low prices. The food is delicious, there's plenty of choice and it's conveniently located near the most popular guesthouses in town.

⭐ **Dee Dee Pohchanah**　　THAI $$
(1155/9 Th Prajak; mains 60-425B; ⊘ 11am-2am; 🔊) How good is Dee Dee? Just look at the dinner-time crowds. But don't be put off by them: despite having a full house every night, this open-air place is a well-oiled machine and you won't be waiting long.

BUSES FROM NONG KHAI

DESTINATION	FARE (B)	DURATION (HR)	FREQUENCY
Bangkok	329-658	10-11	frequent in late afternoon & early evening, hourly during the day
Bangkok (Suvarnabhumi International Airport)	428	9-10	8pm
Nakhon Phanom	200	7-8	11am
Udon Thani (minivan)	50	1	frequent 5.30am-7pm

Shopping

Nong Khai

Walking Street Market MARKET
(⊙4pm-10pm Sat) This weekly street festival
featuring music, handmade items and food
takes over the promenade every Saturday
night. It's smaller, but far more pleasant
than the similar Walking Street markets in
Chiang Mai.

Village Weaver Handicrafts ARTS & CRAFTS
(☑042 422651; 1020 Th Prajak; ⊙8.30am-6pm)
This place sells high-quality, handwoven
fabrics and clothing (ready-made or made to
order) that help fund development projects
around Nong Khai. The *mát·mèe* cotton is
particularly good here.

Information

Nongkhai Hospital (☑042 413456; Th
Meechai; ⊙24hr) Has a 24-hour casualty
department.

Getting There & Away

Nong Khai bus terminal (☑042 421246) is
located just off Th Prajak, about 1.5km from the
main pack of riverside guesthouses. **Nong Khai
train station** (☑042 411637, nationwide 1690;
www.railway.co.th), 2km west of the city centre,
has three evening express trains to Bangkok
(seats from 223B to 607B, sleeper upper/lower
1157B/1357B, 11½ hours).

EASTERN GULF COAST

Two islands – Ko Samet and Ko Chang – are
the magnets that draw travellers to the eastern seaboard. The mainland has the charismatic, old-world charm of Trat and Chanthaburi, as well as the raucous, hedonistic
resort of Pattaya.

Ko Samet, the nearest major island to
Bangkok, is a flashpacker fave where visitors
sip from vodka buckets and admire the fire
jugglers or head for the quieter southern
coves. Further down the coast is Ko Chang,
Thailand's second-largest island, which offers diving, beaches and hiking, as well as a
vibrant party scene.

Ko Samet เกาะเสม็ด

Once the doyen of backpacker destinations,
today Ko Samet shares its charms with a
wider audience. The sandy shores, cosy coves
and aquamarine waters attract ferryloads of
Bangkokians looking to party each weekend,

ⓘ GETTING TO LAOS: NONG KHAI TO VIENTIANE

Getting to the border If you already
have your Lao visa, the easiest way to
Vientiane is the direct bus from Nong
Khai's bus terminal (55B, 1½ hours, six
daily from 7.30am to 6pm). If you're
getting your visa at the border, take a
túk-túk from the town centre (60B) to
the bridge. Don't use a visa agency.

At the border After getting stamped
out of Thailand, take the waiting buses
(15B to 20B) across the bridge. Lao
visas are available on arrival. Bring a
passport photo.

Moving on It's about 20km to Vientiane. Plenty of buses, túk-túk and taxis
will be waiting for you.

while tour groups pack out the main beach
and many resorts. Fire-juggling shows and
beach barbecues are nightly events on the
northern beaches, but the southern parts of
the island are far more secluded and sedate,
while the thick jungle interior is surprisingly
rustic.

Sleeping & Eating

Most resorts and bungalows have their
own restaurants offering mixed Thai and
international menus. Room rates rocket on
weekends and holidays. Early risers should
note that Hat Sai Kaew, Ao Hin Khok, Ao
Phai and Ao Wong Deuan are popular party
beaches.

Apaché BUNGALOW $
(☑081 452 9472; Ao Thian; r 800-1500B; ❈⊜)
Apaché's eclectic, quirky decorations and
cheerfully random colour scheme add character to this super-chilled spot at the southern end of a tranquil strip. Bungalows are
basic but adequate. The on-site restaurant
on stilts is well worthwhile.

⭐**Ao Nuan Bungalows** BUNGALOW $$
(☑081 781 4875; Ao Nuan; bungalows with fan 800-
1200B, with air-con 1500-3000B; ❈⊜) Samet's
one remaining bohemian bay is tucked off
the main road down a dirt track. Running
down a jungle hillside to the sea are cute
wooden bungalows ranging from simple
fan-cooled affairs with shared cold-water
bathroom to romantic air-conditioned re-
treats with elegant deck furniture. There's a

THAILAND KO SAMET

WORTH A TRIP

PHIMAI พิมาย

Phimai, the architectural inspiration for Cambodia's Angkor Wat, is one of the grandest ancient monuments in Thailand. It's an easy day trip from Nakhon Ratchasima (p729). Frequent buses and minivans (50B, 1½ hours) travel here from Khorat's Bus Terminal 1.

Phimai Historical Park (อุทยานประวัติศาสตร์พิมาย; ☑044 471568; Th Ananthajinda; 100B; ⊙7am-6pm, visitors centre 8.30am-4.30pm) Prasat Phimai is one of the most impressive Khmer ruins in Thailand, both in its grand scale and its intricate details. Though built as a Mahayana Buddhist temple, the carvings feature many Hindu deities, and many design elements – most notably the **main shrine**'s distinctive *prang* tower – were later used at Angkor Wat. There has been a temple at this naturally fortified site since at least the 8th century, though most of the existing buildings were erected in the late 11th century by Khmer king Jayavarman VI.

Phimai National Museum (พิพิธภัณฑสถานแห่งชาติพิมาย; ☑044 471167; Th Tha Songkhran; 100B; ⊙9am-4pm) One of the biggest and best museums in Isan, the Phimai National Museum is well worth a visit. Situated on the banks of Sa Kwan, a 12th-century Khmer reservoir, the museum consists of two spacious buildings housing a fine collection of Khmer sculptures from not just Phimai but also many other ruins from around Isan. Though the focus is on the Khmer era, there are also artefacts from Muang Sema, distinctive trumpet-mouthed and black Phimai pottery from Ban Prasat, and Buddha images from various periods.

Sai Ngam (ไทรงาม; ⊙daylight hours) A bit east of town is Thailand's largest and oldest banyan tree, a 350-plus-year-old giant spread over an island. The extensive system of interlocking branches and gnarled trunks makes the 'Beautiful Banyan' look like a small forest.

bar and simple restaurant; if you need more action, Tubtim beach is a few minutes' stroll.

Nice & Easy BUNGALOW $$
(☑038 644370; www.niceandeasysamed.com; Ao Wong Deuan; r 1000-1800B; ❄️🛜) As the name suggests, this is a very amiable place, with comfortable, modern bungalows in four categories set around a garden and carp pool behind the beach, where it runs a cafe-restaurant. It's a great deal for this beach.

❶ Information

There are plenty of ATMs on Ko Samet.
International Clinic Ko Samet (☑038 644414, emergency 086 094 0566; www.sametclinic.in.th; Na Dan; ⊙8am-6pm, emergencies until midnight) This private English-speaking clinic is near the ferry pier.

❶ Getting There & Around

Ko Samet is accessed by boat via the mainland piers in Ban Phe (one-way/return 70B/100B, 40 minutes, hourly, 8am to 5pm). Boats dock at **Na Dan** (usage fee 20B), the main pier on Ko Samet.

Green **sŏrng·tăa·ou** meet boats at the pier and provide drop-offs at the various beaches (20B to 200B, depending on the beach and number of passengers).

To get to Ban Phe from Bangkok, head to Rayong. You'll arrive at bus station 2; there are some minibuses from here to Ban Phe, but it'll usually be quicker to catch a *sŏrng·tăa·ou* to bus station 1, then another from there to Ban Phe.

From Ko Samet, it's easy to arrange minibus transfers to Bangkok (250B), Suvarnabhumi airport (500B), Ko Chang piers (250B) and elsewhere.

Chanthaburi & Trat จันทบุรี / ตราด

Surrounded by palm trees and fruit plantations, Chanthaburi and Trat are mainly transit points for travellers headed to Ko Chang or the Cambodian border. If you stop to catch your breath, you'll find that Chanthaburi dazzles with its weekend gem market, while sleepy Trat is filled with old teak shophouses and genuine small-town living.

🛏️ Sleeping & Eating

🛏️ Chanthaburi

Chernchan Hostel HOSTEL $$
(☑065 573 8841; www.facebook.com/chernchan2017; 43/11-13 Th Tirat; dm 450B, r 900-1500B; ❄️🛜) On a quiet lane close to the river, this boutique hostel has eye-catching modern design and helpful staff. Dorms and rooms are compact but comfortable; downstairs in the cafe an abundant breakfast is

ℹ GETTING TO CAMBODIA: COASTAL BORDERS

Trat to Koh Kong

The Hat Lek/Cham Yeam crossing is the most convenient border crossing between Ko Chang and Sihanoukville in coastal Cambodia.

Getting to the border Take a minivan from Trat's bus station to Hat Lek (120B, 1½ hours, hourly from 5am to 6pm).

At the border Cambodian tourist visas are available at the border for US$30 but over-charging is common. Bring a passport photo. Avoid anyone who says you require a 'med-ical certificate' or other paperwork. The border closes at 8pm.

Moving on Take a taxi (US$10), túk-túk (US$5) or moto (motorcycle taxi; US$3) to Ko Kong where you can catch onward transport to Sihanoukville (four hours, one or two de-partures per day) and Phnom Penh (five hours, two or three departures until 11.30am).

Chanthaburi to Pailin

If you're heading to Siem Reap (or Battambang) from Ko Chang, you don't have to schlep up to the Aranya Prathet/Poipet border. The Ban Pakard/Psar Pruhm crossing isn't crowded and shaves some travel time.

Getting to the border Minivans depart Chanthaburi for Ban Packard (180B, 1½ hours, 10am and noon) from a stop across the river from the River Guest House.

At the border You need a passport photo and US$30 for the visa fee, although over-charging is common.

Moving on Hop on a motorbike taxi to Pailin, where there are shared taxis (US$5 per person, 1½ hours) to Battambang, which has buses to Siem Reap and Phnom Penh.

For information on making this crossing in reverse see p117.

served (included in room but not dorm rates). It rents bikes.

★ Chanthorn   THAI $$

(102/5-8 Th Benchamarachutit; mains 120-250B; ☺9am-9pm; 🖊) This welcoming family-run restaurant in the centre near the waterfront is a great place to try local specialities; the *chamung* leaves with pork and Chanthaburi crab noodles are particularly good, but it's all really excellent quality. It's a fairly early closer at dinner time.

🛏 Trat

★ Ban Jai Dee Guest House   GUESTHOUSE $

(📞039 520678, 083 589 0839; banjaideehouse@yahoo.com; 6 Th Chaimongkol; s/d 250/300B; 🛜) This relaxed traditional wooden house has simple rooms with shared bathrooms (hot-water showers). Paintings and objets d'art made by the artistically inclined own-ers decorate the beautiful common spaces. There are only seven rooms and an addic-tively relaxing ambience so it can fill fast. The owners are full of helpful information and understand a budget traveller's needs.

Night Market   MARKET $

(off Th Sukhumvit; mains from 30B; ☺5-9pm) Trat's busy night market is a good destina-tion for cheap eats, with lots of grill stalls doing fish and other seafood, plenty of *sôm·dam* (spicy green papaya salad), a cor-nucopia of fruit and numerous other delec-tables. Things start to pack up around 8pm, so you're better off arriving before then.

ℹ Getting There & Away

CHANTHABURI

Chanthaburi's **bus station** (Th Saritidet) is west of the river. Minivans also leave from the bus station.

DESTINATION	BUS	MINIVAN
Bangkok's Eastern Bus Terminal (Ekamai)	184B; 4hr; 25 daily	210B; frequent
Bangkok's Northern Bus Terminal (Mo Chit)	187B; 4hr; 4 daily	215B; frequent
Trat		52-70B; 1hr; frequent

TRAT

Bangkok Airways (☏ 039 525767; www.bang-kokair.com; Trat Airport; ◷ 8.30am-6.30pm) operates three daily flights to/from Bangkok's Suvarnabhumi International Airport (one hour). The airport is 40km from Trat. A taxi into town is 600B.

Trat's **bus station** is 2km outside town. Minivans leave from Th Sukhumvit. **Family Tour** (☏ 081 940 7380; Th Sukhumvit) run minivans to Bangkok, as well as Phnom Penh and Siem Reap.

Ko Chang   เกาะช้าง

☏ 039 / POPULATION 10,000

With steep, jungle-covered peaks, picturesque Ko Chang (Elephant Island) retains its remote and rugged spirit – despite the transformation of some parts into a package-tour destination. Cambodia-bound backpackers and island-hopping couples still pass through, drawn by the sweeping bays along the west coast, an accessible forested interior and a thriving party scene.

◉ Sights & Activities

Ko Chang's west coast is by far the most developed stretch of the island thanks to the beaches that line the coast. **Hat Sai Khao** is the biggest and busiest beach, while **Lonely Beach** is the backpacker fave and the liveliest place come nightfall. **Hat Khlong Kloi** is popular but still feels a little hidden away. **Ban Bang Bao** in the southwest of the island is a former fishing village now packed with seafood restaurants and souvenir shops.

In contrast, the east coast remains quiet with hidden bays, mangrove forests and low-key fishing villages. The hilly, forested interior of the island has a few waterfalls and is fine for day treks, although you'll need a guide. **Mr Tan** (☏ 089 645 2019; hikes 600-1400B) speaks good English and comes recommended.

The dive sites near Ko Chang offer a variety of coral, fish and beginner-friendly shallow waters. **BB Divers** (☏ 039 558040; www.bbdivers.com; Bang Bao; 2 boat dives 3000B) can take you to them. Ko Chang is also a decent spot for kayaking: **KayakChang** (☏ 097 182 8319; www.kayakchang.com; Emerald Cove Resort, Khlong Prao; kayaks per day from 1000B) is a professional outfit.

🛌 Sleeping

★**Pajamas Hostel**   HOSTEL $
(☏ 039 510789; www.pajamaskohchang.com; Khlong Prao; dm/r incl breakfast 570/2600B;

☏⌨) A couple of kilometres north of the main Khlong Prao strip and by the beach, this superb hostel oozes relaxation, with an open-plan lounge and bar overlooking the swimming pool. Good modern air-con dorms are upstairs, while the private rooms are really excellent, with platform beds, a cool, light feel and your own terrace/balcony. It's all spotless, and exceedingly well run.

★**Paradise Cottage**   BUNGALOW $
(☏ 081 773 9337; www.paradisecottageresort.com; 104/1 Mu 1, Lonely Beach; r basic 450-990B, sea view 1700B; ❄🛜) With house music as a backdrop, hammock-clad pavilions facing the sea and compact, handsome rooms, well-run Paradise Cottage is a gloriously relaxing retreat. The sea-view rooms have air-con and a marvellous outlook, while the cheapest ones have fans but lack hot water and sockets. At low tide a sandbank just beyond the rocks can be reached. Off-season prices are great.

Independent Bo's   GUESTHOUSE $
(☏ 039 551165; Hat Sai Khao; r 300-800B; 🛜) Quirky and enchanting, this is an old-school bohemian budget place right on the sand. It's a striking sight and experience: a warren of driftwood cabins, common areas and quirky signs with a communal, hippie feel and the sea at your feet. The fan-only rooms are simple and mostly rather charming; bathrooms range from extremely basic to modernised. No reservations (and no children).

Little Eden   BUNGALOW $
(☏ 084 867 7459; www.littleedenkohchang.com; Soi 3, Lonely Beach; r with fan/air-con 950/1500B; ❄🛜) On the quiet side of the main road, but still close to the beach, Little Eden has a series of wooden bungalows, all connected by an intricate lattice of wooden walkways. Rooms are comfortable with a terrace, wooden floors and mosquito nets: expect plenty of chirping noise from forest critters. There are good breakfasts and other meals, a pleasant communal area and friendly staff.

Porn's Bungalows   BUNGALOW $
(☏ 080 613 9266; www.pornsbungalows-kohchang.com; Hat Kaibae; r 600-1600B; 🛜) This is a very chilled spot at the far western end of Kaibae beach, with a popular on-site restaurant. All of the wooden bungalows are fan-only. The beachfront bungalows are larger, have a great outlook, and are a fab deal at around 1000B. They can't be booked ahead, so you might have to find somewhere else first in busy periods.

THAILAND KO CHANG

BUILDING THE DEATH RAILWAY

The so-called 'Death Railway' was an astonishing but brutal feat of engineering. Over 12,000 Allied prisoners of war and as many as 90,000 forced Asian labourers died due to disease, poor hygiene, lack of medical equipment and brutal treatment by the Japanese camp guards.

The 415km railway was built during the WWII Japanese occupation of Thailand (1941–45). Its objective was to secure an overland supply route to Burma (Myanmar) for the Japanese conquest of other west Asian countries.

The bridge that spans the 'River Kwai' near Kanchanaburi city – now referred to as the Death Railway Bridge (p722) – was the only steel bridge built in Thailand; Burma had seven. It was bombed several times by the Allies, but the POWs were sent to rebuild it. When the war's tide turned, the railway became an escape path for Japanese troops.

On the Thai side, the State Railway of Thailand (SRT) assumed control and continues to operate trains on 130km of the original route between Nong Pladuk, southeast of Kanchanaburi, and Nam Tok.

Starbeach Bungalows GUESTHOUSE $
(☑089 574 9486; www.starbeach-kohchang.com; Hat Sai Khao; bungalows 600-750B; ☜) Right on the prime part of the beach, this ramshackle-looking spot is a glorious place for no-frills sand-and-sea sleeping. Fan-cooled rooms are simple but decent and all look out towards the water. There's a friendly on-site bar and restaurant. No reservations: text to see if there's a vacancy. Head towards the beach down the side of the 7-Eleven and turn right.

BB Lonely Beach HOSTEL $
(☑089 504 0543; www.bblonelybeach.com; Lonely Beach; dm 250B; r with fan 500-700B; ☜☒) One of the only dorms within reach of the beach, this has basic and stuffy – but decent – shared and private rooms at bargain rates. There's plenty to do here, with a dive school, a gym, Belgian beers and a pool: it's a great spot to meet fellow travellers. It's surrounded by bars so this is definitely one for party folk.

★**Mangrove Hideaway** GUESTHOUSE $$
(☑080 133 6600; www.themangrovehideaway.com; Ban Salak Phet; r 1900-2700B; ☒☜) 🌿 Facing the mangrove forest, this environmentally friendly guesthouse is a fabulous spot. Crisp, attractive rooms face the verdant front garden, while the sumptuous superior suites have gorgeous wooden floors and overlook the dining area and mangroved river estuary. There's an open-air jacuzzi and massage area upstairs; the resort was made using locally sourced wood and employs local villagers

★**Barrio Bonito** MEXICAN $$
(☑080 092 8208; www.barriobonito.com; Hat Kaibae; mains 160-280B; ☺5-10pm Jul-late May; ☜☑) Fab fajitas and cracking cocktails are served by a charming French-Mexican couple at this roadside spot in the middle of Kaibae. Offering authentic, delicious, beautifully presented food and stylish surroundings, this is one of the island's finest places to eat.

Baan Rim Nam GUESTHOUSE $$
(☑087 005 8575; www.iamkohchang.com; Khlong Prao; r 1000-1900B; ☒☜) This marvellously converted fishers house is right over the mangrove-lined river estuary and makes a supremely peaceful place to stay. Cool, appealing rooms open onto a wonderful waterside deck. The owner is a mine of information and keen that visitors enjoy what the region has to offer. Free kayaks and canoes are provided – the beach is a three-minute paddle away.

Bang Bao Beach Resort BUNGALOW $$
(☑093 327 2788; www.bangbaobeachresort.com; Hat Khlong Koi; r 1700-2500B) Very sprucely set along green lawn right on super Khlong Koi beach, just east of Bang Bao, this is a marvellous spot. Old and new bungalows are available; both are attractively wooden and air-conditioned. It's a very efficiently run place with easy access to beach bars and restaurants alongside. Walk along the beach from the canal bridge or drive the long way round.

🍴 Eating

Virtually all of the island's accommodation choices have attached restaurants with adequate but not outstanding fare.

★**Blues Blues Restaurant** THAI $
(☑087 144 6412; Ban Khlong Son; mains 80-170B; ☺9am-9pm) Through the green screen of

THAILAND KO CHANG

tropical plants is an arty stir-fry hut that is beloved for its expertise, efficiency and economy. The owner's delicate watercolour paintings are on display too. Take the road to Ban Kwan Chang; it's 600m ahead on the right.

Phu-Talay   SEAFOOD $$
(☑ 039 551300; 4/2 Mu 4, Khlong Prao; mains 120-320B; ☺ 10am-10pm) A beautiful place right on the *klorng*, Phu-Talay has cute wooden-floored, blue-and-white decor, a picturesque deck and its own boat (for pick-up up from nearby accommodations). It specialises in seafood, with standout softshell crab, prawns and other fish dishes. It's far more reasonably priced than many other seafood places.

Kung Kra Ta   BARBECUE $$
(☑ 091 738 7429; Hat Kaibae; all-you-can-eat 229B; ☺ 6-11pm) This open-air place packs in locals and tourists alike for its all-you-can-eat hotpot and grill offer. Help yourself to ingredients and get dunking and sizzling. The quality isn't sky-high but it's a fun way to enjoy a big feed without breaking the bank.

Chow Lay   SEAFOOD $$
(Ban Bang Bao; dishes 120-500B; ☺ 10am-midnight) 'If it swims, we have it' is its motto, and this restaurant in the middle of the pier does indeed have a huge seafood menu as well as great bay views. Let yourself be guided by whatever is fresh that day.

❶ Information

Ko Chang Hospital (☑ 039 586131; Ban Dan Mai) Public hospital with a good reputation

and affordably priced care; south of the ferry terminal.
Tourist Police Office (☑ 1155; Khlong Prao) Next to the temple in Khlong Prao. Also has smaller police boxes in Hat Sai Khao and Hat Kaibae.

❶ Getting There & Away

Be aware of the cheap minibus tickets from Siem Reap to Ko Chang; these usually involve some sort of time- and money-wasting commission scam.

Ferries (80B, 40min, frequent from 6am to 7pm) from the mainland leave from the piers collectively known as Laem Ngop, southwest of Trat . You'll arrive at either Tha Sapparot or Tha Centrepoint, depending on which pier you departed from. Tha Sapparot is closest to the west coast beaches.
Bang Bao Boat (☑ 084 567 8765; www. kohchangbangbaoboat.com; Ban Bang Bao; ☺ Nov-Apr) runs boats from Bang Bao in the southwest of the island to nearby islands.

There are two daily buses (269B, 6 hours) from Bangkok's Eastern Bus Terminal (Ekamai) to Laem Ngop. They travel via Chanthaburi and Trat. There are also direct bus and minivan services from Bangkok's Suvarnabhumi Airport.

The nearest airport is in Trat.

❶ Getting Around

Shared *sŏrng·tăa·ou* will shuttle you from the pier to the various beaches (100B to 200B).

Motorbikes can be hired from 200B per day. Ko Chang's hilly and winding roads are dangerous; make sure the bike is in good working order, drive slowly and wear a helmet.

---

❶ GETTING TO CAMBODIA
∙∙

Many travellers undertaking the Angkor pilgrimage take the direct bus from Bangkok through the Aranya Prathet/Poipet border. We do not recommend the tourist buses that leave from Th Khao San road.

Bangkok To Siem Reap

Getting to the border There is a daily bus (750B, seven hours, 9am) from Bangkok's Northern and Northeastern (Mo Chit) bus terminal to the Aranya Prathet/Poipet border.

At the border Thai immigration is open 7am to 8pm. Expect long queues at weekends, so get here early. Cambodian visas are available on arrival (US$30), but officials may overcharge. Ignore any touts or money-exchange services on both sides of the border; watch out for pickpockets.

Moving on If you're not on the direct bus, the best way to Siem Reap is by share taxi, departing from the main bus station in Poipet, 1km from the border. A motorcycle taxi here will cost around 2000r. Don't go to the international bus station, 9km east of town, where prices are double.

For information on making the crossing in reverse see p101.

SOUTHERN GULF COAST

Palm-fringed beaches, warm lazy days, jewel-toned seas: the southern gulf coast pours an intoxicating draught of paradise that attracts a steady crowd of sun worshippers. Most are bound for one or more of the islands in the Samui archipelago: resort-y Ko Samui, hippie Ko Pha-Ngan and dive-centric Ko Tao.

But you can also stop off at the mild-mannered provincial capitals for a glimpse at the rhythms of coastal Thailand. Further south, Thailand starts to merge with Malaysia: with the minarets of mosques peeping over the palm trees. The best time to visit Thailand's southern reaches is from February to June, when the rest of the country is practically melting from the angry sun.

Hua Hin
หัวหิน

032 / POPULATION 59,369

Thailand's original beach resort, Hua Hin is no tree-peppered castaway island. Instead, it's a refreshing mix of city and sea with an almost cosmopolitan ambience, lively markets, water parks, international cuisine and excellent accommodation.

Hua Hin traces its aristocratic roots to 1911 when the railroad arrived from Bangkok and members of the royal family built vacation homes here. There's a lot of money swirling around Hua Hin, but it's still a good budget destination: seafood is plentiful and cheap, there's convenient public transport and it's easy to get here from Bangkok.

Activities

★ Wildlife Friends Foundation Thailand Rescue Centre and Elephant Refuge
ANIMAL SANCTUARY

(มูลนิธิเพื่อนสัตว์ป่า; ☑ 032 458135; www.wfft. org; full-access tours incl lunch half-/full day 1100/1800B) The centre, 45km west of Hua Hin, cares for over 500 animals, including bears, tigers, gibbons, macaques, loris and birds. There's also an affiliated elephant rescue program where the elephants live out their lives chain-free. A visit here is a great day out – far better than the elephant and tiger tourist traps featured on many tours out of Hua Hin. The centre offers full-access tours introducing animals and discussing rescue histories. The full-day option includes walking and bathing elephants. Drop-in visits are not allowed.

Sleeping

Chanchala Hostel
HOSTEL $

(☑ 086 331 6763; www.chanchalahostelhuahin. com; 1/5 Th Sasong; dm incl breakfast 340B; ※ ⦿) This spick and span three-room dorm five minutes' walk from the train station does things right. Each bed in the six- and eight-bed rooms (one for women only) comes with its own locker, reading light and power outlet. Guests mingle with the friendly staff in the coffee shop and with each other at the rooftop lounge.

★ King's Home
GUESTHOUSE $$

(☑ 089 052 0490; www.huahinkingshome.blog-spot.com; off Th Phunsuk; r 750-950B; ※ ⦿ ⊠) Family-run guesthouse with great prices and loads of character – you're greeted at the front door by a crystal chandelier and a statue of a German Shepherd wearing a floral lei on its head. The rest of the house, including the six small guest rooms, are also crammed with antiques and kitsch providing a real homely atmosphere.

Lemon House 51
HOTEL $$

(lemonhouse51@gmail.com; Th Damrongraj (Soi 51); r 800-1200B; ※ ⦿) Making no effort to be stylish or trendy, the Lemon just delivers good value. Rooms are large, clean and quiet and the Thai-French couple running it is eager to please. Plus, it's on a really good eating street.

Hua Hin Place
GUESTHOUSE $$

(☑ 032 516640; www.huahin-place.com; 43/21 Th Naebkehardt; d & tw 400-1500 f 1200-1500B; ※ ⦿) Straddling a fine line between hotel and guesthouse, this fairly large place still falls into the latter thanks to the breezy ground-floor lounge – full of a museum's worth of shells, photos and other knick-knacks – where you can chat with the charming owner and other guests.

Tong-Mee House
GUESTHOUSE $$

(☑ 081 274 5676; tongmeehuahin@hotmail.com; 1 Soi Raumpow, Th Naebkehardt; r 700-1000B; ※ @ ⦿) Down a quiet residential soi, this long-running guesthouse has no character, just decent clean rooms with balconies – the 1000B versions are on the top floor and have a view. Book ahead.

Mod Guesthouse
HOTEL $$

(☑ 032 512296; www.modguesthouse.com; Th Naresdamri; r with fan & cold-water bath/air-con 600-700/900-1500B; ※ @ ⦿) This hotel has tiny noisy rooms with minimal decor and noticeable aging, but it's usually full throughout the high season. Of the half-dozen pier guesthouses (all of which suffer the same faults), this two-storey wooden behemoth sticking out into the ocean has the most historic charm, and has fairly decent beds.

✗ Eating

★ Jek Pia
THAI $

(51/6 Th Dechanuchit; mains 35-150B; ⊙6.30am-12.30pm & 5.30-8pm) Once just a coffee shop, this 50-plus-year-old restaurant is one of Hua Hin's top culinary destinations. The late mother of the current owner invited her favourite cooks to come join her and it's now a gourmet food court of sorts, hence the stack of menus you get when you arrive.

Sôm·dam Tanontok 51
THAI $

(Th Damrongraj/Soi 51; mains 40-190B; ⊙10am-8pm; 🔊) A stand-out restaurant in a great dining neighbourhood, this is real Isan food cooked by a family from Khorat. There's everything you'd expect to find including grilled catfish, *gaang orm* (coconut-milk-less herbal curry) and many versions of *sôm·dam* other than papaya, including cucumber and bamboo shoot. It also does a squid *lâhp*.

Baan Khrai Wang
THAI, COFFEE $

(Th Naebkehardt; mains 65-285B; ⊙9am-6pm) The palm trees, flower garden, historic wooden beach homes and the sound of the surf make the setting at 'The House Near the Palace' pretty much perfect. For many, it's a place to lounge with coffee and coconut cake, but there's also a small menu of massaman curry, crab fried rice, *kôw châe* (moist chilled rice) and Caesar salad wrap.

★ Koti
CHINESE, THAI $$

(☑032 511252; 16/1 Th Dechanuchit; mains 40-400B; ⊙11am-10pm) This Thai-Chinese restaurant, opened in 1932, is a national culinary luminary. Thais adore the stir-fried oyster with flour and egg, while foreigners frequently aim for the *đôm yam gûng*. Everyone loves the *yam tá-lair* (spicy seafood salad) and classic green curry. Be prepared to wait for a table.

ℹ Information

San Paolo Hospital (☑032 532576; www.sanpaulo.co.th; 222 Th Phetkasem, South Hua Hin) A small private hospital south of town at Soi 86; it's a good option for ordinary illnesses and injuries.

Tourism Authority of Thailand (TAT; ☑032 513854; www.tourismthailand.org/hua-hin; 39/4 Th Phetkasem, at Soi 55; ⊙8.30am-4.30pm) Staff here speak English and are quite helpful, though they rarely open on time.

Tourist Police (☑032 516219; Th Damnoen Kasem) At the eastern end of the street just before the beach.

Tuk Tours (☑032 514281, mobile 080 544 2465; www.tuktours.net; 2/1 Th Chomsin; ⊙9.30am-6pm) Helpful, no-pressure place that can book activities and transport all around Thailand.

ℹ Getting There

Minivans going north (including Kanchanaburi and Bangkok) use the new **Hua Hin Van Station** (Soi 51) while minivans going south stop in the road next to the clock tower. Ordinary buses north leave from Th Phetkasem opposite the Esso petrol station.

Go to **Hua Hin Bus Station** (Th Phetkasem, at Soi 96, South Hua Hin) for long-distance buses to destinations north and south. **Hua Hin-Pran Tour** (☑032 511654; Th Sasong) on Th Sasong near the night market has buses to Bangkok's Southern Bus Terminal.

Lomprayah (☑032 532761; www.lomprayah. com; Th Phetkasem; ⊙8am-10pm) offers bus-boat combinations to Ko Tao (1050B, six to nine hours), Ko Pha-Ngan (1300B, nine to 12 hours) and Ko Samui (1400B, 10 to 13 hours).

Hua Hin's dinky and historic **train station** (☑032 511073; Th Liap Thang Rot Fai) has 12 daily departures to Bangkok (44B to 402B, 4½ hours), as well as trains south to Chumphon, Hat Yai and Prachuap Khiri Khan.

ℹ Getting Around

Green *sŏrng·tăa·ou* (10B) depart from the corner of Th Sasong & Th Dechanuchit, by the night market. They travel from 6am to 9pm along Th Phetkasem south to Khao Takiab.

Túk-túk fares in Hua Hin are outrageous (starting at 100B). Motorcycle taxis are much more reasonable (30B to 50B) for short hops.

Motorcycles (200B to 250B per day) and bicycles (100B to 200B per day) can be rented all over town.

Prachuap Khiri Khan
ประจวบคีรีขันธ์

☑032 / POPULATION 33,500

A sleepy seaside town, Prachuap Khiri Khan is a delightfully relaxed place. The broad bay is a tropical turquoise punctuated by bobbing fishing boats and overlooked by honeycombed limestone mountains – scenery that you usually have to travel to the southern Andaman to find.

In recent years foreigners have discovered Prachuap's charms. But their numbers are still very small, leaving plenty of room on the beaches, at the hilltop temples and in the many excellent seafood restaurants.

🛏 Sleeping & Eating

Safehouse Hostel   HOSTEL $

(☑ 087 909 4770; 28 Soi 6, Th Salacheep; dm 250, r 450-650B; ❄ 🛜) Safehouse has fairly frumpy though very tidy rooms: the host Sherry is the real reason this small hostel has become popular. She goes out of her way to please guests and leads good tours to **Kuiburi National Park** (อุทยานแห่งชาติกุยบุรี; ☑ 085 266 1601; Rte 4024; adult/child 200/100B, wildlife-spotting trip per truck 850B; ⊙ wildlife trips 2-6pm) and elsewhere. There's a communal kitchen.

★ Prachuap Beach Hotel   HOTEL $$

(☑ 032 601288; www.prachuapbeach.com; 123 Th Suseuk; d & tw 800-900, tr 1200B; ❄ 🛜) The best located, and possibly quietest, hotel in the city is near lots of good restaurants, opens up to the promenade and has great views from upper floors. The 2nd-floor rooms are cheapest, but it's worth paying the extra 100B to be up higher – the 5th floor is the top. The rooms are old-fashioned, though very good for the price.

Krua Chaiwat   THAI $

(Th Salacheep; mains 40-160B; ⊙ 9am-3pm & 4.30-8pm Mon-Sat; 🛜 🍴) With good food at low prices, this small restaurant serves a mix of locals and expats. While Thai food is its strength – the *dôm yam* and *mêe·ang kam* (an assemble-it-yourself snack with wild pepper leaves) are quite good – there are also steaks and a few fusion foods like the stir-fried spaghetti with salted mackerel.

★ In Town Seafood   THAI $$

(Th Chai Thaleh; mains 50-350B; ⊙ 3-11pm) A go-to place for discerning locals, here you can eat streetside under a utilitarian tent while gazing at the squid boats in the bay. Great range of fresh seafood on display – barracuda, crab and shellfish – so you can point and pick if you don't recognise the names on the menu. Service can be slow.

ℹ Getting There & Around

Minivans form the backbone of Prachuap transport and they all depart from **kew rót dôo** (Th Prachuap Khiri Khan/Rte 326) minivan station at the junction of Rte 326 and Hwy 4 near the main bus stop.

There are four daily buses to Bangkok's Southern Bus Terminal (200B) from Th Pihitak Chat. Pick up buses to other destinations at a **bus stop** (sà·tǎh·nee dern rót; Phetkasem Hwy) on Th Phetkasem, 4km northwest of the city centre. Tickets are sold on the northbound side of the road; buy your ticket the day before.

The **train station** (☑ 032 611175; Th Maharat) is in town on Th Maharat. There are nine daily departures to Bangkok (168B to 455B, 5½ hours), as well as daily trains to destinations south.

Most hotels have motorcycle hire for 200B to 250B per day. A few also do bicycles for 50B. Motorcycle taxis hop around town for 30B to 50B.

Chumphon   ชุมพร

☑ 077 / POPULATION 33,500

A transit town funnelling travellers to and from Ko Tao or southwards to Ranong or Phuket, Chumphon is where the south of Thailand starts proper; Muslim headscarves are a common sight here.

The surrounding beaches are alternative sun-and-sand stops far off the backpacker bandwagon. Beautiful **Hat Thung Wua Laen**, 15km northeast of town, is the best known and during the week you'll have it mostly to yourself.

🛏 Sleeping & Eating

★ Salsa Hostel   HOSTEL $

(☑ 077 505005; www.salsachumphon.com; 25/42 Th Krumluang Chumphon; incl breakfast dm 300-330, tw/d 650/750B; ❄ @ 🛜) East of the train station near the night market, this is one of the best addresses in Chumphon. It's clean, friendly, not too big and a reliable source of local info in excellent English. The private rooms are some of the best in town, regardless of the price.

Kook Noy Kitchen   THAI $

(Th Suksamur; mains 40-180B; ⊙ 4pm-4am Mon-Sat; 🛜) Just a concrete floor, a corrugated roof and a chaotic kitchen turning out central and southern Thai dishes you know like *dôm yam* with free-range chicken and crab fried rice, plus many you probably don't, including fried duck beak and *pàt pèt gòp* (curry fried frog).

ℹ Getting There & Away

AIR

Chumphon's airport has two daily flights to Bangkok's Don Mueang Airport with Nok Air (from 1200B, 1hr).

CHUMPHON TRANSPORT CONNECTIONS

DESTINATION	BOAT	BUS	MINIVAN	TRAIN
Bangkok Hualamphong				seat 192-510B, sleeper 620-1194B, 6½-8hr, 11 daily
Bangkok Southern Bus Terminal		155-510B, 8hr, 11 daily 9am-10pm		
Hat Yai		328-355B, 7hr, 8 daily 7am-midnight		79-502B, 8-10½hr, 7 daily
Hua Hin				49-423B, 4-5hr, 12 daily
Ko Pha-Ngan (Lomprayah)	1000B, 3¼-3¾hr, 7am, 1pm			
Ko Pha-Ngan (Songserm)	900B, 4½hr, 7am			
Ko Samui (Lomprayah)	1100B, 3¾-4¼hr, 7am, 1pm			
Ko Samui (Songserm)	1000B, 6¼hr, 7am			
Ko Tao (car ferry)	400B, 6hr, 11pm Mon-Sat			
Ko Tao (Lomprayah)	600B, 1¾hr, 7am, 1pm			
Ko Tao (Songserm)	500B, 2¾hr, 7am			
Ko Tao (Sunday night boat)	450B, 6hr, midnight Sun			
Phuket		350-600B, 6-7hr, 7 daily 5am-2.30pm		
Prachuap Khiri Khan		220B, 4hr, hourly 7am-10pm	180B, 3½hr, every 50min 5.30am-6pm	16-347B, 2½-3hr, 10 daily
Ranong		120B, 2½hr, 4 daily	120B, 2½hr, hourly 6am-5pm	
Surat Thani			170B, 3½hr, hourly, 6am-5.30pm	34-388B, 2-3hr, 12 daily

BOAT

Lomprayah (☎City 081 956 5644, Pier 077 558214; www.lomprayah.com; Th Krumluang Chumphon; ⊙4.30am-6pm) and **Songserm** (☎077 506205; www.songserm.com) have modern ferries sailing during the day to Ko Tao and onto Ko Pha-Ngan and Ko Samui. Lomprayah is the best and most popular. Songserm has a poor reputation. There are also nightly car ferries. Boats leave from different piers and transfer costs 50B to 100B. If you have a combination ticket, make sure you have a ticket for both the bus and boat.

BUS

Chumphon's main **bus station** (☎077 576 796; Rte 41) is an inconvenient 12km out of town. There are many in-town bus stops offering buses to Bangkok and Phuket, including **Choke Anan Tour** (☎077 511480; off Soi 1, Th Pracha Uthit) and **Suwannatee Tour** (☎077 504901; Th Nawamin Ruamjai).

Minivans to Surat Thani and Prachuap Khiri Khan leave from the night bazaar, close to the Salsa Hostel. Minivans to Ranong leave from Tha Taphao.

TRAIN

There are frequent trains to Bangkok and the far south. The train station is near the centre of town.

Ko Samui   เกาะสมุย

POPULATION 62,000

Whether you're sun-seeking, dozing in a hammock, feasting on world-class cuisine, beach partying or discovering wellness in an exclusive spa, Ko Samui has it covered.

One of the original backpacker hang-outs in Thailand, Samui is now an all-purpose resort island, popular with everyone from honeymooners to package tourists and where everything you might want is in easy reach. Peak season especially can be a bit of a carnival. But Samui is a large island, and on the northern beaches and quieter west coast you can still find the laid-back vibe of old. Ko Samui is also home to a thriving local community, whose life you can easily experience by eating at roadside shacks or exploring morning markets.

🏃 Activities

What can't you do on Samui? While the **diving** is more expensive than on neighbouring Ko Tao, there are plenty of operators who'll take you underwater or on **snorkelling trips**. **Spas** are everywhere, there are many **cooking schools**, you can **hike**, **bike** and **zipline** through the interior to waterfalls and splendid viewpoints, or you can satisfy your martial urges at a **Muay Thai** boxing camp. Alternatively, just lie on the beach or by the pool with a cocktail to hand.

🛏 Sleeping

🛏 Chaweng

Samui Hostel   HOSTEL $
(📞 089 874 3737; Chaweng Beach Rd; dm 200-300B; d 850B; ❄@) It doesn't look like much from the front, but this neat, tidy, friendly and popular place is very central, with clean fan and air-con dorm rooms and spruce air-con doubles on the non-beach side of the road. Service is a cut above the rest and there's a popular room at the front with wooden tables for lounging and chatting.

Pott Guesthouse   GUESTHOUSE $
(Chaweng Beach Rd; r with fan/air-con from 300/600B; ❄🛜) The big, bright cement rooms all with attached hot-water bathrooms and balcony in this nondescript apartment block are a steal, but that's about it. Reception is at an unnamed restaurant on the main drag right opposite, across the alley.

P Chaweng   HOTEL $
(📞 077 230684; Chaweng Beach Rd; r from 600B; ❄@🛜) At the end of a road off the main drag, this vine-covered cheapie has clean, pink-tiled rooms and wood-floored family rooms (1000B) in two blocks, all decked out with air-con, hot water, TVs and fridges. It's a 10-minute walk to the bar zone and not particularly hip, but good luck finding a better room in the area for this price.

🛏 Lamai

New Hut   BUNGALOW $
(📞 077 230437; Lamai North; huts 250-800B; 🛜) A-frame huts right on the beach all share a big, clean block of bathrooms, with a lively restaurant and friendly enough staff. With one of the simplest and happiest backpacker vibes around, it's pretty much the best value in Lamai.

WHICH KO SAMUI BEACH?

Samui is just about small enough to beach-hop, but deciding which beach to stay at, or near, is all about whether you're looking for crowds or a more tranquil life. **Chaweng** and **Lamai** are the longest and most renowned spots, which means many more people but also tons of restaurants and bars to choose from. If you want to party, head here.

Mae Nam is the best swimming beach on the north coast and along with **Bang Po**, just around the tiny peninsula, retains a reasonably chilled-out vibe, but also has all the traveller facilities you'll need. **Ao Thong Sai** in the northeastern corner of Samui is also lovely.

The less-visited west coast has pleasant beaches at **Taling Ngam** and **Lipa Noi**. For a total escape, head down to **Ao Phang Ka** in the southwest where there is little in the way of tourist infrastructure.

THAILAND KO SAMUI

Ko Samui

Ko Samui

THAILAND KO SAMUI

Amarina Residence HOTEL $$
(📞 077 418073; www.amarinaresidence.com; La-
mai; r 1200-1800B; ❄🔊) A two-minute walk
to the beach, this excellent-value small hotel
has two storeys of big, tastefully furnished,
tiled rooms encircling the lobby and an in-
congruous dipping pool.

Spa Resort BUNGALOW $$
(📞 077 230855; www.thesparesorts.com; Lamai
North; bungalows 720-1200B; ❄🔊🏊) Programs at this friendly, practical and simple
spa include colonics, massage, aqua detox,
hypnotherapy and yoga, just to name a few.
With rattan furniture, traditional wall art

and balconies, rooms are comfortable and excellent value, but book up quickly. Non-guests are welcome to partake in the spa programs and dine at the excellent (and healthy) open-air **restaurant** (off Rte 4169; meals 100-400B; ☺7am-10pm; ☎⚹) by the beach.

Northern Beaches

Shangri-la   BUNGALOW **$**
(☎077 425189; Mae Nam; bungalows with fan/air-con from 500/1300B; ❄☎) A backpacker's Shangri La indeed – these are some of the cheapest huts around and they occupy a sublime stretch of the beach. Grounds are sparsely landscaped but the basic concrete bungalows, all with attached bathrooms (only air-con rooms have hot water), are well kept and the staff are pleasant.

Castaway Guesthouse   GUESTHOUSE **$$**
(☎081 968 5811; www.castawaysamui.com; Fisherman's Village; r with fan/air-con 650-1500B; ❄☎) A block away from the beach, Castaway has 15 rooms that are all clean, bright and cheery.

Eating & Drinking

Chaweng

Laem Din Market   MARKET **$**
(Chaweng; dishes from 35B; ☺4am-6pm, night market 6pm-2am) A busy day market, Laem Din is packed with stalls that sell fresh fruits, vegetables and meats and stock local Thai kitchens. Pick up a kilo of sweet green oranges or wander the stalls trying to spot the ingredients in last night's curry. For dinner, check out the adjacent night market to sample tasty southern-style fried chicken and curries.

Tuk Tuk Backpackers   CAFE **$**
(☎087 268 2575; Chaweng Beach Rd; mains from 120B; ☺10am-2am) This full-on, no-holds-barred, high-impact, brazen and voluminous saloon-style Western cafe/restaurant/bar on Chaweng Beach Rd does good hangover-cure brekkies, with multiple TV screens, pool tables and all the usual trappings.

★Stacked   STEAK **$$**
(www.stacked-samui.com; Chaweng Beach Rd; mains from 295B; ☺noon-midnight; ☎) All sharp lines, open kitchen/grill, a team of busy and super-efficient staff plus a cracker of a menu,

ANG THONG MARINE NATIONAL PARK

The 40-some jagged jungle islands of **Ang Thong Marine National Park** (adult/child 300/150B) stretch across the cerulean sea like a shattered emerald necklace – each piece a virgin realm featuring sheer limestone cliffs, hidden lagoons and perfect peach-coloured sands. These dream-inducing islets inspired Alex Garland's 1996 novel *The Beach*.

The best way to reach the park is on a day tour from Ko Samui. **Blue Stars** (☎077 300615; www.bluestars.info; tours adult/child 2500/1600B) has a deserved reputation for leading excellent excursions here. The park entrance fee (300B) should be included in the price of any tour you take.

February, March and April are the best months to visit this ethereal preserve of greens and blues; crashing monsoon waves mean that the park is almost always closed during November and December.

this awesome burger restaurant remains a visual and culinary feast. Burgers and steaks – bursting with flavour – are served up on slate slabs in generous portions. Go with a sizeable hunger as the inclination is to simply keep on ordering.

Ark Bar   BAR
(www.ark-bar.com; Hat Chaweng; ☺7am-1am) Drinks are dispensed from the multi-coloured bar to an effusive crowd, guests recline on loungers on the beach, and the party is on day and night, with fire shows lighting up the sands after sundown and DJs providing house music from the afternoon onwards.

Reggae Pub   BAR
(Laem Din Rd; ☺6pm-3am) This fortress of fun sports an open-air dance floor with music spun by foreign DJs. It's a towering two-storey affair with long bars, pool tables and a live-music stage. The whole place doubles as a shrine to Bob Marley; it's often empty early in the evening, getting going around midnight. The long road up to Reggae Pub is ladyboy central.

SPLURGE

Ko Samui is as good a place as anywhere in Thailand to bust your budget for a few days. If you're in the mood for a taste of the luxe life, try the following places. And remember, prices drop outside the high-season months of December to February.

Library (☑ 077 422767; www.thelibrary.co.th; Chaweng Beach Rd; studio/ste incl breakfast from 11,900/13,600B; ❀@☎☀) This library is too cool for school. The entire resort is a sparkling white mirage accented with black trimming and slatted curtains. Besides the futuristic iMac computer in each page (rooms are 'pages' here), our favourite feature is the large monochromatic wall art – it glows brightly in the evening and you can adjust the colour to your mood.

Code (☑ 077 602122; www.samuicode.com; Mae Nam; ste 3300-11,100B; ❀☎☀) Sleek modern lines and dust-free white contrast against the turquoise sea and the hotel's large infinity pool, making for a stunning piece of architecture. The all-ocean-view suites are spacious and efficient, and the service is just as neat. Of course, everything you require is there at your fingertips, including a gym, spa, steam room, tennis court and restaurant.

Rocky's Resort (☑ 077 418367; www.rockyresort.com; off Rte 4169; r 8000-20,000B; ❀☎☀) With a supremely calm reception area and two swimming pools, Rocky effortlessly finds the right balance between an upmarket ambience and an unpretentious, sociable vibe. During quieter months prices are a steal, since ocean views abound, and each room (some with pool) has been furnished with beautiful Thai-inspired furniture that seamlessly incorporates a modern twist.

🍴 Lamai

Pad Thai   THAI $
(☑ 077 458560-4; www.manathai.com/samui/phad-thai; Rte 4169; mains from 70B; ☺11am-9.30pm) On the corner of the huge Manathai hotel by the road, this highly affordable, semi-alfresco and smart restaurant is a fantastic choice for stir-fried and soup noodles, rounded off with a coconut ice cream.

★ Baobab   FRENCH $$
(☑ 084 838 3040; Hat Lamai; mains 150-380B; ☺8am-6pm) Grab a free beach towel and crash out on a sun lounger after a full meal at breezy Baobab, or have a massage next door, but seize one of the beach tables (if you can). You'll need two hands to turn over the hefty menu, with its all-day breakfasts, French/Thai dishes, grills, pastas and popular specials, including red tuna steak (350B).

Black Pearl   THAI $$
(Hat Lamai; mains 140-450B; ☺8am-10.30pm; ☎) This decent restaurant has a gorgeous perspective on the sea, from a lovely stretch of Lamai sand peppered with boulders. It's lovely throughout the day, but twilight and evening with cocktails and the lapping of the surf is a very pleasant time to arrive.

Bear Cocktails   BAR
(Lamai Beach Rd; ☺5pm-2am) It's not a traditional bar, but a fun, open-air cocktail stall on the road run by some friendly girls (Bear and Lek); buy a strawberry daiquiri, grab a plastic seat and chat to whoever's at hand. It's not far from the McDonald's; cocktails are 79B.

🍴 Northern Beaches

Fish Restaurant   INTERNATIONAL $
(☑ 087 472 4097; Rte 4169, Mae Nam; mains from 50B; ☺11am-11pm) With elegant Thai tablecloths and a well-priced, tasty menu of Thai seafood and pan-Asian dishes and international appetisers, this popular wood-floored eatery pulls in a regular stream of diners for its charming setting, winning spring rolls, gorgeous seafood curries, steamed sea bass and much more.

★ Pepenero   ITALIAN $$
(☑ 077 963353; www.pepenerosamui.com; Mae Nam; mains from 250B; ☺6-10pm Mon-Sat) Pepenero continues to cause a stir on Ko Samui, moving to this more accessible Mae Nam location. What this excellent and neatly designed Italian restaurant lacks in views is more than made up for by a terrific menu (including cutting boards with cheese and cold cuts) and the care and attention dis-

played to customers by the very sociable, hard-working hosts. Put this one in your planner.

69

(☑081 978 1945; Route 4169, near Fisherman's Village; mains from 150B; ☺1-10pm; ☏) The simply roaring roadside setting puts it on the wrong side of the tracks, and the dated, eclectic decor is limp and tired; that said, almost unanimous rave reviews for its creative twists on Thai favourites make this a really popular choice, though not all dishes dazzle.

ℹ Information

The road accident fatality rate on Ko Samui is high. The combination of inexperienced tourist drivers, winding roads, sudden tropical rains, frenzied traffic and sand on the roads can be lethal. If you've never driven a motorcycle before, Samui is not the place to learn.

Watch out for strong riptides at Chaweng and Lamai between December and April.

Bangkok Hospital Samui (☑077 429500, emergency 077 429555; www.bangkokhospitalsamui.com) Your best bet for just about any medical problem.

Immigration Office (☑077 423440; Soi 1 Mu 1, Mae Nam; ☺8.30am-4.30pm Mon-Fri) Offers seven-day tourist visa extensions. Located south of the 4169 in Mae Nam.

Main Post Office (Na Thon) Near the TAT office; not always reliable.

Tourist Police (☑077 421281, emergency 1155) Based south of Na Thon.

ℹ Getting There & Away

AIR

Ko Samui's **airport** (www.samuiairportonline.com) is in the north-east of the island near Big Buddha Beach.

Bangkok Airways (www.bangkokair.com) operates flights roughly every 30 minutes between Samui and Bangkok's Suvarnabhumi International Airport (65 minutes). There are also flights to Chiang Mai, Singapore, Kuala Lumpur, Hong Kong and other destinations in Thailand, Southeast Asia and China.

If the Samui flights are full, try flying into Surat Thani on the mainland and catching the ferry from there to Samui.

BOAT

Between Samui and the mainland there are frequent boat services, including the high-speed **Lomprayah** (p762; 400B) and the slower, stinkier **Raja** (☑022 768211-2, 092 274 3423-5; www.rajaferryport.com; adult 130B) car ferry (130B). Ferries take one to five hours, depending on the

boat. There is also a slow night boat to Samui (300B, six hours, 11pm) from Surat Thani. It returns at 9pm, arriving at around 3am. Watch your bags on this boat.

There are combination ticket options that arrange transport all the way to Bangkok either by bus or by train. Lomprayah has the best bus-boat combination. Phun Phin is the closest train station to the mainland pier in Surat Thani.

Boats to Ko Pha-Ngan (200B to 300B, 20 minutes to one hour, frequent) and Ko Tao depart from various piers across Samui. When booking tickets, tell the agent where you're staying on Samui and where you'll be staying on Ko Pha-Ngan to reduce transit time to the various piers.

The Haad Rin Queen is a handy service during Full Moon Parties; it travels from Big Buddha Beach (Ko Samui) to Hat Rin (Ko Pha-Ngan, 200B, 50 minutes) four times daily, with extra boats after the Full Moon Party. The last boat leaves at 6.30pm.

ℹ Getting Around

You can rent motorcycles (150B to 200B) from almost every resort on the island. *Sŏrng·tăa·ou* (50B to 100B) run a loop between the popular beaches during daylight hours. Taxis typically charge around 500B for an airport transfer.

Ko Pha-Ngan เกาะพะงัน

POPULATION 12,500

There's far more to Ko Pha-Ngan than the Full Moon Parties that have made it famous. When the moon isn't round, and even during the smaller but still-raucous half-moon party periods, the island's charms – turquoise waters and spectacular beaches, backed by a mountainous, jungly interior – are brought to the fore. It's also easier to get a room, prices are more reasonable and life is far more serene.

⊙ Sights & Activities

Ko Pha-Ngan is fringed with some delightful beaches. Try the isolated beaches on the east coast, which include **Hat Yuan**, **Hat Thian** and teeny-tiny **Hat Thong Reng**. The west-coast beaches, **Hat Yao**, **Hat Salad** and **Ao Mae Hat**, are the place for sunset views. Inland are many waterfalls to discover and there are some exhilarating trekking opportunities.

Ko Ma is the best snorkelling spot and there's the chance to dive **Sail Rock**, the finest dive site in the Gulf of Thailand. Two-dive trips cost 2500B to 2800B.

Ko Pha-Ngan

THAILAND KO PHA-NGAN

Ko Pha-Ngan

⊙ Sights
1 Hat Khom	B1
2 Hat Leela	D4
3 Than Prawet Waterfall	C2
4 Wat Paa Sang Tham	B2

🛏 Sleeping
5 Bamboo Hut	D4
6 Boom's Cafe Bungalows	C4
7 Chills Resort	A2
8 Coco Garden	B3

9 Cookies Salad	A1
10 Fantasea	B1
11 Hacienda Resort	B3
12 Longtail Beach Resort	C2
13 Smile Bungalows	C1

✕ Eating
14 Crave	A2
15 Fisherman's Restaurant	B3
16 Food Market	B3
17 Nira's	B3

Chaloklum Diving DIVING
(☏ 077 374025; www.chaloklum-diving.com; from
1000B; ☺ 6am-8pm) One of the longer-estab-
lished dive shops on the island, these guys
(on the main drag in Ban Chalok Lam) have
quality equipment and provide high standards in all they do, whether scuba-diving,
free-diving, night diving or snorkelling trips.

Haad Yao Divers DIVING
(☏ 086 279 3085; www.haadyaodivers.com; from
1400B) Established in 1997, this dive operator has garnered a strong reputation by
maintaining European standards of safety
and customer service. Prices start at 1400B
for a beach dive at Hat Yao, but there's a
huge selection of courses and options.

🛌 Sleeping

🛏 Hat Rin

During Full Moon festivities, Hat Rin bungalow operators expect you to stay for a minimum of five nights. Booking ahead is obligatory. Room rates rocket too.

Same Same   GUESTHOUSE $
(Map p754; ☑ 077 375200; www.same-same.com; Ban Hat Rin; dm 400B, r 650B; ❄ 🗟) Run by two Danish girls (Christina and Heidi), this sociable spot offers simple but bright rooms and plenty of party preparation fun for the Full Moon beach shenanigans. It's very lethargic outside lunar-lunacy periods, but that's a good time to pitch up. The restaurant and bar is a solid choice.

Seaview Sunrise   BUNGALOW $
(Map p754; ☑ 077 375160; www.seaviewsunrise. com; Hat Rin Nok; r 500-1400B; ❄ 🗟) Budget Full Moon revellers who want to sleep inches from the tide should apply here (but note the minimum five-day policy during the lunar lunacy). Some of the options back in the jungle are sombre and musty, but the solid beachfront models have bright, polished wooden interiors facing onto a line of coconut trees and the sea.

Jungle Gym & Ecolodge   RESORT $
(Map p754; ☑ 077 375115; www.junglegymandecolodge.com; Hat Rin; dm/d 400/1500B; ❄ 🗟 ➿) Now that the old Jungle Gym has been converted to a five-a-side football pitch, this new place – just around the corner from the old one – combines health, a gym, *moo·ay tai* (Thai boxing) with a big pool and a fine bar (Palms Cafe). There's clean four-bed dorms with outside terrace and garden-view doubles, plus lots of outdoor space, too.

Tommy Resort   RESORT $$
(Map p754; ☑ 077 375215; www.tommyresort.com; Hat Rin Nok; r incl breakfast 2200-8500B; ❄ 🗟 ➿) This trendy address at the heart of Hat Rin strikes a balance between chic boutique and carefree flashpacker hang-out, with standard rooms, bungalows and pool villas. Wander down to a lovely strip of white sand, past flowering trees, to a resort with an azure slab of a pool at the heart of things and helpful, obliging staff. Rooms come with air-con, fridge and safe.

🏖 Southern Beaches

The southern beaches don't have the post-card-worthy turquoise waters you might be longing for, but they are close to Hat Rin.

★Coco Garden   BUNGALOW $
(Map p752; ☑ 077 377721, 086 073 1147; www.cocogardens.com; Thong Sala; bungalows 450-1100B; ❄ 🗟) 🌿 One of the best budget hang-outs along the southern coast and superpopular with the backpacker set, fantastic Coco Garden one-ups the nearby resorts with well-manicured grounds and 25 neat bungalows plus a funtastic beach bar, where hammocks await and a beachfront restaurant supplies breakfast, lunch and dinner with views.

Boom's Cafe Bungalows   BUNGALOW $
(Map p752; ☑ 081 979 3814; www.boomscafe. com; Ban Khai; bungalows 600-1000B; ❄) Staying at Boom's is like visiting the Thai family you never knew you had. Superfriendly and helpful owner Nok takes care of all her guests and keeps things looking good. No one seems to mind that there's no swimming pool, since the curling tide rolls right up to your doorstep. At the far eastern corner of Ban Khai, near Hat Rin.

★Divine Comedie   RESORT $$$
(☑ 077 377869, 080 885 8789; www.divinecomedyhotel.com; Ban Tai; r 2700-4300B, ste 4500-5600B; ❄ 🗟 ➿) A stunning mix of 1920s Chinese and perhaps Mexican hacienda architecture with a colour palette that shifts from mint to ochre, this 15-room (10 bungalows and five bedrooms) boutique oasis not only works, it's beguiling. Junior suites have rooftop terraces, while standard rooms have modest balconies, and the elongated infinity pool runs to the slim beach. No kids under 12.

🏖 West Coast Beaches

The west coast atmosphere is a pleasant mix between the east coast's quiet seclusion and Hat Rin's sociable vibe.

Shiralea   BUNGALOW $
(☑ 080 719 9256; www.shiralea.com; Hat Yao; dm 275B, bungalows 645-1400B; ❄ 🗟 ➿) The fresh-faced poolside bungalows are simple but the air-con dorms are great, and the ambience, with an on-site bar with draught beer, is fun and convivial. It's about 100m away from the

Hat Rin

⊙ 0 ————— 200 m
0 ————— 0.1 miles

Hat Rin

🛏 **Sleeping**
1 Jungle Gym & Ecolodge A2
2 Same Same... B2
3 Seaview Sunrise B1
4 Tommy Resort.. B1

🍴 **Eating**
5 Lazy House.. A2

🍸 **Drinking & Nightlife**
6 Mellow Mountain B1
7 Rock B2
8 Sunrise.. B1

beach and it fills up every few weeks with Contiki student tour groups.

Hacienda Resort   BUNGALOW $
(Map p752; ☎ 077 238825; www.beachresortha-cienda.com; Thong Sala; dm 300B, r 500-1500B; ❄🖥🏊) With good-looking blue-and-white painted bungalows, rooms in two-storey blocks further down and beachfront air-con dorms, the Hacienda is a spruce and efficient outfit, although the poolside bar can get noisy at night. There's a Phangan International Diving School office and an open-air gym.

Chills Resort   RESORT $$
(Map p752; ☎ 089 875 2100; www.chillsresort.ho-tel.phanganbungalows.com; Ao Sri Thanu; r 1000-2300B; ❄🖥🏊) Set along a stunning and secluded stretch of stony outcrops north of Ao Hin Kong, Chills' cluster of delightfully simple but modern rooms all have peaceful ocean views letting in plenty of sunlight, sea breezes and gorgeous sunset views.

🏖 Northern Beaches

The dramatic northern coast is a wild jungle with several stunning and secluded beaches – it's the most scenic coast on the island.

Smile Bungalows   BUNGALOW $
(Map p752; ☎ 085 429 4995; www.smilebungalows.com; Hat Khuat; bungalows 520-920B; ⊙ closed Nov) For real remoteness and seclusion, it's hard to beat this place at the far western corner of Bottle Beach. Family-run Smile features an assortment of all-fan wooden huts climbing up a forested hill: the two-storey bungalows (920B) are our favourite.

Longtail Beach Resort   BUNGALOW $
(Map p752; ☎ 077 445018; www.longtailbeachre-sort.com; Thong Nai Pan; bungalows with fan/air-con from 690/990B; ❄🖥) Tucked away by the forest at the lovely southern end of Thong Nai Pan – and a long way from Full Moon Ko Pha-Ngan madness – Longtail offers backpackers charming thatch-and-bamboo abodes that wind up a lush garden path. There's plenty of choice, too, for larger groups and families. The sand is fantastic and the lush, green setting is adorable.

Fantasea   BUNGALOW $
(Map p752; ☎ 089 443 0785; www.fantasea-re-sort-phangan.info; Chalok Lam; bungalows with fan/air-con from 600/1200B; 🖥) This friendly place far from the Full Moon mayhem on the other side of the island is one of the better of a string of family-run bungalow operations along the quiet eastern part of Chalok Lam. There's a thin beach out front, OK swimming and an elevated Thai-style restaurant area to chill out in.

Cookies Salad   RESORT $$$
(Map p752; ☎ 083 181 7125, 077 349125; www.cookies-phangan.com; Hat Salad; bungalows 1700-3300B; 🖥🏊) Sling out on a hammock at this resort with private Balinese-style bungalows on a steep hill, orbiting a two-tiered lap pool tiled in various shades of blue. Shaggy thatching and dense tropical foliage give the place a certain rustic quality, although you won't want for creature comforts. It's super-friendly and books up fast.

🏖 East Coast Beaches

The east coast is the ultimate hermit hangout. For some of these isolated stretches of sand, you'll have to hire a boat (or trek on foot) to get to these beaches, but water taxis are available in Thong Sala and Hat Rin.

Bamboo Hut
BUNGALOW $

(Map p752; ☑ 087 888 8592; Hat Yuan; bungalows 400-1000B; ☜) Beautifully lodged up on the bouldery outcrops that overlook Hat Yuan and the jungle, groovy, friendly, hippie-village Bamboo Hut is a favourite for yoga retreats, meditative relaxation and some serious chilling out. The dark wood bungalows are small, with terraces, while the restaurant serves up superb views and reasonable food.

Mai Pen Rai
BUNGALOW $$

(☑ 093 959 8073; www.thansadet.com; Than Sadet; bungalows 683-1365B; ☜) By the river at the south end of leisurely Than Sadet, this lovely, secluded retreat elicits sedate smiles. Bungalows – some temptingly right on the rocks by the sea – also mingle with Plaa's next door on the hilly headland, and sport panels of straw weaving with gabled roofs. Family bungalows are available and a friendly on-site restaurant rounds out an appealing choice.

🍴 Eating

Most visitors wind up eating at their accommodation, which is a shame as Ko Pha-Ngan has some excellent restaurants scattered around the island.

★ Food Market
MARKET $

(Map p752; Thong Sala; dishes 25-180B; ☺1-11pm) A heady mix of steam and snacking locals, Thong Sala's terrific food market is a must for those looking for doses of culture while nibbling on low-priced snacks. Wander the stalls for a galaxy of Thai street food, from vegetable curry puffs to corn on the cob, spicy sausages, kebabs, spring rolls, Hainanese chicken rice or coconut ice cream.

Nira's
BAKERY $

(Map p752; Thong Sala; snacks from 80B; ☺7am-7pm; ☜) With lots of busy staff offering outstanding service, a big and bright interconnected two-room interior, scrummy baked goodies, tip-top coffee (and exotic rarities such as Marmite and Vegemite) and trendy furniture, Nira's is second to none in Thong Sala, and perhaps the entire island. This is *the* place for breakfast. Music is cool, jazzy chill-out. There's another (small) branch in Hat Rin.

★ Fisherman's Restaurant
SEAFOOD $$

(Map p752; ☑ 084 454 7240; Ban Tai; dishes 50-600B; ☺1.30-10pm) Sit in a long-tail boat looking out over the sunset and a rocky pier. Lit up at night, it's one of the island's prettiest settings, and the food, from the addictive yellow curry crab to the massive seafood platter to share, is as wonderful as the ambience. Reserve ahead, especially when the island is hopping during party time.

Crave
BURGERS $$

(Map p752; ☑ 098 838 7268; www.cravekohphang-an.com; Sri Thanu; mains from 200B; ☺6-10pm Wed-Mon; ☜) Attractively bedecked with glowing lanterns at night, this excellent, very popular and atmospheric choice in Sri Thanu puts together some fine burgers in a cosy and charming setting. Cocktails are great too, starting at 170B. Shame it's only open evenings.

Lazy House
INTERNATIONAL $$

(Map p754; Hat Rin Nai; dishes 90-270B; ☺lunch & dinner) Back in the day, this joint was the owner's apartment – everyone liked his cooking so much that he decided to turn the place into a restaurant and hang-out spot. Today, Lazy House is one of Hat Rin's best places to veg out in front of a movie with a scrumptious shepherd's pie.

🍸 Drinking & Nightlife

Hat Rin is the beating heart of the legendary Full Moon fun. When the moon isn't lighting up the night sky, party-goers flock to other spots on the island's south side. **Rock** (Map p754; ☑ 093 725 7989; Hat Rin Nok; ☺8am-late)

THAILAND KO PHA-NGAN

THE TEN COMMANDMENTS OF FULL MOON FUN

On the eve of every full moon, tens of thousands of bodies converge on Sunrise Beach for an epic trance-a-thon. Though people come for fun, having a good time is serious business. There is a 100B entrance fee for much-needed beach clean-up and security.

➡ Thou shalt arrive in Hat Rin at least three days early to nail down accommodation during the pre-full-moon rush of backpackers.

➡ Thou shalt double-check the party dates as sometimes they coincide with Buddhist holidays and are rescheduled.

➡ Thou shalt secure all valuables, especially when staying in budget bungalows.

➡ Thou shalt savour some delicious fried fare in Chicken Corner before the revelry begins.

➡ Thou shalt wear protective shoes during the sandy celebration, unless thou wants a tetanus shot.

➡ Thou shalt cover thyself with swirling patterns of neon body paint.

➡ Thou shalt visit the Rock for killer views of the heathens below.

➡ Thou shalt not sample the drug buffet, nor shalt thou swim in the ocean under the influence of alcohol.

➡ Thou shalt stay in a group of two or more people, especially if thou art a woman, and especially when returning home at the end of the evening.

➡ Thou shalt party until the sun comes up and have a great time.

and **Sunrise** (Map p754; ☑ 077 375144; Hat Rin Nok) are popular spots.

★ **Secret Beach Bar**   BAR
(Hat Son; ⊗9am-7pm) There are few better ways to unwind at the end of a Ko Pha-Ngan day than watching the sun slide into an azure sea from this bar on the north-west sands of the island. Grab a table, order up a mojito and take in the sunset through the palm fronds.

Mellow Mountain   BAR
(Map p754; Hat Rin Nok; ⊗24hr; ☏) Also called 'Mushy Mountain' (you'll know when you get there), this trippy hang-out sits at the northern end of Hat Rin Nok, delivering stellar views of the shenanigans below.

ⓘ Information

Ko Pha-Ngan Hospital (Map p752; ☑ 077 377034; Thong Sala; ⊗24hr) About 2.5km north of Thong Sala, this government hospital offers 24-hour emergency services.

Main Police Station (Map p752; ☑191, 077 377114; Thong Sala) Located about 2km north of Thong Sala. Come here to file a report. You might be charged between 110B and 200B to file the report, which is for insurance – refusing to pay may lead to complications. If you are arrested you have the right to an embassy phone

call; you don't have to accept the 'interpreter' you are offered.

Main Post Office (Map p752; Thong Sala; ⊗8.30am-4.30pm Mon-Fri, 9am-noon Sat)

ⓘ Getting There & Away

Ko Pha-Ngan's new airport has yet to open.

The main pier on Ko Pha-Ngan is Thong Sala, though some companies run boats to Hat Rin and the east coast from northern piers on Samui (200B to 300B, 20 minutes to one hour, frequently 7am to 6pm). Bus-boat combinations connect all the way to Bangkok (1300B, 17 hours).

The **Haad Rin Queen** (Map p754; ☑ 077 484668) goes back and forth between Hat Rin and Big Buddha Beach on Ko Samui (200B, 50 minutes, four times a day). Service increases during the Full Moon Parties. The wobbly Thong Nai Pan Express connects Hat Rin and east coast beaches, including Thong Nai Pan, to Mae Hat on Ko Samui (200B to 400B, once a day). The boat won't run in bad weather.

ⓘ Getting Around

Motorbike rental is widely available for 200B to 250B. It is not recommended to rent a motorbike on the island if you're a novice.

Sŏrng·tăa·ou chug along the island's major roads, charging 100B between Thong Sala to Hat Rin and 150B to 200B for other beaches. Rates double after sunset. Ask your accommodation about free or discount transfers when you leave the island.

Long-tail boats depart from Thong Sala to various beaches throughout the day. Rates range from 50B to 300B.

Ko Tao

เกาะเต่า

POPULATION 2032

The smallest of the Samui islands, Ko Tao has long attracted visitors for its near-shore reefs, cheap dive certificates and jungle-clad coves. It has firmly moved into upscale terri-

tory but it still remains one of the cheapest places to learn how to scuba.

🏃 Activities

Ko Tao is *the* place in Thailand to lose your scuba virginity. The shallow bays scalloping the island are perfect for newbie divers to take their first stab at scuba; the waters are crystal clear, there are loads of neon reefs and the temperatures are bathwater warm.

Scores of dive centres are ready to teach you the ropes in a 3½-day Open Water certification course. The intense competition means prices are unbeatably low and stand-

Ko Tao

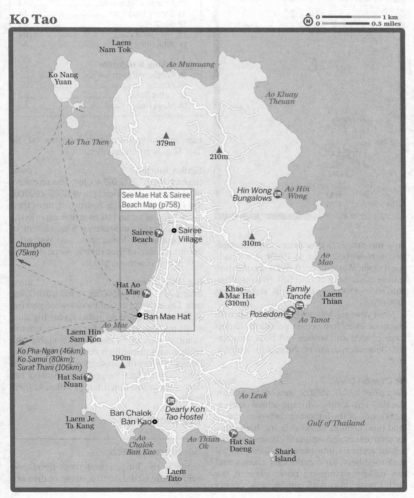

Mae Hat & Sairee Beach

GULF OF THAILAND

Sairee Beach

Ko Tao

Chumphon (75km)

Ao Mae Hat Ao Mae

Ko Pha-Ngan (46km)

Surat Thani (106km)

ATM

Ko Tao Hospital

MAE HAT

into marine conservation projects on Ko Tao. Highly recommended.

Scuba Junction   DIVING
(Scuba J; Map p758; ☎077 456164; www.scubajunctiondiving.com; Sairee Beach; dives 1100B-29,000B) This team of outgoing instructors lures travellers looking for an intimate dive experience. Scuba Junction guarantees a maximum of four people per diving group, so you get a decent amount of time diving. A one-day Discover Scuba course is 2100B.

Big Blue Diving   DIVING
(Map p758; ☎077 456050; www.bigbluediving.com; Sairee Beach) If Goldilocks were picking a dive school, she'd probably go for Big Blue – this midsize operation (not too big, not too small) is popular for fostering a sociable vibe while maintaining high standards of service. Divers of every ilk can score accommodation across the budget ranges, from backpacker dorms up to top-notch family villas, at their resort.

🛏 Sleeping

🛏 Sairee Beach

Sairee is the longest and most developed strip on the island, with a string of dive op-

ards top-notch. Diving prices are standardised across the island. A **PADI** (www.padi.com) Open Water Diver (OWD) certification course costs 9800B; an **SSI** (www.ssithailand.com) OWD certificate is slightly less (9000B).

Most dive schools will hook you up with cheap or even free accommodation. Expect large crowds and booked-out beds throughout December, January, June, July and August.

★ Crystal Dive   DIVING
(Map p758; ☎077 456106; www.crystaldive.com; Mae Hat) This award-winning school (and resort) is one of the largest operators on the island (and around the world), but high-quality instructors and intimate classes keep the school feeling quite personal. Multilingual staff members, air-conditioned classes and two on-site swimming pools sweeten the deal. Crystal also puts considerable energy

erations, bungalows, travel agencies, mini-markets and internet cafes.

Spicytao Backpackers
HOSTEL $

(Map p758; ☑ 082 278 7115; www.spicyhostels.com/Home.html; Sairee Village; dm 230-280B; ✳ 🛜) With bargain prices, no-frills Spicytao is like your own supersocial country hangout; it is hidden off the main drag in a rustic garden setting. Backpackers rave about the ambience and staff who are always organising activities. Book in advance!

Ko Tao Central Hostel
HOSTEL $

(Map p758; ☑ 077 456925; www.kohtaohostel.com; Mae Hat; dm 310B; ✳ 🛜) Identified by its London Underground–style logo and decorated with Banksy murals and Tube-line stripes, this clean, central and friendly hostel has good 14-bed dorms, if all you need is a handy bed near to the pier. Check out is at 11am. Reception is in Island Travel next door; no towel service, so bring your own.

★ Ban's Diving Resort
RESORT $$

(Map p758; ☑ 077 456466; www.bansdivingresort.com; Sairee Beach; r 700-10,000B; ✳ @ 🛜 ⛱) This dive-centric party palace offers a wide range of quality accommodation, from basic backpacker digs to sleek hillside villas, and it's growing all the time. Post-scuba chill sessions take place on Ban's prime slice of beach or at one of the two swimming pools tucked within the strip of jungle between the two-storey, pillared and terraced white hotel blocks.

Chalok Ban Tao

This is the quietest of the main beaches but there's still a mellow yet fun nightlife scene.

★ Dearly Koh Tao Hostel
HOSTEL $$

(Map p757; ☑ 077 332494; www.thedearlykohtao-hostel.com; 14/55 Mu 3, Chalok Ban Kao; dm 600-700B, d 1700-3000B, tr 2400B; 🛜 ⛱) Located on the road that leads inland from Chalok Ban Kao, this new hostel has all the right ingredients: clean, comfortable, contemporary (but also traditional) rooms, bubbly and friendly staff, rattan furniture and a rooftop terrace. There's a mix of dorms and private rooms, and a swimming pool was going in when we visited. Breakfast is included.

Buddha View Dive Resort
BUNGALOW $$

(☑ 077 456074; www.buddhaview-diving.com; Chalok Ban Kao; r 800-1300B; ☺ 7am-6.30pm; ✳ @ 🛜 ⛱) Like other large diving opera-

tions on the island, **Buddha View** (☑ 077 456074; www.buddhaview-diving.com; Chalok Ban Kao; r from 1000B; ☺ 7am-6.30pm) offers its divers discounted on-site digs in a super-social atmosphere.

New Heaven Resort
BUNGALOW $$

(☑ 077 456422; www.newheavendiveschool.com; Chalok Ban Kao; dm 300B; r & bungalows 800-3500B; ✳ 🛜) New Heaven – part of the diving operation of the same name – delivers colourful huts perched on a hill over impossibly clear waters, air-con beachfront rooms, family sea-view bungalows and budget dorm beds.

East Coast Beaches

The serene eastern coast offers stunning views, yet all of your creature comforts are within 10 minutes' reach.

Hin Wong Bungalows
BUNGALOW $

(Map p757; ☑ 077 456006; Hin Wong; bungalows 400-700B; 🛜) Above boulders strewn to the sea, these decent enough but basic corrugated-roof huts are scattered across a lot of untamed tropical terrain. A rickety dock, jutting out just beyond the breezy restaurant, is the perfect place to dangle your legs and watch schools of black sardines slide through the cerulean water; or why not hop in with a snorkel?

Poseidon
BUNGALOW $

(Map p757; ☑ 077 456735; poseidonkohtao@hotmail.com; Ao Tanot; bungalows 800-1500B; 🛜) Poseidon keeps the tradition of the budget bamboo bungalow alive with basic but sleepable fan huts scattered near the sand. There's a reasonable restaurant here which is also a good spot for a drink.

Family Tanote
BUNGALOW $$

(Map p757; ☑ 077 456757; Ao Tanot; bungalows 1000-3800B; ✳ @ 🛜) This family-run scatter of hillside bungalows is a so-so choice for solitude-seekers. Strap on a snorkel mask and swim around with the fish at your doorstep, or climb up to the restaurant for a tasty meal and beautiful views of the bay.

✗ Eating

Sairee Beach

★ 995 Roasted Duck
CHINESE $

(Map p758; Sairee Village; mains from 70B; ☺ 9am-9pm) You may have to queue a while to get a

THAILAND KO TAO

seat at this glorified shack, wondering what all the fuss is about. The fuss is excellent roast duck, from 70B for a steaming bowl of roasted waterfowl with noodles to 700B for a whole bird, served in a jiffy. You'd be quackers to miss out.

Bang Burgers
BURGERS $

(Map p758; ☑ 081 136 6576; Sairee Village; mains from 130B; ⊙ 10am-10pm) You may have to dig your heels in and wait in line at this terrific burger bar that does a roaring trade in Sairee. There's around a half-dozen burgers (cheese, double cheese, red chilli cheese) on the menu, including a veggie choice for meat-free diners; chips are 50B.

Su Chili
THAI $

(Map p758; Sairee Village; dishes 85-225B; ⊙ 10am-10.30pm) Inviting and bustling, Su Chili serves fresh and tasty Thai dishes, with friendly staff always asking how spicy you want your food and somehow getting it right. Try the delicious northern Thai specialities or Penang curries. There's a smattering of Western comfort food for homesick diners.

★ Barracuda Restaurant & Bar
FUSION $$

(Map p758; ☑ 080 146 3267; www.barracuda-kohtao.com; Sairee Village; mains 240-380B; ⊙ 6-10.30pm; ☎) Sociable chef Ed Jones caters for the Thai princess when she's in town, but you can sample his exquisite cuisine for mere pennies in comparison to her budget. Locally sourced ingredients are turned into creative, fresh, fusion masterpieces. Try the seafood platter, pan-fried barracuda fillet or vegetarian falafel platter – then wash it down with a passionfruit mojito.

The Gallery
THAI $$

(Map p758; ☑ 077 456547; www.thegallerykohtao.com; Sairee Village; mains 120-420B; ⊙ noon-10pm) At one of the most pleasant settings in town, the food here is equally special. The signature dish is *hor mok maprao on* (chicken, shrimp and fish curry served in a young coconut; 420B), but the white snapper fillet in creamy red curry sauce is also excellent and there's a choice of vegetarian dishes.

✕ Mae Hat

Pranee's Kitchen
THAI $

(Map p758; Mae Hat; dishes 50-150B; ⊙ 7am-10pm; ☎) An old Mae Hat fave, Pranee's serves scrumptious curries and other Thai treats in an open-air pavilion sprinkled with lounging pillows, wooden tables and TVs. English-language movies are shown nightly at 6pm.

Safety Stop Pub
INTERNATIONAL $

(Map p758; ☑ 077 456209; Mae Hat; mains 60-250B; ⊙ 7am-11pm; ☎) A haven for homesick Brits, this pier-side restaurant and bar feels like a tropical beer garden. Stop by on Sundays to stuff your face with an endless supply of barbecued goodness; the Thai dishes also aren't half bad.

★ Whitening
INTERNATIONAL $$

(Map p758; ☑ 077 456199; Mae Hat; dishes 160-480B; ⊙ 1pm-1am; ☎) This starched, white, beachy spot falls somewhere between being a restaurant and a chic seaside bar – foodies will appreciate the tasty twists on indigenous and international dishes. Dine amid dangling white Christmas lights while keeping your bare feet tucked into the

---

❶ GETTING TO MALAYSIA: SUNGAI KOLOK TO RANTAU PANJANG

This border is within Thailand's Deep South, an area that has had a small-scale insurgent war for over a decade. Exercise caution when travelling overland in this area.

Getting to the border The Thai border (open 5am to 9pm) is about 1.5km from the centre of Sungai Kolok. Motorbike taxis charge around 30B.

At the border This is a hassle-free border crossing. After completing formalities, walk across the Harmony Bridge to the Malaysian border post.

Moving on Shared taxis and buses to Kota Bharu, the capital of Malaysia's Kelantan State, can be caught 200m beyond the Malaysian border post. Shared taxis cost RM$10 per person (90B) or RM$50 (450B) to charter the whole car yourself. The ride takes around 40 minutes. Buses make the hour-long journey for RM$5.10 (45B).

For information on making the crossing in reverse see p432

THAILAND KO TAO

sand. And the best part? It's comparatively easy on the wallet.

✗ Chalok Ban Kao

South Beach Cafe
CAFE $
(☏094 369 1979; Chalok Ban Kao; mains from 100B; ⊙6am-10pm) Service is rather slack, but the coffee is good, as are the breakfasts at this fresh addition to Chalok Ban Kao, with an early kick-off and a long day. The menu spans paninis, salads, pizzas, burgers, vegan dishes, cheesecake and glasses of house wine (99B), plus there's the obligatory full English breakfast (plus a full vegan).

I (Heart) Salad
CAFE $$
(Chalok Ban Kao; mains from 120B; ⊙8am-9pm; 🔊) This rustic choice offers a healthy array of salads using fresh ingredients, with a good supply of vegetarian and vegan dishes and sticky desserts to follow. There are also real fruit juices and healthy egg-white-only breakfasts.

🍷 Drinking & Nightlife

★ Fizz
BAR
(Map p758; Sairee Beach; ⊙noon-1am) Come sunset, sink into a green beanbag, order up a designer cocktail and let the hypnotic surf roll in amid a symphony of ambient sounds. Fantastic.

Lotus Bar
BAR
(Map p758; ☏087 069 6078; Sairee Beach) Lotus is the leading late-night hang-out spot along the northern end of Sairee; it also affords front-row seats to some spectacular sunsets. Muscular fire-twirlers toss around flaming batons, and the drinks are so large there should be a lifeguard on duty.

Maya Beach Club
BAR
(Map p758; ☏080 578 2225; www.mayabeachclub-kohtao.com; Sairee Beach; ⊙noon-9pm Sat-Thu, to 2am Fri) Rivalling Fizz (p761) for its entrancing sunset visuals and relaxing mood, Maya has nightly DJs and party nights. Make a move for a beach lounger and stay put.

Fishbowl Beach Bar
BAR
(Map p758; ☏062 046 8996; Sairee Beach; ⊙noon-2am) This buzzin' and hoppin' bar gazes out at sunset onto killer views; enjoy fire shows, live music kicking off from 8pm and DJs casting their spell.

ℹ Information

Ko Tao is not the place to learn how to drive a motorcycle. Roads can be treacherous. Wear a helmet at all times.

Ko Tao Hospital (Map p758; ☏077 456490; ⊙24hr) For general medical and dental treatment.

Post Office (Map p758; ☏077 456170; Mae Hat; ⊙9am-5pm Mon-Fri, 9am-noon Sat) A 10-to 15-minute walk from the pier; at the corner of Ko Tao's main inner-island road and Mae Hat's 'down road'.

ℹ Getting There & Away

Chumphon is the mainland jumping-off point for Ko Tao. Inter-island ferries connect Tao to its neighbours and on to Surat Thani. Mae Hat is the island's primary pier. Book your tickets in advance around Ko Pha-Ngan's Full Moon Parties. Pier-transfer costs should be included in the price of the ticket.

Services to Ko Pha-Ngan include Lomprayah (500B to 600B, one hour, three daily), Seatran Discovery Ferry (430B, one hour, three daily) and Songserm (350B, two hours).

Services to Samui include Lomprayah (600B, two hours, twice daily), Seatran Discovery Ferry (600B, three daily) and Songserm (500B, 3½ hours, once daily).

ℹ Getting Around

Sŏrng·tǎa·ou and motorbikes haul passengers from the pier in Mae Hat to their hotels. Rates to Sairee Beach and Chalok Ban Kao are 200B per person, depending on the number of passengers. Water taxis leave from Mae Hat to Chalok Ban Kao to the northern part of Sairee Beach for about 100B. Chartered boats start at 1500B per day.

Motorcycles can be rented from 150B per day.

Surat Thani อำเภอเมืองสุราษฎร์ธานี
☏077 / POPULATION 128,990

Surat Thani is a busy transport hub moving cargo and people around the country. Travellers rarely linger here as they make their way to the Samui archipelago and the Andaman coast.

Night Market
MARKET $
(Sarn Chao Ma; Th Ton Pho; dishes from 35B; ⊙6-11pm) A smorgasbord of food including masses of melt-in-your-mouth marinated meats on sticks, fresh fruit juices, noodle dishes and desserts.

My Place @ Surat Hotel
HOTEL $
(☏077 272288; 247/5 Th Na Muang; d 490-590B, f 620B; ❄🔊) All smiles and nary a speck of

BUSES & MINIVANS FROM SURAT THANI

DESTINATION	FARE (B)	DURATION (HR)
Bangkok	425–860	10
Hat Yai	165–300	5
Khanom	100	1
Krabi	170	2½
Phuket	270	6
Trang	180	2hr 10min

dust, this excellent central hotel offers spacious, clean rooms, bright paint, colourful throw cushions, modern art on the walls, power showers and value for money. It may be budget, but it doesn't seem that way and will suit almost anyone. Breakfast is served in the so-so cafe next door.

ⓘ Getting There & Away

If you are coming from points north (such as Bangkok or Hua Hin) for the Samui islands, it's generally easier to use Chumphon rather than Surat as a jumping-off point to the islands.

AIR

Use Surat Thani's airport as an alternative to flying to/from Bangkok, if you can't get a flight to Samui. Transferring from Surat's airport to the pier adds significant time and hassle to the trip. Surat's airport is serviced by Air Asia, which has transfer shuttles to the boat pier, Nok Air, Thai Smile and Thai Lion.

BOAT

Various ferry companies offer services to the islands. Try **Lomprayah** (☏ 077 4277 656; www.lomprayah.com), **Seatran Discovery** (☏ 077 275063; www.seatrandiscovery.com) or **Songserm** (☏ 077 377704; www.songserm-expressboat.com).

From the centre of Surat there are nightly ferries to **Ko Tao** (600B, eight hours, 11pm), Ko Pha-Ngan (400B, seven hours, 11pm) and Ko Samui (300B, six hours, 11pm). These are cargo ships, not luxury boats, so bring supplies and watch your bags.

TRAIN

Surat's train station is in Phun Phin, 14km west of town. From Phun Phin there are buses to Phuket, Phang-Nga and Krabi, some via Takua Pa, the stopping point for Khao Sok National Park. There are also train-boat combinations that connect arriving train passengers to the Samui islands.

BUS & MINIVAN

Frequent buses and minivans depart from two main locations in town: Talat Kaset 1 and Talat Kaset 2. Go to Talat Kaset 2 for transport to Phuket.

The bus terminal is 7km south of town and has buses to Bangkok.

ⓘ Getting Around

Airport minivans will drop you off at your hotel for 100B per person. Sŏrng·tǎa·ou around town cost 10B to 30B. Orange ordinary buses run from Phun Phin train station to Surat Thani (15B, 25 minutes). Taxis from the train station charge 200B for a maximum of four people.

Hat Yai   หาดใหญ่
☏ 074 / POPULATION 191,696

Hat Yai is southern Thailand's urban hub and the unofficial capital of delicious southern Thai cuisine. In addition to its shopping malls and modern amenities, it is also a favourite weekend trip for Malaysian men looking for prostitutes, giving it a slightly rough border-town image. Occasionally, the low-scale insurgent war in Thailand's nearby Deep South provinces spills over to Hat Yai with bomb attacks on high-profile targets (such as shopping malls, hotels and the airport). The most recent bombing occurred in 2014 and Hat Yai is generally a safe place to pass through.

The very helpful staff at the local **Tourism Authority of Thailand** (TAT; www.tourismthailand.org/hatyai; 1/1 Soi 2, Th Niphat Uthit 3; ⏰8.30am-4.30pm) office speak excellent English and have loads of info on the entire region.

Hat Yai Backpackers   HOSTEL $
(www.hatyaibackpackershostel.com; 226 Th Niphat Uthit 1; dm 240B; 🕸) With four-bed women's dorms and eight-bed mixed dorms, this

BUSES & MINIVANS FROM HAT YAI

DESTINATION	FARE (B)	DURATION (HR)
Bangkok	688–1130	15
Krabi	182–540	5
Nakhon Si Thammarat	140	4
Pak Bara	130	2
Phuket	370	7
Songkhla	40	1½
Sungai Kolok	220	4
Surat Thani	240	5
Trang	110	2

central choice is a decent bet, and there are helpful staff at hand for Hat Yai pointers.

Night Market   MARKET $

(Th Montri 1) The night market boasts heaps of local eats including several stalls selling the famous Hat Yai–style deep-fried chicken and *kà·nŏm jeen* (fresh rice noodles served with curry), as well as a couple of stalls peddling grilled seafood.

ℹ Getting There & Away

AIR

Hat Yai International Airport (📞 074 227131; www.hatyaiairportthai.com) is around 14km south-west of town. Air Asia (www.airasia.com), Nok Air (www.nokair.com), Thai Lion Air (www.lionairthai.com) and Thai Airways have daily flights to and from Bangkok. There are also flights to Kuala Lumpur in Malaysia. A taxi to/from the airport is around 320B.

BUS

Most interprovincial buses and southbound minivans leave from the bus terminal 2km southeast of the town centre, while most northbound minivans now leave from a minivan terminal 5km west of town at Talat Kaset, a 60B túk-túk ride from the centre of town. Buses link Hat Yai to almost any location in southern Thailand.

TRAIN

Four overnight trains run to/from Bangkok via Surat Thani each day (259B to 945B, 16 hours). There are also seven trains daily to Sungai Kolok (92B) and two daily trains to Butterworth (332B) and Padang Besar (57B), both in Malaysia.

THE ANDAMAN COAST

The Andaman is Thailand's dream coast, that place on a 'Travel to Paradise' poster that makes you want to leave your job and live in flip-flops forever. White-sand beaches, turquoise sea, cathedral-like limestone cliffs, neon corals and hundreds of jungle-covered isles extend down the Andaman Sea from the border of Myanmar to Malaysia. It is a postcard-perfect destination thoroughly serviced by the package-tourist industry, so finding budget spots takes some searching.

Ranong   ระนอง

📞 077 / POPULATION 17,500

Ranong lies just a 45-minute boat ride from Myanmar. This border town *par excellence* (shabby, frenetic, slightly seedy) has a thriving population from Myanmar, bubbling hot springs, crumbling historical buildings and some sensational street food.

It's an increasingly popular border crossing; dive operators specialising in live-aboard trips to the Surin Islands and Myanmar's Mergui Archipelago are now establishing themselves here.

Rueangrat Hotel   HOTEL $

(📞 092 279 9919; rueangratranong@gmail.com; 240/10 Th Ruangrat; r 690B; ❄ 🛜) Bright, shiny rooms are set back from the road at this new place close to restaurants and shops. All come with fridges, TVs and decent bathrooms. There's free coffee in the lobby area, friendly staff and good wi-fi.

Night Market   MARKET $

(Th Kamlangsap, off Hwy 4; mains 30-70B; ⏱ 2-7pm) The night market, just north-west off the highway, sizzles up brilliant Thai dishes at killer prices.

BUSES FROM RANONG

DESTINATION	FARE (B)	DURATION (HR)	FREQUENCY
Bangkok	403-627	9-10	7.30am, 8.10am, 10.30am, 1.30pm, 3.30pm, 7.30pm, 8pm (VIP), 8.30pm (VIP)
Chumphon	150	2	hourly 7am-5pm
Hat Yai	380	7	6am, 10am, 8pm
Khao Lak	165	3½	hourly 6.30am-5.45pm
Krabi	210	6	7am, 10am, 2pm
Phang-Nga	180	5	7am, 10am, 2pm
Phuket	225	5-6	hourly 6.30am-5.45pm
Surat Thani	190	4-5	hourly 6am-4pm

A-One-Diving   DIVING
(☑ 077 832984; www.a-one-diving.com; 256 Th Ru-angrat; ⊘ Oct-Apr) Specialises in live-aboards to the Surin Islands and Myanmar's Mergui Archipelago (from 34,900B), plus PADI diving certification courses.

ℹ Getting There & Away

Ranong Airport is 22km south of town. Nok Air (www.nokair.com) flies twice daily to Bangkok (Don Muang). The **bus terminal** (Th Phetkasem) is 1km south-east of the centre. The blue *Sŏrng·tăa·ou* 2 (pick-up minibus) passes the terminal.

Ko Chang

This little-visited rustic isle is a long way (in every respect) from its much more popular Trat Province namesake. The speciality here is no-frills living, and electricity and wi-fi are still scarce. An all-pervading quiet lies over the island. Between May and October (low season) it's beyond mellow and many places shut down.

🛏 Sleeping

★ Crocodile Rock   GUESTHOUSE $
(☑ 080 533 4138; tonn1970@yahoo.com; Ao Yai; bungalows 400-700B; ⊘ Oct-Apr; 🐾) Simple metal-roofed bamboo bungalows with hammocks perched on Ao Yai's serene southern headland have superb bay views. The classy kitchen turns out home-made yoghurt, breads, cookies, good espresso, and a variety of veggie and seafood dishes. It's popular, so book ahead.

Sangsuree Bungalows   BUNGALOW $
(☑ 081 2511 7726; bungalow.sangsuree@gmail.com; Ao Takien; bungalows 300-500B; 🐾) Ko

Chang's northwest coast is dotted with hidden bays; Sangsuree's seven basic bungalows are positioned just above one of them, commanding fine sea views. Run by a charming husband-and-wife team, this is a classic, old-school Thai island chill-out spot, with communal meals and much lazing around. It's a 10-minute walk to a sandy swimming beach.

ℹ Getting There & Away

From Ranong, *sŏrng·tăa·ou* (20B) or motorcycle taxis (50B) go from Th Ruangrat to Tha Ko Phayam near Saphan Plaa. Long-tail taxi boats (200B, two hours, 9.30am and 2pm) leave for Ko Chang. In high season they stop at the west-coast beaches, returning to the mainland at approximately 8.30am and 1pm. During the monsoon, only morning long-tails make the crossing (weather permitting) from the northeast's main pier. During the November-to-April high season, two daily speedboats (350B, 30 minutes, 8.30am and 10.30am) run between Ranong's Tha Ko Phayam and Ko Chang's northeast-coast pier. In low season, only the 8.30am speedboat runs.

Motorcycle taxis meet boats, charging 100B to Ao Yai.

Ko Phayam

Ko Phayam is fringed with beautiful soft-white beaches and is becoming increasingly popular as a family destination. If you're coming from Phuket or Ko Phi-Phi, it'll feel refreshingly wild and dozy. The spectacular northwest and southwest coasts are dotted with rustic bungalows, small-scale resorts, breezy sand-side restaurants and barefoot beach bars.

Snorkelling here isn't great, but the sensational Surin Islands are close enough to visit.

🛏 Sleeping

Sabai Sabai BUNGALOW $
(📞 087 895 4653; www.sabai-bungalows.com; Ao Mea Mai; bungalow 400-1000B; 🛜) Five minutes' walk south of the east-coast pier, this long-standing and social travellers hideaway has clean, fan-cooled, budget-friendly bungalows. Simple doubles come with sea views, sunken bathrooms and a bit of style. Best is the two-floor, loft-style room with balcony. There's a chilled-out bar, plus hammocks and movie nights. The cheapest bungalows share bathrooms.

Bamboo Bungalows BUNGALOW $$
(📞 077 820012; www.bamboo-bungalows.com; Ao Yai; bungalows 750-2600B; 🛜) Smart, rustic bungalows come with indoor/outdoor bathrooms, some decoration and balconies with hammocks. All are scattered throughout a leafy garden set just back from the middle of lovely Ao Yai. The beachfront restaurant is pretty good and kayaks and boogie boards can be hired. It has 24-hour electricity in high season.

🏃 Activities

Phayam Divers DIVING
(📞 086 995 2598; www.phayamlodge.com; Ao Yai; 2 dives 4900B; ⏰ Nov-Apr) At the north end of Ao Yai. Offers dive trips to the Surins, plus multi-day live-aboards to the Surins, Ko Tachai and Ko Bon. Snorkellers are welcome too. Also runs PADI Open Water courses (14,900B).

ℹ️ Getting There & Around

From Ranong, two daily ferries go to Ko Phayam's main pier (200B, two hours, 9.30am and 2pm), returning at 8.30am and 3pm. During the high season, speedboats go to Ko Phayam (350B, 35 minutes, almost hourly from 7.30am to 5.30pm); they make eight return trips. A motorcycle taxi from the pier to the main beaches costs 50B to 70B per person. Motorcycle and bicycle rentals are available in the village and from most of the larger resorts.

Khao Sok National Park

If you've had enough of beach-bumming, venture inland to the wondrous 738-sq-km **Khao Sok National Park** (อุทยานแห่งชาติเขาสก; 📞 077 395154; www.khaosok.com; Khao Sok; adult/child 300/150B; ⏰ 6am-6pm). Many believe this lowland jungle (Thailand's rainiest spot) dates back 160 million years, making it one of the world's oldest rainforests. It's interspersed by hidden waterfalls and caves.

Rainy season (June to October) is the best time to spot the many animal species who live here, and to see the waterfalls in full flow, although the hiking trails get slippery.

🛏 Sleeping & Activities

Kayaking (800B) and tubing (500B; rainy season) are popular activities. We recommend a two-day, one-night canoeing and hiking trip (per person 2500B) to **Chiaw Lan** (เขื่อนเชี่ยวหลาน; day/overnight trip 1500/2500B), where you sleep on the lake in floating huts.

ℹ️ GETTING TO MYANMAR: RANONG TO KAWTHOUNG

If you're looking to renew your visa, the easiest way to do it is on one of the 'visa trips' (1300B) offered by Ranong travel agencies, including **Pon's Place** (📞 081 597 4549; www.ponplace-ranong.com; Th Ruangrat; ⏰ 8am-7.30pm). Myanmar visas are not available at the border, but if you have an e-visa you can enter Myanmar here.

Getting to the border Boats to Kawthoung leave from the Saphan Plaa pier, 5km from Ranong. Red *sŏrng·tăa·ou* from Ranong go to the pier (20B).

At the border Long-tail boat drivers will meet you at the pier. A trip to Myanmar should cost 100B/200B one way/return. Get photocopies of your passport at the pier for 5B. After Thai immigration, board the boat to the other side and go through Myanmar's checkpoint. Touts may await you offering to 'help': you don't need them. If you are a day visitor, you will pay a US$10 fee (crisp, untorn bills) for a border pass; your passport will be kept at the pier.

Moving on You can tour Kawthoung for the day or continue on to destinations within Myanmar with a pre-arranged visa.

For information on making this crossing in reverse see p505.

Jungle Huts BUNGALOW $
(☎077 395160; www.khaosokjunglehuts.com; 242 Mu 6, Khao Sok; r fan/air-con 400/1200B; ❄️🛜) This popular hang-out contains a collection of decent, individually styled bungalows, all with bathrooms and porches. Choose from plain stilted bamboo huts, bigger wooden editions, pink-washed concrete bungalows, or rooms set along vertiginous walkways.

Khao Sok Hostel 1 HOSTEL $
(☎096 142 6539; www.khaosokcentertour.net; 53/7 Mu 6, Khao Sok; dm 200B; ❄️🛜) The dorms at this new hostel are really just beds in a room rather than conventional dorms. Nor is there a communal area. But the mattresses are thick, there's hot water and small lockers. There's a second, identical **branch** (☎096 142 6539; 53/7 Mu 6, Khao Sok; dm 200B; ❄️🛜) 100m down the road.

ⓘ Information

Khao Sok National Park Headquarters
(☎077 395154; www.khaosok.com; ⏰6am-6pm) About 1.8km northeast off Rte 401, exiting near the Km 109 marker; helpful maps and information.

ⓘ Getting There & Away

From Surat catch a bus going towards Takua Pa; from the Andaman Coast, take a Surat Thani–bound bus. Buses stop on Rte 401, 1.8km southwest of the visitors centre. If touts don't meet you, you'll have to walk to your chosen guesthouse (50m to 2km). Most minivans will drop you at your accommodation.

There is a daily bus to Bangkok (1000B, 11 hours) at 6pm.

Daily minivan departures include the following:

DESTINATION	FARE (B)	DURATION (HR)
Khao Lak	200	1¼
Ko Lanta	800	5
Ko Tao	1000	8
Krabi	350	3
Phang-Nga	250	2
Surat Thani	200	1

Hat Khao Lak & Around

When people refer to Khao Lak, they're usually talking about a series of beaches hugging Phang-Nga's west coastline, about 70km north of Phuket. With easy day trips to the Similan and Surin Islands, Khao Sok and Khao Lak/Lam Ru National Parks, or even Phuket, the area makes a central base for exploring the northern Andaman.

🏃 Activities

Diving and snorkelling day excursions to the Similan and Surin Islands are immensely popular but, if you can, go for a live-aboard as the islands are around 70km from the mainland. Dive shops, such as **Wicked** (☎085 795 2221; www.wickeddiving.com; Th Nangthong, Khao Lak; 2 dives 5700B; ⏰Oct-May) and **Sea Dragon** (☎076 485420; www.seadragondivecenter.com; Th Phetkasem, Khao Lak; 2 dives 6000B; ⏰9am-9pm), offer live-aboard package trips from around 19,000B for three days, 35,000B for six days, and day trips for 5000B to 6000B.

The Similan and Surin dive seasons run from mid-October to mid-May.

🛏️ Sleeping & Eating

Bed Hostel HOSTEL $
(☎087 387 4050; krittayakorn.d@gmail.com; 6/3 Mu 5, Hat Bang Niang; dm fan/air-con 370/450B, r 1600B; ❄️🛜) This modest, family-run hostel lacks a communal area, but the compact dorms are clean and come with lockers. It's fine if you just want a place to lay your head, after a day's diving or lazing on the sand. It's a 15-minute walk to the beach.

Fasai House GUESTHOUSE $$
(☎076 485867; www.fasaihouse.com; 5/54 Mu 7, Khao Lak; r 950B; ❄️@🛜) One of Khao Lak's best budget choices, Fasai wins us over with its delightful staff and simple but immaculate, motel-style air-con rooms set in a warm yellow-washed block framing a little pool. It makes a good divers crash-pad. Look for the sign off Hwy 4 towards the northern end of Khao Lak.

Go Pong THAI $
(Th Phetkasem, Khao Lak; mains 50-140B; ⏰10am-11pm) Get a real taste of local flavours at this terrific streetside diner where the stir-fry noodles and sensational spicy rice dishes and aromatic noodle soups attract a loyal lunch following. Dishes are packed full of flavour.

Jai THAI $$
(☎076 485390; 5/1 Mu 7 Th Phetkasem, Khao Lak; mains 90-300B; ⏰8am-midnight; 🛜) Under a soaring peaked roof at the northern end of central Khao Lak, this semi-open-air, family-run eatery has a big menu of fresh grilled

THAILAND HAT KHAO LAK & AROUND

seafood, spiced stir fries and all the usual curries, rices and noodles. Satisfying, friendly and convenient.

ⓘ Getting There & Away

Any bus between Takua Pa (60B, 45 minutes) and Phuket (100B, two hours) will stop at Hat Khao Lak if you ask. **Khao Lak Land Discovery** (☑ 076 485411; www.khaolaklanddiscovery. com; 21/5 Mu 7, Th Phetkasem, Khao Lak; ⊗ 8am-8.30pm) runs shared minibuses to Phuket International Airport (600B, 1¼ hours). Alternatively, you can take **Cheaper Than Hotel** (☑ 085 786 1378, 086 276 6479; cheaperkhaolak1@gmail.com; Hwy 4) taxis to Phuket airport (1000B) and points south.

Numerous travel agencies and guesthouses rent motorbikes by the day (200B to 250B).

Surin Islands Marine National Park

The five gorgeous islands that make up this **national park** (อุทยานแห่งชาติหมู่เกาะ สุรินทร์; ☑ 076 491378; www.dnp.go.th; adult/ child 500/300B; ⊗ mid-Oct–mid-May) sit about 60km offshore and 5km from the Thai–Myanmar marine border. Healthy rainforests, pockets of white-sand beach in sheltered bays and rocky headlands that jut into the ocean characterise these granite-outcrop islands. The clearest of water makes for great marine life, with underwater visibility often up to 20m. Park headquarters and all visitor facilities are on Ko Surin Neua, near the jetty. Khuraburi, on the mainland, is the jumping-off point for the park. The pier is 9km north of town, as is the **national park office** (Ko Surin Neua; ⊗ 7.30am-8.30pm mid-Oct–mid-May).

Dive sites in the park include **Ko Surin Tai** and **HQ Channel**. Richelieu Rock (a seamount 14km southeast) is also technically in the park and happens to be one of the best, if not the best, dive site on the Andaman Coast. There's no dive facility in the park itself, so dive trips must be booked from the mainland. Bleaching has damaged some of the hard corals but you'll see plenty of fish and soft corals.

Half-day snorkelling trips (150B per person, snorkel hire 160B) leave the island headquarters at 9am and 2pm. You can also charter a long-tail from the national park (3000B per day), or from **Ban Moken**, a village that is home to a community of *chow lair* (sea gypsies; also spelt *chao leh*).

Surin Islands Marine National Park

Accommodation   BUNGALOW, CAMPGROUND **$$**

(☑ 076 472145; www.dnp.go.th; Ko Surin Neua; r 2000-3000B, campsite per person 80B, with tent hire 300B; ⊗ mid-Oct–mid-May; ❋) Bungalows, at Ao Chong Khad, have wooden floors, private bathrooms, terraces, and fans (from 9.30pm to 7am) or air-con (from 6pm to 9.30pm). Electricity runs 6pm to 7am. You can camp on Ao Chong Khad and Ao Mai Ngam. The former has the more spectacular beach; the latter is more secluded and, with its narrow, shallow white-sand bay, feels wilder.

ⓘ Getting There & Away

If you're not visiting on an organised tour, tour operator speedboats (return 1800B, 1¼ hours one-way) leave around 9am, return between 1pm and 4pm and honour open tickets. Confirm your return ticket with Ko Surin Neua's park office the night before.

Similan Islands Marine National Park

Known to divers the world over, beautiful **Similan Islands Marine National Park** (อุทยานแห่งชาติหมู่เกาะสิมิลัน; ☑ 076 453272; www. dnp.go.th; adult/child 500/300B; ⊗ mid-Oct–mid-May) is 70km offshore. Its smooth granite islands are as impressive above water as below, topped with rainforests, edged with white-sand beaches and fringed with coral reefs.

Two of the nine islands, Island 4 (Ko Miang) and Island 8 (Ko Similan), have ranger stations and accommodation; park headquarters and most visitor activity centres are on Island 4. Khao Lak is the jumping-off point for the park. The pier is at Thap Lamu, about 10km south of town

The Similans offer diving for all levels, at depths from 2m to 30m. No facilities for divers exist in the national park, so you'll be taking a dive tour from Hat Khao Lak. Agencies in Khao Lak offer snorkelling-only day trips that visit three or four sites, from 3200B.

Coral bleaching has killed off many hard corals, but soft corals are still intact and there's plenty of fish. The Similans see many day trippers these days, so some snorkelling sites get very crowded.

The islands also have some lovely walking trails and there's lots of animal and bird life to spot.

Similan Islands Marine National Park Accommodation
BUNGALOW $$

(076 453272, in Bangkok 02 562 0760; www. dnp.go.th; Ko Miang (Island 4); r fan/air-con 1000/2000B, campsite with tent hire 570B; ⊗mid-Oct–mid-May; ❄) On Ko Miang there are 20 bungalows, the best with balconies, or tents. You are paying for the location: the bungalows are simple. During the day, many tour groups will drop by. Electricity operates from 6pm to 6am. Book ahead online, by phone or through the mainland **park headquarters** (076 453272; www. dnp.go.th; 93 Mu 5, Thap Lamu; ⊗8am-5pm mid-Oct–mid-May) at Thap Lamu. If you are camping, bring repellent: the mosquitoes are ferocious.

❶ Getting There & Away

There's no official public transport to the Similans. Almost everyone visits on tours from Hat Khao Lak and Phuket.

Phuket
ภูเก็ต

First, let's get the pronunciation right. The 'h' in Phuket is silent. And then remember that this is the largest Thai island, so you rarely feel surrounded by water. But that means there is space for everyone. Phuket offers such a rich variety of experiences – beach-bumming, culture, diving, kite-boarding and surfing, fabulous food, hedonistic or holistic pleasures – that visitors are spoilt for choice.

Of course, the white-sand beaches that ring the southern and western coasts are the principal draw. But there's also the culturally rich east-coast capital Phuket Town, as well as wildlife sanctuaries and national parks in the north.

❂ Sights & Activities

Phuket's stunning west coast, scalloped by sandy bays, faces the crystal Andaman Sea. **Patong** is the eye of the tourist storm, with **Kata** and **Karon** – Patong's little brothers – to the south. **Phuket Town** is the provincial capital and home to wonderful Sino-Portuguese architecture, some of which has been revitalised by artsy entrepreneurs.

★ Phuket Elephant Sanctuary
WILDLIFE, VOLUNTEERING

(Map p770; 094 990 3649; www.phuketelephantsanctuary.org; 100 Mu 2, Pa Klok, on 4027 Hwy; adult/child 3000/1500B; ⊗9.30am-1pm & 2-5.30pm) Phuket's only genuine elephant sanctuary is a refuge for animals who were mistreated for decades while working in the logging and tourism industries. During the morning tour, you get to feed them, before tagging along a few metres away as the aged pachyderms wander the forest, bathe and hang out. It's a rare opportunity that almost all visitors rave about.

★ John Gray's Seacanoe
KAYAKING

(Map p770; 076 254505; www.johngray-seacanoe.com; 86 Soi 2/3, Th Yaowarat; adult/child from 3950/1975B) ⊘ The original, the most reputable and by far the most ecologically sensitive kayaking company on Phuket. The 'Hong by Starlight' trip dodges the crowds, involves sunset paddling and will introduce you to Ao Phang-Nga's famed after-dark bioluminescence. Like any good brand in Thailand, John Gray's 'Seacanoe' name and itineraries have been frequently copied. Located 3.5km north of Phuket Town.

Kite Zone
KITESURFING

(Map p770; 083 395 2005; www.kitesurfthailand.com; Hat Friendship; 1hr lesson 1100B, 3-day course 10,000B) Rawai is a fine place to tackle kitesurfing and this cool young school has a tremendous perch on Hat Friendship. Courses range from one-hour tasters to three-day, 10-hour courses. From April to October, classes happen at **Hat Nai Yang** (หาดในยาง; Map p770) on the northwest side of the island. Also rents kit (per hour/day 1200/3500B) and runs stand-up paddle trips (from 700B).

Sea Fun Divers
DIVING

(076 330124; www.seafundivers.com; 14 Th Kata Noi, Katathani; 2-/3-dive day trip 3900/4400B; ⊗9am-6pm) An outstanding and very professional diving operation, albeit rather more expensive than the competition. Standards are extremely high, service is impeccable and instructors are keen and knowledgeable. Open Water Diver certification costs 18,400B. Sea Fun also has a **branch** (Map p770; 076 340480; www.seafundivers.com; 29 Soi Karon Nui; 2-/3-dive trip 3900/4400B, Open Water Diver certification 18,400B; ⊗9am-6pm) at Le Meridien resort at the southern end of Patong.

Phuket Surf
SURFING

(063 870280; www.phuketsurfing.com; Hat Kata Yai; lessons 1500B, board rental per hour/day 150/500B; ⊗8am-7pm Apr-late Oct) Offers pri-

vate 1½-hour surf lessons plus board rentals. Check the website for info on local surf breaks.

Tours

Amazing Bike Tours CYCLING
(☑ 076 283436, 087 263 2031; www.amazingbike-toursthailand.asia; 32/4 Th Chaofa; half-/full-day trip 1900/3200B) This highly popular adventure outfitter leads small groups on half-day bicycle tours through the villages of northeast Phuket, as well as on terrific full-day trips around Ko Yao Noi and more challenging three-day adventure rides around Khao Sok National Park (14,900B) and Krabi Province (15,900B). Prices include bikes, helmets, meals, water and national-park entry fees.

⭐⭐ Festivals

Vegetarian Festival RELIGIOUS
(www.phuketvegetarian.com; ☺ late Sep-Oct) Firecrackers pop, the air is thick with smoke and people parade through Phuket Town, some with their cheeks pierced with skewers and knives or, more surprisingly, lamps and tree branches. Welcome to the Vegetarian Festival, one of Phuket's most colourful celebrations, where residents of Chinese ancestry adopt a vegetarian diet for 10 days for the purpose of spiritual cleansing.

🛏 Sleeping

🛏 Phuket Town

Phuket Town is a treasure trove of affordable lodging, but you'll have to commute to the beach.

Ai Phuket Hostel HOSTEL **$**
(Map p772; ☑ 076 212881; www.aiphukethostel.com; 88 Th Yaowarat; dm 299B, d 700-900B; ❄ @ 🛜) Popular, well-organised hostel in the heart of town. Doubles are tight but come with wood floors, black-and-white photos and, for two rooms, private bathrooms. Not all have windows, something of an Old Town trait. Dorms lack windows also but are colourful and clean, sleeping six (women-only) to eight. All share polished-concrete hot-water bathrooms and a small downstairs hang-out lounge.

Art-C House GUESTHOUSE **$**
(Map p772; ☑ 082 420 3911; ArtCphuket@hotmail.com; 288 Th Phuket; d 800B; 🛜) Not many guesthouses have their own climbing wall

---

---

and a (smaller) bouldering wall inside. Art-C does, along with 10 tidy private rooms that are a good deal for pricey Phuket. There's a downstairs cafe and friendly staff; non-guests can access the climbing wall for 350B per day. There's no lift: you climb to your room (ropes provided free).

Box Poshtel HOSTEL **$**
(Map p772; ☑ 076 602367; boxposhtel@gmail.com; 151 Th Phang-Nga; dm 350, d 1000B; ❄ 🛜) The dorms and the few private rooms (all sharing bathrooms) at this new hostel are really boxes: they're places to crash only. But they are spotless with comfortable beds, and there's a downstairs bar and communal area and plans for a rooftop terrace. The staff and the place get good feedback, so book ahead.

🛏 Patong

If you can't score a bed in a hostel, you'll struggle to find a room for under 1000B between November and April.

★Wire Hostel HOSTEL **$**
(☑ 076 604066; 66/10 Th Bangla; dm 340-550B; ❄ @ 🛜) Patong's hostel of the moment is right in the belly of the beast: a minute's walk from the Bangla nightlife. There's some stylish design on display, three floors of dorms (none with doors but you can get a double bed if you fancy getting intimate in public). Downstairs bar, clean shared bathrooms but, unsurprisingly, it can get noisy. Book ahead.

Phuket

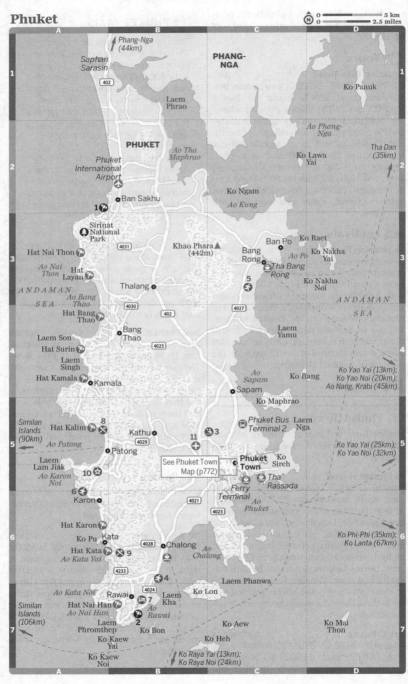

Phang-Nga (44km)

PHANG-NGA

Ko Panuk

Saphan Sarasin

402

Laem Phrao

PHUKET

Ao Tha Maphrao

Ao Phang-Nga

Tha Dan (35km)

Ko Lawa Yai

Phuket International Airport

Ban Sakhu

Ko Ngam

Ao Kung

Ban Po

Ko Raet

Sirinat National Park

Khao Phara (442m)

Bang Rong

Ko Nakha Yai

Ao Po

Hat Nai Thon

Tha Bang Rong

Ko Nakha Noi

Ao Nai Thon

Hat Layan

ANDAMAN SEA

4031

Thalang

5

ANDAMAN SEA

Ao Bang Thao

4030

402

4027

Laem Yamu

Hat Bang Thao

Bang Thao

4025

Laem Son

Ko Yao Yai (13km); Ko Yao Noi (20km); Ao Nang, Krabi (45km)

Hat Surin

Laem Singh

Ao Sapam

Ko Rang

Hat Kamala

Kamala

Sapam

Ko Maphrao

Similan Islands (90km)

Hat Kalim

8

Phuket Bus Terminal 2

Laem Nga

Ao Patong

Kathu

11

3

Phuket Town

Ko Yao Yai (25km); Ko Yao Noi (32km)

4029

See Phuket Town Map (p772)

Ko Sireh

Patong

Laem Lam Jiak

10

Ferry Terminal

Tha Rassada

Ao Karon Noi

6

4021

Ao Phuket

Ko Phi-Phi (35km); Ko Lanta (67km)

Karon

4023

Hat Karon

Ko Pu

Kata

4028

Chalong

Ao Chalong

Hat Kata

9

Ao Kata Yai

4233

4

Laem Phanwa

Ao Kata Noi

4024

Rawai

Laem Kha

Ko Lon

Similan Islands (106km)

Hat Nai Han

7

Ao Rawai

Ko Bon

2

Ko Aew

Ko Mai Thon

Laem Phromthep

Ko Kaew Yai

Ko Heh

Ko Kaew Noi

Ko Raya Yai (13km); Ko Raya Noi (24km)

Phuket

Hip Hostel   HOSTEL $
(📞076 636998; hiphostelpatong@gmail.com; 202/3 Th Rat Uthit; dm 320-380B, d 990B; ❋ 🛜) There's no communal area and it's not that hip, but the four- and six-bed dorms are comfortable enough and have their own bathrooms inside. Private rooms are big with stone floors and small balconies and are a reasonable deal. Efficient staff. It's down a small soi: look for the sign.

Priew Wan Guesthouse   GUESTHOUSE $$
(📞076 344441; info@priewwanguesthouse.com; 83/9 Th Rat Uthit; d 1600B; 🛜) This long-running and reliable family-run guesthouse is hidden down a mostly residential soi, but is still only a 10-minute walk to the northern end of Hat Patong. Clean, sizeable rooms come with balconies, safes, fridges and TVs and are a good deal. Friendly staff and great low-season (April to October) discounts.

🛌 Southern Beaches

South of Patong, the vibe mellows out in increments. Hat Karon is the most hyperactive of the bunch. Hat Kata is more well-heeled yet still social, and Hat Nai Han is a beautiful beach, best for a day's ocean frolic rather than a budget sleep. Way down south, Rawai is carved out of lush rolling hills.

★ Fin Hostel   HOSTEL $
(📞088 753 1162; www.finhostelphuket.com; 100/20 Th Kata/Patak West; dm/capsules/d 400/600/2000B; ❋ 🛜 ☒) This well-kept, efficient hostel, set back from the road, spreads across two buildings. Dorms are spotless with comfy mattresses. The capsules are a step up – curtained spaces with either single or double mattresses – while private rooms have some quirky decoration, beanbags, TVs and fridges. There's a decent communal area, a small rooftop pool and you're walking distance to Kata beach.

Doolay Hostel   HOSTEL $
(📞062 451 9546; www.doolayhostel.com; 164 Th Karon/Patak West; dm 450-600B; ❋ 🛜) There are 40 beds spread across six compact, four- and eight-bed dorms at this newish place that's a mere stroll across the road to the sand. Mattresses are good and the bathrooms are clean. There's a nice communal area and, best of all, a long 2nd-floor seafront terrace strewn with bean bags that's fine for lounging. Helpful staff. Book ahead.

Good 9 at Home   GUESTHOUSE $
(Map p770; 📞088 457 6969; www.facebook.com/good9athome; 62 Mu 6, Soi Wassana, Hat Rawai; d 900B; ❋ 🛜) Set beside a cute patio, these seven fresh, gleaming contemporary-style rooms spiced up with colour accent walls, tiled bathrooms and the odd bit of artwork make for good-value digs, 300m up the street from **Hat Rawai** (หาดราไวย์; Map p770). The lime-green-and-grey house is kept clean, cosy and friendly, with a thoughtful little coffee corner thrown into the mix.

Pineapple Guesthouse   GUESTHOUSE $
(📞076 396223; www.pineapplephuket.com; 291/4 Karon Plaza, Hat Karon; dm/d 300/1100B; ❋ @ 🛜) Pocketed away 400m inland from Hat Karon, Pineapple is a decent budget choice under warm Thai-English management. Rooms are old-fashioned, but clean and comfortable enough with colourful feature walls, fridges and, in some cases, small balconies. There's a simple 10-bed dorm (closed low season April to October) with its own bathroom and big lockers.

🛌 Northern Beaches

The northern beaches are sublime and so are the luxury rates. But there are a few budget options.

Phuket Town

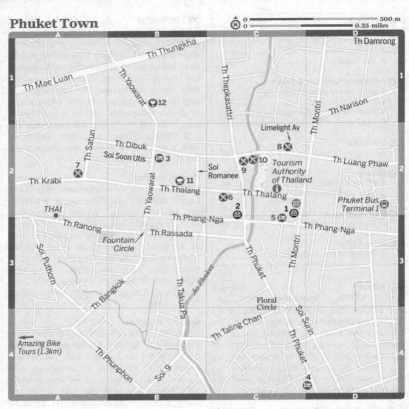

0 500 m
0 0.25 miles

THAILAND PHUKET

Phuket Town

Pensiri House   GUESTHOUSE $

(☏ 076 327683; www.pensirihouse.com; 112 Mu 5, Hat Nai Yang; d 800-1200B; ❋ 🛜) 300m inland from Hat Nai Yang, this friendly place is the best budget option in the area. Rooms are spread across two buildings. The nicest are in the new block: sizeable, light, modern and with balconies. All come with TVs, fridges and safes.

Baan Kamala   GUESTHOUSE $

(☏ 076 279053; www.baankamalaphuket.com; 74/42 Mu 3, Hat Kamala; dm 450-550B, d 2000B; ❋ 🛜) A cross between a guesthouse and a hostel, welcoming Baan Kamala offers big and light six-bed dorms for backpackers and a collection of individually designed private rooms for flashpackers. The concrete walls of the spacious rooms are livened up with paintings and beds are comfortable, although bathrooms are a little poky. The communal area features its very own long-tail boat.

Eating

Phuket Town

There's great food in Phuket Town, and meals cost a lot less than at the beach.

★ Abdul's Roti Shop   BREAKFAST $
(Map p772; Th Thalang; mains from 40B; ⊙7am-4pm Mon-Sat, to noon Sun) Time to try Abdul's legendary, delicious *roti*. At 75-years-plus, Abdul has been cooking flaky *roti* at the front of his shop for years. Whether you're a fan of sweet or savoury, this place has it covered, with sticky banana *roti* or plain served with spicy chicken, beef or fish massaman (curry).

Indy Market   MARKET $
(Map p772; Limelight Av; mains 30-100B; ⊙4-10.30pm Wed-Fri) Local families, schoolkids and students flock to this smallish central market for the excellent array of food stalls, ranging from barbecue and dumplings to sushi and sweet snacks. There's also a couple of outdoor bars, live music and clothes and jewellery stalls.

★ One Chun   THAI $$
(Map p772; ✆076 355909; 48/1 Th Thepkasattri; mains 90-350B; ⊙10am-10pm; 🔊) A sister restaurant to **Raya** (Map p772; ✆076 218155; rayarestaurant@gmail.com; 48/1 Th Dibuk; mains 180-650B; ⊙10am-10pm), only the dishes here are cheaper and that's why the locals crowd it out every night. Superb seafood – the crabmeat curry in coconut milk is the best in Phuket Town – but also a great roasted-duck red curry. The atmospheric shophouse setting, with 1950s decor and tiled floors, adds to the experience.

Patong

Patong has loads of restaurants for all budgets. Bargain seafood and noodle stalls pop up at night. Try the sois around Th Bangla.

Patong Food Park   THAI $
(Th Rat Uthit; mains 50-200B; ⊙4.30pm-midnight) This cheap, local foodie's dream world is jammed with stalls offering all kinds of fresh fish, crab, lobster, roasted pork leg, steamed chicken, satay and *sôm-dam* (spicy green papaya salad), plus sticky rice with mango for dessert. All delicious.

★ No.9 2nd Restaurant   ASIAN $$
(✆076 624445; 143 Th Phra Barami; mains 165-800B; ⊙11.30am-11.30pm, closed 5th & 20th of every month) Deceptively simple, with wooden tables and photo-strewn walls, this is one of the best, busiest restaurants in Patong, thanks to the inventive and delicious mix of Thai, Japanese and Western dishes. It's a rare feat for a kitchen to be able to turn out authentic sushi, vegetarian versions of Thai curries and a lamb shank without any dip in quality.

THAILAND PHUKET

SPLURGE

If you want to flash the cash, Phuket has plenty of excellent international eateries who'll happily oblige you.

Eat Bar & Grill (✆085 292 5652; www.eatbargrill.com; 250/1 Th Patak East; mains 200-800B; ⊙11am-10pm; 🔊) Awesome burgers and superb steaks contend for the best on Phuket, at this laid-back place with a wooden bar and limited space (make sure to book ahead). The menu includes other dishes, including a great lamb shank, but beef is the thing here: prepared to your taste, stylishly presented and reasonably priced, given the quality. Proper cocktails too.

Home Kitchen (Map p770; ✆093 764 6753; www.facebook.com/home.kitchen.bar.bed; 314 Th Phra Barami, Hat Kalim; mains 195-695B; ⊙4-11pm, closed Sun; 🔊) White leather, faded tables, floaty fabrics, burning lanterns and neon lighting make this crazily beautiful, quirky-chic dining room/cocktail bar shaped like a ship's hull the coolest eatery in Patong. And the creative Thai-Mediterranean food is fab too. Try avocado and crabmeat salad, squid-ink pasta with salmon, massaman (curry) Wagyu beef, deep-fried *pá·naang*-curry sea bass and perfectly crispy Parmesan-coated chips.

PHUKET TOWN'S SINO-PORTUGUESE ARCHITECTURE

Stroll along Ths Thalang, Dibuk, Yaowarat, Ranong, Phang-Nga, Rassada and Krabi for a glimpse of Phuket Town's Sino-Portuguese architectural treasures. The most magnificent examples are the **Standard Chartered Bank** (ธนาคารสแตนดาร์ดชาร์เตอร์ด; Map p772; Th Phang-Nga), Thailand's oldest foreign bank; the **THAI office** (Map p772; ☑ 076 360444; www.thaiairways.com; 78/1 Th Ranong, Phuket Town; ⊗8am-4.30pm); and the **old post office building**, which now houses the **Phuket Philatelic Museum** (พิพิธภัณฑ์ ตราไปรษณียากรภูเก็ต; Map p772; ☑ 076 211020; Th Montri; ⊗9am-4.30pm Mon-Fri, to noon Sat) FREE. Some of the most colourfully revamped buildings line Soi Romanee, off Th Thalang, once home to brothels, gambling and opium dens.

The best-restored residential properties lie along Ths Thalang, Dibuk and Krabi. The fabulous 1903 **Phra Phitak Chyn Pracha Mansion** has been refurbished into the upscale **Blue Elephant restaurant** (Map p772; ☑ 076 354355; www.blueelephant.com; 96 Th Krabi; mains 420-980B; set menus 1150-2050B; ⊗11.30am-2pm & 6.30-10pm; ☎ ☑) and **cooking school** (Map p772; ☑ 076 354355; www.blueelephantcookingschool.com; 96 Th Krabi; half-day classes 3296B; ⊗Mon-Sun).

Ella　　　　　　　　　INTERNATIONAL **$$**
(☑ 076 344253; 100/19-20 Soi Post Office; mains 150-400B; ⊗9am-midnight; ☎) This moulded-concrete, industrial-feel bistro-cafe is a lovely surprise. Inventive all-day breakfasts feature spicy Rajasthani scrambled eggs, massaman (curry) chicken tacos, omelettes stuffed with chicken and veg, and baguette French toast with caramelised banana. At night, it's also a bar and a cool spot for a cocktail. There are similarly styled rooms (d2200-4000B) for rent upstairs.

✕ Southern Beaches

★ Pad Thai Shop　　　　　　THAI **$**
(Th Patak East, Hat Karon; mains 50-80B; ⊗8am-7pm, closed Fri) This glorified roadside food shack makes rich, savoury chicken stew and absurdly good *kôw pàt boo* (fried rice with crab), *pàt see·éw* (fried noodles) and noodle soup. It also serves up some of the best *pàt tai* we've ever tasted: spicy and sweet, packed with tofu, egg and peanuts, and plated with spring onions, bean sprouts and lime.

Kata Mama　　　　　　　　THAI **$**
(☑ 076 284006; Hat Kata Yai; mains 100-200B; ⊗8am-10pm) Our pick of several cheapie seafood places at the southern end of Hat Kata Yai, long-standing Kata Mama keeps busy thanks to its charming management, reliably tasty Thai standards and low-key beachside setting.

★ Istanbul Restaurant　　　TURKISH **$$**
(Map p770; ☑ 091 820 7173; www.istanbulrestaurantphuket.com; 100/87 Th Koktanod, Hat Kata; mains 210-320B; ⊗8am-10pm) This delightful, family-run place is the most popular foreign restaurant in Kata and for good reason. The food is simply splendid, ranging from big Western- or Turkish-style breakfasts to completely authentic and super-tasty mains such as *hünkar beğendi* (beef stew on a bed of eggplant puree), kebabs and Turkish-style pizza. Then there are the superb soups, salads and delectable desserts.

✕ Northern Beaches

Mr Kobi　　　　　　　　　THAI **$$**
(Hat Nai Yang; mains 150-350B; ⊗10am-11pm) The sign says 'Broken English spoken here perfect', but the ever-popular Mr Kobi speaks English very well. He handles the drinks, while Malee deals with the seafood and Thai faves served up in refreshingly unpretentious surroundings. One wall is dedicated to telling the story of the 2004 tsunami.

Phen's Restaurant　　　THAI, SEAFOOD **$$**
(☑ 081 895 9489; www.facebook.com/PhensRestaurant; Hat Nai Yang; mains 80-280B; ⊗9am-10pm; ☎) Turquoise-on-white tablecloths and attentive staff make Phen's a popular beachside choice. It's one of the few spots where you can still dine with sand between your toes. Expect masses of barbecued fresh seafood (lemon-fried crab, red-curry snapper, chilli-smoked shrimp), as well as a few Phuket dishes, such as *gaeng som pla*, a sour and spicy fish curry.

Drinking & Entertainment

 Phuket Town

★**Bookhemian** CAFE

(Map p772; ☑098 090 0657; www.bookhemian. com; 61 Th Thalang; ☺9am-7pm Mon-Fri, to 8.30pm Sat & Sun; ☜) Every town should have a coffee house this cool, with a split-level design that enables it to be both a cafe and an art exhibition space. Used books (for sale) line the front room, bicycles hang from the wall, and the offerings include gourmet coffee, tea and cakes, as well as all-day breakfasts, salads, sandwiches and pasta.

Timber Hut CLUB

(Map p772; ☑076 211839; 118/1 Th Yaowarat; ☺6pm-2am) Locals, expats and visitors have been packing out this two-floor pub-club nightly for 27 years, downing beers and whisky while swaying to live bands that swing from hard rock to pure pop to hip-hop. No cover charge.

 Patong

Th Bangla is Patong's beer and bar-girl mecca and features a number of spectacular gogo extravaganzas, where you can expect the usual mix of gyrating Thai girls and often red-faced Western men.

Illuzion CLUB

(www.illuzionphuket.com; 31 Th Bangla; ☺9pm-late) Still the most popular of Patong's megaclubs, Illuzion is a multi-level mishmash of dance and gymnastics shows, international DJs, regular ladies' nights, all-night electronic beats, LED screens and more bars than you could ever count.

Bangla Boxing Stadium SPECTATOR SPORT

(☑076 273416; www.banglaboxingstadiumpatong. com; Th Pangmuang Sai Kor; stadium/ringside 1700/2500B; ☺9pm Wed, Fri & Sun) A packed line-up of competitive *moo·ay tai* (Thai boxing) bouts featuring Thai and foreign fighters.

Phuket Simon Cabaret CABARET

(Map p770; ☑076 342114; www.phuket-simon-cabaret.com; 8 Th Sirirach; adult 800-1000B, child 600-800B; ☺shows 6pm, 7.30pm & 9pm) About 500m south of town, Simon puts on fun, colourful trans cabarets that are wildly popular with Asian tourists. The 600-seat theatre is grand, the costumes are glittery, feathery extravaganzas, and the ladyboys are convincing. The house is usually full – book ahead.

Southern Beaches

★**Ska Bar** BAR

(www.skabar-phuket.com; 186/12 Th Koktanod; ☺1pm-2am) Tucked into the rocks on the southernmost curl of Hat Kata Yai and seemingly intertwined with the trunk of a grand old banyan tree, Ska is our choice for seaside sundowners. The Thai bartenders add to the laid-back Rasta vibe, and buoys, paper lanterns and flags dangle from the canopy. There's normally a fire show on Friday nights.

★**Art Space Cafe & Gallery** BAR

(☑090 156 0677; Th Kade Kwan, Hat Kata; ☺11am-1am) Hands down the most fabulously quirky bar in Phuket, this trippy, multi-use space bursts with colour and is smothered in uniquely brushed canvases and sculptures celebrating, especially, the feminine form. It's the work of an eccentric creative and his tattoo-artist wife, who whip up both decent cocktails and veggie meals (160B to 400B). There's normally live music around 8pm.

ℹ **Information**

Phuket International Hospital (Map p770; ☑076 361818, 076 249400; www.phuketinternationalhospital.com; 44 Th Chalermprakiat) International doctors rate this hospital as the island's best. Diving emergencies are normally brought here.

Tourism Authority of Thailand (TAT; Map p772; ☑076 211036; www.tourismthailand.org/Phuket; 191 Th Thalang; ☺8.30am-4.30pm) Has maps, brochures, transport advice and info on boat trips to nearby islands.

ℹ **PHUKET DANGERS & ANNOYANCES**

During May to October, large waves and fierce undertows can make it too dangerous to swim, especially at certain beaches; red-flag warnings are posted when conditions are rough.

Phuket's roads are congested and road rules are erratic. It is not advised to rent a motorcycle, especially for inexperienced drivers, as vehicle accidents and fatalities are common. If you do drive a motorbike, wear a helmet and protective clothing and keep your belongings on your person, not in the basket. Do not drink and drive.

THAILAND PHUKET

BUSES FROM PHUKET BUS TERMINAL 2

DESTINATION	FARE (B)	DURATION (HR)	FREQUENCY	BUS TYPE
Bangkok	913	13	5pm, 6.30pm	VIP
	587	13-14	6.30am, 7am, 1.30pm, 3.30pm, 5.30pm, 6pm, 6.30pm	air-con
Chiang Mai	1646	22	12.30pm	VIP
Hat Yai	507	7	9.45pm	VIP
	326	7	hourly 7.30am-12.30pm, 7.30pm & 9.30pm	air-con
Ko Samui	450	8 (bus/boat)	9am	air-con
Ko Pha-Ngan	550	9½ (bus/boat)	9am	air-con
Krabi	140	3½	hourly 4.50am-7pm	air-con
Phang-Nga	80	2½	hourly 4.50am-7pm	air-con
Ranong	225	6	hourly 5.30am-6.10pm	air-con
Satun	329	7	8.15am, 10.15am, 12.15pm, 8.15pm	air-con
Surat Thani	195	5	8am, 10am, noon, 2pm	air-con
Trang	230	5	hourly 4.50am-7pm	air-con

Tourist Police (☑1669, 076 342719; cnr Th Thawiwong & Th Bangla) Tourist police outpost by the beach.

ⓘ Getting There & Away

AIR
Phuket International Airport (Map p770; ☑ 076 632 7230; www.phuketairportthai.com) is 30km northwest of Phuket Town; it takes around 45 minutes to an hour to reach the southern beaches from here. An orange government airport bus runs between the airport and Phuket Town (100B, one hour, from 8am to 8.30pm); taxis to the airport start at 450B, depending which beach you are on. There are many flights to Bangkok and other domestic and international destinations.

BOAT
Phuket's **Tha Rassada** (Map p770; Tha Rassada), 3km southeast of Phuket Town, is the main pier for boats to Ko Phi-Phi and the other southern Andaman islands. Additional services to Krabi and Ao Nang via Ko Yao leave from **Tha Bang Rong** (Map p770; Tha Bang Rong), 26km north of Tha Rassada.

BUS & MINIVAN
Interstate buses depart from **Phuket Bus Terminal 2** (Map p770; Th Thepkrasattri), 4km north of Phuket Town. Minivans to destinations across southern Thailand leave from **Phuket Bus Terminal 1** (Map p772; Th Phang-Nga), 500m east of Phuket Town centre.

ⓘ Getting Around

Large *sŏrng·tăa·ou* run from Th Ranong near Phuket Town's day market to the beaches (20B to 40B, regularly 7am to 5pm). Túk-túk and taxis should cost about 400B to 600B from Phuket Town to the beaches. Motorcycle rentals (300B) are widely available but are not recommended for novice riders.

Krabi Town   กระบี่
☑075 / POPULATION 31,475
Bustling Krabi Town is a key transport hub for the nearby islands, around which a busy traveller scene continues to evolve. There's no shortage of restaurants, or guesthouses, while just down the road Ao Nang has more upmarket accommodation..

🛏 Sleeping & Eating

★**Pak-Up Hostel**   HOSTEL $
(☑075 611955; www.pakuphostel.com; 87 Th Utarakit; dm/r 380/850B; 🕸@🤏) Still the hostel of choice in Krabi, Pak-Up has contemporary, polished-cement air-con dorms with big wooden bunks built into the wall, each with its own locker. Massive, modern shared bathrooms have cold-water stalls and hot-water rain showers. The two doubles share bathrooms and women-only dorms are available. The bar gets busy and there's a young, fun-loving vibe here.

Chan Cha Lay
GUESTHOUSE $$

(☑075 620952; www.lovechanchalay.com; 55 Th Utarakit; r 400-1400B; ❋@☎) The en-suite, air-con rooms at long-standing Chan Cha Lay, done up in Mediterranean blues and whites with white-pebble and polished-concrete open-air bathrooms, are among Krabi's most comfortable and charming for the price. There's a range of cheaper rooms with shared-bathroom, and fan or air-con, which are plain and compact but spotless.

Night Market
MARKET, THAI $

(Th Khong Kha; mains 30-70B; ☺4-10pm) Beside Tha Khong Kha, this market is a popular place for an evening meal. Try authentic *sôm·dam* (spicy green papaya salad), wok-fried noodles, *dôm yam gûng* (prawn and lemongrass soup), grilled snapper and all things satay, plus creamy Thai desserts and freshly pressed juices. English menus are a bonus.

★ May & Mark's
INTERNATIONAL, THAI $$

(☑081 396 6114; 34 Th Sukhon; mains 75-250B; ☺7am-10pm; ☎) A classic travellers meeting spot with a bold varnished-concrete coffee bar, May and Mark's is always busy. We love it for the excellent espresso and the big choice of delicious omelettes, pancakes and home-baked bread. It also does popular Thai meals, plus international salads, sandwiches and mains. Good vegetarian selection.

❶ Information

Krabi Immigration Office (☑075 611097; 382 Mu 7, Saithai; ☺8.30am-4.30pm Mon-Fri) Handles visa extensions; 4km southwest of Krabi.
Krabi Nakharin International Hospital (☑075 626555; www.krabinakharin.co.th; 1 Th Pisanpob) Located 2km northwest of town.

❶ Getting There & Away

The airport is 14km northeast of Krabi on Hwy 4. A taxi to/from town is 350B. Most domestic carriers fly between Bangkok and Krabi. Bangkok Air flies daily to Ko Samui and Air Asia to Chiang Mai.

Krabi bus terminal (☑075 663503; cnr Th Utarakit & Hwy 4) is about 5km north of Krabi. *Sŏrng·tăa·ou* run from the bus station to central Krabi (30B, frequently 6am to 6.30pm) and onto Ao Nang (60B). Travel agencies run minivans to popular southern destinations, but they are often overcrowded. The cheaper minivans that leave from the bus terminal are a better deal.

BOAT

Boats to Ko Phi-Phi (300B to 350B, 1½ to two hours, four daily) and Ko Lanta (400B, two hours, one daily) leave from the passenger pier at **Tha Khlong Chilat**, about 4km southwest of Krabi. Travel agencies will arrange free transfers. Schedules vary in the low season. Take a long-tail boat from Krabi's Khong Kha pier to Hat Raily (150B, 45 minutes, between 7.45am and 6pm).

Railay
ไร่เล

Krabi's fairytale limestone formations come to a dramatic climax at Railay, the ultimate Andaman gym for rock-climbing fanatics. Monkeys gamble alongside climbers on the gorgeous crags, while down below some of the prettiest beaches in all Thailand are backed by proper jungle.

Railay is more crowded than it was but, thankfully, it remains much less-developed than Ko Phi-Phi.

❄ Activities

With more than 1000 routes in 51 areas, ranging from beginner to challenging advanced climbs, all with unparalleled clifftop vistas, Railay is among the world's top

BUSES FROM KRABI

DESTINATION	FARE (B)	DURATION (HR)	FREQUENCY
Bangkok (VIP)	862	12	5pm
Bangkok (air-con)	587	12	8am, 8.20am, 4pm, 5pm, 6pm
Hat Yai	255	4½	hourly 8.30am-7.20pm
Phuket	140	3	every 30min 8.30am-7.20pm
Ranong	210	5	8.30am & noon
Satun	212	5	11am, 1pm, 2pm, 3pm
Surat Thani	150	2½	hourly 4.30am-4.30pm
Trang	110	2	every 30min 7.30am-5pm

climbing spots. Deep-water soloing, where free-climbers scramble up ledges over deep water, is incredibly popular here. Climbing courses cost 800B to 1000B for a half day and 1500B to 1800B for a full day. Snorkelling, diving and kayaking trips are also available.

King Climbers
CLIMBING

(☎081 797 8923; www.railay.com; Walking St; half/full day 1000/1800B, 3-day course 6000B; ☻8.30am-9pm Mon-Fri, to 6pm Sat & Sun) One of the biggest, oldest and most reputable climbing schools.

Basecamp Tonsai
CLIMBING

(☎081 149 9745; www.tonsaibasecamp.com; Hat Ton Sai; half/full day 800/1500B, 3-day course 6000B; ☻8am-5pm & 7-9pm) Long-established, laid-back climbing outfit. Big on deep-water soloing (700B).

Hot Rock
CLIMBING

(☎085 641 9842; www.railayadventure.com; Hat Railay East; half/full day 1000/1800B, 3-day course 6000B; ☻9am-8pm) Owned by one of the granddaddies of Railay climbing, Hot Rock has a good reputation.

🛏 Sleeping & Eating

Hat Ton Sai, the most isolated beach, is where you'll find the best budget choices and a buzzing backpacker/climber scene. Hat Railay East and Railay Highlands have many midrange options.

Chill Out
BUNGALOW $$

(☎087 699 4527, 084 186 8138; www.chilloutkrabi. com; Hat Ton Sai; dm 300B, bungalows 600-1200B; ☎) While no more luxurious than Ton Sai's other offerings, Chill Out's bungalows bring a sociable, laid-back atmosphere and a pinch more style. Vibrantly painted international flags are plastered across the doors of basic tin-topped, wood-floored huts, which have terraces, cold-water bathrooms and mosquito nets. The dorm is functional with bunk beds. The **bar** (Hat Ton Sai; ☻11am-late; ☎) gets busy. Electricity and wi-fi in evenings only.

Rapala Rockwood Resort
BUNGALOW $$

(☎080 973 7778; kritrailay1@gmail.com; Hat Railay East; bungalow 600-1200B; ❄☎) These simple wooden bungalows have been spruced up with gleaming paint and hammocks on verandahs. Inside are cold-water bathrooms, mosquito nets and fans. The most expensive are bigger and have air-con. There's a teensy paddling pool beside a couple of sun loung-

ers. The hilltop location means breezes, sea panoramas and some steep steps.

Mama's Chicken
THAI $

(Hat Ton Sai; mains 70-100B; ☻7am-10pm; 🖉) Relocated to the jungle path leading inland to Hat Railay East and West, Mama's remains one of Ton Sai's favourite food stops for its international breakfasts, fruit smoothies and extensive range of cheap Thai dishes, including a rare massaman tofu and other vegetarian-friendly adaptations.

Mangrove Restaurant
THAI $$

(Walking St; mains 80-350B; ☻10am-10pm; ☎) This humble, heaving, local-style place, set beneath a stilted thatched roof between east and west beaches, turns out all the Thai favourites, from glass-noodle salad and cashew-nut stir-fry to curries, spicy *sôm đam* and the wonderful creation that is egg-grilled sticky rice. Praise goes to the kitchen's matriarch.

❶ Getting There & Away

Long-tail boats to Railay run from Khong Kha pier in Krabi (150B, 45 minutes, 7.45am to 6pm) when full (eight passengers). The Ao Nang Princess stops at Hat Railay West en route to Ko Phi-Phi (450B, two hours, daily November to April; service is less frequent from May to October).

The next bay over from Railay is Ao Nang, which has land access to Krabi Town. Ao Nang is accessible by boat from Hat Railay West and Hat Ton Sai (100B/150B day/night, 15 minutes, with eight passengers). From Ao Nang, *sŏrng·tăa·ou* and buses go to Krabi Town (60B, 20 minutes) and Krabi airport (150B, hourly from 9am to 5pm). There are also minivans to other southern Thai locations from Ao Nang.

North of Ao Nang is Hat Noppharat, a national park with speedboat access to Phuket (1200B, 1¼ hours, 11am from November to April).

Ko Phi-Phi
เกาะพีพี

With their curvy, bleached beaches and stunning jungle interiors, Phi-Phi Don and Phi-Phi Leh (collectively known as Ko Phi-Phi) are the darlings of the Andaman Coast. Phi-Phi Don is a hedonistic paradise where visitors cavort by day in azure seas and party all night on soft sand. In contrast, smaller Phi-Phi Leh, the setting of the book and movie *The Beach*, is undeveloped and can only be visited only on day or sunset cruises.

Phi-Phi Don is no peaceful island paradise. Rampant development has rendered its centre a chaotic, noisy mess. But the east

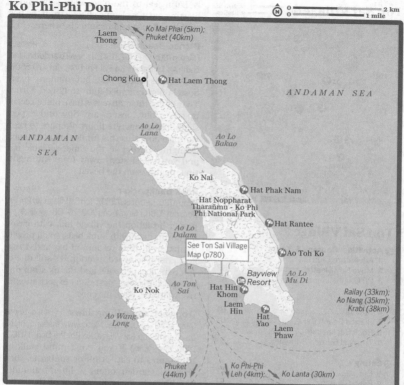

coast and Hat Yao in the south remain relatively tranquil.

🏃 Activities & Tours

Crystalline water and abundant marine life make the perfect recipe for top-notch scuba diving. Prices are stadardised across the island. Open Water certification costs 13,800B, while standard two-dive trips cost 2500B to 3500B. Day snorkelling trips go from 600B to 1500B.

You can also rock climb on Ko Phi-Phi, but most operators are based on Railay.

★ Adventure Club
DIVING

(Map p780; 📞 081 895 1334; www.diving-in-thailand.net; 125/19 Mu 7, Ton Sai Village, Ko Phi-Phi Don; 2 dives 2500B; ⏱ 7am-10pm) 🌿 Our favourite Phi-Phi diving operation runs an excellent assortment of educational and responsible diving and snorkelling tours. You won't mind getting up at 6am for the popu-

lar shark-watching snorkel trips (1100B) on which you're guaranteed to cavort with at least one reef shark. Open Water certification 13,800B.

PP Original Sunset Tour
BOATING

(Map p780; Ton Sai Village, Ko Phi-Phi Don; per person 900B; ⏱ tours 1pm) A sensational sunset cruise that sees you bobbing around Phi-Phi Leh aboard a double-decker boat to mellow beats, snorkelling and kayaking between Ao Pi Leh's sheer-sided cliffs and dining on fried rice off Maya Beach. Led by an enthusiastic, organised team. Bliss.

Maya Bay Sleepaboard
BOATING

(Map p780; www.mayabaytours.com; Ton Sai Village, Ko Phi-Phi Don; per person 3500B) You can no longer camp on Phi-Phi Leh's Maya Beach, but Maya Bay Sleepaboard can arrange for you to spend the night just offshore. Prices include food, sleeping bags and national park entry fees; tours depart at 3pm, re-

Ton Sai Village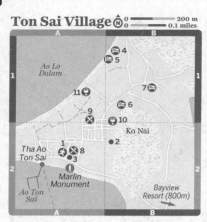

0 | 200 m
0 | 0.1 miles

turning at 10am the following morning. The same team runs the popular **Plankton Sunset Cruise** (www.mayabaytours.com; Ko Phi-Phi Leh; per person 1700B; ⊙3-8pm) to Phi-Phi Leh.

🛏 Sleeping

Book in advance during holiday periods and secure your windows and doors to deter break-ins.

Apache HOSTEL $
(Map p780; ☑ 081 535 4613; apachebar_2008@ hotmail.com; Ao Lo Dalam, Ko Phi-Phi Don; dm 500-550B, r 1500B; ❋🔊) One of several bar/hostel combos on kicking Ao Lo Dalam, Apache has compact dorms and rooms that are comfortable enough, given that you won't be spending too much time in them, and an amenable vibe. At night, there's a vague-

ly Latin feel to the place with salsa music blasting out, a welcome change from the bog standard house and techno elsewhere.

Blanco Beach Bar HOSTEL $
(Map p780; ☑ 061 231 4101; www.blancothailand. com; Ao Lo Dalam, Ko Phi-Phi Don; dm 470-550B; ❋🔊) This bare-bones but modern party hostel offers cramped four- to 12-bed dorms. Thankfully, the mattresses have had a recent upgrade, but lockers are tiny and expect sand on the concrete floors. Prepare to keep vampire hours, as this fun-loving place stages nightly parties in the super-sociable bar and you're just steps away from the night-time madness on the beach.

Rock Backpacker HOSTEL $
(Map p780; ☑ 081 607 3897; Ton Sai Village, Ko Phi-Phi Don; dm 300B, r fan/air-con 900/2000B; ❋@🔊) A proper hostel on the village hill, with clean, big dorms lined with bunk beds, small private rooms, an inviting restaurant-bar and a rugged, graffiti-scrawled exterior. It's still one of Ton Sai's cheaper pads and there's a buzzing backpacker scene – just don't expect an effusive welcome. Walk-ins only.

Tropical Garden Bungalows BUNGALOW $$
(Map p780; ☑ 089 729 1436; www.thailandphiphi-travel.com; Ton Sai Village, Ko Phi-Phi Don; r 1100-1800B; ❋🔊🏊) If you don't mind walking 10 minutes to eat, drink or sunbathe, then Tropical Garden offers a little tranquillity (although you're in earshot of the bars). Near the viewpoint path, the simple bungalows are set close together in a shady garden and come with balconies and hammocks. The cheapest are fan-only. There's a small flower-fringed pool with a swim-up bar.

Bayview Resort RESORT $$$
(Map p779; ☑ 075 601127; www.phiphibayview. com; 69/1 Mu 7, Hat Laem Hin, Ko Phi-Phi Don; r 1500-3600B; ❋@🔊🏊) This vast place sprawls uphill from an OK beach and is strategically located about halfway between Ton Sai Village and Hat Yao. There are 200 bungalows here in different sizes, all modern with wood floors and big balconies and all mod cons. Some have decent sea views. It feels a little soulless, but it's efficient and is open year round.

🍽 Eating, Drinking & Nightlife

⭐ **Esan Ganeang** THAI $
(Map p780; Ton Sai Village, Ko Phi-Phi Don; mains 70-150B; ⊙10am-midnight) On an alley jammed with hole-in-the-wall places favoured by the

locals, family-run Esan Ganeang has fantastic and authentic dishes from the Isan region in northeast Thailand. Come here for fiery salads and soups, as well as more mild curries and noodle dishes packed with flavour. Make sure to order sticky rice to accompany your meal.

★ Efe
TURKISH $$

(Map p780; ☑ 095 150 4434; Ton Sai Village, Ko Phi-Phi Don; mains 170-640B; ☺ noon-10.30pm; 🛜) This Mediterranean newcomer has swiftly become the restaurant of choice for discerning travellers and expats, thanks to its super selection of kebabs served on sizzling plates, salads and wraps. Also does fine burgers and pizzas. It's a cosy place, with a few tables inside and a tiny patio, so expect to wait for a table during the dinner rush.

Banana Bar
BAR

(Map p780; Ton Sai Village, Ko Phi-Phi Don; ☺ 11am-2pm; 🛜) The 'alt' bar destination in Ton Sai Village, inland for those seeking to escape the house and techno barrage on the beach, Banana is spread over multiple levels. Climb to the rooftop, or lounge on cushions on the raised decks around the bar. Solid sounds and popular with people who like to roll their own cigarettes. Also does Mexican food.

Slinky
CLUB

(Map p780; Ao Lo Dalam, Ko Phi-Phi Don; ☺ 9pm-2am) Still the best fire show on Ao Lo Dalam and still the beach dancefloor of the moment. Expect throbbing bass, buckets of liquor (from 350B) and throngs of tourists mingling, flirting and flailing to the music.

ⓘ Getting There & Around

Ko Phi-Phi Don can be reached from Ao Nang, Krabi, Phuket, Railay and Ko Lanta. Most boats moor at **Ao Ton Sai** (Map p780; Ton Sai Village, Ko Phi-Phi Don). Ferries operate year round, although not always every day.

There are also combined boat and minivan tickets to destinations across Thailand, including Bangkok, Ko Samui and Ko Pha-Ngan.

There are no real roads on Ko Phi-Phi. Transport is by foot. Long-tail boats can run you to the different beaches, as well as Ko Phi-Phi Leh, for 100B to 1200B.

Ko Lanta
เกาะลันตา

Once the domain of sea gypsies, Lanta has morphed from a luscious Thai backwater

into a midrange getaway for both Asian and European visitors who come for the divine miles-long beaches. Charming Lanta remains calmer and more real than its brash neighbour Ko Phi-Phi, although the backpacker party scene is growing.

Ko Lanta is technically called Ko Lanta Yai. Flatter and bigger than surrounding islands with reasonable roads, it's easily explored by motorbike.

⊙ Sights & Activities

Some of Thailand's top diving spots are within arm's reach of Lanta. The best diving can be found at the undersea pinnacles of Hin Muang and Hin Daeng, two hours away by boat. Lanta's dive season is November to April. Dive trips cost 3100B to 4500B. **Lanta Diver** (☑ 075 668058; www.lantadiver.com; 197/3 Mu 1, Ban Sala Dan; 2 dives 3600B; ☺ 10am-6pm) and **Scubafish** (☑ 075 665095; www.scubafish.com; Ao Kantiang; 2 dives 3500B; ☺ 8am-8pm) are both recommended dive operators.

From mid-October to April, agencies across Lanta offer four-island snorkelling and kayaking tours (1200B to 1900B) to Ko Rok Nok, the Trang Islands and other nearby isles.

★ Ban Si Raya
VILLAGE

(บ้านศรีรายา, Lanta Old Town) Halfway down Lanta's eastern coast, Ban Si Raya was the island's original port and commercial centre, providing a safe harbour for Arab and Chinese trading vessels sailing between Phuket, Penang and Singapore. Known to the locals as Lanta Old Town, the vibe here is very different from the rest of the island, with wooden century-old stilt houses and shopfronts transformed into charming, characterful guesthouses. Pier restaurants offer fresh catch overlooking the sea, and there are some cute bohemian shops dotted around.

🛏 Sleeping

Hat Phra Ae and Hat Khlong Khong are the backpacker enclaves on Lanta.

Chill Out House
HOSTEL $

(☑ 082 183 2258; www.chillouthouselanta.com; Hat Phra Ae; dm 220B, d 280-320B; ☺ Sep-Apr; 🛜 ☒) This buzzing backpacker 'treehouse community' set back from the beach has three different and simple dorms, shared bathrooms, chalkboard doors and rickety doubles with bathrooms. It's basic, but you can't beat the laid-back vibe (or the price): swings at the bar, a communal iPod dock, and a wonderful (yes) chill-out lounge heavy on hammocks.

★**Bee Bee Bungalows** BUNGALOW $$
(📱081 537 9932; Hat Khlong Khong; bungalows 700-1000B; ⏰Oct-Apr; 📶) Bee Bee's is comprised of a dozen creative bamboo cabins managed by super-friendly staff. Each bungalow is unique; a few are stilted in the trees. The on-site restaurant has a library of tattered paperbacks to keep you occupied while you wait for your delicious Thai staples.

★**Old Times** GUESTHOUSE $$
(📱075 697255, 075 697288; www.theoldtimeslanta.com; Ban Si Raya; r 500-1700B; ❄📶) Tucked into two artfully revamped 100-year-old teak houses facing each other across the street, this is an excellent choice. Impeccably-styled rooms grace various sizes and budgets, under music-inspired names such as 'Yellow Submarine'. The best – bright and decked with black-and-white photos – jut out over the sea on the jetty, where there's a cushioned communal chill-out area. Fun, fresh and friendly.

Lanta Baan Nok Resort BUNGALOW $$
(📱075 684459; lantabaannokresort@gmail.com; Hat Phra Ae; bungalows 1500B; ❄📶) New resort with eight spotless, comfortable bungalows with modern bathrooms, beds raised up off the floor on platforms, balconies with ham-

---

ℹ **GETTING TO MALAYSIA: KO LIPE TO PULAU LANGKAWI**

It's easy to island-hop from Ko Lipe to the Malaysian island of Pulau Langkawi. Note: Malaysia is one hour ahead of Thailand.

Getting to the border From Ko Lipe, ferries travel twice daily to Pulau Langkawi (1000B to 1200B, 1½ hours, 10.30am and 3.30pm from mid-October to mid-April).

At the border Before departing, get stamped out of Thailand from the immigration office (8am to 6pm) on Pattaya Beach next to the Bundhaya Resort. Border formalities on Pulau Langkawi are straightforward and most European nationals receive a visa on arrival.

Moving on Pulau Langkawi has transport connections to the mainland and to Penang.

For information on making this crossing in reverse see p420.

---

mocks and an agreeably laid-back vibe. A decent deal for the price. It's a short walk to the beach.

Where Else! BUNGALOW $$
(📱092 942 6554, 093 293 6545; where-else-lanta@hotmail.com; Hat Khlong Khong; bungalows 600-1500B; 📶) One of Lanta's hippie outposts – thatched bungalows with semi-outdoor cold-water bathrooms. If you're trying to avoid late-night parties and tropical critters look elsewhere. Still, the place buzzes with backpackers, the owner is cool and there's a fun barefoot beach vibe centred on the popular **Feeling Bar** (Hat Khlong Khong; ⏰11am-late; 📶). Pricier bungalows are multi-level abodes sleeping up to four.

🍴 Eating & Drinking

★**Drunken Sailors** INTERNATIONAL, THAI $$
(📱075 665076; www.facebook.com/drunkensailors; Ao Kantiang; mains 130-200B; ⏰9am-3pm & 6-10pm; 📶🍴) This super-relaxed place features beanbags, hammocks and low-lying tables spilling out onto a terrace. The global, want-to-eat-it-all menu employs quality ingredients and roams from handmade pasta, baguettes and burgers to top-notch Thai, including perfectly spiced ginger stir-fries and red curries cooked to personal taste. Coffees, cakes and juices are also excellent. It closes for a couple of months in the low season.

★**Kung Restaurant** SEAFOOD $$
(📱075 656086; 413 Mu 1, Ban Sala Dan; mains 90-220B; ⏰5-11pm) Highly rated by both visiting Thais and locals, this Thai-Chinese place offers a delectable range of fresh fish (pay by the weight) in a simple setting close to the pier in Sala Dan. The sea bass, snapper and barracuda go quick, so get here early in the evening. There's also a large menu of Thai standards and some Chinese-style dishes.

Why Not Bar BAR
(Ao Kantiang; ⏰11am-2am; 📶) Tap into Ao Kantiang's laid-back scene at this driftwood-clad beachfront hang-out. It keeps things simple but fun with a killer mix of fire twirlers, sturdy cocktails, bubbly bar-staff and fantastic nightly live-music jams, best enjoyed at low-slung wooden tables on a raised deck.

ℹ Information

Ko Lanta Hospital (📱075 697017; Ban Si Raya) About 1km south of the Ban Si Raya Old Town.

ⓘ Getting There & Around

Transport to Ko Lanta is by boat or minivan. The **passenger jetty** (Ban Sala Dan) is 300m from the main strip of shops in Ban Sala Dan.

From mid-October to mid-April, the high-speed **Tigerline** (📞 075 590490, 081 358 8989; www.tigerlinetravel.com) ferry runs between Phuket (1500B, two hours) and Ko Lanta and on to Ko Lipe (1700B, five hours), via the Trang Islands.

There are two daily boats to Ko Phi-Phi at 8am and 1pm (300B 1½ hours), as well as high-season speedboats. There is also a daily boat to Krabi at 8.30am (400B, two hours) from November to late April.

Minivans to Krabi (300B, frequent) and other destinations in southern Thailand run year-round but are often packed.

Most resorts provide free transfers from the pier. Motorbike taxis run to the beaches from the pier for 50B to 400B.

Motorbikes (250B) can be rented everywhere.

Ko Tarutao Maritime National Park

อุทยานแห่งชาติหมู่เกาะตะรุเตา

One of Thailand's most exquisite, unspoilt regions, **Ko Tarutao Marine National Park** (📞 074 783485; www.dnp.go.th; adult/child 200/100B; ⊙ mid-Oct–mid-May) encompasses 51 islands blanketed by well-preserved rainforest teeming with fauna, surrounded by healthy coral reefs and radiant white beaches.

Ko Lipe has become a high-profile tourist destination and it's where most travellers stay. The only other islands you can stay on are Ko Tarutao, the biggest island and home to the **park headquarters** (Ao Pante Malacca, Ko Tarutao; ⊙ 8am-5pm), and Ko Adang. Apart from Ko Lipe, the park officially shuts from mid-October to mid-May.

🏃 Activities

There's decent snorkelling and diving off Ko Adang and Ko Lipe; you can also kitesurf off Ko Lipe when the wind is right. Ko Tarutao has hiking, mountain-biking and kayaking options.

🛏 Sleeping

On Ko Tarutao and Ko Adang your only choices are national park accommodation. Budget digs are limited on Ko Lipe.

🛏 Ko Lipe

Bila Beach BUNGALOW $$
(📞 087 570 3684; www.bilabeachresort.com; Hat Sunset; bungalows 1500B) A killer bamboo reggae bar and beachfront restaurant lurk below stylish, shaggy-haired cliff-side bungalows set above a tiny, secluded white-sand cove, which is strewn with boulders and adjacent to Hat Sunset. It's the perfect setting for your hippie honeymoon and a short sweaty walk over the hill from Hat Pattaya.

Koh Lipe Backpackers Hostel HOSTEL $$
(📞 085 361 7923; www.kohlipebackpackers.com; Hat Pattaya; dm 500B, r 2500-3000B; ❄ 🛜) There's a slightly random, spacey feel to Lipe's only hostel. Rooms and dorms are housed in a contemporary-style concrete block on west Hat Pattaya. Showers are shared, but you get private lockers, wi-fi, the on-site **Davy Jones' Locker dive school** (📞 085 361 7923; www.scubadivekohlipe.com; Hat Pattaya; dives from 2500B) (divers get a discount) and the beach location is ace. Upstairs are simple but comfortable enough air-con private rooms.

Gecko Lipe BUNGALOW $$$
(📞 087 810 7257; www.geckolipe.com; 61 Mu 7, Walking St; r 1600-2500, family rooms 7000B; ❄ 🛜) One of the better accommodation deals on Ko Lipe, the bamboo and wood bungalows here nestle in a jungle garden perched just above Walking Street. The cheapest are basic and compact: fan-only and with cold-water bathrooms. The two newest rooms house four people on two floors and are much smarter, coming with air-con and TVs. Good low-season discounts.

ⓘ Getting There & Away

Pak Bara on the mainland is the departure point for the national park.

Boats from Pak Bara stop at Ko Tarutao (450B, four daily) and Ko Lipe (650B, 1½ hours). Service runs from mid-October to mid-May with five daily trips. During low season, there's normally at least one boat daily to Ko Lipe.

Tigerline (p783) runs high-season (November to late April) ferries from Phuket to Ko Lipe (2400B, eight hours) with stops in Ko Lanta (1700B) and Ko Phi-Phi (1950B).

Satun Pak Bara Speedboat Club (📞 099 404 0409, 099 414 4994; www.spcthailand.com) and **Bundhaya Speedboat** (📞 074 750389, 074 750388; www.bundhayaspeedboat.com) run from Ko Lanta to Ko Lipe (1900B, three hours, one daily).

UNDERSTAND THAILAND

Thailand Today

Many of the political loose ends that have caused instability and uncertainty in Thailand for nearly a decade are now being tied up. The death of the revered King Bhumibol Adulyadej (Rama IX) in October 2016 after a 70-year reign brought about a sense of national unity. The transfer of the crown to his son King Maha Vajiralongkorn (Rama X) occurred peacefully. And a new constitution has cemented the role of the military in the government. These changes mark the end of an era.

Thailand ratified a draft version of its 20th constitution on 7 August 2016 by popular vote. The new constitution dilutes democracy in the kingdom and gives formal governing powers to the military. The 250-member Senate (upper house) will be solely appointed with no direct elections, and includes seats reserved for the military. There is also a provision for an unelected council to have authority to remove an elected government and for the Senate to appoint a prime minister.

The military-drafted constitution was described by the regime as a road map to democracy and a stable, corruption-free government. At 55%, voter turnout was low but it passed with a 61% majority. Public information about the constitution was limited and criticisms of the provisions were repressed by the ruling military junta. Some polled voters supported the measure because the military has brought about an end to street protests in Bangkok.

Prayuth Chan-o-cha, the current prime minister, has suggested there will be a general election in 2019, the first since the military coup in 2014.

History

Rise of Thai Kingdoms

It is believed that the first Thais migrated southwest from modern-day Yúnnán and Guangxi, China, to what is today known as Thailand. They settled along river valleys and formed small farming communities that eventually fell under the dominion of the expansionist Khmer empire of present-day Cambodia. What is now southern Thailand, along the Malay peninsula, was under the sway of the Srivijaya empire based in Sumatra. By the 13th and 14th centuries, what is considered to be the first Thai kingdom – Sukhothai (meaning 'Rising Happiness') – emerged and began to chip away at the crumbling Khmer empire. The Sukhothai kingdom is regarded as the cultural and artistic kernel of the modern Thai state.

Sukhothai was soon eclipsed by another Thai power, Ayuthaya, established by King U Thong in 1350. This new centre developed into a cosmopolitan port on the Asian trade route, courted by various European nations. The small nation managed to thwart foreign takeovers, including one orchestrated by a Thai court official – a Greek man named Constantine Phaulkon – to advance French interests. For 400 years and 34 successive reigns, Ayuthaya dominated Thailand until the Burmese led a successful invasion in 1765, ousting the monarch and destroying the capital.

The Thais eventually rebuilt their capital in present-day Bangkok, established by the Chakri dynasty, which continues to occupy the throne today. As Western imperialism marched across the region, King Mongkut (Rama IV, r 1851–68) and his son and successor, King Chulalongkorn (Rama V, r 1868–1910), successfully steered the country into the modern age without becoming a colonial vassal. In return for the country's continued independence, King Chulalongkorn ceded huge tracts of Laos and Cambodia to French-controlled Indochina – an unprecedented territorial loss in Thai history.

A Struggling Democracy

In 1932 a peaceful coup converted the country into a constitutional monarchy, loosely based on the British model. What followed has been a near-continuous cycle of power struggles among three factions – the elected government, military leaders and the monarchy backed by the aristocrats. These groups occasionally form tenuous allegiances based on mutual dislike for the opposition, and the resulting power grab is often a peaceful military takeover sometimes dubbed the 'smooth as silk' coup.

During the mid-20th century the military dominated the political sphere with an anticommunist position widely regarded as being ineffectual, except in the suppression of democratic representation and civil rights.

In 1973 student activists staged demonstrations calling for a real constitution and the release of political dissidents. A brief respite came, with reinstated voting rights and relaxed censorship. But in October 1976 a demonstration on the campus of Thammasat University in Bangkok was brutally quashed, resulting in hundreds of casualties and the reinstatement of authoritarian rule. Many activists went underground to join armed communist insurgency groups hiding in the northeast.

In the 1980s, as the regional threat of communism subsided, the military-backed Prime Minister Prem Tinsulanonda stabilised the country and moved towards a representative democracy. The military reemerged in 1991 to overthrow the democratically elected government; this was the country's 10th successful coup since 1932. In May 1992 huge demonstrations led by Bangkok's charismatic governor Chamlong Srimuang erupted throughout the city and the larger provincial capitals. The bloodiest confrontation occurred at Bangkok's Democracy Monument, resulting in nearly 50 deaths, but it eventually led to the reinstatement of a civilian government.

Same Same But Different

Straddling the new millennium, Thailand seemed to have entered an age of democracy. Elected governments oversaw the 1997 enactment of Thailand's 16th constitution, the first charter in the nation's history not written under military order. The country pulled through the 1997 Asian currency crisis and entered a stable period of prosperity in the early 2000s. Telecommunications tycoon Thaksin Shinawatra and his populist Thai Rak Thai party were elected in 2001 and, with little political opposition, Thaksin consolidated his power over the next five years in all ranks of government, stifling press criticism and scrutiny of his administration.

In 2006 Thaksin was accused of conflicts of interest with his family's sale of their Shin Corporation to the Singaporean government for 73 billion baht (US$1.88 billion), a tax-free gain thanks to legislation that he helped craft. Meanwhile Thaksin's working-class and rural base rallied behind him, spotlighting longstanding class divides within Thai society.

Behind the scenes the military and the aristocrats forged an allegiance that resulted in the 2006 coup of the Thaksin government. The military banned Thaksin's political party (Thai Rak Thai), only to have the regenerated party, now named Pheu Thai, win the 2007 elections. In response, the aristocrats staged massive protests in Bangkok that took over the parliament building and closed down the city's two airports for a week in November 2008.

The Constitutional Court sided with the elites and dissolved Pheu Thai due to a technicality. This decision by the courts was viewed by pro-Thaksin factions as a silent coup. A new coalition was formed in December 2008, led by Oxford-educated Abhisit Vejjajiva, leader of the Democrat party and Thailand's fourth prime minister for the year.

THAI ETIQUETTE

Thais are generally very understanding and hospitable, but there are some important taboos and social conventions.

Monarchy It is a criminal offence to disrespect the royal family; treat objects depicting the king (like money) with respect.

Temples Wear clothing that covers to your knees and elbows. Remove all footwear before entering. Sit with your feet tucked behind you, so they are not facing the Buddha image. Women should never touch a monk or a monk's belongings; step out of the way on footpaths and don't sit next to them on public transport.

Modesty At the beach, avoid public nudity or topless sunbathing. Cover up going to and from the beach.

Body language Avoid touching anyone on the head and be careful where you point your feet; they're the lowest part of the body literally and metaphorically.

Keep your cool Thailand is a non-confrontational culture. Don't get angry, smile and things will work out.

The pro-Thaksin faction (known as 'Red Shirts') retaliated with a crippling, two-month demonstration in Bangkok's central shopping district that was ended in May 2010 through military force. The crackdown resulted in 91 deaths and US$1.5 billion in arson damage.

Elections were held again in 2011 and Pheu Thai won a clear majority. Thaksin's sister, Yingluck Shinawatra, became Thailand's first female prime minister. She raised the minimum wage to 300B per day and introduced a populist rice-pledging scheme intended to boost farmers' incomes, only to see it become an expensive flop. But it was her government's attempt to introduce an amnesty bill that would have allowed Thaksin's return that led to her becoming the second member of the Shinawatra clan to be overthrown in a coup. On 7 May 2014 Yingluck stepped down and on 22nd May the military, under General Prayuth Chan-o-cha, took over.

Prayuth's government is known as the National Council for Peace and Order (NCPO). The NCPO has aggressively silenced critics of military rule: the media are under orders to refrain from dissent and more than 1000 people – opposition politicians, academics, journalists, bloggers and students – have been detained or tried in military courts.

KING RAMA IX'S FUNERAL

After the death of King Bhumibol Adulyadej (Rama IX) in October 2016, Thailand entered into a state-mandated and personal grieving period. The government requested a month-long hiatus from 'joyful' events, and even Thailand's sex tourism industry obliged with curtailed hours and no scantily clad promoters. The demand for mourning clothes outpaced supply and the government supplied eight million free black shirts to low-income people.

In October 2017, after Rama IX's body had been lying in state at Bangkok's Grand Palace for a year, one of the most lavish funerals in modern history was held. A 50m-high funeral pyre was built at Sanam Luang, and mourners from across the country lined the streets of the capital for the various ceremonies, which allegedly cost US$90 million.

While the NCPO was busy silencing critics, it failed to address Thailand's slumping economy. Foreign investment, exports and GDP all contracted after the coup. In 2016 a much-needed infrastructure investment plan was announced to help bolster the downturn. Tourism continues to be the bright spot in the economy.

The Monarchy

On 13 October 2016 the beloved King Bhumibol Adulyadej (Rama IX) passed away at the age of 88 after many years of failing health. Claiming a 70-year reign, King Bhumibol was the world's longest-serving monarch and the only king that the majority of the Thai population had ever known. He was regarded as a national father figure and benevolent ruler, undertaking many poverty-alleviation programs during his lifetime.

The late king's son, the crown prince, ascended the throne as King Maha Vajiralongkorn (Rama X) on 1 December 2016. It is unclear what kind of monarch he will be and if he will measure up to the larger-than-life persona of his father. Prior to his coronation, the new king, who is 64 years old and three times divorced, was not favourably viewed due to a variety of personal scandals and a jet-setting lifestyle. But strict *lèse-majesté* laws ensure that the Thai public is reluctant to express candid sentiments, and they are hopeful for stability and decorum.

People & Culture

Thailand's cohesive national identity provides a unifying patina for ethnic and regional differences that evolved through historical migrations and geographic kinships with ethnically diverse neighbours.

The National Psyche

Paramount to the Thai philosophy of life is *sà·nùk* (fun) – each day is celebrated with food and conversation, foreign festivals are readily adopted as an excuse for a party and every task is measured on the *sà·nùk* meter.

The social dynamics of Thai culture can be perplexing. The ideals of the culture are based on Buddhist principles and include humility, gratitude and filial piety. These golden rules are translated into such social conventions as saving face *(nâa)*, in which confrontation is avoided and people endeavour not to embarrass themselves or other people.

An important component of saving face is knowing one's place in society: all relationships in Thai society are governed by conventions of social rank defined by age, wealth, status, and personal and political power. Thais 'size up' a Westerner's social status with a list of common questions: Where are you from? How old are you? Are you married? To a Thai these questions are matters of public record and aren't considered impolite.

Religion and the monarchy, which is still regarded by many as divine, are the culture's sacred cows. Whatever you do, don't insult the king or disrespect his image, especially in the current era of ultra-sensitivity towards the institution of the monarchy.

Lifestyle

Thailand straddles the divide between the highly Westernised urban life in major cities and the traditional rhythms of rural, agricultural life. But several persisting customs offer a rough snapshot of daily life. Thais wake up early, thanks in part to the roosters that start crowing some time after sunrise. In the grey stillness of early morning, barefoot monks carrying large round bowls travel through the town to collect their daily meals from the faithful. The housewives are already awake steaming rice and sweeping their front porches with stiff bristled brooms. Soon business is in full swing: the vendors have arrived at their favourite corner to feed the uniformed masses, be they khaki-clad civil servants or white-and-black wearing university students.

Eating appears to make up the rest of the day. Notice the shop girls, ticket vendors or even the office workers: they can be found in a tight circle swapping gossip and snacking (or *gin lên*, literally 'eat for fun'). Then there is dinner and after-dinner and the whole seemingly chaotic, yet highly ordered, affair starts all over again.

Population

About 75% of citizens are ethnic Thais, further divided by geography (north, central, south and northeast). Each group speaks its own Thai dialect and to a certain extent practises customs unique to its region or influenced by neighbouring countries. Politically and economically, the central Thais are the dominant group. People of Chinese ancestry make up roughly 14% of the population, many of whom have been in Thailand for generations. Other large minority groups include the Malays in the far south, the Khmers in the northeast and the Lao, spread throughout the north and east. Smaller non-Thai-speaking groups include the hill tribes living in the northern mountains. An increasing community of economic migrants, predominately from Myanmar, are changing the racial and cultural demographics of Thailand.

Religion

Alongside the Thai national flag flies the yellow flag of Buddhism – Theravada Buddhism (as opposed to the Mahayana schools found in East Asia and the Himalayas). Country, family and daily life are all married to religion. Every Thai male is expected to become a monk for a short period in his life, since a family earns great merit when a son 'takes robe and bowl'.

More evident than the philosophical aspects of Buddhism is the everyday fusion with animist rituals. Monks are consulted to determine an auspicious date for a wedding or the likelihood of success for a business. Spirit houses *(phrá phuum)* are constructed outside buildings and homes to encourage

SAVING FACE

Thais believe strongly in the concept of saving face, ie avoiding confrontation and endeavouring not to embarrass themselves or other people (except when it's *sà·nùk* to do so). The ideal face-saver doesn't bring up negative topics in conversation, doesn't express firm convictions or opinions and doesn't claim to have any expertise. Agreement and harmony are considered to be the most important social graces.

While Westerners might think of heated discussion as social sport, Thais regard any instance where voices are raised as rude and potentially volatile. Losing your temper causes a loss of face for everyone, and Thais who have been crossed may react in extreme ways. Minor embarrassments, such as tripping or falling, might elicit giggles from a crowd of Thais. In this case they aren't taking delight in your mishap, but helping you save face by laughing it off.

THAILAND PEOPLE & CULTURE

THAILAND'S HILL-TRIBE COMMUNITIES

Thailand's hill-tribe communities (referred to in Thai as *chao khao*, literally 'mountain people') are ethnic minorities who have traditionally lived in the country's mountainous frontier. Most tribes migrated from Tibet and parts of China some 200 years ago and settled along Southeast Asia's mountain belt from Myanmar to Vietnam. The Tribal Research Institute in Chiang Mai recognises 10 different hill tribes, but there may be up to 20 in Thailand. Increasing urban migration has significantly altered the hill tribes' cultural independence.

Hill-Tribe Groups

The Karen are the largest hill-tribe group in Thailand and number about 47% of the total tribal population. They tend to live in lowland valleys and practise crop rotation rather than swidden (slash and burn) agriculture. Their numbers and proximity to mainstream society have made them the most integrated and financially successful of the hill-tribe groups. Thickly woven V-neck tunics of various colours are their traditional dress.

The Hmong are Thailand's second-largest hill-tribe group and are especially numerous in Chiang Mai Province. They usually live on mountain peaks or plateaus above 1000m. Traditional dress is a simple black jacket and indigo or black baggy trousers. Sashes may be worn around the waist, and embroidered aprons draped front and back.

The Akha are among the poorest of Thailand's ethnic minorities and live mainly in Chiang Mai and Chiang Rai Provinces, along mountain ridges or steep slopes 1000m to 1400m in altitude. They are regarded as skilled farmers but are often displaced from arable land by government intervention. Their traditional garb includes a headdress of beads, feathers and dangling silver ornaments.

Other minority groups include the Lisu, Lahu and Mien.

Village Etiquette

If you're planning on visiting hill-tribe villages, talk to your guide about dos and don'ts. Here are some general guidelines.

➡ Always ask permission before taking photos, especially at private moments inside dwellings. Many traditional belief systems view photography with suspicion. Some tribespeople will ask for money in exchange for a photo; honour their request.

➡ Show respect for religious symbols and rituals. Don't touch totems at village entrances or sacred items. Don't participate in ceremonies unless invited to join.

➡ Avoid cultivating a tradition of begging, especially among children. Instead talk to your guide about donating to a local school.

➡ Avoid public nudity and be careful not to undress near an open window where village children might be able to peep in.

➡ Don't flirt with members of the opposite sex unless you plan to marry them. Don't drink or do drugs with the villagers; altered states sometimes lead to culture clashes.

➡ Smile at villagers even if they stare at you; ask your guide how to say 'hello' in the tribal language.

➡ Avoid public displays of affection, which in some traditional systems are viewed as offensive to the spirit world.

➡ Don't interact with the villagers' livestock; these creatures are valuable possessions, not entertainment.

the spirits to live independently from the family, but to remain comfortable so as to bring good fortune to the site.

Roughly 95% of the population practises Buddhism, but in southern Thailand there is a significant Muslim minority community.

Arts

Music

Classical Thai music was developed for the royal court as an accompaniment to classical dance-drama and other forms of theatre. Traditional instruments have more pedestrian applications and can often be heard at temple fairs or provincial festivals. Whether used in the high or low arts, traditional Thai music has an incredible range of textures and subtleties, hair-raising tempos and pastoral melodies.

In the north and northeast there are several popular wind instruments with multiple reed pipes, which function like a mouth organ. Chief among these is the *kaan*, which originated in Laos; when played by an adept musician it sounds like a calliope organ. It is used chiefly in *mŏr lam* music, a rural folk tradition often likened to the American blues. A near cousin to *mŏr lam* is *lôok tûng* (literally 'children of the fields'), which enjoys a working-class fan base much like country music does in the US.

Popular Thai music has borrowed rock-and-roll's instruments to create perky teeny-bop hits, hippie protest ballads, garage rock and urban indie anthems. It is an easy courtship with Thai classic rock, like the decades-old group Carabao and the folk style known as *pleng pêu·a chee·wít* (songs for life). These days, guitar-based rock bands have been joined by many hip-hop acts and electronic music outfits.

Sculpture & Architecture

Thailand's most famous sculptural output has been its bronze Buddha images, coveted the world over for their originality and grace. Traditional architecture is more visible as it is applied to simple homes and famous temples. Ancient Thai homes consisted of a single-room teak structure raised on stilts, since most Thais once lived along river banks or canals. The space underneath also served as the living room, kitchen, garage and barn. Rooflines in Thailand are steeply pitched and often decorated at the corners or along the gables with motifs related to the *naga* (mythical sea serpent), long believed to be a spiritual protector. Temple buildings demonstrate more formal aspects of traditional architecture and artistic styles.

Theatre & Dance

Traditional Thai theatre consists of six dramatic forms, including *kŏhn*, a formal masked dance-drama depicting scenes from the Ramakian (the *Thakŏhi* version of India's *Ramayana*), that were originally performed only for the royal court. Popular in rural villages, *lí·gair* is a partly improvised, often bawdy folk play featuring dancing, comedy, melodrama and music. The southern Thai equivalent is *má·noh·rah*, which is based on a 2000-year-old Indian story. Shadow puppet plays *(năng)* found in southern Thailand demonstrate that region's shared cultural heritage with Malaysia and Indonesia.

Food & Drink

Food

Thai food is a complex balance of spicy, salty, sweet and sour. The ingredients are fresh and zesty with lots of lemongrass, basil, coriander and mint. Chilli peppers pack a nose-running, tongue-searing burn. And pungent *nám blah* (fish sauce; generally made from anchovies) adds a touch of the sea. Throw in a little lime and a pinch of sugar and you've got the true taste of Thailand.

Day and night markets, pushcart vendors, makeshift stalls, open-air restaurants – Thais eat most of their meals outside of the home as prices are relatively low and local cooks are famous for a particular dish. No self-respecting shoestringer would shy away

THAILAND FOOD & DRINK

TEMPLE ARCHITECTURE

Planning to conquer Thailand's temples and ruins? With this handy guide, you'll be able to sort out your wát (Thai temple complex) from your what's that.

Chedi Large bell-shaped tower usually containing five structural elements symbolising (from bottom to top) earth, water, fire, wind and void; relics of Buddha or a Thai king are housed inside the chedi; also known as a stupa.

Prang Towering phallic spire of Khmer origin serving the same religious purpose as a chedi.

Wí·hăhn Main sanctuary for the temple's Buddha sculpture and where laypeople come to make offerings; sometimes it is translated as the 'assembly hall'. Typically the building has a three-tiered roofline representing the triple gems (Buddha, the teacher; Dharma, the teaching; and Sangha, the followers).

HOW TO EAT LIKE A THAI

In Thailand, chopsticks are used for noodle dishes and a spoon and fork for rice dishes. Many curries and soups are served in bowls but should be ladled on to a bed of rice, rather than eaten directly from the bowl.

from the pushcarts in Thailand for fear of stomach troubles.

For breakfast and late-night snacks, Thais nosh on *gŏo·ay đĕe·o*, a noodle soup with chicken or pork and vegetables. There are two major types of noodles: *sên lék* (thin) and *sên yài* (wide and flat). Before you dig into your steaming bowl, first use the chopsticks and a spoon to cut the noodles into smaller segments so they are easier to pick up. Then add to taste a few teaspoonfuls of the provided spices: dried red chilli, sugar, fish sauce and vinegar. It's a combination that is pure Thai. The weapons of choice when eating noodles are chopsticks and a rounded soup spoon.

Thais are social eaters: meals are rarely taken alone and dishes are meant to be shared. Usually a small army of plates will be placed in the centre of the table, with individual servings of rice for each diner. The protocol goes like this – ladle a spoonful of food at a time on to your plate of rice. Dishes aren't passed in Thailand; instead you reach across the table to the different items. When you are full, leave a little rice on your plate (an empty plate is a silent request for more rice) and place your fork so that it is cradled by the spoon in the centre of the plate.

Even when eating with *fà·ràng*, it is wise to order 'family style', as dishes are rarely synchronised. Ordering individually will leave one person staring politely at a hot plate and another staring wistfully at the kitchen.

Drink

Water purified for drinking is simply called *náam dèum* (drinking water), whether boiled or filtered. All water offered in restaurants, offices or homes will be purified. Ice is generally safe in Thailand. *Châa* (tea) and *gah·faa* (coffee) are prepared strong, milky and sweet – an instant morning buzz.

Thanks to the tropical bounty, fruit juices are sold on every corner. Thais prefer a little salt to cut the sweetness of the juice; the salt also has some mystical power to make a hot day tolerable.

Cheap beer appears hand-in-hand with backpacker ghettos. Beer Chang, Beer Singha (pronounced 'sing', not 'sing-ha') and Beer Leo are a few local brands. Thais have created yet another innovative method for beating the heat; they drink their beer with ice to keep the beverage cool and crisp.

More of a ritual than a beverage, Thai whisky usually runs with a distinct crowd – soda water, Coke and ice. Fill the short glass with ice cubes, two-thirds whisky, one-third soda and a splash of Coke. Thai tradition dictates the youngest in the crowd is responsible for filling the other drinkers' glasses. Many travellers prefer to go straight to the ice bucket with shared straws, not forgetting a dash of Red Bull in cocktails to keep them going.

Environment

Thailand spans a distance of 1650km from its northern tip to its southern tail, a distance that encompasses 16 latitudinal degrees and a variety of ecological zones, making it one of the most environmentally diverse countries in Southeast Asia.

The Land

Thailand's odd shape is often likened to the head of an elephant, with the trunk being the Malay peninsula and the head being the northern mountains. Starting at the crown of the country, northern Thailand is dominated by the Dawna-Tenasserim mountain range. Dropping into the central region, the topography mellows into rice-producing plains fed by rivers that are as revered as the national monarchy. Thailand's most exalted river is Chao Phraya.

Tracing the contours of Thailand's northern and northeastern border is another imposing watercourse: the Mekong, which both physically separates and culturally fuses Thailand with its neighbours. The landscape of Thailand's northeastern border is occupied by the arid Khorat Plateau rising some 300m above the central plain.

The kingdom's eastern rivers dump their waters into the Gulf of Thailand. Sliding further south is the Malay peninsula, a long trunk-like landmass. On the western side extends the Andaman Sea, a splendid tropical setting of stunning blue waters and dramatic limestone islands.

Wildlife

Thailand is particularly rich in bird life: more than 1000 resident and migrating species have been recorded and approximately 10% of all world bird species dwell here.

Thailand's most revered indigenous mammal, the elephant, once ran wild in the country's dense virgin forests. Integral to Thai culture, the elephant symbolises wisdom, strength and good fortune. White elephants are even more auspicious and by tradition are donated to the king. Sadly, elephants are now endangered, having lost their traditional role in society and much of their habitat, as have the dwindling numbers of tigers.

The animals visitors are most likely to see or encounter are the 12 different species of monkeys and gibbons indigenous to Thailand.

Environmental Issues

Like all countries with a high population density, there is enormous pressure on Thailand's ecosystems: natural forest cover in 1961 was 53.5%; by 2016 that had declined to about 31.6% of land area, according to the World Bank.

In response to environmental degradation, the Thai government created protected natural areas and outlawed logging. Thailand designated its first national park (Khao Yai) in the 1960s and has added over 100 parks, including marine environments, to the list since. Together these cover 15% of the country's land and sea area, one of the highest ratios of protected to unprotected areas of any nation in the world. Since the turn of the millennium, forest loss has slowed to about 0.6% per year (according to the World Bank).

Though the conservation efforts are laudable, Thailand's national parks are poorly funded and poorly protected from commercial development, illegal hunting and logging, and swidden agriculture. The passing of the 1992 Environmental Act was an encouraging move by the government, but standards still lag behind Western nations. Thailand is a signatory to the UN Convention on International Trade in Endangered Species (CITES), but the country remains an important transport link and marketplace for the global wildlife trade.

SURVIVAL GUIDE

❶ Directory A–Z

ACCOMMODATION

Finding a place to stay in Thailand is easy. For peace of mind, book a room for your arrival night; after that, you can wing it. Bear in mind, however, vacancies can become scarce during certain holidays and peak travel periods.

Guesthouses Family-run options are the best. Rooms run from basic (bed and fan) to plush (private bathroom and air-con).

Hotels From boutique to stodgy, hotels offer comfortable, mostly modern rooms, with extra services like breakfast included in the rate and sometimes a swimming pool.

Hostels As the cost and standard of Thailand's guesthouses have increased, dorms have become better value.

CUSTOMS REGULATIONS

Thailand allows the following items to enter duty-free:

➔ reasonable amount of personal effects (clothing and toiletries)

➔ professional instruments

➔ 200 cigarettes

➔ 1L of wine or spirits

Thailand prohibits the import of the following items:

➔ firearms and ammunition (unless registered in advance with the police department)

➔ illegal drugs

➔ pornographic media

An export licence is required for any antique reproductions or newly cast Buddha images.

ELECTRICITY

Thailand uses 220V AC electricity. Power outlets most commonly feature two-prong round or flat sockets.

THAILAND DIRECTORY A–Z

SLEEPING PRICE RANGES

In big cities and resorts, the following price ranges refer to a double room and are the high-season walk-in rates.

$ less than 1000B

$$ 1000B–4000B

$$$ more than 4000B

In small towns, the following price ranges are used:

$ less than 600B

$$ 600B–1500B

$$$ more than 1500B

EATING PRICES RANGES

The following price ranges refer to a main dish.

$ less than 150B

$$ 150B–350B

$$$ more than 350B

EMBASSIES & CONSULATES

Foreign embassies are located in Bangkok; some nations also have consulates in Chiang Mai, Pattaya, Phuket and Songkhla.

Australian Embassy (Map p664; ☑ 02 344 6300; www.thailand.embassy.gov.au; 181 Th Witthayu/Wireless Rd, Bangkok; ☺ 8.30am-4.30pm Mon-Fri; Ⓜ Lumphini exit 2) Consulates in Chiang Mai, Ko Samui and Phuket.

Cambodian Embassy (☑ 02 957 5851; 518/4 Soi Ramkhamhaeng 39, Th Pracha Uthit, Bangkok; ☺ 8.30am-noon & 2-5pm Mon-Fri; Ⓜ Phra Ram 9 exit 3 & taxi) Consulate in Sa Kaew.

Canadian Embassy (Map p664; ☑ 02 646 4300; www.thailand.gc.ca; 15th fl, Abdulrahim Pl, 990 Rama IV, Bangkok; ☺ 9am-noon Mon-Fri; Ⓜ Si Lom exit 2, Ⓢ Sala Daeng exit 4) Consulate in Chiang Mai (☑ 05 3850147; 151 Superhighway, Tambon Tahsala; ☺ 9am-noon Mon-Fri).

French Embassy (Map p664; ☑ 02 657 5100; www.ambafrance-th.org; 35 Soi 36/Rue de Brest, Th Charoen Krung, Bangkok; ☺ 8.30am-noon Mon-Fri; ⛴ Oriental Pier) Consulates in Chiang Mai (☑ 053 281466; 138 Th Charoen Prathet, Chiang Mai; ☺ 10am-noon Mon-Fri), Chiang Rai and Pattaya.

German Embassy (Map p664; ☑ 02 287 9000; www.bangkok.diplo.de; 9 Th Sathon Tai/South, Bangkok; ☺ 7.30-11.30am Mon-Fri; Ⓜ Lumphini exit 2)

Irish Embassy (Map p674; ☑ 02 016 1360; www.dfa.ie/irish-embassy/thailand; 12th fl, 208 Th Witthayu/Wireless Rd, Bangkok; ☺ 9.30am-12.30pm & 2.30-3.30pm Mon-Thu, 9.30am-noon Fri; Ⓢ Phloen Chit exit 1)

Laotian Embassy (☑ 02 539 6667; 502/1-3 Soi Sahakarnpramoon, Th Pracha Uthit/Soi Ramkhamhaeng 39, Bangkok; ☺ 8am-noon & 1-4pm Mon-Fri; Ⓜ Phra Ram 9 exit 3 & taxi)

Malaysian Embassy (Map p664; ☑ 02 629 6800; www.kln.gov.my/web/tha_bangkok/home; 33-35 Th Sathon Tai/South, Bangkok; ☺ 8am-4pm Mon-Fri; Ⓜ Lumphini exit 2) Consulate in Songkhla.

Myanmar Embassy (Map p664; ☑ 02 233 7250; www.myanmarembassybkk.com; 132 Th Sathon Neua/North, Bangkok; ☺ 9am-noon & 1-3pm Mon-Fri; Ⓢ Surasak exit 3)

Netherlands Embassy (Map p674; ☑ 02 309 5200; www.netherlandsworldwide.nl/countries/thailand; 15 Soi Ton Son; ☺ 8.30am-noon & 1.30-4.30pm Mon-Thu, 8.30-11.30am Fri; Ⓢ Chit Lom exit 4)

New Zealand Embassy (Map p674; ☑ 02 254 2530; www.nzembassy.com/thailand; 14th fl, M Thai Tower, All Seasons Pl, 87 Th Witthayu/Wireless Rd, Bangkok; ☺ 8am-noon & 1-2.30pm Mon-Fri; Ⓢ Phloen Chit exit 5)

UK Embassy (Map p674; ☑ 02 305 8333; www.gov.uk/government/world/organisations/british-embassy-bangkok; 14 Th Witthayu/Wireless Rd, Bangkok; ☺ 8am-4.30pm Mon-Thu, to 1pm Fri; Ⓢ Phloen Chit exit 5)

US Embassy (Map p674; ☑ 02 205 4000; https://th.usembassy.gov; 95 Th Witthayu/Wireless Rd, Bangkok; ☺ 8am-4pm Mon-Fri; Ⓢ Phloen Chit exit 5) Consulate in Chiang Mai (☑ 05 3107700; https://th.usembassy.gov; 387 Th Wichayanon; ☺ 8am-3.30pm Tue & Thu).

FESTIVALS & EVENTS

Many Thai festivals are linked to Buddhist holy days and follow the lunar calendar. Thus they fall on different dates each year. Businesses typically close and transport becomes difficult preceding any public holiday or national festival. The following are popular national festivals:

Songkran Festival From 12 to 14 April, Buddha images are 'bathed', monks and elders have their hands respectfully sprinkled with water and a lot of water is wildly tossed about on everyone else. Bangkok and Chiang Mai are major battlegrounds.

Loi Krathong On the night of the full moon in November, small lotus-shaped boats made of banana leaves and decorated with flowers and candles are floated on waterways in honour of the river goddess.

INTERNET ACCESS

Wi-fi is almost standard in hotels, guesthouses and cafes. Signal strength deteriorates in the upper floors of a multi-storey building; request a room near a router if wi-fi is essential. Cellular data networks continue to expand and increase in capability.

LEGAL MATTERS

In general Thai police don't hassle foreigners, especially tourists. One major exception is drugs – there are strict drug laws for the possession and trafficking of narcotics.

If you are arrested for any offence, the police will allow you the opportunity to make a phone call, either to your embassy or consulate in Thailand if you have one, or to a friend or relative if not. Thai law does not presume an indicted detainee to be either guilty or innocent but rather a 'suspect', whose guilt or innocence will be decided in court. Trials are usually speedy.

LGBT TRAVELLERS

Thai culture is relatively tolerant of both male and female homosexuality. There is a fairly prominent LGBT scene in Bangkok, Pattaya and Phuket. With regard to dress or mannerism, the LGBT community are generally accepted without comment. However, public displays of affection – whether heterosexual or homosexual – are frowned upon.

Utopia (www.utopia-asia.com) posts lots of Thailand information for LGBT travellers and publishes a gay guidebook to the kingdom.

MONEY

Most places in Thailand deal only with cash. Some foreign credit cards are accepted in high-end establishments. ATMs are everywhere, but charge a 200B withdrawal fee.

Coins come in 1B, 2B (gold-coloured), 5B and 10B denominations. There are 100 satang to 1B and occasionally you'll see 25 and 50 satang coins.

Notes are denominations of 20B, 50B, 100B, 500B and 1000B.

OPENING HOURS

Banks and government offices close for national holidays. Some bars and clubs close during elections and certain religious holidays when alcohol sales are banned. Shopping centres have banks that open late.

Banks 8.30am to 4.30pm; 24hr ATMs

Bars 6pm to midnight or 1am

Clubs 8pm to 2am

Government Offices 8.30am to 4.30pm Monday to Friday; some close for lunch

Restaurants 8am to 10pm

Shops 10am to 7pm

POST

Thailand has a very efficient postal service and local postage is inexpensive. Don't send cash or other valuables through the mail.

PUBLIC HOLIDAYS

Government offices and banks close their doors on the following public holidays.

1 January New Year's Day

February (date varies) Makha Bucha Day, Buddhist holy day

6 April Chakri Day, commemorating the founder of the Chakri dynasty, Rama I

13–15 April Songkran Festival

1 May Labour Day

5 May Coronation Day

May/June (date varies) Visakha Bucha, Buddhist holy day

July 28 King Maha Vajiralongkorn's Birthday

July/August (date varies) Asanha Bucha, Buddhist holy day

12 August Queen Sirikit's Birthday/Mother's Day

23 October Chulalongkorn Day

5 December Commemoration of Late King Bhumiphol/Father's Day

10 December Constitution Day

31 December New Year's Eve

SAFE TRAVEL

Thailand is generally a safe country to visit, but it's smart to exercise caution, especially when it comes to dealing with strangers (both Thai and foreigners) and travelling alone.

➡ Assault of travellers is relatively rare in Thailand, but it does happen.

➡ Possession of drugs can result in a year or more of prison time. Drug smuggling carries considerably higher penalties, including execution.

➡ Disregard all offers of free shopping or sightseeing help from strangers. These are scams that invariably take a commission from your purchases.

The **tourist police** (📞1155) are a useful point of call if you are in trouble.

Ongoing violence in the Deep South has made the crossing at Sungai Kolok into Malaysia dangerous, and most Muslim-majority provinces (Yala, Pattani, Narathiwat and Songkhla) should be avoided by casual visitors.

TELEPHONE

The telephone country code for Thailand is 66 and is used when calling the country from abroad. All Thai telephone numbers are preceded by a '0' if you're dialling domestically (the '0' is omitted when calling from overseas). After the initial '0', the next three numbers represent the provincial area code, which is now integral to the telephone number. If the initial '0' is followed by a '6', an '8' or a '9' then you're dialling a mobile phone.

TOILETS

Increasingly, the Asian-style squat toilet is less of the norm in Thailand. There are still specimens in rural places, provincial bus stations, older homes and modest restaurants, but the Western-style toilet is becoming more prevalent and appears wherever foreign tourists can be found. Some toilets also come with a small spray hose – Thailand's version of the bidet.

TOURIST INFORMATION

The Tourism Authority of Thailand (TAT) has offices throughout the country that distribute maps and sightseeing advice. TAT offices do not book accommodation, transport or tours.

TRAVELLERS WITH DISABILITIES

Thailand presents one large, ongoing obstacle course for the mobility-impaired. The following organisations might be useful:

Asia Pacific Development Centre on Disability (www.apcdfoundation.org)
Society for Accessible Travel & Hospitality (www.sath.org)
Wheelchair Holidays @ Thailand (www.wheelchairtours.com)

VISAS

Thailand has visa-exemption and visa-on-arrival agreements with most nations (including European countries, Australia, New Zealand and the USA). Depending on nationality, these citizens are issued a 14- or 90-day visa exemption. Note that for some nationalities, less time (15 days rather than 30 days) is given if arriving by land rather than air. Check the **Ministry of Foreign Affairs** (02 203 5000; www.mfa.go.th) website for more details.

Without proof of an onward ticket and sufficient funds for your projected stay, you can be denied entry, but in practice this is a formality that is rarely checked.

If you plan to stay in Thailand longer than 30 days, you should apply for the 60-day tourist visa from a Thai consulate or embassy before your trip. Recent changes to this visa now allow multiple entries within a six-month period.

Visa Extensions

You can extend your visa by applying at any immigration office in Thailand. The usual fee for a visa extension is 1900B. Those issued with a standard stay of 15 or 30 days can extend their stay for 30 days if the extension is handled before the visa expires. The 60-day tourist visa can be extended by up to 30 days at the discretion of Thai immigration authorities.

Another visa-renewal option is to cross a land border. A new 15- or 30-day visa exemption, depending on the nationality, will be issued upon your return.

If you overstay your visa, the usual penalty is a fine of 500B per day, with a 20,000B limit. Fines can be paid at the airport, or in advance at an immigration office. If you've overstayed only one day, you don't have to pay.

VOLUNTEERING

There are many wonderful volunteering organisations in Thailand that provide meaningful work and cultural engagement. Volunteer Work Thailand (www.volunteerworkthailand.org) maintains a database of opportunities.

WORK

Thailand is a huge destination for temporary work stints, especially those involving English teaching. To work legally in the country, you need a non-immigrant visa and a work permit – which legitimate institutions should be able to provide. An excellent resource for background

on teaching in Thailand, as well as a resource for jobs, is Ajarn (www.ajarn.com).

ℹ Getting There & Away

AIR

Bangkok has one primary international airport (Suvarnabhumi International Airport) plus a budget carrier airport (Don Muang Airport) with international connections mainly to Asian countries. Chiang Mai, Chiang Rai, Hat Yai, Krabi, Samui, Pattaya and Phuket also have some international flights from nearby countries, especially China.

LAND

Thailand shares land borders with Cambodia, Laos, Malaysia and Myanmar (Burma). Visas on arrival are available for land-crossings into Cambodia, Laos and Malaysia. Pre-arranged visas are required for land entry into Myanmar. Improved highways and bridges have made it easier to travel overland to/from China via Laos.

ℹ Getting Around

AIR

Hopping around the country by air continues to be affordable. Most routes originate from Bangkok (both Don Mueang and Suvarnabhumi International Airports), but Chiang Mai, Hat Yai, Ko Samui, Phuket and Udon Thani all have a few routes to other Thai towns.

BICYCLE

Bicycles are a great way to explore the more rural, less-trafficked corners of Thailand. They can usually be hired from guesthouses for as little as 50B per day, though they aren't always high quality.

A good resource for cycling in the country is Bicycle Thailand (www.bicyclethailand.com).

BOAT

Long-tail boats are a staple of transport on rivers and canals in Bangkok and neighbouring provinces, and between islands.

Between the mainland and small, less-touristed islands, the standard craft is a wooden boat, 8m to 10m long, with an inboard engine, a wheelhouse and a simple roof to shelter passengers and cargo. To more popular destinations, faster hovercraft (jetfoils) and speedboats are the norm.

BUS & MINIVAN

The Thai bus service is widespread, convenient and fast. Reputable companies operate out of the government bus stations, not the tourist centres such as Bangkok's Th Khao San. Starting at the top, VIP buses are the closest you will come to a rock star's tour bus. The seats recline, the air-con is frosty and an 'air hostess' dispenses refreshments. Various diminishing classes of air-con buses strip away the extras until you're left with a fairly beat-up bus with an asthmatic cooling system.

Minivans are a convenient option for trips to nearby cities. They depart from the market instead of an out-of-town bus station and, in some cases, offer hotel drop-off.

For long-distance trips, purchase tickets the day before.

CAR & MOTORCYCLE

Cars and motorcycles can be rented in most tourist towns. Inspect the vehicle before committing. Document any existing damage to avoid being charged for it. Always verify that the vehicle is insured for liability before signing a rental contract, and ask to see the dated insurance documents.

Motorcycle travel is a popular way to do local sightseeing. Motorcycle rental usually requires that you leave your passport as a deposit.

Thais drive on the left-hand side of the road – most of the time. Every two-lane road has an invisible third lane in the middle that all drivers use as a passing lane. The main rule to be aware of is that 'might makes right' and smaller vehicles always yield to bigger ones. Drivers usually use their horns to indicate that they are passing.

An International Driving Permit is necessary to drive vehicles in Thailand, but this is rarely enforced for motorcycle hire.

HITCHING

It is uncommon to see people hitching, since bus travel is inexpensive and reliable. Hitching becomes an option where public transport isn't available. In this case you can usually catch a ride, but remember to use the Asian style of beckoning: hold your arm out towards the road, palm-side down and wave towards the ground.

Hitching is never entirely safe, and travellers who do so should understand that they are taking a small but potentially serious risk.

LOCAL TRANSPORT

Săhm·lór & Túk-Túk

Săhm·lór (also spelt *'săamláw'*), meaning 'three wheels', are pedal rickshaws found mainly in small towns for short hops. Their modern replacements are the motorised túk-túk, named for the throaty cough of their two-stroke engines. In Bangkok and other tourist centres, túk-túk drivers often grossly overcharge foreigners.

You must bargain and agree on a fare before accepting a ride.

Sŏrng·tăa·ou

Sŏrng·tăa·ou (literally, 'two benches') are small pick-up trucks with a row of seats down each

① ROAD SAFETY

Thailand's roads are dangerous: in 2015 the WHO declared Thailand the second-deadliest country in the world for road fatalities.

Fatal bus crashes make headlines, but nearly 75% of vehicle accidents in Thailand involve motorcycles. Many tourists are injured riding motorcycles because they don't know how to handle the vehicles and are unfamiliar with local driving conventions.

If you are a novice motorcyclist, familiarise yourself with the vehicle in an uncongested area of town and stick to the smaller 100cc automatic bikes. Drive slowly, especially when roads are slick or when there is loose gravel or sand. Remember to distribute weight as evenly as possible across the frame of the bike to improve handling. And don't expect other vehicles to look out for you. Always wear a helmet.

side. In some towns, *sŏrng·tăa·ou* serve as public buses running regular, fixed-fare routes. But in tourist towns, they act as shared taxis or private charter; in this case agree on a fare beforehand.

TRAIN

The **State Railway of Thailand** (SRT; ☑ nationwide 1690; www.railway.co.th) operates comfortable and moderately priced, but rather slow, services. All rail travel originates in Bangkok and radiates north, south and northeast. Trains are convenient for overnight travel between Bangkok and Chiang Mai and south to Chumphon or Surat Thani. The train can also dodge Bangkok traffic to Ayuthaya.

The SRT operates passenger trains in three classes – 1st, 2nd and 3rd – but each class varies depending on the train type (ordinary, rapid or express). Rapid and express trains make fewer stops than ordinary trains.

Fares are calculated from a base price with surcharges added for distance, class and train type. Extra charges are added for air-con and for sleeping berths (either upper or lower).

Advance bookings can be made from one to 60 days before your intended date of departure. You can make bookings in person from any train station. Train tickets can also be purchased at travel agencies, which usually add a service charge to the ticket price. If you are making an advance reservation from outside the country, contact a licensed travel agent: the SRT no longer operates its own online ticket service.

Timor-Leste

⏎ 670 / POP 1,167,242

Best for Culture

➡ Resistance Museum (p799)

➡ Chega! Exhibition (p799)

➡ Balibó Flag House (p811)

➡ Santa Cruz Cemetery (p801)

➡ Dare Memorial Museum (p801)

Top Tetun Phrases

Hello *Bondia*

Thank you *Obrigadu/a (m/f)*

Do you speak English? *Ita koalia Inglés?*

Why Go?

With hardly-touched 'best-in-the-world' reefs to dive, dugongs to spot, mountains to climb, and ancient traditions that have survived the ravages of war, Asia's newest country offers some of the world's last great off-the-beaten-track adventures.

Get an insight into Timor-Leste's dark history in Dili's museums, then venture out of the capital. Hike to jungle caves, wander through misty mountain village markets, and sip local coffee on the terrace of grand Portuguese *pousadas*. Bump along diabolical roads, stopping for photos of the seascapes as you grip the cliffs along the coast.

Strap on a snorkel and marvel at the pristine reefs that fringe the north coast and Ataúro, or delve deeper with dive companies that are proud to show off sites with superlative reef fish biodiversity. Trailblaze your way through this amazing country, and find out what everyone else has been missing.

When to Go
Dili

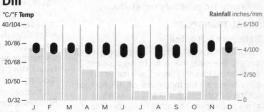

May–Nov (Dry season) There's little rainfall and lots of sun, though it can get very dusty.

Sep–Dec It's whale-watching season as pods migrate through the Wetar Strait.

Dec–Apr (Wet season) Heavy rain makes the landscape lush but many district-roads impassable.

Entering the Country

You can fly to Dili from Denpasar (Bali), Jakarta, Darwin and Singapore. There are flights from Kupang to Dili three times a week (Monday, Wednesday & Friday). A taxi into Dili from Presidente Nicolau Lobato International Airport is US$10.

Land border arrivals from Indonesia require a visa in advance; those flying in can get a visa on arrival. The land border at Batugade is about five hours by local bus (US$5) from Dili.

REGIONS AT A GLANCE

Central Timor-Leste features coffee groves in rainforest, picturesque hilltop villages as well as waterfalls and mountains. The East is best known for the beaches of Baucau and Jaco and the seascapes along the road to both. The West has the border with Indonesia, the up-and-coming resort towns of Liquica, historic Balibó and hot springs. North of Dili is the island of Atauro, best known for its great reefs and abundance of accommodation.

Essential Food & Drink

Locally grown coffee Served in Dili's on-trend cafes

Coconut water Fresh coconut juice

Tropical fruits From roadside stalls

Burgers and fries Not what you were expecting, but an essential from the bars lining Dili's foreshore

International food Dili offers an abundance of multi-cultural restaurants

Paun (bread) A breakfast staple in the districts

Things on a stick Fish or chicken, from roadside stalls

Top Tips

➡ Bring your own sunscreen and insect repellent.

➡ Expect long and often frustrating delays using public transport. Locals use buses to transport livestock and produce as well as themselves.

➡ Take care driving; many roads are in serious states of disrepair. Pigs and kids cross major roads at random times.

➡ Most small towns have informal budget homestay accommodation at around $US10 per night – ask around.

➡ Bring your own snorkelling equipment.

➡ Women moving around Dili alone should be on alert; there are frequent reports of harassment occurring day and night.

➡ Take metered blue taxis rather than unmetered yellow taxis.

➡ Paying a local to guide you up a mountain, to a waterfall or rock art spreads the tourist dollar and stops you inadvertently crossing onto sacred land.

AT A GLANCE

Currency US dollars (US$). Anything under US$2 can be paid in centavos (cv).

Visas Australian, Irish and British visitors must pay for a visa on arrival at Dili's airport or seaport; US$30 for 30 days. Most other EU nationals are free.

Money There are few ATMs outside Dili.

Language Portuguese and Tetun (official languages), local dialects. Use of English and Indonesian is decreasing.

Exchange Rates

Australia	A$1	US$0.80
Euro	€1	US$1.18
Indonesia	10,000 Rp	US$0.74
Singapore	S$1	US$0.74
UK	UK£1	US$1.30

For current exchange rates, see www.xe.com

TIMOR-LESTE

Daily Costs

Dorm bed US$14 to US$20

Local restaurant meal US$3

Short taxi trip US$2

Bus trip to the districts US$6

Resources

Official tourism website www.timorleste.tl

Guide Post Timor www.guideposttimor.com

Agora Food Studio www.timorlestefoodlab.com

Timor-Leste Highlights

1 Atauro (p806) Checking out the world's best reefs on this island a short trip from Dili.

2 Mt Ramelau (p811) Climbing to the peak of Timor-Leste's highest mountain at dawn to watch the sun rise over the clouds.

3 Jaco Island (p809) Enjoying a day lazing about on the powder-white sands,

with dazzling snorkelling just offshore.

4 Balibó (p811) Making the pilgrimage to the place where five Australian-based journalists were killed in 1975,

and staying in the Balibó Fort Hotel opposite.

5 Maubisse (p810) Enjoying the accommodation and food of this misty mountain town.

6 Loi Hunu (p808) Relaxing in a riverside bungalow, climbing to see former guerilla hideouts and trekking up **Mundo Perdido** (p808)

DILI

POP 252,884

Dili is a city by the sea, locked in by hills that lead to the districts beyond. The island of Ataúro glimmers to its north, on the other side of one of the deepest channels in Asia. Dili itself spreads from the airport, along the waterfront and all the way to the Cristo Rei statue (p801) in the east. The city's foreshore is popular with runners and walkers in the morning and evening, when the weather is cooler. Most of the action occurs here on the waterfront, and one or two blocks south of it, though sadly the western section has recently been populated by oversized embassies.

Dili is a great place to recharge batteries (literally) between jaunts into the districts. Pick accommodation with a pool and its own restaurant for the ideal escape from the dust and noise that can overload the senses. Travellers tend to hang out in the bars along Av de Portugal (also known as Beach Rd) and at Areia Branca, near the Cristo Rei statue. Timor Plaza (p803), closeish to the airport, is a surprisingly good spot for food, bars and air-con. Dili's biggest jewel? World-class dive sites are just minutes from town.

◉ Sights

★ Chega! Exhibition
MUSEUM

(Centro Nacional Chega; ☏ 33 1003; www.cavr-timorleste.org; Estrada de Balide; ⊙ 9am-noon & 2-5pm Mon-Fri) FREE Set in the buildings and cells of a Portuguese-era prison where resistance figures were interned by the Indonesian military, Chega! (*chega* means 'stop' or 'no more' in Portuguese) houses the results of the Commission for Reception, Truth and Reconciliation (CAVR) process – documenting human rights abuses from 1974 to 1999. It's hard to find and navigate; best to head here with Dili History Tours (p802).

★ Resistance Museum
MUSEUM

(Resistência Timorense; ☏ 7713 1903; www.amrtimor.org; Rua de Cidade de Lisboa; admission US$1; ⊙ 9am-4.30pm Tue-Sat) An excellent museum, established in 2005, which commemorates Timor-Leste's 24-year struggle against the Indonesian occupation. Falintil's resistance is brought to life with a timeline, photos, video recordings and exhibits of the weapons and tools of communication that the East Timorese used in their fight for independence. You can watch harrowing footage of the Santa Cruz Massacre here before heading to Santa Cruz Cemetery (p801).

Motael Church
CHURCH

(The Church de São António de Motael; Av Salazar) This church, the oldest Catholic church in Timor-Leste, was one of the most important places in the story of the fight for Timorese independence. Sebastião Gomes was shot dead here in 1991 by the Indonesian military; his funeral parade to Santa Cruz Cemetery (p801) attracted thousands, and resulted in the Santa Cruz Massacre.

ITINERARIES

One Week

From Dili, lunch in Baucau before continuing to Loi Hunu (p808) to stay at Hotel Comunitaria Wailakurini and climb past the Guerilla Hideout. Wake early and head through Ossu to hike **Mundo Perdido** (Lost World; p808) with a guide. Next up, check out the **cave art** (p809) on the way down to sacred Jaco Island (p809). Stay in a simple hut on the mainland for two nights, spending a day on Jaco, snorkelling. Return to Dili, via a night in Baucau (p807) to explore museums and markets, before heading out to Ataúro (p806) for a couple of nights. Cap off your adventure with a dawn climb of Mt Ramelau (p811).

One Month

Complete the one-week itinerary (p799), then return to Dili for some diving before heading west to Liquiçá (p810) for luxury beachside camping at Caimeo Beach or beach games at Lauhata Beach Escape. Continue towards the Indonesian border, stopping at Maubara Fort for souvenirs. Be reminded of the tragic story of the Balibó Five in Balibó (p811), and overnight at the terrific Balibó Fort Hotel, before heading south past Maliana to soak in the **hot springs** (be manis; p810) at Marobo. Finally, fly from Dili to Oecusse (p812) for a night to witness the rapid development of this once sleepy town (and maybe spot a dugong, too).

Dili

Oecusse
(170km)

Atauro Island
(40km)

Dili
Harbour

WETAR
STRAIT

Santana River

Bemori River

Santana River

Fish on a Stick' Stalls (3km);
Aquatica Dive Resort (3.5km)

Caz Bar (2.5km);
Beachside Hotel (2.6km);
Cristo Rei (4.6km)

Becora
(1.4km)

Av de Portugal (Beach Rd)

Av de Sant'Ana

Av dos Direitos Humanos

Estrada de Bidau

Av Liberdade Emprensa

LECIDERE

Rua Cidade Viana do Castelo

Rua Belarmino Lobo

Rua Circunvalação

Taibessi Bus
Terminal

MOTAEL

Av dos Mártires de Pátria

Landmark Plaza (600m);
Timor Plaza (2.1km);
Arte Moris (4.4km)

Av Alves Aldeia

Rua de Colmera

Rua de Cidade
de Lisboa

Resistance
Museum

Rua Colmera

COLMERA

Western
Union

DHL

Av Bispo
de Medeiros

Rua Jacinto de Candido

Rua Caicoli

CAICOLI

MATADOURO

BAIRO
PITE

Timor Tour
& Travel

Rua Quinze de Outubro

Estrada de Balide

Chega!
Exhibition

1 km
0.5 miles

N

16
11
14
23
19
24
17
10
3
28
6
5
8
31
30 18
21 22
13
27 15
29
26
9
12
4
7
20
25
1
2

Dili

TIMOR-LESTE DILI

Santa Cruz Massacre Memorial Monument   MONUMENT

(Av Salazar) It lacks an inscription or an official name, but the monument's location opposite Motael Church (p799) offers a clue: independence supporter Sebastião Gomes was shot by Indonesian forces near here on 28 October 1991. Built to remember those who lost their lives in the resulting Santa Cruz Massacre, it shows survivors Agustinho, now living in Portugal, and Amali, who remains in Timor-Leste.

Cristo Rei   STATUE

(Jesus Statue; Av de Areia Branca) The hard-to-miss Cristo Rei, 7km east of town, has 570 steps leading to the statue of Jesus, a gift from the Indonesian government in 1996. It's a popular morning and evening exercise spot, with mountain and water views. Catch blue *mikrolet* number 12 or a taxi (US$7) to get here (ask the taxi driver to wait).

Santa Cruz Cemetery   CEMETERY

(Rua de Santa Cruz) On 12 November 1991 Indonesian soldiers fired on a peaceful memorial procession for Sebastião Gomes from Motael Church (p799) to Santa Cruz Cemetery. More than 250 civilians (mostly students)

died. British journalist Max Stahl filmed the bloody attack and the smuggled footage was beamed around the world, empowering the nation's independence struggle.

Dili Waterfront   AREA

Watch kids kicking soccer balls around on the patches of sandy beach, and runners sweating it out while you're strolling the decent walking path that runs along the waterfront. The grand **Palácio do Governo** (Rua 30 de Agosta) (Government House) is a highlight, as is **Farol Lighthouse** (Av de Portugal) to the west. Further west, oversized embassies take up space next to small expat-owned bars.

Dare Memorial Museum   MEMORIAL

(☎726 6517; https://darememorialmuseum.com; Rua Fatunaba, Dare; ☉10am-4pm Sat & Sun) **FREE** There are two great things about Dare (pronounced da-ray) Memorial Museum, but you'll have to ask for them. First, ask for a cup of Timorese coffee, then to watch the excellent video documenting Timor-Leste's involvement in WWII including the Timorese who helped Australian troops before being left to face the repercussions from the Japanese once the Australians departed.

🏃 Activities & Tours

Get to know Timor-Leste's fascinating history by checking out Dili's museums and cultural centres. An organised tour will help you get bearings to start. The diving is great in town, too; choose a dive company and get under the water to check out incredible coral and fish biodiversity just offshore – or head a little further afield to legendary dive site K41. Adventurous cyclists come to Timor-Leste to test out their skills in the dry, harsh conditions promised by Tour de Timor (p802).

Compass Charters   DIVING
(☑ 7723 0964, 7723 0965; www.compassadventuretours.com; Av dos Mártires de Pátria; snorkelling US$140, two-dive day trip US$210, two-night trip to Ataúro US$500) Specialises in multi-day trips to Ataúro's spectacular north coast sites (eg two nights at its tented Adara or Beloi Beach ecocamps), as well as two-dive day trips to Ataúro, plus local and coast dives, a water-taxi service to Ataúro and snorkelling day trips. Located next to Tiger Fuel.

Aquatica Dive Resort   DIVING
(☑ 7700 5121, 7803 8885; www.aquaticadiveresort.com; Aldeia Metin, Bebonuk, Comoro; local dives US$60, two-dive coast trip US$120, Ataúro US$170) Aussies Desmond and Jennifer are the go-to people for heading out on a local dive to find Dili's dugong, Douglas. They also offer other local dives, two-dive coast trips and visits to Ataúro. It's east of the Comoro River and a bit out of town; there is also accommodation here.

Dive Timor Lorosae   DIVING
(☑ 7723 7092; www.divetimor.com; Av de Portugal; shore dive US$45, day trip US$110, two-dive trip US$165, whale-watching US$85; ⊙ 7.30am-7.30pm) 🐾 This dive centre has been operating since 2000, offering shore dives, two-dive day trips to sites along the north coast (including legendary K41) and two-dive trips to sites around Ataúro. Also has its own training pool and backpackers (p803). Runs beach clean-up days and offers whale watching from September to November.

★ Eco Discovery   TOURS
(☑ 7726 9829, 332 2454; www.ecodiscovery-east-timor.com; Landmark Plaza, Av Nicolau Lobato; 4WD and guide/driver US$235 per day, all inclusive; ⊙ 9am-5pm Mon-Fri, to noon Sat) 🐾 It's not cheap to tour Timor-Leste, but hiring a 4WD and guide (split the cost with others if possible) and planning your big rural adventure can be worth the expense. Eco Discovery's English-speaking guides are often matched to their home territory, and are fonts of information and assistance. Highly recommended.

★ Dili History Tours   TOURS
(☑ 7824 5891, 7797 6473; www.jdntimorleste.weebly.com; Rua Metiaut; US$21; ⊙ Tours begin at 9am or 2pm) Run by Timorese students in the Juventude ba Dezenvolvimentu Násional (JDN), these tours cover the story of Timor-Leste's independence, travelling around by *mikrolet*. An excellent way to see and understand the city's history.

✨ Festivals & Events

Darwin Dili Yacht Rally   SAILING
(www.sailtimorleste.org; AUD$250 per yacht; ⊙ Jul) Yachts and their crew make their way from Darwin in Australia to Dili and Oecussi in this popular annual event. See the Sail Timor-Leste website for entry details and general information about sailing to Timor-Leste.

Dili City of Peace Marathon   SPORTS
(⊙ Aug) Running is huge in Dili, and it's celebrated annually with a marathon and half marathon. In 2017 the full marathon (42km) saw a winning time of 2:26, with almost half the field of 50 not finishing (it's tough!). The half marathon (21km) is more popular.

Tour de Timor   CYCLING
(www.tourdetimor.com; registration US$1000; ⊙ Sep) Adventure cyclists from around the world bring their own bikes to test them on the tough and challenging conditions of Timor-Leste's roads in this five-day, 500km cycling adventure. It began in 2009 as part of the 'City of Peace' initiative, and the months before the (usually) annual event see expats and locals zooming around Dili in Lycra as dawn breaks.

DUGONGS OF TIMOR-LESTE

Each day at Tasi Tolu, just west of Dili's airport, Douglas the dugong has his (or her; there are rumours) lunch in the sea grass. Sightings of Douglas (and other dugongs) are never guaranteed, but these huge placid beasts are often spotted by divers and snorkellers at various sites along the coast east of Dili. Local dive operators can show you where to point your GoPro.

🛏 Sleeping

A host of new backpacker options have opened Dili up to visa-renewers flying in from Bali. Hotels have been bringing their prices down, so it's always worth trying to negotiate a better rate. Life in Dili is better with a pool, but unfortunately only a few places to stay have one.

★ Dive Timor Lorosae Backpackers
HOSTEL $

(🗷 7723 7092; www.divetimor.com; Av de Portugal; dm US$20, r US$40-100; �🤶🎇) 🍴 Offering air-con, free wi-fi and pool access, plus sunrise and sunset views across the road, you'd be hard-pressed to find better budget accom in Dili. If you can splash out, opt for one of the stylish apartments set around the pool, which are good value if shared. You can grab a pre-dive feed at Castaway Bar (p804) upstairs.

Hostel daTerra
HOSTEL $

(🗷 7784 5678, 7730 6030; Rua do Colégio Militar; dm US$14, s/d US$22/35, incl breakfast; 🌃🤶) 🍴 A popular cafe in a luscious front garden helps Hostel daTerra claim its spot as Dili's greenest and most 'backpacker' place to stay. The rooms (one dorm and one single/double) are bright and share a bathroom. Movie night is on Thursday, and neighbour, Timorese singer Ego Lemos, keeps the vibe musical.

Dili Central Backpackers
HOSTEL $

(🗷 7355 4433; www.dtceasttimor.com; Rua de Nu Laran 28; dm from US$15 incl breakfast) Bland dorms with fans or air-con ($US5 more). Lockers and breakfast are included, and owner Kym is a font of local knowledge, having lived in Timor-Leste for nearly two decades. The cafe serves great juices and snacks. Dive, Trek & Camp (🗷 7350 6279; www.dtceasttimor.com; Rua de Nu Laran 28; bike US$10 per day, motorbike US$20 per day, motorbike and rider US$50 per day, mikrolet tour US$95, nightlife/music tour US$135) runs from here. Bike hire is US$10 per day.

Beachside Hotel
HOTEL $$

(🗷 7750 2184, 7754 9681; www.beachsidehoteldili.com; Areia Branca; dm US$30, d from US$85, incl breakfast; 🤶) Opposite Areia Branca beach, this is one of Dili's best beachside accommodation options. Tastefully decorated rooms have kitchenettes; more expensive ones overlook the beach, and there's also a bunk room. Rates include breakfast and laundry. There's a great on-site cafe (7.30am to 7pm) serving organic food. Connected to town by blue *mikrolet* No.12.

Esplanada
HOTEL $$

(🗷 331 3088; www.hotelesplanada.com; Av de Portugal; d US$99 incl breakfast; 🌃🤶🎇) This boutique hotel is a favourite spot for repeat visitors to Timor-Leste: its pleasant accommodation blocks surround a palm-tree-shaded pool. The upstairs bar-restaurant serves pricey meals (US$12) to go with its water views, but come during an event, or when there's live music on a Thursday night, and be swept up in the fun of Dili. Rates can often be negotiated.

Hotel Timor
HOTEL $$

(🗷 332 4502; www.timortur.com; Rua Mártires da Pátria; r US$85; 🌃🤶) A stay in Hotel Timor, in the heart of Dili, is a dip into colonial times. The foyer shops, including the NGO gift shop Things and Stories, are good, and you can soak up the Portuguese influence while eating your *pastel de nata* (custard tart) in its colonial-esque cafe. Rooms are a blend of luxurious dark timber and good linen.

🍴 Eating

Most of Dili's places to eat are concentrated along Av de Portugal (Beach Rd) and along Rua Presidente Nicolau Lobato, with another cluster at Metiaut, about 2km east of the centre towards Cristo Rei. **Timor Plaza** (www.timorplaza.com; Av Nicolau Lobato, Comoro; ⏱9am-6pm; 🤶) offers a wide range of meals in its food court.

Rolls N Bowls
VIETNAMESE $

(🗷 7796 0909; Grand Diocesse, Av Alves Aldela; mains US$6; ⏱7am-10pm Mon-Thu, to 11pm Fri, 10am-10pm Sat & Sun; 🌃) Sit down in air-con comfort and get your *pho* fix at this popular Vietnamese restaurant in the heart of Dili's foreshore precinct. As well as *pho*, you can enjoy spring rolls and salad bowls. There's a view of Dili's container-ship yard from its rooftop lounge (Thursday and Friday from 5pm).

Kaffè U'ut
CAFE $

(kaffeuut@gmail.com; Rua Gov. José Celestino da Silva; mains US$3.80-6.90; ⏱7am-9pm Mon-Sat; from 9am Sun; 🌃✏) Hard-to-resist cheesecakes and Brazilian *brigadeiro* (fudge balls) go down well with the Timorese coffee (US$3) served in this modern cafe with air-con. Lunch-seekers can enjoy burgers, paninis or vegan pasta. Also at Páteo (p804).

Letefoho Specialty Coffee Roaster
CAFE $

(🗷 7807 3264; Av de Portugal; drinks $US1.50-4; ⏱7am-7pm) The super-friendly baristas at Timor-Leste's first speciality coffee shop transform house-roasted Timorese beans into perfect flat whites, iced lattes, or whichever way you like it. A calm spot to while away the hours.

Lita Supermarket SUPERMARKET $
(Av dos Direitos Humanos; ☺8.30am-8.30pm) Sells a wide range of groceries; good for grabbing supplies before trips to the districts. There's a fresh fruit and veg market across the road.

★ **Agora Food Studio** CAFE $$
(📞7785 9912; www.timorlestefoodlab.com; Kampung Alor, behind the Mosque; mains US$6-14; ☺8am-6pm Tue-Sat; ❄️🍴) 🍴 House-made yoghurt breakfast bowls, *kombucha* (fermented tea) and barista-made coffee set this cafe, upstairs in the LELI English school, apart. Staff transform local staples like fresh ginger, turmeric and sweet potato into tasty meals. Don't miss the Timorese speciality Foho Roots Salad. Friendly staff welcome you loudly, and the mellow music helps you settle in.

Castaway Bar INTERNATIONAL $$
(📞7723 5449; Av de Portugal; mains US$6-16; ☺6.30am-midnight) Crowds of locals, tourists and expats enjoy Aussie comfort food staples as well as gourmet pizzas and burgers at this popular two-storey place overlooking the waterfront. Check the blackboard for lunch and dinner specials – and giggle at the listed 'today sorry no haves' (jalapeños and muffins when we visitied). Bands play Friday night.

🍷 Drinking & Nightlife

Dili's bar scene is great: there's usually something happening after dark – ask around or look for posters offering deals like dinner and five beers for US$10. Heineken opened a flash new brewery in Dili in 2016, so it's likely your Tiger or Bintang has been locally brewed.

Skybar ROOFTOP BAR
(📞7825 7091; Level 4, Timor Plaza, Av Nicolau Lobato, Comoro; ☺5pm-late; 🛜) Cheap Bintang beer and live music draws the expat crowds to this rooftop bar on Friday nights in particular. The views over Dili are excellent.

DiZa BAR
(📞7785 3222; Av Marginal, Metiaut; ☺10am-midnight Tue-Sun) Dili's expat crowd vie for the best seats to watch the sun set over the harbour here – passionfruit mojito in hand – at this beautifully appointed, Balinese-inspired beachside bar. It's no longer the most popular spot to eat, but the vibe is still good.

Caz Bar BAR
(Areia Branca; ☺7am-9pm Mon-Fri, to 10pm Sat & Sun) Sink back in your chair on the sand at this popular place near the statue of Jesus – the perfect place to recover with a beer or fresh coconut water after running up and down its steps. The menu is good: eggs benedict suits Sunday mornings. Catch blue *mikrolet* no. 12, or pay around US$7 for a taxi to get there.

🛍️ Shopping

Boneca de Ataúro ARTS & CRAFTS
(📞7797 6508; www.bonecadeatauro.com; Páteo, Rua D Fernando) This small outlet sells well-designed, modern and handmade laptop bags, Christmas tree decorations, tea towels and soft toys. The work is done by formerly disadvantaged women on Ataúro – you can see them in action on old Singer sewing machines at the Boneca de Ataúro (p806) workshop on the island.

Páteo AREA
(Rua D Fernando; ☺8am-9pm) This new shopping area is home to some of Dili's best cafes and shops, as well as a Portuguese supermarket with a great, cheap deli and plenty of Portuguese products.

Alola Foundation ARTS & CRAFTS
(📞332 3855; www.alolafoundation.org; Rua Bispo de Medeiros; ☺8.45am-5.30pm Mon-Fri, 10am-3pm Sat) Sells *tais* (woven cloth), sculptures, soaps and other crafts from around the country to support its work with the women and children of Timor-Leste.

ℹ️ Information

There's no proper tourist office. Tourism websites www.turismo.gov.tl and www.visiteast timor.com are unfortunately out of date.

DANGERS & ANNOYANCES

Violent outbreaks can and do occur, often quickly, so stay clear of gathering groups of people and political rallies. There are frequent reports of foreign women being groped and sexually assaulted in broad daylight and in public places; as a result, it's probably safer to travel around with others. Avoid yellow taxis and the city after dark if travelling alone.

INTERNET ACCESS

Most internet is provided through mobile phones, with companies offering unlimited data for US$1 per day; bring an unlocked phone and buy a local SIM. Wi-fi is rare.

Telemor (📞7551 1555; www.telmor.tl; Timor Plaza, Av Nicolau Lobato, Comoro; ☺8am-8pm)

Telkomsel (☑ 7373 7373; www.telkomcel.tl; Timor Plaza; ☺ 9am-7pm; 🛜)

Timor Telecom (☑ 330 3357; www.timor telecom.tl; Hotel Timor; ☺ 8am-6pm Mon-Fri, 9am-3pm Sat; 🛜)

MEDICAL SERVICES

Australian Embassy Clinic (☑ 331 1555; www. timorleste.embassy.gov.au; ☺ 8.30am-4.30pm Mon-Fri) You have to be Australian to see the doctor at this fee-per-service clinic. Its location will be changing in late 2017 – check the embassy's website for the new location.

Clínica Portuguesa (☑ 7741 8969; www. clinicaportuguesa.com; Timor Plaza, Avenida Luro Mata entrance, Comoro; ☺ 8.30am-6pm Mon-Fri, 9am-1pm Sat) This modern fee-per-service clinic outside **Timor Plaza** (p803) has GPs and dental services.

Hospital Nacional Guido Valadares (Dili National Hospital; ☑ 331 1008; Rua Cidade Viana do Castelo, Bidau) A cadre of Western volunteers assists locals at this busy national hospital just east of Estrada de Bidau. It's best to bring someone to look out for you.

Stamford Medical Clinic (☑ 331 0141, emergencies 7772 1111; Rua D Boa 17, Ventura; ☺ 9am-6pm Mon-Fri, to 1pm Sat) This spotless Western clinic also opens after hours for emergencies.

MONEY

ANZ (☑ 330 6100; www.anz.com/timorleste; Timor Plaza, Av Nicolau Lobato, Comoro; ☺ 8am-5pm Mon-Fri) has eight ATMs in Dili, including one at the airport. ATMs dispense US dollars.

Western Union (☑ 332 1586; www.western union.com; Sang Tai Hoo Building, Rua de Colmera, Colmera; ☺ 9am-4.30pm Mon-Fri, 9am-noon Sat) in Colmera and Páteo; transfers funds internationally.

POSTAL SERVICES

Central Post Office (Av Bishop de Medeiros; ☺ 9am-noon Mon-Sat, 2-5pm Mon-Fri) The only place you can receive/send mail in Dili (aside from trying your luck at **DHL** (Timor Air Services, Colmera Plaza, Estrada Balide; ☺ 8.30am-5.30pm Mon-Fri, to noon Sat) in Colmera Plaza), opposite the Alola Foundation.

ⓘ Getting There & Away

Presidente Nicolau Lobato International Airport (code: DIL; Rua Nicolau Lobato; 🛜) is situated towards Tasi Tolu, a US$10 taxi journey from the city centre, or a cheaper *mikrolet* journey (number 11; walk 600m from the airport to the main road).

The **Nakroma Ferry Office** (☑ 331 7264; Av de Portugal; ☺ 8am-5pm) is in the large building at the port. Ferries for Oecusse (12 hours, US$8) leave at 4pm Monday and Thursday, departing Oecusse at 2pm Tuesday and Friday. The **Laju Laju** (☑ Dili office 332 2266; Grand Diocesse, Av Alves Aldeia, Dili; ☺ 7am-5pm Mon-Fri, to 1pm Sat) also does the trip to Oecusse, departing Dili at 2.45pm Tuesday and Friday, and returning from Oecusse at 2.45pm Wednesday and Saturday (US$10).

Ferries headed for Ataúro are the Nakroma (8am Saturday; US$4; returning to Dili at 3pm), Laju Laju (8am Thursday, departing Ataúro for Dili at 3pm) and **Dragon Star Shipping** (☑ 332 2266, 7622 2000; dragonstarshippinglda@gmail.com; Grand Diocesse, Av Alves Aldeia; ☺ 7am-5pm Mon-Fri, to 1pm Sat) goes at 8am Monday and Friday to Sunday, departing Ataúro 2.30pm Monday and Friday, 3pm Saturday and Sunday; US$15. **Compass Charters** (☑ 7723 0965; www.compassadventuretours.com; Av dos Mártires de Pátria) heads to the island daily at 7.30am (adult/child one-way US$45/25), from right of the front of Palácio Do Governo and returns at 9.30am to depart from Barry's Place.

Dili's bus 'terminals' (more like shabby shelters) are served by taxis and *mikrolet* (small minibuses). Buses are more frequent in the morning. **Tasi Tolu Terminal**, west of the airport, is the hub for destinations to the west of the country (Ermera, Maliana and Liquiçá). Buses travelling to the east (Baucau, Lospalos, Viqueque) leave from **Becora Bus Terminal** (Av de Becora). The **Taibessi Bus Terminal**, next to the huge Taibessi market, is the stop for transport to Maubisse, Same and Suai.

Timor Tour & Travel (☑ 7723 5093, Kupang office +62 8 12379 4199; Rua Quinze de Outubro 17) runs a daily minibus service to Kupang (US$23, 12 hours) in Indonesian West Timor. Be at the office by 8am to check in, and note that you'll switch buses at the border. Seats can book out in advance.

ⓘ Getting Around

Mikrolet (small minibuses) are like moving stereos: they buzz about loudly on designated routes during daylight hours, stopping frequently over short distances.

Cars are useful for night travel in Dili, though drivers must carry car registration papers and their drivers license at all times. Otherwise, walking, cycling and using taxis should suffice. The addition of the metered **Blue Taxi** (☑ 7742 7777, 331 1110) to Dili's streets means you can book ahead and have an element of safety. Avoid the decrepit yellow (unmetered) taxis; if you must take one, negotiate a price before you get in – most trips cost US$2. If you find a good driver, ask for their mobile number and see if they'll be your regular driver. Streets are usually taxi-free by 9pm.

Both motorbike and scooter riders and passengers are required by law to wear helmets.

TIMOR-LESTE DILI

ATAÚRO

This island, some 24km from Dili over a 3km-deep channel, hit the spotlight in 2016 after Conservation International announced that it had the most biodiverse waters in the world. According to their research, Ataúro has the most species of reef fish per site, with globally superlative reef fish biodiversity.

Many of the reefs are accessible from the shore, or you can share the cost of a charter to get a bit further out for around US$10. As well as the diving and snorkelling day trips run here from Dili, Ataúro now has its own dive backpackers, so you can make the most of the relaxed island vibe and get your fill of pretty coral and fish, too.

🏃 Activities

Dili's dive shops arrange underwater tours of the island's technicolour coral drop-offs, as does island-based operator Ataúro Dive Resort (p806). Guesthouses and local fishermen can arrange boat transport for snorkelling the outer reef or you can stick to the reefs just offshore.

Hike across the island's hilly interior to reach a white-sand beach at **Adara** (three to four hours), where you'll find some of the best snorkelling on the island, and simple hut or tent accommodation. On the east coast, Barry's Place (p806) and **Beloi Beach Hotel** (☑7558 3421; www.beloibeachhoteltimorleste.com; Beloi; r per person incl meals with/without boat transfers US$160/$80; ❄🛜🏊) 🍴 can organise lunch and a fishing boat charter (US$50 one way; two hours) from **Beloi**. You'll chug over azure waters past white-sand beaches (including stunning **Akrema** beach) and caves.

You can also hike to **Mt Manucoco** (995m, around three hours up from **Vila**), the island's highest peak.

🛌 Sleeping & Eating

Compass Charters (p802) has two tented camps on the island (one at Beloi and one at Adara).

Ataúro Dive Resort   BUNGALOW **$**
(☑323 2455, 7738 6166; www.ataurodiveresort.com; Beloi; s/d US$35/50, dorm bed US$18 incl breakfast) Volker and Saffy run this dive centre and backpackers, which offers comfortable island-style bungalows with shared bathrooms, as well as a simple thatched six-bed dorm. The best diving spots are two minutes away by boat, or you can snorkel and dive out from the beach. Saffy makes a mean bowl of ice cream (US$1).

You can learn to dive from US$450; after this, dives are US$50 each. Night dives are also available.

⭐ **Barry's Place**   BUNGALOW **$$**
(☑7723 6084; www.barrysplaceatauro.com; Beloi; r per person incl meals US$35-45) 🍴 Australian owner Barry is almost clocking up two decades in Timor-Leste, and can be credited for some of the sustainable, income-producing development on Ataúro. This spot, once a stark desert-like block, is now a tropical delight. Don't miss a stay in one of the thatched bungalows, and a swing in your own hammock (each bungalow has one). Book ahead.

Mario's Place   BUNGALOW **$$**
(☑7795 7272; Adara; r per person incl meals US$25) Adara, on the west side of Ataúro, is a quiet, palm-tree-fringed area with terrific snorkelling and diving. Mario's has four basic bungalows with lights, fans and mosquito nets and shared drop toilet. You can hike here from Beloi (three hours), or charter a boat (two hours; US$100 return).

Day-trippers are welcome for lunch (US$5): bring your own snorkel (and pay the US$1.50 reef tax).

🛍 Shopping

Boneca de Ataúro   GIFTS & SOUVENIRS
(Vila de Maumeta; ⊙9am-5pm) Calling this a doll shop doesn't do it justice: here, in a simple building by the beach, marginalised women sew modern, well-designed laptop bags and pencil cases as well as dolls and toys (check out the resistance leaders in camouflage). You can also purchase their items at the Boneca de Ataúro (p804) shop in Dili, too.

Empreza Di'ak
ARTS & CRAFTS

(☑ Ataúro 7730 3698, Dili 7726 6204; geral@
empreza-diak.com; Beloi) 🏍 This eco-friendly
NGO sells locally carved crocodiles, bamboo
straws and pottery. The pottery is an Ataúro
tradition remembered, and brought to life
again, by two local women in their late 90s.

ℹ Getting There & Around

The most convenient way to get to/from Ataúro
is with **Compass Charters** (p802)' water-taxi
service, which departs Dili daily at 7.30am from
just east of the Palácio do Governo (US$45 one
way, 90 minutes) and lands at Barry's Place. It
departs Barry's Place for Dili at 9.30am daily
and sometimes again around 3pm.

The Nakroma ferry (p805) departs Dili Port
on Saturday at 8am arriving at Beloi on Ataúro,
just south of Barry's Place, and returns at 3pm,
taking two hours each way. Buy tickets from Dili
dock on Friday (US$4 one way).

The Laju Laju (p805) car ferry leaves Dili for
Beloi on Thursday at 8am and departs with a
great deal of horn blowing the same day at 3pm
(US$5 one way).

Kevin runs the MV *Ataúro* (US$35 one way;
+670 7733 6611). He also offers whale sightseeing trips between September and December, or
alternatively try Beloi Beach Hotel (p806), which
can get you to and from the island on a charter
for US$45 per person.

Dragon Star Shipping (p805) sends a river
boat to Ataúro on Friday, Saturday, Sunday
and Monday at 8am, departing Ataúro at 3pm
(2.30pm Monday and Friday). However, we don't
recommend it: it often does not leave in rough
weather and is not designed for sea travel. Fares
for foreigners are US$15 one way, and it takes an
hour. Accommodation hosts can help you to get
around, whether by motorbike or boat.

EASTERN TIMOR-LESTE

With your own wheels (or on painfully slow
public transport) you'll stumble across lime-
green rice paddies, mangroves and idyllic
beaches where buffaloes (and the occasional
crocodile) roam. You're essentially on the
long road east to check out two things: Mundo Perdido (p808) and the resistance centre
of Loi Hunu, and the isolated white sands
and coral reef of Jaco Island (p809), a short
trip from the mainland. En route, you'll
pass reminders of the various occupiers of
this land, including Portuguese forts and
churches, and Japanese WWII hillside tunnels, as well as a monument to three nuns
who were murdered by Indonesian militia

VENILALE

It takes an hour to drive the 28km of rugged road to the crumbling colonial buildings of Venilale, a town wedged between
Mt Matebian (p809) in the east and
Mundo Perdido (p808; 1775m) in the
west. Almost halfway between the two,
look for the seven caves tunnelled out of
the hillside by Japanese forces in WWII;
you can stop and have a wander through.
In Venilale, check out the resistance
monument – painted in the Timor-Leste
colours of yellow, black and white.

Built in 1933, Escola do Reino could
win prizes for its have-to-see-to-believe
colour scheme. Unfortunately the school,
and its library, is not faring well, but the
blue and pink stripes remain bright.

---

in 1999. This is also the direction to head for
some the country's best diving spots, while
Baucau is certainly worth stopping at for its
beaches, historic accommodation and lovely
pool.

Baucau
POP 16,000

Perched on a steep hillside 123km east of
Dili, Baucau is a tale of two cities (or, rather, large towns): the Old Town with its sea
views and Portuguese-era relics, and the
bland, Indonesian-built New Town (Kota
Baru), up the hill. A road leads downhill
from the *pousada* through a lush ravine to
the palm-fringed seaside village of Osolata.

Don't miss the roundabout with its fresh
food (and fish) market, the towering pousada (p808) and the picturesque **swimming
pool** (Old Town Roundabout, on the road to the
beach and Los Palos; US$1), which is fed by a
clear natural spring. It's a further 4km down
to Baucau's white-sand beach (keep a look
out for crocodiles).

🛏 Sleeping

Baucau Beach Bungalow
BUNGALOW $

(☑ 7770 4585; Osolata; r per person incl breakfast bungalow/house US$15/25; camping US$5)
Choose between a thatched bungalow that
sleeps five, or one of three rooms in a nearby house (with shared facilities) closer to
the beach. Meals can be arranged for US$8,
with fish sourced from local boats. It's 4km

from Baucau's Old Town; take a *mikrolet* (small minibus; 50cv) from the roundabout. A grassy patch is perfect for camping.

Book ahead for weekend stays.

Melita Guesthouse   GUESTHOUSE **$**
(☑ 7725 0267; menobruno@yahoo.com; Rua Vao Redi Bahu, Old Town; s/d US$20/30; ❄ 🛜) With clean rooms, friendly staff and a huge open-air balcony, Melita is one of Baucau's best budget options. Add US$5 per night per room for air-con, and an extra US$2.50 for breakfast. Often booked up with school groups and aid workers. To find it, take a left downhill at the Pousada roundabout.

★ **Pousada de Baucau**   HOTEL **$$**
(☑ 7724 1111; www.pousadadebaucau.com; Rua de Catedral, Old Town; s/d incl breakfast US$70/75; ❄ 🛜) An eerie history as a torture centre during the Indonesian occupation doesn't stop this large, salmon-pink building from topping the best hotels of Timor-Leste list. Comfortable rooms have views, mini bars, *tais* (woven cloth) bedheads, timber floorboards and antique furniture. A block of new rooms (without views) were being built when we visited. There's also a fancy (and expensive) restaurant.

✗ Eating & Drinking

A few restaurants sit on the main road in the Old Town, and there are cheap *warungs* (food stalls) in the New Town. The road to Baucau is lined with roadside stalls selling *ai manas* (chilli paste), coconut oil and peanuts.

Tato-Toty   INDONESIAN **$**
(☑ 7848 4478; by the roundabout, Old Town; ☺ 9am-10pm) This upstairs restaurant offers a tongue-twisting name, eye-busting colour scheme and delicious food. The chicken-ball soup *(soto ayam)* for US$2.50 is the best around. Rooms are also available (from US$35) and the swimming pool is just next door.

Restaurante Amalia   PORTUGUESE **$**
(☑ 7691 0908; Rua Vila Antiga, Old Town; mains US$4-7; ☺ 9am-10pm) This Baucau old-timer still looks welcoming with its luscious, shady and cool outdoor terrace. However, while it's the perfect spot for a coffee or Bintang, the meals themselves can be disappointing. Still, enjoy the sea views outside, and pop your head inside and admire the wonderfully decorated altars.

ℹ Getting There & Away

Many buses drive the 123km between Dili and Baucau (US$5, four hours). Most of the road was being dug up and replaced in 2017, which hopefully will pave the way for a shorter journey in future. Buses also head towards Lospalos (US$5, four hours); hop off at the Tutuala turn-off if you're heading to Jaco.

Loi Hunu & Mundo Perdido

Loi Hunu was one of the main resistance areas of Timor-Leste, and it's where many of today's leaders came from, or hid, during Indonesian occupation. It's still an area full of mystery, home to bat caves and hot springs.

You can learn how to cook traditional food in bamboo in an open fire at Hotel Comunitaria Wailakurini. If you're doing the dawn climb up Mundo Perdido, purchase snacks beforehand in Baucau.

Mundo Perdido   MOUNTAIN
Crashing through foliage under the squawks of bats and lorikeets as you climb Mundo Perdido (1775m) – which translates to 'Lost World' – is one of the country's highlights. The view of sunrise from the grassy plateau near the top (1380m) is worth the 4am wake-up call. Local guide Xisto (7786 7272) charges US$10 a group. The starting point is near Ossu, 20 to 30 minutes from Loi Hunu. From there, the 6km hike takes two hours return.

Guerilla Hideout   HIKING
(Wasu-Diga; Loi Hunu; US$5 per person plus US$5 per group for a guide) ✿ Local veterans have come together to build steps up Wasa-Diga hill so that visitors can check out the rock ledges where resistance heroes, including Ossu local Lu-Olo (Francisco Guterres), and the proceeding President Taur Matan Ruak (José Maria Vasconcelos), hid. The almost vertical climb is worth it for the peaceful view from the platform at the top.

Hotel Comunitaria Wailakurini   GUESTHOUSE **$$**
(☑ 7832 6687; hotelcomunitariawailakurini@gmail.com; Loi Hunu; r incl breakfast US$45) This friendly guesthouse is located on a hillside near a swimming hole and waterfall. Let staff know you're coming and you can learn to cook food in bamboo, then feast on it (US$7). Rooms are named after resistance leaders. A traditional wooden hut with

carved doors and balcony costs US$5 extra – though it's a little worse-for-wear.

❶ Getting There & Away

It takes two hours in a 4WD to reach Loi Hunu from Baucau. Buses to and from Baucau (US$2) head for Viqueque and Ossu and don't pass the accommodation in Loi Hunu, but tell the driver where you're going and you can possibly flag down a lift from where they drop you. It's another 20- to 30-minute drive from the accommodation to the start of the hike up Mundo Perdido.

Mt Matebian & Around

Mt Matebian (2315m) was the main target of Indonesia's aerial bombing in the late 1970s and the last liberated area to be conquered by the invading forces. Stories abound of the ferociousness of the attacks, with entire families wiped out when the caves they were hiding in collapsed under fire. It's also known as 'Mountain of the Dead' and remains a sacred place where the 'souls of the good' rest. Timor-Leste's newer political parties are sending young recruits up the mountain to commit themselves to the spirits if they are tempted by corruption.

Matebian is topped with a statue of Christ and attracts thousands of pilgrims annually for All Souls Day (2 November).

Climbing here is no day trip: parts are dangerous, it takes a lot of time and you definitely need a local guide. It's closed to most climbers from November to February. If you are determined to climb it, the best bet is starting out from **Quelicai** and walking 8km to the saddle, bedding down in tents for some rest before setting off to the summit to watch the sunrise.

You'll need to bring your own 4WD to get here. BYO food supplies; accommodation requires local connections.

Tutuala & Jaco Island

Tutuala village is set on a bluff, with sweeping views out to sea from a renovated Portuguese pousada (p809). Nearby, just off the road to **Valu**, are **rock art caves** (Along the road from Tutuala to Valu). They're signposted, but it's best to go with a guide. Down the hill, Valu has a picturesque white-sand beach, while a left after the 8km descent will take you to the thatched cabins of community-run Valu Sere (p809). Fall asleep listening to waves lapping and wake to the stunning vision of Jaco Island, just across the turquoise waters. Development (and overnight stays) are prohibited on this sacred isle, but fishers will take you across for US$10 return. Once you arrive, you're officially on a deserted tropical island. The water is crystal clear and there's excellent snorkelling along the coral drop-off.

It's a long way from Dili to Jaco (nine hours); there are a couple of sleeping options in Tutuala if you don't make it down to Valu in one day.

★ Valu Sere   BUNGALOW $
(✆ 7791 2657; Valu beach; camping with own/rented tent US$5/10, r US$20) 🅿 Listen to the waves crash on to the beach from these basic, open-air bungalows (with mosquito nets) in the shaded grounds (also a campsite) of this community-run guesthouse; 25% of profits go to national park projects. Basic meals are served in a central hut. You can also purchase fish from the local fishers (US$15) and they'll do the rest.

Gracinda's Homestay   APARTMENT $
(Homestay Ranu Painu; ✆ 7807 7722; Tutuala; r US$10) This room-above-a-shop is a great relief if you've almost made it to Jaco but it's too dark to continue the 6km down. The kiosk does a brisk trade in the local brandy *Tua Sabu*. Give Gracinda a call before arriving so she can tidy things up. It's just opposite where the road turns down to Valu.

Tutuala Pousada   HOTEL $$
(Pousada de Tutuala; ✆ 7746 3880; top of the hill, Tutuala.; r per person incl breakfast US$30) This colonial-era *pousada* sits high up on a hill, ignoring the rather shabby village of Tutuala behind it. With no beach access, there's nothing to do apart from relax into the views; most visitors pass through on their way to must-see Jaco Island. Rooms are decent, with fans. Meals can be arranged for US$10.

❶ Getting There & Away

You can't get to Valu by public transport. Your best bet is to catch the bus heading for Lospalos from Baucau (US$4; four hours) and get dropped off at the Tutuala turn-off in Fuiloro. Call your accommodation to see if it can organise an *ojek* (motorcycle taxi) to pick you up from here – it's an hour to Tutuala.

Once at Tutuala you'll have to walk the last 8km down to the beach.

Local fishers will whisk you off for the short journey by boat to Jaco Island for US$10 (return; per group). Let them know your return time and they'll come and get you.

WESTERN TIMOR-LESTE

Western Timor-Leste encompasses everything from bare, winding passes through the interior, and its coffee-bean shading rainforest, to the coast-hugging road that leads to the Indonesian border. Inland from Dili is excellent coffee country: Aileu (p812) is a good place to stop and eat before you hit the misty mountain town of Maubisse. Come for a weekend, hopefully spending a morning climbing Timor-Leste's highest mountain, Mt Ramelau. The coast road leads you past the resort town of Liquiçá.

Back up into the hills is Balibó (p811) and Marobo's **Be Manis** (Marobo Hot Springs; Marobo; per car/motorbike US$5/1; ⊙ 9am-5pm) hot springs, a former Portuguese mountain resort that has been renovated into a fairly large complex. It's a bumpy 18km road from Maliana to Marobo, and normal cars won't make the steep 6km track down from the signed turn-off to the springs.

Buses to Maliana via Balibó (US$6) depart from Tasi Tolu Terminal in Dili. It's possible to organise an *ojek* from Balibó to the hot springs (US$10).

THE ROAD TO THE BORDER

The border with Indonesian West Timor is almost four hours west of Dili along a newly built but rapidly deteriorating coastal road.

You'll spot the picturesque seaside ruins of the Portuguese-era **Prisão do Apelo** around 20km from Dili. Another 14km will take you to Liquiçá, which has some grand old buildings; its church was the site of one of the worst massacres of 1999. You'll find **glamping** by the water here, but head to **Lauhata Beach Escape** if you'd prefer to relax on a sandy beach.

Beachside **Maubara**, 49km from Dili, features a 17th-century Dutch **fort** with a small restaurant and a handicraft market. *Mikrolets* (small minibuses) from Dili stop at both Liquiçá and Maubara (US$2). Buses from Dili pass through the tiny border town of **Batugade** (US$6; 113km from Dili) and head inland to Balibó and Maliana.

Liquiçá

POP 5000

Beachside Liquiçá has morphed from a pretty place to visit to a great place to stay. There's nothing much to do in the town itself, so most visitors just lounge around soaking up the sun from where they're staying. It makes an excellent mid-week escape from Dili (though at weekends prices go up and it gets very busy).

Mikrolets (small minibuses) leave Dili from Tasi Tolu Bus Terminal (p805) during daylight hours and take an hour (US$2).

🛏 Sleeping & Eating

★ **Caimeo Beach Resort**   TENTED CAMP $$
(☏7798 8305; www.caimeobeach.com; Caimeo Beach Road; per tent US$30-115) Eight luxurious tents (four with private bathrooms) come with ready-made beds, fans, lights and hot showers. Rates drop during the week. It's worth coming here for the restaurant alone. The occasionally choppy sea is accessible via steps rather than sand. To get here, follow the signs off the main road just before Liquiçá.

Lauhata Beach Escape   HOTEL $$
(☏7740 1111; lauhata@flybus.tl; Liquiçá; r US$75; ❊ 🛜) Expat families love this spot, which is designed for relaxing. There's plenty to do here: sip cold coconut water under the palm trees, chill in the restaurant or get the black Liquiçá sand between your toes while playing volleyball. The eight rooms don't really have views, and they're better value mid-week, but friendly host Carlos runs the place well.

Black Rock Restaurant   TIMORESE $$
(☏7798 8305; Caimeo Beach Resort, Caimeo Beach Road; mains US$8-18; ⊙ 8am-8pm) All-day toasted sandwiches, local plunger coffee and banana pancake breakfasts mean you can pop in anytime for a quick meal. If you're staying for longer, check out the fish-of-the-day specials on the whiteboard, or try Timorese specialities like 'bok choy Timor style'. Breakfast runs until 10am. The vegetarian pizza gets good reviews.

Maubisse

POP 6229 / ELEV 1400M

Waking up in the chilly village of Maubisse and watching clouds rising, uncovering the village below, is a real highlight. A waterfall you can swim in and two excellent dining

BALIBÓ

Inland from Batugade is the pleasant mountain town of Balibó. Terrific views and the old trees lining the good road down to Maliana give the area a cool mountain feel, but it's best known as the town where five Australia-based journalists were killed by Indonesian soldiers in October 1975.

The Australian flag the journalists painted for protection is still visible (just) on **Balibó Flag House** (www.balibohouse.com; ⊘ 8am-noon & 2pm-5pm Mon-Sat, from 10am Sun) **FREE**, which now houses a memorial, cafe and community facilities. Here, you can watch Greg Shackleton's final, chilling broadcast. The Australian film *Balibo* (2009) was based on these tragic, and still unresolved, murders.

A restored 18th-century Portuguese fort stands on the hill opposite, housing a small gallery and the excellent **Balibó Fort Hotel** (☑ 7709 1555; www.baliboforthotel.com; d/tw incl buffet breakfast US$95; ⊘ restaurant 8am-9pm; ❋ ⬚), which opened in 2015.

Buses to Maliana via Balibó (US$6) depart from **Tasi Tolu Terminal** (p805) in Dili. The long-winded trip is punctuated by cargo-loading and lunch breaks so it takes six hours (it's four hours by car).

options nearby add to Maubisse's appeal. Improved roads from Dili (though the climb out of Dili is intense) make this an ideal weekend destination for expats.

On the hill behind Hakmatek you'll find a number of still-lived-in traditional Timorese homes, where you'll catch a glimpse of locals, both young and old, living a more bucolic life.

🛏 Sleeping & Eating

The Pousada de Maubisse, once a highlight of Timor-Leste's accommodation scene, was closed for renovations at the time of research, but if it opens again it'll probably claw back the old title (as long as the price is right).

★ **Hakmatek Cooperative**   BUNGALOW $$
(☑ 7771 4410, 7514 9808; turismo_etico@yahoo.com; Tartehi, Maubisse; s/d US$15/30) 🥾 The simple thatched huts at this community-run enterprise, ten minutes south of Maubisse, offer unmissable sweeping views of the surrounding mountains. A guided visit to the *uma lulik* (sacred house) behind the guesthouse gives a glimpse of traditional life; afterwards, swim in the cold, blue waterhole nearby (guides charge US$10 per person).

The Timorese meals are excellent, too, just book ahead so they know you're coming.

Green School   BUNGALOW $$
(Escola Verde; ☑ 7620 9936; www.santanatimorleste.com; r US$35) 🥾 Steps lead down through terraced organic vegetable gardens to two thatched villas (with hot and cold water), though you'll need to book ahead. Give

plenty of notice if you'd like to indulge in a terrific meal (US$12) in its delightful restaurant, which serves organic and free-range food with views. It's signposted off the main road.

❶ Getting There & Away

It takes 40 minutes on a good road to travel the 24km from Aileu to Maubisse. Buses depart from Taibessi Bus Terminal (p805) in Dili for Maubisse via Aileu (US$5, around three hours) each morning. Travellers continuing on to Hatubuilico can catch a bus heading to Same (US$4) and hop out at the turn-off.

Hatubuilico & Mt Ramelau

Wild roses grow by the road and mountain streams trickle through the teeny town of Hatubuilico, located at the base of Mt Ramelau (2963m). While here, the *pousada* is worth a wander, but the real reason to head here is to watch the sun rise over the clouds from the top of Mt Ramelau – undoubtedly a highlight of travelling in Timor-Leste.

Hiking from the village to the Na'i Feto Ramelau (Virgin Mary) statue at the top takes up to three hours; leave at 4am if you want to see the sunrise. With a 4WD you can drive 2.5km to a car park from where it'll take about 90 minutes to reach the peak on foot. After ascending 724 steps you'll find a wide, easy-to-follow walking path. An open-air church sits on a plateau at the 2700m mark. From the peak, the south and north coasts are visible.

AILEU

Aileu is scenic coffee country. The drive here is pleasant, with new roads making it a fairly straightforward trip from Dili. Be sure to organise a visit to **Wild Timor Coffee** (www.wildtimorcoffee.com; Aileu), which is just before Aileu itself.

Restaurante da Montanha (✔7725 2527; Aileu; mains US$6-12; ⊗8am-5pm) is one of Timor-Leste's best casual restaurants, and worth a day trip out here alone.

Buses from Taibessi Bus Terminal (p805) pass through Aileu (US$4, one hour) before heading on to Maubisse and Same.

Ask at your accommodation for a guide (US$20 per group); hiring one helps support the local community. Remember to dress warmly - it's cold at the top.

Ovalido Garden   HOTEL **$**
(✔7618 3577, 7741 3468; main road into Hatubuilico; r US$35) You may have to fight for hot water (all rooms have bathrooms but not all have hot water), but this new place is a comfortable spot to rest up before your 4am wake-up call to climb Mt Ramelau. Ask for the fried-egg roll breakfast and coffee to be ready when you wake. The dinner (US$5) is the best around.

Pousada da Alecrim   GUESTHOUSE **$**
(✔7611 3821, 7730 4366; Rua Gruta Ramelau Hun No. 1; r per person incl breakfast US$15) This dark and gloomy guesthouse on the main road is rather rundown. Let them know you're coming and book ahead for meals (US$5), or you'll go hungry. Staff can arrange a guide (US$20 per group) to assist you up Mt Ramelau.

❶ Getting There & Away

Buses to Same or Ainaro from Maubisse (US$4) can drop you at the Hatubuilico turn-off. From here, it's 18km to Hatubuilico (around one hour in your own 4WD). If the road is passable (it turns to fudge at the hint of rain), *angguna* (tray trucks) travel from Maubisse to Hatubuilico on Wednesday and Saturday. The price depends on the number of passengers, but the trip should cost around US$4 and take two hours. As it's a popular weekend trip for locals you may be able to share a ride.

OECUSSE

POP 72,000

Since being named a Special Zone of Social Market Economy (ZEESM) in 2015, Oecusse has undergone rapid development. The capital has new roads (though not many cars), a huge new **bridge** (west of Oecusse Town), 24/7 electricity and a US$120 million international airport due to open in 2018. With marine biodiversity similar to Ataúro (bring your own snorkels and diving equipment) and easy access from Dili, Oecusse is a place worth spending a few days in.

◉ Sights & Activities

Pantemakassar, aka Oecusse Town, has a palm-fringed foreshore that provides great sunsets. November sees pilot whales swimming by, and divers are likely to spot a turtle or two underwater each time they hit the seas. The coral cover here is very good; enlist someone to watch for crocodiles and you can snorkel out from in front of the beachfront church.

Oecusse's seagrass meadows are home to dugongs. The best beach begins 2km east of town on **Pantai Mahata**, which ends at a stunning red-rock headland.

Fonte Sagrada Trail   WATERFALL
(Sacred Waterfall Walk; ✔7734 0023; US$5 per person) A push for community tourism has led to the creation of the 3km Fonte Sagrada Trail. Local guides will clear the way for you to enter this special and sacred place where a traditional ritual – including the sacrifice of a buffalo – is held when a local man marries a woman from outside the area. Don't swim in the waterfall.

Mud Geyser   HOT SPRINGS
(Oesilo) Watch volcanic mud bubbling up from this geyser. The spot is five minutes from Oesilo, which is around 90 minutes' drive south-east of Pantemakassar and close to the Indonesian border. Take an *ojek* (motorcycle taxi) out here.

🛏 Sleeping & Eating

Most visitors stay in Oecusse Town. The tiny expat scene here is vibrant, with a number of Spanish and Portuguese folk setting up restaurants and bars in good locations.

Hotel Tony   GUESTHOUSE **$**
(✔7568 4457; Rua Sikluli Aldeia Sanane; per person incl breakfast US$17.50; P❄) A local Timorese family keeps these four no-frills motel-style

rooms in good nick, and pretty gardens out the front of rooms add to the appeal. Each room has a bathroom and air-con.

Alegria   HOMESTAY $$

(⌨ 7761 0000; Rua Sikluli Aldeia Sanan, Pantema-cassar; r incl breakfast US$50; ❄) Alegria is otherwise known as 'the cocktail lounge' thanks to its on-site bar and restaurant. Eight new rooms have turned this into *the* place to stay in Pantemacassar. They're beautifully presented, with *tais* (woven cloth) decorations and Western-style en suites; expect plenty of rock features and attention to detail.

Dominican Cafe   CAFE $

(main road down to beach in Oecusse Town; ⊙ 7.30am-9.30pm) On the main road to the beach and well signposted, this outdoor social enterprise cafe has palm-fringed huts in lovely botanic surroundings. It serves up good coffee, cheap fresh juices and rather dry cake. It's a popular hang-out for local expats (mostly Portuguese teachers) and others doing business in Oecusse.

Moxito   CAFE $$

(beachfront in Oecusse Town; mains US$8.50; ⊙ 7am-9pm) Enter through the large circular concrete sculpture and enjoy a G&T while watching the sun set at beachfront Moxito. This expat-owned cafe/bar offers burgers and pizzas, and rather delicious chocolate puddings, too.

❶ Getting There & Around

Oecusse is easy to reach from Dili, with flights Thursday to Tuesday with **STAT-ZEESM** (⌨ Dili office 7762 5771, Oecusse office 7752 4697; Presidente Nicolau Lobato International Airport; 40 minutes) and regular ferries from Laju Laju (p805) and **Nakroma** (⌨ Dili office 331 7264; 12 hours).

The fancy Wini Timor-Leste/Indonesian border crossing is 20 minutes from Pantemakassar on a new road; catch an *ojek* (motorcycle taxi; US$2). Most travellers do not need an Indonesian visa to travel overland from Oecusse to Indonesian West Timor, but if you are heading back to Timor-Leste overland through Mota'Ain, you will need to get an authorisation from the office in Kupang, West Timor. Alternatively, apply through www.migracao.gov.tl to get one emailed to you (takes over 10 days).

If you depart the Timor-Leste border at Wini at 8.30am you can travel by pre-organised taxi (try ⌨ +62 8 23420 77777) to Atambua, West Timor, and catch the daily 12.30pm flight to Kupang, West Timor on Wings Air (www.lionair.co.id), arriving around 1.15pm.

Hop on the back of an *ojek* (motorcycle taxi) for 25cv to get around Oecusse Town. **RentLo** (⌨ 7723 2351, 7732 9755; oe-cusseamasat@ hotmail.com) has 4WDs for hire for the rest of Oecusse. There is no bus service.

UNDERSTAND TIMOR-LESTE

Timor-Leste Today

A development boom in Suai and Oecusse is being financed by revenue from offshore oil and gas reserves, but many Timorese remain in poor health, with 40% living below the poverty line. Timor-Leste's dusty dry seasons give way to wet seasons that cut entire villages off and see wide rivers pouring out into the coral reefs surrounding the country. The politicians in power since independence (2002) have maintained their grip on the country, despite regular allegations of corruption and nepotism.

Who controls the oil and gas resources in the waters between Timor-Leste and Australia has been a topic of debate since before Indonesian occupation in the 1970s. After independence, Australia signed several treaties with Timor-Leste, including one that shared the revenue from the oil and gas deposits evenly (US$40 billion from the Greater Sunrise field – which lies about 150km from Timor-Leste and 450km from Darwin – alone). However, Timor-Leste argued that the maritime border should be halfway between the two countries, which would put most of Greater Sunrise in its territory.

In January 2017 espionage allegations against the Australian government led Timor-Leste to tear up the 2006 agreement, and eight months later Timor-Leste's chief negotiator, former president and resistance hero Xanana Gusmão signed what he called a 'historic' deal in the Permanent Court of Arbitration in Copenhagen, addressing the issues of the Greater Sunrise field. He returned to the cheers of thousands, but outside observers say Timor-Leste still may have been short-changed in the deal.

In the meantime, revenue from oil and gas is quickly being spent on large infrastructure projects in Suai and Oecusse. While money is being poured into projects like a US$120 million international airport in Oecusse (with a view to attracting international visitors for, among other things, medical tourism and casinos), commentators are concerned that Timor-Leste's oil and gas revenue may be completely depleted within a decade.

Peaceful presidential and parliamentary elections were held in 2017 and saw Francisco 'Lu Olo' Guterres elected president, and former prime minister Mari Alkatiri elected to the position once again – a decade after his last stint (he was Timor-Leste's first prime minister from 2002–2006). Nobel-prize winner and former president and prime minister José Ramos-Horta took up a new post as Minister of State and Counsellor for National Security.

Alkatiri's Fretilin party led a minority government for the first time in Timor-Leste's history, after winning just 23 seats in the 65-seat parliament. Original plans to form a coalition with new youth party Khunto (which surprised many by winning five seats) failed, and Fretilin formed a coalition with the PD (Democratic Party), with which it had had a longstanding antagonistic relationship. The minority government failed to pass the budget, and adhering to the constitution, called fresh elections for March 2018. Many debate whether this minority government will be able to pass the next budget and last the five-year term.

History

Portugal Settles In

Little is known of Timor before AD 1500, although Chinese and Javanese traders visited the island from at least the 13th century, and possibly as early as the 7th century. These traders searched the coastal settlements for aromatic sandalwood and beeswax. Portuguese traders arrived between 1509 and 1511, and in 1556 a handful of Dominican friars established the first Portuguese settlement at Lifau in Oecusse and set about converting the Timorese to Catholicism.

To counter the Portuguese, the Dutch established a base at Kupang in western Timor in 1653. The Portuguese appointed an administrator to Lifau in 1656, but the Topasses (people from the region who claimed Portuguese ancestry and/or identified with the culture) went on to become a law unto themselves, driving out the Portuguese governor in 1705.

By 1749 the Topasses controlled central Timor and marched on Kupang, but the Dutch won the ensuing battle, expanding their control of western Timor in the process. On the Portuguese side, after more attacks from the Topasses in Lifau, the colonial base was moved east to Dili in 1769.

The 1859 Treaty of Lisbon divided Timor, giving Portugal the eastern half, together with the north-coast pocket of Oecusse; this was formalised in 1904. Portuguese Timor was a sleepy and neglected outpost ruled through a traditional system of *liurai* (local chiefs). Control outside Dili was limited and it wasn't until the 20th century that the Portuguese intervened in a major way in the interior.

World War II

In 1941 Australia sent a small commando force (known as Sparrow Force) into Portuguese Timor to counter the Japanese. Although the military initiative angered neutral Portugal and dragged the colony into the Pacific War, it slowed the Japanese expansion. In February 1942 the Japanese forced the surrender of the Allies following the bloody Battle of Timor, but several hundred commandos stayed on for another year, waging many successful raids on Japanese forces with the help of locals, including *creados* (Timorese boys who assisted Australian servicemen during WWII). The Japanese retaliated by razing villages, seizing food and killing Timorese in areas where Australians were operating. By the end of the war, up to 60,000 Timorese had died.

Portugal Pulls Out, Indonesia Invades

After WWII the colony reverted to Portuguese rule, but following the Carnation Revolution in Portugal in April 1974, Lisbon began a program of decolonisation. Within a few weeks, political parties had formed in Timor-Leste and the Timorese Democratic Union (UDT) attempted to seize power in August 1975. A brief but brutal civil war saw UDT's rival Fretilin (previously known as the Association of Timorese Social Democrats) come out on top, and it urgently declared the independent existence of the Democratic Republic of Timor-Leste on 28 November, amid an undeclared invasion by Indonesia. On 7 December Indonesia officially launched a full-scale attack on Dili after months of incursions (including at Balibó, where five Australia-based journalists were killed on 16 October).

Anti-communist Indonesia feared an independent Timor-Leste governed by a left-leaning Fretilin would bring communism to its door, and commenced its invasion of Timor-Leste just a day after Henry Kissinger and Gerald Ford departed Jakarta, having tacitly given their assent. (Indeed, the Americans urged the Indonesians to conduct a swift campaign so that the world wouldn't see them using weapons the US had provided). Australia and Britain also sided with Indonesia.

Falintil, the military wing of Fretilin, fought a guerrilla war against Indonesian troops (which numbered 35,000 by 1976) with marked success in the first few years, but weakened considerably thereafter, though the resistance continued. The cost of the takeover to the Timorese was huge; it's estimated that up to 183,000 died in the hostilities, and the ensuing disease and famine.

By 1989 Indonesia had things firmly under control and opened Timor-Leste to limited controlled tourism. On 12 November 1991 Indonesian troops fired on protesters who'd gathered at the Santa Cruz Cemetery in Dili to commemorate the killing of an independence activist. With the event captured on film and aired around the world, the Indonesian government admitted to 19 killings (later increased to more than 50), although it's estimated that over 250 died in the massacre. While Indonesia introduced a civilian administration, the military remained in control. Aided by secret police and civilian pro-Indonesian militia to crush dissent, reports of arrest, torture and murder were commonplace.

Independence

After Indonesia's President Soeharto resigned in May 1998, his replacement BJ Habibie unexpectedly announced a referendum for autonomy in Timor-Leste. January 1999 marked the commencement of attacks by militias backed by the Indonesian National Armed Forces (TNI), who began terrorising the population to coerce them into rejecting independence.

Attacks peaked in April 1999, just prior to the arrival of the UN Electoral Mission, when, according to a report commissioned by the UN Office of the High Commissioner for Human Rights, up to 60 people were massacred near Liquiçá church. Other attacks occurred in Dili and Maliana while Indonesian authorities looked on. Attacks escalated in the weeks prior to the vote, with thousands seeking refuge in the hills away from the reach of the TNI and militia.

Despite threats, intimidation and brutality, on 30 August 1999 Timor-Leste voted overwhelmingly (78.5%) for independence from, rather than autonomy within, Indonesia. Though the Indonesian government promised to respect the results of the UN-sponsored vote, militias and Indonesian forces went on a rampage, killing people, burning and looting buildings and destroying infrastructure.

While the world watched in horror, the UN was attacked and forced to evacuate, leaving the East Timorese defenceless. On 20 September, weeks after the main massacres in Suai, Dili, Maliana and Oecusse, the Australian-led International Force for East Timor (INTERFET) arrived in Dili. The Indonesian forces and their militia supporters left for West Timor, leaving behind scenes of devastation. Half a million people had been displaced, and telecommunications, power installations, bridges, government buildings, shops and houses were destroyed.

The UN set up a temporary administration during the transition to independence, and aid and foreign workers flooded into the country. As well as physically rebuilding the country, Timor-Leste had to create a civil service, police, judiciary, education, health system and so on, with staff recruited and trained from scratch.

The UN handed over government to Timor-Leste on 20 May 2002 with Falintil leader Xanana Gusmão elected president, and long-time leader of Fretilin, Mari Alkatiri, chosen as prime minister.

Birth Pangs

The early years of independence have been rocky ones for Timor-Leste, due in large part to the challenges involved with creating a new nation from the ground up. Poverty and frustration, not to mention rather rocky elections, have led to numerous riots taking place since 2002. However, since 2008 Timor-Leste has been a much safer and more stable country and the most recent elections – in 2012 and 2017 – were peaceful.

TIMOR-LESTE HISTORY

People & Culture

The National Psyche

Timor-Leste's identity is firmly rooted in its survival of extreme hardship and foreign occupation. As a consequence of the long and difficult struggle for independence, the people of Timor-Leste are profoundly politically aware – not to mention proud and loyal. While there is great respect for elders and church and community leaders, there lurks a residual suspicion surrounding foreign occupiers, most recently in the form of the UN (not to mention Australian oil bosses). Religious beliefs (Catholic and animist) also greatly inform the national consciousness.

Lifestyle

Most Timorese lead a subsistence lifestyle: what is farmed (or caught) is eaten. While the birth rate continues to decline, large families (with an average of 5.5 children per mother) are still common, and infant mortality remains high. Malnutrition and food insecurity is widespread. Infrastructure remains limited.

Outside of Dili, family life often exists in simple thatched huts, though more stable brick structures are becoming common. NGOs and aid projects have had mostly limited lifetimes and the ability to rise above poverty is a huge challenge for many as bad roads and drought or floods play havoc. Family cars and utility trucks are often full to the brim on weekends with those heading to the family events that form the backbone of Timorese life.

Population

Timor-Leste has at least a dozen indigenous groups, the largest being the Tetun, who live around Suai, Dili and Viqueque. The next largest group is the Mambai, who live in the mountains of Maubisse, Ainaro and Same. The Kemak live in the Ermera and Bobonaro districts; the Bunak also live in Bobonaro, and their territory extends into West Timor and the Suai area. The Baikeno live in the area around Pantemakassar, and the Fataluku people are famous for their high-peaked houses in the area around Lospalos. More groups are scattered among the interior mountains.

Religion

Religion is an integral part of daily life for most Timorese. Recent estimates indicate 98% of Timor-Leste's population is Catholic (though many also hold animist beliefs), 1% Protestant and less than 1% Muslim.

Indigenous beliefs revolve around an earth mother, from whom all humans are born and shall return after death, and her male counterpart, the god of the sky or sun. These are accompanied by a complex web of spirits from ancestors and nature. The *matan d'ok* (medicine man) is the village mediator with the spirits; he can divine the future and cure illness. Many people believe in various forms of black magic.

Arts

The Timorese love a party, and celebrate with *tebe* (dancing) and singing. Music has been passed down through the years and changed little during Indonesian times. Traditional trance-like drumming is used in ceremonies, while local rock and hip-hop groups are popular. Country-and-western style is popular, too, and features plenty of guitar use and the usual lovelorn themes.

Each region has its own style of *tais* (woven cloth) and they're usually used as skirts or shawls for men *(tais mane)* or sewn up to form a tube skirt/dress for women *(tais feto)*.

Environment

The Land

Timor-Leste consists of the eastern half of the island of Timor, Ataúro and Jaco Islands, and the exclave of Oecusse on the north coast, 70km to the west and surrounded by Indonesian West Timor.

Once part of the Australian continental shelf, Timor fully emerged from the ocean only four million years ago, and is therefore composed mainly of marine sediment, principally limestone. Rugged mountains, a product of the collision with the Banda Trench to the north, run the length of the country, the highest of which is Mt Ramelau (2963m).

Wildlife

Timor-Leste is squarely in the area known as Wallacea, a kind of crossover zone between Asian and Australian plants and animals, and one of the most biologically distinctive areas on earth.

The north coast is a global hot spot for whale and dolphin activity, and its coral reefs are home to a diverse range of marine life. Species spotted include dugongs, blue whales and dolphins. More than 260 species of bird have been recorded in its skies. The eastern fringe of the nation was declared a national park partly because of its rich bird life: it's home to honeyeaters, critically endangered yellow-crested cockatoos and endangered *wetar* ground-doves. The number of mammals and reptiles in the wild is limited, though monkeys, civets, crocodiles and snakes make appearances.

Environmental Issues

Timor-Leste's only national park, the Nino Konis Santana National Park, was declared in 2008 – a 123,000-hectare parcel of land (including some tropical forest) and sea at the country's eastern tip, also incorporating Jaco Island and Tutuala. Most of the country, however, is suffering from centuries of deforestation, and erosion is a huge problem: roads and even villages have been known to slip away.

In 2017 marine conservation organisation Sea Shepherd found Chinese-owned boats targeting sharks for their fins in Timor-Leste's waters, and brought international attention to the issue. Criticism was centered on officials who defended the practice, and the contracts that allowed it. Much of Timor-Leste's waters remain unprotected, including seagrass areas – home to dugongs – and country's reefs and mangrove areas.

SURVIVAL GUIDE

ⓘ Directory A–Z

ACCOMMODATION

In Dili, expect sit-down loos, air-conditioning, wi-fi and not much more. Accommodation with adjoining restaurants/bars is a good choice for those who'd prefer not to travel around at night. In the regions, you're doing well if you get a clean room with hole-free mosquito nets and electricity. Basic homestay accommodation with *mandi* washing facilities is found in most towns (offer from US$10 per night).

CUSTOMS REGULATIONS

You can bring the following into Timor-Leste:

Alcohol 2.5L of any type
Cigarettes 200
Money Declare amounts between US$5,000 and US$10,000. Higher amounts require authorisation from the Central Bank of Timor-Leste (info@bancocentral). For restrictions on taking cash out of the country, contact the Central Bank.

DANGERS & ANNOYANCES

There are frequent reports of foreign women being sexually assaulted in Dili – this often happens during the day and in public areas, so travel with others if possible.

Dengue fever is rife – avoid mosquitoes bites by covering up as much as possible.

Crocodiles occasionally swim in the ocean near river mouths.

Drive with extreme caution on the nation's notoriously bad roads; hiring a driver is recommended.

ELECTRICITY

Plug types E,G and I are common.

EMBASSIES & CONSULATES

More than a dozen countries have embassies, consulates or representative offices in Dili.

Australian Embassy (☑ 332 2111; www.timorleste.embassy.gov.au; Rua Mártires de Pátria) Also assists Canadian citizens.

British Honorary Consul (☑ 7723 4273)

Indonesian Embassy (☑ 331 7107; www.kemlu.go.id/dili; Rua Gov. Maria de Serpa Rosa, Farol; ☺ Visa service 9am-noon, 2pm-6pm Mon-Fri)

New Zealand Embassy (☑ 331 0087, emergency 7732 1015; dili@mfat.govt.nz; Rua Geremias Do Amaral, Motael; ☺ 8.30am-12.30pm & 1.30pm-5pm Mon-Fri) Also assists British citizens.

Portuguese Embassy (☑ 331 0050, 331 1520; embaixador@embaixadaportugal.tl; Rua 30 de agosto 2; ☺ 8.30am-12.30pm & 2pm-6pm Mon-Fri)

US Embassy (☑ 332 4684; https://tl.usembassy.gov; Av de Portugal)

INSURANCE

Travel insurance is vital in Timor-Leste. Medical facilities outside Dili are limited and any serious cases generally get evacuated to Darwin or Singapore. Accordingly, travellers need to ensure that they have full evacuation coverage.

SLEEPING PRICE RANGES

The following price ranges refer to the price of a room:

$ less than US$25

$$ US$25–100

$$$ more than US$100

INTERNET ACCESS

Many hotels in Dili have slow wi-fi access, but the best bet is bringing an unlocked phone and using a local SIM for internet – it costs around US$1 a day. A Telemor (p804) dongle offers unlimited data for US$1 a day.

LEGAL MATTERS

If you are the victim of a serious crime, go to the nearest police station and notify your embassy. If arrested, you have the right to a phone call and legal representation, which your embassy can help locate. The **National Police Headquarters** (☑ 7723 0635, 112; www.pntl.tl; Rua Jacinto de Cândido) is in Dili.

Foreigners have been imprisoned for carrying small amounts of drugs or being in vehicles with others carrying drugs, so be aware of what is legal in Timor-Leste as well as who you're travelling with, what they're carrying or may be involved with. Laws can change quickly; recently codeine was banned and pharmacists supplying or storing the drug were jailed.

You can be jailed for up to 72 hours for not wearing a helmet on a motorbike. Carry registration papers and your license with you while driving.

LGBT TRAVELLERS

The LGBT community held its first Gay Pride Day rally in Dili in 2017, with public support from then Prime Minister Rui Maria de Araújo. Fundasaun Codiva is a local NGO with a focus on diversity and action. Public displays of affection between couples of any orientation are not usual in Timor-Leste.

MEDICAL SERVICES

Medical services in Timor-Leste are limited. Serious cases usually require evacuation to Australia or Singapore. Check with your embassy for other options. Australians can see the doctor at the Australian Embassy Clinic (p805) for a fee.

MONEY

There are few ATMs outside Dili. Expensive hotels sometimes accept credit cards.

Tipping is not obligatory. If you are asked to tip excessively post (an expensive) tour, you can politely decline.

EATING PRICE RANGES

As an approximate guide, the following price ranges refer to the cost of a main course.

$ less than US$5

$$ US$5–10

$$$ more than US$10

Bargain with Dili's yellow taxi drivers before you start your journey. If you don't like bargaining, catch a metered blue taxi (p805) instead. There is a *malae* (foreigner) price for goods at roadside stalls – bargain for the local price.

OPENING HOURS

Budget and midrange restaurants and cafes morning until late

High-end restaurants noon to 2pm and 6 to 10pm

Small shops 9am to 6pm Monday to Friday

Supermarkets 8am to 8pm

Banks 9am to 4pm Monday to Friday

PUBLIC HOLIDAYS

Timor-Leste has a long list of public holidays.

New Year's Day 1 January

Veterans Day 3 March

Good Friday March/April (date varies)

World Labour Day 1 May

Restoration of Independence Day 20 May (the day in 2002 when sovereignty was transferred from the UN)

Corpus Christi Day May/June (date varies)

Idul Fitri End of Ramadan (date varies)

Popular Consultation Day 30 August (marks the start of independence in 1999)

Idul Adha Muslim day of sacrifice (date varies, usually September)

All Saints' Day 1 November

All Souls' Day 2 November

National Youth Day 12 November (commemorates the Santa Cruz Cemetery massacre)

Proclamation of Independence Day 28 November

Memorial Day 7 December

Day of Our Lady of Immaculate Conception and Timor-Leste Patroness 8 December

Christmas Day 25 December

National Heroes Day 31 December

TELEPHONE
Mobile Phones

Easy-to-obtain Timor Telecom, Telkomsel and Telemor SIM cards can be used in unlocked phones. Coverage is good, though occasionally drops out.

Phone Codes

International access code 0011

International country code 670

Landline numbers 7 digits, starting with a 3

Mobile numbers 8 digits, starting with a 7

TOILETS

Hotels and restaurants have toilet facilities ranging from modern Western flush toilets to *mandi*-style (a hole in the ground with a bucket of water to flush). There are public facilities (often broken) at food stops in the districts. You may need to hunt down a key. Your best bet for regional travel is 'going bush' or asking at restaurants.

TOURIST INFORMATION

Timor-Leste doesn't have a central tourist office, but Dili's expat community is especially generous with information. Language barriers aside, locals are often happy to help.

TRAVEL WITH CHILDREN

Travelling with children is a big adventure in Timor-Leste (as if it's not adventurous enough!). Supplies (nappies, formula etc) are good in Dili but you'll need to stock up if you're travelling with children in the districts.

TRAVELLERS WITH DISABILITIES

Timor-Leste's footpaths pose problems for people with disabilities; local wheelchair users tend to use the road.

The tour companies operating in Dili (p799) should be able to take visitors' needs on board and suggest itineraries and places that are more accessible than others.

VISAS

Australian, Irish and British visitors must pay for a visa on arrival at Dili's airport or seaport (US$30 for 30 days). Most other EU nationals are free. Most nationalities need a visa in advance for land border arrivals.

Always ask for a 30-day visa, even if you don't plan on staying that long – extending can be difficult. Tourist visas can be extended for 30 days (US$35) or 60 days (US$75). If needing a multiple-entry visa or to stay between 30 and 90 days, you can apply for Visa Application Authorisation online before arrival.

VOLUNTEERING

Many NGOs and local organisations take on volunteers to assist in a wide variety of roles.
Blue Ventures (☑ +44 (0)207 697 8598; www. blueventures.org; Barry's Place, Beloi, Ataúro; from US$3070) runs regular six-week Marine Conservation Expeditions at Ataúro, which is a pay-for 'volunteer' diving course.

It is essential to do your homework about the organisations and their work. Lonely Planet does not endorse any organisations that we do not work with directly.

WOMEN TRAVELLERS

Sanitary products are available in Dili, but can be scarce in the districts.

WORK

There are still employment opportunities for foreigners in Timor-Leste; check www.jobs.creativebridgedili.com for opportunities. In order to work in Timor-Leste, you'll need to apply for the appropriate Work Permit or Residence Visa, which can be downloaded from www.migracao. gov.tl and lodged with the Ministry of Interior at the **Immigration Service of Timor-Leste** (☑ 331 0369; www.migracao.gov.tl; Estr de Balide, Vila Verde, Ministry of Security Bldg; ⊗ 9am-noon & 2-4pm Mon-Fri).

❶ Getting There & Away

There are no passenger boat services to Timor-Leste from other countries.

AIR

You can fly to Dili from Denpasar (Bali), Jakarta, Darwin and Singapore. Dili's **Presidente Nicolau Lobato International Airport** (p805) is a 10-minute drive from town. A taxi there is US$10. *Mikrolets* charge 25cv (US$0.25) from the main road (600m from the airport) into town. The airport has an outdoor cafe, bar and a duty-free shop for those departing.

Air North (www.airnorth.com.au) Usually flies daily between Dili and Darwin (Australia). There's no office in Dili; book online.

Air Timor (☑ 331 2777; www.air-timor.com; President Nicolau Lobato International Airport; ⊗ 8am-5pm Mon-Sat, to noon Sun) The national airline charters Silkair flights to fly between Dili and Singapore on Tuesdays and Saturdays.

Citilink (☑ 7750 2881; www.citilink.co.id; Timor Plaza, Av Nicolau Lobato, Comoro; ⊗ 9am-5.30am) Flies Jakarta to Dili and Denpasar (Bali) to Dili daily.

Sriwijaya Air (Nam Air; ☑ 331 1777, 331 1355; www.sriwijayaair.co.id; Timor Plaza, Av Nicolau Lobato, Comoro; ⊗ 9am-5pm) Flies daily between Dili and Denpasar (Bali).

❶ Getting Around

AIR

Confirm domestic **STAT** (p813) flights to and from Oecusse on the morning of your flight; sometimes they change times. These flights depart daily except Wednesday.

BICYCLE

Dili's roads are fine for cycling, and there are cyclists on the road training before the Tour de Timor (p802). Road conditions away from the north coast call for proper mountain bikes. Hire bikes in Dili at **Dili Central Backpackers** (p803), or in Balibó at **Balibó Fort Hotel** (p811).

BOAT

Ferry transport is available between Dili and Oecusse on the Nakroma ferry (p805) and Laju Laju (p805) car ferry. Compass Charters (p805) run daily water-taxi services to/from Ataúro; the

ℹ BORDER CROSSINGS: GETTING TO INDONESIA

Getting to the border Catch a direct daily Dili–Kupang (Indonesia) minibus (US$23, 12 hours) through Timor Tour & Travel (p805). It's slightly cheaper but harder work to catch a local bus to Batugade (US$5) at the border. You can then walk through both border checkpoints and catch local transport to West Timor destinations (US$3 to Atambua, then US$7 Kupang; eight hours). Start early, and expect to wait for transport connections. The Wini border is 20 minutes from Oecusse Town (p812).

At the border Most passport holders can get an Indonesian visa on arrival.

Moving on It's complicated to head through to Oecusse after travelling through Indonesia: you'll need to already have a visa for Timor-Leste, which is available in Kupang (Indonesia).

For information on making the crossing in reverse see p254.

Nakroma (p805) services Ataúro on Saturday, and the Laju Laju (p805) on Thursday. Dragon Star (p805) sends its riverboat over daily, unless the weather is bad (though the boat that was being used at the time of research is designed for river crossings, not sea crossings, and is therefore not recommended).

BUS

Mikrolet (small minibuses) operate around Dili and other large towns. Larger buses leave when they are full (both of people and livestock) and serve the main routes from Dili. The Taibessi Bus Terminal (p805) is the stop for transport to Maubisse, Same and Suai. Buses from Becora Bus Terminal (p805) head to destinations in the east, including Baucau and Lospalos. Tasi Tolu Bus Terminal (p805) has buses heading to Ermera and Maliana. More rugged routes are covered by *angguna* (tray trucks where passengers, including the odd buffalo or goat, all pile into the back). If *angguna* aren't covering their usual turf you can be assured the road conditions are exceptionally dire. Trip times are a rough guide only – times depend on how bad the roads are and the whim of the driver when it comes to the frequency and length of stops.

CAR & MOTORCYCLE

Vehicle accidents are a serious risk in Timor-Leste. The notoriously bad roads are a minefield of animals and school children, while dips, ditches and entire missing sections of road are common. There are plenty of blind coastal corners with large sections missing from them. Good stretches include Aileu to Maubisse, Dili to Dare (perfect until after you reach Xanana Gusmão's house) and Balibo to Maliana. The trip to Baucau may return to a two-hour trip once roadworks are completed in late 2018 (it currently takes four hours).

Conventional cars can handle Dili, but a 4WD is recommended elsewhere. We recommend a 4WD and driver for trips to the districts; try **EDS** (📞 7723 0881, 7723 0880); US$130 per day. There's usually compulsory insurance (US$15 per day) on top of the price. You can rent motorbikes from Hostel daTerra (p803) or Dili Central Backpackers (p803); US$35 per day.

Drivers must carry registration papers and their license – police checkpoints are common. The International Drivers Permit is not technically valid in Timor-Leste; if you're staying for a while, it's worth getting a local driving licence.

HITCHING

A foreigner recently spent months in jail after hitching a lift in Timor-Leste in a car that was subsequently involved in a crime. Hitching is never entirely safe, and we don't recommend it. Travellers who hitch should understand that they are taking a small but potentially serious risk.

Vietnam

📞 84 / POP 95.7 MILLION

Includes ➡

Why Go?

A kaleidoscope of dazzling colours and subtle shades, limestone highlands and endless rice paddies, full-on cities and laid-back beach resorts, deeply moving war sites and grand colonial-era architecture – Vietnam has a unique appeal.

The nation is a budget traveller's dream, with inexpensive transport, outstanding street food, good-value accommodation and *bia hoi* – perhaps the world's cheapest beer.

Nature has gifted Vietnam with soaring mountains in the north, tropical islands in the south and a sensational curvaceous coastline of ravishing sandy beaches. Travelling here you'll witness children riding buffalo, see the impossibly intricate textiles of hill-tribe communities, taste the super-fresh and incredibly subtle flavours of Vietnamese cuisine and hear the buzz of a million motorbikes.

This is a dynamic nation on the move, where life is lived at speed. Prepare yourself for the ride of your life.

Best Beaches

➡ Sao Beach (p907)

➡ Long Beach (p907)

➡ Bai Dai Beach (p883)

➡ An Bang Beach (p879)

Top Phrases

Hello Xin chào (sin jòw)

Thank you Cảm ơn (ğaảm ern)

How much is this? Cái này giá bao nhiêu? (ğaí này zaá bow nyee·oo)

When to Go
Hanoi

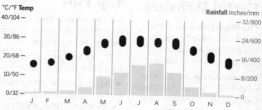

Dec–Mar Expect cool weather north of Hue as the winter monsoon brings cloud, mist and drizzle.

May–Jun Danang's riverfront explodes with colour and noise during the city's fireworks festival.

Jul & Aug Perfect beach time on the central coastline, with balmy sea and air temperatures.

AT A GLANCE

Currency Dong (d)

Visas Tourist visas are available for 30 or 90 days.

Money ATMs are widely available.

Language Vietnamese

Emergency Police ☑113

Exchange Rates

Australia	A$1	17,925d
Canada	C$1	18,222d
Euro	€1	26,845d
Japan	¥100	20,345d
New Zealand	NZ$1	16,297d
UK	£1	30,170d
US	US$1	22,709d

For current exchange rates, see www.xe.com.

Daily Costs

➡ Glass of *bia hoi* (draught beer): from US$0.50

➡ One hour on a local bus: US$1.50-2

➡ Cheap hotel: US$10–120 a night, dorms less

➡ Noodle dish: US$2-3

Useful Websites

The Word (www.wordhcmc. com) This superb magazine has comprehensive coverage and excellent features.

Vietnam Coracle (http://vietnamcoracle.com) Excellent independent travel advice; lots of backroads content.

Vietnam Online (www. vietnamonline.com) Good all-rounder.

Entering the Country

Most travellers enter Vietnam by plane or bus, but there are also train links from China and boat connections from Cambodia via the Mekong River. Flights, cars and tours can be booked online at lonelyplanet.com/bookings.

REGIONS AT A GLANCE

Vietnam is incredibly physically, climatically and culturally varied. Jagged alpine peaks define the northern provinces and a pancake-flat river delta enriches the endless rice paddies of the far south. Cave-riddled limestone hills loom over the central belt and there are dense rainforests along its western border.

The northern half of the nation experiences a much cooler winter, and the cuisine, lifestyle and character of the people reflect this. As you head south, the country has more of a tropical feel, with coconut trees outnumbering bamboo plants and fish sauce replacing soy sauce on the menu. The southern provinces are always humid, hot and sticky, their food sweet, spicy, aromatic and complex.

Essential Food & Drink

White rose An incredibly delicate, subtly flavoured shrimp dumpling topped with crispy onions.

Pho Rice-noodle soup. A good *pho bo* (beef noodle soup) hinges on the broth, which is made from beef bones boiled for hours in water with shallots, ginger, fish sauce, black cardamom, star anise and cassia.

Banh xeo This giant crispy, chewy rice crêpe is made in 12in or 14in skillets or woks and amply filled with pork, shrimp, mung beans and bean sprouts.

Bia hoi 'Fresh' or draught beer brewed daily, without additives or preservatives, to be drunk within hours.

Vietnamese coffee Often served iced, with condensed milk.

Top Tips

➡ Expect crazy driving: traffic can come at you every which way. When crossing busy urban roads maintain a slow, deliberate walking pace.

➡ Try not to lose your temper; shouting and aggression cause a loss of face for both parties.

➡ Vietnam has more than its fair share of scams; most concern overcharging. Though very rare, more serious dangers (such as unexploded ordnance) can be a real concern.

➡ In towns such as Hue and Sapa, and on beaches popular with tourists, expect plenty of hustle from street vendors, *cyclo* (pedicab or bicycle rickshaw) drivers and the like.

➡ Few locals speak English away from tourist centres; try to learn a few words of Vietnamese.

HANOI

024 / POP 7.58 MILLION

Vietnam's capital races to make up for time lost to the ravages of war and a government that as recently as the 1990s kept the outside world at bay. Its streets surge with scooters vying for right of way amid the din of constantly blaring horns, and all around layers of history reveal periods of French and Chinese occupation – offering a glimpse into the resilience of ambitious, proud Hanoians.

Negotiate a passage past the ubiquitous knock-off merchants and you'll find the original streets of the Old Quarter. Defiant real-deal farmers hawk their wares, while city folk breakfast on noodles, practise t'ai chi at dawn or play chess with goateed grandfathers.

Dine on the wild and wonderful at every corner, sample market wares, uncover an evolving arts scene, then sleep soundly in luxury for very little cost. Meet the people, delve into the past and witness the awakening of a Hanoi on the move.

Sights

Note that some museums are closed on Mondays and take a two-hour lunch break on other days of the week. Check opening hours carefully before setting off.

Old Quarter

Steeped in history, pulsating with life, bubbling with commerce, buzzing with motorbikes and rich in exotic scents, the Old Quarter is Hanoi's historic heart and soul. Hawkers pound the streets bearing sizzling, smoking baskets that hide a cheap meal. *Pho* (noodle soup) stalls and *bia hoi* (draught beer) dens hug every corner, resonant with the sound of gossip and laughter. Take your time and experience this captivating warren of lanes – this is Asian street life at its purest and most atmospheric. The flip side is that it's also a notoriously chaotic and polluted enclave, and tough to explore on foot, as you pick your way through an urban assault course of motorbikes (parked and speeding) and cracked pavements. One day the authorities will get round to a pedestrianisation program, but for now enjoy the anarchy.

★ Bach Ma Temple
BUDDHIST TEMPLE

(Den Bach Ma; Map p828; cnr P Hang Buom & P Hang Giay; ⊙8-11am & 2-5pm Tue-Sun) FREE In the heart of the Old Quarter, the small Bach Ma Temple is said to be the oldest temple in the city, though much of the current structure dates from the 18th century and a shrine to Confucius was added in 1839. It was originally built by Emperor Ly Thai To in the 11th century to honour a white horse that guided him to this site, where he chose to construct his city walls.

★ Heritage House
HISTORIC BUILDING

(Ngoi Nha Di San; Map p828; 87 P Ma May; 10,000d; ⊙9am-noon & 1-6pm) One of the Old Quarter's best-restored properties, this traditional merchants' house is sparsely but beautifully decorated, with rooms set around two courtyards and filled with fine furniture. Note the high steps between rooms, a traditional design incorporated to stop the flow of bad energy around the property.

Around Hoan Kiem Lake

★ Hoa Lo Prison Museum
HISTORIC BUILDING

(Map p830; 024-3934 2253; cnr P Hoa Lo & P Hai Ba Trung; adult/child 30,000d/free; ⊙8am-5pm) This thought-provoking site is all that remains of the former Hoa Lo Prison, ironically nicknamed the 'Hanoi Hilton' by US prisoners of war (POWs) during the American War. Most exhibits relate to the prison's use up to the mid-1950s, focusing on the Vietnamese struggle for independence from France. A gruesome relic is the ominous French guillotine, used to behead Vietnamese revolutionaries. There are also displays focusing on the American pilots who were incarcerated at Hoa Lo during the American War.

Hoan Kiem Lake
LAKE

(Map p830) Legend claims that, in the mid-15th century, Heaven sent Emperor Ly Thai To a magical sword, which he used to drive the Chinese from Vietnam. After the war a giant golden turtle grabbed the sword and disappeared into the depths of this lake to restore the sword to its divine owners, inspiring the name Ho Hoan Kiem (Lake of the Restored Sword). The area is best on Friday to Sunday when nearby traffic is banned from 7pm to midnight and a public-square, funfair vibe takes over.

National Museum of Vietnamese History
MUSEUM

(Bao Tang Lich Su Quoc Gia; Map p830; 024-3825 2853; http://baotanglichsu.vn; 1 P Trang Tien; adult/student 40,000/10,000d; ⊙8am-noon & 1.30-5pm Tue-Sun) Built between 1925 and 1932, this architecturally impressive museum was formerly home to the École

VIETNAM HANOI

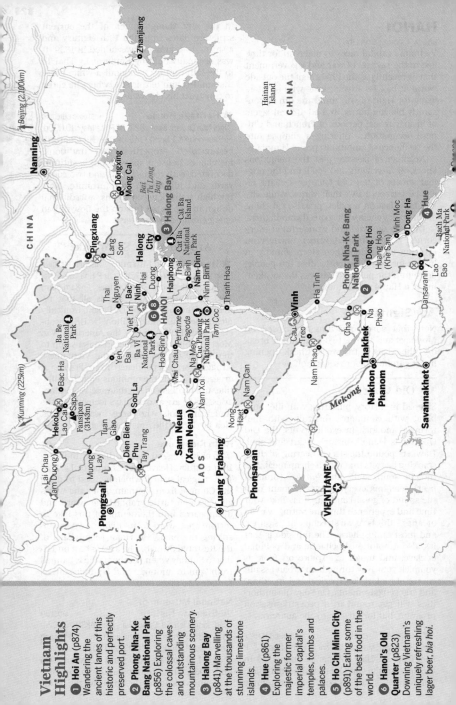

Vietnam Highlights

1 Hoi An (p874)
Wandering the ancient lanes of this historic and perfectly preserved port.

2 Phong Nha-Ke Bang National Park (p856) Exploring the colossal caves and outstanding mountainous scenery.

3 Halong Bay (p841) Marvelling at the thousands of stunning limestone islands.

4 Hue (p861) Exploring the majestic former imperial capital's temples, tombs and palaces.

5 Ho Chi Minh City (p891) Eating some of the best food in the world.

6 Hanoi's Old Quarter (p823) Downing Vietnam's uniquely refreshing lager beer, *bia hoi*.

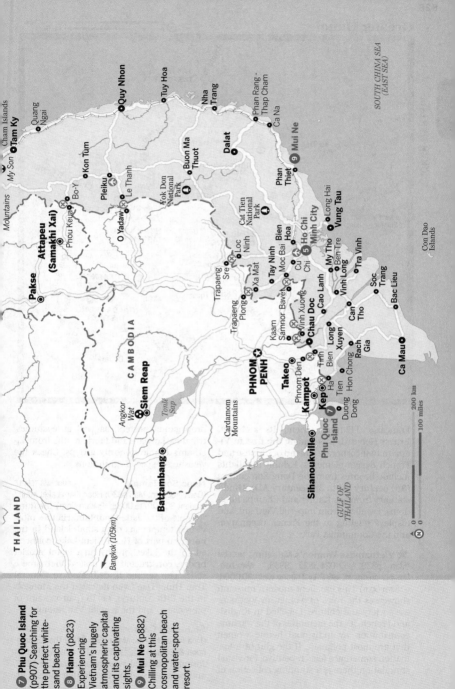

THAILAND

CAMBODIA

Siem Reap

Angkor Wat

Tonlé Sap

Battambang

Cardamom Mountains

PHNOM PENH

Takeo

Kampot

Kep 7

Phu Quoc Island

Sihanoukville

GULF OF THAILAND

Bangkok (105km)

Phnom Den

Ha Tien

Duong Dong

Tinh Bien

Hon Chong

Rach Gia

Bien Long Xuyen

Chau Doc

Cao Lanh

Kaam Samnor

Vinh Xuong

Bavet

Trapaeng Plong

Trapaeng Sre

Xa Mat

Moc Bai

Tay Ninh

Cu Chi

Loc Ninh

O Yadaw

Le Thanh

Yok Don National Park

Kon Tum

Pleiku

Bo-Y

Phou Keua

Attapeu (Samakhi Xai)

Pakse

Mountains

My Son

Tam Ky

Quang Ngai

Quy Nhon

Tuy Hoa

Buon Ma Thuot

Dalat

Phan Thiet

Mui Ne 9

Phan Rang - Thap Cham

Ca Na

Nha Trang

Cham Islands

Bien Hoa

Ho Chi Minh City 5

Long Hai

Vung Tau

Cat Tien National Park 4

My Tho

Ben Tre

Vinh Long

Tra Vinh

Can Tho

Soc Trang

Bac Lieu

Ca Mau

Con Dao Islands

SOUTH CHINA SEA (EAST SEA)

0   200 km
0   100 miles

Greater Hanoi

VIETNAM HANOI

Française d'Extrême-Orient. Its architect, Ernest Hebrard, was among the first in Vietnam to incorporate a blend of Chinese and French design elements. Exhibit highlights include bronzes from the Dong Son culture (3rd century BC to 3rd century AD), Hindu statuary from the Khmer and Champa kingdoms, jewellery from imperial Vietnam, and displays relating to the French occupation and the Communist Party.

★ Vietnamese Women's Museum   MUSEUM
(Map p830; ☎024-3825 9936; www.baotangphunu.org.vn; 36 P Ly Thuong Kiet; 30,000d; ☺8am-5pm) This excellent modern museum showcases the roles of women in Vietnamese society and culture. Labelled in English and French, it's the memories of the wartime contribution by individual heroic women that are most poignant. If the glut of information sometimes feels repetitive, for visual stimulation there is a stunning collection of propaganda posters, as well as costumes, tribal basketware and fabric motifs from Vietnam's ethnic minority groups. Check the website for special exhibitions.

Ngoc Son Temple   BUDDHIST TEMPLE
(Den Ngoc Son; Map p830; Hoan Kiem Lake; adult/student 30,000/15,000d; ☺8am-6pm) Meaning 'Temple of the Jade Mountain', Hanoi's most visited temple sits on a small island in the northern part of Hoan Kiem Lake, connected to the lakeshore by an elegant scarlet bridge, constructed in classical Vietnamese style. The temple is dedicated to General Tran Hung Dao (who defeated the Mongols in the 13th century), La To (patron saint of physicians) and the scholar Van Xuong.

St Joseph Cathedral   CHURCH
(Nha To Lon Ha Noi; Map p830; P Nha Tho; ☺8am-noon & 2-6pm) FREE Hanoi's neo-Gothic St Joseph Cathedral was inaugurated in 1886, and boasts a soaring facade that faces a lit-

Greater Hanoi

tle plaza. Its most noteworthy features are its twin bell towers, elaborate altar and fine stained-glass windows. Entrance via the main gate is only permitted during Mass: times are listed on a sign on the gates to the left of the cathedral.

◉ West of the Old Quarter

★ **Temple of Literature**   CONFUCIAN TEMPLE
(Van Mieu Quoc Tu Giam; Map p834; ☑ 024-3845 2917; P Quoc Tu Giam; adult/student 30,000/15,000d; ☺ 8am-6pm) A rare example of well-preserved traditional Vietnamese architecture, the Temple of Literature honours Vietnam's finest scholars. Founded in 1070 by Emperor Ly Thanh Tong, the attractive complex is dedicated to Confucius (Khong Tu) and was the site of Vietnam's first university (1076). The altars are popular with students praying for good grades; while the pagodas, ponds and gardens of the five courtyards make picturesque backdrops for student graduation photos. It is depicted on the 100,000d note.

Ho Chi Minh's Mausoleum   MAUSOLEUM
(Lang Chu Tich Ho Chi Minh; Map p834; ☑ 024-3845 5128; www.bqllang.gov.vn; Ba Dinh Sq; ☺ 8-11am Tue-Thu, Sat & Sun Dec-Aug, last entry 10.15am) FREE In the tradition of Lenin, Stalin and Mao, Ho Chi Minh's Mausoleum is a monumental marble edifice. Contrary to

his desire for a simple cremation, the mausoleum was constructed from materials gathered from all over Vietnam between 1973 and 1975. Set deep in the bowels of the building in a glass sarcophagus is the frail, pale body of Ho Chi Minh. The mausoleum is usually closed from 4 September to 4 November while his embalmed body goes to Russia for maintenance.

**Vietnam Military
History Museum**   MUSEUM
(Bao Tang Lich Su Quan Su Viet Nam; Map p834; ☑ 024-733 6453; www.btlsqsvn.org.vn; 28a P Dien Bien Phu; 40,000d, camera fee 20,000d; ☺ 8-11.30am daily & 1-4.30pm Tue-Thu, Sat & Sun) Easy to spot thanks to a large collection of weaponry at the front, the Military Museum displays Soviet and Chinese equipment alongside French- and US-made weapons captured during years of warfare. The centrepiece is a Soviet-built MiG-21 jet fighter, triumphant amid the wreckage of French aircraft downed at Dien Bien Phu, and a US F-111.

Fine Arts Museum of Vietnam   MUSEUM
(Bao Tang My Thuat Viet Nam; Map p834; ☑ 024-3733 2131; http://vnfam.vn; 66 P Nguyen Thai Hoc; adult/child 40,000/20,000d; ☺ 8.30am-5pm) The excellent Fine Arts Museum is housed in two buildings that were once the French Ministry of Information. Treasures abound, including ancient Champa stone carvings and some astonishing effigies of Quan Am, the thousand-eyed, thousand-armed Goddess of Compassion. Look out for the lacquered statues of Buddhist monks from the Tay Son dynasty and the collection of contemporary art and folk-naive paintings. Most pieces have English explanations, but guided tours (150,000d) are useful.

Ho Chi Minh's Stilt House   HISTORIC SITE
(Nha San Bac Ho & Phu Chu Tich Tai; Map p834; So 1 Ngo Bach Thao; 25,000d; ☺ 8-11.30am daily & 2-4pm Tue-Thu, Sat & Sun) This humble, traditional stilt house where Ho lived intermittently from 1958 until 1969 is set in a well-tended garden adjacent to a carp-filled pond and has been preserved just as Ho left it. The clear views through the open doorways and windows give an insight more fascinating than most museum mementos. It's now used for official receptions and isn't open to the public, but visitors may wander the grounds if sticking to the paths.

From here, you look out on to the opulent beaux-arts Presidential Palace. There is a combined entrance gate to the stilt house

Old Quarter

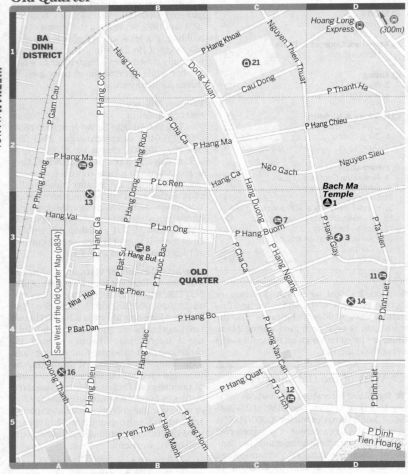

and palace grounds on P Ong Ich Kiem inside the Ho Chi Minh Mausoleum Complex. When the main entrance is closed, enter from Đ Hung Vuong.

Ho Chi Minh Museum   MUSEUM
(Bao Tang Ho Chi Minh; Map p834; ☎ 024-3845 5435; www.baotanghochiminh.vn; 19 P Ngoc Ha; 40,000d; ⊙ 8am-noon daily & 2-4.30pm Tue-Thu, Sat & Sun) The huge concrete Soviet-style Ho Chi Minh Museum is a triumphalist monument dedicated to the life of the founder of modern Vietnam. The often-confusing exhibition is a mixed bag; highlights include

mementos of Ho's life, and some fascinating photos and dusty official documents relating to the overthrow of the French and the onward march of revolutionary socialism. Photography is forbidden and you may be asked to check your bag at reception.

One Pillar Pagoda   BUDDHIST TEMPLE
(Chua Mot Cot; Map p834; P Ong Ich Kiem; 25,000d; ⊙ 8-11.30am daily & 2-4pm Tue-Thu, Sat & Sun) The One Pillar Pagoda was originally built by the Emperor Ly Thai Tong who ruled from 1028 to 1054. According to the annals, the heirless emperor dreamed that he met

namese military power for over 1000 years. Ongoing archaeological digs of ancient palaces, grandiose pavilions and imperial gates are complemented by fascinating military command bunkers from the American War – complete with maps and 1960s communications equipment – used by the legendary Vietnamese general Vo Nguyen Giap.

The leafy grounds are also an easygoing and quiet antidote to Hanoi's bustle.

Greater Hanoi

★ **Vietnam Museum of Ethnology** MUSEUM (☑ 024-3756 2193; www.vme.org.vn; Đ Nguyen Van Huyen; adult/concession 40,000/15,000d, guide 100,000d; ⊙ 8.30am-5.30pm Tue-Sun) This fabulous collection relating to Vietnam's ethnic minorities features well-presented tribal art, artefacts and everyday objects gathered from across the nation, and examples of traditional village houses. Displays are well labelled in Vietnamese, French and English. If you're into anthropology, it's well worth the

Quan The Am Bo Tat, the Goddess of Mercy, who handed him a male child. Ly Thai Tong then married a young peasant girl and had a son and heir by her. As a way of expressing his gratitude for this event, he constructed a pagoda here in 1049.

Imperial Citadel of Thang Long HISTORIC SITE (Hoang Thanh Thang Long; Map p834; www. hoangthanhthanglong.vn; 19c P Hoang Dieu; adult/ child 30,000d/free; ⊙ 8-11.30am daily & 2-4pm Tue-Thu, Sat & Sun) Added to Unesco's World Heritage List in 2010 and reopened in 2012, Hanoi's Imperial Citadel was the hub of Viet-

Around Hoan Kiem Lake

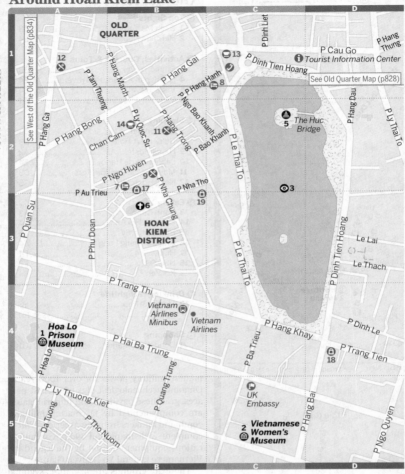

approximately 200,000d-each-way taxi fares to the Cau Giay district, about 7km from the city centre, where the museum is located.

West Lake LAKE
(Ho Tay; Map p826) The city's largest lake, known as both Ho Tay and West Lake, is 15km in circumference and ringed by upmarket suburbs, including the predominantly expat Tay Ho district. On the south side, along Đ Thuy Khue, are seafood restaurants, and to the east, the Xuan Dieu strip is lined with restaurants, cafes, boutiques and luxury hotels. The atmosphere makes a calm change from

the chaos of the Old Quarter. A pathway circles the lake, making for a great bicycle ride.

🎣 Courses & Tours

⭐ **Hanoi Free Tour Guides** WALKING
(📱0988 979 174; http://hanoifreetourguides.com) **FREE** There's no better way to experience the real Hanoi than with this not-for-profit social organisation run by a team of over 400 volunteer staff and guides comprising students and ex-students, speaking a multitude of languages. A variety of suggested tours are available, or work with your guide to tailor your own itinerary. Book online.

the eastern side of West Lake (Ho Tay). Options include seafood and village-food menus. Walking tours (per person US$25) exploring Hanoi street food are available. Hidden Hanoi also offers a language-study program (per person from $US200), including two field trips.

🛏 Sleeping

Many good budget places are in the Old Quarter or neighbouring Hoan Kiem lake area.

🛏 Old Quarter

★ **Cocoon Inn** HOSTEL $
(Map p828; ☑024-388 5333; https://cocooninn.com; 116-118 P Hang Buom; dm/tw from US$8/30; ❄@⚓) This luxury hostel shows off boutique good looks in its dorms and slick bar. Privacy curtains create a cocoon around plush, clean beds, with personal lamps, fans and powerpoints. An entourage of helpful staff can organise tours, airport transfer and visa extensions. It's on a busy street full of restaurants and bars.

Vietnam Awesome Travel WALKING
(Map p828; ☑0904 123 217; www.vietnamawesometravel.com; 19b P Hang Be; tours from US$18) A wide range of good-value walking tours, including the popular Food on Foot (US$25) street-food walking tours around the Old Quarter. A wide range of day trips and longer guided tours are available. See the website for details.

Hidden Hanoi COOKING, LANGUAGE
(Map p826; ☑0912 254 045; www.hiddenhanoi.com.vn; 147 P Nghi Tam, Tay Ho; per class with/without market tour US$55/45; ☺11am-2pm Mon-Sat) Offers cooking classes from its kitchen near

HANOI STREET EATS

When in Hanoi, chow down with the masses. Most of these stalls specialise in just one dish and have somewhat flexible opening hours.

Bun Cha 34 (Map p826; ☑0948 361 971; 34 P Hang Than; meals 35,000d; ⊗8.30am-5pm; 🛜) Best *bun cha* in Vietnam? Many say 34 is up there. No presidents have eaten at the plastic tables, but you get perfectly moist chargrilled pork, zesty fresh herbs and delicious broth to dip everything in. The *nem* (seafood spring rolls) are great too. Aim for midday for patties straight off the coals.

Bun Rieu Cua (Map p830; 40 P Hang Tre; bun rieu 25,000d; ⊗7-9:30am) Get to this incredibly popular spot early, as its sole dish of *bun rieu cua* (noodle soup with beef in a spicy crab broth) is only served for a couple of hours from 7am. A Hanoi classic.

Banh Cuon (Map p828; 14 P Hang Ga; meals from 35,000d; ⊗8am-3pm) Don't even bother ordering here; just squeeze in and a plate of gossamer-light *banh cuon* (steamed rice pancakes filled with minced pork, mushrooms and shrimp) will be placed in front of you.

Banh Goi (Map p830; 52 P Ly Quoc Su; snacks 35,000d; ⊗10am-7pm) Nestled under a banyan tree near St Joseph Cathedral, this humble stall turns out *banh goi*, moreish deepfried pastries crammed with pork, vermicelli and mushrooms.

Banh Mi Hoi An (Bami Bread; Map p828; ☑0981 043 144; 98 P Hang Bac; banh mi 15,000-25,000d; ⊗6.30am-10.30pm) Dense, toasted baguettes with flavoursome pâté and fillings like *ga nuong xa* (grilled chicken, chili and lemongrass) is what keeps this tiny *banh mi* branch busy into the night. They often sell out before closing time.

Mien Xao Luon (Map p830; 87 P Hang Dieu; meals from 25,000d; ⊗7am-2pm) Head to this humble stall trimmed with mini-mountains of fried eels for three different ways of eating the crisp little morsels. Try them stir-fried in vermicelli with egg, bean sprouts and shallots. The fishy flavour is milder than you might expect.

Pho Thin (Map p826; 13 P Lo Duc; pho 50,000d; ⊗6am-8.30pm) Negotiate your way to the rear of this narrow, rustic establishment and sit down to some excellent *pho bo* (beef noodle soup). A classic Hanoi experience that hasn't changed in decades.

Xoi Yen (Map p828; cnr P Nguyen Huu Huan & P Hang Mam; sticky rice from 10,000d; ⊗7am-11pm) Equally good for breakfast or as a stodgy hangover cure, Xoi Yen specialises in sticky rice topped with goodies, including sweet Asian sausage, gooey fried egg and slow-cooked pork. Watching it being prepared is half the fun.

★**Tomodachi House** HOSTEL **$**
(Map p834; ☑024-3266 9493; http://hanoi.tomodachihouse.com; 5a Tong Duy Tan; dm/d from US$9/27; 🌐@🛜) This quiet Japanese-styled flashpacker is on the snazzier western edge of the Old Quarter, near hip all-night eating and drinking. Large, restful dorm beds have their own USB charging, shelf space, privacy curtain and chunky locker. Great breakfast (included) and helpful staff seal the deal, and acoustic guitar livens up the restaurant every Saturday night.

May De Ville Backpackers HOSTEL **$**
(Map p828; ☑024-3935 2468; www.maydevillebackpackershostelvietnam.com; 1 Hai Tuong, near P Ta Hien; dm/d from US$10/30; 🌐@🛜) A short walk from Ta Hien's bars, May De Ville is one of Hanoi's best hostels. Dorms have firm beds but are spotless and there's also a movie room. Doubles are also good value.

Hanoi Hostel HOSTEL **$**
(Map p828; ☑0972 844 804; www.vietnam-hostel.com; 91c P Hang Ma; dm/d/tr US$6/25/30; 🌐🛜) This small, quiet, privately owned hostel is nicely located away from Hanoi's conglomeration of hostels. It's well run and clean, with tours on tap and plenty of information about onward travel to China or Laos.

★**La Beauté de Hanoi** HOTEL **$$**
(Map p828; ☑024-3935 1626; www.la-beautehanoihotel.com; 15 Ngo Trung Yen; d/ste from US$61/96; 🌐🛜) Renovated in 2017, this 18-room hotel has a fresh white-and-cream palette with red accents, cable TV, fast wi-fi, and the larger suites and family rooms have small private balconies. It's in an excellent

location on a quiet lane just a hop, skip and a jump from all the action on P Ma May.

★ Golden Art Hotel
HOTEL **$$**

(Map p828; ☎024-3923 4294; www.goldenarthotel.com; 6a P Hang But; d & tw US$45; ❀❅@❧) Golden Art enjoys a quiet location on the western edge of the Old Quarter. Rooms are stylish and relatively spacious, and there's a real can-do attitude from the exceptional and friendly staff. Each room has a laptop, and breakfast (included in the price) includes warm baguettes, omelettes, *pho* (noodle soup) and fresh fruit.

Around Hoan Kiem Lake

★ Nexy Hostel
HOSTEL **$**

(Map p828; ☎024-7300 6399; www.nexyhostels.com; 12 P To Tich; dm/tw/tr from $9/35/40; ❅❧) A new wave of flashpackers has arrived, looking for modern, clean dorms and bathrooms, soft beds with privacy curtains, quality linen and ample locked storage, plus staff who speak excellent English. Boutique hostel Nexy has all this, plus a standout location near Hoan Kiem Lake. Nexy also boasts a calm bar, games room, small lounge and rooftop zones.

Especen Hotel
HOTEL **$**

(Map p830; ☎024-3824 4401; www.especen.vn; 28 P Tho Xuong; d US$13-25; ❅@❧) This budget hotel near St Joseph Cathedral has spacious and light rooms, excellent rates and an almost-tranquil location (by Old Quarter standards). There are two annexes within walking distance.

Madame Moon Hotel
GUESTHOUSE **$$**

(Map p830; ☎024-3938 1255; www.madammoonguesthouse.com; 17 P Hang Hanh; d & tw from US$28; ❅@❧) Keeping it simple just one block from Hoan Kiem Lake, Madame Moon has surprisingly chic rooms and a (relatively) traffic-free location in a street filled with local cafes and bars. Note that there are three hotels belonging to Madame Moon. This review is for the Hang Hanh property.

✗ Eating

Hanoi offers cuisine from all over the world but as the capital's grub is so tasty, fragrantly spiced and inexpensive, you're best sticking to local fare. Don't miss the street food either.

✗ Old Quarter

★ New Day
VIETNAMESE **$**

(Map p828; ☎024-3828 0315; http://newdayrestaurant.com; 72 P Ma May; meals 50,000-100,000d; ❧8am-late) Busy New Day attracts locals, expats and travellers alike with its broad menu. The eager staff always find space for new diners, so look forward to sharing a table with some like-minded fans of Vietnamese food. It's not advertised, but evening diners can point and choose from dishes for a mixed plate for about 100,000d.

★ Blue Butterfly
VIETNAMESE **$$**

(Map p828; ☎024-3926 3845; http://bluebutterflyrestaurant.com; 69 P Ma May; meals 100,000-300,000d; ❧8am-10.30pm) Blue Butterfly floats above its weight with the lamp-lit dark-wood stylings of a heritage house and a good-value menu of Vietnamese classics. Staff offer knowledgeable suggestions and demonstrate how to tackle dishes such as *nem lui,* pork grilled on lemongrass skewers, wrapped in rice paper and dipped in peanut sauce. Set menus (from 350,000d) are available.

Cha Ca Thang Long
VIETNAMESE **$$**

(Map p828; ☎024-3824 5115; www.chacathanglong.com; 19-31 P Duong Thanh; cha ca fish meal 180,000d; ❧10am-3pm & 5-10pm) Bring along your DIY cooking skills and grill your own succulent fish with a little shrimp paste and plenty of herbs. *Cha ca* (fish burger) is an iconic Hanoi dish heavy on turmeric and dill; while another nearby more-famous *cha ca* eatery gets all the tour-bus traffic, the food here is actually better.

Highway 4
VIETNAMESE **$$**

(Map p828; ☎024-3926 0639; www.highway4.com; 3 P Hang Tre; meals 110,000-290,000d; ❧noon-late) This is the original location of a restaurant family famed for adapting

---

SPLURGE

The stylish bistro **La Badiane** (Map p834; ☎024-3942 4509; www.labadiane-hanoi.com; 10 Nam Ngu; mains from 280,000d; ❧11.30am-2pm & 6-10pm Mon-Sat) is set in a restored, whitewashed French villa arrayed around a breezy central courtyard. French cuisine underpins the menu – La Badiane translates as 'star anise' – but Asian and Mediterranean flavours also feature. Menu highlights include sea-bass tagliatelle with smoked paprika, and prawn bisque with wasabi tomato bruschetta. Three-course lunches (385,000d) are excellent value, and there's an evening degustation (1,490,000d).

West of the Old Quarter

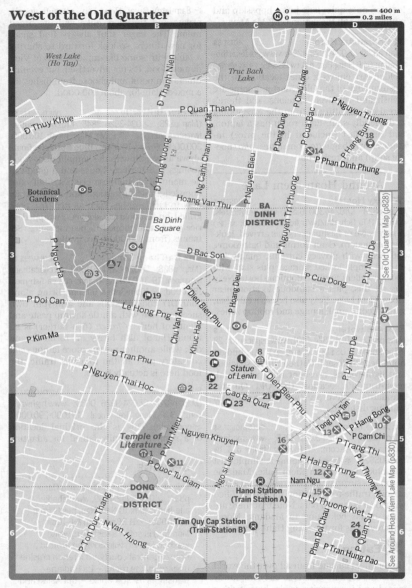

Vietnamese cuisine to Western palates, although with increasing popularity it becomes harder to please everybody. There are now four other branches in Hanoi: check the website for locations. Come for small plates to share, cold beer, cocktails and funky decor.

✗ Around Hoan Kiem Lake

Jalus Vegan Kitchen   VEGAN **$**
(Map p830; ☑ 024-3266 9730; 2nd fl, 46 Hang Trong; meals 30,000-60,000d; ⊙ 8am-10pm Tue-Sun; ✻ ⊛ ⊘) Pull up a pine table at this modern,

West of the Old Quarter

hidden restaurant and try some delicious coconut and chia smoothies and veggie burgers, or pizza, quiche and ravioli made with vegan cheese. There are definite Vietnamese twists with lemongrass and spice, and sometimes special all-Vietnamese menus.

★ **Hanoi Social Club**   CAFE $$
(Map p834; ☏ 024-3938 2117; www.facebook.com/TheHanoiSocialClub; 6 Hoi Vu; meals 95,000-175,000d; ☺ 8am-11pm) On three funky levels with retro furniture, the Hanoi Social Club is the city's most cosmopolitan cafe and an artist hub. Dishes include potato fritters with chorizo for breakfast, and pasta, burgers and wraps for lunch or dinner. Vegetarian options feature a tasty mango curry, and the quiet laneway location is a good spot for an end-of-day coffee, beer or wine.

West of the Old Quarter

Ray Quan   VIETNAMESE $
(Map p834; ☏ 0913 578 588; 48 Le Duan; dishes 30,000-120,000d) Popular with expats in the know, this quirky spot directly on the train tracks won't be for everyone, but those who like it, will love it. A wide range of delicious Vietnamese cuisine is cooked to order by the eccentric owner-chef who ferments her own rice wine: it's strong and delicious.

Net Hue   VIETNAMESE $
(Map p834; ☏ 024-3938 1795; http://nethue.com.vn; 198 P Hang Bong; snacks & meals from 35,000d; ☺ 11am-9pm) One of a small chain, Net Hue is well priced for such comfortable surroundings. Head to the top floor for the

nicest ambience and enjoy Hue-style dishes like *banh nam* (steamed rice pancake with minced shrimp).

Quan An Ngon   VIETNAMESE $
(Map p834; ☏ 024-3942 8162; http://quananngon.com.vn; 18 Phan Boi Chau; meals 70,000-150,000d; ☺ 7am-11pm) This branch of a number of small same-named kitchens turns out street-food specialities from across Vietnam. Try to visit just outside the busy lunch and dinner periods, or consider Quan An Ngon's newest branch (Map p834; ☏ 024-3734 9777; www.ngon-hanoi.com.vn; 34 P Phan Đinh Phung; meals 70,000-150,000d; ☺ 11am-11pm) in a lovely French villa just north of the Old Quarter.

Koto   CAFE $$
(Nha Hang Koto Van Mieu; Map p834; ☏ 024-3747 0338; www.koto.com.au; 59 P Van Mieu; meals 120,000-160,000d; ☺ 7.30am-10pm, closed dinner Mon) Stunning four-storey modernist cafe-bar-restaurant overlooking the Temple of Literature, where the interior design has been taken very seriously, from the stylish seating to the fresh flowers by the till. Daily specials are chalked up on a blackboard, and the short menu has everything from excellent Vietnamese food to yummy pita wraps and beer-battered fish and chips.

🍷 Drinking & Nightlife

With dive bars, congenial pubs, sleek lounges and clubs, and *bia hoi* joints by the barrel-load, you won't go thirsty in Hanoi. Ha Tien in the Old Quarter has a choice of bars and is a good starting or finishing point for a crawl. Cafes come in every persuasion too.

SCAM ALERT

Hanoi is a very safe city on the whole and crimes against tourists are extremely rare. That said, the city certainly has its share of scams. Make sure you report any to the **Vietnam National Administration of Tourism** (Map p834; ☑ 024-3942 3760; www. vietnamtourism.gov.vn; 80 P Quan Su), who might well pressure the cowboys into cleaning up their act.

Fake hotels The taxi and minibus mafia at the airport take unwitting tourists to the wrong hotel. Invariably, the hotel has appropriated the name of another popular property and will then attempt to swindle as much of your money as possible. Check out a room before you check in. And walk on if you have any suspicions.

Hotel tours Some budget hotel staff have been verbally aggressive and threatened physical violence towards guests who've declined to book tours through their in-house tour agency. Don't feel pressured, and if it persists, find another place to stay.

After midnight Walking alone at night is generally safe in the Old Quarter, but you should always be aware of your surroundings. Hailing a taxi is a good idea if it's late and you have a long walk home.

The kindness of strangers There's a scam going on around Hoan Kiem Lake where a friendly local approaches you offering to take you out. Your new friend may then suggest a visit to a karaoke bar or a snake-meat restaurant, and before you know it you're presented with a bill for hundreds of dollars. Be careful and follow your instincts.

Coffee meccas include P Trieu Viet Vuong, around 1km south of Hoan Kiem Lake, which has scores of cafes.

★ **Tadioto**   BAR
(Map p830; ☑ 024-6680 9124; www.fb.me/tadiototongdan; 24b P Tong Dan; ☺ 8am-midnight) Nguyen Qui Duc's unofficial clubhouse for the underground art scene's latest incarnation is this dark and quirky colonial bar in the French Quarter. Obligatory red accents (seat covers, wrought-iron grill on the doors), reworkings of art deco furniture and plenty of recycled ironwork feature heavily. It attracts many well-dressed visitors. The highlight of the cool cocktail list is the sweet mojito.

★ **Nola**   BAR
(Map p828; 89 P Ma May; ☺ 9am-midnight) Retro furniture and art are mixed and matched in this bohemian multilevel labyrinth tucked away from Ma May's tourist bustle. Pop in for a coffee and banana bread in a quiet section, or return after dark for one of Hanoi's best little bars.

Moose & Roo   PUB
(Map p828; ☑ 024-3200 1289; www.mooseandroo. com; 42b P Ma May; ☺ 11am-midnight Mon-Fri, 10am-midnight Sat, 10am-11pm Sun) This jovial Canadian-Aussie-themed pub and grill serves excellent home-style comfort food (burgers, pulled pork, wings, fish and chips)

in a fun and friendly environment. One for the homesick or those looking to meet other travellers.

Bia Hoi Ha Noi   BIA HOI
(Map p834; 2 P Duong Thanh) A *bia hoi* junction that is local in flavour is where P Nha Hoa meets P Duong Thanh on the western edge of the Old Quarter. Bia Hoi Ha Noi does the best spare ribs in town for a little something to go with the beer.

Quan Ly   BAR
(Map p826; ☑ 024-3822 5276; 82 P Le Van Hu; ☺ 10am-9pm) Owner Pham Xuan Ly has lived on this block since 1950, and now runs one of Hanoi's most traditional *ruou* (Vietnamese wine) bars. Kick off with the ginseng one, and work your way up. An English-language menu makes it easy to choose, and there's also cheap beer and good Vietnamese food on offer.

Café Duy Tri   CAFE
(Map p826; ☑ 024-3829 1386; 43a P Yen Phu; ☺ 8am-6pm) In the same location since 1936, this caffeine-infused labyrinth is a Hanoi classic. You'll feel like Gulliver as you negotiate the tiny ladders and stairways to reach the 3rd-floor balcony. Delicious *caphe sua chua* (iced coffee with yoghurt) may be your new favourite summertime drink. You'll find P Yen Phu a couple of blocks east of Truc Bach Lake.

Cafe Pho Co   CAFE
(Map p830; 4th fl, 11 P Hang Gai; ⊙8am-11pm) One of Hanoi's most hidden cafes, this place has plum views over Hoan Kiem Lake. Enter through the silk shop, and continue through the antique-bedecked courtyard up to the top floor for the mother of all vistas. You'll need to order coffee and snacks before tackling the final winding staircase. Try sweet *caphe trung da,* coffee topped with silky-smooth beaten egg yolk.

Manzi Art Space   BAR
(Map p834; ☑ 024-3716 3397; www.facebook.com/manzihanoi; 14 Phan Huy Ich; ⊙cafe 9am-midnight, shop 10am-6pm) Part cool art gallery, part chic cafe and bar, Manzi is worth seeking out north of the Old Quarter. A restored French villa hosts diverse exhibitions of painting, sculpture and photography, and the compact courtyard garden is perfect for a cup of coffee or glass of wine. There's also a small shop selling works by contemporary Vietnamese artists.

Cong Caphe   CAFE
(Map p826; http://congcaphe.com; 152 P Trieu Viet Vuong) Settle in to the eclectic beats and kitsch Communist memorabilia at the hip Cong Caphe with a *caphe sua da* (iced coffee with condensed milk). You'll notice a bunch of branches around the city; a full list appears on its website.

Loading T Cafe   CAFE
(Map p830; ☑ 0122-786 8686; 2nd fl, 8 Chan Cam; ⊙8am-6pm; 📶) Architecture lovers will especially love this cafe converted from a room in a dilapidated French colonial house. The ornate tiled floor, vintage fans and other design gems capture Hanoi's faded glamour. Homemade cakes, fresh juices and coconut or yoghurt coffee are on the menu.

☆ Entertainment

★ Binh Minh Jazz Club   LIVE MUSIC
(Map p830; www.minhjazzvietnam.com; 1 P Trang Tien; ⊙performances 9pm-midnight) **FREE** This atmospheric venue tucked behind the Opera House is the place in Hanoi to catch live jazz. There's a full bar, food menu and high-quality gigs featuring father-and-son team Minh and Dac, plus other local and international jazz acts. Free admission means the small, smoky venue fills quickly, so get there early.

The club is owned by the local saxophonist legend Quyen Van Minh. Check the website for listings.

Hanoi Rock City   LIVE MUSIC
(☑ 0943 571 984; www.hanoirockcity.com; 27/52 To Ngoc Van, Tay Ho) Hanoi Rock City is tucked away down a residential lane about 7km north of the city near Tay Ho, but it's a journey well worth taking for reggae, Hanoi punk and regular electronica nights. A few international acts swing by, so check the website or https://tnhvietnam.xemzi.com for listings.

🔒 Shopping

The Old Quarter is brimming with temptations: fake sunglasses, T-shirts, musical instruments, herbal medicines, jewellery, spices, propaganda art, fake English Premier League football kits and much, much more.

For ethnic minority garb and handicrafts, P Hang Bac and P To Tich are good hunting grounds. North and northwest of Hoan Kiem Lake around P Hang Gai, P To Tich, P Hang Khai and P Cau Go are dozens of shops offering handicrafts, artwork and antiques.

Dong Xuan Market   MARKET
(Map p828; Dong Xuan; ⊙6am-7pm) This is a large, non-touristy market located in the Old Quarter of Hanoi, 900m north of Hoan Kiem Lake. There are hundreds of stalls here and much of it is household items or tat, but it's a fascinating place to explore if you want to catch a flavour of local Hanoian life. The area around it also has loads of bustling shops, and stalls appear when night falls.

Things of Substance   CLOTHING
(Map p830; ☑ 024-3828 6965; 5 P Nha Tho; ⊙9am-9pm) Tailored fashions and some off-the-rack items at moderate prices. The staff are professional and speak decent English.

HANOI ON THE WEB

Hanoi has some great online resources:

TNH Vietnam (tnhvietnam.xemzi.com) Premier resource with useful restaurant reviews.

Hanoi Grapevine (www.hanoigrapevine.com) What's on in Hanoi.

Sticky Rice (www.stickyrice.typepad.com) Brilliant foodie website.

The Word (www.wordhanoi.com) Great articles.

And Of Other Things (www.andofotherthings.com) All things arty.

ℹ CATCHING THE BUS TO CHINA

Two daily services (at 7.30am and 9.30am) to China's Nanning ('Nam Ninh' in Vietnamese; 480,000d, nine hours) leave from 206 Đ Tran Quang Khai. Tickets should be purchased in advance through a reputable travel agency. Be sure you have the correct Chinese visa.

The bus runs to the border at Dong Dang, where you pass through Chinese immigration. You then change to a Chinese bus, which continues to the Lang Dong bus station in Nanning. Reports from Nanning-bound travellers indicate that this route is less hassle and quicker than the 13-hour trip by sleeper train from **Gia Lam Railway Station** (Ga Gia Lam), which is an eight-minute walk north of Gia Lam Bus Station (p840).

Indigenous   ARTS & CRAFTS
(Map p830; ☑ 024-3938 1263; 36 P Au Trieu; ☺9am-6pm) A top spot for quirky ethnic-style gifts and excellent fair-trade coffee. There's a great little cafe too, so you can choose your favourite Vietnamese java before you buy.

ℹ Information

INTERNET ACCESS

➔ Most budget and midrange hotels offer free access to a computer and the internet: at fancier places in the rooms, at cheaper places in the lobby.

➔ Free wi-fi access is virtually ubiquitous in the city's cafes and bars, but dedicated internet cafes are largely a thing of the past, so pack a tablet or smartphone.

➔ If you are staying longer than a week, consider getting a prepaid SIM card to stay connected on your (unlocked) device. **Viettel** (Map p830; http://international.viettel.vn; 51 Luong Van Can; ☺8am-8pm) will sell and set up a SIM for about US$8 with 1GB, after which you get unlimited data at slower speeds for the month. Passport required as ID.

MEDICAL SERVICES

Hanoi Family Medical Practice (Map p826; ☑ 024-3843 0748; www.vietnammedicalpractice.com; Van Phuc Diplomatic Compound, 298 P Kim Ma; ☺24hr) Located a few hundred metres west of the Ho Chi Minh Mausoleum Complex, this practice includes a team of well-respected international physicians and dentists, and has 24-hour emergency cover. Prices are high, so check that your medical travel insurance is in order.

MONEY

Hanoi has many ATMs. On the main roads around Hoan Kiem Lake are international banks where you can change money and get cash advances on credit cards.

TOURIST INFORMATION

In the cafes and bars of the Old Quarter, look for the excellent local magazine *The Word*.

Tourist Information & Support Center (Map p826; ☑24hr English hotline 0941 336 677, Vietnamese 0911 081 968; 28 P Hang Dau; ☺8am-5pm Wed-Sun) Hanoi finally has an official tourist information desk, although the location near the Long Bien bridge might put off those staying south around Hoan Kiem Lake. They offer four free walking tours, themed by architecture, history, Hoan Kiem Lake and Hanoi's craft streets.

Tourist Information Center (Map p830; ☑ 024-3926 3366; P Dinh Tien Hoang; ☺9am-7pm) City maps and brochures, but privately run with an emphasis on selling tours.

TRAVEL AGENCIES

Hanoi has hundreds of budget travel agencies. The agencies we recommend have professional, knowledgeable staff and coordinate well-organised trips with a high rate of guest satisfaction. Most run smaller groups and use their own vehicles and guides.

It's not advisable to book trips or tickets through guesthouses and hotels.

Ethnic Travel (Map p828; ☑ 024-3926 1951; www.ethnictravel.com.vn; 35 P Hang Giay; ☺9am-6pm Mon-Sat, 10am-5pm Sun) Off-the-beaten-track trips across the north in small groups. Some trips are low-impact using public transport and homestays, others are activity based (including hiking, cycling and cooking). Offers Bai Tu Long Bay tours and also has an office in Sapa.

Handspan Adventure Travel (Map p828; ☑ 024-3926 2828; www.handspan.com; 78 P Ma May; ☺9am-8pm) Sea-kayaking trips in Halong Bay and around Cat Ba Island, plus 4WD, mountain-biking and trekking tours. Other options include remote areas such as Moc Chau and Ba Be National Park, community-based tourism projects in northern Vietnam, and the *Treasure Junk*, the only true sailing craft cruising Halong Bay. Handspan also has offices in Sapa and Ho Chi Minh City.

Mr Linh's Adventure Tours (Map p828; ☑ 024-3642 5420; www.mrlinhadventure.com; 83 P Ma May) A professional, friendly outfit specialising in off-the-beaten-track and adventure travel in Vietnam's remote north. Ba Be Lakes homestay trips are recommended.

Vega Travel (Map p828; ☑ 024-3926 2092; www.vegatravel.vn; cnr P Ma May & 24a P Hang Bac; ☺8am-8pm) Family-owned-and-operated company offering well-run tours around the north of the country and throughout Vietnam. Excellent guides and drivers, and it also financially supports ethnic minority kindergartens and schools around Sapa and Bac Ha. Halong Bay tours on a private boat are excellent value and bespoke touring is available.

ℹ Getting There & Away

AIR

Hanoi has fewer direct international flights than Ho Chi Minh City (HCMC), but with excellent connections through Singapore, Hong Kong or Bangkok you can get almost anywhere easily.

Vietnam Airlines (Map p830; ☑1900 545 486; www.vietnamair.com.vn; 25 P Trang Thi; ⊗8am-5pm Mon-Fri) Links Hanoi to destinations throughout Vietnam. Popular routes include Hanoi to Dalat, Danang, Dien Bien Phu,

Ho Chi Minh City, Hue, Nha Trang and Phu Quoc Island, all served daily.

Jetstar Airways (www.jetstar.com) Operates low-cost flights to Danang, Ho Chi Minh City and Nha Trang.

VietJet Air (www.vietjetair.com) This low-cost airline has flights to Hanoi, Nha Trang, Danang, Dalat and Bangkok.

BUS

Hanoi has three main long-distance bus stations of interest to travellers (a fourth – Luong Yen – was closed in late 2016). They are fairly well organised, with ticket offices, fixed prices and schedules, though can be crowded and at times chaotic. Consider buying tickets the day before you plan to travel on the longer-distance routes, to ensure a seat. It's often easier to book through a travel agent, but you'll obviously be charged a commission.

BUSES FROM HANOI
Gia Lam Bus Station

DESTINATION	DURATION (HR)	COST (D)	FREQUENCY
Ba Be	5	150,000	noon daily
Bai Chay (Halong City)	3½	130,000	every 30min
Haiphong	2	70,000	frequent
Lang Son	5	90,000	every 45min
Lao Cai	9	320,000	6.30pm & 7pm (sleeper)
Mong Cai	9	200,000	hourly (approx)
Sapa	10	250,000	6.30pm & 7pm (sleeper)

My Dinh Bus Station

DESTINATION	DURATION (HR)	COST (D)	FREQUENCY
Cao Bang	10	260,000	9pm
Dien Bien Phu	8	365,000	11am & 6pm
Ha Giang	8	300,000	six daily
Hoa Binh	2	40,000	frequent
Son La	7	200,000	frequent

Giap Bat Bus Station

DESTINATION	DURATION (HR)	COST (D)	FREQUENCY
Dalat	35	470,000	9am & 11am
Danang	12	380,000	frequent sleepers noon-6pm
Dong Ha	8	380,000	frequent sleepers noon-6pm
Dong Hoi	8	380,000	frequent sleepers noon-6pm
Hue	10	365,000	frequent sleepers noon-6pm
Nha Trang	32	710,000	10am, 3pm, 6pm
Ninh Binh	2	70,000	frequent 7am-6pm

Tourist-style minibuses can be booked through most hotels and travel agents. Popular destinations include Halong Bay and Sapa. Prices are usually about 30% to 40% higher than the regular public bus, but include a hotel pick-up.

Many open-ticket tours through Vietnam start or finish in Hanoi.

Giap Bat Bus Station (☑ 024-3864 1467; Đ Giai Phong) Serves points south of Hanoi, and offers more comfortable sleeper buses. It is 7km south of Hanoi train station.

Gia Lam Bus Station (☑ 024-3827 1569; 132 Ngo Gia Kham) Has buses to regions north and northeast of Hanoi. It's located 3km northeast of the city centre across the Song Hong (Red River).

My Dinh Bus Station (☑ 024-3768 5549; Đ Pham Hung) This station 7km west of the city provides services to the west and the north, including sleeper buses to Dien Bien Phu for onward travel to Laos. It's also the best option for buses to Ha Giang and Mai Chau.

CAR & MOTORCYCLE

Car hire is best arranged via a travel agency or tour operator. The roads in the north are in pretty good shape but expect an average speed of 35km to 40km per hour. You'll definitely need a 4WD. Daily rates start at about US$110 a day (including driver and petrol).

TRAIN

The main **Hanoi Train Station** (Ga Hang Co, Train Station A; ☑ 024-3825 3949; 120 Đ Le Duan; ⊙ ticket office 7.30am-12.30pm & 1.30-7.30pm) is at the western end of P Tran Hung Dao. Trains from here go to destinations south.

To the right of the main entrance of the train station is a separate ticket office for northbound trains to Lao Cai (for Sapa) and China. Note that all northbound trains leave from a separate station (just behind the main station) called **Tran Quy Cap Station** (Train Station B; ☑ 024-3825 2628; P Tran Quy Cap; ⊙ ticket office 4-6am & 4-10pm).

To make things even more complicated, some northbound (Lao Cai and Lang Son included) and eastbound (Haiphong) trains depart from Gia Lam on the eastern side of the Song Hong (Red River), and Long Bien on the western (city) side of the river. Be sure to ask just where you need to go to catch your train.

Schedules, fares, information and advance bookings are available at Bau Lau (www.baolau.vn). Travel agents will also book train tickets for a commission.

It's best to buy tickets at least one day before departure to ensure a seat or sleeper.

❶ Getting Around

Hanoi's **Noi Bai International Airport** (HAN; www.hanoiairportonline.com; ☑ 024-3827 1513) is 35km north of the city. Don't use freelance taxi drivers touting for business – the chances of a rip-off are too high. Here are the transport options:

Airport Taxi (☑ 024-3873 3333) US$20 for a door-to-door taxi ride.

Public bus 17 (9000d, 1½ hours) To/from Long Bien bus station.

Express bus 86 (30,000) To/from north side of Hoan Kiem Lake.

TRAINS FROM HANOI

Eastern & Northbound Trains

DESTINATION	STATION	DURATION (HR)	HARD SEAT/ SLEEPER	SOFT SEAT/ SLEEPER	FREQUENCY
Beijing	Tran Quy Cap	18	US$240	US$352	6.30pm Tue & Fri
Haiphong	Gia Lam	2	60,000d	70,000d	6am
Haiphong	Long Bien	2½-3	60,000d	70,000d	9.20am, 3.30pm & 6.10pm
Nanning	Gia Lam	12	US$28	US$42	9.40pm

Southbound Trains

DESTINATION	HARD SEAT	SOFT SEAT	HARD SLEEPER	SOFT SLEEPER
Danang	from 430,000d	from 630,000d	from 782,000d	from 954,000d
HCMC	from 790,000d	from 1,160,000d	from 1,340,000d	from 1,692,000d
Hue	from 374,000d	from 545,000d	from 675,000d	from 894,000d
Nha Trang	from 692,000d	from 998,000d	from 1,240,000d	from 1,647,000d

CRUISING THE KARSTS: TOURS TO HALONG BAY

Halong Bay tours sold in Hanoi start from US$60 per person for a dodgy day trip, rising to around US$220 for two nights on the bay with kayaking. For around US$110 to US$130 you should get a worthwhile overnight cruise. Some tips:

➡ We get many complaints about poor service, bad food and rats running around on the boats, but these tend to be on the ultra-budget tours.

➡ Most tours include transport, meals and, sometimes, island hikes or kayaking. Cruises tend to follow a strict itinerary, with stops at touristy caves. On an overnight trip there's simply not time to stray far from Halong City.

➡ Boat tours are sometimes cancelled in bad weather – ascertain in advance what refund will be given.

➡ Take care with your valuables on day trips; most overnight cruises have lockable cabins.

➡ If you want to experience Halong Bay without the crowds, consider heading to Cat Ba Island. From there, tour operators concentrate on Lan Ha Bay, which is relatively untouched and has sublime sandy beaches.

Vietnam Airlines minibus (Map p830; 1 Quang Trung) (40,000d, every 45 minutes 5am-7pm) To/from the Vietnam Airlines office on Quang Trung. Departs when full and can be unreliable.

BICYCLE

Many Old Quarter guesthouses and cafes offer bike hire for about US$3 per day.

BUS

Hanoi has an extensive public bus system, though few tourists take advantage of the rock-bottom fares (3000d). If you're game, pick up the *Xe Buyt Ha Noi* (Hanoi bus map; 5000d) from the **Thang Long bookshop** (Hieu Sach Thang Long; Map p830; ☑ 024-825 7043; 53-55 P Trang Tien; ⊘ 9am-6pm).

CYCLO

A few *cyclo* (pedicab) drivers still frequent the Old Quarter but they tend to charge more than taxis, around 60,000d for a shortish journey.

MOTORCYCLE TAXI

You'll easily find a *xe om* (motorbike taxi) in Hanoi. An average journey in the city centre costs around 15,000d to 20,000d, while a trip further to Ho Chi Minh's Mausoleum is around 35,000d to 40,000d. For two or more people, a metered taxi is usually cheaper than a convoy of *xe om*.

TAXIS

Several reliable companies offer metered taxis. All charge fairly similar rates. Flag fall is around 20,000d, which takes you 1km to 2km; every kilometre thereafter costs around 15,000d. Some dodgy operators have high-speed meters, so use these more reliable companies and beware of copycats with similar colours. App-based companies Uber (uber.com) and Grab

(grab.com) operate taxi-like cars and motorbikes in Hanoi, even from the airport.
Hanoi Taxi (☑ 024-3853 5353)
Mai Linh (☑ 024-3822 2666)
Thanh Nga Taxi (☑ 024-3821 5215)
Van Xuan (☑ 024-3822 2888)

NORTHERN VIETNAM

Vistas. This is Vietnam's big-sky country; a place of rippling mountains, cascading rice terraces and karst topography. Halong Bay's seascape of limestone towers is the view everyone's here to see, but the karst connection continues inland to Ba Be's sprawling lakes until it segues into the evergreen hills of the northwest highlands. And right on the Chinese border, everything you've heard about Ha Giang province is true. It really is that spectacular.

Not to be outdone by the scenery, northern Vietnam's cultural kaleidoscope is just as diverse. In this heartland of hill-tribe culture, villages snuggle between paddy field patchworks outside of Sapa and the scarlet headdresses of the Dzao and the Black Hmong's indigo fabrics add dizzying colour to chaotic highland markets. If you're up for some road-tripping, this is the place to do it.

Halong Bay

Towering limestone pillars and tiny islets topped by forest rise from the emerald waters of the Gulf of Tonkin. Designated a

World Heritage Site in 1994, Halong Bay's scatter of islands, dotted with wind- and wave-eroded grottoes, is a vision of ethereal beauty and, unsurprisingly, northern Vietnam's number one-tourism hub.

Sprawling Halong City (also known as Bai Chay) is the bay's main gateway, but its high-rises are a disappointing doorstep to this site. Most visitors opt for cruise tours that include sleeping on board within the bay, while a growing number are deciding to eschew the main bay completely, heading straight for Cat Ba Island from where trips to less-visited but equally alluring Lan Ha Bay are easily set up.

All visitors must purchase entry tickets for the national park (40,000d) and there are also separate admission tickets for attractions in the bay, such as caves and fishing villages (30,000d to 50,000d).

Cat Ba Island

📋 0225 / POP 13,500

Rugged, craggy and jungle-clad Cat Ba, the largest island in Halong Bay, has experienced a tourism surge in recent years. The central hub of Cat Ba Town is now framed by a chain of low-rise concrete hotels along its once-lovely bay, but the rest of the island is largely untouched and as wild as ever. With idyllic Lan Ha Bay just offshore, you'll soon overlook Cat Ba Town's overdevelopment.

Almost half of Cat Ba Island (with a total area of 354 sq km) and 90 sq km of the adjacent waters were declared a national park in 1986 to protect the island's diverse ecosystems. Most of the coastline consists of rocky cliffs, but there are some sandy beaches and tiny fishing villages hidden away in small coves.

Lakes, waterfalls and grottoes dot the spectacular limestone hills, the highest rising 331m above sea level. The island's largest body of water is Ech Lake (3 hectares).

◉ Sights

★ Lan Ha Bay   BAY

(40,000d) Lying south and east of Cat Ba Town, the 300 or so karst islands and limestone outcrops of Lan Ha are just as beautiful as those of Halong Bay and have the additional attraction of numerous white-sand beaches. Due to it being a fair way from Halong City, not so many tourist boats venture here, meaning Lan Ha Bay has a more

isolated appeal. Sailing and kayak trips here are best organised in Cat Ba Town.

★ Cannon Fort   HISTORIC SITE

(40,000d; ◉ sunrise-sunset) For one of the best views in Vietnam – no, we're not kidding – head to Cannon Fort where there are astounding panoramas of Cat Ba Island's jungle-clad hills rolling down to colourful tangles of fishing boats in the harbour and out to the karst-punctuated sea beyond.

The entrance gate is a steep 10-minute walk from Cat Ba Town and from the gate it's another stiff 20-minute walk to the fort, or take a *xe om* from Cat Ba Town (15,000d).

Cat Ba National Park   NATIONAL PARK

(📋 0225-216 350; 40,000d; ◉ sunrise-sunset) Cat Ba's beautiful national park is home to 32 types of mammal, including most of the world's 65 remaining golden-headed langur, the world's most endangered primate. There are some good hiking trails here, including a hard-core 18km route up to a mountain summit. To reach the **park headquarters** at Trung Trang, hop on the green QH public bus from the docks at Cat Ba Town (25,000d, 7am, 11am and 3pm), hire a *xe om* (around 80,000d one way) or hire a motorbike for the day.

Hospital Cave   HISTORIC SITE

(admission 40,000d; ◉ 7am-4.30pm) Hospital Cave served both as a secret bomb-proof hospital during the American War and as a safe house for Viet Cong (VC) leaders. Built between 1963 and 1965 (with assistance from China), this incredibly well constructed three-storey feat of engineering was in constant use until 1975. The cave is about 10km north of Cat Ba Town on the road to Cat Ba National Park entrance.

Cat Co Cove   BEACH

A 10-minute walk southeast from Cat Ba Town, the three Cat Co Cove beaches boast the nearest sand to town, although rubbish in the water can be problematic some days. **Cat Co 3** is the closest, with a blink-and-you-miss-it sliver of sand. From there a walking trail, cut into the cliff and offering gorgeous sea views, winds its way to **Cat Co 1** dominated by a rather ugly resort, then onwards to the pretty white-sand swath of **Cat Co 2**.

🏃 Activities

Cat Ba is a superb base for adventure sports – on the island, and in, on and over the water.

Mountain Biking

Hotels can arrange Chinese mountain bikes (around US$6 per day). Blue Swimmer offers better-quality mountain bikes for US$15 per day. One possible route traverses the heart of the island, past Hospital Cave down to the west coast's mangroves and crab farms, and then in a loop back to Cat Ba Town past tidal mud flats and deserted beaches.

Rock Climbing

Cat Ba Island and Lan Ha Bay's spectacular limestone cliffs make for world-class rock climbing amid stunning scenery. Asia Outdoors uses fully licensed and certified instructors and is the absolute authority. Half-day climbing trips including instruction, transport, lunch and gear start at US$44 per person. Climbing and boat trips incorporate kayaking, beach stops and exploring the amazing karst landscape.

Sailing, Kayaking & SUP

Plenty of places in Cat Ba Town have kayaks for hire (half-day around US$8) that are ideal for exploring the coastline independently. SUP (stand-up paddle-boarding) trips are run by Asia Outdoors. Blue Swimmer offers sailing excursions to myriad islands around Cat Ba, often including kayaking and sleeping on a private beach.

Trekking

Most of Cat Ba Island consists of protected tropical forest. Cat Ba National Park has the most hiking opportunities.

⟳ Tours

Boat trips around Lan Ha Bay are offered by nearly every hotel on Cat Ba Island. Typical prices start at around US$80 for overnight tours, but it is usually worth spending a bit more as we receive unfavourable feedback – cramped conditions and dodgy food – about some of these trips.

★ **Asia Outdoors**   CLIMBING
(☑ 0225-368 8450; www.asiaoutdoors.com.vn; 229, Đ 1/4 Street, Cat Ba Town; half-/full-day climbing US$44/59; ⊙ 8am-9pm) Climbing is Asia Outdoors' real expertise, with fully licensed and certified instructors leading trips; advanced climbers can hire gear here and talk shop. Also on offer are climbing and kayaking packages with an overnight on its boat (from US$90). It has also launched stand-up paddle-boarding (SUP) trips (US$36) and trekking excursions in the national park.

WORTH A TRIP

BAI TU LONG BAY

The area immediately northeast of Halong Bay is part of **Bai Tu Long National Park** (100,000d), which is blessed with spectacular limestone islands every bit as beautiful as its more famous neighbour Halong. Hanoi travel agencies including **Ethnic Travel** (p838) and **Vega Travel** (p838) run trips into the Bai Tu Long area. Or for more flexibility head overland to Cai Rong and visit the outlying islands by boat from there.

★ **Cat Ba Ventures**   BOATING
(☑ 0225-388 8755, 0912 467 016; www.catbaventures.com; 223 Đ 1-4, Cat Ba Town; overnight boat tour per person from US$128; ⊙ 7.30am-8pm) Locally owned and operated company offering boat trips around Lan Ha and Halong Bays, one-day kayaking trips (US$29) and guided hikes in Cat Ba National Park. Excellent service from Mr Tung is reinforced by multiple reader recommendations. These guys are a font of knowledge on everything Cat Ba and a great source of information on onward transport options.

Blue Swimmer   ADVENTURE
(☑ 0915 063 737, 0225-368 8237; www.blueswimmersailing.com; Ben Beo Harbour; overnight sailing trip per person from US$190; ⊙ 8am-8pm) This environmentally conscious outfit was established by Vinh, one of the founders of respected tour operator Handspan Adventure Travel. Superb sailing and kayaking trips, and trekking and mountain-biking excursions (some with overnight homestay accommodation) are offered.

🛏 Sleeping

Most hotels are in Cat Ba Town. Room rates fluctuate greatly between high-season summertime (May to August) and the slower winter months.

🛏 Cat Ba Town

Cat Ba Central Hostel   HOSTEL $
(☑ 0913 311 006; www.catbacentralhostel.com; 240 Đ 1-4; dm incl breakfast US$5-7; ⊛ ❄ ⊚) This friendly hostel is fast becoming the heart of Cat Ba's backpacker action. Clean dorms (one with 28 beds, one with 14 beds and two with six beds, including a female-only room) come with lockers built into beds, and power points.

Hai Long Hotel
HOTEL **$**

(☑0225-388 8635; www.hailongcatba.com; 234 Đ 1-4; r US$14-30; ❋❂🛈) A new-ish-feeling place with 60 rooms, neither huge nor sexy, but entirely capable. Opt for the more expensive rooms, which have more leg room, natural light and bay-front balconies.

Thu Ha
HOTEL **$**

(☑0225-388 8343; Đ 1-4; r US$12-15; ❋❂🛈) This small family-run place has basically furnished, clean rooms, some boasting four beds. Negotiate hard for a front room and wake up to sea views. Communicating in English might be a problem.

Sea Pearl Hotel
HOTEL **$$**

(☑0225-368 8567; www.seapearlcatbahotel. vn; 219 Đ 1-4; r incl breakfast 900,000-1,200,000d; ❋@❂🛈) As indicated in the grand, tidy lobby, the Sea Pearl is a solid choice. Classically styled rooms are comfortable and a decent size, and staff are professional and helpful.

🛏 Around Cat Ba Island

Lan Homestay
GUESTHOUSE **$**

(☑0989 419 098; Viet Hai village; r & bungalows incl breakfast 400,000d; ❋🛈) This pretty compound wasn't quite finished when we stopped by, but if the existing rooms are anything to go by, it will be a clever budget choice. Expect 10 spacious, if somewhat dark, brick bungalows, all with en suite bathrooms, in a quiet corner of Viet Hai village.

Ancient House Homestay
HOMESTAY **$**

(☑0916 645 858, 0915 063 737; www.cat-ba-homestay.com; Ang Soi village; dm incl breakfast US$12, bungalow incl breakfast US$50; 🛈) Located around 3km from Cat Ba Town, down an unmarked alley in the village of Ang Soi, this heritage house was carefully moved here from the outskirts of Hanoi. As impressive and atmospheric as the house and grounds are, the accommodation is basic, with simple beds in a long room, or a couple of bungalows. Lunch and dinner set menus (US$12 per person) are available on request.

Cat Ba Mountain View Guesthouse
BUNGALOW **$$**

(☑0225-368 8641; 452 Đ Ha Sen, Ang Soi village; dm 222,000d, bungalow 700,000-1,000,000d; ❋) One step removed from the hustle of town, this collection of gaily decorated bungalows (both private and dorm options) is backed by a cliff. The spacious, thatch-roofed restau-rant area is a great social spot for hanging out and meeting fellow travellers. It's on the main road, 3km from Cat Ba Town.

🍴 Eating & Drinking

For a cheap feed, head to the food stalls in front of the market. You'll find **bia hoi stalls** (Đ 1-4; ⏰4-10pm) near the entrance to the fishing harbour.

Family Bakery
BAKERY **$**

(196 Đ 1-4; pastries 10,000-15,000d, sandwiches 30,000-40,000d; ⏰7am-4pm) Friendly spot that opens early for almost-passable Western-style pastries. Pop in for a coffee, crème caramel or croissant before the bus-ferry-bus combo back to Hanoi.

Phuong Nhung
VIETNAMESE **$**

(184 Đ 1-4; meals from 45,000d; ⏰7-10am) Bustling breakfast spot that's a popular place for a hearty bowl of *pho bo* (beef noodle soup) – just the thing you need before a day of climbing or kayaking.

Vien Duong
VIETNAMESE **$$**

(12 Đ Nui Ngoc; meals from 120,000d; ⏰11am-11pm) Justifiably one of the most popular of the seafood spots lining Đ Nui Ngoc, and often heaving with Vietnamese tourists diving into local crab, squid and steaming seafood hotpots. Definitely not the place to come if you're looking for a quiet night.

Quang Anh
SEAFOOD **$$**

(☑0255-388 8485; Ben Beo Pier; meals from 200,000d) At this 'floating' fish-farm-meets-restaurant at Ben Beo Pier, select your seafood from the pen and it will be grilled, fried or steamed in no time. Prices go by weight and type of seafood; you can eat your fill of a selection of fish for around 200,000d per person.

Oasis Bar
BAR

(Đ 1-4; ⏰noon-11pm; 🛈) A free-use pool table, occasional karaoke, smiley staff and a location slap in the centre of the seafront strip make Oasis a popular spot to plonk yourself down for a beer or two.

ℹ Information

For tourist information, the best impartial advice is at Asia Outdoors (p843). Cat Ba Ventures (p843) is also very helpful. Both companies have websites with local information.

ℹ Getting There & Away

Cat Ba Island is 45km east of Haiphong and 50km south of Halong City. Various boat and bus combinations make the journey from Hanoi, or there are ferries from Haiphong and Halong City.

FROM HANOI

Departing from Hanoi's Nuoc Ngam bus station, **Hoang Long** ([phone] 0225-387 7224; http://hoanglongasia.com; Đ 1-4, Cat Ba Town; [hours] 7.30am-6pm) operates an efficient bus-boat-bus combo to Cat Ba Town. A bus takes you to Haiphong, followed by a minibus to nearby Dinh Vu port, then a 40-minute ferry to Cai Vieng Harbour (also known as Phu Long) on Cat Ba Island. From there, another minibus whisks passengers to Cat Ba Town (220,000d, four hours).

Buses depart Hanoi at 7.30am and 11.30am, and return from Cat Ba Town at 9.30am, 1.30pm and 3.30pm; there are additional departures during the high season, from May to August.

If you're travelling independently from Hanoi, this is the most hassle-free way.

🛈 Getting Around

Bicycle and motorbike hire is available from most Cat Ba hotels (both around US$5 per day). If you're heading out to the beaches or national park, pay the parking fee for security.

Ba Be National Park

[phone] 0209

Boasting mountains high, rivers deep, and waterfalls, lakes and caves, **Ba Be National Park** ([phone] 0281-389 4721; 46,000d; [hours] 5am-9pm) is an incredibly scenic spot. The region is surrounded by steep peaks (up to 1554m) while the park contains tropical rainforest with more than 550 plant species. Wildlife in the forest includes bears, monkeys, bats and lots of butterflies. Surrounding the park are Tay minority villages.

Ba Be (Three Bays) is in fact three linked lakes, with a total length of 8km and a width of about 400m. The Nang River is navigable for 23km between a point 4km above Cho Ra and the **Dau Dang Waterfall** (Thac Dau Dang), which is a series of spectacular cascades between sheer walls of rock. River cave **Puong Cave** (Hang Puong) is about 30m high and 300m long.

Park staff can organise **tours**, starting at about US$30 per day for solo travellers, less for a group. Boat trips (650,000d per boat) take around seven hours to take in most sights. **Mr Sinh** ([phone] 0653 224 214) is a keen, English-speaking boat conductor. There's also opportunities for kayaking, cycling and trekking. Tay-owned **Ba Be Tourism Centre** ([phone] 0209-389 4721; www.babenationalpark.com.vn; Bo Lu village) arranges homestays, boat trips,

trekking, cycling and kayaking (or a combo of all four) for around US$45 per day.

Homestays in Pac Ngoi village are very popular with travellers; there's also accommodation near the national park entrance. Recommended in Pac Ngoi is **Hoa Son Guesthouse** ([phone] 0947 150 154; Pac Ngoi village; per person 70,000d) where excellent home-cooked meals (50,000d to 120,000d) can include fresh fish from the lake. **Mr Linh's Homestay** ([phone] 0989 587 400, 0209-389 4894; www.mrlinhhomestay.com; Coc Toc village; dm incl breakfast US$8, r with shared bathroom incl breakfast US$22-42; [icons]) in Coc Toc village is a step up from most and has kayaks for hire.

🛈 Getting There & Away

Ba Be National Park is 240km from Hanoi and 18km from Cho Ra. Most travellers come on pre-arranged tours from Hanoi. For independent travel from Hanoi, the most direct route to Ba Be's lakeside homestay villages is the local bus to Cho Don, via Thai Nguyen, run by Thuong Nga bus company. It leaves My Dinh (p840) bus station gate 33 at 10am (130,000d, four hours). At Cho Don, you hop on a connecting minibus (run by the same company) to Pac Ngoi, Bo Lu and Coc Toc (40,000d)

Mai Chau

[phone] 0218 / POP 12,000

In an idyllic valley, Mai Chau is surrounded by lush paddy fields and the rural soundtrack is defined by gurgling irrigation streams and birdsong.

Dozens of local families have signed up to a highly successful homestay initiative, and for visitors the chance to sleep in a traditional stilt house is a real appeal – though note that the villages are on the tour-group agenda.

Mai Chau is also an extremely popular weekend getaway for locals from Hanoi; try to come midweek if possible.

💿 Sights & Activities

You can walk or cycle past rice fields and trek to minority villages; a local guide costs about US$10. Many travel agencies in Hanoi run inexpensive trips to Mai Chau.

Ask around in Mai Chau about longer treks of three to seven days. Other options include rock climbing, kayaking and mountain-biking excursions; enquire at **Asia Outdoors** ([phone] 0218-386 8859; www.asiaoutdoors.com.vn; Mai Chau Lodge; [hours] 8am-8pm).

🛏 Sleeping & Eating

Most visitors stay in **Thai stilt houses** (Mai Chau; per person 100,000-250,000d) in the villages of Lac or Pom Coong. All homestays have electricity, running water, hot showers, mosquito nets and roll-up mattresses. **Mai Chau Sunrise Village** (☑0914 788 884; www.maichausunrisevillage.com; Lac village; bungalow US$35-65; 🛜) in Lac village offers private bungalows with bamboo furniture and free bikes. Grab a bungalow at the back to wake up to verdant rice-field views.

Most people eat where they stay; note that some families charge up to 200,000d for dinner.

❶ Getting There & Away

Direct buses to Mai Chau (90,000d, 3¾ hours) leave Hanoi's My Dinh Bus Station (p840) at 6am, 8.30am and 11am. If you want to stay in Lac or Pom Coong villages, just ask the bus driver to drop you off there. You'll be dropped off at the crossroads, just a short stroll from both villages.

To Hanoi, buses leave from Mai Chau's **bus station** (Hwy 15), 2km south of town, at 7.15am, 8am, 8.45am, 12.30pm and 1pm. Homestay owners can book these buses for you and arrange for you to be picked up from the village.

Lao Cai

☑0214 / POP 98,360

One of the gateways to the north, Lao Cai lies at the end of the train line, 3km from the Chinese border. The town has no sights but is a major hub for travellers journeying between Hanoi, Sapa and the Chinese city of Kunming. There are hotels and ATMs next to the train station.

❶ Getting There & Away

Lao Cai's **inter-provincial bus station** (off Hwy 4E; ⊙24hr) is a whopping 10km southeast of town; a taxi there will cost about 150,000d.

Yellow-and-red minibuses and larger buses for Sapa (30,000d, 30 minutes) leave at least hourly between 5.10am and 6pm from the car park in front of Lao Cai train station. Touts will try to push you to their private minibuses for an inflated 100,000d. Minibuses to Bac Ha (60,000d, 2½ hours) leave from the **provincial bus station** (Pha Dinh Phung), located just west of the train station; there are frequent departures from 4.45am to 5.30pm.

Bac Ha

☑0214 / POP 7400

An unhurried and friendly town, Bac Ha makes a relaxed base to explore the northern highlands and hill-tribe villages. The climate here is also noticeably warmer than in Sapa.

Bac Ha has a certain charm, though its stock of traditional old adobe houses is dwindling and being replaced by concrete structures. Wood smoke fills the morning air and chickens and pigs poke around the back lanes. For six days a week Bac Ha slumbers, but its lanes fill up to choking point each Sunday when tourists and Flower Hmong flood in for the weekly market.

◉ Sights & Activities

Bac Ha's **Sunday market** (off Đ Tran Bac; ⊙sunrise-2pm Sun) is a riot of colour and commerce, with an entire area devoted to *ruoc* (corn hooch).

While you're here, check out the outlandish **Vua Meo** ('Cat King' House; ĐT 153; 20,000d; ⊙7.30-11.30am & 1.30-5pm), a palace that has been built in a kind of bizarre 'oriental baroque' architectural style.

Beyond town lie several interesting markets; tour operators in Bac Ha can arrange day trips to surrounding markets in villages including **Co Ly** (Tuesday), **Sin Cheng** (Wednesday), and **Lung Phin** (Sunday).

Contact **Green Sepa Tour** (☑0912 005 952; www.bachatourist.com; Đ Tran Bac; ⊙6am-10pm), operated by English-speaking Mr Nghe, for tours.

BUSES FROM LAO CAI

DESTINATION	COST (D)	DURATION (HR)	FREQUENCY
Dien Bien Phu	200,000-250,000	8	6.45am, 5pm, 5.30pm & 10pm
Ha Giang	130,000	5-6	6am & 11.30am
Halong City (Bai Chay)	360,000	12	7.15pm, 6pm & 8.15pm
Hanoi	230,000	10	frequent 5am-12.30am

Sleeping & Eating

Room rates increase on weekends.

Ngan Nga Bac Ha Hotel   HOTEL $
(📞0214-880 286; www.nganngabachahotel.com; 117 P Ngoc Uyen; r incl breakfast US$18-27; ❋ 🛜) Rooms here are a solid budget deal; they are a decent size and are decked out with a few homey touches that give them some character. Bag a front room for a balcony.

Saturday Hotel   HOTEL $
(📞0868 138 290; 126 P Ngoc Uyen; dm 100,000d, r 400,000-500,000; ❋ 🛜) Right in the middle of all the action in Bac Ha is this tidy, pleasant place. Rooms are clean and inviting, if plain, while the dorms, little more than mattresses separated by curtains, feel somewhat clinical.

Thanh Cong   VIETNAMESE $$
(P Ngoc Uyen; meals from 150,000d; ⊙7am-8pm) A favourite dish in northern Vietnam is grilled duck. Come to this simple restaurant (look for the rotisserie out the front) for a half (100,000d) or a full (200,000d) bird and a beer, and feel like a local. A broad menu of other dishes is also available.

ℹ Information

Located at Vua Meo, the English-speaking staff at the local **tourist information center** (ĐT 153; ⊙7.30-11.30am & 1.30-5pm) can offer advice on trekking, tours and buses, although one gets the impression that there's a tendency to steer visitors towards businesses run by friends and family.

ℹ Getting There & Away

Tours to Bac Ha from Sapa cost from around US$20 per person; on the way back you can bail out in Lao Cai and catch the night train to Hanoi.

If you're heading east to Ha Giang, there are two options – we recommend checking the latest information with either Mr Dong at Ngan Nga Bac Ha Hotel or Mr Nighe at Green Sapa Tour (p846) as Ha Giang schedules change regularly.

A *xe om*/taxi to Lao Cai costs US$25/70, or to Sapa US$30/80.

> **ℹ GETTING TO CHINA: LAO CAI TO KUNMING**
>
> **Getting to the border** The Lao Cai–Hekou crossing connects northern Vietnam with Yunnan Province in China. The border is about 3km from the Lao Cai train station; *xe om* charge 25,000d.
>
> **At the border** The border crossing is open from 7am to 10pm. Visas must be arranged in advance. Note that China is one hour ahead of Vietnam.
>
> **Moving on** The new Hekou bus station is around 6km from the border post. There are regular departures to Kunming, including sleeper buses which leave at 7.20pm and 7.30pm, getting into Kunming at around 7am. There are also four daily trains.

Sapa
📞0214 / POP 52,899 / ELEV 1650M

Established as a hill station by the French in 1922, Sapa today is the tourism centre of the northwest.

Sapa is oriented to make the most of the spectacular views emerging on clear days; it overlooks a plunging valley, with mountains towering above on all sides. Views are often subdued by thick mist rolling across the peaks, but even when it's cloudy, local hill-tribe people fill the town with colour.

If you were expecting a quaint alpine town, recalibrate your expectations. Modern tourism development has mushroomed haphazardly. Thanks to rarely enforced building-height restrictions, Sapa's skyline is continually thrusting upwards.

But you're not here to hang out in town. This is northern Vietnam's premier trekking base, from where hikers launch themselves into a surrounding countryside of cascading rice terraces and tiny hill-tribe villages that seem a world apart. Once you've stepped out into the lush fields, you'll understand the Sapa area's real charm.

BUSES FROM BAC HA

DESTINATION	COST (D)	DURATION (HR)	FREQUENCY
Haiphong	300,000	9	8am & 4.30pm
Hanoi	300,000	8	12.30pm & 8.30pm
Lao Cai	60,000	2	frequent 7am-2pm

◎ Sights & Activities

Surrounding Sapa are the Hoang Lien Mountains, including **Fansipan**, which at 3143m is Vietnam's highest peak. The trek from Sapa to the summit and back can take several days, although a new cable car to the summit and mountain-top shopping have changed the experience forever.

Some of the better-known sights around Sapa include the epic **Tram Ton Pass**; the pretty **Thac Bac** (Silver Falls); and **Cau May** (Cloud Bridge), which spans the Muong Hoa River. Treks can be arranged at many guesthouses and tour operators. **Sapa O'Chau** (☑0214-377 1166; www.sapaochau.org; 8 Đ Thac Bac; ☺6.30am-6.30pm) 🖉 is one excellent outfit which benefits Hmong children, and Hmong-owned **Sapa Sisters** (☑0214-773 388; www.sapasisters.com; Sapa Graceful Hotel, 9 Đ Phan Si; ☺7am-5pm) is another good operator.

As well as hiking tours, also on offer are culturally focused trips including visits to the Hmong village of **Sin Chai**, staying overnight in the village to learn about textiles or music. Other popular communities to visit include the Giay village of **Ta Van** and the Hmong village of **Matra**.

★ Sapa Museum
MUSEUM
(103 P Cau May; ☺7.30-11.30am & 1.30-5pm) **FREE** Excellent showcase of the history and ethnology of the Sapa area, including the colonial times of the French. Dusty exhibitions demonstrate the differences between the various ethnic minority people of the area, so it's definitely worth a quick visit when you first arrive in town, even if some descriptions are too faded to read. Located above a handicrafts shop behind the Tourist Information Center (p850).

Sapa Market
MARKET
(Đ Ngu Chi Son; ☺6am-2pm) Unfortunately turfed out of central Sapa, and now in a purpose-built modern building near the bus station, Sapa Market is still a hive of colourful activity outside, with fresh produce, a butcher's section not for the squeamish and hill-tribe people from surrounding villages heading here most days to sell handicrafts. Saturday is the busiest day.

🛏 Sleeping

Go Sapa Hostel
HOSTEL $
(☑0214-871 198; www.gosapahostel.com; 25 Đ Thac Bac; dm 110,000-130,000đ, r 400,000đ; @☎) Up the hill from central Sapa, this setup has a multitude of eight-bed dorms (with lockers) set around a communal courtyard. More expensive dorm options come with private bathroom and some have tiny balconies. There are free computers and bike hire.

Luong Thuy Family Guesthouse
GUESTHOUSE $
(☑0214-872 310; www.familysapa.com; 28 Đ Muong Hoa; dm US$5, r US$15-20; ❄@☎) This friendly guesthouse has a decent, though dark, dorm and snug private rooms. Motorcycles and bikes can be hired, trekking and transport arranged, and there are valley views from front balconies.

Sapa Auberge
HOTEL $
(☑0214-387 1243; www.sapaauberge.com; 31 P Cau May; r incl breakfast US$21; ☎) A bright yellow villa boasting 21 comfy, homey rooms. Unlike most places in Sapa, there's not much in the way of views, but it's just off the main strip, so you're compensated with peace and quiet.

★ Sapa Dragon Hotel
HOTEL $$
(☑0214-871 363; www.sapadragonhotel.com; 1a Đ Thac Bac; r incl breakfast US$55-105; ❄☎) This new kid in town offers 20 handsome, spacious rooms with thoughtful touches such as laptops and locally influenced design, as well as friendly, but not overbearing, service. One of the wiser options if you want to stay in Sapa proper.

🍴 Eating & Drinking

For eating on a budget, humble Vietnamese restaurants huddle on Đ Tue Tinh, and the stalls south of the church can't be beaten for *bun cha* (barbecued pork).

Co Lich
VIETNAMESE $
(Đ Phan Si; meals from 70,000đ; ☺noon-11pm) This rowdy place brings all the local faves – grilled skewers, roast piglet, dried beef, hotpot – together in one venue. Pull up a pew at one of the simple tables and tuck in.

Sapa O'Chau
CAFE $
(www.sapaochau.org; 8 Đ Thac Bac; snacks from 40,000đ; ☺6.30am-6.30pm; ☎) Don't miss warming up with a cup of ginger tea sweetened with Sapa mountain honey at this simple cafe attached to the Sapa O'Chau tour company. Also does good breakfasts and a few simple snacks and light meals.

★ Hill Station Signature Restaurant
VIETNAMESE $$
(www.thehillstation.com; 37 Đ Phan Si; meals from 150,000đ; ☺7am-11pm; ❄☎🖉) A showcase of

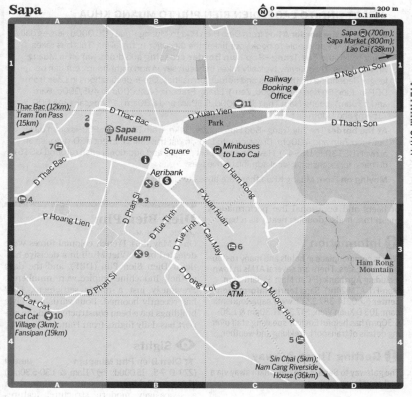

Sapa

Hmong cuisine with cool Zen decor and superb views. Dishes include flash-cooked pork with lime, ash-baked trout in banana leaves, and traditional Hmong-style black pudding. Tasting sets of local rice and corn wine are also of interest to curious travelling foodies. Don't miss trying the delicate rainbow-trout rice-paper rolls; think of them as 'Sapa sushi'.

Cafe in the Clouds   BEER GARDEN
(☑0214-377 1011; 60 Đ Phan Si; ⊙6am-11pm; ☜) The large terrace of this bar is a great corner of Sapa (and the planet) to pause and ponder the valley or, often, the wandering mist at eye level. The crisp air must come with lofty prices? Actually drinks are priced very reasonably, plus wi-fi is zippy for logging in to electronic clouds. The food isn't bad either.

Cong Ca Phe   CAFE
(Đ Xuan Vien; ⊙7am-11pm; ☜) Sapa is home to a branch of everybody's favourite Communist/retro-themed coffee shop. A selection

Sapa

◎ Top Sights
1 Sapa Museum..B2

✪ Activities, Courses & Tours
2 Sapa O'Chau...A2
3 Sapa Sisters..B2

⊜ Sleeping
4 Go Sapa Hostel...A2
5 Luong Thuy Family Guesthouse........C4
6 Sapa Auberge...C3
7 Sapa Dragon Hotel....................................A2

✗ Eating
8 Co Lich...B2
9 Hill Station Signature Restaurant......B3
Sapa O'Chau.......................................(see 2)

⊜ Drinking & Nightlife
10 Cafe in the Clouds...................................A4
11 Cong Ca Phe...C1

ℹ GETTING TO LAOS: DIEN BIEN PHU TO MUANG KHUA

Getting to the border A bus from Dien Bien Phu to Muang Khua (115,000đ) leaves daily at 5.30am. It's advisable to book your ticket the day prior to travelling. This bus takes you through the **Tay Trang–Sop Hun border crossing** and drops you off in Muang Khua in Laos. The journey typically takes between seven and eight hours, but can be longer depending on the roads and border formalities. Other destinations in Laos from DBP include Bo Keo (560,000đ, 7am), Luang Prabang (402,000đ to 495,000đ, 6am and 7.30am), Luang Nam Tha (350,000đ, 6.30am and 8.30am), Phongsali (345,000, 7.15am) and Udomxai (230,000đ, 6am).

At the border The Tay Trang–Sop Hun border, 34km from Dien Bien Phu, is open daily between 7am and 4.30pm. Crossing into Laos, most travellers can get a 30-day visa on arrival (US$30 to US$42). Have two passport photos and additional cash (around US$5) on hand for occasional local administrative fees.

Moving on From Muang Khua there are buses to Udomxai.

of beers and occasional live performances mean that it also doubles neatly as a bar.

ℹ Information

Wi-fi is commonplace in hotels and many restaurants and cafes. There are several ATMs in town including **Agribank** (P Cau May; ⊗8am-3pm Mon-Fri, ATM 24hr). Sapa **tourist information center** (☑0214-387 3239; www.sapa-tourism. com; 103 Đ Xuan Vien; ⊗7.30-11.30am & 1.30-5.30pm) has helpful English-speaking staff offering details of transport, trekking and weather.

ℹ Getting There & Away

The gateway to Sapa is Lao Cai, 38km away via a well-maintained highway.

BUS

Sapa's **bus station** (Đ Luong Dinh Cua) is northeast of the town centre, near the market. To Hanoi there are frequent departures between 7am and 10.30pm (200,000đ to 250,000đ, 10 hours); to Mong Cai, there's a daily bus at 4pm (450,000đ).

There is no direct service to Bac Ha, Dien Bien Phu or Lai Chau. You need to take a minibus to Lao Cai and change there.

Minibuses (Đ Ham Rong) and buses to Lao Cai (30,000đ, 30 minutes) leave every 30 minutes between 6am and 6pm, from a bus stop near Sapa Church. Look for yellow-and-red buses with price lists in the window.

TRAIN

There's no direct train line to Sapa, but there are regular services between Hanoi and Lao Cai. Most hotels and travel agencies can book train tickets back to Hanoi.

You can book tickets at the **Railway Booking Office** (☑0214-387 1480; P Cau May; ⊗7.30-11am & 1.30-4pm) on P Cau May, which charges a small commission.

Dien Bien Phu

☑0215 / POP 46,362

On 7 May 1954 French colonial forces were defeated by the Viet Minh in a decisive battle at Dien Bien Phu (DBP), and the days of their Indochine empire were numbered. Previously just a minor settlement, DBP has recently boomed. Boulevards and civic buildings have been constructed and the airport has daily flights from Hanoi.

◉ Sights

★**Dien Bien Phu Museum**   MUSEUM
(279 Đ 7-5; 15,000đ; ⊗7-11am & 1.30-5.30pm) This well-laid-out museum, contained in a space-agey modern structure, features an eclectic collection that commemorates the 1954 battle. Alongside weaponry and guns, there's a bath-tub that belonged to the French commander Colonel de Castries, a bicycle capable of carrying 330kg of ordnance, and photographs and documents, some with English translations.

Bunker of Colonel de Castries   MONUMENT
(off P Nguyen Huu Tho; 15,000đ; ⊗7-11am & 1.30-6pm) West of the Ron River, the command bunker of Colonel Christian de Castries has been recreated. A few discarded tanks linger nearby, and you might see Vietnamese tourists mounting the bunker and waving the Vietnamese flag, re-enacting an iconic photograph taken at the battle's conclusion.

★**A1 Hill**   MONUMENT
(Đ 7-5; 15,000đ; ⊗7-11am & 1.30-5pm) This vantage point was crucial in the battle of Dien Bien Phu. There are tanks and a monument to Viet Minh casualties on this former French position, known to the French as Eli-

ane and to the Vietnamese as A1 Hill. The elaborate trenches at the heart of the French defences have also been re-created. Little background information is given on-site.

🛏 Sleeping & Eating

Nam Ron Hotel
HOTEL $

(☎ 0946 251 967; Đ Trang Dang Ninh; r 400,000-450,000d; ❊ 🛜) At the edge of the Ron River is this characterless but tidy place. By Vietnamese standards, the rooms feel tight, but are functional and comfortable, and come decked out with retro furniture.

★ Ruby Hotel
HOTEL $$

(☎ 0913 655 793; www.rubyhoteldienbien.com; off Đ Nguyen Chi Thanh; r incl breakfast 560,000-900,000d; ❊ 🛜) The best deal in Dien Bien Phu is this friendly hotel, down a signposted alleyway. The 31 rooms are comfortably fitted out with good beds, flat-screen TVs and bathrooms featuring rain shower heads. If you're travelling solo, treat yourself to a double room as the singles are quite small.

Pho Stalls
VIETNAMESE $

(P Thanh Binh; meals from 40,000d; ⊘ 8am-10pm) There's good-value eating at these inexpensive *pho* stalls and simple restaurants opposite the bus station; some serve delicious fresh sugar-cane juice.

Bia Hoi Restaurants
VIETNAMESE $

(Đ Hoang Van Thai; meals from 30,000d; ⊘ noon-10pm) You're probably only in town for a night, so meet the locals at the *bia hoi* gardens along Đ Hoang Van Thai. There's decent and cheap grilled food as well, if you're tired of rice and noodles.

ℹ Information

DBP has many ATMs including **Agribank** (Đ 7-5; ⊘ 8am-3pm Mon-Fri, to 11.30am Sat, ATM 24hr).

ℹ Getting There & Away

AIR

Dien Bien Phu Airport is 1.5 km north of the town centre along the road to Muong Lay. **Vasco**

Airlines (☎ 0215-382 4948; www.vasco.com.vn; Dien Bien Phu Airport; ⊘ 7.30-11.30am & 1.30-5pm) operates two flights daily to/from Hanoi (from 1,113,000d, one hour).

BUS

DBP's bus station is at the corner of Đ Tran Dang Ninh and Hwy 12.

Ha Giang Province

POP 750,000

Ha Giang is the final frontier in northern Vietnam, an amazing landscape of limestone pinnacles and granite outcrops. The far north of the province has some of the most spectacular scenery in the country – if not the region – and the trip between Yen Minh and Dong Van, and then across the Mai Pi Leng Pass to Meo Vac, is quite mindblowing. Ha Giang should be one of the most popular destinations in this region, but its distance from just about everywhere else keeps visitor numbers at a low level.

Travel permits (US$10) are required to travel on the road north from Tam Son to Dong Van and Meo Vac, but these are simply paid directly with whichever hotel you choose to overnight in along the way.

👁 Sights

Dong Van is the Ha Giang region's most popular overnight stop and, not coincidentally, is home to some solid accommodation and food. But the real reason to come is for the **Sunday market** (Đ Vao Cho; ⊘ 6am-2pm Sun), one of the region's biggest and most colourful. The town is also a good base for day treks around nearby minority villages and nearby sights such as the **Lung Cu** (25,000d; ⊘ 8am-5pm) flag tower.

Meo Vac is a small but charming district capital hemmed in by steep karst mountains and, like many towns in the northwest, it is steadily being settled by Vietnamese from elsewhere. The journey here along the spectacular Mai Pi Leng Pass, which winds for 22km from Dong Van, is the main attraction.

BUSES FROM DIEN BIEN PHU

DESTINATION	COST (D)	DURATION (HR)	FREQUENCY
Hanoi	255,000-570,000	11½	frequent 4.30am-9.15pm
Muang Khua (Laos)	115,000	7-8	5.30am
Muong Lay	60,000	3-4	2.30pm, 3pm & 4pm
Muong Te	130,000	6	6 departures 5-8.15am
Son La	97,000-100,000	4	9 departures 4.30am-2pm

ℹ GETTING TO CHINA: LANG SON TO NANNING

Getting to the border The Friendship Pass at the **Dong Dang–Pingxiang border crossing** is the most popular crossing in the far north. The border post itself is at Huu Nghi Quan (Friendship Pass), 3km north of Dong Dang town. From Lang Son, a train heads to Dong Dang daily at 11.15am (15,000d, 30 minutes), or you can count on about 160,000d for a taxi and 70,000d for a *xe om* directly to the border.

At the border The border is open from 7am to 8pm daily Vietnam time. Note that China is one hour ahead of Vietnam. To cross 500m to the Chinese side you'll need to catch one of the electric cars (12,000d). You'll also need a pre-arranged visa for China.

Moving on On the Chinese side, it's a 20-minute drive to Pingxiang by bus or shared taxi. Pingxiang is connected by train and bus to Nanning (three hours).

The road has been cut into the side of a cliff with a view of rippling hills tumbling down to the distant waters of the Nho Que River far below. At the top of the pass is a lookout point where you can stop to take in the scenery.

🛏 Sleeping

⭐ **Lam Tung Hotel**   HOTEL $
(📱0219-385 6789; Đ Vao Cho; r 350,000-450,000d; ❋📶) Just off Dong Van's main road, and overlooking the plaza that hosts the Sunday market, the Lam Tung has surprisingly smart modern rooms with soft mattresses, and friendly English-speaking staff. It has motorbikes for hire for 150,000d to 200,000d per day.

⭐ **Auberge de Meo Vac**   GUESTHOUSE $$
(📱0219-387 1686; aubergemeovac@gmail.com; dm/r with shared bathroom 330,000/1,320,000d; 📶) This is a unique stay in a lovingly restored ethnic-minority house dating from the 19th century, with to clay walls, lots of natural timber and a spacious inner courtyard. Breakfast (US$5) and dinner (US$12) are available. It's located northeast of the town centre, just east of Hwy 4C.

ℹ Getting There & Around

The province is best managed with a car and driver or by motorbike. If you're going to splurge on private transport once during your trip, this is the time to do it.

Public transport is improving and it's relatively simple to journey by bus from Ha Giang city to Dong Van, but at the time of writing there was still no public transport from Dong Van onward to Meo Vac. However, there are buses, along the low road, between Meo Vac and Ha Giang city, so by hiring a *xe om* or taxi in Dong Van for the stretch to Meo Vac, it is entirely possible to do a loop back to Ha Giang city. Heading east from Meo Vac to Cao Bang continues to be a headache, as there is no public transport from Meo Vac to Bao Lac.

NORTH CENTRAL VIETNAM

The extraordinary cave systems of the Phong Nha-Ke Bang National Park and the karst scenery around Ninh Binh make north central Vietnam an essential destination for intrepid visitors. Beyond the caves of Phong Nha, it's also very easy to spend a few days mountain biking around the laidback Bong Lai valley, or kicking back in some of the region's more interesting bars and cafes.

Factor in wildlife watching and trekking opportunities in Cuc Phuong National Park and it's definitely the right decision not to rush through this region while heading north or south.

Ninh Binh

📱 0229 / POP 160,000

The city of Ninh Binh isn't a destination in itself, but it's a good base for exploring some quintessentially Vietnamese karst scenery and bucolic countryside (including Tam Coc and Cuc Phuong National Park). However, many attractions are heavily commercialised.

👁 Sights

Trang An   CAVE
(🕑7.30am-4pm) Rowboats bob along the Sao Khe River through limestone caves. It's a relaxing trip, but many caves have also been enlarged to accommodate boats. Boat trips (150,000d per person, or 800,000d for your own boat) take two hours, and there are two possible routes, both visiting caves and temples. Bring a hat and sunscreen as the boats lack shade. Trang An is 7km northwest of Ninh Binh. You'll pass it on the way to the Chua Bai Dinh.

Chua Bai Dinh
BUDDHIST SITE

(⊙7am-5.45pm) **FREE** Chua Bai Dinh is a bombastic Buddhist complex, built on a vast scale, that rises up a hillside near Ninh Binh. Construction was completed in 2014, and it's now a huge attraction for Vietnamese tourists. The entrance leads to cloistered walkways past 500 stone *arhats* (enlightened Buddhists) lining the route to the main triple-roofed Phap Chu Pagoda. This contains a 10m, 100-tonne bronze Buddha, flanked by two more gilded Buddha figures.

🛏 Sleeping & Eating

Restaurant choices are limited, try the local speciality, *de* (goat meat).

Go Ninh Binh Hostel
HOSTEL $

(📞0229-387 1186; www.goninhbinhhostel.com; Đ Ngo Gia Tu; dm US$5, d US$20-24; ❋@🛜) Recently opened in the city's former railway station, Go Ninh Binh has colourful dorms, doubles with en suite bathrooms, and plenty of shared areas including hammocks and a foosball table. A library, bar, pool table and darts board are also all popular, and the team at reception has plenty of ideas for exploring the broader Ninh Binh area.

Trung Tuyet
VIETNAMESE $

(14 Đ Hoang Hoa Tham; meals 40,000-90,000d; ⊙8.30am-9.30pm; 🖊) Expect filling portions, options for vegetarians, and a warm welcome from the host family at this busy little place that's popular with travellers. The owners will even drop you off at the nearby train station if you're kicking on after your meal.

Bia Hoi
BAR

For drinking *bia hoi* (draught beer), try the riverside places near the local brewery.

👉 Tours

Truong Nguyen
TOURS

(📞0915 666 211, 0165 348 8778; www.ninhbinhtour.vn) Freelance guide Truong offers escorted motorbike trips around Ninh Binh using country back roads, and also trekking in Pu Luong Nature Reserve, a forested area across two mountain ridges, where you can stay in Thai and Hmong homestays. He also runs trips to the northern Ha Giang province, and operates an excellent new **hotel** (📞0229-388 3588; www.friendlyhome.vn; 5 60/45 Đ Hai Thuong Lang On; s US$16, d US$22-35, f $42; ❋@🛜) in Ninh Binh City.

Chookie's Tours
OUTDOORS

(📞0948 346 026; www.facebook.com/chookiesninhbinh; 17 Đ Luong Van Tuy; per person 300,000-1,210,000d; ⊙9am-10pm) Regular departures exploring the area's attractions by motorbike, tours to Trang An grottoes, and a nature discovery tour taking in Van Long Nature Reserve and the Cuc Phuong National Park.

ℹ Getting There & Away

The city is connected by very regular buses from Giap Bat bus station in Hanoi (from 75,000d, 2½ hours). Ninh Binh is a scheduled stop for both opentour buses and some trains travelling between Hanoi and Ho Chi Minh City (HCMC).

Tam Coc

Famed for huge limestone rock formations that loom over rice paddies, this famous, though touristy, site is 9km southwest of Ninh Binh. **Tam Coc Boat Trips** (boat base fare 150,000d, plus adult/child 120,000/60,000d; ⊙7am-3.30pm) take in some breathtaking scenery, passing through karst caves on the beautiful two-hour tour. Boats seat two passengers (and have no shade). Prepare yourself for pushy vendors.

The surrounding karst limestone landscapes are also excellent for cycling and most accommodation has bikes on offer.

🛏 Sleeping & Eating

The largely rural area around Tam Coc has several good accommodation options, and it is a good and quieter alternative to staying in Ninh Binh city.

Nguyen Shack
BUNGALOW $$

(📞0229-361 8678; www.nguyenshack.com; near Mua Cave, Hoa Lu district; bungalows US$22-55; 🛜) With a riverside setting around 5km from Tam Coc, Nguyen Shack's easygoing, lazy-days thatched bungalows are the perfect antidote to the bustle of Hanoi. Lie in a hammock, drop a fishing rod off your rustic terrace, or grab a bicycle and go exploring. There's an on-site restaurant and bar, too.

Chookies Beer Garden
BEER GARDEN

(www.facebook.com/pg/chookiesninhbinh; Tam Coc–Bich Dong Rd; ⊙9am-10pm) The comfy deckchairs and rustic shared tables at Chookies Beer Garden are the place to be after a day boating or mountain biking around the Tam Coc and Trang An areas. As well as

Scenes of Vietnam

Towering mountains define the north. Stunning beaches and tropical islands spoil travellers along the country's coast. And French colonial charm and iconic skyscrapers are highlights in the buzzing big cities.

EFIRED/SHUTTERSTOCK ©

DINO GEROMELLA/SHUTTERSTOCK ©

1. Sao Beach (p907)
Just a few kilometres from An Thoi, Sao Beach has picture-pefect white sand and crystal clear waters

2. Tam Coc (p853)
Boat trips at Tam Coc take in breathtaking scenery, with limestone rock formations looming over rice paddies.

3. Notre Dame Cathedral (p891)
The Notre Dame Cathedral in Ho Chi Minh City features 40m-high, neo-Romanesque square towers.

4. Hanoi (p823)
Hawkers are a common sight on Hanoi's streets..

ANDREW V MARCUS/SHUTTERSTOCK ©

frosty beers, there's also a small menu of burgers, salads and falafel wraps.

❶ Getting There & Away

Tam Coc is 9km southwest of Ninh Binh. Hotels in Ninh Binh run tours, or make your own way by bicycle or motorbike (your hotel can advise on beautiful back roads). Hanoi tour operators offer day trips from around US$25.

Cuc Phuong National Park

📞 030 / ELEV 150-656M

This impressive national park (📞 030-384 8006; www.cucphuongtourism.com; adult/child 40,000/20,000d) was declared the nation's first national park in 1963 and is home to 307 bird, 133 mammal and 122 reptile species, plus more than 2000 different plants. However, due to illegal poaching, little wildlife is encountered. Trekking opportunities are good, including a hike (8km return) to an enormous 1000-year-old tree (*Tetrameles nudiflora*, for botany geeks), and to a Muong village, where you can also go rafting. A guide is mandatory for longer treks.

The Endangered Primate Rescue Center (📞 0229-384 8002; www.eprc.asia; 30,000d; ⏱ 9-11.30am & 1.30-4pm) is home to around 150 rare primates bred in captivity or confiscated from illegal traders. These gibbons, langurs and lorises are rehabilitated, studied and, whenever possible, released into semiwild protected areas. There's also a Turtle Conservation Center (📞 030-384 8090; www.asianturtleprogram.org; 30,000d; ⏱ 9-11am & 2-4.45pm). You'll find excellent information displays, and there are incubation and hatchling viewing areas. The centre successfully breeds and releases turtles of 11 different species.

During the rainy season (July to September) leeches are common in Cuc Phuong. There are several accommodation areas inside the park. At the park headquarters (s US$16-35, d US$27-50, stilt house US$14, bungalow US$23) you'll find standard rooms redecorated 'deluxe' rooms, a stilt house and a private bungalow. There's a simple restaurant here too.

❶ Getting There & Away

Cuc Phuong National Park is 45km west of Ninh Binh and is best visited with your own wheels. Tour companies based in Ninh Binh and Hanoi can arrange transport, activities and accommodation.

Phong Nha-Ke Bang National Park

📞 0232

Designated a Unesco World Heritage Site in 2003, the remarkable Phong Nha-Ke Bang National Park (📞 052-367 7021; http://phongnhakebang.vn/en) 🎟 FREE contains the oldest karst mountains in Asia, formed approximately 400 million years ago. Riddled with hundreds of cave systems – many of extraordinary scale and length – and spectacular underground rivers, Phong Nha is a speleologists' heaven on earth.

The Phong Nha region is changing fast. Son Trach town (population 3000) is the main centre, with an ATM, a growing range of accommodation and eating options, and improving transport links with other parts of central Vietnam.

The caves are the region's absolute highlights, but the above-ground attractions of forest trekking, the area's war history, and rural mountain biking mean it deserves a stay of around three days.

◉ Sights

The Phong Nha region is exploding in popularity, and it's recommended that you book overnight caving tours for Tu Lan, Hang Va and Hang En in advance if possible. Note that most of the adventure caves are closed during the wet season from around mid-September to either late November or late December.

★ Tu Lan Cave   CAVE
(www.oxalis.com.vn; 2-day tours per person 5,500,000d; ⏱ Nov–mid-Sep) The Tu Lan cave trip begins with a countryside hike, then a swim (with headlamps and life jackets) through two spectacular river caves, before emerging in an idyllic valley. Then there's more hiking through dense forest to a 'beach' where rivers merge; this is an ideal campsite. There's more wonderful swimming here in vast caverns. Moderate fitness levels are necessary. Tu Lan is 65km north of Son Trach and can only be visited on a guided tour.

Hang Toi   CAVE
(Dark Cave; per person 350,000d) Incorporating an above-water zipline, followed by a swim into the cave and then exploration of a pitch-black passageway of oozing mud, it's little wonder Hang Toi is the cave experience you've probably already heard about from other travellers. Upon exiting the cave, a leisurely kayak

paddle heads to a jetty where there are more into-the-water zipline thrills to be had.

★ **Hang En**   CAVE
(per person 1,100,000d; ⊘ late Dec-Aug) This gigantic cave is very close to **Hang Son Doong** (⊘ Feb-Aug), and both featured in a *National Geographic* photographic spread in 2011. Getting here involves a trek through dense jungle, valleys and the Ban Doong minority village, a very remote tribal settlement (with no electricity or roads). You stay overnight in the cave or in a minority village. Tours can be booked via Oxalis or local accommodation.

Paradise Cave   CAVE
(Thien Dong; adult/child under 1.3m 250,000/125,000d; ⊘ 7.30am-4.30pm) Surrounded by forested karst peaks, this remarkable cave system extends for 31km, though most people only visit the first kilometre. The scale is breathtaking, as wooden staircases descend into a cathedral-like space with colossal stalagmites and glimmering stalactites. Get here early to beat the crowds, as during peak times (early afternoon) tour guides shepherd groups using megaphones. Paradise Cave is about 14km southwest of Son Trach. Electric buggies (per person one way/return 15,000/25,000d) ferry visitors from the car park to the entrance.

Phong Nha Cave & Boat Trip   CAVE
(adult/child under 1.3m 150,000/25,000d, boat up to 14 people 320,000d; ⊘ 7am-4pm) The spectacular boat trip through Phong Nha Cave is an enjoyable, though touristy, experience beginning in Son Trach town. Boats cruise along past buffalo, limestone peaks and church steeples to the cave's gaping mouth. The engine is then cut and the boats are nego-

tiated silently through cavern after garishly illuminated cavern. On the return leg there's the option to climb (via 330 steps) up to the mountainside Tien Son Cave (80,000d) with the remains of 9th-century Cham altars.

 Tours

Beyond the attractions of the caves, there's a growing range of options to explore the jungle scenery and history of this interesting area. Most activities can be booked through your accommodation.

★ **Oxalis Adventure Tours**   ADVENTURE
(☎ 0232-367 7678; www.oxalis.com.vn; Son Trach; ⊘ 7.30am-noon & 1.30-5.30pm Mon-Sat) Oxalis is unquestionably *the* expert in caving and trekking expeditions, and is the only outfit licensed to conduct tours to Hang Son Doong. Staff are all fluent English-speakers, and trained by world-renowned British cavers Howard and Deb Limbert.

Phong Nha Farmstay Tours   ADVENTURE
(☎ 0232-367 5135; www.phong-nha-cave.com; Cu Nam) Phong Nha Farmstay's popular National Park Tour (per person 1,350,000d) incorporates the Ho Chi Minh Trail with Paradise Cave and Hang Toi (p856); there's also the option of negotiating the recently opened Tra Ang Cave. Ask about exciting customised tours (per person 2,500,000d), bouncing around in the farmstay's vintage Ural motorbike and sidecar.

Hai's Eco Tours   HIKING
(☎ 0962 606 844; www.ecophongnha.com; Bamboo Cafe, Son Trach; per person 1,450,000d) Interesting day tours combining hiking in the jungle – you'll need to be relatively fit – with a visit to Phong Nha's Wildlife Rescue and Rehabilitation Centre, which rehabilitates

---

HANG SON DOONG

Ho Khanh, a hunter, stumbled across gargantuan **Hang Son Doong** (Mountain River Cave) in the early 1990s, but the sheer scale and majesty of the principal cavern (more than 5km long, 200m high and, in some places, 150m wide) was only confirmed as the world's biggest cave when British explorers returned with him in 2009.

Sections of the cave are pierced by skylights that reveal formations of ethereal stalagmites (some up to 80m high) that cavers have called the Cactus Garden. Colossal cave pearls have been discovered, measuring 10cm in diameter. Magnificent rimstone pools are present too.

Hang Son Doong is one of the most spectacular sights in Southeast Asia, and the only specialist operator permitted (by the Vietnamese president no less) to lead tours here is Son Trach–based **Oxalis Adventure Tours**. Four-night/three day expeditions cost a backpacking blowout of US$3000 per person.

rescued animals (mainly macaques from nearby regions, but also snakes and birds). Prices include a barbecue lunch, and there's an opportunity to cool off at the end of the day in a natural swimming hole. A two-day/one-night option (3,200,000d) camping overnight in the Weapon Cave is also available.

Jungle Boss Trekking HIKING
(☑ 0917 800 805; www.jungle-boss.com; Phong Nha village, Son Trach; per person from 1,350,000d) Dzung ('Jungle Boss') is an experienced guide to the area. He speaks excellent English and runs one- and two-day tours around the Ho Chi Minh Trail and the Abandoned Valley area of the national park. A recent addition exploring the remote Ma Da Valley includes a swim in the Tra Ang river cave. You'll need moderate to high fitness levels.

🛏 Sleeping

Easy Tiger HOSTEL $
(☑ 0232-367 7844; www.easytigerphongnha.com; Son Trach; dm 160,000d; ✳@🛜🏊) In Son Trach town, this very popular hostel has four- and six-bed dorms, the great **Jungle Bar** (Son Trach; ⊘ 7am-midnight; 🛜), a pool table and excellent travel information. A swimming pool and beer garden make it ideal for relaxation after trekking and caving. Ask about free bicycles and a map to explore the interesting Bong Lai valley. Email reservations preferred.

Shambalaa HOSTEL $
(☑ 0232-367 7889; www.shambalaa.com; dm 160,000d; ❄✳🛜) One of Phong Nha's newest hostels, Shambalaa is brightly decorated with Asian-style wall hangings, and features spotless dorms and a rooftop lounge area. It has a more chilled and laid-back ambience than at other more social hostels around town. Use of the pool and bar facilities at the Easy Tiger hostel is included. Email is preferred for bookings.

Phong Nha Mountain House GUESTHOUSE $$
(☑ 0935 931 009; www.phongnhamountainhouse.com; d US$40; @🛜) Owned by a hardworking local family, the Phong Nha Mountain House features four comfortable wooden stilt houses with private bathrooms and views of surrounding farmland. Pristine white bed linen contrasts with the warm sheen of the timber walls, and the elevated position means the rooms are light and breezy. It's a flat 3km bike ride into Son Trach town.

★ Phong Nha Farmstay GUESTHOUSE $$
(☑ 0232-367 5135; www.phong-nha-cave.com; Cu Nam; r 910,000-1,170,000d, f 1,300,000-1,950,000d; ❄✳@🛜🏊) The place that really put Phong Nha on the map, the Farmstay has peaceful views overlooking an ocean of rice paddies. Rooms are smallish but neat, with high ceilings and shared balconies. The bar-restaurant serves up Asian and Western meals, and there's a social vibe and occasional movies and live music. Local tours are excellent and there's free bicycle hire.

Jungle Boss Homestay GUESTHOUSE $$
(☑ 0886 077 780; www.jungle-boss.com; Son Trach; d/f 800,000/1,000,000d; ✳🛜) Run by the friendly Dzung – a local trekking guide with excellent English – and his wife Huong, this place has simple but stylish rooms, and two edge-of-the-village locations with rice-paddy views and an organic farm. Rates include breakfast and free use of bicycles, and Dzung's Jungle Boss Trekking also offers caving and jungle trekking trips. Family rooms are good value.

🍴 Eating & Drinking

Eating options in the town of Son Trach now include everything from bakeries and simple Vietnamese restaurants through to pizza, Indian cuisine and Western-style cafes. Explore the nearby Bong Lai valley by mountain bike for simple places selling barbecue duck and pork.

Bamboo Cafe CAFE $
(www.phong-nha-bamboo-cafe.com; Son Trach; meals 40,00-80,000d; ⊘ 7am-10.30pm; 🛜🍴) This laid-back haven on Son Trach's main drag has colourful decor, and well-priced food and drink, including excellent fresh-fruit smoothies and varied vegetarian options.

Mountain Goat Restaurant VIETNAMESE $$
(Son Trach; goat from 150,000d; ⊘ 11am-9pm) Dine on grilled and steamed *de* (goat) – try the goat with lemongrass – at this riverside spot in Son Trach. Other options include spicy chicken and ice-cold beer. From the Phong Nha Cave boat station, walk 150m along the river, just past the church.

Bomb Crater Bar BAR
(☑ 0166 541 0230; www.bombcraterbar.com; Cu Lac village; ⊘ 9am-7pm) Ride a bike 3km from Son Trach to this riverside spot for cold beers, robust gin and tonics, and tasty Vietnamese snacks. Lying in a hammock, kayaking on the river, or chilling with the bar's resident

water buffalo are all added attractions at this great place for a sundowner drink. And, yes, there is a 1970s bomb crater just nearby.

East Hill CAFE, BAR
(☑0948 953 925; www.facebook.com/East-Hill-Phong-Nha-237868583268158/; ⊙11am-8pm) High on a grassy hillock, the open-sided East Hill is a laid-back spot for a sunset beer and Vietnamese snacks, and equally popular with travellers, and students from nearby Dong Hoi. Sit at the rustic shared wooden tables and take in great rural views. East Hill is around 8km east of Son Trach en route to the Bong Lai valley.

❶ Information

Hai at the Bamboo Cafe (p858) is a superb source of independent travel information, and the helpful staff at the Phong Nha Farmstay (p858) and Easy Tiger (p858) can assist with tours, information and transport. There's a tourist office opposite the jetty in Son Trach, but staff are not well versed regarding independent travel.

❶ Getting There & Away

The coastal city of Dong Hoi, 166km north of Hue on Hwy 1 and on the north–south train line, is the main gateway to Phong Nha. The national park abuts Son Trach village, which is 50km northwest of Dong Hoi.

Hotels can organise lifts in private cars from Dong Hoi (500,000d); they work together so rides can be shared between travellers to cut costs. Local buses (35,000d, 90 minutes) shuttle between Dong Hoi's bus station and Son Trach, leaving regularly from 6am to 5pm. Dong Hoi's railway station is around 1.3km from the bus station and the city is on the main north–south line.

From Hue (around 180,000d, five hours), the Hung Thanh open-tour bus leaves 49 Đ Chu Van An at 4.30pm, and the Tan Nha bus leaves from the Why Not? bar on Đ Vo Thi Sau around 6.30am. Also convenient is a daily bus (150,000d) leaving the DMZ bar in Hue at 2pm.

Open-tour buses also link Hanoi and Hoi An to Son Trach and it's now a regular stop on motorbike transfer services operating from Hanoi, Hue and Hoi An. Sit back and enjoy the ride.

❶ Getting Around

Bicycling is recommended to explore Phong Nha's rural back roads, especially the quirky collection of rustic local restaurants and activities popping up around the nearby Bong Lai valley. Easy Tiger (p858) hires out bikes and can supply a handy map.

Motorcycling or scootering around the national park is not recommended for inexperienced drivers – the area is not well signposted and every year there's an increasing number of injuries to travellers.

A good option is to book a tour with **Thang's Phong Nha Riders** (www.easytigerhostel.com/thangs-phong-nha-riders; beside Easy Tiger hostel, Son Trach). A day's hire of a bike and driver is around 400,000d, they're well-versed in the sights of the area, and you'll be providing work for enthusiastic locals. Thang's can also arrange motorbike transfers through absolutely stunning scenery to Hue or Khe Sanh.

Demilitarised Zone (DMZ)

From 1954 until 1975 the Ben Hai River served as the dividing line between South Vietnam and North Vietnam. The DMZ, 90km north of Hue, consisted of the area 5km on either side of the line. Many of the 'sights' around the DMZ may not be worthwhile unless you're into war history. To make sense of it all, and to avoid areas where there's still unexploded ordnance, a guide is essential. Group day tours from Hue cost from US$15 for a budget bus trip to as much as US$120 for a specialised car tour with a Viet vet.

⊙ Sights

★**Vinh Moc Tunnels** HISTORIC SITE
(30,000d; ⊙7am-4.30pm) A highly impressive complex of tunnels, Vinh Moc is the remains of a coastal North Vietnamese village that literally went underground in response to unremitting American bombing. More than 90 families disappeared into three levels of tunnels running for almost 2km, and continued to live and work while bombs rained down around them. Most of the tunnels are open to visitors and are kept in their original form (except for electric lights, a recent addition).

Ben Hai River MONUMENT
(museum 20,000d; ⊙7am-4.30pm) Once the border between North and South Vietnam, Ben Hai River's southern bank now has a grandiose reunification monument, its stylised palm leaves oddly resembling missiles. Cua Tung Beach's fine golden sands are just east of here. Ben Hai's northern bank is dominated by a reconstructed flag tower and small museum full of war mementoes. Ben Hai is 22km north of Dong Ha on Hwy 1.

🛈 GETTING TO LAOS: CENTRAL BORDERS

Vinh to Lak Sao

Getting to the border The **Cau Treo–Nam Phao border** (96km west of Vinh and 30km from Lak Sao in Laos) has a dodgy reputation with independent travellers. Chronic overcharging on local buses is the norm; stick to direct services. Buses leave Vinh at 6am on Monday, Wednesday, Friday and Saturday for Vieng Khan in Laos (280,000d).

At the border The border is open from 7am to 6pm; 30-day Laos visas (US$30 to US$40) are available on arrival.

Moving on On the Laos side, a jumbo or *sawngthaew* (small pick-up truck) between the border and Lak Sao costs about 60,000K (bargain hard).

Vinh to Phonsavan

Getting to the border The **Nam Can–Nong Haet border crossing** is 250km north-west of Vinh. Buses leave at 6am Monday, Wednesday, Friday and Saturday for Luang Prabang (750,000d, 22 hours) via Phonsavan (410,000d, 12 hours).

At the border Lao visas are available for most nationalities for between US$30 and US$40.

Moving on Transport on the Laos side to Nong Haet is erratic, but once you get there you can pick up a bus to Phonsavan.

Dong Hoi to Tha Khaek

For Laos, buses leave for Vientiane daily (400,000d) and for Thakhek from Tuesday to Sunday (300,000d). Both nine-hour services run via the **Cha Lo–Na Phao border crossing**, where Lao visas are available. For all up-to-date transport information, see Sy at the **Nam Long Hotel** (📞0918 923 595; www.namlonghotels.com; 22 Đ Ho Xuan Huong).

For information on doing this crossing in the opposite direction, see p360.

Truong Son National Cemetery   CEMETERY
An evocative memorial to the legions of North Vietnamese soldiers who died along the Ho Chi Minh Trail, this cemetery is a sobering sight. More than 10,000 graves dot these hillsides, each marked by a simple white tombstone headed by the inscription *liet si* (martyr). Many graves lie empty, simply bearing names, representing a fraction of Vietnam's 300,000 soldiers missing in action. It's 27km northwest of Dong Ha; the turn-off from Hwy 1 is close to Doc Mieu.

Khe Sanh Combat Base   HISTORIC SITE
(museum 20,000d; ☺7am-5pm) The site of the most famous siege of the American War, the USA's Khe Sanh Combat Base was never overrun, but saw the bloodiest battle of the war. About 500 Americans, 10,000 North Vietnamese troops and uncounted civilian bystanders died around this remote highland base. It's eerily peaceful today, but in 1968 the hillsides trembled with the impact of 1000kg bombs, white phosphorus shells, napalm, mortars and endless artillery rounds, as desperate American forces sought to repel the NVA.

🛈 Getting There & Around

Virtually everyone explores the DMZ on a tour. Standard tours are cheap (around US$15 for a group day trip) and can be arranged in Hue. Most take in the Rockpile, Khe Sanh, Vinh Moc and Doc Mieu, and leave Hue at 7am, returning by about 5pm. From Hue, much more time is spent driving around 300km than sightseeing.

Tours can also be arranged in Dong Ha, at the intersection of Hwys 1 and 9 – try **Tam's Tours** (📞0905 425 912; http://tamscafe.jimdo.com; 211 Đ Ba Trieu, Tam's DMZ Guesthouse & Cafe) or **Annam Tour** (📞0905 140 600; www.annam-tour.com).

A superior experience is to see the DMZ independently. Reckon on US$120 for a car and expert guide. Leaving from Dong Ha rather than Hue means less time on the road.

SOUTH-CENTRAL VIETNAM

With ancient history and compelling culture, south-central Vietnam has real allure. This is an area that packs in the serene city of Hue (Vietnam's former imperial capital), booming and energetic Danang, and Hoi An, an exquisite architectural gem that time forgot.

There's excellent beach action at An Bang and Phu Thuan, and both Hue and Hoi An feature superb dining scenes. Feast on excellent street food, or take a cooking class so you can recreate the local flavours back home. For snorkelling and diving fans, the Cham Islands are an easy day trip from Hoi An, and history buffs can soak up the heritage ambience of My Son.

Hue

📵 0234 / POP 361,000

Palaces and pagodas, tombs and temples, culture and cuisine, history and heartbreak – there's no shortage of poetic pairings to describe the graceful city of Hue. A World Heritage Site, the capital of the Nguyen emperors is where tourists come to see opulent royal tombs and the grand, crumbling Citadel. Most of these architectural attractions lie along the northern side of the Song Huong (Perfume River). For rest and recreation the south bank is where it's at.

The city hosts a biennial arts festival, the **Festival of Hue** (www.huefestival.com; ☺ late Apr–early May 2018 and 2020), featuring local and international artists and performers.

◉ Sights & Activities

Most of Hue's principal sights lie within the moats of its Citadel and Imperial Enclosure. Other museums and pagodas are dotted around the city. The royal tombs (p867) are south of Hue. A good-value 'package tour ticket' (adult/child 360,000/70,000d) is available that includes admission to the Citadel and the tombs of **Gia Long** FREE, Khai Dinh (p867) and Minh Mang (p867).

◉ Inside the Citadel

Built between 1804 and 1833, the Citadel (Kinh Thanh) is still the heart of Hue. Heavily fortified, it consists of 2m-thick, 10km-long walls, a moat (30m across and 4m deep), and 10 gateways.

The Citadel has distinct sections. The Imperial Enclosure and **Forbidden Purple City** (Tu Cam Thanh) formed the epicentre of Vietnamese royal life. On the southwestern side were temple compounds. There were residences in the northwest, gardens in the northeast and, in the north, the Mang Ca Fortress (still a military base).

Note that if you're planning to visit the Royal Tombs (p867) too, combination tickets including the Citadel and the tombs are available.

★**Imperial Enclosure**   HISTORIC SITE
(adult/child 150,000/30,000d; ☺ 7am-5.30pm, to 10pm mid-Apr–mid-Sep) The Imperial Enclosure is a citadel-within-a-citadel, housing the emperor's residence, temples and palaces, and the main buildings of state, within 6m-high, 2.5km-long walls. What's left is only a fraction of the original – the enclosure was badly bombed during the French and American Wars, and only 20 of its 148 buildings survived. This is a fascinating site easily worth half a day, but poor signage can make navigation a bit difficult. Restoration and reconstruction is ongoing.

Expect a lot of broken masonry, rubble, cracked tiling and weeds as you work your way around. Nevertheless it's enjoyable as a leisurely stroll and some of the less-visited areas are highly atmospheric. There are little cafes and souvenir stands dotted around. It's best to approach the sights starting from Ngo Mon Gate and moving anticlockwise around the enclosure.

Starting in 2017, from mid-April to mid-September the Citadel opens until 10pm, and visitors can enjoy a nightly program of dance and cultural performances. At the time of writing, evening openings were only being trialled, however, so check with your accommodation for the latest information. Visiting at night is an excellent option as it is cooler, and the spectacular lighting showcases the best of the historic complex.

Ngo Mon Gate   GATE
The principal entrance to the Imperial Enclosure is Ngo Mon Gate, which faces the Flag Tower. The central passageway with its yellow doors was reserved for the use of the emperor, as was the bridge across the lotus pond. Others had to use the gates to either side and the paths around the pond. On top of the gate is Ngu Phung (Belvedere of the Five Phoenixes); on its upper level is a huge drum and bell.

Thai Hoa Palace   PALACE
(Palace of Supreme Harmony) This 1803 palace is a spacious hall with an ornate timber roof supported by 80 carved and lacquered columns. It was used for the emperor's official receptions and important ceremonies. On state occasions the emperor sat on his

Hue's Imperial Enclosure

EXPLORING THE SITE

An incongruous combination of meticulously restored palaces and pagodas, ruins and rubble, the Imperial Enclosure is approached from the south through the outer walls of the Citadel. It's best to tackle the site as a walking tour, winding your way around the structures in an anticlockwise direction.

You'll pass through the monumental **❶ Ngo Mon Gateway**, where the ticket office is located. This dramatic approach quickens the pulse as you enter this citadel-within-a-citadel. Directly ahead is the **❷ Thai Hoa Palace**, where the emperor would greet offical visitors from his elevated throne. Continuing north you'll cross a small courtyard to the twin **❸ Halls of the Mandarins**, where mandarins once had their offices and prepared for ceremonial occasions.

To the northeast is the Royal Theatre, where traditional dance performances are held several times daily. Next you'll be able to get a glimpse of the Emperor's Reading Room built by Thieu Tri and used as a place of retreat. Just east of here are the lovely Co Ha Gardens. Wander their pathways, dotted with hundreds of bonsai trees and potted plants, which have been recently restored.

Guarding the far north of the complex is the Tu Vo Phuong Pavilion, from where you can follow a moat to the Truong San residence. Then loop back south via the **❹ Dien Tho Residence** and finally view the beautifully restored temple compound of To Mieu, perhaps the most rewarding part of the entire enclosure to visit, including its fabulous **❺ Nine Dynastic Urns**.

TOP TIPS

➡ Allow half a day to explore the Citadel.

➡ Drink vendors are dotted around the site, but the best places to take a break are the delightful Co Ha Gardens, the Tu Vo Phuong Pavilion and the Dien Tho Residence (the latter two also serve food).

➡ Consider visiting after dark, when the site is spectacularly illuminated.

Dien Tho Residence
This pretty corner of the complex, with its low structures and pond, was the residence of many Queen Mothers. The earliest structures here date from 1804.

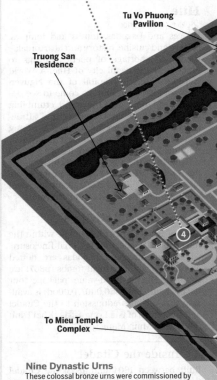

Tu Vo Phuong Pavilion

Truong San Residence

To Mieu Temple Complex

Nine Dynastic Urns
These colossal bronze urns were commissioned by Emperor Minh Mang and cast between 1835 and 1836. They're embellished with decorative elements including landscapes, rivers, flowers and animals.

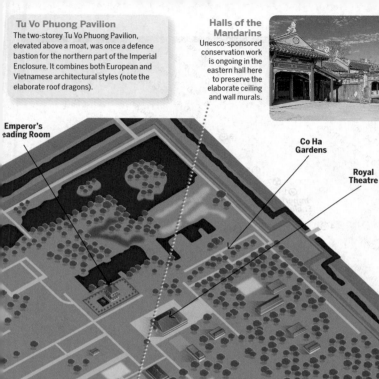

Tu Vo Phuong Pavilion
The two-storey Tu Vo Phuong Pavilion, elevated above a moat, was once a defence bastion for the northern part of the Imperial Enclosure. It combines both European and Vietnamese architectural styles (note the elaborate roof dragons).

Halls of the Mandarins
Unesco-sponsored conservation work is ongoing in the eastern hall here to preserve the elaborate ceiling and wall murals.

Emperor's Reading Room

Co Ha Gardens

Royal Theatre

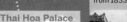

Ngo Mon Gateway
A huge, grandiose structure that guards the main approach to the Imperial Enclosure, this gateway has a fortified lower level and a more architecturally elaborate upper part. It dates from 1833.

Thai Hoa Palace
Be sure to check out this palace's incredible ironwood columns, painted in 12 coats of brilliant scarlet and gold lacquer. The structure was saved from collapse by restoration work in the 1990s.

Hue

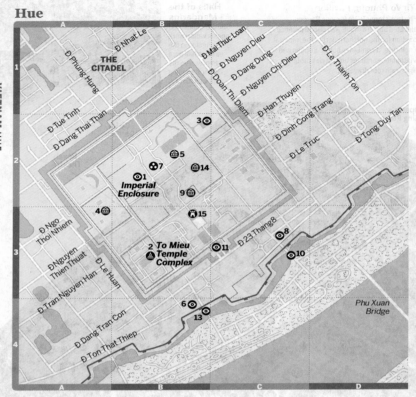

elevated throne, facing visitors entering via the Ngo Mon Gate. No photos are permitted, but be sure to see the impressive audiovisual display, which gives an excellent overview of the entire Citadel, its architecture and the historical context.

Halls of the Mandarins   HISTORIC BUILDING
Located immediately behind Thai Hoa Palace, on either side of a courtyard, these halls were used by mandarins as offices and to prepare for court ceremonies. The hall on the right showcases fascinating old photographs (including boy-king Vua Duya Tan's coronation), gilded Buddha statues and assorted imperial curios. Behind the courtyard are the ruins of the Can Chanh Palace, where two wonderful long galleries, painted in gleaming scarlet lacquer, have been reconstructed.

Emperor's Reading Room   HISTORIC BUILDING
(Royal Library; Thai Binh Lau) The exquisite (though crumbling) little two-storey Em-

peror's Reading Room was the only part of the Forbidden Purple City to escape damage during the French reoccupation of Hue in 1947. The Gaudí-esque, yin-yang roof mosaics outside are in stark contrast to the sombre, recently renovated interior, the circular hallway of which you can now walk around on the small ground level. The exterior features poems by Emperor Khai Dinh on either side, and three Chinese characters that translate as 'Emperor's Reading Room'.

Royal Theatre   HISTORIC BUILDING
(Duyen Thi Duong; ☎ 054-351 4989; www.nhanhac. com.vn; performances 200,000d; ⊗ performances 10.40am & 3.40pm) The Royal Theatre, begun in 1826 and later home to the National Conservatory of Music, has been rebuilt on its former foundations. When performances aren't on, it's free to sit in the plush chairs or examine the fascinating display of masks and musical instruments from Vietnamese

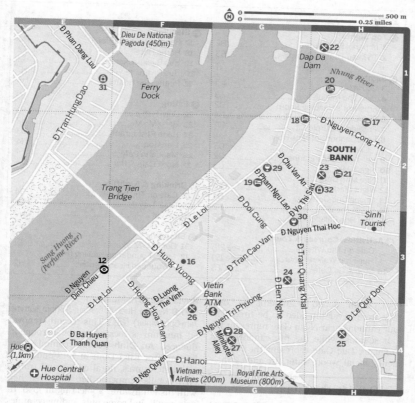

theatre, with English descriptions. Cultural performances here last 45 minutes.

Co Ha Gardens
GARDENS

(Royal Gardens) Occupying the northeast corner of the Imperial Enclosure, these delightful gardens were developed by the first four emperors of the Nguyen dynasty but fell into disrepair. They've been beautifully recreated in the last few years, and are dotted with little gazebo-style pavilions and ponds. This is one of the most peaceful spots in the entire Citadel. The latest section to be discovered, excavated and restored was completed in early 2017.

Dien Tho Residence
HISTORIC BUILDING

The stunning, partially ruined Dien Tho Residence (1804) once comprised the apartments and audience hall of the queen mothers of the Nguyen dynasty. The audience hall houses an exhibition of photos illustrating its former use, and there is a display of embroidered royal garments. Just outside, a pleasure pavilion above a lily pond has been transformed into a cafe worthy of a refreshment stop.

★ To Mieu Temple Complex
BUDDHIST TEMPLE

Taking up the southwest corner of the Imperial Enclosure, this highly impressive walled complex has been beautifully restored. The imposing three-tiered Hien Lam Pavilion sits on the south side of the complex; it dates from 1824. On the other side of a courtyard is the solemn To Mieu Temple, housing shrines to each of the emperors, topped by their photos. Between these two temples are Nine Dynastic Urns (dinh) cast between 1835 and 1836, each dedicated to one Nguyen sovereign.

Nine Holy Cannons
HISTORIC SITE

Located just inside the Citadel ramparts, near the gates to either side of the Flag Tower, are the Nine Holy Cannons (1804), symbolic protectors of the palace and king-

Hue

dom. Commissioned by Emperor Gia Long, they were never intended to be fired. The four cannons near Ngan Gate represent the four seasons, while the five cannons next to Quang Duc Gate represent the five elements: metal, wood, water, fire and earth.

◉ Outside the Citadel

★ Thien Mu Pagoda   BUDDHIST TEMPLE
FREE Built on a hill overlooking the Song Huong (Perfume River), 4km southwest of the Citadel, this pagoda is an icon of Vietnam and as potent a symbol of Hue as the Citadel. The 21m-high octagonal tower, **Thap Phuoc Duyen**, was constructed under the reign of Emperor Thieu Tri in 1844. Each of its seven storeys is dedicated to a *manushi-buddha* (a Buddha that appeared in human form). Visit in the morning before tour groups show up.

Dieu De National Pagoda   BUDDHIST TEMPLE
(Quoc Tu Dieu De; 102 Đ Bach Dang) **FREE** Overlooking Dong Ba Canal, this pagoda was built under Emperor Thieu Tri's rule (1841–47) and is famous for its four low towers, one either side of the gate and two flanking the sanctuary. The pavilions on either side of the main sanctuary entrance contain the 18 La Ha, whose rank is just below that of Bodhisattva, and the eight Kim Cang, protectors of Buddha. In the back row of the main dais is Thich Ca Buddha, flanked by two assistants.

Royal Fine Arts Museum   MUSEUM
(150 Đ Nguyen Hue; ⊙ 6.30am-5.30pm summer, 7am-5pm winter) **FREE** This recently renovated museum is located in the baroque-influenced **An Dinh Palace**, commissioned by Emperor Khai Dinh in 1918 and full of elaborate murals, floral motifs and *trompe l'œil* details. Emperor Bao Dai lived here with his family after abdicating in 1945. Inside, you'll find some outstanding ceramics, paintings, furniture, silverware, porcelain and royal clothing, though information is a little lacking.

Night Market   MARKET
(Đ Nguyen Dinh Chieu; ⊙ 7-10pm) This nightly market is mainly focused on local arts and crafts, but there are also simple cafes and bars perfect for a riverside snack and a drink.

☞ Tours

Most hotels and travellers' cafes offer shared tours covering the main sights (from as little as US$5 to around US$20 per person). There are many different itineraries; some of the better ones start with a morning river cruise, stopping at pagodas and temples, then after lunch you transfer to a minibus to hit the main tombs and then return to Hue by road. On the cheaper options you'll often have to hire a motorbike to get from the moorings to the tombs, or walk (in the intense heat of the day). It's perfectly possible to hire a *xe om* or your own bike and do a DIY tour.

Tran Van Thinh   TOURS
(☑0905 731 537; www.tranvanthinhtours.com; half-day tours from US$15 per person) Knowledgeable local motorbike guide who can arrange local city tours and explorations of the royal tombs. Thinh is a long-time resident of Hue and speaks excellent English.

Ton That Quy   TOURS
(☑0935 782 533; www.facebook.com/ton.t.quy) Quy is a friendly and trustworthy motorbike guide who can arrange scenic transfers via the Hai Van Pass to Hoi An, local sightseeing around Hue and the DMZ, and longer trips exploring all parts of Vietnam.

Stop & Go Café   DRIVING
(☑0234-382 7051; www.stopandgo-hue.com; 3 Đ Hung Vuong) Customised motorbike and car tours. A full-day DMZ car tour guided by a Vietnamese war veteran costs around US$30 per person for four people, representing a good deal. Guided trips to Hoi An stopping at beaches are also recommended. Note, there are similarly named, unrelated

businesses at other addresses. Also has a travellers' cafe with good food.

Café on Thu Wheels   TOURS
(☑054-383 2241; minhthuhue@yahoo.com; 3/34 Nguyen Tri Phuong) Inexpensive cycle hire, and motorbike, minibus and car tours around Hue and the DMZ. Can also arrange transfers to Hoi An by motorbike (US$45) or car (US$55). The establishment also serves a small selection of burgers, sandwiches and local dishes.

Hue Flavor   FOOD & DRINK
(☑0905 937 006; www.hueflavor.com; per person US$49) Excellent street-food tours exploring the delights of Hue cuisine. Transport is by *cyclo* and around 15 different dishes are sampled across four hours.

Hue Free Walking Tour   WALKING
(☑0935 616 090; www.beebeetravel.com; 9 Đ Pham Nhu Lao, Le's Garden; ⊘10am) Daily tours – donate what you wish at the tour's end – and also other paid tours exploring Hue food and the city's imperial history.

VIETNAM HUE

ROYAL TOMBS

The tombs of the rulers of the Nguyen dynasty (1802–1945) are extravagant mausoleums, spread out along the banks of the Song Huong (Perfume River) between 2km and 16km south of Hue. Almost all were planned by the emperors during their lifetimes, and some were even used as residences while they were still alive.

Some tombs are included in boat tours, but you'll have more time to enjoy them by hiring a bicycle, motorbike or *xe om* for the day. These three are particularly impressive, but there are many more:

Tomb of Tu Duc (adult/child 150,000/30,000d) This tomb, constructed between 1864 and 1867, is the most popular and impressive of the royal mausoleums. Emperor Tu Duc designed it himself to use before and after his death. The enormous expense of the tomb and the forced labour used in its construction spawned a coup plot that was discovered and suppressed. Tu Duc's tomb is 5km south of Hue on Van Nien Hill in Duong Xuan Thuong village.

Tomb of Minh Mang (adult/child 150,000/30,000d) This majestic tomb is renowned for its architecture and sublime forest setting. The tomb was planned during Minh Mang's reign (1820–40) but built by his successor, Thieu Tri. Minh Mang's tomb is in An Bang village, on the west bank of the Perfume River, 12km from Hue.

Tomb of Khai Dinh (adult/child 150,000/30,000d) This hillside monument is a synthesis of Vietnamese and European elements. Most of the tomb's grandiose exterior is covered in blackened concrete, creating an unexpectedly Gothic air, while the interiors resemble an explosion of colourful mosaic. Khai Dinh was the penultimate emperor of Vietnam, from 1916 to 1925, and widely seen as a puppet of the French. The construction of his flamboyant tomb took 11 years. The tomb of Khai Dinh is 10km from Hue in Chau Chu village.

SPLURGE

A short walk from good restaurants, the **Hue Riverside Villa** (☑0905 771 602; www.hueriversidevilla.com; 16/7 Đ Nguyen Cong Tru; r $45-60; ☀✳✷) combines five whitewashed and red-brick bungalows with a relaxing shared garden and a quiet, absolute edge-of-the-river location. Decor is crisp and modern – adorned with warm timber, the bathrooms are especially pleasant – and the switched-on English-speaking owner offers tours and plenty of local information.

🛏 Sleeping

Home Hotel   HOTEL **$**
(☑0234-383 0014; www.huehomehotel.com; 8 Đ Nguyen Cong Tru; r US$17-25; ✳@✷) Run by a really friendly team, the welcoming Home Hotel has a young, hip vibe, and spacious rooms arrayed across several levels. Ask to book a room looking over Đ Nguyen Cong Tru for a compact balcony, French doors and views of the river. No lift.

Beach Bar Hue   HOTEL **$**
(☑0908 993 584; www.beachbarhue.com; Phu Thuan Beach; dm US$9-12; ☀✷) At glorious Phu Thuan Beach (about 7km southeast of Thuan An), the Beach Bar Hue has excellent shared four-bed bungalows and sits pretty on a sublime stretch of sand (with no hawkers...for now). There's a funky bamboo-and-thatch bar for drinks and snacks.

Poetic Hue Hostel   HOSTEL **$**
(☑0918 342 138; www.poetichuehostel.com; 24/26 Đ Vo Thi Sau; dm/d/f from US$7/13/25; ☀✳✷) This spotless recent opening in a whitewashed villa in a quiet back lane is a good alternative to Hue's other busier and more social hostels. Local families and birdsong give the location a neighbourhood ambience, and the rooms are spacious and relaxing. Good eating – including Hue's famous royal rice cakes – is just metres away. Some rooms have balconies.

Hue Backpackers   HOSTEL **$**
(☑0234-382 6567; www.vietnambackpackerhostels.com; 10 Đ Pham Ngu Lao; incl breakfast dm US$8-12/r US$18; ✳@✷) Backpackers' mecca thanks to its central location, eager-to-please staff, good info and sociable bar-restaurant that hosts happy hour and big sporting events. Dorms are well designed, and have air-conditioning and lockers.

Canary Boutique Hotel   BOUTIQUE HOTEL **$**
(☑0906 416 331; http://canaryboutiquehotel.com; Lane 8, 43 Đ Nguyen Cong Tru; r US$16-24; ☀✳@✷) You don't need a bath-tub. Then again, with a budget price for such cleanliness, professional staff, a great breakfast menu with free seconds, and competitively priced tours, a bath-tub is just the cherry on top after a long day at the Citadel or nearby bars. If you can't find the hotel's small lane, enquire at the sister Canary Hotel on the main road.

ⓘ GETTING TO LAOS: DONG HA TO SAVANNAKHET

Getting to the border The **Lao Bao–Dansavanh border crossing**, on the Sepon River (Song Xe Pon), is one of the most popular and least problematic border crossings between Laos and Vietnam. Buses to Savannakhet in Laos run from Hue via Dong Ha and Lao Bao. From Hue, there's a daily 7am air-conditioned bus (350,000d, 9½ hours) that stops at the Dong Ha bus station around 9.30am to pick up more passengers. It's also easy to cross the border on your own; Dong Ha is the gateway. Buses leave the town to Lao Bao (60,000d, two hours) roughly every 15 minutes. From here xe om charge 15,000d to the border. You can check schedules and book tickets at **Tam's DMZ Cafe & Guesthouse** (☑0905 425 912; http://tamscafe.jimdo.com; 211 Đ Ba Trieu; s/d/tr US$7/10/15; ✳✷). Tam's also book tickets to Vientiane (14 hours), Thakhek (10 hours) and Pakse (10 hours). It's not possible to cross on motorbikes from Vietnam at the Lao Bao border.

At the border The border posts (7am to 6pm) are a few hundred metres apart. Lao visas are available on arrival, but Vietnamese visas need to be arranged in advance. There are several serviceable hotels on the Vietnamese side. Try not to change currency in Lao Bao: money changers offer terrible rates.

Moving on Sawngthaew head regularly to Sepon, from where you can get a bus or another sawngthaew to Savannakhet.

TOMBS & DUNES

From the centre of Hue it's only 15km north to the coast, the road shadowing the Perfume River before you hit the sands of **Thuan An Beach**. Southeast from here there's a beautiful, quiet coastal road to follow with very light traffic (so it's ideal for bikers). The route traverses a narrow coastal island, with views of the Tam Giang-Cau Hai lagoon on the inland side, and stunning sandy beaches and dunes on the other. This coastal strip is virtually undeveloped, but between September and March the water's often too rough for swimming.

From Thuan An the road winds past villages alternating between shrimp lagoons and vegetable gardens. Thousands of garishly colourful and opulent graves and family temples line the beach, most the final resting places of Viet Kieu (overseas Vietnamese) who wanted to be buried in their homeland. Tracks cut through the tombs and sand dunes to the beach. Pick a spot and you'll probably have a beach to yourself.

At glorious **Phu Thuan Beach** (about 7km southeast of Thuan An) are the funky Beach Bar Hue (p868) and charming **Villa Louise** (☑ 0917 673 656; www.villalouisehue. com; Phu Thuan beach; d US$75-149, villas US$140-244; ☀ ☃ ⚊). The restaurant and beach can be used by outside guests – there's an entrance fee of 100,000d, which can be offset against food and beverage purchases in the beachfront bar. For 250,000d per person, guests can also use the lovely pool area at Villa Louise. A taxi from Hue to Phu Thuan is around 250,000d and a *xe om* (motorbike taxi) around 100,000d. Ask at backpacker hostels in Hue about occasional shared shuttles to Beach Bar Hue.

Around 8km past Beach Bar Hue, the remains of **Phu Dien**, a small Cham temple, lie protected by a glass pavilion in the dunes just off the beach. There are seafood shacks here too.

Continuing southeast, a narrow paved road weaves past fishing villages, shrimp farms, giant sand dunes and the settlement of Vinh Hung until it reaches the mouth of another river estuary at Thuon Phu An, where there's a row of seafood restaurants. This spot is 40km from Thuan An. Cross the Tu Hien Bridge here and you can continue around the eastern lip of the huge Cau Hai lagoon and link up with Hwy 1.

🍴 Eating

Hue's culinary variety is amazing, with many unique local dishes, including lots of veggie creations. Royal rice cakes, the most common of which is *banh khoai,* are well worth seeking out.

★ Hanh Restaurant
VIETNAMESE $

(☑ 0905 520 512; 11 Pho Duc Chinh; meals 30,000-100,000d; ⊙ 10am-9pm) Newbies to Hue specialities should start at this busy restaurant. Order the five-dish set menu (120,000d) for a speedy lesson of *banh khoai* (savoury prawn pancakes), *banh beo* (steamed rice cakes topped with shrimp and spring onions), and divine *nem lui* (grilled pork on lemongrass skewers) wrapped in rice paper and herbs. Ask the patient staff how to devour everything.

Hang Me Me
VIETNAMESE $

(16 Đ Vo Thi Sau; meals from 40,000d; ⊙ 8am-11pm; ☑) A top, unfussy spot to try Hue's dizzying menu of royal rice cakes. Serving portions are pretty big, so rustle up a few friends to try the different variations. Our favourite is the *banh beo*, perfect little mouthfuls topped with spring onions and dried shrimp.

Com Hen
VIETNAMESE $

(17 Đ Han Mac Tu; meals from 10,000d; ⊙ 7am-11pm) Tuck into bowls of rice *(com hen)* or noodles *(bun hen)* combining fresh herbs and tasty local clams from a nearby island in the middle of the Song Huong.

Lien Hoa
VEGETARIAN $

(☑ 054-381 2456; 3 Đ Le Quy Don; meals 50,000-80,000d; ⊙ 6.30am-9pm; ☑) No-nonsense Viet vegetarian restaurant renowned for filling food at bargain prices. Fresh *banh beo*, noodle dishes, crispy fried jackfruit and aubergine with ginger all deliver. The menu has very rough English translations to help you order (staff speak little or no English).

Nook Cafe & Bar
VIETNAMESE, CAFE $

(☑ 0935 069 741; www.facebook.com/nookcafebarhue; 7/34 Đ Nguyen Tri Phuong; meals 50,000-120,000d; ⊙ 8am-10pm; ☃ ☑) Tucked away near a tangle of cheaper accommodation and travel agencies, Nook's breezy upstairs location is a good spot for well-executed

Vietnamese dishes and Western comfort food like veggie burgers and toasted sandwiches. Top marks for the quirky decor, good music, and refreshing juices and smoothies.

Mandarin Café VIETNAMESE $
(054-382 1281; www.mrcumandarin.com; 24 Đ Tran Cao Van; meals 25,000-69,000d; ⊙6am-10pm; 🛜🌿) Owner-photographer Mr Cu, whose inspirational pictures adorn the walls, has been hosting backpackers for years, and his relaxed restaurant has lots of vegetarian and breakfast choices. Also operates as a tour agency for in and outside of Hue.

🍷 Drinking & Nightlife

DMZ Travel BAR
(www.dmz.com.vn; 60 Đ Le Loi; ⊙7am-1am; 🛜) Ever-popular bar near the river with a free pool table, cold Huda beer, cocktails (try a watermelon mojito) and antics most nights. Also serves Western and local food till midnight, plus smoothies and juices. Happy hour is 3pm to 8pm. Check out the upside-down map of the DMZ – complete with a US chopper – on the ceiling of the bar.

Ta Vet BAR
(0914 833 679; 11 Đ Vo Thi Sau; ⊙6.30am-1am; 🛜) One part beer bar and one part cafe, this spacious spot with rustic wooden furniture, a short walk from Hue's backpacker strip, is a good location to meet younger English-speaking locals. There's a decent beer selection beyond the usual suspects, and the Vietnamese food is also affordable and tasty.

Café on Thu Wheels BAR
(054-383 2241; lnhin60@yahoo.com; 3/34 Đ Nguyen Tri Phuong; ⊙7am-11pm; 🛜) Graffiti-splattered walls, a sociable vibe, excellent food and smoothies all combine at this welcoming spot owned by a friendly family. It also offers good tours (p867), and has books and mags to browse.

🛍 Shopping

Hue produces the finest conical hats in Vietnam and is renowned for rice paper and silk paintings. As ever, bargain hard. Also check out the city's riverside night market. (p866)

Spiral Foundation Healing the Wounded Heart Center ARTS & CRAFTS
(0234-381 7643; www.spiralfoundation.org; 23 Đ Vo Thi Sau; ⊙8am-10pm) Generating cash from trash, this shop stocks lovely handicrafts – such as quirky bags made from plastic, and picture frames made from recycled beer cans – all crafted by artists with disabilities. Profits aid heart surgery for children in need.

Dong Ba Market MARKET
(Đ Tran Hung Dao; ⊙6.30am-8pm) Just north of Trang Tien Bridge, this is Hue's largest market, selling anything and everything.

ℹ Information

Wi-fi is very widespread at cafes, bars and accommodation.

Hue Central Hospital (Benh Vien Trung Uong Hue; 0234-382 2325; 16 Đ Le Loi; ⊙6am-10pm) Well-regarded local hospital.

Post Office (8 Đ Hoang Hoa Tham; ⊙7am-5.30pm Mon-Sat) A short walk from Hue's main street.

Sinh Tourist (0234-384 5022; www.thesinhtourist.vn; 37 Đ Nguyen Thai Hoc; ⊙6.30am-8.30pm) Books open-tour buses, and buses to Laos and many other destinations in Vietnam.

ℹ Getting There & Away

AIR

Jetstar (www.jetstar.com) and **VietJet** (www.vietjetair.com) offer flights to/from HCMC.
Vietnam Airlines (0234-382 4709; www.vietnamairlines.com; 23 Đ Nguyen Van Cu; ⊙8am-5pm Mon-Sat) has services to/from Hanoi and HCMC.

TRAINS FROM HUE

The **Hue train station** (0234-382 2175; 2 Đ Phan Chu Trinh) is at the southwestern end of Đ Le Loi. A taxi here from the hotel area costs about 70,000d.

DESTINATION	COST (US$)	DURATION (HR)	FREQUENCY
Danang	4-8	2½-4	7 daily
Dong Hoi	5-11	3-5½	7 daily
Hanoi	25-42	12-15½	6 daily
HCMC	33-55	19½-23	5 daily
Ninh Binh	19-35	10-13	5 daily

BUSES FROM HUE

DESTINATION	COST (D)	DURATION (HR)	FREQUENCY
Danang	80,000	3	frequent
Dong Ha	44,000	2	every 30 minutes
Dong Hoi	100,000	4	frequent
Hanoi	320,000	13-16	9 daily
HCMC	500,000	19-24	9 daily
Ninh Binh	270,000	10½-12	8 daily

BUS

The main bus station, 4km southeast of the centre, has connections to Danang and south to HCMC. **An Hoa bus station** (Hwy 1), northwest of the Citadel, serves northern destinations.

For Phong Nha (around 135,000d, five hours), the Hung Thanh open-tour bus leaves 49 Đ Chu Van An at 4.30pm, and the Tan Nhat bus leaves from the Why Not? Bar on Đ Vo Thi Sau around 6.30am. Also convenient is a daily bus (150,000d) leaving the DMZ Travel bar in Hue at 2pm. This departure travels directly to Phong Nha, but there is also the option of incorporating a tour of the DMZ en route.

Hue is a regular stop on open-tour bus routes. Most drop off and pick up passengers at central hotels. Expect some hassle from persistent hotel touts when you arrive.

Mandarin Cafe (p870), Sinh Tourist (p870) and Stop & Go Café (p867) can arrange bookings for buses to Savannakhet, Laos.

ⓘ Getting Around

Bicycles (US$3), motorbikes (US$5 to US$10) and cars (from US$50 per day) can be hired through hotels all over town. **Mai Linh** (☑ 0234-389 8989) has taxis with meters. Cyclos and xe om will fi nd you whether you need them or not.

Danang

☑ 0236 / POP 1,052,000

Nowhere in Vietnam is changing as fast as Danang. For decades it had a reputation as a provincial backwater, but big changes are ongoing. The Han riverfront is resplendent with gleaming hotels, bustling restaurants and spectacular bridges. Beachside, five-star hotel developments are emerging, and Danang has a great street-food scene.

Except for a decent museum, the city itself has few conventional sightseeing spots, but it's a fun city and a couple of days of eating well and enjoying the beach are recommended before or after visiting Hoi An, less than an hour down the coast.

◉ Sights

★ **Dragon Bridge**   BRIDGE
(Cau Rong; ⊘ 24hr) FREE Welcome to the biggest show in town every Saturday and Sunday night. At 9pm, this impressive drag-on sculpture spouts fire and water from its head near the Han River's eastern bank. The best observation spots are the cafes lining the eastern bank to the north of the bridge; boat trips taking in the action also depart from Đ Bach Dang on the river's western bank. The colour-changing Dragon Bridge sees selfie-takers parking their scooters on the bridge every night.

★ **Museum of Cham Sculpture**   MUSEUM
(Bao Tang; 1 Đ Trung Nu Vuong; 40,000d; ⊘ 7am-5pm) This fine, small museum has the world's largest collection of Cham artefacts, housed in buildings marrying French-colonial architecture with Cham elements. Founded in 1915 by the École Française d'Extrême Orient, it displays more than 300 pieces including altars, *lingas* (stylised phalluses that represent Shiva), garudas (griffin-like sky beings), *apsaras* (heavenly nymphs), Ganeshes and images of Shiva, Brahma and Vishnu, all dating from the 5th to 15th centuries. Explanations are slim. To hire an MP3 audio guide (20,000d), you'll need to show ID – passport or driving licence – or leave a refundable US$50 bond.

ⓖ Tours

Danang Free Walking Tour   WALKING
(☑ 0905 631 419; www.danangfreewalkingtour.com; 108 Đ Bach Dang; ⊘ 9am & 3pm) Run by local English-speaking students, these walking tours are a good introduction to the city. Donate what you think is appropriate at the end of the tour, and maybe sign up for one of the other (paid) specialised tours, including street food. Tours leave from the Danang Visitor Centre, and booking ahead is recommended.

WORTH A TRIP

BACH MA NATIONAL PARK

A French-era hill station known for its cool weather, **Bach Ma National Park** (Vuon Quoc Gia Bach Ma; ☑0234-387 1330; www.bachmapark.com.vn; adult/child 40,000/20,000d) is 45km southeast of Hue. There's some decent trekking in the lower levels through subtropical forest to villages on the fringes of the park. You can book village and birdwatching tours and English- or French-speaking guides (500,000d per day) at the visitor centre. Unexploded ordnance is still in the area, so stick to the trails.

There's a **guesthouse** (☑054-387 1330; www.bachmapark.com.vn; campsite per person 20,000d, r 300,000d) at the park entrance.

Danang Food Tour   FOOD & DRINK
(www.danangfoodtour.com; per person US$45) Excellent morning and evening explorations of the local food scene by passionate foodies. Check the website for the great blog on the best of Danang.

Hoi An Jeep Adventures   TOURS
(☑0905 101 930; www.vietnamjeeps.com; per person from US$96) Based in nearby Hoi An, but also offering jeep explorations of Danang's street-food and after-dark scenes. Other Danang options are discovering Monkey Mountain by jeep or a day trip to the Hai Van Pass. Look forward to really interesting street-food discoveries for curious travelling foodies.

🛏 Sleeping

Recent openings have improved Danang's range of budget accommodation, both in the city, and also east across the Han River nearer the beach.

Memory Hostel   HOSTEL $
(☑0236-374 7797; http://memoryhostel.com; 3 Đ Tran Quoc Toan; dm US$7-8; ❄🛜) Sweet memories are made of casual strolls to the Dragon Bridge, good restaurants and nightlife, all near this hostel. If you just want to stay in, the decor is arty, eclectic and clean, and beds have privacy curtains. An excellent budget option.

Barney's Hostel   HOSTEL $
(☑0126 520 6103; www.barneyhostel.com; 169 Đ Tran Hung Dao; dm US$8-10; ❄🛜) With a quieter northern location near the river's eastern bank, Barney's gets good reviews from

travellers for its combination of modern and spotless rooms, and a great little bar and restaurant. Tours and onward transport can be booked, and it can also hook up travellers with scooters (half/full day 80,000/120,000d) for getting out and about to the nearby Son Tra peninsula.

Funtastic Danang Hostel   HOSTEL $
(☑0236-389 2024; www.funtasticdanang.com; 115 Đ Hai Phong; dm US$6.50, d & tw US$19; ❄@🛜) Danang's original specialist hostel is a goodie, with young and energetic owners, colourful rooms and dorms, and a comfortable lounge area for when all you want to do is chill and watch a movie. Ask about the street food tours (☑0905 272 921; www.funtasticdanang.com; per person US$45).

Frangipani Boutique Hotel   BOUTIQUE HOTEL $$
(☑0236-393 8368; www.frangipaniboutiquehotel.com; 8 Nguyen Huu Thong; d US$45-50; ♨❄@🛜🖥) With just 11 rooms, and stylish shared areas, the Frangipani is more like a classy European guesthouse. Rooms are spacious and modern with elegant decor, and it's just a short stroll to the sands of Danang Beach. A small indoor pool is available downstairs, bicycles are free to use, and there's also a pleasant on-site restaurant with courtyard seating.

🍴 Eating & Drinking

⭐**Taco Ngon**   TACOS $
(☑0906 504 284; www.facebook.com/tacongon; 2 My Da Dong 8; tacos 35,000d; ⏱10.30am-10pm Tue-Sun) Worth seeking out down a quiet lane, this spot with just a few tables serves up quite possibly Vietnam's best tacos. Cool down with a bargain-priced can of La Rue beer and tuck into fusion flavour combos like pork with wasabi coleslaw, fish with ginger and lime, or chicken with a tamarind barbecue sauce. Tequila shots are just 25,000d. Dangerous...

BBQ Un In   BARBECUE, VIETNAMESE $$
(☑0236-654 5357; www.bbqunin.com; 379 Đ Tran Hung Dao; meals 100,000-210,000d; ⏱11.30am-10.30pm) Vietnamese flavours and American barbecue combine at this fun new opening along the fast-expanding restaurant strip on the Han River's eastern bank. Shipping containers daubed with colourful street art provide the backdrop for fall-off-the-bone ribs, spicy grilled sausages, and hearty side dishes including sweetcorn and grilled pineapple. Order up a good-value beer tower if you're dining in a group.

Happy Heart
INTERNATIONAL **$$**

(☎0236-388 8384; www.facebook.com/hap-pyheartdanang; 9 Đ Ly Tu Trong; meals 95,000-160,000d; ◷7.30am-9pm Mon-Sat; 🛜🅿) 🖉
Hearing-impaired wait staff deliver brilliant service at this cafe that helps to provide opportunities for people with disabilities in Danang. The food's also excellent with Western comfort food including burgers, lasagne and a terrific breakfast burrito. Good coffee and fruit-and-yoghurt smoothies are other fine reasons to linger.

Minsk Bar
BAR

(59 Ngo Thi Si; ◷8am-2am; 🛜) Traditionally a hangout of expats negotiating Russian Minsk motorbikes around Vietnam, the Minsk Bar has now evolved to also include a more local customer base. Loping reggae beats are often the preferred soundtrack of choice, and the rustic corner location is a great place to hang out. Nearby, An Thong 4 St has an expanding range of interesting dining options.

❶ Information

Consult www.danangexperience.com and www.indanang.com for reviews and local information.

Danang Family Medical Practice (☎0236-358 2700; www.vietnammedicalpractice.com; 50-52 Đ Nguyen Van Linh; ◷7am-6pm) With in-patient facilities; run by an Australian doctor.

Danang Visitor Centre (☎0236-389 8196; www.tourism.danang.vn; 32a Đ Phan Dinh Phung; ◷7.30am-9pm) Really helpful, with English spoken, and good maps and brochures. Danang's official tourism website is one of Vietnam's best. Bicycles can be hired for venturing across the bridge to Danang's beaches.

Sinh Tourist (☎0511-384 3258; www.thesinhtourist.vn; 16 Đ 3 Thang 2; ◷7am-10pm) Books open-tour buses and tours.

❶ Getting There & Away

AIR
Danang's busy airport (p922), 2km west of the city centre, has international flights to cities including Kuala Lumpur, Hong Kong and Singapore.

Domestic services to HCMC, Hanoi, Dalat, Nha Trang, Can Tho and Haiphong are operated by **Vietnam Airlines** (☎0236-382 1130; www.vietnamairlines.com), **VietJet Air** (http://bookvietjetair.com) and Jetstar (p902).

BUS
Danang's **intercity bus station** (☎0236-382 1265; Đ Dien Bien Phu) is 3km west of the city centre. A metered taxi to the riverside will cost around 90,000d. Frequent buses leave for all

SPLURGE

The stylish restaurant and lounge bar **Fatfish** (☎0236-394 5707; www.fatfish-danang.com; 439 Đ Tran Hung Dao; meals 110,000-330,000d; ◷11am-10pm; 🛜) is leading the eating and drinking charge across the river on the Han's eastern shore. Innovative Asian fusion dishes, pizza and wood-fired barbecue all partner with flavour-packed craft beers from Ho Chi Minh City's **Pasteur Street Brewing** (Map p894; www.pasteurstreet.com). Fatfish is good for a few snacks or a more leisurely full meal.

major centres including Dong Hoi (140,000d, six hours), Hanoi (320,000d, 16 hours), HCMC (400,000d, 22 hours), Hue (60,000d, three hours), and Nha Trang (250,000d, 12 hours).

Yellow public buses to Hoi An (20,000d, one hour, every 30 minutes to 6pm) travel along Đ Bach Dang. The price is usually posted inside the door; check it if you think the bus driver is attempting to overcharge.

Sinh Tourist open-tour buses pick up from the company office in the northern part of downtown twice daily to both Hue (90,000d, 2½ hours) and Hoi An (80,000d, one hour). Sinh Tourist can also advise on travel to Laos.

TAXI & MOTORCYCLE
A car to Hoi An costs around 550,000d via your hotel or a local travel agency; a xe om will cost around 150,000d. Shared shuttle buses are a good budget option at around 300,000d, and can be booked through hotels.

TRAIN
Danang's **train station** (202 Đ Hai Phong) has services to all destinations on the north–south main line. The train ride to Hue is one of the best in the country – it's worth taking as an excursion in itself for the stunning coastline

Around Danang

About 10km south of Danang are the striking Marble Mountains, which consist of five craggy marble outcrops topped with jungle and pagodas. With natural caves sheltering small Hindu and Buddhist sanctuaries and stunning views of the ocean and surrounding countryside, they're worth taking the time to explore. **Thuy Son** (15,000d; ◷7am-5pm) is the largest and most famous of the five mountains.

Danang Beach (Bai Non Nuoc), once an R'n'R hangout for US soldiers during the war, is actually a series of beaches stretching 30km between Hoi An and Danang.

For surfers, Danang Beach's break gets a decent swell from mid-September to December. There's a mean undertow, so take care.

Hoi An

📞 0235 / POP 134,000

Graceful, historic Hoi An is Vietnam's most atmospheric and delightful town. Once a major port, it boasts the grand architecture and beguiling riverside setting that befits its heritage, and the 21st-century curses of traffic and pollution are almost entirely absent.

The face of the Old Town has preserved its incredible legacy of tottering Japanese merchant houses, Chinese temples and ancient tea warehouses – though, of course, residents and rice fields have been gradually replaced by tourist businesses. Lounge bars, boutique hotels, travel agents and a glut of tailor shops are very much part of the scene here. And yet, down by the market and over on Cam Nam Island, you'll find life has changed little. Travel a few kilometres further – you'll find some superb bicycle, motorbike and boat trips – and some of central Vietnam's most enticingly laid-back scenery and beaches are within easy reach.

⊙ Sights

⊙ Hoi An Old Town

A Unesco World Heritage Site (www.hoianworldheritage.org.vn), Hoi An Old Town levies an admission fee to most of its historic buildings, which goes towards funding the preservation of the town's architecture. Buying the **ticket** (120,000d) gives you a choice of five heritage sites to visit – Chinese Assembly Halls, pagodas and temples, historic houses and museums. Booths dotted around the Old Town sell tickets. Tickets are valid for 10 days. You won't normally be checked if you're just dining or shopping in the area, but keep your ticket with you just in case.

★ **Japanese Covered Bridge**   BRIDGE
(Cau Nhat Ban; admission by Old Town ticket; ⊙24hr) This beautiful little bridge is emblematic of Hoi An. A bridge was first constructed here in the 1590s by the Japanese community to link it with the Chinese quarters. Over the centuries the ornamen-

tation has remained relatively faithful to the original Japanese design. The French flattened out the roadway for cars, but the original arched shape was restored in 1986. The bridge is due for a complete removal for repair, so check it's open before you travel, if making a special trip.

Assembly Hall of the Fujian
Chinese Congregation   TEMPLE
(Phuc Kien Hoi Quan; opposite 35 Ð Tran Phu; admission by Old Town ticket; ⊙7am-5.30pm) 🏮 Originally a traditional assembly hall, this structure was later transformed into a temple for the worship of Thien Hau, a deity from Fujian province. The green-tiled triple gateway dates from 1975. The mural on the right-hand wall depicts Thien Hau, her way lit by lantern light as she crosses a stormy sea to rescue a foundering ship. Opposite is a mural of the heads of the six Fujian families who fled from China to Hoi An in the 17th century.

★ **Tan Ky House**   HISTORIC BUILDING
(101 Ð Nguyen Thai Hoc; admission by Old Town ticket; ⊙8am-noon & 2-4.30pm) Built two centuries ago by an ethnically Vietnamese family, this gem of a house has been lovingly preserved through seven generations. Look out for signs of Japanese and Chinese influences on the architecture. Japanese elements include the ceiling (in the sitting area), which is supported by three progressively shorter beams, one on top of the other. Under the crab-shell ceiling are carvings of crossed sabres wrapped in silk ribbon. The sabres symbolise force; the silk represents flexibility.

Tran Family Chapel   HISTORIC BUILDING
(21 Ð Le Loi; admission by Old Town ticket; ⊙7.30am-noon & 2-5.30pm) Built for worshipping family ancestors, this chapel dates back to 1802. It was commissioned by Tran Tu, one of the clan who ascended to the rank of mandarin and served as an ambassador to China. His picture is to the right of the chapel. The architecture of the building reflects the influence of Chinese (the 'turtle' style roof), Japanese (triple beam) and vernacular (look out for the bow-and-arrow detailing) styles.

Precious Heritage   MUSEUM, GALLERY
(📞0235 6558 382; www.facebook.com/precious. heritage.museum.art.gallery; 26 Ð Phan Boi Chau; ⊙8.30am-8.30pm) FREE The latest project from Hoi An–based French photographer Réhahn, this cross between a museum and a gallery combines his superb photos of Vietnam's hill tribes with artefacts and cloth-

ing he collected from each group during his wide-ranging travels in remote areas. If you're planning on visiting the north of the country or the Central Highlands, Precious Heritage is an essential detour.

Museum of Trading Ceramics MUSEUM
(80 Đ Tran Phu; admission by Old Town ticket; ◷ 7am-5.30pm) Occupies a restored wooden house and contains a small collection of artefacts from all over Asia, with oddities from as far afield as Egypt. While this reveals that Hoi An had some rather impressive trading links, it takes an expert's eye to appreciate the display. The exhibition on the restoration of Hoi An's old houses provides a useful crash course in Old Town architecture.

Arts & Crafts Villages

All those neat fake antiques sold in Hoi An's shops are manufactured in nearby villages. Cross the An Hoi footbridge to reach the **An Hoi Peninsula**, noted for boat building and mat weaving. **Cam Kim Island** is renowned for its woodcarvers. Cross the Cam Nam bridge to **Cam Nam** village, a lovely spot also noted for arts and crafts.

🏃 Activities

Two reputable dive schools, **Cham Island Diving Center** (☑ 0235-391 0782; www.vietnamscubadiving.com; 88 Đ Nguyen Thai Hoc; snorkelling day trips US$44, overnight snorkelling/diving trips US$82/112) and **Blue Coral Diving** (☑ 0235-627 9297; www.divehoian.com; 33 Đ Trung Hung Dao) offer trips to the Cham Islands. Many dive schools charge almost exactly the same rates: two fun dives are US$80. The diving is not world class, but can be intriguing, with good macro life – and the day trip to the Cham Islands is superb. Snorkellers pay about US$40. Trips only leave between February and September; conditions are best in June, July and August.

Eat Hoi An FOOD & DRINK
(Coconut Tours; ☑ 0905 411 184; www.eathoian.com; 37 Đ Phan Chau Trinh; per person US$45) Lots of really authentic cuisine and the infectious enthusiasm of host Phuoc make this an excellent choice if you really want to explore the grassroots local street-food scene. Be prepared for lots of different foods and flavours; check the website for details of cooking classes held in Phuoc's home village.

Grasshopper Adventures CYCLING
(☑ 0932 034 286; www.grasshopperadventures.com; 62 Đ Hai Ba Trung; per person US$37-47)

Highly recommended biking tours on very well-maintained bikes. Options include a daytime countryside tour and an excellent sunset food tour. Longer multiday tours exploring Vietnam are also available.

🥢 Courses

Green Bamboo Cooking School COOKING
(☑ 0905 815 600; www.greenbamboo-hoian.com; 21 Đ Truong Minh Hung, Cam An; per person US$45) Directed by Van, a charming local chef and English-speaker, these courses are more personalised than most. Groups are limited to a maximum of 10, and classes take place in Van's spacious kitchen. Choose what to cook from a diverse menu including vegetarian choices. It's 5km east of the centre, near Cu Dai beach; transport from Hoi An is included.

Herbs and Spices COOKING
(☑ 0235-393 6868; www.herbsandspicesvn.com; 2/6 Đ Le Loi; per person US$35-58; ◷ 10.30am, 4.30pm & 8pm) Excellent classes with three different options, and smaller, more hands-on groups than some other cookery classes.

🛏 Sleeping

Lazy Bear Hostel HOSTEL $
(☑ 0905 025 491; www.facebook.com/lazybearhostel; 12 Đ Tran Quuc Toan; dm/d US$8/20; ❉ ⑉) This small family-owned hostel has a good location – the Old Town and Cua Dai beach are both around 2.5km away – and lots of free inclusions, such as breakfast, bicycles and the occasional bar crawl and food tour. A relaxing garden and modern bathrooms in the private en-suite rooms seal the deal at one of Hoi An's best-value accommodation options.

Hoi An Backpackers Hostel HOSTEL $
(☑ 0235-391 4400; www.vietnambackpackerhostels.com; 252 Đ Cua Dai; dm/tw/d incl breakfast US$12/40/40; ❀❉@⑉) Purpose-built and brand new, this is the spectacular Hoi An location for a hostel empire spanning Vietnam. Accommodation ranges from dorms to private en-suite rooms. There's a poolside bar and restaurant, and plenty of quiet common areas for some private time. Location-wise, you're handily placed between the Old Town and the beach, and bikes are available to hire for exploring.

⭐ **Nu Ni Homestay** GUESTHOUSE $$
(☑ 0235-392 7979; www.nunihomestayhoian.com; 131/12 Đ Tran Hung Dao; d/tr/f US$20/28/36; ❀❉⑉) Hidden down a quiet lane just north of the Old Town, the Nu Ni Homestay has

Hoi An

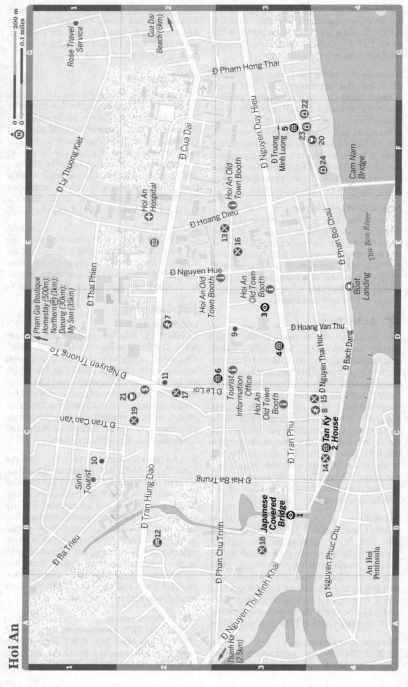

0 — 200 m
0 — 0.1 miles

Rose Travel Service

Đ Pham Hong Thai

Cua Dai Beach (6km)

Đ Ly Thuong Kiet

Đ Cua Dai

Hoi An Hospital

Đ Nguyen Duy Hieu

22
23
5
20
24

Đ Truong Minh Luong

Cam Nam Bridge

Hoi An Old Town Booth

Đ Hoang Dieu

13
16

Đ Thai Phien

Đ Nguyen Hue

Hoi An Old Town Booth

Hoi An Old Town Booth

3

Đ Phan Boi Chau

Thu Bon River

Pham Gia Boutique Homestay (500m); Northern (1km); Danang (30km); My Son (35km)

7

9

4

Đ Hoang Van Thu

Đ Nguyen Truong To

Boat Landing

6

11

21
19
17

Đ Le Loi

Tourist Information Office

Hoi An Old Town Booth

Đ Nguyen Thai Hoc

Đ Bach Dang

Đ Tran Cao Van

Sinh Tourist

10

Đ Tran Hung Dao

Đ Tran Phu

14
8 15

Tan Ky House
2

Đ Hai Ba Trung

Đ Ba Trieu

12

Japanese Covered Bridge

1

Đ Phan Chu Trinh

18

Đ Nguyen Phuc Chu

An Hoi Peninsula

Đ Nguyen Thi Minh Khai

Thanh Ha (2.5km)

Hoi An

VIETNAM HOI AN

spacious and sparkling new rooms – some with large balconies – and a real can-do attitude from the friendly family owners. Flat screen TVs, modern bathrooms and a comfortable shared downstairs area all make Nu Ni a great choice. Breakfast is additional.

Pham Gia Boutique Homestay GUESTHOUSE $$
(☎0914 085 075; www.phamgiahoian.com; 73/1 Phan Dinh Phung; d/ste from US$35/42; ✆❀ 🛜) Another excellent homestay, Pham Gia easily edges into the boutique guesthouse category. Blending colonial and local design, rooms are spacious and sunny, and the friendly owner is a Hoi An local with plenty of experience in the travel industry. Bikes are provided free of charge, and both the Old Town and An Bang Beach are just a short ride away.

✕ Eating

Hoi An offers a culinary tour de force, including several amazing local specialities. Be sure to try *banh beo* ('white rose'), an incredibly delicate dish of steamed dumplings stuffed with minced shrimp. *Cao lau* – doughy flat noodles mixed with croutons, bean sprouts and greens, topped with pork slices and served in a savoury broth – is also delicious. The other two culinary treats are fried *hoanh thanh* (wonton) and *banh xeo* (savoury pancakes rolled with herbs in fresh rice paper).

Banh Mi Phuong VIETNAMESE $
(2b Đ Phan Chu Trinh; banh mi 20,000-30,000d) What makes the *banh mi* at this cramped joint draw the crowds? It's the dense, chewy bread, the freshness of the greens and the generous serves of *thit nuong* (chargrilled pork), beef or other meat that seals the deal. A celebrity-chef endorsement helps too.

Cocobox CAFE $
(http://fb.me/cocoboxvietnam; 94 Đ Le Loi; juices & smoothies 60,000-75,000d; ⊙7am-10pm) Refreshing cold-press juices are the standout at this compact combo of cafe and deli. Our favourite is the Watermelon Man juice combining watermelon, passionfruit, lime and mint. Coffee, salads and snacks are also good – try the chicken pesto sandwich. The attached 'farm shop' sells Vietnamese artisan produce including local honey and cider from Ho Chi Minh City.

Nu Eatery FUSION $
(www.facebook.com/NuEateryHoiAn; 10a Đ Nguyen Th[] Minh Khai; meals 90,000d; ⊙noon-9pm Mon-Sat) Don't be deceived by the humble decor at this compact eatery tucked away near the Japanese Bridge. There's a real wow factor to the seasonal small plates at this Hoi An favourite. Combine the pork-belly steamed buns with a salad of grilled pineapple, coconut and pomelo, and don't miss the homemade lemongrass, ginger or chilli ice cream.

★ Cargo Club INTERNATIONAL $$
(☎0235-391 1227; www.msvy-tastevietnam.com/cargo-club; 107 Đ Nguyen Thai Hoc; meals 70,000-160,000d; ⊙8am-11pm; 🛜) Remarkable cafe-restaurant, serving Vietnamese and Western food, with a terrific riverside location (the

upper terrace has stunning views). A relaxing day here munching your way around the menu would be a day well spent. The breakfasts are legendary (try the eggs Benedict), the patisserie and cakes are superb, and fine-dining dishes and good cocktails also deliver.

Hola Taco
MEXICAN $$

(www.facebook.com/pg/holataco; 9 Đ Phan Chau Trinh; snacks & meals 75,0000-160,000d; ⊙11am-10pm; 🛜🍽) Mexican flavours come to Hoi An at the excellent Hola Taco. The standouts are the tacos and enchiladas, both well spiced and ideal with a couple of Tiger beers or frosty margaritas. Here you'll find some of Hoi An's most colourful food and decent options for vegetarians.

Little Menu
VIETNAMESE $$

(www.thelittlemenu.com; 12 Đ Le Loi; meals 60,000-150,000d; ⊙9.30am-11pm; 🛜) 🍽 English-speaking owner Son is a fantastic host at this popular little restaurant with an open kitchen and short menu – try the fish in banana leaf or duck spring rolls, which feature on the set menu (225,000d). Almost all of the ingredients are strictly local from around Hoi An.

🍷 Drinking & Nightlife

3 Dragons
PUB

(www.facebook.com/3Dragonshoian; 51 Đ Phan Boi Chau; ⊙8am-midnight; 🛜) Half sports bar (where you can watch everything from Aussie Rules to Indian cricket) and half restaurant (burgers, steaks and local food).

Espresso Station
CAFE

(📞0905 691 164; www.facebook.com/TheEspressoStation; 28/2 Đ Tran Hung Dao; coffee 30,000-50,000d; ⊙7.30am-5pm; 🛜) A slice of Melbourne-style coffee culture – albeit in a

---

---

heritage Hoi An residence – the Espresso Station is where to go for the best flat whites and cold-brew coffees in town. There's a compact food menu with granola, muesli and sandwiches; relaxing in the arty courtyard is where you'll want to be.

🛍 Shopping

Tailor-made clothing is one of Hoi An's best trades, and there are more than 200 tailor shops in town that can whip up suits, shirts, dresses and much more.

★ Villagecraft Planet
ARTS & CRAFTS

(www.facebook.com/VillagecraftPlanet; 59 Đ Phan Boi Chau; ⊙10am-6pm) 🍽 Shop here for interesting homewares and fashion, often using natural hemp and indigo, and crafted with fair-trade practices by the Hmong, Black Thai and Lolo ethnic minority people in the north of Vietnam.

★ Reaching Out
SOUVENIRS, CLOTHING

(www.reachingoutvietnam.com; 103 Đ Nguyen Thai Hoc; ⊙8.30am-9.30pm Mon-Fri, 9.30am-8.30pm Sat & Sun) 🍽 Excellent fair-trade gift shop that stocks good-quality silk scarves, clothes, jewellery, hand-painted Vietnamese hats, handmade toys and teddy bears. The shop employs and supports artisans with disabilities, and staff are happy to show visitors through the workshop.

★ Rue des Arts
ARTS & CRAFTS

(Đ Phan Boi Chau) This mid-2017 initiative focuses attention on Đ Phan Boi Chau, east of Đ Hoang Dieu, as a dedicated arts street with galleries, museums and cafes housed mainly in the heritage buildings of Hoi An's former French Quarter. Pick up a walking map from the **March Gallery** (📞0122 377 9074; www.marchgallery-hoian.com; 25 Đ Phan Boi Chau; ⊙9am-6pm), Precious Heritage (p874) or **Mia Coffee House** (www.facebook.com/miacoffeehouse; 20 Đ Phan Boi Chau; ⊙8am-5pm) and start exploring.

ⓘ Information

Coast Vietnam (www.coastvietnam.com) features lots of eating, drinking and activities information from savvy Hoi An expats. Look for the free *Hoi An Travel Guide* map too. Wi-fi is widespread at cafes, bars and accommodation.

Hoi An Hospital (📞0235-386 1364; 4 Đ Tran Hung Dao; ⊙6am-10pm) For serious problems, go to Danang.

Rose Travel Service (📞0235-391 7567; www.rosetravelservice.com; 37-39 Đ Ly Thai To;

⊘7.30am-5.30pm) Tours around the area and Vietnam, plus car hire and buses.

Sinh Tourist (🖵 0235-386 3948; www.thesinhtourist.vn; 587 Đ Hai Ba Trung; ⊘6am-10pm) Books reputable open-tour buses.

Tourist Information Office (🖵 0235-391 6961; www.quangnamtourism.com.vn; 47 Đ Phan Chau Trinh; ⊘8am-5pm) Helpful office with good English spoken.

❶ Getting There & Away

Most north–south bus services do not stop at Hoi An, as Hwy 1 passes 10km west of the town, but you can head for the town of Vinh Dien and flag down a bus there. More convenient open-tour buses offer regular connections for Hue and Nha Trang.

Yellow buses to Danang (20,000d) leave from the **northern bus station** just off Đ Le Hong Phong, a 15-minute walk or a 15,000d xe om ride from central Hoi An.

The nearest airport and train station are both in Danang. A car to Hoi An costs around 550,000d via your hotel or a local travel agency, while xe om will do it for around 150,000d. Bargain hard if you want to stop at the Marble Mountains or Danang Beach en route. Shared shuttle buses cost around 300,000d and can be booked through hotels.

❶ Getting Around

Metered taxis and motorbike drivers wait for business over the footbridge in An Hoi. Call **Hoi An Taxi** (🖵 0510-391 9919) or **Mai Linh** (🖵 0235-392 5925) for a pick-up.

Many hotels offer bicycles/motorbikes for hire from 20,000/100,000d per day. Hoi An's compact Old Town is best explored on foot.

Around Hoi An

An Bang Beach

An Bang is one of Vietnam's most happening and enjoyable beaches. At present there's a wonderful stretch of fine sand and an enormous horizon, with less of the serious erosion evident at Cua Dai, and with only the distant Cham Islands interrupting the seaside symmetry. Staying at the beach and visiting Hoi An on day trips is a good strategy for a relaxing visit to the area.

There is a growing band of vendors selling souvenirs and food on the beach, and at the end of the day the beach gets very busy with local families heading down for a swim. A few watersports operators are also now offering parasailing and jet-ski hire. Note that safety standards for these activities may not be enforced as strongly as in other countries.

🍴 Sleeping & Eating

Under the Coconut Tree   BUNGALOW **$**
(🖵0168 245 5666; www.underthecoconuttree-hoian.com; An Bang; dm US$9, d US$30-40; 🛜) The funkiest place to stay in An Bang is this ramshackle garden collection of wooden and bamboo lodges and bungalows. For thrifty travellers, the Coconut Dorm House has outdoor showers and simple, shared accommodation in a breezy, open-sided pavilion, while the Bamboo Family House accommodates four. The cosy Mushroom House is couples-friendly and has a private bathroom.

★**Sea Shell**   FRENCH, SEAFOOD **$**
(119 Đ Tran Cao Van; meals 90,000d; ⊘noon-9pm) Shaded by a decades-old banyan tree, Sea Shell is a flavour-packed offshoot of Nu Eatery in Hoi An's Old Town. Try snacks like tempura-prawn rolls and turmeric-catfish wraps, or mains like spicy pork noodles with a refreshing calamari and green-apple salad. A decent wine list covers Australia, France, Italy and South Africa.

Sound of Silence   CAFE
(www.facebook.com/soundofsilencecoffee; coffee from 25,000d; ⊘7am-5pm; 🛜) An Bang's best spot for a coffee, Sound of Silence combines a rustic garden setting, ocean views and the best barista skills in the village. Fresh coconuts and crêpes crammed with tropical fruit are other distractions while you wonder about going for a swim.

❶ Getting There & Away

Access to/from Hoi An is easy – it's just a 20-minute bike ride or a five-minute (70,000d) taxi journey. Parking your bicycle will cost around 5000d, a good investment to guarantee its security while you're on the beach

My Son

Set under the shadow of Cat's Tooth Mountain are the enigmatic ruins of **My Son** (150,000d; ⊘6.30am-4pm), the most important remains of the ancient Cham empire and a Unesco World Heritage Site. Although Vietnam has better-preserved Cham sites, none are as extensive and few have such beautiful surroundings, with brooding mountains and clear streams running between the temples.

VIETNAM AROUND HOI AN

The ruins are 55km southwest of Hoi An. Day tours to My Son can be arranged in Hoi An for between US$10 and US$15, not including admission, and some trips return to Hoi An by boat.

Independent travellers can hire a motorbike, *xe om* or car. Get here early in order to beat the tour groups, or later in the afternoon.

SOUTHEAST COAST

Vietnam has an incredibly curvaceous coastline and on this coast it's defined by sweeping sands, towering cliffs and concealed bays. Nha Trang and Mui Ne are key destinations, but the beach breaks come thick and fast here.

If your idea of paradise is reclining in front of turquoise waters, weighing up the merits of a massage or a mojito, then you have come to the right place. On hand to complement the sedentary delights are activities to set the pulse racing, including scuba diving, snorkelling, surfing, windsurfing and kitesurfing. Action or inaction, this coast bubbles with opportunities.

Nha Trang

📞 0258426,000 / POP 426,000

Welcome to the beach capital of Vietnam. The high-rise, high-energy resort of Nha Trang enjoys a stunning setting, ringed by a necklace of hills, with a sweeping crescent beach and turquoise bay dotted with tropical islands.

Central Nha Trang is a party town at heart. Until relatively recently a lot of the bar action was geared towards the backpacker market, but today it's mainly aimed at the burgeoning numbers of well-heeled Russian and Asian tourists.

If vodka shooters, cocktail buckets and karaoke are not your scene, try the natural mud baths or visit the imposing Cham towers.

🅾 Sights

★Nha Trang Beach   BEACH

Forming a magnificent sweeping arc, Nha Trang's 6km-long golden-sand beach is the city's trump card. Sections are roped off and designated for safe swimming (where you won't be bothered by jet skis or boats). The turquoise water is very inviting, and the promenade a delight to stroll.

Two popular lounging spots are the **Sailing Club** (www.sailingclubnhatrang.com; 72-74 Đ

Tran Phu; ⏱ 7am-2am; 📶) and Louisiane Brewhouse (p881). If you head south of here, the beach gets quieter and it's possible to find a quiet stretch of sand.

★**Po Nagar Cham Towers**   BUDDHIST TEMPLE

(Thap Ba, Lady of the City; north side of Xom Bong Bridge; admission 22,000d, guide 50,000d; ⏱ 6am-6pm) Built between the 7th and 12th centuries, these impressive Cham towers are still actively used for worship by Cham, Chinese and Vietnamese Buddhists. Originally the complex had seven or eight towers, but only four remain, of which the 28m-high North Tower (Thap Chinh; AD 817), with a terraced pyramidal roof, vaulted interior masonry and vestibule, is the most magnificent.

The towers stand on a granite knoll 3km north of central Nha Trang, on the northern bank of the Cai River.

🏃 Activities

Nha Trang is Vietnam's most popular scuba-diving centre. February to September is considered the best time to dive, while October to December is the worst time of year.

There are around 25 dive sites in the area. Some sites have good drop-offs and there are small underwater caves to explore. It's not world-class diving, but the waters support a reasonable number of small reef fish.

A two-dive boat trip costs between US$60 and US$85; snorkellers typically pay US$20.

Most dive operators also offer a range of dive courses. Watch out for dodgy dive shops not following responsible diving practices and even using fake PADI/SSI accreditation – stick to reputable operators including **Oceans 5** (📞 0258-381 1969, 0258-352 2012; www.oceans5.co; 49/06 Đ Hung Vuong; 2 dives US$75) and **Angel Dive** (📞 0258-352 2461; www.angeldivevietnam.info; 10 Đ Nguyen Thien Thuat; fun dive from US$30).

★**Lanterns Tours**   CULTURAL

(📞 0258-247 1674; www.lanternsvietnam.com; 30a Đ Nguyen Thien Thuat; tour from US$29) This nonprofit restaurant offers fine-value street-food tours (250,000d) of Nha Trang featuring seven dishes including *banh tai vac* (tapioca shrimp dumplings). It also offers a tour to Ninh Hoa (from US$29), a nontouristy town, which includes a local market and lunch with a family.

★**Vietnam Active**   ADVENTURE SPORTS

(📞 0258-352 8119; www.vietnamactive.com; 115 Đ Hung Vuong) Offers a diverse range of excellent activities: rafting, kayaking, mountain biking, yoga (150,000d per class), scuba-diving (two dives US$65) and freediving. Exact prices depend upon numbers for most activities.

Shamrock Adventures RAFTING
(📞 0905 150 978; www.shamrockadventures.vn; Đ Phan Dinh Giot; trips per person incl lunch from US$45) Specialises in fishing trips (including deep-sea and fly) and also runs white-water rafting excursions (which can be combined with some mountain biking) along the Serapok River.

🛏 Sleeping

⭐Sunny Sea HOTEL $
(📞 0258-352 2286; sunnyseahotel@gmail.com; 64b/9 Đ Tran Phu; r 250,000-330,000d; ❄@🛜) This very welcoming mini-hotel is run by a local couple (a doctor and nurse) and their super-friendly staff who delight in helping out travellers. Rooms are in great shape: very clean, with springy mattresses, minibar and modern bathrooms; some have a balcony. It's fine value and just off the beach.

⭐Mojzo Inn HOSTEL $
(📞 0988 879 069; www.facebook.com/mojzoInn; 120/36 Đ Nguyen Thien Thuat; dm US$7, r US$19-23; ❄@🛜) This funky hostel gets most things right, with well-designed dorms, a lovely cushion-scattered lounge area, huge breakfasts and even free beer served on the rooftop! Staff really go the extra mile to help out with travel info and connections.

Binh An Hotel GUESTHOUSE $
(📞 090 514 3548; www.binhanhotel.com; 28h Đ Hoang Hoa Tham; r 350,000-380,000d; ❄@🛜) A family-run, welcoming place where the owners look after guests with pride and provide travel tips and fresh fruit daily. Rooms are spotless, spacious and boast good air-conditioning and fast wi-fi. A good breakfast is available for 60,000d.

🍴 Eating

For inexpensive, authentic Vietnamese food, head to **Dam Market** (Đ Trang Nu Vuong; meals 15,000-50,000d; ⏰6am-4pm) which has good stalls and lots of veggie choices.

Au Lac VEGETARIAN $
(28c Đ Hoang Hoa Tham; meals 15,000-32,000d; ⏰10am-7pm; 🍴) No-frills vegan/vegetarian place where a mixed plate (20,000d) is just about the best-value meal you can find in Nha Trang. Just take a seat and a plate will

arrive. Surrounds are simple, with steel tables and plastic stools.

⭐Lac Canh Restaurant VIETNAMESE $$
(44 Đ Nguyen Binh Khiem; meals 50,000-150,000d; ⏰11am-8.45pm) A unique experience, this scruffy, unadulterated barbecue place is where locals go to feast on meat (beef, richly marinated with spices, is the speciality, but there are other meats and seafood, too). It's DIY: you grill ingredients on your own charcoal burner. Note: it closes quite early.

79 Dung Lin VIETNAMESE $$
(29 Đ Phan Chu Trinh; meals 75,000-130,000d; ⏰6-9.30pm) Simple local joint that's famous for its wonderfully flavoursome barbecued duck (half a duck with salad, dips and rice 100,000d).

🍷 Drinking & Nightlife

⭐Alpaca Homestyle Cafe CAFE
(www.facebook.com/alpacanhatrang; 10/1b Đ Nguyen Thien Thuat; ⏰8am-9.30pm Mon-Sat; 🛜) This hip little cafe with an artistic interior is famous for its coffee (sourced in Dalat), which comes in espresso, French press or cold-brewed options. Iced teas, juices (45,000d) and great Mediterranean and Mexican food are also offered.

⭐Louisiane Brewhouse BREWERY
(29 Đ Tran Phu; ⏰7am-midnight; 🛜) This shorefront microbrewery has it all – you can cool off in the swimming pool or enjoy the sea breeze before sampling one of the six craft brews, which include red ale and dark lager. There's a full food menu here, too.

Crazy Kim Bar BAR
(http://crazykimvietnam.wordpress.com; 19 Đ Biet Thu; ⏰9am-late; 🛜) This place is home to the commendable 'Hands off the Kids!' campaign, working to prevent paedophilia – part of the profits go towards the cause. Crazy Kim's has regular themed party nights, cheap beer and tasty pub grub. There are happy hour promos

---

DRINK SPIKING

Periodically, we receive reports of laced cocktail buckets in popular nightspots. This might mean staff using homemade moonshine instead of legal spirits or it could mean the addition of drugs by other punters. While buckets can be fun and communal, consider the risks.

throughout the night, including two-for-one cocktails between 4.30pm and 10.30pm.

Information

Though Nha Trang is generally a safe place, be very careful on the beach during the day (theft) and at night (robbery). Pickpocketing is a perennial problem. Bags with valuables left behind bars for 'safekeeping' are regularly relieved of cash and phones, and there have been reports of spiked cocktail buckets.

Most hotels and bars have free wi-fi, and ATMs are widespread.

Khanh Hoa Tourist Information (☑ 0258-382 9357; www.nhatrang-travel.com; Tran Phu; ◷ 8am-5.30pm) Small office staffed by helpful English-speaking staff.

Main Post Office (4 Đ Le Loi; ◷ 6.30am-8pm Mon-Fri, to 1pm Sat) Post office in Nha Trang.

Pasteur Institute (☑ 0258-382 2355; www. pasteur-nhatrang.org.vn; 8-10 Đ Tran Phu; ◷ 7-11am & 1-4.30pm) Offers medical consultations and vaccinations.

Sinh Tourist (☑ 0258-352 2982; www.thesinhtourist.vn; 90C Đ Hung Vuong; ◷ 6am-10pm) Reliable, professional agency for inexpensive local trips, including a city tour for 279,000d (excluding entrance fees) as well as open-tour buses, train and flight bookings.

❶ Getting There & Away

AIR

Cam Ranh International Airport (☑ 0258-398 9913) is 35km south of the city via a beautiful coastal road.

Vietnam Airlines (☑ 0258-352 6768; www. vietnamairlines.com; 91 Đ Nguyen Thien Thuat) connects Nha Trang with Hanoi, HCMC and Danang daily and also has flights to several Chinese cities including Chengdu and Kunming. Vietjet Air (www.vietjetair.com) has links to Hanoi and HCMC daily and also flights to several cities in China including Shanghai. Jetstar (www.jetstar.com) offers good connections with Hanoi and HCMC and also operates flights to Hue, Bangkok and Siem Riep.

Other usual international links include an Air Asia flight to Kuala Lumpur and a Korean Air flight to Seoul.

BUS

Phia Nam Nha Trang Bus Station (Đ 23 Thang 10) The main intercity bus terminal. Regular daily buses north to Danang and south towards Phan Rang and HCMC.

TRAIN

The **Nha Trang Train Station** (☑ 0258-382 2113; Đ Thai Nguyen; ◷ ticket office 7-11.30am, 1.30-6pm & 7-9pm) is in the centre of town. It's on the main north–south line with good connections to destinations including Dieu Tri (for Quy Nhon), Danang and HCMC. There's no line to Dalat.

❶ Getting Around

Shuttle buses (50,000d, 45 minutes) connect the airport with Nha Trang roughly every 30 minutes between 6am and 6.30pm. They pass through the heart of town, stopping at points along the coastal road Đ Tran Phu.

Nha Trang city is pretty flat, so it's easy to get around all the sights by bicycle. Hotels have bikes for hire from 30,000d per day. Use a metered taxi from a reputable company such as **Mai Linh** (☑ 0258-382 2266).

Mui Ne

☑ 0252 / POP 17,600

Once upon a time, Mui Ne was an isolated stretch of sand, but it was too beautiful to be ignored – now it's a string of resorts spread along a 10km stretch of highway. Mercifully, most of these are low-rise and set amid pretty gardens by the sea.

Windsurfing and kitesurfing are huge here – surf's up from August to December. It's

TRANSPORT FROM NHA TRANG

DESTINATION	AIR	BUS	CAR/ MOTORCYCLE	TRAIN
Dalat	N/A	US$7, 5hr, 12 daily	4-5hr	N/A
Danang	from US$40, 1hr, 1 daily	US$11-16, 11-12hr, 15 daily	11hr	US$13-18, 9-11hr, 7 daily
Ho Chi Minh City	from US$25, 1hr, 12 daily	US$9-14, 10-12hr, 16 daily	10hr	US$11-16, 7-9hr, 7 daily
Mui Ne	N/A	US$8, 5½hr, 4 daily	5hr	N/A
Quy Nhon	N/A	US$6.50, 6hr, every 2½hr	6hr	US$5.50-7, 3½-4½hr, 7 daily

WORTH A TRIP

BAI DAI BEACH

South of Nha Trang, a spectacular coastal road leads to Cam Ranh Bay, a gorgeous natural harbour, and the airport. Virtually the entire shoreline south of Mia Resort forms Bai Dai (Long Beach), a breathtaking sandy coast.

Until very recently, the Vietnamese military controlled the entire area, restricting access to all but the odd fishing boat. However, times have changed and now the entire strip has been earmarked for development. Several giant resort hotels have already opened and many others are under construction.

You may not find virgin sands any longer, but some of the best surf breaks in Vietnam are still found on Bai Dai. At the northern tip of the coastline, Shack Vietnam (www.shackvietnam.com) offers one-hour board hire and surf instruction in English for 600,000d (board hire only is 200,000d per hour). It also offers kayak hire, beers and grub. The Shack sits in the middle of a strip of 20 or so seafood restaurants, all with near-identical menus.

A one-way journey in a taxi to the north end of Bai Dai costs around 275,000d, or you can catch an airport-bound bus (50,000d, every 30 minutes) and jump off anywhere along the coast.

also the 'Sahara' of Vietnam, with the most dramatic sand dunes in the region looming large.

⊙ Sights

Sand Dunes   BEACH
Mui Ne is famous for its enormous red and white sand dunes. The 'red dunes' (*doi hong*) are convenient to Hai Long, but the 'white dunes' (*doi cat trang*), 24km northeast, are the more impressive – the near-constant oceanic winds sculpt the pale yellow sands into wonderful Saharaesque formations. But as this is Vietnam there's little chance of experiencing the silence of the desert.

🏃 Activities

★ Manta Sail Training Centre   BOATING
(☑ 0908 400 108; http://mantasailing.org; 108 Đ Huynh Thuc Khang; sailing instruction per hr US$66) One of Southeast Asia's best sailing schools, Manta offers instruction and training (from beginner to advanced racing). Speak to staff about wakeboarding (US$100 per hour), SUP hire (US$10 per hour) and boat tours. The centre also has budget rooms available right by the beach.

★ Mui Ne Hot Air Balloon   BALLOONING
(☑ 0120 853 6828; www.vietnamballoons.com; from US$136) The first hot-air balloon experience in Vietnam is a professionally run, European-owned operation that sees you either soaring over the spectacular white sand dunes and desert lakes east of Mui Ne, or alternatively over the bustling fishing harbour of Phan Thiet. Prepare yourself for a magical flight at sunrise.

Jibes   KITESURFING
(☑ 0252-384 7405; www.jibesbeachclub.com; 84-90 Đ Nguyen Dinh Chieu; ⊙ 7.30am-6pm) Mui Ne's original kitesurfing school, Jibes offers instruction (US$60 per hour) and gear including windsurfs (US$55 per day), SUPs (US$20 per half day), surfboards, kitesurfs and kayaks for hire.

**Surfpoint
Kiteboarding School**   KITESURFING, SURFING
(☑ 0167 342 2136; www.surfpoint-vietnam.com; 52a Đ Nguyen Dinh Chieu; 5hr course incl all gear US$250; ⊙ 7am-6pm) One of Mui Ne's best-regarded kite schools. A three-hour starter course costs US$150. Surfing lessons on soft boards are also offered (from US$50) when waves permit.

★ Festivals

Mui Ne Street Food Festival   FOOD & DRINK
(www.facebook.com/muinestreetfoodfestival) Mui Ne hosts a popular street food festival three times a year (usually January, April and July), featuring local dishes from Phan Thiet in addition to national and international classics. It's held on the main drag by Blue Ocean Resort and Coco Beach Resort; there's also live music and DJs.

🛏 Sleeping

Mui Ne Backpacker Village   HOSTEL **$**
(☑ 0252-374 1047; www.muinebackpackervillage. com; 137 Đ Nguyen Dinh Chieu; dm/r from US$6/20; ⊖✹🛜⊠) This huge, well-designed modern hostel is wildly popular with its inviting swimming pool. Thanks to the bar-restaurant, pool table, darts, and table football and ten-

nis, there's a social, party vibe. All dorms have air-conditioning, individual beds and lockers while the private rooms all have a balcony or patio. The hostel runs lots of good-value tours.

Coco Sand Hotel
GUESTHOUSE $

(📞 0127 364 3446; http://cocosandhotel.com; 119 Đ Nguyen Dinh Chieu; r US$16-27; ❋ 🛜) Down a little lane, Coco Sand has excellent-value rooms with air-conditioning, cable TV, fridge and private bathroom. There's a shady courtyard garden (with hammocks) to enjoy and the friendly owners hire out motorbikes at fair rates.

Mui Ne Hills Budget Hotel
HOTEL $

(📞 0252-374 1707; www.muinehills.com; 69 Đ Nguyen Dinh Chieu; dm/r from US$6/30; ❋ 🛜 ⊠) Around 300m off the main strip, via an incredibly steep access road, this popular spot has several air-conditioned dorms with en suites and lockers. Private rooms have quality furnishings and contemporary design touches. During quiet times guests are often upgraded to upmarket sister accommodation over the road.

★ Cat Sen Auberge
B&B $$

(📞 0122 323 3673; http://catsen.simdif.com; 195 Đ Nguyen Dinh Chieu; r/bungalow US$23/36; ❋ 🛜 ⊠) A wonderfully relaxing place to stay, Cat Sen Auberge has well-constructed rooms and lovely bungalows (with gorgeous verandahs) dotted around extensive, coconut treetstudded grounds. There's a great pool and lots of space, with hammocks for lounging and free drinking water. Book ahead in high season.

🍴 Eating

★ Dong Vui Food Court
FOOD HALL $

(www.facebook.com/FoodCourtDongVui; 246 Đ Nguyen Dinh Chieu; meals 30,000-170,000d; ⊘ 5-11pm) A brilliant new concept, this attractive open-air food court has loads of independently run cook stations offering everything from Punjabi cuisine to paella, German sausages and Thai curries – plus plenty of Vietnamese options. Just grab a seat and order what you fancy. There's also great craft beer on tap and live music some weekends. Located on the eastern side of the strip.

Mui Ne Beach

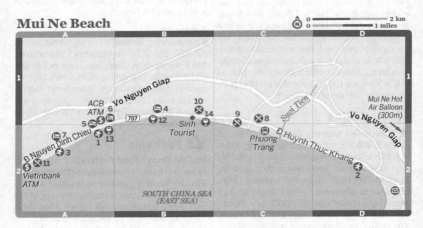

Mui Ne Beach

BAI XEP

An isolated fishing village just a few years back, the pretty bay of Bai Xep is fast emerging as one of coastal Vietnam's most popular spots with independent travellers. It's still quite remote, 13km south of Quy Nhon, but this beach's relaxed appeal is considerable and its beauty undeniable.

Bai Xep consists of two small coves. The northernmost cove, Bai Truoc ('Front Beach'), is a busy little fishing port with a warren of lanes of tightly packed houses and a small bay strewn with fishing tackle and boats. Just to the south is larger, more attractive Bai Sau ('Back Beach'), which has an expanding range of accommodation, each place facing a stunning crescent-shaped sandy bay that offers wonderful swimming. It's easy to lose track of time here, chilling in a hammock, socialising with locals and fellow travellers and exploring the stunning coastline and islands offshore.

Bai Xep is 13km south of Quy Nhon and connected by local buses: T11 (9000d) runs roughly hourly from the Metro mall between 5.30am and 5pm (with a break for lunch). A taxi from Quy Nhon is 180,000d. Many travellers arrive by motorbike.

Recommended accommodation includes **Life's A Beach Backpackers** (☑086-895 8843; http://lifesabeachvietnam.com; 2km north of Xuan Hai; dm/hut/r from US$6/15/20; ✷ ❒) and **Haven** (☑0982 114 906; www.havenvietnam.com; To 2, Khu Vuc 1, Bai Sau, Bai Xep; r incl breakfast 720,000-1,000,000d; ✷ ❒).

Com Chay Vi Dieu VEGETARIAN $
(15B Đ Huynh Thuc Khang; meals 25,000d; ⊘7am-9pm;) A simple roadside place perfect for inexpensive Vietnamese vegetarian dishes (curries, noodle soup and fried rice dishes); it also serves great smoothies (20,000d). It's opposite the Eiffel Tower of the Little Paris resort. Almost no English is spoken.

Phat Hamburgers INTERNATIONAL $
(253 Đ Nguyen Dinh Chieu; burgers 80,000-165,000d; ⊘9am-10pm; ❒) This casual roadside joint has many meaty burger options (try a Phatarella, spread with cashew-nut pesto and served with mozzarella), and it's rightly proud of its veggie versions as well. Hot dogs hit the spot, too.

🍸 Drinking & Nightlife

★**PoGo** BAR
(☑0912 000 751; www.thepogobar.com; 138 Đ Nguyen Dinh Chieu; ⊘8.30am-2am) This casual bar has a great beachfront location, day beds for lounging, DJs on weekends and regular movie nights. Staff are very friendly; happy hour runs from 6pm to 8pm.

Joe's Café BAR
(http://joescafemuine.com; 86 Đ Nguyen Dinh Chieu; ⊘7am-1am; ❒) This very popular pub-like place has live music (every night at 7.30pm) and a gregarious vibe. During the day it's a good place to hang, too, with seats set under a giant mango tree, magazines to browse, a pool table and an extensive food menu.

Dragon Beach BAR, CLUB
(120-121 Đ Nguyen Dinh Chieu; ⊘1pm-4am) Mui Ne's main nightclub has a cool shoreside location with a chill-out deck scattered with cushions and a lively dance floor. Musically, expect commercial EDM, house and banging techno. Staff are notoriously unprofessional – don't expect much in the way of service.

❶ Information

Internet and wi-fi are available at pretty much all hotels and resorts, as well as at most restaurants and bars.

Main Post Office (348 Đ Huynh Thuc Khang; ⊘7am-5pm) In the fishing village.

Sinh Tourist (☑098 925 8060; www.thesinhtourist.vn; 144 Đ Nguyen Dinh Chieu; ⊘7am-10pm) Reliable and trustworthy agency for open-tour buses, trips around Mui Ne and also credit-card cash advances.

ⓘ Getting There & Away

Open-tour buses are the most convenient option for Mui Ne, as most public buses only serve Phan Thiet. Several companies have daily services to/from HCMC (110,000d to 135,000d, six hours), Nha Trang (from 112,000d, 5½ hours) and Dalat (125,000d, four hours). Sleeper open-tour night buses usually cost more.

Phuong Trang (http://futabus.vn; 97 Đ Nguyen Dinh Chieu) has regular, comfortable buses running between Mui Ne and HCMC (130,000d). Its depot is just west of the fairy spring river. Sinh Tourist (p885) operates three daily buses on this route.

Local buses (9000d, 45 minutes, frequent) make trips between Phan Thiet Bus Station and Mui Ne, departing from the Coopmart, on the corner of Đ Nguyen Tat Thanh and Đ Tran Hung Dao.

SOUTHWEST HIGHLANDS

There's a rugged charm to this distinctly rural region, with pine-studded hilltops soaring over intensively farmed fields and remote, bumpy roads meandering through coffee plantations. Looking for big nature? Check out Cat Tien National Park (p887), where there are gibbons, crocodiles and elusive tigers. Dalat, a former French hill station that still boasts plenty of colonial-era charm, makes a great base.

Dalat

📞 0263 / POP 184,755 / ELEV 1475M

Dalat is the alter-ego of lowland Vietnam. The weather is springlike cool instead of tropical hot. The town is dotted with elegant French-colonial villas, and farms are thick with strawberries and flowers, not rice.

Dalat is small enough to remain charming, and the surrounding countryside is blessed with lakes, waterfalls, evergreen forests and gardens. The town is a big draw for domestic tourists.

For travellers, the moderate climate is ideal for adrenaline-fuelled activities – mountain biking, forest hiking, canyoning and climbing.

⊙ Sights

Perhaps there's something in the cool mountain air that fosters the distinctly artistic vibe that veers towards cute kitsch in Dalat.

★ **Hang Nga Crazy House** ARCHITECTURE
(📞 0263-382 2070; 3 Đ Huynh Thuc Khang; 50,000d; ⊙ 8.30am-7pm Mon-Fri) A free-wheeling architectural exploration of surrealism, Hang Nga Crazy House is a joyously designed, outrageously artistic private home. Imagine sculptured rooms connected by superslim bridges rising out of a tangle of greenery, an excess of cascading lava-flow-like shapes, wild colours, spiderweb windows and an almost organic quality to it all, with the swooping hand rails resembling jungle vines. Think of Gaudí and Tolkien dropping acid together.

King Palace PALACE
(Dinh 1; 📞 0263-358 0558; Hung Vuong; adult/child 30,000/10,000d; ⊙ 7am-5pm) Tastefully revamped, the main palace of Bao Dai, Vietnam's last emperor, beckons visitors with its beautiful tree-lined avenue and a surprisingly modest but attractive royal residence. It was home to Bao Dai and his family until they went into exile in France in 1954. The house was subsequently taken over by then Prime Minister Ngo Dinh Diem. Highlights are undoubtedly the family photos: Bao Dai playing with a dog, and riding a horse, and well-scrubbed royal children with serious faces.

Crémaillère Railway Station HISTORIC BUILDING
(Ga Da Lat; 1 Đ Quang Trung; 5000d; ⊙ 6.30am-5pm) **FREE** From Dalat's wonderful art deco train station you can ride one of the nine scheduled trains that run to Trai Mat (return 108,000d, 30 minutes) daily between 6.55am and 4.39pm; a minimum of 25 passengers is required. A *crémaillère* (cog railway) linking Dalat and Thap Cham from 1928 to 1964 was closed due to VC attacks. A Japanese steam train is on display.

☞ Tours

★ **Phat Tire Ventures** ADVENTURE
(📞 063-382 9422; www.ptv-vietnam.com; 109 Đ Nguyen Van Troi; ⊙ 8am-7pm) A highly professional and experienced operator with mountain-biking trips from US$49, trekking from US$39, kayaking from US$39, canyoning (US$75) and rapelling (US$57), and white-water rafting (US$67) in the rainy season. Multiday cycling trips are available and it also ventures into Cat Tien National Park.

Groovy Gecko Adventure Tours ADVENTURE
(📞 0263-383 6521; www.groovygeckotours.net; 65 Đ Truong Cong Dinh; ⊙ 7.30am-8.30pm)

CAT TIEN NATIONAL PARK

Unesco-listed **Cat Tien National Park** (☑0251-366 9228; www.namcattien.org; adult/child 60,000/10,000d; ⊘7am-10pm) 🏍 comprises an amazingly biodiverse area of lowland tropical rainforest. The hiking, mountain biking and birdwatching are outstanding.

Fauna in the park includes 326 bird species, 100 mammals (including elephants) and 79 reptiles, though the last rhino was killed by poachers in 2010.

Call headquarters for reservations and to book a guide, as the park can accommodate only a limited number of visitors.

Sights & Activities

Cat Tien National Park can be explored on foot, by mountain bike, by 4WD and also by boat. There are 14 well-established hiking trails in the park. A guide (from 800,000d) is only mandatory for three difficult trails.

Trips to the **Crocodile Lake** (Bau Sau; Cat Tien National Park; admission 200,000d, guide fee 550,000d, boat trip from 200,000d) taking in a three-hour jungle trek, are popular.

Dao Tien Endangered Primate Species Centre (www.go-east.org; Cat Tien National Park; adult/child incl boat ride 300,000/150,000d; ⊘tours 8.30am & 2pm) is located on an island in the Dong Nai River. This rehabilitation centre hosts gibbons, langurs and lorises. The **Bear & Wild Cat Rescue Station** (Cat Tien National Park; 150,000d; ⊘7.30am-4pm) is also worth a visit.

Wild Gibbon Trek (www.go-east.org; Cat Tien National Park; per person 1,050,000d, maximum 4 people; ⊘4.30am) involves a 4.30am start to hear the gibbons' dawn chorus and a fully guided tour of the Primate Species Centre. Book ahead.

Sleeping & Eating

Accommodation options include the riverside **Green Hope Lodge** (☑0251-366 9919, 0972 184 683; www.greenhopelodge.com; Nam Cat Tien; r US$5-35; ❄🏠), a five-minute walk from the ferry crossing, and **Ta Lai Long House** (☑0974 160 827; www.talai-adventure.vn; Cat Tien National Park; dm 450,000d; 🏠) is another goodie, but 12km away. There are small restaurants near the park HQ, and many people eat at their guesthouse accommodation.

Getting There & Around

Cat Tien is 175km south of Dalat; turn off Hwy 20 at Tan Phu and it's another 24km up a paved access road to the entrance. Buses between Dalat and HCMC (210,000d, every 30 minutes) pass the access road. Waiting motorbikes (around 150,000d) will then take you to the park entrance. Guesthouses either rent bicycles or provide them free of charge.

Long-running agency offering a canyoning adventure that includes abseiling down a remote 65m waterfall (US$55). Also does mountain-bike trips (from US$28) and day treks (from US$28), as well as a one-day downhill cycle to Nha Trang (US$75).

Pine Track Adventures   ADVENTURE
(☑0263-383 1916; www.pinetrackadventures.com; 72b Đ Truong Cong Dinh; ⊘8am-8.30pm) Run by an enthusiastic and experienced local team, this operator offers canyoning (from US$55), white-water rafting (US$60), trekking (from US$35), biking (from US$41) and some excellent multisport packages. A seven-day bike tour from Dalat to Hoi An is US$595.

Dalat Happy Tours   FOOD & DRINK
(☑0163 654 6450; www.dalathappytours.com; street-food tour US$4) After all the active exertions around Dalat, replenish your calories by going on an entertaining, nightly street-food tour with friendly Lao. Start from the central Hoa Binh cinema at 6.30pm and proceed to sample *banh xeo* (filled pancakes), buffalo-tail hotpot, delectable grilled skewers, 'Dalat pizza', rabbit curry, hot rice wine and more. Food costs are not included.

🛏 Sleeping

★**Dalat Central Hostel**   HOSTEL $
(Hotel Phuong Hanh; ☑0989 878 879, 0263-383 8839; phuonghanhhotel@gmail.com; 80 Đ Ba Thang Hai; mixed/female dm US$5/6, r US$20-25; ❄🏠) More budget hotel than hostel, although it's a popular traveller hub. The vast eight- and 12-bed dorms come with comfy bunks and privacy curtains (a

Central Dalat

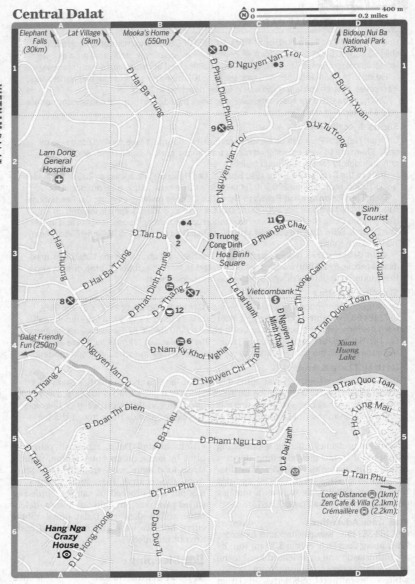

Elephant Falls (30km)
Lat Village (5km)
Mooka's Home (550m)
Bidoup Nui Ba National Park (32km)

Đ Nguyen Van Troi

Đ Hai Ba Trung

Đ Phan Dinh Phung

Đ Nguyen Van Troi

Đ Bui Thi Xuan

Đ Ly Tu Trong

Lam Dong General Hospital

Sinh Tourist

Đ Bui Thi Xuan

Đ Hai Thuong

Đ Tan Da

Đ Truong Cong Dinh

Hoa Binh Square

Đ Phan Boi Chau

Đ Hai Ba Trung

Đ Phan Dinh Phung

Đ 3 Thang 2

Đ Le Dai Hanh

Vietcombank

Đ Le Thi Hong Gam

Đ Tran Quoc Toan

Xuan Huong Lake

Dalat Friendly Fun (250m)

Đ Nguyen Van Cu

Đ Nam Ky Khoi Nghia

Đ Nguyen Chi Thanh

Đ Nguyen Thi Minh Khai

Đ Tran Quoc Toan

Đ 3 Thang 2

Đ Doan Thi Diem

Đ Ba Trieu

Đ Pham Ngu Lao

Đ Le Dai Hanh

Đ Ho Tung Mau

Đ Tran Phu

Đ Tran Phu

Đ Tran Phu

Đ Dao Duy Tu

Long-Distance (1km);
Zen Cafe & Villa (2.1km);
Crémaillère (2.2km);

Hang Nga Crazy House

Đ Le Hong Phong

women-only dorm is available), while the private rooms are also huge. The most expensive are equipped with triangular bathtubs. Staff is helpful and knowledgeable, and motorbikes (100,000d per day) can be hired.

★ **Dalat Friendly Fun**   HOSTEL **$**
(📱 0919 124 137; youthactiontour@gmail.com; 18 Mac Dinh Chi; dm US$5; 🛜) This place lives up to its name with a warm welcome and helpful staff who organise nightly group dinners (US$3), as well as recommending decent tour

Central Dalat

operators. Dorms are huge and bright, with curtained beds and inside bathrooms. There's one private room (US$15), and a couple of tents on the roof for when it's really busy.

★**Mooka's Home**   HOSTEL $
(☑0932 579 752; mookahome@gmail.com; 2 Co Loa; dm 100,000d; ☺@🛇) Big and light dorms come with sparkly inside bathrooms at this popular place. There are two four-bed female dorms, as well as a roof terrace and downstairs communal area. Nightly group dinners or barbecues are on offer (50,000d), and the friendly staff can arrange tours.

★**Villa Doc May**   GUESTHOUSE $
(☑0263-382 5754; villadocmaydalat@gmail.com; 16B Đ Nam Ky Khoi Nghia; r 450,000-790,000d; ❋🛇) More of a homestay than a guesthouse, there are just four individually decorated rooms here, all comfortable, as well as two pleasant communal areas with sofas and a kitchen for guests to use. It's run by a charming family. Find it up a steep alley off the street; look for the sign.

Zen Cafe & Villa   GUESTHOUSE $$
(☑0994 799 518; www.zencafedalat.com; 27c Pham Hong Thai; r US$28-48; 🛇) Lodge in spacious, characterful rooms in a century-old French villa with a tranquil garden, sufficiently high up to give you mountain views. Owners Axel and Mai Dung regale you with local anecdotes and the coffee served at their cafe is wonderful.

✖ Eating

There are vegetarian food stalls and cheap eats in the market area on Cho Da Lat.

★**Tau Cao Wonton Noodles**   NOODLES $
(217 Đ Phan Dinh Phung; noodles 35,000-40,000d; ☺6am-8pm) This humble eatery is famed throughout Dalat and is always heaving with locals, who come for the noodle wonton soup.

It's served with thin slices of pork on top and a sprinkling of mincemeat. Add chilli, lime and bean sprouts to taste and you're good to go. Classic Asian street eats. No English spoken.

★**Trong Dong**   VIETNAMESE $
(☑0263-382 1889; 220 Đ Phan Dinh Phung; meals 75,000-150,000d; ☺11am-3pm & 5-9pm; 🛇) Intimate restaurant run by a very hospitable team where the creative menu includes spins on Vietnamese delights such as shrimp paste on a sugar-cane stick, beef wrapped in *la lut* leaf, and fiery lemongrass-and-chilli squid.

★**Restaurant Ichi**   JAPANESE $$
(☑0263-355 5098; 1 Đ Hoang Dieu; sushi 30,000-130,000d, meals from 160,000d; ☺5.30-10pm Tue-Sun, closed every 2nd Tue) Dalat's only truly genuine Japanese restaurant is compact, with subdued lighting and jazz in the background. Spicy tuna rolls, chicken yakitori and tempura are all fantastic, the bento boxes are a bargain and there's even *natto* (fermented soybeans) for aficionados. Perch in front of the bar (with extensive whisky offerings from around the world) to watch sushi-master Tomo at work.

Oz Burgers   BURGERS $
(☑0902 475 923; 61 Đ Ba Thang Hai; meals 70,000-180,000d; ☺11am-2pm & 5.30-9pm Wed-Mon) Packed out every night with backpackers, Asian tourists and even a few locals, this Australian-run joint serves up delicious burgers on wooden platters, along with fries and imported beers. Various set meal options are available, but they all involve burgers.

🍷 Drinking & Entertainment

★**100 Roofs Café**   BAR
(Duong Len Trang; ☑0263-837 518; 57 Đ Phan Boi Chau; ☺8am-midnight; 🛇) This is a surreal drinking experience. The owners claim Gandalf and his hobbit friends have drunk here,

OFF THE BEATEN TRACK

MOTORBIKE RIDES IN THE CENTRAL HIGHLANDS

It's easy to get off the beaten track in the wonderfully scenic highlands. This is a great part of the country to see from the back of a motorbike. Indeed, for many travellers, the highlight of their central highlands trip is a motorcycle tour with an Easy Rider (driver-guide). The flip side to the popularity of the Easy Riders is that now everyone claims to be one. In central Dalat, you can't walk down the street without being invited (sometimes harassed) for a tour.

Rider-guides can be found in hotels and cafes in Dalat. Read testimonials from past clients. Check the bike over. Test-drive a rider first before committing to a longer trip. Then discuss the route in detail – for scenery, the new coastal highways that link Dalat to Mui Ne and Nha Trang, plus the old road to the coast via Phan Rang, are wonderful. Rates start at US$25 for a day tour, or around US$75 per day for longer journeys. Here are some tips for exploring :

➡ The upgrading of the historic **Ho Chi Minh Trail** has made it easier to visit out-of-the way places such as **Kon Tum**, one of the friendliest cities in Vietnam.

➡ Buon Ma Thuot is the major city in the region, but the biggest buzz you'll get is from the coffee beans. Nearby **Yok Don National Park** (☑ 0262-378 3049; www. yokdonnationalpark.vn; Buon Don; adult/child 60,000/10,000d; ⊙ 7am-10pm) is home to 38 endangered mammal species, including plenty of elephants. Stunning waterfalls in this area include **Dray Sap**, **Gia Long** (☑ 0262-321 3194; 40,000d; ⊙ 8am-6pm) and **Dray Nur Falls** (30,000d; ⊙ 8am-6pm) along the Krong Ana River.

➡ Northeast of Dalat, the high road to **Nha Trang** offers spectacular views, hitting 1700m at Hon Giao mountain, following a breathtaking 33km pass.

➡ And 43km southeast of Dalat, it's possible to see the ocean from the spectacular **Ngoan Muc Pass**.

and this dim labyrinth of rooms with multiple nooks and crannies and art and sculptures that range from the cool to the kitsch does resemble a Middle-earth location. A cheap happy hour and Wonderland-like rooftop garden add to the fun.

★ **An Cafe**   CAFE
(☑ 0975 735 521; www.ancafe.vn; 63bis Ba Thang Hai; ⊙ 7am-10pm; 🛜) Perched high above the street, this cafe feels like a hip treehouse. Sip good lattes, healthy juices and smoothies or artichoke tea at the wood-chic booths inside or on garden-bench swings outside. If you tire of people-watching, there are crayons and paper for doodling, and an atrium filled with coffee beans for sniffing.

🛍 Shopping

Hoa Binh Sq and the market building adjacent to it are the places to purchase ethnic handicrafts, including Lat rush baskets that roll up when empty.

ℹ Information

Lam Dong General Hospital (☑ 0263-382 1369; 4 Đ Pham Ngoc Thach; ⊙ 24hr) Emergency medical care.

Main Post Office (14 Đ Tran Phu; ⊙ 7am-6pm)
Sinh Tourist (☑ 0263-382 2663; www.thesinhtourist.vn; 22 Đ Bui Thi Xuan; ⊙ 8am-7pm) Reliable tours, including city sightseeing trips, and open-tour bus bookings.

ℹ Getting There & Around

There are regular flights with Vietnam Airlines (p902), **VietJet Air** (Cat Bi International Airport; www.vietjetair.com; ☑ 1900 1886; 7am-10pm) and Jetstar (p902), including four flights a week to Danang and four daily to Hanoi and HCMC. Lien Khuong Airport is 30km south of the city.

Dalat is a major stop for open-tour buses. The Sinh Tourist has daily buses to Mui Ne, Nha Trang and Ho Chi Minh City.

Dalat's **long-distance bus station** (Ben Xe Lien Tinh Da Lat; Đ 3 Thang 4) is 1.5km south of Xuan Huong Lake, and is dominated by reputable **Phuong Trang** (☑ 0263-358 5858; https://futabus.vn) buses that offer free hotel pick-ups and drop-offs and cover all main regional destinations.

For short trips around town (around 20,000d), *xe om* drivers can be found around the Central Market area. Motorbike hire starts at 120,000d per day.

Around Dalat

Truc Lam Pagoda
& Cable Car   BUDDHIST TEMPLE

(Ho Tuyen Lam; cable car one way/return adult 60,000/80,000d, child 30,000/40,000d; ☉cable car 7.30-11.30am & 1.30-5pm) The Truc Lam Pagoda enjoys a hilltop setting and has splendid gardens. It's an active monastery, though the grounds frequently teem with tour groups. Be sure to arrive by cable car (the terminus is 3km south of the centre, up a short road next to the long-distance bus station), which soars over majestic pine forests.

The pagoda can be reached by road via turn-offs from Hwy 20.

HO CHI MINH CITY

◢ 028 / POP 8.2 MILLION

Ho Chi Minh City (HCMC) is Vietnam at its most dizzying: a high-octane city of commerce and culture that has driven the country forward with its pulsating energy. A chaotic whirl, the city breathes life and vitality into all who settle here, and visitors cannot help but be hauled along for the ride.

From the finest of hotels to the cheapest of guesthouses, the classiest of restaurants to the tastiest of street stalls, the choicest of boutiques to the scrum of the markets, HCMC is a city of energy and discovery.

Wander through timeless alleys to incense-infused temples before negotiating chic designer malls beneath sleek 21st-century skyscrapers. The ghosts of the past live on in buildings that one generation ago witnessed a city in turmoil, but now the real beauty of the former Saigon's urban collage is the seamless blending of these two worlds into one exciting mass.

◉ Sights

◉ Dong Khoi Area

This well-heeled area, immediately west of the Saigon River, is a swish enclave of designer stores and fashionable restaurants, concrete towers and tree-lined boulevards.

★**Notre Dame Cathedral**   CHURCH

(Map p894; Đ Han Thuyen) Built between 1877 and 1883, Notre Dame Cathedral enlivens the heart of Ho Chi Minh City's government quarter, facing Đ Dong Khoi. A brick,

---

ⓘ GETTING TO CAMBODIA:
PLEIKU TO BAN LUNG
....

Getting to the border Remote and rarely used by foreigners, the **Le Thanh–O Yadaw border crossing** lies 90km from Pleiku and 64km from Ban Lung, Cambodia. From Pleiku, there's a daily minivan at 7am (75,000d, two hours) from the main market car park on Đ Tran Phu direct to the Cambodian border at Le Thanh.

At the border Cambodian visas (US$30) are issued at the border; you may end up overpaying by a few dollars or be made to wait. Vietnamese visas need to be organised in advance.

Moving on From O Yadaw, on the Cambodia side of the border, local buses (around US$10) or motorbikes (around US$25) head to Ban Lung. There are far fewer transport options in the afternoon.

---

neo-Romanesque church with 40m-high square towers tipped with iron spires, the Catholic cathedral is named after the Virgin Mary. Interior walls are inlaid with devotional tablets and some stained glass survives. English-speaking staff dispense tourist information from 9am to 11am Monday to Saturday. Mass is 9.30am Sunday. If the front gates are locked, try the door on the side facing the Reunification Palace.

★**Bitexco Financial Tower**   VIEWPOINT

(Map p894; www.ticketbox.vn/saigon-skydeck/en; 2 Đ Hai Trieu; adult/child 200,000/130,000d; ☉9.30am-9.30pm) The 68-storey, 262m-high, Carlos Zapata–designed skyscraper dwarfs all around it. It's reportedly shaped like a lotus bulb, but also resembles a CD rack with a tambourine shoved into it. That tambourine is the 48th-floor **Saigon Skydeck**, with a helipad on its roof. Choose a clear day and aim for sunset – or down a drink in the **EON Heli Bar** (Map p894; http://eon51.com/eon-heli-bar; ☉10.30am-2am) on the 52nd floor instead.

HCMC Museum   MUSEUM

(Bao Tang Thanh Pho Ho Chi Minh; Map p894; www.hcmc-museum.edu.vn; 65 Đ Ly Tu Trong; 30,000d; ☉8am-5pm) A grand neoclassical structure built in 1885 and once known as Gia Long Palace (and later the Revolutionary Museum), HCMC's city museum is a singularly beautiful and impressive building, telling

Ho Chi Minh City

the story of the city through archaeological artefacts, ceramics, old city maps and displays on the marriage traditions of its various ethnicities. The struggle for independence is extensively covered, with most of the upper floor devoted to it.

Central Post Office
HISTORIC BUILDING

(Map p894; 2 Cong Xa Paris; ⊙ 7am-7pm Mon-Fri, to 6pm Sat, 8am-6pm Sun) Right across the way from Notre Dame Cathedral, Ho Chi Minh City's striking French post office is a period classic, designed by Marie-Alfred Foulhoux (though often credited to Gustave Eiffel) and built between 1886 and 1891. Painted on the walls of its grand concourse are fascinating historic maps of South Vietnam, Saigon and Cholon, while a mosaic of Ho Chi Minh takes pride of place at the end of its barrel-vaulted hall. Note the magnificent tiled floor of the interior and the copious green-painted wrought iron.

Opera House
THEATRE

(Nha Hat Thanh Pho; Map p894; ☑ 028-3823 7419; www.hbso.org.vn; Lam Son Sq) Gracing the intersection of Đ Dong Khoi and ĐL Le Loi, this grand colonial edifice with a sweeping staircase was built in 1897 and is one of the city's most recognisable buildings. Officially known as the Municipal Theatre, the Opera House captures the flamboyance of France's belle époque. Performances range from ballet and opera to modern dance and musicals. Check the website for English-language listings and booking information.

◉ Da Kao & Around

★ Jade Emperor Pagoda
TAOIST TEMPLE

(Phuoc Hai Tu, Chua Ngoc Hoang; Map p896; 73 Đ Mai Thi Luu; ⊙ 7am-6pm daily, plus 5am-7pm 1st & 15th of lunar month) FREE Built in 1909 in honour of the supreme Taoist god (the Jade Emperor or King of Heaven, Ngoc Hoang), this is one of the most spectacularly atmospheric temples in Ho Chi Minh City, stuffed with statues of phantasmal divinities and grotesque heroes. The pungent smoke of incense *(huong)* fills the air, obscuring the exquisite woodcarvings. Its roof is encrusted with elaborate tile work, and the temple's statues, depicting characters from both Buddhist and Taoist lore, are made from reinforced papier mâché.

History Museum   MUSEUM
(Bao Tang Lich Su; Map p896; Đ Nguyen Binh Khiem; 15,000đ; ⊙8-11.30am & 1.30-5pm Tue-Sun) Built in 1929 by the Société des Études Indochinoises, this notable Sino-French museum houses a rewarding collection of artefacts illustrating the evolution of the cultures of Vietnam, from the Bronze Age Dong Son civilisation (which emerged in 2000 BC) and the Funan civilisation (1st to 6th centuries AD), to the Cham, Khmer and Vietnamese. The museum is just inside the main gate to the city's botanic gardens and zoo.

⊙ Reunification Palace & Around

★War Remnants Museum   MUSEUM
(Bao Tang Chung Tich Chien Tranh; Map p898; ☑028-3930 5587; http://warremnantsmuseum.com; 28 Đ Vo Van Tan, cnr Đ Le Quy Don; 40,000đ; ⊙7.30am-noon & 1.30-5pm) Formerly the Museum of Chinese and American War Crimes, the War Remnants Museum is consistently popular with Western tourists. Few museums anywhere convey the brutal effects of war on its civilian victims so powerfully. Many of the atrocities documented here were well publicised, but rarely do Westerners hear the victims of US military action tell their own stories. While some displays are one-sided, many of the most disturbing photographs illustrating US atrocities are from US sources, including those of the infamous My Lai Massacre.

★Reunification Palace   HISTORIC BUILDING
(Dinh Thong Nhat; Map p898; ☑028-3829 4117; www.dinhdoclap.gov.vn; Đ Nam Ky Khoi Nghia; adult/child 40,000/20,000đ; ⊙7.30-11am & 1-4pm) Surrounded by royal palm trees, the dissonant 1960s architecture of this government building and the eerie mood that accompanies a walk through its deserted halls make it an intriguing spectacle. The first Communist tanks to arrive in Saigon rumbled here on 30 April 1975 and it's as if time has stood still since then. The building is deeply associated with the fall of the city

in 1975, yet it's the kitsch detailing and period motifs that steal the show.

Fine Arts Museum   GALLERY
(Bao Tang My Thuat; Map p894; www.baotangmythuattphcm.com; 97a Đ Pho Duc Chinh; 10,000đ; ⊙9am-5pm Tue-Sun) With its airy corridors and verandahs, this elegant 1929 colonial-era, yellow-and-white building is stuffed with period details; it is exuberantly tiled throughout and home to some fine (albeit deteriorated) stained glass, as well as one of the city's oldest lifts. Hung from the walls is an impressive selection of art, including thoughtful pieces from the modern period. As well as contemporary art, much of it (unsurprisingly) inspired by war, the museum displays historical pieces dating back to the 4th century.

⊙ Cholon

Cholon, 5km southwest of the centre, forms the city's Chinatown. The district has a wealth of wonderful Chinese temples including **Thien Hau Pagoda** (Ba Mieu, Pho Mieu, Chua Ba Thien Hau; 710 Đ Nguyen Trai) FREE, dedicated to Thien Hau (Tianhou), the Chinese goddess of the sea, and the fabulously ornamental **Phuoc An Hoi Quan Pagoda** (Quan De Mieu; 184 Đ Hong Bang) FREE, built in 1902 by the Fujian Chinese congregation.

★Binh Tay Market   MARKET
(Cho Binh Tay; www.chobinhtay.gov.vn; 57a ĐL Thap Muoi; ⊙6am-7.30pm) Cholon's main market has a great clock tower and a central courtyard with gardens. Much of the business here is wholesale but it's popular with tour groups. The market was originally built by the French in the 1880s; Guangdong-born philanthropist Quach Dam paid for its rebuilding and was commemorated by a statue that is now in the Fine Arts Museum. Expect a friendly welcome when you sit down for breakfast or coffee with the market's street-food vendors.

🍜 Courses

Saigon Cooking Class   COOKING
(Map p894; ☑028-3825 8485; www.saigoncookingclass.com; 74/7 ĐL Hai Ba Trung; adult/child under 12yr US$39/25; ⊙10am & 2pm Tue-Sun) Watch and learn from the chefs at Hoa Tuc restaurant as they prepare three mains (including *pho bo* – beef noodle soup – and some of their signature dishes) and one dessert. A market visit is optional (per adult/child under 12 years US$45/28, including a three-hour class).

Dong Khoi

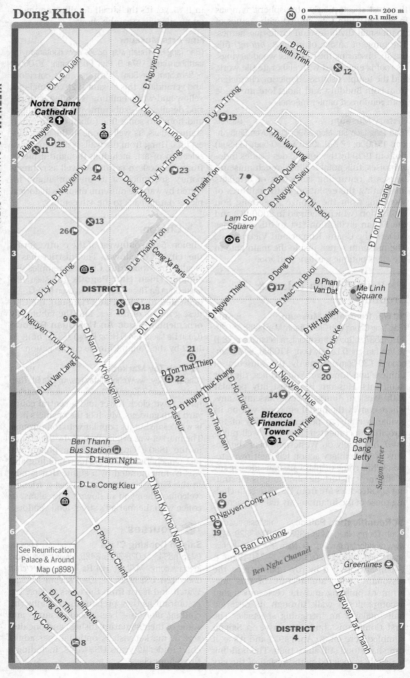

0   200 m
0   0.1 miles

Đ Chu Minh Trinh
✕ 12

ĐL Le Duan
Đ Nguyen Du
Đ Ly Tu Trong
✕ 15

Notre Dame Cathedral
2 🛈
ĐL Hai Ba Trung
Đ Thai Van Lung

3 🏛
Đ Han Thuyen
✕ 11 25
Đ Nguyen Du
Đ Ly Tu Trong
🅿 24
Đ Dong Khoi
Đ Ly Tu Trong
🅿 23
Đ Le Thanh Ton
Đ Cao Ba Quat
Đ Nguyen Sieu
Đ Thi Sach

7 ●

26 🅿
✕ 13
Đ Ly Tu Trong
Đ Le Thanh Ton
Cong Xa Paris

Lam Son Square
◉ 6

Đ Ton Duc Thang

DISTRICT 1
🏛 5
Đ Nguyen Trung Truc
9 ✕
✕ 10
🅿 18
ĐL Le Loi
Đ Nam Ky Khoi Nghia
Đ Nguyen Thiep
Đ Dong Du
🅿 17
Đ Mac Thi Buoi
Đ Phan Van Dat
● Me Linh Square

Đ Luu Van Lang
Đ HH Nghiep
Đ Ngo Duc Ke
21 🏛
Đ Ton That Thiep
🅿 22
Đ Pasteur
Đ Huynh Thuc Khang
Đ Ton That Dam
Đ Ho Tung Mau
💲
ĐL Nguyen Hue
14 🅿
🏛 20

Bitexco Financial Tower
🏛 1
Đ Hai Trieu

Ben Thanh Bus Station 🏢
Đ Ham Nghi
Đ Le Cong Kieu
Đ Nam Ky Khoi Nghia

🏛 4
Bach Dang Jetty 🛥

Saigon River

See Reunification Palace & Around Map (p898)

Đ Pho Duc Chinh
16 🅿
Đ Nguyen Cong Tru
🅿 19
Đ Ban Chuong

Ben Nghe Channel
Greenlines 🛥

Đ Ky Con
Đ Le Thi Hong Gam
Đ Calmette
Đ Nguyen Tat Thanh

DISTRICT 4

🅿 8

Dong Khoi

👉 Tours

HCMC has some excellent tours, with themes as diverse as street food, craft beer and the city's art scene.

Street Foodies Saigon   FOOD
(📱093 210 3985; www.streetfoodiessaigon.com; per person US$59) Excellent after-dark walking tours exploring the great street-food scene of the alleys and byways of the less-visited Co Giang neighbourhood. Look forward to around four hours of very tasty snacking.

XO Tours   CULTURAL
(📱0933 083 727; www.xotours.vn; from US$48) Wearing *ao-dai* (traditional dress), these women run scooter/motorbike foodie, sights and Saigon by Night tours: super-hospitable and fantastic fun.

Vespa Adventures   TOURS
(Map p898; 📱0122 299 3585; www.vespaadventures.com; 169a Đ De Tham; per person from US$73) Zooming out of **Café Zoom** (Map p898; www.facebook.com/cafezoomsaigon; 169a Đ De Tham; meals 65,000-150,000d; ⊘7am-2am), Vespa Adventures offers entertaining guided city tours on vintage scooters, as well as multiday trips around southern Vietnam. Embracing food, drink and music, the Saigon After Dark tour is brilliant fun, and the new Saigon Craft Beer Tour is essential for travelling hopheads.

★ Sophie's Art Tour   TOURS
(📱0933 752 402; www.sophiesarttour.com; per person US$65; ⊘9am-1pm Tue-Sat) Highly engaging four-hour tours from art experts Sophie Hughes and Stu Palmer who have their fingers on the pulse of the HCMC art scene. Tours visit private collections and contemporary art spaces, explaining the influence of Vietnamese history on artistic style and technique. Especially poignant is learning about 'combat art' crafted in the heat of battle during the American War.

🛏 Sleeping

Virtually all budget travellers head straight to the Pham Ngu Lao (PNL) area. HCMC's backpacker precinct has more than 100 places to stay, most with rooms between US$15 and US$40, and there's also a good range of hostels. Some hotels with Đ Pham Ngu Lao or Đ Bui Vien addresses are located in alleys off those main streets.

Lily's Hostel   HOSTEL $
(Map p898; 📱0948 213 181; lilyshostel.hcm@gmail.com; 35/5 Đ Bui Vien; dm/d US$8/26; ⊛☀@🛜) One of the new breed of modern hostels popping up in Pham Ngu Lao, Lily's has a warm and welcoming ambience courtesy of the elegant and soothing decor. Located in a quiet lane just off bustling Đ Bui Vien, Lily's easily bridges the gap between hostel and boutique guesthouse. Some private rooms have a flatscreen TV and minibar.

Da Kao & Around

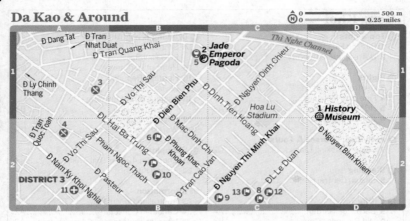

Da Kao & Around

◎ Top Sights
1 History Museum.....................................D1
2 Jade Emperor Pagoda..........................B1

⊗ Eating
3 Banh Xeo 46A..A1
4 Pho Hoa..A2

⊖ Drinking & Nightlife
5 Indika Saigon..B1

ⓘ Information
6 Cambodian Consulate...........................B2
7 Chinese Consulate.................................B2
8 Dutch Consulate....................................C2
9 French Consulate...................................C2
10 German Consulate.................................B2
11 Raffles Medical Group...........................A2
12 UK Consulate...C2
13 US Consulate...C2

Saigon Central Hostel   HOSTEL $
(Map p894; ☎028-3914 1107; saigoncentralhostel@ gmail.com; 54/6 Đ Ky Con; dm/d US$6/26; ❄@🖥) Friendly, family-owned guesthouse located in a quiet lane in a more local area of town – still just a short walk to Pham Ngu Lao, Dong Khoi and Ben Thanh Market, though.

Town House 50   GUESTHOUSE, HOSTEL $
(Map p898; ☎028-3925 0210; www.townhousesai- gon.com; 50e Đ Bui Thi Xuan; dm US$11, r US$35-39; ⊖❄@🖥) Part guesthouse and part boutique hotel, Town House 50 offers stylish accommodation down a quiet laneway on a street with good restaurants and cafes. All dorms and rooms are nonsmoking, and the decor is clean and modern. Rates include a cooked breakfast, and the team at reception have loads of local information on offer.

Diep Anh   GUESTHOUSE $
(Map p898; ☎028-3836 7920; dieptheanh@ hcm.vnn.vn; 241/31 Đ Pham Ngu Lao; r US$21-26; ❄@🖥) A step above most PNL guesthouses, figuratively and literally (think thousand-yard stairs), Diep Anh's tall and narrow shape makes for light and airy upper rooms. The gracious staff ensure they're kept in good nick.

Flipside   HOSTEL $
(Map p898; ☎028-3920 5656; www.flipsidead- venturetravel.com; 175/24 Đ Pham Ngu Lao; dm US$9; ❄🖥🛏) Located in a lane with good restaurants, one of HCMC's most popular and sociable hostels includes modern dorms with personal charging stations and lockers, a rooftop bar and plunge pool, and plenty of experience in planning travel and tours around the country. Ask about the three-day True North motorbike adventure exploring Vietnam's spectacular Ha Giang province on the Chinese border.

Hideout Hostel   HOSTEL $
(Map p898; ☎028-3838 9147; www.vietnamhide- outhostels.com; 281 Đ Pham Ngu Lao; dm US$9; ❄@🖥) A modern PNL hostel with an emphasis on good times and meeting other travellers. Dorms are spick and span with bright colours, a free beer per day is on offer at the Hideout Bar next door, and the hostel runs bar crawls six nights a week that

are free for guests. Nearby is Hideout's new Hangout annex.

★ Nguyen Shack
GUESTHOUSE $$

(Map p898; ☏ 028-3822 0501; www.nguyenshack. com; 6/15 Đ Cach Mang Thang Tam; r US$30-50; ◕❋☎) Down a quiet residential lane a short walk or motorbike taxi from Pham Ngu Lao or Ben Thanh Market, Nguyen Shack's first city opening incorporates rustic, country-style decor, spotless and spacious rooms, and a leafy, shared downstairs area. Breakfast is included but there are good cafes just metres away.

✖ Eating

HCMC is the reigning culinary king of Vietnam. Restaurants here range from dirt-cheap sidewalk stalls to atmospheric villas. Besides brilliant Vietnamese fare, world cuisine – Indian, Japanese, Thai, French, Spanish and Korean – are all on offer. The Dong Khoi area has many top-quality restaurants. Pham Ngu Lao's eateries are generally less memorable, though there are exceptions. To really discover more of the city's great street food, a tour is an excellent option.

✖ Dong Khoi Area

Secret Garden
VIETNAMESE $

(Map p894; 8th fl, 158 Đ Pasteur; meals 55,000-90,000d; ◷8am-10pm; 🖉) Negotiate the stairs in this faded HCMC apartment building to arrive at Secret Garden's wonderful rooftop restaurant. Rogue chickens peck away in the herb garden, Buddhist statues add Asian ambience, and delicious homestyle dishes are served up with city views. Service can sometimes be a little *too* casual, but it's worth persevering for the great flavours.

Old Compass Cafe
CAFE $$

(Map p894; ☏ 090 390 0841; www.facebook.com/oldcompasscafe; 63 Đ Pasteur, 3rd fl; meals 150,000d; ◷10.30am-10pm Sun-Thu, 10.30am-11pm Fri & Sat; ☎) Concealed off busy Pasteur St down an alley and up narrow staircases, Old Compass is a relaxed all-day cafe that often segues into an interesting live music and performance space later at night. Relax over a coffee, wine or craft beer on the comfy sofas, or take advantage of good value, three-course lunch deals. Check Facebook for listings of events.

Propaganda
VIETNAMESE $$

(Map p894; ☏ 028-3822 9048; www.propagandasaigon.com; 21 Đ Han Thuyen; meals 105,000-185,000d; ◷7.30am-10.30pm) Colourful murals and retro socialist posters brighten up this popular bistro with park views. The menu focuses on street-food classics from around Vietnam, all enjoyed with a bustling and energetic ambience. Salads are particularly good: try the wild pepper and green-mango salad with barbecue chicken. Retreat to the 1st floor if downstairs is too crowded.

Barbecue Garden
VIETNAMESE $$

(Map p894; www.barbecuegarden.com; 135 Đ Nam Ky Khoi Nghia; meals 80,000-200,000d; ◷11am-11pm) Trees festooned with fairy lights, outdoor tables, and a laid-back ambience make this the ideal spot for groups. Fire up the table-top grills to barbecue different meats and seafood, and partner it all with tasty Vietnamese salads and cold beer. Friday nights are popular with locals celebrating the end of the week, and weekday lunch specials are good value.

✖ Da Kao & Around

Pho Hoa
VIETNAMESE $

(Map p896; 260c Đ Pasteur; meals 60,000-75,000d; ◷6am-midnight) This long-running establishment is more upmarket than most but is definitely the real deal – as evidenced by its popularity with regular local patrons. Tables come laden with herbs, chilli and lime, as well as *gio chao quay* (fried Chinese bread), *banh xu xe* (glutinous coconut cakes with mung-bean paste) and *cha lua* (pork-paste sausages wrapped in banana leaves).

Banh Xeo 46A
VIETNAMESE $

(Map p896; ☏ 028-3824 1110; 46a Đ Dinh Cong Trang; regular/extra large 70,000/110,000d; ◷10am-9pm; 🖉) Locals will always hit the

---

> ## SPLURGE
>
> Stylish Indochinese decor features at the slick eatery **Quan Bui** (Map p894; ☏ 028-3829 1545; http://quan-bui.com; 17a Đ Ngo Van Nam; meals 69,000-169,000d; ◷8am-11pm; ❋) in up-and-coming Đ Ngo Van Nam. Nearby restaurants offer Japanese flavours, but Quan Bui's focus is on authentic Vietnamese cuisine and many dishes feature the more hearty flavours of northern Vietnam. Cocktails – from the associated bar across the lane – are among HCMC's best, and upstairs there's an air-conditioned and smoke-free dining room.

Reunification Palace & Around

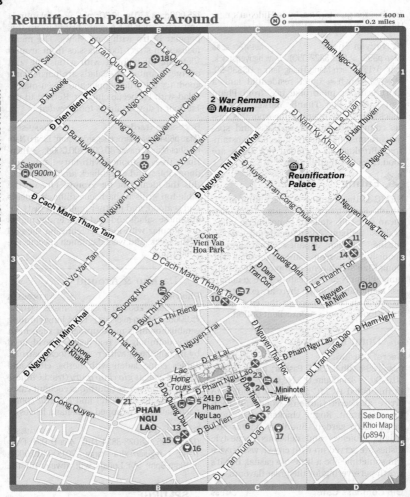

restaurants that specialise in a single dish and this renowned spot serves some of the best *banh xeo* in town. These Vietnamese rice-flour pancakes stuffed with bean sprouts, prawns and pork (vegetarian versions available) are legendary. Other dishes available include excellent *goi cuon* (fresh summer rolls with pork and prawn).

✕ Pham Ngu Lao Area

Asiana Food Town   STREET FOOD $

(Map p898; ☑090 377 0836; www.facebook.com/asianafoodtown; 4 Đ Pham Ngu Lao; meals 50,000-

100,000d; ⊗8.30am-10pm; ❄☑) Cooling aircon, a handy location near accommodation in Pham Ngu Lao, and a huge selection of street food from around Vietnam and the rest of the Asia are the highlights of this excellent new undercover food court. There's a convenient supermarket, pharmacy and English-language bookshop as well.

Five Oysters   VIETNAMESE $

(Map p898; ☑09 0301 2123; www.fiveoysters.com; 234 Đ Bui Vien; meals from 45,000d; ⊗9am-11pm) With a strong seafood slant and friendly service, light and bright Five Oysters in back-

Reunification Palace & Around

VIETNAM HO CHI MINH CITY

packerland is frequently packed with travellers feasting on oysters (30,000d), grilled octopus, seafood soup, snail pie, *pho*, fried noodles, grilled mackerel with chilli oil and more. Bargain-priced beer also makes it a popular spot along the PNL strip.

✕ **Reunification Palace & Around**

Banh Mi Huynh Hoa   VIETNAMESE $
(Map p898; 26 Le Thi Rieng; banh mi 33,000d; ⊙2.30-11pm) This hole-in-the-wall *banh mi* joint is busy day and night with locals zipping up on motorbikes for stacks of excellent baguettes stuffed with pork, pork and more pork in tasty ways you may not have known existed. Street standing room only.

**Ben Thanh
Street Food Market**   STREET FOOD $
(Map p898; ☎090 688 1707; www.facebook.com/pg/BenThanhstreetfoodmarket; 26-30 Đ Thu Khoa Huan; meals from 40,000d; ⊙9am-11pm) Grab a table at the front of the market, order up some cold beers from the adjacent bar, and then go exploring to put together a minifeast of well-priced street food. Highlights include fresh oysters from Nha Trang – optional dipping sauces include fiery wasabi – and fragrant *bun bo Hue* noodles.

Pizza 4P's   PIZZA $$
(Map p898; ☎028-3622-0500; www.pizza4ps.com; 8 Thu Khoa Huan; pizza & pasta 150,000-330,000d; ⊙10am-2am Mon-Sat, 10am-11pm Sun)

Recently opened close to Ben Thanh Market, Pizza 4P's interesting mix of pasta and Japanese-influenced pizza – trust us, the combinations work – is partnered with excellent craft beer from Ho Chi Minh City's Heart of Darkness brewery. Booking ahead is recommended as this new branch is very popular.

🍷 **Drinking & Nightlife**

Happening HCMC is concentrated around the Dong Khoi area, with everything from dives to designer bars open to 1am. Pham Ngu Lao stays open later, and PNL's Bui Vien is a pedestrians-only street from 7pm to 2am on Saturday and Sunday nights. Dance clubs usually kick off after 10pm; ask around at popular bars about the latest greatest places.

🍸 **Dong Khoi Area**

★ **Heart of Darkness**   CRAFT BEER
(Map p894; ☎090 301 7596; www.heartofdarknessbrewery.com; 31D Đ Ly Tu Trong; ⊙10am-midnight) Our pick for the best of HCMC's craft breweries, with an always interesting selection of innovative beers on tap. The selection varies as Heart of Darkness brewers are always trying something, but the hoppy 7.1% Kurtz's Insane IPA is a great drop. Secure a wooden table out the front and order up excellent pizza from Pizza 4P's.

★ **Rogue Saigon**   CRAFT BEER
(Map p894; ☎090 236 5780; www.facebook.com/roguesaigon; 11 Đ Pasteur; ⊙4pm-midnight Sun-

Thu, 4pm-2am Fri & Sat) Live music and Vietnamese craft beers combine on Rogue's rooftop terrace in a pleasantly rundown building on the riverside edge of District 1. You'll find good beers such as Lac Brewing's Devil's Lake IPA and music with a blues, country or rock vibe. The after-dark, shadowy views from this off-the-radar location are pretty cool, too.

Broma: Not a Bar BAR
(Map p894; ☑ 0126 387 2603; www.facebook.com/bromabar; 41 ĐL Nguyen Hue; ⊙5pm-2am Sun-Thu, 5pm-4am Fri & Sat) Compact and bohemian rooftop bar overlooking the busy pedestrian mall of Đ Nguyen Hue. It has a good selection of international beers, live gigs, and DJs with a funk, hip-hop and electronica edge.

Heritage Republic LOUNGE
(Map p894; ☑ 0906 227 576; http://fb.me/heritagerepublic; 10 Đ Pasteur; ⊙24hr; ⓢ) It's easy to lose track of time in tiny Heritage. By day, relax on a vintage sofa with a smoothie, snuggling up to the resident bulldogs. Suddenly it's evening and this 24-hour lounge transforms into one of HCMC's most chilled bars, with a hip crowd spilling onto the streets for beer and cocktails. Discount days for patrons dressed in black.

Workshop COFFEE
(Map p894; www.facebook.com/the.workshop.coffee; 10 Đ Ngo Duc Ke; coffee from 45,000đ; ⊙8am-9pm; ⓢ) Coffee-geek culture comes to HCMC at this spacious upstairs warehouse space that's also perfect if you need to do some writing or other work. Single-origin, fair-trade roasts from Dalat feature, and there's a great display of black-and-white photos of old Saigon to peruse while you're waiting for your Chemex or cold brew.

Layla COCKTAIL BAR
(Map p894; ☑ 028-3827 2279; www.facebook.com/LaylaEateryandBarHCM; 2nd fl, 63 Đ Dong Du; ⊙4pm-1am Mon-Sat, 12.30pm-1am Sun) With an effortlessly long bar – we're talking 10 metres plus here – Layla is a laid-back spot that's perfect for the first or last cocktails of the night. Don't be surprised if the combination of a chic ambience, super-comfy sofas and Med-style bar snacks – think Italian flatbreads and Spanish tortilla – sees you staying longer then planned.

Pham Ngu Lao Area

View BAR
(Map p898; www.ducvuonghotel.com; 8th fl, Duc Vuong Hotel, 195 Đ Bui Vien; ⊙10am-midnight Mon-Fri, to 2am Sat & Sun) Not as elevated as other rooftop bars around town, but less pretentious and a whole lot easier on the wallet. It's still a good escape to look down on the heaving backpacker bustle of Pham Ngu Lao, and the food menu is also good value.

Ong Cao BAR
(Map p898; ☑ 091 199 6160; www.facebook.com/ongcaosaigon; 240 Đ Bui Vien; ⊙5-11pm Tue-Sun; ⓢ) A hoppy cut above the backpacker bars lining Bui Vien, Ong Cao is your best bet for craft brews in Pham Ngu Lao. Bar snacks, including cheese and charcuterie plates, partner well with 16 taps serving mainly local HCMC beers. Yes, it is more expensive than that 10,000đ Bia Saigon along the road, but it's worth it.

Whiskey & Wares BAR
(Map p898; ☑ 0163 279 4179; www.facebook.com/WhiskeyandWares; 196 Đ De Tham; ⊙4.30pm-2am Tue-Sun; ⓢ) ⍟ Just a short stroll from Đ Bui Vien, Whiskey & Wares' blend of fine whiskey, good cocktails and local craft beer is a more sophisticated but still relaxed alternative to Pham Ngu Lao's backpacker bars. It's also a top spot to purchase local artisanal goods, and products for sale include hip T-shirts, fragrant soaps and cool prints and postcards.

Da Kao & Around

Indika Saigon BAR
(Map p896; ☑ 0122 399 4260; www.facebook.com/IndikaSaigon; 43 Đ Nguyen Van Giai; ⊙9am-midnight) Tucked down a narrow laneway, the off-the-radar Indika Saigon is definitely worth venturing to. Negotiate past the hipster barbecue joint and beer bar at the front to Indika's raffish multiroom labyrinth that's used for concerts, open-mic sessions, movie nights and DJs. Check out the Facebook page for listings, and be surprised at the emerging energy of the new Saigon.

☆ Entertainment

Pick up *The Word HCMC*, *Asialife HCMC* or *The Guide* to find out what's on during your stay in Ho Chi Minh City, or log on to www.anyarena.com or www.wordhcmc.com.

Yoko   LIVE MUSIC
(Map p898; ☎028-3933 0577; www.facebook.com/
Yokocafesaigon; 22a Đ Nguyen Thi Dieu; ⊙8am-late;
☎) Portraits of John Lennon, Jim Morrison
and James Brown look on at this cool shrine
to live music. The environment: exposed
T-beam joists and concrete floor; the music:
anything from funk rock to metal, kicking off
around 9pm nightly. New owners have proudly re-energised one of the city's best live venues. Check Facebook for what's on.

Acoustic   LIVE MUSIC
(Map p898; ☎028-3930 2239; www.facebook.com/
acousticbarpage; 6e1 Đ Ngo Thoi Nhiem; ⊙7pm-
midnight; ☎) Don't be misled by the name:
most of the musicians are fully plugged in
and dangerous when they take to the intimate
stage of the city's leading live-music venue.
And judging by the numbers that pack in, the
local crowd just can't get enough. It's at the
end of the alley by the upended VW Beetle;
the cocktails are deceptively strong.

Observatory   LIVE MUSIC
(www.facebook.com/theobservatoryhcmc; ⊙6pm-
6am Wed-Sun) Following the redevelopment
of its venue in late 2017, this excellent entertainment cooperative pops up at different
locations around town. Check the Facebook
page for where to see everything from live
bands to DJs from around the globe.

🛍 Shopping

Among the tempting wares to be found in
HCMC are embroidered silk shoes, miniature cyclos and fake Zippos engraved with
GI philosophy. Boutiques along Đ Le Thanh
Ton and Đ Pasteur sell handmade ready-to-
wear fashion. In Pham Ngu Lao, shops sell
ethnic-minority fabrics, handicrafts, T-shirts
and various appealing accessories.

Chung Cu 42 Ton That Thiep   CLOTHING
(Map p894; 42 Đ Ton That Thiep; ⊙most shops
9am-9pm) Come for the apartment building
partially converted into cool boutique shops,
and linger for the young, social-media-
savvy fashion labels that produce stylish
(but affordable) clothing. There is a sense
that HCMC's hipster boom starts here. Head
upstairs, and also through to the back to the
second building.

Mai Handicrafts   ARTS & CRAFTS
(☎028-3844 0988; www.maihandicrafts.com; 298
Đ Nguyen Trong Tuyen, Tan Binh District; ⊙9am-
5pm Mon-Sat) 🌱 A fair-trade shop dealing in
ceramics, ethnic fabrics and other gift items

that, in turn, support disadvantaged families
and street children. To get here, head northwest on ĐL Hai Ba Trung, which becomes
Đ Phan Dinh Phung, and turn left on Đ
Nguyen Trong Tuyen.

Saigon Kitsch   GIFTS & SOUVENIRS
(Map p894; 33 Đ Ton That Thiep; ⊙9am-10pm)
This colourful French-run shop specialises
in reproduction propaganda items, embla-
zoning its revolutionary motifs on coffee
mugs, coasters, jigsaws and T-shirts. Also
stocks cool laptop and tablet covers fashioned from recycled Vietnamese packaging.

Ben Thanh Market   MARKET
(Cho Ben Thanh; Map p898; ĐL Le Loi, ĐL Ham Nghi,
ĐL Tran Hung Dao & Đ Le Lai; ⊙5am-6pm) Centrally located, Ben Thanh and its surrounding streets comprise one of HCMC's liveliest
areas. Everything that's commonly eaten,
worn or used by the Saigonese is piled high,
and souvenirs can be found in equal abundance. Vendors are determined and prices
usually higher than elsewhere (restaurant
stalls are reasonable), so bargain vigorously
and ignore any 'Fixed Price' signs.

ℹ Information

DANGERS & ANNOYANCES
Be careful in the Dong Khoi area and along the
riverfront, where motorbike 'cowboys' operate
and specialise in bag, phone, tablet and camera
snatching. It's best to leave your passport in
your hotel room, and be prudent when you use
your smartphone on the street.

INTERNET ACCESS
Free wi-fi access is virtually ubiquitous in all
HCMC accommodation and cafes and bars, and
if you're in town for an extended period, securing
4G mobile access with a local SIM card is recommended. Costs are very reasonable, and any
one of a number of shops in the backpacker area
of Pham Ngu Lao can sort out access for your
mobile device of choice.

MEDICAL SERVICES
International Medical Centre (Map p894;
☎028-3827 2366; www.cmi-vietnam.com; 1
Đ Han Thuyen; ⊙8.30am-7pm Mon-Fri, 9am-
1pm Sat) A nonprofit organisation with English-speaking French doctors.

MONEY
Citibank (Map p894; 115 ĐL Nguyen Hue)
Citibank in the foyer of the Sun Wah Tower dispenses up to 8,000,000d, but only for Citibank
cards (2,000,000d maximum for other cards).

GETTING TO CAMBODIA: HCMC TO PHNOM PENH

Getting to the border The busy Moc Bai–Bavet border crossing is the fastest land route between HCMC and Phnom Penh. Pham Ngu Lao travel agencies sell through bus tickets (US$10 to US$15) to Phnom Penh. Allow six hours for the trip.

At the border Cambodian visas (US$30) are issued at the border (you'll need a passport-sized photo).

Moving on Most travellers have a through ticket.

POST

Post Office (Buu Dien Quan 5; ☎ 028-3855 1763; 3 Đ Mac Cuu, District 5; ☉7am-7pm Mon-Fri, to 6pm Sat, 8am-6pm Sun) Look for the light-yellow building with a clock.

TRAVEL AGENCIES

Dozens of travel agents offer tours of the Mekong Delta and other jaunts beyond HCMC. Some of the better ones include the following:

Sinh Tourist (Map p898; ☎ 028-3838 9593; www.thesinhtourist.vn; 246 Đ De Tham; ☉6.30am-10.30pm) Popular budget travel agency.

Handspan Adventure Travel (Map p898; ☎ 028-3925 7605; www.handspan.com; Central Park Bldg, 208 Đ Nguyen Trai, 10th fl) Excellent, high-quality tours are available from this HCMC branch of the Hanoi-based travel agency.

Kim Tran Travel (Map p898; ☎ 028-3836 5489; www.thekimtourist.com; 270 Đ De Tham; ☉7am-9.30pm) Arranges day trips and overnighters around HCMC and Mekong area.

❶ Getting There & Away

AIR

Ho Chi Minh City is served by **Tan Son Nhat International Airport** (☎ 028-3848 5383; www.tsnairport.hochiminhcity.com.vn/vn; Tan Binh District), located 7km northwest of central Ho Chi Minh City. A number of airlines offer domestic routes from HCMC.

Jetstar Pacific Airlines (☎1900 1550; www.jetstar.com/vn/en/home) Flies to/from Hanoi, Haiphong, Vinh, Hue, Phu Quoc, Nha Trang, Buon Ma Thuot, Dong Hoi, Dalat and Danang.

VietJet Air (www.vietjetair.com) Flies to/from Hanoi, Haiphong, Vinh, Dong Hoi, Hue, Danang, Quy Nhon, Nha Trang, Dalat, Buon Ma Thuot and Phu Quoc Island.

Vietnam Air Service Company (Vasco; ☎ 028-3845 8017; www.vasco.com.vn) Flies to/from Ca Mau, Con Dao Islands and Rach Gia.

Vietnam Airlines (☎ 028-3832 0320; www.vietnamairlines.com) Flies to/from Hanoi, Haiphong, Vinh, Dong Hoi, Hue, Danang, Quy Nhon, Nha Trang, Dalat, Buon Ma Thuot, Phu Quoc and Thuy Hoa.

BUS

Intercity buses operate from three large stations on the city outskirts, all well served by local bus services from near Ben Thanh Market. Ho Chi Minh City is one place where the open-tour buses really come into their own, as they depart and arrive in the very convenient Pham Ngu Lao area, saving the extra local bus journey or taxi fare.

Any of the travel agencies around town can book open-tour buses. Indicative fares: Mui Ne US$6, Dalat US$10, Nha Trang US$13, Hoi An US$21, Hue US$26 and Hanoi US$47.

Mien Dong bus station (Ben Xe Mien Dong; ☎ 028-3829 4056) Buses to locations north of HCMC leave from this huge and busy station in Binh Thanh district, about 5km from central HCMC on Hwy 13 (Quoc Lo 13; the continuation of Đ Xo Viet Nghe Tinh). The station is just under 2km north of the intersection of Đ Xo Viet Nghe Tinh and Đ Dien Bien Phu. Note that express buses depart from the east side, and local buses connect with the west side of the complex.

Mien Tay bus station (Ben Xe Mien Tay; ☎ 028-3825 5955; Đ Kinh Duong Vuong) Serves all areas south of HCMC, essentially the Mekong Delta. This huge station is about 10km west of HCMC in An Lac, a part of Binh Chanh district (Huyen Binh Chanh). A taxi here from Pham Ngu Lao costs around 200,000d. Buses and minibuses from Mien Tay serve most towns in the Mekong Delta using air-con express buses and premium minibuses.

TRANSPORT FROM HCMC

DESTINATION	AIR	BUS	TRAIN
Dalat	50min; from US$41	7hr; from US$10	N/A
Hanoi	2hr; from US$50	41hr; from US47	30hr; US$18-40
Hue	80min; from US$30	29hr; from US$26	18hr; US$15-27
Nha Trang	55min; from US$26	12hr; from US$13	6½hr; US$7-27

TRAIN

Trains from **Saigon Train Station** (Ga Sai Gon; ☑ 028-3823 0105; 1 Đ Nguyen Thong, District 3; ⊙ ticket office 7.15-11am & 1-3pm) head north to many destinations. Purchase tickets from travel agents for a small booking fee at the train station.

❶ Getting Around

TO/FROM THE AIRPORT

Tan Son Nhat Airport is 7km northwest of central HCMC. Metered taxis cost around 180,000d to/from the centre. Stick to either **Mai Linh** (☑ 028-3838 3838) or **Vinasun** (☑ 028-3827 2727) taxis.

There are two dedicated airport buses:

Route 109 (20,000d, 50 minutes, 5.30am to 1.30am, every 15 to 20 minutes) goes to the 'backpacker district' of Pham Ngu Lao via Ben Thanh Bus Station.

Route 49 (40,000d, 40 minutes, 5.30am to 1.30am, every 15 to 30 minutes) also stops at the Pham Ngu Lao area, via Ben Thanh Market.

MOTORBIKE TAXI

Short hops are around 30,000d. Rides can be booked via the Uber and Grab apps and are usually cheaper.

TAXI

Metered taxis are very affordable; a 2km ride is about 30,000d. Mai Linh Taxi (p903) and Vinasun Taxi (p903) are reliable. Journeys can also be booked on Uber and Grab.

AROUND HO CHI MINH CITY

Cu Chi

☑ 028 / POP 19,573

If the tenacious spirit of the Vietnamese could be symbolised by a single place, then Cu Chi might be it. Its fame is such that it's become a place of pilgrimage for many Vietnamese, and a must-see for travellers.

Cu Chi Tunnels   HISTORIC SITE
(adult/child 110,000/30,000d) Two sections of this remarkable tunnel network (which are enlarged and upgraded versions of the real thing) are open to the public. One is near the village of **Ben Dinh** and the other is 15km beyond at **Ben Duoc**, where admission is slightly cheaper. Most tourists visiting the tunnels end up at Ben Dinh, as it's easier for tour buses to reach. Even if you stay above ground, it's still an interesting experience learning about the region's ingenious and brave resistance activities.

Cu Chi
Wildlife Rescue Station   WILDLIFE RESERVE
(www.wildlifeatrisk.org; adult/child US\$5/free; ⊙ 7.30-11.30am & 1-4.30pm) Just a few kilometres from the Ben Dinh tunnels, this centre is dedicated to the protection of wildlife that has been confiscated from owners or illegal traders. Animals include bears, otters and gibbons. There is an informative display on the rather depressing state of wildlife in Vietnam, including the 'room of death' featuring traps and baits. It's tough to navigate these back roads solo, so talk to a travel agent about incorporating it into a Cu Chi Tunnels trip. Phoning ahead before a visit is recommended to ensure centre staff are on hand.

❶ Getting There & Away

By far the easiest way to get to the tunnels is by guided tour from HCMC City. As the competition is stiff, prices are reasonable (around US\$15 per person), and vary depending on group size and choice of tunnels. Most tours also visit the **Cao Dai Temple** in Tay Ninh.

Tay Ninh

☑ 0276 / POP 153,500

Tay Ninh town serves as the headquarters of Cao Dai, one of Vietnam's most interesting indigenous religions. The **Cao Dai Great Temple** was built between 1933 and 1955. Victor Hugo is among the Westerners especially revered by the Cao Dai; look for his likeness at the Great Temple. Tay Ninh is 96km northwest of HCMC. The Cao Dai Holy See complex is 4km east of Tay Ninh. One-day tours from HCMC, including Tay Ninh and the Cu Chi Tunnels, cost from around US\$7.

MEKONG DELTA

The 'rice bowl' of Vietnam, the Mekong Delta is a landscape carpeted in a dizzying variety of greens. It's also a water world where boats, houses, restaurants and even markets float upon the innumerable rivers, canals and streams that flow through like arteries.

Visitors can experience southern charm in riverside homestays, while Phu Quoc is a tropical island lined with white-sand beaches.

Delta tours are very convenient (book through travel agencies in Ho Chi Minh

Mekong Delta

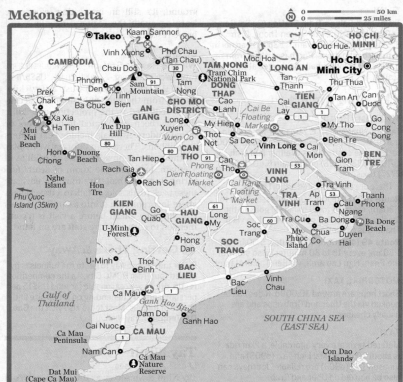

City) but independent travel is perfectly feasible, if sometimes time-consuming.

Vinh Long

📞 0270 / POP 147,000

Vinh Long is a noisy, chaotic transit hub, but the riverfront has plenty of cafes and restaurants. Close by are several worthwhile sites including the Cai Be floating market, beautiful islands, abundant orchards and atmospheric homestays.

Cuu Long Tourist (📞 0270-382 3616; www. cuulongtourist.com; 2 Đ Phan B Chau; ⏰ 7am-5pm) offers boat tours ranging from three hours (from US$15 per person) to three days. Bustling **Cai Be Floating Market** (⏰ 5am-noon) is worth including on a boat tour from Vinh Long.

Arrive early in the morning to see huge boats packed with tropical fruit and vegetables. We suggest you don't stay in town;

instead opt for a homestay. Frequent buses go to HCMC (105,000d, three hours) and Can Tho (50,000d) from a bus station 2.5km south of town.

Can Tho

📞 0292 / POP 1.2 MILLION

Can Tho is the political, economic, cultural and transportation epicentre of the Mekong Delta. It's a buzzing city with a waterfront lined with sculpted gardens and an appealing blend of narrow backstreets and wide boulevards.

English-speaking **Hieu** (📞 0939 666 156; www.hieutour.com; 27a Đ Le Thanh Ton) offers excellent trips to floating markets (from US$25), cycling excursions and food tours.

Cai Rang (⏰ 5am-noon) **FREE** is the biggest floating market in the Mekong Delta, 6km from Can Tho; it's a morning affair. You can hire boats (about 120,000d per hour) on the river near the Can Tho market. Cai Rang is one hour away by boat, or you can drive to Cau Dau Sau boat landing, where you can get a rowing boat (per hour around 100,000d) to the market, 10 minutes away.

Less crowded and less motorised is the **Phong Dien Market** (☉5am-noon) **FREE**, 20km from Can Tho by road, which has more stand-up rowboats. It's best between 6am and 8am. You can hire a boat on arrival.

🛏 Sleeping & Eating

⭐ **Xoai Hotel**   HOTEL $
(☏0907 652 927; http://hotelxoai.com; 93 Đ Mau Than; s/d from US$10.50/14.50; ✱◉🛜) Fantastic value at this friendly, efficient hotel with bright, mango-coloured (the hotel name means 'Mango Hotel'), airy rooms. Helpful staff speak excellent English and there's a roof terrace with hammocks.

⭐ **Nguyen Shack Can Tho**   GUESTHOUSE $$
(☏0966 550 016; www.nguyenshack.com; Ong Tim Bridge, Thanh My, Thuong Thanh; dm/d with shared bathroom US$9/25, bungalows US$45-65; 🛜) 🌿 Not a shack, but rather a clutch of rustic thatched bungalows with fans, this great place overlooks the Ong Tim River, 6km from Can Tho. It's the kind of place where backpackers are inspired to linger longer, thanks to the camaraderie between English-speaking staff and guests. The engaging boat and bicycle tours and the proximity to Cai Rang floating market are bonuses.

⭐ **Nem Nuong Thanh Van**   VIETNAMESE $
(☏0292-0382 7255; cnr Nam Ky Khoi Nghia & 30 Thang 4; meals 45,000d; ☉8am-9pm) The only dish this locally acclaimed spot does is the best *nem nuong* in town. Roll your own rice rolls using the ingredients provided: pork sausage, rice paper, green banana, star fruit (*carambola*), cucumber and a riot of fresh herbs, then dip into the peanut-and-something-else sauce, its secret jealously guarded. Simple and fantastic!

ℹ Getting There & Away

AIR

Can Tho International Airport (www.canthoairport.com; Đ Le Hong Phong) is served by **Vietnam Airlines** (☏0292-384 4320; 64 Đ Nguyen An Ninh), **Vietjet Air** (www.vietjetair.com) and **Vasco** (☏038 422 790), with flights to Dalat (one hour, twice weekly), Danang (1½ hours, daily), Hanoi (2¼ hours, three daily) and Phu Quoc (one hour, daily). There are no direct flights to HCMC; the nearest connecting flight is through Phu Quoc.

The airport is 10km northwest of the city centre. A taxi into town will cost around 220,000d.

BUS

All buses depart from a new **bus station** (Ben Xe 91B; Đ Nguyen Van Linh) in the southwest of town. Destinations include HCMC Mien Tay terminal (110,000d, 3½ hours, every 30 minutes) and Chau Doc (from 95,000d, 3¼ hours, hourly).

Chau Doc

☏0296 / POP 157,000

Perched on the banks of the Bassac River, Chau Doc is a charming town near the Cambodian border, with sizeable Chinese, Khmer and Cham communities. Its cultural diversity – apparent in the mosques, temples, churches and nearby pilgrimage sites – makes it a fascinating place to explore.

A NIGHT ON THE MEKONG

For many travellers, the chance to experience river life and to share a home-cooked meal with a local family is a highlight of a Mekong visit. Vinh Long offers many homestay options.

Ngoc Sang (☏0270-385 8694; 95/8 Binh Luong, Dao Trinh Nhat, An Binh; per person 250,000d; 🛜) Most travellers love this friendly, canal-facing rustic homestay. The grandmother cooks up some wonderful local dishes, free bikes are available, the owner runs decent early-morning boat tours and there's a languid atmosphere about the place. The family seems shy when it comes to hanging out with the guests, though. Free pick-up from the ferry pier 15 minutes' walk away.

Ba Linh Homestay (☏0270-385 8683, 0939 138 142; balinhhomestay@gmail.com; 95 An Thanh, An Binh; r 500,000d) Run by friendly Mr Truong, this traditional-looking and popular place has six simple, high-roofed, partitioned rooms in a line, all with fan. Breakfast and dinner is included in the price and you may get to try such local specialities as rice-field rat.

WORTH A TRIP

CON DAO ISLANDS

Isolated from the mainland, the Con Dao Islands are one of Vietnam's star attractions. Long the preserve of political prisoners and undesirables, they now turn heads thanks to their striking natural beauty. Con Son, the largest of this chain of 15 islands and islets, is ringed with lovely beaches, coral reefs and scenic bays, and remains partially covered in tropical forests. In addition to hiking, diving and exploring deserted coastal roads there are excellent wildlife-watching opportunities.

Standout beaches include **Bai Dat Doc** and **Bau Dram Trau**, and to the east of Con Son Island, **Bay Canh** island has lovely beaches, old-growth forest, mangroves, coral reefs and sea turtles (seasonal). There is a fantastic two-hour walk to a functioning French-era lighthouse on Bay Canh's eastern tip; a steep climb of 325m. At the summit, the panoramic views are breathtaking.

Until 2017, getting to Con Dao involved buying a pricey air ticket or a long journey at sea on an ancient ferry, but a new fast boat link means the islands are now far more accessible.

Superdong (☑ 029 9384 3888; http://superdong.com.vn; Ben Dam port) schedules a daily 8am ferry (310,000d, 2½ hours) from Tran De, Soc Trang province in the Mekong Delta; it returns from Ben Dam at 1pm. This service began in July 2017 and its reliability is untested.

Note that sea connections to Con Dao are not reliable; sailings on all routes are frequently cancelled in heavy seas.

The popular nearby river crossing between Vietnam and Cambodia means many travellers pass through. Nearby Sam Mountain is a local beauty spot with terrific views over Cambodia, while the **Tra Su Bird Sanctuary** (Rung Tram Tra Su; admission 120,000d, boat rides per person 75,000d; ⊙7am-4pm) 23km west of town is worth a visit for avian buffs.

War remnants near Chau Doc include **Ba Chuc**, the site of a Khmer Rouge massacre with a bone pagoda, and **Tuc Dup Hill**, where an expensive American bombing campaign in 1963 earned it the nickname Two Million Dollar Hill.

It's also possible to visit fish farms set up underneath floating houses on the river. **Mekong Tours** (☑ 098 308 6355; 41 Đ Quang Trung) is a reliable travel agent offering boat or bus transport to Phnom Penh, car hire and boat trips on the Mekong. Good budget places to stay include **Trung Nguyen Hotel** (☑0296-356 1561; 86 Đ Bach Dang; s/d US$12/15; P ꙮ ꙮ) and **Murray Guesthouse** (☑0296-356 2108; www.themurrayguesthouse.com; 11 Truong Dinh; s/d from US$26/32; ꙮꙮꙮ) while **Bay Bong** (20 Đ Suong Nguyet Anh; meals 50,000-150,000d; ⊙9am-8pm) has excellent hotpots and soups. For vegetarian options, head to **Tam Tinh** (Com Chay Tam Tinh; ☑0296-386 5064; Quang Trung near Chi Lang; meals 25,000d; ꙮ)

There are very regular buses to both Can Tho (100,000d, four hours) and HCMC (140,000, 6½ hours) from the main bus station.

Ha Tien

☑ 0297 / POP 30,100

Ha Tien's location on the Gulf of Thailand makes it feels a world away from the rice fields and rivers that typify the region. Dramatic limestone formations define the area, pepper tree plantations dot the hillsides and the town itself has a sleepy tropical charm. It's a transport hub for road links to the Cambodia border at Xa Xia/Prek Chak and boats to Phu Quoc.

For hotels, the **Bao Anh** (Nga Nhi Bao Anh; ☑ 0166 223 8440; cnr Đ Hong Van Tu & waterfront; r Mon-Fri/Sat & Sun from 350,000/400,000d; ꙮꙮ) is good value, while **Hai Van Hotel** (☑0297-385 2872; www.khachsanhaivan.com; 55 Đ Lam Son; s/d from 250,000/300,000d; ꙮꙮ) offers smart, if featureless rooms with polished floors. Some English is spoken.

For cheap grub the **night market** (Đ Lam Son; meals from 20,000d; ⊙5-9pm) can't be beat, while **Oasis** (☑0297-370 1553; www.oasisbarhatien.com; 30 Đ Tran Hau; meals 60,000-150,000d; ⊙9am-9pm; ꙮ) is a popular expat-run bar-restaurant; the owner provides good travel advice.

ⓘ Getting There & Away

Buses connect HCMC (200,000d, eight hours) and Ha Tien; they also run to destinations including Chau Doc (160,000d to 200,000d), Rach Gia (70,000d) and Can Tho (200,000d).

The bus station is located 1.5km south of the bridge next to a hospital.

Phu Quoc Island

☑ 0297 / POP 112,000

Fringed with idyllic beaches and with large tracts still covered in dense tropical jungle, Phu Quoc has morphed from a sleepy backwater into a favoured escape.

Beyond the resorts lining Long Beach there's still ample room for exploration and escaping. Dive the reefs, kayak the bays, eat up back-road miles on a motorbike, dine on fresh seafood or just lounge on the beach.

Despite increasing development (including an international airport), close to 70% of the island is protected as Phu Quoc National Park.

Phu Quoc's rainy season is from late May to October; the peak season for tourism is between December and March.

◉ Sights

Deserted white-sand beaches ring Phu Quoc.

Duong Dong   VILLAGE
The island's main town and chief fishing port on the central west coast is a tangle of budget hotels catering to domestic tourists (though foreigners are allowed), streetside stalls, bars and shops. The old bridge in town is a great vantage point to photograph the island's scruffy fishing fleet crammed into the narrow channel, and the filthy, bustling produce market makes for an interesting stroll. Most visitors come for the night market, seafood and the best glimpse at local life on the island.

Long Beach   BEACH
(Bai Truong) Long Beach is draped invitingly along the west coast from Duong Dong almost to An Thoi port. Development concentrates in the north near Duong Dong, where the recliners and rattan umbrellas of the various resorts rule; these are the only stretches that are kept garbage-free. With its west-facing aspect, sunsets can be stupendous.

Although not the prettiest, Long Beach is a good budget choice for accommodation and socialising; and, from its north end, Duong Dong and its night market are in walking distance.

★ An Thoi Islands   ISLAND
(Quan Dao An Thoi) Just off the southern tip of Phu Quoc, these 15 islands and islets are a paradise of white sand and blue waters. They can be visited by chartered boat for a fine day of sightseeing, fishing, swimming and snorkelling. Hon Thom (Pineapple Island) is about 3km in length and is the largest island in the group.

Most boats depart from An Thoi on Phu Quoc, but you can make arrangements through hotels on Long Beach, as well as dive operators.

★ Sao Beach   BEACH
(Bai Sao) With picture-perfect white sand, the delightful curve of beautiful Sao Beach bends out alongside a sea of mineral-water clarity just a few kilometres from An Thoi, the main shipping port at the southern tip of the island. There are a couple of beachfront restaurants, where you can settle into a deckchair (50,000d for nonguests), change into bathers (10,000d fee) or partake in water sports. If heading down to Sao Beach by motorbike, fill up with petrol before the trip.

VIETNAM PHU QUOC ISLAND

OFF THE BEATEN TRACK

MORE OF THE MEKONG DELTA

Most tourists are on hit-and-run day trips from HCMC or passing through on their way to or from Cambodia, but it's not hard to get off the beaten track in the Mekong Delta. Here are some lesser-known regional gems:

Check out some Khmer culture in **Tra Vinh,** home to a significant population of Cambodians and their beautiful temples.

The Khmer kingdom of Funan once held sway over much of the lower Mekong; its principal port was at **Oc-Eo,** located near Long Xuyen. Archaeologists have found ancient Persian and Roman artefacts here.

Birdwatching enthusiasts will want to make a diversion to **Tram Chin National Park** (⊗6am-8pm) near Cao Lanh, a habitat for the rare eastern sarus crane. These huge birds are depicted on the bas-reliefs at Angkor and are only found here and in northwest Cambodia.

The small and secluded beach resort of **Hon Chong** has the most scenic stretch of coastline on the Mekong Delta mainland. The big attractions here are Chua Hang Grotto, Duong Beach and Nghe Island.

ℹ️ GETTING TO CAMBODIA: SOUTHERN BORDERS

Chau Doc to Phnom Penh

Getting to the border The Vinh Xuong–Kaam Samnor border crossing is located northwest of Chau Doc along the Mekong River. Several companies in Chau Doc sell boat journeys to Phnom Penh via the Vinh Xuong border. **Hang Chau** (📞 Chau Doc 0296-356 2771, Phnom Penh 855-12-883 542; www.hangchautourist.com.vn; per person US$25) boats depart Chau Doc at 7.30am from a pier at 18 Đ Tran Hung Dao, arriving at 12.30pm.

At the border Cambodian visas are available, but minor overcharging is common.

For information on doing this crossing in the opposite direction, see p87.

Ha Tien to Kep

Getting to the border The Xa Xia–Prek Chak border crossing connects Ha Tien with Kep and Kampot on Cambodia's south coast. Several minibus companies leave Ha Tien for Cambodia at around 1pm, heading to Kep (US$9, one hour), Kampot (US$12, 1½ hours), Sihanoukville (US$15, four hours) and Phnom Penh (US$15, four hours). Book via Ha Tien Tourism.

At the border Cambodian visas are available at the border.

Moving on Most travellers opt for a through minibus ticket.

For information on doing this crossing in the opposite direction, see p135.

Chau Doc to Takeo

Getting to the border The Tinh Bien–Phnom Den border crossing is rarely used by travellers. A bus to Phnom Penh (US$25, five to six hours) passes through Chau Doc at around 7.30am; book through Mekong Tours (p906) in Chau Doc.

At the border Cambodian visas can be obtained here, although it's not uncommon to be charged US$35, several dollars more than the official rate.

Moving on Most travellers opt for a through bus ticket from Chau Doc.

For information on doing this crossing in the opposite direction, see p87.

Phu Quoc National Park NATURE RESERVE
About 90% of Phu Quoc is forested and the trees and adjoining marine environment enjoy official protection. This is the last large stand of forest in the south, and in 2010 the park was declared a Unesco Biosphere Reserve. The forest is densest in northern Phu Quoc, in the Khu Rung Nguyen Sinh forest reserve; you'll need a motorbike or mountain bike to tackle the bumpy dirt roads that cut through it. There are no real hiking trails.

🏃 Activities

Jerry's Jungle Tours BOAT TOUR, HIKING
(📞 0938 226 021; www.jerrystours.wixsite.com/jerrystours; 106 Đ Tran Hung Dao; day trips from US$30) Archipelago explorations by boat, with snorkelling, fishing, one-day and multiday trips to islands, motorbike tours, bouldering, birdwatching, hiking and cultural tours around Phu Quoc.

Flipper Diving Club DIVING
(📞 0297-399 4924; www.flipperdiving.com; 60 Đ Tran Hung Dao; ⏰ 7am-7pm) Centrally located, multilingual PADI dive centre for everything from novice dive trips to full instructor courses. Very professional, with plenty of diving experience worldwide, and with instructors who put you at ease if you're a newbie.

🛏️ Sleeping

Most beachside accommodation options are at Long Beach. Expect to pay more here than elsewhere in Vietnam; accommodation prices also yo-yo depending on the season.

🛏️ Long Beach

⭐ **Langchia Hostel** HOSTEL $
(📞 0939 132 613; www.langchia-village.com; 84 Đ Tran Hung Dao; dm US$5-7, d US$15; ❄️ 🛜 🏊) A favourite with solo travellers, this hostel gets plenty of praise for the friendliness and helpfulness of its staff, the lively bar with pool table and the swimming pool to cool down in. Dorm beds come with mozzie nets and individual fans; it's worth paying extra for the decent breakfast.

Q Hao Hostel HOSTEL $
(☏0297-359 7999; http://q-hao.com; 122 Tran Hung Dao; dm/d from US$13/35; ✴@☎) Oh, how Q Hao raises the hostel standard on Phuo Quoc. It boasts the stylings of a Hoi An family mansion but feels modern with comfy dorm beds, privacy curtains, rain shower, air-con, and immaculate cleanliness. And the social aspects remain – nightly free beer, events, pool table, Jacuzzi, and walk to Rory's Beach Bar. Phu Quoc isn't just for lovebirds and families.

Sunshine Bungalow HOTEL $
(☏0297-397 5777; www.sunshinephuquoc.com; Đ Tran Hung Dao; bungalows US$23-48; ✴☎) Friendly place run by a Vietnamese family, just 80m from the sea and sand. Large bright rooms nestle amid lush vegetation and the owners do their best to help. Some English and German spoken.

🛏 Around the Island

Freedomland HOMESTAY $$
(☏0297-399 4891; www.freedomlandphuquoc.com; 2 Ap Ong Lang, Xa Cua Duong; bungalows US$57-86; ☎) 🏖 With an emphasis on switching off (no TV, wi-fi or air-conditioning in rooms) and socialising – fun communal dinners are a mainstay – Freedomland has 11 basic but elegant bungalows (mosquito nets, fans, solar-heated showers) scattered around a shady plot. The beach is a five-minute walk away, or you can slump in the hammocks strung between the trees. Popular with solo travellers; call ahead.

🍴 Eating & Drinking

Most hotels have on-site cafes or restaurants. The seafood restaurants in the fishing village of Ham Ninh also offer an authentic local experience.

🍴 Duong Dong

★Phu Quoc Night Market SEAFOOD $
(Cho Dem Phu Quoc; Đ Bach Dang; meals from 50,000d; ⊙4.30pm-3am; 🍴) The most atmospheric and best-value place to dine on the island, Duong Dong's busy night market has stalls of snacks, coconut ice cream and a parade of outdoor restaurants serving a delicious range of Vietnamese seafood, grills and vegetarian options. Quality can be a mixed bag, so follow the discerning local crowd. Riverside tables can be a bit whiffy.

Khanh Ly Vegetarian VEGAN $
(☏0297-281 0180; 35 Đ Nguyen Trai; meals 20,000-45,000d; ⊙8am-8pm; 🍴) Pick and choose from a buffet of Vietnamese vegan-vegetarian dishes, such as mock shrimp on sugar cane, to accompany green veg and rice for an excellent value, delicious plate. Staff are friendly, and there are also hearty noodle soups to tempt carnivores.

Buddy Ice Cream & Info Cafe INTERNATIONAL $$
(☏0297-399 4181; 6 Đ Bach Dang; meals 80,000-180,000d; ⊙8am-10pm; 🍴) With the coolest music in town, this cafe is excellent for sides of tourist info with its New Zealand ice-cream combos, toasted sandwiches, fish 'n' chips, thirst-busting fruit juices, shakes, smoothies, all-day breakfasts, comfy sofas and book exchange. The owner speaks English and is generous with travel advice.

🍴 Long Beach

Heaven Restaurant VIETNAMESE $
(☏0975 542 769; 141 Đ Tran Hung Dao; meals 40,000-90,000d; ⊙8am-11pm; 🍴) You may not expect heaven to have basic wooden tables opening onto a road, but it does at this good-value family joint. With fresh, generous servings of Vietnamese dishes such as lemongrass chicken, and a very long list of vegetarian options, this is paradise for every taste.

Winston's Burgers & Beer BURGERS $
(☏0126 390 1093; 121 Đ Tran Hung Dao; burgers from 135,000d; ⊙12.30-10.30pm) The name says it all: this bar is about really good burgers, beer and a large selection of cocktails,

---

SPLURGE

Nab a sea-view table, order a papaya salad, grilled garlic prawns, *banh xeo* (Vietnamese pancake), cinnamon-infused okra, a delectable Khmer fish curry or grilled beef skewers wrapped in betel leaves and time dinner to catch the sunset at the excellent restaurant at **Spice House at Cassia Cottage** (www.cassiacottage.com; 100c Đ Tran Hung Dao; meals 190,000-300,000d; ⊙7-10am & 11am-10pm) . There's even a single romantic cabana table right on the sand. It's the best option nearby, attracting plenty of nonresort guests.

mixed by the eponymous Winston. Linger for a chat or challenge your drinking companions to a game of Connect 4. It has few vegetarian options.

Alanis Deli CAFE $
(☑ 0297-399 4931; 98 Đ Tran Hung Dao; meals from 60,000d; ☺ 8am-10.30pm; ☎) Fab caramel pancakes, American breakfast combos, plus good (if pricey) coffee and wonderfully friendly service.

★ Rory's Beach Bar BAR
(☑ 0919 333 950; 118/10 Đ Tran Hung Dao; ☺ 9am-1am) Phu Quoc's liveliest and most fun beach bar draws a steady torrent of travellers and island residents down the path to its seaside perch. Expect bonfires on the beach, great happy-hour specials and staff ready to chat.

❶ Getting There & Away

AIR
There are international flights to Singapore and Bangkok. **Vietnam Airlines** (☑ 0297-399 6677; www.vietnamairlines.com; 122 Đ Nguyen Trung Truc), **VietJet Air** (www.vietjetair.com) and Jetstar (p902) between them offer daily flights to Can Tho, Hanoi, HCMC, Haiphong and Rach Gia. Demand can be high in peak season, so book ahead

BOAT
Fast boats connect Phu Quoc to both Ha Tien (1½ hours) and Rach Gia (2½ hours). Phu Quoc travel agents have the most up-to-date schedules and can book tickets. Five virtually identical operators, including **Duong Dong Express** (☑ Phu Quoc 0297-398 1648, Rach Gia 0297-387 9765; 4 Đ Tran Hung Dao) and **Superdong** (p906) run fast boats from Rach Gia to Phu Quoc's Bai Vong on the east coast, most departing at 8am and making the return journey at 1pm (250,000d).

Three daily fast ferries (230,000d) from Ha Tien arrive at the Ham Ninh port, just north of Bai Vong. There are also car ferries to/from Ha Tien and Phu Quoc's Da Chong port.

❶ Getting Around

The island's airport is 10km from Duong Dong; a taxi costs around 100,000d to Long Beach. Bicycles/motorbikes are available through most hotels from 70,000/120,000d per day. There is a skeletal bus service (every hour or two) between An Thoi and Duong Dong. A bus (20,000d) waits for the ferry at Bai Vong to take passengers to Duong Dong. Motorbike taxis are everywhere. Short hops cost 20,000d; figure on around 60,000d for about 5km.

UNDERSTAND VIETNAM

Vietnam Today

Two decades of rising, sustained growth has transformed Vietnam. Change is most apparent in the big cities, where steel-and-glass high-rises define skylines and a burgeoning middle class now has the spending power to enjoy air-conditioned living and overseas travel. Yet in rural areas the nation's new-found prosperity is less evident, and up in the highlands life remains a day-to-day struggle for millions of minority people.

The Big Picture

In the 40 years since the end of the American War, Vietnam has made giant strides. A victorious, though bankrupt, nation has worked around the clock, grafting its way forward, overcoming a series of formidable hurdles (including a 19-year US trade embargo). Per-capita income grew from US$98 in 1993 to over US$2000 by 2015, and today Vietnam is one of the 10 fastest-growing economies in the world, boosted by strong manufacturing. Start-up business numbers are booming. And yet this rapid development is disjointed. The state sector remains huge, controlling around two-fifths of the economy – 100 of the 200 biggest Vietnamese companies are state-owned (including oil production, shipbuilding, cement and coal). Many of these operations haemorrhage money.

The spectre of corruption casts a shadow over development every step of the way. Transparency International ranked Vietnam the lowest of all the Asia Pacific countries it measured in 2014. Corruption scandals emerge on a daily basis, such as the nine Vinashin shipbuilding execs jailed following the company's near-collapse under US$4.5 billion of debt. For most Vietnamese people corruption is simply a part of day-to-day life, as they have to pay backhanders for everything from securing a civil service job to an internet connection.

North & South

The Vietnamese economy has been buoyant for 20 years, but some areas are more buoyant than others. In 2015 Ho Chi Minh City's economy was growing at 8.6%, well above that in the north. It's the south that's benefited most from inward investment as Viet Kieu (overseas Vietnamese, the vast majority of whom are southerners) have returned and invested in the region.

The government is aware of these divisions and tries to balance the offices of state, so if the prime minister is from the south, the head of the Communist Party is from the north.

When it comes to the older generation, the south has never forgiven the north for bulldozing their war cemeteries, imposing communism and blackballing whole families. The north has never forgiven the south for siding with the Americans against their own people. Luckily for Vietnam, the new generation seems to have less interest in the country's harrowing history.

Uneasy Neighbours

On the surface, Vietnam and its northern neighbour China have much in common, with a shared heritage, common frontier and all-powerful ruling Communist parties. But for the Vietnamese, China represents something of an overbearing big brother (and 1000 years of subordination). The nations fought a recent on-off border war which rumbled on for years, only ending in 1990. In a 2014 survey, over 80% of Vietnamese were concerned that another conflict could erupt over offshore islands in the South China Sea (always the 'East Sea' in Vietnam). China claims virtually the whole area, and is busy constructing port facilities and airstrips. In May 2014 anti-Chinese riots erupted in several provinces, resulting in at least 21 deaths, in response to China deploying an oil rig in the Paracel Islands. Thousands of Chinese nationals fled the country. By November 2015 tensions remained but the situation had calmed enough for President Xi Jinping to visit Hanoi as the countries sought to repair ties.

The two nations have plenty of common ground. Trade has continued to boom (though it is more one way than the Vietnamese would like), reaching US$58 billion in 2014, and Chinese is the second most popular foreign language studied in Vietnam. Ultimately, Presidents Trong and Xi signed various cooperation agreements concerning investment and infrastructure but little progress was evident over territorial disputes.

History

Early Vietnam

The Vietnamese trace their roots back to the Red River Delta where farmers first cultivated rice. Millennia of struggle against the Chinese then followed. Vietnam only became a united state in the 19th century, but quickly faced the ignominy of French colonialism and then the devastation of the American intervention. The Vietnamese nation has survived tempestuous, troubled times, but its strength of character has served it well. Today, the signs are it's continuing to grow with some promise.

The sophisticated Indianised kingdom of Funan flourished from the 1st to 6th centuries AD in the Mekong Delta area. Archaeological evidence reveals that Funan's busy trading port of Oc-Eo had contact with China, India, Persia and even the Mediterranean. Between the mid-6th century and the 9th century, the Funan empire was absorbed by the pre-Angkorian kingdom of Chenla.

Meanwhile, around present-day Danang, the Hindu kingdom of Champa emerged in the late 2nd century AD. Like Funan, it adopted Sanskrit as a sacred language and borrowed heavily from Indian art and culture. By the 8th century Champa had expanded to include what is now Nha Trang and Phan Rang. The Cham warred constantly with the Vietnamese to the north and the Khmers to the south and ultimately found themselves squeezed between these two great powers.

Chinese Occupation

The Chinese conquered the Red River Delta in the 2nd century BC and over the following centuries attempted to impress a centralised state system on the Vietnamese.

UNCLE OF THE PEOPLE

Father of the nation, Ho Chi Minh (Bringer of Light) was the son of a fiercely nationalistic scholar-official. Born Nguyen Tat Thanh near Vinh in 1890, he was educated in Hue and adopted many pseudonyms during his momentous life. Many Vietnamese affectionately refer to him as Bac Ho (Uncle Ho) today.

In 1911 he signed up as a cook's apprentice on a French ship, sailing the seas to North America, Africa and Europe. While he was odd-jobbing in England and France as a gardener, snow sweeper, waiter, photo-retoucher and stoker, his political consciousness developed.

Ho Chi Minh moved to Paris, where he mastered languages including English, French, German and Mandarin and began to promote the issue of Indochinese independence. He was a founding member of the French Communist Party in 1920.

In 1941 Ho Chi Minh returned to Vietnam for the first time in 30 years, and established the Viet Minh (whose goal was independence from France). As Japan prepared to surrender in August 1945, Ho Chi Minh led the August Revolution, and his forces then established control throughout much of Vietnam.

The return of the French compelled the Viet Minh to conduct a guerrilla war, which ultimately led to victory against the colonists at Dien Bien Phu in 1954. Ho then led North Vietnam until his death in September 1969 – he never lived to see the North's victory over the South.

Since then the party has worked hard to preserve the image and reputation of Bac Ho. His image dominates contemporary Vietnam. This cult of personality is in stark contrast to the simplicity with which Ho lived his life. For more Ho, check out *Ho Chi Minh,* the excellent biography by William J Duiker.

There were numerous small-scale rebellions against Chinese rule – which was characterised by tyranny, forced labour and insatiable demands for tribute – between the 3rd and 6th centuries, but all were defeated.

However, the early Viets learned much from the Chinese, including advanced irrigation for rice cultivation and medical knowledge as well as Confucianism, Taoism and Mahayana Buddhism. Much of the 1000-year period of Chinese occupation was typified by both Vietnamese resistance and the adoption of many Chinese cultural traits.

In AD 938 Ngo Quyen destroyed Chinese forces on the Bach Dang River, winning independence and signalling the start of a dynastic tradition. During subsequent centuries the Vietnamese successfully repulsed foreign invaders, including the Mongols, and absorbed the kingdom of Champa in 1471 as they expanded south.

Contact with the West

In 1858 a joint military force from France and the Spanish colony of the Philippines stormed Danang after several missionaries were killed. Early the next year, Saigon was seized. By 1883 the French had imposed a Treaty of Protectorate on Vietnam. French rule often proved cruel and arbitrary. Ultimately, the most successful resistance came from the communists, first organised by Ho Chi Minh in 1925.

During WWII the only group that significantly resisted the Japanese occupation was the communist-dominated Viet Minh. When WWII ended, Ho Chi Minh – whose Viet Minh forces already controlled large parts of the country – declared Vietnam independent. French efforts to reassert control soon led to violent confrontations and full-scale war. In May 1954 Viet Minh forces overran the French garrison at Dien Bien Phu.

The Geneva Accords of mid-1954 provided for a temporary division of Vietnam at the Ben Hai River. When Ngo Dinh Diem, the anti-communist, Catholic leader of the southern zone, refused to hold the 1956 elections, the Ben Hai line became the border between North and South Vietnam.

The War in Vietnam

Around 1960 the Hanoi government changed its policy of opposition to the Diem regime from one of 'political struggle' to one of 'armed struggle'. The National Liberation Front (NLF), a communist guerrilla group better known as the Viet Cong (VC), was founded to fight against Diem.

An unpopular ruler, Diem was assassinated in 1963 by his own troops. When the Hanoi government ordered North Vietnamese Army (NVA) units to infiltrate the South in 1964, the situation for the Saigon regime became desperate. In 1965 the USA committed its first combat troops, soon joined by soldiers from South Korea, Australia, Thailand and New Zealand in an effort to bring global legitimacy to the conflict.

As Vietnam celebrated the Lunar New Year in 1968, the VC launched a surprise attack, known as the Tet Offensive, marking a crucial turning point in the war. Many Americans, who had for years believed their government's insistence that the USA was winning, started demanding a negotiated end to the war. The Paris Agreements, signed in 1973, provided for a ceasefire, the total withdrawal of US combat forces and the release of American prisoners of war.

Reunification

Saigon surrendered to the NVA on 30 April 1975. Vietnam's reunification by the communists meant liberation from more than a century of colonial oppression, but was soon followed by large-scale internal repression. Hundreds of thousands of southerners fled Vietnam, creating a flood of refugees for the next 15 years.

Vietnam's campaign of repression against the ethnic Chinese, plus its invasion of Cambodia at the end of 1978, prompted China to attack Vietnam in 1979. The war lasted only 17 days, but Chinese–Vietnamese mistrust lasted for well over a decade.

Post-Cold War

After the collapse of the Soviet Union in 1991, Vietnam and Western nations sought rapprochement. The 1990s brought foreign investment and Association of Southeast Asian Nations (Asean) membership. The US established diplomatic relations with Vietnam in 1995, and Bill Clinton and George W Bush visited Hanoi. Vietnam was welcomed into the World Trade Organization (WTO) in 2007.

In recent years friction has grown between Vietnam and China over territorial claims in the South China Sea, and there were anti-Chinese riots in 2014. Conversely, relations between the USA and Vietnam have become much warmer, with booming bilateral trade.

People & Culture

The Vietnamese are battle-hardened, proud and nationalist, as they have earned their stripes in successive skirmishes with the world's mightiest powers. But that's the older generation, who remember every inch of the territory for which they fought. For the new generation, Vietnam is a place to succeed, a place to ignore the staid structures set in stone by the communists, and a place to go out and have some fun.

As in other parts of Asia, life revolves around the family; there are often several generations living under one roof. Poverty, and the transition from a largely agricultural society to that of a more industrialised nation, sends many people seeking their fortune to the bigger cities, and is changing the structure of the modern family unit. Women make up 52% of the nation's workforce but are not well represented in positions of power.

Vietnam's population is 84% ethnic Vietnamese (Kinh) and 2% ethnic Chinese; the rest is made up of Khmers, Chams and members of more than 50 minority peoples, who mainly live in highland areas.

Religion

Over the centuries, Confucianism, Taoism and Buddhism have fused with popular Chinese beliefs and ancient Vietnamese animism to form what's collectively known as the Triple Religion (Tam Giao). Most Viet-

BEST FILMS

Apocalypse Now (1979) The American War depicted as an epic 'heart of darkness' adventure.

The Deer Hunter (1978) Examines the psychological breakdown suffered by small-town servicemen.

Cyclo (1995) Visually stunning masterpiece that cuts to the core of HCMC's underworld.

The Quiet American (2002) Atmospherically set in Saigon during the French colonial period, with rebellion in the air.

The Vietnam War (2017) Definitive documentary series, which examines the roots of the conflict, war itself, and consequences.

namese people identify with this belief system, but, if asked, they'll usually say they're Buddhist. Vietnam also has a significant percentage of Catholics (8% to 10% of the total population).

Cao Daism is a unique and colourful Vietnamese sect that was founded in the 1920s. It combines secular and religious philosophies of the East and West, and is based on seance messages revealed to the group's founder, Ngo Minh Chieu.

There are also small numbers of Muslims (around 65,000) and Hindus (50,000).

Etiquette

Take your time to learn a little about the local culture in Vietnam.

→ Respect local dress standards: shorts to the knees, women's tops covering the shoulders, particularly at religious sites. Remove your shoes before entering a temple. Topless or nude sunbathing is totally inappropriate.

→ Exchanging business cards is an important part of even the smallest transaction or business contact. Hand them out like confetti.

→ Leaving a pair of chopsticks sitting vertically in a rice bowl looks very much like the incense sticks that are burned for the dead. This is not appreciated anywhere in Asia.

BEST BOOKS

The Quiet American (Graham Greene) Classic novel set in the 1950s as the French empire is collapsing.

The Sorrow of War (Bao Ninh) The North Vietnamese perspective, retold in novel form via flashbacks.

Vietnam: Rising Dragon (Bill Hayton) A candid assessment of the nation that's one of the most up-to-date sources available.

Catfish & Mandala (Andrew X Pham) Beautifully written and thought-provoking biographical tale of a Vietnamese-American.

The Sympathizer (Viet Thanh Nguyen) Superbly written spy novel dealing with the aftermath of the American War; 2016 Pulitzer Prize–winner.

→ Remove shoes when entering somebody's home. Don't point the bottom of your feet towards other people. Never, ever point your feet towards anything sacred, such as a Buddha image.

→ As a form of respect to elderly or other esteemed people, such as monks, take off your hat and bow your head politely when addressing them. The head is the symbolic highest point – never pat or touch a person on the head.

Arts

Contemporary Art & Music

It is possible to catch modern dance, classical ballet and stage plays in Hanoi and Ho Chi Minh City.

The work of contemporary painters and photographers covers a wide swath of styles and gives a glimpse into the modern Vietnamese psyche; there are good galleries in Hanoi, HCMC and Hoi An.

Youth culture is most vibrant in HCMC and Hanoi, where there's more freedom for musicians and artists. There's a small but growing hip-hop scene, with HCMC-born Suboi acknowledged as Vietnam's leading female artist; she raps to eclectic beats including dubstep rhythms. Hot bands include HCMC's The Children, metal merchants Black Infinity, punk band Giao Chi and alt-roots band 6789.

Viet-American Trace is an emerging artist whose moody, indie-tronic album *Low* received rave reviews upon release in 2017.

Architecture

The Vietnamese were not great builders like their neighbours the Khmer. Early Vietnamese structures were made of wood and other materials that proved highly vulnerable in the tropical climate. The grand exceptions are the stunning towers built by Vietnam's ancient Cham culture. These are most numerous in central Vietnam. The Cham ruins at My Son are a major draw.

Sculpture

Vietnamese sculpture has traditionally centred on religious themes and has functioned as an adjunct to architecture, especially that of pagodas, temples and tombs.

The Cham civilisation produced exquisite carved sandstone figures for its Hindu and Buddhist sanctuaries. The largest single collection of Cham sculpture is at the Museum of Cham Sculpture in Danang.

Water Puppetry

Vietnam's ancient art of *roi nuoc* (water puppetry) originated in northern Vietnam at least 1000 years ago. Developed by rice farmers, the wooden puppets were manipulated by puppeteers using water-flooded rice paddies as their stage. Hanoi is the best place to see water-puppetry performances, which are accompanied by music played on traditional instruments.

Food & Drink

Food

Vietnamese food is one of the world's greatest cuisines; there are said to be nearly 500 traditional dishes. It varies a lot between the north, centre and south. Soy sauce, Chinese influence and hearty soups like *pho* typify northern cuisine. Central Vietnamese food is known for its prodigious use of fresh herbs and intricate flavours; Hue imperial cuisine and Hoi An specialities are key to this area. Southern food is sweet, spicy and tropical – its curries will be familiar to lovers of Thai and Cambodian food. Everywhere you'll find that Vietnamese meals are superbly prepared and excellent value.

Most restaurants trade seven days a week, opening around 7am or 8am and closing around 9pm, often later in the big cities.

FRUIT

Aside from the usual delightful Southeast Asian fruits, Vietnam has its own unique *trai thanh long* (green dragon fruit), a bright fuchsia-coloured fruit with green scales. Grown mainly in the coastal region near Nha Trang, it has white flesh flecked with edible black seeds, and tastes something like a mild kiwifruit.

MEALS

Pho is the noodle soup that built a nation and is eaten at all hours of the day, but especially for breakfast. *Com* are rice dishes. You'll see signs saying *pho* and *com* everywhere. Other noodle soups to try are *bun bo Hue* (rice-noodle soup with beef and pork) and *hu tieu.*

THERE'S SOMETHING FISHY AROUND HERE...

Nuoc mam (fish sauce) is the one ingredient that is quintessentially Vietnamese, and it lends a distinctive character to Vietnamese cooking. The sauce is made by fermenting highly salted fish in large ceramic vats for four to 12 months. Connoisseurs insist high-grade sauce has a much milder aroma than the cheaper variety. Dissenters insist it is a chemical weapon. It's very often used as a dipping sauce, and takes the place occupied by salt on a Western table.

Spring rolls (*nem* in the north, *cha gio* in the south) are a speciality. These are normally dipped in *nuoc mam* (fish sauce), though many foreigners prefer soy sauce (*xi dau* in the north, *nuoc tuong* in the south).

Because Buddhist monks of the Mahayana tradition are strict vegetarians, *an chay* (vegetarian cooking) is an integral part of Vietnamese cuisine.

SNACKS

Street stalls or roaming vendors are everywhere, selling steamed sweet potatoes, rice porridge and ice-cream bars even in the wee hours.

There are also many other Vietnamese nibbles to try, including the following:

Bap xao Made from stir-fried fresh corn, chillies and tiny shrimp.

Bo bia Nearly microscopic shrimp, fresh lettuce and thin slices of Vietnamese sausage, rolled up in rice paper and dipped in a spicy-sweet peanut sauce.

Sinh to Shakes made with milk and sugar or yoghurt, and fresh tropical fruit.

SWEETS

Many sticky confections are made from sticky rice, like *banh it nhan dau,* which also contains sugar and bean paste and is sold wrapped in banana leaf.

Most foreigners prefer *kem* (ice cream) or *yaourt* (yoghurt), which is generally of good quality. Try *che,* a cold, refreshing sweet soup made with sweetened black bean, green bean or corn. It's served in a glass with ice and sweet coconut cream on top.

Drink

VIETNAMESE COFFEE CULTURE

Enjoying a Vietnamese coffee is a tradition that can't be rushed. A glass tumbler, topped with a curious aluminium lid is placed before you while you crouch on a tiny blue plastic chair. A layer of condensed milk on the bottom of the glass is gradually infused with coffee lazily drip, drip, dripping from the aluminium top. Minutes pass, and eventually a darker caffeine-laden layer floats atop the condensed milk. Stir it together purposefully – maybe pouring it over ice in a separate glass – and it's definitely an energising ritual worth waiting for. And while you're drip-watching, consider the *caphe* variations usually on offer in a Vietnamese cafe.

Caphe sua da Iced coffee with condensed milk.

Caphe da Iced coffee without milk.

Caphe den Black coffee.

Caphe sua chua Iced coffee with yoghurt.

Caphe trung da Coffee topped with a beaten egg yolk.

ALCOHOLIC DRINKS

Memorise the words *bia hoi,* which mean 'draught beer'. Probably the cheapest beer in the world, *bia hoi* starts at around 5000d a glass, so anyone can afford a round. Places that serve *bia hoi* usually also serve cheap food.

Several foreign labels brewed in Vietnam under licence include Tiger, Carlsberg and Heineken. National and regional brands include Halida and Hanoi in the North, Huda and Larue in the centre, and BGI and 333 *(ba ba ba)* in the south. Craft beer is also increasingly popular, and both HCMC and Hanoi have excellent craft breweries and specialist beer bars.

Wine and spirits are available but at higher prices. Local brews are cheaper but not always drinkable.

NONALCOHOLIC DRINKS

Whatever you drink, make sure that it's been boiled or bottled. Ice is generally safe on the tourist trail, but may not be elsewhere.

Foreign soft drinks are widely available in Vietnam. An excellent local treat is *soda chanh* (carbonated mineral water with lemon and sugar) or *nuoc chanh nong* (hot, sweetened lemon juice).

Environment

Environmental consciousness is low in Vietnam. Rapid industrialisation, deforestation and pollution are major problems facing the country.

Unsustainable logging and farming practices, as well as the extensive spraying of defoliants by the US during the war, have contributed to deforestation. This has resulted not only in significant loss of biological diversity, but also in a harder existence for many minority people.

The country's rapid economic and population growth over the last decade – demonstrated by the dramatic increase in industrial production, motorbike numbers and helter-skelter construction – has put additional pressure on the already-stressed environment.

The Land

Vietnam stretches more than 1600km along the east coast of the Indochinese peninsula. The country's land area is 329,566 sq km, making it slightly larger than Italy and a bit smaller than Japan.

As the Vietnamese are quick to point out, it resembles a *don ganh,* the ubiquitous bamboo pole with a basket of rice slung from each end. The baskets represent the main rice-growing regions of the Red River Delta in the north and the Mekong Delta in the south.

Of several interesting geological features found in Vietnam, the most striking are its spectacular karst formations (limestone peaks with caves and underground streams). The northern half of Vietnam has a spectacular array of karst areas, particularly around Halong Bay and Phong Nha.

Wildlife

We'll start with the good news. Despite some disastrous bouts of deforestation, Vietnam's flora and fauna is still incredibly exotic and varied. The nation has an estimated 12,000 plant species, only 7000 of which have been identified; more than 275 species of mammal; 800 species of bird; 180 species of reptile; and 80 species of amphibian. The other side of the story is that, despite this outstanding diversity, the threat to Vietnam's remaining wildlife has never been greater, due to poaching, hunting and habitat loss. Three of the nation's iconic animals – the elephant, the saola and the tiger – are on the brink. It's virtually certain that the last wild Vietnamese rhino was killed inside Cat Tien National Park in 2010. And for every trophy animal there are hundreds of other less 'headline' species that are being cleared from forests and reserves for the sake of profit (or hunger).

Many officials still turn a blind eye to the trade in wildlife for export and domestic consumption, though laws are in place to protect the animals. Poachers continue to profit from meeting the demand for exotic animals for pets and traditional medicines.

National Parks

There are 31 national parks and over 150 nature reserves; officially, 9% of the nation's territory is protected. In the north the most interesting and accessible include Cat Ba, Bai Tu Long, Ba Be and Cuc Phuong. Heading south Phong Nha-Ke Bang, Bach Ma National Park, Yok Don National Park and Cat Tien National Park are well worth investigating.

SURVIVAL GUIDE

❶ Directory A–Z

ACCOMMODATION

Accommodation is superb value for money in Vietnam. As tourism is booming it's usually best to book your accommodation a day or two in advance, or several weeks ahead in the high season (the Tet holiday in late January to mid-February, July to August, and around Christmas).

Hotels Range from simple, functional minihotels to uber-luxurious spa resorts.

Hostels Popular in the main tourism centres, but rare elsewhere.

Guesthouses Usually family run and less formal than hotels.

Camping Options are extremely limited, but new facilities are opening in southern Vietnam.

CHILDREN

Children will have a good time in Vietnam, mainly because of the overwhelming amount of attention they attract and the fact that almost everybody wants to play with them.

➤ Big cities usually have plenty to keep kids interested, though traffic safety is a serious concern.

➤ Watch out for rip tides along the main coastline. Some popular beaches have warning flags and lifeguards.

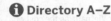

➤ Local cuisine is rarely too spicy for kids and the range of fruit is staggering. International food (pizzas, pasta, burgers and ice cream) is available, too.

➤ Breastfeeding in public is perfectly acceptable in Vietnam.

Check out Lonely Planet's *Travel with Children* for more information and advice.

ELECTRICITY

Voltage is 220V, 50 cycles. Sockets are two pin, round head.

EMBASSIES & CONSULATES

Generally speaking, embassies won't be that sympathetic if you end up in jail after committing a crime. In genuine emergencies you might get some assistance.

If you have your passport stolen, it can take some time to replace it as many embassies in Vietnam do not issue new passports, which have to be sent from a regional embassy.

Australian Embassy (Map p826; ☎ 024-3774 0100; www.vietnam.embassy.gov.au; 8 Đ Dao Tan, Ba Dinh District, Hanoi)

Australian Consulate (Map p894; ☎ 028-3521 8100; www.hcmc.vietnam.embassy.gov.au; 20th fl, Đ 47 Ly Tu Truong, Vincom Center, HCMC)

Cambodian Embassy (Map p826; ☎ 024-3825 6473; camemb.vnm@mfa.gov.kh; 71a P Tran Hung Dao, Hanoi; ⏱ 8.00-11.30am & 2-5.30pm Mon-Fri)

Cambodian Consulate (Map p896; ☑ 028-3829 2751; camcg.hcm@mfa.gov.kh; 41 Đ Phung Khac Khoan, HCMC)

Canadian Embassy (Map p834; www.canadainternational.gc.ca/vietnam; 31 Đ Hung Vuong, Hanoi)

Canadian Consulate (Map p894; ☑ 028-3827 9899; www.canadainternational.gc.ca; 10th fl, 235 Đ Dong Khoi, HCMC)

Chinese Embassy (Map p834; ☑ 024-8845 3736; http://vn.china-embassy.org; 46 P Hoang Dieu, Hanoi)

Chinese Consulate (Map p896; ☑ 028-3829 2457; http://hcmc.chineseconsulate.org; 175 Đ Hai Ba Trung, HCMC)

French Embassy (Map p826; ☑ 024-3944 5700; www.ambafrance-vn.org; P Tran Hung Dao, Hanoi)

French Consulate (Map p896; ☑ 028-3520 6800; www.consulfrance-hcm.org; 27 Đ Nguyen Thi Minh Khai, HCMC)

German Embassy (Map p834; ☑ 024-3845 3836; www.hanoi.diplo.de; 29 Đ Tran Phu, Hanoi)

German Consulate (Map p896; ☑ 028-3829 1967; www.ho-chi-minh-stadt.diplo.de; 126 Đ Nguyen Dinh Chieu, HCMC)

Japanese Embassy (Map p826; ☑ 024-3846 3000; www.vn.emb-japan.go.jp; 27 P Lieu Giai, Ba Dinh District, Hanoi)

Japanese Consulate (Map p898; ☑ 028-3933 3510; www.hcmcgj.vn.emb-japan.go.jp; 261 Đ Dien Bien Phu, HCMC)

Laotian Embassy (Map p826; ☑ 024-3942 4576; 40 Quang Trung, Hanoi; ⊙ 8.30-11.30am & 1-4pm Mon-Fri)

Laotian Consulate (Map p894; ☑ 028-3829 7667; 93 Đ Pasteur, HCMC)

Netherlands Embassy (Map p830; ☑ 024-3831-5650; www.nederlandwereldwijd.nl/landen/vietnam; 7th fl, BIDV Tower, 194 Đ Tran Quang Khai, Hanoi)

Netherlands Consulate (Map p896; ☑ 028-3823 5932; www.nederlandwereldwijd.nl/landen/vietnam; Saigon Tower, 29 ĐL Le Duan, HCMC)

New Zealand Embassy (Map p830; ☑ 024-3824 1481; www.mfat.govt.nz; Level 5, 63 P Ly Thai To, Hanoi)

New Zealand Consulate (Map p894; ☑ 028-3822 6907; www.mfat.govt.nz/en/countries-and-regions/south-east-asia/viet-nam/new-zealand-embassy/; 8th fl, The Metropolitan, 235 Đ Dong Khoi, HCMC)

Singaporean Embassy (Map p834; ☑ 024-3848 9168; www.mfa.gov.sg/hanoi; 41-43 Đ Tran Phu, Hanoi)

Thai Embassy (Map p834; ☑ 024-3823 5092; www.thaiembassy.org; 3-65 P Hoang Dieu, Hanoi)

Thai Consulate (Map p898; ☑ 028-3932 7637; www.thaiembassy.org/hochiminh; 77 Đ Tran Quoc Thao, HCMC)

UK Embassy (Map p830; ☑ 024-3936 0500; http://ukinvietnam.fco.gov.uk; 4th fl, Central Bldg, 31 P Hai Ba Trung, Hanoi)

UK Consulate (Map p896; ☑ 028-3825 1380; www.gov.uk/world/organisations/british-consulate-general-ho-chi-minh-city; 25 ĐL Le Duan, HCMC)

US Embassy (Map p826; ☑ 024-3850 5000; https://vn.usembassy.gov; 7 P Lang Ha, Ba Dinh District, Hanoi)

US Consulate (Map p896; ☑ 028-3520 4200; https://vn.usembassy.gov/embassy-consulates/ho-chi-minh-city; 4 ĐL Le Duan, HCMC)

INSURANCE

Insurance is a must for Vietnam, as the cost of major medical treatment is prohibitive. A travel insurance policy to cover theft, loss and medical problems is the best bet.

Some insurance policies specifically exclude such 'dangerous activities' as riding motorbikes, diving and even trekking. Check that your policy covers an emergency evacuation in the event of serious injury.

If you're driving a vehicle, you need a Vietnamese insurance policy.

Worldwide travel insurance is available at www.lonelyplanet.com/travel-insurance. You can buy, extend and claim online anytime – even if you're already on the road.

INTERNET ACCESS

Internet and wi-fi are widely available throughout Vietnam. Something like 98% of hotels and guesthouses have wi-fi; only in very remote places (such as national parks) is it not standard. Wi-fi is almost always free of charge. Many cafes and restaurants also have (free) wi-fi. Connection speeds are normally good. Internet cafes are also available, costing 3000d to 8000d per hour.

Most travellers also surf the net using 3G or 4G mobile phone connections.

EATING PRICE RANGES

The following price ranges refer to a typical meal (excluding drinks). Unless otherwise stated, taxes are included in the price.

Budget less than US$5 (115,000d)

Midrange US$5 (115,000d) to US$15 (340,000d)

Top end more than US$15 (340,000d)

LEGAL MATTERS

Very few foreigners experience any hassle from police. If you lose something really valuable such as your passport or visa, you'll need to contact them. Note you may face imprisonment and/or large fines for drug offences, and drug trafficking can be punishable by death.

LGBT TRAVELLERS

Vietnam is pretty hassle-free for gay travellers. There's not much in the way of harassment, nor are there official laws on same-sex relationships. VietPride (www.facebook.com/vietpride.vn) marches have been held in Hanoi and HCMC since 2012. Gay weddings were officially authorised in 2015 (though their legal status has not yet been recognised). Checking into hotels as a same-sex couple is perfectly OK. But be discreet – public displays of affection are not socially acceptable whatever your sexual orientation.

Check out Utopia (www.utopia-asia.com) to obtain contacts and useful travel information. The gay dating app Grindr is popular in Vietnam.

MONEY

The Vietnamese currency is the dong (abbreviated to 'd'). US dollars are also widely used.

For the last few years the dong has been fairly stable at around 22,000d to the US dollar.

ATMs are widespread and present in virtually every town in the country.

Tipping is not expected, but is appreciated.

Credit & Debit Cards

Visa and MasterCard are accepted in many tourist centres, but don't expect noodle bars to take plastic. Commission charges (around 3%) sometimes apply.

For cash advances, try branches of Vietcombank in most cities around the country. Expect to pay at least a 3% commission for this service.

OPENING HOURS

Hours vary little throughout the year.

Banks 8am–3pm weekdays, to 11.30am Saturday; some take a lunch break

Offices and museums 7am or 7.30am–5pm or 6pm; museums generally close on Monday; most take a lunch break (roughly 11am–1.30pm)

Restaurants 11am–9pm

Shops 8am–6pm

Temples and pagodas 5am–9pm

PUBLIC HOLIDAYS

If a public holiday falls on a weekend, it is observed on the Monday.

New Year's Day (Tet Duong Lich) 1 January
Vietnamese New Year (Tet) January or February; a three-day national holiday

Founding of the Vietnamese Communist Party (Thanh Lap Dang CSVN) 3 February; the date the party was founded in 1930
Hung Kings Commemorations (Hung Vuong) 10th day of the 3rd lunar month (March or April)
Liberation Day (Saigon Giai Phong) 30 April; the date of Saigon's 1975 surrender is commemorated nationwide
International Workers' Day (Quoc Te Lao Dong) 1 May
Ho Chi Minh's Birthday (Sinh Nhat Bac Ho) 19 May
Buddha's Birthday (Phat Dan) Eighth day of the fourth moon (usually June)
National Day (Quoc Khanh) 2 September; commemorates the Declaration of Independence by Ho Chi Minh in 1945

SAFE TRAVEL

All in all, Vietnam is an extremely safe country to travel in.

➡ The police keep a pretty tight grip on social order and there are rarely reports of muggings, robberies or sexual assaults.

➡ Scams and hassles do exist, particularly in Hanoi, HCMC and Nha Trang (and to a lesser degree in Hoi An).

➡ Be extra careful if you're travelling on two wheels on Vietnam's anarchic roads; traffic accident rates are woeful and driving standards are pretty appalling.

TELEPHONE

A mobile phone with a local SIM card (and an internet-based calls and messaging app) will allow you to get online and make phone calls in Vietnam.

Local calls

Domestic calls are very inexpensive using a Vietnamese SIM.

Phone numbers in Hanoi, HCMC and Haiphong have eight digits. Elsewhere around the country phone numbers have seven digits. Telephone area codes are assigned according to the province.

International calls

It's usually easiest to use wi-fi and a calling app such as Skype. Mobile phone rates for international phone calls can be less than US$0.10 a minute.

Mobile Phones

If you have an unlocked phone, it's virtually essential to get a local SIM card for longer visits in Vietnam. 3G and 4G data packages are some of the cheapest in the world at around 150,000d for 3GB and will enable you to use the net if wi-fi is weak; some packages include call time, too. Many SIM card deals allow you to call abroad cheaply (from 2000d a minute).

Get the shop owner (or someone at your hotel) to set up your phone in English or your native language. The three main mobile-phone companies are Viettel, Vinaphone and Mobifone.

Phone Codes

Most regional phone codes (59 of Vietnam's 63 provinces) changed in 2017. Many publications and web pages will take some time to update numbers using new codes.

TIME

Vietnam is seven hours ahead of Greenwich Mean Time/Universal Time Coordinated (GMT/UTC). There's no daylight saving or summer time.

TOILETS

➡ The issue of toilets and what to do with used toilet paper can cause confusion. In general, if there's a wastepaper basket next to the toilet, that is where the toilet paper goes (many sewage systems cannot handle toilet paper). If there's no basket, flush paper down the toilet.

➡ Toilet paper is usually provided though it's wise to keep a stash of your own while on the move.

➡ There are still some squat toilets in public places and out in the countryside.

➡ The scarcity of public toilets is more of a problem for women than for men. Vietnamese men often urinate in public. Women might find roadside toilet stops easier if wearing a sarong. You usually have to pay a few dong to an attendant to access a public toilet.

TOURIST INFORMATION

Tourist offices in Vietnam have a different philosophy from the majority of tourist offices worldwide. These government-owned enterprises are really travel agencies whose primary interests are booking tours and turning a profit. Don't expect much independent travel information.

Vietnam Tourism (www.vietnamtourism.com)

Saigon Tourist (www.saigon-tourist.com)

Travel agents, backpacker cafes and your fellow travellers are usually a much better source of information.

Other Useful Websites

The Word (www.wordhcmc.com) This superb magazine has comprehensive coverage and excellent features.

Vietnam Coracle (http://vietnamcoracle.com) Excellent independent travel advice, including lots of backroads content.

Vietnam Online (www.vietnamonline.com) Good all-rounder.

Coast Vietnam (www.coastvietnam.com) Classy website concentrating on Vietnam's central coast.

Rusty Compass (www.rustycompass.com) Useful online travel guide with itineraries and videos.

Lonely Planet (www.lonelyplanet.com/vietnam) Destination information, hotel bookings, traveller forum and more.

TRAVELLERS WITH DISABILITIES

Vietnam is not the easiest of places for travellers with disabilities. Tactical problems include the chaotic traffic, a lack of lifts (elevators) in smaller hotels, and pavements (sidewalks) that are routinely blocked by parked motorbikes and food stalls.

That said, with some careful planning it is possible to enjoy your trip. Find a reliable company to make the travel arrangements. Many hotels in the midrange and above category have elevators, and disabled access is improving. Bus and train travel is tough, but hire a private vehicle with a driver and almost anywhere becomes instantly accessible.

The hazards for blind travellers in Vietnam are acute, with traffic coming at you from all directions, so you'll definitely need a sighted companion.

The Travellers With Disabilities forum on Lonely Planet's Thorn Tree (www.lonelyplanet.com/thorntree/forums/travellers-with-disabilities) is a good place to seek the advice of other travellers.

Alternatively, you could try organisations such as Mobility International USA (www.miusa.org), the Royal Association for Disability Rights (www.disabilityrightsuk.org) or the Society for Accessible Travel & Hospitality (www.sath.org).

VISAS

The (very complicated) visa situation has recently changed for many nationalities, and is fluid – always check the latest regulations.

Firstly, if you are staying more than 15 days and from a Western country, you'll still need a visa (or approval letter from an agent) in advance. If your visit is less than 15 days, some nationalities are now visa-exempt (for a single visit, not multiple-entry trips).

Tourist visas are valid for either 30 days or 90 days. A single-entry 30-day visa costs US$20, a three-month multiple-entry visa is US$70. Only United States nationals are able to arrange one-year visas.

Until recently there have been two methods of applying for a visa: a Visa on Arrival (VOA) via online visa agents; or via a Vietnamese embassy or consulate. That is changing as e-visas have been rolled out (for a limited number of nationalities).

Visa on Arrival (VOA)

Visa on Arrival (VOA) is the preferred method for most travellers arriving by air, since it's cheaper, faster and you don't have to part with your passport by posting it to an embassy. Online visa agencies email the VOA to you directly.

It can only be used if you are flying into any of Vietnam's six international airports, not at land crossings. The process is straightforward: you fill out an online application form and pay the agency fee (around US$20). You'll then receive by email a VOA approval letter signed by Vietnamese immigration that you print out and show on arrival, where you pay your visa stamping fee in US dollars, cash only. The single-entry stamping fee is US$25, a multiple-entry stamping fee is US$50.

There are many visa agents, but there are some inefficient cut-priced operators out there. It's recommended to stick to well-established companies; the following two are professional and efficient:

Vietnam Visa Choice (www.vietnamvisachoice.com) Online support from native English-speakers. This agency also guarantees your visa will be issued within the time specified.

Vietnam Visa Center (www.vietnamvisacenter.org) Competent all-rounder with helpful staff well briefed on the latest visa situation. Offers a two-hour express service for last-minute trips.

Visas via an Embassy or Consulate

You can also obtain visas through Vietnamese embassies and consulates around the world, but fees are normally much higher than using a visa agent and (depending on the country) the process can be slow. In Asia, Vietnamese visas tend to be issued in two to three working days in Cambodia. In Europe and North America it takes around a week.

E-visas

A pilot e-visa program introduced in early 2017 allows visitors to apply for visas online through the Vietnam Immigration Department. Citizens of 40 countries are eligible, including those from the UK and the USA (though not Australians, Canadians or New Zealanders).

E-visas are single-entry only, valid for 30 days (nonextendable), and cost US$25. Processing takes three to five days.

However this e-visa system has not exactly been efficiently implemented. The official website is glitch-prone and often fails to load. We've also heard of several cases where applications have gone AWOL and photos rejected for not being picture-perfect.

There have been reports of visitors being deported due to incorrect details (such as wrong date of birth or mispelt names) on the online application form. If you do apply for an e-visa, double-check that all the information you provide is 100% accurate.

E-visas can be applied for online at www.immigration.gov.vn.

Multiple-Entry Visas

It's possible to enter Cambodia or Laos from Vietnam and then re-enter Vietnam without having to apply for another visa. However, you must hold a multiple-entry visa before you leave Vietnam.

Single-entry visas can no longer be changed to multiple-entry visas inside Vietnam.

Visa Extensions

Tourist visa extensions officially cost as little as US$10, and have to be organised via agents. The procedure takes seven to ten days and you can only extend the visa for 30 (US$40) or 60 (US$60) days depending on the visa you hold.

You can extend your visa in big cities, but if it's done in a different city from the one you arrived in, it'll cost you US$50 to $70. In practice, extensions work most smoothly in HCMC, Hanoi, Danang and Hue.

VOLUNTEERING

Opportunities for voluntary work are quite limited in Vietnam.

The **NGO Resource Centre** (☑ 024-3832 8570; www.ngocentre.org.vn; Room 201, Bldg E3, 6 Dang Van Ngu, Trung Tu Diplomatic Compound, Dong Da, Hanoi) keeps a database of all of the NGOs assisting Vietnam.

WORK

At least 90% of foreign travellers seeking work in Vietnam end up teaching English, though some dive centres and hostels need workers.

ℹ Getting There & Away

Most travellers enter Vietnam by plane or bus, but there are also train links from China and boat connections from Cambodia via the Mekong River.

ENTERING VIETNAM

Formalities at Vietnam's international airports are generally smoother than at land borders. Crossing the border between Vietnam and Laos can be particularly slow.

Passport

Your passport must be valid for six months upon arrival in Vietnam. Many nationalities have to arrange a visa in advance.

AIR
Airports

There are three main international airports in Vietnam. Phu Quoc also has international flights including Singapore, Bangkok and some charters to Europe. Located 36km south of Nha Trang, Cam Ranh has an expanding range of flights including Hong Kong and Seoul.

Tan Son Nhat International Airport (www.tsnairport.hochiminhcity.gov.vn/vn) For Ho Chi Minh City.

Noi Bai Airport (www.hanoiairportonline.com) Serves the capital, Hanoi.

Danang Airport (www.danangairport.vn/en) International flights to China, South Korea, Japan, Hong Kong, Thailand, Cambodia and Singapore.

BORDER CROSSINGS

Vietnam shares land borders with Cambodia, China and Laos and there are plenty of border crossings open to foreigners with each.

Officials at border crossings occasionally ask for an 'immigration fee' of a dollar or two.

Cambodia

Cambodia and Vietnam share a long frontier with seven border crossings. One-month Cambodian visas are issued at all border crossings for US$30, but overcharging is common at all borders except Bavet.

Cambodian border crossings are officially open daily between 8am and 8pm.

China

There are three main borders where foreigners are permitted to cross between Vietnam and China: Dong Dang–Pingxiang (the Friendship Pass), Lao Cai and Mong Cai.

In most cases it's necessary to arrange a Chinese visa in advance but some nationalities (including Australians) can get their visas on the Vietnamese side of the Lao Cai–Hekou border.

Time in China is one hour ahead.

Laos

There are seven overland crossings between Vietnam and Laos. Thirty-day Lao visas are available at all borders.

The golden rule is to try to use direct city-to-city bus connections between the countries, as potential hassle will be greatly reduced. If you travel step by step using local buses, expect transport scams (eg serious overcharging) on the Vietnamese side. Devious drivers have even stopped in the middle of nowhere to renegotiate the price.

Transport links on both sides of the border can be hit-and-miss, so don't use the more remote borders unless you have plenty of time, and patience, to spare.

ℹ️ Getting Around

AIR

Vietnam has excellent domestic flight connections, with new routes opening up all the time, and very affordable prices (if you book early). Airlines accept bookings on international credit and debit cards. Note, however, that cancellations are quite common. It's safest not to rely on a flight from a small regional airport to make an international connection the same day – travel a day early if you can. Vietnam Airlines is the least likely to cancel flights.

Jetstar Airways (www.jetstar.com)
Vasco (www.vasco.com.vn)
VietJet Air (www.vietjetair.com)
Vietnam Airlines (www.vietnamairlines.com.vn)

BICYCLE

Bikes are a great way to get around Vietnam, particularly when you get off the main highways.

The main hazard is the traffic, and it's wise to avoid certain areas (notably Hwy 1). Some of the best cycling is along quiet coastal roads in Central Vietnam, in the Southwest Highlands and up in the northern mountains (although you'll have to cope with some big hills here). The Mekong Delta is a rewarding option for those who like it flat.

Bicycles can be hired from guesthouses from US$1 per day, while good-quality mountain bikes cost from US$10.

BOAT

In the North, cruises on Halong Bay or Lan Ha Bay are extremely popular and should not be missed. Hydrofoils also connect Haiphong with Cat Ba Island (near Halong Bay). Day trips by boat to islands off the coast of Nha Trang and to the Chams off Hoi An are also worthwhile.

The extensive network of canals in the Mekong Delta makes getting around by boat feasible. Travellers to Phu Quoc Island can catch ferries from Ha Tien or Rach Gia.

BUS

Vietnam has an extensive network of buses that reach the far-flung corners of the country. Modern buses, operated by myriad companies, run on all the main highways.

Many travellers (perhaps the majority) never actually visit a Vietnamese bus station at all, preferring to stick to the convenient, tourist-friendly open-tour bus network.

Whichever class of bus you're on, bus travel in Vietnam is never speedy; reckon on just 50km/h on major routes including Hwy 1.

Bus Stations

Many cities have several bus stations – make sure you go to the right one! Bus stations all look chaotic, but many now have ticket offices with official prices and departure times displayed.

Reservations & Costs

Reservations aren't required for most of the frequent, popular services between towns and cities, and it doesn't hurt to purchase the ticket the day before. Always buy a ticket from the office, as bus drivers are notorious for overcharging.

On many rural runs foreigners are typically overcharged anywhere from twice to 10 times the going rate. As a benchmark, a typical 100km ride *should* be between US$2 and US$3.

Bus Types

On most popular routes, modern air-conditioned buses offer comfortable reclining seats, while sleeper buses have flat beds for really long trips.

Deluxe buses are nonsmoking. On the flip side, most of them are equipped with blaring TVs and even karaoke.

Connecting backpacker haunts across the nation, open-tour buses are wildly popular in Vietnam. These air-con buses use convenient, centrally located departure points and allow you to hop on and hop off at any major city along the main north–south route. Prices are reasonable. An open-tour ticket from Ho Chi Minh City to Hanoi costs from US$35 and US$70; the more stops you add, the higher the price. Sinh Tourist (www.thesinhtourist.vn) has a good reputation, with online seat reservations and comfortable buses.

Local buses in the countryside are slow and stop frequently. Conductors tend to routinely overcharge foreigners on these local services.

CAR & MOTORCYCLE

Having your own set of wheels gives you maximum flexibility to visit remote regions and stop when and where you please. Car hire always includes a driver. Motorbike hire is good value and this can be self-drive or with a driver.

Driving Licence

Foreigners are now permitted to drive in Vietnam with an International Driving Permit (IDP). This must be combined with local insurance for it to be valid. In reality on the ground virtually no car-hire agency will provide a car to a foreign visitor without including a driver. If you do manage to acquire a car without a driver an IDP is technically required.

Car & Minibus

Hiring a vehicle with a driver is a realistic option (even for budget travellers) if you share the cost.
Costs per day:
Standard model US$80 to US$120
4WD/minibus US$100 to US$130

Motorbike

Motorbikes can be hired from virtually anywhere, including cafes, hotels and travel agencies. Some places will ask to keep your passport until you return the bike. Try to sign some sort of agreement, clearly stating what you are hiring, how much it costs, the extent of compensation and so on.

To tackle the mountains of the north, it is best to get a slightly more powerful model such as a road or trail bike. Plenty of local drivers are

willing to act as chauffeur and guide for around US$20 to US$30 per day.

The approximate costs per day without a driver are between US$5 and US$8 for a moped or US$20 and up for trail and road bikes.

Insurance

If you're travelling in a tourist vehicle with a driver, the car-hire company organises insurance. If you're using a hired bike, the owners should have some insurance. Many rental places will make you sign a contract agreeing to a valuation for the bike if it is stolen. Use guarded parking where available.

If you're considering buying a vehicle, try HSBC (www.hsbc.com.vn) for cover.

Travel insurance is essential if you're planning to travel by motorbike. However, check your policy carefully as some exclude cover for two-wheeled travel. The cost of treating serious injuries can be bankrupting for budget travellers.

Road Conditions & Hazards

Road safety is definitely not one of Vietnam's strong points. Vehicles drive on the right-hand side (in theory). Size matters and small vehicles get out of the way of big vehicles. Accidents are common.

In general, the major highways are hard-surfaced and reasonably well maintained, but seasonal flooding can be a problem. Unsealed roads are best tackled with a 4WD vehicle or motorbike. Mountain roads are particularly dangerous: landslides, falling rocks and runaway vehicles can add an unwelcome edge to your journey.

LOCAL TRANSPORT

Cyclos

These are bicycle rickshaws. Drivers hang out in touristy areas and some speak broken English. Bargaining is imperative; settle on a fare before going anywhere. A short ride should be 12,000d to 25,000d.

Taxis

Metered taxis are found in all cities and are very, very cheap by international standards and a safe way to travel around at night. Average tariffs are about 12,000d to 15,000d per kilometre. Mai Linh (www.mailinh.vn) and Vinasun (www.vinasuntaxi.com) are two excellent nationwide firms.

App-based taxis (both car and motorbike) including Uber and Grab are available in several Vietnamese cities including HCMC, Hanoi and Danang.

Xe Om

Motorbike taxis are everywhere. Fares should be about half that of a taxi. Drivers usually hang around street corners, markets, hotels and bus stations. To avoid overcharging, it's a good idea to use Uber or Grab in HCMC, Hanoi and Danang.

TOURS

These Vietnam-based travel agencies offer great tours:

Buffalo Tours (www.buffalotours.com) Offers diverse and customised trips.

Handspan Travel Indochina (www.handspan. com) A wide range of innovative, interesting tours to seldom-visited regions.

Ocean Tours (www.ocean tours.com.vn) Heads to Ba Be National Park and has a great Thousand Island tour of Halong Bay.

TRAIN

Operated by national carrier, Vietnam Railways (www.vr.com.vn), the Vietnamese railway system is an ageing but pretty dependable service, and offers a relaxing way to get around the nation. Travelling in an air-conditoned sleeping berth sure beats a hairy overnight bus journey along Hwy 1. And, of course, there's some spectacular scenery to lap up, too.

Routes

Aside from the main HCMC–Hanoi run, three rail-spur lines link Hanoi with the other parts of northern Vietnam: one runs east to the port city of Haiphong; a second heads northeast to Lang Son and continues across the border to Nanning, China; a third runs northwest to Lao Cai (for trains on to Kunming, China).

'Fast' trains between Hanoi and HCMC take between 32 and 35 hours.

Classes & Costs

Trains classified as SE are the smartest and fastest. There are four main ticket classes: hard seat, soft seat, hard sleeper and soft sleeper. These classes are further split according to whether or not they have air-conditioning. Presently, air-con is only available on the faster express trains. Some SE trains now have wi-fi (though connection speeds, like Vietnamese trains, are not the quickest).

Hard-seat class is usually packed. It's tolerable for day travel, but expect plenty of cigarette smoke.

Ticket prices vary depending on the train; the fastest trains are the most expensive.

Reservations

You can can buy tickets in advance from the Vietnam Railways bookings site (http://dsvn. vn); however, at the time of writing only Vietnamese credit cards were accepted. You can also book online using the travel agency Bao Lau (www.baolau.vn), which has an efficient website, details seat and sleeper-berth availability, and accepts international cards. E-tickets are emailed to you; there's a 40,000d commission per ticket.

You can reserve seats/berths on long trips 60 to 90 days in advance (less on shorter trips). Most of the time you can book train tickets a day or two ahead without a problem, except during peak holiday times. For sleeping berths book a week or more before the date of departure.

Schedules, fares, information and advance bookings are available on Bao Lau's website. Vietnam Impressive (www.vietnamimpressive. com) is another dependable online agent; it charges US$2 per ticket.

Many travel agencies, hotels and cafes will also buy you train tickets for a small commission.

Understand Southeast Asia

Southeast Asia Today

Southeast Asia in the 21st century is a dynamic region with a strong sense of possibility as millions move into the middle class. It is also a flashpoint for many pressing global issues: urbanisation, human rights, religious extremism and environmental degradation. For each country it is a careful balancing act, between growth and sustainability, autocracy and autonomy, self-determination and the strings attached to foreign investments. Increasingly, countries are working together, under the umbrella of ASEAN (Association of Southeast Asian Nations).

Best in Print

The Quiet American (Graham Greene; 1955) Classic portrayal of Saigon as the US slowly descends into war in Vietnam.

The Beach (Alex Garland; 1998) Now-legendary tale about a backpacker utopia in southern Thailand.

Smaller and Smaller Circles (F H Bataclan; 2016) Nuanced crime novel set in the gritty slums of Manila.

Married to the Demon King (Sri Daoruang; 2005) The ancient Hindu epic, the *Ramayana*, set in modern Bangkok.

Burmese Days (George Orwell; 1934) Account of close-minded colonials living in Myanmar.

Best on Film

Ilo Ilo (2013) Moving meditation on middle-class family life in Singapore, with an international cast.

First They Killed My Father (2017) Haunting adaption of Loung Ung's personal account of life under the Khmer Rouge.

Cemetery of Splendour (2015) The living world and the spirit world collide in northern Thailand when soldiers succumb to a weird sleeping illness.

Apocalypse Now (1979) Set in Vietnam, filmed in the Philippines, this psychological thriller is the ultimate anti-war film.

Myanmar Falters

After decades of international-pariah status things were looking up for Myanmar. A landmark election in 2015 resulted in a sweeping victory for the National League for Democracy (NLD), the party of pro-democracy activist Aung San Suu Kyi. Foreign investment was flowing in; between 2010 and 2015 international arrivals rose by 490%.

In 2017, however, skirmishes between the military and the Arakan Rohingya Salvation Army (ARSA) escalated into a full-blown humanitarian crisis. The Rohingya, who are Muslim, are one of Myanmar's largest ethnic minorities, with an estimated population of 1 million. The official government view is that they are illegal immigrants from Bangladesh – both countries were common territories under the British crown – and that ARSA is a terrorist organisation. Denied citizenship, the Rohingya are a stateless people, without access to healthcare or education.

Following a deadly ARSA attack on a police station, the military launched a crackdown that, according to human rights groups, targeted civilians and rebels with equal ferocity. Villages burned and hundreds of thousands of Rohingya refugees fled to Bangladesh. Under Myanmar's constitution, written by the military junta that ruled the country for decades, the commander-in-chief has full autonomy; still, de facto political leader and Nobel-laureate Aung San Suu Kyi has come under criticism for equivocating on the issue of the violence.

China's Shadow

The 2016 election of American president Donald Trump saw the global superpower pivot abruptly inward – causing many in Southeast Asia to wonder if an increasingly assertive China would succeed in supplanting American hegemony in the region with its own. Under its ambitious One Belt One Road scheme, which seeks to revive the old overland and maritime Silk Road trade routes, China is already spearheading numerous infrastructure projects across the whole of Asia. Proponents say the project will promote growth; critics, notably India, have called it neocolonialism in disguise.

China has also been a bullish presence in the South China Sea (the East Sea, to Vietnam), fortifying its claims to disputed uninhabited territories – the Paracel Islands, the Spratly Islands and the Scarborough Shoal – with land reclamation projects and military outposts. What's at stake is not only control of a strategic shipping lane but also fishing rights and potentially lucrative underground stores of natural gas. The Philippines took its claims against China to a UN tribunal and, in 2016, won, but has since backed down. Which raises the question: can countries in Southeast Asia afford not to do business with China?

Optimism & the Middle Class

Global market research firm Nielsen estimated that in 2015, 150 million Southeast Asians, or 25% of the population, could be classified as middle class. It expects that number to reach 400 million – more than half of the projected population – by 2020. While critics are quick to point out that upward mobility is patchy, hamstrung by corruption, cronyism and identity politics, in general, studies show consumer confidence is high – especially among millennials (and this in a region where the median age is 29). The new middle class wants to live in air-conditioned city apartments and have the latest mobile phones but is also keen to travel. And while many aspire to visit cities like Paris, most are in fact travelling within the region – getting to know their neighbours for the first time ever on such a large scale.

Damming the Mekong

The mighty Mekong River, which runs through China, Laos, Cambodia, Thailand and Vietnam, is seen as a huge potential source of hydropower. China has already built several dams on the Upper Mekong. Laos, down river, has already begun construction on two dams, Xayaburi and Don Sahong (near Si Phan Don, where the rare Irrawaddy dolphin lives). More are in the planning stages.

Hydropower is considered a source of clean energy, but comes with concerns. The Mekong supplies a quarter of the world's fresh fish and has the world's second-most diverse river ecosystem, after the Amazon; the Mekong Delta in Vietnam is among the world's largest rice-growing regions. If the dams disrupt this, a crucial source of sustenance and livelihood for millions of people could be at risk.

POPULATION: **636 MILLION**

GDP: **US$2.71 TRILLION**

GDP PER CAPITA:
**SINGAPORE US$52,961;
CAMBODIA US$1270**

INFLATION: **BRUNEI 0.4%;
MYANMAR 8.5%**

UNEMPLOYMENT:
**CAMBODIA 0.5%;
PHILIPPINES 5.6%**

if South East Asia were 100 people

39 would be Muslim
36 would be Buddhist
18 would be other
7 would be Christian

economy
(% of GDP)

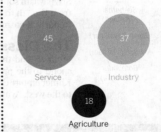

45 Service
37 Industry
18 Agriculture

population per sq km

SOUTH EAST ASIA   USA   UK

≈ 30 people

History

The countries of Southeast Asia have played a part in every great historical movement of the last two millennia. They have borne witness to the great era of empire building; the golden age of sea trade (and its dark side, colonialism); the subsequent tides of religion (first Hinduism, then Buddhism, Islam and Christianity); the ugly, bloody realities of Cold War politics; and now, in the 21st century, the spectre of global terrorism and the rise of the megacity.

Early Kingdoms

At the dawn of the last millennium, trading ships were sailing between India in the west and China in the east, across the Bay of Bengal and through the Straits of Malacca. Along the way, traders spread Indian culture – notably Hinduism and Buddhism, but also advances in the sciences and arts, the Sanskrit writing system and sophisticated models of statehood – across mainland Southeast Asia, as far east as the southern half of Vietnam, and down through the islands of Indonesia.

The empires that arose in the region over the next several centuries embraced many (and varying) elements of this new culture, tailoring it to local customs and beliefs. The most impressive empire was that of the Khmer, which developed in the 8th century. At its peak, it covered most of present-day Cambodia, Laos and Thailand. The Khmer built the temples of Angkor to their god-kings *(devaraja)* and also created a sophisticated irrigation system across vast tracts of land around Tonlé Sap (Great Lake). Meanwhile, in maritime Southeast Asia, the powerful kingdom of Srivijaya, in southeast Sumatra, controlled shipping through the Java Sea from the 7th to the 12th centuries. Srivijaya's capital, Palembang, was an important cosmopolitan centre for trade and Buddhist study.

Ancient Capitals

Angkor
(Cambodia)

Sukhothai
(Thailand)

Bagan (Myanmar)

My Son (Vietnam)

Borobodur
(Indonesia)

The Classical Age

From around the 14th century, the regional identities that roughly correspond to the present-day map of Southeast Asia began to crystalise. The Khmer empire crumbled under pressure from emerging Thai city-kingdoms to the west. Ayutthaya (also called Siam; 14th–18th centuries), the strongest

TIMELINE	2800–100 BC	1st century AD	AD 802
	Ancestors of modern Southeast Asians begin to migrate south from China and Tibet, populating river valleys and coastal areas and organising small city-states.	Funan, believed to be the first of the Indianised empires in Southeast Asia, is established in the Mekong River Delta.	King Jayavarman consolidates the Khmer empire in present-day Cambodia, supplanting the Funan state.

of the Thai polities, grew to cover most of modern-day Thailand and part of Myanmar. The Majapahit kingdom (13th–15th centuries) unified Indonesia from Sumatra to New Guinea, effectively controlling the seas. The kingdom of Dai Viet, long antagonised by the Chinese to the north, came into its own under the Later Le dynasty (15th–18th centuries), extending its border south to form a state that resembled present-day Vietnam.

By as early as the 10th century, the trade winds were bringing a new cultural force from India and the Middle East: Islam. It spread slowly, and relatively peacefully: converting to Islam meant access to a vast trade network throughout the Muslim world and escape from the inflexible caste system of Hindu-Buddhist Srivijaya. By the 17th century, the new religion was well-established throughout Malaysia, Indonesia, southern Thailand and the Philippine island of Mindanao. This period is also marked by the waning influence of Hinduism. While the ancient religion still echoed through the arts, Theravada Buddhism, which spread from Sri Lanka, had become the dominant faith throughout most of the kingdoms of continental Southeast Asia.

Colonialism

European traders began appearing in the seas of Southeast Asia in the 16th century in search of the legendary 'Spice Islands' (the Maluka Islands of eastern Indonesia). The Portuguese were the first to arrive, followed by the Dutch. Initially they caused little alarm: the region was long accustomed to trading with diverse peoples. If the Europeans did have one thing on their side, however, it was timing: the empires of the classical age had become stretched and brittle. The Dutch aggressively sought trade monopolies and their efforts embroiled them in Indonesian politics; eventually the Dutch would win control over Java and then, by the early 19th century, all of Indonesia (which was called the Dutch East Indies).

The industrial revolution raised the stakes, increasing European demand for the raw materials (such as rubber, petroleum and tin) and commodities (like coffee, sugar, and tobacco) that Southeast Asia could supply. In the 19th century, the British fought their way to power on the Malay Peninsula and across Myanmar; the French, using gunboat diplomacy, took over Vietnam, Cambodia and Laos (collectively called French Indochina). The Spanish, meanwhile, had set their sights on the Philippines, then a diverse collection of islands with little political or cultural connection to each other. When they arrived in the 16th century they were able to impose rule – and Catholicism – in quick succession.

Although its sphere of influence was diminished, Thailand was the only Southeast Asian nation to remain independent. Credit is often given to the Thai kings who remodeled their country in the western image and played competing European powers against each other.

ASEAN, the Association for Southeast Asian Nations, was formed in 1967 by Indonesia, Malaysia, the Philippines, Singapore and Thailand to promote regional growth and stability; Brunei, Vietnam, Laos, Myanmar and Cambodia have since joined. In 2015, the group established a common market, the ASEAN Economic Community. Collectively, the ASEAN members form the world's seventh largest economy.

AD 938	13th century	13th–15th century	1511
The Vietnamese reclaim the Red River Delta after over 1000 years of Chinese occupation.	The beginning of the decline of the Khmer empire and rise of powerful states in modern-day Thailand and Vietnam.	City-states in northern Sumatra and later Melaka, on the Malay Peninsula, adopt Islam as their religion, with rulers claiming the title of Sultan.	The sultanate of Melaka falls to the Portuguese and marks the beginning of colonial expansion in the region by European powers.

The 20th Century: War, Revolution & Independence

On the eve of the outbreak of WWII, anticolonial sentiment was bubbling across Southeast Asia. During the war, the Japanese Imperial Army swept briskly through the region. While some locals may have been initially optimistic about the ousting of the European imperialists, the Japanese proved to be brutal rulers; millions were conscripted into harsh labour. In an attempt to win local cooperation, the Japanese fanned the flames of resentment to the west; as an unintended consequence, at the war's end, when the Japanese withdrew and the Europeans returned, nationalist sentiment was not only high but also organised.

One by one, the former colonies won or were granted independence, only to face new challenges: civilian rioters, minority insurgents and communist guerrillas – often acting at the instigation of the Cold War powers, China, the Soviet Union and the USA – frequently undermined stability.

Vietnam, following liberation from the French, was initially partitioned in two, with the North going to resistance leader and Marxist Ho Chi Minh and the south going to anti-communist Ngo Dinh Diem. The USA feared a communist Vietnam and stepped in – first surreptitiously and then in all-out war – to thwart the North's efforts to unite the country under communist rule. The North won, but only after catastrophic loses on both sides.

Meanwhile a shadow war was taking place in Cambodia and Laos as American bombers tried to root out Vietnamese communist guerrillas using passage through Vietnam's neighbours. Cambodia dissolved into civil war and the Khmer Rouge seized power. The new regime, under Pol Pot, aspired to an ethnically Khmer, agrarian communist society. Large numbers of the population – an estimated 1.5 million Cambodians (20% of the population) – were killed in purges before Vietnamese forces brought an end to the Khmer Rouge's cruel and terrifying four-year reign in 1979.

Anti-communist purges in Indonesia in the 1960s resulted in hundreds of thousands dead and the three-decades long dictatorship of Suharto. A 1962 coup ushered in a half-century of mostly unbroken military rule in Myanmar. Thailand has had a dozen military coups since 1932. Malaysia and especially Singapore are hailed as the region's postwar success stories, though order has often been kept at the expense of civil liberties, through anti-sedition laws and restrictions on press freedoms.

European Hill Stations

Sapa (Vietnam)

Cameron Highlands (Malaysia)

Pyin Oo Lwin (Myanmar)

Bokor National Park (Cambodia)

1939–45	1965	1975	1999
WWII; Japan occupies much of Southeast Asia using Thailand as a cooperative base and Malaysia and Indonesia as a source of conscripts.	Singapore splits from Malaysia and forms an independent country, which goes on to become the most successful economy in the region.	Saigon (today's Ho Chi Minh City) falls to northern Vietnamese forces, reuniting the country and ending the Vietnam War; the Khmer Rouge seize power in Cambodia.	Timor-Leste votes for independence from Indonesian occupiers. An international peacekeeping force enters the country to prevent violence.

The 1990s and Beyond

On the whole, things were looking up for the region by the 1990s. Thailand, Malaysia, Indonesia and the Philippines seemed destined to follow in the footsteps of the 'Asian Tigers' – Singapore, Hong Kong, Taiwan and South Korea – whose economies had soared in recent decades. On the back of market-minded reforms, the formerly closed countries of Vietnam and Cambodia were beginning to open up. The upward trend was derailed, however, in 1997 when the collapse of the Thai baht sparked a financial crisis throughout Asia. The value of the Indonesian rupiah plummeted, destablising Indonesia to the point that long-time dictator Sukarno stepped down. More than two decades later, following intervention from the international finance community, the region is in a better place than before the crisis – though corruption, inefficiencies and political tensions continue to throw wrenches.

Whereas the 20th century had been dominated by long-standing leaders, by the start of the 21st century most had stepped down or been replaced. This changing of the guard has created uncertainty but also optimism – that perhaps real democracy could flourish.

This century has so far avoided out-and out-war, but blood has been shed. In the southern border provinces of Thailand, where the population is mostly ethnic Malay Muslims, separatist groups have bombed malls and marketplaces. In Myanmar – which has the largest percentage of ethnic minorities in the region at 30% of the total population – armed conflicts continue between minority insurgents seeking greater autonomy and the national army trying to repress them. Acts of terrorism in Indonesia, notably in Jakarta and Bali, have been linked to international organisations such as Al Qaeda, Jemaah Islamiyah and the Islamic State.

Stability can feel, at times, desperately just out of reach. Decades of violence on the island of Mindanao in the Philippines looked to be finally winding down, with the 2014 signing of a peace treaty that promised the establishment of a Muslim autonomous region, Bangsamoro. However, in 2017, militants pledging allegiance to the Islamic State laid siege to the Mindanao city of Marawi and the whole of the island was placed under military rule.

Historical Reads

Southeast Asia: An Introductory History (Milton Osborne)

In Search of Southeast Asia: A Modern History (David P Chandler, et al)

Southeast Asia: Past and Present (DR SarDesai)

HISTORY THE 1990S AND BEYOND

2004	2009	2015	2016
An Indian Ocean earthquake with its epicentre near Sumatra (Indonesia) triggers a giant tsunami that kills thousands in Indonesia and Thailand.	Tribunals of surviving members of Cambodia's Khmer Rouge senior leadership begin, 30 years after the genocidal reign was toppled.	ASEAN Economic Community (AEC) goes into effect, uniting the region into a common marketplace. Myanmar holds historic elections ushering Suu Kyi and her National League for Democracy party into power.	After reigning for 70 years, Thai King Bhumibol (Rama IX) dies at the age of 88. He was the world's longest-serving present-day head of state.

People & Culture

The map of Southeast Asia does little to convey the diversity – of ethnicity, religion, culture and lifestyle – found throughout this region. Southeast Asia, a key node on an ancient trade route that spanned the eastern hemisphere, has long been a cultural crossroads frequented by traders, wandering ascetics and kingmakers who brought with them new beliefs, customs and tastes. Hardly passive, the people here have absorbed these influences, combined them with native traditions and made them their own.

People

Southeast Asia has hundreds and hundreds of ethnic groups. Indonesia – the world's fourth largest country – has more than 300 alone (and at least as many languages). Some countries, such as Cambodia, Thailand and Vietnam, have high levels of homogeneity and thus a strong national, ethnic identity (though this often masks regional differences). Others, such as Indonesia, Malaysia and the Philippines, have tried to make their very diversity their identity (though this may not reflect real power distribution). The balancing act between cohesion and representation is a common struggle throughout the region, as these still relatively young countries try to live up to the awkward borders bequeathed to them by colonialism.

Chinese make up significant minority populations in most Southeast Asian countries, going back hundreds of years. In Malaysia and Singapore, Chinese traders intermarrying with local Malay created a distinct identity, called Straits Chinese. While most countries derive cultural and commercial strength from Chinese immigrants, in times of economic hardship, especially in Malaysia and Indonesia, ethnic Chinese have been targets of abuse for their prosperity and ethnic differences. Ethnic Indians, mostly from the southern state of Tamil Nadu, also have well-established communities in many cities in the region.

City Life, Country Life

Social harmony is valued across Southeast Asia. Crucial to this is the concept of 'face' – one's honour and reputation in social standing. To 'save face' (both yours and others), avoid causing embarrassment and confrontation (even if you feel you're getting the short end of the stick).

Perhaps greater than the difference between national cultures is the difference between life in the city and life in the country. Rates of urbanisation vary greatly across the region: Singapore is, of course, one big city; Malaysia and Brunei also have predominantly urban populations. In Indonesia, Thailand and the Philippines, roughly half of the population lives in cities; in Laos, Myanmar, Vietnam and Timor-Leste, the number is somewhere between 30% and 40%; in Cambodia, the number is just 20%.

If there is one constant, however, it is that the rate is rapidly increasing. As of 2015, Southeast Asia had 21 cities with a population of more than one million; the UN predicts it will have 15 more by 2025. While cities are nothing new for the region – Hanoi, for example, is over 1000 years old – this mass migration is. In 1950, just 15.5% of the population was urban; today it's over 40%. Local infrastructure and economies have struggled to keep up, resulting in chaotic cities, where some live in air-conditioned towers and others live in off-the-grid slums (but everyone has to deal with the cacophonous traffic). In between is the middle class, usually educated government workers who can afford terraced apartments.

Meanwhile, for the more than half of the population who live in rural areas, life remains deeply rooted in the village and tied to the agricultural calendar. In these communities, multi-generational households are the norm and distinct animistic customs are part of daily life. Rice farming, especially with crude tools such as ploughs drawn by water buffalo, is difficult work that typically affords only a subsistence lifestyle.

Highland Indigenous Peoples

The mountainous stretch of continental Southeast Asia, from Myanmar's western border across northern Thailand, Laos and Cambodia and through Vietnam's central and northern highlands, is home to hundreds of indigenous minorities – sometimes called 'hill tribes' – totalling some several million people. Today they live in varying degrees of assimilation, conflict and isolation from the majority populations who occupy the fertile lowlands, and largely in poverty.

Some have territorial claims that go back hundreds of years (or longer); others arrived more recently, most likely from the Himalayas or southern China. Before the colonial era, when borders were less fixed, they lived largely autonomously, subsisting on farming and animal husbandry. Some groups are relatively sedentary; others practise a kind of slash-and-burn agriculture that requires regular relocation. Some grew opium as a cash crop, though this has largely been shut down.

In the 19th and 20th centuries, the British and French colonialists – and later the Americans during the Vietnam War – occasionally sought to make allies of the tribes, pitting them against a recalcitrant majority. At the same time, missionaries converted some communities to Christianity. During the latter half of the 20th century, when the newly independent nations were dominated by strongmen and a forceful ethno-nationalist rhetoric, many indigenous peoples found themselves persecuted, stripped of their lands or pressured to assimilate.

In recent decades, tourism and conservation have complicated the issue. Tribal villages have proved popular with overseas visitors, which can be an economic boon for communities but also puts them at risk of exploitation. There are also tribes with historic ties to land that has since been converted into protected national parks; as a result, certain traditional farming and hunting practices were made illegal and tribes have been forced to relocate.

The Arts

Much of Southeast Asia's ancient and classical art is religious in nature. The regions' temples (p936), mosques (p937) and churches are great repositories of architectural design and sculpture. There are also strong artisan traditions that remain to this day, resulting in the vivid batik (cloth dyed with a wax-resist technique) of Indonesia; the woodcarvings of totems by the Ifugao people of northern Luzon; and the lacquerware polished to a high gloss in the workshops of Bagan, Myanmar.

Southeast Asia's most iconic art form, however, has to be Javanese shadow puppetry (*wayang kulit*). The two-dimensional puppets are made of leather, finely carved and rich in detail. What appears before the audience is the shadow cast by the puppet (ideally from an atmospheric oil lamp). Stories are taken from Hindu epics, Islamic tales and Javanese legends; one puppet master (the *dalang*) tells the whole story, which is set to the music of a *gamelan* orchestra, composed of gongs, metallophones and hand drums. Traditionally, shows go on all night. Yogyakarta and Solo are the best places to see *wayang kulit*.

Top Five Museums

Asian Civilisations Museum (Singapore)

Islamic Arts Museum (Malaysia)

Jim Thompson's House (Thailand)

National Museum of Cambodia (Cambodia)

Vietnam Museum of Ethnology (Vietnam)

PEOPLE & CULTURE THE ARTS

The small island of Bali has a rich culture of dance, originally performed as part of religious rituals but now often staged for tourists. The two most common styles seen today are captivating *legong*, a stylised form of dance-drama traditionally performed by preteen girls (but now also adult women) with graceful, precise gestures and witchy eyes; and *kecak*, performed by men who chant and sing hypnotically. Bali, and particularly the town of Ubud, has a sizeable community of working artists and artisans, including many expats.

As for contemporary art, Singapore's scene stands out. The new National Gallery opened in 2015 to showcase the largest collection of modern and contemporary Southeast Asian art. Singapore also has numerous commercial galleries and hosts an art biennale on even-numbered years.

Food

Rice is the staple food across Southeast Asia. Meals are often eaten family-style, with an assortment of shared side dishes served all at once to accompany rice (which may be steamed in bamboo baskets or cooked with a modern, electric rice cooker). It's hard to overestimate the importance of rice in the region. In several languages, the word for 'eat' is literally 'eat rice'; many folk religions have a rice goddess. Village festivals mark the beginning of rice-planting season, with rituals and customs designed to ensure a bountiful harvest. Noodles, made of rice or wheat, make up for what they lack in symbolism with their popularity.

Southeast Asia's history as a global crossroads is evident through its cuisine: there are curries and flat breads from India; stir-fries from China; baguette sandwiches – like Vietnam's *banh mi* – from France; and ingredients from the Americas such as peanuts. And while it's hard to imagine the food here without chillies, it's likely the Spanish introduced them in the 1600s. The region's geography is also a big factor: fish – from the sea, the Mekong River, Tonlé Sap (Great Lake) or water-logged rice paddies – is more prevalent than meat. As dictated by the strictures of Islam, Muslim communities throughout the region don't eat pork (creating a culinary culture clash with their Chinese neighbours who adore pork dishes).

Herbs and spices play a big part in local cooking: common aromatics include lemongrass, pandan leaf, galangal (a stronger, earthier kind of ginger), shallots and turmeric. Creamy coconut is often added to curries. It's typical for single dishes to combine sour, sweet and salty flavours. The sweet element usually comes from palm sugar; kaffir lime or tamarind adds a touch of sour. Rather than just salt, many dishes are seasoned instead with a salty fermented fish sauce (usually made of anchovies), which also adds a crucial umami element. Southeast Asian food is also known for its spicy kick – which can show up where you may not expect it (such as in the salads of Thailand and Laos).

In the cities, meals are often eaten out – which will make sense once you see the wealth of cheap options available from street carts and simple canteens. Noodle soups and rice porridge are popular for breakfast. Dessert is not typically eaten after a meal, but sweets are common as snacks or with tea. Tropical Southeast Asia produces a rainbow cornucopia of fruit; in addition to your standard bananas and pineapples, you'll see market stalls and smoothie stands offering mangosteens, rambutans, jackfruits, custard apples, star fruits and durian – a large spikey fruit that people either love or loathe.

Religion

Throughout Southeast Asia, religion is a fundamental component of the national and ethnic identities. Islam is the majority religion in Indonesia, Malaysia and Brunei, and a significant minority religion in Thailand, Myanmar, Singapore and the Philippines. Across continental Southeast Asia – in Thailand, Myanmar, Cambodia, Laos and Vietnam – Buddhism is the dominant faith. The Philippines and Timor-Leste are largely Catholic. Singapore, meanwhile, is the world's most religiously diverse country, with significant populations of Buddhists, Christians, Muslims, Taoists and Hindus.

Buddhism

Buddhism begins in the 6th century BC with the story of a sheltered Indian prince named Siddhartha Gautama who, at the age of 29, left his life of privilege on a spiritual quest. After years of experimenting with different ascetic practices, he meditated under a fig tree for 49 days and reached a state of enlightenment. The prince became a Buddha, an 'Awakened One'.

Buddhism builds on many Hindu beliefs, chiefly *samsara*, the cycle of death and rebirth governed by karma, the law of cause and effect. The Buddha taught what came to be known as the Four Noble Truths: that life is suffering; that suffering is caused by attachments; that ending attachments ends suffering; and that ending attachments is possible by following the 'middle way', which steered clear of both sensual indulgences and the opposite extreme of asceticism. The end goal is nirvana, a final emancipation from the world of desires and suffering and an end to the cycle of rebirth (both moment-to-moment and life-to-life).

Folk religions are still practised around the region, often alongside, or intertwined with, Islam, Buddhism and Christianity – meaning a faith with which you are familiar might appear, in practice, markedly different here.

Buddhism in Practice

As Buddhism spread it evolved, splitting into two principle branches: Theravada and Mahayana. Theravada ('Teaching of the Elders') is the more conservative of the two, based on what are believed to be the earliest teachings of the Buddha. It emphasises the individual's path to liberation. Meditation is a big part of Theravada practice; to master one's mind is a step towards eliminating attachments. Monastic life is held up as the ideal, though the laity can 'make merit' through devotional acts.

Theravada, also called the Southern School, reached Southeast Asia via Sri Lanka and is practised in Cambodia, Laos, Myanmar and Thailand. In these countries, monks, with their shaved heads and saffron robes, are a visible presence, especially when they make their morning rounds to receive alms of rice. It's expected that all male Buddhists take vows for a period of time (for some weeks or months), usually after finishing school. Though orders of nuns existed in the past, women who aspire to monastic life are no longer granted full ordination (though there are women fighting this).

Mahayana ('Greater Vehicle') Buddhism takes a more expansive approach, seeking a universal liberation for all sentient creatures (all of whom are believed to possess an inherent Buddha nature and interconnectivity). A central figure in this tradition is the bodhisattva, a being

BUDDHA IMAGES

Buddha images are visual sermons. Elongated earlobes, no evidence of bone or muscle, arms that reach to the knees, a third eye: these non-human elements express Buddha's divine nature. Periods within Buddha's life are also depicted in the figure's 'posture' or pose:

Reclining Exact moment of Buddha's enlightenment and death.

Sitting Buddha teaching or meditating. If the right hand is pointed towards the earth, Buddha is shown subduing the demons of desire; if the hands are folded in the lap, Buddha is turning the wheel of law.

Standing Buddha bestowing blessings or taming evil forces.

Walking Buddha after his return to earth from heaven.

who, on the cusp of achieving enlightenment, chooses instead to stay back and help unburden others. Mahayana, also called the Northern School, spread through Tibet, China, Japan and Vietnam – though in reality, most Vietnamese practise a fusion of Confucianism, Taoism and Buddhism, collectively known as Tam Giao (Triple Religion).

Temple Art & Architecture

The influence of South Asian art and architecture, as well as the doctrine of Theravada Buddhism, can be seen in the temples of Cambodia, Laos, Myanmar and Thailand (called wat or in Myanmar, *paya*). The most important structure is the stupa, a kind of monument that originally functioned as a reliquary but could also be built to commemorate a place or an event (and building a stupa was a good way to earn cosmic merit). Early stupa were often shaped like half-globes, topped by a single, parasol-shaped spire; over time different cultures developed different styles. Traditional Khmer-style stupas look a bit like corncobs; in Myanmar they are often bulbous or bell-shaped; Thailand, too, has many bell-shaped stupa, but with facets and tiers; stupa in Laos are often tall, thin and angular. Temples usually also have a hall of worship containing a central image of the historical Buddha, Gautama.

Mahayana temples typically conform to Chinese aesthetics and may have several images of the Buddha (illustrating the many faces of the Buddha that are worshipped in the Mahayana tradition) and bodhisattvas. In China, the stupa evolved into the pagoda, a tower with multiple tiered roofs, which also appears in some Vietnamese temples.

Christianity

Christianity was brought by the Europeans during the colonial period. Catholicism was introduced to Vietnam by the French, to the Philippines by the Spanish and to Timor-Leste by the Portuguese. Today, the Philippines has the world's third largest Catholic population. Parts of Indonesia are Christian, mainly Protestant, due to the efforts of Western missionary groups. In each of these populations there are remnants of earlier beliefs and customs and an almost personal emphasis on preferred aspects of the liturgy or the ideology. Local variations of Christianity can often be so pronounced that Westerners of the same faith might still observe the practice as foreign.

Buddhist Monuments

Temples of Angkor (Cambodia)

Borobudur (Indonesia)

Bagan (Myanmar)

Sukhothai Historical Park (Thailand)

Hinduism

Hinduism is an ancient, amorphous religion; it's more a way of life, built up over thousands of years, than a doctrine. It has no origin story, but it belongs to India. It is both pantheistic – meaning god and the universe are one and the same – and polytheistic: the limitless eternal god (Brahman) appears in many forms, which are worshipped by followers. The three principle incarnations of Brahman are Brahma (the creator), Vishnu (the preserver) and Shiva (the destroyer or reproducer). In art they are often represented as having multiple arms or heads to express their multifaceted nature.

Hinduism, alongside Buddhism, was an important influence on the culture and society of Southeast Asia during the first millennium. The Mataram kingdom of Java and the Khmer kingdom of Cambodia built grand temples (at Prambanan and Angkor, respectively) to the Hindu gods. Hindu temples are typically constructed on plinths with towers rising like mountains, which symbolise cosmic Mt Meru, the home of the gods. Exteriors are often covered in relief sculptures of divinities, such as the curvaceous *apsara* (celestial nymphs). Even after Hinduism faded as a religion, many deities continue to live on, often having merged with a local spirit. One example is *naga*, a Hindu serpent deity associated with water, who is a common sight at Buddhist temples throughout Southeast Asia.

Islam

Islam originated in Arabia in the 7th century, when the prophet Mohammed received the word of God (the Quran, the holy book of the faith). Islam means 'submission' in Arabic, and it is the duty of every Muslim to submit to the all-knowing, omnipresent Allah (God). This profession of faith is the first of the five pillars of Islam; the other four are to pray five times a day, give alms to the poor, fast during Ramadan (ninth month of the lunar calendar) and make the pilgrimage (hajj) to Mecca.

When Islam arrived in Southeast Asia, it didn't so much supplant existing beliefs – the Hindu-Buddhism of the previous centuries and the folk religions of even earlier – as absorb them. For example, chanting and drumming remain a component of the region's Islamic prayer tradition. Sufism, a mystical strand of Islam, is often credited for the particularly syncretic brand of Islam that developed in Southeast Asia. Sufis were itinerant holy men (suf is an Arabic word for the coarse wool worn by a religious ascetic) who encouraged a personal expression of the religion instead of a strict orthodoxy and adherence to the law. Scholars believe that they played a part in adapting traditional practices to Islamic beliefs.

Mosque Design

All mosques (*masjid* in Indonesian, Malaya and Arabic) have a large prayer hall, often partitioned by gender. There are no seats; worshippers pray on the floor facing towards the *mihrab*, a wall niche that indicates the direction of Mecca. In the courtyard there will be a fountain for the ritual ablutions required before prayer and a minaret (tower)

A HINDU EPIC'S LASTING LEGACY

The Ramayana is an ancient Hindu epic that has been played out – in traditional dance and puppetry, on temple carvings and in modern comic books – countless times over the centuries in Southeast Asia. It is the story of Prince Rama (an incarnation of the Hindu god Vishnu) who falls in love with the beautiful Sita, winning her hand in marriage – by completing the challenge of stringing a magic bow. Before they can ascend the throne, the couple are banished to the jungle (by a scheming stepmother), where Sita is kidnapped by Ravana, a demon king. With the help of his loyal brother, Laksmana, and the resourceful monkey king, Hanuman, Rama defeats Ravana, Sita is rescued and peace and goodness are restored. Different cultures have interpreted the story in different ways, with Rama most often manifesting the ideals held by that particular culture.

from where the call to prayer is announced. Beyond these fundamental elements, there is great variation in mosque design around Southeast Asia. The oldest mosques have peaked or tiered roofs reminiscent of Hindu temples. Others, particularly those built in the late 18th and early 19th centuries, are modelled on mosques in the Middle East, with domes, arched porticoes and slender minarets. Some have latticework or mosaics in geometric patterns that are typical of Islamic art (which eschews veneration of people or objects). The Masjid Negara, Malaysia's national mosque, is an example of modernist, 20th-century mosque design.

Political Islam

Historically, Islam makes no distinction between the spiritual and secular worlds. Sharia (Islamic law), which is based on the Quran, the words and deeds of the prophet (collectively known as sunnah) and the interpretations of scholars, regulates criminal, civil and personal conduct. A major discussion in the Muslim world is how to define, follow and apply Sharia within the context of the modern, pluralistic state. Some instructions are clear-cut, such as abstinence from pork products, drinking and gambling; yet, should those who partake be legally punished? Other requirements, like modesty in dress, leave much room for debate.

Compared to the Middle East, Southeast Asia has typically practised a more moderate form of Islam. Women have never been cloistered and with few exceptions are not required to cover their heads – though recently more women are choosing to do so. Malaysia has long maintained a parallel Sharia system that applied to Muslim Malays only, but it is largely concerned with family matters. Indonesia does not have national Sharia, but it does allow the province of Aceh to enforce partial Sharia under the terms of the 2005 peace deal. There is a Sharia family court in the Philippines for Muslims.

Fundamentalism has been on the rise throughout the Muslim world and Southeast Asia has been no exception. In Indonesia and Malaysia, conservative movements have been calling for an expanded implementation of Sharia. Local critics deride this as an Arabisation of their culture; others point to the growing income gap as a reason for the recent surge of hardline populism. While changes on the national level have so far been minor – for example, Indonesia has banned the sale of alcohol in convenience stores – religious moderates worry that this is only the beginning.

The small sultanate of Brunei has the strictest Sharia law of any country in the region. In 2014, it was announced that the country would begin phasing in a Sharia criminal code that would include corporal punishments, such as the severing of limbs for theft.

Survival Guide

Responsible Travel

In Southeast Asia, tourism brings mixed blessings and curses. Small-scale, locally focused tourism supports family-owned businesses and one-on-one cultural exchanges that broaden people's perspectives, helping to preserve cultural and environmental assets. But tourism also adds to the environmental and cultural pressures on local people and habitats.

To ensure that your trip is a gift, not a burden, consider your impact on the host country, seek out operators who support rather than exploit, and always be respectful to people and the natural environment.

ENVIRONMENTAL CONCERNS

Southeast Asia has some of the richest biodiversity on the planet, and its dense jungles and marine reserves contain species that do not exist anywhere else. Indeed, new, never-before-seen species are being discovered every year.

Among other things, this amazing region is home to 75% of the world's coral species, particularly in the 6-million-sq-km Coral Triangle, which stretches all the way from Malaysia to the Solomon Islands. Here you'll also find the world's largest fish (the whale shark), the largest

lizard (the Komodo dragon) and the largest flower (the dustbin-sized rafflesia). Then there's the mighty Mekong River, which rivals the Amazon for biodiversity.

But the region is also densely populated, and environmental degradation and forest loss are accelerating problems. Every year, smoke chokes the skies as forests are cleared for logging and to make space for tourist resorts, farms and palm-oil plantations. Traffic and industry fill the cities with pollution, and waterways are clogged with rubbish and polluted by chemical waste and sewerage.

Travellers contribute to all these problems, so it's helpful to know about the problems and how to minimise your impact.

Deforestation

Due to deforestation and associated forest fires, Indonesia is the world's third-largest greenhouse-gas emitter. Smoke from Indonesian forest fires regularly cloaks Singapore and parts of Malaysia in a choking haze, causing air-travel chaos and increasing rates of respiratory disease. Loss of mangrove forests, which act as tidal buffer zones and provide nurseries for marine fish, has decimated fish stocks and increased the

severity of coastal storms, contributing to the carnage of the 2004 Boxing Day tsunami, Cyclone Nargis in 2008 and Typhoon Haiyan in 2013.

Water Systems

The aquatic environment is suffering. Coral reefs are being degraded by overfishing and fishing with poison and dynamite, by sediment run-off from coastal developments, by rising sea temperatures due to climate change, and directly by the anchors of tourist boats and by contact with tourists themselves. Along the Mekong River, hydroelectric dams are significantly altering the river's ecosystem, from sediment movement to fish migration, as well as water levels downstream.

Habitat Loss

Habitat loss is a serious threat to the region's indigenous wildlife. Though national parks and nature reserves abound, these preserve just a small part of the total land area, and human encroachment is nibbling away at their edges. Poaching is a major problem, and Thailand is one of the primary conduits through which live wildlife and harvested wildlife parts travel to overseas markets.

Solutions

Though the environmental problems are obvious, answers are not. The movement to conserve natural areas faces a constant challenge from business and commercial interests, political corruption and the desperation of people living in poverty in rural areas.

Of all of the Southeast Asian nations, Brunei leads the conservationist charge, with approximately 70% of its original forest cover still intact, but its oil wealth allows it to overlook the potential profit of undeveloped lands. Other nations are often forced by necessity to see their environmental resources in purely financial terms.

What You Can Do

There are many environmental problems that the average tourist has no control over, but you can strive to reduce your individual footprint by putting as little pressure on the natural environment and the local infrastructure as possible. Here are some modest steps:

➡ Live like a local: opt for a fan instead of an air-con room; shower with cold water instead of hot.

➡ Use biodegradable soap to reduce water pollution.

➡ Eat locally sourced meals instead of imported products.

➡ Avoid plastic packaging where you can; where you can't, make sure it is disposed of properly.

➡ Dispose of cigarette butts in rubbish bins, not on the beach or in the water.

➡ Choose unplugged modes of transit (walking tour over minivan tour, bicycle over motorbike, kayak over jet ski).

➡ Volunteer with a local conservation or animal-welfare group.

➡ Be a responsible diver.

➡ Dispose of your litter in a proper receptacle, even if the locals don't.

➡ Don't eat, drink or buy products made from endangered animals or plants.

➡ Avoid plastic bottles: take a reusable water bottle and treat water.

➡ Patronise businesses that promote sustainable tourism, responsible tourism and ecotourism.

WILDLIFE ENCOUNTERS

Southeast Asia offers some incredible opportunities for wildlife encounters and animal interaction. You can walk with elephants, zipline through the jungle canopy with gibbons, dive with whale sharks and get perilously close to the world's largest lizard, the Komodo dragon. However, it is important to remember that these are wild animals in their natural habitat, so always behave in an appropriate manner. Some tips:

➡ Do not leave any litter in the natural environment in case it enters the food chain, particularly in a marine location.

➡ Do not smoke anywhere near wild animals.

➡ Do not use flash photography near animals in case it disturbs them.

➡ Do listen to rangers and guides and keep a safe and respectful distance from animals at all times.

➡ Do choose responsible wildlife encounters such as walking with an elephant herd instead of taking an elephant ride, which can directly harm the creatures.

CULTURAL & SOCIAL CONCERNS

The people of Southeast Asia are gracious hosts, and are prepared to overlook innocent breaches of social etiquette, but each culture has its own taboos and sacred beliefs that should not be disrespected. Before arriving, read up on the touchy subjects and show them the appropriate respect.

One mistake many visitors make is underestimating the significance of 'losing face' in Asian cultures. Public displays of anger and aggression bring shame on everyone involved, and should be avoided. Locals go out of their way to avoid causing embarrassment to others, and your travels will go more smoothly if you do the same.

Money disputes are the most common cause of conflict between travellers and locals, but never let disagreements over prices turn into arguments – if the price is too high, don't buy, or shop elsewhere.

Poverty & Economic Disparity

Although wealth and opportunity is growing in Southeast Asia, the gap between rich and poor shows no signs of narrowing. Few countries in the region have well-developed social safety nets to support people left homeless or jobless by illness, death of family members, debt, discrimination and other causes of hardship and poverty.

In rural areas, most live precarious subsistence lives without access to modern health care, education or opportunities for economic advancement. Often, traditional lifestyles are incompatible with modern aspirations, and many villages lose their young people to the cities, where they find themselves trapped in a new cycle of urban poverty.

Rural people flocking to Asia's primate cities often do menial labour for menial wages, and some are pushed into prostitution, crime and modern-day slavery. When a family is financially compromised, children are often expected to work, either formally, or informally as street hawkers and in domestic service. Education often comes second to the need to make money to survive.

Then there is the ongoing problem of human trafficking, with economic migrants lured to cities and neighbouring countries with promises of work, only to find themselves forced into slavery and prostitution. War also casts a long shadow in the region, with large numbers of victims of landmines and unexploded ordnance, particularly in Vietnam and Cambodia.

Begging is commonplace. Whether or not to give is a very personal decision, but donating to an established community program is likely to do more good than dropping coins into a cup. Many child welfare organisations counsel against giving money to children to avoid creating a culture of dependency, and a lifestyle that lures other impoverished children onto the streets.

Personal Space

Southeast Asia is a pressure cooker when it comes to personal space. Locals think nothing of being crammed shoulder to shoulder in public transport, and most would smile at the notion of having your own area of inviolable personal space. Be ready to be in close physical contact with total strangers for large parts of your stay.

The idea of a queue is a novelty in Southeast Asia. While some offices have a 'take a number and wait' policy, getting served is more commonly a case of jostling for attention with a crowd of like-minded rivals. The trick is to do as locals do and compete for your place at the counter; if you wait politely for your turn, you may never get served.

Etiquette

Here are some pointers to keep you on everyone's good side:

➡ Respect local dress standards, particularly at religious sites. Remove shoes and hats before entering religious buildings.

➡ Additional rules apply for women at some religious sites – check if your head should be covered, and dress modestly to avoid offense.

➡ Treat all religious objects, no matter how old or decrepit, with the utmost respect; don't clamber on temple ruins or pose behind headless Buddha statues.

➡ Learn the local greetings and basic pleasantries in each country, or even better, take a language course.

➡ Always ask for permission before you take a photo of someone; asking in the local language is even better.

➡ Do not raise your voice in anger or be aggressive; this will lead to a 'loss of face' for everyone and can have serious repercussions.

➡ It's good manners to share your snacks or cigarettes with your neighbour on long bus rides.

➡ Tip fairly where possible, as daily wages are very low.

➡ Don't take haggling too seriously; a bit of give and take is part of the game, and fighting to the bitter end

RESOURCES

Responsible Travel (www.responsible-travel.org) Tips on how to be a 'better' tourist regarding environmental issues, begging and bargaining, as well as ethical holidays.

Mekong Responsible Tourism (www.mekongresponsibletourism.org) Online guide promoting community-based and socially responsible tourism in the Mekong region, including homestays and ecolodges.

WWF International (www.panda.org) Read up on WWF's environmental campaigns to protect Southeast Asia's threatened species and landscapes.

Elephant Asia Rescue & Survival Foundation (www.earsasia.org) Encourages responsible elephant tourism and elephant welfare.

Wildlife Alliance (www.wildlifealliance.org) Supports direct conservation projects across the region.

Mongabay (www.mongabay.com) Environmental science and conservation news site with a focus on tropical rainforests, including in Indonesia.

Ecology Asia (www.ecologyasia.com) Facts and figures about Southeast Asia's flora and fauna.

Sealang Projects (sealang.net) Academic resource for learning Southeast Asian languages.

Travelers Against Plastic (www.travelersagainstplastic.org) Promotes the use of reusable water bottles to help the environment.

over a few pennies will cause everyone to lose face.

Volunteering & Voluntourism

Voluntourism is a booming business in Southeast Asia, but it is important to be aware that this is a commercial enterprise, and it is essential to do some proper research to make sure that your efforts and money make a real difference to local people, rather than line the pockets of travel companies.

The golden rule is to find a placement that utilises your existing skills, for a reasonable period of time, doing work that needs doing, in a way that supports local people on a path towards independence. Any project that offers the opportunity to do whatever you like, wherever you like, for as long as you like, is unlikely to be putting the needs of local people first.

It is essential to do some research on the hundreds of organisations that offer volunteer work to find an ethical and sustainable project that will give you a chance to use your existing skills. For any organisation working with children, background checks on volunteers should be mandatory; avoid any organisation that doesn't vet volunteers.

Lonely Planet does not endorse any organisations that we do not work with directly, so it is essential that you do your own thorough research before agreeing to volunteer with or donating to any organisation. Consider the following:

➡ Short-term volunteering is rarely beneficial; experts recommend that a month should be the minimum time commitment; three months at a minimum for volunteering with children.

➡ Look for programs that use your existing skills; if you have no teaching experience, volunteering as a teacher is unlikely to be a good use of your time.

➡ Is the program sustainable? Seek out projects that help people towards an independent life, rather than creating dependency.

➡ Never hand over large fees for a placement without checking where the money goes. Is the host project the beneficiary, or the sending organisation?

➡ Don't volunteer with children without thoroughly researching the project. Is it regulated? Do they require background checks on volunteers?

Orphanage Tourism

Visiting orphanages has become a popular activity in Asia, but this is becoming increasingly discredited, as investigations have found many orphanages being run as businesses to harvest money from well-meaning tourists, while doing nothing to help the children in their care. There are even reports of children being kidnapped, or borrowed from parents and local schools, to make money for the host orphanage. There are concerns even when orphanages are legitimate – strangers

dropping in and out on tours and short stays can be detrimental to a child's emotional well-being and development.

Friends International and Unicef joined forces to launch the 'Think Before Visiting' campaign. Learn more at www.thinkchildsafe.org/ thinkbeforevisiting before you inadvertently contribute to the problem.

What You Can Do

The way you travel can have a positive effect on the countries you visit. Consider the following tips:

➡ Support businesses that make a social contribution, such as fair-trade cooperatives and job-skills development projects.

➡ Stay at village homestays to support rural communities.

➡ Make a donation to a local school or charity instead of handing out money or gifts to beggars, especially children.

➡ Hire local guides to support village-based employment opportunities.

➡ Avoid all-inclusive packages (lodging, transport, tours, food); instead, spread your spending so that more local people benefit.

Directory A–Z

Accommodation

Book ahead during high season or around festivals or holidays, when rooms fill up in popular destinations.

Hostels Dormitories provide cheap and social lodging for solo travellers. Amenities sometimes include pool, restaurant or rooftop hang-out space.

Homestays Live like a villager in a family home; set-ups are simple but come with bonus cultural immersion.

Guesthouses These backpacker favourites have a range of rooms from basic to plush – and offer loads of local information.

Hotels From stuffy to snazzy, hotels have modern amenities (refrigerators, TVs, air-con) and private bathrooms.

Bathrooms

In remote corners or basic accommodation, you'll meet the Southeast Asian version of a shower: a large basin that holds water for bathing. Water should be scooped out of the basin with a smaller bowl and poured over the body. Resist the urge to climb in like a bath-tub and avoid washing directly over the basin, as this is your source for clean water.

Modern places usually have a cold-water shower. In more expensive accommodation, large cities and colder regions, rooms may come with hot-water showers at a higher price.

Many rural people bathe in rivers or streams. If you choose to do the same, be aware that public nudity is not acceptable. Do as the locals do and bathe while wearing a sarong.

Children

Southeast Asia can be a wonderful place to travel with children. Children are the focus of life for most people, and they're warmly welcomed in restaurants and other public places.

Dedicated children's menus are rarely available, but most countries offer simple dishes such as fried rice and grilled chicken that will appeal to less adventurous palates. Kids will also love Southeast Asia's abundant and varied tropical fruit.

Challenges include health concerns, difficulties with public transport and the climate, which can sap energy from younger travellers. It pays to be conservative about how much ground you can cover, and to stick close to water – the sea, hotel swimming pools or waterfalls – to give children somewhere to cool down. Bring plenty of sunscreen and mosquito repellent and put children to sleep under a mosquito net.

Thailand is far and away the most child-friendly destination in Southeast Asia, but Malaysia, Indonesia (particularly Bali) and the Philippines also have good family-friendly beach options. Cities tend to be less child-friendly, in part because of the high levels of atmospheric pollution. Be wary of travelling with children at times when forest fires are blowing smog across the region.

Be sure to investigate the health considerations for children, including any required immunisations. For more tips, see Lonely Planet's *Travel with Children*.

Practicalities

➡ Child seats are rarely available locally, so bring one from home.

➡ Hotels can usually provide an extra bed, but cots for infants are harder to find. Consider bringing a travel 'pod' infant bed with an integrated mosquito screen.

BOOK YOUR STAY ONLINE

For more accommodation reviews by Lonely Planet authors, check out http://lonelyplanet.com/hotels/. You'll find independent reviews, as well as recommendations on the best places to stay. Best of all, you can book online.

➡ Restaurants rarely have high chairs or children's menus, except in major cities.

➡ As well as simple local dishes such as fried rice, Western-style fast food is easy to find in cities and tourist areas.

➡ Disposable nappies are easy to find, but nappy-changing facilities are limited; however, no one will bat an eyelid if you do a change in public.

➡ Sunscreen and mosquito repellent are easy to find. Carry an antiseptic cream and antihistamine cream to stop itching and prevent mosquito bites from becoming infected.

Discount Cards

The International Student Identity Card (ISIC) is moderately useful in Southeast Asia, and can secure some discounts. Domestic and international airlines may provide discounts to ISIC cardholders, but many companies no longer honour the cards because fake cards are so widely available.

Electricity

Most countries work on a voltage of 220V to 240V at 50Hz (cycles); note that 240V appliances will happily run on 220V. Adaptors are available in electrical stops and markets in most Southeast Asian cities.

Embassies & Consulates

Most foreign governments maintain embassies, consulates or similar missions in the capital cities of Southeast Asia.

However, it's important to realise what your own embassy – the embassy of the country of which you are a citizen – can and can't do

to help you if you get into trouble. Generally speaking, your embassy won't be much help if you break the laws of the country you are in, even if your actions would be legal in your own country. The best you could hope for would be assistance finding a lawyer.

In genuine emergencies, an embassy may be able to provide assistance if other channels have been exhausted – for example, arranging evacuation for its citizens in the event of a coup. Do not expect financial assistance from your embassy. If you have all your money and documents stolen, staff may assist with getting a new passport, but a loan for onward travel is out of the question.

Most travellers should have no need to contact their embassy while in Southeast Asia. However, if you are travelling in unstable regions or going into remote areas, it may be worth letting your embassy know when you are leaving, where you are going and when you plan to return.

Insurance

A travel-insurance policy to cover theft, loss and medical problems is a necessity. If you can't afford travel insurance, you certainly can't afford the costs in the event of a crisis. There's a wide variety of policies available; most insurance companies offer travel policies, and these are also available through travel agencies.

Always check the small print: some policies specifically exclude 'dangerous activities', which can include scuba diving, motorcycling and even trekking. Make sure any activities you plan to get involved in are covered. Ensure that your driving licence is valid for any vehicle you hire, or this may invalidate your insurance. Check that any insurance policy covers ambulance rides, emergency flights home and, in the case of death, repatriation of a body.

Worldwide travel insurance is available at www.lonely-planet.com/travel-insurance. You can buy, extend and claim online anytime – even if you're already on the road.

Internet Access

Southeast Asia is incredibly well connected, with abundant wi-fi access, plentiful internet cafes, fast connections and low prices, though service dips outside of tourist resorts and cities. Internet connections normally mirror the destination's road network: well-sealed highways usually mean speedy travel through the information superhighway. 3G and even 4G mobile access is available in large urban centres.

Censorship of some websites is in effect across the region, particularly in Vietnam and Myanmar. You may need to use proxy servers or other tricks to get around the censors.

Legal Matters

Each country in Southeast Asia has its own laws, so never assume that something is legal in one country just because it's legal in the country next door. Read up on the national laws so that you don't unwittingly commit a crime.

If you are a victim of a crime, contact the tourist police, if available; they are usually better trained to deal with foreigners and foreign languages than the regular police force.

Drugs

Although Southeast Asia has a reputation as a playground for users of recreational drugs, it is also infamous for the severity of the penalties for those caught using, selling or trafficking drugs.

The death penalty is the standard punishment for drug trafficking, and even possession for personal use can lead to prison sentences and huge fines; no one has ever evaded punishment because of ignorance of local laws. In Indonesia in 2005, nine Australians (dubbed the 'Bali Nine') were arrested on charges of heroin possession: seven received life sentences, while the other two were executed by firing squad in 2015.

In Indonesia, you can be jailed because your travel companions had drugs and you didn't report them. In Malaysia and Singapore, possession of certain quantities of banned drugs can lead to hanging. Customs officials are zealous in their screening of both luggage and passengers, so the chances of getting caught are extremely high; it's just not worth it.

LGBT Travellers

Some areas of Southeast Asia rank among the most progressive regions in the world regarding homosexuality; Thailand and the Philippines in particular. However, attitudes are less tolerant in other regions, particularly in Muslim-dominated Indonesia, Brunei and Malaysia.

In general most urban centres have gay communities, and attitudes towards same-sex relationships are tolerant, though travellers should still mind the region-wide prescription of refraining from public displays of affection. More caution is required in Muslim nations where homosexuality is a social taboo. Homosexual sex between men is technically illegal in Brunei and Malaysia.

Utopia Asian Gay & Lesbian Resources (www.utopia-asia. com) has an excellent profile of each country's record on acceptance, as well as short reviews on gay nightspots and handy travel guides to the various Southeast Asian countries.

Money

Each country has its own currency. Cash is king, but ATMs are widespread and credit cards are increasingly accepted in cities in Thailand, Malaysia and Indonesia.

Bargaining

Haggling is a way of life in Southeast Asia. Always remember that bargaining should be a good-natured rather than angry process. Step one is to ask the price and then counter with a lower offer. Suggesting half the asked price is a reasonable starting point, but expect to go higher to reach a final agreed price. After a few offers and counter-offers, you should reach a price that works for everyone. Don't start to haggle unless you're serious about buying. If you become angry or visibly frustrated, you've lost the game.

It is also customary (and mandatory) to bargain for chartered transport. Tourists are often taken advantage of by drivers so ask at your guesthouse how much a trip should cost before chartering a vehicle. Expect a bit of back and forth before you agree on a price. If the driver won't budge, then politely decline the service and move on.

Opening Hours

Opening hours vary from country to country; the following is an overview.

Banks & Government Offices Open Monday to Friday, from around 9am to about 5pm (most close for an hour for lunch).

Restaurants Open early morning to late at night; only expensive restaurants have separate lunch and dinner opening times.

Bar & Nightclubs Closing times depend on local licensing laws, but tend to be earlier than in Western countries.

Shops These often double as the proprietor's home, so they open

early and stay open late into the night, seven days a week.

Passports

To enter most countries your passport must be valid for at least six months from your date of entry, even if you're only staying for a few days. It's probably best to have at least a year left on your passport if heading off on a big trip around Southeast Asia.

Border guards may refuse entry if your passport doesn't have enough blank pages available. If you are reaching the end of your passport pages, get more pages added before you travel (if this is a service offered by your home country), or apply for a new passport. Once on the road, you can apply for a new passport in most Southeast Asian capitals at your home embassy or consulate.

Photography

You should always ask permission before taking a person's photograph. Many hill-tribe villagers seriously object to being photographed, or they may ask for money in exchange; if you want the photo, you should honour their wishes. Also respect people's privacy even if they are in public; guesthouses and small restaurants serve double-duty as the owner's living space and they deserve to have family time without being a photo opportunity.

The best places to buy camera equipment or have repairs done are Singapore, Bangkok and Kuala Lumpur, and prices can be very low if you avail of duty-free-tax refund programs. However, remember that the more equipment you travel with, the more vulnerable you are to theft.

Before leaving home, check if your battery charger will require a power adapter.

Camera memory cards are widely available and many photography shops still stock film for traditionalists.

Lonely Planet's Guide to Travel Photography is full of helpful tips for photography while on the road.

Post

Government-run national postal services are generally reliable across the region, and most post offices have dedicated parcel-packing services. For cash or more valuable items, it's better to use a trusted international courier company such as DHL or TNT.

There's always an element of risk in sending parcels home by sea, though as a rule they eventually reach their destination. If it's something of value, you're better off mailing home your dirty clothes to make room in your luggage for precious keepsakes.

Poste restante is widely available (although infrequently used) and is the best way of receiving mail.

Public Holidays

Every country has its own set of public holidays, marking religious festivals and key events in history (such as independence days and birthdays of royalty). Some events are based on lunar calendars and change date every year. Banks and government offices close for holidays; shops and public transport generally operate as normal. During religious holidays, additional restrictions may be in place, such as a ban on the sale of alcohol, or restrictions on the times during which food may be sold.

Safe Travel

Southeast Asia is generally a safe place for travellers, but you still need to keep your wits about you to avoid scams and other problems on the road.

➡ The most serious risk to travellers is from traffic accidents; take care if you rent a vehicle.

➡ Theft is typically opportunistic; keep your belongings secure and your valuables out of sight.

➡ Political violence is a risk across the region; monitor the local news and avoid political rallies and demonstrations.

➡ Southeast Asia is prone to earthquakes, volcanic eruptions, severe storms and other environmental hazards; follow local advice in the event of a disaster.

Assaults

Violent assaults in Southeast Asia are not common, but attacks on foreigners generate media attention and corresponding anxiety. Travellers should exercise basic street smarts: avoid quiet areas at night, avoid excessive drinking and avoid getting into angry arguments with locals.

Police enforcement of local laws and investigations into crimes are often inadequate, and police have been known to collude with criminals, so don't assume that a country's general friendliness equates to a crime-free zone.

Avoid confrontations with locals, especially when alcohol is involved. What might seem like harmless verbal sparring to you might provoke disproportionately violent acts of retribution thanks to the complicated concept of 'saving face'.

Special caution should be exercised at big parties like Thailand's Full Moon raves, where criminal gangs with political connections take advantage of intoxicated revellers. Other party places such as Manila, Sihanoukville and Bali also have seedy underbellies that should be avoided.

Political Unrest

Avoid political demonstrations, no matter how benign or celebratory they may appear. Mass rallies can quickly turn into violent clashes with rival factions or the military.

That said, unrest is normally localised, and a rally in one corner of a city does not mean that the whole country, or even the whole city, is off-limits. Your home country's embassy will issue the safest possible travel warnings, which should be balanced with coverage in the local press in order to gauge the actual political temperature.

No-go areas experiencing low-scale independence wars exist in parts of eastern and northwestern Myanmar, southern Thailand and the southern Philippines.

Scams

Every year we get emails from travellers reporting that they've been scammed in Southeast Asia. In most cases the scams are petty rip-offs, in which a naive traveller is tricked into paying too much for a ride to the bus station or a hotel room, short-changed while changing money, or conned into buying overpriced souvenirs.

Rip-offs are in full force at border crossings, popular tourist attractions, bus and rail stations and anywhere else where newly arrived travellers might be an easy target for con artists.

Here are some tips for avoiding common scams:

➡ Be politely suspicious of over-friendly locals; these individuals are often touts.

➡ Avoid super-cheap, inclusive transport packages, which often include extra commission-generating fees.

➡ Don't accept invitations to play cards or go shopping with a friendly stranger; this is a prelude to a well-rehearsed scam to strip you of your cash.

→ Understand that commissions are common business practices in the region and are levied whenever a third party is involved in a transaction.

Theft

Theft in Southeast Asia is usually by stealth rather than by force – bag and camera snatching and theft from backpacks being the most common forms. Violent theft is rare but it can occur late at night and often after the victim has been drinking. Travel in groups after a night of carousing, to ensure safety in numbers, and be wary of groups of friendly seeming locals gathering round if you have been drinking. Women should be especially careful about returning home late at night from a bar.

Clandestine theft is a concern, especially on overnight buses, in communal dorms or in lodgings with inadequate locks. In Malaysia, petty thieves have been known to check into a guesthouse and then rob the other guests in the middle of the night.

Bag snatching is an increasing problem, especially in Vietnam and Cambodia. Typically, thieves pull up alongside a tourist just long enough to grab a bag, phone or camera, and then speed away. This can happen when you are walking along the street or riding in a vehicle like a *moto* or *túk-túk*.

Here are some tips for keeping your possessions safe:

→ Keep your money and valuables in a money belt (worn underneath your clothes).

→ Don't carry valuables in a bag that can easily be grabbed and don't carry your camera by its strap.

→ Place your bag in between you and the driver when riding on a motorcycle or between your legs when riding in a *túk-túk* to deter bag snatchers.

→ Don't store valuables in easily accessible places such as backpack pockets or packs that are stored in the luggage compartment of buses.

→ Don't put valuables in the baskets of a motorcycle or bicycle, where they are easy pickings for bag snatchers.

→ Be especially careful about your belongings when sleeping in dorms.

Unexploded Ordnance & Landmines

The legacy of war lingers on in Cambodia, Laos and Vietnam. Laos suffers the fate of being the most heavily bombed country per capita in the world, while all three countries were on the receiving end of more bombs than were dropped by all sides during WWII.

There are still many undetonated bombs and explosives out there, so be careful walking off the trail in areas near the Laos/Vietnam border or around the Demilitarised Zone (DMZ). Cambodia suffers the additional affliction of landmines, some four to six million of them according to surveys. It pays to stick to marked paths anywhere in Cambodia.

Government Travel Advice

Government advisories are often so general that they seem intended to provide bureaucratic cover for the government should trouble occur. However, the following sites have useful tips:

Australia (www.smartraveller. gov.au)

Canada (http://travel.gc.ca)

New Zealand (www.safetravel. govt.nz)

UK (www.gov.uk/foreign-travel-advice)

US (https://travel.state.gov)

Telephone

Mobile-phone use is huge in Southeast Asia, and many people use a mobile in place of a landline, though networks are more limited in Myanmar, Cambodia and Laos. You can expect an excellent signal in cities, but coverage is patchy in rural areas.

Payphones (which may take cash or phonecards) and call offices with metered phones are also widespread, and in rural areas, shops may have a phone that customers can use for a fee. Dialling codes and international access numbers vary from country to country.

Local mobile-phone companies offer cheap pay-as-you-go SIM packages, and low-price local and international calls, often at much better rates than companies in the Western world. If your mobile from home is locked into a network, it may be better to buy a cheap handset locally, rather than risking damaging your phone by trying to have it unlocked by a phone shop.

Toilets

As tourism continues to grow in the region, Western-style sit-down toilets are becoming increasingly common. However, in rural areas, squat toilets are the norm. You'll also find the curious hybrid toilet – a Western-style sit-down toilet with optional foot rests on the seat for squatters.

If you encounter a squat toilet, here's what you should do. Straddle the two footpads and face the door. To flush and for personal cleaning, use the plastic bowl to scoop water out of the adjacent basin and pour into the toilet bowl. Carry a small bar of soap to wash your hands afterwards.

For those who insist on paper, some loos offer toilet

paper for purchase at the entrance; otherwise local pharmacies can provide supplies. Because of the narrow bore of local plumbing, toilet paper and other sanitary waste should be placed in the bin provided and never flushed.

Tourist Information

Most of the Southeast Asian countries have government-funded tourist offices of varying usefulness; the national tourist organisations of Thailand and Malaysia are better than average. Guesthouses and free traveller magazines often provide more useful information than tourist offices. Be aware that official tourist offices don't make accommodation and transport bookings. If a so-called tourist office provides this service, then they are a travel agency that charges a commission.

Travellers with Disabilities

Travellers with serious disabilities will likely find Southeast Asia to be a challenging place to travel. Pavements are rarely wheelchair-friendly and public transport, hotels and public spaces are seldom designed with disabled patrons in mind. Even the more modern cities can be difficult to navigate for mobility- or vision-impaired people because of stairs, steps and narrow sidewalks. On the other hand, hiring a vehicle and a guide who can double as an assistant is inexpensive compared to most Western nations.

Download Lonely Planet's free Accessible Travel guides from http://lptravel.to/AccessibleTravel. Other international organisations that can provide information on mobility-impaired travel include the following:

Disability Alliance (www.disabilityrightsuk.org)

Mobility International USA (www.miusa.org)

Society for Accessible Travel & Hospitality (SATH) (www.sath.org)

Visas

Most nationalities can visit Brunei, Malaysia, Indonesia, the Philippines, Singapore and Thailand without a visa; for other nations, you'll need a visa, which may be available on arrival.

Visa Tips

➡ Plan your trip around the length of stay mandated by your visa.

➡ If you plan to stay longer, apply for a longer visa from the embassy in your home country or from an embassy in a neighbouring country. Alternatively, investigate the ease of extending a visa within the country.

➡ Stock up on passport photos; you'll probably need at least two pictures each time you apply for a visa.

➡ Have the correct amount of local currency (or US dollars) to pay the on-arrival visa fee.

➡ Dress smartly when you're visiting embassies, consulates and borders; you may be judged on your appearance.

➡ If entering by land or sea, check if the border post offers visas on arrival; some do not.

➡ Be aware that travellers are often targeted by transport and foreign-exchange scams at land border crossings.

Women Travellers

While travel in Southeast Asia for women is generally safe, solo women should exercise the usual caution when travelling at night alone. While assaults are rare, harassment is not, and local men may have misguided notions about the behaviour of foreign women. Be especially careful in party towns, particularly in Bali and the Thai islands.

Travelling in Muslim regions introduces additional challenges. In conservative areas, local women rarely go out unaccompanied and are usually modestly dressed, often wearing a hair-covering *hijab* or a face-covering *burka*, and with arms and legs covered. Clothing that would be seen as casual wear back home may be considered immodest and provocative here.

Women with a male companion or women travelling together in a group will experience less unwanted attention than solo women travellers.

Work

Many travellers find casual work teaching English or working in the diving industry.

For short-term English-teaching gigs, Bangkok, Ho Chi Minh City (Saigon), Jakarta and Phnom Penh have language schools and a high turnover of staff. In the Philippines, English-speakers are often needed as language trainers for call centres. A TEFL/TESOL qualification is useful.

In Indonesia and Thailand you may be able to find some dive-school work.

Payaway (www.payaway.co.uk) Provides a handy online list of language schools and volunteer groups looking for recruits for its Southeast Asian programs.

Transitions Abroad (www.transitionsabroad.com) Web portal that covers all aspects of overseas life, including landing a job in a variety of fields.

Transport

GETTING THERE & AWAY

Step one is to get to Southeast Asia; flying is the easiest option. The only overland possibilities from outside the region are from China into Vietnam or Laos, or from Papua New Guinea into Indonesia. Travel agencies can sometimes arrange crossings from India into Myanmar, although this requires a special permit. Flights, cars and tours can be booked online at lonelyplanet.com/bookings.

Air

The major Asian gateways for cheap flights are Bangkok, Kuala Lumpur, Singapore, Denpasar (Bali) and Manila, with regular connections to Europe and Australia. Thanks to the proliferation of budget carriers, it's easy to find cheap fares between these hubs and other Southeast Asian cities and resorts, and flights onwards to China.

When pricing flights, it's worth looking at the cost of flying first to China or Hong Kong, or to a neighbouring Southeast Asian hub, and then connecting to your destination on a budget carrier. Budget carriers may not show up on online booking sites, so you may need to book directly with the airlines.

It pays to be flexible with travel dates. Expect prices to soar and availability to plummet around religious festivals and during the peak holiday season, which usually coincides with the best (and driest) weather. If you don't mind putting up with the odd rain shower, you can save money by travelling out of season.

In Asia, trips longer than two weeks often incur higher fares. When researching airline fares, clear out your web browser's cookies: these track your online activity and can sometimes result in a higher fare upon subsequent searches.

Round-the-World & Circle Asia Tickets

If Southeast Asia is just one stop on a worldwide tour, consider a round-the-world (RTW) ticket, which allows a certain number of stops within a set time period (as long as you don't backtrack). Circle Asia passes are offered by various airline alliances for a circular route that originates in the USA, Europe or Australia and travels to selected destinations in Asia.

Land

Southeast Asia shares land borders with China and India, as well as one land border with Papua New Guinea. Crossing from China into Laos and Vietnam or vice versa is easy; crossing from Myanmar to either China or India (or vice versa) is tricky. Travel agencies may be able to arrange a permit to cross the Mu-Se/Ruili border between Myanmar and China or the Moreh/Tamu border between Myanmar and India, but this depends on the political situation, and both crossings often close down at times of political instability.

The only other international land border crossing is between Indonesia and Papua New Guinea, although this isn't a very practical international gateway, with limited transport options with Port Moresby. Travellers with time and money might consider reaching Asia via the Trans-Manchurian or Trans-Mongolian express trains to China, travelling onwards into Laos or Vietnam by land.

Sea

There are no regular scheduled ferry routes to Southeast Asia from India or China. One adventurous option is to book passage on one of the cargo ships plying routes around the Indian and Pacific Oceans. Some freighters have space for a few noncrew members, who have their own rooms but eat meals with the crew. Prices vary depending on your departure point, but costs start at around US$150 a day plus additional fees.

GETTING AROUND

Border Crossings

Part of the fun of Southeast Asia is being able to hop from one country to the next, clocking up plenty of new stamps in your passport. Some routes have become traveller superhighways, with well-organised transport links across borders and plenty of travellers to share the experience with. Other routes require more planning, and involve getting a visa in advance rather than on arrival at the border. However, it can sometimes be cheaper to find a budget flight between neighbouring countries, compared to the costs of crossing overland.

With the inception of the Asean Economic Community (AEC), border relations between most countries have normalised, but there are still visa requirements, and transport scams to look out for. Be aware that some border crossings are located in areas of political instability, and crossings may shut down at short notice. Routes to be wary of include the west-coast route from southern Thailand to Malaysia (Sungai Kolok to Rantau Panjang), boat crossings from Malaysian Borneo to the southern Philippines, and overland crossings into Myanmar.

Ask around or check the Lonely Planet Thorn Tree (lonelyplanet.com/thorntree) for border-cross-ing reports with further information and transport recommendations. Here's a checklist of things to consider when travelling across borders:

➡ Know which borders offer visas on arrival and which require prearranged visas.

➡ For borders that do issue visas upon arrival, travel with two passport photos and enough cash in the required currency to pay the visa fee.

➡ Plan your travel to arrive when the border post is open to avoid being stranded overnight at the border.

➡ While moneychangers, both legal and illegal, operate at most border crossings, always carry some small-denomination US dollars as a backup.

➡ Black-market moneychangers abound at border crossings, but many offer unfavourable exchange rates, and scams like short-changing customers or straightforward theft are not unheard of.

➡ Be aware of border-crossing scams, like dodgy transport schemes that do not cover the entire journey, or deliver you to a commission-paying hotel miles from where you want to go.

➡ At some border crossings staff may request or demand extra 'fees', in addition to the legitimate visa-issuing fees. Resisting might result in some savings but it will not make the crossing speedier or smoother.

Whatever approach you take, remember to stay calm and don't get angry.

Air

Thanks to the proliferation of budget airlines, flights can be a bargain within the region, especially between major hubs such as Bangkok, Singapore and Kuala Lumpur. Some budget carriers are better than others, so check reputations before committing, but almost all offer online booking, with cheaper fares the further in advance you book.

Some airports in Southeast Asia charge a departure tax, particularly small regional hubs, so make sure you have a bit of local currency left. The following are useful for local air travel in the region:

Air Asia (www.airasia.com) Leading regional budget airline with hubs in Bangkok, Kuala Lumpur and Manila.

Attitude Travel (www.attitudetravel.com) A guide to low-cost carriers in Asia.

Cebu Pacific Air (www.cebupacificair.com) Popular Filipino budget carrier flying in/out of Manila.

Jetstar Asia (www.jetstar.com) Subsidiary of Australian-owned Jetstar, with its main hub in Singapore.

Lion Air (www.lionair.co.id) Indonesia's leading budget carrier.

Scoot (www.flyscoot.com) Low-cost carrier based out of Singapore.

CLIMATE CHANGE & TRAVEL

Every form of transport that relies on carbon-based fuel generates CO_2, the main cause of human-induced climate change. Modern travel is dependent on aeroplanes, which might use less fuel per kilometre per person than most cars but travel much greater distances. The altitude at which aircraft emit gases (including CO_2) and particles also contributes to their climate change impact. Many websites offer 'carbon calculators' that allow people to estimate the carbon emissions generated by their journey and, for those who wish to do so, to offset the impact of the greenhouse gases emitted with contributions to portfolios of climate-friendly initiatives throughout the world. Lonely Planet offsets the carbon footprint of all staff and author travel.

SOUTHEAST ASIAN BORDER CROSSINGS

From Brunei Darussalam

TO	BORDER CROSSING	CONNECTING TOWNS
Malaysia	Kuala Belait (B)/Miri (M)	Bandar Seri Begawan (B)/Miri (M)
Malaysia	Muara (B)/Bandar Labuan (M)	Bandar Seri Begawan (B)/Kota Kinabalu (M)

From Cambodia

TO	BORDER CROSSING	CONNECTING TOWNS
Laos	Trapeang Kriel (C)/Nong Nok Khiene (L)	Stung Treng (C)/Don Det (L)
Thailand	Cham Yeam (C)/Hat Lek (T)	Koh Kong (C)/Trat (T)
Thailand	Choam (C)/Chong Sa-Ngam (T)	Anlong Veng (C)/Phusing (T)
Thailand	O Smach (C)/Chong Chom (T)	Samraong (C)/Surin (T)
Thailand	Poipet (C)/Aranya Prathet (T)	Siem Reap (C)/Bangkok (T)
Thailand	Psar Pruhm (C)/Pong Nam Ron (T)	Pailin (C)/Chanthaburi (T)
Vietnam	Bavet (C)/Moc Bai (V)	Phnom Penh (C)/Ho Chi Minh City (V)
Vietnam	Kaam Samnor (C)/Vinh Xuong (V)	Phnom Penh (C)/Chau Doc (V)
Vietnam	O Yadaw (C)/Le Thanh (V)	Ban Lung (C)/Pleiku (V)
Vietnam	Phnom Den (C)/Tinh Bien (V)	Takeo (C)/Chau Doc (V)
Vietnam	Prek Chak (C)/Xa Xia (V)	Kep (C)/Ha Tien (V)
Vietnam	Trapeang Plong (C)/Xa Mat (V)	Kompong Cham (C)/Tay Ninh (V)
Vietnam	Trapeang Sre (C)/Loc Ninh (V)	Kratie (C)/Binh Long (V)

From Indonesia

TO	BORDER CROSSING	CONNECTING TOWNS
Malaysia	Bintan & Batam (Riau Islands) (I)/Johor Bahru (M)	Riau Islands (I)/Johor Bahru (M)
Malaysia	Dumai (I)/Melaka (M)	Pekanbaru (I)/Melaka (M)
Malaysia	Entikong (I)/Tebedu (M)	Pontianak (I)/Kuching (M)
Malaysia	Tarakan & Nunukan (I)/Tawau (M)	Tarakan & Nunukan (I)/Tawau (M)
Papua New Guinea	Pasar Skouw (I)/Wutung (P)	Jayapura (I)/Vanimo (P)
Singapore	Bintan & Batam (Riau Islands) (I)/Singapore	Riau Islands (I)/Singapore
Timor-Leste	Mota'ain (I)/Batugade (T)	Kupang (I)/Dili (T)

From Laos

TO	BORDER CROSSING	CONNECTING TOWNS
Cambodia	Nong Nok Khiene (L)/Trapeang Kriel (C)	Si Phan Don (L)/Stung Treng (C)
China	Boten (L)/Mohan (Ch)	Luang Namtha (L)/Mengla (Ch)
Thailand	Huay Xai (L)/Chiang Khong (T)	Huay Xai (L)/Chiang Rai (T)
Thailand	Kaen Thao (L)/Tha Li (T)	Pak Lai (L)/Loei (T)

From Laos *(continued)*

TO	BORDER CROSSING	CONNECTING TOWNS
Thailand	Muang Ngeun (L)/Ban Huay Kon (T)	Hongsa (L)/Phrae (T)
Thailand	Paksan (L)/Bueng Kan (T)	Paksan (L)/Bueng Kan (T)
Thailand	Savannakhet (L)/Mukdahan (T)	Savannakhet (L)/Mukdahan (T)
Thailand	Tha Khaek (L)/Nakhon Phanom (T)	Tha Khaek (L)/Nakhon Phanom (T)
Thailand	Tha Na Long (L)/Nong Khai (T)	Vientiane (L)/Nong Khai (T)
Thailand	Vang Tao (L)/Chong Mek (T)	Pakse (L)/Ubon Ratchathani (T)
Vietnam	Dansavanh (L)/Lao Bao (V)	Savannakhet (L)/Dong Ha (V)
Vietnam	Na Phao (L)/Cha Lo (V)	Tha Khaek (L)/Dong Hoi (V)
Vietnam	Nam Phao (L)/Cau Treo (V)	Lak Sao (L)/Vinh (V)
Vietnam	Nam Soi (L)/Na Meo (V)	Sam Neua (L)/Thanh Hoa (V)
Vietnam	Nong Haet (L)/Nam Can (V)	Phonsavan (L)/Vinh (V)
Vietnam	Pang Hok (L)/Tay Trang (V)	Muang Khua (L)/Dien Bien Phu (V)
Vietnam	Phou Keua (L)/Bo Y (V)	Attapeu (L)/Kon Tum (V)

From Malaysia

TO	BORDER CROSSING	CONNECTING TOWNS
Brunei Darussalam	Bandar Labuan (M)/Muara (B)	Pulau Labuan (M)/Bandar Seri Begawan (B)
Brunei Darussalam	Miri (M)/Kuala Berait (B)	Miri (M)/Bandar Seri Begawan (B)
Indonesia	Johor Bahru (M)/Riau Islands (I)	Johor Bahru (M)/Riau Islands (I)
Indonesia	Melaka (M)/Dumai (I)	Melaka (M)/Bukittinggi (I)
Indonesia	Tawau (M)/Tarakan & Nunukan (I)	Tawau (M)/Tarakan & Nunukan (I)
Indonesia	Tebedu (M)/Entikong (I)	Kuching (M)/Pontianak (I)
Philippines	Sandakan (M)/Zamboanga (P)	Sandakan (M)/Zamboanga (P)
Singapore	Johor Bahru (M)/Singapore	Johor Bahru (M)/Singapore
Thailand	Bukit Kayu Hitam (M)/Sadao (T)	Alor Setar (M)/Hat Yai (T)
Thailand	Padang Besar (M)/Hat Yai (T)	Kangar (M)/Hat Yai (T)
Thailand	Pulau Langkawi (M)/ Ko Lipe & Satun (T)	Pulau Langkawi (M)/ Ko Lipe & Satun (T)
Thailand	Rantau Panjang (M)/ Sungai Kolok (T)	Kota Bharu (M)/ Bangkok (T)

From Myanmar

TO	BORDER CROSSING	CONNECTING TOWNS
China	Mu-Se (My)/Ruili (Ch)	Mu-Se (My)/Ruili (Ch)
India	Tamu (My)/Moreh (India)	Mawlaik (My)/Imphal (India)
Thailand	Hteke (My)/Phu Nam Ron (T)	Dawei (My)/Kanchanaburi (T)
Thailand	Kawthoung (My)/Saphan Pla Pier (T)	Kawthoung (My)/Ranong (T)
Thailand	Myawaddy (My)/Mae Sot (T)	Hpa-an (My)/Mae Sot (T)
Thailand	Tachileik (My)/Mae Sai (T)	Kyaingtong (My)/Mae Sai (T)

TRANSPORT

From Thailand

TO	BORDER CROSSING	CONNECTING TOWNS
Cambodia	Aranya Prathet (T)/Poipet (C)	Bangkok (T)/Siem Reap (C)
Cambodia	Ban Pakard (T)/Psar Pruhm (C)	Chanthaburi (T)/Pailin (C)
Cambodia	Chong Chom (T)/O Smach (C)	Surin (T)/Samraong (C)
Cambodia	Chong Sa-Ngam (T)/Choam (C)	Chong Sa-Ngam (T)/Anlong Veng (C)
Cambodia	Hat Lek (T)/Cham Yeam (C)	Trat (T)/Koh Kong (C)
Laos	Ban Huay Kon (T)/Muang Ngeun (L)	Nan (T)/Hongsa (L)
Laos	Bueng Kan (T)/Paksan (L)	Bueng Kan (T)/Paksan (L)
Laos	Chiang Khong (T)/Huay Xai (L)	Chiang Rai (T)/Huay Xai (L)
Laos	Chong Mek (T)/Vang Tao (L)	Ubon Ratchathani (T)/Pakse (L)
Laos	Mukdahan (T)/Savannakhet (L)	Mukdahan (T)/Savannakhet (L)
Laos	Nakhon Phanom (T)/Tha Khaek (L)	Nakhon Phanom (T)/Tha Khaek (L)
Laos	Nong Khai (T)/Tha Na Long (L)	Nong Khai (T)/Vientiane (L)
Laos	Tha Li (T)/Kaen Thao (L)	Loei (T)/Pak Lai (L)
Malaysia	Hat Yai (T)/Padang Besar (M)	Hat Yai (T)/Kangar (M)
Malaysia	Ko Lipe & Satun (T)/Pulau Langkawi (M)	Ko Lipe & Satun (T)/Pulau Langkawi (M)
Malaysia	Sadao (T)/Bukit Kayu Hitam (M)	Hat Yai (T)/Alor Setar (M)
Malaysia	Sungai Kolok (T)/Rantau Panjang (M)	Sungai Kolok (T)/Kota Bharu (M)
Myanmar	Mae Sai (T)/Tachileik (My)	Mae Sai (T)/Kyaingtong (My)
Myanmar	Mae Sot (T)/Myawaddy (My)	Mae Sot (T)/Hpa-an (My)
Myanmar	Phu Nam Rom (T)/Hteke (My)	Kanchanaburi (T)/Dawei (My)
Myanmar	Saphan Pla Pier (T)/Kawthoung (My)	Ranong (T)/Kawthoung (My)

From Vietnam

TO	BORDER CROSSING	CONNECTING TOWNS
Cambodia	Le Thanh (V)/O Yadaw (C)	Pleiku (V)/Ban Lung (C)
Cambodia	Loc Ninh (V)/Trapeang Sre (C)	Binh Long (V)/Snuol (C)
Cambodia	Moc Bai (V)/Bavet (C)	Ho Chi Minh City (V)/Phnom Penh (C)
Cambodia	Tinh Bien (V)/Phnom Den (C)	Chau Doc (V)/Takeo (C)
Cambodia	Vinh Xuong (V)/Kaam Samnor (C)	Chau Doc (V)/Phnom Penh (C)
Cambodia	Xa Mat (V)/Trapeang Plong (C)	Tay Ninh (V)/Kompong Cham (C)
Cambodia	Xa Xia (V)/Prek Chak (C)	Ha Tien (V)/Kep (C)
China	Huu Nghi Quan (V)/Youyi Guan (Ch)	Dong Dang (V)/Pingxiang (Ch)
China	Lao Cai (V)/Hekou (Ch)	Hanoi (V)/Kunming (Ch)
China	Mong Cai (V)/Dongxing (Ch)	Mong Cai (V)/Dongxing (Ch)
Laos	Bo Y (V)/Phou Keua (L)	Kon Tum (V)/Attapeu (L)
Laos	Cau Treo (V)/Nam Phao (L)	Vinh (V)/Lak Sao (L)
Laos	Cha Lo (V)/Na Phao (L)	Dong Hoi (V)/Tha Khaek (L)
Laos	Lao Bao (V)/Dansavanh (L)	Dong Ha (V)/Savannakhet (L)
Laos	Nam Can (V)/Nong Haet (L)	Vinh (V)/Phonsavan (L)
Laos	Nam Soi (V)/Na Meo (L)	Thanh Hoa (V)/Sam Neua (L)
Laos	Tay Trang (V)/Sop Hun (L)	Dien Bien Phu (V)/Muang Khua (L)

Air Passes

Most of Southeast Asia's national flag carriers run promotional deals to and from specific Western cities or for regional deals, and you can also find passes that work across airlines in the same alliance. Search online for 'air passes' and your chosen destination to find the most up-to-date information, or contact airlines directly.

Bicycle

Southeast Asia loves the humble bicycle, so visiting cyclists will feel right at home. Many long-distance cyclists start in Thailand and head south through Malaysia to Singapore, but there are spectacular routes across the region, from Myanmar to Indonesia. Major roads are generally suitable for touring bikes but a hybrid or mountain bike is recommended if you want to get off the beaten track.

Vietnam is a great place to travel by bicycle – you can take bikes on buses, and the coastal route from Hanoi to Ho Chi Minh City is a worthy goal. For more challenging terrain, consider northern Thailand, or island-hopping routes through Indonesia. Roads are often in poor repair in Cambodia, Myanmar and Laos.

Basic bicycle repair shops are found everywhere. High-quality bicycles and their components can be bought in major cities such as Bangkok. Bicycles can travel by air; check with airlines about charges and specifications.

Boat

A vast flotilla of pumpboats and car and passenger ferries connects the various islands of Southeast Asia, as well as linking ports on larger land masses and towns along major rivers. International boat travel is possible between Singapore

and Indonesia, Malaysia and Indonesia, Thailand and Malaysia, and the Philippines and Malaysia. You also have the option of crossing the Mekong River from Thailand to Laos and from Cambodia to Vietnam. Guesthouses or travel agents sell tickets and provide travellers with updated departure times. Check visa regulations at port cities: some crossings will not issue visas on arrival.

Bus

Buses are almost always the most hassle-free way to cross land borders. In some cases, direct buses connect towns on either side of the border, with a well-organised stop for border formalities. If not, you'll have to take one bus to the border, go through departure and immigration formalities, and then board another bus on the other side.

Bus travellers will enjoy a higher standard of luxury in Thailand, the Philippines and Malaysia, where roads are well paved and reliable schedules exist. Be aware that theft does occur on some long-distance buses – keep all valuables on your person, not in a stowed bag.

Car & Motorcycle

What is the sound of freedom in Southeast Asia? The 'put-put' noise of a motorcycle. For visitors, motorbikes are convenient for

getting around beaches or touring the countryside. Car hire is also available in most countries, and handy for local sightseeing.

You can hit Thailand and Malaysia by car or motorcycle pretty easily, enjoying well-signposted, well-paved roads. Road conditions in Cambodia, Laos and Myanmar vary, although sealed roads are becoming the norm. Indonesia and the Philippines have roads that vary between islands, but most are in need of repair. Vietnam's major highways are in relatively good health.

Driving Licenses

If you plan to do any driving, it pays to get an International Driving Permit (IDP) from your local automobile association before you leave your home country; IDPs are inexpensive and valid for one year.

Motorcycle and scooter rental firms in Southeast Asia have a reputation for renting out vehicles without asking to see paperwork, but the law generally requires you have an appropriate driving licence.

Insurance

When renting a car, motorcycle or scooter, always make sure you have at least the legally required minimum insurance cover in that country, and be aware of the excess you may be liable to pay in the event of damage to the rental vehicle or another vehicle. If more comprehensive insurance is available, it is often worthwhile paying the higher cost for peace of mind.

Hire

Western car-rental chains are found at Southeast Asian airports, capitals and major tourist destinations. Local shops also rent motorcycles and cars, but vehicles are sometimes poorly maintained, so check any vehicle thoroughly before renting.

Take a walk around the vehicle with the proprietor, noting any existing damage so you won't be charged for old knocks. Taking pictures of the vehicle before driving it off the premises is another safeguard. Check the tyre treads, brakes and lights to make sure that the vehicle is in good working order.

Hitching

Hitching is never entirely safe, and we don't recommend it. Travellers who hitch should understand that they are taking a small but potentially serious risk. Many people do it without incident, however. People who do choose to hitch will be safer if they travel in pairs and let someone know where they are planning to go.

Local Transport

Most towns have local buses and larger cities also have mass transit networks, using underground trains, overland trains, overhead trains, or sometimes all three. Taxis buzz around in incredible numbers, often joined by autorickshaws (*túk-túk*) and cycle-rickshaws, which come in a remarkable variety of configurations under a remarkable variety of names.

Trains and buses – including the jeepneys that serve as buses in the Philippines – have fixed fares, and taxis in larger cities are metered (though getting drivers to use their meters can be a challenge). For any form of transport without fixed fares, agree on the fare before the start of the journey, usually with some haggling to reach a fair price.

Train

Thailand and Malaysia have the most extensive rail systems, although trains rarely run on time and extended journey times are commonplace. Myanmar, Laos, Cambodia and Indonesia have more limited train networks that still provide a fascinating vantage point from which to view the countryside. The only international train service of note is the *International Express*, which runs from Bangkok through the Malay peninsula to Singapore.

Health

Health issues and the quality of medical facilities vary enormously depending on where you travel in Southeast Asia, but due to the climate and local standards of hygiene, the risks of illness are generally higher than in more developed parts of the world.

Travellers tend to worry about contracting infectious diseases, but serious infections are a rare cause of illness or death in travellers. Traffic accidents and drowning are comparatively more serious risks. However, minor illnesses are relatively common and may include respiratory infections, diarrhoea and dengue fever. Fortunately, most common illnesses can be either prevented or treated.

BEFORE YOU GO

Pack medications in their original, clearly labelled containers. A signed, dated letter from your physician describing your medical conditions and medications, including generic names, is recommended. If carrying syringes or needles, have a physician's letter stating their medical necessity. If you have a heart condition, bring a copy of your ECG.

If you take any regular medication, bring a double supply in case of loss or theft. In most Southeast Asian countries, excluding Singapore, you can buy many medications over the counter, but it can be difficult to find some of the newer drugs, particularly the latest anti-depressants, blood pressure medications and contraceptive pills.

Insurance

Even if you are fit and healthy, don't travel without health insurance – accidents happen. Adventure activities, such as scuba diving and rock climbing, may require extra coverage. If your existing health insurance doesn't cover you for medical expenses abroad, consider purchasing travel insurance that includes provision for emergency evacuation.

Find out in advance if your insurance plan will make payments directly to providers or reimburse you later for overseas health expenditures (in some countries doctors expect advance payment in cash). If you have to claim later, make sure you keep all receipts. Some policies ask you to call a centre in your home country, where an immediate assessment of your problem is made.

Divers should ensure their insurance covers them for decompression sickness – get specialised dive insurance through an organisation such as Divers Alert Network (www.diversalertnetwork. org). Have a dive medical before you leave your home country; note that there are certain medical conditions that are incompatible with diving.

IN SOUTHEAST ASIA

Availability of Health Care

The standard of health care in Southeast Asia varies from country to country. Most capital cities have clinics that cater specifically to travellers and expats. Costs for medical treatment tend to be higher than at local medical facilities but these centres offer a superior standard of care and staff will speak English.

It is difficult to find reliable medical care in rural areas. Your embassy and insurance company are good contacts for finding reputable medical centres. Here are some considerations for each country.

Brunei Darussalam General medical care is reasonable. There is no local medical university, so expats and foreign-trained locals run the health-care system. Serious illness is better managed in Singapore.

Cambodia There are international clinics in Phnom Penh and Siem Reap and an NGO-run surgical hospital in Battambang that offer high-quality primary care and emergency stabilisation. Local government hospitals should be avoided; for more

MEDICAL CHECKLIST

Recommended items for a personal medical kit:

➡ antibacterial cream, eg mupirocin

➡ antibiotic for skin infections, eg amoxicillin/clavulanate or cephalexin

➡ antibiotics for diarrhoea, eg norfloxacin or ciprofloxacin; azithromycin for bacterial diarrhoea; tinidazole for giardiasis or amoebic dysentery

➡ antifungal cream, eg clotrimazole

➡ antihistamine, eg cetirizine for daytime and promethazine for night

➡ anti-inflammatory, eg ibuprofen

➡ antiseptic, eg Betadine

➡ antispasmodic for stomach cramps, eg Buscopan

➡ contraceptives

➡ decongestant, eg pseudoephedrine

➡ DEET-based insect repellent

➡ diarrhoea treatment, including an oral rehydration solution (eg Gastrolyte), diarrhoea 'stopper' (eg loperamide) and antinausea medication (eg prochlorperazine)

➡ first-aid items, eg scissors, plasters, bandages, gauze, thermometer (but not one with mercury), sterile needles and syringes, safety pins and tweezers

➡ indigestion medication, eg Quick-Eze or Mylanta

➡ iodine tablets to purify water

➡ laxative, eg Coloxyl

➡ paracetamol

➡ permethrin to impregnate clothing and mosquito nets

➡ steroid cream for allergic or itchy rashes, eg 1% to 2% hydrocortisone

➡ sunscreen and hat

➡ throat lozenges

➡ thrush (vaginal yeast infection) treatment, eg clotrimazole pessaries or Diflucan tablet

➡ Ural or equivalent if you're prone to urine infections

Divers and surfers should seek specialised advice on stocking medical kits for coral cuts and tropical ear infection treatments.

serious conditions, it is better to seek treatment in Bangkok.

Indonesia Local medical care falls short of international standards. Foreign doctors are not allowed to work in Indonesia and most Indonesian doctors work at government hospitals during the day and in private practices at night, so standards of care vary depending on the time of day. For serious illness, consider evacuating to Australia or Singapore.

Laos There are no facilities in Laos that meet international standards; the best facilities nearby are in northern Thailand.

The Australian Embassy Clinic in Vientiane treats citizens of Commonwealth countries.

Malaysia Medical care is of a high standard in major urban centres, and serious problems can be dealt with in Kuala Lumpur.

Myanmar Local medical care is dismal and local hospitals should be used only as a last resort. There is an international medical clinic in Yangon.

Philippines Good medical care is available in most major cities, but ambulance services are poor and it may be quicker to get to hospital by taxi.

Singapore Excellent medical facilities; Singapore is the referral centre for most of Southeast Asia.

Thailand After Singapore, Bangkok is the city of choice for expats living in Southeast Asia who require specialised care.

Timor-Leste Private clinics are available in Dili. The government hospital is basic and should be avoided.

Vietnam Government hospitals are overcrowded and basic. Only licensed facilities can treat foreigners; the private clinics in Hanoi, Ho Chi Minh City and Danang should be your first choices.

Environmental Hazards

Heat

Many parts of Southeast Asia are hot and humid. For most people it takes at least two weeks to adapt to the climate. Swelling of the feet and ankles is common, as are muscle cramps caused by excessive sweating. You can prevent these by avoiding dehydration and excessive activity; you should also take it easy when you first arrive. Treat cramps by stopping activity, resting, rehydrating with double-strength rehydration solution and gently stretching. Salted soda water with lime juice is an excellent electrolyte replenisher.

Dehydration is the main contributor to heat exhaustion. Symptoms include weakness, headache, irritability, nausea or vomiting, sweaty skin, a fast pulse and a slightly elevated body temperature. Treatment involves getting out of the heat, fanning and applying cool wet cloths to the skin, lying flat with legs raised, and rehydrating with water containing a quarter of a teaspoon of salt per litre. Recovery is usually rapid, though it is common to feel weak afterwards.

Heat stroke is a serious medical emergency. Symptoms come on suddenly and include weakness, nausea, a hot dry body with a body temperature of over 41°C, dizziness, confusion, loss of coordination, seizures, and eventually collapse and loss of consciousness. Unless the body temperature is reduced, heart failure can follow. Seek medical help and commence cooling by getting out of the heat, removing clothes, fanning and applying cool wet cloths or ice to the body, especially to the groin and armpits.

Prickly heat is a common skin rash in the tropics caused by sweat being trapped under the skin. The result is an itchy rash of tiny lumps. Treat by moving out of the heat and into an air-conditioned area for a few hours and by having cool showers. Creams and ointments clog the skin so they should be avoided. Locally bought prickly heat powder can be helpful.

Insect Bites & Stings

Bedbugs don't carry disease but their bites are very itchy. They live in the cracks of furniture and walls, and then migrate to the bed at night to feed on you. You can treat the itch with an antihistamine. Bed linen with blood spots in cheaper hotels is a warning that bed bugs may be present.

Lice inhabit various parts of your body, but most commonly your head and pubic area. Transmission is via close contact with an infected person. Lice can be difficult to treat and you may need numerous applications of an anti-lice shampoo. Pubic lice are usually contracted from sexual contact.

Tick bites are usually contracted after walking in long grass in rural areas, particularly where wildlife or livestock are common. Bites are commonly found behind the ears, on the belly and in armpits. The bites themselves are harmless, but ticks can carry some potentially dangerous diseases. If you have had a tick bite and experience symptoms such as a rash at the site of the bite or elsewhere, or fever or muscle aches, you should see a doctor. Doxycycline prevents tick-borne diseases.

Leeches are found in humid rainforest areas. They do not transmit any disease but their bites are often intensely itchy for weeks afterwards and can easily become infected. Apply an iodine-based antiseptic to any leech bite to help prevent infection. Salt can encourage a biting leech to let go; don't pull it off as this can leave leech mouth parts in the wound, increasing the risk of infection.

Bee and wasp stings mainly cause problems for people who are allergic to them. Anyone with a serious bee or wasp allergy should carry an

RARE BUT BE AWARE

The following diseases are common in the local population (in all countries except Singapore) but rare in travellers.

Filariasis A mosquito-borne disease that can cause disfiguring swellings; prevented by mosquito-avoidance measures.

Typhus Murine typhus is spread by the bite of a flea and scrub typhus is spread via a mite; symptoms include fever, muscle pains and a rash. Prevention is through general insect-avoidance measures or doxycycline.

Tuberculosis Medical and aid workers and long-term travellers should take precautions against this deadly respiratory disease and consider pre- and post-travel testing; symptoms are fever, cough, weight loss and tiredness.

Melioidosis (Thailand only) An infection contracted by skin contact with soil; symptoms similar to tuberculosis.

Japanese B Encephalitis (Vietnam, Thailand and Indonesia are highest risk areas) A viral disease, transmitted by mosquitoes; most cases occur in rural areas and vaccination is recommended for travellers spending more than one month outside cities.

injection of adrenaline (eg an EpiPen) for emergency treatment. For others, pain is the main problem – apply ice to the sting and take painkillers.

Most jellyfish in Southeast Asian waters are not dangerous, but stings can be painful. First aid for jellyfish stings involves pouring vinegar onto the affected area to neutralise the poison. Do not rub sand or water onto the stings. Take painkillers, and if you feel ill in any way after being stung, seek medical advice. Take local advice if there are dangerous jellyfish around and keep out of the water.

Sandflies inhabit beaches (usually the more remote ones) across Southeast Asia. They have a nasty bite that is extremely itchy and can easily become infected. Use an antihistamine to quell the itching, and, if you have to itch, use the palm of your hand and not your nails or infection may follow.

Parasites

Numerous parasites are common in local populations in Southeast Asia; however, most of these are rare in travellers. The two rules for avoiding parasitic infections are to wear shoes and to avoid eating raw food, especially fish, pork and vegetables. A number of parasites are transmitted via the skin by walking barefoot, including *Strongyloides*, hookworm and cutaneous larva migrans.

Skin Problems

Fungal rashes are common in humid climates. There are two common fungal rashes that tend to affect travellers. The first occurs in moist areas that get less air, such as the groin, armpits and between the toes. It starts as a red patch that slowly spreads and is usually itchy. Treatment involves keeping the skin dry, avoiding chafing and using an antifungal cream such as clotrimazole or Lamisil. *Tinea versicolor* is also common – this fungus causes small, light-coloured patches, most commonly on the back, chest and shoulders. Consult a doctor for treatment.

Cuts and scratches become easily infected in humid climates. Take meticulous care of them to prevent complications such as abscesses. Immediately wash all wounds in clean water and apply antiseptic. If you develop signs of infection (increasing pain and redness), see a doctor. Divers and surfers should be particularly careful with coral cuts as they can be easily infected.

Snakes

Southeast Asia is home to many species of both poison-

RECOMMENDED VACCINATIONS

Specialised travel-medicine clinics can advise on which vaccines are recommended for your trip. Some vaccines require multiple injections spaced out over a certain period of time; start the process six weeks prior to departure.

The only vaccine *required* by international regulations is for yellow fever. Proof of vaccination will be required only if you have visited a country in the yellow-fever zone within the six days before entering Southeast Asia. If you are travelling to Southeast Asia from Africa or South America you should check to see if you require proof of vaccination.

The World Health Organization (WHO) recommends the following vaccinations for travellers to Southeast Asia:

→ Adult diphtheria and tetanus

→ Hepatitis A

→ Hepatitis B

→ Measles, mumps and rubella (MMR)

→ Polio

→ Typhoid

→ Varicella

The following immunisations are recommended for long-term travellers (more than one month) or those at special risk:

→ Japanese B Encephalitis

→ Meningitis

→ Rabies

→ Tuberculosis (TB)

Note that there is no vaccination for dengue fever; the best way to avoid infection is to take steps to avoid mosquito bites.

ous and harmless snakes. Assume that all snakes are poisonous and never try to catch one. Wear boots and long pants if walking in an area that may have snakes. Antivenins are available for most species.

First aid in the event of a snakebite involves pressure immobilisation using an elastic bandage firmly wrapped around the affected limb, starting at the bite site and working up towards the chest. The bandage should not be so tight that the circulation is cut off, and the fingers or toes should be kept free so the circulation can be checked. Immobilise the limb with a splint and carry the victim to medical attention. Do not use tourniquets or try to suck the venom out.

Sunburn

Even on a cloudy day sunburn can occur rapidly. Always use a strong sunscreen (at least factor 30), making sure to reapply after a swim, and always wear a wide-brimmed hat and sunglasses outdoors. Avoid lying in the sun during the hottest part of the day (10am to 2pm). If you become sunburnt, stay out of the sun until you have recovered, apply cool compresses and take painkillers for the discomfort; 1% hydrocortisone cream applied twice daily is also helpful.

Infectious Diseases

Cutaneous Larva Migrans

Risk areas All countries except Singapore.
This disease, caused by dog hookworm, is particularly common on the beaches of Thailand. The rash starts as a small lump then slowly spreads in a linear fashion. It is intensely itchy, especially at night. It is easily treated with medications and should not be cut out or frozen.

Dengue Fever

Risk areas All countries.
This mosquito-borne disease is increasingly problematic throughout Southeast Asia, especially in the cities. There is no vaccine, only prevention. The mosquito that carries dengue bites day and night, so use DEET-mosquito cream periodically throughout the day. Symptoms include high fever, severe headache and body ache (dengue used to be known as breakbone fever). Some people develop a rash and experience diarrhoea. There is no specific treatment, just rest and paracetamol – do not take aspirin as it increases the likelihood of haemorrhaging. See a doctor to be diagnosed and monitored.

Don't assume this is a rural issue: Southeast Asia's cities, such as Bangkok and Singapore, as well as Thailand's southern islands and Chiang Mai province are high-risk areas.

Hepatitis A

Risk areas All countries.
A problem throughout the region, this food- and water-borne virus infects the liver, causing jaundice (yellow skin and eyes), nausea and lethargy. There is no specific treatment for hepatitis A; you just need to allow time for the liver to heal. All travellers to Southeast Asia should be vaccinated against hepatitis A.

Hepatitis B

Risk areas All countries.
The only serious sexually transmitted disease that can be prevented by vaccination, hepatitis B is spread by body fluids. In some parts of Southeast Asia, up to 20% of the population carry hepatitis B, and usually are unaware of it. The long-term consequences can include liver cancer and cirrhosis.

Hepatitis E

Risk areas All countries.
Hepatitis E is transmitted through contaminated food

and water, and has similar symptoms to hepatitis A but is far less common. It is a severe problem in pregnant women, and can result in the deaths of both mother and baby. There is currently no vaccine; prevention is by following safe eating and drinking guidelines.

HIV

Risk areas All countries.
HIV is now one of the most common causes of death in people under the age of 50 in Thailand. The Southeast Asian countries with the worst and most rapidly increasing HIV problem are Myanmar, Thailand and Vietnam. Heterosexual sex is now the main method of transmission in these countries.

Influenza

Risk areas All countries.
Present year-round in the tropics, influenza (flu) symptoms include high fever, muscle aches, runny nose, cough and sore throat. It can be very severe in people over the age of 65, and in those with underlying medical conditions such as heart disease or diabetes; vaccination is recommended for these individuals. There is no specific treatment, just rest and paracetamol. Follow local advice about outbreaks of potentially pandemic flu strains such as swine flu and avian flu.

Leptospirosis

Risk areas Thailand and Malaysia.
Leptospirosis is most commonly contracted after river rafting or canyoning. Early

symptoms are very similar to the flu, and include headache and fever. The disease can vary from very mild to fatal. Diagnosis is through blood tests and it is easily treated with doxycycline.

Malaria

Risk areas All countries except Singapore and Brunei. Many parts of Southeast Asia, particularly city and resort areas, have minimal to no risk of malaria, and the risk of side effects from the prevention tablets may outweigh the risk of getting the disease.

For most rural areas, however, the risk of contracting the disease is increased and malaria can be fatal. Before you travel, seek medical advice on the right medication and dosage.

Malaria is caused by a parasite transmitted by the bite of an infected mosquito. The most important symptom of malaria is fever, but general symptoms such as headache, diarrhoea, cough or chills may also occur. Diagnosis can only be made by taking a blood sample.

Two strategies are combined to prevent malaria – mosquito avoidance and anti-malarial medications. Which anti-malarial drug you take will depend on where you are travelling – speak to your doctor for specific advice. Most courses of anti-malarial tablets need to start before you travel to the destination.

Travellers are advised to prevent mosquito bites by taking the following steps:

➡ Use an insect repellent containing DEET.

➡ Sleep under a mosquito net that is impregnated with permethrin.

➡ Choose accommodation with screens and fans (if not air-conditioned).

➡ Impregnate clothing with permethrin when in high-risk areas.

➡ Wear long sleeves and trousers in light colours.

➡ Use mosquito coils.

➡ Spray your room with insect repellent before going out for your evening meal.

Measles

Risk areas All countries except Singapore and Brunei. Measles remains a problem in some parts of Southeast Asia. This highly contagious bacterial infection is spread via coughing and sneezing. Most people born before 1966 are immune as they had the disease during childhood, and most people born since then in developed countries will have been immunised in childhood. Measles starts with a high fever and rash, and can be complicated by pneumonia and brain disease. There is no specific treatment.

Rabies

Risk areas All countries except Singapore and Brunei. Still a common problem in most parts of Southeast Asia, this deadly disease is spread by the bite or lick of an infected animal, most commonly a dog or monkey. Without treatment, rabies is typically fatal. Seek medical advice immediately after any animal bite and commence post-exposure treatment. Having a pre-travel vaccination means the post-bite treatment is greatly simplified. If an animal bites you, gently wash the wound with soap and water, and apply iodine-based antiseptic. If you are not pre-vaccinated you will need to receive rabies immunoglobulin as soon as possible.

Schistosomiasis

Risk areas Laos, Philippines, Vietnam and Sulawesi (Indonesia). Schistosomiasis is a tiny parasite that enters your skin after you've been swimming in contaminated water. Travellers usually only get a light infection and hence develop no symptoms. On rare occasions, travellers may develop 'Katayama fever'. This occurs some weeks after exposure, as the parasite passes through the lungs and causes an allergic reaction; symptoms are coughing and fever. Schistosomiasis is easily treated with medications.

STIs

Risk areas All countries. As well as HIV, sexually transmitted diseases commonly found in Southeast Asia include herpes, warts, syphilis, gonorrhoea and chlamydia. People carrying these diseases often have no signs of infection. Condoms will prevent gonorrhoea and chlamydia but not warts or herpes. If after a sexual encounter you develop any rash, lumps, discharge or pain when passing urine, seek immediate medical attention. If you have been sexually active during your

FOOD & WATER

Food and water contamination are the biggest risk factors for contracting traveller's diarrhoea.

➡ Eat only freshly cooked food and peelable fruit.

➡ Avoid food that has been sitting around for hours.

➡ Eat in busy restaurants with a high turnover of customers.

➡ Never drink tap water; opt for bottled or filtered water.

➡ Avoid ice unless it's been made with purified water.

➡ Avoid fresh juices that may have been watered down.

➡ Boil water or use iodine tablets as a means of purification; pregnant women or those with thyroid problems should avoid iodine use.

travels, have an STI check on your return home.

Strongyloides

Risk areas Cambodia, Myanmar and Thailand.
This parasite, transmitted by skin contact with soil, is common in travellers but rarely affects them. It is characterised by an unusual skin rash called larva currens – a linear rash on the trunk that comes and goes. Most people don't have other symptoms until their immune system becomes severely suppressed, when the parasite can cause an overwhelming infection. It can be treated with medications.

Typhoid

Risk areas All countries except Singapore.
This serious bacterial infection is spread via food and water. It gives a high and slowly progressive fever and a headache, and may be accompanied by a dry cough and stomach pain. It is diagnosed by blood tests and treated with antibiotics. Vaccination is recommended for all travellers spending more than a week in Southeast Asia, or travelling outside the major cities. Vaccination is not 100% effective so you must still be careful about what you eat and drink.

Traveller's Diarrhoea

Traveller's diarrhoea is by far the most common problem that affects travellers – between 30% and 50% of people will suffer from it within two weeks of starting their trip. In over 80% of cases, traveller's diarrhoea is caused by bacteria (there are numerous potential culprits), and therefore responds promptly to treatment with antibiotics. Treatment will depend on your situation – how sick you are, how quickly you need to get better and so on.

Traveller's diarrhoea is defined as the passage of more than three watery bowel actions within 24 hours, plus at least one other symptom such as fever, cramps, nausea, vomiting or feeling generally unwell.

Treatment consists of staying well hydrated; rehydration solutions such as Gastrolyte are the best for this. Antibiotics such as norfloxacin, ciprofloxacin or azithromycin will kill the bacteria quickly.

Loperamide is just a 'stopper'. It can be helpful if you have to go on a long bus ride. Don't take loperamide if you have a fever, or blood in your stools. Seek medical attention quickly if you do not respond to an appropriate antibiotic.

Amoebic Dysentery

Amoebic dysentery is very rare in travellers but is often misdiagnosed by labs in Southeast Asia. Symptoms are similar to bacterial diarrhoea – fever, bloody diarrhoea and generally feeling unwell. You should always seek reliable medical care if you have blood in your diarrhoea. Treatment involves two drugs: tinidazole or metronidazole to kill the parasite in your gut, and then a second drug to kill the cysts. If left untreated, complications such as liver or gut abscesses can occur.

Giardiasis

Giardia lamblia is a relatively common parasite in travellers. Symptoms include nausea, bloating, excess gas, fatigue and intermittent diarrhoea. 'Eggy' burps are often attributed solely to giardiasis, but work in Nepal has shown that they are not specific to this infection. The parasite will eventually go away if left untreated but this can take months. The treatment of choice is tinidazole, with metronidazole being a second option.

Women's Health

In urban areas, supplies of sanitary products are readily available. Birth-control options may be limited so bring adequate supplies of your favoured form of contraception. Heat, humidity and antibiotics can all contribute to thrush. Treatment is with antifungal creams and pessaries such as clotrimazole. A practical alternative is a single tablet of fluconazole (Diflucan). Urinary tract infections can be precipitated by dehydration or long bus journeys without toilet stops; bring suitable antibiotics.

Pregnant women should receive specialised advice before travelling. Avoid rural travel in areas with poor transport and medical facilities. Malaria is a high-risk disease during pregnancy. The WHO recommends that pregnant women do *not* travel to areas with chloroquine-resistant malaria. None of the more effective anti-malarial drugs are completely safe in pregnancy. Traveller's diarrhoea can quickly lead to dehydration and result in inadequate blood flow to the placenta. Many of the drugs used to treat various diarrhoea bugs are not recommended in pregnancy. Azithromycin is considered safe.

FURTHER READING

Centers for Disease Control & Prevention (www.cdc.gov) Country-specific advice.

International Travel & Health (www.who.int/ith) Health guide published by the WHO.

MD Travel Health (www.mdtravelhealth.com) Travel-health recommendations for every country.

Language

This chapter offers basic vocabulary to help you get around Southeast Asia. Read our coloured pronunciation guides as if they were English, and you'll be understood. The stressed syllables are in italics. The polite and informal forms are indicated by the abbreviations 'pol' and 'inf' where needed. The abbreviations 'm' and 'f' indicate masculine and feminine gender respectively.

BURMESE

In Burmese, there's a difference between aspirated consonants (pronounced with a puff of air) and unaspirated ones. These consonants are said with a puff of air after the sound: ch (as in 'church'), k (as in 'kite'), ş (as in 'sick'), t (as in 'talk'); the following ones are pronounced with a puff of air before the sound: hl (as in 'life'), hm (as in 'me'), hn (as in 'not'), hng (as in 'sing'), hny (as in 'canyon'). Note also that the apostrophe (') represents the sound heard between 'uh-oh', th is pronounced as in 'thin' and ţh as in 'their'.

There are three distinct tones in Burmese (the raising and lowering of pitch on certain syllables). They are indicated in our pronunciation guides by the accent mark above the vowel: high creaky tone, as in 'heart' (á), plain high tone, as in 'car' (à), and the low tone (a). Note also that ai is pronounced as in 'aisle', aw as in 'law', and au as in 'brown'.

WANT MORE?

For in-depth language information and handy phrases, check out Lonely Planet's *Southeast Asia Phrasebook*. You'll find it at **shop.lonelyplanet.com**, or you can buy Lonely Planet's iPhone phrasebooks at the Apple App Store.

Basics

Hello.	မင်္ဂလာပါ။	ming·guh·la·ba
Goodbye.	သွားမယ်နော်။	thwà·me·naw
Excuse me.	ဆောရီးနော်။	sàw·rì·naw
Sorry.	ဆောရီးနော်။	sàw·rì·naw
Please.	တစ်ဆိတ်လောက်။	duh·şay'·lau'
Thank you.	ကျေးဇူး	jày·zù
	တင်ပါတယ်။	ding·ba·de
Yes.	ဟုတ်ကဲ့။	hoh'·gé
No.	ဟင့်အင်း။	híng·ìn
Help!	ကယ်ပါ။	ge·ba

NUMBERS – BURMESE

1	တစ်	di'
2	နှစ်	hni'
3	သုံး	thòhng
4	လေး	lày
5	ငါး	ngà
6	ခြောက်	chau'
7	ခုနစ်	kung·ni'
8	ရှစ်	shi'
9	ကိုး	gòh
10	တစ်ဆယ်	duh·şe

What's your name?

နာမည် ဘယ်လို	nang·me be·loh
ခေါ်သလဲ။	kaw·ţhuh·lè

My name is ...

ကျနော်/ကျမ	juh·náw/juh·má
နာမည်က- - - ပါ။	nang·me·gá ... ba (m/f)

Do you speak English?
အင်္ဂလိပ်လိုလ္ simple | ìng·guh·lay'·loh
ပြောတတ်သလား။ | byàw·da'·thuh·là

I don't understand.
နားမလည်ဘူး။ | nà·muh·le·bòo

How much is it?
ဒါဘယ်လောက်လဲ။ | da be·lau'·lè

Where are the toilets?
အိမ်သာ ဘယ်မှာလဲ။ | ayng·ṭha be·hma·lè

I'd like the ..., please.
- - - ပေးပါ။ | ... bày·ba

bill | ဘောက်ချာ | bau'·cha
menu | မီးနူး | mì·nù

Call ...
- - - ခေါ်ပေးပါ။ | ... kaw·bày·ba

a doctor | ဆရာဝန် | ṣuh·ya·wung
the police | ရဲ | yèh

FILIPINO

Filipino is easy to pronounce and most sounds are familiar to English speakers. In addition, the relationship between Filipino sounds and their spelling is straightforward and consistent, meaning that each letter is always pronounced the same way. Note that ai is pronounced as in 'aisle', ay as in 'say', ew like ee with rounded lips, oh as the 'o' in 'go', ow as in 'how' and ooy as the 'wea' in 'tweak'. The r sound is stronger than in English and rolled. The glottal stop, pronounced like the pause between the two syllables in 'uh-oh', is indicated in our pronunciation guides by an apostrophe (').

Basics

Good day.
Magandáng | ma·gan·dang
araw pô. (pol) | a·row po'
Magandáng | ma·gan·dang
araw. (inf) | a·row

NUMBERS – FILIPINO

1	isá	ee·sa
2	dalawá	da·la·wa
3	tatló	tat·lo
4	apat	a·pat
5	limá	lee·ma
6	anim	a·neem
7	pitó	pee·to
8	waló	wa·lo
9	siyám	see·yam
10	sampû	sam·poo'

Goodbye.
Paalam na pô. (pol) | pa·a·lam na po'
Babay. (inf) | ba·bai

Yes.
Opò. (pol) | o·po'
Oo. (inf) | o·o

No.
Hindí pô. (pol) | heen·dee' po'
Hindî. (inf) | heen·dee'

Thank you.
Salamat pô. (pol) | sa·la·mat po'
Salamat. (inf) | sa·la·mat

Help!
Saklolo! | sak·lo·lo

What's your name?
Anó pô ang pangalan ninyó? | a·no po' ang pa·nga·lan neen·yo

My name is ...
Ang pangalan ko pô ay ... | ang pa·nga·lan ko po' ai ...

Do you speak English?
Marunong ka ba ng Inglés? | ma·roo·nong ka ba nang eeng·gles

I don't understand.
Hindí ko náiintindihán. | heen·dee ko na·ee·een·teen·dee·han

How much is it?
Magkano? | mag·ka·no

Where are the toilets?
Násaán ang kubeta? | na·sa·an ang koo·be·ta

I'd like the menu.
Gustó ko ng menú. | goos·to ko nang me·noo

Please bring the bill.
Pakidalá ang tsit. | pa·kee·da·la ang tseet

Call ...!
Tumawag ka ng ...! | too·ma·wag ka nang ...

a doctor | doktór | dok·tor
the police | pulís | poo·lees

INDONESIAN & MALAY

Indonesian and Malay are very similar, so in this section we've provided translations in both languages – indicated by (I) and (M) respectively – only where the differences are significant enough to cause confusion. Most letters are pronounced more or less the same as their English counterparts, except for the letter c which is always pronounced as the 'ch' in 'chair'. Nearly all syllables carry equal emphasis, but a good approximation is to lightly stress the second-last syllable.

Basics

Hello. | Salam./Helo. (I/M)
Goodbye. | Selamat tinggal/jalan. (by person leaving/staying)
Excuse me. | Maaf.
Sorry. | Maaf.

NUMBERS – INDONESIAN/MALAY

1	satu
2	dua
3	tiga
4	empat
5	lima
6	enam
7	tujuh
8	delapan (I)
	lapan (M)
9	sembilan
10	sepuluh

Please.	Silakan.
Thank you.	Terima kasih.
Yes.	Ya.
No.	Tidak.
Help!	Tolong!
What's your name?	Siapa nama anda/kamu? (I/M)
My name is ...	Nama saya ...
Do you speak English?	Anda bisa Bahasa Inggris? (I) Adakah anda berbahasa Inggeris? (M)
I don't understand.	Saya tidak mengerti. (I) Saya tidak faham. (M)
How much is it?	Berapa harganya?
Where are the toilets?	Kamar kecil di mana? (I) Tandas di mana? (M)
I'd like the menu.	Saya minta daftar makanan.
Bring the bill, please.	Tolong bawa kuitansi/bil. (I/M)
Call a doctor!	Panggil doktor!
Call the police!	Panggil polis!

KHMER

In our pronunciation guides, vowels and vowel combinations with an h at the end are pronounced hard and aspirated (with a puff of air). The symbols for vowels are read as follows: aa as the 'a' in 'father'; a and ah shorter and harder than aa; i as in 'kit'; uh as the 'u' in 'but'; ii as the 'ee' in 'feet'; eu like 'oo' (with the lips spread flat); euh as eu (short and hard); oh as the 'o' in 'hose' (short and hard); ow as in 'glow'; u as the 'u' in 'flute' (short and hard); uu as the 'oo' in 'zoo'; ua as the 'ou' in 'tour'; uah as ua (short and hard); œ as 'er' in 'her' (more open); ia as the 'ee' in 'beer' (without the 'r'); e as in 'they'; ai

as in 'aisle'; ae as the 'a' in 'cat'; ay as ai (slightly more nasal); ey as in 'prey'; o as the 'ow' in 'cow'; av like a nasal ao (without the 'v'); euv like a nasal eu (without the 'v'); ohm as the 'ome' in 'home'; am as the 'um' in 'glum'; ih as the 'ee' in 'teeth' (short and hard); eh as the 'a' in 'date' (short and hard); awh as the 'aw' in 'jaw' (short and hard); and aw as the 'aw' in 'jaw'.

Some consonant combinations in our pronunciation guides are separated with an apostrophe for ease of pronunciation, eg 'j-r' in j'rook and 'ch-ng' in ch'ngain. Also note that k is pronounced as the 'g' in 'go'; kh as the 'k' in 'kind'; p as the final 'p' in 'puppy'; ph as the 'p' in 'pond'; r as in 'rum' but hard and rolling; t as the 't' in 'stand'; and th as the 't' in 'two'.

Basics

Hello.	ជម្រាបសួរ	johm riab sua
Goodbye.	លាសិនហើយ	lia suhn hao-y
Excuse me.	សូមទោស	sohm toh
Sorry.	សូមទោស	sohm toh
Please.	សូម	sohm
Thank you.	អរគុណ	aw kohn
Yes.	បាទ/ចាស	baat/jaa (m/f)
No.	ទេ	te
Help!	ជួយខ្ញុំផង!	juay kh'nyohm phawng

What's your name?

អ្នកឈ្មោះអ្វី? niak ch'muah ei

My name is ...

ខ្ញុំឈ្មោះ... kh'nyohm ch'muah ...

Does anyone speak English?

ទីនេះមានអ្នកចេះ tii nih mian niak jeh
ភាសាអង់គ្លេសទេ? phiasaa awngle te

NUMBERS – KHMER

1	មួយ	muy
2	ពីរ	pii
3	បី	bei
4	បួន	buan
5	ប្រាំ	bram
6	ប្រាំមួយ	bram muy
7	ប្រាំពីរ	bram pii
8	ប្រាំបី	bram bei
9	ប្រាំបួន	bram buan
10	ដប់	dawp

I don't understand.

ຂ້ອຍມິນຍວລ់ເຫ   kh'nyohm muhn yuhl te

How much is it?

ເນະໄຖ່ບ៉ុຖ្ฐาถ?   nih th'lay pohnmaan

Where are the toilets?

ບຂ្ណ្នៃ2เ2ฒา?   bawngkohn neuv ai naa

Do you have a menu in English?

มาถม្ปุ้ยเ2   mien menui jea

ฤาสาถ2រ̌ត្ธ？   piasaa awnglay te

The bill, please.

ຊຸมฝิตฉุย   sohm kuht lui

Call a doctor!

ญูยเ2ร្ดุเ2ฉฏม2ฏ!   juay hav kruu paet mok

Call the police!

ญูยเ2ฏ្ด៉ฉิสม2ฏ!   juay hav police mok

LAO

Lao is a tonal language, meaning that many identical sounds are differentiated only by changes in the pitch of a speaker's voice. Pitch variations are relative to the speaker's natural vocal range, so that one person's low tone isn't necessarily the same pitch as another person's. There are six tones in Lao, indicated in our pronunciation guides by accent marks on letters: low tone (eg dẹe), high (eg héu·a), rising (eg sǎhm), high falling (eg sôw) and low falling (eg kòw). Note that no accent mark is used for the mid tone (eg het).

The pronunciation of vowels goes like this: i as in 'it'; ee as in 'feet'; ai as in 'aisle'; ah as the 'a' in 'father'; a as the short 'a' in 'about'; aa as in 'bad'; air as in 'air'; er as in 'fur'; eu as in 'sir'; u as in 'put'; oo as in 'food'; ow as in 'now'; or as in 'jaw'; o as in 'phone'; oh as in 'toe'; ee·a as in 'lan'; oo·a as in 'tour'; ew as in 'yew'; and oy as in 'boy'. Most consonants correspond to their English counterparts. The exceptions are đ (a hard 't' sound, a bit like 'dt') and ɓ (a hard 'p' sound, a bit like 'bp').

In our pronunciation guides, the hyphens indicate syllable breaks, eg àng-gìt (English). Some syllables are divided with a dot to help pronounce compound vowels, eg kẽe·an (write).

Basics

Hello.	ສะบายถิ	sábại-děe
Goodbye.	ສะบายถิ	sábại-děe
Excuse me.	ຂໍໂທถ	kǒr tôht
Sorry.	ຂໍໂທถ	kǒr tôht
Please.	ฤะฉุຖๆ	ga-lú-náh

NUMBERS – LAO

1	ทຖ្่ๆ	neung
2	ສຍๆ	sǒrng
3	ສาม	sǎhm
4	ສ็	see
5	ท้า	hàh
6	ทຖ	hók
7	ເจิด	jét
8	แฤด	ɓàat
9	เฏ้า	gôw
10	ສิบ	síp

Thank you.	ຂอบใจ	kòrp jại
Yes.	แมຖ	maan
No.	บ่	bor
Help!	ຂ้อยแด่	soo·ay daa

What's your name?

เจั้าຂ้ทยัๆ   jôw seu nyǎng

My name is ...

ຂ้อยຂ้ ...   kòy seu ...

Do you speak English?

เจั้าปๆา   jôw ɓàhk

ฤาสาຍัๆฏิดໄถ้บ่   páh-sǎh ạng·kít dâi bor

I don't understand.

บ่ຂ้าใจ   bor kòw jại

How much (for) ...?

... เท้าใด   ... tow dại

Where are the toilets?

ຂ้อๆบ้ๆยู่ใส   hòrng nâm yoo sǎii

Menu

ฉายฤาຖอาຍาຖ   lái-gạhn ạh-hǎhn

Please bring the bill.

ຂ้แຊ้ฤาฏแถ้   kǒr saak daa

Call a doctor!

ຂ้อยตาຖຂาຒ̌   soo·ay đạhm hǎh mǒr

ใท้แถ่   hài daa

Call the police!

ຂ้อยเฬ็มฏำฉอดแถ่   soo·ay êrn đam-lòo·at daa

TETUN

Tetun pronunciation is pretty straightforward. Letters always have the same sound value, and are generally pronounced just like in English, with the following exceptions: *j* is

NUMBERS – TETUN

1	ida
2	rua
3	tolu
4	hat
5	lima
6	nen
7	hitu
8	ualu
9	sia
10	sanulu

pronounced as the 's' in 'pleasure' (and sometimes as the 'z' in 'zebra'), x is pronounced as the 'sh' in 'ship' (sometimes as the 's' in 'summer'), while lh and nh are pronounced as the 'ly' in 'million' and the 'ny' in 'canyon' respectively (and outside Dili they are often reduced to l and n respectively).

Word stress is fairly regular and usually falls on the second-last syllable of a word; if it falls on another syllable, we've indicated this with an accent mark on the vowel (eg polísia).

Basics

Hello.	Haló./Olá. (pol/inf)
Goodbye.	Adeus.
Excuse me.	Kolisensa.
Sorry.	Disculpa.
Please.	Favór ida./Faz favór.
Thank you.	Obrigadu/a. (m/f)
Yes.	Sin./Diak./Los.
No.	Lae.
Help!	Ajuda!
What's your name?	Ita-nia naran saida?
My name is ...	Hau-nia naran ...
Do you speak English?	Ita koalia Inglés?
I don't understand.	Hau la kompriende.
How much is it?	Folin hira?
Where are the toilets?	Sintina iha nebé?
Please bring the menu/bill.	Favór ida lori hela menu/konta mai.
Call a doctor!	Bolu dotór!
Call the police!	Bolu polísia!

THAI

In Thai the meaning of a syllable may be altered by means of tones. In standard Thai there are five tones: low (eg bàht), mid (eg dee), falling (eg mâi), high (eg máh) and rising (eg săhm). The range of all tones is relative to each speaker's vocal range, so there is no fixed 'pitch' intrinsic to the language.

In our pronunciation guides, the hyphens indicate syllable breaks within words, and for ease of pronunciation some compound vowels are divided with a dot (eg mêu·a·rai).

The vowel a is pronounced as in 'about', aa as the 'a' in 'bad', ah as the 'a' in 'father', ai as in 'aisle', air as in 'flair' (without the 'r'), eu as the 'er' in 'her' (without the 'r'), ew as in 'new' (with rounded lips), oh as the 'o' in 'toe', or as in 'torn' (without the 'r') and ow as in 'now'.

Note also the pronunciation of the following consonants: b (a hard 'p' sound, almost like a 'b', eg in 'hip-bag'); d (a hard 't' sound, like a sharp 'd', eg in 'mid-tone'); and r (as in 'run' but flapped; often pronounced like 'l').

Basics

Hello.	สวัสดี	sà·wàt·dee
Goodbye.	ลาก่อน	lah gòrn
Excuse me.	ขออภัย	kŏr à·pai
Sorry.	ขอโทษ	kŏr tôht
Please.	ขอ	kŏr
Thank you.	ขอบคุณ	kòrp kun
Yes.	ใช่	châi
No.	ไม่	mâi
Help!	ช่วยด้วย	chôo·ay dôo·ay

NUMBERS – THAI

1	หนึ่ง	nèung
2	สอง	sŏrng
3	สาม	săhm
4	สี่	sèe
5	ห้า	hâh
6	หก	hòk
7	เจ็ด	jèt
8	แปด	bàat
9	เก้า	gôw
10	สิบ	sìp

What's your name?

คุณชื่ออะไร — kun chêu à-rai

My name is ...

ผม/ดิฉัน — pŏm/dì-chăn

ชื่อ... — chêu ... (m/f)

Do you speak English?

คุณพูดภาษา — kun pôot pah-săh

อังกฤษได้ไหม — ang-grìt dâi măi

I don't understand.

ผม/ดิฉันไม่ — pŏm/dì-chăn mâi

เข้าใจ — kôw jai (m/f)

How much is it?

เท่าไร — tôw-rai

Where are the toilets?

ห้องน้ำอยู่ที่ไหน — hôrng nám yòo têe năi

I'd like the menu, please.

ขอรายการ — kŏr rai gahn

อาหารหน่อย — ah-hăhn nòy

Please bring the bill.

ขอบิลหน่อย — kŏr bin nòy

Call a doctor!

เรียกหมอหน่อย — rêe·ak mŏr nòy

Call the police!

เรียกตำรวจหน่อย — rêe·ak đam·ròo·at nòy

VIETNAMESE

Vietnamese is written in a Latin-based phonetic alphabet, which was declared the official written form in 1910.

In our pronunciation guides, a is pronounced as in 'at', aa as in 'father', aw as in 'law', er as in 'her', oh as in 'doh!', ow as in 'cow', u as in 'book', uh as in 'but' and uhr as in 'fur' (without the 'r'). We've used dots (eg dee·úh-ng) to separate the combined vowel sounds. Note also that d is pronounced as in 'stop', đ as in 'dog', and ğ as in 'skill'.

Vietnamese uses a system of tones to make distinctions between words – so some vowels are pronounced with a high or low pitch. There are six tones in Vietnamese, indicated in the written language (and in our pronunciation guides) by accent marks on the vowel: mid (ma), low falling (mà), low rising (mả), high broken (mã), high rising (má) and low broken (mạ). The mid tone is flat.

The variation in vocabulary between the Vietnamese of the north and the south is indicated by (N) and (S) respectively.

NUMBERS – VIETNAMESE

1	một	mạwt
2	hai	hai
3	ba	baa
4	bốn	báwn
5	năm	nuhm
6	sáu	sóh
7	bảy	bảy
8	tám	dúhm
9	chín	jín
10	mười	muhr·eè

Basics

Hello.	Xin chào.	sin jòw
Goodbye.	Tạm biệt.	daạm bee·ụht
Excuse me.	Xin lỗi.	sin lõy
Sorry.	Xin lỗi.	sin lõy
Please.	Làm ơn.	laàm ern
Thank you.	Cảm ơn.	ğaảm ern
Yes.	Vâng./Dạ. (N/S)	vuhng/yạ
No.	Không.	kawm
Help!	Cứu tôi!	ğuhr·oó doy

What's your name?
Tên là gì? — den laà zeè

My name is ...
Tên tôi là ... — den doy laà ...

Do you speak English?
Bạn có nói tiếng — baạn ğó nóy dee·úhng
Anh không? — aang kawm

I don't understand.
Tôi không hiểu. — doy kawm heẻ·oo

How much is this?
Cái này giá bao nhiêu? — ğaí này zaá bow nyee·oo

Where is the toilet?
Nhà vệ sinh ở đâu? — nyaà vẹ sing ẻr đoh

I'd like the menu.
Tôi muốn thực đơn. — doy moo·úhn tụhrk đern

The bill, please.
Xin tính tiền. — sin díng dee·ùhn

Please call a doctor.
Làm ơn gọi bác sĩ. — laàm ern gọy baák seẻ

Please call the police.
Làm ơn gọi công an. — laàm ern gọy ğawm aan

Behind the Scenes

SEND US YOUR FEEDBACK

We love to hear from travellers – your comments keep us on our toes and help make our books better. Our well-travelled team reads every word on what you loved or loathed about this book. Although we cannot reply individually to your submissions, we always guarantee that your feedback goes straight to the appropriate authors, in time for the next edition. Each person who sends us information is thanked in the next edition – the most useful submissions are rewarded with a selection of digital PDF chapters.

Visit **lonelyplanet.com/contact** to submit your updates and suggestions or to ask for help. Our award-winning website also features inspirational travel stories, news and discussions.

Note: We may edit, reproduce and incorporate your comments in Lonely Planet products such as guidebooks, websites and digital products, so let us know if you don't want your comments reproduced or your name acknowledged. For a copy of our privacy policy visit lonelyplanet.com/privacy.

OUR READERS

Many thanks to the travellers who used the last edition and wrote to us with helpful hints, useful advice and interesting anecdotes:
Laura Child, Francesca Harber, Andy Hughes, Tom Jeffcoate, Oliver Neff, Kajsa Nilsson, Carina Pellar and Sheila Robinson.

WRITER THANKS

Brett Atkinson

It's always a thrill and pleasure to return to one of my favourite countries, and my thanks go to Mark Zazula in HCMC, Ben, Bich, Seamus and the gang in Phong Nha, and the Hoi An crew of Neil, Caroline, Mark and Leanne. Cheers also to Tam in Dong Ha and Sy in Dong Hoi, and it was great for my wife Carol to finally meet my good friend Kien and his family in Hanoi.

Lindsay Brown

I am very grateful for the assistance provided by numerous friendly folks across Borneo. In particular, I thank Carmalita Goh and the excellent staff at the Sabah Tourism Board in Kota Kinabalu, Leslie Chiang and the friendly folks at Borneo Guide in Brunei, Johnny Lim in Sandakan, and Jacqueline Fong in Kuching. Last but not least, thanks to Jenny for being the best travelling companion.

Jayne D'Arcy

Massive appreciation to Dora Ball and Clifton Wilkinson for the opportunity to return to Timor-Leste. Thanks to my dear friends Atoy and Julio: watching the magical journey of your country through you is a joy. Thanks to oracle Tracey Morgan, Nela Slezak in Oecussi and Matt Wilkinson on his bike. Thanks again Professor Damien Kingsbury. Thanks Rich, the dugong hunter, for keeping the kettle warm, and to Miles and Ruby, who, one day, I'll bring to the country I love.

David Eimer

Thanks to the other Myanmar writers for their sterling work and to Laura Crawford and all the LP crew. Thanks also to Htwe Htwe in Hsipaw, John in Tiddim and Jochen in Yangon for their assistance. As ever, much gratitude to everyone I met on the road who passed on tips, whether knowingly or unwittingly. Thanks to my fellow island writers and all the LP crew in London. Thanks also to Alex and co for the nights out on Phuket.

Paul Harding

Thanks to the many people who helped with advice and information during my travels in Indonesia, including Johan and Lola in Medan, Leisa in Kalimantan, Michael in Maluku and Roni and Michael in Bukittinggi. Big thanks to Laura Crawford, Dora and Clifton at Lonely

Planet, and to fellow writer Greg Bloom for help and support. In the Philippines, thanks to Jay, Elvie and friends, Meann and Martine in Legazpi and Harvey in Caramoan. But most of all, thanks to my patient and supportive wife Hannah and my super intrepid travelling daughter Layla.

Nick Ray

A huge and heartfelt thanks to the people of Cambodia, whose warmth and humour, stoicism and spirit make it such a fascinating place to live. Biggest thanks are reserved for my lovely wife Kulikar Sotho and our children Julian and Belle, as without their support and encouragement the adventures would not be possible. Thanks also to Mum and Dad for giving me a taste for travel from a young age. Thanks to fellow travellers and residents, friends and contacts in Cambodia who have helped shaped my knowledge and experience in this country. Finally, thanks my fellow Cambodia author Ashley Harrell and to the Lonely Planet team who have worked on this title. The author may be the public face, but a huge amount of work goes into making this a better book behind the scenes and I thank everyone for their hard work.

Tim Bewer

A hearty *kòrp jai* to the many people along the way who answered my incessant questions or helped me out in other ways during this update. In particular Nicolas Papon-Phalaphanh, Latanakone Keokhamphoui, Yves Verlaine, Khun Buasone, and Prapaporn Sompakdee provided great assistance while Laura, Nick, Rich and the rest of the Lonely Planet team were a pleasure to work with, as always. Finally, a special thanks to my wife Suttawan for help on this book and much more.

Joe Bindloss

I'd like to dedicate my work on this project to my son Benjamin, who arrived while I was working on this update. Thanks to all of my co-writers on this project, who provided invaluable tips and recommendations for their varied corners of Southeast Asia, often squeezing this in around their own deadlines.

Greg Bloom

A giant thanks to my crack research assistants in Manila: Windi (fountain of knowledge on all things drinking and dining), Anna ('Manila for Kids' guinea pig) and Callie (baby-related stress relief and laughs). Couldn't have done it without you guys. Also to Will and LT for the (costly) casino research. To Bart for accommodating LP writers when needed. To Pia for

Palawan tips. And to Luc for doing yeoman's work post-hockey on QC nightlife.

Celeste Brash

Thanks to Chiang Mai University and my beloved professors; to Samui Steve, Iain Leonard, Frans Betgem, Lee at Akha Ama and Catherine Bodry. A huge hug to Janine Brown of the Smithsonian Conservation Biology Institute for passion and insight on a tricky subject; and my family, Josh, Jasmine and Tevai who I wish could come with me on every trip. Thanks to Andrea, Raf and Rafael. To Mon in Pagudpud; Francis and Archie Baccoy and his family in Kalinga; Grail in Batad; Siegrid and Ryan in Sagada; Ryan Baldino and his uncle in Kabayan; policeman Peter in Abatan; and a huge thanks to Tuvyan Savoy in Baguio. Mostly thanks to my coauthor Greg and DE Laura for dedication and know-how, to my family for understanding and the people of North Luzon for unfaltering friendliness.

Austin Bush

A big thanks to DEs Dora Ball and Clifton Wilkinson, as well as to all the people on the ground in Bangkok and northern Thailand. I'm grateful for all the wonderful people on the ground in northern Vietnam, but my trip was made especially easier and more enjoyable by Mr Tung at Cat Ba Ventures, James and Mr Minh at Vision Travel, and the villagers of Na Hu, as well as my helpful Destination Editor, Laura Crawford.

Ria de Jong

Thank you to my destination editors Clifton Wilkinson and Tanya Parker for all their help guiding me through my Lonely Planet adventure, and to all those I met along my travels who kindly shared their knowledge, time and Singapore secrets with me. To Craig, Cisca and William, my travelling circus tribe.

Michael Grosberg

Thanks to all the kind people I met on the road. Especially to folks at the Iloilo provincial tourism office; Jac Señagan in Dumaguete; Ulrika, Julia and Fiona in Dauin; Mike of Coco Grove on Siquijor; Arno and Kaisa on Camiguin; Gerry and Susan for their warmth and friendship in Siargao; Princess Villarama, Sarah Sapo, Angelo Balao and Joaquin de Jesus on Boracay for their insight on Filipino music. To Carly, Rosie and Boone for making me never feel far from home.

Damian Harper

Huge thanks to the late Neil Bambridge, much gratitude for everything, may you rest in peace. Also thanks to Neil's wife Ratchi, to Maurice Senseit, the jolly staff at Nira's in Thong Sala, Piotr, Gemma, James Horton,

George W, Celeste Brash and everyone else who helped along the way, in whatever fashion.

Ashley Harrell

Thanks to: wise editors Laura Crawford and Clifton Wilkinson, and coauthor Nick Ray for the faith and guidance; Lauren Gurfein for introducing me to Cambodia; Andy Lavender for the dog-sitting; Peyton Bowsher for the dog-tolerating; Jess in Kampot for going above and beyond; Nicole and Alex for excellent company on Koh Totang; Ben, Sharyon, Amelie, Jarrah and Georgie for my favourite 'research' day, Lim for the hospitality/volcano sauce, and Nick Berry for showing me real Cambodia and teaching me to ride a motorbike. Thanks also to beautiful surfer Shaina Miller, monkey harasser Andy Wright, safety patrol Sean Abrams, penis gourd model Dustin Weatherford, magical Baliem Valley guide Antoni Sitepu, expert Raja Ampat guy Stuart Wilkinson, Lonely Planet loyalists Mac and John, parents Ronni and Mack, brothers Evan and Alex, and grandmother Adele Fox, the best Gumpy a girl could have asked for, who refused to depart this world before I could return home for a proper goodbye. Love you always.

Trent Holden

First up thanks very much for Dora Ball for giving me an opportunity to cover such a cool destination like Java. Thanks also to all the production team for putting this book together. On the ground a massive thanks goes to Gusri Tri Patra and Zulfindo 'Ajou' Koto for helping me getting around, and the many laughs along the way. Also thanks to Laura from Laura's Backpacker 523 in Yogyakarta and Yoppie from the Attic in Bandung for your help in piecing together vital travel info. Finally lots of love to my family and my partner Kate.

Anita Isalska

Huge thanks to everyone who generously gave time, tips or a warm welcome during my time in Malaysia. I'm especially grateful to Isabel Albiston, Alex Yong, Marco Ferrarese, Narelle McMurtrie and Howard Tan. Big thanks to Dora and Cliff. And endless gratitude to my write-up champion, Normal Matt.

Mark Johanson

I owe a huge debt of gratitude to the lovely people in Laos who not only made the country such a joy to revisit but either knowingly or (more often) unwittingly helped me along.

Special thanks go out to Miss Noy, Mr Ping, Kaz Kumrunrotschna, Michel Marcel Saada, Lara Picavet and Tom Chanthaphone for unlocking the secrets of their respective regions. Thanks to Felipe Bascuñán for tolerating my long absences and to Laura Crawford for taking a chance on a guidebook newbie.

Hugh McNaughtan

I'd like to thank Agus, Hernan, Edwin and all the other kind people who helped me get to grips with Nusa Tenggara and Sulawesi; Cliff and everyone I worked with at LP for the opportunity and support; and, most of all, Tas, Maise and Willa for their endless forbearance.

Rebecca Milner

I am indebted to the journalists, scholars and bloggers who cover the region with insight, fearlessness and compassion.

Iain Stewart

I was lucky to have a wonderful research trip along Vietnam's stunning coastline. Thanks to Mark, Lu and Matt Cowan in Saigon, Caroline Mills, Neil Fraser and Travis in Hoi An, team Nha Trang and Grazina, Thomas and Julia. My appreciation as well to Laura Crawford and my coauthors. Thanks to Laura for the commission, to Greg Bloom for help and contacts in the region, to Jamie Marshall for sharing some of the hard yards on the road, to Gino and Nikki in Bantayan and Cebu, Jacques and Lucia in Tacloban for expert advice and to the good folk of Calicoan Island, particularly Luna Beach resort. Many tourist information staff helped me on the way across the region, and I am grateful to you all.

Andy Symington

A great number of people, from taxi drivers to information officers, gave me excellent advice and help along the way; I'm very grateful to all of them. Specific thanks go to Siriporn Chiangpoon, Ian on Ko Chang, Maitri in Si Racha, Chayanan in Chanthaburi and the friendly Ang Sila volunteers.

Phillip Tang

Many thanks to the Vietnamese people and friends, especially Pham Hoang Manh in Hanoi, Nam, Tri and Liam Le in Saigon, Mr The for Ha Tien and Hon Chong, Nghiêm Nguyen and Anthony in Can Tho, Phuc Anh for the adventure to Tra Vinh. Thank you Laura Crawford for having me on board again. Thanks to Daniel Belfield for dressing gowns, bao, cocktails and *xe om* teaming.

ACKNOWLEDGEMENTS

Climate map data adapted from Peel MC, Finlayson BL & McMahon TA (2007) 'Updated World Map of the Köppen-Geiger Climate Classification', Hydrology and Earth System Sciences, 11, 163344.

Illustrations pp106-7, pp662-3, pp862-3 by Michael Weldon.

Cover photograph: Traditional puppet show, Thailand, saravutvanset/Getty©

THIS BOOK

This 19th edition of Lonely Planet's *Southeast Asia on a Shoestring* guidebook was researched and written by Brett Atkinson, Lindsay Brown, Jayne D'Arcy, David Eimer, Paul Harding, Nick Ray, Tim Bewer, Joe Bindloss, Greg Bloom, Celeste Brash, Austin Bush, Ria de Jong, Michael Grosberg, Damian Harper, Ashley Harrell, Trent Holden, Anita Isalska, Mark Johanson, Hugh McNaughtan, Rebecca Milner, Simon Richmond, Iain Stewart, Andy Symington and Phillip Tang. The previous edition was written by Nick Ray, Isabel Albiston, Greg Bloom, Ria de Jong, David Eimer, Sarah Reid, Simon Richmond, Iain Stewart, Ryan Ver Berkmoes, Richard Waters and China Williams. This guidebook was produced by the following:

Destination Editors Dora Ball, Laura Crawford, Tanya Parker, Clifton Wilkinson
Senior Product Editor Kate Chapman
Product Editor Kate Kiely
Senior Cartographer Diana Von Holdt
Book Designer Clara Monitto
Assisting Editors Sarah Bailey, James Bainbridge, Judith Bamber, Imogen Bannister, Janice Bird, Nigel Chin, Katie Connolly, Melanie Dankel, Andrea Dobbin, Emma Gibbs, Carly Hall, Jennifer Hattam, Gabrielle Innes, Helen Koehne, Kellie Langdon, Jodie Martire, Lou McGregor, Kate Morgan, Rosie Nicholson, Kristin Odijk, Monique Perrin, Christopher Pitts, Tamara Sheward, Sarah Stewart, Fionnuala Twomey, Simon Williamson
Assisting Cartographers Michael Garrett, Rachel Imeson
Assisting Book Designer Virginia Moreno
Cover Researcher Naomi Parker
Thanks to Carolyn Boicos, Barbara Delissen, Bruce Evans, Shona Gray, Liz Heynes, Andi Jones, Elizabeth Jones, Sandie Kestell, Anne Mason, Mao Monkolransey, Niamh O'Brien, Lauren O'Connell, Martine Power, Moe Pwint Phyu, Kirsten Rawlings, Kathryn Rowan, Vicky Smith, Gabrielle Stefanos, Branislava Vladisavljevic, Tracy Whitmey

Index

Map Legend

Sights

- Beach
- Bird Sanctuary
- Buddhist
- Castle/Palace
- Christian
- Confucian
- Hindu
- Islamic
- Jain
- Jewish
- Monument
- Museum/Gallery/Historic Building
- Ruin
- Shinto
- Sikh
- Taoist
- Winery/Vineyard
- Zoo/Wildlife Sanctuary
- Other Sight

Activities, Courses & Tours

- Bodysurfing
- Diving
- Canoeing/Kayaking
- Course/Tour
- Sento Hot Baths/Onsen
- Skiing
- Snorkelling
- Surfing
- Swimming/Pool
- Walking
- Windsurfing
- Other Activity

Sleeping

- Sleeping
- Camping
- Hut/Shelter

Eating

- Eating

Drinking & Nightlife

- Drinking & Nightlife
- Cafe

Entertainment

- Entertainment

Shopping

- Shopping

Information

- Bank
- Embassy/Consulate
- Hospital/Medical
- Internet
- Police
- Post Office
- Telephone
- Toilet
- Tourist Information
- Other Information

Geographic

- Beach
- Gate
- Hut/Shelter
- Lighthouse
- Lookout
- Mountain/Volcano
- Oasis
- Park
- Pass
- Picnic Area
- Waterfall

Population

- Capital (National)
- Capital (State/Province)
- City/Large Town
- Town/Village

Transport

- Airport
- Border crossing
- Bus
- Cable car/Funicular
- Cycling
- Ferry
- Metro/MRT/MTR station
- Monorail
- Parking
- Petrol station
- Skytrain/Subway station
- Taxi
- Train station/Railway
- Tram
- Underground station
- Other Transport

Routes

- Tollway
- Freeway
- Primary
- Secondary
- Tertiary
- Lane
- Unsealed road
- Road under construction
- Plaza/Mall
- Steps
- Tunnel
- Pedestrian overpass
- Walking Tour
- Walking Tour detour
- Path/Walking Trail

Boundaries

- International
- State/Province
- Disputed
- Regional/Suburb
- Marine Park
- Cliff
- Wall

Hydrography

- River, Creek
- Intermittent River
- Canal
- Water
- Dry/Salt/Intermittent Lake
- Reef

Areas

- Airport/Runway
- Beach/Desert
- Cemetery (Christian)
- Cemetery (Other)
- Glacier
- Mudflat
- Park/Forest
- Sight (Building)
- Sportsground
- Swamp/Mangrove

Note: Not all symbols displayed above appear on the maps in this book

Hugh McNaughtan

Indonesia A former English lecturer, Hugh swapped grant applications for visa applications, and turned his love of travel intro a full-time thing. Having done a bit of restaurant-reviewing in his home town (Melbourne) he's now eaten his way across four continents. He's never happier than when on the road with his two daughters. Except perhaps on the cricket field...

Rebecca Milner

Southeast Asia regional content California born, longtime Tokyo resident (15 years and counting!), Rebecca has coauthored Lonely Planet guides to Tokyo, Japan, Korea and China. She is also a freelance writer covering travel, food and culture, published in *The Guardian*, the *Independent*, the *Sunday Times Travel Magazine*, the *Japan Times* and more. After spending the better part of her twenties working to travel – doing odd jobs in Tokyo to make money to spend months at a time backpacking around Asia – Rebecca was fortunate enough to turn the tables in 2010, joining the Lonely Planet team of freelance authors.

Simon Richmond

Malaysia Journalist and photographer Simon Richmond has specialised as a travel writer since the early 1990s and first worked for Lonely Planet in 1999 on their Central Asia guide. He's long since stopped counting the number of guidebooks he's researched and written for the company, but countries covered including Australia, China, India, Iran, Japan, Korea, Malaysia, Mongolia, Myanmar (Burma), Russia, Singapore, South Africa and Turkey. His travel features have been published in newspapers and magazines around the world, including in the UK's Independent, Guardian, Times, Daily Telegraph and Royal Geographical Society Magazine; and Australia's Sydney Morning Herald and Australian newspapers and Australian Financial Review Magazine.

Iain Stewart

Vietnam Iain trained as journalist in the 1990s and then worked as a news reporter and a restaurant critic in London. He started writing travel guides in 1997 and has since penned more than 60 books for destinations as diverse as Ibiza and Cambodia. Iain's contributed to Lonely Planet titles including Mexico, Indonesia, Central America, Croatia, Vietnam, Bali & Lombok and Southeast Asia. He also writes regularly for the *Independent*, *The Observer* and *The Daily Telegraph* and tweets at @iaintravel. He'll consider working anywhere there's a palm tree or two and a beach of a generally sandy persuasion. Iain lives in Brighton (UK) within firing range of the city's wonderful south-facing horizon.

Andy Symington

Thailand Andy has written or worked on more than a hundred books and other updates for Lonely Planet (especially in Europe and Latin America) and other publishing companies, and has published articles on numerous subjects for a variety of newspapers, magazines and websites. He part-owns and operates a rock bar, has written a novel, and is currently working on several fiction and nonfiction writing projects. Originally from Australia, Andy moved to northern Spain many years ago. When he's not off with a backpack in some far-flung corner of the world, he can probably be found watching the tragically poor local football side or tasting local wines after a long walk in the nearby mountains.

Phillip Tang

Vietnam Phillip Tang grew up on a typically Australian diet of pho and fish'n'chips before moving to Mexico City. A degree in Chinese- and Latin-American cultures launched him into travel and then writing about it for Lonely Planet's Canada, China, Japan, Korea, Mexico, Peru and Vietnam guides. Writing at hellophillip.com, photos @mrtangtangtang, and tweets @philliptang.

Contributing Writers & Researchers
Isabel Albiston, Ryan Ver Berkmoes, Adam Skolnick

Michael Grosberg

Philippines Michael has worked on more than 45 Lonely Planet guidebooks. Whether covering Myanmar or New Jersey, each project has added to his rich and complicated psyche and taken years from his (still?) relatively young life. Prior to his freelance writing career, other international work included development on the island of Rota in the western Pacific; time in South Africa where he investigated and wrote about political violence and helped train newly elected government representatives; and a stint teaching in Quito, Ecuador. He received a Masters in Comparative Literature and taught literature and writing as an adjunct professor at several New York City area colleges.

Damian Harper

Thailand With two degrees (one in modern and classical Chinese from SOAS), Damian has been writing for Lonely Planet for more than two decades, contributing to titles as covering destinations as diverse as China, Beijing, Shanghai, Vietnam, Thailand, Ireland, London, Mallorca, Malaysia, Singapore & Brunei, Hong Kong, China's Southwest and the UK. A seasoned guidebook writer, Damian has penned articles for numerous newspapers and magazines, including The Guardian and The Daily Telegraph, and currently makes Surrey, England, his home. A self-taught trumpet novice, his other hobbies include collecting modern first editions, photography and Taekwondo. Follow Damian on Instagram (damian.harper).

Ashley Harrell

Cambodia, Indonesia After a brief stint selling day spa coupons door-to-door in South Florida, Ashley decided she'd rather be a writer. She went to journalism grad school, convinced a newspaper to hire her, and starting covering wildlife, crime and tourism, sometimes all in the same story. Fuelling her zest for storytelling and the unknown, she travelled widely and moved often, from a tiny NYC apartment to a vast California ranch to a jungle cabin in Costa Rica, where she started writing for Lonely Planet. From there her travels became more exotic and farther flung, and she still laughs when paychecks arrive.

Trent Holden

Indonesia A Geelong-based writer, located just outside Melbourne, Trent has worked for Lonely Planet since 2005. He's contributed to 30-plus guidebooks covering Asia, Africa and Australia. With a penchant for megacities, Trent's in his element when assigned to cover a nation's capital – the more chaotic the better – to unearth cool bars, art, street food and underground subculture. On the flipside he also writes books to idyllic tropical islands across Asia, in between going on safari to national parks in Africa and the subcontinent. When not travelling, Trent works as a freelance editor, reviewer and spending all his money catching live gigs. You can catch him on Twitter @hombreholden.

Anita Isalska

Malaysia, Thailand Anita Isalska is a travel journalist, editor and copywriter. After several merry years as a staff writer and editor – a few of them in Lonely Planet's London office – Anita now works freelance between Australia, the UK and any Alpine chalet with good wi-fi. Anita writes about France, Eastern Europe, Southeast Asia and off-beat travel. Read her stuff on www.anitaisalska.com.

Mark Johanson

Laos Mark Johanson grew up in Virginia and has called five different countries home over the last decade. His travel-writing career began as something of a quarter-life crisis, and he's happily spent the past eight years circling the globe reporting for Australian travel magazines (such as Get Lost), British newspapers (such as The Guardian), American lifestyles (such as Men's Journal) and global media outlets (such as CNN and BBC). When not on the road, you'll find him gazing at the Andes from his home in Santiago, Chile. Follow the adventure at www.markjohanson.com.

Nick Ray

Cambodia A Londoner of sorts, Nick comes from Watford, the sort of town that makes you want to travel. He lives in Phnom Penh with his wife, Kulikar, and children, Julian and Belle. He has written for countless guidebooks on the Mekong region, including Lonely Planet's *Vietnam, Cambodia, Laos & Northern Thailand* and *Myanmar* books, as well as *Southeast Asia on a Shoestring*. When not writing, he is often out exploring the remote parts of Cambodia as a location scout and manager for the world of television and film, including everything from *Tomb Raider* to *Top Gear*. Motorbikes are a part-time passion and he has travelled through most of Indochina on two wheels.

Tim Bewer

Thailand After university Tim worked as a legislative assistant before quitting capitol life to backpack around West Africa. It was during this trip that the idea of becoming a travel writer and photographer was hatched, and he's been at it ever since. He has visited more than 80 countries, including most in Southeast Asia. His first journey to Laos was in 1997, before the highway from Vientiane to the south was paved, and he's returned nearly a dozen times since. He lives in Khon Kaen, Thailand.

Joe Bindloss

Southeast Asia regional content Joe first got the travel bug on a grand tour of Asia in the early 1990s, and he's been roaming around its temples and paddy fields ever since on dozens of assignments for Lonely Planet and other publishers, covering everywhere from Myanmar and Thailand to India and Nepal. When not on the road, Joe works as Lonely Planet's Destination Editor for the Indian Subcontinent.

Greg Bloom

Philippines Greg is a freelance writer, tour operator and travel planner based out of Siem Reap, Cambodia, and Manila, Philippines. Greg began his writing career in the late '90s in Ukraine, working as a journalist and later editor-in-chief of the Kyiv Post, an English-language weekly. As a freelance travel writer, he has contributed to some 35 Lonely Planet titles, mostly in Eastern Europe and Asia. Greg also researched the Plan Your Trip section and the Survival Guide section.

Celeste Brash

Thailand Like many California natives, Celeste now lives in Portland, Oregon. She arrived however after 15 years in French Polynesia, a year and a half in Southeast Asia and a stint teaching English as a second language (in an American accent) in Brighton, England – among other things. She's been writing guidebooks for Lonely Planet since 2005 and her travel articles have appeared in publications from BBC Travel to National Geographic. She's currently writing a book about her five years on a remote pearl farm in the Tuamotu Atolls and is represented by the Donald Maass Agency, New York.

Austin Bush

Vietnam, Thailand Austin originally came to Thailand in 1999 as part of a language study program hosted by Chiang Mai University. The lure of city life, employment and spicy food eventually led him to Bangkok and have managed to keep him there since. Austin works as a writer and photographer, and has contributed text and photos to more than 20 Lonely Planet titles including *Bangkok*; *The Food Book*; *Food Lover's Guide to the World*; *Ko Samui Encounter*; *Laos*; *Malaysia, Singapore & Brunei*; *Myanmar (Burma)*; *Pocket Bangkok*; *Phuket Encounter*; *Thailand*; *Thailand's Islands & Beaches*; *Vietnam, Cambodia, Laos & Northern Thailand*; and *The World's Best Street Food*.

Ria de Jong

Singapore Born in Sri Lanka to Dutch/Australian parents, Ria has always relished the hustle and excitement of this continent of contrasts. After growing up in Townsville, Australia, Ria moved to Sydney as a features writer before packing her bags for a five-year stint in the Philippines. Having moved to Singapore in 2015 with her husband and two small children, Ria is loving discovering every nook and cranny of this tiny nation. This is Ria's second *Southeast Asia on a Shoestring* update.

OUR STORY

A beat-up old car, a few dollars in the pocket and a sense of adventure. In 1972 that's all Tony and Maureen Wheeler needed for the trip of a lifetime – across Europe and Asia overland to Australia. It took several months, and at the end – broke but inspired – they sat at their kitchen table writing and stapling together their first travel guide, *Across Asia on the Cheap*. Within a week they'd sold 1500 copies. Lonely Planet was born.

Today, Lonely Planet has offices in Franklin, London, Melbourne, Oakland, Dublin, Beijing and Delhi, with more than 600 staff and writers. We share Tony's belief that 'a great guidebook should do three things: inform, educate and amuse'.

OUR WRITERS

Brett Atkinson

Central Vietnam Brett Atkinson is based in Auckland, New Zealand, but is frequently on the road for Lonely Planet. He's a full-time travel and food writer specialising in adventure travel, unusual destinations and surprising angles on more well-known destinations. He is featured regularly on the Lonely Planet website, and in newspapers, magazines and websites across New Zealand and Australia. Brett has covered areas as diverse as Vietnam, Sri Lanka, the Czech Republic, New Zealand, Morocco, California and the South Pacific.

Lindsay Brown

Brunei Darussalam, Indonesia, Malaysia Lindsay started travelling as young bushwalker exploring the Blue Mountains west of Sydney. Then, as a marine biologist, he dived the coastal and island waters of southeastern Australia. He continued travelling whenever he could while employed at Lonely Planet as an editor and publishing manager. Since becoming a freelance writer and photographer he has coauthored more than 35 Lonely Planet guides to Australia, Bhutan, India, Malaysia, Nepal, Pakistan and Papua New Guinea

Jayne D'Arcy

Timor-Leste Taking the first step on a new country's soil used to send shivers of excitement up Jayne's spine: now everything about new sights and activities does. Keen to research by bike, she also loves checking out a new town's early morning scene with a quick dawn run. Recent winner of an Australian award for best adventure travel story, she plans to keep on trekking. She's worked in Ireland and Timor-Leste, and is now based in Melbourne, Australia. Instagram: @jayne.darcy.

David Eimer

Myanmar (Burma), Thailand David has been a journalist and writer ever since abandoning the idea of a law career in 1990. After spells working in his native London and in Los Angeles, he moved to Beijing in 2005, where he contributed to a variety of newspapers and magazines in the UK. Since then, he has travelled and lived across China and in numerous cities in Southeast Asia, including Bangkok, Phnom Penh and Yangon. He has been covering China, Myanmar and Thailand for Lonely Planet since 2006. David also wrote the Plan Your Trip, Understand and Survival Guide chapters.

Paul Harding

Indonesia, Laos, Philippines As a writer and photographer, Paul has been travelling the globe for the best part of two decades, with an interest in remote and offbeat places, islands and cultures. He's an author and contributor to more than 50 Lonely Planet guides to countries and regions as diverse as India, Belize, Vanuatu, Iran, Indonesia, New Zealand, Iceland, Finland, Philippines and – his home patch – Australia.

OVER PAGE MORE WRITERS

Published by Lonely Planet Global Limited
CRN 554153
19th edition – October 2018
ISBN 978 1 78657 175 5
© Lonely Planet 2018   Photographs © as indicated 2018
10 9 8 7 6 5 4 3 2 1
Printed in Singapore

Although the authors and Lonely Planet have taken all reasonable care in preparing this book, we make no warranty about the accuracy or completeness of its content and, to the maximum extent permitted, disclaim all liability arising from its use.